✓ **W9-DEW-730**

PETERSON'S®
GRADUATE PROGRAMS
IN ENGINEERING & APPLIED
SCIENCES

2020

About Peterson's®

Peterson's® has been your trusted educational publisher for over 50 years. It's a milestone we're quite proud of, as we continue to offer the most accurate, dependable, high-quality educational content in the field, providing you with everything you need to succeed. No matter where you are on your academic or professional path, you can rely on Peterson's for its books, online information, expert test-prep tools, the most up-to-date education exploration data, and the highest quality career success resources—everything you need to achieve your education goals. For our complete line of products, visit **www.petersons.com**.

For more information about Peterson's range of educational products, contact Peterson's, 8740 Lucent Blvd., Suite 400 Highlands Ranch, CO 80129, or find us online at **www.petersons.com.**

ISSN 1093-8443
ISBN: 978-0-7689-4320-7

Printed in the United States of America

10 9 8 7 6 5 4 3 2 1   21 20 19

Fifty-fourth Edition

CONTENTS

CONTENTS

A Note from the Peterson's Editors

The six volumes of Peterson's *Graduate and Professional Programs*, the only annually updated reference work of its kind, provide wide-ranging information on the graduate and professional programs offered by accredited colleges and universities in the United States, U.S. territories, and Canada and by those institutions outside the United States that are accredited by U.S. accrediting bodies. More than 44,000 individual academic and professional programs at nearly 2,300 institutions are listed. Peterson's *Graduate and Professional Programs* have been used for more than fifty years by prospective graduate and professional students, placement counselors, faculty advisers, and all others interested in postbaccalaureate education.

Graduate & Professional Programs: An Overview contains information on institutions as a whole, while the other books in the series are devoted to specific academic and professional fields:

* *Graduate Programs in the Biological/Biomedical Sciences & Health-Related Medical Professions*

* *Graduate Programs in Business, Education, Information Studies, Law & Social Work*

* *Graduate Programs in Engineering & Applied Sciences*

* *Graduate Programs in the Humanities, Arts & Social Sciences*

* *Graduate Programs in the Physical Sciences, Mathematics, Agricultural Sciences, the Environment & Natural Resources*

The books may be used individually or as a set. For example, if you have chosen a field of study but do not know what institution you want to attend or if you have a college or university in mind but have not chosen an academic field of study, it is best to begin with the Overview guide.

Graduate & Professional Programs: An Overview presents several directories to help you identify programs of study that might interest you; you can then research those programs further in the other books in the series by using the Directory of Graduate and Professional Programs by Field, which lists 500 fields and gives the names of those institutions that offer graduate degree programs in each.

For geographical or financial reasons, you may be interested in attending a particular institution and will want to know what it has to offer. You should turn to the Directory of Institutions and Their Offerings, which lists the degree programs available at each institution. As in the Directory of Graduate and Professional Programs by Field, the level of degrees offered is also indicated.

All books in the series include advice on graduate education, including topics such as admissions tests, financial aid, and accreditation. **The Graduate Adviser** includes two essays and information about accreditation. The first essay, "The Admissions Process," discusses general admission requirements, admission tests, factors to consider when selecting a graduate school or program, when and how to apply, and how admission decisions are made. Special information for international students and tips for minority students are also included. The second essay, "Financial Support," is an overview of the broad range of support available at the graduate level. Fellowships, scholarships, and grants; assistantships and internships; federal and private loan programs, as well as Federal Work-Study; and the GI bill are detailed. This essay concludes with advice on applying for need-based financial aid. "Accreditation and Accrediting Agencies" gives information on accreditation and its purpose and lists institutional accrediting agencies first and then specialized accrediting agencies relevant to each volume's specific fields of study.

With information on more than 40,000 graduate programs in more than 500 disciplines, Peterson's *Graduate and Professional Programs* give you all the information you need about the programs that are of interest to you in three formats: **Profiles** (capsule summaries of basic information), **Displays** (information that an institution or program wants to emphasize), and **Close-Ups** (written by administrators, with more expansive information than the **Profiles**, emphasizing different aspects of the programs). By using these various formats of program information, coupled with **Appendixes** and **Indexes** covering directories and subject areas for all six books, you will find that these guides provide the most comprehensive, accurate, and up-to-date graduate study information available.

Peterson's publishes a full line of resources with information you need to guide you through the graduate admissions process. Peterson's publications can be found at college libraries and career centers and your local bookstore or library—or visit us on the Web at www.petersons.com.

Colleges and universities will be pleased to know that Peterson's helped you in your selection. Admissions staff members are more than happy to answer questions, address specific problems, and help in any way they can. The editors at Peterson's wish you great success in your graduate program search!

THE GRADUATE ADVISER

The Admissions Process

Generalizations about graduate admissions practices are not always helpful because each institution has its own set of guidelines and procedures. Nevertheless, some broad statements can be made about the admissions process that may help you plan your strategy.

Factors Involved in Selecting a Graduate School or Program

Selecting a graduate school and a specific program of study is a complex matter. Quality of the faculty; program and course offerings; the nature, size, and location of the institution; admission requirements; cost; and the availability of financial assistance are among the many factors that affect one's choice of institution. Other considerations are job placement and achievements of the program's graduates and the institution's resources, such as libraries, laboratories, and computer facilities. If you are to make the best possible choice, you need to learn as much as you can about the schools and programs you are considering before you apply.

The following steps may help you narrow your choices.

- Talk to alumni of the programs or institutions you are considering to get their impressions of how well they were prepared for work in their fields of study.
- Remember that graduate school requirements change, so be sure to get the most up-to-date information possible.
- Talk to department faculty members and the graduate adviser at your undergraduate institution. They often have information about programs of study at other institutions.
- Visit the websites of the graduate schools in which you are interested to request a graduate catalog. Contact the department chair in your chosen field of study for additional information about the department and the field.
- Visit as many campuses as possible. Call ahead for an appointment with the graduate adviser in your field of interest and be sure to check out the facilities and talk to students.

General Requirements

Graduate schools and departments have requirements that applicants for admission must meet. Typically, these requirements include undergraduate transcripts (which provide information about undergraduate grade point average and course work applied toward a major), admission test scores, and letters of recommendation. Most graduate programs also ask for an essay or personal statement that describes your personal reasons for seeking graduate study. In some fields, such as art and music, portfolios or auditions may be required in addition to other evidence of talent. Some institutions require that the applicant have an undergraduate degree in the same subject as the intended graduate major.

Most institutions evaluate each applicant on the basis of the applicant's total record, and the weight accorded any given factor varies widely from institution to institution and from program to program.

The Application Process

You should begin the application process at least one year before you expect to begin your graduate study. Find out the application deadline for each institution (many are provided in the **Profile** section of this guide). Go to the institution's website and find out if you can apply online. If not, request a paper application form. Fill out this form thoroughly and neatly. Assume that the school needs all the information it is requesting and that the admissions officer will be sensitive to the neatness and overall quality of what you submit. Do not supply more information than the school requires.

The institution may ask at least one question that will require a three- or four-paragraph answer. Compose your response on the assumption that the admissions officer is interested in both what you think and how you express yourself. Keep your statement brief and to the point, but, at the same time, include all pertinent information about your past experiences and your educational goals. Individual statements vary greatly in style and content, which helps admissions officers differentiate among applicants. Many graduate departments give considerable weight to the statement in making their admissions decisions, so be sure to take the time to prepare a thoughtful and concise statement.

If recommendations are a part of the admissions requirements, carefully choose the individuals you ask to write them. It is generally best to ask current or former professors to write the recommendations, provided they are able to attest to your intellectual ability and motivation for doing the work required of a graduate student. It is advisable to provide stamped, preaddressed envelopes to people being asked to submit recommendations on your behalf.

Completed applications, including references, transcripts, and admission test scores, should be received at the institution by the specified date.

Be advised that institutions do not usually make admissions decisions until all materials have been received. Enclose a self-addressed postcard with your application, requesting confirmation of receipt. Allow at least ten days for the return of the postcard before making further inquiries.

If you plan to apply for financial support, it is imperative that you file your application early.

ADMISSION TESTS

The major testing program used in graduate admissions is the Graduate Record Examinations (GRE®) testing program, sponsored by the GRE Board and administered by Educational Testing Service, Princeton, New Jersey.

The Graduate Record Examinations testing program consists of a General Test and six Subject Tests. The General Test measures critical thinking, verbal reasoning, quantitative reasoning, and analytical writing skills. It is offered as an Internet-based test (iBT) in the United States, Canada, and many other countries.

The GRE® revised General Test's questions were designed to reflect the kind of thinking that students need to do in graduate or business school and demonstrate that students are indeed ready for graduate-level work.

- **Verbal Reasoning**—Measures ability to analyze and evaluate written material and synthesize information obtained from it, analyze relationships among component parts of sentences, and recognize relationships among words and concepts.
- **Quantitative Reasoning**—Measures problem-solving ability, focusing on basic concepts of arithmetic, algebra, geometry, and data analysis.
- **Analytical Writing**—Measures critical thinking and analytical writing skills, specifically the ability to articulate and support complex ideas clearly and effectively.

The computer-delivered GRE® revised General Test is offered year-round at Prometric™ test centers and on specific dates at testing locations outside of the Prometric test center network. Appointments are scheduled on a first-come, first-served basis. The GRE® revised General Test is also offered as a paper-based test three times a year in areas where computer-based testing is not available.

You can take the computer-delivered GRE® revised General Test once every twenty-one days, up to five times within any continuous rolling twelve-month period (365 days)—even if you canceled your scores on a previously taken test. You may take the paper-based GRE® revised General Test as often as it is offered.

Three scores are reported on the revised General Test:

1. A **Verbal Reasoning score** is reported on a 130–170 score scale, in 1-point increments.

2. A **Quantitative Reasoning score** is reported on a 130–170 score scale, in 1-point increments.

3. An **Analytical Writing score** is reported on a 0–6 score level, in half-point increments.

The GRE® Subject Tests measure achievement and assume undergraduate majors or extensive background in the following six disciplines:

- Biology
- Chemistry
- Literature in English
- Mathematics
- Physics
- Psychology

The Subject Tests are available three times per year as paper-based administrations around the world. Testing time is approximately 2 hours and 50 minutes. You can obtain more information about the GRE® by visiting the ETS website at **www.ets.org** or consulting the *GRE® Information Bulletin*. The *Bulletin* can be obtained at many undergraduate colleges. You can also download it from the ETS website or obtain it by contacting Graduate Record Examinations, Educational Testing Service, P.O. Box 6000, Princeton, NJ 08541-6000; phone: 609-771-7670 or 866-473-4373.

If you expect to apply for admission to a program that requires any of the GRE® tests, you should select a test date well in advance of the application deadline. Scores on the computer-based General Test are reported within ten to fifteen days; scores on the paper-based Subject Tests are reported within six weeks.

Another testing program, the Miller Analogies Test® (MAT®), is administered at more than 500 Controlled Testing Centers in the United States, Canada, and other countries. The MAT® computer-based test is now available. Testing time is 60 minutes. The test consists of 120 partial analogies. You can obtain the *Candidate Information Booklet,* which contains a list of test centers and instructions for taking the test, from **www.milleranalogies.com** or by calling 800-328-5999 (toll-free).

Check the specific requirements of the programs to which you are applying.

How Admission Decisions Are Made

The program you apply to is directly involved in the admissions process. Although the final decision is usually made by the graduate dean (or an associate) or the faculty admissions committee, recommendations from faculty members in your intended field are important. At some institutions, an interview is incorporated into the decision process.

A Special Note for International Students

In addition to the steps already described, there are some special considerations for international students who intend to apply for graduate study in the United States. All graduate schools require an indication of competence in English. The purpose of the Test of English as a Foreign Language (TOEFL®) is to evaluate the English proficiency of people who are nonnative speakers of English and want to study at colleges and universities where English is the language of instruction. The TOEFL® is administered by Educational Testing Service (ETS) under the general direction of a policy board established by the College Board and the Graduate Record Examinations Board.

The TOEFL iBT® assesses four basic language skills: listening, reading, writing, and speaking. The Internet-based test is administered at secure, official test centers. The testing time is approximately 4 hours.

The TOEFL® is also offered in a paper-based format in areas of the world where internet-based testing is not available. In 2017, ETS launched a revised TOEFL® paper-based Test, that more closely aligned to the TOEFL iBT® test. This revised paper-based test consists of three sections—listening, reading, and writing. The testing time is approximately 3 hours.

You can obtain more information for both versions of the TOEFL® by visiting the ETS website at **www.ets.org/toefl**. Information can also be obtained by contacting TOEFL® Services, Educational Testing Service, P.O. Box 6151, Princeton, NJ 08541-6151. Phone: 609-771-7100 or 877-863-3546 (toll free).

International students should apply especially early because of the number of steps required to complete the admissions process. Furthermore, many United States graduate schools have a limited number of spaces for international students, and many more students apply than the schools can accommodate.

International students may find financial assistance from institutions very limited. The U.S. government requires international applicants to submit a certification of support, which is a statement attesting to the applicant's financial resources. In addition, international students *must* have health insurance coverage.

Tips for Minority Students

Indicators of a university's values in terms of diversity are found both in its recruitment programs and its resources directed to student success. Important questions: Does the institution vigorously recruit minorities for its graduate programs? Is there funding available to help with the costs associated with visiting the school? Are minorities represented in the institution's brochures or website or on their faculty rolls? What campus-based resources or services (including assistance in locating housing or career counseling and placement) are available? Is funding available to members of underrepresented groups?

At the program level, it is particularly important for minority students to investigate the "climate" of a program under consideration. How many minority students are enrolled and how many have graduated? What opportunities are there to work with diverse faculty and mentors whose research interests match yours? How are conflicts resolved or concerns addressed? How interested are faculty in building strong and supportive relations with students? "Climate" concerns should be addressed by posing questions to various individuals, including faculty members, current students, and alumni.

Information is also available through various organizations, such as the Hispanic Association of Colleges & Universities (HACU), and publications such as *Diverse Issues in Higher Education* and *Hispanic Outlook* magazine. There are also books devoted to this topic, such as *The Multicultural Student's Guide to Colleges* by Robert Mitchell.

Financial Support

The range of financial support at the graduate level is very broad. The following descriptions will give you a general idea of what you might expect and what will be expected of you as a financial support recipient.

Fellowships, Scholarships, and Grants

These are usually outright awards of a few hundred to many thousands of dollars with no service to the institution required in return. Fellowships and scholarships are usually awarded on the basis of merit and are highly competitive. Grants are made on the basis of financial need or special talent in a field of study. Many fellowships, scholarships, and grants not only cover tuition, fees, and supplies but also include stipends for living expenses with allowances for dependents. However, the terms of each should be examined because some do not permit recipients to supplement their income with outside work. Fellowships, scholarships, and grants may vary in the number of years for which they are awarded.

In addition to the availability of these funds at the university or program level, many excellent fellowship programs are available at the national level and may be applied for before and during enrollment in a graduate program. A listing of many of these programs can be found at the Council of Graduate Schools' website, **https://cgsnet.org/**. There is a wealth of information in the "Programs" and "Awards" sections.

Assistantships and Internships

Many graduate students receive financial support through assistantships, particularly involving teaching or research duties. It is important to recognize that such appointments should not be viewed simply as employment relationships but rather should constitute an integral and important part of a student's graduate education. As such, the appointments should be accompanied by strong faculty mentoring and increasingly responsible apprenticeship experiences. The specific nature of these appointments in a given program should be considered in selecting that graduate program.

TEACHING ASSISTANTSHIPS

These usually provide a salary and full or partial tuition remission and may also provide health benefits. Unlike fellowships, scholarships, and grants, which require no service to the institution, teaching assistantships require recipients to provide the institution with a specific amount of undergraduate teaching, ideally related to the student's field of study. Some teaching assistants are limited to grading papers, compiling bibliographies, taking notes, or monitoring laboratories. At some graduate schools, teaching assistants must carry lighter course loads than regular full-time students.

RESEARCH ASSISTANTSHIPS

These are very similar to teaching assistantships in the manner in which financial assistance is provided. The difference is that recipients are given basic research assignments in their disciplines rather than teaching responsibilities. The work required is normally related to the student's field of study; in most instances, the assistantship supports the student's thesis or dissertation research.

ADMINISTRATIVE INTERNSHIPS

These are similar to assistantships in application of financial assistance funds, but the student is given an assignment on a part-time basis, usually as a special assistant with one of the university's administrative offices. The assignment may not necessarily be directly related to the recipient's discipline.

RESIDENCE HALL AND COUNSELING ASSISTANTSHIPS

These assistantships are frequently assigned to graduate students in psychology, counseling, and social work, but they may be offered to students in other disciplines, especially if the student has worked in this capacity during his or her undergraduate years. Duties can vary from being available in a dean's office for a specific number of hours for consultation with undergraduates to living in campus residences and being responsible for both counseling and administrative tasks or advising student activity groups. Residence hall assistantships often include a room and board allowance and, in some cases, tuition assistance and stipends. Contact the Housing and Student Life Office for more information.

Health Insurance

The availability and affordability of health insurance is an important issue and one that should be considered in an applicant's choice of institution and program. While often included with assistantships and fellowships, this is not always the case and, even if provided, the benefits may be limited. It is important to note that the U.S. government requires international students to have health insurance.

The GI Bill

This provides financial assistance for students who are veterans of the United States armed forces. If you are a veteran, contact your local Veterans Administration office to determine your eligibility and to get full details about benefits. There are a number of programs that offer educational benefits to current military enlistees. Some states have tuition assistance programs for members of the National Guard. Contact the VA office at the college for more information.

Federal Work-Study Program (FWS)

Employment is another way some students finance their graduate studies. The federally funded Federal Work-Study Program provides eligible students with employment opportunities, usually in public and private nonprofit organizations. Federal funds pay up to 75 percent of the wages, with the remainder paid by the employing agency. FWS is available to graduate students who demonstrate financial need. Not all schools have these funds, and some only award them to undergraduates. Each school sets its application deadline and workstudy earnings limits. Wages vary and are related to the type of work done. You must file the Free Application for Federal Student Aid (FAFSA) to be eligible for this program.

Loans

Many graduate students borrow to finance their graduate programs when other sources of assistance (which do not have to be repaid) prove insufficient. You should always read and understand the terms of any loan program before submitting your application.

FEDERAL DIRECT LOANS

Federal Direct Loans. The Federal Direct Loan Program offers a variable-fixed interest rate loan to graduate students with the Department of Education acting as the lender. Students receive a new rate with each new loan, but that rate is fixed for the life of the loan. Beginning with loans made on or after July 1, 2013, the interest rate for loans made each July 1st to June 30th period are determined based on the last 10-year Treasury note auction prior to June 1st of that year, plus an added percentage. The interest rate can be no higher than 9.5%.

Beginning July 1, 2012, the Federal Direct Loan for graduate students is an unsubsidized loan. Under the *unsubsidized* program, the grad borrower pays the interest on the loan from the day proceeds are issued and is responsible for paying interest during all periods. If the borrower chooses not to pay the interest while in school, or during the grace periods, deferment, or forbearance, the interest accrues and will be capitalized.

Graduate students may borrow up to $20,500 per year through the Direct Loan Program, up to a cumulative maximum of $138,500, including undergraduate borrowing. No more than $65,500 of the $138,500 can be from subsidized loans, including loans the grad borrower may have received for periods of enrollment that began before July 1, 2012, or for prior undergraduate borrowing. You may borrow up to the cost of attendance at the school in which you are enrolled or will attend, minus estimated financial assistance from other federal, state, and private sources, up to a maximum of $20,500. Grad borrowers who reach the aggregate loan limit over the course of their education cannot receive additional loans; however, if they repay some of their loans to bring the outstanding balance below the aggregate limit, they could be eligible to borrow again, up to that limit.

Under the *subsidized* Federal Direct Loan Program, repayment begins six months after your last date of enrollment on at least a half-time basis. Under the *unsubsidized* program, repayment of interest begins within thirty days from disbursement of the loan proceeds, and repayment of the principal begins six months after your last enrollment on at least a half-time basis. Some borrowers may choose to defer interest payments while they are in school. The accrued interest is added to the loan balance when the borrower begins repayment. There are several repayment options.

Federal Perkins Loans. The Federal Perkins Loan is available to students demonstrating financial need and is administered directly by the school. Not all schools have these funds, and some may award them to undergraduates only. Eligibility is determined from the information you provide on the FAFSA. The school will notify you of your eligibility.

Eligible graduate students may borrow up to $8,000 per year, up to a maximum of $60,000, including undergraduate borrowing (even if your previous Perkins Loans have been repaid). The interest rate for Federal Perkins Loans is 5 percent, and no interest accrues while you remain in school at least half-time. Students who are attending less than half-time need to check with their school to determine the length of their grace period. There are no guarantee, loan, or disbursement fees. Repayment begins nine months after your last date of enrollment on at least a half-time basis and may extend over a maximum of ten years with no prepayment penalty.

Federal Direct Graduate PLUS Loans. Effective July 1, 2006, graduate and professional students are eligible for Graduate PLUS loans. This program allows students to borrow up to the cost of attendance, less any other aid received. These loans have a fixed interest rate (7.08% for loans first disbursed on or after July 1, 2019, and before July 1, 2020) and interest begins to accrue at the time of disbursement. Beginning with loans made on or after July 1, 2013, the interest rate for loans made each July 1st to June 30th period are determined based on the last 10-year Treasury note auction prior to June 1st of that year. The interest rate can be no higher than 10.5%. The PLUS loans do involve a credit check; a PLUS borrower may obtain a loan with a cosigner if his or her credit is not good enough. Grad PLUS loans may be deferred while a student is in school and for the six months following a drop below half-time enrollment. For more information, you should contact a representative in your college's financial aid office.

Deferring Your Federal Loan Repayments. If you borrowed under the Federal Direct Loan Program, Federal Direct PLUS Loan Program, or the Federal Perkins Loan Program for previous undergraduate or graduate study, your payments may be deferred when you return to graduate school, depending on when you borrowed and under which program.

There are other deferment options available if you are temporarily unable to repay your loan. Information about these deferments is provided at your entrance and exit interviews. If you believe you are eligible for a deferment of your loan payments, you must contact your lender or loan servicer to request a deferment. The deferment must be filed prior to the time your payment is due, and it must be re-filed when it expires if you remain eligible for deferment at that time.

SUPPLEMENTAL (PRIVATE) LOANS

Many lending institutions offer supplemental loan programs and other financing plans, such as the ones described here, to students seeking additional assistance in meeting their education expenses. Some loan programs target all types of graduate students; others are designed specifically for business, law, or medical students. In addition, you can use private loans not specifically designed for education to help finance your graduate degree.

If you are considering borrowing through a supplemental or private loan program, you should carefully consider the terms and be sure to read the fine print. Check with the program sponsor for the most current terms that will be applicable to the amounts you intend to borrow for graduate study. Most supplemental loan programs for graduate study offer unsubsidized, credit-based loans. In general, a credit-ready borrower is one who has a satisfactory credit history or no credit history at all. A creditworthy borrower generally must pass a credit test to be eligible to borrow or act as a cosigner for the loan funds.

Many supplemental loan programs have minimum and maximum annual loan limits. Some offer amounts equal to the cost of attendance minus any other aid you will receive for graduate study. If you are planning to borrow for several years of graduate study, consider whether there is a cumulative or aggregate limit on the amount you may borrow. Often this cumulative or aggregate limit will include any amounts you borrowed and have not repaid for undergraduate or previous graduate study.

The combination of the annual interest rate, loan fees, and the repayment terms you choose will determine how much you will repay over time. Compare these features in combination before you decide which loan program to use. Some loans offer interest rates that are adjusted monthly, quarterly, or annually. Some offer interest rates that are lower during the in-school, grace, and deferment periods and then increase when you begin repayment. Some programs include a loan origination fee, which is usually deducted from the principal amount you receive when the loan is disbursed and must be repaid along with the interest and other principal when you graduate, withdraw from school, or drop below half-time study. Sometimes the loan fees are reduced if you borrow with a qualified cosigner. Some programs allow you to defer interest and/or principal payments while you are enrolled in graduate school. Many programs allow you to capitalize your interest payments; the interest due on your loan is added to the outstanding balance of your loan, so you don't have to repay immediately, but this increases the amount you owe. Other programs allow you to pay the interest as you go, which reduces the amount you later have to repay. The private loan market is very competitive, and your financial aid office can help you evaluate these programs.

Applying for Need-Based Financial Aid

Schools that award federal and institutional financial assistance based on need will require you to complete the FAFSA and, in some cases, an institutional financial aid application.

If you are applying for federal student assistance, you **must** complete the FAFSA. A service of the U.S. Department of Education, the FAFSA is free to all applicants. Most applicants apply online at **www.fafsa.ed.gov**. Paper applications are available at the financial aid office of your local college.

After your FAFSA information has been processed, you will receive a Student Aid Report (SAR). If you provided an e-mail address on the FAFSA, this will be sent to you electronically; otherwise, it will be mailed to your home address.

Follow the instructions on the SAR if you need to correct information reported on your original application. If your situation changes after you file your FAFSA, contact your financial aid officer to discuss amending your information. You can also appeal your financial aid award if you have extenuating circumstances.

If you would like more information on federal student financial aid, visit the FAFSA website or download the most recent version of *Do You Need Money for College* at www.studentaid.ed.gov/sa/sites/default/files/2018-19-do-you-need-money.pdf. This guide is also available in Spanish.

The U.S. Department of Education also has a toll-free number for questions concerning federal student aid programs. The number is 1-800-4-FED AID (1-800-433-3243). If you are hearing impaired, call toll-free, 1-800-730-8913.

Summary

Remember that these are generalized statements about financial assistance at the graduate level. Because each institution allots its aid differently, you should communicate directly with the school and the specific department of interest to you. It is not unusual, for example, to find that an endowment vested within a specific department supports one or more fellowships. You may fit its requirements and specifications precisely.

Accreditation and Accrediting Agencies

Colleges and universities in the United States, and their individual academic and professional programs, are accredited by nongovernmental agencies concerned with monitoring the quality of education in this country. Agencies with both regional and national jurisdictions grant accreditation to institutions as a whole, while specialized bodies acting on a nationwide basis—often national professional associations—grant accreditation to departments and programs in specific fields.

Institutional and specialized accrediting agencies share the same basic concerns: the purpose an academic unit—whether university or program—has set for itself and how well it fulfills that purpose, the adequacy of its financial and other resources, the quality of its academic offerings, and the level of services it provides. Agencies that grant institutional accreditation take a broader view, of course, and examine university-wide or college-wide services with which a specialized agency may not concern itself.

Both types of agencies follow the same general procedures when considering an application for accreditation. The academic unit prepares a self-evaluation, focusing on the concerns mentioned above and usually including an assessment of both its strengths and weaknesses; a team of representatives of the accrediting body reviews this evaluation, visits the campus, and makes its own report; and finally, the accrediting body makes a decision on the application. Often, even when accreditation is granted, the agency makes a recommendation regarding how the institution or program can improve. All institutions and programs are also reviewed every few years to determine whether they continue to meet established standards; if they do not, they may lose their accreditation.

Accrediting agencies themselves are reviewed and evaluated periodically by the U.S. Department of Education and the Council for Higher Education Accreditation (CHEA). Recognized agencies adhere to certain standards and practices, and their authority in matters of accreditation is widely accepted in the educational community.

This does not mean, however, that accreditation is a simple matter, either for schools wishing to become accredited or for students deciding where to apply. Indeed, in certain fields the very meaning and methods of accreditation are the subject of a good deal of debate. For their part, those applying to graduate school should be aware of the safeguards provided by regional accreditation, especially in terms of degree acceptance and institutional longevity. Beyond this, applicants should understand the role that specialized accreditation plays in their field, as this varies considerably from one discipline to another. In certain professional fields, it is necessary to have graduated from a program that is accredited in order to be eligible for a license to practice, and in some fields the federal government also makes this a hiring requirement. In other disciplines, however, accreditation is not as essential, and there can be excellent programs that are not accredited. In fact, some programs choose not to seek accreditation, although most do.

Institutions and programs that present themselves for accreditation are sometimes granted the status of candidate for accreditation, or what is known as "preaccreditation." This may happen, for example, when an academic unit is too new to have met all the requirements for accreditation. Such status signifies initial recognition and indicates that the school or program in question is working to fulfill all requirements; it does not, however, guarantee that accreditation will be granted.

Institutional Accrediting Agencies—Regional

MIDDLE STATES COMMISSION ON HIGHER EDUCATION

Accredits institutions in Delaware, District of Columbia, Maryland, New Jersey, New York, Pennsylvania, Puerto Rico, and the Virgin Islands.

Dr. Elizabeth Sibolski, President
Middle States Commission on Higher Education
3624 Market Street, Second Floor West
Philadelphia, Pennsylvania 19104
Phone: 267-284-5000
Fax: 215-662-5501
E-mail: info@msche.org
Website: www.msche.org

NEW ENGLAND ASSOCIATION OF SCHOOLS AND COLLEGES

Accredits institutions in Connecticut, Maine, Massachusetts, New Hampshire, Rhode Island, and Vermont.

Dr. Barbara E. Brittingham, President/Director
Commission on Institutions of Higher Education
3 Burlington Woods Drive, Suite 100
Burlington, Massachusetts 01803-4531
Phone: 855-886-3272 or 781-425-7714
Fax: 781-425-1001
E-mail: cihe@neasc.org
Website: https://cihe.neasc.org

THE HIGHER LEARNING COMMISSION

Accredits institutions in Arizona, Arkansas, Colorado, Illinois, Indiana, Iowa, Kansas, Michigan, Minnesota, Missouri, Nebraska, New Mexico, North Dakota, Ohio, Oklahoma, South Dakota, West Virginia, Wisconsin, and Wyoming.

Dr. Barbara Gellman-Danley, President
The Higher Learning Commission
230 South LaSalle Street, Suite 7-500
Chicago, Illinois 60604-1413
Phone: 800-621-7440 or 312-263-0456
Fax: 312-263-7462
E-mail: info@hlcommission.org
Website: www.hlcommission.org

NORTHWEST COMMISSION ON COLLEGES AND UNIVERSITIES

Accredits institutions in Alaska, Idaho, Montana, Nevada, Oregon, Utah, and Washington.

Dr. Sandra E. Elman, President
8060 165th Avenue, NE, Suite 100
Redmond, Washington 98052
Phone: 425-558-4224
Fax: 425-376-0596
E-mail: selman@nwccu.org
Website: www.nwccu.org

SOUTHERN ASSOCIATION OF COLLEGES AND SCHOOLS

Accredits institutions in Alabama, Florida, Georgia, Kentucky, Louisiana, Mississippi, North Carolina, South Carolina, Tennessee, Texas, and Virginia.

Dr. Belle S. Wheelan, President
Commission on Colleges
1866 Southern Lane
Decatur, Georgia 30033-4097
Phone: 404-679-4500 Ext. 4504
Fax: 404-679-4558
E-mail: questions@sacscoc.org
Website: www.sacscoc.org

WESTERN ASSOCIATION OF SCHOOLS AND COLLEGES

Accredits institutions in California, Guam, and Hawaii.

Jamienne S. Studley, President
WASC Senior College and University Commission
985 Atlantic Avenue, Suite 100
Alameda, California 94501
Phone: 510-748-9001
Fax: 510-748-9797
E-mail: wasc@wscuc.org
Website: https://www.wscuc.org/

Institutional Accrediting Agencies—Other

ACCREDITING COUNCIL FOR INDEPENDENT COLLEGES AND SCHOOLS
Michelle Edwards, President
750 First Street NE, Suite 980
Washington, DC 20002-4223
Phone: 202-336-6780
Fax: 202-842-2593
E-mail: info@acics.org
Website: www.acics.org

DISTANCE EDUCATION ACCREDITING COMMISSION (DEAC)
Leah Matthews, Executive Director
1101 17th Street NW, Suite 808
Washington, DC 20036-4704
Phone: 202-234-5100
Fax: 202-332-1386
E-mail: info@deac.org
Website: www.deac.org

Specialized Accrediting Agencies

ACUPUNCTURE AND ORIENTAL MEDICINE
Mark S. McKenzie, LAc MsOM DiplOM, Executive Director
Accreditation Commission for Acupuncture and Oriental Medicine
8941 Aztec Drive, Suite 2
Eden Prairie, Minnesota 55347
Phone: 952-212-2434
Fax: 301-313-0912
E-mail: info@acaom.org
Website: www.acaom.org

ALLIED HEALTH
Kathleen Megivern, Executive Director
Commission on Accreditation of Allied Health Education Programs (CAAHEP)
25400 US Hwy 19 North, Suite 158
Clearwater, Florida 33763
Phone: 727-210-2350
Fax: 727-210-2354
E-mail: mail@caahep.org
Website: www.caahep.org

ART AND DESIGN
Karen P. Moynahan, Executive Director
National Association of Schools of Art and Design (NASAD)
Commission on Accreditation
11250 Roger Bacon Drive, Suite 21
Reston, Virginia 20190-5248
Phone: 703-437-0700
Fax: 703-437-6312
E-mail: info@arts-accredit.org
Website: http://nasad.arts-accredit.org

ATHLETIC TRAINING EDUCATION
Pamela Hansen, CAATE Director of Accreditation
Commission on Accreditation of Athletic Training Education (CAATE)
6850 Austin Center Blvd., Suite 100
Austin, Texas 78731-3184
Phone: 512-733-9700
E-mail: pamela@caate.net
Website: www.caate.net

AUDIOLOGY EDUCATION
Meggan Olek, Director
Accreditation Commission for Audiology Education (ACAE)
11480 Commerce Park Drive, Suite 220
Reston, Virginia 20191
Phone: 202-986-9500
Fax: 202-986-9550
E-mail: info@acaeaccred.org
Website: https://acaeaccred.org/

AVIATION
Dr. Gary J. Northam, President
Aviation Accreditation Board International (AABI)
3410 Skyway Drive
Auburn, Alabama 36830
Phone: 334-844-2431
Fax: 334-844-2432
E-mail: gary.northam@auburn.edu
Website: www.aabi.aero

BUSINESS
Stephanie Bryant, Executive Vice President and Chief Accreditation Officer
AACSB International—The Association to Advance Collegiate Schools of Business
777 South Harbour Island Boulevard, Suite 750
Tampa, Florida 33602
Phone: 813-769-6500
Fax: 813-769-6559
E-mail: stephanie.bryant@aacsb.edu
Website: www.aacsb.edu

BUSINESS EDUCATION
Dr. Phyllis Okrepkie, President
International Assembly for Collegiate Business Education (IACBE)
11374 Strang Line Road
Lenexa, Kansas 66215
Phone: 913-631-3009
Fax: 913-631-9154
E-mail: iacbe@iacbe.org
Website: www.iacbe.org

CHIROPRACTIC
Dr. Craig S. Little, President
Council on Chiropractic Education (CCE)
Commission on Accreditation
8049 North 85th Way
Scottsdale, Arizona 85258-4321
Phone: 480-443-8877 or 888-443-3506
Fax: 480-483-7333
E-mail: cce@cce-usa.org
Website: www.cce-usa.org

CLINICAL LABORATORY SCIENCES
Dianne M. Cearlock, Ph.D., Chief Executive Officer
National Accrediting Agency for Clinical Laboratory Sciences
5600 North River Road, Suite 720
Rosemont, Illinois 60018-5119
Phone: 773-714-8880 or 847-939-3597
Fax: 773-714-8886
E-mail: info@naacls.org
Website: www.naacls.org

CLINICAL PASTORAL EDUCATION
Trace Haythorn, Ph.D., Executive Director/CEO
Association for Clinical Pastoral Education, Inc.
One West Court Square, Suite 325
Decatur, Georgia 30030-2576
Phone: 678-363-6226
Fax: 404-320-0849
E-mail: acpe@acpe.edu
Website: www.acpe.edu

DANCE
Karen P. Moynahan, Executive Director
National Association of Schools of Dance (NASD)
Commission on Accreditation
11250 Roger Bacon Drive, Suite 21
Reston, Virginia 20190-5248
Phone: 703-437-0700
Fax: 703-437-6312
E-mail: info@arts-accredit.org
Website: http://nasd.arts-accredit.org

DENTISTRY
Dr. Kathleen T. O'Loughlin, Executive Director
Commission on Dental Accreditation
American Dental Association
211 East Chicago Avenue
Chicago, Illinois 60611
Phone: 312-440-2500
E-mail: accreditation@ada.org
Website: www.ada.org

DIETETICS AND NUTRITION
Mary B. Gregoire, Ph.D., Executive Director; RD, FADA, FAND
Academy of Nutrition and Dietetics
Accreditation Council for Education in Nutrition and Dietetics (ACEND)
120 South Riverside Plaza
Chicago, Illinois 60606-6995
Phone: 800-877-1600 or 312-899-0040
E-mail: acend@eatright.org
Website: www.eatright.org/cade

EDUCATION PREPARATION
Christopher Koch, President
Council for the Accreditation of Educator Preparation (CAEP)
1140 19th Street NW, Suite 400
Washington, DC 20036
Phone: 202-223-0077
Fax: 202-296-6620
E-mail: caep@caepnet.org
Website: www.caepnet.org

ENGINEERING
Michael Milligan, Ph.D., PE, Executive Director
Accreditation Board for Engineering and Technology, Inc. (ABET)
415 North Charles Street
Baltimore, Maryland 21201
Phone: 410-347-7700
E-mail: accreditation@abet.org
Website: www.abet.org

FORENSIC SCIENCES
Nancy J. Jackson, Director of Development and Accreditation
American Academy of Forensic Sciences (AAFS)
Forensic Science Education Program Accreditation Commission (FEPAC)
410 North 21st Street
Colorado Springs, Colorado 80904
Phone: 719-636-1100
Fax: 719-636-1993
E-mail: njackson@aafs.org
Website: www.fepac-edu.org

FORESTRY
Carol L. Redelsheimer
Director of Science and Education
Society of American Foresters
10100 Laureate Way
Bethesda, Maryland 20814-2198
Phone: 301-897-8720 or 866-897-8720
Fax: 301-897-3690
E-mail: membership@safnet.org
Website: www.eforester.com

HEALTHCARE MANAGEMENT
Commission on Accreditation of Healthcare Management Education (CAHME)
Anthony Stanowski, President and CEO
6110 Executive Boulevard, Suite 614
Rockville, Maryland 20852
Phone: 301-298-1820
E-mail: info@cahme.org
Website: www.cahme.org

HEALTH INFORMATICS AND HEALTH MANAGEMENT
Angela Kennedy, EdD, MBA, RHIA, Chief Executive Officer
Commission on Accreditation for Health Informatics and Information Management Education (CAHIIM)
233 North Michigan Avenue, 21st Floor
Chicago, Illinois 60601-5800
Phone: 312-233-1134
Fax: 312-233-1948
E-mail: info@cahiim.org
Website: www.cahiim.org

HUMAN SERVICE EDUCATION
Dr. Elaine Green, President
Council for Standards in Human Service Education (CSHSE)
3337 Duke Street
Alexandria, Virginia 22314
Phone: 571-257-3959
E-mail: info@cshse.org
Website: www.cshse.org

INTERIOR DESIGN
Holly Mattson, Executive Director
Council for Interior Design Accreditation
206 Grandview Avenue, Suite 350
Grand Rapids, Michigan 49503-4014
Phone: 616-458-0400
Fax: 616-458-0460
E-mail: info@accredit-id.org
Website: www.accredit-id.org

JOURNALISM AND MASS COMMUNICATIONS
Patricia Thompson, Executive Director
Accrediting Council on Education in Journalism and Mass Communications (ACEJMC)
201 Bishop Hall
P.O. Box 1848
University, MS 38677-1848
Phone: 662-915-5504
E-mail: pthomps1@olemiss.edu
Website: www.acejmc.org

LANDSCAPE ARCHITECTURE
Nancy Somerville, Executive Vice President, CEO
American Society of Landscape Architects (ASLA)
636 Eye Street, NW
Washington, DC 20001-3736
Phone: 202-898-2444
Fax: 202-898-1185
E-mail: info@asla.org
Website: www.asla.org

LAW
Barry Currier, Managing Director of Accreditation & Legal Education
American Bar Association
321 North Clark Street, 21st Floor
Chicago, Illinois 60654
Phone: 312-988-6738
Fax: 312-988-5681
E-mail: legaled@americanbar.org
Website: https://www.americanbar.org/groups/legal_education/accreditation.html

LIBRARY
Karen O'Brien, Director
Office for Accreditation
American Library Association
50 East Huron Street
Chicago, Illinois 60611-2795
Phone: 800-545-2433, ext. 2432 or 312-280-2432
Fax: 312-280-2433
E-mail: accred@ala.org
Website: http://www.ala.org/aboutala/offices/accreditation/

MARRIAGE AND FAMILY THERAPY
Tanya A. Tamarkin, Director of Educational Affairs
Commission on Accreditation for Marriage and Family Therapy
    Education (COAMFTE)
American Association for Marriage and Family Therapy
112 South Alfred Street
Alexandria, Virginia 22314-3061
Phone: 703-838-9808
Fax: 703-838-9805
E-mail: coa@aamft.org
Website: www.aamft.org

MEDICAL ILLUSTRATION
Kathleen Megivern, Executive Director
Commission on Accreditation of Allied Health Education Programs
    (CAAHEP)
25400 US Highway 19 North, Suite 158
Clearwater, Florida 33756
Phone: 727-210-2350
Fax: 727-210-2354
E-mail: mail@caahep.org
Website: www.caahep.org

MEDICINE
Liaison Committee on Medical Education (LCME)
Robert B. Hash, M.D., LCME Secretary
American Medical Association
Council on Medical Education
330 North Wabash Avenue, Suite 39300
Chicago, Illinois 60611-5885
Phone: 312-464-4933
E-mail: lcme@aamc.org
Website: www.ama-assn.org

Liaison Committee on Medical Education (LCME)
Heather Lent, M.A., Director
Accreditation Services
Association of American Medical Colleges
655 K Street, NW
Washington, DC 20001-2399
Phone: 202-828-0596
E-mail: lcme@aamc.org
Website: www.lcme.org

MUSIC
Karen P. Moynahan, Executive Director
National Association of Schools of Music (NASM)
Commission on Accreditation
11250 Roger Bacon Drive, Suite 21
Reston, Virginia 20190-5248
Phone: 703-437-0700
Fax: 703-437-6312
E-mail: info@arts-accredit.org
Website: http://nasm.arts-accredit.org/

NATUROPATHIC MEDICINE
Daniel Seitz, J.D., Ed.D., Executive Director
Council on Naturopathic Medical Education
P.O. Box 178
Great Barrington, Massachusetts 01230
Phone: 413-528-8877
E-mail: https://cnme.org/contact-us/
Website: www.cnme.org

NURSE ANESTHESIA
Francis R.Gerbasi, Ph.D., CRNA, COA Executive Director
Council on Accreditation of Nurse Anesthesia Educational Programs
    (CoA-NAEP)
American Association of Nurse Anesthetists
222 South Prospect Avenue
Park Ridge, Illinois 60068-4001
Phone: 847-655-1160
Fax: 847-692-7137
E-mail: accreditation@coa.us.com
Website: http://www.coacrna.org

NURSE EDUCATION
Jennifer L. Butlin, Executive Director
Commission on Collegiate Nursing Education (CCNE)
One Dupont Circle, NW, Suite 530
Washington, DC 20036-1120
Phone: 202-887-6791
Fax: 202-887-8476
E-mail: jbutlin@aacn.nche.edu
Website: www.aacn.nche.edu/accreditation

Marsal P. Stoll, Chief Executive Officer
Accreditation Commission for Education in Nursing (ACEN)
3343 Peachtree Road, NE, Suite 850
Atlanta, Georgia 30326
Phone: 404-975-5000
Fax: 404-975-5020
E-mail: mstoll@acenursing.org
Website: www.acenursing.org

NURSE MIDWIFERY
Heather L. Maurer, M.A., Executive Director
Accreditation Commission for Midwifery Education (ACME)
American College of Nurse-Midwives
8403 Colesville Road, Suite 1550
Silver Spring, Maryland 20910
Phone: 240-485-1800
Fax: 240-485-1818
E-mail: info@acnm.org
Website: www.midwife.org/Program-Accreditation

NURSE PRACTITIONER
Gay Johnson, CEO
National Association of Nurse Practitioners in Women's Health
Council on Accreditation
505 C Street, NE
Washington, DC 20002
Phone: 202-543-9693 Ext. 1
Fax: 202-543-9858
E-mail: info@npwh.org
Website: www.npwh.org

NURSING
Marsal P. Stoll, Chief Executive Officer
Accreditation Commission for Education in Nursing (ACEN)
3343 Peachtree Road, NE, Suite 850
Atlanta, Georgia 30326
Phone: 404-975-5000
Fax: 404-975-5020
E-mail: info@acenursing.org
Website: www.acenursing.org

OCCUPATIONAL THERAPY
Heather Stagliano, DHSc, OTR/L, Executive Director
The American Occupational Therapy Association, Inc.
4720 Montgomery Lane, Suite 200
Bethesda, Maryland 20814-3449
Phone: 301-652-6611 Ext. 2682
TDD: 800-377-8555
Fax: 240-762-5150
E-mail: accred@aota.org
Website: www.aoteonline.org

OPTOMETRY
Joyce L. Urbeck, Administrative Director
Accreditation Council on Optometric Education (ACOE)
American Optometric Association
243 North Lindbergh Boulevard
St. Louis, Missouri 63141-7881
Phone: 314-991-4100, Ext. 4246
Fax: 314-991-4101
E-mail: accredit@aoa.org
Website: www.theacoe.org

OSTEOPATHIC MEDICINE
Director, Department of Accreditation
Commission on Osteopathic College Accreditation (COCA)
American Osteopathic Association
142 East Ontario Street
Chicago, Illinois 60611
Phone: 312-202-8048
Fax: 312-202-8202
E-mail: predoc@osteopathic.org
Website: www.aoacoca.org

PHARMACY
Peter H. Vlasses, PharmD, Executive Director
Accreditation Council for Pharmacy Education
135 South LaSalle Street, Suite 4100
Chicago, Illinois 60603-4810
Phone: 312-664-3575
Fax: 312-664-4652
E-mail: csinfo@acpe-accredit.org
Website: www.acpe-accredit.org

PHYSICAL THERAPY
Sandra Wise, Senior Director
Commission on Accreditation in Physical Therapy Education (CAPTE)
American Physical Therapy Association (APTA)
1111 North Fairfax Street
Alexandria, Virginia 22314-1488
Phone: 703-706-3245
Fax: 703-706-3387
E-mail: accreditation@apta.org
Website: www.capteonline.org

PHYSICIAN ASSISTANT STUDIES
Sharon L. Luke, Executive Director
Accredittion Review Commission on Education for the Physician
    Assistant, Inc. (ARC-PA)
12000 Findley Road, Suite 275
Johns Creek, Georgia 30097
Phone: 770-476-1224
Fax: 770-476-1738
E-mail: arc-pa@arc-pa.org
Website: www.arc-pa.org

PLANNING
Jesmarie Soto Johnson, Executive Director
American Institute of Certified Planners/Association of Collegiate
    Schools of Planning/American Planning Association
Planning Accreditation Board (PAB)
2334 West Lawrence Avenue, Suite 209
Chicago, Illinois 60625
Phone: 773-334-7200
E-mail: smerits@planningaccreditationboard.org
Website: www.planningaccreditationboard.org

PODIATRIC MEDICINE
Heather Stagliano, OTR/L, DHSc, Executive Director
Council on Podiatric Medical Education (CPME)
American Podiatric Medical Association (APMA)
9312 Old Georgetown Road
Bethesda, Maryland 20814-1621
Phone: 301-581-9200
Fax: 301-571-4903
Website: www.cpme.org

PSYCHOLOGY AND COUNSELING
Jacqueline Remondet, Associate Executive Director, CEO of the
Accrediting Unit,
Office of Program Consultation and Accreditation
American Psychological Association
750 First Street, NE
Washington, DC 20002-4202
Phone: 202-336-5979 or 800-374-2721
TDD/TTY: 202-336-6123
Fax: 202-336-5978
E-mail: apaaccred@apa.org
Website: www.apa.org/ed/accreditation

Kelly Coker, Executive Director
Council for Accreditation of Counseling and Related Educational
    Programs (CACREP)
1001 North Fairfax Street, Suite 510
Alexandria, Virginia 22314
Phone: 703-535-5990
Fax: 703-739-6209
E-mail: cacrep@cacrep.org
Website: www.cacrep.org

Richard M. McFall, Executive Director
Psychological Clinical Science Accreditation System (PCSAS)
1101 East Tenth Street
IU Psychology Building
Bloomington, Indiana 47405-7007
Phone: 812-856-2570
Fax: 812-322-5545
E-mail: rmmcfall@pcsas.org
Website: www.pcsas.org

PUBLIC HEALTH
Laura Rasar King, M.P.H., MCHES, Executive Director
Council on Education for Public Health
1010 Wayne Avenue, Suite 220
Silver Spring, Maryland 20910
Phone: 202-789-1050
Fax: 202-789-1895
E-mail: Lking@ceph.org
Website: www.ceph.org

PUBLIC POLICY, AFFAIRS AND ADMINISTRATION
Crystal Calarusse, Chief Accreditation Officer
Commission on Peer Review and Accreditation
Network of Schools of Public Policy, Affairs, and Administration
(NASPAA-COPRA)
1029 Vermont Avenue, NW, Suite 1100
Washington, DC 20005
Phone: 202-628-8965
Fax: 202-626-4978
E-mail: copra@naspaa.org
Website: accreditation.naspaa.org

RADIOLOGIC TECHNOLOGY
Leslie Winter, Chief Executive Officer Joint Review Committee on
Education in Radiologic Technology (JRCERT)
20 North Wacker Drive, Suite 2850
Chicago, Illinois 60606-3182
Phone: 312-704-5300
Fax: 312-704-5304
E-mail: mail@jrcert.org
Website: www.jrcert.org

REHABILITATION EDUCATION
Frank Lane, Ph.D., Executive Director
Council for Accreditation of Counseling and Related Educational
    Programs (CACREP)
1001 North Fairfax Street, Suite 510
Alexandria, Virginia 22314
Phone: 703-535-5990
Fax: 703-739-6209
E-mail: cacrep@cacrep.org
Website: www.cacrep.org

RESPIRATORY CARE
Thomas Smalling, Executive Director
Commission on Accreditation for Respiratory Care (CoARC)
1248 Harwood Road
Bedford, Texas 76021-4244
Phone: 817-283-2835
Fax: 817-354-8519
E-mail: tom@coarc.com
Website: www.coarc.com

SOCIAL WORK
Dr. Stacey Borasky, Director of Accreditation
Office of Social Work Accreditation
Council on Social Work Education
1701 Duke Street, Suite 200
Alexandria, Virginia 22314
Phone: 703-683-8080
Fax: 703-519-2078
E-mail: info@cswe.org
Website: www.cswe.org

SPEECH-LANGUAGE PATHOLOGY AND AUDIOLOGY
Kimberlee Moore, Accreditation Executive Director
American Speech-Language-Hearing Association
Council on Academic Accreditation in Audiology and Speech-Language
    Pathology
2200 Research Boulevard #310
Rockville, Maryland 20850-3289
Phone: 301-296-5700
Fax: 301-296-8750
E-mail: accreditation@asha.org
Website: http://caa.asha.org

TEACHER EDUCATION
Christopher A. Koch, President
National Council for Accreditation of Teacher Education (NCATE)
Teacher Education Accreditation Council (TEAC)
1140 19th Street, Suite 400
Washington, DC 20036
Phone: 202-223-0077
Fax: 202-296-6620
E-mail: caep@caepnet.org
Website: www.ncate.org

TECHNOLOGY
Michale S. McComis, Ed.D., Executive Director
Accrediting Commission of Career Schools and Colleges
2101 Wilson Boulevard, Suite 302
Arlington, Virginia 22201
Phone: 703-247-4212
Fax: 703-247-4533
E-mail: mccomis@accsc.org
Website: www.accsc.org

TECHNOLOGY, MANAGEMENT, AND APPLIED ENGINEERING
Kelly Schild, Director of Accreditation
The Association of Technology, Management, and Applied Engineering
(ATMAE)
275 N. York Street, Suite 401
Elmhurst, Illinois 60126
Phone: 630-433-4514
Fax: 630-563-9181
E-mail: Kelly@atmae.org
Website: www.atmae.org

THEATER
Karen P. Moynahan, Executive Director
National Association of Schools of Theatre Commission on
    Accreditation
11250 Roger Bacon Drive, Suite 21
Reston, Virginia 20190
Phone: 703-437-0700
Fax: 703-437-6312
E-mail: info@arts-accredit.org
Website: http://nast.arts-accredit.org/

THEOLOGY
Dr. Bernard Fryshman, Executive VP
Emeritus and Interim Executive Director
Association of Advanced Rabbinical and Talmudic Schools (AARTS)
Accreditation Commission
11 Broadway, Suite 405
New York, New York 10004
Phone: 212-363-1991
Fax: 212-533-5335
E-mail: k.sharfman.aarts@gmail.com

Frank Yamada, Executive Director
Association of Theological Schools in the United States and Canada
    (ATS)
Commission on Accrediting
10 Summit Park Drive
Pittsburgh, Pennsylvania 15275
Phone: 412-788-6505
Fax: 412-788-6510
E-mail: ats@ats.edu
Website: www.ats.edu

Dr. Timothy Eaton, President
Transnational Association of Christian Colleges and Schools (TRACS)
Accreditation Commission
15935 Forest Road
Forest, Virginia 24551
Phone: 434-525-9539
Fax: 434-525-9538
E-mail: info@tracs.org
Website: www.tracs.org

VETERINARY MEDICINE
Dr. Karen Brandt, Director of Education and Research
American Veterinary Medical Association (AVMA)
Council on Education
1931 North Meacham Road, Suite 100
Schaumburg, Illinois 60173-4360
Phone: 847-925-8070 Ext. 6674
Fax: 847-285-5732
E-mail: info@avma.org
Website: www.avma.org

How to Use These Guides

As you identify the particular programs and institutions that interest you, you can use both the *Graduate & Professional Programs: An Overview* volume and the specialized volumes in the series to obtain detailed information.

- *Graduate Programs in the Biological/Biomedical Sciences & Health-Related Professions*
- *Graduate Programs in Business, Education, Information Studies, Law & Social Work*
- *Graduate Programs in Engineering & Applied Sciences*
- *Graduate Programs the Humanities, Arts & Social Sciences*
- *Graduate Programs in the Physical Sciences, Mathematics, Agricultural Sciences, the Environment & Natural Resources*

Each of the specialized volumes in the series is divided into sections that contain one or more directories devoted to programs in a particular field. If you do not find a directory devoted to your field of interest in a specific volume, consult "Directories and Subject Areas" (located at the end of each volume). After you have identified the correct volume, consult the "Directories and Subject Areas in This Book" index, which shows (as does the more general directory) what directories cover subjects not specifically named in a directory or section title.

Each of the specialized volumes in the series has a number of general directories. These directories have entries for the largest unit at an institution granting graduate degrees in that field. For example, the general Engineering and Applied Sciences directory in the *Graduate Programs in Engineering & Applied Sciences* volume consists of **Profiles** for colleges, schools, and departments of engineering and applied sciences.

General directories are followed by other directories, or sections, that give more detailed information about programs in particular areas of the general field that has been covered. The general Engineering and Applied Sciences directory, in the previous example, is followed by nineteen sections with directories in specific areas of engineering, such as Chemical Engineering, Industrial/Management Engineering, and Mechanical Engineering.

Because of the broad nature of many fields, any system of organization is bound to involve a certain amount of overlap. Environmental studies, for example, is a field whose various aspects are studied in several types of departments and schools. Readers interested in such studies will find information on relevant programs in the *Graduate Programs in the Biological/Biomedical Sciences & Health-Related Professions* volume under Ecology and Environmental Biology and Environmental and Occupational Health; in the *Graduate Programs in the Physical Sciences, Mathematics, Agricultural Sciences, the Environment & Natural Resources* volume under Environmental Management and Policy and Natural Resources; and in the *Graduate Programs in Engineering & Applied Sciences* volume under Energy Management and Policy and Environmental Engineering. To help you find all of the programs of interest to you, the introduction to each section within the specialized volumes includes, if applicable, a paragraph suggesting other sections and directories with information on related areas of study.

Directory of Institutions with Programs in the Physical Sciences, Mathematics, Agricultural Sciences, the Environment & Natural Resources

This directory lists institutions in alphabetical order and includes beneath each name the academic fields in which each institution offers graduate programs. The degree level in each field is also indicated, provided that the institution has supplied that information in response to Peterson's Annual Survey of Graduate and Professional Institutions.

An M indicates that a master's degree program is offered; a D indicates that a doctoral degree program is offered; an O signifies that other advanced degrees (e.g., certificates or specialist degrees) are offered; and an * (asterisk) indicates that a **Close-Up** and/or **Display** is located in this volume. See the index, "Close-Ups and Displays," for the specific page number.

Profiles of Academic and Professional Programs in the Specialized Volumes

Each section of **Profiles** has a table of contents that lists the Program Directories, **Displays**, and **Close-Ups.** Program Directories consist of the **Profiles** of programs in the relevant fields, with **Displays** following if programs have chosen to include them. **Close-Ups,** which are more individualized statements, are also listed for those graduate schools or programs that have chosen to submit them.

The **Profiles** found in the 500 directories in the specialized volumes provide basic data about the graduate units in capsule form for quick reference. To make these directories as useful as possible, **Profiles** are generally listed for an institution's smallest academic unit within a subject area. In other words, if an institution has a College of Liberal Arts that administers many related programs, the **Profile** for the individual program (e.g., Program in History), not the entire College, appears in the directory.

There are some programs that do not fit into any current directory and are not given individual **Profiles.** The directory structure is reviewed annually in order to keep this number to a minimum and to accommodate major trends in graduate education.

The following outline describes the **Profile** information found in the guides and explains how best to use that information. Any item that does not apply to or was not provided by a graduate unit is omitted from its listing. The format of the **Profiles** is constant, making it easy to compare one institution with another and one program with another.

A ★ graphic next to the school's name indicates the institution has additional detailed information in a "Premium Profile" on Petersons.com. After reading their information here, you can learn more about the school by visiting www.petersons.com and searching for that particular college or university's graduate program.

Identifying Information. The institution's name, in boldface type, is followed by a complete listing of the administrative structure for that field of study. (For example, University of Akron, Buchtel College of Arts and Sciences, Department of Theoretical and Applied Mathematics, Program in Mathematics.) The last unit listed is the one to which all information in the **Profile** pertains. The institution's city, state, and ZIP code follow.

Offerings. Each field of study offered by the unit is listed with all postbaccalaureate degrees awarded. Degrees that are not preceded by a specific concentration are awarded in the general field listed in the unit name. Frequently, fields of study are broken down into subspecializations, and those appear following the degrees awarded; for example, "Offerings in secondary education (M.Ed.), including English education, mathematics education, science education." Students enrolled in the M.Ed. program would be able to specialize in any of the three fields mentioned.

Professional Accreditation. Some **Profiles** indicate whether a program is professionally accredited. Because it is possible for a program to receive or lose professional accreditation at any time, students entering fields in which accreditation is important to a career should verify the status of programs by contacting either the chairperson or the appropriate accrediting association.

Jointly Offered Degrees. Explanatory statements concerning programs that are offered in cooperation with other institutions are included in the list of degrees offered. This occurs most commonly on a regional basis (for example, two state universities offering a cooperative Ph.D. in special education) or where the specialized nature of the institutions encourages joint efforts (a J.D./M.B.A. offered by a law school at an institution with no formal business programs and an institution with a business school but lacking a law school). Only programs that are truly cooperative are listed; those involving only limited course work at another institution are not. Interested students should contact the heads of such units for further information.

Program Availability. This may include the following: part-time, evening/weekend, online only, blended/hybrid learning, and/or minimal on-campus study. When information regarding the availability of part-time or evening/weekend study appears in the **Profile**, it means that students are able to earn a degree exclusively through such study. Blended/hybrid learning describes those courses in which some traditional in-class time has been replaced by online learning activities. Hybrid courses take advantage of the best features of both face-to-face and online learning.

Faculty. Figures on the number of faculty members actively involved with graduate students through teaching or research are separated into full- and part-time as well as men and women whenever the information has been supplied.

Students. Figures for the number of students enrolled in graduate and professional programs pertain to the semester of highest enrollment from the 2018–19 academic year. These figures are broken down into full- and part-time and men and women whenever the data have been supplied. Information on the number of matriculated students enrolled in the unit who are members of a minority group or are international students appears here. The average age of the matriculated students is followed by the number of applicants, the percentage accepted, and the number enrolled for fall 2018.

Degrees Awarded. The number of degrees awarded in the calendar year is listed. Many doctoral programs offer a terminal master's degree if students leave the program after completing only part of the requirements for a doctoral degree; that is indicated here. All degrees are classified into one of four types: master's, doctoral, first professional, and other advanced degrees. A unit may award one or several degrees at a given level; however, the data are only collected by type and may therefore represent several different degree programs.

Degree Requirements. The information in this section is also broken down by type of degree, and all information for a degree level pertains to all degrees of that type unless otherwise specified. Degree requirements are collected in a simplified form to provide some very basic information on the nature of the program and on foreign language, thesis or dissertation, comprehensive exam, and registration requirements. Many units also provide a short list of additional requirements, such as fieldwork or an internship. For complete information on graduation requirements, contact the graduate school or program directly.

Entrance Requirements. Entrance requirements are broken down into the four degree levels of master's, doctoral, first professional, and other advanced degrees. Within each level, information may be provided in two basic categories: entrance exams and other requirements. The entrance exams are identified by the standard acronyms used by the testing agencies, unless they are not well known. Other entrance requirements are quite varied, but they often contain an undergraduate or graduate grade point average (GPA). Unless otherwise stated, the GPA is calculated on a 4.0 scale and is listed as a minimum required for admission. Additional exam requirements/recommendations for international students may be listed here. Application deadlines for domestic and international students, the application fee, and whether electronic applications are accepted may be listed here. Note that the deadline should be used for reference only; these dates are subject to change, and students interested in applying should always contact the graduate unit directly about application procedures and deadlines.

Expenses. The typical cost of study for the 2018–2019 academic year (2017–18 if 2018–19 figures were not available) is given in two basic categories: tuition and fees. Cost of study may be quite complex at a graduate institution. There are often sliding scales for part-time study, a different cost for first-year students, and other variables that make it impossible to completely cover the cost of study for each graduate program. To provide the most usable information, figures are given for full-time study for a full year where available and for part-time study in terms of a per-unit rate (per credit, per semester hour, etc.). Occa-

sionally, variances may be noted in tuition and fees for reasons such as the type of program, whether courses are taken during the day or evening, whether courses are at the master's or doctoral level, or other institution-specific reasons. Respondents were also given the opportunity to provide more specific and detailed tuition and fees information at the unit level. When provided, this information will appear in place of any typical costs entered elsewhere on the university-level survey. Expenses are usually subject to change; for exact costs at any given time, contact your chosen schools and programs directly. Keep in mind that the tuition of Canadian institutions is usually given in Canadian dollars.

Financial Support. This section contains data on the number of awards administered by the institution and given to graduate students during the 2018–19 academic year. The first figure given represents the total number of students receiving financial support enrolled in that unit. If the unit has provided information on graduate appointments, these are broken down into three major categories: fellowships give money to graduate students to cover the cost of study and living expenses and are not based on a work obligation or research commitment, research assistantships provide stipends to graduate students for assistance in a formal research project with a faculty member, and teaching assistantships provide stipends to graduate students for teaching or for assisting faculty members in teaching undergraduate classes. Within each category, figures are given for the total number of awards, the average yearly amount per award, and whether full or partial tuition reimbursements are awarded. In addition to graduate appointments, the availability of several other financial aid sources is covered in this section. Tuition waivers are routinely part of a graduate appointment, but units sometimes waive part or all of a student's tuition even if a graduate appointment is not available. Federal Work Study is made available to students who demonstrate need and meet the federal guidelines; this form of aid normally includes 10 or more hours of work per week in an office of the institution. Institutionally sponsored loans are low-interest loans available to graduate students to cover both educational and living expenses. Career-related internships or fieldwork offer money to students who are participating in a formal off-campus research project or practicum. Grants, scholarships, traineeships, unspecified assistantships, and other awards may also be noted. The availability of financial support to part-time students is also indicated here.

Some programs list the financial aid application deadline and the forms that need to be completed for students to be eligible for financial awards. There are two forms: FAFSA, the Free Application for Federal Student Aid, which is required for federal aid, and the CSS PROFILE®.

Faculty Research. Each unit has the opportunity to list several keyword phrases describing the current research involving faculty members and graduate students. Space limitations prevent the unit from listing complete information on all research programs. The total expenditure for funded research from the previous academic year may also be included.

Unit Head and Application Contact. The head of the graduate program for each unit may be listed with academic title, phone and fax numbers, and e-mail address. In addition to the unit head's contact information, many graduate programs also list a separate contact for application and admission information, followed by the graduate school, program, or department's website. If no unit head or application contact is given, you should contact the overall institution for information on graduate admissions.

Displays and Close-Ups

The **Displays** and **Close-Ups** are supplementary insertions submitted by deans, chairs, and other administrators who wish to offer an additional, more individualized statement to readers. A number of graduate school and program administrators have attached a **Display** ad near the **Profile** listing. Here you will find information that an institution or program wants to emphasize. The **Close-Ups** are by their very nature more expansive and flexible than the **Profiles**, and the administrators who have written them may emphasize different aspects of their programs. All of the **Close-Ups** are organized in the same way (with the exception of a few that describe research and training opportunities instead of degree programs), and in each one you will find information on the same basic topics, such as programs of study, research facilities, tuition and fees, financial aid, and application procedures. If an institution or program has submitted a **Close-Up**, a boldface cross-reference appears below its **Profile**. As with the **Displays**, all of the **Close-Ups** in the guides have been submitted by choice; the absence of a **Display** or **Close-Up** does not reflect any type of editorial judgment on the part of Peterson's, and their presence in the guides should not be taken as an indication of status, quality, or approval. Statements regarding a university's objectives and accomplishments are a reflection of its own beliefs and are not the opinions of the Peterson's editors.

Appendixes

This section contains two appendixes. The first, "Institutional Changes Since the 2018 Edition," lists institutions that have closed, merged, or changed their name or status since the last edition of the guides. The second, "Abbreviations Used in the Guides," gives abbreviations of degree names, along with what those abbreviations stand for. These appendixes are identical in all six volumes of *Peterson's Graduate and Professional Programs*.

Indexes

There are three indexes presented here. The first index, "Close-Ups and Displays," gives page references for all programs that have chosen to place **Close-Ups** and **Displays** in this volume. It is arranged alphabetically by institution; within institutions, the arrangement is alphabetical by subject area. It is not an index to all programs in the book's directories of **Profiles**; readers must refer to the directories themselves for **Profile** information on programs that have not submitted the additional, more individualized statements. The second index, "Directories and Subject Areas in Other Books in This Series", gives book references for the directories in the specialized volumes and also includes cross-references for subject area names not used in the directory structure, for example, "Computing Technology (see Computer Science)." The third index, "Directories and Subject Areas in This Book," gives page references for the directories in this volume and cross-references for subject area names not used in this volume's directory structure.

Data Collection Procedures

The information published in the directories and Profiles of all the books is collected through Peterson's Annual Survey of Graduate and Professional Institutions. The survey is sent each spring to nearly 2,300 institutions offering postbaccalaureate degree programs, including accredited institutions in the United States, U.S. territories, and Canada and those institutions outside the United States that are accredited by U.S. accrediting bodies. Deans and other administrators complete these surveys, providing information on programs in the 500 academic and professional fields covered in the guides as well as overall institutional information. While every effort has been made to ensure the accuracy and completeness of the data, information is sometimes unavailable or changes occur after publication deadlines. All usable information received in time for publication has been included. The omission of any particular item from a directory or Profile signifies either that the item is not applicable to the institution or program or that information was not available. Profiles of programs scheduled to begin during the 2018–19 academic year cannot, obviously, include statistics on enrollment or, in many cases, the number of faculty members. If no usable data were submitted by an institution, its name, address, and program name appear in order to indicate the availability of graduate work.

Criteria for Inclusion in This Guide

To be included in this guide, an institution must have full accreditation or be a candidate for accreditation (preaccreditation) status by an institutional or specialized accrediting body recognized by the U.S. Department of Education or the Council for Higher Education Accreditation (CHEA). Institutional accrediting bodies, which review each institution as a whole, include the six regional associations of schools and colleges (Middle States, New England, North Central, Northwest, Southern, and Western), each of which is responsible for a specified portion of the United States and its territories. Other institutional accrediting bodies are national in scope and accredit specific kinds of institutions (e.g., Bible colleges, independent colleges, and rabbinical and Talmudic schools). Program registration by the New York State Board of Regents is considered to be the equivalent of institutional accreditation, since the board requires that all programs offered by an institution meet its standards before recognition is granted. A Canadian institution must be chartered and authorized to grant degrees by the provincial government, affiliated with a chartered institution, or accredited by a recognized U.S. accrediting body. This guide also includes institutions outside the United States that are accredited by these U.S. accrediting bodies. There are recognized specialized or professional accrediting bodies in more than fifty different fields, each of which is authorized to accredit institutions or specific programs in its particular field. For specialized institutions that offer programs in one field only, we designate this to be the equivalent of institutional accreditation. A full explanation of the accrediting process and complete information on recognized institutional (regional and national) and specialized accrediting bodies can be found online at **www.chea.org** or at **www.ed.gov/admins/finaid/accred/index.html**.

DIRECTORY OF INSTITUTIONS WITH PROGRAMS IN ENGINEERING & APPLIED SCIENCES

ACADEMY OF ART UNIVERSITY
Game Design and
    Development   M

ACADIA UNIVERSITY
Computer Science   M

ADELPHI UNIVERSITY
Biotechnology   M
Health Informatics   M,D,O

AIR FORCE INSTITUTE OF TECHNOLOGY
Aerospace/Aeronautical
    Engineering   M,D
Computer Engineering   M,D
Computer Science   M,D
Electrical Engineering   M,D
Engineering and Applied
    Sciences—General   M,D
Engineering Management   M
Engineering Physics   M,D
Environmental Engineering   M
Management of Technology   M,D
Materials Sciences   M,D
Nuclear Engineering   M,D
Operations Research   M,D
Systems Engineering   M,D

ALABAMA AGRICULTURAL AND MECHANICAL UNIVERSITY
Computer Science   M
Engineering and Applied
    Sciences—General   M,D
Materials Engineering   M
Materials Sciences   M,D

ALASKA PACIFIC UNIVERSITY
Telecommunications
    Management   M

ALCORN STATE UNIVERSITY
Computer Science   M
Information Science   M

ALFRED UNIVERSITY
Bioengineering   M,D
Ceramic Sciences and
    Engineering   M,D
Electrical Engineering   M,D
Engineering and Applied
    Sciences—General   M,D
Materials Sciences   M,D
Mechanical Engineering   M,D

AMERICAN COLLEGE DUBLIN
Energy Management and
    Policy   M

AMERICAN INTERCONTINENTAL UNIVERSITY ATLANTA
Information Science   M

AMERICAN INTERCONTINENTAL UNIVERSITY ONLINE
Computer and Information
    Systems Security   M
Information Science   M

AMERICAN PUBLIC UNIVERSITY SYSTEM
Computer and Information
    Systems Security   M,D
Health Informatics   M,D

AMERICAN SENTINEL UNIVERSITY
Computer Science   M
Health Informatics   M

AMERICAN UNIVERSITY
Biotechnology   M
Data Science/Data Analytics   M,O

THE AMERICAN UNIVERSITY IN CAIRO
Artificial Intelligence/Robotics   M,D,O
Biotechnology   M,D,O
Computer Science   M,D,O
Construction Engineering   M,D,O
Electrical Engineering   M,D,O
Engineering and Applied
    Sciences—General   M,D,O
Environmental Engineering   M,D,O
Mechanical Engineering   M,D,O
Nanotechnology   M,D,O

THE AMERICAN UNIVERSITY IN DUBAI
Construction Management   M

AMERICAN UNIVERSITY OF ARMENIA
Computer Science   M
Energy Management and
    Policy   M
Industrial/Management
    Engineering   M
Information Science   M
Manufacturing Engineering   M

AMERICAN UNIVERSITY OF BEIRUT
Biomedical Engineering   M,D
Civil Engineering   M,D
Computer Engineering   M,D
Computer Science   M,D
Electrical Engineering   M,D
Engineering and Applied
    Sciences—General   M,D
Engineering Management   M,D
Mechanical Engineering   M,D
Water Resources Engineering   M,D

AMERICAN UNIVERSITY OF SHARJAH
Biomedical Engineering   M,D
Chemical Engineering   M,D
Civil Engineering   M,D
Computer Engineering   M,D
Electrical Engineering   M,D
Engineering Management   M,D
Mechanical Engineering   M,D

APPALACHIAN STATE UNIVERSITY
Computer Science   M
Energy and Power
    Engineering   M

ARIZONA STATE UNIVERSITY AT THE TEMPE CAMPUS
Aerospace/Aeronautical
    Engineering   M,D
Bioinformatics   M,D
Biomedical Engineering   M,D
Biotechnology   M,D
Chemical Engineering   M,D
Civil Engineering   M,D
Computer Engineering   M,D
Computer Science   M,D
Construction Engineering   M,D
Construction Management   M,D
Electrical Engineering   M,D,O
Energy and Power
    Engineering   M,D
Engineering and Applied
    Sciences—General   M,D,O
Environmental Engineering   M,D
Ergonomics and Human
    Factors   M
Geological Engineering   M,D

Industrial/Management
    Engineering   M,D
Information Science   M
Management of Technology   M
Manufacturing Engineering   M
Materials Engineering   M,D
Materials Sciences   M,D
Mechanical Engineering   M,D
Medical Informatics   M,D
Modeling and Simulation   M,D
Nanotechnology   M,D
Nuclear Engineering   M,D,O
Reliability Engineering   M
Software Engineering   M,D
Systems Engineering   M
Systems Science   M,D
Technology and Public Policy   M
Transportation and Highway
    Engineering   M,D,O

ARKANSAS STATE UNIVERSITY
Biotechnology   M,O
Computer Science   M
Engineering and Applied
    Sciences—General   M
Engineering Management   M

ARKANSAS TECH UNIVERSITY
Electrical Engineering   M
Engineering and Applied
    Sciences—General   M
Health Informatics   M
Information Science   M
Mechanical Engineering   M

ARTCENTER COLLEGE OF DESIGN
Transportation and Highway
    Engineering   M

ASPEN UNIVERSITY
Information Science   M,O

ATHABASCA UNIVERSITY
Management of Technology   M,D,O

ATLANTIS UNIVERSITY
Computer Engineering   M
Engineering and Applied
    Sciences—General   M
Management of Technology   M

AUBURN UNIVERSITY
Aerospace/Aeronautical
    Engineering   M,D
Biosystems Engineering   M,D
Chemical Engineering   M,D
Civil Engineering   M,D
Computer Engineering   M,D
Computer Science   M,D
Construction Engineering   M
Electrical Engineering   M,D
Engineering and Applied
    Sciences—General   M,D,O
Industrial/Management
    Engineering   M,D,O
Materials Engineering   M,D
Mechanical Engineering   M,D
Polymer Science and
    Engineering   M,D
Software Engineering   M,D
Systems Engineering   M,D,O

AUGUSTA UNIVERSITY
Computer and Information
    Systems Security   M
Health Informatics   M

AUSTIN PEAY STATE UNIVERSITY
Computer and Information
    Systems Security   M

Data Science/Data Analytics   M
Engineering and Applied
    Sciences—General   M

AZUSA PACIFIC UNIVERSITY
Biotechnology   M
Data Science/Data Analytics   M

BALL STATE UNIVERSITY
Computer Science   M
Information Science   M,O
Telecommunications   M

BARRY UNIVERSITY
Health Informatics   O
Information Science   M

BARUCH COLLEGE OF THE CITY UNIVERSITY OF NEW YORK
Financial Engineering   M

BAYLOR COLLEGE OF MEDICINE
Bioengineering   D
Biomedical Engineering   D

BAYLOR UNIVERSITY
Biomedical Engineering   M,D
Computer Engineering   M,D
Computer Science   M,D
Electrical Engineering   M,D
Mechanical Engineering   M,D

BAY PATH UNIVERSITY
Computer and Information
    Systems Security   M
Health Informatics   M

BELLEVUE UNIVERSITY
Information Science   M

BELMONT UNIVERSITY
Health Informatics   D

BENEDICTINE UNIVERSITY
Computer and Information
    Systems Security   M
Health Informatics   M

BENTLEY UNIVERSITY
Ergonomics and Human
    Factors   M
Information Science   M

BINGHAMTON UNIVERSITY, STATE UNIVERSITY OF NEW YORK
Biomedical Engineering   M,D
Computer Science   M,D
Electrical Engineering   M,D
Engineering and Applied
    Sciences—General   M,D
Industrial/Management
    Engineering   M,D
Materials Engineering   M,D
Materials Sciences   M,D
Mechanical Engineering   M,D
Systems Science   M,D

BOISE STATE UNIVERSITY
Civil Engineering   M
Computer Engineering   M,D
Computer Science   M,O
Electrical Engineering   M,D
Engineering and Applied
    Sciences—General   M,D,O
Materials Engineering   M,D
Mechanical Engineering   M

BOSTON UNIVERSITY
Bioinformatics	M,D
Biomedical Engineering	M,D
Computer and Information Systems Security	M,D,O
Computer Engineering	M,D,O
Computer Science	M,D,O
Data Science/Data Analytics	M,D
Electrical Engineering	M,D
Energy Management and Policy	M,D
Engineering and Applied Sciences—General	M,D
Health Informatics	M,O
Management of Technology	M
Manufacturing Engineering	M,D
Materials Engineering	M,D
Materials Sciences	M,D
Mechanical Engineering	M,D
Software Engineering	M,O
Systems Engineering	M,D
Telecommunications Management	M,O
Telecommunications	M,O

BOWIE STATE UNIVERSITY
Computer Science	M,D

BOWLING GREEN STATE UNIVERSITY
Computer Science	M
Operations Research	M
Software Engineering	M

BRADLEY UNIVERSITY
Civil Engineering	M
Computer Science	M
Construction Engineering	M
Electrical Engineering	M
Engineering and Applied Sciences—General	M
Industrial/Management Engineering	M
Information Science	M
Manufacturing Engineering	M
Mechanical Engineering	M

BRANDEIS UNIVERSITY
Artificial Intelligence/Robotics	M
Bioinformatics	M
Biotechnology	M
Computer and Information Systems Security	M
Computer Science	M,D
Health Informatics	M
Human-Computer Interaction	M
Medical Informatics	M
Software Engineering	M

BRANDMAN UNIVERSITY
Data Science/Data Analytics	M

BRIDGEWATER STATE UNIVERSITY
Computer Science	M

BRIGHAM YOUNG UNIVERSITY
Biotechnology	M,D
Chemical Engineering	M,D
Civil Engineering	M,D
Computer Engineering	M,D
Computer Science	M,D
Construction Management	M
Electrical Engineering	M,D
Engineering and Applied Sciences—General	M,D
Information Science	M
Manufacturing Engineering	M
Mechanical Engineering	M,D

BROCK UNIVERSITY
Biotechnology	M,D
Computer Science	M

BROOKLYN COLLEGE OF THE CITY UNIVERSITY OF NEW YORK
Computer Science	M,O
Health Informatics	M,O
Information Science	M,O

BROWN UNIVERSITY
Biochemical Engineering	M,D
Biomedical Engineering	M,D
Biotechnology	M,D
Chemical Engineering	M,D
Computer Engineering	M,D
Computer Science	M,D
Electrical Engineering	M,D
Engineering and Applied Sciences—General	M,D
Materials Sciences	M,D
Mechanical Engineering	M,D
Mechanics	M,D

BUCKNELL UNIVERSITY
Chemical Engineering	M
Civil Engineering	M
Computer Engineering	M
Electrical Engineering	M
Engineering and Applied Sciences—General	M
Mechanical Engineering	M

BUFFALO STATE COLLEGE, STATE UNIVERSITY OF NEW YORK
Data Science/Data Analytics	M
Industrial/Management Engineering	M
Manufacturing Engineering	M
Mechanical Engineering	M

CALIFORNIA BAPTIST UNIVERSITY
Civil Engineering	M
Construction Management	M
Mechanical Engineering	M
Software Engineering	M

CALIFORNIA INSTITUTE OF TECHNOLOGY
Aerospace/Aeronautical Engineering	M,D,O
Bioengineering	M,D
Chemical Engineering	M,D
Civil Engineering	M,D,O
Computer Science	M,D
Electrical Engineering	M,D,O
Engineering and Applied Sciences—General	M,D,O
Environmental Engineering	M,D
Materials Sciences	M,D
Mechanical Engineering	M,D,O
Mechanics	M,D
Systems Engineering	M,D

CALIFORNIA LUTHERAN UNIVERSITY
Management of Technology	M,O

CALIFORNIA MIRAMAR UNIVERSITY
Telecommunications Management	M
Telecommunications	M

CALIFORNIA POLYTECHNIC STATE UNIVERSITY, SAN LUIS OBISPO
Aerospace/Aeronautical Engineering	M
Architectural Engineering	M
Biomedical Engineering	M
Civil Engineering	M
Computer Science	M
Electrical Engineering	M
Environmental Engineering	M
Industrial/Management Engineering	M
Mechanical Engineering	M
Polymer Science and Engineering	M

CALIFORNIA STATE POLYTECHNIC UNIVERSITY, POMONA
Aerospace/Aeronautical Engineering	M
Civil Engineering	M
Computer Science	M
Electrical Engineering	M
Engineering Management	M
Mechanical Engineering	M
Systems Engineering	M

CALIFORNIA STATE UNIVERSITY CHANNEL ISLANDS
Bioinformatics	M
Biotechnology	M
Computer Science	M

CALIFORNIA STATE UNIVERSITY, CHICO
Computer Engineering	M
Computer Science	M
Construction Management	M
Electrical Engineering	M
Engineering and Applied Sciences—General	M

CALIFORNIA STATE UNIVERSITY, DOMINGUEZ HILLS
Bioinformatics	M
Computer Science	M

CALIFORNIA STATE UNIVERSITY, EAST BAY
Computer Science	M
Construction Management	M
Engineering and Applied Sciences—General	M
Engineering Management	M

CALIFORNIA STATE UNIVERSITY, FRESNO
Civil Engineering	M
Computer Engineering	M
Computer Science	M
Electrical Engineering	M
Engineering and Applied Sciences—General	M
Industrial/Management Engineering	M
Mechanical Engineering	M

CALIFORNIA STATE UNIVERSITY, FULLERTON
Architectural Engineering	M
Biotechnology	M
Civil Engineering	M
Computer Engineering	M
Computer Science	M
Electrical Engineering	M
Engineering and Applied Sciences—General	M

CALIFORNIA STATE UNIVERSITY, LONG BEACH
Civil Engineering	M
Computer Engineering	M
Computer Science	M
Electrical Engineering	M
Engineering Management	M,D
Ergonomics and Human Factors	M
Mechanical Engineering	M,D

CALIFORNIA STATE UNIVERSITY, LOS ANGELES
Civil Engineering	M
Computer Science	M
Electrical Engineering	M
Engineering and Applied Sciences—General	M
Management of Technology	M
Mechanical Engineering	M

CALIFORNIA STATE UNIVERSITY MARITIME ACADEMY
Engineering Management	M

CALIFORNIA STATE UNIVERSITY, NORTHRIDGE
Artificial Intelligence/Robotics	M
Civil Engineering	M
Computer Science	M
Construction Management	M
Electrical Engineering	M
Engineering and Applied Sciences—General	M
Engineering Management	M
Industrial/Management Engineering	M
Manufacturing Engineering	M
Materials Engineering	M
Mechanical Engineering	M
Software Engineering	M
Structural Engineering	M
Systems Engineering	M

CALIFORNIA STATE UNIVERSITY, SACRAMENTO
Civil Engineering	M
Computer Science	M
Electrical Engineering	M
Engineering and Applied Sciences—General	M
Mechanical Engineering	M
Software Engineering	M

CALIFORNIA STATE UNIVERSITY, SAN BERNARDINO
Computer and Information Systems Security	M
Computer Science	M

CALIFORNIA STATE UNIVERSITY, SAN MARCOS
Biotechnology	M
Computer and Information Systems Security	M
Computer Science	M

CALIFORNIA UNIVERSITY OF PENNSYLVANIA
Computer and Information Systems Security	M

M—masters degree; D—doctorate; O—other advanced degree; *—Close-Up and/or Display

CAMBRIDGE COLLEGE
Management of Technology M

CAMPBELLSVILLE UNIVERSITY
Management of Technology M,D

CANISIUS COLLEGE
Health Informatics M,O

CAPELLA UNIVERSITY
Computer and Information
    Systems Security M,D
Health Informatics M
Management of Technology M,D
Operations Research M

CAPITOL TECHNOLOGY UNIVERSITY
Computer and Information
    Systems Security M
Computer Science M
Electrical Engineering M
Information Science M
Telecommunications
    Management M

CARDINAL STRITCH UNIVERSITY
Computer and Information
    Systems Security M

CARLETON UNIVERSITY
Aerospace/Aeronautical
    Engineering M,D
Biomedical Engineering M
Civil Engineering M,D
Computer Science M,D
Electrical Engineering M,D
Engineering and Applied
    Sciences—General M,D
Environmental Engineering M,D
Information Science M,D
Management of Technology M
Materials Engineering M,D
Mechanical Engineering M,D
Systems Engineering M,D
Systems Science M,D

CARNEGIE MELLON UNIVERSITY
Architectural Engineering M,D
Artificial Intelligence/Robotics M,D
Bioengineering M,D
Biomedical Engineering M,D
Biotechnology M
Chemical Engineering M,D
Civil Engineering M,D
Computer and Information
    Systems Security M
Computer Engineering M,D
Computer Science M,D
Construction Management M,D
Electrical Engineering M,D
Energy and Power
    Engineering M,D
Environmental Engineering M,D
Human-Computer Interaction M,D
Information Science M,D
Materials Engineering M,D
Materials Sciences M,D
Mechanical Engineering M,D
Mechanics M,D
Modeling and Simulation M,D
Nanotechnology D
Operations Research D
Polymer Science and
    Engineering M
Software Engineering M,D
Systems Engineering M,D
Technology and Public Policy M,D
Telecommunications
    Management M
Water Resources Engineering M,D

CARROLL UNIVERSITY
Software Engineering M

CASE WESTERN RESERVE UNIVERSITY
Aerospace/Aeronautical
    Engineering M,D
Biomedical Engineering M,D
Chemical Engineering M,D
Civil Engineering M,D
Computer Engineering M,D
Computer Science M,D
Electrical Engineering M,D
Engineering and Applied
    Sciences—General M,D
Engineering Management M
Information Science M,D
Materials Engineering M,D
Materials Sciences M,D
Mechanical Engineering M,D
Operations Research M,D
Polymer Science and
    Engineering M,D
Systems Engineering M,D

THE CATHOLIC UNIVERSITY OF AMERICA
Biomedical Engineering M,D
Biotechnology M,D
Civil Engineering M,D,O
Computer Science M,D
Electrical Engineering M,D
Energy and Power
    Engineering M,D
Engineering and Applied
    Sciences—General M,D,O
Engineering Management M,O
Environmental Engineering M,D
Ergonomics and Human
    Factors M,D
Management of Technology M,O
Materials Engineering M
Materials Sciences M
Mechanical Engineering M,D
Systems Engineering M,O
Transportation and Highway
    Engineering M,D,O

CENTRAL CONNECTICUT STATE UNIVERSITY
Computer Science M,O
Construction Management M,O
Engineering and Applied
    Sciences—General M
Management of Technology M,O

CENTRAL EUROPEAN UNIVERSITY
Data Science/Data Analytics D
Management of Technology M,D

CENTRAL MICHIGAN UNIVERSITY
Computer and Information
    Systems Security O
Computer Science M
Engineering and Applied
    Sciences—General M
Engineering Management M,O
Materials Sciences D

CHAMPLAIN COLLEGE
Computer and Information
    Systems Security M
Management of Technology M

CHATHAM UNIVERSITY
Health Informatics M

CHICAGO STATE UNIVERSITY
Computer Science M

CHRISTIAN BROTHERS UNIVERSITY
Engineering and Applied
    Sciences—General M

CHRISTOPHER NEWPORT UNIVERSITY
Computer Science M

THE CITADEL, THE MILITARY COLLEGE OF SOUTH CAROLINA
Aerospace/Aeronautical
    Engineering M,O
Civil Engineering M,O
Computer Engineering M,O
Electrical Engineering M,O
Engineering and Applied
    Sciences—General M,O
Engineering Management M,O
Geotechnical Engineering M,O
Information Science M
Manufacturing Engineering M,O
Mechanical Engineering M,O
Structural Engineering M,O
Systems Engineering M,O
Transportation and Highway
    Engineering M,O

CITY COLLEGE OF THE CITY UNIVERSITY OF NEW YORK
Biomedical Engineering M,D
Chemical Engineering M,D
Civil Engineering M,D
Computer Science M,D
Electrical Engineering M,D
Engineering and Applied
    Sciences—General M,D
Mechanical Engineering M,D

CITY UNIVERSITY OF SEATTLE
Computer and Information
    Systems Security M,O
Computer Science M,O
Management of Technology M,O

CLAFLIN UNIVERSITY
Biotechnology M

CLAREMONT GRADUATE UNIVERSITY
Computer and Information
    Systems Security M,D,O
Data Science/Data Analytics M,D,O
Financial Engineering M
Health Informatics M,D,O
Information Science M,D,O
Operations Research M,D
Systems Science M,D,O
Telecommunications M,D,O

CLARION UNIVERSITY OF PENNSYLVANIA
Data Science/Data Analytics M
Information Science M

CLARK ATLANTA UNIVERSITY
Computer Science M
Information Science M

CLARKSON UNIVERSITY
Biotechnology M,D
Chemical Engineering M,D
Civil Engineering M,D
Computer Science M,D
Electrical Engineering M
Energy and Power
    Engineering M,D
Energy Management and
    Policy M,O
Engineering and Applied
    Sciences—General M,D,O

Engineering Management M
Environmental Engineering M,D
Health Informatics M
Materials Engineering D
Materials Sciences D
Mechanical Engineering M,D
Systems Engineering M

CLARK UNIVERSITY
Information Science M

CLEMSON UNIVERSITY
Automotive Engineering M,D,O
Bioengineering M,D,O
Bioinformatics M,D,O
Biomedical Engineering M,D,O
Biosystems Engineering M,D
Chemical Engineering M,D
Civil Engineering M,D
Computer Engineering M,D
Computer Science M,D
Construction Engineering M,D
Construction Management M,D
Electrical Engineering M,D
Engineering and Applied
    Sciences—General M,D,O
Environmental Engineering M,D
Ergonomics and Human
    Factors M,D
Geotechnical Engineering M,D
Industrial/Management
    Engineering M,D
Materials Engineering M,D
Materials Sciences M,D
Mechanical Engineering M,D
Structural Engineering M,D
Transportation and Highway
    Engineering M,D
Water Resources Engineering M,D

CLEVELAND STATE UNIVERSITY
Biomedical Engineering D
Chemical Engineering M,D
Civil Engineering M,D
Electrical Engineering M,D
Engineering and Applied
    Sciences—General M,D
Environmental Engineering M,D
Mechanical Engineering M,D
Software Engineering M,D

COASTAL CAROLINA UNIVERSITY
Computer Science M,D,O

COLLEGE FOR CREATIVE STUDIES
Automotive Engineering M
Transportation and Highway
    Engineering M

COLLEGE OF CHARLESTON
Computer Science M

COLLEGE OF SAINT ELIZABETH
Computer and Information
    Systems Security M,O
Data Science/Data Analytics M

THE COLLEGE OF SAINT ROSE
Computer Science M,O
Information Science M,O

THE COLLEGE OF ST. SCHOLASTICA
Health Informatics M,O

COLLEGE OF STATEN ISLAND OF THE CITY UNIVERSITY OF NEW YORK
Artificial Intelligence/Robotics M

Biotechnology	M
Computer and Information Systems Security	M
Computer Science	M
Data Science/Data Analytics	M,O
Electrical Engineering	M
Software Engineering	M

COLORADO CHRISTIAN UNIVERSITY

Computer and Information Systems Security	M

COLORADO MESA UNIVERSITY

Health Informatics	M,D,O

COLORADO SCHOOL OF MINES

Bioengineering	M,D
Chemical Engineering	M,D
Civil Engineering	M,D
Computer Science	M,D
Construction Engineering	M,D
Electrical Engineering	M,D
Electronic Materials	M,D
Energy Management and Policy	M,D
Engineering and Applied Sciences—General	M,D,O
Engineering Management	M,D
Environmental Engineering	M,D
Geological Engineering	M,D
Management of Technology	M,D
Materials Engineering	M,D
Materials Sciences	M,D
Mechanical Engineering	M,D
Metallurgical Engineering and Metallurgy	M,D
Mineral/Mining Engineering	M,D
Nuclear Engineering	M,D
Operations Research	M,D
Petroleum Engineering	M,D

COLORADO STATE UNIVERSITY

Bioengineering	M,D
Biomedical Engineering	M,D
Chemical Engineering	M,D
Civil Engineering	M,D
Computer Science	M,D
Construction Management	M
Electrical Engineering	M,D
Energy Management and Policy	M
Engineering and Applied Sciences—General	M,D
Materials Sciences	M,D
Mechanical Engineering	M,D
Systems Engineering	M,D

COLORADO STATE UNIVERSITY–PUEBLO

Applied Science and Technology	M
Engineering and Applied Sciences—General	M
Industrial/Management Engineering	M
Systems Engineering	M

COLORADO TECHNICAL UNIVERSITY AURORA

Computer and Information Systems Security	M
Computer Engineering	M
Computer Science	M
Data Science/Data Analytics	M
Electrical Engineering	M
Management of Technology	M
Software Engineering	M
Systems Engineering	M

COLORADO TECHNICAL UNIVERSITY COLORADO SPRINGS

Computer and Information Systems Security	M,D
Computer Engineering	M
Computer Science	M,D
Data Science/Data Analytics	M
Electrical Engineering	M
Management of Technology	M,D
Software Engineering	M,D
Systems Engineering	M

COLUMBIA UNIVERSITY

Biomedical Engineering	M,D
Biotechnology	M,D
Chemical Engineering	M,D
Civil Engineering	M,D
Computer Engineering	M,D
Computer Science	M,D
Construction Engineering	M,D
Construction Management	M,D
Data Science/Data Analytics	M
Electrical Engineering	M,D
Engineering and Applied Sciences—General	M,D
Environmental Engineering	M,D
Financial Engineering	M,D
Industrial/Management Engineering	M,D
Management of Technology	M
Materials Engineering	M,D
Materials Sciences	M,D
Mechanical Engineering	M,D
Mechanics	M,D
Medical Informatics	M,D,O
Operations Research	M,D

COLUMBUS STATE UNIVERSITY

Computer and Information Systems Security	M,O
Computer Science	M,O
Modeling and Simulation	M,O

CONCORDIA UNIVERSITY (CANADA)

Aerospace/Aeronautical Engineering	M
Biotechnology	M,D,O
Civil Engineering	M,D,O
Computer and Information Systems Security	M,D,O
Computer Engineering	M,D
Computer Science	M,D,O
Construction Engineering	M,D,O
Electrical Engineering	M,D
Engineering and Applied Sciences—General	M,D,O
Environmental Engineering	M,D,O
Game Design and Development	M,D,O
Industrial/Management Engineering	M,D,O
Mechanical Engineering	M,D,O
Software Engineering	M,D,O
Systems Engineering	M,D,O
Telecommunications Management	M,D,O

CONCORDIA UNIVERSITY, NEBRASKA

Computer and Information Systems Security	M
Computer Science	M

CONCORDIA UNIVERSITY OF EDMONTON

Computer and Information Systems Security	M

CONCORDIA UNIVERSITY, ST. PAUL

Computer and Information Systems Security	M

COOPER UNION FOR THE ADVANCEMENT OF SCIENCE AND ART

Chemical Engineering	M
Civil Engineering	M
Electrical Engineering	M
Engineering and Applied Sciences—General	M
Mechanical Engineering	M

CORNELL UNIVERSITY

Aerospace/Aeronautical Engineering	M,D
Agricultural Engineering	M,D
Artificial Intelligence/Robotics	M,D
Biochemical Engineering	M,D
Bioengineering	M,D
Biomedical Engineering	M,D
Biotechnology	M,D
Chemical Engineering	M,D
Civil Engineering	M,D
Computer Engineering	M,D
Computer Science	M,D
Electrical Engineering	M,D
Energy and Power Engineering	M,D
Engineering and Applied Sciences—General	M,D
Engineering Management	M,D
Engineering Physics	M,D
Environmental Engineering	M,D
Ergonomics and Human Factors	M
Geotechnical Engineering	M,D
Human-Computer Interaction	M,D
Industrial/Management Engineering	M,D
Information Science	D
Manufacturing Engineering	M,D
Materials Engineering	M,D
Materials Sciences	M,D
Mechanical Engineering	M,D
Mechanics	M,D
Nanotechnology	M,D
Operations Research	M,D
Polymer Science and Engineering	M,D
Structural Engineering	M,D
Systems Engineering	M,D
Textile Sciences and Engineering	M,D
Transportation and Highway Engineering	M,D
Water Resources Engineering	M,D

DAKOTA STATE UNIVERSITY

Computer Science	M,D,O
Health Informatics	M,D,O
Information Science	M,D,O

DALHOUSIE UNIVERSITY

Bioengineering	M,D
Bioinformatics	M,D
Biomedical Engineering	M,D
Chemical Engineering	M,D
Civil Engineering	M,D
Computer Engineering	M,D
Computer Science	M,D
Electrical Engineering	M,D
Engineering and Applied Sciences—General	M,D
Environmental Engineering	M,D
Human-Computer Interaction	M,D
Industrial/Management Engineering	M,D

Internet Engineering	M,D
Mechanical Engineering	M,D
Medical Informatics	M,D
Mineral/Mining Engineering	M,D

DARTMOUTH COLLEGE

Biomedical Engineering	M,D
Chemical Engineering	M,D
Computer Engineering	M,D
Computer Science	M,D
Electrical Engineering	M,D
Energy and Power Engineering	M,D
Engineering and Applied Sciences—General	M,D
Engineering Management	M
Health Informatics	M,D
Materials Engineering	M,D
Materials Sciences	M,D
Mechanical Engineering	M,D
Systems Engineering	M,D

DAVENPORT UNIVERSITY

Computer and Information Systems Security	M

DEPAUL UNIVERSITY

Computer and Information Systems Security	M,D
Computer Science	M,D
Data Science/Data Analytics	M,D
Game Design and Development	M,D
Health Informatics	M,D
Human-Computer Interaction	M,D
Information Science	M,D
Polymer Science and Engineering	M,D
Software Engineering	M,D

DESALES UNIVERSITY

Computer and Information Systems Security	M,O
Data Science/Data Analytics	M,O
Health Informatics	M,O

DIGIPEN INSTITUTE OF TECHNOLOGY

Computer Science	M

DREXEL UNIVERSITY

Architectural Engineering	M,D
Biochemical Engineering	M
Biomedical Engineering	M,D
Chemical Engineering	M,D
Civil Engineering	M,D
Computer Engineering	M
Computer Science	M,D,O*
Construction Management	M
Electrical Engineering	M
Engineering and Applied Sciences—General	M,D,O
Engineering Management	M,O
Environmental Engineering	M,D
Geotechnical Engineering	M,D
Hydraulics	M,D
Information Science	M,D,O
Materials Engineering	M,D
Mechanical Engineering	M,D
Mechanics	M,D
Software Engineering	M,D,O
Structural Engineering	M,D
Telecommunications	M

DRURY UNIVERSITY

Computer and Information Systems Security	O

M—masters degree; D—doctorate; O—other advanced degree; *—Close-Up and/or Display

DUKE UNIVERSITY

Bioinformatics	D,O
Biomedical Engineering	M,D
Civil Engineering	M,D
Computer Engineering	M,D
Computer Science	M,D
Electrical Engineering	M,D
Energy Management and Policy	M,O
Engineering and Applied Sciences—General	M
Engineering Management	M
Environmental Engineering	M,D
Health Informatics	M
Management of Technology	M,O
Materials Engineering	M
Materials Sciences	M,D
Mechanical Engineering	M,D

DUQUESNE UNIVERSITY

Biotechnology	M

EAST CAROLINA UNIVERSITY

Biomedical Engineering	M
Biotechnology	M
Computer and Information Systems Security	M,D,O
Computer Engineering	M,D,O
Computer Science	M,D,O
Construction Management	M,O
Health Informatics	M,O
Management of Technology	M,D,O
Software Engineering	M
Telecommunications Management	M,D,O

EASTERN ILLINOIS UNIVERSITY

Computer and Information Systems Security	M
Computer Science	M
Energy Management and Policy	M
Engineering and Applied Sciences—General	M,O
Systems Science	M,O

EASTERN KENTUCKY UNIVERSITY

Industrial/Management Engineering	M
Manufacturing Engineering	M

EASTERN MICHIGAN UNIVERSITY

Computer and Information Systems Security	O
Computer Science	M,O
Construction Management	M,O
Engineering and Applied Sciences—General	M
Engineering Management	M
Management of Technology	D
Polymer Science and Engineering	M,O
Technology and Public Policy	M

EASTERN VIRGINIA MEDICAL SCHOOL

Biotechnology	M

EASTERN WASHINGTON UNIVERSITY

Computer Science	M

EAST STROUDSBURG UNIVERSITY OF PENNSYLVANIA

Computer Science	M

EAST TENNESSEE STATE UNIVERSITY

Computer Science	M,O

Information Science	M,O
Manufacturing Engineering	M

EC-COUNCIL UNIVERSITY

Computer and Information Systems Security	M

ÉCOLE POLYTECHNIQUE DE MONTRÉAL

Aerospace/Aeronautical Engineering	M,D,O
Biomedical Engineering	M,D,O
Chemical Engineering	M,D,O
Civil Engineering	M,D,O
Computer Engineering	M,D,O
Computer Science	M,D,O
Electrical Engineering	M,D,O
Engineering and Applied Sciences—General	M,D,O
Engineering Physics	M,D,O
Environmental Engineering	M,D,O
Geotechnical Engineering	M,D,O
Hydraulics	M,D,O
Industrial/Management Engineering	M,D,O
Management of Technology	M,D,O
Mechanical Engineering	M,D,O
Mechanics	M,D,O
Nuclear Engineering	M,D,O
Operations Research	M,D,O
Structural Engineering	M,D,O
Transportation and Highway Engineering	M,D,O

ECPI UNIVERSITY

Computer and Information Systems Security	M

ELIZABETH CITY STATE UNIVERSITY

Computer Science	M

ELMHURST COLLEGE

Data Science/Data Analytics	M

EMBRY-RIDDLE AERONAUTICAL UNIVERSITY–DAYTONA

Aerospace/Aeronautical Engineering	M,D
Aviation	M
Civil Engineering	M
Computer and Information Systems Security	M
Electrical Engineering	M
Engineering Physics	M,D
Ergonomics and Human Factors	M,D
Mechanical Engineering	M,D
Software Engineering	M
Systems Engineering	M

EMBRY-RIDDLE AERONAUTICAL UNIVERSITY–PRESCOTT

Aviation	M
Safety Engineering	M

EMBRY-RIDDLE AERONAUTICAL UNIVERSITY–WORLDWIDE

Aerospace/Aeronautical Engineering	M
Computer and Information Systems Security	M
Engineering Management	M
Management of Technology	M
Systems Engineering	M

EMORY UNIVERSITY

Bioinformatics	M,D
Computer Science	M,D
Health Informatics	M,D

ENDICOTT COLLEGE

Bioinformatics	M
Computer and Information Systems Security	M,O

EVERGLADES UNIVERSITY

Aviation	M

FAIRFIELD UNIVERSITY

Computer and Information Systems Security	M,O
Computer Engineering	M,O
Data Science/Data Analytics	M,O
Electrical Engineering	M,O
Engineering and Applied Sciences—General	M,O
Management of Technology	M,O
Mechanical Engineering	M,O
Software Engineering	M,O
Telecommunications	M,O

FAIRLEIGH DICKINSON UNIVERSITY, FLORHAM CAMPUS

Chemical Engineering	M,O
Computer Science	M
Management of Technology	M,O

FAIRLEIGH DICKINSON UNIVERSITY, METROPOLITAN CAMPUS

Computer Engineering	M
Computer Science	M
Electrical Engineering	M
Engineering and Applied Sciences—General	M
Systems Science	M

FARMINGDALE STATE COLLEGE

Construction Management	M
Electrical Engineering	M
Management of Technology	M
Mechanical Engineering	M

FITCHBURG STATE UNIVERSITY

Computer Science	M
Data Science/Data Analytics	M

FLORIDA AGRICULTURAL AND MECHANICAL UNIVERSITY

Biomedical Engineering	M,D
Chemical Engineering	M,D
Civil Engineering	M,D
Electrical Engineering	M,D
Engineering and Applied Sciences—General	M,D
Industrial/Management Engineering	M,D
Mechanical Engineering	M,D
Software Engineering	

FLORIDA ATLANTIC UNIVERSITY

Bioengineering	M,D
Civil Engineering	M
Computer Engineering	M,D
Computer Science	M,D
Electrical Engineering	M,D
Engineering and Applied Sciences—General	M,D
Environmental Engineering	M
Mechanical Engineering	M,D
Ocean Engineering	M,D

FLORIDA INSTITUTE OF TECHNOLOGY

Aerospace/Aeronautical Engineering	M,D
Aviation	M,D
Biomedical Engineering	M,D
Biotechnology	M,D
Chemical Engineering	M,D

Civil Engineering	M,D
Computer and Information Systems Security	M
Computer Engineering	M,D
Computer Science	M,D
Electrical Engineering	M,D
Engineering and Applied Sciences—General	M,D
Engineering Management	M
Information Science	M
Mechanical Engineering	M,D
Ocean Engineering	M,D
Operations Research	M,D
Software Engineering	M
Systems Engineering	M,D

FLORIDA INTERNATIONAL UNIVERSITY

Biomedical Engineering	M,D
Civil Engineering	M,D
Computer and Information Systems Security	M,D
Computer Engineering	M,D
Computer Science	M,D
Construction Management	M
Data Science/Data Analytics	M,D
Electrical Engineering	M,D
Engineering and Applied Sciences—General	M,D
Engineering Management	M
Environmental Engineering	M,D
Information Science	M,D
Materials Engineering	M,D
Materials Sciences	M,D
Mechanical Engineering	M,D
Telecommunications	M,D

FLORIDA POLYTECHNIC UNIVERSITY

Computer Science	M
Engineering and Applied Sciences—General	M

FLORIDA STATE UNIVERSITY

Biomedical Engineering	M,D
Chemical Engineering	M,D
Civil Engineering	M,D
Computer and Information Systems Security	M,D
Electrical Engineering	M,D
Energy and Power Engineering	M,D
Engineering and Applied Sciences—General	M,D
Environmental Engineering	M,D
Industrial/Management Engineering	M,D
Manufacturing Engineering	M,D
Materials Engineering	M,D
Materials Sciences	M,D
Mechanical Engineering	M,D

FONTBONNE UNIVERSITY

Computer Science	M

FORDHAM UNIVERSITY

Computer Science	M
Data Science/Data Analytics	M

FRANKLIN PIERCE UNIVERSITY

Energy Management and Policy	M,D,O
Telecommunications	M,D,O

FRANKLIN UNIVERSITY

Computer Science	M

FROSTBURG STATE UNIVERSITY

Computer Science	M

FULL SAIL UNIVERSITY

Game Design and Development	M

GANNON UNIVERSITY

Computer Science	M
Electrical Engineering	M
Engineering Management	M
Environmental Engineering	M
Information Science	M
Mechanical Engineering	M
Software Engineering	M

GEORGE MASON UNIVERSITY

Bioengineering	D
Bioinformatics	M,D,O
Civil Engineering	M,D
Computer and Information Systems Security	M
Computer Engineering	M,D,O
Computer Science	M,D,O
Construction Engineering	M,D
Data Science/Data Analytics	M,D,O
Electrical Engineering	M,D,O
Engineering and Applied Sciences—General	M,D,O
Health Informatics	M,D,O
Information Science	M,D,O
Management of Technology	M
Operations Research	M,D,O
Systems Engineering	M,D,O
Transportation and Highway Engineering	M,D

GEORGETOWN UNIVERSITY

Bioinformatics	M,O
Computer Science	M
Management of Technology	M,D
Materials Sciences	D
Systems Engineering	M,D

THE GEORGE WASHINGTON UNIVERSITY

Aerospace/Aeronautical Engineering	M,D,O
Biomedical Engineering	M,D
Biotechnology	M,D,O
Civil Engineering	M,D,O
Computer and Information Systems Security	M,D,O
Computer Engineering	M,D,O
Computer Science	M,D,O
Electrical Engineering	M,D,O
Engineering and Applied Sciences—General	M,D,O
Engineering Management	M,D,O
Environmental Engineering	M,D,O
Management of Technology	M,D
Materials Sciences	M,D
Mechanical Engineering	M,D,O
Systems Engineering	M,D,O
Technology and Public Policy	M,O
Telecommunications	M,D,O

GEORGIA INSTITUTE OF TECHNOLOGY

Aerospace/Aeronautical Engineering	M,D
Artificial Intelligence/Robotics	D
Bioengineering	M,D
Bioinformatics	M,D
Biomedical Engineering	D
Chemical Engineering	M,D
Civil Engineering	M,D
Computer and Information Systems Security	M
Computer Engineering	M,D
Computer Science	M,D
Electrical Engineering	M,D

Engineering and Applied Sciences—General	M,D
Environmental Engineering	M
Ergonomics and Human Factors	M,D
Human-Computer Interaction	M
Industrial/Management Engineering	M,D
Materials Engineering	M,D
Mechanical Engineering	M,D
Mechanics	M
Nuclear Engineering	M,D
Operations Research	M,D
Paper and Pulp Engineering	M,D
Systems Engineering	M

GEORGIA SOUTHERN UNIVERSITY

Civil Engineering	M
Computer and Information Systems Security	M,O
Computer Science	M
Construction Management	M
Electrical Engineering	M
Energy and Power Engineering	M
Engineering and Applied Sciences—General	M,O
Engineering Management	M,O
Manufacturing Engineering	M,O
Mechanical Engineering	M
Systems Engineering	M

GEORGIA SOUTHWESTERN STATE UNIVERSITY

Computer Science	M,O
Health Informatics	M,O

GEORGIA STATE UNIVERSITY

Bioinformatics	M,D
Computer Science	M,D
Health Informatics	M,D,O
Information Science	M,D,O
Operations Research	M,D

GOLDEN GATE UNIVERSITY

Management of Technology	M,D,O

GONZAGA UNIVERSITY

Engineering and Applied Sciences—General	M,O

GOVERNORS STATE UNIVERSITY

Computer Science	M

THE GRADUATE CENTER, CITY UNIVERSITY OF NEW YORK

Computer Science	D
Data Science/Data Analytics	M

GRAND CANYON UNIVERSITY

Data Science/Data Analytics	D
Health Informatics	M,D,O
Management of Technology	M

GRAND VALLEY STATE UNIVERSITY

Bioinformatics	M
Computer Engineering	M
Computer Science	M
Electrical Engineering	M
Engineering and Applied Sciences—General	M
Information Science	M
Manufacturing Engineering	M
Mechanical Engineering	M
Medical Informatics	M
Software Engineering	M

GRANTHAM UNIVERSITY

Engineering and Applied Sciences—General	M

HAMPTON UNIVERSITY

Computer and Information Systems Security	M
Computer Science	M

HARDIN-SIMMONS UNIVERSITY

Information Science	M

HARRISBURG UNIVERSITY OF SCIENCE AND TECHNOLOGY

Computer and Information Systems Security	M
Human-Computer Interaction	M
Management of Technology	M
Software Engineering	M
Systems Engineering	M
Systems Science	M

HARVARD UNIVERSITY

Applied Science and Technology	M,O
Bioengineering	M,D
Biomedical Engineering	D
Biotechnology	M,O
Computer Science	M,D
Electrical Engineering	M,D
Engineering and Applied Sciences—General	M,D
Engineering Design	M,D
Environmental Engineering	M,D
Ergonomics and Human Factors	M,D
Information Science	M,D,O
Management of Technology	D
Materials Sciences	M,D
Mechanical Engineering	M,D

HEC MONTREAL

Data Science/Data Analytics	D
Financial Engineering	M,D
Operations Research	O

HERZING UNIVERSITY ONLINE

Management of Technology	M

HOFSTRA UNIVERSITY

Computer and Information Systems Security	M
Engineering and Applied Sciences—General	M
Health Informatics	M,O

HOOD COLLEGE

Bioinformatics	M,O
Computer and Information Systems Security	M,O
Computer Science	M,O
Information Science	M,O
Systems Science	M

HOWARD UNIVERSITY

Biotechnology	M,D
Chemical Engineering	M
Civil Engineering	M
Computer Science	M
Electrical Engineering	M,D
Engineering and Applied Sciences—General	M,D
Mechanical Engineering	M,D

HUMBOLDT STATE UNIVERSITY

Hazardous Materials Management	M

HUNTER COLLEGE OF THE CITY UNIVERSITY OF NEW YORK

Bioinformatics	M

HUSSON UNIVERSITY

Biotechnology	M

IDAHO STATE UNIVERSITY

Civil Engineering	M
Engineering and Applied Sciences—General	M,D,O
Environmental Engineering	M
Mechanical Engineering	M
Nuclear Engineering	M,D
Operations Research	M

IGLOBAL UNIVERSITY

Data Science/Data Analytics	M

ILLINOIS INSTITUTE OF TECHNOLOGY

Aerospace/Aeronautical Engineering	M,D
Agricultural Engineering	M
Architectural Engineering	M,D
Artificial Intelligence/Robotics	M,D
Bioengineering	M,D
Biomedical Engineering	M,D
Chemical Engineering	M,D
Civil Engineering	M,D
Computer and Information Systems Security	M,D
Computer Engineering	M,D
Computer Science	M,D
Construction Engineering	M,D
Construction Management	M,D
Data Science/Data Analytics	M,D
Electrical Engineering	M,D
Engineering and Applied Sciences—General	M,D
Environmental Engineering	M,D
Geotechnical Engineering	M,D
Manufacturing Engineering	M,D
Materials Engineering	M,D
Materials Sciences	M,D
Mechanical Engineering	M,D
Software Engineering	M,D
Structural Engineering	M,D
Telecommunications	M,D
Transportation and Highway Engineering	M,D

ILLINOIS STATE UNIVERSITY

Biotechnology	M
Industrial/Management Engineering	M
Management of Technology	M

INDIANA STATE UNIVERSITY

Computer Engineering	M
Computer Science	M
Engineering and Applied Sciences—General	M
Management of Technology	M,D

INDIANA TECH

Engineering Management	M

INDIANA UNIVERSITY BLOOMINGTON

Artificial Intelligence/Robotics	D
Bioinformatics	M,D,O
Biotechnology	M,D
Computer and Information Systems Security	M,D
Computer Science	M,D,O
Data Science/Data Analytics	M,O
Energy Management and Policy	M,D,O

M—masters degree; D—doctorate; O—other advanced degree; *—Close-Up and/or Display

Ergonomics and Human
  Factors M,D
Hazardous Materials
  Management M,D,O
Health Informatics M,D
Human-Computer Interaction M,D
Information Science M,D,O
Materials Sciences M,D
Safety Engineering M,D
Systems Engineering D
Water Resources Engineering M,D,O

**INDIANA UNIVERSITY OF
PENNSYLVANIA**
Nanotechnology M

**INDIANA UNIVERSITY–PURDUE
UNIVERSITY INDIANAPOLIS**
Bioinformatics M,D
Biomedical Engineering M,D
Computer and Information
  Systems Security M,D,O
Computer Engineering M,D
Computer Science M,D,O
Data Science/Data Analytics M,D,O
Electrical Engineering M,D
Health Informatics M,D
Human-Computer Interaction M,D
Information Science M
Management of Technology M
Mechanical Engineering M,D
Software Engineering M,D,O

**INDIANA UNIVERSITY SOUTH
BEND**
Computer Science M,O

**THE INSTITUTE OF WORLD
POLITICS**
Computer and Information
  Systems Security M,D,O

**INSTITUTO CENTROAMERICANO
DE ADMINISTRACIÓN DE
EMPRESAS**
Management of Technology M

**INSTITUTO TECNOLOGICO DE
SANTO DOMINGO**
Construction Management M,O
Energy and Power
  Engineering M,D,O
Energy Management and
  Policy M,D,O
Engineering and Applied
  Sciences—General M,O
Environmental Engineering M,O
Industrial/Management
  Engineering M,O
Information Science M,O
Software Engineering M,O
Structural Engineering M,O
Telecommunications M,O

**INSTITUTO TECNOLÓGICO Y DE
ESTUDIOS SUPERIORES DE
MONTERREY, CAMPUS CENTRAL
DE VERACRUZ**
Computer Science M

**INSTITUTO TECNOLÓGICO Y DE
ESTUDIOS SUPERIORES DE
MONTERREY, CAMPUS
CHIHUAHUA**
Computer Engineering M,O
Electrical Engineering M,O
Engineering Management M,O
Industrial/Management
  Engineering M,O
Mechanical Engineering M,O
Systems Engineering M,O

**INSTITUTO TECNOLÓGICO Y DE
ESTUDIOS SUPERIORES DE
MONTERREY, CAMPUS CIUDAD
DE MÉXICO**
Computer Science M,D
Environmental Engineering M,D
Industrial/Management
  Engineering M,D
Telecommunications
  Management M

**INSTITUTO TECNOLÓGICO Y DE
ESTUDIOS SUPERIORES DE
MONTERREY, CAMPUS CIUDAD
OBREGÓN**
Engineering and Applied
  Sciences—General M
Telecommunications
  Management M

**INSTITUTO TECNOLÓGICO Y DE
ESTUDIOS SUPERIORES DE
MONTERREY, CAMPUS
CUERNAVACA**
Computer Science M,D
Information Science M,D
Management of Technology M,D

**INSTITUTO TECNOLÓGICO Y DE
ESTUDIOS SUPERIORES DE
MONTERREY, CAMPUS ESTADO
DE MÉXICO**
Computer Science M,D
Information Science M,D
Materials Engineering M,D
Materials Sciences M,D
Telecommunications
  Management M,D

**INSTITUTO TECNOLÓGICO Y DE
ESTUDIOS SUPERIORES DE
MONTERREY, CAMPUS IRAPUATO**
Computer Science M,D
Information Science M,D
Management of Technology M,D
Telecommunications
  Management M,D

**INSTITUTO TECNOLÓGICO Y DE
ESTUDIOS SUPERIORES DE
MONTERREY, CAMPUS LAGUNA**
Industrial/Management
  Engineering M

**INSTITUTO TECNOLÓGICO Y DE
ESTUDIOS SUPERIORES DE
MONTERREY, CAMPUS
MONTERREY**
Agricultural Engineering M,D
Artificial Intelligence/Robotics M,D
Biotechnology M,D
Chemical Engineering M,D
Civil Engineering M,D
Computer Science M,D
Electrical Engineering M,D
Engineering and Applied
  Sciences—General M,D
Environmental Engineering M,D
Industrial/Management
  Engineering M,D
Information Science M,D
Manufacturing Engineering M,D
Mechanical Engineering M,D
Systems Engineering M,D

**INSTITUTO TECNOLÓGICO Y DE
ESTUDIOS SUPERIORES DE
MONTERREY, CAMPUS SONORA
NORTE**
Information Science M

**INTER AMERICAN UNIVERSITY OF
PUERTO RICO, BARRANQUITAS
CAMPUS**
Biotechnology M

**INTER AMERICAN UNIVERSITY OF
PUERTO RICO, BAYAMÓN
CAMPUS**
Aerospace/Aeronautical
  Engineering M
Biotechnology M
Electrical Engineering M
Energy and Power
  Engineering M
Mechanical Engineering M

**INTER AMERICAN UNIVERSITY OF
PUERTO RICO, FAJARDO
CAMPUS**
Computer Science M

**INTER AMERICAN UNIVERSITY OF
PUERTO RICO, GUAYAMA
CAMPUS**
Computer and Information
  Systems Security M
Computer Science M

**INTER AMERICAN UNIVERSITY OF
PUERTO RICO, METROPOLITAN
CAMPUS**
Computer Science M

**INTERNATIONAL
TECHNOLOGICAL UNIVERSITY**
Computer Engineering M
Electrical Engineering M,D
Engineering Management M
Software Engineering M

**THE INTERNATIONAL UNIVERSITY
OF MONACO**
Financial Engineering M

IONA COLLEGE
Computer and Information
  Systems Security M,O
Computer Science M
Game Design and
  Development M
Management of Technology M,O

**IOWA STATE UNIVERSITY OF
SCIENCE AND TECHNOLOGY**
Aerospace/Aeronautical
  Engineering M,D
Agricultural Engineering M,D
Bioinformatics M,D
Chemical Engineering M,D
Civil Engineering M,D
Computer Engineering M,D
Computer Science M,D
Construction Engineering M,D
Electrical Engineering M,D
Environmental Engineering M,D
Geotechnical Engineering M,D
Human-Computer Interaction M,D
Industrial/Management
  Engineering M,D
Information Science M
Materials Engineering M,D
Materials Sciences M,D
Mechanical Engineering M,D
Mechanics M,D
Operations Research M,D
Structural Engineering M,D
Systems Engineering M
Transportation and Highway
  Engineering M,D

JACKSON STATE UNIVERSITY
Civil Engineering M,D
Computer Science M
Environmental Engineering M,D
Hazardous Materials
  Management M,D
Materials Sciences M,D

**JACKSONVILLE STATE
UNIVERSITY**
Computer Science M
Software Engineering M

JACKSONVILLE UNIVERSITY
Health Informatics M

JAMES MADISON UNIVERSITY
Computer and Information
  Systems Security M
Computer Science M
Engineering and Applied
  Sciences—General M

JOHN F. KENNEDY UNIVERSITY
Management of Technology M

JOHNS HOPKINS UNIVERSITY
Aerospace/Aeronautical
  Engineering M
Artificial Intelligence/Robotics M
Bioengineering M,D
Bioinformatics M
Biomedical Engineering M,D,O
Biotechnology M
Chemical Engineering M,D
Civil Engineering M,D,O
Computer and Information
  Systems Security M,O
Computer Engineering M,D,O
Computer Science M,D,O
Electrical Engineering M,D,O
Energy Management and
  Policy M,O
Engineering and Applied
  Sciences—General M,D,O
Engineering Management M
Environmental Engineering M,D,O
Management of Technology M,O
Materials Engineering M,D
Materials Sciences M,D
Mechanical Engineering M,D,O
Mechanics M
Nanotechnology M
Operations Research M,D
Systems Engineering M,O

JOHNSON & WALES UNIVERSITY
Computer and Information
  Systems Security M
Data Science/Data Analytics M

KANSAS STATE UNIVERSITY
Agricultural Engineering M,D
Applied Science and
  Technology M,O
Architectural Engineering M
Bioengineering M,D
Chemical Engineering M,D,O
Civil Engineering M,D
Computer Engineering M,D
Computer Science M,D
Data Science/Data Analytics M,O
Electrical Engineering M,D
Energy and Power
  Engineering M,D
Energy Management and
  Policy M,D
Engineering and Applied
  Sciences—General M,D,O
Engineering Management M,D
Environmental Engineering M,D
Geotechnical Engineering M,D

Industrial/Management
    Engineering   M,D
Management of Technology   M
Manufacturing Engineering   M,D
Mechanical Engineering   M,D
Nuclear Engineering   M,D
Operations Research   M,D
Structural Engineering   M,D
Transportation and Highway
    Engineering   M,D
Water Resources Engineering   M,D

KEAN UNIVERSITY
Biotechnology   M

KECK GRADUATE INSTITUTE
Data Science/Data Analytics   M

KEISER UNIVERSITY
Computer and Information
    Systems Security   M
Management of Technology   M

KENNESAW STATE UNIVERSITY
Civil Engineering   M
Computer and Information
    Systems Security   M,O
Computer Science   M
Construction Management   M
Data Science/Data Analytics   M,D,O
Electrical Engineering   M
Engineering and Applied
    Sciences—General   M
Engineering Management   M
Environmental Engineering   M
Geotechnical Engineering   M
Health Informatics   M,O
Information Science   M,O
Management of Technology   M
Mechanical Engineering   M
Software Engineering   M,O
Structural Engineering   M
Systems Engineering   M
Transportation and Highway
    Engineering   M
Water Resources Engineering   M

KENT STATE UNIVERSITY
Aerospace/Aeronautical
    Engineering   M
Computer and Information
    Systems Security   M
Computer Science   M,D
Health Informatics   M
Information Science   M

KETTERING UNIVERSITY
Electrical Engineering   M
Engineering Management   M
Manufacturing Engineering   M
Mechanical Engineering   M

KUTZTOWN UNIVERSITY OF PENNSYLVANIA
Computer Science   M

LAKEHEAD UNIVERSITY
Computer Engineering   M
Computer Science   M
Electrical Engineering   M
Engineering and Applied
    Sciences—General   M
Environmental Engineering   M

LAMAR UNIVERSITY
Chemical Engineering   M,D
Computer Science   M
Electrical Engineering   M,D

Engineering and Applied
    Sciences—General   M,D
Mechanical Engineering   M,D

LA SALLE UNIVERSITY
Computer Science   M,O
Management of Technology   M,O

LAURENTIAN UNIVERSITY
Engineering and Applied
    Sciences—General   M,D
Mineral/Mining Engineering   M,D

LAWRENCE TECHNOLOGICAL UNIVERSITY
Architectural Engineering   M,D
Artificial Intelligence/Robotics   M,O
Automotive Engineering   M,D
Bioinformatics   M,O
Biomedical Engineering   M,D
Civil Engineering   M,D
Computer and Information
    Systems Security   M,D,O
Computer Engineering   M,D
Computer Science   M,O
Construction Engineering   M,D
Data Science/Data Analytics   M,O
Electrical Engineering   M,D
Energy and Power
    Engineering   M,D
Engineering and Applied
    Sciences—General   M,D
Engineering Management   M,D
Industrial/Management
    Engineering   M,D
Information Science   M,D,O
Manufacturing Engineering   M,D
Mechanical Engineering   M,D
Water Resources Engineering   M,D

LEBANESE AMERICAN UNIVERSITY
Computer Science   M

LEHIGH UNIVERSITY
Biochemical Engineering   M,D
Bioengineering   M,D
Chemical Engineering   M,D
Civil Engineering   M,D
Computer Engineering   M,D
Computer Science   M,D
Electrical Engineering   M,D
Energy and Power
    Engineering   M
Engineering and Applied
    Sciences—General   M,D,O
Engineering Management   M,D,O
Environmental Engineering   M,D
Industrial/Management
    Engineering   M,D,O
Information Science   M
Materials Engineering   M,D
Materials Sciences   M,D
Mechanical Engineering   M,D
Mechanics   M,D
Polymer Science and
    Engineering   M,D
Systems Engineering   M,D,O

LEHMAN COLLEGE OF THE CITY UNIVERSITY OF NEW YORK
Computer Science   M

LETOURNEAU UNIVERSITY
Engineering and Applied
    Sciences—General   M
Engineering Management   M

LEWIS UNIVERSITY
Aviation   M
Bioinformatics   M
Computer and Information
    Systems Security   M
Computer Science   M
Data Science/Data Analytics   M
Management of Technology   M
Software Engineering   M

LIBERTY UNIVERSITY
Computer and Information
    Systems Security   M,D
Health Informatics   M,D

LINDENWOOD UNIVERSITY
Computer and Information
    Systems Security   M,O

LIPSCOMB UNIVERSITY
Computer and Information
    Systems Security   M,O
Data Science/Data Analytics   M,O
Health Informatics   M,D
Management of Technology   M,O
Software Engineering   M,O

LOGAN UNIVERSITY
Health Informatics   M,D

LONDON METROPOLITAN UNIVERSITY
Computer and Information
    Systems Security   M,D
Data Science/Data Analytics   M,D
Management of Technology   M,D

LONG ISLAND UNIVERSITY–LIU BROOKLYN
Computer Science   M,O

LONG ISLAND UNIVERSITY–LIU POST
Engineering Management   M
Game Design and
    Development   M

LONG ISLAND UNIVERSITY–RIVERHEAD
Computer and Information
    Systems Security   M,O

LOUISIANA STATE UNIVERSITY AND AGRICULTURAL & MECHANICAL COLLEGE
Agricultural Engineering   M,D
Applied Science and
    Technology   M
Bioengineering   M,D
Chemical Engineering   M,D
Civil Engineering   M,D
Computer Engineering   M,D
Computer Science   M,D
Construction Management   M,D
Electrical Engineering   M,D
Engineering and Applied
    Sciences—General   M,D
Environmental Engineering   M,D
Geotechnical Engineering   M,D
Mechanical Engineering   M,D
Mechanics   M,D
Petroleum Engineering   M,D
Structural Engineering   M,D
Systems Science   M,D
Transportation and Highway
    Engineering   M,D
Water Resources Engineering   M,D

LEWIS UNIVERSITY *(see above)*

LOUISIANA STATE UNIVERSITY IN SHREVEPORT
Computer Science   M
Systems Science   M

LOUISIANA TECH UNIVERSITY
Biomedical Engineering   M,D,O
Computer and Information
    Systems Security   M,D
Computer Science   M,D,O
Engineering and Applied
    Sciences—General   M,D,O
Engineering Management   M,D,O
Engineering Physics   M,D,O
Health Informatics   M,D,O
Management of Technology   M,D,O
Materials Sciences   M,D,O
Nanotechnology   M,D,O

LOYOLA MARYMOUNT UNIVERSITY
Civil Engineering   M
Electrical Engineering   M
Engineering Management
Mechanical Engineering   M
Systems Engineering   M

LOYOLA UNIVERSITY CHICAGO
Bioinformatics   M
Computer Science   M
Information Science   M
Software Engineering   M

MAHARISHI UNIVERSITY OF MANAGEMENT
Computer Science   M

MANHATTAN COLLEGE
Chemical Engineering   M
Civil Engineering   M
Computer Engineering   M
Construction Management   M
Data Science/Data Analytics   M
Electrical Engineering   M
Engineering and Applied
    Sciences—General   M
Environmental Engineering   M
Mechanical Engineering   M

MARIST COLLEGE
Computer Science   M,O
Software Engineering   M,O

MARQUETTE UNIVERSITY
Bioinformatics   M,D
Biomedical Engineering   M,D
Civil Engineering   M,D,O
Computer Engineering   M,D,O
Computer Science   M,D
Construction Engineering   M,D,O
Construction Management   M,D,O
Electrical Engineering   M,D,O
Engineering and Applied
    Sciences—General   M,D,O
Engineering Management   M
Environmental Engineering   M,D,O
Hazardous Materials
    Management   M,D,O
Management of Technology   M,D
Mechanical Engineering   M,D,O
Structural Engineering   M,D,O
Transportation and Highway
    Engineering   M,D,O
Water Resources Engineering   M,D,O

MARSHALL UNIVERSITY
Computer Engineering   M
Computer Science   M
Electrical Engineering   M

*M—masters degree; D—doctorate; O—other advanced degree; *—Close-Up and/or Display*

Engineering and Applied
   Sciences—General — M,O
Engineering Management — M
Environmental Engineering — M
Health Informatics — M
Information Science — M
Management of Technology — M,O
Mechanical Engineering — M
Transportation and Highway
   Engineering — M

MARYMOUNT UNIVERSITY
Computer and Information
   Systems Security — M,D,O
Health Informatics — M,O
Software Engineering — M,O

MARYVILLE UNIVERSITY OF SAINT LOUIS
Computer and Information
   Systems Security — M,O
Data Science/Data Analytics — M
Information Science — M,O

MARYWOOD UNIVERSITY
Biotechnology — M
Computer and Information
   Systems Security — M

MASSACHUSETTS INSTITUTE OF TECHNOLOGY
Aerospace/Aeronautical
   Engineering — M,D,O
Bioengineering — M,D
Bioinformatics — M,D
Biomedical Engineering — M,D
Chemical Engineering — M,D
Civil Engineering — M,D,O
Computer Engineering — M,D,O
Computer Science — M,D,O
Construction Engineering — M,D,O
Electrical Engineering — M,D,O
Engineering and Applied
   Sciences—General — M,D,O
Engineering Management — M
Environmental Engineering — M,D,O
Geotechnical Engineering — M,D,O
Information Science — M,D,O
Manufacturing Engineering — M,D,O
Materials Engineering — M,D,O
Materials Sciences — M,D,O
Mechanical Engineering — M,D,O
Nuclear Engineering — M,D,O
Ocean Engineering — M,D,O
Operations Research — M,D
Structural Engineering — M,D,O
Systems Engineering — M,D
Technology and Public Policy — M,D
Transportation and Highway
   Engineering — M,D,O

MAYO CLINIC GRADUATE SCHOOL OF BIOMEDICAL SCIENCES
Biomedical Engineering — M,D

MCGILL UNIVERSITY
Aerospace/Aeronautical
   Engineering — M,D
Agricultural Engineering — M,D
Bioengineering — M,D
Bioinformatics — M,D
Biomedical Engineering — M,D
Biotechnology — M,D,O
Chemical Engineering — M,D
Civil Engineering — M,D
Computer Engineering — M,D
Computer Science — M,D
Electrical Engineering — M,D
Engineering and Applied
   Sciences—General — M,D,O
Environmental Engineering — M,D

Geotechnical Engineering — M,D
Hydraulics — M,D
Materials Engineering — M,D,O
Mechanical Engineering — M,D
Mechanics — M,D
Mineral/Mining Engineering — M,D,O
Structural Engineering — M,D
Water Resources Engineering — M,D

MCMASTER UNIVERSITY
Chemical Engineering — M,D
Civil Engineering — M,D
Computer Science — M,D
Electrical Engineering — M,D
Engineering and Applied
   Sciences—General — M,D
Engineering Physics — M,D
Materials Engineering — M,D
Materials Sciences — M,D
Mechanical Engineering — M,D
Nuclear Engineering — M,D
Software Engineering — M,D

MCNEESE STATE UNIVERSITY
Chemical Engineering — M
Civil Engineering — M
Computer Science — M
Electrical Engineering — M
Engineering and Applied
   Sciences—General — M
Engineering Management — M
Mechanical Engineering — M

MEMORIAL UNIVERSITY OF NEWFOUNDLAND
Civil Engineering — M,D
Computer Engineering — M,D
Computer Science — M,D
Electrical Engineering — M,D
Engineering and Applied
   Sciences—General — M,D
Environmental Engineering — M
Mechanical Engineering — M,D
Ocean Engineering — M,D

MERCER UNIVERSITY
Biomedical Engineering — M
Computer Engineering — M
Electrical Engineering — M
Engineering and Applied
   Sciences—General — M
Engineering Management — M
Environmental Engineering — M
Health Informatics — M,D
Management of Technology — M
Mechanical Engineering — M
Software Engineering — M

MERCY COLLEGE
Computer and Information
   Systems Security — M

MERCYHURST UNIVERSITY
Computer and Information
   Systems Security — M

MERRIMACK COLLEGE
Civil Engineering — M
Computer Science — M
Data Science/Data Analytics — M
Engineering and Applied
   Sciences—General — M
Engineering Management — M
Mechanical Engineering — M

METROPOLITAN STATE UNIVERSITY
Computer and Information
   Systems Security — M,D,O
Computer Science — M
Data Science/Data Analytics — M,D,O

MIAMI UNIVERSITY
Chemical Engineering — M
Computer Engineering — M
Electrical Engineering — M
Engineering and Applied
   Sciences—General — M
Mechanical Engineering — M
Systems Science — M

MICHIGAN STATE UNIVERSITY
Biosystems Engineering — M,D
Chemical Engineering — M,D
Civil Engineering — M,D
Computer Science — M,D
Construction Management — M,D
Electrical Engineering — M,D
Engineering and Applied
   Sciences—General — M,D
Environmental Engineering — M,D
Game Design and
   Development — M
Manufacturing Engineering — M,D
Materials Engineering — M,D
Materials Sciences — M,D
Mechanical Engineering — M,D
Mechanics — M,D

MICHIGAN TECHNOLOGICAL UNIVERSITY
Biomedical Engineering — M,D
Chemical Engineering — M,D
Civil Engineering — M,D
Computer Engineering — M,D,O
Data Science/Data Analytics — M,D,O
Electrical Engineering — M,D,O
Engineering and Applied
   Sciences—General — M,D,O
Environmental Engineering — M,D
Ergonomics and Human
   Factors — M,D,O
Materials Engineering — M,D
Mechanical Engineering — M,D,O
Mechanics — M,D,O
Metallurgical Engineering and
   Metallurgy — M,D

MIDDLE GEORGIA STATE UNIVERSITY
Computer and Information
   Systems Security — M
Health Informatics — M

MIDDLE TENNESSEE STATE UNIVERSITY
Aerospace/Aeronautical
   Engineering — M
Biotechnology — M
Computer Science — M
Engineering Management — M
Medical Informatics — M

MIDWESTERN STATE UNIVERSITY
Computer Science — M
Health Informatics — M,O

MILLENNIA ATLANTIC UNIVERSITY
Health Informatics — M

MILLS COLLEGE
Computer Science — M,O

MILWAUKEE SCHOOL OF ENGINEERING
Architectural Engineering — M
Civil Engineering — M
Engineering and Applied
   Sciences—General — M
Engineering Management — M

MINNESOTA STATE UNIVERSITY MANKATO
Automotive Engineering — M
Computer Science — M,O
Information Science — M,O
Manufacturing Engineering — M

MISSISSIPPI COLLEGE
Computer and Information
   Systems Security — M
Computer Science — M

MISSISSIPPI STATE UNIVERSITY
Aerospace/Aeronautical
   Engineering — M,D
Bioengineering — M,D
Biomedical Engineering — M,D
Chemical Engineering — M,D
Civil Engineering — M,D
Computer Engineering — M,D
Computer Science — M,D
Electrical Engineering — M,D
Engineering and Applied
   Sciences—General — M,D
Ergonomics and Human
   Factors — M,D
Industrial/Management
   Engineering — M,D
Mechanical Engineering — M,D
Operations Research — M,D
Systems Engineering — M,D

MISSOURI STATE UNIVERSITY
Applied Science and
   Technology — M,O
Computer Science — M
Construction Management — M
Materials Sciences — M

MISSOURI UNIVERSITY OF SCIENCE AND TECHNOLOGY
Aerospace/Aeronautical
   Engineering — M,D
Ceramic Sciences and
   Engineering — M,D
Chemical Engineering — M,D
Civil Engineering — M,D
Computer Engineering — M,D
Computer Science — M,D
Electrical Engineering — M,D
Engineering Management — M,D
Environmental Engineering — M,D
Geological Engineering — M,D
Geotechnical Engineering — M
Information Science — M
Manufacturing Engineering — M,D
Materials Engineering — M,D
Materials Sciences — M,D
Mechanical Engineering — M,D
Metallurgical Engineering and
   Metallurgy — M,D
Mineral/Mining Engineering — M,D
Nuclear Engineering — M,D
Petroleum Engineering — M,D
Systems Engineering — M,D

MISSOURI WESTERN STATE UNIVERSITY
Computer and Information
   Systems Security — M
Engineering and Applied
   Sciences—General — M

MONMOUTH UNIVERSITY
Computer Science — M
Software Engineering — M,O

MONROE COLLEGE
Computer Science — M
Information Science — M

MONTANA STATE UNIVERSITY
Chemical Engineering	M,D
Civil Engineering	M,D
Computer Engineering	M,D
Computer Science	M,D
Construction Engineering	M,D
Electrical Engineering	M,D
Engineering and Applied Sciences—General	M,D
Environmental Engineering	M,D
Industrial/Management Engineering	M,D
Mechanical Engineering	M,D
Mechanics	M,D

MONTANA TECH OF THE UNIVERSITY OF MONTANA
Electrical Engineering	M
Engineering and Applied Sciences—General	M
Environmental Engineering	M
Geological Engineering	M
Health Informatics	O
Industrial/Management Engineering	M
Materials Sciences	D
Metallurgical Engineering and Metallurgy	M
Mineral/Mining Engineering	M
Petroleum Engineering	M

MONTCLAIR STATE UNIVERSITY
Computer Science	M,O
Data Science/Data Analytics	O
Management of Technology	M

MORGAN STATE UNIVERSITY
Bioinformatics	M
Civil Engineering	M,D,O
Computer Science	M
Electrical Engineering	M,D,O
Engineering and Applied Sciences—General	M,D,O
Industrial/Management Engineering	M,D,O
Transportation and Highway Engineering	M,D,O

MOUNT ST. MARY'S UNIVERSITY (MD)
Biotechnology	M

MURRAY STATE UNIVERSITY
Computer Science	M
Safety Engineering	M
Telecommunications Management	M

NATIONAL TEST PILOT SCHOOL
Aviation	M

NATIONAL UNIVERSITY
Computer and Information Systems Security	M
Computer Science	M
Data Science/Data Analytics	M
Electrical Engineering	M
Engineering and Applied Sciences—General	M
Engineering Management	M
Health Informatics	M,O
Management of Technology	M

NAVAL POSTGRADUATE SCHOOL
Aerospace/Aeronautical Engineering	M,D,O
Applied Science and Technology	M,D

Computer and Information Systems Security	M,D
Computer Engineering	M,D,O
Computer Science	M,D,O
Electrical Engineering	M,D,O
Engineering Management	M,D,O
Information Science	M,D,O
Mechanical Engineering	M,D,O
Modeling and Simulation	M,D
Operations Research	M,D
Software Engineering	M,D
Systems Engineering	M,D,O

NEW COLLEGE OF FLORIDA
Data Science/Data Analytics	M

NEW ENGLAND INSTITUTE OF TECHNOLOGY
Construction Management	M
Engineering Management	M

NEW JERSEY CITY UNIVERSITY
Computer and Information Systems Security	M,D,O

NEW JERSEY INSTITUTE OF TECHNOLOGY
Biomedical Engineering	M,D
Chemical Engineering	M,D
Computer and Information Systems Security	M,D,O
Computer Engineering	M,D
Computer Science	M,D,O
Data Science/Data Analytics	M,D,O
Electrical Engineering	M,D
Energy and Power Engineering	M,D
Engineering and Applied Sciences—General	M,D
Engineering Management	M,D
Environmental Engineering	M,D
Industrial/Management Engineering	M,D
Information Science	M,D,O
Internet Engineering	M,D
Management of Technology	M,D,O
Manufacturing Engineering	M,D
Materials Engineering	M,D,O
Materials Sciences	M,D,O
Mechanical Engineering	M,D
Pharmaceutical Engineering	M,D
Safety Engineering	M,D
Software Engineering	M,D,O
Telecommunications	M,D
Transportation and Highway Engineering	M,D

NEW MEXICO HIGHLANDS UNIVERSITY
Computer Science	M

NEW MEXICO INSTITUTE OF MINING AND TECHNOLOGY
Computer Science	M,D
Electrical Engineering	M
Engineering Management	M
Environmental Engineering	M
Geological Engineering	M
Hazardous Materials Management	M
Materials Engineering	M,D
Mechanical Engineering	M
Mechanics	M
Mineral/Mining Engineering	M,D
Operations Research	M,D
Petroleum Engineering	M,D
Systems Engineering	M
Water Resources Engineering	M

NEW MEXICO STATE UNIVERSITY
Bioinformatics	M,D
Biotechnology	M,D
Engineering and Applied Sciences—General	M,D,O
Environmental Engineering	M,D
Systems Engineering	M,D,O

THE NEW SCHOOL
Data Science/Data Analytics	M

NEWSCHOOL OF ARCHITECTURE AND DESIGN
Construction Management	M

NEW YORK INSTITUTE OF TECHNOLOGY
Bioengineering	M
Computer and Information Systems Security	M
Computer Engineering	M
Computer Science	M
Electrical Engineering	M
Energy and Power Engineering	O
Energy Management and Policy	O
Engineering and Applied Sciences—General	M,O
Environmental Engineering	M
Mechanical Engineering	M

NEW YORK UNIVERSITY
Artificial Intelligence/Robotics	M,D
Bioinformatics	M,D,O
Civil Engineering	M,D
Computer and Information Systems Security	M
Computer Engineering	M,D
Computer Science	M,D,O
Construction Management	M
Data Science/Data Analytics	M
Electrical Engineering	M,D
Engineering and Applied Sciences—General	M,D,O
Game Design and Development	M
Manufacturing Engineering	M,D
Mechanical Engineering	M,D
Software Engineering	O
Transportation and Highway Engineering	M,D

NIAGARA UNIVERSITY
Computer and Information Systems Security	M

NORFOLK STATE UNIVERSITY
Computer Engineering	M
Computer Science	M
Electrical Engineering	M
Materials Sciences	M

NORTH CAROLINA AGRICULTURAL AND TECHNICAL STATE UNIVERSITY
Bioengineering	M
Chemical Engineering	M
Civil Engineering	M
Computer Engineering	M,D
Computer Science	M,D
Electrical Engineering	M,D
Energy and Power Engineering	M,D
Engineering and Applied Sciences—General	M,D
Industrial/Management Engineering	M,D
Mechanical Engineering	M,D

NORTH CAROLINA STATE UNIVERSITY
Aerospace/Aeronautical Engineering	M,D
Agricultural Engineering	M,D,O
Bioengineering	M,D,O
Chemical Engineering	M,D
Civil Engineering	M,D
Computer Engineering	M,D
Computer Science	M,D
Electrical Engineering	M,D
Engineering and Applied Sciences—General	M,D
Ergonomics and Human Factors	D
Financial Engineering	M
Industrial/Management Engineering	M,D
Management of Technology	M,D
Manufacturing Engineering	M
Materials Engineering	M,D
Materials Sciences	M,D
Mechanical Engineering	M,D
Nuclear Engineering	M,D
Operations Research	M,D
Polymer Science and Engineering	M,D
Textile Sciences and Engineering	M,D

NORTH CENTRAL COLLEGE
Computer Science	M

NORTHCENTRAL UNIVERSITY
Computer and Information Systems Security	M,D,O
Computer Science	M,D,O
Data Science/Data Analytics	M,D,O

NORTH DAKOTA STATE UNIVERSITY
Agricultural Engineering	M,D
Bioinformatics	M,D
Biosystems Engineering	M,D
Civil Engineering	M,D
Computer Engineering	M,D
Computer Science	M,D,O
Construction Management	M,O
Electrical Engineering	M,D
Engineering and Applied Sciences—General	M,D,O
Environmental Engineering	M,D
Industrial/Management Engineering	M,D
Manufacturing Engineering	M,D
Materials Sciences	M,D
Mechanical Engineering	M,D
Nanotechnology	M,D
Polymer Science and Engineering	M,D
Software Engineering	M,D,O
Transportation and Highway Engineering	D

NORTHEASTERN ILLINOIS UNIVERSITY
Computer Science	M

NORTHEASTERN UNIVERSITY
Bioengineering	M,D,O
Bioinformatics	M,D
Biotechnology	M,D
Chemical Engineering	M,D,O
Civil Engineering	M,D,O
Computer and Information Systems Security	M,D,O
Computer Engineering	M,D,O
Computer Science	M,D

Data Science/Data Analytics	M,D
Electrical Engineering	M,D,O
Energy and Power Engineering	M,D,O
Engineering and Applied Sciences—General	M,D,O
Engineering Management	M,D,O
Environmental Engineering	M,D,O
Health Informatics	M,D
Industrial/Management Engineering	M,D,O
Mechanical Engineering	M,D,O
Operations Research	M,D,O
Systems Engineering	M,D,O
Telecommunications	M,D,O

NORTHERN ARIZONA UNIVERSITY

Bioengineering	M,D
Civil Engineering	M
Computer Engineering	M,D
Computer Science	M,D
Electrical Engineering	M,D
Engineering and Applied Sciences—General	M,D,O
Mechanical Engineering	M,D

NORTHERN ILLINOIS UNIVERSITY

Computer Science	M
Electrical Engineering	M
Engineering and Applied Sciences—General	M
Industrial/Management Engineering	M
Mechanical Engineering	M

NORTHERN KENTUCKY UNIVERSITY

Computer and Information Systems Security	M,O
Computer Science	M,O
Health Informatics	M,O
Information Science	M,O
Management of Technology	M
Software Engineering	M,O

NORTHWESTERN POLYTECHNIC UNIVERSITY

Computer Engineering	M,D
Computer Science	M,D
Electrical Engineering	M,D
Engineering and Applied Sciences—General	M,D

NORTHWESTERN UNIVERSITY

Artificial Intelligence/Robotics	M
Bioengineering	D
Biomedical Engineering	M,D
Biotechnology	M,D
Chemical Engineering	M,D
Civil Engineering	M,D
Computer and Information Systems Security	M
Computer Engineering	M,D
Computer Science	M,D
Data Science/Data Analytics	M
Electrical Engineering	M,D
Engineering and Applied Sciences—General	M,D,O
Engineering Design	M
Engineering Management	M
Environmental Engineering	M,D
Geotechnical Engineering	M,D
Health Informatics	M,D
Industrial/Management Engineering	M,D
Information Science	M
Materials Engineering	M,D,O
Materials Sciences	M,D,O
Mechanical Engineering	M,D
Mechanics	M,D
Medical Informatics	M,D
Software Engineering	M
Structural Engineering	M,D

Transportation and Highway Engineering	M,D

NORTHWEST MISSOURI STATE UNIVERSITY

Computer Science	M

NORWICH UNIVERSITY

Civil Engineering	M
Computer and Information Systems Security	M
Construction Management	M
Energy Management and Policy	M
Environmental Engineering	M
Geotechnical Engineering	M
Structural Engineering	M

NOTRE DAME COLLEGE (OH)

Computer Science	M,O

NOVA SOUTHEASTERN UNIVERSITY

Bioinformatics	M,D,O
Computer and Information Systems Security	M,D
Computer Science	M,D
Health Informatics	M,D,O
Information Science	M,D
Medical Informatics	M,D,O

OAKLAND UNIVERSITY

Computer Engineering	M,D
Computer Science	M,D
Electrical Engineering	M,D
Engineering and Applied Sciences—General	M,D,O
Engineering Management	M
Mechanical Engineering	M,D
Software Engineering	M,D
Systems Engineering	M,D
Systems Science	M,D

OHIO DOMINICAN UNIVERSITY

Data Science/Data Analytics	M
Engineering Design	M

THE OHIO STATE UNIVERSITY

Aerospace/Aeronautical Engineering	M,D
Agricultural Engineering	M,D
Bioengineering	M,D
Biomedical Engineering	M,D
Chemical Engineering	M,D
Civil Engineering	M,D
Computer Engineering	M,D
Computer Science	M,D
Electrical Engineering	M,D
Engineering and Applied Sciences—General	M,D
Industrial/Management Engineering	M,D
Materials Engineering	M,D
Materials Sciences	M,D
Mechanical Engineering	M,D
Metallurgical Engineering and Metallurgy	M,D
Nuclear Engineering	M,D
Operations Research	M
Systems Engineering	M,D

OHIO UNIVERSITY

Biomedical Engineering	M
Chemical Engineering	M,D
Civil Engineering	M,D
Computer Science	M,D
Construction Engineering	M,D
Electrical Engineering	M,D
Engineering and Applied Sciences—General	M,D
Environmental Engineering	M,D

Geotechnical Engineering	M,D
Industrial/Management Engineering	M
Mechanical Engineering	M
Mechanics	M,D
Structural Engineering	M,D
Systems Engineering	M
Telecommunications	M,D
Transportation and Highway Engineering	M,D
Water Resources Engineering	M,D

OKLAHOMA BAPTIST UNIVERSITY

Energy Management and Policy	M

OKLAHOMA CHRISTIAN UNIVERSITY

Computer Engineering	M
Computer Science	M
Electrical Engineering	M
Engineering and Applied Sciences—General	M
Engineering Management	M
Mechanical Engineering	M
Software Engineering	M

OKLAHOMA CITY UNIVERSITY

Computer Science	M
Energy Management and Policy	M

OKLAHOMA STATE UNIVERSITY

Agricultural Engineering	M,D
Aviation	M,D,O
Bioengineering	M,D
Chemical Engineering	M,D
Civil Engineering	M,D
Computer Engineering	M,D
Computer Science	M,D
Electrical Engineering	M,D
Engineering and Applied Sciences—General	M,D
Environmental Engineering	M,D
Fire Protection Engineering	M,D
Industrial/Management Engineering	M,D
Information Science	M,D
Materials Engineering	M,D
Materials Sciences	M,D
Mechanical Engineering	M,D
Telecommunications Management	M,D,O

OLD DOMINION UNIVERSITY

Aerospace/Aeronautical Engineering	M,D
Biomedical Engineering	M,D
Civil Engineering	M,D
Computer Engineering	M,D
Computer Science	M,D
Electrical Engineering	M,D
Engineering and Applied Sciences—General	M,D
Engineering Management	M,D
Environmental Engineering	M,D
Ergonomics and Human Factors	D
Geotechnical Engineering	M
Hydraulics	M
Information Science	D
Mechanical Engineering	M,D
Modeling and Simulation	M,D
Structural Engineering	M
Systems Engineering	M,D
Transportation and Highway Engineering	M

OPEN UNIVERSITY

Engineering and Applied Sciences—General	M

OREGON HEALTH & SCIENCE UNIVERSITY

Bioinformatics	M,D,O
Biomedical Engineering	M,D
Computer Engineering	M,D
Computer Science	M,D
Electrical Engineering	M,D
Environmental Engineering	M,D
Health Informatics	M,D,O
Medical Informatics	M,D,O

OREGON INSTITUTE OF TECHNOLOGY

Manufacturing Engineering	M

OREGON STATE UNIVERSITY

Agricultural Engineering	M,D
Artificial Intelligence/Robotics	M,D
Bioengineering	M,D
Bioinformatics	D
Biotechnology	M,D
Chemical Engineering	M,D
Civil Engineering	M,D
Computer Engineering	M,D
Computer Science	M,D
Construction Engineering	M,D
Data Science/Data Analytics	M
Electrical Engineering	M,D
Engineering and Applied Sciences—General	M,D
Engineering Management	M,D
Environmental Engineering	M,D
Geotechnical Engineering	M,D
Industrial/Management Engineering	M,D
Manufacturing Engineering	M,D
Materials Sciences	M,D
Mechanical Engineering	M,D
Nuclear Engineering	M,D
Ocean Engineering	M,D
Structural Engineering	M,D
Systems Engineering	M,D
Transportation and Highway Engineering	M,D
Water Resources Engineering	M,D

OUR LADY OF THE LAKE UNIVERSITY

Computer and Information Systems Security	M

PACE UNIVERSITY

Computer and Information Systems Security	M,D,O
Computer Science	M,D,O
Information Science	M,D,O
Software Engineering	M,D,O
Telecommunications	M,D,O

PACIFIC STATES UNIVERSITY

Computer Science	M
Management of Technology	M,O

PENN STATE GREAT VALLEY

Computer and Information Systems Security	M,O
Data Science/Data Analytics	M,O
Engineering and Applied Sciences—General	M,O
Engineering Management	M,O
Information Science	M,O
Software Engineering	M,O
Systems Engineering	M,O

PENN STATE HARRISBURG

Civil Engineering	M,O
Computer Science	M,O
Electrical Engineering	M,O
Engineering and Applied Sciences—General	M,O
Engineering Management	M,O
Environmental Engineering	M,O

Mechanical Engineering — M,O
Structural Engineering — M,O

PENN STATE HERSHEY MEDICAL CENTER
Bioinformatics — M,D

PENN STATE UNIVERSITY PARK
Aerospace/Aeronautical Engineering — M,D
Agricultural Engineering — M,D
Architectural Engineering — M,D
Bioengineering — M,D
Biotechnology — M,D
Chemical Engineering — M,D
Civil Engineering — M,D
Computer Engineering — M,D
Computer Science — M,D*
Electrical Engineering — M,D
Engineering and Applied Sciences—General — M,D
Engineering Design — M
Environmental Engineering — M,D
Geotechnical Engineering — M,D
Industrial/Management Engineering — M,D
Information Science — M,D
Materials Engineering — M,D
Materials Sciences — M,D
Mechanical Engineering — M,D
Mechanics — M,D
Mineral/Mining Engineering — M,D
Nuclear Engineering — M,D

PITTSBURG STATE UNIVERSITY
Construction Engineering — M
Construction Management — M,O
Electrical Engineering — M
Management of Technology — M,O
Manufacturing Engineering — M
Mechanical Engineering — M
Polymer Science and Engineering — M

POINT PARK UNIVERSITY
Engineering Management — M

POLYTECHNIC UNIVERSITY OF PUERTO RICO
Civil Engineering — M
Computer Engineering — M
Computer Science — M
Electrical Engineering — M
Engineering Management — M
Management of Technology — M
Manufacturing Engineering — M
Mechanical Engineering — M

POLYTECHNIC UNIVERSITY OF PUERTO RICO, MIAMI CAMPUS
Construction Management — M
Environmental Engineering — M

POLYTECHNIC UNIVERSITY OF PUERTO RICO, ORLANDO CAMPUS
Construction Management — M
Engineering Management — M
Environmental Engineering — M
Management of Technology — M

PONTIFICAL JOHN PAUL II INSTITUTE FOR STUDIES ON MARRIAGE AND FAMILY
Biotechnology — M,D,O

PONTIFICIA UNIVERSIDAD CATOLICA MADRE Y MAESTRA
Engineering and Applied Sciences—General — M
Structural Engineering — M

PORTLAND STATE UNIVERSITY
Artificial Intelligence/Robotics — M,D,O
Civil Engineering — M,D,O
Computer and Information Systems Security — M,D,O
Computer Engineering — M,D
Computer Science — M,D,O
Electrical Engineering — M,D
Energy Management and Policy — M,D,O
Engineering and Applied Sciences—General — M,D,O
Engineering Management — M,D,O
Environmental Engineering — M,D
Management of Technology — M,D
Materials Engineering — M,D
Mechanical Engineering — M,D,O
Modeling and Simulation — M,D,O
Systems Science — M,D,O

PRAIRIE VIEW A&M UNIVERSITY
Computer Science — M,D
Electrical Engineering — M,D
Engineering and Applied Sciences—General — M,D

PRINCETON UNIVERSITY
Aerospace/Aeronautical Engineering — M,D
Bioengineering — M,D
Chemical Engineering — M,D
Civil Engineering — M,D
Computer Science — M,D
Electrical Engineering — M,D
Electronic Materials — D
Engineering and Applied Sciences—General — M,D
Environmental Engineering — M,D
Financial Engineering — M,D
Materials Sciences — D
Mechanical Engineering — M,D
Ocean Engineering — D
Operations Research — M,D

PURDUE UNIVERSITY
Aerospace/Aeronautical Engineering — M,D
Agricultural Engineering — M,D
Biomedical Engineering — M,D
Biotechnology — D
Chemical Engineering — M,D
Civil Engineering — M,D
Computer and Information Systems Security — M
Computer Engineering — M,D
Computer Science — M,D
Construction Management — M
Electrical Engineering — M,D
Engineering and Applied Sciences—General — M,D,O
Environmental Engineering — M,D
Ergonomics and Human Factors — M,D
Industrial/Management Engineering — M,D
Management of Technology — M,D
Materials Engineering — M,D
Mechanical Engineering — M,D,O
Nuclear Engineering — M,D

PURDUE UNIVERSITY FORT WAYNE
Civil Engineering — M
Computer Engineering — M

Computer Science — M
Construction Management — M
Electrical Engineering — M
Engineering and Applied Sciences—General — M,O
Industrial/Management Engineering — M
Information Science — M
Mechanical Engineering — M
Operations Research — M,O
Systems Engineering — M

PURDUE UNIVERSITY GLOBAL
Computer and Information Systems Security — M

PURDUE UNIVERSITY NORTHWEST
Biotechnology — M
Computer Engineering — M
Computer Science — M
Electrical Engineering — M
Engineering and Applied Sciences—General — M
Mechanical Engineering — M

QUEENS COLLEGE OF THE CITY UNIVERSITY OF NEW YORK
Computer Science — M
Data Science/Data Analytics — M

QUEEN'S UNIVERSITY AT KINGSTON
Artificial Intelligence/Robotics — M
Chemical Engineering — M,D
Civil Engineering — M,D
Computer Engineering — M,D
Computer Science — M,D
Electrical Engineering — M,D
Engineering and Applied Sciences—General — M,D
Engineering Physics — M,D
Ergonomics and Human Factors — M,D
Materials Engineering — M,D
Mechanical Engineering — M,D
Mineral/Mining Engineering — M,D

QUINNIPIAC UNIVERSITY
Computer and Information Systems Security — M

RADFORD UNIVERSITY
Data Science/Data Analytics — M

REGENT UNIVERSITY
Computer and Information Systems Security — M

REGIS UNIVERSITY
Computer and Information Systems Security — M,O
Computer Science — M,O
Data Science/Data Analytics — M,O
Health Informatics — M,O
Information Science — M,O
Medical Informatics — M,O
Software Engineering — M,O
Systems Engineering — M,O

RENSSELAER AT HARTFORD
Computer Engineering — M
Computer Science — M
Electrical Engineering — M
Engineering and Applied Sciences—General — M
Information Science — M
Mechanical Engineering — M

Systems Science — M

RENSSELAER POLYTECHNIC INSTITUTE
Aerospace/Aeronautical Engineering — M,D
Biomedical Engineering — M,D
Chemical Engineering — M,D
Civil Engineering — M,D
Computer Engineering — M,D
Computer Science — M,D
Electrical Engineering — M,D
Engineering and Applied Sciences—General — M,D
Engineering Physics — M,D
Environmental Engineering — M,D
Financial Engineering — M
Industrial/Management Engineering — M,D
Information Science — M
Materials Engineering — M,D
Mechanical Engineering — M,D
Nuclear Engineering — M,D
Systems Engineering — M,D
Technology and Public Policy — M,D
Transportation and Highway Engineering — M,D

RICE UNIVERSITY
Bioengineering — M,D
Bioinformatics — M,D
Biomedical Engineering — M,D
Chemical Engineering — M,D
Civil Engineering — M,D
Computer Engineering — M,D
Computer Science — M,D
Electrical Engineering — M,D
Energy Management and Policy — M,D
Engineering and Applied Sciences—General — M,D
Environmental Engineering — M,D
Materials Sciences — M,D
Mechanical Engineering — M,D

RIVIER UNIVERSITY
Computer Science — M

ROBERT MORRIS UNIVERSITY
Computer and Information Systems Security — M,D
Data Science/Data Analytics — M,D
Engineering and Applied Sciences—General — M
Engineering Management — M
Information Science — M,D

ROBERT MORRIS UNIVERSITY ILLINOIS
Computer and Information Systems Security — M

ROBERTS WESLEYAN COLLEGE
Health Informatics — M

ROCHESTER INSTITUTE OF TECHNOLOGY
Bioinformatics — M
Computer and Information Systems Security — M,O
Computer Engineering — M
Computer Science — M,D
Data Science/Data Analytics — O
Electrical Engineering — M
Engineering and Applied Sciences—General — M,D,O
Engineering Design — M
Engineering Management — M

*M—masters degree; D—doctorate; O—other advanced degree; *—Close-Up and/or Display*

Game Design and Development	M
Health Informatics	M
Human-Computer Interaction	M
Industrial/Management Engineering	M
Information Science	M,D
Manufacturing Engineering	M
Materials Engineering	M
Materials Sciences	M
Mechanical Engineering	M
Modeling and Simulation	D
Safety Engineering	M
Software Engineering	M
Systems Engineering	M,D
Technology and Public Policy	M
Telecommunications	M

ROCKHURST UNIVERSITY

Data Science/Data Analytics	M,O

ROGER WILLIAMS UNIVERSITY

Computer and Information Systems Security	M

ROOSEVELT UNIVERSITY

Biotechnology	M
Computer Science	M

ROSE-HULMAN INSTITUTE OF TECHNOLOGY

Biomedical Engineering	M
Chemical Engineering	M
Civil Engineering	M
Computer Engineering	M
Electrical Engineering	M
Engineering and Applied Sciences—General	M
Engineering Management	M
Environmental Engineering	M
Mechanical Engineering	M
Systems Engineering	M

ROWAN UNIVERSITY

Bioinformatics	M
Chemical Engineering	M
Civil Engineering	M
Computer and Information Systems Security	O
Computer Science	M
Electrical Engineering	M
Engineering and Applied Sciences—General	M
Mechanical Engineering	M

ROYAL MILITARY COLLEGE OF CANADA

Chemical Engineering	M,D
Civil Engineering	M,D
Computer Engineering	M,D
Computer Science	M
Electrical Engineering	M,D
Engineering and Applied Sciences—General	M,D
Mechanical Engineering	M,D
Software Engineering	M,D

RUTGERS UNIVERSITY–CAMDEN

Computer Science	M

RUTGERS UNIVERSITY–NEWARK

Bioinformatics	M,D
Biomedical Engineering	O
Management of Technology	D
Medical Informatics	M,D,O

RUTGERS UNIVERSITY–NEW BRUNSWICK

Aerospace/Aeronautical Engineering	M,D
Biochemical Engineering	M,D
Biomedical Engineering	M,D
Chemical Engineering	M,D
Civil Engineering	M,D
Computer Engineering	M,D
Computer Science	M,D
Electrical Engineering	M,D
Environmental Engineering	M,D
Hazardous Materials Management	M,D
Health Informatics	M
Industrial/Management Engineering	M,D
Information Science	M
Materials Engineering	M,D
Materials Sciences	M,D
Mechanical Engineering	M,D
Mechanics	M,D
Operations Research	D
Reliability Engineering	M,D
Systems Engineering	M,D

RYERSON UNIVERSITY

Management of Technology	M

SACRED HEART UNIVERSITY

Computer and Information Systems Security	M
Computer Science	M
Game Design and Development	M
Health Informatics	M
Information Science	M

SAGINAW VALLEY STATE UNIVERSITY

Computer and Information Systems Security	M
Computer Science	M
Energy and Power Engineering	M
Engineering and Applied Sciences—General	M

ST. AMBROSE UNIVERSITY

Management of Technology	M

ST. CATHERINE UNIVERSITY

Health Informatics	M

ST. CLOUD STATE UNIVERSITY

Biomedical Engineering	M,O
Computer and Information Systems Security	M
Computer Science	M,O
Electrical Engineering	M
Engineering and Applied Sciences—General	M,O

ST. FRANCIS XAVIER UNIVERSITY

Computer Science	M

ST. JOHN'S UNIVERSITY (NY)

Biotechnology	M
Data Science/Data Analytics	M
Information Science	

ST. JOSEPH'S COLLEGE, LONG ISLAND CAMPUS

Health Informatics	M

ST. JOSEPH'S COLLEGE, NEW YORK

Health Informatics	M

SAINT JOSEPH'S UNIVERSITY

Computer Science	M,O
Health Informatics	M

SAINT LEO UNIVERSITY

Computer and Information Systems Security	M,D

SAINT LOUIS UNIVERSITY

Bioinformatics	M
Biomedical Engineering	M,D
Computer Science	M
Software Engineering	M

SAINT MARTIN'S UNIVERSITY

Civil Engineering	M
Engineering Management	M
Mechanical Engineering	M

SAINT MARY'S COLLEGE

Data Science/Data Analytics	M

SAINT MARY'S UNIVERSITY (CANADA)

Applied Science and Technology	M

ST. MARY'S UNIVERSITY (UNITED STATES)

Computer and Information Systems Security	M,O
Computer Engineering	M
Computer Science	M
Electrical Engineering	M
Engineering Management	M
Industrial/Management Engineering	M
Information Science	M
Software Engineering	M,O

SAINT MARY'S UNIVERSITY OF MINNESOTA

Computer and Information Systems Security	M
Data Science/Data Analytics	M

SAINT PETER'S UNIVERSITY

Data Science/Data Analytics	M

SAINT XAVIER UNIVERSITY

Computer Science	M

SALEM INTERNATIONAL UNIVERSITY

Computer and Information Systems Security	M

SALVE REGINA UNIVERSITY

Computer and Information Systems Security	M,O

SAMFORD UNIVERSITY

Energy Management and Policy	M
Health Informatics	M

SAM HOUSTON STATE UNIVERSITY

Computer and Information Systems Security	M,D
Computer Science	M,D
Information Science	M,D

SAN DIEGO STATE UNIVERSITY

Aerospace/Aeronautical Engineering	M,D
Civil Engineering	M
Computer Science	M
Electrical Engineering	M
Engineering and Applied Sciences—General	M,D
Engineering Design	M,D
Mechanical Engineering	M,D

Mechanics	M,D
Telecommunications Management	M

SAN FRANCISCO STATE UNIVERSITY

Biotechnology	M
Computer Science	M
Electrical Engineering	M
Energy and Power Engineering	M
Engineering and Applied Sciences—General	M

SAN JOSE STATE UNIVERSITY

Aerospace/Aeronautical Engineering	M
Chemical Engineering	M
Civil Engineering	M
Computer Engineering	M
Electrical Engineering	M
Industrial/Management Engineering	M
Materials Engineering	M
Mechanical Engineering	M
Software Engineering	M
Systems Engineering	M

THE SANS TECHNOLOGY INSTITUTE

Computer and Information Systems Security	M

SANTA CLARA UNIVERSITY

Bioengineering	M,D,O
Civil Engineering	M,D,O
Computer Engineering	M,D,O
Computer Science	M,D,O
Electrical Engineering	M,D,O
Energy and Power Engineering	M,D,O
Engineering and Applied Sciences—General	M,D,O
Engineering Management	M,D,O
Mechanical Engineering	M,D,O
Software Engineering	M,D,O

SAVANNAH COLLEGE OF ART AND DESIGN

Game Design and Development	M

SEATTLE PACIFIC UNIVERSITY

Computer and Information Systems Security	M
Data Science/Data Analytics	M

SEATTLE UNIVERSITY

Computer Science	M
Engineering and Applied Sciences—General	M

SETON HALL UNIVERSITY

Management of Technology	M,O

SHIPPENSBURG UNIVERSITY OF PENNSYLVANIA

Computer Science	M,O
Information Science	M,O
Software Engineering	M,O

SIMON FRASER UNIVERSITY

Bioinformatics	M,D,O
Biotechnology	M,D,O
Computer Science	M,D
Engineering and Applied Sciences—General	M,D
Management of Technology	M,D,O
Mechanical Engineering	M,D
Operations Research	M,D

Systems Engineering	M,D

SIT GRADUATE INSTITUTE

Energy Management and Policy	M

SLIPPERY ROCK UNIVERSITY OF PENNSYLVANIA

Data Science/Data Analytics	M
Health Informatics	M

SOFIA UNIVERSITY

Computer Science	M,D

SOUTH CAROLINA STATE UNIVERSITY

Civil Engineering	M
Mechanical Engineering	M
Transportation and Highway Engineering	M

SOUTH DAKOTA SCHOOL OF MINES AND TECHNOLOGY

Artificial Intelligence/Robotics	M
Bioengineering	D
Biomedical Engineering	M,D
Chemical Engineering	M,D
Civil Engineering	M,D
Construction Management	M
Electrical Engineering	M
Engineering and Applied Sciences—General	M,D
Engineering Management	M
Geological Engineering	M,D
Management of Technology	M
Materials Engineering	M,D
Materials Sciences	M,D
Mechanical Engineering	M,D
Mineral/Mining Engineering	M
Nanotechnology	D

SOUTH DAKOTA STATE UNIVERSITY

Agricultural Engineering	M,D
Biosystems Engineering	M,D
Civil Engineering	M
Electrical Engineering	M,D
Engineering and Applied Sciences—General	M,D
Mechanical Engineering	M,D
Operations Research	M

SOUTHEASTERN LOUISIANA UNIVERSITY

Applied Science and Technology	M

SOUTHEASTERN OKLAHOMA STATE UNIVERSITY

Aviation	M
Biotechnology	M

SOUTHEAST MISSOURI STATE UNIVERSITY

Management of Technology	M

SOUTHERN ADVENTIST UNIVERSITY

Computer Science	M

SOUTHERN ARKANSAS UNIVERSITY–MAGNOLIA

Computer and Information Systems Security	M
Computer Science	M
Data Science/Data Analytics	M

SOUTHERN CONNECTICUT STATE UNIVERSITY

Computer Science	M

SOUTHERN ILLINOIS UNIVERSITY CARBONDALE

Biomedical Engineering	M
Civil Engineering	M,D
Computer Engineering	M,D
Computer Science	M,D
Electrical Engineering	M,D
Energy and Power Engineering	D
Engineering and Applied Sciences—General	M,D
Engineering Management	M
Environmental Engineering	D
Mechanical Engineering	M,D
Mechanics	M
Mineral/Mining Engineering	M,D

SOUTHERN ILLINOIS UNIVERSITY EDWARDSVILLE

Civil Engineering	M
Computer Science	M
Electrical Engineering	M
Engineering and Applied Sciences—General	M
Environmental Engineering	M
Geotechnical Engineering	M
Health Informatics	M
Industrial/Management Engineering	M
Mechanical Engineering	M
Operations Research	M
Structural Engineering	M
Transportation and Highway Engineering	M

SOUTHERN METHODIST UNIVERSITY

Civil Engineering	M,D
Computer Engineering	M,D
Computer Science	M,D
Data Science/Data Analytics	M,D
Electrical Engineering	M,D
Engineering and Applied Sciences—General	M,D
Engineering Management	M,D
Environmental Engineering	M,D
Geotechnical Engineering	M,D
Information Science	M,D
Manufacturing Engineering	M,D
Mechanical Engineering	M,D
Operations Research	M,D
Software Engineering	M,D
Structural Engineering	M,D
Systems Engineering	M,D
Telecommunications	M,D
Transportation and Highway Engineering	M,D

SOUTHERN NEW HAMPSHIRE UNIVERSITY

Computer and Information Systems Security	M
Data Science/Data Analytics	M,D,O
Engineering Management	M,D,O
Health Informatics	M,D,O

SOUTHERN OREGON UNIVERSITY

Computer Science	M

SOUTHERN STATES UNIVERSITY

Information Science	M

SOUTHERN UNIVERSITY AND AGRICULTURAL AND MECHANICAL COLLEGE

Computer Science	M
Engineering and Applied Sciences—General	M

SOUTHERN UTAH UNIVERSITY

Computer and Information Systems Security	M

STANFORD UNIVERSITY

Bioengineering	M,D
Biomedical Engineering	M,D,O
Chemical Engineering	M,D
Computer Science	M,D
Construction Engineering	M,D,O
Electrical Engineering	M,D
Energy and Power Engineering	M,D,O
Engineering and Applied Sciences—General	M,D,O
Engineering Design	M,D,O
Engineering Management	M,D
Engineering Physics	M,D
Geotechnical Engineering	M,D,O
Industrial/Management Engineering	M,D
Materials Engineering	M,D,O
Materials Sciences	M,D,O
Mechanical Engineering	M,D,O
Mechanics	M,D,O
Medical Informatics	M,D
Structural Engineering	M,D,O

STATE UNIVERSITY OF NEW YORK AT OSWEGO

Bioinformatics	M
Health Informatics	M
Human-Computer Interaction	M

STATE UNIVERSITY OF NEW YORK COLLEGE OF ENVIRONMENTAL SCIENCE AND FORESTRY

Environmental Engineering	M,D
Materials Sciences	M,D,O
Paper and Pulp Engineering	M,D,O
Water Resources Engineering	M,D

STATE UNIVERSITY OF NEW YORK DOWNSTATE MEDICAL CENTER

Biomedical Engineering	M,D

STATE UNIVERSITY OF NEW YORK POLYTECHNIC INSTITUTE

Computer and Information Systems Security	M
Computer Science	M
Information Science	M
Management of Technology	M
Nanotechnology	M,D

STEPHEN F. AUSTIN STATE UNIVERSITY

Biotechnology	M
Computer and Information Systems Security	M

STEPHENS COLLEGE

Health Informatics	M,O

STEVENS INSTITUTE OF TECHNOLOGY

Aerospace/Aeronautical Engineering	M,O
Artificial Intelligence/Robotics	M,D,O
Biomedical Engineering	M,D,O
Chemical Engineering	M,D,O
Civil Engineering	M,D,O
Computer and Information Systems Security	M,O
Computer Engineering	M,D,O
Computer Science	M,D,O
Construction Engineering	M,O
Construction Management	M,O
Electrical Engineering	M,D,O
Engineering and Applied Sciences—General	M,D,O
Engineering Design	M
Engineering Management	M,D,O
Environmental Engineering	M,D,O
Financial Engineering	M,D,O
Hydraulics	M
Information Science	M,O
Management of Technology	M,D,O
Manufacturing Engineering	M
Materials Engineering	M,D,O
Materials Sciences	M,D
Mechanical Engineering	M,D,O
Modeling and Simulation	M,D,O
Ocean Engineering	M,D
Software Engineering	M,O
Structural Engineering	M,D,O
Systems Engineering	M,D,O
Systems Science	M,D
Telecommunications Management	M,D,O
Telecommunications	M,D,O
Transportation and Highway Engineering	M,D,O
Water Resources Engineering	M,D,O

STEVENSON UNIVERSITY

Computer and Information Systems Security	M
Management of Technology	M

STOCKTON UNIVERSITY

Data Science/Data Analytics	M

STONY BROOK UNIVERSITY, STATE UNIVERSITY OF NEW YORK

Bioinformatics	M,D,O
Biomedical Engineering	M,D,O
Civil Engineering	M,D,O
Computer Engineering	M,D
Computer Science	M,D,O
Electrical Engineering	M,D
Energy Management and Policy	M
Engineering and Applied Sciences—General	M,D,O
Health Informatics	M,D,O
Management of Technology	M
Materials Engineering	M,D
Materials Sciences	M,D
Mechanical Engineering	M,D
Systems Engineering	M,D
Telecommunications	M,D,O

STRATFORD UNIVERSITY (VA)

Computer and Information Systems Security	M,D
Computer Science	M,D
Management of Technology	M,D
Software Engineering	M,D
Telecommunications	M,D

STRAYER UNIVERSITY

Computer and Information Systems Security	M
Information Science	M
Software Engineering	M
Systems Science	M

*M—masters degree; D—doctorate; O—other advanced degree; *—Close-Up and/or Display*

Telecommunications
  Management — M

SUFFOLK UNIVERSITY
Data Science/Data Analytics — M

SYRACUSE UNIVERSITY
Aerospace/Aeronautical
  Engineering — M,D
Bioengineering — M,D
Chemical Engineering — M,D
Civil Engineering — M,D
Computer and Information
  Systems Security — M,O
Computer Engineering — M,D
Computer Science — M
Data Science/Data Analytics — M,O
Electrical Engineering — M,D
Engineering and Applied
  Sciences—General — M,D,O
Engineering Management — M
Environmental Engineering — M
Information Science — M,D
Mechanical Engineering — M,D

TARLETON STATE UNIVERSITY
Engineering Management — M

TÉLÉ-UNIVERSITÉ
Computer Science — M,D

TEMPLE UNIVERSITY
Artificial Intelligence/Robotics — M,D
Bioengineering — M,D
Biotechnology — M,D
Civil Engineering — M,D,O
Computer and Information
  Systems Security — M,D
Computer Science — M,D
Electrical Engineering — M,D
Engineering and Applied
  Sciences—General — D*
Engineering Management — M,O
Environmental Engineering — M,D,O
Financial Engineering — M
Health Informatics — M,D
Information Science — M,D
Mechanical Engineering — M,D

TENNESSEE STATE UNIVERSITY
Biomedical Engineering — M,D
Biotechnology — M,D
Civil Engineering — M,D
Computer Engineering — M,D
Electrical Engineering — M,D
Engineering and Applied
  Sciences—General — M,D
Environmental Engineering — M,D
Manufacturing Engineering — M,D
Mechanical Engineering — M,D
Systems Engineering — M,D

TENNESSEE TECHNOLOGICAL UNIVERSITY
Chemical Engineering — M
Civil Engineering — M
Computer Science — M,D
Electrical Engineering — M
Engineering and Applied
  Sciences—General — M,D
Mechanical Engineering — M

TEXAS A&M UNIVERSITY
Aerospace/Aeronautical
  Engineering — M,D
Agricultural Engineering — M,D
Bioengineering — M,D
Biomedical Engineering — M,D
Chemical Engineering — M,D
Civil Engineering — M,D
Computer Engineering

Computer Science — M,D
Construction Management — M
Electrical Engineering — M,D
Engineering Management — M,D
Industrial/Management
  Engineering — M,D
Manufacturing Engineering — M
Materials Engineering — M,D
Materials Sciences — M,D
Mechanical Engineering — M,D
Nuclear Engineering — M,D
Petroleum Engineering — M,D

TEXAS A&M UNIVERSITY–COMMERCE
Management of Technology — M,O

TEXAS A&M UNIVERSITY–CORPUS CHRISTI
Computer Science — M

TEXAS A&M UNIVERSITY–KINGSVILLE
Chemical Engineering — M
Civil Engineering — M
Computer Science — M
Electrical Engineering — M
Energy and Power
  Engineering — D
Engineering and Applied
  Sciences—General — M,D
Environmental Engineering — M,D
Industrial/Management
  Engineering — M
Mechanical Engineering — M
Petroleum Engineering — M
Systems Engineering — D

TEXAS SOUTHERN UNIVERSITY
Computer Science — M
Industrial/Management
  Engineering — M
Transportation and Highway
  Engineering — M

TEXAS STATE UNIVERSITY
Civil Engineering — M
Computer Science — M,D
Electrical Engineering — M
Engineering and Applied
  Sciences—General — M
Health Informatics — M
Industrial/Management
  Engineering — M
Management of Technology — M
Manufacturing Engineering — M
Materials Engineering — D
Materials Sciences — D
Mechanical Engineering — M
Software Engineering — M

TEXAS TECH UNIVERSITY
Biotechnology — M,D
Data Science/Data Analytics — M,D
Energy and Power
  Engineering — M,D
Engineering and Applied
  Sciences—General — M,D
Engineering Management — M,D
Software Engineering — M,D

TEXAS TECH UNIVERSITY HEALTH SCIENCES CENTER
Biotechnology — M

TEXAS WOMAN'S UNIVERSITY
Information Science — M

THOMAS EDISON STATE UNIVERSITY
Applied Science and
  Technology — M,O
Computer and Information
  Systems Security — M,O
Information Science — M,O

THOMAS JEFFERSON UNIVERSITY
Biotechnology — M
Construction Management — M
Textile Sciences and
  Engineering — M,D

TOWSON UNIVERSITY
Computer Science — M
Information Science — M,D,O
Management of Technology — M,O

TOYOTA TECHNOLOGICAL INSTITUTE AT CHICAGO
Computer Science — D

TRENT UNIVERSITY
Computer Science — M
Materials Sciences — M
Modeling and Simulation — M,D

TREVECCA NAZARENE UNIVERSITY
Information Science — M,O

TRIDENT UNIVERSITY INTERNATIONAL
Computer and Information
  Systems Security — M,D
Health Informatics — M,D,O

TRINE UNIVERSITY
Engineering Management — M

TROY UNIVERSITY
Computer Science — M

TUFTS UNIVERSITY
Artificial Intelligence/Robotics — M,D
Bioengineering — M,D,O
Bioinformatics — M,D
Biomedical Engineering — M,D
Biotechnology — M,D,O
Chemical Engineering — M,D
Civil Engineering — M,D
Computer Science — M,D,O
Data Science/Data Analytics — M,D
Electrical Engineering — M,D,O
Engineering and Applied
  Sciences—General — M,D
Engineering Management — M
Environmental Engineering — M,D
Ergonomics and Human
  Factors — M,D
Geotechnical Engineering — M,D
Human-Computer Interaction — O
Manufacturing Engineering — O
Mechanical Engineering — M,D
Structural Engineering — M,D
Water Resources Engineering — M,D

TULANE UNIVERSITY
Biomedical Engineering — M,D
Chemical Engineering — M,D
Energy Management and
  Policy — M,D

TUSKEGEE UNIVERSITY
Computer and Information
  Systems Security — M
Electrical Engineering — M

Engineering and Applied
  Sciences—General — M,D
Materials Engineering — D
Mechanical Engineering — M

UNITED STATES MERCHANT MARINE ACADEMY
Civil Engineering — M

UNIVERSIDAD AUTONOMA DE GUADALAJARA
Computer Science — M,D
Energy and Power
  Engineering — M,D
Manufacturing Engineering — M,D
Systems Science — M,D

UNIVERSIDAD CENTRAL DEL ESTE
Environmental Engineering — M

UNIVERSIDAD DE LAS AMÉRICAS PUEBLA
Biotechnology — M
Chemical Engineering — M
Computer Science — M,D
Construction Management — M
Electrical Engineering — M
Engineering and Applied
  Sciences—General — M,D
Industrial/Management
  Engineering — M
Manufacturing Engineering — M

UNIVERSIDAD DEL ESTE
Computer and Information
  Systems Security — M

UNIVERSIDAD DEL TURABO
Computer Engineering — M
Electrical Engineering — M
Engineering and Applied
  Sciences—General — M
Mechanical Engineering — M
Telecommunications — M

UNIVERSIDAD NACIONAL PEDRO HENRIQUEZ URENA
Environmental Engineering — M

UNIVERSITÉ DE MONCTON
Civil Engineering — M
Computer Science — M,O
Electrical Engineering — M
Engineering and Applied
  Sciences—General — M
Industrial/Management
  Engineering — M
Mechanical Engineering — M

UNIVERSITÉ DE MONTRÉAL
Bioinformatics — M,D
Biomedical Engineering — M,D,O
Computer Science — M,D
Ergonomics and Human
  Factors — O

UNIVERSITÉ DE SHERBROOKE
Chemical Engineering — M,D
Civil Engineering — M,D
Computer and Information
  Systems Security — M
Electrical Engineering — M,D
Engineering and Applied
  Sciences—General — M,D,O
Engineering Management — M,O
Environmental Engineering — M
Information Science — M,D
Mechanical Engineering — M,D

UNIVERSITÉ DU QUÉBEC À CHICOUTIMI
Engineering and Applied Sciences—General — M,D

UNIVERSITÉ DU QUÉBEC À MONTRÉAL
Ergonomics and Human Factors — O

UNIVERSITÉ DU QUÉBEC À RIMOUSKI
Engineering and Applied Sciences—General — M

UNIVERSITÉ DU QUÉBEC À TROIS-RIVIÈRES
Computer Science — M
Electrical Engineering — M,D
Industrial/Management Engineering — M,O

UNIVERSITÉ DU QUÉBEC, ÉCOLE DE TECHNOLOGIE SUPÉRIEURE
Engineering and Applied Sciences—General — M,D,O

UNIVERSITÉ DU QUÉBEC EN ABITIBI-TÉMISCAMINGUE
Engineering and Applied Sciences—General — M,O
Mineral/Mining Engineering — M,O

UNIVERSITÉ DU QUÉBEC EN OUTAOUAIS
Computer Science — M,D,O

UNIVERSITÉ DU QUÉBEC, INSTITUT NATIONAL DE LA RECHERCHE SCIENTIFIQUE
Energy Management and Policy — M,D
Materials Sciences — M,D
Telecommunications — M,D

UNIVERSITÉ LAVAL
Aerospace/Aeronautical Engineering — M
Agricultural Engineering — M
Chemical Engineering — M,D
Civil Engineering — M,D,O
Computer Science — M,D
Electrical Engineering — M,D
Engineering and Applied Sciences—General — M,D,O
Environmental Engineering — M,D
Industrial/Management Engineering — O
Mechanical Engineering — M,D
Metallurgical Engineering and Metallurgy — M,D
Mineral/Mining Engineering — M,D
Modeling and Simulation — M,O
Software Engineering — O

UNIVERSITY AT ALBANY, STATE UNIVERSITY OF NEW YORK
Computer and Information Systems Security — M,D,O
Computer Science — M,D
Engineering and Applied Sciences—General — M,D,O
Information Science — M,D

UNIVERSITY AT BUFFALO, THE STATE UNIVERSITY OF NEW YORK
Aerospace/Aeronautical Engineering — M,D
Bioengineering — M,D,O
Bioinformatics — M,D
Biomedical Engineering — M,D
Biotechnology — M
Chemical Engineering — M,D,O
Civil Engineering — M,D
Computer Science — M,D,O
Data Science/Data Analytics — M,D
Electrical Engineering — M,D
Energy and Power Engineering — M,D
Engineering and Applied Sciences—General — M,D,O
Engineering Management — M,D,O
Environmental Engineering — M,D
Industrial/Management Engineering — M,D,O
Manufacturing Engineering — M,D,O
Materials Sciences — M,D
Mechanical Engineering — M,D
Medical Informatics — M,D
Modeling and Simulation — M,D
Nanotechnology — M,D,O
Structural Engineering — M,D
Water Resources Engineering — M,D

UNIVERSITY OF ADVANCING TECHNOLOGY
Computer and Information Systems Security — M
Computer Science — M
Game Design and Development — M
Management of Technology — M

THE UNIVERSITY OF AKRON
Biomedical Engineering — M,D
Chemical Engineering — M,D
Civil Engineering — M,D
Computer Engineering — M,D
Computer Science — M
Electrical Engineering — M,D
Engineering and Applied Sciences—General — M,D
Geological Engineering — M
Mechanical Engineering — M,D
Polymer Science and Engineering — M,D

THE UNIVERSITY OF ALABAMA
Aerospace/Aeronautical Engineering — M,D
Chemical Engineering — M,D
Civil Engineering — M,D
Computer Engineering — M,D
Computer Science — M,D
Construction Engineering — M,D
Electrical Engineering — M,D
Engineering and Applied Sciences—General — M,D
Environmental Engineering — M,D
Ergonomics and Human Factors — M
Materials Engineering — M,D
Materials Sciences — D
Mechanical Engineering — M,D
Mechanics — M,D
Metallurgical Engineering and Metallurgy — M,D

THE UNIVERSITY OF ALABAMA AT BIRMINGHAM
Bioinformatics — D
Biomedical Engineering — M,D
Biotechnology — M
Civil Engineering — M,D

Computer and Information Systems Security — M
Computer Engineering — M,D
Computer Science — M,D
Construction Engineering — M
Construction Management — M
Electrical Engineering — M,D
Engineering and Applied Sciences—General — D
Engineering Design — M
Engineering Management — M
Health Informatics — M
Information Science — M,D
Materials Engineering — M,D
Mechanical Engineering — M
Safety Engineering — M
Structural Engineering — M

THE UNIVERSITY OF ALABAMA IN HUNTSVILLE
Aerospace/Aeronautical Engineering — M,D
Biotechnology — M,D
Chemical Engineering — M,D
Civil Engineering — M,D
Computer and Information Systems Security — M,D,O
Computer Engineering — M,D
Computer Science — M,D,O
Electrical Engineering — M,D
Engineering and Applied Sciences—General — M,D
Environmental Engineering — M,D
Industrial/Management Engineering — M,D
Management of Technology — M,O
Materials Sciences — M,D
Mechanical Engineering — M,D
Modeling and Simulation — M,D,O
Operations Research — M,D
Software Engineering — M,D,O
Systems Engineering — M,D

UNIVERSITY OF ALASKA FAIRBANKS
Civil Engineering — M,D,O
Computer Science — M
Construction Management — M,D,O
Electrical Engineering — M
Engineering and Applied Sciences—General — D
Environmental Engineering — M,D,O
Geological Engineering — M
Mechanical Engineering — M
Mineral/Mining Engineering — M
Petroleum Engineering — M

UNIVERSITY OF ALBERTA
Biomedical Engineering — M,D
Biotechnology — M,D
Chemical Engineering — M,D
Civil Engineering — M,D
Computer Engineering — M,D
Computer Science — M,D
Construction Engineering — M,D
Electrical Engineering — M,D
Energy and Power Engineering — M,D
Engineering Management — M,D
Environmental Engineering — M,D
Geotechnical Engineering — M,D
Materials Engineering — M,D
Mechanical Engineering — M,D
Mineral/Mining Engineering — M,D
Nanotechnology — M,D
Petroleum Engineering — M,D
Structural Engineering — M,D
Systems Engineering — M,D
Telecommunications — M,D
Water Resources Engineering — M,D

THE UNIVERSITY OF ARIZONA
Aerospace/Aeronautical Engineering — M,D
Agricultural Engineering — M,D
Biomedical Engineering — M,D
Biosystems Engineering — M,D
Chemical Engineering — M,D
Computer Engineering — M,D
Computer Science — M,D
Data Science/Data Analytics — M
Electrical Engineering — M,D
Engineering and Applied Sciences—General — M,D,O
Engineering Management — M,D,O
Environmental Engineering — M,D
Geological Engineering — M,D,O
Industrial/Management Engineering — M,D,O
Materials Engineering — M,D
Materials Sciences — M,D
Mechanical Engineering — M,D
Medical Informatics — M,D,O
Mineral/Mining Engineering — M,D,O
Systems Engineering — M,D,O

UNIVERSITY OF ARKANSAS
Agricultural Engineering — M,D
Bioengineering — M
Biomedical Engineering — M
Chemical Engineering — M,D
Civil Engineering — M,D
Computer Engineering — M,D
Computer Science — M,D
Electrical Engineering — M,D
Electronic Materials — M,D
Engineering and Applied Sciences—General — M,D
Environmental Engineering — M,D
Industrial/Management Engineering — M,D
Mechanical Engineering — M,D
Telecommunications — M,D
Transportation and Highway Engineering — M,D

UNIVERSITY OF ARKANSAS AT LITTLE ROCK
Applied Science and Technology — M,D
Bioinformatics — M,D
Computer Science — M,D
Construction Management — M
Information Science — M,D,O
Systems Engineering — M,D,O

UNIVERSITY OF ARKANSAS FOR MEDICAL SCIENCES
Bioinformatics — M,D,O

UNIVERSITY OF BALTIMORE
Human-Computer Interaction — M

UNIVERSITY OF BRIDGEPORT
Biomedical Engineering — M
Computer Engineering — M,D
Computer Science — M,D
Electrical Engineering — M
Engineering and Applied Sciences—General — M,D
Management of Technology — M,D
Mechanical Engineering — M

THE UNIVERSITY OF BRITISH COLUMBIA
Bioengineering — M,D
Bioinformatics — M,D
Biomedical Engineering — M,D
Chemical Engineering — M,D
Civil Engineering — M,D
Computer Engineering — M,D

M—masters degree; D—doctorate; O—other advanced degree; *—Close-Up and/or Display

Computer Science	M,D
Electrical Engineering	M,D
Energy and Power Engineering	M
Engineering and Applied Sciences—General	M,D
Geological Engineering	M,D
Materials Engineering	M,D
Mechanical Engineering	M,D
Mineral/Mining Engineering	M,D

UNIVERSITY OF CALGARY

Biomedical Engineering	M,D
Biotechnology	M
Chemical Engineering	M,D
Civil Engineering	M,D
Computer Engineering	M,D
Computer Science	M,D
Electrical Engineering	M,D
Energy and Power Engineering	M,D
Energy Management and Policy	M,D
Engineering and Applied Sciences—General	M,D
Environmental Engineering	M,D
Geotechnical Engineering	M,D
Manufacturing Engineering	M,D
Materials Sciences	M,D
Mechanical Engineering	M,D
Mechanics	M,D
Petroleum Engineering	M,D
Software Engineering	M,D
Structural Engineering	M,D
Transportation and Highway Engineering	M,D

UNIVERSITY OF CALIFORNIA, BERKELEY

Applied Science and Technology	D
Bioengineering	M,D
Chemical Engineering	M,D
Civil Engineering	M,D
Computer Science	M,D
Construction Management	O
Data Science/Data Analytics	M
Electrical Engineering	M,D
Energy Management and Policy	M,D
Engineering and Applied Sciences—General	M,D,O
Engineering Management	M,D
Environmental Engineering	M,D
Financial Engineering	M
Geotechnical Engineering	M,D
Industrial/Management Engineering	M,D
Materials Engineering	M,D
Materials Sciences	M,D
Mechanical Engineering	M,D
Mechanics	M,D
Nuclear Engineering	M,D
Operations Research	M,D
Structural Engineering	M,D
Transportation and Highway Engineering	M,D
Water Resources Engineering	M,D

UNIVERSITY OF CALIFORNIA, DAVIS

Aerospace/Aeronautical Engineering	M,D,O
Applied Science and Technology	M,D
Bioengineering	M,D
Biomedical Engineering	M,D
Chemical Engineering	M,D
Civil Engineering	M,D,O
Computer Engineering	M,D
Computer Science	M,D
Electrical Engineering	M,D

Engineering and Applied Sciences—General	M,D,O
Environmental Engineering	M,D,O
Materials Engineering	M,D
Materials Sciences	M,D
Mechanical Engineering	M,D,O
Medical Informatics	M
Transportation and Highway Engineering	M,D

UNIVERSITY OF CALIFORNIA, IRVINE

Aerospace/Aeronautical Engineering	M,D
Biochemical Engineering	M,D
Biomedical Engineering	M,D
Biotechnology	M
Chemical Engineering	M,D
Civil Engineering	M,D
Computer Science	M,D
Electrical Engineering	M,D
Engineering and Applied Sciences—General	M,D
Engineering Management	M
Environmental Engineering	M,D
Information Science	M,D
Manufacturing Engineering	M,D
Materials Engineering	M,D
Materials Sciences	M,D
Mechanical Engineering	M,D
Transportation and Highway Engineering	M,D

UNIVERSITY OF CALIFORNIA, LOS ANGELES

Aerospace/Aeronautical Engineering	M,D
Bioengineering	M,D
Bioinformatics	M,D
Biomedical Engineering	M,D
Chemical Engineering	M,D
Civil Engineering	M,D
Computer Engineering	M,D
Computer Science	M,D
Electrical Engineering	M,D
Engineering and Applied Sciences—General	M,D
Environmental Engineering	M,D
Financial Engineering	M,D
Management of Technology	M,D
Manufacturing Engineering	M
Materials Engineering	M,D
Materials Sciences	M,D
Mechanical Engineering	M,D

UNIVERSITY OF CALIFORNIA, MERCED

Bioengineering	M,D
Computer Science	M,D
Electrical Engineering	M,D
Engineering and Applied Sciences—General	M,D
Environmental Engineering	M,D
Information Science	M,D
Mechanical Engineering	M,D
Mechanics	M,D
Systems Engineering	M,D

UNIVERSITY OF CALIFORNIA, RIVERSIDE

Artificial Intelligence/Robotics	M,D
Bioengineering	M,D
Bioinformatics	D
Chemical Engineering	M,D
Computer Engineering	M
Computer Science	M,D
Electrical Engineering	M,D
Environmental Engineering	M,D
Materials Engineering	M
Materials Sciences	M
Mechanical Engineering	M,D
Nanotechnology	M

UNIVERSITY OF CALIFORNIA, SAN DIEGO

Aerospace/Aeronautical Engineering	M,D
Architectural Engineering	M
Artificial Intelligence/Robotics	M,D
Bioengineering	M,D
Bioinformatics	D
Chemical Engineering	M,D
Computer Engineering	M,D
Computer Science	M,D
Data Science/Data Analytics	M
Electrical Engineering	M,D
Energy Management and Policy	M
Engineering Physics	M,D
Materials Sciences	M,D
Mechanical Engineering	M,D
Mechanics	M,D
Modeling and Simulation	M,D
Nanotechnology	M,D
Ocean Engineering	M,D
Structural Engineering	M,D
Telecommunications	M,D

UNIVERSITY OF CALIFORNIA, SAN FRANCISCO

Bioengineering	D
Bioinformatics	D

UNIVERSITY OF CALIFORNIA, SANTA BARBARA

Bioengineering	M,D
Chemical Engineering	M,D
Computer Engineering	M,D
Computer Science	M,D
Electrical Engineering	M,D
Engineering and Applied Sciences—General	M,D
Management of Technology	M
Materials Engineering	M,D
Materials Sciences	M,D
Mechanical Engineering	M,D

UNIVERSITY OF CALIFORNIA, SANTA CRUZ

Bioinformatics	M,D
Computer Engineering	M,D
Computer Science	M,D
Electrical Engineering	M,D
Engineering and Applied Sciences—General	M,D
Game Design and Development	M,D

UNIVERSITY OF CENTRAL ARKANSAS

Computer Science	M

UNIVERSITY OF CENTRAL FLORIDA

Aerospace/Aeronautical Engineering	M
Civil Engineering	M,D,O
Computer Engineering	M,D
Computer Science	M,D
Electrical Engineering	M,D
Engineering and Applied Sciences—General	M,D,O
Environmental Engineering	M,D
Health Informatics	M,O
Industrial/Management Engineering	M,D,O
Materials Engineering	M,D
Materials Sciences	M,D
Mechanical Engineering	M,D
Modeling and Simulation	M,D,O
Structural Engineering	M,D,O
Transportation and Highway Engineering	M,D,O

UNIVERSITY OF CENTRAL MISSOURI

Aerospace/Aeronautical Engineering	M,D,O
Computer Science	M,D,O
Information Science	M,D,O
Management of Technology	M,D,O

UNIVERSITY OF CENTRAL OKLAHOMA

Biomedical Engineering	M
Computer Science	M
Electrical Engineering	M
Engineering and Applied Sciences—General	M
Engineering Physics	M
Mechanical Engineering	M

UNIVERSITY OF CHICAGO

Bioengineering	D
Bioinformatics	M
Computer Science	M,D

UNIVERSITY OF CINCINNATI

Aerospace/Aeronautical Engineering	M,D
Bioinformatics	D,O
Biomedical Engineering	M,D
Chemical Engineering	M,D
Civil Engineering	M,D
Computer Engineering	M,D
Computer Science	M,D
Electrical Engineering	M,D
Engineering and Applied Sciences—General	M,D
Environmental Engineering	M,D
Ergonomics and Human Factors	M,D
Health Informatics	M
Industrial/Management Engineering	M,D
Information Science	M,O
Materials Engineering	M,D
Materials Sciences	M,D
Mechanical Engineering	M,D
Mechanics	M,D
Nuclear Engineering	M,D

UNIVERSITY OF COLORADO BOULDER

Aerospace/Aeronautical Engineering	M,D
Architectural Engineering	M,D
Chemical Engineering	M,D
Civil Engineering	M,D
Computer Engineering	M,D
Computer Science	M,D
Electrical Engineering	M,D
Engineering and Applied Sciences—General	M,D
Engineering Management	M
Environmental Engineering	M,D
Information Science	D
Materials Engineering	M,D
Materials Sciences	M,D
Mechanical Engineering	M,D
Telecommunications Management	M
Telecommunications	M

UNIVERSITY OF COLORADO COLORADO SPRINGS

Aerospace/Aeronautical Engineering	M,D
Computer and Information Systems Security	M,D
Energy and Power Engineering	M,D
Engineering and Applied Sciences—General	M,D
Software Engineering	M,D
Systems Engineering	M,D

UNIVERSITY OF COLORADO DENVER

Applied Science and Technology	M
Bioengineering	M,D
Bioinformatics	D
Civil Engineering	M,D
Computer Science	M,D
Data Science/Data Analytics	M
Electrical Engineering	M,D
Energy Management and Policy	M
Engineering and Applied Sciences—General	M,D
Environmental Engineering	M,D
Geotechnical Engineering	M,D
Hazardous Materials Management	M
Health Informatics	M
Hydraulics	M,D
Information Science	M,D
Management of Technology	M
Mechanical Engineering	M
Mechanics	M
Medical Informatics	M,D
Operations Research	M,D
Structural Engineering	M,D
Transportation and Highway Engineering	M,D

UNIVERSITY OF CONNECTICUT

Biochemical Engineering	M,D
Biomedical Engineering	M,D
Chemical Engineering	M,D
Civil Engineering	M,D
Computer Engineering	M,D
Computer Science	M,D
Electrical Engineering	M,D
Engineering and Applied Sciences—General	M,D
Environmental Engineering	M,D
Materials Engineering	M
Materials Sciences	M,D
Mechanical Engineering	M,D
Polymer Science and Engineering	M,D
Software Engineering	M,D

UNIVERSITY OF DALLAS

Computer and Information Systems Security	M,D
Management of Technology	M,D

UNIVERSITY OF DAYTON

Aerospace/Aeronautical Engineering	M,D
Bioengineering	M
Chemical Engineering	M
Civil Engineering	M
Computer and Information Systems Security	M
Computer Engineering	M,D
Computer Science	M
Electrical Engineering	M,D
Engineering Management	M
Environmental Engineering	M
Geotechnical Engineering	M
Materials Engineering	M,D
Mechanical Engineering	M,D
Mechanics	M
Structural Engineering	M
Transportation and Highway Engineering	M
Water Resources Engineering	M

UNIVERSITY OF DELAWARE

Biotechnology	M,D
Chemical Engineering	M,D
Civil Engineering	M,D
Computer Engineering	M,D
Computer Science	M,D

Electrical Engineering	M,D
Energy Management and Policy	M,D
Engineering and Applied Sciences—General	M,D
Environmental Engineering	M,D
Geotechnical Engineering	M,D
Information Science	M,D
Management of Technology	M
Materials Engineering	M,D
Materials Sciences	M,D
Mechanical Engineering	M,D
Ocean Engineering	M,D
Operations Research	M
Structural Engineering	M,D
Transportation and Highway Engineering	M,D
Water Resources Engineering	M,D

UNIVERSITY OF DENVER

Bioengineering	M,D
Computer and Information Systems Security	M,D
Computer Engineering	M,D
Computer Science	M,D
Construction Management	M
Data Science/Data Analytics	M,D
Electrical Engineering	M,D
Engineering and Applied Sciences—General	M,D
Engineering Management	M,D
Information Science	M,O
Materials Engineering	M,D
Materials Sciences	M,D
Mechanical Engineering	M,D

UNIVERSITY OF DETROIT MERCY

Architectural Engineering	M
Civil Engineering	M,D
Computer and Information Systems Security	M,D,O
Computer Engineering	M,D
Computer Science	M,D,O
Electrical Engineering	M,D
Engineering and Applied Sciences—General	M,D
Engineering Management	M,D
Environmental Engineering	M,D
Mechanical Engineering	M,D
Software Engineering	M,D

UNIVERSITY OF FAIRFAX

Computer and Information Systems Security	M,D
Computer Science	M,D
Information Science	M,D

THE UNIVERSITY OF FINDLAY

Health Informatics	M,D

UNIVERSITY OF FLORIDA

Aerospace/Aeronautical Engineering	M,D
Agricultural Engineering	M,D,O
Bioengineering	M,D,O
Biomedical Engineering	M,D,O
Chemical Engineering	M,D,O
Civil Engineering	M,D
Computer Engineering	M,D
Computer Science	M,D
Construction Management	M,D
Electrical Engineering	M,D
Engineering and Applied Sciences—General	M,D,O
Environmental Engineering	M,D,O
Industrial/Management Engineering	M,D,O
Information Science	M,D
Materials Engineering	M,D
Materials Sciences	M,D

Mechanical Engineering	M,D
Nuclear Engineering	M,D
Ocean Engineering	M,D
Systems Engineering	M,D,O
Telecommunications	M,D

UNIVERSITY OF GEORGIA

Artificial Intelligence/Robotics	M
Biochemical Engineering	M
Bioinformatics	M,D
Computer Science	M,D
Environmental Engineering	M

UNIVERSITY OF GUELPH

Bioengineering	M,D
Biotechnology	M,D
Computer Science	M,D
Engineering and Applied Sciences—General	M,D
Environmental Engineering	M,D
Water Resources Engineering	M,D

UNIVERSITY OF HARTFORD

Engineering and Applied Sciences—General	M

UNIVERSITY OF HAWAII AT MANOA

Bioengineering	M
Civil Engineering	M,D
Computer Science	M,D,O
Electrical Engineering	M,D
Engineering and Applied Sciences—General	M,D
Environmental Engineering	M,D
Geological Engineering	M,D
Information Science	M,D
Mechanical Engineering	M,D
Ocean Engineering	M,D
Telecommunications	O

UNIVERSITY OF HOUSTON

Biomedical Engineering	D
Chemical Engineering	M,D
Civil Engineering	M,D
Computer and Information Systems Security	M
Computer Science	M,D
Construction Management	M
Electrical Engineering	M,D
Engineering and Applied Sciences—General	M,D
Industrial/Management Engineering	M,D
Information Science	M,D
Mechanical Engineering	M,D
Petroleum Engineering	M,D
Telecommunications	M

UNIVERSITY OF HOUSTON–CLEAR LAKE

Biotechnology	M
Computer Engineering	M
Computer Science	M
Information Science	M
Software Engineering	M
Systems Engineering	M

UNIVERSITY OF HOUSTON–DOWNTOWN

Data Science/Data Analytics	M

UNIVERSITY OF HOUSTON–VICTORIA

Computer Science	M

UNIVERSITY OF IDAHO

Bioengineering	M,D

Bioinformatics	M,D
Chemical Engineering	M,D
Civil Engineering	M,D
Computer Science	M,D
Electrical Engineering	M,D
Engineering and Applied Sciences—General	M,D
Geological Engineering	M,D
Materials Sciences	M,D
Mechanical Engineering	M,D
Nuclear Engineering	M,D
Water Resources Engineering	M,D

UNIVERSITY OF ILLINOIS AT CHICAGO

Bioengineering	M,D
Bioinformatics	M,D
Chemical Engineering	M,D
Civil Engineering	M,D
Computer Engineering	M,D
Computer Science	M,D
Electrical Engineering	M,D
Engineering and Applied Sciences—General	M,D
Health Informatics	M,O
Industrial/Management Engineering	M,D
Materials Engineering	M,D
Mechanical Engineering	M,D
Operations Research	M,D

UNIVERSITY OF ILLINOIS AT SPRINGFIELD

Computer Science	M
Data Science/Data Analytics	M

UNIVERSITY OF ILLINOIS AT URBANA–CHAMPAIGN

Aerospace/Aeronautical Engineering	M,D
Agricultural Engineering	M,D
Bioengineering	M,D
Bioinformatics	M,D,O
Chemical Engineering	M,D
Civil Engineering	M,D
Computer Engineering	M,D
Computer Science	M,D
Electrical Engineering	M,D
Energy and Power Engineering	M,D
Energy Management and Policy	M
Engineering and Applied Sciences—General	M,D
Environmental Engineering	M,D
Financial Engineering	M
Health Informatics	M,D,O
Human-Computer Interaction	M,D,O
Industrial/Management Engineering	M,D
Information Science	M,D,O
Management of Technology	M,D
Materials Engineering	M,D
Materials Sciences	M,D
Mechanical Engineering	M,D
Mechanics	M,D
Medical Informatics	M,D,O
Nuclear Engineering	M,D
Systems Engineering	M,D

THE UNIVERSITY OF IOWA

Biochemical Engineering	M,D
Bioinformatics	M,D,O
Biomedical Engineering	M,D
Chemical Engineering	M,D
Civil Engineering	M,D
Computer Engineering	M,D
Computer Science	M,D
Electrical Engineering	M,D
Energy and Power Engineering	M,D

*M—masters degree; D—doctorate; O—other advanced degree; *—Close-Up and/or Display*

Engineering and Applied
   Sciences—General — M,D
Environmental Engineering — M,D
Ergonomics and Human
   Factors — M,D,O
Health Informatics — M,D,O
Hydraulics — M,D
Industrial/Management
   Engineering — M,D
Information Science — M,D,O
Manufacturing Engineering — M,D
Materials Engineering — M,D
Mechanical Engineering — M,D
Operations Research — M,D
Transportation and Highway
   Engineering — M,D
Water Resources Engineering — M,D

THE UNIVERSITY OF KANSAS
Aerospace/Aeronautical
   Engineering — M,D
Architectural Engineering — M
Bioengineering — M,D
Biotechnology — M
Chemical Engineering — M,D,O
Civil Engineering — M,D
Computer Engineering — M
Computer Science — M,D
Construction Management — M
Electrical Engineering — M,D
Engineering and Applied
   Sciences—General — M,D,O
Engineering Management — M,O
Environmental Engineering — M,D
Health Informatics — M,O
Mechanical Engineering — M,D
Medical Informatics — M,D,O
Petroleum Engineering — M,D,O

UNIVERSITY OF KENTUCKY
Agricultural Engineering — M,D
Biomedical Engineering — M,D
Chemical Engineering — M,D
Civil Engineering — M,D
Computer Science — M,D
Electrical Engineering — M,D
Engineering and Applied
   Sciences—General — M,D
Information Science — M,D
Manufacturing Engineering — M
Materials Engineering — M,D
Materials Sciences — M,D
Mechanical Engineering — M,D
Mineral/Mining Engineering — M,D

UNIVERSITY OF LETHBRIDGE
Computer Science — M,D

**UNIVERSITY OF LOUISIANA AT
LAFAYETTE**
Architectural Engineering — M
Chemical Engineering — M
Civil Engineering — M
Electrical Engineering — M,D
Mechanical Engineering — M
Petroleum Engineering — M
Systems Engineering — M,D

UNIVERSITY OF LOUISVILLE
Bioengineering — M,D
Bioinformatics — M,D
Chemical Engineering — M,D
Civil Engineering — M,D
Computer and Information
   Systems Security — M,D,O
Computer Engineering — M,D,O
Computer Science — M,D
Data Science/Data Analytics — M,D,O
Electrical Engineering — M,D
Engineering and Applied
   Sciences—General — M,D,O
Engineering Management — M,D,O

Industrial/Management
   Engineering — M,D,O
Mechanical Engineering — M,D

UNIVERSITY OF LYNCHBURG
Health Informatics — O

UNIVERSITY OF MAINE
Bioinformatics — M,D
Biomedical Engineering — M,D
Chemical Engineering — M,D
Civil Engineering — M,D
Computer Engineering — M,D
Computer Science — M,D,O
Electrical Engineering — M,D
Engineering and Applied
   Sciences—General — M,D
Information Science — M,D,O
Mechanical Engineering — M,D

**UNIVERSITY OF MANAGEMENT
AND TECHNOLOGY**
Computer Science — M,O
Engineering Management — M
Software Engineering — M,O

**THE UNIVERSITY OF
MANCHESTER**
Aerospace/Aeronautical
   Engineering — M,D
Biochemical Engineering — M,D
Bioinformatics — M,D
Biotechnology — M,D
Chemical Engineering — M,D
Civil Engineering — M,D
Computer Science — M,D
Electrical Engineering — M,D
Engineering Management — M,D
Environmental Engineering — M,D
Hazardous Materials
   Management — M,D
Materials Sciences — M,D
Mechanical Engineering — M,D
Metallurgical Engineering and
   Metallurgy — M,D
Modeling and Simulation — M,D
Nuclear Engineering — M,D
Paper and Pulp Engineering — M,D
Polymer Science and
   Engineering — M,D
Structural Engineering — M,D

UNIVERSITY OF MANITOBA
Biosystems Engineering — M,D
Civil Engineering — M,D
Computer Engineering — M,D
Computer Science — M,D
Electrical Engineering — M,D
Engineering and Applied
   Sciences—General — M,D
Industrial/Management
   Engineering — M,D
Manufacturing Engineering — M,D
Mechanical Engineering — M,D

UNIVERSITY OF MARY
Energy Management and
   Policy — M

**UNIVERSITY OF MARYLAND,
BALTIMORE COUNTY**
Biochemical Engineering — M,D,O
Biotechnology — M,O
Chemical Engineering — M,D
Computer and Information
   Systems Security — M,O
Computer Engineering — M,D
Computer Science — M,D
Data Science/Data Analytics — M
Electrical Engineering — M,D
Engineering and Applied
   Sciences—General — M,D,O

Engineering Management — M,O
Environmental Engineering — M,D
Health Informatics — M
Information Science — M
Management of Technology — M
Mechanical Engineering — M,D
Mechanics — O
Systems Engineering — M,O

**UNIVERSITY OF MARYLAND,
COLLEGE PARK**
Aerospace/Aeronautical
   Engineering — M,D
Bioengineering — M,D
Bioinformatics — D
Chemical Engineering — M,D
Civil Engineering — M,D
Computer Engineering — M,D
Computer Science — M,D
Electrical Engineering — M,D
Engineering and Applied
   Sciences—General — M
Environmental Engineering — M,D
Fire Protection Engineering — M
Manufacturing Engineering — M,D
Materials Engineering — M,D
Materials Sciences — M,D
Mechanical Engineering — M,D
Mechanics — M,D
Nuclear Engineering — M,D
Reliability Engineering — M,D
Systems Engineering — M
Telecommunications — M

**UNIVERSITY OF MARYLAND
EASTERN SHORE**
Computer Science — M

**UNIVERSITY OF MARYLAND
UNIVERSITY COLLEGE**
Biotechnology — M,O
Computer and Information
   Systems Security — M,O
Data Science/Data Analytics — M,O
Health Informatics — M
Information Science — M

**UNIVERSITY OF
MASSACHUSETTS AMHERST**
Architectural Engineering — M,D
Biotechnology — M,D
Chemical Engineering — M,D
Civil Engineering — M,D
Computer Engineering — M,D
Computer Science — M,D
Electrical Engineering — M,D
Engineering and Applied
   Sciences—General — M,D
Environmental Engineering — M,D
Geotechnical Engineering — M,D
Industrial/Management
   Engineering — M,D
Mechanical Engineering — M,D
Mechanics — M,D
Operations Research — M,D
Polymer Science and
   Engineering — M,D
Structural Engineering — M,D
Transportation and Highway
   Engineering — M,D
Water Resources Engineering — M,D

**UNIVERSITY OF
MASSACHUSETTS BOSTON**
Biomedical Engineering — D
Biotechnology — M,D
Computer Science — M,D

**UNIVERSITY OF
MASSACHUSETTS DARTMOUTH**
Biomedical Engineering — D
Biotechnology — D

Civil Engineering — M
Computer Engineering — M,D,O
Computer Science — M,O
Data Science/Data Analytics — M
Electrical Engineering — M,D,O
Engineering and Applied
   Sciences—General — D
Industrial/Management
   Engineering — M,O
Management of Technology — M
Mechanical Engineering — M,O
Software Engineering — M,O
Systems Engineering — M,O
Telecommunications — M,D,O

**UNIVERSITY OF
MASSACHUSETTS LOWELL**
Chemical Engineering — M,D
Civil Engineering — M,D
Computer Engineering — M,D
Computer Science — M,D
Electrical Engineering — M,D
Energy and Power
   Engineering — M,D
Engineering and Applied
   Sciences—General — M,D
Environmental Engineering — M,D
Industrial/Management
   Engineering — D
Mechanical Engineering — M,D
Nuclear Engineering — M,D
Polymer Science and
   Engineering — M,D

**UNIVERSITY OF
MASSACHUSETTS MEDICAL
SCHOOL**
Bioinformatics — M,D

UNIVERSITY OF MEMPHIS
Bioinformatics — M,D
Biomedical Engineering — M,D
Civil Engineering — M,D,O
Computer Engineering — M,D,O
Computer Science — M,D
Electrical Engineering — M,D,O
Electronic Materials — M,O
Energy and Power
   Engineering — M,D,O
Engineering and Applied
   Sciences—General — M,D,O
Environmental Engineering — M,D,O
Geotechnical Engineering — M,D,O
Mechanical Engineering — M,D,O
Structural Engineering — M,D,O
Transportation and Highway
   Engineering — M,D,O
Water Resources Engineering — M,D,O

UNIVERSITY OF MIAMI
Aerospace/Aeronautical
   Engineering — M,D
Architectural Engineering — M,D
Biomedical Engineering — M,D
Civil Engineering — M,D
Computer Engineering — M,D
Computer Science — M,D
Electrical Engineering — M,D
Engineering and Applied
   Sciences—General — M,D
Ergonomics and Human
   Factors — M
Industrial/Management
   Engineering — M,D
Management of Technology — M,D
Mechanical Engineering — M,D

UNIVERSITY OF MICHIGAN
Aerospace/Aeronautical
   Engineering — M,D
Artificial Intelligence/Robotics — M,D
Automotive Engineering — M,D
Bioinformatics — M,D

Industrial/Management
   Engineering — M,D,O
Mechanical Engineering — M,D

Biomedical Engineering M,D
Chemical Engineering M,D,O
Civil Engineering M,D,O
Computer Engineering M,D
Computer Science M,D
Construction Engineering M,D,O
Data Science/Data Analytics M,D,O
Electrical Engineering M,D
Energy and Power
   Engineering M,D
Engineering and Applied
   Sciences—General M,D,O
Engineering Design M,D
Environmental Engineering M,D,O
Health Informatics M,D
Industrial/Management
   Engineering M,D
Information Science M,D
Manufacturing Engineering M,D
Materials Engineering M,D
Materials Sciences M,D
Mechanical Engineering M,D
Nuclear Engineering M,D,O
Ocean Engineering M,D,O
Operations Research M,D
Pharmaceutical Engineering M,D
Structural Engineering M,D,O
Systems Engineering M,D
Systems Science M,D

**UNIVERSITY OF
MICHIGAN–DEARBORN**
Automotive Engineering M
Bioengineering M
Computer and Information
   Systems Security D
Computer Engineering M,D
Computer Science D
Data Science/Data Analytics M,D
Electrical Engineering M,D
Energy and Power
   Engineering M
Engineering and Applied
   Sciences—General M,D
Engineering Management M
Health Informatics M
Industrial/Management
   Engineering M,D
Information Science M,D
Manufacturing Engineering M
Mechanical Engineering M,D
Software Engineering M,D
Systems Engineering M,D

UNIVERSITY OF MICHIGAN–FLINT
Computer Science M
Health Informatics M
Information Science M
Mechanical Engineering M

**UNIVERSITY OF MINNESOTA,
DULUTH**
Computer Engineering M
Computer Science M
Electrical Engineering M
Engineering Management M
Safety Engineering M

**UNIVERSITY OF MINNESOTA
ROCHESTER**
Bioinformatics M,D

**UNIVERSITY OF MINNESOTA,
TWIN CITIES CAMPUS**
Aerospace/Aeronautical
   Engineering M,D
Biomedical Engineering M,D
Biosystems Engineering M,D
Biotechnology M
Chemical Engineering M,D

Civil Engineering M,D,O
Computer and Information
   Systems Security M
Computer Engineering M,D
Computer Science M,D
Data Science/Data Analytics M
Electrical Engineering M,D
Engineering and Applied
   Sciences—General M,D,O
Geological Engineering M,D,O
Health Informatics M,D
Industrial/Management
   Engineering M,D
Management of Technology M
Materials Engineering M,D
Materials Sciences M,D
Mechanical Engineering M,D
Mechanics M,D
Paper and Pulp Engineering M,D
Software Engineering M,D
Technology and Public Policy M

UNIVERSITY OF MISSISSIPPI
Applied Science and
   Technology M,D
Chemical Engineering M,D
Civil Engineering M,D
Computer Science M,D
Data Science/Data Analytics M,D
Electrical Engineering M,D
Engineering and Applied
   Sciences—General M,D
Environmental Engineering M,D
Geological Engineering M,D
Mechanical Engineering M,D
Telecommunications M,D

**UNIVERSITY OF MISSISSIPPI
MEDICAL CENTER**
Materials Sciences M,D

UNIVERSITY OF MISSOURI
Aerospace/Aeronautical
   Engineering M,D
Bioengineering M,D
Bioinformatics M
Chemical Engineering M,D
Civil Engineering M,D
Computer Engineering M,D
Computer Science M,D
Electrical Engineering M,D
Engineering and Applied
   Sciences—General M,D,O
Environmental Engineering M,D
Health Informatics M,O
Industrial/Management
   Engineering M,D
Manufacturing Engineering M,D
Mechanical Engineering M,D

**UNIVERSITY OF
MISSOURI–KANSAS CITY**
Bioinformatics M,D,O
Civil Engineering M,D,O
Computer Engineering M,D,O
Computer Science M,D,O
Construction Engineering M,D,O
Electrical Engineering M,D,O
Engineering and Applied
   Sciences—General M,D,O
Engineering Management M,D,O
Mechanical Engineering M,D,O
Polymer Science and
   Engineering M,D
Software Engineering M,D,O
Telecommunications M,D,O

**UNIVERSITY OF MISSOURI–ST.
LOUIS**
Biotechnology M,D

Computer and Information
   Systems Security M,D,O
Computer Science M,D

UNIVERSITY OF MONTANA
Computer Science M

**UNIVERSITY OF NEBRASKA AT
OMAHA**
Artificial Intelligence/Robotics M,O
Bioinformatics M,D
Computer and Information
   Systems Security M,D,O
Computer Science M,O
Data Science/Data Analytics M,D,O
Information Science M,D,O
Software Engineering M,O
Systems Engineering M,O

**UNIVERSITY OF
NEBRASKA–LINCOLN**
Agricultural Engineering M,D
Architectural Engineering M,D
Bioengineering M,D
Bioinformatics M,D
Biomedical Engineering M,D
Chemical Engineering M,D
Civil Engineering M,D
Computer Engineering M,D
Computer Science M,D
Electrical Engineering M,D
Engineering and Applied
   Sciences—General M,D
Engineering Management M,D
Environmental Engineering M,D
Industrial/Management
   Engineering M,D
Information Science M,D
Manufacturing Engineering M,D
Materials Engineering M,D
Materials Sciences M,D
Mechanical Engineering M,D
Mechanics M,D
Metallurgical Engineering and
   Metallurgy M,D

**UNIVERSITY OF NEBRASKA
MEDICAL CENTER**
Bioinformatics M,D

**UNIVERSITY OF NEVADA, LAS
VEGAS**
Aerospace/Aeronautical
   Engineering M,D,O
Biomedical Engineering M,D,O
Computer and Information
   Systems Security M,D,O
Data Science/Data Analytics M,O
Engineering and Applied
   Sciences—General M,D,O
Materials Engineering M,D,O
Nuclear Engineering M,D,O
Transportation and Highway
   Engineering M,D

UNIVERSITY OF NEVADA, RENO
Biomedical Engineering M,D
Biotechnology M
Chemical Engineering M,D
Civil Engineering M,D
Computer Engineering M,D
Computer Science M,D
Electrical Engineering M,D
Engineering and Applied
   Sciences—General M,D
Geological Engineering M,D
Materials Engineering M,D
Mechanical Engineering M,D
Metallurgical Engineering and
   Metallurgy M,D

Mineral/Mining Engineering M,D

**UNIVERSITY OF NEW BRUNSWICK
FREDERICTON**
Chemical Engineering M,D
Civil Engineering M,D
Computer Engineering M,D
Computer Science M,D
Construction Engineering M,D
Electrical Engineering M,D
Engineering and Applied
   Sciences—General M,D,O
Engineering Management M
Environmental Engineering M,D
Geotechnical Engineering M,D
Materials Sciences M,D
Mechanical Engineering M,D
Mechanics M,D
Structural Engineering M,D
Surveying Science and
   Engineering M,D
Transportation and Highway
   Engineering M,D

UNIVERSITY OF NEW ENGLAND
Health Informatics M,D,O

UNIVERSITY OF NEW HAMPSHIRE
Chemical Engineering M,D
Civil Engineering M,D
Computer and Information
   Systems Security M,O
Computer Science M,D
Electrical Engineering M,D,O
Environmental Engineering M,D
Materials Engineering M,D
Materials Sciences M,D
Mechanical Engineering M,D
Ocean Engineering M,D,O

UNIVERSITY OF NEW HAVEN
Biomedical Engineering M
Civil Engineering M
Computer and Information
   Systems Security M
Computer Engineering M
Computer Science M,O
Electrical Engineering M
Engineering and Applied
   Sciences—General M,O
Engineering Management M,O
Environmental Engineering M
Fire Protection Engineering M,O
Hazardous Materials
   Management M
Industrial/Management
   Engineering M,O
Mechanical Engineering M
Software Engineering M,O
Water Resources Engineering M

UNIVERSITY OF NEW MEXICO
Biomedical Engineering M,D
Chemical Engineering M,D
Civil Engineering M,D
Computer and Information
   Systems Security M
Computer Engineering M,D
Computer Science M,D
Construction Management M,D
Electrical Engineering M,D
Engineering and Applied
   Sciences—General M,D
Management of Technology M
Manufacturing Engineering M
Mechanical Engineering M,D
Nanotechnology M,D
Nuclear Engineering M,D
Systems Engineering M,D

*M—masters degree; D—doctorate; O—other advanced degree; *—Close-Up and/or Display*

UNIVERSITY OF NEW ORLEANS

Civil Engineering	M
Computer Science	M,D
Electrical Engineering	M
Engineering and Applied Sciences—General	M,D
Engineering Management	M
Mechanical Engineering	M

UNIVERSITY OF NORTH ALABAMA

Information Science	M

THE UNIVERSITY OF NORTH CAROLINA AT CHAPEL HILL

Bioinformatics	D
Biomedical Engineering	M,D
Computer Science	M,D
Environmental Engineering	M,D
Operations Research	M,D
Telecommunications	M,D,O

THE UNIVERSITY OF NORTH CAROLINA AT CHARLOTTE

Bioinformatics	M,D,O
Civil Engineering	M,D
Computer and Information Systems Security	M,D,O
Computer Engineering	M,D
Computer Science	M,D
Construction Management	M,O
Data Science/Data Analytics	M,O
Electrical Engineering	M,D
Energy and Power Engineering	M,O
Engineering and Applied Sciences—General	M,D,O
Engineering Management	M,O
Environmental Engineering	M,D
Fire Protection Engineering	M,O
Game Design and Development	M,O
Health Informatics	M,O
Information Science	M,O
Mechanical Engineering	M,D
Systems Engineering	M,D,O

THE UNIVERSITY OF NORTH CAROLINA AT GREENSBORO

Computer Science	M

THE UNIVERSITY OF NORTH CAROLINA WILMINGTON

Computer Science	M
Data Science/Data Analytics	M

UNIVERSITY OF NORTH DAKOTA

Aviation	M
Chemical Engineering	M,D
Civil Engineering	M,D
Computer Science	M
Electrical Engineering	M,D
Engineering and Applied Sciences—General	D
Environmental Engineering	M,D
Geological Engineering	M,D
Mechanical Engineering	M,D

UNIVERSITY OF NORTHERN BRITISH COLUMBIA

Computer Science	M,D,O

UNIVERSITY OF NORTH FLORIDA

Civil Engineering	M
Computer Science	M
Construction Management	M
Electrical Engineering	M
Mechanical Engineering	M
Software Engineering	M

UNIVERSITY OF NORTH TEXAS

Biomedical Engineering	M,D,O
Computer Engineering	M,D,O
Computer Science	M,D,O
Electrical Engineering	M,D,O
Energy and Power Engineering	M,D,O
Engineering and Applied Sciences—General	M,D,O
Information Science	M,D,O
Mechanical Engineering	M,D,O

UNIVERSITY OF NORTH TEXAS HEALTH SCIENCE CENTER AT FORT WORTH

Biotechnology	M,D

UNIVERSITY OF NOTRE DAME

Aerospace/Aeronautical Engineering	M,D
Bioengineering	M,D
Chemical Engineering	M,D
Civil Engineering	M,D
Computer Engineering	M,D
Computer Science	M,D
Electrical Engineering	M,D
Engineering and Applied Sciences—General	M,D
Environmental Engineering	M,D
Mechanical Engineering	M,D

UNIVERSITY OF OKLAHOMA

Aerospace/Aeronautical Engineering	M,D
Civil Engineering	M,D
Computer Engineering	M,D
Electrical Engineering	M,D
Engineering Physics	M,D
Environmental Engineering	M,D
Geological Engineering	M,D,O
Mechanical Engineering	M,D
Petroleum Engineering	M,D,O
Telecommunications	M,D

UNIVERSITY OF OREGON

Computer Science	M,D
Information Science	M,D

UNIVERSITY OF OTTAWA

Aerospace/Aeronautical Engineering	M,D
Bioengineering	M,D
Biomedical Engineering	M
Chemical Engineering	M,D
Civil Engineering	M,D
Computer Engineering	M,D
Computer Science	M,D
Electrical Engineering	M,D
Engineering and Applied Sciences—General	M,D,O
Engineering Management	M,O
Information Science	M,O
Mechanical Engineering	M,D
Systems Science	M,D,O

UNIVERSITY OF PENNSYLVANIA

Artificial Intelligence/Robotics	M
Bioengineering	M,D
Biotechnology	M
Chemical Engineering	M,D
Computer Science	M,D
Data Science/Data Analytics	M
Electrical Engineering	M,D
Engineering and Applied Sciences—General	M,D*
Game Design and Development	M,D
Information Science	M,D
Materials Engineering	M,D
Materials Sciences	M,D
Mechanical Engineering	M,D
Mechanics	M,D

Nanotechnology	M
Systems Engineering	M,D

UNIVERSITY OF PHOENIX–BAY AREA CAMPUS

Energy Management and Policy	M,D
Management of Technology	M,D

UNIVERSITY OF PHOENIX–CENTRAL VALLEY CAMPUS

Management of Technology	M

UNIVERSITY OF PHOENIX–DALLAS CAMPUS

Management of Technology	M

UNIVERSITY OF PHOENIX–HAWAII CAMPUS

Management of Technology	M

UNIVERSITY OF PHOENIX–HOUSTON CAMPUS

Management of Technology	M

UNIVERSITY OF PHOENIX–LAS VEGAS CAMPUS

Management of Technology	M

UNIVERSITY OF PHOENIX–ONLINE CAMPUS

Energy Management and Policy	M,O
Health Informatics	M,O
Management of Technology	M,O

UNIVERSITY OF PHOENIX–PHOENIX CAMPUS

Energy Management and Policy	M,O
Management of Technology	M,O
Medical Informatics	M,O

UNIVERSITY OF PHOENIX–SACRAMENTO VALLEY CAMPUS

Management of Technology	M

UNIVERSITY OF PHOENIX–SAN ANTONIO CAMPUS

Management of Technology	M

UNIVERSITY OF PHOENIX–SAN DIEGO CAMPUS

Management of Technology	M

UNIVERSITY OF PITTSBURGH

Artificial Intelligence/Robotics	M,D
Bioengineering	M,D
Bioinformatics	M,D,O
Chemical Engineering	M,D
Civil Engineering	M,D
Computer Engineering	M,D
Computer Science	M,D
Data Science/Data Analytics	M,D,O
Electrical Engineering	M,D
Energy Management and Policy	M
Engineering and Applied Sciences—General	M,D
Environmental Engineering	M,D
Health Informatics	M
Industrial/Management Engineering	M,D
Information Science	M,D,O
Materials Sciences	M,D
Mechanical Engineering	M,D
Modeling and Simulation	M,D

Petroleum Engineering	M,D

UNIVERSITY OF PORTLAND

Biomedical Engineering	M
Civil Engineering	M
Computer Science	M
Electrical Engineering	M
Engineering and Applied Sciences—General	M
Management of Technology	M
Mechanical Engineering	M

UNIVERSITY OF PUERTO RICO–MAYAGÜEZ

Aerospace/Aeronautical Engineering	M,D
Bioengineering	M,D
Chemical Engineering	M,D
Civil Engineering	M,D
Computer Engineering	M,D
Computer Science	M,D
Construction Engineering	M,D
Electrical Engineering	M,D
Energy and Power Engineering	M,D
Engineering and Applied Sciences—General	M,D
Engineering Management	M,D
Environmental Engineering	M,D
Geotechnical Engineering	M,D
Industrial/Management Engineering	M
Information Science	M,D
Manufacturing Engineering	M,D
Materials Engineering	M,D
Materials Sciences	M,D
Mechanical Engineering	M,D
Structural Engineering	M,D
Transportation and Highway Engineering	M,D

UNIVERSITY OF PUERTO RICO–MEDICAL SCIENCES CAMPUS

Health Informatics	M

UNIVERSITY OF PUERTO RICO–RÍO PIEDRAS

Information Science	M,O

UNIVERSITY OF REGINA

Computer Engineering	M,D
Computer Science	M,D
Engineering and Applied Sciences—General	M,D
Engineering Management	M,O
Environmental Engineering	M,D
Industrial/Management Engineering	M,D
Petroleum Engineering	M,D
Software Engineering	M,D
Systems Engineering	M,D

UNIVERSITY OF RHODE ISLAND

Biomedical Engineering	M,D
Biotechnology	M,D
Chemical Engineering	M,D,O
Civil Engineering	M,D
Computer and Information Systems Security	M,D,O
Computer Engineering	M,D
Computer Science	M,D,O
Electrical Engineering	M,D
Engineering and Applied Sciences—General	M,D,O
Environmental Engineering	M,D
Geotechnical Engineering	M,D
Industrial/Management Engineering	M,D
Ocean Engineering	M,D
Systems Engineering	M,D

UNIVERSITY OF ROCHESTER
Artificial Intelligence/Robotics M,D
Bioinformatics M,D
Biomedical Engineering M,D
Chemical Engineering M,D*
Computer Engineering M,D
Computer Science M,D
Data Science/Data Analytics M
Electrical Engineering M,D
Engineering and Applied
    Sciences—General M,D
Human-Computer Interaction M,D
Materials Sciences M,D
Mechanical Engineering M,D

UNIVERSITY OF ST. AUGUSTINE FOR HEALTH SCIENCES
Health Informatics M

UNIVERSITY OF ST. THOMAS (MN)
Data Science/Data Analytics M,O
Electrical Engineering M,O
Engineering and Applied
    Sciences—General M,O
Engineering Management M,O
Information Science M,O
Management of Technology M,O
Manufacturing Engineering M,O
Mechanical Engineering M,O
Software Engineering M,O
Systems Engineering M,O

UNIVERSITY OF SAN DIEGO
Computer and Information
    Systems Security M
Computer Engineering M
Health Informatics M,D

UNIVERSITY OF SAN FRANCISCO
Biotechnology M
Computer Science M
Data Science/Data Analytics M
Energy Management and
    Policy M
Health Informatics M

UNIVERSITY OF SASKATCHEWAN
Bioengineering M,D
Biomedical Engineering M,D,O
Chemical Engineering M,D
Civil Engineering M,D
Computer Science M,D
Electrical Engineering M,D,O
Engineering and Applied
    Sciences—General M,D,O
Engineering Physics M,D
Geological Engineering M,D
Mechanical Engineering M,D

THE UNIVERSITY OF SCRANTON
Software Engineering M

UNIVERSITY OF SOUTH AFRICA
Chemical Engineering M
Engineering and Applied
    Sciences—General M
Information Science M,D
Technology and Public Policy M,D
Telecommunications
    Management M,D

UNIVERSITY OF SOUTH ALABAMA
Chemical Engineering M
Civil Engineering M
Computer Engineering M
Computer Science M,D
Electrical Engineering M
Engineering and Applied
    Sciences—General M,D

Environmental Engineering M
Mechanical Engineering M
Systems Engineering D

UNIVERSITY OF SOUTH CAROLINA
Chemical Engineering M,D
Civil Engineering M,D
Computer Engineering M,D
Computer Science M,D
Electrical Engineering M,D
Engineering and Applied
    Sciences—General M,D
Hazardous Materials
    Management M,D
Mechanical Engineering M,D
Nuclear Engineering M,D
Software Engineering M,D

UNIVERSITY OF SOUTH CAROLINA UPSTATE
Health Informatics M
Information Science M

UNIVERSITY OF SOUTH DAKOTA
Computer Science M

UNIVERSITY OF SOUTHERN CALIFORNIA
Aerospace/Aeronautical
    Engineering M,D,O
Artificial Intelligence/Robotics M,D
Bioinformatics D
Biomedical Engineering M,D
Biotechnology M
Chemical Engineering M,D,O
Civil Engineering M,D,O
Computer and Information
    Systems Security M,D
Computer Engineering M,D,O
Computer Science M,D
Construction Management M,D,O
Electrical Engineering M,D,O
Engineering and Applied
    Sciences—General M,D,O
Engineering Management M,D,O
Environmental Engineering M,D,O
Game Design and
    Development M,D
Geotechnical Engineering M,D,O
Hazardous Materials
    Management M,D,O
Industrial/Management
    Engineering M,D,O
Manufacturing Engineering M,D,O
Materials Engineering M,D,O
Materials Sciences M,D,O
Mechanical Engineering M,D,O
Mechanics M,D,O
Modeling and Simulation M,D
Operations Research M,D,O
Petroleum Engineering M,D,O
Safety Engineering M,D,O
Software Engineering M,D
Systems Engineering M,D,O
Telecommunications M,D,O
Transportation and Highway
    Engineering M,D,O

UNIVERSITY OF SOUTHERN INDIANA
Data Science/Data Analytics M
Engineering and Applied
    Sciences—General M,D
Engineering Management M

UNIVERSITY OF SOUTHERN MAINE
Computer Science M,O
Software Engineering M,O

UNIVERSITY OF SOUTHERN MISSISSIPPI
Computer Science M,D
Construction Engineering M
Information Science M,O
Polymer Science and
    Engineering M,D

UNIVERSITY OF SOUTH FLORIDA
Bioinformatics M,D,O
Biomedical Engineering M,D,O
Biotechnology M,D,O
Chemical Engineering M,D,O
Civil Engineering M,D,O
Computer and Information
    Systems Security M,D
Computer Engineering M,D
Computer Science M,D
Data Science/Data Analytics M,D,O
Electrical Engineering M,D
Engineering and Applied
    Sciences—General M,D,O
Engineering Management M,D
Environmental Engineering M,D
Geotechnical Engineering M,D
Health Informatics M,D,O
Industrial/Management
    Engineering M,D,O
Information Science M
Management of Technology O
Materials Engineering M,D,O
Materials Sciences M,D,O
Mechanical Engineering M,D
Nanotechnology M,D
Structural Engineering M,D
Systems Engineering O
Transportation and Highway
    Engineering M,D,O
Water Resources Engineering M,D,O

THE UNIVERSITY OF TAMPA
Computer and Information
    Systems Security M,O

THE UNIVERSITY OF TENNESSEE
Aerospace/Aeronautical
    Engineering M,D
Agricultural Engineering M
Aviation M
Biomedical Engineering M,D
Biosystems Engineering M,D
Chemical Engineering M,D
Civil Engineering M,D
Computer Engineering M,D
Computer Science M,D
Data Science/Data Analytics D
Electrical Engineering M,D
Energy and Power
    Engineering D
Engineering and Applied
    Sciences—General M,D
Engineering Management M,D
Environmental Engineering M
Industrial/Management
    Engineering M,D
Information Science M,D
Materials Engineering M,D
Materials Sciences M,D
Mechanical Engineering M,D
Nuclear Engineering M,D
Reliability Engineering M,D

THE UNIVERSITY OF TENNESSEE AT CHATTANOOGA
Automotive Engineering M
Bioinformatics M,O
Chemical Engineering M
Civil Engineering M
Computer Science M,O
Construction Management M,O
Electrical Engineering M

Energy and Power
    Engineering M,O
Engineering Management M,O
Mechanical Engineering M

THE UNIVERSITY OF TENNESSEE HEALTH SCIENCE CENTER
Biomedical Engineering M,D
Health Informatics M,D

THE UNIVERSITY OF TEXAS AT ARLINGTON
Aerospace/Aeronautical
    Engineering M,D
Bioengineering M,D
Civil Engineering M,D
Computer Engineering M,D
Computer Science M,D
Construction Management M,D
Electrical Engineering M,D
Engineering and Applied
    Sciences—General M,D
Engineering Management M
Industrial/Management
    Engineering M,D
Materials Engineering M,D
Materials Sciences M,D
Mechanical Engineering M,D
Software Engineering M,D
Systems Engineering M

THE UNIVERSITY OF TEXAS AT AUSTIN
Aerospace/Aeronautical
    Engineering M,D
Architectural Engineering M
Biomedical Engineering M,D
Chemical Engineering M,D
Civil Engineering M,D
Computer and Information
    Systems Security M,D
Computer Engineering M,D
Computer Science M,D
Electrical Engineering M,D
Engineering and Applied
    Sciences—General M,D
Environmental Engineering M,D
Geotechnical Engineering M,D
Industrial/Management
    Engineering M,D
Materials Engineering M,D
Materials Sciences M,D
Mechanical Engineering M,D
Mechanics M
Mineral/Mining Engineering M,D
Operations Research M,D
Petroleum Engineering M,D
Technology and Public Policy M
Textile Sciences and
    Engineering M
Water Resources Engineering M,D

THE UNIVERSITY OF TEXAS AT DALLAS
Biomedical Engineering M,D
Biotechnology M,D
Computer Engineering M,D
Computer Science M,D
Data Science/Data Analytics M,D
Electrical Engineering M,D
Engineering and Applied
    Sciences—General M,D
Management of Technology M
Materials Engineering M,D
Materials Sciences M,D
Mechanical Engineering M,D
Software Engineering M,D
Systems Engineering M,D
Telecommunications M,D

*M—masters degree; D—doctorate; O—other advanced degree; *—Close-Up and/or Display*

THE UNIVERSITY OF TEXAS AT EL PASO

Bioinformatics	M,D
Civil Engineering	M,D,O
Computer and Information Systems Security	M,D,O
Computer Engineering	M,D,O
Computer Science	M,D,O
Construction Management	M,D,O
Electrical Engineering	M,D,O
Energy and Power Engineering	M,D,O
Engineering and Applied Sciences—General	M,D,O
Environmental Engineering	M,D,O
Industrial/Management Engineering	M
Information Science	M,D,O
Manufacturing Engineering	M
Materials Engineering	M,D
Materials Sciences	M,D
Mechanical Engineering	M,D
Metallurgical Engineering and Metallurgy	M,D
Software Engineering	M,D,O
Systems Engineering	M

THE UNIVERSITY OF TEXAS AT SAN ANTONIO

Biomedical Engineering	M,D
Biotechnology	M,D
Civil Engineering	M,D
Computer and Information Systems Security	M,D,O
Computer Engineering	M,D
Computer Science	M,D
Electrical Engineering	M,D
Engineering and Applied Sciences—General	M,D
Environmental Engineering	M,D
Information Science	M,D,O
Management of Technology	M,D,O
Manufacturing Engineering	M,D
Materials Engineering	M,D
Mechanical Engineering	M,D

THE UNIVERSITY OF TEXAS AT TYLER

Civil Engineering	M
Computer and Information Systems Security	M
Computer Science	M
Electrical Engineering	M
Energy Management and Policy	M
Engineering Management	M
Environmental Engineering	M
Mechanical Engineering	M
Structural Engineering	M
Transportation and Highway Engineering	M
Water Resources Engineering	M

THE UNIVERSITY OF TEXAS HEALTH SCIENCE CENTER AT HOUSTON

Bioinformatics	M,D,O
Data Science/Data Analytics	M,D,O
Health Informatics	M,D,O

THE UNIVERSITY OF TEXAS HEALTH SCIENCE CENTER AT SAN ANTONIO

Biomedical Engineering	M,D

THE UNIVERSITY OF TEXAS HEALTH SCIENCE CENTER AT TYLER

Biotechnology	M

THE UNIVERSITY OF TEXAS MEDICAL BRANCH

Bioinformatics	D

THE UNIVERSITY OF TEXAS OF THE PERMIAN BASIN

Computer Science	M

THE UNIVERSITY OF TEXAS RIO GRANDE VALLEY

Computer Science	M
Electrical Engineering	M
Engineering Management	M
Manufacturing Engineering	M
Mechanical Engineering	M
Systems Engineering	M

THE UNIVERSITY OF TEXAS SOUTHWESTERN MEDICAL CENTER

Biomedical Engineering	M,D

UNIVERSITY OF THE DISTRICT OF COLUMBIA

Computer Science	M
Electrical Engineering	M
Engineering and Applied Sciences—General	M

UNIVERSITY OF THE PACIFIC

Engineering and Applied Sciences—General	M

UNIVERSITY OF THE SACRED HEART

Information Science	O

UNIVERSITY OF THE SCIENCES

Bioinformatics	M
Biotechnology	M

THE UNIVERSITY OF TOLEDO

Bioengineering	M,D
Bioinformatics	M,O
Biomedical Engineering	D
Chemical Engineering	M,D
Civil Engineering	M,D
Computer Science	M,D
Electrical Engineering	M,D
Engineering and Applied Sciences—General	M
Industrial/Management Engineering	M,D
Materials Sciences	M,D
Mechanical Engineering	M,D

UNIVERSITY OF TORONTO

Aerospace/Aeronautical Engineering	M,D
Biomedical Engineering	M,D
Biotechnology	M
Chemical Engineering	M,D
Civil Engineering	M,D
Computer Engineering	M,D
Computer Science	M,D
Electrical Engineering	M,D
Engineering and Applied Sciences—General	M,D
Health Informatics	M
Industrial/Management Engineering	M,D
Management of Technology	M
Manufacturing Engineering	M
Materials Engineering	M,D
Materials Sciences	M,D
Mechanical Engineering	M,D

THE UNIVERSITY OF TULSA

Chemical Engineering	M,D

Computer and Information Systems Security	M,D
Computer Science	M,D
Electrical Engineering	M,D
Energy Management and Policy	M
Engineering and Applied Sciences—General	M,D
Mechanical Engineering	M,D
Petroleum Engineering	M,D

UNIVERSITY OF UTAH

Bioengineering	M,D
Bioinformatics	M,D,O
Biotechnology	M
Chemical Engineering	M,D
Civil Engineering	M,D
Computer and Information Systems Security	M,O
Computer Engineering	M,D
Computer Science	M,D
Electrical Engineering	M,D
Engineering and Applied Sciences—General	M,D
Environmental Engineering	M,D
Game Design and Development	M
Geological Engineering	M,D
Materials Engineering	M,D
Materials Sciences	M,D
Mechanical Engineering	M,D
Metallurgical Engineering and Metallurgy	M,D
Mineral/Mining Engineering	M,D
Nuclear Engineering	M,D
Petroleum Engineering	M,D
Software Engineering	M,D,O
Systems Engineering	M,O

UNIVERSITY OF VERMONT

Bioengineering	D
Biomedical Engineering	M
Civil Engineering	M,D
Computer Science	M,D
Data Science/Data Analytics	M,D
Electrical Engineering	M,D
Engineering and Applied Sciences—General	M,D
Engineering Management	M
Environmental Engineering	M,D
Materials Sciences	M,D
Mechanical Engineering	M,D

UNIVERSITY OF VICTORIA

Computer Engineering	M,D
Computer Science	M,D
Electrical Engineering	M,D
Engineering and Applied Sciences—General	M,D
Health Informatics	M
Mechanical Engineering	M,D

UNIVERSITY OF VIRGINIA

Aerospace/Aeronautical Engineering	M,D
Biomedical Engineering	M,D
Chemical Engineering	M,D
Civil Engineering	M,D
Computer Engineering	M,D
Computer Science	M,D
Construction Engineering	D
Data Science/Data Analytics	M
Electrical Engineering	M,D
Engineering and Applied Sciences—General	M,D
Engineering Physics	M,D
Health Informatics	M
Management of Technology	M
Materials Sciences	M,D
Mechanical Engineering	M,D
Systems Engineering	M,D

UNIVERSITY OF WASHINGTON

Aerospace/Aeronautical Engineering	M,D
Bioengineering	M,D
Bioinformatics	M,D
Biotechnology	D
Chemical Engineering	M,D
Civil Engineering	M,D
Computer and Information Systems Security	M,D
Computer Engineering	M,D
Computer Science	M,D
Construction Engineering	M,D
Construction Management	M
Data Science/Data Analytics	M,D
Electrical Engineering	M,D
Engineering and Applied Sciences—General	M,D,O
Environmental Engineering	M,D
Geotechnical Engineering	M,D
Health Informatics	M,D
Human-Computer Interaction	M,D,O
Industrial/Management Engineering	M,D
Information Science	M,D
Management of Technology	M,D
Materials Engineering	M,D
Materials Sciences	M,D
Mechanical Engineering	M,D
Mechanics	M,D
Medical Informatics	M,D
Nanotechnology	M,D
Structural Engineering	M,D
Systems Engineering	M,D
Transportation and Highway Engineering	M,D

UNIVERSITY OF WASHINGTON, BOTHELL

Computer Engineering	M
Software Engineering	M

UNIVERSITY OF WASHINGTON, TACOMA

Computer Engineering	M
Software Engineering	M

UNIVERSITY OF WATERLOO

Chemical Engineering	M,D
Civil Engineering	M,D
Computer Engineering	M,D
Computer Science	M,D
Electrical Engineering	M,D
Engineering and Applied Sciences—General	M,D
Engineering Management	M,D
Environmental Engineering	M,D
Health Informatics	M,D
Information Science	M,D
Management of Technology	M,D
Mechanical Engineering	M,D
Operations Research	M,D
Software Engineering	M,D
Systems Engineering	M,D

THE UNIVERSITY OF WESTERN ONTARIO

Biochemical Engineering	M,D
Chemical Engineering	M,D
Civil Engineering	M,D
Computer Engineering	M,D
Computer Science	M,D
Electrical Engineering	M,D
Engineering and Applied Sciences—General	M,D
Environmental Engineering	M,D
Materials Engineering	M,D
Mechanical Engineering	M,D

UNIVERSITY OF WEST FLORIDA

Computer and Information Systems Security	M
Computer Science	M

Data Science/Data Analytics	M
Software Engineering	M

UNIVERSITY OF WEST GEORGIA

Computer Science	M,O

UNIVERSITY OF WINDSOR

Civil Engineering	M,D
Computer Science	M,D
Electrical Engineering	M,D
Engineering and Applied Sciences—General	M,D
Environmental Engineering	M,D
Industrial/Management Engineering	M,D
Manufacturing Engineering	M,D
Materials Engineering	M,D
Mechanical Engineering	M,D

UNIVERSITY OF WISCONSIN–LA CROSSE

Data Science/Data Analytics	M
Software Engineering	M

UNIVERSITY OF WISCONSIN–MADISON

Agricultural Engineering	M,D
Automotive Engineering	M,D
Bioinformatics	M,D
Biomedical Engineering	M,D
Chemical Engineering	D
Civil Engineering	M
Computer and Information Systems Security	M
Computer Science	M,D
Construction Engineering	M
Electrical Engineering	M,D
Engineering and Applied Sciences—General	M,D
Engineering Physics	M,D
Environmental Engineering	M
Ergonomics and Human Factors	M,D
Geological Engineering	M,D
Geotechnical Engineering	M
Industrial/Management Engineering	M,D
Management of Technology	M
Manufacturing Engineering	M
Materials Engineering	M,D
Mechanical Engineering	M,D
Mechanics	M,D
Nuclear Engineering	M,D
Structural Engineering	M
Systems Engineering	M,D
Transportation and Highway Engineering	M
Water Resources Engineering	M

UNIVERSITY OF WISCONSIN–MILWAUKEE

Biomedical Engineering	M,D
Civil Engineering	M,D
Computer Engineering	M,D
Computer Science	M,D
Electrical Engineering	M,D
Engineering and Applied Sciences—General	M,D
Ergonomics and Human Factors	M
Health Informatics	M,D
Industrial/Management Engineering	M,D
Management of Technology	M,O
Manufacturing Engineering	M,D
Materials Engineering	M,D
Mechanical Engineering	M,D
Mechanics	M,D
Medical Informatics	M

UNIVERSITY OF WISCONSIN–PARKSIDE

Computer Science	M
Information Science	M

UNIVERSITY OF WISCONSIN–PLATTEVILLE

Computer Science	M
Engineering and Applied Sciences—General	M

UNIVERSITY OF WISCONSIN–STEVENS POINT

Data Science/Data Analytics	M

UNIVERSITY OF WISCONSIN–STOUT

Construction Management	M
Industrial/Management Engineering	M
Information Science	M
Manufacturing Engineering	M
Telecommunications Management	M

UNIVERSITY OF WYOMING

Architectural Engineering	M,D
Biotechnology	D
Chemical Engineering	M,D
Civil Engineering	M,D
Computer Science	M,D
Electrical Engineering	M,D
Engineering and Applied Sciences—General	M,D
Environmental Engineering	M
Mechanical Engineering	M,D
Petroleum Engineering	M,D

UTAH STATE UNIVERSITY

Aerospace/Aeronautical Engineering	M,D
Bioengineering	M,D
Civil Engineering	M,D,O
Computer Science	M,D
Electrical Engineering	M,D
Engineering and Applied Sciences—General	M,D,O
Environmental Engineering	M,D,O
Mechanical Engineering	M,D

UTAH VALLEY UNIVERSITY

Computer and Information Systems Security	O

UTICA COLLEGE

Computer and Information Systems Security	M

VALPARAISO UNIVERSITY

Computer and Information Systems Security	M
Engineering Management	M,O

VANDERBILT UNIVERSITY

Bioinformatics	M,D
Biomedical Engineering	M,D
Chemical Engineering	M,D
Civil Engineering	M,D
Computer and Information Systems Security	M
Computer Science	M,D
Electrical Engineering	M,D
Engineering and Applied Sciences—General	M,D
Environmental Engineering	M,D
Materials Sciences	M,D
Mechanical Engineering	M,D

VERMONT LAW SCHOOL

Energy Management and Policy	M

VERMONT TECHNICAL COLLEGE

Software Engineering	M

VILLANOVA UNIVERSITY

Artificial Intelligence/Robotics	M,O
Biochemical Engineering	M,O
Chemical Engineering	M,O
Civil Engineering	M
Computer Engineering	M,O
Computer Science	M,O
Electrical Engineering	M,O
Engineering and Applied Sciences—General	M,D,O
Environmental Engineering	M,O
Manufacturing Engineering	M,O
Mechanical Engineering	M,O
Water Resources Engineering	M,O

VIRGINIA COMMONWEALTH UNIVERSITY

Biomedical Engineering	M,D
Computer Science	M,D
Engineering and Applied Sciences—General	M,D
Mechanical Engineering	M,D
Nanotechnology	M,D
Nuclear Engineering	M,D

VIRGINIA INTERNATIONAL UNIVERSITY

Computer and Information Systems Security	M,O
Computer Science	M,O
Data Science/Data Analytics	M,O
Game Design and Development	M,O
Health Informatics	M,O
Software Engineering	M,O

VIRGINIA POLYTECHNIC INSTITUTE AND STATE UNIVERSITY

Aerospace/Aeronautical Engineering	M,D,O
Agricultural Engineering	M,D
Bioengineering	M,D
Bioinformatics	M,D
Biomedical Engineering	M,D
Biotechnology	M,D
Chemical Engineering	M,D
Civil Engineering	M,D,O
Computer and Information Systems Security	M,O
Computer Engineering	M,D,O
Computer Science	M,D,O
Electrical Engineering	M,D,O
Engineering and Applied Sciences—General	M,D
Engineering Management	M,O
Environmental Engineering	M,O
Industrial/Management Engineering	M,O
Ocean Engineering	M,O
Software Engineering	M,O
Systems Engineering	M,O
Transportation and Highway Engineering	M,O

WAKE FOREST UNIVERSITY

Biomedical Engineering	M,D
Computer Science	M

WALDEN UNIVERSITY

Computer and Information Systems Security	M,D,O

Health Informatics	M,D,O

WALSH COLLEGE OF ACCOUNTANCY AND BUSINESS ADMINISTRATION

Computer and Information Systems Security	M
Data Science/Data Analytics	M

WASHINGTON STATE UNIVERSITY

Agricultural Engineering	M,D
Bioengineering	M,D
Chemical Engineering	M,D
Civil Engineering	M,D
Computer Engineering	M,D
Computer Science	M,D
Electrical Engineering	M,D
Energy and Power Engineering	M,D
Engineering and Applied Sciences—General	M,D,O
Engineering Management	M,O
Environmental Engineering	M,D
Management of Technology	M,O
Materials Engineering	M,D
Materials Sciences	M,D
Mechanical Engineering	M,D

WASHINGTON UNIVERSITY IN ST. LOUIS

Aerospace/Aeronautical Engineering	M,D
Biomedical Engineering	M,D
Chemical Engineering	M,D
Computer Engineering	M,D
Computer Science	M,D
Data Science/Data Analytics	M
Engineering and Applied Sciences—General	M,D
Environmental Engineering	M,D
Materials Sciences	M,D
Mechanical Engineering	M,D

WAYNESBURG UNIVERSITY

Energy Management and Policy	M,D

WAYNE STATE UNIVERSITY

Automotive Engineering	M,O
Bioinformatics	M,D
Biomedical Engineering	M,D,O
Chemical Engineering	M,D,O
Civil Engineering	M,D
Computer Engineering	M,D
Computer Science	M,D
Data Science/Data Analytics	M,D,O
Electrical Engineering	M,D
Electronic Materials	M
Energy and Power Engineering	M,O
Engineering and Applied Sciences—General	M,D,O
Engineering Management	M,D,O
Industrial/Management Engineering	M,D,O
Manufacturing Engineering	M,D,O
Materials Sciences	M,D,O
Mechanical Engineering	M,D
Polymer Science and Engineering	M,D,O
Systems Engineering	M,D,O

WEBER STATE UNIVERSITY

Computer Engineering	M

WEBSTER UNIVERSITY

Aerospace/Aeronautical Engineering	M,D,O

*M—masters degree; D—doctorate; O—other advanced degree; *—Close-Up and/or Display*

Computer and Information Systems Security — M
Computer Science — M
Management of Technology — M,D,O

WEILL CORNELL MEDICINE

Data Science/Data Analytics — M
Health Informatics — M

WENTWORTH INSTITUTE OF TECHNOLOGY

Civil Engineering — M
Computer Science — M
Construction Engineering — M
Construction Management — M
Management of Technology — M
Transportation and Highway Engineering — M

WESLEYAN UNIVERSITY

Bioinformatics — D
Computer Science — M,D

WEST CHESTER UNIVERSITY OF PENNSYLVANIA

Computer and Information Systems Security — M,O
Computer Science — M,O

WESTERN CAROLINA UNIVERSITY

Construction Management — M
Industrial/Management Engineering — M

WESTERN GOVERNORS UNIVERSITY

Computer and Information Systems Security — M
Data Science/Data Analytics — M
Information Science — M

WESTERN ILLINOIS UNIVERSITY

Computer Science — M
Manufacturing Engineering — M

WESTERN KENTUCKY UNIVERSITY

Computer Science — M
Management of Technology — M

WESTERN MICHIGAN UNIVERSITY

Aerospace/Aeronautical Engineering — M,D
Chemical Engineering — M,D
Civil Engineering — M
Computer Engineering — M,D
Computer Science — M,D
Electrical Engineering — M,D
Engineering and Applied Sciences—General — M,D
Engineering Management — M,D
Industrial/Management Engineering — M,D

Manufacturing Engineering — M
Mechanical Engineering — M,D
Paper and Pulp Engineering — M,D

WESTERN NEW ENGLAND UNIVERSITY

Civil Engineering — M
Electrical Engineering — M
Engineering and Applied Sciences—General — M,D
Engineering Management — M,D
Industrial/Management Engineering — M
Manufacturing Engineering — M
Mechanical Engineering — M

WESTERN WASHINGTON UNIVERSITY

Computer Science — M

WEST TEXAS A&M UNIVERSITY

Engineering and Applied Sciences—General — M

WEST VIRGINIA STATE UNIVERSITY

Biotechnology — M

WEST VIRGINIA UNIVERSITY

Aerospace/Aeronautical Engineering — M,D
Chemical Engineering — M,D
Civil Engineering — M,D
Computer and Information Systems Security — M,D,O
Computer Engineering — M,D
Computer Science — M,D
Electrical Engineering — M,D
Energy and Power Engineering — M,D
Engineering and Applied Sciences—General — M,D
Industrial/Management Engineering — M,D
Materials Engineering — M,D
Materials Sciences — M,D
Mechanical Engineering — M,D
Mineral/Mining Engineering — M,D
Petroleum Engineering — M,D
Safety Engineering — M,D
Software Engineering — M,D

WICHITA STATE UNIVERSITY

Aerospace/Aeronautical Engineering — M,D
Biomedical Engineering — M
Computer Engineering — M,D
Computer Science — M,D
Electrical Engineering — M,D
Engineering and Applied Sciences—General — M,D
Engineering Management — M,D
Industrial/Management Engineering — M,D
Manufacturing Engineering — M,D

Mechanical Engineering — M,D

WIDENER UNIVERSITY

Biomedical Engineering — M
Chemical Engineering — M
Civil Engineering — M
Electrical Engineering — M
Engineering and Applied Sciences—General — M
Engineering Management — M
Mechanical Engineering — M

WILFRID LAURIER UNIVERSITY

Management of Technology — M,D

WILKES UNIVERSITY

Bioengineering — M
Electrical Engineering — M
Engineering and Applied Sciences—General — M
Engineering Management — M
Mechanical Engineering — M

WILLIAM PATERSON UNIVERSITY OF NEW JERSEY

Biotechnology — M,D,O
Materials Sciences — M,D,O

WILMINGTON UNIVERSITY

Computer and Information Systems Security — M
Internet Engineering — M

WINSTON-SALEM STATE UNIVERSITY

Computer Science — M

WOODS HOLE OCEANOGRAPHIC INSTITUTION

Ocean Engineering — D

WORCESTER POLYTECHNIC INSTITUTE

Aerospace/Aeronautical Engineering — M,D
Artificial Intelligence/Robotics — M,D
Bioinformatics — M,D
Biomedical Engineering — M,D,O
Biotechnology — M,D
Chemical Engineering — M,D
Civil Engineering — M,D,O
Computer Engineering — M,D,O
Computer Science — M,D,O
Data Science/Data Analytics — M,D,O
Electrical Engineering — M,D,O
Energy and Power Engineering — M,D,O
Engineering and Applied Sciences—General — M,D,O
Engineering Design — M,D,O
Environmental Engineering — M,D,O
Fire Protection Engineering — M,D,O
Game Design and Development — M

Manufacturing Engineering — M,D,O
Materials Engineering — M,D,O
Materials Sciences — M,D,O
Mechanical Engineering — M,D,O
Modeling and Simulation — M,D,O
Nuclear Engineering — M,D,O
Systems Engineering — M,D,O
Systems Science — M,D,O

WORCESTER STATE UNIVERSITY

Biotechnology — M

WRIGHT STATE UNIVERSITY

Aerospace/Aeronautical Engineering — M
Biomedical Engineering — M
Computer Engineering — M,D
Computer Science — M,D
Electrical Engineering — M
Engineering and Applied Sciences—General — M,D
Ergonomics and Human Factors — M,D
Industrial/Management Engineering — M
Materials Engineering — M
Materials Sciences — M
Mechanical Engineering — M

YALE UNIVERSITY

Bioinformatics — D
Biomedical Engineering — M,D
Chemical Engineering — M,D
Computer Science — M,D
Electrical Engineering — M,D
Engineering and Applied Sciences—General — M,D
Engineering Physics — M,D
Environmental Engineering — M,D
Mechanical Engineering — M,D

YESHIVA UNIVERSITY

Biotechnology — M
Data Science/Data Analytics — M

YORK UNIVERSITY

Computer Science — M,D

YOUNGSTOWN STATE UNIVERSITY

Civil Engineering — M
Computer Engineering — M
Computer Science — M
Electrical Engineering — M
Engineering and Applied Sciences—General — M,O
Environmental Engineering — M
Industrial/Management Engineering — M
Information Science — M
Mechanical Engineering — M
Systems Engineering — M

ACADEMIC AND PROFESSIONAL PROGRAMS IN ENGINEERING & APPLIED SCIENCES

Section 1
Engineering and Applied Sciences

This section contains a directory of institutions offering graduate work in engineering and applied sciences, followed by in-depth entries submitted by institutions that chose to prepare detailed program descriptions. Additional information about programs listed in the directory but not augmented by an in-depth entry may be obtained by writing directly to the dean of a graduate school or chair of a department at the address given in the directory.

For programs in specific areas of engineering, see all other sections in this book. In the other guides in this series:

Graduate Programs in the Humanities, Arts & Social Sciences

See *Applied Arts and Design (Industrial Design)* and *Architecture (Environmental Design)*

Graduate Programs in the Biological/Biomedical Sciences & Health-Related Medical Professions

See *Ecology, Environmental Biology,* and *Evolutionary Biology*

Graduate Programs in the Physical Sciences, Mathematics, Agricultural Sciences, the Environment & Natural Resources

See *Agricultural and Food Sciences* and *Natural Resources*

CONTENTS

Engineering and Applied Sciences—General

Air Force Institute of Technology, Graduate School of Engineering and Management, Dayton, OH 45433-7765. Offers MS, PhD. *Accreditation:* ABET (one or more programs are accredited). *Program availability:* Part-time. *Degree requirements:* For master's, thesis; for doctorate, thesis/dissertation. *Entrance requirements:* For master's, GRE General Test, minimum GPA of 3.0; for doctorate, GRE General Test.

Alabama Agricultural and Mechanical University, School of Graduate Studies, College of Engineering, Technology, and Physical Sciences, Huntsville, AL 35811. Offers M Eng, MS, PhD. *Program availability:* Part-time, evening/weekend. *Degree requirements:* For master's, comprehensive exam, thesis optional. *Entrance requirements:* For master's, GRE General Test. Additional exam requirements/ recommendations for international students: Required—TOEFL (minimum score 500 paper-based; 61 iBT). Electronic applications accepted. *Faculty research:* Ionized gases, hypersonic flow phenomenology, robotics systems development.

Alfred University, Graduate School, College of Ceramics, Inamori School of Engineering, Alfred, NY 14802. Offers biomaterials engineering (MS); ceramic engineering (MS, PhD); electrical engineering (MS); glass science (MS, PhD); materials science and engineering (MS, PhD); mechanical engineering (MS). *Program availability:* Part-time. *Degree requirements:* For master's, thesis; for doctorate, thesis/dissertation. *Entrance requirements:* Additional exam requirements/recommendations for international students: Required—TOEFL (minimum score 590 paper-based; 90 iBT), IELTS (minimum score 6.5). Electronic applications accepted. *Expenses:* Contact institution. *Faculty research:* X-ray diffraction, biomaterials and polymers, thin-film processing, electronic and optical ceramics, solid-state chemistry.

The American University in Cairo, School of Sciences and Engineering, Cairo, Egypt. Offers biotechnology (MS); chemistry (MS); computer science (MS); computing (M Comp); construction engineering (M Eng, MS); electronics and communications engineering (M Eng); environmental engineering (MS); environmental system design (M Eng); mechanical engineering (M Eng, MS); nanotechnology (MS); physics (MS); robotics, control and smart systems (MS); sciences and engineering (PhD); sustainable development (MS, Graduate Diploma). *Program availability:* Part-time, evening/ weekend. *Degree requirements:* For master's, comprehensive exam (for some programs), thesis (for some programs); for doctorate, comprehensive exam (for some programs), thesis/dissertation. *Entrance requirements:* Additional exam requirements/ recommendations for international students: Required—TOEFL (minimum score 450 paper-based; 45 iBT), IELTS (minimum score 5). Electronic applications accepted. *Faculty research:* Construction, mechanical, and electronics engineering; physics; computer science; biotechnology; nanotechnology; chemistry; robotics.

American University of Beirut, Graduate Programs, Maroun Semaan Faculty of Engineering and Architecture, Beirut, Lebanon. Offers applied energy (ME); civil engineering (PhD); electrical and computer engineering (PhD); energy studies (MS); engineering management (MEM); environmental and water resources (ME); environmental technology (MSES); mechanical engineering (ME, PhD); urban design (MUD); urban planning and policy (MUPP). For progreen diploma: LAU/AUC. *Program availability:* Part-time, 100% online. *Faculty:* 105 full-time (25 women), 102 part-time/ adjunct (33 women). *Students:* 380 full-time (186 women), 100 part-time (38 women). Average age 27. 489 applicants, 64% accepted, 127 enrolled. In 2018, 109 master's, 14 doctorates awarded. Terminal master's awarded for partial completion of doctoral program. *Degree requirements:* For master's, one foreign language, comprehensive exam, thesis optional; for doctorate, one foreign language, comprehensive exam, thesis/ dissertation. *Entrance requirements:* For doctorate, GRE. Additional exam requirements/recommendations for international students: Required—TOEFL (minimum score 575 paper-based; 88 iBT), AUB-EN; Recommended—IELTS (minimum score 7). *Application deadline:* For fall admission, 4/4 for domestic and international students; for spring admission, 11/3 for domestic and international students; for summer admission, 4/4 for domestic and international students. Application fee: $50. *Expenses: Tuition:* Full-time $17,748; part-time $986 per credit. *Required fees:* $762. Tuition and fees vary according to course load and program. *Financial support:* In 2018–19, 15 students received support, including 92 fellowships with full tuition reimbursements available (averaging $14,400 per year), 80 research assistantships with full and partial tuition reimbursements available (averaging $5,300 per year), 162 teaching assistantships with full and partial tuition reimbursements available (averaging $1,400 per year); scholarships/grants, tuition waivers (full and partial), and unspecified assistantships also available. Financial award application deadline: 4/4. *Faculty research:* All areas in engineering, architecture and design. *Total annual research expenditures:* $1.5 million. *Unit head:* Prof. Alan Shihade, Dean, 961-1-374374 Ext. 3400, Fax: 961-1-744462, E-mail: as20@aub.edu.lb. *Application contact:* Dr. Salim Kanaan, Director, Admissions Office, 961-1-374374 Ext. 2590, Fax: 961-1-750775, E-mail: sk00@aub.edu.lb. Website: https://www.aub.edu.lb/msfea/pages/default.aspx

Arizona State University at the Tempe campus, Ira A. Fulton Schools of Engineering, Tempe, AZ 85287-9309. Offers M Eng, MA, MCS, MS, MSE, PSM, PhD, Graduate Certificate. *Program availability:* Part-time, evening/weekend, online learning. Terminal master's awarded for partial completion of doctoral program. *Degree requirements:* For master's, comprehensive exam (for some programs), thesis (for some programs), interactive Program of Study (iPOS) submitted before completing 50 percent of required credit hours; for doctorate, comprehensive exam, thesis/dissertation, interactive Program of Study (iPOS) submitted before completing 50 percent of required credit hours. *Entrance requirements:* For master's and doctorate, GRE, minimum GPA of 3.0 or equivalent in last 2 years of work leading to bachelor's degree. Additional exam requirements/recommendations for international students: Required—TOEFL, IELTS, or PTE. Electronic applications accepted. *Expenses:* Contact institution.

Arkansas State University, Graduate School, College of Engineering, State University, AR 72467. Offers engineering (MS Eng); engineering management (MEM). *Program availability:* Part-time. *Degree requirements:* For master's, comprehensive exam. *Entrance requirements:* For master's, GRE, appropriate bachelor's degree, official transcript, letters of recommendation, resume, immunization records. Additional exam requirements/recommendations for international students: Required—TOEFL (minimum score 550 paper-based; 79 iBT), IELTS (minimum score 6), PTE (minimum score 56). Electronic applications accepted. *Expenses:* Contact institution.

Arkansas Tech University, College of Engineering and Applied Sciences, Russellville, AR 72801. Offers electrical engineering (M Engr); emergency management (MS); information technology (MS); mechanical engineering (M Engr). *Program availability:* Part-time, evening/weekend, 100% online, blended/hybrid learning. *Students:* 46 full-time (17 women), 39 part-time (16 women); includes 12 minority (7 Black or African American, non-Hispanic/Latino; 1 American Indian or Alaska Native, non-Hispanic/ Latino; 1 Asian, non-Hispanic/Latino; 2 Hispanic/Latino; 1 Two or more races, non-Hispanic/Latino), 29 international. Average age 31. In 2018, 54 master's awarded. *Degree requirements:* For master's, comprehensive exam (for some programs), thesis

(for some programs). *Entrance requirements:* Additional exam requirements/ recommendations for international students: Required—TOEFL (minimum score 550 paper-based; 79 iBT), IELTS (minimum score 6.5), PTE (minimum score 58). *Application deadline:* For fall admission, 3/1 priority date for domestic students, 5/1 priority date for international students; for spring admission, 10/1 priority date for domestic and international students. Applications are processed on a rolling basis. Application fee: $40 ($90 for international students). Electronic applications accepted. *Expenses: Tuition, area resident:* Full-time $6816; part-time $284 per credit hour. Tuition, state resident: full-time $6816; part-time $284 per credit hour. Tuition, nonresident: full-time $13,632; part-time $568 per credit hour. *International tuition:* $13,632 full-time. *Required fees:* $457.50 per semester. Tuition and fees vary according to course load and degree level. *Financial support:* In 2018–19, research assistantships with full and partial tuition reimbursements (averaging $4,800 per year), teaching assistantships with full and partial tuition reimbursements (averaging $4,800 per year) were awarded; career-related internships or fieldwork, Federal Work-Study, scholarships/grants, health care benefits, and unspecified assistantships also available. Support available to part-time students. Financial award application deadline: 4/15; financial award applicants required to submit FAFSA. *Unit head:* Dr. Judy Cezeaux, Dean, 479-968-0353, E-mail: jcezeaux@atu.edu. *Application contact:* Dr. Jeff Robertson, Interim Dean of Graduate College, 479-968-0398, Fax: 479-964-0542, E-mail: gradcollege@atu.edu.
Website: http://www.atu.edu/appliedsci/

Atlantis University, School of Engineering, Miami, FL 33132. Offers computer engineering (MS).

Auburn University, Graduate School, Ginn College of Engineering, Auburn University, AL 36849. Offers M Ch E, M Mtl E, MAE, MCE, MEE, MISE, MME, MS, MSWE, PhD, Graduate Certificate. *Program availability:* Part-time. *Degree requirements:* For master's, thesis (for some programs); for doctorate, thesis/dissertation. *Entrance requirements:* For master's and doctorate, GRE General Test. Electronic applications accepted. *Expenses:* Tuition, state resident: full-time $11,282; part-time $535 per credit hour. Tuition, nonresident: full-time $30,542; part-time $1605 per credit hour. *Required fees:* $826 per semester. Tuition and fees vary according to degree level and program.

Austin Peay State University, College of Graduate Studies, College of Science, Technology, Engineering and Mathematics, Department of Engineering Technology, Clarksville, TN 37044. Offers MS. *Program availability:* Part-time. *Faculty:* 2 full-time (0 women). *Students:* 4 part-time (1 woman), 1 international. Average age 31. 5 applicants, 80% accepted, 2 enrolled. In 2018, 1 master's awarded. *Entrance requirements:* For master's, minimum GPA of 2.5. Additional exam requirements/recommendations for international students: Required—TOEFL (minimum score 500 paper-based). *Application deadline:* For fall admission, 8/21 for domestic students. Applications are processed on a rolling basis. Application fee: $45 ($55 for international students). Electronic applications accepted. *Expenses: Tuition, area resident:* Part-time $450 per credit hour. Tuition, state resident: full-time $5987; part-time $450 per credit hour. Tuition, nonresident: full-time $8757; part-time $806 per credit hour. *Required fees:* $1583; $79.15 per credit hour. *Financial support:* Career-related internships or fieldwork, Federal Work-Study, institutionally sponsored loans, scholarships/grants, and unspecified assistantships available. Support available to part-time students. Financial award application deadline: 7/1; financial award applicants required to submit FAFSA. *Unit head:* Adel Salama, Graduate Program Coordinator, 931-221-1427, E-mail: salamaa@apsu.edu. *Application contact:* Megan Mitchell, Coordinator of Graduate Admissions, 800-859-4723, Fax: 931-221-7641, E-mail: gradadmissions@apsu.edu.

Binghamton University, State University of New York, Graduate School, Thomas J. Watson School of Engineering and Applied Science, Binghamton, NY 13902-6000. Offers M Eng, MS, PhD. *Program availability:* Part-time, evening/weekend, online learning. *Degree requirements:* For master's, comprehensive exam (for some programs), thesis (for some programs); for doctorate, comprehensive exam (for some programs), thesis/dissertation. *Entrance requirements:* For master's and doctorate, GRE General Test. Additional exam requirements/recommendations for international students: Required—TOEFL (minimum score 550 paper-based; 80 iBT). Electronic applications accepted. *Expenses:* Contact institution.

Boise State University, College of Engineering, Boise, ID 83725-0399. Offers M Engr, MS, PhD, Graduate Certificate. *Program availability:* Part-time, online learning. *Degree requirements:* For master's, comprehensive exam (for some programs), thesis (for some programs); for doctorate, comprehensive exam, thesis/dissertation. *Entrance requirements:* For master's, GRE General Test, minimum GPA of 3.0. Additional exam requirements/recommendations for international students: Required—TOEFL (minimum score 550 paper-based; 80 iBT), IELTS (minimum score 6). Electronic applications accepted.

Boston University, College of Engineering, Boston, MA 02215. Offers M Eng, MS, PhD, MD/PhD, MS/MBA. *Program availability:* Part-time, blended/hybrid learning. *Faculty:* 112 full-time (12 women), 9 part-time/adjunct (1 woman). *Students:* 872 full-time (279 women), 174 part-time (48 women); includes 125 minority (11 Black or African American, non-Hispanic/Latino; 72 Asian, non-Hispanic/Latino; 24 Hispanic/Latino; 18 Two or more races, non-Hispanic/Latino), 602 international. Average age 24. 3,733 applicants, 40% accepted, 389 enrolled. In 2018, 322 master's, 55 doctorates awarded. Terminal master's awarded for partial completion of doctoral program. *Degree requirements:* For master's, thesis (for some programs); for doctorate, comprehensive exam, thesis/dissertation. *Entrance requirements:* For master's and doctorate, GRE General Test. Additional exam requirements/recommendations for international students: Required—TOEFL (minimum score 90 iBT), IELTS (minimum score 7). *Application deadline:* For fall admission, 12/15 for domestic and international students; for spring admission, 10/1 for domestic and international students. Application fee: $95. Electronic applications accepted. *Expenses:* Contact institution. *Financial support:* In 2018–19, 458 students received support, including 115 fellowships with full tuition reimbursements available (averaging $33,000 per year), 246 research assistantships with full tuition reimbursements available (averaging $33,000 per year), 7 teaching assistantships with full tuition reimbursements available (averaging $22,000 per year); scholarships/grants and unspecified assistantships also available. Support available to part-time students. Financial award application deadline: 1/15; financial award applicants required to submit FAFSA. *Faculty research:* Photonics, bioengineering, computer and information systems, nanotechnology, materials science and engineering. *Unit head:* Dr. Kenneth R. Lutchen, Dean, 617-353-2800, Fax: 617-358-3468, E-mail: klutch@bu.edu. *Application contact:* Andrew Butler, Assistant Director, Enrollment Operations, 617-353-9760, E-mail: enggrad@bu.edu.
Website: http://www.bu.edu/eng/

Bradley University, The Graduate School, Caterpillar College of Engineering and Technology, Peoria, IL 61625-0002. Offers MS, MSCE, MSEE, MSME. *Program*

availability: Part-time, evening/weekend. *Faculty:* 45 full-time (6 women), 1 part-time/adjunct (0 women). *Students:* 44 full-time (6 women), 21 part-time (5 women); includes 3 minority (2 Black or African American, non-Hispanic/Latino; 1 Hispanic/Latino), 53 international. Average age 26. 195 applicants, 85% accepted, 14 enrolled. In 2018, 34 master's awarded. *Degree requirements:* For master's, comprehensive exam, thesis optional. *Entrance requirements:* Additional exam requirements/recommendations for international students: Required—TOEFL (minimum score 550 paper-based; 79 iBT), IELTS (minimum score 6.5). *Application deadline:* For fall admission, 5/15 priority date for domestic and international students; for spring admission, 10/15 priority date for domestic and international students. Applications are processed on a rolling basis. Application fee: $40 ($50 for international students). Electronic applications accepted. *Expenses:* $16,020 tuition (18 credit hours), $280 fees, $50 per credit hour additional tuition for College of Engineering and Technology courses. *Financial support:* In 2018–19, 66 students received support, including 26 research assistantships with full and partial tuition reimbursements available (averaging $5,032 per year); teaching assistantships, institutionally sponsored loans, scholarships/grants, tuition waivers (partial), and unspecified assistantships also available. Support available to part-time students. Financial award application deadline: 4/1. *Unit head:* Lex Akers, Dean, 309-677-2721, E-mail: lakers@bradley.edu. *Application contact:* Rachel Webb, Director of On-Campus Graduate Admissions & International Student and Scholar Services, 309-677-2375, E-mail: rkwebb@bradley.edu.
Website: http://www.bradley.edu/academic/colleges/egt/

Brigham Young University, Graduate Studies, Ira A. Fulton College of Engineering, Provo, UT 84602. Offers MS, PhD. *Faculty:* 113 full-time (4 women), 8 part-time/adjunct (2 women). *Students:* 354 full-time (44 women); includes 28 minority (7 Asian, non-Hispanic/Latino; 4 Hispanic/Latino; 1 Native Hawaiian or other Pacific Islander, non-Hispanic/Latino; 16 Two or more races, non-Hispanic/Latino), 58 international. Average age 28. 155 applicants, 48% accepted, 73 enrolled. In 2018, 121 master's, 17 doctorates awarded. *Degree requirements:* For master's, comprehensive exam (for some programs), thesis (for some programs); for doctorate, comprehensive exam (for some programs), thesis/dissertation (for some programs). *Entrance requirements:* For master's and doctorate, GRE, At least 3 letters of recommendation, transcripts from each institution attended, ecclesiastical endorsement, minimum cumulative GPA of 3.0 in last 60 hours of coursework. Additional exam requirements/recommendations for international students: Required—TOEFL (minimum score 580 paper-based; 85 iBT), IELTS (minimum score 7). *Application deadline:* For fall admission, 1/15 for domestic and international students; for winter admission, 6/15 for domestic and international students; for spring admission, 2/5 for domestic and international students; for summer admission, 2/5 for domestic and international students. Application fee: $50. Electronic applications accepted. *Financial support:* In 2018–19, 337 students received support, including 14 fellowships with full and partial tuition reimbursements available (averaging $19,559 per year), 364 research assistantships with full and partial tuition reimbursements available (averaging $14,564 per year), 152 teaching assistantships with full and partial tuition reimbursements available (averaging $11,021 per year); scholarships/grants and health care benefits also available. Financial award application deadline: 1/1; financial award applicants required to submit FAFSA. *Faculty research:* Combustion, microwave remote sensing, structural optimization, biomedical engineering, networking. *Total annual research expenditures:* $15.6 million. *Unit head:* Dr. Michael A. Jensen, Dean, 801-422-5736, Fax: 801-422-0218, E-mail: college@et.byu.edu. *Application contact:* Claire A. DeWitt, Adviser, 801-422-4541, Fax: 801-422-0270, E-mail: gradstudies@byu.edu.
Website: http://www.et.byu.edu/

Brown University, Graduate School, School of Engineering, Providence, RI 02912. Offers biomedical engineering (Sc M, PhD); chemical and biochemical engineering (Sc M, PhD); electrical sciences and computer engineering (Sc M, PhD); fluid and thermal sciences (Sc M, PhD); materials science and engineering (Sc M, PhD); mechanics of solids and structures (Sc M, PhD). *Degree requirements:* For doctorate, thesis/dissertation, preliminary exam.

Bucknell University, Graduate Studies, College of Engineering, Lewisburg, PA 17837. Offers MS Ch E, MSCE, MSEE, MSEV, MSME. *Program availability:* Part-time. *Degree requirements:* For master's, thesis. *Entrance requirements:* For master's, GRE General Test, minimum GPA of 3.0. Additional exam requirements/recommendations for international students: Required—TOEFL (minimum score 600 paper-based).

California Institute of Technology, Division of Engineering and Applied Science, Pasadena, CA 91125. Offers aeronautics (MS, PhD, Engr); applied and computational mathematics (MS, PhD); applied mechanics (MS, PhD); applied physics (MS, PhD); bioengineering (MS, PhD); civil engineering (MS, PhD, Engr); computation and neural systems (MS, PhD); computer science (MS, PhD); control and dynamical systems (MS, PhD); electrical engineering (MS, PhD, Engr); environmental science and engineering (MS, PhD); materials science (MS, PhD); mechanical engineering (MS, PhD, Engr). Terminal master's awarded for partial completion of doctoral program. *Degree requirements:* For doctorate, thesis/dissertation. *Entrance requirements:* For master's and doctorate, GRE (strongly recommended), minimum GPA of 3.5. Additional exam requirements/recommendations for international students: Required—TOEFL; Recommended—TWE (minimum score 5). Electronic applications accepted.

California State University, Chico, Office of Graduate Studies, College of Engineering, Computer Science, and Construction Management, Chico, CA 95929-0722. Offers MS. *Program availability:* Part-time, online learning. *Faculty:* 7 full-time (1 woman), 3 part-time/adjunct (1 woman). *Students:* 1 full-time (0 women), 4 part-time (0 women); includes 3 minority (2 Asian, non-Hispanic/Latino; 1 Hispanic/Latino). 21 applicants. In 2018, 20 master's awarded. *Degree requirements:* For master's, thesis or project or comprehensive exam. *Entrance requirements:* For master's, GRE, fall admissions only; 2 letters of recommendation, statement of purpose, departmental letter of recommendation access waiver form. Additional exam requirements/recommendations for international students: Required—TOEFL (minimum score 550 paper-based; 80 iBT), IELTS (minimum score 6.5), PTE (minimum score 59). *Application deadline:* For fall admission, 4/1 priority date for domestic and international students. Application fee: $55. Electronic applications accepted. *Expenses: Tuition, area resident:* Full-time $4622; part-time $3116 per unit. *Tuition, state resident:* full-time $4622; part-time $3116 per unit. *Tuition, nonresident:* full-time $10,634. *Required fees:* $2160; $1620 per year. Tuition and fees vary according to class time and program. *Financial support:* Fellowships, research assistantships, teaching assistantships, career-related internships or fieldwork, Federal Work-Study, scholarships/grants, traineeships, health care benefits, unspecified assistantships, and stipends available. Support available to part-time students. Financial award application deadline: 3/2; financial award applicants required to submit FAFSA. *Unit head:* Melody Stapleton, Interim Dean, 530-898-5963, Fax: 530-898-4070, E-mail: ecc@csuchico.edu. *Application contact:* Micah Lehner, Graduate Admissions Counselor, 530-898-5416, Fax: 530-898-3342, E-mail: mlehner@csuchico.edu.
Website: http://www.csuchico.edu/ecc/

California State University, East Bay, Office of Graduate Studies, College of Science, School of Engineering, Hayward, CA 94542-3000. Offers construction management (MS); engineering management (MS). *Degree requirements:* For master's,

comprehensive exam (for some programs), research project or exam. *Entrance requirements:* For master's, GRE or GMAT, minimum GPA of 2.5; personal statement; 2 letters of recommendation; resume; college algebra/trigonometry or equivalent. Additional exam requirements/recommendations for international students: Required—TOEFL (minimum score 550 paper-based). Electronic applications accepted. *Faculty research:* Operations research, production planning, simulation, human factors/ergonomics, quality assurance, sustainability.

California State University, Fresno, Division of Research and Graduate Studies, Lyles College of Engineering, Fresno, CA 93740-8027. Offers MS, MSE. *Program availability:* Part-time, evening/weekend. *Degree requirements:* For master's, thesis or alternative. *Entrance requirements:* For master's, GRE General Test, minimum GPA of 2.7. Additional exam requirements/recommendations for international students: Required—TOEFL. Electronic applications accepted. *Faculty research:* Exhaust emission, blended fuel testing, waste management.

California State University, Fullerton, Graduate Studies, College of Engineering and Computer Science, Fullerton, CA 92831-3599. Offers MS. *Program availability:* Part-time. *Degree requirements:* For master's, comprehensive exam, project or thesis. *Entrance requirements:* For master's, minimum undergraduate GPA of 2.5.

California State University, Los Angeles, Graduate Studies, College of Engineering, Computer Science, and Technology, Los Angeles, CA 90032-8530. Offers MA, MS. *Program availability:* Part-time, evening/weekend. *Entrance requirements:* Additional exam requirements/recommendations for international students: Required—TOEFL (minimum score 550 paper-based). Electronic applications accepted.

California State University, Northridge, Graduate Studies, College of Engineering and Computer Science, Northridge, CA 91330. Offers MS. *Program availability:* Part-time, evening/weekend. *Entrance requirements:* For master's, GRE General Test, minimum GPA of 2.5. Additional exam requirements/recommendations for international students: Required—TOEFL.

California State University, Sacramento, College of Engineering and Computer Science, Sacramento, CA 95819. Offers MS. *Program availability:* Part-time, evening/weekend. *Degree requirements:* For master's, comprehensive exam, thesis/project; writing proficiency exam. *Entrance requirements:* Additional exam requirements/recommendations for international students: Required—TOEFL (minimum score 550 paper-based; 80 iBT); Recommended—IELTS, TSE. Electronic applications accepted. *Expenses:* Contact institution.

Carleton University, Faculty of Graduate Studies, Faculty of Engineering and Design, Ottawa, ON K1S 5B6, Canada. Offers M Arch, M Des, M Eng, M Sc, MA Sc, PhD. *Degree requirements:* For doctorate, thesis/dissertation. *Entrance requirements:* For master's, honors degree; for doctorate, MA Sc or M Eng. Additional exam requirements/recommendations for international students: Required—TOEFL.

Case Western Reserve University, School of Graduate Studies, Case School of Engineering, Cleveland, OH 44106. Offers ME, MEM, MS, PhD, MD/MS, MD/PhD. *Program availability:* Part-time, evening/weekend, 100% online, blended/hybrid learning. *Faculty:* 110 full-time (17 women). *Students:* 628 full-time (178 women), 43 part-time (9 women); includes 96 minority (5 Black or African American, non-Hispanic/Latino; 66 Asian, non-Hispanic/Latino; 18 Hispanic/Latino; 7 Two or more races, non-Hispanic/Latino), 410 international. 1,280 applicants, 40% accepted, 119 enrolled. In 2018, 169 master's, 60 doctorates awarded. Terminal master's awarded for partial completion of doctoral program. *Degree requirements:* For master's, thesis (for some programs); for doctorate, thesis/dissertation, qualifying exam, teaching experience. *Entrance requirements:* For master's and doctorate, GRE General Test. Additional exam requirements/recommendations for international students: Required—TOEFL (minimum score 577 paper-based; 90 iBT), IELTS (minimum score 7). *Application deadline:* Applications are processed on a rolling basis. Application fee: $50. Electronic applications accepted. *Expenses: Tuition:* Full-time $45,168; part-time $1939 per credit hour. *Required fees:* $36; $18 per semester. $18 per semester. *Financial support:* In 2018–19, 333 students received support, including 36 fellowships with tuition reimbursements available, 252 research assistantships with tuition reimbursements available, 45 teaching assistantships; career-related internships or fieldwork, Federal Work-Study, and institutionally sponsored loans also available. Support available to part-time students. Financial award applicants required to submit FAFSA. *Faculty research:* Advanced materials, biomedical engineering and human health, electrical engineering and computer science, civil engineering, engineering management. *Total annual research expenditures:* $42.1 million. *Unit head:* Venkataramanan "Ragu" Balakrishnan, Charles H. Phipps Dean, 216-368-4436, Fax: 216-368-6939, E-mail: ragu@case.edu. *Application contact:* Dr. Marc Buchner, Associate Dean, Academics, 216-368-4096, Fax: 216-368-6939, E-mail: marc.buchner@case.edu.
Website: http://www.engineering.case.edu

The Catholic University of America, School of Engineering, Washington, DC 20064. Offers MBE, MCE, MEE, MME, MS, MSCS, MSE, PhD, Certificate. *Program availability:* Part-time. *Faculty:* 31 full-time (2 women), 34 part-time/adjunct (3 women). *Students:* 72 full-time (26 women), 147 part-time (45 women); includes 37 minority (9 Black or African American, non-Hispanic/Latino; 5 Asian, non-Hispanic/Latino; 8 Hispanic/Latino; 15 Two or more races, non-Hispanic/Latino), 104 international. Average age 31. 176 applicants, 81% accepted, 67 enrolled. In 2018, 71 master's, 14 doctorates awarded. *Degree requirements:* For master's, thesis optional; for doctorate, comprehensive exam, thesis/dissertation. *Entrance requirements:* For master's and doctorate, statement of purpose, official copies of academic transcripts, three letters of recommendation. Additional exam requirements/recommendations for international students: Required—TOEFL (minimum score 550 paper-based; 80 iBT). *Application deadline:* For fall admission, 7/15 priority date for domestic students, 7/1 for international students; for spring admission, 11/15 priority date for domestic students, 11/1 for international students. Applications are processed on a rolling basis. Application fee: $55. Electronic applications accepted. *Expenses:* Contact institution. *Financial support:* Fellowships, research assistantships, teaching assistantships, Federal Work-Study, scholarships/grants, tuition waivers (full and partial), and unspecified assistantships available. Financial award application deadline: 2/1; financial award applicants required to submit FAFSA. *Faculty research:* Rehabilitation engineering, cardiopulmonary biomechanics, geotechnical engineering, signal and image processing, fluid mechanics. *Unit head:* Dr. John Judge, Dean, 202-319-5127, Fax: 202-319-4499, E-mail: judge@cua.edu. *Application contact:* Dr. Steven Brown, Director of Graduate Admissions, 202-319-5057, Fax: 202-319-6533, E-mail: cua-admissions@cua.edu.
Website: https://engineering.catholic.edu/

Central Connecticut State University, School of Graduate Studies, School of Engineering, Science and Technology, Department of Engineering, New Britain, CT 06050-4010. Offers MS. *Program availability:* Part-time, evening/weekend. *Faculty:* 1 full-time (0 women). *Students:* 1 part-time (0 women); minority (Asian, non-Hispanic/Latino). Average age 32. In 2018, 2 master's awarded. *Degree requirements:* For master's, thesis or alternative, special project. *Entrance requirements:* For master's, minimum undergraduate GPA of 2.7; four-year BS program in engineering technology, engineering or other programs with specific courses. Additional exam requirements/

recommendations for international students: Required—TOEFL (minimum score 550 paper-based; 79 iBT); Recommended—IELTS (minimum score 6.5). *Application deadline:* For fall admission, 6/1 for domestic students, 5/1 for international students; for spring admission, 11/1 for domestic and international students. Applications are processed on a rolling basis. Application fee: $50. Electronic applications accepted. *Expenses: Tuition, area resident:* Full-time $7027; part-time $388 per credit. Tuition, state resident: full-time $9750; part-time $388 per credit. Tuition, nonresident: full-time $18,102; part-time $388 per credit. *International tuition:* $18,102 full-time. *Required fees:* $266 per semester. *Financial support:* Application deadline: 3/1. *Unit head:* Dr. Peter Baumann, Chair, 860-832-1815, E-mail: baumannp@ccsu.edu. *Application contact:* Patricia Gardner, Associate Director of Graduate Studies, 860-832-2350, Fax: 860-832-2362.
Website: http://www.ccsu.edu/engineering/

Central Connecticut State University, School of Graduate Studies, School of Engineering, Science and Technology, Department of Technology and Engineering Education, New Britain, CT 06050-4010. Offers MS. *Program availability:* Part-time, evening/weekend. *Faculty:* 3 full-time (1 woman), 2 part-time/adjunct (0 women). *Students:* 8 full-time (3 women), 34 part-time (22 women); includes 3 minority (all Hispanic/Latino). Average age 34. 30 applicants, 87% accepted, 18 enrolled. In 2018, 11 master's awarded. *Degree requirements:* For master's, thesis or alternative, special project. *Entrance requirements:* For master's, minimum undergraduate GPA of 2.7. Additional exam requirements/recommendations for international students: Required—TOEFL (minimum score 550 paper-based; 79 iBT); Recommended—IELTS (minimum score 6.5). *Application deadline:* For fall admission, 6/1 for domestic students, 5/1 for international students; for spring admission, 11/1 for domestic and international students. Applications are processed on a rolling basis. Application fee: $50. Electronic applications accepted. *Expenses: Tuition, area resident:* Full-time $7027; part-time $388 per credit. Tuition, state resident: full-time $9750; part-time $388 per credit. Tuition, nonresident: full-time $18,102; part-time $388 per credit. *International tuition:* $18,102 full-time. *Required fees:* $266 per semester. *Financial support:* In 2018–19, 8 students received support. Career-related internships or fieldwork, Federal Work-Study, scholarships/grants, and unspecified assistantships available. Support available to part-time students. Financial award application deadline: 3/1; financial award applicants required to submit FAFSA. *Faculty research:* Instruction, curriculum development, administration, occupational training. *Unit head:* Dr. James DeLaura, Chair, 860-832-1850, E-mail: delaura@ccsu.edu. *Application contact:* Patricia Gardner, Associate Director of Graduate Studies, 860-832-2350, Fax: 860-832-2362.
Website: http://www.ccsu.edu/teched/

Central Michigan University, College of Graduate Studies, College of Science and Engineering, School of Engineering and Technology, Mount Pleasant, MI 48859. Offers industrial management and technology (MA). *Program availability:* Part-time. *Degree requirements:* For master's, thesis or alternative. Electronic applications accepted. *Faculty research:* Computer applications, manufacturing process control, mechanical engineering automation, industrial technology.

Christian Brothers University, School of Engineering, Memphis, TN 38104-5581. Offers MEM, MSEM. *Program availability:* Part-time, evening/weekend, online learning. *Degree requirements:* For master's, engineering management project. *Entrance requirements:* For master's, GRE. Additional exam requirements/recommendations for international students: Required—TOEFL.

The Citadel, The Military College of South Carolina, Citadel Graduate College, School of Engineering, Charleston, SC 29409. Offers MS, Graduate Certificate. *Program availability:* Part-time, evening/weekend. *Entrance requirements:* Additional exam requirements/recommendations for international students: Required—TOEFL (minimum score 550 paper-based; 79 iBT). Electronic applications accepted. *Expenses:* Tuition, state resident: part-time $595 per credit hour. Tuition, nonresident: part-time $1020 per credit hour. *Required fees:* $90 per term.

City College of the City University of New York, Graduate School, Grove School of Engineering, New York, NY 10031-9198. Offers ME, MIS, MS, PhD. *Program availability:* Part-time. Terminal master's awarded for partial completion of doctoral program. *Degree requirements:* For master's, thesis optional; for doctorate, one foreign language, comprehensive exam, thesis/dissertation. *Entrance requirements:* For master's, GRE General Test, minimum B average in undergraduate coursework; for doctorate, GRE General Test, minimum GPA of 3.5. Additional exam requirements/recommendations for international students: Required—TOEFL (minimum score 500 paper-based; 61 iBT). *Faculty research:* Robotics, network systems, structures.

Clarkson University, Wallace H. Coulter School of Engineering, Potsdam, NY 13699. Offers ME, MS, PhD, Advanced Certificate. *Faculty:* 73 full-time (15 women), 34 part-time/adjunct (5 women). *Students:* 152 full-time (33 women), 119 part-time (15 women); includes 25 minority (4 Black or African American, non-Hispanic/Latino; 10 Asian, non-Hispanic/Latino; 9 Hispanic/Latino; 2 Two or more races, non-Hispanic/Latino), 90 international. In 2018, 72 master's, 31 doctorates, 4 other advanced degrees awarded. *Expenses: Tuition:* Full-time $24,984; part-time $1388 per credit hour. *Required fees:* $225. Tuition and fees vary according to campus/location and program. *Unit head:* Dr. William Jemison, Dean of Engineering, 315-268-6446, E-mail: wjemison@clarkson.edu. *Application contact:* Dan Capogna, Director of Graduate Admissions & Recruitment, 518-631-9910, E-mail: graduate@clarkson.edu.
Website: https://www.clarkson.edu/academics/graduate

Clemson University, Graduate School, College of Engineering, Computing and Applied Sciences, Clemson, SC 29634. Offers M Engr, MFA, MS, PhD, Certificate. *Program availability:* Part-time, 100% online. *Faculty:* 273 full-time (62 women), 15 part-time/adjunct (5 women). *Students:* 1,221 full-time (298 women), 291 part-time (66 women); includes 118 minority (39 Black or African American, non-Hispanic/Latino; 2 American Indian or Alaska Native, non-Hispanic/Latino; 30 Asian, non-Hispanic/Latino; 28 Hispanic/Latino; 2 Native Hawaiian or other Pacific Islander, non-Hispanic/Latino; 17 Two or more races, non-Hispanic/Latino), 853 international. Average age 27. 2,871 applicants, 52% accepted, 593 enrolled. In 2018, 399 master's, 87 doctorates, 36 other advanced degrees awarded. Terminal master's awarded for partial completion of doctoral program. *Degree requirements:* For master's, comprehensive exam (for some programs), thesis (for some programs); for doctorate, comprehensive exam (for some programs), thesis/dissertation. *Entrance requirements:* For master's, doctorate, and Certificate, GRE General Test, unofficial transcripts, letters of recommendation; personal statement/portfolio/writing sample (depending on program). Additional exam requirements/recommendations for international students: Required—TOEFL (minimum score 80 paper-based; 80 iBT), IELTS (minimum score 6.5), PTE (minimum score 54). *Application deadline:* For fall admission, 4/15 for international students; for spring admission, 10/15 for international students. Applications are processed on a rolling basis. Application fee: $80 ($90 for international students). Electronic applications accepted. *Expenses:* $6823 per semester full-time resident, $14023 per semester full-time non-resident, $833 per credit hour part-time resident, $1731 per credit hour part-time non-resident, online $1264 per credit hour, $4938 doctoral programs resident, $10405 doctoral programs non-resident, $1144 full-time graduate assistant, other fees may apply per session. *Financial support:* In 2018–19, 866 students received support, including 80 fellowships with full and partial tuition reimbursements available (averaging $4,130 per year), 398 research assistantships with full and partial tuition reimbursements available (averaging $18,301 per year), 198 teaching assistantships with full and partial tuition reimbursements available (averaging $18,423 per year); career-related internships or fieldwork and unspecified assistantships also available. *Faculty research:* Engineering, computing, engineering and science education. *Total annual research expenditures:* $37.5 million. *Unit head:* Dr. Anand Gramopadhye, Dean, 864-656-3200, E-mail: agrampo@clemson.edu. *Application contact:* Dr. Douglas Hirt, Associate Dean for Research and Graduate Studies, 864-656-3201, E-mail: hirtd@clemson.edu.
Website: http://www.clemson.edu/cecas/

Cleveland State University, College of Graduate Studies, Fenn College of Engineering, Cleveland, OH 44115. Offers MS, D Eng. *Program availability:* Part-time, evening/weekend. *Faculty:* 54 full-time (5 women), 12 part-time/adjunct (0 women). *Students:* 200 full-time (61 women), 179 part-time (41 women); includes 39 minority (6 Black or African American, non-Hispanic/Latino; 20 Asian, non-Hispanic/Latino; 8 Hispanic/Latino; 5 Two or more races, non-Hispanic/Latino), 197 international. Average age 26. 1,037 applicants, 48% accepted, 143 enrolled. In 2018, 245 master's, 9 doctorates awarded. *Entrance requirements:* For master's, GRE General Test, BS in engineering, minimum GPA of 3.0 (2.75 for students from ABET-/EAC-accredited programs from the U.S. and Canada); for doctorate, GRE General Test, MS in engineering, minimum GPA of 3.25. Additional exam requirements/recommendations for international students: Required—TOEFL (minimum score 550 paper-based; 78 iBT). *Application deadline:* Applications are processed on a rolling basis. Application fee: $30. Electronic applications accepted. *Expenses:* Tuition, state resident: full-time $7232.55; part-time $6676 per credit hour. Tuition, nonresident: full-time $12,375. *International tuition:* $18,914 full-time. *Required fees:* $80; $80 $40. Tuition and fees vary according to program. *Financial support:* In 2018–19, 93 students received support. Fellowships, research assistantships, teaching assistantships, career-related internships or fieldwork, institutionally sponsored loans, scholarships/grants, tuition waivers (full and partial), and unspecified assistantships available. Support available to part-time students. Financial award application deadline: 3/30; financial award applicants required to submit FAFSA. *Faculty research:* Structural analysis and design, dynamic system and controls, applied biomedical engineering, transportation, water resources, telecommunication, power electronics, computer engineering, industrial automation, engineering management, mechanical design, thermodynamics and fluid mechanics, material engineering, tribology. *Total annual research expenditures:* $7.2 million. *Unit head:* Dr. Paul P. Lin, Associate Dean, 216-687-2556, Fax: 216-687-9280, E-mail: p.lin@csuohio.edu. *Application contact:* Deborah L. Brown, Interim Assistant Director, Graduate Admissions, 216-523-7572, Fax: 216-687-9214, E-mail: d.l.brown@csuohio.edu.
Website: http://www.csuohio.edu/engineering/

Colorado School of Mines, Office of Graduate Studies, Golden, CO 80401. Offers ME, MIPER, MP, MS, PMS, PhD, Graduate Certificate. *Program availability:* Part-time. *Faculty:* 426 full-time (135 women), 181 part-time/adjunct (64 women). *Students:* 1,115 full-time (325 women), 171 part-time (40 women); includes 159 minority (14 Black or African American, non-Hispanic/Latino; 3 American Indian or Alaska Native, non-Hispanic/Latino; 36 Asian, non-Hispanic/Latino; 70 Hispanic/Latino; 1 Native Hawaiian or other Pacific Islander, non-Hispanic/Latino; 35 Two or more races, non-Hispanic/Latino), 398 international. Average age 28. 2,016 applicants, 52% accepted, 425 enrolled. In 2018, 296 master's, 86 doctorates awarded. *Degree requirements:* For master's, thesis (for some programs); for doctorate, comprehensive exam, thesis/dissertation. *Entrance requirements:* For master's, doctorate, and Graduate Certificate, GRE General Test. Additional exam requirements/recommendations for international students: Required—TOEFL (minimum score 550 paper-based; 79 iBT). *Application deadline:* For fall admission, 12/15 priority date for domestic and international students; for spring admission, 9/1 priority date for domestic and international students. Application fee: $60 ($80 for international students). Electronic applications accepted. *Expenses:* Tuition, state resident: full-time $16,650; part-time $925 per contact hour. Tuition, nonresident: full-time $36,270; part-time $2015 per contact hour. *International tuition:* $36,270 full-time. *Required fees:* $2314; $2314 per semester. *Financial support:* In 2018–19, 439 research assistantships with full tuition reimbursements, 194 teaching assistantships with full tuition reimbursements were awarded; fellowships, career-related internships or fieldwork, Federal Work-Study, institutionally sponsored loans, scholarships/grants, health care benefits, and unspecified assistantships also available. Financial award application deadline: 12/15; financial award applicants required to submit FAFSA. *Faculty research:* Energy, environment, materials, minerals, engineering systems. *Total annual research expenditures:* $50.8 million. *Unit head:* Dr. Wendy Zhou, Dean of Graduate Studies, 303-384-2181, E-mail: wzhou@mines.edu. *Application contact:* Kim Medina, Executive Director, Admissions, 303-273-3000, E-mail: admit@mines.edu.
Website: http://mines.edu/graduate_admissions

Colorado State University, Walter Scott, Jr. College of Engineering, Fort Collins, CO 80523-1301. Offers ME, MS, PhD. *Program availability:* Part-time, evening/weekend, 100% online, blended/hybrid learning. Terminal master's awarded for partial completion of doctoral program. *Degree requirements:* For master's, comprehensive exam (for some programs), thesis (for some programs); for doctorate, comprehensive exam (for some programs), thesis/dissertation. Electronic applications accepted. *Expenses:* Contact institution. *Faculty research:* Atmospheric science; chemical and biological engineering; civil and environmental engineering; electrical and computer engineering; mechanical and biomedical engineering.

Colorado State University–Pueblo, College of Education, Engineering and Professional Studies, Pueblo, CO 81001-4901. Offers M Ed, MS. *Program availability:* Part-time, evening/weekend. *Degree requirements:* For master's, thesis optional. *Entrance requirements:* For master's, GRE General Test. Additional exam requirements/recommendations for international students: Required—TOEFL (minimum score 500 paper-based). Electronic applications accepted. *Expenses:* Contact institution. *Faculty research:* Nanotechnology, applied operations, research transportation, decision analysis.

Columbia University, Fu Foundation School of Engineering and Applied Science, New York, NY 10027. Offers MS, Eng Sc D, PhD, MS/MBA, MS/PhD. *Program availability:* Part-time, 100% online. Terminal master's awarded for partial completion of doctoral program. *Degree requirements:* For master's, comprehensive exam (for some programs), thesis (for some programs); for doctorate, comprehensive exam (for some programs), thesis/dissertation, qualifying exam. *Entrance requirements:* For master's, GRE General Test; for doctorate, GRE General Test, GRE Subject Test (applied physics program only). Additional exam requirements/recommendations for international students: Required—TOEFL (minimum score 590 paper-based; 96 iBT), IELTS (minimum score 6.5), PTE. Electronic applications accepted.

Concordia University, School of Graduate Studies, Faculty of Engineering and Computer Science, Montréal, QC H3G 1M8, Canada. Offers M App Comp Sc, M Comp Sc, M Eng, MA Sc, PhD, Certificate, Diploma. *Degree requirements:* For doctorate, comprehensive exam, thesis/dissertation. *Expenses:* Contact institution.

Cooper Union for the Advancement of Science and Art, Albert Nerken School of Engineering, New York, NY 10003. Offers chemical engineering (ME); civil engineering

(ME); electrical engineering (ME); mechanical engineering (ME). *Program availability:* Part-time. *Degree requirements:* For master's, thesis (for some programs), thesis or special project. *Entrance requirements:* For master's, BE or BS in an engineering discipline; official copies of school transcripts including secondary (high school), college and university work; two letters of recommendation; resume. Additional exam requirements/recommendations for international students: Required—TOEFL (minimum score 600 paper-based; 100 iBT). Electronic applications accepted. *Faculty research:* Analytics, bioengineering, dynamic systems, nanoscience, sustainability, STEM education.

Cornell University, Graduate School, Graduate Fields of Engineering, Ithaca, NY 14853. Offers M Eng, MPS, MS, PhD, M Eng/MBA. *Degree requirements:* For doctorate, comprehensive exam, thesis/dissertation. *Entrance requirements:* Additional exam requirements/recommendations for international students: Required—TOEFL. Electronic applications accepted.

Dalhousie University, Faculty of Engineering, Halifax, NS B3H 4R2, Canada. Offers M Eng, M Sc, MA Sc, PhD, M Eng/M Plan, MA Sc/M Plan, MBA/M Eng. *Entrance requirements:* Additional exam requirements/recommendations for international students: Required—1 of 5 approved tests: TOEFL, IELTS, CANTEST, CAEL, Michigan English Language Assessment Battery.

Dartmouth College, Thayer School of Engineering, Hanover, NH 03755. Offers M Eng, MEM, MS, PhD, MD/MS, MD/PhD. *Faculty:* 59 full-time (10 women), 9 part-time/adjunct (0 women). *Students:* 221 full-time (79 women); includes 29 minority (3 Black or African American, non-Hispanic/Latino; 22 Asian, non-Hispanic/Latino; 2 Hispanic/Latino; 2 Two or more races, non-Hispanic/Latino), 120 international. Average age 24. 606 applicants, 28% accepted, 92 enrolled. In 2018, 65 master's, 22 doctorates awarded. *Degree requirements:* For doctorate, thesis/dissertation, candidacy oral exam. *Entrance requirements:* For master's and doctorate, GRE General Test. Additional exam requirements/recommendations for international students: Required—TOEFL, IELTS. *Application deadline:* For fall admission, 1/1 priority date for domestic and international students. Applications are processed on a rolling basis. Application fee: $45. Electronic applications accepted. *Expenses:* $17832 tuition per term, $203 in fees. *Financial support:* In 2018–19, 200 students received support, including 25 fellowships with full tuition reimbursements available (averaging $27,720 per year), 98 research assistantships with full tuition reimbursements available (averaging $27,720 per year), 27 teaching assistantships with partial tuition reimbursements available (averaging $8,640 per year); career-related internships or fieldwork, institutionally sponsored loans, scholarships/grants, and tuition waivers (full and partial) also available. Financial award application deadline: 2/15; financial award applicants required to submit CSS PROFILE. *Faculty research:* Biomedical engineering, biological and chemical engineering, electrical and computer engineering, energy engineering, materials science and engineering, mechanical and systems engineering. *Total annual research expenditures:* $24.7 million. *Unit head:* Dr. Alexis R. Abramson, Dean, 603-646-2238, Fax: 603-646-2580, E-mail: Alexis.R.Abramson@Dartmouth.edu. *Application contact:* Candace S. Potter, Graduate Admissions & Financial Aid Administrator, 603-646-3844, Fax: 603-646-1620, E-mail: candace.s.potter@dartmouth.edu. Website: http://engineering.dartmouth.edu/

Drexel University, College of Engineering, Philadelphia, PA 19104-2875. Offers MS, MSEE, MSSE, PhD, Certificate. *Program availability:* Part-time, evening/weekend. *Degree requirements:* For doctorate, thesis/dissertation. *Entrance requirements:* Additional exam requirements/recommendations for international students: Required—TOEFL. Electronic applications accepted.

Drexel University, Goodwin College of Professional Studies, School of Technology and Professional Studies, Philadelphia, PA 19104-2875. Offers construction management (MS); creativity and innovation (MS); engineering technology (MS); food science (MS); hospitality management (MS); professional studies: creativity studies (MS); professional studies: e-learning leadership (MS); professional studies: homeland security management (MS); project management (MS); property management (MS); sport management (MS). *Program availability:* Part-time, evening/weekend. *Entrance requirements:* Additional exam requirements/recommendations for international students: Required—TOEFL, IELTS. Electronic applications accepted. Application fee is waived when completed online.

Duke University, Graduate School, Pratt School of Engineering, Master of Engineering Program, Durham, NC 27708-0271. Offers biomedical engineering (M Eng); civil engineering (M Eng); computational mechanics and scientific computing (M Eng); electrical and computer engineering (M Eng); environmental engineering (M Eng); materials science and engineering (M Eng); mechanical engineering (M Eng); photonics and optical sciences (M Eng); risk engineering (M Eng). *Program availability:* Part-time. *Entrance requirements:* For master's, GRE General Test, resume, 3 letters of recommendation, statement of purpose, transcripts. Additional exam requirements/recommendations for international students: Required—TOEFL. Electronic applications accepted.

Eastern Illinois University, Graduate School, Lumpkin College of Business and Technology, School of Technology, Charleston, IL 61920. Offers computer technology (Certificate); cybersecurity (MS); quality systems (Certificate); sustainable energy (MS); technology (MS); technology security (Certificate); work performance improvement (Certificate); MS/MBA; MS/MS. *Program availability:* Part-time, evening/weekend. *Expenses:* Tuition, state resident: part-time $299 per credit hour. Tuition, nonresident: part-time $718 per credit hour. *Required fees:* $214.50 per credit hour.

Eastern Michigan University, Graduate School, College of Engineering and Technology, School of Engineering, Programs in Computer Aided Engineering, Ypsilanti, MI 48197. Offers CAD/CAM (MS); computer-aided technology (MS). *Program availability:* Part-time, evening/weekend, online learning. *Students:* 10 full-time (2 women), 6 part-time (1 woman); includes 3 minority (2 Asian, non-Hispanic/Latino; 1 Hispanic/Latino), 9 international. Average age 30. 23 applicants, 57% accepted, 2 enrolled. In 2018, 9 master's awarded. *Entrance requirements:* Additional exam requirements/recommendations for international students: Required—TOEFL. *Application deadline:* Applications are processed on a rolling basis. Application fee: $45. *Financial support:* Fellowships, research assistantships with full tuition reimbursements, teaching assistantships with full tuition reimbursements, and tuition waivers (partial) available. Financial award applicants required to submit FAFSA. *Application contact:* Dr. Tony Shay, Program Coordinator, 734-487-2040, Fax: 734-487-8755, E-mail: tshay@emich.edu.

École Polytechnique de Montréal, Graduate Programs, Montréal, QC H3C 3A7, Canada. Offers M Eng, M Sc A, PhD, DESS. *Program availability:* Part-time, evening/weekend. Terminal master's awarded for partial completion of doctoral program. *Degree requirements:* For master's, one foreign language, thesis; for doctorate, one foreign language, thesis/dissertation. *Entrance requirements:* For master's, minimum GPA of 2.75; for doctorate, minimum GPA of 3.0. Electronic applications accepted. *Faculty research:* Chemical engineering, environmental engineering, microelectronics and communications, biomedical engineering, engineering physics.

Fairfield University, School of Engineering, Fairfield, CT 06824. Offers database management (CAS); electrical and computer engineering (MS); information security

(CAS); management of technology (MS); mechanical engineering (MS); network technology (CAS); software engineering (MS); Web application development (CAS). *Program availability:* Part-time, evening/weekend. *Degree requirements:* For master's, capstone course. *Entrance requirements:* For master's, resume, 2 recommendations. Additional exam requirements/recommendations for international students: Required—TOEFL (minimum score 550 paper-based; 80 iBT) or IELTS (minimum score 6.5). Electronic applications accepted. *Expenses:* Contact institution. *Faculty research:* Artificial intelligence and information visualization, natural language processing, thermofluids, microwaves and electromagnetics, micro-/nano-manufacturing.

Fairleigh Dickinson University, Metropolitan Campus, University College: Arts, Sciences, and Professional Studies, School of Computer Sciences and Engineering, Teaneck, NJ 07666-1914. Offers computer engineering (MS); computer science (MS); e-commerce (MS); electrical engineering (MSEE); management information systems (MS); mathematical foundation (MS).

Florida Agricultural and Mechanical University, Division of Graduate Studies, Research, and Continuing Education, FAMU-FSU College of Engineering, Tallahassee, FL 32307-3200. Offers M Eng, MS, PhD. College administered jointly by Florida State University. *Entrance requirements:* For master's, GRE General Test, minimum GPA of 3.0. Additional exam requirements/recommendations for international students: Required—TOEFL (minimum score 550 paper-based).

Florida Atlantic University, College of Engineering and Computer Science, Boca Raton, FL 33431-0991. Offers MS, PhD. *Program availability:* Part-time, evening/weekend, online learning. *Faculty:* 73 full-time (8 women), 4 part-time/adjunct (0 women). *Students:* 140 full-time (31 women), 222 part-time (47 women); includes 6,506 minority (31 Black or African American, non-Hispanic/Latino; 20 Asian, non-Hispanic/Latino; 6,447 Hispanic/Latino; 8 Two or more races, non-Hispanic/Latino), 121 international. Average age 31. 288 applicants, 47% accepted, 107 enrolled. In 2018, 133 master's, 15 doctorates awarded. Terminal master's awarded for partial completion of doctoral program. *Degree requirements:* For master's, thesis optional; for doctorate, thesis/dissertation, qualifying exam. *Entrance requirements:* For master's, GRE General Test, minimum GPA of 3.0; for doctorate, GRE General Test. Additional exam requirements/recommendations for international students: Required—TOEFL (minimum score 500 paper-based; 61 iBT), IELTS (minimum score 6). *Application deadline:* For fall admission, 7/1 for domestic students, 2/15 for international students; for spring admission, 11/1 for domestic students, 7/15 for international students. Applications are processed on a rolling basis. Application fee: $30. *Expenses: Tuition, area resident:* Full-time $7400; part-time $369.82 per credit. Tuition, state resident: full-time $7400; part-time $369.82 per credit. Tuition, nonresident: full-time $20,496; part-time $1024.81 per credit. *Financial support:* Fellowships, research assistantships with partial tuition reimbursements, teaching assistantships with partial tuition reimbursements, career-related internships or fieldwork, Federal Work-Study, and unspecified assistantships available. Support available to part-time students. Financial award applicants required to submit FAFSA. *Faculty research:* Automated underwater vehicles, communication systems, computer networks, materials, neural networks. *Unit head:* Dr. Stella Batalama, Dean, 561-297-3426, E-mail: sbatalama@fau.edu. *Application contact:* Dr. Stella Batalama, Dean, 561-297-3426, E-mail: sbatalama@fau.edu. Website: http://www.eng.fau.edu/

Florida Institute of Technology, College of Engineering and Science, Melbourne, FL 32901-6975. Offers MS, PhD. *Program availability:* Part-time. *Faculty:* 169 full-time (18 women), 42 part-time/adjunct (3 women). *Students:* 638 full-time (226 women), 310 part-time (69 women); includes 103 minority (24 Black or African American, non-Hispanic/Latino; 2 American Indian or Alaska Native, non-Hispanic/Latino; 22 Asian, non-Hispanic/Latino; 44 Hispanic/Latino; 1 Native Hawaiian or other Pacific Islander, non-Hispanic/Latino; 10 Two or more races, non-Hispanic/Latino), 498 international. Average age 28. 601 applicants, 70% accepted, 150 enrolled. In 2018, 290 master's, 74 doctorates awarded. Terminal master's awarded for partial completion of doctoral program. *Degree requirements:* For master's, comprehensive exam (for some programs), thesis (for some programs), thesis or final exam; for doctorate, thesis/dissertation. *Entrance requirements:* For master's, GRE, minimum GPA of 3.0, 3 letters of recommendation, resume, statement of objectives; for doctorate, GRE, minimum GPA of 3.2, 3 letters of recommendation, resume, statement of objectives. Additional exam requirements/recommendations for international students: Required—TOEFL (minimum score 550 paper-based; 79 iBT). *Application deadline:* For fall admission, 4/1 for international students; for spring admission, 9/30 for international students. Applications are processed on a rolling basis. Application fee: $50. Electronic applications accepted. *Expenses: Tuition:* Full-time $22,338; part-time $1241 per credit hour. Tuition and fees vary according to degree level, campus/location and program. *Financial support:* In 2018–19, 109 research assistantships with partial tuition reimbursements, 129 teaching assistantships with partial tuition reimbursements were awarded; career-related internships or fieldwork, institutionally sponsored loans, unspecified assistantships, and tuition remissions also available. Support available to part-time students. Financial award application deadline: 3/1; financial award applicants required to submit FAFSA. *Faculty research:* Electrical and computer science and engineering; aerospace, chemical, civil, mechanical, and ocean engineering; environmental science and oceanography. *Total annual research expenditures:* 12.2 million. *Unit head:* Dr. Marco Carvalho, Dean, 321-674-7150, E-mail: mcarvalho@fit.edu. *Application contact:* Mike Perry, Executive Director of Admissions, 321-674-7127, E-mail: perrymj@fit.edu. Website: www.fit.edu/engineering-and-science/

Florida International University, College of Engineering and Computing, Miami, FL 33175. Offers MS, PMS, PhD. *Program availability:* Part-time, evening/weekend, online learning. *Faculty:* 149 full-time (30 women), 81 part-time/adjunct (13 women). *Students:* 642 full-time (197 women), 295 part-time (76 women); includes 418 minority (47 Black or African American, non-Hispanic/Latino; 1 American Indian or Alaska Native, non-Hispanic/Latino; 30 Asian, non-Hispanic/Latino; 324 Hispanic/Latino; 16 Two or more races, non-Hispanic/Latino), 443 international. Average age 30. 1,138 applicants, 47% accepted, 267 enrolled. In 2018, 288 master's, 50 doctorates awarded. Terminal master's awarded for partial completion of doctoral program. *Degree requirements:* For master's, thesis (for some programs); for doctorate, comprehensive exam, thesis/dissertation. *Entrance requirements:* For master's, GRE (depending on program), minimum GPA of 3.0; for doctorate, GRE General Test, minimum GPA of 3.0. Additional exam requirements/recommendations for international students: Required—TOEFL (minimum score 550 paper-based; 80 iBT). *Application deadline:* For fall admission, 6/1 for domestic students, 4/1 for international students; for spring admission, 10/1 for domestic students, 9/1 for international students. Applications are processed on a rolling basis. Application fee: $30. Electronic applications accepted. *Financial support:* Career-related internships or fieldwork, Federal Work-Study, institutionally sponsored loans, scholarships/grants, and unspecified assistantships available. Financial award application deadline: 3/1; financial award applicants required to submit FAFSA. *Faculty research:* Databases, informatics, computing systems, software engineering, security, biosensors, imaging, tissue engineering, biomaterials and bionanotechnology, transportation, wind engineering, hydrology, environmental engineering, engineering management, sustainability and green construction, risk management and decision systems, infrastructure systems, digital signal processing, power systems, nanophotonics, embedded systems, image processing, nanotechnology. *Unit head:* Dr. John Volakis, Dean, 305-348-0273, Fax: 305-348-0127, E-mail: grad_eng@fiu.edu. *Application contact:* Nanett Rojas, Manager, Admissions Operations, 305-348-7464, Fax: 305-348-7441, E-mail: gradadm@fiu.edu.

Florida Polytechnic University, Graduate Programs, Lakeland, FL 33805. Offers computer science (MS); engineering (MS).

Florida State University, The Graduate School, FAMU-FSU College of Engineering, Tallahassee, FL 32310-6046. Offers M Eng, MS, PhD. *Program availability:* Part-time. *Degree requirements:* For master's, comprehensive exam (for some programs), thesis (for some programs); for doctorate, thesis/dissertation, preliminary exam, qualifying exam. *Entrance requirements:* For master's and doctorate, GRE General Test. Additional exam requirements/recommendations for international students: Required—TOEFL (minimum score 550 paper-based; 80 iBT). Electronic applications accepted. *Expenses: Tuition, area resident:* Part-time $479.32 per credit hour. Tuition and fees vary according to campus/location and program. *Faculty research:* Advanced digital signal processing architecture, composite materials, electrochemical engineering, nanomaterial processing, polymer blends.

George Mason University, Volgenau School of Engineering, Fairfax, VA 22030. Offers MS, PhD, Certificate. *Program availability:* Part-time, evening/weekend, 100% online. *Faculty:* 194 full-time (52 women), 177 part-time/adjunct (30 women). *Students:* 816 full-time (323 women), 923 part-time (242 women); includes 454 minority (92 Black or African American, non-Hispanic/Latino; 1 American Indian or Alaska Native, non-Hispanic/Latino; 256 Asian, non-Hispanic/Latino; 86 Hispanic/Latino; 19 Two or more races, non-Hispanic/Latino), 674 international. Average age 30. 1,684 applicants, 71% accepted, 462 enrolled. In 2018, 575 master's, 51 doctorates, 89 other advanced degrees awarded. *Degree requirements:* For master's, thesis optional; for doctorate, thesis/dissertation, comprehensive oral and written exams. *Entrance requirements:* For master's, minimum GPA of 3.0 in last 60 hours of course work; for doctorate, GRE General Test, minimum graduate GPA of 3.5. Additional exam requirements/ recommendations for international students: Required—TOEFL (minimum score 575 paper-based; 88 iBT), IELTS (minimum score 6.5), PTE (minimum score 59). Application fee: $75 ($80 for international students). Electronic applications accepted. *Expenses:* $589 per credit in-state, $1,346.75 per credit out-of-state. *Financial support:* In 2018–19, 382 students received support, including 6 fellowships (averaging $12,267 per year), 148 research assistantships with tuition reimbursements available (averaging $18,707 per year), 232 teaching assistantships with tuition reimbursements available (averaging $12,405 per year); career-related internships or fieldwork, Federal Work-Study, scholarships/grants, unspecified assistantships, and health care benefits (for full-time research or teaching assistantship recipients) also available. Support available to part-time students. Financial award application deadline: 3/1; financial award applicants required to submit FAFSA. *Faculty research:* Systems management, quality assurance, decision support systems, cognitive ergonomics. *Total annual research expenditures:* $22.1 million. *Unit head:* Kenneth S. Ball, Dean, 703-993-1498, Fax: 703-993-1734, E-mail: vsdean@gmu.edu. *Application contact:* Suddaf Ismail, Director, Graduate Admissions and Recruitment, 703-993-9115, Fax: 703-993-1242, E-mail: sismail@gmu.edu.
Website: http://volgenau.gmu.edu

The George Washington University, School of Engineering and Applied Science, Washington, DC 20052. Offers MS, D Sc, PhD, App Sc, Engr, Graduate Certificate. *Program availability:* Part-time, evening/weekend. *Students:* 919 full-time (217 women), 1,149 part-time (318 women); includes 408 minority (194 Black or African American, non-Hispanic/Latino; 8 American Indian or Alaska Native, non-Hispanic/Latino; 145 Asian, non-Hispanic/Latino; 40 Hispanic/Latino; 2 Native Hawaiian or other Pacific Islander, non-Hispanic/Latino; 19 Two or more races, non-Hispanic/Latino), 838 international. Average age 32. 3,123 applicants, 74% accepted, 678 enrolled. In 2018, 609 master's, 165 doctorates, 50 other advanced degrees awarded. *Degree requirements:* For master's, thesis optional; for doctorate, thesis/dissertation, qualifying exam. *Entrance requirements:* For master's, appropriate bachelor's degree; for doctorate, GRE (if highest earned degree is BS), appropriate bachelor's or master's degree; for other advanced degree, appropriate master's degree. Additional exam requirements/recommendations for international students: Required—TOEFL or The George Washington University English as a Foreign Language Test. *Application deadline:* For fall admission, 3/1 for domestic students; for spring admission, 10/1 for domestic students. Applications are processed on a rolling basis. Application fee: $75. *Financial support:* In 2018–19, 216 students received support. Fellowships, research assistantships, teaching assistantships, career-related internships or fieldwork, Federal Work-Study, institutionally sponsored loans, and tuition waivers (full and partial) available. Financial award application deadline: 3/1; financial award applicants required to submit FAFSA. *Faculty research:* Fatigue fracture and structural reliability, computer-integrated manufacturing, materials engineering, artificial intelligence and expert systems, quality assurance. *Total annual research expenditures:* $6.3 million. *Unit head:* David S. Dolling, Dean, 202-994-6080, E-mail: dolling@gwu.edu. *Application contact:* Adina Lav, Marketing, Recruiting and Admissions, 202-994-5827, Fax: 202-994-0909, E-mail: engineering@gwu.edu.
Website: http://www.seas.gwu.edu/

Georgia Institute of Technology, Graduate Studies, College of Engineering, Atlanta, GA 30332-0001. Offers MS, MSMP, MSNE, PhD, MD/PhD. *Program availability:* Part-time, online learning. Terminal master's awarded for partial completion of doctoral program. *Degree requirements:* For doctorate, thesis/dissertation. *Entrance requirements:* For master's and doctorate, GRE. Additional exam requirements/ recommendations for international students: Required—TOEFL (minimum score 550 paper-based; 79 iBT). Electronic applications accepted.

Georgia Southern University, Jack N. Averitt College of Graduate Studies, Allen E. Paulson College of Engineering and Computing, Statesboro, GA 30458. Offers MS, MSAE, Graduate Certificate. *Program availability:* Part-time, blended/hybrid learning. *Degree requirements:* For master's, comprehensive exam, thesis optional. *Entrance requirements:* For master's, GRE, undergraduate major or equivalent in proposed study area. Additional exam requirements/recommendations for international students: Required—TOEFL (minimum score 550 paper-based; 80 iBT), IELTS (minimum score 6). Electronic applications accepted. *Expenses: Tuition, area resident:* Part-time $3324 per semester. Tuition, state resident: full-time $5814; part-time $3324 per semester. Tuition, nonresident: full-time $23,204; part-time $13,260 per semester. *Required fees:* $2092; $2092. Tuition and fees vary according to course load, degree level, campus/ location and program. *Faculty research:* Electromagnetics, biomechatronics, cyber physical systems, big data, nanocomposite material science, renewable energy and engines, robotics.

Gonzaga University, School of Engineering and Applied Science, Spokane, WA 99258. Offers transmission and distribution engineering (M Eng, Certificate). *Program availability:* Part-time-only, evening/weekend, online only, 100% online. *Degree requirements:* For master's, portfolio, capstone course. *Entrance requirements:* For master's, GRE, letter of intent, two letters of recommendation, transcripts, resume/ curriculum vitae. Electronic applications accepted. *Expenses:* Contact institution.

Grand Valley State University, Padnos College of Engineering and Computing, School of Engineering, Allendale, MI 49401-9403. Offers electrical and computer engineering (MSE); manufacturing operations (MSE); mechanical engineering (MSE); product design and manufacturing engineering (MSE). *Program availability:* Part-time, evening/weekend. *Faculty:* 19 full-time (5 women). *Students:* 26 full-time (5 women), 50 part-time (7 women); includes 6 minority (1 Black or African American, non-Hispanic/Latino; 2 Asian, non-Hispanic/Latino; 1 Hispanic/Latino; 2 Two or more races, non-Hispanic/Latino), 39 international. Average age 26. 52 applicants, 62% accepted, 13 enrolled. In 2018, 32 master's awarded. *Entrance requirements:* For master's, engineering degree, minimum GPA of 3.0, resume, 3 confidential letters of recommendation, 1-2 page essay, base of underlying relevant knowledge/evidence from academic records or relevant wok experience. Additional exam requirements/recommendations for international students: Required—Michigan English Language Assessment Battery (minimum score 77), TOEFL (minimum iBT score of 80), or IELTS (6.5); GRE. *Application deadline:* Applications are processed on a rolling basis. Application fee: $30. Electronic applications accepted. *Expenses:* $712 per credit hour, 33 credit hours. *Financial support:* In 2018–19, 40 students received support, including 8 fellowships, 34 research assistantships with full and partial tuition reimbursements available (averaging $4,000 per year); career-related internships or fieldwork, Federal Work-Study, institutionally sponsored loans, scholarships/ grants, and unspecified assistantships also available. *Faculty research:* Digital signal processing, computer aided design, computer aided manufacturing, manufacturing simulation, biomechanics, product design. *Total annual research expenditures:* $300,000. *Unit head:* Dr. Wael Mokhtar, Director, 616-331-6015, Fax: 616-331-7215, E-mail: mokhtarw@gvsu.edu. *Application contact:* Dr. Shabbir Choudhuri, Graduate Program Director, 616-331-6845, Fax: 616-331-7215, E-mail: choudhus@gvsu.edu.
Website: http://www.engineer.gvsu.edu/

Grantham University, College of Engineering and Computer Science, Lenexa, KS 66219. Offers information management (MS), including project management; information management technology (MS); information technology (MS). *Program availability:* Part-time, evening/weekend, online only, 100% online. *Students:* 168 full-time (40 women), 65 part-time (19 women); includes 102 minority (73 Black or African American, non-Hispanic/Latino; 1 American Indian or Alaska Native, non-Hispanic/ Latino; 10 Asian, non-Hispanic/Latino; 10 Hispanic/Latino; 8 Two or more races, non-Hispanic/Latino). Average age 40. 52 applicants, 96% accepted, 44 enrolled. In 2018, 84 master's awarded. *Degree requirements:* For master's, comprehensive exam (for some programs), Project Management: PMP Prep Exam (for information management). *Entrance requirements:* For master's, baccalaureate or master's degree with minimum cumulative GPA of 2.5 from institution accredited by agency recognized by U.S. ED or foreign equivalent; official transcripts showing proof of degree. Additional exam requirements/recommendations for international students: Required—TOEFL (minimum score 530 paper-based; 71 iBT), IELTS (minimum score 6.5), PTE (minimum score 50). *Application deadline:* Applications are processed on a rolling basis. Application fee: $0. Electronic applications accepted. *Expenses:* $350 per credit hour plus $50 per credit hour technology fee and books. Military, first responders and their families receive reduced tuition ($250 per credit hour) and technology fee and books fees are waived. *Financial support:* Scholarships/grants available. Financial award applicants required to submit FAFSA. *Faculty research:* Sensor networks and security, grid technologies, cloud computing. *Unit head:* Dr. Nancy Miller, Dean of the College of Engineering and Computer Science, 913-309-4738, Fax: 855-681-5201, E-mail: nmiller@grantham.edu. *Application contact:* Lauren Cook, Director of Admissions, 800-955-2527 Ext. 803, Fax: 877-304-4467, E-mail: admissions@grantham.edu.
Website: http://www.grantham.edu/engineering-and-computer-science/

Harvard University, Graduate School of Arts and Sciences, Harvard John A. Paulson School of Engineering and Applied Sciences, Cambridge, MA 02138. Offers applied mathematics (PhD); applied physics (PhD); computational science and engineering (ME, SM); computer science (PhD); data science (SM); design engineering (MDE); engineering science (ME), including electrical engineering (ME, SM, PhD); engineering sciences (SM, PhD), including bioengineering (PhD), electrical engineering (ME, SM, PhD), environmental science and engineering (PhD), materials science and mechanical engineering (PhD). MDE offered in collaboration with Graduate School of Design. *Program availability:* Part-time. Terminal master's awarded for partial completion of doctoral program. *Degree requirements:* For master's, thesis (for ME); for doctorate, comprehensive exam, thesis/dissertation. *Entrance requirements:* For master's and doctorate, GRE General Test, GRE Subject Test (recommended), 3 letters of recommendation. Additional exam requirements/recommendations for international students: Required—TOEFL (minimum score 80 iBT). Electronic applications accepted. *Expenses:* Contact institution. *Faculty research:* Applied mathematics, applied physics, computer science and electrical engineering, environmental engineering, mechanical and biomedical engineering.

Hofstra University, Fred DeMatteis School of Engineering and Applied Sciences, Hempstead, NY 11549. Offers computer science (MS). *Program availability:* Part-time, evening/weekend, blended/hybrid learning. *Faculty:* 10 full-time (4 women), 5 part-time/ adjunct. *Students:* 30 full-time (9 women), 13 part-time (1 woman); includes 11 minority (1 Black or African American, non-Hispanic/Latino; 5 Asian, non-Hispanic/Latino; 5 Hispanic/Latino), 15 international. Average age 27. 82 applicants, 66% accepted, 19 enrolled. In 2018, 18 master's awarded. *Degree requirements:* For master's, thesis optional, 30 credits, minimum GPA of 3.0. *Entrance requirements:* For master's, GRE, minimum GPA of 3.0. Additional exam requirements/recommendations for international students: Required—TOEFL (minimum score 550 paper-based; 80 iBT). *Application deadline:* Applications are processed on a rolling basis. Application fee: $75. Electronic applications accepted. *Financial support:* In 2018–19, 24 students received support, including 11 fellowships with full and partial tuition reimbursements available (averaging $4,482 per year); research assistantships with full and partial tuition reimbursements available, career-related internships or fieldwork, Federal Work-Study, institutionally sponsored loans, scholarships/grants, tuition waivers (full and partial), unspecified assistantships, and scholarships and endowed scholarships also available. Support available to part-time students. Financial award applicants required to submit FAFSA. *Faculty research:* Cognitive neuroscience and artificial intelligence; cyber-security and privacy; cell and tissue engineering; experimental fluid mechanics; STEM education. *Total annual research expenditures:* $716,770. *Unit head:* Dr. Sina Rabbany, Dean, 516-463-6672, E-mail: sina.y.rabbany@hofstra.edu. *Application contact:* Sunil Samuel, Assistant Vice President of Admissions, 516-463-4723, Fax: 516-463-4664, E-mail: graduateadmission@hofstra.edu.
Website: http://www.hofstra.edu/academics/colleges/seas/

Howard University, College of Engineering, Architecture, and Computer Sciences, School of Engineering and Computer Science, Washington, DC 20059-0002. Offers M Eng, MCS, MS, PhD. *Program availability:* Part-time. Terminal master's awarded for partial completion of doctoral program. *Degree requirements:* For doctorate, one foreign language, thesis/dissertation, preliminary exam. *Entrance requirements:* For master's and doctorate, GRE General Test, minimum GPA of 3.0. Additional exam requirements/ recommendations for international students: Required—TOEFL. Electronic applications accepted. *Faculty research:* Environmental engineering, solid-state electronics, dynamics and control of large flexible space structures, power systems, reaction kinetics.

Idaho State University, Graduate School, College of Science and Engineering, Pocatello, ID 83209-8060. Offers MA, MNS, MS, DA, PhD, Postbaccalaureate Certificate. *Program availability:* Part-time. *Degree requirements:* For master's, comprehensive exam (for some programs), thesis, thesis project, 2 semesters of seminar; for doctorate, comprehensive exam, thesis/dissertation, oral presentation and defense of research, oral examination; for Postbaccalaureate Certificate, comprehensive exam (for some programs), thesis optional, oral exam or thesis defense. *Entrance requirements:* For master's, GRE General Test, minimum GPA of 3.0 in upper-division undergraduate classes; for doctorate, GRE General Test, master's degree in engineering or physics, 1-page statement of research interests, resume, 3 letters of reference, 1-page statement of career interests; for Postbaccalaureate Certificate, GRE (if GPA between 2.0 and 3.0), bachelor's degree, minimum GPA of 3.0 in upper-division courses. Additional exam requirements/recommendations for international students: Required—TOEFL (minimum score 550 paper-based; 80 iBT). Electronic applications accepted. *Faculty research:* Nuclear engineering, biomedical engineering, robotics, measurement and control, structural systems.

Illinois Institute of Technology, Graduate College, Armour College of Engineering, Chicago, IL 60616. Offers M Arch E, M Env E, M Geoenv E, M Trans E, MAS, MCEM, MGE, MPW, MS, MSE, PhD, MS/MAS, MS/MS. *Program availability:* Part-time, evening/weekend, online learning. Terminal master's awarded for partial completion of doctoral program. *Degree requirements:* For master's, comprehensive exam (for some programs), thesis (for some programs); for doctorate, comprehensive exam, thesis/ dissertation. *Entrance requirements:* For master's and doctorate, GRE General Test, minimum undergraduate GPA of 3.0. Additional exam requirements/recommendations for international students: Required—TOEFL (minimum score 550 paper-based; 80 iBT); Recommended—IELTS (minimum score 5.5). Electronic applications accepted.

Indiana State University, College of Graduate and Professional Studies, College of Technology, Terre Haute, IN 47809. Offers MS, MA/MS. *Entrance requirements:* For master's, bachelor's degree in industrial technology or related field. Additional exam requirements/recommendations for international students: Required—TOEFL. Electronic applications accepted.

Instituto Tecnologico de Santo Domingo, Graduate School, Area of Engineering, Santo Domingo, Dominican Republic. Offers construction administration (MS, Certificate); data telecommunications (M Eng, MS, Certificate); industrial engineering (M Eng, Certificate); industrial management (M Mgmt); information technology (Certificate); maintenance engineering (M Eng); occupational hazard prevention (M Mgmt); production management (Certificate); quantitative methods (Certificate); sanitary and environmental engineering (M Eng); structural engineering (M Eng); systems engineering and electronic data processing (Certificate); transportation (Certificate).

Instituto Tecnológico y de Estudios Superiores de Monterrey, Campus Ciudad Obregón, Program in Engineering, Ciudad Obregón, Mexico. Offers ME.

Instituto Tecnológico y de Estudios Superiores de Monterrey, Campus Monterrey, Graduate and Research Division, Programs in Engineering, Monterrey, Mexico. Offers applied statistics (M Eng); artificial intelligence (PhD); automation engineering (M Eng); chemical engineering (M Eng); civil engineering (M Eng); electrical engineering (M Eng); electronic engineering (M Eng); environmental engineering (M Eng); industrial engineering (M Eng, PhD); manufacturing engineering (M Eng); mechanical engineering (M Eng); systems and quality engineering (M Eng). M Eng program offered jointly with University of Waterloo; PhD in industrial engineering with Texas A&M University. *Program availability:* Part-time, evening/weekend. Terminal master's awarded for partial completion of doctoral program. *Degree requirements:* For master's, one foreign language, thesis; for doctorate, one foreign language, thesis/dissertation. *Entrance requirements:* For master's, EXADEP; for doctorate, GRE, master's degree in related field. Additional exam requirements/recommendations for international students: Required—TOEFL. *Faculty research:* Flexible manufacturing cells, materials, statistical methods, environmental prevention, control and evaluation.

James Madison University, The Graduate School, College of Integrated Science and Engineering, Harrisonburg, VA 22807. Offers MS. *Accreditation:* AOTA. *Program availability:* Part-time, evening/weekend, 100% online, blended/hybrid learning, study abroad. *Faculty:* 75. *Students:* 3 full-time (0 women), 51 part-time (11 women); includes 13 minority (7 Black or African American, non-Hispanic/Latino; 3 Asian, non-Hispanic/Latino; 2 Hispanic/Latino; 1 Two or more races, non-Hispanic/Latino), 2 international. Average age 30. In 2018, 20 master's awarded. Application fee: $60. Electronic applications accepted. *Expenses:* Tuition, state resident: full-time $10,848. Tuition, nonresident: full-time $27,888. *Required fees:* $1128. *Financial support:* In 2018–19, 2 students received support. Career-related internships or fieldwork, Federal Work-Study, and 4 assistantships (averaging $7911) available. Financial award application deadline: 3/1; financial award applicants required to submit FAFSA. *Unit head:* Dr. Robert A. Kolvoord, Dean, 540-568-2752, E-mail: kolvoora@jmu.edu. *Application contact:* Lynette D. Michael, Director of Graduate Admissions, 540-568-6395, Fax: 540-568-7860, E-mail: michaeld@jmu.edu.
Website: http://www.jmu.edu/cise/

Johns Hopkins University, Engineering Program for Professionals, Baltimore, MD 21218. Offers M Ch E, M Mat SE, MCE, MEE, MEM, MME, MS, MSE, D Eng, Graduate Certificate, Post Master's Certificate, Post-Master's Certificate. *Program availability:* Part-time, evening/weekend, 100% online, blended/hybrid learning. *Faculty:* 13 full-time (4 women), 305 part-time/adjunct (48 women). *Students:* 2,455 part-time (630 women). 1,379 applicants, 46% accepted, 406 enrolled. In 2018, 770 master's, 14 other advanced degrees awarded. *Degree requirements:* For master's, thesis optional, 10 courses. *Entrance requirements:* For master's, Applicants typically have earned a grade point average of at least 3.0 on a 4.0 scale (B or above) in the latter half of their undergraduate studies. Significant relevant work experience or a graduate degree in a relevant technical discipline may be considered in lieu of meeting the GPA guideline. Additional exam requirements/recommendations for international students: Required— TOEFL (minimum score 600 paper-based; 100 iBT). *Application deadline:* Applications are processed on a rolling basis. Application fee: $0. Electronic applications accepted. *Expenses:* Contact institution. *Unit head:* Dr. Daniel Horn, Associate Dean, 410-516-2300, Fax: 410-579-8049, E-mail: dhorn@jhu.edu. *Application contact:* Doug Schiller, Director of Admissions & Student Services, 410-516-2300, Fax: 410-579-8049, E-mail: schiller@jhu.edu.
Website: http://www.ep.jhu.edu

Johns Hopkins University, G. W. C. Whiting School of Engineering, Baltimore, MD 21218. Offers M Ch E, M Mat SE, MA, MEE, MME, MS, MSE, MSEM, MSSI, PhD, Certificate, Post-Master's Certificate. *Faculty:* 269 full-time (57 women). *Students:* 1,697 full-time (548 women), 143 part-time (55 women). 5,304 applicants, 34% accepted, 734 enrolled. In 2018, 622 master's, 105 doctorates, 1 other advanced degree awarded. Terminal master's awarded for partial completion of doctoral program. *Degree requirements:* For master's, comprehensive exam (for some programs), thesis (for some programs); for doctorate, comprehensive exam, thesis/dissertation, oral exam. *Entrance requirements:* For master's, GRE General Test, letters of recommendation, transcripts; for doctorate, GRE General Test, letters of recommendation. Additional exam

requirements/recommendations for international students: Required—TOEFL (minimum score 600 paper-based; 100 iBT) or IELTS (minimum score 7). Application fee: $75. Electronic applications accepted. *Expenses:* Contact institution. *Financial support:* In 2018–19, 953 students received support, including 165 fellowships with full and partial tuition reimbursements available, 695 research assistantships with full and partial tuition reimbursements available, 93 teaching assistantships with full and partial tuition reimbursements available; Federal Work-Study, institutionally sponsored loans, scholarships/grants, health care benefits, tuition waivers (full and partial), and unspecified assistantships also available. Support available to part-time students. Financial award applicants required to submit FAFSA. *Faculty research:* Biomedical engineering, environmental systems and engineering, materials science and engineering, signal and image processing, structural dynamics and geomechanics. *Unit head:* Dr. T. E. Schlesinger, Dean, 410-516-8350 Ext. 3, Fax: 410-516-8627. *Application contact:* Lauren McGhee, Director of Engineering Graduate Admissions, 410-516-0505, Fax: 410-516-0780, E-mail: lauren.mcghee@jhu.edu.
Website: http://engineering.jhu.edu/

Kansas State University, Graduate School, College of Engineering, Manhattan, KS 66506. Offers MEM, MS, MSE, PhD, Graduate Certificate. *Program availability:* Part-time, online learning. *Degree requirements:* For doctorate, thesis/dissertation. *Entrance requirements:* For master's and doctorate, GRE. Additional exam requirements/ recommendations for international students: Required—TOEFL. Electronic applications accepted.

Kennesaw State University, Southern Polytechnic College of Engineering and Engineering Technology, Kennesaw, GA 30144. Offers MS. *Program availability:* Part-time, evening/weekend, online learning. *Students:* 31 full-time (9 women), 158 part-time (46 women); includes 80 minority (39 Black or African American, non-Hispanic/Latino; 17 Asian, non-Hispanic/Latino; 16 Hispanic/Latino; 8 Two or more races, non-Hispanic/Latino), 8 international. Average age 35. 178 applicants, 44% accepted, 53 enrolled. In 2018, 47 master's awarded. *Degree requirements:* For master's, comprehensive exam (for some programs), thesis (for some programs). *Entrance requirements:* For master's, GMAT, GRE, references, statement of purpose. Additional exam requirements/ recommendations for international students: Required—TOEFL (minimum score 550 paper-based; 80 iBT), IELTS (minimum score 6.5). *Application deadline:* For fall admission, 7/1 priority date for domestic students, 5/1 priority date for international students; for spring admission, 11/1 priority date for domestic students, 9/1 priority date for international students. Applications are processed on a rolling basis. Application fee: $60. Electronic applications accepted. *Expenses: Tuition, area resident:* Full-time $6960; part-time $290 per credit hour. Tuition, state resident: full-time $6960; part-time $290 per credit hour. Tuition, nonresident: full-time $25,080; part-time $1045 per credit hour. *International tuition:* $25,080 full-time. *Required fees:* $2006; $1706 per semester. $853 per semester. *Financial support:* Research assistantships with tuition reimbursements, teaching assistantships with partial tuition reimbursements, career-related internships or fieldwork, scholarships/grants, and unspecified assistantships available. Support available to part-time students. Financial award applicants required to submit FAFSA. *Application contact:* Admissions Counselor, 470-578-4377, E-mail: ksugrad@kennesaw.edu.
Website: http://engineering.kennesaw.edu/

Lakehead University, Graduate Studies, Faculty of Engineering, Thunder Bay, ON P7B 5E1, Canada. Offers control engineering (M Sc Engr); electrical/computer engineering (M Sc Engr); environmental engineering (M Sc Engr). *Program availability:* Part-time. *Degree requirements:* For master's, thesis. *Entrance requirements:* For master's, bachelor's degree in chemical, electrical or mechanical engineering, minimum B average. Additional exam requirements/recommendations for international students: Required—TOEFL. *Faculty research:* Pulp and paper, adaptive/process control, robust/ interactive learning control, vibration control.

Lamar University, College of Graduate Studies, College of Engineering, Beaumont, TX 77710. Offers ME, MEM, MES, MS, DE, PhD. *Program availability:* Part-time, evening/ weekend. *Faculty:* 53 full-time (6 women), 2 part-time/adjunct (0 women). *Students:* 152 full-time (19 women), 100 part-time (18 women); includes 13 minority (1 Black or African American, non-Hispanic/Latino; 1 American Indian or Alaska Native, non-Hispanic/ Latino; 8 Asian, non-Hispanic/Latino; 2 Hispanic/Latino; 1 Two or more races, non-Hispanic/Latino), 220 international. Average age 28. 359 applicants, 74% accepted, 56 enrolled. In 2018, 185 master's, 15 doctorates awarded. Terminal master's awarded for partial completion of doctoral program. *Degree requirements:* For doctorate, thesis/ dissertation. *Entrance requirements:* For master's and doctorate, GRE General Test. Additional exam requirements/recommendations for international students: Required— TOEFL (minimum score 550 paper-based; 79 iBT), IELTS (minimum score 6.5). *Application deadline:* Applications are processed on a rolling basis. Application fee: $25 ($50 for international students). Electronic applications accepted. *Expenses:* Tuition, state resident: full-time $6234; part-time $346 per credit hour. Tuition, nonresident: full-time $6852; part-time $761 per credit hour. *International tuition:* $6852 full-time. *Required fees:* $1940; $327 per credit hour. Tuition and fees vary according to course load, campus/location, program and reciprocity agreements. *Financial support:* In 2018–19, 15 students received support. Fellowships with partial tuition reimbursements available, research assistantships with partial tuition reimbursements available, teaching assistantships with partial tuition reimbursements available, career-related internships or fieldwork, Federal Work-Study, institutionally sponsored loans, scholarships/grants, tuition waivers (full and partial), and laboratory assistantships available. Support available to part-time students. Financial award applicants required to submit FAFSA. *Faculty research:* Energy alternatives; process analysis, design, and control; pollution prevention. *Total annual research expenditures:* $1.4 million. *Unit head:* Dr. Brian Craig, Dean, 409-880-8784, Fax: 409-880-2197. *Application contact:* Celeste Contreas, Director, Admissions and Academic Services, 409-880-8888, Fax: 409-880-7419, E-mail: gradmissions@lamar.edu.
Website: http://engineering.lamar.edu

Laurentian University, School of Graduate Studies and Research, School of Engineering, Sudbury, ON P3E 2C6, Canada. Offers mineral resources engineering (M Eng, MA Sc); natural resources engineering (PhD). *Program availability:* Part-time. *Faculty research:* Mining engineering, rock mechanics (tunneling, rockbursts, rock support), metallurgy (mineral processing, hydro and pyrometallurgy), simulations and remote mining, simulations and scheduling.

Lawrence Technological University, College of Engineering, Southfield, MI 48075-1058. Offers architectural engineering (MS); automotive engineering (MS); biomedical engineering (MS); civil engineering (MA, MS, PhD), including environmental engineering (MS), geotechnical engineering (MS), structural engineering (MS), transportation engineering (MS), water resource engineering (MS); construction engineering management (MA); electrical and computer engineering (MS); engineering management (MEM); engineering technology (MS); fire engineering (MS); industrial engineering (MS), including healthcare systems; manufacturing systems (ME); mechanical engineering (MS, DE, PhD), including automotive engineering (MS), energy engineering (MS), manufacturing (DE), solid mechanics (MS), thermal/fluid systems (MS); mechatronic systems engineering (MS). *Program availability:* Part-time, evening/weekend. Terminal master's awarded for partial completion of doctoral program. *Degree requirements:* For master's, thesis optional; for doctorate, comprehensive exam, thesis/dissertation optional. *Entrance requirements:* Additional exam requirements/recommendations for international students: Required—TOEFL (minimum score 550 paper-based; 79 iBT), IELTS (minimum score 6.5). Electronic applications accepted. *Faculty research:* Innovative infrastructure and building structures and materials; connectivity and mobility; automotive systems modeling, simulation and testing; biomedical devices and materials; building mechanical/electrical systems.

Lehigh University, P.C. Rossin College of Engineering and Applied Science, Bethlehem, PA 18015. Offers M Eng, MS, PhD, Certificate, MBA/E. MBA & E - Rossin College of Engineering & Applied Science/College of Business; MS Fin engineering (Formerly AFIN) - RCEAS/College of Bus/Coll of Arts & Sc. *Program availability:* Part-time, 100% online, blended/hybrid learning. *Faculty:* 145 full-time (26 women), 9 part-time/adjunct (1 woman). *Students:* 562 full-time (125 women), 121 part-time (46 women); includes 58 minority (13 Black or African American, non-Hispanic/Latino; 18 Asian, non-Hispanic/Latino; 19 Hispanic/Latino; 2 Native Hawaiian or other Pacific Islander, non-Hispanic/Latino; 6 Two or more races, non-Hispanic/Latino), 425 international. Average age 29. 1,598 applicants, 37% accepted, 188 enrolled. In 2018, 284 master's, 60 doctorates awarded. Terminal master's awarded for partial completion of doctoral program. *Degree requirements:* For master's, comprehensive exam (for some programs), thesis (for some programs); for doctorate, comprehensive exam (for some programs), thesis/dissertation. *Entrance requirements:* For master's and doctorate, GRE General Test, BS. Additional exam requirements/recommendations for international students: Required—TOEFL (minimum score 79 iBT), IELTS (minimum score 6.5). *Application deadline:* For fall admission, 7/15 for domestic students, 6/15 for international students; for spring admission, 12/1 for domestic and international students. Application fee: $75. Electronic applications accepted. Tuition and fees vary according to program. *Financial support:* In 2018–19, 257 students received support, including 42 fellowships with tuition reimbursements available (averaging $22,050 per year), 160 research assistantships with tuition reimbursements available (averaging $29,400 per year), 55 teaching assistantships with tuition reimbursements available (averaging $22,050 per year); scholarships/grants, tuition waivers (full and partial), and unspecified assistantships also available. Financial award application deadline: 1/15. *Faculty research:* Engineered bio and health systems, energy and the environment, cyber physical infrastructure, materials, matter, devices & systems, data science and intelligent systems. *Unit head:* Dr. Stephen P. DeWeerth, Dean, 610-758-5308, Fax: 610-758-5623, E-mail: steve.deweerth@lehigh.edu. *Application contact:* Brianne Lisk, Manager of Graduate Programs, 610-758-6310, Fax: 610-758-5623, E-mail: brie.lisk@lehigh.edu.
Website: https://engineering.lehigh.edu

LeTourneau University, Graduate Programs, Longview, TX 75607-7001. Offers business administration (MBA); counseling (MA); curriculum and instruction (M Ed); educational administration (M Ed); engineering (ME, MS); engineering management (MEM); health care administration (MS); marriage and family therapy (MA); psychology (MA); strategic leadership (MSL); teacher leadership (M Ed); teaching and learning (M Ed). *Program availability:* Part-time, 100% online, blended/hybrid learning. *Students:* 61 full-time (47 women), 311 part-time (248 women); includes 184 minority (117 Black or African American, non-Hispanic/Latino; 3 American Indian or Alaska Native, non-Hispanic/Latino; 1 Asian, non-Hispanic/Latino; 35 Hispanic/Latino; 28 Two or more races, non-Hispanic/Latino), 2 international. Average age 37. In 2018, 97 master's awarded. *Entrance requirements:* Additional exam requirements/recommendations for international students: Required—TOEFL (minimum score 525 paper-based; 80 iBT), IELTS (minimum score 6), Either a TOEFL or IELTS is required for graduate students. One or the other. *Application deadline:* Applications are processed on a rolling basis. Electronic applications accepted. *Financial support:* Research assistantships, teaching assistantships, unspecified assistantships, and employee tuition waivers and institutionally sponsored loans available. Financial award applicants required to submit FAFSA.
Website: http://www.letu.edu

Louisiana State University and Agricultural & Mechanical College, Graduate School, College of Engineering, Department of Biological and Agricultural Engineering, Baton Rouge, LA 70803. Offers biological and agricultural engineering (MSBAE); engineering science (MS, PhD).

Louisiana State University and Agricultural & Mechanical College, Graduate School, College of Engineering, Interdepartmental Program in Engineering Science, Baton Rouge, LA 70803. Offers MSES, PhD.

Louisiana Tech University, Graduate School, College of Engineering and Science, Ruston, LA 71272. Offers applied physics (MS); biomedical engineering (PhD); computer science (MS); engineering (MS, PhD), including cyberspace engineering (PhD), engineering education (PhD), engineering physics (PhD), materials and infrastructure systems (PhD), micro/nanoscale systems (PhD); engineering and technology management (MS); mathematics (MS); molecular science and nanotechnology (MS, PhD). *Program availability:* Part-time-only. Terminal master's awarded for partial completion of doctoral program. *Degree requirements:* For master's, thesis (for some programs); for doctorate, thesis/dissertation. *Entrance requirements:* For master's and Graduate Certificate, GRE General Test, minimum GPA of 3.0 in last 60 hours. Additional exam requirements/recommendations for international students: Required—TOEFL (minimum score 550 paper-based; 80 iBT), IELTS (minimum score 6.5). Electronic applications accepted. *Faculty research:* Trenchless technology, micromanufacturing, radionuclide transport, microbial liquefaction, hazardous waste treatment.

Manhattan College, Graduate Programs, School of Engineering, Riverdale, NY 10471. Offers chemical engineering (MS), including chemical engineering, cosmetic engineering; civil engineering (MS); computer engineering (MS); construction management (MS); electrical engineering (MS); environmental engineering (ME, MS); mechanical engineering (MS). *Program availability:* Part-time, evening/weekend. *Degree requirements:* For master's, thesis or alternative. *Entrance requirements:* For master's, GRE (recommended), minimum GPA of 3.0. Additional exam requirements/recommendations for international students: Required—TOEFL (minimum score 550 paper-based; 80 iBT), IELTS (minimum score 6). *Expenses:* Contact institution. *Faculty research:* Environmental/water, nucleation, environmental/management, heat transfer.

Marquette University, Graduate School, College of Engineering, Milwaukee, WI 53201-1881. Offers ME, MS, MSEM, PhD, Certificate. *Program availability:* Part-time, evening/weekend. *Degree requirements:* For doctorate, thesis/dissertation. *Entrance requirements:* For master's, minimum GPA of 3.0; for doctorate, GRE General Test, minimum GPA of 3.0. Additional exam requirements/recommendations for international students: Required—TOEFL (minimum score 530 paper-based). Electronic applications accepted. *Faculty research:* Urban watershed management, micro sensors for environmental pollutants, orthopedic rehabilitation engineering, telemedicine, ergonomics.

Marshall University, Academic Affairs Division, College of Information Technology and Engineering, Huntington, WV 25755. Offers MS, MSE, MSEE, MSME, Certificate. *Program availability:* Part-time, evening/weekend. *Expenses:* Contact institution.

Massachusetts Institute of Technology, School of Engineering, Cambridge, MA 02139. Offers M Eng, SM, PhD, Sc D, CE, EAA, ECS, EE, Mat E, Mech E, NE, Naval E, SM/MBA. *Degree requirements:* For master's, thesis (for some programs); for doctorate, comprehensive exam, thesis/dissertation; for other advanced degree, thesis. Electronic applications accepted. *Expenses: Tuition:* Full-time $51,520; part-time $800 per credit hour. *Required fees:* $312.

McGill University, Faculty of Graduate and Postdoctoral Studies, Faculty of Engineering, Montréal, QC H3A 2T5, Canada. Offers M Arch I, M Arch II, M Eng, M Sc, MMM, MUP, PhD, Diploma.

McGill University, Faculty of Graduate and Postdoctoral Studies, Faculty of Science, Department of Mathematics and Statistics, Montréal, QC H3A 2T5, Canada. Offers computational science and engineering (M Sc); mathematics and statistics (M Sc, MA, PhD), including applied mathematics (M Sc, MA), pure mathematics (M Sc, MA), statistics (M Sc, MA).

McMaster University, School of Graduate Studies, Faculty of Engineering, Hamilton, ON L8S 4M2, Canada. Offers M Eng, M Sc, MA Sc, PhD. *Program availability:* Part-time. *Degree requirements:* For doctorate, comprehensive exam, thesis/dissertation. *Entrance requirements:* Additional exam requirements/recommendations for international students: Required—TOEFL (minimum score 550 paper-based). *Faculty research:* Computer process control, water resources engineering, elasticity, flow induced vibrations, microelectronics.

McNeese State University, Doré School of Graduate Studies, College of Engineering and Computer Science, Lake Charles, LA 70609. Offers chemical engineering (M Eng). *Program availability:* Part-time, evening/weekend. *Entrance requirements:* For master's, GRE, minimum undergraduate GPA of 3.0. Additional exam requirements/recommendations for international students: Required—TOEFL (minimum score 560 paper-based; 83 iBT).

Memorial University of Newfoundland, School of Graduate Studies, Faculty of Engineering and Applied Science, St. John's, NL A1C 5S7, Canada. Offers civil engineering (M Eng, PhD); electrical and computer engineering (M Eng, PhD); mechanical engineering (M Eng, PhD); ocean and naval architecture engineering (M Eng, PhD). *Program availability:* Part-time. *Degree requirements:* For master's, thesis; for doctorate, comprehensive exam, thesis/dissertation, oral thesis defense. *Entrance requirements:* For master's, 2nd class degree; for doctorate, master's degree in engineering. Electronic applications accepted. *Faculty research:* Engineering analysis, environmental and hydrotechnical studies, manufacturing and robotics, mechanics, structures and materials.

Mercer University, Graduate Studies, Macon Campus, School of Engineering, Macon, GA 31207. Offers biomedical engineering (MSE); computer engineering (MSE); electrical engineering (MSE); engineering management (MSE); environmental engineering (MSE); environmental systems (MS); mechanical engineering (MSE); software engineering (MSE); software systems (MS); technical communications management (MS); technical management (MS). *Program availability:* Part-time-only, evening/weekend, online learning. *Degree requirements:* For master's, thesis or alternative. *Entrance requirements:* For master's, GRE (minimum score 300), minimum undergraduate GPA of 3.0. Additional exam requirements/recommendations for international students: Required—TOEFL (minimum score 550 paper-based; 80 iBT). *Expenses:* Contact institution. *Faculty research:* Designing prostheses and orthotics, oxygen transfer and limitations in biological systems, low-cost groundwater development, lung airway and transport, autonomous mobile robots.

Merrimack College, School of Science and Engineering, North Andover, MA 01845-5800. Offers civil engineering (MS); computer science (MS); data science (MS); engineering management (MS); mechanical engineering (MS), including engineering management. *Program availability:* Part-time, evening/weekend, 100% online. *Faculty:* 10 full-time (2 women), 6 part-time/adjunct (1 woman). *Students:* 53 full-time (18 women), 17 part-time (5 women); includes 14 minority (6 Black or African American, non-Hispanic/Latino; 6 Asian, non-Hispanic/Latino; 2 Two or more races, non-Hispanic/Latino), 9 international. Average age 34. 183 applicants, 61% accepted, 40 enrolled. In 2018, 27 master's awarded. *Degree requirements:* For master's, comprehensive exam, thesis optional, internship or capstone (for some programs). *Entrance requirements:* For master's, official college transcripts, resume, personal statement, 2 recommendations. Additional exam requirements/recommendations for international students: Required—TOEFL (minimum score 84 iBT), IELTS (minimum score 6.5), PTE (minimum score 56). *Application deadline:* For fall admission, 8/24 for domestic students, 7/30 for international students; for spring admission, 1/10 for domestic students, 12/10 for international students; for summer admission, 5/10 for domestic students, 4/10 for international students. Applications are processed on a rolling basis. Application fee: $0. Electronic applications accepted. Application fee is waived when completed online. *Expenses:* Contact institution. *Financial support:* Career-related internships or fieldwork, scholarships/grants, health care benefits, and unspecified assistantships available. Support available to part-time students. Financial award application deadline: 5/1; financial award applicants required to submit FAFSA. *Unit head:* Dr. Naira Campbell-Kyureghyan, Dean, 978-837-5265, E-mail: campbellnk@merrimack.edu. *Application contact:* Allison Pena, Graduate Admissions Counselor, 978-837-3563, E-mail: penaa@merrimack.edu.
Website: http://www.merrimack.edu/academics/graduate/

Miami University, College of Engineering and Computing, Oxford, OH 45056. Offers MCS, MS. *Faculty:* 60 full-time (10 women). *Students:* 57 full-time (15 women), 7 part-time (1 woman); includes 4 minority (1 Black or African American, non-Hispanic/Latino; 1 Asian, non-Hispanic/Latino; 2 Hispanic/Latino), 34 international. Average age 25. In 2018, 34 master's awarded. *Unit head:* Dr. Marek Dollar, Dean, 513-529-0700, E-mail: cec@miamioh.edu. *Application contact:* Graduate Admission Coordinator, 513-529-3734, E-mail: applygrad@miamioh.edu.
Website: http://miamioh.edu/cec/

Michigan State University, The Graduate School, College of Engineering, East Lansing, MI 48824. Offers MS, PhD. *Program availability:* Part-time. Electronic applications accepted.

Michigan Technological University, Graduate School, College of Engineering, Houghton, MI 49931. Offers MS, PhD, Graduate Certificate. *Program availability:* Part-time, 100% online, blended/hybrid learning. *Faculty:* 261 full-time (48 women), 99 part-time/adjunct (16 women). *Students:* 634 full-time (123 women), 144 part-time (32 women); includes 30 minority (8 Black or African American, non-Hispanic/Latino; 6 Asian, non-Hispanic/Latino; 10 Hispanic/Latino; 6 Two or more races, non-Hispanic/Latino), 537 international. Average age 27. 2,309 applicants, 39% accepted, 228 enrolled. In 2018, 304 master's, 42 doctorates, 61 other advanced degrees awarded. Terminal master's awarded for partial completion of doctoral program. *Degree requirements:* For master's, thesis (for some programs), 30 credits; for doctorate, comprehensive exam, thesis/dissertation, 30 credits beyond master's degree. *Entrance requirements:* For master's and doctorate, GRE, statement of purpose, personal statement, official transcripts, 2-3 letters of recommendation; for Graduate Certificate, statement of purpose, personal statement, official transcripts. Additional exam requirements/recommendations for international students: Required—TOEFL/IELTS.

Application deadline: Applications are processed on a rolling basis. Electronic applications accepted. *Expenses:* $1,143 per credit. *Financial support:* In 2018–19, 546 students received support, including 54 fellowships with tuition reimbursements available (averaging $16,590 per year), 140 research assistantships with tuition reimbursements available (averaging $16,590 per year), 77 teaching assistantships with tuition reimbursements available (averaging $16,590 per year); career-related internships or fieldwork, Federal Work-Study, scholarships/grants, health care benefits, unspecified assistantships, and cooperative program also available. Financial award applicants required to submit FAFSA. *Faculty research:* Engineering, sustainability, energy systems, transportation, health technologies. *Total annual research expenditures:* $17 million. *Unit head:* Dr. Janet Callahan, Dean, 906-487-2005, E-mail: callahan@mtu.edu. *Application contact:* Carol T. Wingerson, Administrative Aide, 906-487-2328, Fax: 906-487-2284, E-mail: gradadms@mtu.edu.
Website: http://www.mtu.edu/engineering/

Milwaukee School of Engineering, MS Program in Engineering, Milwaukee, WI 53202-3109. Offers MS. *Program availability:* Part-time, evening/weekend. *Degree requirements:* For master's, thesis or alternative, design project or capstone. *Entrance requirements:* For master's, GRE General Test if undergraduate GPA is less than 2.8, BS in engineering, engineering technology, or closely-related area; 2 letters of recommendation. Additional exam requirements/recommendations for international students: Required—TOEFL (minimum score 90 iBT), IELTS (minimum score 7). Electronic applications accepted. *Faculty research:* Microprocessors, materials, thermodynamics, artificial intelligence, fluid power/hydraulics.

Mississippi State University, Bagley College of Engineering, Mississippi State, MS 39762. Offers M Eng, MS, PhD. *Program availability:* Part-time, 100% online. *Faculty:* 100 full-time (15 women), 6 part-time/adjunct (2 women). *Students:* 346 full-time (102 women), 335 part-time (77 women); includes 102 minority (46 Black or African American, non-Hispanic/Latino; 25 Asian, non-Hispanic/Latino; 28 Hispanic/Latino; 1 Native Hawaiian or other Pacific Islander, non-Hispanic/Latino; 2 Two or more races, non-Hispanic/Latino), 213 international. Average age 31. 492 applicants, 46% accepted, 131 enrolled. In 2018, 131 master's, 47 doctorates awarded. *Degree requirements:* For master's, comprehensive exam (for some programs), thesis; for doctorate, comprehensive exam (for some programs), thesis/dissertation. *Entrance requirements:* For master's, GRE, minimum GPA of 2.75; for doctorate, GRE. Additional exam requirements/recommendations for international students: Required—TOEFL (minimum score 477 paper-based; 53 iBT); Recommended—IELTS (minimum score 4.5). *Application deadline:* For fall admission, 7/1 for domestic students, 5/1 for international students; for spring admission, 11/1 for domestic students, 9/1 for international students. Applications are processed on a rolling basis. Application fee: $60 ($80 for international students). Electronic applications accepted. *Expenses:* Tuition, state resident: full-time $8450; part-time $360.59 per credit hour. Tuition, nonresident: full-time $23,140; part-time $969.09 per credit hour. *Required fees:* $110. One-time fee: $55 full-time. Part-time tuition and fees vary according to course load, degree level, campus/location and reciprocity agreements. *Financial support:* In 2018–19, 178 research assistantships with full tuition reimbursements (averaging $16,993 per year), 69 teaching assistantships with full tuition reimbursements (averaging $15,123 per year) were awarded; Federal Work-Study, institutionally sponsored loans, scholarships/grants, and unspecified assistantships also available. Financial award application deadline: 4/1; financial award applicants required to submit FAFSA. *Faculty research:* Fluid dynamics, combustion, composite materials, computer design, high-voltage phenomena. *Total annual research expenditures:* $54.7 million. *Unit head:* Dr. Jason Keith, Dean, 662-325-7183, Fax: 662-325-8573, E-mail: keith@bagley.msstate.edu. *Application contact:* Angie Campbell, Admissions and Enrollment Assistant, 662-325-9514, E-mail: acampbell@grad.msstate.edu.
Website: https://www.bagley.msstate.edu/

Missouri Western State University, Program in Applied Science, St. Joseph, MO 64507-2294. Offers chemistry (MAS); engineering technology management (MAS); industrial life science (MAS); sport and fitness management (MAS). *Accreditation:* AACSB. *Program availability:* Part-time. *Students:* 35 full-time (11 women), 14 part-time (5 women); includes 4 minority (1 Black or African American, non-Hispanic/Latino; 1 Asian, non-Hispanic/Latino; 1 Hispanic/Latino; 1 Two or more races, non-Hispanic/Latino), 10 international. Average age 25. 31 applicants, 94% accepted, 20 enrolled. In 2018, 18 master's awarded. *Entrance requirements:* Additional exam requirements/recommendations for international students: Recommended—TOEFL (minimum score 79 iBT), IELTS (minimum score 6). *Application deadline:* For fall admission, 7/15 for domestic and international students; for spring admission, 11/1 for domestic and international students; for summer admission, 4/29 for domestic and international students. Applications are processed on a rolling basis. Application fee: $45 ($50 for international students). Electronic applications accepted. *Expenses: Tuition, area resident:* Part-time $359.39 per credit hour. Tuition, state resident: part-time $359.39 per credit hour. Tuition, nonresident: part-time $643.39 per credit hour. Tuition and fees vary according to program. *Financial support:* Scholarships/grants and unspecified assistantships available. Support available to part-time students. *Unit head:* Dr. Susan Bashinski, Dean of the Graduate School, 816-271-4394, Fax: 816-271-4525, E-mail: graduate@missouriwestern.edu. *Application contact:* Dr. Susan Bashinski, Dean of the Graduate School, 816-271-4394, Fax: 816-271-4525, E-mail: graduate@missouriwestern.edu.

Montana State University, The Graduate School, College of Engineering, Department of Chemical and Biological Engineering, Bozeman, MT 59717. Offers chemical engineering (MS); engineering (PhD), including chemical engineering option, environmental engineering option; environmental engineering (MS). *Program availability:* Part-time. *Degree requirements:* For master's, comprehensive exam, thesis (for some programs); for doctorate, comprehensive exam, thesis/dissertation. *Entrance requirements:* For master's and doctorate, GRE General Test. Additional exam requirements/recommendations for international students: Required—TOEFL (minimum score 550 paper-based). Electronic applications accepted. *Faculty research:* Metabolic network analysis and engineering; magnetic resonance microscopy; modeling of biological systems; the development of protective coatings on planar solid oxide fuel cell (SOFC) metallic interconnects; characterizing corrosion mechanisms of materials in precisely-controlled exposures; testing materials in poly-crystalline silicon production environments; environmental biotechnology and bioremediation.

Montana State University, The Graduate School, College of Engineering, Department of Civil Engineering, Bozeman, MT 59717. Offers civil engineering (MS); construction engineering management (MCEM); engineering (PhD), including applied mechanics option, civil engineering option. *Program availability:* Part-time. *Degree requirements:* For master's, comprehensive exam, thesis (for some programs); for doctorate, comprehensive exam, thesis/dissertation. *Entrance requirements:* For master's and doctorate, GRE General Test. Additional exam requirements/recommendations for international students: Required—TOEFL (minimum score 550 paper-based). Electronic applications accepted. *Faculty research:* Snow and ice mechanics, biofilm engineering, transportation, structural and geo materials, water resources.

Montana State University, The Graduate School, College of Engineering, Department of Mechanical and Industrial Engineering, Bozeman, MT 59717. Offers engineering (PhD), including industrial engineering, mechanical engineering; industrial and management engineering (MS); mechanical engineering (MS). *Program availability:* Part-time. *Degree requirements:* For master's, comprehensive exam, thesis, oral exams; for doctorate, comprehensive exam, thesis/dissertation, qualifying exam. *Entrance requirements:* For master's, GRE, official transcript, minimum GPA of 3.0, demonstrated potential for success, statement of goals, three letters of recommendation, proof of funds affidavit; for doctorate, minimum undergraduate GPA of 3.0, 3.2 graduate; three letters of recommendation; statement of objectives. Additional exam requirements/recommendations for international students: Required—TOEFL or IELTS. Electronic applications accepted. *Faculty research:* Human factors engineering, energy, design and manufacture, systems modeling, materials and structures, measurement systems.

Montana Tech of The University of Montana, Department of General Engineering, Butte, MT 59701-8997. Offers MS. *Program availability:* Part-time. *Degree requirements:* For master's, comprehensive exam (for some programs), thesis optional. *Entrance requirements:* For master's, minimum GPA of 3.0. Additional exam requirements/recommendations for international students: Required—TOEFL (minimum score 545 paper-based; 78 iBT), IELTS (minimum score 6.5). Electronic applications accepted. *Faculty research:* Wind energy and power controls, robotics, concurrent engineering, remotely piloted aircraft, composite materials.

Morgan State University, School of Graduate Studies, Clarence M. Mitchell, Jr. School of Engineering, Baltimore, MD 21251. Offers civil engineering (M Eng, D Eng); electrical and computer engineering (M Eng, MS, D Eng); industrial and systems engineering (M Eng, D Eng); transportation and urban infrastructure studies (MS, PhD, Postbaccalaureate Certificate), including transportation. *Program availability:* Part-time, evening/weekend. *Degree requirements:* For master's, thesis, comprehensive exam or equivalent; for doctorate, thesis/dissertation, comprehensive exam or equivalent. *Entrance requirements:* For master's, GRE, minimum undergraduate GPA of 2.5; for doctorate, GRE, minimum GPA of 3.0. Additional exam requirements/recommendations for international students: Required—TOEFL (minimum score 550 paper-based).

National University, School of Engineering and Computing, La Jolla, CA 92037-1011. Offers computer science (MS), including advanced computing; cyber security and information assurance (MS); data analytics (MS); electrical engineering (MS); engineering management (MS); information technology management (MS); management information systems (MS); sustainability management (MS). *Program availability:* Part-time, evening/weekend, 100% online, blended/hybrid learning. *Degree requirements:* For master's, thesis (for some programs). *Entrance requirements:* For master's, interview, minimum GPA of 2.5. Additional exam requirements/recommendations for international students: Required—TOEFL (minimum score 550 paper-based; 79 iBT), IELTS (minimum score 6). Electronic applications accepted. *Expenses: Tuition:* Full-time $10,320; part-time $430 per unit. Tuition and fees vary according to degree level. *Faculty research:* Educational technology, scholarships in science.

New Jersey Institute of Technology, Newark College of Engineering, Newark, NJ 07102. Offers biomedical engineering (MS, PhD); biopharmaceutical engineering (MS); chemical engineering (MS, PhD); civil engineering (MS, PhD); computer engineering (MS); critical infrastructure systems (MS); electrical engineering (MS, PhD); engineering management (MS); engineering science (MS); environmental engineering (MS, PhD); healthcare systems management (MS); industrial engineering (MS, PhD); internet engineering (MS); manufacturing systems engineering (MS); materials science & engineering (PhD); materials science and engineering (MS); mechanical engineering (MS, PhD); occupational safety and health engineering (MS). *Program availability:* Part-time, evening/weekend. *Faculty:* 147 full-time (26 women), 133 part-time/adjunct (16 women). *Students:* 690 full-time (163 women), 594 part-time (130 women); includes 427 minority (79 Black or African American, non-Hispanic/Latino; 181 Asian, non-Hispanic/Latino; 140 Hispanic/Latino; 27 Two or more races, non-Hispanic/Latino), 553 international. Average age 27. 2,334 applicants, 57% accepted, 452 enrolled. In 2018, 418 master's, 31 doctorates awarded. Terminal master's awarded for partial completion of doctoral program. *Degree requirements:* For master's, thesis (for some programs); for doctorate, thesis/dissertation. *Entrance requirements:* For master's, GRE General Test, minimum GPA 2.8, personal statement, 1 letter of recommendation, transcripts; for doctorate, GRE General Test, minimum GPA of 3.5, personal statement, 3 letters of recommendation, transcripts. Additional exam requirements/recommendations for international students: Required—TOEFL (minimum score 550 paper-based; 79 iBT), IELTS (minimum score 6.5). *Application deadline:* For fall admission, 6/1 priority date for domestic students, 5/1 priority date for international students; for spring admission, 11/15 priority date for domestic and international students. Applications are processed on a rolling basis. Application fee: $75. Electronic applications accepted. *Expenses:* $22,690 per year (in-state), $32,136 per year (out-of-state). *Financial support:* In 2018–19, 396 students received support, including 52 fellowships with full tuition reimbursements available (averaging $22,000 per year), 113 research assistantships with full tuition reimbursements available (averaging $22,000 per year), 101 teaching assistantships with full tuition reimbursements available (averaging $22,000 per year); career-related internships or fieldwork, Federal Work-Study, scholarships/grants, and unspecified assistantships also available. Financial award application deadline: 1/15. *Faculty research:* Nonlinear signal processing, intelligent medical image analysis, calibration issues in coherent localization, computer-aided design, neural network for tool wear measurement. *Total annual research expenditures:* $41.7 million. *Unit head:* Dr. Moshe Kam, Dean, 973-596-5534, Fax: 973-596-2316, E-mail: moshe.kam@njit.edu. *Application contact:* Stephen Eck, Director of Admissions, 973-596-3300, Fax: 973-596-3461, E-mail: admissions@njit.edu.
Website: http://engineering.njit.edu/

New Mexico State University, College of Engineering, Las Cruces, NM 88003-8001. Offers aerospace engineering (MSAE); chemical engineering (MS Ch E); civil engineering (MSCE); electrical & computer engineering (MSEE); environmental engineering (MS Env E); industrial engineering (MSIE); mechanical engineering (MSME). *Program availability:* Part-time, online learning. *Faculty:* 63 full-time (12 women), 2 part-time/adjunct (0 women). *Students:* 218 full-time (56 women), 162 part-time (39 women); includes 132 minority (9 Black or African American, non-Hispanic/Latino; 3 American Indian or Alaska Native, non-Hispanic/Latino; 12 Asian, non-Hispanic/Latino; 100 Hispanic/Latino; 8 Two or more races, non-Hispanic/Latino), 137 international. Average age 31. 292 applicants, 56% accepted, 79 enrolled. In 2018, 111 master's, 21 doctorates, 6 other advanced degrees awarded. *Degree requirements:* For master's, comprehensive exam; for doctorate, comprehensive exam, thesis/dissertation. *Entrance requirements:* For master's and doctorate, GRE (for some engineering programs). Additional exam requirements/recommendations for international students: Required—TOEFL (minimum score 550 paper-based; 79 iBT), IELTS (minimum score 6.5). *Application deadline:* For fall admission, 7/1 priority date for domestic students; for spring admission, 11/1 for domestic students. Applications are processed on a rolling basis. Application fee: $40 ($50 for international students). Electronic applications accepted. *Expenses: Tuition, area resident:* Full-time $4216.70; part-time $252.70 per credit hour. Tuition, state resident: full-time $4216.70; part-time $252.70 per credit hour. Tuition, nonresident: full-time $12,769; part-time $881.10 per credit hour. *International tuition:* $12,769.30 full-time. *Required fees:* $878.40; $48.80 per credit hour. Full-time tuition and fees vary according to course load

and reciprocity agreements. *Financial support:* In 2018–19, 237 students received support, including 18 fellowships (averaging $3,125 per year), 82 research assistantships (averaging $14,613 per year), 70 teaching assistantships (averaging $13,034 per year); career-related internships or fieldwork, Federal Work-Study, scholarships/grants, traineeships, health care benefits, and unspecified assistantships also available. Support available to part-time students. Financial award application deadline: 3/1. *Faculty research:* Energy, environment, and water research; data and information science including communications and signal processing, machine learning, and sensors and sensing applications; infrastructure and structures including construction materials, nondestructive testing, and structural monitoring. *Total annual research expenditures:* $9.8 million. *Unit head:* Dr. Lakshmi Reddi, Dean, 575-646-7234, Fax: 575-646-3549, E-mail: engrdean@nmsu.edu. *Application contact:* Graduate Admissions, 575-646-3121, E-mail: admissions@nmsu.edu.
Website: http://engr.nmsu.edu/

New York Institute of Technology, College of Engineering and Computing Sciences, Old Westbury, NY 11568-8000. Offers MS, Advanced Certificate. *Program availability:* Part-time, evening/weekend, 100% online, blended/hybrid learning. *Students:* 350 full-time (97 women), 209 part-time (60 women); includes 120 minority (29 Black or African American, non-Hispanic/Latino; 55 Asian, non-Hispanic/Latino; 30 Hispanic/Latino; 1 Native Hawaiian or other Pacific Islander, non-Hispanic/Latino; 5 Two or more races, non-Hispanic/Latino), 353 international. Average age 27. 1,673 applicants, 59% accepted, 159 enrolled. In 2018, 400 master's awarded. *Degree requirements:* For master's, thesis (for some programs). *Entrance requirements:* Additional exam requirements/recommendations for international students: Required—TOEFL (minimum score 79 iBT), IELTS (minimum score 6), PTE (minimum score 53). *Application deadline:* For fall admission, 7/1 for international students; for spring admission, 12/15 for international students. Applications are processed on a rolling basis. Application fee: $50. Electronic applications accepted. *Expenses: Tuition:* Full-time $1285; part-time $1285 per credit. *Required fees:* $215; $175 per unit. Tuition and fees vary according to course load, degree level and campus/location. *Financial support:* Fellowships with partial tuition reimbursements, teaching assistantships with partial tuition reimbursements, career-related internships or fieldwork, Federal Work-Study, scholarships/grants, tuition waivers (full and partial), and unspecified assistantships available. Support available to part-time students. Financial award application deadline: 2/15; financial award applicants required to submit FAFSA. *Unit head:* Dr. Babek Beheshti, Dean, 516-686-7437, E-mail: deanofengineering@nyit.edu. *Application contact:* Alice Dolitsky, Director, Graduate Admissions, 516-686-7520, Fax: 516-686-1116, E-mail: admissions@nyit.edu.
Website: http://www.nyit.edu/engineering

New York University, Tandon School of Engineering, Brooklyn, NY 11201. Offers applied physics (Advanced Certificate); biomedical engineering (MS); biotechnology (PhD). *Program availability:* Part-time, 100% online, blended/hybrid learning. *Faculty:* 179 full-time (41 women), 232 part-time/adjunct (32 women). *Students:* 2,157 full-time (707 women), 523 part-time (148 women); includes 334 minority (41 Black or African American, non-Hispanic/Latino; 180 Asian, non-Hispanic/Latino; 90 Hispanic/Latino; 23 Two or more races, non-Hispanic/Latino), 1,987 international. Average age 25. 9,976 applicants, 38% accepted, 1241 enrolled. In 2018, 1,316 master's, 40 doctorates, 6 other advanced degrees awarded. *Entrance requirements:* Additional exam requirements/recommendations for international students: Required—TOEFL (minimum score 550 paper-based; 90 iBT); Recommended—IELTS (minimum score 7). *Application deadline:* For fall admission, 2/15 for domestic and international students; for spring admission, 11/1 for domestic and international students. Applications are processed on a rolling basis. Application fee: $75. Electronic applications accepted. *Expenses:* Contact institution. *Financial support:* Application deadline: 2/15. *Total annual research expenditures:* $52.4 million. *Unit head:* Dr. Jelena Kovacevic, Dean of NYU Tandon School of Engineering, 646-997-3503, E-mail: jk184@nyu.edu. *Application contact:* Elizabeth Ensweiler, Senior Director of Graduate Enrollment and Graduate Admissions, 646-997-3182, E-mail: elizabeth.ensweiler@nyu.edu.
Website: http://engineering.nyu.edu/

North Carolina Agricultural and Technical State University, The Graduate College, College of Engineering, Greensboro, NC 27411. Offers MS, MSCE, MSCS, MSE, MSEE, MSIE, MSME, PhD. *Program availability:* Part-time.

North Carolina State University, Graduate School, College of Engineering, Raleigh, NC 27695. Offers M Ch E, M Eng, MC Sc, MCE, MIE, MIMS, MMSE, MNAE, MNE, MOR, MS, PhD. *Program availability:* Part-time. Terminal master's awarded for partial completion of doctoral program. *Degree requirements:* For doctorate, thesis/dissertation. Electronic applications accepted.

North Dakota State University, College of Graduate and Interdisciplinary Studies, College of Engineering, Fargo, ND 58102. Offers M Eng, MCM, MS, PhD, Graduate Certificate. *Program availability:* Part-time. Terminal master's awarded for partial completion of doctoral program. *Degree requirements:* For master's, thesis; for doctorate, comprehensive exam, thesis/dissertation. *Entrance requirements:* For master's and doctorate, minimum GPA of 3.0. Additional exam requirements/recommendations for international students: Required—TOEFL. Electronic applications accepted. *Expenses:* Contact institution. *Faculty research:* Theoretical mechanics, robotics, automation, environmental engineering, man-made materials.

Northeastern University, College of Engineering, Boston, MA 02115-5096. Offers bioengineering (MS, PhD); chemical engineering (MS, PhD); civil engineering (MS, PhD); computer engineering (PhD); computer systems engineering (MS); electrical and computer engineering (MS); electrical and computer engineering leadership (MS); electrical engineering (PhD); energy systems (MS); engineering and public policy (MS); engineering management (MS, Certificate); environmental engineering (MS); industrial engineering (MS, PhD); information assurance (PhD); information systems (MS); interdisciplinary engineering (PhD); mechanical engineering (PhD); operations research (MS); telecommunication systems management (MS). *Program availability:* Part-time, online learning. Electronic applications accepted. *Expenses:* Contact institution.

Northern Arizona University, College of Environment, Forestry, and Natural Sciences, Flagstaff, AZ 86011. Offers M Eng, MA, MAT, MF, MS, MSF, PhD, Graduate Certificate. *Program availability:* Part-time, 100% online, blended/hybrid learning. *Degree requirements:* For master's, variable foreign language requirement, comprehensive exam (for some programs), thesis (for some programs); for doctorate, variable foreign language requirement, comprehensive exam (for some programs), thesis/dissertation (for some programs); for Graduate Certificate, comprehensive exam (for some programs). *Entrance requirements:* Additional exam requirements/recommendations for international students: Required—TOEFL (minimum score 80 iBT), IELTS (minimum score 6.5). Electronic applications accepted.

Northern Illinois University, Graduate School, College of Engineering and Engineering Technology, De Kalb, IL 60115-2854. Offers MS. *Program availability:* Part-time, evening/weekend. *Faculty:* 36 full-time (2 women), 2 part-time/adjunct (0 women). *Students:* 125 full-time (29 women), 125 part-time (18 women); includes 34 minority (11 Black or African American, non-Hispanic/Latino; 12 Asian, non-Hispanic/Latino; 8 Hispanic/Latino; 3 Native Hawaiian or other Pacific Islander, non-Hispanic/Latino), 147 international. Average age 28. 329 applicants, 62% accepted, 65 enrolled. In 2018, 125 master's awarded. *Degree requirements:* For master's, comprehensive exam, thesis optional. *Entrance requirements:* For master's, GRE General Test, minimum GPA of 2.75. Additional exam requirements/recommendations for international students: Required—TOEFL (minimum score 550 paper-based). *Application deadline:* For fall admission, 6/1 for domestic students, 5/1 for international students; for spring admission, 11/1 for domestic students, 10/1 for international students. Applications are processed on a rolling basis. Application fee: $40. Electronic applications accepted. *Financial support:* In 2018–19, 1 research assistantship with full tuition reimbursement was awarded; fellowships with full tuition reimbursements, teaching assistantships with full tuition reimbursements, career-related internships or fieldwork, Federal Work-Study, scholarships/grants, tuition waivers (full), and unspecified assistantships also available. Support available to part-time students. Financial award applicants required to submit FAFSA. *Unit head:* Dr. Donald R Peterson, Dean, 815-753-1281, Fax: 815-753-1310, E-mail: drpeterson@niu.edu. *Application contact:* Graduate School Office, 815-753-0395, E-mail: gradsch@niu.edu.
Website: http://www.niu.edu/CEET/

Northwestern Polytechnic University, School of Engineering, Fremont, CA 94539-7482. Offers computer engineering (DCE); computer science (MS); computer systems engineering (MS); electrical engineering (MS). *Program availability:* Part-time, evening/weekend. *Degree requirements:* For master's, thesis optional; for doctorate, thesis/dissertation. *Entrance requirements:* For master's, minimum GPA of 3.0. Additional exam requirements/recommendations for international students: Required—TOEFL (minimum score 550 paper-based; 79 iBT). *Faculty research:* Computer networking, database design, Internet technology, software engineering, digital signal processing.

Northwestern University, McCormick School of Engineering and Applied Science, Evanston, IL 60208. Offers MBA, MEM, MIT, MME, MMM, MPD, MS, PhD, Certificate, MBA/MEM. MS and PhD admissions and degrees offered through The Graduate School. *Program availability:* Part-time, evening/weekend. Terminal master's awarded for partial completion of doctoral program. *Degree requirements:* For master's, comprehensive exam (for some programs), thesis (for some programs); for doctorate, comprehensive exam, thesis/dissertation. *Entrance requirements:* For master's and doctorate, GRE General Test. Additional exam requirements/recommendations for international students: Required—TOEFL (minimum score 577 paper-based; 90 iBT) or IELTS (minimum score 7). Electronic applications accepted.

Oakland University, Graduate Study and Lifelong Learning, School of Engineering and Computer Science, Rochester, MI 48309-4401. Offers MS, PhD, Graduate Certificate. *Program availability:* Part-time, evening/weekend. *Degree requirements:* For doctorate, thesis/dissertation. *Entrance requirements:* For master's and doctorate, minimum GPA of 3.0. Additional exam requirements/recommendations for international students: Required—TOEFL (minimum score 550 paper-based). Electronic applications accepted. *Expenses:* Contact institution.

The Ohio State University, Graduate School, College of Engineering, Columbus, OH 43210. Offers M Arch, M Land Arch, MCRP, MS, PhD. *Program availability:* Part-time, evening/weekend. *Faculty:* 364. *Students:* 1,749 full-time (406 women), 156 part-time (32 women). Average age 26. In 2018, 496 master's, 159 doctorates awarded. *Entrance requirements:* For master's and doctorate, GRE. Additional exam requirements/recommendations for international students: Required—TOEFL (minimum score 600 paper-based; 100 iBT), Michigan English Language Assessment Battery (minimum score 86); Recommended—IELTS (minimum score 8). *Application deadline:* For fall admission, 11/30 priority date for domestic and international students. Applications are processed on a rolling basis. Application fee: $60 ($70 for international students). Electronic applications accepted. *Financial support:* Fellowships with tuition reimbursements, research assistantships with tuition reimbursements, teaching assistantships with tuition reimbursements, career-related internships or fieldwork, Federal Work-Study, institutionally sponsored loans, and unspecified assistantships available. Support available to part-time students. *Unit head:* Dr. David B. Williams, Dean, 614-292-2836, Fax: 614-292-9615, E-mail: williams.4219@osu.edu. *Application contact:* Graduate and Professional Admissions, 614-292-9444, Fax: 614-292-3895, E-mail: gpadmissions@osu.edu.
Website: http://engineering.osu.edu/

Ohio University, Graduate College, Russ College of Engineering and Technology, Athens, OH 45701-2979. Offers M Eng Mgt, MS, PhD. *Program availability:* Part-time. *Degree requirements:* For master's, comprehensive exam (for some programs), thesis (for some programs); for doctorate, comprehensive exam, thesis/dissertation. *Entrance requirements:* For master's, GRE General Test, BS in engineering or related field; for doctorate, GRE General Test, MS in engineering or related field. Additional exam requirements/recommendations for international students: Required—TOEFL or IELTS. Electronic applications accepted. *Expenses:* Contact institution. *Faculty research:* Avionics engineering, coal research, transportation engineering, software systems integration, materials processing.

Oklahoma Christian University, Graduate School of Engineering and Computer Science, Oklahoma City, OK 73136-1100. Offers electrical and computer engineering (MSE); engineering management (MSE); mechanical engineering (MSE); software engineering (MSCS, MSE). *Program availability:* Part-time. *Entrance requirements:* Additional exam requirements/recommendations for international students: Required—TOEFL (minimum score 550 paper-based). Electronic applications accepted. *Expenses:* Contact institution.

Oklahoma State University, College of Engineering, Architecture and Technology, Stillwater, OK 74078. Offers MS, PhD. *Program availability:* Online learning. *Degree requirements:* For master's, thesis (for some programs); for doctorate, comprehensive exam, thesis/dissertation. *Entrance requirements:* For master's and doctorate, GRE or GMAT. Additional exam requirements/recommendations for international students: Required—TOEFL (minimum score 550 paper-based; 79 iBT). Electronic applications accepted. *Expenses: Tuition, area resident:* Full-time $4148. Tuition, state resident: full-time $4148. Tuition, nonresident: full-time $10,517. *International tuition:* $10,517 full-time. *Required fees:* $4394; $2929 per credit hour. Tuition and fees vary according to course load and program.

Old Dominion University, Frank Batten College of Engineering and Technology, Norfolk, VA 23529. Offers ME, MS, D Eng, PhD. *Program availability:* Part-time, evening/weekend, 100% online, blended/hybrid learning. *Degree requirements:* For master's, comprehensive exam, thesis (for some programs); for doctorate, comprehensive exam, thesis/dissertation, candidacy exam. *Entrance requirements:* For master's, GRE, minimum GPA of 3.0; for doctorate, GRE, minimum GPA of 3.5. Additional exam requirements/recommendations for international students: Required—TOEFL (minimum score 550 paper-based). Electronic applications accepted. *Expenses:* Contact institution. *Faculty research:* Physical electronics, computational applied mechanics, structural dynamics, computational fluid dynamics, coastal engineering of water resources, modeling and simulation.

Open University, Graduate Programs, Milton Keynes, United Kingdom. Offers business (MBA); education (M Ed); engineering (M Eng); history (MA); music (MA); philosophy (MA).

Oregon State University, College of Engineering, Corvallis, OR 97331. Offers M Eng, MHP, MMP, MS, PhD. *Program availability:* Part-time, 100% online. Terminal master's awarded for partial completion of doctoral program. *Expenses:* Contact institution.

Penn State Great Valley, Graduate Studies, Engineering Division, Malvern, PA 19355-1488. Offers engineering management (MEM); software engineering (MSE); systems engineering (M Eng, Certificate).

Penn State Harrisburg, Graduate School, School of Science, Engineering and Technology, Middletown, PA 17057. Offers civil engineering (MS); computer science (MS); electrical engineering (M Eng, MS); engineering management (MPS); engineering science (M Eng); environmental engineering (M Eng); environmental pollution control (MEPC, MS); mechanical engineering (MS); structural engineering (Certificate). *Program availability:* Part-time, evening/weekend.

Penn State University Park, Graduate School, College of Engineering, University Park, PA 16802. Offers M Eng, MAE, MFR, MS, PhD. *Program availability:* Part-time, evening/weekend. *Entrance requirements:* Additional exam requirements/recommendations for international students: Required—TOEFL (minimum score 550 paper-based; 80 iBT), IELTS. Electronic applications accepted. *Expenses:* Contact institution.

Pontificia Universidad Catolica Madre y Maestra, Graduate School, Faculty of Engineering Sciences, Santiago, Dominican Republic. Offers earthquake engineering (ME); logistics management (ME).

Portland State University, Graduate Studies, Maseeh College of Engineering and Computer Science, Portland, OR 97207-0751. Offers M Eng, MS, MSME, MSMSE, PhD, Certificate, MS/MBA, MS/MS. *Program availability:* Part-time, evening/weekend. *Degree requirements:* For doctorate, one foreign language, thesis/dissertation. *Entrance requirements:* Additional exam requirements/recommendations for international students: Required—TOEFL (minimum score 550 paper-based; 80 iBT). *Expenses:* Contact institution.

Prairie View A&M University, College of Engineering, Prairie View, TX 77446. Offers computer information systems (MSCIS); computer science (MSCS); electrical engineering (MSEE, PhDEE); general engineering (MS Engr). *Program availability:* Part-time, evening/weekend. *Faculty:* 29 full-time (8 women), 1 part-time/adjunct (0 women). *Students:* 134 full-time (34 women), 67 part-time (24 women); includes 84 minority (67 Black or African American, non-Hispanic/Latino; 12 Asian, non-Hispanic/Latino; 5 Hispanic/Latino), 102 international. Average age 31. 130 applicants, 80% accepted, 52 enrolled. In 2018, 67 master's, 3 doctorates awarded. *Degree requirements:* For master's, thesis optional; for doctorate, comprehensive exam, thesis/dissertation. *Entrance requirements:* For master's, GRE General Test (minimum score of 900), bachelor's degree in engineering from ABET-accredited institution; for doctorate, minimum GPA of 3.0. Additional exam requirements/recommendations for international students: Required—TOEFL (minimum score 550 paper-based; 79 iBT). *Application deadline:* For fall admission, 5/1 priority date for domestic and international students; for spring admission, 10/1 priority date for domestic students, 9/1 priority date for international students; for summer admission, 3/1 priority date for domestic students, 2/1 priority date for international students. Applications are processed on a rolling basis. Application fee: $50. Electronic applications accepted. *Expenses: Tuition, area resident:* Full-time $3172; part-time $317 per credit. Tuition, state resident: full-time $3172; part-time $317 per credit. Tuition, nonresident: full-time $7965; part-time $796 per credit. *Required fees:* $4847; $485 per credit. *Financial support:* Fellowships, research assistantships, teaching assistantships, career-related internships or fieldwork, institutionally sponsored loans, scholarships/grants, health care benefits, tuition waivers (full), and unspecified assistantships available. Financial award application deadline: 4/1; financial award applicants required to submit FAFSA. *Faculty research:* Electrical and computer engineering: big data analysis, wireless communications, bioinformatics and computational biology, space radiation; computer science: cloud computing, cyber security; chemical engineering: thermochemical processing of biofuel, photochemical modeling; civil and environmental engineering: environmental sustainability, water resources, structure; mechanical engineering: thermal science, nanocomposites, computational fluid dynamics. *Unit head:* Dr. Pamela H Obiomon, Dean, 936-261-9890, Fax: 936-261-9868, E-mail: phobiomon@pvamu.edu. *Application contact:* Pauline Walker, Administrative Assistant II, Research and Graduate Studies, 936-261-3521, Fax: 936-261-3529, E-mail: gradadmissions@pvamu.edu.

Princeton University, Graduate School, School of Engineering and Applied Science, Princeton, NJ 08544-1019. Offers M Eng, MSE, PhD. Terminal master's awarded for partial completion of doctoral program. *Degree requirements:* For master's, thesis (for some programs); for doctorate, thesis/dissertation, research requirement, teaching requirement, general exam. *Entrance requirements:* For master's and doctorate, GRE General Test, official transcript(s), 3 letters of recommendation, personal statement. Additional exam requirements/recommendations for international students: Required—TOEFL. Electronic applications accepted.

Purdue University, College of Engineering, West Lafayette, IN 47907-2045. Offers MS, MSABE, MSBME, MSCE, MSChE, MSE, MSECE, MSIE, MSME, MSMSE, MSNE, PhD, Certificate, MD/PhD. *Program availability:* Part-time, 100% online, blended/hybrid learning. Terminal master's awarded for partial completion of doctoral program. *Degree requirements:* For doctorate, thesis/dissertation. Electronic applications accepted. *Expenses:* Contact institution. *Faculty research:* Aerospace, biomed engineering, chemical phenomena and processes, civil infrastructure and the environment, communications, computational science and engineering, computer engineering, computer networks, electrical systems, electronics, energy and power, environment and ecology, human in the loop engineering, imaging, manufacturing and materials processing, materials, measurement, mechanical systems, micro- and nano-science and engineering, optics, systems engineering, thermal and transport.

Purdue University Fort Wayne, College of Engineering, Technology, and Computer Science, Fort Wayne, IN 46805-1499. Offers MS, MSE, Certificate. *Program availability:* Part-time. *Entrance requirements:* For master's, GRE General Test, minimum GPA of 3.0. Additional exam requirements/recommendations for international students: Required—TOEFL (minimum score 550 paper-based; 79 iBT); Recommended—TWE. Electronic applications accepted. *Faculty research:* Software-defined radios, embedded system software, wireless cloud architecture.

Purdue University Northwest, Graduate Studies Office, School of Engineering, Mathematics, and Science, Department of Engineering, Hammond, IN 46323-2094. Offers computer engineering (MSE); electrical engineering (MSE); engineering (MS); mechanical engineering (MSE). *Program availability:* Evening/weekend. *Entrance requirements:* Additional exam requirements/recommendations for international students: Required—TOEFL.

Purdue University Northwest, Graduate Studies Office, School of Technology, Hammond, IN 46323-2094. Offers MS.

Queen's University at Kingston, School of Graduate Studies, Faculty of Engineering and Applied Science, Kingston, ON K7L 3N6, Canada. Offers M Eng, M Sc, M Sc Eng, PhD. *Program availability:* Part-time. *Degree requirements:* For doctorate, comprehensive exam, thesis/dissertation. *Entrance requirements:* Additional exam

requirements/recommendations for international students: Required—TOEFL. Electronic applications accepted.

Rensselaer at Hartford, Department of Engineering, Hartford, CT 06120-2991. Offers ME, MS. *Program availability:* Part-time, evening/weekend. *Entrance requirements:* For master's, GRE. Additional exam requirements/recommendations for international students: Required—TOEFL (minimum score 600 paper-based; 100 iBT). Electronic applications accepted.

Rensselaer Polytechnic Institute, Graduate School, School of Engineering, Troy, NY 12180-3590. Offers M Eng, MS, D Eng, PhD. *Program availability:* Part-time. *Faculty:* 179 full-time (28 women), 8 part-time/adjunct (0 women). *Students:* 533 full-time (137 women), 84 part-time (11 women); includes 76 minority (12 Black or African American, non-Hispanic/Latino; 1 American Indian or Alaska Native, non-Hispanic/Latino; 29 Asian, non-Hispanic/Latino; 13 Hispanic/Latino; 21 Two or more races, non-Hispanic/Latino; 298 international. Average age 26. 1,413 applicants, 36% accepted, 162 enrolled. In 2018, 127 master's, 89 doctorates awarded. Terminal master's awarded for partial completion of doctoral program. *Degree requirements:* For master's, comprehensive exam (for some programs), thesis (for some programs); for doctorate, comprehensive exam (for some programs), thesis/dissertation. *Entrance requirements:* For master's and doctorate, GRE. Additional exam requirements/recommendations for international students: Required—TOEFL (minimum score 570 paper-based; 88 iBT), IELTS (minimum score 6.5), PTE (minimum score 60). *Application deadline:* For fall admission, 1/1 priority date for domestic and international students; for spring admission, 8/15 priority date for domestic and international students. Applications are processed on a rolling basis. Application fee: $75. Electronic applications accepted. *Financial support:* In 2018–19, 462 students received support, including research assistantships (averaging $23,000 per year), teaching assistantships (averaging $23,000 per year); fellowships also available. Financial award application deadline: 1/1. *Faculty research:* Aeronautical, biomedical, chemical, civil, computer and systems, engineering physics, environmental, industrial and management, materials science, mechanical, nuclear, systems engineering and technology management, transportation. *Total annual research expenditures:* $35 million. *Unit head:* Shekhar Garde, Dean, 518-276-6298, E-mail: gardes@rpi.edu. *Application contact:* Jarron Decker, Director of Graduate Admissions, 518-276-6216, Fax: 518-276-4072, E-mail: gradadmissions@rpi.edu.
Website: http://www.eng.rpi.edu/

Rice University, Graduate Programs, George R. Brown School of Engineering, Houston, TX 77251-1892. Offers M Ch E, M Stat, MA, MBE, MCAM, MCE, MCS, MEE, MEE, MES, MME, MMS, MS, PhD, MBA/M Stat, MBA/ME, MBA/MEE, MD/PhD. MD/PhD offered jointly with Baylor College of Medicine, The University of Texas Health Science Center at Houston. *Program availability:* Part-time. Terminal master's awarded for partial completion of doctoral program. *Degree requirements:* For master's, comprehensive exam (for some programs), thesis (for some programs); for doctorate, comprehensive exam (for some programs), thesis/dissertation. *Entrance requirements:* For master's and doctorate, GRE General Test. Additional exam requirements/recommendations for international students: Required—TOEFL (minimum score 600 paper-based). Electronic applications accepted. *Faculty research:* Digital signal processing, tissue engineering, groundwater remediation, computational engineering and high performance computing, nanoscale science and technology.

Robert Morris University, School of Engineering, Mathematics and Science, Moon Township, PA 15108-1189. Offers engineering management (MS). *Program availability:* Part-time-only, evening/weekend, 100% online. *Faculty:* 7 full-time (1 woman), 1 part-time/adjunct (0 women). *Students:* 20 part-time (4 women); includes 1 minority (Black or African American, non-Hispanic/Latino), 9 international. Average age 28. 34 applicants, 18% accepted, 6 enrolled. In 2018, 33 master's awarded. *Degree requirements:* For master's, Completion of 30 credits. *Entrance requirements:* For master's, letters of recommendation. Additional exam requirements/recommendations for international students: Required—TOEFL (minimum score 550 paper-based; 79 iBT). *Application deadline:* For fall admission, 7/1 priority date for domestic and international students; for spring admission, 11/1 priority date for domestic and international students. Applications are processed on a rolling basis. Application fee: $35. Electronic applications accepted. *Expenses:* $980 per credit tuition, $80 per credit fees for 2018-2019. *Financial support:* Federal Work-Study, institutionally sponsored loans, and unspecified assistantships available. Financial award application deadline: 5/1; financial award applicants required to submit FAFSA. *Unit head:* Dr. Maria V. Kalevitch, Dean, 412-397-4020, E-mail: kalevitch@rmu.edu. *Application contact:* Dr. Maria V. Kalevitch, Dean, 412-397-4020, E-mail: kalevitch@rmu.edu.
Website: https://www.rmu.edu/academics/schools/sems

Rochester Institute of Technology, Graduate Enrollment Services, Kate Gleason College of Engineering, Rochester, NY 14623-5603. Offers ME, MS, PhD, Advanced Certificate. *Program availability:* Part-time, evening/weekend, 100% online. *Students:* 409 full-time (82 women), 182 part-time (29 women); includes 29 minority (4 Black or African American, non-Hispanic/Latino; 12 Asian, non-Hispanic/Latino; 12 Hispanic/Latino; 1 Two or more races, non-Hispanic/Latino), 315 international. Average age 26. 1,355 applicants, 39% accepted, 166 enrolled. In 2018, 200 master's, 5 doctorates, 10 other advanced degrees awarded. Terminal master's awarded for partial completion of doctoral program. *Entrance requirements:* For master's and doctorate, GRE, minimum GPA of 3.0 (recommended); for Advanced Certificate, minimum GPA of 3.0 (recommended). *Application deadline:* For fall admission, 2/15 priority date for domestic and international students. Applications are processed on a rolling basis. Application fee: $65. Electronic applications accepted. *Expenses:* Contact institution. *Financial support:* In 2018–19, 489 students received support. Fellowships, research assistantships, teaching assistantships, career-related internships or fieldwork, scholarships/grants, tuition waivers (full and partial), unspecified assistantships, and health care benefits (for PhD program only) available. Support available to part-time students. Financial award applicants required to submit FAFSA. *Faculty research:* Advanced materials, computer vision, embedded systems and control, high performance computing, operations, photonics, semiconductor processing, supply chain and logistics, sustainability, transportation, energy, communications, and healthcare. *Unit head:* Dr. Doreen Edwards, Dean, 585-475-2145, Fax: 585-475-6879, E-mail: coe@rit.edu. *Application contact:* Diane Ellison, Senior Associate Vice President, Graduate Enrollment Services, 585-475-2229, Fax: 585-475-7164, E-mail: gradinfo@rit.edu.
Website: http://www.rit.edu/kgcoe/

Rose-Hulman Institute of Technology, Graduate Studies, Terre Haute, IN 47803-3999. Offers M Eng, MS, MD/MS. *Program availability:* Part-time. *Faculty:* 110 full-time (28 women), 5 part-time/adjunct (1 woman). *Students:* 30 full-time (6 women), 27 part-time (5 women); includes 8 minority (4 Asian, non-Hispanic/Latino; 3 Hispanic/Latino; 1 Two or more races, non-Hispanic/Latino), 21 international. Average age 25. 57 applicants, 60% accepted, 21 enrolled. In 2018, 33 master's awarded. *Degree requirements:* For master's, thesis (for some programs). *Entrance requirements:* For master's, GRE, minimum GPA of 3.0. Additional exam requirements/recommendations for international students: Required—TOEFL (minimum score 580 paper-based; 94 iBT), IELTS (minimum score 7). *Application deadline:* For fall admission, 2/1 priority date for

domestic and international students; for winter admission, 10/1 for domestic students, 8/1 for international students; for spring admission, 1/15 for domestic students, 11/1 for international students. Applications are processed on a rolling basis. Application fee: $0. Electronic applications accepted. *Expenses: Tuition:* Full-time $46,641. *Financial support:* In 2018–19, 49 students received support. Fellowships with tuition reimbursements available, research assistantships with tuition reimbursements available, institutionally sponsored loans, scholarships/grants, and tuition waivers (full and partial) available. Financial award application deadline: 2/1; financial award applicants required to submit FAFSA. *Faculty research:* Optical instrument design and prototypes, biomaterials, adsorption and adsorption-based separations, image and speech processing, groundwater, solid and hazardous waste. *Total annual research expenditures:* $698,884. *Unit head:* Dr. Craig Downing, Associate Dean of Lifelong Learning, 812-877-8822, E-mail: downing@rose-hulman.edu. *Application contact:* Dr. Craig Downing, Associate Dean of Lifelong Learning, 812-877-8822, E-mail: downing@rose-hulman.edu.
Website: https://www.rose-hulman.edu/academics/degrees-and-programs/graduate-studies/index.html

Rowan University, Graduate School, College of Engineering, Program in Engineering, Glassboro, NJ 08028-1701. Offers MSE. *Program availability:* Part-time, evening/weekend. *Degree requirements:* For master's, thesis (for some programs). *Entrance requirements:* For master's, GRE General Test. Additional exam requirements/recommendations for international students: Required—TOEFL. Electronic applications accepted.

Royal Military College of Canada, Division of Graduate Studies, Faculty of Engineering, Kingston, ON K7K 7B4, Canada. Offers M Eng, M Sc, MA Sc, PhD. *Degree requirements:* For master's, thesis; for doctorate, comprehensive exam, thesis/dissertation. *Entrance requirements:* For master's, honours degree with second-class standing; for doctorate, master's degree. Electronic applications accepted.

Saginaw Valley State University, College of Science, Engineering, and Technology, University Center, MI 48710. Offers computer science and information systems (MS); energy and materials (MS). *Program availability:* Part-time, evening/weekend. *Faculty:* 5 full-time (0 women), 1 part-time/adjunct (0 women). *Students:* 10 full-time (1 woman), 12 part-time (3 women); includes 1 minority (Asian, non-Hispanic/Latino), 8 international. Average age 32. 35 applicants, 80% accepted, 8 enrolled. *Degree requirements:* For master's, field project or thesis work. *Entrance requirements:* For master's, minimum GPA of 3.0. Additional exam requirements/recommendations for international students: Required—TOEFL (minimum score 550 paper-based; 79 iBT). *Application deadline:* For fall admission, 7/15 for international students; for winter admission, 11/15 for international students; for spring admission, 4/15 for international students. Applications are processed on a rolling basis. Application fee: $30 ($90 for international students). Electronic applications accepted. *Expenses: Tuition, area resident:* Full-time $6225; part-time $623 per credit hour. Tuition, state resident: full-time $6225; part-time $623 per credit hour. Tuition, nonresident: full-time $14,215; part-time $1185 per credit hour. *International tuition:* $14,215 full-time. *Required fees:* $263; $14.60 per credit hour. Tuition and fees vary according to degree level. *Financial support:* Federal Work-Study and scholarships/grants available. Support available to part-time students. Financial award application deadline: 4/1; financial award applicants required to submit FAFSA. *Unit head:* Dr. Robert Tuttle, Program Coordinator, 989-964-4144, Fax: 989-964-2717. *Application contact:* Jenna Briggs, Director, Graduate and International Admissions, 989-964-6096, Fax: 989-964-2788, E-mail: gradadm@svsu.edu.
Website: http://www.svsu.edu/collegeofscienceengineeringtechnology/

St. Cloud State University, School of Graduate Studies, College of Science and Engineering, St. Cloud, MN 56301-4498. Offers MA, MS, Graduate Certificate. *Degree requirements:* For master's, thesis or alternative. *Entrance requirements:* For master's, GRE General Test, minimum GPA of 2.75. Additional exam requirements/recommendations for international students: Required—TOEFL (minimum score 550 paper-based). Electronic applications accepted.

San Diego State University, Graduate and Research Affairs, College of Engineering, San Diego, CA 92182. Offers MS, PhD. *Program availability:* Part-time, evening/weekend. Terminal master's awarded for partial completion of doctoral program. *Degree requirements:* For master's, thesis optional; for doctorate, thesis/dissertation. *Entrance requirements:* For master's, GRE General Test; for doctorate, GRE, 3 letters of recommendation. Additional exam requirements/recommendations for international students: Required—TOEFL. Electronic applications accepted.

San Francisco State University, Division of Graduate Studies, College of Science and Engineering, School of Engineering, San Francisco, CA 94132-1722. Offers embedded electrical and computer systems (MS); energy systems (MS); structural/earthquake engineering (MS). *Program availability:* Part-time. *Application deadline:* Applications are processed on a rolling basis. Electronic applications accepted. *Unit head:* Dr. Kwok-Siong Teh, Director, 415-338-1228, Fax: 415-338-0525, E-mail: ksteh@sfsu.edu. *Application contact:* Dr. Hamid Shahnasser, Graduate Coordinator, 415-338-2124, Fax: 415-338-0525, E-mail: hamid@sfsu.edu.
Website: http://engineering.sfsu.edu/

Santa Clara University, School of Engineering, Santa Clara, CA 95053. Offers applied mathematics (MS); bioengineering (MS); civil, environmental, and sustainable engineering (MS); computer science and engineering (MS, PhD, Engineer); electrical engineering (MS, PhD, Engineer); engineering management and leadership (MS); mechanical engineering (MS, PhD, Engineer); power systems and sustainable energy (MS); software engineering (MS). *Program availability:* Part-time. *Faculty:* 72 full-time (24 women), 52 part-time/adjunct (9 women). *Students:* 555 full-time (211 women), 269 part-time (91 women); includes 208 minority (8 Black or African American, non-Hispanic/Latino; 1 American Indian or Alaska Native, non-Hispanic/Latino; 145 Asian, non-Hispanic/Latino; 28 Hispanic/Latino; 26 Two or more races, non-Hispanic/Latino), 472 international. Average age 27. 1,309 applicants, 36% accepted, 269 enrolled. In 2018, 320 master's, 7 doctorates awarded. *Entrance requirements:* For master's, GRE, official transcript; for doctorate, GRE, Official transcript, 500 word statement of purpose, three letters of recommendation. Additional exam requirements/recommendations for international students: Required—TOEFL (minimum score 79 iBT), IELTS (minimum score 6.5). *Application deadline:* For fall admission, 6/1 for domestic students; for winter admission, 9/6 for domestic students; for spring admission, 1/10 for domestic students; for summer admission, 3/6 for domestic students. Application fee: $60. Electronic applications accepted. *Financial support:* Fellowships, Federal Work-Study, and scholarships/grants available. Support available to part-time students. Financial award applicants required to submit FAFSA. *Unit head:* Dr. Elaine Scott, Dean, 408-554-3512, E-mail: epscott@scu.edu. *Application contact:* Stacey Tinker, Director of Admissions and Marketing, 408-554-4748, Fax: 408-554-4323, E-mail: stinker@scu.edu.
Website: http://www.scu.edu/engineering/graduate/

Seattle University, College of Science and Engineering, Seattle, WA 98122-1090. Offers MSCS. *Program availability:* Part-time, evening/weekend. *Faculty:* 104 full-time (42 women), 15 part-time/adjunct (7 women). *Students:* 75 full-time (30 women), 80 part-time (26 women); includes 37 minority (1 Black or African American, non-Hispanic/Latino; 19 Asian, non-Hispanic/Latino; 12 Hispanic/Latino; 5 Two or more races, non-Hispanic/Latino), 51 international. Average age 28. 136 applicants, 57% accepted, 56 enrolled. In 2018, 32 master's awarded. *Degree requirements:* For master's, thesis. *Entrance requirements:* For master's, GRE General Test, 2 years of related work experience. *Application deadline:* For fall admission, 7/1 for domestic students. Application fee: $55. *Expenses:* Contact institution. *Financial support:* In 2018–19, 17 students received support. Career-related internships or fieldwork and Federal Work-Study available. Support available to part-time students. Financial award applicants required to submit FAFSA. *Unit head:* Dr. Michael Quinn, Dean, 206-296-5500, Fax: 206-296-2071. *Application contact:* Janet Shandley, Director of Graduate Admissions, 206-296-5900, Fax: 206-298-5656, E-mail: grad_admissions@seattleu.edu.
Website: https://www.seattleu.edu/scieng/

Simon Fraser University, Office of Graduate Studies and Postdoctoral Fellows, Faculty of Applied Sciences, School of Engineering Science, Burnaby, BC V5A 1S6, Canada. Offers M Eng, MA Sc, PhD. *Program availability:* Part-time. *Degree requirements:* For master's, thesis (for some programs); for doctorate, thesis/dissertation, qualifying exam, seminar presentations. *Entrance requirements:* For master's, minimum GPA of 3.0 (on scale of 4.33) or 3.33 based on last 60 credits of undergraduate courses; for doctorate, minimum GPA of 3.5 (on scale of 4.33). Additional exam requirements/recommendations for international students: Recommended—TOEFL (minimum score 580 paper-based; 93 iBT), IELTS (minimum score 7), TWE (minimum score 5). Electronic applications accepted. *Faculty research:* Biomedical engineering, communications, microelectronics, systems and robotics.

South Dakota School of Mines and Technology, Graduate Division, College of Engineering, Rapid City, SD 57701-3995. Offers MS, PhD. *Program availability:* Part-time, online learning. *Degree requirements:* For doctorate, thesis/dissertation. *Entrance requirements:* For doctorate, minimum graduate GPA of 3.0. Additional exam requirements/recommendations for international students: Required—TOEFL (minimum score 520 paper-based; 68 iBT), TWE. Electronic applications accepted. *Faculty research:* Contaminants in soil, nitrate leaching, environmental changes, fracture formations, greenhouse effect.

South Dakota State University, Graduate School, Jerome J. Lohr College of Engineering, Brookings, SD 57007. Offers MS, PhD. *Program availability:* Part-time. *Degree requirements:* For master's, thesis, oral exam; for doctorate, thesis/dissertation, preliminary oral and written exams. *Entrance requirements:* Additional exam requirements/recommendations for international students: Required—TOEFL. *Faculty research:* Process control and management, ground source heat pumps, water quality, heat transfer, power systems.

Southern Illinois University Carbondale, Graduate School, College of Engineering, Carbondale, IL 62901-4701. Offers ME, MS, PhD, JD/MS. *Degree requirements:* For master's, comprehensive exam; for doctorate, thesis/dissertation. *Entrance requirements:* For master's, GRE, minimum GPA of 2.7; for doctorate, GRE General Test, minimum GPA of 3.5. Additional exam requirements/recommendations for international students: Required—TOEFL. *Faculty research:* Electrical systems, all facets of fossil energy, mechanics.

Southern Illinois University Edwardsville, Graduate School, School of Engineering, Edwardsville, IL 62026. Offers MS. *Program availability:* Part-time, evening/weekend. *Degree requirements:* For master's, thesis (for some programs), research paper, final exam. *Entrance requirements:* Additional exam requirements/recommendations for international students: Required—TOEFL (minimum score 550 paper-based; 79 iBT), IELTS (minimum score 6.5). Electronic applications accepted.

Southern Methodist University, Lyle School of Engineering, Dallas, TX 75275. Offers MA, MS, MSIEM, DE, PhD. *Program availability:* Part-time, evening/weekend, online learning. Terminal master's awarded for partial completion of doctoral program. *Degree requirements:* For master's, thesis optional; for doctorate, thesis/dissertation, oral and written qualifying exams. *Entrance requirements:* For master's, GRE General Test, minimum GPA of 3.0 in last 2 years; bachelor's degree in engineering, mathematics, or sciences; for doctorate, bachelor's degree in related field. Additional exam requirements/recommendations for international students: Required—TOEFL (minimum score 550 paper-based). *Expenses:* Contact institution. *Faculty research:* Mobile and fault-tolerant computing, manufacturing systems, telecommunications, solid state devices and materials, fluid and thermal sciences.

Southern University and Agricultural and Mechanical College, Graduate School, College of Sciences and Engineering, Baton Rouge, LA 70813. Offers MA, ME, MS. *Program availability:* Part-time. *Entrance requirements:* For master's, GRE General Test. Additional exam requirements/recommendations for international students: Required—TOEFL (minimum score 525 paper-based). *Faculty research:* Molecular mechanisms, enzymology, metalloenzymes, phytostrogens, porphyrins.

Stanford University, School of Engineering, Stanford, CA 94305-2004. Offers MS, MSE, PhD, Engr. *Expenses: Tuition:* Full-time $50,703; part-time $32,970 per year. *Required fees:* $651.
Website: http://soe.stanford.edu/

Stevens Institute of Technology, Graduate School, Charles V. Schaefer Jr. School of Engineering and Science, Hoboken, NJ 07030. Offers M Eng, MS, PhD, Certificate, Engr. *Program availability:* Part-time, evening/weekend, 100% online, blended/hybrid learning. *Faculty:* 179 full-time (40 women), 72 part-time/adjunct (8 women). *Students:* 1,258 full-time (286 women), 271 part-time (65 women); includes 133 minority (29 Black or African American, non-Hispanic/Latino; 3 American Indian or Alaska Native, non-Hispanic/Latino; 96 Asian, non-Hispanic/Latino; 5 Hispanic/Latino), 1,069 international. Average age 26. In 2018, 783 master's, 36 doctorates, 124 other advanced degrees awarded. Terminal master's awarded for partial completion of doctoral program. *Entrance requirements:* For master's, GRE/GMAT scores: GRE scores are required for all applicants applying to a full-time graduate program in the Schaefer School of Engineering and Science (SES). International applicants must submit TOEFL/IELTS scores and fulfill the English Language Proficiency Requirements in order to be considered. Additional exam requirements/recommendations for international students: Required—TOEFL (minimum score 74 iBT), IELTS (minimum score 6). *Application deadline:* For fall admission, 4/15 for domestic and international students; for spring admission, 11/1 for domestic and international students; for summer admission, 5/1 for domestic students. Applications are processed on a rolling basis. Application fee: $60. Electronic applications accepted. *Expenses: Tuition:* Full-time $35,960; part-time $1620 per credit. *Required fees:* $1290; $600 per semester. Tuition and fees vary according to course load. *Financial support:* Fellowships, research assistantships, teaching assistantships, career-related internships or fieldwork, Federal Work-Study, scholarships/grants, and unspecified assistantships available. Financial award application deadline: 2/15; financial award applicants required to submit FAFSA. *Unit head:* Dr. Jean Zu, Dean, 201-216-2833, E-mail: jean.zu@stevens.edu. *Application contact:* Graduate Admissions, 888-783-8367, Fax: 888-555-1306, E-mail: graduate@stevens.edu.
Website: http://www.stevens.edu/ses/

Stony Brook University, State University of New York, Graduate School, College of Engineering and Applied Sciences, Stony Brook, NY 11794. Offers MS, PhD, AGC, Advanced Certificate, Certificate, Graduate Certificate. *Program availability:* Part-time,

evening/weekend. *Faculty:* 171 full-time (28 women), 38 part-time/adjunct (11 women). *Students:* 1,225 full-time (313 women), 367 part-time (108 women); includes 173 minority (18 Black or African American, non-Hispanic/Latino; 104 Asian, non-Hispanic/Latino; 40 Hispanic/Latino; 11 Two or more races, non-Hispanic/Latino), 1,194 international. Average age 26. 3,381 applicants, 46% accepted, 485 enrolled. In 2018, 396 master's, 87 doctorates, 4 other advanced degrees awarded. *Degree requirements:* For doctorate, comprehensive exam, thesis/dissertation. *Entrance requirements:* For doctorate, GRE General Test. Additional exam requirements/recommendations for international students: Required—TOEFL (minimum score 90 iBT). *Application deadline:* For fall admission, 1/15 for domestic students; for spring admission, 10/1 for domestic students. Application fee: $100. *Expenses:* Contact institution. *Financial support:* In 2018–19, 9 fellowships, 255 research assistantships, 226 teaching assistantships were awarded; career-related internships or fieldwork also available. *Total annual research expenditures:* $32.6 million. *Unit head:* Dr. Fotis Sotiropoulos, Dean, 631-632-8380, Fax: 631-632-8205, E-mail: fotis.sotiropoulos@stonybrook.edu. *Application contact:* Melissa Jordan, Assistant Dean for Records and Admission, 631-632-9712, Fax: 631-632-7243, E-mail: gradadmissions@stonybrook.edu.
Website: http://www.ceas.sunysb.edu/

Syracuse University, College of Engineering and Computer Science, Syracuse, NY 13244. Offers MS, PhD, CAS. *Program availability:* Part-time, evening/weekend. *Faculty:* 88 full-time (24 women), 21 part-time/adjunct (2 women). *Students:* 927 full-time (242 women), 362 part-time (63 women); includes 126 minority (37 Black or African American, non-Hispanic/Latino; 62 Asian, non-Hispanic/Latino; 15 Hispanic/Latino; 12 Two or more races, non-Hispanic/Latino), 914 international. Average age 27. 2,999 applicants, 40% accepted, 450 enrolled. In 2018, 365 master's, 35 doctorates, 2 other advanced degrees awarded. *Degree requirements:* For master's, comprehensive exam (for some programs), thesis (for some programs); for doctorate, comprehensive exam, thesis/dissertation. *Entrance requirements:* For master's, doctorate, and CAS, GRE General Test, resume, official transcripts, personal statement, three letters of recommendation. Additional exam requirements/recommendations for international students: Required—TOEFL, IELTS. *Application deadline:* For fall admission, 7/1 priority date for domestic students, 6/1 priority date for international students; for spring admission, 11/15 priority date for domestic students, 10/15 priority date for international students. Applications are processed on a rolling basis. Application fee: $75. Electronic applications accepted. *Financial support:* Fellowships with full tuition reimbursements, research assistantships with tuition reimbursements, teaching assistantships with tuition reimbursements, scholarships/grants, and tuition waivers (partial) available. Financial award application deadline: 1/1; financial award applicants required to submit FAFSA. *Faculty research:* Environmental systems, information assurance, biomechanics, solid mechanics and materials, software engineering. *Unit head:* Dr. Teresa Dahlberg, Dean, College of Engineering and Computer Science, 315-443-2545, E-mail: dahlberg@syr.edu. *Application contact:* Kathleen Joyce, Assistant Dean, 314-443-2219, E-mail: topgrads@syr.edu.
Website: http://eng-cs.syr.edu/

Temple University, College of Engineering, PhD in Engineering Program, Philadelphia, PA 19122-6096. Offers bioengineering (PhD); civil engineering (PhD); electrical engineering (PhD); environmental engineering (PhD); mechanical engineering (PhD). *Program availability:* Part-time, evening/weekend. *Degree requirements:* For doctorate, thesis/dissertation, preliminary exam, dissertation proposal and defense. *Entrance requirements:* For doctorate, GRE, minimum undergraduate GPA of 3.0; MS in engineering from ABET-accredited or equivalent institution (preferred); resume; goals statement; three letters of reference; official transcripts. Additional exam requirements/recommendations for international students: Required—TOEFL (minimum score 550 paper-based; 79 iBT), IELTS (minimum score 6.5), PTE (minimum score 53). Electronic

applications accepted. *Expenses:* Contact institution. *Faculty research:* Advanced/computer-aided manufacturing and advanced materials processing; bioengineering; computer engineering; construction engineering and management; dynamics, controls, and systems; energy and environmental science; engineering physics and engineering mathematics; green engineering; signal processing and communication; transportation engineering; water resources, hydrology, and environmental engineering.
See Display below and Close-Up on page 73.

Tennessee State University, The School of Graduate Studies and Research, College of Engineering, Nashville, TN 37209-1561. Offers biomedical engineering (ME); civil engineering (ME); computer and information systems engineering (MS, PhD); electrical engineering (ME); environmental engineering (ME); manufacturing engineering (ME); mathematical sciences (MS); mechanical engineering (ME). *Program availability:* Part-time, evening/weekend. *Degree requirements:* For master's, project; for doctorate, comprehensive exam, thesis/dissertation. *Entrance requirements:* For doctorate, minimum GPA of 3.3. *Faculty research:* Robotics, intelligent systems, human-computer interaction software systems, biomedical engineering, signal/image processing, probabilistic design, intelligent manufacturing, cooperative mobile robots, condition based maintenance, sensor fusion.

Tennessee Technological University, College of Graduate Studies, College of Engineering, Cookeville, TN 38505. Offers MS, PhD. *Program availability:* Part-time. *Faculty:* 76 full-time (2 women). *Students:* 68 full-time (11 women), 156 part-time (24 women); includes 9 minority (3 Black or African American, non-Hispanic/Latino; 3 Asian, non-Hispanic/Latino; 2 Hispanic/Latino; 1 Two or more races, non-Hispanic/Latino), 99 international. 273 applicants, 58% accepted, 52 enrolled. In 2018, 50 master's, 8 doctorates awarded. *Degree requirements:* For master's, comprehensive exam, thesis; for doctorate, comprehensive exam, thesis/dissertation. *Entrance requirements:* For master's, GRE General Test; for doctorate, GRE, minimum GPA of 3.5. Additional exam requirements/recommendations for international students: Required—TOEFL (minimum score 550 paper-based; 79 iBT), IELTS (minimum score 5.5), PTE (minimum score 53), or TOEIC (Test of English as an International Communication). *Application deadline:* For fall admission, 8/1 for domestic students, 5/1 for international students; for spring admission, 12/1 for domestic students, 10/1 for international students. Applications are processed on a rolling basis. Application fee: $35 ($40 for international students). Electronic applications accepted. *Financial support:* Fellowships, research assistantships, teaching assistantships, and career-related internships or fieldwork available. Support available to part-time students. Financial award application deadline: 4/1. *Unit head:* Dr. Darrell Hoy, Interim Dean, 931-372-3172, Fax: 931-372-6172, E-mail: dhoy@tntech.edu. *Application contact:* Shelia K. Kendrick, Coordinator of Graduate Studies, 931-372-3808, Fax: 931-372-3497, E-mail: skendrick@tntech.edu.

Texas A&M University–Kingsville, College of Graduate Studies, Frank H. Dotterweich College of Engineering, Kingsville, TX 78363. Offers ME, MS, PhD. *Degree requirements:* For master's, variable foreign language requirement, comprehensive exam, thesis (for some programs); for doctorate, variable foreign language requirement, comprehensive exam, thesis/dissertation (for some programs). *Entrance requirements:* For master's and doctorate, GRE, MAT, GMAT. Additional exam requirements/recommendations for international students: Required—TOEFL (minimum score 550 paper-based; 79 iBT). Electronic applications accepted.

Texas State University, The Graduate College, College of Science and Engineering, Program in Engineering, San Marcos, TX 78666. Offers civil engineering (MS); electrical engineering (MS); industrial engineering (MS); mechanical and manufacturing engineering (MS). *Program availability:* Part-time. *Faculty:* 15 full-time (2 women). *Students:* 46 full-time (14 women), 41 part-time (13 women); includes 11 minority (3

1969

Bioengineering
Civil Engineering
Computer & Systems Security
Electrical Engineering

Engineering Management
Environmental Engineering
Mechanical Engineering

DON'T JUST IMAGINE A BETTER WAY

build it

engineering.temple.edu/petersons
Temple University
College of Engineering

Asian, non-Hispanic/Latino; 7 Hispanic/Latino; 1 Two or more races, non-Hispanic/Latino), 67 international. Average age 27. 105 applicants, 64% accepted, 31 enrolled. In 2018, 13 master's awarded. *Degree requirements:* For master's, comprehensive exam, thesis (for some programs), thesis or research project. *Entrance requirements:* For master's, official GRE (general test only) required with competitive scores in the verbal reasoning and quantitative reasoning sections, baccalaureate degree from regionally-accredited university in engineering, computer science, physics, technology, or closely-related field with minimum GPA of 3.0 on last 60 undergraduate semester hours; resume or curriculum vitae; 2 letters of recommendation; statement of purpose conveying research interest and professional aspirations. Additional exam requirements/recommendations for international students: Required—TOEFL (minimum score 550 paper-based; 78 iBT), IELTS (minimum score 6.5). *Application deadline:* For fall admission, 2/15 priority date for domestic students, 2/1 priority date for international students. Application fee: $55 ($90 for international students). Electronic applications accepted. *Expenses:* Tuition, state resident: full-time $8102; part-time $4051 per semester. Tuition, nonresident: full-time $18,229; part-time $9115 per semester. *International tuition:* $18,229 full-time. *Required fees:* $2116; $120 per credit hour. Tuition and fees vary according to course load. *Financial support:* In 2018–19, 52 students received support, including 14 research assistantships (averaging $12,742 per year), 34 teaching assistantships (averaging $12,483 per year); Federal Work-Study, institutionally sponsored loans, scholarships/grants, health care benefits, and unspecified assistantships also available. Support available to part-time students. Financial award application deadline: 1/15; financial award applicants required to submit FAFSA. *Faculty research:* Computer Architecture & Digital Image Processing; Industrial robotics on a mobile platform; supply chain management optimization modeling and algorithms; Modeling and analysis of manufacturing systems especially semiconductor manufacturing; smart grids for big data analytics and demand response; Digital Signal/Image/Speach Processing & Data Compression; Health care systems engineering and anaylsis of patient flow. *Total annual research expenditures:* $920,229. *Unit head:* Dr. Vishu Viswanathan, Graduate Advisor, 512-245-1826, Fax: 512-245-8365, E-mail: v_v42@txstate.edu. *Application contact:* Dr. Andrea Golato, Dean of Graduate School, 512-245-2581, Fax: 512-245-8365, E-mail: gradcollege@txstate.edu.
Website: http://www.engineering.txstate.edu/Programs/Graduate.html

Texas Tech University, Graduate School, Edward E. Whitacre Jr. College of Engineering, Lubbock, TX 79409-3103. Offers engineering (M Engr); JD/M Engr. *Program availability:* Part-time, evening/weekend, 100% online, blended/hybrid learning. *Faculty:* 182 full-time (31 women), 19 part-time/adjunct (3 women). *Students:* 545 full-time (149 women), 226 part-time (38 women); includes 110 minority (22 Black or African American, non-Hispanic/Latino; 1 American Indian or Alaska Native, non-Hispanic/Latino; 29 Asian, non-Hispanic/Latino; 48 Hispanic/Latino; 10 Two or more races, non-Hispanic/Latino), 446 international. Average age 30. 914 applicants, 45% accepted, 185 enrolled. In 2018, 235 master's, 62 doctorates awarded. *Degree requirements:* For master's, comprehensive exam, thesis (for some programs); for doctorate, comprehensive exam, thesis/dissertation. *Entrance requirements:* For master's, GRE (Verbal and Quantitative), minimum GPA of 3.0. Additional exam requirements/recommendations for international students: Required—TOEFL (minimum score 550 paper-based; 79 iBT), IELTS (minimum score 6.5). *Application deadline:* For fall admission, 6/1 priority date for domestic students, 1/15 priority date for international students; for spring admission, 9/1 priority date for domestic students, 6/15 priority date for international students. Applications are processed on a rolling basis. Application fee: $65. Electronic applications accepted. *Expenses:* Contact institution. *Financial support:* In 2018–19, 622 students received support, including 585 fellowships (averaging $4,151 per year), 265 research assistantships (averaging $23,462 per year), 140 teaching assistantships (averaging $20,404 per year); scholarships/grants, health care benefits, and unspecified assistantships also available. Financial award application deadline: 4/15; financial award applicants required to submit FAFSA. *Faculty research:* Bioengineering, interdisciplinary studies, health care engineering, intellectual property, law and engineering. *Total annual research expenditures:* $19.6 million. *Unit head:* Dr. Albert Sacco, Jr., Dean, Edward E. Whitacre Jr. College of Engineering, 806-742-3451, Fax: 806-742-3493, E-mail: al.sacco-jr@ttu.edu. *Application contact:* Dr. Brandon Weeks, Associate Dean of Research and Graduate Programs, Edward E. Whitacre Jr. College of Engineering, 806-834-7450, Fax: 806-742-3493, E-mail: brandon.weeks@ttu.edu.
Website: www.depts.ttu.edu/coe/

Tufts University, School of Engineering, Medford, MA 02155. Offers MS, MSEM, PhD, PhD/PhD. *Program availability:* Part-time. Terminal master's awarded for partial completion of doctoral program. *Degree requirements:* For master's, thesis (for some programs); for doctorate, thesis/dissertation. *Entrance requirements:* For master's and doctorate, GRE General Test. Additional exam requirements/recommendations for international students: Required—TOEFL (minimum score 550 paper-based; 90 iBT), IELTS (minimum score 6.5). Electronic applications accepted. *Expenses: Tuition:* Full-time $51,288; part-time $1710 per credit hour. *Required fees:* $904. Full-time tuition and fees vary according to degree level, program and student level. Part-time tuition and fees vary according to course load.

Tuskegee University, Graduate Programs, College of Engineering, Tuskegee, AL 36088. Offers MSEE, MSME, PhD. *Degree requirements:* For master's, thesis or alternative. *Entrance requirements:* For master's, GRE General Test, GRE Subject Test. Additional exam requirements/recommendations for international students: Required—TOEFL (minimum score 500 paper-based).

Universidad de las Américas Puebla, Division of Graduate Studies, School of Engineering, Puebla, Mexico. Offers M Adm, MS, PhD. *Program availability:* Part-time, evening/weekend. *Degree requirements:* For master's, one foreign language, thesis. *Faculty research:* Artificial intelligence, food technology, construction, telecommunications, computers in education, operations research.

Universidad del Turabo, Graduate Programs, School of Engineering, Gurabo, PR 00778-3030. Offers computer engineering (M Eng); electrical engineering (M Eng); mechanical engineering (M Eng); telecommunications and network systems administration (M Eng). *Entrance requirements:* For master's, GRE, EXADEP or GMAT, interview, essay, official transcript, recommendation letters. Electronic applications accepted.

Université de Moncton, Faculty of Engineering, Moncton, NB E1A 3E9, Canada. Offers civil engineering (M Sc A); electrical engineering (M Sc A); industrial engineering (M Sc A); mechanical engineering (M Sc A). *Degree requirements:* For master's, thesis, proficiency in French. *Faculty research:* Structures, energy, composite materials, quality control, geo-environment, telecommunications, instrumentation, analog and digital electronics.

Université de Sherbrooke, Faculty of Engineering, Sherbrooke, QC J1K 2R1, Canada. Offers M Eng, M Env, M Sc A, PhD, Diploma. *Program availability:* Part-time. *Degree requirements:* For master's, one foreign language, thesis; for doctorate, comprehensive exam, thesis/dissertation. *Entrance requirements:* For master's, bachelor's degree in engineering or equivalent. Electronic applications accepted.

Université du Québec à Chicoutimi, Graduate Programs, Program in Engineering, Chicoutimi, QC G7H 2B1, Canada. Offers M Sc A, PhD. *Program availability:* Part-time. *Degree requirements:* For master's, thesis; for doctorate, thesis/dissertation. *Entrance requirements:* For master's, appropriate bachelor's degree, proficiency in French.

Université du Québec à Rimouski, Graduate Programs, Program in Engineering, Rimouski, QC G5L 3A1, Canada. Offers M Sc A. Program offered jointly with Université du Québec à Chicoutimi.

Université du Québec, École de technologie supérieure, Graduate Programs, Montréal, QC H3C 1K3, Canada. Offers M Eng, PhD, Diploma. *Program availability:* Online learning. *Entrance requirements:* For master's and Diploma, appropriate bachelor's degree, proficiency in French; for doctorate, appropriate master's degree, proficiency in French.

Université du Québec en Abitibi-Témiscamingue, Graduate Programs, Program in Engineering, Rouyn-Noranda, QC J9X 5E4, Canada. Offers engineering (ME); mineral engineering (ME); mining engineering (DESS).

Université Laval, Faculty of Sciences and Engineering, Québec, QC G1K 7P4, Canada. Offers M Sc, PhD, Diploma. *Program availability:* Part-time. *Degree requirements:* For doctorate, thesis/dissertation. Electronic applications accepted.

University at Albany, State University of New York, College of Engineering and Applied Sciences, Albany, NY 12222-0001. Offers MS, PhD, CAS. *Accreditation:* ALA (one or more programs are accredited). *Program availability:* Part-time. *Faculty:* 29 full-time (8 women), 19 part-time/adjunct (3 women). *Students:* 188 full-time (48 women), 69 part-time (22 women); includes 14 minority (1 Black or African American, non-Hispanic/Latino; 9 Asian, non-Hispanic/Latino; 3 Hispanic/Latino; 1 Two or more races, non-Hispanic/Latino), 228 international. Average age 27. 552 applicants, 51% accepted, 193 enrolled. In 2018, 84 master's, 3 doctorates awarded. *Degree requirements:* For doctorate, thesis/dissertation. *Entrance requirements:* For doctorate, GRE General Test. Additional exam requirements/recommendations for international students: Required—TOEFL (minimum score 550 paper-based). *Application deadline:* For fall admission, 3/1 for domestic students. Applications are processed on a rolling basis. Application fee: $75. Electronic applications accepted. *Financial support:* Fellowships and Federal Work-Study available. Financial award application deadline: 4/1. *Faculty research:* Human-computer interaction, government information management, library information science, Web development, social implications of technology. *Unit head:* Kim L. Boyer, Dean, 518-956-8240, Fax: 518-442-5367, E-mail: ceasinfo@albany.edu. *Application contact:* Kim L. Boyer, Dean, 518-956-8240, Fax: 518-442-5367, E-mail: ceasinfo@albany.edu.
Website: http://www.albany.edu/ceas/

University at Buffalo, the State University of New York, Graduate School, School of Engineering and Applied Sciences, Buffalo, NY 14260. Offers ME, MS, PhD, Certificate. *Program availability:* Part-time, evening/weekend, 100% online, blended/hybrid learning. *Faculty:* 236 full-time (35 women), 28 part-time/adjunct (3 women). *Students:* 2,062 full-time (512 women); includes 127 minority (22 Black or African American, non-Hispanic/Latino; 66 Asian, non-Hispanic/Latino; 23 Hispanic/Latino; 16 Two or more races, non-Hispanic/Latino), 1,663 international. Average age 25. 7,143 applicants, 38% accepted, 683 enrolled. In 2018, 613 master's, 76 doctorates awarded. Terminal master's awarded for partial completion of doctoral program. *Degree requirements:* For master's, minimum of 30 credits; for doctorate, minimum of 72 credits; for Certificate, minimum of 12 credits. *Entrance requirements:* For master's and doctorate, GRE General Test, transcripts, curriculum vitae/resume, statement of purpose, letters of recommendation. Additional exam requirements/recommendations for international students: Required—TOEFL (minimum score 79 iBT), IELTS. *Application deadline:* For fall admission, 12/15 priority date for domestic and international students; for spring admission, 10/15 priority date for domestic and international students. Applications are processed on a rolling basis. Application fee: $85. Electronic applications accepted. *Financial support:* In 2018–19, 520 students received support, including 38 fellowships with full and partial tuition reimbursements available (averaging $26,734 per year), 215 research assistantships with full and partial tuition reimbursements available (averaging $21,800 per year), 185 teaching assistantships with full and partial tuition reimbursements available (averaging $21,875 per year); scholarships/grants and unspecified assistantships also available. Support available to part-time students. *Total annual research expenditures:* $74 million. *Application contact:* Jennifer Gammell, Associate Director of Graduate Enrollment Management, 716-645-9099, E-mail: gradeng@buffalo.edu.
Website: http://engineering.buffalo.edu

The University of Akron, Graduate School, College of Engineering, Akron, OH 44325. Offers MS, PhD. *Program availability:* Part-time, evening/weekend. Terminal master's awarded for partial completion of doctoral program. *Degree requirements:* For master's, thesis optional; for doctorate, one foreign language, thesis/dissertation, candidacy exam, qualifying exam. *Entrance requirements:* For master's, GRE, minimum GPA of 2.75, letters of recommendation, statement of purpose, resume; for doctorate, GRE, minimum GPA of 3.0 with bachelor's degree, 3.5 with master's degree; letters of recommendation; personal statement; resume. Additional exam requirements/recommendations for international students: Required—TOEFL (minimum score 550 paper-based; 79 iBT), IELTS (minimum score 6.5). Electronic applications accepted. *Faculty research:* Engineering materials, energy research, nano and microelectromechanical systems (NEMS and MEMS), bio-engineering, computational methods.

The University of Alabama, Graduate School, College of Engineering, Tuscaloosa, AL 35487. Offers MS, MS Ch E, MS Met E, MSAEM, MSCE, PhD. *Program availability:* Part-time, online learning. Terminal master's awarded for partial completion of doctoral program. *Degree requirements:* For master's, comprehensive exam; for doctorate, thesis/dissertation. *Entrance requirements:* For master's and doctorate, minimum GPA of 3.0. Additional exam requirements/recommendations for international students: Required—TOEFL (minimum score 550 paper-based). Electronic applications accepted. *Faculty research:* Materials and biomaterials networks and sensors, transportation, energy.

The University of Alabama at Birmingham, School of Engineering, Program in Interdisciplinary Engineering, Birmingham, AL 35294. Offers computational engineering (PhD). *Program availability:* Part-time. *Faculty:* 1 full-time (0 women), 1 (woman) part-time/adjunct. *Students:* 11 full-time (0 women), 18 part-time (3 women); includes 7 minority (5 Black or African American, non-Hispanic/Latino; 1 Asian, non-Hispanic/Latino; 1 Two or more races, non-Hispanic/Latino), 7 international. Average age 40. 4 applicants, 50% accepted. In 2018, 1 doctorate awarded. *Degree requirements:* For doctorate, comprehensive exam, thesis/dissertation, publication of three first-author original research articles in peer-reviewed journal. *Entrance requirements:* For doctorate, The GRE general test is required for all applicants. Applicants must score a 156 or higher on the quantitative section of the GRE to be considered for admission., Undergraduate or graduate degree in Engineering. Minimum 3.0 on a 4.0 scale on most recent degree. Personal statement identifying research interest. CV/résumé. 3 recommendations from academic or professional contact. Additional exam requirements/recommendations for international students: Required—TOEFL (minimum score 80 iBT); Recommended—IELTS (minimum score 6.5). *Application deadline:* For

fall admission, 8/1 for domestic and international students; for spring admission, 12/1 for domestic and international students; for summer admission, 5/1 for domestic and international students. Applications are processed on a rolling basis. Application fee: $50 ($60 for international students). Electronic applications accepted. *Expenses:* Contact institution. *Faculty research:* Aerospace systems, environmental engineering, mathematical foundations of quantum electronics, digital circuits and systems design, CO2 enhanced oil production. *Unit head:* Dr. Gregg Janowski, Program Director, 205-934-8524, E-mail: janowski@uab.edu. *Application contact:* Jesse Keppley, Director of Student and Academic Services, 205-996-5696, E-mail: gradschool@uab.edu.
Website: http://www.uab.edu/engineering/home/degrees-cert/phd?id-189:phd-in-interdisciplinary-engineering&catid-3

The University of Alabama in Huntsville, School of Graduate Studies, College of Engineering, Huntsville, AL 35899. Offers MS, MSE, MSOR, MSSE, PhD. *Program availability:* Part-time. *Faculty:* 59 full-time (9 women), 6 part-time/adjunct (0 women). *Students:* 192 full-time (44 women), 302 part-time (46 women); includes 58 minority (21 Black or African American, non-Hispanic/Latino; 7 American Indian or Alaska Native, non-Hispanic/Latino; 20 Asian, non-Hispanic/Latino; 7 Hispanic/Latino; 3 Two or more races, non-Hispanic/Latino), 127 international. Average age 31. 511 applicants, 63% accepted, 113 enrolled. In 2018, 114 master's, 22 doctorates awarded. *Degree requirements:* For master's, comprehensive exam, thesis or alternative, oral and written exams; for doctorate, comprehensive exam, thesis/dissertation, oral and written exams. *Entrance requirements:* For master's and doctorate, GRE General Test, minimum GPA of 3.0. Additional exam requirements/recommendations for international students: Required—TOEFL (minimum score 500 paper-based; 80 iBT), IELTS (minimum score 6.5). *Application deadline:* For fall admission, 7/15 priority date for domestic students, 4/1 priority date for international students; for spring admission, 11/30 priority date for domestic students, 9/1 priority date for international students. Applications are processed on a rolling basis. Application fee: $50. Electronic applications accepted. *Expenses: Tuition, area resident:* Full-time $10,632; part-time $412 per credit hour. Tuition, state resident: full-time $10,632. Tuition, nonresident: full-time $23,604; part-time $412 per credit hour. *Required fees:* $582; $582. Tuition and fees vary according to course load and program. *Financial support:* In 2018–19, 149 students received support, including 83 research assistantships with full tuition reimbursements available (averaging $6,729 per year), 66 teaching assistantships with full tuition reimbursements available (averaging $5,765 per year); career-related internships or fieldwork, Federal Work-Study, institutionally sponsored loans, scholarships/grants, health care benefits, tuition waivers (full and partial), and unspecified assistantships also available. Support available to part-time students. Financial award application deadline: 4/1; financial award applicants required to submit FAFSA. *Faculty research:* Transport technology, biotechnology, advanced computer architecture and systems, systems and engineering process, rocket propulsion and plasma engineering. *Unit head:* Dr. Shankar Mahalingam, Dean, 256-824-6474, Fax: 256-824-6843, E-mail: coedean@uah.edu. *Application contact:* Kim Gray, Graduate Studies Admissions Coordinator, 256-824-6002, Fax: 256-824-6405, E-mail: deangrad@uah.edu.
Website: http://www.uah.edu/eng

University of Alaska Fairbanks, College of Engineering and Mines, PhD Programs in Engineering, Fairbanks, AK 99775-7520. Offers PhD. *Program availability:* Part-time. *Faculty:* 43 full-time (7 women), 3 part-time/adjunct (0 women). *Students:* 6 full-time (1 woman), 7 part-time (2 women); includes 2 minority (1 Black or African American, non-Hispanic/Latino; 1 Two or more races, non-Hispanic/Latino), 5 international. Average age 35. 12 applicants, 8% accepted, 1 enrolled. In 2018, 3 doctorates awarded. *Degree requirements:* For doctorate, comprehensive exam, thesis/dissertation, oral defense of dissertation. *Entrance requirements:* For doctorate, GRE General Test, minimum cumulative GPA of 3.0. Additional exam requirements/recommendations for international students: Required—TOEFL (minimum score 550 paper-based; 79 iBT), IELTS (minimum score 6.5). *Application deadline:* For fall admission, 6/1 for domestic students, 3/1 for international students; for spring admission, 10/15 for domestic students, 9/1 for international students. Applications are processed on a rolling basis. Application fee: $60. Electronic applications accepted. *Expenses:* College of Engineering and Mines (CEM) tuition has a 20% surcharge per credit hour over that for credits of most other UAF colleges. Assuming 60 credits for PhD and 32 for Master's, this augments costs by $6,180 for in-state PhD, $3,296 for in-state Master's, $12,948 for non-resident PhD and $6,912 for non-resident Master's students, respectively. *Financial support:* In 2018–19, 3 research assistantships (averaging $6,562 per year), 5 teaching assistantships (averaging $7,208 per year) were awarded; career-related internships or fieldwork, Federal Work-Study, scholarships/grants, health care benefits, and unspecified assistantships also available. Support available to part-time students. Financial award application deadline: 7/1; financial award applicants required to submit FAFSA. *Faculty research:* Transportation, energy, housing, and climate change. *Unit head:* Dr. Bill Schnabel, Dean, 907-474-7730, E-mail: fycem@uaf.edu. *Application contact:* Samara Taber, Director of Admissions, 907-474-7500, E-mail: uaf-admissions@alaska.edu.
Website: http://cem.uaf.edu/

The University of Arizona, College of Engineering, Tucson, AZ 85721. Offers ME, MS, PhD, Certificate. *Program availability:* Part-time, online learning. *Degree requirements:* For doctorate, thesis/dissertation. *Entrance requirements:* Additional exam requirements/recommendations for international students: Required—TOEFL (minimum score 550 paper-based; 79 iBT). Electronic applications accepted.

University of Arkansas, Graduate School, College of Engineering, Fayetteville, AR 72701. Offers MS, MS Cmp E, MS Ch E, MS En E, MS Tc E, MSBE, MSBME, MSCE, MSE, MSEE, MSIE, MSME, MSTE, PhD. In 2018, 273 master's, 27 doctorates awarded. *Degree requirements:* For doctorate, one foreign language, thesis/dissertation. *Application deadline:* For fall admission, 8/1 for domestic students, 4/1 for international students; for spring admission, 12/1 for domestic students, 10/1 for international students; for summer admission, 4/15 for domestic students, 3/1 for international students. Applications are processed on a rolling basis. Application fee: $60. Electronic applications accepted. *Financial support:* In 2018–19, 198 research assistantships, 21 teaching assistantships were awarded; fellowships with tuition reimbursements, career-related internships or fieldwork, and Federal Work-Study also available. Support available to part-time students. Financial award application deadline: 4/1; financial award applicants required to submit FAFSA. *Unit head:* Dr. John R. English, Dean, 479-575-7455, E-mail: jre@uark.edu. *Application contact:* Dr. Norman Dennis, Senior Associate Dean and University Professor, 479-575-6011, E-mail: ndennis@uark.edu.
Website: https://engineering.uark.edu

University of Bridgeport, School of Engineering, Bridgeport, CT 06604. Offers MS, PhD. *Program availability:* Part-time, evening/weekend, online learning. *Degree requirements:* For master's, thesis optional; for doctorate, thesis/dissertation. *Entrance requirements:* Additional exam requirements/recommendations for international students: Recommended—TOEFL (minimum score 550 paper-based; 80 iBT), IELTS (minimum score 6.5). Electronic applications accepted. *Expenses:* Contact institution.

The University of British Columbia, Faculty of Applied Science, Vancouver, BC V6T 1Z4, Canada. Offers M Arch, M Eng, M Sc, M Sc P, MA Sc, MAP, MASA, MASLA, MCRP, MEL, MLA, MN, MSN, MUD, PhD, M Arch/MLA. *Program availability:* Part-time. *Degree requirements:* For master's, comprehensive exam (for some programs), thesis (for some programs); for doctorate, comprehensive exam, thesis/dissertation. *Entrance requirements:* Additional exam requirements/recommendations for international students: Required—TOEFL (minimum score 550 paper-based; 90 iBT), IELTS. Electronic applications accepted. *Expenses:* Contact institution. *Faculty research:* Architecture, nursing, engineering, landscape architecture, health leadership and policy.

University of Calgary, Faculty of Graduate Studies, Schulich School of Engineering, Calgary, AB T2N 1N4, Canada. Offers M Eng, M Sc, MPM, PhD. *Program availability:* Part-time, evening/weekend. *Degree requirements:* For doctorate, comprehensive exam, thesis/dissertation. *Entrance requirements:* Additional exam requirements/recommendations for international students: Required—TOEFL, IELTS. Electronic applications accepted. *Faculty research:* Chemical and petroleum engineering, civil engineering, electrical and computer engineering, geomatics engineering, mechanical engineering and computer-integrated manufacturing.

University of California, Berkeley, Graduate Division, College of Engineering, Berkeley, CA 94720. Offers M Eng, MS, MTM, PhD, M Arch/MS, MCP/MS, MPP/MS. *Program availability:* Part-time, 100% online, blended/hybrid learning. Terminal master's awarded for partial completion of doctoral program. *Degree requirements:* For master's, comprehensive exam (for some programs), thesis (for some programs); for doctorate, thesis/dissertation, qualifying exam. *Entrance requirements:* For master's and doctorate, GRE General Test, minimum GPA of 3.0, 3 letters of recommendation. Additional exam requirements/recommendations for international students: Required—TOEFL (minimum score 570 paper-based; 90 iBT). Electronic applications accepted.

University of California, Berkeley, UC Berkeley Extension, Certificate Programs in Engineering, Construction and Facilities Management, Berkeley, CA 94720. Offers construction management (Certificate); HVAC (Certificate); integrated circuit design and techniques (online) (Certificate). *Program availability:* Online learning.

University of California, Davis, College of Engineering, Davis, CA 95616. Offers M Engr, MS, D Engr, PhD, Certificate, M Engr/MBA. *Program availability:* Part-time. Terminal master's awarded for partial completion of doctoral program. *Degree requirements:* For master's, comprehensive exam (for some programs), thesis (for some programs); for doctorate, comprehensive exam, thesis/dissertation. *Entrance requirements:* For doctorate, GRE. Additional exam requirements/recommendations for international students: Required—TOEFL (minimum score 550 paper-based). Electronic applications accepted.

University of California, Irvine, Samueli School of Engineering, Irvine, CA 92697. Offers MS, PhD. *Program availability:* Part-time. *Students:* 863 full-time (287 women), 63 part-time (14 women); includes 164 minority (12 Black or African American, non-Hispanic/Latino; 106 Asian, non-Hispanic/Latino; 31 Hispanic/Latino; 15 Two or more races, non-Hispanic/Latino), 566 international. Average age 26. 3,561 applicants, 28% accepted, 288 enrolled. In 2018, 262 master's, 97 doctorates awarded. Terminal master's awarded for partial completion of doctoral program. *Entrance requirements:* For master's and doctorate, GRE General Test, minimum GPA of 3.0, 3 letters of recommendation. Additional exam requirements/recommendations for international students: Required—TOEFL (minimum score 550 paper-based). *Application deadline:* For fall admission, 1/15 priority date for domestic students, 1/15 for international students. Applications are processed on a rolling basis. Application fee: $105 ($125 for international students). Electronic applications accepted. *Financial support:* Fellowships with tuition reimbursements, research assistantships with full tuition reimbursements, teaching assistantships with tuition reimbursements, institutionally sponsored loans, traineeships, health care benefits, and unspecified assistantships available. Financial award application deadline: 3/1; financial award applicants required to submit FAFSA. *Faculty research:* Biomedical, chemical and biochemical, civil and environmental, electrical and computer, mechanical and aerospace engineering. *Unit head:* Gregory N. Washington, Dean, 949-824-4333, Fax: 949-824-8200, E-mail: engineering@uci.edu. *Application contact:* Jean Bennett, Director of Graduate Student Affairs, 949-824-6475, Fax: 949-824-8200, E-mail: jean.bennett@uci.edu.
Website: http://www.eng.uci.edu/

University of California, Los Angeles, Graduate Division, Henry Samueli School of Engineering and Applied Science, Los Angeles, CA 90095-1601. Offers MS, PhD, MBA/MS. *Program availability:* Evening/weekend, blended/hybrid learning. *Degree requirements:* For master's, comprehensive exam or thesis; for doctorate, thesis/dissertation, qualifying exams. *Entrance requirements:* For master's, GRE General Test, minimum GPA of 3.0 depending on department/major; for doctorate, GRE General Test, minimum GPA of 3.25 (depending on department/major). Additional exam requirements/recommendations for international students: Required—TOEFL (minimum score 560 paper-based; 87 iBT), IELTS (minimum score 7). Electronic applications accepted.

University of California, Merced, Graduate Division, School of Engineering, Merced, CA 95343. Offers biological engineering and small scale technologies (MS, PhD); electrical engineering and computer science (MS, PhD); environmental systems (MS, PhD); management of innovation, sustainability, and technology (MM); mechanical engineering (MS); mechanical engineering and applied mechanics (PhD). *Faculty:* 60 full-time (16 women). *Students:* 219 full-time (72 women), 1 part-time (0 women); includes 43 minority (2 Black or African American, non-Hispanic/Latino; 17 Asian, non-Hispanic/Latino; 20 Hispanic/Latino; 1 Native Hawaiian or other Pacific Islander, non-Hispanic/Latino; 3 Two or more races, non-Hispanic/Latino), 145 international. Average age 28. 371 applicants, 46% accepted, 75 enrolled. In 2018, 30 master's, 17 doctorates awarded. Terminal master's awarded for partial completion of doctoral program. *Degree requirements:* For master's, variable foreign language requirement, comprehensive exam, thesis or alternative, oral defense; for doctorate, variable foreign language requirement, comprehensive exam, thesis/dissertation, oral defense. *Entrance requirements:* For master's and doctorate, GRE. Additional exam requirements/recommendations for international students: Required—TOEFL (minimum score 550 paper-based; 80 iBT); Recommended—IELTS (minimum score 6.5). *Application deadline:* For fall admission, 1/15 priority date for domestic and international students. Application fee: $105 ($125 for international students). Electronic applications accepted. *Expenses:* In-state tuition $11442 per year; Out-of-state tuition $26544 per year; Student Fees $1765 per year. *Financial support:* In 2018–19, 200 students received support, including 14 fellowships with full tuition reimbursements available (averaging $20,851 per year), 70 research assistantships with full tuition reimbursements available (averaging $18,334 per year), 116 teaching assistantships with full tuition reimbursements available (averaging $19,841 per year); scholarships/grants, traineeships, and health care benefits also available. *Faculty research:* Sustainability systems engineering and resource management: food, energy, water; biomolecular engineering and biotechnology; computational science and data analytics; artificial intelligence, machine learning, internet of things, human computer interface; cyber-physical systems and automation. *Total annual research expenditures:* $3.1 million. *Unit head:* Dr. Mark Matsumoto, Dean, 209-228-4047, Fax: 209-228-4047, E-mail: mmatsumoto@ucmerced.edu. *Application contact:* Tsu Ya, Director of Admissions and Academic Services, 209-228-4521, Fax: 209-228-6906, E-mail: tya@ucmerced.edu.

University of California, Santa Barbara, Graduate Division, College of Engineering, Santa Barbara, CA 93106-5130. Offers MS, MTM, PhD, MS/PhD. Terminal master's awarded for partial completion of doctoral program. *Degree requirements:* For doctorate, thesis/dissertation. *Entrance requirements:* For master's, GRE, 3 letters of recommendation, resume/curriculum vitae; for doctorate, GRE, 3 letters of recommendation, statement of purpose, personal achievements/contributions statement, resume/curriculum vitae, transcripts for post-secondary institutions attended. Additional exam requirements/recommendations for international students: Required—TOEFL, IELTS. Electronic applications accepted.

University of California, Santa Cruz, Jack Baskin School of Engineering, Santa Cruz, CA 95064. Offers MS, PhD. *Program availability:* Part-time. *Entrance requirements:* For master's and doctorate, GRE General Test. Additional exam requirements/recommendations for international students: Required—TOEFL (minimum score 570 paper-based; 89 iBT); Recommended—IELTS (minimum score 8). Electronic applications accepted.

University of Central Florida, College of Engineering and Computer Science, Orlando, FL 32816. Offers MS, MS Cp E, MS Env E, MSAE, MSCE, MSEE, MSEM, MSIE, MSME, MSMSE, PhD, Certificate. *Program availability:* Part-time, evening/weekend. *Faculty:* 205 full-time (31 women), 55 part-time/adjunct (4 women). *Students:* 953 full-time (215 women), 738 part-time (196 women); includes 456 minority (88 Black or African American, non-Hispanic/Latino; 2 American Indian or Alaska Native, non-Hispanic/Latino; 106 Asian, non-Hispanic/Latino; 241 Hispanic/Latino; 19 Two or more races, non-Hispanic/Latino), 648 international. Average age 30. 1,762 applicants, 61% accepted, 517 enrolled. In 2018, 401 master's, 100 doctorates, 23 other advanced degrees awarded. *Degree requirements:* For master's, thesis or alternative; for doctorate, thesis/dissertation, candidacy exam, departmental qualifying exam. *Entrance requirements:* For master's, resume, letters of recommendation; for doctorate, GRE, resume, letters of recommendation. Additional exam requirements/recommendations for international students: Required—TOEFL. *Application deadline:* For fall admission, 7/15 for domestic students; for spring admission, 12/1 for domestic students. Application fee: $30. Electronic applications accepted. *Financial support:* In 2018–19, 599 students received support, including 182 fellowships with partial tuition reimbursements available (averaging $10,579 per year), 454 research assistantships with partial tuition reimbursements available (averaging $12,376 per year), 216 teaching assistantships with partial tuition reimbursements available (averaging $11,537 per year); career-related internships or fieldwork, Federal Work-Study, institutionally sponsored loans, tuition waivers (partial), and unspecified assistantships also available. Financial award application deadline: 3/1; financial award applicants required to submit FAFSA. *Faculty research:* Electro-optics, lasers, materials, simulation, microelectronics. *Unit head:* Dr. Michael Georgiopoulos, Dean, 407-823-2156, E-mail: michaelg@ucf.edu. *Application contact:* Associate Director, Graduate Admissions, 407-823-2766, Fax: 407-823-6442, E-mail: gradadmissions@ucf.edu.
Website: http://www.cecs.ucf.edu/

University of Central Oklahoma, The Jackson College of Graduate Studies, College of Mathematics and Science, Department of Engineering and Physics, Edmond, OK 73034-5209. Offers engineering physics (MS), including biomedical engineering, electrical engineering, mechanical systems, physics. *Program availability:* Part-time. *Degree requirements:* For master's, thesis optional. *Entrance requirements:* For master's, GRE, 24 hours of course work in physics or equivalent, mathematics through differential equations, minimum GPA of 2.75 overall and 3.0 in last 60 hours attempted, two letters of recommendation. Additional exam requirements/recommendations for international students: Required—TOEFL (minimum score 550 paper-based; 79 iBT), IELTS (minimum score 6.5). Electronic applications accepted.

University of Cincinnati, Graduate School, College of Engineering and Applied Science, Cincinnati, OH 45221. Offers M Eng, MS, PhD. *Program availability:* Part-time, 100% online. *Faculty:* 119 full-time (16 women), 15 part-time/adjunct (0 women). *Students:* 1,192 full-time (305 women), 65 part-time (6 women); includes 41 minority (15 Black or African American, non-Hispanic/Latino; 1 American Indian or Alaska Native, non-Hispanic/Latino; 14 Asian, non-Hispanic/Latino; 9 Hispanic/Latino; 2 Two or more races, non-Hispanic/Latino), 986 international. Average age 26. 1,803 applicants, 41% accepted, 448 enrolled. In 2018, 414 master's, 58 doctorates awarded. Terminal master's awarded for partial completion of doctoral program. *Degree requirements:* For master's, thesis or alternative, Thesis for MS students; capstone for MEng students; for doctorate, comprehensive exam, thesis/dissertation. *Entrance requirements:* For master's and doctorate, GRE General Test-some students may be exempt. Additional exam requirements/recommendations for international students: Required—Required to take one exam to demonstrate proficiency: TOEFL (minimum score 92 iBT), IELTS (6.5), or PTE (47). *Application deadline:* For fall admission, 3/15 priority date for domestic students, 1/15 priority date for international students. Applications are processed on a rolling basis. Application fee: $75 ($80 for international students). Electronic applications accepted. *Expenses:* 7738. *Financial support:* In 2018–19, 733 students received support, including 16 fellowships with tuition reimbursements available (averaging $23,400 per year), 396 research assistantships with tuition reimbursements available (averaging $23,400 per year), 248 teaching assistantships with tuition reimbursements available (averaging $23,400 per year); career-related internships or fieldwork, Federal Work-Study, scholarships/grants, tuition waivers (full and partial), and unspecified assistantships also available. Support available to part-time students. Financial award application deadline: 1/15. *Total annual research expenditures:* $17.8 million. *Unit head:* Dr. Frank M. Gerner, Senior Associate Dean, 513-556-3647, E-mail: frank.gerner@uc.edu. *Application contact:* Julie Muenchen, Director, Academics, 513-556-3647, E-mail: julie.muenchen@uc.edu.
Website: http://www.ceas.uc.edu/

University of Colorado Boulder, Graduate School, College of Engineering and Applied Science, Boulder, CO 80309. Offers ME, MS, PhD, JD/MS, MBA/MS. *Degree requirements:* For doctorate, thesis/dissertation. *Entrance requirements:* For master's, minimum undergraduate GPA of 2.75. Electronic applications accepted. Application fee is waived when completed online. *Expenses:* Contact institution. *Faculty research:* Chemical engineering, civil engineering, computer science, materials engineering, mechanical engineering.

University of Colorado Colorado Springs, College of Engineering and Applied Science, Colorado Springs, CO 80918. Offers computer science (PhD). *Program availability:* Part-time, evening/weekend. *Faculty:* 41 full-time (11 women), 48 part-time/adjunct (9 women). *Students:* 26 full-time (4 women), 267 part-time (50 women); includes 61 minority (6 Black or African American, non-Hispanic/Latino; 22 Asian, non-Hispanic/Latino; 20 Hispanic/Latino; 1 Native Hawaiian or other Pacific Islander, non-Hispanic/Latino; 12 Two or more races, non-Hispanic/Latino), 73 international. Average age 33. 162 applicants, 84% accepted, 52 enrolled. In 2018, 58 master's, 15 doctorates awarded. *Degree requirements:* For master's, comprehensive exam (for some programs), thesis or alternative; for doctorate, comprehensive exam, thesis/dissertation. *Entrance requirements:* For master's, GRE General Test, minimum GPA of 3.0; for doctorate, GRE General Test, minimum GPA of 3.3. Additional exam requirements/recommendations for international students: Required—TOEFL (minimum score 80 iBT), IELTS (minimum score 6.5). *Application deadline:* For fall admission, 6/1 for domestic students, 4/1 for international students; for spring admission, 11/1 for domestic students, 10/1 for international students. Applications are processed on a rolling basis. Application fee: $60 ($100 for international students). *Expenses:* Tuition and fees vary by program, course load, and residency type. Please visit the University of Colorado Colorado Springs Student Financial Service website to estimate current program costs: https://www.uccs.edu/bursar/index.php/estimate-your-bill. *Financial support:* In 2018–19, 22 students received support, including 33 teaching assistantships (averaging $5,800 per year); career-related internships or fieldwork, Federal Work-Study, scholarships/grants, and unspecified assistantships also available. Support available to part-time students. Financial award application deadline: 3/1; financial award applicants required to submit FAFSA. *Faculty research:* Synthesis and modeling of digital systems, microelectronics, superconductive thin films, sol-gel processes, linear and nonlinear adaptive filtering, wireless communications networks, computer architecture. *Total annual research expenditures:* $3.2 million. *Unit head:* Dr. Donald Rabern, Dean, 719-255-3543, E-mail: drabern@uccs.edu. *Application contact:* Ali Langfels, Office of Student Support, 719-255-3544, E-mail: alangfel@uccs.edu.
Website: https://www.uccs.edu/eas/

University of Colorado Denver, College of Engineering, Design and Computing, Denver, CO 80217. Offers comp sci and info systems, bioengineering, civil engineering (PhD); electrical, mechanical, civil engineering (M Eng); electrical, mechanical, civil, computer science, bioengineering (MS). *Program availability:* Part-time, evening/weekend. *Students:* 296 full-time (88 women), 132 part-time (36 women); includes 74 minority (12 Black or African American, non-Hispanic/Latino; 22 Asian, non-Hispanic/Latino; 30 Hispanic/Latino; 10 Two or more races, non-Hispanic/Latino), 162 international. Average age 30. 702 applicants, 52% accepted, 111 enrolled. In 2018, 118 master's, 12 doctorates awarded. Application fee: $50 ($75 for international students). Electronic applications accepted. *Expenses:* Contact institution. *Financial support:* In 2018–19, 180 students received support. Federal Work-Study and scholarships/grants available. Support available to part-time students. Financial award applicants required to submit FAFSA. *Total annual research expenditures:* $11.6 million. *Unit head:* Martin Dunn, Dean, 303-315-7170, Fax: 303-315-7173, E-mail: martin.dunn@ucdenver.edu. *Application contact:* Graduate School Admissions, 303-556-2704, E-mail: admissions@ucdenver.edu.
Website: http://www.ucdenver.edu/academics/colleges/Engineering/Pages/EngineeringAppliedScience.aspx

University of Connecticut, Graduate School, School of Engineering, Storrs, CT 06269. Offers M Eng, MS, PhD. Terminal master's awarded for partial completion of doctoral program. *Degree requirements:* For master's, comprehensive exam; for doctorate, thesis/dissertation. *Entrance requirements:* For master's and doctorate, GRE General Test. Additional exam requirements/recommendations for international students: Required—TOEFL (minimum score 550 paper-based). Electronic applications accepted.

University of Delaware, College of Engineering, Newark, DE 19716. Offers M Ch E, MAS, MCE, MEM, MMSE, MS, MSECE, MSME, PhD. *Program availability:* Part-time, evening/weekend, online learning. Terminal master's awarded for partial completion of doctoral program. *Degree requirements:* For master's, thesis (for some programs); for doctorate, thesis/dissertation. *Entrance requirements:* For master's and doctorate, GRE General Test. Additional exam requirements/recommendations for international students: Required—TOEFL (minimum score 550 paper-based). Electronic applications accepted. *Faculty research:* Biotechnology, photonics, transportation, composite materials, materials science.

University of Denver, Daniel Felix Ritchie School of Engineering and Computer Science, Denver, CO 80208. Offers MS, PhD. *Faculty:* 39 full-time (6 women), 5 part-time/adjunct (2 women). *Students:* 32 full-time (9 women), 184 part-time (46 women); includes 30 minority (4 Black or African American, non-Hispanic/Latino; 1 American Indian or Alaska Native, non-Hispanic/Latino; 10 Asian, non-Hispanic/Latino; 6 Hispanic/Latino; 1 Native Hawaiian or other Pacific Islander, non-Hispanic/Latino; 8 Two or more races, non-Hispanic/Latino), 85 international. Average age 29. 425 applicants, 59% accepted, 113 enrolled. In 2018, 39 master's, 14 doctorates awarded. *Degree requirements:* For master's, thesis (for some programs); for doctorate, variable foreign language requirement, comprehensive exam, thesis/dissertation. *Entrance requirements:* For master's, GRE General Test, bachelor's degree, transcripts, three letters of recommendation, personal statement, resume; for doctorate, GRE General Test, master's degree, transcripts, three letters of recommendation, personal statement, resume. Additional exam requirements/recommendations for international students: Required—TOEFL (minimum score 550 paper-based; 80 iBT). *Application deadline:* Applications are processed on a rolling basis. Application fee: $65. Electronic applications accepted. *Expenses:* $33,183 per year full-time. *Financial support:* In 2018–19, 156 students received support, including 14 research assistantships with tuition reimbursements available (averaging $13,848 per year), 34 teaching assistantships with tuition reimbursements available (averaging $16,054 per year); Federal Work-Study, institutionally sponsored loans, scholarships/grants, health care benefits, and unspecified assistantships also available. Financial award application deadline: 2/15; financial award applicants required to submit FAFSA. *Unit head:* JB Holston, Dean, 303-871-3787, E-mail: jb.holston@du.edu. *Application contact:* Information Contact, 303-871-3787, E-mail: ritchieschool@du.edu.
Website: http://ritchieschool.du.edu/

University of Detroit Mercy, College of Engineering and Science, Detroit, MI 48221. Offers chemistry (MS); civil and environmental engineering (DE); electrical and computer engineering (ME); electrical engineering (DE); engineering management (M Eng Mgt); environmental engineering (MEE); mechanical engineering (MME, DE); product development (MS); software engineering (MSSE); teaching of mathematics (MATM). *Program availability:* Part-time, evening/weekend. *Degree requirements:* For doctorate, thesis/dissertation. Electronic applications accepted. Application fee is waived when completed online. *Expenses:* Contact institution.

University of Florida, Graduate School, Herbert Wertheim College of Engineering, Gainesville, FL 32611. Offers ME, MS, PhD, Certificate, Engr, JD/MS, MD/PhD, MSM/MS. *Program availability:* Part-time, online learning. *Degree requirements:* For doctorate, thesis/dissertation. *Entrance requirements:* For master's and doctorate, minimum GPA of 3.0; for other advanced degree, GRE General Test. Additional exam requirements/recommendations for international students: Required—TOEFL (minimum score 550 paper-based; 80 iBT), IELTS (minimum score 6). Electronic applications accepted.

University of Guelph, Office of Graduate and Postdoctoral Studies, College of Physical and Engineering Science, School of Engineering, Guelph, ON N1G 2W1, Canada. Offers biological engineering (M Eng, M Sc, MA Sc, PhD); engineering systems and computing (M Eng, M Sc, MA Sc, PhD); environmental engineering (M Eng, M Sc, MA Sc, PhD); water resources engineering (M Eng, M Sc, MA Sc, PhD). *Program availability:* Part-time. *Degree requirements:* For master's, thesis (for some programs); for doctorate, comprehensive exam, thesis/dissertation. *Entrance requirements:* For master's, minimum B- average during previous 2 years of course work; for doctorate, minimum B average. Additional exam requirements/recommendations for international students: Required—TOEFL (minimum score 550 paper-based; 89 iBT), IELTS (minimum score 6.5). Electronic applications accepted. *Faculty research:* Water and food safety, environmental contaminant fates and mechanisms, computer systems, robotics and mechatronics, waste treatment.

University of Hartford, College of Engineering, Technology and Architecture, Program in Engineering, West Hartford, CT 06117-1599. Offers M Eng. *Entrance requirements:* Additional exam requirements/recommendations for international students: Required—TOEFL.

University of Hawaii at Manoa, Office of Graduate Education, College of Engineering, Honolulu, HI 96822. Offers MS, PhD. *Accreditation:* ABET (one or more programs are accredited). *Program availability:* Part-time. *Entrance requirements:* Additional exam requirements/recommendations for international students: Required—TOEFL or IELTS.

University of Houston, Cullen College of Engineering, Houston, TX 77204. Offers M Pet E, MCE, MCHE, MEE, MIE, MME, MSEE, MSME, PhD. *Program availability:* Part-time. Terminal master's awarded for partial completion of doctoral program. *Degree requirements:* For master's, thesis (for some programs); for doctorate, thesis/dissertation, departmental qualifying exam. *Entrance requirements:* For master's and doctorate, GRE General Test. *Faculty research:* Superconducting materials, microantennas for space packs, direct numerical simulation of pairing vortices.

University of Idaho, College of Graduate Studies, College of Engineering, Moscow, ID 83844-101. Offers M Engr, MS, PhD. *Faculty:* 81 full-time, 8 part-time/adjunct. *Students:* 220 full-time (32 women), 182 part-time (30 women). Average age 32. 390 applicants, 56% accepted, 116 enrolled. In 2018, 81 master's, 11 doctorates awarded. *Degree requirements:* For doctorate, thesis/dissertation. *Entrance requirements:* For master's, minimum GPA of 3.0. Additional exam requirements/recommendations for international students: Required—TOEFL. *Application deadline:* For fall admission, 8/1 for domestic students; for spring admission, 12/15 for domestic students. Applications are processed on a rolling basis. Application fee: $60. Electronic applications accepted. *Expenses:* Tuition, state resident: full-time $7266.44; part-time $474.50 per credit hour. Tuition, nonresident: full-time $24,902; part-time $1453.50 per credit hour. *Required fees:* $2085.56; $45.50 per credit hour. *Financial support:* Fellowships, research assistantships, teaching assistantships, career-related internships or fieldwork, and Federal Work-Study available. Support available to part-time students. Financial award applicants required to submit FAFSA. *Faculty research:* Robotics, micro-electronic packaging, water resources engineering and science, oscillating flows in macro- and micro-scale methods of mechanical separation, nuclear energy. *Unit head:* Dr. Larry Stauffer, Dean, 208-885-6470, E-mail: deanengr@uidaho.edu. *Application contact:* Dr. Larry Stauffer, Dean, 208-885-6470, E-mail: deanengr@uidaho.edu.
Website: https://www.uidaho.edu/engr

University of Illinois at Chicago, College of Engineering, Chicago, IL 60607-7128. Offers M Eng, MEE, MS, PhD. *Program availability:* Part-time, evening/weekend. Terminal master's awarded for partial completion of doctoral program. *Degree requirements:* For doctorate, thesis/dissertation. *Entrance requirements:* For doctorate, GRE. Additional exam requirements/recommendations for international students: Required—TOEFL. Electronic applications accepted. *Expenses:* Contact institution.

University of Illinois at Urbana–Champaign, Graduate College, College of Engineering, Champaign, IL 61820. Offers M Eng, MCS, MS, PhD, M Arch/MS, MBA/MS, MCS/JD, MCS/M Arch, MCS/MBA, MS/MBA, PhD/MBA. *Program availability:* Part-time, evening/weekend, online learning. *Expenses:* Contact institution.

The University of Iowa, Graduate College, College of Engineering, Iowa City, IA 52242-1527. Offers MS, PhD. *Degree requirements:* For master's, comprehensive exam (for some programs), oral exam and/or thesis; for doctorate, comprehensive exam, thesis/dissertation. *Entrance requirements:* For master's and doctorate, GRE, official academic records/transcripts, 3 letters of recommendation, resume, statement of purpose. Additional exam requirements/recommendations for international students: Required—TOEFL (minimum score 550 paper-based; 81 iBT), IELTS (minimum score 7). Electronic applications accepted. *Expenses:* Contact institution.

The University of Kansas, Graduate Studies, School of Engineering, Lawrence, KS 66045. Offers MCE, MCM, ME, MS, DE, PhD, Certificate. *Program availability:* Part-time, evening/weekend, online learning. *Students:* 401 full-time (99 women), 239 part-time (58 women); includes 86 minority (24 Black or African American, non-Hispanic/Latino; 1 American Indian or Alaska Native, non-Hispanic/Latino; 24 Asian, non-Hispanic/Latino; 20 Hispanic/Latino; 17 Two or more races, non-Hispanic/Latino), 262 international. Average age 29. 585 applicants, 61% accepted, 150 enrolled. In 2018, 164 master's, 32 doctorates, 2 other advanced degrees awarded. Terminal master's awarded for partial completion of doctoral program. *Entrance requirements:* For master's and doctorate, GRE, minimum GPA of 3.0, 3 letters of recommendation, official transcripts, statement of purpose. Additional exam requirements/recommendations for international students: Required—TOEFL, IELTS. Application fee: $65 ($85 for international students). Electronic applications accepted. *Financial support:* Fellowships, research assistantships, teaching assistantships, career-related internships or fieldwork, Federal Work-Study, scholarships/grants, and unspecified assistantships available. *Faculty research:* Global change, transportation, water, energy, healthcare, information technology, sustainable infrastructure, remote sensing, environmental sustainability, telecommunications, oil recovery, airplane design, structured materials, robotics, sustainable fuels and chemicals, radar systems, composite materials and structures, precision particles, tissue engineering, chemo-enzymatic catalysis, communication systems and networks, intelligent systems, data mining, fuel cells, imaging. *Unit head:* Dr. Arvin Agah, Dean, 785-864-2930, E-mail: agah@ku.edu. *Application contact:* Amy Wierman, Assistant to the Dean, 785-864-2930, E-mail: awierman@ku.edu.
Website: http://www.engr.ku.edu/

University of Kentucky, Graduate School, College of Engineering, Lexington, KY 40506-0032. Offers M Eng, MCE, MME, MS, MS Ch E, MS Min, MSCE, MSEE, MSEM, MSMAE, MSME, MSMSE, PhD. *Program availability:* Part-time. *Degree requirements:* For master's, comprehensive exam; for doctorate, comprehensive exam, thesis/dissertation. *Entrance requirements:* For master's, GRE General Test, minimum undergraduate GPA of 2.75; for doctorate, GRE General Test, minimum undergraduate GPA of 3.0. Additional exam requirements/recommendations for international students: Required—TOEFL (minimum score 550 paper-based). Electronic applications accepted.

University of Louisville, J. B. Speed School of Engineering, Louisville, KY 40292-0001. Offers M Eng, MS, PhD, Certificate. *Accreditation:* ABET (one or more programs are accredited). *Program availability:* 100% online, blended/hybrid learning. *Faculty:* 111 full-time (21 women), 23 part-time/adjunct (4 women). *Students:* 296 full-time (73 women), 396 part-time (93 women); includes 105 minority (26 Black or African American, non-Hispanic/Latino; 38 Asian, non-Hispanic/Latino; 21 Hispanic/Latino; 20 Two or more races, non-Hispanic/Latino), 201 international. Average age 29. 266 applicants, 51% accepted, 108 enrolled. In 2018, 122 master's, 15 doctorates, 8 other advanced degrees awarded. Terminal master's awarded for partial completion of doctoral program. *Degree requirements:* For master's, thesis optional; for doctorate, thesis/dissertation. *Entrance requirements:* For master's and doctorate, GRE, letters of recommendation, official transcripts, personal statement. Additional exam requirements/recommendations for international students: Required—TOEFL (minimum score 550 paper-based; 80 iBT), IELTS (minimum score 6.5), GRE. *Application deadline:* For fall admission, 5/1 priority date for domestic and international students; for spring admission, 11/1 priority date for domestic and international students; for summer admission, 3/1 priority date for domestic students, 4/1 priority date for international students. Applications are processed on a rolling basis. Application fee: $65. Electronic applications accepted. *Expenses: Tuition, area resident:* Full-time $6500; part-time $723 per credit hour. Tuition, state resident: full-time $6500. Tuition, nonresident: full-time $13,557; part-time $1507 per credit hour. Tuition and fees vary according to course load and program. *Financial support:* In 2018–19, 293 students received support. Fellowships, research assistantships, teaching assistantships, scholarships/grants, health care benefits, tuition waivers (full), and unspecified assistantships available. Financial award application deadline: 2/1. *Faculty research:* Energy and sustainability; advanced manufacturing and logistics; engineering human health; materials science and engineering, including nanoscience, cyber-enabled discovery. *Total annual research expenditures:* $18.3 million. *Unit head:* Dr. Kevin Walsh, Associate Dean for Research and Graduate Studies, 502-852-0826, E-mail: kevin.walsh@louisville.edu. *Application contact:* Dr. Katherine Markuson, Director of Graduate Affairs, 502-852-6278, E-mail: katherine.markuson@louisville.edu.
Website: http://louisville.edu/speed/

University of Maine, Graduate School, College of Engineering, Orono, ME 04469. Offers ME, MS, PSM, PhD. *Program availability:* Part-time. *Faculty:* 52 full-time (8 women), 5 part-time/adjunct (0 women). *Students:* 111 full-time (30 women), 29 part-time (2 women); includes 11 minority (1 Black or African American, non-Hispanic/Latino; 2 American Indian or Alaska Native, non-Hispanic/Latino; 4 Asian, non-Hispanic/Latino; 3 Hispanic/Latino; 1 Two or more races, non-Hispanic/Latino), 50 international. Average age 29. 123 applicants, 70% accepted, 34 enrolled. In 2018, 42 master's, 9 doctorates awarded. Terminal master's awarded for partial completion of doctoral program. *Degree requirements:* For master's, thesis (for some programs); for doctorate, comprehensive exam, thesis/dissertation. *Entrance requirements:* For master's and doctorate, GRE General Test. Additional exam requirements/recommendations for international students: Required—TOEFL. *Application deadline:* For fall admission, 2/1 priority date for domestic students. Applications are processed on a rolling basis. Application fee: $65. Electronic applications accepted. *Financial support:* In 2018–19, 120 students received support, including 4 fellowships (averaging $22,650 per year), 48 research assistantships (averaging $20,700 per year), 22 teaching assistantships (averaging $16,300 per year); Federal Work-Study, institutionally sponsored loans, scholarships/grants, tuition waivers (full and partial), and unspecified assistantships also available. Financial award application deadline: 3/1. *Total annual research expenditures:* $17.7 million. *Unit head:* Dr. Dana Humphrey, Dean, 207-581-2217, Fax: 207-581-2220, E-mail: dana.humphrey@umit.maine.edu. *Application contact:* Scott G. Delcourt, Assistant Vice President for Graduate Studies and Senior Associate Dean, 207-581-3291, Fax: 207-581-3232, E-mail: graduate@maine.edu.
Website: http://engineering.umaine.edu

University of Manitoba, Faculty of Graduate Studies, Faculty of Engineering, Winnipeg, MB R3T 2N2, Canada. Offers M Eng, M Sc, PhD.

University of Maryland, Baltimore County, The Graduate School, College of Engineering and Information Technology, Baltimore, MD 21250. Offers MPS, MS, PhD, Postbaccalaureate Certificate. *Program availability:* Part-time. Terminal master's awarded for partial completion of doctoral program. *Degree requirements:* For master's, comprehensive exam (for some programs), thesis (for some programs); for doctorate, comprehensive exam, thesis/dissertation. *Entrance requirements:* Additional exam requirements/recommendations for international students: Required—TOEFL (minimum score 550 paper-based; 80 iBT). Electronic applications accepted. *Expenses:* Contact institution. *Faculty research:* Biochemical/biomedical engineering, environmental engineering, computer science/cybersecurity/electrical engineering, information systems, mechanical engineering.

University of Maryland, College Park, Academic Affairs, A. James Clark School of Engineering and School of Public Policy, Program in Engineering and Public Policy, College Park, MD 20742. Offers MS.

University of Massachusetts Amherst, Graduate School, College of Engineering, Amherst, MA 01003. Offers MS, MS Env E, MSCE, MSChE, MSECE, MSEM, MSIE, MSME, PhD. *Program availability:* Part-time. Terminal master's awarded for partial completion of doctoral program. *Degree requirements:* For master's, thesis (for some programs); for doctorate, comprehensive exam, thesis/dissertation. *Entrance requirements:* For master's and doctorate, GRE General Test. Additional exam requirements/recommendations for international students: Required—TOEFL (minimum score 550 paper-based; 80 iBT), IELTS (minimum score 6.5). Electronic applications accepted.

University of Massachusetts Dartmouth, Graduate School, College of Engineering, Program in Engineering and Applied Science, North Dartmouth, MA 02747-2300. Offers engineering and applied science (PhD). *Program availability:* Part-time. *Students:* 21 full-time (6 women), 19 part-time (6 women); includes 3 minority (1 Black or African American, non-Hispanic/Latino; 2 Hispanic/Latino), 21 international. Average age 31. 24 applicants, 83% accepted, 7 enrolled. In 2018, 6 doctorates awarded. *Degree requirements:* For doctorate, comprehensive exam, thesis/dissertation. *Entrance requirements:* For doctorate, GRE, statement of purpose (minimum of 300 words), resume, 3 letters of recommendation, official transcripts. Additional exam requirements/recommendations for international students: Required—TOEFL (minimum score 550 paper-based; 79 iBT). *Application deadline:* For fall admission, 2/15 priority date for domestic students, 1/15 priority date for international students; for spring admission, 11/15 priority date for domestic students, 10/15 priority date for international students. Application fee: $60. Electronic applications accepted. *Financial support:* In 2018–19, 8 fellowships (averaging $16,875 per year), 19 research assistantships (averaging $12,214 per year), 12 teaching assistantships (averaging $8,793 per year) were awarded; tuition waivers (full and partial) and doctoral support also available. Financial award application deadline: 3/1; financial award applicants required to submit FAFSA. *Faculty research:* Tissue/cell engineering, transport applications related to micro fabrication, heat mass transfer, resilient infrastructure robotics, computational fluid dynamics and renewable energy. *Total annual research expenditures:* $96,000. *Unit head:* Gaurav Khanna, Graduate Program Director, Engineering and Applied Science, 508-910-6605, Fax: 508-999-9115, E-mail: gkhanna@umassd.edu. *Application contact:* Scott Webster, Director of Graduate Studies & Admissions, 508-999-8604, Fax: 508-999-8183, E-mail: graduate@umassd.edu.
Website: http://www.umassd.edu/engineering/graduate/doctoraldegreeprograms/egrandappliedsciencephd/

University of Massachusetts Lowell, Francis College of Engineering, Lowell, MA 01854. Offers MS, MS Eng, PhD. *Program availability:* Part-time, evening/weekend. Terminal master's awarded for partial completion of doctoral program. *Degree requirements:* For doctorate, thesis/dissertation. *Entrance requirements:* For master's and doctorate, GRE General Test.

University of Memphis, Graduate School, Herff College of Engineering, Memphis, TN 38152. Offers MS, PhD, Graduate Certificate. *Program availability:* Part-time. *Faculty:* 31 full-time (5 women), 4 part-time/adjunct (0 women). *Students:* 90 full-time (22 women), 75 part-time (20 women); includes 29 minority (8 Black or African American, non-Hispanic/Latino; 1 American Indian or Alaska Native, non-Hispanic/Latino; 15

Asian, non-Hispanic/Latino; 4 Hispanic/Latino; 1 Two or more races, non-Hispanic/Latino), 86 international. Average age 31. 151 applicants, 68% accepted, 38 enrolled. In 2018, 27 master's, 7 doctorates, 3 other advanced degrees awarded. *Degree requirements:* For master's, comprehensive exam, thesis optional, 30-36 hours of course work, completion of course work within 6 years, continuous enrollment; for doctorate, comprehensive exam, thesis/dissertation, completion of degree within 12 years, residency, continuous enrollment. *Entrance requirements:* For master's and doctorate, GRE, MAT, GMAT, three letters of recommendation. Additional exam requirements/recommendations for international students: Required—TOEFL (minimum score 550 paper-based; 79 iBT). *Application deadline:* For fall admission, 8/1 for domestic students, 5/1 for international students; for spring admission, 12/1 for domestic students, 9/15 for international students; for summer admission, 5/1 for domestic students. Application fee: $35 ($60 for international students). Electronic applications accepted. *Expenses: Tuition, area resident:* Full-time $10,240; part-time $503 per credit hour. Tuition, state resident: full-time $10,464. Tuition, nonresident: full-time $20,224; part-time $991 per credit hour. *Required fees:* $850; $106 per credit hour. *Financial support:* Fellowships with full tuition reimbursements, research assistantships with full tuition reimbursements, teaching assistantships with full tuition reimbursements, career-related internships or fieldwork, Federal Work-Study, scholarships/grants, tuition waivers (full and partial), and unspecified assistantships available. Financial award application deadline: 2/1; financial award applicants required to submit FAFSA. *Faculty research:* Medical and biological applications of engineering; infrastructure, including transportation, ground water and GPS studies; computational intelligence and modeling; sensors. *Unit head:* Dr. Richard Joseph Sweigard, Dean, 901-678-4306, Fax: 901-678-4180, E-mail: rjswgard@memphis.edu. *Application contact:* Dr. Russell Deaton, Associate Dean of Academic Affairs and Administration, 901-678-2175, Fax: 901-678-5030, E-mail: rjdeaton@memphis.edu.
Website: https://www.memphis.edu/herff/

University of Miami, Graduate School, College of Engineering, Coral Gables, FL 33124. Offers MS, MSAE, MSBE, MSCE, MSECE, MSIE, MSME, MSOES, PhD, MBA/MSIE. *Program availability:* Part-time, evening/weekend. *Degree requirements:* For master's, thesis (for some programs); for doctorate, comprehensive exam, thesis/dissertation. *Entrance requirements:* For master's and doctorate, GRE General Test, minimum GPA of 3.0. Additional exam requirements/recommendations for international students: Required—TOEFL (minimum score 550 paper-based; 59 iBT). Electronic applications accepted.

University of Michigan, College of Engineering, Ann Arbor, MI 48109. Offers M Eng, MS, MSE, D Eng, PhD, CE, Certificate, Ch E, Mar Eng, Nav Arch, Nuc E, M Arch/M Eng, M Arch/MSE, MBA/M Eng, MBA/MS, MBA/MSE, MSE/MS. *Program availability:* Part-time, 100% online, blended/hybrid learning. *Faculty:* 426 full-time (86 women). *Students:* 3,285 full-time (888 women), 323 part-time (56 women). 11,153 applicants, 26% accepted, 1099 enrolled. In 2018, 1,244 master's, 289 doctorates awarded. *Application deadline:* Applications are processed on a rolling basis. Electronic applications accepted. *Expenses:* Contact institution. *Financial support:* Fellowships, research assistantships, teaching assistantships, career-related internships or fieldwork, Federal Work-Study, institutionally sponsored loans, scholarships/grants, traineeships, health care benefits, tuition waivers (full and partial), and unspecified assistantships available. Support available to part-time students. Financial award applicants required to submit FAFSA. *Total annual research expenditures:* $303.6 million. *Unit head:* Prof. Alec D. Gallimore, Dean of Engineering, 734-647-7008, Fax: 734-647-7009, E-mail: alec.gallimore@umich.edu. *Application contact:* Jeanne Murabito, Executive Director for Student Affairs, 734-647-7118, E-mail: coe-studentaffairs@umich.edu.
Website: http://www.engin.umich.edu/

University of Michigan–Dearborn, College of Engineering and Computer Science, Dearborn, MI 48128. Offers MS, MSE, PhD, MBA/MSE. *Program availability:* Part-time, evening/weekend, 100% online. *Faculty:* 80 full-time (11 women), 42 part-time/adjunct (4 women). *Students:* 343 full-time (98 women), 1,023 part-time (189 women); includes 193 minority (46 Black or African American, non-Hispanic/Latino; 3 American Indian or Alaska Native, non-Hispanic/Latino; 90 Asian, non-Hispanic/Latino; 38 Hispanic/Latino; 1 Native Hawaiian or other Pacific Islander, non-Hispanic/Latino; 15 Two or more races, non-Hispanic/Latino), 514 international. Average age 28. 1,641 applicants, 47% accepted, 369 enrolled. In 2018, 471 master's, 4 doctorates awarded. *Degree requirements:* For master's, thesis optional; for doctorate, comprehensive exam, thesis/dissertation. *Entrance requirements:* For doctorate, GRE. Additional exam requirements/recommendations for international students: Required—TOEFL (minimum score 560 paper-based; 84 iBT), IELTS (minimum score 6.5). *Application deadline:* For fall admission, 8/1 priority date for domestic students, 5/1 priority date for international students; for winter admission, 12/1 priority date for domestic students, 9/1 priority date for international students; for spring admission, 4/1 priority date for domestic students, 1/1 priority date for international students. Applications are processed on a rolling basis. Application fee: $60. Electronic applications accepted. *Expenses:* Tuition, state resident: full-time $15,380; part-time $88 per credit hour. Tuition, nonresident: full-time $23,948; part-time $1377 per credit hour. *Required fees:* $780; $780 $390. Tuition and fees vary according to course level, course load, degree level, program, reciprocity agreements and student level. *Financial support:* In 2018–19, 327 students received support. Research assistantships with full tuition reimbursements available, teaching assistantships with full tuition reimbursements available, career-related internships or fieldwork, scholarships/grants, health care benefits, and non-residential student scholarships available. Support available to part-time students. Financial award application deadline: 3/1; financial award applicants required to submit FAFSA. *Faculty research:* Microelectronics, advance automotive and manufacturing engineering, robotics, cybersecurity, machine learning and artificial intelligence. *Unit head:* Dr. Anthony England, Dean, 313-593-5290, E-mail: cecsdeansoffice@umich.edu. *Application contact:* Office of Graduate Studies Staff, 313-583-6321, E-mail: umd-graduatestudies@umich.edu.
Website: http://umdearborn.edu/cecs/

University of Minnesota, Twin Cities Campus, College of Science and Engineering, Minneapolis, MN 55455. Offers M Ch E, M Geo E, M Mat SE, MA, MCE, MCS, MFM, MS, MS Ch E, MS Mat SE, MSEE, MSME, MSMOT, MSSE, MSST, PhD, Certificate, MD/PhD. *Program availability:* Part-time, evening/weekend, 100% online, blended/hybrid learning. *Faculty:* 428 full-time (67 women). *Students:* 2,250 full-time, 379 part-time; includes 273 minority (38 Black or African American, non-Hispanic/Latino; 5 American Indian or Alaska Native, non-Hispanic/Latino; 114 Asian, non-Hispanic/Latino; 73 Hispanic/Latino; 1 Native Hawaiian or other Pacific Islander, non-Hispanic/Latino; 42 Two or more races, non-Hispanic/Latino), 1,286 international. Average age 25. 5,478 applicants, 32% accepted, 721 enrolled. In 2018, 586 master's, 255 doctorates awarded. Terminal master's awarded for partial completion of doctoral program. *Degree requirements:* For master's, thesis (for some programs); for doctorate, thesis/dissertation. *Entrance requirements:* Additional exam requirements/recommendations for international students: Required—TOEFL (minimum score 550 paper-based; 79 iBT). *Application deadline:* Applications are processed on a rolling basis. Application fee: $75 ($95 for international students). Electronic applications accepted. *Financial support:* Fellowships, research assistantships, teaching assistantships, and unspecified assistantships available. Financial award applicants required to submit FAFSA. *Total annual research expenditures:* $170 million. *Unit head:* Mostafa Kaveh, Dean, 612-624-2006, Fax: 612-624-2841, E-mail: mos@umn.edu. *Application contact:* Graduate Admissions Office, 612-625-3014.
Website: http://cse.umn.edu/

University of Mississippi, Graduate School, School of Engineering, University, MS 38677. Offers aeroacoustics (MS, PhD); chemical engineering (MS, PhD); civil engineering (MS, PhD); computational hydroscience (MS, PhD); computer science (MS, PhD); electrical engineering (MS, PhD); electromagnetics (MS, PhD); environmental engineering (MS, PhD); geology and geological engineering (MS, PhD); hydrology (MS); material science (MS); mechanical engineering (MS, PhD); telecommunications (MS). *Faculty:* 76 full-time (16 women), 3 part-time/adjunct (1 woman). *Students:* 129 full-time (33 women), 21 part-time (5 women); includes 15 minority (7 Black or African American, non-Hispanic/Latino; 6 Asian, non-Hispanic/Latino; 1 Hispanic/Latino; 1 Two or more races, non-Hispanic/Latino), 73 international. Average age 29. In 2018, 36 master's, 17 doctorates awarded. *Entrance requirements:* For master's, GRE General Test, minimum GPA of 3.0; for doctorate, GRE General Test. Additional exam requirements/recommendations for international students: Required—TOEFL. *Application deadline:* Applications are processed on a rolling basis. Application fee: $50. Electronic applications accepted. *Financial support:* Scholarships/grants available. Financial award application deadline: 3/1; financial award applicants required to submit FAFSA. *Unit head:* Dr. David Puleo, Dean, 662-915-5780, Fax: 662-915-5387, E-mail: engineer@olemiss.edu. *Application contact:* Temeka Smith, Graduate Activities Specialist for Admissions, 662-915-7474, Fax: 662-915-7577, E-mail: gschool@olemiss.edu.

University of Missouri, Office of Research and Graduate Studies, College of Engineering, Columbia, MO 65211. Offers ME, MS, MSCE, MSEE, PhD, Certificate, MS/MHA. *Program availability:* Part-time. *Entrance requirements:* For master's and doctorate, GRE General Test. Additional exam requirements/recommendations for international students: Required—TOEFL, IELTS.

University of Missouri–Kansas City, School of Computing and Engineering, Kansas City, MO 64110-2499. Offers civil engineering (MS); computer and electrical engineering (PhD); computer science (MS), including bioinformatics, software engineering, telecommunications networking; computer science and informatics (PhD); computing (PhD); electrical engineering (MS); engineering (PhD); engineering and construction management (Graduate Certificate); mechanical engineering (MS); telecommunications and computer networking (PhD). PhD (interdisciplinary) offered through the School of Graduate Studies. *Program availability:* Part-time. *Degree requirements:* For doctorate, thesis/dissertation. *Entrance requirements:* For master's, GRE General Test, minimum GPA of 3.0, 3 letters of recommendation from professors; for doctorate, GRE General Test, minimum GPA of 3.5. Additional exam requirements/recommendations for international students: Required—TOEFL (minimum score 550 paper-based; 80 iBT). *Faculty research:* Algorithms, bioinformatics and medical informatics, biomechanics/biomaterials, civil engineering materials, networking and telecommunications, thermal science.

University of Nebraska–Lincoln, Graduate College, College of Engineering, Lincoln, NE 68588. Offers M Eng, MAE, MEE, MS, PhD. *Degree requirements:* For doctorate, comprehensive exam, thesis/dissertation. *Entrance requirements:* For master's and doctorate, GRE General Test. Additional exam requirements/recommendations for international students: Required—TOEFL. Electronic applications accepted.

University of Nevada, Las Vegas, Graduate College, Howard R. Hughes College of Engineering, Las Vegas, NV 89154-4005. Offers civil & environmental engineering and construction, computer science, electrical and computer engineering, mechanical engineering (PhD); MS/MS; MS/PhD. *Program availability:* Part-time. *Faculty:* 62 full-time (9 women), 5 part-time/adjunct (0 women). *Students:* 162 full-time (44 women), 84 part-time (17 women); includes 64 minority (6 Black or African American, non-Hispanic/Latino; 1 American Indian or Alaska Native, non-Hispanic/Latino; 20 Asian, non-Hispanic/Latino; 27 Hispanic/Latino; 10 Two or more races, non-Hispanic/Latino), 110 international. Average age 30. 178 applicants, 66% accepted, 58 enrolled. In 2018, 50 master's, 17 doctorates, 2 other advanced degrees awarded. *Degree requirements:* For master's, comprehensive exam (for some programs), thesis (for some programs); for doctorate, comprehensive exam, thesis/dissertation. *Entrance requirements:* For master's, GRE General Test; for doctorate, GRE General Test, 3 letters of recommendation; statement of purpose. Additional exam requirements/recommendations for international students: Required—TOEFL (minimum score 550 paper-based; 80 iBT), IELTS (minimum score 7). Application fee: $60 ($95 for international students). Electronic applications accepted. *Expenses:* Contact institution. *Financial support:* In 2018–19, 156 students received support, including 2 fellowships with full tuition reimbursements available (averaging $20,000 per year), 48 research assistantships with full tuition reimbursements available (averaging $16,373 per year), 108 teaching assistantships with full tuition reimbursements available (averaging $15,832 per year); institutionally sponsored loans, scholarships/grants, health care benefits, and unspecified assistantships also available. Financial award application deadline: 3/15; financial award applicants required to submit FAFSA. *Faculty research:* Batteries, big data, biomedical engineering, environmental engineering, water resources, security, renewable energy, transportation, unmanned aerial system, functional and energy materials. *Total annual research expenditures:* $10.9 million. *Unit head:* Dr. Rama Venkat, Dean, 702-895-3699, Fax: 702-895-4059, E-mail: engineering.dean@unlv.edu. *Application contact:* Dr. Rama Venkat, Dean, 702-895-3699, Fax: 702-895-4059, E-mail: engineering.dean@unlv.edu.
Website: http://engineering.unlv.edu/

University of Nevada, Reno, Graduate School, College of Engineering, Reno, NV 89557. Offers MS, PhD. Terminal master's awarded for partial completion of doctoral program. *Degree requirements:* For master's, thesis optional; for doctorate, thesis/dissertation. *Entrance requirements:* For master's, GRE General Test, minimum GPA of 2.75; for doctorate, GRE General Test, minimum GPA of 3.0. Additional exam requirements/recommendations for international students: Required—TOEFL (minimum score 500 paper-based; 61 iBT), IELTS (minimum score 6). Electronic applications accepted. *Faculty research:* Fabrication, development of new materials, structural and earthquake engineering, computer vision/virtual reality, acoustics, smart materials.

University of New Brunswick Fredericton, School of Graduate Studies, Faculty of Engineering, Fredericton, NB E3B 5A3, Canada. Offers M Eng, M Sc E, PhD, Certificate. *Program availability:* Part-time. *Degree requirements:* For master's, thesis; for doctorate, comprehensive exam, thesis/dissertation, qualifying exam. *Entrance requirements:* For master's, minimum GPA of 3.0. Additional exam requirements/recommendations for international students: Required—TOEFL, TWE. Electronic applications accepted.

University of New Haven, Graduate School, Tagliatela College of Engineering, West Haven, CT 06516. Offers MS, MSIE, Graduate Certificate, MBA/MSIE. *Program availability:* Part-time, evening/weekend. *Students:* 463 full-time (129 women), 143 part-time (41 women); includes 50 minority (16 Black or African American, non-Hispanic/Latino; 1 American Indian or Alaska Native, non-Hispanic/Latino; 22 Asian, non-Hispanic/Latino; 10 Hispanic/Latino; 1 Two or more races, non-Hispanic/Latino), 445

international. Average age 26. 1,825 applicants, 72% accepted, 188 enrolled. In 2018, 213 master's, 1 other advanced degree awarded. *Degree requirements:* For master's, thesis or alternative. *Entrance requirements:* Additional exam requirements/recommendations for international students: Required—TOEFL (minimum score 75 iBT), IELTS, PTE (minimum score 50). *Application deadline:* Applications are processed on a rolling basis. Application fee: $50. Electronic applications accepted. Application fee is waived when completed online. *Expenses: Tuition:* Full-time $16,470; part-time $915 per credit hour. *Required fees:* $230; $95 per term. *Financial support:* Research assistantships with partial tuition reimbursements, teaching assistantships with partial tuition reimbursements, Federal Work-Study, scholarships/grants, and unspecified assistantships available. Support available to part-time students. Financial award applicants required to submit FAFSA. *Unit head:* Dr. Ronald Harichandran, Dean and Vice Provost for Research, 203-932-7167, E-mail: rharichandran@newhaven.edu. *Application contact:* Selina O'Toole, Senior Associate Director of Graduate Admissions, 203-932-7337, E-mail: SOToole@newhaven.edu.
Website: http://www.newhaven.edu/engineering/

University of New Mexico, Graduate Studies, School of Engineering, Albuquerque, NM 87131. Offers M Eng, MCM, MEME, MS, MSCE, PhD, MBA/MEME. *Program availability:* Part-time. Terminal master's awarded for partial completion of doctoral program. *Degree requirements:* For master's, comprehensive exam, thesis or alternative; for doctorate, comprehensive exam, thesis/dissertation. *Entrance requirements:* For master's, GRE, GMAT, letters of recommendation; letter of intent; for doctorate, GRE, letters of recommendation; letter of intent. Additional exam requirements/recommendations for international students: Required—TOEFL (minimum score 550 paper-based). Electronic applications accepted. *Faculty research:* Emerging energy technologies, biomedical engineering and biocomputing, water resources and environmental engineering, optical engineering and optoelectronic materials, graphics and digital imaging.

University of New Orleans, Graduate School, College of Engineering, New Orleans, LA 70148. Offers MS, PhD. *Program availability:* Part-time. Terminal master's awarded for partial completion of doctoral program. *Degree requirements:* For master's, comprehensive exam, thesis optional; for doctorate, comprehensive exam, thesis/dissertation. *Entrance requirements:* For master's, GRE General Test, minimum GPA of 3.0; for doctorate, GRE General Test. Additional exam requirements/recommendations for international students: Required—TOEFL (minimum score 550 paper-based; 79 iBT). Electronic applications accepted.

The University of North Carolina at Charlotte, William States Lee College of Engineering, Charlotte, NC 28223-0001. Offers MS, MSCE, MSE, MSEE, MSEM, MSME, PhD, Graduate Certificate. *Program availability:* Part-time, evening/weekend, blended/hybrid learning. *Students:* 393 full-time (89 women), 198 part-time (35 women); includes 47 minority (13 Black or African American, non-Hispanic/Latino; 1 American Indian or Alaska Native, non-Hispanic/Latino; 16 Asian, non-Hispanic/Latino; 11 Hispanic/Latino; 6 Two or more races, non-Hispanic/Latino), 370 international. Average age 28. 738 applicants, 72% accepted, 150 enrolled. In 2018, 193 master's, 33 doctorates, 3 other advanced degrees awarded. Terminal master's awarded for partial completion of doctoral program. *Entrance requirements:* For master's, bachelor's degree, or its U.S. equivalent, from regionally-accredited college or university; minimum overall GPA of 3.0 on all previous work beyond high school; statement of purpose (essay); at least three recommendation forms; for doctorate, bachelor's degree (or its U.S. equivalent) from regionally-accredited college or university; minimum overall GPA of 3.5 in master's degree program; for Graduate Certificate, bachelor's degree from regionally-accredited university; minimum GPA of 2.75 on all post-secondary work attempted; transcripts; personal statement outlining why the applicant seeks admission to the program. Additional exam requirements/recommendations for international students: Required—TOEFL (minimum score 523 paper-based; 70 iBT), IELTS (minimum score 6), TOEFL (minimum score 523 paper-based, 70 iBT) or IELTS (6). *Application deadline:* Applications are processed on a rolling basis. Application fee: $75. Electronic applications accepted. Tuition and fees vary according to course load and program. *Financial support:* Fellowships, research assistantships, teaching assistantships, career-related internships or fieldwork, institutionally sponsored loans, scholarships/grants, and unspecified assistantships available. Support available to part-time students. Financial award application deadline: 3/1; financial award applicants required to submit FAFSA. *Faculty research:* Environmental engineering, structures and geotechnical engineering, precision engineering and precision metrology, optoelectronics and microelectronics, communications. *Total annual research expenditures:* $10.6 million. *Unit head:* Dr. Robert E. Johnson, Dean, 704-687-8242, E-mail: robejohn@uncc.edu. *Application contact:* Kathy B. Giddings, Director of Graduate Admissions, 704-687-5503, Fax: 704-687-1668, E-mail: gradadm@uncc.edu. Website: http://engr.uncc.edu/

University of North Dakota, Graduate School, School of Engineering and Mines, Program in Engineering, Grand Forks, ND 58202. Offers PhD. *Degree requirements:* For doctorate, comprehensive exam, thesis/dissertation, final exam. *Entrance requirements:* For doctorate, minimum GPA of 3.0. Additional exam requirements/recommendations for international students: Required—TOEFL (minimum score 550 paper-based; 79 iBT), IELTS (minimum score 6.5). Electronic applications accepted. *Faculty research:* Combustion science, energy conversion, power transmission, environmental engineering.

University of North Texas, Toulouse Graduate School, Denton, TX 76203-5459. Offers accounting (MS); applied anthropology (MA, MS); applied behavior analysis (Certificate); applied geography (MA); applied technology and performance improvement (M Ed, MS); art education (MA); art history (MA); arts leadership (Certificate); audiology (Au D); behavior analysis (MS); behavioral science (PhD); biochemistry and molecular biology (MS); biology (MA, MS); biomedical engineering (MS); business analysis (MS); chemistry (MS); clinical health psychology (PhD); communication studies (MA, MS); computer engineering (MS); computer science (MS); counseling (M Ed, MS), including clinical mental health counseling (MS), college and university counseling, elementary school counseling, secondary school counseling; creative writing (MA); criminal justice (MS); curriculum and instruction (M Ed); decision sciences (MBA); design (MA, MFA), including fashion design (MFA), innovation studies, interior design (MFA); early childhood studies (MS); economics (MS); educational leadership (M Ed, Ed D); educational psychology (MS, PhD), including family studies (MS), gifted and talented (MS), human development (MS), learning and cognition (MS), research, measurement and evaluation (MS); electrical engineering (MS); emergency management (MPA); engineering technology (MS); English (MA); English as a second language (MA); environmental science (MS); finance (MBA, MS); financial management (MPA); French (MA); health services management (MBA); higher education (M Ed, Ed D); history (MA, MS); hospitality management (MS); human resources management (MPA); information science (MS); information systems (PhD); information technologies (MBA); interdisciplinary studies (MA, MS); international studies (MA); international sustainable tourism (MS); jazz studies (MM); journalism (MA, MJ, Graduate Certificate), including interactive and virtual digital communication (Graduate Certificate), narrative journalism (Graduate Certificate), public relations (Graduate Certificate); kinesiology (MS); linguistics (MA); local government management (MPA); logistics (PhD); logistics

and supply chain management (MBA); long-term care, senior housing, and aging services (MA); management (PhD); marketing (MBA); mathematics (MA, MS); mechanical and energy engineering (MS, PhD); music (MA), including ethnomusicology, music theory, musicology, performance; music composition (PhD); music education (MM Ed, PhD); nonprofit management (MPA); operations and supply chain management (MBA); performance (MM, DMA); philosophy (MA); political science (MA); professional and technical communication (MA); radio, television and film (MA, MFA); rehabilitation counseling (Certificate); sociology (MA); Spanish (MA); special education (M Ed); speech-language pathology (MA); strategic management (MBA); studio art (MFA); teaching (M Ed); MBA/MS. *Program availability:* Part-time, evening/weekend, online learning. Terminal master's awarded for partial completion of doctoral program. *Degree requirements:* For master's, variable foreign language requirement, comprehensive exam (for some programs), thesis (for some programs); for doctorate, variable foreign language requirement, comprehensive exam (for some programs), thesis/dissertation; for other advanced degree, variable foreign language requirement, comprehensive exam (for some programs). *Entrance requirements:* For master's and doctorate, GRE, GMAT. Additional exam requirements/recommendations for international students: Required—TOEFL (minimum score 550 paper-based; 79 iBT). Electronic applications accepted.

University of Notre Dame, The Graduate School, College of Engineering, Notre Dame, IN 46556. Offers M Eng, MEME, MS, MS Aero E, MS Bio E, MS Ch E, MS Env E, MSCE, MSCSE, MSEE, MSME, PhD. Terminal master's awarded for partial completion of doctoral program. *Degree requirements:* For master's, comprehensive exam; for doctorate, thesis/dissertation. *Entrance requirements:* For master's and doctorate, GRE General Test. Additional exam requirements/recommendations for international students: Required—TOEFL. Electronic applications accepted.

University of Ottawa, Faculty of Graduate and Postdoctoral Studies, Faculty of Engineering, Ottawa, ON K1N 6N5, Canada. Offers M Eng, MA Sc, MCS, PhD, Certificate. *Degree requirements:* For master's, thesis or alternative; for doctorate, thesis/dissertation. *Entrance requirements:* For master's, honors degree or equivalent, minimum B average. Electronic applications accepted.

University of Pennsylvania, School of Engineering and Applied Science, Philadelphia, PA 19104. Offers MBT, MCIT, MIPD, MSE, PhD, MSE/MBA, PhD/MD, VMD/PhD. *Program availability:* Part-time. *Faculty:* 124 full-time (22 women), 27 part-time/adjunct (4 women). *Students:* 1,283 full-time (420 women), 407 part-time (131 women); includes 234 minority (15 Black or African American, non-Hispanic/Latino; 1 American Indian or Alaska Native, non-Hispanic/Latino; 141 Asian, non-Hispanic/Latino; 45 Hispanic/Latino; 32 Two or more races, non-Hispanic/Latino), 1,048 international. Average age 25. 9,042 applicants, 20% accepted, 928 enrolled. In 2018, 647 master's, 73 doctorates awarded. Terminal master's awarded for partial completion of doctoral program. *Degree requirements:* For master's, comprehensive exam, thesis optional; for doctorate, comprehensive exam, thesis/dissertation. *Entrance requirements:* For master's and doctorate, GRE, bachelor's degree, letters of recommendation, resume, personal statement. Additional exam requirements/recommendations for international students: Required—TOEFL (minimum score 100 iBT), IELTS (minimum score 7). *Application deadline:* For fall admission, 12/15 for domestic and international students. Application fee: $80. Electronic applications accepted. *Expenses:* Contact institution. *Application contact:* William Fenton, Assistant Director of Graduate Admissions, 215-898-4542, Fax: 215-573-5577, E-mail: gradstudies@seas.upenn.edu.
Website: http://www.seas.upenn.edu

See Display on the next page and Close-Up on page 75.

University of Pittsburgh, Katz Graduate School of Business, MBA/Master of Science in Engineering Joint Degree Program, Pittsburgh, PA 15260. Offers MBA/MSE. *Accreditation:* AACSB. *Program availability:* Part-time, evening/weekend. *Entrance requirements:* Additional exam requirements/recommendations for international students: Required—TOEFL (minimum score 100 iBT) or IELTS (minimum score 7.0). Electronic applications accepted. *Faculty research:* Accounting systems/financial reporting, corporate finance, shopper marketing/consumer behavior, management information systems, organizational behavior and entrepreneurship.

University of Pittsburgh, Swanson School of Engineering, Pittsburgh, PA 15260. Offers MS, MS Ch E, MSBENG, MSCEE, MSIE, MSME, MSNE, MSPE, PhD, MD/PhD, MS Ch E/MSPE. *Program availability:* Part-time. Terminal master's awarded for partial completion of doctoral program. *Degree requirements:* For doctorate, comprehensive exam, thesis/dissertation, final oral exams. *Entrance requirements:* For master's and doctorate, minimum GPA of 3.0. Additional exam requirements/recommendations for international students: Required—TOEFL (minimum score 550 paper-based; 80 iBT). Electronic applications accepted. *Expenses:* Contact institution. *Faculty research:* Artificial organs, biotechnology, signal processing, construction management, fluid dynamics.

University of Portland, Shiley School of Engineering, Portland, OR 97203-5798. Offers biomedical engineering (MBME); civil engineering (ME); computer science (ME); electrical engineering (ME); mechanical engineering (ME). *Program availability:* Part-time, evening/weekend. *Students:* 12 full-time (4 women), 2 part-time (both women); includes 1 minority (Black or African American, non-Hispanic/Latino), 2 international. Average age 24. 43 applicants, 49% accepted, 10 enrolled. In 2018, 6 master's awarded. *Degree requirements:* For master's, thesis optional. *Entrance requirements:* For master's, GRE General Test, minimum GPA of 3.0, 2 letters of recommendation, resume, statement of goals, official transcripts. Additional exam requirements/recommendations for international students: Required—TOEFL (minimum score 80 iBT), IELTS (minimum score 7). *Application deadline:* For fall admission, 7/15 priority date for domestic and international students; for spring admission, 12/15 priority date for domestic and international students; for summer admission, 4/15 for domestic and international students. Applications are processed on a rolling basis. Electronic applications accepted. *Expenses:* $1,326 per credit plus $50 professional tuition per credit. *Financial support:* Research assistantships, career-related internships or fieldwork, Federal Work-Study, and scholarships/grants available. Support available to part-time students. Financial award application deadline: 3/1; financial award applicants required to submit FAFSA. *Unit head:* Dr. Matthew Kuhn, Dean, 503-943-7361, E-mail: kuhn@up.edu. *Application contact:* Caitlin Biddulph, Graduate Programs and Admissions Specialist, 503-943-7107.
Website: http://engineering.up.edu/default.aspx?cid-6464&pid-2432

University of Puerto Rico–Mayagüez, Graduate Studies, College of Engineering, Mayagüez, PR 00681-9000. Offers ME, MS, PhD. *Program availability:* Part-time. *Degree requirements:* For master's, one foreign language, comprehensive exam, thesis. Electronic applications accepted. *Faculty research:* Structural dynamics, plastic materials, fluid mechanics, computer graphics, computer programming.

University of Regina, Faculty of Graduate Studies and Research, Faculty of Engineering and Applied Science, Regina, SK S4S 0A2, Canada. Offers electronic systems engineering (M Eng, MA Sc, PhD), including electronic systems; environmental systems engineering (M Eng, MA Sc, PhD), including environmental systems; industrial systems engineering (M Eng, MA Sc, PhD), including industrial systems; petroleum systems engineering (M Eng, MA Sc, PhD), including petroleum systems; process systems

engineering (M Eng, MA Sc, PhD), including process systems; software systems engineering (M Eng, MA Sc, PhD), including software systems. *Program availability:* Part-time. *Faculty:* 44 full-time (6 women), 26 part-time/adjunct (2 women). *Students:* 255 full-time (69 women), 32 part-time (7 women). Average age 30. 154 applicants, 33% accepted. In 2018, 88 master's, 14 doctorates awarded. *Degree requirements:* For master's, thesis, project, report; for doctorate, comprehensive exam, thesis/dissertation. *Entrance requirements:* Additional exam requirements/recommendations for international students: Required—TOEFL (minimum score 550 paper-based; 80 iBT), IELTS (minimum score 6.5), PTE (minimum score 59). *Application deadline:* For fall admission, 3/31 for domestic and international students; for winter admission, 7/31 for domestic and international students; for spring admission, 11/30 for domestic and international students. Application fee: $100. Electronic applications accepted. *Expenses:* 16,000.00. *Financial support:* In 2018–19, 24 fellowships (averaging $6,000 per year), 70 teaching assistantships (averaging $2,562 per year) were awarded; research assistantships, career-related internships or fieldwork, scholarships/grants, and unspecified assistantships also available. Financial award application deadline: 6/15. *Faculty research:* Curriculum and instruction, educational administration, educational psychology, adult education, or human resource development. *Unit head:* Dr. Amr Henni, Acting Dean, 306-585-4960, Fax: 306-585-4556, E-mail: Amr.Henni@uregina.ca. *Application contact:* Colleen Walsh, Graduate and Co-operative Education Coordinator, 306-585-5416, Fax: 306-585-4556, E-mail: colleen.walsh@uregina.ca.
Website: http://www.uregina.ca/engineering/

University of Rhode Island, Graduate School, College of Engineering, Kingston, RI 02881. Offers MS, PhD, Graduate Certificate, Postbaccalaureate Certificate. *Program availability:* Part-time. *Faculty:* 72 full-time (14 women), 1 part-time/adjunct (0 women). *Students:* 137 full-time (35 women), 88 part-time (13 women); includes 26 minority (6 Black or African American, non-Hispanic/Latino; 1 American Indian or Alaska Native, non-Hispanic/Latino; 9 Asian, non-Hispanic/Latino; 9 Hispanic/Latino; 1 Two or more races, non-Hispanic/Latino; 78 international. 170 applicants, 68% accepted, 67 enrolled. In 2018, 49 master's, 16 doctorates, 1 other advanced degree awarded. *Entrance requirements:* Additional exam requirements/recommendations for international students: Required—TOEFL. Application fee: $65. Electronic applications accepted. *Expenses: Tuition, area resident:* Full-time $13,226; part-time $735 per credit. Tuition, state resident: full-time $13,226; part-time $735 per credit. Tuition, nonresident: full-time $25,854; part-time $1436 per credit. *International tuition:* $25,854 full-time. *Required fees:* $1698; $50 per credit. $35 per semester. One-time fee: $165. *Financial support:* In 2018–19, 50 research assistantships with full tuition reimbursements (averaging $10,164 per year), 30 teaching assistantships with full tuition reimbursements (averaging $9,283 per year) were awarded. Financial award applicants required to submit FAFSA. *Unit head:* Dr. Raymond Wright, Dean, 401-874-2186, Fax: 401-782-1066, E-mail: dean@egr.uri.edu. *Application contact:* Dr. Raymond Wright, Dean, 401-874-2186, Fax: 401-782-1066, E-mail: dean@egr.uri.edu.
Website: http://www.egr.uri.edu/

University of Rochester, Hajim School of Engineering and Applied Sciences, Rochester, NY 14627. Offers MS, PhD. *Faculty:* 97 full-time (13 women). *Students:* 630 full-time (159 women), 21 part-time (4 women); includes 73 minority (18 Black or African American, non-Hispanic/Latino; 1 American Indian or Alaska Native, non-Hispanic/Latino; 29 Asian, non-Hispanic/Latino; 18 Hispanic/Latino; 7 Two or more races, non-Hispanic/Latino; 411 international. Average age 26. 2,490 applicants, 40% accepted, 245 enrolled. In 2018, 167 master's, 49 doctorates awarded. Terminal master's awarded for partial completion of doctoral program. *Degree requirements:* For master's, comprehensive exam (for some programs), thesis (for some programs); for doctorate, comprehensive exam (for some programs), thesis/dissertation. *Entrance requirements:* For master's, personal statement, three letters of recommendation, transcripts; for doctorate, GRE, personal statement, three letters of recommendation, transcripts. Additional exam requirements/recommendations for international students: Required—TOEFL. Application fee: $60. Electronic applications accepted. *Expenses:* Contact institution. *Financial support:* Fellowships, research assistantships, teaching assistantships, career-related internships or fieldwork, scholarships/grants, traineeships, health care benefits, tuition waivers, and unspecified assistantships available. Support available to part-time students. *Total annual research expenditures:* $31.5 million. *Unit head:* Dr. Wendi Heinzelman, Dean, Hajim School of Engineering and Applied Sciences/ Professor of Electrical and Computer Engineering, 585-273-3958, E-mail: wendi.heinzelman@rochester.edu. *Application contact:* Gretchen Briscoe, Director of Graduate Enrollment, 585-275-2059, E-mail: gretchen.briscoe@rochester.edu.
Website: https://www.hajim.rochester.edu/

University of St. Thomas, School of Engineering, St. Paul, MN 55105. Offers data science (MS); electrical engineering (MS); information technology (MS); manufacturing engineering (MS); manufacturing systems (Certificate); mechanical engineering (MS); medical device development (Certificate); regulatory science (MS); software engineering (MS); software management (MS); systems engineering (MS); technology leadership (Certificate); technology management (MS). *Program availability:* Part-time, evening/ weekend. *Entrance requirements:* For master's, resume, official transcripts. Additional exam requirements/recommendations for international students: Required—TOEFL (minimum score 80 iBT), IELTS (minimum score 6.5). Electronic applications accepted. *Expenses:* Contact institution.

University of Saskatchewan, College of Graduate and Postdoctoral Studies, College of Engineering, Saskatoon, SK S7N 5E5, Canada. Offers M Eng, M Sc, PhD, PGD. *Program availability:* Part-time. *Degree requirements:* For master's, 30 credits (for M Eng); thesis and 12 credits (for MS); for doctorate, comprehensive exam, thesis/ dissertation, qualifying exam, 18 credits. *Entrance requirements:* For master's and doctorate, GRE. Additional exam requirements/recommendations for international students: Required—TOEFL (minimum iBT score of 80), IELTS (6.5), CanTEST (4.5), or PTE (59). Electronic applications accepted.

University of South Africa, College of Science, Engineering and Technology, Pretoria, South Africa. Offers chemical engineering (M Tech); information technology (M Tech).

University of South Alabama, College of Engineering, Mobile, AL 36688. Offers MS Ch E, MSCE, MSEE, MSME, D Sc. *Program availability:* Part-time. *Degree requirements:* For master's, comprehensive exam, project or thesis; for doctorate, comprehensive exam, thesis/dissertation. *Entrance requirements:* For master's, GRE General Test, BS in engineering, minimum GPA of 3.0; for doctorate, GRE, MS in engineering, minimum graduate GPA of 3.0. Additional exam requirements/ recommendations for international students: Required—TOEFL (minimum score 550 paper-based; 79 iBT). Electronic applications accepted. *Expenses:* Contact institution.

University of South Carolina, The Graduate School, College of Engineering and Computing, Columbia, SC 29208. Offers ME, MS, PhD. *Program availability:* Part-time, evening/weekend, online learning. *Degree requirements:* For master's, thesis (for some programs); for doctorate, thesis/dissertation. *Entrance requirements:* For master's and doctorate, GRE General Test. Additional exam requirements/recommendations for international students: Required—TOEFL. Electronic applications accepted. *Faculty research:* Electrochemical engineering/fuel cell technology, fracture mechanics and nondestructive evaluation, virtual prototyping for electric power systems, wideband-gap electronics materials behavior/composites and smart materials.

University of Southern California, Graduate School, Viterbi School of Engineering, Los Angeles, CA 90089. Offers MCM, ME, MS, PhD, Engr, Graduate Certificate, MS/MBA. *Program availability:* Part-time, online learning. Terminal master's awarded for partial completion of doctoral program. *Degree requirements:* For doctorate, comprehensive exam, thesis/dissertation. *Entrance requirements:* For master's and doctorate, GRE. Additional exam requirements/recommendations for international students: Recommended—TOEFL. Electronic applications accepted. *Expenses:* Contact institution. *Faculty research:* Mechanics and materials, aerodynamics of air/ground vehicles, gas dynamics, aerosols, astronautics and space science, geophysical and microgravity flows, planetary physics, power MEMs and MEMS vacuum pumps, heat transfer and combustion, health systems, transportation and logistics, manufacturing and automation, engineering systems design, risk and economic analysis, electromagnetic devices circuits and VLSI, MEMS and nanotechnology, electromagnetics and plasmas.

University of Southern Indiana, Graduate Studies, Pott College of Science, Engineering, and Education, Evansville, IN 47712-3590. Offers MSE, MSIM, MSSM, Ed D. *Program availability:* Part-time, evening/weekend. *Degree requirements:* For master's, project. *Entrance requirements:* For master's, GRE General Test, NTE, PRAXIS I, minimum GPA of 2.5 and BS in engineering or engineering technology (MSIM); minimum GPA of 3.0 and teaching license (MSE). Additional exam requirements/recommendations for international students: Required—TOEFL (minimum score 550 paper-based; 79 iBT), IELTS (minimum score 6). Electronic applications accepted.

University of South Florida, College of Engineering, Tampa, FL 33620-9951. Offers MCE, MEVE, MSBE, MSCE, MSCH, MSCP, MSCS, MSEE, MSEM, MSEV, MSIE, MSIT, MSME, MSMSE, PhD, Graduate Certificate, MSBE/MS. *Program availability:* Part-time, evening/weekend. *Faculty:* 136 full-time (22 women), 1 part-time/adjunct (0 women). *Students:* 879 full-time (221 women), 302 part-time (66 women); includes 141 minority (35 Black or African American, non-Hispanic/Latino; 27 Asian, non-Hispanic/Latino; 69 Hispanic/Latino; 10 Two or more races, non-Hispanic/Latino), 832 international. Average age 27. 1,773 applicants, 50% accepted, 311 enrolled. In 2018, 450 master's, 62 doctorates awarded. Terminal master's awarded for partial completion of doctoral program. *Degree requirements:* For master's, comprehensive exam, thesis (for some programs); for doctorate, comprehensive exam, thesis/dissertation. *Entrance requirements:* For master's, GRE General Test, minimum GPA of 3.0 in last 60 hours of coursework; for doctorate, GRE General Test, minimum GPA of 3.3 in last 60 hours of coursework. Additional exam requirements/recommendations for international students: Required—TOEFL (minimum score 550 paper-based; 79 iBT), IELTS (minimum score 6.5). *Application deadline:* For fall admission, 2/15 for domestic students, 1/2 priority date for international students; for spring admission, 10/15 for domestic students, 6/1 priority date for international students. Applications are processed on a rolling basis. Application fee: $30. Electronic applications accepted. *Expenses:* Tuition, state resident: full-time $6350. Tuition, nonresident: full-time $19,048. International tuition: $19,048 full-time. Required fees: $2079. *Financial support:* In 2018–19, 169 students received support. Career-related internships or fieldwork, Federal Work-Study, scholarships/grants, health care benefits, and unspecified assistantships available. Financial award application deadline: 3/1. *Faculty research:* Biomedical engineering and sustainability, particularly in water resources and energy; electrical engineering; civil/environmental engineering; industrial/management systems engineering; chemical engineering; computer science and engineering; mechanical engineering. *Total annual research expenditures:* $14.8 million. *Unit head:* Dr. Robert Bishop, Dean, 813-974-3864, Fax: 813-974-5094, E-mail: robertbishop@usf.edu. *Application contact:* Dr. Sanjukta Bhanja, Associate Dean for Academic Affairs, 813-974-4755, Fax: 813-974-5094, E-mail: bhanja@usf.edu.
Website: http://www2.eng.usf.edu/

The University of Tennessee, Graduate School, Tickle College of Engineering, Knoxville, TN 37996. Offers MS, PhD, MS/MBA, MS/PhD. *Program availability:* Part-time, online learning. *Faculty:* 222 full-time (28 women), 24 part-time/adjunct (4 women). *Students:* 847 full-time (192 women), 264 part-time (51 women); includes 120 minority (26 Black or African American, non-Hispanic/Latino; 1 American Indian or Alaska Native, non-Hispanic/Latino; 42 Asian, non-Hispanic/Latino; 37 Hispanic/Latino; 1 Native Hawaiian or other Pacific Islander, non-Hispanic/Latino; 13 Two or more races, non-Hispanic/Latino), 388 international. Average age 28. 1,139 applicants, 50% accepted, 272 enrolled. In 2018, 234 master's, 116 doctorates awarded. *Degree requirements:* For master's, thesis or alternative; for doctorate, comprehensive exam, thesis/dissertation. *Entrance requirements:* For master's, GRE General Test (for MS students pursuing research thesis), minimum GPA of 2.7 (for U.S. degree holders), 3.0 (for international degree holders); 3 references; statement of purpose; for doctorate, GRE General Test, minimum GPA of 3.0 on previous graduate course work; 3 references; statement of purpose. Additional exam requirements/recommendations for international students: Required—TOEFL (minimum score 550 paper-based; 80 iBT), IELTS (minimum score 6.5). *Application deadline:* For fall admission, 2/1 priority date for domestic and international students; for spring admission, 6/15 for domestic and international students; for summer admission, 10/15 for domestic and international students. Applications are processed on a rolling basis. Application fee: $60. Electronic applications accepted. *Expenses:* Contact institution. *Financial support:* In 2018–19, 949 students received support, including 176 fellowships with full tuition reimbursements available (averaging $18,134 per year), 561 research assistantships with full tuition reimbursements available (averaging $23,396 per year), 212 teaching assistantships with full tuition reimbursements available (averaging $19,998 per year); career-related internships or fieldwork, Federal Work-Study, institutionally sponsored loans, health care benefits, and unspecified assistantships also available. Financial award application deadline: 2/1; financial award applicants required to submit FAFSA. *Faculty research:* Chemical and biomolecular engineering; civil and environmental engineering; electrical engineering and computer science; nuclear engineering; materials science and engineering; mechanical, aerospace, and biomedical engineering; industrial and information engineering. *Total annual research expenditures:* $73.9 million. *Unit head:* Dr. Janis P. Terpenny, Dean, 865-974-5321, Fax: 865-974-8890, E-mail: terpenny@utk.edu. *Application contact:* Dr. Ozlem Kilic, Associate Dean of Student Affairs, 865-974-2454, Fax: 865-974-9871, E-mail: okilic@utk.edu.
Website: http://www.engr.utk.edu/

The University of Texas at Arlington, Graduate School, College of Engineering, Arlington, TX 76019. Offers M Engr, MCM, MS, PhD. *Program availability:* Part-time, evening/weekend, online learning. Terminal master's awarded for partial completion of doctoral program. *Degree requirements:* For master's, thesis optional; for doctorate, thesis/dissertation. *Entrance requirements:* For master's, GRE General Test, minimum GPA of 3.0 in last 60 hours of coursework; for doctorate, GRE General Test. Additional exam requirements/recommendations for international students: Required—TOEFL (minimum score 550 paper-based). *Faculty research:* Nanotechnology, mobile pervasive computing, bioinformatics intelligent systems.

The University of Texas at Austin, Graduate School, Cockrell School of Engineering, Austin, TX 78712-1111. Offers MA, MS, MSE, PhD, MBA/MSE, MD/PhD, MP Aff/MSE. *Program availability:* Part-time, evening/weekend. *Entrance requirements:* For master's and doctorate, GRE General Test. Additional exam requirements/recommendations for international students: Required—TOEFL (minimum score 550 paper-based). Electronic applications accepted.

The University of Texas at Dallas, Erik Jonsson School of Engineering and Computer Science, Richardson, TX 75080. Offers MS, MSCS, MSEE, MSTE, PhD. *Program availability:* Part-time, evening/weekend. *Faculty:* 151 full-time (16 women), 40 part-time/adjunct (7 women). *Students:* 1,726 full-time (487 women), 530 part-time (142 women); includes 177 minority (18 Black or African American, non-Hispanic/Latino; 96 Asian, non-Hispanic/Latino; 49 Hispanic/Latino; 14 Two or more races, non-Hispanic/Latino), 1,851 international. Average age 27. 5,913 applicants, 40% accepted, 709 enrolled. In 2018, 825 master's, 89 doctorates awarded. *Degree requirements:* For master's, thesis optional; for doctorate, thesis/dissertation. *Entrance requirements:* For master's, GRE General Test, minimum GPA of 3.0 in related bachelor's course work; for doctorate, GRE General Test, minimum GPA of 3.5. Additional exam requirements/recommendations for international students: Required—TOEFL (minimum score 550 paper-based). *Application deadline:* For fall admission, 7/15 for domestic students, 5/1 priority date for international students; for spring admission, 11/15 for domestic students, 9/1 priority date for international students. Applications are processed on a rolling basis. Application fee: $50 ($100 for international students). Electronic applications accepted. *Expenses:* Tuition, area resident: Full-time $13,458. Tuition, state resident: full-time $13,458. Tuition, nonresident: full-time $26,852. International tuition: $26,852 full-time. Tuition and fees vary according to course load. *Financial support:* In 2018–19, 494 students received support, including 34 fellowships (averaging $3,054 per year), 382 research assistantships with partial tuition reimbursements available (averaging $24,085 per year), 186 teaching assistantships with partial tuition reimbursements available (averaging $17,393 per year); career-related internships or fieldwork, Federal Work-Study, institutionally sponsored loans, scholarships/grants, and unspecified assistantships also available. Support available to part-time students. Financial award application deadline: 4/30; financial award applicants required to submit FAFSA. *Faculty research:* Semiconducting materials, nano-fabrication and bio-nanotechnology, biomedical devices and organic electronics, signal processing and language technology, cloud computing and IT security. *Total annual research expenditures:* $34.5 million. *Unit head:* Dr. Stephanie G Adams, Dean, 972-883-2557, Fax: 972-883-2813. *Application contact:* Leiane Davis, Administrative Associate, 972-883-6851, Fax: 972-883-2813, E-mail: leiane.davis@utdallas.edu.
Website: http://engineering.utdallas.edu/

The University of Texas at El Paso, Graduate School, College of Engineering, El Paso, TX 79968-0001. Offers M Eng, MEENE, MS, MSENE, MSIT, PhD, Certificate, Graduate Certificate. *Program availability:* Part-time, evening/weekend. *Degree requirements:* For master's, thesis optional; for doctorate, thesis/dissertation. *Entrance requirements:* For master's, GRE, minimum GPA of 3.0, letters of reference; for doctorate, GRE, statement of purpose, letters of reference. Additional exam requirements/recommendations for international students: Required—TOEFL; Recommended—IELTS. Electronic applications accepted. *Expenses:* Contact institution.

The University of Texas at San Antonio, College of Engineering, San Antonio, TX 78249-0617. Offers MCE, MS, MSCE, MSEE, PhD. *Program availability:* Part-time, evening/weekend. Terminal master's awarded for partial completion of doctoral program. *Degree requirements:* For master's, variable foreign language requirement, comprehensive exam, thesis optional, completion of all course work requirements within six-year time limit; no courses with grade of less than C; minimum GPA of 3.0; for doctorate, variable foreign language requirement, comprehensive exam, thesis/dissertation, continuous enrollment until time of graduation; all completed coursework included in the final program of study must have been taken within the preceding eight years to include successful completion and defense of the dissertation. *Entrance requirements:* For master's, GRE, baccalaureate degree in related field from regionally-accredited college or university in the U.S. or proof of equivalent training at foreign institution; minimum GPA of 3.0 in last 60 semester credit hours or foreign institution equivalent of coursework taken; for doctorate, GRE, baccalaureate degree or MS in related field from regionally-accredited college or university in the U.S. or proof of equivalent training at foreign institution; minimum GPA of 3.0, 3.3 in upper-division/graduate courses. Additional exam requirements/recommendations for international students: Required—TOEFL (minimum score 550 paper-based; 79 iBT), IELTS (minimum score 6.5). Electronic applications accepted. *Expenses:* Contact institution. *Faculty research:* Biomedical engineering, civil and environmental science engineering, electrical and computer engineering, advanced materials engineering, mechanical engineering.

University of the District of Columbia, School of Engineering and Applied Sciences, Washington, DC 20008-1175. Offers MSCS, MSEE.

University of the Pacific, School of Engineering and Computer Science, Stockton, CA 95211-0197. Offers engineering science (MS). *Entrance requirements:* For master's, GRE, three references; official transcripts; personal statement; bachelor's degree in engineering, computer science, or a closely related discipline. Additional exam requirements/recommendations for international students: Required—TOEFL. Electronic applications accepted.

The University of Toledo, College of Graduate Studies, College of Engineering, Program in Engineering, Toledo, OH 43606-3390. Offers general engineering (MS). *Entrance requirements:* For master's, GRE General Test, minimum GPA of 2.7, industrial experience.

University of Toronto, School of Graduate Studies, Faculty of Applied Science and Engineering, Toronto, ON M5S 1A1, Canada. Offers M Eng, MA Sc, MH Sc, PhD. *Program availability:* Part-time. *Degree requirements:* For doctorate, thesis/dissertation. *Expenses:* Contact institution.

The University of Tulsa, Graduate School, College of Engineering and Natural Sciences, Tulsa, OK 74104-3189. Offers ME, MS, MSE, MTA, PhD, JD/MS, MBA/MS, MSF/MSAM. *Program availability:* Part-time. *Faculty:* 102 full-time (11 women), 2 part-time/adjunct (1 woman). *Students:* 210 full-time (46 women), 96 part-time (23 women); includes 29 minority (6 Black or African American, non-Hispanic/Latino; 7 American Indian or Alaska Native, non-Hispanic/Latino; 2 Asian, non-Hispanic/Latino; 8 Hispanic/Latino; 6 Two or more races, non-Hispanic/Latino), 151 international. Average age 28. 563 applicants, 40% accepted, 71 enrolled. In 2018, 92 master's, 22 doctorates awarded. Terminal master's awarded for partial completion of doctoral program. *Degree requirements:* For master's, thesis (for some programs); for doctorate, comprehensive exam, thesis/dissertation. *Entrance requirements:* For master's and doctorate, GRE General Test. Additional exam requirements/recommendations for international students: Required—TOEFL (minimum score 550 paper-based), IELTS (minimum score 6). *Application deadline:* Applications are processed on a rolling basis. Application fee: $55. Electronic applications accepted. *Expenses:* Tuition: Full-time $22,230; part-time $1235 per credit hour. Required fees: $2100; $6 per credit hour. One-time fee: $400 full-time. Tuition and fees vary according to course level, course load and program. *Financial support:* Fellowships with full tuition reimbursements, research assistantships with full tuition reimbursements, teaching assistantships with full tuition reimbursements,

career-related internships or fieldwork, Federal Work-Study, scholarships/grants, health care benefits, tuition waivers (full and partial), and unspecified assistantships available. Support available to part-time students. Financial award application deadline: 2/1; financial award applicants required to submit FAFSA. *Unit head:* Dr. James Sorem, Dean, 918-631-2288, E-mail: james-sorem@utulsa.edu. *Application contact:* Graduate School, 918-631-2336, Fax: 918-631-2156, E-mail: grad@utulsa.edu.
Website: http://engineering.utulsa.edu/

University of Utah, Graduate School, College of Engineering, Salt Lake City, UT 84112. Offers ME, MEAE, MS, PhD, MS/MBA. *Faculty:* 177 full-time (28 women), 90 part-time/adjunct (13 women). *Students:* 966 full-time (214 women), 301 part-time (47 women); includes 135 minority (12 Black or African American, non-Hispanic/Latino; 59 Asian, non-Hispanic/Latino; 40 Hispanic/Latino; 1 Native Hawaiian or other Pacific Islander, non-Hispanic/Latino; 23 Two or more races, non-Hispanic/Latino), 528 international. Average age 28. In 2018, 332 master's, 88 doctorates awarded. *Degree requirements:* For master's, comprehensive exam (for some programs), thesis (for some programs); for doctorate, comprehensive exam (for some programs), thesis/dissertation (for some programs). *Entrance requirements:* For master's and doctorate, minimum GPA of 3.0. Additional exam requirements/recommendations for international students: Required—TOEFL. Electronic applications accepted. *Expenses:* Contact institution. *Financial support:* Research assistantships with tuition reimbursements, career-related internships or fieldwork, Federal Work-Study, institutionally sponsored loans, scholarships/grants, and unspecified assistantships available. Financial award application deadline: 2/1; financial award applicants required to submit FAFSA. *Faculty research:* Surface analysis, energy and fuels, transportation, solid mechanics, environmental sustainability. *Unit head:* Dr. Richard B. Brown, Dean, 801-585-7498, E-mail: brown@utah.edu. *Application contact:* Jeff Bates, Assistant Professor, 801-581-8737, E-mail: jeff.bates@utah.edu.
Website: http://www.coe.utah.edu/

University of Vermont, Graduate College, College of Engineering and Mathematical Sciences, Burlington, VT 05405-0156. Offers MS, MST, PhD. *Program availability:* Part-time. *Degree requirements:* For master's, thesis (for some programs); for doctorate, thesis/dissertation. *Entrance requirements:* Additional exam requirements/recommendations for international students: Required—TOEFL (minimum score 550 paper-based; 90 iBT), IELTS (minimum score 6.5). Electronic applications accepted.

University of Victoria, Faculty of Graduate Studies, Faculty of Engineering, Victoria, BC V8W 2Y2, Canada. Offers M Eng, M Sc, MA Sc, PhD.

University of Virginia, School of Engineering and Applied Science, Charlottesville, VA 22903. Offers MCS, ME, MEP, MMSE, MS, PhD, ME/MBA. *Program availability:* Part-time, online learning. Terminal master's awarded for partial completion of doctoral program. *Degree requirements:* For doctorate, comprehensive exam, thesis/dissertation. *Entrance requirements:* For master's, GRE General Test, 3 letters of recommendation; for doctorate, GRE General Test, 3 letters of recommendation, essay. Additional exam requirements/recommendations for international students: Required—TOEFL (minimum score 600 paper-based; 90 iBT), IELTS (minimum score 7). Electronic applications accepted. *Expenses:* Contact institution.

University of Washington, Graduate School, College of Engineering, Seattle, WA 98195-2180. Offers MAB, MAE, MISE, MS, MSAA, MSCE, MSE, MSME, PhD, Certificate. *Program availability:* Part-time, online learning. *Faculty:* 264 full-time (64 women). *Students:* 1,679 full-time (535 women), 989 part-time (298 women); includes 575 minority (39 Black or African American, non-Hispanic/Latino; 5 American Indian or Alaska Native, non-Hispanic/Latino; 323 Asian, non-Hispanic/Latino; 121 Hispanic/Latino; 3 Native Hawaiian or other Pacific Islander, non-Hispanic/Latino; 84 Two or more races, non-Hispanic/Latino), 996 international. Average age 27. 7,345 applicants, 32% accepted, 838 enrolled. In 2018, 736 master's, 112 doctorates awarded. Terminal master's awarded for partial completion of doctoral program. *Degree requirements:* For master's, comprehensive exam (for some programs), thesis (for some programs); for doctorate, comprehensive exam, thesis/dissertation. *Entrance requirements:* Additional exam requirements/recommendations for international students: Required—TOEFL. *Application deadline:* For fall admission, 12/1 for domestic and international students. Application fee: $85. Electronic applications accepted. *Expenses:* Research-focused Master's and PhD: $18,852 resident, $32,760 nonresident. Applied/Professional Master's degrees have a range of rates. *Financial support:* In 2018–19, 1,126 students received support, including 130 fellowships with full tuition reimbursements available (averaging $33,722 per year), 727 research assistantships with full tuition reimbursements available (averaging $33,722 per year), 312 teaching assistantships with full tuition reimbursements available (averaging $33,722 per year); career-related internships or fieldwork, Federal Work-Study, institutionally sponsored loans, scholarships/grants, traineeships, health care benefits, tuition waivers (full), unspecified assistantships, and stipend supplements also available. Financial award application deadline: 2/28; financial award applicants required to submit FAFSA. *Total annual research expenditures:* $153.4 million. *Unit head:* Dr. Greg Miller, Interim Dean of Engineering, 206-543-1829, Fax: 206-685-0666, E-mail: gmiller@uw.edu. *Application contact:* Mike Engh, Assistant Director, Academic Affairs, 206-685-3714, Fax: 206-685-0666, E-mail: enghmw@uw.edu.
Website: http://www.engr.washington.edu/

University of Waterloo, Graduate Studies and Postdoctoral Affairs, Faculty of Engineering, Waterloo, ON N2L 3G1, Canada. Offers M Arch, M Eng, MA Sc, MBET, MMS, PhD. *Program availability:* Part-time, evening/weekend, online learning. *Degree requirements:* For master's, research paper or thesis; for doctorate, comprehensive exam, thesis/dissertation. *Entrance requirements:* For master's, honors degree; for doctorate, master's degree, minimum A- average. Additional exam requirements/recommendations for international students: Required—TOEFL, IELTS, PTE. *Application deadline:* Applications are processed on a rolling basis. Application fee: $125 Canadian dollars. Electronic applications accepted. *Financial support:* Fellowships, research assistantships, teaching assistantships, career-related internships or fieldwork, Federal Work-Study, and institutionally sponsored loans available.
Website: https://uwaterloo.ca/engineering/

The University of Western Ontario, School of Graduate and Postdoctoral Studies, Physical Sciences Division, Faculty of Engineering, London, ON N6A 3K7, Canada. Offers chemical and biochemical engineering (ME Sc, PhD); civil and environmental engineering (M Eng, ME Sc, PhD); electrical and computer engineering (M Eng, ME Sc, PhD); mechanical and materials engineering (M Eng, ME Sc, PhD). *Program availability:* Part-time. Terminal master's awarded for partial completion of doctoral program. *Degree requirements:* For master's, thesis; for doctorate, thesis/dissertation. *Entrance requirements:* For master's, minimum B average; for doctorate, minimum B+ average. *Faculty research:* Wind, geotechnical, chemical reactor engineering, applied electrostatics, biochemical engineering.

University of Windsor, Faculty of Graduate Studies, Faculty of Engineering, Windsor, ON N9B 3P4, Canada. Offers M Eng, MA Sc, PhD. *Program availability:* Part-time. *Degree requirements:* For doctorate, comprehensive exam, thesis/dissertation. *Entrance requirements:* For master's, minimum B average; for doctorate, master's degree. Additional exam requirements/recommendations for international students: Required—TOEFL. Electronic applications accepted.

University of Wisconsin–Madison, Graduate School, College of Engineering, Madison, WI 53706-1380. Offers MS, PhD. *Program availability:* Part-time, 100% online, blended/hybrid learning. *Faculty:* 194 full-time (40 women). *Students:* 1,384 full-time (334 women), 460 part-time (102 women); includes 208 minority (31 Black or African American, non-Hispanic/Latino; 1 American Indian or Alaska Native, non-Hispanic/Latino; 77 Asian, non-Hispanic/Latino; 74 Hispanic/Latino; 2 Native Hawaiian or other Pacific Islander, non-Hispanic/Latino; 23 Two or more races, non-Hispanic/Latino), 902 international. Average age 27. 5,591 applicants, 25% accepted, 453 enrolled. In 2018, 416 master's, 157 doctorates awarded. Terminal master's awarded for partial completion of doctoral program. *Degree requirements:* For master's, thesis (for some programs); for doctorate, thesis/dissertation. *Entrance requirements:* For master's and doctorate, GRE. Additional exam requirements/recommendations for international students: Required—TOEFL (minimum score 580 paper-based; 92 iBT), IELTS (minimum score 7). *Application deadline:* Applications are processed on a rolling basis. Application fee: $75 ($81 for international students). Electronic applications accepted. *Financial support:* In 2018–19, 1,199 students received support, including 64 fellowships with full tuition reimbursements available, 765 research assistantships with full tuition reimbursements available, 335 teaching assistantships with full tuition reimbursements available; career-related internships or fieldwork, Federal Work-Study, institutionally sponsored loans, scholarships/grants, health care benefits, and unspecified assistantships also available. Support available to part-time students. Financial award application deadline: 12/1; financial award applicants required to submit FAFSA. *Total annual research expenditures:* $137 million. *Unit head:* Dr. Ian M. Robertson, Dean, 608-262-3482, Fax: 608-262-6400, E-mail: engr-dean_engr@wisc.edu. *Application contact:* Information Contact, 608-262-2433, Fax: 608-265-9505, E-mail: admissions@grad.wisc.edu.
Website: http://www.engr.wisc.edu/

University of Wisconsin–Milwaukee, Graduate School, College of Engineering and Applied Science, Milwaukee, WI 53201. Offers MS, PhD. *Program availability:* Part-time. *Students:* 219 full-time (54 women), 177 part-time (34 women); includes 42 minority (4 Black or African American, non-Hispanic/Latino; 1 American Indian or Alaska Native, non-Hispanic/Latino; 21 Asian, non-Hispanic/Latino; 5 Hispanic/Latino; 11 Two or more races, non-Hispanic/Latino), 243 international. Average age 31. 485 applicants, 54% accepted, 98 enrolled. In 2018, 87 master's, 25 doctorates awarded. *Degree requirements:* For master's, comprehensive exam (for some programs), thesis or alternative; for doctorate, thesis/dissertation, internship. *Entrance requirements:* For master's, GRE, minimum GPA of 2.75; for doctorate, GRE, minimum GPA of 3.5. Additional exam requirements/recommendations for international students: Required—TOEFL (minimum score 550 paper-based; 79 iBT), IELTS (minimum score 6.5). *Application deadline:* For fall admission, 1/1 for domestic students; for spring admission, 9/1 for domestic students. Applications are processed on a rolling basis. Application fee: $56 ($96 for international students). Electronic applications accepted. *Financial support:* Fellowships, research assistantships, teaching assistantships, career-related internships or fieldwork, Federal Work-Study, and unspecified assistantships available. Support available to part-time students. Financial award application deadline: 4/15. *Unit head:* Dr. Brett Peters, Dean, 414-229-4126, E-mail: ceas-deans-office@uwm.edu. *Application contact:* Betty Warras, General Information Contact, 414-229-6169, Fax: 414-229-6958, E-mail: ceas-graduate@uwm.edu.
Website: http://uwm.edu/engineering/

University of Wisconsin–Platteville, School of Graduate Studies, Distance Learning Center, Online Master of Science in Engineering Program, Platteville, WI 53818-3099. Offers MS. *Program availability:* Part-time. *Degree requirements:* For master's, thesis or alternative. *Entrance requirements:* Additional exam requirements/recommendations for international students: Required—TOEFL (minimum score 550 paper-based; 79 iBT), IELTS (minimum score 6.5). Electronic applications accepted. *Expenses:* Contact institution.

University of Wyoming, College of Engineering and Applied Science, Laramie, WY 82071. Offers MS, PhD. *Program availability:* Part-time. *Entrance requirements:* For master's and doctorate, GRE General Test, minimum GPA of 3.0. Additional exam requirements/recommendations for international students: Required—TOEFL. Electronic applications accepted. *Expenses: Tuition, area resident:* Full-time $6504; part-time $271 per credit hour. Tuition, state resident: full-time $6504; part-time $271 per credit hour. Tuition, nonresident: full-time $19,464; part-time $811 per credit hour. *International tuition:* $19,464 full-time. *Required fees:* $1410.94; $343.82 per semester. $343.82 per semester. Tuition and fees vary according to course load, program and reciprocity agreements.

Utah State University, School of Graduate Studies, College of Engineering, Logan, UT 84322. Offers MCS, ME, MS, PhD, CE. *Program availability:* Part-time, evening/weekend. Terminal master's awarded for partial completion of doctoral program. *Degree requirements:* For master's, thesis (for some programs); for doctorate, thesis/dissertation. *Entrance requirements:* For master's and doctorate, GRE General Test, minimum GPA of 3.0. Additional exam requirements/recommendations for international students: Required—TOEFL. Electronic applications accepted. *Faculty research:* Crop-yield modeling, earthquake engineering, digital signal processing, technology and the public school, cryogenic cooling.

Vanderbilt University, School of Engineering, Nashville, TN 37235. Offers M Eng, MS, PhD, MD/PhD. MS and PhD offered through the Graduate School. *Program availability:* Part-time. Terminal master's awarded for partial completion of doctoral program. *Degree requirements:* For master's, comprehensive exam (for some programs), thesis (for some programs); for doctorate, comprehensive exam (for some programs), thesis/dissertation. *Entrance requirements:* For master's and doctorate, GRE General Test. Additional exam requirements/recommendations for international students: Required—TOEFL. Electronic applications accepted. Application fee is waived when completed online. *Expenses: Tuition:* Full-time $47,208; part-time $2026 per credit hour. *Required fees:* $478. *Faculty research:* Robotics, microelectronics, reliability in design, software engineering, medical imaging.

Villanova University, College of Engineering, Villanova, PA 19085-1699. Offers MSCPE, MSChE, MSEE, MSME, MSWREE, PhD, Certificate. *Program availability:* Part-time, evening/weekend, online learning. Terminal master's awarded for partial completion of doctoral program. *Degree requirements:* For master's, thesis optional; for doctorate, thesis/dissertation. *Entrance requirements:* For master's, GRE General Test (for applicants with degrees from foreign universities), minimum GPA of 3.0; for doctorate, GRE General Test. Additional exam requirements/recommendations for international students: Required—TOEFL (minimum score 600 paper-based; 100 iBT). Electronic applications accepted. *Expenses:* Contact institution. *Faculty research:* Composite materials, economy and risk, heat transfer, signal detection.

Virginia Commonwealth University, Graduate School, School of Engineering, Richmond, VA 23284-9005. Offers MS, PhD. *Degree requirements:* For doctorate, thesis/dissertation, comprehensive oral and written exams. *Entrance requirements:* For master's and doctorate, GRE General Test. Additional exam requirements/

recommendations for international students: Required—TOEFL (minimum score 600 paper-based; 100 iBT). Electronic applications accepted. *Faculty research:* Artificial hearts, orthopedic implants, medical imaging, medical instrumentation and sensors, cardiac monitoring.

Virginia Polytechnic Institute and State University, Graduate School, College of Engineering, Blacksburg, VA 24061. Offers aerospace engineering (PhD, M Eng/MS); biological systems engineering (PhD); biomedical engineering (MS, PhD); chemical engineering (PhD); civil engineering (PhD); computer engineering (PhD); computer science and applications (MS); electrical engineering (PhD); engineering education (PhD); M Eng/MS. *Faculty:* 446 full-time (87 women), 7 part-time/adjunct (3 women). *Students:* 1,776 full-time (471 women), 367 part-time (62 women); includes 260 minority (50 Black or African American, non-Hispanic/Latino; 3 American Indian or Alaska Native, non-Hispanic/Latino; 99 Asian, non-Hispanic/Latino; 67 Hispanic/Latino; 41 Two or more races, non-Hispanic/Latino), 1,178 international. Average age 27. 3,798 applicants, 37% accepted, 507 enrolled. In 2018, 489 master's, 200 doctorates awarded. *Degree requirements:* For master's, comprehensive exam (for some programs), thesis (for some programs); for doctorate, comprehensive exam (for some programs), thesis/dissertation (for some programs). *Entrance requirements:* For master's and doctorate, GRE/GMAT. Additional exam requirements/recommendations for international students: Required—TOEFL (minimum score 90 iBT). *Application deadline:* For fall admission, 8/1 for domestic students, 4/1 for international students; for spring admission, 1/1 for domestic students, 9/1 for international students. Applications are processed on a rolling basis. Application fee: $75. Electronic applications accepted. *Expenses:* Tuition, state resident: full-time $15,510; part-time $739.50 per credit hour. Tuition, nonresident: full-time $29,629; part-time $1490.25 per credit hour. *Required fees:* $2804; $550 per semester. Tuition and fees vary according to course load, campus/location and program. *Financial support:* In 2018–19, 37 fellowships with full tuition reimbursements (averaging $24,951 per year), 1,110 research assistantships with full tuition reimbursements (averaging $20,129 per year), 486 teaching assistantships with full tuition reimbursements (averaging $16,192 per year) were awarded; scholarships/grants and unspecified assistantships also available. Financial award application deadline: 3/1; financial award applicants required to submit FAFSA. *Total annual research expenditures:* $96.3 million. *Unit head:* Dr. Julia Ross, Dean, 540-231-9752, Fax: 540-231-3031, E-mail: rjulie@vt.edu. *Application contact:* Linda Perkins, Executive Assistant, 540-231-9752, Fax: 540-231-3031, E-mail: lperkins@vt.edu. Website: http://www.eng.vt.edu/

Washington State University, Voiland College of Engineering and Architecture, Pullman, WA 99164-2714. Offers M Arch, METM, MS, PhD, Certificate. Terminal master's awarded for partial completion of doctoral program. *Degree requirements:* For master's, comprehensive exam (for some programs), thesis (for some programs), oral exam; for doctorate, comprehensive exam, thesis/dissertation, oral exam. *Entrance requirements:* For master's, GRE, minimum GPA of 3.0, 3 letters of recommendation; for doctorate, GRE, minimum GPA of 3.4, 3 letters of recommendation. Additional exam requirements/recommendations for international students: Required—TOEFL (minimum score 520 paper-based).

Washington University in St. Louis, School of Engineering and Applied Science, Saint Louis, MO 63130-4899. Offers M Eng, MCE, MCM, MEM, MIM, MPM, MS, MSEE, MSEE, MSI, D Sc, PhD. *Program availability:* Part-time, evening/weekend. Terminal master's awarded for partial completion of doctoral program. *Degree requirements:* For master's, comprehensive exam (for some programs), thesis (for some programs); for doctorate, comprehensive exam, thesis/dissertation. *Entrance requirements:* For master's and doctorate, GRE. Additional exam requirements/recommendations for international students: Required—TOEFL (minimum score 550 paper-based; 90 iBT), IELTS (minimum score 6.5) or TWE. Electronic applications accepted.

Wayne State University, College of Engineering, Detroit, MI 48202. Offers MS, MSET, PhD, Certificate, Graduate Certificate, Postbaccalaureate Certificate. *Program availability:* Part-time, evening/weekend. *Faculty:* 110. *Students:* 741 full-time (196 women), 390 part-time (99 women); includes 139 minority (49 Black or African American, non-Hispanic/Latino; 65 Asian, non-Hispanic/Latino; 21 Hispanic/Latino; 4 Two or more races, non-Hispanic/Latino), 655 international. Average age 28. 1,916 applicants, 40% accepted, 289 enrolled. In 2018, 584 master's, 47 doctorates, 1 other advanced degree awarded. Terminal master's awarded for partial completion of doctoral program. *Degree requirements:* For master's, thesis (for some programs), project (engineering management and engineering technology); for doctorate, thesis/dissertation. *Entrance requirements:* For master's, minimum GPA of 2.8 from ABET-accredited institution and in all upper-division courses; for doctorate, minimum overall GPA of 3.2, 3.5 in last two years as undergraduate student if being admitted directly from a bachelor's program, or master's degree with minimum GPA of 3.5 (preferred); for other advanced degree, minimum GPA of 3.0 from ABET-accredited institution and in all upper-division courses. Additional exam requirements/recommendations for international students: Required—TOEFL (minimum score 550 paper-based; 79 iBT), TWE (minimum score 5.5); Recommended—IELTS (minimum score 6.5). *Application deadline:* For fall admission, 7/15 priority date for domestic students, 5/15 priority date for international students; for winter admission, 11/1 priority date for domestic students, 10/1 priority date for international students; for spring admission, 2/1 priority date for domestic students, 1/1 priority date for international students. Applications are processed on a rolling basis. Application fee: $50. Electronic applications accepted. *Expenses:* $1500 per credit out-of-state; $780 per credit in-state. *Financial support:* In 2018–19, 538 students received support, including 23 fellowships with tuition reimbursements available (averaging $20,935 per year), 66 research assistantships with tuition reimbursements available (averaging $20,907 per year), 82 teaching assistantships with tuition reimbursements available (averaging $20,204 per year); Federal Work-Study, scholarships/grants, health care benefits, tuition waivers (full and partial), and unspecified assistantships also available. Support available to part-time students. Financial award applicants required to submit FAFSA. *Faculty research:* Biomedical research, integrated automotive safety, energy solutions, advanced manufacturing and materials, big data and business analytics. *Total annual research expenditures:* $12 million. *Unit head:* Dr. Farshad Fotouhi, Dean, 313-577-3776, E-mail: fotouhi@wayne.edu. *Application contact:* Graduate Program Coordinator, E-mail: engineeringgradadmissions@eng.wayne.edu. Website: http://engineering.wayne.edu/

Western Michigan University, Graduate College, College of Engineering and Applied Sciences, Kalamazoo, MI 49008. Offers MS, MSE, PhD. *Program availability:* Part-time. *Degree requirements:* For doctorate, thesis/dissertation.

Western New England University, College of Engineering, Springfield, MA 01119. Offers MS, MSEE, MSEM, MSME, PhD, MSEM/MBA. *Program availability:* Part-time, evening/weekend, online learning. *Faculty:* 33 full-time (3 women). *Students:* 78 part-time (13 women); includes 6 minority (1 Black or African American, non-Hispanic/Latino; 2 Asian, non-Hispanic/Latino; 3 Hispanic/Latino), 18 international. Average age 29. 300 applicants, 73% accepted, 37 enrolled. In 2018, 41 master's, 2 doctorates awarded. *Degree requirements:* For master's, comprehensive exam (for some programs), thesis optional; for doctorate, comprehensive exam, thesis/dissertation. *Entrance requirements:* For master's, bachelor's degree in engineering or related field, official

transcript, two letters of recommendation, resume; for doctorate, GRE, official transcript, master's or bachelor's degree in engineering or closely-related discipline, two letters of recommendation. Additional exam requirements/recommendations for international students: Required—TOEFL (minimum score 79 iBT). *Application deadline:* For fall admission, 1/15 priority date for domestic students. Applications are processed on a rolling basis. Application fee: $30. Electronic applications accepted. *Expenses:* Contact institution. *Financial support:* In 2018–19, 6 fellowships with tuition reimbursements were awarded. Financial award application deadline: 4/15; financial award applicants required to submit FAFSA. *Faculty research:* Fluid mechanics, control systems. *Unit head:* Dr. S. Hossein Cheraghi, Dean, 413-796-2302, Fax: 413-796-2116, E-mail: cheraghi@wne.edu. *Application contact:* Matthew Fox, Executive Director of Graduate Admissions, 413-782-1410, Fax: 413-782-1777, E-mail: study@wne.edu. Website: https://www1.wne.edu/academics/graduate/index.cfm#?category=5

West Texas A&M University, School of Engineering, Computer Science and Mathematics, Program in Engineering Technology, Canyon, TX 79015. Offers MS. *Program availability:* Part-time, evening/weekend. *Degree requirements:* For master's, comprehensive exam, thesis optional. *Entrance requirements:* For master's, GRE General Test. Additional exam requirements/recommendations for international students: Required—TOEFL (minimum score 550 paper-based). Electronic applications accepted. *Faculty research:* Stochastic temporal series, fuzzy network, computer-assisted/introductory physics classes, development of photorefractive polymers, central nervous system.

West Virginia University, Statler College of Engineering and Mineral Resources, Morgantown, WV 26506. Offers aerospace engineering (MSAE, PhD); chemical engineering (MS Ch E, PhD); civil engineering (MSCE, PhD); computer engineering (PhD); computer science (MSCS, PhD); electrical engineering (MSEE, PhD); energy systems engineering (MSESE); engineering (MSE); industrial engineering (MSIE, PhD); industrial hygiene (MS); material science and engineering (MSMSE, PhD); mechanical engineering (MSME, PhD); mining engineering (MS Min E, PhD); petroleum and natural gas engineering (MSPNGE, PhD); safety management (MS); software engineering (MSSE). *Program availability:* Part-time. *Students:* 466 full-time (113 women), 154 part-time (27 women); includes 57 minority (22 Black or African American, non-Hispanic/Latino; 1 American Indian or Alaska Native, non-Hispanic/Latino; 8 Asian, non-Hispanic/Latino; 12 Hispanic/Latino; 14 Two or more races, non-Hispanic/Latino), 283 international. In 2018, 179 master's, 39 doctorates awarded. Terminal master's awarded for partial completion of doctoral program. *Degree requirements:* For master's, thesis optional; for doctorate, comprehensive exam, thesis/dissertation. *Entrance requirements:* Additional exam requirements/recommendations for international students: Required—TOEFL (minimum score 550 paper-based). *Application deadline:* For fall admission, 4/1 for international students; for winter admission, 4/1 for international students; for spring admission, 10/1 for international students. Applications are processed on a rolling basis. Application fee: $60. Electronic applications accepted. *Expenses:* Contact institution. *Financial support:* Fellowships, research assistantships, teaching assistantships, career-related internships or fieldwork, Federal Work-Study, institutionally sponsored loans, health care benefits, tuition waivers (full and partial), unspecified assistantships, and administrative assistantships available. Financial award application deadline: 2/1; financial award applicants required to submit FAFSA. *Faculty research:* Composite materials, software engineering, information systems, aerodynamics, vehicle propulsion and emission. *Unit head:* Dr. Earl Scime, Interim Dean, 304-293-4157 Ext. 2237, Fax: 304-293-2037, E-mail: earl.scime@mail.wvu.edu. *Application contact:* Dr. David A. Wyrick, Associate Dean, Academic Affairs, 304-293-4334, Fax: 304-293-5024, E-mail: david.wyrick@mail.wvu.edu. Website: https://www.statler.wvu.edu

Wichita State University, Graduate School, College of Engineering, Wichita, KS 67260. Offers MEM, MS, PhD. *Program availability:* Part-time, evening/weekend. *Unit head:* Dr. Dennis R. Livesay, Dean, 316-978-3400, Fax: 316-978-3853, E-mail: dennis.livesay@wichita.edu. *Application contact:* Jordan Oleson, Admissions Coordinator, 316-978-3095, Fax: 316-978-3253, E-mail: jordan.oleson@wichita.edu. Website: http://www.wichita.edu/engineering

Widener University, Graduate Programs in Engineering, Chester, PA 19013. Offers M Eng, ME/MBA. *Program availability:* Part-time, evening/weekend. *Degree requirements:* For master's, thesis optional. *Entrance requirements:* Additional exam requirements/recommendations for international students: Required—TOEFL (minimum score 550 paper-based). Electronic applications accepted. *Expenses:* Contact institution. *Faculty research:* Image and signal processing, drug delivery, therapeutics, nanotechnology, brain computer interface, cancer and Alzheimer's research, biomechanics, numerical computation, geotechnics, solid waste disposal, hemodialysis.

Wilkes University, College of Graduate and Professional Studies, College of Science and Engineering, Wilkes-Barre, PA 18766-0002. Offers MS, MSEE. *Program availability:* Part-time. *Students:* 12 full-time (2 women), 7 part-time (1 woman); includes 5 minority (2 Asian, non-Hispanic/Latino; 3 Hispanic/Latino), 1 international. Average age 26. In 2018, 28 master's awarded. *Entrance requirements:* Additional exam requirements/recommendations for international students: Required—TOEFL (minimum score 550 paper-based; 79 iBT). *Application deadline:* Applications are processed on a rolling basis. Application fee: $45 ($65 for international students). Electronic applications accepted. Tuition and fees vary according to course load, degree level and program. *Financial support:* Unspecified assistantships available. Financial award application deadline: 3/1; financial award applicants required to submit FAFSA. *Unit head:* Dr. Prahlad Murthy, Interim Dean, 570-408-4600, Fax: 570-408-7860, E-mail: prahlad.murthy@wilkes.edu. *Application contact:* Kristin Donati, Associate Director of Graduate Admissions, 570-408-3338, Fax: 570-408-7846, E-mail: kristin.donati@wilkes.edu. Website: http://www.wilkes.edu/academics/colleges/science-and-engineering/index.aspx

Worcester Polytechnic Institute, Graduate Admissions, Worcester, MA 01609-2280. Offers M Eng, MBA, ME, MME, MS, PhD, Advanced Certificate, Graduate Certificate. *Program availability:* Part-time, evening/weekend, 100% online, blended/hybrid learning. *Students:* 839 full-time (291 women), 1,247 part-time (331 women); includes 278 minority (55 Black or African American, non-Hispanic/Latino; 2 American Indian or Alaska Native, non-Hispanic/Latino; 106 Asian, non-Hispanic/Latino; 87 Hispanic/Latino; 1 Native Hawaiian or other Pacific Islander, non-Hispanic/Latino; 27 Two or more races, non-Hispanic/Latino), 839 international. Average age 29. 4,194 applicants, 54% accepted, 735 enrolled. In 2018, 791 master's, 60 doctorates, 67 other advanced degrees awarded. Terminal master's awarded for partial completion of doctoral program. *Degree requirements:* For master's, thesis (for some programs); for doctorate, comprehensive exam, thesis/dissertation. *Entrance requirements:* For master's and doctorate, 3 letters of recommendation. Additional exam requirements/recommendations for international students: Required—TOEFL (minimum score 563 paper-based; 84 iBT), IELTS (minimum score 7). *Application deadline:* For fall admission, 1/1 priority date for domestic and international students; for spring admission, 10/1 priority date for domestic and international students. Applications are processed on a rolling basis. Application fee: $70. Electronic applications accepted. *Financial support:* Fellowships, research assistantships, teaching assistantships,

career-related internships or fieldwork, institutionally sponsored loans, scholarships/grants, health care benefits, tuition waivers, and unspecified assistantships available. Financial award application deadline: 1/1. *Faculty research:* Health and biotechnology; robotics and cyberphysical systems; advanced materials, manufacturing and mobility; cyber, data, and security systems engineering; learning sciences and technology. *Unit head:* Dr. Terri Camesano, Dean of Graduate Studies, 508-831-5380, E-mail: grad@wpi.edu. *Application contact:* Lynne Dougherty, Administrative Assistant, 508-831-5301, Fax: 508-831-5717, E-mail: grad@wpi.edu.
Website: http://grad.wpi.edu/

Wright State University, Graduate School, College of Engineering and Computer Science, Dayton, OH 45435. Offers MS, PhD. *Program availability:* Part-time, evening/weekend. *Degree requirements:* For master's, thesis optional; for doctorate, thesis/dissertation, candidacy and general exams. *Entrance requirements:* For doctorate, GRE General Test, minimum GPA of 3.3. Additional exam requirements/recommendations for international students: Required—TOEFL. *Faculty research:* Robotics, heat transfer, fluid dynamics, microprocessors, mechanical vibrations.

Yale University, Graduate School of Arts and Sciences, School of Engineering and Applied Science, New Haven, CT 06520. Offers MS, PhD. *Program availability:* Part-time. Terminal master's awarded for partial completion of doctoral program. *Degree requirements:* For doctorate, thesis/dissertation, exam. *Entrance requirements:* For master's and doctorate, GRE General Test. Additional exam requirements/recommendations for international students: Required—TOEFL.

Youngstown State University, College of Graduate Studies, College of Science, Technology, Engineering and Mathematics, Youngstown, OH 44555-0001. Offers MCIS, MS, MSE, Certificate. *Program availability:* Part-time, evening/weekend. *Degree requirements:* For master's, thesis optional. *Entrance requirements:* For master's, minimum GPA of 2.75 in field. Additional exam requirements/recommendations for international students: Required—TOEFL. *Faculty research:* Structural mechanics, water quality, wetlands engineering, control systems, power systems, heat transfer, kinematics and dynamics.

Applied Science and Technology

Colorado State University–Pueblo, College of Science and Mathematics, Pueblo, CO 81001-4901. Offers applied natural science (MS), including biochemistry, biology, chemistry. *Program availability:* Part-time, evening/weekend. *Degree requirements:* For master's, comprehensive exam (for some programs), thesis (for some programs), internship report (if non-thesis). *Entrance requirements:* For master's, GRE General Test (minimum score 1000), 2 letters of reference, minimum GPA of 3.0. Additional exam requirements/recommendations for international students: Required—TOEFL (minimum score 500 paper-based), IELTS (minimum score 5). *Faculty research:* Fungal cell walls, molecular biology, bioactive materials synthesis, atomic force microscopy-surface chemistry, nanoscience.

Harvard University, Extension School, Cambridge, MA 02138-3722. Offers applied sciences (CAS); biotechnology (ALM); educational technologies (ALM); educational technology (CET); English for graduate and professional studies (DGP); environmental management (ALM, CEM); information technology (ALM); journalism (ALM); liberal arts (ALM); management (ALM, CM); mathematics for teaching (ALM); museum studies (ALM); premedical studies (Diploma); publication and communication (CPC). *Program availability:* Part-time, evening/weekend. *Degree requirements:* For master's, thesis. *Entrance requirements:* For master's, 3 completed graduate courses with grade of B or higher. Additional exam requirements/recommendations for international students: Required—TOEFL (minimum score 600 paper-based), TWE (minimum score 5). *Expenses:* Contact institution.

Kansas State University, Graduate School, School of Applied and Interdisciplinary Studies, Olathe, KS 66061. Offers applied science and technology (PSM); professional interdisciplinary sciences (Graduate Certificate); professional skills for STEM practitioners (Graduate Certificate). *Program availability:* Part-time, 100% online, blended/hybrid learning. *Degree requirements:* For master's, capstone experience and/or internship. *Entrance requirements:* Additional exam requirements/recommendations for international students: Required—TOEFL (minimum score 550 paper-based; 79 iBT), IELTS (minimum score 6.5), PTE (minimum score 58). Electronic applications accepted. *Faculty research:* Applied and interdisciplinary science, food science, diagnostic medicine and pathobiology, adult education and leadership dynamics, horticulture and urban food systems.

Louisiana State University and Agricultural & Mechanical College, Graduate School, College of Science, Master of Natural Sciences Program, Baton Rouge, LA 70803. Offers MNS.

Missouri State University, Graduate College, College of Natural and Applied Sciences, Department of Biology, Springfield, MO 65897. Offers biology (MS); natural and applied science (MNAS), including biology (MNAS, MS Ed); secondary education (MS Ed), including biology (MNAS, MS Ed). *Faculty:* 18 full-time (3 women), 7 part-time/adjunct (2 women). *Students:* 23 full-time (12 women), 21 part-time (13 women); includes 2 minority (1 Black or African American, non-Hispanic/Latino; 1 Two or more races, non-Hispanic/Latino), 8 international. Average age 24. 28 applicants, 46% accepted. In 2018, 17 master's awarded. *Degree requirements:* For master's, comprehensive exam, thesis or alternative. *Entrance requirements:* For master's, GRE (MS, MNAS), 24 hours of course work in biology (MS); minimum GPA of 3.0 (MS, MNAS); 9-12 teacher certification (MS Ed). Additional exam requirements/recommendations for international students: Required—TOEFL (minimum score 550 paper-based; 79 iBT), IELTS (minimum score 6). *Application deadline:* For fall admission, 7/20 priority date for domestic students, 5/1 for international students; for spring admission, 12/20 priority date for domestic students, 9/1 for international students; for summer admission, 5/20 priority date for domestic students. Applications are processed on a rolling basis. Application fee: $55 ($60 for international students). Electronic applications accepted. Tuition and fees vary according to class time, course level, course load, degree level, campus/location, program and student level. *Financial support:* In 2018–19, 2 research assistantships with full tuition reimbursements (averaging $10,672 per year), 26 teaching assistantships with full tuition reimbursements (averaging $9,746 per year) were awarded; Federal Work-Study, institutionally sponsored loans, scholarships/grants, and unspecified assistantships also available. Financial award application deadline: 1/31; financial award applicants required to submit FAFSA. *Faculty research:* Hibernation physiology of bats, behavioral ecology of salamanders, mussel conservation, plant evolution and systematics, cellular/molecular mechanisms involved in migraine pathology. *Unit head:* Dr. S. Alicia Mathis, Department Head, 417-836-5126, Fax: 417-836-6934, E-mail: biology@missouristate.edu. *Application contact:* Lakan Drinker, Director, Graduate Enrollment Management, 417-836-5330, Fax: 417-836-6200, E-mail: lakandrinker@missouristate.edu.
Website: http://biology.missouristate.edu/

Missouri State University, Graduate College, College of Natural and Applied Sciences, Department of Chemistry, Springfield, MO 65897. Offers chemistry (MS); natural and applied science (MNAS), including chemistry (MNAS, MS Ed); secondary education (MS Ed), including chemistry (MNAS, MS Ed). *Program availability:* Part-time. *Faculty:* 15 full-time (2 women). *Students:* 12 full-time (5 women), 9 part-time (4 women); includes 2 minority (1 Hispanic/Latino; 1 Two or more races, non-Hispanic/Latino), 5 international. Average age 23. 11 applicants, 45% accepted. In 2018, 8 master's awarded. *Degree requirements:* For master's, comprehensive exam, thesis. *Entrance requirements:* For master's, GRE General Test (MS, MNAS), minimum undergraduate GPA of 3.0 (MS and MNAS), 9-12 teacher certification (MS Ed). Additional exam requirements/recommendations for international students: Required—TOEFL (minimum score 550 paper-based; 79 iBT), IELTS (minimum score 6). *Application deadline:* For fall admission, 7/20 priority date for domestic students, 5/1 for international students; for spring admission, 12/20 priority date for domestic students, 9/1 for international students; for summer admission, 5/20 priority date for domestic students. Applications are processed on a rolling basis. Application fee: $55 ($60 for international students). Electronic applications accepted. Tuition and fees vary according to class time, course level, course load, degree level, campus/location, program and student level. *Financial support:* In 2018–19, 17 teaching assistantships with full tuition reimbursements (averaging $8,772 per year) were awarded; Federal Work-Study, institutionally sponsored loans, scholarships/grants, and unspecified assistantships also available. Financial award application deadline: 1/31; financial award applicants required to submit FAFSA. *Faculty research:* Polyethylene glycol derivatives, electrochemiluminescence of environmental systems, enzymology, environmental organic pollutants, DNA repair via nuclear magnetic resonance (NMR). *Unit head:* Dr. Bryan Breyfogle, Department Head, 417-836-5601, Fax: 417-836-5507, E-mail: chemistry@missouristate.edu. *Application contact:* Lakan Drinker, Director, Graduate Enrollment Management, 417-836-5330, Fax: 417-836-6200, E-mail: lakandrinker@missouristate.edu.
Website: http://chemistry.missouristate.edu/

Missouri State University, Graduate College, College of Natural and Applied Sciences, Department of Computer Science, Springfield, MO 65897. Offers natural and applied science (MNAS), including computer science. *Program availability:* Part-time. *Faculty:* 6 full-time (1 woman). *Students:* 14 full-time (1 woman), 7 part-time (2 women); includes 3 minority (1 Asian, non-Hispanic/Latino; 1 Hispanic/Latino; 1 Two or more races, non-Hispanic/Latino), 12 international. Average age 25. 21 applicants, 67% accepted. In 2018, 3 master's awarded. *Degree requirements:* For master's, comprehensive exam, thesis or alternative. *Entrance requirements:* For master's, GRE, minimum GPA of 3.0. Additional exam requirements/recommendations for international students: Required—TOEFL (minimum score 550 paper-based; 79 iBT), IELTS (minimum score 6). *Application deadline:* For fall admission, 7/20 priority date for domestic students, 5/1 for international students; for spring admission, 12/20 priority date for domestic students, 9/1 for international students. Applications are processed on a rolling basis. Application fee: $55 ($60 for international students). Electronic applications accepted. Tuition and fees vary according to class time, course level, course load, degree level, campus/location, program and student level. *Financial support:* In 2018–19, 1 teaching assistantship with partial tuition reimbursement (averaging $2,150 per year) was awarded; Federal Work-Study, institutionally sponsored loans, scholarships/grants, and unspecified assistantships also available. Financial award application deadline: 1/31; financial award applicants required to submit FAFSA. *Faculty research:* Floating point numbers, data compression, graph theory. *Unit head:* Dr. Ajay Katangur, Department Head, 417-836-4157, Fax: 417-836-6659, E-mail: computerscience@missouristate.edu. *Application contact:* Lakan Drinker, Director, Graduate Enrollment Management, 417-836-5330, Fax: 417-836-6200, E-mail: lakandrinker@missouristate.edu.
Website: http://computerscience.missouristate.edu/

Missouri State University, Graduate College, College of Natural and Applied Sciences, Department of Geography, Geology, and Planning, Springfield, MO 65897. Offers geography, geology, and planning (Certificate); natural and applied science (MNAS), including geography, geology and planning; secondary education (MS Ed), including earth science, physical geography. *Program availability:* Part-time, evening/weekend. *Faculty:* 18 full-time (4 women), 1 part-time/adjunct (0 women). *Students:* 24 full-time (10 women), 10 part-time (5 women); includes 2 minority (1 Hispanic/Latino; 1 Two or more races, non-Hispanic/Latino), 5 international. Average age 25. 26 applicants, 50% accepted. In 2018, 8 master's awarded. *Degree requirements:* For master's, comprehensive exam, thesis (for some programs). *Entrance requirements:* For master's, GRE General Test (MS, MNAS), minimum undergraduate GPA of 3.0 (MS, MNAS), 9-12 teacher certification (MS Ed). Additional exam requirements/recommendations for international students: Required—TOEFL (minimum score 550 paper-based; 79 iBT), IELTS (minimum score 6). *Application deadline:* For fall admission, 7/20 priority date for domestic students, 5/1 for international students; for spring admission, 12/20 priority date for domestic students, 9/1 for international students. Applications are processed on a rolling basis. Application fee: $55 ($60 for international students). Electronic applications accepted. Tuition and fees vary according to class time, course level, course load, degree level, campus/location, program and student level. *Financial support:* In 2018–19, 3 research assistantships with full tuition reimbursements (averaging $11,574 per year), 15 teaching assistantships with full tuition reimbursements (averaging $9,365 per year) were awarded; career-related internships or fieldwork, Federal Work-Study, institutionally sponsored loans, scholarships/grants, and unspecified assistantships also available. Financial award application deadline: 1/31; financial award applicants required to submit FAFSA. *Faculty research:* Stratigraphy and ancient meteorite impacts, environmental geochemistry of karst, hyperspectral image processing, water quality, small town planning. *Unit head:* Dr. Toby Dogwiler, Department Head, 417-836-5800, Fax: 417-836-6934, E-mail: tobydogwiler@missouristate.edu. *Application contact:* Lakan Drinker, Director, Graduate Enrollment Management, 417-836-5330, Fax: 417-836-6200, E-mail: lakandrinker@missouristate.edu.
Website: http://geosciences.missouristate.edu/

Missouri State University, Graduate College, College of Natural and Applied Sciences, Department of Mathematics, Springfield, MO 65897. Offers mathematics (MS); natural and applied science (MNAS), including mathematics (MNAS, MS Ed); secondary education (MS Ed), including mathematics (MNAS, MS Ed). *Program availability:* Part-time. *Faculty:* 21 full-time (4 women). *Students:* 13 full-time (4 women), 15 part-time (10 women); includes 2 minority (1 American Indian or Alaska Native, non-Hispanic/Latino; 1

Hispanic/Latino), 6 international. Average age 24. 18 applicants, 56% accepted. In 2018, 11 master's awarded. *Degree requirements:* For master's, comprehensive exam, thesis or alternative. *Entrance requirements:* For master's, GRE (MS, MNAS), minimum undergraduate GPA of 3.0 (MS, MNAS), 9-12 teacher certification (MS Ed). Additional exam requirements/recommendations for international students: Required—TOEFL (minimum score 550 paper-based; 79 iBT), IELTS (minimum score 6). *Application deadline:* For fall admission, 7/20 priority date for domestic students, 5/1 for international students; for spring admission, 12/20 priority date for domestic students, 9/1 for international students. Applications are processed on a rolling basis. Application fee: $55 ($60 for international students). Electronic applications accepted. Tuition and fees vary according to class time, course level, course load, degree level, campus/location, program and student level. *Financial support:* In 2018–19, 11 teaching assistantships with full tuition reimbursements (averaging $10,672 per year) were awarded; Federal Work-Study, institutionally sponsored loans, scholarships/grants, and unspecified assistantships also available. Financial award application deadline: 1/31; financial award applicants required to submit FAFSA. *Faculty research:* Harmonic analysis, commutative algebra, number theory, K-theory, probability. *Unit head:* Dr. William Bray, Department Head, 417-836-5112, Fax: 417-836-6966, E-mail: mathematics@missouristate.edu. *Application contact:* Lakan Drinker, Director, Graduate Enrollment Management, 417-836-5330, Fax: 417-836-6200, E-mail: lakandrinker@missouristate.edu.
Website: http://math.missouristate.edu/

Missouri State University, Graduate College, College of Natural and Applied Sciences, Department of Physics, Astronomy, and Materials Science, Springfield, MO 65897. Offers materials science (MS); natural and applied science (MNAS), including physics (MNAS, MS Ed); secondary education (MS Ed), including physics (MNAS, MS Ed). *Program availability:* Part-time. *Faculty:* 9 full-time (0 women). *Students:* 11 full-time (1 woman), 4 part-time (1 woman); includes 1 minority (Hispanic/Latino), 13 international. Average age 26. 12 applicants, 92% accepted. In 2018, 9 master's awarded. *Degree requirements:* For master's, comprehensive exam, thesis. *Entrance requirements:* For master's, GRE (MS, MNAS), minimum undergraduate GPA of 3.0 (MS and MNAS), 9-12 teaching certification (MS Ed). Additional exam requirements/recommendations for international students: Required—TOEFL (minimum score 550 paper-based; 79 iBT), IELTS (minimum score 6). *Application deadline:* For fall admission, 7/20 priority date for domestic students, 5/1 for international students; for spring admission, 12/20 priority date for domestic students, 9/1 for international students. Applications are processed on a rolling basis. Application fee: $55 ($60 for international students). Electronic applications accepted. Tuition and fees vary according to class time, course level, course load, degree level, campus/location, program and student level. *Financial support:* In 2018–19, 6 research assistantships with full tuition reimbursements (averaging $10,672 per year), 11 teaching assistantships with full tuition reimbursements (averaging $10,672 per year) were awarded; Federal Work-Study, institutionally sponsored loans, scholarships/grants, and unspecified assistantships also available. Financial award application deadline: 1/31; financial award applicants required to submit FAFSA. *Faculty research:* Nanocomposites, ferroelectricity, infrared focal plane array sensors, biosensors, pulsating stars. *Unit head:* Dr. Robert Mayanovic, Department Head, 417-836-5131, Fax: 417-836-6226, E-mail: physics@missouristate.edu. *Application contact:* Lakan Drinker, Director, Graduate Enrollment Management, 417-836-5330, Fax: 417-836-6200, E-mail: lakandrinker@missouristate.edu.
Website: http://physics.missouristate.edu/

Naval Postgraduate School, Departments and Academic Groups, Department of Operations Research, Monterey, CA 93943. Offers applied science (MS), including operations research; cost estimating analysis (MS); human systems integration (MS); operations research (MS, PhD); systems analysis (MS). Program only open to commissioned officers of the United States and friendly nations and selected United States federal civilian employees. *Program availability:* Part-time. *Degree requirements:* For master's, thesis (for some programs); for doctorate, thesis/dissertation. *Faculty research:* Next generation network science, performance analysis of ground solider mobile ad-hoc networks, irregular warfare methods and tools, human social cultural behavior modeling, large-scale optimization.

Naval Postgraduate School, Departments and Academic Groups, Undersea Warfare Academic Group, Monterey, CA 93943. Offers applied mathematics (MS); applied physics (MS); applied science (MS), including acoustics, operations research, physical oceanography, signal processing; electrical engineering (MS); engineering acoustics (MS, PhD); engineering science (MS), including electrical engineering, mechanical engineering; mechanical engineer (ME); mechanical engineering (MS, MSME); meteorology (MS); operations research (MS); physical oceanography (MS). Program only open to commissioned officers of the United States and friendly nations and selected United States federal civilian employees. *Program availability:* Part-time. *Degree requirements:* For master's, thesis. *Faculty research:* Unmanned/autonomous vehicles, sea mines and countermeasures, submarine warfare in the twentieth and twenty-first centuries.

Saint Mary's University, Faculty of Science, Interdisciplinary Program in Applied Science, Halifax, NS B3H 3C3, Canada. Offers M Sc.

Southeastern Louisiana University, College of Science and Technology, Program in Integrated Science and Technology, Hammond, LA 70402. Offers integrated science and technology (MS). *Program availability:* Part-time, evening/weekend. *Faculty:* 5 full-time (2 women). *Students:* 12 full-time (5 women), 7 part-time (1 woman); includes 5 minority (1 Black or African American, non-Hispanic/Latino; 4 Hispanic/Latino), 5 international. Average age 27. 10 applicants, 40% accepted, 3 enrolled. In 2018, 3 master's awarded. *Degree requirements:* For master's, thesis optional, 33-36 hours. *Entrance requirements:* For master's, GRE (minimum combined Verbal and Quantitative score of 280), undergraduate degree; at least 30 semester hours in any combination of chemistry, computer science, industrial technology, mathematics, or physics; letter of introduction; 3 letters of recommendation; cumulative undergraduate GPA of 2.75.

Additional exam requirements/recommendations for international students: Required—TOEFL (minimum score 500 paper-based; 61 iBT). *Application deadline:* For fall admission, 7/15 priority date for domestic students, 6/1 priority date for international students; for spring admission, 12/1 priority date for domestic students, 10/1 priority date for international students. Applications are processed on a rolling basis. Application fee: $20 ($30 for international students). Electronic applications accepted. *Expenses: Tuition, area resident:* Full-time $6684. Tuition, state resident: full-time $6684. Tuition, nonresident: full-time $19,162. *Required fees:* $2097. *Financial support:* In 2018–19, 14 students received support, including 4 research assistantships with tuition reimbursements available (averaging $19,047 per year); career-related internships or fieldwork, Federal Work-Study, institutionally sponsored loans, scholarships/grants, and unspecified assistantships also available. Support available to part-time students. Financial award application deadline: 5/1; financial award applicants required to submit FAFSA. *Faculty research:* Organic medicinal chemistry, computer architecture, robotics, CAD solid modeling, matrix analysis. *Unit head:* Dr. Daniel McCarthy, 985-549-3943, E-mail: dmccarthy@southeastern.edu. *Application contact:* Dr. Daniel McCarthy, 985-549-3943, E-mail: dmccarthy@southeastern.edu.
Website: http://www.southeastern.edu/acad_research/programs/isat/index.html

Thomas Edison State University, School of Applied Science and Technology, Trenton, NJ 08608. Offers clinical trials management (MS); cybersecurity (Graduate Certificate); information technology (MS); nuclear energy technology management (MS); technical studies (MS). *Program availability:* Part-time, online learning. *Degree requirements:* For master's, project. *Entrance requirements:* Additional exam requirements/recommendations for international students: Required—TOEFL (minimum score 550 paper-based; 79 iBT). Electronic applications accepted.

University of Arkansas at Little Rock, Graduate School, George W. Donaghey College of Engineering and Information Technology, Department of Applied Science, Little Rock, AR 72204-1099. Offers MS, PhD. *Program availability:* Part-time. *Degree requirements:* For master's, comprehensive exam, thesis optional, oral exams; for doctorate, thesis/dissertation, 2 semesters of residency, candidacy exams. *Entrance requirements:* For master's, GRE General Test, interview, minimum GPA of 3.0; for doctorate, GRE General Test, interview, minimum graduate GPA of 3.5. Additional exam requirements/recommendations for international students: Required—TOEFL. *Faculty research:* Particle and powder science and technology, optical sensors, process control and automation, signal and image processing, biomedical measurement systems.

University of California, Berkeley, Graduate Division, College of Engineering, Group in Applied Science and Technology, Berkeley, CA 94720. Offers PhD. Terminal master's awarded for partial completion of doctoral program. *Degree requirements:* For doctorate, thesis/dissertation, preliminary exam, qualifying exam. *Entrance requirements:* For doctorate, GRE General Test, BA or BS in engineering, physics, mathematics, chemistry, or related field; minimum GPA of 3.0, 3 letters of recommendation. Additional exam requirements/recommendations for international students: Required—TOEFL (minimum score 570 paper-based; 90 iBT). Electronic applications accepted. Application fee is waived when completed online.

University of California, Davis, College of Engineering, Program in Applied Science, Davis, CA 95616. Offers MS, PhD. Terminal master's awarded for partial completion of doctoral program. *Degree requirements:* For master's, comprehensive exam (for some programs), thesis (for some programs); for doctorate, thesis/dissertation. *Entrance requirements:* For master's and doctorate, GRE General Test, minimum GPA of 3.3. Additional exam requirements/recommendations for international students: Required—TOEFL (minimum score 550 paper-based). Electronic applications accepted. *Faculty research:* Plasma physics, scientific computing, fusion technology, laser physics and nonlinear optics.

University of Colorado Denver, College of Liberal Arts and Sciences, Program in Integrated Sciences, Denver, CO 80217. Offers applied science (MIS); computer science (MIS); mathematics (MIS). *Program availability:* Part-time, evening/weekend. *Entrance requirements:* For master's, GRE if undergraduate GPA is 3.0 or less, minimum of 40 semester hours in mathematics, computer science, physics, biology, chemistry and/or geology; essay; three letters of recommendation. *Expenses:* Tuition, state resident: full-time $6786; part-time $337 per credit hour. Tuition, nonresident: full-time $22,590; part-time $1255 per credit hour. *Required fees:* $1231; $137 per credit hour. Tuition and fees vary according to program and reciprocity agreements. *Faculty research:* Computer science, applied science, mathematics.

University of Mississippi, Graduate School, School of Applied Sciences, University, MS 38677. Offers communicative disorders (MS); criminal justice (MCJ); exercise science (MS); food and nutrition services (MS); health and kinesiology (PhD); health promotion (MS); nutrition and hospitality management (PhD); park and recreation management (MA); social welfare (PhD); social work (MSW). *Faculty:* 66 full-time (36 women), 27 part-time/adjunct (13 women). *Students:* 192 full-time (148 women), 40 part-time (25 women); includes 50 minority (41 Black or African American, non-Hispanic/Latino; 1 American Indian or Alaska Native, non-Hispanic/Latino; 1 Asian, non-Hispanic/Latino; 5 Hispanic/Latino; 2 Two or more races, non-Hispanic/Latino), 16 international. Average age 26. In 2018, 72 master's, 5 doctorates awarded. *Entrance requirements:* For master's, GRE General Test, minimum GPA of 3.0. Additional exam requirements/recommendations for international students: Required—TOEFL. *Application deadline:* Applications are processed on a rolling basis. Application fee: $50. Electronic applications accepted. *Financial support:* Scholarships/grants available. Financial award application deadline: 3/1; financial award applicants required to submit FAFSA. *Unit head:* Dr. Peter Grandjean, Dean of Applied Sciences, 662-915-7900, Fax: 662-915-7901, E-mail: applsci@olemiss.edu. *Application contact:* Temeka Smith, Graduate Activities Specialist for Admissions, 662-915-7474, Fax: 662-915-7577, E-mail: gschool@olemiss.edu.

TEMPLE UNIVERSITY
College of Engineering

College of Engineering

Programs of Study

Established in 1969, the College of Engineering at Temple University is a rising institution with an intimate and diverse community. You will have access to faculty performing top-tier research, both within the College and collaboratively with Temple's dental, medical and other professional schools. Temple Engineers show their work, demonstrating their skills and reaching their goals in engineering and in their careers.

- Bioengineering, M.S. and Ph.D.
- Civil Engineering, M.S. and Ph.D.
- Computer & Systems Security, P.S.M. and Graduate Certificate
- Electrical Engineering, M.S. and Ph.D.
- Engineering Management, M.S. and Graduate Certificate
- Environmental Engineering, M.S. and Ph.D.
- Mechanical Engineering, M.S. and Ph.D.
- Stormwater Management, Graduate Certificate

The M.S. programs require 30 semester hours that can be completed on a part-time or full-time basis. Each program has core coursework with the remainder completed with elective course work, allowing for customization for your interests. Students enrolled in the program can choose to complete coursework only, project, or thesis study tracks.

The Ph.D. degree requires 30 semester hours beyond the master's degree -- 15 semester hours are associated with didactic coursework and the remaining 15 semester hours are associated with Ph.D. examinations and dissertation research. The programs are highly individualized; students work closely with their adviser on creating a plan of study through to the conclusion of their dissertation proposal, dissertation writing, and then defense of the dissertation.

Research Facilities

Faculty members engage in cutting-edge research funded by grants through such organizations as the National Institutes of Health, the American Heart Association, the National Science Foundation, and PennDOT. The College's faculty work in the 15+ advanced laboratories and centers supported by a thriving graduate student population and team of post-doctoral fellows and research scientists.

Research is critical in graduate-level education. It is through research activities that graduate students can apply what they have learned in their undergraduate- and graduate-level coursework to solve real-world problems. Graduate students have opportunities to participate at the College in addition to interdisciplinary research being conducted with other colleges and schools at Temple University, such as the College of Science and Technology, School of Podiatry, College of Public Health, and the Lewis Katz School of Medicine.

Financial Aid

The College of Engineering makes every effort to provide graduate students with the resources necessary for an affordable education. Eligible Ph.D. students are awarded teaching and research assistantships and are automatically reviewed at the time of application. Students awarded an assistantship receive a stipend, tuition remission, and health insurance in exchange for conducting research or assisting faculty in the classroom. Preference is given to those applicants who already have M.S. degrees. In addition, Ph.D. students are eligible for University-wide fellowships, which typically provide a stipend, tuition remission, and health insurance coverage.

In the master's programs there are a limited amount of merit-based scholarships available for competitive applicants. Students are automatically considered and will be notified at time of admission if they have received such an award.

All U.S. citizens and permanent residents are eligible to apply for need-based aid by completing the Free Application for Federal Student Aid (FAFSA) at www.fafsa.ed.gov.

Cost of Study

Tuition for the 2019–20 academic year is $1,135 per semester credit for Pennsylvania residents and $1,490 per semester credit for out-of-state residents.

Location

The College of Engineering is located at Temple University's main campus, in the thriving city of Philadelphia—a city at the forefront of science and technology. Graduate students can take advantage of a vibrant arts and culture scene, restaurants, sports and recreation activities in a city easily navigated by walking, biking, or through an array of public transportation options.

Philadelphia is a multicultural city, providing numerous opportunities for students to immerse themselves in the city's diverse neighborhoods and traditions. With a thriving student culture, the Greater Philadelphia region is home to over 25 colleges and universities and boasts an affordable cost of living.

The University

Temple University is many things to many people. A place to pursue life's passions. A nurturing learning environment. A hotbed of research. An engine of employment. A melting pot of ideas and innovation. An incubator for tomorrow's leaders. The University is a R1 rated Carnegie classification for research activity.

Temple's 17 schools and colleges, eight campuses, hundreds of degree programs, and more than 39,000 students combine to create one of the nation's most comprehensive and diverse learning environments. In neighborhoods, across disciplines, and on a global stage, members of the Temple community are making things happen.

The Faculty

Graduate-level instruction and research are guided by a talented faculty. College of Engineering graduate faculty members explore new and innovative research, publish in peer-reviewed journals, participate in top conference proceedings, and receive grants from prestigious funding sources such as the U.S. Army, the National Science Foundation, the National Institutes of Health, and many others. Faculty members are engaged in areas of research including, but not limited to water resources engineering, sustainability, network securities, artificial intelligence, rehabilitation engineering, tissue engineering, targeted drug delivery, biomaterials, and materials science engineering.

Temple University

A complete list of faculty members and their areas of research can be found at https://engineering.temple.edu.

Applying

The College of Engineering at Temple University welcomes applications to its doctoral, master's, and certificate programs. The College of Engineering admits for both the fall and spring semesters with the following recommended deadlines:

Ph.D. PROGRAMS

Fall Entry
- December 15—Fellowship Consideration Deadline
- January 15—Priority Deadline for Departmental Funding Consideration*
- March 1—Regular Decision Deadline

Spring Entry
- August 1

MASTER'S PROGRAMS

Fall Entry
- June 1—Domestic Students
- March 1—International Students

Spring Entry
- November 1—Domestic Students
- August 1—International Students

Upon receiving all of the required credentials, the application will be reviewed individually by the appropriate department. Please note that the PSM and Certificate in Computer and Systems Security admits for Fall only.

To apply for a Ph.D. or M.S. degree program, students must have:
- An undergraduate degree in engineering from an ABET-accredited or equivalent institution.
- For applicants to the doctoral program, a master's degree is preferred, though not required.
- A minimum undergraduate GPA of a 3.0 (on a 4.0 scale).
- Minimum GRE scores as follows: Verbal—150, Quantitative—151, Analytical Writing—4.5
- For applicants whose native language is not English, the TOEFL or IELTS exam is required with the following minimum scores: 79 on the internet based TOEFL or 6.5 on the academic version of the IELTS.

The following credentials must be submitted for doctoral or master's degree programs:
- Completed graduate application and submission of the application fee.
- Official transcripts from all post-secondary institutions attended;
- Three letters of reference
- Statement of Goals
- Resume/CV
- Official GRE score report sent directly from the Educational Testing Agency (ETS). Temple University's institutional code is 2906.
- For applicants whose native language is not English, the TOEFL or the academic version of the IELTS exam is required. TOEFL scores must be submitted directly from the testing agency.

Correspondence and Information

Office of Admissions and Graduate Student Services
College of Engineering
Temple University
1947 N. 12th Street
Philadelphia, Pennsylvania 19122
Phone: 215-204-7800
E-mail: gradengr@temple.edu
Website: engineering.temple.edu

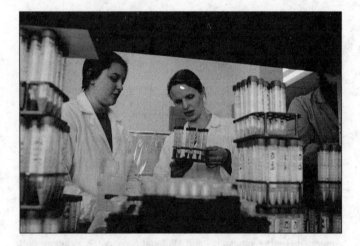

UNIVERSITY OF PENNSYLVANIA
School of Engineering and Applied Science

Programs of Study

Penn Engineering's collaborative research and learning environment truly distinguish the School from its peers, as research and education form its dynamic, creative graduate mission. The excitement and discovery of research is open to all students and is the keystone of the School's world-renowned doctoral programs. These programs are augmented by a diverse array of master's degree offerings.

Students work with and learn from faculty mentors within the core disciplinary programs as well as through scholarly interactions involving the School of Medicine, the School of Arts and Sciences, and the Wharton School, to note a few. This environment is further enriched by Penn's many institutes, centers, and laboratories. For more than 100 years, Penn Engineering has been at the forefront of innovation, just like the University's founder was in his day: Benjamin Franklin, America's first scientist and engineer.

The six Doctor of Philosophy (Ph.D.) programs are research-oriented degree programs for students of superior caliber who will make original contributions to theory and practice in their fields of interest. The programs prepare them for a research career in academe, government, or industry. Curricula are purposely designed to develop the intellectual skills essential for the rapidly changing character of research.

Penn Engineering's seventeen master's programs (Master of Science in Engineering, unless otherwise noted) serve a wide range of highly qualified students such as those expanding on their undergraduate training for professional engineering practice, preparing for doctoral studies, or working toward greater expertise to advance their careers. The School's constantly evolving curricula is grounded in up-to-the-minute research findings and industrial priorities that focus on practical applications of knowledge and responses to career and professional interests, as well as to the needs of today's high-tech society and economy. These include the M.S.E. in Data Science, which just graduated its first cohort, and the first-in-the-Ivy League Online Master of Computer Information Technology (OMCIT) that began classes in January of 2019.

Research Facilities

Shared research laboratories and facilities are an integral part of research and education at Penn Engineering. The School's collection of labs and facilities share a physical connectivity that enables collaborations with faculty, students, and postdoctoral scholars across Penn. It includes interdisciplinary research centers and institutes, such as the new Pennovation Center, Singh Center for Nanotechnology, GRASP Lab, Nano/Bio Interface Center (NBIC), SIG Center for Computer Graphics, and PRECISE Lab (http://www.seasupenn.edu/research/centers-institutes.php).

Cost of Study

The cost for four on-campus courses in the academic year 2019–20 is $29,240. This includes tuition and general and technology fees. Students are charged per registered course unit. Additional information can be found at http://www.seas.upenn.edu/prospective-students/graduate/admissions/pay.php. The cost for OMCIT courses in the 2019–20 academic is as follows: $2,500 per course unit and $130 for fees.

Living and Housing Costs

On-campus housing is available for both single and married students. There are also numerous privately-owned apartments for rent in the immediate area. More information can be found on the Graduate Housing website at http://cms.business-services.upenn.edu/residential-services/applications-a-assignments/graduate-students.html.

Student Population

There are approximately 21,000 students at the University, around 11,000 of whom are enrolled in graduate and professional schools. Of these, approximately 1,500 are in graduate engineering programs.

Location

The University of Pennsylvania is located in West Philadelphia, just a few blocks from the heart of the city. Philadelphia is a twenty-first-century city with seventeenth-century origins, a patchwork of distinctive neighborhoods ranging from Society Hill to Chinatown. Renowned museums, concert halls, theaters, and sports arenas provide cultural and recreational outlets for students. Fairmount Park, the largest urban park network in the country, extends through large sections of Philadelphia. Not far away are the Jersey shore to the east, Pennsylvania Dutch country to the west, and the Pocono Mountains to the north. The city is also less than a 3-hour drive from New York City and Washington, D.C.

The School

The School of Engineering and Applied Science has a distinguished reputation for the quality of its programs. The School's alumni have achieved international distinction in research, higher education, management, entrepreneurship and industrial development, and government service. Research is led by faculty members at the forefront of modern technology and makes major contributions in a wide variety of fields.

The University of Pennsylvania was founded in 1740 by Benjamin Franklin. A member of the Ivy League and one of the world's leading universities, Penn is renowned for its graduate schools, faculty, research centers, and institutes. Conveniently situated on a compact and attractive campus, Penn offers an abundance of multidisciplinary educational programs with exceptional opportunities for individually tailored graduate education.

Applying

Candidates may apply directly to the School of Engineering through an online application system. Applicants should visit the admissions website for detailed application requirements and access to the online application system. Ph.D. applications for fall admission must be received by December 15, 2019. Master's applications for six of the programs will have two application deadlines: November 15, 2019 or March 15, 2020. All other master's program applications are due by February 1, 2020. The application for Spring 2020 for the OMCIT program is due by October 1, 2019. All test scores, and letters of recommendation must be received by the deadline for applications to be considered. Graduate Record Examinations (GRE) are required for all masters and PhD programs except the OMCIT; they are optional for this program. All students whose native language is not English must arrange to take either the Test of English as a Foreign Language (TOEFL) or International English Language Testing System (IELTS) test prior to the application process unless you qualify for a waiver by having graduated from an institution where English is the language of instruction. The admissions website can be found at http://www.seas.upenn.edu/grad.

Correspondence and Information

Graduate Admissions
School of Engineering and Applied Science
109 Towne Building
University of Pennsylvania
220 South 33rd Street
Philadelphia, Pennsylvania 19104-6391
Phone: 215-898-4542
E-mail: gradstudies@seas.upenn.edu
Website: http://www.seas.upenn.edu/grad
         @PennEngGradAdm (Twitter)

AREAS OF RESEARCH

Bioengineering: The Master of Science in Bioengineering program has an inter-disciplinary focus on scientific and engineering fundamentals, specifically new developments in bioengineering. The Bioengineering Ph.D. program is designed to train individuals for academic, government, or industrial research careers. Research interests for these programs include: bioengineered therapeutics (device and drug delivery), biomaterials, cardiovascular and pulmonary cell and tissue mechanics, cell mechanics, cellular and molecular imaging, cellular engineering, hhmi-nibib, imaging theory and analysis, injury biomechanics, medical imaging and imagining instrumentation, molecular engineering, neuroengineering, orthopaedic bioengineering, systems and synthetic bioengineering, theoretical and computational bioengineering, and tissue engineering. (http://www.be.seas.upenn.edu)

Biotechnology: The Master of Biotechnology (M.B.) program prepares students for leadership in the critically important and dynamic industries of biotechnology and pharmaceuticals. Strongly interdisciplinary, this program draws its faculty and courses from the Schools of Engineering, Arts and Sciences, and Medicine. Research interests are: biomedical technologies, biopharmaceutical/engineering biotechnology, and molecular biology. (http://www.upenn.edu/biotech)

Chemical and Biomolecular Engineering: The M.S.E. program in Chemical and Biomolecular Engineering (CBE) provides students with the firm theoretical foundation and interdisciplinary skills that are essential in the rapidly changing field of chemical and biomolecular engineering. The Ph.D. CBE program is a research-oriented degree for students showing exceptional promise for original contributions to the theory and practice of chemical and biomolecular engineering. Research interests are: advanced materials and nanotechnology, catalysis and reaction engineering, cellular and biomolecular engineering, energy and environmental engineering, molecular simulation and thermodynamics, soft matter and complex fluids, and systems engineering. (http://www.cbe.seas.upenn.edu)

Computer Graphics and Game Technology: The M.S.E. program in Computer Graphics and Game Technology is nationally recognized for preparing students for leadership careers as designers, technical animators, directors, and game programmers. Students receive first-hand experience in the latest graphics and animation technologies, interactive media design principles, product development methodologies, and entrepreneurship. Courses utilize Penn's Center for Human Modeling and Simulation, internationally recognized for cutting-edge research in 3-D computer graphics, human simulation, and the behavioral animation of embodied intelligent agents. (http://www.cis.upenn.edu/grad)

Computer and Information Science: The M.S.E. program in Computer and Information Science (CIS) is one of the nation's top programs, preparing students to be innovators, leaders, and visionaries. M.S.E. students develop their own advanced study focus and arrange interdisciplinary programs such as CIS and telecommunications, CIS and computational linguistics, CIS and biomedical computation. The Ph.D. CIS program is designed for candidates with strong training in disciplines related to modern information processing, with an emphasis on computer science and mathematics. The curriculum is intended to develop intellectual skills essential for the rapidly changing character of research and to meet the demands of academe and industry. Research interests include: architecture and compilers, artificial intelligence, bioinformatics and computational biology, computational linguistics, databases and data management, embedded and real-time systems, formal methods and software engineering, graphics, machine learning, networks and distributed systems, programming languages, robotics, security and information assurance, theory, and vision. There are also interdisciplinary collaborations with fields such as biology, genetics, linguistics, mathematics, and electrical engineering. (http://www.cis.upenn.edu/grad)

Computer and Information Technology: The master's program in Computer and Information Technology (MCIT) is specifically designed for students and professionals with minimal or no prior computing experience or formal training in computer science. This program gives students the expertise needed to understand and succeed in today's highly innovative and competitive workplace. It benefits students and industry professionals who want to begin or advance a career in information technology or prepare for doctoral studies in computer science (http://www.cis.upenn.edu/grad). In addition to the on-campus program, the Master of Computer and Information Technology degree is also offered as a fully online program. (https://onlinelearning.seas.upenn.edu/mcit)

Electrical and Systems Engineering: The graduate group in electrical and systems engineering offers a Ph.D. in Electrical and Systems Engineering (ESE), an M.S.E. in Electrical Engineering (EE), and an M.S.E. in Systems Engineering (SE). The EE program enables students to tailor their own interests and goals, from circuits and computer engineering, information and decision systems, to nanodevices and nanosystems. It gives students the theoretical foundation and interdisciplinary skills needed to deal with the new ideas and new applications that are the hallmarks of modern electroscience. The SE program, grounded in the intersection of electrical and systems engineering, gives students in-depth theoretical foundation and interdisciplinary skills required by the growing complexity of technological systems. In addition, students are also able to complete a Certificate in Engineering Entrepreneurship, where they take cross degree courses at Wharton, including leadership and Fundamentals of High-Tech Ventures.

The Ph.D. program focuses on the development of research skills to prepare the student for scholarship in their field of interest. These research themes are: circuits and computer engineering, information and decision systems, and nanodevices and nanosystems. (http://www.ese.upenn.edu)

Integrated Product Design: Two integrated product design degree programs are offered: the Master of Integrated Product Design (M:IPD) and the Master of Science in Engineering in Integrated Product Design (M.S.E. in IPD). The M:IPD is intended for students with a non-engineering background or students with an engineering background who wish to build their skills in other disciplines. Students gain an interdisciplinary perspective of product design, building skills in conceptualization, ideation, manufacturing, marketing, and business planning. The M.S.E. in IPD is intended for students who have an undergraduate degree in engineering. The degree emphasizes technology and manufacturing processes, including coursework in advanced CAD/CAM and mechatronics. (http://ipd.me.upenn.edu)

Materials Science and Engineering: The M.S.E and Ph.D. programs in Materials Science and Engineering prepare students to be leaders, innovators, and visionaries in the materials revolution. Students have access to a broad range of state-of-the-art instrumentation in the department and the Laboratory for Research on the Structure of Matter (LRSM). Research interests include: computational materials science, electronic/optical/magnetic materials, materials for energy, materials for the health sciences, polymers and soft matter, and structural materials and mechanical behavior. (http://www.mse.seas.upenn.edu)

Mechanical Engineering and Applied Mechanics: The M.S.E in Mechanical Engineering and Applied Mechanics (MEAM) is nationally recognized for its excellence. Research interests are: design and manufacturing, heat transfer/fluid mechanics/energy, mechanics of materials, mechatronic and robotic systems, and micro and nano systems. The MEAM Ph.D. is an interdisciplinary, hands-on, research-focused program that collaborates with material sciences, computer sciences, electrical and systems engineering, chemical and biomolecular engineering, and the School of Medicine. Research interests:

advanced manufacturing, computational and data science and engineering, design, energy science and engineering, fluid mechanics, mechanics and materials, mechanical engineering in biology and medicine, micro and nano scale science and engineering, robotics and controls, and thermal sciences. (http://www.me.upenn.edu)

Nanotechnology: The M.S.E. program in Nanotechnology prepares students for leadership roles in emerging high-tech industries as well as traditional industries that utilize nanoscale phenomena. Nanotechnology is a highly interdisciplinary field and students are able to take courses from the Schools of Engineering, Arts and Sciences, and Wharton. Technical courses are organized into three research interests: synthesis, materials, and nanofabrication; devices and fundamental properties; and biotechnology. (https://masters.nano.upenn.edu/)

Robotics: The M.S.E. program in Robotics is a unique program administered by Penn's General Robotics, Automation, Sensing and Perception (GRASP) Laboratory, recognized as one of the nation's premier robotics research centers. Multidisciplinary in scope, it provides an ideal foundation for what today's experts in robotics and intelligent systems need to know. Research interests are: artificial intelligence, computer vision, control systems, dynamics and machine learning, design, programming, and prototyping of robotic systems. (https://www.grasp.upenn.edu)

Scientific Computing and Data Science: The M.S.E. in Data Science focuses on the use of statistical and data analytics techniques across a variety of disciplines, including business, public policy, medicine, social science, and the humanities. It is a cross-disciplinary program aimed at students with a computational, mathematical, or statistical background. The M.S.E. in Scientific Computing focuses on computational techniques for engineering and the physical sciences and expects a background in these disciplines. Both programs provide graduate training in the fundamentals of computational science, hypothesis testing, data analytics, and machine learning, and they give an opportunity for students to choose a specialization and receive practical experience. (http://pics.upenn.edu/masters-of-engineering-in-scientific-computing) (https://dats.seas.upenn.edu/)

Smith Walk in the Penn Engineering Quad.

Dr. George J. Pappas, Joseph Moore Professor and Chair of the Department of Electrical and Systems Engineering, with students.

Section 2
Aerospace/Aeronautical Engineering

This section contains a directory of institutions offering graduate work in aerospace/aeronautical engineering. Additional information about programs listed in the directory may be obtained by writing directly to the dean of a graduate school or chair of a department at the address given in the directory.

For programs offering related work, see also in this book *Engineering and Applied Sciences* and *Mechanical Engineering and Mechanics.* In another guide in this series:

Graduate Programs in the Physical Sciences, Mathematics, Agricultural Sciences, the Environment & Natural Resources
See *Geosciences* and *Physics*

CONTENTS

Program Directories

Aerospace/Aeronautical Engineering

Air Force Institute of Technology, Graduate School of Engineering and Management, Department of Aeronautics and Astronautics, Dayton, OH 45433-7765. Offers aeronautical engineering (MS, PhD); astronautical engineering (MS, PhD); materials science (MS, PhD); space operations (MS); systems engineering (MS, PhD). *Accreditation:* ABET (one or more programs are accredited). *Program availability:* Part-time. *Degree requirements:* For master's, thesis; for doctorate, thesis/dissertation. *Entrance requirements:* For master's and doctorate, GRE General Test, minimum GPA of 3.0, U.S. citizenship. *Faculty research:* Computational fluid dynamics, experimental aerodynamics, computational structural mechanics, experimental structural mechanics, aircraft and spacecraft stability and control.

Arizona State University at the Tempe campus, Ira A. Fulton Schools of Engineering, School for Engineering of Matter, Transport and Energy, Tempe, AZ 85281. Offers aerospace engineering (MS, PhD); chemical engineering (MS, PhD); materials science and engineering (MS, PhD); mechanical engineering (MS, PhD); solar energy engineering and commercialization (PSM). *Program availability:* Part-time, evening/weekend, online learning. Terminal master's awarded for partial completion of doctoral program. *Degree requirements:* For master's, thesis and oral defense (MS); applied project or comprehensive exam (MSE); interactive Program of Study (iPOS) submitted before completing 50 percent of required credit hours; for doctorate, comprehensive exam, thesis/dissertation, interactive Program of Study (iPOS) submitted before completing 50 percent of required credit hours. *Entrance requirements:* For master's, GRE, minimum GPA of 3.0 or equivalent in last 2 years of work leading to bachelor's degree; for doctorate, GRE, minimum GPA of 3.0 in last 2 years of work leading to bachelor's degree. Additional exam requirements/recommendations for international students: Required—TOEFL, IELTS, or PTE. Electronic applications accepted. *Expenses:* Contact institution. *Faculty research:* Electronic materials and packaging, materials for energy (batteries), adaptive/intelligent materials and structures, multiscale fluid mechanics, membranes, therapeutics and bioseparations, flexible structures, nanostructured materials, micro-/nano-transport.

Auburn University, Graduate School, Ginn College of Engineering, Department of Aerospace Engineering, Auburn University, AL 36849. Offers MAE, MS, PhD. *Program availability:* Part-time. *Degree requirements:* For master's, thesis (MS), exam; for doctorate, thesis/dissertation, exams. *Entrance requirements:* For master's and doctorate, GRE General Test. Electronic applications accepted. *Expenses:* Tuition, state resident: full-time $11,282; part-time $535 per credit hour. Tuition, nonresident: full-time $30,542; part-time $1605 per credit hour. *Required fees:* $826 per semester. Tuition and fees vary according to degree level and program. *Faculty research:* Aerodynamics, flight dynamics and simulation, propulsion, structures and aero elasticity, aerospace smart structures.

California Institute of Technology, Division of Engineering and Applied Science, Option in Aeronautics, Pasadena, CA 91125-0001. Offers MS, PhD, Engr. Terminal master's awarded for partial completion of doctoral program. *Degree requirements:* For doctorate, thesis/dissertation. *Faculty research:* Computational fluid dynamics, technical fluid dynamics, structural mechanics, mechanics of fracture, aeronautical engineering and propulsion.

California Polytechnic State University, San Luis Obispo, College of Engineering, Department of Aerospace Engineering, San Luis Obispo, CA 93407. Offers MS. *Program availability:* Part-time. *Faculty:* 8 full-time (3 women). *Students:* 15 full-time (2 women), 15 part-time (0 women); includes 8 minority (3 Hispanic/Latino; 5 Two or more races, non-Hispanic/Latino), 1 international. Average age 23. 46 applicants, 52% accepted, 17 enrolled. In 2018, 20 master's awarded. *Degree requirements:* For master's, thesis. *Entrance requirements:* For master's, GRE. Additional exam requirements/recommendations for international students: Required—TOEFL (minimum score 80 iBT). *Application deadline:* For fall admission, 1/4 for domestic and international students. Applications are processed on a rolling basis. Application fee: $55. Electronic applications accepted. *Expenses: Tuition, area resident:* Full-time $7176; part-time $4164 per year. Tuition, state resident: full-time $10,965. Tuition, nonresident: full-time $10,965. *Required fees:* $6336; $3711. *Financial support:* Fellowships, research assistantships, teaching assistantships, career-related internships or fieldwork, scholarships/grants, and unspecified assistantships available. Financial award application deadline: 3/2; financial award applicants required to submit FAFSA. *Faculty research:* Space systems engineering, space vehicle design, aerodynamics, aerospace propulsion, dynamics and control. *Unit head:* Dr. Aaron Drake, Graduate Coordinator, 805-756-2577, E-mail: agdrake@calpoly.edu. *Application contact:* Dr. Aaron Drake, Graduate Coordinator, 805-756-2577, E-mail: agdrake@calpoly.edu.
Website: http://aero.calpoly.edu

California State Polytechnic University, Pomona, Program in Engineering, Pomona, CA 91768-2557. Offers engineering (MSE). *Program availability:* Part-time, evening/weekend. *Students:* 1 full-time (0 women), 43 part-time (9 women); includes 24 minority (1 Black or African American, non-Hispanic/Latino; 11 Asian, non-Hispanic/Latino; 10 Hispanic/Latino; 2 Two or more races, non-Hispanic/Latino), 4 international. Average age 27. 61 applicants, 34% accepted, 15 enrolled. In 2018, 1 master's awarded. *Entrance requirements:* Additional exam requirements/recommendations for international students: Required—TOEFL (minimum score 550 paper-based). *Application deadline:* Applications are processed on a rolling basis. Application fee: $55. Electronic applications accepted. *Expenses:* Contact institution. *Financial support:* Application deadline: 3/2; applicants required to submit FAFSA. *Faculty research:* Aerospace engineering, materials engineering. *Unit head:* Dr. Ali R. Ahmadi, Department Chair/Professor, 909-869-2470, Fax: 909-869-6920, E-mail: arahmadi@cpp.edu. *Application contact:* Dr. Ali R. Ahmadi, Department Chair/Professor, 909-869-2470, Fax: 909-869-6920, E-mail: arahmadi@cpp.edu.
Website: http://www.cpp.edu/~engineering/ARO/masters.shtml

Carleton University, Faculty of Graduate Studies, Faculty of Engineering and Design, Department of Mechanical and Aerospace Engineering, Ottawa, ON K1S 5B6, Canada. Offers aerospace engineering (M Eng, MA Sc, PhD); materials engineering (M Eng, MA Sc); mechanical engineering (M Eng, MA Sc, PhD). *Degree requirements:* For master's, thesis optional; for doctorate, thesis/dissertation. *Entrance requirements:* For master's, honors degree; for doctorate, MA Sc or M Eng. Additional exam requirements/recommendations for international students: Required—TOEFL. *Faculty research:* Thermal fluids engineering, heat transfer, vehicle engineering.

Case Western Reserve University, School of Graduate Studies, Case School of Engineering, Department of Mechanical and Aerospace Engineering, Cleveland, OH 44106. Offers MS, PhD. *Program availability:* Part-time, 100% online. *Faculty:* 15 full-time (5 women). *Students:* 86 full-time (17 women), 3 part-time (1 woman); includes 10 minority (2 Black or African American, non-Hispanic/Latino; 5 Asian, non-Hispanic/Latino; 3 Hispanic/Latino), 55 international. In 2018, 24 master's, 9 doctorates awarded.

Degree requirements: For master's, thesis (for some programs); for doctorate, thesis/dissertation, qualifying exam, teaching experience. *Entrance requirements:* For master's and doctorate, GRE General Test. Additional exam requirements/recommendations for international students: Required—TOEFL. *Application deadline:* For fall admission, 7/1 priority date for domestic students. Applications are processed on a rolling basis. Application fee: $50. *Expenses: Tuition:* Full-time $45,168; part-time $1939 per credit hour. *Required fees:* $36; $18 per semester. $18 per semester. *Financial support:* In 2018–19, 60 students received support, including 4 fellowships with tuition reimbursements available, 26 research assistantships with tuition reimbursements available, 30 teaching assistantships; institutionally sponsored loans and tuition waivers (full and partial) also available. Financial award application deadline: 3/1; financial award applicants required to submit FAFSA. *Faculty research:* Musculoskeletal biomechanics, combustion diagnostics and computation, mechanical behavior of advanced materials and nanostructures, biorobotics. *Total annual research expenditures:* $6.2 million. *Unit head:* Dr. Robert Gao, Department Chair, 216-368-6045, Fax: 216-368-6445, E-mail: robert.gao@case.edu. *Application contact:* Carla Wilson, Student Affairs Coordinator, 216-368-4580, Fax: 216-368-3007, E-mail: cxw75@case.edu.
Website: http://www.engineering.case.edu/emae

The Citadel, The Military College of South Carolina, Citadel Graduate College, School of Engineering, Department of Mechanical Engineering, Charleston, SC 29409. Offers aeronautical engineering (Graduate Certificate); composites engineering (Graduate Certificate); manufacturing engineering (Graduate Certificate); mechanical engineering (MS); mechatronics engineering (Graduate Certificate); power and energy (Graduate Certificate). *Program availability:* Part-time, evening/weekend. *Degree requirements:* For master's, 30 hours of coursework with minimum GPA of 3.0 on hours earned at The Citadel. *Entrance requirements:* For master's, GRE, 2 letters of recommendation; official transcript of baccalaureate degree from an ABET accredited engineering program or approved alternative. Additional exam requirements/recommendations for international students: Required—TOEFL (minimum score 550 paper-based; 79 iBT). Electronic applications accepted. *Expenses:* Tuition, state resident: part-time $595 per credit hour. Tuition, nonresident: part-time $1020 per credit hour. *Required fees:* $90 per term.

Concordia University, School of Graduate Studies, Faculty of Engineering and Computer Science, Program in Aerospace Engineering, Montréal, QC H3G 1M8, Canada. Offers M Eng. Program offered jointly with École Polytechnique de Montréal and McGill University. *Degree requirements:* For master's, thesis or alternative. *Faculty research:* Aeronautics and propulsion avionics and control, structures and materials, space engineering.

Cornell University, Graduate School, Graduate Fields of Engineering, Field of Aerospace Engineering, Ithaca, NY 14853. Offers M Eng, MS, PhD. Terminal master's awarded for partial completion of doctoral program. *Degree requirements:* For master's, thesis (MS); for doctorate, one foreign language, comprehensive exam, thesis/dissertation. *Entrance requirements:* For master's and doctorate, GRE General Test, 3 letters of recommendation. Additional exam requirements/recommendations for international students: Required—TOEFL (minimum score 550 paper-based; 77 iBT). Electronic applications accepted. *Faculty research:* Aerodynamics, fluid mechanics, turbulence, combustion/propulsion, aeroacoustics.

École Polytechnique de Montréal, Graduate Programs, Department of Mechanical Engineering, Montréal, QC H3C 3A7, Canada. Offers aerothermics (M Eng, M Sc A, PhD); applied mechanics (M Eng, M Sc A, PhD); tool design (M Eng, M Sc A, PhD). *Program availability:* Part-time, evening/weekend. *Degree requirements:* For master's, one foreign language, thesis; for doctorate, one foreign language, thesis/dissertation. *Entrance requirements:* For master's, minimum GPA of 2.75; for doctorate, minimum GPA of 3.0. *Faculty research:* Noise control and vibration, fatigue and creep, aerodynamics, composite materials, biomechanics, robotics.

Embry-Riddle Aeronautical University–Daytona, Department of Aerospace Engineering, Daytona Beach, FL 32114-3900. Offers aerodynamics and propulsion (MS, PhD); dynamics and control (MS, PhD); structures and materials (MS, PhD). *Degree requirements:* For master's, thesis optional; for doctorate, thesis/dissertation. *Entrance requirements:* For doctorate, GRE, minimum master's cumulative GPA of 3.5. Additional exam requirements/recommendations for international students: Required—TOEFL (minimum score 550 paper-based, 79 iBT) or IELTS (6). Electronic applications accepted.

Embry-Riddle Aeronautical University–Daytona, School of Graduate Studies, Daytona Beach, FL 32114-3900. Offers aeronautics (MSA), including air traffic management, aviation safety systems, aviation/aerospace education technology, aviation/aerospace management, aviation/aerospace operations, small unmanned aircraft systems operation; aviation (PhD), including human factors in aviation systems. Application fee for PhD is $100. *Degree requirements:* For master's, thesis or capstone project; for doctorate, comprehensive exam, thesis/dissertation. *Entrance requirements:* Additional exam requirements/recommendations for international students: Required—TOEFL (minimum score 550 paper-based, 79 iBT) or IELTS (6). Electronic applications accepted.

Embry-Riddle Aeronautical University–Worldwide, Department of Aeronautics, Graduate Studies, Daytona Beach, FL 32114-3900. Offers aeronautics (MSA); aeronautics and design (MS); aviation & aerospace sustainability (MS); aviation maintenance (MAM); aviation/aerospace research (MS); education (MS); human factors (MSHFS); occupational safety management (MS); operations (MS); safety/emergency response (MS); space systems (MS); unmanned systems (MS). *Program availability:* Part-time, evening/weekend, 100% online. *Faculty:* 30 full-time (11 women), 124 part-time/adjunct (19 women). *Students:* 663 full-time (149 women), 877 part-time (191 women); includes 420 minority (144 Black or African American, non-Hispanic/Latino; 6 American Indian or Alaska Native, non-Hispanic/Latino; 58 Asian, non-Hispanic/Latino; 168 Hispanic/Latino; 3 Native Hawaiian or other Pacific Islander, non-Hispanic/Latino; 41 Two or more races, non-Hispanic/Latino), 126 international. Average age 37. 602 applicants, 71% accepted, 272 enrolled. In 2018, 499 master's awarded. *Degree requirements:* For master's, comprehensive exam, thesis (for some programs), capstone or thesis dependent on degree program. *Entrance requirements:* For master's, GRE required for MSHF. Additional exam requirements/recommendations for international students: Required—TOEFL (minimum score 550 paper-based; 79 iBT), IELTS (minimum score 6), TOEFL or IELTS required for Applicants for whom English is not the primary language. *Application deadline:* Applications are processed on a rolling basis. Application fee: $50. Electronic applications accepted. *Expenses: Tuition:* Full-time $7980; part-time $665 per credit hour. Tuition and fees vary according to course load, degree level and program. *Financial support:* Career-related internships or fieldwork and scholarships/grants available. Financial award applicants required to submit FAFSA. *Unit head:* Kenneth Witcher, PhD, Associate Professor and Dean,

College of Aeronautics, E-mail: kenneth.witcher@erau.edu. *Application contact:* Worldwide Campus, 800-522-6787, E-mail: worldwide@erau.edu. Website: http://worldwide.erau.edu/colleges/aeronautics/department-aeronautics-graduate-studies/

Embry-Riddle Aeronautical University–Worldwide, Department of Engineering and Technology, Daytona Beach, FL 32114-3900. Offers aerospace engineering (MS); entrepreneurship in technology (MS); systems engineering (M Sys E), including engineering management, technical. *Program availability:* Part-time, evening/weekend, 100% online, blended/hybrid learning. *Entrance requirements:* For master's, GRE (for MS in aerospace engineering). Additional exam requirements/recommendations for international students: Required—TOEFL (minimum score 550 paper-based; 79 iBT), IELTS (minimum score 6). Electronic applications accepted. *Expenses:* Contact institution.

Florida Institute of Technology, College of Aeronautics, Melbourne, FL 32901-6975. Offers aviation human factors (MS); aviation safety, applied (MSA); aviation sciences (PhD). *Program availability:* Part-time, evening/weekend, 100% online. *Faculty:* 20 full-time (7 women), 13 part-time/adjunct (2 women). *Students:* 46 full-time (17 women), 5 part-time (0 women); includes 7 minority (1 Black or African American, non-Hispanic/Latino; 2 Asian, non-Hispanic/Latino; 2 Hispanic/Latino; 2 Two or more races, non-Hispanic/Latino), 35 international. 25 applicants, 96% accepted, 14 enrolled. In 2018, 18 master's awarded. *Degree requirements:* For master's, thesis (for some programs), thesis or capstone project; for doctorate, thesis/dissertation (for some programs). *Entrance requirements:* For master's, GRE, minimum GPA of 3.0, 3 letters of recommendation, resume, statement of objectives; for doctorate, GRE, minimum GPA of 3.2; master's degree in an aviation field (for international applicants). Additional exam requirements/recommendations for international students: Required—TOEFL (minimum score 550 paper-based; 79 iBT). *Application deadline:* Applications are processed on a rolling basis. Application fee: $50. Electronic applications accepted. *Expenses:* Tuition: Full-time $22,338; part-time $1241 per credit hour. Tuition and fees vary according to degree level, campus/location and program. *Financial support:* In 2018–19, 7 students received support, including 7 research assistantships with partial tuition reimbursements available; teaching assistantships with partial tuition reimbursements available, career-related internships or fieldwork, institutionally sponsored loans, tuition waivers (partial), and tuition remissions also available. Financial award application deadline: 3/1; financial award applicants required to submit FAFSA. *Faculty research:* Aircraft cockpit design, medical human factors, operating room human factors, hypobaric chamber operations and effects, aviation professional education. *Total annual research expenditures:* $846,073. *Unit head:* Dr. Ulreen Jones, Interim Dean, 321-674-7472, Fax: 321-674-7368, E-mail: ujones@fit.edu. *Application contact:* Cheryl A. Brown, Associate Director of Graduate Admissions, 321-674-7581, Fax: 321-723-9468, E-mail: cbrown@fit.edu. Website: www.fit.edu/aeronautics

Florida Institute of Technology, College of Engineering and Science, Program in Aerospace Engineering, Melbourne, FL 32901-6975. Offers MS, PhD. *Program availability:* Part-time. *Students:* 30 full-time (7 women), 29 part-time (7 women); includes 9 minority (3 Asian, non-Hispanic/Latino; 6 Hispanic/Latino), 19 international. Average age 27. 42 applicants, 60% accepted, 10 enrolled. In 2018, 22 master's, 1 doctorate awarded. Terminal master's awarded for partial completion of doctoral program. *Degree requirements:* For master's, comprehensive exam, 30 credit hours; thesis or additional courses plus final exam; for doctorate, comprehensive exam, thesis/dissertation, 42 credit hours. *Entrance requirements:* For master's, GRE General Test, minimum GPA of 3.0; for doctorate, GRE General Test, minimum GPA of 3.2, 3 letters of recommendation. Additional exam requirements/recommendations for international students: Required—TOEFL (minimum score 550 paper-based; 79 iBT). *Application deadline:* Applications are processed on a rolling basis. Application fee: $50. Electronic applications accepted. *Expenses:* Tuition: Full-time $22,338; part-time $1241 per credit hour. Tuition and fees vary according to degree level, campus/location and program. *Financial support:* Research assistantships, teaching assistantships, career-related internships or fieldwork, institutionally sponsored loans, and tuition remissions available. Financial award application deadline: 3/1; financial award applicants required to submit FAFSA. *Faculty research:* Propulsion, flight mechanics and control, mechatronics, robotics, fluid mechanics, aerodynamics, computational methods, composite structures, lasers, and hurricane and wind damage. *Unit head:* Dr. Chelakara Subramanian, Program Chair, 321-674-7614, Fax: 321-674-8813, E-mail: subraman@fit.edu. *Application contact:* Mike Perry, Executive Director of Admissions, 321-674-7127, E-mail: perrymj@fit.edu. Website: www.fit.edu/programs/aerospace-engineering-ms/

The George Washington University, School of Engineering and Applied Science, Department of Mechanical and Aerospace Engineering, Washington, DC 20052. Offers MS, PhD, App Sc, Engr, Graduate Certificate. *Program availability:* Part-time, evening/weekend. *Faculty:* 23 full-time (4 women), 11 part-time/adjunct (1 woman). *Students:* 92 full-time (11 women), 37 part-time (6 women); includes 8 minority (1 Black or African American, non-Hispanic/Latino; 1 American Indian or Alaska Native, non-Hispanic/Latino; 2 Asian, non-Hispanic/Latino; 2 Hispanic/Latino; 2 Two or more races, non-Hispanic/Latino), 98 international. Average age 26. 301 applicants, 73% accepted, 42 enrolled. In 2018, 40 master's, 13 doctorates awarded. *Degree requirements:* For master's, thesis optional; for doctorate, thesis/dissertation, final and qualifying exams. *Entrance requirements:* For master's, appropriate bachelor's degree, minimum GPA of 3.0; for doctorate, GRE (if highest earned degree is BS), appropriate bachelor's or master's degree, minimum GPA of 3.4; for other advanced degree, appropriate master's degree, minimum GPA of 3.0. Additional exam requirements/recommendations for international students: Required—TOEFL or The George Washington University English as a Foreign Language Test. *Application deadline:* For fall admission, 3/1 priority date for domestic students; for spring admission, 10/1 for domestic students. Applications are processed on a rolling basis. Application fee: $75. *Financial support:* In 2018–19, 51 students received support. Fellowships, research assistantships, teaching assistantships, career-related internships or fieldwork, and institutionally sponsored loans available. Financial award application deadline: 3/1; financial award applicants required to submit FAFSA. *Unit head:* Dr. Michael Plesniak, Chair, 202-994-9800, E-mail: maeng@gwu.edu. *Application contact:* Adina Lav, Marketing, Recruiting and Admissions, 202-994-5827, Fax: 202-994-0909, E-mail: engineering@gwu.edu.

Georgia Institute of Technology, Graduate Studies, College of Engineering, School of Aerospace Engineering, Atlanta, GA 30332-0001. Offers MS, PhD. *Program availability:* Part-time. Terminal master's awarded for partial completion of doctoral program. *Degree requirements:* For master's, thesis optional; for doctorate, thesis/dissertation. *Entrance requirements:* For master's and doctorate, GRE. Additional exam requirements/recommendations for international students: Required—TOEFL (minimum score 550 paper-based; 79 iBT). Electronic applications accepted. *Faculty research:* Structural mechanics and dynamics, fluid mechanics, flight mechanics and controls, combustion and propulsion, system design and optimization.

Illinois Institute of Technology, Graduate College, Armour College of Engineering, Department of Mechanical, Materials and Aerospace Engineering, Chicago, IL 60616. Offers manufacturing engineering (MAS, MS); materials science and engineering (MAS, MS, PhD); mechanical and aerospace engineering (MAS, MS, PhD), including

economics (MS), energy (MS), environment (MS). *Program availability:* Part-time, evening/weekend, online learning. Terminal master's awarded for partial completion of doctoral program. *Degree requirements:* For master's, comprehensive exam (for some programs), thesis (for some programs); for doctorate, comprehensive exam, thesis/dissertation. *Entrance requirements:* For master's and doctorate, GRE General Test (minimum score 1000 Quantitative and Verbal, 3.0 Analytical Writing), minimum undergraduate GPA of 3.0. Additional exam requirements/recommendations for international students: Required—TOEFL (minimum score 550 paper-based; 80 iBT). Electronic applications accepted. *Faculty research:* Fluid dynamics, metallurgical and materials engineering, solids and structures, computational mechanics, computer added design and manufacturing, thermal sciences, dynamic analysis and control of complex systems.

Inter American University of Puerto Rico, Bayamón Campus, Graduate School, Bayamón, PR 00957. Offers biology (MS), including environmental sciences and ecology, molecular biotechnology; electrical engineering (ME), including control system, potence system; human resources (MBA); mechanical engineering (ME, MS), including aerospace, energy. *Program availability:* Part-time, evening/weekend. *Degree requirements:* For master's, comprehensive exam, research project. *Entrance requirements:* For master's, EXADEP, GRE General Test, letters of recommendation. *Expenses:* Tuition: Full-time $3816; part-time $1908 per trimester. *Required fees:* $735; $642.

Iowa State University of Science and Technology, Department of Aerospace Engineering and Engineering Mechanics, Ames, IA 50011. Offers aerospace engineering (M Eng, MS, PhD); engineering mechanics (M Eng, MS, PhD). *Degree requirements:* For master's, thesis (for some programs); for doctorate, thesis/dissertation. *Entrance requirements:* For master's and doctorate, GRE General Test, resume. Additional exam requirements/recommendations for international students: Required—TOEFL (minimum score 550 paper-based; 80 iBT), IELTS (minimum score 6.5). Electronic applications accepted.

Johns Hopkins University, Engineering Program for Professionals, Part-time Program in Space Systems Engineering, Baltimore, MD 21218. Offers MS. *Program availability:* 100% online, blended/hybrid learning. *Faculty:* 6 part-time/adjunct. *Students:* 143 part-time (38 women). 63 applicants, 75% accepted, 22 enrolled. In 2018, 33 master's awarded. *Entrance requirements:* For master's, undergraduate degree in a technical discipline; at least two years of experience in the space technology or space science field; minimum of two years of relevant work experience; resume; official transcripts from all college studies. Additional exam requirements/recommendations for international students: Required—TOEFL (minimum score 600 paper-based; 100 iBT). Application fee: $0. Electronic applications accepted. *Unit head:* Dr. Patrick Binning, Program Chair, E-mail: patrick.binning@jhu.edu. *Application contact:* Doug Schiller, Admissions Director, 410-516-2300, Fax: 410-579-8049, E-mail: schiller@jhu.edu. Website: http://ep.jhu.edu/graduate-programs/space-systems-engineering

Kent State University, College of Aeronautics and Engineering, Kent, OH 44242-0001. Offers technology (MTC). *Program availability:* Part-time, 100% online. *Faculty:* 11 full-time (0 women), 2 part-time/adjunct (1 woman). *Students:* 27 full-time (5 women), 21 part-time (3 women); includes 2 minority (both Hispanic/Latino), 27 international. Average age 27. 49 applicants, 82% accepted, 14 enrolled. In 2018, 63 master's awarded. *Degree requirements:* For master's, thesis optional. *Entrance requirements:* For master's, 4-year undergraduate (bachelor's) degree in science or related field from accredited college, university, or institute. Additional exam requirements/recommendations for international students: Required—TOEFL (minimum score 550 paper-based; 79 iBT), IELTS (minimum score 6.5), PTE (minimum score 58), Michigan English Language Assessment Battery (minimum score 71). *Application deadline:* For fall admission, 7/23 for domestic and international students; for spring admission, 12/14 for domestic and international students; for summer admission, 4/30 for domestic and international students. Applications are processed on a rolling basis. Application fee: $45 ($70 for international students). Electronic applications accepted. *Expenses:* Tuition, state resident: full-time $11,766; part-time $536 per credit. Tuition, nonresident: full-time $21,952; part-time $999 per credit. *International tuition:* $21,952 full-time. Tuition and fees vary according to course load. *Financial support:* Research assistantships, teaching assistantships, career-related internships or fieldwork, Federal Work-Study, scholarships/grants, and unspecified assistantships available. Financial award application deadline: 2/1; financial award applicants required to submit FAFSA. *Unit head:* Christina Bloebaum, Dean, 330-672-9780, E-mail: cbloebau@kent.edu. *Application contact:* Richard Mangrum, Coordinator, Graduate Program, 330-672-1933, E-mail: rmangum@kent.edu. Website: https://www.kent.edu/cae

Massachusetts Institute of Technology, School of Engineering, Department of Aeronautics and Astronautics, Cambridge, MA 02139. Offers aeronautics and astronautics (SM, PhD, Sc D, EAA); aerospace computational engineering (PhD, Sc D); air transportation systems (PhD, Sc D); air-breathing propulsion (PhD, Sc D); aircraft systems engineering (PhD, Sc D); autonomous systems (PhD, Sc D); communications and networks (PhD, Sc D); controls (PhD, Sc D); humans in aerospace (PhD, Sc D); materials and structures (PhD, Sc D); space propulsion (PhD, Sc D); space systems (PhD, Sc D); SM/MBA. *Degree requirements:* For master's, thesis; for doctorate, comprehensive exam, thesis/dissertation, minimum cumulative GPA of 4.4 on 5.0 scale; for EAA, comprehensive exam, thesis. *Entrance requirements:* For master's and doctorate, GRE General Test. Additional exam requirements/recommendations for international students: Required—TOEFL, IELTS. Electronic applications accepted. *Expenses:* Tuition: Full-time $51,520; part-time $800 per credit hour. *Required fees:* $312. *Faculty research:* Vehicle design; information sciences; computation; human-system collaboration; atmosphere and space sciences; complex systems.

McGill University, Faculty of Graduate and Postdoctoral Studies, Faculty of Engineering, Department of Mechanical Engineering, Montréal, QC H3A 2T5, Canada. Offers aerospace (M Eng); manufacturing management (MMM); mechanical engineering (M Eng, M Sc, PhD).

Middle Tennessee State University, College of Graduate Studies, College of Basic and Applied Sciences, Department of Aerospace, Murfreesboro, TN 37132. Offers aerospace education (M Ed); aviation administration (MS). *Program availability:* Part-time, evening/weekend, online learning. *Degree requirements:* For master's, comprehensive exam, thesis optional. *Entrance requirements:* For master's, GRE General Test or MAT. Additional exam requirements/recommendations for international students: Required—TOEFL (minimum score 525 paper-based; 71 iBT) or IELTS (minimum score 6). Electronic applications accepted.

Mississippi State University, Bagley College of Engineering, Department of Aerospace Engineering, Mississippi State, MS 39762. Offers aerospace engineering (MS); engineering (PhD), including aerospace engineering. *Program availability:* Part-time. *Faculty:* 12 full-time (1 woman), 3 part-time/adjunct (2 women). *Students:* 47 full-time (13 women), 23 part-time (6 women); includes 6 minority (4 Black or African American, non-Hispanic/Latino; 2 Hispanic/Latino), 36 international. Average age 28. 33 applicants, 82% accepted, 13 enrolled. In 2018, 29 master's, 3 doctorates awarded. *Degree requirements:* For master's, comprehensive exam, thesis optional, oral exam;

for doctorate, comprehensive exam, thesis/dissertation. *Entrance requirements:* For master's, GRE (for graduates from program not accredited by EAC/ABET), bachelor's degree in engineering with minimum GPA of 3.0 from junior and senior years; for doctorate, GRE, bachelor's or master's degree in aerospace engineering or closely-related field. Additional exam requirements/recommendations for international students: Required—TOEFL (minimum score 550 paper-based; 79 iBT); Recommended—IELTS (minimum score 6.5). *Application deadline:* For fall admission, 7/1 for domestic students, 5/1 for international students; for spring admission, 11/1 for domestic students, 9/1 for international students. Applications are processed on a rolling basis. Application fee: $60 ($80 for international students). Electronic applications accepted. *Expenses:* Tuition, state resident: full-time $8450; part-time $360.59 per credit hour. Tuition, nonresident: full-time $23,140; part-time $969.09 per credit hour. *Required fees:* $110. One-time fee: $55 full-time. Part-time tuition and fees vary according to course load, degree level, campus/location and reciprocity agreements. *Financial support:* In 2018–19, 14 research assistantships with partial tuition reimbursements (averaging $15,811 per year), 12 teaching assistantships with partial tuition reimbursements (averaging $15,476 per year) were awarded; Federal Work-Study, institutionally sponsored loans, and unspecified assistantships also available. Financial award application deadline: 4/1; financial award applicants required to submit FAFSA. *Faculty research:* Computational fluid dynamics, flight mechanics, aerodynamics, composite structures, prototype development. *Total annual research expenditures:* $5.1 million. *Unit head:* Dr. Davy Belk, Department Head and Professor, 662-325-3623, Fax: 662-325-7730, E-mail: davy.belk@ae.msstate.edu. *Application contact:* Ryan King, Admissions and Enrollment Assistant, 662-325-8951, E-mail: rjk101@grad.msstate.edu.
Website: http://www.ae.msstate.edu/

Missouri University of Science and Technology, Department of Mechanical and Aerospace Engineering, Rolla, MO 65401. Offers aerospace engineering (MS, PhD); manufacturing engineering (M Eng, MS); mechanical engineering (MS, PhD). *Program availability:* Part-time, evening/weekend. Terminal master's awarded for partial completion of doctoral program. *Degree requirements:* For master's, thesis optional; for doctorate, comprehensive exam, thesis/dissertation. *Entrance requirements:* For master's, GRE General Test (minimum score 1100 verbal and quantitative, writing 3.5), minimum GPA of 3.0; for doctorate, GRE General Test (minimum score: verbal and quantitative 1100, writing 3.5), minimum GPA of 3.5. Additional exam requirements/recommendations for international students: Required—TOEFL (minimum score 550 paper-based). Electronic applications accepted. *Expenses:* Tuition, state resident: full-time $7545.60; part-time $419.20 per credit hour. Tuition, nonresident: full-time $22,169; part-time $1231.60 per credit hour. *International tuition:* $23,518.80 full-time. *Required fees:* $4523.05. Full-time tuition and fees vary according to course load, campus/location, program and reciprocity agreements. *Faculty research:* Dynamics and controls, acoustics, computational fluid dynamics, space mechanics, hypersonics.

Naval Postgraduate School, Departments and Academic Groups, Department of Defense Analysis, Monterey, CA 93943. Offers command and control (MS); communications (MS); defense analysis (MS), including astronautics; financial management (MS); information operations (MS); irregular warfare (MS); national security affairs (MS); operations analysis (MS); special operations (MA, MS), including command and control (MS), communications (MS), financial management (MS), information operations (MS), irregular warfare (MS), national security affairs, operations analysis (MS), tactile missiles (MS), terrorist operations and financing (MS); tactile missiles (MS); terrorist operations and financing (MS). Program only open to commissioned officers of the United States and friendly nations and selected United States federal civilian employees. *Program availability:* Part-time. *Degree requirements:* For master's, thesis. *Faculty research:* CTF Global Ecco Project, Afghanistan endgames, core lab Philippines project, Defense Manpower Data Center (DMDC) data vulnerability.

Naval Postgraduate School, Departments and Academic Groups, Department of Mechanical and Aerospace Engineering, Monterey, CA 93943. Offers astronautical engineer (AstE); astronautical engineering (MS); engineering science (MS), including astronautical engineering, mechanical engineering; mechanical and aerospace engineering (PhD); mechanical engineering (MS). Program only open to commissioned officers of the United States and friendly nations and selected United States federal civilian employees. *Program availability:* Part-time, online learning. *Degree requirements:* For master's, thesis (for some programs), capstone or research/dissertation paper (for some programs); for doctorate, thesis/dissertation; for AstE, thesis. *Faculty research:* Sensors and actuators, new materials and methods, mechanics of materials, laser and material interaction, energy harvesting and storage.

Naval Postgraduate School, Departments and Academic Groups, Space Systems Academic Group, Monterey, CA 93943. Offers applied physics (MS); astronautical engineering (MS); computer science (MS); electrical engineering (MS); mechanical engineering (MS); space systems (Engr); space systems operations (MS). Program only open to commissioned officers of the United States and friendly nations and selected United States federal civilian employees. *Program availability:* Part-time. *Degree requirements:* For master's and Engr, thesis; for doctorate, thesis/dissertation. *Faculty research:* Military applications for space; space reconnaissance and remote sensing; radiation-hardened electronics for space; design, construction and operations of small satellites; satellite communications systems.

North Carolina State University, Graduate School, College of Engineering, Department of Mechanical and Aerospace Engineering, Program in Aerospace Engineering, Raleigh, NC 27695. Offers MS, PhD. *Program availability:* Online learning. *Degree requirements:* For master's, thesis (for some programs), oral exam; for doctorate, thesis/dissertation, oral and preliminary exams. *Entrance requirements:* For master's and doctorate, GRE General Test. Additional exam requirements/recommendations for international students: Required—TOEFL (minimum score 550 paper-based). Electronic applications accepted. *Faculty research:* Aerodynamics, computational fluid dynamics, flight research, smart structures, propulsion.

The Ohio State University, Graduate School, College of Engineering, Department of Mechanical and Aerospace Engineering, Columbus, OH 43210. Offers aerospace engineering (MS, PhD); mechanical engineering (MS, PhD); nuclear engineering (MS, PhD). *Faculty:* 67. *Students:* 367 (56 women). Average age 25. In 2018, 100 master's, 29 doctorates awarded. *Entrance requirements:* For master's and doctorate, GRE. Additional exam requirements/recommendations for international students: Required—TOEFL (minimum score 550 paper-based; 79 iBT), Michigan English Language Assessment Battery (minimum score 82); Recommended—IELTS (minimum score 7). *Application deadline:* For fall admission, 11/30 priority date for domestic and international students; for spring admission, 10/1 for domestic and international students. Applications are processed on a rolling basis. Application fee: $60 ($70 for international students). Electronic applications accepted. *Financial support:* Fellowships, research assistantships, teaching assistantships, career-related internships or fieldwork, Federal Work-Study, institutionally sponsored loans, and unspecified assistantships available. Support available to part-time students. *Unit head:* Dr. Vish Subramaniam, Chair, 614-292-6096, E-mail: subramaniam.1@osu.edu. *Application contact:* Janeen Sands, Graduate Program Administrator, 614-247-6605, Fax: 614-292-3656, E-mail: maegradadmissions@osu.edu.
Website: http://mae.osu.edu/

Old Dominion University, Frank Batten College of Engineering and Technology, Programs in Aerospace Engineering, Norfolk, VA 23529. Offers ME, MS, D Eng, PhD. *Program availability:* Part-time, 100% online, blended/hybrid learning. *Degree requirements:* For master's, comprehensive exam (for some programs), thesis (MS), exam/project (ME); for doctorate, comprehensive exam, thesis/dissertation, candidacy exam, proposal, exam. *Entrance requirements:* For master's, GRE, minimum GPA of 3.0; for doctorate, GRE, minimum GPA of 3.5. Additional exam requirements/recommendations for international students: Required—TOEFL (minimum score 550 paper-based; 79 iBT), IELTS (minimum score 6.5). Electronic applications accepted. *Expenses:* Contact institution. *Faculty research:* Computational fluid dynamics, experimental fluid dynamics, structural mechanics, dynamics and control, microfluidics.

Penn State University Park, Graduate School, College of Engineering, Department of Aerospace Engineering, University Park, PA 16802. Offers M Eng, MS, PhD.

Princeton University, Graduate School, School of Engineering and Applied Science, Department of Mechanical and Aerospace Engineering, Princeton, NJ 08544. Offers M Eng, MSE, PhD. Terminal master's awarded for partial completion of doctoral program. *Degree requirements:* For master's, thesis (MSE); for doctorate, thesis/dissertation, general exam. *Entrance requirements:* For master's, GRE General Test, 3 letters of recommendation; for doctorate, GRE General Test, official transcript(s), 3 letters of recommendation, personal statement. Additional exam requirements/recommendations for international students: Required—TOEFL. Electronic applications accepted. *Faculty research:* Bioengineering and biomechanics; combustion, energy conversion, and climate; fluid mechanics, dynamics, and control systems; lasers and applied physics; materials and mechanical systems.

Purdue University, College of Engineering, School of Aeronautics and Astronautics, West Lafayette, IN 47907. Offers MS, PhD. *Program availability:* Part-time, 100% online. Terminal master's awarded for partial completion of doctoral program. *Degree requirements:* For master's, thesis optional; for doctorate, thesis/dissertation. *Entrance requirements:* For master's, GRE General Test, minimum GPA of 3.25; for doctorate, GRE General Test, minimum GPA of 3.5. Electronic applications accepted. *Faculty research:* Aerodynamics, aerospace systems, astrodynamics and space applications, dynamics and control, propulsion, structures and materials.

Rensselaer Polytechnic Institute, Graduate School, School of Engineering, Program in Aeronautical Engineering, Troy, NY 12180-3590. Offers M Eng, MS, PhD. *Faculty:* 55 full-time (6 women), 1 part-time/adjunct (0 women). *Students:* 50 full-time (8 women), 1 part-time; includes 4 minority (1 Black or African American, non-Hispanic/Latino; 1 Asian, non-Hispanic/Latino; 2 Two or more races, non-Hispanic/Latino), 15 international. Average age 25. 69 applicants, 55% accepted, 18 enrolled. In 2018, 11 master's, 10 doctorates awarded. *Degree requirements:* For master's, thesis (for some programs); for doctorate, thesis/dissertation. *Entrance requirements:* For master's and doctorate, GRE. Additional exam requirements/recommendations for international students: Required—TOEFL (minimum score 600 paper-based; 100 iBT), IELTS (minimum score 7), PTE (minimum score 68). *Application deadline:* For fall admission, 1/1 priority date for domestic and international students; for spring admission, 8/15 priority date for domestic and international students. Applications are processed on a rolling basis. Application fee: $75. Electronic applications accepted. *Financial support:* In 2018–19, research assistantships with full tuition reimbursements (averaging $23,000 per year), teaching assistantships with full tuition reimbursements (averaging $23,000 per year) were awarded; fellowships also available. Financial award application deadline: 1/1. *Faculty research:* Advanced nuclear materials, aerodynamics, design, dynamics and vibrations, fission systems and radiation transport, fluid mechanics (computational, theoretical, and experimental), heat transfer and energy conversion, manufacturing, medical imaging, health physics, multiscale/computational modeling, nanostructured materials and properties, nuclear physics/nuclear reactor, propulsion. *Total annual research expenditures:* $1.6 million. *Unit head:* Dr. Theo Borca-Tasciuc, Graduate Program Director, 518-276-2627, E-mail: borcat@rpi.edu. *Application contact:* Jarron Decker, Director of Graduate Admissions, 518-276-6216, Fax: 518-276-4072, E-mail: gradadmissions@rpi.edu.
Website: http://mane.rpi.edu/graduate/aeronautical-engineering

Rutgers University–New Brunswick, Graduate School-New Brunswick, Program in Mechanical and Aerospace Engineering, Piscataway, NJ 08854-8097. Offers design and control (MS, PhD); fluid mechanics (MS, PhD); solid mechanics (MS, PhD); thermal sciences (MS, PhD). *Program availability:* Part-time, evening/weekend. *Degree requirements:* For master's, thesis (for some programs); for doctorate, thesis/dissertation. *Entrance requirements:* For master's, GRE General Test, BS in mechanical/aerospace engineering or related field; for doctorate, GRE General Test, MS in mechanical/aerospace engineering or related field. Additional exam requirements/recommendations for international students: Required—TOEFL. Electronic applications accepted. *Faculty research:* Combustion, propulsion, thermal transport, crystal plasticity, optimization, fabrication, nanoidentation.

San Diego State University, Graduate and Research Affairs, College of Engineering, Department of Aerospace Engineering and Engineering Mechanics, San Diego, CA 92182. Offers aerospace engineering (MS); engineering mechanics (MS); engineering sciences and applied mechanics (PhD); flight dynamics (MS); fluid dynamics (MS). PhD offered jointly with University of California, San Diego and Department of Mechanical Engineering. Terminal master's awarded for partial completion of doctoral program. *Degree requirements:* For master's, comprehensive exam (for some programs), thesis (for some programs); for doctorate, thesis/dissertation. *Entrance requirements:* For master's, GRE General Test; for doctorate, GRE, 3 letters of recommendation. Additional exam requirements/recommendations for international students: Required—TOEFL. Electronic applications accepted. *Faculty research:* Organized structures in post-stall flow over wings/three dimensional separated flow, airfoil growth effect, probabilities, structural mechanics.

San Jose State University, Program in Mechanical and Aerospace Engineering, San Jose, CA 95192-0001. Offers aerospace engineering (MS); mechanical engineering (MS). *Program availability:* Part-time. *Entrance requirements:* For master's, GRE. Electronic applications accepted.

Stevens Institute of Technology, Graduate School, School of Systems and Enterprises, Program in Space Systems Engineering, Hoboken, NJ 07030. Offers M Eng, Certificate. *Program availability:* Part-time, evening/weekend. *Faculty:* 28 full-time (8 women), 5 part-time/adjunct (1 woman). *Students:* 5 full-time (0 women), 17 part-time (4 women); includes 4 minority (3 Black or African American, non-Hispanic/Latino; 1 Asian, non-Hispanic/Latino), 2 international. Average age 30. In 2018, 8 master's awarded. *Degree requirements:* For master's, thesis optional, minimum B average in major field and overall; for Certificate, minimum B average. *Entrance requirements:* For master's, GRE/GMAT scores: GRE scores are required for all applicants applying to a full-time graduate program in the Schaefer School of Engineering and Science (SES). International applicants must submit TOEFL/IELTS scores and fulfill the English Language Proficiency Requirements in order to be considered. Additional exam requirements/recommendations for international students: Required—TOEFL (minimum score 74 iBT), IELTS (minimum score 6). *Application deadline:* For fall admission, 4/15 for domestic and international students; for spring admission, 11/1 for domestic and

international students; for summer admission, 5/1 for domestic students. Applications are processed on a rolling basis. Application fee: $60. Electronic applications accepted. *Expenses: Tuition:* Full-time $35,960; part-time $1620 per credit. *Required fees:* $1290; $600 per semester. Tuition and fees vary according to course load. *Financial support:* Fellowships, research assistantships, teaching assistantships, career-related internships or fieldwork, Federal Work-Study, scholarships/grants, and unspecified assistantships available. Financial award application deadline: 2/15; financial award applicants required to submit FAFSA. *Unit head:* Dr. Yehia Massoud, Dean of SSE, 201-216.8025, E-mail: yehia.massoud@stevens.edu. *Application contact:* Graduate Admissions, 888-783-8367, Fax: 888-511-1306, E-mail: graduate@stevens.edu.
Website: https://www.stevens.edu/school-systems-enterprises/masters-degree-programs/space-systems-engineering

Syracuse University, College of Engineering and Computer Science, Programs in Mechanical and Aerospace Engineering, Syracuse, NY 13244. Offers MS, PhD. *Program availability:* Part-time. *Students:* Average age 25. In 2018, 55 master's, 8 doctorates awarded. *Degree requirements:* For master's, project or thesis; for doctorate, comprehensive exam, thesis/dissertation. *Entrance requirements:* For master's and doctorate, GRE General Test, official transcripts, personal statement, three letters of recommendation, resume. Additional exam requirements/recommendations for international students: Required—TOEFL (minimum score 100 iBT). *Application deadline:* For fall admission, 7/1 priority date for domestic students, 6/1 priority date for international students; for spring admission, 11/15 priority date for domestic students, 10/15 priority date for international students. Applications are processed on a rolling basis. Application fee: $75. Electronic applications accepted. *Financial support:* Fellowships with full tuition reimbursements, research assistantships, teaching assistantships, scholarships/grants, and tuition waivers (partial) available. Financial award application deadline: 1/1. *Faculty research:* Solid mechanics and materials, fluid mechanics, thermal sciences, controls and robotics. *Unit head:* Dr. Young Bai Moon, III, Department Chair, 315-443-4366, E-mail: gradinfo@syr.edu. *Application contact:* Kathleen Joyce, Assistant Dean, 315-443-2219, E-mail: topgrads@syr.edu.
Website: http://eng-cs.syr.edu/our-departments/mechanical-and-aerospace-engineering/

Texas A&M University, College of Engineering, Department of Aerospace Engineering, College Station, TX 77843. Offers aerospace engineering (M Eng). *Faculty:* 40. *Students:* 156 full-time (24 women), 19 part-time (1 woman); includes 19 minority (1 Black or African American, non-Hispanic/Latino; 6 Asian, non-Hispanic/Latino; 9 Hispanic/Latino; 3 Two or more races, non-Hispanic/Latino), 66 international. Average age 26. 282 applicants, 28% accepted, 49 enrolled. In 2018, 14 master's, 10 doctorates awarded. *Degree requirements:* For master's, thesis (MS); for doctorate, thesis/dissertation. *Entrance requirements:* For master's and doctorate, GRE General Test. Additional exam requirements/recommendations for international students: Required—TOEFL (minimum score 550 paper-based; 80 iBT), IELTS (minimum score 6), PTE (minimum score 53). *Application deadline:* For fall admission, 1/1 priority date for domestic students; for spring admission, 7/1 priority date for domestic students; for summer admission, 12/1 priority date for domestic students. Applications are processed on a rolling basis. Application fee: $50 ($90 for international students). Electronic applications accepted. *Expenses:* Contact institution. *Financial support:* In 2018–19, 159 students received support, including 11 fellowships with tuition reimbursements available (averaging $18,909 per year), 127 research assistantships with tuition reimbursements available (averaging $15,646 per year), 32 teaching assistantships with tuition reimbursements available (averaging $9,530 per year); career-related internships or fieldwork, institutionally sponsored loans, scholarships/grants, traineeships, health care benefits, tuition waivers (full and partial), and unspecified assistantships also available. Support available to part-time students. Financial award application deadline: 3/15; financial award applicants required to submit FAFSA. *Faculty research:* Materials and structures, aerodynamics and computational fluid dynamics (CFD), flight dynamics and control. *Unit head:* Dr. Rodney Bowersox, Department Head, 979-854-4184, E-mail: bowersox@tamu.edu. *Application contact:* Gail Rowe, Senior Academic Advisor II, Graduate Programs, 979-845-5520, Fax: 979-845-6051, E-mail: lgrowe@tamu.edu.
Website: http://engineering.tamu.edu/aerospace

Université Laval, Faculty of Sciences and Engineering, Department of Mechanical Engineering, Program in Aerospace Engineering, Québec, QC G1K 7P4, Canada. Offers M Sc. Program offered jointly with Concordia University, École Polytechnique de Montréal, McGill University, and Université de Sherbrooke. *Program availability:* Part-time. *Entrance requirements:* For master's, knowledge of French and English. Electronic applications accepted.

University at Buffalo, the State University of New York, Graduate School, School of Engineering and Applied Sciences, Department of Mechanical and Aerospace Engineering, Buffalo, NY 14260. Offers aerospace engineering (MS, PhD); mechanical engineering (MS, PhD). *Program availability:* Part-time. Terminal master's awarded for partial completion of doctoral program. *Degree requirements:* For master's, comprehensive exam, project or thesis; for doctorate, thesis/dissertation. *Entrance requirements:* For master's and doctorate, GRE General Test, GRE Subject Test. Additional exam requirements/recommendations for international students: Required—TOEFL (minimum score 79 iBT). Electronic applications accepted. *Faculty research:* Fluid and thermal sciences; computational and applied mechanics; materials; bioengineering; design and manufacturing; dynamics, control and mechatronics.

The University of Alabama, Graduate School, College of Engineering, Department of Aerospace Engineering and Mechanics, Tuscaloosa, AL 35487. Offers aerospace engineering (MSAEM); engineering science and mechanics (PhD). *Program availability:* Part-time, online learning. Terminal master's awarded for partial completion of doctoral program. *Degree requirements:* For master's, comprehensive exam (for some programs), thesis (for some programs); for doctorate, comprehensive exam, thesis/dissertation, 1-year residency. *Entrance requirements:* For master's, GRE, BS in engineering or physics; for doctorate, GRE, BS or MS in engineering or physics. Additional exam requirements/recommendations for international students: Required—TOEFL (minimum score 550 paper-based; 79 iBT). Electronic applications accepted. *Faculty research:* Aeronautics, astronautics, solid mechanics, fluid mechanics, computational modeling.

The University of Alabama in Huntsville, School of Graduate Studies, College of Engineering, Department of Mechanical and Aerospace Engineering, Huntsville, AL 35899. Offers aerospace systems engineering (MS, PhD). *Program availability:* Part-time. *Faculty:* 18 full-time (1 woman), 1 part-time/adjunct. *Students:* 75 full-time (11 women), 87 part-time (8 women); includes 20 minority (6 Black or African American, non-Hispanic/Latino; 4 American Indian or Alaska Native, non-Hispanic/Latino; 8 Asian, non-Hispanic/Latino; 1 Hispanic/Latino; 1 Two or more races, non-Hispanic/Latino), 31 international. Average age 29. 167 applicants, 57% accepted, 40 enrolled. In 2018, 33 master's, 7 doctorates awarded. *Degree requirements:* For master's, comprehensive exam, thesis or alternative, oral and written exams; for doctorate, comprehensive exam, thesis/dissertation, oral and written exams. *Entrance requirements:* For master's, GRE General Test, BSE, minimum GPA of 3.0; for doctorate, GRE General Test, minimum GPA of 3.0. Additional exam requirements/recommendations for international students: Required—TOEFL (minimum score 500 paper-based; 80 iBT), IELTS (minimum score 6.5). *Application deadline:* For fall admission, 7/15 priority date for domestic students, 4/1 for international students; for spring admission, 11/30 for domestic students, 9/1 for international students. Applications are processed on a rolling basis. Application fee: $50. Electronic applications accepted. *Expenses: Tuition, area resident:* Full-time $10,632; part-time $412 per credit hour. Tuition, state resident: full-time $10,632. Tuition, nonresident: full-time $23,604; part-time $412 per credit hour. *Required fees:* $582; $582. Tuition and fees vary according to course load and program. *Financial support:* In 2018–19, 70 students received support, including 43 research assistantships with full tuition reimbursements available (averaging $6,736 per year), 27 teaching assistantships with full tuition reimbursements available (averaging $5,609 per year); career-related internships or fieldwork, Federal Work-Study, institutionally sponsored loans, scholarships/grants, health care benefits, and unspecified assistantships also available. Support available to part-time students. Financial award application deadline: 4/1; financial award applicants required to submit FAFSA. *Faculty research:* Rocket propulsion and plasma engineering, materials engineering and solid mechanics, energy conversion, transport, and storage. *Unit head:* Dr. Keith Hollingsworth, Chair, 256-824-5421, Fax: 256-824-6758, E-mail: keith.hollingsworth@uah.edu. *Application contact:* Kim Gray, Graduate Studies Admissions Coordinator, 256-824-6002, Fax: 256-824-6405, E-mail: deangrad@uah.edu.
Website: http://www.mae.uah.edu/graduate.shtml

The University of Arizona, College of Engineering, Department of Aerospace and Mechanical Engineering, Tucson, AZ 85721. Offers aerospace engineering (MS, PhD); mechanical engineering (MS, PhD). *Program availability:* Part-time. *Degree requirements:* For master's, thesis or alternative; for doctorate, thesis/dissertation. *Entrance requirements:* For master's, GRE General Test, 3 letters of recommendation; for doctorate, GRE General Test, 3 letters of recommendation, statement of purpose. Additional exam requirements/recommendations for international students: Required—TOEFL (minimum score 550 paper-based; 79 iBT). Electronic applications accepted.

University of California, Davis, College of Engineering, Program in Mechanical and Aeronautical Engineering, Davis, CA 95616. Offers aeronautical engineering (M Engr, MS, D Engr, PhD, Certificate); mechanical engineering (M Engr, MS, D Engr, PhD, Certificate); M Engr/MBA. *Degree requirements:* For master's, comprehensive exam (for some programs), thesis (for some programs); for doctorate, thesis/dissertation. *Entrance requirements:* For master's and doctorate, GRE General Test, minimum GPA of 3.0. Additional exam requirements/recommendations for international students: Required—TOEFL (minimum score 550 paper-based). Electronic applications accepted.

University of California, Irvine, Samueli School of Engineering, Department of Mechanical and Aerospace Engineering, Irvine, CA 92697. Offers MS, PhD. *Program availability:* Part-time. *Students:* 137 full-time (37 women), 12 part-time (2 women); includes 30 minority (4 Black or African American, non-Hispanic/Latino; 13 Asian, non-Hispanic/Latino; 9 Hispanic/Latino; 4 Two or more races, non-Hispanic/Latino), 90 international. Average age 27. 517 applicants, 25% accepted, 46 enrolled. In 2018, 29 master's, 5 doctorates awarded. Terminal master's awarded for partial completion of doctoral program. *Entrance requirements:* For master's and doctorate, GRE General Test, minimum GPA of 3.0, 3 letters of recommendation. Additional exam requirements/recommendations for international students: Required—TOEFL (minimum score 550 paper-based). *Application deadline:* For fall admission, 1/15 priority date for domestic students, 1/15 for international students. Applications are processed on a rolling basis. Application fee: $105 ($125 for international students). Electronic applications accepted. *Financial support:* Fellowships, research assistantships with full tuition reimbursements, teaching assistantships, institutionally sponsored loans, traineeships, health care benefits, and unspecified assistantships available. Financial award application deadline: 3/1; financial award applicants required to submit FAFSA. *Faculty research:* Thermal and fluid sciences, combustion and propulsion, control systems, robotics, lightweight structures. *Unit head:* Prof. Kenneth Mease, Chair, 949-824-5855, Fax: 949-824-8585, E-mail: kmease@uci.edu. *Application contact:* Prof. Roger Rangel, Graduate Admissions Advisor, 949-824-4033, Fax: 949-824-8585, E-mail: rhrangel@uci.edu.
Website: http://mae.eng.uci.edu/

University of California, Los Angeles, Graduate Division, Henry Samueli School of Engineering and Applied Science, Department of Mechanical and Aerospace Engineering, Program in Aerospace Engineering, Los Angeles, CA 90095-1597. Offers MS, PhD. *Degree requirements:* For master's, comprehensive exam or thesis; for doctorate, thesis/dissertation, qualifying exams. *Entrance requirements:* For master's, GRE General Test, minimum GPA of 3.0; for doctorate, GRE General Test, minimum GPA of 3.25. Additional exam requirements/recommendations for international students: Required—TOEFL (minimum score 560 paper-based; 87 iBT), IELTS (minimum score 7). Electronic applications accepted. *Faculty research:* Applied mathematics, applied plasma physics, dynamics, fluid mechanics, heat and mass transfer, design, robotics and manufacturing, nanoelectromechanical/microelectromechanical systems (NEMS/MEMS), structural and solid mechanics, systems and control.

University of California, San Diego, Graduate Division, Department of Mechanical and Aerospace Engineering, Program in Aerospace Engineering, La Jolla, CA 92093. Offers MS, PhD. *Students:* 18 full-time (3 women), 3 part-time (0 women). 111 applicants, 30% accepted, 8 enrolled. In 2018, 10 master's, 3 doctorates awarded. *Degree requirements:* For master's, comprehensive exam (for some programs), thesis (for some programs), comprehensive exam or thesis; for doctorate, comprehensive exam, thesis/dissertation. *Entrance requirements:* For master's and doctorate, GRE General Test, minimum GPA of 3.0. Additional exam requirements/recommendations for international students: Required—TOEFL (minimum score 550 paper-based; 80 iBT), IELTS (minimum score 7). *Application deadline:* For fall admission, 3/2 for domestic students. Application fee: $105 ($125 for international students). Electronic applications accepted. *Financial support:* Fellowships, research assistantships, teaching assistantships, scholarships/grants, and unspecified assistantships available. Financial award applicants required to submit FAFSA. *Faculty research:* Aerodynamics, turbulence and fluid mechanics. *Unit head:* Carlos Coimbra, Chair, 858-534-4285, E-mail: mae-chair-l@ucsd.edu. *Application contact:* Joana Halnez, Graduate Coordinator, 858-534-4387, E-mail: mae-gradadm-l@ucsd.edu.
Website: http://maeweb.ucsd.edu/

University of Central Florida, College of Engineering and Computer Science, Department of Mechanical and Aerospace Engineering, Program in Aerospace Engineering, Orlando, FL 32816. Offers MSAE. *Students:* 29 full-time (3 women), 36 part-time (5 women); includes 30 minority (7 Asian, non-Hispanic/Latino; 18 Hispanic/Latino; 5 Two or more races, non-Hispanic/Latino), 1 international. Average age 26. 50 applicants, 62% accepted, 17 enrolled. In 2018, 14 master's awarded. *Entrance requirements:* For master's, resume, goal statement. Additional exam requirements/recommendations for international students: Required—TOEFL. *Application deadline:* For fall admission, 7/15 for domestic students; for spring admission, 12/1 for domestic students. Application fee: $30. Electronic applications accepted. *Financial support:* In 2018–19, 9 students received support, including 3 fellowships with partial tuition reimbursements available (averaging $1,067 per year), 8 research assistantships with partial tuition reimbursements available (averaging $9,332 per year), 5 teaching assistantships with partial tuition reimbursements available (averaging $5,740 per year); career-related internships or fieldwork, institutionally sponsored loans, scholarships/

grants, tuition waivers (partial), and unspecified assistantships also available. Financial award application deadline: 3/1; financial award applicants required to submit FAFSA. *Unit head:* Dr. Jihua Gou, Program Coordinator, 407-823-2155, E-mail: jihua.gou@ucf.edu. *Application contact:* Associate Director, Graduate Admissions, 407-823-2766, Fax: 407-823-6442, E-mail: gradadmissions@ucf.edu.
Website: http://mae.ucf.edu/academics/graduate/

University of Central Missouri, The Graduate School, Warrensburg, MO 64093. Offers accountancy (MA); accounting (MBA); applied mathematics (MS); aviation safety (MA); biology (MS); business administration (MBA); career and technical education leadership (MS); college student personnel administration (MS); communication (MA); computer science (MS); counseling (MS); criminal justice (MS); educational leadership (Ed D); educational technology (MS); elementary and early childhood education (MSE); English (MA); environmental studies (MA); finance (MBA); history (MA); human services/educational technology (Ed S); human services/learning resources (Ed S); human services/professional counseling (Ed S); industrial hygiene (MS); industrial management (MS); information systems (MBA); information technology (MS); kinesiology (MS); library science and information services (MS); literacy education (MSE); marketing (MBA); mathematics (MS); music (MA); occupational safety management (MS); psychology (MS); rural family nursing (MS); school administration (MSE); social gerontology (MS); sociology (MA); special education (MSE); speech language pathology (MS); superintendency (Ed S); teaching (MAT); teaching English as a second language (MA); technology (MS); technology management (PhD); theatre (MA). *Accreditation:* ASHA. *Program availability:* Part-time, 100% online, blended/hybrid learning. *Degree requirements:* For master's and Ed S, comprehensive exam (for some programs), thesis (for some programs). *Entrance requirements:* Additional exam requirements/recommendations for international students: Required—TOEFL (minimum score 550 paper-based; 79 iBT). Electronic applications accepted.

University of Cincinnati, Graduate School, College of Engineering and Applied Science, Department of Aerospace Engineering and Engineering Mechanics, Cincinnati, OH 45221-0070. Offers M Eng, MS, PhD. *Program availability:* Part-time. Terminal master's awarded for partial completion of doctoral program. *Degree requirements:* For master's, thesis; for doctorate, thesis/dissertation. *Entrance requirements:* For master's and doctorate, GRE General Test. Additional exam requirements/recommendations for international students: Required—TOEFL (minimum iBT score 90), IELTS (6.5), or PTE (47). Electronic applications accepted. *Faculty research:* Computational fluid mechanics/propulsion, large space structures, dynamics and guidance of VTOL vehicles, unmanned aerial vehicles, space robotics, aero-acoustics, thermal management, gas turbine simulation, combustion and rocket propulsion, ultrasonic imaging, nondestructive evaluation, finite element simulation.

University of Colorado Boulder, Graduate School, College of Engineering and Applied Science, Department of Aerospace Engineering Sciences, Boulder, CO 80309. Offers MS, PhD. Terminal master's awarded for partial completion of doctoral program. *Degree requirements:* For master's, comprehensive exam, thesis or alternative; for doctorate, comprehensive exam, thesis/dissertation. *Entrance requirements:* For master's, GRE General Test, minimum undergraduate GPA of 3.0; for doctorate, minimum undergraduate GPA of 3.25. Electronic applications accepted. Application fee is waived when completed online. *Faculty research:* Aeronautical/astronautical engineering; aerospace engineering; earth satellite applications; astronautics; atmospheric sciences.

University of Colorado Colorado Springs, College of Engineering and Applied Science, Program in General Engineering, Colorado Springs, CO 80918. Offers computer science (PhD); cybersecurity (ME); energy engineering (ME); engineering management (ME); engineering systems (ME); software engineering (ME); space operations (ME). *Program availability:* Part-time, evening/weekend, blended/hybrid learning. *Faculty:* 1 full-time (0 women), 20 part-time/adjunct (6 women). *Students:* 12 full-time (1 woman), 177 part-time (39 women); includes 38 minority (4 Black or African American, non-Hispanic/Latino; 12 Asian, non-Hispanic/Latino; 12 Hispanic/Latino; 1 Native Hawaiian or other Pacific Islander, non-Hispanic/Latino; 9 Two or more races, non-Hispanic/Latino), 54 international. Average age 35. 44 applicants, 93% accepted, 21 enrolled. In 2018, 24 master's, 15 doctorates awarded. *Degree requirements:* For master's, thesis, portfolio, or project; for doctorate, comprehensive exam, thesis/dissertation. *Entrance requirements:* For master's, GRE may be required based on past academic performance., Professional recommendation letters are required for all applicants.; for doctorate, GRE (minimum score of 148 new grading scale on the quantitative portion if the applicant has not graduated from a program of recognized standing), minimum GPA of 3.3 in the bachelor's or master's degree program attempted. Additional exam requirements/recommendations for international students: Required—TOEFL (minimum score 80 iBT), IELTS (minimum score 6). *Application deadline:* For fall admission, 6/1 for domestic and international students; for spring admission, 11/1 for domestic and international students; for summer admission, 4/15 for domestic and international students. Applications are processed on a rolling basis. Application fee: $60 ($100 for international students). Electronic applications accepted. *Expenses:* Program tuition and fees vary by course load and residency classification. Please visit the University of Colorado Colorado Springs Student Financial Services website to see current program costs: https://www.uccs.edu/bursar/index.php/estimate-your-bill. *Financial support:* In 2018–19, 1 student received support. Career-related internships or fieldwork, Federal Work-Study, scholarships/grants, traineeships, and unspecified assistantships available. Support available to part-time students. Financial award application deadline: 3/1; financial award applicants required to submit FAFSA. *Total annual research expenditures:* $22,249. *Unit head:* Dr. Donald Rabern, Dean of Engineering and Applied Science, 719-255-3543, E-mail: drabern@uccs.edu. *Application contact:* Dawn House, Extended Studies Coordinator, 719-255-3246, E-mail: dhouse@uccs.edu.

University of Dayton, Department of Mechanical and Aerospace Engineering, Dayton, OH 45469. Offers aerospace engineering (MSAE, PhD); mechanical engineering (MSME, PhD); renewable and clean energy (MS). *Program availability:* Part-time, 100% online, blended/hybrid learning. *Degree requirements:* For master's, variable foreign language requirement, comprehensive exam (for some programs), thesis; for doctorate, variable foreign language requirement, comprehensive exam, thesis/dissertation, departmental qualifying exam. *Entrance requirements:* For master's, BS in engineering, math, or physics; minimum GPA of 3.0; for doctorate, GRE. Additional exam requirements/recommendations for international students: Required—TOEFL (minimum score 550 paper-based; 80 iBT), IELTS (minimum score 6.5). Electronic applications accepted. *Faculty research:* Biomechanics, combustion, renewable energy, mechatronics, aerodynamics.

University of Florida, Graduate School, Herbert Wertheim College of Engineering, Department of Mechanical and Aerospace Engineering, Gainesville, FL 32611. Offers aerospace engineering (ME, MS, PhD); mechanical engineering (ME, MS, PhD). *Program availability:* Part-time, online learning. *Degree requirements:* For master's, thesis (for some programs); for doctorate, comprehensive exam, thesis/dissertation. *Entrance requirements:* For master's and doctorate, minimum GPA of 3.0. Additional exam requirements/recommendations for international students: Required—TOEFL (minimum score 550 paper-based; 80 iBT), IELTS (minimum score 6). Electronic applications accepted. *Faculty research:* Thermal sciences, design, controls and robotics, manufacturing, energy transport and utilization.

University of Illinois at Urbana–Champaign, Graduate College, College of Engineering, Department of Aerospace Engineering, Champaign, IL 61820. Offers MS, PhD. *Program availability:* Part-time, online learning.

The University of Kansas, Graduate Studies, School of Engineering, Program in Aerospace Engineering, Lawrence, KS 66045. Offers ME, MS, DE, PhD. *Program availability:* Part-time. *Students:* 38 full-time (6 women), 6 part-time (0 women); includes 2 minority (both Hispanic/Latino), 21 international. Average age 27. 24 applicants, 79% accepted, 11 enrolled. In 2018, 7 master's, 3 doctorates awarded. *Entrance requirements:* For master's, GRE, minimum GPA of 3.0, official transcripts, statement of objectives, three letters of recommendation; Statement of Financial Resources (for international students only); for doctorate, GRE, minimum GPA of 3.5, official transcripts, statement of objectives, three letters of recommendation; Statement of Financial Resources (for international students only). Additional exam requirements/recommendations for international students: Required—TOEFL, IELTS. *Application deadline:* For fall admission, 12/1 priority date for domestic and international students; for spring admission, 9/15 priority date for domestic and international students; for summer admission, 9/15 priority date for domestic and international students. Application fee: $65 ($85 for international students). Electronic applications accepted. *Financial support:* Fellowships, research assistantships, teaching assistantships, career-related internships or fieldwork, scholarships/grants, tuition waivers (full and partial), and unspecified assistantships available. Financial award application deadline: 12/1. *Faculty research:* Artificial intelligence, composite materials and structures, computational fluid dynamics and computational aeroacoustics, structural vibrations of high performance structures, flight test engineering. *Unit head:* Richard Hale, Chair, 785-864-2949, E-mail: rhale@ku.edu. *Application contact:* Amy Borton, Administrative Assistant, 785-864-2963, E-mail: aborton@ku.edu.
Website: http://www.ae.engr.ku.edu/

The University of Manchester, School of Materials, Manchester, United Kingdom. Offers advanced aerospace materials engineering (M Sc); advanced metallic systems (PhD); biomedical materials (M Phil, M Sc, PhD); ceramics and glass (M Phil, M Sc, PhD); composite materials (M Sc, PhD); corrosion and protection (M Phil, M Sc, PhD); materials (M Phil, PhD); metallic materials (M Phil, M Sc, PhD); nanostructural materials (M Phil, M Sc, PhD); paper science (M Phil, M Sc, PhD); polymer science and engineering (M Phil, M Sc, PhD); technical textiles (M Sc); textile design, fashion and management (M Phil, M Sc, PhD); textile science and technology (M Phil, M Sc, PhD); textiles (M Phil, PhD); textiles and fashion (M Ent).

The University of Manchester, School of Mechanical, Aerospace and Civil Engineering, Manchester, United Kingdom. Offers advanced manufacturing technology (M Ent); aerospace engineering (M Phil, M Sc, PhD); civil engineering (M Phil, M Sc, PhD); environmental engineering (M Phil, PhD); management of projects (M Phil, M Sc, PhD); mechanical engineering (M Phil, M Sc, PhD); mechanical engineering design (M Ent); nuclear engineering (M Phil, D Eng, PhD).

University of Maryland, College Park, Academic Affairs, A. James Clark School of Engineering, Department of Aerospace Engineering, College Park, MD 20742. Offers M Eng, MS, PhD. *Program availability:* Part-time, evening/weekend, online learning. *Degree requirements:* For master's, thesis optional; for doctorate, thesis/dissertation. *Entrance requirements:* For master's and doctorate, GRE General Test (recommended), 3 letters of recommendation. Electronic applications accepted. *Faculty research:* Aerodynamics and propulsion, structural mechanics, flight dynamics, rotor craft, space robotics.

University of Miami, Graduate School, College of Engineering, Department of Mechanical and Aerospace Engineering, Coral Gables, FL 33124. Offers MSME, PhD. *Program availability:* Part-time. *Degree requirements:* For master's, thesis (for some programs); for doctorate, comprehensive exam, thesis/dissertation. *Entrance requirements:* For master's and doctorate, GRE General Test, minimum GPA of 3.0. Additional exam requirements/recommendations for international students: Required—TOEFL (minimum score 550 paper-based). Electronic applications accepted. *Faculty research:* Internal combustion engines, heat transfer, hydrogen energy, controls, fuel cells.

University of Michigan, College of Engineering, Department of Aerospace Engineering, Ann Arbor, MI 48109. Offers M Eng, MS, MSE, PhD. *Program availability:* Part-time. *Students:* 219 full-time (31 women), 6 part-time (1 woman). 506 applicants, 41% accepted, 94 enrolled. In 2018, 61 master's, 33 doctorates awarded. *Degree requirements:* For doctorate, thesis/dissertation, oral defense of dissertation, preliminary exams. *Entrance requirements:* For master's, GRE General Test; for doctorate, GRE General Test, master's degree. *Application deadline:* Applications are processed on a rolling basis. Electronic applications accepted. *Financial support:* Fellowships, research assistantships, teaching assistantships, Federal Work-Study, and tuition waivers (full and partial) available. *Faculty research:* Turbulent flows and combustion, advanced spacecraft control, helicopter aeroelasticity, experimental fluid dynamics, space propulsion, optimal structural design, interactive materials, computational fluid and solid dynamics. *Total annual research expenditures:* $14.2 million. *Unit head:* Anthony Waas, Department Chair, 734-764-7320, Fax: 734-763-0578, E-mail: awaas@umich.edu. *Application contact:* Denise Phelps, Graduate Student Services Coordinator, 734-615-4406, Fax: 734-763-0578, E-mail: dphelps@umich.edu.
Website: https://aero.engin.umich.edu/

University of Michigan, College of Engineering, Department of Climate and Space Sciences and Engineering, Ann Arbor, MI 48109. Offers applied climate (M Eng); atmospheric, oceanic and space sciences (MS, PhD); geoscience and remote sensing (PhD); space and planetary sciences (PhD); space engineering (M Eng). *Program availability:* Part-time. *Students:* 83 full-time (29 women). 103 applicants, 19% accepted, 9 enrolled. In 2018, 42 master's, 10 doctorates awarded. Terminal master's awarded for partial completion of doctoral program. *Degree requirements:* For master's, thesis (for some programs); for doctorate, thesis/dissertation, oral defense of dissertation, preliminary exams. *Entrance requirements:* For master's and doctorate, GRE General Test. Additional exam requirements/recommendations for international students: Required—TOEFL. *Application deadline:* Applications are processed on a rolling basis. Electronic applications accepted. *Financial support:* Fellowships, research assistantships, teaching assistantships, career-related internships or fieldwork, Federal Work-Study, institutionally sponsored loans, and health care benefits available. Support available to part-time students. Financial award applicants required to submit FAFSA. *Faculty research:* Planetary environments, space instrumentation, air pollution meteorology, global climate change, sun-earth connection, space weather. *Total annual research expenditures:* $29.9 million. *Unit head:* Tuija Pulkkinen, Department Chair, 734-780-4079, Fax: 734-763-0437, E-mail: tuija@umich.edu. *Application contact:* Sandra Pytlinski, Graduate Student Services Coordinator, 734-936-0482, Fax: 734-763-0437, E-mail: sanpyt@umich.edu.
Website: https://clasp.engin.umich.edu/

University of Minnesota, Twin Cities Campus, College of Science and Engineering, Department of Aerospace Engineering and Mechanics, Minneapolis, MN 55455-0213.

Offers MS, PhD. *Program availability:* Part-time. *Degree requirements:* For doctorate, thesis/dissertation. *Entrance requirements:* Additional exam requirements/recommendations for international students: Required—TOEFL (minimum score 550 paper-based). Electronic applications accepted. *Faculty research:* Fluid mechanics, solid mechanics and materials, aerospace systems, nanotechnology.

University of Missouri, Office of Research and Graduate Studies, College of Engineering, Department of Mechanical and Aerospace Engineering, Columbia, MO 65211. Offers ME, MS, PhD. *Entrance requirements:* For master's and doctorate, GRE General Test, minimum GPA of 3.0.

University of Nevada, Las Vegas, Graduate College, Howard R. Hughes College of Engineering, Department of Mechanical Engineering, Las Vegas, NV 89154-4027. Offers aerospace engineering (MS); biomedical engineering (MS); materials and nuclear engineering (MS); mechanical engineering (MS, PhD); nuclear criticality safety engineering (Certificate); nuclear safeguards and security (Certificate). *Program availability:* Part-time. *Faculty:* 17 full-time (2 women). *Students:* 50 full-time (18 women), 19 part-time (4 women); includes 19 minority (4 Black or African American, non-Hispanic/Latino; 1 American Indian or Alaska Native, non-Hispanic/Latino; 4 Asian, non-Hispanic/Latino; 7 Hispanic/Latino; 3 Two or more races, non-Hispanic/Latino), 21 international. Average age 29. 63 applicants, 73% accepted, 23 enrolled. In 2018, 15 master's, 5 doctorates, 1 other advanced degree awarded. *Degree requirements:* For master's, thesis optional, design project; for doctorate, comprehensive exam, thesis/dissertation. *Entrance requirements:* For master's, GRE General Test, statement of purpose; 2 letters of recommendation; for doctorate, GRE General Test, 3 letters of recommendation; statement of purpose; bachelor's degree with minimum GPA of 3.5/master's degree with minimum GPA of 3.3. Additional exam requirements/recommendations for international students: Required—TOEFL (minimum score 550 paper-based; 80 iBT), IELTS (minimum score 7). *Application deadline:* For fall admission, 8/1 for domestic students, 5/1 for international students; for spring admission, 12/1 for domestic students, 10/1 for international students. Application fee: $60 ($95 for international students). Electronic applications accepted. *Expenses:* Contact institution. *Financial support:* In 2018–19, 40 students received support, including 1 fellowship with full tuition reimbursement available (averaging $15,000 per year), 17 research assistantships with full tuition reimbursements available (averaging $16,910 per year), 23 teaching assistantships with full tuition reimbursements available (averaging $16,467 per year); institutionally sponsored loans, scholarships/grants, health care benefits, and unspecified assistantships also available. Financial award application deadline: 3/15; financial award applicants required to submit FAFSA. *Faculty research:* Dynamics and control systems; energy systems including renewable and nuclear; computational fluid and solid mechanics; structures, materials and manufacturing; vibrations and acoustics. *Total annual research expenditures:* $4.5 million. *Unit head:* Dr. Brendan O'Toole, Chair/Professor, 702-895-3885, Fax: 702-895-3936, E-mail: mechanical.chair@unlv.edu. *Application contact:* Dr. Hui Zhao, Graduate Coordinator, 702-895-1463, Fax: 702-895-3936, E-mail: mechanical.gradcoord@unlv.edu.
Website: http://me.unlv.edu/

University of Notre Dame, The Graduate School, College of Engineering, Department of Aerospace and Mechanical Engineering, Notre Dame, IN 46556. Offers aerospace and mechanical engineering (M Eng, PhD); aerospace engineering (MS Aero E); mechanical engineering (MEME, MSME). Terminal master's awarded for partial completion of doctoral program. *Degree requirements:* For master's, comprehensive exam, thesis or alternative; for doctorate, thesis/dissertation, candidacy exam. *Entrance requirements:* For master's and doctorate, GRE General Test. Additional exam requirements/recommendations for international students: Required—TOEFL (minimum score 600 paper-based; 80 iBT). Electronic applications accepted. *Faculty research:* Aerodynamics/fluid dynamics, design and manufacturing, controls/robotics, solid mechanics or biomechanics/biomaterials.

University of Oklahoma, Gallogly College of Engineering, School of Aerospace and Mechanical Engineering, Norman, OK 73019. Offers aerospace engineering (MS, PhD), including aerospace engineering-general; mechanical engineering (MS, PhD), including mechanical engineering-general. *Program availability:* Part-time. *Faculty:* 28 full-time (3 women). *Students:* 46 full-time (12 women), 18 part-time (5 women); includes 8 minority (1 Black or African American, non-Hispanic/Latino; 1 American Indian or Alaska Native, non-Hispanic/Latino; 2 Asian, non-Hispanic/Latino; 1 Hispanic/Latino; 3 Two or more races, non-Hispanic/Latino), 38 international. Average age 28. 33 applicants, 73% accepted, 14 enrolled. In 2018, 15 master's, 8 doctorates awarded. *Degree requirements:* For master's, comprehensive exam (for some programs), thesis (for some programs); for doctorate, comprehensive exam, thesis/dissertation, general exam. *Entrance requirements:* For master's and doctorate, GRE, letters of reference, resume, statement of purpose. Additional exam requirements/recommendations for international students: Required—TOEFL (minimum score 79 iBT) or IELTS (minimum score 6.5). *Application deadline:* For fall admission, 1/15 for domestic and international students; for spring admission, 9/1 for domestic and international students. Application fee: $50 ($100 for international students). Electronic applications accepted. *Expenses:* Tuition, state resident: full-time $5683.20; part-time $236.80 per credit hour. Tuition, nonresident: full-time $20,342; part-time $847.60 per credit hour. International tuition: $20,342.40 full-time. *Required fees:* $2894.20; $110.05 per credit hour. $126.50 per semester. Tuition and fees vary according to course load and program. *Financial support:* Fellowships, research assistantships, teaching assistantships, and scholarships/grants available. Financial award application deadline: 6/1; financial award applicants required to submit FAFSA. *Faculty research:* Unmanned aerial vehicles, advanced materials, energy systems, design and manufacturing, biomechanics. *Unit head:* Zahed Siddique, Director, 405-325-5011, Fax: 405-325-1088, E-mail: zsiddique@ou.edu. *Application contact:* Bethany Burklund, AME Student Services Coordinator, 405-325-5013, Fax: 405-325-1088, E-mail: bethanyhb@ou.edu.
Website: http://www.ou.edu/coe/ame.html

University of Ottawa, Faculty of Graduate and Postdoctoral Studies, Faculty of Engineering, Ottawa-Carleton Institute for Mechanical and Aerospace Engineering, Ottawa, ON K1N 6N5, Canada. Offers M Eng, MA Sc, PhD. MA Sc, M Eng, PhD offered jointly with Carleton University. *Degree requirements:* For master's, thesis or alternative; for doctorate, thesis/dissertation, seminar series, qualifying exam. *Entrance requirements:* For master's, honors degree or equivalent, minimum B average; for doctorate, master's degree, minimum B+ average. Electronic applications accepted. *Faculty research:* Fluid mechanics-heat transfer, solid mechanics, design, manufacturing and control.

University of Puerto Rico–Mayagüez, Graduate Studies, College of Engineering, Department of Mechanical Engineering, Mayagüez, PR 00681-9000. Offers mechanical engineering (ME, MS, PhD), including aerospace and unmanned vehicles (ME), automation/mechatronics, bioengineering, fluid mechanics, heat transfer/energy systems, manufacturing, mechanics of materials, micro and nano engineering. *Program availability:* Part-time. Terminal master's awarded for partial completion of doctoral program. *Degree requirements:* For master's, one foreign language, comprehensive exam, thesis; for doctorate, one foreign language, comprehensive exam, thesis/dissertation. *Entrance requirements:* For master's, BS in mechanical engineering or its

equivalent; for doctorate, GRE, BS or MS in mechanical engineering or its equivalent; minimum GPA of 3.0. Additional exam requirements/recommendations for international students: Required—TOEFL (minimum score 80 iBT). Electronic applications accepted. *Faculty research:* Computational fluid dynamics, thermal sciences, mechanical design, material health, microfluidics.

University of Southern California, Graduate School, Viterbi School of Engineering, Department of Aerospace and Mechanical Engineering, Los Angeles, CA 90089. Offers aerospace and mechanical engineering: computational fluid and solid mechanics (MS); aerospace and mechanical engineering: dynamics and control (MS); aerospace engineering (MS, PhD, Engr), including aerospace engineering (PhD, Engr); green technologies (MS); mechanical engineering (MS, PhD, Engr), including energy conversion (MS); mechanical engineering (PhD, Engr), nuclear power (MS); product development engineering (MS). *Program availability:* Part-time, evening/weekend, online learning. Terminal master's awarded for partial completion of doctoral program. *Degree requirements:* For master's, thesis optional; for doctorate, thesis/dissertation. *Entrance requirements:* For master's, doctorate, and Engr, GRE General Test. Additional exam requirements/recommendations for international students: Recommended—TOEFL. Electronic applications accepted. *Faculty research:* Mechanics and materials, aerodynamics of air/ground vehicles, gas dynamics, aerosols, astronautics and space science, geophysical and microgravity flows, planetary physics, power MEMs and MEMS vacuum pumps, heat transfer and combustion.

University of Southern California, Graduate School, Viterbi School of Engineering, Department of Astronautical Engineering, Los Angeles, CA 90089. Offers MS, PhD, Engr, Graduate Certificate. *Program availability:* Part-time, evening/weekend, online learning. Terminal master's awarded for partial completion of doctoral program. *Degree requirements:* For master's, thesis optional; for doctorate, thesis/dissertation; for other advanced degree, comprehensive exam (for some programs). *Entrance requirements:* For master's, doctorate, and other advanced degree, GRE General Test. Additional exam requirements/recommendations for international students: Recommended—TOEFL. Electronic applications accepted. *Faculty research:* Space technology, space science and applications, space instrumentation, advanced propulsion, fundamental processes in gases and plasmas.

The University of Tennessee, Graduate School, Tickle College of Engineering, Department of Mechanical, Aerospace and Biomedical Engineering, Program in Aerospace Engineering, Knoxville, TN 37996. Offers MS, PhD, MS/MBA. *Program availability:* Part-time, online learning. *Faculty:* 16 full-time (2 women), 1 part-time/adjunct (0 women). *Students:* 29 full-time (4 women), 12 part-time (0 women); includes 7 minority (2 Asian, non-Hispanic/Latino; 3 Hispanic/Latino; 2 Two or more races, non-Hispanic/Latino), 4 international. Average age 26. 35 applicants, 60% accepted, 11 enrolled. In 2018, 14 master's, 2 doctorates awarded. *Degree requirements:* For master's, thesis or alternative; for doctorate, comprehensive exam, thesis/dissertation. *Entrance requirements:* For master's, GRE General Test (for MS students pursuing research thesis), minimum GPA of 2.7 (for U.S. degree holders), 3.0 (for international degree holders); 3 references; statement of purpose; for doctorate, GRE General Test, minimum GPA of 3.0 on previous graduate course work; 3 references; statement of purpose. Additional exam requirements/recommendations for international students: Required—TOEFL (minimum score 550 paper-based; 80 iBT), IELTS (minimum score 6.5). *Application deadline:* For fall admission, 2/1 priority date for domestic and international students; for spring admission, 6/15 for domestic and international students; for summer admission, 10/15 for domestic and international students. Applications are processed on a rolling basis. Application fee: $60. Electronic applications accepted. *Financial support:* In 2018–19, 34 students received support, including 5 fellowships with full tuition reimbursements available (averaging $9,616 per year), 19 research assistantships with full tuition reimbursements available (averaging $22,554 per year), 10 teaching assistantships with full tuition reimbursements available (averaging $20,828 per year); career-related internships or fieldwork, Federal Work-Study, institutionally sponsored loans, health care benefits, and unspecified assistantships also available. Financial award application deadline: 2/1; financial award applicants required to submit FAFSA. *Faculty research:* Atmospheric re-entry mechanics, hybrid rocket propulsion, laser-induced plasma spectroscopy, unsteady aerodynamics and aeroelasticity. *Unit head:* Dr. Matthew Mench, Head, 865-974-5115, Fax: 865-974-5274, E-mail: mmench@utk.edu. *Application contact:* Dr. Kivanc Ekici, Associate Professor/Graduate Program Director, 865-974-6016, Fax: 865-974-5274, E-mail: ekici@utk.edu.
Website: http://www.engr.utk.edu/mabe/

The University of Tennessee, The University of Tennessee Space Institute, Tullahoma, TN 37388. Offers aerospace engineering (MS, PhD); biomedical engineering (MS, PhD); engineering science (MS, PhD); industrial and systems engineering/engineering management (MS, PhD); mechanical engineering (MS, PhD); physics (MS, PhD). *Program availability:* Part-time, blended/hybrid learning. Terminal master's awarded for partial completion of doctoral program. *Degree requirements:* For doctorate, one foreign language, thesis/dissertation. *Entrance requirements:* Additional exam requirements/recommendations for international students: Required—TOEFL (minimum score 550 paper-based; 80 iBT), IELTS (minimum score 6.5). Electronic applications accepted. *Expenses:* Contact institution. *Faculty research:* Fluid mechanics/aerodynamics, chemical and electric propulsion and laser diagnostics, computational mechanics and simulations, carbon fiber production and composite materials.

The University of Texas at Arlington, Graduate School, College of Engineering, Department of Mechanical and Aerospace Engineering, Program in Aerospace Engineering, Arlington, TX 76019. Offers M Engr, MS, PhD. *Program availability:* Part-time, evening/weekend, online learning. Terminal master's awarded for partial completion of doctoral program. *Degree requirements:* For master's, thesis optional; for doctorate, comprehensive exam, thesis/dissertation. *Entrance requirements:* For master's and doctorate, GRE General Test, minimum GPA of 3.0. Additional exam requirements/recommendations for international students: Required—TOEFL (minimum score 550 paper-based).

The University of Texas at Austin, Graduate School, Cockrell School of Engineering, Department of Aerospace Engineering and Engineering Mechanics, Program in Aerospace Engineering, Austin, TX 78712-1111. Offers MSE, PhD. *Entrance requirements:* For master's and doctorate, GRE General Test. Electronic applications accepted.

University of Toronto, School of Graduate Studies, Faculty of Applied Science and Engineering, Institute for Aerospace Studies, Toronto, ON M5S 1A1, Canada. Offers M Eng, MA Sc, PhD. *Program availability:* Part-time. *Degree requirements:* For master's, thesis (for some programs); for doctorate, thesis/dissertation, formal manuscript for publication. *Entrance requirements:* For master's, BA Sc or equivalent in engineering (M Eng); bachelor's degree in physics, mathematics, engineering or chemistry (MA Sc); 2 letters of reference; for doctorate, master's degree in applied science, engineering, mathematics, physics, or chemistry; demonstrated ability to perform advanced research, 2 letters of reference. Additional exam requirements/recommendations for international students: Required—TOEFL (minimum score 580 paper-based), TWE (minimum score 5). Electronic applications accepted.

Aerospace/Aeronautical Engineering

University of Virginia, School of Engineering and Applied Science, Department of Mechanical and Aerospace Engineering, Charlottesville, VA 22903. Offers ME, MS, PhD. *Program availability:* Online learning. *Degree requirements:* For master's, thesis (MS); for doctorate, comprehensive exam, thesis/dissertation. *Entrance requirements:* For master's and doctorate, GRE General Test, 3 letters of recommendation. Additional exam requirements/recommendations for international students: Required—TOEFL (minimum score 650 paper-based; 90 iBT), IELTS (minimum score 7). Electronic applications accepted. *Faculty research:* Solid mechanics, dynamical systems and control, thermofluids.

University of Washington, Graduate School, College of Engineering, William E. Boeing Department of Aeronautics and Astronautics, Seattle, WA 98195-2400. Offers MAE, MSAA, PhD. *Program availability:* Part-time, online learning. *Faculty:* 15 full-time (1 woman). *Students:* 109 full-time (21 women), 111 part-time (22 women); includes 63 minority (6 Black or African American, non-Hispanic/Latino; 30 Asian, non-Hispanic/Latino; 18 Hispanic/Latino; 9 Two or more races, non-Hispanic/Latino), 40 international. Average age 27. 396 applicants, 44% accepted, 70 enrolled. In 2018, 78 master's, 5 doctorates awarded. Terminal master's awarded for partial completion of doctoral program. *Degree requirements:* For master's, thesis optional, completion of all work within 6 years; for doctorate, comprehensive exam, thesis/dissertation, qualifying, general and final exams; completion of all work within 10 years. *Entrance requirements:* For master's and doctorate, GRE General Test, minimum GPA of 3.0, letters of recommendation, statement of objectives, undergraduate degree in aerospace or mechanical engineering. Additional exam requirements/recommendations for international students: Required—TOEFL (minimum score 580 paper-based; 92 iBT); Recommended—IELTS (minimum score 7). *Application deadline:* For fall admission, 12/15 for domestic and international students. Application fee: $85. Electronic applications accepted. *Expenses:* Regular/research-focused master's degrees and Ph.D.s: resident, $18,852, non-resident, $32,760. *Financial support:* In 2018–19, 82 students received support, including 39 research assistantships with full tuition reimbursements available (averaging $33,900 per year), 21 teaching assistantships with full tuition reimbursements available (averaging $33,900 per year); fellowships, career-related internships or fieldwork, Federal Work-Study, health care benefits, tuition waivers (full), and unspecified assistantships also available. Financial award application deadline: 1/15; financial award applicants required to submit FAFSA. *Faculty research:* Space systems, aircraft systems, energy systems, aerospace control systems, advanced composite materials and structures, fluid mechanics. *Total annual research expenditures:* $9.5 million. *Unit head:* Dr. AnthonyKristi Morgansen, Professor and Chair, 206-543-5950, Fax: 206-543-0217, E-mail: morgansn@uw.edu. *Application contact:* Ed Connery, Advisor/Admissions Coordinator, 206-543-6725, Fax: 206-543-0217, E-mail: econnery@uw.edu.
Website: http://www.aa.washington.edu/

Utah State University, School of Graduate Studies, College of Engineering, Department of Mechanical and Aerospace Engineering, Logan, UT 84322. Offers aerospace engineering (MS, PhD); mechanical engineering (ME, MS, PhD). Terminal master's awarded for partial completion of doctoral program. *Degree requirements:* For master's, thesis (for some programs); for doctorate, thesis/dissertation. *Entrance requirements:* For master's, GRE General Test, minimum GPA of 3.0; for doctorate, GRE General Test, minimum GPA of 3.3. Additional exam requirements/recommendations for international students: Required—TOEFL. *Faculty research:* In-space instruments, cryogenic cooling, thermal science, space structures, composite materials.

Virginia Polytechnic Institute and State University, Graduate School, College of Engineering, Blacksburg, VA 24061. Offers aerospace engineering (PhD, M Eng/MS); biological systems engineering (PhD); biomedical engineering (MS, PhD); chemical engineering (PhD); civil engineering (PhD); computer engineering (PhD); computer science and applications (MS); electrical engineering (PhD); engineering education (PhD); M Eng/MS. *Faculty:* 446 full-time (87 women), 7 part-time/adjunct (3 women). *Students:* 1,776 full-time (471 women), 367 part-time (62 women); includes 260 minority (50 Black or African American, non-Hispanic/Latino; 3 American Indian or Alaska Native, non-Hispanic/Latino; 99 Asian, non-Hispanic/Latino; 67 Hispanic/Latino; 41 Two or more races, non-Hispanic/Latino), 1,178 international. Average age 27. 3,798 applicants, 37% accepted, 507 enrolled. In 2018, 489 master's, 200 doctorates awarded. *Degree requirements:* For master's, comprehensive exam (for some programs), thesis (for some programs); for doctorate, comprehensive exam (for some programs), thesis/dissertation (for some programs). *Entrance requirements:* For master's and doctorate, GRE/GMAT. Additional exam requirements/recommendations for international students: Required—TOEFL (minimum score 90 iBT). *Application deadline:* For fall admission, 8/1 for domestic students, 4/1 for international students; for spring admission, 1/1 for domestic students, 9/1 for international students. Applications are processed on a rolling basis. Application fee: $75. Electronic applications accepted. *Expenses:* Tuition, state resident: full-time $15,510; part-time $739.50 per credit hour. Tuition, nonresident: full-time $29,629; part-time $1490.25 per credit hour. *Required fees:* $2804; $550 per semester. Tuition and fees vary according to course load, campus/location and program. *Financial support:* In 2018–19, 37 fellowships with full tuition reimbursements (averaging $24,951 per year), 1,110 research assistantships with full tuition reimbursements (averaging $20,129 per year), 486 teaching assistantships with full tuition reimbursements (averaging $16,192 per year) were awarded; scholarships/grants and unspecified assistantships also available. Financial award application deadline: 3/1; financial award applicants required to submit FAFSA. *Total annual research expenditures:* $96.3 million. *Unit head:* Dr. Julia Ross, Dean, 540-231-9752, Fax: 540-231-3031, E-mail: rjulie@vt.edu. *Application contact:* Linda Perkins, Executive Assistant, 540-231-9752, Fax: 540-231-3031, E-mail: lperkins@vt.edu.
Website: http://www.eng.vt.edu/

Virginia Polytechnic Institute and State University, VT Online, Blacksburg, VA 24061. Offers advanced transportation systems (Certificate); aerospace engineering (MS); agricultural and life sciences (MSLFS); business information systems (Graduate Certificate); career and technical education (MS); civil engineering (MS); computer engineering (M Eng, MS); decision support systems (Graduate Certificate); eLearning leadership (MA); electrical engineering (M Eng, MS); engineering administration (MEA); environmental engineering (Certificate); environmental politics and policy (Graduate Certificate); environmental sciences and engineering (MS); foundations of political analysis (Graduate Certificate); health product risk management (Graduate Certificate); industrial and systems engineering (MS); information policy and society (Graduate Certificate); information security (Graduate Certificate); information technology (MIT); instructional technology (MA); integrative STEM education (MA Ed); liberal arts (Graduate Certificate); life sciences: health product risk management (MS); natural resources (MNR, Graduate Certificate); networking (Graduate Certificate); nonprofit and nongovernmental organization management (Graduate Certificate); ocean engineering (MS); political science (MA); security studies (Graduate Certificate); software

development (Graduate Certificate). *Expenses:* Tuition, state resident: full-time $15,510; part-time $739.50 per credit hour. Tuition, nonresident: full-time $29,629; part-time $1490.25 per credit hour. *Required fees:* $2804; $550 per semester. Tuition and fees vary according to course load, campus/location and program. *Application contact:* Graduate Admissions and Academic Progress, 540-231-8636, E-mail: grads@vt.edu. Website: http://www.vto.vt.edu/

Washington University in St. Louis, School of Engineering and Applied Science, Department of Mechanical Engineering and Materials Science, St. Louis, MO 63130-4899. Offers aerospace engineering (MS, PhD); materials science (MS); mechanical engineering (M Eng, MS, PhD). *Program availability:* Part-time. Terminal master's awarded for partial completion of doctoral program. *Degree requirements:* For master's, thesis optional; for doctorate, thesis/dissertation optional. *Entrance requirements:* For master's, GRE; for doctorate, GRE General Test, departmental qualifying exam. *Faculty research:* Aerosols science and technology, applied mechanics, biomechanics and biomedical engineering, design, dynamic systems, combustion science, composite materials, materials science.

Webster University, George Herbert Walker School of Business and Technology, Department of Management, St. Louis, MO 63119-3194. Offers business and organizational security management (MA); digital marketing management (Graduate Certificate); government contracting (Graduate Certificate); health administration (MHA); health care management (MA); health services management (MA); human resources development (MA); human resources management (MA); information technology management (MA, MS); management (D Mgt); management and leadership (MA); marketing (MA); nonprofit leadership (MA); nonprofit revenue development (Graduate Certificate); organizational development (Graduate Certificate); procurement and acquisitions management (MA); public administration (MPA); space systems operations management (MS). *Program availability:* Part-time, evening/weekend, online learning. *Degree requirements:* For master's, thesis (for some programs); for doctorate, thesis/dissertation, written exam. *Entrance requirements:* For doctorate, GMAT, 3 years of work experience, MBA. Additional exam requirements/recommendations for international students: Required—TOEFL. *Expenses:* Tuition: Full-time $22,500; part-time $750 per credit hour. Tuition and fees vary according to degree level, campus/location and program.

Western Michigan University, Graduate College, College of Engineering and Applied Sciences, Department of Mechanical and Aerospace Engineering, Kalamazoo, MI 49008. Offers mechanical engineering (MSE, PhD). *Program availability:* Part-time. *Degree requirements:* For master's, thesis optional; for doctorate, thesis/dissertation.

West Virginia University, Statler College of Engineering and Mineral Resources, Morgantown, WV 26506. Offers aerospace engineering (MSAE, PhD); chemical engineering (MS Ch E, PhD); civil engineering (MSCE, PhD); computer engineering (PhD); computer science (MSCS, PhD); electrical engineering (MSEE, PhD); energy systems engineering (MSESE); engineering (MSE); industrial engineering (MSIE, PhD); industrial hygiene (MS); material science and engineering (MSMSE, PhD); mechanical engineering (MSME, PhD); mining engineering (MS Min E, PhD); petroleum and natural gas engineering (MSPNGE, PhD); safety management (MS); software engineering (MSSE). *Program availability:* Part-time. *Students:* 466 full-time (113 women), 154 part-time (27 women); includes 57 minority (22 Black or African American, non-Hispanic/Latino; 1 American Indian or Alaska Native, non-Hispanic/Latino; 8 Asian, non-Hispanic/Latino; 12 Hispanic/Latino; 14 Two or more races, non-Hispanic/Latino), 283 international. In 2018, 179 master's, 39 doctorates awarded. Terminal master's awarded for partial completion of doctoral program. *Degree requirements:* For master's, thesis optional; for doctorate, comprehensive exam, thesis/dissertation. *Entrance requirements:* Additional exam requirements/recommendations for international students: Required—TOEFL (minimum score 550 paper-based). *Application deadline:* For fall admission, 4/1 for international students; for winter admission, 4/1 for international students; for spring admission, 10/1 for international students. Applications are processed on a rolling basis. Application fee: $60. Electronic applications accepted. *Expenses:* Contact institution. *Financial support:* Fellowships, research assistantships, teaching assistantships, career-related internships or fieldwork, Federal Work-Study, institutionally sponsored loans, health care benefits, tuition waivers (full and partial), unspecified assistantships, and administrative assistantships available. Financial award application deadline: 2/1; financial award applicants required to submit FAFSA. *Faculty research:* Composite materials, software engineering, information systems, aerodynamics, vehicle propulsion and emission. *Unit head:* Dr. Earl Scime, Interim Dean, 304-293-4157 Ext. 2237, Fax: 304-293-2037, E-mail: earl.scime@mail.wvu.edu. *Application contact:* Dr. David A. Wyrick, Associate Dean, Academic Affairs, 304-293-4334, Fax: 304-293-5024, E-mail: david.wyrick@mail.wvu.edu. Website: https://www.statler.wvu.edu

Wichita State University, Graduate School, College of Engineering, Department of Aerospace Engineering, Wichita, KS 67260. Offers MS, PhD. *Program availability:* Part-time. *Unit head:* Dr. L. Scott Miller, Chairperson, 316-978-3410, E-mail: scott.miller@wichita.edu. *Application contact:* Jordan Oleson, Admission Coordinator, 316-978-3095, E-mail: jordan.oleson@wichita.edu.
Website: http://www.wichita.edu/ae

Worcester Polytechnic Institute, Graduate Admissions, Program in Aerospace Engineering, Worcester, MA 01609-2280. Offers aerospace engineering (MS). *Program availability:* Part-time, evening/weekend. *Students:* 20 full-time (3 women), 15 part-time (3 women); includes 5 minority (1 Black or African American, non-Hispanic/Latino; 2 Asian, non-Hispanic/Latino; 1 Hispanic/Latino; 1 Two or more races, non-Hispanic/Latino), 10 international. Average age 26. 58 applicants, 78% accepted, 16 enrolled. In 2018, 23 master's, 2 doctorates awarded. *Entrance requirements:* For master's and doctorate, 3 letters of recommendation. Additional exam requirements/recommendations for international students: Required—TOEFL (minimum score 563 paper-based; 84 iBT), IELTS (minimum score 7). *Application deadline:* For fall admission, 1/1 for domestic and international students; for spring admission, 10/1 for domestic and international students. Applications are processed on a rolling basis. Application fee: $70. Electronic applications accepted. *Financial support:* Research assistantships and teaching assistantships available. Financial award application deadline: 1/1. *Unit head:* Dr. Nikolas Gatsonis, Director, 508-831-5221, Fax: 508-831-5680, E-mail: gatsonis@wpi.edu. *Application contact:* Donna Hughes, Administrative Assistant, 508-831-5221, E-mail: dmhughes@wpi.edu. Website: https://www.wpi.edu/academics/departments/aerospace-engineering

Wright State University, Graduate School, College of Engineering and Computer Science, Department of Mechanical and Materials Engineering, Dayton, OH 45435. Offers aerospace systems engineering (MS); materials science and engineering (MS); mechanical engineering (MS); renewable and clean energy (MS). *Degree requirements:* For master's, thesis or course option alternative. *Entrance requirements:* Additional exam requirements/recommendations for international students: Required—TOEFL.

Aviation

Embry-Riddle Aeronautical University–Daytona, College of Business, Daytona Beach, FL 32114-3900. Offers airline management (MBA); airport management (MBA); aviation finance (MSAF); aviation human resources (MBA); aviation management (MBA-AM); aviation system management (MBA); finance (MBA). *Accreditation:* ACBSP. *Degree requirements:* For master's, thesis (for some programs). *Entrance requirements:* For master's, GRE (for some programs). Additional exam requirements/recommendations for international students: Required—TOEFL (minimum score 550 paper-based, 79 iBT) or IELTS (6). Electronic applications accepted.

Embry-Riddle Aeronautical University–Prescott, Behavioral and Safety Sciences Department, Prescott, AZ 86301-3720. Offers aviation safety (MSSS). *Degree requirements:* For master's, research project, capstone, or thesis. *Entrance requirements:* For master's, transcripts, statement of goals, letters of recommendation, resume. Additional exam requirements/recommendations for international students: Required—TOEFL (minimum score 550 paper-based; 79 iBT), IELTS (minimum score 6). Electronic applications accepted.

Everglades University, Graduate Programs, Program in Aviation Science, Boca Raton, FL 33431. Offers aviation operations management (MSA); aviation security (MSA); business administration (MSA). *Program availability:* Part-time, evening/weekend, 100% online. *Entrance requirements:* For master's, GMAT (minimum score of 400) or GRE (minimum score of 290), bachelor's or graduate degree from college accredited by an agency recognized by the U.S. Department of Education; minimum cumulative GPA of 2.0 at the baccalaureate level, 3.0 at the master's level. Additional exam requirements/recommendations for international students: Recommended—TOEFL (minimum score 500 paper-based). Electronic applications accepted. *Expenses:* Contact institution.

Florida Institute of Technology, College of Aeronautics, Melbourne, FL 32901-6975. Offers aviation human factors (MS); aviation safety, applied (MSA); aviation sciences (PhD). *Program availability:* Part-time, evening/weekend, 100% online. *Faculty:* 20 full-time (7 women), 13 part-time/adjunct (2 women). *Students:* 46 full-time (17 women), 5 part-time (0 women); includes 7 minority (1 Black or African American, non-Hispanic/Latino; 2 Asian, non-Hispanic/Latino; 2 Hispanic/Latino; 2 Two or more races, non-Hispanic/Latino), 35 international. 25 applicants, 96% accepted, 14 enrolled. In 2018, 18 master's awarded. *Degree requirements:* For master's, thesis (for some programs), thesis or capstone project; for doctorate, thesis/dissertation (for some programs). *Entrance requirements:* For master's, GRE, minimum GPA of 3.0, 3 letters of recommendation, resume, statement of objectives; for doctorate, GRE, minimum GPA of 3.2; master's degree in an aviation field (for international applicants). Additional exam requirements/recommendations for international students: Required—TOEFL (minimum score 550 paper-based; 79 iBT). *Application deadline:* Applications are processed on a rolling basis. Application fee: $50. Electronic applications accepted. *Expenses:* Tuition: Full-time $22,338; part-time $1241 per credit hour. Tuition and fees vary according to degree level, campus/location and program. *Financial support:* In 2018–19, 7 students received support, including 7 research assistantships with partial tuition reimbursements available; teaching assistantships with partial tuition reimbursements available, career-related internships or fieldwork, institutionally sponsored loans, tuition waivers (partial), and tuition remissions also available. Financial award application deadline: 3/1; financial award applicants required to submit FAFSA. *Faculty research:* Aircraft cockpit design, medical human factors, operating room human factors, hypobaric chamber operations and effects, aviation professional education. *Total annual research expenditures:* $846,073. *Unit head:* Dr. Ulreen Jones, Interim Dean, 321-674-7472, Fax: 321-674-7368, E-mail: ujones@fit.edu. *Application contact:* Cheryl A. Brown, Associate Director of Graduate Admissions, 321-674-7581, Fax: 321-723-9468, E-mail: cbrown@fit.edu. Website: www.fit.edu/aeronautics/

Lewis University, College of Arts and Sciences, Program in Aviation and Transportation, Romeoville, IL 60446. Offers MS. *Program availability:* Part-time, evening/weekend, 100% online, blended/hybrid learning. *Students:* 22 full-time (7 women), 26 part-time (8 women); includes 11 minority (3 Black or African American, non-Hispanic/Latino; 1 Asian, non-Hispanic/Latino; 7 Hispanic/Latino), 10 international. Average age 30. *Degree requirements:* For master's, comprehensive exam (for some programs). *Entrance requirements:* For master's, bachelor's degree, minimum GPA of 3.0, personal statement, 2 letters of recommendation. Additional exam requirements/recommendations for international students: Required—TOEFL (minimum score 550 paper-based; 79 iBT), IELTS (minimum score 6). *Application deadline:* For fall admission, 5/1 priority date for international students; for spring admission, 11/15 priority date for international students. Applications are processed on a rolling basis. Application fee: $40. Electronic applications accepted. *Financial support:* Federal Work-Study and unspecified assistantships available. Financial award application deadline: 5/1; financial award applicants required to submit FAFSA. *Total annual research expenditures:* $30. *Unit head:* Dr. Erik Baker, Program Chair, E-mail: bakerer@lewisu.edu. *Application contact:* Linda Campbell, Graduate Admissions Counselor, 815-836-5610, E-mail: grad@lewisu.edu.

National Test Pilot School, National Flight Institute, Mojave, CA 93502-0658. Offers flight test and evaluation (MS); flight test engineering (MS). *Accreditation:* ABET. *Degree requirements:* For master's, final project. *Entrance requirements:* For master's, undergraduate degree in engineering, physical or computer science, mathematics or technical management.

Oklahoma State University, College of Education, Health and Aviation, Stillwater, OK 74078. Offers MS, Ed D, PhD, Ed S. *Accreditation:* NCATE. *Program availability:* Part-time, online learning. *Degree requirements:* For master's, thesis or alternative; for doctorate, comprehensive exam, thesis/dissertation. *Entrance requirements:* For master's and doctorate, GRE or GMAT. Additional exam requirements/recommendations for international students: Required—TOEFL (minimum score 550 paper-based; 79 iBT). Electronic applications accepted. *Expenses: Tuition, area resident:* Full-time $4148. Tuition, state resident: full-time $4148. Tuition, nonresident: full-time $10,517. *International tuition:* $10,517 full-time. *Required fees:* $4394; $2929 per credit hour. Tuition and fees vary according to course load and program.

Southeastern Oklahoma State University, Department of Aviation Science, Durant, OK 74701-0609. Offers aerospace administration and logistics (MS). *Program availability:* Part-time, evening/weekend. *Entrance requirements:* For master's, minimum GPA of 3.0 in last 60 hours or 2.75 overall. Additional exam requirements/recommendations for international students: Required—TOEFL (minimum score 550 paper-based; 79 iBT). Electronic applications accepted.

University of North Dakota, Graduate School, John D. Odegard School of Aerospace Sciences, Department of Aviation, Grand Forks, ND 58202. Offers MS. *Program availability:* Part-time, online learning. *Degree requirements:* For master's, comprehensive exam. *Entrance requirements:* For master's, GRE General Test, FAA private pilot certificate or foreign equivalent. Additional exam requirements/recommendations for international students: Required—TOEFL (minimum score 550 paper-based; 79 iBT), IELTS (minimum score 6.5). Electronic applications accepted.

The University of Tennessee, Graduate School, Intercollegiate Programs, Program in Aviation Systems, Knoxville, TN 37996. Offers MS. *Program availability:* Part-time, online learning. *Degree requirements:* For master's, thesis optional. *Entrance requirements:* For master's, minimum GPA of 2.7. Additional exam requirements/recommendations for international students: Required—TOEFL. Electronic applications accepted.

Section 3
Agricultural Engineering and Bioengineering

This section contains a directory of institutions offering graduate work in agricultural engineering and bioengineering, followed by an in-depth entry submitted by an institution that chose to prepare a detailed program description. Additional information about programs listed in the directory but not augmented by an in-depth entry may be obtained by writing directly to the dean of a graduate school or chair of a department at the address given in the directory.

For programs offering related work, see also in this book *Biomedical Engineering and Biotechnology; Civil and Environmental Engineering; Engineering and Applied Sciences;* and *Management of Engineering and Technology.* In the other guides in this series:

Graduate Programs in the Biological/Biomedical Sciences & Health-Related Medical Professions
See *Biological and Biomedical Sciences; Ecology, Environmental Biology, and Evolutionary Biology; Marine Biology; Nutrition;* and *Zoology*

Graduate Programs in the Physical Sciences, Mathematics, Agricultural Sciences, the Environment & Natural Resources
See *Agricultural and Food Sciences* and *Natural Resources*

CONTENTS

Program Directories

Featured School: Display and Close-Up

See:

Agricultural Engineering

Cornell University, Graduate School, Graduate Fields of Agriculture and Life Sciences and Graduate Fields of Engineering, Field of Biological and Environmental Engineering, Ithaca, NY 14853. Offers bioenergy and integrated energy systems (M Eng, MPS, MS, PhD); biological engineering (M Eng, MPS, MS, PhD); bioprocess engineering (M Eng, MPS, MS, PhD); ecohydrology (M Eng, MPS, MS, PhD); environmental engineering (M Eng, MPS, MS, PhD); environmental management (MPS); food engineering (M Eng, MPS, MS, PhD); industrial biotechnology (M Eng, MPS, MS, PhD); nanobiotechnology (M Eng, MPS, MS, PhD); sustainable systems (M Eng, MPS, MS, PhD); synthetic biology (MS); syntheticbiology (M Eng, MPS, PhD). Terminal master's awarded for partial completion of doctoral program. *Degree requirements:* For master's, thesis (MS); for doctorate, comprehensive exam, thesis/dissertation. *Entrance requirements:* For master's, letters of recommendation (3 for MS, 2 for M Eng and MPS); for doctorate, GRE General Test, 3 letters of recommendation. Additional exam requirements/recommendations for international students: Required—TOEFL (minimum score 550 paper-based; 77 iBT). Electronic applications accepted. *Faculty research:* Biological and food engineering, environmental, soil and water engineering, international agricultural engineering, structures and controlled environments, machine systems and energy.

Illinois Institute of Technology, Graduate College, School of Applied Technology, Institute for Food Safety and Health, Bedford Park, IL 60501-1957. Offers food process engineering (MFPE, MS); food safety and technology (MFST, MS). *Program availability:* Part-time. *Degree requirements:* For master's, comprehensive exam (for some programs), thesis (for some programs). *Entrance requirements:* For master's, GRE (minimum score 304), minimum undergraduate GPA of 3.0. Additional exam requirements/recommendations for international students: Required—TOEFL (minimum score 550 paper-based; 80 iBT). Electronic applications accepted. *Faculty research:* Microbial food safety and security, food virology, interfacial colloidal phenomena, development of DNA-based methods for detection, differentiation and tracking of food borne pathogens in food systems and environment, appetite and obesity management and vascular disease.

Instituto Tecnológico y de Estudios Superiores de Monterrey, Campus Monterrey, Graduate and Research Division, Program in Agriculture, Monterrey, Mexico. Offers agricultural parasitology (PhD); agricultural sciences (MS); farming productivity (MS); food processing engineering (MS); phytopathology (MS). *Program availability:* Part-time. *Degree requirements:* For master's, one foreign language, thesis; for doctorate, one foreign language, thesis/dissertation. *Entrance requirements:* For master's, EXADEP; for doctorate, GMAT or GRE, master's degree in related field. Additional exam requirements/recommendations for international students: Required—TOEFL. *Faculty research:* Animal embryos and reproduction, crop entomology, tropical agriculture, agricultural productivity, induced mutation in oleaginous plants.

Iowa State University of Science and Technology, Program in Agricultural and Biosystems Engineering, Ames, IA 50011. Offers M En, MS, PhD. *Degree requirements:* For master's, thesis (for some programs); for doctorate, thesis/dissertation. *Entrance requirements:* For master's and doctorate, GRE. Additional exam requirements/recommendations for international students: Required—TOEFL (minimum score 550 paper-based; 79 iBT), IELTS (minimum score 6.5). Electronic applications accepted. *Faculty research:* Grain processing and quality, tillage systems, simulation and controls, water management, environmental quality.

Kansas State University, Graduate School, College of Agriculture, Department of Grain Science and Industry, Manhattan, KS 66506. Offers MS, PhD. *Program availability:* Part-time. Terminal master's awarded for partial completion of doctoral program. *Degree requirements:* For master's, thesis, oral exam; for doctorate, thesis/dissertation, preliminary exam. *Entrance requirements:* For master's and doctorate, GRE General Test, minimum undergraduate GPA of 3.0. Additional exam requirements/recommendations for international students: Required—TOEFL (minimum score 550 paper-based; 79 iBT), IELTS (minimum score 7). Electronic applications accepted. *Faculty research:* Cereal science, bakery science and management, feed science and management, milling science and management.

Kansas State University, Graduate School, College of Engineering, Department of Biological and Agricultural Engineering, Manhattan, KS 66506. Offers MS, PhD. Terminal master's awarded for partial completion of doctoral program. *Degree requirements:* For master's, thesis; for doctorate, thesis/dissertation, preliminary exam. *Entrance requirements:* For master's, GRE, bachelor's degree in biological and agricultural engineering; for doctorate, GRE. Additional exam requirements/recommendations for international students: Required—TOEFL (minimum score 550 paper-based; 79 iBT). Electronic applications accepted. *Faculty research:* Ecological engineering, watershed modeling, air quality, bioprocessing, bio-fuel, sensors and controls, 3D engineered biomaterials and biomedical devices, mobile health, point-of-care diagnosis, protein biomarker discovery, cancer early detection.

Louisiana State University and Agricultural & Mechanical College, Graduate School, College of Engineering, Department of Biological and Agricultural Engineering, Baton Rouge, LA 70803. Offers biological and agricultural engineering (MSBAE); engineering science (MS, PhD).

McGill University, Faculty of Graduate and Postdoctoral Studies, Faculty of Agricultural and Environmental Sciences, Department of Bioresource Engineering, Montréal, QC H3A 2T5, Canada. Offers computer applications (M Sc, M Sc A, PhD); food engineering (M Sc, M Sc A, PhD); grain drying (M Sc, M Sc A, PhD); irrigation and drainage (M Sc, M Sc A, PhD); machinery (M Sc, M Sc A, PhD); pollution control (M Sc, M Sc A, PhD); post-harvest technology (M Sc, M Sc A, PhD); soil dynamics (M Sc, M Sc A, PhD); structure and environment (M Sc, M Sc A, PhD); vegetable and fruit storage (M Sc, M Sc A, PhD).

North Carolina State University, Graduate School, College of Agriculture and Life Sciences, Department of Biological and Agricultural Engineering, Raleigh, NC 27695. Offers MBAE, MS, PhD, Certificate. *Program availability:* Part-time, online learning. *Degree requirements:* For master's, thesis (for some programs); for doctorate, thesis/dissertation. *Entrance requirements:* For master's and doctorate, GRE. Additional exam requirements/recommendations for international students: Required—TOEFL. Electronic applications accepted. *Faculty research:* Bioinstrumentation, animal waste management, water quality engineering, machine systems, controlled environment agriculture.

North Dakota State University, College of Graduate and Interdisciplinary Studies, College of Engineering, Department of Agricultural and Biosystems Engineering, Fargo, ND 58102. Offers MS, PhD. *Program availability:* Part-time. *Degree requirements:* For master's, thesis; for doctorate, thesis/dissertation. *Entrance requirements:* For master's and doctorate, BS in engineering or the equivalent, minimum undergraduate GPA of 3.0. Additional exam requirements/recommendations for international students: Required—TOEFL (minimum score 550 paper-based; 79 iBT). Electronic applications accepted.

Faculty research: Irrigation, crop processing, food engineering, environmental resources, sensors and instrumentation.

The Ohio State University, Graduate School, College of Food, Agricultural, and Environmental Sciences, Department of Food, Agricultural, and Biological Engineering, Columbus, OH 43210. Offers MS, PhD. Program offered jointly with College of Engineering. *Faculty:* 15. *Students:* 47 (19 women). Average age 27. In 2018, 10 master's, 5 doctorates awarded. *Entrance requirements:* For master's and doctorate, GRE General Test, GRE Subject Test in engineering (recommended). Additional exam requirements/recommendations for international students: Required—TOEFL (minimum score 550 paper-based; 79 iBT), Michigan English Language Assessment Battery (minimum score 82); Recommended—IELTS (minimum score 7). *Application deadline:* For fall admission, 12/13 priority date for domestic students, 11/30 priority date for international students; for spring admission, 12/12 for domestic students, 11/10 for international students; for summer admission, 4/10 for domestic students, 3/13 for international students. Applications are processed on a rolling basis. Application fee: $60 ($70 for international students). Electronic applications accepted. *Financial support:* Fellowships with tuition reimbursements, research assistantships with tuition reimbursements, teaching assistantships with tuition reimbursements, career-related internships or fieldwork, Federal Work-Study, and institutionally sponsored loans available. Support available to part-time students. *Unit head:* Dr. Scott Shearer, Chair, 614-292-7284, E-mail: shearer.95@osu.edu. *Application contact:* Graduate and Professional Admissions, 614-292-9444, Fax: 614-292-3895, E-mail: gpadmissions@osu.edu.
Website: http://fabe.osu.edu/

Oklahoma State University, College of Agricultural Science and Natural Resources, Department of Biosystems and Agricultural Engineering, Stillwater, OK 74078. Offers biosystems engineering (MS, PhD); environmental and natural resources (MS, PhD). *Faculty:* 22 full-time (5 women), 2 part-time/adjunct (0 women). *Students:* 8 full-time (0 women), 17 part-time (8 women); includes 5 minority (1 Black or African American, non-Hispanic/Latino; 1 Asian, non-Hispanic/Latino; 2 Hispanic/Latino; 1 Two or more races, non-Hispanic/Latino), 15 international. Average age 30. 19 applicants, 32% accepted, 3 enrolled. In 2018, 4 master's, 7 doctorates awarded. *Entrance requirements:* For master's and doctorate, GRE or GMAT. Additional exam requirements/recommendations for international students: Required—TOEFL (minimum score 550 paper-based; 79 iBT). *Application deadline:* For fall admission, 3/1 priority date for international students; for spring admission, 8/1 priority date for international students. Applications are processed on a rolling basis. Application fee: $40 ($75 for international students). Electronic applications accepted. *Expenses: Tuition, area resident:* Full-time $4148. Tuition, state resident: full-time $4148. Tuition, nonresident: full-time $10,517. *International tuition:* $10,517 full-time. *Required fees:* $4394; $2929 per credit hour. Tuition and fees vary according to course load and program. *Financial support:* Research assistantships, teaching assistantships, career-related internships or fieldwork, Federal Work-Study, scholarships/grants, health care benefits, tuition waivers (partial), and unspecified assistantships available. Support available to part-time students. Financial award application deadline: 3/1; financial award applicants required to submit FAFSA. *Unit head:* Dr. John Veenstra, Department Head, 405-744-5431, Fax: 405-744-6059, E-mail: jveenst@okstate.edu. *Application contact:* Dr. Ning Wang, Professor/Graduate Coordinator, 405-744-2877, E-mail: ning.wang@okstate.edu.
Website: http://bae.okstate.edu/

Oregon State University, College of Agricultural Sciences, Program in Food Science and Technology, Corvallis, OR 97331. Offers brewing (MS, PhD); enology (MS, PhD); flavor chemistry (MS, PhD); food and seafood processing (MS, PhD); food chemistry/biochemistry (MS, PhD); food engineering (MS, PhD); food microbiology/biotechnology (MS, PhD); sensory evaluation (MS, PhD). *Entrance requirements:* For master's and doctorate, GRE (minimum Verbal and Quantitative scores of 300), minimum GPA of 3.0 in last 90 hours. Additional exam requirements/recommendations for international students: Required—TOEFL (minimum score 80 iBT), IELTS (minimum score 6.5).

Penn State University Park, Graduate School, College of Agricultural Sciences, Department of Agricultural and Biological Engineering, University Park, PA 16802. Offers agricultural and biological engineering (MS, PhD); biorenewable systems (MS, PhD).

Purdue University, College of Engineering, School of Agricultural and Biological Engineering, West Lafayette, IN 47907-2093. Offers MS, MSABE, MSE, PhD. *Program availability:* Part-time. Terminal master's awarded for partial completion of doctoral program. *Degree requirements:* For master's, thesis (for some programs); for doctorate, thesis/dissertation. *Entrance requirements:* For master's and doctorate, GRE General Test, minimum GPA of 3.0. Electronic applications accepted. *Faculty research:* Agricultural systems management, food process engineering, environmental and natural resources engineering, biological engineering, machine systems engineering.

South Dakota State University, Graduate School, Jerome J. Lohr College of Engineering, Department of Agricultural and Biosystems Engineering, Brookings, SD 57007. Offers biological sciences (MS, PhD); engineering (MS). PhD offered jointly with Iowa State University of Science and Technology. *Program availability:* Part-time. *Degree requirements:* For master's, thesis (for some programs), oral exam; for doctorate, thesis/dissertation, preliminary oral and written exams. *Entrance requirements:* For master's and doctorate, engineering degree. Additional exam requirements/recommendations for international students: Required—TOEFL (minimum score 550 paper-based; 79 iBT). *Faculty research:* Water resources, food engineering, natural resources engineering, machine design, bioprocess engineering.

Texas A&M University, College of Agriculture and Life Sciences, Department of Biological and Agricultural Engineering, College Station, TX 77843. Offers agricultural systems management (M Agr, MS); biological and agricultural engineering (MS, PhD). *Program availability:* Part-time. *Faculty:* 19. *Students:* 59 full-time (20 women), 18 part-time (5 women); includes 12 minority (4 Black or African American, non-Hispanic/Latino; 1 Asian, non-Hispanic/Latino; 5 Hispanic/Latino; 2 Two or more races, non-Hispanic/Latino), 50 international. Average age 31. 16 applicants, 100% accepted, 11 enrolled. In 2018, 26 master's, 5 doctorates awarded. *Degree requirements:* For master's, thesis (MS); preliminary and final exams; for doctorate, thesis/dissertation, preliminary and final exams. *Entrance requirements:* For master's and doctorate, GRE General Test. Additional exam requirements/recommendations for international students: Required—TOEFL (minimum score 550 paper-based; 80 iBT), IELTS (minimum score 6), PTE (minimum score 53). *Application deadline:* For fall admission, 12/15 priority date for domestic students. Applications are processed on a rolling basis. Application fee: $50 ($90 for international students). Electronic applications accepted. *Expenses:* Contact institution. *Financial support:* In 2018–19, 61 students received support, including 8 fellowships with tuition reimbursements available (averaging $8,618 per year), 39 research assistantships with tuition reimbursements available (averaging $13,984 per

year), 20 teaching assistantships with tuition reimbursements available (averaging $10,945 per year); career-related internships or fieldwork, institutionally sponsored loans, scholarships/grants, traineeships, health care benefits, tuition waivers (full and partial), and unspecified assistantships also available. Support available to part-time students. Financial award application deadline: 3/15; financial award applicants required to submit FAFSA. *Faculty research:* Water quality and quantity; air quality; biological, food, ecological engineering; off-road equipment; mechatronics. *Unit head:* Dr. Steve Searcy, Professor and Head, 979-845-3940, Fax: 979-862-3442, E-mail: s-searcy@tamu.edu. *Application contact:* Dr. Sandun Fernando, Director of Graduate Programs, 979-845-9793, E-mail: sfernando@tamu.edu.
Website: http://baen.tamu.edu

Université Laval, Faculty of Agricultural and Food Sciences, Department of Soils and Agricultural Engineering, Programs in Agri-Food Engineering, Québec, QC G1K 7P4, Canada. Offers agri-food engineering (M Sc); environmental technology (M Sc). *Degree requirements:* For master's, thesis (for some programs). *Entrance requirements:* For master's, knowledge of French. Electronic applications accepted.

The University of Arizona, College of Agriculture and Life Sciences, Department of Agricultural and Biosystems Engineering, Tucson, AZ 85721. Offers MS, PhD. Terminal master's awarded for partial completion of doctoral program. *Degree requirements:* For master's, thesis; for doctorate, thesis/dissertation. *Entrance requirements:* For master's, minimum GPA of 3.0 in last 2 years of undergraduate study, 3 letters of recommendation; for doctorate, minimum GPA of 3.0 in last 2 years of undergraduate study, 3 letters of recommendation, statement of purpose. Additional exam requirements/recommendations for international students: Required—TOEFL (minimum score 550 paper-based; 79 iBT). Electronic applications accepted. *Faculty research:* Irrigation system design, energy-use management, equipment for alternative crops, food properties enhancement.

University of Arkansas, Graduate School, College of Engineering, Department of Biological and Agricultural Engineering, Fayetteville, AR 72701. Offers biological and agricultural engineering (MSE, PhD); biological engineering (MSBE); biomedical engineering (MSBME). In 2018, 7 master's, 2 doctorates awarded. *Degree requirements:* For master's, thesis; for doctorate, one foreign language, thesis/dissertation. *Application deadline:* For fall admission, 8/1 for domestic students, 4/1 for international students; for spring admission, 12/1 for domestic students, 10/1 for international students; for summer admission, 4/15 for domestic students, 3/1 for international students. Applications are processed on a rolling basis. Application fee: $60. Electronic applications accepted. *Financial support:* In 2018–19, 21 research assistantships, 3 teaching assistantships were awarded; fellowships with tuition reimbursements, career-related internships or fieldwork, and Federal Work-Study also available. Support available to part-time students. Financial award application deadline: 4/1; financial award applicants required to submit FAFSA. *Unit head:* Dr. Lalit R. Verma, Department Head, 479-575-2351, E-mail: lverma@uark.edu. *Application contact:* Dr. Jin-Woo Kim, Program Coordinator, 479-575-3402, E-mail: jwkim@uark.edu.
Website: https://bio-ag-engineering.uark.edu

University of Florida, Graduate School, Herbert Wertheim College of Engineering and College of Agricultural and Life Sciences, Department of Agricultural and Biological Engineering, Gainesville, FL 32611. Offers agricultural and biological engineering (ME, MS, PhD), including geographic information systems, hydrologic sciences, wetland sciences; biological systems modeling (Certificate). *Program availability:* Part-time. Terminal master's awarded for partial completion of doctoral program. *Degree requirements:* For master's, comprehensive exam, thesis (for some programs); for doctorate, comprehensive exam, thesis/dissertation. *Entrance requirements:* For master's and doctorate, minimum GPA of 3.0, 3 letters of recommendation, statement of purpose. Additional exam requirements/recommendations for international students: Required—TOEFL (minimum score 550 paper-based; 80 iBT), IELTS (minimum score 6). Electronic applications accepted. *Faculty research:* Bioenergy and bioprocessing; hydrological, biological and agricultural modeling; biosensors; precision agriculture and robotics; food packaging and food security.

University of Illinois at Urbana–Champaign, Graduate College, College of Agricultural, Consumer and Environmental Sciences, Department of Agricultural and Biological Engineering, Champaign, IL 61820. Offers agricultural and biological engineering (MS, PhD); technical systems management (MS, PSM).

University of Kentucky, Graduate School, College of Agriculture, Food and Environment, Program in Biosystems and Agricultural Engineering, Lexington, KY 40506-0032. Offers MS, PhD. *Program availability:* Part-time. *Degree requirements:* For master's, comprehensive exam, thesis optional; for doctorate, comprehensive exam, thesis/dissertation. *Entrance requirements:* For master's, GRE General Test, minimum undergraduate GPA of 2.75; for doctorate, GRE General Test, minimum graduate GPA of 3.0. Additional exam requirements/recommendations for international students: Required—TOEFL (minimum score 550 paper-based). Electronic applications accepted. *Faculty research:* Machine systems, food engineering, fermentation, hydrology, water quality.

University of Nebraska–Lincoln, Graduate College, College of Engineering, Department of Biological Systems Engineering, Interdepartmental Area of Agricultural and Biological Systems Engineering, Lincoln, NE 68588. Offers MS, PhD. *Degree requirements:* For master's, thesis optional. *Entrance requirements:* Additional exam requirements/recommendations for international students: Required—TOEFL (minimum score 550 paper-based). Electronic applications accepted. *Faculty research:* Hydrological engineering, tractive performance, biomedical engineering, irrigation systems.

The University of Tennessee, Graduate School, College of Agricultural Sciences and Natural Resources, Department of Biosystems Engineering and Environmental Science, Program in Biosystems Engineering Technology, Knoxville, TN 37996. Offers MS. *Degree requirements:* For master's, thesis or alternative. *Entrance requirements:* For master's, GRE General Test, minimum GPA of 2.7. Additional exam requirements/recommendations for international students: Required—TOEFL. Electronic applications accepted.

University of Wisconsin–Madison, Graduate School, College of Agricultural and Life Sciences, Department of Biological Systems Engineering, Madison, WI 53706. Offers MS, PhD. *Program availability:* Part-time. Terminal master's awarded for partial completion of doctoral program. *Degree requirements:* For master's, thesis; for doctorate, thesis/dissertation. *Entrance requirements:* Additional exam requirements/recommendations for international students: Required—TOEFL. Electronic applications accepted. *Faculty research:* Biomaterials, biosensors, food safety, food engineering, bioprocessing, machinery systems, natural resources and environment, structures engineering.

Virginia Polytechnic Institute and State University, Graduate School, College of Engineering, Blacksburg, VA 24061. Offers aerospace engineering (PhD, M Eng/MS); biological systems engineering (PhD); biomedical engineering (MS, PhD); chemical engineering (PhD); civil engineering (PhD); computer engineering (PhD); computer science and applications (MS); electrical engineering (PhD); engineering education (PhD); M Eng/MS. *Faculty:* 446 full-time (87 women), 7 part-time/adjunct (3 women). *Students:* 1,776 full-time (471 women), 367 part-time (62 women); includes 260 minority (50 Black or African American, non-Hispanic/Latino; 3 American Indian or Alaska Native, non-Hispanic/Latino; 99 Asian, non-Hispanic/Latino; 67 Hispanic/Latino; 41 Two or more races, non-Hispanic/Latino), 1,178 international. Average age 27. 3,798 applicants, 37% accepted, 507 enrolled. In 2018, 489 master's, 200 doctorates awarded. *Degree requirements:* For master's, comprehensive exam (for some programs), thesis (for some programs); for doctorate, comprehensive exam (for some programs), thesis/dissertation (for some programs). *Entrance requirements:* For master's and doctorate, GRE/GMAT. Additional exam requirements/recommendations for international students: Required—TOEFL (minimum score 90 iBT). *Application deadline:* For fall admission, 8/1 for domestic students, 4/1 for international students; for spring admission, 1/1 for domestic students, 9/1 for international students. Applications are processed on a rolling basis. Application fee: $75. Electronic applications accepted. *Expenses:* Tuition, state resident: full-time $15,510; part-time $739.50 per credit hour. Tuition, nonresident: full-time $29,629; part-time $1490.25 per credit hour. *Required fees:* $2804; $550 per semester. Tuition and fees vary according to course load, campus/location and program. *Financial support:* In 2018–19, 37 fellowships with full tuition reimbursements (averaging $24,951 per year), 1,110 research assistantships with full tuition reimbursements (averaging $20,129 per year), 486 teaching assistantships with full tuition reimbursements (averaging $16,192 per year) were awarded; scholarships/grants and unspecified assistantships also available. Financial award application deadline: 3/1; financial award applicants required to submit FAFSA. *Total annual research expenditures:* $96.3 million. *Unit head:* Dr. Julia Ross, Dean, 540-231-9752, Fax: 540-231-3031, E-mail: rjulie@vt.edu. *Application contact:* Linda Perkins, Executive Assistant, 540-231-9752, Fax: 540-231-3031, E-mail: lperkins@vt.edu.
Website: http://www.eng.vt.edu/

Washington State University, College of Agricultural, Human, and Natural Resource Sciences, Department of Biological Systems Engineering, Pullman, WA 99164-6120. Offers biological and agricultural engineering (MS, PhD). Program applications must be made through the Pullman campus. *Degree requirements:* For master's, comprehensive exam, thesis (for some programs), written and oral exam; for doctorate, comprehensive exam, thesis/dissertation, written and oral exam. *Entrance requirements:* For master's and doctorate, minimum GPA of 3.0, bachelor's degree in engineering or closely-related subject. Additional exam requirements/recommendations for international students: Required—TOEFL. Electronic applications accepted. *Faculty research:* Agricultural automation engineering; bioenergy and bioproducts engineering; food engineering; land, air, and water resources and environmental engineering.

Bioengineering

Alfred University, Graduate School, College of Ceramics, Inamori School of Engineering, Alfred, NY 14802. Offers biomaterials engineering (MS); ceramic engineering (MS, PhD); electrical engineering (MS); glass science (MS, PhD); materials science and engineering (MS, PhD); mechanical engineering (MS). *Program availability:* Part-time. *Degree requirements:* For master's, thesis; for doctorate, thesis/dissertation. *Entrance requirements:* Additional exam requirements/recommendations for international students: Required—TOEFL (minimum score 590 paper-based; 90 iBT), IELTS (minimum score 6.5). Electronic applications accepted. *Expenses:* Contact institution. *Faculty research:* X-ray diffraction, biomaterials and polymers, thin-film processing, electronic and optical ceramics, solid-state chemistry.

Baylor College of Medicine, Graduate School of Biomedical Sciences, Program in Translational Biology and Molecular Medicine, Houston, TX 77030-3498. Offers PhD. *Degree requirements:* For doctorate, thesis/dissertation, public defense. *Entrance requirements:* For doctorate, GRE, minimum GPA of 3.0. Additional exam requirements/recommendations for international students: Required—TOEFL. Electronic applications accepted. *Faculty research:* Molecular medicine, translational biology, human disease biology and therapy.

California Institute of Technology, Division of Engineering and Applied Science, Option in Bioengineering, Pasadena, CA 91125-0001. Offers MS, PhD. *Degree requirements:* For master's, thesis; for doctorate, thesis/dissertation. *Faculty research:* Biosynthesis and analysis, biometrics.

Carnegie Mellon University, Carnegie Institute of Technology, Biomedical and Health Engineering Program, Pittsburgh, PA 15213-3891. Offers bioengineering (MS, PhD); MD/PhD. *Degree requirements:* For master's, thesis; for doctorate, thesis/dissertation, qualifying exam. *Entrance requirements:* For master's and doctorate, GRE General Test. Additional exam requirements/recommendations for international students: Required—TOEFL. Electronic applications accepted. *Faculty research:* Cellular and molecular systematics, signal and image processing, materials and mechanics.

Clemson University, Graduate School, College of Engineering, Computing and Applied Sciences, Department of Bioengineering, Clemson, SC 29634-0905. Offers bioengineering (MS, PhD); biomedical engineering (M Engr); medical device recycling and reprocessing (Certificate). *Program availability:* Part-time. *Faculty:* 27 full-time (9 women), 1 (woman) part-time/adjunct. *Students:* 122 full-time (53 women), 13 part-time (5 women); includes 19 minority (4 Black or African American, non-Hispanic/Latino; 8 Asian, non-Hispanic/Latino; 4 Hispanic/Latino; 3 Two or more races, non-Hispanic/Latino), 31 international. Average age 25. 159 applicants, 68% accepted, 62 enrolled. In 2018, 36 master's, 15 doctorates, 2 other advanced degrees awarded. *Degree requirements:* For master's, thesis optional; for doctorate, comprehensive exam, thesis/dissertation. *Entrance requirements:* For master's, doctorate, and Certificate, GRE General Test, unofficial transcripts, letters of recommendation. Additional exam requirements/recommendations for international students: Required—TOEFL (minimum score 100 paper-based; 100 iBT); Recommended—IELTS (minimum score 7), TSE (minimum score 54). *Application deadline:* For fall admission, 2/15 priority date for domestic students, 1/15 priority date for international students. Applications are processed on a rolling basis. Application fee: $80 ($90 for international students). Electronic applications accepted. *Expenses:* $6823 per semester full-time resident, $14023 per semester full-time non-resident, $833 per credit hour part-time resident, $1731 per credit hour part-time non-resident, online $1264 per credit hour, $4938 doctoral programs resident, $10405 doctoral programs non-resident, $1144 full-time graduate assistant, other fees may apply per session. *Financial support:* In 2018–19, 96

students received support, including 8 fellowships with full and partial tuition reimbursements available (averaging $1,958 per year), 45 research assistantships with full and partial tuition reimbursements available (averaging $18,444 per year), 30 teaching assistantships with full and partial tuition reimbursements available (averaging $18,803 per year); career-related internships or fieldwork and unspecified assistantships also available. Financial award application deadline: 2/15; financial award applicants required to submit FAFSA. *Faculty research:* Biomaterials, biomechanics, bioinstrumentation, tissue engineering, vascular engineering. *Total annual research expenditures:* $4.8 million. *Unit head:* Dr. Martine LaBerge, Department Chair, 864-656-5557, E-mail: laberge@clemson.edu. *Application contact:* Dr. Agneta Simionescu, Graduate Coordinator, 864-650-2575, E-mail: agneta@clemson.edu.
Website: https://www.clemson.edu/cecas/departments/bioe/

Colorado School of Mines, Office of Graduate Studies, Department of Chemical and Biological Engineering, Golden, CO 80401. Offers chemical engineering (MS, PhD). *Program availability:* Part-time. *Faculty:* 34 full-time (12 women), 6 part-time/adjunct (2 women). *Students:* 56 full-time (20 women), 5 part-time (2 women); includes 6 minority (3 Asian, non-Hispanic/Latino; 1 Hispanic/Latino; 2 Two or more races, non-Hispanic/Latino), 21 international. Average age 26. 126 applicants, 44% accepted, 10 enrolled. In 2018, 12 master's, 10 doctorates awarded. Terminal master's awarded for partial completion of doctoral program. *Degree requirements:* For master's, thesis (for some programs); for doctorate, comprehensive exam, thesis/dissertation. *Entrance requirements:* For master's and doctorate, GRE General Test. Additional exam requirements/recommendations for international students: Required—TOEFL (minimum score 550 paper-based; 79 iBT). *Application deadline:* For fall admission, 12/15 priority date for domestic and international students; for spring admission, 9/1 for domestic and international students. Application fee: $60 ($80 for international students). Electronic applications accepted. *Expenses:* Tuition, state resident: full-time $16,650; part-time $925 per contact hour. Tuition, nonresident: full-time $36,270; part-time $2015 per contact hour. *International tuition:* $36,270 full-time. *Required fees:* $2314; $2314 per semester. *Financial support:* In 2018–19, 26 research assistantships with tuition reimbursements, 19 teaching assistantships with full tuition reimbursements were awarded; fellowships, scholarships/grants, health care benefits, and unspecified assistantships also available. Financial award application deadline: 12/15; financial award applicants required to submit FAFSA. *Faculty research:* Liquid fuels for the future, responsible management of hazardous substances, surface and interfacial engineering, advanced computational methods and process control, gas hydrates. *Unit head:* Dr. Anuj Chauhan, Department Head, 303-273-3720, E-mail: chauhan@mines.edu. *Application contact:* Jennie Gambach, Program Assistant, 303-273-3246, E-mail: jgambach@mines.edu.
Website: http://chemeng.mines.edu/

Colorado State University, Walter Scott, Jr. College of Engineering, School of Biomedical Engineering, Fort Collins, CO 80523-1376. Offers bioengineering (MS, PhD). *Program availability:* Part-time, online learning. Terminal master's awarded for partial completion of doctoral program. *Degree requirements:* For master's, thesis, minimum of two presentations in seminar series; for doctorate, thesis/dissertation, minimum of two presentations in seminar series. *Entrance requirements:* For master's and doctorate, GRE General Test, minimum GPA of 3.0, resume, statement of purpose, official transcripts, three letters of recommendation. Additional exam requirements/recommendations for international students: Required—TOEFL (minimum score 550 paper-based; 80 iBT), IELTS (minimum score 6). Electronic applications accepted. *Expenses:* Contact institution. *Faculty research:* Regenerative and rehabilitative medicine, imaging and diagnostics, medical devices and therapeutics.

Cornell University, Graduate School, Graduate Fields of Agriculture and Life Sciences and Graduate Fields of Engineering, Field of Biological and Environmental Engineering, Ithaca, NY 14853. Offers bioenergy and integrated energy systems (M Eng, MPS, MS, PhD); biological engineering (M Eng, MPS, MS, PhD); bioprocess engineering (M Eng, MPS, MS, PhD); ecohydrology (M Eng, MPS, MS, PhD); environmental engineering (M Eng, MPS, MS, PhD); environmental management (MPS); food engineering (M Eng, MPS, MS, PhD); industrial biotechnology (M Eng, MPS, MS, PhD); nanobiotechnology (M Eng, MPS, MS, PhD); sustainable systems (M Eng, MPS, MS, PhD); synthetic biology (MS); syntheticbiology (M Eng, MPS, PhD). Terminal master's awarded for partial completion of doctoral program. *Degree requirements:* For master's, thesis (MS); for doctorate, comprehensive exam, thesis/dissertation. *Entrance requirements:* For master's, letters of recommendation (3 for MS, 2 for M Eng and MPS); for doctorate, GRE General Test, 3 letters of recommendation. Additional exam requirements/recommendations for international students: Required—TOEFL (minimum score 550 paper-based; 77 iBT). Electronic applications accepted. *Faculty research:* Biological and food engineering, environmental, soil and water engineering, international agricultural engineering, structures and controlled environments, machine systems and energy.

Dalhousie University, Faculty of Engineering, Department of Process Engineering and Applied Science, Halifax, NS B3J 1Z1, Canada. Offers biological engineering (M Eng, MA Sc, PhD); chemical engineering (M Eng, MA Sc, PhD); food science (M Sc, PhD). *Degree requirements:* For master's, thesis; for doctorate, thesis/dissertation. *Entrance requirements:* Additional exam requirements/recommendations for international students: Required—TOEFL, IELTS, CANTEST, CAEL, or Michigan English Language Assessment Battery. Electronic applications accepted. *Faculty research:* Explosions, process optimization, combustion synthesis of materials, waste minimization, treatment of industrial wastewater.

Florida Atlantic University, College of Engineering and Computer Science, Department of Computer and Electrical Engineering and Computer Science, Boca Raton, FL 33431-0991. Offers bioengineering (MS); computer engineering (MS, PhD); computer science (MS, PhD); electrical engineering (MS, PhD). *Program availability:* Part-time, evening/weekend. *Faculty:* 37 full-time (7 women), 2 part-time/adjunct (0 women). *Students:* 85 full-time (18 women), 140 part-time (26 women); includes 86 minority (18 Black or African American, non-Hispanic/Latino; 17 Asian, non-Hispanic/Latino; 43 Hispanic/Latino; 8 Two or more races, non-Hispanic/Latino), 60 international. Average age 32. 185 applicants, 41% accepted, 69 enrolled. In 2018, 89 master's, 11 doctorates awarded. Terminal master's awarded for partial completion of doctoral program. *Degree requirements:* For master's, thesis optional; for doctorate, thesis/dissertation, qualifying exam. *Entrance requirements:* For master's, GRE General Test, minimum GPA of 3.0; for doctorate, GRE General Test, master's degree, minimum GPA of 3.5. Additional exam requirements/recommendations for international students: Required—TOEFL (minimum score 500 paper-based; 61 iBT), IELTS (minimum score 6). *Application deadline:* For fall admission, 7/1 priority date for domestic students, 2/15 for international students; for spring admission, 11/1 for domestic students, 7/15 for international students. Applications are processed on a rolling basis. Application fee: $30. *Expenses: Tuition, area resident:* Full-time $7400; part-time $369.82 per credit. Tuition, state resident: full-time $7400; part-time $369.82 per credit. Tuition, nonresident: full-time $20,496; part-time $1024.81 per credit. *Financial support:* Fellowships, research assistantships with partial tuition reimbursements, teaching assistantships with full tuition reimbursements, career-related internships or fieldwork, and Federal Work-Study available. Support available to part-time students. Financial award application deadline: 4/1; financial award applicants required to submit FAFSA. *Faculty research:* VLSI and neural networks, communication networks, software engineering, computer architecture, multimedia and video processing. *Unit head:* Jean Mangiaracina, Graduate Program Administrator, 561-297-6482, E-mail: jmangiar@fau.edu. *Application contact:* Jean Mangiaracina, Graduate Program Administrator, 561-297-6482, E-mail: jmangiar@fau.edu.
Website: http://www.ceecs.fau.edu/

George Mason University, Volgenau School of Engineering, Department of Bioengineering, Fairfax, VA 22030. Offers PhD. *Faculty:* 15 full-time (8 women), 4 part-time/adjunct (1 woman). *Students:* 14 full-time (5 women), 3 part-time (1 woman); includes 4 minority (1 Black or African American, non-Hispanic/Latino; 2 Asian, non-Hispanic/Latino; 1 Hispanic/Latino), 10 international. Average age 27. 19 applicants, 58% accepted, 3 enrolled. In 2018, 1 doctorate awarded. *Degree requirements:* For doctorate, comprehensive exam, thesis/dissertation, proposal. *Entrance requirements:* For doctorate, GRE General Test, two copies of official transcripts; goals statement (1000 words maximum); three letters of recommendation; resume. Additional exam requirements/recommendations for international students: Required—TOEFL (minimum score 575 paper-based; 88 iBT), IELTS (minimum score 6.5), PTE (minimum score 59). *Application deadline:* For fall admission, 12/15 priority date for domestic and international students; for spring admission, 8/15 priority date for domestic and international students. Application fee: $75 ($80 for international students). Electronic applications accepted. *Expenses:* $589 per credit in-state, $1,346.75 per credit out-of-state. *Financial support:* In 2018–19, 15 students received support, including 10 research assistantships with tuition reimbursements available (averaging $19,772 per year), 5 teaching assistantships with tuition reimbursements available (averaging $18,625 per year); career-related internships or fieldwork, Federal Work-Study, scholarships/grants, unspecified assistantships, and health care benefits (for full-time research or teaching assistantship recipients) also available. Support available to part-time students. Financial award application deadline: 3/1; financial award applicants required to submit FAFSA. *Faculty research:* Biomedical imaging and devices; computational modeling and biomechanics; biomaterials and nano-medicine; neuroengineering and neuroscience. *Total annual research expenditures:* $2.9 million. *Unit head:* Brian L. Mark, Acting Chair, 703-993-4069, Fax: 703-993-1601, E-mail: bmark@gmu.edu. *Application contact:* Claudia Borke, Academic Advisor, 703-993-4190, E-mail: cborke@gmu.edu.
Website: http://bioengineering.gmu.edu

Georgia Institute of Technology, Graduate Studies, Multidisciplinary Program in Bioengineering, Atlanta, GA 30332-0001. Offers MS, PhD. Program offered jointly with College of Computing, School of Aerospace Engineering, Wallace H. Coulter Department of Biomedical Engineering, School of Civil and Environmental Engineering, School of Chemical and Biomolecular Engineering, School of Electrical and Computer Engineering, School of Materials Science and Engineering, and George W. Woodruff School of Mechanical Engineering. *Program availability:* Part-time. *Degree requirements:* For master's, thesis; for doctorate, thesis/dissertation. *Entrance requirements:* For master's and doctorate, GRE General Test. Additional exam requirements/recommendations for international students: Required—TOEFL (minimum score 620 paper-based; 105 iBT). Electronic applications accepted.

Harvard University, Graduate School of Arts and Sciences, Harvard John A. Paulson School of Engineering and Applied Sciences, Cambridge, MA 02138. Offers applied mathematics (PhD); applied physics (PhD); computational science and engineering (ME, SM); computer science (PhD); data science (SM); design engineering (MDE); engineering science (ME), including electrical engineering (ME, SM, PhD); engineering sciences (SM, PhD), including bioengineering (PhD), electrical engineering (ME, SM, PhD), environmental science and engineering (PhD), materials science and mechanical engineering (PhD). MDE offered in collaboration with Graduate School of Design. *Program availability:* Part-time. Terminal master's awarded for partial completion of doctoral program. *Degree requirements:* For master's, thesis (for ME); for doctorate, comprehensive exam, thesis/dissertation. *Entrance requirements:* For master's and doctorate, GRE General Test, GRE Subject Test (recommended), 3 letters of recommendation. Additional exam requirements/recommendations for international students: Required—TOEFL (minimum score 80 iBT). Electronic applications accepted. *Expenses:* Contact institution. *Faculty research:* Applied mathematics, applied physics, computer science and electrical engineering, environmental engineering, mechanical and biomedical engineering.

Illinois Institute of Technology, Graduate College, Armour College of Engineering, Department of Chemical and Biological Engineering, Chicago, IL 60616. Offers biological engineering (MAS); chemical engineering (MAS, MS, PhD); MS/MAS. *Program availability:* Part-time, evening/weekend, online learning. Terminal master's awarded for partial completion of doctoral program. *Degree requirements:* For master's, comprehensive exam (for some programs), thesis (for some programs); for doctorate, comprehensive exam, thesis/dissertation. *Entrance requirements:* For master's, GRE General Test with minimum score of 950 Quantitative and Verbal, 2.5 Analytical Writing (for MAS); GRE General Test with minimum score of 1100 Quantitative and Verbal, 3.0 Analytical Writing (for MS), minimum undergraduate GPA of 3.0; for doctorate, GRE General Test (minimum score 1100 Quantitative and Verbal, 3.0 Analytical Writing), minimum undergraduate GPA of 3.0. Additional exam requirements/recommendations for international students: Required—TOEFL (minimum score 550 paper-based; 80 iBT). Electronic applications accepted. *Faculty research:* Energy and sustainability, biological engineering, advanced materials, systems engineering.

Johns Hopkins University, G. W. C. Whiting School of Engineering and School of Medicine, Department of Biomedical Engineering, Baltimore, MD 21205. Offers bioengineering innovation and design (MSE); biomedical engineering (MSE, PhD). *Faculty:* 34 full-time (9 women). *Students:* 316 full-time (133 women). 337 applicants, 37% accepted, 57 enrolled. In 2018, 57 master's awarded. Terminal master's awarded for partial completion of doctoral program. *Degree requirements:* For master's, thesis; for doctorate, comprehensive exam, thesis/dissertation. *Entrance requirements:* For master's and doctorate, GRE General Test, 3 letters of recommendation, statement of purpose, transcripts. Additional exam requirements/recommendations for international students: Required—TOEFL (minimum score 600 paper-based, 100 iBT) or IELTS (7). *Application deadline:* For fall admission, 1/4 for domestic and international students. Application fee: $75. Electronic applications accepted. *Financial support:* In 2018–19, 198 students received support, including 52 fellowships with partial tuition reimbursements available (averaging $33,383 per year), 146 research assistantships with partial tuition reimbursements available (averaging $32,894 per year); teaching assistantships, Federal Work-Study, institutionally sponsored loans, scholarships/grants, health care benefits, tuition waivers (full), and unspecified assistantships also available. Financial award application deadline: 1/15; financial award applicants required to submit FAFSA. *Faculty research:* Systems neuroscience and neuroengineering, molecular and cellular systems biology, biomedical imaging, cell and tissue engineering, cardiovascular systems engineering. *Unit head:* Dr. Michael Miller, Director, 410-516-2039, Fax: 410-516-4771, E-mail: mim@cis.jhu.edu. *Application contact:* Samuel Bourne, Academic Program Administrator, 410-516-8482, Fax: 410-516-4771, E-mail: sbourne@jhu.edu.
Website: http://www.bme.jhu.edu/

Johns Hopkins University, G. W. C. Whiting School of Engineering, Department of Chemical and Biomolecular Engineering, Baltimore, MD 21218. Offers MSE, PhD. *Faculty:* 26 full-time (9 women). *Students:* 214 full-time (72 women). 358 applicants, 61% accepted, 117 enrolled. In 2018, 81 master's, 17 doctorates awarded. Terminal master's awarded for partial completion of doctoral program. *Degree requirements:* For master's, essay presentation; for doctorate, thesis/dissertation, oral exam; thesis presentation. *Entrance requirements:* For master's and doctorate, GRE General Test, 3 letters of recommendation, statement of purpose, transcripts. Additional exam requirements/recommendations for international students: Required—TOEFL (minimum score 600 paper-based, 100 iBT) or IELTS (7). *Application deadline:* For fall admission, 12/15 for domestic and international students. Application fee: $25. Electronic applications accepted. *Financial support:* In 2018–19, 131 students received support, including 14 fellowships with full and partial tuition reimbursements available (averaging $29,592 per year), 117 research assistantships with full tuition reimbursements available (averaging $31,000 per year); teaching assistantships with full and partial tuition reimbursements available, career-related internships or fieldwork, Federal Work-Study, institutionally sponsored loans, scholarships/grants, health care benefits, tuition waivers (partial), and unspecified assistantships also available. Support available to part-time students. Financial award application deadline: 1/15; financial award applicants required to submit FAFSA. *Faculty research:* Engineering in health and disease, biomolecular design and engineering, materials by design, micro and nanotechnology, alternative energy and sustainability. *Unit head:* Dr. Paulette Clancy, Chair and Professor, 410-516-4312, Fax: 410-516-5510, E-mail: pclancy3@jhu.edu. *Application contact:* Alisha Wells, Academic Program Coordinator, 410-516-2943, Fax: 410-516-5510, E-mail: AWells18@jhu.edu.
Website: http://engineering.jhu.edu/chembe/

Kansas State University, Graduate School, College of Engineering, Department of Biological and Agricultural Engineering, Manhattan, KS 66506. Offers MS, PhD. Terminal master's awarded for partial completion of doctoral program. *Degree requirements:* For master's, thesis; for doctorate, thesis/dissertation, preliminary exam. *Entrance requirements:* For master's, GRE, bachelor's degree in biological and agricultural engineering; for doctorate, GRE. Additional exam requirements/recommendations for international students: Required—TOEFL (minimum score 550 paper-based; 79 iBT). Electronic applications accepted. *Faculty research:* Ecological engineering, watershed modeling, air quality, bioprocessing, bio-fuel, sensors and controls, 3D engineered biomaterials and biomedical devices, mobile health, point-of-care diagnosis, protein biomarker discovery, cancer early detection.

Kansas State University, Graduate School, College of Engineering, Department of Electrical and Computer Engineering, Manhattan, KS 66506. Offers electrical engineering (MS), including bioengineering, communication systems, design of computer systems, electrical engineering, energy and power systems, integrated circuits and devices, real time embedded systems, renewable energy, signal processing. *Program availability:* Part-time, evening/weekend, online learning. *Degree requirements:* For master's, thesis or alternative, final exam; for doctorate, thesis/dissertation, final exam, preliminary exams. *Entrance requirements:* For master's, GRE General Test, bachelor's degree in electrical engineering or computer science, minimum GPA of 3.0; for doctorate, GRE General Test. Additional exam requirements/recommendations for international students: Required—TOEFL (minimum score 600 paper-based; 85 iBT). Electronic applications accepted. *Faculty research:* Energy systems and renewable energy, computer systems and real time embedded systems, communication systems and signal processing, integrated circuits and devices, bioengineering.

Lehigh University, P.C. Rossin College of Engineering and Applied Science, Department of Bioengineering, Bethlehem, PA 18015. Offers MS, PhD. *Faculty:* 11 full-time (4 women). *Students:* 18 full-time (10 women); includes 1 minority (Asian, non-Hispanic/Latino), 14 international. Average age 27. 53 applicants, 40% accepted, 5 enrolled. In 2018, 8 master's, 1 doctorate awarded. Terminal master's awarded for partial completion of doctoral program. *Degree requirements:* For master's, thesis, only thesis based is required; for doctorate, comprehensive exam, thesis/dissertation, must attend seminars. *Entrance requirements:* For master's and doctorate, GRE. Additional exam requirements/recommendations for international students: Required—TOEFL (minimum score 79 iBT), IELTS (minimum score 6.5), Either TOEFL or IELTS required. *Application deadline:* For fall admission, 7/15 for domestic and international students. Application fee: $75. Electronic applications accepted. *Expenses:* $1500 per credit. *Financial support:* Fellowships, research assistantships, teaching assistantships, health care benefits, and unspecified assistantships available. Financial award application deadline: 1/15. *Faculty research:* Biomaterials, biomechanics (biomolecular, cellular, fluid and solid mechanics), BioMEMS Biosensors, bioelectronics/biophotonics, biocomputational engineering. *Unit head:* Dr. Susan Perry, Faculty Graduate Coordinator in Bioengineering, 610-758-4330, E-mail: sup3@lehigh.edu. *Application contact:* Brianne Lisk, Administrative Coordinator of Graduate Studies and Research, 610-758-6310, Fax: 610-758-5623, E-mail: brc3@lehigh.edu.
Website: http://www.lehigh.edu/~inbioe/graduate/index.html

Louisiana State University and Agricultural & Mechanical College, Graduate School, College of Engineering, Department of Biological and Agricultural Engineering, Baton Rouge, LA 70803. Offers biological and agricultural engineering (MSBAE); engineering science (MS, PhD).

Massachusetts Institute of Technology, School of Engineering, Department of Biological Engineering, Cambridge, MA 02139. Offers applied biosciences (PhD, Sc D); bioengineering (PhD, Sc D); biological engineering (PhD, Sc D); biomedical engineering (M Eng); toxicology (SM); SM/MBA. Terminal master's awarded for partial completion of doctoral program. *Degree requirements:* For master's, thesis; for doctorate, comprehensive exam, thesis/dissertation. *Entrance requirements:* For master's and doctorate, GRE General Test. Additional exam requirements/recommendations for international students: Required—IELTS. Electronic applications accepted. *Expenses: Tuition:* Full-time $51,520; part-time $800 per credit hour. *Required fees:* $312. *Faculty research:* Biomaterials; biophysics; cell and tissue engineering; computational modeling of biological and physiological systems; discovery and delivery of molecular therapeutics; new tools for genomics; functional genomics; proteomics and glycomics; macromolecular biochemistry and biophysics; molecular, cell and tissue biomechanics; synthetic biology; systems biology.

McGill University, Faculty of Graduate and Postdoctoral Studies, Faculty of Agricultural and Environmental Sciences, Department of Bioresource Engineering, Montréal, QC H3A 2T5, Canada. Offers computer applications (M Sc, M Sc A, PhD); food engineering (M Sc, M Sc A, PhD); grain drying (M Sc, M Sc A, PhD); irrigation and drainage (M Sc, M Sc A, PhD); machinery (M Sc, M Sc A, PhD); pollution control (M Sc, M Sc A, PhD); post-harvest technology (M Sc, M Sc A, PhD); soil dynamics (M Sc, M Sc A, PhD); structure and environment (M Sc, M Sc A, PhD); vegetable and fruit storage (M Sc, M Sc A, PhD).

Mississippi State University, College of Agriculture and Life Sciences, Department of Agricultural and Biological Engineering, Mississippi State, MS 39762. Offers biological engineering (MS, PhD); biomedical engineering (MS, PhD). *Faculty:* 15 full-time (5 women). *Students:* 30 full-time (14 women), 7 part-time (3 women); includes 4 minority (2 Black or African American, non-Hispanic/Latino; 2 Asian, non-Hispanic/Latino), 13 international. Average age 29. 23 applicants, 70% accepted, 11 enrolled. In 2018, 7 master's, 1 doctorate awarded. *Degree requirements:* For master's, thesis (for some programs); for doctorate, thesis/dissertation, preliminary exam. *Entrance requirements:* For master's, GRE General Test, minimum undergraduate GPA of 2.75 (3.0 for biomedical engineering); for doctorate, GRE General Test, minimum GPA of 3.0 (biomedical engineering). Additional exam requirements/recommendations for international students: Required—TOEFL (minimum score 550 paper-based; 79 iBT); Recommended—IELTS (minimum score 6.5). *Application deadline:* For fall admission, 7/1 for domestic students, 5/1 for international students; for spring admission, 11/1 for domestic students, 9/1 for international students. Applications are processed on a rolling basis. Application fee: $60 ($80 for international students). Electronic applications accepted. *Expenses:* Tuition, state resident: full-time $8450; part-time $360.59 per credit hour. Tuition, nonresident: full-time $23,140; part-time $969.09 per credit hour. *Required fees:* $110. One-time fee: $55 full-time. Part-time tuition and fees vary according to course load, degree level, campus/location and reciprocity agreements. *Financial support:* In 2018–19, 13 research assistantships with partial tuition reimbursements (averaging $16,989 per year), 4 teaching assistantships (averaging $17,423 per year) were awarded; Federal Work-Study, institutionally sponsored loans, and unspecified assistantships also available. Financial award application deadline: 4/1; financial award applicants required to submit FAFSA. *Faculty research:* Bioenvironmental engineering, bioinstrumentation, biomechanics/biomaterials, precision agriculture, tissue engineering, ergonomics human factors, biosimulation and modeling. *Total annual research expenditures:* $85.6 million. *Unit head:* Dr. Jonathan Pote, Professor/Head/Executive Director, 662-325-3280, Fax: 662-325-3853, E-mail: jpote@abe.msstate.edu. *Application contact:* Ryan King, Admissions and Enrollment Assistant, 662-325-8951, E-mail: rjk101@grad.msstate.edu.
Website: http://www.abe.msstate.edu/

New York Institute of Technology, College of Engineering and Computing Sciences, Department of Bioengineering, Old Westbury, NY 11568-8000. Offers MS. *Program availability:* Part-time. *Students:* 2 full-time (both women), 8 part-time (5 women); includes 3 minority (2 Black or African American, non-Hispanic/Latino; 1 Asian, non-Hispanic/Latino), 2 international. Average age 28. 47 applicants, 66% accepted, 7 enrolled. *Degree requirements:* For master's, design project. *Entrance requirements:* For master's, BS in computer science, life science, electrical engineering, physics, or related area; minimum undergraduate GPA of 2.85; meet pre-requisites. Additional exam requirements/recommendations for international students: Required—TOEFL (minimum score 79 iBT), IELTS (minimum score 6), PTE (minimum score 53). *Application deadline:* For fall admission, 7/1 for domestic students, 6/1 for international students; for spring admission, 12/1 for domestic and international students. Applications are processed on a rolling basis. Application fee: $50. Electronic applications accepted. *Expenses: Tuition:* Full-time $1285; part-time $1285 per credit. *Required fees:* $215; $175 per unit. Tuition and fees vary according to course load, degree level and campus/location. *Financial support:* Fellowships with partial tuition reimbursements, career-related internships or fieldwork, Federal Work-Study, scholarships/grants, tuition waivers (full and partial), and unspecified assistantships available. Financial award application deadline: 2/15; financial award applicants required to submit FAFSA. *Unit head:* Dr. Aydin Farajidavar, Program Director, 516-686-4014, E-mail: afarajid@nyit.edu. *Application contact:* Alice Dolitsky, Director, Graduate Admissions, 516-686-7520, Fax: 516-686-1116, E-mail: admissions@nyit.edu.
Website: https://www.nyit.edu/degrees/bioengineering_ms

North Carolina Agricultural and Technical State University, The Graduate College, College of Engineering, Department of Chemical, Biological and Bio Engineering, Greensboro, NC 27411. Offers bioengineering (MS); biological engineering (MS); chemical engineering (MS).

North Carolina State University, Graduate School, College of Agriculture and Life Sciences, Department of Biological and Agricultural Engineering, Raleigh, NC 27695. Offers MBAE, MS, PhD, Certificate. *Program availability:* Part-time, online learning. *Degree requirements:* For master's, thesis (for some programs); for doctorate, thesis/dissertation. *Entrance requirements:* For master's and doctorate, GRE. Additional exam requirements/recommendations for international students: Required—TOEFL. Electronic applications accepted. *Faculty research:* Bioinstrumentation, animal waste management, water quality engineering, machine systems, controlled environment agriculture.

Northeastern University, College of Engineering, Boston, MA 02115-5096. Offers bioengineering (MS, PhD); chemical engineering (MS, PhD); civil engineering (MS, PhD); computer engineering (PhD); computer systems engineering (MS); electrical and computer engineering (MS); electrical and computer engineering leadership (MS); electrical engineering (PhD); energy systems (MS); engineering and public policy (MS); engineering management (MS, Certificate); environmental engineering (MS); industrial engineering (MS, PhD); information assurance (PhD); information systems (MS); interdisciplinary engineering (PhD); mechanical engineering (PhD); operations research (MS); telecommunication systems management (MS). *Program availability:* Part-time, online learning. Electronic applications accepted. *Expenses:* Contact institution.

Northern Arizona University, College of Engineering, Informatics, and Applied Sciences, Department of Mechanical Engineering, Flagstaff, AZ 86011. Offers bioengineering (PhD); engineering (M Eng), including mechanical engineering. *Program availability:* Part-time. *Degree requirements:* For master's, variable foreign language requirement, comprehensive exam (for some programs), thesis (for some programs); for doctorate, variable foreign language requirement, comprehensive exam (for some programs), thesis/dissertation (for some programs). *Entrance requirements:* For master's and doctorate, GRE General Test. Additional exam requirements/recommendations for international students: Required—TOEFL (minimum score 80 iBT), IELTS (minimum score 6.5). Electronic applications accepted.

Northwestern University, The Graduate School, Interdisciplinary Biological Sciences Program (IBiS), Evanston, IL 60208. Offers biochemistry (PhD); bioengineering and biotechnology (PhD); biotechnology (PhD); cell and molecular biology (PhD); developmental and systems biology (PhD); nanotechnology (PhD); neurobiology (PhD); structural biology and biophysics (PhD). *Degree requirements:* For doctorate, thesis/dissertation, qualifying exam. *Entrance requirements:* For doctorate, GRE General Test. Additional exam requirements/recommendations for international students: Required—TOEFL (minimum score 600 paper-based). Electronic applications accepted. *Faculty research:* Biophysics/structural biology, cell/molecular biology, synthetic biology, developmental systems biology, chemical biology/nanotechnology.

The Ohio State University, Graduate School, College of Food, Agricultural, and Environmental Sciences, Department of Food, Agricultural, and Biological Engineering, Columbus, OH 43210. Offers MS, PhD. Program offered jointly with College of Engineering. *Faculty:* 15. *Students:* 47 (19 women). Average age 27. In 2018, 10 master's, 5 doctorates awarded. *Entrance requirements:* For master's and doctorate, GRE General Test, GRE Subject Test in engineering (recommended). Additional exam requirements/recommendations for international students: Required—TOEFL (minimum score 550 paper-based; 79 iBT), Michigan English Language Assessment Battery (minimum score 82); Recommended—IELTS (minimum score 7). *Application deadline:* For fall admission, 12/13 priority date for domestic students, 11/30 priority date for international students; for

spring admission, 12/12 for domestic students, 11/10 for international students; for summer admission, 4/10 for domestic students, 3/13 for international students. Applications are processed on a rolling basis. Application fee: $60 ($70 for international students). Electronic applications accepted. *Financial support:* Fellowships with tuition reimbursements, research assistantships with tuition reimbursements, teaching assistantships with tuition reimbursements, career-related internships or fieldwork, Federal Work-Study, and institutionally sponsored loans available. Support available to part-time students. *Unit head:* Dr. Scott Shearer, Chair, 614-292-7284, E-mail: shearer.95@osu.edu. *Application contact:* Graduate and Professional Admissions, 614-292-9444, Fax: 614-292-3895, E-mail: gpadmissions@osu.edu.
Website: http://fabe.osu.edu/

Oklahoma State University, College of Agricultural Science and Natural Resources, Department of Biosystems and Agricultural Engineering, Stillwater, OK 74078. Offers biosystems engineering (MS, PhD); environmental and natural resources (MS, PhD). *Faculty:* 22 full-time (5 women), 2 part-time/adjunct (0 women). *Students:* 8 full-time (0 women), 17 part-time (8 women); includes 5 minority (1 Black or African American, non-Hispanic/Latino; 1 Asian, non-Hispanic/Latino; 2 Hispanic/Latino; 1 Two or more races, non-Hispanic/Latino), 15 international. Average age 30. 19 applicants, 32% accepted, 3 enrolled. In 2018, 4 master's, 7 doctorates awarded. *Entrance requirements:* For master's and doctorate, GRE or GMAT. Additional exam requirements/recommendations for international students: Required—TOEFL (minimum score 550 paper-based; 79 iBT). *Application deadline:* For fall admission, 3/1 priority date for international students; for spring admission, 8/1 priority date for international students. Applications are processed on a rolling basis. Application fee: $40 ($75 for international students). Electronic applications accepted. *Expenses: Tuition, area resident:* Full-time $4148. Tuition, state resident: full-time $4148. Tuition, nonresident: full-time $10,517. *International tuition:* $10,517 full-time. *Required fees:* $4394; $2929 per credit hour. Tuition and fees vary according to course load and program. *Financial support:* Research assistantships, teaching assistantships, career-related internships or fieldwork, Federal Work-Study, scholarships/grants, health care benefits, tuition waivers (partial), and unspecified assistantships available. Support available to part-time students. Financial award application deadline: 3/1; financial award applicants required to submit FAFSA. *Unit head:* Dr. John Veenstra, Department Head, 405-744-5431, Fax: 405-744-6059, E-mail: jveenst@okstate.edu. *Application contact:* Dr. Ning Wang, Professor/Graduate Coordinator, 405-744-2877, E-mail: ning.wang@okstate.edu.
Website: http://bae.okstate.edu/

Oregon State University, College of Engineering, Program in Bioengineering, Corvallis, OR 97331. Offers biomaterials (M Eng, MS, PhD); biomedical devices and instrumentation (M Eng, MS, PhD); human performance engineering (M Eng, MS, PhD); medical imaging (M Eng, MS, PhD); systems and computational biology (M Eng, MS, PhD). Electronic applications accepted. *Expenses:* Contact institution. *Faculty research:* Biomaterials, biomedical devices and instrumentation, human performance engineering, medical imaging, systems and computational biology.

Oregon State University, College of Engineering, Program in Biological and Ecological Engineering, Corvallis, OR 97331. Offers bio-based products and fuels (M Eng, MS, PhD); biological systems analysis (M Eng, MS, PhD); bioprocessing (M Eng, MS, PhD); ecosystems analysis and modeling (M Eng, MS, PhD); water quality (M Eng, MS, PhD); water resources (M Eng, MS, PhD). Terminal master's awarded for partial completion of doctoral program. *Entrance requirements:* For master's and doctorate, GRE, minimum GPA of 3.0 in last 90 hours. Additional exam requirements/recommendations for international students: Required—TOEFL (minimum score 80 iBT), IELTS (minimum score 6.5). *Expenses:* Contact institution. *Faculty research:* Bioengineering, water resources engineering, food engineering, cell culture and fermentation, vadose zone transport.

Penn State University Park, Graduate School, College of Agricultural Sciences, Department of Agricultural and Biological Engineering, University Park, PA 16802. Offers agricultural and biological engineering (MS, PhD); biorenewable systems (MS, PhD).

Penn State University Park, Graduate School, Intercollege Graduate Programs, Intercollege Graduate Program in Bioengineering, University Park, PA 16802. Offers MS, PhD.

Princeton University, Graduate School, School of Engineering and Applied Science, Department of Chemical and Biological Engineering, Princeton, NJ 08544-1019. Offers M Eng, MSE, PhD. Terminal master's awarded for partial completion of doctoral program. *Degree requirements:* For master's, thesis (MSE); for doctorate, thesis/dissertation, general exam. *Entrance requirements:* For master's, GRE General Test, 3 letters of recommendation; for doctorate, GRE General Test, official transcript(s), 3 letters of recommendation, personal statement. Additional exam requirements/recommendations for international students: Required—TOEFL. Electronic applications accepted. *Faculty research:* Applied and computational mathematics, bioengineering, environmental and energy science and technology, fluid mechanics and transport phenomena, materials science.

Rice University, Graduate Programs, George R. Brown School of Engineering, Department of Bioengineering, Houston, TX 77251-1892. Offers MBE, MS, PhD, MD/PhD. Terminal master's awarded for partial completion of doctoral program. *Degree requirements:* For master's, thesis; for doctorate, thesis/dissertation, qualifying exam, internship. *Entrance requirements:* For master's and doctorate, GRE General Test. Additional exam requirements/recommendations for international students: Required—TOEFL (minimum score 600 paper-based; 90 iBT). Electronic applications accepted. *Faculty research:* Biomaterials, tissue engineering, laser-tissue interactions, biochemical engineering, gene therapy.

Rice University, Graduate Programs, George R. Brown School of Engineering, Department of Electrical and Computer Engineering, Houston, TX 77251-1892. Offers bioengineering (MS, PhD); circuits, controls, and communication systems (MS, PhD); computer science and engineering (MS, PhD); electrical engineering (MEE); lasers, microwaves, and solid-state electronics (MS, PhD); MBA/MEE. *Program availability:* Part-time. *Degree requirements:* For master's, thesis (for some programs); for doctorate, thesis/dissertation. *Entrance requirements:* For master's and doctorate, GRE General Test, GRE Subject Test, minimum GPA of 3.0. Additional exam requirements/recommendations for international students: Required—TOEFL (minimum score 600 paper-based; 90 iBT). Electronic applications accepted. *Faculty research:* Physical electronics, systems, computer engineering, bioengineering.

Santa Clara University, School of Engineering, Santa Clara, CA 95053. Offers applied mathematics (MS); bioengineering (MS); civil, environmental, and sustainable engineering (MS); computer science and engineering (MS, PhD, Engineer); electrical engineering (MS, PhD, Engineer); engineering management and leadership (MS); mechanical engineering (MS, PhD, Engineer); power systems and sustainable energy (MS); software engineering (MS). *Program availability:* Part-time. *Faculty:* 72 full-time (24 women), 52 part-time/adjunct (9 women). *Students:* 555 full-time (211 women), 269 part-time (91 women); includes 208 minority (8 Black or African American, non-Hispanic/Latino; 1 American Indian or Alaska Native, non-Hispanic/Latino; 145 Asian, non-Hispanic/Latino; 28 Hispanic/Latino; 26 Two or more races, non-Hispanic/Latino), 472 international. Average age 27. 1,309 applicants, 36% accepted, 269 enrolled. In 2018, 320 master's, 7 doctorates awarded. *Entrance requirements:* For master's, GRE, official transcript; for doctorate, GRE, Official transcript, 500 word statement of purpose, three letters of recommendation. Additional exam requirements/recommendations for international students: Required—TOEFL (minimum score 79 iBT), IELTS (minimum score 6.5). *Application deadline:* For fall admission, 6/1 for domestic students; for winter admission, 9/6 for domestic students; for spring admission, 1/10 for domestic students; for summer admission, 3/6 for domestic students. Application fee: $60. Electronic applications accepted. *Financial support:* Fellowships, Federal Work-Study, and scholarships/grants available. Support available to part-time students. Financial award applicants required to submit FAFSA. *Unit head:* Dr. Elaine Scott, Dean, 408-554-3512, E-mail: epscott@scu.edu. *Application contact:* Stacey Tinker, Director of Admissions and Marketing, 408-554-4748, Fax: 408-554-4323, E-mail: stinker@scu.edu.
Website: http://www.scu.edu/engineering/graduate/

South Dakota School of Mines and Technology, Graduate Division, Program in Chemical and Biological Engineering, Rapid City, SD 57701-3995. Offers PhD. *Program availability:* Part-time. *Degree requirements:* For doctorate, thesis/dissertation. *Entrance requirements:* Additional exam requirements/recommendations for international students: Required—TOEFL (minimum score 520 paper-based; 68 iBT). Electronic applications accepted.

Stanford University, School of Medicine, Department of Bioengineering, Stanford, CA 94305-2004. Offers MS, PhD. *Expenses: Tuition:* Full-time $50,703; part-time $32,970 per year. *Required fees:* $651.
Website: http://bioengineering.stanford.edu/

Syracuse University, College of Engineering and Computer Science, Programs in Bioengineering, Syracuse, NY 13244. Offers MS, PhD. *Program availability:* Part-time. *Degree requirements:* For master's, thesis (for some programs); for doctorate, comprehensive exam, thesis/dissertation. *Entrance requirements:* For master's and doctorate, GRE General Test, three letters of recommendation, resume, personal statement, official transcripts. Additional exam requirements/recommendations for international students: Required—TOEFL (minimum score 100 iBT). *Application deadline:* For fall admission, 7/1 priority date for domestic students, 6/1 priority date for international students; for spring admission, 10/15 for domestic students, 11/15 priority date for international students. Applications are processed on a rolling basis. Application fee: $75. Electronic applications accepted. *Financial support:* Fellowships with full tuition reimbursements, research assistantships, teaching assistantships, and tuition waivers (partial) available. Financial award application deadline: 1/1; financial award applicants required to submit FAFSA. *Faculty research:* Biomaterials/tissue engineering, complex fluids, soft condensed matter, rheology. *Unit head:* Dr. James Henderson, Associate Professor/Bioengineering Graduate Program Director, 315-443-9739, E-mail: jhhender@syr.edu. *Application contact:* Kathleen Joyce, Assistant Dean, 315-443-2219, E-mail: topgrads@syr.edu.
Website: http://eng-cs.syr.edu/our-departments/biomedical-and-chemical-engineering/

Temple University, College of Engineering, Department of Bioengineering, Philadelphia, PA 19122-6096. Offers MS, PhD. *Program availability:* Part-time, evening/weekend. Terminal master's awarded for partial completion of doctoral program. *Degree requirements:* For master's, thesis optional; for doctorate, comprehensive exam, thesis/dissertation, preliminary exam, dissertation proposal and defense. *Entrance requirements:* For master's, GRE General Test, minimum undergraduate GPA of 3.0; BS in engineering from ABET-accredited or equivalent institution; resume; goals statement; three letters of reference; official transcripts; for doctorate, GRE General Test, minimum undergraduate GPA of 3.0; MS in engineering from ABET-accredited or equivalent institution (preferred); resume; goals statement; three letters of reference; official transcripts. Additional exam requirements/recommendations for international students: Required—TOEFL (minimum score 550 paper-based; 79 iBT), IELTS (minimum score 6.5), PTE (minimum score 53). Electronic applications accepted. *Expenses:* Contact institution. *Faculty research:* Soft tissue mechanics, injury biomechanics, targeted drug delivery, brain-computer interface, regenerative medicine, smart nanotechnology-based biomaterials, tissue spectroscopy.

Temple University, College of Engineering, PhD in Engineering Program, Philadelphia, PA 19122-6096. Offers bioengineering (PhD); civil engineering (PhD); electrical engineering (PhD); environmental engineering (PhD); mechanical engineering (PhD). *Program availability:* Part-time, evening/weekend. *Degree requirements:* For doctorate, thesis/dissertation, preliminary exam, dissertation proposal and defense. *Entrance requirements:* For doctorate, GRE, minimum undergraduate GPA of 3.0; MS in engineering from ABET-accredited or equivalent institution (preferred); resume; goals statement; three letters of reference; official transcripts. Additional exam requirements/recommendations for international students: Required—TOEFL (minimum score 550 paper-based; 79 iBT), IELTS (minimum score 6.5), PTE (minimum score 53). Electronic applications accepted. *Expenses:* Contact institution. *Faculty research:* Advanced/computer-aided manufacturing and advanced materials processing; bioengineering; computer engineering; construction engineering and management; dynamics, controls, and systems; energy and environmental science; engineering physics and engineering mathematics; green engineering; signal processing and communication; transportation engineering; water resources, hydrology, and environmental engineering.

See Display on page 59 and Close-Up on page 73.

Texas A&M University, College of Agriculture and Life Sciences, Department of Biological and Agricultural Engineering, College Station, TX 77843. Offers agricultural systems management (M Agr, MS); biological and agricultural engineering (MS, PhD). *Program availability:* Part-time. *Faculty:* 19. *Students:* 59 full-time (20 women), 18 part-time (5 women); includes 12 minority (4 Black or African American, non-Hispanic/Latino; 1 Asian, non-Hispanic/Latino; 5 Hispanic/Latino; 2 Two or more races, non-Hispanic/Latino), 50 international. Average age 31. 16 applicants, 100% accepted, 11 enrolled. In 2018, 26 master's, 5 doctorates awarded. *Degree requirements:* For master's, thesis (MS), preliminary and final exams; for doctorate, thesis/dissertation, preliminary and final exams. *Entrance requirements:* For master's and doctorate, GRE General Test. Additional exam requirements/recommendations for international students: Required—TOEFL (minimum score 550 paper-based; 80 iBT), IELTS (minimum score 6), PTE (minimum score 53). *Application deadline:* For fall admission, 12/15 priority date for domestic students. Applications are processed on a rolling basis. Application fee: $50 ($90 for international students). Electronic applications accepted. *Expenses:* Contact institution. *Financial support:* In 2018–19, 61 students received support, including 8 fellowships with tuition reimbursements available (averaging $8,618 per year), 39 research assistantships with tuition reimbursements available (averaging $13,984 per year), 20 teaching assistantships with tuition reimbursements available (averaging $10,945 per year); career-related internships or fieldwork, institutionally sponsored loans, scholarships/grants, traineeships, health care benefits, tuition waivers (full and partial), and unspecified assistantships also available. Support available to part-time students. Financial award application deadline: 3/15; financial award applicants required to submit FAFSA. *Faculty research:* Water quality and quantity; air quality; biological, food, ecological engineering; off-road equipment; mechatronics. *Unit head:* Dr. Steve Searcy, Professor and Head, 979-845-3940, Fax: 979-862-3442, E-mail: s-searcy@tamu.edu. *Application contact:* Dr. Sandun Fernando, Director of Graduate Programs, 979-845-9793, E-mail: sfernando@tamu.edu.
Website: http://baen.tamu.edu

Tufts University, Graduate School of Arts and Sciences, Graduate Certificate Programs, Program in Bioengineering, Medford, MA 02155. Offers Certificate. *Program availability:* Part-time, evening/weekend. Electronic applications accepted. *Expenses: Tuition:* Full-time $51,288; part-time $1710 per credit hour. *Required fees:* $904. Full-time tuition and fees vary according to degree level, program and student level. Part-time tuition and fees vary according to course load.

Tufts University, School of Engineering, Department of Biomedical Engineering, Medford, MA 02155. Offers bioengineering (MS), including biomaterials; biomedical engineering (MS, PhD); PhD/PhD. *Program availability:* Part-time. Terminal master's awarded for partial completion of doctoral program. *Degree requirements:* For master's, thesis (for some programs); for doctorate, thesis/dissertation. *Entrance requirements:* For master's and doctorate, GRE General Test. Additional exam requirements/recommendations for international students: Required—TOEFL (minimum score 550 paper-based; 80 iBT), IELTS (minimum score 6.5). Electronic applications accepted. *Expenses: Tuition:* Full-time $51,288; part-time $1710 per credit hour. *Required fees:* $904. Full-time tuition and fees vary according to degree level, program and student level. Part-time tuition and fees vary according to course load. *Faculty research:* Regenerative medicine with biomaterials and tissue engineering, diffuse optical imaging and spectroscopy, optics in the development of biomedical devices, ultrafast nonlinear optics and biophotonics, optical diagnostics for diseased and engineered tissues.

Tufts University, School of Engineering, Department of Chemical and Biological Engineering, Medford, MA 02155. Offers bioengineering (MS), including cell and bioprocess engineering; biotechnology (PhD); chemical engineering (MS, PhD); PhD/PhD. *Program availability:* Part-time. Terminal master's awarded for partial completion of doctoral program. *Degree requirements:* For master's, thesis (for some programs); for doctorate, thesis/dissertation. *Entrance requirements:* For master's and doctorate, GRE General Test. Additional exam requirements/recommendations for international students: Required—TOEFL (minimum score 550 paper-based; 80 iBT), IELTS (minimum score 6.5). Electronic applications accepted. *Expenses: Tuition:* Full-time $51,288; part-time $1710 per credit hour. *Required fees:* $904. Full-time tuition and fees vary according to degree level, program and student level. Part-time tuition and fees vary according to course load. *Faculty research:* Clean energy with materials, biomaterials, colloids; metabolic engineering, biotechnology; process control; reaction kinetics, catalysis; transport phenomena.

Tufts University, School of Engineering, Department of Civil and Environmental Engineering, Medford, MA 02155. Offers bioengineering (MS), including environmental biotechnology; civil and environmental engineering (MS, PhD), including applied data science, environmental and water resources engineering, environmental health, geosystems engineering, structural engineering and mechanics; PhD/PhD. *Program availability:* Part-time. Terminal master's awarded for partial completion of doctoral program. *Degree requirements:* For master's, thesis (for some programs); for doctorate, thesis/dissertation. *Entrance requirements:* For master's and doctorate, GRE General Test. Additional exam requirements/recommendations for international students: Required—TOEFL (minimum score 550 paper-based; 80 iBT), IELTS (minimum score 6.5). Electronic applications accepted. *Expenses: Tuition:* Full-time $51,288; part-time $1710 per credit hour. *Required fees:* $904. Full-time tuition and fees vary according to degree level, program and student level. Part-time tuition and fees vary according to course load. *Faculty research:* Environmental and water resources engineering, environmental health, geotechnical and geoenvironmental engineering, structural engineering and mechanics, water diplomacy.

Tufts University, School of Engineering, Department of Computer Science, Medford, MA 02155. Offers bioengineering (MS), including bioinformatics; cognitive science/computer science (PhD); computer science (MS, PhD); soft material robotics (PhD). *Program availability:* Part-time. Terminal master's awarded for partial completion of doctoral program. *Entrance requirements:* For master's and doctorate, GRE General Test. Additional exam requirements/recommendations for international students: Required—TOEFL (minimum score 550 paper-based; 80 iBT), IELTS (minimum score 6.5). Electronic applications accepted. *Expenses: Tuition:* Full-time $51,288; part-time $1710 per credit hour. *Required fees:* $904. Full-time tuition and fees vary according to degree level, program and student level. Part-time tuition and fees vary according to course load. *Faculty research:* Computational biology, computational geometry, and computational systems biology; cognitive sciences, human-computer interaction, and human-robotic interaction; visualization and graphics, educational technologies; machine learning and data mining; programming languages and systems.

Tufts University, School of Engineering, Department of Electrical and Computer Engineering, Medford, MA 02155. Offers bioengineering (MS), including signals and systems; electrical engineering (MS, PhD); PhD/PhD. *Program availability:* Part-time. Terminal master's awarded for partial completion of doctoral program. *Degree requirements:* For master's, thesis or alternative; for doctorate, thesis/dissertation. *Entrance requirements:* For master's and doctorate, GRE General Test. Additional exam requirements/recommendations for international students: Required—TOEFL (minimum score 550 paper-based; 80 iBT), IELTS (minimum score 6.5). Electronic applications accepted. *Expenses: Tuition:* Full-time $51,288; part-time $1710 per credit hour. *Required fees:* $904. Full-time tuition and fees vary according to degree level, program and student level. Part-time tuition and fees vary according to course load. *Faculty research:* Communication theory, networks, protocol, and transmission technology; simulation and modeling; digital processing technology; image and signal processing for security and medical applications; integrated circuits and VLSI.

University at Buffalo, the State University of New York, Graduate School, School of Engineering and Applied Sciences, Department of Chemical and Biological Engineering, Buffalo, NY 14260. Offers bioengineering nanotechnology (Certificate); chemical and biological engineering (ME, MS, PhD); nanomaterials and materials informatics (Certificate). *Program availability:* Part-time. *Degree requirements:* For master's, thesis (for some programs); for doctorate, comprehensive exam, thesis/dissertation. *Entrance requirements:* For master's and doctorate, GRE General Test. Additional exam requirements/recommendations for international students: Required—TOEFL (minimum score 550 paper-based; 79 iBT). Electronic applications accepted. *Faculty research:* Biochemical and biomedical engineering, nanoscale science and engineering, computational science and engineering.

University of Arkansas, Graduate School, College of Engineering, Department of Biological and Agricultural Engineering, Program in Biological Engineering, Fayetteville, AR 72701. Offers MSBE. *Application deadline:* For fall admission, 8/1 for domestic students, 4/1 for international students; for spring admission, 12/1 for domestic students, 10/1 for international students; for summer admission, 4/15 for domestic students, 3/1 for international students. Applications are processed on a rolling basis. Application fee: $60. Electronic applications accepted. *Financial support:* In 2018–19, 17 research assistantships, 1 teaching assistantship were awarded; fellowships also available. *Unit head:* Dr. Lalit R. Verma, Department Head, 479-575-6800, E-mail: lverma@uark.edu. *Application contact:* Dr. Jin-Woo Kim, Program Coordinator, 479-575-3402, E-mail: jwkim@uark.edu.
Website: https://bio-ag-engineering.uark.edu

The University of British Columbia, Faculty of Applied Science, Department of Chemical and Biological Engineering, Vancouver, BC V6T 1Z3, Canada. Offers M Eng, M Sc, MA Sc, PhD. *Program availability:* Part-time, evening/weekend. *Degree requirements:* For master's, thesis (for some programs); for doctorate, thesis/dissertation. *Entrance requirements:* Additional exam requirements/recommendations for international students: Required—TOEFL, IELTS. Electronic applications accepted. *Expenses:* Contact institution. *Faculty research:* Biotechnology, catalysis, polymers, fluidization, pulp and paper.

University of California, Berkeley, Graduate Division, Bioengineering Graduate Program Berkeley/UCSF, Berkeley, CA 94720-1762. Offers PhD. Program offered jointly with University of California, San Francisco. *Degree requirements:* For doctorate, comprehensive exam, thesis/dissertation. *Entrance requirements:* For doctorate, GRE General Test, minimum GPA of 3.0. Additional exam requirements/recommendations for international students: Required—TOEFL (minimum score 570 paper-based; 68 iBT). Electronic applications accepted. *Faculty research:* Biomaterials, biomechanics, biomedical imaging and instrumentation, computational biology, drug delivery systems and pharmacogenomics, neural systems engineering and vision science, systems and synthetic biology, tissue engineering and regenerative medicine.

University of California, Berkeley, Graduate Division, College of Engineering, Department of Bioengineering, Berkeley, CA 94720. Offers M Eng, MTM. *Degree requirements:* For master's, comprehensive exam. *Entrance requirements:* Additional exam requirements/recommendations for international students: Required—TOEFL (minimum score 570 paper-based; 90 iBT). Electronic applications accepted.

University of California, Davis, College of Engineering, Program in Biological Systems Engineering, Davis, CA 95616. Offers M Engr, MS, D Engr, PhD, M Engr/MBA. Terminal master's awarded for partial completion of doctoral program. *Degree requirements:* For master's, thesis; for doctorate, thesis/dissertation. *Entrance requirements:* For master's, minimum GPA of 3.0; for doctorate, GRE, minimum graduate GPA of 3.25. Additional exam requirements/recommendations for international students: Required—TOEFL (minimum score 550 paper-based). Electronic applications accepted. *Faculty research:* Forestry, irrigation and drainage, power and machinery, structures and environment, information and energy technologies.

University of California, Los Angeles, Graduate Division, Henry Samueli School of Engineering and Applied Science, Department of Bioengineering, Los Angeles, CA 90095-1600. Offers MS, PhD. *Degree requirements:* For master's, comprehensive exam or thesis; for doctorate, thesis/dissertation, qualifying exams. *Entrance requirements:* For master's, GRE General Test, minimum GPA of 3.0; for doctorate, GRE General Test, minimum GPA of 3.25. Additional exam requirements/recommendations for international students: Required—TOEFL (minimum score 560 paper-based; 87 iBT), IELTS (minimum score 7). Electronic applications accepted. *Faculty research:* Biomedical instrumentation; biomedical signal and image processing; biosystems science and engineering; medical imaging informatics; molecular cellular tissue therapeutics; neuroengineering.

University of California, Merced, Graduate Division, School of Engineering, Merced, CA 95343. Offers biological engineering and small scale technologies (MS, PhD); electrical engineering and computer science (MS, PhD); environmental systems (MS, PhD); management of innovation, sustainability, and technology (MM); mechanical engineering (MS); mechanical engineering and applied mechanics (PhD). *Faculty:* 60 full-time (16 women). *Students:* 219 full-time (72 women), 1 part-time (0 women); includes 43 minority (2 Black or African American, non-Hispanic/Latino; 17 Asian, non-Hispanic/Latino; 20 Hispanic/Latino; 1 Native Hawaiian or other Pacific Islander, non-Hispanic/Latino; 3 Two or more races, non-Hispanic/Latino), 145 international. Average age 28. 371 applicants, 46% accepted, 75 enrolled. In 2018, 30 master's, 17 doctorates awarded. Terminal master's awarded for partial completion of doctoral program. *Degree requirements:* For master's, variable foreign language requirement, comprehensive exam, thesis or alternative, oral defense; for doctorate, variable foreign language requirement, comprehensive exam, thesis/dissertation, oral defense. *Entrance requirements:* For master's and doctorate, GRE. Additional exam requirements/recommendations for international students: Required—TOEFL (minimum score 550 paper-based; 80 iBT); Recommended—IELTS (minimum score 6.5). *Application deadline:* For fall admission, 1/15 priority date for domestic and international students. Application fee: $105 ($125 for international students). Electronic applications accepted. *Expenses:* In-state tuition $11442 per year; Out-of-state tuition $26544 per year; Student Fees $1765 per year. *Financial support:* In 2018–19, 200 students received support, including 14 fellowships with full tuition reimbursements available (averaging $20,851 per year), 70 research assistantships with full tuition reimbursements available (averaging $18,334 per year), 116 teaching assistantships with full tuition reimbursements available (averaging $19,841 per year); scholarships/grants, traineeships, and health care benefits also available. *Faculty research:* Sustainability systems engineering and resource management: food, energy, water; biomolecular engineering and biotechnology; computational science and data analytics; artificial intelligence, machine learning, internet of things, human computer interface; cyber-physical systems and automation. *Total annual research expenditures:* $3.1 million. *Unit head:* Dr. Mark Matsumoto, Dean, 209-228-4047, Fax: 209-228-4047, E-mail: mmatsumoto@ucmerced.edu. *Application contact:* Tsu Ya, Director of Admissions and Academic Services, 209-228-4521, Fax: 209-228-6906, E-mail: tya@ucmerced.edu.

University of California, Riverside, Graduate Division, Department of Bioengineering, Riverside, CA 92521. Offers MS, PhD. *Degree requirements:* For doctorate, thesis/dissertation, qualifying exams. *Entrance requirements:* Additional exam requirements/recommendations for international students: Required—TOEFL (minimum score 550 paper-based; 80 iBT).

University of California, San Diego, Graduate Division, Department of Bioengineering, La Jolla, CA 92093. Offers M Eng, MS, PhD. PhD offered jointly with San Diego State University. *Students:* 214 full-time (76 women), 7 part-time (2 women). 688 applicants, 34% accepted, 76 enrolled. In 2018, 38 master's, 22 doctorates awarded. *Degree requirements:* For doctorate, comprehensive exam, thesis/dissertation, 2 quarters teaching 20 hours a week or 4 quarters teaching 10 hours a week. *Entrance requirements:* For master's, GRE General Test, minimum GPA of 3.0 (for M Eng), 3.4 (for MS); for doctorate, GRE General Test, minimum GPA of 3.4. Additional exam requirements/recommendations for international students: Required—TOEFL (minimum score 550 paper-based; 80 iBT), IELTS (minimum score 7). *Application deadline:* For fall admission, 12/12 for domestic students. Application fee: $105 ($125 for international students). Electronic applications accepted. *Financial support:* Fellowships, research assistantships, teaching assistantships, scholarships/grants, traineeships, and unspecified assistantships available. Financial award applicants required to submit FAFSA. *Faculty research:* Bioinformatics and systems biology, multi-scale biology, quantitative biology, biomaterials, biosensors, neural engineering, integrative genomics, biophotonics. *Unit head:* Kun Zhang, Chair, 858-822-3441, E-mail: chair@bioeng.ucsd.edu. *Application contact:* Jan Lenington, Graduate Coordinator, 858-822-1604, E-mail: jlenington@ucsd.edu.
Website: http://www.be.ucsd.edu/prospective-graduate-students

Bioengineering

University of California, San Francisco, Graduate Division, Program in Bioengineering, Berkeley, CA 94720-1762. Offers PhD. Program offered jointly with University of California, Berkeley. *Degree requirements:* For doctorate, thesis/dissertation, qualifying exam. *Entrance requirements:* For doctorate, GRE General Test, minimum GPA of 3.0. Additional exam requirements/recommendations for international students: Required—TOEFL (minimum score 570 paper-based). Electronic applications accepted. *Faculty research:* Bioengineering, biomaterials, biomedical imaging and instrumentation, biomechanics, microfluidics, computational biology, systems biology, drug delivery systems and pharmacogenomics, neural systems engineering and vision science, synthetic biology, tissue engineering, regenerative medicine.

University of California, Santa Barbara, Graduate Division, College of Engineering, Department of Mechanical Engineering, Santa Barbara, CA 93106-5070. Offers bioengineering (PhD); mechanical engineering (MS); MS/PhD. Terminal master's awarded for partial completion of doctoral program. *Degree requirements:* For master's, thesis optional; for doctorate, comprehensive exam, thesis/dissertation. *Entrance requirements:* For master's and doctorate, GRE. Additional exam requirements/recommendations for international students: Required—TOEFL (minimum score 550 paper-based; 80 iBT), IELTS (minimum score 7). Electronic applications accepted. *Faculty research:* Micro/nanoscale technology; bioengineering and systems biology; computational science and engineering; dynamics systems, controls and robotics; thermofluid sciences; solid mechanics, materials, and structures.

University of California, Santa Barbara, Graduate Division, College of Letters and Sciences, Division of Mathematics, Life, and Physical Sciences, Department of Statistics and Applied Probability, Santa Barbara, CA 93106-3110. Offers bioengineering (PhD); financial mathematics and statistics (PhD); quantitative methods in the social sciences (PhD); statistics (MA), including applied statistics, mathematical statistics; statistics and applied probability (PhD); MA/PhD. Terminal master's awarded for partial completion of doctoral program. *Degree requirements:* For master's, comprehensive exam, thesis optional; for doctorate, comprehensive exam, thesis/dissertation. *Entrance requirements:* For master's and doctorate, GRE General Test. Additional exam requirements/recommendations for international students: Required—TOEFL (minimum score 550 paper-based; 80 iBT), IELTS (minimum score 7). Electronic applications accepted. *Faculty research:* Bayesian inference, financial mathematics, stochastic processes, environmental statistics, biostatistical modeling.

University of California, Santa Barbara, Graduate Division, College of Letters and Sciences, Division of Mathematics, Life, and Physical Sciences, Interdepartmental Graduate Program in Biomolecular Science and Engineering, Santa Barbara, CA 93106-2014. Offers biochemistry and molecular biology (PhD), including biochemistry and molecular biology, biophysics and bioengineering. Terminal master's awarded for partial completion of doctoral program. *Degree requirements:* For doctorate, thesis/dissertation. *Entrance requirements:* For doctorate, GRE General Test. Additional exam requirements/recommendations for international students: Required—TOEFL (minimum score 630 paper-based; 109 iBT), IELTS (minimum score 7). Electronic applications accepted. *Faculty research:* Biochemistry and molecular biology, biophysics, biomaterials, bioengineering, systems biology.

University of Chicago, Institute for Molecular Engineering, Chicago, IL 60637. Offers PhD. *Degree requirements:* For doctorate, thesis/dissertation, qualifying research presentation, teaching requirement. *Entrance requirements:* For doctorate, GRE General Test, transcripts, statement of purpose, 3 letters of recommendation. Additional exam requirements/recommendations for international students: Required—TOEFL (minimum score 90 iBT), IELTS (minimum score 7). Electronic applications accepted. *Faculty research:* Bimolecular engineering, spintronics, nanotechnology, quantum computing, protein folding and aggregation, liquid crystals, theoretical and computational modeling of materials, immunology, nanolithography, directed self-assembly, cancer research.

University of Colorado Denver, College of Engineering, Design and Computing, Department of Bioengineering, Aurora, CO 80045-2560. Offers basic research (MS, PhD); biomedical device design (MS); entrepreneurship (PhD); entrepreneurship and regulatory affairs (MS); translational bioengineering (PhD). *Program availability:* Part-time. Terminal master's awarded for partial completion of doctoral program. *Degree requirements:* For master's, thesis or alternative, 30 credit hours; for doctorate, comprehensive exam, 36 credit hours of classwork (18 core, 18 elective), additional 30 hours of thesis work, three formal examinations, approval of dissertations. *Entrance requirements:* For master's and doctorate, GRE, transcripts, three letters of recommendation, resume, statement of purpose. Additional exam requirements/recommendations for international students: Required—TOEFL (minimum score 550 paper-based; 79 iBT), TOEFL (minimum score 600 paper-based; 100 iBT) for PhD. Electronic applications accepted. *Expenses:* Tuition, state resident: full-time $6786; part-time $337 per credit hour. Tuition, nonresident: full-time $22,590; part-time $1255 per credit hour. *Required fees:* $1231; $137 per credit hour. Tuition and fees vary according to program and reciprocity agreements.

University of Dayton, Department of Chemical Engineering, Dayton, OH 45469. Offers bioengineering (MS); chemical engineering (MS Ch E). *Program availability:* Part-time, online learning. *Degree requirements:* For master's, thesis for 33 credit hours. *Entrance requirements:* For master's, GRE (preferred), minimum GPA of 3.0 as undergraduate, transcript, 3 letters of recommendation, bachelor's degree in chemical engineering (preferred). Additional exam requirements/recommendations for international students: Required—TOEFL (minimum score 550 paper-based; 80 iBT); Recommended—IELTS. Electronic applications accepted. *Expenses:* Contact institution. *Faculty research:* Process control modeling/mixing; multiphase flow data analysis; chemical reaction biocatalysts enhanced in vitro models.

University of Denver, Daniel Felix Ritchie School of Engineering and Computer Science, Department of Mechanical and Materials Engineering, Denver, CO 80208. Offers bioengineering (MS); engineering (MS, PhD), including management; materials science (MS, PhD); mechanical engineering (MS, PhD). *Program availability:* Part-time. *Faculty:* 13 full-time (2 women), 2 part-time/adjunct (1 woman). *Students:* 4 full-time (1 woman), 33 part-time (7 women); includes 5 minority (2 Black or African American, non-Hispanic/Latino; 2 Hispanic/Latino; 1 Two or more races, non-Hispanic/Latino), 11 international. Average age 28. 71 applicants, 63% accepted, 15 enrolled. In 2018, 11 master's, 3 doctorates awarded. Terminal master's awarded for partial completion of doctoral program. *Degree requirements:* For master's, thesis optional; for doctorate, comprehensive exam, thesis/dissertation. *Entrance requirements:* For master's, GRE General Test, bachelor's degree in engineering or closely related field, transcripts, personal statement, resume or curriculum vitae, two letters of recommendation; for doctorate, GRE General Test, master's degree in engineering or closely related field, transcripts, personal statement, resume or curriculum vitae, two letters of recommendation, recommended that applicants find a research advisor before submitting the application. Additional exam requirements/recommendations for international students: Required—TOEFL (minimum score 550 paper-based; 80 iBT). *Application deadline:* For fall admission, 1/15 priority date for domestic and international students; for winter admission, 10/25 for domestic and international students; for spring admission, 2/7 for domestic and international students; for summer admission, 4/24 for domestic and international students. Applications are processed on a rolling basis. Application fee: $65. Electronic applications accepted. *Expenses:* $33,183 per year full-time. *Financial support:* In 2018–19, 25 students received support, including 10 research assistantships with tuition reimbursements available (averaging $12,917 per year), 13 teaching assistantships with tuition reimbursements available (averaging $15,289 per year); Federal Work-Study, institutionally sponsored loans, scholarships/grants, health care benefits, and unspecified assistantships also available. Financial award application deadline: 2/15; financial award applicants required to submit FAFSA. *Faculty research:* Cardiac biomechanics, novel high voltage/temperature materials and structures, high speed stereo radiography, musculoskeletal modeling, composites. *Unit head:* Dr. Matt Gordon, Professor and Chair, 303-871-3580, E-mail: matthew.gordon@du.edu. *Application contact:* Chrissy Alexander, Assistant to the Chair, 303-871-3041, E-mail: Christine.Alexander@du.edu.
Website: http://ritchieschool.du.edu/departments/mme/

University of Florida, Graduate School, Herbert Wertheim College of Engineering and College of Agricultural and Life Sciences, Department of Agricultural and Biological Engineering, Gainesville, FL 32611. Offers agricultural and biological engineering (ME, MS, PhD), including geographic information systems, hydrologic sciences, wetland sciences; biological systems modeling (Certificate). *Program availability:* Part-time. Terminal master's awarded for partial completion of doctoral program. *Degree requirements:* For master's, comprehensive exam, thesis (for some programs); for doctorate, comprehensive exam, thesis/dissertation. *Entrance requirements:* For master's and doctorate, minimum GPA of 3.0, 3 letters of recommendation, statement of purpose. Additional exam requirements/recommendations for international students: Required—TOEFL (minimum score 550 paper-based; 80 iBT), IELTS (minimum score 6). Electronic applications accepted. *Faculty research:* Bioenergy and bioprocessing; hydrological, biological and agricultural modeling; biosensors; precision agriculture and robotics; food packaging and food security.

University of Guelph, Office of Graduate and Postdoctoral Studies, College of Physical and Engineering Science, School of Engineering, Guelph, ON N1G 2W1, Canada. Offers biological engineering (M Eng, M Sc, MA Sc, PhD); engineering systems and computing (M Eng, M Sc, MA Sc, PhD); environmental engineering (M Eng, M Sc, MA Sc, PhD); water resources engineering (M Eng, M Sc, MA Sc, PhD). *Program availability:* Part-time. *Degree requirements:* For master's, thesis (for some programs); for doctorate, comprehensive exam, thesis/dissertation. *Entrance requirements:* For master's, minimum B- average during previous 2 years of course work; for doctorate, minimum B average. Additional exam requirements/recommendations for international students: Required—TOEFL (minimum score 550 paper-based; 89 iBT), IELTS (minimum score 6.5). Electronic applications accepted. *Faculty research:* Water and food safety, environmental contaminant fates and mechanisms, computer systems, robotics and mechatronics, waste treatment.

University of Hawaii at Manoa, Office of Graduate Education, College of Tropical Agriculture and Human Resources, Department of Molecular Biosciences and Bioengineering, Program in Bioengineering, Honolulu, HI 96822. Offers MS. *Program availability:* Part-time. *Degree requirements:* For master's, thesis optional. *Entrance requirements:* For master's, GRE General Test. Additional exam requirements/recommendations for international students: Required—TOEFL (minimum score 500 paper-based; 61 iBT), IELTS (minimum score 5).

University of Idaho, College of Graduate Studies, College of Engineering, Department of Biological Engineering, Moscow, ID 83844-0904. Offers M Engr, MS, PhD. *Faculty:* 7. *Students:* 14. Average age 28. In 2018, 1 master's, 2 doctorates awarded. *Entrance requirements:* For master's, minimum GPA of 3.0. Additional exam requirements/recommendations for international students: Required—TOEFL (minimum score 79 iBT), IELTS (minimum score 6.5), Michigan English Language Assessment Battery (minimum score of 77). *Application deadline:* For fall admission, 8/1 for domestic students; for spring admission, 12/15 for domestic students. Applications are processed on a rolling basis. Application fee: $60. Electronic applications accepted. *Expenses:* Tuition, state resident: full-time $7266.44; part-time $474.50 per credit hour. Tuition, nonresident: full-time $24,902; part-time $1453.50 per credit hour. *Required fees:* $2085.56; $45.50 per credit hour. *Financial support:* Research assistantships, teaching assistantships, and career-related internships or fieldwork available. Financial award applicants required to submit FAFSA. *Faculty research:* Biofuels, biotechnology, liquid plasma technology, nanotechnology, water management. *Unit head:* Dr. Ching-An Peng, Chair, 208-885-6182, E-mail: bioengr@uidaho.edu. *Application contact:* Dr. Ching-An Peng, Chair, 208-885-6182, E-mail: bioengr@uidaho.edu.
Website: http://www.uidaho.edu/engr/departments/be

University of Illinois at Chicago, College of Engineering, Department of Bioengineering, Chicago, IL 60607-7128. Offers MS, PhD. Terminal master's awarded for partial completion of doctoral program. *Degree requirements:* For master's, thesis; for doctorate, thesis/dissertation. *Entrance requirements:* For master's and doctorate, GRE Subject Test, minimum GPA of 3.0. Additional exam requirements/recommendations for international students: Required—TOEFL. Electronic applications accepted. *Expenses:* Contact institution. *Faculty research:* Imaging systems, bioinstrumentation, electrophysiology, biological control, laser scattering.

University of Illinois at Urbana–Champaign, Graduate College, College of Agricultural, Consumer and Environmental Sciences, Department of Agricultural and Biological Engineering, Champaign, IL 61820. Offers agricultural and biological engineering (MS, PhD); technical systems management (MS, PSM).

University of Illinois at Urbana–Champaign, Graduate College, College of Engineering, Department of Bioengineering, Champaign, IL 61820. Offers MS, PhD.

University of Illinois at Urbana–Champaign, Graduate College, College of Liberal Arts and Sciences, School of Chemical Sciences, Department of Chemical and Biomolecular Engineering, Champaign, IL 61820. Offers bioinformatics: chemical and biomolecular engineering (MS); chemical engineering (MS, PhD). *Entrance requirements:* For master's, minimum GPA of 3.0.

The University of Kansas, Graduate Studies, School of Engineering, Program in Bioengineering, Lawrence, KS 66045. Offers MS, PhD. *Program availability:* Part-time. *Students:* 46 full-time (19 women), 5 part-time (2 women); includes 8 minority (2 Black or African American, non-Hispanic/Latino; 1 American Indian or Alaska Native, non-Hispanic/Latino; 2 Hispanic/Latino; 3 Two or more races, non-Hispanic/Latino), 11 international. Average age 25. 52 applicants, 65% accepted, 13 enrolled. In 2018, 4 master's, 5 doctorates awarded. Terminal master's awarded for partial completion of doctoral program. *Entrance requirements:* For master's and doctorate, GRE, statement of academic objectives, curriculum vitae or resume, official transcripts, 3 letters of recommendation. Additional exam requirements/recommendations for international students: Required—TOEFL, IELTS. *Application deadline:* For fall admission, 12/15 for domestic and international students; for spring admission, 9/30 for domestic and international students; for summer admission, 3/15 for domestic and international students. Application fee: $65 ($85 for international students). Electronic applications accepted. *Financial support:* Fellowships, research assistantships, teaching assistantships, and scholarships/grants available. Financial award application deadline: 12/12. *Faculty research:* Biomaterials and tissue engineering, biomechanics and neural engineering, biomedical product design and development, biomolecular engineering,

bioimaging and bioinformatics. *Unit head:* Dr. Ken Fischer, Director, 785-864-2994, E-mail: fischer@ku.edu. *Application contact:* Denise Birdwell, Program Assistant, 785-864-5258, E-mail: dbridwell@ku.edu.
Website: http://bio.engr.ku.edu/

University of Louisville, J. B. Speed School of Engineering, Department of Bioengineering, Louisville, KY 40292-0001. Offers advancing bioengineering technologies through entrepreneurship (PhD); bioengineering (M Eng, PhD). *Accreditation:* ABET. *Students:* 19 full-time (12 women), 21 part-time (8 women); includes 7 minority (1 Black or African American, non-Hispanic/Latino; 3 Asian, non-Hispanic/Latino; 1 Hispanic/Latino; 2 Two or more races, non-Hispanic/Latino). Average age 25. 2 applicants, 100% accepted, 2 enrolled. In 2018, 6 master's awarded. *Degree requirements:* For master's, thesis; for doctorate, comprehensive exam, thesis/dissertation. *Entrance requirements:* For master's, GRE, 2 letters of recommendation; for doctorate, GRE, Three letters of recommendation, written statement describing previous experience related to bioengineering, a written statement as to how the PhD in Bioengineering will allow the applicant to fulfill their career goals. Additional exam requirements/recommendations for international students: Required—TOEFL (minimum score 550 paper-based; 80 iBT), IELTS (minimum score 6.5), GRE. *Application deadline:* For fall admission, 5/1 priority date for domestic and international students; for spring admission, 11/1 priority date for domestic and international students; for summer admission, 3/1 priority date for domestic and international students. Applications are processed on a rolling basis. Application fee: $65. Electronic applications accepted. *Expenses: Tuition, area resident:* Full-time $6500; part-time $723 per credit hour. Tuition, state resident: full-time $6500. Tuition, nonresident: full-time $13,557; part-time $1507 per credit hour. Tuition and fees vary according to course load and program. *Financial support:* In 2018–19, 18 students received support. Fellowships with full tuition reimbursements available, research assistantships with full tuition reimbursements available, teaching assistantships with full tuition reimbursements available, scholarships/grants, and health care benefits available. Financial award application deadline: 2/3. *Faculty research:* Bioimaging, Biomedical Devices, Drug, Gene & Protein Delivery, Bioinstrumentation & Controls Research & Development, Injury Risk Assessment and Prevention. *Total annual research expenditures:* $5.2 million. *Unit head:* Dr. Ayman El-Baz, Chair, 502-852-5092, E-mail: aymen.elbaz@louisville.edu. *Application contact:* Gina Bertocci, Director of Graduate Studies, 502-852-0296, E-mail: gina.bertocci@louisville.edu.
Website: https://louisville.edu/speed/bioengineering/

University of Maryland, College Park, Academic Affairs, A. James Clark School of Engineering, Department of Chemical and Biomolecular Engineering, College Park, MD 20742. Offers bioengineering (MS, PhD); chemical engineering (M Eng, MS, PhD). *Program availability:* Part-time, evening/weekend. *Degree requirements:* For master's, thesis optional; for doctorate, variable foreign language requirement, thesis/dissertation, exam, oral presentation. *Entrance requirements:* For master's and doctorate, GRE General Test, 3 letters of recommendation. Additional exam requirements/recommendations for international students: Required—TOEFL. Electronic applications accepted. *Faculty research:* Applied polymer science, biochemical engineering, thermal properties, bioprocess monitoring.

University of Maryland, College Park, Academic Affairs, A. James Clark School of Engineering, Fischell Department of Bioengineering, College Park, MD 20742. Offers MS, PhD. *Degree requirements:* For master's, thesis optional; for doctorate, thesis/dissertation. *Entrance requirements:* For master's, GRE General Test, minimum GPA of 3.0, 3 letters of recommendation. Electronic applications accepted. *Faculty research:* Bioengineering, bioenvironmental and water resources engineering, natural resources management.

University of Michigan–Dearborn, College of Engineering and Computer Science, MSE Program in Bioengineering, Dearborn, MI 48128. Offers MSE. *Program availability:* Part-time, evening/weekend. *Faculty:* 24 full-time (4 women), 12 part-time/adjunct (2 women). *Students:* 4 full-time (2 women), 2 part-time (1 woman). Average age 24. 14 applicants, 43% accepted, 2 enrolled. In 2018, 2 master's awarded. *Entrance requirements:* Additional exam requirements/recommendations for international students: Required—TOEFL (minimum score 560 paper-based; 84 iBT), IELTS (minimum score 6.5). *Application deadline:* For fall admission, 8/1 for domestic students, 5/1 for international students; for winter admission, 12/1 for domestic students, 9/1 for international students; for spring admission, 4/1 for domestic students, 1/1 for international students. Applications are processed on a rolling basis. Application fee: $60. Electronic applications accepted. *Expenses:* Tuition, state resident: full-time $15,380; part-time $88 per credit hour. Tuition, nonresident: full-time $23,948; part-time $1377 per credit hour. *Required fees:* $780; $780 $390. Tuition and fees vary according to course level, course load, degree level, program, reciprocity agreements and student level. *Financial support:* In 2018–19, 3 students received support. Research assistantships with full tuition reimbursements available, scholarships/grants, and non-resident tuition scholarships available. Financial award application deadline: 3/1; financial award applicants required to submit FAFSA. *Faculty research:* Biomaterials and tissue engineering, cell preservation and biomimetics, microfluidics, drug delivery, biomechanics. *Unit head:* Dr. Alan Argento, Program Director, 313-593-5241, E-mail: aargento@umich.edu. *Application contact:* Office of Graduate Studies Staff, 313-583-6321, E-mail: umd-graduatestudies@umich.edu.
Website: https://umdearborn.edu/cecs/departments/mechanical-engineering/graduate-programs/mse-bioengineering

University of Missouri, Office of Research and Graduate Studies, College of Engineering, Department of Biomedical, Biological and Chemical Engineering, Columbia, MO 65211. Offers biological engineering (MS, PhD); chemical engineering (MS, PhD). *Entrance requirements:* For master's and doctorate, GRE General Test, minimum GPA of 3.0. Additional exam requirements/recommendations for international students: Required—TOEFL.

University of Nebraska–Lincoln, Graduate College, College of Engineering, Department of Biological Systems Engineering, Interdepartmental Area of Agricultural and Biological Systems Engineering, Lincoln, NE 68588. Offers MS, PhD. *Degree requirements:* For master's, thesis optional. *Entrance requirements:* Additional exam requirements/recommendations for international students: Required—TOEFL (minimum score 550 paper-based). Electronic applications accepted. *Faculty research:* Hydrological engineering, tractive performance, biomedical engineering, irrigation systems.

University of Nebraska–Lincoln, Graduate College, College of Engineering, Department of Chemical and Biomolecular Engineering, Lincoln, NE 68588. Offers MS, PhD. *Degree requirements:* For master's, thesis; for doctorate, comprehensive exam, thesis/dissertation. *Entrance requirements:* For master's and doctorate, GRE. Additional exam requirements/recommendations for international students: Required—TOEFL (minimum score 550 paper-based). Electronic applications accepted. *Faculty research:* Fermentation, radioactive waste remediation, chemical fuels from renewable feedstocks.

University of Notre Dame, The Graduate School, College of Engineering, Department of Civil and Environmental Engineering and Earth Sciences, Notre Dame, IN 46556. Offers bioengineering (MS Bio E); civil engineering (MSCE); civil engineering and geological sciences (PhD); earth sciences (MS); environmental engineering (MS Env E). Terminal master's awarded for partial completion of doctoral program. *Degree requirements:* For master's, comprehensive exam; for doctorate, thesis/dissertation, candidacy exam. *Entrance requirements:* For master's and doctorate, GRE General Test. Additional exam requirements/recommendations for international students: Required—TOEFL (minimum score 600 paper-based; 80 iBT). Electronic applications accepted. *Faculty research:* Environmental modeling, biological-waste treatment, petrology, environmental geology, geochemistry.

University of Ottawa, Faculty of Graduate and Postdoctoral Studies, Faculty of Engineering, Department of Chemical and Biological Engineering, Ottawa, ON K1N 6N5, Canada. Offers M Eng, MA Sc, PhD. *Degree requirements:* For master's, thesis or alternative; for doctorate, comprehensive exam, thesis/dissertation. *Entrance requirements:* For master's, honors degree or equivalent, minimum B average; for doctorate, master's degree, minimum B+ average. Electronic applications accepted. *Faculty research:* Material development, process engineering, clean technologies.

University of Pennsylvania, School of Engineering and Applied Science, Department of Bioengineering, Philadelphia, PA 19104. Offers MSE, PhD, PhD/MD, VMD/PhD. *Program availability:* Part-time. *Faculty:* 101 full-time (15 women), 25 part-time/adjunct (3 women). *Students:* 170 full-time (77 women), 39 part-time (19 women); includes 75 minority (4 Black or African American, non-Hispanic/Latino; 43 Asian, non-Hispanic/Latino; 17 Hispanic/Latino; 11 Two or more races, non-Hispanic/Latino), 47 international. Average age 26. 651 applicants, 21% accepted, 66 enrolled. In 2018, 41 master's, 16 doctorates awarded. Terminal master's awarded for partial completion of doctoral program. *Degree requirements:* For master's, comprehensive exam, thesis optional; for doctorate, comprehensive exam, thesis/dissertation. *Entrance requirements:* For master's and doctorate, GRE, bachelor's degree, letters of recommendation, resume, personal statement. Additional exam requirements/recommendations for international students: Required—TOEFL (minimum score 100 iBT), IELTS (minimum score 7). *Application deadline:* For fall admission, 12/15 priority date for domestic and international students. Application fee: $80. Electronic applications accepted. *Expenses:* Contact institution. *Faculty research:* Bioengineering therapeutics, devices and drug delivery, biomaterials, cell mechanics, molecular engineering, theoretical and computational bioengineering. *Application contact:* William Fenton, Assistant Director of Graduate Admissions, 215-898-4542, Fax: 215-573-5577, E-mail: gradstudies@seas.upenn.edu.
Website: http://www.be.seas.upenn.edu/prospective-students/masters/index.php

University of Pennsylvania, School of Engineering and Applied Science, Department of Chemical and Biomolecular Engineering, Philadelphia, PA 19104. Offers MSE, PhD. *Program availability:* Part-time. *Students:* Average age 25. 429 applicants, 31% accepted, 55 enrolled. In 2018, 14 master's, 12 doctorates awarded. Terminal master's awarded for partial completion of doctoral program. *Degree requirements:* For master's, comprehensive exam, thesis optional; for doctorate, comprehensive exam, thesis/dissertation. *Entrance requirements:* For master's and doctorate, GRE, bachelor's degree, letters of recommendation, resume, personal statement. Additional exam requirements/recommendations for international students: Required—TOEFL (minimum score 100 iBT), IELTS (minimum score 7). *Application deadline:* For fall admission, 12/15 priority date for domestic and international students. Application fee: $80. Electronic applications accepted. *Expenses:* Contact institution. *Faculty research:* Advanced materials and nanotechnology, catalysis and reaction engineering, cellular and biomolecular engineering, energy and environmental engineering, soft matter and complex fluids. *Application contact:* William Fenton, Assistant Director of Graduate Admissions, 215-898-4542, Fax: 215-573-5577, E-mail: gradstudies@seas.upenn.edu.
Website: http://www.cbe.seas.upenn.edu/prospective-students/masters/index.php

University of Pittsburgh, Swanson School of Engineering, Department of Bioengineering, Pittsburgh, PA 15260. Offers MSBENG, PhD, MD/PhD. *Program availability:* Part-time, 100% online. Terminal master's awarded for partial completion of doctoral program. *Degree requirements:* For doctorate, comprehensive exam, thesis/dissertation, final oral exams. *Entrance requirements:* For master's and doctorate, GRE General Test, minimum GPA of 3.0. Additional exam requirements/recommendations for international students: Required—TOEFL (minimum score 550 paper-based; 80 iBT). Electronic applications accepted. *Expenses:* Contact institution. *Faculty research:* Artificial organs, biomechanics, biomaterials, signal processing, biotechnology.

University of Puerto Rico–Mayagüez, Graduate Studies, College of Engineering, Department of Mechanical Engineering, Mayagüez, PR 00681-9000. Offers mechanical engineering (ME, MS, PhD), including aerospace and unmanned vehicles (ME), automation/mechatronics, bioengineering, fluid mechanics, heat transfer/energy systems, manufacturing, mechanics of materials, micro and nano engineering. *Program availability:* Part-time. Terminal master's awarded for partial completion of doctoral program. *Degree requirements:* For master's, one foreign language, comprehensive exam, thesis; for doctorate, one foreign language, comprehensive exam, thesis/dissertation. *Entrance requirements:* For master's, BS in mechanical engineering or its equivalent; for doctorate, GRE, BS or MS in mechanical engineering or its equivalent; minimum GPA of 3.0. Additional exam requirements/recommendations for international students: Required—TOEFL (minimum score 80 iBT). Electronic applications accepted. *Faculty research:* Computational fluid dynamics, thermal sciences, mechanical design, material health, microfluidics.

University of Saskatchewan, College of Graduate and Postdoctoral Studies, College of Engineering, Biological Engineering Program, Saskatoon, SK S7N 5E5, Canada. Offers M Sc, PhD. *Program availability:* Part-time. *Degree requirements:* For master's, 30 credits (for M Eng); thesis and 12 credits (for MS); for doctorate, comprehensive exam, thesis/dissertation, qualifying exam, 18 credits. *Entrance requirements:* For master's and doctorate, GRE. Additional exam requirements/recommendations for international students: Required—TOEFL (minimum iBT score of 80), IELTS (6.5), CanTEST (4.5), or PTE (59). Electronic applications accepted. *Faculty research:* Agricultural machinery systems, animal welfare, biomechanical engineering, feed processing, food and bioprocess engineering, irrigation, livestock odor control, post-harvest technologies, soil and water conservation.

The University of Texas at Arlington, Graduate School, College of Engineering, Bioengineering Department, Arlington, TX 76019. Offers MS, PhD. Programs offered jointly with The University of Texas Southwestern Medical Center at Dallas. *Program availability:* Part-time. Terminal master's awarded for partial completion of doctoral program. *Degree requirements:* For master's, comprehensive exam (for some programs), thesis (for some programs); for doctorate, comprehensive exam, thesis/dissertation, qualifying exam. *Entrance requirements:* For master's, GRE General Test (minimum total of 1100 with minimum verbal score of 400), minimum GPA of 3.0 in last 60 hours of course work, 3 letters of recommendation; for doctorate, GRE General Test (minimum total of 1175 with minimum verbal score of 400), minimum GPA of 3.4 in last 60 hours of course work, 3 letters of recommendation. Additional exam requirements/recommendations for international students: Required—TOEFL. *Faculty research:* Instrumentation, mechanics, materials.

Bioengineering

The University of Toledo, College of Graduate Studies, College of Engineering, Department of Bioengineering, Toledo, OH 43606-3390. Offers MS, PhD. Terminal master's awarded for partial completion of doctoral program. *Degree requirements:* For master's, thesis optional; for doctorate, thesis/dissertation, qualifying exam. *Entrance requirements:* For master's, GRE General Test, minimum GPA of 3.0; for doctorate, GRE General Test, minimum GPA of 3.3. Additional exam requirements/recommendations for international students: Required—TOEFL (minimum score 550 paper-based; 80 iBT). Electronic applications accepted. *Faculty research:* Artificial organs, biochemical engineering, bioelectrical systems, biomechanics, cellular engineering.

University of Utah, Graduate School, College of Engineering, Department of Bioengineering, Salt Lake City, UT 84112-9202. Offers MS, PhD, MS/MBA. MS/MBA offered with David Eccles School of Business. *Faculty:* 22 full-time (3 women), 9 part-time/adjunct (1 woman). *Students:* 122 full-time (35 women), 42 part-time (11 women); includes 26 minority (1 Black or African American, non-Hispanic/Latino; 15 Asian, non-Hispanic/Latino; 6 Hispanic/Latino; 4 Two or more races, non-Hispanic/Latino), 13 international. Average age 27. 266 applicants, 42% accepted, 49 enrolled. In 2018, 42 master's, 8 doctorates awarded. Terminal master's awarded for partial completion of doctoral program. *Degree requirements:* For master's, comprehensive exam (for some programs), thesis (for some programs), project presentation, oral exam; for doctorate, comprehensive exam, thesis/dissertation, seminar presentation, TA mentorship. *Entrance requirements:* For master's and doctorate, GRE General Test or MCAT, bachelor's degree from accredited institution, college, or university; minimum undergraduate GPA of 3.0. Additional exam requirements/recommendations for international students: Required—TOEFL (minimum score 575 paper-based; 90 iBT); Recommended—IELTS (minimum score 7.5). *Application deadline:* For fall admission, 4/1 for domestic and international students. Application fee: $55 ($65 for international students). Electronic applications accepted. *Expenses:* Contact institution. *Financial support:* In 2018–19, 126 students received support, including 22 fellowships with full and partial tuition reimbursements available (averaging $30,000 per year), 103 research assistantships with full and partial tuition reimbursements available (averaging $25,000 per year), 1 teaching assistantship with full and partial tuition reimbursement available (averaging $24,250 per year); traineeships, health care benefits, and unspecified assistantships also available. Financial award application deadline: 4/1; financial award applicants required to submit FAFSA. *Faculty research:* Neural engineering and prosthesis; cardiovascular engineering and computer modeling; biomedical imaging and ultrasonic bioinstrumentation; biomedical device innovation and design; cellular, molecular and tissue therapeutics. *Total annual research expenditures:* $7.9 million. *Unit head:* Dr. David W. Grainger, Chair, Bioengineering/Professor of Pharmaceutics and Pharmaceutical Chemistry, 801-581-8528, Fax: 801-585-5361, E-mail: david.grainger@utah.edu. *Application contact:* Laura L. Olsen, Academic Advisor, Graduate Program, 801-581-8559, Fax: 801-585-5361, E-mail: laura.l.olsen@utah.edu. Website: http://www.bioen.utah.edu/

University of Vermont, Graduate College, Cross-College Interdisciplinary Program, Program in Bioengineering, Burlington, VT 05405. Offers PhD. *Entrance requirements:* For doctorate, GRE General Test. Additional exam requirements/recommendations for international students: Required—TOEFL (minimum score 550 paper-based; 90 iBT), IELTS (minimum score 6.5). Electronic applications accepted.

University of Washington, Graduate School, College of Engineering and School of Medicine, Department of Bioengineering, Seattle, WA 98195-5061. Offers applied bioengineering (MAB); bioengineering (MS, PhD); bioengineering and nanotechnology (PhD); pharmaceutical bioengineering (MS). *Program availability:* Part-time. *Faculty:* 50 full-time (15 women), 47 part-time/adjunct (5 women). *Students:* 142 full-time (63 women), 42 part-time (25 women); includes 58 minority (4 Black or African American, non-Hispanic/Latino; 1 American Indian or Alaska Native, non-Hispanic/Latino; 32 Asian, non-Hispanic/Latino; 13 Hispanic/Latino; 8 Two or more races, non-Hispanic/Latino), 42 international. Average age 26. 877 applicants, 19% accepted, 60 enrolled. In 2018, 26 master's, 27 doctorates awarded. *Degree requirements:* For master's, comprehensive exam, thesis; for doctorate, comprehensive exam, thesis/dissertation, qualifying exam, general exam, thesis defense. *Entrance requirements:* For master's and doctorate, GRE General Test, minimum GPA of 3.0, transcripts, statement of purpose, letters of recommendation, resume/curriculum vitae. Additional exam requirements/recommendations for international students: Required—TOEFL (minimum score 500 paper-based; 80 iBT). *Application deadline:* For fall admission, 12/15 for domestic and international students. Application fee: $85. Electronic applications accepted. Application fee is waived when completed online. *Expenses:* Regular/research-focused master's degrees and Ph.D.s: resident, $18,852, non-resident, $32,760; Master's of Applied Bioengineering: $24,719 resident, $29,446 nonresident. *Financial support:* In 2018–19, 135 students received support, including 31 fellowships with full tuition reimbursements available (averaging $37,680 per year), 92 research assistantships with full tuition reimbursements available (averaging $37,680 per year), 4 teaching assistantships with full tuition reimbursements available (averaging $37,680 per year); Federal Work-Study, institutionally sponsored loans, traineeships, health care benefits, and tuition waivers (full) also available. Support available to part-time students. Financial award application deadline: 12/1; financial award applicants required to submit FAFSA. *Faculty research:* Imaging and image guided therapy, molecular and cellular engineering, biomaterials and regenerative medicine, technology for expanding access to healthcare, synthetic and quantitative biology, neural engineering. *Total annual research expenditures:* $25.6 million. *Unit head:* Dr. Cecilia Giachelli, Professor/Chair, 206-685-2000, Fax: 206-685-3300, E-mail: ceci@uw.edu. *Application contact:* Peggy Sharp, Graduate Academic Counselor, 206-685-3494, Fax: 206-685-3300, E-mail: peggys55@uw.edu. Website: https://bioe.uw.edu/

Utah State University, School of Graduate Studies, College of Engineering, Department of Biological Engineering, Logan, UT 84322. Offers MS, PhD. *Program availability:* Part-time. Terminal master's awarded for partial completion of doctoral program. *Degree requirements:* For master's, thesis (for some programs); for doctorate, thesis/dissertation. *Entrance requirements:* For master's and doctorate, GRE General Test, minimum GPA of 3.0. Additional exam requirements/recommendations for international students: Required—TOEFL. *Faculty research:* On-farm water management, crop-water yield modeling, irrigation, biosensors, biological engineering.

Virginia Polytechnic Institute and State University, Graduate School, College of Engineering, Blacksburg, VA 24061. Offers aerospace engineering (PhD, M Eng/MS); biological systems engineering (PhD); biomedical engineering (MS, PhD); chemical engineering (PhD); civil engineering (PhD); computer engineering (PhD); computer science and applications (MS); electrical engineering (PhD); engineering education (PhD); M Eng/MS. *Faculty:* 446 full-time (87 women), 7 part-time/adjunct (3 women). *Students:* 1,776 full-time (471 women), 367 part-time (62 women); includes 260 minority (50 Black or African American, non-Hispanic/Latino; 3 American Indian or Alaska Native, non-Hispanic/Latino; 99 Asian, non-Hispanic/Latino; 67 Hispanic/Latino; 41 Two or more races, non-Hispanic/Latino), 1,178 international. Average age 27. 3,798 applicants, 37% accepted, 507 enrolled. In 2018, 489 master's, 200 doctorates awarded. *Degree requirements:* For master's, comprehensive exam (for some programs), thesis (for some programs); for doctorate, comprehensive exam (for some programs), thesis/dissertation (for some programs). *Entrance requirements:* For master's and doctorate, GRE/GMAT. Additional exam requirements/recommendations for international students: Required—TOEFL (minimum score 90 iBT). *Application deadline:* For fall admission, 8/1 for domestic students, 4/1 for international students; for spring admission, 1/1 for domestic students, 9/1 for international students. Applications are processed on a rolling basis. Application fee: $75. Electronic applications accepted. *Expenses:* Tuition, state resident: full-time $15,510; part-time $739.50 per credit hour. Tuition, nonresident: full-time $29,629; part-time $1490.25 per credit hour. *Required fees:* $2804; $550 per semester. Tuition and fees vary according to course load, campus/location and program. *Financial support:* In 2018–19, 37 fellowships with full tuition reimbursements (averaging $24,951 per year), 1,110 research assistantships with full tuition reimbursements (averaging $20,129 per year), 486 teaching assistantships with full tuition reimbursements (averaging $16,192 per year) were awarded; scholarships/grants and unspecified assistantships also available. Financial award application deadline: 3/1; financial award applicants required to submit FAFSA. *Total annual research expenditures:* $96.3 million. *Unit head:* Dr. Julia Ross, Dean, 540-231-9752, Fax: 540-231-3031, E-mail: rjulie@vt.edu. *Application contact:* Linda Perkins, Executive Assistant, 540-231-9752, Fax: 540-231-3031, E-mail: lperkins@vt.edu. Website: http://www.eng.vt.edu/

Washington State University, College of Agricultural, Human, and Natural Resource Sciences, Department of Biological Systems Engineering, Pullman, WA 99164-6120. Offers biological and agricultural engineering (MS, PhD). Program applications must be made through the Pullman campus. *Degree requirements:* For master's, comprehensive exam, thesis (for some programs), written and oral exam; for doctorate, comprehensive exam, thesis/dissertation, written and oral exam. *Entrance requirements:* For master's and doctorate, minimum GPA of 3.0, bachelor's degree in engineering or closely-related subject. Additional exam requirements/recommendations for international students: Required—TOEFL. Electronic applications accepted. *Faculty research:* Agricultural automation engineering; bioenergy and bioproducts engineering; food engineering; land, air, and water resources and environmental engineering.

Wilkes University, College of Graduate and Professional Studies, College of Science and Engineering, Department of Electrical Engineering and Physics, Wilkes-Barre, PA 18766-0002. Offers bioengineering (MS); electrical engineering (MSEE). *Program availability:* Part-time. *Students:* 8 full-time (2 women), 4 part-time (1 woman); includes 3 minority (1 Asian, non-Hispanic/Latino; 2 Hispanic/Latino), 1 international. Average age 24. In 2018, 15 master's awarded. *Entrance requirements:* For master's, GRE General Test. Additional exam requirements/recommendations for international students: Required—TOEFL (minimum score 550 paper-based; 79 iBT). *Application deadline:* Applications are processed on a rolling basis. Application fee: $45 ($65 for international students). Electronic applications accepted. Tuition and fees vary according to course load, degree level and program. *Financial support:* Unspecified assistantships available. Financial award application deadline: 3/1; financial award applicants required to submit FAFSA. *Unit head:* Dr. Prahlad Murthy, Interim Dean, 570-408-4600, Fax: 570-408-7846, E-mail: prahlad.murthy@wilkes.edu. *Application contact:* Kristin Donati, Associate Director of Graduate Admissions, 570-408-3338, Fax: 570-408-7846, E-mail: kristin.donati@wilkes.edu. Website: http://www.wilkes.edu/academics/colleges/science-and-engineering/engineering-physics/electrical-engineering-physics/index.aspx

Biosystems Engineering

Auburn University, Graduate School, Ginn College of Engineering, Department of Biosystems Engineering, Auburn University, AL 36849. Offers MS, PhD. *Expenses:* Tuition, state resident: full-time $11,282; part-time $535 per credit hour. Tuition, nonresident: full-time $30,542; part-time $1605 per credit hour. *Required fees:* $826 per semester. Tuition and fees vary according to degree level and program.

Clemson University, Graduate School, College of Engineering, Computing and Applied Sciences, Department of Environmental Engineering and Earth Sciences, Anderson, SC 29625. Offers biosystems engineering (MS, PhD); environmental engineering and science (MS, PhD); environmental health physics (MS); hydrogeology (MS). *Program availability:* Part-time. *Faculty:* 20 full-time (4 women). *Students:* 75 full-time (30 women), 16 part-time (5 women); includes 5 minority (1 Black or African American, non-Hispanic/Latino; 1 Native Hawaiian or other Pacific Islander, non-Hispanic/Latino; 3 Two or more races, non-Hispanic/Latino), 30 international. Average age 26. 118 applicants, 72% accepted, 24 enrolled. In 2018, 31 master's, 4 doctorates awarded. *Degree requirements:* For master's, thesis or alternative; for doctorate, comprehensive exam, thesis/dissertation. *Entrance requirements:* For master's and doctorate, GRE General Test, unofficial transcripts, letters of recommendation. Additional exam requirements/recommendations for international students: Required—TOEFL (minimum score 80 paper-based; 80 iBT); Recommended—IELTS (minimum score 6.5), TSE (minimum score 54). *Application deadline:* For fall admission, 2/15 for domestic and international students. Applications are processed on a rolling basis. Application fee: $80 ($90 for international students). Electronic applications accepted. *Expenses:* $6823 per semester full-time resident, $14023 per semester full-time non-resident, $833 per credit hour part-time resident, $1731 per credit hour part-time non-resident, online $1264 per credit hour, $4938 doctoral programs resident, $10405 doctoral programs non-resident, $1144 full-time graduate assistant, other fees may apply per session. *Financial support:* In 2018–19, 60 students received support, including 5 fellowships with full and partial tuition reimbursements available (averaging $3,573 per year), 34 research assistantships with full and partial tuition reimbursements available (averaging $18,464 per year), 19 teaching assistantships with full and partial tuition reimbursements available (averaging $18,021 per year); career-related internships or fieldwork and unspecified assistantships also available. Financial award application deadline: 2/15. *Faculty research:* Environmental engineering, bioprocess and ecological engineering, nuclear environmental engineering and science, hydrogeology, environmental chemistry and microbiology. *Total annual research expenditures:* $5.4 million. *Unit head:* Dr. David Freedman, Department Chair, 864-656-5566, E-mail: dfreedm@clemson.edu. *Application contact:* Dr. Mark Schlautman, Graduate Program Coordinator, 864-656-4059, E-mail: mschlau@clemson.edu. Website: https://www.clemson.edu/cecas/departments/eees/

Michigan State University, The Graduate School, College of Agriculture and Natural Resources and College of Engineering, Department of Biosystems and Agricultural Engineering, East Lansing, MI 48824. Offers biosystems engineering (MS, PhD). *Entrance requirements:* Additional exam requirements/recommendations for international students: Required—TOEFL. Electronic applications accepted.

North Dakota State University, College of Graduate and Interdisciplinary Studies, College of Engineering, Department of Agricultural and Biosystems Engineering, Fargo, ND 58102. Offers MS, PhD. *Program availability:* Part-time. *Degree requirements:* For master's, thesis; for doctorate, thesis/dissertation. *Entrance requirements:* For master's and doctorate, BS in engineering or the equivalent, minimum undergraduate GPA of 3.0. Additional exam requirements/recommendations for international students: Required—TOEFL (minimum score 550 paper-based; 79 iBT). Electronic applications accepted. *Faculty research:* Irrigation, crop processing, food engineering, environmental resources, sensors and instrumentation.

South Dakota State University, Graduate School, College of Agriculture, Food and Environmental Sciences, Department of Agricultural and Biosystems Engineering, Brookings, SD 57007. Offers MS, PhD. *Program availability:* Part-time. *Degree requirements:* For master's, thesis; for doctorate, comprehensive exam, thesis/dissertation, preliminary oral and written exams. *Entrance requirements:* Required—TOEFL (minimum score 525 paper-based; 71 iBT).

South Dakota State University, Graduate School, Jerome J. Lohr College of Engineering, Department of Agricultural and Biosystems Engineering, Brookings, SD 57007. Offers biological sciences (MS, PhD); engineering (MS). PhD offered jointly with Iowa State University of Science and Technology. *Program availability:* Part-time. *Degree requirements:* For master's, thesis (for some programs), oral exam; for doctorate, thesis/dissertation, preliminary oral and written exams. *Entrance requirements:* For master's and doctorate, engineering degree. Additional exam requirements/recommendations for international students: Required—TOEFL (minimum score 550 paper-based; 79 iBT). *Faculty research:* Water resources, food engineering, natural resources engineering, machine design, bioprocess engineering.

The University of Arizona, College of Agriculture and Life Sciences, Department of Agricultural and Biosystems Engineering, Tucson, AZ 85721. Offers MS, PhD. Terminal master's awarded for partial completion of doctoral program. *Degree requirements:* For master's, thesis; for doctorate, thesis/dissertation. *Entrance requirements:* For master's, minimum GPA of 3.0 in last 2 years of undergraduate study, 3 letters of recommendation; for doctorate, minimum GPA of 3.0 in last 2 years of undergraduate study, 3 letters of recommendation, statement of purpose. Additional exam requirements/recommendations for international students: Required—TOEFL (minimum score 550 paper-based; 79 iBT). Electronic applications accepted. *Faculty research:* Irrigation system design, energy-use management, equipment for alternative crops, food properties enhancement.

University of Manitoba, Faculty of Graduate Studies, Faculty of Engineering, Department of Biosystems Engineering, Winnipeg, MB R3T 2N2, Canada. Offers M Eng, M Sc, PhD.

University of Minnesota, Twin Cities Campus, Graduate School, College of Food, Agricultural and Natural Resource Sciences, Bioproducts and Biosystems Science, Engineering and Management Graduate Program, St. Paul, MN 55108. Offers MS, PhD. *Program availability:* Part-time. Terminal master's awarded for partial completion of doctoral program. *Degree requirements:* For master's, comprehensive exam, thesis, written and oral preliminary exams; for doctorate, comprehensive exam, thesis/dissertation, written and oral preliminary exams. *Entrance requirements:* For master's and doctorate, GRE, BS in engineering, mathematics, physical or biological sciences, or related field. Additional exam requirements/recommendations for international students: Required—TOEFL (minimum score 550 paper-based; 79 iBT), IELTS (minimum score 6.5). Electronic applications accepted. *Faculty research:* Water quality, bioprocessing, food engineering, terramechanics, process and machine control.

The University of Tennessee, Graduate School, College of Agricultural Sciences and Natural Resources, Department of Biosystems Engineering and Environmental Science, Program in Biosystems Engineering, Knoxville, TN 37996. Offers MS, PhD. *Degree requirements:* For master's, thesis; for doctorate, thesis/dissertation. *Entrance requirements:* For master's and doctorate, GRE General Test, minimum GPA of 2.7. Additional exam requirements/recommendations for international students: Required—TOEFL. Electronic applications accepted.

The University of Tennessee, Graduate School, College of Agricultural Sciences and Natural Resources, Department of Biosystems Engineering and Environmental Science, Program in Biosystems Engineering Technology, Knoxville, TN 37996. Offers MS. *Degree requirements:* For master's, thesis or alternative. *Entrance requirements:* For master's, GRE General Test, minimum GPA of 2.7. Additional exam requirements/recommendations for international students: Required—TOEFL. Electronic applications accepted.

Section 4
Architectural Engineering

This section contains a directory of institutions offering graduate work in architectural engineering. Additional information about programs listed in the directory may be obtained by writing directly to the dean of a graduate school or chair of a department at the address given in the directory.

For programs offering related work, see also in this book *Engineering and Applied Sciences* and *Management of Engineering and Technology*. In the other guides in this series:

Graduate Programs in the Humanities, Arts & Social Sciences

See *Applied Arts and Design (Industrial Design and Interior Design), Architecture (Environmental Design), Political Science and International Affairs,* and *Public, Regional, and Industrial Affairs (Urban and Regional Planning and Urban Studies)*

Graduate Programs in the Physical Sciences, Mathematics, Agricultural Sciences, the Environment & Natural Resources

See *Environmental Sciences and Management*

CONTENTS

Program Directory

Architectural Engineering

California Polytechnic State University, San Luis Obispo, College of Architecture and Environmental Design, Department of Architectural Engineering, San Luis Obispo, CA 93407. Offers MS. *Program availability:* Part-time. *Faculty:* 3 full-time (1 woman). *Students:* 13 full-time (6 women); includes 4 minority (2 Asian, non-Hispanic/Latino; 2 Hispanic/Latino). Average age 23. 18 applicants, 67% accepted, 11 enrolled. *Entrance requirements:* For master's, GRE. Additional exam requirements/recommendations for international students: Required—TOEFL (minimum score 80 iBT). *Application deadline:* For fall admission, 4/1 for domestic and international students. Applications are processed on a rolling basis. Application fee: $55. Electronic applications accepted. *Expenses: Tuition, area resident:* Full-time $7176; part-time $4164 per year. Tuition, state resident: full-time $10,965. Tuition, nonresident: full-time $10,965. *Required fees:* $6336; $3711. *Financial support:* Fellowships, teaching assistantships, scholarships/grants, tuition waivers, and unspecified assistantships available. Financial award application deadline: 3/2; financial award applicants required to submit FAFSA. *Unit head:* Dr. Allen C. Estes, Head, 805-756-1314, Fax: 805-756-6054, E-mail: acestes@calpoly.edu. *Application contact:* Dr. Allen C. Estes, Head, 805-756-1314, Fax: 805-756-6054, E-mail: acestes@calpoly.edu.
Website: http://www.arce.calpoly.edu

California State University, Fullerton, Graduate Studies, College of Engineering and Computer Science, Department of Civil and Environmental Engineering, Fullerton, CA 92831-3599. Offers civil engineering (MS), including architectural engineering, environmental engineering. *Program availability:* Part-time. *Degree requirements:* For master's, comprehensive exam, project or thesis. *Entrance requirements:* For master's, minimum undergraduate GPA of 2.5. *Faculty research:* Soil-structure interaction, finite-element analysis, computer-aided analysis and design.

Carnegie Mellon University, College of Fine Arts, School of Architecture, Pittsburgh, PA 15213-3891. Offers architecture (MSA); architecture, engineering, and construction management (PhD); building performance and diagnostics (MS, PhD); computational design (MS, PhD); engineering construction management (MSA); tangible interaction design (MTID); urban design (MUD). Terminal master's awarded for partial completion of doctoral program. *Degree requirements:* For doctorate, thesis/dissertation. *Entrance requirements:* For master's and doctorate, GRE General Test. Additional exam requirements/recommendations for international students: Required—TOEFL.

Drexel University, College of Engineering, Department of Civil, Architectural, and Environmental Engineering, Philadelphia, PA 19104-2875. Offers architectural/building systems engineering (MS, PhD); civil engineering (MS, PhD); environmental engineering (MS, PhD); geotechnical, geoenvironmental and geosynthetics engineering (MS, PhD); hydraulics, hydrology and water resources engineering (MS, PhD); structures (MS, PhD). *Program availability:* Part-time, evening/weekend. *Degree requirements:* For master's, thesis optional; for doctorate, thesis/dissertation. *Entrance requirements:* For master's, minimum GPA of 3.0; for doctorate, minimum GPA of 3.5, MS in civil engineering. Additional exam requirements/recommendations for international students: Required—TOEFL. Electronic applications accepted. *Faculty research:* Structural dynamics, hazardous wastes, water resources, pavement materials, groundwater.

Illinois Institute of Technology, Graduate College, Armour College of Engineering, Department of Civil, Architectural and Environmental Engineering, Chicago, IL 60616. Offers architectural engineering (M Arch E); civil engineering (MS, PhD), including architectural engineering (MS), construction engineering and management (MS), geoenvironmental engineering (MS), geotechnical engineering (MS), structural engineering (MS), transportation engineering (MS); construction engineering and management (MCEM); environmental engineering (M Env E, MS, PhD); geoenvironmental engineering (M Geoenv E); geotechnical engineering (MGE); infrastructure engineering and management (MPW); structural engineering (MSE); transportation engineering (M Trans E). *Program availability:* Part-time, evening/weekend, online learning. Terminal master's awarded for partial completion of doctoral program. *Degree requirements:* For master's, thesis (for some programs); for doctorate, comprehensive exam, thesis/dissertation. *Entrance requirements:* For master's, GRE General Test (minimum score 900 Quantitative and Verbal, 2.5 Analytical Writing), minimum undergraduate GPA of 3.0; for doctorate, GRE General Test (minimum score 1000 Quantitative and Verbal, 3.0 Analytical Writing), minimum undergraduate GPA of 3.0. Additional exam requirements/recommendations for international students: Required—TOEFL (minimum score 550 paper-based; 80 iBT). Electronic applications accepted. *Faculty research:* Structural, architectural, geotechnical and geoenvironmental engineering; construction engineering and management; transportation engineering; environmental engineering and public works.

Kansas State University, Graduate School, College of Engineering, Department of Architectural Engineering and Construction Science, Manhattan, KS 66506. Offers MS. *Degree requirements:* For master's, thesis or alternative. *Entrance*

requirements: For master's, GRE, minimum GPA of 3.0, undergraduate degree (BS) from ABET-accredited engineering program. Additional exam requirements/recommendations for international students: Required—TOEFL. Electronic applications accepted. *Faculty research:* Structural systems design and analysis, building electrical and lighting systems, building HVAC and plumbing systems, sustainable engineering.

Lawrence Technological University, College of Engineering, Southfield, MI 48075-1058. Offers architectural engineering (MS); automotive engineering (MS); biomedical engineering (MS); civil engineering (MA, MS, PhD), including environmental engineering (MS), geotechnical engineering (MS), structural engineering (MS), transportation engineering (MS), water resource engineering (MS); construction engineering management (MA); electrical and computer engineering (MS); engineering management (MEM); engineering technology (MS); fire engineering (MS); industrial engineering (MS), including healthcare systems; manufacturing systems (ME); mechanical engineering (MS, DE, PhD), including automotive engineering (MS), energy engineering (MS), manufacturing (DE), solid mechanics (MS), thermal/fluid systems (MS); mechatronic systems engineering (MS). *Program availability:* Part-time, evening/weekend. Terminal master's awarded for partial completion of doctoral program. *Degree requirements:* For master's, thesis optional; for doctorate, comprehensive exam, thesis/dissertation optional. *Entrance requirements:* Additional exam requirements/recommendations for international students: Required—TOEFL (minimum score 550 paper-based; 79 iBT), IELTS (minimum score 6.5). Electronic applications accepted. *Faculty research:* Innovative infrastructure and building structures and materials; connectivity and mobility; automotive systems modeling, simulation and testing; biomedical devices and materials; building mechanical/electrical systems.

Milwaukee School of Engineering, MS Program in Architectural Engineering, Milwaukee, WI 53202-3109. Offers MS. *Program availability:* Part-time, evening/weekend. *Degree requirements:* For master's, thesis. *Entrance requirements:* For master's, GRE General Test if undergraduate GPA is less than 3.0, 2 letters of recommendation; BS in architectural engineering or closely-related area from ABET-accredited program. Additional exam requirements/recommendations for international students: Required—TOEFL (minimum score 90 iBT), IELTS (minimum score 7). Electronic applications accepted. *Faculty research:* Steel, materials.

Penn State University Park, Graduate School, College of Engineering, Department of Architectural Engineering, University Park, PA 16802. Offers architectural engineering (M Eng, MAE, MS, PhD); facilities engineering and management (M Eng).

University of California, San Diego, Graduate Division, Program in Architecture-based Enterprise Systems Engineering, La Jolla, CA 92093. Offers MAS. *Program availability:* Part-time. *Students:* 20 full-time (6 women). 30 applicants, 87% accepted, 21 enrolled. In 2018, 32 master's awarded. *Degree requirements:* For master's, capstone project. *Entrance requirements:* For master's, 2 letters of recommendation, statement of purpose, resume or curriculum vitae. Additional exam requirements/recommendations for international students: Required—TOEFL (minimum score 550 paper-based; 80 iBT), IELTS (minimum score 7). *Application deadline:* For fall admission, 8/10 for domestic students. Application fee: $105 ($125 for international students). Electronic applications accepted. *Expenses:* Contact institution. *Financial support:* Applicants required to submit FAFSA. *Faculty research:* Emerging enterprise solution approaches, globally distributed operations challenges. *Unit head:* Harold Sorenson, Director, 858-534-4406, E-mail: hsorenson@ucsd.edu. *Application contact:* Stacey Williams, Coordinator, 858-534-1069, E-mail: staceyw@eng.ucsd.edu.
Website: http://maseng.ucsd.edu/aese/

University of Colorado Boulder, Graduate School, College of Engineering and Applied Science, Department of Civil, Environmental, and Architectural Engineering, Boulder, CO 80309. Offers MS, PhD. Terminal master's awarded for partial completion of doctoral program. *Degree requirements:* For master's, comprehensive exam, thesis or alternative; for doctorate, thesis/dissertation. *Entrance requirements:* For master's, GRE General Test, minimum undergraduate GPA of 3.0. Electronic applications accepted. Application fee is waived when completed online. *Faculty research:* Civil engineering; environmental engineering; architectural engineering; hydrology; water resources engineering.

University of Detroit Mercy, School of Architecture, Detroit, MI 48221. Offers architecture (M Arch); community development (MA). *Entrance requirements:* For master's, BS in architecture, minimum GPA of 3.0, portfolio.

The University of Kansas, Graduate Studies, School of Engineering, Program in Architectural Engineering, Lawrence, KS 66045. Offers MS. *Program availability:* Part-time. *Students:* 4 full-time (2 women); includes 1 minority (Black or African American, non-Hispanic/Latino), 2 international. Average age 27. 4 applicants, 75% accepted, 1 enrolled. In 2018, 6 master's awarded. *Entrance requirements:*

For master's, GRE, two letters of recommendation, statement of purpose. Additional exam requirements/recommendations for international students: Required—TOEFL, IELTS. *Application deadline:* For fall admission, 8/17 for domestic and international students; for spring admission, 1/14 for domestic and international students; for summer admission, 5/26 for domestic and international students. Application fee: $65 ($85 for international students). Electronic applications accepted. *Financial support:* Fellowships, research assistantships, teaching assistantships, career-related internships or fieldwork, and scholarships/grants available. Financial award application deadline: 12/15. *Faculty research:* Building mechanical systems, energy management, lighting and electrical systems, construction engineering. *Unit head:* David Darwin, Chair, 785-864-3827, E-mail: daved@ku.edu. *Application contact:* Susan Scott, Graduate Secretary, 785-864-3826, Fax: 785-864-5631, E-mail: s523s307@ku.edu. Website: http://www.ceae.ku.edu/

University of Louisiana at Lafayette, College of the Arts, School of Architecture and Design, Lafayette, LA 70504. Offers M Arch. *Entrance requirements:* For master's, GRE General Test. Additional exam requirements/recommendations for international students: Required—TOEFL (minimum score 550 paper-based). Electronic applications accepted.

University of Massachusetts Amherst, Graduate School, College of Natural Sciences, Department of Environmental Conservation, Amherst, MA 01003. Offers building systems (MS, PhD); environmental policy and human dimensions (MS, PhD); forest resources (MS, PhD); sustainability science (MS); water, wetlands and watersheds (MS, PhD); wildlife and fisheries conservation (MS, PhD). *Program availability:* Part-time. Terminal master's awarded for partial completion of doctoral program. *Degree requirements:* For master's, thesis or alternative; for doctorate, comprehensive exam, thesis/dissertation. *Entrance requirements:* For master's and doctorate, GRE General Test. Additional exam requirements/recommendations for international students: Required—TOEFL (minimum score 550 paper-based; 80 iBT), IELTS (minimum score 6.5). Electronic applications accepted.

University of Miami, Graduate School, College of Engineering, Department of Civil, Architectural, and Environmental Engineering, Coral Gables, FL 33124. Offers architectural engineering (MSAE); civil engineering (MSCE, PhD). *Program availability:* Part-time. Terminal master's awarded for partial completion of doctoral program. *Degree requirements:* For master's, thesis (for some programs); for doctorate, comprehensive exam, thesis/dissertation. *Entrance requirements:* For master's, GRE General Test (minimum score 1000 verbal and quantitative), minimum GPA of 3.0; for doctorate, GRE General Test, minimum GPA of 3.5 in preceding degree. Additional exam requirements/recommendations for international students: Required—TOEFL (minimum score 550 paper-based). Electronic applications accepted. *Faculty research:* Structural assessment and wind engineering, sustainable construction and materials, moisture transport and management, wastewater and waste engineering, water management and risk analysis.

University of Nebraska–Lincoln, Graduate College, College of Engineering, Program in Architectural Engineering, Lincoln, NE 68588. Offers M Eng, MAE, MS, PhD. *Entrance requirements:* Additional exam requirements/recommendations for international students: Required—TOEFL (minimum score 550 paper-based).

The University of Texas at Austin, Graduate School, Cockrell School of Engineering, Department of Civil, Architectural and Environmental Engineering, Program in Architectural Engineering, Austin, TX 78712-1111. Offers MSE. *Program availability:* Part-time. *Degree requirements:* For master's, thesis. *Entrance requirements:* For master's, GRE General Test. Additional exam requirements/recommendations for international students: Required—TOEFL. Electronic applications accepted. *Faculty research:* Materials engineering, structural engineering, construction engineering, project management.

University of Wyoming, College of Engineering and Applied Science, Department of Civil and Architectural Engineering, Laramie, WY 82071. Offers architectural engineering (MS); civil engineering (MS, PhD). *Program availability:* Part-time. Terminal master's awarded for partial completion of doctoral program. *Degree requirements:* For master's, thesis (for some programs); for doctorate, variable foreign language requirement, comprehensive exam, thesis/dissertation. *Entrance requirements:* For master's, GRE General Test (minimum combined score 900), minimum GPA of 3.0; for doctorate, GRE General Test (minimum combined score: 1000), minimum GPA of 3.0. Additional exam requirements/recommendations for international students: Required—TOEFL (minimum score 550 paper-based). Electronic applications accepted. *Expenses: Tuition, area resident:* Full-time $6504; part-time $271 per credit hour. Tuition, state resident: full-time $6504; part-time $271 per credit hour. Tuition, nonresident: full-time $19,464; part-time $811 per credit hour. *International tuition:* $19,464 full-time. *Required fees:* $1410.94; $343.82 per semester. $343.82 per semester. Tuition and fees vary according to course load, program and reciprocity agreements. *Faculty research:* Water resources, structures, geotechnical engineering, transportation, architectural engineering.

Section 5
Biomedical Engineering and Biotechnology

This section contains a directory of institutions offering graduate work in biomedical engineering and biotechnology, followed by an in-depth entry submitted by an institution that chose to prepare a detailed program description. Additional information about programs listed in the directory but not augmented by an in-depth entry may be obtained by writing directly to the dean of a graduate school or chair of a department at the address given in the directory.

For programs offering related work, see also in this book *Aerospace/Aeronautical Engineering, Engineering and Applied Sciences, Engineering Design, Engineering Physics, Management of Engineering and Technology,* and *Mechanical Engineering and Mechanics.* In the other guides in this series:

Graduate Programs in the Biological/Biomedical Sciences & Health-Related Medical Professions

See *Allied Health, Biological and Biomedical Sciences,* and *Physiology*
Graduate Programs in the Physical Sciences, Mathematics, Agricultural Sciences, the Environment & Natural Resources
See *Mathematical Sciences (Biometrics and Biostatistics)*

CONTENTS

Program Directories

Biomedical Engineering

American University of Beirut, Graduate Programs, Faculty of Medicine, Beirut, Lebanon. Offers biochemistry (MS); biomedical engineering (MS); biomedical sciences (PhD); health research (MS); human morphology (MS); medicine (MD); microbiology and immunology (MS); neuroscience (MS); orthodontics (clinical) (MS); pharmacology and therapeutics (MS); physiology (MS). *Program availability:* Part-time. *Faculty:* 346 full-time (128 women), 44 part-time/adjunct (5 women). *Students:* 556 full-time (304 women). 463 applicants, 51% accepted, 165 enrolled. In 2018, 23 master's, 101 doctorates awarded. *Degree requirements:* For master's, comprehensive exam, thesis (for some programs); for doctorate, comprehensive exam, thesis/dissertation. *Entrance requirements:* For doctorate, MCAT (for Doctor of Medicine(MD)); GRE (for PhD). Additional exam requirements/recommendations for international students: Required— TOEFL (minimum score 600 paper-based; 100 iBT). *Application deadline:* Applications are processed on a rolling basis. Application fee: $75. Electronic applications accepted. *Expenses: Tuition:* Full-time $17,748; part-time $986 per credit. *Required fees:* $762. Tuition and fees vary according to course load and program. *Financial support:* Fellowships, research assistantships, teaching assistantships, and tuition waivers available. *Unit head:* Dr. Mohamed Sayegh, Dean, 961-1-135000 Ext. 4700, Fax: 961-1-744489, E-mail: msayegh@aub.edu.lb. *Application contact:* Dr. Salim Kanaan, Director, Admission's Office, 961-1-350000 Ext. 2594, Fax: 961-1-750775, E-mail: sk00@aub.edu.lb.
Website: http://www.aub.edu.lb/fm/Pages/default.aspx

American University of Sharjah, Graduate Programs, Sharjah, United Arab Emirates. Offers accounting (MS); biomedical engineering (MSBME); business administration (MBA); chemical engineering (MS Ch E); civil engineering (MSCE); computer engineering (MS); electrical engineering (MSEE); engineering systems management (MS, PhD); mathematics (MS); mechanical engineering (MSME); mechatronics engineering (MS); teaching English to speakers of other languages (MA); translation and interpreting (MA); urban planning (MUP). *Program availability:* Part-time, evening/ weekend. *Degree requirements:* For master's, thesis (for some programs). *Entrance requirements:* For master's, GMAT (for MBA). Additional exam requirements/ recommendations for international students: Required—TOEFL (minimum score 550 paper-based; 80 iBT), TWE (minimum score 5); Recommended—IELTS (minimum score 6.5). Electronic applications accepted. *Faculty research:* Water pollution, management and waste water treatment, energy and sustainability, air pollution, Islamic finance, family business and small and medium enterprises.

Arizona State University at the Tempe campus, Ira A. Fulton Schools of Engineering, School of Biological and Health Systems Engineering, Tempe, AZ 85287-9709. Offers biological design (PhD); biomedical engineering (MS, PhD). *Program availability:* Part-time, evening/weekend. Terminal master's awarded for partial completion of doctoral program. *Degree requirements:* For master's, thesis and oral defense or applied project; interactive Program of Study (iPOS) submitted before completing 50 percent of required credit hours; for doctorate, comprehensive exam, thesis/dissertation, interactive Program of Study (iPOS) submitted before completing 50 percent of required credit hours. *Entrance requirements:* For master's and doctorate, GRE General Test, minimum GPA of 3.0 or equivalent in last 2 years of work leading to bachelor's degree, 3 letters of recommendation, one-page personal statement. Additional exam requirements/ recommendations for international students: Required—TOEFL (minimum score 580 paper-based; 92 iBT). Electronic applications accepted. *Expenses:* Contact institution. *Faculty research:* Cardiovascular engineering; synthetic/computational biology; medical devices and diagnostics; neuroengineering; rehabilitation; regenerative medicine; imaging; molecular, cellular and tissue engineering; virtual reality healthcare delivery systems.

Baylor College of Medicine, Graduate School of Biomedical Sciences, Program in Translational Biology and Molecular Medicine, Houston, TX 77030-3498. Offers PhD. *Degree requirements:* For doctorate, thesis/dissertation, public defense. *Entrance requirements:* For doctorate, GRE, minimum GPA of 3.0. Additional exam requirements/ recommendations for international students: Required—TOEFL. Electronic applications accepted. *Faculty research:* Molecular medicine, translational biology, human disease biology and therapy.

Baylor University, Graduate School, School of Engineering and Computer Science, Department of Engineering, Waco, TX 76798. Offers biomedical engineering (MSBME); electrical and computer engineering (MSECE, PhD); engineering (ME); mechanical engineering (MSME). *Faculty:* 14 full-time (1 woman). *Students:* 7 full-time (3 women), 4 part-time (0 women); includes 4 minority (2 Asian, non-Hispanic/Latino; 2 Hispanic/ Latino), 2 international. In 2018, 14 master's, 8 doctorates awarded. *Unit head:* Dr. Mike Thompson, Graduate Director, 254-710-4188. *Application contact:* Linda Keer, Administrative Assistant, 254-710-4188, Fax: 254-710-3870, E-mail: linda_kerr@ baylor.edu.
Website: http://www.ecs.baylor.edu/engineering

Baylor University, Graduate School, School of Engineering and Computer Science, Department of Mechanical Engineering, Waco, TX 76798. Offers biomedical engineering (MSBME); engineering (ME); mechanical engineering (MS, PhD). *Program availability:* Part-time. *Faculty:* 15 full-time (2 women). *Students:* 25 full-time (4 women), 2 part-time (0 women); includes 3 minority (1 Asian, non-Hispanic/Latino; 2 Two or more races, non-Hispanic/Latino), 10 international. Average age 26. 47 applicants, 40% accepted, 11 enrolled. In 2018, 9 master's awarded. *Degree requirements:* For master's, thesis (for some programs), 30 credits including 24 coursework and 6 research (for MS); 33 coursework credits or 6 project credits and 27 coursework credits (for ME); for doctorate, thesis/dissertation (for some programs), 48 semester hours of approved course work and research hours beyond the master's degree. *Entrance requirements:* For master's, GRE. Additional exam requirements/recommendations for international students: Required—TOEFL (minimum score 550 paper-based; 80 iBT), IELTS (minimum score 6.5). *Application deadline:* For fall admission, 1/15 priority date for domestic and international students; for spring admission, 12/1 priority date for domestic and international students; for summer admission, 5/1 priority date for domestic students. Application fee: $50. Electronic applications accepted. *Expenses:* Contact institution. *Financial support:* In 2018–19, 33 students received support, including 17 research assistantships with full tuition reimbursements available (averaging $16,400 per year), 15 teaching assistantships with full tuition reimbursements available (averaging $17,100 per year); health care benefits and unspecified assistantships also available. Financial award application deadline: 1/15; financial award applicants required to submit FAFSA. *Faculty research:* Bone biomechanics, control strategies for multi-segmented motion, orthopedics and rehabilitation, film cooling for gas turbines, airfoils and combustor liners, convective heat transfer from realistic ice accretion roughness, fiber orientation prediction models for fiber-filled thermoplastic composites, modeling and simulation, the electrical and thermal behavior of carbon nanotube networks. *Unit head:* Dr. Dennis L. O'Neal, Dean, 254-710-3871, Fax: 254-710-3839, E-mail: dennis_oneal@baylor.edu. *Application contact:* Dr. Douglas E. Smith, Associate Professor and Graduate Program Director, 254-710-6830, Fax: 254-710-3360, E-mail: douglas_e_smith@baylor.edu.
Website: http://www.ecs.baylor.edu/mechanicalengineering/

Binghamton University, State University of New York, Graduate School, Thomas J. Watson School of Engineering and Applied Science, Department of Biomedical Engineering, Binghamton, NY 13902-6000. Offers MS, PhD. *Program availability:* Part-time, online learning. *Degree requirements:* For master's, thesis; for doctorate, comprehensive exam, thesis/dissertation. *Entrance requirements:* For master's and doctorate, GRE General Test. Additional exam requirements/recommendations for international students: Required—TOEFL (minimum score 550 paper-based; 80 iBT). Electronic applications accepted. *Expenses:* Contact institution.

Boston University, College of Engineering, Department of Biomedical Engineering, Boston, MA 02215. Offers biomedical engineering (M Eng, MS, PhD); MD/PhD. *Program availability:* Part-time. *Students:* Average age 24. 819 applicants, 34% accepted, 76 enrolled. In 2018, 51 master's, 13 doctorates awarded. Terminal master's awarded for partial completion of doctoral program. *Degree requirements:* For master's, thesis (for some programs); for doctorate, comprehensive exam, thesis/dissertation. *Entrance requirements:* For master's and doctorate, GRE General Test. Additional exam requirements/recommendations for international students: Required—TOEFL (minimum score 90 iBT), IELTS (minimum score 7). *Financial support:* Applicants required to submit FAFSA. *Faculty research:* Biomaterials, tissue engineering and drug delivery; modeling of biological systems; molecular bioengineering and biophysics; neuroscience and neural disease; synthetic biology and systems biology. *Unit head:* Dr. John White, Chairman, 617-353-2805, Fax: 617-353-6766. *Application contact:* Dr. John White, Chairman, 617-353-2805, Fax: 617-353-6766.
Website: http://www.bu.edu/bme/

Brown University, Graduate School, Division of Biology and Medicine, Department of Molecular Pharmacology, Physiology and Biotechnology, Providence, RI 02912. Offers biomedical engineering (Sc M, PhD); biotechnology (PhD); molecular pharmacology and physiology (PhD); MD/PhD. *Degree requirements:* For doctorate, thesis/dissertation, preliminary exam. *Entrance requirements:* For master's and doctorate, GRE General Test, GRE Subject Test. Additional exam requirements/recommendations for international students: Required—TOEFL. Electronic applications accepted. *Faculty research:* Structural biology, antiplatelet drugs, nicotinic receptor structure/function.

Brown University, Graduate School, School of Engineering and Division of Biology and Medicine, Center for Biomedical Engineering, Providence, RI 02912. Offers Sc M, PhD. *Degree requirements:* For master's, thesis.

California Polytechnic State University, San Luis Obispo, College of Engineering, Department of Biomedical Engineering, San Luis Obispo, CA 93407. Offers MS, MBA/ MS, MCRP/MS. *Program availability:* Part-time. *Faculty:* 6 full-time (2 women), 2 part-time/adjunct (0 women). *Students:* 32 full-time (17 women), 14 part-time (8 women); includes 15 minority (9 Asian, non-Hispanic/Latino; 3 Hispanic/Latino; 3 Two or more races, non-Hispanic/Latino). Average age 23. 56 applicants, 55% accepted, 19 enrolled. In 2018, 25 master's awarded. *Degree requirements:* For master's, thesis. *Entrance requirements:* For master's, GRE. Additional exam requirements/recommendations for international students: Required—TOEFL (minimum score 80 iBT). *Application deadline:* For fall admission, 3/1 for domestic and international students. Applications are processed on a rolling basis. Application fee: $55. Electronic applications accepted. *Expenses: Tuition, area resident:* Full-time $7176; part-time $4164 per year. Tuition, state resident: full-time $10,965. Tuition, nonresident: full-time $10,965. *Required fees:* $6336; $3711. *Financial support:* Fellowships, research assistantships, teaching assistantships, and scholarships/grants available. Financial award application deadline: 3/2; financial award applicants required to submit FAFSA. *Faculty research:* Biomedical engineering, materials engineering, water engineering, stem cell research. *Unit head:* Dr. David Clague, Graduate Coordinator, 805-756-5145, E-mail: dclague@calpoly.edu. *Application contact:* Dr. David Clague, Graduate Coordinator, 805-756-5145, E-mail: dclague@calpoly.edu.
Website: http://bmed.calpoly.edu/

Carleton University, Faculty of Graduate Studies, Faculty of Engineering and Design, Ottawa-Carleton Institute for Biomedical Engineering, Ottawa, ON K1S 5B6, Canada. Offers MA Sc. *Degree requirements:* For master's, thesis optional. *Entrance requirements:* For master's, honours degree. Additional exam requirements/ recommendations for international students: Required—TOEFL.

Carnegie Mellon University, Carnegie Institute of Technology, Biomedical and Health Engineering Program, Pittsburgh, PA 15213-3891. Offers bioengineering (MS, PhD); MD/PhD. *Degree requirements:* For master's, thesis; for doctorate, thesis/dissertation, qualifying exam. *Entrance requirements:* For master's and doctorate, GRE General Test. Additional exam requirements/recommendations for international students: Required—TOEFL. Electronic applications accepted. *Faculty research:* Cellular and molecular systematics, signal and image processing, materials and mechanics.

Case Western Reserve University, School of Graduate Studies, Case School of Engineering, Department of Biomedical Engineering, Cleveland, OH 44106. Offers MS, PhD, MD/MS, MD/PhD. *Program availability:* 100% online. *Faculty:* 21 full-time (2 women). *Students:* 117 full-time (49 women), 14 part-time (1 woman); includes 36 minority (28 Asian, non-Hispanic/Latino; 6 Hispanic/Latino; 2 Two or more races, non-Hispanic/Latino), 50 international. In 2018, 23 master's, 11 doctorates awarded. Terminal master's awarded for partial completion of doctoral program. *Degree requirements:* For master's, thesis (for some programs); for doctorate, thesis/ dissertation, qualifying exam, teaching experience. *Entrance requirements:* For master's and doctorate, GRE General Test. Additional exam requirements/recommendations for international students: Required—TOEFL. *Application deadline:* For fall admission, 4/1 priority date for domestic students; for spring admission, 10/1 priority date for domestic students. Applications are processed on a rolling basis. Application fee: $50. *Expenses: Tuition:* Full-time $45,168; part-time $1939 per credit hour. *Required fees:* $36; $18 per semester. $18 per semester. *Financial support:* In 2018–19, 95 students received support, including 28 fellowships with full tuition reimbursements available, 67 research assistantships with tuition reimbursements available; traineeships also available. Financial award application deadline: 2/15; financial award applicants required to submit FAFSA. *Faculty research:* Neuroengineering, biomaterials/tissue engineering, drug delivery, biomedical imaging, biomedical sensors/systems. *Total annual research expenditures:* $15.1 million. *Unit head:* Dr. Robert Kirsch, Department Chair, 216-368-3158, Fax: 216-368-4969, E-mail: robert.kirsch@case.edu. *Application contact:* Carol Adrine, Academic Operations Coordinator, 216-368-4094, Fax: 216-368-4969, E-mail: caa7@case.edu.
Website: http://engineering.case.edu/ebme/

The Catholic University of America, School of Engineering, Department of Biomedical Engineering, Washington, DC 20064. Offers MBE, PhD. *Program availability:* Part-time.

Faculty: 6 full-time (0 women), 2 part-time/adjunct (1 woman). *Students:* 9 full-time (7 women), 18 part-time (7 women); includes 6 minority (1 Black or African American, non-Hispanic/Latino; 3 Hispanic/Latino; 2 Two or more races, non-Hispanic/Latino), 14 international. Average age 29. 23 applicants, 91% accepted, 11 enrolled. In 2018, 10 master's, 5 doctorates awarded. *Degree requirements:* For master's, thesis or alternative; for doctorate, comprehensive exam, thesis/dissertation, oral exams. *Entrance requirements:* For master's, minimum GPA of 3.0, statement of purpose, official copies of academic transcripts, three letters of recommendation; for doctorate, minimum GPA of 3.4, statement of purpose, official copies of academic transcripts, three letters of recommendation. Additional exam requirements/recommendations for international students: Required—TOEFL (minimum score 550 paper-based; 80 iBT). *Application deadline:* For fall admission, 7/15 priority date for domestic students, 7/1 for international students; for spring admission, 11/15 priority date for domestic students, 11/1 for international students. Applications are processed on a rolling basis. Application fee: $55. Electronic applications accepted. *Expenses:* Contact institution. *Financial support:* Fellowships, research assistantships, teaching assistantships, Federal Work-Study, scholarships/grants, tuition waivers (full and partial), and unspecified assistantships available. Financial award application deadline: 2/1; financial award applicants required to submit FAFSA. *Faculty research:* Biomedical optics, robotics and human motor control, cell and tissue engineering, biomechanics, rehabilitation engineering. *Unit head:* Dr. Peter S. Lum, Chair, 202-319-5181, Fax: 202-319-4287, E-mail: lum@cua.edu. *Application contact:* Dr. Steven Brown, Director of Graduate Admissions, 202-319-5057, Fax: 202-319-6533, E-mail: cua-admissions@cua.edu. Website: http://biomedical.cua.edu/

City College of the City University of New York, Graduate School, Grove School of Engineering, Department of Biomedical Engineering, New York, NY 10031-9198. Offers MS, PhD. *Entrance requirements:* For master's, GRE. Additional exam requirements/recommendations for international students: Required—TOEFL (minimum score 550 paper-based).

Clemson University, Graduate School, College of Engineering, Computing and Applied Sciences, Department of Bioengineering, Clemson, SC 29634-0905. Offers bioengineering (MS, PhD); biomedical engineering (M Engr); medical device recycling and reprocessing (Certificate). *Program availability:* Part-time. *Faculty:* 27 full-time (9 women), 1 (woman) part-time/adjunct. *Students:* 122 full-time (53 women), 13 part-time (5 women); includes 19 minority (4 Black or African American, non-Hispanic/Latino; 8 Asian, non-Hispanic/Latino; 4 Hispanic/Latino; 3 Two or more races, non-Hispanic/Latino), 31 international. Average age 25. 159 applicants, 68% accepted, 62 enrolled. In 2018, 36 master's, 15 doctorates, 2 other advanced degrees awarded. *Degree requirements:* For master's, thesis optional; for doctorate, comprehensive exam, thesis/dissertation. *Entrance requirements:* For master's, doctorate, and Certificate, GRE General Test, unofficial transcripts, letters of recommendation. Additional exam requirements/recommendations for international students: Required—TOEFL (minimum score 100 paper-based; 100 iBT); Recommended—IELTS (minimum score 7), TSE (minimum score 54). *Application deadline:* For fall admission, 2/15 priority date for domestic students, 1/15 priority date for international students. Applications are processed on a rolling basis. Application fee: $80 ($90 for international students). Electronic applications accepted. *Expenses:* $6823 per semester full-time resident, $14023 per semester full-time non-resident, $833 per credit hour part-time resident, $1731 per credit hour part-time non-resident, online $1264 per credit hour, $4938 doctoral programs resident, $10405 doctoral programs non-resident, $1144 full-time graduate assistant, other fees may apply per session. *Financial support:* In 2018–19, 96 students received support, including 8 fellowships with full and partial tuition reimbursements available (averaging $1,958 per year), 45 research assistantships with full and partial tuition reimbursements available (averaging $18,444 per year), 30 teaching assistantships with full and partial tuition reimbursements available (averaging $18,803 per year); career-related internships or fieldwork and unspecified assistantships also available. Financial award application deadline: 2/15; financial award applicants required to submit FAFSA. *Faculty research:* Biomaterials, biomechanics, bioinstrumentation, tissue engineering, vascular engineering. *Total annual research expenditures:* $4.8 million. *Unit head:* Dr. Martine LaBerge, Department Chair, 864-656-5557, E-mail: laberge@clemson.edu. *Application contact:* Dr. Agneta Simionescu, Graduate Coordinator, 864-650-2575, E-mail: agneta@clemson.edu. Website: https://www.clemson.edu/cecas/departments/bioe/

Cleveland State University, College of Graduate Studies, Fenn College of Engineering, Department of Chemical and Biomedical Engineering, Program in Applied Biomedical Engineering, Cleveland, OH 44115. Offers D Eng. *Program availability:* Part-time, evening/weekend. *Faculty:* 8 full-time (1 woman), 1 part-time/adjunct (0 women). *Students:* 11 full-time (5 women), 5 part-time (3 women); includes 2 minority (both Black or African American, non-Hispanic/Latino), 11 international. Average age 29. 38 applicants, 18% accepted, 1 enrolled. In 2018, 2 doctorates awarded. *Entrance requirements:* For doctorate, GRE, minimum undergraduate GPA of 2.75, graduate 3.25; degree in engineering. Additional exam requirements/recommendations for international students: Required—TOEFL (minimum score 550 paper-based; 78 iBT). *Application deadline:* Applications are processed on a rolling basis. Application fee: $40. Electronic applications accepted. *Expenses:* Tuition, state resident: full-time $7232.55; part-time $6676 per credit hour. Tuition, nonresident: full-time $12,375. *International tuition:* $18,914 full-time. *Required fees:* $80; $80 $40. Tuition and fees vary according to program. *Financial support:* In 2018–19, 24 research assistantships with tuition reimbursements (averaging $11,800 per year) were awarded; career-related internships or fieldwork, scholarships/grants, and tuition waivers (full and partial) also available. Financial award application deadline: 3/30. *Faculty research:* Biomechanics, drug delivery systems, medical imaging, tissue engineering, artificial heart valves. *Unit head:* Dr. Dhananjai B. Shah, Director, 216-687-3569, Fax: 216-687-9220, E-mail: d.shah@csuohio.edu. *Application contact:* Becky Laird, Administrative Coordinator, 216-687-2571, Fax: 216-687-9220, E-mail: b.laird@csuohio.edu. Website: http://www.csuohio.edu/engineering/chemical/ABE/index.html

Colorado State University, Walter Scott, Jr. College of Engineering, School of Biomedical Engineering, Fort Collins, CO 80523-1376. Offers bioengineering (MS, PhD). *Program availability:* Part-time, online learning. Terminal master's awarded for partial completion of doctoral program. *Degree requirements:* For master's, thesis, minimum of two presentations in seminar series; for doctorate, thesis/dissertation, minimum of two presentations in seminar series. *Entrance requirements:* For master's and doctorate, GRE General Test, minimum GPA of 3.0, resume, statement of purpose, official transcripts, three letters of recommendation. Additional exam requirements/recommendations for international students: Required—TOEFL (minimum score 550 paper-based; 80 iBT), IELTS (minimum score 6). Electronic applications accepted. *Expenses:* Contact institution. *Faculty research:* Regenerative and rehabilitative medicine, imaging and diagnostics, medical devices and therapeutics.

Columbia University, Fu Foundation School of Engineering and Applied Science, Department of Biomedical Engineering, New York, NY 10027. Offers MS, Eng Sc D, PhD. *Program availability:* Part-time, online learning. *Degree requirements:* For doctorate, thesis/dissertation, qualifying exam. *Entrance requirements:* For master's and doctorate, GRE General Test. Additional exam requirements/recommendations for

international students: Required—TOEFL, IELTS, PTE. Electronic applications accepted. *Faculty research:* Biomechanics, biosignal and biomedical imaging, cellular and tissue engineering.

Cornell University, Graduate School, Graduate Fields of Engineering, Field of Biomedical Engineering, Ithaca, NY 14853. Offers M Eng, MS, PhD. *Degree requirements:* For master's, thesis; for doctorate, comprehensive exam, thesis/dissertation. *Entrance requirements:* For master's and doctorate, GRE General Test, GRE Subject Test (engineering), 3 letters of recommendation. Additional exam requirements/recommendations for international students: Required—TOEFL (minimum score 77 iBT). Electronic applications accepted. *Faculty research:* Biomaterials; biomedical instrumentation and diagnostics; biomedical mechanics; drug delivery, design, and metabolism.

Dalhousie University, Faculty of Engineering and Faculty of Medicine, School of Biomedical Engineering, Halifax, NS B3H3J5, Canada. Offers MA Sc, PhD. *Entrance requirements:* Additional exam requirements/recommendations for international students: Required—TOEFL, IELTS, CANTEST, CAEL, or Michigan English Language Assessment Battery. Electronic applications accepted.

Dartmouth College, Thayer School of Engineering, Program in Engineering in Medicine/Biomedical Engineering, Hanover, NH 03755. Offers M Eng, MS, PhD. *Faculty research:* Imaging, physiological modeling, cancer hyperthermia and radiation therapy, bioelectromagnetics, biomedical optics and lasers.

Drexel University, School of Biomedical Engineering, Science and Health Systems, Program in Biomedical Engineering, Philadelphia, PA 19104-2875. Offers MS, PhD. *Degree requirements:* For master's, thesis (for some programs); for doctorate, thesis/dissertation. Electronic applications accepted.

Duke University, Graduate School, Pratt School of Engineering, Department of Biomedical Engineering, Durham, NC 27708. Offers M Eng, MS, PhD. *Degree requirements:* For doctorate, thesis/dissertation. *Entrance requirements:* For master's and doctorate, GRE General Test. Additional exam requirements/recommendations for international students: Required—TOEFL (minimum score 90 iBT), IELTS (minimum score 7). Electronic applications accepted.

Duke University, Graduate School, Pratt School of Engineering, Master of Engineering Program, Durham, NC 27708-0271. Offers biomedical engineering (M Eng); civil engineering (M Eng); computational mechanics and scientific computing (M Eng); electrical and computer engineering (M Eng); environmental engineering (M Eng); materials science and engineering (M Eng); mechanical engineering (M Eng); photonics and optical sciences (M Eng); risk engineering (M Eng). *Program availability:* Part-time. *Entrance requirements:* For master's, GRE General Test, resume, 3 letters of recommendation, statement of purpose, transcripts. Additional exam requirements/recommendations for international students: Required—TOEFL. Electronic applications accepted.

East Carolina University, Graduate School, College of Engineering and Technology, Department of Engineering, Greenville, NC 27858-4353. Offers biomedical engineering (MS). *Expenses: Tuition, area resident:* Full-time $4749. Tuition, state resident: full-time $4749. Tuition, nonresident: full-time $17,898. *International tuition:* $17,898 full-time. *Required fees:* $2787. Part-time tuition and fees vary according to course load and program. *Unit head:* Dr. Barbara Muller-Borer, Chair, 252-744-2546, E-mail: mullerborerb@ecu.edu. *Application contact:* Graduate School Admissions, 252-328-6012, Fax: 252-328-6071, E-mail: gradschool@ecu.edu. Website: http://www.ecu.edu/cs-cet/engineering/index.cfm

École Polytechnique de Montréal, Graduate Programs, Institute of Biomedical Engineering, Montréal, QC H3C 3A7, Canada. Offers M Sc A, PhD, DESS. M Sc A and PhD programs offered jointly with Université de Montréal. *Program availability:* Part-time. *Degree requirements:* For master's, one foreign language, thesis; for doctorate, one foreign language, thesis/dissertation. *Entrance requirements:* For master's, minimum GPA of 2.75; for doctorate, minimum GPA of 3.0. *Faculty research:* Cardiac electrophysiology, biomedical instrumentation, biomechanics, biomaterials, medical imagery.

Florida Agricultural and Mechanical University, Division of Graduate Studies, Research, and Continuing Education, FAMU-FSU College of Engineering, Department of Chemical and Biomedical Engineering, Tallahassee, FL 32307-3200. Offers biomedical engineering (MS, PhD); chemical engineering (MS, PhD). *Degree requirements:* For master's, thesis optional; for doctorate, thesis/dissertation, paper presentation at professional meeting. *Entrance requirements:* For master's, GRE General Test, minimum GPA of 3.3, letters of recommendation (3); for doctorate, minimum GPA of 3.3. Additional exam requirements/recommendations for international students: Required—TOEFL (minimum score 550 paper-based). *Faculty research:* Cellular signaling, cancer therapy, drug delivery, cellular and tissue engineering, brain physiology.

Florida Institute of Technology, College of Engineering and Science, Program in Biomedical Engineering, Melbourne, FL 32901-6975. Offers MS, PhD. *Program availability:* Part-time. *Students:* 25 full-time (10 women), 2 part-time (0 women); includes 4 minority (2 Black or African American, non-Hispanic/Latino; 1 Asian, non-Hispanic/Latino; 1 Hispanic/Latino), 14 international. Average age 28. 15 applicants, 93% accepted, 4 enrolled. In 2018, 7 master's awarded. Terminal master's awarded for partial completion of doctoral program. *Degree requirements:* For master's, thesis optional, thesis or supervised project with 6 credits of elective courses; for doctorate, comprehensive exam, thesis/dissertation, 42 credit hours beyond the master's degree, minimum of GPA of 3.2. *Entrance requirements:* For master's, GRE, 3 letters of recommendation, resume, statement of objectives; for doctorate, GRE, minimum GPA of 3.2, 3 letters of recommendation, resume, statement of objectives. Additional exam requirements/recommendations for international students: Required—TOEFL (minimum score 550 paper-based; 79 iBT). *Application deadline:* For fall admission, 4/1 priority date for international students; for spring admission, 9/30 for international students. Applications are processed on a rolling basis. Application fee: $50. Electronic applications accepted. *Expenses: Tuition:* Full-time $22,338; part-time $1241 per credit hour. Tuition and fees vary according to degree level, campus/location and program. *Financial support:* In 2018–19, 9 research assistantships with partial tuition reimbursements, 6 teaching assistantships with partial tuition reimbursements were awarded; career-related internships or fieldwork, institutionally sponsored loans, tuition waivers (partial), unspecified assistantships, and tuition remissions also available. Support available to part-time students. Financial award application deadline: 3/1; financial award applicants required to submit FAFSA. *Faculty research:* techniques and devices for detection and therapy of cardiovascular diseases, cancer, and tumor tissues; developing bioactive materials for load-bearing orthopedic devices; and implanting micro-stimulators in nerves for restoring function. *Unit head:* Dr. Ted Conway, Department Head, 321-674-8491, Fax: 321-674-7270, E-mail: tconway@fit.edu. *Application contact:* Mike Perry, Executive Director of Admissions, 321-674-7127, E-mail: perrymj@fit.edu. Website: https://www.fit.edu/programs/biomedical-engineering-ms/

Biomedical Engineering

Florida International University, College of Engineering and Computing, Department of Biomedical Engineering, Miami, FL 33175. Offers MS, PhD. *Program availability:* Part-time, evening/weekend. *Faculty:* 15 full-time (3 women), 2 part-time/adjunct (0 women). *Students:* 57 full-time (26 women), 9 part-time (2 women); includes 30 minority (3 Black or African American, non-Hispanic/Latino; 7 Asian, non-Hispanic/Latino; 17 Hispanic/Latino; 3 Two or more races, non-Hispanic/Latino), 26 international. Average age 28. 96 applicants, 49% accepted, 22 enrolled. In 2018, 9 master's, 1 doctorate awarded. *Degree requirements:* For master's, thesis; for doctorate, comprehensive exam, thesis/dissertation. *Entrance requirements:* For master's, GRE General Test (minimum combined score 1000, verbal 350, quantitative 650), minimum GPA of 3.0; for doctorate, GRE General Test (minimum combined score 1150, verbal 450, quantitative 700), minimum GPA of 3.0, letter of intent, letters of recommendation. Additional exam requirements/recommendations for international students: Required—TOEFL (minimum score 550 paper-based; 80 iBT). *Application deadline:* For fall admission, 6/1 for domestic students, 4/1 for international students; for spring admission, 10/1 for domestic students, 9/1 for international students. Applications are processed on a rolling basis. Application fee: $30. Electronic applications accepted. *Financial support:* Institutionally sponsored loans, scholarships/grants, and unspecified assistantships available. Financial award application deadline: 3/1; financial award applicants required to submit FAFSA. *Faculty research:* Bioimaging and biosignal processing, bioinstrumentation, devices and sensors, biomaterials and bio-nanotechnology, cellular and tissue engineering. *Unit head:* Dr. Ranu Jung, Chair, 305-348-3722, E-mail: ranu.jung@fiu.edu. *Application contact:* Nanett Rojas, Manager, Admissions Operations, 305-348-7464, Fax: 305-348-7441, E-mail: gradadm@fiu.edu.
Website: http://cec.fiu.edu/

Florida State University, The Graduate School, FAMU-FSU College of Engineering, Department of Chemical and Biomedical Engineering, Tallahassee, FL 32310-6046. Offers biomedical engineering (MS, PhD); chemical engineering (MS, PhD). *Program availability:* Part-time. Terminal master's awarded for partial completion of doctoral program. *Degree requirements:* For master's, thesis (for some programs); for doctorate, comprehensive exam, thesis/dissertation, qualifying exam. *Entrance requirements:* For master's, GRE General Test (recommended minimum scores: verbal 151/8th percentile; quantitative: 158/75th percentile), BS in chemical engineering or other physical science/engineering, minimum GPA of 3.0; for doctorate, GRE General Test (recommended minimum scores: verbal 151/8th percentile; quantitative: 158/75th percentile), BS in chemical engineering or other physical science/engineering, minimum GPA of 3.0, or MS in chemical or biomedical engineering. Additional exam requirements/recommendations for international students: Required—TOEFL (minimum score 550 paper-based; 80 iBT); Recommended—IELTS (minimum score 6.5). Electronic applications accepted. *Expenses:* Contact institution. *Faculty research:* Macromolecular transport and reaction; polymer characterization and processing; solid NMR-MRI for solid state spectroscopy and cell microscopy; protein, cell, and tissue engineering; electrochemical and fuel cell engineering.

The George Washington University, School of Engineering and Applied Science, Department of Biomedical Engineering, Washington, DC 20052. Offers biomedical engineering (MS, PhD); regulatory biomedical engineering (MS). MS in regulatory biomedical engineering offered in partnership with the School of Medicine and Health Sciences Regulatory Affairs Program. *Faculty:* 5 full-time (2 women), 2 part-time/adjunct (1 woman). *Students:* 40 full-time (23 women), 23 part-time (10 women); includes 19 minority (3 Black or African American, non-Hispanic/Latino; 9 Asian, non-Hispanic/Latino; 6 Hispanic/Latino; 1 Two or more races, non-Hispanic/Latino), 26 international. Average age 26. 155 applicants, 68% accepted, 23 enrolled. In 2018, 20 master's awarded. *Unit head:* Igor Efimov, Chair, 202-994-2152. *Application contact:* Adina Lav, Marketing, Recruiting and Admissions, 202-994-5827, Fax: 202-994-0909, E-mail: engineering@gwu.edu.

Georgia Institute of Technology, Graduate Studies, College of Engineering, Wallace H. Coulter Department of Biomedical Engineering, Atlanta, GA 30332-0001. Offers PhD, MD/PhD. PhD offered jointly with Emory University (Georgia) and Peking University (China). *Program availability:* Part-time. *Degree requirements:* For doctorate, thesis/dissertation. *Entrance requirements:* For doctorate, GRE. Additional exam requirements/recommendations for international students: Required—TOEFL (minimum score 600 paper-based; 100 iBT). Electronic applications accepted. *Expenses:* Contact institution. *Faculty research:* Biomechanics and tissue engineering, bioinstrumentation and medical imaging.

Harvard University, Graduate School of Arts and Sciences, Department of Physics, Cambridge, MA 02138. Offers experimental physics (PhD); medical engineering/medical physics (PhD), including applied physics, engineering sciences, physics; theoretical physics (PhD). *Degree requirements:* For doctorate, thesis/dissertation, final exams, laboratory experience. *Entrance requirements:* For doctorate, GRE General Test, GRE Subject Test. Additional exam requirements/recommendations for international students: Required—TOEFL. *Faculty research:* Particle physics, condensed matter physics, atomic physics.

Illinois Institute of Technology, Graduate College, Armour College of Engineering, Department of Biomedical Engineering, Chicago, IL 60616. Offers MAS, MS, PhD. *Program availability:* Part-time. *Degree requirements:* For doctorate, comprehensive exam, thesis/dissertation. *Entrance requirements:* For master's and doctorate, GRE (minimum 1800 combined; 1200 quantitative and verbal; 3.0 analytical writing), minimum cumulative undergraduate GPA of 3.2. Electronic applications accepted. *Faculty research:* Cell and tissue engineering, medical imaging, neural engineering.

Indiana University–Purdue University Indianapolis, School of Engineering and Technology, Department of Biomedical Engineering, Indianapolis, IN 46202. Offers MS, PhD. *Program availability:* Part-time, evening/weekend. *Degree requirements:* For master's, thesis optional. *Entrance requirements:* For master's, GRE, minimum B average; for doctorate, GRE General Test. Additional exam requirements/recommendations for international students: Required—TOEFL. *Expenses:* Contact institution.

Johns Hopkins University, Engineering Program for Professionals, Part-time Program in Applied Biomedical Engineering, Baltimore, MD 21218. Offers MS, Post-Master's Certificate. *Program availability:* Part-time, evening/weekend, 100% online, blended/hybrid learning. *Faculty:* 4 full-time (2 women), 9 part-time/adjunct (4 women). *Students:* 65 part-time (27 women). 64 applicants, 28% accepted, 12 enrolled. In 2018, 27 master's, 1 other advanced degree awarded. *Entrance requirements:* Additional exam requirements/recommendations for international students: Required—TOEFL (minimum score 600 paper-based; 100 iBT). *Application deadline:* Applications are processed on a rolling basis. Application fee: $75. Electronic applications accepted. *Unit head:* Dr. Eileen Haase, Program Chair, 443-778-6201, E-mail: ehaase1@jhu.edu. *Application contact:* Doug Schiller, Admissions Director, 410-516-2300, Fax: 410-579-8049, E-mail: schiller@jhu.edu.
Website: http://www.ep.jhu.edu

Johns Hopkins University, G. W. C. Whiting School of Engineering and School of Medicine, Department of Biomedical Engineering, Baltimore, MD 21205. Offers bioengineering innovation and design (MSE); biomedical engineering (MSE, PhD). *Faculty:* 34 full-time (9 women). *Students:* 316 full-time (133 women). 337 applicants, 37% accepted, 57 enrolled. In 2018, 57 master's awarded. Terminal master's awarded for partial completion of doctoral program. *Degree requirements:* For master's, thesis; for doctorate, comprehensive exam, thesis/dissertation. *Entrance requirements:* For master's and doctorate, GRE General Test, 3 letters of recommendation, statement of purpose, transcripts. Additional exam requirements/recommendations for international students: Required—TOEFL (minimum score 600 paper-based, 100 iBT) or IELTS (7). *Application deadline:* For fall admission, 1/4 for domestic and international students. Application fee: $75. Electronic applications accepted. *Financial support:* In 2018–19, 198 students received support, including 52 fellowships with partial tuition reimbursements available (averaging $33,383 per year), 146 research assistantships with partial tuition reimbursements available (averaging $32,894 per year); teaching assistantships, Federal Work-Study, institutionally sponsored loans, scholarships/grants, health care benefits, tuition waivers (full), and unspecified assistantships also available. Financial award application deadline: 1/15; financial award applicants required to submit FAFSA. *Faculty research:* Systems neuroscience and neuroengineering, molecular and cellular systems biology, biomedical imaging, cell and tissue engineering, cardiovascular systems engineering. *Unit head:* Dr. Michael Miller, Director, 410-516-2039, Fax: 410-516-4771, E-mail: mim@cis.jhu.edu. *Application contact:* Samuel Bourne, Academic Program Administrator, 410-516-8482, Fax: 410-516-4771, E-mail: sbourne@jhu.edu.
Website: http://www.bme.jhu.edu/

Lawrence Technological University, College of Engineering, Southfield, MI 48075-1058. Offers architectural engineering (MS); automotive engineering (MS); biomedical engineering (MS); civil engineering (MA, MS, PhD), including environmental engineering (MS), geotechnical engineering (MS), structural engineering (MS), transportation engineering (MS), water resource engineering (MS); construction engineering management (MA); electrical and computer engineering (MS); engineering management (MEM); engineering technology (MS); fire engineering (MS); industrial engineering (MS), including healthcare systems; manufacturing systems (ME); mechanical engineering (MS, DE, PhD), including automotive engineering (MS), energy engineering (MS), manufacturing (DE), solid mechanics (MS), thermal/fluid systems (MS); mechatronic systems engineering (MS). *Program availability:* Part-time, evening/weekend. Terminal master's awarded for partial completion of doctoral program. *Degree requirements:* For master's, thesis optional; for doctorate, comprehensive exam, thesis/dissertation optional. *Entrance requirements:* Additional exam requirements/recommendations for international students: Required—TOEFL (minimum score 550 paper-based; 79 iBT), IELTS (minimum score 6.5). Electronic applications accepted. *Faculty research:* Innovative infrastructure and building structures and materials; connectivity and mobility; automotive systems modeling, simulation and testing; biomedical devices and materials; building mechanical/electrical systems.

Louisiana Tech University, Graduate School, College of Engineering and Science, Ruston, LA 71272. Offers applied physics (MS); biomedical engineering (PhD); computer science (MS); engineering (MS, PhD), including cyberspace engineering (PhD), engineering education (PhD), engineering physics (PhD), materials and infrastructure systems (PhD), micro/nanoscale systems (PhD); engineering and technology management (MS); mathematics (MS); molecular science and nanotechnology (MS, PhD). *Program availability:* Part-time-only. Terminal master's awarded for partial completion of doctoral program. *Degree requirements:* For master's, thesis (for some programs); for doctorate, thesis/dissertation. *Entrance requirements:* For master's and Graduate Certificate, GRE General Test, minimum GPA of 3.0 in last 60 hours. Additional exam requirements/recommendations for international students: Required—TOEFL (minimum score 550 paper-based; 80 iBT), IELTS (minimum score 6.5). Electronic applications accepted. *Faculty research:* Trenchless technology, micromanufacturing, radionuclide transport, microbial liquefaction, hazardous waste treatment.

Marquette University, Graduate School, College of Engineering, Department of Biomedical Engineering, Milwaukee, WI 53201-1881. Offers biocomputing (ME); bioimaging (ME); bioinstrumentation (ME); bioinstrumentation/computers (MS, PhD); biomechanics (ME); biomechanics/biomaterials (MS, PhD); biorehabilitation (ME); functional imaging (PhD); healthcare technologies management (MS); rehabilitation bioengineering (PhD); systems physiology (MS, PhD). *Program availability:* Part-time, evening/weekend. Terminal master's awarded for partial completion of doctoral program. *Degree requirements:* For master's, comprehensive exam, thesis; for doctorate, comprehensive exam, thesis/dissertation, dissertation defense, qualifying exam. *Entrance requirements:* For master's, GRE General Test, minimum GPA of 3.0, official transcripts from all current and previous colleges/universities except Marquette, three letters of recommendation, brief statement of purpose that includes proposed area of research specialization, interview with program director (for ME), one year of post-baccalaureate professional work experience; for doctorate, GRE General Test, minimum GPA of 3.0, official transcripts from all current and previous colleges/universities except Marquette, three letters of recommendation, brief statement of purpose that includes proposed area of research specialization. Additional exam requirements/recommendations for international students: Required—TOEFL (minimum score 530 paper-based). Electronic applications accepted. *Faculty research:* Cell and organ physiology, signal processing, gait analysis, orthopedic rehabilitation engineering, telemedicine.

Massachusetts Institute of Technology, School of Engineering, Department of Biological Engineering, Cambridge, MA 02139. Offers applied biosciences (PhD, Sc D); bioengineering (PhD, Sc D); biological engineering (PhD, Sc D); biomedical engineering (M Eng); toxicology (SM); SM/MBA. Terminal master's awarded for partial completion of doctoral program. *Degree requirements:* For master's, thesis; for doctorate, comprehensive exam, thesis/dissertation. *Entrance requirements:* For master's and doctorate, GRE General Test. Additional exam requirements/recommendations for international students: Required—IELTS. Electronic applications accepted. *Expenses: Tuition:* Full-time $51,520; part-time $800 per credit hour. *Required fees:* $312. *Faculty research:* Biomaterials; biophysics; cell and tissue engineering; computational modeling of biological and physiological systems; discovery and delivery of molecular therapeutics; new tools for genomics; functional genomics; proteomics and glycomics; macromolecular biochemistry and biophysics; molecular, cell and tissue biomechanics; synthetic biology; systems biology.

Massachusetts Institute of Technology, School of Engineering, Harvard-MIT Health Sciences and Technology Program, Cambridge, MA 02139. Offers health sciences and technology (SM, PhD, Sc D), including bioastronautics (PhD, Sc D), bioinformatics and integrative genomics (PhD, Sc D), medical engineering and medical physics (PhD, Sc D), speech and hearing bioscience and technology (PhD, Sc D). Terminal master's awarded for partial completion of doctoral program. *Degree requirements:* For doctorate, comprehensive exam, thesis/dissertation. *Entrance requirements:* For doctorate, GRE General Test. Additional exam requirements/recommendations for international students: Required—TOEFL, IELTS. Electronic applications accepted. *Expenses: Tuition:* Full-time $51,520; part-time $800 per credit hour. *Required fees:* $312. *Faculty research:* Biomedical imaging, drug delivery, medical devices, medical diagnostics, regenerative biomedical technologies.

Mayo Clinic Graduate School of Biomedical Sciences, Program in Biomedical Engineering and Physiology, Rochester, MN 55905. Offers MS, PhD. *Faculty:* 77 full-time (10 women). *Students:* 26 full-time (12 women); includes 2 minority (1 American Indian or Alaska Native, non-Hispanic/Latino; 1 Asian, non-Hispanic/Latino). 42 applicants, 36% accepted, 5 enrolled. Terminal master's awarded for partial completion of doctoral program. *Degree requirements:* For master's, thesis; for doctorate, comprehensive exam, thesis/dissertation, oral defense of dissertation, qualifying oral and written exam. *Entrance requirements:* For doctorate, GRE, 1 year of chemistry, biology, calculus, and physics; courses in quantitative science and engineering, e.g., signal processing, computer science, instrumentation (encouraged). Additional exam requirements/recommendations for international students: Required—TOEFL. *Application deadline:* For fall admission, 12/1 for domestic and international students. Application fee: $50. Electronic applications accepted. *Financial support:* Fellowships with full tuition reimbursements available. *Faculty research:* Biomechanics, biomedical imaging, molecular biophysics, physiology, likelihood-based metabolic modeling, tissue engineering and tendon surgery in the hand, role of neurotrophic signaling in restoration of respiratory function after cervical spinal cord injury. *Unit head:* Dr. Carlos B. Mantilla, Director, 507-255-8544, E-mail: mantilla.carlos@mayo.edu. *Application contact:* Sarah E. Giese, Admissions Coordinator, 507-538-1160, E-mail: phd.training@mayo.edu. Website: http://www.mayo.edu/mgs/

McGill University, Faculty of Graduate and Postdoctoral Studies, Faculty of Medicine, Department of Biomedical Engineering, Montréal, QC H3A 2T5, Canada. Offers M Eng, PhD.

Mercer University, Graduate Studies, Macon Campus, School of Engineering, Macon, GA 31207. Offers biomedical engineering (MSE); computer engineering (MSE); electrical engineering (MSE); engineering management (MSE); environmental engineering (MSE); environmental systems (MS); mechanical engineering (MSE); software engineering (MSE); software systems (MS); technical communications management (MS); technical management (MS). *Program availability:* Part-time-only, evening/weekend, online learning. *Degree requirements:* For master's, thesis or alternative. *Entrance requirements:* For master's, GRE (minimum score 300), minimum undergraduate GPA of 3.0. Additional exam requirements/recommendations for international students: Required—TOEFL (minimum score 550 paper-based; 80 iBT). *Expenses:* Contact institution. *Faculty research:* Designing prostheses and orthotics, oxygen transfer and limitations in biological systems, low-cost groundwater development, lung airway and transport, autonomous mobile robots.

Michigan Technological University, Graduate School, College of Engineering, Department of Biomedical Engineering, Houghton, MI 49931. Offers MS, PhD. *Program availability:* Part-time. *Faculty:* 17 full-time (6 women), 4 part-time/adjunct. *Students:* 34 full-time (10 women), 3 part-time; includes 1 minority (Black or African American, non-Hispanic/Latino), 21 international. Average age 26. 104 applicants, 30% accepted, 15 enrolled. In 2018, 10 master's, 1 doctorate awarded. *Degree requirements:* For master's, comprehensive exam (for some programs), thesis (for some programs); for doctorate, comprehensive exam, thesis/dissertation. *Entrance requirements:* For master's, GRE (recommended for students with a Michigan Tech degree), statement of purpose, personal statement, official transcripts, 3 letters of recommendation, resume/curriculum vitae; for doctorate, GRE, statement of purpose, personal statement, official transcripts, 3 letters of recommendation, resume/curriculum vitae. Additional exam requirements/recommendations for international students: Required—TOEFL (recommended minimum score 110 iBT) or IELTS (recommended minimum score of 8.0). *Application deadline:* Applications are processed on a rolling basis. Electronic applications accepted. *Expenses:* $1,143 per credit. *Financial support:* In 2018–19, 32 students received support, including 4 fellowships with tuition reimbursements available (averaging $16,590 per year), 11 research assistantships with tuition reimbursements available (averaging $16,590 per year), 5 teaching assistantships with tuition reimbursements available (averaging $16,590 per year); career-related internships or fieldwork, Federal Work-Study, scholarships/grants, health care benefits, unspecified assistantships, and cooperative program also available. Financial award applicants required to submit FAFSA. *Faculty research:* Biomaterials/tissue engineering, physiology measurement and biosensors, biomechanics, mechanotransduction, biomedical optics, micro devices. *Total annual research expenditures:* $889,106. *Unit head:* Dr. Sean J. Kirkpatrick, Chair, 906-487-2167, Fax: 906-487-1717, E-mail: sjkirkpa@mtu.edu. *Application contact:* Coreen Dompier, Department Coordinator, 906-487-2772, Fax: 906-487-1717, E-mail: biomed@mtu.edu. Website: http://www.mtu.edu/biomedical

Mississippi State University, College of Agriculture and Life Sciences, Department of Agricultural and Biological Engineering, Mississippi State, MS 39762. Offers biological engineering (MS, PhD); biomedical engineering (MS, PhD). *Faculty:* 15 full-time (5 women). *Students:* 30 full-time (14 women), 7 part-time (3 women); includes 4 minority (2 Black or African American, non-Hispanic/Latino; 2 Asian, non-Hispanic/Latino), 13 international. Average age 29. 23 applicants, 70% accepted, 11 enrolled. In 2018, 7 master's, 1 doctorate awarded. *Degree requirements:* For master's, thesis (for some programs); for doctorate, thesis/dissertation, preliminary exam. *Entrance requirements:* For master's, GRE General Test, minimum undergraduate GPA of 2.75 (3.0 for biomedical engineering); for doctorate, GRE General Test, minimum GPA of 3.0 (biomedical engineering). Additional exam requirements/recommendations for international students: Required—TOEFL (minimum score 550 paper-based; 79 iBT); Recommended—IELTS (minimum score 6.5). *Application deadline:* For fall admission, 7/1 for domestic students, 5/1 for international students; for spring admission, 11/1 for domestic students, 9/1 for international students. Applications are processed on a rolling basis. Application fee: $60 ($80 for international students). Electronic applications accepted. *Expenses:* Tuition, state resident: full-time $8450; part-time $360.59 per credit hour. Tuition, nonresident: full-time $23,140; part-time $969.09 per credit hour. *Required fees:* $110. One-time fee: $55 full-time. Part-time tuition and fees vary according to course load, degree level, campus/location and reciprocity agreements. *Financial support:* In 2018–19, 13 research assistantships with partial tuition reimbursements (averaging $16,989 per year), 4 teaching assistantships (averaging $17,423 per year) were awarded; Federal Work-Study, institutionally sponsored loans, and unspecified assistantships also available. Financial award application deadline: 4/1; financial award applicants required to submit FAFSA. *Faculty research:* Bioenvironmental engineering, bioinstrumentation, biomechanics/biomaterials, precision agriculture, tissue engineering, ergonomics human factors, biosimulation and modeling. *Total annual research expenditures:* $85.6 million. *Unit head:* Dr. Jonathan Pote, Professor/Head/Executive Director, 662-325-3280, Fax: 662-325-3853, E-mail: jpote@abe.msstate.edu. *Application contact:* Ryan King, Admissions and Enrollment Assistant, 662-325-8951, E-mail: rjk101@grad.msstate.edu. Website: http://www.abe.msstate.edu/

New Jersey Institute of Technology, Newark College of Engineering, Newark, NJ 07102. Offers biomedical engineering (MS, PhD); biopharmaceutical engineering (MS); chemical engineering (MS, PhD); civil engineering (MS, PhD); computer engineering (MS); critical infrastructure systems (MS); electrical engineering (MS, PhD); engineering management (MS); engineering science (MS); environmental engineering (MS, PhD); healthcare systems management (MS); industrial engineering (MS, PhD); internet engineering (MS); manufacturing systems engineering (MS); materials science & engineering (PhD); materials science and engineering (MS); mechanical engineering (MS, PhD); occupational safety and health engineering (MS). *Program availability:* Part-time, evening/weekend. *Faculty:* 147 full-time (26 women), 133 part-time/adjunct (16 women). *Students:* 690 full-time (163 women), 594 part-time (130 women); includes 427 minority (79 Black or African American, non-Hispanic/Latino; 181 Asian, non-Hispanic/Latino; 140 Hispanic/Latino; 27 Two or more races, non-Hispanic/Latino), 553 international. Average age 27. 2,334 applicants, 57% accepted, 452 enrolled. In 2018, 418 master's, 31 doctorates awarded. Terminal master's awarded for partial completion of doctoral program. *Degree requirements:* For master's, thesis (for some programs); for doctorate, thesis/dissertation. *Entrance requirements:* For master's, GRE General Test, minimum GPA 2.8, personal statement, 1 letter of recommendation, transcripts; for doctorate, GRE General Test, minimum GPA of 3.5, personal statement, 3 letters of recommendation, transcripts. Additional exam requirements/recommendations for international students: Required—TOEFL (minimum score 550 paper-based; 79 iBT), IELTS (minimum score 6.5). *Application deadline:* For fall admission, 6/1 priority date for domestic students, 5/1 priority date for international students; for spring admission, 11/15 priority date for domestic and international students. Applications are processed on a rolling basis. Application fee: $75. Electronic applications accepted. *Expenses:* $22,690 per year (in-state), $32,136 per year (out-of-state). *Financial support:* In 2018–19, 396 students received support, including 52 fellowships with full tuition reimbursements available (averaging $22,000 per year), 113 research assistantships with full tuition reimbursements available (averaging $22,000 per year), 101 teaching assistantships with full tuition reimbursements available (averaging $22,000 per year); career-related internships or fieldwork, Federal Work-Study, scholarships/grants, and unspecified assistantships also available. Financial award application deadline: 1/15. *Faculty research:* Nonlinear signal processing, intelligent medical image analysis, calibration issues in coherent localization, computer-aided design, neural network for tool wear measurement. *Total annual research expenditures:* $41.7 million. *Unit head:* Dr. Moshe Kam, Dean, 973-596-5534, Fax: 973-596-2316, E-mail: moshe.kam@njit.edu. *Application contact:* Stephen Eck, Director of Admissions, 973-596-3300, Fax: 973-596-3461, E-mail: admissions@njit.edu. Website: http://engineering.njit.edu/

Northwestern University, McCormick School of Engineering and Applied Science, Department of Biomedical Engineering, Evanston, IL 60208. Offers MS, PhD. Admissions and degrees offered through The Graduate School. *Program availability:* Part-time. Terminal master's awarded for partial completion of doctoral program. *Degree requirements:* For master's, comprehensive exam, thesis (for some programs); for doctorate, comprehensive exam, thesis/dissertation. *Entrance requirements:* For master's and doctorate, GRE General Test. Additional exam requirements/recommendations for international students: Required—TOEFL (minimum score 577 paper-based; 90 iBT), IELTS (minimum score 7). Electronic applications accepted. *Faculty research:* Imaging and biophotonics; biomaterials and regenerative medicine; neural engineering and rehabilitation.

The Ohio State University, Graduate School, College of Engineering, Department of Biomedical Engineering, Columbus, OH 43210. Offers MS, PhD. *Program availability:* Evening/weekend. *Faculty:* 24. *Students:* 80 (32 women). Average age 26. In 2018, 20 master's, 8 doctorates awarded. *Entrance requirements:* For master's and doctorate, GRE General Test. Additional exam requirements/recommendations for international students: Required—TOEFL (minimum score 550 paper-based; 79 iBT), Michigan English Language Assessment Battery (minimum score 82); Recommended—IELTS (minimum score 7). *Application deadline:* For fall admission, 12/13 priority date for domestic students, 11/29 priority date for international students; for spring admission, 11/1 for domestic and international students. Applications are processed on a rolling basis. Application fee: $60 ($70 for international students). Electronic applications accepted. *Financial support:* Fellowships, research assistantships, career-related internships or fieldwork, Federal Work-Study, and institutionally sponsored loans available. Support available to part-time students. *Unit head:* Dr. Samir Ghadiali, Chair, 614-292-7742, E-mail: ghadiali.1@osu.edu. *Application contact:* Graduate and Professional Admissions, 614-292-9444, Fax: 614-292-3895, E-mail: gpadmissions@osu.edu. Website: http://bme.osu.edu

Ohio University, Graduate College, Russ College of Engineering and Technology, Department of Chemical and Biomolecular Engineering, Program in Biomedical Engineering, Athens, OH 45701-2979. Offers MS. *Program availability:* Part-time. *Degree requirements:* For master's, thesis. *Entrance requirements:* For master's, GRE General Test. Additional exam requirements/recommendations for international students: Required—TOEFL (minimum score 590 paper-based; 96 iBT), IELTS (minimum score 7). Electronic applications accepted. *Faculty research:* Molecular mechanisms of human disease, molecular therapeutics, biomedical information analysis and management, image analysis, biomechanics.

Ohio University, Graduate College, Russ College of Engineering and Technology, Department of Mechanical Engineering, Athens, OH 45701-2979. Offers biomedical engineering (MS); mechanical engineering (MS), including CAD/CAM, design, energy, manufacturing, materials, robotics, thermofluids. *Program availability:* Part-time. *Degree requirements:* For master's, comprehensive exam (for some programs), thesis. *Entrance requirements:* For master's, GRE, BS in engineering or science, minimum GPA of 2.8. Additional exam requirements/recommendations for international students: Required—TOEFL (minimum score 550 paper-based; 80 iBT) or IELTS (minimum score 6.5). Electronic applications accepted. *Faculty research:* Biomedical, energy and the environment, materials and manufacturing, bioengineering.

Old Dominion University, Frank Batten College of Engineering and Technology, Program in Biomedical Engineering, Norfolk, VA 23529. Offers ME, MS, PhD. *Program availability:* Part-time, evening/weekend. Terminal master's awarded for partial completion of doctoral program. *Degree requirements:* For master's, thesis (for some programs); for doctorate, thesis/dissertation, candidacy exam. *Entrance requirements:* For master's, GRE, master's degree, minimum graduate GPA of 3.0, two letters of recommendation, statement of purpose; for doctorate, GRE, master's degree, minimum graduate GPA of 3.5, three letters of recommendation, statement of purpose. Additional exam requirements/recommendations for international students: Required—TOEFL (minimum score 550 paper-based; 79 iBT). Electronic applications accepted. *Faculty research:* Cellular and molecular bioengineering, cardiovascular engineering, musculoskeletal biomechanics, neural engineering, systems biology and computational bioengineering.

Oregon Health & Science University, School of Medicine, Graduate Programs in Medicine, Department of Biomedical Engineering, Portland, OR 97239-3098. Offers MBI, MS, PhD. *Program availability:* Part-time. *Faculty:* 28 full-time (13 women), 5 part-time/adjunct (0 women). *Students:* 47 full-time (18 women); includes 14 minority (7 Asian, non-Hispanic/Latino; 4 Hispanic/Latino; 3 Two or more races, non-Hispanic/Latino). Average age 27. 41 applicants, 22% accepted, 9 enrolled. In 2018, 6 doctorates awarded. *Degree requirements:* For doctorate, comprehensive exam, thesis/dissertation, qualifying exam. *Entrance requirements:* For doctorate, GRE General Test (minimum scores: 153 Verbal/148 Quantitative/4.5 Analytical). *Application deadline:* For fall admission, 1/15 for domestic students, 1/15 priority date for international students; for winter admission, 10/15 for domestic students, 9/15 for international students; for spring admission, 1/15 for domestic students, 12/15 for international students. Applications are processed on a rolling basis. Application fee: $70. Electronic applications accepted. *Financial support:* Health care benefits, tuition waivers (full), and full-tuition and stipends (for PhD students) available. Financial award applicants required to submit FAFSA. *Faculty research:* Blood cells in cancer and cancer biology, smart homes and machine learning, computational mechanics and multiscale modeling, tissue optics and biophotonics, nanomedicine and nano-biotechnology. *Unit head:* Dr. Monica Hinds, Program Director, 503-418-9309, E-mail: somgrad@ohsu.edu. *Application contact:* Nermina Radaslic, Administrative Coordinator, 503-418-9462, E-mail: somgrad@ohsu.edu.

Purdue University, College of Engineering, Weldon School of Biomedical Engineering, West Lafayette, IN 47907-2032. Offers MSBME, PhD, MD/PhD. Programs offered jointly with School of Mechanical Engineering, School of Electrical and Computer Engineering, and School of Chemical Engineering. *Degree requirements:* For master's, thesis optional; for doctorate, thesis/dissertation. *Entrance requirements:* For master's and doctorate, GRE General Test, minimum GPA of 3.25. Electronic applications accepted. *Faculty research:* Engineered biomaterials and biomechanics, imaging, instrumentation, quantitative cellular and systems engineering.

Rensselaer Polytechnic Institute, Graduate School, School of Engineering, Program in Biomedical Engineering, Troy, NY 12180-3590. Offers M Eng, MS, D Eng, PhD. *Faculty:* 19 full-time (5 women). *Students:* 62 full-time (28 women), 3 part-time (1 woman); includes 19 minority (2 Black or African American, non-Hispanic/Latino; 10 Asian, non-Hispanic/Latino; 5 Hispanic/Latino; 2 Two or more races, non-Hispanic/Latino), 14 international. Average age 24. 142 applicants, 56% accepted, 17 enrolled. In 2018, 19 master's, 10 doctorates awarded. Terminal master's awarded for partial completion of doctoral program. *Degree requirements:* For master's, thesis optional; for doctorate, thesis/dissertation. *Entrance requirements:* For master's and doctorate, GRE. Additional exam requirements/recommendations for international students: Required—TOEFL (minimum score 570 paper-based; 88 iBT), IELTS (minimum score 6.5), PTE (minimum score 60). *Application deadline:* For fall admission, 1/1 priority date for domestic and international students; for spring admission, 8/15 priority date for domestic and international students. Applications are processed on a rolling basis. Application fee: $75. Electronic applications accepted. *Financial support:* In 2018–19, research assistantships with full tuition reimbursements (averaging $23,000 per year), teaching assistantships with full tuition reimbursements (averaging $23,000 per year) were awarded; fellowships also available. Financial award application deadline: 1/1. *Faculty research:* Biomolecular science and engineering, biomedical imaging, musculoskeletal engineering, neural engineering, systems biology and biocomputation, vascular engineering. *Total annual research expenditures:* $2.3 million. *Unit head:* Dr. Leo Wan, Graduate Program Director, 518-276-2505, E-mail: wanq@rpi.edu. *Application contact:* Jarron Decker, Director of Graduate Admissions, 518-276-6216, Fax: 518-276-4072, E-mail: gradadmissions@rpi.edu.
Website: http://www.bme.rpi.edu/

Rice University, Graduate Programs, George R. Brown School of Engineering, Department of Chemical and Biomolecular Engineering, Houston, TX 77251-1892. Offers chemical and biomolecular engineering (MS, PhD); chemical engineering (M Ch E). *Program availability:* Part-time. *Degree requirements:* For master's, thesis (for some programs); for doctorate, thesis/dissertation. *Entrance requirements:* For master's and doctorate, GRE General Test, minimum GPA of 3.0. Additional exam requirements/recommendations for international students: Required—TOEFL (minimum score 600 paper-based; 90 iBT). Electronic applications accepted. *Faculty research:* Thermodynamics, phase equilibria, rheology, fluid mechanics, polymers, biomedical engineering, interfacial phenomena, process control, petroleum engineering, reaction engineering and catalysis, biomaterials, metabolic engineering.

Rose-Hulman Institute of Technology, Graduate Studies, Department of Biology and Biomedical Engineering, Terre Haute, IN 47803-3999. Offers MS, MD/MS. *Program availability:* Part-time. *Faculty:* 9 full-time (5 women). *Students:* 2 full-time (both women). Average age 24. 4 applicants, 50% accepted, 1 enrolled. In 2018, 1 master's awarded. *Degree requirements:* For master's, thesis. *Entrance requirements:* For master's, GRE, minimum GPA of 3.0. Additional exam requirements/recommendations for international students: Required—TOEFL (minimum score 580 paper-based; 94 iBT), IELTS (minimum score 7). *Application deadline:* For fall admission, 2/1 priority date for domestic and international students; for winter admission, 10/1 for domestic students, 8/1 for international students; for spring admission, 1/15 for domestic students, 11/1 for international students. Applications are processed on a rolling basis. Application fee: $0. Electronic applications accepted. *Expenses: Tuition:* Full-time $46,641. *Financial support:* In 2018–19, 2 students received support. Fellowships with tuition reimbursements available, research assistantships with tuition reimbursements available, institutionally sponsored loans, scholarships/grants, and tuition waivers (full and partial) available. *Faculty research:* Biomedical instrumentation, biomechanics, biomedical fluid mechanics, biomedical materials, quantitative physiology, soft tissue biomechanics, tissue-biomaterial interaction, biomaterials, biomedical instrumentation, biomedical fluid mechanics. *Total annual research expenditures:* $2,534. *Unit head:* Dr. Jameel Ahmed, Department Head, 812-872-6033, Fax: 812-877-8545, E-mail: ahmed@rose-hulman.edu. *Application contact:* Dr. Craig Downing, Associate Dean of Lifelong Learning, 812-877-8822, E-mail: downing@rose-hulman.edu.
Website: https://www.rose-hulman.edu/academics/academic-departments/biology-and-biomedical-engineering/index.html

Rutgers University–Newark, Graduate School of Biomedical Sciences, Department of Biomedical Engineering, Newark, NJ 07107. Offers Certificate. *Entrance requirements:* Additional exam requirements/recommendations for international students: Required—TOEFL. Electronic applications accepted.

Rutgers University–New Brunswick, Graduate School of Biomedical Sciences, Program in Biomedical Engineering, Piscataway, NJ 08854-5635. Offers MS, PhD, MD/PhD. MS, PhD offered jointly with Rutgers, The State University of New Jersey, New Brunswick. *Degree requirements:* For master's, thesis, qualifying exam; for doctorate, thesis/dissertation, qualifying exam. *Entrance requirements:* For master's and doctorate, GRE General Test. Additional exam requirements/recommendations for international students: Required—TOEFL. Electronic applications accepted.

St. Cloud State University, School of Graduate Studies, College of Science and Engineering, Program in Regulatory Affairs and Services, St. Cloud, MN 56301-4498. Offers MS, Graduate Certificate. *Program availability:* Part-time. *Degree requirements:* For master's, final paper. *Entrance requirements:* For master's, GRE General Test, minimum GPA of 2.75. Additional exam requirements/recommendations for international students: Required—TOEFL (minimum score 550 paper-based; 79 iBT), IELTS (minimum score 6.5). *Expenses:* Contact institution.

Saint Louis University, Graduate Programs, Parks College of Engineering, Aviation, and Technology, Department of Biomedical Engineering, St. Louis, MO 63103. Offers MS, MS-R, PhD. *Degree requirements:* For master's, thesis optional; for doctorate, thesis/dissertation. *Entrance requirements:* For master's, GRE General Test, letters of recommendation, resume, interview; for doctorate, GRE General Test, letters of recommendation, resumé, interview, transcripts, goal statement. Additional exam requirements/recommendations for international students: Required—TOEFL (minimum score 525 paper-based). *Faculty research:* Tissue engineering and biomaterials/neural cardiovascular and orthopedic tissue engineering; tissue engineering/airway remodeling, vasculopathy, and elastic, biodegradable scaffolds; biomechanics/orthopedics, trauma biomechanics and biomechanical modeling; biosignals/electrophysiology, signal processing, and biomechanical instrumentation.

South Dakota School of Mines and Technology, Graduate Division, Program in Biomedical Engineering, Rapid City, SD 57701-3995. Offers MS, PhD. *Program availability:* Part-time. *Degree requirements:* For master's, thesis (for some programs); for doctorate, thesis/dissertation. *Entrance requirements:* For doctorate, GRE General Test, 3 letters of recommendation, minimum GPA of 3.0. Additional exam requirements/recommendations for international students: Required—TOEFL (minimum score 520 paper-based; 68 iBT). Electronic applications accepted.

Southern Illinois University Carbondale, Graduate School, College of Engineering, Program in Biomedical Engineering, Carbondale, IL 62901-4701. Offers ME, MS. *Degree requirements:* For master's, thesis. *Entrance requirements:* For master's, GRE. Additional exam requirements/recommendations for international students: Required—TOEFL.

Stanford University, School of Engineering, Department of Mechanical Engineering, Stanford, CA 94305-2004. Offers biomechanical engineering (MSE); design impact (MSE); mechanical engineering (MS, PhD, Engr). *Expenses: Tuition:* Full-time $50,703; part-time $32,970 per year. *Required fees:* $651.
Website: http://me.stanford.edu/

State University of New York Downstate Medical Center, School of Graduate Studies, Program in Biomedical Engineering, Brooklyn, NY 11203-2098. Offers bioimaging and neuroengineering (PhD); biomedical engineering (MS); MD/PhD. *Degree requirements:* For doctorate, comprehensive exam, thesis/dissertation.

Stevens Institute of Technology, Graduate School, Charles V. Schaefer Jr. School of Engineering and Science, Department of Chemistry, Chemical Biology and Biomedical Engineering, Program in Biomedical Engineering, Hoboken, NJ 07030. Offers M Eng, PhD, Certificate. *Program availability:* Part-time, evening/weekend. *Faculty:* 12 full-time (5 women), 3 part-time/adjunct (1 woman). *Students:* 41 full-time (13 women), 15 part-time (6 women); includes 8 minority (2 Black or African American, non-Hispanic/Latino; 1 American Indian or Alaska Native, non-Hispanic/Latino; 5 Asian, non-Hispanic/Latino), 23 international. Average age 28. In 2018, 27 master's, 3 doctorates awarded. Terminal master's awarded for partial completion of doctoral program. *Degree requirements:* For master's, thesis optional, minimum B average in major field and overall; for doctorate, comprehensive exam (for some programs), thesis/dissertation; for Certificate, minimum B average. *Entrance requirements:* For master's, GRE/GMAT scores: GRE scores are required for all applicants applying to a full-time graduate program in the Schaefer School of Engineering and Science (SES). International applicants must submit TOEFL/IELTS scores and fulfill the English Language Proficiency Requirements in order to be considered. Additional exam requirements/recommendations for international students: Required—TOEFL (minimum score 74 iBT), IELTS (minimum score 6). *Application deadline:* For fall admission, 4/15 for domestic and international students; for spring admission, 11/1 for domestic and international students; for summer admission, 6/1 for domestic students. Applications are processed on a rolling basis. Application fee: $60. Electronic applications accepted. *Expenses: Tuition:* Full-time $35,960; part-time $1620 per credit. *Required fees:* $1290; $600 per semester. Tuition and fees vary according to course load. *Financial support:* Fellowships, research assistantships, teaching assistantships, career-related internships or fieldwork, Federal Work-Study, scholarships/grants, and unspecified assistantships available. Financial award application deadline: 2/15; financial award applicants required to submit FAFSA. *Unit head:* Dr. Jean Zu, Dean of SES, 201-216.8233, Fax: 201-216.8372, E-mail: Jean.Zu@stevens.edu. *Application contact:* Graduate Admissions, 888-783-8367, Fax: 888-511-1306, E-mail: graduate@stevens.edu.

Stony Brook University, State University of New York, Graduate School, College of Engineering and Applied Sciences, Department of Biomedical Engineering, Stony Brook, NY 11794. Offers biomedical engineering (MS, PhD, Certificate); medical physics (MS, PhD). *Faculty:* 10 full-time (2 women), 1 part-time/adjunct (0 women). *Students:* 85 full-time (32 women), 5 part-time (2 women); includes 22 minority (3 Black or African American, non-Hispanic/Latino; 15 Asian, non-Hispanic/Latino; 2 Hispanic/Latino; 2 Two or more races, non-Hispanic/Latino), 27 international. Average age 26. 149 applicants, 38% accepted, 22 enrolled. In 2018, 22 master's, 7 doctorates awarded. *Degree requirements:* For doctorate, thesis/dissertation, qualifying exams. *Entrance requirements:* For master's and doctorate, GRE General Test. Additional exam requirements/recommendations for international students: Required—TOEFL (minimum score 90 iBT). *Application deadline:* For fall admission, 1/15 for domestic students; for spring admission, 10/1 for domestic students. Application fee: $100. *Expenses:* Contact institution. *Financial support:* In 2018–19, 2 fellowships, 28 research assistantships, 17 teaching assistantships were awarded. *Faculty research:* Bioimaging, tissue engineering, biomedical engineering, carbon nanotubes, chemistry. *Total annual research expenditures:* $4.2 million. *Unit head:* Dr. Stefan Judex, Professor and Interim Chair, 631-632-1549, E-mail: stefan.judex@stonybrook.edu. *Application contact:* Erica Valdez, Graduate Program Coordinator, 631-632-8375, Fax: 631-632-8577, E-mail: Erica.Valdez@stonybrook.edu.
Website: https://www.stonybrook.edu/bme/

Tennessee State University, The School of Graduate Studies and Research, College of Engineering, Nashville, TN 37209-1561. Offers biomedical engineering (ME); civil engineering (ME); computer and information systems engineering (MS, PhD); electrical engineering (ME); environmental engineering (ME); manufacturing engineering (ME); mathematical sciences (MS); mechanical engineering (ME). *Program availability:* Part-time, evening/weekend. *Degree requirements:* For master's, project; for doctorate, comprehensive exam, thesis/dissertation. *Entrance requirements:* For doctorate, minimum GPA of 3.3. *Faculty research:* Robotics, intelligent systems, human-computer interaction software systems, biomedical engineering, signal/image processing, probabilistic design, intelligent manufacturing, cooperative mobile robots, condition based maintenance, sensor fusion.

Texas A&M University, College of Engineering, Department of Biomedical Engineering, College Station, TX 77843. Offers biomedical engineering (PhD). *Program availability:* Part-time. *Faculty:* 27. *Students:* 118 full-time (46 women), 8 part-time (5 women); includes 28 minority (3 Black or African American, non-Hispanic/Latino; 12 Asian, non-Hispanic/Latino; 11 Hispanic/Latino; 2 Two or more races, non-Hispanic/Latino), 41 international. Average age 26. 203 applicants, 33% accepted, 27 enrolled. In 2018, 12 master's, 13 doctorates awarded. *Degree requirements:* For master's, thesis (for MS); for doctorate, dissertation (for PhD). *Entrance requirements:* For master's and doctorate, GRE General Test, leveling courses if non-engineering undergraduate major. Additional exam requirements/recommendations for international students: Required—TOEFL (minimum score 550 paper-based; 80 iBT), TWE, PTE (minimum score 53). *Application deadline:* For fall admission, 5/1 for domestic students, 3/1 for international students; for spring admission, 10/1 for domestic students, 7/1 for international students. Applications are processed on a rolling basis. Application fee: $50 ($90 for international students). Electronic applications accepted. *Expenses:* Contact institution. *Financial support:* In 2018–19, 115 students received support, including 18 fellowships with tuition reimbursements available (averaging $18,835 per year), 84 research assistantships with tuition reimbursements available (averaging $17,477 per year), 16 teaching assistantships with tuition reimbursements available (averaging $10,776 per year); career-related internships or fieldwork, institutionally sponsored loans, scholarships/grants, traineeships, health care benefits, tuition waivers (full and partial), and unspecified assistantships also available. Support available to part-time students. Financial award application deadline: 3/15; financial award applicants required to submit FAFSA. *Faculty research:* Medical devices, cardiovascular biomechanics, biomedical optics and sensing, imaging, tissue engineering, biomaterials. *Unit head:* Dr. Gerard L. Cote, Department Head, 979-845-4196, Fax: 979-845-4450, E-mail: gcote@tamu.edu. *Application contact:* Dr. John C. Criscione, Assistant Dean for Graduate Programs, 979-845-5428, Fax: 979-845-4450, E-mail: jccriscione@tamu.edu. Website: http://engineering.tamu.edu/biomedical

Tufts University, School of Engineering, Department of Biomedical Engineering, Medford, MA 02155. Offers bioengineering (MS), including biomaterials; biomedical engineering (MS, PhD); PhD/PhD. *Program availability:* Part-time. Terminal master's awarded for partial completion of doctoral program. *Degree requirements:* For master's, thesis (for some programs); for doctorate, thesis/dissertation. *Entrance requirements:* For master's and doctorate, GRE General Test. Additional exam requirements/recommendations for international students: Required—TOEFL (minimum score 550 paper-based; 80 iBT), IELTS (minimum score 6.5). Electronic applications accepted. *Expenses: Tuition:* Full-time $51,288; part-time $1710 per credit hour. *Required fees:* $904. Full-time tuition and fees vary according to degree level, program and student level. Part-time tuition and fees vary according to course load. *Faculty research:* Regenerative medicine with biomaterials and tissue engineering, diffuse optical imaging and spectroscopy, optics in the development of biomedical devices, ultrafast nonlinear optics and biophotonics, optical diagnostics for diseased and engineered tissues.

Tulane University, School of Science and Engineering, Department of Biomedical Engineering, New Orleans, LA 70118-5669. Offers MS, PhD. MS and PhD offered through the Graduate School. *Program availability:* Part-time. Terminal master's awarded for partial completion of doctoral program. *Degree requirements:* For master's, thesis (for some programs); for doctorate, thesis/dissertation. *Entrance requirements:* For master's and doctorate, GRE General Test, minimum B average in undergraduate course work. Additional exam requirements/recommendations for international students: Required—TOEFL. Electronic applications accepted. *Expenses: Tuition:* Full-time $52,856; part-time $2937 per credit hour. *Required fees:* $2040; $44.50 per credit hour. $580 per term. Tuition and fees vary according to course load, degree level and program. *Faculty research:* Pulmonary and biofluid mechanics and biomechanics of bone, biomaterials science, finite element analysis, electric fields of the brain.

Université de Montréal, Faculty of Medicine, Institute of Biomedical Engineering, Montréal, QC H3C 3J7, Canada. Offers M Sc A, PhD, DESS. M Sc A and PhD programs offered jointly with École Polytechnique de Montréal. *Degree requirements:* For master's, thesis; for doctorate, thesis/dissertation, general exam. *Entrance requirements:* For master's and doctorate, proficiency in French, knowledge of English. Electronic applications accepted. *Faculty research:* Electrophysiology, biomechanics, instrumentation, imaging, simulation.

University at Buffalo, the State University of New York, Graduate School, School of Engineering and Applied Sciences, Department of Biomedical Engineering, Buffalo, NY 14260. Offers MS, PhD. *Program availability:* Part-time. *Degree requirements:* For master's, thesis (for some programs); for doctorate, comprehensive exam, thesis/dissertation. *Entrance requirements:* For master's and doctorate, GRE General Test. Additional exam requirements/recommendations for international students: Required—TOEFL (minimum score 550 paper-based; 79 iBT). Electronic applications accepted. *Faculty research:* Biomedical devices, sensors, instrumentation and diagnostics; computational engineering and modeling; medical imaging and analysis; molecular, cellular, and tissue engineering.

The University of Akron, Graduate School, College of Engineering, Department of Biomedical Engineering, Akron, OH 44325. Offers biomedical engineering (MS); engineering (PhD). *Program availability:* Part-time, evening/weekend. *Degree requirements:* For master's, thesis; for doctorate, one foreign language, thesis/dissertation, candidacy exam, qualifying exam. *Entrance requirements:* For master's, GRE, minimum GPA of 2.75, three letters of recommendation, statement of purpose; for doctorate, GRE, minimum GPA of 3.0 with bachelor's degree, 3.5 with master's degree; three letters of recommendation; statement of purpose; resume. Additional exam requirements/recommendations for international students: Required—TOEFL (minimum score 590 paper-based; 96 iBT). Electronic applications accepted. *Faculty research:* Signal and image processing, physiological controls and instrumentation, biomechanics - orthopedic and hemodynamic, biomaterials for gene and drug delivery systems, telemedicine.

The University of Alabama at Birmingham, School of Engineering, Program in Biomedical Engineering, Birmingham, AL 35294. Offers MSBME, PhD. *Faculty:* 6 full-time (2 women), 7 part-time/adjunct (1 woman). *Students:* 28 full-time (14 women), 7 part-time (1 woman); includes 3 minority (1 Black or African American, non-Hispanic/Latino; 2 Two or more races, non-Hispanic/Latino), 12 international. Average age 26. 57 applicants, 33% accepted, 8 enrolled. In 2018, 3 master's, 2 doctorates awarded. *Degree requirements:* For master's, thesis or alternative; for doctorate, comprehensive exam, thesis/dissertation. *Entrance requirements:* For master's and doctorate, GRE General Test. Additional exam requirements/recommendations for international students: Required—TOEFL (minimum score 80 iBT); Recommended—IELTS (minimum score 6.5). *Application deadline:* For fall admission, 1/15 for domestic students. Application fee: $50 ($60 for international students). Electronic applications accepted. *Expenses:* Contact institution. *Financial support:* In 2018–19, 29 students received support, including 13 fellowships with full tuition reimbursements available (averaging $26,000 per year), 16 research assistantships with full tuition reimbursements available. *Faculty research:* Biomedical imaging, biomedical implants and devices, cardiac electrophysiology, tissue engineering and regenerative medicine. *Total annual research expenditures:* $6.6 million. *Unit head:* Dr. Jianyi Zhang, Chair, 205-934-8420, E-mail: jayzhang@uab.edu. *Application contact:* Jesse Keppley, Director of Student and Academic Services, 205-996-5696, E-mail: gradschool@uab.edu. Website: https://www.uab.edu/engineering/home/departments-research/bme

University of Alberta, Faculty of Medicine and Dentistry and Faculty of Graduate Studies and Research, Graduate Programs in Medicine, Department of Biomedical Engineering, Edmonton, AB T6G 2E1, Canada. Offers biomedical engineering (M Sc); medical sciences (PhD). *Degree requirements:* For master's, thesis; for doctorate, thesis/dissertation. Electronic applications accepted. *Faculty research:* Medical imaging, rehabilitation engineering, biomaterials and tissue engineering, biomechanics, cryobiology.

The University of Arizona, Graduate Interdisciplinary Programs, Graduate Interdisciplinary Program in Biomedical Engineering, Tucson, AZ 85721. Offers MS, PhD. *Entrance requirements:* For master's, GRE, 3 letters of recommendation; for doctorate, GRE, 3 letters of recommendation, statement of purpose. Additional exam requirements/recommendations for international students: Required—TOEFL (minimum score 600 paper-based). Electronic applications accepted.

University of Arkansas, Graduate School, College of Engineering, Department of Biological and Agricultural Engineering, Program in Biomedical Engineering, Fayetteville, AR 72701. Offers MSBME. In 2018, 7 master's awarded. *Application deadline:* For fall admission, 8/1 for domestic students, 4/1 for international students; for spring admission, 12/1 for domestic students, 10/1 for international students; for summer admission, 4/15 for domestic students, 3/1 for international students. Applications are processed on a rolling basis. Application fee: $60. Electronic applications accepted. *Financial support:* In 2018–19, 4 research assistantships, 2 teaching assistantships were awarded; fellowships also available. *Unit head:* Dr. Raj Raghavendra Rao, Department Head, 479-575-8610, E-mail: rajrao@uark.edu. *Application contact:* Dr. Kartik Balachandran, Program Coordinator, 479-575-3376, E-mail: kbalacha@uark.edu. Website: https://biomedical-engineering.uark.edu/

University of Bridgeport, School of Engineering, Department of Biomedical Engineering, Bridgeport, CT 06604. Offers MS. *Program availability:* Part-time, evening/weekend. *Degree requirements:* For master's, thesis optional. *Entrance requirements:* Additional exam requirements/recommendations for international students: Recommended—TOEFL (minimum score 550 paper-based; 80 iBT), IELTS (minimum score 6.5). *Expenses:* Contact institution.

The University of British Columbia, Faculty of Applied Science, School of Biomedical Engineering, Vancouver, BC V6T 1Z1, Canada. Offers M Eng, MA Sc, PhD. *Degree requirements:* For master's, internship (for M Eng); thesis (for MA Sc); for doctorate, thesis/dissertation.

University of Calgary, Faculty of Graduate Studies, Schulich School of Engineering, Program in Biomedical Engineering, Calgary, AB T2N 1N4, Canada. Offers M Sc, PhD. *Degree requirements:* For master's, comprehensive exam, thesis, defense exam; for doctorate, comprehensive exam, thesis/dissertation, defense exam. *Entrance requirements:* For master's, B Sc, minimum GPA of 3.2, confirmed faculty supervisor; for doctorate, M Sc, minimum GPA of 3.5, confirmed faculty supervisor. Additional exam requirements/recommendations for international students: Required—TOEFL, IELTS. *Faculty research:* Bioelectricity, biomechanics, cell and tissue engineering (or biomaterials), imaging, bioinstrumentation, clinical engineering, rehabilitation engineering.

University of California, Davis, College of Engineering, Graduate Group in Biomedical Engineering, Davis, CA 95616. Offers MS, PhD. *Degree requirements:* For master's, thesis; for doctorate, thesis/dissertation. *Entrance requirements:* For master's and doctorate, GRE General Test, minimum GPA of 3.25. Additional exam requirements/recommendations for international students: Required—TOEFL (minimum score 550 paper-based), IELTS (minimum score 7). Electronic applications accepted. *Faculty research:* Orthopedic biomechanics, cell/molecular biomechanics and transport, biosensors and instrumentation, human movement, biomedical image analysis, spectroscopy.

University of California, Irvine, Samueli School of Engineering, Department of Biomedical Engineering, Irvine, CA 92697. Offers MS, PhD. *Program availability:* Part-time. *Students:* 132 full-time (49 women), 6 part-time (1 woman); includes 40 minority (2 Black or African American, non-Hispanic/Latino; 29 Asian, non-Hispanic/Latino; 6 Hispanic/Latino; 3 Two or more races, non-Hispanic/Latino), 50 international. Average age 26. 387 applicants, 31% accepted, 37 enrolled. In 2018, 44 master's, 22 doctorates awarded. Terminal master's awarded for partial completion of doctoral program. *Entrance requirements:* For master's and doctorate, GRE General Test, minimum GPA of 3.0, 3 letters of recommendation. Additional exam requirements/recommendations for international students: Required—TOEFL (minimum score 550 paper-based). *Application deadline:* For fall admission, 1/15 priority date for domestic students, 1/15 for international students. Applications are processed on a rolling basis. Application fee: $105 ($125 for international students). Electronic applications accepted. *Financial support:* Fellowships, research assistantships with full tuition reimbursements, teaching assistantships, institutionally sponsored loans, traineeships, health care benefits, and unspecified assistantships available. Financial award application deadline: 3/1; financial award applicants required to submit FAFSA. *Faculty research:* Biomedical photonics, biomedical imaging, biomedical nano- and micro-scale systems, biomedical computation/modeling, neuroengineering, tissue engineering. *Unit head:* Prof. Abraham P. Lee, Chair, 949-824-8155, Fax: 949-824-1727, E-mail: aplee@uci.edu. *Application contact:* Connie Cheng, Assistant Director of Graduate Student Affairs, 949-824-3562, Fax: 949-824-9096, E-mail: connie.cheng@uci.edu. Website: http://www.eng.uci.edu/dept/bme

University of California, Los Angeles, Graduate Division, Henry Samueli School of Engineering and Applied Science, Department of Chemical and Biomolecular Engineering, Los Angeles, CA 90095-1592. Offers MS, PhD. *Degree requirements:* For master's, comprehensive exam (for some programs), thesis (for some programs); for doctorate, thesis/dissertation, qualifying exams. *Entrance requirements:* For master's, GRE General Test, minimum GPA of 3.0; for doctorate, GRE General Test, minimum GPA of 3.25. Additional exam requirements/recommendations for international students: Required—TOEFL (minimum score 560 paper-based; 87 iBT), IELTS (minimum score 7). Electronic applications accepted. *Faculty research:* Biomolecular engineering, renewable energy, water technology, advanced materials processing, process systems engineering.

University of Central Oklahoma, The Jackson College of Graduate Studies, College of Mathematics and Science, Department of Engineering and Physics, Edmond, OK 73034-5209. Offers engineering physics (MS), including biomedical engineering, electrical engineering, mechanical systems, physics. *Program availability:* Part-time. *Degree requirements:* For master's, thesis optional. *Entrance requirements:* For master's, GRE, 24 hours of course work in physics or equivalent, mathematics through differential equations, minimum GPA of 2.75 overall and 3.0 in last 60 hours attempted, two letters of recommendation. Additional exam requirements/recommendations for international students: Required—TOEFL (minimum score 550 paper-based; 79 iBT), IELTS (minimum score 6.5). Electronic applications accepted.

University of Cincinnati, Graduate School, College of Engineering and Applied Science, Department of Biomedical, Chemical and Environmental Engineering, Cincinnati, OH 45221. Offers biomechanics (PhD); chemical engineering (MS, PhD); environmental engineering (MS, PhD); environmental sciences (MS, PhD); medical imaging (PhD); tissue engineering (PhD). *Program availability:* Part-time. *Degree requirements:* For master's, thesis or alternative; for doctorate, one foreign language, thesis/dissertation. *Entrance requirements:* For master's and doctorate, GRE General Test. Additional exam requirements/recommendations for international students: Required—TOEFL (minimum score 600 paper-based).

University of Connecticut, Graduate School, School of Engineering, Department of Biomedical Engineering, Storrs, CT 06269. Offers MS, PhD. Terminal master's awarded for partial completion of doctoral program. *Degree requirements:* For master's, comprehensive exam, thesis or alternative; for doctorate, thesis/dissertation. *Entrance requirements:* For master's and doctorate, GRE General Test. Additional exam requirements/recommendations for international students: Required—TOEFL (minimum score 550 paper-based). Electronic applications accepted.

University of Florida, Graduate School, Herbert Wertheim College of Engineering, J. Crayton Pruitt Family Department of Biomedical Engineering, Gainesville, FL 32611. Offers biomedical engineering (ME, MS, PhD, Certificate); clinical and translational science (PhD); medical physics (MS, PhD); MD/PhD. Terminal master's awarded for partial completion of doctoral program. *Degree requirements:* For master's, comprehensive exam (for some programs), thesis (for some programs); for doctorate, comprehensive exam (for some programs), thesis/dissertation (for some programs). *Entrance requirements:* Additional exam requirements/recommendations for international students: Required—TOEFL (minimum score 550 paper-based; 80 iBT), IELTS (minimum score 6). Electronic applications accepted. *Faculty research:* Neural engineering, imaging and medical physics, biomaterials and regenerative medicine, biomedical informatics and modeling.

University of Houston, Cullen College of Engineering, Department of Biomedical Engineering, Houston, TX 77204. Offers PhD. *Program availability:* Part-time. *Degree requirements:* For doctorate, seminar. *Entrance requirements:* For doctorate, GRE, BS or MS in biomedical engineering or related field, minimum GPA of 3.3 on last 60 hours. Additional exam requirements/recommendations for international students: Required—TOEFL (minimum score 580 paper-based; 92 iBT), IELTS (minimum score 6). Electronic applications accepted.

The University of Iowa, Graduate College, College of Engineering, Department of Biomedical Engineering, Iowa City, IA 52242-1316. Offers MS, PhD. *Program availability:* Part-time. Terminal master's awarded for partial completion of doctoral program. *Degree requirements:* For master's, thesis (for some programs), written and oral exam; for doctorate, comprehensive exam, thesis/dissertation, written and oral exam. *Entrance requirements:* For master's, GRE (minimum combined score of 310 on verbal and quantitative), minimum undergraduate GPA of 3.0; for doctorate, GRE (minimum combined score of 310 on verbal and quantitative), minimum undergraduate GPA of 3.25. Additional exam requirements/recommendations for international students: Required—TOEFL (minimum score 553 paper-based; 85 iBT), IELTS (minimum score 7). Electronic applications accepted. *Faculty research:* Biomaterials, tissue engineering and cellular mechanics; cell motion analysis and modeling; spinal and joint biomechanics, digital human modeling, and biomedical imaging; bioinformatics and computational biology; fluid and cardiovascular biomechanics; wound healing; mechanobiology.

University of Kentucky, Graduate School, College of Engineering, Program in Biomedical Engineering, Lexington, KY 40506-0032. Offers MSBE, PBME, PhD. *Degree requirements:* For master's, comprehensive exam, thesis optional; for doctorate, comprehensive exam, thesis/dissertation. *Entrance requirements:* For master's, GRE General Test, minimum undergraduate GPA of 2.75; for doctorate, GRE General Test, minimum graduate GPA of 3.0. Additional exam requirements/recommendations for international students: Required—TOEFL (minimum score 550 paper-based). Electronic applications accepted. *Faculty research:* Signal processing and dynamical systems, cardiopulmonary mechanics and systems, bioelectromagnetics, neuromotor control and electrical stimulation, biomaterials and musculoskeletal biomechanics.

University of Maine, Graduate School, Graduate School of Biomedical Science and Engineering, Orono, ME 04469. Offers bioinformatics (PSM); biomedical engineering (PhD); biomedical science (PhD). *Faculty:* 182 full-time (60 women). *Students:* 46 full-time (25 women), 6 part-time (3 women); includes 2 minority (1 Asian, non-Hispanic/Latino; 1 Two or more races, non-Hispanic/Latino), 9 international. Average age 30. 54 applicants, 20% accepted, 8 enrolled. In 2018, 5 doctorates awarded. *Degree requirements:* For doctorate, comprehensive exam, thesis/dissertation. *Entrance requirements:* For doctorate, GRE General Test, master's degree. Additional exam requirements/recommendations for international students: Required—TOEFL (minimum score 80 iBT), IELTS (minimum score 6.5), PTE (minimum score 60). *Application deadline:* For fall admission, 1/1 priority date for domestic and international students. Applications are processed on a rolling basis. Application fee: $65. Electronic applications accepted. *Financial support:* In 2018–19, 4 students received support, including 1 research assistantship with full tuition reimbursement available (averaging $18,000 per year), 4 teaching assistantships with full tuition reimbursements available (averaging $15,600 per year); scholarships/grants and unspecified assistantships also available. Financial award application deadline: 3/1. *Faculty research:* Molecular and Cellular Biology, Developmental Biology, Genomics, Neuroscience, Stem Cell Research. *Total annual research expenditures:* $1.6 million. *Unit head:* Dr. David Neivandt, Director, 207-581-2803. *Application contact:* Scott G. Delcourt, Assistant Vice President for Graduate Studies and Senior Associate Dean, 207-581-3291, Fax: 207-581-3232, E-mail: graduate@maine.edu.
Website: http://gsbse.umaine.edu/

University of Massachusetts Boston, College of Science and Mathematics, Program in Biomedical Engineering and Biotechnology, Boston, MA 02125-3393. Offers PhD. *Students:* 3 part-time (1 woman), 2 international. Average age 30. 6 applicants. In 2018, 1 doctorate awarded. *Application deadline:* For fall admission, 1/2 for domestic students; for spring admission, 10/15 for domestic students. *Expenses: Tuition, area resident:* Full-time $17,896. Tuition, state resident: full-time $17,896. Tuition, nonresident: full-time $34,932. *International tuition:* $34,932 full-time. *Required fees:* $355. *Unit head:* Dr. Greg Beck, Associate Professor of Biology, 617-287.6619, E-mail: Greg.Beck@umb.ed. *Application contact:* Graduate Admissions Coordinator, 617-287-6400, Fax: 617-287-6236, E-mail: graduate.admissions@umb.edu.

University of Massachusetts Dartmouth, Graduate School, College of Engineering, Program in Biomedical Engineering and Biotechnology, North Dartmouth, MA 02747-2300. Offers biomedical engineering/biotechnology (PhD). *Program availability:* Part-time. *Faculty:* 6 full-time (3 women), 1 part-time/adjunct (0 women). *Students:* 10 full-time (4 women), 12 part-time (8 women); includes 5 minority (2 Asian, non-Hispanic/Latino; 3 Hispanic/Latino), 8 international. Average age 29. 15 applicants, 80% accepted, 6 enrolled. Terminal master's awarded for partial completion of doctoral program. *Degree requirements:* For doctorate, comprehensive exam, thesis/dissertation. *Entrance requirements:* For doctorate, GRE, statement of purpose (minimum of 300 words), resume, 3 letters of recommendation, official transcripts. Additional exam requirements/recommendations for international students: Required—TOEFL (minimum score 550 paper-based; 79 iBT), IELTS (minimum score 6.5). *Application deadline:* For fall admission, 2/15 priority date for domestic students, 1/15 priority date for international students; for spring admission, 11/15 priority date for domestic students, 10/15 priority date for international students. Application fee: $60. Electronic applications accepted. *Financial support:* In 2018–19, 3 fellowships (averaging $24,000 per year), 6 research assistantships (averaging $13,633 per year), 2 teaching assistantships (averaging $4,038 per year) were awarded; tuition waivers (full and partial) and doctoral support also available. Financial award application deadline: 3/1; financial award applicants required to submit FAFSA. *Faculty research:* Anti-oxidants, anti-cancer, anti-microbial agents; mechanisms of anti-microbial resistance; synthesis and modification of nano-structures; self-assembled bio-molecular networks; tissue regeneration. *Total annual research expenditures:* $809,000. *Unit head:* Tracie Ferreira, Graduate Program Co-Director, 508-999-8604, E-mail: bmebtphd@umassd.edu. *Application contact:* Scott Webster, Director of Graduate Studies & Admissions, 508-999-8604, Fax: 508-999-8183, E-mail: graduate@umassd.edu.
Website: http://www.umassd.edu/engineering/graduate/doctoraldegreeprograms/biomedicalengineeringandbiotechnology/

University of Memphis, Graduate School, Herff College of Engineering, Program in Biomedical Engineering, Memphis, TN 38152. Offers MS, PhD. *Students:* 18 full-time (6 women), 9 part-time (3 women); includes 7 minority (2 Black or African American, non-Hispanic/Latino; 1 American Indian or Alaska Native, non-Hispanic/Latino; 2 Asian, non-Hispanic/Latino; 2 Hispanic/Latino), 6 international. Average age 31. 22 applicants, 45% accepted, 6 enrolled. In 2018, 2 master's awarded. *Degree requirements:* For master's, thesis or alternative, oral exam; for doctorate, comprehensive exam, thesis/dissertation. *Entrance requirements:* For master's, GRE, minimum undergraduate GPA of 3.0, three letters of recommendation; for doctorate, GRE, minimum undergraduate GPA of 3.25 or master's degree in biomedical engineering, three letters of recommendation. Additional exam requirements/recommendations for international students: Required—TOEFL (minimum score 550 paper-based; 79 iBT). *Application deadline:* For fall admission, 8/1 priority date for domestic students; for spring admission, 12/1 for domestic students. Applications are processed on a rolling basis. Application fee: $35 ($60 for international students). Electronic applications accepted. *Expenses: Tuition, area resident:* Full-time $10,240; part-time $503 per credit hour. Tuition, state resident: full-time $10,464. Tuition, nonresident: full-time $20,224; part-time $991 per credit hour. *Required fees:* $850; $106 per credit hour. *Financial support:* Fellowships with full tuition reimbursements, research assistantships with full tuition reimbursements, career-related internships or fieldwork, Federal Work-Study, scholarships/grants, and unspecified assistantships available. Financial award application deadline: 2/1; financial award applicants required to submit FAFSA. *Faculty research:* Biomaterials and cell/tissue engineering, especially for orthopedic applications; biosensors; biomechanics (hemodynamics, soft tissue, lung, gait); electrophysiology; novel medical image-acquisition devices. *Unit head:* Dr. Eugene Eckstein, Chair, 901-678-3733, E-mail: eckstein@memphis.edu. *Application contact:* Dr. Amy de Jongh Curry, Coordinator of Graduate Studies, 901-678-2017, E-mail: adejongh@memphis.edu.
Website: http://www.memphis.edu/bme

University of Miami, Graduate School, College of Engineering, Department of Biomedical Engineering, Coral Gables, FL 33124. Offers MSBE, PhD. *Program availability:* Part-time. *Degree requirements:* For master's, thesis (for some programs); for doctorate, comprehensive exam, thesis/dissertation. *Entrance requirements:* For master's and doctorate, GRE General Test, minimum GPA of 3.0. Additional exam requirements/recommendations for international students: Required—TOEFL (minimum score 550 paper-based). Electronic applications accepted. *Faculty research:* Biomedical signal processing and instrumentation, cardiovascular engineering, optics and lasers, rehabilitation engineering, tissue mechanics.

University of Michigan, College of Engineering, Department of Biomedical Engineering, Ann Arbor, MI 48109. Offers MS, MSE, PhD. *Program availability:* Part-time. *Students:* 216 full-time (103 women), 4 part-time (1 woman). 672 applicants, 33% accepted, 97 enrolled. In 2018, 79 master's, 17 doctorates awarded. *Degree requirements:* For master's, thesis optional; for doctorate, comprehensive exam, oral defense of dissertation. *Entrance requirements:* For master's, GRE General Test; for doctorate, GRE General Test, master's degree. Additional exam requirements/recommendations for international students: Required—TOEFL. *Application deadline:* Applications are processed on a rolling basis. Electronic applications accepted. *Financial support:* Fellowships, research assistantships, teaching assistantships, Federal Work-Study, scholarships/grants, traineeships, and tuition waivers (partial) available. Financial award applicants required to submit FAFSA. *Faculty research:* Cellular and tissue engineering, biotechnology, biomedical materials, biomechanics, biomedical imaging, rehabilitation engineering. *Total annual research expenditures:* $44.7 million. *Unit head:* Lonnie Shea, Department Chair, 734-647-6319, Fax: 734-936-1905, E-mail: ldshea@umich.edu. *Application contact:* Maria Steele, Graduate Student Program Coordinator, 734-647-1091, Fax: 734-936-1905, E-mail: msteele@umich.edu.
Website: https://bme.umich.edu/

University of Minnesota, Twin Cities Campus, College of Science and Engineering and Medical School, Department of Biomedical Engineering, Minneapolis, MN 55455-0213. Offers MS, PhD, MD/PhD. *Program availability:* Part-time. Terminal master's awarded for partial completion of doctoral program. *Degree requirements:* For master's, thesis optional; for doctorate, thesis/dissertation. *Entrance requirements:* For master's and doctorate, GRE General Test. Additional exam requirements/recommendations for international students: Required—TOEFL. Electronic applications accepted. *Faculty research:* Bioinstrumentation and medical devices; biomaterials; biomechanics; biomedical optics and imaging; biomolecular, cellular, and tissue engineering; cardiovascular engineering; neural engineering.

University of Nebraska–Lincoln, Graduate College, College of Engineering, Department of Mechanical and Materials Engineering, Lincoln, NE 68588-0526. Offers biomedical engineering (PhD); engineering mechanics (MS); materials engineering (PhD); mechanical engineering (MS), including materials science engineering, metallurgical engineering; mechanical engineering and applied mechanics (PhD); MS/MS. MS/MS offered with University of Rouen-France. *Degree requirements:* For master's, thesis optional; for doctorate, comprehensive exam, thesis/dissertation. *Entrance requirements:* For master's and doctorate, GRE General Test. Additional exam requirements/recommendations for international students: Required—TOEFL (minimum score 550 paper-based). Electronic applications accepted. *Faculty research:* Medical robotics, rehabilitation dynamics, and design; combustion, fluid mechanics, and heat transfer; nano-materials, manufacturing, and devices; fiber, tissue, bio-polymer, and adaptive composites; blast, impact, fracture, and failure; electro-active and magnetic materials and devices; functional materials, design, and added manufacturing; materials characterization, modeling, and computational simulation.

University of Nevada, Las Vegas, Graduate College, Howard R. Hughes College of Engineering, Department of Mechanical Engineering, Las Vegas, NV 89154-4027. Offers aerospace engineering (MS); biomedical engineering (MS); materials and nuclear engineering (MS); mechanical engineering (MS, PhD); nuclear criticality safety engineering (Certificate); nuclear safeguards and security (Certificate). *Program availability:* Part-time. *Faculty:* 17 full-time (2 women). *Students:* 50 full-time (18 women), 19 part-time (4 women); includes 19 minority (4 Black or African American, non-Hispanic/Latino; 1 American Indian or Alaska Native, non-Hispanic/Latino; 4 Asian, non-Hispanic/Latino; 7 Hispanic/Latino; 3 Two or more races, non-Hispanic/Latino), 21 international. Average age 29. 63 applicants, 73% accepted, 23 enrolled. In 2018, 15 master's, 5 doctorates, 1 other advanced degree awarded. *Degree requirements:* For master's, thesis optional, design project; for doctorate, comprehensive exam, thesis/dissertation. *Entrance requirements:* For master's, GRE General Test, statement of purpose; 2 letters of recommendation; for doctorate, GRE General Test, 3 letters of recommendation; statement of purpose; bachelor's degree with minimum GPA of 3.5/master's degree with minimum GPA of 3.3. Additional exam requirements/

recommendations for international students: Required—TOEFL (minimum score 550 paper-based; 80 iBT), IELTS (minimum score 7). *Application deadline:* For fall admission, 8/1 for domestic students, 5/1 for international students; for spring admission, 12/1 for domestic students, 10/1 for international students. Application fee: $60 ($95 for international students). Electronic applications accepted. *Expenses:* Contact institution. *Financial support:* In 2018–19, 40 students received support, including 1 fellowship with full tuition reimbursement available (averaging $15,000 per year), 17 research assistantships with full tuition reimbursements available (averaging $16,910 per year), 23 teaching assistantships with full tuition reimbursements available (averaging $16,467 per year); institutionally sponsored loans, scholarships/grants, health care benefits, and unspecified assistantships also available. Financial award application deadline: 3/15; financial award applicants required to submit FAFSA. *Faculty research:* Dynamics and control systems; energy systems including renewable and nuclear; computational fluid and solid mechanics; structures, materials and manufacturing; vibrations and acoustics. *Total annual research expenditures:* $4.5 million. *Unit head:* Dr. Brendan O'Toole, Chair/Professor, 702-895-3885, Fax: 702-895-3936, E-mail: mechanical.chair@unlv.edu. *Application contact:* Dr. Hui Zhao, Graduate Coordinator, 702-895-1463, Fax: 702-895-3936, E-mail: mechanical.gradcoord@unlv.edu.
Website: http://me.unlv.edu/

University of Nevada, Reno, Graduate School, College of Engineering, Department of Electrical and Biomedical Engineering, Reno, NV 89557. Offers MS, PhD. Terminal master's awarded for partial completion of doctoral program. *Degree requirements:* For master's, thesis optional; for doctorate, thesis/dissertation. *Entrance requirements:* For master's, GRE General Test, minimum GPA of 2.75; for doctorate, GRE General Test, minimum GPA of 3.0. Additional exam requirements/recommendations for international students: Required—TOEFL (minimum score 500 paper-based; 61 iBT), IELTS (minimum score 6). Electronic applications accepted. *Faculty research:* Acoustics, neural networking, synthetic aperture radar simulation, optical fiber communications and sensors.

University of Nevada, Reno, Graduate School, Interdisciplinary Program in Biomedical Engineering, Reno, NV 89557. Offers MS, PhD. Terminal master's awarded for partial completion of doctoral program. *Degree requirements:* For master's, thesis optional; for doctorate, thesis/dissertation. *Entrance requirements:* For master's, GRE General Test (recommended), minimum GPA of 2.75; for doctorate, GRE General Test (recommended), minimum GPA of 3.0. Additional exam requirements/recommendations for international students: Required—TOEFL (minimum score 500 paper-based; 61 iBT), IELTS (minimum score 6). Electronic applications accepted. *Faculty research:* Bioengineering, biophysics, biomedical instrumentation, biosensors.

University of New Haven, Graduate School, Tagliatela College of Engineering, Program in Biomedical Engineering, West Haven, CT 06516. Offers MS. *Students:* 24 full-time (11 women), 9 part-time (5 women); includes 7 minority (5 Black or African American, non-Hispanic/Latino; 2 Asian, non-Hispanic/Latino), 19 international. Average age 26. 47 applicants, 83% accepted, 13 enrolled. In 2018, 18 master's awarded. *Application deadline:* Applications are processed on a rolling basis. Application fee: $50. Electronic applications accepted. *Expenses: Tuition:* Full-time $16,470; part-time $915 per credit hour. *Required fees:* $230; $95 per term. *Financial support:* Applicants required to submit FAFSA. *Unit head:* Dr. Kagya Amoako, Assistant Professor, 203-479-4877, E-mail: kamoako@newhaven.edu. *Application contact:* Selina O'Toole, Senior Associate Director of Graduate Admissions, 203-932-7337, E-mail: sotoole@newhaven.edu.
Website: http://www.newhaven.edu/engineering/graduate-programs/biomedical-engineering/index.php

University of New Mexico, Graduate Studies, School of Engineering, Program in Biomedical Engineering, Albuquerque, NM 87131-2039. Offers MS, PhD. *Program availability:* Part-time. Terminal master's awarded for partial completion of doctoral program. *Degree requirements:* For master's, thesis (for some programs); for doctorate, comprehensive exam, thesis/dissertation. *Entrance requirements:* For master's and doctorate, GRE General Test, letters of recommendation, letter of intent.

The University of North Carolina at Chapel Hill, School of Medicine and Graduate School, Graduate Programs in Medicine, Joint Department of Biomedical Engineering UNC-Chapel Hill and NC State, Chapel Hill, NC 27599. Offers MS, PhD. Terminal master's awarded for partial completion of doctoral program. *Degree requirements:* For master's, comprehensive exam, thesis, ethics seminar; for doctorate, comprehensive exam, thesis/dissertation, qualifying exam, teaching and ethics seminar. *Entrance requirements:* For master's, GRE General Test, minimum GPA of 3.0; for doctorate, GRE General Test, minimum GPA of 3.3. Additional exam requirements/recommendations for international students: Required—TOEFL. Electronic applications accepted. *Faculty research:* Biomedical imaging, rehabilitation engineering, microsystems engineering.

University of North Texas, Toulouse Graduate School, Denton, TX 76203-5459. Offers accounting (MS); applied anthropology (MA, MS); applied behavior analysis (Certificate); applied geography (MA); applied technology and performance improvement (M Ed, MS); art education (MA); art history (MA); arts leadership (Certificate); audiology (Au D); behavior analysis (MS); behavioral science (PhD); biochemistry and molecular biology (MS); biology (MA, MS); biomedical engineering (MS); business analysis (MS); chemistry (MS); clinical health psychology (PhD); communication studies (MA, MS); computer engineering (MS); computer science (MS); counseling (M Ed, MS), including clinical mental health counseling (MS), college and university counseling, elementary school counseling, secondary school counseling; creative writing (MA); criminal justice (MS); curriculum and instruction (M Ed); decision sciences (MBA); design (MA, MFA), including fashion design (MFA), innovation studies, interior design (MFA); early childhood studies (MS); economics (MS); educational leadership (M Ed, Ed D); educational psychology (MS, PhD), including family studies (MS), gifted and talented (MS), human development (MS), learning and cognition (MS), research, measurement and evaluation (MS); electrical engineering (MS); emergency management (MPA); engineering technology (MS); English (MA); English as a second language (MA); environmental science (MS); finance (MBA, MS); financial management (MPA); French (MA); health services management (MBA); higher education (M Ed, Ed D); history (MA, MS); hospitality management (MS); human resources management (MPA); information science (MS); information systems (PhD); information technologies (MBA); interdisciplinary studies (MA, MS); international studies (MA); international sustainable tourism (MS); jazz studies (MM); journalism (MA, MJ, Graduate Certificate), including interactive and virtual digital communication (Graduate Certificate), narrative journalism (Graduate Certificate), public relations (Graduate Certificate); kinesiology (MS); linguistics (MA); local government management (MPA); logistics (PhD); logistics and supply chain management (MBA); long-term care, senior housing, and aging services (MA); management (PhD); marketing (MBA); mathematics (MA, MS); mechanical and energy engineering (MS, PhD); music (MA), including ethnomusicology, music theory, musicology, performance; music composition (PhD); music education (MM Ed, PhD); nonprofit management (MPA); operations and supply chain management (MBA); performance (MM, DMA); philosophy (MA); political science (MA); professional and technical communication (MA); radio, television and film (MA, MFA);

rehabilitation counseling (Certificate); sociology (MA); Spanish (MA); special education (M Ed); speech-language pathology (MA); strategic management (MBA); studio art (MFA); teaching (M Ed); MBA/MS. *Program availability:* Part-time, evening/weekend, online learning. Terminal master's awarded for partial completion of doctoral program. *Degree requirements:* For master's, variable foreign language requirement, comprehensive exam (for some programs), thesis (for some programs); for doctorate, variable foreign language requirement, comprehensive exam (for some programs), thesis/dissertation; for other advanced degree, variable foreign language requirement, comprehensive exam (for some programs). *Entrance requirements:* For master's and doctorate, GRE, GMAT. Additional exam requirements/recommendations for international students: Required—TOEFL (minimum score 550 paper-based; 79 iBT). Electronic applications accepted.

University of Ottawa, Faculty of Graduate and Postdoctoral Studies, Ottawa—Carlton Joint Program in Biomedical Engineering, Ottawa, ON K1N 6N5, Canada. Offers MA Sc. *Degree requirements:* For master's, thesis or alternative. *Entrance requirements:* For master's, honors degree or equivalent, minimum B average.

University of Portland, Shiley School of Engineering, Portland, OR 97203-5798. Offers biomedical engineering (MBME); civil engineering (ME); computer science (ME); electrical engineering (ME); mechanical engineering (ME). *Program availability:* Part-time, evening/weekend. *Students:* 12 full-time (4 women), 2 part-time (both women); includes 1 minority (Black or African American, non-Hispanic/Latino), 2 international. Average age 24. 43 applicants, 49% accepted, 10 enrolled. In 2018, 6 master's awarded. *Degree requirements:* For master's, thesis optional. *Entrance requirements:* For master's, GRE General Test, minimum GPA of 3.0, 2 letters of recommendation, resume, statement of goals, official transcripts. Additional exam requirements/recommendations for international students: Required—TOEFL (minimum score 80 iBT), IELTS (minimum score 7). *Application deadline:* For fall admission, 7/15 priority date for domestic and international students; for spring admission, 12/15 priority date for domestic and international students; for summer admission, 4/15 for domestic and international students. Applications are processed on a rolling basis. Electronic applications accepted. *Expenses:* $1,326 per credit plus $50 professional tuition per credit. *Financial support:* Research assistantships, career-related internships or fieldwork, Federal Work-Study, and scholarships/grants available. Support available to part-time students. Financial award application deadline: 3/1; financial award applicants required to submit FAFSA. *Unit head:* Dr. Matthew Kuhn, Dean, 503-943-7361, E-mail: kuhn@up.edu. *Application contact:* Caitlin Biddulph, Graduate Programs and Admissions Specialist, 503-943-7107.
Website: http://engineering.up.edu/default.aspx?cid=6464&pid=2432

University of Rhode Island, Graduate School, College of Engineering, Department of Electrical, Computer and Biomedical Engineering, Kingston, RI 02881. Offers acoustics and underwater acoustics (MS, PhD); biomedical engineering (MS, PhD); circuits and devices (MS); communication theory (MS, PhD); computer architectures and digital systems (MS, PhD); computer networks (MS, PhD); digital signal processing (MS); embedded systems and computer applications (MS, PhD); fault-tolerant computing (MS, PhD); materials and optics (MS, PhD); systems theory (MS, PhD). *Program availability:* Part-time. *Faculty:* 23 full-time (4 women), 1 part-time/adjunct (0 women). *Students:* 41 full-time (7 women), 17 part-time (2 women); includes 8 minority (1 Black or African American, non-Hispanic/Latino; 1 American Indian or Alaska Native, non-Hispanic/Latino; 4 Asian, non-Hispanic/Latino; 2 Hispanic/Latino), 26 international. 44 applicants, 75% accepted, 20 enrolled. In 2018, 14 master's, 3 doctorates awarded. *Entrance requirements:* Additional exam requirements/recommendations for international students: Required—TOEFL. *Application deadline:* For fall admission, 7/15 for domestic students, 2/1 for international students; for spring admission, 11/15 for domestic students, 7/15 for international students; for summer admission, 4/15 for domestic students. Application fee: $65. Electronic applications accepted. *Expenses: Tuition, area resident:* Full-time $13,226; part-time $735 per credit. Tuition, state resident: full-time $13,226; part-time $735 per credit. Tuition, nonresident: full-time $25,854; part-time $1436 per credit. *International tuition:* $25,854 full-time. *Required fees:* $1698; $50 per credit. $35 per semester. One-time fee: $165. *Financial support:* In 2018–19, 22 research assistantships with tuition reimbursements (averaging $10,249 per year), 9 teaching assistantships with tuition reimbursements (averaging $8,477 per year) were awarded. Financial award application deadline: 2/1; financial award applicants required to submit FAFSA. *Unit head:* Dr. Haibo He, Chair, 401-874-5844, E-mail: he@ele.uri.edu. *Application contact:* Dr. Frederick J. Vetter, Graduate Director, 401-874-5141, E-mail: vetter@ele.uri.edu.
Website: http://www.ele.uri.edu/

University of Rochester, Hajim School of Engineering and Applied Sciences, Department of Biomedical Engineering, Rochester, NY 14627. Offers MS, PhD. *Faculty:* 14 full-time (7 women). *Students:* 85 full-time (45 women), 2 part-time (1 woman); includes 23 minority (4 Black or African American, non-Hispanic/Latino; 11 Asian, non-Hispanic/Latino; 5 Hispanic/Latino; 3 Two or more races, non-Hispanic/Latino), 29 international. Average age 26. 282 applicants, 44% accepted, 41 enrolled. In 2018, 23 master's, 6 doctorates awarded. Terminal master's awarded for partial completion of doctoral program. *Degree requirements:* For master's, comprehensive exam (for some programs), thesis (for some programs), teaching assistantship; for doctorate, thesis/dissertation, 1st-year preliminary exam, qualifying exam, 2 teaching assistantships, 3 lab rotations, 39 required course credits. *Entrance requirements:* For master's and doctorate, GRE General Test, curriculum vitae, three letters of recommendations, official transcripts, personal statement. Additional exam requirements/recommendations for international students: Required—TOEFL (minimum score 600 paper-based; 100 iBT), IELTS. *Application deadline:* For fall admission, 4/15 for domestic and international students. Application fee: $60. Electronic applications accepted. *Expenses: Tuition:* Full-time $52,974; part-time $1654 per credit hour. *Required fees:* $612. One-time fee: $30 part-time. Tuition and fees vary according to campus/location and program. *Financial support:* In 2018–19, 59 students received support, including 21 fellowships with full tuition reimbursements available (averaging $28,656 per year), 38 research assistantships with full and partial tuition reimbursements available (averaging $28,764 per year); traineeships, health care benefits, tuition waivers (full and partial), and unspecified assistantships also available. Financial award application deadline: 4/15. *Faculty research:* Biomechanics, biomedical acoustics, biomedical nanotechnology, biomedical optics, regenerative medicine. *Total annual research expenditures:* $5.1 million. *Unit head:* Diane Dalecki, Professor and Chair, 585-275-7378, E-mail: diane.dalecki@rochester.edu. *Application contact:* Ania Dworzanski, Graduate Program Coordinator, 585-275-3891, E-mail: adworzan@ur.rochester.edu.
Website: http://www.hajim.rochester.edu/bme/graduate/index.html

University of Rochester, Hajim School of Engineering and Applied Sciences, Master of Science in Technical Entrepreneurship and Management Program, Rochester, NY 14627. Offers biomedical engineering (MS). Program offered in collaboration with the Simon School of Business and administered by the University of Rochester Ain Center for Entrepreneurship. *Program availability:* Part-time. *Students:* 39 full-time (13 women), 6 part-time (2 women); includes 5 minority (3 Black or African American, non-Hispanic/Latino; 1 Asian, non-Hispanic/Latino; 1 Hispanic/Latino), 30 international. Average age 25. 220 applicants, 73% accepted, 23 enrolled. In 2018, 14 master's awarded. *Degree*

requirements: For master's, comprehensive exam. *Entrance requirements:* For master's, GRE or GMAT (strongly recommended), 3 letters of recommendation, personal statement, official transcript. Additional exam requirements/recommendations for international students: Required—TOEFL (minimum score 90 paper-based), IELTS (minimum score 6.5). *Application deadline:* For fall admission, 2/1 for domestic and international students. Application fee: $60. Electronic applications accepted. *Expenses: Tuition:* Full-time $52,974; part-time $1654 per credit hour. *Required fees:* $612. One-time fee: $30 part-time. Tuition and fees vary according to campus/location and program. *Financial support:* Career-related internships or fieldwork, scholarships/grants, health care benefits, and tuition waivers (partial) available. Support available to part-time students. Financial award application deadline: 2/1. *Unit head:* Duncan T. Moore, Vice Provost for Entrepreneurship, 585-275-5248, E-mail: duncan.moore@rochester.edu. *Application contact:* Andrea Barrett, Executive Director, 585-276-3407, E-mail: andrea.barrett@rochester.edu.
Website: http://www.rochester.edu/team/

University of Saskatchewan, College of Graduate and Postdoctoral Studies, College of Engineering, Biomedical Engineering Program, Saskatoon, SK S7N 5E5, Canada. Offers M Eng, M Sc, PhD, PGD. *Program availability:* Part-time. *Degree requirements:* For master's, 30 credits (for M Eng); thesis and 12 credits (for MS); for doctorate, comprehensive exam, thesis/dissertation, qualifying exam, 18 credits. *Entrance requirements:* For master's and doctorate, GRE. Additional exam requirements/recommendations for international students: Required—TOEFL (minimum iBT score of 80), IELTS (6.5), CanTEST (4.5), or PTE (59). Electronic applications accepted. *Faculty research:* Bioinformatics, biomechanics, biomedical signal and image processing, biosensor, medical instrumentation, medical imaging, nano-drug delivery system, systems biology, tissue engineering.

University of Southern California, Graduate School, Viterbi School of Engineering, Department of Biomedical Engineering, Los Angeles, CA 90089. Offers biomedical engineering (PhD); medical device and diagnostic engineering (MS); medical imaging and imaging informatics (MS). *Program availability:* Online learning. Terminal master's awarded for partial completion of doctoral program. *Degree requirements:* For master's, thesis optional; for doctorate, thesis/dissertation. *Entrance requirements:* For master's and doctorate, GRE General Test. Additional exam requirements/recommendations for international students: Recommended—TOEFL. Electronic applications accepted. *Faculty research:* Medical ultrasound, BioMEMS, neural prosthetics, computational bioengineering, bioengineering of vision, medical devices.

University of South Florida, College of Engineering, Department of Chemical and Biomedical Engineering, Tampa, FL 33620. Offers biomedical engineering (MSBE), including pharmacy; chemical engineering (MSCH, PhD). *Program availability:* Part-time. *Faculty:* 18 full-time (2 women). *Students:* 50 full-time (13 women), 10 part-time (3 women); includes 5 minority (1 Black or African American, non-Hispanic/Latino; 2 Asian, non-Hispanic/Latino; 1 Hispanic/Latino; 1 Two or more races, non-Hispanic/Latino), 42 international. Average age 27. 61 applicants, 59% accepted, 20 enrolled. In 2018, 19 master's, 2 doctorates awarded. Terminal master's awarded for partial completion of doctoral program. *Degree requirements:* For master's, comprehensive exam, thesis (for some programs); for doctorate, comprehensive exam, thesis/dissertation. *Entrance requirements:* For master's, GRE (preferred minimum scores of Verbal greater than 50% percentile, Quantitative greater than 75th percentile, Analytical Writing of 3.0 or greater; applicants who have successfully completed the Fundamentals of Engineering (FE) Exam offered by the Society of Professional Engineers will be exempted from the GRE requirement, Bachelors or equivalent in Chemical Engineering; 2 letters of reference; statement of research interests; for doctorate, (preferred scores: Verbal greater than 50% percentile, Quantitative greater than 75% percentile, Analytical Writing greater than 4.0), bachelors or equivalent in Chemical Engineering; 3 letters of reference; statement of research interests. Additional exam requirements/recommendations for international students: Required—TOEFL, TOEFL (minimum score 550 paper-based; 79 iBT) or IELTS (minimum score 6.5). *Application deadline:* For fall admission, 2/15 for domestic and international students; for spring admission, 10/15 for domestic students, 9/15 for international students; for summer admission, 2/15 for domestic students, 1/15 for international students. Application fee: $30. Electronic applications accepted. *Expenses:* Tuition, state resident: full-time $6350. Tuition, nonresident: full-time $19,048. *International tuition:* $19,048 full-time. *Required fees:* $2079. *Financial support:* In 2018–19, 10 students received support, including 29 research assistantships with tuition reimbursements available (averaging $13,171 per year), 12 teaching assistantships with tuition reimbursements available (averaging $14,017 per year); unspecified assistantships also available. Financial award applicants required to submit FAFSA. *Faculty research:* Neuroengineering, tissue engineering, biomedicine and biotechnology, engineering education, functional materials and nanotechnology, energy, environment/sustainability. *Total annual research expenditures:* $1.6 million. *Unit head:* Dr. Venkat R. Bhethanabotla, Professor and Department Chair, 813-974-3997, E-mail: bhethana@usf.edu. *Application contact:* Dr. Robert Frisina, Jr., Professor and Graduate Program Director, 813-974-4013, Fax: 813-974-3651, E-mail: rfrisina@usf.edu.
Website: http://che.eng.usf.edu/

University of South Florida, Innovative Education, Tampa, FL 33620-9951. Offers adult, career and higher education (Graduate Certificate), including college teaching, leadership in developing human resources, leadership in higher education; Africana studies (Graduate Certificate), including diasporas and health disparities, genocide and human rights; aging studies (Graduate Certificate), including gerontology; art research (Graduate Certificate), including museum studies; business foundations (Graduate Certificate); chemical and biomedical engineering (Graduate Certificate), including materials science and engineering, water, health and sustainability; child and family studies (Graduate Certificate), including positive behavior support; civil and industrial engineering (Graduate Certificate), including transportation systems analysis; community and family health (Graduate Certificate), including maternal and child health, social marketing and public health, violence and injury: prevention and intervention, women's health; criminology (Graduate Certificate), including criminal justice administration; data science for public administration (Graduate Certificate); digital humanities (Graduate Certificate); educational measurement and research (Graduate Certificate), including evaluation; English (Graduate Certificate), including comparative literary studies, creative writing, professional and technical communication; entrepreneurship (Graduate Certificate); environmental health (Graduate Certificate), including safety management; epidemiology and biostatistics (Graduate Certificate), including applied biostatistics, biostatistics, concepts and tools of epidemiology, epidemiology, epidemiology of infectious diseases; geography, environment and planning (Graduate Certificate), including community development, environmental policy and management, geographical information systems; geology (Graduate Certificate), including hydrogeology; global health (Graduate Certificate), including disaster management, global health and Latin American and Caribbean studies, global health practice, humanitarian assistance, infection control; government and international affairs (Graduate Certificate), including Cuban studies, globalization studies; health policy and management (Graduate Certificate), including health management and leadership, public health policy and programs; hearing specialist: early intervention (Graduate Certificate); industrial and management systems engineering (Graduate Certificate), including systems engineering, technology management; information studies (Graduate Certificate), including school library media specialist; information systems/decision sciences (Graduate Certificate), including analytics and business intelligence; instructional technology (Graduate Certificate), including distance education, Florida digital/virtual educator, instructional design, multimedia design, Web design; internal medicine, bioethics and medical humanities (Graduate Certificate), including biomedical ethics; Latin American and Caribbean studies (Graduate Certificate); leadership for coastal resiliency planning (Graduate Certificate); mass communications (Graduate Certificate), including multimedia journalism; mathematics and statistics (Graduate Certificate), including mathematics; medicine (Graduate Certificate), including aging and neuroscience, bioinformatics, biotechnology, brain fitness and memory management, clinical investigation, hand and upper limb rehabilitation, health informatics, health sciences, integrative weight management, intellectual property, medicine and gender, metabolic and nutritional medicine, metabolic cardiology, pharmacy sciences; national and competitive intelligence (Graduate Certificate); nursing (Graduate Certificate), including simulation based academic fellowship in advanced pain management; psychological and social foundations (Graduate Certificate), including career counseling, college teaching, diversity in education, mental health counseling, school counseling; public affairs (Graduate Certificate), including nonprofit management, public management, research administration; public health (Graduate Certificate), including assessing chemical toxicity and public health risks, health equity, pharmacoepidemiology, public health generalist, toxicology, translational research in adolescent behavioral health; public health practices (Graduate Certificate), including planning for healthy-communities; rehabilitation and mental health counseling (Graduate Certificate), including integrative mental health care, marriage and family therapy, rehabilitation technology; secondary education (Graduate Certificate), including ESOL, foreign language education: culture and content, foreign language education: professional; social work (Graduate Certificate), including geriatric social work/clinical gerontology; special education (Graduate Certificate), including autism spectrum disorder, disabilities education: severe/profound; world languages (Graduate Certificate), including teaching English as a second language (TESL) or foreign language. *Expenses:* Tuition, state resident: full-time $6350. Tuition, nonresident: full-time $19,048. *International tuition:* $19,048 full-time. *Required fees:* $2079. *Unit head:* Dr. Cynthia DeLuca, Associate Vice President and Assistant Vice Provost, 813-974-3077, Fax: 813-974-7061, E-mail: deluca@usf.edu. *Application contact:* Owen Hooper, Director, Summer and Alternative Calendar Programs, 813-974-6917, E-mail: hooper@usf.edu.
Website: http://www.usf.edu/innovative-education/

University of South Florida, Taneja College of Pharmacy, Tampa, FL 33620-9951. Offers pharmaceutical nanotechnology (MS), including biomedical engineering, drug discovery, delivery, development and manufacturing; pharmacy (Pharm D), including pharmacy and health education. *Accreditation:* ACPE. *Faculty:* 32 full-time (18 women), 1 part-time/adjunct (0 women). *Students:* 398 full-time (234 women), 7 part-time (3 women); includes 180 minority (33 Black or African American, non-Hispanic/Latino; 72 Asian, non-Hispanic/Latino; 59 Hispanic/Latino; 2 Native Hawaiian or other Pacific Islander, non-Hispanic/Latino; 14 Two or more races, non-Hispanic/Latino), 13 international. Average age 25. 465 applicants, 44% accepted, 112 enrolled. In 2018, 11 master's, 91 doctorates awarded. *Degree requirements:* For master's, comprehensive exam, thesis optional, capstone or thesis; for doctorate, internship/field experience. *Entrance requirements:* For master's, GRE, MCAT or DAT, Bachelor's preferably in biomedical, biological, chemical sciences or engineering; 2 letters of recommendation; resume; professional statement; interview; for doctorate, PCAT, minimum GPA of 2.75 overall (preferred); completion of 72 prerequisite credit hours; U.S. citizenship or permanent resident; interviews; criminal background check and drug screen. Additional exam requirements/recommendations for international students: Required—TOEFL (minimum score 550 paper-based; 79 iBT), IELTS (minimum score 6.5). *Application deadline:* For fall admission, 6/1 for domestic and international students; for spring admission, 10/15 for domestic students, 9/15 for international students; for summer admission, 2/15 for domestic and international students. Electronic applications accepted. *Expenses:* Tuition, state resident: full-time $6350. Tuition, nonresident: full-time $19,048. *International tuition:* $19,048 full-time. *Required fees:* $2079. *Financial support:* In 2018–19, 159 students received support. *Total annual research expenditures:* $1.4 million. *Unit head:* James Lambert, 813-974-4562, E-mail: jlambert2@usf.edu. *Application contact:* Dr. Amy Schwartz, Associate Dean, 813-974-2251, E-mail: aschwar1@health.usf.edu.

The University of Tennessee, Graduate School, Tickle College of Engineering, Department of Mechanical, Aerospace and Biomedical Engineering, Program in Biomedical Engineering, Knoxville, TN 37996. Offers MS, PhD, MS/PhD. *Program availability:* Part-time, online learning. *Faculty:* 15 full-time (2 women). *Students:* 20 full-time (3 women), 1 part-time (0 women); includes 2 minority (both Asian, non-Hispanic/Latino), 3 international. Average age 25. 34 applicants, 44% accepted, 9 enrolled. In 2018, 6 master's, 3 doctorates awarded. *Degree requirements:* For master's, thesis or alternative; for doctorate, comprehensive exam, thesis/dissertation. *Entrance requirements:* For master's, GRE General Test (for MS students pursuing research thesis), minimum GPA of 2.7 (for U.S. degree holders), 3.0 (for international degree holders); 3 references; statement of purpose; for doctorate, GRE General Test, minimum GPA of 3.0 on previous graduate course work; 3 references; statement of purpose. Additional exam requirements/recommendations for international students: Required—TOEFL (minimum score 550 paper-based; 80 iBT), IELTS (minimum score 6.5). *Application deadline:* For fall admission, 2/1 priority date for domestic and international students; for spring admission, 6/15 for domestic and international students; for summer admission, 10/15 for domestic and international students. Applications are processed on a rolling basis. Application fee: $60. Electronic applications accepted. *Financial support:* In 2018–19, 15 students received support, including 1 fellowship with full tuition reimbursement available (averaging $9,616 per year), 7 research assistantships with full tuition reimbursements available (averaging $20,025 per year), 7 teaching assistantships with full tuition reimbursements available (averaging $20,400 per year); career-related internships or fieldwork, Federal Work-Study, institutionally sponsored loans, health care benefits, and unspecified assistantships also available. Financial award application deadline: 2/1; financial award applicants required to submit FAFSA. *Faculty research:* Bioimaging, biomechanics, biorobotics, biosensors, biomaterials. *Unit head:* Dr. Matthew Mench, Head, 865-974-5115, Fax: 865-974-5274, E-mail: mmench@utk.edu. *Application contact:* Dr. Kivanc Ekici, Associate Professor/Graduate Program Director, 865-974-6016, Fax: 865-974-5274, E-mail: ekici@utk.edu.
Website: http://www.engr.utk.edu/mabe

The University of Tennessee, The University of Tennessee Space Institute, Tullahoma, TN 37388. Offers aerospace engineering (MS, PhD); biomedical engineering (MS, PhD); engineering science (MS, PhD); industrial and systems engineering/engineering management (MS, PhD); mechanical engineering (MS, PhD); physics (MS, PhD). *Program availability:* Part-time, blended/hybrid learning. Terminal master's awarded for partial completion of doctoral program. *Degree requirements:* For doctorate, one foreign language, thesis/dissertation. *Entrance requirements:* Additional exam requirements/recommendations for international students: Required—TOEFL (minimum score 550 paper-based; 80 iBT), IELTS (minimum score 6.5). Electronic applications accepted. *Expenses:* Contact institution. *Faculty research:* Fluid mechanics/aerodynamics, chemical and electric propulsion and laser diagnostics, computational mechanics and simulations, carbon fiber production and composite materials.

The University of Tennessee Health Science Center, College of Graduate Health Sciences, Memphis, TN 38163. Offers biomedical engineering (MS, PhD); biomedical sciences (PhD); dental sciences (MDS); epidemiology (MS); health outcomes and policy research (PhD); laboratory research and management (MS); nursing science (PhD); pharmaceutical sciences (PhD); pharmacology (MS); speech and hearing science (PhD); DDS/PhD; DNP/PhD; MD/PhD; Pharm D/PhD. MS and PhD programs in biomedical engineering offered jointly with University of Memphis. Terminal master's awarded for partial completion of doctoral program. *Degree requirements:* For master's, comprehensive exam, thesis; for doctorate, thesis/dissertation, oral and written preliminary and comprehensive exams. *Entrance requirements:* For master's and doctorate, GRE General Test, minimum GPA of 3.0. Additional exam requirements/ recommendations for international students: Recommended—TOEFL (minimum score 79 iBT), IELTS (minimum score 6.5). Electronic applications accepted. *Expenses:* Contact institution. *Faculty research:* Cell biology, epidemiology, biomedical engineering, speech and hearing science, health policy, pharmaceutical sciences, dental sciences, nursing science, pharmacology.

The University of Texas at Austin, Graduate School, Cockrell School of Engineering, Department of Biomedical Engineering, Austin, TX 78712-1111. Offers MS, PhD, MD/ PhD. MD/PhD offered jointly with The University of Texas Medical Branch. *Program availability:* Part-time. *Degree requirements:* For master's, thesis optional; for doctorate, comprehensive exam, thesis/dissertation. *Entrance requirements:* For master's and doctorate, GRE General Test. Additional exam requirements/recommendations for international students: Required—TOEFL (minimum score 550 paper-based). Electronic applications accepted. *Faculty research:* Biomechanics, bioengineering, tissue engineering, tissue optics, biothermal studies.

The University of Texas at Dallas, Erik Jonsson School of Engineering and Computer Science, Department of Bioengineering, Richardson, TX 75080. Offers biomedical engineering (MS, PhD). *Faculty:* 17 full-time (3 women), 3 part-time/adjunct (1 woman). *Students:* 110 full-time (61 women), 12 part-time (5 women); includes 27 minority (3 Black or African American, non-Hispanic/Latino; 11 Asian, non-Hispanic/Latino; 12 Hispanic/Latino; 1 Two or more races, non-Hispanic/Latino), 63 international. Average age 28. 146 applicants, 42% accepted, 23 enrolled. In 2018, 36 master's, 4 doctorates awarded. *Degree requirements:* For master's, thesis (for some programs); for doctorate, comprehensive exam, thesis/dissertation. *Entrance requirements:* For master's, GRE (minimum scores of 500 in verbal, 700 in quantitative and 4 in analytical writing), minimum GPA of 3.0 in upper-division quantitative course work; for doctorate, GRE (minimum scores of 500 in verbal, 700 in quantitative and 4 in analytical writing), minimum GPA of 3.5 in upper-division quantitative course work. Additional exam requirements/recommendations for international students: Required—TOEFL (minimum score 550 paper-based). *Application deadline:* For fall admission, 7/15 for domestic students, 5/1 priority date for international students; for spring admission, 11/15 for domestic students, 9/1 priority date for international students. Applications are processed on a rolling basis. Application fee: $50 ($100 for international students). Electronic applications accepted. *Expenses: Tuition, area resident:* Full-time $13,458. Tuition, state resident: full-time $13,458. Tuition, nonresident: full-time $26,852. *International tuition:* $26,852 full-time. Tuition and fees vary according to course load. *Financial support:* In 2018–19, 67 students received support, including 9 fellowships (averaging $4,222 per year), 50 research assistantships with partial tuition reimbursements available (averaging $25,012 per year), 19 teaching assistantships with partial tuition reimbursements available (averaging $17,503 per year); career-related internships or fieldwork, Federal Work-Study, institutionally sponsored loans, scholarships/grants, and unspecified assistantships also available. Support available to part-time students. Financial award application deadline: 4/30; financial award applicants required to submit FAFSA. *Faculty research:* Bio-nanotechnology, organic electronics, system-level design for medical devices, computational geometry and biomedical computing. *Unit head:* Dr. Shalini Prasad, Interim Department Head, 972-883-4247, E-mail: shalini.prasad@utdallas.edu. *Application contact:* Dr. Shalini Prasad, Interim Department Head, 972-883-4247, E-mail: shalini.prasad@utdallas.edu.
Website: http://be.utdallas.edu/

The University of Texas at San Antonio, College of Engineering, Department of Biomedical Engineering, San Antonio, TX 78249. Offers MS, PhD. *Program availability:* Part-time. Terminal master's awarded for partial completion of doctoral program. *Degree requirements:* For master's, comprehensive exam, thesis; for doctorate, comprehensive exam, thesis/dissertation. *Entrance requirements:* For master's, GRE, three letters of recommendation, statement of purpose, BS in any of the science or engineering disciplines; for doctorate, GRE, resume, three letters of recommendation, statement of purpose, BS in any of the science or engineering disciplines. Additional exam requirements/recommendations for international students: Required—TOEFL (minimum score 550 paper-based; 79 iBT), IELTS (minimum score 6.5). Electronic applications accepted. *Expenses:* Contact institution. *Faculty research:* Tissue engineering and biomaterials, ocular biomechanics and cardiovascular biomechanics, biophotonics, cellular bioengineering, nano-biomaterials and nano-biotechnology.

The University of Texas Health Science Center at San Antonio, Graduate School of Biomedical Sciences, Biomedical Engineering Program, San Antonio, TX 78229-3900. Offers MS, PhD. Program offered jointly with The University of Texas at San Antonio. *Program availability:* Part-time. Terminal master's awarded for partial completion of doctoral program. *Degree requirements:* For master's, comprehensive exam, thesis; for doctorate, comprehensive exam, thesis/dissertation.

The University of Texas Southwestern Medical Center, Southwestern Graduate School of Biomedical Sciences, Division of Basic Science, Biomedical Engineering Program, Dallas, TX 75390. Offers MS, PhD. Programs offered jointly with The University of Texas at Arlington. *Degree requirements:* For master's, comprehensive exam or thesis; for doctorate, comprehensive exam, thesis/dissertation. *Entrance requirements:* For master's, GRE General Test, minimum GPA of 3.0; for doctorate, GRE General Test, minimum GPA of 3.4. Additional exam requirements/ recommendations for international students: Required—TOEFL. Electronic applications accepted. *Faculty research:* Noninvasive image analysis, biomaterials development, rehabilitation engineering, biomechanics, bioinstrumentation.

The University of Toledo, College of Graduate Studies, College of Engineering and College of Medicine and Life Sciences, PhD Program in Biomedical Engineering, Toledo, OH 43606-3390. Offers PhD. *Degree requirements:* For doctorate, thesis/ dissertation, qualifying exam. *Entrance requirements:* For doctorate, GRE General Test, minimum GPA of 3.3. Additional exam requirements/recommendations for international students: Required—TOEFL (minimum score 550 paper-based; 80 iBT). Electronic applications accepted. *Faculty research:* Biomechanics, biomaterials, tissue engineering, artificial organs, biosensors.

University of Toronto, School of Graduate Studies, Faculty of Applied Science and Engineering, Institute of Biomaterials and Biomedical Engineering, Toronto, ON M5S 1A1, Canada. Offers biomedical engineering (MA Sc, PhD); clinical engineering (MH Sc, PhD). *Program availability:* Part-time. *Degree requirements:* For master's, thesis (for some programs), research project (MH Sc), oral presentation (MA Sc); for doctorate, thesis/dissertation, qualifying exam. *Entrance requirements:* For master's, minimum A-average; bachelor's degree or equivalent in engineering, physical or biological science (for MA Sc), applied science or engineering (for MH Sc); for doctorate, master's degree in engineering, engineering science, medicine, dentistry, or a physical or biological science. Additional exam requirements/recommendations for international students: Required—TOEFL (minimum score 600 paper-based), TWE (minimum score 4), IELTS, Michigan English Language Assessment Battery, or COPE. Electronic applications accepted.

University of Vermont, Graduate College, College of Engineering and Mathematical Sciences, Program in Biomedical Engineering, Burlington, VT 05405. Offers MS. *Entrance requirements:* For master's, GRE. Additional exam requirements/ recommendations for international students: Required—TOEFL (minimum iBT score of 90) or IELTS (6.5). Electronic applications accepted. *Faculty research:* Engineered biomaterials, musculoskeletal imaging and orthopedic biomechanics, wearable and mobile devices.

University of Virginia, School of Engineering and Applied Science, Department of Biomedical Engineering, Charlottesville, VA 22903. Offers ME, MS, PhD. *Degree requirements:* For master's, project or thesis; for doctorate, thesis/dissertation. *Entrance requirements:* For master's, GRE General Test, 3 letters of recommendation; for doctorate, GRE General Test, 3 letters of recommendation, essay. Additional exam requirements/recommendations for international students: Required—TOEFL (minimum score 600 paper-based; 90 iBT), IELTS (minimum score 7). Electronic applications accepted. *Faculty research:* Cardiopulmonary and neural engineering, cellular engineering, image processing, orthopedics and rehabilitation engineering.

University of Wisconsin–Madison, Graduate School, College of Engineering, Department of Biomedical Engineering, Madison, WI 53706. Offers MS, PhD. *Program availability:* Part-time. *Faculty:* 16 full-time (7 women). *Students:* 104 full-time (43 women), 4 part-time (2 women); includes 21 minority (3 Black or African American, non-Hispanic/Latino; 7 Asian, non-Hispanic/Latino; 6 Hispanic/Latino; 5 Two or more races, non-Hispanic/Latino), 18 international. Average age 25. 309 applicants, 21% accepted, 37 enrolled. In 2018, 31 master's, 6 doctorates awarded. Terminal master's awarded for partial completion of doctoral program. *Degree requirements:* For master's, thesis optional, at least 30 credits of coursework; for doctorate, comprehensive exam, thesis/ dissertation, 60 credits total, 30 additional credits of coursework beyond MS. *Entrance requirements:* For master's and doctorate, GRE, bachelor degree in engineering (biomedical, chemical, electrical, industrial, mechanical, etc.) or science (biology, biochemistry, chemistry, genetics, immunology, physics, etc.). Additional exam requirements/recommendations for international students: Required—TOEFL (minimum score 625 paper-based; 92 iBT). *Application deadline:* For fall admission, 12/1 for domestic and international students; for spring admission, 10/1 for domestic and international students; for summer admission, 12/1 for domestic and international students. Application fee: $75 ($81 for international students). Electronic applications accepted. *Financial support:* In 2018–19, 61 students received support, including 3 fellowships with full tuition reimbursements available (averaging $30,180 per year), 46 research assistantships with full tuition reimbursements available (averaging $25,824 per year), 11 teaching assistantships with full tuition reimbursements available (averaging $18,156 per year); career-related internships or fieldwork, Federal Work-Study, scholarships/grants, traineeships, and health care benefits also available. Financial award application deadline: 12/1; financial award applicants required to submit FAFSA. *Faculty research:* Cellular and molecular engineering; bioinstrumentation; biomedical imaging; cancer research; biomechanics; biomaterials and tissue engineering. *Total annual research expenditures:* $11.6 million. *Unit head:* Dr. Justin Williams, Professor and Chair, 608-263-4660, E-mail: info@bme.wisc.edu. *Application contact:* Janna Pollock, Graduate Student Services Coordinator, 608-890-2756, E-mail: janna.pollock@wisc.edu.
Website: https://www.engr.wisc.edu/department/biomedical-engineering/

University of Wisconsin–Milwaukee, Graduate School, College of Engineering and Applied Science, Program in Engineering, Milwaukee, WI 53201-0413. Offers biomedical engineering (MS); civil engineering (MS, PhD); computer science (PhD); electrical and computer engineering (MS); electrical engineering (PhD); engineering mechanics (MS); industrial and management engineering (MS); industrial engineering (PhD); manufacturing engineering (MS); materials (PhD); materials engineering (MS); mechanical engineering (MS). *Program availability:* Part-time. *Students:* 174 full-time (41 women), 149 part-time (27 women); includes 31 minority (2 Black or African American, non-Hispanic/Latino; 1 American Indian or Alaska Native, non-Hispanic/ Latino; 16 Asian, non-Hispanic/Latino; 4 Hispanic/Latino; 8 Two or more races, non-Hispanic/Latino), 207 international. Average age 31. 343 applicants, 57% accepted, 78 enrolled. In 2018, 73 master's, 24 doctorates awarded. *Degree requirements:* For master's, comprehensive exam (for some programs), thesis or alternative; for doctorate, comprehensive exam, thesis/dissertation, internship. *Entrance requirements:* For master's, GRE, minimum GPA of 2.75; for doctorate, GRE, minimum GPA of 3.5. Additional exam requirements/recommendations for international students: Required—TOEFL (minimum score 550 paper-based; 79 iBT), IELTS (minimum score 6.5). *Application deadline:* For fall admission, 1/1 priority date for domestic students; for spring admission, 9/1 for domestic students. Applications are processed on a rolling basis. Application fee: $56 ($96 for international students). *Financial support:* Fellowships, research assistantships, teaching assistantships, career-related internships or fieldwork, Federal Work-Study, unspecified assistantships, and project assistantships available. Support available to part-time students. Financial award application deadline: 4/15. *Unit head:* David Yu, Representative, 414-229-6169, E-mail: yu@uwm.edu. *Application contact:* Betty Warras, General Information Contact, 414-229-6169, Fax: 414-229-6967, E-mail: bwarras@uwm.edu.
Website: http://www4.uwm.edu/ceas/academics/graduate_programs/

Vanderbilt University, School of Engineering, Department of Biomedical Engineering, Nashville, TN 37240-1001. Offers M Eng, MS, PhD, MD/PhD. *Degree requirements:* For master's, thesis (for some programs); for doctorate, thesis/dissertation. *Entrance requirements:* For master's, GRE General Test (for all except M Eng); for doctorate, GRE General Test. Additional exam requirements/recommendations for international students: Required—TOEFL. Electronic applications accepted. *Expenses: Tuition:* Full-time $47,208; part-time $2026 per credit hour. *Required fees:* $478. *Faculty research:* Bio-medical imaging, cell bioengineering, biomedical optics, technology-guided therapy, laser-tissue interaction and spectroscopy.

Virginia Commonwealth University, Graduate School, School of Engineering, Department of Biomedical Engineering, Richmond, VA 23284-9005. Offers MS, PhD. *Degree requirements:* For master's, thesis; for doctorate, thesis/dissertation, comprehensive oral and written exams. *Entrance requirements:* For master's and doctorate, GRE General Test. Additional exam requirements/recommendations for international students: Required—TOEFL (minimum score 600 paper-based; 100 iBT). Electronic applications accepted. *Faculty research:* Clinical instrumentation, mathematical modeling, neurosciences, radiation physics and rehabilitation.

Virginia Polytechnic Institute and State University, Graduate School, College of Engineering, Blacksburg, VA 24061. Offers aerospace engineering (PhD, M Eng/MS); biological systems engineering (PhD); biomedical engineering (MS, PhD); chemical engineering (PhD); civil engineering (PhD); computer engineering (PhD); computer science and applications (MS); electrical engineering (PhD); engineering education (PhD); M Eng/MS. *Faculty:* 446 full-time (87 women), 7 part-time/adjunct (3 women). *Students:* 1,776 full-time (471 women), 367 part-time (62 women); includes 260 minority (50 Black or African American, non-Hispanic/Latino; 3 American Indian or Alaska Native, non-Hispanic/Latino; 99 Asian, non-Hispanic/Latino; 67 Hispanic/Latino; 41 Two or more races, non-Hispanic/Latino), 1,178 international. Average age 27. 3,798 applicants, 37% accepted, 507 enrolled. In 2018, 489 master's, 200 doctorates awarded. *Degree requirements:* For master's, comprehensive exam (for some programs), thesis (for some programs); for doctorate, comprehensive exam (for some programs), thesis/dissertation (for some programs). *Entrance requirements:* For master's and doctorate, GRE/GMAT. Additional exam requirements/recommendations for international students: Required—TOEFL (minimum score 90 iBT). *Application deadline:* For fall admission, 8/1 for domestic students, 4/1 for international students; for spring admission, 1/1 for domestic students, 9/1 for international students. Applications are processed on a rolling basis. Application fee: $75. Electronic applications accepted. *Expenses:* Tuition, state resident: full-time $15,510; part-time $739.50 per credit hour. Tuition, nonresident: full-time $29,629; part-time $1490.25 per credit hour. *Required fees:* $2804; $550 per semester. Tuition and fees vary according to course load, campus/location and program. *Financial support:* In 2018–19, 37 fellowships with full tuition reimbursements (averaging $24,951 per year), 1,110 research assistantships with full tuition reimbursements (averaging $20,129 per year), 486 teaching assistantships with full tuition reimbursements (averaging $16,192 per year) were awarded; scholarships/grants and unspecified assistantships also available. Financial award application deadline: 3/1; financial award applicants required to submit FAFSA. *Total annual research expenditures:* $96.3 million. *Unit head:* Dr. Julia Ross, Dean, 540-231-9752, Fax: 540-231-3031, E-mail: rjulie@vt.edu. *Application contact:* Linda Perkins, Executive Assistant, 540-231-9752, Fax: 540-231-3031, E-mail: lperkins@vt.edu.
Website: http://www.eng.vt.edu/

Wake Forest University, Virginia Tech-Wake Forest University School of Biomedical Engineering and Sciences, Winston-Salem, NC 27109. Offers biomedical engineering (MS, PhD); DVM/PhD; MD/PhD. Terminal master's awarded for partial completion of doctoral program. *Degree requirements:* For master's, comprehensive exam, thesis; for doctorate, comprehensive exam, thesis/dissertation. *Entrance requirements:* For master's and doctorate, GRE, 3 letters of recommendation. Additional exam requirements/recommendations for international students: Required—TOEFL (minimum score 603 paper-based). Electronic applications accepted. *Faculty research:* Biomechanics, cell and tissue engineering, medical imaging, medical physics.

Washington University in St. Louis, School of Engineering and Applied Science, Department of Biomedical Engineering, St. Louis, MO 63130-4899. Offers MS, D Sc, PhD. Terminal master's awarded for partial completion of doctoral program. *Degree requirements:* For master's, thesis optional; for doctorate, thesis/dissertation. *Entrance requirements:* For master's, GRE, minimum GPA of 3.0; for doctorate, GRE General Test, minimum GPA of 3.5. Additional exam requirements/recommendations for international students: Required—TOEFL. Electronic applications accepted. *Faculty research:* Cell and tissue engineering, molecular engineering, neural engineering.

Wayne State University, College of Engineering, Department of Biomedical Engineering, Detroit, MI 48202. Offers biomedical engineering (MS, PhD), including biomedical imaging (PhD); injury biomechanics (Graduate Certificate). *Faculty:* 16. *Students:* 66 full-time (33 women), 38 part-time (19 women); includes 19 minority (6 Black or African American, non-Hispanic/Latino; 11 Asian, non-Hispanic/Latino; 2 Hispanic/Latino), 37 international. Average age 27. 113 applicants, 42% accepted, 29 enrolled. In 2018, 44 master's, 9 doctorates awarded. Terminal master's awarded for partial completion of doctoral program. *Entrance requirements:* For master's, GRE (recommended), bachelor's degree, minimum undergraduate GPA of 3.0, one-page statement of purpose, completion of prerequisite coursework in calculus and engineering physics; for doctorate, GRE, bachelor's degree in biomedical engineering with minimum undergraduate GPA of 3.5, or master's degree in biomedical engineering with minimum GPA of 3.3; personal statement; three letters of recommendation; for Graduate Certificate, minimum undergraduate GPA of 3.0, bachelor's degree in engineering or in a mathematics-based science program. Additional exam requirements/recommendations for international students: Required—TOEFL (minimum score 550 paper-based; 79 iBT), TWE; Recommended—IELTS (minimum score 6.5). *Application deadline:* For fall admission, 6/1 priority date for domestic students, 5/1 priority date for international students; for winter admission, 10/1 priority date for domestic students, 9/1 priority date for international students; for spring admission, 2/1 priority date for domestic students, 1/1 priority date for international students. Applications are processed on a rolling basis. Application fee: $50. Electronic applications accepted. *Expenses:* Contact institution. *Financial support:* In 2018–19, 50 students received support, including 5 fellowships with tuition reimbursements available (averaging $21,500 per year), 5 research assistantships with tuition reimbursements available (averaging $22,620 per year), 8 teaching assistantships with tuition reimbursements available (averaging $20,166 per year); Federal Work-Study, scholarships/grants, health care benefits, and unspecified assistantships also available. Support available to part-time students. Financial award applicants required to submit FAFSA. *Faculty research:* Injury and orthopedic biomechanics, neurophysiology of pain, smart sensors, biomaterials and imaging. *Unit head:* Dr. John Cavanaugh, Interim Department Chair, 313-577-3916, E-mail: jmc@wayne.edu. *Application contact:* Ellen Cope, Graduate Program Coordinator, 313-577-0409, Fax: 313-577-8333, E-mail: escope@wayne.edu.
Website: http://engineering.wayne.edu/bme/

Wichita State University, Graduate School, College of Engineering, Department of Biomedical Engineering, Wichita, KS 67260. Offers MS. *Entrance requirements:* For master's, GRE, bachelor's degree, transcript, minimum undergraduate GPA of 3.0, statement of purpose, three letters of recommendation. Additional exam requirements/recommendations for international students: Required—TOEFL. *Unit head:* Dr. Michael Jorgensen, Chairperson, 316-978-5904, E-mail: michael.jorgensen@wichita.edu. *Application contact:* Jordan Oleson, Admissions Coordinator, 316-978-3095, Fax: 316-978-3253, E-mail: jordan.oleson@wichita.edu.

Widener University, Graduate Programs in Engineering, Program in Biomedical Engineering, Chester, PA 19013. Offers M Eng. *Entrance requirements:* For master's, BS in engineering. Electronic applications accepted.

Worcester Polytechnic Institute, Graduate Admissions, Department of Biomedical Engineering, Worcester, MA 01609-2280. Offers M Eng, MS, PhD, Graduate Certificate. *Program availability:* Part-time, evening/weekend. *Students:* 30 full-time (16 women), 19 part-time (10 women); includes 7 minority (2 Black or African American, non-Hispanic/Latino; 2 Asian, non-Hispanic/Latino; 2 Hispanic/Latino; 1 Two or more races, non-Hispanic/Latino), 10 international. Average age 26. 156 applicants, 56% accepted, 22 enrolled. In 2018, 13 master's, 3 doctorates awarded. Terminal master's awarded for partial completion of doctoral program. *Degree requirements:* For master's, thesis optional; for doctorate, comprehensive exam, thesis/dissertation. *Entrance requirements:* For master's and doctorate, GRE General Test, 3 letters of recommendation, statement of purpose. Additional exam requirements/recommendations for international students: Required—TOEFL (minimum score 563 paper-based; 84 iBT), IELTS (minimum score 7). *Application deadline:* For fall admission, 1/1 priority date for domestic and international students. Application fee: $70. Electronic applications accepted. *Financial support:* Fellowships, research assistantships, teaching assistantships, career-related internships or fieldwork, institutionally sponsored loans, scholarships/grants, and unspecified assistantships available. Financial award application deadline: 1/1. *Unit head:* Dr. Kristen Billiar, Head, 508-831-5447, Fax: 508-831-4121, E-mail: kbilliar@wpi.edu. *Application contact:* Dr. Songbi Ji, Graduate Coordinator, 508-831-5447, Fax: 508-831-4121, E-mail: sji@wpi.edu.
Website: https://www.wpi.edu/academics/departments/biomedical-engineering

Wright State University, Graduate School, College of Engineering and Computer Science, Department of Biomedical, Industrial and Human Factors Engineering, Dayton, OH 45435. Offers biomedical engineering (MS); industrial and human factors engineering (MS). *Program availability:* Part-time. *Degree requirements:* For master's, thesis or course option alternative. *Entrance requirements:* Additional exam requirements/recommendations for international students: Required—TOEFL. *Faculty research:* Medical imaging, functional electrical stimulation, implantable aids, man-machine interfaces, expert systems.

Yale University, Graduate School of Arts and Sciences, School of Engineering and Applied Science, Department of Biomedical Engineering, New Haven, CT 06520. Offers MS, PhD. *Faculty research:* Biomedical imaging and biosignals; biomechanics; biomolecular engineering and biotechnology.

Biotechnology

Adelphi University, College of Arts and Sciences, Department of Biology, Garden City, NY 11530-0701. Offers biology (MS); biotechnology (MS). *Program availability:* Part-time, evening/weekend. *Faculty:* 17 full-time (8 women), 28 part-time/adjunct (14 women). *Students:* 37 full-time (27 women), 10 part-time (8 women); includes 17 minority (7 Black or African American, non-Hispanic/Latino; 1 American Indian or Alaska Native, non-Hispanic/Latino; 4 Asian, non-Hispanic/Latino; 4 Hispanic/Latino; 1 Two or more races, non-Hispanic/Latino), 17 international. Average age 26. 121 applicants, 43% accepted, 25 enrolled. In 2018, 21 master's awarded. *Degree requirements:* For master's, thesis or alternative. *Entrance requirements:* For master's, bachelor's degree in biology or allied sciences, essay, 3 letters of recommendation, official transcripts. Additional exam requirements/recommendations for international students: Required—TOEFL (minimum score 550 paper-based; 80 iBT), IELTS (minimum score 6.5). *Application deadline:* For fall admission, 5/1 for international students; for spring admission, 12/1 for international students. Applications are processed on a rolling basis. Application fee: $50. Electronic applications accepted. *Expenses:* Contact institution. *Financial support:* Research assistantships with full and partial tuition reimbursements, teaching assistantships, career-related internships or fieldwork, institutionally sponsored loans, scholarships/grants, traineeships, and unspecified assistantships available. Support available to part-time students. Financial award application deadline: 1/1; financial award applicants required to submit FAFSA. *Faculty research:* Plant-animal interactions, physiology (plant, cornea), reproductive behavior, topics in evolution, fish biology. *Unit head:* Dr. Andrea Ward, Chair, 516-877-4204, E-mail: award@adelphi.edu. *Application contact:* Dr. Andrea Ward, Chair, 516-877-4204, E-mail: award@adelphi.edu.
Website: http://academics.adelphi.edu/artsci/bio/index.php

American University, College of Arts and Sciences, Department of Biology, Washington, DC 20016-8007. Offers biology (MS); biotechnology (MA). *Program availability:* Part-time. *Faculty:* 19 full-time (10 women). *Students:* 15 full-time (9 women), 6 part-time (3 women); includes 3 minority (1 Black or African American, non-Hispanic/Latino; 1 Asian, non-Hispanic/Latino; 1 Hispanic/Latino), 4 international. Average age 25. 24 applicants, 63% accepted, 9 enrolled. In 2018, 12 master's awarded. *Degree requirements:* For master's, comprehensive exam, thesis (for some programs). *Entrance requirements:* For master's, GRE General Test, GRE Subject Test, Please see website : https://www.american.edu/cas/biology/, statement of purpose, transcripts, 2 letters of recommendation, resume. Additional exam requirements/recommendations for international students: Required—TOEFL. Application fee: $55. Electronic applications accepted. *Expenses:* Contact institution. *Financial support:* Research assistantships, teaching assistantships, institutionally sponsored loans, and unspecified assistantships available. Financial award applicants required to submit FAFSA. *Faculty research:* Neurobiology, cave biology, population genetics, vertebrate physiology. *Unit head:* Dr. Katie DeCicco-Skinner, Chair, Department of Art, 202-885-2176, E-mail: biology@american.edu. *Application contact:* Jonathan Harper, Assistant Director, Graduate Recruitment, 202-855-3620, E-mail: casgrad@american.edu.
Website: http://www.american.edu/cas/biology/

The American University in Cairo, School of Sciences and Engineering, Cairo, Egypt. Offers biotechnology (MS); chemistry (MS); computer science (MS); computing (M Comp); construction engineering (M Eng, MS); electronics and communications engineering (M Eng); environmental engineering (MS); environmental system design (M Eng); mechanical engineering (M Eng, MS); nanotechnology (MS); physics (MS); robotics, control and smart systems (MS); sciences and engineering (PhD); sustainable development (MS, Graduate Diploma). *Program availability:* Part-time, evening/weekend. *Degree requirements:* For master's, comprehensive exam (for some programs), thesis (for some programs); for doctorate, comprehensive exam (for some programs), thesis/dissertation. *Entrance requirements:* Additional exam requirements/recommendations for international students: Required—TOEFL (minimum score 450 paper-based; 45 iBT), IELTS (minimum score 5). Electronic applications accepted. *Faculty research:* Construction, mechanical, and electronics engineering; physics; computer science; biotechnology; nanotechnology; chemistry; robotics.

Arizona State University at the Tempe campus, Sandra Day O'Connor College of Law, Phoenix, AZ 85287-7906. Offers biotechnology and genomics (LL M); law (JD);

legal studies (MLS); patent practice (MLS); sports law and business (MSLB); tribal policy, law and government (LL M); JD/MBA; JD/MD; JD/MSW; JD/PhD. JD/MD offered jointly with Mayo Medical School. *Accreditation:* ABA. *Program availability:* 100% online. *Faculty:* 62 full-time (26 women), 146 part-time/adjunct (40 women). *Students:* 812 full-time (372 women); includes 201 minority (16 Black or African American, non-Hispanic/Latino; 15 American Indian or Alaska Native, non-Hispanic/Latino; 37 Asian, non-Hispanic/Latino; 97 Hispanic/Latino; 3 Native Hawaiian or other Pacific Islander, non-Hispanic/Latino; 33 Two or more races, non-Hispanic/Latino), 16 international. Average age 28. 3,363 applicants, 34% accepted, 271 enrolled. In 2018, 131 master's, 276 doctorates awarded. *Entrance requirements:* For master's, bachelor's degree and JD (for LL M); for doctorate, LSAT, bachelor's degree. Additional exam requirements/recommendations for international students: Required—TOEFL (minimum score 550 paper-based; 80 iBT). *Application deadline:* For fall admission, 3/1 priority date for domestic and international students. Applications are processed on a rolling basis. Application fee: $0. Electronic applications accepted. *Expenses:* $27,584 resident tuition and fees (for JD), $45,940 non-resident tuition and fees (for JD). *Financial support:* In 2018–19, 579 students received support. Institutionally sponsored loans and scholarships/grants available. Financial award application deadline: 3/15; financial award applicants required to submit FAFSA. *Faculty research:* Emerging technologies and the law, Indian law, international law, intellectual property, health law, sports law and business. *Total annual research expenditures:* $2.8 million. *Unit head:* Douglas Sylvester, Dean/Professor, 480-965-6188, Fax: 480-965-6521, E-mail: douglas.sylvester@asu.edu. *Application contact:* Chitra Damania, Director, 480-965-1474, Fax: 480-727-7930, E-mail: law.admissions@asu.edu.
Website: http://www.law.asu.edu/

Arkansas State University, Graduate School, College of Sciences and Mathematics, Department of Biological Sciences, State University, AR 72467. Offers biological sciences (MA); biology (MS); biology education (MSE, SCCT); biotechnology (PSM). *Program availability:* Part-time. *Degree requirements:* For master's, comprehensive exam, thesis (for some programs); for SCCT, comprehensive exam. *Entrance requirements:* For master's, GRE General Test, appropriate bachelor's degree, letters of reference, interview, official transcripts, immunization records, statement of educational objectives and career goals, teaching certificate (for MSE); for SCCT, GRE General Test or MAT, interview, master's degree, letters of reference, official transcript, personal statement, immunization records. Additional exam requirements/recommendations for international students: Required—TOEFL (minimum score 550 paper-based; 79 iBT), IELTS (minimum score 6), PTE (minimum score 56). Electronic applications accepted.

Azusa Pacific University, College of Liberal Arts and Sciences, Program in Biotechnology, Azusa, CA 91702-7000. Offers MS.

Brandeis University, Graduate School of Arts and Sciences, Department of Biotechnology, Waltham, MA 02454-9110. Offers PSM, MS/MBA. Offered jointly with The Heller School for Social Policy and Management. *Faculty:* 8 full-time (5 women), 2 part-time/adjunct (0 women). *Students:* 20 full-time (14 women); includes 4 minority (1 Black or African American, non-Hispanic/Latino; 2 Hispanic/Latino; 1 Two or more races, non-Hispanic/Latino), 11 international. Average age 24. 68 applicants, 54% accepted, 12 enrolled. In 2018, 13 master's awarded. *Degree requirements:* For master's, poster presentation; summer internship. *Entrance requirements:* For master's, GRE or GMAT, transcripts, recommendation letters, resume, statement of purpose. Additional exam requirements/recommendations for international students: Required—TOEFL, IELTS, PTE. *Application deadline:* For fall admission, 1/15 priority date for domestic students. Applications are processed on a rolling basis. Application fee: $75. Electronic applications accepted. *Financial support:* Fellowships, career-related internships or fieldwork, scholarships/grants, and health care benefits available. *Faculty research:* Biotechnology, biotechnology and business administration. *Unit head:* Dr. Neil Simister, Director of Graduate Studies, 781-736-2520, E-mail: simister@brandeis.edu. *Application contact:* Maryanna Aldrich, Administrator, 781-736-2352, E-mail: scigradoffice@brandeis.edu.
Website: http://www.brandeis.edu/gsas/programs/biotech.html

Brigham Young University, Graduate Studies, College of Life Sciences, Department of Plant and Wildlife Sciences, Provo, UT 84602-1001. Offers environmental science (MS); genetics and biotechnology (MS); wildlife and wildlands conservation (MS, PhD). *Faculty:* 24 full-time (1 woman). *Students:* 12 full-time (7 women), 42 part-time (12 women); includes 2 minority (both Hispanic/Latino). Average age 30. 29 applicants, 59% accepted, 17 enrolled. In 2018, 18 master's, 1 doctorate awarded. *Degree requirements:* For master's, thesis, no C grades or below, 30 hours (24 coursework, 6 thesis); for doctorate, comprehensive exam, thesis/dissertation, no C grades or below, 54 hours (18 dissertation, 36 coursework). *Entrance requirements:* For master's, GRE General Test, minimum GPA of 3.2; for doctorate, GRE, minimum GPA of 3.2. Additional exam requirements/recommendations for international students: Required—TOEFL (minimum score 580 paper-based; 85 iBT). *Application deadline:* 2/1 for domestic and international students; for summer admission, 2/1 for domestic and international students. Application fee: $50. Electronic applications accepted. *Financial support:* In 2018–19, 54 students received support, including 71 research assistantships with partial tuition reimbursements available (averaging $18,081 per year), 42 teaching assistantships with partial tuition reimbursements available (averaging $16,478 per year); scholarships/grants and tuition waivers (partial) also available. Financial award application deadline: 3/1. *Faculty research:* Environmental science, plant genetics, plant ecology, plant nutrition and pathology, wildlife and wildlands conservation. *Total annual research expenditures:* $2.1 million. *Unit head:* Neil Hansen, Chair, 801-422-2491, E-mail: neil_hansen@byu.edu. *Application contact:* Bradley D. Geary, Graduate Coordinator, 801-422-1228, Fax: 801-422-0008, E-mail: bradley_geary@byu.edu.
Website: http://pws.byu.edu

Brock University, Faculty of Graduate Studies, Faculty of Mathematics and Science, Program in Biotechnology, St. Catharines, ON L2S 3A1, Canada. Offers M Sc, PhD. *Program availability:* Part-time. *Degree requirements:* For master's, thesis; for doctorate, thesis/dissertation. *Entrance requirements:* For master's, honors B Sc; for doctorate, M Sc. Additional exam requirements/recommendations for international students: Required—TOEFL (minimum score 550 paper-based; 80 iBT), IELTS (minimum score 6.5), TWE (minimum score 4). Electronic applications accepted. *Faculty research:* Bioorganic chemistry, structural chemistry, electrochemistry, cell and molecular biology, plant sciences, oenology, and viticulture.

Brown University, Graduate School, Division of Biology and Medicine, Department of Molecular Pharmacology, Physiology and Biotechnology, Providence, RI 02912. Offers biomedical engineering (Sc M, PhD); biotechnology (PhD); molecular pharmacology and physiology (PhD); MD/PhD. *Degree requirements:* For doctorate, thesis/dissertation, preliminary exam. *Entrance requirements:* For master's and doctorate, GRE General Test, GRE Subject Test. Additional exam requirements/recommendations for international students: Required—TOEFL. Electronic applications accepted. *Faculty research:* Structural biology, antiplatelet drugs, nicotinic receptor structure/function.

California State University Channel Islands, Extended University and International Programs, MS Biotechnology & Bioinformatics, Camarillo, CA 93012. Offers biotechnology and bioinformatics (MS); MS/MBA. *Program availability:* Part-time, evening/weekend. *Students:* 66 full-time (33 women); includes 44 minority (1 Black or African American, non-Hispanic/Latino; 28 Asian, non-Hispanic/Latino; 7 Hispanic/Latino; 2 Native Hawaiian or other Pacific Islander, non-Hispanic/Latino; 6 Two or more races, non-Hispanic/Latino). *Degree requirements:* For master's, thesis. *Entrance requirements:* For master's, GRE/GMAT; GMAT can be waived based on certain requirements. Additional exam requirements/recommendations for international students: Required—TOEFL (minimum score 550 paper-based; 80 iBT), IELTS (minimum score 6.5). *Application deadline:* For fall admission, 5/1 for domestic students; for spring admission, 11/1 for domestic students. Application fee: $55. Electronic applications accepted. *Financial support:* Applicants required to submit FAFSA. *Unit head:* Dr. Nitika Parmar, Program Director, 805-437-8873, E-mail: nitika.parmar@csuci.edu. *Application contact:* Andrew Conley, Graduate Program Recruiter, 805-437-2652, E-mail: andrew.conley@csuci.edu.
Website: https://ext.csuci.edu/

California State University, Fullerton, Graduate Studies, College of Natural Science and Mathematics, Department of Biological Science, Fullerton, CA 92831-3599. Offers biology (MS); biotechnology (MBT). *Program availability:* Part-time. *Entrance requirements:* For master's, GRE General and Subject Tests, MCAT, or DAT, minimum GPA of 3.0 in biology. *Faculty research:* Glycosidase release and the block to polyspermy in ascidian eggs.

California State University, San Marcos, Program in Biotechnology, San Marcos, CA 92096-0001. Offers PSM. *Unit head:* Dr. Betsy Read, Director, 760-750-4129, E-mail: bread@csusm.edu. *Application contact:* JoAnne Mendez, Coordinator, 760-750-8797, E-mail: jmendez@csusm.edu.
Website: https://www.csusm.edu/el/degreeprograms/psmbiotech/

Carnegie Mellon University, Heinz College, School of Public Policy and Management, Master of Science Program in Biotechnology and Management, Pittsburgh, PA 15213-3891. Offers MS. *Accreditation:* AACSB. *Entrance requirements:* For master's, GRE or GMAT, college-level course in advanced algebra/pre-calculus; college-level courses in economics and statistics (recommended). Additional exam requirements/recommendations for international students: Required—TOEFL or IELTS.

The Catholic University of America, School of Arts and Sciences, Department of Biology, Washington, DC 20064. Offers biotechnology (MS); cell and microbial biology (MS, PhD), including cell biology; clinical laboratory science (MS, PhD); MSLS/MS. MSLS/MS offered jointly with Department of Library and Information Science. *Program availability:* Part-time. *Faculty:* 8 full-time (3 women), 4 part-time/adjunct (0 women). *Students:* 25 full-time (21 women), 37 part-time (23 women); includes 10 minority (3 Black or African American, non-Hispanic/Latino; 2 Asian, non-Hispanic/Latino; 5 Two or more races, non-Hispanic/Latino), 41 international. Average age 31. 40 applicants, 55% accepted, 9 enrolled. In 2018, 9 master's, 2 doctorates awarded. Terminal master's awarded for partial completion of doctoral program. *Degree requirements:* For master's and doctorate, comprehensive exam. *Entrance requirements:* For master's and doctorate, GRE General Test, GRE Subject Test, statement of purpose, official copies of academic transcripts, three letters of recommendation. Additional exam requirements/recommendations for international students: Required—TOEFL (minimum score 550 paper-based; 80 iBT). *Application deadline:* For fall admission, 7/15 priority date for domestic students, 7/1 for international students; for spring admission, 11/15 priority date for domestic students, 11/1 for international students. Applications are processed on a rolling basis. Application fee: $55. Electronic applications accepted. *Expenses:* Contact institution. *Financial support:* Fellowships, research assistantships, teaching assistantships, Federal Work-Study, scholarships/grants, tuition waivers (full and partial), and unspecified assistantships available. Financial award application deadline: 2/1; financial award applicants required to submit FAFSA. *Faculty research:* Virus structure and assembly, hepatic and epithelial cell biology, drug resistance and genome stabilization in yeast, biophysics of ion-conductive nanostructures, eukaryotic gene regulation, cancer and vaccine research. *Unit head:* Dr. Venigalla Rao, Chair, 202-319-5271, Fax: 202-319-5721, E-mail: rao@cua.edu. *Application contact:* Dr. Steven Brown, Director of Graduate Admissions, 202-319-5057, Fax: 202-319-6533, E-mail: cua-admissions@cua.edu.
Website: http://biology.cua.edu/

Claflin University, Graduate Programs, Orangeburg, SC 29115. Offers biotechnology (MS); business administration (MBA). *Program availability:* Part-time. *Degree requirements:* For master's, comprehensive exam, thesis. *Entrance requirements:* For master's, GRE, GMAT, baccalaureate degree, 3 letters of recommendation, resume, statement of purpose. Additional exam requirements/recommendations for international students: Recommended—TOEFL (minimum score 550 paper-based).

Clarkson University, School of Arts and Sciences, Program in Interdisciplinary Bioscience and Biotechnology, Potsdam, NY 13699. Offers MS, PhD. *Students:* 14 full-time (8 women); includes 2 minority (1 Black or African American, non-Hispanic/Latino; 1 Hispanic/Latino), 7 international. 23 applicants, 43% accepted, 7 enrolled. In 2018, 2 doctorates awarded. *Degree requirements:* For doctorate, comprehensive exam, thesis/dissertation. *Entrance requirements:* For doctorate, GRE. Additional exam requirements/recommendations for international students: Required—TOEFL (minimum score 550 paper-based, 80 iBT) or IELTS (6.5). *Application deadline:* Applications are processed on a rolling basis. Application fee: $50. Electronic applications accepted. *Expenses: Tuition:* Full-time $24,984; part-time $1388 per credit hour. *Required fees:* $225. Tuition and fees vary according to campus/location and program. *Financial support:* Scholarships/grants and unspecified assistantships available. *Unit head:* Dr. Tom Langen, Chair of Biology, 315-268-2342, E-mail: tlangen@clarkson.edu. *Application contact:* Dan Capogna, Director of Graduate Admissions & Recruitment, 518-631-9910, E-mail: graduate@clarkson.edu.
Website: https://www.clarkson.edu/academics/graduate

College of Staten Island of the City University of New York, Graduate Programs, Division of Science and Technology, Program in Biology, Staten Island, NY 10314-6600. Offers biology (MS), including biotechnology, general biology. *Program availability:* Part-time, evening/weekend. *Students:* 29. 35 applicants, 46% accepted, 6 enrolled. In 2018, 9 master's awarded. *Degree requirements:* For master's, 30 credits (for general biology and biotechnology tracks). *Entrance requirements:* For master's, GRE (recommended), BS in Biology degree from an accredited college, overall GPA of 2.75 (B-), GPA of 3.0 (B) in undergraduate science and mathematics courses, 2 letters of recommendation. Additional exam requirements/recommendations for international students: Required—TOEFL (minimum score 550 paper-based; 79 iBT), IELTS (minimum score 6.5). *Application deadline:* For fall admission, 7/1 for domestic students, 4/25 for international students; for spring admission, 11/25 for domestic and international students. Applications are processed on a rolling basis. Application fee: $75. Electronic applications accepted. *Expenses: Tuition, area resident:* Full-time $10,770; part-time $455 per credit. Tuition, state resident: full-time $10,770; part-time $455 per credit. Tuition, nonresident: full-time $19,920; part-time $830 per credit. *International tuition:* $19,920 full-time. *Required fees:* $559.20; $181.10 per semester. Tuition and fees vary according to program. *Faculty research:* Gene regulatory network, transcriptional regulation and epigenetics; developmental biology and evolution; biogeography, conservation, species responses and abundance; ecological process and computational biology; cancer biology. *Unit head:* Dr. Jianying Gu, Biotechnology Coordinator, 718-982-4123, E-mail: jianying.gu@csi.cuny.edu. *Application contact:* Sasha Spence,

Associate Director for Graduate Admissions, 718-982-2019, Fax: 718-982-2500, E-mail: sasha.spence@csi.cuny.edu.
Website: https://www.csi.cuny.edu/sites/default/files/pdf/admissions/grad/pdf/Biology%20Fact%20Sheet.pdf

Columbia University, Graduate School of Arts and Sciences, New York, NY 10027. Offers African-American studies (MA); American studies (MA); anthropology (MA, PhD); art history and archaeology (MA, PhD); astronomy (PhD); biological sciences (PhD); biotechnology (MA); chemical physics (PhD); chemistry (PhD); classical studies (MA, PhD); classics (MA, PhD); climate and society (MA); conservation biology (MA); earth and environmental sciences (PhD); East Asia: regional studies (MA); East Asian languages and cultures (MA, PhD); ecology, evolution and environmental biology (MA), including conservation biology; ecology, evolution, and environmental biology (PhD), including ecology and evolutionary biology, evolutionary primatology; economics (MA, PhD); English and comparative literature (MA, PhD); French and Romance philology (MA, PhD); Germanic languages (MA, PhD); global French studies (MA); global thought (MA); Hispanic cultural studies (MA); history (PhD); history and literature (MA); human rights studies (MA); Islamic studies (MA); Italian (MA, PhD); Japanese pedagogy (MA); Jewish studies (MA); Latin America and the Caribbean: regional studies (MA); Latin American and Iberian cultures (PhD); mathematics (MA, PhD), including finance (MA); medieval and Renaissance studies (MA); Middle Eastern, South Asian, and African studies (MA, PhD); modern art: critical and curatorial studies (MA); modern European studies (MA); museum anthropology (MA); music (DMA, PhD); oral history (MA); philosophical foundations of physics (MA); philosophy (MA, PhD); physics (PhD); political science (MA, PhD); psychology (PhD); quantitative methods in the social sciences (MA); religion (MA, PhD); Russia, Eurasia and East Europe: regional studies (MA); Russian translation (MA); Slavic cultures (MA); Slavic languages (MA, PhD); sociology (MA, PhD); South Asian studies (MA); statistics (MA, PhD); theatre (PhD). Dual-degree programs require admission to both Graduate School of Arts and Sciences and another Columbia school. *Program availability:* Part-time. Terminal master's awarded for partial completion of doctoral program. *Degree requirements:* For master's, variable foreign language requirement, comprehensive exam (for some programs), thesis (for some programs); for doctorate, variable foreign language requirement, comprehensive exam (for some programs), thesis/dissertation. *Entrance requirements:* For master's and doctorate, GRE General Test, GRE Subject Test (for some programs). Additional exam requirements/recommendations for international students: Required—TOEFL, IELTS. Electronic applications accepted.

Concordia University, School of Graduate Studies, Faculty of Arts and Science, Department of Biology, Montréal, QC H3G 1M8, Canada. Offers biology (M Sc, PhD); biotechnology and genomics (Diploma). *Degree requirements:* For master's, thesis; for doctorate, thesis/dissertation, pedagogical training. *Entrance requirements:* For master's, honors degree in biology; for doctorate, M Sc in life science. *Faculty research:* Cell biology, animal physiology, ecology, microbiology/molecular biology, plant physiology/biochemistry and biotechnology.

Cornell University, Graduate School, Graduate Fields of Agriculture and Life Sciences and Graduate Fields of Engineering, Field of Biological and Environmental Engineering, Ithaca, NY 14853. Offers bioenergy and integrated energy systems (M Eng, MPS, MS, PhD); biological engineering (M Eng, MPS, MS, PhD); bioprocess engineering (M Eng, MPS, MS, PhD); ecohydrology (M Eng, MPS, MS, PhD); environmental engineering (M Eng, MPS, MS, PhD); environmental management (MPS); food engineering (M Eng, MPS, MS, PhD); industrial biotechnology (M Eng, MPS, MS, PhD); nanobiotechnology (M Eng, MPS, MS, PhD); sustainable systems (M Eng, MPS, MS, PhD); synthetic biology (MS); syntheticbiology (M Eng, MPS, PhD). Terminal master's awarded for partial completion of doctoral program. *Degree requirements:* For master's, thesis (MS); for doctorate, comprehensive exam, thesis/dissertation. *Entrance requirements:* For master's, letters of recommendation (3 for MS, 2 for M Eng and MPS); for doctorate, GRE General Test, 3 letters of recommendation. Additional exam requirements/recommendations for international students: Required—TOEFL (minimum score 550 paper-based; 77 iBT). Electronic applications accepted. *Faculty research:* Biological and food engineering, environmental, soil and water engineering, international agricultural engineering, structures and controlled environments, machine systems and energy.

Duquesne University, Bayer School of Natural and Environmental Sciences, Program in Biotechnology, Pittsburgh, PA 15282-0001. Offers MS. *Program availability:* Part-time, evening/weekend. *Faculty:* 1 full-time (0 women), 2 part-time/adjunct (0 women). *Students:* 7 full-time (2 women), 5 part-time (2 women); includes 1 minority (Black or African American, non-Hispanic/Latino), 5 international. Average age 24. 21 applicants, 100% accepted, 7 enrolled. In 2018, 5 master's awarded. *Entrance requirements:* For master's, GRE General Test, statement of purpose, 2 letters of recommendation, official transcripts. Additional exam requirements/recommendations for international students: Required—TOEFL (minimum score 80 iBT), TOEFL (minimum score 80 iBT) or IELTS. *Application deadline:* For fall admission, 7/1 priority date for domestic students, 5/1 for international students; for spring admission, 10/1 priority date for domestic students, 10/1 for international students. Applications are processed on a rolling basis. Application fee: $0. Electronic applications accepted. *Expenses:* $1376 per credit hour. *Financial support:* In 2018–19, 10 students received support, including 1 fellowship with full tuition reimbursement available (averaging $17,500 per year); career-related internships or fieldwork and tuition waivers (partial) also available. *Unit head:* Dr. Alan W. Seadler, Director, 412-396-1568, E-mail: seadlera@duq.edu. *Application contact:* Heather Costello, Senior Graduate Academic Advisor, 412-396-6339, E-mail: costelloh@duq.edu.
Website: http://www.duq.edu/academics/schools/natural-and-environmental-sciences/academic-programs/biotechnology

East Carolina University, Graduate School, Thomas Harriot College of Arts and Sciences, Department of Biology, Greenville, NC 27858-4353. Offers biology (MS); molecular biology and biotechnology (MS). *Program availability:* Part-time. *Application deadline:* For fall admission, 6/1 priority date for domestic students, 3/1 priority date for international students; for spring admission, 10/15 priority date for domestic students. *Expenses: Tuition, area resident:* Full-time $4749. Tuition, state resident: full-time $4749. Tuition, nonresident: full-time $17,898. *International tuition:* $17,898 full-time. *Required fees:* $2787. Part-time tuition and fees vary according to course load and program. *Financial support:* Application deadline: 3/1. *Unit head:* Dr. Jeff McKinnon, Chair, 252-328-6718, E-mail: mckinnonj@ecu.edu. *Application contact:* graduate School Admissions, 252-328-6012, Fax: 252-328-6071, E-mail: gradschool@ecu.edu.
Website: http://www.ecu.edu/cs-cas/biology/

Eastern Virginia Medical School, Biotechnology Program, Norfolk, VA 23501-1980. Offers MS. *Entrance requirements:* For master's, GRE. Additional exam requirements/recommendations for international students: Required—TOEFL. Electronic applications accepted.

Florida Institute of Technology, College of Engineering and Science, Program in Biological Sciences, Melbourne, FL 32901-6975. Offers biological sciences (PhD); biotechnology (MS); ecology (MS). *Program availability:* Part-time. *Students:* 21 full-time (18 women); includes 1 minority (Hispanic/Latino), 6 international. Average age 30. 9 applicants, 44% accepted, 1 enrolled. In 2018, 2 doctorates awarded. *Degree requirements:* For doctorate, comprehensive exam, thesis/dissertation, dissertations seminar, publications. *Entrance requirements:* For doctorate, GRE General Test, resume, 3 letters of recommendation, minimum GPA of 3.2, statement of objectives. Additional exam requirements/recommendations for international students: Required—TOEFL (minimum score 550 paper-based; 79 iBT). *Application deadline:* For fall admission, 3/1 for domestic students, 4/1 for international students; for spring admission, 9/1 for domestic and international students. Applications are processed on a rolling basis. Application fee: $50. Electronic applications accepted. *Expenses: Tuition:* Full-time $22,338; part-time $1241 per credit hour. Tuition and fees vary according to degree level, campus/location and program. *Financial support:* Career-related internships or fieldwork, institutionally sponsored loans, tuition waivers (partial), unspecified assistantships, and tuition remissions available. Support available to part-time students. Financial award application deadline: 3/1; financial award applicants required to submit FAFSA. *Faculty research:* Initiation of protein synthesis in eukaryotic cells, fixation of radioactive carbon, changes in DNA molecule, endangered or threatened avian and mammalian species, hydro acoustics and feeding preference of the West Indian manatee. *Unit head:* Dr. Ted Conway, Department Head, 321-674-8491, E-mail: tconway@fit.edu. *Application contact:* Mike Perry, Executive Director of Admission, 321-674-7127, E-mail: perrymj@fit.edu.
Website: https://www.fit.edu/programs/biological-sciences-phd/

Florida Institute of Technology, College of Engineering and Science, Program in Biotechnology, Melbourne, FL 32901-6975. Offers MS. *Program availability:* Part-time. *Students:* 29 full-time (23 women), 2 part-time (1 woman); includes 1 minority (Black or African American, non-Hispanic/Latino), 30 international. Average age 26. 14 applicants, 79% accepted, 4 enrolled. In 2018, 23 master's awarded. *Degree requirements:* For master's, comprehensive exam, thesis, internship. *Entrance requirements:* For master's, GRE General Test, 3 letter of recommendation, stated objectives. Additional exam requirements/recommendations for international students: Required—TOEFL (minimum score 550 paper-based; 79 iBT). *Application deadline:* Applications are processed on a rolling basis. Application fee: $50. Electronic applications accepted. *Expenses: Tuition:* Full-time $22,338; part-time $1241 per credit hour. Tuition and fees vary according to degree level, campus/location and program. *Financial support:* Research assistantships, teaching assistantships, and career-related internships or fieldwork available. Financial award application deadline: 3/1; financial award applicants required to submit FAFSA. *Faculty research:* Molecular medicine, diagnostics, agriculture, environmental science. *Unit head:* Dr. Ted Conway, Department Head, 321-674-8491, E-mail: tconway@fit.edu. *Application contact:* Mike Perry, Executive Director of Admissions, 321-674-7127, E-mail: perrymj@fit.edu.
Website: https://www.fit.edu/programs/biotechnology-ms/

The George Washington University, School of Medicine and Health Sciences, Health Sciences Programs, Washington, DC 20052. Offers clinical practice management (MSHS); clinical research administration (MSHS); emergency services management (MSHS); end-of-life care (MSHS); immunohematology (MSHS); immunohematology and biotechnology (MSHS); physical therapy (DPT); physician assistant (MSHS). *Program availability:* Online learning. *Students:* 315 full-time (237 women), 326 part-time (259 women); includes 229 minority (74 Black or African American, non-Hispanic/Latino; 81 Asian, non-Hispanic/Latino; 54 Hispanic/Latino; 3 Native Hawaiian or other Pacific Islander, non-Hispanic/Latino; 17 Two or more races, non-Hispanic/Latino), 11 international. Average age 33. 2,865 applicants, 14% accepted, 238 enrolled. In 2018, 177 master's, 43 doctorates, 5 other advanced degrees awarded. *Entrance requirements:* Additional exam requirements/recommendations for international students: Required—TOEFL (minimum score 550 paper-based). *Application deadline:* Applications are processed on a rolling basis. Application fee: $75. *Expenses:* Contact institution. *Unit head:* Jean E. Johnson, Senior Associate Dean, 202-994-3725, E-mail: jejohns@gwu.edu. *Application contact:* Joke Ogundiran, Director of Admission, 202-994-1668, Fax: 202-994-0870, E-mail: jokeogun@gwu.edu.

Harvard University, Extension School, Cambridge, MA 02138-3722. Offers applied sciences (CAS); biotechnology (ALM); educational technologies (ALM); educational technology (CET); English for graduate and professional studies (DGP); environmental management (ALM, CEM); information technology (ALM); journalism (ALM); liberal arts (ALM); management (ALM, CM); mathematics for teaching (ALM); museum studies (ALM); premedical studies (Diploma); publication and communication (CPC). *Program availability:* Part-time, evening/weekend. *Degree requirements:* For master's, thesis. *Entrance requirements:* For master's, 3 completed graduate courses with grade of B or higher. Additional exam requirements/recommendations for international students: Required—TOEFL (minimum score 600 paper-based), TWE (minimum score 5). *Expenses:* Contact institution.

Howard University, College of Medicine, Department of Biochemistry and Molecular Biology, Washington, DC 20059-0002. Offers biochemistry and molecular biology (PhD); biotechnology (MS); MD/PhD. *Program availability:* Part-time. *Degree requirements:* For master's, externship; for doctorate, comprehensive exam, thesis/dissertation. *Entrance requirements:* For master's and doctorate, GRE General Test, minimum GPA of 3.0. *Faculty research:* Cellular and molecular biology of olfaction, gene regulation and expression, enzymology, NMR spectroscopy of molecular structure, hormone regulation/metabolism.

Husson University, Master of Business Administration Program, Bangor, ME 04401-2999. Offers athletic administration (MBA); biotechnology and innovation (MBA); general business administration (MBA); healthcare management (MBA); hospitality and tourism management (MBA); organizational management (MBA); risk management (MBA). *Program availability:* Part-time, evening/weekend, 100% online, blended/hybrid learning. *Degree requirements:* For master's, comprehensive exam (for some programs), thesis optional. *Entrance requirements:* For master's, minimum GPA of 3.0, letter of recommendation. Additional exam requirements/recommendations for international students: Required—TOEFL (minimum score 550 paper-based; 80 iBT), IELTS (minimum score 6.5). Electronic applications accepted. *Expenses:* Contact institution.

Illinois State University, Graduate School, College of Arts and Sciences, School of Biological Sciences, Program in Biotechnology, Normal, IL 61790. Offers MS. *Faculty:* 27 full-time (8 women), 7 part-time/adjunct (4 women). *Students:* 3 full-time (2 women). Average age 26. 13 applicants, 23% accepted, 3 enrolled. In 2018, 4 master's awarded. *Degree requirements:* For master's, thesis or alternative. *Entrance requirements:* For master's, GRE General Test, minimum GPA of 2.6 in last 60 hours of course work. *Application deadline:* Applications are processed on a rolling basis. Application fee: $40. *Expenses: Tuition, area resident:* Full-time $7264.62. Tuition, state resident: full-time $9466. Tuition, nonresident: full-time $17,290. *International tuition:* $15,089.40 full-time. *Required fees:* $1481.04. *Financial support:* Application deadline: 4/1. *Unit head:* Dr. Craig Gatto, School Director, 309-438-3087, E-mail: cgatto@IllinoisState.edu. *Application contact:* Dr. Ben Sadd, Assistant Chair for Graduate Studies, 309-438-5151, E-mail: bmsadd@IllinoisState.edu.
Website: http://www.bio.ilstu.edu/biotech/

Indiana University Bloomington, University Graduate School, College of Arts and Sciences, Department of Biology, Bloomington, IN 47405. Offers biology teaching (MAT); biotechnology (MA); evolution, ecology, and behavior (MA, PhD); genetics (PhD); microbiology (MA, PhD); molecular, cellular, and developmental biology (PhD); plant sciences (MA, PhD); zoology (MA, PhD). Terminal master's awarded for partial completion of doctoral program. *Degree requirements:* For master's, thesis, oral defense; for doctorate, thesis/dissertation, oral defense. *Entrance requirements:* For master's and doctorate, GRE General Test. Additional exam requirements/recommendations for international students: Required—TOEFL (minimum score 100 iBT). Electronic applications accepted. *Faculty research:* Evolution, ecology and behavior; microbiology; molecular biology and genetics; plant biology.

Instituto Tecnológico y de Estudios Superiores de Monterrey, Campus Monterrey, Graduate and Research Division, Program in Natural and Social Sciences, Monterrey, Mexico. Offers biotechnology (MS); chemistry (MS, PhD); communications (MS); education (MA). *Program availability:* Part-time. *Degree requirements:* For master's, one foreign language, thesis; for doctorate, one foreign language, thesis/dissertation. *Entrance requirements:* For master's, EXADEP; for doctorate, EXADEP, master's degree in related field. Additional exam requirements/recommendations for international students: Required—TOEFL. *Faculty research:* Cultural industries, mineral substances, bioremediation, food processing, CQ in industrial chemical processing.

Inter American University of Puerto Rico, Barranquitas Campus, Program in Biotechnology, Barranquitas, PR 00794. Offers general biotechnology (MSB); plants biotechnology (MSB). *Program availability:* Part-time, evening/weekend. *Degree requirements:* For master's, 2 foreign languages, comprehensive exam (for some programs), project research and thesis or additional 9 credits in biotechnology and comprehensive exam. *Entrance requirements:* For master's, GRE or EXADEP, bachelor's degree in natural science or related area, official academic transcript from institution that conferred bachelor's degree, minimum GPA of 2.5, two recommendations letters, interview (for some programs). Electronic applications accepted. *Expenses:* Contact institution. *Faculty research:* Plants in danger of extinction with medicinal activity, molecular genetics, somatic embryogenesis and micro-propagation of plants of agricultural interest, epigenetics and heavy metal homeostasis, metallothionein and myosin mRNA levels with tolerance of heavy metals in plants, unraveling the core and variable bacterial communities of evolutionarily distant marine macroalgae.

Inter American University of Puerto Rico, Bayamón Campus, Graduate School, Bayamón, PR 00957. Offers biology (MS), including environmental sciences and ecology, molecular biotechnology; electrical engineering (ME), including control system, potence system; human resources (MBA); mechanical engineering (ME, MS), including aerospace, energy. *Program availability:* Part-time, evening/weekend. *Degree requirements:* For master's, comprehensive exam, research project. *Entrance requirements:* For master's, EXADEP, GRE General Test, letters of recommendation. *Expenses: Tuition:* Full-time $3816; part-time $1908 per trimester. *Required fees:* $735; $642.

Johns Hopkins University, Advanced Academic Programs, Program in Biotechnology, Washington, DC 21218. Offers MS, MS/MBA. *Program availability:* Part-time, evening/weekend, 100% online. *Students:* 130 full-time (76 women), 573 part-time (353 women). 195 applicants, 75% accepted, 80 enrolled. In 2018, 236 master's awarded. *Entrance requirements:* For master's, minimum GPA of 3.0; coursework in biology and chemistry. Additional exam requirements/recommendations for international students: Required—TOEFL (minimum score 100 iBT). *Application deadline:* For fall admission, 5/31 priority date for domestic students, 4/30 priority date for international students; for spring admission, 10/31 priority date for domestic and international students. Applications are processed on a rolling basis. Application fee: $75. Electronic applications accepted. *Financial support:* Applicants required to submit FAFSA. *Unit head:* Dr. Kristina Obom, Program Director, 301-294-7159, E-mail: kobom@jhu.edu. *Application contact:* Melissa Edwards, Admissions Manager, 202-452-1941, Fax: 202-452-1970, E-mail: aapadmissions@jhu.edu.
Website: http://advanced.jhu.edu/academics/graduate-degree-programs/biotechnology/

Johns Hopkins University, Advanced Academic Programs, Program in Biotechnology Enterprise and Entrepreneurship, Washington, DC 21218. Offers MBEE. *Program availability:* Part-time, evening/weekend, online learning. *Students:* 23 applicants, 78% accepted, 12 enrolled. In 2018, 30 master's awarded. *Entrance requirements:* For master's, minimum GPA of 3.0, coursework in biochemistry and cell biology. Additional exam requirements/recommendations for international students: Required—TOEFL (minimum score 100 iBT). *Application deadline:* For fall admission, 5/31 for domestic students, 4/30 for international students; for spring admission, 10/31 for domestic students, 10/15 for international students. Applications are processed on a rolling basis. Application fee: $75. Electronic applications accepted. *Financial support:* Applicants required to submit FAFSA. *Unit head:* Dr. Kristina Obom, Program Director, 301-294-7159, E-mail: kobom@jhu.edu. *Application contact:* Melissa Edwards, Admissions Manager, 202-452-1941, Fax: 202-452-1970, E-mail: aapadmissions@jhu.edu.
Website: http://advanced.jhu.edu/academic/biotechnology/m-in-bee/index.htm

Johns Hopkins University, G. W. C. Whiting School of Engineering, Master of Science in Engineering Management Program, Baltimore, MD 21218. Offers biomaterials (MSEM); civil engineering (MSEM); communications science (MSEM); computer science (MSEM); environmental systems analysis, economics and public policy (MSEM); fluid mechanics (MSEM); materials science and engineering (MSEM); mechanical engineering (MSEM); mechanics and materials (MSEM); nano-biotechnology (MSEM); nanomaterials and nanotechnology (MSEM); operations research (MSEM); probability and statistics (MSEM); smart product and device design (MSEM). *Students:* 34 full-time (12 women), 18 part-time (7 women). 233 applicants, 39% accepted, 33 enrolled. In 2018, 27 master's awarded. *Entrance requirements:* For master's, GRE, 3 letters of recommendation, statement of purpose, transcripts. Additional exam requirements/recommendations for international students: Required—TOEFL (minimum score 600 paper-based, 100 iBT) or IELTS (7). *Application deadline:* For fall admission, 2/15 for domestic and international students. Application fee: $75. Electronic applications accepted. *Financial support:* In 2018–19, 43 research assistantships (averaging $43,344 per year) were awarded; health care benefits also available. *Unit head:* Dr. Pamela Sheff, Director, 410-516-7056, Fax: 410-516-4880, E-mail: pamsheff@gmail.com. *Application contact:* Lindsey Conklin, Sr. Academic Program Coordinator, 410-516-1108, Fax: 410-516-0780, E-mail: lconkli4@jhu.edu.
Website: http://engineering.jhu.edu/msem/

Kean University, New Jersey Center for Science, Technology and Mathematics, Program in Biotechnology Science, Union, NJ 07083. Offers MS. *Program availability:* Part-time. *Faculty:* 7 full-time (1 woman). *Students:* 18 full-time (15 women), 6 part-time (4 women); includes 16 minority (6 Black or African American, non-Hispanic/Latino; 3 Asian, non-Hispanic/Latino; 7 Hispanic/Latino), 3 international. Average age 28. 15 applicants, 87% accepted, 6 enrolled. In 2018, 9 master's awarded. *Degree requirements:* For master's, written research project paper, presentation of research. *Entrance requirements:* For master's, GRE General Test, minimum GPA of 3.0 cumulative and in all science and math courses; official transcripts from all institutions attended; three letters of recommendation; professional resume/curriculum vitae; personal statement. Additional exam requirements/recommendations for international students: Required—TOEFL (minimum score 550 paper-based; 79 iBT), IELTS. *Application deadline:* For fall admission, 6/30 for domestic and international students; for spring admission, 12/1 for domestic and international students. Applications are processed on a rolling basis. Application fee: $75. Electronic applications accepted. *Expenses:* Tuition, state resident: full-time $15,025; part-time $733.50 per credit. Tuition, nonresident: full-time $19,890; part-time $884.50 per credit. *Required fees:*

$2107.50; $89.50 per credit. Tuition and fees vary according to course level, course load, degree level and program. *Financial support:* Scholarships/grants and unspecified assistantships available. Financial award applicants required to submit FAFSA. *Unit head:* Dr. Salvatore Coniglio, Program Coordinator, 908-737-7216, E-mail: coniglsa@kean.edu. *Application contact:* Pedro Lopes, Graduate Admissions Counselor, 908-737-7100, E-mail: gradadmissions@kean.edu.
Website: http://grad.kean.edu/masters-programs/biotechnology

Marywood University, Academic Affairs, Munley College of Liberal Arts and Sciences, Science Department, Scranton, PA 18509-1598. Offers biotechnology (MS). *Program availability:* Part-time. Electronic applications accepted.

McGill University, Faculty of Graduate and Postdoctoral Studies, Faculty of Agricultural and Environmental Sciences, Institute of Parasitology, Montréal, QC H3A 2T5, Canada. Offers biotechnology (M Sc A, Certificate); parasitology (M Sc, PhD).

Middle Tennessee State University, College of Graduate Studies, College of Basic and Applied Sciences, Program in Professional Science, Murfreesboro, TN 37132. Offers actuarial sciences (MS); biostatistics (MS); biotechnology (MS); engineering management (MS); health care informatics (MS). *Program availability:* Part-time, evening/weekend, online learning. *Degree requirements:* For master's, comprehensive exam. *Entrance requirements:* For master's, GRE. Additional exam requirements/recommendations for international students: Required—TOEFL (minimum score 525 paper-based; 71 iBT) or IELTS (minimum score 6).

Mount St. Mary's University, Program in Biotechnology and Management, Emmitsburg, MD 21727-7799. Offers MS. *Program availability:* Part-time-only, evening/weekend. *Degree requirements:* For master's, capstone experience (written paper and formal oral presentation of the project outcomes). *Entrance requirements:* For master's, bachelor's degree in biology or related field, undergraduate transcripts from accredited four-year institution with minimum GPA of 2.75, two letters of recommendation. Additional exam requirements/recommendations for international students: Required—TOEFL (minimum score 550 paper-based; 83 iBT). Electronic applications accepted. *Expenses:* Contact institution.

New Mexico State University, College of Arts and Sciences, Department of Biology, Las Cruces, NM 88003-8001. Offers behavioral, ecological & evolutionary biology (PhD); biology (MS); biotechnology (MS). *Program availability:* Part-time. *Faculty:* 20 full-time (10 women). *Students:* 48 full-time (25 women), 6 part-time (3 women); includes 16 minority (2 American Indian or Alaska Native, non-Hispanic/Latino; 2 Asian, non-Hispanic/Latino; 10 Hispanic/Latino; 2 Two or more races, non-Hispanic/Latino), 15 international. Average age 31. 33 applicants, 52% accepted, 10 enrolled. In 2018, 10 master's, 4 doctorates awarded. *Degree requirements:* For master's, thesis (for some programs), defense or oral exam; for doctorate, comprehensive exam, thesis/dissertation, qualifying exam. *Entrance requirements:* For master's and doctorate, GRE. Additional exam requirements/recommendations for international students: Required—TOEFL (minimum score 550 paper-based; 79 iBT), IELTS (minimum score 6.5). *Application deadline:* For fall admission, 1/15 priority date for domestic and international students; for spring admission, 9/30 priority date for domestic and international students. Applications are processed on a rolling basis. Application fee: $40 ($50 for international students). Electronic applications accepted. *Expenses: Tuition, area resident:* Full-time $4216.70; part-time $252.70 per credit hour. Tuition, state resident: full-time $4216.70; part-time $252.70 per credit hour. Tuition, nonresident: full-time $12,769; part-time $881.10 per credit hour. *International tuition:* $12,769.30 full-time. *Required fees:* $878.40; $48.80 per credit hour. Full-time tuition and fees vary according to course load and reciprocity agreements. *Financial support:* In 2018–19, 50 students received support, including 6 fellowships (averaging $4,548 per year), 12 research assistantships (averaging $19,333 per year), 33 teaching assistantships (averaging $19,106 per year); career-related internships or fieldwork, Federal Work-Study, scholarships/grants, traineeships, health care benefits, and unspecified assistantships also available. Support available to part-time students. Financial award application deadline: 3/1. *Faculty research:* Microbiology, cell and organismal physiology, ecology and ethology, evolution, genetics, developmental biology. *Total annual research expenditures:* $2.4 million. *Unit head:* Dr. Michele K. Nishiguchi, Department Head, 575-646-3611, Fax: 575-646-5665, E-mail: nish@nmsu.edu. *Application contact:* Dr. Jennifer Curtiss, Associate Professor, 575-646-3611, Fax: 575-646-5665, E-mail: curtij01@nmsu.edu.
Website: http://bio.nmsu.edu

Northeastern University, College of Science, Boston, MA 02115-5096. Offers applied mathematics (MS); bioinformatics (MS); biology (PhD); biotechnology (MS); chemistry and chemical biology (MS, PhD); environmental science and policy (MS); marine and environmental sciences (PhD); marine biology (MS); mathematics (MS, PhD); operations research (MSOR); physics (MS, PhD); psychology (PhD). *Program availability:* Part-time. Terminal master's awarded for partial completion of doctoral program. *Degree requirements:* For master's, comprehensive exam (for some programs), thesis; for doctorate, comprehensive exam (for some programs), thesis/dissertation. *Entrance requirements:* For master's, GRE General Test. Electronic applications accepted. *Expenses:* Contact institution.

Northwestern University, The Graduate School, Interdisciplinary Biological Sciences Program (IBiS), Evanston, IL 60208. Offers biochemistry (PhD); bioengineering and biotechnology (PhD); biotechnology (PhD); cell and molecular biology (PhD); developmental and systems biology (PhD); nanotechnology (PhD); neurobiology (PhD); structural biology and biophysics (PhD). *Degree requirements:* For doctorate, thesis/dissertation, qualifying exam. *Entrance requirements:* For doctorate, GRE General Test. Additional exam requirements/recommendations for international students: Required—TOEFL (minimum score 600 paper-based). Electronic applications accepted. *Faculty research:* Biophysics/structural biology, cell/molecular biology, synthetic biology, developmental systems biology, chemical biology/nanotechnology.

Northwestern University, McCormick School of Engineering and Applied Science, Department of Chemical and Biological Engineering, MS in Biotechnology Program, Evanston, IL 60208. Offers MS. *Entrance requirements:* For master's, GRE General Test. Additional exam requirements/recommendations for international students: Required—TOEFL, IELTS. Electronic applications accepted.

Oregon State University, College of Agricultural Sciences, Program in Food Science and Technology, Corvallis, OR 97331. Offers brewing (MS, PhD); enology (MS, PhD); flavor chemistry (MS, PhD); food and seafood processing (MS, PhD); food chemistry/biochemistry (MS, PhD); food engineering (MS, PhD); food microbiology/biotechnology (MS, PhD); sensory evaluation (MS, PhD). *Entrance requirements:* For master's and doctorate, GRE (minimum Verbal and Quantitative scores of 300), minimum GPA of 3.0 in last 90 hours. Additional exam requirements/recommendations for international students: Required—TOEFL (minimum score 80 iBT), IELTS (minimum score 6.5).

Oregon State University, College of Agricultural Sciences, Program in Horticulture, Corvallis, OR 97331. Offers breeding, genetics, and biotechnology (MS, PhD); community and landscape horticultural systems (MS, PhD); sustainable crop production (MS, PhD). *Degree requirements:* For master's, thesis (for some programs); for doctorate, thesis/dissertation. *Entrance requirements:* For master's and doctorate, GRE General Test, minimum GPA of 3.0 in last 90 hours. Additional exam requirements/recommendations for international students: Required—TOEFL (minimum score 80 iBT), IELTS (minimum score 6.5).

Biotechnology

Oregon State University, Interdisciplinary/Institutional Programs, Program in Molecular and Cellular Biology, Corvallis, OR 97331. Offers bioinformatics (PhD); biotechnology (PhD); genome biology (PhD); molecular virology (PhD); plant molecular biology (PhD). *Degree requirements:* For doctorate, thesis/dissertation, oral and written qualifying exams. *Entrance requirements:* For doctorate, GRE. Additional exam requirements/recommendations for international students: Required—TOEFL (minimum score 80 iBT), IELTS (minimum score 6.5).

Penn State University Park, Graduate School, Eberly College of Science, Department of Biochemistry and Molecular Biology, University Park, PA 16802. Offers biochemistry, microbiology, and molecular biology (MS, PhD); biotechnology (MBIOT).

Pontifical John Paul II Institute for Studies on Marriage and Family, Graduate Programs, Washington, DC 20064. Offers biotechnology and ethics (MTS); marriage and family (MTS, STD, STL); theology (PhD).

Purdue University, Graduate School, PULSe - Purdue University Life Sciences Program, West Lafayette, IN 47907. Offers biomolecular structure and biophysics (PhD); biotechnology (PhD); chemical biology (PhD); chromatin and regulation of gene expression (PhD); integrative neuroscience (PhD); integrative plant sciences (PhD); membrane biology (PhD); microbiology (PhD); molecular evolutionary and cancer biology (PhD); molecular evolutionary genetics (PhD); molecular virology (PhD). *Students:* 43 full-time (24 women); includes 8 minority (1 Black or African American, non-Hispanic/Latino; 2 Asian, non-Hispanic/Latino; 2 Hispanic/Latino; 3 Two or more races, non-Hispanic/Latino), 25 international. Average age 25. 181 applicants, 25% accepted, 17 enrolled. *Entrance requirements:* For doctorate, GRE, minimum undergraduate GPA of 3.0. Additional exam requirements/recommendations for international students: Required—TOEFL (minimum score 550 paper-based; 77 iBT). *Application deadline:* For fall admission, 1/15 priority date for domestic and international students. Applications are processed on a rolling basis. Application fee: $60 ($75 for international students). Electronic applications accepted. *Financial support:* In 2018–19, research assistantships with tuition reimbursements (averaging $22,500 per year), teaching assistantships with tuition reimbursements (averaging $22,500 per year) were awarded. *Unit head:* Dr. Jason R. Cannon, Head of the Graduate Program, 765-494-0794, E-mail: cannonjr@purdue.edu. *Application contact:* Lindsey Springer, Graduate Contact for Admissions, 765-496-9667, E-mail: lbcampbe@purdue.edu.
Website: http://www.gradschool.purdue.edu/pulse

Purdue University Northwest, Graduate Studies Office, School of Engineering, Mathematics, and Science, Department of Biological Sciences, Program in Biotechnology, Hammond, IN 46323-2094. Offers MS. *Degree requirements:* For master's, thesis (for some programs). *Entrance requirements:* For master's, GRE General Test, 3 letters of recommendation.

Roosevelt University, Graduate Division, College of Arts and Sciences, Department of Biological, Chemical, and Physical Sciences, Chicago, IL 60605. Offers biology (MS); biomedical sciences (MA); biotechnology and chemical science (MS), including biotechnology, biotechnology management, chemical science. *Program availability:* Part-time, evening/weekend. *Degree requirements:* For master's, thesis optional. Electronic applications accepted. *Expenses:* Contact institution.

St. John's University, Institute for Biotechnology, Queens, NY 11439. Offers biological and pharmaceutical biotechnology (MS). *Entrance requirements:* For master's, GRE General Test, letters of recommendation, transcripts, resume, personal statement. Additional exam requirements/recommendations for international students: Required—TOEFL (minimum score 80 iBT), IELTS (minimum score 6.5). Electronic applications accepted. *Expenses:* Contact institution.

San Francisco State University, Division of Graduate Studies, College of Science and Engineering, Department of Biology, Professional Science Master's Program, San Francisco, CA 94132-1722. Offers biotechnology (PSM); stem cell science (PSM). *Unit head:* Dr. Lily Chen, Director, 415-338-6763, Fax: 415-338-2295, E-mail: lilychen@sfsu.edu. *Application contact:* Dr. Linda H. Chen, Associate Director and Program Coordinator, 415-338-1696, Fax: 415-338-2295, E-mail: psm@sfsu.edu.
Website: http://psm.sfsu.edu/

Simon Fraser University, Office of Graduate Studies and Postdoctoral Fellows, Faculty of Business Administration, Vancouver, BC V6B 5K3, Canada. Offers business administration (EMBA, PhD, Graduate Diploma); finance (M Sc); management of technology (MBA); management of technology/biotechnology (MBA). *Program availability:* Online learning. *Degree requirements:* For master's, thesis (for some programs); for doctorate, comprehensive exam, thesis/dissertation. *Entrance requirements:* For master's, GMAT, minimum GPA of 3.0 (on scale of 4.33) or 3.33 based on last 60 credits of undergraduate courses; for doctorate, minimum GPA of 3.5 (on scale of 4.33); for Graduate Diploma, minimum GPA of 2.5 (on scale of 4.33) or 2.67 based on last 60 credits of undergraduate courses. Additional exam requirements/recommendations for international students: Recommended—TOEFL (minimum score 580 paper-based; 93 iBT), IELTS (minimum score 7), TWE (minimum score 5). *Expenses:* Contact institution. *Faculty research:* Accounting, management and organizational studies, technology and operations management, finance, international business.

Southeastern Oklahoma State University, School of Arts and Sciences, Durant, OK 74701-0609. Offers biology (MT); computer information systems (MT); occupational safety and health (MT). *Program availability:* Part-time, evening/weekend. *Degree requirements:* For master's, thesis optional. *Entrance requirements:* For master's, minimum GPA of 3.0 in last 60 hours or 2.75 overall. Additional exam requirements/recommendations for international students: Required—TOEFL (minimum score 550 paper-based; 79 iBT). Electronic applications accepted.

Stephen F. Austin State University, Graduate School, College of Sciences and Mathematics, Division of Biotechnology, Nacogdoches, TX 75962. Offers MS. *Degree requirements:* For master's, comprehensive exam, thesis. *Entrance requirements:* For master's, GRE General Test, minimum GPA of 2.8 in last 60 hours, 2.5 overall. Additional exam requirements/recommendations for international students: Required—TOEFL.

Temple University, College of Science and Technology, Department of Biology, Philadelphia, PA 19122-6078. Offers biology (MS, PSM, PhD); biotechnology (MS). *Program availability:* Part-time. *Faculty:* 45 full-time (15 women), 2 part-time/adjunct (1 woman). *Students:* 88 full-time (44 women), 20 part-time (9 women); includes 30 minority (3 Black or African American, non-Hispanic/Latino; 17 Asian, non-Hispanic/Latino; 8 Hispanic/Latino; 2 Two or more races, non-Hispanic/Latino), 22 international. 106 applicants, 58% accepted, 38 enrolled. In 2018, 29 master's, 4 doctorates awarded. *Degree requirements:* For master's, thesis (for some programs); for doctorate, thesis/dissertation. *Entrance requirements:* For master's, GRE (optional for P.S.M. in Biotechnology), baccalaureate degree in a related discipline, statement of goals, letters of recommendation; for doctorate, GRE, statement of goals, baccalaureate degree in a related discipline, 3 letters of recommendation. Additional exam requirements/recommendations for international students: Required—TOEFL (minimum score 90 iBT), IELTS (minimum score 6.5), PTE (minimum score 61), one of three is required. Application fee: $60. *Expenses:* Contact institution. *Financial support:* Fellowships, research assistantships, teaching assistantships, Federal Work-Study, and health care benefits available. Financial award applicants required to submit FAFSA. *Faculty research:* Protein-protein interactions; treatment of HIV infection; ecology of specialized deep-sea habitats; plant evolutionary ecology. *Unit head:* Robert W Sanders, Chairperson/Professor, 215-204-2056, E-mail: robert.sanders@temple.edu. *Application contact:* Richard Waring, Graduate Chair, 215-204-7119, E-mail: richard.waring@temple.edu.
Website: https://bio.cst.temple.edu/

Tennessee State University, The School of Graduate Studies and Research, College of Agriculture, Human and Natural Sciences, Nashville, TN 37209-1561. Offers agricultural sciences (MS), including agribusiness, agricultural and extension education, animal science, plant and soil science; biological sciences (MS, PhD); biotechnology (PhD); chemistry (MS). *Program availability:* Part-time, evening/weekend. *Degree requirements:* For master's, thesis. *Entrance requirements:* For master's, GRE General Test, GRE Subject Test, MAT. *Faculty research:* Small farm economics, ornamental horticulture, beef cattle production, rural elderly.

Texas Tech University, Graduate School, Interdisciplinary Programs, Lubbock, TX 79409-1030. Offers arid land studies (MS); biotechnology (MS); heritage and museum sciences (MA); interdisciplinary studies (MA, MS); wind science and engineering (PhD); JD/MS. *Program availability:* Part-time, 100% online, blended/hybrid learning. *Faculty:* 10 full-time (5 women). *Students:* 98 full-time (50 women), 82 part-time (52 women); includes 75 minority (33 Black or African American, non-Hispanic/Latino; 1 American Indian or Alaska Native, non-Hispanic/Latino; 7 Asian, non-Hispanic/Latino; 31 Hispanic/Latino; 3 Two or more races, non-Hispanic/Latino), 19 international. Average age 30. 96 applicants, 76% accepted, 55 enrolled. In 2018, 64 master's, 1 doctorate awarded. Terminal master's awarded for partial completion of doctoral program. *Degree requirements:* For master's, comprehensive exam (for some programs), thesis (for some programs); for doctorate, comprehensive exam, thesis/dissertation (for some programs). *Entrance requirements:* Additional exam requirements/recommendations for international students: Required—TOEFL (minimum score 550 paper-based; 79 iBT), IELTS (minimum score 6.5), PTE (minimum score 60), Cambridge Advanced (B), Cambridge Proficiency (C), ELS English for Academic Purposes (Level 112). *Application deadline:* For fall admission, 6/1 priority date for domestic students, 1/15 priority date for international students; for spring admission, 9/1 priority date for domestic students, 6/15 priority date for international students. Applications are processed on a rolling basis. Application fee: $65. Electronic applications accepted. *Expenses:* Tuition, state resident: full-time $7776; part-time $324 per credit hour. Tuition, nonresident: full-time $17,736; part-time $739 per credit hour. *Required fees:* $2504; $53.50 per credit hour. $610 per semester. Tuition and fees vary according to program. *Financial support:* In 2018–19, 124 students received support, including 111 fellowships (averaging $4,942 per year), 27 research assistantships (averaging $17,595 per year), 8 teaching assistantships (averaging $13,758 per year); scholarships/grants and unspecified assistantships also available. Financial award application deadline: 4/15; financial award applicants required to submit FAFSA. *Total annual research expenditures:* $2.3 million. *Unit head:* Dr. Mark A. Sheridan, Vice Provost for Graduate and Postdoctoral Affairs/Dean of the Graduate School, 806-742-2787, Fax: 806-742-1746, E-mail: mark.sheridan@ttu.edu. *Application contact:* David Doerfert, Associate Dean, 806-834-4477, Fax: 806-742-4038, E-mail: david.doerfert@ttu.edu.
Website: www.depts.ttu.edu/gradschool/

Texas Tech University Health Sciences Center, Graduate School of Biomedical Sciences, Program in Biotechnology, Lubbock, TX 79430. Offers MS. *Entrance requirements:* For master's, GRE General Test, minimum GPA of 3.0. Additional exam requirements/recommendations for international students: Required—TOEFL (minimum score 550 paper-based). *Faculty research:* Reproductive endocrinology, immunology, molecular biology and developmental biochemistry, biology of developing systems.

Thomas Jefferson University, Jefferson College of Health Professions, Department of Medical Laboratory Sciences and Biotechnology, Philadelphia, PA 19107. Offers biotechnology (MS); cytotechnology (MS); medical laboratory science (MS). *Accreditation:* NAACLS. *Program availability:* Part-time. *Degree requirements:* For master's, comprehensive exam. *Entrance requirements:* Additional exam requirements/recommendations for international students: Required—TOEFL (minimum score 87 iBT), IELTS (minimum score 6.5). Electronic applications accepted. *Expenses:* Contact institution. *Faculty research:* Women's health; transportation of islet cells to remedy diabetes/insulin deficiency; bone regeneration; the use of stem cells to remedy cardiac injuries.

Tufts University, Graduate School of Arts and Sciences, Department of Chemistry, Medford, MA 02155. Offers chemical physics (PhD); chemistry (MS, PhD); chemistry/biotechnology (PhD). Terminal master's awarded for partial completion of doctoral program. *Degree requirements:* For master's, thesis optional; for doctorate, comprehensive exam, thesis/dissertation. *Entrance requirements:* For master's and doctorate, GRE General Test; GRE Subject Test (recommended). Additional exam requirements/recommendations for international students: Required—TOEFL (minimum score 550 paper-based; 80 iBT), IELTS (minimum score 6.5). Electronic applications accepted. *Expenses:* Contact institution.

Tufts University, Graduate School of Arts and Sciences, Graduate Certificate Programs, Biotechnology Engineering Program, Medford, MA 02155. Offers Certificate. *Program availability:* Part-time, evening/weekend. Electronic applications accepted. *Expenses: Tuition:* Full-time $51,288; part-time $1710 per credit hour. *Required fees:* $904. Full-time tuition and fees vary according to degree level, program and student level. Part-time tuition and fees vary according to course load.

Tufts University, Graduate School of Arts and Sciences, Graduate Certificate Programs, Biotechnology Program, Medford, MA 02155. Offers Certificate. *Program availability:* Part-time, evening/weekend. Electronic applications accepted. *Expenses: Tuition:* Full-time $51,288; part-time $1710 per credit hour. *Required fees:* $904. Full-time tuition and fees vary according to degree level, program and student level. Part-time tuition and fees vary according to course load.

Tufts University, School of Engineering, Department of Chemical and Biological Engineering, Medford, MA 02155. Offers bioengineering (MS), including cell and bioprocess engineering; biotechnology (PhD); chemical engineering (MS, PhD); PhD/PhD. *Program availability:* Part-time. Terminal master's awarded for partial completion of doctoral program. *Degree requirements:* For master's, thesis (for some programs); for doctorate, thesis/dissertation. *Entrance requirements:* For master's and doctorate, GRE General Test. Additional exam requirements/recommendations for international students: Required—TOEFL (minimum score 550 paper-based; 80 iBT), IELTS (minimum score 6.5). Electronic applications accepted. *Expenses: Tuition:* Full-time $51,288; part-time $1710 per credit hour. *Required fees:* $904. Full-time tuition and fees vary according to degree level, program and student level. Part-time tuition and fees vary according to course load. *Faculty research:* Clean energy with materials, biomaterials, colloids; metabolic engineering, biotechnology; process control; reaction kinetics, catalysis; transport phenomena.

Tufts University, School of Engineering, Department of Civil and Environmental Engineering, Medford, MA 02155. Offers bioengineering (MS), including environmental biotechnology; civil and environmental engineering (MS, PhD), including applied data science, environmental and water resources engineering, environmental health, geosystems engineering, structural engineering and mechanics; PhD/PhD. *Program availability:* Part-time. Terminal master's awarded for partial completion of doctoral program. *Degree requirements:* For master's, thesis (for some programs); for doctorate, thesis/dissertation. *Entrance requirements:* For master's and doctorate, GRE General Test. Additional exam requirements/recommendations for international students: Required—TOEFL (minimum score 550 paper-based; 80 iBT), IELTS (minimum score 6.5). Electronic applications accepted. *Expenses: Tuition:* Full-time $51,288; part-time $1710 per credit hour. *Required fees:* $904. Full-time tuition and fees vary according to degree level, program and student level. Part-time tuition and fees vary according to course load. *Faculty research:* Environmental and water resources engineering, environmental health, geotechnical and geoenvironmental engineering, structural engineering and mechanics, water diplomacy.

Universidad de las Américas Puebla, Division of Graduate Studies, School of Sciences, Program in Biotechnology, Puebla, Mexico. Offers MS. *Degree requirements:* For master's, one foreign language, thesis.

University at Buffalo, the State University of New York, Graduate School, Jacobs School of Medicine and Biomedical Sciences, Graduate Programs in Medicine and Biomedical Sciences, Department of Biotechnical and Clinical Laboratory Sciences, Buffalo, NY 14214. Offers biotechnology (MS). *Accreditation:* NAACLS. *Program availability:* Part-time. *Degree requirements:* For master's, thesis. *Entrance requirements:* For master's, GRE General Test, minimum GPA of 3.0 or equivalent. Additional exam requirements/recommendations for international students: Required—TOEFL (minimum score 79 iBT), IELTS. Electronic applications accepted. *Faculty research:* Immunology, cancer biology, toxicology, analytical clinical chemistry, hematology, chemistry, microbial genomics.

The University of Alabama at Birmingham, School of Health Professions, Program in Biotechnology, Birmingham, AL 35294. Offers MS. *Entrance requirements:* For master's, GRE (minimum score of 500 in each area), minimum GPA of 3.0 overall or on last 60 hours attempted, interview. Additional exam requirements/recommendations for international students: Required—TOEFL, TWE. *Expenses: Tuition, area resident:* Full-time $8100; part-time $8100 per year. Tuition, state resident: full-time $8100. Tuition, nonresident: full-time $19,188; part-time $19,188 per year. Tuition and fees vary according to program.

The University of Alabama in Huntsville, School of Graduate Studies, College of Engineering, Department of Chemical and Materials Engineering, Huntsville, AL 35899. Offers biotechnology science and engineering (PhD); chemical and materials engineering (MSE); materials science (PhD); mechanical engineering (PhD), including chemical engineering. *Program availability:* Part-time. *Faculty:* 3 full-time (1 woman), 1 part-time/adjunct. *Students:* 5 full-time (1 woman), 4 part-time (1 woman); includes 1 minority (Asian, non-Hispanic/Latino), 1 international. Average age 25. 12 applicants, 25% accepted, 2 enrolled. In 2018, 2 master's awarded. *Degree requirements:* For master's, comprehensive exam, thesis or alternative, oral and written exams; for doctorate, comprehensive exam, thesis/dissertation. *Entrance requirements:* For master's, GRE General Test, appropriate bachelor's degree, minimum GPA of 3.0; for doctorate, GRE General Test, minimum GPA of 3.0. Additional exam requirements/recommendations for international students: Required—TOEFL (minimum score 500 paper-based; 80 iBT), IELTS (minimum score 6.5). *Application deadline:* For fall admission, 7/15 priority date for domestic students, 4/1 priority date for international students; for spring admission, 11/30 priority date for domestic students, 9/1 priority date for international students. Applications are processed on a rolling basis. Application fee: $50. Electronic applications accepted. *Expenses: Tuition, area resident:* Full-time $10,632; part-time $412 per credit hour. Tuition, state resident: full-time $10,632. Tuition, nonresident: full-time $23,604; part-time $412 per credit hour. *Required fees:* $582; $582. Tuition and fees vary according to course load and program. *Financial support:* In 2018–19, 4 students received support, including 1 research assistantship with full tuition reimbursement available (averaging $2,500 per year), 3 teaching assistantships with full tuition reimbursements available (averaging $5,500 per year); career-related internships or fieldwork, Federal Work-Study, institutionally sponsored loans, scholarships/grants, health care benefits, and unspecified assistantships also available. Support available to part-time students. Financial award application deadline: 4/1; financial award applicants required to submit FAFSA. *Faculty research:* Ultrathin films for optical, sensor and biological applications; materials processing including low gravity; hypergolic reactants; computational fluid dynamics; biofuels and renewable resources. *Unit head:* Dr. Anuradha Subramanian, Chair, 256-824-6194, Fax: 256-824-6839, E-mail: anu.subramanian@uah.edu. *Application contact:* Kim Gray, Graduate Studies Admissions Coordinator, 256-824-6002, Fax: 256-824-6405, E-mail: deangrad@uah.edu.
Website: http://www.cme.uah.edu/

The University of Alabama in Huntsville, School of Graduate Studies, College of Science, Department of Biological Sciences, Huntsville, AL 35899. Offers biology (MS); biotechnology science and engineering (PhD); education (MS). *Program availability:* Part-time. *Faculty:* 14 full-time (2 women), 3 part-time/adjunct. *Students:* 43 full-time (30 women), 12 part-time (7 women); includes 8 minority (3 Black or African American, non-Hispanic/Latino; 2 Asian, non-Hispanic/Latino; 3 Hispanic/Latino), 11 international. Average age 33. 36 applicants, 64% accepted, 14 enrolled. In 2018, 2 master's, 5 doctorates awarded. *Degree requirements:* For master's, comprehensive exam, thesis or alternative, oral and written exams. *Entrance requirements:* For master's, GRE General Test, previous course work in biochemistry and organic chemistry, minimum GPA of 3.0. Additional exam requirements/recommendations for international students: Required—TOEFL (minimum score 550 paper-based; 80 iBT), IELTS (minimum score 6.5). *Application deadline:* For fall admission, 7/15 priority date for domestic students, 4/1 priority date for international students; for spring admission, 11/30 for domestic students, 9/1 priority date for international students. Applications are processed on a rolling basis. Application fee: $50. Electronic applications accepted. *Expenses: Tuition, area resident:* Full-time $10,632; part-time $412 per credit hour. Tuition, state resident: full-time $10,632. Tuition, nonresident: full-time $23,604; part-time $412 per credit hour. *Required fees:* $582; $582. Tuition and fees vary according to course load and program. *Financial support:* In 2018–19, 11 students received support, including 1 research assistantship with full tuition reimbursement available (averaging $2,500 per year), 10 teaching assistantships with full tuition reimbursements available (averaging $6,000 per year); career-related internships or fieldwork, Federal Work-Study, institutionally sponsored loans, scholarships/grants, health care benefits, tuition waivers (full and partial), and unspecified assistantships also available. Support available to part-time students. Financial award application deadline: 4/1; financial award applicants required to submit FAFSA. *Faculty research:* Physiology, microbiology, genomics and proteomics, ecology and evolution, drug discovery. *Unit head:* Dr. Bruce W. Stallsmith, Associate Professor and Interim Chair, 256-824-6260, Fax: 256-824-6305, E-mail: stallsb@uah.edu. *Application contact:* Kim Gray, Graduate Studies Admissions Manager, 256-824-6002, Fax: 256-824-6405, E-mail: deangrad@uah.edu.
Website: http://www.uah.edu/science/departments/biology

The University of Alabama in Huntsville, School of Graduate Studies, College of Science, Department of Chemistry, Huntsville, AL 35899. Offers biotechnology science and engineering (PhD); chemistry (MS); education (MS); materials science (MS, PhD). *Program availability:* Part-time. *Faculty:* 5 full-time (3 women). *Students:* 14 full-time (5 women), 8 part-time (5 women); includes 5 minority (all Black or African American, non-Hispanic/Latino), 4 international. Average age 29. 26 applicants, 77% accepted, 9 enrolled. In 2018, 3 master's awarded. *Degree requirements:* For master's, comprehensive exam, thesis or alternative, oral and written exams. *Entrance requirements:* For master's, GRE General Test, minimum GPA of 3.0. Additional exam requirements/recommendations for international students: Required—TOEFL (minimum score 550 paper-based; 80 iBT), IELTS (minimum score 6.5). *Application deadline:* For fall admission, 7/15 priority date for domestic students, 4/1 priority date for international students; for spring admission, 11/30 priority date for domestic students, 9/1 priority date for international students. Applications are processed on a rolling basis. Application fee: $50. Electronic applications accepted. *Expenses: Tuition, area resident:* Full-time $10,632; part-time $412 per credit hour. Tuition, state resident: full-time $10,632. Tuition, nonresident: full-time $23,604; part-time $412 per credit hour. *Required fees:* $582; $582. Tuition and fees vary according to course load and program. *Financial support:* In 2018–19, 8 students received support, including 1 research assistantship with full tuition reimbursement available (averaging $6,000 per year), 7 teaching assistantships with full tuition reimbursements available (averaging $6,000 per year); career-related internships or fieldwork, Federal Work-Study, institutionally sponsored loans, scholarships/grants, health care benefits, tuition waivers (full and partial), and unspecified assistantships also available. Support available to part-time students. Financial award application deadline: 4/1; financial award applicants required to submit FAFSA. *Faculty research:* Natural products drug discovery, protein biochemistry, macromolecular biophysics, polymer synthesis, surface modification and analysis of materials. *Unit head:* Dr. John Foster, Professor and Chair, 256-824-6253, Fax: 256-824-6349, E-mail: john.foster@uah.edu. *Application contact:* Kim Gray, Graduate Studies Admissions Coordinator, 256-824-6002, Fax: 256-824-6405, E-mail: deangrad@uah.edu.
Website: http://chemistry.uah.edu

University of Alberta, Faculty of Graduate Studies and Research, Department of Biological Sciences, Edmonton, AB T6G 2E1, Canada. Offers environmental biology and ecology (M Sc, PhD); microbiology and biotechnology (M Sc, PhD); molecular biology and genetics (M Sc, PhD); physiology and cell biology (M Sc, PhD); plant biology (M Sc, PhD); systematics and evolution (M Sc, PhD). Terminal master's awarded for partial completion of doctoral program. *Degree requirements:* For master's, thesis; for doctorate, thesis/dissertation. *Entrance requirements:* Additional exam requirements/recommendations for international students: Required—TOEFL.

University of Calgary, Cumming School of Medicine and Faculty of Graduate Studies, Masters Program in Biomedical Technology, Calgary, AB T2N 1N4, Canada. Offers MBT. *Program availability:* Part-time. *Degree requirements:* For master's, comprehensive exam, practicum. *Entrance requirements:* For master's, minimum GPA of 3.2 in last 2 years, B Sc in biological science. Additional exam requirements/recommendations for international students: Required—TOEFL (minimum score 600 paper-based). Electronic applications accepted. *Expenses:* Contact institution. *Faculty research:* Patent law, intellectual proprietorship.

University of California, Irvine, School of Biological Sciences, Department of Molecular Biology and Biochemistry, Program in Biotechnology, Irvine, CA 92697. Offers MS. *Students:* 26 full-time (14 women); includes 16 minority (9 Asian, non-Hispanic/Latino; 3 Hispanic/Latino; 4 Two or more races, non-Hispanic/Latino), 6 international. Average age 25. 108 applicants, 18% accepted, 12 enrolled. In 2018, 14 master's awarded. *Entrance requirements:* For master's, GRE General Test, GRE Subject Test, minimum GPA of 3.0. *Application deadline:* For fall admission, 3/1 priority date for domestic and international students. Applications are processed on a rolling basis. Application fee: $105 ($125 for international students). Electronic applications accepted. *Financial support:* Application deadline: 3/1; applicants required to submit FAFSA. *Unit head:* Michael G. Cumsky, Director, 949-824-7766, Fax: 949-824-8551, E-mail: mgcumsky@uci.edu. *Application contact:* Morgan Oldham, Administrative Contact, 949-824-6034, Fax: 949-824-8551, E-mail: morgano@uci.edu.

University of California, Irvine, School of Biological Sciences, Department of Molecular Biology and Biochemistry, Program in Biotechnology Management, Irvine, CA 92697. Offers MS. Program offered jointly with The Paul Merage School of Business and the Department of Biomedical Engineering. *Students:* 34 full-time (22 women); includes 7 minority (6 Asian, non-Hispanic/Latino; 1 Two or more races, non-Hispanic/Latino), 23 international. Average age 25. 43 applicants, 81% accepted, 18 enrolled. In 2018, 17 master's awarded. *Application deadline:* For fall admission, 3/15 for domestic students. Application fee: $105 ($125 for international students). *Unit head:* Michael G. Cumsky, Program Director, 949-824-7766, Fax: 949-824-8551, E-mail: mgcumsky@uci.edu. *Application contact:* Morgan Oldham, Student Affairs Assistant, 949-826-6034, Fax: 949-824-8551, E-mail: morgano@uci.edu.
Website: http://mbb.bio.uci.edu/graduates/masters-science-degree-biotechnology-management/

University of Delaware, College of Arts and Sciences, Department of Biological Sciences, Newark, DE 19716. Offers biotechnology (MS); cancer biology (MS, PhD); cell and extracellular matrix biology (MS, PhD); cell and systems physiology (MS, PhD); developmental biology (MS, PhD); ecology and evolution (MS, PhD); microbiology (MS, PhD); molecular biology and genetics (MS, PhD). Terminal master's awarded for partial completion of doctoral program. *Degree requirements:* For master's, thesis, preliminary exam; for doctorate, comprehensive exam, thesis/dissertation, preliminary exam. *Entrance requirements:* For master's and doctorate, GRE General Test. Additional exam requirements/recommendations for international students: Required—TOEFL (minimum score 600 paper-based); Recommended—TWE. Electronic applications accepted. *Faculty research:* Microorganisms, bone, cancer metastasis, developmental biology, cell biology, DNA.

University of Guelph, Office of Graduate and Postdoctoral Studies, Ontario Agricultural College, Department of Environmental Biology, Guelph, ON N1G 2W1, Canada. Offers entomology (M Sc, PhD); environmental microbiology and biotechnology (M Sc, PhD); environmental toxicology (M Sc, PhD); plant and forest systems (M Sc, PhD); plant pathology (M Sc, PhD). *Program availability:* Part-time. *Degree requirements:* For master's, thesis; for doctorate, comprehensive exam, thesis/dissertation. *Entrance requirements:* For master's, minimum 75% average during previous 2 years of course work; for doctorate, minimum 75% average. Additional exam requirements/recommendations for international students: Required—TOEFL or IELTS. Electronic applications accepted. *Faculty research:* Entomology, environmental microbiology and biotechnology, environmental toxicology, forest ecology, plant pathology.

University of Houston–Clear Lake, School of Science and Computer Engineering, Program in Biotechnology, Houston, TX 77058-1002. Offers MS.

The University of Kansas, University of Kansas Medical Center, School of Health Professions, Program in Molecular Biotechnology, Kansas City, KS 66045. Offers MS. *Faculty:* 9. *Students:* 2 part-time (both women). Average age 25. 5 applicants, 20%

accepted. *Degree requirements:* For master's, comprehensive exam. *Entrance requirements:* For master's, GRE General Test. Additional exam requirements/recommendations for international students: Required—TOEFL, TOEFL or IELTS. *Application deadline:* For fall admission, 2/1 priority date for domestic and international students. Application fee: $60. Electronic applications accepted. *Financial support:* Career-related internships or fieldwork and scholarships/grants available. Financial award application deadline: 3/1; financial award applicants required to submit FAFSA. *Faculty research:* Diabetes, obesity, polycystic kidney disease, protein structure and function, cell signaling pathways. *Total annual research expenditures:* $457,261. *Unit head:* Dr. Eric Elsinghorst, Director of Graduate Studies, 913-588-1089, E-mail: eelsinghorst@kumc.edu. *Application contact:* Valerie Noack, Senior Coordinator, 913-945-7347, Fax: 913-588-4697, E-mail: vnoack@kumc.edu.
Website: http://www.mb.kumc.edu

The University of Manchester, School of Biological Sciences, Manchester, United Kingdom. Offers adaptive organismal biology (M Phil, PhD); animal biology (M Phil, PhD); biochemistry (M Phil, PhD); bioinformatics (M Phil, PhD); biomolecular sciences (M Phil, PhD); biotechnology (M Phil, PhD); cell biology (M Phil, PhD); cell matrix research (M Phil, PhD); channels and transporters (M Phil, PhD); developmental biology (M Phil, PhD); environmental biology (M Phil, PhD); evolutionary biology (M Phil, PhD); gene expression (M Phil, PhD); genetics (M Phil, PhD); history of science, technology and medicine (M Phil, PhD); immunology (M Phil, PhD); integrative neurobiology and behavior (M Phil, PhD); membrane trafficking (M Phil, PhD); microbiology (M Phil, PhD); molecular and cellular neuroscience (M Phil, PhD); molecular biology (M Phil, PhD); molecular cancer studies (M Phil, PhD); neuroscience (M Phil, PhD); ophthalmology (M Phil, PhD); optometry (M Phil, PhD); organelle function (M Phil, PhD); pharmacology (M Phil, PhD); physiology (M Phil, PhD); plant sciences (M Phil, PhD); stem cell research (M Phil, PhD); structural biology (M Phil, PhD); systems neuroscience (M Phil, PhD); toxicology (M Phil, PhD).

University of Maryland, Baltimore County, The Graduate School, College of Natural and Mathematical Sciences, Department of Biological Sciences, Programs in Biotechnology, Baltimore, MD 21227. Offers biotechnology (MPS); biotechnology management (Graduate Certificate). *Program availability:* Part-time, evening/weekend. *Entrance requirements:* Additional exam requirements/recommendations for international students: Required—TOEFL (minimum score 99 iBT). Electronic applications accepted. *Expenses:* Contact institution.

University of Maryland University College, The Graduate School, Program in Biotechnology, Adelphi, MD 20783. Offers MS, Certificate. *Program availability:* Part-time, evening/weekend, online learning. *Students:* 11 full-time (9 women), 503 part-time (302 women); includes 266 minority (158 Black or African American, non-Hispanic/Latino; 1 American Indian or Alaska Native, non-Hispanic/Latino; 57 Asian, non-Hispanic/Latino; 39 Hispanic/Latino; 11 Two or more races, non-Hispanic/Latino), 18 international. Average age 33. 148 applicants, 100% accepted, 93 enrolled. In 2018, 113 master's, 6 other advanced degrees awarded. *Degree requirements:* For master's, thesis or alternative, capstone course. *Application deadline:* Applications are processed on a rolling basis. Application fee: $50. Electronic applications accepted. *Financial support:* Scholarships/grants available. Support available to part-time students. Financial award application deadline: 6/1; financial award applicants required to submit FAFSA. *Unit head:* James Coker, Program Chair, 240-684-2014, E-mail: james.coker@umuc.edu. *Application contact:* Admissions, 800-888-8682, E-mail: studentsfirst@umuc.edu.
Website: http://www.umuc.edu/academic-programs/masters-degrees/biotechnology.cfm

University of Massachusetts Amherst, Graduate School, College of Natural Sciences, Department of Animal Biotechnology and Biomedical Sciences, Amherst, MA 01003. Offers MS, PhD. *Program availability:* Part-time. Terminal master's awarded for partial completion of doctoral program. *Degree requirements:* For master's, thesis or alternative; for doctorate, comprehensive exam, thesis/dissertation. *Entrance requirements:* For doctorate, GRE General Test. Additional exam requirements/recommendations for international students: Required—TOEFL (minimum score 550 paper-based; 80 iBT), IELTS (minimum score 6.5). Electronic applications accepted.

University of Massachusetts Boston, College of Science and Mathematics, Program in Biomedical Engineering and Biotechnology, Boston, MA 02125-3393. Offers PhD. *Students:* 3 part-time (1 woman), 2 international. Average age 30. 6 applicants. In 2018, 1 doctorate awarded. *Application deadline:* For fall admission, 1/2 for domestic students; for spring admission, 10/15 for domestic students. *Expenses: Tuition, area resident:* Full-time $17,896. Tuition, state resident: full-time $17,896. Tuition, nonresident: full-time $34,932. *International tuition:* $34,932 full-time. *Required fees:* $355. *Unit head:* Dr. Greg Beck, Associate Professor of Biology, 617-287.6619, E-mail: Greg.Beck@umb.ed. *Application contact:* Graduate Admissions Coordinator, 617-287-6400, Fax: 617-287-6236, E-mail: graduate.admissions@umb.edu.

University of Massachusetts Boston, College of Science and Mathematics, Program in Biotechnology and Biomedical Sciences, Boston, MA 02125-3393. Offers MS. *Program availability:* Part-time, evening/weekend. *Students:* 1 (woman) full-time, 1 part-time (0 women), 1 international. Average age 28. 16 applicants, 6% accepted. In 2018, 2 master's awarded. *Entrance requirements:* For master's, GRE General Test, GRE Subject Test, minimum GPA of 2.75, 3.0 in science and math. *Application deadline:* For fall admission, 1/2 for domestic students; for spring admission, 10/15 for domestic students. *Expenses: Tuition, area resident:* Full-time $17,896. Tuition, state resident: full-time $17,896. Tuition, nonresident: full-time $34,932. *International tuition:* $34,932 full-time. *Required fees:* $355. *Financial support:* Research assistantships, teaching assistantships, career-related internships or fieldwork, Federal Work-Study, and unspecified assistantships available. Support available to part-time students. Financial award application deadline: 3/1; financial award applicants required to submit FAFSA. *Faculty research:* Evolutionary and molecular immunology, molecular genetics, tissue culture, computerized laboratory technology. *Unit head:* Dr. Greg Beck, Director, 617-287-6619, E-mail: Greg.Beck@umb.edu. *Application contact:* Graduate Admissions Coordinator, 617-287-6400, Fax: 617-287-6236, E-mail: graduate.admissions@umb.edu.

University of Massachusetts Dartmouth, Graduate School, College of Engineering, Program in Biomedical Engineering and Biotechnology, North Dartmouth, MA 02747-2300. Offers biomedical engineering/biotechnology (PhD). *Program availability:* Part-time. *Faculty:* 6 full-time (3 women), 1 part-time/adjunct (0 women). *Students:* 10 full-time (4 women), 12 part-time (8 women); includes 5 minority (2 Asian, non-Hispanic/Latino; 3 Hispanic/Latino), 8 international. Average age 29. 15 applicants, 80% accepted, 6 enrolled. Terminal master's awarded for partial completion of doctoral program. *Degree requirements:* For doctorate, comprehensive exam, thesis/dissertation. *Entrance requirements:* For doctorate, GRE, statement of purpose (minimum of 300 words), resume, 3 letters of recommendation, official transcripts. Additional exam requirements/recommendations for international students: Required—TOEFL (minimum score 550 paper-based; 79 iBT), IELTS (minimum score 6.5). *Application deadline:* For fall admission, 2/15 priority date for domestic students, 1/15 priority date for international students; for spring admission, 11/15 priority date for domestic students, 10/15 priority date for international students. Application fee: $60. Electronic applications accepted. *Financial support:* In 2018–19, 3 fellowships (averaging $24,000 per year), 6 research assistantships (averaging $13,633 per year), 2 teaching assistantships (averaging $4,038 per year) were awarded; tuition waivers (full and partial) and doctoral support also available. Financial award application deadline: 3/1; financial award applicants required to submit FAFSA. *Faculty research:* Anti-oxidants, anti-cancer, anti-microbial agents; mechanisms of anti-microbial resistance; synthesis and modification of nano-structures; self-assembled bio-molecular networks; tissue regeneration. *Total annual research expenditures:* $809,000. *Unit head:* Tracie Ferreira, Graduate Program Co-Director, 508-999-8604, E-mail: bmebtphd@umassd.edu. *Application contact:* Scott Webster, Director of Graduate Studies & Admissions, 508-999-8604, Fax: 508-999-8183, E-mail: graduate@umassd.edu.
Website: http://www.umassd.edu/engineering/graduate/doctoraldegreeprograms/biomedicalengineeringandbiotechnology/

University of Minnesota, Twin Cities Campus, Graduate School, Program in Microbial Engineering, Minneapolis, MN 55455-0213. Offers MS. *Program availability:* Part-time. *Degree requirements:* For master's, thesis. *Entrance requirements:* For master's, GRE General Test. Additional exam requirements/recommendations for international students: Required—TOEFL. *Faculty research:* Microbial genetics, oncogenesis, gene transfer, fermentation, bioreactors, genetics of antibiotic biosynthesis.

University of Missouri–St. Louis, College of Arts and Sciences, Department of Chemistry and Biochemistry, St. Louis, MO 63121. Offers biochemistry and biotechnology (MS); chemistry (MS, PhD). *Program availability:* Part-time, evening/weekend. Terminal master's awarded for partial completion of doctoral program. *Degree requirements:* For master's, thesis optional; for doctorate, thesis/dissertation. *Entrance requirements:* For master's, 2 letters of recommendation; for doctorate, GRE General Test, 3 letters of recommendation. Additional exam requirements/recommendations for international students: Required—TOEFL (minimum score 550 paper-based; 79 iBT), IELTS (minimum score 6.5). Electronic applications accepted. *Faculty research:* Metallaborane chemistry, serum transferrin chemistry, natural products chemistry, organic synthesis.

University of Nevada, Reno, Graduate School, College of Agriculture, Biotechnology and Natural Resources, Program in Biotechnology, Reno, NV 89557. Offers MS. 5 year degree; students are admitted to as undergraduates. *Degree requirements:* For master's, thesis. *Entrance requirements:* For master's, GRE, minimum GPA of 2.75. Additional exam requirements/recommendations for international students: Required—TOEFL (minimum score 500 paper-based; 61 iBT), IELTS (minimum score 6). Electronic applications accepted. *Faculty research:* Cancer biology, plant virology.

University of North Texas Health Science Center at Fort Worth, Graduate School of Biomedical Sciences, Fort Worth, TX 76107-2699. Offers biochemistry and cancer biology (MS, PhD); biotechnology (MS); cell biology, immunology and microbiology (MS, PhD); clinical research management (MS); forensic genetics (MS); genetics (MS, PhD); integrative physiology (MS, PhD); medical sciences (MS); pharmaceutical sciences and pharmacotherapy (MS, PhD); pharmacology and neuroscience (MS, PhD); structural anatomy and rehabilitation sciences (MS, PhD); DO/MS; DO/PhD. Terminal master's awarded for partial completion of doctoral program. *Degree requirements:* For master's, thesis; for doctorate, thesis/dissertation. *Entrance requirements:* For master's and doctorate, GRE General Test. Additional exam requirements/recommendations for international students: Required—TOEFL. *Expenses:* Contact institution. *Faculty research:* Alzheimer's disease, aging, eye diseases, cancer, cardiovascular disease.

University of Pennsylvania, School of Engineering and Applied Science, Program in Biotechnology, Philadelphia, PA 19104. Offers MBT. *Program availability:* Part-time. *Students:* 61 full-time (40 women), 28 part-time (12 women); includes 7 minority (6 Asian, non-Hispanic/Latino; 1 Two or more races, non-Hispanic/Latino), 57 international. Average age 24. 177 applicants, 55% accepted, 62 enrolled. In 2018, 45 master's awarded. *Degree requirements:* For master's, comprehensive exam, thesis optional. *Entrance requirements:* For master's, GRE, bachelor's degree, 3 letters of recommendation, resume, personal statement. Additional exam requirements/recommendations for international students: Required—TOEFL (minimum score 100 iBT), IELTS (minimum score 7). *Application deadline:* For fall admission, 3/15 priority date for domestic and international students. Application fee: $80. Electronic applications accepted. *Expenses:* Contact institution. *Faculty research:* Biopharmaceuticals, biomedical technologies, engineering biotechnology, molecular biology. *Application contact:* William Fenton, Assistant Director of Graduate Admissions, 215-898-4542, Fax: 215-573-5577, E-mail: gradstudies@seas.upenn.edu.
Website: http://www.upenn.edu/biotech/

University of Rhode Island, Graduate School, College of the Environment and Life Sciences, Department of Cell and Molecular Biology, Kingston, RI 02881. Offers biochemistry (MS, PhD); clinical laboratory sciences (MS), including biotechnology, clinical laboratory science, cytopathology; microbiology (MS, PhD); molecular genetics (MS, PhD). *Program availability:* Part-time. *Faculty:* 16 full-time (7 women). *Students:* 3 full-time (1 woman), 15 part-time (11 women); includes 5 minority (3 Black or African American, non-Hispanic/Latino; 2 Hispanic/Latino), 5 international. 26 applicants, 62% accepted, 6 enrolled. In 2018, 28 master's awarded. *Entrance requirements:* Additional exam requirements/recommendations for international students: Required—TOEFL. *Application deadline:* For fall admission, 1/15 for domestic and international students. Application fee: $65. Electronic applications accepted. *Expenses: Tuition, area resident:* Full-time $13,226; part-time $735 per credit. Tuition, state resident: full-time $13,226; part-time $735 per credit. Tuition, nonresident: full-time $25,854; part-time $1436 per credit. *International tuition:* $25,854 full-time. *Required fees:* $1698; $50 per credit. $35 per semester. One-time fee: $165. *Financial support:* In 2018–19, 11 teaching assistantships with tuition reimbursements (averaging $10,985 per year) were awarded; traineeships also available. Financial award application deadline: 1/15; financial award applicants required to submit FAFSA. *Unit head:* Dr. Gongqing Sun, Chair and Professor, 401-874-5937, Fax: 401-874-2202, E-mail: gsun@mail.uri.edu. *Application contact:* Bethany Jenkins, Professor, 401-874-7551, E-mail: bjenkins@uri.edu.
Website: https://web.uri.edu/cmb/

University of San Francisco, College of Arts and Sciences, Biotechnology Program, San Francisco, CA 94117. Offers PSM. *Program availability:* Part-time, evening/weekend. *Students:* 25 full-time (14 women), 2 part-time (both women); includes 14 minority (6 Asian, non-Hispanic/Latino; 6 Hispanic/Latino; 1 Native Hawaiian or other Pacific Islander, non-Hispanic/Latino; 1 Two or more races, non-Hispanic/Latino), 5 international. Average age 25. 80 applicants, 68% accepted, 13 enrolled. In 2018, 14 master's awarded. *Entrance requirements:* For master's, GRE or MCAT, Upper division biology coursework. Additional exam requirements/recommendations for international students: Required—TOEFL (minimum score 90 iBT), IELTS (minimum score 6.5), PTE (minimum score 61). *Application deadline:* For fall admission, 4/15 for domestic and international students. Applications are processed on a rolling basis. Application fee: $55. Electronic applications accepted. *Financial support:* In 2018–19, 14 students received support. Fellowships with partial tuition reimbursements available, career-related internships or fieldwork, and scholarships/grants available. Financial award applicants required to submit FAFSA. *Unit head:* Dr. Cary Lai, Graduate Director, 415-422-6755, E-mail: cklai2@usfca.edu. *Application contact:* Information Contact, 415-422-5101, Fax: 422-, E-mail: asgraduate@usfca.edu.
Website: https://www.usfca.edu/arts-sciences/graduate-programs/biotechnology

University of Southern California, Keck School of Medicine and Graduate School, Graduate Programs in Medicine, Master of Science Program in Translational Biotechnology, Los Angeles, CA 90089. Offers biotechnology (MS). *Program availability:* Part-time. *Faculty:* 8 full-time (3 women), 3 part-time/adjunct (0 women). *Students:* 13 full-time (10 women), 8 part-time (7 women); includes 2 minority (both Hispanic/Latino), 15 international. Average age 22. 63 applicants, 59% accepted, 14 enrolled. In 2018, 7 master's awarded. *Degree requirements:* For master's, experiential projects. *Entrance requirements:* For master's, GRE or MCAT. Additional exam requirements/recommendations for international students: Recommended—TOEFL (minimum score 90 iBT), IELTS (minimum score 6.5). *Application deadline:* For fall admission, 8/1 for domestic students, 6/15 for international students; for spring admission, 12/1 for domestic students, 11/1 for international students. Applications are processed on a rolling basis. Application fee: $90. Electronic applications accepted. *Faculty research:* Stem cells, cell biology, oncogenesis, drug discovery and development. *Unit head:* Dr. Carol S. Lin, Director, 323-442-3237, E-mail: carollin@usc.edu. *Application contact:* Dr. Carol S. Lin, Director, 323-442-3237, E-mail: carollin@usc.edu.
Website: http://keck.usc.edu/translational-biotechnology-program/

University of South Florida, Innovative Education, Tampa, FL 33620-9951. Offers adult, career and higher education (Graduate Certificate), including college teaching, leadership in developing human resources, leadership in higher education; Africana studies (Graduate Certificate), including diasporas and health disparities, genocide and human rights; aging studies (Graduate Certificate), including gerontology; art research (Graduate Certificate), including museum studies; business foundations (Graduate Certificate); chemical and biomedical engineering (Graduate Certificate), including materials science and engineering, water, health and sustainability; child and family studies (Graduate Certificate), including positive behavior support; civil and industrial engineering (Graduate Certificate), including transportation systems analysis; community and family health (Graduate Certificate), including maternal and child health, social marketing and public health, violence and injury: prevention and intervention, women's health; criminology (Graduate Certificate), including criminal justice administration; data science for public administration (Graduate Certificate); digital humanities (Graduate Certificate); educational measurement and research (Graduate Certificate), including evaluation; English (Graduate Certificate), including comparative literary studies, creative writing, professional and technical communication; entrepreneurship (Graduate Certificate); environmental health (Graduate Certificate), including safety management; epidemiology and biostatistics (Graduate Certificate), including applied biostatistics, biostatistics, concepts and tools of epidemiology, epidemiology, epidemiology of infectious diseases; geography, environment and planning (Graduate Certificate), including community development, environmental policy and management, geographical information systems; geology (Graduate Certificate), including hydrogeology; global health (Graduate Certificate), including disaster management, global health and Latin American and Caribbean studies, global health practice, humanitarian assistance, infection control; government and international affairs (Graduate Certificate), including Cuban studies, globalization studies; health policy and management (Graduate Certificate), including health management and leadership, public health policy and programs; hearing specialist: early intervention (Graduate Certificate); industrial and management systems engineering (Graduate Certificate), including systems engineering, technology management; information studies (Graduate Certificate), including school library media specialist; information systems/decision sciences (Graduate Certificate), including analytics and business intelligence; instructional technology (Graduate Certificate), including distance education, Florida digital/virtual educator, instructional design, multimedia design, Web design; internal medicine, bioethics and medical humanities (Graduate Certificate), including biomedical ethics; Latin American and Caribbean studies (Graduate Certificate); leadership for coastal resiliency planning (Graduate Certificate); mass communications (Graduate Certificate), including multimedia journalism; mathematics and statistics (Graduate Certificate), including mathematics; medicine (Graduate Certificate), including aging and neuroscience, bioinformatics, biotechnology, brain fitness and memory management, clinical investigation, hand and upper limb rehabilitation, health informatics, health sciences, integrative weight management, intellectual property, medicine and gender, metabolic and nutritional medicine, metabolic cardiology, pharmacy sciences; national and competitive intelligence (Graduate Certificate); nursing (Graduate Certificate), including simulation based academic fellowship in advanced pain management; psychological and social foundations (Graduate Certificate), including career counseling, college teaching, diversity in education, mental health counseling, school counseling; public affairs (Graduate Certificate), including nonprofit management, public management, research administration; public health (Graduate Certificate), including assessing chemical toxicity and public health risks, health equity, pharmacoepidemiology, public health generalist, toxicology, translational research in adolescent behavioral health; public health practices (Graduate Certificate), including planning for healthy communities; rehabilitation and mental health counseling (Graduate Certificate), including integrative mental health care, marriage and family therapy, rehabilitation technology; secondary education (Graduate Certificate), including ESOL, foreign language education: culture and content, foreign language education: professional; social work (Graduate Certificate), including geriatric social work/clinical gerontology; special education (Graduate Certificate), including autism spectrum disorder, disabilities education: severe/profound; world languages (Graduate Certificate), including teaching English as a second language (TESL) or foreign language. *Expenses:* Tuition, state resident: full-time $6350. Tuition, nonresident: full-time $19,048. *International tuition:* $19,048 full-time. *Required fees:* $2079. *Unit head:* Dr. Cynthia DeLuca, Associate Vice President and Assistant Vice Provost, 813-974-3077, Fax: 813-974-7061, E-mail: deluca@usf.edu. *Application contact:* Owen Hooper, Director, Summer and Alternative Calendar Programs, 813-974-6917, E-mail: hooper@usf.edu.
Website: http://www.usf.edu/innovative-education/

University of South Florida, Morsani College of Medicine and College of Graduate Studies, Graduate Programs in Medical Sciences, Tampa, FL 33620-9951. Offers advanced athletic training (MS); athletic training (MS); bioinformatics and computational biology (MSBCB); biotechnology (MSB); health informatics (MSHI); medical sciences (MSMS, PhD), including aging and neuroscience (MSMS), allergy, immunology and infectious disease (PhD), anatomy, biochemistry and molecular biology, clinical and translational research, health science (MSMS), interdisciplinary medical sciences (MSMS), medical microbiology and immunology (MSMS), metabolic and nutritional medicine (MSMS), microbiology and immunology (PhD), molecular medicine, molecular pharmacology and physiology (PhD), neuroscience (PhD), pathology and cell biology (PhD), women's health (MSMS). *Faculty:* 1 (woman) full-time. *Students:* 355 full-time (207 women), 229 part-time (145 women); includes 283 minority (71 Black or African American, non-Hispanic/Latino; 2 American Indian or Alaska Native, non-Hispanic/Latino; 89 Asian, non-Hispanic/Latino; 103 Hispanic/Latino; 2 Native Hawaiian or other Pacific Islander, non-Hispanic/Latino; 16 Two or more races, non-Hispanic/Latino), 48 international. Average age 28. 898 applicants, 57% accepted, 323 enrolled. In 2018, 227 master's, 13 doctorates awarded. Terminal master's awarded for partial completion of doctoral program. *Degree requirements:* For master's, comprehensive exam, thesis; for doctorate, comprehensive exam, thesis/dissertation. *Entrance requirements:* For

master's, GRE General Test or GMAT, bachelor's degree or equivalent from regionally-accredited university with minimum GPA of 3.0 in upper-division sciences coursework; prerequisites in general biology, general chemistry, general physics, organic chemistry, quantitative analysis, and integral and differential calculus; for doctorate, GRE General Test, bachelor's degree from regionally-accredited university with minimum GPA of 3.0 in upper-division sciences coursework; 3 letters of recommendation; personal interview; 1-2 page personal statement; prerequisites in biology, chemistry, physics, organic chemistry, quantitative analysis, and integral/differential calculus. Additional exam requirements/recommendations for international students: Required—TOEFL (minimum score 550 paper-based; 79 iBT) or IELTS (minimum score 6.5). *Application deadline:* For fall admission, 2/1 priority date for domestic students, 2/1 for international students. Application fee: $30. Electronic applications accepted. *Expenses:* Contact institution. *Financial support:* In 2018–19, 106 students received support. *Faculty research:* Anatomy, biochemistry, cancer biology, cardiovascular disease, cell biology, immunology, microbiology, molecular biology, neuroscience, pharmacology, physiology. *Total annual research expenditures:* $50.9 million. *Unit head:* Dr. Michael Barber, Professor/Associate Dean for Graduate and Postdoctoral Affairs, 813-974-9908, Fax: 813-974-4317, E-mail: mbarber@health.usf.edu. *Application contact:* Dr. Eric Bennett, Graduate Director, PhD Program in Medical Sciences, 813-974-1545, Fax: 813-974-4317, E-mail: esbennet@health.usf.edu.
Website: http://health.usf.edu/nocms/medicine/graduatestudies/

The University of Texas at Dallas, School of Natural Sciences and Mathematics, Department of Biological Sciences, Richardson, TX 75080. Offers bioinformatics and computational biology (MS); biotechnology (MS); molecular and cell biology (MS, PhD). *Program availability:* Part-time, evening/weekend. *Faculty:* 20 full-time (4 women), 5 part-time/adjunct (3 women). *Students:* 120 full-time (74 women), 23 part-time (14 women); includes 29 minority (2 Black or African American, non-Hispanic/Latino; 18 Asian, non-Hispanic/Latino; 7 Hispanic/Latino; 2 Two or more races, non-Hispanic/Latino), 78 international. Average age 28. 332 applicants, 24% accepted, 43 enrolled. In 2018, 31 master's, 10 doctorates awarded. *Degree requirements:* For master's, thesis optional; for doctorate, thesis/dissertation, publishable paper. *Entrance requirements:* For master's and doctorate, GRE (minimum combined score of 1000 on verbal and quantitative). Additional exam requirements/recommendations for international students: Required—TOEFL (minimum score 550 paper-based; 80 iBT). *Application deadline:* For fall admission, 7/15 for domestic students, 5/1 priority date for international students; for spring admission, 11/15 for domestic students, 9/1 priority date for international students. Applications are processed on a rolling basis. Application fee: $50 ($100 for international students). Electronic applications accepted. *Expenses:* Tuition, area resident: Full-time $13,458. Tuition, state resident: full-time $13,458. Tuition, nonresident: full-time $26,852. *International tuition:* $26,852 full-time. Tuition and fees vary according to course load. *Financial support:* In 2018–19, 57 students received support, including 11 research assistantships with partial tuition reimbursements available (averaging $24,273 per year), 63 teaching assistantships with partial tuition reimbursements available (averaging $17,100 per year); fellowships with partial tuition reimbursements available, career-related internships or fieldwork, Federal Work-Study, institutionally sponsored loans, scholarships/grants, and unspecified assistantships also available. Support available to part-time students. Financial award application deadline: 4/30; financial award applicants required to submit FAFSA. *Faculty research:* Role of mitochondria in neurodegenerative diseases, protein-DNA interactions in site-specific recombination, eukaryotic gene expression, bio-nanotechnology, sickle cell research. *Unit head:* Dr. Tae Hoon Kim, Department Head, 972-883-6032, Fax: 972-883-4551, E-mail: biology@utdallas.edu. *Application contact:* Dr. Lawrence Reitzer, Graduate Advisor, 972-883-2502, Fax: 972-883-4551, E-mail: reitzer@utdallas.edu.
Website: http://www.utdallas.edu/biology/

The University of Texas at San Antonio, College of Sciences, Department of Biology, San Antonio, TX 78249-0617. Offers biology (MS); biotechnology (MS); cell and molecular biology (PhD); neurobiology (PhD). Terminal master's awarded for partial completion of doctoral program. *Degree requirements:* For master's, comprehensive exam, thesis or alternative; for doctorate, comprehensive exam, thesis/dissertation. *Entrance requirements:* For master's, GRE General Test, bachelor's degree with 18 credit hours in field of study or in another appropriate field of study; for doctorate, GRE General Test, 3 letters of recommendation, statement of purpose, resume. Additional exam requirements/recommendations for international students: Required—TOEFL (minimum score 500 paper-based; 100 iBT), IELTS (minimum score 5). Electronic applications accepted. *Faculty research:* Development of human and veterinary vaccines against a fungal disease, mammalian germ cells and stem cells, dopamine neuron physiology and addiction, plant biochemistry, dendritic computation and synaptic plasticity.

The University of Texas Health Science Center at Tyler, School of Medical Biological Sciences, Tyler, TX 75708. Offers biotechnology (MS).

University of the Sciences, Program in Cell Biology and Biotechnology, Philadelphia, PA 19104-4495. Offers MS. *Program availability:* Part-time, evening/weekend. *Degree requirements:* For master's, thesis optional. *Entrance requirements:* For master's, GRE General Test. Additional exam requirements/recommendations for international students: Required—TOEFL, TWE. *Expenses:* Contact institution.

University of Toronto, School of Graduate Studies, Program in Biotechnology, Toronto, ON M5S 1A1, Canada. Offers MBiotech. *Entrance requirements:* For master's, minimum B+ average in the last two years of study and/or GRE. Additional exam requirements/recommendations for international students: Required—TOEFL (minimum score 580 paper-based; 93 iBT), TWE (minimum score 5). Electronic applications accepted.

University of Utah, Graduate School, Professional Master of Science and Technology Program, Salt Lake City, UT 84112-9016. Offers biotechnology (PSM); computational science (PSM); environmental science (PSM); science instrumentation (PSM). *Program availability:* Part-time. *Degree requirements:* For master's, professional experience project (internship). *Entrance requirements:* For master's, GRE (recommended), minimum undergraduate GPA of 3.0, bachelor's degree from accredited university or college. Additional exam requirements/recommendations for international students: Required—TOEFL (minimum score 550 paper-based; 80 iBT), IELTS (minimum score 6.5). Electronic applications accepted. *Expenses:* Contact institution.

University of Washington, Graduate School, School of Medicine, Graduate Programs in Medicine, Department of Genome Sciences, Seattle, WA 98195. Offers PhD. *Degree requirements:* For doctorate, thesis/dissertation, general exam. *Entrance requirements:* For doctorate, GRE General Test, minimum GPA of 3.0. Additional exam requirements/recommendations for international students: Required—TOEFL. Electronic applications accepted. *Faculty research:* Model organism genetics, human and medical genetics, genomics and proteomics, computational biology.

University of Wyoming, Graduate Program in Molecular and Cellular Life Sciences, Laramie, WY 82071. Offers PhD. *Degree requirements:* For doctorate, thesis/dissertation, four eight-week laboratory rotations, comprehensive basic practical exam, two-part qualifying exam, seminars, symposium. *Expenses: Tuition, area resident:* Full-time $6504; part-time $271 per credit hour. Tuition, state resident: full-time $6504; part-time $271 per credit hour. Tuition, nonresident: full-time $19,464; part-time $811 per credit hour. *International tuition:* $19,464 full-time. *Required fees:* $1410.94; $343.82 per semester. $343.82 per semester. Tuition and fees vary according to course load, program and reciprocity agreements.

Virginia Polytechnic Institute and State University, Graduate School, College of Science, Blacksburg, VA 24061. Offers biological sciences (MS, PhD); biomedical technology development and management (MS); chemistry (MS, PhD); data analysis and applied statistics (MA); economics (PhD); geosciences (MS, PhD); mathematics (MS, PhD); physics (MS, PhD); psychology (MS, PhD); statistics (MS, PhD). *Faculty:* 349 full-time (109 women), 3 part-time/adjunct (2 women). *Students:* 542 full-time (202 women), 39 part-time (19 women); includes 71 minority (11 Black or African American, non-Hispanic/Latino; 1 American Indian or Alaska Native, non-Hispanic/Latino; 18 Asian, non-Hispanic/Latino; 32 Hispanic/Latino; 9 Two or more races, non-Hispanic/Latino), 220 international. Average age 27. 977 applicants, 25% accepted, 110 enrolled. In 2018, 75 master's, 69 doctorates awarded. *Degree requirements:* For master's, comprehensive exam (for some programs), thesis (for some programs); for doctorate, comprehensive exam (for some programs), thesis/dissertation (for some programs). *Entrance requirements:* For master's and doctorate, GRE/GMAT. Additional exam requirements/recommendations for international students: Required—TOEFL (minimum score 90 iBT). *Application deadline:* For fall admission, 8/1 for domestic students, 4/1 for international students; for spring admission, 1/1 for domestic students, 9/1 for international students. Applications are processed on a rolling basis. Application fee: $75. Electronic applications accepted. *Expenses:* Tuition, state resident: full-time $15,510; part-time $739.50 per credit hour. Tuition, nonresident: full-time $29,629; part-time $1490.25 per credit hour. *Required fees:* $2804; $550 per semester. Tuition and fees vary according to course load, campus/location and program. *Financial support:* In 2018–19, 7 fellowships with full tuition reimbursements (averaging $29,657 per year), 260 research assistantships with full tuition reimbursements (averaging $15,888 per year), 383 teaching assistantships with full tuition reimbursements (averaging $18,063 per year) were awarded; unspecified assistantships also available. Financial award application deadline: 3/1; financial award applicants required to submit FAFSA. *Total annual research expenditures:* $27.3 million. *Unit head:* Dr. Sally C. Morton, Dean, 540-231-5422, Fax: 540-231-3380, E-mail: scmorton@vt.edu. *Application contact:* Allison Craft, Executive Assistant, 540-231-6394, Fax: 540-231-3380, E-mail: crafta@vt.edu.
Website: http://www.science.vt.edu/

West Virginia State University, Biotechnology Graduate Program, Institute, WV 25112-1000. Offers MA, MS. *Degree requirements:* For master's, comprehensive exam. *Entrance requirements:* For master's, GRE (Verbal 140, Quantitative 150), International Students: Affidavit of Support, Proof of Immunization, TOEFL (80), evaluation of academic transcripts. Additional exam requirements/recommendations for international students: Required—TOEFL. Electronic applications accepted. *Faculty research:* Plant physiology, microbiology, molecular biology, social insect biology, insect population biology, ecology, fish biology, aquaculture, nutrigenomics, nutritional immunology, tumor biology, gene therapy, muscle physiology, environmental microbiology, microbial genomics, biofilms, anaeromic digestion, plant genomics, parasitic platyhelminths, environmental parasitology, horticulture, plant breeding and genetics, plant reproductive barriers, sustainable agriculture, DNA-assisted plant breeding.

William Paterson University of New Jersey, College of Science and Health, Wayne, NJ 07470-8420. Offers adult gerontology nurse practitioner (Certificate); adult nurse practitioner (Certificate); biology (MS); biotechnology (MS); communication disorders (MS); exercise and sport studies (MS); materials chemistry (MS); nursing (MSN); nursing education (Certificate); nursing practice (DNP); school nurse instructional (Certificate). *Accreditation:* ASHA. *Program availability:* Part-time. *Faculty:* 34 full-time (20 women), 24 part-time/adjunct (19 women). *Students:* 62 full-time (49 women), 236 part-time (203 women); includes 135 minority (22 Black or African American, non-Hispanic/Latino; 48 Asian, non-Hispanic/Latino; 57 Hispanic/Latino; 8 Two or more races, non-Hispanic/Latino), 4 international. Average age 33. 546 applicants, 47% accepted, 151 enrolled. In 2018, 75 master's, 8 doctorates awarded. *Degree requirements:* For master's, Programs Differ see: https://academiccatalog.wpunj.edu/content.php?catoid=1&navoid=68. *Entrance requirements:* For master's, program details: https://www.wpunj.edu/admissions/graduate/admission-deadlines-and-requirements/. Additional exam requirements/recommendations for international students: Required—TOEFL (minimum score 550 paper-based; 79 iBT), IELTS (minimum score 6). *Application deadline:* For fall admission, 6/1 for domestic students, 3/1 for international students; for spring admission, 11/1 for domestic students, 10/1 for international students. Applications are processed on a rolling basis. Application fee: $50. Electronic applications accepted. *Expenses: Tuition, area resident:* Full-time $14,714; part-time $727 per credit. Tuition, state resident: full-time $14,714; part-time $727 per credit. Tuition, nonresident: full-time $22,952; part-time $727 per credit. *International tuition:* $22,952 full-time. *Required fees:* $4 per semester. Tuition and fees vary according to course load, degree level and program. *Financial support:* In 2018–19, 18 students received support. Career-related internships or fieldwork, Federal Work-Study, scholarships/grants, tuition waivers, and unspecified assistantships available. Support available to part-time students. Financial award application deadline: 3/15; financial award applicants required to submit FAFSA. *Faculty research:* Behaviors of American long-eared bats, postpartum fatigue, methodologies for coating carbon nanotubes, paleo climatology, prelinguistic gestures in children with language disorders. *Total annual research expenditures:* $248,283. *Unit head:* Dr. Venkat Sharma, Dean, 973-720-2194, Fax: 973-720-3414, E-mail: sharmav@wpunj.edu. *Application contact:* Christina Aiello, Assistant Director, Graduate Admissions, 973-720-2506, Fax: 973-720-2035, E-mail: aielloc@wpunj.edu.
Website: http://www.wpunj.edu/cosh

Worcester Polytechnic Institute, Graduate Admissions, Department of Biology and Biotechnology, Worcester, MA 01609-2280. Offers MS, PhD. *Program availability:* Part-time, blended/hybrid learning. *Students:* 15 full-time (9 women), 48 part-time (25 women); includes 8 minority (2 Black or African American, non-Hispanic/Latino; 3 Asian, non-Hispanic/Latino; 2 Hispanic/Latino; 1 Two or more races, non-Hispanic/Latino), 8 international. Average age 29. 113 applicants, 30% accepted, 21 enrolled. In 2018, 1 master's, 1 doctorate awarded. Terminal master's awarded for partial completion of doctoral program. *Degree requirements:* For master's, thesis (for some programs); for doctorate, comprehensive exam, thesis/dissertation, qualifying exam. *Entrance requirements:* For master's and doctorate, GRE General Test, 3 letters of recommendation, statement of purpose. Additional exam requirements/recommendations for international students: Required—TOEFL (minimum score 563 paper-based; 84 iBT), IELTS (minimum score 7). *Application deadline:* For fall admission, 1/1 priority date for domestic and international students. Application fee: $70. Electronic applications accepted. *Financial support:* Fellowships, research assistantships, teaching assistantships, career-related internships or fieldwork, institutionally sponsored loans, scholarships/grants, and unspecified assistantships available. Financial award application deadline: 1/1. *Unit head:* Dr. Joseph Duffy, Head, 508-831-5543, Fax: 508-831-5936, E-mail: jduffy@wpi.edu. *Application contact:* Dr. Luis Vidali, Graduate Coordinator, 508-831-5543, Fax: 508-831-5936, E-mail: lvidali@wpi.edu.
Website: https://www.wpi.edu/academics/departments/biology-biotechnology

Worcester State University, Graduate School, Program in Biotechnology, Worcester, MA 01602-2597. Offers MS. *Program availability:* Part-time, evening/weekend. *Faculty:* 7 full-time (4 women), 1 part-time/adjunct (0 women). *Students:* 4 full-time (2 women), 15 part-time (10 women); includes 8 minority (1 Black or African American, non-Hispanic/Latino; 1 American Indian or Alaska Native, non-Hispanic/Latino; 2 Asian, non-Hispanic/Latino; 4 Hispanic/Latino), 1 international. Average age 34. 8 applicants, 100% accepted, 8 enrolled. In 2018, 1 master's awarded. *Degree requirements:* For master's, comprehensive exam, thesis, For a detail list in Degree Completion requirements please see the graduate catalog at catalog.worcester.edu. *Entrance requirements:* For master's, GRE General Test or MAT, For a detail list of entrance requirements please see the graduate catalog at catalog.worcester.edu. Additional exam requirements/recommendations for international students: Required—TOEFL (minimum score 550 paper-based; 79 iBT), IELTS (minimum score 6). *Application deadline:* For fall admission, 3/1 for domestic and international students; for spring admission, 11/1 for domestic and international students; for summer admission, 3/1 for domestic and international students. Applications are processed on a rolling basis. Application fee: $50. Electronic applications accepted. *Expenses: Tuition, area resident:* Full-time $3042; part-time $169 per credit hour. Tuition, state resident: full-time $3042; part-time $169 per credit hour. Tuition, nonresident: full-time $3042; part-time $169 per credit hour. *International tuition:* $3042 full-time. *Required fees:* $2754; $153 per credit hour. *Financial support:* Career-related internships or fieldwork, scholarships/grants, and unspecified assistantships available. Financial award application deadline: 3/1; financial award applicants required to submit FAFSA. *Unit head:* Dr. Ellen Fynan, Program Coordinator, 508-929-8596, Fax: 508-929-8148, E-mail: efynan@worcester.edu. *Application contact:* Sara Grady, Associate Dean, Graduate and Professional Development, 508-929-8130, Fax: 508-929-8100, E-mail: sara.grady@worcester.edu.

Yeshiva University, The Katz School, Program in Biotechnology Management and Entrepreneurship, New York, NY 10033-3201. Offers MS. *Program availability:* Part-time.

Nanotechnology

The American University in Cairo, School of Sciences and Engineering, Cairo, Egypt. Offers biotechnology (MS); chemistry (MS); computer science (MS); computing (M Comp); construction engineering (M Eng, MS); electronics and communications engineering (M Eng); environmental engineering (MS); environmental system design (M Eng); mechanical engineering (M Eng, MS); nanotechnology (MS); physics (MS); robotics, control and smart systems (MS); sciences and engineering (PhD); sustainable development (MS, Graduate Diploma). *Program availability:* Part-time, evening/weekend. *Degree requirements:* For master's, comprehensive exam (for some programs), thesis (for some programs); for doctorate, comprehensive exam (for some programs), thesis/dissertation. *Entrance requirements:* Additional exam requirements/recommendations for international students: Required—TOEFL (minimum score 450 paper-based; 45 iBT), IELTS (minimum score 5). Electronic applications accepted. *Faculty research:* Construction, mechanical, and electronics engineering; physics; computer science; biotechnology; nanotechnology; chemistry; robotics.

Arizona State University at the Tempe campus, College of Liberal Arts and Sciences, Department of Chemistry and Biochemistry, Tempe, AZ 85287-1604. Offers biochemistry (MS, PhD); chemistry (MS, PhD); nanoscience (PSM). Terminal master's awarded for partial completion of doctoral program. *Degree requirements:* For master's, thesis, interactive Program of Study (iPOS) submitted before completing 50 percent of required credit hours; for doctorate, comprehensive exam, thesis/dissertation, interactive Program of Study (iPOS) submitted before completing 50 percent of required credit hours. *Entrance requirements:* For master's and doctorate, GRE, minimum GPA of 3.0 or equivalent in last 2 years of work leading to bachelor's degree. Additional exam requirements/recommendations for international students: Required—TOEFL, IELTS, or PTE. Electronic applications accepted.

Arizona State University at the Tempe campus, College of Liberal Arts and Sciences, Department of Physics, Tempe, AZ 85287-1504. Offers nanoscience (PSM); physics (MNS, PhD). *Program availability:* Part-time. Terminal master's awarded for partial completion of doctoral program. *Degree requirements:* For master's, comprehensive exam, thesis or alternative, interactive Program of Study (iPOS) submitted before completing 50 percent of required credit hours; for doctorate, comprehensive exam, thesis/dissertation, interactive Program of Study (iPOS) submitted before completing 50 percent of required credit hours. *Entrance requirements:* For master's and doctorate, GRE, minimum GPA of 3.0 or equivalent in last 2 years of work leading to bachelor's degree. Additional exam requirements/recommendations for international students: Required—TOEFL, IELTS, or PTE. Electronic applications accepted. *Expenses:* Contact institution.

Carnegie Mellon University, Mellon College of Science, Department of Chemistry, Pittsburgh, PA 15213-3891. Offers atmospheric chemistry (PhD); bioinorganic chemistry (PhD); bioorganic chemistry and chemical biology (PhD); biophysical chemistry (PhD); catalysis (PhD); green and environmental chemistry (PhD); materials and nanoscience (PhD); renewable energy (PhD); sensors, probes, and imaging (PhD); spectroscopy and single molecule analysis (PhD); theoretical and computational chemistry (PhD). *Program availability:* Part-time. Terminal master's awarded for partial completion of doctoral program. *Degree requirements:* For doctorate, thesis/dissertation, departmental qualifying and oral exams, teaching experience. *Entrance requirements:* For doctorate, GRE General Test, GRE Subject Test. Additional exam requirements/recommendations for international students: Required—TOEFL. Electronic applications accepted. *Faculty research:* Physical and theoretical chemistry, chemical synthesis, biophysical/bioinorganic chemistry.

Cornell University, Graduate School, Graduate Fields of Agriculture and Life Sciences and Graduate Fields of Engineering, Field of Biological and Environmental Engineering, Ithaca, NY 14853. Offers bioenergy and integrated energy systems (M Eng, MPS, MS, PhD); biological engineering (M Eng, MPS, MS, PhD); bioprocess engineering (M Eng, MPS, MS, PhD); ecohydrology (M Eng, MPS, MS, PhD); environmental engineering (M Eng, MPS, MS, PhD); environmental management (MPS); food engineering (M Eng,

MPS, MS, PhD); industrial biotechnology (M Eng, MPS, MS, PhD); nanobiotechnology (M Eng, MPS, MS, PhD); sustainable systems (M Eng, MPS, MS, PhD); synthetic biology (MS); syntheticbiology (M Eng, MPS, PhD). Terminal master's awarded for partial completion of doctoral program. *Degree requirements:* For master's, thesis (MS); for doctorate, comprehensive exam, thesis/dissertation. *Entrance requirements:* For master's, letters of recommendation (3 for MS, 2 for M Eng and MPS); for doctorate, GRE General Test, 3 letters of recommendation. Additional exam requirements/recommendations for international students: Required—TOEFL (minimum score 550 paper-based; 77 iBT). Electronic applications accepted. *Faculty research:* Biological and food engineering, environmental, soil and water engineering, international agricultural engineering, structures and controlled environments, machine systems and energy.

Indiana University of Pennsylvania, School of Graduate Studies and Research, College of Natural Sciences and Mathematics, Department of Physics, Program in Nanoscience/Industrial Materials, Indiana, PA 15705. Offers PSM. *Program availability:* Part-time. *Faculty:* 4 full-time (0 women). *Students:* 2 full-time (1 woman), 1 international. Average age 25. 6 applicants, 50% accepted, 6 enrolled. In 2018, 1 master's awarded. *Entrance requirements:* Additional exam requirements/recommendations for international students: Required—TOEFL (minimum score 540 paper-based). *Application deadline:* Applications are processed on a rolling basis. Application fee: $50. Electronic applications accepted. *Expenses:* Tuition, state resident: full-time $12,384; part-time $516 per credit hour. Tuition, nonresident: full-time $18,576; part-time $774 per credit hour. *Required fees:* $4454; $186 per credit hour. $65 per semester. Tuition and fees vary according to program and reciprocity agreements. *Financial support:* In 2018–19, 2 research assistantships (averaging $3,173 per year) were awarded; fellowships, career-related internships or fieldwork, Federal Work-Study, and scholarships/grants also available. Support available to part-time students. Financial award application deadline: 4/15; financial award applicants required to submit FAFSA. *Unit head:* Dr. John Bradshaw, Graduate Coordinator, 724-357-7731, E-mail: bradshaw@iup.edu. *Application contact:* Dr. John Bradshaw, Graduate Coordinator, 724-357-7731, E-mail: bradshaw@iup.edu.

Johns Hopkins University, Engineering Program for Professionals, Part-time Program in Materials Science and Engineering, Baltimore, MD 21218. Offers nanotechnology (M Mat SE). *Program availability:* Part-time, evening/weekend. *Faculty:* 1 full-time, 4 part-time/adjunct (2 women). *Students:* 13 part-time (5 women). 14 applicants, 29% accepted, 3 enrolled. In 2018, 8 master's awarded. *Entrance requirements:* Additional exam requirements/recommendations for international students: Required—TOEFL (minimum score 600 paper-based; 100 iBT). *Application deadline:* Applications are processed on a rolling basis. Application fee: $0. Electronic applications accepted. *Unit head:* Dr. James Spicer, Program Chair, 410-516-8524, E-mail: spicer@jhu.edu. *Application contact:* Doug Schiller, Admissions Director, 410-516-2300, Fax: 410-579-8049, E-mail: schiller@jhu.edu.
Website: http://www.ep.jhu.edu

Johns Hopkins University, G. W. C. Whiting School of Engineering, Master of Science in Engineering Management Program, Baltimore, MD 21218. Offers biomaterials (MSEM); civil engineering (MSEM); communications science (MSEM); computer science (MSEM); environmental systems analysis, economics and public policy (MSEM); fluid mechanics (MSEM); materials science and engineering (MSEM); mechanical engineering (MSEM); mechanics and materials (MSEM); nanobiotechnology (MSEM); nanomaterials and nanotechnology (MSEM); operations research (MSEM); probability and statistics (MSEM); smart product and device design (MSEM). *Students:* 34 full-time (12 women), 18 part-time (7 women). 233 applicants, 39% accepted, 33 enrolled. In 2018, 27 master's awarded. *Entrance requirements:* For master's, GRE, 3 letters of recommendation, statement of purpose, transcripts. Additional exam requirements/recommendations for international students: Required—TOEFL (minimum score 600 paper-based, 100 iBT) or IELTS (7). *Application deadline:* For fall admission, 2/15 for domestic and international students. Application fee: $75. Electronic applications accepted. *Financial support:* In 2018–19, 43 research assistantships (averaging $43,344 per year) were awarded; health care benefits also available. *Unit head:* Dr. Pamela Sheff, Director, 410-516-7056, Fax: 410-516-4880, E-mail: pamsheff@gmail.com. *Application contact:* Lindsey Conklin, Sr. Academic Program Coordinator, 410-516-1108, Fax: 410-516-0780, E-mail: lconkli4@jhu.edu.
Website: http://engineering.jhu.edu/msem/

Louisiana Tech University, Graduate School, College of Applied and Natural Sciences, Ruston, LA 71272. Offers biology (MS); dietetics (Graduate Certificate); health informatics (MHI); molecular science and nanotechnology (MS, PhD). *Program availability:* Part-time. *Degree requirements:* For master's, comprehensive exam (for some programs), thesis (for some programs); for doctorate, comprehensive exam, thesis/dissertation. *Entrance requirements:* For master's and doctorate, GRE General Test, transcript with bachelor's degree awarded; for Graduate Certificate, transcript with bachelor's degree awarded. Additional exam requirements/recommendations for international students: Required—TOEFL (minimum score 550 paper-based; 80 iBT), IELTS (minimum score 6.5). Electronic applications accepted. *Faculty research:* Developmentally appropriate practices in early childhood education, maternal and child nutrition, nutrition and cardiovascular disease, and early intervention for infants and toddlers; research in cell and molecular biology; health promotion in emerging adults, insulin pump use, forensic nursing, qualitative research, empathy in nursing students, civility in nursing education, and STI education; gene expression data analysis and data mining, knowledge discovery for health related data.

Louisiana Tech University, Graduate School, College of Engineering and Science, Ruston, LA 71272. Offers applied physics (MS); biomedical engineering (PhD); computer science (MS); engineering (MS, PhD), including cyberspace engineering (PhD), engineering education (PhD), engineering physics (PhD), materials and infrastructure systems (PhD), micro/nanoscale systems (PhD); engineering and technology management (MS); mathematics (MS); molecular science and nanotechnology (MS, PhD). *Program availability:* Part-time-only. Terminal master's awarded for partial completion of doctoral program. *Degree requirements:* For master's, thesis (for some programs); for doctorate, thesis/dissertation. *Entrance requirements:* For master's and Graduate Certificate, GRE General Test, minimum GPA of 3.0 in last 60 hours. Additional exam requirements/recommendations for international students: Required—TOEFL (minimum score 550 paper-based; 80 iBT), IELTS (minimum score 6.5). Electronic applications accepted. *Faculty research:* Trenchless technology, micromanufacturing, radionuclide transport, microbial liquefaction, hazardous waste treatment.

North Dakota State University, College of Graduate and Interdisciplinary Studies, College of Engineering, Doctoral Program in Engineering, Fargo, ND 58102. Offers environmental and conservation science (PhD); materials and nanotechnology (PhD); natural resource management (PhD); STEM education (PhD); transportation and logistics (PhD). *Degree requirements:* For doctorate, comprehensive exam, thesis/dissertation. *Entrance requirements:* For doctorate, bachelor's degree in engineering, minimum GPA of 3.0. Additional exam requirements/recommendations for international students: Required—TOEFL. Electronic applications accepted. *Expenses:* Contact institution.

North Dakota State University, College of Graduate and Interdisciplinary Studies, Interdisciplinary Program in Materials and Nanotechnology, Fargo, ND 58102. Offers MS, PhD. *Entrance requirements:* For doctorate, GRE General Test. Additional exam requirements/recommendations for international students: Required—TOEFL.

South Dakota School of Mines and Technology, Graduate Division, Program in Nanoscience and Nanoengineering, Rapid City, SD 57701-3995. Offers PhD. *Program availability:* Part-time. *Degree requirements:* For doctorate, thesis/dissertation. *Entrance requirements:* Additional exam requirements/recommendations for international students: Required—TOEFL (minimum score 520 paper-based; 68 iBT). Electronic applications accepted.

State University of New York Polytechnic Institute, College of Nanoscale Science and Engineering, Albany, NY 13502. Offers nanoscale engineering (PhD); nanoscale science (MS); MD/PhD. *Students:* 34 full-time (10 women), 36 part-time (14 women); includes 27 minority (17 Asian, non-Hispanic/Latino; 4 Hispanic/Latino; 6 Two or more races, non-Hispanic/Latino), 13 international. Average age 28. 65 applicants, 31% accepted, 10 enrolled. In 2018, 8 master's, 5 doctorates awarded. *Degree requirements:* For master's, comprehensive exam, thesis, Research Project; for doctorate, comprehensive exam, thesis/dissertation. *Entrance requirements:* For master's, GRE (preferred, not required), background in sciences. Additional exam requirements/recommendations for international students: Required—TOEFL (minimum score 79 paper-based), IELTS (minimum score 6.5), PTE (minimum score 53), TOEFL, IELTS, or PTE; GRE. *Application deadline:* For fall admission, 7/1 for domestic and international students; for spring admission, 12/1 for domestic students, 11/1 for international students. Applications are processed on a rolling basis. Application fee: $60. Electronic applications accepted. *Expenses:* Contact institution. *Financial support:* Fellowships, research assistantships, teaching assistantships, and tuition waivers available. Financial award application deadline: 6/1; financial award applicants required to submit FAFSA. *Faculty research:* Mems/nems, theranostics, biomedical engineering, nanoelectronics and quantum computing, materials characterization and metrology, power electronics, energy, sensors. *Unit head:* Dr. Alain Diebold, 518-956-7363, E-mail: adiebold@sunypoly.edu. *Application contact:* Krista Thompson, Assistant Dean of Graduate Studies, 518-956-7011, E-mail: kthompson@sunypoly.edu.

University at Buffalo, the State University of New York, Graduate School, School of Engineering and Applied Sciences, Department of Chemical and Biological Engineering, Buffalo, NY 14260. Offers bioengineering nanotechnology (Certificate); chemical and biological engineering (ME, MS, PhD); nanomaterials and materials informatics (Certificate). *Program availability:* Part-time. *Degree requirements:* For master's, thesis (for some programs); for doctorate, comprehensive exam, thesis/dissertation. *Entrance requirements:* For master's and doctorate, GRE General Test. Additional exam requirements/recommendations for international students: Required—TOEFL (minimum score 550 paper-based; 79 iBT). Electronic applications accepted. *Faculty research:* Biochemical and biomedical engineering, nanoscale science and engineering, computational science and engineering.

University of Alberta, Faculty of Graduate Studies and Research, Department of Electrical and Computer Engineering, Edmonton, AB T6G 2E1, Canada. Offers communications (M Eng, M Sc, PhD); computer engineering (M Eng, M Sc, PhD); electromagnetics (M Eng, M Sc, PhD); nanotechnology and microdevices (M Eng, M Sc, PhD); power/power electronics (M Eng, M Sc, PhD); systems (M Eng, M Sc, PhD). Terminal master's awarded for partial completion of doctoral program. *Degree requirements:* For master's, thesis; for doctorate, thesis/dissertation. *Entrance requirements:* Additional exam requirements/recommendations for international students: Required—TOEFL. Electronic applications accepted. *Faculty research:* Controls, communications, microelectronics, electromagnetics.

University of California, Riverside, Graduate Division, Materials Science and Engineering Program, Riverside, CA 92521. Offers MS. *Entrance requirements:* For master's, GRE. Additional exam requirements/recommendations for international students: Required—TOEFL (minimum score 550 paper-based; 80 iBT). Electronic applications accepted.

University of California, San Diego, Graduate Division, Department of Electrical and Computer Engineering, La Jolla, CA 92093. Offers applied ocean science (MS, PhD); applied physics (MS, PhD); communication theory and systems (MS, PhD); computer engineering (MS, PhD); electronic circuits and systems (MS, PhD); intelligent systems, robotics and control (MS, PhD); medical devices and systems (MS, PhD); nanoscale devices and systems (MS, PhD); photonics (MS, PhD); signal and image processing (MS, PhD). Program offered jointly with San Diego State University. *Students:* 830 full-time (174 women), 69 part-time (8 women). 2,810 applicants, 40% accepted, 399 enrolled. In 2018, 226 master's, 42 doctorates awarded. Terminal master's awarded for partial completion of doctoral program. *Degree requirements:* For master's, comprehensive exam (for some programs), thesis (for some programs); for doctorate, comprehensive exam, thesis/dissertation. *Entrance requirements:* For master's and doctorate, GRE General Test, minimum GPA of 3.0, resume or curriculum vitae (recommended). Additional exam requirements/recommendations for international students: Required—TOEFL (minimum score 550 paper-based; 80 iBT), IELTS (minimum score 7), PTE (minimum score 65). *Application deadline:* For fall admission, 12/13 for domestic students. Application fee: $105 ($125 for international students). Electronic applications accepted. *Financial support:* Fellowships, research assistantships, teaching assistantships, scholarships/grants, traineeships, and unspecified assistantships available. Financial award applicants required to submit FAFSA. *Faculty research:* Applied ocean science; applied physics; communication theory and systems; computer engineering; electronic circuits and systems; intelligent systems, robotics and control; medical devices and systems; nanoscale devices and systems; photonics; signal and image processing. *Unit head:* Bill Lin, Chair, 858-822-1383, E-mail: billin@ucsd.edu. *Application contact:* Sean Jones, Graduate Admissions Coordinator, 858-534-3213, E-mail: ecegradapps@ece.ucsd.edu.
Website: http://ece.ucsd.edu/

University of California, San Diego, Graduate Division, Department of Nanoengineering, La Jolla, CA 92093. Offers MS, PhD. *Students:* 104 full-time (34 women), 5 part-time (3 women). 214 applicants, 33% accepted, 23 enrolled. In 2018, 40 master's, 7 doctorates awarded. *Degree requirements:* For master's, comprehensive exam (for some programs), thesis (for some programs), comprehensive exam or thesis; for doctorate, comprehensive exam, thesis/dissertation, 1-quarter teaching assistantship. *Entrance requirements:* For master's and doctorate, GRE General Test, 3 letters of recommendation, statement of purpose, resume. Additional exam requirements/recommendations for international students: Required—TOEFL (minimum score 550 paper-based; 80 iBT), IELTS (minimum score 7). *Application deadline:* For fall admission, 2/25 for domestic students. Application fee: $105 ($125 for international students). Electronic applications accepted. *Financial support:* Fellowships, research assistantships, teaching assistantships, and scholarships/grants available. Financial award applicants required to submit FAFSA. *Faculty research:* Biomedical nanotechnology, molecular and nanomaterials, nanotechnologies for energy and the environment. *Unit head:* Shaochen Chen, Chair, 858-822-7856, E-mail: chen168@ucsd.edu. *Application contact:* Dana Jimenez, Graduate Coordinator, 858-822-7981, E-mail: dljimenez@ucsd.edu.
Website: http://nanoengineering.ucsd.edu

Nanotechnology

University of New Mexico, Graduate Studies, School of Engineering, Program in Nanoscience and Microsystems Engineering, Albuquerque, NM 87131. Offers MS, PhD. *Program availability:* Part-time. *Degree requirements:* For master's, comprehensive exam, thesis; for doctorate, comprehensive exam, thesis/dissertation. *Entrance requirements:* For master's and doctorate, GRE. Additional exam requirements/recommendations for international students: Required—TOEFL. Electronic applications accepted.

University of Pennsylvania, School of Engineering and Applied Science, Program in Nanotechnology, Philadelphia, PA 19104. Offers MSE. *Program availability:* Part-time. *Students:* 9 full-time (2 women), 10 part-time (3 women); includes 3 minority (1 Black or African American, non-Hispanic/Latino; 1 Asian, non-Hispanic/Latino; 1 Hispanic/Latino), 14 international. Average age 25. 24 applicants, 71% accepted, 13 enrolled. In 2018, 10 master's awarded. *Degree requirements:* For master's, comprehensive exam, thesis optional. *Entrance requirements:* For master's, GRE, bachelor's degree, letters of recommendation, resume, personal statement. Additional exam requirements/recommendations for international students: Required—TOEFL (minimum score 100 iBT), IELTS (minimum score 7). *Application deadline:* For fall admission, 3/15 priority date for domestic and international students. Application fee: $80. Electronic applications accepted. *Expenses:* Contact institution. *Faculty research:* Synthesis, materials and nanofabrication, devices and fundamental properties, biotechnology. *Application contact:* William Fenton, Assistant Director of Graduate Admissions, 215-898-4542, Fax: 215-573-5577, E-mail: gradstudies@seas.upenn.edu. Website: http://www.masters.nano.upenn.edu/

University of South Florida, Taneja College of Pharmacy, Tampa, FL 33620-9951. Offers pharmaceutical nanotechnology (MS), including biomedical engineering, drug discovery, delivery, development and manufacturing; pharmacy (Pharm D), including pharmacy and health education. *Accreditation:* ACPE. *Faculty:* 32 full-time (18 women), 1 part-time/adjunct (0 women). *Students:* 398 full-time (234 women), 7 part-time (3 women); includes 180 minority (33 Black or African American, non-Hispanic/Latino; 72 Asian, non-Hispanic/Latino; 59 Hispanic/Latino; 2 Native Hawaiian or other Pacific Islander, non-Hispanic/Latino; 14 Two or more races, non-Hispanic/Latino), 13 international. Average age 25. 465 applicants, 44% accepted, 112 enrolled. In 2018, 11 master's, 91 doctorates awarded. *Degree requirements:* For master's, comprehensive exam, thesis optional, capstone or thesis; for doctorate, internship/field experience. *Entrance requirements:* For master's, GRE, MCAT or DAT, Bachelor's preferably in biomedical, biological, chemical sciences or engineering; 2 letters of recommendation; resume; professional statement; interview; for doctorate, PCAT, minimum GPA of 2.75 overall (preferred); completion of 72 prerequisite credit hours; U.S. citizenship or permanent resident; interviews; criminal background check and drug screen. Additional exam requirements/recommendations for international students: Required—TOEFL (minimum score 550 paper-based; 79 iBT), IELTS (minimum score 6.5). *Application deadline:* For fall admission, 6/1 for domestic and international students; for spring admission, 10/15 for domestic students, 9/15 for international students; for summer admission, 2/15 for domestic and international students. Electronic applications accepted. *Expenses:* Tuition, state resident: full-time $6350. Tuition, nonresident: full-time $19,048. *International tuition:* $19,048 full-time. *Required fees:* $2079. *Financial support:* In 2018–19, 159 students received support. *Total annual research expenditures:* $1.4 million. *Unit head:* James Lambert, 813-974-4562, E-mail: jlambert2@usf.edu. *Application contact:* Dr. Amy Schwartz, Associate Dean, 813-974-2251, E-mail: aschwar1@health.usf.edu.

University of Washington, Graduate School, College of Engineering and School of Medicine, Department of Bioengineering, Seattle, WA 98195-5061. Offers applied bioengineering (MAB); bioengineering (MS, PhD); bioengineering and nanotechnology (PhD); pharmaceutical bioengineering (MS). *Program availability:* Part-time. *Faculty:* 50 full-time (15 women), 47 part-time/adjunct (5 women). *Students:* 142 full-time (63 women), 42 part-time (25 women); includes 58 minority (4 Black or African American, non-Hispanic/Latino; 1 American Indian or Alaska Native, non-Hispanic/Latino; 32 Asian, non-Hispanic/Latino; 13 Hispanic/Latino; 8 Two or more races, non-Hispanic/Latino), 42 international. Average age 26. 877 applicants, 19% accepted, 60 enrolled. In 2018, 26 master's, 27 doctorates awarded. *Degree requirements:* For master's, comprehensive exam, thesis; for doctorate, comprehensive exam, thesis/dissertation, qualifying exam, general exam, thesis defense. *Entrance requirements:* For master's and doctorate, GRE General Test, minimum GPA of 3.0, transcripts, statement of purpose, letters of recommendation, resume/curriculum vitae. Additional exam requirements/recommendations for international students: Required—TOEFL (minimum score 500 paper-based; 80 iBT). *Application deadline:* For fall admission, 12/15 for domestic and international students. Application fee: $85. Electronic applications accepted. Application fee is waived when completed online. *Expenses:* Regular/research-focused master's degrees and Ph.D.s: resident, $18,852, non-resident, $32,760; Master's of Applied Bioengineering: $24,719 resident, $29,446 nonresident. *Financial support:* In 2018–19, 135 students received support, including 31 fellowships with full tuition reimbursements available (averaging $37,680 per year), 92 research assistantships with full tuition reimbursements available (averaging $37,680 per year), 4 teaching assistantships with full tuition reimbursements available (averaging $37,680 per year); Federal Work-Study, institutionally sponsored loans, traineeships, health care benefits, and tuition waivers (full) also available. Support available to part-time students. Financial award application deadline: 12/1; financial award applicants required to submit FAFSA. *Faculty research:* Imaging and image guided therapy, molecular and cellular engineering, biomaterials and regenerative medicine, technology for expanding access to healthcare, synthetic and quantitative biology, neural engineering. *Total annual research expenditures:* $25.6 million. *Unit head:* Dr. Cecilia Giachelli, Professor/Chair, 206-685-2000, Fax: 206-685-3300, E-mail: ceci@uw.edu. *Application contact:* Peggy Sharp, Graduate Academic Counselor, 206-685-3494, Fax: 206-685-3300, E-mail: peggys55@uw.edu. Website: https://bioe.uw.edu/

University of Washington, Graduate School, College of Engineering, Department of Chemical Engineering, Seattle, WA 98195-1750. Offers chemical engineering (MS, PhD); chemical engineering and advanced data science (PhD); chemical engineering and nanotechnology (PhD). *Faculty:* 19 full-time (3 women). *Students:* 90 full-time (30 women), 15 part-time (7 women); includes 15 minority (1 Black or African American, non-Hispanic/Latino; 6 Asian, non-Hispanic/Latino; 6 Hispanic/Latino; 2 Two or more races, non-Hispanic/Latino), 49 international. Average age 25. 423 applicants, 28% accepted, 28 enrolled. In 2018, 29 master's, 12 doctorates awarded. Terminal master's awarded for partial completion of doctoral program. *Degree requirements:* For master's, comprehensive exam, thesis optional, final exam, research project, degree completed in 6 years; for doctorate, comprehensive exam, thesis/dissertation, general and final exams, research project, completion of all work within 10 years. *Entrance requirements:* For master's and doctorate, GRE General Test (minimum Quantitative score of 159), minimum GPA of 3.0, official transcripts, personal statement, confidential evaluations by 3 professors or other technical professional, high rank (top 5%) in respected chemical engineering program. Additional exam requirements/recommendations for international

students: Required—TOEFL (minimum score 580 paper-based; 92 iBT); Recommended—IELTS (minimum score 7). *Application deadline:* For fall admission, 1/1 priority date for domestic students, 12/15 priority date for international students. Applications are processed on a rolling basis. Application fee: $85. Electronic applications accepted. *Expenses:* Research-focused Master's and PhD: $18,852 resident; $32,760 nonresident. Applied/Professional Master's: $23,070 resident; $35,571 nonresident. *Financial support:* In 2018–19, 73 students received support, including 16 fellowships with full tuition reimbursements available (averaging $32,640 per year), 38 research assistantships with full tuition reimbursements available (averaging $32,640 per year), 17 teaching assistantships with full tuition reimbursements available (averaging $32,640 per year); career-related internships or fieldwork, Federal Work-Study, health care benefits, and unspecified assistantships also available. Financial award application deadline: 1/15; financial award applicants required to submit FAFSA. *Faculty research:* Materials processing and characterization, optical and electronic polymers, surface science, biochemical engineering and bioengineering, computational chemistry, environmental studies. *Total annual research expenditures:* $13.5 million. *Unit head:* Dr. Francois Baneyx, Professor/Chair, 206-543-2250, Fax: 206-543-3778, E-mail: baneyx@uw.edu. *Application contact:* Allison Sherrill, Graduate Program Advisor, 206-685-9785, E-mail: sherra@uw.edu. Website: http://www.cheme.washington.edu/

University of Washington, Graduate School, College of Engineering, Department of Electrical and Computer Engineering, Seattle, WA 98195-2500. Offers electrical engineering (MS, PhD); electrical engineering and nanotechnology (PhD). *Program availability:* Part-time, evening/weekend. *Faculty:* 40 full-time (8 women), 39 part-time/adjunct (8 women). *Students:* 247 full-time (59 women), 135 part-time (23 women); includes 67 minority (9 Black or African American, non-Hispanic/Latino; 43 Asian, non-Hispanic/Latino; 10 Hispanic/Latino; 5 Two or more races, non-Hispanic/Latino), 192 international. Average age 27. 1,392 applicants, 34% accepted, 132 enrolled. In 2018, 83 master's, 30 doctorates awarded. Terminal master's awarded for partial completion of doctoral program. *Degree requirements:* For master's, thesis optional; for doctorate, thesis/dissertation, qualifying, general, and final exams. *Entrance requirements:* For master's and doctorate, GRE General Test - Optional (not required), minimum GPA of 3.5 (recommended); resume or curriculum vitae, statement of purpose, 3 letters of recommendation, undergraduate and graduate transcripts. Additional exam requirements/recommendations for international students: Required—TOEFL (minimum score 600 paper-based; 92 iBT). *Application deadline:* For fall admission, 12/15 for domestic and international students. Application fee: $85. Electronic applications accepted. *Expenses:* Research-focused Master's and PhD: $18,852 resident; $32,760 nonresident. *Financial support:* In 2018–19, 154 students received support, including 8 fellowships with full tuition reimbursements available (averaging $32,880 per year), 99 research assistantships with full tuition reimbursements available (averaging $32,880 per year), 47 teaching assistantships with full tuition reimbursements available (averaging $32,880 per year); career-related internships or fieldwork, Federal Work-Study, institutionally sponsored loans, health care benefits, and tuition waivers (full) also available. Financial award application deadline: 12/15; financial award applicants required to submit FAFSA. *Faculty research:* Computing and networking, data sciences, and biosystems, photonics and nano-devices, power and energy systems, robotics and controls. *Total annual research expenditures:* $29 million. *Unit head:* Dr. Radha Poovendran, Professor/Chair, 206-543-6515, Fax: 206-543-3842, E-mail: chair@ece.uw.edu. *Application contact:* Brenda Larson, Lead Academic Counselor, Graduate Programs, 206-616-1351, Fax: 206-543-3842, E-mail: grad@ece.uw.edu. Website: http://www.ece.uw.edu

University of Washington, Graduate School, College of Engineering, Department of Materials Science and Engineering, Seattle, WA 98195-2120. Offers applied materials science and engineering (MS); materials science and engineering (MS, PhD); materials science and engineering and nanotechnology (PhD); materials science and engineering, nanotechnology, and molecular engineering (PhD). *Program availability:* Part-time. *Faculty:* 12 full-time (2 women). *Students:* 110 full-time (32 women), 24 part-time (9 women); includes 34 minority (3 Black or African American, non-Hispanic/Latino; 14 Asian, non-Hispanic/Latino; 9 Hispanic/Latino; 1 Native Hawaiian or other Pacific Islander, non-Hispanic/Latino; 7 Two or more races, non-Hispanic/Latino), 60 international. Average age 25. 456 applicants, 37% accepted, 57 enrolled. In 2018, 35 master's, 12 doctorates awarded. Terminal master's awarded for partial completion of doctoral program. *Degree requirements:* For master's, comprehensive exam, final paper or thesis and presentation; for doctorate, comprehensive exam, thesis/dissertation, qualifying evaluation, general and final exams. *Entrance requirements:* For master's and doctorate, GRE General Test, minimum GPA of 3.0, resume/curriculum vitae, letters of recommendation, statement of purpose, transcripts. Additional exam requirements/recommendations for international students: Required—TOEFL (minimum score 92 iBT). *Application deadline:* For fall admission, 1/4 for domestic and international students. Application fee: $85. Electronic applications accepted. *Expenses:* Contact institution. *Financial support:* In 2018–19, 65 students received support, including 42 research assistantships with full tuition reimbursements available (averaging $30,660 per year), 20 teaching assistantships with full tuition reimbursements available (averaging $30,660 per year); fellowships with full tuition reimbursements available, career-related internships or fieldwork, Federal Work-Study, institutionally sponsored loans, scholarships/grants, health care benefits, unspecified assistantships, and stipend supplements also available. Financial award application deadline: 1/1; financial award applicants required to submit FAFSA. *Faculty research:* Synthesis/structure/property and processing, biomaterials and biomimetics, solar energy and battery materials, materials chemistry and characterization, optical and electronic materials. *Total annual research expenditures:* $6.5 million. *Unit head:* Dr. Jihui Yang, Professor/Chair, 206-543-7090, Fax: 206-221-4934, E-mail: jihuiy@uw.edu. *Application contact:* Karen Wetterhahn, Academic Counselor, 206-543-2740, Fax: 206-543-3100, E-mail: karenlw@uw.edu. Website: http://mse.washington.edu

Virginia Commonwealth University, Graduate School, College of Humanities and Sciences, Department of Physics, Richmond, VA 23284-9005. Offers medical physics (MS, PhD); nanoscience and nanotechnology (PhD); physics and applied physics (MS). *Program availability:* Part-time. *Degree requirements:* For master's, comprehensive exam, thesis optional. *Entrance requirements:* For master's, GRE. Additional exam requirements/recommendations for international students: Required—TOEFL (minimum score 600 paper-based; 100 iBT); Recommended—IELTS (minimum score 6.5). Electronic applications accepted. *Faculty research:* Condensed-matter theory and experimentation, electronic instrumentation, relativity.

Virginia Commonwealth University, Graduate School, College of Humanities and Sciences, Program in Nanosciences, Richmond, VA 23284-9005. Offers PhD. *Entrance requirements:* For doctorate, GRE General Test. Additional exam requirements/recommendations for international students: Required—TOEFL (minimum score 600 paper-based; 100 iBT); Recommended—IELTS (minimum score 6.5). Electronic applications accepted. *Faculty research:* Nanotechnology, nanoscience.

Section 6
Chemical Engineering

This section contains a directory of institutions offering graduate work in chemical engineering, followed by an in-depth entry submitted by an institution that chose to prepare a detailed program description. Additional information about programs listed in the directory but not augmented by an in-depth entry may be obtained by writing directly to the dean of a graduate school or chair of a department at the address given in the directory.

For programs offering related work, see also in this book *Engineering and Applied Sciences; Geological, Mineral/Mining, and Petroleum Engineering; Management of Engineering and Technology;* and *Materials Sciences and Engineering.* In the other guides in this series:

Graduate Programs in the Humanities, Arts & Social Sciences
See *Family and Consumer Sciences (Clothing and Textiles)*

Graduate Programs in the Biological/Biomedical Sciences & Health-Related Medical Professions
See *Biochemistry*

Graduate Programs in the Physical Sciences, Mathematics, Agricultural Sciences, the Environment & Natural Resources
See *Chemistry* and *Geosciences (Geochemistry* and *Geology)*

CONTENTS

Program Directories

Featured School: Display and Close-Up

Biochemical Engineering

Brown University, Graduate School, School of Engineering, Providence, RI 02912. Offers biomedical engineering (Sc M, PhD); chemical and biochemical engineering (Sc M, PhD); electrical sciences and computer engineering (Sc M, PhD); fluid and thermal sciences (Sc M, PhD); materials science and engineering (Sc M, PhD); mechanics of solids and structures (Sc M, PhD). *Degree requirements:* For doctorate, thesis/dissertation, preliminary exam.

Cornell University, Graduate School, Graduate Fields of Engineering, Field of Chemical Engineering, Ithaca, NY 14853. Offers advanced materials processing (M Eng, MS, PhD); applied mathematics and computational methods (M Eng, MS, PhD); biochemical engineering (M Eng, MS, PhD); chemical reaction engineering (M Eng, MS, PhD); classical and statistical thermodynamics (M Eng, MS, PhD); fluid dynamics, rheology and biorheology (M Eng, MS, PhD); heat and mass transfer (M Eng, MS, PhD); kinetics and catalysis (M Eng, MS, PhD); polymers (M Eng, MS, PhD); surface science (M Eng, MS, PhD). *Degree requirements:* For master's, thesis (MS); for doctorate, comprehensive exam, thesis/dissertation. *Entrance requirements:* For master's and doctorate, GRE General Test, 2 letters of recommendation. Additional exam requirements/recommendations for international students: Required—TOEFL (minimum score 600 paper-based; 77 iBT). Electronic applications accepted. *Faculty research:* Biochemical, biomedical and metabolic engineering; fluid and polymer dynamics; surface science and chemical kinetics; electronics materials; microchemical systems and nanotechnology.

Drexel University, College of Engineering, Department of Chemical and Biological Engineering, Program in Biochemical Engineering, Philadelphia, PA 19104-2875. Offers MS. *Program availability:* Part-time, evening/weekend. *Degree requirements:* For master's, thesis. *Entrance requirements:* For master's, minimum GPA of 3.0 in chemical engineering or biological sciences. Additional exam requirements/recommendations for international students: Required—TOEFL. Electronic applications accepted. *Faculty research:* Monitoring and control of bioreactors, sensors for bioreactors, large-scale production of monoclonal antibodies.

Lehigh University, P.C. Rossin College of Engineering and Applied Science, Department of Chemical and Biomolecular Engineering, Bethlehem, PA 18015. Offers biological chemical engineering (M Eng); chemical energy engineering (M Eng); chemical engineering (M Eng, MS, PhD); MBA/E. *Program availability:* Part-time, 100% online. *Faculty:* 19 full-time (2 women), 1 part-time/adjunct (0 women). *Students:* 41 full-time (15 women), 21 part-time (10 women); includes 9 minority (2 Black or African American, non-Hispanic/Latino; 4 Asian, non-Hispanic/Latino; 3 Hispanic/Latino), 31 international. Average age 27. 127 applicants, 35% accepted, 12 enrolled. In 2018, 19 master's, 10 doctorates awarded. Terminal master's awarded for partial completion of doctoral program. *Degree requirements:* For master's, thesis (for some programs); for doctorate, comprehensive exam, thesis/dissertation. *Entrance requirements:* For master's and doctorate, GRE General Test. Additional exam requirements/recommendations for international students: Required—TOEFL (minimum score 79 iBT), IELTS (minimum score 6.5). *Application deadline:* For fall admission, 7/15 for domestic students, 7/15 priority date for international students; for spring admission, 12/1 for domestic and international students. Applications are processed on a rolling basis. Application fee: $75. Electronic applications accepted. Tuition and fees vary according to program. *Financial support:* In 2018–19, 43 students received support, including 4 fellowships with full tuition reimbursements available (averaging $29,400 per year), 30 research assistantships with full tuition reimbursements available (averaging $29,400 per year), 3 teaching assistantships with full tuition reimbursements available (averaging $29,400 per year); career-related internships or fieldwork, institutionally sponsored loans, scholarships/grants, health care benefits, and unspecified assistantships also available. Financial award application deadline: 1/15. *Faculty research:* Process control, energy, biotechnology, catalysis, polymers. *Total annual research expenditures:* $2.8 million. *Unit head:* Dr. Mayuresh V. Kothare, Chairman, 610-758-6654, Fax: 610-758-5057, E-mail: mvk2@lehigh.edu. *Application contact:* Janine Jekels, Academic Coordinator, 610-758-4260, Fax: 610-758-5057, E-mail: inchegs@lehigh.edu. Website: https://www.che.lehigh.edu/

Rutgers University–New Brunswick, Graduate School-New Brunswick, Program in Chemical and Biochemical Engineering, Piscataway, NJ 08854-8097. Offers MS, PhD. *Program availability:* Part-time, evening/weekend. Terminal master's awarded for partial completion of doctoral program. *Degree requirements:* For master's, thesis or alternative; for doctorate, thesis/dissertation. *Entrance requirements:* For master's and doctorate, GRE General Test. Additional exam requirements/recommendations for international students: Required—TOEFL. *Faculty research:* Biotechnology, pharmaceutical engineering, nanotechnology, process system engineering, materials and polymer science, chemical engineering sciences.

University of California, Irvine, Samueli School of Engineering, Department of Chemical Engineering and Materials Science, Irvine, CA 92697. Offers chemical and biochemical engineering (MS, PhD); materials science and engineering (MS, PhD). *Program availability:* Part-time. *Students:* 133 full-time (57 women), 2 part-time (0 women); includes 36 minority (3 Black or African American, non-Hispanic/Latino; 26 Asian, non-Hispanic/Latino; 5 Hispanic/Latino; 2 Two or more races, non-Hispanic/Latino), 51 international. Average age 26. 417 applicants, 35% accepted, 36 enrolled. In 2018, 30 master's, 26 doctorates awarded. Terminal master's awarded for partial completion of doctoral program. *Entrance requirements:* For master's and doctorate, GRE General Test, minimum GPA of 3.0, 3 letters of recommendation. Additional exam requirements/recommendations for international students: Required—TOEFL (minimum score 550 paper-based). *Application deadline:* For fall admission, 1/15 priority date for domestic students, 1/15 for international students. Applications are processed on a rolling basis. Application fee: $105 ($125 for international students). Electronic applications accepted. *Financial support:* Fellowships, research assistantships with full tuition reimbursements, teaching assistantships, institutionally sponsored loans, traineeships, health care benefits, and unspecified assistantships available. Financial award application deadline: 3/1; financial award applicants required to submit FAFSA. *Faculty research:* Molecular biotechnology, nanobiomaterials, biophotonics, synthesis, super plasticity and mechanical behavior, characterization of advanced and nanostructural materials. *Unit head:* Prof. Vasan Venugopalan, Chair, 949-824-5802, Fax: 949-824-2541, E-mail: vvenugop@uci.edu. *Application contact:* Grace Chau, Academic Program and Graduate Admission Coordinator, 949-824-3887, Fax: 949-824-2541, E-mail: chaug@uci.edu.
Website: http://www.eng.uci.edu/dept/chems

University of Connecticut, Graduate School, School of Engineering, Department of Chemical and Biomolecular Engineering, Storrs, CT 06269. Offers MS, PhD. Terminal master's awarded for partial completion of doctoral program. *Degree requirements:* For master's, comprehensive exam, thesis or alternative; for doctorate, thesis/dissertation. *Entrance requirements:* For master's and doctorate, GRE General Test. Additional exam requirements/recommendations for international students: Required—TOEFL (minimum score 550 paper-based). Electronic applications accepted.

University of Georgia, College of Engineering, Athens, GA 30602. Offers MS.

The University of Iowa, Graduate College, College of Engineering, Department of Chemical and Biochemical Engineering, Iowa City, IA 52242-1316. Offers MS, PhD. *Program availability:* Part-time. *Degree requirements:* For master's, comprehensive exam (for some programs), thesis (for some programs); for doctorate, comprehensive exam, thesis/dissertation. *Entrance requirements:* For master's and doctorate, GRE (minimum combined score of 310 on verbal and quantitative), minimum undergraduate GPA of 3.0. Additional exam requirements/recommendations for international students: Required—TOEFL (minimum score 600 paper-based; 100 iBT), IELTS (minimum score 7). Electronic applications accepted. *Faculty research:* Polymeric materials, photo polymerization, atmospheric chemistry and air pollution, biochemical engineering, bioprocessing and biomedical engineering.

The University of Manchester, School of Chemical Engineering and Analytical Science, Manchester, United Kingdom. Offers biocatalysis (M Phil, PhD); chemical engineering (M Phil, PhD); chemical engineering and analytical science (M Phil, D Eng, PhD); colloids, crystals, interfaces and materials (M Phil, PhD); environment and sustainable technology (M Phil, PhD); instrumentation (M Phil, PhD); multi-scale modeling (M Phil, PhD); process integration (M Phil, PhD); systems biology (M Phil, PhD).

University of Maryland, Baltimore County, The Graduate School, College of Engineering and Information Technology, Department of Chemical, Biochemical, and Environmental Engineering, Post Baccalaureate Certificate Program in Biochemical Regulatory Engineering, Baltimore, MD 21250. Offers Postbaccalaureate Certificate. *Program availability:* Part-time. Electronic applications accepted. *Expenses:* Contact institution.

University of Maryland, Baltimore County, The Graduate School, College of Engineering and Information Technology, Department of Chemical, Biochemical, and Environmental Engineering, Program in Chemical and Biochemical Engineering, Baltimore, MD 21250. Offers MS, PhD. *Program availability:* Part-time. *Degree requirements:* For master's, comprehensive exam (for some programs), thesis (for some programs); for doctorate, comprehensive exam, thesis/dissertation. *Entrance requirements:* For master's, GRE General Test, minimum GPA of 3.0, strong mathematical background; for doctorate, GRE General Test (taken within last 5 years), minimum GPA of 3.0. Additional exam requirements/recommendations for international students: Required—TOEFL (minimum score 550 paper-based; 80 iBT). Electronic applications accepted. Application fee is waived when completed online. *Expenses:* Contact institution. *Faculty research:* Biomedical engineering; biochemical engineering.

The University of Western Ontario, School of Graduate and Postdoctoral Studies, Physical Sciences Division, Faculty of Engineering, London, ON N6A 3K7, Canada. Offers chemical and biochemical engineering (ME Sc, PhD); civil and environmental engineering (M Eng, ME Sc, PhD); electrical and computer engineering (M Eng, ME Sc, PhD); mechanical and materials engineering (M Eng, ME Sc, PhD). *Program availability:* Part-time. Terminal master's awarded for partial completion of doctoral program. *Degree requirements:* For master's, thesis; for doctorate, thesis/dissertation. *Entrance requirements:* For master's, minimum B average; for doctorate, minimum B+ average. *Faculty research:* Wind, geotechnical, chemical reactor engineering, applied electrostatics, biochemical engineering.

Villanova University, College of Engineering, Department of Chemical Engineering, Villanova, PA 19085-1699. Offers biochemical engineering (Certificate); chemical engineering (MSChE); environmental protection in the chemical process industries (Certificate). *Program availability:* Part-time, evening/weekend. *Degree requirements:* For master's, comprehensive exam, thesis optional. *Entrance requirements:* For master's, GRE General Test (for applicants with degrees from foreign universities), B Ch E, minimum GPA of 3.0. Additional exam requirements/recommendations for international students: Required—TOEFL (minimum score 600 paper-based; 100 iBT). *Faculty research:* Heat transfer, advanced materials, chemical vapor deposition, pyrolysis and combustion chemistry, industrial waste treatment.

Chemical Engineering

American University of Sharjah, Graduate Programs, Sharjah, United Arab Emirates. Offers accounting (MS); biomedical engineering (MSBME); business administration (MBA); chemical engineering (MS Ch E); civil engineering (MSCE); computer engineering (MS); electrical engineering (MSEE); engineering systems management (MS, PhD); mathematics (MS); mechanical engineering (MSME); mechatronics engineering (MS); teaching English to speakers of other languages (MA); translation and interpreting (MA); urban planning (MUP). *Program availability:* Part-time, evening/weekend. *Degree requirements:* For master's, thesis (for some programs). *Entrance requirements:* For master's, GMAT (for MBA). Additional exam requirements/recommendations for international students: Required—TOEFL (minimum score 550 paper-based; 80 iBT), TWE (minimum score 5); Recommended—IELTS (minimum score 6.5). Electronic applications accepted. *Faculty research:* Water pollution, management and waste water treatment, energy and sustainability, air pollution, Islamic finance, family business and small and medium enterprises.

Arizona State University at the Tempe campus, Ira A. Fulton Schools of Engineering, School for Engineering of Matter, Transport and Energy, Tempe, AZ 85281. Offers aerospace engineering (MS, PhD); chemical engineering (MS, PhD); materials science and engineering (MS, PhD); mechanical engineering (MS, PhD); solar energy engineering and commercialization (PSM). *Program availability:* Part-time, evening/weekend, online learning. Terminal master's awarded for partial completion of doctoral program. *Degree requirements:* For master's, thesis and oral defense (MS); applied project or comprehensive exam (MSE); interactive Program of Study (iPOS) submitted before completing 50 percent of required credit hours; for doctorate, comprehensive exam, thesis/dissertation, interactive Program of Study (iPOS) submitted before completing 50 percent of required credit hours. *Entrance requirements:* For master's, GRE, minimum GPA of 3.0 or equivalent in last 2 years of work leading to bachelor's degree; for doctorate, GRE, minimum GPA of 3.0 in last 2 years of work leading to bachelor's degree. Additional exam requirements/recommendations for international students: Required—TOEFL, IELTS, or PTE. Electronic applications accepted. *Expenses:* Contact institution. *Faculty research:* Electronic materials and packaging, materials for energy (batteries), adaptive/intelligent materials and structures, multiscale fluid mechanics, membranes, therapeutics and bioseparations, flexible structures, nanostructured materials, micro-/nano-transport.

Auburn University, Graduate School, Ginn College of Engineering, Department of Chemical Engineering, Auburn University, AL 36849. Offers M Ch E, MS, PhD. *Program availability:* Part-time. *Degree requirements:* For master's, thesis (for some programs); for doctorate, comprehensive exam, thesis/dissertation. *Entrance requirements:* For master's and doctorate, GRE General Test. Electronic applications accepted. *Expenses:* Tuition, state resident: full-time $11,282; part-time $535 per credit hour. Tuition, nonresident: full-time $30,542; part-time $1605 per credit hour. *Required fees:* $826 per semester. Tuition and fees vary according to degree level and program. *Faculty research:* Coal liquefaction, asphalt research, pulp and paper engineering, surface science, biochemical engineering.

Brigham Young University, Graduate Studies, Ira A. Fulton College of Engineering, Department of Chemical Engineering, Provo, UT 84602. Offers chemical engineering (MS). *Faculty:* 18 full-time (1 woman). *Students:* 58 full-time (12 women); includes 1 minority (Two or more races, non-Hispanic/Latino), 21 international. Average age 29. 23 applicants, 43% accepted, 10 enrolled. In 2018, 3 master's, 6 doctorates awarded. *Degree requirements:* For master's, comprehensive exam, thesis; for doctorate, comprehensive exam, thesis/dissertation. *Entrance requirements:* For master's and doctorate, GRE, BS in chemical engineering or related engineering field, minimum GPA of 3.3. Additional exam requirements/recommendations for international students: Required—TOEFL (minimum score 580 paper-based; 85 iBT), IELTS (minimum score 7). *Application deadline:* For fall admission, 1/31 for domestic and international students; for winter admission, 6/15 for domestic and international students; for spring admission, 10/15 for domestic and international students; for summer admission, 10/15 for domestic and international students. Application fee: $50. Electronic applications accepted. *Financial support:* In 2018–19, 57 students received support, including 4 fellowships (averaging $24,996 per year), 62 research assistantships with full and partial tuition reimbursements available (averaging $22,836 per year), 21 teaching assistantships with full and partial tuition reimbursements available (averaging $22,500 per year); scholarships/grants also available. Financial award application deadline: 1/15; financial award applicants required to submit FAFSA. *Faculty research:* Energy and combustion, thermodynamics and thermophysical properties, biochemical and biomedical engineering, nano- and micro-technology, molecular modeling. *Total annual research expenditures:* $2.4 million. *Unit head:* Dr. Thomas H. Fletcher, Chair, 801-422-6236, Fax: 801-422-0151, E-mail: cheme@byu.edu. *Application contact:* Dr. William G. Pitt, Graduate Coordinator, 801-422-2588, Fax: 801-422-0151, E-mail: pitt@byu.edu.
Website: http://www.chemicalengineering.byu.edu

Brown University, Graduate School, School of Engineering, Providence, RI 02912. Offers biomedical engineering (Sc M, PhD); chemical and biochemical engineering (Sc M, PhD); electrical sciences and computer engineering (Sc M, PhD); fluid and thermal sciences (Sc M, PhD); materials science and engineering (Sc M, PhD); mechanics of solids and structures (Sc M, PhD). *Degree requirements:* For doctorate, thesis/dissertation, preliminary exam.

Bucknell University, Graduate Studies, College of Engineering, Department of Chemical Engineering, Lewisburg, PA 17837. Offers MS Ch E. *Degree requirements:* For master's, thesis. *Entrance requirements:* For master's, GRE General Test, minimum GPA of 3.0. Additional exam requirements/recommendations for international students: Required—TOEFL (minimum score 600 paper-based). *Faculty research:* Computer-aided design, software engineering, applied mathematics and modeling, polymer science, digital process control.

California Institute of Technology, Division of Chemistry and Chemical Engineering, Program in Chemical Engineering, Pasadena, CA 91106. Offers MS, PhD. Terminal master's awarded for partial completion of doctoral program. *Degree requirements:* For master's, thesis; for doctorate, thesis/dissertation. *Entrance requirements:* For doctorate, GRE, BS. Additional exam requirements/recommendations for international students: Required—TOEFL; Recommended—IELTS, TWE. Electronic applications accepted. *Faculty research:* Fluids, biomolecular engineering, atmospheric chemistry, polymers/materials, catalysis.

Carnegie Mellon University, Carnegie Institute of Technology, Department of Chemical Engineering, Pittsburgh, PA 15213-3891. Offers chemical engineering (M Ch E, MS, PhD); colloids, polymers and surfaces (MS). *Program availability:* Part-time, evening/weekend. Terminal master's awarded for partial completion of doctoral program. *Degree requirements:* For doctorate, thesis/dissertation, qualifying exam. *Entrance requirements:* For master's and doctorate, GRE General Test, GRE Subject Test. Additional exam requirements/recommendations for international students: Required—TOEFL. *Faculty research:* Computer-aided design in process engineering, biomedical engineering, biotechnology, complex fluids.

Case Western Reserve University, School of Graduate Studies, Case School of Engineering, Department of Chemical and Biomolecular Engineering, Cleveland, OH 44106. Offers MS, PhD. *Program availability:* Part-time, evening/weekend, blended/hybrid learning. *Faculty:* 12 full-time (4 women). *Students:* 45 full-time (12 women); includes 5 minority (all Asian, non-Hispanic/Latino), 28 international. In 2018, 15 master's, 6 doctorates awarded. Terminal master's awarded for partial completion of doctoral program. *Degree requirements:* For master's, thesis (for some programs); for doctorate, thesis/dissertation, qualifying exam, research proposal, teaching experience. *Entrance requirements:* For master's and doctorate, GRE General Test. Additional exam requirements/recommendations for international students: Required—TOEFL. *Application deadline:* For fall admission, 2/15 priority date for domestic students; for spring admission, 11/1 for domestic students. Applications are processed on a rolling basis. Application fee: $50. *Expenses: Tuition:* Full-time $45,168; part-time $1939 per credit hour. *Required fees:* $36; $18 per semester. $18 per semester. *Financial support:* In 2018–19, 23 students received support, including 23 research assistantships with tuition reimbursements available; Federal Work-Study and institutionally sponsored loans also available. Financial award application deadline: 3/1; financial award applicants required to submit FAFSA. *Faculty research:* Advanced separation methods; design, synthesis, processing and characterization of advanced materials; biotransport and bioprocessing; electrochemical engineering; materials engineering; energy storage and fuel cells. *Total annual research expenditures:* $2.6 million. *Unit head:* Daniel Lacks, Department Chair, 216-368-4238, Fax: 216-368-3016, E-mail: daniel.lacks@case.edu. *Application contact:* Theresa Claytor, Student Affairs Coordinator, 216-368-8555, E-mail: theresa.claytor@case.edu.
Website: http://engineering.case.edu/eche

City College of the City University of New York, Graduate School, Grove School of Engineering, Department of Chemical Engineering, New York, NY 10031-9198. Offers ME, PhD. PhD program offered jointly with Graduate School and University Center of the City University of New York. *Program availability:* Part-time. *Degree requirements:* For master's, thesis optional; for doctorate, one foreign language, comprehensive exam, thesis/dissertation. *Entrance requirements:* For master's and doctorate, GRE General Test. Additional exam requirements/recommendations for international students: Required—TOEFL (minimum score 500 paper-based; 61 iBT). *Faculty research:* Theoretical turbulences, bio-fluid dynamics, polymers, fluidization, transport phenomena.

Clarkson University, Wallace H. Coulter School of Engineering, Department of Chemical and Biomolecular Engineering, Potsdam, NY 13699. Offers chemical engineering (ME). *Faculty:* 11 full-time (4 women), 2 part-time/adjunct (0 women). *Students:* 23 full-time (3 women), 22 international. 33 applicants, 45% accepted, 5 enrolled. In 2018, 1 master's, 8 doctorates awarded. *Degree requirements:* For master's, thesis (for MS); project (for ME); for doctorate, comprehensive exam, thesis/dissertation. *Entrance requirements:* For master's and doctorate, GRE. Additional exam requirements/recommendations for international students: Required—TOEFL (minimum score 550 paper-based, 80 iBT) or IELTS (6.5). *Application deadline:* Applications are processed on a rolling basis. Application fee: $50. Electronic applications accepted. *Expenses: Tuition:* Full-time $24,984; part-time $1388 per credit hour. *Required fees:* $225. Tuition and fees vary according to campus/location and program. *Financial support:* Scholarships/grants and unspecified assistantships available. *Unit head:* Dr. Elizabeth Podlaha-Murphy, Chair of Chemical and Biomolecular Engineering, 315-268-6650, E-mail: epodlaha@clarkson.edu. *Application contact:* Dan Capogna, Director of Graduate Admissions & Recruitment, 518-631-9910, E-mail: graduate@clarkson.edu.
Website: https://www.clarkson.edu/academics/graduate

Clemson University, Graduate School, College of Engineering, Computing and Applied Sciences, Department of Chemical and Biomolecular Engineering, Clemson, SC 29634. Offers chemical engineering (MS, PhD). *Faculty:* 14 full-time (3 women). *Students:* 63 full-time (16 women); includes 5 minority (1 Black or African American, non-Hispanic/Latino; 4 Asian, non-Hispanic/Latino), 31 international. Average age 26. 90 applicants, 43% accepted, 17 enrolled. In 2018, 1 master's, 6 doctorates awarded. *Degree requirements:* For master's, thesis; for doctorate, comprehensive exam, thesis/dissertation. *Entrance requirements:* For master's and doctorate, GRE General Test, unofficial transcripts, letters of recommendation. Additional exam requirements/recommendations for international students: Required—TOEFL (minimum score 80 iBT); Recommended—IELTS (minimum score 6.5), TSE (minimum score 54). *Application deadline:* For fall admission, 2/1 for domestic and international students. Applications are processed on a rolling basis. Application fee: $80 ($90 for international students). Electronic applications accepted. *Expenses:* $6823 per semester full-time resident, $14023 per semester full-time non-resident, $833 per credit hour part-time resident, $1731 per credit hour part-time non-resident, online $1264 per credit hour, $4938 doctoral programs resident, $10405 doctoral programs non-resident, $1144 full-time graduate assistant, other fees may apply per session. *Financial support:* In 2018–19, 34 students received support, including 3 fellowships with full and partial tuition reimbursements available (averaging $9,467 per year), 19 research assistantships with full and partial tuition reimbursements available (averaging $24,237 per year), 12 teaching assistantships with full and partial tuition reimbursements available (averaging $21,829 per year); career-related internships or fieldwork also available. Financial award application deadline: 2/1. *Faculty research:* Advanced materials, biotechnology, energy, molecular simulation, chemical and biochemical processing. *Total annual research expenditures:* $2.4 million. *Unit head:* Dr. David Bruce, Department Chair, 864-656-5425, E-mail: dbruce@clemson.edu. *Application contact:* Dr. Mark Roberts, Graduate Coordinator, 864-656-6307, E-mail: mrober9@clemson.edu.
Website: https://www.clemson.edu/cecas/departments/chbe/

Cleveland State University, College of Graduate Studies, Fenn College of Engineering, Department of Chemical and Biomedical Engineering, Cleveland, OH 44115. Offers MS, D Eng. *Program availability:* Part-time, evening/weekend. *Faculty:* 12 full-time (1 woman), 26 part-time/adjunct (3 women). *Students:* 23 full-time (7 women), 29 part-time (12 women); includes 7 minority (1 Black or African American, non-Hispanic/Latino; 2 Asian, non-Hispanic/Latino; 3 Hispanic/Latino; 1 Two or more races, non-Hispanic/Latino), 18 international. Average age 26. 126 applicants, 60% accepted, 22 enrolled. In 2018, 37 master's, 2 doctorates awarded. *Entrance requirements:* For master's, GRE General Test, minimum GPA of 2.75; for doctorate, GRE General Test, minimum GPA of 3.25. Additional exam requirements/recommendations for international students: Required—TOEFL (minimum score 550 paper-based; 78 iBT). *Application deadline:* Applications are processed on a rolling basis. Application fee: $40. Electronic applications accepted. *Expenses:* Tuition, state resident: full-time $7232.55; part-time $6676 per credit hour. Tuition, nonresident: full-time $12,375. *International tuition:* $18,914 full-time. *Required fees:* $80; $80 $40. Tuition and fees vary according to program. *Financial support:* In 2018–19, 34 students received support, including 2 research assistantships with tuition reimbursements available (averaging $6,960 per year), 3 teaching assistantships with tuition reimbursements available (averaging $6,960 per year); fellowships, career-related internships or fieldwork, Federal Work-Study, institutionally sponsored loans, scholarships/grants, tuition waivers (full and partial), and unspecified assistantships also available. Financial award application deadline: 3/30. *Faculty research:* Absorption equilibrium and dynamics, advanced materials processing, biomaterials surface characterization, bioprocessing, cardiovascular mechanics, magnetic resonance imaging, mechanics of biomolecules, metabolic modeling, molecular simulation, process systems engineering, statistical mechanics. *Unit head:* Dr. Joanne M. Belovich, Chairperson, 216-687-3502, Fax: 216-687-9220, E-mail: j.belovich@csuohio.edu. *Application contact:* Becky Laird, Administrative Coordinator, 216-687-2571, Fax: 216-687-9220, E-mail: b.laird@csuohio.edu.
Website: http://www.csuohio.edu/engineering/chemical/

Colorado School of Mines, Office of Graduate Studies, Department of Chemical and Biological Engineering, Golden, CO 80401. Offers chemical engineering (MS, PhD). *Program availability:* Part-time. *Faculty:* 34 full-time (12 women), 6 part-time/adjunct (2 women). *Students:* 56 full-time (20 women), 5 part-time (2 women); includes 6 minority (3 Asian, non-Hispanic/Latino; 1 Hispanic/Latino; 2 Two or more races, non-Hispanic/Latino), 21 international. Average age 26. 126 applicants, 44% accepted, 10 enrolled. In 2018, 12 master's, 10 doctorates awarded. Terminal master's awarded for partial completion of doctoral program. *Degree requirements:* For master's, thesis (for some programs); for doctorate, comprehensive exam, thesis/dissertation. *Entrance requirements:* For master's and doctorate, GRE General Test. Additional exam requirements/recommendations for international students: Required—TOEFL (minimum score 550 paper-based; 79 iBT). *Application deadline:* For fall admission, 12/15 priority date for domestic and international students; for spring admission, 9/1 for domestic and international students. Application fee: $60 ($80 for international students). Electronic applications accepted. *Expenses:* Tuition, state resident: full-time $16,650; part-time $925 per contact hour. Tuition, nonresident: full-time $36,270; part-time $2015 per contact hour. *International tuition:* $36,270 full-time. *Required fees:* $2314; $2314 per semester. *Financial support:* In 2018–19, 26 research assistantships with tuition reimbursements, 19 teaching assistantships with full tuition reimbursements were

awarded; fellowships, scholarships/grants, health care benefits, and unspecified assistantships also available. Financial award application deadline: 12/15; financial award applicants required to submit FAFSA. *Faculty research:* Liquid fuels for the future, responsible management of hazardous substances, surface and interfacial engineering, advanced computational methods and process control, gas hydrates. *Unit head:* Dr. Anuj Chauhan, Department Head, 303-273-3720, E-mail: chauhan@mines.edu. *Application contact:* Jennie Gambach, Program Assistant, 303-273-3246, E-mail: jgambach@mines.edu.
Website: http://chemeng.mines.edu/

Colorado State University, Walter Scott, Jr. College of Engineering, Department of Chemical and Biological Engineering, Fort Collins, CO 80523-1370. Offers MS, PhD. *Program availability:* Part-time. Terminal master's awarded for partial completion of doctoral program. *Degree requirements:* For master's, thesis (for some programs); for doctorate, thesis/dissertation, oral and written preliminary exam. *Entrance requirements:* For master's and doctorate, GRE General Test, minimum GPA of 3.0; relevant degree; recommendations; transcripts. Additional exam requirements/recommendations for international students: Required—TOEFL (minimum score 550 paper-based; 80 iBT), IELTS (minimum score 6.5), PTE (minimum score 58). Electronic applications accepted. *Expenses:* Contact institution. *Faculty research:* Materials, systems biology, synthetic biology, transport phenomena, biosensors.

Columbia University, Fu Foundation School of Engineering and Applied Science, Department of Chemical Engineering, New York, NY 10027. Offers MS, PhD. PhD offered through the Graduate School of Arts and Sciences. *Program availability:* Part-time, online learning. *Degree requirements:* For doctorate, thesis/dissertation, qualifying exam. *Entrance requirements:* For master's and doctorate, GRE General Test. Additional exam requirements/recommendations for international students: Required—TOEFL, IELTS, PTE. Electronic applications accepted. *Faculty research:* Molecular design and modification of material surfaces, biophysics and soft matter physics, genomics engineering, interfacial engineering and electrochemistry, protein and metabolic engineering.

Cooper Union for the Advancement of Science and Art, Albert Nerken School of Engineering, New York, NY 10003. Offers chemical engineering (ME); civil engineering (ME); electrical engineering (ME); mechanical engineering (ME). *Program availability:* Part-time. *Degree requirements:* For master's, thesis (for some programs), thesis or special project. *Entrance requirements:* For master's, BE or BS in an engineering discipline; official copies of school transcripts including secondary (high school), college and university work; two letters of recommendation; resume. Additional exam requirements/recommendations for international students: Required—TOEFL (minimum score 600 paper-based; 100 iBT). Electronic applications accepted. *Faculty research:* Analytics, bioengineering, dynamic systems, nanoscience, sustainability, STEM education.

Cornell University, Graduate School, Graduate Fields of Engineering, Field of Chemical Engineering, Ithaca, NY 14853. Offers advanced materials processing (M Eng, MS, PhD); applied mathematics and computational methods (M Eng, MS, PhD); biochemical engineering (M Eng, MS, PhD); chemical reaction engineering (M Eng, MS, PhD); classical and statistical thermodynamics (M Eng, MS, PhD); fluid dynamics, rheology and biorheology (M Eng, MS, PhD); heat and mass transfer (M Eng, MS, PhD); kinetics and catalysis (M Eng, MS, PhD); polymers (M Eng, MS, PhD); surface science (M Eng, MS, PhD). *Degree requirements:* For master's, thesis (MS); for doctorate, comprehensive exam, thesis/dissertation. *Entrance requirements:* For master's and doctorate, GRE General Test, 2 letters of recommendation. Additional exam requirements/recommendations for international students: Required—TOEFL (minimum score 600 paper-based; 77 iBT). Electronic applications accepted. *Faculty research:* Biochemical, biomedical and metabolic engineering; fluid and polymer dynamics; surface science and chemical kinetics; electronics materials; microchemical systems and nanotechnology.

Dalhousie University, Faculty of Engineering, Department of Process Engineering and Applied Science, Halifax, NS B3J 1Z1, Canada. Offers biological engineering (M Eng, MA Sc, PhD); chemical engineering (M Eng, MA Sc, PhD); food science (M Sc, PhD). *Degree requirements:* For master's, thesis; for doctorate, thesis/dissertation. *Entrance requirements:* Additional exam requirements/recommendations for international students: Required—TOEFL, IELTS, CANTEST, CAEL, or Michigan English Language Assessment Battery. Electronic applications accepted. *Faculty research:* Explosions, process optimization, combustion synthesis of materials, waste minimization, treatment of industrial wastewater.

Dartmouth College, Thayer School of Engineering, Program in Biological and Chemical Engineering, Hanover, NH 03755. Offers MS, PhD. *Degree requirements:* For master's, thesis; for doctorate, thesis/dissertation, candidacy oral exam. *Entrance requirements:* For master's and doctorate, GRE General Test. *Faculty research:* Biomass processing, metabolic engineering, kinetics and reactor design, applied microbiology, resource and environmental analysis.

Drexel University, College of Engineering, Department of Chemical and Biological Engineering, Program in Chemical Engineering, Philadelphia, PA 19104-2875. Offers MS, PhD. *Degree requirements:* For doctorate, thesis/dissertation. *Entrance requirements:* For master's, minimum GPA of 3.0; for doctorate, minimum GPA of 3.5, MS in chemical engineering. Additional exam requirements/recommendations for international students: Required—TOEFL. Electronic applications accepted.

École Polytechnique de Montréal, Graduate Programs, Department of Chemical Engineering, Montréal, QC H3C 3A7, Canada. Offers M Eng, M Sc A, PhD, DESS. *Program availability:* Part-time, evening/weekend. Terminal master's awarded for partial completion of doctoral program. *Degree requirements:* For master's, one foreign language, thesis; for doctorate, one foreign language, thesis/dissertation. *Entrance requirements:* For master's, minimum GPA of 2.75; for doctorate, minimum GPA of 3.0. Electronic applications accepted. *Faculty research:* Polymer engineering, biochemical and food engineering, reactor engineering and industrial processes pollution control engineering, gas technology.

Fairleigh Dickinson University, Florham Campus, Silberman College of Business, Program in Pharmaceutical Studies, Madison, NJ 07940-1099. Offers MBA, Certificate.

Florida Agricultural and Mechanical University, Division of Graduate Studies, Research, and Continuing Education, FAMU-FSU College of Engineering, Department of Chemical and Biomedical Engineering, Tallahassee, FL 32307-3200. Offers biomedical engineering (MS, PhD); chemical engineering (MS, PhD). *Degree requirements:* For master's, thesis optional; for doctorate, thesis/dissertation, paper presentation at professional meeting. *Entrance requirements:* For master's, GRE General Test, minimum GPA of 3.3, letters of recommendation (3); for doctorate, minimum GPA of 3.3. Additional exam requirements/recommendations for international students: Required—TOEFL (minimum score 550 paper-based). *Faculty research:* Cellular signaling, cancer therapy, drug delivery, cellular and tissue engineering, brain physiology.

Florida Institute of Technology, College of Engineering and Science, Program in Chemical Engineering, Melbourne, FL 32901-6975. Offers MS, PhD. *Program availability:* Part-time. *Students:* 15 full-time (6 women), 2 part-time (1 woman); includes 2 minority (both Asian, non-Hispanic/Latino), 8 international. Average age 25. 10 applicants, 90% accepted, 3 enrolled. In 2018, 9 master's, 1 doctorate awarded. Terminal master's awarded for partial completion of doctoral program. *Degree requirements:* For master's, comprehensive exam, thesis, 30 credit hours thesis or capstone project with final exam; for doctorate, comprehensive exam, thesis/dissertation, publication in refereed journals, oral and written exams, research project, minimum of 72 credit hours. *Entrance requirements:* For master's, GRE, resume, 3 letters of recommendation, statement of objectives, undergraduate transcripts; for doctorate, GRE, minimum GPA of 3.5, resume, 3 letters of recommendation, statement of objectives. Additional exam requirements/recommendations for international students: Required—TOEFL (minimum score 550 paper-based; 79 iBT). *Application deadline:* For fall admission, 4/1 for international students; for spring admission, 9/30 for international students. Applications are processed on a rolling basis. Application fee: $50. Electronic applications accepted. *Expenses: Tuition:* Full-time $22,338; part-time $1241 per credit hour. Tuition and fees vary according to degree level, campus/location and program. *Financial support:* Research assistantships, teaching assistantships, career-related internships or fieldwork, institutionally sponsored loans, tuition waivers (partial), unspecified assistantships, and tuition remissions available. Support available to part-time students. Financial award application deadline: 3/1; financial award applicants required to submit FAFSA. *Faculty research:* Reverse osmosis; materials synthesis, characterization, and failure prevention, transport and separation processes, computer-aided modeling, processing, and control. *Unit head:* Dr. Ted Conway, Department Head, 321-674-8491, E-mail: tconway@fit.edu. *Application contact:* Mike Perry, Executive Director of Admissions, 321-674-7127, E-mail: perrymj@fit.edu.
Website: https://www.fit.edu/programs/chemical-engineering-ms/

Florida State University, The Graduate School, FAMU-FSU College of Engineering, Department of Chemical and Biomedical Engineering, Tallahassee, FL 32310-6046. Offers biomedical engineering (MS, PhD); chemical engineering (MS, PhD). *Program availability:* Part-time. Terminal master's awarded for partial completion of doctoral program. *Degree requirements:* For master's, thesis (for some programs); for doctorate, comprehensive exam, thesis/dissertation, qualifying exam. *Entrance requirements:* For master's, GRE General Test (recommended minimum scores: verbal 151/8th percentile; quantitative: 158/75th percentile), BS in chemical engineering or other physical science/engineering, minimum GPA of 3.0; for doctorate, GRE General Test (recommended minimum scores: verbal 151/8th percentile; quantitative: 158/75th percentile), BS in chemical engineering or other physical science/engineering, minimum GPA of 3.0, or MS in chemical or biomedical engineering. Additional exam requirements/recommendations for international students: Required—TOEFL (minimum score 550 paper-based; 80 iBT); Recommended—IELTS (minimum score 6.5). Electronic applications accepted. *Expenses:* Contact institution. *Faculty research:* Macromolecular transport and reaction; polymer characterization and processing; solid NMR-MRI for solid state spectroscopy and cell microscopy; protein, cell, and tissue engineering; electrochemical and fuel cell engineering.

Georgia Institute of Technology, Graduate Studies, College of Engineering, School of Chemical and Biomolecular Engineering, Atlanta, GA 30332-0001. Offers chemical engineering (MS, PhD). Terminal master's awarded for partial completion of doctoral program. *Degree requirements:* For master's, thesis; for doctorate, comprehensive exam, thesis/dissertation. *Entrance requirements:* For master's and doctorate, GRE. Additional exam requirements/recommendations for international students: Required—TOEFL (minimum score 550 paper-based; 85 iBT). Electronic applications accepted. *Faculty research:* Biochemical engineering; process modeling, synthesis, and control; polymer science and engineering; thermodynamics and separations; surface and particle science.

Howard University, College of Engineering, Architecture, and Computer Sciences, School of Engineering and Computer Science, Department of Chemical Engineering, Washington, DC 20059-0002. Offers MS. Offered through the Graduate School of Arts and Sciences. *Program availability:* Part-time. *Degree requirements:* For master's, thesis. *Entrance requirements:* For master's, GRE General Test, minimum GPA of 2.75. Additional exam requirements/recommendations for international students: Required—TOEFL. *Faculty research:* Bioengineering, reactor modeling, environmental engineering, nanotechnology, fuel cells.

Illinois Institute of Technology, Graduate College, Armour College of Engineering, Department of Chemical and Biological Engineering, Chicago, IL 60616. Offers biological engineering (MAS); chemical engineering (MAS, MS, PhD); MS/MAS. *Program availability:* Part-time, evening/weekend, online learning. Terminal master's awarded for partial completion of doctoral program. *Degree requirements:* For master's, comprehensive exam (for some programs), thesis (for some programs); for doctorate, comprehensive exam, thesis/dissertation. *Entrance requirements:* For master's, GRE General Test with minimum score of 950 Quantitative and Verbal, 2.5 Analytical Writing (for MAS); GRE General Test with minimum score of 1100 Quantitative and Verbal, 3.0 Analytical Writing (for MS), minimum undergraduate GPA of 3.0; for doctorate, GRE General Test (minimum score 1100 Quantitative and Verbal, 3.0 Analytical Writing), minimum undergraduate GPA of 3.0. Additional exam requirements/recommendations for international students: Required—TOEFL (minimum score 550 paper-based; 80 iBT). Electronic applications accepted. *Faculty research:* Energy and sustainability, biological engineering, advanced materials, systems engineering.

Instituto Tecnológico y de Estudios Superiores de Monterrey, Campus Monterrey, Graduate and Research Division, Programs in Engineering, Monterrey, Mexico. Offers applied statistics (M Eng); artificial intelligence (PhD); automation engineering (M Eng); chemical engineering (M Eng); civil engineering (M Eng); electrical engineering (M Eng); electronic engineering (M Eng); environmental engineering (M Eng); industrial engineering (M Eng, PhD); manufacturing engineering (M Eng); mechanical engineering (M Eng); systems and quality engineering (M Eng). M Eng program offered jointly with University of Waterloo; PhD in industrial engineering with Texas A&M University. *Program availability:* Part-time, evening/weekend. Terminal master's awarded for partial completion of doctoral program. *Degree requirements:* For master's, one foreign language, thesis; for doctorate, one foreign language, thesis/dissertation. *Entrance requirements:* For master's, EXADEP; for doctorate, GRE, master's degree in related field. Additional exam requirements/recommendations for international students: Required—TOEFL. *Faculty research:* Flexible manufacturing cells, materials, statistical methods, environmental prevention, control and evaluation.

Iowa State University of Science and Technology, Department of Chemical and Biological Engineering, Ames, IA 50011-2230. Offers M Eng, MS, PhD. *Degree requirements:* For master's, thesis (for some programs); for doctorate, thesis/dissertation. *Entrance requirements:* For master's and doctorate, GRE General Test. Additional exam requirements/recommendations for international students: Recommended—TOEFL (minimum score 587 paper-based; 94 iBT), IELTS (minimum score 7). Electronic applications accepted.

Johns Hopkins University, Engineering Program for Professionals, Part-time Program in Chemical and Biomolecular Engineering, Baltimore, MD 21218. Offers M Ch E. *Program availability:* Part-time, evening/weekend. *Faculty:* 2 full-time (1 woman), 2 part-time/adjunct. *Students:* 7 part-time (3 women). 5 applicants, 80% accepted, 3 enrolled.

In 2018, 3 master's awarded. *Entrance requirements:* Additional exam requirements/recommendations for international students: Required—TOEFL (minimum score 600 paper-based; 100 iBT). *Application deadline:* Applications are processed on a rolling basis. Application fee: $0. Electronic applications accepted. *Unit head:* Dr. Michael Betenbaugh, Program Chair, 410-516-5461, E-mail: beten@jhu.edu. *Application contact:* Doug Schiller, Admissions Director, 410-516-2300, Fax: 410-579-8049, E-mail: schiller@jhu.edu.
Website: http://www.ep.jhu.edu

Johns Hopkins University, G. W. C. Whiting School of Engineering, Department of Chemical and Biomolecular Engineering, Baltimore, MD 21218. Offers MSE, PhD. *Faculty:* 26 full-time (9 women). *Students:* 214 full-time (72 women). 358 applicants, 61% accepted, 117 enrolled. In 2018, 81 master's, 17 doctorates awarded. Terminal master's awarded for partial completion of doctoral program. *Degree requirements:* For master's, essay presentation; for doctorate, thesis/dissertation, oral exam; thesis presentation. *Entrance requirements:* For master's and doctorate, GRE General Test, 3 letters of recommendation, statement of purpose, transcripts. Additional exam requirements/recommendations for international students: Required—TOEFL (minimum score 600 paper-based, 100 iBT) or IELTS (7). *Application deadline:* For fall admission, 12/15 for domestic and international students. Application fee: $25. Electronic applications accepted. *Financial support:* In 2018–19, 131 students received support, including 14 fellowships with full and partial tuition reimbursements available (averaging $29,592 per year), 117 research assistantships with full tuition reimbursements available (averaging $31,000 per year); teaching assistantships with full and partial tuition reimbursements available, career-related internships or fieldwork, Federal Work-Study, institutionally sponsored loans, scholarships/grants, health care benefits, tuition waivers (partial), and unspecified assistantships also available. Support available to part-time students. Financial award application deadline: 1/15; financial award applicants required to submit FAFSA. *Faculty research:* Engineering in health and disease, biomolecular design and engineering, materials by design, micro and nanotechnology, alternative energy and sustainability. *Unit head:* Dr. Paulette Clancy, Chair and Professor, 410-516-4312, Fax: 410-516-5510, E-mail: pclancy3@jhu.edu. *Application contact:* Alisha Wells, Academic Program Coordinator, 410-516-2943, Fax: 410-516-5510, E-mail: AWells18@jhu.edu.
Website: http://engineering.jhu.edu/chembe/

Kansas State University, Graduate School, College of Engineering, Department of Chemical Engineering, Manhattan, KS 66506. Offers MS, PhD, Graduate Certificate. *Program availability:* Online learning. Terminal master's awarded for partial completion of doctoral program. *Degree requirements:* For master's, thesis, 24 hours of coursework; 6 hours of thesis; for doctorate, thesis/dissertation, 90 hours of credit. *Entrance requirements:* For doctorate, GRE. Additional exam requirements/recommendations for international students: Required—TOEFL. Electronic applications accepted. *Faculty research:* Renewable sustainable energy, molecular engineering, advanced materials.

Lamar University, College of Graduate Studies, College of Engineering, Dan F. Smith Department of Chemical Engineering, Beaumont, TX 77710. Offers ME, PhD. *Faculty:* 11 full-time (1 woman). *Students:* 34 full-time (8 women), 21 part-time (6 women); includes 5 minority (1 Black or African American, non-Hispanic/Latino; 2 Asian, non-Hispanic/Latino; 1 Hispanic/Latino; 1 Two or more races, non-Hispanic/Latino), 46 international. Average age 28. 30 applicants, 70% accepted, 5 enrolled. In 2018, 38 master's, 7 doctorates awarded. *Degree requirements:* For master's, comprehensive exam (for some programs), thesis (for some programs); for doctorate, comprehensive exam, thesis/dissertation. *Entrance requirements:* For master's and doctorate, GRE General Test. Additional exam requirements/recommendations for international students: Required—TOEFL (minimum score 550 paper-based; 79 iBT), IELTS (minimum score 6.5). *Application deadline:* Applications are processed on a rolling basis. Application fee: $25 ($50 for international students). Electronic applications accepted. *Expenses:* Tuition, state resident: full-time $6234; part-time $346 per credit hour. Tuition, nonresident: full-time $6852; part-time $761 per credit hour. *International tuition:* $6852 full-time. *Required fees:* $1940; $327 per credit hour. Tuition and fees vary according to course load, campus/location, program and reciprocity agreements. *Financial support:* In 2018–19, 3 students received support, including 32 fellowships with partial tuition reimbursements available (averaging $1,000 per year), 15 research assistantships with partial tuition reimbursements available (averaging $6,000 per year), 8 teaching assistantships with partial tuition reimbursements available (averaging $12,600 per year); tuition waivers (full and partial) also available. Financial award applicants required to submit FAFSA. *Faculty research:* Flare minimization, process optimization, process integration. *Unit head:* Dr. Thomas C. Ho, Chair, 409-880-8784, Fax: 409-880-2197, E-mail: che_dept@lamar.edu. *Application contact:* Celeste Contreas, Director, Admissions and Academic Services, 409-880-8888, Fax: 409-880-7419, E-mail: gradmissions@lamar.edu.
Website: http://engineering.lamar.edu/chemical

Lehigh University, P.C. Rossin College of Engineering and Applied Science, Department of Chemical and Biomolecular Engineering, Bethlehem, PA 18015. Offers biological chemical engineering (M Eng); chemical energy engineering (M Eng); chemical engineering (M Eng, MS, PhD); MBA/E. *Program availability:* Part-time, 100% online. *Faculty:* 19 full-time (2 women), 1 part-time/adjunct (0 women). *Students:* 41 full-time (15 women), 21 part-time (10 women); includes 9 minority (2 Black or African American, non-Hispanic/Latino; 4 Asian, non-Hispanic/Latino; 3 Hispanic/Latino), 31 international. Average age 27. 127 applicants, 35% accepted, 12 enrolled. In 2018, 19 master's, 10 doctorates awarded. Terminal master's awarded for partial completion of doctoral program. *Degree requirements:* For master's, thesis (for some programs); for doctorate, comprehensive exam, thesis/dissertation. *Entrance requirements:* For master's and doctorate, GRE General Test. Additional exam requirements/recommendations for international students: Required—TOEFL (minimum score 79 iBT), IELTS (minimum score 6.5). *Application deadline:* For fall admission, 7/15 for domestic students, 7/15 priority date for international students; for spring admission, 12/1 for domestic and international students. Applications are processed on a rolling basis. Application fee: $75. Electronic applications accepted. Tuition and fees vary according to program. *Financial support:* In 2018–19, 43 students received support, including 4 fellowships with full tuition reimbursements available (averaging $29,400 per year), 30 research assistantships with full tuition reimbursements available (averaging $29,400 per year), 3 teaching assistantships with full tuition reimbursements available (averaging $29,400 per year); career-related internships or fieldwork, institutionally sponsored loans, scholarships/grants, health care benefits, and unspecified assistantships also available. Financial award application deadline: 1/15. *Faculty research:* Process control, energy, biotechnology, catalysis, polymers. *Total annual research expenditures:* $2.8 million. *Unit head:* Dr. Mayuresh V. Kothare, Chairman, 610-758-6654, Fax: 610-758-5057, E-mail: mvk2@lehigh.edu. *Application contact:* Janine Jekels, Academic Coordinator, 610-758-4260, Fax: 610-758-5057, E-mail: inchegs@lehigh.edu.
Website: https://www.che.lehigh.edu/

Louisiana State University and Agricultural & Mechanical College, Graduate School, College of Engineering, Cain Department of Chemical Engineering, Baton Rouge, LA 70803. Offers MS Ch E, PhD.

Manhattan College, Graduate Programs, School of Engineering, Program in Chemical Engineering, Riverdale, NY 10471. Offers chemical engineering (MS). *Program availability:* Part-time, evening/weekend. *Degree requirements:* For master's, 30 credits with minimum GPA of 3.0. *Entrance requirements:* For master's, GRE (recommended), minimum GPA of 3.0. Additional exam requirements/recommendations for international students: Required—TOEFL (minimum score 550 paper-based; 80 iBT), IELTS (minimum score 6). Electronic applications accepted. *Expenses:* Contact institution. *Faculty research:* Department of energy, collagen.

Massachusetts Institute of Technology, School of Engineering, Department of Chemical Engineering, Cambridge, MA 02139. Offers chemical engineering (PhD, Sc D); chemical engineering practice (SM, PhD); SM/MBA. *Degree requirements:* For master's, thesis (for some programs), one-semester industrial internship; for doctorate, comprehensive exam, thesis/dissertation. *Entrance requirements:* For master's and doctorate, GRE General Test. Additional exam requirements/recommendations for international students: Required—TOEFL, IELTS. Electronic applications accepted. *Expenses: Tuition:* Full-time $51,520; part-time $800 per credit hour. *Required fees:* $312. *Faculty research:* Catalysis and reaction engineering, biological engineering, materials and polymers, surfaces and nanostructures, thermodynamics and molecular computation.

McGill University, Faculty of Graduate and Postdoctoral Studies, Faculty of Engineering, Department of Chemical Engineering, Montréal, QC H3A 2T5, Canada. Offers chemical engineering (M Eng, PhD); environmental engineering (M Eng).

McMaster University, School of Graduate Studies, Faculty of Engineering, Department of Chemical Engineering, Hamilton, ON L8S 4M2, Canada. Offers M Eng, MA Sc, PhD. *Degree requirements:* For master's, thesis; for doctorate, comprehensive exam, thesis/dissertation. *Entrance requirements:* For master's, minimum B average in the last two years. Additional exam requirements/recommendations for international students: Required—TOEFL (minimum score 550 paper-based). *Faculty research:* Biomaterials, computer process control, polymer processing, environmental biotechnology, reverse osmosis.

McNeese State University, Doré School of Graduate Studies, College of Engineering and Computer Science, Master of Engineering Program, Lake Charles, LA 70609. Offers chemical engineering (M Eng); civil engineering (M Eng); electrical engineering (M Eng); engineering management (M Eng); mechanical engineering (M Eng). *Program availability:* Part-time, evening/weekend. *Entrance requirements:* For master's, GRE, baccalaureate degree, minimum overall GPA of 3.0. Additional exam requirements/recommendations for international students: Required—TOEFL (minimum score 560 paper-based; 83 iBT).

Miami University, College of Engineering and Computing, Department of Chemical, Paper and Biomedical Engineering, Oxford, OH 45056. Offers MS. *Faculty:* 14 full-time (4 women). *Students:* 10 full-time (4 women), 2 part-time (1 woman); includes 2 minority (1 Asian, non-Hispanic/Latino; 1 Hispanic/Latino), 6 international. Average age 25. In 2018, 7 master's awarded. *Unit head:* Dr. Shashi Lalvani, Chair, 513-529-0763, E-mail: lalvansb@miamioh.edu. *Application contact:* Department of Chemical, Paper and Biomedical Engineering, 513-529-0760, E-mail: paper@miamioh.edu.
Website: http://miamioh.edu/cec/academics/departments/cpb/

Michigan State University, The Graduate School, College of Engineering, Department of Chemical Engineering and Materials Science, East Lansing, MI 48824. Offers chemical engineering (MS, PhD); materials science and engineering (MS, PhD). *Entrance requirements:* Additional exam requirements/recommendations for international students: Required—TOEFL. Electronic applications accepted.

Michigan Technological University, Graduate School, College of Engineering, Department of Chemical Engineering, Houghton, MI 49931. Offers MS, PhD. *Program availability:* Part-time. *Faculty:* 18 full-time (5 women), 2 part-time/adjunct. *Students:* 33 full-time (11 women), 1 part-time; includes 1 minority (Asian, non-Hispanic/Latino), 26 international. Average age 27. 127 applicants, 35% accepted, 10 enrolled. In 2018, 10 master's, 6 doctorates awarded. Terminal master's awarded for partial completion of doctoral program. *Degree requirements:* For master's, comprehensive exam (for some programs), thesis (for some programs); for doctorate, comprehensive exam, thesis/dissertation. *Entrance requirements:* For master's and doctorate, GRE, statement of purpose, personal statement, official transcripts, 2 letters of recommendation. Additional exam requirements/recommendations for international students: Required—TOEFL (minimum score 94 iBT) or IELTS (recommended minimum score of 7.0). *Application deadline:* For fall admission, 1/15 priority date for domestic and international students. Applications are processed on a rolling basis. Electronic applications accepted. *Expenses:* $1,143 per credit. *Financial support:* In 2018–19, 31 students received support, including 6 fellowships with tuition reimbursements available (averaging $16,590 per year), 10 research assistantships with tuition reimbursements available (averaging $16,590 per year), 9 teaching assistantships with tuition reimbursements available (averaging $16,590 per year); career-related internships or fieldwork, Federal Work-Study, scholarships/grants, health care benefits, unspecified assistantships, and cooperative program also available. Financial award applicants required to submit FAFSA. *Faculty research:* Polymer engineering, thermodynamics, chemical process safety, surface science/catalysis, environmental chemical engineering. *Total annual research expenditures:* $1 million. *Unit head:* Dr. Pradeep K. Agrawal, Chair, 906-487-1870, Fax: 906-487-3213, E-mail: pkagrawa@mtu.edu. *Application contact:* Taana Kalliainen, Staff Assistant, 906-487-3211, Fax: 906-487-3213, E-mail: taana@mtu.edu.
Website: http://www.mtu.edu/chemical/

Mississippi State University, Bagley College of Engineering, Dave C. Swalm School of Chemical Engineering, Mississippi State, MS 39762. Offers MS, PhD. *Faculty:* 10 full-time (2 women). *Students:* 16 full-time (7 women), 4 part-time (1 woman); includes 2 minority (both Asian, non-Hispanic/Latino), 15 international. Average age 29. 21 applicants, 29% accepted, 5 enrolled. In 2018, 1 master's, 3 doctorates awarded. *Degree requirements:* For master's, comprehensive exam or thesis; for doctorate, comprehensive exam, thesis/dissertation. *Entrance requirements:* For master's, GRE, minimum GPA of 3.0 on last 64 undergraduate hours; for doctorate, GRE, minimum GPA of 3.2 on last 64 undergraduate hours. Additional exam requirements/recommendations for international students: Required—TOEFL (minimum score 550 paper-based; 79 iBT); Recommended—IELTS (minimum score 6.5). *Application deadline:* For fall admission, 4/1 priority date for domestic students, 5/1 for international students; for spring admission, 8/1 priority date for domestic students, 9/1 for international students. Applications are processed on a rolling basis. Application fee: $60 ($80 for international students). Electronic applications accepted. *Expenses:* Tuition, state resident: full-time $8450; part-time $360.59 per credit hour. Tuition, nonresident: full-time $23,140; part-time $969.09 per credit hour. *Required fees:* $110. One-time fee: $55 full-time. Part-time tuition and fees vary according to course load, degree level, campus/location and reciprocity agreements. *Financial support:* In 2018–19, 13 research assistantships with full tuition reimbursements (averaging $17,669 per year), 1 teaching assistantship with full tuition reimbursement (averaging $17,669 per year) were awarded; Federal Work-Study, institutionally sponsored loans, and unspecified assistantships also available. Financial award application deadline: 4/1; financial award applicants required to submit FAFSA. *Faculty research:*

Chemical Engineering

Thermodynamics, composite materials, catalysis, surface science, environmental engineering. *Total annual research expenditures:* $1.9 million. *Unit head:* Dr. Bill Elmore, Director/Earnest W. Deavenport Jr. Chair, 662-325-2480, Fax: 662-325-2482, E-mail: elmore@che.msstate.edu. *Application contact:* Angie Campbell, Admissions and Enrollment Assistant, 662-325-9514, E-mail: acampbell@grad.msstate.edu. Website: http://www.che.msstate.edu/

Missouri University of Science and Technology, Department of Chemical and Biochemical Engineering, Rolla, MO 65409. Offers chemical engineering (MS, PhD). *Degree requirements:* For master's, thesis optional; for doctorate, comprehensive exam. *Entrance requirements:* For master's, GRE (minimum score 1100 verbal and quantitative, 4 writing); for doctorate, GRE (minimum score: verbal and quantitative 1200, writing 4). Additional exam requirements/recommendations for international students: Required—TOEFL (minimum score 550 paper-based). Electronic applications accepted. *Expenses:* Tuition, state resident: full-time $7545.60; part-time $419.20 per credit hour. Tuition, nonresident: full-time $22,169; part-time $1231.60 per credit hour. *International tuition:* $23,518.80 full-time. *Required fees:* $4523.05. Full-time tuition and fees vary according to course load, campus/location, program and reciprocity agreements. *Faculty research:* Mixing, fluid mechanics, bioengineering, freeze-drying, extraction.

Montana State University, The Graduate School, College of Engineering, Department of Chemical and Biological Engineering, Bozeman, MT 59717. Offers chemical engineering (MS); engineering (PhD), including chemical engineering option, environmental engineering option; environmental engineering (MS). *Program availability:* Part-time. *Degree requirements:* For master's, comprehensive exam, thesis (for some programs); for doctorate, comprehensive exam, thesis/dissertation. *Entrance requirements:* For master's and doctorate, GRE General Test. Additional exam requirements/recommendations for international students: Required—TOEFL (minimum score 550 paper-based). Electronic applications accepted. *Faculty research:* Metabolic network analysis and engineering; magnetic resonance microscopy; modeling of biological systems; the development of protective coatings on planar solid oxide fuel cell (SOFC) metallic interconnects; characterizing corrosion mechanisms of materials in precisely-controlled exposures; testing materials in poly-crystalline silicon production environments; environmental biotechnology and bioremediation.

New Jersey Institute of Technology, Newark College of Engineering, Newark, NJ 07102. Offers biomedical engineering (MS, PhD); biopharmaceutical engineering (MS); chemical engineering (MS, PhD); civil engineering (MS, PhD); computer engineering (MS); critical infrastructure systems (MS); electrical engineering (MS, PhD); engineering management (MS); engineering science (MS); environmental engineering (MS, PhD); healthcare systems management (MS); industrial engineering (MS, PhD); internet engineering (MS); manufacturing systems engineering (MS); materials science & engineering (PhD); materials science and engineering (MS); mechanical engineering (MS, PhD); occupational safety and health engineering (MS). *Program availability:* Part-time, evening/weekend. *Faculty:* 147 full-time (26 women), 133 part-time/adjunct (16 women). *Students:* 690 full-time (163 women), 594 part-time (130 women); includes 427 minority (79 Black or African American, non-Hispanic/Latino; 181 Asian, non-Hispanic/Latino; 140 Hispanic/Latino; 27 Two or more races, non-Hispanic/Latino; 553 international. Average age 27. 2,334 applicants, 57% accepted, 452 enrolled. In 2018, 418 master's, 31 doctorates awarded. Terminal master's awarded for partial completion of doctoral program. *Degree requirements:* For master's, thesis (for some programs); for doctorate, thesis/dissertation. *Entrance requirements:* For master's, GRE General Test, minimum GPA 2.8, personal statement, 1 letter of recommendation, transcripts; for doctorate, GRE General Test, minimum GPA of 3.5, personal statement, 3 letters of recommendation, transcripts. Additional exam requirements/recommendations for international students: Required—TOEFL (minimum score 550 paper-based; 79 iBT), IELTS (minimum score 6.5). *Application deadline:* For fall admission, 6/1 priority date for domestic students, 5/1 priority date for international students; for spring admission, 11/15 priority date for domestic and international students. Applications are processed on a rolling basis. Application fee: $75. Electronic applications accepted. *Expenses:* $22,690 per year (in-state), $32,136 per year (out-of-state). *Financial support:* In 2018–19, 396 students received support, including 52 fellowships with full tuition reimbursements available (averaging $22,000 per year), 113 research assistantships with full tuition reimbursements available (averaging $22,000 per year), 101 teaching assistantships with full tuition reimbursements available (averaging $22,000 per year); career-related internships or fieldwork, Federal Work-Study, scholarships/grants, and unspecified assistantships also available. Financial award application deadline: 1/15. *Faculty research:* Nonlinear signal processing, intelligent medical image analysis, calibration issues in coherent localization, computer-aided design, neural network for tool wear measurement. *Total annual research expenditures:* $41.7 million. *Unit head:* Dr. Moshe Kam, Dean, 973-596-5534, Fax: 973-596-2316, E-mail: moshe.kam@njit.edu. *Application contact:* Stephen Eck, Director of Admissions, 973-596-3300, Fax: 973-596-3461, E-mail: admissions@njit.edu. Website: http://engineering.njit.edu/

North Carolina Agricultural and Technical State University, The Graduate College, College of Engineering, Department of Chemical, Biological and Bio Engineering, Greensboro, NC 27411. Offers bioengineering (MS); biological engineering (MS); chemical engineering (MS).

North Carolina State University, Graduate School, College of Engineering, Department of Chemical and Biomolecular Engineering, Raleigh, NC 27695. Offers chemical engineering (M Ch E, MS, PhD). *Program availability:* Part-time. Terminal master's awarded for partial completion of doctoral program. *Degree requirements:* For master's, thesis optional; for doctorate, thesis/dissertation. *Entrance requirements:* For master's and doctorate, GRE General Test. Additional exam requirements/recommendations for international students: Required—TOEFL. Electronic applications accepted. *Faculty research:* Molecular thermodynamics and computer simulation, catalysis, kinetics, electrochemical reaction engineering, biochemical engineering.

Northeastern University, College of Engineering, Boston, MA 02115-5096. Offers bioengineering (MS, PhD); chemical engineering (MS, PhD); civil engineering (MS, PhD); computer engineering (PhD); computer systems engineering (MS); electrical and computer engineering (MS); electrical and computer engineering leadership (MS); electrical engineering (PhD); energy systems (MS); engineering and public policy (MS); engineering management (MS, Certificate); environmental engineering (MS); industrial engineering (MS, PhD); information assurance (PhD); information systems (MS); interdisciplinary engineering (PhD); mechanical engineering (PhD); operations research (MS); telecommunication systems management (MS). *Program availability:* Part-time, online learning. Electronic applications accepted. *Expenses:* Contact institution.

Northwestern University, McCormick School of Engineering and Applied Science, Department of Chemical and Biological Engineering, Evanston, IL 60208. Offers biotechnology (MS); chemical engineering (MS, PhD). Admissions and degrees offered through The Graduate School. *Program availability:* Part-time. Terminal master's awarded for partial completion of doctoral program. *Degree requirements:* For master's, comprehensive exam (for some programs), thesis optional; for doctorate, comprehensive exam, thesis/dissertation. *Entrance requirements:* For master's and doctorate, GRE General Test. Additional exam requirements/recommendations for

international students: Required—TOEFL (minimum score 577 paper-based; 90 iBT), IELTS (minimum score 7). Electronic applications accepted. *Faculty research:* Biotechnology, bioengineering, complexity, energy, sustainability, materials, nanoengineering, and synthetic biology.

The Ohio State University, Graduate School, College of Engineering, Department of Chemical and Biomolecular Engineering, Columbus, OH 43210. Offers chemical engineering (MS, PhD). *Faculty:* 23. *Students:* 114 (36 women). Average age 25. In 2018, 21 master's, 20 doctorates awarded. *Entrance requirements:* For master's, GRE; for doctorate, GRE (highly recommend minimum score of 75% in Verbal and Quantitative and 4.0 in Analytical Writing). Additional exam requirements/recommendations for international students: Required—TOEFL (minimum score 600 paper-based; 100 iBT), Michigan English Language Assessment Battery (minimum score 86); Recommended—IELTS (minimum score 8). *Application deadline:* For fall admission, 12/13 priority date for domestic students, 11/30 priority date for international students; for spring admission, 10/1 for domestic and international students. Applications are processed on a rolling basis. Application fee: $60 ($70 for international students). Electronic applications accepted. *Financial support:* Fellowships with tuition reimbursements, research assistantships with tuition reimbursements, teaching assistantships with tuition reimbursements, career-related internships or fieldwork, Federal Work-Study, institutionally sponsored loans, and unspecified assistantships available. Support available to part-time students. *Unit head:* Dr. Umit Ozkan, Chair, 614-292-6623, E-mail: ozkan.1@osu.edu. *Application contact:* Graduate and Professional Admissions, 614-292-9444, Fax: 614-292-3895, E-mail: gpadmissions@osu.edu. Website: http://www.cbe.osu.edu

Ohio University, Graduate College, Russ College of Engineering and Technology, Department of Chemical and Biomolecular engineering, Athens, OH 45701-2979. Offers biomedical engineering (MS); chemical engineering (MS, PhD). *Program availability:* Part-time. *Degree requirements:* For master's, comprehensive exam (for some programs), thesis; for doctorate, comprehensive exam, thesis/dissertation, qualifying exams. *Entrance requirements:* For master's and doctorate, GRE General Test. Additional exam requirements/recommendations for international students: Required—TOEFL (minimum score 590 paper-based; 96 iBT) or IELTS (minimum score 7). Electronic applications accepted. *Faculty research:* Corrosion and multiphase flow, biochemical engineering, thin film materials, air pollution modeling and control, biomedical engineering.

Oklahoma State University, College of Engineering, Architecture and Technology, School of Chemical Engineering, Stillwater, OK 74078. Offers MS, PhD. *Faculty:* 12 full-time (2 women), 1 part-time/adjunct (0 women). *Students:* 13 full-time (2 women), 29 part-time (6 women); includes 3 minority (1 Asian, non-Hispanic/Latino; 2 Two or more races, non-Hispanic/Latino), 26 international. Average age 29. 64 applicants, 20% accepted, 13 enrolled. In 2018, 8 master's, 2 doctorates awarded. *Entrance requirements:* For master's and doctorate, GRE or GMAT. Additional exam requirements/recommendations for international students: Required—TOEFL (minimum score 550 paper-based; 79 iBT). *Application deadline:* For fall admission, 3/1 priority date for international students; for spring admission, 8/1 priority date for international students. Applications are processed on a rolling basis. Application fee: $40 ($75 for international students). Electronic applications accepted. *Expenses:* Tuition, area resident: Full-time $4148. Tuition, state resident: full-time $4148. Tuition, nonresident: full-time $10,517. *International tuition:* $10,517 full-time. *Required fees:* $4394; $2929 per credit hour. Tuition and fees vary according to course load and program. *Financial support:* Research assistantships, teaching assistantships, career-related internships or fieldwork, Federal Work-Study, scholarships/grants, health care benefits, tuition waivers (partial), and unspecified assistantships available. Support available to part-time students. Financial award application deadline: 3/1; financial award applicants required to submit FAFSA. *Unit head:* Dr. Gier Hareland, Head, 405-744-5280, Fax: 405-744-6338. *Application contact:* Dr. Sheryl Tucker, Dean, 405-744-6368, Fax: 405-744-0355, E-mail: gradi@okstate.edu. Website: http://che.okstate.edu/

Oregon State University, College of Engineering, Program in Chemical Engineering, Corvallis, OR 97331. Offers M Eng, MS, PhD. *Entrance requirements:* For master's, GRE. Additional exam requirements/recommendations for international students: Required—TOEFL (minimum score 92 iBT). *Expenses:* Contact institution.

Penn State University Park, Graduate School, College of Engineering, Department of Chemical Engineering, University Park, PA 16802. Offers MS, PhD.

Princeton University, Graduate School, School of Engineering and Applied Science, Department of Chemical and Biological Engineering, Princeton, NJ 08544-1019. Offers M Eng, MSE, PhD. Terminal master's awarded for partial completion of doctoral program. *Degree requirements:* For master's, thesis (MSE); for doctorate, thesis/dissertation, general exam. *Entrance requirements:* For master's, GRE General Test, 3 letters of recommendation; for doctorate, GRE General Test, official transcript(s), 3 letters of recommendation, personal statement. Additional exam requirements/recommendations for international students: Required—TOEFL. Electronic applications accepted. *Faculty research:* Applied and computational mathematics, bioengineering, environmental and energy science and technology, fluid mechanics and transport phenomena, materials science.

Purdue University, College of Engineering, Davidson School of Chemical Engineering, West Lafayette, IN 47907-2050. Offers MSChE, PhD. Terminal master's awarded for partial completion of doctoral program. *Degree requirements:* For master's, thesis optional; for doctorate, thesis/dissertation. *Entrance requirements:* For master's and doctorate, GRE, minimum GPA of 3.0. Electronic applications accepted. *Faculty research:* Biomedical and biomolecular engineering, catalysis and reaction engineering, fluid mechanics and interfacial phenomena, mass transfer and separations, nanoscale science and engineering, polymers and materials, product and process systems engineering, thermodynamics, molecular and nanoscale modeling.

Queen's University at Kingston, School of Graduate Studies, Faculty of Engineering and Applied Science, Department of Chemical Engineering, Kingston, ON K7L 3N6, Canada. Offers M Sc, PhD. *Program availability:* Part-time. *Degree requirements:* For master's, thesis or alternative; for doctorate, comprehensive exam, thesis/dissertation. *Entrance requirements:* Additional exam requirements/recommendations for international students: Required—TOEFL (minimum score 580 paper-based). Electronic applications accepted. *Faculty research:* Polymers and reaction engineering, process control and applied statistics, combustion, fermentation and bioremediation, biomaterials.

Rensselaer Polytechnic Institute, Graduate School, School of Engineering, Program in Chemical Engineering, Troy, NY 12180-3590. Offers M Eng, MS, PhD. *Faculty:* 17 full-time (2 women). *Students:* 69 full-time (21 women); includes 10 minority (1 Black or African American, non-Hispanic/Latino; 4 Asian, non-Hispanic/Latino; 5 Two or more races, non-Hispanic/Latino), 40 international. Average age 25. 191 applicants, 24% accepted, 14 enrolled. In 2018, 5 master's, 15 doctorates awarded. Terminal master's awarded for partial completion of doctoral program. *Entrance requirements:* For master's and doctorate, GRE. Additional exam requirements/recommendations for international students: Required—TOEFL (minimum score 570 paper-based; 88 iBT), IELTS (minimum score 6.5), PTE (minimum score 60). *Application deadline:* For fall admission, 1/1 priority date for domestic and international students; for spring admission, 8/15 priority date for domestic and international students. Applications are processed on a rolling basis. Application fee: $75. Electronic applications accepted. *Financial support:* In 2018–19, research assistantships with full tuition reimbursements (averaging $23,000 per year), teaching assistantships with full tuition reimbursements (averaging $23,000 per year) were awarded; fellowships also available. Financial award application deadline: 1/1. *Faculty research:* Advanced materials, biochemical engineering; biomedical engineering; biotechnology; drug delivery; energy; fluid mechanics; interfacial phenomena; mass transport; molecular simulations; molecular thermodynamics; nanotechnology; polymers; process control, design, and optimization; separation and bioseparation processes; systems biology; systems engineering; transport phenomena. *Total annual research expenditures:* $6.2 million. *Unit head:* Dr. Patrick Underhill, Graduate Program Director, 518-276-3032, E-mail: underhill@rpi.edu. *Application contact:* Jarron Decker, Director of Graduate Admissions, 518-276-6216, Fax: 518-276-4072, E-mail: gradadmissions@rpi.edu. Website: http://cbe.rpi.edu/graduate

Rice University, Graduate Programs, George R. Brown School of Engineering, Department of Chemical and Biomolecular Engineering, Houston, TX 77251-1892. Offers chemical and biomolecular engineering (MS, PhD); chemical engineering (M Ch E). *Program availability:* Part-time. *Degree requirements:* For master's, thesis (for some programs); for doctorate, thesis/dissertation. *Entrance requirements:* For master's and doctorate, GRE General Test, minimum GPA of 3.0. Additional exam requirements/recommendations for international students: Required—TOEFL (minimum score 600 paper-based; 90 iBT). Electronic applications accepted. *Faculty research:* Thermodynamics, phase equilibria, rheology, fluid mechanics, polymers, biomedical engineering, interfacial phenomena, process control, petroleum engineering, reaction engineering and catalysis, biomaterials, metabolic engineering.

Rose-Hulman Institute of Technology, Graduate Studies, Department of Chemical Engineering, Terre Haute, IN 47803-3999. Offers M Eng, MS. *Program availability:* Part-time. *Faculty:* 11 full-time (5 women), 1 part-time/adjunct (0 women). *Students:* 2 full-time (1 woman), 4 part-time (0 women), 1 international. Average age 23. 6 applicants, 50% accepted, 3 enrolled. In 2018, 8 master's awarded. *Degree requirements:* For master's, thesis. *Entrance requirements:* For master's, GRE, minimum GPA of 3.0. Additional exam requirements/recommendations for international students: Required—TOEFL (minimum score 580 paper-based; 94 iBT), IELTS (minimum score 7). *Application deadline:* For fall admission, 2/1 priority date for domestic and international students; for winter admission, 10/1 for domestic students, 4/1 for international students; for spring admission, 1/15 for domestic students, 11/1 for international students. Applications are processed on a rolling basis. Application fee: $0. Electronic applications accepted. *Expenses: Tuition:* Full-time $46,641. *Financial support:* In 2018–19, 4 students received support. Fellowships with tuition reimbursements available, research assistantships with tuition reimbursements available, institutionally sponsored loans, scholarships/grants, and tuition waivers (full and partial) available. *Faculty research:* Thermodynamics and interfacial phenomena, reaction kinetics and separations, particle technology and materials, process systems and control, petrochemical processes. *Total annual research expenditures:* $5,859. *Unit head:* Dr. Adam Nolte, Department Head, 812-877-8096, Fax: 812-877-8992, E-mail: nolte@rose-hulman.edu. *Application contact:* Dr. Craig Downing, Associate Dean of Lifelong Learning, 812-877-8822, E-mail: downing@rose-hulman.edu. Website: https://www.rose-hulman.edu/academics/academic-departments/chemical-engineering/index.html

Rowan University, Graduate School, College of Engineering, Department of Chemical Engineering, Glassboro, NJ 08028-1701. Offers MS. Electronic applications accepted.

Royal Military College of Canada, Division of Graduate Studies, Faculty of Science, Department of Chemistry and Chemical Engineering, Kingston, ON K7K 7B4, Canada. Offers chemical engineering (M Eng, MA Sc, PhD); chemistry (M Sc, PhD). *Degree requirements:* For master's, thesis; for doctorate, comprehensive exam, thesis/dissertation. *Entrance requirements:* For master's, honour's degree with second-class standing; for doctorate, master's degree. Electronic applications accepted.

Rutgers University–New Brunswick, Graduate School-New Brunswick, Program in Chemical and Biochemical Engineering, Piscataway, NJ 08854-8097. Offers MS, PhD. *Program availability:* Part-time, evening/weekend. Terminal master's awarded for partial completion of doctoral program. *Degree requirements:* For master's, thesis or alternative; for doctorate, thesis/dissertation. *Entrance requirements:* For master's and doctorate, GRE General Test. Additional exam requirements/recommendations for international students: Required—TOEFL. *Faculty research:* Biotechnology, pharmaceutical engineering, nanotechnology, process system engineering, materials and polymer science, chemical engineering sciences.

San Jose State University, Program in Chemical & Materials Engineering, San Jose, CA 95192-0001. Offers chemical engineering (MS); materials engineering (MS). *Program availability:* Part-time. *Degree requirements:* For master's, thesis or alternative. Electronic applications accepted.

South Dakota School of Mines and Technology, Graduate Division, Program in Chemical and Biological Engineering, Rapid City, SD 57701-3995. Offers PhD. *Program availability:* Part-time. *Degree requirements:* For doctorate, thesis/dissertation. *Entrance requirements:* Additional exam requirements/recommendations for international students: Required—TOEFL (minimum score 520 paper-based; 68 iBT). Electronic applications accepted.

South Dakota School of Mines and Technology, Graduate Division, Program in Chemical Engineering, Rapid City, SD 57701-3995. Offers MS. *Program availability:* Part-time. *Degree requirements:* For master's, thesis. *Entrance requirements:* For master's, GRE General Test. Additional exam requirements/recommendations for international students: Required—TOEFL (minimum score 520 paper-based; 68 iBT), TWE. Electronic applications accepted. *Faculty research:* Incineration chemistry, environmental chemistry, polymer surface chemistry.

Stanford University, School of Engineering, Department of Chemical Engineering, Stanford, CA 94305-2004. Offers MS, PhD. *Expenses: Tuition:* Full-time $50,703; part-time $32,970 per year. *Required fees:* $651. Website: http://cheme.stanford.edu/

Stevens Institute of Technology, Graduate School, Charles V. Schaefer Jr. School of Engineering and Science, Department of Chemical Engineering and Materials Science, Program in Chemical Engineering, Hoboken, NJ 07030. Offers M Eng, PhD, Engr. *Program availability:* Part-time, evening/weekend, 100% online, blended/hybrid learning. *Faculty:* 14 full-time (3 women). *Students:* 28 full-time (8 women), 7 part-time (2 women); includes 1 minority (Hispanic/Latino), 25 international. Average age 26. In 2018, 16 master's, 1 doctorate awarded. Terminal master's awarded for partial completion of doctoral program. *Entrance requirements:* For master's, GRE/GMAT scores: GRE scores are required for all applicants applying to a full-time graduate program in the Schaefer School of Engineering and Science (SES). International applicants must submit TOEFL/IELTS scores and fulfill the English Language

Proficiency Requirements in order to be considered. Additional exam requirements/recommendations for international students: Required—TOEFL (minimum score 74 iBT), IELTS (minimum score 6). *Application deadline:* For fall admission, 4/15 for domestic and international students; for spring admission, 11/1 for domestic and international students; for summer admission, 5/1 for domestic students. Applications are processed on a rolling basis. Application fee: $60. Electronic applications accepted. *Expenses: Tuition:* Full-time $35,960; part-time $1620 per credit. *Required fees:* $1290; $600 per semester. Tuition and fees vary according to course load. *Financial support:* Fellowships, research assistantships, teaching assistantships, career-related internships or fieldwork, Federal Work-Study, scholarships/grants, and unspecified assistantships available. Financial award application deadline: 2/15; financial award applicants required to submit FAFSA. *Unit head:* Dr. Jean Zu, Dean of SES, 201-216.8233, Fax: 201-216.8372, E-mail: Jean.Zu@stevens.edu. *Application contact:* Graduate Admissions, 888-783-8367, Fax: 888-511-1306, E-mail: graduate@stevens.edu.

Syracuse University, College of Engineering and Computer Science, Programs in Chemical Engineering, Syracuse, NY 13244. Offers MS, PhD. *Program availability:* Part-time. *Students:* Average age 25. *Degree requirements:* For master's, comprehensive exam (for some programs), thesis (for some programs); for doctorate, comprehensive exam, thesis/dissertation. *Entrance requirements:* For master's, GRE General Test, official transcripts, three letters of recommendation, resume, personal statement; for doctorate, GRE General Test. Additional exam requirements/recommendations for international students: Required—TOEFL (minimum score 100 iBT). *Application deadline:* For fall admission, 7/1 priority date for domestic students, 6/1 priority date for international students; for spring admission, 11/15 for domestic students, 10/15 priority date for international students. Applications are processed on a rolling basis. Application fee: $75. Electronic applications accepted. *Financial support:* Fellowships with full tuition reimbursements, research assistantships, teaching assistantships, and tuition waivers (partial) available. Financial award application deadline: 1/1; financial award applicants required to submit FAFSA. *Faculty research:* Complex fluids, soft condensed matter, rheology, energy sources, conversion and conservation, multiple phase systems, nanotechnology, rehabilitative and regenerative engineering, smart materials for healthcare, sustainable energy production, systems biology/metabolic engineering. *Unit head:* Dr. Dacheng Ren, Professor, Chemical Engineering/Graduate Program Director, 315-443-4409, E-mail: dren@syr.edu. *Application contact:* Kathleen Joyce, Assistant Dean, 315-443-2219, E-mail: topgrads@syr.edu. Website: http://eng-cs.syr.edu/

Tennessee Technological University, College of Graduate Studies, College of Engineering, Department of Chemical Engineering, Cookeville, TN 38505. Offers MS. *Program availability:* Part-time. *Faculty:* 8 full-time (0 women). *Students:* 3 full-time (0 women), 11 part-time (5 women); includes 1 minority (Hispanic/Latino), 7 international. 20 applicants, 50% accepted, 2 enrolled. In 2018, 7 master's awarded. *Degree requirements:* For master's, thesis. *Entrance requirements:* For master's, GRE General Test. Additional exam requirements/recommendations for international students: Required—TOEFL (minimum score 550 paper-based; 79 iBT), IELTS (minimum score 5.5), PTE (minimum score 53), or TOEIC (Test of English as an International Communication). *Application deadline:* For fall admission, 8/1 for domestic students, 5/1 for international students; for spring admission, 12/1 for domestic students, 10/1 for international students; for summer admission, 5/1 for domestic students, 2/1 for international students. Applications are processed on a rolling basis. Application fee: $35 ($40 for international students). Electronic applications accepted. *Financial support:* Fellowships, research assistantships, teaching assistantships, and career-related internships or fieldwork available. Financial award application deadline: 4/1. *Faculty research:* Biochemical conversion, insulation, fuel reprocessing. *Unit head:* Dr. Pedro Arce, Chairperson, 931-372-3297, Fax: 931-372-6372, E-mail: parce@tntech.edu. *Application contact:* Shelia K. Kendrick, Coordinator of Graduate Studies, 931-372-3808, Fax: 931-372-3497, E-mail: skendrick@tntech.edu.

Texas A&M University, College of Engineering, Artie McFerrin Department of Chemical Engineering, College Station, TX 77843. Offers chemical engineering (MS). *Faculty:* 32. *Students:* 198 full-time (62 women), 30 part-time (6 women); includes 29 minority (5 Black or African American, non-Hispanic/Latino; 16 Asian, non-Hispanic/Latino; 4 Hispanic/Latino; 4 Two or more races, non-Hispanic/Latino), 164 international. Average age 27. 368 applicants, 45% accepted, 68 enrolled. In 2018, 57 master's, 16 doctorates awarded. Terminal master's awarded for partial completion of doctoral program. *Degree requirements:* For master's, thesis (MS); for doctorate, thesis/dissertation. *Entrance requirements:* For master's and doctorate, GRE General Test. Additional exam requirements/recommendations for international students: Required—TOEFL (minimum score 550 paper-based; 80 iBT), IELTS (minimum score 6), PTE (minimum score 53). *Application deadline:* For fall admission, 12/1 for domestic students, 12/1 priority date for international students; for spring admission, 10/1 for domestic and international students. Applications are processed on a rolling basis. Application fee: $50 ($90 for international students). Electronic applications accepted. *Expenses:* Contact institution. *Financial support:* In 2018–19, 209 students received support, including 14 fellowships with tuition reimbursements available (averaging $18,097 per year), 165 research assistantships with tuition reimbursements available (averaging $18,782 per year); career-related internships or fieldwork, institutionally sponsored loans, scholarships/grants, traineeships, health care benefits, tuition waivers (full and partial), and unspecified assistantships also available. Support available to part-time students. Financial award application deadline: 3/15; financial award applicants required to submit FAFSA. *Faculty research:* Reaction engineering, interface phenomena, environmental applications, biochemical engineering, polymers. *Unit head:* Dr. M. Nazmul Karim, Head, 979-845-9806, E-mail: nazkarim@che.tamu.edu. *Application contact:* Dr. Hae-Kwon Jeong, Graduate Recruitment and Admissions Coordinator, 979-862-4850, E-mail: jeong@chemail.tamu.edu. Website: http://engineering.tamu.edu/chemical

Texas A&M University–Kingsville, College of Graduate Studies, Frank H. Dotterweich College of Engineering, Wayne H. King Department of Chemical and Natural Gas Engineering, Program in Chemical Engineering, Kingsville, TX 78363. Offers ME, MS. *Degree requirements:* For master's, variable foreign language requirement, comprehensive exam, thesis (for some programs). *Entrance requirements:* For master's, GRE (minimum quantitative score of 150, verbal 145), MAT, GMAT, minimum GPA of 2.75. Additional exam requirements/recommendations for international students: Required—TOEFL (minimum score 550 paper-based; 79 iBT). Electronic applications accepted.

Tufts University, School of Engineering, Department of Chemical and Biological Engineering, Medford, MA 02155. Offers bioengineering (MS), including cell and bioprocess engineering; biotechnology (PhD); chemical engineering (MS, PhD); PhD/PhD. *Program availability:* Part-time. Terminal master's awarded for partial completion of doctoral program. *Degree requirements:* For master's, thesis (for some programs); for doctorate, thesis/dissertation. *Entrance requirements:* For master's and doctorate, GRE General Test. Additional exam requirements/recommendations for international students: Required—TOEFL (minimum score 550 paper-based; 80 iBT), IELTS (minimum score 6.5). Electronic applications accepted. *Expenses: Tuition:* Full-time

$51,288; part-time $1710 per credit hour. *Required fees:* $904. Full-time tuition and fees vary according to degree level, program and student level. Part-time tuition and fees vary according to course load. *Faculty research:* Clean energy with materials, biomaterials, colloids; metabolic engineering, biotechnology; process control; reaction kinetics, catalysis; transport phenomena.

Tulane University, School of Science and Engineering, Department of Chemical and Biomolecular Engineering, New Orleans, LA 70118-5669. Offers MS, PhD. *Program availability:* Part-time. Terminal master's awarded for partial completion of doctoral program. *Degree requirements:* For master's, thesis (for some programs); for doctorate, thesis/dissertation. *Entrance requirements:* For master's and doctorate, GRE General Test, minimum B average in undergraduate course work. Additional exam requirements/recommendations for international students: Required—TOEFL. Electronic applications accepted. *Expenses: Tuition:* Full-time $52,856; part-time $2937 per credit hour. *Required fees:* $2040; $44.50 per credit hour. $580 per term. Tuition and fees vary according to course load, degree level and program. *Faculty research:* Interfacial phenomena catalysis, electrochemical engineering, environmental science.

Universidad de las Américas Puebla, Division of Graduate Studies, School of Engineering, Program in Chemical Engineering, Puebla, Mexico. Offers chemical engineering (MS); food technology (MS). *Program availability:* Part-time, evening/weekend. *Degree requirements:* For master's, one foreign language, thesis. *Faculty research:* Food science, reactors, oil industry, biotechnology.

Université de Sherbrooke, Faculty of Engineering, Department of Chemical Engineering, Sherbrooke, QC J1K 2R1, Canada. Offers M Sc A, PhD. *Degree requirements:* For master's, one foreign language, thesis; for doctorate, comprehensive exam, thesis/dissertation. *Entrance requirements:* For doctorate, master's degree in engineering or equivalent. Electronic applications accepted. *Faculty research:* Conversion processes, high-temperature plasma technologies, system engineering, environmental engineering, textile technologies.

Université Laval, Faculty of Sciences and Engineering, Department of Chemical Engineering, Programs in Chemical Engineering, Québec, QC G1K 7P4, Canada. Offers M Sc, PhD. Terminal master's awarded for partial completion of doctoral program. *Degree requirements:* For master's, thesis (for some programs); for doctorate, comprehensive exam, thesis/dissertation. *Entrance requirements:* Additional exam requirements/recommendations for international students: Required—TOEFL (minimum score 500 paper-based). Electronic applications accepted.

University at Buffalo, the State University of New York, Graduate School, School of Engineering and Applied Sciences, Department of Chemical and Biological Engineering, Buffalo, NY 14260. Offers bioengineering nanotechnology (Certificate); chemical and biological engineering (ME, MS, PhD); nanomaterials and materials informatics (Certificate). *Program availability:* Part-time. *Degree requirements:* For master's, thesis (for some programs); for doctorate, comprehensive exam, thesis/dissertation. *Entrance requirements:* For master's and doctorate, GRE General Test. Additional exam requirements/recommendations for international students: Required—TOEFL (minimum score 550 paper-based; 79 iBT). Electronic applications accepted. *Faculty research:* Biochemical and biomedical engineering, nanoscale science and engineering, computational science and engineering.

The University of Akron, Graduate School, College of Engineering, Department of Chemical and Biomolecular Engineering, Akron, OH 44325. Offers chemical engineering (MS); engineering (PhD). *Program availability:* Part-time, evening/weekend. *Degree requirements:* For master's, thesis optional; for doctorate, one foreign language, thesis/dissertation, candidacy exam, qualifying exam. *Entrance requirements:* For master's, GRE, minimum GPA of 2.75, letters of recommendation, statement of purpose; for doctorate, GRE, minimum GPA of 3.0 with bachelor's degree, 3.5 with master's degree; letters of recommendation; personal statement; resume. Additional exam requirements/recommendations for international students: Required—TOEFL (minimum score 79 iBT), IELTS (minimum score 6.5). Electronic applications accepted. *Faculty research:* Renewable energy, fuel cell and CO2 sequestration, nanofiber synthesis and applications, materials for biomedical applications, engineering, surface characterization and modification.

The University of Alabama, Graduate School, College of Engineering, Department of Chemical and Biological Engineering, Tuscaloosa, AL 35487. Offers MS Ch E, PhD. Terminal master's awarded for partial completion of doctoral program. *Degree requirements:* For master's, comprehensive exam, thesis; for doctorate, comprehensive exam, thesis/dissertation. *Entrance requirements:* For master's, GRE, minimum GPA of 3.0 overall; for doctorate, GRE, minimum GPA of 3.0. Additional exam requirements/recommendations for international students: Required—TOEFL (minimum score 550 paper-based); Recommended—IELTS (minimum score 6.5). Electronic applications accepted. *Faculty research:* Nanotechnology, materials, electrochemistry, alternative energy, biological.

The University of Alabama in Huntsville, School of Graduate Studies, College of Engineering, Department of Chemical and Materials Engineering, Huntsville, AL 35899. Offers biotechnology science and engineering (PhD); chemical and materials engineering (MSE); materials science (PhD); mechanical engineering (PhD), including chemical engineering. *Program availability:* Part-time. *Faculty:* 3 full-time (1 woman), 1 part-time/adjunct. *Students:* 5 full-time (1 woman), 4 part-time (1 woman); includes 1 minority (Asian, non-Hispanic/Latino), 1 international. Average age 25. 12 applicants, 25% accepted, 2 enrolled. In 2018, 2 master's awarded. *Degree requirements:* For master's, comprehensive exam, thesis or alternative, oral and written exams; for doctorate, comprehensive exam, thesis/dissertation. *Entrance requirements:* For master's, GRE General Test, appropriate bachelor's degree, minimum GPA of 3.0; for doctorate, GRE General Test, minimum GPA of 3.0. Additional exam requirements/recommendations for international students: Required—TOEFL (minimum score 500 paper-based; 80 iBT), IELTS (minimum score 6.5). *Application deadline:* For fall admission, 7/15 priority date for domestic students, 4/1 priority date for international students; for spring admission, 11/30 priority date for domestic students, 9/1 priority date for international students. Applications are processed on a rolling basis. Application fee: $50. Electronic applications accepted. *Expenses: Tuition, area resident:* Full-time $10,632; part-time $412 per credit hour. Tuition, state resident: full-time $10,632. Tuition, nonresident: full-time $23,604; part-time $412 per credit hour. *Required fees:* $582; $582. Tuition and fees vary according to course load and program. *Financial support:* In 2018–19, 4 students received support, including 1 research assistantship with full tuition reimbursement available (averaging $2,500 per year), 3 teaching assistantships with full tuition reimbursements available (averaging $5,500 per year); career-related internships or fieldwork, Federal Work-Study, institutionally sponsored loans, scholarships/grants, health care benefits, and unspecified assistantships also available. Support available to part-time students. Financial award application deadline: 4/1; financial award applicants required to submit FAFSA. *Faculty research:* Ultrathin films for optical, sensor and biological applications; materials processing including low gravity; hypergolic reactants; computational fluid dynamics; biofuels and renewable resources. *Unit head:* Dr. Anuradha Subramanian, Chair, 256-824-6194, Fax: 256-824-6839, E-mail: anu.subramanian@uah.edu. *Application contact:* Kim Gray, Graduate Studies Admissions Coordinator, 256-824-6002, Fax: 256-824-6405, E-mail: deangrad@uah.edu.
Website: http://www.cme.uah.edu/

University of Alberta, Faculty of Graduate Studies and Research, Department of Chemical and Materials Engineering, Edmonton, AB T6G 2E1, Canada. Offers chemical engineering (M Eng, M Sc, PhD); materials engineering (M Eng, M Sc, PhD); process control (M Eng, M Sc, PhD); welding (M Eng). *Program availability:* Part-time, online learning. Terminal master's awarded for partial completion of doctoral program. *Degree requirements:* For master's, thesis; for doctorate, thesis/dissertation. *Faculty research:* Advanced materials and polymers, catalytic and reaction engineering, mineral processing, physical metallurgy, fluid mechanics.

The University of Arizona, College of Engineering, Department of Chemical and Environmental Engineering, Tucson, AZ 85721-0011. Offers chemical engineering (MS, PhD); environmental engineering (MS, PhD). *Program availability:* Part-time. *Degree requirements:* For master's, thesis; for doctorate, comprehensive exam, thesis/dissertation, departmental qualifying exams. *Entrance requirements:* For master's and doctorate, GRE General Test, 3 letters of recommendation, resume, statement of purpose. Additional exam requirements/recommendations for international students: Required—TOEFL (minimum score 550 paper-based; 79 iBT). Electronic applications accepted. *Faculty research:* Energy and environment-hazardous waste incineration, sustainability, kinetics, bioremediation, semiconductor processing.

University of Arkansas, Graduate School, College of Engineering, Department of Chemical Engineering, Fayetteville, AR 72701. Offers MS Ch E, MSE, PhD. *Program availability:* Part-time. In 2018, 7 master's, 4 doctorates awarded. *Degree requirements:* For master's, thesis optional; for doctorate, one foreign language, thesis/dissertation. *Entrance requirements:* For master's and doctorate, GRE General Test. *Application deadline:* For fall admission, 8/1 for domestic students, 4/1 for international students; for spring admission, 12/1 for domestic students, 10/1 for international students; for summer admission, 4/15 for domestic students, 3/1 for international students. Applications are processed on a rolling basis. Application fee: $60. Electronic applications accepted. *Financial support:* In 2018–19, 18 research assistantships were awarded; fellowships with tuition reimbursements, teaching assistantships, career-related internships or fieldwork, and Federal Work-Study also available. Support available to part-time students. Financial award application deadline: 4/1; financial award applicants required to submit FAFSA. *Unit head:* Dr. David M. Ford, Department Head, 479-575-4951, E-mail: daveford@uark.edu. *Application contact:* Dr. Christa Hestekin, Graduate Coordinator, 479-575-3416, E-mail: chesteki@uark.edu.
Website: https://chemical-engineering.uark.edu/

The University of British Columbia, Faculty of Applied Science, Department of Chemical and Biological Engineering, Vancouver, BC V6T 1Z3, Canada. Offers M Eng, M Sc, MA Sc, PhD. *Program availability:* Part-time, evening/weekend. *Degree requirements:* For master's, thesis (for some programs); for doctorate, thesis/dissertation. *Entrance requirements:* Additional exam requirements/recommendations for international students: Required—TOEFL, IELTS. Electronic applications accepted. *Expenses:* Contact institution. *Faculty research:* Biotechnology, catalysis, polymers, fluidization, pulp and paper.

University of Calgary, Faculty of Graduate Studies, Schulich School of Engineering, Program in Chemical and Petroleum Engineering, Calgary, AB T2N 1N4, Canada. Offers chemical engineering (M Eng, M Sc, PhD); energy and environment engineering (M Eng, M Sc, PhD); energy and environmental systems (M Eng, M Sc, PhD); environmental engineering (M Eng, M Sc, PhD); petroleum engineering (M Eng, M Sc, PhD); reservoir characterization (M Eng, M Sc). *Program availability:* Part-time. *Degree requirements:* For master's, thesis (for some programs); for doctorate, comprehensive exam, thesis/dissertation, candidacy exam. *Entrance requirements:* For master's, minimum GPA of 3.0 or equivalent; for doctorate, minimum GPA of 3.5 or equivalent. Additional exam requirements/recommendations for international students: Required—TOEFL (minimum score 550 paper-based; 80 iBT), IELTS (minimum score 7). Electronic applications accepted. *Faculty research:* Environmental engineering, biomedical engineering modeling, simulation and control, petroleum recovery and reservoir engineering, phase equilibria and transport properties.

University of California, Berkeley, Graduate Division, College of Chemistry, Department of Chemical and Biomolecular Engineering, Berkeley, CA 94720. Offers chemical engineering (PhD); product development (MS). Terminal master's awarded for partial completion of doctoral program. *Degree requirements:* For master's, comprehensive exam (for some programs), thesis (for some programs); for doctorate, thesis/dissertation, qualifying exam. *Entrance requirements:* For master's and doctorate, GRE General Test, minimum GPA of 3.0, 3 letters of recommendation. Additional exam requirements/recommendations for international students: Required—TOEFL (minimum score 570 paper-based; 90 iBT). Electronic applications accepted. *Faculty research:* Biochemical engineering, electrochemical engineering, electronic materials, heterogeneous catalysis and reaction engineering, complex fluids.

University of California, Davis, College of Engineering, Program in Chemical Engineering, Davis, CA 95616. Offers MS, PhD. Terminal master's awarded for partial completion of doctoral program. *Degree requirements:* For master's, comprehensive exam (for some programs), thesis (for some programs); for doctorate, thesis/dissertation. *Entrance requirements:* For master's and doctorate, GRE General Test, minimum GPA of 3.0. Additional exam requirements/recommendations for international students: Required—TOEFL (minimum score 550 paper-based). Electronic applications accepted. *Faculty research:* Transport phenomena, colloid science, catalysis, biotechnology, materials.

University of California, Irvine, Samueli School of Engineering, Department of Chemical Engineering and Materials Science, Irvine, CA 92697. Offers chemical and biochemical engineering (MS, PhD); materials science and engineering (MS, PhD). *Program availability:* Part-time. *Students:* 133 full-time (57 women), 2 part-time (0 women); includes 36 minority (3 Black or African American, non-Hispanic/Latino; 26 Asian, non-Hispanic/Latino; 5 Hispanic/Latino; 2 Two or more races, non-Hispanic/Latino), 51 international. Average age 26. 417 applicants, 35% accepted, 36 enrolled. In 2018, 30 master's, 26 doctorates awarded. Terminal master's awarded for partial completion of doctoral program. *Entrance requirements:* For master's and doctorate, GRE General Test, minimum GPA of 3.0, 3 letters of recommendation. Additional exam requirements/recommendations for international students: Required—TOEFL (minimum score 550 paper-based). *Application deadline:* For fall admission, 1/15 priority date for domestic students, 1/15 for international students. Applications are processed on a rolling basis. Application fee: $105 ($125 for international students). Electronic applications accepted. *Financial support:* Fellowships, research assistantships with full tuition reimbursements, teaching assistantships, institutionally sponsored loans, traineeships, health care benefits, and unspecified assistantships available. Financial award application deadline: 3/1; financial award applicants required to submit FAFSA. *Faculty research:* Molecular biotechnology, nanobiomaterials, biophotonics, synthesis, super plasticity and mechanical behavior, characterization of advanced and nanostructural materials. *Unit head:* Prof. Vasan Venugopalan, Chair, 949-824-5802, Fax: 949-824-2541, E-mail: vvenugop@uci.edu. *Application contact:* Grace Chau, Academic Program and Graduate Admission Coordinator, 949-824-3887, Fax: 949-824-2541, E-mail: chaug@uci.edu.
Website: http://www.eng.uci.edu/dept/chems

University of California, Los Angeles, Graduate Division, Henry Samueli School of Engineering and Applied Science, Department of Chemical and Biomolecular Engineering, Los Angeles, CA 90095-1592. Offers MS, PhD. *Degree requirements:* For master's, comprehensive exam (for some programs), thesis (for some programs); for doctorate, thesis/dissertation, qualifying exams. *Entrance requirements:* For master's, GRE General Test, minimum GPA of 3.0; for doctorate, GRE General Test, minimum GPA of 3.25. Additional exam requirements/recommendations for international students: Required—TOEFL (minimum score 560 paper-based; 87 iBT), IELTS (minimum score 7). Electronic applications accepted. *Faculty research:* Biomolecular engineering, renewable energy, water technology, advanced materials processing, process systems engineering.

University of California, Riverside, Graduate Division, Department of Chemical and Environmental Engineering, Riverside, CA 92521-0102. Offers MS, PhD. *Program availability:* Part-time. Terminal master's awarded for partial completion of doctoral program. *Degree requirements:* For master's, thesis (for some programs); for doctorate, comprehensive exam, thesis/dissertation. *Entrance requirements:* For master's and doctorate, GRE General Test, minimum GPA of 3.0. Additional exam requirements/recommendations for international students: Required—TOEFL (minimum score 550 paper-based; 80 iBT). Electronic applications accepted. *Faculty research:* Air quality systems, water quality systems, advanced materials and nanotechnology, energy systems/alternative fuels, theory and molecular modeling.

University of California, San Diego, Graduate Division, Program in Chemical Engineering, La Jolla, CA 92093. Offers MS, PhD. *Students:* 54 full-time (10 women), 7 part-time (1 woman). 228 applicants, 44% accepted, 24 enrolled. In 2018, 43 master's, 1 doctorate awarded. *Degree requirements:* For master's, comprehensive exam (for some programs), thesis (for some programs); for doctorate, comprehensive exam, thesis/dissertation, 1-quarter teaching assistantship. *Entrance requirements:* For master's, GRE General Test; for doctorate, GRE General Test, statement of purpose. Additional exam requirements/recommendations for international students: Required—TOEFL (minimum score 550 paper-based; 80 iBT), IELTS (minimum score 7). *Application deadline:* For fall admission, 3/21 for domestic students. Application fee: $105 ($125 for international students). Electronic applications accepted. *Financial support:* Fellowships, research assistantships, teaching assistantships, scholarships/grants, and readerships available. Financial award applicants required to submit FAFSA. *Faculty research:* Regenerative medicine, development of new microfluidic devices, biomedical modeling, solar thermochemical hydrogen production. *Unit head:* Joseph Wang, Chair, 858-882-7640, E-mail: josephwang@ucsd.edu. *Application contact:* Dana Jimenez, Graduate Coordinator, 858-822-7981, E-mail: dljimenez@ucsd.edu.
Website: http://nanoengineering.ucsd.edu/graduate-programs/degree/chemical-engineering

University of California, Santa Barbara, Graduate Division, College of Engineering, Department of Chemical Engineering, Santa Barbara, CA 93106. Offers MS, PhD. *Degree requirements:* For master's, thesis or comprehensive exam; for doctorate, thesis/dissertation, research progress reports (prior to candidacy), candidacy exam, thesis defense, seminar. *Entrance requirements:* For doctorate, GRE. Additional exam requirements/recommendations for international students: Required—TOEFL (minimum score 560 paper-based; 83 iBT), IELTS (minimum score 7). Electronic applications accepted. *Faculty research:* Biomaterials and bioengineering; energy, catalysis and reaction engineering; complex fluids and polymers; electronic and optical materials; fluids and transport phenomena; molecular thermodynamics and simulation; process systems engineering; surfaces and interfacial phenomena.

University of Cincinnati, Graduate School, College of Engineering and Applied Science, Department of Biomedical, Chemical and Environmental Engineering, Program in Chemical Engineering, Cincinnati, OH 45221. Offers MS, PhD. *Program availability:* Part-time, evening/weekend. Terminal master's awarded for partial completion of doctoral program. *Degree requirements:* For master's, thesis; for doctorate, thesis/dissertation. *Entrance requirements:* For master's and doctorate, GRE General Test. Additional exam requirements/recommendations for international students: Required—TOEFL (minimum score 600 paper-based).

University of Colorado Boulder, Graduate School, College of Engineering and Applied Science, Department of Chemical and Biological Engineering, Boulder, CO 80309. Offers ME, MS, PhD. Terminal master's awarded for partial completion of doctoral program. *Degree requirements:* For master's, comprehensive exam, thesis; for doctorate, thesis/dissertation. *Entrance requirements:* For master's, minimum undergraduate GPA of 3.0. Electronic applications accepted. Application fee is waived when completed online. *Faculty research:* Chemical engineering; materials engineering; interfacial phenomena; bioengineering; catalysis/kinetics.

University of Connecticut, Graduate School, School of Engineering, Department of Chemical and Biomolecular Engineering, Storrs, CT 06269. Offers MS, PhD. Terminal master's awarded for partial completion of doctoral program. *Degree requirements:* For master's, comprehensive exam, thesis or alternative; for doctorate, thesis/dissertation. *Entrance requirements:* For master's and doctorate, GRE General Test. Additional exam requirements/recommendations for international students: Required—TOEFL (minimum score 550 paper-based). Electronic applications accepted.

University of Dayton, Department of Chemical Engineering, Dayton, OH 45469. Offers bioengineering (MS); chemical engineering (MS Ch E). *Program availability:* Part-time, online learning. *Degree requirements:* For master's, thesis for 33 credit hours. *Entrance requirements:* For master's, GRE (preferred), minimum GPA of 3.0 as undergraduate, transcript, 3 letters of recommendation, bachelor's degree in chemical engineering (preferred). Additional exam requirements/recommendations for international students: Required—TOEFL (minimum score 550 paper-based; 80 iBT); Recommended—IELTS. Electronic applications accepted. *Expenses:* Contact institution. *Faculty research:* Process control modeling/mixing; multiphase flow data analysis; chemical reaction biocatalysts enhanced in vitro models.

University of Delaware, College of Engineering, Department of Chemical Engineering, Newark, DE 19716. Offers M Ch E, PhD. *Program availability:* Part-time, evening/weekend, online learning. Terminal master's awarded for partial completion of doctoral program. *Degree requirements:* For master's, thesis (for some programs); for doctorate, thesis/dissertation. *Entrance requirements:* For master's and doctorate, GRE General Test. Additional exam requirements/recommendations for international students: Required—TOEFL. Electronic applications accepted. *Faculty research:* Biochemical/biomedical engineer, thermodynamics, polymers/composites, materials, catalysis/reactions, colloid/interfaces, expert systems/process control.

University of Florida, Graduate School, Herbert Wertheim College of Engineering, Department of Chemical Engineering, Gainesville, FL 32611. Offers ME, MS, PhD, Engr. *Program availability:* Part-time. Terminal master's awarded for partial completion of doctoral program. *Degree requirements:* For master's, thesis optional; for doctorate, comprehensive exam, thesis/dissertation. *Entrance requirements:* For master's and doctorate, minimum GPA of 3.0. Additional exam requirements/recommendations for international students: Required—TOEFL (minimum score 550 paper-based; 80 iBT), IELTS (minimum score 6). Electronic applications accepted. *Faculty research:* Complex fluids and interfacial and colloidal phenomena; materials for biological, energy and

microelectronic applications; catalysis and reaction kinetics; transport and electrochemistry; biomolecular research including biomechanics, signal transduction, and tissue engineering.

University of Houston, Cullen College of Engineering, Department of Chemical and Biomolecular Engineering, Houston, TX 77204. Offers chemical engineering (MCHE, PhD); petroleum engineering (M Pet E). *Program availability:* Part-time. Terminal master's awarded for partial completion of doctoral program. *Entrance requirements:* For master's and doctorate, GRE General Test. Additional exam requirements/recommendations for international students: Required—TOEFL (minimum score 550 paper-based; 79 iBT), IELTS (minimum score 6.5). *Faculty research:* Chemical engineering.

University of Idaho, College of Graduate Studies, College of Engineering, Department of Chemical and Materials Engineering, Moscow, ID 83844-1021. Offers chemical engineering (M Engr, MS, PhD); materials science and engineering (PhD). *Faculty:* 14. *Students:* 27 full-time (5 women), 6 part-time (0 women). Average age 30. In 2018, 7 master's, 1 doctorate awarded. *Entrance requirements:* For master's and doctorate, GRE, minimum GPA of 3.0. Additional exam requirements/recommendations for international students: Required—TOEFL (minimum score 79 iBT). *Application deadline:* For fall admission, 8/1 for domestic students; for spring admission, 12/15 for domestic students. Applications are processed on a rolling basis. Application fee: $60. Electronic applications accepted. *Expenses:* Tuition, state resident: full-time $7266.44; part-time $474.50 per credit hour. Tuition, nonresident: full-time $24,902; part-time $1453.50 per credit hour. *Required fees:* $2085.56; $45.50 per credit hour. *Financial support:* Fellowships, research assistantships, and teaching assistantships available. Financial award applicants required to submit FAFSA. *Faculty research:* High temperature mechanical behavior of materials, polyampholyte polymers, multi-scale modeling of materials. *Unit head:* Dr. Eric Aston, Department Chair, 208-885-7572, E-mail: che@uidaho.edu. *Application contact:* Dr. Eric Aston, Department Chair, 208-885-7572, E-mail: che@uidaho.edu.
Website: https://www.uidaho.edu/engr/departments/cme

University of Illinois at Chicago, College of Engineering, Department of Chemical Engineering, Chicago, IL 60607-7128. Offers MS, PhD. *Program availability:* Part-time. *Degree requirements:* For master's, thesis or project; for doctorate, thesis/dissertation, departmental qualifying exam. *Entrance requirements:* For master's and doctorate, GRE General Test, minimum GPA of 2.75. Additional exam requirements/recommendations for international students: Required—TOEFL. *Expenses:* Contact institution. *Faculty research:* Multiphase flows, interfacial transport, heterogeneous catalysis, coal technology, molecular and static thermodynamics.

University of Illinois at Urbana–Champaign, Graduate College, College of Liberal Arts and Sciences, School of Chemical Sciences, Department of Chemical and Biomolecular Engineering, Champaign, IL 61820. Offers bioinformatics: chemical and biomolecular engineering (MS); chemical engineering (MS, PhD). *Entrance requirements:* For master's, minimum GPA of 3.0.

The University of Iowa, Graduate College, College of Engineering, Department of Chemical and Biochemical Engineering, Iowa City, IA 52242-1316. Offers MS, PhD. *Program availability:* Part-time. *Degree requirements:* For master's, comprehensive exam (for some programs), thesis (for some programs); for doctorate, comprehensive exam, thesis/dissertation. *Entrance requirements:* For master's and doctorate, GRE (minimum combined score of 310 on verbal and quantitative), minimum undergraduate GPA of 3.0. Additional exam requirements/recommendations for international students: Required—TOEFL (minimum score 600 paper-based; 100 iBT), IELTS (minimum score 7). Electronic applications accepted. *Faculty research:* Polymeric materials, photo polymerization, atmospheric chemistry and air pollution, biochemical engineering, bioprocessing and biomedical engineering.

The University of Kansas, Graduate Studies, School of Engineering, Program in Chemical and Petroleum Engineering, Lawrence, KS 66045. Offers chemical and petroleum engineering (PhD); chemical engineering (MS); petroleum engineering (MS); petroleum management (Certificate). *Program availability:* Part-time. *Students:* 37 full-time (13 women), 2 part-time (1 woman); includes 1 minority (Black or African American, non-Hispanic/Latino), 31 international. Average age 28. 29 applicants, 41% accepted, 3 enrolled. In 2018, 3 doctorates awarded. *Entrance requirements:* For master's, GRE General Test, minimum GPA of 3.0, resume, personal statement, transcripts, three letters of recommendation; for doctorate, GRE General Test, minimum GPA of 3.5, resume, personal statement, transcripts, three letters of recommendation. Additional exam requirements/recommendations for international students: Required—TOEFL, IELTS. *Application deadline:* For fall admission, 12/15 priority date for domestic and international students; for spring admission, 8/31 priority date for domestic and international students. Application fee: $65 ($85 for international students). Electronic applications accepted. *Financial support:* Fellowships, research assistantships, teaching assistantships, career-related internships or fieldwork, Federal Work-Study, scholarships/grants, traineeships and unspecified assistantships available. Financial award application deadline: 12/15; financial award applicants required to submit FAFSA. *Faculty research:* Enhanced oil recovery, catalysis and kinetics, electrochemical engineering, biomedical engineering, semiconductor materials processing. *Unit head:* Laurence R Weatherley, Chair, 785-864-3553, E-mail: lweather@ku.edu. *Application contact:* Martha Kehr, Graduate Admission Contact, 785-864-2900, E-mail: cpegrad@ku.edu.
Website: http://www.cpe.engr.ku.edu

The University of Kansas, Graduate Studies, School of Engineering, Program in Chemical Engineering, Lawrence, KS 66045. Offers MS. *Program availability:* Part-time. *Students:* 9 full-time (4 women), 2 part-time (0 women), 5 international. Average age 25. 9 applicants, 33% accepted, 1 enrolled. In 2018, 1 master's awarded. *Entrance requirements:* For master's, GRE, resume, personal statement, transcripts, three letters of recommendation. Additional exam requirements/recommendations for international students: Required—TOEFL, IELTS. *Application deadline:* For fall admission, 12/15 priority date for domestic and international students; for spring admission, 8/31 for domestic and international students. Application fee: $65 ($85 for international students). Electronic applications accepted. *Financial support:* Fellowships, research assistantships, teaching assistantships, Federal Work-Study, and scholarships/grants available. Financial award application deadline: 12/15. *Unit head:* Laurence R Weatherley, Chair, 785-864-3553, E-mail: lweather@ku.edu. *Application contact:* Martha Kehr, Graduate Admissions Contact, 785-864-2900, E-mail: cpegrad@ku.edu.
Website: http://www.cpe.engr.ku.edu/

University of Kentucky, Graduate School, College of Engineering, Program in Chemical Engineering, Lexington, KY 40506-0032. Offers MS, PhD. *Degree requirements:* For master's, comprehensive exam, thesis optional; for doctorate, comprehensive exam, thesis/dissertation. *Entrance requirements:* For master's, GRE General Test, minimum undergraduate GPA of 2.75; for doctorate, GRE General Test, minimum undergraduate GPA of 3.0. Additional exam requirements/recommendations for international students: Required—TOEFL (minimum score 550 paper-based). Electronic applications accepted. *Faculty research:* Aerosol physics and chemistry, biocellular engineering fuel science, poly and membrane science.

Chemical Engineering

University of Louisiana at Lafayette, College of Engineering, Department of Chemical Engineering, Lafayette, LA 70504. Offers MSE. *Program availability:* Evening/weekend. *Degree requirements:* For master's, comprehensive exam, thesis or alternative. *Entrance requirements:* For master's, GRE General Test, BS in chemical engineering, minimum GPA of 2.85. Additional exam requirements/recommendations for international students: Required—TOEFL (minimum score 550 paper-based). Electronic applications accepted. *Faculty research:* Corrosion, transport phenomena and thermodynamics in the oil and gas industry.

University of Louisville, J. B. Speed School of Engineering, Department of Chemical Engineering, Louisville, KY 40292-0001. Offers M Eng, MS, PhD. *Accreditation:* ABET (one or more programs are accredited). *Faculty:* 10 full-time (1 woman). *Students:* 34 full-time (7 women), 7 part-time (2 women); includes 6 minority (1 Black or African American, non-Hispanic/Latino; 1 Asian, non-Hispanic/Latino; 1 Hispanic/Latino; 3 Two or more races, non-Hispanic/Latino), 14 international. Average age 28. 21 applicants, 24% accepted, 5 enrolled. In 2018, 14 master's awarded. Terminal master's awarded for partial completion of doctoral program. *Degree requirements:* For master's, thesis optional; for doctorate, comprehensive exam, thesis/dissertation. *Entrance requirements:* For master's and doctorate, GRE, Two letters of recommendation. All final official transcripts. Additional exam requirements/recommendations for international students: Required—TOEFL (minimum score 550 paper-based; 80 iBT), IELTS (minimum score 6.5), GRE. *Application deadline:* For fall admission, 5/1 priority date for domestic and international students; for spring admission, 11/1 priority date for domestic and international students; for summer admission, 3/1 priority date for domestic and international students. Applications are processed on a rolling basis. Application fee: $65. Electronic applications accepted. *Expenses: Tuition, area resident:* Full-time $6500; part-time $723 per credit hour. Tuition, state resident: full-time $6500. Tuition, nonresident: full-time $13,557; part-time $1507 per credit hour. Tuition and fees vary according to course load and program. *Financial support:* In 2018–19, 33 students received support. Fellowships, research assistantships, teaching assistantships, scholarships/grants, and health care benefits available. Financial award application deadline: 1/1. *Faculty research:* Biomaterials, Biofuels & Bio-Products, Bioprocessing, Fuel Cells, Membranes, Polymers. *Total annual research expenditures:* $926,743. *Unit head:* Dr. Joel R. Fried, Chair, 502-852-6347, Fax: 502-852-6355, E-mail: joel.fried@louisville.edu. *Application contact:* R. Eric Berson, Director of Graduate Studies, 502-852-1567, E-mail: eric.berson@louisville.edu.
Website: http://louisville.edu/speed/chemical/

University of Maine, Graduate School, College of Engineering, Chemical and Biomedical Engineering, Orono, ME 04469. Offers chemical engineering (MS, PhD). *Program availability:* Part-time. *Faculty:* 14 full-time (2 women). *Students:* 23 full-time (12 women), 1 part-time (0 women); includes 2 minority (both Asian, non-Hispanic/Latino), 9 international. Average age 26. 27 applicants, 41% accepted, 5 enrolled. In 2018, 9 master's, 2 doctorates awarded. Terminal master's awarded for partial completion of doctoral program. *Degree requirements:* For master's, thesis; for doctorate, comprehensive exam, thesis/dissertation. *Entrance requirements:* For master's and doctorate, GRE General Test. Additional exam requirements/recommendations for international students: Required—TOEFL. *Application deadline:* For fall admission, 5/1 priority date for domestic students, 3/1 priority date for international students; for spring admission, 10/1 priority date for domestic students, 9/1 priority date for international students; for summer admission, 3/1 for domestic students, 1/1 for international students. Applications are processed on a rolling basis. Application fee: $65. Electronic applications accepted. *Financial support:* In 2018–19, 40 students received support, including 27 research assistantships with full tuition reimbursements available (averaging $18,700 per year), 7 teaching assistantships with full tuition reimbursements available (averaging $15,600 per year); Federal Work-Study, tuition waivers (full and partial), and unspecified assistantships also available. Financial award application deadline: 3/1. *Faculty research:* Catalysts, pulp and paper, cellulose nanomaterials, coatings, biological interactions. *Total annual research expenditures:* $5.8 million. *Unit head:* Dr. Hemant Pendse, Chair, 207-581-2290, Fax: 207-581-2323, E-mail: pendse@maine.edu. *Application contact:* Scott G. Delcourt, Assistant Vice President for Graduate Studies and Senior Associate Dean, 207-581-3291, Fax: 207-581-3232, E-mail: graduate@maine.edu.
Website: https://umaine.edu/chb/

The University of Manchester, School of Chemical Engineering and Analytical Science, Manchester, United Kingdom. Offers biocatalysis (M Phil, PhD); chemical engineering (M Phil, PhD); chemical engineering and analytical science (M Phil, D Eng, PhD); colloids, crystals, interfaces and materials (M Phil, PhD); environment and sustainable technology (M Phil, PhD); instrumentation (M Phil, PhD); multi-scale modeling (M Phil, PhD); process integration (M Phil, PhD); systems biology (M Phil, PhD).

University of Maryland, Baltimore County, The Graduate School, College of Engineering and Information Technology, Department of Chemical, Biochemical, and Environmental Engineering, Program in Chemical and Biochemical Engineering, Baltimore, MD 21250. Offers MS, PhD. *Program availability:* Part-time. *Degree requirements:* For master's, comprehensive exam (for some programs), thesis (for some programs); for doctorate, comprehensive exam, thesis/dissertation. *Entrance requirements:* For master's, GRE General Test, minimum GPA of 3.0, strong mathematical background; for doctorate, GRE General Test (taken within last 5 years), minimum GPA of 3.0. Additional exam requirements/recommendations for international students: Required—TOEFL (minimum score 550 paper-based; 80 iBT). Electronic applications accepted. Application fee is waived when completed online. *Expenses:* Contact institution. *Faculty research:* Biomedical engineering; biochemical engineering.

University of Maryland, College Park, Academic Affairs, A. James Clark School of Engineering, Department of Chemical and Biomolecular Engineering, College Park, MD 20742. Offers bioengineering (MS, PhD); chemical engineering (M Eng, MS, PhD). *Program availability:* Part-time, evening/weekend. *Degree requirements:* For master's, thesis optional; for doctorate, variable foreign language requirement, thesis/dissertation, exam, oral presentation. *Entrance requirements:* For master's and doctorate, GRE General Test, 3 letters of recommendation. Additional exam requirements/recommendations for international students: Required—TOEFL. Electronic applications accepted. *Faculty research:* Applied polymer science, biochemical engineering, thermal properties, bioprocess monitoring.

University of Massachusetts Amherst, Graduate School, College of Engineering, Department of Chemical Engineering, Amherst, MA 01003. Offers MSChE, PhD. *Program availability:* Part-time. Terminal master's awarded for partial completion of doctoral program. *Degree requirements:* For master's, thesis; for doctorate, comprehensive exam, thesis/dissertation. *Entrance requirements:* For master's and doctorate, GRE General Test. Additional exam requirements/recommendations for international students: Required—TOEFL (minimum score 550 paper-based; 80 iBT), IELTS (minimum score 6.5). Electronic applications accepted.

University of Massachusetts Lowell, Francis College of Engineering, Department of Chemical Engineering, Lowell, MA 01854. Offers MS Eng, PhD. *Program availability:* Part-time. *Degree requirements:* For master's, thesis; for doctorate, thesis/dissertation, seminar, qualifying examination. *Entrance requirements:* For master's, GRE General Test. Electronic applications accepted. *Faculty research:* Biotechnology/bioprocessing, nanomaterials, ceramic materials, materials characterization.

University of Michigan, College of Engineering, Department of Chemical Engineering, Ann Arbor, MI 48109. Offers MSE, PhD, Ch E. *Program availability:* Part-time. *Students:* 162 full-time (61 women), 2 part-time (1 woman). 505 applicants, 25% accepted, 47 enrolled. In 2018, 36 master's, 21 doctorates awarded. Terminal master's awarded for partial completion of doctoral program. *Degree requirements:* For doctorate, thesis/dissertation, oral defense of dissertation, preliminary exams. *Entrance requirements:* For master's and doctorate, GRE General Test. Additional exam requirements/recommendations for international students: Required—TOEFL. *Application deadline:* Applications are processed on a rolling basis. Electronic applications accepted. *Financial support:* Fellowships, research assistantships, teaching assistantships, scholarships/grants, traineeships, health care benefits, tuition waivers (partial), and unspecified assistantships available. Financial award applicants required to submit FAFSA. *Faculty research:* Life sciences and biotechnology, energy and environment, complex fluids and nanostructured materials. *Total annual research expenditures:* $19.7 million. *Unit head:* Sharon Glotzer, Department Chair, 734-936-3314, E-mail: glotzerchair@umich.edu. *Application contact:* Susan Hamlin, Graduate Program Coordinator, 734-763-1148, Fax: 734-764-7453, E-mail: hamlins@umich.edu.
Website: https://che.engin.umich.edu/

University of Minnesota, Twin Cities Campus, College of Science and Engineering, Department of Chemical Engineering and Materials Science, Program in Chemical Engineering, Minneapolis, MN 55455-0132. Offers M Ch E, MS Ch E, PhD. *Program availability:* Part-time. Terminal master's awarded for partial completion of doctoral program. *Degree requirements:* For master's, thesis; for doctorate, thesis/dissertation. *Entrance requirements:* For master's and doctorate, GRE General Test. Additional exam requirements/recommendations for international students: Required—TOEFL. Electronic applications accepted. *Faculty research:* Biotechnology and bioengineering, chemical kinetics, reaction engineering and chemical process synthesis.

University of Mississippi, Graduate School, School of Engineering, University, MS 38677. Offers aeroacoustics (MS, PhD); chemical engineering (MS, PhD); civil engineering (MS, PhD); computational hydroscience (MS, PhD); computer science (MS, PhD); electrical engineering (MS, PhD); electromagnetics (MS, PhD); environmental engineering (MS, PhD); geology and geological engineering (MS, PhD); hydrology (MS); material science (MS); mechanical engineering (MS, PhD); telecommunications (MS). *Faculty:* 76 full-time (16 women), 3 part-time/adjunct (1 woman). *Students:* 129 full-time (33 women), 21 part-time (5 women); includes 15 minority (7 Black or African American, non-Hispanic/Latino; 6 Asian, non-Hispanic/Latino; 1 Hispanic/Latino; 1 Two or more races, non-Hispanic/Latino), 73 international. Average age 29. In 2018, 36 master's, 17 doctorates awarded. *Entrance requirements:* For master's, GRE General Test, minimum GPA of 3.0; for doctorate, GRE General Test. Additional exam requirements/recommendations for international students: Required—TOEFL. *Application deadline:* Applications are processed on a rolling basis. Application fee: $50. Electronic applications accepted. *Financial support:* Scholarships/grants available. Financial award application deadline: 3/1; financial award applicants required to submit FAFSA. *Unit head:* Dr. David Puleo, Dean, 662-915-5780, Fax: 662-915-5387, E-mail: engineer@olemiss.edu. *Application contact:* Temeka Smith, Graduate Activities Specialist for Admissions, 662-915-7474, Fax: 662-915-7577, E-mail: gschool@olemiss.edu.

University of Missouri, Office of Research and Graduate Studies, College of Engineering, Department of Biomedical, Biological and Chemical Engineering, Columbia, MO 65211. Offers biological engineering (MS, PhD); chemical engineering (MS, PhD). *Entrance requirements:* For master's and doctorate, GRE General Test, minimum GPA of 3.0. Additional exam requirements/recommendations for international students: Required—TOEFL.

University of Nebraska–Lincoln, Graduate College, College of Engineering, Department of Chemical and Biomolecular Engineering, Lincoln, NE 68588. Offers MS, PhD. *Degree requirements:* For master's, thesis; for doctorate, comprehensive exam, thesis/dissertation. *Entrance requirements:* For master's and doctorate, GRE. Additional exam requirements/recommendations for international students: Required—TOEFL (minimum score 550 paper-based). Electronic applications accepted. *Faculty research:* Fermentation, radioactive waste remediation, chemical fuels from renewable feedstocks.

University of Nevada, Reno, Graduate School, College of Engineering, Department of Chemical and Materials Engineering, Program in Chemical Engineering, Reno, NV 89557. Offers MS, PhD. Terminal master's awarded for partial completion of doctoral program. *Degree requirements:* For master's, comprehensive exam, thesis optional; for doctorate, thesis/dissertation. *Entrance requirements:* For master's, GRE General Test, minimum GPA of 2.75; for doctorate, GRE General Test, minimum GPA of 3.0. Additional exam requirements/recommendations for international students: Required—TOEFL (minimum score 500 paper-based; 61 iBT), IELTS (minimum score 6). Electronic applications accepted. *Faculty research:* Energy conservation, fuel efficiency, development and fabrication of new materials.

University of New Brunswick Fredericton, School of Graduate Studies, Faculty of Engineering, Department of Chemical Engineering, Fredericton, NB E3B 5A3, Canada. Offers chemical engineering (M Eng, M Sc E, PhD); environmental studies (M Eng). *Program availability:* Part-time. *Degree requirements:* For master's, thesis; for doctorate, comprehensive exam, thesis/dissertation, qualifying exam. *Entrance requirements:* For master's and doctorate, minimum GPA of 3.0. Additional exam requirements/recommendations for international students: Required—TOEFL (minimum score 580 paper-based), TWE (minimum score 5), Michigan English Language Assessment Battery (minimum score 85) or CanTest (minimum score 4.5). Electronic applications accepted. *Faculty research:* Processing and characterizing nanoengineered composite materials based on carbon nanotubes, enhanced oil recovery processes and oil sweep strategies for conventional and heavy oils, pulp and paper, waste-water treatment, chemistry and corrosion of high and lower temperature water systems, adsorption, aquaculture systems, bioprocessing and biomass refining, nanotechnologies, nuclear, oil and gas, polymer and recirculation.

University of New Hampshire, Graduate School, College of Engineering and Physical Sciences, Department of Chemical Engineering, Durham, NH 03824. Offers M Engr, MS, PhD. *Entrance requirements:* For master's and doctorate, GRE. Additional exam requirements/recommendations for international students: Required—TOEFL (minimum score 550 paper-based; 80 iBT). Electronic applications accepted.

University of New Mexico, Graduate Studies, School of Engineering, Program in Chemical Engineering, Albuquerque, NM 87131-2039. Offers MS, PhD. *Program availability:* Part-time. Terminal master's awarded for partial completion of doctoral program. *Degree requirements:* For master's, thesis (for some programs); for doctorate, comprehensive exam, thesis/dissertation, qualifying exam. *Entrance requirements:* For master's, GRE General Test, minimum GPA of 3.0, 3 letters of reference, letter of intent; for doctorate, GRE General Test, 3 letters of reference, minimum GPA of 3.0, letter of intent. Additional exam requirements/recommendations for international students: Required—TOEFL. Electronic applications accepted. *Faculty research:* Bioanalytical systems, ceramics, catalysis, colloidal science, bioengineering, biomaterials, fuel cells, protein engineering, semiconductors, tissue engineering.

University of North Dakota, Graduate School, School of Engineering and Mines, Department of Chemical Engineering, Grand Forks, ND 58202. Offers M Engr, MS, PhD. *Program availability:* Part-time. *Degree requirements:* For master's, comprehensive exam, thesis or alternative. *Entrance requirements:* For master's, GRE General Test, minimum GPA of 3.0 (MS), 2.5 (M Engr). Additional exam requirements/recommendations for international students: Required—TOEFL (minimum score 550 paper-based; 79 iBT), IELTS (minimum score 6.5). Electronic applications accepted. *Faculty research:* Catalysis, fluid flow and heat transfer, application of fractals, modeling and simulation, reaction engineering.

University of Notre Dame, The Graduate School, College of Engineering, Department of Chemical and Biomolecular Engineering, Notre Dame, IN 46556. Offers MS Ch E, PhD. *Degree requirements:* For master's, comprehensive exam, thesis; for doctorate, comprehensive exam, thesis/dissertation, candidacy exam. *Entrance requirements:* For master's, GRE General Test; for doctorate, GRE General Test, GRE Subject Test (strongly recommended). Additional exam requirements/recommendations for international students: Required—TOEFL (minimum score 600 paper-based; 80 iBT). Electronic applications accepted. *Faculty research:* Biomolecular engineering, green chemistry and engineering for the environment, advanced materials, nanoengineering, catalysis and reaction engineering.

University of Ottawa, Faculty of Graduate and Postdoctoral Studies, Faculty of Engineering, Department of Chemical and Biological Engineering, Ottawa, ON K1N 6N5, Canada. Offers M Eng, MA Sc, PhD. *Degree requirements:* For master's, thesis or alternative; for doctorate, comprehensive exam, thesis/dissertation. *Entrance requirements:* For master's, honors degree or equivalent, minimum B average; for doctorate, master's degree, minimum B+ average. Electronic applications accepted. *Faculty research:* Material development, process engineering, clean technologies.

University of Pennsylvania, School of Engineering and Applied Science, Department of Chemical and Biomolecular Engineering, Philadelphia, PA 19104. Offers MSE, PhD. *Program availability:* Part-time. *Students:* Average age 25. 429 applicants, 31% accepted, 55 enrolled. In 2018, 14 master's, 12 doctorates awarded. Terminal master's awarded for partial completion of doctoral program. *Degree requirements:* For master's, comprehensive exam, thesis optional; for doctorate, comprehensive exam, thesis/dissertation. *Entrance requirements:* For master's and doctorate, GRE, bachelor's degree, letters of recommendation, resume, personal statement. Additional exam requirements/recommendations for international students: Required—TOEFL (minimum score 100 iBT), IELTS (minimum score 7). *Application deadline:* For fall admission, 12/15 priority date for domestic and international students. Application fee: $80. Electronic applications accepted. *Expenses:* Contact institution. *Faculty research:* Advanced materials and nanotechnology, catalysis and reaction engineering, cellular and biomolecular engineering, energy and environmental engineering, soft matter and complex fluids. *Application contact:* William Fenton, Assistant Director of Graduate Admissions, 215-898-4542, Fax: 215-573-5577, E-mail: gradstudies@seas.upenn.edu. Website: http://www.cbe.seas.upenn.edu/prospective-students/masters/index.php

University of Pittsburgh, Swanson School of Engineering, Department of Chemical and Petroleum Engineering, Pittsburgh, PA 15260. Offers chemical engineering (MS Ch E, PhD); petroleum engineering (MSPE); MS Ch E/MSPE. *Program availability:* Part-time, 100% online. Terminal master's awarded for partial completion of doctoral program. *Degree requirements:* For doctorate, comprehensive exam, thesis/dissertation, final oral exams. *Entrance requirements:* For master's and doctorate, GRE General Test, minimum GPA of 3.0. Additional exam requirements/recommendations for international students: Required—TOEFL (minimum score 550 paper-based; 80 iBT). Electronic applications accepted. *Expenses:* Contact institution. *Faculty research:* Biotechnology, polymers, catalysis, energy and environment, computational modeling.

University of Puerto Rico–Mayagüez, Graduate Studies, College of Engineering, Department of Chemical Engineering, Mayagüez, PR 00681-9000. Offers ME, MS, PhD. *Program availability:* Part-time. Terminal master's awarded for partial completion of doctoral program. *Degree requirements:* For master's, one foreign language, comprehensive exam, thesis; for doctorate, one foreign language, comprehensive exam, thesis/dissertation. *Entrance requirements:* For master's, BS in chemical engineering or its equivalent; minimum GPA of 3.0; for doctorate, MS in chemical engineering or its equivalent; minimum GPA of 3.0. Electronic applications accepted. *Faculty research:* Process simulation and optimization, air and water pollution control, mass transport, biochemical engineering, colloids and interfaces.

University of Rhode Island, Graduate School, College of Engineering, Department of Chemical Engineering, Kingston, RI 02881. Offers chemical engineering (MS, PhD); polymer (Postbaccalaureate Certificate). *Program availability:* Part-time. *Faculty:* 9 full-time (2 women). *Students:* 19 full-time (8 women), 5 part-time (2 women); includes 2 minority (1 Black or African American, non-Hispanic/Latino; 1 Hispanic/Latino), 13 international. 23 applicants, 22% accepted, 4 enrolled. In 2018, 3 master's, 3 doctorates awarded. *Entrance requirements:* Additional exam requirements/recommendations for international students: Required—TOEFL. *Application deadline:* For fall admission, 12/1 for domestic and international students; for spring admission, 7/15 for domestic and international students; for summer admission, 12/1 for domestic students. Application fee: $65. Electronic applications accepted. *Expenses: Tuition, area resident:* Full-time $13,226; part-time $735 per credit. *Tuition, state resident:* full-time $13,226; part-time $735 per credit. *Tuition, nonresident:* full-time $25,854; part-time $1436 per credit. *International tuition:* $25,854 full-time. *Required fees:* $1698; $50 per credit. $35 per semester. One-time fee: $165. *Financial support:* In 2018–19, 6 research assistantships with tuition reimbursements (averaging $8,317 per year), 4 teaching assistantships with tuition reimbursements (averaging $7,907 per year) were awarded. Financial award application deadline: 12/1; financial award applicants required to submit FAFSA. *Unit head:* Dr. Angelo Lucia, Chair, 401-874-4689, E-mail: alucia@uri.edu. *Application contact:* Dr. Michael Greenfield, Associate Professor/Chair of Polymer Engineering, 401-874-9289, E-mail: greenfield@uri.edu.
Website: http://egr.uri.edu/che/

University of Rochester, Hajim School of Engineering and Applied Sciences, Department of Chemical Engineering, Rochester, NY 14627. Offers MS, PhD. *Faculty:* 11 full-time (1 woman). *Students:* 44 full-time (12 women), 2 part-time (0 women); includes 4 minority (1 Black or African American, non-Hispanic/Latino; 1 Asian, non-Hispanic/Latino; 2 Hispanic/Latino), 30 international. Average age 28. 110 applicants, 57% accepted, 10 enrolled. In 2018, 13 master's, 3 doctorates awarded. Terminal master's awarded for partial completion of doctoral program. *Degree requirements:* For master's, comprehensive exam, thesis or alternative; for doctorate, comprehensive exam, thesis/dissertation, qualifying exam. *Entrance requirements:* For master's and doctorate, GRE, curriculum vitae, personal and research statement, three letters of recommendation, official transcript. Additional exam requirements/recommendations for international students: Recommended—TOEFL (minimum score 90 iBT), IELTS (minimum score 7). *Application deadline:* For fall admission, 1/15 for domestic and international students. Application fee: $60. Electronic applications accepted. *Expenses: Tuition:* Full-time $52,974; part-time $1654 per credit hour. *Required fees:* $612. One-time fee: $30 part-time. Tuition and fees vary according to campus/location and program. *Financial support:* In 2018–19, 48 students received support, including 25 fellowships with full tuition reimbursements available (averaging $27,996 per year), 4

research assistantships, 19 teaching assistantships with full tuition reimbursements available; career-related internships or fieldwork, health care benefits, tuition waivers (full and partial), and unspecified assistantships also available. Financial award application deadline: 4/15. *Faculty research:* Advanced materials, biotechnology, electrochemistry, theory and simulation, functional interfaces. *Total annual research expenditures:* $549,008. *Unit head:* Mitch Anthamatten, Department Chair, 585-273-5526, E-mail: mitchell.anthamatten@rochester.edu. *Application contact:* Victoria Heberling, Graduate Program Coordinator, 585-275-4913, E-mail: victoria.heberling@rochester.edu.
Website: http://www.hajim.rochester.edu/che/graduate/index.html
See Display on the next page and Close-Up on page 139.

University of Saskatchewan, College of Graduate and Postdoctoral Studies, College of Engineering, Chemical Engineering Program, Saskatoon, SK S7N 5E5, Canada. Offers M Eng, M Sc, PhD. *Program availability:* Part-time. *Degree requirements:* For master's, 30 credits (for M Eng); thesis and 12 credits (for MS); for doctorate, comprehensive exam, thesis/dissertation, qualifying exam, 18 credits. *Entrance requirements:* For master's and doctorate, GRE. Additional exam requirements/recommendations for international students: Required—TOEFL (minimum iBT score of 80), IELTS (6.5), CanTEST (4.5), or PTE (59). Electronic applications accepted. *Faculty research:* Applied thermodynamics, biochemical engineering, biosorption, chemical reaction engineering and catalysis, corrosion, environmental remediation, fluidization, fuel cell and microbial fuel cell technology, mineral processing, petroleum processing, process engineering, renewable energy.

University of South Africa, College of Science, Engineering and Technology, Pretoria, South Africa. Offers chemical engineering (M Tech); information technology (M Tech).

University of South Alabama, College of Engineering, Department of Chemical and Biomolecular Engineering, Mobile, AL 36688. Offers MS Ch E. *Degree requirements:* For master's, comprehensive exam, project or thesis. *Entrance requirements:* For master's, GRE General Test, BS in engineering, minimum GPA of 3.0. Additional exam requirements/recommendations for international students: Required—TOEFL (minimum score 550 paper-based; 79 iBT). Electronic applications accepted. *Expenses:* Contact institution. *Faculty research:* Molecular imaging, novel catalyst synthesis, lepidic ionic liquids, microscopy and endoscopy, and silver bullet therapy.

University of South Carolina, The Graduate School, College of Engineering and Computing, Department of Chemical Engineering, Columbia, SC 29208. Offers ME, MS, PhD. *Program availability:* Part-time, evening/weekend, online learning. *Degree requirements:* For master's, comprehensive exam, thesis (for some programs); for doctorate, comprehensive exam, thesis/dissertation. *Entrance requirements:* For master's and doctorate, GRE General Test. Additional exam requirements/recommendations for international students: Required—TOEFL. Electronic applications accepted. *Faculty research:* Rheology, liquid and supercritical extractions, electrochemistry, corrosion, heterogeneous and homogeneous catalysis.

University of Southern California, Graduate School, Viterbi School of Engineering, Mork Family Department of Chemical Engineering and Materials Science, Los Angeles, CA 90089. Offers chemical engineering (MS, PhD, Engr); geoscience technologies (MS); materials engineering (MS); materials science (MS, PhD, Engr); petroleum engineering (MS, PhD, Engr); smart oilfield technologies (MS, Graduate Certificate). Terminal master's awarded for partial completion of doctoral program. *Degree requirements:* For master's, thesis optional; for doctorate, thesis/dissertation. *Entrance requirements:* For master's and doctorate, GRE General Test. Additional exam requirements/recommendations for international students: Recommended—TOEFL. Electronic applications accepted. *Expenses:* Contact institution. *Faculty research:* Heterogeneous materials and porous media, statistical mechanics, molecular simulation, polymer science and engineering, advanced materials, reaction engineering and catalysis, membrane processes and separation, biochemical engineering, cell culture, bioreactor modeling, petroleum engineering.

University of South Florida, College of Engineering, Department of Chemical and Biomedical Engineering, Tampa, FL 33620. Offers biomedical engineering (MSBE), including pharmacy; chemical engineering (MSCH, PhD). *Program availability:* Part-time. *Faculty:* 18 full-time (2 women). *Students:* 50 full-time (13 women), 10 part-time (3 women); includes 5 minority (1 Black or African American, non-Hispanic/Latino; 2 Asian, non-Hispanic/Latino; 1 Hispanic/Latino; 1 Two or more races, non-Hispanic/Latino), 42 international. Average age 27. 61 applicants, 59% accepted, 20 enrolled. In 2018, 19 master's, 2 doctorates awarded. Terminal master's awarded for partial completion of doctoral program. *Degree requirements:* For master's, comprehensive exam, thesis (for some programs); for doctorate, comprehensive exam, thesis/dissertation. *Entrance requirements:* For master's, GRE (preferred minimum scores of Verbal greater than 50% percentile, Quantitative greater than 75th percentile, Analytical Writing of 3.0 or greater; applicants who have successfully completed the Fundamentals of Engineering (FE) Exam offered by the Society of Professional Engineers will be exempted from the GRE requirement, Bachelors or equivalent in Chemical Engineering; 2 letters of reference; statement of research interests; for doctorate, (preferred scores: Verbal greater than 50% percentile, Quantitative greater than 75% percentile, Analytical Writing greater than 4.0), bachelors or equivalent in Chemical Engineering; 3 letters of reference; statement of research interests. Additional exam requirements/recommendations for international students: Required—TOEFL, TOEFL (minimum score 550 paper-based; 79 iBT) or IELTS (minimum score 6.5). *Application deadline:* For fall admission, 2/15 for domestic and international students; for spring admission, 10/15 for domestic students, 9/15 for international students; for summer admission, 2/15 for domestic students, 1/15 for international students. Application fee: $30. Electronic applications accepted. *Expenses: Tuition, state resident:* full-time $6350. *Tuition, nonresident:* full-time $19,048. *International tuition:* $19,048 full-time. *Required fees:* $2079. *Financial support:* In 2018–19, 10 students received support, including 29 research assistantships with tuition reimbursements available (averaging $13,171 per year), 12 teaching assistantships with tuition reimbursements available (averaging $14,017 per year); unspecified assistantships also available. Financial award applicants required to submit FAFSA. *Faculty research:* Neuroengineering, tissue engineering, biomedicine and biotechnology, engineering education, functional materials and nanotechnology, energy, environment/sustainability. *Total annual research expenditures:* $1.6 million. *Unit head:* Dr. Venkat R. Bhethanabotla, Professor and Department Chair, 813-974-3997, E-mail: bhethana@usf.edu. *Application contact:* Dr. Robert Frisina, Jr., Professor and Graduate Program Director, 813-974-4013, Fax: 813-974-3651, E-mail: rfrisina@usf.edu.
Website: http://che.eng.usf.edu/

University of South Florida, Innovative Education, Tampa, FL 33620-9951. Offers adult, career and higher education (Graduate Certificate), including college teaching, leadership in developing human resources, leadership in higher education; Africana studies (Graduate Certificate), including diasporas and health disparities, genocide and human rights; aging studies (Graduate Certificate), including gerontology; art research (Graduate Certificate), including museum studies; business foundations (Graduate Certificate); chemical and biomedical engineering (Graduate Certificate), including materials science and engineering, water, health and sustainability; child and family studies (Graduate Certificate), including positive behavior support; civil and industrial

Chemical Engineering

engineering (Graduate Certificate), including transportation systems analysis; community and family health (Graduate Certificate), including maternal and child health, social marketing and public health, violence and injury: prevention and intervention, women's health; criminology (Graduate Certificate), including criminal justice administration; data science for public administration (Graduate Certificate); digital humanities (Graduate Certificate); educational measurement and research (Graduate Certificate), including evaluation; English (Graduate Certificate), including comparative literary studies, creative writing, professional and technical communication; entrepreneurship (Graduate Certificate); environmental health (Graduate Certificate), including safety management; epidemiology and biostatistics (Graduate Certificate), including applied biostatistics, biostatistics, concepts and tools of epidemiology, epidemiology, epidemiology of infectious diseases; geography, environment and planning (Graduate Certificate), including community development, environmental policy and management, geographical information systems; geology (Graduate Certificate), including hydrogeology; global health (Graduate Certificate), including disaster management, global health and Latin American and Caribbean studies, global health practice, humanitarian assistance, infection control; government and international affairs (Graduate Certificate), including Cuban studies, globalization studies; health policy and management (Graduate Certificate), including health management and leadership, public health policy and programs; hearing specialist: early intervention (Graduate Certificate); industrial and management systems engineering (Graduate Certificate), including systems engineering, technology management; information studies (Graduate Certificate), including school library media specialist; information systems/decision sciences (Graduate Certificate), including analytics and business intelligence; instructional technology (Graduate Certificate), including distance education, Florida digital/virtual educator, instructional design, multimedia design, Web design; internal medicine, bioethics and medical humanities (Graduate Certificate), including biomedical ethics; Latin American and Caribbean studies (Graduate Certificate); leadership for coastal resiliency planning (Graduate Certificate); mass communications (Graduate Certificate), including multimedia journalism; mathematics and statistics (Graduate Certificate), including mathematics; medicine (Graduate Certificate), including aging and neuroscience, bioinformatics, biotechnology, brain fitness and memory management, clinical investigation, hand and upper limb rehabilitation, health informatics, health sciences, integrative weight management, intellectual property, medicine and gender, metabolic and nutritional medicine, metabolic cardiology, pharmacy sciences; national and competitive intelligence (Graduate Certificate); nursing (Graduate Certificate), including simulation based academic fellowship in advanced pain management; psychological and social foundations (Graduate Certificate), including career counseling, college teaching, diversity in education, mental health counseling, school counseling; public affairs (Graduate Certificate), including nonprofit management, public management, research administration; public health (Graduate Certificate), including assessing chemical toxicity and public health risks, health equity, pharmacoepidemiology, public health generalist, toxicology, translational research in adolescent behavioral health; public health practices (Graduate Certificate), including planning for healthy communities; rehabilitation and mental health counseling (Graduate Certificate), including integrative mental health care, marriage and family therapy, rehabilitation technology; secondary education (Graduate Certificate), including ESOL, foreign language education: culture and content, foreign language education: professional; social work (Graduate Certificate), including geriatric social work/clinical gerontology; special education (Graduate Certificate), including autism spectrum disorder, disabilities education: severe/profound; world languages (Graduate Certificate), including teaching English as a second language (TESL) or foreign language. *Expenses:* Tuition, state resident: full-time $6350. Tuition, nonresident: full-time $19,048. *International tuition:* $19,048 full-time. *Required fees:* $2079. *Unit head:* Dr. Cynthia DeLuca, Associate Vice President and Assistant Vice Provost, 813-974-3077, Fax: 813-974-7061, E-mail: deluca@usf.edu. *Application contact:* Owen Hooper, Director, Summer and Alternative Calendar Programs, 813-974-6917, E-mail: hooper@usf.edu.
Website: http://www.usf.edu/innovative-education/

The University of Tennessee, Graduate School, Tickle College of Engineering, Department of Chemical and Biomolecular Engineering, Knoxville, TN 37996. Offers chemical engineering (MS, PhD); reliability and maintainability engineering (MS); MS/MBA. *Program availability:* Part-time. *Faculty:* 17 full-time (1 woman), 4 part-time/adjunct (0 women). *Students:* 46 full-time (9 women), 4 part-time (3 women); includes 5 minority (1 Black or African American, non-Hispanic/Latino; 4 Hispanic/Latino), 20 international. Average age 27. 64 applicants, 27% accepted, 7 enrolled. In 2018, 5 master's, 8 doctorates awarded. *Degree requirements:* For master's, thesis or alternative; for doctorate, comprehensive exam, thesis/dissertation. *Entrance requirements:* For master's, GRE General Test (for MS students pursuing research thesis), minimum GPA of 2.7 (for U.S. degree holders), 3.0 (for international degree holders); for doctorate, GRE General Test, minimum GPA of 3.0 on previous graduate course work. Additional exam requirements/recommendations for international students: Required—TOEFL (minimum score 550 paper-based; 80 iBT), IELTS (minimum score 6.5). *Application deadline:* For fall admission, 2/1 priority date for domestic and international students; for spring admission, 6/15 for domestic and international students; for summer admission, 10/15 for domestic and international students. Applications are processed on a rolling basis. Application fee: $60. Electronic applications accepted. *Financial support:* In 2018–19, 72 students received support, including 8 fellowships (averaging $11,544 per year), 43 research assistantships with full tuition reimbursements available (averaging $26,976 per year), 21 teaching assistantships with full tuition reimbursements available (averaging $22,893 per year); career-related internships or fieldwork, Federal Work-Study, institutionally sponsored loans, health care benefits, and unspecified assistantships also available. Financial award application deadline: 2/1; financial award applicants required to submit FAFSA. *Faculty research:* Bio-fuels; engineering of soft, functional and structural materials; fuel cells and energy storage devices; molecular and cellular bioengineering; molecular modeling and simulations. *Total annual research expenditures:* $5.8 million. *Unit head:* Dr. Bamin Khomami, Head, 865-974-2421, Fax: 865-974-7076, E-mail: bkhomami@utk.edu. *Application contact:* Dr. Cong Trinh, Graduate Recruiting Director, 865-974-2421, Fax: 865-974-7076, E-mail: ctrinh@utk.edu.
Website: http://www.engr.utk.edu/cbe/

The University of Tennessee at Chattanooga, Program in Engineering, Chattanooga, TN 37403. Offers automotive (MS Engr); chemical (MS Engr); civil (MS Engr); electrical (MS Engr); mechanical (MS Engr). *Program availability:* Part-time. *Degree requirements:* For master's, comprehensive exam, thesis or alternative, engineering project. *Entrance requirements:* For master's, GRE General Test, minimum undergraduate GPA of 2.7 or 3.0 in last two years of undergraduate coursework. Additional exam requirements/recommendations for international students: Required—TOEFL (minimum score 550 paper-based; 79 iBT), IELTS (minimum score 6). Electronic applications accepted. *Expenses:* Contact institution. *Faculty research:* Quality control and reliability engineering, financial management, thermal science, energy conservation, structural analysis.

The University of Texas at Austin, Graduate School, Cockrell School of Engineering, Department of Chemical Engineering, Austin, TX 78712-1111. Offers MSE, PhD. Terminal master's awarded for partial completion of doctoral program. *Degree requirements:* For master's, thesis (for some programs); for doctorate, comprehensive exam, thesis/dissertation. *Entrance requirements:* For master's and doctorate, GRE General Test. Electronic applications accepted.

The University of Toledo, College of Graduate Studies, College of Engineering, Department of Chemical and Environmental Engineering, Toledo, OH 43606-3390. Offers chemical engineering (MS, PhD). *Program availability:* Part-time, evening/weekend. *Degree requirements:* For master's, thesis optional; for doctorate, thesis/dissertation, qualifying exam. *Entrance requirements:* For master's, GRE General Test, minimum GPA of 3.0; for doctorate, GRE General Test, minimum GPA of 3.3. Additional exam requirements/recommendations for international students: Required—TOEFL (minimum score 550 paper-based; 80 iBT). Electronic applications accepted. *Faculty research:* Polymers, applied computing, membranes, alternative energy (fuel cells).

University of Toronto, School of Graduate Studies, Faculty of Applied Science and Engineering, Department of Chemical Engineering and Applied Chemistry, Toronto, ON M5S 1A1, Canada. Offers M Eng, MA Sc, PhD. *Program availability:* Part-time. *Degree requirements:* For master's, thesis (for some programs); for doctorate, thesis/dissertation. *Entrance requirements:* For master's, minimum B+ average in final 2 years, four-year degree in engineering (M Eng, MA Sc) or physical sciences (MA Sc), 2 letters of reference; for doctorate, research master's degree, minimum B+ average, 2 letters of reference. Additional exam requirements/recommendations for international students: Required—TOEFL (minimum score 580 paper-based; 93 iBT), TWE (minimum score 4). Electronic applications accepted.

The University of Tulsa, Graduate School, College of Engineering and Natural Sciences, Department of Chemical Engineering, Tulsa, OK 74104-3189. Offers ME, MSE, PhD. *Program availability:* Part-time. *Faculty:* 11 full-time (3 women), 5 part-time/adjunct (2 women). *Students:* 13 full-time (3 women), 6 part-time (1 woman); includes 2 minority (1 Black or African American, non-Hispanic/Latino; 1 American Indian or Alaska Native, non-Hispanic/Latino), 14 international. Average age 28. 16 applicants, 88% accepted, 4 enrolled. In 2018, 6 master's awarded. Terminal master's awarded for partial completion of doctoral program. *Degree requirements:* For master's, thesis (for some programs); for doctorate, comprehensive exam, thesis/dissertation. *Entrance requirements:* For master's and doctorate, GRE General Test. Additional exam requirements/recommendations for international students: Required—TOEFL (minimum score 550 paper-based; 80 iBT), IELTS (minimum score 6). *Application deadline:* Applications are processed on a rolling basis. Application fee: $55. Electronic applications accepted. *Expenses: Tuition:* Full-time $22,230; part-time $1235 per credit hour. *Required fees:* $2100; $6 per credit hour. One-time fee: $400 full-time. Tuition and fees vary according to course level, course load and program. *Financial support:* In 2018–19, 15 students received support, including 8 fellowships with full tuition reimbursements available (averaging $6,927 per year), 8 research assistantships with full tuition reimbursements available (averaging $17,653 per year), 6 teaching assistantships with full tuition reimbursements available (averaging $13,290 per year); career-related internships or fieldwork, Federal Work-Study, scholarships/grants, health care benefits, tuition waivers (full and partial), and unspecified assistantships also available. Support available to part-time students. Financial award application deadline: 2/1; financial award applicants required to submit FAFSA. *Faculty research:* Environment, surface science, catalysis, transport phenomena, process systems engineering, bioengineering, alternative energy, petrochemical processes. *Unit head:* Dr. Geoffrey Price, Chairperson, 918-631-2575, Fax: 918-631-3268, E-mail: chegradadvisor@utulsa.edu. *Application contact:* Dr. Ty Johannes, Advisor, 918-631-2947, Fax: 918-631-3268, E-mail: ty-johannes@utulsa.edu.
Website: http://engineering.utulsa.edu/academics/chemical-engineering/

University of Utah, Graduate School, College of Engineering, Department of Chemical Engineering, Salt Lake City, UT 84112-1107. Offers chemical engineering (MS, PhD); petroleum engineering (MS); MS/MBA. *Program availability:* Blended/hybrid learning. *Faculty:* 19 full-time (2 women), 10 part-time/adjunct (2 women). *Students:* 62 full-time (15 women), 32 part-time (5 women); includes 8 minority (1 Black or African American, non-Hispanic/Latino; 2 Asian, non-Hispanic/Latino; 4 Hispanic/Latino; 1 Two or more races, non-Hispanic/Latino), 46 international. Average age 29. 145 applicants, 18% accepted, 23 enrolled. In 2018, 18 master's, 11 doctorates awarded. *Degree requirements:* For master's, comprehensive exam (for some programs), thesis optional; for doctorate, comprehensive exam, thesis/dissertation. *Entrance requirements:* For master's, GRE General Test, minimum GPA of 3.0; for doctorate, GRE General Test, minimum GPA of 3.0, degree or course work in chemical engineering. Additional exam requirements/recommendations for international students: Required—TOEFL (minimum score 550 paper-based; 80 iBT), IELTS (minimum score 6.5). *Application deadline:* For fall admission, 1/15 priority date for domestic and international students; for spring admission, 10/1 priority date for domestic and international students; for summer admission, 2/1 priority date for domestic and international students. Applications are processed on a rolling basis. Application fee: $0 ($15 for international students). Electronic applications accepted. *Expenses:* Contact institution. *Financial support:* In 2018–19, 53 students received support, including 10 fellowships with full tuition reimbursements available (averaging $28,000 per year), 53 research assistantships with full tuition reimbursements available (averaging $28,000 per year), 1 teaching assistantship (averaging $6,848 per year); Federal Work-Study, institutionally sponsored loans, scholarships/grants, health care benefits, and unspecified assistantships also available. Financial award application deadline: 4/15; financial award applicants required to submit FAFSA. *Faculty research:* Drug delivery, fossil fuel and biomass combustion and gasification, oil and gas reservoir characteristics and management, multi-scale simulation, micro-scale synthesis. *Unit head:* Dr. Eric G. Eddings, Chair, 801-581-6915, Fax: 801-585-9291, E-mail: eric.eddings@utah.edu. *Application contact:* Wanda Brown, Graduate Coordinator, 801-585-1181, Fax: 801-585-9291, E-mail: wanda.brown@chemeng.utah.edu.
Website: http://www.che.utah.edu/

University of Virginia, School of Engineering and Applied Science, Department of Chemical Engineering, Charlottesville, VA 22903. Offers ME, MS, PhD. *Program availability:* Online learning. *Degree requirements:* For master's, thesis (for some programs); for doctorate, thesis/dissertation. *Entrance requirements:* For master's, GRE General Test, 3 recommendations; for doctorate, GRE General Test, 3 recommendations, essay. Additional exam requirements/recommendations for international students: Required—TOEFL (minimum score 600 paper-based; 90 iBT), IELTS (minimum score 7). Electronic applications accepted. *Faculty research:* Fluid mechanics, heat and mass transfer, chemical reactor analysis and engineering, biochemical engineering and biotechnology.

University of Washington, Graduate School, College of Engineering, Department of Chemical Engineering, Seattle, WA 98195-1750. Offers chemical engineering (MS, PhD); chemical engineering and advanced data science (PhD); chemical engineering and nanotechnology (PhD). *Faculty:* 19 full-time (3 women). *Students:* 90 full-time (30 women), 15 part-time (7 women); includes 15 minority (1 Black or African American, non-Hispanic/Latino; 6 Asian, non-Hispanic/Latino; 6 Hispanic/Latino; 2 Two or more races, non-Hispanic/Latino), 49 international. Average age 25. 423 applicants, 28% accepted, 28 enrolled. In 2018, 29 master's, 12 doctorates awarded. Terminal master's awarded for partial completion of doctoral program. *Degree requirements:* For master's, comprehensive exam, thesis optional, final exam, research project, degree completed in 6 years; for doctorate, comprehensive exam, thesis/dissertation, general and final exams, research project, completion of all work within 10 years. *Entrance requirements:* For master's and doctorate, GRE General Test (minimum Quantitative score of 159), minimum GPA of 3.0, official transcripts, personal statement, confidential evaluations by 3 professors or other technical professional, high rank (top 5%) in respected chemical engineering program. Additional exam requirements/recommendations for international students: Required—TOEFL (minimum score 580 paper-based; 92 iBT); Recommended—IELTS (minimum score 7). *Application deadline:* For fall admission, 1/1 priority date for domestic students, 12/15 priority date for international students. Applications are processed on a rolling basis. Application fee: $85. Electronic applications accepted. *Expenses:* Research-focused Master's and PhD: $18,852 resident; $32,760 nonresident. Applied/Professional Master's: $23,070 resident; $35,571 nonresident. *Financial support:* In 2018–19, 73 students received support, including 16 fellowships with full tuition reimbursements available (averaging $32,640 per year), 38 research assistantships with full tuition reimbursements available (averaging $32,640 per year), 17 teaching assistantships with full tuition reimbursements available (averaging $32,640 per year); career-related internships or fieldwork, Federal Work-Study, health care benefits, and unspecified assistantships also available. Financial award application deadline: 1/15; financial award applicants required to submit FAFSA. *Faculty research:* Materials processing and characterization, optical and electronic polymers, surface science, biochemical engineering and bioengineering, computational chemistry, environmental studies. *Total annual research expenditures:* $13.5 million. *Unit head:* Dr. Francois Baneyx, Professor/Chair, 206-543-2250, Fax: 206-543-3778, E-mail: baneyx@uw.edu. *Application contact:* Allison Sherrill, Graduate Program Advisor, 206-685-9785, E-mail: sherra@uw.edu.
Website: http://www.cheme.washington.edu/

University of Waterloo, Graduate Studies and Postdoctoral Affairs, Faculty of Engineering, Department of Chemical Engineering, Waterloo, ON N2L 3G1, Canada. Offers M Eng, MA Sc, PhD. *Program availability:* Part-time. *Degree requirements:* For master's, research project or thesis, seminar; for doctorate, comprehensive exam, thesis/dissertation. *Entrance requirements:* For master's, honors degree, minimum B average; for doctorate, master's degree, minimum A- average. Additional exam requirements/recommendations for international students: Required—TOEFL, IELTS, PTE. *Application deadline:* Applications are processed on a rolling basis. Application fee: $125 Canadian dollars. Electronic applications accepted. *Financial support:* Research assistantships and teaching assistantships available. *Faculty research:* Biotechnical and environmental engineering, mathematical analysis, statistics and control, polymer science and engineering.
Website: https://uwaterloo.ca/chemical-engineering/

The University of Western Ontario, School of Graduate and Postdoctoral Studies, Physical Sciences Division, Faculty of Engineering, London, ON N6A 3K7, Canada. Offers chemical and biochemical engineering (ME Sc, PhD); civil and environmental engineering (M Eng, ME Sc, PhD); electrical and computer engineering (M Eng, ME Sc, PhD); mechanical and materials engineering (M Eng, ME Sc, PhD). *Program availability:* Part-time. Terminal master's awarded for partial completion of doctoral program. *Degree requirements:* For master's, thesis; for doctorate, thesis/dissertation. *Entrance requirements:* For master's, minimum B average; for doctorate, minimum B+ average. *Faculty research:* Wind, geotechnical, chemical reactor engineering, applied electrostatics, biochemical engineering.

University of Wisconsin–Madison, Graduate School, College of Engineering, Department of Chemical and Biological Engineering, Madison, WI 53706-0607. Offers chemical engineering (PhD). *Faculty:* 18 full-time (2 women). *Students:* 101 full-time (19 women); includes 14 minority (1 Black or African American, non-Hispanic/Latino; 4 Asian, non-Hispanic/Latino; 8 Hispanic/Latino; 1 Two or more races, non-Hispanic/Latino), 46 international. Average age 25. 386 applicants, 21% accepted, 17 enrolled. In 2018, 17 doctorates awarded. *Degree requirements:* For doctorate, comprehensive exam, thesis/dissertation, at least 18 credits of coursework, 2 semesters of teaching assistantship. *Entrance requirements:* For doctorate, GRE General Test, bachelor's degree with strong background in chemical engineering; minimum GPA of 3.0 in last 60 semester hours. Additional exam requirements/recommendations for international students: Required—TOEFL (minimum score 580 paper-based; 92 iBT). *Application deadline:* For fall admission, 12/15 for domestic and international students; for spring admission, 10/15 for domestic and international students. Application fee: $75 ($81 for international students). Electronic applications accepted. *Financial support:* In 2018–19, 129 students received support, including 6 fellowships with full tuition reimbursements available (averaging $27,816 per year), 96 research assistantships with full tuition reimbursements available (averaging $27,156 per year), 27 teaching assistantships with full tuition reimbursements available (averaging $15,384 per year); traineeships and health care benefits also available. Financial award application deadline: 12/1; financial award applicants required to submit FAFSA. *Faculty research:* Fluid mechanics, colloids, bioengineering, reaction and systems engineering, materials and nanotechnology, polymer science and engineering, process control, optimization and scheduling, catalysis. *Total annual research expenditures:* $12.6 million. *Unit head:* Prof. Regina Murphy, Chair, 608-262-1092, E-mail: che@che.wisc.edu. *Application contact:* Kate Fanis, Associate Student Services Coordinator, 608-263-3138, Fax: 608-262-5434, E-mail: gradrecruit@che.wisc.edu.
Website: https://www.engr.wisc.edu/department/cbe/

University of Wyoming, College of Engineering and Applied Science, Department of Chemical Engineering, Program in Chemical Engineering, Laramie, WY 82071. Offers MS, PhD. *Program availability:* Part-time. Terminal master's awarded for partial completion of doctoral program. *Degree requirements:* For master's, thesis; for doctorate, thesis/dissertation. *Entrance requirements:* For master's and doctorate, GRE General Test, minimum GPA of 3.0. Additional exam requirements/recommendations for international students: Required—TOEFL (minimum score 600 paper-based; 76 iBT). Electronic applications accepted. *Expenses: Tuition, area resident:* Full-time $6504; part-time $271 per credit hour. Tuition, state resident: full-time $6504; part-time $271 per credit hour. Tuition, nonresident: full-time $19,464; part-time $811 per credit hour. *International tuition:* $19,464 full-time. *Required fees:* $1410.94; $343.82 per semester. $343.82 per semester. Tuition and fees vary according to course load, program and reciprocity agreements. *Faculty research:* Microwave reactor systems, synthetic fuels, fluidization, coal combustion/gasification, flue-gas cleanup.

Vanderbilt University, School of Engineering, Department of Chemical and Biomolecular Engineering, Nashville, TN 37240-1001. Offers M Eng, MS, PhD. MS and PhD offered through the Graduate School. *Program availability:* Part-time. *Degree requirements:* For master's, thesis; for doctorate, thesis/dissertation. *Entrance requirements:* For master's and doctorate, GRE General Test. Additional exam requirements/recommendations for international students: Required—TOEFL. Electronic applications accepted. *Expenses: Tuition:* Full-time $47,208; part-time $2026 per credit hour. *Required fees:* $478. *Faculty research:* Adsorption and surface chemistry; biochemical engineering and biotechnology; chemical reaction engineering, environment, materials, process modeling and control; molecular modeling and thermodynamics.

Villanova University, College of Engineering, Department of Chemical Engineering, Villanova, PA 19085-1699. Offers biochemical engineering (Certificate); chemical engineering (MSChE); environmental protection in the chemical process industries

Chemical Engineering

(Certificate). *Program availability:* Part-time, evening/weekend. *Degree requirements:* For master's, comprehensive exam, thesis optional. *Entrance requirements:* For master's, GRE General Test (for applicants with degrees from foreign universities), B Ch E, minimum GPA of 3.0. Additional exam requirements/recommendations for international students: Required—TOEFL (minimum score 600 paper-based; 100 iBT). *Faculty research:* Heat transfer, advanced materials, chemical vapor deposition, pyrolysis and combustion chemistry, industrial waste treatment.

Virginia Polytechnic Institute and State University, Graduate School, College of Engineering, Blacksburg, VA 24061. Offers aerospace engineering (PhD, M Eng/MS); biological systems engineering (PhD); biomedical engineering (MS, PhD); chemical engineering (PhD); civil engineering (PhD); computer engineering (PhD); computer science and applications (MS); electrical engineering (PhD); engineering education (PhD); M Eng/MS. *Faculty:* 446 full-time (87 women), 7 part-time/adjunct (3 women). *Students:* 1,776 full-time (471 women), 367 part-time (62 women); includes 260 minority (50 Black or African American, non-Hispanic/Latino; 3 American Indian or Alaska Native, non-Hispanic/Latino; 99 Asian, non-Hispanic/Latino; 67 Hispanic/Latino; 41 Two or more races, non-Hispanic/Latino), 1,178 international. Average age 27. 3,798 applicants, 37% accepted, 507 enrolled. In 2018, 489 master's, 200 doctorates awarded. *Degree requirements:* For master's, comprehensive exam (for some programs), thesis (for some programs); for doctorate, comprehensive exam (for some programs), thesis/dissertation (for some programs). *Entrance requirements:* For master's and doctorate, GRE/GMAT. Additional exam requirements/recommendations for international students: Required—TOEFL (minimum score 90 iBT). *Application deadline:* For fall admission, 8/1 for domestic students, 4/1 for international students; for spring admission, 1/1 for domestic students, 9/1 for international students. Applications are processed on a rolling basis. Application fee: $75. Electronic applications accepted. *Expenses:* Tuition, state resident: full-time $15,510; part-time $739.50 per credit hour. Tuition, nonresident: full-time $29,629; part-time $1490.25 per credit hour. *Required fees:* $2804; $550 per semester. Tuition and fees vary according to course load, campus/location and program. *Financial support:* In 2018–19, 37 fellowships with full tuition reimbursements (averaging $24,951 per year), 1,110 research assistantships with full tuition reimbursements (averaging $20,129 per year), 486 teaching assistantships with full tuition reimbursements (averaging $16,192 per year) were awarded; scholarships/grants and unspecified assistantships also available. Financial award application deadline: 3/1; financial award applicants required to submit FAFSA. *Total annual research expenditures:* $96.3 million. *Unit head:* Dr. Julia Ross, Dean, 540-231-9752, Fax: 540-231-3031, E-mail: rjulie@vt.edu. *Application contact:* Linda Perkins, Executive Assistant, 540-231-9752, Fax: 540-231-3031, E-mail: lperkins@vt.edu. Website: http://www.eng.vt.edu/

Washington State University, Voiland College of Engineering and Architecture, The Gene and Linda Voiland School of Chemical Engineering and Bioengineering, Pullman, WA 99164-6515. Offers MS, PhD. Terminal master's awarded for partial completion of doctoral program. *Degree requirements:* For master's, comprehensive exam, thesis (for some programs), oral exam; for doctorate, one foreign language, comprehensive exam, thesis/dissertation, oral exam. *Entrance requirements:* For master's and doctorate, minimum GPA of 3.0, 3 letters of recommendation by faculty. Additional exam requirements/recommendations for international students: Required—TOEFL (minimum score 580 paper-based). *Faculty research:* Kinetics and catalysis, biofilm engineering, muscle systems, engineering education.

Washington University in St. Louis, School of Engineering and Applied Science, Department of Energy, Environmental and Chemical Engineering, St. Louis, MO 63130-4899. Offers chemical engineering (MS, D Sc); environmental engineering (MS, D Sc). *Program availability:* Part-time. Terminal master's awarded for partial completion of doctoral program. *Degree requirements:* For master's, thesis optional; for doctorate, thesis/dissertation, preliminary exam, qualifying exam. *Entrance requirements:* For master's and doctorate, GRE, minimum B average during final 2 years of course work. Additional exam requirements/recommendations for international students: Required—TOEFL, TWE. Electronic applications accepted. *Faculty research:* Reaction engineering, materials processing, catalysis, process control, air pollution control.

Wayne State University, College of Engineering, Department of Chemical Engineering and Materials Science, Detroit, MI 48202. Offers chemical engineering (MS, PhD); materials science and engineering (MS, PhD), including materials science and engineering; polymer engineering (Graduate Certificate), including polymer engineering. *Program availability:* Part-time. *Faculty:* 15. *Students:* 39 full-time (11 women), 32 part-time (10 women); includes 6 minority (2 Black or African American, non-Hispanic/Latino; 2 Asian, non-Hispanic/Latino; 1 Hispanic/Latino; 1 Two or more races, non-Hispanic/Latino), 36 international. Average age 27. 127 applicants, 28% accepted, 16 enrolled. In 2018, 7 master's, 5 doctorates awarded. *Entrance requirements:* For master's, three letters of recommendation (at least two from the applicant's academic institution); personal statement; resume; for doctorate, GRE, three letters of recommendation (at least two from the applicant's academic institution); personal statement; resume; for Graduate Certificate, bachelor's degree in engineering or other mathematics-based sciences in exceptional cases. Additional exam requirements/recommendations for international students: Required—TOEFL (minimum score 550 paper-based; 79 iBT), TWE (minimum score 5.5), Michigan English Language Assessment Battery (minimum score 85); Recommended—IELTS (minimum score 6.5). *Application deadline:* For fall admission, 3/1 priority date for domestic and international students; for winter admission, 10/1 priority date for domestic students, 9/1 priority date for international students; for spring admission, 2/1 priority date for domestic and international students; for summer admission, 2/1 priority date for domestic and international students. Application fee: $50. Electronic applications accepted. *Expenses:* Contact institution. *Financial support:* In 2018–19, 36 students received support, including 3 fellowships with tuition reimbursements available (averaging $20,000 per year), 16 research assistantships with tuition reimbursements available (averaging $21,307 per year), 6 teaching assistantships with tuition reimbursements available (averaging $20,166 per year); scholarships/grants, health care benefits, and unspecified assistantships also available. Support available to part-time students. Financial award applicants required to submit FAFSA. *Faculty research:* Environmental transport and management of hazardous waste; process design and synthesis based on waste minimization; biocatalysis in multiphase systems; biomaterials and tissue engineering. *Total annual research expenditures:* $1.6 million. *Unit head:* Dr. Guangzhao Mao, Professor and Chair, 313-577-3804, E-mail: gzmao@eng.wayne.edu. *Application contact:* Ellen Cope, Graduate Program Coordinator, 313-577-0409, E-mail: escope@wayne.edu. Website: http://engineering.wayne.edu/che/

Western Michigan University, Graduate College, College of Engineering and Applied Sciences, Department of Chemical and Paper Engineering, Kalamazoo, MI 49008. Offers MS, MSE, PhD. *Degree requirements:* For master's, thesis optional; for doctorate, one foreign language, comprehensive exam, thesis/dissertation.

West Virginia University, Statler College of Engineering and Mineral Resources, Morgantown, WV 26506. Offers aerospace engineering (MSAE, PhD); chemical engineering (MS Ch E, PhD); civil engineering (MSCE, PhD); computer engineering (PhD); computer science (MSCS, PhD); electrical engineering (MSEE, PhD); energy systems engineering (MSESE); engineering (MSE); industrial engineering (MSIE, PhD); industrial hygiene (MS); material science and engineering (MSMSE, PhD); mechanical engineering (MSME, PhD); mining engineering (MS Min E, PhD); petroleum and natural gas engineering (MSPNGE, PhD); safety management (MS); software engineering (MSSE). *Program availability:* Part-time. *Students:* 466 full-time (113 women), 154 part-time (27 women); includes 57 minority (22 Black or African American, non-Hispanic/Latino; 1 American Indian or Alaska Native, non-Hispanic/Latino; 8 Asian, non-Hispanic/Latino; 12 Hispanic/Latino; 14 Two or more races, non-Hispanic/Latino), 283 international. In 2018, 179 master's, 39 doctorates awarded. Terminal master's awarded for partial completion of doctoral program. *Degree requirements:* For master's, thesis optional; for doctorate, comprehensive exam, thesis/dissertation. *Entrance requirements:* Additional exam requirements/recommendations for international students: Required—TOEFL (minimum score 550 paper-based). *Application deadline:* For fall admission, 4/1 for international students; for winter admission, 4/1 for international students; for spring admission, 10/1 for international students. Applications are processed on a rolling basis. Application fee: $60. Electronic applications accepted. *Expenses:* Contact institution. *Financial support:* Fellowships, research assistantships, teaching assistantships, career-related internships or fieldwork, Federal Work-Study, institutionally sponsored loans, health care benefits, tuition waivers (full and partial), unspecified assistantships, and administrative assistantships available. Financial award application deadline: 2/1; financial award applicants required to submit FAFSA. *Faculty research:* Composite materials, software engineering, information systems, aerodynamics, vehicle propulsion and emission. *Unit head:* Dr. Earl Scime, Interim Dean, 304-293-4157 Ext. 2237, Fax: 304-293-2037, E-mail: earl.scime@mail.wvu.edu. *Application contact:* Dr. David A. Wyrick, Associate Dean, Academic Affairs, 304-293-4334, Fax: 304-293-5024, E-mail: david.wyrick@mail.wvu.edu. Website: https://www.statler.wvu.edu

Widener University, Graduate Programs in Engineering, Program in Chemical Engineering, Chester, PA 19013. Offers M Eng. *Program availability:* Part-time, evening/weekend. *Degree requirements:* For master's, thesis optional. Electronic applications accepted. *Faculty research:* Biotechnology, environmental engineering, computational fluid mechanics, reaction kinetics, process design.

Worcester Polytechnic Institute, Graduate Admissions, Department of Chemical Engineering, Worcester, MA 01609-2280. Offers MS, PhD. *Program availability:* Part-time, evening/weekend. *Students:* 24 full-time (8 women), 10 part-time (4 women); includes 6 minority (4 Asian, non-Hispanic/Latino; 1 Hispanic/Latino; 1 Two or more races, non-Hispanic/Latino), 11 international. Average age 25. 100 applicants, 60% accepted, 20 enrolled. In 2018, 1 master's, 3 doctorates awarded. Terminal master's awarded for partial completion of doctoral program. *Degree requirements:* For master's, thesis (for some programs); for doctorate, comprehensive exam, thesis/dissertation. *Entrance requirements:* For master's and doctorate, GRE (recommended). GRE is required for International students, 3 letters of recommendation. Additional exam requirements/recommendations for international students: Required—TOEFL (minimum score 563 paper-based; 84 iBT), IELTS (minimum score 7). *Application deadline:* For fall admission, 1/1 priority date for domestic and international students; for spring admission, 10/1 for domestic students, 10/1 priority date for international students. Applications are processed on a rolling basis. Application fee: $70. Electronic applications accepted. *Financial support:* Fellowships, research assistantships, career-related internships or fieldwork, institutionally sponsored loans, scholarships/grants, and unspecified assistantships available. Financial award application deadline: 1/1. *Unit head:* Dr. Susan Roberts, Head, 508-831-5250, Fax: 508-831-5853, E-mail: scroberts@wpi.edu. *Application contact:* Dr. Nick Kazantzis, Graduate Coordinator, 508-831-5250, Fax: 508-831-5853, E-mail: nikolas@wpi.edu. Website: https://www.wpi.edu/academics/departments/chemical-engineering

Yale University, Graduate School of Arts and Sciences, School of Engineering and Applied Science, Department of Chemical Engineering, New Haven, CT 06520. Offers MS, PhD. Terminal master's awarded for partial completion of doctoral program. *Degree requirements:* For doctorate, thesis/dissertation, exam. *Entrance requirements:* For master's and doctorate, GRE General Test. Additional exam requirements/recommendations for international students: Required—TOEFL. *Faculty research:* Biochemical engineering, heterogeneous catalysis, high-temperature chemical reaction engineering, separation science and technology, colloids and complex fluids.

UNIVERSITY OF ROCHESTER

Edmund A. Hajim School of Engineering and Applied Sciences
Department of Chemical Engineering

Programs of Study

The interdisciplinary nature of the University of Rochester's chemical engineering program manifests itself in active collaborations with other departments at the school. The faculty enjoys generous research support from government agencies and private industries. The University's graduate programs are among the highest ranked in the nation according to the 2010 National Research Council survey report (www.nap.edu/rdp).

To earn a Ph.D., students must complete 90 credit hours. It typically takes five years to complete the program, which includes successful defense of a dissertation. The first two semesters are devoted to graduate courses in chemical engineering and other sciences. Students are expected to provide undergraduate teaching assistance. At the end of this period, students take a first-year examination as a transition from classroom to full-time research.

Students without prior backgrounds in chemical engineering are encouraged to apply. The Department has a graduate curriculum devised for students with a background in science, such as chemistry, physics, and biology. The curriculum combines courses at the undergraduate and graduate levels and is designed to foster interdisciplinary research in advanced materials, nanotechnology, alternative energy, and biotechnology.

The Master of Science degree may be obtained through either a full-time or a part-time program. Graduate students may complete a thesis (Plan A) or choose a non-thesis (Plan B) option. All students who pursue Plan A are expected to earn 30 hours of credit, of which a minimum of 18 and a maximum of 24 hours should be formal course work. The balance of credit hours required for the degree is earned through M.S. research and/or reading courses. Satisfactory completion of the master thesis is also required. All students who pursue Plan B must earn a minimum of 32 credits of course work. At least 18 credits should be taken from courses within the Department. Overall, no more than 6 credits toward a degree may be earned by research and/or reading courses. Plan B students are required to pass a comprehensive oral exam toward the end of their program.

The Department of Chemical Engineering also awards the Master of Science degree in Alternative Energy. Courses and research projects focus on the fundamentals and applications of the generation, storage, and utilization of various forms of alternative energy as well as their impact on sustainability and energy conservation. This program is designed for graduate students with a bachelor's degree in engineering or science who are interested in pursuing a technical career in alternative energy. As with the other M.S. programs, the M.S. degree in Alternative Energy is available as a full- or part-time program, with a thesis (Plan A) or non-thesis (Plan B) option. All students who pursue Plan A are expected to earn 30 hours of credit; at least 18 should be attributed to 400-level courses. The balance of the credit-hour requirement can be satisfied through independent reading (no more than 4 credit hours) and thesis research (at least 6 credit hours), culminating in a master thesis. All students who pursue Plan B must earn a minimum of 32 credits of course work, with at least 18 credits from 400-level courses and no more than 4 through independent reading. Students may opt for industrial internship (1 credit hour), for which a final essay must be submitted as a part of their degree requirements. In addition to course work and the essay, all Plan B students must pass a comprehensive oral exam toward the end of their program.

Research Facilities

The River Campus Libraries hold approximately 2.5 million volumes and provide access to an extensive collection of electronic, multimedia, and interlibrary loan resources. Miner Library includes more than 230,000 volumes of journals, books, theses, and government documents for healthcare and medical research. Located at the Medical Center, the library also maintains access to online databases and electronic resources.

The Laboratory for Laser Energetics and the Center for Optoelectronics and Imaging are two state-of-the-art facilities in which specialized material science research is conducted. The Laboratory for Laser Energetics was established in 1970 for the investigation of the interaction of intense radiation with matter, to conduct experiments in support of the National Inertial Confinement Fusion (ICF) program; develop new laser and materials technologies; provide education in electro-optics, high-power lasers, high-energy-density physics, plasma physics, and nuclear fusion technology; operate the National Laser User's Facility; and conduct research in advanced technology related to high-energy-density phenomena.

The renowned Medical Center, which is a few minutes' walk from the River Campus, houses the Peptide Sequencing/Mass Spectrometry Facilities, Cell Sorting Facility, Nucleic Acid Laboratory, Real-Time and Static Confocal Imaging Facility, Functional Genomics Center, and a network of nearly 1,000 investigators providing research, clinical trial, and education services. In addition, a recently founded research institute, the Aab Institute of Biomedical Sciences, is the centerpiece of a ten-year, $400-million strategic plan to expand the Medical Center's research programs in the basic sciences. It is headquartered in a 240,000-square-foot research building on the Medical Center campus.

Financial Aid

The University offers fellowships, scholarships, and assistantships for full-time graduate students and individual departments provide support through research assistantships. Applicants are encouraged to apply for outside funding such as NSF or New York State fellowships. Full-time Ph.D. students receive an annual stipend of $28,000 plus full graduate tuition.

Cost of Study

In the 2019-20 academic year, tuition is $1,718 per credit hour. Students must also pay additional yearly fees of $612 for health services and $2,292 for optional health insurance. Fees can be found at: https://www.rochester.edu/adminfinance/bursar/tuition2019-20.html. All amounts are subject to change.

Living and Housing Costs

Students are eligible to lease a University apartment if enrolled as a full-time graduate student or postgraduate trainee. In the 2019-20 academic year, rent, utilities, food, and supplies are estimated at $18,000 per year; books at $1,500; and personal expenses at $2,900. All amounts are subject to change.

Student Group

The chemical engineering discipline appeals to students who are proficient at both analytical and descriptive sciences and are intrigued by the prospect of investigating new phenomena and devising new materials and devices for the technologies of the future. Students in the master's degree program should have acquired technical background in chemistry, mathematics, and physics. For students interested in biotechnology, a technical background in biology is desirable.

Student Outcomes

In addition to the traditional jobs in the chemical process and petrochemical industries, chemical engineers work in pharmaceuticals, health care, pulp and paper, food processing, polymers, biotechnology, and environmental health and safety industries. Their expertise is also applied in law, education, publishing, finance, and medicine. Chemical engineers also are well equipped to analyze environmental issues and develop solutions to environmental problems, such as pollution control and remediation.

Location

Located at a bend of the Genesee River, the 85-acre River Campus is about 2 miles south of downtown Rochester, New York. Rochester has been ranked as one of the Northeast's ten "Best Places to Live in America" by *Money* magazine; Rochester has also been listed as one of the "Most Livable Cities" in America by the Partners for Livable Communities. Rochester claims more sites on the National Register of Historic Places than any other city its size. With Lake Ontario on its northern border and the scenic Finger Lakes to the south, the Rochester area of about 1 million people offers a wide variety of cultural and recreational opportunities through its museums, parks, orchestras, planetarium, theater companies, and professional sports teams.

The University

Founded in 1850, the University of Rochester ranks among the most highly regarded universities in the country, offering degree programs at the bachelor's, master's, and doctoral levels, as well as in several professional disciplines. In the last eighteen years, 27 faculty members have been named Guggenheim Fellows. Present faculty members include a MacArthur Foundation fellowship recipient and 6 National Endowment for the Humanities Senior Fellows. Past alumni have included 7 Nobel Prize winners and 11 Pulitzer Prize winners. The University's Eastman School of Music is consistently ranked as one of the top music schools in the nation.

University of Rochester

Applying

The official graduate application can be found online at **https://apply.grad. rochester.edu**. The entire application must be received by January 15 for fall admission. Late applications are considered for exceptional applicants only if scholarship slots are available. Applicants are required to send college transcripts, letters of recommendation, personal/research statement, curriculum vitae, and standardized test results along with a $60 application fee to the Department of Chemical Engineering.

Correspondence and Information

Graduate Program Coordinator
Department of Chemical Engineering
University of Rochester
4510 Wegman Hall, Box 270166
Rochester, New York 14627-0166
United States
Phone: 585-275-4913
Fax: 585-273-1348
E-mail: chegradinfo@che.rochester.edu
Website: http://www.che.rochester.edu

THE FACULTY AND THEIR RESEARCH

Mitchell Anthamatten, Professor, Chair, and Scientist, LLE; Ph.D., MIT, 2001. Macromolecular self-assembly, associative and functional polymers, nanostructured materials, liquid crystals, interfacial phenomena, optoelectronic materials, vapor deposition polymerization, fuel cell membranes.

Danielle S. W. Benoit, Associate Professor Biomedical Engineering and Chemical Engineering; Ph.D., Colorado, 2006. The rational design, synthesis, characterization, and employment of materials to treat diseases or control cell behavior for applications in drug therapy, regenerative medicine, and tissue engineering.

Shaw H. Chen, Professor and Senior Scientist, LLE; Ph.D., Minnesota, 1981. Organic semiconductors, green chemical engineering, glassy liquid crystals, photoalignment of conjugated molecules, bipolar hosts for phosphorescent OLEDs, geometric surfactancy for bulk heterojunction solar cells.

Eldred H. Chimowitz, Professor; Ph.D., Connecticut, 1982. Critical phenomena, statistical mechanics of fluids, computer-aided design, supercritical fluids.

David G. Foster, Associate Professor; Ph.D., Rochester, 1999. Principles of transport phenomena, classic chemical engineering as well as biomedical engineering research, creation of nanoparticle coatings for enhanced capture of flowing cells in microtubes, capture cancer cells in blood flow, creating state-of-the-art videos for curricular purposes of fundamental fluid mechanics principles.

David R. Harding, Professor of Chemical Engineering and Senior Scientist, LLE; Ph.D., Cambridge, 1986. Thin-film deposition, properties of films and composite structures, and developing cryogenic fuel capsules for nuclear fusion experiments.

Jacob Jornè, Professor; Ph.D., Berkeley, 1972. Electrochemical engineering, microelectronics processing, fuel cells, polymer electrolyte membrane fuel cell, lithium batteries, green energy, copper electrodeposition, and reaction-diffusion interactions.

F. Douglas Kelley, Associate Professor; Ph.D., Rochester, 1990. Ways to exploit the divergent transport properties of fluids near the critical point, energy storage technologies that can be useful in balancing energy demand with sustainable energy generation, polymer mixtures and composites.

Tanya Z. Kosc, Lecturer of Chemical Engineering and Scientist, LLE; Ph.D., Rochester, 2003. Polymer cholesteric liquid crystals, optical materials.

Mark F. Mathias, Associate Professor, Ph.D., University of Wisconsin, 1987. Application of novel materials and design to electrochemical devices, technology and economics of electrochemical systems.

Astrid M. Müller, Assistant Professor, Ph.D., Max-Plank Institute of Quantum Optics & Ludwig-Maximilians-Universität München, 2000. Heterogeneous electrocatalysis, pulsed-laser-in-liquids preparation of controlled nanomaterials, nanocatalyst property-functionality relationships, selective CO_2 reduction catalysis, integrated solar fuels photoelectrodes, nanomaterials for anti-cancer applications.

Marc D. Porosoff, Assistant Professor, Ph.D. Columbia University, 2015. CO_2 reduction, heterogeneous catalysis, catalyst structure-property relationships, C1 chemistry, upgrading light alkanes.

Lewis Rothberg, Professor of Chemistry and Chemical Engineering; Ph.D., Harvard, 1984. Polymer electronics, optoelectronic devices, light-emitting diodes, thin-film transistors, organic photovoltaics and solar cells, biomolecular sensors, plasmon-enhanced devices.

Yonathon Shapir, Professor of Physics and Chemical Engineering; Ph.D., Tel-Aviv, 1981. Critical phenomena in ordered and disordered systems, classical and quantum transport in dirty metals and the metal-insulator transition, statistical properties of different polymer configurations, fractal properties of percolation and other clusters, kinetic models of growth and aggregation.

Alexander A. Shestopalov, Associate Professor; Ph.D., Duke, 2009. Development of new unconventional fabrication and patterning techniques and their use in preparation of functional micro- and nanostructured devices, organic chemistry and colloidal self-assembly.

Ching W. Tang, Emeritus Professor of Chemical Engineering; Ph.D., Cornell, 1975. Applications of organic electronic devices—organic light-emitting diodes, solar cells, photoconductors, image sensors, photoreceptors; basic studies of organic thin-film devices: charge injection, transport, recombination and luminescence properties; metal-organic and organic-organic junction phenomena; development of flat-panel display technology based on organic light-emitting diodes.

Wyatt Tenhaeff, Assistant Professor; Ph.D., MIT, 2009. Electrochemical energy storage, solid-state lithium batteries, solid electrolytes, polymer thin films and interfaces, thin film synthesis and characterization, vacuum deposition techniques.

Andrew D. White, Assistant Professor; Ph.D., Washington (Seattle), 2013. Computer simulation and data informatics design of material design for self-assembly, machine learning.

J. H. David Wu, Professor of Chemical Engineering and Biomedical Engineering and Associate Professor of Microbiology and Immunology; Ph.D., MIT, 1987. Biofuels development, molecular enzymology, transcriptional network, genomics and systems biology of biomass degradation for bioenergy conversion, artificial bone marrow and lymphoid tissue engineering, molecular control of hematopoiesis and immune response, stem cell and lymphocyte culture, biochemical engineering, fermentation, molecular biology.

Matthew Z. Yates, Professor and Scientist, LLE; Ph.D., Texas, 1999. Particle synthesis and assembly, crystallization, fuel cell membranes, microemulsions and microencapsulation, supercritical fluids, microencapsulation, colloids and interfaces.

Meliora—"Ever Better"

Rochester fall colors.

Section 7
Civil and Environmental Engineering

This section contains a directory of institutions offering graduate work in civil and environmental engineering. Additional information about programs listed in the directory may be obtained by writing directly to the dean of a graduate school or chair of a department at the address given in the directory.

For programs offering related work, see also in this book *Agricultural Engineering and Bioengineering, Biomedical Engineering and Biotechnology, Engineering and Applied Sciences, Management of Engineering and Technology,* and *Ocean Engineering.* In the other guides in this series:

Graduate Programs in the Humanities, Arts & Social Sciences

See *Public, Regional, and Industrial Affairs (Urban and Regional Planning and Urban Studies)*

Graduate Programs in the Biological/Biomedical Sciences & Health-Related Medical Professions

See *Ecology, Environmental Biology,* and *Evolutionary Biology*

Graduate Programs in the Physical Sciences, Mathematics, Agricultural Sciences, the Environment & Natural Resources

See *Agricultural and Food Sciences, Environmental Sciences and Management, Geosciences,* and *Marine Sciences and Oceanography*

CONTENTS

Program Directories

Featured School: Display and Close-Up

See:

Civil Engineering

American University of Beirut, Graduate Programs, Maroun Semaan Faculty of Engineering and Architecture, Beirut, Lebanon. Offers applied energy (ME); civil engineering (PhD); electrical and computer engineering (PhD); energy studies (MS); engineering management (MEM); environmental and water resources (ME); environmental technology (MSES); mechanical engineering (ME, PhD); urban design (MUD); urban planning and policy (MUPP). For progreen diploma: LAU/AUC. *Program availability:* Part-time, 100% online. *Faculty:* 105 full-time (25 women), 102 part-time/adjunct (33 women). *Students:* 380 full-time (186 women), 100 part-time (38 women). Average age 27. 489 applicants, 64% accepted, 127 enrolled. In 2018, 109 master's, 14 doctorates awarded. Terminal master's awarded for partial completion of doctoral program. *Degree requirements:* For master's, one foreign language, comprehensive exam, thesis optional; for doctorate, one foreign language, comprehensive exam, thesis/dissertation. *Entrance requirements:* For doctorate, GRE. Additional exam requirements/recommendations for international students: Required—TOEFL (minimum score 575 paper-based; 88 iBT), AUB-EN; Recommended—IELTS (minimum score 7). *Application deadline:* For fall admission, 4/4 for domestic and international students; for spring admission, 11/3 for domestic and international students; for summer admission, 4/4 for domestic and international students. Application fee: $50. *Expenses: Tuition:* Full-time $17,748; part-time $986 per credit. *Required fees:* $762. Tuition and fees vary according to course load and program. *Financial support:* In 2018–19, 15 students received support, including 92 fellowships with full tuition reimbursements available (averaging $14,400 per year), 80 research assistantships with full and partial tuition reimbursements available (averaging $5,300 per year), 162 teaching assistantships with full and partial tuition reimbursements available (averaging $1,400 per year); scholarships/grants, tuition waivers (full and partial), and unspecified assistantships also available. Financial award application deadline: 4/4. *Faculty research:* All areas in engineering, architecture and design. *Total annual research expenditures:* $1.5 million. *Unit head:* Prof. Alan Shihade, Dean, 961-1-374374 Ext. 3400, Fax: 961-1-744462, E-mail: as20@aub.edu.lb. *Application contact:* Dr. Salim Kanaan, Director, Admissions Office, 961-1-374374 Ext. 2590, Fax: 961-1-750775, E-mail: sk00@aub.edu.lb.
Website: https://www.aub.edu.lb/msfea/pages/default.aspx

American University of Sharjah, Graduate Programs, Sharjah, United Arab Emirates. Offers accounting (MS); biomedical engineering (MSBME); business administration (MBA); chemical engineering (MS Ch E); civil engineering (MSCE); computer engineering (MS); electrical engineering (MSEE); engineering systems management (MS, PhD); mathematics (MS); mechanical engineering (MSME); mechatronics engineering (MS); teaching English to speakers of other languages (MA); translation and interpreting (MA); urban planning (MUP). *Program availability:* Part-time, evening/weekend. *Degree requirements:* For master's, thesis (for some programs). *Entrance requirements:* For master's, GMAT (for MBA). Additional exam requirements/recommendations for international students: Required—TOEFL (minimum score 550 paper-based; 80 iBT), TWE (minimum score 5); Recommended—IELTS (minimum score 6.5). Electronic applications accepted. *Faculty research:* Water pollution, management and waste water treatment, energy and sustainability, air pollution, Islamic finance, family business and small and medium enterprises.

Arizona State University at the Tempe campus, Ira A. Fulton Schools of Engineering, School of Sustainable Engineering and the Built Environment, Tempe, AZ 85287-5306. Offers civil, environmental and sustainable engineering (MS, MSE, PhD); construction engineering (MSE); construction management (MS, PhD). *Program availability:* Part-time, evening/weekend, online learning. Terminal master's awarded for partial completion of doctoral program. *Degree requirements:* For master's, thesis optional, comprehensive exams (MSE); interactive Program of Study (iPOS) submitted before completing 50 percent of required credit hours; for doctorate, comprehensive exam, thesis/dissertation, interactive Program of Study (iPOS) submitted before completing 50 percent of required credit hours. *Entrance requirements:* For master's, GRE, minimum GPA of 3.0 or equivalent in last 2 years of work leading to bachelor's degree; for doctorate, GRE, minimum GPA of 3.0 in last 2 years of work leading to bachelor's degree, 3.2 in all graduate-level coursework with master's degree; 3 letters of recommendation; resume/curriculum vitae; letter of intent; thesis (if applicable); statement of research interests. Additional exam requirements/recommendations for international students: Required—TOEFL, IELTS, or PTE. Electronic applications accepted. *Expenses:* Contact institution. *Faculty research:* Water purification, transportation (safety and materials), construction management, environmental biotechnology, environmental nanotechnology, earth systems engineering and management, SMART innovations, project performance metrics, and underground infrastructure.

Auburn University, Graduate School, Ginn College of Engineering, Department of Civil Engineering, Auburn University, AL 36849. Offers MCE, MS, PhD. *Program availability:* Part-time. *Degree requirements:* For master's, project (MCE), thesis (MS); for doctorate, comprehensive exam, thesis/dissertation. *Entrance requirements:* For master's and doctorate, GRE General Test. Electronic applications accepted. *Expenses:* Tuition, state resident: full-time $11,282; part-time $535 per credit hour. Tuition, nonresident: full-time $30,542; part-time $1605 per credit hour. *Required fees:* $826 per semester. Tuition and fees vary according to degree level and program.

Boise State University, College of Engineering, Department of Civil Engineering, Boise, ID 83725-0399. Offers civil engineering (M Engr, MS). *Program availability:* Part-time. *Degree requirements:* For master's, comprehensive exam, thesis (for some programs). *Entrance requirements:* For master's, GRE General Test, minimum GPA of 3.0. Additional exam requirements/recommendations for international students: Required—TOEFL (minimum score 550 paper-based; 80 iBT), IELTS (minimum score 6). Electronic applications accepted.

Bradley University, The Graduate School, Caterpillar College of Engineering and Technology, Department of Civil Engineering and Construction, Peoria, IL 61625-0002. Offers construction management, structural engineering, geo-environmental engineering (MSCE). *Program availability:* Part-time, evening/weekend. *Faculty:* 11 full-time (2 women). *Students:* 16 full-time (4 women), 7 part-time (1 woman); includes 2 minority (1 Black or African American, non-Hispanic/Latino; 1 Hispanic/Latino), 18 international. Average age 25. 62 applicants, 90% accepted, 5 enrolled. In 2018, 11 master's awarded. *Degree requirements:* For master's, comprehensive exam, thesis or alternative, 30 hours. *Entrance requirements:* For master's, minimum GPA of 2.5, Essays, Recommendation letters, Transcripts. Additional exam requirements/recommendations for international students: Required—TOEFL (minimum score 550 paper-based; 79 iBT), IELTS (minimum score 6.5). *Application deadline:* For fall admission, 5/15 priority date for domestic and international students; for spring admission, 10/15 priority date for domestic and international students. Applications are processed on a rolling basis. Application fee: $40 ($50 for international students). Electronic applications accepted. *Expenses: Tuition:* Part-time $890 per credit. *Required fees:* $50 per unit. *Financial support:* In 2018–19, 26 students received support, including 12 research assistantships with full and partial tuition reimbursements available (averaging $4,895 per year); teaching assistantships with tuition reimbursements available, scholarships/grants, tuition waivers (full and partial), and unspecified assistantships also available. Support available to part-time students. Financial award application deadline: 4/1. *Unit head:* Souhail Elhouar, Chairman, 309-677-3830, E-mail: selhouar@bradley.edu. *Application contact:* Rachel Webb, Director of On-Campus Graduate Admissions, 309-677-2375, E-mail: bugrad@bradley.edu.
Website: http://www.bradley.edu/academic/departments/cec/

Brigham Young University, Graduate Studies, Ira A. Fulton College of Engineering, Department of Civil and Environmental Engineering, Provo, UT 84602. Offers civil engineering (MS, PhD). *Faculty:* 16 full-time (0 women), 3 part-time/adjunct (2 women). *Students:* 54 full-time (14 women); includes 7 minority (4 Asian, non-Hispanic/Latino; 1 Hispanic/Latino; 2 Two or more races, non-Hispanic/Latino), 13 international. Average age 29. 19 applicants, 53% accepted, 10 enrolled. In 2018, 27 master's awarded. *Degree requirements:* For master's, thesis (for some programs), Fundamentals of Engineering (FE) Exam; for doctorate, comprehensive exam, thesis/dissertation. *Entrance requirements:* For master's, GRE General Test, minimum cumulative GPA of 3.0 in last 60 hours of upper-division course work; for doctorate, GRE General Test, Minimum cumulative GPA of 3.0 in last 60 hours of upper-division course work. Additional exam requirements/recommendations for international students: Required—TOEFL (minimum score 580 paper-based; 85 iBT), IELTS (minimum score 7). *Application deadline:* For fall admission, 2/15 for domestic and international students; for winter admission, 9/5 for domestic and international students; for spring admission, 2/5 for domestic and international students; for summer admission, 2/5 for domestic and international students. Application fee: $50. Electronic applications accepted. *Financial support:* In 2018–19, 63 students received support, including 74 research assistantships (averaging $13,080 per year), 42 teaching assistantships (averaging $3,372 per year); fellowships and scholarships/grants also available. Financial award application deadline: 1/15; financial award applicants required to submit FAFSA. *Faculty research:* Structural optimization; finite element modeling and earthquake resistant analysis; groundwater, surface water, watershed and hydrologic modeling and visualization; subsurface environmental issues including transport, remediation, monitoring and characterization; capacity of deep foundations under static and dynamic loading and the behavior and mitigation of liquefiable soils. *Total annual research expenditures:* $1.4 million. *Unit head:* Dr. Norman L. Jones, Department Chair, 801-422-2811, Fax: 801-422-0159, E-mail: njones@byu.edu. *Application contact:* Dr. Fernando S. Fonseca, Graduate Coordinator, 801-422-2811, Fax: 801-422-0159, E-mail: ffonseca@byu.edu.
Website: http://ceen.et.byu.edu/

Bucknell University, Graduate Studies, College of Engineering, Department of Civil and Environmental Engineering, Lewisburg, PA 17837. Offers MSCE, MSEV. *Degree requirements:* For master's, thesis. *Entrance requirements:* For master's, GRE General Test, minimum GPA of 3.0. Additional exam requirements/recommendations for international students: Required—TOEFL (minimum score 600 paper-based). *Faculty research:* Pile foundations, rehabilitation of bridges, deep-shaft biological-waste treatment, pre-cast concrete structures.

California Baptist University, Program in Civil Engineering, Riverside, CA 92504-3206. Offers MS. *Program availability:* Part-time. *Faculty:* 7 full-time (1 woman), 1 part-time/adjunct (0 women). *Students:* 7 full-time (1 woman), 1 part-time (0 women); includes 3 minority (all Hispanic/Latino), 3 international. Average age 28. 3 applicants, 100% accepted, 1 enrolled. In 2018, 4 master's awarded. *Entrance requirements:* For master's, minimum undergraduate GPA of 3.0, bachelor's transcripts, three letters of recommendation, essay, resume, interview. Additional exam requirements/recommendations for international students: Required—TOEFL (minimum score 80 iBT). *Application deadline:* For fall admission, 8/1 priority date for domestic students, 7/1 priority date for international students; for spring admission, 12/1 priority date for domestic students, 11/1 priority date for international students. Applications are processed on a rolling basis. Application fee: $45. Electronic applications accepted. *Expenses:* $858 per unit. *Financial support:* In 2018–19, 1 student received support. Federal Work-Study and scholarships/grants available. Financial award applicants required to submit CSS PROFILE or FAFSA. *Faculty research:* Resilient infrastructure, probabilistic capacity/demand model, pavement performance behavior, environmental nanotechnology, nanofabrication. *Unit head:* Dr. Anthony Donaldson, Dean, College of Engineering, 951-343-4841, E-mail: adonaldson@calbaptist.edu. *Application contact:* Dr. Jong-Wha Bai, Department Chair, Civil Engineering and Construction Management, 951-343-4935, E-mail: jbai@calbaptist.edu.

California Institute of Technology, Division of Engineering and Applied Science, Option in Civil Engineering, Pasadena, CA 91125-0001. Offers MS, PhD, Engr. *Degree requirements:* For doctorate, thesis/dissertation. *Faculty research:* Earthquake engineering, soil mechanics, finite-element analysis, hydraulics, coastal engineering.

California Polytechnic State University, San Luis Obispo, College of Engineering, Department of Civil and Environmental Engineering, San Luis Obispo, CA 93407. Offers MS. *Program availability:* Part-time. *Faculty:* 11 full-time (3 women), 2 part-time/adjunct (0 women). *Students:* 36 full-time (16 women), 5 part-time (0 women); includes 16 minority (8 Asian, non-Hispanic/Latino; 5 Hispanic/Latino; 3 Two or more races, non-Hispanic/Latino), 3 international. Average age 23. 73 applicants, 59% accepted, 24 enrolled. In 2018, 48 master's awarded. *Degree requirements:* For master's, comprehensive exam (for some programs), thesis (for some programs). *Entrance requirements:* For master's, GRE. Additional exam requirements/recommendations for international students: Required—TOEFL (minimum score 80 iBT). *Application deadline:* For fall admission, 1/1 for domestic students, 3/1 priority date for international students. Applications are processed on a rolling basis. Application fee: $55. Electronic applications accepted. *Expenses: Tuition, area resident:* Full-time $7176; part-time $4164 per year. Tuition, state resident: full-time $10,965. Tuition, nonresident: full-time $10,965. *Required fees:* $6336; $3711. *Financial support:* Fellowships, research assistantships, teaching assistantships, career-related internships or fieldwork, and scholarships/grants available. Financial award application deadline: 3/2; financial award applicants required to submit FAFSA. *Faculty research:* Transportation and traffic, environmental protection, geotechnology, water engineering. *Unit head:* Dr. Robb Moss, Graduate Coordinator, 805-756-6427, E-mail: rmoss@calpoly.edu. *Application contact:* Dr. Robb Moss, Graduate Coordinator, 805-756-6427, E-mail: rmoss@calpoly.edu.
Website: http://ceenve.calpoly.edu

California State Polytechnic University, Pomona, Program in Civil Engineering, Pomona, CA 91768-2557. Offers civil engineering (MS), including environmental and water resources engineering, geotechnical engineering, structural engineering, transportation engineering. *Program availability:* Part-time, evening/weekend. *Students:* 34 full-time (11 women), 63 part-time (15 women); includes 62 minority (3 Black or African American, non-Hispanic/Latino; 25 Asian, non-Hispanic/Latino; 32 Hispanic/

Latino; 2 Two or more races, non-Hispanic/Latino), 20 international. Average age 28. 116 applicants, 66% accepted, 45 enrolled. In 2018, 51 master's awarded. *Degree requirements:* For master's, project or thesis. *Entrance requirements:* Additional exam requirements/recommendations for international students: Required—TOEFL (minimum score 550 paper-based). *Application deadline:* Applications are processed on a rolling basis. Application fee: $55. Electronic applications accepted. *Expenses:* Contact institution. *Financial support:* Application deadline: 3/2; applicants required to submit FAFSA. *Faculty research:* Environmental and water resources engineering, geotechnical engineering, structural engineering, transportation engineering. *Unit head:* Dr. Lisa Wang, Professor/Graduate Coordinator, 909-869-4641, Fax: 909-869-4342, E-mail: ylwang@cpp.edu. *Application contact:* Dr. Lisa Wang, Professor/Graduate Coordinator, 909-869-4641, Fax: 909-869-4342, E-mail: ylwang@cpp.edu.
Website: http://www.cpp.edu/~engineering/CE/msce.shtml

California State University, Fresno, Division of Research and Graduate Studies, Lyles College of Engineering, Department of Civil and Geomatics Engineering, Fresno, CA 93740-8027. Offers MS. *Program availability:* Part-time, evening/weekend. *Degree requirements:* For master's, thesis or alternative. *Entrance requirements:* For master's, GRE General Test, minimum GPA of 2.75. Additional exam requirements/recommendations for international students: Required—TOEFL. Electronic applications accepted. *Faculty research:* Surveying, water damage, instrumentation equipment, agricultural drainage, aerial triangulation, dairy manure particles.

California State University, Fullerton, Graduate Studies, College of Engineering and Computer Science, Department of Civil and Environmental Engineering, Fullerton, CA 92831-3599. Offers civil engineering (MS), including architectural engineering, environmental engineering. *Program availability:* Part-time. *Degree requirements:* For master's, comprehensive exam, project or thesis. *Entrance requirements:* For master's, minimum undergraduate GPA of 2.5. *Faculty research:* Soil-structure interaction, finite-element analysis, computer-aided analysis and design.

California State University, Long Beach, Graduate Studies, College of Engineering, Department of Civil Engineering and Construction Engineering Management, Long Beach, CA 90840. Offers civil engineering (MSCE). *Program availability:* Part-time. *Degree requirements:* For master's, comprehensive exam or thesis. *Entrance requirements:* Additional exam requirements/recommendations for international students: Required—TOEFL. *Application deadline:* For fall admission, 3/1 for domestic students. Application fee: $55. Electronic applications accepted. *Expenses: Required fees:* $2628 per term. Tuition and fees vary according to class time, course level, course load, degree level, campus/location and program. *Financial support:* Career-related internships or fieldwork, Federal Work-Study, institutionally sponsored loans, scholarships/grants, and unspecified assistantships available. Financial award application deadline: 3/2; financial award applicants required to submit FAFSA. *Faculty research:* Soils, hydraulics, seismic structures, composite metals, computer-aided manufacturing. *Unit head:* Antonella Sciortino, Chair, 562-985-5118, Fax: 562-985-2380, E-mail: antonella.sciortino@csulb.edu. *Application contact:* Vesna Terzic, Graduate Advisor, 562-985-7816, E-mail: vesna.terzic@csulb.edu.
Website: www.csulb.edu/colleges/coe/cecem/

California State University, Los Angeles, Graduate Studies, College of Engineering, Computer Science, and Technology, Department of Civil Engineering, Los Angeles, CA 90032-8530. Offers MS. *Program availability:* Part-time, evening/weekend. *Degree requirements:* For master's, comprehensive exam or thesis. *Entrance requirements:* For master's, GRE or minimum GPA of 2.4. Additional exam requirements/recommendations for international students: Required—TOEFL (minimum score 550 paper-based). *Faculty research:* Structure, hydraulics, hydrology, soil mechanics.

California State University, Northridge, Graduate Studies, College of Engineering and Computer Science, Department of Civil Engineering and Construction Management, Northridge, CA 91330. Offers engineering (MS), including structural engineering. *Program availability:* Part-time, evening/weekend. *Degree requirements:* For master's, thesis. *Entrance requirements:* Additional exam requirements/recommendations for international students: Required—TOEFL. *Faculty research:* Composite study.

California State University, Sacramento, College of Engineering and Computer Science, Department of Civil Engineering, Sacramento, CA 95819. Offers MS. *Program availability:* Part-time, evening/weekend. *Degree requirements:* For master's, thesis, project, or comprehensive exam; writing proficiency exam. *Entrance requirements:* Additional exam requirements/recommendations for international students: Required—TOEFL (minimum score 550 paper-based; 80 iBT); Recommended—IELTS, TSE. Electronic applications accepted. *Expenses:* Contact institution.

Carleton University, Faculty of Graduate Studies, Faculty of Engineering and Design, Department of Civil and Environmental Engineering, Ottawa, ON K1S 5B6, Canada. Offers M Eng, MA Sc, PhD. *Degree requirements:* For master's, thesis optional; for doctorate, thesis/dissertation. *Entrance requirements:* For master's, honors degree; for doctorate, MA Sc or M Eng. Additional exam requirements/recommendations for international students: Required—TOEFL. *Faculty research:* Pollution and wastewater management, fire safety engineering, earthquake engineering, structural design, bridge engineering.

Carnegie Mellon University, Carnegie Institute of Technology, Department of Civil and Environmental Engineering, Pittsburgh, PA 15213. Offers advanced infrastructure systems (MS, PhD); advanced infrastructure systems technology development and application (MS); air quality engineering and science (MS); civil and environmental engineering (MS, PhD); civil and environmental engineering/engineering and public policy (PhD); civil engineering (MS, PhD); computational mechanics (MS, PhD); computational modeling and monitoring for resilient structural and material systems (MS); energy infrastructure systems (MS); environmental engineering (MS, PhD); environmental management and science (MS, PhD); IT-based sustainable global infrastructure and construction management (MS); sustainability and green design (MS); water quality engineering and science (MS). *Program availability:* Part-time. *Faculty:* 23 full-time (5 women), 12 part-time/adjunct (3 women). *Students:* 264 full-time (109 women); includes 24 minority (6 Black or African American, non-Hispanic/Latino; 13 Asian, non-Hispanic/Latino; 5 Hispanic/Latino), 208 international. Average age 25. 630 applicants, 64% accepted, 114 enrolled. In 2018, 112 master's, 15 doctorates awarded. Terminal master's awarded for partial completion of doctoral program. *Degree requirements:* For master's, thesis optional; for doctorate, comprehensive exam, thesis/dissertation, two-part qualifying exam, public defense of dissertation. *Entrance requirements:* For master's, GRE General Test, BS in engineering, science or mathematics; for doctorate, GRE General Test, BS or MS in engineering, science or mathematics. Additional exam requirements/recommendations for international students: Required—TOEFL (minimum score 84 iBT), TOEFL (minimum score 84 iBT) or IELTS (7.0). *Application deadline:* For fall admission, 1/5 priority date for domestic and international students; for spring admission, 9/15 priority date for domestic and international students. Applications are processed on a rolling basis. Application fee: $75. Electronic applications accepted. *Expenses:* Contact institution. *Financial support:* In 2018–19, 137 students received support. Fellowships with tuition reimbursements available, research assistantships with tuition reimbursements available, scholarships/grants, health care benefits, tuition waivers (full and partial), unspecified assistantships,

and service assistantships available. Financial award application deadline: 1/5. *Faculty research:* Advanced infrastructure systems; environmental engineering, sustainability, and science; mechanics, materials, and computing. *Total annual research expenditures:* $7.4 million. *Unit head:* Dr. David A. Dzombak, Professor and Department Head, 412-268-2941, Fax: 412-268-7813, E-mail: dzombak@cmu.edu. *Application contact:* David A. Vey, Director of Graduate Programs, 412-268-2292, Fax: 412-268-7813, E-mail: dvey@andrew.cmu.edu.
Website: http://www.cmu.edu/cee/

Case Western Reserve University, School of Graduate Studies, Case School of Engineering, Department of Civil Engineering, Cleveland, OH 44106. Offers civil engineering (MS, PhD). *Program availability:* Part-time. *Faculty:* 8 full-time (2 women). *Students:* 19 full-time (3 women), 16 international. In 2018, 7 master's, 2 doctorates awarded. *Degree requirements:* For master's, thesis (for some programs); for doctorate, thesis/dissertation, qualifying exam, teaching experience. *Entrance requirements:* For master's and doctorate, GRE General Test. Additional exam requirements/recommendations for international students: Required—TOEFL. *Application deadline:* For fall admission, 8/1 priority date for domestic students; for spring admission, 1/1 for domestic students. Application fee: $50. *Expenses: Tuition:* Full-time $45,168; part-time $1939 per credit hour. *Required fees:* $36; $18 per semester. $18 per semester. *Financial support:* In 2018–19, 12 students received support, including 2 fellowships, 5 research assistantships with tuition reimbursements available, 5 teaching assistantships; institutionally sponsored loans also available. Financial award application deadline: 8/1; financial award applicants required to submit FAFSA. *Faculty research:* Infrastructure performance and reliability, environmental, geotechnical, infrastructure reliability, mechanics, structures. *Total annual research expenditures:* $900,000. *Unit head:* Xiong "Bill" Yu, Interim chair, 216-368-6247, Fax: 216-368-5229, E-mail: xxy21@case.edu. *Application contact:* Carla Wilson, Student Affairs Coordinator, 216-368-4580, Fax: 216-368-3007, E-mail: cxw75@case.edu.
Website: http://engineering.case.edu/eciv/

The Catholic University of America, School of Engineering, Department of Civil Engineering, Washington, DC 20064. Offers civil engineering (MS, PhD); transportation and infrastructure systems (Certificate). *Program availability:* Part-time. *Faculty:* 6 full-time (0 women), 4 part-time/adjunct (1 woman). *Students:* 15 full-time (3 women), 15 part-time (4 women); includes 8 minority (3 Black or African American, non-Hispanic/Latino; 5 Two or more races, non-Hispanic/Latino), 20 international. Average age 33. 36 applicants, 75% accepted, 13 enrolled. In 2018, 15 master's, 2 doctorates awarded. *Degree requirements:* For master's, thesis optional; for doctorate, comprehensive exam, thesis/dissertation. *Entrance requirements:* For master's and doctorate, GRE General Test, statement of purpose, official copies of academic transcripts, three letters of recommendation. Additional exam requirements/recommendations for international students: Required—TOEFL (minimum score 550 paper-based; 80 iBT). *Application deadline:* For fall admission, 7/15 priority date for domestic students, 7/1 for international students; for spring admission, 11/15 priority date for domestic students, 11/1 for international students. Applications are processed on a rolling basis. Application fee: $55. Electronic applications accepted. *Expenses:* Contact institution. *Financial support:* Fellowships, research assistantships, teaching assistantships, Federal Work-Study, scholarships/grants, tuition waivers (full and partial), and unspecified assistantships available. Financial award application deadline: 2/1; financial award applicants required to submit FAFSA. *Faculty research:* Transportation engineering, solid mechanics, construction engineering and management, environmental engineering and water resources, structural engineering. *Unit head:* Dr. Arash Massoudieh, Chair, 202-319-5671, Fax: 202-319-6677, E-mail: massoudieh@cua.edu. *Application contact:* Dr. Steven Brown, Director of Graduate Admissions, 202-319-5057, Fax: 202-319-6533, E-mail: cua-admissions@cua.edu.
Website: https://engineering.catholic.edu/civil/index.html

The Citadel, The Military College of South Carolina, Citadel Graduate College, School of Engineering, Department of Civil and Environmental Engineering, Charleston, SC 29409. Offers built environment and public health (Graduate Certificate); civil engineering (MS); geotechnical engineering (Graduate Certificate); structural engineering (Graduate Certificate); transportation engineering (Graduate Certificate). *Program availability:* Part-time, evening/weekend. *Degree requirements:* For master's, plan of study outlining intended areas of interest and top four corresponding courses of interest. *Entrance requirements:* For master's, official transcript of baccalaureate degree from ABET-accredited engineering program or approved alternative; 2 letters of recommendation; for Graduate Certificate, official transcript of baccalaureate degree directly from an accredited college or university. Additional exam requirements/recommendations for international students: Required—TOEFL (minimum score 550 paper-based; 79 iBT). Electronic applications accepted. *Expenses:* Tuition, state resident: part-time $595 per credit hour. Tuition, nonresident: part-time $1020 per credit hour. *Required fees:* $90 per term.

City College of the City University of New York, Graduate School, Grove School of Engineering, Department of Civil Engineering, New York, NY 10031-9198. Offers ME, MS, PhD. PhD program offered jointly with Graduate School and University Center of the City University of New York. *Program availability:* Part-time. *Degree requirements:* For master's, thesis optional; for doctorate, one foreign language, comprehensive exam, thesis/dissertation. *Entrance requirements:* For master's and doctorate, GRE General Test. Additional exam requirements/recommendations for international students: Required—TOEFL (minimum score 500 paper-based; 61 iBT). *Faculty research:* Earthquake engineering, transportation systems, groundwater, environmental systems, highway systems.

Clarkson University, Wallace H. Coulter School of Engineering, Department of Civil and Environmental Engineering, Potsdam, NY 13699. Offers ME, MS, PhD. *Faculty:* 18 full-time (3 women), 6 part-time/adjunct (1 woman). *Students:* 27 full-time (12 women), 2 part-time (1 woman); includes 1 minority (Hispanic/Latino), 17 international. 47 applicants, 55% accepted, 11 enrolled. In 2018, 7 master's, 4 doctorates awarded. *Degree requirements:* For master's, thesis (for MS); project (for ME); for doctorate, comprehensive exam, thesis/dissertation. *Entrance requirements:* For master's and doctorate, GRE. Additional exam requirements/recommendations for international students: Required—TOEFL (minimum score 550 paper-based, 80 iBT) or IELTS (6.5). *Application deadline:* Applications are processed on a rolling basis. Application fee: $50. Electronic applications accepted. *Expenses: Tuition:* Full-time $24,984; part-time $1388 per credit hour. *Required fees:* $225. Tuition and fees vary according to campus/location and program. *Financial support:* Scholarships/grants and unspecified assistantships available. *Unit head:* Dr. John Dempsey, Chair of Civil and Environmental Engineering, 315-268-6529, E-mail: jdempsey@clarkson.edu. *Application contact:* Dan Capogna, Director of Graduate Admissions, 518-631-9910, E-mail: graduate@clarkson.edu.
Website: https://www.clarkson.edu/academics/graduate

Clemson University, Graduate School, College of Engineering, Computing and Applied Sciences, Glenn Department of Civil Engineering, Clemson, SC 29634. Offers civil engineering (MS, PhD), including construction engineering and management, construction materials, geotechnical engineering, structural engineering, transportation engineering, water resources engineering. *Program availability:* Part-time. *Faculty:* 20 full-time (3 women). *Students:* 109 full-time (23 women), 55 part-time (11 women);

includes 9 minority (2 Black or African American, non-Hispanic/Latino; 2 Asian, non-Hispanic/Latino; 4 Hispanic/Latino; 1 Two or more races, non-Hispanic/Latino), 111 international. Average age 28. 283 applicants, 59% accepted, 53 enrolled. In 2018, 31 master's, 11 doctorates awarded. *Degree requirements:* For master's, thesis or alternative, oral exam, seminar; for doctorate, comprehensive exam, thesis/dissertation, oral exam, seminar. *Entrance requirements:* For master's and doctorate, GRE General Test, unofficial transcripts, letters of recommendation, statement of purpose. Additional exam requirements/recommendations for international students: Required—TOEFL (minimum score 80 paper-based; 80 iBT), PTE (minimum score 54); Recommended—IELTS (minimum score 6.5). *Application deadline:* For fall admission, 4/15 for domestic and international students; for spring admission, 9/15 for domestic and international students. Applications are processed on a rolling basis. Application fee: $80 ($90 for international students). Electronic applications accepted. *Expenses:* $6823 per semester full-time resident, $14023 per semester full-time non-resident, $833 per credit hour part-time resident, $1731 per credit hour part-time non-resident, online $1264 per credit hour, $4938 doctoral programs resident, $10405 doctoral programs non-resident, $1144 full-time graduate assistant, other fees may apply per session. *Financial support:* In 2018–19, 104 students received support, including 20 fellowships with full and partial tuition reimbursements available (averaging $4,491 per year), 43 research assistantships with full and partial tuition reimbursements available (averaging $16,364 per year), 1 teaching assistantship with full and partial tuition reimbursement available (averaging $12,750 per year); career-related internships or fieldwork and unspecified assistantships also available. Financial award application deadline: 4/15. *Faculty research:* Applied fluid mechanics, construction materials, project management, structural and geotechnical engineering, transportation. *Total annual research expenditures:* $4.9 million. *Unit head:* Dr. Ronald Andrus, Interim Department Chair, 864-656-0488, E-mail: randrus@clemson.edu. *Application contact:* Dr. Abdul Khan, Graduate Program Coordinator, 864-656-3327, E-mail: abdkhan@clemson.edu.
Website: https://www.clemson.edu/cecas/departments/ce/

Cleveland State University, College of Graduate Studies, Fenn College of Engineering, Department of Civil and Environmental Engineering, Cleveland, OH 44115. Offers MS, D Eng. *Program availability:* Part-time, evening/weekend. *Faculty:* 8 full-time (2 women). *Students:* 25 full-time (9 women), 30 part-time (5 women); includes 3 minority (2 Asian, non-Hispanic/Latino; 1 Hispanic/Latino), 33 international. Average age 25. 214 applicants, 61% accepted, 21 enrolled. In 2018, 42 master's, 1 doctorate awarded. *Entrance requirements:* For master's, GRE General Test, GRE Subject Test, minimum GPA of 2.75; for doctorate, GRE General Test, GRE Subject Test, minimum GPA of 3.25. Additional exam requirements/recommendations for international students: Required—TOEFL (minimum score 550 paper-based; 78 iBT). *Application deadline:* Applications are processed on a rolling basis. Application fee: $40. Electronic applications accepted. *Expenses:* Tuition, state resident: full-time $7232.55; part-time $6676 per credit hour. Tuition, nonresident: full-time $12,375. *International tuition:* $18,914 full-time. *Required fees:* $80; $80 $40. Tuition and fees vary according to program. *Financial support:* Research assistantships, teaching assistantships, career-related internships or fieldwork, scholarships/grants, and unspecified assistantships available. Financial award application deadline: 9/1. *Faculty research:* Solid-waste disposal, constitutive modeling, transportation, safety engineering, concrete materials. *Total annual research expenditures:* $800,000. *Unit head:* Dr. Norbert Joseph Delatte, Chairperson, 216-687-9259, Fax: 216-687-5395, E-mail: n.delatte@csuohio.edu. *Application contact:* Deborah L. Brown, Interim Assistant Director, Graduate Admissions, 216-523-7572, Fax: 216-687-9214, E-mail: d.l.brown@csuohio.edu.
Website: http://www.csuohio.edu/engineering/civil

Colorado School of Mines, Office of Graduate Studies, Department of Civil and Environmental Engineering, Golden, CO 80401. Offers civil and environmental engineering (MS, PhD); environmental engineering science (MS, PhD); hydrologic science and engineering (MS, PhD); underground construction and tunneling (MS, PhD). *Program availability:* Part-time. *Faculty:* 44 full-time (16 women), 11 part-time/adjunct (6 women). *Students:* 99 full-time (46 women), 23 part-time (10 women); includes 15 minority (2 Black or African American, non-Hispanic/Latino; 3 Asian, non-Hispanic/Latino; 4 Hispanic/Latino; 6 Two or more races, non-Hispanic/Latino), 21 international. Average age 28. 171 applicants, 60% accepted, 47 enrolled. In 2018, 45 master's, 13 doctorates awarded. *Degree requirements:* For master's, thesis (for some programs); for doctorate, comprehensive exam, thesis/dissertation. *Entrance requirements:* For master's and doctorate, GRE General Test. Additional exam requirements/recommendations for international students: Required—TOEFL (minimum score 550 paper-based; 79 iBT). *Application deadline:* For fall admission, 12/15 priority date for domestic students, 1/15 priority date for international students; for spring admission, 9/1 priority date for domestic and international students. Application fee: $60 ($80 for international students). Electronic applications accepted. *Expenses:* Tuition, state resident: full-time $16,650; part-time $925 per contact hour. Tuition, nonresident: full-time $36,270; part-time $2015 per contact hour. *International tuition:* $36,270 full-time. *Required fees:* $2314; $2314 per semester. *Financial support:* In 2018–19, 62 research assistantships with full tuition reimbursements, 2 teaching assistantships with full tuition reimbursements were awarded; scholarships/grants, health care benefits, and unspecified assistantships also available. Financial award application deadline: 12/15; financial award applicants required to submit FAFSA. *Faculty research:* Treatment of water and wastes, environmental law: policy and practice, natural environment systems, hazardous waste management, environmental data analysis. *Unit head:* Dr. Terri Hogue, Department Head, 303-384-2588, E-mail: thogue@mines.edu. *Application contact:* Dr. Tim VanHaverbeke, Research Faculty/Program Manager, 303-273-3467, E-mail: tvanhave@mines.edu.

Colorado State University, Walter Scott, Jr. College of Engineering, Department of Civil and Environmental Engineering, Fort Collins, CO 80523-1372. Offers MS, PhD. *Program availability:* Part-time, online learning. Terminal master's awarded for partial completion of doctoral program. *Degree requirements:* For master's, thesis, publication (for MS); for doctorate, comprehensive exam, thesis/dissertation, journal paper publication. *Entrance requirements:* For master's, GRE, minimum GPA of 3.0; resume; statement of purpose; three letters of recommendation; transcripts; for doctorate, GRE, master's degree; minimum GPA of 3.0; resume; statement of purpose; three letters of recommendation; transcripts. Additional exam requirements/recommendations for international students: Required—TOEFL (minimum score 550 paper-based; 80 iBT), IELTS (minimum score 6.5), PTE (minimum score 58). Electronic applications accepted. *Expenses:* Contact institution. *Faculty research:* Environmental and energy systems, infrastructure resiliency and sustainability, water engineering and science.

Columbia University, Fu Foundation School of Engineering and Applied Science, Department of Civil Engineering and Engineering Mechanics, New York, NY 10027. Offers civil engineering (MS, Eng Sc D, PhD); construction engineering and management (MS); engineering mechanics (MS, Eng Sc D, PhD). *Program availability:* Part-time, online learning. Terminal master's awarded for partial completion of doctoral program. *Degree requirements:* For doctorate, thesis/dissertation, qualifying exam. *Entrance requirements:* For master's and doctorate, GRE General Test. Additional exam requirements/recommendations for international students: Required—TOEFL, IELTS, PTE. Electronic applications accepted. *Faculty research:* Structural dynamics, structural health and monitoring, fatigue and fracture mechanics, geo-environmental engineering, multiscale science and engineering.

Concordia University, School of Graduate Studies, Faculty of Engineering and Computer Science, Department of Building, Civil and Environmental Engineering, Montréal, QC H3G 1M8, Canada. Offers building engineering (M Eng, MA Sc, PhD, Certificate); civil engineering (M Eng, MA Sc, PhD); environmental engineering (Certificate). *Degree requirements:* For master's, thesis or alternative; for doctorate, comprehensive exam, thesis/dissertation. *Faculty research:* Structural engineering, geotechnical engineering, water resources and fluid engineering, transportation engineering, systems engineering.

Cooper Union for the Advancement of Science and Art, Albert Nerken School of Engineering, New York, NY 10003. Offers chemical engineering (ME); civil engineering (ME); electrical engineering (ME); mechanical engineering (ME). *Program availability:* Part-time. *Degree requirements:* For master's, thesis (for some programs), thesis or special project. *Entrance requirements:* For master's, BE or BS in an engineering discipline; official copies of school transcripts including secondary (high school), college and university work; two letters of recommendation; resume. Additional exam requirements/recommendations for international students: Required—TOEFL (minimum score 600 paper-based; 100 iBT). Electronic applications accepted. *Faculty research:* Analytics, bioengineering, dynamic systems, nanoscience, sustainability, STEM education.

Cornell University, Graduate School, Graduate Fields of Engineering, Field of Civil and Environmental Engineering, Ithaca, NY 14853. Offers engineering management (M Eng, MS, PhD); environmental engineering (M Eng, MS, PhD); environmental fluid mechanics and hydrology (M Eng, MS, PhD); environmental systems engineering (M Eng, MS, PhD); geotechnical engineering (M Eng, MS, PhD); remote sensing (M Eng, MS, PhD); structural engineering (M Eng, MS, PhD); structural mechanics (M Eng, MS); transportation engineering (MS, PhD); transportation systems engineering (M Eng); water resource systems (M Eng, MS, PhD). Terminal master's awarded for partial completion of doctoral program. *Degree requirements:* For master's, thesis (MS); for doctorate, comprehensive exam, thesis/dissertation. *Entrance requirements:* For master's and doctorate, GRE General Test (recommended), 2 letters of recommendation. Additional exam requirements/recommendations for international students: Required—TOEFL (minimum score 600 paper-based; 77 iBT). Electronic applications accepted. *Faculty research:* Environmental engineering, geotechnical engineering, remote sensing, environmental fluid mechanics and hydrology, structural engineering.

Dalhousie University, Faculty of Engineering, Department of Civil and Resource Engineering, Halifax, NS B3J 2X4, Canada. Offers civil engineering (M Eng, MA Sc, PhD); environmental engineering (M Eng, MA Sc); mineral resource engineering (M Eng, MA Sc, PhD). *Degree requirements:* For master's, thesis; for doctorate, thesis/dissertation. *Entrance requirements:* Additional exam requirements/recommendations for international students: Required—TOEFL, IELTS, CANTEST, CAEL, or Michigan English Language Assessment Battery. Electronic applications accepted. *Faculty research:* Environmental/water resources, bridge engineering, geotechnical engineering, pavement design and management/highway materials, composite materials.

Drexel University, College of Engineering, Department of Civil, Architectural, and Environmental Engineering, Program in Civil Engineering, Philadelphia, PA 19104-2875. Offers MS, PhD. *Program availability:* Part-time, evening/weekend. *Degree requirements:* For master's, thesis optional; for doctorate, thesis/dissertation. *Entrance requirements:* For master's, minimum GPA of 3.0; for doctorate, minimum GPA of 3.5, MS in civil engineering. Additional exam requirements/recommendations for international students: Required—TOEFL. Electronic applications accepted.

Duke University, Graduate School, Pratt School of Engineering, Department of Civil and Environmental Engineering, Durham, NC 27708. Offers civil and environmental engineering (MS, PhD); civil engineering (M Eng); computational mechanics and scientific computing (M Eng); environmental engineering (M Eng, MS, PhD); risk engineering (M Eng). Terminal master's awarded for partial completion of doctoral program. *Degree requirements:* For doctorate, thesis/dissertation. *Entrance requirements:* For master's and doctorate, GRE General Test. Additional exam requirements/recommendations for international students: Required—TOEFL (minimum score 550 paper-based; 90 iBT), IELTS (minimum score 7). Electronic applications accepted. *Faculty research:* Environmental process engineering, hydrology and fluid dynamics, materials, structures and geo-systems.

Duke University, Graduate School, Pratt School of Engineering, Master of Engineering Program, Durham, NC 27708-0271. Offers biomedical engineering (M Eng); civil engineering (M Eng); computational mechanics and scientific computing (M Eng); electrical and computer engineering (M Eng); environmental engineering (M Eng); materials science and engineering (M Eng); mechanical engineering (M Eng); photonics and optical sciences (M Eng); risk engineering (M Eng). *Program availability:* Part-time. *Entrance requirements:* For master's, GRE General Test, resume, 3 letters of recommendation, statement of purpose, transcripts. Additional exam requirements/recommendations for international students: Required—TOEFL. Electronic applications accepted.

École Polytechnique de Montréal, Graduate Programs, Department of Civil, Geological and Mining Engineering, Montréal, QC H3C 3A7, Canada. Offers civil, geological and mining engineering (DESS); environmental engineering (M Eng, M Sc A, PhD); geotechnical engineering (M Eng, M Sc A, PhD); hydraulics engineering (M Eng, M Sc A, PhD); structural engineering (M Eng, M Sc A, PhD); transportation engineering (M Eng, M Sc A, PhD). *Program availability:* Part-time. *Degree requirements:* For master's, one foreign language, thesis; for doctorate, one foreign language, thesis/dissertation. *Entrance requirements:* For master's, minimum GPA of 2.75; for doctorate, minimum GPA of 3.0. *Faculty research:* Water resources management, characteristics of building materials, aging of dams, pollution control.

Embry-Riddle Aeronautical University–Daytona, Department of Civil Engineering, Daytona Beach, FL 32114-3900. Offers MS. *Degree requirements:* For master's, thesis optional. *Entrance requirements:* For master's, GRE, minimum cumulative GPA of 3.0. Additional exam requirements/recommendations for international students: Required—TOEFL (minimum score 550 paper-based, 79 iBT) or IELTS (6). Electronic applications accepted.

Florida Agricultural and Mechanical University, Division of Graduate Studies, Research, and Continuing Education, FAMU-FSU College of Engineering, Department of Civil and Environmental Engineering, Tallahassee, FL 32307-3200. Offers civil engineering (M Eng, MS, PhD). *Degree requirements:* For master's, comprehensive exam, thesis optional; for doctorate, comprehensive exam, thesis/dissertation. *Entrance requirements:* For master's, GRE General Test, minimum GPA of 3.0; for doctorate, GRE General Test, minimum GPA of 3.0, letters of recommendation (3). Additional exam requirements/recommendations for international students: Required—TOEFL (minimum score 550 paper-based). *Faculty research:* Geotechnical, environmental, hydraulic, construction materials, and structures.

Florida Atlantic University, College of Engineering and Computer Science, Department of Civil, Environmental and Geomatics Engineering, Boca Raton, FL 33431-0991. Offers civil engineering (MS); environmental engineering (MS). *Program availability:* Part-time, evening/weekend. *Faculty:* 13 full-time (0 women), 1 part-time/adjunct (0 women). *Students:* 13 full-time (7 women), 23 part-time (10 women); includes 9 minority (2 Black or African American, non-Hispanic/Latino; 7 Hispanic/Latino), 18 international. Average age 28. 36 applicants, 44% accepted, 10 enrolled. In 2018, 10 master's awarded. *Degree requirements:* For master's, thesis optional. *Entrance requirements:* For master's, GRE General Test, minimum GPA of 3.0 in last 60 hours of undergraduate course work. Additional exam requirements/recommendations for international students: Required—TOEFL (minimum score 550 paper-based; 61 iBT), IELTS (minimum score 6). *Application deadline:* For fall admission, 7/1 priority date for domestic students, 2/15 for international students; for spring admission, 11/1 for domestic students, 7/15 for international students. Applications are processed on a rolling basis. Application fee: $30. *Expenses: Tuition, area resident:* Full-time $7400; part-time $369.82 per credit. Tuition, state resident: full-time $7400; part-time $369.82 per credit. Tuition, nonresident: full-time $20,496; part-time $1024.81 per credit. *Financial support:* Research assistantships with full tuition reimbursements, teaching assistantships with full tuition reimbursements, career-related internships or fieldwork, Federal Work-Study, scholarships/grants, and unspecified assistantships available. Financial award applicants required to submit FAFSA. *Faculty research:* Structures, geotechnical engineering, environmental and water resources engineering, transportation engineering, materials. *Unit head:* Dr. Yan Yong, Chair, 561-297-3445, Fax: 561-297-0493, E-mail: cege@fau.edu. *Application contact:* Dr. Frederick Bloetscher, Associate Dean & Professor, 561-297-0744, E-mail: fbloetsch@fau.edu. Website: http://www.cege.fau.edu/

Florida Institute of Technology, College of Engineering and Science, Program in Civil Engineering, Melbourne, FL 32901-6975. Offers MS, PhD. *Program availability:* Part-time. *Students:* 29 full-time (6 women), 6 part-time (0 women); includes 1 minority (Black or African American, non-Hispanic/Latino), 29 international. Average age 29. 24 applicants, 83% accepted, 9 enrolled. In 2018, 15 master's, 4 doctorates awarded. *Degree requirements:* For master's, comprehensive exam (for some programs), thesis optional, 30 credit hours; teaching/internship (for thesis) or final examinations (for non-thesis); for doctorate, comprehensive exam, thesis/dissertation, 42 credit hours of coursework beyond the master's degree. *Entrance requirements:* For master's, GRE, 2 letters of recommendation, statement of objectives; for doctorate, GRE, 3 letters of recommendation, minimum GPA of 3.2, resume, statement of objectives, degree from accredited institution. Additional exam requirements/recommendations for international students: Required—TOEFL (minimum score 550 paper-based; 79 iBT). *Application deadline:* For fall admission, 4/1 for international students; for spring admission, 9/30 for international students. Applications are processed on a rolling basis. Electronic applications accepted. *Expenses: Tuition:* Full-time $22,338; part-time $1241 per credit hour. Tuition and fees vary according to degree level, campus/location and program. *Financial support:* Research assistantships, teaching assistantships, career-related internships or fieldwork, institutionally sponsored loans, tuition waivers (partial), unspecified assistantships, and tuition remissions available. Support available to part-time students. Financial award application deadline: 3/1; financial award applicants required to submit FAFSA. *Faculty research:* Groundwater and surface water modeling, pavements, waste materials, in situ soil testing, fiber optic sensors. *Unit head:* Dr. Ashok Pandit, Department Head, 321-674-7151, Fax: 321-768-7565, E-mail: apandit@fit.edu. *Application contact:* Mike Perry, Executive Director of Admissions, 321-674-7127, E-mail: perrymj@fit.edu. Website: https://www.fit.edu/programs/civil-engineering-ms/

Florida International University, College of Engineering and Computing, Department of Civil and Environmental Engineering, Miami, FL 33175. Offers civil engineering (MS, PhD); environmental engineering (MS). *Program availability:* Part-time, evening/weekend, online learning. *Faculty:* 24 full-time (7 women), 11 part-time/adjunct (2 women). *Students:* 82 full-time (28 women), 22 part-time (6 women); includes 33 minority (4 Black or African American, non-Hispanic/Latino; 27 Hispanic/Latino; 2 Two or more races, non-Hispanic/Latino), 66 international. Average age 30. 119 applicants, 43% accepted, 18 enrolled. In 2018, 21 master's, 10 doctorates awarded. Terminal master's awarded for partial completion of doctoral program. *Degree requirements:* For master's, thesis or alternative; for doctorate, comprehensive exam, thesis/dissertation. *Entrance requirements:* For master's, bachelor's degree in related field, 3 letters of recommendation, minimum GPA of 3.0; for doctorate, GRE General Test, minimum graduate GPA of 3.3, 3 letters of recommendation, master's degree, resume, statement of purpose. Additional exam requirements/recommendations for international students: Required—TOEFL (minimum score 550 paper-based; 80 iBT). *Application deadline:* For fall admission, 6/1 for domestic students, 4/1 for international students; for spring admission, 10/1 for domestic students, 9/1 for international students. Applications are processed on a rolling basis. Application fee: $30. Electronic applications accepted. *Financial support:* Federal Work-Study, institutionally sponsored loans, scholarships/grants, health care benefits, and unspecified assistantships available. Financial award application deadline: 3/1; financial award applicants required to submit FAFSA. *Faculty research:* Structural engineering, wind engineering, water resources engineering, transportation engineering, environmental engineering. *Unit head:* Dr. Atorod Azizinamini, Chair, 305-348-2824, Fax: 305-348-2802, E-mail: aazizina@fiu.edu. *Application contact:* Nanett Rojas, Manager, Admissions Operations, 305-348-7464, Fax: 305-348-7441, E-mail: gradadm@fiu.edu. Website: http://cec.fiu.edu

Florida State University, The Graduate School, FAMU-FSU College of Engineering, Department of Civil and Environmental Engineering, Tallahassee, FL 32310. Offers M Eng, MS, PhD. *Program availability:* Part-time. *Degree requirements:* For master's, comprehensive exam, thesis optional; for doctorate, thesis/dissertation. *Entrance requirements:* For master's, GRE General Test (minimum score 1000 in old version), BS in engineering or related field, minimum GPA of 3.0; for doctorate, GRE General Test, master's degree in engineering or related field, minimum GPA of 3.0. Additional exam requirements/recommendations for international students: Required—TOEFL (minimum score 550 paper-based; 80 iBT); Recommended—IELTS (minimum score 6.5). Electronic applications accepted. *Expenses: Tuition, area resident:* Part-time $479.32 per credit hour. Tuition and fees vary according to campus/location and program. *Faculty research:* Tidal hydraulics, temperature effects on bridge girders, codes for coastal construction, field performance of pine bridges, river basin management, transportation pavement design, soil dynamics, structural analysis.

George Mason University, Volgenau School of Engineering, Sid and Reva Dewberry Department of Civil, Environmental, and Infrastructure Engineering, Fairfax, VA 22030. Offers construction project management (MS); transportation engineering (PhD). *Faculty:* 16 full-time (4 women), 15 part-time/adjunct (4 women). *Students:* 59 full-time (20 women), 69 part-time (19 women); includes 34 minority (9 Black or African American, non-Hispanic/Latino; 14 Asian, non-Hispanic/Latino; 11 Hispanic/Latino), 46 international. Average age 28. 117 applicants, 75% accepted, 31 enrolled. In 2018, 39 master's, 8 doctorates awarded. *Degree requirements:* For master's, thesis (for some programs), 30 credits, departmental seminars; for doctorate, thesis/dissertation, qualifying exams. *Entrance requirements:* For master's, GRE, photocopy of passport; 2

official college transcripts; resume; official bank statement; proof of financial support; expanded goals statement; self-evaluation form; BS in engineering or other related science; 3 letters of recommendation; for doctorate, GRE (for those who received degree outside of the U.S.), photocopy of passport; 2 official college transcripts; resume; official bank statement; proof of financial support; expanded goals statement; self-evaluation form; baccalaureate degree in engineering or related science; master's degree (preferred); 3 letters of recommendation. Additional exam requirements/recommendations for international students: Required—TOEFL (minimum score 575 paper-based; 88 iBT), IELTS (minimum score 6.5), PTE (minimum score 59). *Application deadline:* For fall admission, 12/15 priority date for domestic and international students; for spring admission, 8/15 priority date for domestic and international students. Application fee: $75 ($80 for international students). Electronic applications accepted. *Expenses:* $589 per credit in-state, $1,346.75 per credit out-of-state. *Financial support:* In 2018–19, 37 students received support, including 25 research assistantships with tuition reimbursements available (averaging $19,626 per year), 13 teaching assistantships with tuition reimbursements available (averaging $17,449 per year); career-related internships or fieldwork, Federal Work-Study, scholarships/grants, unspecified assistantships, and health care benefits (for full-time research or teaching assistantship recipients) also available. Support available to part-time students. Financial award application deadline: 3/1; financial award applicants required to submit FAFSA. *Faculty research:* Evolutionary design, infrastructure security, intelligent transportation systems, national transportation networks, water quality modeling. *Total annual research expenditures:* $1.6 million. *Unit head:* Liza Wilson Durant, Acting Chair, 703-993-1687, Fax: 703-993-9790, E-mail: ldurant2@gmu.edu. *Application contact:* Laura Kosoglu, Director, Graduate Program, 703-993-1675, Fax: 703-993-9790, E-mail: ceiegrad@gmu.edu. Website: http://civil.gmu.edu/

The George Washington University, School of Engineering and Applied Science, Department of Civil and Environmental Engineering, Washington, DC 20052. Offers MS, PhD, App Sc, Engr, Graduate Certificate. *Program availability:* Part-time, evening/weekend. *Faculty:* 13 full-time (3 women), 5 part-time/adjunct (0 women). *Students:* 31 full-time (14 women), 17 part-time (6 women); includes 3 minority (2 Black or African American, non-Hispanic/Latino; 1 Asian, non-Hispanic/Latino), 41 international. Average age 27. 156 applicants, 51% accepted, 13 enrolled. In 2018, 13 master's, 2 doctorates awarded. *Degree requirements:* For master's, thesis optional; for doctorate, thesis/dissertation, final and qualifying exams. *Entrance requirements:* For master's, appropriate bachelor's degree, minimum GPA of 3.0; for doctorate, GRE (if highest earned degree is BS), appropriate bachelor's or master's degree, minimum GPA of 3.4; for other advanced degree, appropriate master's degree, minimum GPA of 3.0. Additional exam requirements/recommendations for international students: Required—TOEFL or The George Washington University English as a Foreign Language Test. *Application deadline:* For fall admission, 3/1 priority date for domestic students; for spring admission, 10/1 for domestic students. Applications are processed on a rolling basis. Application fee: $75. *Financial support:* In 2018–19, 42 students received support. Fellowships, research assistantships, teaching assistantships, career-related internships or fieldwork, Federal Work-Study, institutionally sponsored loans, and tuition waivers available. Financial award application deadline: 3/1; financial award applicants required to submit FAFSA. *Faculty research:* Computer-integrated manufacturing, materials engineering, electronic materials, fatigue and fracture, reliability. *Unit head:* Dr. Majid T. Manzari, Chair, 202-994-4901, Fax: 202-994-0127, E-mail: manzari@gwu.edu. *Application contact:* Adina Lav, Marketing, Recruiting and Admissions, 202-994-5827, Fax: 202-994-0909, E-mail: engineering@gwu.edu. Website: http://www.cee.seas.gwu.edu/

Georgia Institute of Technology, Graduate Studies, College of Engineering, School of Civil and Environmental Engineering, Program in Civil Engineering, Atlanta, GA 30332-0001. Offers MS, PhD. *Program availability:* Part-time. Terminal master's awarded for partial completion of doctoral program. *Degree requirements:* For master's, thesis optional; for doctorate, comprehensive exam, thesis/dissertation. *Entrance requirements:* For master's and doctorate, GRE. Additional exam requirements/recommendations for international students: Required—TOEFL (minimum score 550 paper-based; 79 iBT). Electronic applications accepted. *Faculty research:* Structural analysis, fluid mechanics, geotechnical engineering, construction management, transportation engineering.

Georgia Southern University, Jack N. Averitt College of Graduate Studies, Allen E. Paulson College of Engineering and Computing, Department of Civil Engineering and Construction, Statesboro, GA 30458. Offers MSAE. *Degree requirements:* For master's, comprehensive exam, thesis (for some programs). *Entrance requirements:* For master's, undergraduate major or equivalent in proposed study area. Additional exam requirements/recommendations for international students: Required—TOEFL (minimum score 550 paper-based; 80 iBT), IELTS (minimum score 6). Electronic applications accepted. *Expenses: Tuition, area resident:* Part-time $3324 per semester. Tuition, state resident: full-time $5814; part-time $3324 per semester. Tuition, nonresident: full-time $23,204; part-time $13,260 per semester. *Required fees:* $2092; $2092. Tuition and fees vary according to course load, degree level, campus/location and program.

Howard University, College of Engineering, Architecture, and Computer Sciences, School of Engineering and Computer Science, Department of Civil Engineering, Washington, DC 20059-0002. Offers M Eng. Offered through the Graduate School of Arts and Sciences. *Degree requirements:* For master's, comprehensive exam, thesis. *Entrance requirements:* For master's, GRE General Test, minimum GPA of 3.0, bachelor's degree in engineering or related field. Additional exam requirements/recommendations for international students: Required—TOEFL. Electronic applications accepted. *Faculty research:* Modeling of concrete, structures, transportation planning, structural analysis, environmental and water resources.

Idaho State University, Graduate School, College of Science and Engineering, Department of Civil and Environmental Engineering, Pocatello, ID 83209-8060. Offers civil engineering (MS); environmental engineering (MS); environmental science and management (MS). *Program availability:* Part-time. *Degree requirements:* For master's, comprehensive exam (for some programs), thesis optional, thesis project, 2 semesters of seminar. *Entrance requirements:* For master's, GRE. Additional exam requirements/recommendations for international students: Required—TOEFL (minimum score 550 paper-based; 80 iBT). Electronic applications accepted. *Faculty research:* Floor vibration investigations, earthquake engineering, base isolation systems and seismic risk assessment, infrastructure revitalization (building foundations and damage, bridge structures, highways, and dams), slope stability and soil erosion, pavement rehabilitation, computational fluid dynamics and flood control structures, microbial fuel cells, water treatment and water quality modeling, environmental risk assessment, biotechnology, nanotechnology.

Illinois Institute of Technology, Graduate College, Armour College of Engineering, Department of Civil, Architectural and Environmental Engineering, Chicago, IL 60616. Offers architectural engineering (M Arch E); civil engineering (MS, PhD), including architectural engineering (MS), construction engineering and management (MS), geoenvironmental engineering (MS), geotechnical engineering (MS), structural engineering (MS), transportation engineering (MS); construction engineering and management (MCEM); environmental engineering (M Env E, MS, PhD); geoenvironmental engineering (M Geoenv E); geotechnical engineering (MGE); infrastructure engineering and management (MPW); structural engineering (MSE); transportation engineering (M Trans E). *Program availability:* Part-time, evening/weekend, online learning. Terminal master's awarded for partial completion of doctoral program. *Degree requirements:* For master's, thesis (for some programs); for doctorate, comprehensive exam, thesis/dissertation. *Entrance requirements:* For master's, GRE General Test (minimum score 900 Quantitative and Verbal, 2.5 Analytical Writing), minimum undergraduate GPA of 3.0; for doctorate, GRE General Test (minimum score 1000 Quantitative and Verbal, 3.0 Analytical Writing), minimum undergraduate GPA of 3.0. Additional exam requirements/recommendations for international students: Required—TOEFL (minimum score 550 paper-based; 80 iBT). Electronic applications accepted. *Faculty research:* Structural, architectural, geotechnical and geoenvironmental engineering; construction engineering and management; transportation engineering; environmental engineering and public works.

Instituto Tecnológico y de Estudios Superiores de Monterrey, Campus Monterrey, Graduate and Research Division, Programs in Engineering, Monterrey, Mexico. Offers applied statistics (M Eng); artificial intelligence (PhD); automation engineering (M Eng); chemical engineering (M Eng); civil engineering (M Eng); electrical engineering (M Eng); electronic engineering (M Eng); environmental engineering (M Eng); industrial engineering (M Eng, PhD); manufacturing engineering (M Eng); mechanical engineering (M Eng); systems and quality engineering (M Eng). M Eng program offered jointly with University of Waterloo; PhD in industrial engineering with Texas A&M University. *Program availability:* Part-time, evening/weekend. Terminal master's awarded for partial completion of doctoral program. *Degree requirements:* For master's, one foreign language, thesis; for doctorate, one foreign language, thesis/dissertation. *Entrance requirements:* For master's, EXADEP; for doctorate, GRE, master's degree in related field. Additional exam requirements/recommendations for international students: Required—TOEFL. *Faculty research:* Flexible manufacturing cells, materials, statistical methods, environmental prevention, control and evaluation.

Iowa State University of Science and Technology, Department of Civil and Construction Engineering, Ames, IA 50011. Offers civil engineering (MS, PhD), including civil engineering materials, construction engineering and management, environmental engineering, geotechnical engineering, structural engineering, transportation engineering. *Degree requirements:* For master's, thesis or alternative; for doctorate, thesis/dissertation. *Entrance requirements:* For master's and doctorate, GRE General Test. Additional exam requirements/recommendations for international students: Required—TOEFL (minimum score 550 paper-based; 82 iBT), IELTS (minimum score 6.5). Electronic applications accepted.

Jackson State University, Graduate School, College of Science, Engineering and Technology, Department of Civil and Environmental Engineering and Industrial Systems and Technology, Jackson, MS 39217. Offers civil engineering (MS, PhD); coastal engineering (MS, PhD); environmental engineering (MS, PhD); hazardous materials management (MS); technology education (MS Ed). *Program availability:* Part-time, evening/weekend. *Degree requirements:* For master's, comprehensive exam, thesis or alternative. *Entrance requirements:* For master's, GRE General Test. Additional exam requirements/recommendations for international students: Required—TOEFL (minimum score 520 paper-based; 67 iBT).

Johns Hopkins University, Engineering Program for Professionals, Part-time Program in Civil Engineering, Baltimore, MD 21218. Offers MCE, Graduate Certificate. *Program availability:* Part-time, evening/weekend, 100% online, blended/hybrid learning. *Faculty:* 8 part-time/adjunct (2 women). *Students:* 22 part-time (4 women). 15 applicants, 67% accepted, 6 enrolled. In 2018, 7 master's, 1 other advanced degree awarded. *Entrance requirements:* Additional exam requirements/recommendations for international students: Required—TOEFL (minimum score 600 paper-based; 100 iBT). *Application deadline:* Applications are processed on a rolling basis. Application fee: $0. Electronic applications accepted. *Unit head:* Dr. Rachel Sangree, Chair, 410-516-7138, E-mail: sangree@jhu.edu. *Application contact:* Doug Schiller, Admissions Director, 410-516-2300, Fax: 410-579-8049, E-mail: schiller@jhu.edu.
Website: http://www.ep.jhu.edu

Johns Hopkins University, G. W. C. Whiting School of Engineering, Department of Civil Engineering, Baltimore, MD 21218. Offers MSE, PhD. *Faculty:* 10 full-time (2 women). *Students:* 71 full-time (20 women). 120 applicants, 53% accepted, 24 enrolled. In 2018, 18 master's, 10 doctorates awarded. *Degree requirements:* For master's, thesis (for some programs); for doctorate, comprehensive exam, thesis/dissertation, qualifying and oral exams. *Entrance requirements:* For master's and doctorate, GRE General Test, 3 letters of recommendation, statement of purpose, transcripts. Additional exam requirements/recommendations for international students: Required—TOEFL (minimum score 600 paper-based, 100 iBT) or IELTS (7). *Application deadline:* For fall admission, 12/31 for domestic and international students. Application fee: $25. Electronic applications accepted. *Financial support:* In 2018–19, 42 students received support, including 8 fellowships with full tuition reimbursements available (averaging $30,000 per year), 34 research assistantships with full tuition reimbursements available (averaging $29,968 per year); teaching assistantships with full tuition reimbursements available and tuition waivers (full and partial) also available. Financial award application deadline: 2/1. *Faculty research:* Mechanics of materials, structural engineering, systems engineering, probabilistic modeling, computational mechanics. *Unit head:* Dr. Lori Brady, Chair, 410-516-8167, E-mail: lori@jhu.edu. *Application contact:* Lisa Wetzelberger, Academic Program Coordinator, 410-516-0617, Fax: 410-516-7473, E-mail: lawetzel@jhu.edu.
Website: http://www.ce.jhu.edu/

Johns Hopkins University, G. W. C. Whiting School of Engineering, Master of Science in Engineering Management Program, Baltimore, MD 21218. Offers biomaterials (MSEM); civil engineering (MSEM); communications science (MSEM); computer science (MSEM); environmental systems analysis, economics and public policy (MSEM); fluid mechanics (MSEM); materials science and engineering (MSEM); mechanical engineering (MSEM); mechanics and materials (MSEM); nanobiotechnology (MSEM); nanomaterials and nanotechnology (MSEM); operations research (MSEM); probability and statistics (MSEM); smart product and device design (MSEM). *Students:* 34 full-time (12 women), 18 part-time (7 women). 233 applicants, 39% accepted, 33 enrolled. In 2018, 27 master's awarded. *Entrance requirements:* For master's, GRE, 3 letters of recommendation, statement of purpose, transcripts. Additional exam requirements/recommendations for international students: Required—TOEFL (minimum score 600 paper-based, 100 iBT) or IELTS (7). *Application deadline:* For fall admission, 2/15 for domestic and international students. Application fee: $75. Electronic applications accepted. *Financial support:* In 2018–19, 43 research assistantships (averaging $43,344 per year) were awarded; health care benefits also available. *Unit head:* Dr. Pamela Sheff, Director, 410-516-7056, Fax: 410-516-4880, E-mail: pamsheff@gmail.com. *Application contact:* Lindsey Conklin, Sr. Academic Program Coordinator, 410-516-1108, Fax: 410-516-0780, E-mail: lconkli4@jhu.edu.
Website: http://engineering.jhu.edu/msem/

Kansas State University, Graduate School, College of Engineering, Department of Civil Engineering, Manhattan, KS 66506. Offers civil engineering (MS, PhD); environmental engineering (MS, PhD); geotechnical engineering (MS, PhD); structural engineering (MS, PhD); transportation engineering (MS, PhD); water resources engineering (MS, PhD). *Program availability:* Part-time, evening/weekend, online learning. *Degree requirements:* For master's, thesis or alternative; for doctorate, thesis/dissertation. *Entrance requirements:* For master's, GRE General Test, bachelor's degree or course work in related engineering fields; for doctorate, GRE General Test. Additional exam requirements/recommendations for international students: Required—TOEFL (minimum score 550 paper-based; 79 iBT). Electronic applications accepted. *Faculty research:* Transportation and materials engineering, water resources engineering, environmental engineering, geotechnical engineering, structural engineering.

Kennesaw State University, Southern Polytechnic College of Engineering and Engineering Technology, Program in Civil Engineering, Kennesaw, GA 30144. Offers environmental engineering (MS); geotechnical engineering (MS); structural engineering (MS); transportation and pavement engineering (MS); water resources engineering (MS). *Program availability:* Online learning. *Students:* 13 full-time (2 women), 24 part-time (5 women); includes 20 minority (8 Black or African American, non-Hispanic/Latino; 5 Asian, non-Hispanic/Latino; 4 Hispanic/Latino; 3 Two or more races, non-Hispanic/Latino), 2 international. Average age 33. 21 applicants, 57% accepted, 1 enrolled. In 2018, 6 master's awarded. *Degree requirements:* For master's, thesis optional. *Entrance requirements:* Additional exam requirements/recommendations for international students: Required—TOEFL (minimum score 550 paper-based; 80 iBT), IELTS (minimum score 6.5). *Application deadline:* For fall admission, 11/1 for domestic and international students; for spring admission, 4/1 for domestic and international students. Applications are processed on a rolling basis. Application fee: $60. Electronic applications accepted. *Expenses: Tuition, area resident:* Full-time $6960; part-time $290 per credit hour. Tuition, state resident: full-time $6960; part-time $290 per credit hour. Tuition, nonresident: full-time $25,080; part-time $1045 per credit hour. *International tuition:* $25,080 full-time. *Required fees:* $2006; $1706 per semester. $853 per semester. *Unit head:* Metin Oguzmert, Coordinator, 470-578-5083, E-mail: moguzmer@kennesaw.edu. *Application contact:* Admissions Counselor, 470-578-4377, E-mail: ksugrad@kennesaw.edu.
Website: http://engineering.kennesaw.edu/civil-construction/degrees/ms-civil-engineering.php

Lawrence Technological University, College of Engineering, Southfield, MI 48075-1058. Offers architectural engineering (MS); automotive engineering (MS); biomedical engineering (MS); civil engineering (MA, MS, PhD), including environmental engineering (MS), geotechnical engineering (MS), structural engineering (MS), transportation engineering (MS), water resource engineering (MS); construction engineering management (MA); electrical and computer engineering (MS); engineering management (MEM); engineering technology (MS); fire engineering (MS); industrial engineering (MS), including healthcare systems; manufacturing systems (ME); mechanical engineering (MS, DE, PhD), including automotive engineering (MS), energy engineering (MS), manufacturing (DE), solid mechanics (MS), thermal/fluid systems (MS); mechatronic systems engineering (MS). *Program availability:* Part-time, evening/weekend. Terminal master's awarded for partial completion of doctoral program. *Degree requirements:* For master's, thesis optional; for doctorate, comprehensive exam, thesis/dissertation optional. *Entrance requirements:* Additional exam requirements/recommendations for international students: Required—TOEFL (minimum score 550 paper-based; 79 iBT), IELTS (minimum score 6.5). Electronic applications accepted. *Faculty research:* Innovative infrastructure and building structures and materials; connectivity and mobility; automotive systems modeling, simulation and testing; biomedical devices and materials; building mechanical/electrical systems.

Lehigh University, P.C. Rossin College of Engineering and Applied Science, Department of Civil and Environmental Engineering, Bethlehem, PA 18015. Offers M Eng, MS, PhD. *Program availability:* Part-time. *Faculty:* 21 full-time (4 women), 1 part-time/adjunct (0 women). *Students:* 73 full-time (20 women), 8 part-time (2 women); includes 6 minority (1 Black or African American, non-Hispanic/Latino; 1 Asian, non-Hispanic/Latino; 3 Hispanic/Latino; 1 Two or more races, non-Hispanic/Latino), 52 international. Average age 27. 162 applicants, 31% accepted, 11 enrolled. In 2018, 30 master's, 6 doctorates awarded. Terminal master's awarded for partial completion of doctoral program. *Degree requirements:* For master's, thesis (for some programs); for doctorate, comprehensive exam, thesis/dissertation. *Entrance requirements:* For master's and doctorate, GRE. Additional exam requirements/recommendations for international students: Required—TOEFL (minimum score 550 paper-based; 79 iBT), IELTS (minimum score 6.5). *Application deadline:* For fall admission, 7/15 for domestic and international students; for spring admission, 12/1 for domestic and international students; for summer admission, 5/30 for domestic and international students. Application fee: $75. Electronic applications accepted. Tuition and fees vary according to program. *Financial support:* In 2018–19, 15 students received support, including 4 fellowships with full tuition reimbursements available (averaging $22,050 per year), 49 research assistantships with full and partial tuition reimbursements available (averaging $21,000 per year), 8 teaching assistantships with full tuition reimbursements available (averaging $20,440 per year); unspecified assistantships also available. Financial award application deadline: 1/15; financial award applicants required to submit FAFSA. *Faculty research:* Structural engineering, geotechnical engineering, water resources engineering, environmental engineering. *Total annual research expenditures:* $6.6 million. *Unit head:* Dr. Panayiotis Diplas, Chair, 610-758-3554, E-mail: pad313@lehigh.edu. *Application contact:* Prisca Vidanage, Graduate Coordinator, 610-758-3530, E-mail: pmv1@lehigh.edu.
Website: http://www.lehigh.edu/~incee/

Louisiana State University and Agricultural & Mechanical College, Graduate School, College of Engineering, Department of Civil and Environmental Engineering, Baton Rouge, LA 70803. Offers environmental engineering (MSCE, PhD); geotechnical engineering (MSCE, PhD); structural engineering and mechanics (MSCE, PhD); transportation engineering (MSCE, PhD); water resources (MSCE, PhD).

Loyola Marymount University, Frank R. Seaver College of Science and Engineering, Program in Civil Engineering, Los Angeles, CA 90045. Offers MSE. *Unit head:* Dr. Jeremy Pal, Graduate Program Director, Civil Engineering and Environmental Science, 310-568-6241, E-mail: jpal@lmu.edu. *Application contact:* Ammar Dalal, Assistant Vice Provost for Graduate Enrollment, 310-338-2721, Fax: 310-338-6086, E-mail: graduateinfo@lmu.edu.

Manhattan College, Graduate Programs, School of Engineering, Program in Civil Engineering, Riverdale, NY 10471. Offers MS. *Program availability:* Part-time, evening/weekend. *Degree requirements:* For master's, thesis or alternative. *Entrance requirements:* For master's, GRE (recommended), minimum GPA of 3.0. Additional exam requirements/recommendations for international students: Required—TOEFL (minimum score 550 paper-based; 80 iBT), IELTS (minimum score 6). *Faculty research:* Compressible-inclusion function for geofoams used with rigid walls under static loading, validation of sediment criteria.

Marquette University, Graduate School, College of Engineering, Department of Civil and Environmental Engineering, Milwaukee, WI 53201-1881. Offers construction engineering and management (MS, PhD, Certificate); environmental engineering (MS, PhD); structural design (Certificate); structural engineering and structural mechanics

(MS, PhD); transportation (Certificate); transportation engineering and materials (MS, PhD); waste and wastewater treatment processes (Certificate); water resources engineering (Certificate). *Program availability:* Part-time, evening/weekend. Terminal master's awarded for partial completion of doctoral program. *Degree requirements:* For master's, comprehensive exam (for some programs), thesis or alternative; for doctorate, thesis/dissertation. *Entrance requirements:* For master's, GRE General Test (recommended), minimum GPA of 3.0, official transcripts from all current and previous colleges/universities except Marquette, three letters of recommendation; for doctorate, GRE General Test, minimum GPA of 3.0, official transcripts from all current and previous colleges/universities except Marquette, three letters of recommendation, brief statement of purpose, submission of any English language publications authored by applicant (strongly recommended). Additional exam requirements/recommendations for international students: Required—TOEFL (minimum score 530 paper-based). Electronic applications accepted. *Faculty research:* Highway safety, highway performance, and intelligent transportation systems; surface mount technology; watershed management.

Massachusetts Institute of Technology, School of Engineering, Department of Civil and Environmental Engineering, Cambridge, MA 02139. Offers biological oceanography (PhD, Sc D); chemical oceanography (PhD, Sc D); civil and environmental engineering (M Eng, SM, PhD, Sc D); civil and environmental systems (PhD, Sc D); civil engineering (PhD, Sc D, CE); civil engineering and computation (PhD); coastal engineering (PhD, Sc D); construction engineering and management (PhD, Sc D); environmental biology (PhD, Sc D); environmental chemistry (PhD, Sc D); environmental engineering (PhD, Sc D); environmental engineering and computation (PhD); environmental fluid mechanics (PhD, Sc D); geotechnical and geoenvironmental engineering (PhD, Sc D); hydrology (PhD, Sc D); information technology (PhD, Sc D); oceanographic engineering (PhD, Sc D); structures and materials (PhD, Sc D); transportation (PhD, Sc D); SM/MBA. *Degree requirements:* For master's, thesis; for doctorate, comprehensive exam, thesis/dissertation; for CE, comprehensive exam, thesis. *Entrance requirements:* For master's, doctorate, and CE, GRE General Test. Additional exam requirements/recommendations for international students: Required—TOEFL, IELTS. Electronic applications accepted. *Expenses:* Tuition: Full-time $51,520; part-time $800 per credit hour. *Required fees:* $312. *Faculty research:* Environmental chemistry, environmental fluid mechanics and coastal engineering, environmental microbiology, geotechnical engineering and geomechanics, hydrology and hydro climatology, infrastructure systems, mechanics of materials and structures, transportation systems.

McGill University, Faculty of Graduate and Postdoctoral Studies, Faculty of Engineering, Department of Civil Engineering and Applied Mechanics, Montréal, QC H3A 2T5, Canada. Offers environmental engineering (M Eng, M Sc, PhD); fluid mechanics (M Sc); fluid mechanics and hydraulic engineering (M Eng, PhD); materials engineering (M Eng, PhD); rehabilitation of urban infrastructure (M Eng, PhD); soil behavior (M Eng, PhD); soil mechanics and foundations (M Eng, PhD); structures and structural mechanics (M Eng, PhD); water resources (M Sc); water resources engineering (M Eng, PhD).

McMaster University, School of Graduate Studies, Faculty of Engineering, Department of Civil Engineering, Hamilton, ON L8S 4M2, Canada. Offers M Eng, MA Sc, PhD. *Degree requirements:* For master's, thesis; for doctorate, comprehensive exam, thesis/dissertation. *Entrance requirements:* Additional exam requirements/recommendations for international students: Required—TOEFL (minimum score 550 paper-based). *Faculty research:* Building science, environmental hydrology, bolted steel connections, research on highway materials, earthquake engineering.

McNeese State University, Doré School of Graduate Studies, College of Engineering and Computer Science, Master of Engineering Program, Lake Charles, LA 70609. Offers chemical engineering (M Eng); civil engineering (M Eng); electrical engineering (M Eng); engineering management (M Eng); mechanical engineering (M Eng). *Program availability:* Part-time, evening/weekend. *Entrance requirements:* For master's, GRE, baccalaureate degree, minimum overall GPA of 3.0. Additional exam requirements/recommendations for international students: Required—TOEFL (minimum score 560 paper-based; 83 iBT).

Memorial University of Newfoundland, School of Graduate Studies, Faculty of Engineering and Applied Science, St. John's, NL A1C 5S7, Canada. Offers civil engineering (M Eng, PhD); electrical and computer engineering (M Eng, PhD); mechanical engineering (M Eng, PhD); ocean and naval architecture engineering (M Eng, PhD). *Program availability:* Part-time. *Degree requirements:* For master's, thesis; for doctorate, comprehensive exam, thesis/dissertation, oral thesis defense. *Entrance requirements:* For master's, 2nd class degree; for doctorate, master's degree in engineering. Electronic applications accepted. *Faculty research:* Engineering analysis, environmental and hydrotechnical studies, manufacturing and robotics, mechanics, structures and materials.

Merrimack College, School of Science and Engineering, North Andover, MA 01845-5800. Offers civil engineering (MS); computer science (MS); data science (MS); engineering management (MS); mechanical engineering (MS), including engineering management. *Program availability:* Part-time, evening/weekend, 100% online. *Faculty:* 10 full-time (2 women), 6 part-time/adjunct (1 woman). *Students:* 53 full-time (18 women), 17 part-time (5 women); includes 14 minority (6 Black or African American, non-Hispanic/Latino; 6 Asian, non-Hispanic/Latino; 2 Two or more races, non-Hispanic/Latino), 9 international. Average age 34. 183 applicants, 61% accepted, 40 enrolled. In 2018, 27 master's awarded. *Degree requirements:* For master's, comprehensive exam, thesis optional, internship or capstone (for some programs). *Entrance requirements:* For master's, official college transcripts, resume, personal statement, 2 recommendations. Additional exam requirements/recommendations for international students: Required—TOEFL (minimum score 84 iBT), IELTS (minimum score 6.5), PTE (minimum score 56). *Application deadline:* For fall admission, 8/24 for domestic students, 7/30 for international students; for spring admission, 1/10 for domestic students, 12/10 for international students; for summer admission, 5/10 for domestic students, 4/10 for international students. Applications are processed on a rolling basis. Application fee: $0. Electronic applications accepted. Application fee is waived when completed online. *Expenses:* Contact institution. *Financial support:* Career-related internships or fieldwork, scholarships/grants, health care benefits, and unspecified assistantships available. Support available to part-time students. Financial award application deadline: 5/1; financial award applicants required to submit FAFSA. *Unit head:* Dr. Naira Campbell-Kyureghyan, Dean, 978-837-5265, E-mail: campbellnk@merrimack.edu. *Application contact:* Allison Pena, Graduate Admissions Counselor, 978-837-3563, E-mail: penaa@merrimack.edu.
Website: http://www.merrimack.edu/academics/graduate/

Michigan State University, The Graduate School, College of Engineering, Department of Civil and Environmental Engineering, East Lansing, MI 48824. Offers civil engineering (MS, PhD); environmental engineering (MS, PhD); environmental engineering-environmental toxicology (PhD). *Program availability:* Part-time. *Entrance requirements:* Additional exam requirements/recommendations for international students: Required—TOEFL. Electronic applications accepted.

Michigan Technological University, Graduate School, College of Engineering, Department of Civil and Environmental Engineering, Houghton, MI 49931. Offers civil

engineering (MS, PhD); environmental engineering (MS, PhD); environmental engineering science (MS). *Program availability:* Part-time, 100% online. *Faculty:* 39 full-time, 8 part-time/adjunct. *Students:* 65 full-time (26 women), 12 part-time (5 women); includes 8 minority (2 Black or African American, non-Hispanic/Latino; 2 Hispanic/Latino; 4 Two or more races, non-Hispanic/Latino), 31 international. Average age 27. 276 applicants, 40% accepted, 24 enrolled. In 2018, 55 master's, 4 doctorates awarded. *Degree requirements:* For master's, comprehensive exam (for some programs), thesis (for some programs); for doctorate, comprehensive exam, thesis/dissertation. *Entrance requirements:* For master's and doctorate, GRE (Michigan Tech students exempt), statement of purpose, personal statement, official transcripts, 2 letters of recommendation. Additional exam requirements/recommendations for international students: Required—TOEFL, TOEFL (recommended minimum score 100 iBT) or IELTS (recommended minimum score of 7.0). *Application deadline:* For fall admission, 1/15 priority date for domestic and international students; for spring admission, 9/15 priority date for domestic and international students; for summer admission, 2/15 priority date for domestic and international students. Applications are processed on a rolling basis. Electronic applications accepted. *Expenses:* $1,143 per credit. *Financial support:* In 2018–19, 51 students received support, including 6 fellowships with tuition reimbursements available (averaging $16,590 per year), 22 research assistantships with tuition reimbursements available (averaging $16,590 per year), 5 teaching assistantships with tuition reimbursements available (averaging $16,590 per year); career-related internships or fieldwork, Federal Work-Study, scholarships/grants, health care benefits, unspecified assistantships, and cooperative program also available. Financial award applicants required to submit FAFSA. *Faculty research:* Water resources, environment engineering, transportation engineering, structural engineering, geotechnical engineering. *Total annual research expenditures:* $2.5 million. *Unit head:* Dr. Audra N. Morse, Chair, 906-487-3240, Fax: 906-487-2943, E-mail: anmorse@mtu.edu. *Application contact:* Angela Keranen, Administrative Aide, 906-487-2474, Fax: 906-487-2943, E-mail: amkerane@mtu.edu.
Website: http://www.mtu.edu/cee/

Milwaukee School of Engineering, MS Program in Civil Engineering, Milwaukee, WI 53202-3109. Offers MS. *Program availability:* Part-time, evening/weekend. *Degree requirements:* For master's, thesis. *Entrance requirements:* For master's, GRE General Test if undergraduate GPA is less than 3.0, 2 letters of recommendation; BS in civil engineering or closely-related area from ABET-accredited program. Additional exam requirements/recommendations for international students: Required—TOEFL (minimum score 90 iBT), IELTS (minimum score 7). Electronic applications accepted.

Mississippi State University, Bagley College of Engineering, Department of Civil and Environmental Engineering, Mississippi State, MS 39762. Offers MS, PhD. *Program availability:* Part-time, blended/hybrid learning. *Faculty:* 10 full-time (0 women). *Students:* 19 full-time (6 women), 77 part-time (18 women); includes 19 minority (8 Black or African American, non-Hispanic/Latino; 2 Asian, non-Hispanic/Latino; 9 Hispanic/Latino), 12 international. Average age 33. 44 applicants, 32% accepted, 9 enrolled. In 2018, 17 master's, 2 doctorates awarded. Terminal master's awarded for partial completion of doctoral program. *Degree requirements:* For master's, thesis optional; for doctorate, thesis/dissertation, research on an approved topic, minimum 20 hours of dissertation research. *Entrance requirements:* For master's and doctorate, GRE (for graduates from program not accredited by EAC/ABET), minimum GPA of 3.0. Additional exam requirements/recommendations for international students: Required—TOEFL (minimum score 550 paper-based; 79 iBT); Recommended—IELTS (minimum score 6.5). *Application deadline:* For fall admission, 7/1 for domestic students, 5/1 for international students; for spring admission, 11/1 for domestic students, 9/1 for international students. Applications are processed on a rolling basis. Application fee: $60 ($80 for international students). Electronic applications accepted. *Expenses:* Tuition, state resident: full-time $8450; part-time $360.59 per credit hour. Tuition, nonresident: full-time $23,140; part-time $969.09 per credit hour. *Required fees:* $110. One-time fee: $55 full-time. Part-time tuition and fees vary according to course load, degree level, campus/location and reciprocity agreements. *Financial support:* In 2018–19, 7 research assistantships with full tuition reimbursements (averaging $16,001 per year), 4 teaching assistantships with full tuition reimbursements (averaging $14,356 per year) were awarded; Federal Work-Study, institutionally sponsored loans, and unspecified assistantships also available. Financial award application deadline: 4/1; financial award applicants required to submit FAFSA. *Faculty research:* Transportation, water modeling, construction materials, structures. *Total annual research expenditures:* $2.2 million. *Unit head:* Dr. Dennis D. Truax, Department Head, 662-325-7187, Fax: 662-325-7189, E-mail: truax@cee.msstate.edu. *Application contact:* Angie Campbell, Admissions and Enrollment Assistant, 662-325-9514, E-mail: acampbell@grad.msstate.edu.
Website: http://www.cee.msstate.edu/

Missouri University of Science and Technology, Department of Civil, Architectural, and Environmental Engineering, Rolla, MO 65401. Offers civil engineering (MS, DE, PhD); environmental engineering (MS). *Program availability:* Part-time, evening/weekend. Terminal master's awarded for partial completion of doctoral program. *Degree requirements:* For master's, thesis optional; for doctorate, comprehensive exam, thesis/dissertation. *Entrance requirements:* For master's, GRE General Test (minimum combined score 1100), minimum GPA of 3.0; for doctorate, GRE General Test (minimum score: verbal and quantitative 400, writing 3.5), minimum GPA of 3.0. Additional exam requirements/recommendations for international students: Required—TOEFL (minimum score 550 paper-based). Electronic applications accepted. *Expenses:* Tuition, state resident: full-time $7545.60; part-time $419.20 per credit hour. Tuition, nonresident: full-time $22,169; part-time $1231.60 per credit hour. *International tuition:* $23,518.80 full-time. *Required fees:* $4523.05. Full-time tuition and fees vary according to course load, campus/location, program and reciprocity agreements. *Faculty research:* Earthquake engineering, structural optimization and control systems, structural health monitoring/damage detection, soil-structure interaction, soil mechanics and foundation engineering.

Montana State University, The Graduate School, College of Engineering, Department of Civil Engineering, Bozeman, MT 59717. Offers civil engineering (MS); construction engineering management (MCEM); engineering (PhD), including applied mechanics option, civil engineering option. *Program availability:* Part-time. *Degree requirements:* For master's, comprehensive exam, thesis (for some programs); for doctorate, comprehensive exam, thesis/dissertation. *Entrance requirements:* For master's and doctorate, GRE General Test. Additional exam requirements/recommendations for international students: Required—TOEFL (minimum score 550 paper-based). Electronic applications accepted. *Faculty research:* Snow and ice mechanics, biofilm engineering, transportation, structural and geo materials, water resources.

Morgan State University, School of Graduate Studies, Clarence M. Mitchell, Jr. School of Engineering, Baltimore, MD 21251. Offers civil engineering (M Eng, D Eng); electrical and computer engineering (M Eng, MS, D Eng); industrial and systems engineering (M Eng, D Eng); transportation and urban infrastructure studies (MS, PhD, Postbaccalaureate Certificate), including transportation. *Program availability:* Part-time, evening/weekend. *Degree requirements:* For master's, thesis, comprehensive exam or equivalent; for doctorate, thesis/dissertation, comprehensive exam or equivalent.

Civil Engineering

Entrance requirements: For master's, GRE, minimum undergraduate GPA of 2.5; for doctorate, GRE, minimum GPA of 3.0. Additional exam requirements/recommendations for international students: Required—TOEFL (minimum score 550 paper-based).

New York University, Tandon School of Engineering, Department of Civil and Urban Engineering, Major in Civil Engineering, New York, NY 10012-1019. Offers MS, PhD. *Program availability:* Part-time, evening/weekend. *Students:* 61 full-time (13 women), 35 part-time (8 women); includes 17 minority (2 Black or African American, non-Hispanic/ Latino; 7 Asian, non-Hispanic/Latino; 7 Hispanic/Latino; 1 Two or more races, non-Hispanic/Latino), 48 international. Average age 27. 272 applicants, 42% accepted, 28 enrolled. In 2018, 32 master's, 6 doctorates awarded. *Degree requirements:* For master's, comprehensive exam (for some programs), thesis (for some programs); for doctorate, comprehensive exam, thesis/dissertation, qualifying exam. *Entrance requirements:* For doctorate, MS in civil engineering. Additional exam requirements/ recommendations for international students: Required—TOEFL (minimum score 550 paper-based; 90 iBT); Recommended—IELTS (minimum score 7). *Application deadline:* For fall admission, 2/15 priority date for domestic and international students; for spring admission, 11/1 priority date for domestic and international students. Applications are processed on a rolling basis. Application fee: $75. Electronic applications accepted. *Financial support:* Fellowships, research assistantships, teaching assistantships, institutionally sponsored loans, scholarships/grants, and unspecified assistantships available. Support available to part-time students. Financial award applicants required to submit FAFSA. *Total annual research expenditures:* $2.5 million. *Unit head:* Dr. Mohsen Hossein, Academic Director, 646-997-3766, Fax: 718-260-3433, E-mail: mhossein@ nyu.edu. *Application contact:* Elizabeth Ensweiler, Senior Director of Graduate Enrollment and Graduate Admissions, 646-997-3182, E-mail: elizabeth.ensweiler@ nyu.edu.

North Carolina Agricultural and Technical State University, The Graduate College, College of Engineering, Department of Civil, Architectural and Environmental Engineering, Greensboro, NC 27411. Offers civil engineering (MSCE). *Program availability:* Part-time. *Degree requirements:* For master's, thesis optional. *Entrance requirements:* For master's, GRE General Test, GRE Subject Test (recommended). Additional exam requirements/recommendations for international students: Required—TOEFL. *Faculty research:* Lightning, indoor air quality, material behavior HVAC controls, structural masonry systems.

North Carolina State University, Graduate School, College of Engineering, Department of Civil, Construction, and Environmental Engineering, Raleigh, NC 27695. Offers civil engineering (MCE, MS, PhD); environmental engineering (MS). *Program availability:* Part-time, online learning. *Degree requirements:* For master's, thesis optional, oral exams; for doctorate, thesis/dissertation, oral exams. *Entrance requirements:* For master's, GRE General Test, minimum B average in major; for doctorate, GRE General Test. Additional exam requirements/recommendations for international students: Required—TOEFL. Electronic applications accepted. *Faculty research:* Materials; systems, environmental, geotechnical, structural, transportation and water rescue engineering.

North Dakota State University, College of Graduate and Interdisciplinary Studies, College of Engineering, Department of Civil and Environmental Engineering, Fargo, ND 58102. Offers civil engineering (MS, PhD); environmental engineering (MS). *Program availability:* Part-time, online learning. *Degree requirements:* For master's, thesis; for doctorate, comprehensive exam, thesis/dissertation. *Entrance requirements:* Additional exam requirements/recommendations for international students: Required—TOEFL (minimum score 525 paper-based; 71 iBT). Electronic applications accepted. *Faculty research:* Wastewater, solid waste, composites, nanotechnology.

Northeastern University, College of Engineering, Boston, MA 02115-5096. Offers bioengineering (MS, PhD); chemical engineering (MS, PhD); civil engineering (MS, PhD); computer engineering (PhD); computer systems engineering (MS); electrical and computer engineering (MS); electrical and computer engineering leadership (MS); electrical engineering (PhD); energy systems (MS); engineering and public policy (MS); engineering management (MS, Certificate); environmental engineering (MS); industrial engineering (MS, PhD); information assurance (PhD); information systems (MS); interdisciplinary engineering (PhD); mechanical engineering (PhD); operations research (MS); telecommunication systems management (MS). *Program availability:* Part-time, online learning. Electronic applications accepted. *Expenses:* Contact institution.

Northern Arizona University, College of Engineering, Informatics, and Applied Sciences, Department of Civil Engineering, Construction Management and Environmental Engineering, Flagstaff, AZ 86011. Offers engineering (M Eng), including civil engineering, environmental engineering. *Program availability:* Part-time. *Degree requirements:* For master's, variable foreign language requirement, comprehensive exam (for some programs), thesis, individualized research. *Entrance requirements:* Additional exam requirements/recommendations for international students: Required—TOEFL (minimum score 80 iBT), IELTS (minimum score 6.5). Electronic applications accepted.

Northwestern University, McCormick School of Engineering and Applied Science, Department of Civil and Environmental Engineering, Evanston, IL 60208-3109. Offers environmental engineering and science (MS, PhD); geotechnical engineering (MS, PhD); mechanics of materials and solids (MS, PhD); project management (MS); structural engineering and materials (MS, PhD); transportation systems analysis and planning (MS, PhD). MS and PhD admissions and degrees offered through The Graduate School. *Program availability:* Part-time. Terminal master's awarded for partial completion of doctoral program. *Degree requirements:* For master's, comprehensive exam (for some programs), thesis (for some programs); for doctorate, comprehensive exam, thesis/dissertation. *Entrance requirements:* For master's and doctorate, GRE General Test, minimum 2 letters of recommendation, transcripts from all academic institutions attended. Additional exam requirements/recommendations for international students: Required—TOEFL (minimum score 577 paper-based; 90 iBT), IELTS (minimum score 7). Electronic applications accepted. *Faculty research:* Environmental engineering and science, geotechnics, mechanics, materials, structures, and transportation systems analysis and planning.

Norwich University, College of Graduate and Continuing Studies, Master of Civil Engineering Program, Northfield, VT 05663. Offers construction management (MCE); environmental (MCE); geotechnical (MCE); structural (MCE). *Program availability:* Evening/weekend, online only, mostly all online with a week-long residency requirement. *Degree requirements:* For master's, capstone. *Entrance requirements:* For master's, minimum undergraduate GPA of 2.75. Additional exam requirements/recommendations for international students: Required—TOEFL (minimum score 550 paper-based; 80 iBT), IELTS (minimum score 6.5). Electronic applications accepted. *Expenses:* Contact institution.

The Ohio State University, Graduate School, College of Engineering, Department of Civil, Environmental and Geodetic Engineering, Columbus, OH 43210. Offers civil engineering (MS, PhD). *Faculty:* 29. *Students:* 51 (11 women). Average age 31. In 2018, 8 doctorates awarded. *Entrance requirements:* For master's and doctorate, GRE General Test (for all applicants whose undergraduate GPA is below 3.0 or whose undergraduate degree is not from an accredited U.S.-ABET or Canadian-CEAB institution). Additional exam requirements/recommendations for international students: Required—TOEFL (minimum score 550 paper-based; 79 iBT), Michigan English Language Assessment Battery (minimum score 82); Recommended—IELTS (minimum score 7). *Application deadline:* For fall admission, 12/13 priority date for domestic students, 11/30 priority date for international students. Applications are processed on a rolling basis. Application fee: $60 ($70 for international students). Electronic applications accepted. *Financial support:* Fellowships, research assistantships, teaching assistantships, institutionally sponsored loans, and unspecified assistantships available. *Unit head:* Dr. Allison MacKay, Chair, 614-247-7652, E-mail: mackay.49@osu.edu. *Application contact:* Graduate and Professional Admissions, 614-292-9444, Fax: 614-292-3895, E-mail: gpadmissions@osu.edu.
Website: http://ceg.osu.edu/

Ohio University, Graduate College, Russ College of Engineering and Technology, Department of Civil Engineering, Athens, OH 45701-2979. Offers civil engineering (PhD); construction engineering and management (MS); environmental (MS); geoenvironmental (MS); geotechnical (MS); mechanics (MS); structures (MS); transportation (MS); water resources (MS). *Program availability:* Part-time. *Degree requirements:* For master's, comprehensive exam (for some programs), thesis or alternative; for doctorate, comprehensive exam, thesis/dissertation. *Entrance requirements:* For master's, GRE General Test, minimum GPA of 3.0, 3 letters of recommendation; for doctorate, GRE General Test. Additional exam requirements/ recommendations for international students: Required—TOEFL (minimum score 550 paper-based; 80 iBT) or IELTS (minimum score 6.5). Electronic applications accepted. *Faculty research:* Noise abatement, materials and environment, highway infrastructure, subsurface investigation (pavements, pipes, bridges).

Oklahoma State University, College of Engineering, Architecture and Technology, School of Civil and Environmental Engineering, Stillwater, OK 74078. Offers civil engineering (MS, PhD). *Faculty:* 21 full-time (2 women), 2 part-time/adjunct (0 women). *Students:* 20 full-time (5 women), 41 part-time (12 women); includes 6 minority (3 American Indian or Alaska Native, non-Hispanic/Latino; 1 Hispanic/Latino; 2 Two or more races, non-Hispanic/Latino), 31 international. Average age 29. 74 applicants, 26% accepted, 11 enrolled. In 2018, 17 master's, 4 doctorates awarded. *Entrance requirements:* For master's and doctorate, GRE or GMAT. Additional exam requirements/recommendations for international students: Required—TOEFL (minimum score 550 paper-based; 79 iBT). *Application deadline:* For fall admission, 3/1 priority date for international students; for spring admission, 8/1 priority date for international students. Applications are processed on a rolling basis. Application fee: $40 ($75 for international students). Electronic applications accepted. *Expenses: Tuition, area resident:* Full-time $4148. Tuition, state resident: full-time $4148. Tuition, nonresident: full-time $10,517. *International tuition:* $10,517 full-time. *Required fees:* $4394; $2929 per credit hour. Tuition and fees vary according to course load and program. *Financial support:* Research assistantships, teaching assistantships, career-related internships or fieldwork, Federal Work-Study, scholarships/grants, health care benefits, tuition waivers (partial), and unspecified assistantships available. Support available to part-time students. Financial award application deadline: 3/1; financial award applicants required to submit FAFSA. *Unit head:* Dr. Norb Delatte, Department Head, 405-744-5190, Fax: 405-744-7554, E-mail: norb.delatte@okstate.edu. *Application contact:* Dr. Sheryl Tucker, Dean, 405-744-6368, Fax: 405-744-0355, E-mail: gradi@okstate.edu.
Website: http://cive.okstate.edu

Old Dominion University, Frank Batten College of Engineering and Technology, Program in Civil and Environmental Engineering, Norfolk, VA 23529. Offers D Eng, PhD. *Program availability:* Part-time, evening/weekend, blended/hybrid learning. *Degree requirements:* For doctorate, comprehensive exam, thesis/dissertation, candidacy exam. *Entrance requirements:* For doctorate, GRE, minimum GPA of 3.5. Electronic applications accepted. *Expenses:* Contact institution. *Faculty research:* Structural engineering, coastal engineering, environmental engineering, geotechnical engineering, water resources, transportation engineering.

Old Dominion University, Frank Batten College of Engineering and Technology, Program in Civil Engineering, Norfolk, VA 23529. Offers civil engineering (ME, MS), including coastal engineering, geotechnical engineering, hydraulics and water resources, structural engineering, transportation engineering. *Program availability:* Part-time, evening/weekend, blended/hybrid learning. *Degree requirements:* For master's, comprehensive exam, thesis optional. *Entrance requirements:* For master's, GRE, minimum GPA of 3.0. Additional exam requirements/recommendations for international students: Required—TOEFL (minimum score 550 paper-based, 80 iBT) or IELTS (6.5). Electronic applications accepted. *Expenses:* Contact institution. *Faculty research:* Structural engineering, coastal engineering, geotechnical engineering, water resources, transportation engineering.

Oregon State University, College of Engineering, Program in Civil Engineering, Corvallis, OR 97331. Offers civil engineering (M Eng, MS, PhD); coastal and ocean engineering (M Eng, MS, PhD); construction engineering management (M Eng, MS, PhD); engineering education (M Eng, MS, PhD); geomatics (M Eng, MS, PhD); geotechnical engineering (M Eng, MS, PhD); infrastructure materials (M Eng, MS, PhD); structural engineering (M Eng, MS, PhD); transportation engineering (M Eng). *Entrance requirements:* For master's and doctorate, GRE. Additional exam requirements/ recommendations for international students: Required—TOEFL (minimum score 80 iBT), IELTS (minimum score 6.5). *Expenses:* Contact institution.

Penn State Harrisburg, Graduate School, School of Science, Engineering and Technology, Middletown, PA 17057. Offers civil engineering (MS); computer science (MS); electrical engineering (M Eng, MS); engineering management (MPS); engineering science (M Eng); environmental engineering (M Eng); environmental pollution control (MEPC, MS); mechanical engineering (MS); structural engineering (Certificate). *Program availability:* Part-time, evening/weekend.

Penn State University Park, Graduate School, College of Engineering, Department of Civil and Environmental Engineering, University Park, PA 16802. Offers civil engineering (M Eng, MS, PhD); environmental engineering (M Eng, MS, PhD).

Polytechnic University of Puerto Rico, Graduate School, Hato Rey, PR 00918. Offers business administration (MBA), including computer information systems, general management, management of information systems, management of international enterprises; civil engineering (ME, MS); computer engineering (ME, MS); computer science (MCS, MS); electrical engineering (ME, MS); engineering management (MEM); environmental management (MEM); landscape architecture (M Land Arch); manufacturing competitiveness (MMC, MS); manufacturing engineering (ME, MS); mechanical engineering (M Mech E). *Accreditation:* ASLA. *Program availability:* Part-time, evening/weekend. *Entrance requirements:* For master's, 3 letters of recommendation.

Portland State University, Graduate Studies, College of Liberal Arts and Sciences, Systems Science Program, Portland, OR 97207-0751. Offers computational intelligence (Certificate); computer modeling and simulation (Certificate); systems science (MS); systems science/anthropology (PhD); systems science/business administration (PhD); systems science/civil engineering (PhD); systems science/economics (PhD); systems science/engineering management (PhD); systems science/general (PhD); systems science/mathematical sciences (PhD); systems science/mechanical engineering (PhD); systems science/psychology (PhD); systems science/sociology (PhD). *Degree requirements:* For master's, comprehensive exam (for some programs), thesis optional; for doctorate, variable foreign language requirement, comprehensive exam (for some programs), thesis/dissertation. *Entrance requirements:* For master's, GRE/GMAT (recommended), minimum GPA of 3.0 on undergraduate or graduate work, 2 letters of recommendation, statement of interest; for doctorate, GMAT, GRE General Test, minimum GPA of 3.0 undergraduate, 3.25 graduate; 3 letters of recommendation; statement of interest. Additional exam requirements/recommendations for international students: Required—TOEFL (minimum score 550 paper-based; 80 iBT). Electronic applications accepted. *Faculty research:* Systems theory and methodology, artificial intelligence neural networks, information theory, nonlinear dynamics/chaos, modeling and simulation.

Portland State University, Graduate Studies, Maseeh College of Engineering and Computer Science, Department of Civil and Environmental Engineering, Portland, OR 97207-0751. Offers civil and environmental engineering (M Eng, MS, PhD). *Program availability:* Part-time, evening/weekend. *Degree requirements:* For master's, comprehensive exam (for some programs), thesis (for some programs); for doctorate, one foreign language, comprehensive exam, thesis/dissertation, oral and written exams. *Entrance requirements:* For master's, BS in an engineering field, science, or closely-related area with minimum GPA of 3.0; for doctorate, MS in an engineering field, science, or closely-related area. Additional exam requirements/recommendations for international students: Required—TOEFL (minimum score 550 paper-based). *Expenses:* Contact institution. *Faculty research:* Structures, water resources, geotechnical engineering, environmental engineering, transportation.

Princeton University, Graduate School, School of Engineering and Applied Science, Department of Civil and Environmental Engineering, Princeton, NJ 08544-1019. Offers M Eng, MSE, PhD. Terminal master's awarded for partial completion of doctoral program. *Degree requirements:* For master's, thesis (MSE); for doctorate, thesis/dissertation, general exam. *Entrance requirements:* For master's, GRE General Test, 3 letters of recommendation; for doctorate, GRE General Test, official transcript(s), 3 letters of recommendation, personal statement. Additional exam requirements/recommendations for international students: Required—TOEFL. Electronic applications accepted. *Faculty research:* Carbon mitigation; civil engineering materials and structures; climate and atmospheric dynamics; computational mechanics and risk assessment; hydrology, remote sensing, and sustainability.

Purdue University, College of Engineering, Lyles School of Civil Engineering, West Lafayette, IN 47907-2051. Offers MS, MSCE, MSE, PhD. *Program availability:* Part-time. Terminal master's awarded for partial completion of doctoral program. *Degree requirements:* For master's, thesis optional; for doctorate, thesis/dissertation. *Entrance requirements:* For master's and doctorate, GRE General Test, minimum GPA of 3.0. Electronic applications accepted. *Faculty research:* Architectural engineering, construction engineering, environmental engineering, geomatics engineering, geotechnical engineering, hydraulic and hydrologic engineering, materials engineering, structural engineering, transportation and infrastructure systems engineering.

Purdue University Fort Wayne, College of Engineering, Technology, and Computer Science, Department of Civil and Mechanical Engineering, Fort Wayne, IN 46805-1499. Offers civil engineering (MSE); mechanical engineering (MSE). *Program availability:* Part-time. *Entrance requirements:* For master's, minimum GPA of 3.0, bachelor's degree in engineering discipline. Additional exam requirements/recommendations for international students: Required—TOEFL (minimum score 550 paper-based; 79 iBT); Recommended—TWE. Electronic applications accepted. *Faculty research:* Continuous space language model, sensor networks, wireless cloud architecture.

Queen's University at Kingston, School of Graduate Studies, Faculty of Engineering and Applied Science, Department of Civil Engineering, Kingston, ON K7L 3N6, Canada. Offers M Eng, M Sc Eng, PhD. *Program availability:* Part-time. *Degree requirements:* For master's, thesis (for some programs); for doctorate, comprehensive exam, thesis/dissertation. *Entrance requirements:* Additional exam requirements/recommendations for international students: Required—TOEFL. *Faculty research:* Structural, geotechnical, transportation, hydrotechnical, and environmental engineering.

Rensselaer Polytechnic Institute, Graduate School, School of Engineering, Program in Civil Engineering, Troy, NY 12180-3590. Offers M Eng, MS, PhD. *Program availability:* Part-time. *Faculty:* 18 full-time (3 women), 4 part-time/adjunct (0 women). *Students:* 25 full-time (11 women), 1 part-time (0 women); includes 4 minority (1 Asian, non-Hispanic/Latino; 1 Hispanic/Latino; 2 Two or more races, non-Hispanic/Latino), 11 international. Average age 25. 66 applicants, 11% accepted, 4 enrolled. In 2018, 6 master's, 1 doctorate awarded. Terminal master's awarded for partial completion of doctoral program. *Degree requirements:* For master's, thesis (for some programs); for doctorate, thesis/dissertation. *Entrance requirements:* For master's and doctorate, GRE. Additional exam requirements/recommendations for international students: Required—TOEFL (minimum score 570 paper-based; 88 iBT), IELTS (minimum score 6.5), PTE (minimum score 60). *Application deadline:* For fall admission, 1/1 priority date for domestic and international students; for spring admission, 8/15 priority date for domestic and international students. Applications are processed on a rolling basis. Application fee: $75. Electronic applications accepted. *Financial support:* In 2018–19, 16 students received support, including research assistantships (averaging $23,000 per year), teaching assistantships (averaging $23,000 per year); fellowships also available. Financial award application deadline: 1/1. *Faculty research:* Geotechnical, structural, transportation. Total annual research expenditures: $843,952. *Unit head:* Dr. Michael O'Rourke, Graduate Program Director, 518-276-6933, E-mail: orourm@rpi.edu. *Application contact:* Jarron Decker, Director of Graduate Admissions, 518-276-6216, Fax: 518-276-4072, E-mail: gradadmissions@rpi.edu. Website: http://cee.rpi.edu/graduate

Rice University, Graduate Programs, George R. Brown School of Engineering, Department of Civil and Environmental Engineering, Houston, TX 77251-1892. Offers civil engineering (MCE, MS, PhD); environmental engineering (MEE, MES, MS, PhD); environmental science (MEE, MES, MS, PhD). *Program availability:* Part-time. *Degree requirements:* For master's, thesis (for some programs); for doctorate, thesis/dissertation. *Entrance requirements:* For master's and doctorate, GRE General Test, GRE Subject Test, minimum GPA of 3.25. Additional exam requirements/recommendations for international students: Required—TOEFL (minimum score 600 paper-based; 90 iBT). Electronic applications accepted. *Faculty research:* Biology and chemistry of groundwater, pollutant fate in groundwater systems, water quality monitoring, urban storm water runoff, urban air quality.

Rose-Hulman Institute of Technology, Graduate Studies, Department of Civil and Environmental Engineering, Terre Haute, IN 47803-3999. Offers civil engineering (MS); environmental engineering (MS). *Program availability:* Part-time. *Faculty:* 8 full-time (2 women), 1 part-time/adjunct (0 women). *Students:* 2 full-time (0 women), 1 part-time (0 women); includes 1 minority (Hispanic/Latino), 1 international. Average age 23. 5 applicants, 80% accepted, 1 enrolled. In 2018, 2 master's awarded. *Degree requirements:* For master's, thesis (for some programs). *Entrance requirements:* For master's, GRE, minimum GPA of 3.0. Additional exam requirements/recommendations

for international students: Required—TOEFL (minimum score 580 paper-based; 94 iBT), IELTS (minimum score 7). *Application deadline:* For fall admission, 2/1 priority date for domestic and international students; for winter admission, 10/1 for domestic students, 4/1 for international students; for spring admission, 1/15 for domestic students, 11/1 for international students. Applications are processed on a rolling basis. Application fee: $0. Electronic applications accepted. *Expenses: Tuition:* Full-time $46,641. *Financial support:* In 2018–19, 3 students received support. Fellowships with tuition reimbursements available, research assistantships with tuition reimbursements available, institutionally sponsored loans, scholarships/grants, and tuition waivers (full and partial) available. *Faculty research:* Transportation, hydraulics/hydrology, environmental, construction, geotechnical, structural. Total annual research expenditures: $6,927. *Unit head:* Dr. Kevin Sutterer, Department Head, 812-877-8959, E-mail: sutterer@rose-hulman.edu. *Application contact:* Dr. Craig Downing, Associate Dean of Lifelong Learning, 812-877-8822, E-mail: downing@rose-hulman.edu. Website: https://www.rose-hulman.edu/academics/academic-departments/civil-and-environmental-engineering/index.html

Rowan University, Graduate School, College of Engineering, Department of Civil Engineering, Glassboro, NJ 08028-1701. Offers MEM, MS. Electronic applications accepted.

Royal Military College of Canada, Division of Graduate Studies, Faculty of Engineering, Department of Civil Engineering, Kingston, ON K7K 7B4, Canada. Offers M Eng, MA Sc, PhD. *Degree requirements:* For master's, thesis; for doctorate, comprehensive exam, thesis/dissertation. *Entrance requirements:* For master's, honours degree with second-class standing; for doctorate, master's degree. Electronic applications accepted.

Rutgers University–New Brunswick, Graduate School-New Brunswick, Department of Civil and Environmental Engineering, Piscataway, NJ 08854-8097. Offers MS, PhD. *Program availability:* Part-time, evening/weekend. Terminal master's awarded for partial completion of doctoral program. *Degree requirements:* For master's, comprehensive exam, thesis or alternative; for doctorate, comprehensive exam, thesis/dissertation. *Entrance requirements:* For master's and doctorate, GRE General Test. Additional exam requirements/recommendations for international students: Required—TOEFL (minimum score 580 paper-based). Electronic applications accepted. *Faculty research:* Civil engineering materials research, non-destructive evaluation of transportation infrastructure, transportation planning, intelligent transportation systems.

Saint Martin's University, Office of Graduate Studies, Program in Civil Engineering, Lacey, WA 98503. Offers MCE. *Program availability:* Part-time. *Faculty:* 2 full-time (1 woman), 3 part-time/adjunct (0 women). *Students:* 2 full-time (0 women), 9 part-time (3 women); includes 4 minority (3 Asian, non-Hispanic/Latino; 1 Two or more races, non-Hispanic/Latino). Average age 40. 11 applicants, 55% accepted, 4 enrolled. In 2018, 3 master's awarded. *Degree requirements:* For master's, thesis optional. *Entrance requirements:* For master's, minimum GPA of 2.8 in undergraduate work; BS in civil engineering or other engineering/science with completion of calculus, differential equations, physics, chemistry, statistics, mechanics of materials and dynamics. Additional exam requirements/recommendations for international students: Required—TOEFL (minimum score 550 paper-based; 79 iBT); Recommended—IELTS (minimum score 6.5). *Application deadline:* For fall admission, 4/1 priority date for domestic students, 4/1 for international students; for spring admission, 11/1 priority date for domestic students, 11/1 for international students. Applications are processed on a rolling basis. Application fee: $50. Electronic applications accepted. *Expenses: Tuition:* Full-time $22,950; part-time $1275 per credit. Tuition and fees vary according to course load, campus/location and program. *Financial support:* Scholarships/grants and tuition waivers (partial) available. Support available to part-time students. Financial award application deadline: 3/1; financial award applicants required to submit FAFSA. *Faculty research:* Transportation engineering, metal fatigue and fracture, environmental engineering. *Unit head:* Dr. Dintie S. Mahamah, Program Chair, 360-688-2755, Fax: 360-438-4548, E-mail: dmahamah@stmartin.edu. *Application contact:* Chantelle Petron Marker, Senior Recruiter, 360-412-6128, E-mail: cmarker@stmartin.edu. Website: https://www.stmartin.edu/directory/office-graduate-studies

San Diego State University, Graduate and Research Affairs, College of Engineering, Department of Civil and Environmental Engineering, San Diego, CA 92182. Offers civil engineering (MS). *Program availability:* Part-time, evening/weekend. *Degree requirements:* For master's, thesis optional. *Entrance requirements:* For master's, GRE General Test. Additional exam requirements/recommendations for international students: Required—TOEFL. Electronic applications accepted. *Faculty research:* Hydraulics, hydrology, transportation, smart material, concrete material.

San Jose State University, Program in Civil & Environmental Engineering, San Jose, CA 95192-0001. Offers civil engineering (MS). *Degree requirements:* For master's, thesis or alternative. *Entrance requirements:* For master's, minimum GPA of 2.7. Electronic applications accepted.

Santa Clara University, School of Engineering, Santa Clara, CA 95053. Offers applied mathematics (MS); bioengineering (MS); civil, environmental, and sustainable engineering (MS); computer science and engineering (MS, PhD, Engineer); electrical engineering (MS, PhD, Engineer); engineering management and leadership (MS); mechanical engineering (MS, PhD, Engineer); power systems and sustainable energy (MS); software engineering (MS). *Program availability:* Part-time. *Faculty:* 72 full-time (24 women), 52 part-time/adjunct (9 women). *Students:* 555 full-time (211 women), 269 part-time (91 women); includes 208 minority (8 Black or African American, non-Hispanic/Latino; 1 American Indian or Alaska Native, non-Hispanic/Latino; 145 Asian, non-Hispanic/Latino; 28 Hispanic/Latino; 26 Two or more races, non-Hispanic/Latino), 472 international. Average age 27. 1,309 applicants, 36% accepted, 269 enrolled. In 2018, 320 master's, 7 doctorates awarded. *Entrance requirements:* For master's, GRE, official transcript; for doctorate, GRE, Official transcript, 500 word statement of purpose, three letters of recommendation. Additional exam requirements/recommendations for international students: Required—TOEFL (minimum score 79 iBT), IELTS (minimum score 6.5). *Application deadline:* For fall admission, 6/1 for domestic students; for winter admission, 9/6 for domestic students; for spring admission, 1/10 for domestic students; for summer admission, 3/6 for domestic students. Application fee: $60. Electronic applications accepted. *Financial support:* Fellowships, Federal Work-Study, and scholarships/grants available. Support available to part-time students. Financial award applicants required to submit FAFSA. *Unit head:* Dr. Elaine Scott, Dean, 408-554-3512, E-mail: epscott@scu.edu. *Application contact:* Stacey Tinker, Director of Admissions and Marketing, 408-554-4748, Fax: 408-554-4323, E-mail: stinker@scu.edu. Website: http://www.scu.edu/engineering/graduate/

South Carolina State University, College of Graduate and Professional Studies, Department of Civil and Mechanical Engineering Technology, Orangeburg, SC 29117-0001. Offers transportation (MS). *Program availability:* Part-time, evening/weekend. *Faculty:* 4 full-time (2 women). *Students:* 11 full-time (1 woman); includes 10 minority (9 Black or African American, non-Hispanic/Latino; 1 Asian, non-Hispanic/Latino), 1 international. Average age 27. 8 applicants, 88% accepted, 7 enrolled. In 2018, 1 master's awarded. *Degree requirements:* For master's, comprehensive exam, thesis, departmental qualifying exam. *Entrance requirements:* For master's, GRE. Additional

exam requirements/recommendations for international students: Recommended—TOEFL. *Application deadline:* For fall admission, 6/15 for domestic and international students; for spring admission, 11/1 for domestic and international students. Application fee: $25. Electronic applications accepted. *Expenses: Tuition, area resident:* Full-time $9928; part-time $552 per credit hour. Tuition, state resident: full-time $9928. Tuition, nonresident: full-time $21,038; part-time $1169 per credit hour. *Required fees:* $1532; $85 per credit hour. *Financial support:* Fellowships, research assistantships, career-related internships or fieldwork, Federal Work-Study, scholarships/grants, and unspecified assistantships available. Financial award application deadline: 6/1. *Unit head:* Dr. Stanley Ihekweazu, Chair, 803-536-7117, Fax: 803-516-4607, E-mail: sihekwea@scsu.edu. *Application contact:* Curtis Foskey, Coordinator of Graduate Admission, 803-536-8419, Fax: 803-536-8812, E-mail: cfoskey@scsu.edu.
Website: http://www.scsu.edu/schoolofgraduatestudies.aspx

South Dakota School of Mines and Technology, Graduate Division, Program in Civil and Environmental Engineering, Rapid City, SD 57701-3995. Offers MS, PhD. *Program availability:* Part-time, online learning. *Degree requirements:* For master's, thesis (for some programs). *Entrance requirements:* Additional exam requirements/recommendations for international students: Required—TOEFL (minimum score 520 paper-based; 68 iBT), TWE. Electronic applications accepted.

South Dakota State University, Graduate School, Jerome J. Lohr College of Engineering, Department of Civil and Environmental Engineering, Brookings, SD 57007. Offers engineering (MS). *Program availability:* Part-time, online learning. *Degree requirements:* For master's, thesis (for some programs), oral exam. *Entrance requirements:* Additional exam requirements/recommendations for international students: Required—TOEFL (minimum score 525 paper-based). *Faculty research:* Structural, environmental, geotechnical, transportation engineering and water resources.

Southern Illinois University Carbondale, Graduate School, College of Engineering, Department of Civil and Environmental Engineering, Carbondale, IL 62901-4701. Offers civil and environmental engineering (ME); civil engineering (MS). *Degree requirements:* For master's, comprehensive exam, thesis. *Entrance requirements:* For master's, GRE, minimum GPA of 2.7. Additional exam requirements/recommendations for international students: Required—TOEFL. *Faculty research:* Composite materials, wastewater treatment, solid waste disposal, slurry transport, geotechnical engineering.

Southern Illinois University Carbondale, Graduate School, College of Engineering, Program in Engineering Science, Carbondale, IL 62901-4701. Offers engineering science (PhD), including civil and environmental engineering, electrical and computer engineering, mechanical engineering and energy processes, mining and mineral resources engineering. *Degree requirements:* For doctorate, thesis/dissertation. *Entrance requirements:* For doctorate, GRE General Test, minimum GPA of 3.5. Additional exam requirements/recommendations for international students: Required—TOEFL.

Southern Illinois University Edwardsville, Graduate School, School of Engineering, Department of Civil Engineering, Edwardsville, IL 62026. Offers environmental engineering (MS); geotechnical engineering (MS); structural engineering (MS); transportation engineering (MS). *Program availability:* Part-time, evening/weekend. *Degree requirements:* For master's, thesis (for some programs), research paper. *Entrance requirements:* For master's, minimum undergraduate GPA of 2.75 in science, math, and engineering courses. Additional exam requirements/recommendations for international students: Required—TOEFL (minimum score 550 paper-based; 79 iBT), IELTS (minimum score 6.5). Electronic applications accepted.

Southern Methodist University, Lyle School of Engineering, Department of Civil and Environmental Engineering, Dallas, TX 75275-0340. Offers civil and environmental engineering (PhD); civil engineering (MS), including geotechnical engineering, structural engineering, transportation systems; environmental engineering (MS); sustainability and development (MA). *Program availability:* Part-time, evening/weekend, online learning. Terminal master's awarded for partial completion of doctoral program. *Degree requirements:* For master's, thesis optional; for doctorate, thesis/dissertation, oral and written qualifying exams. *Entrance requirements:* For master's, GRE General Test, minimum GPA of 3.0 in last 2 years; bachelor's degree in engineering, mathematics, or sciences; for doctorate, GRE, BS and MS in related field, minimum GPA of 3.3. Additional exam requirements/recommendations for international students: Required—TOEFL. Electronic applications accepted. *Faculty research:* Human and environmental health effects of endocrine disrupters, development of air pollution control systems for diesel engines, structural analysis and design, modeling and design of waste treatment systems.

Stevens Institute of Technology, Graduate School, Charles V. Schaefer Jr. School of Engineering and Science, Department of Civil, Environmental, and Ocean Engineering, Program in Civil Engineering, Hoboken, NJ 07030. Offers civil engineering (PhD, Certificate), including geotechnical engineering (Certificate); geotechnical/geoenvironmental engineering (M Eng, Engr); hydrologic modeling (M Eng); stormwater management (M Eng); structural engineering (M Eng, Engr); transportation engineering (M Eng); water resources engineering (M Eng). *Program availability:* Part-time, evening/weekend. *Faculty:* 28 full-time (7 women), 2 part-time/adjunct (1 woman). *Students:* 37 full-time (8 women), 27 part-time (8 women); includes 8 minority (1 Black or African American, non-Hispanic/Latino; 1 American Indian or Alaska Native, non-Hispanic/Latino; 6 Asian, non-Hispanic/Latino), 30 international. Average age 25. In 2018, 44 master's awarded. Terminal master's awarded for partial completion of doctoral program. *Degree requirements:* For master's, thesis optional, minimum B average in major field and overall; for doctorate, comprehensive exam (for some programs), thesis/dissertation; for other advanced degree, minimum B average. *Entrance requirements:* For master's, GRE/GMAT scores: GRE scores are required for all applicants applying to a full-time graduate program in the Schaefer School of Engineering and Science (SES). International applicants must submit TOEFL/IELTS scores and fulfill the English Language Proficiency Requirements in order to be considered. Additional exam requirements/recommendations for international students: Required—TOEFL (minimum score 74 iBT), IELTS (minimum score 6). *Application deadline:* For fall admission, 4/15 for domestic and international students; for spring admission, 11/1 for domestic and international students; for summer admission, 5/1 for domestic students. Applications are processed on a rolling basis. Application fee: $60. Electronic applications accepted. *Expenses: Tuition:* Full-time $35,960; part-time $1620 per credit. *Required fees:* $1290; $600 per semester. Tuition and fees vary according to course load. *Financial support:* Fellowships, research assistantships, teaching assistantships, career-related internships or fieldwork, Federal Work-Study, scholarships/grants, and unspecified assistantships available. Financial award application deadline: 2/15; financial award applicants required to submit FAFSA. *Unit head:* Dr. Jean Zu, Dean of SES, 201-216.8233, Fax: 201-216.8372, E-mail: Jean.Zu@stevens.edu. *Application contact:* Graduate Admission, 888-783-8367, Fax: 888-511-1306, E-mail: graduate@stevens.edu.

Stony Brook University, State University of New York, Graduate School, College of Engineering and Applied Sciences, Department of Civil Engineering, Stony Brook, NY 11794. Offers MS, PhD, Graduate Certificate. *Program availability:* Part-time. *Faculty:* 9 full-time (2 women), 2 part-time/adjunct (1 woman). *Students:* 16 full-time (7 women), 2 part-time (0 women), 16 international. Average age 27. 32 applicants, 56% accepted, 6 enrolled. In 2018, 2 master's awarded. Terminal master's awarded for partial completion of doctoral program. *Degree requirements:* For doctorate, thesis/dissertation, preliminary examination, qualifying examination, teaching requirement. *Entrance requirements:* For doctorate, GRE General Test. Additional exam requirements/recommendations for international students: Required—TOEFL (minimum score 90 iBT). *Application deadline:* For fall admission, 1/15 for domestic students; for spring admission, 10/1 for domestic students. Application fee: $100. *Expenses:* Contact institution. *Financial support:* In 2018–19, 5 research assistantships, 5 teaching assistantships were awarded; fellowships also available. *Faculty research:* Air transportation, civil engineering, public transportation, transportation, transportation energy use, transportation engineering. *Total annual research expenditures:* $1.5 million. *Unit head:* Dr. Burgueño Rigoberto, Chair, 631-632-8315, Fax: 631-632-8110, E-mail: Rigoberto.Burgueno@stonybrook.edu. *Application contact:* Dr. Burgueño Rigoberto, 631-632-8315, E-mail: Rigoberto.Burgueno@stonybrook.edu.
Website: http://www.stonybrook.edu/commcms/civileng/

Syracuse University, College of Engineering and Computer Science, Programs in Civil Engineering, Syracuse, NY 13244. Offers MS, PhD. *Program availability:* Part-time. *Students:* Average age 26. *Degree requirements:* For master's, comprehensive exam (for some programs), thesis (for some programs); for doctorate, comprehensive exam, thesis/dissertation. *Entrance requirements:* For master's and doctorate, GRE General Test, official transcripts, resume, three letters of recommendation, personal statement. Additional exam requirements/recommendations for international students: Required—TOEFL (minimum score 100 iBT). *Application deadline:* For fall admission, 7/1 priority date for domestic students, 6/1 priority date for international students; for spring admission, 11/15 priority date for domestic students, 10/15 priority date for international students. Applications are processed on a rolling basis. Application fee: $75. Electronic applications accepted. *Financial support:* Fellowships with full tuition reimbursements, research assistantships, teaching assistantships, and tuition waivers (partial) available. Financial award application deadline: 1/1. *Faculty research:* Fate and transport of pollutants, methods for characterization and remediation of hazardous wastes, response of eco-systems to disturbances, water quality and engineering. *Unit head:* Dr. Dawit Negussey, Professor/Graduate Program Director, 315-443-2311, E-mail: negussey@syr.edu. *Application contact:* Kathleen Joyce, Assistant Dean, 315-443-2219, E-mail: topgrads@syr.edu.
Website: http://eng-cs.syr.edu/our-departments/civil-and-environmental-engineering/

Temple University, College of Engineering, Department of Civil and Environmental Engineering, Philadelphia, PA 19122-6096. Offers civil engineering (MSCE); environmental engineering (MS Env E); storm water management (Graduate Certificate). *Program availability:* Part-time, evening/weekend. Terminal master's awarded for partial completion of doctoral program. *Degree requirements:* For master's, thesis optional. *Entrance requirements:* For master's, GRE General Test, minimum GPA of 3.0; BS in engineering from ABET-accredited or equivalent institution; resume; goals statement; three letters of reference; official transcripts. Additional exam requirements/recommendations for international students: Required—TOEFL (minimum score 550 paper-based; 79 iBT), IELTS (minimum score 6.5), PTE (minimum score 53). Electronic applications accepted. *Expenses:* Contact institution. *Faculty research:* Analysis of the effect of scour on bridge stability, design of sustainable buildings, development of new highway pavement material using plastic waste, characterization of by-products and waste materials for pavement and geotechnical engineering applications, development of effective traffic signals in urban and rural settings, development of techniques for effective construction management.

Temple University, College of Engineering, PhD in Engineering Program, Philadelphia, PA 19122-6096. Offers bioengineering (PhD); civil engineering (PhD); electrical engineering (PhD); environmental engineering (PhD); mechanical engineering (PhD). *Program availability:* Part-time, evening/weekend. *Degree requirements:* For doctorate, thesis/dissertation, preliminary exam, dissertation proposal and defense. *Entrance requirements:* For doctorate, GRE, minimum undergraduate GPA of 3.0; MS in engineering from ABET-accredited or equivalent institution (preferred); resume; goals statement; three letters of reference; official transcripts. Additional exam requirements/recommendations for international students: Required—TOEFL (minimum score 550 paper-based; 79 iBT), IELTS (minimum score 6.5), PTE (minimum score 53). Electronic applications accepted. *Expenses:* Contact institution. *Faculty research:* Advanced/computer-aided manufacturing and advanced materials processing; bioengineering; computer engineering; construction engineering and management; dynamics, controls, and systems; energy and environmental science; engineering physics and engineering mathematics; green engineering; signal processing and communication; transportation engineering; water resources, hydrology, and environmental engineering.

See Display on page 59 and Close-Up on page 73.

Tennessee State University, The School of Graduate Studies and Research, College of Engineering, Nashville, TN 37209-1561. Offers biomedical engineering (ME); civil engineering (ME); computer and information systems engineering (MS, PhD); electrical engineering (ME); environmental engineering (ME); manufacturing engineering (ME); mathematical sciences (MS); mechanical engineering (ME). *Program availability:* Part-time, evening/weekend. *Degree requirements:* For master's, project; for doctorate, comprehensive exam, thesis/dissertation. *Entrance requirements:* For doctorate, minimum GPA of 3.3. *Faculty research:* Robotics, intelligent systems, human-computer interaction software systems, biomedical engineering, signal/image processing, probabilistic design, intelligent manufacturing, cooperative mobile robots, condition based maintenance, sensor fusion.

Tennessee Technological University, College of Graduate Studies, College of Engineering, Department of Civil and Environmental Engineering, Cookeville, TN 38505. Offers MS. *Program availability:* Part-time. *Faculty:* 17 full-time (0 women). *Students:* 13 full-time (2 women), 11 part-time (1 woman); includes 2 minority (1 Black or African American, non-Hispanic/Latino; 1 Hispanic/Latino), 6 international. 25 applicants, 52% accepted, 8 enrolled. In 2018, 9 master's awarded. *Degree requirements:* For master's, thesis. *Entrance requirements:* For master's, GRE. Additional exam requirements/recommendations for international students: Required—TOEFL (minimum score 550 paper-based; 79 iBT), IELTS (minimum score 5.5), PTE (minimum score 53), or TOEIC (Test of English as an International Communication). *Application deadline:* For fall admission, 8/1 for domestic students, 5/1 for international students; for spring admission, 12/1 for domestic students, 10/1 for international students; for summer admission, 5/1 for domestic students, 2/1 for international students. Applications are processed on a rolling basis. Application fee: $35 ($40 for international students). Electronic applications accepted. *Financial support:* Research assistantships, teaching assistantships, and career-related internships or fieldwork available. Financial award application deadline: 4/1. *Faculty research:* Environmental engineering, transportation, structural engineering, water resources. *Unit head:* Dr. Ben Mohr, Chairperson, 931-372-3454, Fax: 931-372-6352, E-mail: bmohr@tntech.edu. *Application contact:* Shelia K. Kendrick, Coordinator of Graduate Studies, 931-372-3808, Fax: 931-372-3497, E-mail: skendrick@tntech.edu.

Texas A&M University, College of Engineering, Zachry Department of Civil Engineering, College Station, TX 77843. Offers civil engineering (M Eng, MS, PhD). *Program availability:* Part-time. *Faculty:* 63. *Students:* 374 full-time (99 women), 57 part-time (10 women); includes 44 minority (6 Black or African American, non-Hispanic/Latino; 11 Asian, non-Hispanic/Latino; 24 Hispanic/Latino; 3 Two or more races, non-Hispanic/Latino), 301 international. Average age 28. 705 applicants, 47% accepted, 107 enrolled. In 2018, 130 master's, 21 doctorates awarded. *Degree requirements:* For master's, thesis (MS); for doctorate, dissertation (PhD), internship (D Eng). *Entrance requirements:* For master's and doctorate, GRE General Test. Additional exam requirements/recommendations for international students: Required—TOEFL (minimum score 550 paper-based; 80 iBT), IELTS (minimum score 6), PTE (minimum score 53). *Application deadline:* For fall admission, 7/15 for domestic students, 4/15 for international students; for spring admission, 10/15 for domestic students, 9/15 for international students. Applications are processed on a rolling basis. Application fee: $50 ($90 for international students). Electronic applications accepted. *Expenses:* Contact institution. *Financial support:* In 2018–19, 337 students received support, including 140 fellowships with tuition reimbursements available (averaging $3,033 per year), 150 research assistantships with tuition reimbursements available (averaging $13,775 per year), 63 teaching assistantships with tuition reimbursements available (averaging $12,781 per year); career-related internships or fieldwork, institutionally sponsored loans, scholarships/grants, traineeships, health care benefits, tuition waivers (full and partial), and unspecified assistantships also available. Support available to part-time students. Financial award application deadline: 3/15; financial award applicants required to submit FAFSA. *Unit head:* Dr. Robin Autenrieth, Department Head, 979-845-2438, E-mail: rautenrieth@civil.tamu.edu. *Application contact:* Laura Byrd, Program Assistant, Graduate Student Services, 979-845-2498, E-mail: lbyrd@civil.tamu.edu.
Website: http://engineering.tamu.edu/civil/

Texas A&M University–Kingsville, College of Graduate Studies, Frank H. Dotterweich College of Engineering, Department of Civil and Architectural Engineering, Kingsville, TX 78363. Offers civil engineering (ME, MS). *Degree requirements:* For master's, variable foreign language requirement, comprehensive exam, thesis (for some programs). *Entrance requirements:* For master's, GRE (minimum Quantitative and Verbal score of 950 on old scale), MAT, GMAT, minimum GPA of 2.6. Additional exam requirements/recommendations for international students: Required—TOEFL (minimum score 550 paper-based; 79 iBT). Electronic applications accepted. *Faculty research:* Dam restoration.

Texas State University, The Graduate College, College of Science and Engineering, Program in Engineering, San Marcos, TX 78666. Offers civil engineering (MS); electrical engineering (MS); industrial engineering (MS); mechanical and manufacturing engineering (MS). *Program availability:* Part-time. *Faculty:* 15 full-time (2 women). *Students:* 46 full-time (14 women), 41 part-time (13 women); includes 11 minority (3 Asian, non-Hispanic/Latino; 7 Hispanic/Latino; 1 Two or more races, non-Hispanic/Latino), 67 international. Average age 27. 105 applicants, 64% accepted, 31 enrolled. In 2018, 13 master's awarded. *Degree requirements:* For master's, comprehensive exam, thesis (for some programs), thesis or research project. *Entrance requirements:* For master's, official GRE (general test only) required with competitive scores in the verbal reasoning and quantitative reasoning sections, baccalaureate degree from regionally-accredited university in engineering, computer science, physics, technology, or closely-related field with minimum GPA of 3.0 on last 60 undergraduate semester hours; resume or curriculum vitae; 2 letters of recommendation; statement of purpose conveying research interest and professional aspirations. Additional exam requirements/recommendations for international students: Required—TOEFL (minimum score 550 paper-based; 78 iBT), IELTS (minimum score 6.5). *Application deadline:* For fall admission, 2/15 priority date for domestic students, 2/1 priority date for international students. Application fee: $55 ($90 for international students). Electronic applications accepted. *Expenses:* Tuition, state resident: full-time $8102; part-time $4051 per semester. Tuition, nonresident: full-time $18,229; part-time $9115 per semester. *International tuition:* $18,229 full-time. *Required fees:* $2116; $120 per credit hour. Tuition and fees vary according to course load. *Financial support:* In 2018–19, 52 students received support, including 14 research assistantships (averaging $12,742 per year), 34 teaching assistantships (averaging $12,483 per year); Federal Work-Study, institutionally sponsored loans, scholarships/grants, health care benefits, and unspecified assistantships also available. Support available to part-time students. Financial award application deadline: 1/15; financial award applicants required to submit FAFSA. *Faculty research:* Computer Architecture & Digital Image Processing; Industrial robotics on a mobile platform; supply chain management optimization modeling and algorithms; Modeling and analysis of manufacturing systems especially semiconductor manufacturing; smart grids for big data analytics and demand response; Digital Signal/Image/Speach Processing & Data Compression; Health care systems engineering and anaylsis of patient flow. *Total annual research expenditures:* $920,229. *Unit head:* Dr. Vishu Viswanathan, Graduate Advisor, 512-245-1826, Fax: 512-245-8365, E-mail: v_v42@txstate.edu. *Application contact:* Dr. Andrea Golato, Dean of Graduate School, 512-245-2581, Fax: 512-245-8365, E-mail: gradcollege@txstate.edu.
Website: http://www.engineering.txstate.edu/Programs/Graduate.html

Tufts University, School of Engineering, Department of Civil and Environmental Engineering, Medford, MA 02155. Offers bioengineering (MS), including environmental biotechnology; civil and environmental engineering (MS, PhD), including applied data science, environmental and water resources engineering, environmental health, geosystems engineering, structural engineering and mechanics; PhD/PhD. *Program availability:* Part-time. Terminal master's awarded for partial completion of doctoral program. *Degree requirements:* For master's, thesis (for some programs); for doctorate, thesis/dissertation. *Entrance requirements:* For master's and doctorate, GRE General Test. Additional exam requirements/recommendations for international students: Required—TOEFL (minimum score 550 paper-based; 80 iBT), IELTS (minimum score 6.5). Electronic applications accepted. *Expenses: Tuition:* Full-time $51,288; part-time $1710 per credit hour. *Required fees:* $904. Full-time tuition and fees vary according to degree level, program and student level. Part-time tuition and fees vary according to course load. *Faculty research:* Environmental and water resources engineering, environmental health, geotechnical and geoenvironmental engineering, structural engineering and mechanics, water diplomacy.

United States Merchant Marine Academy, Graduate Program, Kings Point, NY 11024-1699. Offers MS.

Université de Moncton, Faculty of Engineering, Program in Civil Engineering, Moncton, NB E1A 3E9, Canada. Offers M Sc A. *Degree requirements:* For master's, thesis, proficiency in French. *Faculty research:* Structures and materials, hydrology and water resources, soil mechanics and statistical analysis, environment, transportation.

Université de Sherbrooke, Faculty of Engineering, Department of Civil Engineering, Sherbrooke, QC J1K 2R1, Canada. Offers M Sc A, PhD. *Degree requirements:* For master's, one foreign language, thesis; for doctorate, comprehensive exam, thesis/dissertation. *Entrance requirements:* For master's, bachelor's degree in engineering or equivalent; for doctorate, master's degree in engineering or equivalent. Electronic applications accepted. *Faculty research:* High-strength concrete, dynamics of structures, solid mechanics, geotechnical engineering, wastewater treatment.

Université Laval, Faculty of Sciences and Engineering, Department of Civil Engineering, Program in Urban Infrastructure Engineering, Québec, QC G1K 7P4, Canada. Offers Diploma. *Program availability:* Part-time, evening/weekend. *Entrance requirements:* For degree, knowledge of French. Electronic applications accepted.

Université Laval, Faculty of Sciences and Engineering, Department of Civil Engineering, Programs in Civil Engineering, Québec, QC G1K 7P4, Canada. Offers civil engineering (M Sc, PhD); environmental technology (M Sc). Terminal master's awarded for partial completion of doctoral program. *Degree requirements:* For master's, thesis (for some programs); for doctorate, comprehensive exam, thesis/dissertation. *Entrance requirements:* For master's and doctorate, knowledge of French and English. Electronic applications accepted.

University at Buffalo, the State University of New York, Graduate School, School of Engineering and Applied Sciences, Department of Civil, Structural, and Environmental Engineering, Buffalo, NY 14260. Offers civil engineering (MS, PhD); engineering science (MS), including data sciences, green energy, Internet of Things, nanoelectronics; environmental and water resources engineering (MS). *Program availability:* Part-time, online learning. Terminal master's awarded for partial completion of doctoral program. *Degree requirements:* For master's, project, thesis, or comprehensive exam; for doctorate, thesis/dissertation. *Entrance requirements:* For master's and doctorate, GRE General Test, letters of reference. Additional exam requirements/recommendations for international students: Required—TOEFL (minimum score 550 paper-based; 79 iBT). Electronic applications accepted. *Faculty research:* Structural and earthquake engineering; geomechanics, geotechnical and geoenvironmental engineering; computational engineering mechanics; bridge engineering; environmental and water resources engineering; transportation systems engineering.

The University of Akron, Graduate School, College of Engineering, Department of Civil Engineering, Akron, OH 44325. Offers civil engineering (MS); engineering (PhD). *Program availability:* Evening/weekend. *Degree requirements:* For master's, thesis optional; for doctorate, thesis/dissertation, candidacy exam, qualifying exam. *Entrance requirements:* For master's, GRE, minimum GPA of 2.75, statement of purpose, three letters of recommendation; for doctorate, GRE, minimum GPA of 3.0 with bachelor's degree, 3.5 with master's degree; three letters of recommendation; statement of purpose; resume. Additional exam requirements/recommendations for international students: Required—TOEFL (minimum score 79 iBT), IELTS (minimum score 6.5). Electronic applications accepted. *Faculty research:* Development of constitutive laws for numerical analysis of nonlinear problems in structural mechanics, multiscale modeling and simulation of novel materials, water quality and distribution system analysis, safety-related traffic control, dynamic pile testing and analysis.

The University of Alabama, Graduate School, College of Engineering, Department of Civil, Construction and Environmental Engineering, Tuscaloosa, AL 35487-0205. Offers civil engineering (MSCE, PhD); environmental engineering (MS). *Program availability:* Part-time. Terminal master's awarded for partial completion of doctoral program. *Degree requirements:* For master's, thesis or alternative; for doctorate, comprehensive exam, thesis/dissertation. *Entrance requirements:* For master's and doctorate, GRE General Test (minimum combined score of 300), minimum overall GPA of 3.0 in last hours of course work. Additional exam requirements/recommendations for international students: Required—TOEFL (minimum score 550 paper-based; 79 iBT), IELTS (minimum score 6.5), PTE (minimum score 59). Electronic applications accepted. *Faculty research:* Experimental structures, modeling of structures, bridge management systems, geotechnological engineering, environmental remediation.

The University of Alabama at Birmingham, School of Engineering, Program in Civil Engineering, Birmingham, AL 35294. Offers MSCE, PhD. Program offered jointly with The University of Alabama in Huntsville. *Program availability:* Part-time, evening/weekend, 100% online. *Faculty:* 6 full-time (1 woman), 1 part-time/adjunct (0 women). *Students:* 17 full-time (7 women), 17 part-time (7 women); includes 3 minority (1 Black or African American, non-Hispanic/Latino; 2 Two or more races, non-Hispanic/Latino), 23 international. Average age 30. 42 applicants, 55% accepted, 5 enrolled. In 2018, 9 master's, 1 doctorate awarded. *Degree requirements:* For master's, comprehensive exam, thesis optional; for doctorate, comprehensive exam, thesis/dissertation. *Entrance requirements:* For master's, GRE General Test, minimum GPA of 3.0 in all undergraduate degree major courses attempted, letters of evaluation. Additional exam requirements/recommendations for international students: Required—TOEFL (minimum score 80 iBT), TWE (minimum score 3.5); Recommended—IELTS (minimum score 6.5). *Application deadline:* For fall admission, 8/1 for domestic and international students; for spring admission, 12/1 for domestic and international students; for summer admission, 5/1 for domestic and international students. Applications are processed on a rolling basis. Application fee: $50 ($60 for international students). Electronic applications accepted. *Expenses:* Contact institution. *Financial support:* In 2018–19, 22 students received support, including 12 fellowships with full tuition reimbursements available (averaging $22,883 per year), 9 research assistantships with full and partial tuition reimbursements available. *Faculty research:* Health monitoring of structures; high performance concrete materials; structural behavior and testing of bridge and building components; sustainable water and energy conservation; sustainable transportation systems. *Total annual research expenditures:* $871,687. *Unit head:* Dr. Fouad H. Fouad, Chair, 205-934-8430, Fax: 205-934-9855, E-mail: ffouad@uab.edu. *Application contact:* Jesse Keppley, Director of Student and Academic Services, 205-996-5696, Fax: 205-934-8413, E-mail: gradschool@uab.edu.
Website: https://www.uab.edu/engineering/home/graduate-civil

The University of Alabama in Huntsville, School of Graduate Studies, College of Engineering, Department of Civil and Environmental Engineering, Huntsville, AL 35899. Offers civil and environmental engineering (PhD); civil engineering (MSE), including civil engineering. PhD offered jointly with The University of Alabama at Birmingham. *Program availability:* Part-time. *Faculty:* 6 full-time (1 woman). *Students:* 18 full-time (7 women), 13 part-time (4 women); includes 6 minority (4 Black or African American, non-Hispanic/Latino; 2 Hispanic/Latino), 15 international. Average age 32. 43 applicants, 72% accepted, 11 enrolled. In 2018, 11 master's, 1 doctorate awarded. *Degree requirements:* For master's, comprehensive exam, thesis or alternative, oral and written exams; for doctorate, comprehensive exam, thesis/dissertation, oral and written exams. *Entrance requirements:* For master's, GRE General Test, BSE, minimum GPA of 3.0; for doctorate, GRE General Test, minimum GPA of 3.0. Additional exam requirements/recommendations for international students: Required—TOEFL (minimum score 500 paper-based; 80 iBT), IELTS (minimum score 6.5). *Application deadline:* For fall admission, 7/15 priority date for domestic students, 4/1 priority date for international students; for spring admission, 11/30 priority date for domestic students, 9/1 priority date for international students. Applications are processed on a rolling basis. Application fee: $50. Electronic applications accepted. *Expenses: Tuition, area resident:* Full-time $10,632; part-time $412 per credit hour. Tuition, state resident: full-time $10,632. Tuition, nonresident: full-time $23,604; part-time $412 per credit hour. *Required fees:* $582; $582. Tuition and fees vary according to course load and program. *Financial support:* In 2018–19, 14 students received support, including 8 research assistantships with full tuition reimbursements available (averaging $7,825 per year), 6 teaching assistantships with full tuition reimbursements available (averaging $5,316 per year);

career-related internships or fieldwork, Federal Work-Study, institutionally sponsored loans, scholarships/grants, health care benefits, and unspecified assistantships also available. Support available to part-time students. Financial award application deadline: 4/1; financial award applicants required to submit FAFSA. *Faculty research:* Smart materials and smart structures, fiber-reinforced cementitious composites, processing and mechanics of composites, geographic information systems, environmental engineering. *Unit head:* Dr. Michael Anderson, Interim Chair, 256-824-5028, Fax: 256-824-6724, E-mail: andersmd@uah.edu. *Application contact:* Kim Gray, Graduate Studies Admissions Coordinator, 256-824-6002, Fax: 256-824-6405, E-mail: deangrad@uah.edu.
Website: http://www.uah.edu/eng/departments/cee

University of Alaska Fairbanks, College of Engineering and Mines, Department of Civil and Environmental Engineering, Fairbanks, AK 99775-5900. Offers civil engineering (MS); design and construction management (Graduate Certificate); environmental engineering (PhD). *Program availability:* Part-time. *Faculty:* 6 full-time (1 woman), 1 (woman) part-time/adjunct. *Students:* 8 full-time (2 women), 7 part-time (2 women); includes 4 minority (1 Black or African American, non-Hispanic/Latino; 1 Asian, non-Hispanic/Latino; 2 Two or more races, non-Hispanic/Latino), 2 international. Average age 27. 10 applicants, 30% accepted, 3 enrolled. In 2018, 4 master's awarded. *Degree requirements:* For master's, comprehensive exam, thesis (for some programs), oral defense of project or thesis; for doctorate, comprehensive exam, thesis/dissertation. *Entrance requirements:* For master's, bachelor's degree from accredited institution with minimum cumulative undergraduate and major GPA of 3.0. Additional exam requirements/recommendations for international students: Required—TOEFL (minimum score 550 paper-based; 79 iBT), IELTS (minimum score 6.5). *Application deadline:* For fall admission, 6/1 for domestic students, 3/1 for international students; for spring admission, 10/15 for domestic students, 9/1 for international students. Applications are processed on a rolling basis. Application fee: $60. Electronic applications accepted. *Expenses:* CEM tuition has a 20% surcharge per credit hour over that for credits of most other UAF colleges. Assuming 60 credits for PhD and 32 for Master's, this augments costs by $6,180 for in-state PhD, $3,296 for in-state Master's, $12,948 for non-resident PhD and $6,912 for non-resident Masters students, respectively. *Financial support:* In 2018–19, 7 research assistantships with full tuition reimbursements (averaging $4,557 per year), 6 teaching assistantships with full tuition reimbursements (averaging $5,086 per year) were awarded; fellowships with full tuition reimbursements, career-related internships or fieldwork, Federal Work-Study, scholarships/grants, health care benefits, and unspecified assistantships also available. Support available to part-time students. Financial award application deadline: 7/1; financial award applicants required to submit FAFSA. *Faculty research:* Soils, structures, culvert thawing with solar power, pavement drainage, contaminant hydrogeology. *Unit head:* Dr. Robert Perkins, Department Chair, 907-474-7694, E-mail: fycee@uaf.edu. *Application contact:* Samara Taber, Director of Admissions, 907-474-7500, E-mail: uaf-admissions@alaska.edu.
Website: http://cem.uaf.edu/cee

University of Alberta, Faculty of Graduate Studies and Research, Department of Civil and Environmental Engineering, Edmonton, AB T6G 2E1, Canada. Offers construction engineering and management (M Eng, M Sc, PhD); environmental engineering (M Eng, M Sc, PhD); environmental science (M Sc, PhD); geoenvironmental engineering (M Eng, M Sc, PhD); geotechnical engineering (M Eng, M Sc, PhD); mining engineering (M Eng, M Sc, PhD); petroleum engineering (M Eng, M Sc, PhD); structural engineering (M Eng, M Sc, PhD); water resources (M Eng, M Sc, PhD). *Program availability:* Part-time, online learning. *Degree requirements:* For master's, thesis (for some programs); for doctorate, thesis/dissertation. *Entrance requirements:* For master's, minimum GPA of 3.0 in last 2 years of undergraduate studies; for doctorate, minimum GPA of 3.0. Additional exam requirements/recommendations for international students: Required—TOEFL (minimum score 550 paper-based). Electronic applications accepted. *Faculty research:* Mining.

University of Arkansas, Graduate School, College of Engineering, Department of Civil Engineering, Program in Civil Engineering, Fayetteville, AR 72701. Offers MSCE, MSE, PhD. In 2018, 14 master's, 5 doctorates awarded. *Degree requirements:* For master's, thesis optional; for doctorate, one foreign language, thesis/dissertation. *Application deadline:* For fall admission, 8/1 for domestic students, 4/1 for international students; for spring admission, 12/1 for domestic students, 10/1 for international students; for summer admission, 4/15 for domestic students, 3/1 for international students. Applications are processed on a rolling basis. Application fee: $60. Electronic applications accepted. *Financial support:* In 2018–19, 33 research assistantships, 1 teaching assistantship were awarded; fellowships, career-related internships or fieldwork, and Federal Work-Study also available. Support available to part-time students. Financial award application deadline: 4/1; financial award applicants required to submit FAFSA. *Unit head:* Dr. Micah Hale, Department Head, 479-575-6348, E-mail: micah@uark.edu. *Application contact:* Dr. Julian Fairey, Graduate Coordinator, 479-575-4023, E-mail: julianf@uark.edu.
Website: https://civil-engineering.uark.edu/

The University of British Columbia, Faculty of Applied Science, Department of Civil Engineering, Vancouver, BC V6T 1Z4, Canada. Offers M Eng, MA Sc, PhD. *Program availability:* Part-time. *Degree requirements:* For master's, thesis; for doctorate, thesis/dissertation. *Entrance requirements:* Additional exam requirements/recommendations for international students: Required—TOEFL (minimum score 100 iBT), IELTS. Electronic applications accepted. *Expenses:* Contact institution. *Faculty research:* Geotechnology; structural, water, and environmental engineering; transportation; materials and construction engineering.

University of Calgary, Faculty of Graduate Studies, Schulich School of Engineering, Program in Civil Engineering, Calgary, AB T2N 1N4, Canada. Offers avalanche mechanics (M Sc, PhD); civil engineering (M Eng, M Sc, PhD); energy and environment engineering (M Eng, M Sc, PhD); environmental engineering (M Eng, M Sc, PhD); geotechnical engineering (M Eng, M Sc, PhD); materials science (M Eng, M Sc, PhD); project management (M Eng, M Sc, PhD); structures and solid mechanics (M Eng, M Sc, PhD); transportation engineering (M Eng, M Sc, PhD); water resources (M Eng, M Sc, PhD). *Program availability:* Part-time. *Degree requirements:* For master's, thesis; for doctorate, thesis/dissertation, written and oral candidacy exam. *Entrance requirements:* For master's, minimum GPA of 3.0; for doctorate, minimum GPA of 3.5. Additional exam requirements/recommendations for international students: Required—TOEFL (minimum score 580 paper-based; 93 iBT), IELTS (minimum score 7). Electronic applications accepted. *Faculty research:* Geotechnical engineering, energy and environment, transportation, project management, structures and solid mechanics.

University of California, Berkeley, Graduate Division, College of Engineering, Department of Civil and Environmental Engineering, Berkeley, CA 94720. Offers engineering and project management (M Eng, MS, PhD); environmental engineering (M Eng, MS, PhD); geoengineering (M Eng, MS, PhD); structural engineering, mechanics and materials (M Eng, MS, PhD); transportation engineering (M Eng, MS, PhD); M Arch/MS; MCP/MS; MPP/MS. Terminal master's awarded for partial completion of doctoral program. *Degree requirements:* For master's, comprehensive exam (for some programs), thesis (for some programs), comprehensive exam or thesis (MS); for doctorate, thesis/dissertation, qualifying exam. *Entrance requirements:* For master's, GRE General Test, minimum GPA of 3.0, 3 letters of recommendation; for doctorate, GRE General Test, minimum GPA of 3.5, 3 letters of recommendation. Additional exam requirements/recommendations for international students: Required—TOEFL (minimum score 570 paper-based; 90 iBT). Electronic applications accepted.

University of California, Davis, College of Engineering, Program in Civil and Environmental Engineering, Davis, CA 95616. Offers M Engr, MS, D Engr, PhD, Certificate, M Engr/MBA. *Degree requirements:* For master's, comprehensive exam (for some programs), thesis (for some programs); for doctorate, thesis/dissertation. *Entrance requirements:* For master's, GRE General Test, minimum GPA of 3.0; for doctorate, GRE, minimum graduate GPA of 3.5. Additional exam requirements/recommendations for international students: Required—TOEFL (minimum score 550 paper-based). Electronic applications accepted. *Faculty research:* Environmental water resources, transportation, structural mechanics, structural engineering, geotechnical engineering.

University of California, Irvine, Samueli School of Engineering, Department of Civil and Environmental Engineering, Irvine, CA 92697. Offers MS, PhD. *Program availability:* Part-time. *Students:* 133 full-time (53 women), 19 part-time (8 women); includes 23 minority (1 Black or African American, non-Hispanic/Latino; 14 Asian, non-Hispanic/Latino; 5 Hispanic/Latino; 3 Two or more races, non-Hispanic/Latino), 96 international. Average age 27. 433 applicants, 45% accepted, 45 enrolled. In 2018, 49 master's, 16 doctorates awarded. Terminal master's awarded for partial completion of doctoral program. *Entrance requirements:* For master's and doctorate, GRE General Test, minimum GPA of 3.0, 3 letters of recommendation. Additional exam requirements/recommendations for international students: Required—TOEFL (minimum score 550 paper-based). *Application deadline:* For fall admission, 1/15 priority date for domestic students, 1/15 for international students. Applications are processed on a rolling basis. Application fee: $105 ($125 for international students). Electronic applications accepted. *Financial support:* Fellowships, research assistantships with full tuition reimbursements, teaching assistantships, institutionally sponsored loans, traineeships, health care benefits, and unspecified assistantships available. Financial award application deadline: 3/1; financial award applicants required to submit FAFSA. *Faculty research:* Intelligent transportation systems and transportation economics, risk and reliability, fluid mechanics, environmental hydrodynamics, hydrological and climate systems, water resources. *Unit head:* Prof. Brett F. Sanders, Chair and Professor, 949-824-4327, Fax: 949-824-3672, E-mail: bsanders@uci.edu. *Application contact:* Connie Cheng, Assistant Director, 949-824-3562, Fax: 949-824-8200, E-mail: connie.cheng@uci.edu.
Website: http://www.eng.uci.edu/dept/cee

University of California, Los Angeles, Graduate Division, Henry Samueli School of Engineering and Applied Science, Department of Civil and Environmental Engineering, Los Angeles, CA 90095-1593. Offers MS, PhD. *Degree requirements:* For master's, comprehensive exam or thesis; for doctorate, thesis/dissertation, qualifying exams. *Entrance requirements:* For master's, GRE General Test, minimum GPA of 3.0; for doctorate, GRE General Test, minimum GPA of 3.25. Additional exam requirements/recommendations for international students: Required—TOEFL (minimum score 560 paper-based; 87 iBT), IELTS (minimum score 7). Electronic applications accepted. *Faculty research:* Civil engineering materials, environmental engineering, geotechnical engineering, hydrology and water resources, structures.

University of Central Florida, College of Engineering and Computer Science, Department of Civil, Environmental, and Construction Engineering, Program in Civil Engineering, Orlando, FL 32816. Offers MS, MSCE, PhD, Certificate. *Program availability:* Part-time, evening/weekend. *Students:* 93 full-time (19 women), 64 part-time (19 women); includes 38 minority (5 Black or African American, non-Hispanic/Latino; 6 Asian, non-Hispanic/Latino; 27 Hispanic/Latino), 79 international. Average age 31. 122 applicants, 72% accepted, 44 enrolled. In 2018, 29 master's, 17 doctorates, 1 other advanced degree awarded. *Degree requirements:* For master's, thesis or alternative; for doctorate, thesis/dissertation, departmental qualifying exam, candidacy exam. *Entrance requirements:* For master's, minimum GPA of 3.0 in last 60 hours, letters of recommendation, goal statement, resume; for doctorate, GRE General Test, minimum GPA of 3.5 in last 60 hours, letters of recommendation, goal statement, resume. Additional exam requirements/recommendations for international students: Required—TOEFL. *Application deadline:* For fall admission, 7/15 priority date for domestic students; for spring admission, 12/1 priority date for domestic students. Application fee: $30. Electronic applications accepted. *Financial support:* In 2018–19, 66 students received support, including 32 fellowships with partial tuition reimbursements available (averaging $13,256 per year), 42 research assistantships with partial tuition reimbursements available (averaging $12,964 per year), 16 teaching assistantships with partial tuition reimbursements available (averaging $9,890 per year); career-related internships or fieldwork, Federal Work-Study, institutionally sponsored loans, health care benefits, tuition waivers (partial), and unspecified assistantships also available. Financial award application deadline: 3/1; financial award applicants required to submit FAFSA. *Unit head:* Dr. Andrew Randall, Graduate Director, 407-823-2841, E-mail: andrew.randall@ucf.edu. *Application contact:* Associate Director, Graduate Admissions, 407-823-2766, Fax: 407-823-6442, E-mail: gradadmissions@ucf.edu.
Website: http://cece.ucf.edu/

University of Cincinnati, Graduate School, College of Engineering and Applied Science, Department of Civil and Architectural Engineering and Construction Management, Program in Civil Engineering, Cincinnati, OH 45221. Offers M Eng, MS, PhD. *Program availability:* Part-time. Terminal master's awarded for partial completion of doctoral program. *Degree requirements:* For master's, comprehensive exam, thesis; for doctorate, comprehensive exam, thesis/dissertation. *Entrance requirements:* For master's and doctorate, GRE General Test. Additional exam requirements/recommendations for international students: Required—TOEFL (minimum iBT score 90), IELTS (6.5), or PTE (47). Electronic applications accepted. *Faculty research:* Sustainable infrastructure, asset management, decision analysis, integrated construction technologies, foundation engineering, slope stability, consolidation and settlement, geosynthetics, pavements, rock mechanics, earthquake engineering, steel, concrete, precast structures, structural connections, fire engineering, large-scale experimental testing and numerical simulations, connected and autonomous vehicles, intelligent traffic signal control, roadway design, multi-modal travel.

University of Colorado Boulder, Graduate School, College of Engineering and Applied Science, Department of Civil, Environmental, and Architectural Engineering, Boulder, CO 80309. Offers MS, PhD. Terminal master's awarded for partial completion of doctoral program. *Degree requirements:* For master's, comprehensive exam, thesis or alternative; for doctorate, thesis/dissertation. *Entrance requirements:* For master's, GRE General Test, minimum undergraduate GPA of 3.0. Electronic applications accepted. Application fee is waived when completed online. *Faculty research:* Civil engineering; environmental engineering; architectural engineering; hydrology; water resources engineering.

University of Colorado Denver, College of Engineering, Design and Computing, Department of Civil Engineering, Denver, CO 80217. Offers civil engineering (EASPh D); civil engineering systems (PhD); environmental and sustainability engineering (MS, PhD); geographic information systems (MS); geotechnical engineering (MS, PhD); hydrology and hydraulics (MS, PhD); structural engineering (MS, PhD); transportation engineering (MS, PhD). *Program availability:* Part-time, evening/

weekend. *Degree requirements:* For master's, comprehensive exam, 30 credit hours, project or thesis; for doctorate, comprehensive exam, thesis/dissertation, 60 credit hours (30 of which are dissertation research). *Entrance requirements:* For master's, GRE, statement of purpose, transcripts, three references; for doctorate, GRE, statement of purpose, transcripts, references, letter of support from faculty stating willingness to serve as dissertation advisor and outlining plan for financial support. Additional exam requirements/recommendations for international students: Required—TOEFL (minimum score 537 paper-based; 75 iBT); Recommended—IELTS (minimum score 6.5). Electronic applications accepted. *Expenses:* Tuition, state resident: full-time $6786; part-time $337 per credit hour. Tuition, nonresident: full-time $22,590; part-time $1255 per credit hour. *Required fees:* $1231; $137 per credit hour. Tuition and fees vary according to program and reciprocity agreements.

University of Colorado Denver, College of Engineering, Design and Computing, Master of Engineering Program, Denver, CO 80217-3364. Offers civil engineering (M Eng), including civil engineering, geographic information systems, transportation systems; electrical engineering (M Eng); mechanical engineering (M Eng). *Program availability:* Part-time. *Entrance requirements:* For master's, GRE (for those with GPA below 2.75), transcripts, references, statement of purpose. *Expenses:* Tuition, state resident: full-time $6786; part-time $337 per credit hour. Tuition, nonresident: full-time $22,590; part-time $1255 per credit hour. *Required fees:* $1231; $137 per credit hour. Tuition and fees vary according to program and reciprocity agreements.

University of Connecticut, Graduate School, School of Engineering, Department of Civil and Environmental Engineering, Field of Civil Engineering, Storrs, CT 06269. Offers MS, PhD. Terminal master's awarded for partial completion of doctoral program. *Degree requirements:* For master's, comprehensive exam, thesis or alternative; for doctorate, thesis/dissertation. *Entrance requirements:* Additional exam requirements/recommendations for international students: Required—TOEFL (minimum score 550 paper-based). Electronic applications accepted.

University of Dayton, Department of Civil and Environmental Engineering and Engineering Mechanics, Dayton, OH 45469. Offers engineering mechanics (MSEM); environmental engineering (MSCE); geotechnical engineering (MSCE); structural engineering (MSCE); transportation engineering (MSCE); water resources engineering (MSCE). *Program availability:* Part-time, blended/hybrid learning. *Degree requirements:* For master's, thesis or alternative. *Entrance requirements:* For master's, minimum GPA of 3.0 in undergraduate work. Additional exam requirements/recommendations for international students: Required—TOEFL (minimum score 550 paper-based; 80 iBT); Recommended—IELTS (minimum score 6.5), TSE (minimum score 60). Electronic applications accepted. *Faculty research:* Infrastructure, environmental composite, reliability, computer simulation.

University of Delaware, College of Engineering, Department of Civil and Environmental Engineering, Newark, DE 19716. Offers environmental engineering (MAS, MCE, PhD); geotechnical engineering (MAS, MCE, PhD); ocean engineering (MAS, MCE, PhD); structural engineering (MAS, MCE, PhD); transportation engineering (MAS, MCE, PhD); water resource engineering (MAS, MCE, PhD). *Program availability:* Part-time. Terminal master's awarded for partial completion of doctoral program. *Degree requirements:* For master's, thesis; for doctorate, thesis/dissertation. *Entrance requirements:* For master's and doctorate, GRE General Test. Additional exam requirements/recommendations for international students: Required—TOEFL. Electronic applications accepted. *Faculty research:* Structural engineering and mechanics; transportation engineering; ocean engineering; soil mechanics and foundation; water resources and environmental engineering.

University of Detroit Mercy, College of Engineering and Science, Detroit, MI 48221. Offers chemistry (MS); civil and environmental engineering (DE); electrical and computer engineering (ME); electrical engineering (DE); engineering management (M Eng Mgt); environmental engineering (MEE); mechanical engineering (MME, DE); product development (MS); software engineering (MSSE); teaching of mathematics (MATM). *Program availability:* Part-time, evening/weekend. *Degree requirements:* For doctorate, thesis/dissertation. Electronic applications accepted. Application fee is waived when completed online. *Expenses:* Contact institution.

University of Florida, Graduate School, Herbert Wertheim College of Engineering, Department of Civil and Coastal Engineering, Gainesville, FL 32611. Offers civil engineering (ME, MS, PhD); coastal and oceanographic engineering (ME, MS, PhD); geographic information systems (ME, MS, PhD); hydrologic sciences (ME, MS, PhD); structural engineering (ME, MS); wetland sciences (ME, MS, PhD). *Program availability:* Part-time, online learning. Terminal master's awarded for partial completion of doctoral program. *Degree requirements:* For master's, thesis (for some programs); for doctorate, comprehensive exam, thesis/dissertation. *Entrance requirements:* For master's and doctorate, minimum GPA of 3.0. Additional exam requirements/recommendations for international students: Required—TOEFL (minimum score 550 paper-based; 80 iBT), IELTS (minimum score 6). Electronic applications accepted. *Faculty research:* Traffic congestion mitigation, wind mitigation, sustainable infrastructure materials, improved sensors for in situ measurements, storm surge modeling.

University of Hawaii at Manoa, Office of Graduate Education, College of Engineering, Department of Civil and Environmental Engineering, Honolulu, HI 96822. Offers MS, PhD. *Program availability:* Part-time. *Degree requirements:* For master's, comprehensive exam, thesis; for doctorate, comprehensive exam, thesis/dissertation. *Entrance requirements:* For master's and doctorate, GRE General Test or EIT Exam. Additional exam requirements/recommendations for international students: Required—TOEFL (minimum score 540 paper-based; 76 iBT), IELTS (minimum score 5). *Faculty research:* Structures, transportation, environmental engineering, geotechnical engineering, construction.

University of Houston, Cullen College of Engineering, Department of Civil and Environmental Engineering, Houston, TX 77204. Offers civil engineering (MCE, PhD). *Program availability:* Part-time. Terminal master's awarded for partial completion of doctoral program. *Entrance requirements:* For master's and doctorate, GRE General Test. Additional exam requirements/recommendations for international students: Required—TOEFL (minimum score 550 paper-based; 79 iBT), IELTS (minimum score 6.5). Electronic applications accepted. *Faculty research:* Civil engineering.

University of Idaho, College of Graduate Studies, College of Engineering, Department of Civil and Environmental Engineering, Moscow, ID 83844-1022. Offers civil and environmental engineering (M Engr, PhD); geological engineering (MS). *Faculty:* 15. *Students:* 27 full-time, 38 part-time. Average age 33. In 2018, 21 master's, 1 doctorate awarded. *Entrance requirements:* For master's and doctorate, minimum GPA of 3.0. Additional exam requirements/recommendations for international students: Required—TOEFL (minimum score 550 paper-based; 79 iBT). *Application deadline:* For fall admission, 8/1 for domestic students; for spring admission, 12/15 for domestic students. Applications are processed on a rolling basis. Application fee: $60. Electronic applications accepted. *Expenses:* Tuition, state resident: full-time $7266.44; part-time $474.50 per credit hour. Tuition, nonresident: full-time $24,902; part-time $1453.50 per credit hour. *Required fees:* $2085.56; $45.50 per credit hour. *Financial support:* Fellowships, research assistantships, teaching assistantships, and career-related internships or fieldwork available. Financial award applicants required to submit FAFSA.

Faculty research: Transportation cyber security, highway maintenance management systems, river restoration, remediation of organic and metal contaminants in the subsurface, pipeline leak detection. *Unit head:* Patricia Colberg, Department Chair, 208-885-6782, E-mail: cee@uidaho.edu. *Application contact:* Patricia Colberg, Department Chair, 208-885-6782, E-mail: cee@uidaho.edu. Website: http://www.uidaho.edu/engr/cee

University of Illinois at Chicago, College of Engineering, Department of Civil and Materials Engineering, Chicago, IL 60607-7128. Offers MS, PhD. *Program availability:* Evening/weekend. *Degree requirements:* For master's, thesis (for some programs); for doctorate, thesis/dissertation, preliminary and qualifying exams. *Entrance requirements:* For master's and doctorate, GRE General Test, minimum GPA of 3.0. Additional exam requirements/recommendations for international students: Required—TOEFL. Electronic applications accepted. *Expenses:* Contact institution. *Faculty research:* Integrated fiber optic, acoustic emission and MEMS-based sensors development; monitoring the state of repaired and strengthened structures; development of weigh-in-motion (WIM) systems; image processing techniques for characterization of concrete entrained air bubble systems.

University of Illinois at Urbana–Champaign, Graduate College, College of Engineering, Department of Civil and Environmental Engineering, Champaign, IL 61820. Offers civil engineering (MS, PhD); environmental engineering in civil engineering (MS, PhD); M Arch/MS; MBA/MS. *Program availability:* Part-time, evening/weekend, online learning.

The University of Iowa, Graduate College, College of Engineering, Department of Civil and Environmental Engineering, Iowa City, IA 52242-1316. Offers environmental engineering and science (MS, PhD); hydraulics and water resources (MS, PhD); structures, mechanics and materials (MS, PhD); sustainable water development (MS, PhD); transportation engineering (MS, PhD). *Program availability:* Part-time. Terminal master's awarded for partial completion of doctoral program. *Degree requirements:* For master's, thesis optional, exam; for doctorate, comprehensive exam, thesis/dissertation, exam. *Entrance requirements:* For master's, GRE (minimum combined score of 301 on verbal and quantitative), minimum undergraduate GPA of 3.0; for doctorate, GRE (minimum combined score of 301 on verbal and quantitative), minimum graduate GPA of 3.0. Additional exam requirements/recommendations for international students: Required—TOEFL (minimum score 550 paper-based; 81 iBT), IELTS (minimum score 7). Electronic applications accepted. *Faculty research:* Water resources; environmental engineering and science; hydraulics and hydrology; structures, mechanics, and materials; transportation engineering.

The University of Kansas, Graduate Studies, School of Engineering, Program in Civil Engineering, Lawrence, KS 66045. Offers MCE, MS, PhD. *Program availability:* Part-time, evening/weekend. *Students:* 72 full-time (17 women), 38 part-time (10 women); includes 8 minority (3 Black or African American, non-Hispanic/Latino; 1 Asian, non-Hispanic/Latino; 1 Hispanic/Latino; 3 Two or more races, non-Hispanic/Latino), 62 international. Average age 28. 79 applicants, 71% accepted, 19 enrolled. In 2018, 38 master's, 5 doctorates awarded. *Entrance requirements:* For master's and doctorate, GRE, BS in engineering, two letters of recommendation, statement of purpose. Additional exam requirements/recommendations for international students: Required—TOEFL, IELTS. *Application deadline:* For fall admission, 8/17 priority date for domestic and international students; for spring admission, 1/14 priority date for domestic and international students; for summer admission, 5/26 for domestic and international students. Application fee: $65 ($85 for international students). Electronic applications accepted. *Financial support:* Fellowships, research assistantships, teaching assistantships, and career-related internships or fieldwork available. Financial award application deadline: 12/15. *Faculty research:* Structural engineering, geotechnical engineering, transportation engineering, water resources engineering, construction engineering. *Unit head:* David Darwin, Chair, 785-864-3827, E-mail: daved@ku.edu. *Application contact:* Susan Scott, Graduate Secretary, 785-864-3826, E-mail: s523s307@ku.edu. Website: http://www.ceae.ku.edu/

University of Kentucky, Graduate School, College of Engineering, Program in Civil Engineering, Lexington, KY 40506-0032. Offers MSCE, PhD. *Degree requirements:* For master's, comprehensive exam, thesis optional; for doctorate, comprehensive exam, thesis/dissertation. *Entrance requirements:* For master's, GRE General Test, minimum undergraduate GPA of 2.75; for doctorate, GRE General Test, minimum undergraduate GPA of 3.0. Additional exam requirements/recommendations for international students: Required—TOEFL (minimum score 550 paper-based). Electronic applications accepted. *Faculty research:* Geotechnical engineering, structures, construction engineering and management, environmental engineering and water resources, transportation and materials.

University of Louisiana at Lafayette, College of Engineering, Department of Civil Engineering, Lafayette, LA 70504. Offers MSE. *Program availability:* Evening/weekend. *Degree requirements:* For master's, comprehensive exam, thesis or alternative. *Entrance requirements:* For master's, GRE General Test, BS in civil engineering, minimum GPA of 2.85. *Faculty research:* Structural mechanics, computer-aided design, environmental engineering.

University of Louisville, J. B. Speed School of Engineering, Department of Civil and Environmental Engineering, Louisville, KY 40292-0001. Offers civil engineering (M Eng, MS, PhD). *Accreditation:* ABET (one or more programs are accredited). *Program availability:* 100% online, blended/hybrid learning. *Faculty:* 11 full-time (1 woman), 6 part-time/adjunct (0 women). *Students:* 25 full-time (7 women), 24 part-time (3 women); includes 4 minority (1 Black or African American, non-Hispanic/Latino; 1 Asian, non-Hispanic/Latino; 2 Two or more races, non-Hispanic/Latino), 16 international. Average age 28. 16 applicants, 13% accepted, 1 enrolled. In 2018, 20 master's, 1 doctorate awarded. Terminal master's awarded for partial completion of doctoral program. *Degree requirements:* For master's, thesis optional; for doctorate, comprehensive exam, thesis/dissertation. *Entrance requirements:* For master's and doctorate, GRE, Two letters of recommendation, official transcripts. Additional exam requirements/recommendations for international students: Required—TOEFL (minimum score 550 paper-based; 80 iBT); Recommended—IELTS (minimum score 6.5). *Application deadline:* For fall admission, 5/1 priority date for domestic and international students; for spring admission, 11/1 priority date for domestic and international students; for summer admission, 3/1 priority date for domestic and international students. Applications are processed on a rolling basis. Application fee: $65. Electronic applications accepted. *Expenses: Tuition, area resident:* Full-time $6500; part-time $723 per credit hour. Tuition, state resident: full-time $6500. Tuition, nonresident: full-time $13,557; part-time $1507 per credit hour. Tuition and fees vary according to course load and program. *Financial support:* In 2018–19, 24 students received support. Fellowships, research assistantships, teaching assistantships, scholarships/grants, health care benefits, and tuition waivers (full) available. Financial award application deadline: 1/1. *Faculty research:* Structural/material engineering, geotechnical engineering, water resources, transportation engineering. *Total annual research expenditures:* $648,296. *Unit head:* Zhihui Sun, Chair, 502-852-4583, Fax: 502-852-8851, E-mail: z.sun@louisville.edu. *Application contact:* Nageshar R Bhaskar, Director of Graduate Studies, 502-852-4547, Fax: 502-852-7294, E-mail: nageshar.bhaskar@louisville.edu. Website: http://louisville.edu/speed/civil/

Civil Engineering

University of Maine, Graduate School, College of Engineering, Department of Civil and Environmental Engineering, Orono, ME 04469. Offers MS, PSM, PhD. *Faculty:* 14 full-time (5 women), 1 part-time/adjunct (0 women). *Students:* 36 full-time (12 women), 4 part-time (0 women); includes 4 minority (2 American Indian or Alaska Native, non-Hispanic/Latino; 2 Asian, non-Hispanic/Latino), 21 international. Average age 28. 24 applicants, 71% accepted, 9 enrolled. In 2018, 16 master's, 3 doctorates awarded. Terminal master's awarded for partial completion of doctoral program. *Degree requirements:* For master's, thesis (for some programs); for doctorate, comprehensive exam, thesis/dissertation. *Entrance requirements:* For master's and doctorate, GRE General Test. Additional exam requirements/recommendations for international students: Required—TOEFL (minimum score 80 iBT), IELTS (minimum score 6.5). *Application deadline:* For fall admission, 2/1 priority date for domestic and international students. Applications are processed on a rolling basis. Application fee: $65. Electronic applications accepted. *Financial support:* In 2018–19, 63 students received support, including 1 fellowship with full tuition reimbursement available (averaging $25,500 per year), 26 research assistantships with full tuition reimbursements available (averaging $16,500 per year), 10 teaching assistantships with full tuition reimbursements available (averaging $13,800 per year); Federal Work-Study, institutionally sponsored loans, scholarships/grants, and tuition waivers (full and partial) also available. Financial award application deadline: 3/1. *Faculty research:* Structural engineering and engineering mechanics; geotechnical engineering; environmental engineering; water resources and coastal engineering; transportation engineering. *Total annual research expenditures:* $9 million. *Unit head:* Dr. Bill Davids, Chair, 207-581-2170, E-mail: william.davids@umit.maine.edu. *Application contact:* Scott G. Delcourt, Assistant Vice President for Graduate Studies and Senior Associate Dean, 207-581-3291, Fax: 207-581-3232, E-mail: graduate@maine.edu.
Website: http://www.civil.umaine.edu/

The University of Manchester, School of Mechanical, Aerospace and Civil Engineering, Manchester, United Kingdom. Offers advanced manufacturing technology (M Ent); aerospace engineering (M Phil, M Sc, PhD); civil engineering (M Phil, M Sc, PhD); environmental engineering (M Phil, PhD); management of projects (M Phil, M Sc, PhD); mechanical engineering (M Phil, M Sc, PhD); mechanical engineering design (M Ent); nuclear engineering (M Phil, D Eng, PhD).

University of Manitoba, Faculty of Graduate Studies, Faculty of Engineering, Department of Civil Engineering, Winnipeg, MB R3T 2N2, Canada. Offers M Eng, M Sc, PhD. *Degree requirements:* For master's, thesis.

University of Maryland, College Park, Academic Affairs, A. James Clark School of Engineering, Department of Civil and Environmental Engineering, College Park, MD 20742. Offers M Eng, MS, PhD. *Program availability:* Part-time, evening/weekend, online learning. *Degree requirements:* For master's, thesis optional; for doctorate, thesis/dissertation, qualifying exam. *Entrance requirements:* For master's and doctorate, GRE General Test, 3 letters of recommendation. Electronic applications accepted. *Faculty research:* Transportation and urban systems, environmental engineering, geotechnical engineering, construction engineering and management, hydraulics.

University of Massachusetts Amherst, Graduate School, College of Engineering, Department of Civil and Environmental Engineering, Amherst, MA 01003. Offers civil engineering (MSCE, PhD); environmental and water resources engineering (MSCE); geotechnical engineering (MSCE); structural engineering and mechanics (MSCE); transportation engineering (MSCE). *Program availability:* Part-time. Terminal master's awarded for partial completion of doctoral program. *Degree requirements:* For master's, thesis or alternative; for doctorate, comprehensive exam, thesis/dissertation. *Entrance requirements:* For master's and doctorate, GRE General Test. Additional exam requirements/recommendations for international students: Required—TOEFL (minimum score 550 paper-based; 80 iBT), IELTS (minimum score 6.5). Electronic applications accepted.

University of Massachusetts Amherst, Graduate School, Interdisciplinary Programs, Dual Degree Programs in Management and Engineering, Amherst, MA 01003. Offers MBA/MIE, MBA/MSEWRE, MSCE/MBA, MSME/MBA. *Program availability:* Part-time. *Entrance requirements:* Additional exam requirements/recommendations for international students: Required—TOEFL (minimum score 600 paper-based; 100 iBT), IELTS (minimum score 7). Electronic applications accepted.

University of Massachusetts Dartmouth, Graduate School, College of Engineering, Department of Civil and Environmental Engineering, North Dartmouth, MA 02747-2300. Offers civil engineering (MS). *Program availability:* Part-time. *Faculty:* 9 full-time (2 women), 1 part-time/adjunct (0 women). *Students:* 6 full-time (0 women), 4 part-time (1 woman), 8 international. Average age 28. 14 applicants, 57% accepted, 2 enrolled. In 2018, 4 master's awarded. *Degree requirements:* For master's, thesis, thesis or project. *Entrance requirements:* For master's, GRE unless UMass Dartmouth graduate in civil engineering, statement of purpose (minimum of 300 words), resume, 3 letters of recommendation, official transcripts. Additional exam requirements/recommendations for international students: Required—TOEFL (minimum score 550 paper-based; 79 iBT), IELTS (minimum score 6.5). *Application deadline:* For fall admission, 2/15 priority date for domestic students, 1/15 priority date for international students; for spring admission, 11/15 priority date for domestic students, 10/15 priority date for international students. Application fee: $60. Electronic applications accepted. *Financial support:* In 2018–19, 5 research assistantships (averaging $16,180 per year), 4 teaching assistantships (averaging $8,075 per year) were awarded; tuition waivers (full) also available. Financial award application deadline: 3/1; financial award applicants required to submit FAFSA. *Faculty research:* Development of marine renewable energy systems, physio-chemical treatment processes in hazardous waste contamination systems, innovative technologies for measuring contaminants, computational solid and structural mechanics, modular low-head hydropower systems. *Total annual research expenditures:* $2.9 million. *Unit head:* Mazdak Tootkaboni, Graduate Program Director, Civil and Environmental Engineering, 508-999-8465, Fax: 508-999-8964, E-mail: mtootkaboni@umassd.edu. *Application contact:* Scott Webster, Director of Graduate Studies and Admissions, 508-999-8406, Fax: 508-999-8183, E-mail: graduate@umassd.edu.
Website: http://www.umassd.edu/engineering/cen/graduate

University of Massachusetts Lowell, Francis College of Engineering, Department of Civil and Environmental Engineering, Lowell, MA 01854. Offers environmental studies (PhD). *Program availability:* Part-time. *Degree requirements:* For master's, thesis optional. *Entrance requirements:* For master's, GRE General Test. *Faculty research:* Bridge design, traffic control, groundwater remediation, pile capacity.

University of Memphis, Graduate School, Herff College of Engineering, Department of Civil Engineering, Memphis, TN 38152. Offers civil engineering (PhD); engineering seismology (MS); environmental engineering (MS); freight transportation (Graduate Certificate); geotechnical engineering (MS); structural engineering (MS); transportation engineering (MS); water resources engineering (MS). *Students:* 14 full-time (3 women), 8 part-time (3 women); includes 1 minority (Black or African American, non-Hispanic/Latino), 12 international. Average age 27. 27 applicants, 70% accepted, 13 enrolled. In 2018, 11 master's awarded. Terminal master's awarded for partial completion of doctoral program. *Degree requirements:* For master's, comprehensive exam, thesis optional; for doctorate, comprehensive exam, thesis/dissertation. *Entrance requirements:* For master's, GRE General Test, minimum undergraduate GPA of 2.5; bachelor's degree in engineering or a related science or mathematics program; three letters of reference; for doctorate, GRE General Test, bachelor's degree in engineering or engineering science; three letters of reference; for Graduate Certificate, minimum undergraduate GPA of 2.75; bachelor's degree in engineering or engineering science. Additional exam requirements/recommendations for international students: Required—TOEFL (minimum score 550 paper-based; 79 iBT). *Application deadline:* For fall admission, 8/1 for domestic students; for spring admission, 12/1 for domestic students. Application fee: $35 ($60 for international students). Electronic applications accepted. *Expenses: Tuition, area resident:* Full-time $10,240; part-time $503 per credit hour. Tuition, state resident: full-time $10,464. Tuition, nonresident: full-time $20,224; part-time $991 per credit hour. *Required fees:* $850; $106 per credit hour. *Financial support:* Fellowships with full tuition reimbursements, research assistantships with full tuition reimbursements, career-related internships or fieldwork, Federal Work-Study, scholarships/grants, and unspecified assistantships available. Financial award application deadline: 2/1; financial award applicants required to submit FAFSA. *Faculty research:* Structural response to earthquakes, pavement design, water quality, transportation safety, intermodal transportation. *Unit head:* Dr. Shahram Pezeshk, Chair, 901-678-4727, Fax: 901-678-3026, E-mail: spezeshk@memphis.edu. *Application contact:* Dr. Roger Meier, Coordinator of Graduate Studies, 901-678-3284, E-mail: rwmeier@memphis.edu.
Website: https://www.memphis.edu/ce

University of Miami, Graduate School, College of Engineering, Department of Civil, Architectural, and Environmental Engineering, Coral Gables, FL 33124. Offers architectural engineering (MSAE); civil engineering (MSCE, PhD). *Program availability:* Part-time. Terminal master's awarded for partial completion of doctoral program. *Degree requirements:* For master's, thesis (for some programs); for doctorate, comprehensive exam, thesis/dissertation. *Entrance requirements:* For master's, GRE General Test (minimum score 1000 verbal and quantitative), minimum GPA of 3.0; for doctorate, GRE General Test, minimum GPA of 3.5 in preceding degree. Additional exam requirements/recommendations for international students: Required—TOEFL (minimum score 550 paper-based). Electronic applications accepted. *Faculty research:* Structural assessment and wind engineering, sustainable construction and materials, moisture transport and management, wastewater and waste engineering, water management and risk analysis.

University of Michigan, College of Engineering, Department of Civil and Environmental Engineering, Ann Arbor, MI 48109. Offers civil engineering (MSE, PhD, CE); construction engineering and management (M Eng, MSE); environmental engineering (MSE, PhD); structural engineering (M Eng); MBA/MSE. *Program availability:* Part-time. *Students:* 206 full-time (86 women), 6 part-time (3 women). 690 applicants, 41% accepted, 76 enrolled. In 2018, 65 master's, 18 doctorates awarded. Terminal master's awarded for partial completion of doctoral program. *Degree requirements:* For master's, thesis optional; for doctorate, comprehensive exam, thesis/dissertation, oral defense of dissertation, preliminary and written exams. *Entrance requirements:* For master's and doctorate, GRE General Test. Additional exam requirements/recommendations for international students: Required—TOEFL. *Application deadline:* Applications are processed on a rolling basis. Electronic applications accepted. *Financial support:* Fellowships, research assistantships, teaching assistantships, institutionally sponsored loans, and tuition waivers (partial) available. *Faculty research:* Construction engineering and management, geotechnical engineering, earthquake-resistant design of structures, environmental chemistry and microbiology, cost engineering, environmental and water resources engineering. *Total annual research expenditures:* $11.6 million. *Unit head:* Jerome Lynch, Department Chair, 734-615-5290, Fax: 734-764-4292, E-mail: jerlynch@umich.edu. *Application contact:* Kelley Archer, Graduate Coordinator, 734-647-2703, Fax: 734-764-4292, E-mail: krichko@umich.edu.
Website: https://cee.engin.umich.edu/

University of Michigan, College of Engineering, Department of Naval Architecture and Marine Engineering, Ann Arbor, MI 48109. Offers MS, MSE, PhD, Mar Eng, Nav Arch, MBA/MSE. *Program availability:* Part-time. *Students:* 72 full-time (18 women), 3 part-time (0 women). 80 applicants, 53% accepted, 26 enrolled. In 2018, 25 master's, 7 doctorates awarded. Terminal master's awarded for partial completion of doctoral program. *Degree requirements:* For master's, thesis (for some programs); for doctorate, comprehensive exam, thesis/dissertation, oral defense of dissertation, written and oral preliminary exams; for other advanced degree, comprehensive exam, thesis, oral defense of thesis. *Entrance requirements:* For doctorate, GRE General Test, master's degree; for other advanced degree, GRE General Test. Additional exam requirements/recommendations for international students: Required—TOEFL. *Application deadline:* Applications are processed on a rolling basis. Electronic applications accepted. *Financial support:* Fellowships, research assistantships, teaching assistantships, career-related internships or fieldwork, Federal Work-Study, institutionally sponsored loans, scholarships/grants, and unspecified assistantships available. Financial award applicants required to submit FAFSA. *Faculty research:* System and structural reliability, design and analysis of offshore structures and vehicles, marine systems design, remote sensing of ship wakes and sea surfaces, marine hydrodynamics, nonlinear seakeeping analysis. *Total annual research expenditures:* $8.2 million. *Unit head:* Jing Sun, Department Chair, 734-615-8061, E-mail: jingsun@umich.edu. *Application contact:* Nathalie Fiveland, Graduate Student Advisor/Program Coordinator, 734-936-0566, Fax: 734-936-8820, E-mail: fiveland@umich.edu.
Website: https://name.engin.umich.edu/

University of Minnesota, Twin Cities Campus, College of Science and Engineering, Department of Civil, Environmental, and Geo-Engineering, Minneapolis, MN 55455-0213. Offers civil engineering (MCE, MS, PhD); geological engineering (M Geo E, MS); stream restoration science and engineering (Certificate). *Program availability:* Part-time. *Degree requirements:* For master's, thesis optional; for doctorate, thesis/dissertation. *Entrance requirements:* For master's and doctorate, GRE General Test. Additional exam requirements/recommendations for international students: Required—TOEFL. Electronic applications accepted. *Faculty research:* Environmental engineering, geomechanics, structural engineering, transportation, water resources.

University of Mississippi, Graduate School, School of Engineering, University, MS 38677. Offers aeroacoustics (MS, PhD); chemical engineering (MS, PhD); civil engineering (MS, PhD); computational hydroscience (MS, PhD); computer science (MS, PhD); electrical engineering (MS, PhD); electromagnetics (MS, PhD); environmental engineering (MS, PhD); geology and geological engineering (MS, PhD); hydrology (MS); material science (MS); mechanical engineering (MS, PhD); telecommunications (MS). *Faculty:* 76 full-time (16 women), 3 part-time/adjunct (1 woman). *Students:* 129 full-time (33 women), 21 part-time (5 women); includes 15 minority (7 Black or African American, non-Hispanic/Latino; 6 Asian, non-Hispanic/Latino; 1 Hispanic/Latino; 1 Two or more races, non-Hispanic/Latino), 73 international. Average age 29. In 2018, 36 master's, 17 doctorates awarded. *Entrance requirements:* For master's, GRE General Test, minimum GPA of 3.0; for doctorate, GRE General Test. Additional exam requirements/recommendations for international students: Required—TOEFL. *Application deadline:* Applications are processed on a rolling basis. Application fee: $50. Electronic applications accepted. *Financial support:* Scholarships/grants available. Financial award application deadline: 3/1; financial award applicants required to submit FAFSA. *Unit head:* Dr. David Puleo, Dean, 662-915-5780, Fax: 662-915-5387, E-mail: engineer@olemiss.edu. *Application contact:* Temeka Smith, Graduate Activities Specialist for Admissions, 662-915-7474, Fax: 662-915-7577, E-mail: gschool@olemiss.edu.

University of Missouri, Office of Research and Graduate Studies, College of Engineering, Department of Civil and Environmental Engineering, Columbia, MO 65211. Offers civil engineering (MS, PhD). *Degree requirements:* For master's, report or thesis. *Entrance requirements:* For master's and doctorate, GRE General Test. Additional exam requirements/recommendations for international students: Required—TOEFL (minimum score 550 paper-based; 80 iBT).

University of Missouri–Kansas City, School of Computing and Engineering, Kansas City, MO 64110-2499. Offers civil engineering (MS); computer and electrical engineering (PhD); computer science (MS), including bioinformatics, software engineering, telecommunications networking; computer science and informatics (PhD); computing (PhD); electrical engineering (MS); engineering (PhD); engineering and construction management (Graduate Certificate); mechanical engineering (MS); telecommunications and computer networking (PhD). PhD (interdisciplinary) offered through the School of Graduate Studies. *Program availability:* Part-time. *Degree requirements:* For doctorate, thesis/dissertation. *Entrance requirements:* For master's, GRE General Test, minimum GPA of 3.0, 3 letters of recommendation from professors; for doctorate, GRE General Test, minimum GPA of 3.5. Additional exam requirements/recommendations for international students: Required—TOEFL (minimum score 550 paper-based; 80 iBT). *Faculty research:* Algorithms, bioinformatics and medical informatics, biomechanics/biomaterials, civil engineering materials, networking and telecommunications, thermal science.

University of Nebraska–Lincoln, Graduate College, College of Engineering, Department of Civil Engineering, Lincoln, NE 68588. Offers MS, PhD. *Degree requirements:* For master's, thesis optional; for doctorate, comprehensive exam, thesis/dissertation. *Entrance requirements:* For master's and doctorate, GRE General Test. Additional exam requirements/recommendations for international students: Required—TOEFL (minimum score 550 paper-based). Electronic applications accepted. *Faculty research:* Water resources engineering, sediment transport, steel bridge systems, highway safety.

University of Nevada, Reno, Graduate School, College of Engineering, Department of Civil and Environmental Engineering, Reno, NV 89557. Offers MS, PhD. Terminal master's awarded for partial completion of doctoral program. *Degree requirements:* For master's, thesis optional; for doctorate, thesis/dissertation. *Entrance requirements:* For master's, GRE General Test, minimum GPA of 3.0; for doctorate, GRE General Test, minimum GPA of 3.25. Additional exam requirements/recommendations for international students: Required—TOEFL (minimum score 500 paper-based; 61 iBT), IELTS (minimum score 6). Electronic applications accepted. *Faculty research:* Structural and earthquake engineering, geotechnical engineering, environmental engineering, transportation, pavements/materials.

University of New Brunswick Fredericton, School of Graduate Studies, Faculty of Engineering, Department of Civil Engineering, Fredericton, NB E3B 5A3, Canada. Offers construction engineering and management (M Eng, M Sc E, PhD); environmental engineering (M Eng, M Sc E, PhD); environmental studies (M Eng); geotechnical engineering (M Eng, M Sc E, PhD); groundwater/hydrology (M Eng, M Sc E, PhD); materials (M Eng, M Sc E, PhD); pavements (M Eng, M Sc E, PhD); structures (M Eng, M Sc E, PhD); transportation (M Eng, M Sc E, PhD). *Program availability:* Part-time. *Degree requirements:* For master's, thesis; for doctorate, comprehensive exam, thesis/dissertation, qualifying exam; 27 credit hours of courses. *Entrance requirements:* For master's, minimum GPA of 3.0; B Sc E in civil engineering or related engineering degree; for doctorate, minimum GPA of 3.0; graduate degree in engineering or applied science. Additional exam requirements/recommendations for international students: Required—IELTS (minimum score 7.5), TWE (minimum score 4), Michigan English Language Assessment Battery (minimum score 85) or CanTest (minimum score 4.5); Recommended—TOEFL (minimum score 580 paper-based). Electronic applications accepted. *Faculty research:* Construction engineering and management; engineering materials and infrastructure renewal; highway and pavement research; structures and solid mechanics; geotechnical and geoenvironmental engineering; structure interaction; transportation and planning; environment, solid waste management; structural engineering; water and environmental engineering.

University of New Hampshire, Graduate School, College of Engineering and Physical Sciences, Department of Civil and Environmental Engineering, Durham, NH 03824. Offers M Engr, MS, PhD. *Program availability:* Part-time. *Entrance requirements:* For master's and doctorate, GRE. Additional exam requirements/recommendations for international students: Required—TOEFL (minimum score 550 paper-based; 80 iBT), IELTS (minimum score 6.5). Electronic applications accepted.

University of New Haven, Graduate School, Tagliatela College of Engineering, Program in Civil Engineering, West Haven, CT 06516. Offers MS. *Students:* 42 full-time (6 women), 6 part-time (0 women); includes 3 minority (all Asian, non-Hispanic/Latino), 42 international. Average age 25. 117 applicants, 87% accepted, 16 enrolled. In 2018, 4 master's awarded. *Application deadline:* Applications are processed on a rolling basis. Application fee: $50. Electronic applications accepted. *Expenses: Tuition:* Full-time $16,470; part-time $915 per credit hour. *Required fees:* $230; $95 per term. *Financial support:* Applicants required to submit FAFSA. *Unit head:* Dr. Byungik Chang, Associate Professor, 203-479-4234, E-mail: bchang@newhaven.edu. *Application contact:* Selina O'Toole, Senior Associate Director of Graduate Admissions, 203-932-7337, E-mail: sotoole@newhaven.edu.
Website: http://www.newhaven.edu/engineering/graduate-programs/civil-engineering/index.php

University of New Mexico, Graduate Studies, School of Engineering, Program in Civil Engineering, Albuquerque, NM 87131-0001. Offers civil engineering (M Eng, MSCE); construction management (MCM); engineering (PhD). *Program availability:* Part-time. Terminal master's awarded for partial completion of doctoral program. *Degree requirements:* For master's, comprehensive exam, thesis (for some programs); for doctorate, comprehensive exam, thesis/dissertation. *Entrance requirements:* For master's, GRE General Test (for MSCE and M Eng); GRE or GMAT (for MCM), minimum GPA of 3.0; for doctorate, GRE General Test, minimum GPA of 3.0. Additional exam requirements/recommendations for international students: Required—TOEFL (minimum score 550 paper-based; 80 iBT), IELTS (minimum score 6.5). Electronic applications accepted. *Faculty research:* Integrating design and construction, project delivery methods, sustainable design and construction, leadership and management in construction, project management and project supervision, production management and improvement.

University of New Orleans, Graduate School, College of Engineering, Program in Engineering, New Orleans, LA 70148. Offers civil engineering (MS); electrical engineering (MS); mechanical engineering (MS); naval architecture and marine engineering (MS). *Degree requirements:* For master's, thesis optional. *Entrance requirements:* For master's, GRE General Test, minimum GPA of 3.0. Additional exam requirements/recommendations for international students: Required—TOEFL (minimum score 550 paper-based; 79 iBT). Electronic applications accepted. *Faculty research:* Two-phase flow instabilities, thermal-hydrodynamic modeling, solar energy, heat transfer from sprays, boundary integral techniques in mechanics.

The University of North Carolina at Charlotte, William States Lee College of Engineering, Department of Civil and Environmental Engineering, Charlotte, NC 28223-0001. Offers civil engineering (MSCE); infrastructure and environmental systems (PhD), including infrastructure and environmental systems design. *Program availability:* Part-time, evening/weekend. *Students:* 61 full-time (18 women), 47 part-time (12 women); includes 9 minority (1 Black or African American, non-Hispanic/Latino; 5 Asian, non-Hispanic/Latino; 2 Hispanic/Latino; 1 Two or more races, non-Hispanic/Latino), 51 international. Average age 30. 89 applicants, 47% accepted, 19 enrolled. In 2018, 16 master's, 6 doctorates awarded. *Entrance requirements:* For master's, GRE, undergraduate degree in civil and environmental engineering or a closely-related field; minimum undergraduate GPA of 3.0; for doctorate, GRE General Test, equivalent to U.S. baccalaureate or master's degree from regionally-accredited college or university in engineering, earth science and geology, chemical and biological sciences or a related field with minimum undergraduate GPA of 3.2, graduate 3.5. Additional exam requirements/recommendations for international students: Required—TOEFL (minimum score 523 paper-based; 70 iBT), IELTS (minimum score 6), TOEFL (minimum score 523 paper-based, 70 iBT) or IELTS (6). *Application deadline:* Applications are processed on a rolling basis. Application fee: $75. Electronic applications accepted. *Expenses:* Contact institution. *Financial support:* Fellowships, research assistantships, teaching assistantships, career-related internships or fieldwork, institutionally sponsored loans, scholarships/grants, and unspecified assistantships available. Support available to part-time students. Financial award application deadline: 3/1; financial award applicants required to submit FAFSA. *Total annual research expenditures:* $3.4 million. *Unit head:* Dr. James D. Bowen, Interim Chair, 704-687-1215, E-mail: jdbowen@uncc.edu. *Application contact:* Kathy B. Giddings, Director of Graduate Admissions, 704-687-5503, Fax: 704-687-1668, E-mail: gradadm@uncc.edu.
Website: http://cee.uncc.edu/

University of North Dakota, Graduate School, School of Engineering and Mines, Department of Civil Engineering, Grand Forks, ND 58202. Offers civil engineering (M Engr). *Program availability:* Part-time. *Degree requirements:* For master's, comprehensive exam, thesis or alternative. *Entrance requirements:* For master's, GRE General Test, minimum GPA of 2.5. Additional exam requirements/recommendations for international students: Required—TOEFL (minimum score 550 paper-based; 79 iBT), IELTS (minimum score 6.5). Electronic applications accepted. *Faculty research:* Soil-structures, environmental-water resources.

University of North Florida, College of Computing, Engineering, and Construction, School of Engineering, Jacksonville, FL 32224. Offers MSCE, MSEE, MSME. *Program availability:* Part-time. *Faculty:* 19 full-time (4 women). *Students:* 17 full-time (5 women), 32 part-time (5 women); includes 13 minority (1 Black or African American, non-Hispanic/Latino; 5 Asian, non-Hispanic/Latino; 5 Hispanic/Latino; 2 Two or more races, non-Hispanic/Latino), 9 international. Average age 30. 36 applicants, 58% accepted, 16 enrolled. In 2018, 19 master's awarded. *Application deadline:* For fall admission, 8/1 priority date for domestic students, 5/1 for international students; for spring admission, 12/1 priority date for domestic students, 10/1 for international students; for summer admission, 3/15 priority date for domestic students, 2/1 for international students. Application fee: $30. *Expenses: Tuition, area resident:* Part-time $408.10 per credit hour. Tuition, state resident: part-time $408.10 per credit hour. Tuition, nonresident: part-time $932.61 per credit hour. *Required fees:* $111.81 per credit hour. Tuition and fees vary according to course load, campus/location and program. *Financial support:* In 2018–19, 25 students received support, including 4 research assistantships (averaging $3,161 per year), 2 teaching assistantships (averaging $4,445 per year); Federal Work-Study, scholarships/grants, tuition waivers, and unspecified assistantships also available. Financial award application deadline: 4/1; financial award applicants required to submit FAFSA. *Total annual research expenditures:* $1.1 million. *Unit head:* Dr. Murat Tiryakioglu, Director, 904-620-1393, E-mail: m.tiryakioglu@unf.edu. *Application contact:* Dr. Amanda Pascale, Director, The Graduate School, 904-320-1360, Fax: 904-620-1362, E-mail: graduateschool@unf.edu.
Website: http://www.unf.edu/ccec/engineering/

University of Notre Dame, The Graduate School, College of Engineering, Department of Civil and Environmental Engineering and Earth Sciences, Notre Dame, IN 46556. Offers bioengineering (MS Bio E); civil engineering (MSCE); civil engineering and geological sciences (PhD); earth sciences (MS); environmental engineering (MS Env E). Terminal master's awarded for partial completion of doctoral program. *Degree requirements:* For master's, comprehensive exam; for doctorate, thesis/dissertation, candidacy exam. *Entrance requirements:* For master's and doctorate, GRE General Test. Additional exam requirements/recommendations for international students: Required—TOEFL (minimum score 600 paper-based; 80 iBT). Electronic applications accepted. *Faculty research:* Environmental modeling, biological-waste treatment, petrology, environmental geology, geochemistry.

University of Oklahoma, Gallogly College of Engineering, School of Civil Engineering and Environmental Science, Norman, OK 73019-0390. Offers civil engineering (MS, PhD), including civil engineering; environmental engineering (MS, PhD); environmental science (M Env Sc, PhD), including environmental science. *Program availability:* Part-time. *Faculty:* 24 full-time (4 women), 3 part-time/adjunct (2 women). *Students:* 33 full-time (11 women), 61 part-time (22 women); includes 21 minority (6 Black or African American, non-Hispanic/Latino; 2 American Indian or Alaska Native, non-Hispanic/Latino; 2 Asian, non-Hispanic/Latino; 7 Hispanic/Latino; 4 Two or more races, non-Hispanic/Latino), 27 international. Average age 30. 154 applicants, 68% accepted, 52 enrolled. In 2018, 9 master's, 4 doctorates awarded. Terminal master's awarded for partial completion of doctoral program. *Degree requirements:* For master's, thesis; for doctorate, comprehensive exam, thesis/dissertation, general exam. *Entrance requirements:* For master's and doctorate, GRE. Additional exam requirements/recommendations for international students: Required—TOEFL (minimum score 79 iBT) or IELTS (minimum score 6.5). *Application deadline:* For fall admission, 1/15 for domestic and international students; for spring admission, 5/15 for domestic and international students. Application fee: $50 ($100 for international students). Electronic applications accepted. *Expenses:* Tuition, state resident: full-time $5683.20; part-time $236.80 per credit hour. Tuition, nonresident: full-time $20,342; part-time $847.60 per credit hour. *International tuition:* $20,342.40 full-time. *Required fees:* $2894.20; $110.05 per credit hour. $126.50 per semester. Tuition and fees vary according to course load and program. *Financial support:* Fellowships, research assistantships, teaching assistantships, and scholarships/grants available. Financial award application deadline: 6/1; financial award applicants required to submit FAFSA. *Faculty research:* Intelligent structures, composites, earthquake engineering, intelligent compaction, bridge engineering. *Unit head:* Dr. Randall Kolar, Director, 405-325-4267, Fax: 405-325-4217, E-mail: kolar@ou.edu. *Application contact:* Graduate Studies Coordinator, 405-325-2344, Fax: 405-325-4217, E-mail: ceesgradstudies@ou.edu.
Website: http://www.ou.edu/coe/cees.html

Civil Engineering

University of Ottawa, Faculty of Graduate and Postdoctoral Studies, Faculty of Engineering, Ottawa-Carleton Institute for Civil Engineering, Ottawa, ON K1N 6N5, Canada. Offers M Eng, MA Sc, PhD. PhD, M Eng, MA Sc offered jointly with Carleton University. *Degree requirements:* For master's, thesis or alternative; for doctorate, comprehensive exam, thesis/dissertation, seminar series. *Entrance requirements:* For master's, honors degree or equivalent, minimum B average; for doctorate, master's degree, minimum B+ average. Electronic applications accepted. *Faculty research:* Environmental engineering, geotechnical engineering, structural engineering, transportation engineering, water resources engineering.

University of Pittsburgh, Swanson School of Engineering, Department of Civil and Environmental Engineering, Pittsburgh, PA 15260. Offers MSCEE, PhD. *Program availability:* Part-time, 100% online. Terminal master's awarded for partial completion of doctoral program. *Degree requirements:* For doctorate, comprehensive exam, thesis/dissertation, final oral exams. *Entrance requirements:* For master's and doctorate, minimum GPA of 3.0. Additional exam requirements/recommendations for international students: Required—TOEFL (minimum score 550 paper-based; 80 iBT). Electronic applications accepted. *Expenses:* Contact institution. *Faculty research:* Environmental and water resources, structures and infrastructures, construction management.

University of Portland, Shiley School of Engineering, Portland, OR 97203-5798. Offers biomedical engineering (MBME); civil engineering (ME); computer science (ME); electrical engineering (ME); mechanical engineering (ME). *Program availability:* Part-time, evening/weekend. *Students:* 12 full-time (4 women), 2 part-time (both women); includes 1 minority (Black or African American, non-Hispanic/Latino), 2 international. Average age 24. 43 applicants, 49% accepted, 10 enrolled. In 2018, 6 master's awarded. *Degree requirements:* For master's, thesis optional. *Entrance requirements:* For master's, GRE General Test, minimum GPA of 3.0, 2 letters of recommendation, resume, statement of goals, official transcripts. Additional exam requirements/recommendations for international students: Required—TOEFL (minimum score 80 iBT), IELTS (minimum score 7). *Application deadline:* For fall admission, 7/15 priority date for domestic and international students; for spring admission, 12/15 priority date for domestic and international students; for summer admission, 4/15 for domestic and international students. Applications are processed on a rolling basis. Electronic applications accepted. *Expenses:* $1,326 per credit plus $50 professional tuition per credit. *Financial support:* Research assistantships, career-related internships or fieldwork, Federal Work-Study, and scholarships/grants available. Support available to part-time students. Financial award application deadline: 3/1; financial award applicants required to submit FAFSA. *Unit head:* Dr. Matthew Kuhn, Dean, 503-943-7361, E-mail: kuhn@up.edu. *Application contact:* Caitlin Biddulph, Graduate Programs and Admissions Specialist, 503-943-7107.
Website: http://engineering.up.edu/default.aspx?cid-6464&pid-2432

University of Puerto Rico–Mayagüez, Graduate Studies, College of Engineering, Department of Civil Engineering and Surveying, Mayagüez, PR 00681-9000. Offers civil engineering (ME, MS, PhD), including construction engineering and management (ME, MS), environmental engineering, geotechnical engineering (ME, MS), structural engineering, transportation engineering. *Program availability:* Part-time. Terminal master's awarded for partial completion of doctoral program. *Degree requirements:* For master's, one foreign language, thesis; for doctorate, one foreign language, comprehensive exam, thesis/dissertation, qualifying exams. *Entrance requirements:* For master's, proficiency in English and Spanish; BS in civil engineering or its equivalent; for doctorate, proficiency in English and Spanish. Electronic applications accepted. *Faculty research:* Structural design, concrete structure, finite elements, dynamic analysis, transportation, soils.

University of Rhode Island, Graduate School, College of Engineering, Department of Civil and Environmental Engineering, Kingston, RI 02881. Offers civil and environmental engineering (MS, PhD), including environmental engineering, geotechnical engineering, structural engineering, transportation engineering. *Program availability:* Part-time. *Faculty:* 12 full-time (3 women). *Students:* 22 full-time (7 women), 10 part-time (2 women); includes 2 minority (1 Asian, non-Hispanic/Latino; 1 Hispanic/Latino), 12 international. 26 applicants, 112% accepted, 16 enrolled. In 2018, 9 master's, 3 doctorates awarded. *Entrance requirements:* Additional exam requirements/recommendations for international students: Required—TOEFL. *Application deadline:* For fall admission, 7/15 for domestic students, 2/1 for international students; for spring admission, 11/15 for domestic students, 7/15 for international students. Application fee: $65. Electronic applications accepted. *Expenses: Tuition, area resident:* Full-time $13,226; part-time $735 per credit. Tuition, state resident: full-time $13,226; part-time $735 per credit. Tuition, nonresident: full-time $25,854; part-time $1436 per credit. *International tuition:* $25,854 full-time. *Required fees:* $1698; $50 per credit. $35 per semester. One-time fee: $165. *Financial support:* In 2018–19, 9 research assistantships with tuition reimbursements (averaging $12,684 per year), 5 teaching assistantships with tuition reimbursements (averaging $13,694 per year) were awarded. Financial award application deadline: 2/1; financial award applicants required to submit FAFSA. *Unit head:* Dr. Leon Thiem, Chair, 401-874-2693, Fax: 401-874-2786, E-mail: leonthiem@uri.edu. *Application contact:* Dr. George Tsiatas, Graduate Program Director, 401-874-5117, E-mail: gt@uri.edu.
Website: http://www.uri.edu/cve/

University of Saskatchewan, College of Graduate and Postdoctoral Studies, College of Engineering, Civil and Geological Engineering Program, Saskatoon, SK S7N 5E5, Canada. Offers M Eng, M Sc, PhD. *Program availability:* Part-time. *Degree requirements:* For master's, 30 credits (for M Eng); thesis and 12 credits (for MS); for doctorate, comprehensive exam, thesis/dissertation, qualifying exam, 18 credits. *Entrance requirements:* For master's, GRE, minimum GPA of 5.0 on an 8.0 scale; for doctorate, GRE. Additional exam requirements/recommendations for international students: Required—TOEFL (minimum iBT score of 80), IELTS (6.5), CanTEST (4.5), or PTE (59). Electronic applications accepted. *Faculty research:* Geotechnical/geo-environmental engineering, structural engineering, water resources engineering, civil engineering materials, environmental/sanitary engineering, hydrogeology, rock mechanics and mining, transportation engineering.

University of South Alabama, College of Engineering, Department of Civil, Coastal, and Environmental Engineering, Mobile, AL 36688. Offers MSCE. *Degree requirements:* For master's, comprehensive exam, thesis or project. *Entrance requirements:* For master's, GRE, minimum GPA of 3.0, three references, portfolio. Additional exam requirements/recommendations for international students: Required—TOEFL (minimum score 525 paper-based; 71 iBT), IELTS (minimum score 6.5). Electronic applications accepted. *Expenses:* Contact institution. *Faculty research:* Calibration of simulation model, monitoring coastal processes, reducing crashes, roadway runoff treatment, roundabouts.

University of South Carolina, The Graduate School, College of Engineering and Computing, Department of Civil and Environmental Engineering, Columbia, SC 29208. Offers civil engineering (ME, MS, PhD). *Program availability:* Part-time, evening/weekend, online learning. *Degree requirements:* For master's, comprehensive exam, thesis (for some programs); for doctorate, thesis/dissertation. *Entrance requirements:* For master's and doctorate, GRE General Test, 2 letters of recommendation. Additional exam requirements/recommendations for international students: Required—TOEFL (minimum score 570 paper-based). Electronic applications accepted. *Faculty research:* Structures, water resources.

University of Southern California, Graduate School, Viterbi School of Engineering, Sonny Astani Department of Civil and Environmental Engineering, Los Angeles, CA 90089. Offers applied mechanics (MS); civil engineering (MS, PhD); computer-aided engineering (ME, Graduate Certificate); construction management (MCM); engineering technology commercialization (Graduate Certificate); environmental engineering (MS, PhD); environmental quality management (ME); structural design (ME); sustainable cities (Graduate Certificate); transportation systems (MS, Graduate Certificate); water and waste management (MS). *Program availability:* Part-time, evening/weekend. Terminal master's awarded for partial completion of doctoral program. *Degree requirements:* For master's, thesis optional; for doctorate, thesis/dissertation. *Entrance requirements:* For master's and doctorate, GRE General Test. Additional exam requirements/recommendations for international students: Recommended—TOEFL. Electronic applications accepted. *Faculty research:* Geotechnical engineering, transportation engineering, structural engineering, construction management, environmental engineering, water resources.

University of South Florida, College of Engineering, Department of Civil and Environmental Engineering, Tampa, FL 33620-9951. Offers civil engineering (MCE, MSCE, PhD), including geotechnical engineering, materials science and engineering, structures engineering, transportation engineering, water resources; environmental engineering (MEVE, MSEV, PhD), including engineering for international development (MSEV). *Program availability:* Part-time. *Faculty:* 19 full-time (5 women). *Students:* 144 full-time (46 women), 76 part-time (22 women); includes 35 minority (8 Black or African American, non-Hispanic/Latino; 5 Asian, non-Hispanic/Latino; 18 Hispanic/Latino; 4 Two or more races, non-Hispanic/Latino), 123 international. Average age 28. 220 applicants, 65% accepted, 59 enrolled. In 2018, 82 master's, 15 doctorates awarded. Terminal master's awarded for partial completion of doctoral program. *Degree requirements:* For master's, comprehensive exam, thesis (for some programs); for doctorate, comprehensive exam, thesis/dissertation. *Entrance requirements:* For master's, GRE required, bachelor's degree in appropriate field, minimum GPA of 3.0 in major, letters of reference, statement of purpose, resume, intake form; for doctorate, GRE with V (45th percentile), Q (75th percentile), and AW (55th percentile), letters of recommendation, statement of purpose, resume, intake form. Additional exam requirements/recommendations for international students: Required—TOEFL, TOEFL (minimum score 550 paper-based; 79 iBT) or IELTS (minimum score 6.5). *Application deadline:* For fall admission, 2/15 for domestic students, 2/15 priority date for international students; for spring admission, 10/15 for domestic students, 9/15 priority date for international students. Application fee: $30. Electronic applications accepted. *Expenses:* Tuition, state resident: full-time $6350. Tuition, nonresident: full-time $19,048. *International tuition:* $19,048 full-time. *Required fees:* $2079. *Financial support:* In 2018–19, 45 students received support, including 44 research assistantships (averaging $14,123 per year), 21 teaching assistantships with tuition reimbursements available (averaging $15,329 per year). *Faculty research:* Environmental and water resources engineering, geotechnics and geoenvironmental systems, structures and materials systems, transportation systems. *Total annual research expenditures:* $3.7 million. *Unit head:* Dr. Manjriker Gunaratne, Professor and Department Chair, 813-974-5818, Fax: 813-974-2957, E-mail: gunaratn@usf.edu. *Application contact:* Dr. Sarina J. Ergas, Professor and Graduate Program Coordinator, 813-974-1119, Fax: 813-974-2957, E-mail: sergas@usf.edu.
Website: http://www.usf.edu/engineering/cee/

University of South Florida, Innovative Education, Tampa, FL 33620-9951. Offers adult, career and higher education (Graduate Certificate), including college teaching, leadership in developing human resources, leadership in higher education; Africana studies (Graduate Certificate), including diasporas and health disparities, genocide and human rights; aging studies (Graduate Certificate), including gerontology; art research (Graduate Certificate), including museum studies; business foundations (Graduate Certificate); chemical and biomedical engineering (Graduate Certificate), including materials science and engineering, water, health and sustainability; child and family studies (Graduate Certificate), including positive behavior support; civil and industrial engineering (Graduate Certificate), including transportation systems analysis; community and family health (Graduate Certificate), including maternal and child health, social marketing and public health, violence and injury: prevention and intervention, women's health; criminology (Graduate Certificate), including criminal justice administration; data science for public administration (Graduate Certificate); digital humanities (Graduate Certificate); educational measurement and research (Graduate Certificate), including evaluation; English (Graduate Certificate), including comparative literary studies, creative writing, professional and technical communication; entrepreneurship (Graduate Certificate); environmental health (Graduate Certificate), including safety management; epidemiology and biostatistics (Graduate Certificate), including applied biostatistics, biostatistics, concepts and tools of epidemiology, epidemiology, epidemiology of infectious diseases; geography, environment and planning (Graduate Certificate), including community development, environmental policy and management, geographical information systems; geology (Graduate Certificate), including hydrogeology; global health (Graduate Certificate), including disaster management, global health and Latin American and Caribbean studies, global health practice, humanitarian assistance, infection control; government and international affairs (Graduate Certificate), including Cuban studies, globalization studies; health policy and management (Graduate Certificate), including health management and leadership, public health policy and programs; hearing specialist: early intervention (Graduate Certificate); industrial and management systems engineering (Graduate Certificate), including systems engineering, technology management; information studies (Graduate Certificate), including school library media specialist; information systems/decision sciences (Graduate Certificate), including analytics and business intelligence; instructional technology (Graduate Certificate), including distance education, Florida digital/virtual educator, instructional design, multimedia design, Web design; internal medicine, bioethics and medical humanities (Graduate Certificate), including biomedical ethics; Latin American and Caribbean studies (Graduate Certificate); leadership for coastal resiliency planning (Graduate Certificate); mass communications (Graduate Certificate), including multimedia journalism; mathematics and statistics (Graduate Certificate), including mathematics; medicine (Graduate Certificate), including aging and neuroscience, bioinformatics, biotechnology, brain fitness and memory management, clinical investigation, hand and upper limb rehabilitation, health informatics, health sciences, integrative weight management, intellectual property, medicine and gender, metabolic and nutritional medicine, metabolic cardiology, pharmacy sciences; national and competitive intelligence (Graduate Certificate); nursing (Graduate Certificate), including simulation based academic fellowship in advanced pain management; psychological and social foundations (Graduate Certificate), including career counseling, college teaching, diversity in education, mental health counseling, school counseling; public affairs (Graduate Certificate), including nonprofit management, public management, research administration; public health (Graduate Certificate), including assessing chemical toxicity and public health risks, health equity, pharmacoepidemiology, public health generalist, toxicology, translational research in adolescent behavioral health; public health practices (Graduate Certificate), including planning for healthy communities; rehabilitation and mental health counseling (Graduate Certificate), including integrative mental health care, marriage and family therapy,

rehabilitation technology; secondary education (Graduate Certificate), including ESOL, foreign language education: culture and content, foreign language education: professional; social work (Graduate Certificate), including geriatric social work/clinical gerontology; special education (Graduate Certificate), including autism spectrum disorder, disabilities education: severe/profound; world languages (Graduate Certificate), including teaching English as a second language (TESL) or foreign language. *Expenses:* Tuition, state resident: full-time $6350. Tuition, nonresident: full-time $19,048. *International tuition:* $19,048 full-time. *Required fees:* $2079. *Unit head:* Dr. Cynthia DeLuca, Associate Vice President and Assistant Vice Provost, 813-974-3077, Fax: 813-974-7061, E-mail: deluca@usf.edu. *Application contact:* Owen Hooper, Director, Summer and Alternative Calendar Programs, 813-974-6917, E-mail: hooper@usf.edu.
Website: http://www.usf.edu/innovative-education/

The University of Tennessee, Graduate School, Tickle College of Engineering, Department of Civil and Environmental Engineering, Program in Civil Engineering, Knoxville, TN 37996. Offers MS, PhD, MS/MBA. *Program availability:* Part-time, online learning. *Faculty:* 27 full-time (5 women), 2 part-time/adjunct (1 woman). *Students:* 84 full-time (22 women), 47 part-time (11 women); includes 10 minority (3 Black or African American, non-Hispanic/Latino; 4 Asian, non-Hispanic/Latino; 2 Hispanic/Latino; 1 Native Hawaiian or other Pacific Islander, non-Hispanic/Latino), 60 international. Average age 28. 110 applicants, 61% accepted, 32 enrolled. In 2018, 34 master's, 17 doctorates awarded. *Degree requirements:* For master's, thesis or alternative; for doctorate, comprehensive exam, thesis/dissertation. *Entrance requirements:* For master's, GRE General Test (for MS students pursuing research thesis), minimum GPA of 2.7 (for U.S. degree holders), 3.0 (for international degree holders); 3 references; statement of purpose; resume; for doctorate, GRE General Test, minimum GPA of 3.0 on previous graduate course work; 3 references; statement of purpose; resume. Additional exam requirements/recommendations for international students: Required—TOEFL (minimum score 550 paper-based; 80 iBT), IELTS (minimum score 6.5). *Application deadline:* For fall admission, 2/1 priority date for domestic and international students; for spring admission, 6/15 for domestic and international students; for summer admission, 10/15 for domestic and international students. Applications are processed on a rolling basis. Application fee: $60. Electronic applications accepted. *Financial support:* In 2018–19, 111 students received support, including 16 fellowships (averaging $8,280 per year), 75 research assistantships with full tuition reimbursements available (averaging $22,052 per year), 20 teaching assistantships with full tuition reimbursements available (averaging $21,120 per year); career-related internships or fieldwork, Federal Work-Study, institutionally sponsored loans, health care benefits, and unspecified assistantships also available. Financial award application deadline: 2/1; financial award applicants required to submit FAFSA. *Faculty research:* Multi-functional composites and mechanics of materials, geohydrologic investigations and monitoring, structures and vibrations, geotechnical and earthquake engineering, transportation system planning and design. *Unit head:* Dr. Chris Cox, Head, 865-974-2503, Fax: 865-974-2669, E-mail: ccox9@utk.edu. *Application contact:* Dr. Khalid Alshibli, Associate Head, 865-974-7728, Fax: 865-974-2669, E-mail: alshibli@utk.edu.
Website: http://www.engr.utk.edu/civil

The University of Tennessee at Chattanooga, Program in Engineering, Chattanooga, TN 37403. Offers automotive (MS Engr); chemical (MS Engr); civil (MS Engr); electrical (MS Engr); mechanical (MS Engr). *Program availability:* Part-time. *Degree requirements:* For master's, comprehensive exam, thesis or alternative, engineering project. *Entrance requirements:* For master's, GRE General Test, minimum undergraduate GPA of 2.7 or 3.0 in last two years of undergraduate coursework. Additional exam requirements/recommendations for international students: Required—TOEFL (minimum score 550 paper-based; 79 iBT), IELTS (minimum score 6). Electronic applications accepted. *Expenses:* Contact institution. *Faculty research:* Quality control and reliability engineering, financial management, thermal science, energy conservation, structural analysis.

The University of Texas at Arlington, Graduate School, College of Engineering, Department of Civil Engineering, Arlington, TX 76019. Offers civil engineering (M Engr, MS, PhD); construction management (MCM). *Program availability:* Part-time, evening/weekend, online learning. Terminal master's awarded for partial completion of doctoral program. *Degree requirements:* For master's, comprehensive exam, thesis (for some programs), oral and written exams; for doctorate, comprehensive exam, thesis/dissertation, oral and written defense of dissertation. *Entrance requirements:* For master's, GRE General Test, minimum GPA of 3.0 in last 60 hours of undergraduate course work; for doctorate, GRE General Test, minimum GPA of 3.5. Additional exam requirements/recommendations for international students: Required—TOEFL. Electronic applications accepted. *Faculty research:* Environmental and water resources structures, geotechnical, transportation.

The University of Texas at Austin, Graduate School, Cockrell School of Engineering, Department of Civil, Architectural and Environmental Engineering, Austin, TX 78712-1111. Offers architectural engineering (MSE); civil engineering (MS, PhD); environmental and water resources engineering (MS, PhD). *Program availability:* Part-time. *Degree requirements:* For master's, thesis or alternative; for doctorate, comprehensive exam, thesis/dissertation. *Entrance requirements:* For master's and doctorate, GRE General Test. Additional exam requirements/recommendations for international students: Required—TOEFL. Electronic applications accepted. *Faculty research:* Geotechnical structural engineering, transportation engineering, construction engineering/project management.

The University of Texas at El Paso, Graduate School, College of Engineering, Department of Civil Engineering, El Paso, TX 79968-0001. Offers civil engineering (MS, PhD); construction management (MS, Certificate); environmental engineering (MEENE, MSENE). *Program availability:* Part-time, evening/weekend. *Degree requirements:* For master's, comprehensive exam, thesis optional; for doctorate, comprehensive exam, thesis/dissertation. *Entrance requirements:* For master's, GRE, minimum GPA of 3.0; for doctorate, GRE. Additional exam requirements/recommendations for international students: Required—TOEFL. Electronic applications accepted. *Faculty research:* Non-destructive testing for geotechnical and pavement applications, transportation systems, wastewater treatment systems, air quality, linear and non-linear modeling of structures, structural reliability.

The University of Texas at San Antonio, College of Engineering, Department of Civil and Environmental Engineering, San Antonio, TX 78249-0617. Offers civil engineering (MCE, MSCE); environmental science and engineering (PhD). *Program availability:* Part-time. *Degree requirements:* For master's, comprehensive exam, thesis (for some programs); for doctorate, comprehensive exam, thesis/dissertation, written qualifying exam, dissertation proposal. *Entrance requirements:* For master's, GRE General Test, BS in civil engineering or related field from accredited institution, statement of research/specialization interest, recommendation by the Civil Engineering Master's Program Admissions Committee; for doctorate, GRE, BS and MS from accredited institution, minimum GPA of 3.0 in upper-division and graduate courses, three letters of recommendation, letter of research interest, resume/curriculum vitae. Additional exam requirements/recommendations for international students: Required—TOEFL (minimum score 550 paper-based; 79 iBT), IELTS (minimum score 6.5). Electronic applications accepted. *Expenses:* Contact institution. *Faculty research:* Structures, application of geographic information systems in water resources, geotechnical engineering, pavement traffic loading, hydrogeology.

The University of Texas at Tyler, College of Engineering, Department of Civil Engineering, Tyler, TX 75799-0001. Offers environmental engineering (MS); industrial safety (MS); structural engineering (MS); transportation engineering (MS); water resources engineering (MS). *Program availability:* Part-time, evening/weekend. *Students:* 5 full-time (1 woman), 7 part-time (1 woman); includes 3 minority (1 Black or African American, non-Hispanic/Latino; 1 Asian, non-Hispanic/Latino; 1 Hispanic/Latino), 1 international. Average age 26. 5 applicants, 80% accepted, 3 enrolled. *Entrance requirements:* For master's, GRE General Test, bachelor's degree in engineering, associated science degree. Additional exam requirements/recommendations for international students: Required—TOEFL. *Application deadline:* For fall admission, 8/17 priority date for domestic students, 7/1 priority date for international students; for spring admission, 12/21 priority date for domestic students, 11/1 priority date for international students. Application fee: $25 ($50 for international students). *Financial support:* Application deadline: 7/1. *Faculty research:* Non-destructive strength testing, indoor air quality, transportation routing and signaling, pavement replacement criteria, flood water routing, construction and long-term behavior of innovative geotechnical foundation and embankment construction used in highway construction, engineering education. *Unit head:* Dr. Torey Nalbone, Chair, 903-565-5520, E-mail: tnalbone@uttyler.edu. *Application contact:* Dr. Torey Nalbone, Chair, 903-565-5520, E-mail: tnalbone@uttyler.edu.
Website: https://www.uttyler.edu/ce/

The University of Toledo, College of Graduate Studies, College of Engineering, Department of Civil Engineering, Toledo, OH 43606-3390. Offers MS, PhD. *Program availability:* Part-time. Terminal master's awarded for partial completion of doctoral program. *Degree requirements:* For master's, thesis or alternative; for doctorate, thesis/dissertation, qualifying exam. *Entrance requirements:* For master's, GRE General Test, minimum GPA of 3.0; for doctorate, GRE General Test, minimum GPA of 3.3. Additional exam requirements/recommendations for international students: Required—TOEFL (minimum score 550 paper-based; 80 iBT). Electronic applications accepted. *Faculty research:* Environmental modeling, soil/pavement interaction, structural mechanics, earthquakes, transportation engineering.

University of Toronto, School of Graduate Studies, Faculty of Applied Science and Engineering, Department of Civil Engineering, Toronto, ON M5S 1A1, Canada. Offers M Eng, MA Sc, PhD. *Program availability:* Part-time. *Degree requirements:* For master's, thesis and oral presentation (MA Sc); for doctorate, thesis/dissertation, oral presentation. *Entrance requirements:* For master's, bachelor's degree in civil engineering, proficiency in computer usage, minimum B average in final 2 years, 3 letters of reference; for doctorate, proficiency in computer usage, minimum B average in final 2 years, 3 letters of reference. Additional exam requirements/recommendations for international students: Required—TOEFL (minimum score 580 paper-based; 93 iBT). Electronic applications accepted.

University of Utah, Graduate School, College of Engineering, Department of Civil and Environmental Engineering, Salt Lake City, UT 84112. Offers civil and environmental engineering (MS, PhD); nuclear engineering (MS, PhD). *Program availability:* Part-time. *Faculty:* 21 full-time (5 women), 15 part-time/adjunct (1 woman). *Students:* 65 full-time (12 women), 31 part-time (6 women); includes 9 minority (1 Black or African American, non-Hispanic/Latino; 6 Asian, non-Hispanic/Latino; 1 Hispanic/Latino; 1 Two or more races, non-Hispanic/Latino), 45 international. Average age 29. 88 applicants, 40% accepted, 18 enrolled. In 2018, 20 master's, 8 doctorates awarded. Terminal master's awarded for partial completion of doctoral program. *Degree requirements:* For master's, comprehensive exam (for some programs), thesis (for some programs); for doctorate, comprehensive exam, thesis/dissertation, departmental qualifying exam, preliminary exam. *Entrance requirements:* For master's and doctorate, GRE General Test, minimum GPA of 3.0. Additional exam requirements/recommendations for international students: Required—TOEFL (minimum score 550 paper-based; 80 iBT). *Application deadline:* For fall admission, 1/1 priority date for domestic and international students; for spring admission, 10/1 for domestic and international students. Applications are processed on a rolling basis. Application fee: $0 ($25 for international students). Electronic applications accepted. *Expenses:* Contact institution. *Financial support:* In 2018–19, 77 students received support, including 7 fellowships with full tuition reimbursements available (averaging $27,000 per year), 57 research assistantships with full tuition reimbursements available (averaging $23,500 per year), 14 teaching assistantships with full tuition reimbursements available (averaging $23,400 per year); traineeships, health care benefits, and unspecified assistantships also available. Financial award application deadline: 1/1. *Faculty research:* Structural engineering, geotechnical engineering, transportation engineering, environmental engineering, water resources, construction engineering. *Total annual research expenditures:* $6.3 million. *Unit head:* Dr. Michael Barber, Chair, 801-581-6931, Fax: 801-585-5477, E-mail: barber@civil.utah.edu. *Application contact:* Courtney Phillips, Academic Advisor, 801-581-6678, Fax: 801-585-5477, E-mail: cveen-graduate@utah.edu.
Website: http://www.civil.utah.edu

University of Vermont, Graduate College, College of Engineering and Mathematical Sciences, Department of Civil and Environmental Engineering, Burlington, VT 05405. Offers MS, PhD. *Degree requirements:* For master's, thesis or alternative; for doctorate, thesis/dissertation. *Entrance requirements:* For master's and doctorate, GRE General Test. Additional exam requirements/recommendations for international students: Required—TOEFL (minimum score 550 paper-based, 90 iBT) or IELTS (6.5). Electronic applications accepted.

University of Virginia, School of Engineering and Applied Science, Department of Civil and Environmental Engineering, Charlottesville, VA 22903. Offers ME, MS, PhD. *Program availability:* Part-time, online learning. Terminal master's awarded for partial completion of doctoral program. *Degree requirements:* For master's, thesis (for some programs); for doctorate, comprehensive exam, thesis/dissertation. *Entrance requirements:* For master's and doctorate, GRE General Test, 3 letters of recommendation. Additional exam requirements/recommendations for international students: Required—TOEFL (minimum score 600 paper-based; 90 iBT), IELTS (minimum score 7). Electronic applications accepted. *Faculty research:* Groundwater, surface water, traffic engineering, composite materials.

University of Washington, Graduate School, College of Engineering, Department of Civil and Environmental Engineering, Seattle, WA 98195-2700. Offers construction engineering (MSCE, PhD); environmental engineering (MSCE, PhD); geotechnical engineering (MSCE, PhD); hydrology and hydrodynamics (MSCE, PhD); structural engineering and mechanics (MSCE, PhD); transportation engineering (MSCE, PhD). *Program availability:* Part-time, 100% online. *Faculty:* 38 full-time (10 women). *Students:* 239 full-time (104 women), 172 part-time (51 women); includes 91 minority (3 Black or African American, non-Hispanic/Latino; 2 American Indian or Alaska Native, non-Hispanic/Latino; 42 Asian, non-Hispanic/Latino; 26 Hispanic/Latino; 18 Two or more races, non-Hispanic/Latino), 120 international. Average age 28. 787 applicants, 57% accepted, 163 enrolled. In 2018, 161 master's, 11 doctorates awarded. Terminal master's awarded for partial completion of doctoral program. *Degree requirements:* For

master's, thesis optional; for doctorate, comprehensive exam, thesis/dissertation, qualifying, general and final exams; completion of degree within 10 years. *Entrance requirements:* For master's, GRE General Test, minimum GPA of 3.0, statement of purpose, letters of recommendation, transcripts; for doctorate, GRE General Test, minimum GPA of 3.5, statement of purpose, letters of recommendation, transcripts, resume. Additional exam requirements/recommendations for international students: Required—TOEFL (minimum score 580 paper-based; 92 iBT); Recommended—IELTS (minimum score 7), TSE. *Application deadline:* For fall admission, 12/15 for domestic and international students. Applications are processed on a rolling basis. Application fee: $85. Electronic applications accepted. *Expenses:* Research-focused Master's and PhD: $18,852 resident; $32,760 nonresident. *Financial support:* In 2018–19, 120 students received support, including 23 fellowships with tuition reimbursements available (averaging $30,240 per year), 78 research assistantships with full tuition reimbursements available (averaging $30,240 per year), 28 teaching assistantships with full tuition reimbursements available (averaging $30,240 per year); scholarships/grants also available. Financial award application deadline: 12/15; financial award applicants required to submit FAFSA. *Faculty research:* Structural and geotechnical engineering, transportation and construction engineering, water and environmental engineering. *Total annual research expenditures:* $16.4 million. *Unit head:* Dr. Timothy V. Larson, Professor/Chair, 206-543-6815, Fax: 206-543-1543, E-mail: tlarson@uw.edu. *Application contact:* Melissa Pritchard, Graduate Adviser, 206-543-2574, Fax: 206-543-1543, E-mail: ceginfo@u.washington.edu.
Website: http://www.ce.washington.edu/

University of Waterloo, Graduate Studies and Postdoctoral Affairs, Faculty of Engineering, Department of Civil and Environmental Engineering, Waterloo, ON N2L 3G1, Canada. Offers M Eng, MA Sc, PhD. *Program availability:* Part-time. *Degree requirements:* For master's, research paper or thesis; for doctorate, comprehensive exam, thesis/dissertation. *Entrance requirements:* For master's, honors degree, minimum B average; for doctorate, master's degree, minimum A- average. Additional exam requirements/recommendations for international students: Required—TOEFL, IELTS, PTE. *Application deadline:* Applications are processed on a rolling basis. Application fee: $125 Canadian dollars. Electronic applications accepted. *Financial support:* Research assistantships and teaching assistantships available. *Faculty research:* Water resources, structures, construction management, transportation, geotechnical engineering.
Website: https://uwaterloo.ca/civil-environmental-engineering/

The University of Western Ontario, School of Graduate and Postdoctoral Studies, Physical Sciences Division, Faculty of Engineering, London, ON N6A 3K7, Canada. Offers chemical and biochemical engineering (ME Sc, PhD); civil and environmental engineering (M Eng, ME Sc, PhD); electrical and computer engineering (M Eng, ME Sc, PhD); mechanical and materials engineering (M Eng, ME Sc, PhD). *Program availability:* Part-time. Terminal master's awarded for partial completion of doctoral program. *Degree requirements:* For master's, thesis; for doctorate, thesis/dissertation. *Entrance requirements:* For master's, minimum B average; for doctorate, minimum B+ average. *Faculty research:* Wind, geotechnical, chemical reactor engineering, applied electrostatics, biochemical engineering.

University of Windsor, Faculty of Graduate Studies, Faculty of Engineering, Department of Civil and Environmental Engineering, Windsor, ON N9B 3P4, Canada. Offers civil engineering (M Eng, MA Sc, PhD); environmental engineering (M Eng, MA Sc, PhD). *Program availability:* Part-time. *Degree requirements:* For master's, thesis; for doctorate, comprehensive exam, thesis/dissertation. *Entrance requirements:* For master's, minimum B average; for doctorate, master's degree, minimum A average. Additional exam requirements/recommendations for international students: Required—TOEFL (minimum score 580 paper-based). Electronic applications accepted. *Faculty research:* Odors: sampling, measurement, control; drinking water disinfection, hydrocarbon contaminated soil remediation, structural dynamics, numerical simulation of piezoelectric materials.

University of Wisconsin–Madison, Graduate School, College of Engineering, Department of Civil and Environmental Engineering, Madison, WI 53706-1380. Offers construction engineering and management (MS); environmental science and engineering (MS); geological/geotechnical engineering (MS); structural engineering (MS); transportation engineering (MS); water resources engineering (MS). *Program availability:* Part-time. *Faculty:* 31 full-time (8 women). *Students:* 97 full-time (28 women), 39 part-time (15 women); includes 12 minority (2 Black or African American, non-Hispanic/Latino; 3 Asian, non-Hispanic/Latino; 6 Hispanic/Latino; 1 Two or more races, non-Hispanic/Latino), 62 international. Average age 28. 261 applicants, 45% accepted, 29 enrolled. In 2018, 33 master's awarded. Terminal master's awarded for partial completion of doctoral program. *Degree requirements:* For master's, thesis (for some programs), minimum of 30 credits; minimum overall GPA of 3.0. *Entrance requirements:* For master's, GRE General Test, bachelor's degree; minimum GPA of 3.0 for last 60 credits of course work. Additional exam requirements/recommendations for international students: Required—TOEFL (minimum score 580 paper-based; 92 iBT). *Application deadline:* For fall admission, 12/15 priority date for domestic and international students; for spring admission, 10/1 for domestic and international students. Application fee: $75 ($81 for international students). Electronic applications accepted. *Expenses:* In-state tuition (Full-time): $10,728; Out-of-state tuition (full-time): $24,054; Fees: $1282; In-state tuition (per credit): $670; Out-of-state tuition (per credit): $1503; Fees (per credit): $126. *Financial support:* In 2018–19, 90 students received support, including 8 fellowships with full tuition reimbursements available (averaging $28,704 per year), 54 research assistantships with full tuition reimbursements available (averaging $23,784 per year), 21 teaching assistantships with full tuition reimbursements available (averaging $16,584 per year); Federal Work-Study, scholarships/grants, health care benefits, unspecified assistantships, and project assistantships also available. Support available to part-time students. Financial award application deadline: 12/1; financial award applicants required to submit FAFSA. *Faculty research:* Construction engineering and management; environmental engineering; structural engineering; transportation and city planning; water resources engineering; water chemistry. *Total annual research expenditures:* $12.5 million. *Unit head:* Dr. William Likos, Chair, 608-263-9490, Fax: 608-262-5199, E-mail: frontdesk@cee.wisc.edu. *Application contact:* Cheryl Loschko, Student Services Coordinator, 608-890-2420, E-mail: loschko@wisc.edu.
Website: https://www.engr.wisc.edu/department/civil-environmental-engineering/academics/ms-phd-civil-and-environmental-engineering/

University of Wisconsin–Milwaukee, Graduate School, College of Engineering and Applied Science, Program in Engineering, Milwaukee, WI 53201-0413. Offers biomedical engineering (MS); civil engineering (MS, PhD); computer science (PhD); electrical and computer engineering (MS); electrical engineering (PhD); engineering mechanics (MS); industrial and management engineering (MS); industrial engineering (PhD); manufacturing engineering (MS); materials (PhD); materials engineering (MS); mechanical engineering (MS). *Program availability:* Part-time. *Students:* 174 full-time (41 women), 149 part-time (27 women); includes 31 minority (2 Black or African American, non-Hispanic/Latino; 1 American Indian or Alaska Native, non-Hispanic/Latino; 16 Asian, non-Hispanic/Latino; 4 Hispanic/Latino; 8 Two or more races, non-Hispanic/Latino), 207 international. Average age 31. 343 applicants, 57% accepted, 78 enrolled. In 2018, 73 master's, 24 doctorates awarded. *Degree requirements:* For master's, comprehensive exam (for some programs), thesis or alternative; for doctorate, comprehensive exam, thesis/dissertation, internship. *Entrance requirements:* For master's, GRE, minimum GPA of 2.75; for doctorate, GRE, minimum GPA of 3.5. Additional exam requirements/recommendations for international students: Required—TOEFL (minimum score 550 paper-based; 79 iBT), IELTS (minimum score 6.5). *Application deadline:* For fall admission, 1/1 priority date for domestic students; for spring admission, 9/1 for domestic students. Applications are processed on a rolling basis. Application fee: $56 ($96 for international students). *Financial support:* Fellowships, research assistantships, teaching assistantships, career-related internships or fieldwork, Federal Work-Study, unspecified assistantships, and project assistantships available. Support available to part-time students. Financial award application deadline: 4/15. *Unit head:* David Yu, Representative, 414-229-6169, E-mail: yu@uwm.edu. *Application contact:* Betty Warras, General Information Contact, 414-229-6169, Fax: 414-229-6967, E-mail: bwarras@uwm.edu.
Website: http://www4.uwm.edu/ceas/academics/graduate_programs/

University of Wyoming, College of Engineering and Applied Science, Department of Civil and Architectural Engineering, Laramie, WY 82071. Offers architectural engineering (MS); civil engineering (MS, PhD). *Program availability:* Part-time. Terminal master's awarded for partial completion of doctoral program. *Degree requirements:* For master's, thesis (for some programs); for doctorate, variable foreign language requirement, comprehensive exam, thesis/dissertation. *Entrance requirements:* For master's, GRE General Test (minimum combined score 900), minimum GPA of 3.0; for doctorate, GRE General Test (minimum combined score: 1000), minimum GPA of 3.0. Additional exam requirements/recommendations for international students: Required—TOEFL (minimum score 550 paper-based). Electronic applications accepted. *Expenses: Tuition, area resident:* Full-time $6504; part-time $271 per credit hour. Tuition, state resident: full-time $6504; part-time $271 per credit hour. Tuition, nonresident: full-time $19,464; part-time $811 per credit hour. *International tuition:* $19,464 full-time. *Required fees:* $1410.94; $343.82 per semester. $343.82 per semester. Tuition and fees vary according to course load, program and reciprocity agreements. *Faculty research:* Water resources, structures, geotechnical engineering, transportation, architectural engineering.

Utah State University, School of Graduate Studies, College of Engineering, Department of Civil and Environmental Engineering, Logan, UT 84322. Offers ME, MS, PhD, CE. *Degree requirements:* For master's, thesis (for some programs); for doctorate, thesis/dissertation. *Entrance requirements:* For master's and doctorate, GRE General Test, minimum GPA of 3.0. Additional exam requirements/recommendations for international students: Required—TOEFL. Electronic applications accepted. *Faculty research:* Hazardous waste treatment, large space structures, river basin management, earthquake engineering, environmental impact.

Vanderbilt University, School of Engineering, Department of Civil and Environmental Engineering, Program in Civil Engineering, Nashville, TN 37240-1001. Offers M Eng, MS, PhD. MS and PhD offered through the Graduate School. *Program availability:* Part-time. Terminal master's awarded for partial completion of doctoral program. *Degree requirements:* For master's, thesis; for doctorate, thesis/dissertation. *Entrance requirements:* For master's and doctorate, GRE General Test. Additional exam requirements/recommendations for international students: Required—TOEFL. Electronic applications accepted. *Expenses: Tuition:* Full-time $47,208; part-time $2026 per credit hour. *Required fees:* $478. *Faculty research:* Structural mechanics, finite element analysis, urban transportation, hazardous material transport.

Villanova University, College of Engineering, Department of Civil and Environmental Engineering, Program in Civil Engineering, Villanova, PA 19085-1699. Offers MSCE. *Program availability:* Part-time, evening/weekend. *Degree requirements:* For master's, thesis optional. *Entrance requirements:* For master's, GRE General Test (for applicants with degrees from foreign universities), minimum GPA of 3.0. Additional exam requirements/recommendations for international students: Required—TOEFL (minimum score 600 paper-based; 100 iBT). Electronic applications accepted. *Faculty research:* Bridge inspection, environment maintenance, economy and risk.

Virginia Polytechnic Institute and State University, Graduate School, College of Engineering, Blacksburg, VA 24061. Offers aerospace engineering (PhD, M Eng/MS); biological systems engineering (PhD); biomedical engineering (MS, PhD); chemical engineering (PhD); civil engineering (PhD); computer engineering (PhD); computer science and applications (MS); electrical engineering (PhD); engineering education (PhD); M Eng/MS. *Faculty:* 446 full-time (87 women), 7 part-time/adjunct (3 women). *Students:* 1,776 full-time (471 women), 367 part-time (62 women); includes 260 minority (50 Black or African American, non-Hispanic/Latino; 3 American Indian or Alaska Native, non-Hispanic/Latino; 99 Asian, non-Hispanic/Latino; 67 Hispanic/Latino; 41 Two or more races, non-Hispanic/Latino), 1,178 international. Average age 27. 3,798 applicants, 37% accepted, 507 enrolled. In 2018, 489 master's, 200 doctorates awarded. *Degree requirements:* For master's, comprehensive exam (for some programs), thesis (for some programs); for doctorate, comprehensive exam (for some programs), thesis/dissertation (for some programs). *Entrance requirements:* For master's and doctorate, GRE/GMAT. Additional exam requirements/recommendations for international students: Required—TOEFL (minimum score 90 iBT). *Application deadline:* For fall admission, 8/1 for domestic students, 4/1 for international students; for spring admission, 1/1 for domestic students, 9/1 for international students. Applications are processed on a rolling basis. Application fee: $75. Electronic applications accepted. *Expenses:* Tuition, state resident: full-time $15,510; part-time $739.50 per credit hour. Tuition, nonresident: full-time $29,629; part-time $1490.25 per credit hour. *Required fees:* $2804; $550 per semester. Tuition and fees vary according to course load, campus/location and program. *Financial support:* In 2018–19, 37 fellowships with full tuition reimbursements (averaging $24,951 per year), 1,110 research assistantships with full tuition reimbursements (averaging $20,129 per year), 486 teaching assistantships with full tuition reimbursements (averaging $16,192 per year) were awarded; scholarships/grants and unspecified assistantships also available. Financial award application deadline: 3/1; financial award applicants required to submit FAFSA. *Total annual research expenditures:* $96.3 million. *Unit head:* Dr. Julia Ross, Dean, 540-231-9752, Fax: 540-231-3031, E-mail: rjulie@vt.edu. *Application contact:* Linda Perkins, Executive Assistant, 540-231-9752, Fax: 540-231-3031, E-mail: lperkins@vt.edu.
Website: http://www.eng.vt.edu/

Virginia Polytechnic Institute and State University, VT Online, Blacksburg, VA 24061. Offers advanced transportation systems (Certificate); aerospace engineering (MS); agricultural and life sciences (MSLFS); business information systems (Graduate Certificate); career and technical education (MS); civil engineering (MS); computer engineering (M Eng, MS); decision support systems (Graduate Certificate); eLearning leadership (MA); electrical engineering (M Eng, MS); engineering administration (MEA); environmental engineering (Certificate); environmental politics and policy (Graduate Certificate); environmental sciences and engineering (MS); foundations of political analysis (Graduate Certificate); health product risk management (Graduate Certificate); industrial and systems engineering (MS); information policy and society (Graduate Certificate); information security (Graduate Certificate); information technology (MIT);

instructional technology (MA); integrative STEM education (MA Ed); liberal arts (Graduate Certificate); life sciences: health product risk management (MS); natural resources (MNR, Graduate Certificate); networking (Graduate Certificate); nonprofit and nongovernmental organization management (Graduate Certificate); ocean engineering (MS); political science (MA); security studies (Graduate Certificate); software development (Graduate Certificate). *Expenses:* Tuition, state resident: full-time $15,510; part-time $739.50 per credit hour. Tuition, nonresident: full-time $29,629; part-time $1490.25 per credit hour. *Required fees:* $2804; $550 per semester. Tuition and fees vary according to course load, campus/location and program. *Application contact:* Graduate Admissions and Academic Progress, 540-231-8636, E-mail: grads@vt.edu. Website: http://www.vto.vt.edu/

Washington State University, Voiland College of Engineering and Architecture, Department of Civil and Environmental Engineering, Pullman, WA 99164-2910. Offers civil engineering (MS, PhD); environmental engineering (MS). MS programs also offered at Tri-Cities campus. *Program availability:* Part-time. Terminal master's awarded for partial completion of doctoral program. *Degree requirements:* For master's, comprehensive exam (for some programs), thesis (for some programs), oral exam; for doctorate, comprehensive exam, thesis/dissertation, oral exam, written exam. *Entrance requirements:* For master's, minimum GPA of 3.0, 3 letters of recommendation, statement of purpose; for doctorate, minimum GPA of 3.4, 3 letters of recommendation, statement of purpose. Additional exam requirements/recommendations for international students: Required—TOEFL (minimum score 550 paper-based), IELTS. Electronic applications accepted. *Faculty research:* Environmental engineering, water resources, structural engineering, geotechnical, transportation.

Wayne State University, College of Engineering, Department of Civil and Environmental Engineering, Detroit, MI 48202. Offers civil engineering (MS). *Faculty:* 9. *Students:* 37 full-time (10 women), 34 part-time (11 women); includes 4 minority (3 Black or African American, non-Hispanic/Latino; 1 Asian, non-Hispanic/Latino), 26 international. Average age 28. 96 applicants, 34% accepted, 10 enrolled. In 2018, 38 master's, 2 doctorates awarded. *Entrance requirements:* For master's, BS in civil engineering from ABET-accredited institution with minimum GPA of 3.0, statement of purpose; for doctorate, BS in civil engineering from ABET-accredited institution (or comparable foreign institution) with minimum GPA of 3.3, 3.4 in last two years, or MS in civil engineering with minimum GPA of 3.5 from ABET-accredited institution (or comparable foreign institution). Additional exam requirements/recommendations for international students: Required—TOEFL (minimum score 550 paper-based; 79 iBT), TWE (minimum score 5.5), Michigan English Language Assessment Battery (minimum score 85); Recommended—IELTS (minimum score 6.5). *Application deadline:* For fall admission, 3/1 priority date for domestic and international students; for winter admission, 10/1 priority date for domestic students, 9/1 priority date for international students; for spring admission, 2/1 priority date for domestic students, 1/1 priority date for international students. Applications are processed on a rolling basis. Application fee: $50. Electronic applications accepted. *Expenses:* Contact institution. *Financial support:* In 2018–19, 30 students received support, including 2 fellowships with tuition reimbursements available (averaging $27,000 per year), 7 research assistantships with tuition reimbursements available (averaging $18,615 per year), 5 teaching assistantships with tuition reimbursements available (averaging $20,166 per year); scholarships/grants, health care benefits, and unspecified assistantships also available. Support available to part-time students. Financial award applicants required to submit FAFSA. *Faculty research:* Traffic engineering and safety; infrastructure information systems using geographic information systems; intelligent transportation systems; non-destructive evaluation of structures; infrastructure appraisal and upgrade; geosynthetics; water quality modeling; waste containment systems; liquefaction effects on piles and underground utilities; and construction safety and quality management. *Total annual research expenditures:* $1.9 million. *Unit head:* Dr. Mumtaz Usman, Professor and Chair, 313-577-3608, E-mail: musmen@eng.wayne.edu. *Application contact:* Ellen Cope, Graduate Program Coordinator, 313-577-0409, E-mail: escope@wayne.edu. Website: http://engineering.wayne.edu/cee/

Wentworth Institute of Technology, Master of Engineering in Civil Engineering Program, Boston, MA 02115-5998. Offers construction engineering (M Eng); infrastructure engineering (M Eng). *Program availability:* Part-time only, evening/weekend. *Degree requirements:* For master's, thesis optional, capstone course. *Entrance requirements:* For master's, resume, statement of purpose, official transcripts, two professional recommendations, bachelor's degree, minimum GPA of 3.0, one year of professional experience in a technical role and/or technical organization. Additional exam requirements/recommendations for international students: Recommended—TOEFL (minimum score 550 paper-based). Electronic applications accepted. *Expenses:* Contact institution.

Western Michigan University, Graduate College, College of Engineering and Applied Sciences, Department of Civil and Construction Engineering, Kalamazoo, MI 49008. Offers MSE.

Western New England University, College of Engineering, Department of Civil and Environmental Engineering, Springfield, MA 01119. Offers civil engineering (MS). *Program availability:* Part-time, evening/weekend. *Faculty:* 3 full-time (1 woman). *Students:* 2 part-time (0 women), 1 international. Average age 23. 36 applicants, 92% accepted, 3 enrolled. In 2018, 1 master's awarded. *Degree requirements:* For master's, thesis optional. *Entrance requirements:* For master's, transcript, two letters of recommendations, resume, bachelor's degree in engineering or related field. Additional

exam requirements/recommendations for international students: Required—TOEFL (minimum score 79 iBT). *Application deadline:* Applications are processed on a rolling basis. Application fee: $30. Electronic applications accepted. *Expenses:* Contact institution. *Financial support:* Application deadline: 4/15; applicants required to submit FAFSA. *Unit head:* Kenneth Lee, Chair, 413-782-1739, E-mail: kenneth.lee@wne.edu. *Application contact:* Matthew Fox, Executive Director of Graduate Admissions, 413-782-1410, Fax: 413-782-1777, E-mail: study@wne.edu. Website: http://www1.wne.edu/academics/graduate/civil-engineering-ms.cfm

West Virginia University, Statler College of Engineering and Mineral Resources, Morgantown, WV 26506. Offers aerospace engineering (MSAE, PhD); chemical engineering (MS Ch E, PhD); civil engineering (MSCE, PhD); computer engineering (PhD); computer science (MSCS, PhD); electrical engineering (MSEE, PhD); energy systems engineering (MSESE); engineering (MSE); industrial engineering (MSIE, PhD); industrial hygiene (MS); material science and engineering (MSMSE, PhD); mechanical engineering (MSME, PhD); mining engineering (MS Min E, PhD); petroleum and natural gas engineering (MSPNGE, PhD); safety management (MS); software engineering (MSSE). *Program availability:* Part-time. *Students:* 466 full-time (113 women), 154 part-time (27 women); includes 57 minority (22 Black or African American, non-Hispanic/Latino; 1 American Indian or Alaska Native, non-Hispanic/Latino; 8 Asian, non-Hispanic/Latino; 12 Hispanic/Latino; 14 Two or more races, non-Hispanic/Latino), 283 international. In 2018, 179 master's, 39 doctorates awarded. Terminal master's awarded for partial completion of doctoral program. *Degree requirements:* For master's, thesis optional; for doctorate, comprehensive exam, thesis/dissertation. *Entrance requirements:* Additional exam requirements/recommendations for international students: Required—TOEFL (minimum score 550 paper-based). *Application deadline:* For fall admission, 4/1 for international students; for winter admission, 4/1 for international students; for spring admission, 10/1 for international students. Applications are processed on a rolling basis. Application fee: $60. Electronic applications accepted. *Expenses:* Contact institution. *Financial support:* Fellowships, research assistantships, teaching assistantships, career-related internships or fieldwork, Federal Work-Study, institutionally sponsored loans, health care benefits, tuition waivers (full and partial), unspecified assistantships, and administrative assistantships available. Financial award application deadline: 2/1; financial award applicants required to submit FAFSA. *Faculty research:* Composite materials, software engineering, information systems, aerodynamics, vehicle propulsion and emission. *Unit head:* Dr. Earl Scime, Interim Dean, 304-293-4157 Ext. 2237, Fax: 304-293-2037, E-mail: earl.scime@mail.wvu.edu. *Application contact:* Dr. David A. Wyrick, Associate Dean, Academic Affairs, 304-293-4334, Fax: 304-293-5024, E-mail: david.wyrick@mail.wvu.edu. Website: https://www.statler.wvu.edu

Widener University, Graduate Programs in Engineering, Program in Civil Engineering, Chester, PA 19013. Offers M Eng. *Program availability:* Part-time, evening/weekend. *Degree requirements:* For master's, thesis optional. Electronic applications accepted. *Faculty research:* Environmental engineering, laws and water supply, structural analysis and design.

Worcester Polytechnic Institute, Graduate Admissions, Department of Civil and Environmental Engineering, Worcester, MA 01609-2280. Offers civil engineering (MS); construction project management (Graduate Certificate). *Program availability:* Part-time, evening/weekend, 100% online, blended/hybrid learning. *Students:* 22 full-time (9 women), 51 part-time (19 women); includes 9 minority (1 Black or African American, non-Hispanic/Latino; 1 American Indian or Alaska Native, non-Hispanic/Latino; 5 Asian, non-Hispanic/Latino; 2 Hispanic/Latino), 12 international. Average age 31. 136 applicants, 60% accepted, 22 enrolled. In 2018, 21 master's, 12 other advanced degrees awarded. *Degree requirements:* For master's, thesis optional; for doctorate, comprehensive exam, thesis/dissertation. *Entrance requirements:* For master's, required for all international applicants; recommended for all others, 3 letters of recommendation; for doctorate, required for all international applicants; recommended for all others, 3 letters of recommendation, statement of purpose. Additional exam requirements/recommendations for international students: Required—TOEFL (minimum score 563 paper-based; 84 iBT), IELTS (minimum score 7). *Application deadline:* For fall admission, 1/1 priority date for domestic and international students; for spring admission, 10/1 priority date for domestic and international students. Applications are processed on a rolling basis. Application fee: $70. Electronic applications accepted. *Financial support:* Fellowships, research assistantships, teaching assistantships, career-related internships or fieldwork, institutionally sponsored loans, scholarships/grants, and unspecified assistantships available. Financial award application deadline: 1/1. *Unit head:* Dr. Carrick Eggleston, Department Head, 508-831-5530, Fax: 508-831-5808, E-mail: ceggleston@wpi.edu. *Application contact:* Dr. Nima Rahbar, Graduate Coordinator, 508-831-5530, Fax: 508-831-5808, E-mail: nrahbar@wpi.edu. Website: https://www.wpi.edu/academics/departments/civil-environmental-engineering

Youngstown State University, College of Graduate Studies, College of Science, Technology, Engineering and Mathematics, Department of Civil/Environmental and Chemical Engineering, Youngstown, OH 44555-0001. Offers civil and environmental engineering (MSE). *Program availability:* Part-time, evening/weekend. *Degree requirements:* For master's, thesis optional. *Entrance requirements:* For master's, minimum GPA of 2.75 in field. Additional exam requirements/recommendations for international students: Required—TOEFL. *Faculty research:* Structural mechanics, water quality modeling, surface and ground water hydrology, physical and chemical processes in aquatic systems.

Construction Engineering

The American University in Cairo, School of Sciences and Engineering, Cairo, Egypt. Offers biotechnology (MS); chemistry (MS); computer science (MS); computing (M Comp); construction engineering (M Eng, MS); electronics and communications engineering (M Eng); environmental engineering (MS); environmental system design (M Eng); mechanical engineering (M Eng, MS); nanotechnology (MS); physics (MS); robotics, control and smart systems (MS); sciences and engineering (PhD); sustainable development (MS, Graduate Diploma). *Program availability:* Part-time, evening/weekend. *Degree requirements:* For master's, comprehensive exam (for some programs), thesis (for some programs); for doctorate, comprehensive exam (for some programs), thesis/dissertation. *Entrance requirements:* Additional exam requirements/recommendations for international students: Required—TOEFL (minimum score 450 paper-based); 45 iBT), IELTS (minimum score 5). Electronic applications accepted. *Faculty research:* Construction, mechanical, and electronics engineering; physics; computer science; biotechnology; nanotechnology; chemistry; robotics.

Arizona State University at the Tempe campus, Ira A. Fulton Schools of Engineering, School of Sustainable Engineering and the Built Environment, Tempe, AZ 85287-5306. Offers civil, environmental and sustainable engineering (MS, MSE, PhD); construction

engineering (MSE); construction management (MS, PhD). *Program availability:* Part-time, evening/weekend, online learning. Terminal master's awarded for partial completion of doctoral program. *Degree requirements:* For master's, thesis optional, comprehensive exams (MSE); interactive Program of Study (iPOS) submitted before completing 50 percent of required credit hours; for doctorate, comprehensive exam, thesis/dissertation, interactive Program of Study (iPOS) submitted before completing 50 percent of required credit hours. *Entrance requirements:* For master's, GRE, minimum GPA of 3.0 or equivalent in last 2 years of work leading to bachelor's degree; for doctorate, GRE, minimum GPA of 3.0 in last 2 years of work leading to bachelor's degree, 3.2 in all graduate-level coursework with master's degree; 3 letters of recommendation; resume/curriculum vitae; letter of intent; thesis (if applicable); statement of research interests. Additional exam requirements/recommendations for international students: Required—TOEFL, IELTS, or PTE. Electronic applications accepted. *Expenses:* Contact institution. *Faculty research:* Water purification, transportation (safety and materials), construction management, environmental biotechnology, environmental nanotechnology, earth systems engineering and management, SMART innovations, project performance metrics, and underground infrastructure.

Construction Engineering

Auburn University, Graduate School, College of Architecture, Design, and Construction, McWhorter School of Building Science, Auburn University, AL 36849. Offers MBC. *Entrance requirements:* For master's, GRE General Test. Electronic applications accepted. *Expenses:* Tuition, state resident: full-time $11,282; part-time $535 per credit hour. Tuition, nonresident: full-time $30,542; part-time $1605 per credit hour. *Required fees:* $826 per semester. Tuition and fees vary according to degree level and program.

Bradley University, The Graduate School, Caterpillar College of Engineering and Technology, Department of Civil Engineering and Construction, Peoria, IL 61625-0002. Offers construction management, structural engineering, geo-environmental engineering (MSCE). *Program availability:* Part-time, evening/weekend. *Faculty:* 11 full-time (2 women). *Students:* 16 full-time (4 women), 7 part-time (1 woman); includes 2 minority (1 Black or African American, non-Hispanic/Latino; 1 Hispanic/Latino), 18 international. Average age 25. 62 applicants, 90% accepted, 5 enrolled. In 2018, 11 master's awarded. *Degree requirements:* For master's, comprehensive exam, thesis or alternative, 30 hours. *Entrance requirements:* For master's, minimum GPA of 2.5, Essays, Recommendation letters, Transcripts. Additional exam requirements/recommendations for international students: Required—TOEFL (minimum score 550 paper-based; 79 iBT), IELTS (minimum score 6.5). *Application deadline:* For fall admission, 5/15 priority date for domestic and international students; for spring admission, 10/15 priority date for domestic and international students. Applications are processed on a rolling basis. Application fee: $40 ($50 for international students). Electronic applications accepted. *Expenses: Tuition:* Part-time $890 per credit. *Required fees:* $50 per unit. *Financial support:* In 2018–19, 26 students received support, including 12 research assistantships with full and partial tuition reimbursements available (averaging $4,895 per year); teaching assistantships with tuition reimbursements available, scholarships/grants, tuition waivers (full and partial), and unspecified assistantships also available. Support available to part-time students. Financial award application deadline: 4/1. *Unit head:* Souhail Elhouar, Chairman, 309-677-3830, E-mail: selhouar@bradley.edu. *Application contact:* Rachel Webb, Director of On-Campus Graduate Admissions, 309-677-2375, E-mail: bugrad@bradley.edu.
Website: http://www.bradley.edu/academic/departments/cec/

Clemson University, Graduate School, College of Engineering, Computing and Applied Sciences, Glenn Department of Civil Engineering, Clemson, SC 29634. Offers civil engineering (MS, PhD), including construction engineering and management, construction materials, geotechnical engineering, structural engineering, transportation engineering, water resources engineering. *Program availability:* Part-time. *Faculty:* 20 full-time (3 women). *Students:* 109 full-time (23 women), 55 part-time (11 women); includes 9 minority (2 Black or African American, non-Hispanic/Latino; 2 Asian, non-Hispanic/Latino; 4 Hispanic/Latino; 1 Two or more races, non-Hispanic/Latino), 111 international. Average age 28. 283 applicants, 59% accepted, 53 enrolled. In 2018, 31 master's, 11 doctorates awarded. *Degree requirements:* For master's, thesis or alternative, oral exam, seminar; for doctorate, comprehensive exam, thesis/dissertation, oral exam, seminar. *Entrance requirements:* For master's and doctorate, GRE General Test, unofficial transcripts, letters of recommendation, statement of purpose. Additional exam requirements/recommendations for international students: Required—TOEFL (minimum score 80 paper-based; 80 iBT), PTE (minimum score 54); Recommended—IELTS (minimum score 6.5). *Application deadline:* For fall admission, 4/15 for domestic and international students; for spring admission, 9/15 for domestic and international students. Applications are processed on a rolling basis. Application fee: $80 ($90 for international students). Electronic applications accepted. *Expenses:* $6823 per semester full-time resident, $14023 per semester full-time non-resident, $833 per credit hour part-time resident, $1731 per credit hour part-time non-resident, online $1264 per credit hour, $4938 doctoral programs resident, $10405 doctoral programs non-resident, $1144 full-time graduate assistant, other fees may apply per session. *Financial support:* In 2018–19, 104 students received support, including 20 fellowships with full and partial tuition reimbursements available (averaging $4,491 per year), 43 research assistantships with full and partial tuition reimbursements available (averaging $16,364 per year), 1 teaching assistantship with full and partial tuition reimbursement available (averaging $12,750 per year); career-related internships or fieldwork and unspecified assistantships also available. Financial award application deadline: 4/15. *Faculty research:* Applied fluid mechanics, construction materials, project management, structural and geotechnical engineering, transportation. *Total annual research expenditures:* $4.9 million. *Unit head:* Dr. Ronald Andrus, Interim Department Chair, 864-656-0488, E-mail: randrus@clemson.edu. *Application contact:* Dr. Abdul Khan, Graduate Program Coordinator, 864-656-3327, E-mail: abdkhan@clemson.edu.
Website: https://www.clemson.edu/cecas/departments/ce/

Colorado School of Mines, Office of Graduate Studies, Department of Civil and Environmental Engineering, Golden, CO 80401. Offers civil and environmental engineering (MS, PhD); environmental engineering science (MS, PhD); hydrologic science and engineering (MS, PhD); underground construction and tunneling (MS, PhD). *Program availability:* Part-time. *Faculty:* 44 full-time (16 women), 11 part-time/adjunct (6 women). *Students:* 99 full-time (46 women), 23 part-time (10 women); includes 15 minority (2 Black or African American, non-Hispanic/Latino; 3 Asian, non-Hispanic/Latino; 4 Hispanic/Latino; 6 Two or more races, non-Hispanic/Latino), 21 international. Average age 28. 171 applicants, 60% accepted, 47 enrolled. In 2018, 45 master's, 13 doctorates awarded. *Degree requirements:* For master's, thesis (for some programs); for doctorate, comprehensive exam, thesis/dissertation. *Entrance requirements:* For master's and doctorate, GRE General Test. Additional exam requirements/recommendations for international students: Required—TOEFL (minimum score 550 paper-based; 79 iBT). *Application deadline:* For fall admission, 12/15 priority date for domestic students, 1/15 priority date for international students; for spring admission, 9/1 priority date for domestic and international students. Application fee: $60 ($80 for international students). Electronic applications accepted. *Expenses:* Tuition, state resident: full-time $16,650; part-time $925 per contact hour. Tuition, nonresident: full-time $36,270; part-time $2015 per contact hour. *International tuition:* $36,270 full-time. *Required fees:* $2314; $2314 per semester. *Financial support:* In 2018–19, 62 research assistantships with full tuition reimbursements, 2 teaching assistantships with full tuition reimbursements were awarded; scholarships/grants, health care benefits, and unspecified assistantships also available. Financial award application deadline: 12/15; financial award applicants required to submit FAFSA. *Faculty research:* Treatment of water and wastes, environmental law: policy and practice, natural environment systems, hazardous waste management, environmental data analysis. *Unit head:* Dr. Terri Hogue, Department Head, 303-384-2588, E-mail: thogue@mines.edu. *Application contact:* Dr. Tim VanHaverbeke, Research Faculty/Program Manager, 303-273-3467, E-mail: tvanhave@mines.edu.

Colorado School of Mines, Office of Graduate Studies, Department of Geology and Geological Engineering, Golden, CO 80401. Offers environmental geochemistry (PMS); geochemistry (MS, PhD); geological engineering (ME, MS, PhD); geology (MS, PhD); hydrology (MS, PhD); mineral exploration (PMS); petroleum reservoir systems (PMS); underground construction and tunneling (MS). *Program availability:* Part-time. *Faculty:* 30 full-time (12 women), 6 part-time/adjunct (5 women). *Students:* 129 full-time (44 women), 32 part-time (12 women); includes 20 minority (1 Black or African American, non-Hispanic/Latino; 2 American Indian or Alaska Native, non-Hispanic/Latino; 3 Asian, non-Hispanic/Latino; 10 Hispanic/Latino; 4 Two or more races, non-Hispanic/Latino), 30 international. Average age 29. 244 applicants, 41% accepted, 54 enrolled. In 2018, 39 master's, 11 doctorates awarded. *Degree requirements:* For master's, thesis (for some programs); for doctorate, comprehensive exam, thesis/dissertation. *Entrance requirements:* For master's and doctorate, GRE General Test. Additional exam requirements/recommendations for international students: Required—TOEFL (minimum score 550 paper-based; 79 iBT). *Application deadline:* For fall admission, 12/15 priority date for domestic and international students; for spring admission, 9/1 priority date for domestic and international students. Application fee: $60 ($80 for international students). Electronic applications accepted. *Expenses:* Tuition, state resident: full-time $16,650; part-time $925 per contact hour. Tuition, nonresident: full-time $36,270; part-time $2015 per contact hour. *International tuition:* $36,270 full-time. *Required fees:* $2314; $2314 per semester. *Financial support:* In 2018–19, 48 research assistantships with full tuition reimbursements, 20 teaching assistantships with full tuition reimbursements were awarded; fellowships, scholarships/grants, health care benefits, and unspecified assistantships also available. Financial award application deadline: 12/15; financial award applicants required to submit FAFSA. *Faculty research:* Predictive sediment modeling, petrophysics, aquifer-contaminant flow modeling, water-rock interactions, geotechnical engineering. *Unit head:* Dr. Wendy Bohrson, Head, 303-273-3066, E-mail: bohrson@mines.edu. *Application contact:* Dr. Christian Shorey, Lecturer/Program Manager, 303-273-3556, E-mail: cshorey@mines.edu.
Website: http://geology.mines.edu

Colorado School of Mines, Office of Graduate Studies, Department of Mining Engineering, Golden, CO 80401. Offers mining and earth systems engineering (MS); mining engineering (PhD); underground construction and tunneling (MS, PhD). *Program availability:* Part-time. *Faculty:* 16 full-time (6 women), 10 part-time/adjunct (3 women). *Students:* 34 full-time (8 women), 2 part-time (0 women); includes 3 minority (1 Black or African American, non-Hispanic/Latino; 2 Hispanic/Latino), 25 international. Average age 31. 40 applicants, 75% accepted, 9 enrolled. In 2018, 13 master's, 2 doctorates awarded. *Degree requirements:* For master's, thesis (for some programs); for doctorate, comprehensive exam, thesis/dissertation. *Entrance requirements:* For master's and doctorate, GRE General Test. Additional exam requirements/recommendations for international students: Required—TOEFL (minimum score 550 paper-based; 79 iBT). *Application deadline:* For fall admission, 12/15 priority date for domestic and international students; for spring admission, 9/1 priority date for domestic and international students. Application fee: $60 ($80 for international students). Electronic applications accepted. *Expenses:* Tuition, state resident: full-time $16,650; part-time $925 per contact hour. Tuition, nonresident: full-time $36,270; part-time $2015 per contact hour. *International tuition:* $36,270 full-time. *Required fees:* $2314; $2314 per semester. *Financial support:* In 2018–19, 14 research assistantships with full tuition reimbursements, 5 teaching assistantships with full tuition reimbursements were awarded; fellowships, scholarships/grants, health care benefits, and unspecified assistantships also available. Financial award application deadline: 12/15; financial award applicants required to submit FAFSA. *Faculty research:* Mine evaluation and planning, geostatistics, mining robotics, water jet cutting, rock mechanics. *Unit head:* Dr. Jamal Rostami, Head, 303-273-3041, E-mail: rostami@mines.edu. *Application contact:* Justine Robinson, Program Manager, 303-273-3768, E-mail: justinerobinson@mines.edu.
Website: http://mining.mines.edu

Columbia University, Fu Foundation School of Engineering and Applied Science, Department of Civil Engineering and Engineering Mechanics, New York, NY 10027. Offers civil engineering (MS, Eng Sc D, PhD); construction engineering and management (MS); engineering mechanics (MS, Eng Sc D, PhD). *Program availability:* Part-time, online learning. Terminal master's awarded for partial completion of doctoral program. *Degree requirements:* For doctorate, thesis/dissertation, qualifying exam. *Entrance requirements:* For master's and doctorate, GRE General Test. Additional exam requirements/recommendations for international students: Required—TOEFL, IELTS, PTE. Electronic applications accepted. *Faculty research:* Structural dynamics, structural health and monitoring, fatigue and fracture mechanics, geo-environmental engineering, multiscale science and engineering.

Concordia University, School of Graduate Studies, Faculty of Engineering and Computer Science, Department of Building, Civil and Environmental Engineering, Montréal, QC H3G 1M8, Canada. Offers building engineering (M Eng, MA Sc, PhD, Certificate); civil engineering (M Eng, MA Sc, PhD); environmental engineering (Certificate). *Degree requirements:* For master's, thesis or alternative; for doctorate, comprehensive exam, thesis/dissertation. *Faculty research:* Structural engineering, geotechnical engineering, water resources and fluid engineering, transportation engineering, systems engineering.

George Mason University, Volgenau School of Engineering, Sid and Reva Dewberry Department of Civil, Environmental, and Infrastructure Engineering, Fairfax, VA 22030. Offers construction project management (MS); transportation engineering (PhD). *Faculty:* 16 full-time (4 women), 15 part-time/adjunct (4 women). *Students:* 59 full-time (20 women), 69 part-time (19 women); includes 34 minority (9 Black or African American, non-Hispanic/Latino; 14 Asian, non-Hispanic/Latino; 11 Hispanic/Latino), 46 international. Average age 28. 117 applicants, 75% accepted, 31 enrolled. In 2018, 39 master's, 8 doctorates awarded. *Degree requirements:* For master's, thesis (for some programs), 30 credits, departmental seminars; for doctorate, thesis/dissertation, qualifying exams. *Entrance requirements:* For master's, GRE, photocopy of passport; 2 official college transcripts; resume; official bank statement; proof of financial support; expanded goals statement; self-evaluation form; BS in engineering or other related science; 3 letters of recommendation; for doctorate, GRE (for those who received degree outside of the U.S.), photocopy of passport; 2 official college transcripts; resume; official bank statement; proof of financial support; expanded goals statement; self-evaluation form; baccalaureate degree in engineering or related science; master's degree (preferred); 3 letters of recommendation. Additional exam requirements/recommendations for international students: Required—TOEFL (minimum score 575 paper-based; 88 iBT), IELTS (minimum score 6.5), PTE (minimum score 59). *Application deadline:* For fall admission, 12/15 priority date for domestic and international students; for spring admission, 8/15 priority date for domestic and international students. Application fee: $75 ($80 for international students). Electronic applications accepted. *Expenses:* $589 per credit in-state, $1,346.75 per credit out-of-state. *Financial support:* In 2018–19, 37 students received support, including 25 research assistantships with tuition reimbursements available (averaging $19,626 per year), 13 teaching assistantships with tuition reimbursements available (averaging $17,449 per year); career-related internships or fieldwork, Federal Work-Study, scholarships/grants, unspecified assistantships, and health care benefits (for full-time research or teaching assistantship recipients) also available. Support available to part-time students. Financial award application deadline: 3/1; financial award applicants required to submit FAFSA. *Faculty research:* Evolutionary design, infrastructure security, intelligent transportation systems, national transportation networks, water quality modeling. *Total annual research expenditures:* $1.6 million. *Unit head:* LIza Wilson Durant, Acting Chair, 703-993-1687, Fax: 703-993-9790, E-mail: ldurant2@gmu.edu. *Application contact:* Laura Kosoglu, Director, Graduate Program, 703-993-1675, Fax: 703-993-9790, E-mail: ceiegrad@gmu.edu.
Website: http://civil.gmu.edu/

Illinois Institute of Technology, Graduate College, Armour College of Engineering, Department of Civil, Architectural and Environmental Engineering, Chicago, IL 60616. Offers architectural engineering (M Arch E); civil engineering (MS, PhD), including architectural engineering (MS), construction engineering and management (MS), geoenvironmental engineering (MS), geotechnical engineering (MS), structural engineering (MS), transportation engineering (MS); construction engineering and management (MCEM); environmental engineering (M Env E, MS, PhD); geoenvironmental engineering (M Geoenv E); geotechnical engineering (MGE); infrastructure engineering and management (MPW); structural engineering (MSE); transportation engineering (M Trans E). *Program availability:* Part-time, evening/weekend, online learning. Terminal master's awarded for partial completion of doctoral program. *Degree requirements:* For master's, thesis (for some programs); for doctorate, comprehensive exam, thesis/dissertation. *Entrance requirements:* For master's, GRE General Test (minimum score 900 Quantitative and Verbal, 2.5 Analytical Writing), minimum undergraduate GPA of 3.0; for doctorate, GRE General Test (minimum score 1000 Quantitative and Verbal, 3.0 Analytical Writing), minimum undergraduate GPA of 3.0. Additional exam requirements/recommendations for international students: Required—TOEFL (minimum score 550 paper-based; 80 iBT). Electronic applications accepted. *Faculty research:* Structural, architectural, geotechnical and geoenvironmental engineering; construction engineering and management; transportation engineering; environmental engineering and public works.

Iowa State University of Science and Technology, Department of Civil and Construction Engineering, Ames, IA 50011. Offers civil engineering (MS, PhD), including civil engineering materials, construction engineering and management, environmental engineering, geotechnical engineering, structural engineering, transportation engineering. *Degree requirements:* For master's, thesis or alternative; for doctorate, thesis/dissertation. *Entrance requirements:* For master's and doctorate, GRE General Test. Additional exam requirements/recommendations for international students: Required—TOEFL (minimum score 550 paper-based; 82 iBT), IELTS (minimum score 6.5). Electronic applications accepted.

Lawrence Technological University, College of Engineering, Southfield, MI 48075-1058. Offers architectural engineering (MS); automotive engineering (MS); biomedical engineering (MS); civil engineering (MA, MS, PhD), including environmental engineering (MS), geotechnical engineering (MS), structural engineering (MS), transportation engineering (MS), water resource engineering (MS); construction engineering management (MA); electrical and computer engineering (MS); engineering management (MEM); engineering technology (MS); fire engineering (MS); industrial engineering (MS), including healthcare systems; manufacturing systems (ME); mechanical engineering (MS, DE, PhD), including automotive engineering (MS), energy engineering (MS), manufacturing (DE), solid mechanics (MS), thermal/fluid systems (MS); mechatronic systems engineering (MS). *Program availability:* Part-time, evening/weekend. Terminal master's awarded for partial completion of doctoral program. *Degree requirements:* For master's, thesis optional; for doctorate, comprehensive exam, thesis/dissertation optional. *Entrance requirements:* Additional exam requirements/recommendations for international students: Required—TOEFL (minimum score 550 paper-based; 79 iBT), IELTS (minimum score 6.5). Electronic applications accepted. *Faculty research:* Innovative infrastructure and building structures and materials; connectivity and mobility; automotive systems modeling, simulation and testing; biomedical devices and materials; building mechanical/electrical systems.

Marquette University, Graduate School, College of Engineering, Department of Civil and Environmental Engineering, Milwaukee, WI 53201-1881. Offers construction engineering and management (MS, PhD, Certificate); environmental engineering (MS, PhD); structural design (Certificate); structural engineering and structural mechanics (MS, PhD); transportation (Certificate); transportation engineering and materials (MS, PhD); waste and wastewater treatment processes (Certificate); water resources engineering (Certificate). *Program availability:* Part-time, evening/weekend. Terminal master's awarded for partial completion of doctoral program. *Degree requirements:* For master's, comprehensive exam (for some programs), thesis or alternative; for doctorate, thesis/dissertation. *Entrance requirements:* For master's, GRE General Test (recommended), minimum GPA of 3.0, official transcripts from all current and previous colleges/universities except Marquette, three letters of recommendation; for doctorate, GRE General Test, minimum GPA of 3.0, official transcripts from all current and previous colleges/universities except Marquette, three letters of recommendation, brief statement of purpose, submission of any English language publications authored by applicant (strongly recommended). Additional exam requirements/recommendations for international students: Required—TOEFL (minimum score 530 paper-based). Electronic applications accepted. *Faculty research:* Highway safety, highway performance, and intelligent transportation systems; surface mount technology; watershed management.

Massachusetts Institute of Technology, School of Engineering, Department of Civil and Environmental Engineering, Cambridge, MA 02139. Offers biological oceanography (PhD, Sc D); chemical oceanography (PhD, Sc D); civil and environmental engineering (M Eng, SM, PhD, Sc D); civil and environmental systems (PhD, Sc D); civil engineering (PhD, Sc D, CE); civil engineering and computation (PhD); coastal engineering (PhD, Sc D); construction engineering and management (PhD, Sc D); environmental biology (PhD, Sc D); environmental chemistry (PhD, Sc D); environmental engineering (PhD, Sc D); environmental engineering and computation (PhD); environmental fluid mechanics (PhD, Sc D); geotechnical and geoenvironmental engineering (PhD, Sc D); hydrology (PhD, Sc D); information technology (PhD, Sc D); oceanographic engineering (PhD, Sc D); structures and materials (PhD, Sc D); transportation (PhD, Sc D); SM/MBA. *Degree requirements:* For master's, thesis; for doctorate, comprehensive exam, thesis/dissertation; for CE, comprehensive exam, thesis. *Entrance requirements:* For master's, doctorate, and CE, GRE General Test. Additional exam requirements/recommendations for international students: Required—TOEFL, IELTS. Electronic applications accepted. *Expenses: Tuition:* Full-time $51,520; part-time $800 per credit hour. *Required fees:* $312. *Faculty research:* Environmental chemistry, environmental fluid mechanics and coastal engineering, environmental microbiology, geotechnical engineering and geomechanics, hydrology and hydro climatology, infrastructure systems, mechanics of materials and structures, transportation systems.

Montana State University, The Graduate School, College of Engineering, Department of Civil Engineering, Bozeman, MT 59717. Offers civil engineering (MS); construction engineering management (MCEM); engineering (PhD), including applied mechanics option, civil engineering option. *Program availability:* Part-time. *Degree requirements:* For master's, comprehensive exam, thesis (for some programs); for doctorate, comprehensive exam, thesis/dissertation. *Entrance requirements:* For master's and doctorate, GRE General Test. Additional exam requirements/recommendations for international students: Required—TOEFL (minimum score 550 paper-based). Electronic applications accepted. *Faculty research:* Snow and ice mechanics, biofilm engineering, transportation, structural and geo materials, water resources.

Ohio University, Graduate College, Russ College of Engineering and Technology, Department of Civil Engineering, Athens, OH 45701-2979. Offers civil engineering (PhD); construction engineering and management (MS); environmental (MS); geoenvironmental (MS); geotechnical (MS); mechanics (MS); structures (MS); transportation (MS); water resources (MS). *Program availability:* Part-time. *Degree*

requirements: For master's, comprehensive exam (for some programs), thesis or alternative; for doctorate, comprehensive exam, thesis/dissertation. *Entrance requirements:* For master's, GRE General Test, minimum GPA of 3.0, 3 letters of recommendation; for doctorate, GRE General Test. Additional exam requirements/recommendations for international students: Required—TOEFL (minimum score 550 paper-based; 80 iBT) or IELTS (minimum score 6.5). Electronic applications accepted. *Faculty research:* Noise abatement, materials and environment, highway infrastructure, subsurface investigation (pavements, pipes, bridges).

Oregon State University, College of Engineering, Program in Civil Engineering, Corvallis, OR 97331. Offers civil engineering (M Eng, MS, PhD); coastal and ocean engineering (M Eng, MS, PhD); construction engineering management (M Eng, MS, PhD); engineering education (M Eng, MS, PhD); geomatics (M Eng, MS, PhD); geotechnical engineering (M Eng, MS, PhD); infrastructure materials (M Eng, MS, PhD); structural engineering (M Eng, MS, PhD); transportation engineering (M Eng). *Entrance requirements:* For master's and doctorate, GRE. Additional exam requirements/recommendations for international students: Required—TOEFL (minimum score 80 iBT), IELTS (minimum score 6.5). *Expenses:* Contact institution.

Pittsburg State University, Graduate School, College of Technology, School of Construction, Pittsburg, KS 66762. Offers construction engineering technology (MET); construction management (MS). *Program availability:* Part-time, 100% online, blended/hybrid learning. *Degree requirements:* For master's, thesis or alternative. *Entrance requirements:* Additional exam requirements/recommendations for international students: Required—TOEFL (minimum score 550 paper-based; 79 iBT), IELTS (minimum score 6.5), PTE (minimum score 53). Electronic applications accepted. *Expenses:* Contact institution.

Stanford University, School of Engineering, Department of Civil and Environmental Engineering, Stanford, CA 94305-2004. Offers atmosphere and energy (MS, PhD); construction (MS), including construction engineering and management, design-construction integration, sustainable design and construction; environmental engineering and science (MS, PhD, Eng); environmental fluid mechanics and hydrology (PhD); geomechanics (MS); structural engineering (MS). *Expenses: Tuition:* Full-time $50,703; part-time $32,970 per year. *Required fees:* $651. Website: http://www-ce.stanford.edu/

Stevens Institute of Technology, Graduate School, Charles V. Schaefer Jr. School of Engineering and Science, Department of Civil, Environmental, and Ocean Engineering, Program in Construction Management, Hoboken, NJ 07030. Offers construction management (MS, Certificate), including construction accounting/estimating (Certificate), construction engineering (Certificate), construction law/disputes (Certificate), construction/quality management (Certificate). *Program availability:* Part-time, evening/weekend. *Faculty:* 6 part-time/adjunct (1 woman). *Students:* 109 full-time (19 women), 21 part-time (7 women); includes 12 minority (4 Black or African American, non-Hispanic/Latino; 8 Asian, non-Hispanic/Latino), 100 international. Average age 25. In 2018, 49 master's, 3 other advanced degrees awarded. Terminal master's awarded for partial completion of doctoral program. *Degree requirements:* For master's, thesis optional, minimum B average in major field and overall; for Certificate, minimum B average. *Entrance requirements:* For master's, GRE/GMAT scores: GRE scores are required for all applicants applying to a full-time graduate program in the Schaefer School of Engineering and Science (SES). International applicants must submit TOEFL/IELTS scores and fulfill the English Language Proficiency Requirements in order to be considered. Additional exam requirements/recommendations for international students: Required—TOEFL (minimum score 74 iBT), IELTS (minimum score 6). *Application deadline:* For fall admission, 4/15 for domestic and international students; for spring admission, 11/1 for domestic and international students; for summer admission, 5/1 for domestic students. Applications are processed on a rolling basis. Application fee: $60. Electronic applications accepted. *Expenses: Tuition:* Full-time $35,960; part-time $1620 per credit. *Required fees:* $1290; $600 per semester. Tuition and fees vary according to course load. *Financial support:* Fellowships, research assistantships, teaching assistantships, career-related internships or fieldwork, Federal Work-Study, scholarships/grants, and unspecified assistantships available. Financial award application deadline: 2/15; financial award applicants required to submit FAFSA. *Unit head:* Dr. Jean Zu, Dean of SES, 201-216.8233, Fax: 201-216.8372, E-mail: Jean.Zu@stevens.edu. *Application contact:* Graduate Admission, 888-783-8367, Fax: 888-511-1306, E-mail: graduate@stevens.edu.

The University of Alabama, Graduate School, College of Engineering, Department of Civil, Construction and Environmental Engineering, Tuscaloosa, AL 35487-0205. Offers civil engineering (MSCE, PhD); environmental engineering (MS). *Program availability:* Part-time. Terminal master's awarded for partial completion of doctoral program. *Degree requirements:* For master's, thesis or alternative; for doctorate, comprehensive exam, thesis/dissertation. *Entrance requirements:* For master's and doctorate, GRE General Test (minimum combined score of 300), minimum overall GPA of 3.0 in last hours of course work. Additional exam requirements/recommendations for international students: Required—TOEFL (minimum score 550 paper-based; 79 iBT), IELTS (minimum score 6.5), PTE (minimum score 59). Electronic applications accepted. *Faculty research:* Experimental structures, modeling of structures, bridge management systems, geotechnological engineering, environmental remediation.

The University of Alabama at Birmingham, School of Engineering, Professional Engineering Degrees, Birmingham, AL 35294. Offers advanced safety engineering and management (M Eng); construction engineering management (M Eng); design and commercialization (M Eng); information engineering management (M Eng); structural engineering (M Eng); sustainable smart cities (M Eng). *Program availability:* Part-time, evening/weekend, online only, 100% online, blended/hybrid learning. *Faculty:* 6 full-time (1 woman), 12 part-time/adjunct (2 women). *Students:* 23 full-time (7 women), 315 part-time (63 women); includes 96 minority (73 Black or African American, non-Hispanic/Latino; 1 American Indian or Alaska Native, non-Hispanic/Latino; 8 Asian, non-Hispanic/Latino; 12 Hispanic/Latino; 2 Two or more races, non-Hispanic/Latino), 12 international. Average age 37. 154 applicants, 84% accepted, 91 enrolled. In 2018, 87 master's awarded. *Entrance requirements:* For master's, 3.0 GPA on 4.0 scale, undergraduate degree from a nationally accredited school. Additional exam requirements/recommendations for international students: Required—TOEFL (minimum score 80 iBT); Recommended—IELTS (minimum score 6.5). *Application deadline:* For fall admission, 8/1 for domestic and international students; for spring admission, 12/1 for domestic and international students; for summer admission, 5/1 for domestic and international students. Applications are processed on a rolling basis. Application fee: $50 ($60 for international students). Electronic applications accepted. *Expenses:* Contact institution. *Faculty research:* Orthopedic biomechanics, translational rehabilitation and assistive devices, innovation and entrepreneurship, anthropogenic activities and the natural environment, prestressed and spun concrete. *Application contact:* Jesse Kepply, Director of Student and Academic Services, 205-996-5696, E-mail: gradschool@uab.edu.

University of Alberta, Faculty of Graduate Studies and Research, Department of Civil and Environmental Engineering, Edmonton, AB T6G 2E1, Canada. Offers construction engineering and management (M Eng, M Sc, PhD); environmental engineering (M Eng, M Sc, PhD); environmental science (M Sc, PhD); geoenvironmental engineering

(M Eng, M Sc, PhD); geotechnical engineering (M Eng, M Sc, PhD); mining engineering (M Eng, M Sc, PhD); petroleum engineering (M Eng, M Sc, PhD); structural engineering (M Eng, M Sc, PhD); water resources (M Eng, M Sc, PhD). *Program availability:* Part-time, online learning. *Degree requirements:* For master's, thesis (for some programs); for doctorate, thesis/dissertation. *Entrance requirements:* For master's, minimum GPA of 3.0 in last 2 years of undergraduate studies; for doctorate, minimum GPA of 3.0. Additional exam requirements/recommendations for international students: Required—TOEFL (minimum score 550 paper-based). Electronic applications accepted. *Faculty research:* Mining.

University of Michigan, College of Engineering, Department of Civil and Environmental Engineering, Ann Arbor, MI 48109. Offers civil engineering (MSE, PhD, CE); construction engineering and management (M Eng, MSE); environmental engineering (MSE, PhD); structural engineering (M Eng); MBA/MSE. *Program availability:* Part-time. *Students:* 206 full-time (86 women), 6 part-time (3 women). 690 applicants, 41% accepted, 76 enrolled. In 2018, 65 master's, 18 doctorates awarded. Terminal master's awarded for partial completion of doctoral program. *Degree requirements:* For master's, thesis optional; for doctorate, comprehensive exam, thesis/dissertation, oral defense of dissertation, preliminary and written exams. *Entrance requirements:* For master's and doctorate, GRE General Test. Additional exam requirements/recommendations for international students: Required—TOEFL. *Application deadline:* Applications are processed on a rolling basis. Electronic applications accepted. *Financial support:* Fellowships, research assistantships, teaching assistantships, institutionally sponsored loans, and tuition waivers (partial) available. *Faculty research:* Construction engineering and management, geotechnical engineering, earthquake-resistant design of structures, environmental chemistry and microbiology, cost engineering, environmental and water resources engineering. *Total annual research expenditures:* $11.6 million. *Unit head:* Jerome Lynch, Department Chair, 734-615-5290, Fax: 734-764-4292, E-mail: jerlynch@umich.edu. *Application contact:* Kelley Archer, Graduate Coordinator, 734-647-2703, Fax: 734-764-4292, E-mail: krichko@umich.edu.
Website: https://cee.engin.umich.edu/

University of Missouri–Kansas City, School of Computing and Engineering, Kansas City, MO 64110-2499. Offers civil engineering (MS); computer and electrical engineering (PhD); computer science (MS), including bioinformatics, software engineering, telecommunications networking; computer science and informatics (PhD); computing (PhD); electrical engineering (MS); engineering (PhD); engineering and construction management (Graduate Certificate); mechanical engineering (MS); telecommunications and computer networking (PhD). PhD (interdisciplinary) offered through the School of Graduate Studies. *Program availability:* Part-time. *Degree requirements:* For doctorate, thesis/dissertation. *Entrance requirements:* For master's, GRE General Test, minimum GPA of 3.0, 3 letters of recommendation from professors; for doctorate, GRE General Test, minimum GPA of 3.5. Additional exam requirements/recommendations for international students: Required—TOEFL (minimum score 550 paper-based; 80 iBT). *Faculty research:* Algorithms, bioinformatics and medical informatics, biomechanics/biomaterials, civil engineering materials, networking and telecommunications, thermal science.

University of New Brunswick Fredericton, School of Graduate Studies, Faculty of Engineering, Department of Civil Engineering, Fredericton, NB E3B 5A3, Canada. Offers construction engineering and management (M Eng, M Sc E, PhD); environmental engineering (M Eng, M Sc E, PhD); environmental studies (M Eng); geotechnical engineering (M Eng, M Sc E, PhD); groundwater/hydrology (M Eng, M Sc E, PhD); materials (M Eng, M Sc E, PhD); pavements (M Eng, M Sc E, PhD); structures (M Eng, M Sc E, PhD); transportation (M Eng, M Sc E, PhD). *Program availability:* Part-time. *Degree requirements:* For master's, thesis; for doctorate, comprehensive exam, thesis/dissertation, qualifying exam; 27 credit hours of courses. *Entrance requirements:* For master's, minimum GPA of 3.0; B Sc E in civil engineering or related engineering degree; for doctorate, minimum GPA of 3.0; graduate degree in engineering or applied science. Additional exam requirements/recommendations for international students: Required—IELTS (minimum score 7.5), TWE (minimum score 4), Michigan English Language Assessment Battery (minimum score 85) or CanTest (minimum score 4.5); Recommended—TOEFL (minimum score 580 paper-based). Electronic applications accepted. *Faculty research:* Construction engineering and management; engineering materials and infrastructure renewal; highway and pavement research; structures and solid mechanics; geotechnical and geoenvironmental engineering; structure interaction; transportation and planning; environment, solid waste management; structural engineering; water and environmental engineering.

University of Puerto Rico–Mayagüez, Graduate Studies, College of Engineering, Department of Civil Engineering and Surveying, Mayagüez, PR 00681-9000. Offers civil engineering (ME, MS, PhD), including construction engineering and management (ME, MS), environmental engineering, geotechnical engineering (ME, MS), structural engineering, transportation engineering. *Program availability:* Part-time. Terminal master's awarded for partial completion of doctoral program. *Degree requirements:* For master's, one foreign language, thesis; for doctorate, one foreign language, comprehensive exam, thesis/dissertation, qualifying exams. *Entrance requirements:* For master's, proficiency in English and Spanish; BS in civil engineering or its equivalent; for doctorate, proficiency in English and Spanish. Electronic applications accepted. *Faculty research:* Structural design, concrete structure, finite elements, dynamic analysis, transportation, soils.

University of Southern Mississippi, College of Arts and Sciences, School of Construction and Design, Hattiesburg, MS 39406-0001. Offers logistics, trade and transportation (MS). *Program availability:* Part-time, online learning. *Degree requirements:* For master's, comprehensive exam, thesis optional. *Entrance requirements:* For master's, GMAT or GRE General Test, minimum GPA of 2.75 in last 60 hours. Additional exam requirements/recommendations for international students: Required—TOEFL, IELTS. *Faculty research:* Robotics; CAD/CAM; simulation; computer-integrated manufacturing processes; construction scheduling, estimating, and computer systems.

University of Virginia, School of Architecture, Program in the Constructed Environment, Charlottesville, VA 22903. Offers PhD. *Degree requirements:* For doctorate, thesis/dissertation. *Entrance requirements:* For doctorate, GRE, master's degree or equivalent, official transcripts, sample of academic writing, three letters of recommendation, resume or curriculum vitae, graphic portfolio. Additional exam requirements/recommendations for international students: Required—TOEFL.

University of Washington, Graduate School, College of Engineering, Department of Civil and Environmental Engineering, Seattle, WA 98195-2700. Offers construction engineering (MSCE, PhD); environmental engineering (MSCE, PhD); geotechnical engineering (MSCE, PhD); hydrology and hydrodynamics (MSCE, PhD); structural engineering and mechanics (MSCE, PhD); transportation engineering (MSCE, PhD). *Program availability:* Part-time, 100% online. *Faculty:* 38 full-time (10 women). *Students:* 239 full-time (104 women), 172 part-time (51 women); includes 91 minority (3 Black or African American, non-Hispanic/Latino; 2 American Indian or Alaska Native, non-Hispanic/Latino; 42 Asian, non-Hispanic/Latino; 26 Hispanic/Latino; 18 Two or more races, non-Hispanic/Latino), 120 international. Average age 28. 787 applicants, 57% accepted, 163 enrolled. In 2018, 161 master's, 11 doctorates awarded. Terminal master's awarded for partial completion of doctoral program. *Degree requirements:* For master's, thesis optional; for doctorate, comprehensive exam, thesis/dissertation, qualifying, general and final exams; completion of degree within 10 years. *Entrance requirements:* For master's, GRE General Test, minimum GPA of 3.0, statement of purpose, letters of recommendation, transcripts; for doctorate, GRE General Test, minimum GPA of 3.5, statement of purpose, letters of recommendation, transcripts, resume. Additional exam requirements/recommendations for international students: Required—TOEFL (minimum score 580 paper-based; 92 iBT); Recommended—IELTS (minimum score 7), TSE. *Application deadline:* For fall admission, 12/15 for domestic and international students. Applications are processed on a rolling basis. Application fee: $85. Electronic applications accepted. *Expenses:* Research-focused Master's and PhD: $18,852 resident; $32,760 nonresident. *Financial support:* In 2018–19, 120 students received support, including 23 fellowships with tuition reimbursements available (averaging $30,240 per year), 78 research assistantships with full tuition reimbursements available (averaging $30,240 per year), 28 teaching assistantships with full tuition reimbursements available (averaging $30,240 per year); scholarships/grants also available. Financial award application deadline: 12/15; financial award applicants required to submit FAFSA. *Faculty research:* Structural and geotechnical engineering, transportation and construction engineering, water and environmental engineering. *Total annual research expenditures:* $16.4 million. *Unit head:* Dr. Timothy V. Larson, Professor/Chair, 206-543-6815, Fax: 206-543-1543, E-mail: tlarson@uw.edu. *Application contact:* Melissa Pritchard, Graduate Adviser, 206-543-2574, Fax: 206-543-1543, E-mail: ceginfo@u.washington.edu.
Website: http://www.ce.washington.edu/

University of Wisconsin–Madison, Graduate School, College of Engineering, Department of Civil and Environmental Engineering, Madison, WI 53706-1380. Offers construction engineering and management (MS); environmental science and engineering (MS); geological/geotechnical engineering (MS); structural engineering (MS); transportation engineering (MS); water resources engineering (MS). *Program availability:* Part-time. *Faculty:* 31 full-time (8 women). *Students:* 97 full-time (28 women), 39 part-time (15 women); includes 12 minority (2 Black or African American, non-Hispanic/Latino; 3 Asian, non-Hispanic/Latino; 6 Hispanic/Latino; 1 Two or more races, non-Hispanic/Latino), 62 international. Average age 28. 261 applicants, 45% accepted, 29 enrolled. In 2018, 33 master's awarded. Terminal master's awarded for partial completion of doctoral program. *Degree requirements:* For master's, thesis (for some programs), minimum of 30 credits; minimum overall GPA of 3.0. *Entrance requirements:* For master's, GRE General Test, bachelor's degree; minimum GPA of 3.0 for last 60 credits of course work. Additional exam requirements/recommendations for international students: Required—TOEFL (minimum score 580 paper-based; 92 iBT). *Application deadline:* For fall admission, 12/15 priority date for domestic and international students; for spring admission, 10/1 for domestic and international students. Application fee: $75 ($81 for international students). Electronic applications accepted. *Expenses:* In-state tuition (Full-time): $10,728; Out-of-state tuition (full-time): $24,054; Fees: $1282; In-state tuition (per credit): $670; Out-of-state tuition (per credit): $1503; Fees (per credit): $126. *Financial support:* In 2018–19, 90 students received support, including 8 fellowships with full tuition reimbursements available (averaging $28,704 per year), 54 research assistantships with full tuition reimbursements available (averaging $23,784 per year), 21 teaching assistantships with full tuition reimbursements available (averaging $16,584 per year); Federal Work-Study, scholarships/grants, health care benefits, unspecified assistantships, and project assistantships also available. Support available to part-time students. Financial award application deadline: 12/1; financial award applicants required to submit FAFSA. *Faculty research:* Construction engineering and management; environmental engineering; structural engineering; transportation and city planning; water resources engineering; water chemistry. *Total annual research expenditures:* $12.5 million. *Unit head:* Dr. William Likos, Chair, 608-263-9490, Fax: 608-262-5199, E-mail: frontdesk@cee.wisc.edu. *Application contact:* Cheryl Loschko, Student Services Coordinator, 608-890-2420, E-mail: loschko@wisc.edu.
Website: https://www.engr.wisc.edu/department/civil-environmental-engineering/academics/ms-phd-civil-and-environmental-engineering/

Wentworth Institute of Technology, Master of Engineering in Civil Engineering Program, Boston, MA 02115-5998. Offers construction engineering (M Eng); infrastructure engineering (M Eng). *Program availability:* Part-time-only, evening/weekend. *Degree requirements:* For master's, thesis optional, capstone course. *Entrance requirements:* For master's, resume, statement of purpose, official transcripts, two professional recommendations, bachelor's degree, minimum GPA of 3.0, one year of professional experience in a technical role and/or technical organization. Additional exam requirements/recommendations for international students: Recommended—TOEFL (minimum score 550 paper-based). Electronic applications accepted. *Expenses:* Contact institution.

Environmental Engineering

Air Force Institute of Technology, Graduate School of Engineering and Management, Department of Systems and Engineering Management, Dayton, OH 45433-7765. Offers cost analysis (MS); environmental and engineering management (MS); environmental engineering science (MS); information resource/systems management (MS). *Accreditation:* ABET. *Program availability:* Part-time. *Degree requirements:* For master's, thesis. *Entrance requirements:* For master's, GRE, GMAT, minimum GPA of 3.0.

The American University in Cairo, School of Sciences and Engineering, Cairo, Egypt. Offers biotechnology (MS); chemistry (MS); computer science (MS); computing (M Comp); construction engineering (M Eng, MS); electronics and communications engineering (M Eng); environmental engineering (MS); environmental system design (M Eng); mechanical engineering (M Eng, MS); nanotechnology (MS); physics (MS); robotics, control and smart systems (MS); sciences and engineering (PhD); sustainable development (MS, Graduate Diploma). *Program availability:* Part-time, evening/weekend. *Degree requirements:* For master's, comprehensive exam (for some programs), thesis (for some programs); for doctorate, comprehensive exam (for some programs), thesis/dissertation. *Entrance requirements:* Additional exam requirements/recommendations for international students: Required—TOEFL (minimum score 450 paper-based; 45 iBT), IELTS (minimum score 5). Electronic applications accepted. *Faculty research:* Construction, mechanical, and electronics engineering; physics; computer science; biotechnology; nanotechnology; chemistry; robotics.

Arizona State University at the Tempe campus, Ira A. Fulton Schools of Engineering, School of Sustainable Engineering and the Built Environment, Tempe, AZ 85287-5306. Offers civil, environmental and sustainable engineering (MS, MSE, PhD); construction engineering (MSE); construction management (MS, PhD). *Program availability:* Part-time, evening/weekend, online learning. Terminal master's awarded for partial completion of doctoral program. *Degree requirements:* For master's, thesis optional, comprehensive exams (MSE); interactive Program of Study (iPOS) submitted before completing 50 percent of required credit hours; for doctorate, comprehensive exam, thesis/dissertation, interactive Program of Study (iPOS) submitted before completing 50 percent of required credit hours. *Entrance requirements:* For master's, GRE, minimum GPA of 3.0 or equivalent in last 2 years of work leading to bachelor's degree; for doctorate, GRE, minimum GPA of 3.0 in last 2 years of work leading to bachelor's degree, 3.2 in all graduate-level coursework with master's degree; 3 letters of recommendation; resume/curriculum vitae; letter of intent; thesis (if applicable); statement of research interests. Additional exam requirements/recommendations for international students: Required—TOEFL, IELTS, or PTE. Electronic applications accepted. *Expenses:* Contact institution. *Faculty research:* Water purification, transportation (safety and materials), construction management, environmental biotechnology, environmental nanotechnology, earth systems engineering and management, SMART innovations, project performance metrics, and underground infrastructure.

California Institute of Technology, Division of Engineering and Applied Science, Option in Environmental Science and Engineering, Pasadena, CA 91125-0001. Offers MS, PhD. *Degree requirements:* For doctorate, thesis/dissertation. Electronic applications accepted. *Faculty research:* Chemistry of natural waters, physics and chemistry of particulates, fluid mechanics of the natural environment, pollutant formation and control, environmental modeling systems.

California Institute of Technology, Division of Geological and Planetary Sciences, Pasadena, CA 91125-0001. Offers environmental science and engineering (MS, PhD); geobiology (MS, PhD); geochemistry (MS, PhD); geology (MS, PhD); geophysics (MS, PhD); planetary science (MS, PhD). *Degree requirements:* For doctorate, thesis/dissertation. *Entrance requirements:* For doctorate, GRE General Test. Additional exam requirements/recommendations for international students: Required—TOEFL; Recommended—IELTS, TWE. Electronic applications accepted. *Faculty research:* Planetary surfaces, evolution of anaerobic respiratory processes, structural geology and tectonics, theoretical and numerical seismology, global biogeochemical cycles.

California Polytechnic State University, San Luis Obispo, College of Engineering, Department of Civil and Environmental Engineering, San Luis Obispo, CA 93407. Offers MS. *Program availability:* Part-time. *Faculty:* 11 full-time (3 women), 2 part-time/adjunct (0 women). *Students:* 36 full-time (16 women), 5 part-time (0 women); includes 16 minority (8 Asian, non-Hispanic/Latino; 5 Hispanic/Latino; 3 Two or more races, non-Hispanic/Latino), 3 international. Average age 23. 73 applicants, 59% accepted, 24 enrolled. In 2018, 48 master's awarded. *Degree requirements:* For master's, comprehensive exam (for some programs), thesis (for some programs). *Entrance requirements:* For master's, GRE. Additional exam requirements/recommendations for international students: Required—TOEFL (minimum score 80 iBT). *Application deadline:* For fall admission, 1/1 for domestic students, 3/1 priority date for international students. Applications are processed on a rolling basis. Application fee: $55. Electronic applications accepted. *Expenses: Tuition, area resident:* Full-time $7176; part-time $4164 per year. Tuition, state resident: full-time $10,965. Tuition, nonresident: full-time $10,965. *Required fees:* $6336; $3711. *Financial support:* Fellowships, research assistantships, teaching assistantships, career-related internships or fieldwork, and scholarships/grants available. Financial award application deadline: 3/2; financial award applicants required to submit FAFSA. *Faculty research:* Transportation and traffic, environmental protection, geotechnology, water engineering. *Unit head:* Dr. Robb Moss, Graduate Coordinator, 805-756-6427, E-mail: rmoss@calpoly.edu. *Application contact:* Dr. Robb Moss, Graduate Coordinator, 805-756-6427, E-mail: rmoss@calpoly.edu. Website: http://ceenve.calpoly.edu

California State University, Fullerton, Graduate Studies, College of Engineering and Computer Science, Department of Civil and Environmental Engineering, Fullerton, CA 92831-3599. Offers civil engineering (MS), including architectural engineering, environmental engineering. *Program availability:* Part-time. *Degree requirements:* For master's, comprehensive exam, project or thesis. *Entrance requirements:* For master's, minimum undergraduate GPA of 2.5. *Faculty research:* Soil-structure interaction, finite-element analysis, computer-aided analysis and design.

Carleton University, Faculty of Graduate Studies, Faculty of Engineering and Design, Department of Civil and Environmental Engineering, Ottawa, ON K1S 5B6, Canada. Offers M Eng, MA Sc, PhD. *Degree requirements:* For master's, thesis optional; for doctorate, thesis/dissertation. *Entrance requirements:* For master's, honors degree; for doctorate, MA Sc or M Eng. Additional exam requirements/recommendations for international students: Required—TOEFL. *Faculty research:* Pollution and wastewater management, fire safety engineering, earthquake engineering, structural design, bridge engineering.

Carnegie Mellon University, Carnegie Institute of Technology, Department of Civil and Environmental Engineering, Pittsburgh, PA 15213. Offers advanced infrastructure systems (MS, PhD); advanced infrastructure systems technology development and application (MS); air quality engineering and science (MS); civil and environmental engineering (MS, PhD); civil and environmental engineering/engineering and public policy (PhD); civil engineering (MS, PhD); computational mechanics (MS, PhD); computational modeling and monitoring for resilient structural and material systems (MS); energy infrastructure systems (MS); environmental engineering (MS, PhD); environmental management and science (MS, PhD); IT-based sustainable global infrastructure and construction management (MS); sustainability and green design (MS); water quality engineering and science (MS). *Program availability:* Part-time. *Faculty:* 23 full-time (5 women), 12 part-time/adjunct (3 women). *Students:* 264 full-time (109 women); includes 24 minority (6 Black or African American, non-Hispanic/Latino; 13 Asian, non-Hispanic/Latino; 5 Hispanic/Latino), 208 international. Average age 25. 630 applicants, 64% accepted, 114 enrolled. In 2018, 112 master's, 15 doctorates awarded. Terminal master's awarded for partial completion of doctoral program. *Degree requirements:* For master's, thesis optional; for doctorate, comprehensive exam, thesis/dissertation, two-part qualifying exam, public defense of dissertation. *Entrance requirements:* For master's, GRE General Test, BS in engineering, science or mathematics; for doctorate, GRE General Test, BS or MS in engineering, science or mathematics. Additional exam requirements/recommendations for international students: Required—TOEFL (minimum score 84 iBT), TOEFL (minimum score 84 iBT) or IELTS (7.0). *Application deadline:* For fall admission, 1/5 priority date for domestic and international students; for spring admission, 9/15 priority date for domestic and international students. Applications are processed on a rolling basis. Application fee: $75. Electronic applications accepted. *Expenses:* Contact institution. *Financial support:* In 2018–19, 137 students received support. Fellowships with tuition reimbursements available, research assistantships with tuition reimbursements available, scholarships/grants, health care benefits, tuition waivers (full and partial), unspecified assistantships, and service assistantships available. Financial award application deadline: 1/5. *Faculty research:* Advanced infrastructure systems; environmental engineering, sustainability, and science; mechanics, materials, and computing. *Total annual research expenditures:* $7.4 million. *Unit head:* Dr. David A. Dzombak, Professor and Department Head, 412-268-2941, Fax: 412-268-7813, E-mail: dzombak@cmu.edu. *Application contact:* David A. Vey, Director of Graduate Programs, 412-268-2292, Fax: 412-268-7813, E-mail: dvey@andrew.cmu.edu. Website: http://www.cmu.edu/cee/

Carnegie Mellon University, Tepper School of Business, Pittsburgh, PA 15213-3891. Offers accounting (PhD); business management and software engineering (MBMSE); business technologies (PhD); civil engineering and industrial management (MS); computational finance (MSCF); economics (PhD); environmental engineering and management (MEEM); financial economics (PhD); industrial administration (MBA), including administration and public management; marketing (PhD); mathematical finance (PhD); operations management (PhD); operations research (PhD); organizational behavior and theory (PhD); production and operations management (PhD); public policy and management (MS, MSED); software engineering and business management (MS); JD/MS; JD/MSIA; M Div/MS; MOM/MSIA; MSCF/MSIA. JD/MSIA offered jointly with University of Pittsburgh. *Program availability:* Part-time. Terminal master's awarded for partial completion of doctoral program. *Degree requirements:* For doctorate, thesis/dissertation. *Entrance requirements:* For master's, GMAT. Additional exam requirements/recommendations for international students: Required—TOEFL. *Expenses:* Contact institution.

The Catholic University of America, School of Engineering, Department of Mechanical Engineering, Washington, DC 20064. Offers energy and environment (MME); general (MME); mechanical engineering (MSE, PhD). *Program availability:* Part-time. *Faculty:* 9 full-time (0 women), 7 part-time/adjunct (0 women). *Students:* 11 full-time (4 women), 32 part-time (8 women); includes 7 minority (1 Black or African American, non-Hispanic/Latino; 1 Asian, non-Hispanic/Latino; 1 Hispanic/Latino; 4 Two or more races, non-Hispanic/Latino), 8 international. Average age 31. 27 applicants, 81% accepted, 8 enrolled. In 2018, 13 master's, 1 doctorate awarded. Terminal master's awarded for partial completion of doctoral program. *Degree requirements:* For master's, thesis (for some programs); for doctorate, comprehensive exam, thesis/dissertation. *Entrance requirements:* For master's and doctorate, statement of purpose, official copies of academic transcripts, three letters of recommendation. Additional exam requirements/recommendations for international students: Required—TOEFL (minimum score 550 paper-based; 80 iBT). *Application deadline:* For fall admission, 7/15 priority date for domestic students, 7/1 for international students; for spring admission, 11/15 priority date for domestic students, 11/1 for international students. Applications are processed on a rolling basis. Application fee: $55. Electronic applications accepted. *Expenses:* Contact institution. *Financial support:* Fellowships, research assistantships, teaching assistantships, Federal Work-Study, scholarships/grants, tuition waivers (full and partial), and unspecified assistantships available. Financial award application deadline: 2/1; financial award applicants required to submit FAFSA. *Faculty research:* Energy and environment, acoustics and vibration, biofabrication and lab-on-chip, experimental mechanics, smart materials. *Unit head:* Dr. Sen Nieh, Chair, 202-319-5170, Fax: 202-319-5173, E-mail: nieh@cua.edu. *Application contact:* Dr. Steven Brown, Director of Graduate Admissions, 202-319-5057, Fax: 202-319-6533, E-mail: cua-admissions@cua.edu. Website: https://engineering.catholic.edu/mechanical/index.html

Clarkson University, Institute for a Sustainable Environment, Program in Environmental Science and Engineering, Potsdam, NY 13699. Offers MS, PhD. *Program availability:* Part-time. *Students:* 17 full-time (8 women), 9 international. 18 applicants, 72% accepted, 4 enrolled. In 2018, 1 master's, 3 doctorates awarded. *Degree requirements:* For master's, thesis; for doctorate, comprehensive exam, thesis/dissertation. *Entrance requirements:* For master's and doctorate, GRE. Additional exam requirements/recommendations for international students: Required—TOEFL (minimum score 550 paper-based, 80 iBT) or IELTS (6.5). *Application deadline:* Applications are processed on a rolling basis. Application fee: $50. Electronic applications accepted. *Expenses: Tuition:* Full-time $24,984; part-time $1388 per credit hour. *Required fees:* $225. Tuition and fees vary according to campus/location and program. *Financial support:* Scholarships/grants and unspecified assistantships available. *Unit head:* Dr. Susan Powers, Director of the Institute for a Sustainable Environment/Associate Director of Sustainability, 315-268-6542, E-mail: spowers@clarkson.edu. *Application contact:* Dan Capogna, Director of Graduate Admissions & Recruitment, 518-631-9910, E-mail: graduate@clarkson.edu. Website: https://www.clarkson.edu/academics/graduate

Clarkson University, Wallace H. Coulter School of Engineering, Department of Civil and Environmental Engineering, Potsdam, NY 13699. Offers ME, MS, PhD. *Faculty:* 18 full-time (3 women), 6 part-time/adjunct (1 woman). *Students:* 27 full-time (12 women), 2 part-time (1 woman); includes 1 minority (Hispanic/Latino), 17 international. 47 applicants, 55% accepted, 11 enrolled. In 2018, 7 master's, 4 doctorates awarded. *Degree requirements:* For master's, thesis (for MS); project (for ME); for doctorate, comprehensive exam, thesis/dissertation. *Entrance requirements:* For master's and doctorate, GRE. Additional exam requirements/recommendations for international students: Required—TOEFL (minimum score 550 paper-based, 80 iBT) or IELTS (6.5). *Application deadline:* Applications are processed on a rolling basis. Application fee: $50. Electronic applications accepted. *Expenses: Tuition:* Full-time $24,984; part-time $1388 per credit hour. *Required fees:* $225. Tuition and fees vary according to campus/location and program. *Financial support:* Scholarships/grants and unspecified assistantships available. *Unit head:* Dr. John Dempsey, Chair of Civil and Environmental Engineering, 315-268-6529, E-mail: jdempsey@clarkson.edu. *Application contact:* Dan Capogna, Director of Graduate Admissions, 518-631-9910, E-mail: graduate@clarkson.edu. Website: https://www.clarkson.edu/academics/graduate

Clemson University, Graduate School, College of Engineering, Computing and Applied Sciences, Department of Environmental Engineering and Earth Sciences, Anderson, SC 29625. Offers biosystems engineering (MS, PhD); environmental engineering and science (MS, PhD); environmental health physics (MS); hydrogeology (MS). *Program availability:* Part-time. *Faculty:* 20 full-time (4 women). *Students:* 75 full-time (30 women), 16 part-time (5 women); includes 5 minority (1 Black or African American, non-Hispanic/Latino; 1 Native Hawaiian or other Pacific Islander, non-Hispanic/Latino; 3 Two or more races, non-Hispanic/Latino), 30 international. Average age 26. 118 applicants, 72% accepted, 24 enrolled. In 2018, 31 master's, 4 doctorates awarded. *Degree requirements:* For master's, thesis or alternative; for doctorate, comprehensive exam, thesis/dissertation. *Entrance requirements:* For master's and doctorate, GRE General Test, unofficial transcripts, letters of recommendation. Additional exam requirements/recommendations for international students: Required—TOEFL (minimum score 80 paper-based; 80 iBT); Recommended—IELTS (minimum score 6.5), TSE (minimum score 54). *Application deadline:* For fall admission, 2/15 for domestic and international students. Applications are processed on a rolling basis. Application fee: $80 ($90 for international students). Electronic applications accepted. *Expenses:* $6823 per

semester full-time resident, $14023 per semester full-time non-resident, $833 per credit hour part-time resident, $1731 per credit hour part-time non-resident, online $1264 per credit hour, $4938 doctoral programs resident, $10405 doctoral programs non-resident, $1144 full-time graduate assistant, other fees may apply per session. *Financial support:* In 2018–19, 60 students received support, including 5 fellowships with full and partial tuition reimbursements available (averaging $3,573 per year), 34 research assistantships with full and partial tuition reimbursements available (averaging $18,464 per year), 19 teaching assistantships with full and partial tuition reimbursements available (averaging $18,021 per year); career-related internships or fieldwork and unspecified assistantships also available. Financial award application deadline: 2/15. *Faculty research:* Environmental engineering, bioprocess and ecological engineering, nuclear environmental engineering and science, hydrogeology, environmental chemistry and microbiology. *Total annual research expenditures:* $5.4 million. *Unit head:* Dr. David Freedman, Department Chair, 864-656-5566, E-mail: dfreedm@clemson.edu. *Application contact:* Dr. Mark Schlautman, Graduate Program Coordinator, 864-656-4059, E-mail: mschlau@clemson.edu.
Website: https://www.clemson.edu/cecas/departments/eees/

Cleveland State University, College of Graduate Studies, Fenn College of Engineering, Department of Civil and Environmental Engineering, Cleveland, OH 44115. Offers MS, D Eng. *Program availability:* Part-time, evening/weekend. *Faculty:* 8 full-time (2 women). *Students:* 25 full-time (9 women), 30 part-time (5 women); includes 3 minority (2 Asian, non-Hispanic/Latino; 1 Hispanic/Latino), 33 international. Average age 25. 214 applicants, 61% accepted, 21 enrolled. In 2018, 42 master's, 1 doctorate awarded. *Entrance requirements:* For master's, GRE General Test, GRE Subject Test, minimum GPA of 2.75; for doctorate, GRE General Test, GRE Subject Test, minimum GPA of 3.25. Additional exam requirements/recommendations for international students: Required—TOEFL (minimum score 550 paper-based; 78 iBT). *Application deadline:* Applications are processed on a rolling basis. Application fee: $40. Electronic applications accepted. *Expenses:* Tuition, state resident: full-time $7232.55; part-time $6676 per credit hour. Tuition, nonresident: full-time $12,375. *International tuition:* $18,914 full-time. *Required fees:* $80; $80 $40. Tuition and fees vary according to program. *Financial support:* Research assistantships, teaching assistantships, career-related internships or fieldwork, scholarships/grants, and unspecified assistantships available. Financial award application deadline: 9/1. *Faculty research:* Solid-waste disposal, constitutive modeling, transportation, safety engineering, concrete materials. *Total annual research expenditures:* $800,000. *Unit head:* Dr. Norbert Joseph Delatte, Chairperson, 216-687-9259, Fax: 216-687-5395, E-mail: n.delatte@csuohio.edu. *Application contact:* Deborah L. Brown, Interim Assistant Director, Graduate Admissions, 216-523-7572, Fax: 216-687-9214, E-mail: d.l.brown@csuohio.edu.
Website: http://www.csuohio.edu/engineering/civil

Colorado School of Mines, Office of Graduate Studies, Department of Civil and Environmental Engineering, Golden, CO 80401. Offers civil and environmental engineering (MS, PhD); environmental engineering science (MS, PhD); hydrologic science and engineering (MS, PhD); underground construction and tunneling (MS, PhD). *Program availability:* Part-time. *Faculty:* 44 full-time (16 women), 11 part-time/adjunct (6 women). *Students:* 99 full-time (46 women), 23 part-time (10 women); includes 15 minority (2 Black or African American, non-Hispanic/Latino; 3 Asian, non-Hispanic/Latino; 4 Hispanic/Latino; 6 Two or more races, non-Hispanic/Latino), 21 international. Average age 28. 171 applicants, 60% accepted, 47 enrolled. In 2018, 45 master's, 13 doctorates awarded. *Degree requirements:* For master's, thesis (for some programs); for doctorate, comprehensive exam, thesis/dissertation. *Entrance requirements:* For master's and doctorate, GRE General Test. Additional exam requirements/recommendations for international students: Required—TOEFL (minimum score 550 paper-based; 79 iBT). *Application deadline:* For fall admission, 12/15 priority date for domestic students, 1/15 priority date for international students; for spring admission, 9/1 priority date for domestic and international students. Application fee: $60 ($80 for international students). Electronic applications accepted. *Expenses:* Tuition, state resident: full-time $16,650; part-time $925 per contact hour. Tuition, nonresident: full-time $36,270; part-time $2015 per contact hour. *International tuition:* $36,270 full-time. *Required fees:* $2314; $2314 per semester. *Financial support:* In 2018–19, 62 research assistantships with full tuition reimbursements, 2 teaching assistantships with full tuition reimbursements were awarded; scholarships/grants, health care benefits, and unspecified assistantships also available. Financial award application deadline: 12/15; financial award applicants required to submit FAFSA. *Faculty research:* Treatment of water and wastes, environmental law: policy and practice, natural environment systems, hazardous waste management, environmental data analysis. *Unit head:* Dr. Terri Hogue, Department Head, 303-384-2588, E-mail: thogue@mines.edu. *Application contact:* Dr. Tim VanHaverbeke, Research Faculty/Program Manager, 303-273-3467, E-mail: tvanhave@mines.edu.

Columbia University, Fu Foundation School of Engineering and Applied Science, Department of Earth and Environmental Engineering, New York, NY 10027. Offers earth and environmental engineering (Eng Sc D, PhD); earth resources engineering (MS); MS/PhD. *Program availability:* Part-time, online learning. Terminal master's awarded for partial completion of doctoral program. *Degree requirements:* For master's, thesis; for doctorate, thesis/dissertation, qualifying exam. *Entrance requirements:* For master's and doctorate, GRE General Test. Additional exam requirements/recommendations for international students: Required—TOEFL, IELTS, PTE. Electronic applications accepted. *Faculty research:* Sustainable energy and materials, waste to energy, water resources and climate risks, environmental health engineering, life cycle analysis.

Concordia University, School of Graduate Studies, Faculty of Engineering and Computer Science, Department of Building, Civil and Environmental Engineering, Montréal, QC H3G 1M8, Canada. Offers building engineering (M Eng, MA Sc, PhD, Certificate); civil engineering (M Eng, MA Sc, PhD); environmental engineering (Certificate). *Degree requirements:* For master's, thesis or alternative; for doctorate, comprehensive exam, thesis/dissertation. *Faculty research:* Structural engineering, geotechnical engineering, water resources and fluid engineering, transportation engineering, systems engineering.

Cornell University, Graduate School, Graduate Fields of Engineering, Field of Civil and Environmental Engineering, Ithaca, NY 14853. Offers engineering management (M Eng, MS, PhD); environmental engineering (M Eng, MS, PhD); environmental fluid mechanics and hydrology (M Eng, MS, PhD); environmental systems engineering (M Eng, MS, PhD); geotechnical engineering (M Eng, MS, PhD); remote sensing (M Eng, MS, PhD); structural engineering (M Eng, MS, PhD); structural mechanics (M Eng, MS); transportation engineering (MS, PhD); transportation systems engineering (M Eng); water resource systems (M Eng, MS, PhD). Terminal master's awarded for partial completion of doctoral program. *Degree requirements:* For master's, thesis (MS); for doctorate, comprehensive exam, thesis/dissertation. *Entrance requirements:* For master's and doctorate, GRE General Test (recommended), 2 letters of recommendation. Additional exam requirements/recommendations for international students: Required—TOEFL (minimum score 600 paper-based; 77 iBT). Electronic applications accepted. *Faculty research:* Environmental engineering, geotechnical engineering, remote sensing, environmental fluid mechanics and hydrology, structural engineering.

Dalhousie University, Faculty of Engineering, Department of Civil and Resource Engineering, Halifax, NS B3J 2X4, Canada. Offers civil engineering (M Eng, MA Sc, PhD); environmental engineering (M Eng, MA Sc); mineral resource engineering (M Eng, MA Sc, PhD). *Degree requirements:* For master's, thesis; for doctorate, thesis/dissertation. *Entrance requirements:* Additional exam requirements/recommendations for international students: Required—TOEFL, IELTS, CANTEST, CAEL, or Michigan English Language Assessment Battery. Electronic applications accepted. *Faculty research:* Environmental/water resources, bridge engineering, geotechnical engineering, pavement design and management/highway materials, composite materials.

Drexel University, College of Engineering, Department of Civil, Architectural, and Environmental Engineering, Program in Environmental Engineering, Philadelphia, PA 19104-2875. Offers MS, PhD. *Program availability:* Part-time, evening/weekend. Terminal master's awarded for partial completion of doctoral program. *Degree requirements:* For master's, thesis optional; for doctorate, thesis/dissertation. Electronic applications accepted.

Drexel University, College of Engineering, Department of Civil, Architectural, and Environmental Engineering, Program in Geotechnical, Geoenvironmental and Geosynthetics Engineering, Philadelphia, PA 19104-2875. Offers MS, PhD.

Duke University, Graduate School, Pratt School of Engineering, Department of Civil and Environmental Engineering, Durham, NC 27708. Offers civil and environmental engineering (MS, PhD); civil engineering (M Eng); computational mechanics and scientific computing (M Eng); environmental engineering (M Eng, MS, PhD); risk engineering (M Eng). Terminal master's awarded for partial completion of doctoral program. *Degree requirements:* For doctorate, thesis/dissertation. *Entrance requirements:* For master's and doctorate, GRE General Test. Additional exam requirements/recommendations for international students: Required—TOEFL (minimum score 550 paper-based; 90 iBT), IELTS (minimum score 7). Electronic applications accepted. *Faculty research:* Environmental process engineering, hydrology and fluid dynamics, materials, structures and geo-systems.

Duke University, Graduate School, Pratt School of Engineering, Master of Engineering Program, Durham, NC 27708-0271. Offers biomedical engineering (M Eng); civil engineering (M Eng); computational mechanics and scientific computing (M Eng); electrical and computer engineering (M Eng); environmental engineering (M Eng); materials science and engineering (M Eng); mechanical engineering (M Eng); photonics and optical sciences (M Eng); risk engineering (M Eng). *Program availability:* Part-time. *Entrance requirements:* For master's, GRE General Test, resume, 3 letters of recommendation, statement of purpose, transcripts. Additional exam requirements/recommendations for international students: Required—TOEFL. Electronic applications accepted.

École Polytechnique de Montréal, Graduate Programs, Department of Civil, Geological and Mining Engineering, Montréal, QC H3C 3A7, Canada. Offers civil, geological and mining engineering (DESS); environmental engineering (M Eng, M Sc A, PhD); geotechnical engineering (M Eng, M Sc A, PhD); hydraulics engineering (M Eng, M Sc A, PhD); structural engineering (M Eng, M Sc A, PhD); transportation engineering (M Eng, M Sc A, PhD). *Program availability:* Part-time. *Degree requirements:* For master's, one foreign language, thesis; for doctorate, one foreign language, thesis/dissertation. *Entrance requirements:* For master's, minimum GPA of 2.75; for doctorate, minimum GPA of 3.0. *Faculty research:* Water resources management, characteristics of building materials, aging of dams, pollution control.

Florida Atlantic University, College of Engineering and Computer Science, Department of Civil, Environmental and Geomatics Engineering, Boca Raton, FL 33431-0991. Offers civil engineering (MS); environmental engineering (MS). *Program availability:* Part-time, evening/weekend. *Faculty:* 13 full-time (0 women), 1 part-time/adjunct (0 women). *Students:* 13 full-time (7 women), 23 part-time (10 women); includes 9 minority (2 Black or African American, non-Hispanic/Latino; 7 Hispanic/Latino), 18 international. Average age 28. 36 applicants, 44% accepted, 10 enrolled. In 2018, 10 master's awarded. *Degree requirements:* For master's, thesis optional. *Entrance requirements:* For master's, GRE General Test, minimum GPA of 3.0 in last 60 hours of undergraduate course work. Additional exam requirements/recommendations for international students: Required—TOEFL (minimum score 550 paper-based; 61 iBT), IELTS (minimum score 6). *Application deadline:* For fall admission, 7/1 priority date for domestic students, 2/15 for international students; for spring admission, 11/1 for domestic students, 7/15 for international students. Applications are processed on a rolling basis. Application fee: $30. *Expenses: Tuition, area resident:* Full-time $7400; part-time $369.82 per credit. Tuition, state resident: full-time $7400; part-time $369.82 per credit. Tuition, nonresident: full-time $20,496; part-time $1024.81 per credit. *Financial support:* Research assistantships with full tuition reimbursements, teaching assistantships with full tuition reimbursements, career-related internships or fieldwork, Federal Work-Study, scholarships/grants, and unspecified assistantships available. Financial award applicants required to submit FAFSA. *Faculty research:* Structures, geotechnical engineering, environmental and water resources engineering, transportation engineering, materials. *Unit head:* Dr. Yan Yong, Chair, 561-297-3445, Fax: 561-297-0493, E-mail: cege@fau.edu. *Application contact:* Dr. Frederick Bloetscher, Associate Dean & Professor, 561-297-0744, E-mail: fbloetsch@fau.edu.
Website: http://www.cege.fau.edu/

Florida International University, College of Engineering and Computing, Department of Civil and Environmental Engineering, Miami, FL 33175. Offers civil engineering (MS, PhD); environmental engineering (MS). *Program availability:* Part-time, evening/weekend, online learning. *Faculty:* 24 full-time (7 women), 11 part-time/adjunct (2 women). *Students:* 82 full-time (28 women), 22 part-time (6 women); includes 33 minority (4 Black or African American, non-Hispanic/Latino; 27 Hispanic/Latino; 2 Two or more races, non-Hispanic/Latino), 66 international. Average age 30. 119 applicants, 43% accepted, 18 enrolled. In 2018, 21 master's, 10 doctorates awarded. Terminal master's awarded for partial completion of doctoral program. *Degree requirements:* For master's, thesis or alternative; for doctorate, comprehensive exam, thesis/dissertation. *Entrance requirements:* For master's, bachelor's degree in related field, 3 letters of recommendation, minimum GPA of 3.0; for doctorate, GRE General Test, minimum graduate GPA of 3.3, 3 letters of recommendation, master's degree, resume, statement of purpose. Additional exam requirements/recommendations for international students: Required—TOEFL (minimum score 550 paper-based; 80 iBT). *Application deadline:* For fall admission, 6/1 for domestic students, 4/1 for international students; for spring admission, 10/1 for domestic students, 9/1 for international students. Applications are processed on a rolling basis. Application fee: $30. Electronic applications accepted. *Financial support:* Federal Work-Study, institutionally sponsored loans, scholarships/grants, health care benefits, and unspecified assistantships available. Financial award application deadline: 3/1; financial award applicants required to submit FAFSA. *Faculty research:* Structural engineering, wind engineering, water resources engineering, transportation engineering, environmental engineering. *Unit head:* Dr. Atorod Azizinamini, Chair, 305-348-2824, Fax: 305-348-2802, E-mail: aazizina@fiu.edu. *Application contact:* Nanett Rojas, Manager, Admissions Operations, 305-348-7464, Fax: 305-348-7441, E-mail: gradadm@fiu.edu.
Website: http://cec.fiu.edu

Florida State University, The Graduate School, FAMU-FSU College of Engineering, Department of Civil and Environmental Engineering, Tallahassee, FL 32310. Offers M Eng, MS, PhD. *Program availability:* Part-time. *Degree requirements:* For master's, comprehensive exam, thesis optional; for doctorate, thesis/dissertation. *Entrance requirements:* For master's, GRE General Test (minimum score 1000 in old version), BS in engineering or related field, minimum GPA of 3.0; for doctorate, GRE General Test, master's degree in engineering or related field, minimum GPA of 3.0. Additional exam requirements/recommendations for international students: Required—TOEFL (minimum score 550 paper-based; 80 iBT); Recommended—IELTS (minimum score 6.5). Electronic applications accepted. *Expenses: Tuition, area resident:* Part-time $479.32 per credit hour. Tuition and fees vary according to campus/location and program. *Faculty research:* Tidal hydraulics, temperature effects on bridge girders, codes for coastal construction, field performance of pine bridges, river basin management, transportation pavement design, soil dynamics, structural analysis.

Gannon University, School of Graduate Studies, College of Engineering and Business, School of Engineering and Computer Science, Program in Environmental Science and Engineering, Erie, PA 16541-0001. Offers environmental health (MSEH); environmental health and engineering (MS). *Program availability:* Part-time, evening/weekend. *Degree requirements:* For master's, thesis (for some programs), research paper or project (for some programs). *Entrance requirements:* For master's, GRE, bachelor's degree in science or engineering from an accredited college or university. Additional exam requirements/recommendations for international students: Required—TOEFL (minimum score 79 iBT), GRE. Electronic applications accepted. Application fee is waived when completed online.

The George Washington University, School of Engineering and Applied Science, Department of Civil and Environmental Engineering, Washington, DC 20052. Offers MS, PhD, App Sc, Engr, Graduate Certificate. *Program availability:* Part-time, evening/weekend. *Faculty:* 13 full-time (3 women), 5 part-time/adjunct (0 women). *Students:* 31 full-time (14 women), 17 part-time (6 women); includes 3 minority (2 Black or African American, non-Hispanic/Latino; 1 Asian, non-Hispanic/Latino), 41 international. Average age 27. 156 applicants, 51% accepted, 13 enrolled. In 2018, 13 master's, 2 doctorates awarded. *Degree requirements:* For master's, thesis optional; for doctorate, thesis/dissertation, final and qualifying exams. *Entrance requirements:* For master's, appropriate bachelor's degree, minimum GPA of 3.0; for doctorate, GRE (if highest earned degree is BS), appropriate bachelor's or master's degree, minimum GPA of 3.4; for other advanced degree, appropriate master's degree, minimum GPA of 3.0. Additional exam requirements/recommendations for international students: Required—TOEFL or The George Washington University English as a Foreign Language Test. *Application deadline:* For fall admission, 3/1 priority date for domestic students; for spring admission, 10/1 for domestic students. Applications are processed on a rolling basis. Application fee: $75. *Financial support:* In 2018–19, 42 students received support. Fellowships, research assistantships, teaching assistantships, career-related internships or fieldwork, Federal Work-Study, institutionally sponsored loans, and tuition waivers available. Financial award application deadline: 3/1; financial award applicants required to submit FAFSA. *Faculty research:* Computer-integrated manufacturing, materials engineering, electronic materials, fatigue and fracture, reliability. *Unit head:* Dr. Majid T. Manzari, Chair, 202-994-4901, Fax: 202-994-0127, E-mail: manzari@gwu.edu. *Application contact:* Adina Lav, Marketing, Recruiting and Admissions, 202-994-5827, Fax: 202-994-0909, E-mail: engineering@gwu.edu. Website: http://www.cee.seas.gwu.edu/

Georgia Institute of Technology, Graduate Studies, College of Engineering, School of Civil and Environmental Engineering, Program in Environmental Engineering, Atlanta, GA 30332-0001. Offers MS. *Program availability:* Part-time. Terminal master's awarded for partial completion of doctoral program. *Degree requirements:* For master's, thesis optional. *Entrance requirements:* For master's, GRE. Additional exam requirements/recommendations for international students: Required—TOEFL (minimum score 550 paper-based; 79 iBT). Electronic applications accepted. *Faculty research:* Advanced microbiology of water and wastes, industrial waste treatment and disposal, air pollution measurements and control.

Harvard University, Graduate School of Arts and Sciences, Harvard John A. Paulson School of Engineering and Applied Sciences, Cambridge, MA 02138. Offers applied mathematics (PhD); applied physics (PhD); computational science and engineering (ME, SM); computer science (PhD); data science (SM); design engineering (MDE); engineering science (ME), including electrical engineering (ME, SM, PhD); engineering sciences (SM, PhD), including bioengineering (PhD), electrical engineering (ME, SM, PhD), environmental science and engineering (PhD), materials science and mechanical engineering (PhD). MDE offered in collaboration with Graduate School of Design. *Program availability:* Part-time. Terminal master's awarded for partial completion of doctoral program. *Degree requirements:* For master's, thesis (for ME); for doctorate, comprehensive exam, thesis/dissertation. *Entrance requirements:* For master's and doctorate, GRE General Test, GRE Subject Test (recommended), 3 letters of recommendation. Additional exam requirements/recommendations for international students: Required—TOEFL (minimum score 80 iBT). Electronic applications accepted. *Expenses:* Contact institution. *Faculty research:* Applied mathematics, applied physics, computer science and electrical engineering, environmental engineering, mechanical and biomedical engineering.

Idaho State University, Graduate School, College of Science and Engineering, Department of Civil and Environmental Engineering, Pocatello, ID 83209-8060. Offers civil engineering (MS); environmental engineering (MS); environmental science and management (MS). *Program availability:* Part-time. *Degree requirements:* For master's, comprehensive exam (for some programs), thesis optional, thesis project, 2 semesters of seminar. *Entrance requirements:* For master's, GRE. Additional exam requirements/recommendations for international students: Required—TOEFL (minimum score 550 paper-based; 80 iBT). Electronic applications accepted. *Faculty research:* Floor vibration investigations, earthquake engineering, base isolation systems and seismic risk assessment, infrastructure revitalization (building foundations and damage, bridge structures, highways, and dams), slope stability and soil erosion, pavement rehabilitation, computational fluid dynamics and flood control structures, microbial fuel cells, water treatment and water quality modeling, environmental risk assessment, biotechnology, nanotechnology.

Illinois Institute of Technology, Graduate College, Armour College of Engineering, Department of Civil, Architectural and Environmental Engineering, Chicago, IL 60616. Offers architectural engineering (M Arch E); civil engineering (MS, PhD), including architectural engineering (MS), construction engineering and management (MS), geoenvironmental engineering (MS), geotechnical engineering (MS), structural engineering (MS), transportation engineering (MS); construction engineering and management (MCEM); environmental engineering (M Env E, MS, PhD); geoenvironmental engineering (M Geoenv E); geotechnical engineering (MGE); infrastructure engineering and management (MPW); structural engineering (MSE); transportation engineering (M Trans E). *Program availability:* Part-time, evening/weekend, online learning. Terminal master's awarded for partial completion of doctoral program. *Degree requirements:* For master's, thesis (for some programs); for doctorate, comprehensive exam, thesis/dissertation. *Entrance requirements:* For master's, GRE

General Test (minimum score 900 Quantitative and Verbal, 2.5 Analytical Writing), minimum undergraduate GPA of 3.0; for doctorate, GRE General Test (minimum score 1000 Quantitative and Verbal, 3.0 Analytical Writing), minimum undergraduate GPA of 3.0. Additional exam requirements/recommendations for international students: Required—TOEFL (minimum score 550 paper-based; 80 iBT). Electronic applications accepted. *Faculty research:* Structural, architectural, geotechnical and geoenvironmental engineering; construction engineering and management; transportation engineering; environmental engineering and public works.

Instituto Tecnologico de Santo Domingo, Graduate School, Area of Engineering, Santo Domingo, Dominican Republic. Offers construction administration (MS, Certificate); data telecommunications (M Eng, MS, Certificate); industrial engineering (M Eng, Certificate); industrial management (M Mgmt); information technology (Certificate); maintenance engineering (M Eng); occupational hazard prevention (M Mgmt); production management (Certificate); quantitative methods (Certificate); sanitary and environmental engineering (M Eng); structural engineering (M Eng); systems engineering and electronic data processing (Certificate); transportation (Certificate).

Instituto Tecnológico y de Estudios Superiores de Monterrey, Campus Ciudad de México, Virtual University Division, Ciudad de Mexico, Mexico. Offers administration of information technologies (MA); computer sciences (MA); education (MA, PhD); educational technology (MA); environmental engineering (MA); environmental systems (MA); humanistic studies (MA); industrial engineering (MA); international business for Latin America (MA); quality systems (MA); quality systems and productivity (MA). *Program availability:* Part-time, evening/weekend, online learning. *Entrance requirements:* For master's and doctorate, Instituto entrance exam. Additional exam requirements/recommendations for international students: Required—TOEFL.

Instituto Tecnológico y de Estudios Superiores de Monterrey, Campus Monterrey, Graduate and Research Division, Programs in Engineering, Monterrey, Mexico. Offers applied statistics (M Eng); artificial intelligence (PhD); automation engineering (M Eng); chemical engineering (M Eng); civil engineering (M Eng); electrical engineering (M Eng); electronic engineering (M Eng); environmental engineering (M Eng); industrial engineering (M Eng, PhD); manufacturing engineering (M Eng); mechanical engineering (M Eng); systems and quality engineering (M Eng). M Eng program offered jointly with University of Waterloo; PhD in industrial engineering with Texas A&M University. *Program availability:* Part-time, evening/weekend. Terminal master's awarded for partial completion of doctoral program. *Degree requirements:* For master's, one foreign language, thesis; for doctorate, one foreign language, thesis/dissertation. *Entrance requirements:* For master's, EXADEP; for doctorate, GRE, master's degree in related field. Additional exam requirements/recommendations for international students: Required—TOEFL. *Faculty research:* Flexible manufacturing cells, materials, statistical methods, environmental prevention, control and evaluation.

Iowa State University of Science and Technology, Department of Civil and Construction Engineering, Ames, IA 50011. Offers civil engineering (MS, PhD), including civil engineering materials, construction engineering and management, environmental engineering, geotechnical engineering, structural engineering, transportation engineering. *Degree requirements:* For master's, thesis or alternative; for doctorate, thesis/dissertation. *Entrance requirements:* For master's and doctorate, GRE General Test. Additional exam requirements/recommendations for international students: Required—TOEFL (minimum score 550 paper-based; 82 iBT), IELTS (minimum score 6.5). Electronic applications accepted.

Jackson State University, Graduate School, College of Science, Engineering and Technology, Department of Civil and Environmental Engineering and Industrial Systems and Technology, Jackson, MS 39217. Offers civil engineering (MS, PhD); coastal engineering (MS, PhD); environmental engineering (MS, PhD); hazardous materials management (MS); technology education (MS Ed). *Program availability:* Part-time, evening/weekend. *Degree requirements:* For master's, comprehensive exam, thesis or alternative. *Entrance requirements:* For master's, GRE General Test. Additional exam requirements/recommendations for international students: Required—TOEFL (minimum score 520 paper-based; 67 iBT).

Johns Hopkins University, Engineering Program for Professionals, Part-time Program in Environmental Engineering, Baltimore, MD 21218. Offers MS, Graduate Certificate, Post-Master's Certificate. *Program availability:* Part-time, evening/weekend, online only, 100% online. *Faculty:* 1 full-time, 8 part-time/adjunct (1 woman). *Students:* 41 part-time (19 women). 14 applicants, 50% accepted, 4 enrolled. In 2018, 12 master's awarded. *Entrance requirements:* Additional exam requirements/recommendations for international students: Required—TOEFL (minimum score 600 paper-based; 100 iBT). Application fee: $0. *Unit head:* Dr. Hedy Alavi, Program Chair, 410-516-7091, Fax: 410-516-8996, E-mail: hedy.alavi@jhu.edu. *Application contact:* Doug Schiller, Admissions Director, 410-516-2300, Fax: 410-579-8049, E-mail: schiller@jhu.edu. Website: http://www.ep.jhu.edu

Johns Hopkins University, Engineering Program for Professionals, Part-time Program in Environmental Engineering and Science, Baltimore, MD 21218. Offers MEE, MS, Graduate Certificate, Post-Master's Certificate. *Program availability:* Part-time, evening/weekend, online only, 100% online. *Faculty:* 10 part-time/adjunct (2 women). *Students:* 41 part-time (22 women). 28 applicants, 43% accepted, 9 enrolled. In 2018, 22 master's, 1 other advanced degree awarded. *Entrance requirements:* Additional exam requirements/recommendations for international students: Required—TOEFL (minimum score 600 paper-based; 100 iBT). *Application deadline:* Applications are processed on a rolling basis. Application fee: $0. Electronic applications accepted. *Unit head:* Dr. Hedy Alavi, Program Chair, 410-516-7091, Fax: 410-516-8996, E-mail: hedy.alavi@jhu.edu. *Application contact:* Doug Schiller, Admissions Director, 410-516-2300, Fax: 410-579-8049, E-mail: schiller@jhu.edu. Website: http://www.ep.jhu.edu/

Johns Hopkins University, G. W. C. Whiting School of Engineering, Department of Environmental Health and Engineering, Baltimore, MD 21218. Offers MA, MS, MSE, PhD. *Faculty:* 15 full-time (3 women). *Students:* 124 full-time (77 women), 32 part-time (21 women). 171 applicants, 65% accepted, 37 enrolled. In 2018, 26 master's, 8 doctorates awarded. Terminal master's awarded for partial completion of doctoral program. *Degree requirements:* For master's, thesis optional, 1-year full-time residency; for doctorate, comprehensive exam, thesis/dissertation, oral exam, 2-year full-time residency. *Entrance requirements:* For master's and doctorate, GRE General Test, 3 letters of recommendation, statement of purpose, transcripts. Additional exam requirements/recommendations for international students: Required—TOEFL (minimum score 600 paper-based, 100 iBT) or IELTS (7). *Application deadline:* For fall admission, 1/15 priority date for domestic and international students. Application fee: $75. Electronic applications accepted. *Financial support:* In 2018–19, 30 students received support, including 4 fellowships with full and partial tuition reimbursements available (averaging $34,008 per year), 22 research assistantships with full and partial tuition reimbursements available (averaging $29,000 per year), 4 teaching assistantships with partial tuition reimbursements available (averaging $1,400 per year); Federal Work-Study, scholarships/grants, health care benefits, tuition waivers (full and partial), and unspecified assistantships also available. Financial award application deadline: 1/15.

Environmental Engineering

Faculty research: Environmental engineering and science; water and air resources engineering; geomorphology, hydrology and ecology; systems analysis and economics for public decision making; human geography. *Unit head:* Dr. Marsha Willis-Karp, Chair, 410-516-0760, Fax: 410-516-8996, E-mail: mwkarp@jhu.edu. *Application contact:* Adena Rojas, Senior Academic Program Coordinator, 410-516-5533, Fax: 410-516-8996, E-mail: arojas@jhu.edu.
Website: http://ehe.jhu.edu

Kansas State University, Graduate School, College of Engineering, Department of Civil Engineering, Manhattan, KS 66506. Offers civil engineering (MS, PhD); environmental engineering (MS, PhD); geotechnical engineering (MS, PhD); structural engineering (MS, PhD); transportation engineering (MS, PhD); water resources engineering (MS, PhD). *Program availability:* Part-time, evening/weekend, online learning. *Degree requirements:* For master's, thesis or alternative; for doctorate, thesis/dissertation. *Entrance requirements:* For master's, GRE General Test, bachelor's degree or course work in related engineering fields; for doctorate, GRE General Test. Additional exam requirements/recommendations for international students: Required—TOEFL (minimum score 550 paper-based; 79 iBT). Electronic applications accepted. *Faculty research:* Transportation and materials engineering, water resources engineering, environmental engineering, geotechnical engineering, structural engineering.

Kennesaw State University, Southern Polytechnic College of Engineering and Engineering Technology, Program in Civil Engineering, Kennesaw, GA 30144. Offers environmental engineering (MS); geotechnical engineering (MS); structural engineering (MS); transportation and pavement engineering (MS); water resources engineering (MS). *Program availability:* Online learning. *Students:* 13 full-time (2 women), 24 part-time (5 women); includes 20 minority (8 Black or African American, non-Hispanic/Latino; 5 Asian, non-Hispanic/Latino; 4 Hispanic/Latino; 3 Two or more races, non-Hispanic/Latino), 2 international. Average age 33. 21 applicants, 57% accepted, 1 enrolled. In 2018, 6 master's awarded. *Degree requirements:* For master's, thesis optional. *Entrance requirements:* Additional exam requirements/recommendations for international students: Required—TOEFL (minimum score 550 paper-based; 80 iBT), IELTS (minimum score 6.5). *Application deadline:* For fall admission, 11/1 for domestic and international students; for spring admission, 4/1 for domestic and international students. Applications are processed on a rolling basis. Application fee: $60. Electronic applications accepted. *Expenses: Tuition, area resident:* Full-time $6960; part-time $290 per credit hour. Tuition, state resident: full-time $6960; part-time $290 per credit hour. Tuition, nonresident: full-time $25,080; part-time $1045 per credit hour. *International tuition:* $25,080 full-time. *Required fees:* $2006; $1706 per semester. $853 per semester. *Unit head:* Metin Oguzmert, Coordinator, 470-578-5083, E-mail: moguzmer@kennesaw.edu. *Application contact:* Admissions Counselor, 470-578-4377, E-mail: ksugrad@kennesaw.edu.
Website: http://engineering.kennesaw.edu/civil-construction/degrees/ms-civil-engineering.php

Lakehead University, Graduate Studies, Faculty of Engineering, Thunder Bay, ON P7B 5E1, Canada. Offers control engineering (M Sc Engr); electrical/computer engineering (M Sc Engr); environmental engineering (M Sc Engr). *Program availability:* Part-time. *Degree requirements:* For master's, thesis. *Entrance requirements:* For master's, bachelor's degree in chemical, electrical or mechanical engineering, minimum B average. Additional exam requirements/recommendations for international students: Required—TOEFL. *Faculty research:* Pulp and paper, adaptive/process control, robust/interactive learning control, vibration control.

Lehigh University, P.C. Rossin College of Engineering and Applied Science, Department of Civil and Environmental Engineering, Bethlehem, PA 18015. Offers M Eng, MS, PhD. *Program availability:* Part-time. *Faculty:* 21 full-time (4 women), 1 part-time/adjunct (0 women). *Students:* 73 full-time (20 women), 8 part-time (2 women); includes 6 minority (1 Black or African American, non-Hispanic/Latino; 1 Asian, non-Hispanic/Latino; 3 Hispanic/Latino; 1 Two or more races, non-Hispanic/Latino), 52 international. Average age 27. 162 applicants, 31% accepted, 11 enrolled. In 2018, 30 master's, 6 doctorates awarded. Terminal master's awarded for partial completion of doctoral program. *Degree requirements:* For master's, thesis (for some programs); for doctorate, comprehensive exam, thesis/dissertation. *Entrance requirements:* For master's and doctorate, GRE. Additional exam requirements/recommendations for international students: Required—TOEFL (minimum score 550 paper-based; 79 iBT), IELTS (minimum score 6.5). *Application deadline:* For fall admission, 7/15 for domestic and international students; for spring admission, 12/1 for domestic and international students; for summer admission, 5/30 for domestic and international students. Application fee: $75. Electronic applications accepted. Tuition and fees vary according to program. *Financial support:* In 2018–19, 15 students received support, including 4 fellowships with full tuition reimbursements available (averaging $22,050 per year), 49 research assistantships with full and partial tuition reimbursements available (averaging $21,000 per year), 8 teaching assistantships with full tuition reimbursements available (averaging $20,440 per year); unspecified assistantships also available. Financial award application deadline: 1/15; financial award applicants required to submit FAFSA. *Faculty research:* Structural engineering, geotechnical engineering, water resources engineering, environmental engineering. *Total annual research expenditures:* $6.6 million. *Unit head:* Dr. Panayiotis Diplas, Chair, 610-758-3554, E-mail: pad313@lehigh.edu. *Application contact:* Prisca Vidanage, Graduate Coordinator, 610-758-3530, E-mail: pmv1@lehigh.edu.
Website: http://www.lehigh.edu/~incee/

Louisiana State University and Agricultural & Mechanical College, Graduate School, College of Engineering, Department of Civil and Environmental Engineering, Baton Rouge, LA 70803. Offers environmental engineering (MSCE, PhD); geotechnical engineering (MSCE, PhD); structural engineering and mechanics (MSCE, PhD); transportation engineering (MSCE, PhD); water resources (MSCE, PhD).

Manhattan College, Graduate Programs, School of Engineering, Program in Environmental Engineering, Riverdale, NY 10471. Offers ME, MS. *Program availability:* Part-time, evening/weekend. *Degree requirements:* For master's, thesis optional, 30 credits, minimum GPA of 3.0. *Entrance requirements:* For master's, GRE (recommended), minimum GPA of 3.0. Additional exam requirements/recommendations for international students: Required—TOEFL (minimum score 550 paper-based; 80 iBT), IELTS (minimum score 6). *Faculty research:* Water quality modeling, environmental chemistry, air modeling, biological treatment, environmental chemistry.

Marquette University, Graduate School, College of Engineering, Department of Civil and Environmental Engineering, Milwaukee, WI 53201-1881. Offers construction engineering and management (MS, PhD, Certificate); environmental engineering (MS, PhD); structural design (Certificate); structural engineering and structural mechanics (MS, PhD); transportation (Certificate); transportation engineering and materials (MS, PhD); waste and wastewater treatment processes (Certificate); water resources engineering (Certificate). *Program availability:* Part-time, evening/weekend. Terminal master's awarded for partial completion of doctoral program. *Degree requirements:* For master's, comprehensive exam (for some programs), thesis or alternative; for doctorate, thesis/dissertation. *Entrance requirements:* For master's, GRE General Test (recommended), minimum GPA of 3.0, official transcripts from all current and previous

colleges/universities except Marquette, three letters of recommendation; for doctorate, GRE General Test, minimum GPA of 3.0, official transcripts from all current and previous colleges/universities except Marquette, three letters of recommendation, brief statement of purpose, submission of any English language publications authored by applicant (strongly recommended). Additional exam requirements/recommendations for international students: Required—TOEFL (minimum score 530 paper-based). Electronic applications accepted. *Faculty research:* Highway safety, highway performance, and intelligent transportation systems; surface mount technology; watershed management.

Marshall University, Academic Affairs Division, College of Information Technology and Engineering, Program in Engineering, Huntington, WV 25755. Offers engineering management (MSE); environmental engineering (MSE); transportation and infrastructure engineering (MSE). *Program availability:* Part-time, evening/weekend. *Degree requirements:* For master's, final project, oral exam. *Entrance requirements:* For master's, GMAT or GRE General Test, minimum undergraduate GPA of 2.75.

Massachusetts Institute of Technology, School of Engineering, Department of Civil and Environmental Engineering, Cambridge, MA 02139. Offers biological oceanography (PhD, Sc D); chemical oceanography (PhD, Sc D); civil and environmental engineering (M Eng, SM, PhD, Sc D); civil and environmental systems (PhD, Sc D); civil engineering (PhD, Sc D, CE); civil engineering and computation (PhD); coastal engineering (PhD, Sc D); construction engineering and management (PhD, Sc D); environmental biology (PhD, Sc D); environmental chemistry (PhD, Sc D); environmental engineering (PhD, Sc D); environmental engineering and computation (PhD); environmental fluid mechanics (PhD, Sc D); geotechnical and geoenvironmental engineering (PhD, Sc D); hydrology (PhD, Sc D); information technology (PhD, Sc D); oceanographic engineering (PhD, Sc D); structures and materials (PhD, Sc D); transportation (PhD, Sc D); SM/MBA. *Degree requirements:* For master's, thesis; for doctorate, comprehensive exam, thesis/dissertation; for CE, comprehensive exam, thesis. *Entrance requirements:* For master's, doctorate, and CE, GRE General Test. Additional exam requirements/recommendations for international students: Required—TOEFL, IELTS. Electronic applications accepted. *Expenses: Tuition:* Full-time $51,520; part-time $800 per credit hour. *Required fees:* $312. *Faculty research:* Environmental chemistry, environmental fluid mechanics and coastal engineering, environmental microbiology, geotechnical engineering and geomechanics, hydrology and hydro climatology, infrastructure systems, mechanics of materials and structures, transportation systems.

McGill University, Faculty of Graduate and Postdoctoral Studies, Faculty of Engineering, Department of Chemical Engineering, Montréal, QC H3A 2T5, Canada. Offers chemical engineering (M Eng, PhD); environmental engineering (M Eng).

McGill University, Faculty of Graduate and Postdoctoral Studies, Faculty of Engineering, Department of Civil Engineering and Applied Mechanics, Montréal, QC H3A 2T5, Canada. Offers environmental engineering (M Eng, M Sc, PhD); fluid mechanics (M Sc); fluid mechanics and hydraulic engineering (M Eng, PhD); materials engineering (M Eng, PhD); rehabilitation of urban infrastructure (M Eng, PhD); soil behavior (M Eng, PhD); soil mechanics and foundations (M Eng, PhD); structures and structural mechanics (M Eng, PhD); water resources (M Sc); water resources engineering (M Eng, PhD).

Memorial University of Newfoundland, School of Graduate Studies, Interdisciplinary Program in Environmental Systems Engineering and Management, St. John's, NL A1C 5S7, Canada. Offers MA Sc. *Degree requirements:* For master's, project course. *Entrance requirements:* For master's, 2nd class engineering degree. *Expenses:* Contact institution.

Mercer University, Graduate Studies, Macon Campus, School of Engineering, Macon, GA 31207. Offers biomedical engineering (MSE); computer engineering (MSE); electrical engineering (MSE); engineering management (MSE); environmental engineering (MSE); environmental systems (MS); mechanical engineering (MSE); software engineering (MSE); software systems (MS); technical communications management (MS); technical management (MS). *Program availability:* Part-time-only, evening/weekend, online learning. *Degree requirements:* For master's, thesis or alternative. *Entrance requirements:* For master's, GRE (minimum score 300), minimum undergraduate GPA of 3.0. Additional exam requirements/recommendations for international students: Required—TOEFL (minimum score 550 paper-based; 80 iBT). *Expenses:* Contact institution. *Faculty research:* Designing prostheses and orthotics, oxygen transfer and limitations in biological systems, low-cost groundwater development, lung airway and transport, autonomous mobile robots.

Michigan State University, The Graduate School, College of Engineering, Department of Civil and Environmental Engineering, East Lansing, MI 48824. Offers civil engineering (MS, PhD); environmental engineering (MS, PhD); environmental engineering-environmental toxicology (PhD). *Program availability:* Part-time. *Entrance requirements:* Additional exam requirements/recommendations for international students: Required—TOEFL. Electronic applications accepted.

Michigan Technological University, Graduate School, College of Engineering, Department of Civil and Environmental Engineering, Houghton, MI 49931. Offers civil engineering (MS, PhD); environmental engineering (MS, PhD); environmental engineering science (MS). *Program availability:* Part-time, 100% online. *Faculty:* 39 full-time, 8 part-time/adjunct. *Students:* 65 full-time (26 women), 12 part-time (5 women); includes 8 minority (2 Black or African American, non-Hispanic/Latino; 2 Hispanic/Latino; 4 Two or more races, non-Hispanic/Latino), 31 international. Average age 27. 276 applicants, 40% accepted, 24 enrolled. In 2018, 55 master's, 4 doctorates awarded. *Degree requirements:* For master's, comprehensive exam (for some programs), thesis (for some programs); for doctorate, comprehensive exam, thesis/dissertation. *Entrance requirements:* For master's and doctorate, GRE (Michigan Tech students exempt), statement of purpose, personal statement, official transcripts, 2 letters of recommendation. Additional exam requirements/recommendations for international students: Required—TOEFL, TOEFL (recommended minimum score 100 iBT) or IELTS (recommended minimum score of 7.0). *Application deadline:* For fall admission, 1/15 priority date for domestic and international students; for spring admission, 9/15 priority date for domestic and international students; for summer admission, 2/15 priority date for domestic and international students. Applications are processed on a rolling basis. Electronic applications accepted. *Expenses:* $1,143 per credit. *Financial support:* In 2018–19, 51 students received support, including 6 fellowships with tuition reimbursements available (averaging $16,590 per year), 22 research assistantships with tuition reimbursements available (averaging $16,590 per year), 5 teaching assistantships with tuition reimbursements available (averaging $16,590 per year); career-related internships or fieldwork, Federal Work-Study, scholarships/grants, health care benefits, unspecified assistantships, and cooperative program also available. Financial award applicants required to submit FAFSA. *Faculty research:* Water resources, environment engineering, transportation engineering, structural engineering, geotechnical engineering. *Total annual research expenditures:* $2.5 million. *Unit head:* Dr. Audra N. Morse, Chair, 906-487-3240, Fax: 906-487-2943, E-mail: anmorse@mtu.edu. *Application contact:* Angela Keranen, Administrative Aide, 906-487-2474, Fax: 906-487-2943, E-mail: amkerane@mtu.edu.
Website: http://www.mtu.edu/cee/

Missouri University of Science and Technology, Department of Civil, Architectural, and Environmental Engineering, Rolla, MO 65401. Offers civil engineering (MS, DE, PhD); environmental engineering (MS). *Program availability:* Part-time, evening/weekend. Terminal master's awarded for partial completion of doctoral program. *Degree requirements:* For master's, thesis optional; for doctorate, comprehensive exam, thesis/dissertation. *Entrance requirements:* For master's, GRE General Test (minimum combined score 1100), minimum GPA of 3.0; for doctorate, GRE General Test (minimum score: verbal and quantitative 400, writing 3.5), minimum GPA of 3.0. Additional exam requirements/recommendations for international students: Required—TOEFL (minimum score 550 paper-based). Electronic applications accepted. *Expenses:* Tuition, state resident: full-time $7545.60; part-time $419.20 per credit hour. Tuition, nonresident: full-time $22,169; part-time $1231.60 per credit hour. *International tuition:* $23,518.80 full-time. *Required fees:* $4523.05. Full-time tuition and fees vary according to course load, campus/location, program and reciprocity agreements. *Faculty research:* Earthquake engineering, structural optimization and control systems, structural health monitoring/damage detection, soil-structure interaction, soil mechanics and foundation engineering.

Montana State University, The Graduate School, College of Engineering, Department of Chemical and Biological Engineering, Bozeman, MT 59717. Offers chemical engineering (MS); engineering (PhD), including chemical engineering option, environmental engineering option; environmental engineering (MS). *Program availability:* Part-time. *Degree requirements:* For master's, comprehensive exam, thesis (for some programs); for doctorate, comprehensive exam, thesis/dissertation. *Entrance requirements:* For master's and doctorate, GRE General Test. Additional exam requirements/recommendations for international students: Required—TOEFL (minimum score 550 paper-based). Electronic applications accepted. *Faculty research:* Metabolic network analysis and engineering; magnetic resonance microscopy; modeling of biological systems; the development of protective coatings on planar solid oxide fuel cell (SOFC) metallic interconnects; characterizing corrosion mechanisms of materials in precisely-controlled exposures; testing materials in poly-crystalline silicon production environments; environmental biotechnology and bioremediation.

Montana Tech of The University of Montana, Department of Environmental Engineering, Butte, MT 59701-8997. Offers MS. *Program availability:* Part-time. *Degree requirements:* For master's, thesis. *Entrance requirements:* For master's, GRE General Test, minimum GPA of 3.0. Additional exam requirements/recommendations for international students: Required—TOEFL (minimum score 525 paper-based; 78 iBT), IELTS (minimum score 6.5). Electronic applications accepted. *Faculty research:* Mine waste reclamation, modeling, air pollution control, wetlands, water pollution control.

New Jersey Institute of Technology, Newark College of Engineering, Newark, NJ 07102. Offers biomedical engineering (MS, PhD); biopharmaceutical engineering (MS); chemical engineering (MS, PhD); civil engineering (MS, PhD); computer engineering (MS); critical infrastructure systems (MS); electrical engineering (MS, PhD); engineering management (MS); engineering science (MS); environmental engineering (MS, PhD); healthcare systems management (MS); industrial engineering (MS, PhD); internet engineering (MS); manufacturing systems engineering (MS); materials science & engineering (PhD); materials science and engineering (MS); mechanical engineering (MS, PhD); occupational safety and health engineering (MS). *Program availability:* Part-time, evening/weekend. *Faculty:* 147 full-time (26 women), 133 part-time/adjunct (16 women). *Students:* 690 full-time (163 women), 594 part-time (130 women); includes 427 minority (79 Black or African American, non-Hispanic/Latino; 181 Asian, non-Hispanic/Latino; 140 Hispanic/Latino; 27 Two or more races, non-Hispanic/Latino), 553 international. Average age 27. 2,334 applicants, 57% accepted, 452 enrolled. In 2018, 418 master's, 31 doctorates awarded. Terminal master's awarded for partial completion of doctoral program. *Degree requirements:* For master's, thesis (for some programs); for doctorate, thesis/dissertation. *Entrance requirements:* For master's, GRE General Test, minimum GPA 2.8, personal statement, 1 letter of recommendation, transcripts; for doctorate, GRE General Test, minimum GPA of 3.5, personal statement, 3 letters of recommendation, transcripts. Additional exam requirements/recommendations for international students: Required—TOEFL (minimum score 550 paper-based; 79 iBT), IELTS (minimum score 6.5). *Application deadline:* For fall admission, 6/1 priority date for domestic students, 5/1 priority date for international students; for spring admission, 11/15 priority date for domestic and international students. Applications are processed on a rolling basis. Application fee: $75. Electronic applications accepted. *Expenses:* $22,690 per year (in-state), $32,136 per year (out-of-state). *Financial support:* In 2018–19, 396 students received support, including 52 fellowships with full tuition reimbursements available (averaging $22,000 per year), 113 research assistantships with full tuition reimbursements available (averaging $22,000 per year), 101 teaching assistantships with full tuition reimbursements available (averaging $22,000 per year); career-related internships or fieldwork, Federal Work-Study, scholarships/grants, and unspecified assistantships also available. Financial award application deadline: 1/15. *Faculty research:* Nonlinear signal processing, intelligent medical image analysis, calibration issues in coherent localization, computer-aided design, neural network for tool wear measurement. *Total annual research expenditures:* $41.7 million. *Unit head:* Dr. Moshe Kam, Dean, 973-596-5534, Fax: 973-596-2316, E-mail: moshe.kam@njit.edu. *Application contact:* Stephen Eck, Director of Admissions, 973-596-3300, Fax: 973-596-3461, E-mail: admissions@njit.edu. *Website:* http://engineering.njit.edu/

New Mexico Institute of Mining and Technology, Center for Graduate Studies, Department of Civil and Environmental Engineering, Socorro, NM 87801. Offers environmental engineering (MS), including air quality engineering and science, hazardous waste engineering, water quality engineering and science. *Degree requirements:* For master's, thesis, thesis or independent study. *Entrance requirements:* Additional exam requirements/recommendations for international students: Required—TOEFL (minimum score 540 paper-based). *Faculty research:* Air quality, hazardous waste management, wastewater management and treatment, site remediation.

New Mexico State University, College of Engineering, Department of Civil and Geological Engineering, Las Cruces, NM 88003-8001. Offers civil and geological engineering (PhD); master of science (MS Env E, MSCE). *Program availability:* Part-time. *Faculty:* 15 full-time (3 women). *Students:* 53 full-time (18 women), 12 part-time (2 women); includes 20 minority (3 Black or African American, non-Hispanic/Latino; 1 American Indian or Alaska Native, non-Hispanic/Latino; 1 Asian, non-Hispanic/Latino; 14 Hispanic/Latino; 1 Two or more races, non-Hispanic/Latino), 32 international. Average age 29. 63 applicants, 48% accepted, 12 enrolled. In 2018, 20 master's, 4 doctorates awarded. *Degree requirements:* For master's, thesis optional; for doctorate, comprehensive exam, thesis/dissertation, qualifying exam. *Entrance requirements:* For master's and doctorate, BS in engineering, minimum GPA of 3.0. Additional exam requirements/recommendations for international students: Required—TOEFL (minimum score 550 paper-based; 79 iBT), IELTS (minimum score 6.5). *Application deadline:* For fall admission, 4/1 priority date for domestic and international students; for spring admission, 9/1 priority date for domestic and international students. Applications are processed on a rolling basis. Application fee: $40 ($50 for international students). Electronic applications accepted. *Expenses: Tuition, area resident:* Full-time $4216.70; part-time $252.70 per credit hour. Tuition, state resident: full-time $4216.70; part-time

$252.70 per credit hour. Tuition, nonresident: full-time $12,769; part-time $881.10 per credit hour. *International tuition:* $12,769.30 full-time. *Required fees:* $878.40; $48.80 per credit hour. Full-time tuition and fees vary according to course load and reciprocity agreements. *Financial support:* In 2018–19, 57 students received support, including 10 fellowships (averaging $1,987 per year), 27 research assistantships (averaging $13,305 per year), 22 teaching assistantships (averaging $11,651 per year); career-related internships or fieldwork, Federal Work-Study, scholarships/grants, traineeships, health care benefits, and unspecified assistantships also available. Support available to part-time students. Financial award application deadline: 3/1. *Faculty research:* Structural engineering, water resources engineering, environmental engineering, geotechnical engineering, transportation. *Total annual research expenditures:* $2.4 million. *Unit head:* Dr. David Jauregui, Department Head, 575-646-3801, Fax: 575-646-6049, E-mail: jauregui@nmsu.edu. *Application contact:* Dr. David Jauregui, Department Head, 575-646-3801, Fax: 575-646-6049, E-mail: jauregui@nmsu.edu. *Website:* http://ce.nmsu.edu

New York Institute of Technology, College of Engineering and Computing Sciences, Department of Environmental Technology and Sustainability, Old Westbury, NY 11568-8000. Offers MS. *Program availability:* Part-time, evening/weekend, blended/hybrid learning. *Faculty:* 3 full-time (1 woman), 1 part-time/adjunct (0 women). *Students:* 22 full-time (8 women), 11 part-time (4 women); includes 5 minority (2 Black or African American, non-Hispanic/Latino; 2 Asian, non-Hispanic/Latino; 1 Two or more races, non-Hispanic/Latino), 21 international. Average age 27. 67 applicants, 84% accepted, 12 enrolled. In 2018, 24 master's awarded. *Degree requirements:* For master's, capstone project. *Entrance requirements:* For master's, minimum undergraduate GPA of 2.85; BS in engineering, technology, sciences, or related area. Additional exam requirements/recommendations for international students: Required—TOEFL (minimum score 79 iBT), IELTS (minimum score 6), PTE (minimum score 53). *Application deadline:* For fall admission, 7/1 for domestic students, 6/1 for international students; for spring admission, 12/1 for domestic and international students. Applications are processed on a rolling basis. Application fee: $50. Electronic applications accepted. *Expenses: Tuition:* Full-time $1285; part-time $1285 per credit. *Required fees:* $215; $175 per unit. Tuition and fees vary according to course load, degree level and campus/location. *Financial support:* Fellowships with partial tuition reimbursements, teaching assistantships with partial tuition reimbursements, career-related internships or fieldwork, Federal Work-Study, scholarships/grants, tuition waivers (full and partial), and unspecified assistantships available. Support available to part-time students. Financial award application deadline: 2/15; financial award applicants required to submit FAFSA. *Faculty research:* Clean water, development and testing of methodology to assess health risks and environmental impacts from sanitary sewage, introduction of technology innovation (including geographical information systems and virtual reality); emerging contaminants; occupational health and safety. *Unit head:* Dr. David Nadler, Department Chair, 516-686-1373, Fax: 516-686-7919, E-mail: dnadler@nyit.edu. *Application contact:* Alice Dolitsky, Director, Graduate Admissions, 516-686-7520, Fax: 516-686-1116, E-mail: admissions@nyit.edu. *Website:* http://www.nyit.edu/degrees/environmental_technology_sustainability_ms

North Dakota State University, College of Graduate and Interdisciplinary Studies, College of Engineering, Department of Civil and Environmental Engineering, Fargo, ND 58102. Offers civil engineering (MS, PhD); environmental engineering (MS). *Program availability:* Part-time, online learning. *Degree requirements:* For master's, thesis; for doctorate, comprehensive exam, thesis/dissertation. *Entrance requirements:* Additional exam requirements/recommendations for international students: Required—TOEFL (minimum score 525 paper-based; 71 iBT). Electronic applications accepted. *Faculty research:* Wastewater, solid waste, composites, nanotechnology.

Northeastern University, College of Engineering, Boston, MA 02115-5096. Offers bioengineering (MS, PhD); chemical engineering (MS, PhD); civil engineering (MS, PhD); computer engineering (PhD); computer systems engineering (MS); electrical and computer engineering (MS); electrical and computer engineering leadership (MS); electrical engineering (PhD); energy systems (MS); engineering and public policy (MS); engineering management (MS, Certificate); environmental engineering (MS); industrial engineering (MS, PhD); information assurance (PhD); information systems (MS); interdisciplinary engineering (PhD); mechanical engineering (PhD); operations research (MS); telecommunication systems management (MS). *Program availability:* Part-time, online learning. Electronic applications accepted. *Expenses:* Contact institution.

Northwestern University, McCormick School of Engineering and Applied Science, Department of Civil and Environmental Engineering, Evanston, IL 60208-3109. Offers environmental engineering and science (MS, PhD); geotechnical engineering (MS, PhD); mechanics of materials and solids (MS, PhD); project management (MS); structural engineering and materials (MS, PhD); transportation systems analysis and planning (MS, PhD). MS and PhD admissions and degrees offered through The Graduate School. *Program availability:* Part-time. Terminal master's awarded for partial completion of doctoral program. *Degree requirements:* For master's, comprehensive exam (for some programs), thesis (for some programs); for doctorate, comprehensive exam, thesis/dissertation. *Entrance requirements:* For master's and doctorate, GRE General Test, minimum 2 letters of recommendation, transcripts from all academic institutions attended. Additional exam requirements/recommendations for international students: Required—TOEFL (minimum score 577 paper-based; 90 iBT), IELTS (minimum score 7). Electronic applications accepted. *Faculty research:* Environmental engineering and science, geotechnics, mechanics, materials, structures, and transportation systems analysis and planning.

Norwich University, College of Graduate and Continuing Studies, Master of Civil Engineering Program, Northfield, VT 05663. Offers construction management (MCE); environmental (MCE); geotechnical (MCE); structural (MCE). *Program availability:* Evening/weekend, online only, mostly all online with a week-long residency requirement. *Degree requirements:* For master's, capstone. *Entrance requirements:* For master's, minimum undergraduate GPA of 2.75. Additional exam requirements/recommendations for international students: Required—TOEFL (minimum score 550 paper-based; 80 iBT), IELTS (minimum score 6.5). Electronic applications accepted. *Expenses:* Contact institution.

Ohio University, Graduate College, Russ College of Engineering and Technology, Department of Civil Engineering, Athens, OH 45701-2979. Offers civil engineering (PhD); construction engineering and management (MS); environmental (MS); geoenvironmental (MS); geotechnical (MS); mechanics (MS); structures (MS); transportation (MS); water resources (MS). *Program availability:* Part-time. *Degree requirements:* For master's, comprehensive exam (for some programs), thesis or alternative; for doctorate, comprehensive exam, thesis/dissertation. *Entrance requirements:* For master's, GRE General Test, minimum GPA of 3.0, 3 letters of recommendation; for doctorate, GRE General Test. Additional exam requirements/recommendations for international students: Required—TOEFL (minimum score 550 paper-based; 80 iBT) or IELTS (minimum score 6.5). Electronic applications accepted. *Faculty research:* Noise abatement, materials and environment, highway infrastructure, subsurface investigation (pavements, pipes, bridges).

Oklahoma State University, College of Agricultural Science and Natural Resources, Department of Biosystems and Agricultural Engineering, Stillwater, OK 74078. Offers

biosystems engineering (MS, PhD); environmental and natural resources (MS, PhD). *Faculty:* 22 full-time (5 women), 2 part-time/adjunct (0 women). *Students:* 8 full-time (0 women), 17 part-time (8 women); includes 5 minority (1 Black or African American, non-Hispanic/Latino; 1 Asian, non-Hispanic/Latino; 2 Hispanic/Latino; 1 Two or more races, non-Hispanic/Latino), 15 international. Average age 30. 19 applicants, 32% accepted, 3 enrolled. In 2018, 4 master's, 7 doctorates awarded. *Entrance requirements:* For master's and doctorate, GRE or GMAT. Additional exam requirements/recommendations for international students: Required—TOEFL (minimum score 550 paper-based; 79 iBT). *Application deadline:* For fall admission, 3/1 priority date for international students; for spring admission, 8/1 priority date for international students. Applications are processed on a rolling basis. Application fee: $40 ($75 for international students). Electronic applications accepted. *Expenses: Tuition, area resident:* Full-time $4148. Tuition, state resident: full-time $4148. Tuition, nonresident: full-time $10,517. *International tuition:* $10,517 full-time. *Required fees:* $4394; $2929 per credit hour. Tuition and fees vary according to course load and program. *Financial support:* Research assistantships, teaching assistantships, career-related internships or fieldwork, Federal Work-Study, scholarships/grants, health care benefits, tuition waivers (partial), and unspecified assistantships available. Support available to part-time students. Financial award application deadline: 3/1; financial award applicants required to submit FAFSA. *Unit head:* Dr. John Veenstra, Department Head, 405-744-5431, Fax: 405-744-6059, E-mail: jveenst@okstate.edu. *Application contact:* Dr. Ning Wang, Professor/Graduate Coordinator, 405-744-2877, E-mail: ning.wang@okstate.edu.
Website: http://bae.okstate.edu/

Oklahoma State University, College of Engineering, Architecture and Technology, School of Civil and Environmental Engineering, Stillwater, OK 74078. Offers civil engineering (MS, PhD). *Faculty:* 21 full-time (2 women), 2 part-time/adjunct (0 women). *Students:* 20 full-time (5 women), 41 part-time (12 women); includes 6 minority (3 American Indian or Alaska Native, non-Hispanic/Latino; 1 Hispanic/Latino; 2 Two or more races, non-Hispanic/Latino), 31 international. Average age 29. 74 applicants, 26% accepted, 11 enrolled. In 2018, 17 master's, 4 doctorates awarded. *Entrance requirements:* For master's and doctorate, GRE or GMAT. Additional exam requirements/recommendations for international students: Required—TOEFL (minimum score 550 paper-based; 79 iBT). *Application deadline:* For fall admission, 3/1 priority date for international students; for spring admission, 8/1 priority date for international students. Applications are processed on a rolling basis. Application fee: $40 ($75 for international students). Electronic applications accepted. *Expenses: Tuition, area resident:* Full-time $4148. Tuition, state resident: full-time $4148. Tuition, nonresident: full-time $10,517. *International tuition:* $10,517 full-time. *Required fees:* $4394; $2929 per credit hour. Tuition and fees vary according to course load and program. *Financial support:* Research assistantships, teaching assistantships, career-related internships or fieldwork, Federal Work-Study, scholarships/grants, health care benefits, tuition waivers (partial), and unspecified assistantships available. Support available to part-time students. Financial award application deadline: 3/1; financial award applicants required to submit FAFSA. *Unit head:* Dr. Norb Delatte, Department Head, 405-744-5190, Fax: 405-744-7554, E-mail: norb.delatte@okstate.edu. *Application contact:* Dr. Sheryl Tucker, Dean, 405-744-6368, Fax: 405-744-0355, E-mail: gradi@okstate.edu.
Website: http://cive.okstate.edu

Old Dominion University, Frank Batten College of Engineering and Technology, Program in Civil and Environmental Engineering, Norfolk, VA 23529. Offers D Eng, PhD. *Program availability:* Part-time, evening/weekend, blended/hybrid learning. *Degree requirements:* For doctorate, comprehensive exam, thesis/dissertation, candidacy exam. *Entrance requirements:* For doctorate, GRE, minimum GPA of 3.5. Electronic applications accepted. *Expenses:* Contact institution. *Faculty research:* Structural engineering, coastal engineering, environmental engineering, geotechnical engineering, water resources, transportation engineering.

Old Dominion University, Frank Batten College of Engineering and Technology, Program in Environmental Engineering, Norfolk, VA 23529. Offers ME, MS. *Program availability:* Part-time, evening/weekend, blended/hybrid learning. *Degree requirements:* For master's, comprehensive exam, thesis optional. *Entrance requirements:* For master's, GRE, minimum GPA of 3.0. Additional exam requirements/recommendations for international students: Required—TOEFL (minimum score 550 paper-based, 80 iBT) or IELTS (6.5). Electronic applications accepted. *Expenses:* Contact institution. *Faculty research:* Water quality, water and wastewater treatment, hydrologic processes, water resources, environmental engineering microbiology, air quality, hazardous and solid waste, biofuels, nutrient cycling, pollution prevention.

Oregon Health & Science University, School of Medicine, Graduate Programs in Medicine, Department of Environmental and Biomolecular Systems, Portland, OR 97239-3098. Offers biochemistry and molecular biology (MS, PhD); environmental science and engineering (MS, PhD). This program is no longer admitting new students. *Program availability:* Part-time. *Faculty:* 13 full-time (4 women). *Students:* 5 full-time (4 women), 2 part-time (0 women). Average age 31. In 2018, 13 master's, 3 doctorates awarded. Terminal master's awarded for partial completion of doctoral program. *Degree requirements:* For master's, thesis (for some programs); for doctorate, comprehensive exam, thesis/dissertation, qualifying exam. *Entrance requirements:* For master's and doctorate, GRE General Test (minimum scores: 153 Verbal/148 Quantitative/4.5 Analytical) or MCAT (for some programs). *Application deadline:* For fall admission, 7/15 for domestic students, 5/15 for international students; for winter admission, 10/15 for domestic students, 9/15 for international students; for spring admission, 1/15 for domestic students, 12/15 for international students. Applications are processed on a rolling basis. Application fee: $70. Electronic applications accepted. *Financial support:* Health care benefits and full-tuition and stipends (for PhD students) available. Financial award application deadline: 3/1; financial award applicants required to submit FAFSA. *Faculty research:* Metalloprotein biochemistry, molecular microbiology, environmental microbiology, environmental chemistry, biogeochemistry. *Unit head:* Dr. Michiko Nakano, Program Director. *Application contact:* Dr. Michiko Nakano, Program Director.

Oregon State University, College of Engineering, Program in Environmental Engineering, Corvallis, OR 97331. Offers bioremediation (M Eng, MS, PhD). *Entrance requirements:* For master's and doctorate, GRE. Additional exam requirements/recommendations for international students: Required—TOEFL (minimum score 92 iBT). Electronic applications accepted. *Expenses:* Contact institution.

Penn State Harrisburg, Graduate School, School of Science, Engineering and Technology, Middletown, PA 17057. Offers civil engineering (MS); computer science (MS); electrical engineering (M Eng, MS); engineering management (MPS); engineering science (M Eng); environmental engineering (M Eng); environmental pollution control (MEPC, MS); mechanical engineering (MS); structural engineering (Certificate). *Program availability:* Part-time, evening/weekend.

Penn State University Park, Graduate School, College of Engineering, Department of Civil and Environmental Engineering, University Park, PA 16802. Offers civil engineering (M Eng, MS, PhD); environmental engineering (M Eng, MS, PhD).

Polytechnic University of Puerto Rico, Miami Campus, Graduate School, Miami, FL 33166. Offers accounting (MBA); business administration (MBA); construction management (MEM); environmental management (MEM); finance (MBA); human resources management (MBA); logistics and supply chain management (MBA); management of international enterprises (MBA); manufacturing management (MEM); marketing management (MBA); project management (MBA). *Program availability:* Part-time, evening/weekend, online learning. *Entrance requirements:* For master's, minimum GPA of 3.0. Electronic applications accepted.

Polytechnic University of Puerto Rico, Orlando Campus, Graduate School, Orlando, FL 32825. Offers accounting (MBA); business administration (MBA); construction management (MEM); engineering management (MEM); environmental management (MEM); finance (MBA); human resources management (MBA); management of international enterprises (MBA); management of technology (MBA); manufacturing management (MEM). *Program availability:* Part-time, evening/weekend, online learning. *Entrance requirements:* For master's, minimum GPA of 3.0. Additional exam requirements/recommendations for international students: Recommended—TOEFL. Electronic applications accepted.

Portland State University, Graduate Studies, Maseeh College of Engineering and Computer Science, Department of Civil and Environmental Engineering, Portland, OR 97207-0751. Offers civil and environmental engineering (M Eng, MS, PhD). *Program availability:* Part-time, evening/weekend. *Degree requirements:* For master's, comprehensive exam (for some programs), thesis (for some programs); for doctorate, one foreign language, comprehensive exam, thesis/dissertation, oral and written exams. *Entrance requirements:* For master's, BS in an engineering field, science, or closely-related area with minimum GPA of 3.0; for doctorate, MS in an engineering field, science, or closely-related area. Additional exam requirements/recommendations for international students: Required—TOEFL (minimum score 550 paper-based). *Expenses:* Contact institution. *Faculty research:* Structures, water resources, geotechnical engineering, environmental engineering, transportation.

Princeton University, Graduate School, School of Engineering and Applied Science, Department of Civil and Environmental Engineering, Princeton, NJ 08544-1019. Offers M Eng, MSE, PhD. Terminal master's awarded for partial completion of doctoral program. *Degree requirements:* For master's, thesis (MSE); for doctorate, thesis/dissertation, general exam. *Entrance requirements:* For master's, GRE General Test, 3 letters of recommendation; for doctorate, GRE General Test, official transcript(s), 3 letters of recommendation, personal statement. Additional exam requirements/recommendations for international students: Required—TOEFL. Electronic applications accepted. *Faculty research:* Carbon mitigation; civil engineering materials and structures; climate and atmospheric dynamics; computational mechanics and risk assessment; hydrology, remote sensing, and sustainability.

Purdue University, College of Engineering, Division of Environmental and Ecological Engineering, West Lafayette, IN 47907. Offers MS, PhD. *Degree requirements:* For master's, thesis optional; for doctorate, thesis/dissertation. *Entrance requirements:* For master's and doctorate, GRE, minimum GPA of 3.0. *Faculty research:* Water quality engineering, sustainable energy systems and impacts, greening the built environment, air quality engineering, watershed engineering and management, environmental remediation, life cycle engineering, reducing impacts of chemicals and materials.

Rensselaer Polytechnic Institute, Graduate School, School of Engineering, Program in Environmental Engineering, Troy, NY 12180-3590. Offers M Eng, MS, PhD. *Faculty:* 17 full-time (3 women), 3 part-time/adjunct (0 women). *Students:* 5 full-time (2 women), 3 international. Average age 24. 32 applicants, 16% accepted, 2 enrolled. In 2018, 2 master's awarded. Terminal master's awarded for partial completion of doctoral program. *Degree requirements:* For master's, thesis (for some programs); for doctorate, thesis/dissertation. *Entrance requirements:* For master's and doctorate, GRE. Additional exam requirements/recommendations for international students: Required—TOEFL (minimum score 570 paper-based; 88 iBT), IELTS (minimum score 6.5), PTE (minimum score 60). *Application deadline:* For fall admission, 1/1 priority date for domestic students, 1/1 for international students; for spring admission, 8/15 for domestic and international students. Applications are processed on a rolling basis. Application fee: $75. Electronic applications accepted. *Financial support:* In 2018–19, research assistantships (averaging $23,000 per year), teaching assistantships with full tuition reimbursements (averaging $23,000 per year) were awarded; fellowships also available. Financial award application deadline: 1/1. *Faculty research:* Environmental systems, pollutant fate and transport, site remediation and bioremediation, waste treatment, water treatment. *Total annual research expenditures:* $2,798. *Unit head:* Dr. Marianne Nyman, Graduate Program Director, 518-276-2268, E-mail: nymanm@rpi.edu. *Application contact:* Jarron Decker, Director of Graduate Admissions, 518-276-6216, Fax: 518-276-4072, E-mail: gradadmissions@rpi.edu.
Website: http://cee.rpi.edu/graduate

Rice University, Graduate Programs, George R. Brown School of Engineering, Department of Civil and Environmental Engineering, Houston, TX 77251-1892. Offers civil engineering (MCE, MS, PhD); environmental engineering (MEE, MES, MS, PhD); environmental science (MEE, MES, MS, PhD). *Program availability:* Part-time. *Degree requirements:* For master's, thesis (for some programs); for doctorate, thesis/dissertation. *Entrance requirements:* For master's and doctorate, GRE General Test, GRE Subject Test, minimum GPA of 3.25. Additional exam requirements/recommendations for international students: Required—TOEFL (minimum score 600 paper-based; 90 iBT). Electronic applications accepted. *Faculty research:* Biology and chemistry of groundwater, pollutant fate in groundwater systems, water quality monitoring, urban storm water runoff, urban air quality.

Rose-Hulman Institute of Technology, Graduate Studies, Department of Civil and Environmental Engineering, Terre Haute, IN 47803-3999. Offers civil engineering (MS); environmental engineering (MS). *Program availability:* Part-time. *Faculty:* 8 full-time (2 women), 1 part-time/adjunct (0 women). *Students:* 2 full-time (0 women), 1 part-time (0 women); includes 1 minority (Hispanic/Latino), 1 international. Average age 23. 5 applicants, 80% accepted, 1 enrolled. In 2018, 2 master's awarded. *Degree requirements:* For master's, thesis (for some programs). *Entrance requirements:* For master's, GRE, minimum GPA of 3.0. Additional exam requirements/recommendations for international students: Required—TOEFL (minimum score 580 paper-based; 94 iBT), IELTS (minimum score 7). *Application deadline:* For fall admission, 2/1 priority date for domestic and international students; for winter admission, 10/1 for domestic students, 4/1 for international students; for spring admission, 1/15 for domestic students, 11/1 for international students. Applications are processed on a rolling basis. Application fee: $0. Electronic applications accepted. *Expenses: Tuition:* Full-time $46,641. *Financial support:* In 2018–19, 3 students received support. Fellowships with tuition reimbursements available, research assistantships with tuition reimbursements available, institutionally sponsored loans, scholarships/grants, and tuition waivers (full and partial) available. *Faculty research:* Transportation, hydraulics/hydrology, environmental, construction, geotechnical, structural. *Total annual research expenditures:* $6,927. *Unit head:* Dr. Kevin Sutterer, Department Head, 812-877-8959, E-mail: sutterer@rose-hulman.edu. *Application contact:* Dr. Craig Downing, Associate Dean of Lifelong Learning, 812-877-8822, E-mail: downing@rose-hulman.edu.
Website: https://www.rose-hulman.edu/academics/academic-departments/civil-and-environmental-engineering/index.html

Rutgers University–New Brunswick, Graduate School-New Brunswick, Department of Civil and Environmental Engineering, Piscataway, NJ 08854-8097. Offers MS, PhD. *Program availability:* Part-time, evening/weekend. Terminal master's awarded for partial completion of doctoral program. *Degree requirements:* For master's, comprehensive exam, thesis or alternative; for doctorate, comprehensive exam, thesis/dissertation. *Entrance requirements:* For master's and doctorate, GRE General Test. Additional exam requirements/recommendations for international students: Required—TOEFL (minimum score 580 paper-based). Electronic applications accepted. *Faculty research:* Civil engineering materials research, non-destructive evaluation of transportation infrastructure, transportation planning, intelligent transportation systems.

Southern Illinois University Carbondale, Graduate School, College of Engineering, Program in Engineering Science, Carbondale, IL 62901-4701. Offers engineering science (PhD), including civil and environmental engineering, electrical and computer engineering, mechanical engineering and energy processes, mining and mineral resources engineering. *Degree requirements:* For doctorate, thesis/dissertation. *Entrance requirements:* For doctorate, GRE General Test, minimum GPA of 3.5. Additional exam requirements/recommendations for international students: Required—TOEFL.

Southern Illinois University Edwardsville, Graduate School, School of Engineering, Department of Civil Engineering, Program in Environmental Engineering, Edwardsville, IL 62026. Offers MS. *Program availability:* Part-time, evening/weekend. *Degree requirements:* For master's, thesis (for some programs), research paper. *Entrance requirements:* For master's, minimum undergraduate GPA of 2.75 in science, math, and engineering courses. Additional exam requirements/recommendations for international students: Required—TOEFL (minimum score 550 paper-based, 79 iBT), IELTS (minimum score 6.5), Michigan Test of English Language Proficiency or PTE. Electronic applications accepted.

Southern Methodist University, Lyle School of Engineering, Department of Civil and Environmental Engineering, Dallas, TX 75275-0340. Offers civil and environmental engineering (PhD); civil engineering (MS), including geotechnical engineering, structural engineering, transportation systems; environmental engineering (MS); sustainability and development (MA). *Program availability:* Part-time, evening/weekend, online learning. Terminal master's awarded for partial completion of doctoral program. *Degree requirements:* For master's, thesis optional; for doctorate, thesis/dissertation, oral and written qualifying exams. *Entrance requirements:* For master's, GRE General Test, minimum GPA of 3.0 in last 2 years; bachelor's degree in engineering, mathematics, or sciences; for doctorate, GRE, BS and MS in related field, minimum GPA of 3.3. Additional exam requirements/recommendations for international students: Required—TOEFL. Electronic applications accepted. *Faculty research:* Human and environmental health effects of endocrine disrupters, development of air pollution control systems for diesel engines, structural analysis and design, modeling and design of waste treatment systems.

State University of New York College of Environmental Science and Forestry, Department of Environmental Resources Engineering, Syracuse, NY 13210-2779. Offers ecological engineering (MPS, MS, PhD); environmental management (MPS); environmental resources engineering (MPS, MS, PhD); geospatial information science and engineering (MPS, MS, PhD); water resources engineering (MPS, MS, PhD). *Program availability:* Part-time. *Faculty:* 9 full-time (1 woman), 3 part-time/adjunct (0 women). *Students:* 32 full-time (12 women), 8 part-time (0 women); includes 2 minority (1 Black or African American, non-Hispanic/Latino; 1 Asian, non-Hispanic/Latino), 19 international. Average age 41. 31 applicants, 58% accepted, 7 enrolled. In 2018, 11 master's, 1 doctorate awarded. Terminal master's awarded for partial completion of doctoral program. *Degree requirements:* For master's, thesis (for some programs); for doctorate, comprehensive exam, thesis/dissertation. *Entrance requirements:* For master's and doctorate, GRE General Test, minimum GPA of 3.0. Additional exam requirements/recommendations for international students: Required—TOEFL (minimum score 550 paper-based; 80 iBT), IELTS (minimum score 6). *Application deadline:* For fall admission, 1/15 priority date for domestic and international students; for spring admission, 11/1 priority date for domestic and international students. Applications are processed on a rolling basis. Application fee: $60. Electronic applications accepted. *Expenses: Tuition, area resident:* Full-time $11,090; part-time $462 per credit hour. Tuition, state resident: full-time $11,090; part-time $462 per credit hour. Tuition, nonresident: full-time $22,650; part-time $944 per credit hour. *International tuition:* $22,650 full-time. *Required fees:* $1733; $178.58 per credit hour. *Financial support:* In 2018–19, 9 students received support. Unspecified assistantships available. Financial award application deadline: 6/30; financial award applicants required to submit FAFSA. *Faculty research:* Ecological engineering, environmental resources engineering, geospatial information science and engineering, water resources engineering, environmental science. *Total annual research expenditures:* $508,995. *Unit head:* Dr. Lindi Quackenbush, Chair, 315-470-4727, Fax: 315-470-4710, E-mail: ljquackc@esf.edu. *Application contact:* Scott Shannon, Associate Provost for Instruction/Dean of the Graduate School, 315-470-6599, Fax: 315-470-6978, E-mail: esfgrad@esf.edu.
Website: http://www.esf.edu/ere

Stevens Institute of Technology, Graduate School, Charles V. Schaefer Jr. School of Engineering and Science, Department of Civil, Environmental, and Ocean Engineering, Program in Environmental Engineering, Hoboken, NJ 07030. Offers environmental engineering (PhD, Certificate), including environmental compatibility in engineering (Certificate), environmental hydrology (Certificate), environmental processes (Certificate), hydraulics (Certificate), soil and groundwater pollution control (Certificate), water quality control (Certificate); environmental processes (M Eng); inland and coastal environmental hydrodynamics (M Eng); modeling of environmental systems (M Eng); soil and groundwater pollution control (M Eng). *Program availability:* Part-time, evening/weekend. *Faculty:* 28 full-time (7 women), 1 part-time/adjunct (0 women). *Students:* 58 full-time (24 women), 12 part-time (5 women); includes 6 minority (2 Black or African American, non-Hispanic/Latino; 1 American Indian or Alaska Native, non-Hispanic/Latino; 2 Asian, non-Hispanic/Latino; 1 Hispanic/Latino), 48 international. Average age 25. In 2018, 14 master's, 1 doctorate, 6 other advanced degrees awarded. Terminal master's awarded for partial completion of doctoral program. *Degree requirements:* For master's, thesis optional, minimum B average in major field and overall; for doctorate, comprehensive exam (for some programs), thesis/dissertation; for Certificate, minimum B average. *Entrance requirements:* For master's, GRE/GMAT scores: GRE scores are required for all applicants applying to a full-time graduate program in the Schaefer School of Engineering and Science (SES). International applicants must submit TOEFL/IELTS scores and fulfill the English Language Proficiency Requirements in order to be considered. Additional exam requirements/recommendations for international students: Required—TOEFL (minimum score 74 iBT), IELTS (minimum score 6). *Application deadline:* For fall admission, 4/15 for domestic and international students; for spring admission, 11/1 for domestic and international students; for summer admission, 5/1 for domestic students. Applications are processed on a rolling basis. Application fee: $60. Electronic applications accepted. *Expenses: Tuition:* Full-time $35,960; part-time $1620 per credit. *Required fees:* $1290; $600 per semester. Tuition and fees vary according to course load. *Financial support:* Fellowships, research assistantships, teaching assistantships, career-related internships or fieldwork, Federal Work-Study, scholarships/grants, and unspecified assistantships available. Financial award application deadline: 2/15; financial award applicants required to submit FAFSA. *Unit head:* Dr. Jean Zu, Dean of SES, 201-216.8233, Fax: 201-216.8372, E-mail: Jean.Zu@stevens.edu. *Application contact:* Graduate Admission, 888-783-8367, Fax: 888-511-1306, E-mail: graduate@stevens.edu.

Syracuse University, College of Engineering and Computer Science, MS Program in Environmental Engineering, Syracuse, NY 13244. Offers MS. *Program availability:* Part-time. *Students:* Average age 24. In 2018, 6 master's awarded. *Degree requirements:* For master's, thesis optional. *Entrance requirements:* For master's, GRE General Test, three letters of recommendation, personal statement, resume, official transcripts. Additional exam requirements/recommendations for international students: Required—TOEFL (minimum score 100 iBT). *Application deadline:* For fall admission, 7/1 priority date for domestic students, 6/1 priority date for international students; for spring admission, 11/15 priority date for domestic students, 10/15 priority date for international students. Applications are processed on a rolling basis. Application fee: $75. Electronic applications accepted. *Financial support:* Fellowships with full tuition reimbursements, research assistantships, teaching assistantships, and tuition waivers available. Financial award application deadline: 1/1. *Faculty research:* Environmental transport and fate of pollutants, sources of airborne particles in urban and remote areas, measurement and modeling of atmospheric dry and wet deposition of pollutants, emission inventories for airborne lead, assessment of performance of green infrastructure for storm water management. *Unit head:* Dr. Cliff Davidson, Program Director, 315-443-2311, E-mail: davidson@syr.edu. *Application contact:* Kathleen Joyce, Assistant Dean, 315-443-2219, E-mail: topgrads@syr.edu.
Website: http://eng-cs.syr.edu/program/environmental-engineering/?degree-masters_program

Syracuse University, College of Engineering and Computer Science, MS Program in Environmental Engineering Science, Syracuse, NY 13244. Offers MS. *Program availability:* Part-time. *Students:* Average age 24. In 2018, 2 master's awarded. *Entrance requirements:* For master's, GRE General Test, three letters of recommendation, personal statement, resume, official transcripts. Additional exam requirements/recommendations for international students: Required—TOEFL (minimum score 100 iBT). *Application deadline:* For fall admission, 7/1 for domestic students, 6/1 for international students; for spring admission, 11/15 for domestic students, 10/15 priority date for international students. Applications are processed on a rolling basis. Application fee: $75. Electronic applications accepted. *Financial support:* Fellowships with full tuition reimbursements, research assistantships, teaching assistantships, and tuition waivers available. Financial award application deadline: 1/1. *Faculty research:* Sustainable development in urban areas, human perceptions of energy use from day-to-day activities, emission inventories for airborne ammonia, assessment of performance of green infrastructure for storm water management. *Unit head:* Dr. Cliff Davidson, Program Director, 315-443-2311, E-mail: davidson@syr.edu. *Application contact:* Kathleen Joyce, Assistant Dean, 315-443-2219, E-mail: topgrads@syr.edu.
Website: http://eng-cs.syr.edu/program/environmental-engineering-science/?degree-masters_program

Temple University, College of Engineering, Department of Civil and Environmental Engineering, Philadelphia, PA 19122-6096. Offers civil engineering (MSCE); environmental engineering (MS Env E); storm water management (Graduate Certificate). *Program availability:* Part-time, evening/weekend. Terminal master's awarded for partial completion of doctoral program. *Degree requirements:* For master's, thesis optional. *Entrance requirements:* For master's, GRE General Test, minimum GPA of 3.0; BS in engineering from ABET-accredited or equivalent institution; resume; goals statement; three letters of reference; official transcripts. Additional exam requirements/recommendations for international students: Required—TOEFL (minimum score 550 paper-based; 79 iBT), IELTS (minimum score 6.5), PTE (minimum score 53). Electronic applications accepted. *Expenses:* Contact institution. *Faculty research:* Analysis of the effect of scour on bridge stability, design of sustainable buildings, development of new highway pavement material using plastic waste, characterization of by-products and waste materials for pavement and geotechnical engineering applications, development of effective traffic signals in urban and rural settings, development of techniques for effective construction management.

Temple University, College of Engineering, PhD in Engineering Program, Philadelphia, PA 19122-6096. Offers bioengineering (PhD); civil engineering (PhD); electrical engineering (PhD); environmental engineering (PhD); mechanical engineering (PhD). *Program availability:* Part-time, evening/weekend. *Degree requirements:* For doctorate, thesis/dissertation, preliminary exam, dissertation proposal and defense. *Entrance requirements:* For doctorate, GRE, minimum undergraduate GPA of 3.0; MS in engineering from ABET-accredited or equivalent institution (preferred); resume; goals statement; three letters of reference; official transcripts. Additional exam requirements/recommendations for international students: Required—TOEFL (minimum score 550 paper-based; 79 iBT), IELTS (minimum score 6.5), PTE (minimum score 53). Electronic applications accepted. *Expenses:* Contact institution. *Faculty research:* Advanced/computer-aided manufacturing and advanced materials processing; bioengineering; computer engineering; construction engineering and management; dynamics, controls, and systems; energy and environmental science; engineering physics and engineering mathematics; green engineering; signal processing and communication; transportation engineering; water resources, hydrology, and environmental engineering.

See Display on page 59 and Close-Up on page 73.

Tennessee State University, The School of Graduate Studies and Research, College of Engineering, Nashville, TN 37209-1561. Offers biomedical engineering (ME); civil engineering (ME); computer and information systems engineering (MS, PhD); electrical engineering (ME); environmental engineering (ME); manufacturing engineering (ME); mathematical sciences (MS); mechanical engineering (ME). *Program availability:* Part-time, evening/weekend. *Degree requirements:* For master's, project; for doctorate, comprehensive exam, thesis/dissertation. *Entrance requirements:* For doctorate, minimum GPA of 3.3. *Faculty research:* Robotics, intelligent systems, human-computer interaction software systems, biomedical engineering, signal/image processing, probabilistic design, intelligent manufacturing, cooperative mobile robots, condition based maintenance, sensor fusion.

Texas A&M University–Kingsville, College of Graduate Studies, Frank H. Dotterweich College of Engineering, Department of Environmental Engineering, Kingsville, TX 78363. Offers ME, MS, PhD. *Degree requirements:* For master's, variable foreign language requirement, comprehensive exam, thesis (for some programs); for doctorate, variable foreign language requirement, comprehensive exam, thesis/dissertation (for some programs). *Entrance requirements:* For master's, GRE (minimum quantitative and verbal score of 294), MAT, GMAT, minimum undergraduate GPA of 2.8; for doctorate, GRE, MAT, GMAT. Additional exam requirements/recommendations for international students: Required—TOEFL (minimum score 550 paper-based; 79 iBT). Electronic applications accepted. *Faculty research:* Water sampling in the Lower Rio Grande, urban stormwater management.

Tufts University, School of Engineering, Department of Civil and Environmental Engineering, Medford, MA 02155. Offers bioengineering (MS), including environmental biotechnology; civil and environmental engineering (MS, PhD), including applied data science, environmental and water resources engineering, environmental health, geosystems engineering, structural engineering and mechanics; PhD/PhD. *Program availability:* Part-time. Terminal master's awarded for partial completion of doctoral program. *Degree requirements:* For master's, thesis (for some programs); for doctorate, thesis/dissertation. *Entrance requirements:* For master's and doctorate, GRE General Test. Additional exam requirements/recommendations for international students: Required—TOEFL (minimum score 550 paper-based; 80 iBT), IELTS (minimum score 6.5). Electronic applications accepted. *Expenses: Tuition:* Full-time $51,288; part-time $1710 per credit hour. *Required fees:* $904. Full-time tuition and fees vary according to degree level, program and student level. Part-time tuition and fees vary according to course load. *Faculty research:* Environmental and water resources engineering, environmental health, geotechnical and geoenvironmental engineering, structural engineering and mechanics, water diplomacy.

Universidad Central del Este, Graduate School, San Pedro de Macoris, Dominican Republic. Offers environmental engineering (ME); financial management (M Ad); higher education (M Ed), including higher education management, higher education pedagogy; human resources (M Ad). *Entrance requirements:* For master's, letters of recommendation.

Universidad Nacional Pedro Henriquez Urena, Graduate School, Santo Domingo, Dominican Republic. Offers agricultural diversity (MS), including horticultural/fruit production, tropical animal production; conservation of monuments and cultural assets (M Arch); ecology and environment (MS); environmental engineering (MEE); international relations (MA); natural resource management (MS); political science (MA); project optimization (MPM); project feasibility (MPM); project management (MPM); sanitation engineering (ME); science for teachers (MS); tropical Caribbean architecture (M Arch).

Université de Sherbrooke, Faculty of Engineering, Program in the Environment, Sherbrooke, QC J1K 2R1, Canada. Offers M Env. *Degree requirements:* For master's, thesis.

Université Laval, Faculty of Sciences and Engineering, Department of Civil Engineering, Programs in Civil Engineering, Québec, QC G1K 7P4, Canada. Offers civil engineering (M Sc, PhD); environmental technology (M Sc). Terminal master's awarded for partial completion of doctoral program. *Degree requirements:* For master's, thesis (for some programs); for doctorate, comprehensive exam, thesis/dissertation. *Entrance requirements:* For master's and doctorate, knowledge of French and English. Electronic applications accepted.

University at Buffalo, the State University of New York, Graduate School, School of Engineering and Applied Sciences, Department of Civil, Structural, and Environmental Engineering, Buffalo, NY 14260. Offers civil engineering (MS, PhD); engineering science (MS), including data sciences, green energy, Internet of Things, nanoelectronics; environmental and water resources engineering (MS). *Program availability:* Part-time, online learning. Terminal master's awarded for partial completion of doctoral program. *Degree requirements:* For master's, project, thesis, or comprehensive exam; for doctorate, thesis/dissertation. *Entrance requirements:* For master's and doctorate, GRE General Test, letters of reference. Additional exam requirements/recommendations for international students: Required—TOEFL (minimum score 550 paper-based; 79 iBT). Electronic applications accepted. *Faculty research:* Structural and earthquake engineering; geomechanics, geotechnical and geoenvironmental engineering; computational engineering mechanics; bridge engineering; environmental and water resources engineering; transportation systems engineering.

The University of Alabama, Graduate School, College of Engineering, Department of Civil, Construction and Environmental Engineering, Tuscaloosa, AL 35487-0205. Offers civil engineering (MSCE, PhD); environmental engineering (MS). *Program availability:* Part-time. Terminal master's awarded for partial completion of doctoral program. *Degree requirements:* For master's, thesis or alternative; for doctorate, comprehensive exam, thesis/dissertation. *Entrance requirements:* For master's and doctorate, GRE General Test (minimum combined score of 300), minimum overall GPA of 3.0 in last hours of course work. Additional exam requirements/recommendations for international students: Required—TOEFL (minimum score 550 paper-based; 79 iBT), IELTS (minimum score 6.5), PTE (minimum score 59). Electronic applications accepted. *Faculty research:* Experimental structures, modeling of structures, bridge management systems, geotechnological engineering, environmental remediation.

The University of Alabama in Huntsville, School of Graduate Studies, College of Engineering, Department of Civil and Environmental Engineering, Huntsville, AL 35899. Offers civil and environmental engineering (PhD); civil engineering (MSE), including civil engineering. PhD offered jointly with The University of Alabama at Birmingham. *Program availability:* Part-time. *Faculty:* 6 full-time (1 woman). *Students:* 18 full-time (7 women), 13 part-time (4 women); includes 6 minority (4 Black or African American, non-Hispanic/Latino; 2 Hispanic/Latino), 15 international. Average age 32. 43 applicants, 72% accepted, 11 enrolled. In 2018, 11 master's, 1 doctorate awarded. *Degree requirements:* For master's, comprehensive exam, thesis or alternative, oral and written exams; for doctorate, comprehensive exam, thesis/dissertation, oral and written exams. *Entrance requirements:* For master's, GRE General Test, BSE, minimum GPA of 3.0; for doctorate, GRE General Test, minimum GPA of 3.0. Additional exam requirements/recommendations for international students: Required—TOEFL (minimum score 500 paper-based; 80 iBT), IELTS (minimum score 6.5). *Application deadline:* For fall admission, 7/15 priority date for domestic students, 4/1 priority date for international students; for spring admission, 11/30 priority date for domestic students, 9/1 priority date for international students. Applications are processed on a rolling basis. Application fee: $50. Electronic applications accepted. *Expenses: Tuition, area resident:* Full-time $10,632; part-time $412 per credit hour. Tuition, state resident: full-time $10,632. Tuition, nonresident: full-time $23,604; part-time $412 per credit hour. *Required fees:* $582; $582. Tuition and fees vary according to course load and program. *Financial support:* In 2018–19, 14 students received support, including 8 research assistantships with full tuition reimbursements available (averaging $7,825 per year), 6 teaching assistantships with full tuition reimbursements available (averaging $5,316 per year); career-related internships or fieldwork, Federal Work-Study, institutionally sponsored loans, scholarships/grants, health care benefits, and unspecified assistantships also available. Support available to part-time students. Financial award application deadline: 4/1; financial award applicants required to submit FAFSA. *Faculty research:* Smart materials and smart structures, fiber-reinforced cementitious composites, processing and mechanics of composites, geographic information systems, environmental engineering. *Unit head:* Dr. Michael Anderson, Interim Chair, 256-824-5028, Fax: 256-824-6724, E-mail: andersmd@uah.edu. *Application contact:* Kim Gray, Graduate Studies Admissions Coordinator, 256-824-6002, Fax: 256-824-6405, E-mail: deangrad@uah.edu.
Website: http://www.uah.edu/eng/departments/cee

University of Alaska Fairbanks, College of Engineering and Mines, Department of Civil and Environmental Engineering, Fairbanks, AK 99775-5900. Offers civil engineering (MS); design and construction management (Graduate Certificate); environmental engineering (PhD). *Program availability:* Part-time. *Faculty:* 6 full-time (1 woman), 1 (woman) part-time/adjunct. *Students:* 8 full-time (2 women), 7 part-time (2 women); includes 4 minority (1 Black or African American, non-Hispanic/Latino; 1 Asian, non-Hispanic/Latino; 2 Two or more races, non-Hispanic/Latino), 2 international. Average age 27. 10 applicants, 30% accepted, 3 enrolled. In 2018, 4 master's awarded. *Degree requirements:* For master's, comprehensive exam, thesis (for some programs), oral defense of project or thesis; for doctorate, comprehensive exam, thesis/dissertation. *Entrance requirements:* For master's, bachelor's degree from accredited institution with minimum cumulative undergraduate and major GPA of 3.0. Additional exam requirements/recommendations for international students: Required—TOEFL (minimum score 550 paper-based; 79 iBT), IELTS (minimum score 6.5). *Application deadline:* For fall admission, 6/1 for domestic students, 3/1 for international students; for spring admission, 10/15 for domestic students, 9/1 for international students. Applications are processed on a rolling basis. Application fee: $60. Electronic applications accepted. *Expenses:* CEM tuition has a 20% surcharge per credit hour over that for credits of most other UAF colleges. Assuming 60 credits for PhD and 32 for Master's, this augments costs by $6,180 for in-state PhD, $3,296 for in-state Master's, $12,948 for non-resident PhD and $6,912 for non-resident Masters students, respectively. *Financial support:* In 2018–19, 7 research assistantships with full tuition reimbursements (averaging $4,557 per year), 6 teaching assistantships with full tuition reimbursements (averaging $5,086 per year) were awarded; fellowships with full tuition reimbursements, career-related internships or fieldwork, Federal Work-Study, scholarships/grants, health care benefits, and unspecified assistantships also available. Support available to part-time students. Financial award application deadline: 7/1; financial award applicants required to submit FAFSA. *Faculty research:* Soils, structures, culvert thawing with solar power, pavement drainage, contaminant hydrogeology. *Unit head:* Dr. Robert Perkins, Department Chair, 907-474-7694, E-mail: fycee@uaf.edu. *Application contact:* Samara Taber, Director of Admissions, 907-474-7500, E-mail: uaf-admissions@alaska.edu.
Website: http://cem.uaf.edu/cee

University of Alberta, Faculty of Graduate Studies and Research, Department of Civil and Environmental Engineering, Edmonton, AB T6G 2E1, Canada. Offers construction engineering and management (M Eng, M Sc, PhD); environmental engineering (M Eng, M Sc, PhD); environmental science (M Sc, PhD); geoenvironmental engineering (M Eng, M Sc, PhD); geotechnical engineering (M Eng, M Sc, PhD); mining engineering (M Eng, M Sc, PhD); petroleum engineering (M Eng, M Sc, PhD); structural engineering (M Eng, M Sc, PhD); water resources (M Eng, M Sc, PhD). *Program availability:* Part-time, online learning. *Degree requirements:* For master's, thesis (for some programs); for doctorate, thesis/dissertation. *Entrance requirements:* For master's, minimum GPA of 3.0 in last 2 years of undergraduate studies; for doctorate, minimum GPA of 3.0. Additional exam requirements/recommendations for international students: Required—TOEFL (minimum score 550 paper-based). Electronic applications accepted. *Faculty research:* Mining.

The University of Arizona, College of Engineering, Department of Chemical and Environmental Engineering, Tucson, AZ 85721-0011. Offers chemical engineering (MS, PhD); environmental engineering (MS, PhD). *Program availability:* Part-time. *Degree requirements:* For master's, thesis; for doctorate, comprehensive exam, thesis/dissertation, departmental qualifying exams. *Entrance requirements:* For master's and doctorate, GRE General Test, 3 letters of recommendation, resume, statement of purpose. Additional exam requirements/recommendations for international students: Required—TOEFL (minimum score 550 paper-based; 79 iBT). Electronic applications accepted. *Faculty research:* Energy and environment-hazardous waste incineration, sustainability, kinetics, bioremediation, semiconductor processing.

University of Arkansas, Graduate School, College of Engineering, Department of Civil Engineering, Program in Environmental Engineering, Fayetteville, AR 72701. Offers MS En E, MSE. *Degree requirements:* For master's, thesis optional. *Application deadline:* For fall admission, 8/1 for domestic students, 4/1 for international students; for spring admission, 12/1 for domestic students, 10/1 for international students; for summer admission, 4/15 for domestic students, 3/1 for international students. Applications are processed on a rolling basis. Application fee: $60. Electronic applications accepted. *Financial support:* In 2018–19, 4 research assistantships were awarded; fellowships, teaching assistantships, career-related internships or fieldwork, and Federal Work-Study also available. Support available to part-time students. Financial award application deadline: 4/1; financial award applicants required to submit FAFSA. *Unit head:* Dr. Micah Hale, Department Chair, 479-575-6348, E-mail: micah@uark.edu. *Application contact:* Dr. Julian Fairey, Graduate Coordinator, 479-575-4023, E-mail: julianf@uark.edu.
Website: https://civil-engineering.uark.edu/research/environmental-engineering.php

University of Arkansas, Graduate School, Interdisciplinary Program in Environmental Dynamics, Fayetteville, AR 72701. Offers PhD. In 2018, 4 doctorates awarded. *Application deadline:* For fall admission, 8/1 for domestic students, 4/1 for international students; for spring admission, 12/1 for domestic students, 10/1 for international students; for summer admission, 4/15 for domestic students, 3/1 for international students. Applications are processed on a rolling basis. Application fee: $60. Electronic applications accepted. *Financial support:* In 2018–19, 5 research assistantships, 9 teaching assistantships were awarded; fellowships with tuition reimbursements also available. Financial award application deadline: 4/1. *Unit head:* Dr. Peter S. Ungar, Director, 479-575-6361, Fax: 479-575-3469, E-mail: pungar@uark.edu. *Application contact:* JoAnn Kvamme, Assistant Director, 479-575-6603, Fax: 479-575-3469, E-mail: jkvamme@uark.edu.
Website: https://environmental-dynamics.uark.edu

University of Calgary, Faculty of Graduate Studies, Schulich School of Engineering, Program in Chemical and Petroleum Engineering, Calgary, AB T2N 1N4, Canada. Offers chemical engineering (M Eng, M Sc, PhD); energy and environment engineering (M Eng, M Sc, PhD); energy and environmental systems (M Eng, M Sc, PhD); environmental engineering (M Eng, M Sc, PhD); petroleum engineering (M Eng, M Sc, PhD); reservoir characterization (M Eng, M Sc). *Program availability:* Part-time. *Degree requirements:* For master's, thesis (for some programs); for doctorate, comprehensive exam, thesis/dissertation, candidacy exam. *Entrance requirements:* For master's, minimum GPA of 3.0 or equivalent; for doctorate, minimum GPA of 3.5 or equivalent. Additional exam requirements/recommendations for international students: Required—TOEFL (minimum score 550 paper-based; 80 iBT), IELTS (minimum score 7). Electronic applications accepted. *Faculty research:* Environmental engineering, biomedical engineering modeling, simulation and control, petroleum recovery and reservoir engineering, phase equilibria and transport properties.

University of Calgary, Faculty of Graduate Studies, Schulich School of Engineering, Program in Civil Engineering, Calgary, AB T2N 1N4, Canada. Offers avalanche mechanics (M Sc, PhD); civil engineering (M Eng, M Sc, PhD); energy and environment engineering (M Eng, M Sc, PhD); environmental engineering (M Eng, M Sc, PhD); geotechnical engineering (M Eng, M Sc, PhD); materials science (M Eng, M Sc, PhD); project management (M Eng, M Sc, PhD); structures and solid mechanics (M Eng, M Sc, PhD); transportation engineering (M Eng, M Sc, PhD); water resources (M Eng, M Sc, PhD). *Program availability:* Part-time. *Degree requirements:* For master's, thesis; for doctorate, thesis/dissertation, written and oral candidacy exam. *Entrance* *requirements:* For master's, minimum GPA of 3.0; for doctorate, minimum GPA of 3.5. Additional exam requirements/recommendations for international students: Required—TOEFL (minimum score 580 paper-based; 93 iBT), IELTS (minimum score 7). Electronic applications accepted. *Faculty research:* Geotechnical engineering, energy and environment, transportation, project management, structures and solid mechanics.

University of California, Berkeley, Graduate Division, College of Engineering, Department of Civil and Environmental Engineering, Berkeley, CA 94720. Offers engineering and project management (M Eng, MS, PhD); environmental engineering (M Eng, MS, PhD); geoengineering (M Eng, MS, PhD); structural engineering, mechanics and materials (M Eng, MS, PhD); transportation engineering (M Eng, MS, PhD); M Arch/MS; MCP/MS; MPP/MS. Terminal master's awarded for partial completion of doctoral program. *Degree requirements:* For master's, comprehensive exam (for some programs), thesis (for some programs), comprehensive exam or thesis (MS); for doctorate, thesis/dissertation, qualifying exam. *Entrance requirements:* For master's, GRE General Test, minimum GPA of 3.0, 3 letters of recommendation; for doctorate, GRE General Test, minimum GPA of 3.5, 3 letters of recommendation. Additional exam requirements/recommendations for international students: Required—TOEFL (minimum score 570 paper-based; 90 iBT). Electronic applications accepted.

University of California, Davis, College of Engineering, Program in Civil and Environmental Engineering, Davis, CA 95616. Offers M Engr, MS, D Engr, PhD, Certificate, M Engr/MBA. *Degree requirements:* For master's, comprehensive exam (for some programs), thesis (for some programs); for doctorate, thesis/dissertation. *Entrance requirements:* For master's, GRE General Test, minimum GPA of 3.0; for doctorate, GRE, minimum graduate GPA of 3.5. Additional exam requirements/recommendations for international students: Required—TOEFL (minimum score 550 paper-based). Electronic applications accepted. *Faculty research:* Environmental water resources, transportation, structural mechanics, structural engineering, geotechnical engineering.

University of California, Irvine, Samueli School of Engineering, Department of Civil and Environmental Engineering, Irvine, CA 92697. Offers MS, PhD. *Program availability:* Part-time. *Students:* 133 full-time (53 women), 19 part-time (8 women); includes 23 minority (1 Black or African American, non-Hispanic/Latino; 14 Asian, non-Hispanic/Latino; 5 Hispanic/Latino; 3 Two or more races, non-Hispanic/Latino), 96 international. Average age 27. 433 applicants, 45% accepted, 45 enrolled. In 2018, 49 master's, 16 doctorates awarded. Terminal master's awarded for partial completion of doctoral program. *Entrance requirements:* For master's and doctorate, GRE General Test, minimum GPA of 3.0, 3 letters of recommendation. Additional exam requirements/recommendations for international students: Required—TOEFL (minimum score 550 paper-based). *Application deadline:* For fall admission, 1/15 priority date for domestic students, 1/15 for international students. Applications are processed on a rolling basis. Application fee: $105 ($125 for international students). Electronic applications accepted. *Financial support:* Fellowships, research assistantships with full tuition reimbursements, teaching assistantships, institutionally sponsored loans, traineeships, health care benefits, and unspecified assistantships available. Financial award application deadline: 3/1; financial award applicants required to submit FAFSA. *Faculty research:* Intelligent transportation systems and transportation economics, risk and reliability, fluid mechanics, environmental hydrodynamics, hydrological and climate systems, water resources. *Unit head:* Prof. Brett F. Sanders, Chair and Professor, 949-824-4327, Fax: 949-824-3672, E-mail: bsanders@uci.edu. *Application contact:* Connie Cheng, Assistant Director, 949-824-3562, Fax: 949-824-8200, E-mail: connie.cheng@uci.edu. Website: http://www.eng.uci.edu/dept/cee

University of California, Los Angeles, Graduate Division, Fielding School of Public Health, Department of Environmental Health Sciences, Los Angeles, CA 90095. Offers environmental health sciences (MS, PhD); environmental science and engineering (D Env); molecular toxicology (PhD); JD/MPH. *Accreditation:* ABET (one or more programs are accredited); CEPH. *Degree requirements:* For master's, comprehensive exam or thesis; for doctorate, thesis/dissertation, oral and written qualifying exams. *Entrance requirements:* For master's, GRE General Test, minimum GPA of 3.0; for doctorate, GRE General Test, minimum undergraduate GPA of 3.0. Electronic applications accepted.

University of California, Los Angeles, Graduate Division, Henry Samueli School of Engineering and Applied Science, Department of Civil and Environmental Engineering, Los Angeles, CA 90095-1593. Offers MS, PhD. *Degree requirements:* For master's, comprehensive exam or thesis; for doctorate, thesis/dissertation, qualifying exams. *Entrance requirements:* For master's, GRE General Test, minimum GPA of 3.0; for doctorate, GRE General Test, minimum GPA of 3.25. Additional exam requirements/recommendations for international students: Required—TOEFL (minimum score 560 paper-based; 87 iBT), IELTS (minimum score 7). Electronic applications accepted. *Faculty research:* Civil engineering materials, environmental engineering, geotechnical engineering, hydrology and water resources, structures.

University of California, Los Angeles, Graduate Division, Institute of the Environment and Sustainability, Los Angeles, CA 90095-1496. Offers environmental science and engineering (D Env). *Degree requirements:* For doctorate, thesis/dissertation, oral and written qualifying exams. *Entrance requirements:* For doctorate, GRE General Test, minimum undergraduate GPA of 3.0, master's degree or equivalent in a natural science, engineering, or public health. *Faculty research:* Toxic and hazardous substances, air and water pollution, risk assessment/management, water resources, marine science.

University of California, Merced, Graduate Division, School of Engineering, Merced, CA 95343. Offers biological engineering and small scale technologies (MS, PhD); electrical engineering and computer science (MS, PhD); environmental systems (MS, PhD); management of innovation, sustainability, and technology (MM); mechanical engineering (MS); mechanical engineering and applied mechanics (PhD). *Faculty:* 60 full-time (16 women). *Students:* 219 full-time (72 women), 1 part-time (0 women); includes 43 minority (2 Black or African American, non-Hispanic/Latino; 17 Asian, non-Hispanic/Latino; 20 Hispanic/Latino; 1 Native Hawaiian or other Pacific Islander, non-Hispanic/Latino; 3 Two or more races, non-Hispanic/Latino), 145 international. Average age 28. 371 applicants, 46% accepted, 75 enrolled. In 2018, 30 master's, 17 doctorates awarded. Terminal master's awarded for partial completion of doctoral program. *Degree requirements:* For master's, variable foreign language requirement, comprehensive exam, thesis or alternative, oral defense; for doctorate, variable foreign language requirement, comprehensive exam, thesis/dissertation, oral defense. *Entrance requirements:* For master's and doctorate, GRE. Additional exam requirements/recommendations for international students: Required—TOEFL (minimum score 550 paper-based; 80 iBT); Recommended—IELTS (minimum score 6.5). *Application deadline:* For fall admission, 1/15 priority date for domestic and international students. Application fee: $105 ($125 for international students). Electronic applications accepted. *Expenses:* In-state tuition $11442 per year; Out-of-state tuition $26544 per year; Student Fees $1765 per year. *Financial support:* In 2018–19, 200 students received support, including 14 fellowships with full tuition reimbursements available (averaging $20,851 per year), 70 research assistantships with full tuition reimbursements available (averaging $18,334 per year), 116 teaching assistantships with full tuition reimbursements available (averaging $19,841 per year); scholarships/grants, traineeships, and health care benefits also available. *Faculty research:* Sustainability systems engineering and resource management: food, energy, water; biomolecular

engineering and biotechnology; computational science and data analytics; artificial intelligence, machine learning, internet of things, human computer interface; cyber-physical systems and automation. *Total annual research expenditures:* $3.1 million. *Unit head:* Dr. Mark Matsumoto, Dean, 209-228-4047, Fax: 209-228-4047, E-mail: mmatsumoto@ucmerced.edu. *Application contact:* Tsu Ya, Director of Admissions and Academic Services, 209-228-4521, Fax: 209-228-6906, E-mail: tya@ucmerced.edu.

University of California, Riverside, Graduate Division, Department of Chemical and Environmental Engineering, Riverside, CA 92521-0102. Offers MS, PhD. *Program availability:* Part-time. Terminal master's awarded for partial completion of doctoral program. *Degree requirements:* For master's, thesis (for some programs); for doctorate, comprehensive exam, thesis/dissertation. *Entrance requirements:* For master's and doctorate, GRE General Test, minimum GPA of 3.0. Additional exam requirements/recommendations for international students: Required—TOEFL (minimum score 550 paper-based; 80 iBT). Electronic applications accepted. *Faculty research:* Air quality systems, water quality systems, advanced materials and nanotechnology, energy systems/alternative fuels, theory and molecular modeling.

University of Central Florida, College of Engineering and Computer Science, Department of Civil, Environmental, and Construction Engineering, Program in Environmental Engineering, Orlando, FL 32816. Offers MS, MS Env E, PhD. *Program availability:* Part-time, evening/weekend. *Students:* 22 full-time (11 women), 11 part-time (4 women); includes 10 minority (1 Black or African American, non-Hispanic/Latino; 2 Asian, non-Hispanic/Latino; 7 Hispanic/Latino), 10 international. Average age 28. 38 applicants, 61% accepted, 10 enrolled. In 2018, 10 master's, 3 doctorates awarded. *Degree requirements:* For master's, thesis or alternative; for doctorate, thesis/dissertation, departmental qualifying exam, candidacy exam. *Entrance requirements:* For master's, minimum GPA of 3.0 in last 60 hours of course work, letters of recommendation, goal statement, resume; for doctorate, GRE General Test, minimum GPA of 3.0 in last 60 hours of course work, letters of recommendation, goal statement, resume. Additional exam requirements/recommendations for international students: Required—TOEFL. *Application deadline:* For fall admission, 7/15 for domestic students; for spring admission, 12/1 for domestic students. Application fee: $30. Electronic applications accepted. *Financial support:* In 2018–19, 16 students received support, including 5 fellowships with partial tuition reimbursements available (averaging $15,520 per year), 17 research assistantships with partial tuition reimbursements available (averaging $9,319 per year), 3 teaching assistantships with partial tuition reimbursements available (averaging $8,982 per year); career-related internships or fieldwork, Federal Work-Study, institutionally sponsored loans, health care benefits, tuition waivers (partial), and unspecified assistantships also available. Financial award application deadline: 3/1; financial award applicants required to submit FAFSA. *Unit head:* Dr. Andrew Randall, Graduate Director, 407-823-2841, E-mail: andrew.randall@ucf.edu. *Application contact:* Associate Director, Graduate Admissions, 407-823-2766, Fax: 407-823-6442, E-mail: gradadmissions@ucf.edu. Website: http://cece.ucf.edu/

University of Cincinnati, Graduate School, College of Engineering and Applied Science, Department of Biomedical, Chemical and Environmental Engineering, Program in Environmental Engineering, Cincinnati, OH 45221. Offers MS, PhD. *Program availability:* Part-time. *Degree requirements:* For master's, project or thesis; for doctorate, one foreign language, thesis/dissertation. *Entrance requirements:* For master's and doctorate, GRE General Test. Additional exam requirements/recommendations for international students: Required—TOEFL (minimum score 580 paper-based; 92 iBT). Electronic applications accepted. *Faculty research:* Environmental microbiology, solid-waste management, air pollution control, water pollution control, aerosols.

University of Colorado Boulder, Graduate School, College of Engineering and Applied Science, Department of Civil, Environmental, and Architectural Engineering, Boulder, CO 80309. Offers MS, PhD. Terminal master's awarded for partial completion of doctoral program. *Degree requirements:* For master's, comprehensive exam, thesis or alternative; for doctorate, thesis/dissertation. *Entrance requirements:* For master's, GRE General Test, minimum undergraduate GPA of 3.0. Electronic applications accepted. Application fee is waived when completed online. *Faculty research:* Civil engineering; environmental engineering; architectural engineering; hydrology; water resources engineering.

University of Colorado Denver, College of Engineering, Design and Computing, Department of Civil Engineering, Denver, CO 80217. Offers civil engineering (EASPh D); civil engineering systems (PhD); environmental and sustainability engineering (MS, PhD); geographic information systems (MS); geotechnical engineering (MS, PhD); hydrology and hydraulics (MS, PhD); structural engineering (MS, PhD); transportation engineering (MS, PhD). *Program availability:* Part-time, evening/weekend. *Degree requirements:* For master's, comprehensive exam, 30 credit hours, project or thesis; for doctorate, comprehensive exam, thesis/dissertation, 60 credit hours (30 of which are dissertation research). *Entrance requirements:* For master's, GRE, statement of purpose, transcripts, three references; for doctorate, GRE, statement of purpose, transcripts, references, letter of support from faculty stating willingness to serve as dissertation advisor and outlining plan for financial support. Additional exam requirements/recommendations for international students: Required—TOEFL (minimum score 537 paper-based; 75 iBT); Recommended—IELTS (minimum score 6.5). Electronic applications accepted. *Expenses:* Tuition, state resident: full-time $6786; part-time $337 per credit hour. Tuition, nonresident: full-time $22,590; part-time $1255 per credit hour. *Required fees:* $1231; $137 per credit hour. Tuition and fees vary according to program and reciprocity agreements.

University of Connecticut, Graduate School, School of Engineering, Department of Civil and Environmental Engineering, Field of Environmental Engineering, Storrs, CT 06269. Offers MS, PhD. *Degree requirements:* For master's, comprehensive exam; for doctorate, thesis/dissertation. *Entrance requirements:* For master's and doctorate, GRE General Test. Additional exam requirements/recommendations for international students: Required—TOEFL (minimum score 550 paper-based). Electronic applications accepted.

University of Dayton, Department of Civil and Environmental Engineering and Engineering Mechanics, Dayton, OH 45469. Offers engineering mechanics (MSEM); environmental engineering (MSCE); geotechnical engineering (MSCE); structural engineering (MSCE); transportation engineering (MSCE); water resources engineering (MSCE). *Program availability:* Part-time, blended/hybrid learning. *Degree requirements:* For master's, thesis or alternative. *Entrance requirements:* For master's, minimum GPA of 3.0 in undergraduate work. Additional exam requirements/recommendations for international students: Required—TOEFL (minimum score 550 paper-based; 80 iBT); Recommended—IELTS (minimum score 6.5), TSE (minimum score 60). Electronic applications accepted. *Faculty research:* Infrastructure, environmental composite, reliability, computer simulation.

University of Delaware, College of Engineering, Department of Civil and Environmental Engineering, Newark, DE 19716. Offers environmental engineering (MAS, MCE, PhD); geotechnical engineering (MAS, MCE, PhD); ocean engineering (MAS, MCE, PhD); structural engineering (MAS, MCE, PhD); transportation engineering (MAS, MCE, PhD);

water resource engineering (MAS, MCE, PhD). *Program availability:* Part-time. Terminal master's awarded for partial completion of doctoral program. *Degree requirements:* For master's, thesis; for doctorate, thesis/dissertation. *Entrance requirements:* For master's and doctorate, GRE General Test. Additional exam requirements/recommendations for international students: Required—TOEFL. Electronic applications accepted. *Faculty research:* Structural engineering and mechanics; transportation engineering; ocean engineering; soil mechanics and foundation; water resources and environmental engineering.

University of Detroit Mercy, College of Engineering and Science, Detroit, MI 48221. Offers chemistry (MS); civil and environmental engineering (DE); electrical and computer engineering (ME); electrical engineering (DE); engineering management (M Eng Mgt); environmental engineering (MEE); mechanical engineering (MME, DE); product development (MS); software engineering (MSSE); teaching of mathematics (MATM). *Program availability:* Part-time, evening/weekend. *Degree requirements:* For doctorate, thesis/dissertation. Electronic applications accepted. Application fee is waived when completed online. *Expenses:* Contact institution.

University of Florida, Graduate School, Herbert Wertheim College of Engineering, Department of Environmental Engineering Sciences, Gainesville, FL 32611. Offers environmental engineering sciences (ME, MS, PhD, Engr); geographic information systems (ME, MS, PhD); hydrologic sciences (ME, MS, PhD); wetland sciences (ME, MS, PhD); JD/MS. *Program availability:* Part-time, evening/weekend, online learning. Terminal master's awarded for partial completion of doctoral program. *Degree requirements:* For master's, comprehensive exam (for some programs), thesis (for some programs), project, thesis or coursework; for doctorate, comprehensive exam, thesis/dissertation; for Engr, project or thesis. *Entrance requirements:* For master's and doctorate, minimum GPA of 3.0; for Engr, GRE General Test. Additional exam requirements/recommendations for international students: Required—TOEFL (minimum score 550 paper-based; 80 iBT), IELTS (minimum score 6). Electronic applications accepted. *Faculty research:* Air resources; system ecology and ecological engineering; water systems; geosystems engineering; environmental nanotechnology.

University of Georgia, College of Engineering, Athens, GA 30602. Offers MS.

University of Guelph, Office of Graduate and Postdoctoral Studies, College of Physical and Engineering Science, School of Engineering, Guelph, ON N1G 2W1, Canada. Offers biological engineering (M Eng, M Sc, MA Sc, PhD); engineering systems and computing (M Eng, M Sc, MA Sc, PhD); environmental engineering (M Eng, M Sc, MA Sc, PhD); water resources engineering (M Eng, M Sc, MA Sc, PhD). *Program availability:* Part-time. *Degree requirements:* For master's, thesis (for some programs); for doctorate, comprehensive exam, thesis/dissertation. *Entrance requirements:* For master's, minimum B- average during previous 2 years of course work; for doctorate, minimum B average. Additional exam requirements/recommendations for international students: Required—TOEFL (minimum score 550 paper-based; 89 iBT), IELTS (minimum score 6.5). Electronic applications accepted. *Faculty research:* Water and food safety, environmental contaminant fates and mechanisms, computer systems, robotics and mechatronics, waste treatment.

University of Hawaii at Manoa, Office of Graduate Education, College of Engineering, Department of Civil and Environmental Engineering, Honolulu, HI 96822. Offers MS, PhD. *Program availability:* Part-time. *Degree requirements:* For master's, comprehensive exam, thesis; for doctorate, comprehensive exam, thesis/dissertation. *Entrance requirements:* For master's and doctorate, GRE General Test or EIT Exam. Additional exam requirements/recommendations for international students: Required—TOEFL (minimum score 540 paper-based; 76 iBT), IELTS (minimum score 5). *Faculty research:* Structures, transportation, environmental engineering, geotechnical engineering, construction.

University of Illinois at Urbana–Champaign, Graduate College, College of Engineering, Department of Civil and Environmental Engineering, Champaign, IL 61820. Offers civil engineering (MS, PhD); environmental engineering in civil engineering (MS, PhD); M Arch/MS; MBA/MS. *Program availability:* Part-time, evening/weekend, online learning.

The University of Iowa, Graduate College, College of Engineering, Department of Civil and Environmental Engineering, Iowa City, IA 52242-1316. Offers environmental engineering and science (MS, PhD); hydraulics and water resources (MS, PhD); structures, mechanics and materials (MS, PhD); sustainable water development (MS, PhD); transportation engineering (MS, PhD). *Program availability:* Part-time. Terminal master's awarded for partial completion of doctoral program. *Degree requirements:* For master's, thesis optional, exam; for doctorate, comprehensive exam, thesis/dissertation, exam. *Entrance requirements:* For master's, GRE (minimum combined score of 301 on verbal and quantitative), minimum undergraduate GPA of 3.0; for doctorate, GRE (minimum combined score of 301 on verbal and quantitative), minimum graduate GPA of 3.0. Additional exam requirements/recommendations for international students: Required—TOEFL (minimum score 550 paper-based; 81 iBT), IELTS (minimum score 7). Electronic applications accepted. *Faculty research:* Water resources; environmental engineering and science; hydraulics and hydrology; structures, mechanics, and materials; transportation engineering.

The University of Kansas, Graduate Studies, School of Engineering, Program in Environmental Engineering, Lawrence, KS 66045. Offers MS, PhD. *Program availability:* Part-time. *Students:* 15 full-time (5 women), 4 part-time (3 women); includes 4 minority (1 Black or African American, non-Hispanic/Latino; 2 Asian, non-Hispanic/Latino; 1 Two or more races, non-Hispanic/Latino), 10 international. Average age 27. 18 applicants, 44% accepted, 3 enrolled. In 2018, 2 master's awarded. *Entrance requirements:* For master's and doctorate, GRE, BS in engineering, recommendations, resume, statement of purpose. Additional exam requirements/recommendations for international students: Required—TOEFL, IELTS. *Application deadline:* For fall admission, 12/15 priority date for domestic and international students; for spring admission, 9/15 priority date for domestic and international students. Application fee: $65 ($85 for international students). Electronic applications accepted. *Financial support:* Fellowships, research assistantships, teaching assistantships, career-related internships or fieldwork, and scholarships/grants available. Financial award application deadline: 12/15. *Faculty research:* Water quality, water treatment, wastewater treatment, air quality, air pollution control, solid waste, hazardous waste, water resources engineering. *Unit head:* David Darwin, Chair, 785-864-3827, E-mail: daved@ku.edu. *Application contact:* Susan Scott, Administrative Assistant, 785-864-3826, E-mail: s523s307@ku.edu.
Website: http://ceae.ku.edu/overview-3

The University of Manchester, School of Mechanical, Aerospace and Civil Engineering, Manchester, United Kingdom. Offers advanced manufacturing technology (M Ent); aerospace engineering (M Phil, M Sc, PhD); civil engineering (M Phil, M Sc, PhD); environmental engineering (M Phil, PhD); management of projects (M Phil, M Sc, PhD); mechanical engineering (M Phil, M Sc, PhD); mechanical engineering design (M Ent); nuclear engineering (M Phil, D Eng, PhD).

University of Maryland, Baltimore County, The Graduate School, College of Engineering and Information Technology, Department of Chemical, Biochemical, and Environmental Engineering, Program in Environmental Engineering, Baltimore, MD 21250. Offers MS, PhD. *Program availability:* Part-time. *Degree requirements:* For master's, comprehensive exam (for some programs), thesis (for some programs); for doctorate, comprehensive exam, thesis/dissertation. *Entrance requirements:* For master's and doctorate, GRE General Test, BS in environmental engineering or related field of engineering. Additional exam requirements/recommendations for international students: Required—TOEFL (minimum score 550 paper-based; 80 iBT). Electronic applications accepted. *Expenses:* Contact institution. *Faculty research:* Environmental engineering.

University of Maryland, College Park, Academic Affairs, A. James Clark School of Engineering, Department of Civil and Environmental Engineering, College Park, MD 20742. Offers M Eng, MS, PhD. *Program availability:* Part-time, evening/weekend, online learning. *Degree requirements:* For master's, thesis optional; for doctorate, thesis/dissertation, qualifying exam. *Entrance requirements:* For master's and doctorate, GRE General Test, 3 letters of recommendation. Electronic applications accepted. *Faculty research:* Transportation and urban systems, environmental engineering, geotechnical engineering, construction engineering and management, hydraulics.

University of Massachusetts Amherst, Graduate School, College of Engineering, Department of Civil and Environmental Engineering, Amherst, MA 01003. Offers civil engineering (MSCE, PhD); environmental and water resources engineering (MSCE); geotechnical engineering (MSCE); structural engineering and mechanics (MSCE); transportation engineering (MSCE). *Program availability:* Part-time. Terminal master's awarded for partial completion of doctoral program. *Degree requirements:* For master's, thesis or alternative; for doctorate, comprehensive exam, thesis/dissertation. *Entrance requirements:* For master's and doctorate, GRE General Test. Additional exam requirements/recommendations for international students: Required—TOEFL (minimum score 550 paper-based; 80 iBT), IELTS (minimum score 6.5). Electronic applications accepted.

University of Massachusetts Lowell, Francis College of Engineering, Department of Civil and Environmental Engineering and College of Sciences, Program in Environmental Studies, Lowell, MA 01854. Offers MS, PhD. *Program availability:* Part-time. *Degree requirements:* For master's, thesis optional. *Entrance requirements:* For master's, GRE General Test. *Faculty research:* Remote sensing of air pollutants, atmospheric deposition of toxic metals, contaminant transport in groundwater, soil remediation.

University of Memphis, Graduate School, Herff College of Engineering, Department of Civil Engineering, Memphis, TN 38152. Offers civil engineering (PhD); engineering seismology (MS); environmental engineering (MS); freight transportation (Graduate Certificate); geotechnical engineering (MS); structural engineering (MS); transportation engineering (MS); water resources engineering (MS). *Students:* 14 full-time (3 women), 8 part-time (3 women); includes 1 minority (Black or African American, non-Hispanic/Latino), 12 international. Average age 27. 27 applicants, 70% accepted, 13 enrolled. In 2018, 11 master's awarded. Terminal master's awarded for partial completion of doctoral program. *Degree requirements:* For master's, comprehensive exam, thesis optional; for doctorate, comprehensive exam, thesis/dissertation. *Entrance requirements:* For master's, GRE General Test, minimum undergraduate GPA of 2.5; bachelor's degree in engineering or a related science or mathematics program; three letters of reference; for doctorate, GRE General Test, bachelor's degree in engineering or engineering science; three letters of reference; for Graduate Certificate, minimum undergraduate GPA of 2.75; bachelor's degree in engineering or engineering science. Additional exam requirements/recommendations for international students: Required—TOEFL (minimum score 550 paper-based; 79 iBT). *Application deadline:* For fall admission, 8/1 for domestic students; for spring admission, 12/1 for domestic students. Application fee: $35 ($60 for international students). Electronic applications accepted. *Expenses: Tuition, area resident:* Full-time $10,240; part-time $503 per credit hour. Tuition, state resident: full-time $10,464. Tuition, nonresident: full-time $20,224; part-time $991 per credit hour. *Required fees:* $850; $106 per credit hour. *Financial support:* Fellowships with full tuition reimbursements, research assistantships with full tuition reimbursements, career-related internships or fieldwork, Federal Work-Study, scholarships/grants, and unspecified assistantships available. Financial award application deadline: 2/1; financial award applicants required to submit FAFSA. *Faculty research:* Structural response to earthquakes, pavement design, water quality, transportation safety, intermodal transportation. *Unit head:* Dr. Shahram Pezeshk, Chair, 901-678-4727, Fax: 901-678-3026, E-mail: spezeshk@memphis.edu. *Application contact:* Dr. Roger Meier, Coordinator of Graduate Studies, 901-678-3284, E-mail: rwmeier@memphis.edu.
Website: https://www.memphis.edu/ce

University of Michigan, College of Engineering, Department of Civil and Environmental Engineering, Ann Arbor, MI 48109. Offers civil engineering (MSE, PhD, CE); construction engineering and management (M Eng, MSE); environmental engineering (MSE, PhD); structural engineering (M Eng); MBA/MSE. *Program availability:* Part-time. *Students:* 206 full-time (86 women), 6 part-time (3 women). 690 applicants, 41% accepted, 76 enrolled. In 2018, 65 master's, 18 doctorates awarded. Terminal master's awarded for partial completion of doctoral program. *Degree requirements:* For master's, thesis optional; for doctorate, comprehensive exam, thesis/dissertation, oral defense of dissertation, preliminary and written exams. *Entrance requirements:* For master's and doctorate, GRE General Test. Additional exam requirements/recommendations for international students: Required—TOEFL. *Application deadline:* Applications are processed on a rolling basis. Electronic applications accepted. *Financial support:* Fellowships, research assistantships, teaching assistantships, institutionally sponsored loans, and tuition waivers (partial) available. *Faculty research:* Construction engineering and management, geotechnical engineering, earthquake-resistant design of structures, environmental chemistry and microbiology, cost engineering, environmental and water resources engineering. *Total annual research expenditures:* $11.6 million. *Unit head:* Jerome Lynch, Department Chair, 734-615-5290, Fax: 734-764-4292, E-mail: jerlynch@umich.edu. *Application contact:* Kelley Archer, Graduate Coordinator, 734-647-2703, Fax: 734-764-4292, E-mail: krichko@umich.edu.
Website: https://cee.engin.umich.edu/

University of Mississippi, Graduate School, School of Engineering, University, MS 38677. Offers aeroacoustics (MS, PhD); chemical engineering (MS, PhD); civil engineering (MS, PhD); computational hydroscience (MS, PhD); computer science (MS, PhD); electrical engineering (MS, PhD); electromagnetics (MS, PhD); environmental engineering (MS, PhD); geology and geological engineering (MS, PhD); hydrology (MS); material science (MS); mechanical engineering (MS, PhD); telecommunications (MS). *Faculty:* 76 full-time (16 women), 3 part-time/adjunct (1 woman). *Students:* 129 full-time (33 women), 21 part-time (5 women); includes 15 minority (7 Black or African American, non-Hispanic/Latino; 6 Asian, non-Hispanic/Latino; 1 Hispanic/Latino; 1 Two or more races, non-Hispanic/Latino), 73 international. Average age 29. In 2018, 36 master's, 17 doctorates awarded. *Entrance requirements:* For master's, GRE General Test, minimum GPA of 3.0; for doctorate, GRE General Test. Additional exam requirements/recommendations for international students: Required—TOEFL. *Application deadline:* Applications are processed on a rolling basis. Application fee: $50. Electronic applications accepted. *Financial support:* Scholarships/grants available. Financial award application deadline: 3/1; financial award applicants required to submit FAFSA. *Unit head:* Dr. David Puleo, Dean, 662-915-5780, Fax: 662-915-5387, E-mail:

engineer@olemiss.edu. *Application contact:* Temeka Smith, Graduate Activities Specialist for Admissions, 662-915-7474, Fax: 662-915-7577, E-mail: gschool@olemiss.edu.

University of Missouri, Office of Research and Graduate Studies, College of Engineering, Department of Civil and Environmental Engineering, Columbia, MO 65211. Offers civil engineering (MS, PhD). *Degree requirements:* For master's, report or thesis. *Entrance requirements:* For master's and doctorate, GRE General Test. Additional exam requirements/recommendations for international students: Required—TOEFL (minimum score 550 paper-based; 80 iBT).

University of Nebraska–Lincoln, Graduate College, College of Engineering, Interdepartmental Area of Environmental Engineering, Lincoln, NE 68588. Offers MS, PhD. *Degree requirements:* For master's, thesis optional; for doctorate, comprehensive exam, thesis/dissertation. *Entrance requirements:* For master's and doctorate, GRE General Test. Additional exam requirements/recommendations for international students: Required—TOEFL (minimum score 550 paper-based). Electronic applications accepted. *Faculty research:* Wastewater engineering, hazardous waste management, solid waste management, groundwater engineering.

University of New Brunswick Fredericton, School of Graduate Studies, Faculty of Engineering, Department of Civil Engineering, Fredericton, NB E3B 5A3, Canada. Offers construction engineering and management (M Eng, M Sc E, PhD); environmental engineering (M Eng, M Sc E, PhD); environmental studies (M Eng); geotechnical engineering (M Eng, M Sc E, PhD); groundwater/hydrology (M Eng, M Sc E, PhD); materials (M Eng, M Sc E, PhD); pavements (M Eng, M Sc E, PhD); structures (M Eng, M Sc E, PhD); transportation (M Eng, M Sc E, PhD). *Program availability:* Part-time. *Degree requirements:* For master's, thesis; for doctorate, comprehensive exam, thesis/dissertation, qualifying exam; 27 credit hours of courses. *Entrance requirements:* For master's, minimum GPA of 3.0; B Sc E in civil engineering or related engineering degree; for doctorate, minimum GPA of 3.0; graduate degree in engineering or applied science. Additional exam requirements/recommendations for international students: Required—IELTS (minimum score 7.5), TWE (minimum score 4), Michigan English Language Assessment Battery (minimum score 85) or CanTest (minimum score 4.5); Recommended—TOEFL (minimum score 580 paper-based). Electronic applications accepted. *Faculty research:* Construction engineering and management; engineering materials and infrastructure renewal; highway and pavement research; structures and solid mechanics; geotechnical and geoenvironmental engineering; structure interaction; transportation and planning; environment, solid waste management; structural engineering; water and environmental engineering.

University of New Hampshire, Graduate School, College of Engineering and Physical Sciences, Department of Civil and Environmental Engineering, Durham, NH 03824. Offers M Engr, MS, PhD. *Program availability:* Part-time. *Entrance requirements:* For master's and doctorate, GRE. Additional exam requirements/recommendations for international students: Required—TOEFL (minimum score 550 paper-based; 80 iBT), IELTS (minimum score 6.5). Electronic applications accepted.

University of New Haven, Graduate School, Tagliatela College of Engineering, Program in Environmental Engineering, West Haven, CT 06516. Offers environmental engineering (MS); industrial and hazardous waste (MS); water and wastewater treatment (MS); water resources (MS). *Program availability:* Part-time, evening/weekend, 100% online. *Students:* 15 full-time (7 women), 32 part-time (13 women); includes 7 minority (2 Black or African American, non-Hispanic/Latino; 2 Asian, non-Hispanic/Latino; 3 Hispanic/Latino), 17 international. Average age 30. 67 applicants, 97% accepted, 11 enrolled. In 2018, 15 master's awarded. *Degree requirements:* For master's, thesis or alternative, research project. *Entrance requirements:* For master's, bachelor's degree in engineering. Additional exam requirements/recommendations for international students: Required—TOEFL (minimum score 75 iBT), IELTS, PTE (minimum score 50). *Application deadline:* Applications are processed on a rolling basis. Application fee: $50. Electronic applications accepted. Application fee is waived when completed online. *Expenses: Tuition:* Full-time $16,470; part-time $915 per credit hour. *Required fees:* $230; $95 per term. *Financial support:* Research assistantships with partial tuition reimbursements, teaching assistantships with partial tuition reimbursements, career-related internships or fieldwork, Federal Work-Study, scholarships/grants, and unspecified assistantships available. Support available to part-time students. Financial award application deadline: 5/1; financial award applicants required to submit FAFSA. *Unit head:* Dr. Agamemnon Koutsospyros, Professor, 203-932-7398, E-mail: akoutsospyros@newhaven.edu. *Application contact:* Selina O'Toole, Senior Associate Director of Graduate Admissions, 203-932-7337, E-mail: sotoole@newhaven.edu.
Website: https://www.newhaven.edu/engineering/graduate-programs/environmental-engineering/

The University of North Carolina at Chapel Hill, Graduate School, Gillings School of Global Public Health, Department of Environmental Sciences and Engineering, Chapel Hill, NC 27599-7431. Offers environmental engineering (MPH, MS, MSEE, MSPH); environmental health sciences (MPH, MS, MSPH, PhD); MPH/MCRP; MS/MCRP; MSPH/MCRP. *Faculty:* 26 full-time (10 women), 36 part-time/adjunct (10 women). *Students:* 72 full-time (46 women), 25 part-time (14 women); includes 13 minority (3 Black or African American, non-Hispanic/Latino; 3 Asian, non-Hispanic/Latino; 3 Hispanic/Latino; 4 Two or more races, non-Hispanic/Latino), 16 international. Average age 29. 150 applicants, 43% accepted, 33 enrolled. In 2018, 25 master's, 6 doctorates awarded. Terminal master's awarded for partial completion of doctoral program. *Degree requirements:* For master's, comprehensive exam, thesis (for some programs), research paper; for doctorate, comprehensive exam, thesis/dissertation. *Entrance requirements:* For master's and doctorate, GRE General Test, 3 letters of recommendation (academic and/or professional; at least one academic). Additional exam requirements/recommendations for international students: Required—TOEFL (minimum score 90 iBT), IELTS (minimum score 7). *Application deadline:* For fall admission, 4/9 for domestic and international students. Application fee: $90. Electronic applications accepted. *Financial support:* Fellowships with tuition reimbursements, research assistantships with tuition reimbursements, teaching assistantships with tuition reimbursements, career-related internships or fieldwork, Federal Work-Study, scholarships/grants, traineeships, health care benefits, and unspecified assistantships available. Support available to part-time students. Financial award application deadline: 12/10; financial award applicants required to submit FAFSA. *Faculty research:* Air, radiation and industrial hygiene, aquatic and atmospheric sciences, environmental health sciences, environmental management and policy, water resources engineering. *Unit head:* Dr. Barbara J. Turpin, Professor and Chair, 919-966-1024, Fax: 919-966-7911, E-mail: esechair@unc.edu. *Application contact:* Adia Ware, Academic Coordinator, 919-966-3844, Fax: 919-966-7911, E-mail: aware@unc.edu.
Website: https://sph.unc.edu/envr/environmental-sciences-and-engineering-home/

The University of North Carolina at Charlotte, William States Lee College of Engineering, Department of Civil and Environmental Engineering, Charlotte, NC 28223-0001. Offers civil engineering (MSCE); infrastructure and environmental systems (PhD), including infrastructure and environmental systems design. *Program availability:* Part-time, evening/weekend. *Students:* 61 full-time (18 women), 47 part-time (12 women); includes 9 minority (1 Black or African American, non-Hispanic/Latino; 5 Asian, non-

Hispanic/Latino; 2 Hispanic/Latino; 1 Two or more races, non-Hispanic/Latino), 51 international. Average age 30. 89 applicants, 47% accepted, 19 enrolled. In 2018, 16 master's, 6 doctorates awarded. *Entrance requirements:* For master's, GRE, undergraduate degree in civil and environmental engineering or a closely-related field; minimum undergraduate GPA of 3.0; for doctorate, GRE General Test, equivalent to U.S. baccalaureate or master's degree from regionally-accredited college or university in engineering, earth science and geology, chemical and biological sciences or a related field with minimum undergraduate GPA of 3.2, graduate 3.5. Additional exam requirements/recommendations for international students: Required—TOEFL (minimum score 523 paper-based; 70 iBT), IELTS (minimum score 6), TOEFL (minimum score 523 paper-based, 70 iBT) or IELTS (6). *Application deadline:* Applications are processed on a rolling basis. Application fee: $75. Electronic applications accepted. *Expenses:* Contact institution. *Financial support:* Fellowships, research assistantships, teaching assistantships, career-related internships or fieldwork, institutionally sponsored loans, scholarships/grants, and unspecified assistantships available. Support available to part-time students. Financial award application deadline: 3/1; financial award applicants required to submit FAFSA. *Total annual research expenditures:* $3.4 million. *Unit head:* Dr. James D. Bowen, Interim Chair, 704-687-1215, E-mail: jdbowen@uncc.edu. *Application contact:* Kathy B. Giddings, Director of Graduate Admissions, 704-687-5503, Fax: 704-687-1668, E-mail: gradadm@uncc.edu.
Website: http://cee.uncc.edu/

University of North Dakota, Graduate School, School of Engineering and Mines, Department of Environmental Engineering, Grand Forks, ND 58202. Offers M Engr, MS, PhD. *Degree requirements:* For master's, thesis. *Entrance requirements:* For master's, GRE General Test, minimum GPA of 3.0. Additional exam requirements/recommendations for international students: Required—TOEFL (minimum score 550 paper-based; 79 iBT), IELTS (minimum score 6.5). Electronic applications accepted.

University of Notre Dame, The Graduate School, College of Engineering, Department of Civil and Environmental Engineering and Earth Sciences, Notre Dame, IN 46556. Offers bioengineering (MS Bio E); civil engineering (MSCE); civil engineering and geological sciences (PhD); earth sciences (MS); environmental engineering (MS Env E). Terminal master's awarded for partial completion of doctoral program. *Degree requirements:* For master's, comprehensive exam; for doctorate, thesis/dissertation, candidacy exam. *Entrance requirements:* For master's and doctorate, GRE General Test. Additional exam requirements/recommendations for international students: Required—TOEFL (minimum score 600 paper-based; 80 iBT). Electronic applications accepted. *Faculty research:* Environmental modeling, biological-waste treatment, petrology, environmental geology, geochemistry.

University of Oklahoma, Gallogly College of Engineering, School of Civil Engineering and Environmental Science, Norman, OK 73019-0390. Offers civil engineering (MS, PhD), including civil engineering; environmental engineering (MS, PhD); environmental science (M Env Sc, PhD), including environmental science. *Program availability:* Part-time. *Faculty:* 24 full-time (4 women), 3 part-time/adjunct (2 women). *Students:* 33 full-time (11 women), 61 part-time (22 women); includes 21 minority (6 Black or African American, non-Hispanic/Latino; 2 American Indian or Alaska Native, non-Hispanic/Latino; 2 Asian, non-Hispanic/Latino; 7 Hispanic/Latino; 4 Two or more races, non-Hispanic/Latino), 27 international. Average age 30. 154 applicants, 68% accepted, 52 enrolled. In 2018, 9 master's, 4 doctorates awarded. Terminal master's awarded for partial completion of doctoral program. *Degree requirements:* For master's, thesis; for doctorate, comprehensive exam, thesis/dissertation, general exam. *Entrance requirements:* For master's and doctorate, GRE. Additional exam requirements/recommendations for international students: Required—TOEFL (minimum score 79 iBT) or IELTS (minimum score 6.5). *Application deadline:* For fall admission, 1/15 for domestic and international students; for spring admission, 5/15 for domestic and international students. Application fee: $50 ($100 for international students). Electronic applications accepted. *Expenses: Tuition,* state resident: full-time $5683.20; part-time $236.80 per credit hour. *Tuition,* nonresident: full-time $20,342; part-time $847.60 per credit hour. *International tuition:* $20,342.40 full-time. *Required fees:* $2894.20; $110.05 per credit hour. $126.50 per semester. Tuition and fees vary according to course load and program. *Financial support:* Fellowships, research assistantships, teaching assistantships, and scholarships/grants available. Financial award application deadline: 6/1; financial award applicants required to submit FAFSA. *Faculty research:* Intelligent structures, composites, earthquake engineering, intelligent compaction, bridge engineering. *Unit head:* Dr. Randall Kolar, Director, 405-325-4267, Fax: 405-325-4217, E-mail: kolar@ou.edu. *Application contact:* Graduate Studies Coordinator, 405-325-2344, Fax: 405-325-4217, E-mail: ceesgradstudies@ou.edu.
Website: http://www.ou.edu/coe/cees.html

University of Pittsburgh, Swanson School of Engineering, Department of Civil and Environmental Engineering, Pittsburgh, PA 15260. Offers MSCEE, PhD. *Program availability:* Part-time, 100% online. Terminal master's awarded for partial completion of doctoral program. *Degree requirements:* For doctorate, comprehensive exam, thesis/dissertation, final oral exams. *Entrance requirements:* For master's and doctorate, minimum GPA of 3.0. Additional exam requirements/recommendations for international students: Required—TOEFL (minimum score 550 paper-based; 80 iBT). Electronic applications accepted. *Expenses:* Contact institution. *Faculty research:* Environmental and water resources, structures and infrastructures, construction management.

University of Puerto Rico–Mayagüez, Graduate Studies, College of Engineering, Department of Civil Engineering and Surveying, Mayagüez, PR 00681-9000. Offers civil engineering (ME, MS, PhD), including construction engineering and management (ME, MS), environmental engineering, geotechnical engineering (ME, MS), structural engineering, transportation engineering. *Program availability:* Part-time. Terminal master's awarded for partial completion of doctoral program. *Degree requirements:* For master's, one foreign language, thesis; for doctorate, one foreign language, comprehensive exam, thesis/dissertation, qualifying exams. *Entrance requirements:* For master's, proficiency in English and Spanish; BS in civil engineering or its equivalent; for doctorate, proficiency in English and Spanish. Electronic applications accepted. *Faculty research:* Structural design, concrete structure, finite elements, dynamic analysis, transportation, soils.

University of Regina, Faculty of Graduate Studies and Research, Faculty of Engineering and Applied Science, Program in Environmental Systems Engineering, Regina, SK S4S 0A2, Canada. Offers environmental systems (M Eng, MA Sc, PhD). *Program availability:* Part-time. *Faculty:* 8 full-time (2 women), 2 part-time/adjunct (0 women). *Students:* 57 full-time (28 women), 3 part-time (1 woman). Average age 30. 92 applicants, 22% accepted, 8 enrolled. In 2018, 14 master's, 1 doctorate awarded. *Degree requirements:* For master's, thesis, project, report, co-op; for doctorate, comprehensive exam, thesis/dissertation. *Entrance requirements:* For master's, 4 years bachelor degree, at least 70 per cent from a four-year baccalaureate degree (or equivalent). Additional exam requirements/recommendations for international students: Required—TOEFL (minimum score 580 paper-based; 80 iBT), IELTS (minimum score 6.5), PTE (minimum score 59), other options are CAEL, MELAB, Cantest and U of R ESL. *Application deadline:* For fall admission, 3/31 for domestic and international students; for winter admission, 7/31 for domestic and international students; for spring admission, 11/30 for domestic and international students. Application fee: $100.

Electronic applications accepted. *Expenses:* Estimated tuition and fees for one academic year is 8,379.50 for master's. The fee will vary base on your choice program. For doctoral program one academic year is estimated 14,129.40. International students will pay additional 1,191.75 for international surcharge per semester. *Financial support:* Fellowships, research assistantships, teaching assistantships, career-related internships or fieldwork, Federal Work-Study, scholarships/grants, unspecified assistantships, and travel award and Graduate Scholarship base funds available. Support available to part-time students. Financial award application deadline: 9/30. *Faculty research:* Design of water and wastewater treatment systems, urban and regional transportation planning, environmental fluid mechanics, air quality management, environmental modeling and decision-making. *Unit head:* Dr. Shahid Azam, Program Chair, 306-337-2369, Fax: 306-585-4855, E-mail: shahid.azam@uregina.ca. *Application contact:* Dr. Kelvin Ng, Graduate Coordinator, 306-585-8487, Fax: 306-585-4855, E-mail: kelvin.ng@uregina.ca.
Website: http://www.uregina.ca/engineering/

University of Rhode Island, Graduate School, College of Engineering, Department of Civil and Environmental Engineering, Kingston, RI 02881. Offers civil and environmental engineering (MS, PhD), including environmental engineering, geotechnical engineering, structural engineering, transportation engineering. *Program availability:* Part-time. *Faculty:* 12 full-time (3 women). *Students:* 22 full-time (7 women), 10 part-time (2 women); includes 2 minority (1 Asian, non-Hispanic/Latino; 1 Hispanic/Latino), 12 international. 26 applicants, 112% accepted, 16 enrolled. In 2018, 9 master's, 3 doctorates awarded. *Entrance requirements:* Additional exam requirements/recommendations for international students: Required—TOEFL. *Application deadline:* For fall admission, 7/15 for domestic students, 2/1 for international students; for spring admission, 11/15 for domestic students, 7/15 for international students. Application fee: $65. Electronic applications accepted. *Expenses: Tuition, area resident:* Full-time $13,226; part-time $735 per credit. Tuition, state resident: full-time $13,226; part-time $735 per credit. Tuition, nonresident: full-time $25,854; part-time $1436 per credit. *International tuition:* $25,854 full-time. *Required fees:* $1698; $50 per credit. $35 per semester. One-time fee: $165. *Financial support:* In 2018–19, 9 research assistantships with tuition reimbursements (averaging $12,684 per year), 5 teaching assistantships with tuition reimbursements (averaging $13,694 per year) were awarded. Financial award application deadline: 2/1; financial award applicants required to submit FAFSA. *Unit head:* Dr. Leon Thiem, Chair, 401-874-2693, Fax: 401-874-2786, E-mail: leonthiem@uri.edu. *Application contact:* Dr. George Tsiatas, Graduate Program Director, 401-874-5117, E-mail: gt@uri.edu.
Website: http://www.uri.edu/cve/

University of South Alabama, College of Engineering, Department of Civil, Coastal, and Environmental Engineering, Mobile, AL 36688. Offers MSCE. *Degree requirements:* For master's, comprehensive exam, thesis or project. *Entrance requirements:* For master's, GRE, minimum GPA of 3.0, three references, portfolio. Additional exam requirements/recommendations for international students: Required—TOEFL (minimum score 525 paper-based; 71 iBT), IELTS (minimum score 6.5). Electronic applications accepted. *Expenses:* Contact institution. *Faculty research:* Calibration of simulation model, monitoring coastal processes, reducing crashes, roadway runoff treatment, roundabouts.

University of Southern California, Graduate School, Viterbi School of Engineering, Sonny Astani Department of Civil and Environmental Engineering, Los Angeles, CA 90089. Offers applied mechanics (MS); civil engineering (MS, PhD); computer-aided engineering (ME, Graduate Certificate); construction management (MCM); engineering technology commercialization (Graduate Certificate); environmental engineering (MS, PhD); environmental quality management (ME); structural design (ME); sustainable cities (Graduate Certificate); transportation systems (MS, Graduate Certificate); water and waste management (MS). *Program availability:* Part-time, evening/weekend. Terminal master's awarded for partial completion of doctoral program. *Degree requirements:* For master's, thesis optional; for doctorate, thesis/dissertation. *Entrance requirements:* For master's and doctorate, GRE General Test. Additional exam requirements/recommendations for international students: Recommended—TOEFL. Electronic applications accepted. *Faculty research:* Geotechnical engineering, transportation engineering, structural engineering, construction management, environmental engineering, water resources.

University of South Florida, College of Engineering, Department of Civil and Environmental Engineering, Tampa, FL 33620-9951. Offers civil engineering (MCE, MSCE, PhD), including geotechnical engineering, materials science and engineering, structures engineering, transportation engineering, water resources; environmental engineering (MEVE, MSEV, PhD), including engineering for international development (MSEV). *Program availability:* Part-time. *Faculty:* 19 full-time (5 women). *Students:* 144 full-time (46 women), 76 part-time (22 women); includes 35 minority (8 Black or African American, non-Hispanic/Latino; 5 Asian, non-Hispanic/Latino; 18 Hispanic/Latino; 4 Two or more races, non-Hispanic/Latino), 123 international. Average age 28. 220 applicants, 65% accepted, 59 enrolled. In 2018, 82 master's, 15 doctorates awarded. Terminal master's awarded for partial completion of doctoral program. *Degree requirements:* For master's, comprehensive exam, thesis (for some programs); for doctorate, comprehensive exam, thesis/dissertation. *Entrance requirements:* For master's, GRE required, bachelor's degree in appropriate field, minimum GPA of 3.0 in major, letters of reference, statement of purpose, resume, intake form; for doctorate, GRE with V (45th percentile), Q (75th percentile), and AW (55th percentile), letters of recommendation, statement of purpose, resume, intake form. Additional exam requirements/recommendations for international students: Required—TOEFL, TOEFL (minimum score 550 paper-based; 79 iBT) or IELTS (minimum score 6.5). *Application deadline:* For fall admission, 2/15 for domestic students, 2/15 priority date for international students; for spring admission, 10/15 for domestic students, 9/15 priority date for international students. Application fee: $30. Electronic applications accepted. *Expenses:* Tuition, state resident: full-time $6350. Tuition, nonresident: full-time $19,048. *International tuition:* $19,048 full-time. *Required fees:* $2079. *Financial support:* In 2018–19, 45 students received support, including 44 research assistantships (averaging $14,123 per year), 21 teaching assistantships with tuition reimbursements available (averaging $15,329 per year). *Faculty research:* Environmental and water resources engineering, geotechnics and geoenvironmental systems, structures and materials systems, transportation systems. *Total annual research expenditures:* $3.7 million. *Unit head:* Dr. Manjriker Gunaratne, Professor and Department Chair, 813-974-5818, Fax: 813-974-2957, E-mail: gunaratn@usf.edu. *Application contact:* Dr. Sarina J. Ergas, Professor and Graduate Program Coordinator, 813-974-1119, Fax: 813-974-2957, E-mail: sergas@usf.edu.
Website: http://www.usf.edu/engineering/cee/

The University of Tennessee, Graduate School, Tickle College of Engineering, Department of Civil and Environmental Engineering, Program in Environmental Engineering, Knoxville, TN 37996. Offers MS, MS/MBA. *Program availability:* Part-time, online learning. *Faculty:* 11 full-time (2 women). *Students:* 13 full-time (5 women), 6 part-time (4 women); includes 3 minority (1 Black or African American, non-Hispanic/Latino; 1 Hispanic/Latino; 1 Two or more races, non-Hispanic/Latino). Average age 28. 12 applicants, 83% accepted, 7 enrolled. In 2018, 13 master's awarded. *Degree requirements:* For master's, thesis or alternative. *Entrance requirements:* For master's, GRE General Test (for MS students pursuing research thesis), minimum GPA of 2.7 (for U.S. degree holders), 3.0 (for international degree holders); 3 references; statement of purpose; resume. Additional exam requirements/recommendations for international students: Required—TOEFL (minimum score 550 paper-based; 80 iBT), IELTS (minimum score 6.5). *Application deadline:* For fall admission, 2/1 priority date for domestic and international students; for spring admission, 6/15 for domestic and international students; for summer admission, 10/15 for domestic and international students. Applications are processed on a rolling basis. Application fee: $60. Electronic applications accepted. *Financial support:* In 2018–19, 11 students received support, including 5 research assistantships with full tuition reimbursements available (averaging $21,307 per year), 6 teaching assistantships with full tuition reimbursements available (averaging $20,750 per year); career-related internships or fieldwork, Federal Work-Study, institutionally sponsored loans, health care benefits, and unspecified assistantships also available. Financial award application deadline: 2/1; financial award applicants required to submit FAFSA. *Faculty research:* Air pollution control technologies; climate change and engineering impact on environment; environmental sampling, monitoring, and restoration; soil erosion prediction and control; waste management and utilization. *Unit head:* Dr. Chris Cox, Head, 865-974-2503, Fax: 865-974-2669, E-mail: gdreed@utk.edu. *Application contact:* Dr. Khalid Alshibli, Associate Head, 865-974-7728, Fax: 865-974-2669, E-mail: alshibli@utk.edu.
Website: http://www.engr.utk.edu/civil/

The University of Texas at Austin, Graduate School, Cockrell School of Engineering, Department of Civil, Architectural and Environmental Engineering, Program in Environmental and Water Resources Engineering, Austin, TX 78712-1111. Offers MS, PhD. *Program availability:* Part-time. *Degree requirements:* For master's, thesis or alternative. *Entrance requirements:* For master's, GRE General Test. Additional exam requirements/recommendations for international students: Required—TOEFL. Electronic applications accepted.

The University of Texas at El Paso, Graduate School, College of Engineering, Department of Civil Engineering, El Paso, TX 79968-0001. Offers civil engineering (MS, PhD); construction management (MS, Certificate); environmental engineering (MEENE, MSENE). *Program availability:* Part-time, evening/weekend. *Degree requirements:* For master's, comprehensive exam, thesis optional; for doctorate, comprehensive exam, thesis/dissertation. *Entrance requirements:* For master's, GRE, minimum GPA of 3.0; for doctorate, GRE. Additional exam requirements/recommendations for international students: Required—TOEFL. Electronic applications accepted. *Faculty research:* Non-destructive testing for geotechnical and pavement applications, transportation systems, wastewater treatment systems, air quality, linear and non-linear modeling of structures, structural reliability.

The University of Texas at El Paso, Graduate School, College of Engineering, Department of Mechanical Engineering, El Paso, TX 79968-0001. Offers environmental science and engineering (PhD); mechanical engineering (MS). *Program availability:* Part-time. *Degree requirements:* For master's, thesis optional; for doctorate, thesis/dissertation. *Entrance requirements:* For master's, GRE, minimum GPA of 3.0, letter of reference; for doctorate, GRE, minimum GPA of 3.5, letters of reference, BS or equivalent. Additional exam requirements/recommendations for international students: Required—TOEFL; Recommended—IELTS. Electronic applications accepted. *Faculty research:* Aerospace, energy, combustion and propulsion, design engineering, high temperature materials.

The University of Texas at San Antonio, College of Engineering, Department of Civil and Environmental Engineering, San Antonio, TX 78249-0617. Offers civil engineering (MCE, MSCE); environmental science and engineering (PhD). *Program availability:* Part-time. *Degree requirements:* For master's, comprehensive exam, thesis (for some programs); for doctorate, comprehensive exam, thesis/dissertation, written qualifying exam, dissertation proposal. *Entrance requirements:* For master's, GRE General Test, BS in civil engineering or related field from accredited institution, statement of research/specialization interest, recommendation by the Civil Engineering Master's Program Admissions Committee; for doctorate, GRE, BS and MS from accredited institution, minimum GPA of 3.0 in upper-division and graduate courses, three letters of recommendation, letter of research interest, resume/curriculum vitae. Additional exam requirements/recommendations for international students: Required—TOEFL (minimum score 550 paper-based; 79 iBT), IELTS (minimum score 6.5). Electronic applications accepted. *Expenses:* Contact institution. *Faculty research:* Structures, application of geographic information systems in water resources, geotechnical engineering, pavement traffic loading, hydrogeology.

The University of Texas at Tyler, College of Engineering, Department of Civil Engineering, Tyler, TX 75799-0001. Offers environmental engineering (MS); industrial safety (MS); structural engineering (MS); transportation engineering (MS); water resources engineering (MS). *Program availability:* Part-time, evening/weekend. *Students:* 5 full-time (1 woman), 7 part-time (1 woman); includes 3 minority (1 Black or African American, non-Hispanic/Latino; 1 Asian, non-Hispanic/Latino; 1 Hispanic/Latino), 1 international. Average age 26. 5 applicants, 80% accepted, 3 enrolled. *Entrance requirements:* For master's, GRE General Test, bachelor's degree in engineering, associated science degree. Additional exam requirements/recommendations for international students: Required—TOEFL. *Application deadline:* For fall admission, 8/17 priority date for domestic students, 7/1 priority date for international students; for spring admission, 12/21 priority date for domestic students, 11/1 priority date for international students. Application fee: $25 ($50 for international students). *Financial support:* Application deadline: 7/1. *Faculty research:* Non-destructive strength testing, indoor air quality, transportation routing and signaling, pavement replacement criteria, flood water routing, construction and long-term behavior of innovative geotechnical foundation and embankment construction used in highway construction, engineering education. *Unit head:* Dr. Torey Nalbone, Chair, 903-565-5520, E-mail: tnalbone@uttyler.edu. *Application contact:* Dr. Torey Nalbone, Chair, 903-565-5520, E-mail: tnalbone@uttyler.edu.
Website: https://www.uttyler.edu/ce/

University of Utah, Graduate School, College of Engineering, Department of Civil and Environmental Engineering, Salt Lake City, UT 84112. Offers civil and environmental engineering (MS, PhD); nuclear engineering (MS, PhD). *Program availability:* Part-time. *Faculty:* 21 full-time (5 women), 15 part-time/adjunct (1 woman). *Students:* 65 full-time (12 women), 31 part-time (6 women); includes 9 minority (1 Black or African American, non-Hispanic/Latino; 6 Asian, non-Hispanic/Latino; 1 Hispanic/Latino; 1 Two or more races, non-Hispanic/Latino), 45 international. Average age 29. 88 applicants, 40% accepted, 18 enrolled. In 2018, 20 master's, 8 doctorates awarded. Terminal master's awarded for partial completion of doctoral program. *Degree requirements:* For master's, comprehensive exam (for some programs), thesis (for some programs); for doctorate, comprehensive exam, thesis/dissertation, departmental qualifying exam, preliminary exam. *Entrance requirements:* For master's and doctorate, GRE General Test, minimum GPA of 3.0. Additional exam requirements/recommendations for international students: Required—TOEFL (minimum score 550 paper-based; 80 iBT). *Application deadline:* For fall admission, 1/1 priority date for domestic and international students; for spring admission, 10/1 for domestic and international students. Applications are processed on

a rolling basis. Application fee: $0 ($25 for international students). Electronic applications accepted. *Expenses:* Contact institution. *Financial support:* In 2018–19, 77 students received support, including 7 fellowships with full tuition reimbursements available (averaging $27,000 per year), 57 research assistantships with full tuition reimbursements available (averaging $23,500 per year), 14 teaching assistantships with full tuition reimbursements available (averaging $23,400 per year); traineeships, health care benefits, and unspecified assistantships also available. Financial award application deadline: 1/1. *Faculty research:* Structural engineering, geotechnical engineering, transportation engineering, environmental engineering, water resources, construction engineering. *Total annual research expenditures:* $6.3 million. *Unit head:* Dr. Michael Barber, Chair, 801-581-6931, Fax: 801-585-5477, E-mail: barber@civil.utah.edu. *Application contact:* Courtney Phillips, Academic Advisor, 801-581-6678, Fax: 801-585-5477, E-mail: cveen-graduate@utah.edu.
Website: http://www.civil.utah.edu

University of Vermont, Graduate College, College of Engineering and Mathematical Sciences, Department of Civil and Environmental Engineering, Burlington, VT 05405. Offers MS, PhD. *Degree requirements:* For master's, thesis or alternative; for doctorate, thesis/dissertation. *Entrance requirements:* For master's and doctorate, GRE General Test. Additional exam requirements/recommendations for international students: Required—TOEFL (minimum score 550 paper-based, 90 iBT) or IELTS (6.5). Electronic applications accepted.

University of Washington, Graduate School, College of Engineering, Department of Civil and Environmental Engineering, Seattle, WA 98195-2700. Offers construction engineering (MSCE, PhD); environmental engineering (MSCE, PhD); geotechnical engineering (MSCE, PhD); hydrology and hydrodynamics (MSCE, PhD); structural engineering and mechanics (MSCE, PhD); transportation engineering (MSCE, PhD). *Program availability:* Part-time, 100% online. *Faculty:* 38 full-time (10 women). *Students:* 239 full-time (104 women), 172 part-time (51 women); includes 91 minority (3 Black or African American, non-Hispanic/Latino; 2 American Indian or Alaska Native, non-Hispanic/Latino; 42 Asian, non-Hispanic/Latino; 26 Hispanic/Latino; 18 Two or more races, non-Hispanic/Latino), 120 international. Average age 28. 787 applicants, 57% accepted, 163 enrolled. In 2018, 161 master's, 11 doctorates awarded. Terminal master's awarded for partial completion of doctoral program. *Degree requirements:* For master's, thesis optional; for doctorate, comprehensive exam, thesis/dissertation, qualifying, general and final exams; completion of degree within 10 years. *Entrance requirements:* For master's, GRE General Test, minimum GPA of 3.0, statement of purpose, letters of recommendation, transcripts; for doctorate, GRE General Test, minimum GPA of 3.5, statement of purpose, letters of recommendation, transcripts, resume. Additional exam requirements/recommendations for international students: Required—TOEFL (minimum score 580 paper-based; 92 iBT); Recommended—IELTS (minimum score 7, TSE. *Application deadline:* For fall admission, 12/15 for domestic and international students. Applications are processed on a rolling basis. Application fee: $85. Electronic applications accepted. *Expenses:* Research-focused Master's and PhD: $18,852 resident; $32,760 nonresident. *Financial support:* In 2018–19, 120 students received support, including 23 fellowships with tuition reimbursements available (averaging $30,240 per year), 78 research assistantships with full tuition reimbursements available (averaging $30,240 per year), 28 teaching assistantships with full tuition reimbursements available (averaging $30,240 per year); scholarships/grants also available. Financial award application deadline: 12/15; financial award applicants required to submit FAFSA. *Faculty research:* Structural and geotechnical engineering; transportation and construction engineering, water and environmental engineering. *Total annual research expenditures:* $16.4 million. *Unit head:* Dr. Timothy V. Larson, Professor/Chair, 206-543-6815, Fax: 206-543-1543, E-mail: tlarson@uw.edu. *Application contact:* Melissa Pritchard, Graduate Adviser, 206-543-2574, Fax: 206-543-1543, E-mail: ceginfo@u.washington.edu.
Website: http://www.ce.washington.edu/

University of Waterloo, Graduate Studies and Postdoctoral Affairs, Faculty of Engineering, Department of Civil and Environmental Engineering, Waterloo, ON N2L 3G1, Canada. Offers M Eng, MA Sc, PhD. *Program availability:* Part-time. *Degree requirements:* For master's, research paper or thesis; for doctorate, comprehensive exam, thesis/dissertation. *Entrance requirements:* For master's, honors degree, minimum B average; for doctorate, master's degree, minimum A- average. Additional exam requirements/recommendations for international students: Required—TOEFL, IELTS, PTE. *Application deadline:* Applications are processed on a rolling basis. Application fee: $125 Canadian dollars. Electronic applications accepted. *Financial support:* Research assistantships and teaching assistantships available. *Faculty research:* Water resources, structures, construction management, transportation, geotechnical engineering.
Website: https://uwaterloo.ca/civil-environmental-engineering/

The University of Western Ontario, School of Graduate and Postdoctoral Studies, Physical Sciences Division, Faculty of Engineering, London, ON N6A 3K7, Canada. Offers chemical and biochemical engineering (ME Sc, PhD); civil and environmental engineering (M Eng, ME Sc, PhD); electrical and computer engineering (M Eng, ME Sc, PhD); mechanical and materials engineering (M Eng, ME Sc, PhD). *Program availability:* Part-time. Terminal master's awarded for partial completion of doctoral program. *Degree requirements:* For master's, thesis; for doctorate, thesis/dissertation. *Entrance requirements:* For master's, minimum B average; for doctorate, minimum B+ average. *Faculty research:* Wind, geotechnical, chemical reactor engineering, applied electrostatics, biochemical engineering.

University of Windsor, Faculty of Graduate Studies, Faculty of Engineering, Department of Civil and Environmental Engineering, Windsor, ON N9B 3P4, Canada. Offers civil engineering (M Eng, MA Sc, PhD); environmental engineering (M Eng, MA Sc, PhD). *Program availability:* Part-time. *Degree requirements:* For master's, thesis; for doctorate, comprehensive exam, thesis/dissertation. *Entrance requirements:* For master's, minimum B average; for doctorate, master's degree, minimum A average. Additional exam requirements/recommendations for international students: Required—TOEFL (minimum score 580 paper-based). Electronic applications accepted. *Faculty research:* Odors: sampling, measurement, control; drinking water disinfection; hydrocarbon contaminated soil remediation, structural dynamics, numerical simulation of piezoelectric materials.

University of Wisconsin–Madison, Graduate School, College of Engineering, Department of Civil and Environmental Engineering, Madison, WI 53706-1380. Offers construction engineering and management (MS); environmental science and engineering (MS); geological/geotechnical engineering (MS); structural engineering (MS); transportation engineering (MS); water resources engineering (MS). *Program availability:* Part-time. *Faculty:* 31 full-time (8 women). *Students:* 97 full-time (28 women), 39 part-time (15 women); includes 12 minority (2 Black or African American, non-Hispanic/Latino; 3 Asian, non-Hispanic/Latino; 6 Hispanic/Latino; 1 Two or more races, non-Hispanic/Latino), 62 international. Average age 28. 261 applicants, 45% accepted, 29 enrolled. In 2018, 33 master's awarded. Terminal master's awarded for partial completion of doctoral program. *Degree requirements:* For master's, thesis (for some programs), minimum of 30 credits; minimum overall GPA of 3.0. *Entrance requirements:* For master's, GRE General Test, bachelor's degree; minimum GPA of 3.0

for last 60 credits of course work. Additional exam requirements/recommendations for international students: Required—TOEFL (minimum score 580 paper-based; 92 iBT). *Application deadline:* For fall admission, 12/15 priority date for domestic and international students; for spring admission, 10/1 for domestic and international students. Application fee: $75 ($81 for international students). Electronic applications accepted. *Expenses:* In-state tuition (Full-time): $10,728; Out-of-state tuition (full-time): $24,054; Fees: $1282; In-state tuition (per credit): $670; Out-of-state tuition (per credit): $1503; Fees (per credit): $126. *Financial support:* In 2018–19, 90 students received support, including 8 fellowships with full tuition reimbursements available (averaging $28,704 per year), 54 research assistantships with full tuition reimbursements available (averaging $23,784 per year), 21 teaching assistantships with full tuition reimbursements available (averaging $16,584 per year); Federal Work-Study, scholarships/grants, health care benefits, unspecified assistantships, and project assistantships also available. Support available to part-time students. Financial award application deadline: 12/1; financial award applicants required to submit FAFSA. *Faculty research:* Construction engineering and management; environmental engineering; structural engineering; transportation and city planning; water resources engineering; water chemistry. *Total annual research expenditures:* $12.5 million. *Unit head:* Dr. William Likos, Chair, 608-263-9490, Fax: 608-262-5199, E-mail: frontdesk@cee.wisc.edu. *Application contact:* Cheryl Loschko, Student Services Coordinator, 608-890-2420, E-mail: loschko@wisc.edu.
Website: https://www.engr.wisc.edu/department/civil-environmental-engineering/academics/ms-phd-civil-and-environmental-engineering/

University of Wyoming, College of Engineering and Applied Science, Department of Chemical Engineering, Program in Environmental Engineering, Laramie, WY 82071. Offers MS. *Program availability:* Part-time. *Degree requirements:* For master's, thesis optional. *Entrance requirements:* For master's, GRE General Test, minimum GPA of 3.0. Additional exam requirements/recommendations for international students: Required—TOEFL (minimum score 550 paper-based). Electronic applications accepted. *Expenses:* Tuition, area resident: Full-time $6504; part-time $271 per credit hour. Tuition, state resident: full-time $6504; part-time $271 per credit hour. Tuition, nonresident: full-time $19,464; part-time $811 per credit hour. International tuition: $19,464 full-time. *Required fees:* $1410.94; $343.82 per semester. $343.82 per semester. Tuition and fees vary according to course load, program and reciprocity agreements. *Faculty research:* Water and waste water, solid and hazardous waste management, air pollution control, flue-gas cleanup.

Utah State University, School of Graduate Studies, College of Engineering, Department of Civil and Environmental Engineering, Logan, UT 84322. Offers ME, MS, PhD, CE. *Degree requirements:* For master's, thesis (for some programs); for doctorate, thesis/dissertation. *Entrance requirements:* For master's and doctorate, GRE General Test, minimum GPA of 3.0. Additional exam requirements/recommendations for international students: Required—TOEFL. Electronic applications accepted. *Faculty research:* Hazardous waste treatment, large space structures, river basin management, earthquake engineering, environmental impact.

Vanderbilt University, School of Engineering, Department of Civil and Environmental Engineering, Program in Environmental Engineering, Nashville, TN 37240-1001. Offers environmental engineering (M Eng); environmental management (MS, PhD). MS and PhD offered through the Graduate School. *Program availability:* Part-time. Terminal master's awarded for partial completion of doctoral program. *Degree requirements:* For master's, thesis or alternative; for doctorate, thesis/dissertation. *Entrance requirements:* For master's and doctorate, GRE General Test. Additional exam requirements/recommendations for international students: Required—TOEFL. Electronic applications accepted. *Expenses:* Tuition: Full-time $47,208; part-time $2026 per credit hour. *Required fees:* $478. *Faculty research:* Waste treatment, hazardous waste management, chemical waste treatment, water quality.

Villanova University, College of Engineering, Department of Civil and Environmental Engineering, Program in Water Resources and Environmental Engineering, Villanova, PA 19085-1699. Offers urban water resources design (Certificate); water resources and environmental engineering (MSWREE). *Program availability:* Part-time, evening/weekend, online learning. *Degree requirements:* For master's, thesis optional. *Entrance requirements:* For master's, GRE General Test (for applicants with degrees from foreign universities), BCE or bachelor's degree in science or related engineering field, minimum GPA of 3.0. Additional exam requirements/recommendations for international students: Required—TOEFL (minimum score 600 paper-based; 100 iBT). Electronic applications accepted. *Faculty research:* Photocatalytic decontamination and disinfection of water, urban storm water wetlands, economy and risk, removal and destruction of organic acids in water, sludge treatment.

Virginia Polytechnic Institute and State University, VT Online, Blacksburg, VA 24061. Offers advanced transportation systems (Certificate); aerospace engineering (MS); agricultural and life sciences (MSLFS); business information systems (Graduate Certificate); career and technical education (MS); civil engineering (MS); computer engineering (M Eng, MS); decision support systems (Graduate Certificate); eLearning leadership (MA); electrical engineering (M Eng, MS); engineering administration (MEA); environmental engineering (Certificate); environmental politics and policy (Graduate Certificate); environmental sciences and engineering (MS); foundations of political analysis (Graduate Certificate); health product risk management (Graduate Certificate); industrial and systems engineering (MS); information policy and society (Graduate Certificate); information security (Graduate Certificate); information technology (MIT); instructional technology (MA); integrative STEM education (MA Ed); liberal arts (Graduate Certificate); life sciences: health product risk management (MS); natural resources (MNR, Graduate Certificate); networking (Graduate Certificate); nonprofit and nongovernmental organization management (Graduate Certificate); ocean engineering (MS); political science (MA); security studies (Graduate Certificate); software development (Graduate Certificate). *Expenses:* Tuition, state resident: full-time $15,510; part-time $739.50 per credit hour. Tuition, nonresident: full-time $29,629; part-time $1490.25 per credit hour. *Required fees:* $2804; $550 per semester. Tuition and fees vary according to course load, campus/location and program. *Application contact:* Graduate Admissions and Academic Progress, 540-231-8636, E-mail: grads@vt.edu.
Website: http://www.vto.vt.edu/

Washington State University, Voiland College of Engineering and Architecture, Department of Civil and Environmental Engineering, Pullman, WA 99164-2910. Offers civil engineering (MS, PhD); environmental engineering (MS). MS programs also offered at Tri-Cities campus. *Program availability:* Part-time. Terminal master's awarded for partial completion of doctoral program. *Degree requirements:* For master's, comprehensive exam (for some programs), thesis (for some programs), oral exam; for doctorate, comprehensive exam, thesis/dissertation, oral exam, written exam. *Entrance requirements:* For master's, minimum GPA of 3.0, 3 letters of recommendation, statement of purpose; for doctorate, minimum GPA of 3.4, 3 letters of recommendation, statement of purpose. Additional exam requirements/recommendations for international students: Required—TOEFL (minimum score 550 paper-based), IELTS. Electronic applications accepted. *Faculty research:* Environmental engineering, water resources, structural engineering, geotechnical, transportation.

Environmental Engineering

Washington University in St. Louis, School of Engineering and Applied Science, Department of Energy, Environmental and Chemical Engineering, St. Louis, MO 63130-4899. Offers chemical engineering (MS, D Sc); environmental engineering (MS, D Sc). *Program availability:* Part-time. Terminal master's awarded for partial completion of doctoral program. *Degree requirements:* For master's, thesis optional; for doctorate, thesis/dissertation, preliminary exam, qualifying exam. *Entrance requirements:* For master's and doctorate, GRE, minimum B average during final 2 years of course work. Additional exam requirements/recommendations for international students: Required—TOEFL, TWE. Electronic applications accepted. *Faculty research:* Reaction engineering, materials processing, catalysis, process control, air pollution control.

Worcester Polytechnic Institute, Graduate Admissions, Department of Civil and Environmental Engineering, Worcester, MA 01609-2280. Offers civil engineering (MS); construction project management (Graduate Certificate). *Program availability:* Part-time, evening/weekend, 100% online, blended/hybrid learning. *Students:* 22 full-time (9 women), 51 part-time (19 women); includes 9 minority (1 Black or African American, non-Hispanic/Latino; 1 American Indian or Alaska Native, non-Hispanic/Latino; 5 Asian, non-Hispanic/Latino; 2 Hispanic/Latino), 12 international. Average age 31. 136 applicants, 60% accepted, 22 enrolled. In 2018, 21 master's, 12 other advanced degrees awarded. *Degree requirements:* For master's, thesis optional; for doctorate, comprehensive exam, thesis/dissertation. *Entrance requirements:* For master's, required for all international applicants; recommended for all others, 3 letters of recommendation; for doctorate, required for all international applicants; recommended for all others, 3 letters of recommendation, statement of purpose. Additional exam requirements/recommendations for international students: Required—TOEFL (minimum score 563 paper-based; 84 iBT), IELTS (minimum score 7). *Application deadline:* For fall admission, 1/1 priority date for domestic and international students; for spring admission, 10/1 priority date for domestic and international students. Applications are processed on a rolling basis. Application fee: $70. Electronic applications accepted. *Financial support:* Fellowships, research assistantships, teaching assistantships, career-related internships or fieldwork, institutionally sponsored loans, scholarships/grants, and unspecified assistantships available. Financial award application deadline: 1/1. *Unit head:* Dr. Carrick Eggleston, Department Head, 508-831-5530, Fax: 508-831-5808, E-mail: ceggleston@wpi.edu. *Application contact:* Dr. Nima Rahbar, Graduate Coordinator, 508-831-5530, Fax: 508-831-5808, E-mail: nrahbar@wpi.edu.
Website: https://www.wpi.edu/academics/departments/civil-environmental-engineering

Yale University, Graduate School of Arts and Sciences, School of Engineering and Applied Science, Program in Environmental Engineering, New Haven, CT 06520. Offers MS, PhD.

Youngstown State University, College of Graduate Studies, College of Science, Technology, Engineering and Mathematics, Department of Civil/Environmental and Chemical Engineering, Youngstown, OH 44555-0001. Offers civil and environmental engineering (MSE). *Program availability:* Part-time, evening/weekend. *Degree requirements:* For master's, thesis optional. *Entrance requirements:* For master's, minimum GPA of 2.75 in field. Additional exam requirements/recommendations for international students: Required—TOEFL. *Faculty research:* Structural mechanics, water quality modeling, surface and ground water hydrology, physical and chemical processes in aquatic systems.

Fire Protection Engineering

Oklahoma State University, College of Arts and Sciences, Department of Political Science, Stillwater, OK 74078. Offers fire and emergency management administration (MS, PhD); political science (MA). *Faculty:* 21 full-time (7 women), 2 part-time/adjunct (0 women). *Students:* 7 full-time (4 women), 3 part-time (1 woman); includes 2 minority (1 Black or African American, non-Hispanic/Latino; 1 Hispanic/Latino), 1 international. Average age 36. 33 applicants, 52% accepted, 15 enrolled. In 2018, 19 master's, 3 doctorates awarded. *Entrance requirements:* For master's and doctorate, GRE. Additional exam requirements/recommendations for international students: Required—TOEFL (minimum score 550 paper-based; 79 iBT). *Application deadline:* For fall admission, 3/1 priority date for international students; for spring admission, 8/1 priority date for international students. Applications are processed on a rolling basis. Application fee: $40 ($75 for international students). Electronic applications accepted. *Expenses: Tuition, area resident:* Full-time $4148. Tuition, state resident: full-time $4148. Tuition, nonresident: full-time $10,517. *International tuition:* $10,517 full-time. *Required fees:* $4394; $2929 per credit hour. Tuition and fees vary according to course load and program. *Financial support:* Research assistantships, teaching assistantships, career-related internships or fieldwork, Federal Work-Study, scholarships/grants, health care benefits, tuition waivers (partial), and unspecified assistantships available. Support available to part-time students. Financial award application deadline: 3/1; financial award applicants required to submit FAFSA. *Faculty research:* Fire and emergency management, environmental dispute resolution, voting and elections, women and politics, urban politics. *Unit head:* Dr. Farida Jalalzai, Department Head, 405-744-5607. *Application contact:* Dr. Sheryl Tucker, Dean, 405-744-6368, Fax: 405-744-0355, E-mail: gradi@okstate.edu.
Website: http://polsci.okstate.edu

University of Maryland, College Park, Academic Affairs, A. James Clark School of Engineering, Department of Fire Protection Engineering, College Park, MD 20742. Offers M Eng, MS. *Program availability:* Part-time, evening/weekend. *Degree requirements:* For master's, thesis optional. *Entrance requirements:* For master's, GRE General Test, minimum GPA of 3.0, BS in any engineering or physical science area, 3 letters of recommendation. Electronic applications accepted. *Faculty research:* Fire and thermal degradation of materials, fire modeling, fire dynamics, smoke detection and management, fire resistance.

University of New Haven, Graduate School, Henry C. Lee College of Criminal Justice and Forensic Sciences, Fire and Explosion Investigation, West Haven, CT 06516. Offers fire science (MS); fire/arson investigation (MS, Graduate Certificate); forensic science (Graduate Certificate); public safety management (MS). *Program availability:* Part-time, evening/weekend. *Students:* 9 full-time (2 women), 3 part-time (0 women); includes 1 minority (Hispanic/Latino), 4 international. Average age 30. 12 applicants, 100% accepted, 5 enrolled. In 2018, 8 master's awarded. *Degree requirements:* For master's, thesis or alternative, research project or internship. *Entrance requirements:* Additional exam requirements/recommendations for international students: Required—TOEFL (minimum score 80 iBT), IELTS, PTE (minimum score 53). *Application deadline:* Applications are processed on a rolling basis. Application fee: $50. Electronic applications accepted. Application fee is waived when completed online. *Expenses: Tuition:* Full-time $16,470; part-time $915 per credit hour. *Required fees:* $230; $95 per term. *Financial support:* Research assistantships with partial tuition reimbursements, teaching assistantships with partial tuition reimbursements, Federal Work-Study, scholarships/grants, and unspecified assistantships available. Support available to part-time students. Financial award applicants required to submit FAFSA. *Unit head:* Dr. Sorin Iliescu, Assistant Professor, 203-932-7239, E-mail: silliescu@newhaven.edu. *Application contact:* Selina O'Toole, Senior Associate Director of Graduate Admissions, 203-932-7337, E-mail: SOToole@newhaven.edu.
Website: https://www.newhaven.edu/lee-college/graduate-programs/fire-science/

The University of North Carolina at Charlotte, William States Lee College of Engineering, Department of Engineering Technology and Construction Management, Charlotte, NC 28223-0001. Offers applied energy (Graduate Certificate); applied energy and electromechanical systems (MS); construction and facilities management (MS); fire protection and administration (MS). *Program availability:* Part-time. *Students:* 54 full-time (17 women), 17 part-time (3 women); includes 9 minority (3 Black or African American, non-Hispanic/Latino; 2 Asian, non-Hispanic/Latino; 3 Hispanic/Latino; 1 Two or more races, non-Hispanic/Latino), 40 international. Average age 26. 97 applicants, 81% accepted, 22 enrolled. In 2018, 31 master's awarded. *Entrance requirements:* For master's, GRE, minimum undergraduate GPA of 3.0, recommendations, statistics; integral and differential calculus (for students pursuing fire protection concentration or applied energy and electromechanical systems program); for Graduate Certificate, bachelor's degree in engineering, engineering technology, construction management or a closely-related technical or scientific field; undergraduate coursework of at least 3 semesters in engineering analysis or calculus; minimum GPA of 3.0. Additional exam requirements/recommendations for international students: Required—TOEFL (minimum score 523 paper-based; 70 iBT), IELTS (minimum score 6), TOEFL (minimum score 523 paper-based, 70 iBT) or IELTS (6). *Application deadline:* Applications are processed on a rolling basis. Application fee: $75. Electronic applications accepted. *Expenses:* Contact institution. *Financial support:* Research assistantships, career-related internships or fieldwork, institutionally sponsored loans, scholarships/grants, and unspecified assistantships available. Support available to part-time students. Financial award application deadline: 3/1; financial award applicants required to submit FAFSA. *Total annual research expenditures:* $1.7 million. *Unit head:* Dr. Anthony Brizendine, Chair, 704-687-5050, E-mail: albrizen@uncc.edu. *Application contact:* Kathy B. Giddings, Director of Graduate Admissions, 704-687-5503, Fax: 704-687-1668, E-mail: gradadm@uncc.edu.
Website: http://et.uncc.edu/

Worcester Polytechnic Institute, Graduate Admissions, Department of Fire Protection Engineering, Worcester, MA 01609-2280. Offers MS, PhD, Advanced Certificate, Graduate Certificate. *Program availability:* Part-time, evening/weekend, 100% online, blended/hybrid learning. *Students:* 21 full-time (5 women), 55 part-time (13 women); includes 8 minority (4 Black or African American, non-Hispanic/Latino; 1 American Indian or Alaska Native, non-Hispanic/Latino; 2 Asian, non-Hispanic/Latino; 1 Two or more races, non-Hispanic/Latino), 19 international. Average age 28. 65 applicants, 65% accepted, 25 enrolled. In 2018, 49 master's, 2 other advanced degrees awarded. Terminal master's awarded for partial completion of doctoral program. *Degree requirements:* For master's, thesis optional; for doctorate, comprehensive exam, thesis/dissertation. *Entrance requirements:* For master's, General GRE exam required for international applicants., BS in engineering or physical sciences, 3 letters of recommendation; for doctorate, General GRE exam required., 3 letters of recommendation, statement of purpose. Additional exam requirements/recommendations for international students: Required—TOEFL (minimum score 563 paper-based; 84 iBT), IELTS (minimum score 7), GRE. *Application deadline:* For fall admission, 1/1 priority date for domestic students, 1/1 for international students; for spring admission, 10/1 priority date for domestic students, 10/1 for international students. Applications are processed on a rolling basis. Application fee: $70. Electronic applications accepted. *Financial support:* Fellowships, research assistantships, teaching assistantships, career-related internships or fieldwork, institutionally sponsored loans, scholarships/grants, and unspecified assistantships available. Financial award application deadline: 1/1. *Unit head:* Dr. Albert Simeoni, Interim Head, 508-831-5593, Fax: 508-831-5862, E-mail: asimeoni@wpi.edu. *Application contact:* Dr. Ali Rangwala, Graduate Coordinator, 508-831-5593, Fax: 508-831-5862, E-mail: rangwala@wpi.edu.
Website: https://www.wpi.edu/academics/departments/fire-protection-engineering

Geotechnical Engineering

The Citadel, The Military College of South Carolina, Citadel Graduate College, School of Engineering, Department of Civil and Environmental Engineering, Charleston, SC 29409. Offers built environment and public health (Graduate Certificate); civil engineering (MS); geotechnical engineering (Graduate Certificate); structural engineering (Graduate Certificate); transportation engineering (Graduate Certificate). *Program availability:* Part-time, evening/weekend. *Degree requirements:* For master's, plan of study outlining intended areas of interest and top four corresponding courses of interest. *Entrance requirements:* For master's, official transcript of baccalaureate degree from ABET-accredited engineering program or approved alternative; 2 letters of recommendation; for Graduate Certificate, official transcript of baccalaureate degree directly from an accredited college or university. Additional exam requirements/recommendations for international students: Required—TOEFL (minimum score 550 paper-based; 79 iBT). Electronic applications accepted. *Expenses:* Tuition, state resident: part-time $595 per credit hour. Tuition, nonresident: part-time $1020 per credit hour. *Required fees:* $90 per term.

Clemson University, Graduate School, College of Engineering, Computing and Applied Sciences, Glenn Department of Civil Engineering, Clemson, SC 29634. Offers civil engineering (MS, PhD), including construction engineering and management,

construction materials, geotechnical engineering, structural engineering, transportation engineering, water resources engineering. *Program availability:* Part-time. *Faculty:* 20 full-time (3 women). *Students:* 109 full-time (23 women), 55 part-time (11 women); includes 9 minority (2 Black or African American, non-Hispanic/Latino; 2 Asian, non-Hispanic/Latino; 4 Hispanic/Latino; 1 Two or more races, non-Hispanic/Latino), 111 international. Average age 28. 283 applicants, 59% accepted, 53 enrolled. In 2018, 31 master's, 11 doctorates awarded. *Degree requirements:* For master's, thesis or alternative, oral exam, seminar; for doctorate, comprehensive exam, thesis/dissertation, oral exam, seminar. *Entrance requirements:* For master's and doctorate, GRE General Test, unofficial transcripts, letters of recommendation, statement of purpose. Additional exam requirements/recommendations for international students: Required—TOEFL (minimum score 80 paper-based; 80 iBT), PTE (minimum score 54); Recommended—IELTS (minimum score 6.5). *Application deadline:* For fall admission, 4/15 for domestic and international students; for spring admission, 9/15 for domestic and international students. Applications are processed on a rolling basis. Application fee: $80 ($90 for international students). Electronic applications accepted. *Expenses:* $6823 per semester full-time resident, $14023 per semester full-time non-resident, $833 per credit hour part-time resident, $1731 per credit hour part-time non-resident, online $1264 per credit hour, $4938 doctoral programs resident, $10405 doctoral programs non-resident, $1144 full-time graduate assistant, other fees may apply per session. *Financial support:* In 2018–19, 104 students received support, including 20 fellowships with full and partial tuition reimbursements available (averaging $4,491 per year), 43 research assistantships with full and partial tuition reimbursements available (averaging $16,364 per year), 1 teaching assistantship with full and partial tuition reimbursement available (averaging $12,750 per year); career-related internships or fieldwork and unspecified assistantships also available. Financial award application deadline: 4/15. *Faculty research:* Applied fluid mechanics, construction materials, project management, structural and geotechnical engineering, transportation. *Total annual research expenditures:* $4.9 million. *Unit head:* Dr. Ronald Andrus, Interim Department Chair, 864-656-0488, E-mail: randrus@clemson.edu. *Application contact:* Dr. Abdul Khan, Graduate Program Coordinator, 864-656-3327, E-mail: abdkhan@clemson.edu.
Website: https://www.clemson.edu/cecas/departments/ce/

Cornell University, Graduate School, Graduate Fields of Engineering, Field of Civil and Environmental Engineering, Ithaca, NY 14853. Offers engineering management (M Eng, MS, PhD); environmental engineering (M Eng, MS, PhD); environmental fluid mechanics and hydrology (M Eng, MS, PhD); environmental systems engineering (M Eng, MS, PhD); geotechnical engineering (M Eng, MS, PhD); remote sensing (M Eng, MS, PhD); structural engineering (M Eng, MS, PhD); structural mechanics (M Eng, MS); transportation engineering (MS, PhD); transportation systems engineering (M Eng); water resource systems (M Eng, MS, PhD). Terminal master's awarded for partial completion of doctoral program. *Degree requirements:* For master's, thesis (MS); for doctorate, comprehensive exam, thesis/dissertation. *Entrance requirements:* For master's and doctorate, GRE General Test (recommended), 2 letters of recommendation. Additional exam requirements/recommendations for international students: Required—TOEFL (minimum score 600 paper-based; 77 iBT). Electronic applications accepted. *Faculty research:* Environmental engineering, geotechnical engineering, remote sensing, environmental fluid mechanics and hydrology, structural engineering.

Drexel University, College of Engineering, Department of Civil, Architectural, and Environmental Engineering, Program in Geotechnical, Geoenvironmental and Geosynthetics Engineering, Philadelphia, PA 19104-2875. Offers MS, PhD.

École Polytechnique de Montréal, Graduate Programs, Department of Civil, Geological and Mining Engineering, Montréal, QC H3C 3A7, Canada. Offers civil, geological and mining engineering (DESS); environmental engineering (M Eng, M Sc A, PhD); geotechnical engineering (M Eng, M Sc A, PhD); hydraulics engineering (M Eng, M Sc A, PhD); structural engineering (M Eng, M Sc A, PhD); transportation engineering (M Eng, M Sc A, PhD). *Program availability:* Part-time. *Degree requirements:* For master's, one foreign language, thesis; for doctorate, one foreign language, thesis/dissertation. *Entrance requirements:* For master's, minimum GPA of 2.75; for doctorate, minimum GPA of 3.0. *Faculty research:* Water resources management, characteristics of building materials, aging of dams, pollution control.

Illinois Institute of Technology, Graduate College, Armour College of Engineering, Department of Civil, Architectural and Environmental Engineering, Chicago, IL 60616. Offers architectural engineering (M Arch E); civil engineering (MS, PhD), including architectural engineering (MS), construction engineering and management (MS), geoenvironmental engineering (MS), geotechnical engineering (MS), structural engineering (MS), transportation engineering (MS); construction engineering and management (MCEM); environmental engineering (M Env E, MS, PhD); geoenvironmental engineering (M Geoenv E); geotechnical engineering (MGE); infrastructure engineering and management (MPW); structural engineering (MSE); transportation engineering (M Trans E). *Program availability:* Part-time, evening/weekend, online learning. Terminal master's awarded for partial completion of doctoral program. *Degree requirements:* For master's, thesis (for some programs); for doctorate, comprehensive exam, thesis/dissertation. *Entrance requirements:* For master's, GRE General Test (minimum score 900 Quantitative and Verbal, 2.5 Analytical Writing), minimum undergraduate GPA of 3.0; for doctorate, GRE General Test (minimum score 1000 Quantitative and Verbal, 3.0 Analytical Writing), minimum undergraduate GPA of 3.0. Additional exam requirements/recommendations for international students: Required—TOEFL (minimum score 550 paper-based; 80 iBT). Electronic applications accepted. *Faculty research:* Structural, architectural, geotechnical and geoenvironmental engineering; construction engineering and management; transportation engineering; environmental engineering and public works.

Iowa State University of Science and Technology, Department of Civil and Construction Engineering, Ames, IA 50011. Offers civil engineering (MS, PhD), including civil engineering materials, construction engineering and management, environmental engineering, geotechnical engineering, structural engineering, transportation engineering. *Degree requirements:* For master's, thesis or alternative; for doctorate, thesis/dissertation. *Entrance requirements:* For master's and doctorate, GRE General Test. Additional exam requirements/recommendations for international students: Required—TOEFL (minimum score 550 paper-based; 82 iBT), IELTS (minimum score 6.5). Electronic applications accepted.

Kansas State University, Graduate School, College of Engineering, Department of Civil Engineering, Manhattan, KS 66506. Offers civil engineering (MS, PhD); environmental engineering (MS, PhD); geotechnical engineering (MS, PhD); structural engineering (MS, PhD); transportation engineering (MS, PhD); water resources engineering (MS, PhD). *Program availability:* Part-time, evening/weekend, online learning. *Degree requirements:* For master's, thesis or alternative; for doctorate, thesis/dissertation. *Entrance requirements:* For master's, GRE General Test, bachelor's degree or course work in related engineering fields; for doctorate, GRE General Test. Additional exam requirements/recommendations for international students: Required—TOEFL (minimum score 550 paper-based; 79 iBT). Electronic applications accepted. *Faculty research:* Transportation and materials engineering, water resources engineering, environmental engineering, geotechnical engineering, structural engineering.

Kennesaw State University, Southern Polytechnic College of Engineering and Engineering Technology, Program in Civil Engineering, Kennesaw, GA 30144. Offers environmental engineering (MS); geotechnical engineering (MS); structural engineering (MS); transportation and pavement engineering (MS); water resources engineering (MS). *Program availability:* Online learning. *Students:* 13 full-time (2 women), 24 part-time (5 women); includes 20 minority (8 Black or African American, non-Hispanic/Latino; 5 Asian, non-Hispanic/Latino; 4 Hispanic/Latino; 3 Two or more races, non-Hispanic/Latino), 2 international. Average age 33. 21 applicants, 57% accepted, 1 enrolled. In 2018, 6 master's awarded. *Degree requirements:* For master's, thesis optional. *Entrance requirements:* Additional exam requirements/recommendations for international students: Required—TOEFL (minimum score 550 paper-based; 80 iBT), IELTS (minimum score 6.5). *Application deadline:* For fall admission, 11/1 for domestic and international students; for spring admission, 4/1 for domestic and international students. Applications are processed on a rolling basis. Application fee: $60. Electronic applications accepted. *Expenses: Tuition, area resident:* Full-time $6960; part-time $290 per credit hour. Tuition, state resident: full-time $6960; part-time $290 per credit hour. Tuition, nonresident: full-time $25,080; part-time $1045 per credit hour. *International tuition:* $25,080 full-time. *Required fees:* $2006; $1706 per semester. $853 per semester. *Unit head:* Metin Oguzmert, Coordinator, 470-578-5083, E-mail: moguzmer@kennesaw.edu. *Application contact:* Admissions Counselor, 470-578-4377, E-mail: ksugrad@kennesaw.edu.
Website: http://engineering.kennesaw.edu/civil-construction/degrees/ms-civil-engineering.php

Louisiana State University and Agricultural & Mechanical College, Graduate School, College of Engineering, Department of Civil and Environmental Engineering, Baton Rouge, LA 70803. Offers environmental engineering (MSCE, PhD); geotechnical engineering (MSCE, PhD); structural engineering and mechanics (MSCE, PhD); transportation engineering (MSCE, PhD); water resources (MSCE, PhD).

Massachusetts Institute of Technology, School of Engineering, Department of Civil and Environmental Engineering, Cambridge, MA 02139. Offers biological oceanography (PhD, Sc D); chemical oceanography (PhD, Sc D); civil and environmental engineering (M Eng, SM, PhD, Sc D); civil and environmental systems (PhD, Sc D); civil engineering (PhD, Sc D, CE); civil engineering and computation (PhD); coastal engineering (PhD, Sc D); construction engineering and management (PhD, Sc D); environmental biology (PhD, Sc D); environmental chemistry (PhD, Sc D); environmental engineering (PhD, Sc D); environmental engineering and computation (PhD); environmental fluid mechanics (PhD, Sc D); geotechnical and geoenvironmental engineering (PhD, Sc D); hydrology (PhD, Sc D); information technology (PhD, Sc D); oceanographic engineering (PhD, Sc D); structures and materials (PhD, Sc D); transportation (PhD, Sc D); SM/MBA. *Degree requirements:* For master's, thesis; for doctorate, comprehensive exam, thesis/dissertation; for CE, comprehensive exam, thesis. *Entrance requirements:* For master's, doctorate, and CE, GRE General Test. Additional exam requirements/recommendations for international students: Required—TOEFL, IELTS. Electronic applications accepted. *Expenses: Tuition:* Full-time $51,520; part-time $800 per credit hour. *Required fees:* $312. *Faculty research:* Environmental chemistry, environmental fluid mechanics and coastal engineering, environmental microbiology, geotechnical engineering and geomechanics, hydrology and hydro climatology, infrastructure systems, mechanics of materials and structures, transportation systems.

McGill University, Faculty of Graduate and Postdoctoral Studies, Faculty of Engineering, Department of Civil Engineering and Applied Mechanics, Montréal, QC H3A 2T5, Canada. Offers environmental engineering (M Eng, M Sc, PhD); fluid mechanics (M Sc); fluid mechanics and hydraulic engineering (M Eng, PhD); materials engineering (M Eng, PhD); rehabilitation of urban infrastructure (M Eng, PhD); soil behavior (M Eng, PhD); soil mechanics and foundations (M Eng, PhD); structures and structural mechanics (M Eng, PhD); water resources (M Sc); water resources engineering (M Eng, PhD).

Missouri University of Science and Technology, Program in Geotechnics, Rolla, MO 65409. Offers ME. *Expenses:* Tuition, state resident: full-time $7545.60; part-time $419.20 per credit hour. Tuition, nonresident: full-time $22,169; part-time $1231.60 per credit hour. *International tuition:* $23,518.80 full-time. *Required fees:* $4523.05. Full-time tuition and fees vary according to course load, campus/location, program and reciprocity agreements.

Northwestern University, McCormick School of Engineering and Applied Science, Department of Civil and Environmental Engineering, Evanston, IL 60208-3109. Offers environmental engineering and science (MS, PhD); geotechnical engineering (MS, PhD); mechanics of materials and solids (MS, PhD); project management (MS); structural engineering and materials (MS, PhD); transportation systems analysis and planning (MS, PhD). MS and PhD admissions and degrees offered through The Graduate School. *Program availability:* Part-time. Terminal master's awarded for partial completion of doctoral program. *Degree requirements:* For master's, comprehensive exam (for some programs), thesis (for some programs); for doctorate, comprehensive exam, thesis/dissertation. *Entrance requirements:* For master's and doctorate, GRE General Test, minimum 2 letters of recommendation, transcripts from all academic institutions attended. Additional exam requirements/recommendations for international students: Required—TOEFL (minimum score 577 paper-based; 90 iBT), IELTS (minimum score 7). Electronic applications accepted. *Faculty research:* Environmental engineering and science, geotechnics, mechanics, materials, structures, and transportation systems analysis and planning.

Norwich University, College of Graduate and Continuing Studies, Master of Civil Engineering Program, Northfield, VT 05663. Offers construction management (MCE); environmental (MCE); geotechnical (MCE); structural (MCE). *Program availability:* Evening/weekend, online only, mostly all online with a week-long residency requirement. *Degree requirements:* For master's, capstone. *Entrance requirements:* For master's, minimum undergraduate GPA of 2.75. Additional exam requirements/recommendations for international students: Required—TOEFL (minimum score 550 paper-based; 80 iBT), IELTS (minimum score 6.5). Electronic applications accepted. *Expenses:* Contact institution.

Ohio University, Graduate College, Russ College of Engineering and Technology, Department of Civil Engineering, Athens, OH 45701-2979. Offers civil engineering (PhD); construction engineering and management (MS); environmental (MS); geoenvironmental (MS); geotechnical (MS); mechanics (MS); structures (MS); transportation (MS); water resources (MS). *Program availability:* Part-time. *Degree requirements:* For master's, comprehensive exam (for some programs), thesis or alternative; for doctorate, comprehensive exam, thesis/dissertation. *Entrance requirements:* For master's, GRE General Test, minimum GPA of 3.0, 3 letters of recommendation; for doctorate, GRE General Test. Additional exam requirements/recommendations for international students: Required—TOEFL (minimum score 550 paper-based; 80 iBT) or IELTS (minimum score 6.5). Electronic applications accepted. *Faculty research:* Noise abatement, materials and environment, highway infrastructure, subsurface investigation (pavements, pipes, bridges).

Old Dominion University, Frank Batten College of Engineering and Technology, Program in Civil Engineering, Norfolk, VA 23529. Offers civil engineering (ME, MS), including coastal engineering, geotechnical engineering, hydraulics and water resources, structural engineering, transportation engineering. *Program availability:* Part-time, evening/weekend, blended/hybrid learning. *Degree requirements:* For master's, comprehensive exam, thesis optional. *Entrance requirements:* For master's, GRE, minimum GPA of 3.0. Additional exam requirements/recommendations for international students: Required—TOEFL (minimum score 550 paper-based, 80 iBT) or IELTS (6.5). Electronic applications accepted. *Expenses:* Contact institution. *Faculty research:* Structural engineering, coastal engineering, geotechnical engineering, water resources, transportation engineering.

Oregon State University, College of Engineering, Program in Civil Engineering, Corvallis, OR 97331. Offers civil engineering (M Eng, MS, PhD); coastal and ocean engineering (M Eng, MS, PhD); construction engineering management (M Eng, MS, PhD); engineering education (M Eng, MS, PhD); geomatics (M Eng, MS, PhD); geotechnical engineering (M Eng, MS, PhD); infrastructure materials (M Eng, MS, PhD); structural engineering (M Eng, MS, PhD); transportation engineering (M Eng). *Entrance requirements:* For master's and doctorate, GRE. Additional exam requirements/recommendations for international students: Required—TOEFL (minimum score 80 iBT), IELTS (minimum score 6.5). *Expenses:* Contact institution.

Penn State University Park, Graduate School, College of Earth and Mineral Sciences, John and Willie Leone Family Department of Energy and Mineral Engineering, University Park, PA 16802. Offers MS, PhD.

Southern Illinois University Edwardsville, Graduate School, School of Engineering, Department of Civil Engineering, Program in Geotechnical Engineering, Edwardsville, IL 62026. Offers MS. *Program availability:* Part-time, evening/weekend. *Degree requirements:* For master's, thesis (for some programs), research paper. *Entrance requirements:* For master's, minimum undergraduate GPA of 2.75 in science, math, and engineering courses. Additional exam requirements/recommendations for international students: Required—TOEFL (minimum score 550 paper-based, 79 iBT), IELTS (minimum score 6.5), Michigan Test of English Language Proficiency or PTE. Electronic applications accepted.

Southern Methodist University, Lyle School of Engineering, Department of Civil and Environmental Engineering, Dallas, TX 75275-0340. Offers civil and environmental engineering (PhD); civil engineering (MS), including geotechnical engineering, structural engineering, transportation systems; environmental engineering (MS); sustainability and development (MA). *Program availability:* Part-time, evening/weekend, online learning. Terminal master's awarded for partial completion of doctoral program. *Degree requirements:* For master's, thesis optional; for doctorate, thesis/dissertation, oral and written qualifying exams. *Entrance requirements:* For master's, GRE General Test, minimum GPA of 3.0 in last 2 years; bachelor's degree in engineering, mathematics, or sciences; for doctorate, GRE, BS and MS in related field, minimum GPA of 3.3. Additional exam requirements/recommendations for international students: Required—TOEFL. Electronic applications accepted. *Faculty research:* Human and environmental health effects of endocrine disrupters, development of air pollution control systems for diesel engines, structural analysis and design, modeling and design of waste treatment systems.

Stanford University, School of Engineering, Department of Civil and Environmental Engineering, Stanford, CA 94305-2004. Offers atmosphere and energy (MS, PhD); construction (MS), including construction engineering and management, design-construction integration, sustainable design and construction; environmental engineering and science (MS, PhD, Eng); environmental fluid mechanics and hydrology (PhD); geomechanics (MS); structural engineering (MS). *Expenses: Tuition:* Full-time $50,703; part-time $32,970 per year. *Required fees:* $651.
Website: http://www-ce.stanford.edu/

Tufts University, School of Engineering, Department of Civil and Environmental Engineering, Medford, MA 02155. Offers bioengineering (MS), including environmental biotechnology; civil and environmental engineering (MS, PhD), including applied data science, environmental and water resources engineering, environmental health, geosystems engineering, structural engineering and mechanics; PhD/PhD. *Program availability:* Part-time. Terminal master's awarded for partial completion of doctoral program. *Degree requirements:* For master's, thesis (for some programs); for doctorate, thesis/dissertation. *Entrance requirements:* For master's and doctorate, GRE General Test. Additional exam requirements/recommendations for international students: Required—TOEFL (minimum score 550 paper-based; 80 iBT), IELTS (minimum score 6.5). Electronic applications accepted. *Expenses: Tuition:* Full-time $51,288; part-time $1710 per credit hour. *Required fees:* $904. Full-time tuition and fees vary according to degree level, program and student level. Part-time tuition and fees vary according to course load. *Faculty research:* Environmental and water resources engineering, environmental health, geotechnical and geoenvironmental engineering, structural engineering and mechanics, water diplomacy.

University of Alberta, Faculty of Graduate Studies and Research, Department of Civil and Environmental Engineering, Edmonton, AB T6G 2E1, Canada. Offers construction engineering and management (M Eng, M Sc, PhD); environmental engineering (M Eng, M Sc, PhD); environmental science (M Sc, PhD); geoenvironmental engineering (M Eng, M Sc, PhD); geotechnical engineering (M Eng, M Sc, PhD); mining engineering (M Eng, M Sc, PhD); petroleum engineering (M Eng, M Sc, PhD); structural engineering (M Eng, M Sc, PhD); water resources (M Eng, M Sc, PhD). *Program availability:* Part-time, online learning. *Degree requirements:* For master's, thesis (for some programs); for doctorate, thesis/dissertation. *Entrance requirements:* For master's, minimum GPA of 3.0 in last 2 years of undergraduate studies; for doctorate, minimum GPA of 3.0. Additional exam requirements/recommendations for international students: Required—TOEFL (minimum score 550 paper-based). Electronic applications accepted. *Faculty research:* Mining.

University of Calgary, Faculty of Graduate Studies, Schulich School of Engineering, Program in Civil Engineering, Calgary, AB T2N 1N4, Canada. Offers avalanche mechanics (M Sc, PhD); civil engineering (M Eng, M Sc, PhD); energy and environment engineering (M Eng, M Sc, PhD); environmental engineering (M Eng, M Sc, PhD); geotechnical engineering (M Eng, M Sc, PhD); materials science (M Eng, M Sc, PhD); project management (M Eng, M Sc, PhD); structures and solid mechanics (M Eng, M Sc, PhD); transportation engineering (M Eng, M Sc, PhD); water resources (M Eng, M Sc, PhD). *Program availability:* Part-time. *Degree requirements:* For master's, thesis; for doctorate, thesis/dissertation, written and oral candidacy exam. *Entrance requirements:* For master's, minimum GPA of 3.0; for doctorate, minimum GPA of 3.5. Additional exam requirements/recommendations for international students: Required—TOEFL (minimum score 580 paper-based; 93 iBT), IELTS (minimum score 7). Electronic applications accepted. *Faculty research:* Geotechnical engineering, energy and environment, transportation, project management, structures and solid mechanics.

University of Calgary, Faculty of Graduate Studies, Schulich School of Engineering, Program in Geomatics Engineering, Calgary, AB T2N 1N4, Canada. Offers M Eng, M Sc, PhD. *Program availability:* Part-time. *Degree requirements:* For master's, thesis (for some programs), minimum of 4 half-courses, completion of seminar course; for doctorate, comprehensive exam, thesis/dissertation, minimum of 3 half-courses, completion of two seminar courses, candidacy exam. *Entrance requirements:* For master's, B Sc or equivalent with minimum GPA of 3.0; for doctorate, M Sc or transfer from M Sc program with minimum GPA of 3.5. Additional exam requirements/recommendations for international students: Required—TOEFL (minimum score 550 paper-based; 80 iBT) or IELTS (minimum score 7). Electronic applications accepted. *Faculty research:* Digital imaging systems, earth observation, geospatial information systems, and land tenure positioning, navigation and wireless location.

University of California, Berkeley, Graduate Division, College of Engineering, Department of Civil and Environmental Engineering, Berkeley, CA 94720. Offers engineering and project management (M Eng, MS, PhD); environmental engineering (M Eng, MS, PhD); geoengineering (M Eng, MS, PhD); structural engineering, mechanics and materials (M Eng, MS, PhD); transportation engineering (M Eng, MS, PhD); M Arch/MS; MCP/MS; MPP/MS. Terminal master's awarded for partial completion of doctoral program. *Degree requirements:* For master's, comprehensive exam (for some programs), thesis (for some programs), comprehensive exam or thesis (MS); for doctorate, thesis/dissertation, qualifying exam. *Entrance requirements:* For master's, GRE General Test, minimum GPA of 3.0, 3 letters of recommendation; for doctorate, GRE General Test, minimum GPA of 3.5, 3 letters of recommendation. Additional exam requirements/recommendations for international students: Required—TOEFL (minimum score 570 paper-based; 90 iBT). Electronic applications accepted.

University of Colorado Denver, College of Engineering, Design and Computing, Department of Civil Engineering, Denver, CO 80217. Offers civil engineering (EASPh D); civil engineering systems (PhD); environmental and sustainability engineering (MS, PhD); geographic information systems (MS); geotechnical engineering (MS, PhD); hydrology and hydraulics (MS, PhD); structural engineering (MS, PhD); transportation engineering (MS, PhD). *Program availability:* Part-time, evening/weekend. *Degree requirements:* For master's, comprehensive exam, 30 credit hours, project or thesis; for doctorate, comprehensive exam, thesis/dissertation, 60 credit hours (30 of which are dissertation research). *Entrance requirements:* For master's, GRE, statement of purpose, transcripts, three references; for doctorate, GRE, statement of purpose, transcripts, references, letter of support from faculty stating willingness to serve as dissertation advisor and outlining plan for financial support. Additional exam requirements/recommendations for international students: Required—TOEFL (minimum score 537 paper-based; 75 iBT); Recommended—IELTS (minimum score 6.5). Electronic applications accepted. *Expenses:* Tuition, state resident: full-time $6786; part-time $337 per credit hour. Tuition, nonresident: full-time $22,590; part-time $1255 per credit hour. *Required fees:* $1231; $137 per credit hour. Tuition and fees vary according to program and reciprocity agreements.

University of Dayton, Department of Civil and Environmental Engineering and Engineering Mechanics, Dayton, OH 45469. Offers engineering mechanics (MSEM); environmental engineering (MSCE); geotechnical engineering (MSCE); structural engineering (MSCE); transportation engineering (MSCE); water resources engineering (MSCE). *Program availability:* Part-time, blended/hybrid learning. *Degree requirements:* For master's, thesis or alternative. *Entrance requirements:* For master's, minimum GPA of 3.0 in undergraduate work. Additional exam requirements/recommendations for international students: Required—TOEFL (minimum score 550 paper-based; 80 iBT); Recommended—IELTS (minimum score 6.5), TSE (minimum score 60). Electronic applications accepted. *Faculty research:* Infrastructure, environmental composite, reliability, computer simulation.

University of Delaware, College of Engineering, Department of Civil and Environmental Engineering, Newark, DE 19716. Offers environmental engineering (MAS, MCE, PhD); geotechnical engineering (MAS, MCE, PhD); ocean engineering (MAS, MCE, PhD); structural engineering (MAS, MCE, PhD); transportation engineering (MAS, MCE, PhD); water resource engineering (MAS, MCE, PhD). *Program availability:* Part-time. Terminal master's awarded for partial completion of doctoral program. *Degree requirements:* For master's, thesis; for doctorate, thesis/dissertation. *Entrance requirements:* For master's and doctorate, GRE General Test. Additional exam requirements/recommendations for international students: Required—TOEFL. Electronic applications accepted. *Faculty research:* Structural engineering and mechanics; transportation engineering; ocean engineering; soil mechanics and foundation; water resources and environmental engineering.

University of Massachusetts Amherst, Graduate School, College of Engineering, Department of Civil and Environmental Engineering, Amherst, MA 01003. Offers civil engineering (MSCE, PhD); environmental and water resources engineering (MSCE); geotechnical engineering (MSCE); structural engineering and mechanics (MSCE); transportation engineering (MSCE). *Program availability:* Part-time. Terminal master's awarded for partial completion of doctoral program. *Degree requirements:* For master's, thesis or alternative; for doctorate, comprehensive exam, thesis/dissertation. *Entrance requirements:* For master's and doctorate, GRE General Test. Additional exam requirements/recommendations for international students: Required—TOEFL (minimum score 550 paper-based; 80 iBT), IELTS (minimum score 6.5). Electronic applications accepted.

University of Memphis, Graduate School, Herff College of Engineering, Department of Civil Engineering, Memphis, TN 38152. Offers civil engineering (PhD); engineering seismology (MS); environmental engineering (MS); freight transportation (Graduate Certificate); geotechnical engineering (MS); structural engineering (MS); transportation engineering (MS); water resources engineering (MS). *Students:* 14 full-time (3 women), 8 part-time (3 women); includes 1 minority (Black or African American, non-Hispanic/Latino), 12 international. Average age 27. 27 applicants, 70% accepted, 13 enrolled. In 2018, 11 master's awarded. Terminal master's awarded for partial completion of doctoral program. *Degree requirements:* For master's, comprehensive exam, thesis optional; for doctorate, comprehensive exam, thesis/dissertation. *Entrance requirements:* For master's, GRE General Test, minimum undergraduate GPA of 2.5; bachelor's degree in engineering or a related science or mathematics program; three letters of reference; for doctorate, GRE General Test, bachelor's degree in engineering or engineering science; three letters of reference; for Graduate Certificate, minimum undergraduate GPA of 2.75; bachelor's degree in engineering or engineering science. Additional exam requirements/recommendations for international students: Required—TOEFL (minimum score 550 paper-based; 79 iBT). *Application deadline:* For fall admission, 8/1 for domestic students; for spring admission, 12/1 for domestic students. Application fee: $35 ($60 for international students). Electronic applications accepted. *Expenses: Tuition, area resident:* Full-time $10,240; part-time $503 per credit hour. Tuition, state resident: full-time $10,464. Tuition, nonresident: full-time $20,224; part-time $991 per credit hour. *Required fees:* $850; $106 per credit hour. *Financial support:* Fellowships with full tuition reimbursements, research assistantships with full tuition reimbursements, career-related internships or fieldwork, Federal Work-Study, scholarships/grants, and unspecified assistantships available. Financial award application deadline: 2/1; financial award applicants required to submit FAFSA. *Faculty research:* Structural response to earthquakes, pavement design, water quality, transportation safety, intermodal transportation. *Unit head:* Dr. Shahram Pezeshk, Chair, 901-678-4727, Fax: 901-678-3026, E-mail: spezeshk@memphis.edu. *Application contact:* Dr. Roger Meier, Coordinator of Graduate Studies, 901-678-3284, E-mail: rwmeier@memphis.edu.
Website: https://www.memphis.edu/ce

University of New Brunswick Fredericton, School of Graduate Studies, Faculty of Engineering, Department of Civil Engineering, Fredericton, NB E3B 5A3, Canada. Offers construction engineering and management (M Eng, M Sc E, PhD); environmental engineering (M Eng, M Sc E, PhD); environmental studies (M Eng); geotechnical engineering (M Eng, M Sc E, PhD); groundwater/hydrology (M Eng, M Sc E, PhD); materials (M Eng, M Sc E, PhD); pavements (M Eng, M Sc E, PhD); structures (M Eng, M Sc E, PhD); transportation (M Eng, M Sc E, PhD). *Program availability:* Part-time. *Degree requirements:* For master's, thesis; for doctorate, comprehensive exam, thesis/dissertation, qualifying exam; 27 credit hours of courses. *Entrance requirements:* For master's, minimum GPA of 3.0; B Sc E in civil engineering or related engineering degree; for doctorate, minimum GPA of 3.0; graduate degree in engineering or applied science. Additional exam requirements/recommendations for international students: Required—IELTS (minimum score 7.5), TWE (minimum score 4), Michigan English Language Assessment Battery (minimum score 85) or CanTest (minimum score 4.5); Recommended—TOEFL (minimum score 580 paper-based). Electronic applications accepted. *Faculty research:* Construction engineering and management; engineering materials and infrastructure renewal; highway and pavement research; structures and solid mechanics; geotechnical and geoenvironmental engineering; structure interaction; transportation and planning; environment, solid waste management; structural engineering; water and environmental engineering.

University of Puerto Rico–Mayagüez, Graduate Studies, College of Engineering, Department of Civil Engineering and Surveying, Mayagüez, PR 00681-9000. Offers civil engineering (ME, MS, PhD), including construction engineering and management (ME, MS), environmental engineering, geotechnical engineering (ME, MS), structural engineering, transportation engineering. *Program availability:* Part-time. Terminal master's awarded for partial completion of doctoral program. *Degree requirements:* For master's, one foreign language, thesis; for doctorate, one foreign language, comprehensive exam, thesis/dissertation, qualifying exams. *Entrance requirements:* For master's, proficiency in English and Spanish; BS in civil engineering or its equivalent; for doctorate, proficiency in English and Spanish. Electronic applications accepted. *Faculty research:* Structural design, concrete structure, finite elements, dynamic analysis, transportation, soils.

University of Rhode Island, Graduate School, College of Engineering, Department of Ocean Engineering, Narragansett, RI 02882. Offers ocean engineering (MS, PhD), including acoustics, geomechanics (MS), hydrodynamics (MS), ocean instrumentation (MS), offshore energy (MS), offshore structures (MS), water wave mechanics (MS). *Program availability:* Part-time. *Faculty:* 9 full-time (1 woman). *Students:* 24 full-time (6 women), 19 part-time (4 women); includes 2 minority (both Asian, non-Hispanic/Latino), 6 international. 27 applicants, 70% accepted, 9 enrolled. In 2018, 10 master's, 1 doctorate awarded. *Entrance requirements:* Additional exam requirements/recommendations for international students: Required—TOEFL. *Application deadline:* For fall admission, 7/15 for domestic students, 2/1 for international students; for spring admission, 11/15 for domestic students, 7/15 for international students; for summer admission, 4/15 for domestic students. Application fee: $65. Electronic applications accepted. *Expenses: Tuition, area resident:* Full-time $13,226; part-time $735 per credit. Tuition, state resident: full-time $13,226; part-time $735 per credit. Tuition, nonresident: full-time $25,854; part-time $1436 per credit. *International tuition:* $25,854 full-time. *Required fees:* $1698; $50 per credit. $35 per semester. One-time fee: $165. *Financial support:* In 2018–19, 8 research assistantships with tuition reimbursements (averaging $9,512 per year), 3 teaching assistantships with tuition reimbursements (averaging $13,338 per year) were awarded. Financial award application deadline: 2/1; financial award applicants required to submit FAFSA. *Unit head:* Dr. Stephen Grilli, Chairman, 401-874-6636, E-mail: grilli@uri.edu. *Application contact:* Christopher Baxter, Graduate Program Director, 401-874-6575, E-mail: cbaxter@uri.edu. Website: http://www.oce.uri.edu/

University of Southern California, Graduate School, Viterbi School of Engineering, Mork Family Department of Chemical Engineering and Materials Science, Los Angeles, CA 90089. Offers chemical engineering (MS, PhD, Engr); geoscience technologies (MS); materials engineering (MS); materials science (MS, PhD, Engr); petroleum engineering (MS, PhD, Engr); smart oilfield technologies (MS, Graduate Certificate). Terminal master's awarded for partial completion of doctoral program. *Degree requirements:* For master's, thesis optional; for doctorate, thesis/dissertation. *Entrance requirements:* For master's and doctorate, GRE General Test. Additional exam requirements/recommendations for international students: Recommended—TOEFL. Electronic applications accepted. *Expenses:* Contact institution. *Faculty research:* Heterogeneous materials and porous media, statistical mechanics, molecular simulation, polymer science and engineering, advanced materials, reaction engineering and catalysis, membrane processes and separation, biochemical engineering, cell culture, bioreactor modeling, petroleum engineering.

University of South Florida, College of Engineering, Department of Civil and Environmental Engineering, Tampa, FL 33620-9951. Offers civil engineering (MCE, MSCE, PhD), including geotechnical engineering, materials science and engineering, structures engineering, transportation engineering, water resources; environmental engineering (MEVE, MSEV, PhD), including engineering for international development (MSEV). *Program availability:* Part-time. *Faculty:* 19 full-time (5 women). *Students:* 144 full-time (46 women), 76 part-time (22 women); includes 35 minority (8 Black or African American, non-Hispanic/Latino; 5 Asian, non-Hispanic/Latino; 18 Hispanic/Latino; 4 Two or more races, non-Hispanic/Latino), 123 international. Average age 28. 220 applicants, 65% accepted, 59 enrolled. In 2018, 82 master's, 15 doctorates awarded. Terminal master's awarded for partial completion of doctoral program. *Degree requirements:* For master's, comprehensive exam, thesis (for some programs); for doctorate, comprehensive exam, thesis/dissertation. *Entrance requirements:* For master's, GRE required, bachelor's degree in appropriate field, minimum GPA of 3.0 in major, letters of reference, statement of purpose, resume, intake form; for doctorate, GRE with V (45th percentile), Q (75th percentile), and AW (55th percentile), letters of recommendation, statement of purpose, resume, intake form. Additional exam requirements/recommendations for international students: Required—TOEFL, TOEFL (minimum score 550 paper-based; 79 iBT) or IELTS (minimum score 6.5). *Application deadline:* For fall admission, 2/15 for domestic students, 2/15 priority date for international students; for spring admission, 10/15 for domestic students, 9/15 priority date for international students. Application fee: $30. Electronic applications accepted. *Expenses:* Tuition, state resident: full-time $6350. Tuition, nonresident: full-time $19,048. *International tuition:* $19,048 full-time. *Required fees:* $2079. *Financial support:* In 2018–19, 45 students received support, including 44 research assistantships (averaging $14,123 per year), 21 teaching assistantships with tuition reimbursements available (averaging $15,329 per year). *Faculty research:* Environmental and water resources engineering, geotechnics and geoenvironmental systems, structures and materials systems, transportation systems. *Total annual research expenditures:* $3.7 million. *Unit head:* Dr. Manjriker Gunaratne, Professor and Department Chair, 813-974-5818, Fax: 813-974-2957, E-mail: gunaratn@usf.edu. *Application contact:* Dr. Sarina J. Ergas, Professor and Graduate Program Coordinator, 813-974-1119, Fax: 813-974-2957, E-mail: sergas@usf.edu.
Website: http://www.usf.edu/engineering/cee/

The University of Texas at Austin, Graduate School, Cockrell School of Engineering, Department of Petroleum and Geosystems Engineering, Austin, TX 78712-1111. Offers energy and earth resources (MA); petroleum engineering (MS, PhD). *Program availability:* Evening/weekend, online learning. *Entrance requirements:* For master's and doctorate, GRE General Test. Electronic applications accepted.

University of Washington, Graduate School, College of Engineering, Department of Civil and Environmental Engineering, Seattle, WA 98195-2700. Offers construction engineering (MSCE, PhD); environmental engineering (MSCE, PhD); geotechnical engineering (MSCE, PhD); hydrology and hydrodynamics (MSCE, PhD); structural engineering and mechanics (MSCE, PhD); transportation engineering (MSCE, PhD). *Program availability:* Part-time, 100% online. *Faculty:* 38 full-time (10 women). *Students:* 239 full-time (104 women), 172 part-time (51 women); includes 91 minority (3 Black or African American, non-Hispanic/Latino; 2 American Indian or Alaska Native, non-Hispanic/Latino; 42 Asian, non-Hispanic/Latino; 26 Hispanic/Latino; 18 Two or more races, non-Hispanic/Latino), 120 international. Average age 28. 787 applicants, 57% accepted, 163 enrolled. In 2018, 161 master's, 11 doctorates awarded. Terminal master's awarded for partial completion of doctoral program. *Degree requirements:* For master's, thesis optional; for doctorate, comprehensive exam, thesis/dissertation, qualifying, general and final exams; completion of degree within 10 years. *Entrance requirements:* For master's, GRE General Test, minimum GPA of 3.0, statement of purpose, letters of recommendation, transcripts; for doctorate, GRE General Test, minimum GPA of 3.5, statement of purpose, letters of recommendation, transcripts, resume. Additional exam requirements/recommendations for international students: Required—TOEFL (minimum score 580 paper-based; 92 iBT); Recommended—IELTS (minimum score 7), TSE. *Application deadline:* For fall admission, 12/15 for domestic and international students. Applications are processed on a rolling basis. Application fee: $85. Electronic applications accepted. *Expenses:* Research-focused Master's and PhD: $18,852 resident; $32,760 nonresident. *Financial support:* In 2018–19, 120 students received support, including 23 fellowships with tuition reimbursements available (averaging $30,240 per year), 78 research assistantships with full tuition reimbursements available (averaging $30,240 per year), 28 teaching assistantships with full tuition reimbursements available (averaging $30,240 per year); scholarships/grants also available. Financial award application deadline: 12/15; financial award applicants required to submit FAFSA. *Faculty research:* Structural and geotechnical engineering, transportation and construction engineering, water and environmental engineering. *Total annual research expenditures:* $16.4 million. *Unit head:* Dr. Timothy V. Larson, Professor/Chair, 206-543-6815, Fax: 206-543-1543, E-mail: tlarson@uw.edu. *Application contact:* Melissa Pritchard, Graduate Adviser, 206-543-2574, Fax: 206-543-1543, E-mail: ceginfo@u.washington.edu.
Website: http://www.ce.washington.edu/

University of Wisconsin–Madison, Graduate School, College of Engineering, Department of Civil and Environmental Engineering, Madison, WI 53706-1380. Offers construction engineering and management (MS); environmental science and engineering (MS); geological/geotechnical engineering (MS); structural engineering (MS); transportation engineering (MS); water resources engineering (MS). *Program availability:* Part-time. *Faculty:* 31 full-time (8 women). *Students:* 97 full-time (28 women), 39 part-time (15 women); includes 12 minority (2 Black or African American, non-Hispanic/Latino; 3 Asian, non-Hispanic/Latino; 6 Hispanic/Latino; 1 Two or more races, non-Hispanic/Latino), 62 international. Average age 28. 261 applicants, 45% accepted, 29 enrolled. In 2018, 33 master's awarded. Terminal master's awarded for partial completion of doctoral program. *Degree requirements:* For master's, thesis (for some programs), minimum of 30 credits; minimum overall GPA of 3.0. *Entrance requirements:* For master's, GRE General Test, bachelor's degree; minimum GPA of 3.0 for last 60 credits of course work. Additional exam requirements/recommendations for international students: Required—TOEFL (minimum score 580 paper-based; 92 iBT). *Application deadline:* For fall admission, 12/15 priority date for domestic and international students; for spring admission, 10/1 for domestic and international students. Application fee: $75 ($81 for international students). Electronic applications accepted. *Expenses:* In-state tuition (Full-time): $10,728; Out-of-state tuition (full-time): $24,054; Fees: $1282; In-state tuition (per credit): $670; Out-of-state tuition (per credit): $1503; Fees (per credit): $126. *Financial support:* In 2018–19, 90 students received support, including 8 fellowships with full tuition reimbursements available (averaging $28,704 per year), 54 research assistantships with full tuition reimbursements available (averaging $23,784 per year), 21 teaching assistantships with full tuition reimbursements available (averaging $16,584 per year); Federal Work-Study, scholarships/grants, health care benefits, unspecified assistantships, and project assistantships also available. Support available to part-time students. Financial award application deadline: 12/1; financial award applicants required to submit FAFSA. *Faculty research:* Construction engineering and management; environmental engineering; structural engineering; transportation and city planning; water resources engineering; water chemistry. *Total annual research expenditures:* $12.5 million. *Unit head:* Dr. William Likos, Chair, 608-263-9490, Fax: 608-262-5199, E-mail: frontdesk@cee.wisc.edu. *Application contact:* Cheryl Loschko, Student Services Coordinator, 608-890-2420, E-mail: loschko@wisc.edu.
Website: https://www.engr.wisc.edu/department/civil-environmental-engineering/academics/ms-phd-civil-and-environmental-engineering/

Hazardous Materials Management

Humboldt State University, Academic Programs, College of Natural Resources and Sciences, Programs in Natural Resources, Arcata, CA 95521-8299. Offers natural resources (MS), including fisheries, forestry, natural resources planning and interpretation, rangeland resources and wildland soils, wastewater utilization, watershed management, wildlife. *Faculty:* 22 full-time (5 women), 20 part-time/adjunct (7 women).

Students: 43 full-time (22 women), 45 part-time (21 women); includes 24 minority (1 Black or African American, non-Hispanic/Latino; 2 American Indian or Alaska Native, non-Hispanic/Latino; 1 Asian, non-Hispanic/Latino; 16 Hispanic/Latino; 4 Two or more races, non-Hispanic/Latino), 1 international. Average age 28. 38 applicants, 37% accepted, 14 enrolled. In 2018, 21 master's awarded. *Degree requirements:* For

master's, thesis or alternative. *Entrance requirements:* For master's, GRE, appropriate bachelor's degree, minimum GPA of 2.5, 3 letters of recommendation, resume. Additional exam requirements/recommendations for international students: Required—TOEFL (minimum score 500 paper-based). *Application deadline:* For fall admission, 2/1 for domestic and international students; for spring admission, 9/30 for domestic and international students. Applications are processed on a rolling basis. Application fee: $55. *Expenses: Tuition:* Part-time $4649 per semester. *Required fees:* $2121; $1673. Tuition and fees vary according to program. *Financial support:* Fellowships, career-related internships or fieldwork, and Federal Work-Study available. Support available to part-time students. Financial award application deadline: 3/1; financial award applicants required to submit FAFSA. *Faculty research:* Spotted owl habitat, pre-settlement vegetation, hardwood utilization, tree physiology, fisheries. *Unit head:* Dr. Andrew Stubblefield, Graduate Program Coordinator, 707-826-3258, E-mail: andrew.stubblefield@humboldt.edu. *Application contact:* Dr. Andrew Stubblefield, Graduate Program Coordinator, 707-826-3258, E-mail: andrew.stubblefield@humboldt.edu.
Website: http://www.humboldt.edu/cnrs/graduate_programs

Indiana University Bloomington, School of Public and Environmental Affairs, Environmental Science Programs, Bloomington, IN 47405. Offers applied ecology (MSES); energy (MSES); environmental chemistry, toxicology, and risk assessment (MSES); environmental science (PhD); hazardous materials management (Certificate); specialized environmental science (MSES); water resources (MSES); JD/MSES; MSES/MA; MSES/MPA; MSES/MS. *Program availability:* Part-time. Terminal master's awarded for partial completion of doctoral program. *Degree requirements:* For master's, capstone or thesis; internship; for doctorate, comprehensive exam, thesis/dissertation. *Entrance requirements:* For master's, GRE General Test or GMAT, official transcripts, 3 letters of recommendation, resume, personal statement; for doctorate, GRE General Test or LSAT, official transcripts, 3 letters of recommendation, resume or curriculum vitae, statement of purpose. Additional exam requirements/recommendations for international students: Required—TOEFL (minimum score 600 paper-based; 96 iBT); Recommended—IELTS (minimum score 7). Electronic applications accepted. *Faculty research:* Applied ecology, bio-geochemistry, toxicology, wetlands ecology, environmental microbiology, forest ecology, environmental chemistry.

Jackson State University, Graduate School, College of Science, Engineering and Technology, Department of Civil and Environmental Engineering and Industrial Systems and Technology, Jackson, MS 39217. Offers civil engineering (MS, PhD); coastal engineering (MS, PhD); environmental engineering (MS, PhD); hazardous materials management (MS); technology education (MS Ed). *Program availability:* Part-time, evening/weekend. *Degree requirements:* For master's, comprehensive exam, thesis or alternative. *Entrance requirements:* For master's, GRE General Test. Additional exam requirements/recommendations for international students: Required—TOEFL (minimum score 520 paper-based; 67 iBT).

Marquette University, Graduate School, College of Engineering, Department of Civil and Environmental Engineering, Milwaukee, WI 53201-1881. Offers construction engineering and management (MS, PhD, Certificate); environmental engineering (MS, PhD); structural design (Certificate); structural engineering and structural mechanics (MS, PhD); transportation (Certificate); transportation engineering and materials (MS, PhD); waste and wastewater treatment processes (Certificate); water resources engineering (Certificate). *Program availability:* Part-time, evening/weekend. Terminal master's awarded for partial completion of doctoral program. *Degree requirements:* For master's, comprehensive exam (for some programs), thesis or alternative; for doctorate, thesis/dissertation. *Entrance requirements:* For master's, GRE General Test (recommended), minimum GPA of 3.0, official transcripts from all current and previous colleges/universities except Marquette, three letters of recommendation; for doctorate, GRE General Test, minimum GPA of 3.0, official transcripts from all current and previous colleges/universities except Marquette, three letters of recommendation, brief statement of purpose, submission of any English language publications authored by applicant (strongly recommended). Additional exam requirements/recommendations for international students: Required—TOEFL (minimum score 530 paper-based). Electronic applications accepted. *Faculty research:* Highway safety, highway performance, and intelligent transportation systems; surface mount technology; watershed management.

New Mexico Institute of Mining and Technology, Center for Graduate Studies, Department of Civil and Environmental Engineering, Socorro, NM 87801. Offers environmental engineering (MS), including air quality engineering and science, hazardous waste engineering, water quality engineering and science. *Degree requirements:* For master's, thesis, thesis or independent study. *Entrance requirements:* Additional exam requirements/recommendations for international students: Required—TOEFL (minimum score 540 paper-based). *Faculty research:* Air quality, hazardous waste management, wastewater management and treatment, site remediation.

Rutgers University–New Brunswick, Graduate School-New Brunswick, Department of Environmental Sciences, Piscataway, NJ 08854-8097. Offers air pollution and resources (MS, PhD); aquatic biology (MS, PhD); aquatic chemistry (MS, PhD); atmospheric science (MS, PhD); chemistry and physics of aerosol and hydrosol systems (MS, PhD); environmental chemistry (MS, PhD); environmental microbiology (MS, PhD); environmental toxicology (PhD); exposure assessment (PhD); fate and effects of pollutants (MS, PhD); pollution prevention and control (MS, PhD); water and wastewater treatment (MS, PhD); water resources (MS, PhD). Terminal master's awarded for partial completion of doctoral program. *Degree requirements:* For master's, comprehensive exam, thesis or alternative, oral final exam; for doctorate, comprehensive exam, thesis/dissertation, thesis defense, qualifying exam. *Entrance requirements:* For master's and doctorate, GRE General Test. Additional exam requirements/recommendations for international students: Required—TOEFL. Electronic applications accepted. *Faculty research:* Biological waste treatment; contaminant fate and transport; air, soil and water quality.

University of Colorado Denver, College of Liberal Arts and Sciences, Department of Geography and Environmental Sciences, Denver, CO 80217. Offers environmental sciences (MS), including air quality, ecosystems, environmental health, geospatial analysis, hazardous waste, water quality. *Program availability:* Part-time, evening/weekend. *Degree requirements:* For master's, thesis or alternative, 30 credits including 21 of core requirements and 9 of environmental science electives. *Entrance requirements:* For master's, GRE General Test, BA in one of the natural/physical sciences or engineering (or equivalent background); prerequisite coursework in calculus and physics (one semester each); general chemistry with lab and general biology with lab (two semesters each); three letters of recommendation. Additional exam requirements/recommendations for international students: Required—TOEFL (minimum score 537 paper-based; 75 iBT); Recommended—IELTS (minimum score 6.5). Electronic applications accepted. *Expenses:* Tuition, state resident: full-time $6786; part-time $337 per credit hour. Tuition, nonresident: full-time $22,590; part-time $1255 per credit hour. *Required fees:* $1231; $137 per credit hour. Tuition and fees vary according to program and reciprocity agreements. *Faculty research:* Air quality, environmental health, ecosystems, hazardous waste, water quality, geospatial analysis and environmental science education.

The University of Manchester, School of Materials, Manchester, United Kingdom. Offers advanced aerospace materials engineering (M Sc); advanced metallic systems (PhD); biomedical materials (M Phil, M Sc, PhD); ceramics and glass (M Phil, M Sc, PhD); composite materials (M Sc, PhD); corrosion and protection (M Phil, M Sc, PhD); materials (M Phil, PhD); metallic materials (M Phil, M Sc, PhD); nanostructural materials (M Phil, M Sc, PhD); paper science (M Phil, M Sc, PhD); polymer science and engineering (M Phil, M Sc, PhD); technical textiles (M Sc); textile design, fashion and management (M Phil, M Sc, PhD); textile science and technology (M Phil, M Sc, PhD); textiles (M Phil, PhD); textiles and fashion (M Ent).

University of New Haven, Graduate School, Tagliatela College of Engineering, Program in Environmental Engineering, West Haven, CT 06516. Offers environmental engineering (MS); industrial and hazardous waste (MS); water and wastewater treatment (MS); water resources (MS). *Program availability:* Part-time, evening/weekend, 100% online. *Students:* 15 full-time (7 women), 32 part-time (13 women); includes 7 minority (2 Black or African American, non-Hispanic/Latino; 2 Asian, non-Hispanic/Latino; 3 Hispanic/Latino), 17 international. Average age 30. 67 applicants, 97% accepted, 11 enrolled. In 2018, 15 master's awarded. *Degree requirements:* For master's, thesis or alternative, research project. *Entrance requirements:* For master's, bachelor's degree in engineering. Additional exam requirements/recommendations for international students: Required—TOEFL (minimum score 75 iBT), IELTS, PTE (minimum score 50). *Application deadline:* Applications are processed on a rolling basis. Application fee: $50. Electronic applications accepted. Application fee is waived when completed online. *Expenses: Tuition:* Full-time $16,470; part-time $915 per credit hour. *Required fees:* $230; $95 per term. *Financial support:* Research assistantships with partial tuition reimbursements, teaching assistantships with partial tuition reimbursements, career-related internships or fieldwork, Federal Work-Study, scholarships/grants, and unspecified assistantships available. Support available to part-time students. Financial award application deadline: 5/1; financial award applicants required to submit FAFSA. *Unit head:* Dr. Agamemnon Koutsospyros, Professor, 203-932-7398, E-mail: akoutsospyros@newhaven.edu. *Application contact:* Selina O'Toole, Senior Associate Director of Graduate Admissions, 203-932-7337, E-mail: sotoole@newhaven.edu.
Website: https://www.newhaven.edu/engineering/graduate-programs/environmental-engineering/

University of South Carolina, The Graduate School, Arnold School of Public Health, Department of Environmental Health Sciences, Program in Hazardous Materials Management, Columbia, SC 29208. Offers MPH, MSPH, PhD. *Degree requirements:* For master's, comprehensive exam, thesis (for some programs), practicum (MPH); for doctorate, one foreign language, comprehensive exam, thesis/dissertation. *Entrance requirements:* Additional exam requirements/recommendations for international students: Required—TOEFL (minimum score 570 paper-based). Electronic applications accepted. *Faculty research:* Environmental/human health protection; use and disposal of hazardous materials; site safety; exposure assessment; migration, fate and transformation of materials.

University of Southern California, Graduate School, Viterbi School of Engineering, Sonny Astani Department of Civil and Environmental Engineering, Los Angeles, CA 90089. Offers applied mechanics (MS); civil engineering (MS, PhD); computer-aided engineering (ME, Graduate Certificate); construction management (MCM); engineering technology commercialization (Graduate Certificate); environmental engineering (MS, PhD); environmental quality management (ME); structural design (ME); sustainable cities (Graduate Certificate); transportation systems (MS, Graduate Certificate); water and waste management (MS). *Program availability:* Part-time, evening/weekend. Terminal master's awarded for partial completion of doctoral program. *Degree requirements:* For master's, thesis optional; for doctorate, thesis/dissertation. *Entrance requirements:* For master's and doctorate, GRE General Test. Additional exam requirements/recommendations for international students: Recommended—TOEFL. Electronic applications accepted. *Faculty research:* Geotechnical engineering, transportation engineering, structural engineering, construction management, environmental engineering, water resources.

Hydraulics

Drexel University, College of Engineering, Department of Civil, Architectural, and Environmental Engineering, Philadelphia, PA 19104-2875. Offers architectural/building systems engineering (MS, PhD); civil engineering (MS, PhD); environmental engineering (MS, PhD); geotechnical, geoenvironmental and geosynthetics engineering (MS, PhD); hydraulics, hydrology and water resources engineering (MS, PhD); structures (MS). *Program availability:* Part-time, evening/weekend. *Degree requirements:* For master's, thesis optional; for doctorate, thesis/dissertation. *Entrance requirements:* For master's, minimum GPA of 3.0; for doctorate, minimum GPA of 3.5, MS in civil engineering. Additional exam requirements/recommendations for international students: Required—TOEFL. Electronic applications accepted. *Faculty research:* Structural dynamics, hazardous wastes, water resources, pavement materials, groundwater.

École Polytechnique de Montréal, Graduate Programs, Department of Civil, Geological and Mining Engineering, Montréal, QC H3C 3A7, Canada. Offers civil, geological and mining engineering (DESS); environmental engineering (M Eng, M Sc A, PhD); geotechnical engineering (M Eng, M Sc A, PhD); hydraulics engineering (M Eng, M Sc A, PhD); structural engineering (M Eng, M Sc A, PhD); transportation engineering (M Eng, M Sc A, PhD). *Program availability:* Part-time. *Degree requirements:* For master's, one foreign language, thesis; for doctorate, one foreign language, thesis/dissertation. *Entrance requirements:* For master's, minimum GPA of 2.75; for doctorate, minimum GPA of 3.0. *Faculty research:* Water resources management, characteristics of building materials, aging of dams, pollution control.

McGill University, Faculty of Graduate and Postdoctoral Studies, Faculty of Engineering, Department of Civil Engineering and Applied Mechanics, Montréal, QC H3A 2T5, Canada. Offers environmental engineering (M Eng, M Sc, PhD); fluid mechanics (M Sc); fluid mechanics and hydraulic engineering (M Eng, PhD); materials engineering (M Eng, PhD); rehabilitation of urban infrastructure (M Eng, PhD); soil behavior (M Eng, PhD); soil mechanics and foundations (M Eng, PhD); structures and structural mechanics (M Eng, PhD); water resources (M Sc); water resources engineering (M Eng, PhD).

Old Dominion University, Frank Batten College of Engineering and Technology, Program in Civil Engineering, Norfolk, VA 23529. Offers civil engineering (ME, MS), including coastal engineering, geotechnical engineering, hydraulics and water resources, structural engineering, transportation engineering. *Program availability:* Part-time, evening/weekend, blended/hybrid learning. *Degree requirements:* For master's, comprehensive exam, thesis optional. *Entrance requirements:* For master's, GRE, minimum GPA of 3.0. Additional exam requirements/recommendations for international students: Required—TOEFL (minimum score 550 paper-based, 80 iBT) or IELTS (6.5). Electronic applications accepted. *Expenses:* Contact institution. *Faculty research:* Structural engineering, coastal engineering, geotechnical engineering, water resources, transportation engineering.

Stevens Institute of Technology, Graduate School, Charles V. Schaefer Jr. School of Engineering and Science, Department of Civil, Environmental, and Ocean Engineering, Program in Environmental Engineering, Hoboken, NJ 07030. Offers environmental engineering (PhD, Certificate), including environmental compatibility in engineering (Certificate), environmental hydrology (Certificate), environmental processes (Certificate), hydraulics (Certificate), soil and groundwater pollution control (Certificate), water quality control (Certificate); environmental processes (M Eng); inland and coastal environmental hydrodynamics (M Eng); modeling of environmental systems (M Eng); soil and groundwater pollution control (M Eng). *Program availability:* Part-time, evening/weekend. *Faculty:* 28 full-time (7 women), 1 part-time/adjunct (0 women). *Students:* 58 full-time (24 women), 12 part-time (5 women); includes 6 minority (2 Black or African American, non-Hispanic/Latino; 1 American Indian or Alaska Native, non-Hispanic/Latino; 2 Asian, non-Hispanic/Latino; 1 Hispanic/Latino), 48 international. Average age 25. In 2018, 14 master's, 1 doctorate, 6 other advanced degrees awarded. Terminal master's awarded for partial completion of doctoral program. *Degree requirements:* For master's, thesis optional, minimum B average in major field and overall; for doctorate, comprehensive exam (for some programs), thesis/dissertation; for Certificate, minimum B average. *Entrance requirements:* For master's, GRE/GMAT scores: GRE scores are required for all applicants applying to a full-time graduate program in the Schaefer School of Engineering and Science (SES). International applicants must submit TOEFL/IELTS scores and fulfill the English Language Proficiency Requirements in order to be considered. Additional exam requirements/recommendations for international students: Required—TOEFL (minimum score 74 iBT), IELTS (minimum score 6). *Application deadline:* For fall admission, 4/15 for domestic and international students; for spring admission, 11/1 for domestic and international students; for summer admission, 5/1 for domestic students. Applications are processed on a rolling basis. Application fee: $60. Electronic applications accepted. *Expenses: Tuition:* Full-time $35,960; part-time $1620 per credit. *Required fees:* $1290; $600 per semester. Tuition and fees vary according to course load. *Financial support:* Fellowships, research assistantships, teaching assistantships, career-related internships or fieldwork, Federal Work-Study, scholarships/grants, and unspecified assistantships available. Financial award application deadline: 2/15; financial award applicants required to submit FAFSA. *Unit head:* Dr. Jean Zu, Dean of SES, 201-216.8233, Fax: 201-216.8372, E-mail: Jean.Zu@stevens.edu. *Application contact:* Graduate Admission, 888-783-8367, Fax: 888-511-1306, E-mail: graduate@stevens.edu.

University of Colorado Denver, College of Engineering, Design and Computing, Department of Civil Engineering, Denver, CO 80217. Offers civil engineering (EASPh D); civil engineering systems (PhD); environmental and sustainability engineering (MS, PhD); geographic information systems (MS); geotechnical engineering (MS, PhD); hydrology and hydraulics (MS, PhD); structural engineering (MS, PhD); transportation engineering (MS, PhD). *Program availability:* Part-time, evening/weekend. *Degree requirements:* For master's, comprehensive exam, 30 credit hours, project or thesis; for doctorate, comprehensive exam, thesis/dissertation, 60 credit hours (30 of which are dissertation research). *Entrance requirements:* For master's, GRE, statement of purpose, transcripts, three references; for doctorate, GRE, statement of purpose, transcripts, references, letter of support from faculty stating willingness to serve as dissertation advisor and outlining plan for financial support. Additional exam requirements/recommendations for international students: Required—TOEFL (minimum score 537 paper-based; 75 iBT); Recommended—IELTS (minimum score 6.5). Electronic applications accepted. *Expenses:* Tuition, state resident: full-time $6786; part-time $337 per credit hour. Tuition, nonresident: full-time $22,590; part-time $1255 per credit hour. *Required fees:* $1231; $137 per credit hour. Tuition and fees vary according to program and reciprocity agreements.

The University of Iowa, Graduate College, College of Engineering, Department of Civil and Environmental Engineering, Iowa City, IA 52242-1316. Offers environmental engineering and science (MS, PhD); hydraulics and water resources (MS, PhD); structures, mechanics and materials (MS, PhD); sustainable water development (MS, PhD); transportation engineering (MS, PhD). *Program availability:* Part-time. Terminal master's awarded for partial completion of doctoral program. *Degree requirements:* For master's, thesis optional, exam; for doctorate, comprehensive exam, thesis/dissertation, exam. *Entrance requirements:* For master's, GRE (minimum combined score of 301 on verbal and quantitative), minimum undergraduate GPA of 3.0; for doctorate, GRE (minimum combined score of 301 on verbal and quantitative), minimum graduate GPA of 3.0. Additional exam requirements/recommendations for international students: Required—TOEFL (minimum score 550 paper-based; 81 iBT), IELTS (minimum score 7). Electronic applications accepted. *Faculty research:* Water resources; environmental engineering and science; hydraulics and hydrology; structures, mechanics, and materials; transportation engineering.

Structural Engineering

California State University, Northridge, Graduate Studies, College of Engineering and Computer Science, Department of Civil Engineering and Construction Management, Northridge, CA 91330. Offers engineering (MS), including structural engineering. *Program availability:* Part-time, evening/weekend. *Degree requirements:* For master's, thesis. *Entrance requirements:* Additional exam requirements/recommendations for international students: Required—TOEFL. *Faculty research:* Composite study.

The Citadel, The Military College of South Carolina, Citadel Graduate College, School of Engineering, Department of Civil and Environmental Engineering, Charleston, SC 29409. Offers built environment and public health (Graduate Certificate); civil engineering (MS); geotechnical engineering (Graduate Certificate); structural engineering (Graduate Certificate); transportation engineering (Graduate Certificate). *Program availability:* Part-time, evening/weekend. *Degree requirements:* For master's, plan of study outlining intended areas of interest and top four corresponding courses of interest. *Entrance requirements:* For master's, official transcript of baccalaureate degree from ABET-accredited engineering program or approved alternative; 2 letters of recommendation; for Graduate Certificate, official transcript of baccalaureate degree directly from an accredited college or university. Additional exam requirements/recommendations for international students: Required—TOEFL (minimum score 550 paper-based; 79 iBT). Electronic applications accepted. *Expenses:* Tuition, state resident: part-time $595 per credit hour. Tuition, nonresident: part-time $1020 per credit hour. *Required fees:* $90 per term.

Clemson University, Graduate School, College of Engineering, Computing and Applied Sciences, Glenn Department of Civil Engineering, Clemson, SC 29634. Offers civil engineering (MS, PhD), including construction engineering and management, construction materials, geotechnical engineering, structural engineering, transportation engineering, water resources engineering. *Program availability:* Part-time. *Faculty:* 20 full-time (3 women). *Students:* 109 full-time (23 women), 55 part-time (11 women); includes 9 minority (2 Black or African American, non-Hispanic/Latino; 2 Asian, non-Hispanic/Latino; 4 Hispanic/Latino; 1 Two or more races, non-Hispanic/Latino), 111 international. Average age 28. 283 applicants, 59% accepted, 53 enrolled. In 2018, 31 master's, 11 doctorates awarded. *Degree requirements:* For master's, thesis or alternative, oral exam, seminar; for doctorate, comprehensive exam, thesis/dissertation, oral exam, seminar. *Entrance requirements:* For master's and doctorate, GRE General Test, unofficial transcripts, letters of recommendation, statement of purpose. Additional exam requirements/recommendations for international students: Required—TOEFL (minimum score 80 paper-based; 80 iBT), PTE (minimum score 54); Recommended—IELTS (minimum score 6.5). *Application deadline:* For fall admission, 4/15 for domestic and international students; for spring admission, 9/15 for domestic and international students. Applications are processed on a rolling basis. Application fee: $80 ($90 for international students). Electronic applications accepted. *Expenses:* $6823 per semester full-time resident, $14023 per semester full-time non-resident, $833 per credit hour part-time resident, $1731 per credit hour part-time non-resident, online $1264 per credit hour, $4938 doctoral programs resident, $10405 doctoral programs non-resident, $1144 full-time graduate assistant, other fees may apply per session. *Financial support:* In 2018–19, 104 students received support, including 20 fellowships with full and partial tuition reimbursements available (averaging $4,491 per year), 43 research assistantships with full and partial tuition reimbursements available (averaging $16,364 per year), 1 teaching assistantship with full and partial tuition reimbursement available (averaging $12,750 per year); career-related internships or fieldwork and unspecified assistantships also available. Financial award application deadline: 4/15. *Faculty research:* Applied fluid mechanics, construction materials, project management, structural and geotechnical engineering, transportation. *Total annual research expenditures:* $4.9 million. *Unit head:* Dr. Ronald Andrus, Interim Department Chair, 864-656-0488, E-mail: randrus@clemson.edu. *Application contact:* Dr. Abdul Khan, Graduate Program Coordinator, 864-656-3327, E-mail: abdkhan@clemson.edu. Website: https://www.clemson.edu/cecas/departments/ce/

Cornell University, Graduate School, Graduate Fields of Engineering, Field of Civil and Environmental Engineering, Ithaca, NY 14853. Offers engineering management (M Eng, MS, PhD); environmental engineering (M Eng, MS, PhD); environmental fluid mechanics and hydrology (M Eng, MS, PhD); environmental systems engineering (M Eng, MS, PhD); geotechnical engineering (M Eng, MS, PhD); remote sensing (M Eng, MS, PhD); structural engineering (M Eng, MS, PhD); structural mechanics (M Eng, MS); transportation engineering (MS, PhD); transportation systems engineering (M Eng); water resource systems (M Eng, MS, PhD). Terminal master's awarded for partial completion of doctoral program. *Degree requirements:* For master's, thesis (MS); for doctorate, comprehensive exam, thesis/dissertation. *Entrance requirements:* For master's and doctorate, GRE General Test (recommended), 2 letters of recommendation. Additional exam requirements/recommendations for international students: Required—TOEFL (minimum score 600 paper-based; 77 iBT). Electronic applications accepted. *Faculty research:* Environmental engineering, geotechnical engineering, remote sensing, environmental fluid mechanics and hydrology, structural engineering.

Drexel University, College of Engineering, Department of Civil, Architectural, and Environmental Engineering, Philadelphia, PA 19104-2875. Offers architectural/building systems engineering (MS, PhD); civil engineering (MS, PhD); environmental engineering (MS, PhD); geotechnical, geoenvironmental and geosynthetics engineering (MS, PhD); hydraulics, hydrology and water resources engineering (MS, PhD); structures (MS). *Program availability:* Part-time, evening/weekend. *Degree requirements:* For master's, thesis optional; for doctorate, thesis/dissertation. *Entrance requirements:* For master's, minimum GPA of 3.0; for doctorate, minimum GPA of 3.5, MS in civil engineering. Additional exam requirements/recommendations for international students: Required—TOEFL. Electronic applications accepted. *Faculty research:* Structural dynamics, hazardous wastes, water resources, pavement materials, groundwater.

École Polytechnique de Montréal, Graduate Programs, Department of Civil, Geological and Mining Engineering, Montréal, QC H3C 3A7, Canada. Offers civil, geological and mining engineering (DESS); environmental engineering (M Eng, M Sc A, PhD); geotechnical engineering (M Eng, M Sc A, PhD); hydraulics engineering (M Eng, M Sc A, PhD); structural engineering (M Eng, M Sc A, PhD); transportation engineering (M Eng, M Sc A, PhD). *Program availability:* Part-time. *Degree requirements:* For master's, one foreign language, thesis; for doctorate, one foreign language, thesis/dissertation. *Entrance requirements:* For master's, minimum GPA of 2.75; for doctorate, minimum GPA of 3.0. *Faculty research:* Water resources management, characteristics of building materials, aging of dams, pollution control.

Illinois Institute of Technology, Graduate College, Armour College of Engineering, Department of Civil, Architectural and Environmental Engineering, Chicago, IL 60616. Offers architectural engineering (M Arch E); civil engineering (MS, PhD), including architectural engineering (MS), construction engineering and management (MS), geoenvironmental engineering (MS), geotechnical engineering (MS), structural engineering (MS), transportation engineering (MS); construction engineering and management (MCEM); environmental engineering (M Env E, MS, PhD); geoenvironmental engineering (M Geoenv E); geotechnical engineering (MGE); infrastructure engineering and management (MPW); structural engineering (MSE); transportation engineering (M Trans E). *Program availability:* Part-time, evening/weekend, online learning. Terminal master's awarded for partial completion of doctoral program. *Degree requirements:* For master's, thesis (for some programs); for doctorate, comprehensive exam, thesis/dissertation. *Entrance requirements:* For master's, GRE General Test (minimum score 900 Quantitative and Verbal, 2.5 Analytical Writing), minimum undergraduate GPA of 3.0; for doctorate, GRE General Test (minimum score 1000 Quantitative and Verbal, 3.0 Analytical Writing), minimum undergraduate GPA of 3.0. Additional exam requirements/recommendations for international students:

Required—TOEFL (minimum score 550 paper-based; 80 iBT). Electronic applications accepted. *Faculty research:* Structural, architectural, geotechnical and geoenvironmental engineering; construction engineering and management; transportation engineering; environmental engineering and public works.

Instituto Tecnologico de Santo Domingo, Graduate School, Area of Engineering, Santo Domingo, Dominican Republic. Offers construction administration (MS, Certificate); data telecommunications (M Eng, MS, Certificate); industrial engineering (M Eng, Certificate); industrial management (M Mgmt); information technology (Certificate); maintenance engineering (M Eng); occupational hazard prevention (M Mgmt); production management (Certificate); quantitative methods (Certificate); sanitary and environmental engineering (M Eng); structural engineering (M Eng); systems engineering and electronic data processing (Certificate); transportation (Certificate).

Iowa State University of Science and Technology, Department of Civil and Construction Engineering, Ames, IA 50011. Offers civil engineering (MS, PhD), including civil engineering materials, construction engineering and management, environmental engineering, geotechnical engineering, structural engineering, transportation engineering. *Degree requirements:* For master's, thesis or alternative; for doctorate, thesis/dissertation. *Entrance requirements:* For master's and doctorate, GRE General Test. Additional exam requirements/recommendations for international students: Required—TOEFL (minimum score 550 paper-based; 82 iBT), IELTS (minimum score 6.5). Electronic applications accepted.

Kansas State University, Graduate School, College of Engineering, Department of Civil Engineering, Manhattan, KS 66506. Offers civil engineering (MS, PhD); environmental engineering (MS, PhD); geotechnical engineering (MS, PhD); structural engineering (MS, PhD); transportation engineering (MS, PhD); water resources engineering (MS, PhD). *Program availability:* Part-time, evening/weekend, online learning. *Degree requirements:* For master's, thesis or alternative; for doctorate, thesis/dissertation. *Entrance requirements:* For master's, GRE General Test, bachelor's degree or course work in related engineering fields; for doctorate, GRE General Test. Additional exam requirements/recommendations for international students: Required—TOEFL (minimum score 550 paper-based; 79 iBT). Electronic applications accepted. *Faculty research:* Transportation and materials engineering, water resources engineering, environmental engineering, geotechnical engineering, structural engineering.

Kennesaw State University, Southern Polytechnic College of Engineering and Engineering Technology, Program in Civil Engineering, Kennesaw, GA 30144. Offers environmental engineering (MS); geotechnical engineering (MS); structural engineering (MS); transportation and pavement engineering (MS); water resources engineering (MS). *Program availability:* Online learning. *Students:* 13 full-time (2 women), 24 part-time (5 women); includes 20 minority (8 Black or African American, non-Hispanic/Latino; 5 Asian, non-Hispanic/Latino; 4 Hispanic/Latino; 3 Two or more races, non-Hispanic/Latino), 2 international. Average age 33. 21 applicants, 57% accepted, 1 enrolled. In 2018, 6 master's awarded. *Degree requirements:* For master's, thesis optional. *Entrance requirements:* Additional exam requirements/recommendations for international students: Required—TOEFL (minimum score 550 paper-based; 80 iBT), IELTS (minimum score 6.5). *Application deadline:* For fall admission, 11/1 for domestic and international students; for spring admission, 4/1 for domestic and international students. Applications are processed on a rolling basis. Application fee: $60. Electronic applications accepted. *Expenses: Tuition, area resident:* Full-time $6960; part-time $290 per credit hour. Tuition, state resident: full-time $6960; part-time $290 per credit hour. Tuition, nonresident: full-time $25,080; part-time $1045 per credit hour. *International tuition:* $25,080 full-time. *Required fees:* $2006; $1706 per semester. $853 per semester. *Unit head:* Metin Oguzmert, Coordinator, 470-578-5083, E-mail: moguzmer@kennesaw.edu. *Application contact:* Admissions Counselor, 470-578-4377, E-mail: ksugrad@kennesaw.edu.

Website: http://engineering.kennesaw.edu/civil-construction/degrees/ms-civil-engineering.php

Louisiana State University and Agricultural & Mechanical College, Graduate School, College of Engineering, Department of Civil and Environmental Engineering, Baton Rouge, LA 70803. Offers environmental engineering (MSCE, PhD); geotechnical engineering (MSCE, PhD); structural engineering and mechanics (MSCE, PhD); transportation engineering (MSCE, PhD); water resources (MSCE, PhD).

Marquette University, Graduate School, College of Engineering, Department of Civil and Environmental Engineering, Milwaukee, WI 53201-1881. Offers construction engineering and management (MS, PhD, Certificate); environmental engineering (MS, PhD); structural design (Certificate); structural engineering and structural mechanics (MS, PhD); transportation (Certificate); transportation engineering and materials (MS, PhD); waste and wastewater treatment processes (Certificate); water resources engineering (Certificate). *Program availability:* Part-time, evening/weekend. Terminal master's awarded for partial completion of doctoral program. *Degree requirements:* For master's, comprehensive exam (for some programs), thesis or alternative; for doctorate, thesis/dissertation. *Entrance requirements:* For master's, GRE General Test (recommended), minimum GPA of 3.0, official transcripts from all current and previous colleges/universities except Marquette, three letters of recommendation; for doctorate, GRE General Test, minimum GPA of 3.0, official transcripts from all current and previous colleges/universities except Marquette, three letters of recommendation, brief statement of purpose, submission of any English language publications authored by applicant (strongly recommended). Additional exam requirements/recommendations for international students: Required—TOEFL (minimum score 530 paper-based). Electronic applications accepted. *Faculty research:* Highway safety, highway performance, and intelligent transportation systems; surface mount technology; watershed management.

Massachusetts Institute of Technology, School of Engineering, Department of Civil and Environmental Engineering, Cambridge, MA 02139. Offers biological oceanography (PhD, Sc D); chemical oceanography (PhD, Sc D); civil and environmental engineering (M Eng, SM, PhD, Sc D); civil and environmental systems (PhD, Sc D); civil engineering (PhD, Sc D, CE); civil engineering and computation (PhD); coastal engineering (PhD, Sc D); construction engineering and management (PhD, Sc D); environmental biology (PhD, Sc D); environmental chemistry (PhD, Sc D); environmental engineering (PhD, Sc D); environmental engineering and computation (PhD); environmental fluid mechanics (PhD, Sc D); geotechnical and geoenvironmental engineering (PhD, Sc D); hydrology (PhD, Sc D); information technology (PhD, Sc D); oceanographic engineering (PhD, Sc D); structures and materials (PhD, Sc D); transportation (PhD, Sc D); SM/MBA. *Degree requirements:* For master's, thesis; for doctorate, comprehensive exam, thesis/dissertation; for CE, comprehensive exam, thesis. *Entrance requirements:* For master's, doctorate, and CE, GRE General Test. Additional exam requirements/recommendations for international students: Required—TOEFL, IELTS. Electronic applications accepted. *Expenses: Tuition:* Full-time $51,520; part-time $800 per credit hour. *Required fees:* $312. *Faculty research:* Environmental chemistry, environmental fluid mechanics and coastal engineering, environmental microbiology, geotechnical engineering and geomechanics, hydrology and hydro climatology, infrastructure systems, mechanics of materials and structures, transportation systems.

McGill University, Faculty of Graduate and Postdoctoral Studies, Faculty of Engineering, Department of Civil Engineering and Applied Mechanics, Montréal, QC H3A 2T5, Canada. Offers environmental engineering (M Eng, M Sc, PhD); fluid mechanics (M Sc); fluid mechanics and hydraulic engineering (M Eng, PhD); materials engineering (M Eng, PhD); rehabilitation of urban infrastructure (M Eng, PhD); soil behavior (M Eng, PhD); soil mechanics and foundations (M Eng, PhD); structures and structural mechanics (M Eng, PhD); water resources (M Sc); water resources engineering (M Eng, PhD).

Northwestern University, McCormick School of Engineering and Applied Science, Department of Civil and Environmental Engineering, Evanston, IL 60208-3109. Offers environmental engineering and science (MS, PhD); geotechnical engineering (MS, PhD); mechanics of materials and solids (MS, PhD); project management (MS); structural engineering and materials (MS, PhD); transportation systems analysis and planning (MS, PhD). MS and PhD admissions and degrees offered through The Graduate School. *Program availability:* Part-time. Terminal master's awarded for partial completion of doctoral program. *Degree requirements:* For master's, comprehensive exam (for some programs), thesis (for some programs); for doctorate, comprehensive exam, thesis/dissertation. *Entrance requirements:* For master's and doctorate, GRE General Test, minimum 2 letters of recommendation, transcripts from all academic institutions attended. Additional exam requirements/recommendations for international students: Required—TOEFL (minimum score 577 paper-based; 90 iBT), IELTS (minimum score 7). Electronic applications accepted. *Faculty research:* Environmental engineering and science, geotechnics, mechanics, materials, structures, and transportation systems analysis and planning.

Norwich University, College of Graduate and Continuing Studies, Master of Civil Engineering Program, Northfield, VT 05663. Offers construction management (MCE); environmental (MCE); geotechnical (MCE); structural (MCE). *Program availability:* Evening/weekend, online only, mostly all online with a week-long residency requirement. *Degree requirements:* For master's, capstone. *Entrance requirements:* For master's, minimum undergraduate GPA of 2.75. Additional exam requirements/recommendations for international students: Required—TOEFL (minimum score 550 paper-based; 80 iBT), IELTS (minimum score 6.5). Electronic applications accepted. *Expenses:* Contact institution.

Ohio University, Graduate College, Russ College of Engineering and Technology, Department of Civil Engineering, Athens, OH 45701-2979. Offers civil engineering (PhD); construction engineering and management (MS); environmental (MS); geoenvironmental (MS); geotechnical (MS); mechanics (MS); structures (MS); transportation (MS); water resources (MS). *Program availability:* Part-time. *Degree requirements:* For master's, comprehensive exam (for some programs), thesis or alternative; for doctorate, comprehensive exam, thesis/dissertation. *Entrance requirements:* For master's, GRE General Test, minimum GPA of 3.0, 3 letters of recommendation; for doctorate, GRE General Test. Additional exam requirements/recommendations for international students: Required—TOEFL (minimum score 550 paper-based; 80 iBT) or IELTS (minimum score 6.5). Electronic applications accepted. *Faculty research:* Noise abatement, materials and environment, highway infrastructure, subsurface investigation (pavements, pipes, bridges).

Old Dominion University, Frank Batten College of Engineering and Technology, Program in Civil Engineering, Norfolk, VA 23529. Offers civil engineering (ME, MS), including coastal engineering, geotechnical engineering, hydraulics and water resources, structural engineering, transportation engineering. *Program availability:* Part-time, evening/weekend, blended/hybrid learning. *Degree requirements:* For master's, comprehensive exam, thesis optional. *Entrance requirements:* For master's, GRE, minimum GPA of 3.0. Additional exam requirements/recommendations for international students: Required—TOEFL (minimum score 550 paper-based, 80 iBT) or IELTS (6.5). Electronic applications accepted. *Expenses:* Contact institution. *Faculty research:* Structural engineering, coastal engineering, geotechnical engineering, water resources, transportation engineering.

Oregon State University, College of Engineering, Program in Civil Engineering, Corvallis, OR 97331. Offers civil engineering (M Eng, MS, PhD); coastal and ocean engineering (M Eng, MS, PhD); construction engineering management (M Eng, MS, PhD); engineering education (M Eng, MS, PhD); geomatics (M Eng, MS, PhD); geotechnical engineering (M Eng, MS, PhD); infrastructure materials (M Eng, MS, PhD); structural engineering (M Eng, MS, PhD); transportation engineering (M Eng). *Entrance requirements:* For master's and doctorate, GRE. Additional exam requirements/recommendations for international students: Required—TOEFL (minimum score 80 iBT), IELTS (minimum score 6.5). *Expenses:* Contact institution.

Penn State Harrisburg, Graduate School, School of Science, Engineering and Technology, Middletown, PA 17057. Offers civil engineering (MS); computer science (MS); electrical engineering (M Eng, MS); engineering management (MPS); engineering science (M Eng); environmental engineering (M Eng); environmental pollution control (MEPC, MS); mechanical engineering (MS); structural engineering (Certificate). *Program availability:* Part-time, evening/weekend.

Pontificia Universidad Catolica Madre y Maestra, Graduate School, Faculty of Engineering Sciences, Santiago, Dominican Republic. Offers earthquake engineering (ME); logistics management (ME).

Southern Illinois University Edwardsville, Graduate School, School of Engineering, Department of Civil Engineering, Program in Structural Engineering, Edwardsville, IL 62026. Offers MS. *Program availability:* Part-time, evening/weekend. *Degree requirements:* For master's, thesis (for some programs), research paper. *Entrance requirements:* For master's, minimum undergraduate GPA of 2.75 in science, math, and engineering courses. Additional exam requirements/recommendations for international students: Required—TOEFL (minimum score 550 paper-based, 79 iBT), IELTS (minimum score 6.5), Michigan Test of English Language Proficiency or PTE. Electronic applications accepted.

Southern Methodist University, Lyle School of Engineering, Department of Civil and Environmental Engineering, Dallas, TX 75275-0340. Offers civil and environmental engineering (PhD); civil engineering (MS), including geotechnical engineering, structural engineering, transportation systems; environmental engineering (MS); sustainability and development (MA). *Program availability:* Part-time, evening/weekend, online learning. Terminal master's awarded for partial completion of doctoral program. *Degree requirements:* For master's, thesis optional; for doctorate, thesis/dissertation, oral and written qualifying exams. *Entrance requirements:* For master's, GRE General Test, minimum GPA of 3.0 in last 2 years; bachelor's degree in engineering, mathematics, or sciences; for doctorate, GRE, BS and MS in related field, minimum GPA of 3.3. Additional exam requirements/recommendations for international students: Required—TOEFL. Electronic applications accepted. *Faculty research:* Human and environmental health effects of endocrine disrupters, development of air pollution control systems for diesel engines, structural analysis and design, modeling and design of waste treatment systems.

Stanford University, School of Engineering, Department of Civil and Environmental Engineering, Stanford, CA 94305-2004. Offers atmosphere and energy (MS, PhD); construction (MS), including construction engineering and management, design-construction integration, sustainable design and construction; environmental engineering and science (MS, PhD, Eng); environmental fluid mechanics and hydrology (PhD); geomechanics (MS); structural engineering (MS). *Expenses: Tuition:* Full-time $50,703; part-time $32,970 per year. *Required fees:* $651. Website: http://www-ce.stanford.edu/

Stevens Institute of Technology, Graduate School, Charles V. Schaefer Jr. School of Engineering and Science, Department of Civil, Environmental, and Ocean Engineering, Program in Civil Engineering, Hoboken, NJ 07030. Offers civil engineering (PhD, Certificate), including geotechnical engineering (Certificate); geotechnical/geoenvironmental engineering (M Eng, Engr); hydrologic modeling (M Eng); stormwater management (M Eng); structural engineering (M Eng, Engr); transportation engineering (M Eng); water resources engineering (M Eng). *Program availability:* Part-time, evening/weekend. *Faculty:* 28 full-time (7 women), 2 part-time/adjunct (1 woman). *Students:* 37 full-time (8 women), 27 part-time (8 women); includes 8 minority (1 Black or African American, non-Hispanic/Latino; 1 American Indian or Alaska Native, non-Hispanic/Latino; 6 Asian, non-Hispanic/Latino), 30 international. Average age 25. In 2018, 44 master's awarded. Terminal master's awarded for partial completion of doctoral program. *Degree requirements:* For master's, thesis optional, minimum B average in major field and overall; for doctorate, comprehensive exam (for some programs), thesis/dissertation; for other advanced degree, minimum B average. *Entrance requirements:* For master's, GRE/GMAT scores: GRE scores are required for all applicants applying to a full-time graduate program in the Schaefer School of Engineering and Science (SES). International applicants must submit TOEFL/IELTS scores and fulfill the English Language Proficiency Requirements in order to be considered. Additional exam requirements/recommendations for international students: Required—TOEFL (minimum score 74 iBT), IELTS (minimum score 6). *Application deadline:* For fall admission, 4/15 for domestic and international students; for spring admission, 11/1 for domestic and international students; for summer admission, 5/1 for domestic students. Applications are processed on a rolling basis. Application fee: $60. Electronic applications accepted. *Expenses: Tuition:* Full-time $35,960; part-time $1620 per credit. *Required fees:* $1290; $600 per semester. Tuition and fees vary according to course load. *Financial support:* Fellowships, research assistantships, teaching assistantships, career-related internships or fieldwork, Federal Work-Study, scholarships/grants, and unspecified assistantships available. Financial award application deadline: 2/15; financial award applicants required to submit FAFSA. *Unit head:* Dr. Jean Zu, Dean of SES, 201-216.8233, Fax: 201-216.8372, E-mail: Jean.Zu@stevens.edu. *Application contact:* Graduate Admission, 888-783-8367, Fax: 888-511-1306, E-mail: graduate@stevens.edu.

Tufts University, School of Engineering, Department of Civil and Environmental Engineering, Medford, MA 02155. Offers bioengineering (MS), including environmental biotechnology; civil and environmental engineering (MS, PhD), including applied data science, environmental and water resources engineering, environmental health, geosystems engineering, structural engineering and mechanics; PhD/PhD. *Program availability:* Part-time. Terminal master's awarded for partial completion of doctoral program. *Degree requirements:* For master's, thesis (for some programs); for doctorate, thesis/dissertation. *Entrance requirements:* For master's and doctorate, GRE General Test. Additional exam requirements/recommendations for international students: Required—TOEFL (minimum score 550 paper-based; 80 iBT), IELTS (minimum score 6.5). Electronic applications accepted. *Expenses: Tuition:* Full-time $51,288; part-time $1710 per credit hour. *Required fees:* $904. Full-time tuition and fees vary according to degree level, program and student level. Part-time tuition and fees vary according to course load. *Faculty research:* Environmental and water resources engineering, environmental health, geotechnical and geoenvironmental engineering, structural engineering and mechanics, water diplomacy.

University at Buffalo, the State University of New York, Graduate School, School of Engineering and Applied Sciences, Department of Civil, Structural, and Environmental Engineering, Buffalo, NY 14260. Offers civil engineering (MS, PhD); engineering science (MS), including data sciences, green energy, Internet of Things, nanoelectronics; environmental and water resources engineering (MS). *Program availability:* Part-time, online learning. Terminal master's awarded for partial completion of doctoral program. *Degree requirements:* For master's, project, thesis, or comprehensive exam; for doctorate, thesis/dissertation. *Entrance requirements:* For master's and doctorate, GRE General Test, letters of reference. Additional exam requirements/recommendations for international students: Required—TOEFL (minimum score 550 paper-based; 79 iBT). Electronic applications accepted. *Faculty research:* Structural and earthquake engineering; geomechanics, geotechnical and geoenvironmental engineering; computational engineering mechanics; bridge engineering; environmental and water resources engineering; transportation systems engineering.

The University of Alabama at Birmingham, School of Engineering, Professional Engineering Degrees, Birmingham, AL 35294. Offers advanced safety engineering and management (M Eng); construction engineering management (M Eng); design and commercialization (M Eng); information engineering management (M Eng); structural engineering (M Eng); sustainable smart cities (M Eng). *Program availability:* Part-time, evening/weekend, online only, 100% online, blended/hybrid learning. *Faculty:* 6 full-time (1 woman), 12 part-time/adjunct (2 women). *Students:* 23 full-time (7 women), 315 part-time (63 women); includes 96 minority (73 Black or African American, non-Hispanic/Latino; 1 American Indian or Alaska Native, non-Hispanic/Latino; 8 Asian, non-Hispanic/Latino; 12 Hispanic/Latino; 2 Two or more races, non-Hispanic/Latino), 12 international. Average age 37. 154 applicants, 84% accepted, 91 enrolled. In 2018, 87 master's awarded. *Entrance requirements:* For master's, 3.0 GPA on 4.0 scale, undergraduate degree from a nationally accredited school. Additional exam requirements/recommendations for international students: Required—TOEFL (minimum score 80 iBT); Recommended—IELTS (minimum score 6.5). *Application deadline:* For fall admission, 8/1 for domestic and international students; for spring admission, 12/1 for domestic and international students; for summer admission, 5/1 for domestic and international students. Applications are processed on a rolling basis. Application fee: $50 ($60 for international students). Electronic applications accepted. *Expenses:* Contact institution. *Faculty research:* Orthopedic biomechanics, translational rehabilitation and assistive devices, innovation and entrepreneurship, anthropogenic activities and the natural environment, prestressed and spun concrete. *Application contact:* Jesse Kepply, Director of Student and Academic Services, 205-996-5696, E-mail: gradschool@uab.edu.

University of Alberta, Faculty of Graduate Studies and Research, Department of Civil and Environmental Engineering, Edmonton, AB T6G 2E1, Canada. Offers construction engineering and management (M Eng, M Sc, PhD); environmental engineering (M Eng, M Sc, PhD); environmental science (M Sc, PhD); geoenvironmental engineering (M Eng, M Sc, PhD); geotechnical engineering (M Eng, M Sc, PhD); mining engineering (M Eng, M Sc, PhD); petroleum engineering (M Eng, M Sc, PhD); structural engineering (M Eng, M Sc, PhD); water resources (M Eng, M Sc, PhD). *Program availability:* Part-time, online learning. *Degree requirements:* For master's, thesis (for some programs); for doctorate, thesis/dissertation. *Entrance requirements:* For master's, minimum GPA of 3.0 in last 2 years of undergraduate studies; for doctorate, minimum GPA of 3.0.

Additional exam requirements/recommendations for international students: Required—TOEFL (minimum score 550 paper-based). Electronic applications accepted. *Faculty research:* Mining.

University of Calgary, Faculty of Graduate Studies, Schulich School of Engineering, Program in Civil Engineering, Calgary, AB T2N 1N4, Canada. Offers avalanche mechanics (M Sc, PhD); civil engineering (M Eng, M Sc, PhD); energy and environment engineering (M Eng, M Sc, PhD); environmental engineering (M Eng, M Sc, PhD); geotechnical engineering (M Eng, M Sc, PhD); materials science (M Eng, M Sc, PhD); project management (M Eng, M Sc, PhD); structures and solid mechanics (M Eng, M Sc, PhD); transportation engineering (M Eng, M Sc, PhD); water resources (M Eng, M Sc, PhD). *Program availability:* Part-time. *Degree requirements:* For master's, thesis; for doctorate, thesis/dissertation, written and oral candidacy exam. *Entrance requirements:* For master's, minimum GPA of 3.0; for doctorate, minimum GPA of 3.5. Additional exam requirements/recommendations for international students: Required—TOEFL (minimum score 580 paper-based; 93 iBT), IELTS (minimum score 7). Electronic applications accepted. *Faculty research:* Geotechnical engineering, energy and environment, transportation, project management, structures and solid mechanics.

University of California, Berkeley, Graduate Division, College of Engineering, Department of Civil and Environmental Engineering, Berkeley, CA 94720. Offers engineering and project management (M Eng, MS, PhD); environmental engineering (M Eng, MS, PhD); geoengineering (M Eng, MS, PhD); structural engineering, mechanics and materials (M Eng, MS, PhD); transportation engineering (M Eng, MS, PhD); M Arch/MS; MCP/MS; MPP/MS. Terminal master's awarded for partial completion of doctoral program. *Degree requirements:* For master's, comprehensive exam (for some programs), thesis (for some programs), comprehensive exam or thesis (MS); for doctorate, thesis/dissertation, qualifying exam. *Entrance requirements:* For master's, GRE General Test, minimum GPA of 3.0, 3 letters of recommendation; for doctorate, GRE General Test, minimum GPA of 3.5, 3 letters of recommendation. Additional exam requirements/recommendations for international students: Required—TOEFL (minimum score 570 paper-based; 90 iBT). Electronic applications accepted.

University of California, San Diego, Graduate Division, Department of Structural Engineering, La Jolla, CA 92093. Offers structural engineering (MS, PhD); structural health monitoring, prognosis, and validated simulations (MS). PhD in engineering sciences offered jointly with San Diego State University. *Students:* 169 full-time (46 women), 19 part-time (6 women). 391 applicants, 51% accepted, 74 enrolled. In 2018, 84 master's, 5 doctorates awarded. *Degree requirements:* For master's, comprehensive exam (for some programs), thesis (for some programs); for doctorate, comprehensive exam, thesis/dissertation, 1-quarter teaching assistantship. *Entrance requirements:* For master's and doctorate, GRE General Test. Additional exam requirements/recommendations for international students: Required—TOEFL (minimum score 550 paper-based; 80 iBT), IELTS (minimum score 7). *Application deadline:* For fall admission, 1/9 for domestic students. Application fee: $105 ($125 for international students). Electronic applications accepted. *Financial support:* Fellowships, research assistantships, teaching assistantships, scholarships/grants, and readerships available. Financial award applicants required to submit FAFSA. *Faculty research:* Earthquake engineering, advanced composites and aerospace structural systems, geotechnical, marine/offshore engineering; renewal engineering, structural health monitoring, prognosis and validated simulations, structural materials; computational mechanics; solid mechanics. *Unit head:* John McCartney, Chair, 858-534-9630, E-mail: mccartney@eng.ucsd.edu. *Application contact:* Yvonne C. Wollman, Graduate Coordinator, 858-822-1421, E-mail: se-info@ucsd.edu.
Website: http://www.structures.ucsd.edu/

University of Central Florida, College of Engineering and Computer Science, Department of Civil, Environmental, and Construction Engineering, Orlando, FL 32816. Offers civil engineering (PhD, Certificate), including civil engineering (PhD), structural engineering (Certificate), transportation engineering (Certificate); environmental engineering (MS, PhD). *Program availability:* Part-time, evening/weekend. *Students:* 115 full-time (30 women), 75 part-time (23 women); includes 48 minority (6 Black or African American, non-Hispanic/Latino; 8 Asian, non-Hispanic/Latino; 34 Hispanic/Latino), 89 international. Average age 30. 160 applicants, 69% accepted, 54 enrolled. In 2018, 39 master's, 20 doctorates, 1 other advanced degree awarded. *Degree requirements:* For master's, thesis or alternative; for doctorate, comprehensive exam, thesis/dissertation, departmental qualifying exam, candidacy exam. *Entrance requirements:* For master's, letters of recommendation, resume, goal statement; for doctorate, GRE General Test, letters of recommendation, resume, goal statement. Additional exam requirements/recommendations for international students: Required—TOEFL. *Application deadline:* For fall admission, 7/15 priority date for domestic students; for spring admission, 12/1 priority date for domestic students. Application fee: $30. Electronic applications accepted. *Financial support:* In 2018–19, 82 students received support, including 37 fellowships with partial tuition reimbursements available (averaging $13,562 per year), 59 research assistantships with partial tuition reimbursements available (averaging $11,914 per year), 19 teaching assistantships with partial tuition reimbursements available (averaging $9,747 per year); career-related internships or fieldwork, Federal Work-Study, institutionally sponsored loans, health care benefits, tuition waivers (partial), and unspecified assistantships also available. Financial award application deadline: 3/1; financial award applicants required to submit FAFSA. *Unit head:* Dr. Mohamed Abdel-Aty, Chair, 407-823-2841, E-mail: m.aty@ucf.edu. *Application contact:* Associate Director, Graduate Admissions, 407-823-2766, Fax: 407-823-6442, E-mail: gradadmissions@ucf.edu.
Website: http://cece.ucf.edu/

University of Colorado Denver, College of Engineering, Design and Computing, Department of Civil Engineering, Denver, CO 80217. Offers civil engineering (EASPh D); civil engineering systems (PhD); environmental and sustainability engineering (MS, PhD); geographic information systems (MS); geotechnical engineering (MS, PhD); hydrology and hydraulics (MS, PhD); structural engineering (MS, PhD); transportation engineering (MS, PhD). *Program availability:* Part-time, evening/weekend. *Degree requirements:* For master's, comprehensive exam, 30 credit hours, project or thesis; for doctorate, comprehensive exam, thesis/dissertation, 60 credit hours (30 of which are dissertation research). *Entrance requirements:* For master's, GRE, statement of purpose, transcripts, three references; for doctorate, GRE, statement of purpose, transcripts, references, letter of support from faculty stating willingness to serve as dissertation advisor and outlining plan for financial support. Additional exam requirements/recommendations for international students: Required—TOEFL (minimum score 537 paper-based; 75 iBT); Recommended—IELTS (minimum score 6.5). Electronic applications accepted. *Expenses:* Tuition, state resident: full-time $6786; part-time $337 per credit hour. Tuition, nonresident: full-time $22,590; part-time $1255 per credit hour. *Required fees:* $1231; $137 per credit hour. Tuition and fees vary according to program and reciprocity agreements.

University of Dayton, Department of Civil and Environmental Engineering and Engineering Mechanics, Dayton, OH 45469. Offers engineering mechanics (MSEM); environmental engineering (MSCE); geotechnical engineering (MSCE); structural engineering (MSCE); transportation engineering (MSCE); water resources engineering (MSCE). *Program availability:* Part-time, blended/hybrid learning. *Degree requirements:*

For master's, thesis or alternative. *Entrance requirements:* For master's, minimum GPA of 3.0 in undergraduate work. Additional exam requirements/recommendations for international students: Required—TOEFL (minimum score 550 paper-based; 80 iBT); Recommended—IELTS (minimum score 6.5), TSE (minimum score 60). Electronic applications accepted. *Faculty research:* Infrastructure, environmental composite, reliability, computer simulation.

University of Delaware, College of Engineering, Department of Civil and Environmental Engineering, Newark, DE 19716. Offers environmental engineering (MAS, MCE, PhD); geotechnical engineering (MAS, MCE, PhD); ocean engineering (MAS, MCE, PhD); structural engineering (MAS, MCE, PhD); transportation engineering (MAS, MCE, PhD); water resource engineering (MAS, MCE, PhD). *Program availability:* Part-time. Terminal master's awarded for partial completion of doctoral program. *Degree requirements:* For master's, thesis; for doctorate, thesis/dissertation. *Entrance requirements:* For master's and doctorate, GRE General Test. Additional exam requirements/recommendations for international students: Required—TOEFL. Electronic applications accepted. *Faculty research:* Structural engineering and mechanics; transportation engineering; ocean engineering; soil mechanics and foundation; water resources and environmental engineering.

The University of Manchester, School of Materials, Manchester, United Kingdom. Offers advanced aerospace materials engineering (M Sc); advanced metallic systems (PhD); biomedical materials (M Phil, M Sc, PhD); ceramics and glass (M Phil, M Sc, PhD); composite materials (M Sc, PhD); corrosion and protection (M Phil, M Sc, PhD); materials (M Phil, PhD); metallic materials (M Phil, M Sc, PhD); nanostructural materials (M Phil, M Sc, PhD); paper science (M Phil, M Sc, PhD); polymer science and engineering (M Phil, M Sc, PhD); technical textiles (M Sc); textile design, fashion and management (M Phil, M Sc, PhD); textile science and technology (M Phil, M Sc, PhD); textiles (M Phil, PhD); textiles and fashion (M Ent).

University of Massachusetts Amherst, Graduate School, College of Engineering, Department of Civil and Environmental Engineering, Amherst, MA 01003. Offers civil engineering (MSCE, PhD); environmental and water resources engineering (MSCE); geotechnical engineering (MSCE); structural engineering and mechanics (MSCE); transportation engineering (MSCE). *Program availability:* Part-time. Terminal master's awarded for partial completion of doctoral program. *Degree requirements:* For master's, thesis or alternative; for doctorate, comprehensive exam, thesis/dissertation. *Entrance requirements:* For master's and doctorate, GRE General Test. Additional exam requirements/recommendations for international students: Required—TOEFL (minimum score 550 paper-based; 80 iBT), IELTS (minimum score 6.5). Electronic applications accepted.

University of Memphis, Graduate School, Herff College of Engineering, Department of Civil Engineering, Memphis, TN 38152. Offers civil engineering (PhD); engineering seismology (MS); environmental engineering (MS); freight transportation (Graduate Certificate); geotechnical engineering (MS); structural engineering (MS); transportation engineering (MS); water resources engineering (MS). *Students:* 14 full-time (3 women), 8 part-time (3 women); includes 1 minority (Black or African American, non-Hispanic/Latino), 12 international. Average age 27. 27 applicants, 70% accepted, 13 enrolled. In 2018, 11 master's awarded. Terminal master's awarded for partial completion of doctoral program. *Degree requirements:* For master's, comprehensive exam, thesis optional; for doctorate, comprehensive exam, thesis/dissertation. *Entrance requirements:* For master's, GRE General Test, minimum undergraduate GPA of 2.5; bachelor's degree in engineering or a related science or mathematics program; three letters of reference; for doctorate, GRE General Test, bachelor's degree in engineering or engineering science; three letters of reference; for Graduate Certificate, minimum undergraduate GPA of 2.75; bachelor's degree in engineering or engineering science. Additional exam requirements/recommendations for international students: Required—TOEFL (minimum score 550 paper-based; 79 iBT). *Application deadline:* For fall admission, 8/1 for domestic students; for spring admission, 12/1 for domestic students. Application fee: $35 ($60 for international students). Electronic applications accepted. *Expenses: Tuition, area resident:* Full-time $10,240; part-time $503 per credit hour. Tuition, state resident: full-time $10,464. Tuition, nonresident: full-time $20,224; part-time $991 per credit hour. *Required fees:* $850; $106 per credit hour. *Financial support:* Fellowships with full tuition reimbursements, research assistantships with full tuition reimbursements, career-related internships or fieldwork, Federal Work-Study, scholarships/grants, and unspecified assistantships available. Financial award application deadline: 2/1; financial award applicants required to submit FAFSA. *Faculty research:* Structural response to earthquakes, pavement design, water quality, transportation safety, intermodal transportation. *Unit head:* Dr. Shahram Pezeshk, Chair, 901-678-4727, Fax: 901-678-3026, E-mail: spezeshk@memphis.edu. *Application contact:* Dr. Roger Meier, Coordinator of Graduate Studies, 901-678-3284, E-mail: rwmeier@memphis.edu.
Website: https://www.memphis.edu/ce

University of Michigan, College of Engineering, Department of Civil and Environmental Engineering, Ann Arbor, MI 48109. Offers civil engineering (MSE, PhD, CE); construction engineering and management (M Eng, MSE); environmental engineering (MSE, PhD); structural engineering (M Eng); MBA/MSE. *Program availability:* Part-time. *Students:* 206 full-time (86 women), 6 part-time (3 women). 690 applicants, 41% accepted, 76 enrolled. In 2018, 65 master's, 18 doctorates awarded. Terminal master's awarded for partial completion of doctoral program. *Degree requirements:* For master's, thesis optional; for doctorate, comprehensive exam, thesis/dissertation, oral defense of dissertation, preliminary and written exams. *Entrance requirements:* For master's and doctorate, GRE General Test. Additional exam requirements/recommendations for international students: Required—TOEFL. *Application deadline:* Applications are processed on a rolling basis. Electronic applications accepted. *Financial support:* Fellowships, research assistantships, teaching assistantships, institutionally sponsored loans, and tuition waivers (partial) available. *Faculty research:* Construction engineering and management, geotechnical engineering, earthquake-resistant design of structures, environmental chemistry and microbiology, cost engineering, environmental and water resources engineering. *Total annual research expenditures:* $11.6 million. *Unit head:* Jerome Lynch, Department Chair, 734-615-5290, Fax: 734-764-4292, E-mail: jerlynch@umich.edu. *Application contact:* Kelley Archer, Graduate Coordinator, 734-647-2703, Fax: 734-764-4292, E-mail: krichko@umich.edu.
Website: https://cee.engin.umich.edu/

University of New Brunswick Fredericton, School of Graduate Studies, Faculty of Engineering, Department of Civil Engineering, Fredericton, NB E3B 5A3, Canada. Offers construction engineering and management (M Eng, M Sc E, PhD); environmental engineering (M Eng, M Sc E, PhD); environmental studies (M Eng); geotechnical engineering (M Eng, M Sc E, PhD); groundwater/hydrology (M Eng, M Sc E, PhD); materials (M Eng, M Sc E, PhD); pavements (M Eng, M Sc E, PhD); structures (M Eng, M Sc E, PhD); transportation (M Eng, M Sc E, PhD). *Program availability:* Part-time. *Degree requirements:* For master's, thesis; for doctorate, comprehensive exam, thesis/dissertation, qualifying exam; 27 credit hours of courses. *Entrance requirements:* For master's, minimum GPA of 3.0; B Sc E in civil engineering or related engineering degree; for doctorate, minimum GPA of 3.0; graduate degree in engineering or applied science. Additional exam requirements/recommendations for international students: Required—IELTS (minimum score 7.5), TWE (minimum score 4), Michigan English Language Assessment Battery (minimum score 85) or CanTest (minimum score 4.5); Recommended—TOEFL (minimum score 580 paper-based). Electronic applications accepted. *Faculty research:* Construction engineering and management; engineering materials and infrastructure renewal; highway and pavement research; structures and solid mechanics; geotechnical and geoenvironmental engineering; structure interaction; transportation and planning; environment, solid waste management; structural engineering; water and environmental engineering.

University of Puerto Rico–Mayagüez, Graduate Studies, College of Engineering, Department of Civil Engineering and Surveying, Mayagüez, PR 00681-9000. Offers civil engineering (ME, MS, PhD), including construction engineering and management (ME, MS), environmental engineering, geotechnical engineering (ME, MS), structural engineering, transportation engineering. *Program availability:* Part-time. Terminal master's awarded for partial completion of doctoral program. *Degree requirements:* For master's, one foreign language, thesis; for doctorate, one foreign language, comprehensive exam, thesis/dissertation, qualifying exams. *Entrance requirements:* For master's, proficiency in English and Spanish; BS in civil engineering or its equivalent; for doctorate, proficiency in English and Spanish. Electronic applications accepted. *Faculty research:* Structural design, concrete structure, finite elements, dynamic analysis, transportation, soils.

University of South Florida, College of Engineering, Department of Civil and Environmental Engineering, Tampa, FL 33620-9951. Offers civil engineering (MCE, MSCE, PhD), including geotechnical engineering, materials science and engineering, structures engineering, transportation engineering, water resources; environmental engineering (MEVE, MSEV, PhD), including engineering for international development (MSEV). *Program availability:* Part-time. *Faculty:* 19 full-time (5 women). *Students:* 144 full-time (46 women), 76 part-time (22 women); includes 35 minority (8 Black or African American, non-Hispanic/Latino; 5 Asian, non-Hispanic/Latino; 18 Hispanic/Latino; 4 Two or more races, non-Hispanic/Latino), 123 international. Average age 28. 220 applicants, 65% accepted, 59 enrolled. In 2018, 82 master's, 15 doctorates awarded. Terminal master's awarded for partial completion of doctoral program. *Degree requirements:* For master's, comprehensive exam, thesis (for some programs); for doctorate, comprehensive exam, thesis/dissertation. *Entrance requirements:* For master's, GRE required, bachelor's degree in appropriate field, minimum GPA of 3.0 in major, letters of reference, statement of purpose, resume, intake form; for doctorate, GRE with V (45th percentile), Q (75th percentile), and AW (55th percentile), letters of recommendation, statement of purpose, resume, intake form. Additional exam requirements/recommendations for international students: Required—TOEFL, TOEFL (minimum score 550 paper-based; 79 iBT) or IELTS (minimum score 6.5). *Application deadline:* For fall admission, 2/15 for domestic students, 2/15 priority date for international students; for spring admission, 10/15 for domestic students, 9/15 priority date for international students. Application fee: $30. Electronic applications accepted. *Expenses:* Tuition, state resident: full-time $6350. Tuition, nonresident: full-time $19,048. *International tuition:* $19,048 full-time. *Required fees:* $2079. *Financial support:* In 2018–19, 45 students received support, including 44 research assistantships (averaging $14,123 per year), 21 teaching assistantships with tuition reimbursements available (averaging $15,329 per year). *Faculty research:* Environmental and water resources engineering, geotechnics and geoenvironmental systems, structures and materials systems, transportation systems. *Total annual research expenditures:* $3.7 million. *Unit head:* Dr. Manjriker Gunaratne, Professor and Department Chair, 813-974-5818, Fax: 813-974-2957, E-mail: gunaratn@usf.edu. *Application contact:* Dr. Sarina J. Ergas, Professor and Graduate Program Coordinator, 813-974-1119, Fax: 813-974-2957, E-mail: sergas@usf.edu.
Website: http://www.usf.edu/engineering/cee/

The University of Texas at Tyler, College of Engineering, Department of Civil Engineering, Tyler, TX 75799-0001. Offers environmental engineering (MS); industrial safety (MS); structural engineering (MS); transportation engineering (MS); water resources engineering (MS). *Program availability:* Part-time, evening/weekend. *Students:* 5 full-time (1 woman), 7 part-time (1 woman); includes 3 minority (1 Black or African American, non-Hispanic/Latino; 1 Asian, non-Hispanic/Latino; 1 Hispanic/Latino), 1 international. Average age 26. 5 applicants, 80% accepted, 3 enrolled. *Entrance requirements:* For master's, GRE General Test, bachelor's degree in engineering, associated science degree. Additional exam requirements/recommendations for international students: Required—TOEFL. *Application deadline:* For fall admission, 8/17 priority date for domestic students, 7/1 priority date for international students; for spring admission, 12/21 priority date for domestic students, 11/1 priority date for international students. Application fee: $25 ($50 for international students). *Financial support:* Application deadline: 7/1. *Faculty research:* Non-destructive strength testing, indoor air quality, transportation routing and signaling, pavement replacement criteria, flood water routing, construction and long-term behavior of innovative geotechnical foundation and embankment construction used in highway construction, engineering education. *Unit head:* Dr. Torey Nalbone, Chair, 903-565-5520, E-mail: tnalbone@uttyler.edu. *Application contact:* Dr. Torey Nalbone, Chair, 903-565-5520, E-mail: tnalbone@uttyler.edu.
Website: https://www.uttyler.edu/ce/

University of Washington, Graduate School, College of Engineering, Department of Civil and Environmental Engineering, Seattle, WA 98195-2700. Offers construction engineering (MSCE, PhD); environmental engineering (MSCE, PhD); geotechnical engineering (MSCE, PhD); hydrology and hydrodynamics (MSCE, PhD); structural engineering and mechanics (MSCE, PhD); transportation engineering (MSCE, PhD). *Program availability:* Part-time, 100% online. *Faculty:* 38 full-time (10 women). *Students:* 239 full-time (104 women), 172 part-time (51 women); includes 91 minority (3 Black or African American, non-Hispanic/Latino; 2 American Indian or Alaska Native, non-Hispanic/Latino; 42 Asian, non-Hispanic/Latino; 26 Hispanic/Latino; 18 Two or more races, non-Hispanic/Latino), 120 international. Average age 28. 787 applicants, 57% accepted, 163 enrolled. In 2018, 161 master's, 11 doctorates awarded. Terminal master's awarded for partial completion of doctoral program. *Degree requirements:* For master's, thesis optional; for doctorate, comprehensive exam, thesis/dissertation, qualifying, general and final exams; completion of degree within 10 years. *Entrance requirements:* For master's, GRE General Test, minimum GPA of 3.0, statement of purpose, letters of recommendation, transcripts; for doctorate, GRE General Test, minimum GPA of 3.5, statement of purpose, letters of recommendation, transcripts, resume. Additional exam requirements/recommendations for international students: Required—TOEFL (minimum score 580 paper-based; 92 iBT); Recommended—IELTS (minimum score 7), TSE. *Application deadline:* For fall admission, 12/15 for domestic and international students. Applications are processed on a rolling basis. Application fee: $85. Electronic applications accepted. *Expenses:* Research-focused Master's and PhD: $18,852 resident; $32,760 nonresident. *Financial support:* In 2018–19, 120 students received support, including 23 fellowships with tuition reimbursements available (averaging $30,240 per year), 78 research assistantships with full tuition reimbursements available (averaging $30,240 per year), 28 teaching assistantships with full tuition reimbursements available (averaging $30,240 per year); scholarships/grants also available. Financial award application deadline: 12/15; financial award applicants required to submit FAFSA. *Faculty research:* Structural and geotechnical engineering,

transportation and construction engineering, water and environmental engineering. *Total annual research expenditures:* $16.4 million. *Unit head:* Dr. Timothy V. Larson, Professor/Chair, 206-543-6815, Fax: 206-543-1543, E-mail: tlarson@uw.edu. *Application contact:* Melissa Pritchard, Graduate Adviser, 206-543-2574, Fax: 206-543-1543, E-mail: ceginfo@u.washington.edu.
Website: http://www.ce.washington.edu/

University of Wisconsin–Madison, Graduate School, College of Engineering, Department of Civil and Environmental Engineering, Madison, WI 53706-1380. Offers construction engineering and management (MS); environmental science and engineering (MS); geological/geotechnical engineering (MS); structural engineering (MS); transportation engineering (MS); water resources engineering (MS). *Program availability:* Part-time. *Faculty:* 31 full-time (8 women). *Students:* 97 full-time (28 women), 39 part-time (15 women); includes 12 minority (2 Black or African American, non-Hispanic/Latino; 3 Asian, non-Hispanic/Latino; 6 Hispanic/Latino; 1 Two or more races, non-Hispanic/Latino), 62 international. Average age 28. 261 applicants, 45% accepted, 29 enrolled. In 2018, 33 master's awarded. Terminal master's awarded for partial completion of doctoral program. *Degree requirements:* For master's, thesis (for some programs), minimum of 30 credits; minimum overall GPA of 3.0. *Entrance requirements:* For master's, GRE General Test, bachelor's degree; minimum GPA of 3.0 for last 60 credits of course work. Additional exam requirements/recommendations for international students: Required—TOEFL (minimum score 580 paper-based; 92 iBT). *Application deadline:* For fall admission, 12/15 priority date for domestic and international students; for spring admission, 10/1 for domestic and international students. Application fee: $75 ($81 for international students). Electronic applications accepted. *Expenses:* In-state tuition (Full-time): $10,728; Out-of-state tuition (full-time): $24,054; Fees: $1282; In-state tuition (per credit): $670; Out-of-state tuition (per credit): $1503; Fees (per credit): $126. *Financial support:* In 2018–19, 90 students received support, including 8 fellowships with full tuition reimbursements available (averaging $28,704 per year), 54 research assistantships with full tuition reimbursements available (averaging $23,784 per year), 21 teaching assistantships with full tuition reimbursements available (averaging $16,584 per year); Federal Work-Study, scholarships/grants, health care benefits, unspecified assistantships, and project assistantships also available. Support available to part-time students. Financial award application deadline: 12/1; financial award applicants required to submit FAFSA. *Faculty research:* Construction engineering and management; environmental engineering; structural engineering; transportation and city planning; water resources engineering; water chemistry. *Total annual research expenditures:* $12.5 million. *Unit head:* Dr. William Likos, Chair, 608-263-9490, Fax: 608-262-5199, E-mail: frontdesk@cee.wisc.edu. *Application contact:* Cheryl Loschko, Student Services Coordinator, 608-890-2420, E-mail: loschko@wisc.edu.
Website: https://www.engr.wisc.edu/department/civil-environmental-engineering/academics/ms-phd-civil-and-environmental-engineering/

Surveying Science and Engineering

University of New Brunswick Fredericton, School of Graduate Studies, Faculty of Engineering, Department of Geodesy and Geomatics Engineering, Fredericton, NB E3B 5A3, Canada. Offers M Eng, M Sc E, PhD. *Degree requirements:* For master's, thesis; for doctorate, comprehensive exam, thesis/dissertation, qualifying exam. *Entrance requirements:* For master's and doctorate, minimum GPA of 3.0. Additional exam requirements/recommendations for international students: Required—TOEFL (minimum score 550 paper-based; 80 iBT), IELTS (minimum score 7), TWE (minimum score 4), Michigan English Language Assessment Battery (minimum score 85) or CanTest (minimum score 4.5). Electronic applications accepted. *Faculty research:* GIS, GPS, remote sensing, ocean mapping, land administration, hydrography, engineering surveys.

Transportation and Highway Engineering

Arizona State University at the Tempe campus, College of Liberal Arts and Sciences, School of Geographical Sciences and Urban Planning, Tempe, AZ 85287-5302. Offers geographic information systems (MAS); geographical information science (Graduate Certificate); geography (MA, PhD); transportation systems (Graduate Certificate); urban and environmental planning (MUEP); urban planning (PhD). *Accreditation:* ACSP. Terminal master's awarded for partial completion of doctoral program. *Degree requirements:* For master's, thesis, interactive Program of Study (iPOS) submitted before completing 50 percent of required credit hours; for doctorate, comprehensive exam, thesis/dissertation, interactive Program of Study (iPOS) submitted before completing 50 percent of required credit hours. *Entrance requirements:* For master's and doctorate, GRE, minimum GPA of 3.0 or equivalent in last 2 years of work leading to bachelor's degree. Additional exam requirements/recommendations for international students: Required—TOEFL, IELTS, or PTE. Electronic applications accepted. *Expenses:* Contact institution.

ArtCenter College of Design, Graduate Transportation Systems and Design Program, Pasadena, CA 91103. Offers transportation systems (MS).

The Catholic University of America, School of Engineering, Department of Civil Engineering, Washington, DC 20064. Offers civil engineering (MS, PhD); transportation and infrastructure systems (Certificate). *Program availability:* Part-time. *Faculty:* 6 full-time (0 women), 4 part-time/adjunct (1 woman). *Students:* 15 full-time (3 women), 15 part-time (4 women); includes 8 minority (3 Black or African American, non-Hispanic/Latino; 5 Two or more races, non-Hispanic/Latino), 20 international. Average age 33. 36 applicants, 75% accepted, 13 enrolled. In 2018, 15 master's, 2 doctorates awarded. *Degree requirements:* For master's, thesis optional; for doctorate, comprehensive exam, thesis/dissertation. *Entrance requirements:* For master's and doctorate, GRE General Test, statement of purpose, official copies of academic transcripts, three letters of recommendation. Additional exam requirements/recommendations for international students: Required—TOEFL (minimum score 550 paper-based; 80 iBT). *Application deadline:* For fall admission, 7/15 priority date for domestic students, 7/1 for international students; for spring admission, 11/15 priority date for domestic students, 11/1 for international students. Applications are processed on a rolling basis. Application fee: $55. Electronic applications accepted. *Expenses:* Contact institution. *Financial support:* Fellowships, research assistantships, teaching assistantships, Federal Work-Study, scholarships/grants, tuition waivers (full and partial), and unspecified assistantships available. Financial award application deadline: 2/1; financial award applicants required to submit FAFSA. *Faculty research:* Transportation engineering, solid mechanics, construction engineering and management, environmental engineering and water resources, structural engineering. *Unit head:* Dr. Arash Massoudieh, Chair, 202-319-5671, Fax: 202-319-6677, E-mail: massoudieh@cua.edu. *Application contact:* Dr. Steven Brown, Director of Graduate Admissions, 202-319-5057, Fax: 202-319-6533, E-mail: cua-admissions@cua.edu.
Website: https://engineering.catholic.edu/civil/index.html

The Citadel, The Military College of South Carolina, Citadel Graduate College, School of Engineering, Department of Civil and Environmental Engineering, Charleston, SC 29409. Offers built environment and public health (Graduate Certificate); civil engineering (MS); geotechnical engineering (Graduate Certificate); structural engineering (Graduate Certificate); transportation engineering (Graduate Certificate). *Program availability:* Part-time, evening/weekend. *Degree requirements:* For master's, plan of study outlining intended areas of interest and top four corresponding courses of interest. *Entrance requirements:* For master's, official transcript of baccalaureate degree from ABET-accredited engineering program or approved alternative; 2 letters of recommendation; for Graduate Certificate, official transcript of baccalaureate degree directly from an accredited college or university. Additional exam requirements/recommendations for international students: Required—TOEFL (minimum score 550 paper-based; 79 iBT). Electronic applications accepted. *Expenses:* Tuition, state resident: part-time $595 per credit hour. Tuition, nonresident: part-time $1020 per credit hour. *Required fees:* $90 per term.

Clemson University, Graduate School, College of Engineering, Computing and Applied Sciences, Glenn Department of Civil Engineering, Clemson, SC 29634. Offers civil engineering (MS, PhD), including construction engineering and management, construction materials, geotechnical engineering, structural engineering, transportation engineering, water resources engineering. *Program availability:* Part-time. *Faculty:* 20 full-time (3 women). *Students:* 109 full-time (23 women), 55 part-time (11 women); includes 9 minority (2 Black or African American, non-Hispanic/Latino; 2 Asian, non-Hispanic/Latino; 4 Hispanic/Latino; 1 Two or more races, non-Hispanic/Latino), 111 international. Average age 28. 283 applicants, 59% accepted, 53 enrolled. In 2018, 31 master's, 11 doctorates awarded. *Degree requirements:* For master's, thesis or alternative, oral exam, seminar; for doctorate, comprehensive exam, thesis/dissertation, oral exam, seminar. *Entrance requirements:* For master's and doctorate, GRE General Test, unofficial transcripts, letters of recommendation, statement of purpose. Additional exam requirements/recommendations for international students: Required—TOEFL (minimum score 80 paper-based; 80 iBT), PTE (minimum score 54); Recommended—IELTS (minimum score 6.5). *Application deadline:* For fall admission, 4/15 for domestic and international students; for spring admission, 9/15 for domestic and international students. Applications are processed on a rolling basis. Application fee: $80 ($90 for international students). Electronic applications accepted. *Expenses:* $6823 per semester full-time resident, $14023 per semester full-time non-resident, $833 per credit hour part-time resident, $1731 per credit hour part-time non-resident, online $1264 per credit hour, $4938 doctoral programs resident, $10405 doctoral programs non-resident, $1144 full-time graduate assistant, other fees may apply per session. *Financial support:* In 2018–19, 104 students received support, including 20 fellowships with full and partial tuition reimbursements available (averaging $4,491 per year), 43 research assistantships with full and partial tuition reimbursements available (averaging $16,364 per year), 1 teaching assistantship with full and partial tuition reimbursement available (averaging $12,750 per year); career-related internships or fieldwork and unspecified assistantships also available. Financial award application deadline: 4/15. *Faculty research:* Applied fluid mechanics, construction materials, project management, structural and geotechnical engineering, transportation. *Total annual research expenditures:* $4.9 million. *Unit head:* Dr. Ronald Andrus, Interim Department Chair, 864-656-0488, E-mail: randrus@clemson.edu. *Application contact:* Dr. Abdul Khan, Graduate Program Coordinator, 864-656-3327, E-mail: abdkhan@clemson.edu.
Website: https://www.clemson.edu/cecas/departments/ce/

College for Creative Studies, Graduate Programs, Detroit, MI 48202-4034. Offers color and materials design (MFA); integrated design (MFA); interaction design (MFA); transportation design (MFA). *Accreditation:* NASAD.

Cornell University, Graduate School, Graduate Fields of Engineering, Field of Civil and Environmental Engineering, Ithaca, NY 14853. Offers engineering management (M Eng, MS, PhD); environmental engineering (M Eng, MS, PhD); environmental fluid mechanics and hydrology (M Eng, MS, PhD); environmental systems engineering (M Eng, MS, PhD); geotechnical engineering (M Eng, MS, PhD); remote sensing (M Eng, MS, PhD); structural engineering (M Eng, MS, PhD); structural mechanics (M Eng, MS); transportation engineering (MS, PhD); transportation systems engineering (M Eng); water resource systems (M Eng, MS, PhD). Terminal master's awarded for partial completion of doctoral program. *Degree requirements:* For master's, thesis (MS); for doctorate, comprehensive exam, thesis/dissertation. *Entrance requirements:* For master's and doctorate, GRE General Test (recommended), 2 letters of recommendation. Additional exam requirements/recommendations for international students: Required—TOEFL (minimum score 600 paper-based; 77 iBT). Electronic applications accepted. *Faculty research:* Environmental engineering, geotechnical engineering, remote sensing, environmental fluid mechanics and hydrology, structural engineering.

École Polytechnique de Montréal, Graduate Programs, Department of Civil, Geological and Mining Engineering, Montréal, QC H3C 3A7, Canada. Offers civil, geological and mining engineering (DESS); environmental engineering (M Eng, M Sc A, PhD); geotechnical engineering (M Eng, M Sc A, PhD); hydraulics engineering (M Eng, M Sc A, PhD); structural engineering (M Eng, M Sc A, PhD); transportation engineering (M Eng, M Sc A, PhD). *Program availability:* Part-time. *Degree requirements:* For master's, one foreign language, thesis; for doctorate, one foreign language, thesis/dissertation. *Entrance requirements:* For master's, minimum GPA of 2.75; for doctorate, minimum GPA of 3.0. *Faculty research:* Water resources management, characteristics of building materials, aging of dams, pollution control.

Transportation and Highway Engineering

George Mason University, Volgenau School of Engineering, Sid and Reva Dewberry Department of Civil, Environmental, and Infrastructure Engineering, Fairfax, VA 22030. Offers construction project management (MS); transportation engineering (PhD). *Faculty:* 16 full-time (4 women), 15 part-time/adjunct (4 women). *Students:* 59 full-time (20 women), 69 part-time (19 women); includes 34 minority (9 Black or African American, non-Hispanic/Latino; 14 Asian, non-Hispanic/Latino; 11 Hispanic/Latino), 46 international. Average age 28. 117 applicants, 75% accepted, 31 enrolled. In 2018, 39 master's, 8 doctorates awarded. *Degree requirements:* For master's, thesis (for some programs), 30 credits, departmental seminars; for doctorate, thesis/dissertation, qualifying exams. *Entrance requirements:* For master's, GRE, photocopy of passport; 2 official college transcripts; resume; official bank statement; proof of financial support; expanded goals statement; self-evaluation form; BS in engineering or other related science; 3 letters of recommendation; for doctorate, GRE (for those who received degree outside of the U.S.), photocopy of passport; 2 official college transcripts; resume; official bank statement; proof of financial support; expanded goals statement; self-evaluation form; baccalaureate degree in engineering or related science; master's degree (preferred); 3 letters of recommendation. Additional exam requirements/recommendations for international students: Required—TOEFL (minimum score 575 paper-based; 88 iBT), IELTS (minimum score 6.5), PTE (minimum score 59). *Application deadline:* For fall admission, 12/15 priority date for domestic and international students; for spring admission, 8/15 priority date for domestic and international students. Application fee: $75 ($80 for international students). Electronic applications accepted. *Expenses:* $589 per credit in-state, $1,346.75 per credit out-of-state. *Financial support:* In 2018–19, 37 students received support, including 25 research assistantships with tuition reimbursements available (averaging $19,626 per year), 13 teaching assistantships with tuition reimbursements available (averaging $17,449 per year); career-related internships or fieldwork, Federal Work-Study, scholarships/grants, unspecified assistantships, and health care benefits (for full-time research or teaching assistantship recipients) also available. Support available to part-time students. Financial award application deadline: 3/1; financial award applicants required to submit FAFSA. *Faculty research:* Evolutionary design, infrastructure security, intelligent transportation systems, national transportation networks, water quality modeling. *Total annual research expenditures:* $1.6 million. *Unit head:* Llza Wilson Durant, Acting Chair, 703-993-1687, Fax: 703-993-9790, E-mail: ldurant2@gmu.edu. *Application contact:* Laura Kosoglu, Director, Graduate Program, 703-993-1675, Fax: 703-993-9790, E-mail: ceiegrad@gmu.edu.
Website: http://civil.gmu.edu/

Illinois Institute of Technology, Graduate College, Armour College of Engineering, Department of Civil, Architectural and Environmental Engineering, Chicago, IL 60616. Offers architectural engineering (M Arch E); civil engineering (MS, PhD), including architectural engineering (MS), construction engineering and management (MS), geoenvironmental engineering (MS), geotechnical engineering (MS), structural engineering (MS), transportation engineering (MS); construction engineering and management (MCEM); environmental engineering (M Env E, MS, PhD); geoenvironmental engineering (M Geoenv E); geotechnical engineering (MGE); infrastructure engineering and management (MPW); structural engineering (MSE); transportation engineering (M Trans E). *Program availability:* Part-time, evening/weekend, online learning. Terminal master's awarded for partial completion of doctoral program. *Degree requirements:* For master's, thesis (for some programs); for doctorate, comprehensive exam, thesis/dissertation. *Entrance requirements:* For master's, GRE General Test (minimum score 900 Quantitative and Verbal, 2.5 Analytical Writing), minimum undergraduate GPA of 3.0; for doctorate, GRE General Test (minimum score 1000 Quantitative and Verbal, 3.0 Analytical Writing), minimum undergraduate GPA of 3.0. Additional exam requirements/recommendations for international students: Required—TOEFL (minimum score 550 paper-based; 80 iBT). Electronic applications accepted. *Faculty research:* Structural, architectural, geotechnical and geoenvironmental engineering; construction engineering and management; transportation engineering; environmental engineering and public works.

Iowa State University of Science and Technology, Department of Civil and Construction Engineering, Ames, IA 50011. Offers civil engineering (MS, PhD), including civil engineering materials, construction engineering and management, environmental engineering, geotechnical engineering, structural engineering, transportation engineering. *Degree requirements:* For master's, thesis or alternative; for doctorate, thesis/dissertation. *Entrance requirements:* For master's and doctorate, GRE General Test. Additional exam requirements/recommendations for international students: Required—TOEFL (minimum score 550 paper-based; 82 iBT), IELTS (minimum score 6.5). Electronic applications accepted.

Kansas State University, Graduate School, College of Engineering, Department of Civil Engineering, Manhattan, KS 66506. Offers civil engineering (MS, PhD); environmental engineering (MS, PhD); geotechnical engineering (MS, PhD); structural engineering (MS, PhD); transportation engineering (MS, PhD); water resources engineering (MS, PhD). *Program availability:* Part-time, evening/weekend, online learning. *Degree requirements:* For master's, thesis or alternative; for doctorate, thesis/dissertation. *Entrance requirements:* For master's, GRE General Test, bachelor's degree or course work in related engineering fields; for doctorate, GRE General Test. Additional exam requirements/recommendations for international students: Required—TOEFL (minimum score 550 paper-based; 79 iBT). Electronic applications accepted. *Faculty research:* Transportation and materials engineering, water resources engineering, environmental engineering, geotechnical engineering, structural engineering.

Kennesaw State University, Southern Polytechnic College of Engineering and Engineering Technology, Program in Civil Engineering, Kennesaw, GA 30144. Offers environmental engineering (MS); geotechnical engineering (MS); structural engineering (MS); transportation and pavement engineering (MS); water resources engineering (MS). *Program availability:* Online learning. *Students:* 13 full-time (2 women), 24 part-time (5 women); includes 20 minority (8 Black or African American, non-Hispanic/Latino; 5 Asian, non-Hispanic/Latino; 4 Hispanic/Latino; 3 Two or more races, non-Hispanic/Latino), 2 international. Average age 33. 21 applicants, 57% accepted, 1 enrolled. In 2018, 6 master's awarded. *Degree requirements:* For master's, thesis optional. *Entrance requirements:* Additional exam requirements/recommendations for international students: Required—TOEFL (minimum score 550 paper-based; 80 iBT), IELTS (minimum score 6.5). *Application deadline:* For fall admission, 11/1 for domestic and international students; for spring admission, 4/1 for domestic and international students. Applications are processed on a rolling basis. Application fee: $60. Electronic applications accepted. *Expenses: Tuition, area resident:* Full-time $6960; part-time $290 per credit hour. Tuition, state resident: full-time $6960; part-time $290 per credit hour. Tuition, nonresident: full-time $25,080; part-time $1045 per credit hour. *International tuition:* $25,080 full-time. *Required fees:* $2006; $1706 per semester. $853 per semester. *Unit head:* Metin Oguzmert, Coordinator, 470-578-5083, E-mail: moguzmer@kennesaw.edu. *Application contact:* Admissions Counselor, 470-578-4377, E-mail: ksugrad@kennesaw.edu.
Website: http://engineering.kennesaw.edu/civil-construction/degrees/ms-civil-engineering.php

Louisiana State University and Agricultural & Mechanical College, Graduate School, College of Engineering, Department of Civil and Environmental Engineering, Baton Rouge, LA 70803. Offers environmental engineering (MSCE, PhD); geotechnical engineering (MSCE, PhD); structural engineering and mechanics (MSCE, PhD); transportation engineering (MSCE, PhD); water resources (MSCE, PhD).

Marquette University, Graduate School, College of Engineering, Department of Civil and Environmental Engineering, Milwaukee, WI 53201-1881. Offers construction engineering and management (MS, PhD, Certificate); environmental engineering (MS, PhD); structural design (Certificate); structural engineering and structural mechanics (MS, PhD); transportation (Certificate); transportation engineering and materials (MS, PhD); waste and wastewater treatment processes (Certificate); water resources engineering (Certificate). *Program availability:* Part-time, evening/weekend. Terminal master's awarded for partial completion of doctoral program. *Degree requirements:* For master's, comprehensive exam (for some programs), thesis or alternative; for doctorate, thesis/dissertation. *Entrance requirements:* For master's, GRE General Test (recommended), minimum GPA of 3.0, official transcripts from all current and previous colleges/universities except Marquette, three letters of recommendation; for doctorate, GRE General Test, minimum GPA of 3.0, official transcripts from all current and previous colleges/universities except Marquette, three letters of recommendation, brief statement of purpose, submission of any English language publications authored by applicant (strongly recommended). Additional exam requirements/recommendations for international students: Required—TOEFL (minimum score 530 paper-based). Electronic applications accepted. *Faculty research:* Highway safety, highway performance, and intelligent transportation systems; surface mount technology; watershed management.

Marshall University, Academic Affairs Division, College of Information Technology and Engineering, Program in Engineering, Huntington, WV 25755. Offers engineering management (MSE); environmental engineering (MSE); transportation and infrastructure engineering (MSE). *Program availability:* Part-time, evening/weekend. *Degree requirements:* For master's, final project, oral exam. *Entrance requirements:* For master's, GMAT or GRE General Test, minimum undergraduate GPA of 2.75.

Massachusetts Institute of Technology, School of Engineering, Department of Civil and Environmental Engineering, Cambridge, MA 02139. Offers biological oceanography (PhD, Sc D); chemical oceanography (PhD, Sc D); civil and environmental engineering (M Eng, SM, PhD, Sc D); civil and environmental systems (PhD, Sc D); civil engineering (PhD, Sc D, CE); civil engineering and computation (PhD); coastal engineering (PhD, Sc D); construction engineering and management (PhD, Sc D); environmental biology (PhD, Sc D); environmental chemistry (PhD, Sc D); environmental engineering (PhD, Sc D); environmental engineering and computation (PhD); environmental fluid mechanics (PhD, Sc D); geotechnical and geoenvironmental engineering (PhD, Sc D); hydrology (PhD, Sc D); information technology (PhD, Sc D); oceanographic engineering (PhD, Sc D); structures and materials (PhD, Sc D); transportation (PhD, Sc D); SM/MBA. *Degree requirements:* For master's, thesis; for doctorate, comprehensive exam, thesis/dissertation; for CE, comprehensive exam, thesis. *Entrance requirements:* For master's, doctorate, and CE, GRE General Test. Additional exam requirements/recommendations for international students: Required—TOEFL, IELTS. Electronic applications accepted. *Expenses: Tuition:* Full-time $51,520; part-time $800 per credit hour. *Required fees:* $312. *Faculty research:* Environmental chemistry, environmental fluid mechanics and coastal engineering, environmental microbiology, geotechnical engineering and geomechanics, hydrology and hydro climatology, infrastructure systems, mechanics of materials and structures, transportation systems.

Morgan State University, School of Graduate Studies, Clarence M. Mitchell, Jr. School of Engineering, Department of Transportation and Urban Infrastructure Studies, Baltimore, MD 21251. Offers transportation (MS, PhD, Postbaccalaureate Certificate). *Program availability:* Part-time, evening/weekend. *Degree requirements:* For master's, thesis optional, comprehensive exam or equivalent. *Entrance requirements:* For master's, minimum undergraduate GPA of 2.5. Additional exam requirements/recommendations for international students: Required—TOEFL (minimum score 550 paper-based). *Faculty research:* Distributional impacts of congestion, pricing education and training for intelligent vehicle highway systems.

New Jersey Institute of Technology, Newark College of Engineering, Newark, NJ 07102. Offers biomedical engineering (MS, PhD); biopharmaceutical engineering (MS); chemical engineering (MS, PhD); civil engineering (MS, PhD); computer engineering (MS); critical infrastructure systems (MS); electrical engineering (MS, PhD); engineering management (MS); engineering science (MS); environmental engineering (MS, PhD); healthcare systems management (MS); industrial engineering (MS, PhD); internet engineering (MS); manufacturing systems engineering (MS); materials science & engineering (PhD); materials science and engineering (MS); mechanical engineering (MS, PhD); occupational safety and health engineering (MS). *Program availability:* Part-time, evening/weekend. *Faculty:* 147 full-time (26 women), 133 part-time/adjunct (16 women). *Students:* 690 full-time (163 women), 594 part-time (130 women); includes 427 minority (79 Black or African American, non-Hispanic/Latino; 181 Asian, non-Hispanic/Latino; 140 Hispanic/Latino; 27 Two or more races, non-Hispanic/Latino), 553 international. Average age 27. 2,334 applicants, 57% accepted, 452 enrolled. In 2018, 418 master's, 31 doctorates awarded. Terminal master's awarded for partial completion of doctoral program. *Degree requirements:* For master's, thesis (for some programs); for doctorate, thesis/dissertation. *Entrance requirements:* For master's, GRE General Test, minimum GPA 2.8, personal statement, 1 letter of recommendation, transcripts; for doctorate, GRE General Test, minimum GPA of 3.5, personal statement, 3 letters of recommendation, transcripts. Additional exam requirements/recommendations for international students: Required—TOEFL (minimum score 550 paper-based; 79 iBT), IELTS (minimum score 6.5). *Application deadline:* For fall admission, 6/1 priority date for domestic students, 5/1 priority date for international students; for spring admission, 11/15 priority date for domestic and international students. Applications are processed on a rolling basis. Application fee: $75. Electronic applications accepted. *Expenses:* $22,690 per year (in-state), $32,136 per year (out-of-state). *Financial support:* In 2018–19, 396 students received support, including 52 fellowships with full tuition reimbursements available (averaging $22,000 per year), 113 research assistantships with full tuition reimbursements available (averaging $22,000 per year), 101 teaching assistantships with full tuition reimbursements available (averaging $22,000 per year); career-related internships or fieldwork, Federal Work-Study, scholarships/grants, and unspecified assistantships also available. Financial award application deadline: 1/15. *Faculty research:* Nonlinear signal processing, intelligent medical image analysis, calibration issues in coherent localization, computer-aided design, neural network for tool wear measurement. *Total annual research expenditures:* $41.7 million. *Unit head:* Dr. Moshe Kam, Dean, 973-596-5534, Fax: 973-596-2316, E-mail: moshe.kam@njit.edu. *Application contact:* Stephen Eck, Director of Admissions, 973-596-3300, Fax: 973-596-3461, E-mail: admissions@njit.edu.
Website: http://engineering.njit.edu/

New York University, Tandon School of Engineering, Department of Civil and Urban Engineering, New York, NY 10012-1019. Offers civil engineering (MS, PhD); transportation planning and engineering (MS); urban systems engineering and management (MS). *Program availability:* Part-time, evening/weekend. *Faculty:* 20 full-time (5 women), 23 part-time/adjunct (1 woman). *Students:* 158 full-time (57 women), 90 part-time (27 women); includes 47 minority (8 Black or African American, non-Hispanic/Latino; 23 Asian, non-Hispanic/Latino; 12 Hispanic/Latino; 4 Two or more races, non-Hispanic/Latino), 136 international. Average age 29. 658 applicants, 48% accepted, 71 enrolled. In 2018, 139 master's, 4 doctorates awarded. *Degree requirements:* For master's, comprehensive exam (for some programs), thesis (for some programs); for doctorate, comprehensive exam, thesis/dissertation, qualifying exam. *Entrance requirements:* For doctorate, MS in civil engineering. Additional exam requirements/recommendations for international students: Required—TOEFL (minimum score 550 paper-based; 90 iBT); Recommended—IELTS (minimum score 7). *Application deadline:* For fall admission, 2/15 priority date for domestic and international students; for spring admission, 11/1 priority date for domestic and international students. Applications are processed on a rolling basis. Application fee: $75. Electronic applications accepted. *Expenses:* Contact institution. *Financial support:* In 2018–19, 119 students received support. Fellowships, research assistantships, teaching assistantships, career-related internships or fieldwork, scholarships/grants, tuition waivers, and unspecified assistantships available. Support available to part-time students. Financial award application deadline: 2/15. *Faculty research:* Natural and man-made materials. *Total annual research expenditures:* $2.9 million. *Unit head:* Dr. Magued Iskander, Head, 646-997-3016, E-mail: iskander@nyu.edu. *Application contact:* Elizabeth Ensweiler, Senior Director of Graduate Enrollment and Graduate Admissions, 646-997-3182, E-mail: elizabeth.ensweiler@nyu.edu.

North Dakota State University, College of Graduate and Interdisciplinary Studies, College of Engineering, Doctoral Program in Engineering, Fargo, ND 58102. Offers environmental and conservation science (PhD); materials and nanotechnology (PhD); natural resource management (PhD); STEM education (PhD); transportation and logistics (PhD). *Degree requirements:* For doctorate, comprehensive exam, thesis/dissertation. *Entrance requirements:* For doctorate, bachelor's degree in engineering, minimum GPA of 3.0. Additional exam requirements/recommendations for international students: Required—TOEFL. Electronic applications accepted. *Expenses:* Contact institution.

Northwestern University, McCormick School of Engineering and Applied Science, Department of Civil and Environmental Engineering, Evanston, IL 60208-3109. Offers environmental engineering and science (MS, PhD); geotechnical engineering (MS, PhD); mechanics of materials and solids (MS, PhD); project management (MS); structural engineering and materials (MS, PhD); transportation systems analysis and planning (MS, PhD). MS and PhD admissions and degrees offered through The Graduate School. *Program availability:* Part-time. Terminal master's awarded for partial completion of doctoral program. *Degree requirements:* For master's, comprehensive exam (for some programs), thesis (for some programs); for doctorate, comprehensive exam, thesis/dissertation. *Entrance requirements:* For master's and doctorate, GRE General Test, minimum 2 letters of recommendation, transcripts from all academic institutions attended. Additional exam requirements/recommendations for international students: Required—TOEFL (minimum score 577 paper-based; 90 iBT), IELTS (minimum score 7). Electronic applications accepted. *Faculty research:* Environmental engineering and science, geotechnics, mechanics, materials, structures, and transportation systems analysis and planning.

Ohio University, Graduate College, Russ College of Engineering and Technology, Department of Civil Engineering, Athens, OH 45701-2979. Offers civil engineering (PhD); construction engineering and management (MS); environmental (MS); geoenvironmental (MS); geotechnical (MS); mechanics (MS); structures (MS); transportation (MS); water resources (MS). *Program availability:* Part-time. *Degree requirements:* For master's, comprehensive exam (for some programs), thesis or alternative; for doctorate, comprehensive exam, thesis/dissertation. *Entrance requirements:* For master's, GRE General Test, minimum GPA of 3.0, 3 letters of recommendation; for doctorate, GRE General Test. Additional exam requirements/recommendations for international students: Required—TOEFL (minimum score 550 paper-based; 80 iBT) or IELTS (minimum score 6.5). Electronic applications accepted. *Faculty research:* Noise abatement, materials and environment, highway infrastructure, subsurface investigation (pavements, pipes, bridges).

Old Dominion University, Frank Batten College of Engineering and Technology, Program in Civil Engineering, Norfolk, VA 23529. Offers civil engineering (ME, MS), including coastal engineering, geotechnical engineering, hydraulics and water resources, structural engineering, transportation engineering. *Program availability:* Part-time, evening/weekend, blended/hybrid learning. *Degree requirements:* For master's, comprehensive exam, thesis optional. *Entrance requirements:* For master's, GRE, minimum GPA of 3.0. Additional exam requirements/recommendations for international students: Required—TOEFL (minimum score 550 paper-based, 80 iBT) or IELTS (6.5). Electronic applications accepted. *Expenses:* Contact institution. *Faculty research:* Structural engineering, coastal engineering, geotechnical engineering, water resources, transportation engineering.

Oregon State University, College of Engineering, Program in Civil Engineering, Corvallis, OR 97331. Offers civil engineering (M Eng, MS, PhD); coastal and ocean engineering (M Eng, MS, PhD); construction engineering management (M Eng, MS, PhD); engineering education (M Eng, MS, PhD); geomatics (M Eng, MS, PhD); geotechnical engineering (M Eng, MS, PhD); infrastructure materials (M Eng, MS, PhD); structural engineering (M Eng, MS, PhD); transportation engineering (M Eng). *Entrance requirements:* For master's and doctorate, GRE. Additional exam requirements/recommendations for international students: Required—TOEFL (minimum score 80 iBT), IELTS (minimum score 6.5). *Expenses:* Contact institution.

Rensselaer Polytechnic Institute, Graduate School, School of Engineering, Program in Transportation Engineering, Troy, NY 12180-3590. Offers M Eng, MS, PhD. *Faculty:* 18 full-time (3 women), 4 part-time/adjunct (0 women). *Students:* 11 full-time (7 women), 10 international. Average age 30. 8 applicants, 38% accepted, 1 enrolled. Terminal master's awarded for partial completion of doctoral program. *Degree requirements:* For master's, thesis (for some programs); for doctorate, thesis/dissertation. *Entrance requirements:* For master's and doctorate, GRE. Additional exam requirements/recommendations for international students: Required—TOEFL (minimum score 570 paper-based; 88 iBT), IELTS (minimum score 6.5), PTE (minimum score 60). *Application deadline:* For fall admission, 1/1 priority date for domestic and international students; for spring admission, 8/15 priority date for domestic and international students. Applications are processed on a rolling basis. Application fee: $75. Electronic applications accepted. *Financial support:* In 2018–19, research assistantships (averaging $23,000 per year), teaching assistantships (averaging $23,000 per year) were awarded; fellowships also available. Financial award application deadline: 1/1. *Faculty research:* Advanced econometrics, freight transportation systems: operations and modeling, intelligent transportation systems, traffic simulation and network modeling, transportation economics, transportation planning. *Total annual research expenditures:* $1.1 million. *Unit head:* Dr. Michael O'Rourke, Graduate Program Director, 518-276-6933, E-mail: orourm@rpi.edu. *Application contact:* Jarron Decker, Director of Graduate Admissions, 518-276-6216, Fax: 518-276-4072, E-mail: gradadmissions@rpi.edu.
Website: http://cee.rpi.edu/graduate

South Carolina State University, College of Graduate and Professional Studies, Department of Civil and Mechanical Engineering Technology, Orangeburg, SC 29117-0001. Offers transportation (MS). *Program availability:* Part-time, evening/weekend. *Faculty:* 4 full-time (2 women). *Students:* 11 full-time (1 woman); includes 10 minority (9 Black or African American, non-Hispanic/Latino; 1 Asian, non-Hispanic/Latino), 1 international. Average age 27. 8 applicants, 88% accepted, 7 enrolled. In 2018, 1 master's awarded. *Degree requirements:* For master's, comprehensive exam, thesis, departmental qualifying exam. *Entrance requirements:* For master's, GRE. Additional exam requirements/recommendations for international students: Recommended—TOEFL. *Application deadline:* For fall admission, 6/15 for domestic and international students; for spring admission, 11/1 for domestic and international students. Application fee: $25. Electronic applications accepted. *Expenses:* Tuition, area resident: Full-time $9928; part-time $552 per credit hour. Tuition, state resident: full-time $9928. Tuition, nonresident: full-time $21,038; part-time $1169 per credit hour. *Required fees:* $1532; $85 per credit hour. *Financial support:* Fellowships, research assistantships, career-related internships or fieldwork, Federal Work-Study, scholarships/grants, and unspecified assistantships available. Financial award application deadline: 6/1. *Unit head:* Dr. Stanley Ihekweazu, Chair, 803-536-7117, Fax: 803-516-4607, E-mail: sihekwea@scsu.edu. *Application contact:* Curtis Foskey, Coordinator of Graduate Admission, 803-536-8419, Fax: 803-536-8812, E-mail: cfoskey@scsu.edu. Website: http://www.scsu.edu/schoolofgraduatestudies.aspx

Southern Illinois University Edwardsville, Graduate School, School of Engineering, Department of Civil Engineering, Program in Transportation Engineering, Edwardsville, IL 62026. Offers MS. *Program availability:* Part-time, evening/weekend. *Degree requirements:* For master's, thesis (for some programs), research paper. *Entrance requirements:* For master's, minimum undergraduate GPA of 2.75 in science, math, and engineering courses. Additional exam requirements/recommendations for international students: Required—TOEFL (minimum score 550 paper-based, 79 iBT), IELTS (minimum score 6.5), Michigan Test of English Language Proficiency or PTE. Electronic applications accepted.

Southern Methodist University, Lyle School of Engineering, Department of Civil and Environmental Engineering, Dallas, TX 75275-0340. Offers civil and environmental engineering (PhD); civil engineering (MS), including geotechnical engineering, structural engineering, transportation systems; environmental engineering (MS); sustainability and development (MA). *Program availability:* Part-time, evening/weekend, online learning. Terminal master's awarded for partial completion of doctoral program. *Degree requirements:* For master's, thesis optional; for doctorate, thesis/dissertation, oral and written qualifying exams. *Entrance requirements:* For master's, GRE General Test, minimum GPA of 3.0 in last 2 years; bachelor's degree in engineering, mathematics, or sciences; for doctorate, GRE, BS and MS in related field, minimum GPA of 3.3. Additional exam requirements/recommendations for international students: Required—TOEFL. Electronic applications accepted. *Faculty research:* Human and environmental health effects of endocrine disrupters, development of air pollution control systems for diesel engines, structural analysis and design, modeling and design of waste treatment systems.

Stevens Institute of Technology, Graduate School, Charles V. Schaefer Jr. School of Engineering and Science, Department of Civil, Environmental, and Ocean Engineering, Program in Civil Engineering, Hoboken, NJ 07030. Offers civil engineering (PhD, Certificate), including geotechnical engineering (Certificate); geotechnical/geoenvironmental engineering (M Eng, Engr); hydrologic modeling (M Eng); stormwater management (M Eng); structural engineering (M Eng, Engr); transportation engineering (M Eng); water resources engineering (M Eng). *Program availability:* Part-time, evening/weekend. *Faculty:* 28 full-time (7 women), 2 part-time/adjunct (1 woman). *Students:* 37 full-time (8 women), 27 part-time (8 women); includes 8 minority (1 Black or African American, non-Hispanic/Latino; 1 American Indian or Alaska Native, non-Hispanic/Latino; 6 Asian, non-Hispanic/Latino), 30 international. Average age 25. In 2018, 44 master's awarded. Terminal master's awarded for partial completion of doctoral program. *Degree requirements:* For master's, thesis optional, minimum B average in major field and overall; for doctorate, comprehensive exam (for some programs), thesis/dissertation; for other advanced degree, minimum B average. *Entrance requirements:* For master's, GRE/GMAT scores: GRE scores are required for all applicants applying to a full-time graduate program in the Schaefer School of Engineering and Science (SES). International applicants must submit TOEFL/IELTS scores and fulfill the English Language Proficiency Requirements in order to be considered. Additional exam requirements/recommendations for international students: Required—TOEFL (minimum score 74 iBT), IELTS (minimum score 6). *Application deadline:* For fall admission, 4/15 for domestic and international students; for spring admission, 11/1 for domestic and international students; for summer admission, 5/1 for domestic students. Applications are processed on a rolling basis. Application fee: $60. Electronic applications accepted. *Expenses:* Tuition: Full-time $35,960; part-time $1620 per credit. *Required fees:* $1290; $600 per semester. Tuition and fees vary according to course load. *Financial support:* Fellowships, research assistantships, teaching assistantships, career-related internships or fieldwork, Federal Work-Study, scholarships/grants, and unspecified assistantships available. Financial award application deadline: 2/15; financial award applicants required to submit FAFSA. *Unit head:* Dr. Jean Zu, Dean of SES, 201-216.8233, Fax: 201-216.8372, E-mail: Jean.Zu@stevens.edu. *Application contact:* Graduate Admission, 888-783-8367, Fax: 888-511-1306, E-mail: graduate@stevens.edu.

Texas Southern University, School of Science and Technology, Program in Transportation, Planning and Management, Houston, TX 77004-4584. Offers MS. *Program availability:* Part-time, evening/weekend. *Degree requirements:* For master's, comprehensive exam, thesis optional. *Entrance requirements:* For master's, GRE General Test, minimum GPA of 2.5. Additional exam requirements/recommendations for international students: Required—TOEFL. Electronic applications accepted. *Faculty research:* Highway traffic operations, transportation and policy planning, air quality in transportation, transportation modeling.

University of Arkansas, Graduate School, College of Engineering, Department of Civil Engineering, Fayetteville, AR 72701. Offers civil engineering (MSCE, MSE, PhD); environmental engineering (MS En E, MSE); transportation engineering (MSE, MSTE). In 2018, 14 master's, 5 doctorates awarded. *Degree requirements:* For master's, thesis optional; for doctorate, one foreign language, thesis/dissertation. *Application deadline:* For fall admission, 8/1 for domestic students, 4/1 for international students; for spring admission, 12/1 for domestic students, 10/1 for international students; for summer admission, 4/15 for domestic students, 3/1 for international students. Applications are processed on a rolling basis. Application fee: $60. Electronic applications accepted. *Financial support:* In 2018–19, 37 research assistantships, 1 teaching assistantship were awarded; fellowships with tuition reimbursements, career-related internships or fieldwork, and Federal Work-Study also available. Support available to part-time students. Financial award application deadline: 4/1; financial award applicants required to submit FAFSA. *Unit head:* Dr. Micah Hale, Department Head, 479-575-6348, E-mail: micah@uark.edu. *Application contact:* Dr. Julian Fairey, Graduate Coordinator, 479-575-4023, E-mail: julianf@uark.edu.
Website: https://civil-engineering.uark.edu/

Transportation and Highway Engineering

University of Calgary, Faculty of Graduate Studies, Schulich School of Engineering, Program in Civil Engineering, Calgary, AB T2N 1N4, Canada. Offers avalanche mechanics (M Sc, PhD); civil engineering (M Eng, M Sc, PhD); energy and environment engineering (M Eng, M Sc, PhD); environmental engineering (M Eng, M Sc, PhD); geotechnical engineering (M Eng, M Sc, PhD); materials science (M Eng, M Sc, PhD); project management (M Eng, M Sc, PhD); structures and solid mechanics (M Eng, M Sc, PhD); transportation engineering (M Eng, M Sc, PhD); water resources (M Eng, M Sc, PhD). *Program availability:* Part-time. *Degree requirements:* For master's, thesis; for doctorate, thesis/dissertation, written and oral candidacy exam. *Entrance requirements:* For master's, minimum GPA of 3.0; for doctorate, minimum GPA of 3.5. Additional exam requirements/recommendations for international students: Required—TOEFL (minimum score 580 paper-based; 93 iBT), IELTS (minimum score 7). Electronic applications accepted. *Faculty research:* Geotechnical engineering, energy and environment, transportation, project management, structures and solid mechanics.

University of California, Berkeley, Graduate Division, College of Engineering, Department of Civil and Environmental Engineering, Berkeley, CA 94720. Offers engineering and project management (M Eng, MS, PhD); environmental engineering (M Eng, MS, PhD); geoengineering (M Eng, MS, PhD); structural engineering, mechanics and materials (M Eng, MS, PhD); transportation engineering (M Eng, MS, PhD); M Arch/MS; MCP/MS; MPP/MS. Terminal master's awarded for partial completion of doctoral program. *Degree requirements:* For master's, comprehensive exam (for some programs), thesis (for some programs), comprehensive exam or thesis (MS); for doctorate, thesis/dissertation, qualifying exam. *Entrance requirements:* For master's, GRE General Test, minimum GPA of 3.0, 3 letters of recommendation; for doctorate, GRE General Test, minimum GPA of 3.5, 3 letters of recommendation. Additional exam requirements/recommendations for international students: Required—TOEFL (minimum score 570 paper-based; 90 iBT). Electronic applications accepted.

University of California, Davis, College of Engineering, Graduate Group in Transportation Technology and Policy, Davis, CA 95616. Offers MS, PhD. Terminal master's awarded for partial completion of doctoral program. *Degree requirements:* For master's, comprehensive exam (for some programs), thesis (for some programs); for doctorate, thesis/dissertation. *Entrance requirements:* For master's, GRE General Test, minimum GPA of 3.0; for doctorate, GRE General Test, minimum GPA of 3.5. Additional exam requirements/recommendations for international students: Required—TOEFL (minimum score 550 paper-based). Electronic applications accepted.

University of California, Irvine, Institute of Transportation Studies, Irvine, CA 92697. Offers MA, PhD. *Students:* 12 full-time (5 women), 11 international. Average age 29. 26 applicants, 35% accepted, 5 enrolled. In 2018, 2 master's, 1 doctorate awarded. *Entrance requirements:* For master's and doctorate, GRE General Test, minimum GPA of 3.0. *Application deadline:* For fall admission, 1/15 for domestic and international students. Application fee: $105 ($125 for international students). *Financial support:* Fellowships, research assistantships with full tuition reimbursements, teaching assistantships, institutionally sponsored loans, traineeships, health care benefits, and unspecified assistantships available. Financial award application deadline: 3/1. *Unit head:* Stephen G. Ritchie, Director, 949-824-4214, E-mail: sritchie@uci.edu. *Application contact:* Amelia Regan, Director, Transportation Science Program, 949-824-2611, E-mail: aregan@uci.edu.
Website: http://www.its.uci.edu/

University of Central Florida, College of Engineering and Computer Science, Department of Civil, Environmental, and Construction Engineering, Orlando, FL 32816. Offers civil engineering (PhD, Certificate), including civil engineering (PhD), structural engineering (Certificate), transportation engineering (Certificate); environmental engineering (MS, PhD). *Program availability:* Part-time, evening/weekend. *Students:* 115 full-time (30 women), 75 part-time (23 women); includes 48 minority (6 Black or African American, non-Hispanic/Latino; 8 Asian, non-Hispanic/Latino; 34 Hispanic/Latino), 89 international. Average age 30. 160 applicants, 69% accepted, 54 enrolled. In 2018, 39 master's, 20 doctorates, 1 other advanced degree awarded. *Degree requirements:* For master's, thesis or alternative; for doctorate, comprehensive exam, thesis/dissertation, departmental qualifying exam, candidacy exam. *Entrance requirements:* For master's, letters of recommendation, resume, goal statement; for doctorate, GRE General Test, letters of recommendation, resume, goal statement. Additional exam requirements/recommendations for international students: Required—TOEFL. *Application deadline:* For fall admission, 7/15 priority date for domestic students; for spring admission, 12/1 priority date for domestic students. Application fee: $30. Electronic applications accepted. *Financial support:* In 2018–19, 82 students received support, including 37 fellowships with partial tuition reimbursements available (averaging $13,562 per year), 59 research assistantships with partial tuition reimbursements available (averaging $11,914 per year), 19 teaching assistantships with partial tuition reimbursements available (averaging $9,747 per year); career-related internships or fieldwork, Federal Work-Study, institutionally sponsored loans, health care benefits, tuition waivers (partial), and unspecified assistantships also available. Financial award application deadline: 3/1; financial award applicants required to submit FAFSA. *Unit head:* Dr. Mohamed Abdel-Aty, Chair, 407-823-2841, E-mail: m.aty@ucf.edu. *Application contact:* Associate Director, Graduate Admissions, 407-823-2766, Fax: 407-823-6442, E-mail: gradadmissions@ucf.edu.
Website: http://cece.ucf.edu/

University of Colorado Denver, College of Engineering, Design and Computing, Department of Civil Engineering, Denver, CO 80217. Offers civil engineering (EASPh D); civil engineering systems (PhD); environmental and sustainability engineering (MS, PhD); geographic information systems (MS); geotechnical engineering (MS, PhD); hydrology and hydraulics (MS, PhD); structural engineering (MS, PhD); transportation engineering (MS, PhD). *Program availability:* Part-time, evening/weekend. *Degree requirements:* For master's, comprehensive exam, 30 credit hours, project or thesis; for doctorate, comprehensive exam, thesis/dissertation, 60 credit hours (30 of which are dissertation research). *Entrance requirements:* For master's, GRE, statement of purpose, transcripts, three references; for doctorate, GRE, statement of purpose, transcripts, references, letter of support from faculty stating willingness to serve as dissertation advisor and outlining plan for financial support. Additional exam requirements/recommendations for international students: Required—TOEFL (minimum score 537 paper-based; 75 iBT); Recommended—IELTS (minimum score 6.5). Electronic applications accepted. *Expenses:* Tuition, state resident: full-time $6786; part-time $337 per credit hour. Tuition, nonresident: full-time $22,590; part-time $1255 per credit hour. *Required fees:* $1231; $137 per credit hour. Tuition and fees vary according to program and reciprocity agreements.

University of Colorado Denver, College of Engineering, Design and Computing, Master of Engineering Program, Denver, CO 80217-3364. Offers civil engineering (M Eng), including civil engineering, geographic information systems, transportation systems; electrical engineering (M Eng); mechanical engineering (M Eng). *Program availability:* Part-time. *Entrance requirements:* For master's, GRE (for those with GPA below 2.75), transcripts, references, statement of purpose. *Expenses:* Tuition, state resident: full-time $6786; part-time $337 per credit hour. Tuition, nonresident: full-time $22,590; part-time $1255 per credit hour. *Required fees:* $1231; $137 per credit hour. Tuition and fees vary according to program and reciprocity agreements.

University of Dayton, Department of Civil and Environmental Engineering and Engineering Mechanics, Dayton, OH 45469. Offers engineering mechanics (MSEM); environmental engineering (MSCE); geotechnical engineering (MSCE); structural engineering (MSCE); transportation engineering (MSCE); water resources engineering (MSCE). *Program availability:* Part-time, blended/hybrid learning. *Degree requirements:* For master's, thesis or alternative. *Entrance requirements:* For master's, minimum GPA of 3.0 in undergraduate work. Additional exam requirements/recommendations for international students: Required—TOEFL (minimum score 550 paper-based; 80 iBT); Recommended—IELTS (minimum score 6.5), TSE (minimum score 60). Electronic applications accepted. *Faculty research:* Infrastructure, environmental composite, reliability, computer simulation.

University of Delaware, College of Engineering, Department of Civil and Environmental Engineering, Newark, DE 19716. Offers environmental engineering (MAS, MCE, PhD); geotechnical engineering (MAS, MCE, PhD); ocean engineering (MAS, MCE, PhD); structural engineering (MAS, MCE, PhD); transportation engineering (MAS, MCE, PhD); water resource engineering (MAS, MCE, PhD). *Program availability:* Part-time. Terminal master's awarded for partial completion of doctoral program. *Degree requirements:* For master's, thesis; for doctorate, thesis/dissertation. *Entrance requirements:* For master's and doctorate, GRE General Test. Additional exam requirements/recommendations for international students: Required—TOEFL. Electronic applications accepted. *Faculty research:* Structural engineering and mechanics; transportation engineering; ocean engineering; soil mechanics and foundation; water resources and environmental engineering.

The University of Iowa, Graduate College, College of Engineering, Department of Civil and Environmental Engineering, Iowa City, IA 52242-1316. Offers environmental engineering and science (MS, PhD); hydraulics and water resources (MS, PhD); structures, mechanics and materials (MS, PhD); sustainable water development (MS, PhD); transportation engineering (MS, PhD). *Program availability:* Part-time. Terminal master's awarded for partial completion of doctoral program. *Degree requirements:* For master's, thesis optional, exam; for doctorate, comprehensive exam, thesis/dissertation, exam. *Entrance requirements:* For master's, GRE (minimum combined score of 301 on verbal and quantitative), minimum undergraduate GPA of 3.0; for doctorate, GRE (minimum combined score of 301 on verbal and quantitative), minimum graduate GPA of 3.0. Additional exam requirements/recommendations for international students: Required—TOEFL (minimum score 550 paper-based; 81 iBT), IELTS (minimum score 7). Electronic applications accepted. *Faculty research:* Water resources; environmental engineering and science; hydraulics and hydrology; structures, mechanics, and materials; transportation engineering.

University of Massachusetts Amherst, Graduate School, College of Engineering, Department of Civil and Environmental Engineering, Amherst, MA 01003. Offers civil engineering (MSCE, PhD); environmental and water resources engineering (MSCE); geotechnical engineering (MSCE); structural engineering and mechanics (MSCE); transportation engineering (MSCE). *Program availability:* Part-time. Terminal master's awarded for partial completion of doctoral program. *Degree requirements:* For master's, thesis or alternative; for doctorate, comprehensive exam, thesis/dissertation. *Entrance requirements:* For master's and doctorate, GRE General Test. Additional exam requirements/recommendations for international students: Required—TOEFL (minimum score 550 paper-based; 80 iBT), IELTS (minimum score 6.5). Electronic applications accepted.

University of Memphis, Graduate School, Herff College of Engineering, Department of Civil Engineering, Memphis, TN 38152. Offers civil engineering (PhD); engineering seismology (MS); environmental engineering (MS); freight transportation (Graduate Certificate); geotechnical engineering (MS); structural engineering (MS); transportation engineering (MS); water resources engineering (MS). *Students:* 14 full-time (3 women), 8 part-time (3 women); includes 1 minority (Black or African American, non-Hispanic/Latino), 12 international. Average age 27. 27 applicants, 70% accepted, 13 enrolled. In 2018, 11 master's awarded. Terminal master's awarded for partial completion of doctoral program. *Degree requirements:* For master's, comprehensive exam, thesis optional; for doctorate, comprehensive exam, thesis/dissertation. *Entrance requirements:* For master's, GRE General Test, minimum undergraduate GPA of 2.5; bachelor's degree in engineering or a related science or mathematics program; three letters of reference; for doctorate, GRE General Test, bachelor's degree in engineering or engineering science; three letters of reference; for Graduate Certificate, minimum undergraduate GPA of 2.75; bachelor's degree in engineering or engineering science. Additional exam requirements/recommendations for international students: Required—TOEFL (minimum score 550 paper-based; 79 iBT). *Application deadline:* For fall admission, 8/1 for domestic students; for spring admission, 12/1 for domestic students. Application fee: $35 ($60 for international students). Electronic applications accepted. *Expenses: Tuition, area resident:* Full-time $10,240; part-time $503 per credit hour. Tuition, state resident: full-time $10,464. Tuition, nonresident: full-time $20,224; part-time $991 per credit hour. *Required fees:* $850; $106 per credit hour. *Financial support:* Fellowships with full tuition reimbursements, research assistantships with full tuition reimbursements, career-related internships or fieldwork, Federal Work-Study, scholarships/grants, and unspecified assistantships available. Financial award application deadline: 2/1; financial award applicants required to submit FAFSA. *Faculty research:* Structural response to earthquakes, pavement design, water quality, transportation safety, intermodal transportation. *Unit head:* Dr. Shahram Pezeshk, Chair, 901-678-4727, Fax: 901-678-3026, E-mail: spezeshk@memphis.edu. *Application contact:* Dr. Roger Meier, Coordinator of Graduate Studies, 901-678-3284, E-mail: rwmeier@memphis.edu.
Website: https://www.memphis.edu/ce

University of Nevada, Las Vegas, Graduate College, Howard R. Hughes College of Engineering, Department of Civil and Environmental Engineering and Construction, Las Vegas, NV 89154-4015. Offers civil and environmental engineering (MS, PhD); civil and environmental engineering /transportation (MS). *Program availability:* Part-time. *Faculty:* 16 full-time (3 women), 4 part-time/adjunct (0 women). *Students:* 44 full-time (14 women), 39 part-time (8 women); includes 22 minority (2 Black or African American, non-Hispanic/Latino; 7 Asian, non-Hispanic/Latino; 9 Hispanic/Latino; 4 Two or more races, non-Hispanic/Latino), 39 international. Average age 30. 34 applicants, 68% accepted, 10 enrolled. In 2018, 11 master's, 7 doctorates awarded. *Degree requirements:* For master's, thesis (for some programs); for doctorate, comprehensive exam, thesis/dissertation, preliminary exam. *Entrance requirements:* For master's, GRE General Test, bachelor's degree with minimum GPA of 3.0; statement of purpose; letter of recommendation; for doctorate, GRE General Test, master's degree; statement of purpose; 3 letters of recommendation. Additional exam requirements/recommendations for international students: Required—TOEFL (minimum score 550 paper-based; 80 iBT), IELTS (minimum score 7). *Application deadline:* For fall admission, 6/15 for domestic students, 3/15 for international students; for spring admission, 11/15 for domestic students, 8/30 for international students. Application fee: $60 ($95 for international students). Electronic applications accepted. *Expenses:* Contact institution. *Financial support:* In 2018–19, 45 students received support, including 14 research assistantships with full tuition reimbursements available (averaging $16,710 per year), 31 teaching assistantships with full tuition reimbursements available (averaging $17,569

per year); institutionally sponsored loans, scholarships/grants, health care benefits, and unspecified assistantships also available. Financial award application deadline: 3/15; financial award applicants required to submit FAFSA. *Faculty research:* Construction performance improvement, water and waste water treatment, intelligent transportation, resilient infrastructure, hydroinformatics. *Total annual research expenditures:* $2.4 million. *Unit head:* Dr. Sajjad Ahmad, Chair/Professor, 702-895-5456, Fax: 702-895-3936, E-mail: ceec.chair@unlv.edu. *Application contact:* Dr. Pramen P. Shrestha, Graduate Coordinator, 702-895-3841, Fax: 702-895-3936, E-mail: ceec.gradcoord@unlv.edu.
Website: http://www.unlv.edu/ceec

University of New Brunswick Fredericton, School of Graduate Studies, Faculty of Engineering, Department of Civil Engineering, Fredericton, NB E3B 5A3, Canada. Offers construction engineering and management (M Eng, M Sc E, PhD); environmental engineering (M Eng, M Sc E, PhD); environmental studies (M Eng); geotechnical engineering (M Eng, M Sc E, PhD); groundwater/hydrology (M Eng, M Sc E, PhD); materials (M Eng, M Sc E, PhD); pavements (M Eng, M Sc E, PhD); structures (M Eng, M Sc E, PhD); transportation (M Eng, M Sc E, PhD). *Program availability:* Part-time. *Degree requirements:* For master's, thesis; for doctorate, comprehensive exam, thesis/dissertation, qualifying exam; 27 credit hours of courses. *Entrance requirements:* For master's, minimum GPA of 3.0; B Sc E in civil engineering or related engineering degree; for doctorate, minimum GPA of 3.0; graduate degree in engineering or applied science. Additional exam requirements/recommendations for international students: Required—IELTS (minimum score 7.5), TWE (minimum score 4), Michigan English Language Assessment Battery (minimum score 85) or CanTest (minimum score 4.5); Recommended—TOEFL (minimum score 580 paper-based). Electronic applications accepted. *Faculty research:* Construction engineering and management; engineering materials and infrastructure renewal; highway and pavement research; structures and solid mechanics; geotechnical and geoenvironmental engineering; structure interaction; transportation and planning; environment, solid waste management; structural engineering; water and environmental engineering.

University of Puerto Rico–Mayagüez, Graduate Studies, College of Engineering, Department of Civil Engineering and Surveying, Mayagüez, PR 00681-9000. Offers civil engineering (ME, MS, PhD), including construction engineering and management (ME, MS), environmental engineering, geotechnical engineering (ME, MS), structural engineering, transportation engineering. *Program availability:* Part-time. Terminal master's awarded for partial completion of doctoral program. *Degree requirements:* For master's, one foreign language, thesis; for doctorate, one foreign language, comprehensive exam, thesis/dissertation, qualifying exams. *Entrance requirements:* For master's, proficiency in English and Spanish; BS in civil engineering or its equivalent; for doctorate, proficiency in English and Spanish. Electronic applications accepted. *Faculty research:* Structural design, concrete structure, finite elements, dynamic analysis, transportation, soils.

University of Southern California, Graduate School, Sol Price School of Public Policy, Master of Planning Program, Los Angeles, CA 90089. Offers sustainable cities (Graduate Certificate); transportation systems (Graduate Certificate); urban planning (M Pl); M Arch/M Pl; M Pl/MA; M Pl/MPP; M Pl/MRED; M Pl/MS; M Pl/MSW; MBA/M Pl; ML Arch/M Pl; MPA/M Pl. *Accreditation:* ACSP. *Program availability:* Part-time. *Degree requirements:* For master's, comprehensive exam, internship. *Entrance requirements:* For master's, GRE, GMAT. Additional exam requirements/recommendations for international students: Required—TOEFL (minimum score 600 paper-based; 100 iBT). Electronic applications accepted. *Faculty research:* Transportation and infrastructure, comparative international development, healthy communities, social economic development, sustainable community planning.

University of Southern California, Graduate School, Viterbi School of Engineering, Daniel J. Epstein Department of Industrial and Systems Engineering, Los Angeles, CA 90089. Offers digital supply chain management (MS); engineering management (MS); engineering technology communication (Graduate Certificate); health systems operations (Graduate Certificate); industrial and systems engineering (MS, PhD, Engr); manufacturing engineering (MS); operations research engineering (MS); optimization and supply chain management (Graduate Certificate); product development engineering (MS); safety systems and security (MS); systems architecting and engineering (MS, Graduate Certificate); systems safety and security (Graduate Certificate); transportation systems (Graduate Certificate); MS/MBA. *Program availability:* Part-time, evening/weekend, online learning. Terminal master's awarded for partial completion of doctoral program. *Degree requirements:* For master's, thesis optional; for doctorate, thesis/dissertation. *Entrance requirements:* For master's and doctorate, GRE General Test. Additional exam requirements/recommendations for international students: Recommended—TOEFL. Electronic applications accepted. *Faculty research:* Health systems, music cognition and retrieval, transportation and logistics, manufacturing and automation, engineering systems design, risk and economic analysis.

University of Southern California, Graduate School, Viterbi School of Engineering, Sonny Astani Department of Civil and Environmental Engineering, Los Angeles, CA 90089. Offers applied mechanics (MS); civil engineering (MS, PhD); computer-aided engineering (ME, Graduate Certificate); construction management (MCM); engineering technology commercialization (Graduate Certificate); environmental engineering (MS, PhD); environmental quality management (ME); structural design (ME); sustainable cities (Graduate Certificate); transportation systems (MS, Graduate Certificate); water and waste management (MS). *Program availability:* Part-time, evening/weekend. Terminal master's awarded for partial completion of doctoral program. *Degree requirements:* For master's, thesis optional; for doctorate, thesis/dissertation. *Entrance requirements:* For master's and doctorate, GRE General Test. Additional exam requirements/recommendations for international students: Recommended—TOEFL. Electronic applications accepted. *Faculty research:* Geotechnical engineering, transportation engineering, structural engineering, construction management, environmental engineering, water resources.

University of South Florida, College of Engineering, Department of Civil and Environmental Engineering, Tampa, FL 33620-9951. Offers civil engineering (MCE, MSCE, PhD), including geotechnical engineering, materials science and engineering, structures engineering, transportation engineering, water resources; environmental engineering (MEVE, MSEV, PhD), including engineering for international development (MSEV). *Program availability:* Part-time. *Faculty:* 19 full-time (5 women). *Students:* 144 full-time (46 women), 76 part-time (22 women); includes 35 minority (8 Black or African American, non-Hispanic/Latino; 5 Asian, non-Hispanic/Latino; 18 Hispanic/Latino; 4 Two or more races, non-Hispanic/Latino), 123 international. Average age 28. 220 applicants, 65% accepted, 59 enrolled. In 2018, 82 master's, 15 doctorates awarded. Terminal master's awarded for partial completion of doctoral program. *Degree requirements:* For master's, comprehensive exam, thesis (for some programs); for doctorate, comprehensive exam, thesis/dissertation. *Entrance requirements:* For master's, GRE required, bachelor's degree in appropriate field, minimum GPA of 3.0 in major, letters of reference, statement of purpose, resume, intake form; for doctorate, GRE with V (45th percentile), Q (75th percentile), and AW (55th percentile), letters of recommendation, statement of purpose, resume, intake form. Additional exam requirements/recommendations for international students: Required—TOEFL, TOEFL (minimum score 550 paper-based; 79 iBT) or IELTS (minimum score 6.5). *Application deadline:* For fall admission, 2/15 for domestic students, 2/15 priority date for international students; for spring admission, 10/15 for domestic students, 9/15 priority date for international students. Application fee: $30. Electronic applications accepted. *Expenses:* Tuition, state resident: full-time $6350. Tuition, nonresident: full-time $19,048. *International tuition:* $19,048 full-time. *Required fees:* $2079. *Financial support:* In 2018–19, 45 students received support, including 44 research assistantships (averaging $14,123 per year), 21 teaching assistantships with tuition reimbursements available (averaging $15,329 per year). *Faculty research:* Environmental and water resources engineering, geotechnics and geoenvironmental systems, structures and materials systems, transportation systems. *Total annual research expenditures:* $3.7 million. *Unit head:* Dr. Manjriker Gunaratne, Professor and Department Chair, 813-974-5818, Fax: 813-974-2957, E-mail: gunaratn@usf.edu. *Application contact:* Dr. Sarina J. Ergas, Professor and Graduate Program Coordinator, 813-974-1119, Fax: 813-974-2957, E-mail: sergas@usf.edu.
Website: http://www.usf.edu/engineering/cee/

University of South Florida, Innovative Education, Tampa, FL 33620-9951. Offers adult, career and higher education (Graduate Certificate), including college teaching, leadership in developing human resources, leadership in higher education; Africana studies (Graduate Certificate), including diasporas and health disparities, genocide and human rights; aging studies (Graduate Certificate), including gerontology; art research (Graduate Certificate), including museum studies; business foundations (Graduate Certificate); chemical and biomedical engineering (Graduate Certificate), including materials science and engineering, water, health and sustainability; child and family studies (Graduate Certificate), including positive behavior support; civil and industrial engineering (Graduate Certificate), including transportation systems analysis; community and family health (Graduate Certificate), including maternal and child health, social marketing and public health, violence and injury: prevention and intervention, women's health; criminology (Graduate Certificate), including criminal justice administration; data science for public administration (Graduate Certificate); digital humanities (Graduate Certificate); educational measurement and research (Graduate Certificate), including evaluation; English (Graduate Certificate), including comparative literary studies, creative writing, professional and technical communication; entrepreneurship (Graduate Certificate); environmental health (Graduate Certificate), including safety management; epidemiology and biostatistics (Graduate Certificate), including applied biostatistics, biostatistics, concepts and tools of epidemiology, epidemiology, epidemiology of infectious diseases; geography, environment and planning (Graduate Certificate), including community development, environmental policy and management, geographical information systems; geology (Graduate Certificate), including hydrogeology; global health (Graduate Certificate), including disaster management, global health and Latin American and Caribbean studies, global health practice, humanitarian assistance, infection control; government and international affairs (Graduate Certificate), including Cuban studies, globalization studies; health policy and management (Graduate Certificate), including health management and leadership, public health policy and programs; hearing specialist: early intervention (Graduate Certificate); industrial and management systems engineering (Graduate Certificate), including systems engineering, technology management; information studies (Graduate Certificate), including school library media specialist; information systems/decision sciences (Graduate Certificate), including analytics and business intelligence; instructional technology (Graduate Certificate), including distance education, Florida digital/virtual educator, instructional design, multimedia design, Web design; internal medicine, bioethics and medical humanities (Graduate Certificate), including biomedical ethics; Latin American and Caribbean studies (Graduate Certificate); leadership for coastal resiliency planning (Graduate Certificate); mass communications (Graduate Certificate), including multimedia journalism; mathematics and statistics (Graduate Certificate), including mathematics; medicine (Graduate Certificate), including aging and neuroscience, bioinformatics, biotechnology, brain fitness and memory management, clinical investigation, hand and upper limb rehabilitation, health informatics, health sciences, integrative weight management, intellectual property, medicine and gender, metabolic and nutritional medicine, metabolic cardiology, pharmacy sciences; national and competitive intelligence (Graduate Certificate); nursing (Graduate Certificate), including simulation based academic fellowship in advanced pain management; psychological and social foundations (Graduate Certificate), including career counseling, college teaching, diversity in education, mental health counseling, school counseling; public affairs (Graduate Certificate), including nonprofit management, public management, research administration; public health (Graduate Certificate), including assessing chemical toxicity and public health risks, health equity, pharmacoepidemiology, public health generalist, toxicology, translational research in adolescent behavioral health; public health practices (Graduate Certificate), including planning for healthy communities; rehabilitation and mental health counseling (Graduate Certificate), including integrative mental health care, marriage and family therapy, rehabilitation technology; secondary education (Graduate Certificate), including ESOL, foreign language education: culture and content, foreign language education: professional; social work (Graduate Certificate), including geriatric social work/clinical gerontology; special education (Graduate Certificate), including autism spectrum disorder, disabilities education: severe/profound; world languages (Graduate Certificate), including teaching English as a second language (TESL) or foreign language. *Expenses:* Tuition, state resident: full-time $6350. Tuition, nonresident: full-time $19,048. *International tuition:* $19,048 full-time. *Required fees:* $2079. *Unit head:* Dr. Cynthia DeLuca, Associate Vice President and Assistant Vice Provost, 813-974-3077, Fax: 813-974-7061, E-mail: deluca@usf.edu. *Application contact:* Owen Hooper, Director, Summer and Alternative Calendar Programs, 813-974-6917, E-mail: hooper@usf.edu.
Website: http://www.usf.edu/innovative-education/

The University of Texas at Tyler, College of Engineering, Department of Civil Engineering, Tyler, TX 75799-0001. Offers environmental engineering (MS); industrial safety (MS); structural engineering (MS); transportation engineering (MS); water resources engineering (MS). *Program availability:* Part-time, evening/weekend. *Students:* 5 full-time (1 woman), 7 part-time (1 woman); includes 3 minority (1 Black or African American, non-Hispanic/Latino; 1 Asian, non-Hispanic/Latino; 1 Hispanic/Latino), 1 international. Average age 26. 5 applicants, 80% accepted, 3 enrolled. *Entrance requirements:* For master's, GRE General Test, bachelor's degree in engineering, associated science degree. Additional exam requirements/recommendations for international students: Required—TOEFL. *Application deadline:* For fall admission, 8/17 priority date for domestic students, 7/1 priority date for international students; for spring admission, 12/21 priority date for domestic students, 11/1 priority date for international students. Application fee: $25 ($50 for international students). *Financial support:* Application deadline: 7/1. *Faculty research:* Non-destructive strength testing, indoor air quality, transportation routing and signaling, pavement replacement criteria, flood water routing, construction and long-term behavior of innovative geotechnical foundation and embankment construction used in highway construction, engineering education. *Unit head:* Dr. Torey Nalbone, Chair, 903-565-5520, E-mail: tnalbone@uttyler.edu. *Application contact:* Dr. Torey Nalbone, Chair, 903-565-5520, E-mail: tnalbone@uttyler.edu.
Website: https://www.uttyler.edu/ce/

University of Washington, Graduate School, College of Engineering, Department of Civil and Environmental Engineering, Seattle, WA 98195-2700. Offers construction

engineering (MSCE, PhD); environmental engineering (MSCE, PhD); geotechnical engineering (MSCE, PhD); hydrology and hydrodynamics (MSCE, PhD); structural engineering and mechanics (MSCE, PhD); transportation engineering (MSCE, PhD). *Program availability:* Part-time, 100% online. *Faculty:* 38 full-time (10 women). *Students:* 239 full-time (104 women), 172 part-time (51 women); includes 91 minority (3 Black or African American, non-Hispanic/Latino; 2 American Indian or Alaska Native, non-Hispanic/Latino; 42 Asian, non-Hispanic/Latino; 26 Hispanic/Latino; 18 Two or more races, non-Hispanic/Latino), 120 international. Average age 28. 787 applicants, 57% accepted, 163 enrolled. In 2018, 161 master's, 11 doctorates awarded. Terminal master's awarded for partial completion of doctoral program. *Degree requirements:* For master's, thesis optional; for doctorate, comprehensive exam, thesis/dissertation, qualifying, general and final exams; completion of degree within 10 years. *Entrance requirements:* For master's, GRE General Test, minimum GPA of 3.0, statement of purpose, letters of recommendation, transcripts; for doctorate, GRE General Test, minimum GPA of 3.5, statement of purpose, letters of recommendation, transcripts, resume. Additional exam requirements/recommendations for international students: Required—TOEFL (minimum score 580 paper-based; 92 iBT); Recommended—IELTS (minimum score 7), TSE. *Application deadline:* For fall admission, 12/15 for domestic and international students. Applications are processed on a rolling basis. Application fee: $85. Electronic applications accepted. *Expenses:* Research-focused Master's and PhD: $18,852 resident; $32,760 nonresident. *Financial support:* In 2018–19, 120 students received support, including 23 fellowships with tuition reimbursements available (averaging $30,240 per year), 78 research assistantships with full tuition reimbursements available (averaging $30,240 per year), 28 teaching assistantships with full tuition reimbursements available (averaging $30,240 per year); scholarships/grants also available. Financial award application deadline: 12/15; financial award applicants required to submit FAFSA. *Faculty research:* Structural and geotechnical engineering, transportation and construction engineering, water and environmental engineering. *Total annual research expenditures:* $16.4 million. *Unit head:* Dr. Timothy V. Larson, Professor/Chair, 206-543-6815, Fax: 206-543-1543, E-mail: tlarson@uw.edu. *Application contact:* Melissa Pritchard, Graduate Adviser, 206-543-2574, Fax: 206-543-1543, E-mail: ceginfo@u.washington.edu.
Website: http://www.ce.washington.edu/

University of Wisconsin–Madison, Graduate School, College of Engineering, Department of Civil and Environmental Engineering, Madison, WI 53706-1380. Offers construction engineering and management (MS); environmental science and engineering (MS); geological/geotechnical engineering (MS); structural engineering (MS); transportation engineering (MS); water resources engineering (MS). *Program availability:* Part-time. *Faculty:* 31 full-time (8 women). *Students:* 97 full-time (28 women), 39 part-time (15 women); includes 12 minority (2 Black or African American, non-Hispanic/Latino; 3 Asian, non-Hispanic/Latino; 6 Hispanic/Latino; 1 Two or more races, non-Hispanic/Latino), 62 international. Average age 28. 261 applicants, 45% accepted, 29 enrolled. In 2018, 33 master's awarded. Terminal master's awarded for partial completion of doctoral program. *Degree requirements:* For master's, thesis (for some programs), minimum of 30 credits; minimum overall GPA of 3.0. *Entrance requirements:* For master's, GRE General Test, bachelor's degree; minimum GPA of 3.0 for last 60 credits of course work. Additional exam requirements/recommendations for international students: Required—TOEFL (minimum score 580 paper-based; 92 iBT). *Application deadline:* For fall admission, 12/15 priority date for domestic and international students; for spring admission, 10/1 for domestic and international students. Application fee: $75 ($81 for international students). Electronic applications accepted. *Expenses:* In-state tuition (Full-time): $10,728; Out-of-state tuition (full-time): $24,054; Fees: $1282; In-state tuition (per credit): $670; Out-of-state tuition (per credit): $1503; Fees (per credit): $126. *Financial support:* In 2018–19, 90 students received support, including 8 fellowships with full tuition reimbursements available (averaging $28,704 per year), 54 research assistantships with full tuition reimbursements available (averaging $23,784 per year), 21 teaching assistantships with full tuition reimbursements available (averaging $16,584 per year); Federal Work-Study, scholarships/grants, health care benefits, unspecified assistantships, and project assistantships also available. Support available to part-time students. Financial award application deadline: 12/1; financial award applicants required to submit FAFSA. *Faculty research:* Construction engineering and management; environmental engineering; structural engineering; transportation and city planning; water resources engineering; water chemistry. *Total annual research expenditures:* $12.5 million. *Unit head:* Dr. William Likos, Chair, 608-263-9490, Fax: 608-262-5199, E-mail: frontdesk@cee.wisc.edu. *Application contact:* Cheryl Loschko, Student Services Coordinator, 608-890-2420, E-mail: loschko@wisc.edu.
Website: https://www.engr.wisc.edu/department/civil-environmental-engineering/academics/ms-phd-civil-and-environmental-engineering/

Virginia Polytechnic Institute and State University, VT Online, Blacksburg, VA 24061. Offers advanced transportation systems (Certificate); aerospace engineering (MS); agricultural and life sciences (MSLFS); business information systems (Graduate Certificate); career and technical education (MS); civil engineering (MS); computer engineering (M Eng, MS); decision support systems (Graduate Certificate); eLearning leadership (MA); electrical engineering (M Eng, MS); engineering administration (MEA); environmental engineering (Certificate); environmental politics and policy (Graduate Certificate); environmental sciences and engineering (MS); foundations of political analysis (Graduate Certificate); health product risk management (Graduate Certificate); industrial and systems engineering (MS); information policy and society (Graduate Certificate); information security (Graduate Certificate); information technology (MIT); instructional technology (MA); integrative STEM education (MA Ed); liberal arts (Graduate Certificate); life sciences: health product risk management (MS); natural resources (MNR, Graduate Certificate); networking (Graduate Certificate); nonprofit and nongovernmental organization management (Graduate Certificate); ocean engineering (MS); political science (MA); security studies (Graduate Certificate); software development (Graduate Certificate). *Expenses:* Tuition, state resident: full-time $15,510; part-time $739.50 per credit hour. Tuition, nonresident: full-time $29,629; part-time $1490.25 per credit hour. *Required fees:* $2804; $550 per semester. Tuition and fees vary according to course load, campus/location and program. *Application contact:* Graduate Admissions and Academic Progress, 540-231-8636, E-mail: grads@vt.edu.
Website: http://www.vto.vt.edu/

Wentworth Institute of Technology, Master of Engineering in Civil Engineering Program, Boston, MA 02115-5998. Offers construction engineering (M Eng); infrastructure engineering (M Eng). *Program availability:* Part-time-only, evening/weekend. *Degree requirements:* For master's, thesis optional, capstone course. *Entrance requirements:* For master's, resume, statement of purpose, official transcripts, two professional recommendations, bachelor's degree, minimum GPA of 3.0, one year of professional experience in a technical role and/or technical organization. Additional exam requirements/recommendations for international students: Recommended—TOEFL (minimum score 550 paper-based). Electronic applications accepted. *Expenses:* Contact institution.

Water Resources Engineering

American University of Beirut, Graduate Programs, Maroun Semaan Faculty of Engineering and Architecture, Beirut, Lebanon. Offers applied energy (ME); civil engineering (PhD); electrical and computer engineering (PhD); energy studies (MS); engineering management (MEM); environmental and water resources (ME); environmental technology (MSES); mechanical engineering (ME, PhD); urban design (MUD); urban planning and policy (MUPP). For progreen diploma: LAU/AUC. *Program availability:* Part-time, 100% online. *Faculty:* 105 full-time (25 women), 102 part-time/adjunct (33 women). *Students:* 380 full-time (186 women), 100 part-time (38 women). Average age 27. 489 applicants, 64% accepted, 127 enrolled. In 2018, 109 master's, 14 doctorates awarded. Terminal master's awarded for partial completion of doctoral program. *Degree requirements:* For master's, one foreign language, comprehensive exam, thesis optional; for doctorate, one foreign language, comprehensive exam, thesis/dissertation. *Entrance requirements:* For doctorate, GRE. Additional exam requirements/recommendations for international students: Required—TOEFL (minimum score 575 paper-based; 88 iBT), AUB-EN; Recommended—IELTS (minimum score 7). *Application deadline:* For fall admission, 4/4 for domestic and international students; for spring admission, 11/3 for domestic and international students; for summer admission, 4/4 for domestic and international students. Application fee: $50. *Expenses: Tuition:* Full-time $17,748; part-time $986 per credit. *Required fees:* $762. Tuition and fees vary according to course load and program. *Financial support:* In 2018–19, 15 students received support, including 92 fellowships with full tuition reimbursements available (averaging $14,400 per year), 80 research assistantships with full and partial tuition reimbursements available (averaging $5,300 per year), 162 teaching assistantships with full and partial tuition reimbursements available (averaging $1,400 per year); scholarships/grants, tuition waivers (full and partial), and unspecified assistantships also available. Financial award application deadline: 4/4. *Faculty research:* All areas in engineering, architecture and design. *Total annual research expenditures:* $1.5 million. *Unit head:* Prof. Alan Shihade, Dean, 961-1-374374 Ext. 3400, Fax: 961-1-744462, E-mail: as20@aub.edu.lb. *Application contact:* Dr. Salim Kanaan, Director, Admissions Office, 961-1-374374 Ext. 2590, Fax: 961-1-750775, E-mail: sk00@aub.edu.lb.
Website: https://www.aub.edu.lb/msfea/pages/default.aspx

Carnegie Mellon University, Carnegie Institute of Technology, Department of Civil and Environmental Engineering, Pittsburgh, PA 15213. Offers advanced infrastructure systems (MS, PhD); advanced infrastructure systems technology development and application (MS); air quality engineering and science (MS); civil and environmental engineering (MS, PhD); civil and environmental engineering/engineering and public policy (PhD); civil engineering (MS, PhD); computational mechanics (MS, PhD); computational modeling and monitoring for resilient structural and material systems (MS); energy infrastructure systems (MS); environmental engineering (MS, PhD); environmental management and science (MS, PhD); IT-based sustainable global infrastructure and construction management (MS); sustainability and green design (MS); water quality engineering and science (MS). *Program availability:* Part-time. *Faculty:* 23 full-time (5 women), 12 part-time/adjunct (3 women). *Students:* 264 full-time (109 women); includes 24 minority (6 Black or African American, non-Hispanic/Latino; 13 Asian, non-Hispanic/Latino; 5 Hispanic/Latino), 208 international. Average age 25. 630 applicants, 64% accepted, 114 enrolled. In 2018, 112 master's, 15 doctorates awarded. Terminal master's awarded for partial completion of doctoral program. *Degree requirements:* For master's, thesis optional; for doctorate, comprehensive exam, thesis/dissertation, two-part qualifying exam, public defense of dissertation. *Entrance requirements:* For master's, GRE General Test, BS in engineering, science or mathematics; for doctorate, GRE General Test, BS or MS in engineering, science or mathematics. Additional exam requirements/recommendations for international students: Required—TOEFL (minimum score 84 iBT), TOEFL (minimum score 84 iBT) or IELTS (7.0). *Application deadline:* For fall admission, 1/5 priority date for domestic and international students; for spring admission, 9/15 priority date for domestic and international students. Applications are processed on a rolling basis. Application fee: $75. Electronic applications accepted. *Expenses:* Contact institution. *Financial support:* In 2018–19, 137 students received support. Fellowships with tuition reimbursements available, research assistantships with tuition reimbursements available, scholarships/grants, health care benefits, tuition waivers (full and partial), unspecified assistantships, and service assistantships available. Financial award application deadline: 1/5. *Faculty research:* Advanced infrastructure systems; environmental engineering, sustainability, and science; mechanics, materials, and computing. *Total annual research expenditures:* $7.4 million. *Unit head:* Dr. David A. Dzombak, Professor and Department Head, 412-268-2941, Fax: 412-268-7813, E-mail: dzombak@cmu.edu. *Application contact:* David A. Vey, Director of Graduate Programs, 412-268-2292, Fax: 412-268-7813, E-mail: dvey@andrew.cmu.edu.
Website: http://www.cmu.edu/cee/

Clemson University, Graduate School, College of Engineering, Computing and Applied Sciences, Glenn Department of Civil Engineering, Clemson, SC 29634. Offers civil engineering (MS, PhD), including construction engineering and management, construction materials, geotechnical engineering, structural engineering, transportation engineering, water resources engineering. *Program availability:* Part-time. *Faculty:* 20 full-time (3 women). *Students:* 109 full-time (23 women), 55 part-time (11 women); includes 9 minority (2 Black or African American, non-Hispanic/Latino; 2 Asian, non-Hispanic/Latino; 4 Hispanic/Latino; 1 Two or more races, non-Hispanic/Latino), 111 international. Average age 28. 283 applicants, 59% accepted, 53 enrolled. In 2018, 31 master's, 11 doctorates awarded. *Degree requirements:* For master's, thesis or alternative, oral exam, seminar; for doctorate, comprehensive exam, thesis/dissertation, oral exam, seminar. *Entrance requirements:* For master's and doctorate, GRE General Test, unofficial transcripts, letters of recommendation, statement of purpose. Additional exam requirements/recommendations for international students: Required—TOEFL (minimum score 80 paper-based; 80 iBT), PTE (minimum score 54); Recommended—IELTS (minimum score 6.5). *Application deadline:* For fall admission, 4/15 for domestic and international students; for spring admission, 9/15 for domestic and international students. Applications are processed on a rolling basis. Application fee: $80 ($90 for international students). Electronic applications accepted. *Expenses:* $6823 per semester full-time resident, $14023 per semester full-time non-resident, $833 per credit hour part-time resident, $1731 per credit hour part-time non-resident, online $1264 per credit hour, $4938 doctoral programs resident, $10405 doctoral programs non-resident,

$1144 full-time graduate assistant, other fees may apply per session. *Financial support:* In 2018–19, 104 students received support, including 20 fellowships with full and partial tuition reimbursements available (averaging $4,491 per year), 43 research assistantships with full and partial tuition reimbursements available (averaging $16,364 per year), 1 teaching assistantship with full and partial tuition reimbursement available (averaging $12,750 per year); career-related internships or fieldwork and unspecified assistantships also available. Financial award application deadline: 4/15. *Faculty research:* Applied fluid mechanics, construction materials, project management, structural and geotechnical engineering, transportation. *Total annual research expenditures:* $4.9 million. *Unit head:* Dr. Ronald Andrus, Interim Department Chair, 864-656-0488, E-mail: randrus@clemson.edu. *Application contact:* Dr. Abdul Khan, Graduate Program Coordinator, 864-656-3327, E-mail: abdkhan@clemson.edu.
Website: https://www.clemson.edu/cecas/departments/ce/

Cornell University, Graduate School, Graduate Fields of Engineering, Field of Civil and Environmental Engineering, Ithaca, NY 14853. Offers engineering management (M Eng, MS, PhD); environmental engineering (M Eng, MS, PhD); environmental fluid mechanics and hydrology (M Eng, MS, PhD); environmental systems engineering (M Eng, MS, PhD); geotechnical engineering (M Eng, MS, PhD); remote sensing (M Eng, MS, PhD); structural engineering (M Eng, MS, PhD); structural mechanics (M Eng, MS); transportation engineering (MS, PhD); transportation systems engineering (M Eng); water resource systems (M Eng, MS, PhD). Terminal master's awarded for partial completion of doctoral program. *Degree requirements:* For master's, thesis (MS); for doctorate, comprehensive exam, thesis/dissertation. *Entrance requirements:* For master's and doctorate, GRE General Test (recommended), 2 letters of recommendation. Additional exam requirements/recommendations for international students: Required—TOEFL (minimum score 600 paper-based; 77 iBT). Electronic applications accepted. *Faculty research:* Environmental engineering, geotechnical engineering, remote sensing, environmental fluid mechanics and hydrology, structural engineering.

Indiana University Bloomington, School of Public and Environmental Affairs, Environmental Science Programs, Bloomington, IN 47405. Offers applied ecology (MSES); energy (MSES); environmental chemistry, toxicology, and risk assessment (MSES); environmental science (PhD); hazardous materials management (Certificate); specialized environmental science (MSES); water resources (MSES); JD/MSES; MSES/MA; MSES/MPA; MSES/MS. *Program availability:* Part-time. Terminal master's awarded for partial completion of doctoral program. *Degree requirements:* For master's, capstone or thesis; internship; for doctorate, comprehensive exam, thesis/dissertation. *Entrance requirements:* For master's, GRE General Test or GMAT, official transcripts, 3 letters of recommendation, resume, personal statement; for doctorate, GRE General Test or LSAT, official transcripts, 3 letters of recommendation, resume or curriculum vitae, statement of purpose. Additional exam requirements/recommendations for international students: Required—TOEFL (minimum score 600 paper-based; 96 iBT); Recommended—IELTS (minimum score 7). Electronic applications accepted. *Faculty research:* Applied ecology, bio-geochemistry, toxicology, wetlands ecology, environmental microbiology, forest ecology, environmental chemistry.

Kansas State University, Graduate School, College of Engineering, Department of Civil Engineering, Manhattan, KS 66506. Offers civil engineering (MS, PhD); environmental engineering (MS, PhD); geotechnical engineering (MS, PhD); structural engineering (MS, PhD); transportation engineering (MS, PhD); water resources engineering (MS, PhD). *Program availability:* Part-time, evening/weekend, online learning. *Degree requirements:* For master's, thesis or alternative; for doctorate, thesis/dissertation. *Entrance requirements:* For master's, GRE General Test, bachelor's degree or course work in related engineering fields; for doctorate, GRE General Test. Additional exam requirements/recommendations for international students: Required—TOEFL (minimum score 550 paper-based; 79 iBT). Electronic applications accepted. *Faculty research:* Transportation and materials engineering, water resources engineering, environmental engineering, geotechnical engineering, structural engineering.

Kennesaw State University, Southern Polytechnic College of Engineering and Engineering Technology, Program in Civil Engineering, Kennesaw, GA 30144. Offers environmental engineering (MS); geotechnical engineering (MS); structural engineering (MS); transportation and pavement engineering (MS); water resources engineering (MS). *Program availability:* Online learning. *Students:* 13 full-time (2 women), 24 part-time (5 women); includes 20 minority (8 Black or African American, non-Hispanic/Latino; 5 Asian, non-Hispanic/Latino; 4 Hispanic/Latino; 3 Two or more races, non-Hispanic/Latino), 2 international. Average age 33. 21 applicants, 57% accepted, 1 enrolled. In 2018, 6 master's awarded. *Degree requirements:* For master's, thesis optional. *Entrance requirements:* Additional exam requirements/recommendations for international students: Required—TOEFL (minimum score 550 paper-based; 80 iBT), IELTS (minimum score 6.5). *Application deadline:* For fall admission, 11/1 for domestic and international students; for spring admission, 4/1 for domestic and international students. Applications are processed on a rolling basis. Application fee: $60. Electronic applications accepted. *Expenses: Tuition, area resident:* Full-time $6960; part-time $290 per credit hour. Tuition, state resident: full-time $6960; part-time $290 per credit hour. Tuition, nonresident: full-time $25,080; part-time $1045 per credit hour. *International tuition:* $25,080 full-time. *Required fees:* $2006; $1706 per semester. $853 per semester. *Unit head:* Metin Oguzmert, Coordinator, 470-578-5083, E-mail: moguzmer@kennesaw.edu. *Application contact:* Admissions Counselor, 470-578-4377, E-mail: ksugrad@kennesaw.edu.
Website: http://engineering.kennesaw.edu/civil-construction/degrees/ms-civil-engineering.php

Lawrence Technological University, College of Engineering, Southfield, MI 48075-1058. Offers architectural engineering (MS); automotive engineering (MS); biomedical engineering (MS); civil engineering (MA, MS, PhD), including environmental engineering (MS), geotechnical engineering (MS), structural engineering (MS), transportation engineering (MS), water resource engineering (MS); construction engineering management (MA); electrical and computer engineering (MS); engineering management (MEM); engineering technology (MS); fire engineering (MS); industrial engineering (MS), including healthcare systems; manufacturing systems (ME); mechanical engineering (MS, DE, PhD), including automotive engineering (MS), energy engineering (MS), manufacturing (DE), solid mechanics (MS), thermal/fluid systems (MS); mechatronic systems engineering (MS). *Program availability:* Part-time, evening/weekend. Terminal master's awarded for partial completion of doctoral program. *Degree requirements:* For master's, thesis optional; for doctorate, comprehensive exam, thesis/dissertation optional. *Entrance requirements:* Additional exam requirements/recommendations for international students: Required—TOEFL (minimum score 550 paper-based; 79 iBT), IELTS (minimum score 6.5). Electronic applications accepted. *Faculty research:* Innovative infrastructure and building structures and materials; connectivity and mobility; automotive systems modeling, simulation and testing; biomedical devices and materials; building mechanical/electrical systems.

Louisiana State University and Agricultural & Mechanical College, Graduate School, College of Engineering, Department of Civil and Environmental Engineering, Baton Rouge, LA 70803. Offers environmental engineering (MSCE, PhD); geotechnical engineering (MSCE, PhD); structural engineering and mechanics (MSCE, PhD); transportation engineering (MSCE, PhD); water resources (MSCE, PhD).

Marquette University, Graduate School, College of Engineering, Department of Civil and Environmental Engineering, Milwaukee, WI 53201-1881. Offers construction engineering and management (MS, PhD, Certificate); environmental engineering (MS, PhD); structural design (Certificate); structural engineering and structural mechanics (MS, PhD); transportation (Certificate); transportation engineering and materials (MS, PhD); waste and wastewater treatment processes (Certificate); water resources engineering (Certificate). *Program availability:* Part-time, evening/weekend. Terminal master's awarded for partial completion of doctoral program. *Degree requirements:* For master's, comprehensive exam (for some programs), thesis or alternative; for doctorate, thesis/dissertation. *Entrance requirements:* For master's, GRE General Test (recommended), minimum GPA of 3.0, official transcripts from all current and previous colleges/universities except Marquette, three letters of recommendation; for doctorate, GRE General Test, minimum GPA of 3.0, official transcripts from all current and previous colleges/universities except Marquette, three letters of recommendation, brief statement of purpose, submission of any English language publications authored by applicant (strongly recommended). Additional exam requirements/recommendations for international students: Required—TOEFL (minimum score 530 paper-based). Electronic applications accepted. *Faculty research:* Highway safety, highway performance, and intelligent transportation systems; surface mount technology; watershed management.

McGill University, Faculty of Graduate and Postdoctoral Studies, Faculty of Engineering, Department of Civil Engineering and Applied Mechanics, Montréal, QC H3A 2T5, Canada. Offers environmental engineering (M Eng, M Sc, PhD); fluid mechanics (M Sc); fluid mechanics and hydraulic engineering (M Eng, PhD); materials engineering (M Eng, PhD); rehabilitation of urban infrastructure (M Eng, PhD); soil behavior (M Eng, PhD); soil mechanics and foundations (M Eng, PhD); structures and structural mechanics (M Eng, PhD); water resources (M Sc); water resources engineering (M Eng, PhD).

New Mexico Institute of Mining and Technology, Center for Graduate Studies, Department of Civil and Environmental Engineering, Socorro, NM 87801. Offers environmental engineering (MS), including air quality engineering and science, hazardous waste engineering, water quality engineering and science. *Degree requirements:* For master's, thesis, thesis or independent study. *Entrance requirements:* Additional exam requirements/recommendations for international students: Required—TOEFL (minimum score 540 paper-based). *Faculty research:* Air quality, hazardous waste management, wastewater management and treatment, site remediation.

Ohio University, Graduate College, Russ College of Engineering and Technology, Department of Civil Engineering, Athens, OH 45701-2979. Offers civil engineering (PhD); construction engineering and management (MS); environmental (MS); geoenvironmental (MS); geotechnical (MS); mechanics (MS); structures (MS); transportation (MS); water resources (MS). *Program availability:* Part-time. *Degree requirements:* For master's, comprehensive exam (for some programs), thesis or alternative; for doctorate, comprehensive exam, thesis/dissertation. *Entrance requirements:* For master's, GRE General Test, minimum GPA of 3.0, 3 letters of recommendation; for doctorate, GRE General Test. Additional exam requirements/recommendations for international students: Required—TOEFL (minimum score 550 paper-based; 80 iBT) or IELTS (minimum score 6.5). Electronic applications accepted. *Faculty research:* Noise abatement, materials and environment, highway infrastructure, subsurface investigation (pavements, pipes, bridges).

Oregon State University, College of Engineering, Program in Biological and Ecological Engineering, Corvallis, OR 97331. Offers bio-based products and fuels (M Eng, MS, PhD); biological systems analysis (M Eng, MS, PhD); bioprocessing (M Eng, MS, PhD); ecosystems analysis and modeling (M Eng, MS, PhD); water quality (M Eng, MS, PhD); water resources (M Eng, MS, PhD). Terminal master's awarded for partial completion of doctoral program. *Entrance requirements:* For master's and doctorate, GRE, minimum GPA of 3.0 in last 90 hours. Additional exam requirements/recommendations for international students: Required—TOEFL (minimum score 80 iBT), IELTS (minimum score 6.5). *Expenses:* Contact institution. *Faculty research:* Bioengineering, water resources engineering, food engineering, cell culture and fermentation, vadose zone transport.

Oregon State University, Interdisciplinary/Institutional Programs, Program in Water Resources Engineering, Corvallis, OR 97331. Offers MS, PhD, JD/MS. *Entrance requirements:* For master's and doctorate, GRE. Additional exam requirements/recommendations for international students: Required—TOEFL (minimum score 80 iBT), IELTS (minimum score 6.5).

State University of New York College of Environmental Science and Forestry, Department of Environmental Resources Engineering, Syracuse, NY 13210-2779. Offers ecological engineering (MPS, MS, PhD); environmental management (MPS); environmental resources engineering (MPS, MS, PhD); geospatial information science and engineering (MPS, MS, PhD); water resources engineering (MPS, MS, PhD). *Program availability:* Part-time. *Faculty:* 9 full-time (1 woman), 3 part-time/adjunct (0 women). *Students:* 32 full-time (12 women), 8 part-time (0 women); includes 2 minority (1 Black or African American, non-Hispanic/Latino; 1 Asian, non-Hispanic/Latino), 19 international. Average age 41. 31 applicants, 58% accepted, 7 enrolled. In 2018, 11 master's, 1 doctorate awarded. Terminal master's awarded for partial completion of doctoral program. *Degree requirements:* For master's, thesis (for some programs); for doctorate, comprehensive exam, thesis/dissertation. *Entrance requirements:* For master's and doctorate, GRE General Test, minimum GPA of 3.0. Additional exam requirements/recommendations for international students: Required—TOEFL (minimum score 550 paper-based; 80 iBT), IELTS (minimum score 6). *Application deadline:* For fall admission, 1/15 priority date for domestic and international students; for spring admission, 11/1 priority date for domestic and international students. Applications are processed on a rolling basis. Application fee: $60. Electronic applications accepted. *Expenses: Tuition, area resident:* Full-time $11,090; part-time $462 per credit hour. Tuition, state resident: full-time $11,090; part-time $462 per credit hour. Tuition, nonresident: full-time $22,650; part-time $944 per credit hour. *International tuition:* $22,650 full-time. *Required fees:* $1733; $178.58 per credit hour. *Financial support:* In 2018–19, 9 students received support. Unspecified assistantships available. Financial award application deadline: 6/30; financial award applicants required to submit FAFSA. *Faculty research:* Ecological engineering, environmental resources engineering, geospatial information science and engineering, water resources engineering, environmental science. *Total annual research expenditures:* $508,995. *Unit head:* Dr. Lindi Quackenbush, Chair, 315-470-4727, Fax: 315-470-4710, E-mail: ljquackc@esf.edu. *Application contact:* Scott Shannon, Associate Provost for Instruction/Dean of the Graduate School, 315-470-6599, Fax: 315-470-6978, E-mail: esfgrad@esf.edu.
Website: http://www.esf.edu/ere

Stevens Institute of Technology, Graduate School, Charles V. Schaefer Jr. School of Engineering and Science, Department of Civil, Environmental, and Ocean Engineering, Program in Civil Engineering, Hoboken, NJ 07030. Offers civil engineering (PhD, Certificate), including geotechnical engineering (Certificate); geotechnical/geoenvironmental engineering (M Eng, Engr); hydrologic modeling (M Eng); stormwater management (M Eng); structural engineering (M Eng, Engr); transportation engineering (M Eng); water resources engineering (M Eng). *Program availability:* Part-time, evening/weekend. *Faculty:* 28 full-time (7 women), 2 part-time/adjunct (1 woman). *Students:* 37 full-time (8 women), 27 part-time (8 women); includes 8 minority (1 Black or African American, non-Hispanic/Latino; 1 American Indian or Alaska Native, non-Hispanic/Latino; 6 Asian, non-Hispanic/Latino), 30 international. Average age 25. In 2018, 44 master's awarded. Terminal master's awarded for partial completion of doctoral program. *Degree requirements:* For master's, thesis optional, minimum B average in major field and overall; for doctorate, comprehensive exam (for some programs), thesis/dissertation; for other advanced degree, minimum B average. *Entrance requirements:* For master's, GRE/GMAT scores: GRE scores are required for all applicants applying to a full-time graduate program in the Schaefer School of Engineering and Science (SES). International applicants must submit TOEFL/IELTS scores and fulfill the English Language Proficiency Requirements in order to be considered. Additional exam requirements/recommendations for international students: Required—TOEFL (minimum score 74 iBT), IELTS (minimum score 6). *Application deadline:* For fall admission, 4/15 for domestic and international students; for spring admission, 11/1 for domestic and international students; for summer admission, 5/1 for domestic students. Applications are processed on a rolling basis. Application fee: $60. Electronic applications accepted. *Expenses: Tuition:* Full-time $35,960; part-time $1620 per credit. *Required fees:* $1290; $600 per semester. Tuition and fees vary according to course load. *Financial support:* Fellowships, research assistantships, teaching assistantships, career-related internships or fieldwork, Federal Work-Study, scholarships/grants, and unspecified assistantships available. Financial award application deadline: 2/15; financial award applicants required to submit FAFSA. *Unit head:* Dr. Jean Zu, Dean of SES, 201-216.8233, Fax: 201-216.8372, E-mail: Jean.Zu@stevens.edu. *Application contact:* Graduate Admission, 888-783-8367, Fax: 888-511-1306, E-mail: graduate@stevens.edu.

Tufts University, School of Engineering, Department of Civil and Environmental Engineering, Medford, MA 02155. Offers bioengineering (MS), including environmental biotechnology; civil and environmental engineering (MS, PhD), including applied data science, environmental and water resources engineering, environmental health, geosystems engineering, structural engineering and mechanics; PhD/PhD. *Program availability:* Part-time. Terminal master's awarded for partial completion of doctoral program. *Degree requirements:* For master's, thesis (for some programs); for doctorate, thesis/dissertation. *Entrance requirements:* For master's and doctorate, GRE General Test. Additional exam requirements/recommendations for international students: Required—TOEFL (minimum score 550 paper-based; 80 iBT), IELTS (minimum score 6.5). Electronic applications accepted. *Expenses: Tuition:* Full-time $51,288; part-time $1710 per credit hour. *Required fees:* $904. Full-time tuition and fees vary according to degree level, program and student level. Part-time tuition and fees vary according to course load. *Faculty research:* Environmental and water resources engineering, environmental health, geotechnical and geoenvironmental engineering, structural engineering and mechanics, water diplomacy.

University at Buffalo, the State University of New York, Graduate School, School of Engineering and Applied Sciences, Department of Civil, Structural, and Environmental Engineering, Buffalo, NY 14260. Offers civil engineering (MS, PhD); engineering science (MS), including data sciences, green energy, Internet of Things, nanoelectronics; environmental and water resources engineering (MS). *Program availability:* Part-time, online learning. Terminal master's awarded for partial completion of doctoral program. *Degree requirements:* For master's, project, thesis, or comprehensive exam; for doctorate, thesis/dissertation. *Entrance requirements:* For master's and doctorate, GRE General Test, letters of reference. Additional exam requirements/recommendations for international students: Required—TOEFL (minimum score 550 paper-based; 79 iBT). Electronic applications accepted. *Faculty research:* Structural and earthquake engineering; geomechanics, geotechnical and geoenvironmental engineering; computational engineering mechanics; bridge engineering; environmental and water resources engineering; transportation systems engineering.

University of Alberta, Faculty of Graduate Studies and Research, Department of Civil and Environmental Engineering, Edmonton, AB T6G 2E1, Canada. Offers construction engineering and management (M Eng, M Sc, PhD); environmental engineering (M Eng, M Sc, PhD); environmental science (M Sc, PhD); geoenvironmental engineering (M Eng, M Sc, PhD); geotechnical engineering (M Eng, M Sc, PhD); mining engineering (M Eng, M Sc, PhD); petroleum engineering (M Eng, M Sc, PhD); structural engineering (M Eng, M Sc, PhD); water resources (M Eng, M Sc, PhD). *Program availability:* Part-time, online learning. *Degree requirements:* For master's, thesis (for some programs); for doctorate, thesis/dissertation. *Entrance requirements:* For master's, minimum GPA of 3.0 in last 2 years of undergraduate studies; for doctorate, minimum GPA of 3.0. Additional exam requirements/recommendations for international students: Required—TOEFL (minimum score 550 paper-based). Electronic applications accepted. *Faculty research:* Mining.

University of California, Berkeley, Graduate Division, College of Engineering, Department of Civil and Environmental Engineering, Berkeley, CA 94720. Offers engineering and project management (M Eng, MS, PhD); environmental engineering (M Eng, MS, PhD); geoengineering (M Eng, MS, PhD); structural engineering, mechanics and materials (M Eng, MS, PhD); transportation engineering (M Eng, MS, PhD); M Arch/MS; MCP/MS; MPP/MS. Terminal master's awarded for partial completion of doctoral program. *Degree requirements:* For master's, comprehensive exam (for some programs), thesis (for some programs), comprehensive exam or thesis (MS); for doctorate, thesis/dissertation, qualifying exam. *Entrance requirements:* For master's, GRE General Test, minimum GPA of 3.0, 3 letters of recommendation; for doctorate, GRE General Test, minimum GPA of 3.5, 3 letters of recommendation. Additional exam requirements/recommendations for international students: Required—TOEFL (minimum score 570 paper-based; 90 iBT). Electronic applications accepted.

University of Dayton, Department of Civil and Environmental Engineering and Engineering Mechanics, Dayton, OH 45469. Offers engineering mechanics (MSEM); environmental engineering (MSCE); geotechnical engineering (MSCE); structural engineering (MSCE); transportation engineering (MSCE); water resources engineering (MSCE). *Program availability:* Part-time, blended/hybrid learning. *Degree requirements:* For master's, thesis or alternative. *Entrance requirements:* For master's, minimum GPA of 3.0 in undergraduate work. Additional exam requirements/recommendations for international students: Required—TOEFL (minimum score 550 paper-based; 80 iBT); Recommended—IELTS (minimum score 6.5), TSE (minimum score 60). Electronic applications accepted. *Faculty research:* Infrastructure, environmental composite, reliability, computer simulation.

University of Delaware, College of Engineering, Department of Civil and Environmental Engineering, Newark, DE 19716. Offers environmental engineering (MAS, MCE, PhD); geotechnical engineering (MAS, MCE, PhD); ocean engineering (MAS, MCE, PhD); structural engineering (MAS, MCE, PhD); transportation engineering (MAS, MCE, PhD); water resource engineering (MAS, MCE, PhD). *Program availability:* Part-time. Terminal master's awarded for partial completion of doctoral program. *Degree requirements:* For master's, thesis; for doctorate, thesis/dissertation. *Entrance requirements:* For master's

and doctorate, GRE General Test. Additional exam requirements/recommendations for international students: Required—TOEFL. Electronic applications accepted. *Faculty research:* Structural engineering and mechanics; transportation engineering; ocean engineering; soil mechanics and foundation; water resources and environmental engineering.

University of Guelph, Office of Graduate and Postdoctoral Studies, College of Physical and Engineering Science, School of Engineering, Guelph, ON N1G 2W1, Canada. Offers biological engineering (M Eng, M Sc, MA Sc, PhD); engineering systems and computing (M Eng, M Sc, MA Sc, PhD); environmental engineering (M Eng, M Sc, MA Sc, PhD); water resources engineering (M Eng, M Sc, MA Sc, PhD). *Program availability:* Part-time. *Degree requirements:* For master's, thesis (for some programs); for doctorate, comprehensive exam, thesis/dissertation. *Entrance requirements:* For master's, minimum B- average during previous 2 years of course work; for doctorate, minimum B average. Additional exam requirements/recommendations for international students: Required—TOEFL (minimum score 550 paper-based; 89 iBT), IELTS (minimum score 6.5). Electronic applications accepted. *Faculty research:* Water and food safety, environmental contaminant fates and mechanisms, computer systems, robotics and mechatronics, waste treatment.

University of Idaho, College of Graduate Studies, College of Agricultural and Life Sciences, Water Resources Program, Moscow, ID 83844-300. Offers engineering and science (MS, PhD); law, management and policy (MS, PhD); science and management (MS, PhD). *Faculty:* 20 full-time (5 women). *Students:* 23 full-time, 7 part-time. Average age 32. In 2018, 7 master's, 2 doctorates awarded. *Entrance requirements:* For master's, minimum GPA of 3.0. Additional exam requirements/recommendations for international students: Required—TOEFL (minimum score 550 paper-based; 79 iBT), IELTS (minimum score 6.5), Michigan English Language Assessment Battery (minimum score of 77). *Application deadline:* For fall admission, 8/1 for domestic students; for spring admission, 12/15 for domestic students. Applications are processed on a rolling basis. Application fee: $60. Electronic applications accepted. *Expenses:* Tuition, state resident: full-time $7266.44; part-time $474.50 per credit hour. Tuition, nonresident: full-time $24,902; part-time $1453.50 per credit hour. *Required fees:* $2085.56; $45.50 per credit hour. *Financial support:* Applicants required to submit FAFSA. *Faculty research:* Water management, biological wastewater treatment and water reclamation, invasive species, aquatics ecosystem restoration, Fish ecology.
Website: https://www.uidaho.edu/cals/water-resources

The University of Iowa, Graduate College, College of Engineering, Department of Civil and Environmental Engineering, Iowa City, IA 52242-1316. Offers environmental engineering and science (MS, PhD); hydraulics and water resources (MS, PhD); structures, mechanics and materials (MS, PhD); sustainable water development (MS, PhD); transportation engineering (MS, PhD). *Program availability:* Part-time. Terminal master's awarded for partial completion of doctoral program. *Degree requirements:* For master's, thesis optional, exam; for doctorate, comprehensive exam, thesis/dissertation, exam. *Entrance requirements:* For master's, GRE (minimum combined score of 301 on verbal and quantitative), minimum undergraduate GPA of 3.0; for doctorate, GRE (minimum combined score of 301 on verbal and quantitative), minimum graduate GPA of 3.0. Additional exam requirements/recommendations for international students: Required—TOEFL (minimum score 550 paper-based; 81 iBT), IELTS (minimum score 7). Electronic applications accepted. *Faculty research:* Water resources; environmental engineering and science; hydraulics and hydrology; structures, mechanics, and materials; transportation engineering.

University of Massachusetts Amherst, Graduate School, College of Engineering, Department of Civil and Environmental Engineering, Amherst, MA 01003. Offers civil engineering (MSCE, PhD); environmental and water resources engineering (MSCE); geotechnical engineering (MSCE); structural engineering and mechanics (MSCE); transportation engineering (MSCE). *Program availability:* Part-time. Terminal master's awarded for partial completion of doctoral program. *Degree requirements:* For master's, thesis or alternative; for doctorate, comprehensive exam, thesis/dissertation. *Entrance requirements:* For master's and doctorate, GRE General Test. Additional exam requirements/recommendations for international students: Required—TOEFL (minimum score 550 paper-based; 80 iBT), IELTS (minimum score 6.5). Electronic applications accepted.

University of Memphis, Graduate School, Herff College of Engineering, Department of Civil Engineering, Memphis, TN 38152. Offers civil engineering (PhD); engineering seismology (MS); environmental engineering (MS); freight transportation (Graduate Certificate); geotechnical engineering (MS); structural engineering (MS); transportation engineering (MS); water resources engineering (MS). *Students:* 14 full-time (3 women), 8 part-time (3 women); includes 1 minority (Black or African American, non-Hispanic/Latino), 12 international. Average age 27. 27 applicants, 70% accepted, 13 enrolled. In 2018, 11 master's awarded. Terminal master's awarded for partial completion of doctoral program. *Degree requirements:* For master's, comprehensive exam, thesis optional; for doctorate, comprehensive exam, thesis/dissertation. *Entrance requirements:* For master's, GRE General Test, minimum undergraduate GPA of 2.5; bachelor's degree in engineering or a related science or mathematics program; three letters of reference; for doctorate, GRE General Test, bachelor's degree in engineering or engineering science; three letters of reference; for Graduate Certificate, minimum undergraduate GPA of 2.75; bachelor's degree in engineering or engineering science. Additional exam requirements/recommendations for international students: Required—TOEFL (minimum score 550 paper-based; 79 iBT). *Application deadline:* For fall admission, 8/1 for domestic students; for spring admission, 12/1 for domestic students. Application fee: $35 ($60 for international students). Electronic applications accepted. *Expenses: Tuition, area resident:* Full-time $10,240; part-time $503 per credit hour. Tuition, state resident: full-time $10,464. Tuition, nonresident: full-time $20,224; part-time $991 per credit hour. *Required fees:* $850; $106 per credit hour. *Financial support:* Fellowships with full tuition reimbursements, research assistantships with full tuition reimbursements, career-related internships or fieldwork, Federal Work-Study, scholarships/grants, and unspecified assistantships available. Financial award application deadline: 2/1; financial award applicants required to submit FAFSA. *Faculty research:* Structural response to earthquakes, pavement design, water quality, transportation safety, intermodal transportation. *Unit head:* Dr. Shahram Pezeshk, Chair, 901-678-4727, Fax: 901-678-3026, E-mail: spezeshk@memphis.edu. *Application contact:* Dr. Roger Meier, Coordinator of Graduate Studies, 901-678-3284, E-mail: rwmeier@memphis.edu.
Website: https://www.memphis.edu/ce

University of New Haven, Graduate School, Tagliatela College of Engineering, Program in Environmental Engineering, West Haven, CT 06516. Offers environmental engineering (MS); industrial and hazardous waste (MS); water and wastewater treatment (MS); water resources (MS). *Program availability:* Part-time, evening/weekend, 100% online. *Students:* 15 full-time (7 women), 32 part-time (13 women); includes 7 minority (2 Black or African American, non-Hispanic/Latino; 2 Asian, non-Hispanic/Latino; 3 Hispanic/Latino), 17 international. Average age 30. 67 applicants, 97% accepted, 11 enrolled. In 2018, 15 master's awarded. *Degree requirements:* For master's, thesis or alternative, research project. *Entrance requirements:* For master's, bachelor's degree in engineering. Additional exam requirements/recommendations for

international students: Required—TOEFL (minimum score 75 iBT), IELTS, PTE (minimum score 50). *Application deadline:* Applications are processed on a rolling basis. Application fee: $50. Electronic applications accepted. Application fee is waived when completed online. *Expenses: Tuition:* Full-time $16,470; part-time $915 per credit hour. *Required fees:* $230; $95 per term. *Financial support:* Research assistantships with partial tuition reimbursements, teaching assistantships with partial tuition reimbursements, career-related internships or fieldwork, Federal Work-Study, scholarships/grants, and unspecified assistantships available. Support available to part-time students. Financial award application deadline: 5/1; financial award applicants required to submit FAFSA. *Unit head:* Dr. Agamemnon Koutsospyros, Professor, 203-932-7398, E-mail: akoutsospyros@newhaven.edu. *Application contact:* Selina O'Toole, Senior Associate Director of Graduate Admissions, 203-932-7337, E-mail: sotoole@newhaven.edu.
Website: https://www.newhaven.edu/engineering/graduate-programs/environmental-engineering/

University of South Florida, College of Engineering, Department of Civil and Environmental Engineering, Tampa, FL 33620-9951. Offers civil engineering (MCE, MSCE, PhD), including geotechnical engineering, materials science and engineering, structures engineering, transportation engineering, water resources; environmental engineering (MEVE, MSEV, PhD), including engineering for international development (MSEV). *Program availability:* Part-time. *Faculty:* 19 full-time (5 women). *Students:* 144 full-time (46 women), 76 part-time (22 women); includes 35 minority (8 Black or African American, non-Hispanic/Latino; 5 Asian, non-Hispanic/Latino; 18 Hispanic/Latino; 4 Two or more races, non-Hispanic/Latino), 123 international. Average age 28. 220 applicants, 65% accepted, 59 enrolled. In 2018, 82 master's, 15 doctorates awarded. Terminal master's awarded for partial completion of doctoral program. *Degree requirements:* For master's, comprehensive exam, thesis (for some programs); for doctorate, comprehensive exam, thesis/dissertation. *Entrance requirements:* For master's, GRE required, bachelor's degree in appropriate field, minimum GPA of 3.0 in major, letters of reference, statement of purpose, resume, intake form; for doctorate, GRE with V (45th percentile), Q (75th percentile), and AW (55th percentile), letters of recommendation, statement of purpose, resume, intake form. Additional exam requirements/recommendations for international students: Required—TOEFL, TOEFL (minimum score 550 paper-based; 79 iBT) or IELTS (minimum score 6.5). *Application deadline:* For fall admission, 2/15 for domestic students, 2/15 priority date for international students; for spring admission, 10/15 for domestic students, 9/15 priority date for international students. Application fee: $30. Electronic applications accepted. *Expenses:* Tuition, state resident: full-time $6350. Tuition, nonresident: full-time $19,048. *International tuition:* $19,048 full-time. *Required fees:* $2079. *Financial support:* In 2018–19, 45 students received support, including 44 research assistantships (averaging $14,123 per year), 21 teaching assistantships with tuition reimbursements available (averaging $15,329 per year). *Faculty research:* Environmental and water resources engineering, geotechnics and geoenvironmental systems, structures and materials systems, transportation systems. *Total annual research expenditures:* $3.7 million. *Unit head:* Dr. Manjriker Gunaratne, Professor and Department Chair, 813-974-5818, Fax: 813-974-2957, E-mail: gunaratn@usf.edu. *Application contact:* Dr. Sarina J. Ergas, Professor and Graduate Program Coordinator, 813-974-1119, Fax: 813-974-2957, E-mail: sergas@usf.edu.
Website: http://www.usf.edu/engineering/cee/

University of South Florida, Innovative Education, Tampa, FL 33620-9951. Offers adult, career and higher education (Graduate Certificate), including college teaching, leadership in developing human resources, leadership in higher education; Africana studies (Graduate Certificate), including diasporas and health disparities, genocide and human rights; aging studies (Graduate Certificate), including gerontology; art research (Graduate Certificate), including museum studies; business foundations (Graduate Certificate); chemical and biomedical engineering (Graduate Certificate), including materials science and engineering, water, health and sustainability; child and family studies (Graduate Certificate), including positive behavior support; civil and industrial engineering (Graduate Certificate), including transportation systems analysis; community and family health (Graduate Certificate), including maternal and child health, social marketing and public health, violence and injury: prevention and intervention, women's health; criminology (Graduate Certificate), including criminal justice administration; data science for public administration (Graduate Certificate); digital humanities (Graduate Certificate); educational measurement and research (Graduate Certificate), including evaluation; English (Graduate Certificate), including comparative literary studies, creative writing, professional and technical communication; entrepreneurship (Graduate Certificate); environmental health (Graduate Certificate), including safety management; epidemiology and biostatistics (Graduate Certificate), including applied biostatistics, biostatistics, concepts and tools of epidemiology, epidemiology, epidemiology of infectious diseases; geography, environment and planning (Graduate Certificate), including community development, environmental policy and management, geographical information systems; geology (Graduate Certificate), including hydrogeology; global health (Graduate Certificate), including disaster management, global health and Latin American and Caribbean studies, global health practice, humanitarian assistance, infection control; government and international affairs (Graduate Certificate), including Cuban studies, globalization studies; health policy and management (Graduate Certificate), including health management and leadership, public health policy and programs; hearing specialist: early intervention (Graduate Certificate); industrial and management systems engineering (Graduate Certificate), including systems engineering, technology management; information studies (Graduate Certificate), including school library media specialist; information systems/decision sciences (Graduate Certificate), including analytics and business intelligence; instructional technology (Graduate Certificate), including distance education, Florida digital/virtual educator, instructional design, multimedia design, Web design; internal medicine, bioethics and medical humanities (Graduate Certificate), including biomedical ethics; Latin American and Caribbean studies (Graduate Certificate); leadership for coastal resiliency planning (Graduate Certificate); mass communications (Graduate Certificate), including multimedia journalism; mathematics and statistics (Graduate Certificate), including mathematics; medicine (Graduate Certificate), including aging and neuroscience, bioinformatics, biotechnology, brain fitness and memory management, clinical investigation, hand and upper limb rehabilitation, health informatics, health sciences, integrative weight management, intellectual property, medicine and gender, metabolic and nutritional medicine, metabolic cardiology, pharmacy sciences; national and competitive intelligence (Graduate Certificate); nursing (Graduate Certificate), including simulation based academic fellowship in advanced pain management; psychological and social foundations (Graduate Certificate), including career counseling, college teaching, diversity in education, mental health counseling, school counseling; public affairs (Graduate Certificate), including nonprofit management, public management, research administration; public health (Graduate Certificate), including assessing chemical toxicity and public health risks, health equity, pharmacoepidemiology, public health generalist, toxicology, translational research in adolescent behavioral health; public health practices (Graduate Certificate), including planning for healthy communities; rehabilitation and mental health counseling (Graduate Certificate), including integrative mental health care, marriage and family therapy, rehabilitation technology; secondary education (Graduate Certificate), including ESOL, foreign language education: culture and content, foreign language education: professional; social work (Graduate Certificate), including geriatric social work/clinical gerontology; special education (Graduate Certificate), including autism spectrum disorder, disabilities education: severe/profound; world languages (Graduate Certificate), including teaching English as a second language (TESL) or foreign language. *Expenses:* Tuition, state resident: full-time $6350. Tuition, nonresident: full-time $19,048. *International tuition:* $19,048 full-time. *Required fees:* $2079. *Unit head:* Dr. Cynthia DeLuca, Associate Vice President and Assistant Vice Provost, 813-974-3077, Fax: 813-974-7061, E-mail: deluca@usf.edu. *Application contact:* Owen Hooper, Director, Summer and Alternative Calendar Programs, 813-974-6917, E-mail: hooper@usf.edu.
Website: http://www.usf.edu/innovative-education/

University of South Florida, Patel College of Global Sustainability, Tampa, FL 33620-9951. Offers energy, global, water and sustainable tourism (Graduate Certificate); global sustainability (MA), including building sustainable enterprise, climate change and sustainability, coastal sustainability, entrepreneurship, food sustainability and security, sustainability policy, sustainable energy, sustainable tourism, water. *Faculty:* 1 full-time (0 women). *Students:* 64 full-time (33 women), 92 part-time (57 women); includes 32 minority (8 Black or African American, non-Hispanic/Latino; 3 Asian, non-Hispanic/Latino; 15 Hispanic/Latino; 6 Two or more races, non-Hispanic/Latino), 50 international. Average age 29. 119 applicants, 75% accepted, 60 enrolled. In 2018, 91 master's awarded. *Degree requirements:* For master's, comprehensive exam (for some programs), thesis or alternative, internship. *Entrance requirements:* For master's, GPA of at least 3.25 or greater; alternatively a GPA of at least 3.00 along with a GRE Verbal score of 153 (61 percentile) or higher, Quantitative of 153 (51 percentile) or higher and Analytical Writing of 3.5 or higher, all taken within 5 years of application; at least 2 letters of recommendation from professors or supervisors. Additional exam requirements/recommendations for international students: Required—TOEFL (minimum score 550 paper-based; 79 iBT). *Application deadline:* For fall admission, 6/1 for domestic students, 5/1 for international students; for spring admission, 10/15 for domestic students, 9/15 for international students. Electronic applications accepted. *Expenses:* Tuition, state resident: full-time $6350. Tuition, nonresident: full-time $19,048. *International tuition:* $19,048 full-time. *Required fees:* $2079. *Financial support:* In 2018–19, 35 students received support. *Faculty research:* Global sustainability, integrated resource management, systems thinking, green communities, entrepreneurship, ecotourism. *Total annual research expenditures:* $174,608. *Unit head:* Dr. Govindan Parayil, Dean, 813-974-9694, E-mail: gparayil@usf.edu. *Application contact:* Dr. Govindan Parayil, Dean, 813-974-9694, E-mail: gparayil@usf.edu.
Website: http://psgs.usf.edu/

The University of Texas at Austin, Graduate School, Cockrell School of Engineering, Department of Civil, Architectural and Environmental Engineering, Program in Environmental and Water Resources Engineering, Austin, TX 78712-1111. Offers MS, PhD. *Program availability:* Part-time. *Degree requirements:* For master's, thesis or alternative. *Entrance requirements:* For master's, GRE General Test. Additional exam requirements/recommendations for international students: Required—TOEFL. Electronic applications accepted.

The University of Texas at Tyler, College of Engineering, Department of Civil Engineering, Tyler, TX 75799-0001. Offers environmental engineering (MS); industrial safety (MS); structural engineering (MS); transportation engineering (MS); water resources engineering (MS). *Program availability:* Part-time, evening/weekend. *Students:* 5 full-time (1 woman), 7 part-time (1 woman); includes 3 minority (1 Black or African American, non-Hispanic/Latino; 1 Asian, non-Hispanic/Latino; 1 Hispanic/Latino), 1 international. Average age 26. 5 applicants, 80% accepted, 3 enrolled. *Entrance requirements:* For master's, GRE General Test, bachelor's degree in engineering, associated science degree. Additional exam requirements/recommendations for international students: Required—TOEFL. *Application deadline:* For fall admission, 8/17 priority date for domestic students, 7/1 priority date for international students; for spring admission, 12/21 priority date for domestic students, 11/1 priority date for international students. Application fee: $25 ($50 for international students). *Financial support:* Application deadline: 7/1. *Faculty research:* Non-destructive strength testing, indoor air quality, transportation routing and signaling, pavement replacement criteria, flood water routing, construction and long-term behavior of innovative geotechnical foundation and embankment construction used in highway construction, engineering education. *Unit head:* Dr. Torey Nalbone, Chair, 903-565-5520, E-mail: tnalbone@uttyler.edu. *Application contact:* Dr. Torey Nalbone, Chair, 903-565-5520, E-mail: tnalbone@uttyler.edu.
Website: https://www.uttyler.edu/ce/

University of Wisconsin–Madison, Graduate School, College of Engineering, Department of Civil and Environmental Engineering, Madison, WI 53706-1380. Offers construction engineering and management (MS); environmental science and engineering (MS); geological/geotechnical engineering (MS); structural engineering (MS); transportation engineering (MS); water resources engineering (MS). *Program availability:* Part-time. *Faculty:* 31 full-time (8 women). *Students:* 97 full-time (28 women), 39 part-time (15 women); includes 12 minority (2 Black or African American, non-Hispanic/Latino; 3 Asian, non-Hispanic/Latino; 6 Hispanic/Latino; 1 Two or more races, non-Hispanic/Latino), 62 international. Average age 28. 261 applicants, 45% accepted, 29 enrolled. In 2018, 33 master's awarded. Terminal master's awarded for partial completion of doctoral program. *Degree requirements:* For master's, thesis (for some programs), minimum of 30 credits; minimum overall GPA of 3.0. *Entrance requirements:* For master's, GRE General Test, bachelor's degree; minimum GPA of 3.0 for last 60 credits of course work. Additional exam requirements/recommendations for international students: Required—TOEFL (minimum score 580 paper-based; 92 iBT). *Application deadline:* For fall admission, 12/15 priority date for domestic and international students; for spring admission, 10/1 for domestic and international students. Application fee: $75 ($81 for international students). Electronic applications accepted. *Expenses:* In-state tuition (Full-time): $10,728; Out-of-state tuition (full-time): $24,054; Fees: $1282; In-state tuition (per credit): $670; Out-of-state tuition (per credit): $1503; Fees (per credit): $126. *Financial support:* In 2018–19, 90 students received support, including 8 fellowships with full tuition reimbursements available (averaging $28,704 per year), 54 research assistantships with full tuition reimbursements available (averaging $23,784 per year), 21 teaching assistantships with full tuition reimbursements available (averaging $16,584 per year); Federal Work-Study, scholarships/grants, health care benefits, unspecified assistantships, and project assistantships also available. Support available to part-time students. Financial award application deadline: 12/1; financial award applicants required to submit FAFSA. *Faculty research:* Construction engineering and management; environmental engineering; structural engineering; transportation and city planning; water resources engineering; water chemistry. *Total annual research expenditures:* $12.5 million. *Unit head:* Dr. William Likos, Chair, 608-263-9490, Fax: 608-262-5199, E-mail: frontdesk@cee.wisc.edu. *Application contact:* Cheryl Loschko, Student Services Coordinator, 608-890-2420, E-mail: loschko@wisc.edu.
Website: https://www.engr.wisc.edu/department/civil-environmental-engineering/academics/ms-phd-civil-and-environmental-engineering/

Water Resources Engineering

Villanova University, College of Engineering, Department of Civil and Environmental Engineering, Program in Water Resources and Environmental Engineering, Villanova, PA 19085-1699. Offers urban water resources design (Certificate); water resources and environmental engineering (MSWREE). *Program availability:* Part-time, evening/weekend, online learning. *Degree requirements:* For master's, thesis optional. *Entrance requirements:* For master's, GRE General Test (for applicants with degrees from foreign universities), BCE or bachelor's degree in science or related engineering field, minimum GPA of 3.0. Additional exam requirements/recommendations for international students: Required—TOEFL (minimum score 600 paper-based; 100 iBT). Electronic applications accepted. *Faculty research:* Photocatalytic decontamination and disinfection of water, urban storm water wetlands, economy and risk, removal and destruction of organic acids in water, sludge treatment.

Section 8
Computer Science and Information Technology

This section contains a directory of institutions offering graduate work in computer science and information technology, followed by in-depth entries submitted by institutions that chose to prepare detailed program descriptions. Additional information about programs listed in the directory but not augmented by an in-depth entry may be obtained by writing directly to the dean of a graduate school or chair of a department at the address given in the directory.

For programs offering related work, see also in this book *Electrical and Computer Engineering, Engineering and Applied Sciences,* and *Industrial Engineering.* In the other guides in this series:

Graduate Programs in the Humanities, Arts & Social Sciences
See *Communication and Media*

Graduate Programs in the Biological/Biomedical Sciences & Health-Related Medical Professions
See *Allied Health*

Graduate Programs in the Physical Sciences, Mathematics, Agricultural Sciences, the Environment & Natural Resources
See *Mathematical Sciences*

Graduate Programs in Business, Education, Information Studies, Law & Social Work
See *Business Administration and Management* and *Library and Information Studies*

CONTENTS

Artificial Intelligence/Robotics

The American University in Cairo, School of Sciences and Engineering, Cairo, Egypt. Offers biotechnology (MS); chemistry (MS); computer science (MS); computing (M Comp); construction engineering (M Eng, MS); electronics and communications engineering (M Eng); environmental engineering (MS); environmental system design (M Eng); mechanical engineering (M Eng, MS); nanotechnology (MS); physics (MS); robotics, control and smart systems (MS); sciences and engineering (PhD); sustainable development (MS, Graduate Diploma). *Program availability:* Part-time, evening/weekend. *Degree requirements:* For master's, comprehensive exam (for some programs), thesis (for some programs); for doctorate, comprehensive exam (for some programs), thesis/dissertation. *Entrance requirements:* Additional exam requirements/recommendations for international students: Required—TOEFL (minimum score 450 paper-based; 45 iBT), IELTS (minimum score 5). Electronic applications accepted. *Faculty research:* Construction, mechanical, and electronics engineering; physics; computer science; biotechnology; nanotechnology; chemistry; robotics.

Brandeis University, Rabb School of Continuing Studies, Division of Graduate Professional Studies, Master of Science in Robotic Software Engineering Program, Waltham, MA 02454-9110. Offers MS. *Program availability:* Part-time-only. *Entrance requirements:* For master's, bachelor's degree in computer science or software engineering, or 2-3 years of experience in software engineering and undergraduate courses in linear algebra, calculus, and probability/statistics, official transcripts, resume, statement of goals, letter of recommendation. Additional exam requirements/recommendations for international students: Required—TOEFL (minimum score 600 paper-based; 100 iBT), IELTS (minimum score 7), TWE (minimum score 4.5), PTE (minimum score 68). Electronic applications accepted. *Expenses:* Contact institution.

California State University, Northridge, Graduate Studies, College of Engineering and Computer Science, Department of Manufacturing Systems Engineering and Management, Northridge, CA 91330. Offers engineering automation (MS); engineering management (MS); manufacturing systems engineering (MS); materials engineering (MS). *Program availability:* Online learning. *Entrance requirements:* For master's, GRE (if cumulative undergraduate GPA less than 3.0).

Carnegie Mellon University, Dietrich College of Humanities and Social Sciences, Department of Statistics, Pittsburgh, PA 15213-3891. Offers machine learning and statistics (PhD); mathematical finance (PhD); statistics (MS, PhD), including applied statistics (PhD), computational statistics (PhD), theoretical statistics (PhD); statistics and public policy (PhD). Terminal master's awarded for partial completion of doctoral program. *Degree requirements:* For doctorate, comprehensive exam, thesis/dissertation. *Entrance requirements:* For master's and doctorate, GRE General Test. Additional exam requirements/recommendations for international students: Required—TOEFL. *Faculty research:* Stochastic processes, Bayesian statistics, statistical computing, decision theory, psychiatric statistics.

Carnegie Mellon University, School of Computer Science, Department of Machine Learning, Pittsburgh, PA 15213-3891. Offers MS, PhD.

Carnegie Mellon University, School of Computer Science, Program in Automated Science: Biological Experimentation, Pittsburgh, PA 15213-3891. Offers MS.

Carnegie Mellon University, School of Computer Science, Robotics Institute, Pittsburgh, PA 15213-3891. Offers computer vision (MS); robotic systems development (MS); robotics (MS, PhD); robotics technology (MS). *Degree requirements:* For doctorate, thesis/dissertation. *Entrance requirements:* For doctorate, GRE General Test, GRE Subject Test. Additional exam requirements/recommendations for international students: Required—TOEFL. *Faculty research:* Perception, cognition, manipulation, robot systems, manufacturing.

College of Staten Island of the City University of New York, Graduate Programs, Division of Science and Technology, Program in Computer Science, Staten Island, NY 10314-6600. Offers computer science (MS), including artificial intelligence and data analytics, cloud computing and software engineering, cybersecurity and networks. *Program availability:* Part-time, evening/weekend. *Students:* 35. 48 applicants, 48% accepted, 14 enrolled. In 2018, 17 master's awarded. *Degree requirements:* For master's, thesis optional, a program of 10 courses (30 credits) with at least a 3.0 (B) average. Exceptional students may be permitted to satisfy six credits of the total credit requirement with a master's thesis. *Entrance requirements:* For master's, GRE General Test, BS in Computer Science or related area with a B average (3.0 out of 4.0) overall and in the major. Additional exam requirements/recommendations for international students: Required—TOEFL (minimum score 550 paper-based; 79 iBT), IELTS (minimum score 6.5). *Application deadline:* For fall admission, 7/20 priority date for domestic students, 4/25 for international students; for spring admission, 11/2 priority date for domestic students, 11/2 for international students. Applications are processed on a rolling basis. Application fee: $75. Electronic applications accepted. *Expenses:* Tuition, area resident: Full-time $10,770; part-time $455 per credit. Tuition, state resident: full-time $10,770; part-time $455 per credit. Tuition, nonresident: full-time $19,920; part-time $830 per credit. International tuition: $19,920 full-time. Required fees: $559.20; $181.10 per semester. Tuition and fees vary according to program. *Faculty research:* Big data, pattern recognition, text mining and frequent pattern mining; graph theory; computer vision, image processing pattern recognition and serious game; parallel computing and stimulation; high performance computing and modeling simulation; serious games; security, cryptography and communication networks; scheduling algorithms; scheduling, operations research and graph theory. *Unit head:* Dr. Xiaowen Zhang, Associate Professor, 718-982-3262, E-mail: xiaowen.zhang@csi.cuny.edu. *Application contact:* Sasha Spence, Associate Director for Graduate Admissions, 718-982-2019, Fax: 718-982-2500, E-mail: sasha.spence@csi.cuny.edu. Website: https://www.csi.cuny.edu/sites/default/files/pdf/admissions/grad/pdf/Computer%20Science%20Fact%20Sheet.pdf

Cornell University, Graduate School, Graduate Fields of Engineering, Field of Computer Science, Ithaca, NY 14853. Offers algorithms (M Eng, PhD); applied logic and automated reasoning (M Eng, PhD); artificial intelligence (M Eng, PhD); computer graphics (M Eng, PhD); computer science (M Eng, PhD); computer vision (M Eng, PhD); concurrency and distributed computing (M Eng, PhD); information organization and retrieval (M Eng, PhD); operating systems (M Eng, PhD); parallel computing (M Eng, PhD); programming environments (M Eng, PhD); programming languages and methodology (M Eng, PhD); robotics (M Eng, PhD); scientific computing (M Eng, PhD); theory of computation (M Eng, PhD). *Degree requirements:* For doctorate, comprehensive exam, thesis/dissertation. *Entrance requirements:* For master's, GRE General Test, 2 letters of recommendation; for doctorate, GRE General Test, GRE Subject Test (computer science or mathematics), 3 letters of recommendation. Additional exam requirements/recommendations for international students: Required—TOEFL (minimum score 505 paper-based; 77 iBT). Electronic applications accepted. *Faculty research:* Artificial intelligence, operating systems and databases, programming languages and security, scientific computing, theory of computing, computational biology and graphics.

Georgia Institute of Technology, Graduate Studies, College of Computing, Multidisciplinary Program in Robotics, Atlanta, GA 30332-0001. Offers PhD. Program offered jointly with College of Computing, School of Aerospace Engineering, Wallace H. Coulter Department of Biomedical Engineering, George W. Woodruff School of Mechanical Engineering, and School of Electrical and Computer Engineering. *Program availability:* Part-time. *Degree requirements:* For doctorate, comprehensive exam, thesis/dissertation. *Entrance requirements:* For doctorate, GRE General Test. Additional exam requirements/recommendations for international students: Required—TOEFL (minimum score 600 paper-based; 100 iBT). Electronic applications accepted.

Illinois Institute of Technology, Graduate College, College of Science, Department of Computer Science, Chicago, IL 60616. Offers business (MCS); computational intelligence (MCS); computer science (MCS, MS, PhD); cyber-physical systems (MCS); data analytics (MCS); data science (MAS); database systems (MCS); distributed and cloud computing (MCS); education (MCS); finance (MCS); information security and assurance (MCS); networking and communications (MCS); software engineering (MCS); telecommunications and software engineering (MAS); MS/MAS. *Program availability:* Part-time, evening/weekend, online learning. Terminal master's awarded for partial completion of doctoral program. *Degree requirements:* For master's, thesis optional; for doctorate, comprehensive exam, thesis/dissertation. *Entrance requirements:* For master's, GRE General Test with minimum scores of 298 Quantitative and Verbal, 3.0 Analytical Writing (for MS); GRE General Test with minimum scores of 292 Quantitative and Verbal, 2.5 Analytical Writing (for MAS), minimum undergraduate GPA of 3.0; for doctorate, GRE General Test (minimum scores: 304 Quantitative and Verbal, 3.5 Analytical Writing), minimum undergraduate GPA of 3.0. Additional exam requirements/recommendations for international students: Required—TOEFL (minimum score 523 paper-based; 70 iBT). Electronic applications accepted. *Faculty research:* Parallel and distributed processing, high-performance computing, computational linguistics, information retrieval, data mining, grid computing.

Indiana University Bloomington, School of Informatics, Computing, and Engineering, Program in Intelligent Systems Engineering, Bloomington, IN 47405-7000. Offers PhD. *Program availability:* Part-time. *Degree requirements:* For doctorate, thesis/dissertation, qualifying exam. *Entrance requirements:* For doctorate, GRE, statement of purpose, curriculum vitae, 3 letters of recommendation, transcripts. Additional exam requirements/recommendations for international students: Required—TOEFL. Electronic applications accepted. *Faculty research:* Data mining, data modeling, computer networks, biophysics, biocomplexity, high performance computing, large scale computing, parallel and distributed computing, bioengineering, systems biology, computational, toxicology, experimental imaging analysis, medical modeling and data analysis, cyberinfrastructure, neuroengineering, 3D pranging, nanoengineering, high performance hardware, computer engineering, intelligent systems multimedia.

Instituto Tecnológico y de Estudios Superiores de Monterrey, Campus Monterrey, Graduate and Research Division, Program in Computer Science, Monterrey, Mexico. Offers artificial intelligence (PhD); computer science (MS); information systems (MS); information technology (MS). *Program availability:* Part-time. *Degree requirements:* For master's, one foreign language, thesis; for doctorate, one foreign language, thesis/dissertation. *Entrance requirements:* For master's, EXADEP; for doctorate, master's degree in related field. Additional exam requirements/recommendations for international students: Required—TOEFL. *Faculty research:* Distributed systems, software engineering, decision support systems.

Instituto Tecnológico y de Estudios Superiores de Monterrey, Campus Monterrey, Graduate and Research Division, Programs in Engineering, Monterrey, Mexico. Offers applied statistics (M Eng); artificial intelligence (PhD); automation engineering (M Eng); chemical engineering (M Eng); civil engineering (M Eng); electrical engineering (M Eng); electronic engineering (M Eng); environmental engineering (M Eng); industrial engineering (M Eng, PhD); manufacturing engineering (M Eng); mechanical engineering (M Eng); systems and quality engineering (M Eng). M Eng program offered jointly with University of Waterloo; PhD in industrial engineering with Texas A&M University. *Program availability:* Part-time, evening/weekend. Terminal master's awarded for partial completion of doctoral program. *Degree requirements:* For master's, one foreign language, thesis; for doctorate, one foreign language, thesis/dissertation. *Entrance requirements:* For master's, EXADEP; for doctorate, GRE, master's degree in related field. Additional exam requirements/recommendations for international students: Required—TOEFL. *Faculty research:* Flexible manufacturing cells, materials, statistical methods, environmental prevention, control and evaluation.

Johns Hopkins University, G. W. C. Whiting School of Engineering, Master of Science in Engineering in Robotics Program, Baltimore, MD 21218. Offers robotics (MSE). *Students:* 54 full-time (13 women), 4 part-time (1 woman). 150 applicants, 54% accepted, 45 enrolled. In 2018, 44 master's awarded. *Degree requirements:* For master's, thesis optional, 10 courses or 8 courses and an essay. *Entrance requirements:* For master's, GRE, proficiencies in multivariable integral and differential calculus, linear algebra, ordinary differential equations, physics, probability and statistics, basic numerical methods using existing programming environments, and standard programming languages (C++, Java, or MATLAB); 3 letters of recommendation; statement of purpose; transcripts. Additional exam requirements/recommendations for international students: Required—IELTS preferred (minimum score 7) or TOEFL (minimum score 600 paper-based; 100 iBT). *Application deadline:* For fall admission, 12/17 for domestic and international students. Application fee: $75. Electronic applications accepted. *Financial support:* Scholarships/grants available. *Faculty research:* Perception and cognitive systems; medical robotics; dynamical systems and controls; biorobotics; aerospace and marine robotics systems. *Unit head:* Dr. Russ Taylor, Director, 410-516-4639, E-mail: rht@jhu.edu. *Application contact:* Alison Morrow, Robotics Academic Manager, 410-516-4639, E-mail: alison.morrow@jhu.edu. Website: https://www.lcsr.jhu.edu/

Lawrence Technological University, College of Arts and Sciences, Southfield, MI 48075-1058. Offers bioinformatics (Graduate Certificate); computer science (MS), including data science, big data, and data mining, intelligent systems; educational technology (MA), including robotics; instructional design, communication, and presentation (Graduate Certificate); integrated science (MA); science education (MA); technical and professional communication (MS, Graduate Certificate); writing for the digital age (Graduate Certificate). *Program availability:* Part-time, evening/weekend. *Degree requirements:* For master's, thesis (for some programs). *Entrance requirements:* Additional exam requirements/recommendations for international students: Required—TOEFL (minimum score 550 paper-based; 79 iBT), IELTS (minimum score 6.5). Electronic applications accepted. *Faculty research:* Computer analysis of music, machine learning of literature and lyrics, customer sentiments and response analysis through social media, peta-scale computing in astronomical databases, early detection of diseases with pattern recognition.

New York University, Tandon School of Engineering, Department of Mechanical and Aerospace Engineering, New York, NY 10012-1019. Offers mechanical engineering (MS, PhD); mechatronics and robotics (MS). *Program availability:* Part-time, evening/weekend. *Faculty:* 18 full-time (2 women), 11 part-time/adjunct (3 women). *Students:* 116 full-time (22 women), 15 part-time (3 women); includes 12 minority (8 Asian, non-Hispanic/Latino; 3 Hispanic/Latino; 1 Two or more races, non-Hispanic/Latino), 98 international. Average age 25. 563 applicants, 45% accepted, 59 enrolled. In 2018, 66 master's, 3 doctorates awarded. *Degree requirements:* For master's, comprehensive exam (for some programs), thesis (for some programs); for doctorate, comprehensive exam, thesis/dissertation. *Entrance requirements:* Additional exam requirements/recommendations for international students: Required—TOEFL (minimum score 550 paper-based; 90 iBT); Recommended—IELTS (minimum score 7). *Application deadline:* For fall admission, 2/15 priority date for domestic and international students; for spring admission, 11/1 priority date for domestic and international students. Applications are processed on a rolling basis. Application fee: $75. Electronic applications accepted. *Expenses:* Contact institution. *Financial support:* In 2018–19, 74 students received support. Fellowships, research assistantships, teaching assistantships, career-related internships or fieldwork, scholarships/grants, tuition waivers, and unspecified assistantships available. Support available to part-time students. Financial award application deadline: 2/15. *Faculty research:* Underwater applications of dynamical systems, systems science approaches to understanding variation in state traffic and alcohol policies, development of ankle instability rehabilitation robot, synthetic osteochondral grafts for knee osteoarthritis. *Total annual research expenditures:* $11.8 million. *Unit head:* Dr. Richard S. Thorsen, Department Chair, 646-997-3090, E-mail: rthorsen@nyu.edu. *Application contact:* Elizabeth Ensweiler, Senior Director of Graduate Enrollment and Graduate Admissions, 646-997-3182, E-mail: elizabeth.ensweiler@nyu.edu.

Northwestern University, McCormick School of Engineering and Applied Science, Department of Mechanical Engineering, MS in Robotics Program, Evanston, IL 60208. Offers MS. *Entrance requirements:* For master's, GRE General Test (recommended). Additional exam requirements/recommendations for international students: Required—TOEFL (minimum score 100 iBT), IELTS (minimum score 7). Electronic applications accepted.

Oregon State University, College of Engineering, Program in Robotics, Corvallis, OR 97331. Offers M Eng, MS, PhD. *Entrance requirements:* For master's and doctorate, GRE. *Expenses:* Contact institution.

Portland State University, Graduate Studies, College of Liberal Arts and Sciences, Systems Science Program, Portland, OR 97207-0751. Offers computational intelligence (Certificate; computer modeling and simulation (Certificate); systems science (MS); systems science/anthropology (PhD); systems science/business administration (PhD); systems science/civil engineering (PhD); systems science/economics (PhD); systems science/engineering management (PhD); systems science/general (PhD); systems science/mathematical sciences (PhD); systems science/mechanical engineering (PhD); systems science/psychology (PhD); systems science/sociology (PhD). *Degree requirements:* For master's, comprehensive exam (for some programs), thesis optional; for doctorate, variable foreign language requirement, comprehensive exam (for some programs), thesis/dissertation. *Entrance requirements:* For master's, GRE/GMAT (recommended), minimum GPA of 3.0 on undergraduate or graduate work, 2 letters of recommendation, statement of interest; for doctorate, GMAT, GRE General Test, minimum GPA of 3.0 undergraduate, 3.25 graduate; 3 letters of recommendation; statement of interest. Additional exam requirements/recommendations for international students: Required—TOEFL (minimum score 550 paper-based; 80 iBT). Electronic applications accepted. *Faculty research:* Systems theory and methodology, artificial intelligence neural networks, information theory, nonlinear dynamics/chaos, modeling and simulation.

Queen's University at Kingston, Smith School of Business, Master of Management in Artificial Intelligence Program, Kingston, ON K7L 3N6, Canada. Offers MM.

South Dakota School of Mines and Technology, Graduate Division, Program in Computational Sciences and Robotics, Rapid City, SD 57701-3995. Offers MS. *Program availability:* Part-time. *Entrance requirements:* Additional exam requirements/recommendations for international students: Required—TOEFL (minimum score 520 paper-based; 68 iBT), TWE. Electronic applications accepted.

Stevens Institute of Technology, Graduate School, Charles V. Schaefer Jr. School of Engineering and Science, Department of Electrical and Computer Engineering, Program in Electrical Engineering, Hoboken, NJ 07030. Offers autonomous robotics (Certificate); electrical engineering (M Eng, PhD, Certificate), including computer architecture and digital systems (M Eng), microelectronics and photonics science and technology (M Eng), signal processing for communications (M Eng), telecommunications systems engineering (M Eng), wireless communications (M Eng, Certificate). *Program availability:* Part-time, evening/weekend. *Faculty:* 19 full-time (5 women), 5 part-time/adjunct (1 woman). *Students:* 149 full-time (25 women), 23 part-time (4 women); includes 8 minority (1 Black or African American, non-Hispanic/Latino; 6 Asian, non-Hispanic/Latino; 1 Hispanic/Latino), 143 international. Average age 25. In 2018, 68 master's, 1 doctorate, 29 other advanced degrees awarded. Terminal master's awarded for partial completion of doctoral program. *Degree requirements:* For master's, thesis optional, minimum B average in major field and overall; for doctorate, comprehensive exam (for some programs), thesis/dissertation; for Certificate, minimum B average. *Entrance requirements:* For master's, GRE/GMAT scores: GRE scores are required for all applicants applying to a full-time graduate program in the Schaefer School of Engineering and Science (SES). International applicants must submit TOEFL/IELTS scores and fulfill the English Language Proficiency Requirements in order to be considered. Additional exam requirements/recommendations for international students: Required—TOEFL (minimum score 74 iBT), IELTS (minimum score 6). *Application deadline:* For fall admission, 4/15 for domestic and international students; for spring admission, 11/1 for domestic and international students; for summer admission, 5/1 for domestic students. Applications are processed on a rolling basis. Application fee: $60. Electronic applications accepted. *Expenses: Tuition:* Full-time $35,960; part-time $1620 per credit. *Required fees:* $1290; $600 per semester. Tuition and fees vary according to course load. *Financial support:* Fellowships, research assistantships, teaching assistantships, career-related internships or fieldwork, Federal Work-Study, scholarships/grants, and unspecified assistantships available. Financial award application deadline: 2/15; financial award applicants required to submit FAFSA. *Unit head:* Dr. Jean Zu, Dean of SES, 201-216.8233, Fax: 201-216.8372, E-mail: Jean.Zu@stevens.edu. *Application contact:* Graduate Admissions, 888-783-8367, Fax: 888-511-1306, E-mail: graduate@stevens.edu.

Temple University, College of Science and Technology, Department of Computer and Information Sciences, Philadelphia, PA 19122. Offers computational data science (MS); computer and information sciences (PhD), including artificial intelligence, computer and network systems, information systems, software systems; computer science (MS); cyber defense and information assurance (PSM); information science and technology (MS). *Program availability:* Part-time, evening/weekend, online learning. *Faculty:* 31 full-time (7 women), 10 part-time/adjunct (2 women). *Students:* 92 full-time (28 women), 15 part-time (3 women); includes 7 minority (2 Black or African American, non-Hispanic/Latino; 4 Asian, non-Hispanic/Latino; 1 Hispanic/Latino), 82 international. 119 applicants, 43% accepted, 21 enrolled. In 2018, 20 master's, 5 doctorates awarded. *Degree requirements:* For doctorate, thesis/dissertation. *Entrance requirements:* For master's, GRE, 3 letters of recommendation, statement of goals; for doctorate, GRE, 3 letters of recommendation, bachelor's degree in related field, statement of goals, resume. Additional exam requirements/recommendations for international students: Required—TOEFL (minimum score 85 iBT), IELTS (minimum score 6.5), PTE (minimum score 58), one of three is required. *Application deadline:* Applications are processed on a rolling basis. Application fee: $60. Electronic applications accepted. *Expenses:* Contact institution. *Financial support:* Research assistantships, teaching assistantships, health care benefits, and unspecified assistantships available. Financial award applicants required to submit FAFSA. *Faculty research:* Data mining, machine learning, knowledge discovery, computer networks and systems, cyberspace security. *Unit head:* Jamie Payton, Department Chairperson, 215-204-8245, E-mail: Jamie.payton@temple.edu. *Application contact:* Eduard Dragut, Graduate Chair, 215-204-0521, E-mail: cisadmit@temple.edu. Website: https://cis.temple.edu/

Tufts University, School of Engineering, Department of Computer Science, Medford, MA 02155. Offers bioengineering (MS), including bioinformatics; cognitive science/computer science (PhD); computer science (MS, PhD); soft material robotics (PhD). *Program availability:* Part-time. Terminal master's awarded for partial completion of doctoral program. *Entrance requirements:* For master's and doctorate, GRE General Test. Additional exam requirements/recommendations for international students: Required—TOEFL (minimum score 550 paper-based; 80 iBT), IELTS (minimum score 6.5). Electronic applications accepted. *Expenses: Tuition:* Full-time $51,288; part-time $1710 per credit hour. *Required fees:* $904. Full-time tuition and fees vary according to degree level, program and student level. Part-time tuition and fees vary according to course load. *Faculty research:* Computational biology, computational geometry, and computational systems biology; cognitive sciences, human-computer interaction, and human-robotic interaction; visualization and graphics, educational technologies; machine learning and data mining; programming languages and systems.

University of California, Riverside, Graduate Division, Department of Electrical Engineering, Riverside, CA 92521-0102. Offers electrical engineering (MS, PhD), including computer engineering (MS), control and robotics (PhD). Terminal master's awarded for partial completion of doctoral program. *Degree requirements:* For master's, thesis optional; for doctorate, thesis/dissertation, qualifying exams. *Entrance requirements:* For master's and doctorate, GRE General Test, minimum GPA of 3.25. Additional exam requirements/recommendations for international students: Required—TOEFL (minimum score 550 paper-based; 80 iBT). Electronic applications accepted. *Faculty research:* Solid state devices, integrated circuits, signal processing.

University of California, San Diego, Graduate Division, Department of Electrical and Computer Engineering, La Jolla, CA 92093. Offers applied ocean science (MS, PhD); applied physics (MS, PhD); communication theory and systems (MS, PhD); computer engineering (MS, PhD); electronic circuits and systems (MS, PhD); intelligent systems, robotics and control (MS, PhD); medical devices and systems (MS, PhD); nanoscale devices and systems (MS, PhD); photonics (MS, PhD); signal and image processing (MS, PhD). Program offered jointly with San Diego State University. *Students:* 830 full-time (174 women), 69 part-time (8 women). 2,810 applicants, 40% accepted, 399 enrolled. In 2018, 226 master's, 42 doctorates awarded. Terminal master's awarded for partial completion of doctoral program. *Degree requirements:* For master's, comprehensive exam (for some programs), thesis (for some programs); for doctorate, comprehensive exam, thesis/dissertation. *Entrance requirements:* For master's and doctorate, GRE General Test, minimum GPA of 3.0, resume or curriculum vitae (recommended). Additional exam requirements/recommendations for international students: Required—TOEFL (minimum score 550 paper-based; 80 iBT), IELTS (minimum score 7), PTE (minimum score 65). *Application deadline:* For fall admission, 12/13 for domestic students. Application fee: $105 ($125 for international students). Electronic applications accepted. *Financial support:* Fellowships, research assistantships, teaching assistantships, scholarships/grants, traineeships, and unspecified assistantships available. Financial award applicants required to submit FAFSA. *Faculty research:* Applied ocean science; applied physics; communication theory and systems; computer engineering; electronic circuits and systems; intelligent systems, robotics and control; medical devices and systems; nanoscale devices and systems; photonics; signal and image processing. *Unit head:* Bill Lin, Chair, 858-822-1383, E-mail: billin@ucsd.edu. *Application contact:* Sean Jones, Graduate Admissions Coordinator, 858-534-3213, E-mail: ecegradapps@ece.ucsd.edu. Website: http://ece.ucsd.edu/

University of Georgia, Franklin College of Arts and Sciences, Artificial Intelligence Center, Athens, GA 30602. Offers MS. *Degree requirements:* For master's, thesis. *Entrance requirements:* For master's, GRE General Test. Electronic applications accepted.

University of Michigan, College of Engineering, Department of Integrative Systems and Design, Ann Arbor, MI 48109. Offers automotive engineering (M Eng); design science (MS, PhD); energy systems engineering (M Eng, MS); global automotive and manufacturing engineering (M Eng); manufacturing engineering (M Eng, D Eng); pharmaceutical engineering (M Eng); robotics and autonomous vehicles (M Eng); systems engineering and design (M Eng); MBA/M Eng; MSE/MS. *Program availability:* Part-time, online learning. *Students:* 163 full-time (38 women), 251 part-time (40 women). 282 applicants, 12% accepted, 15 enrolled. In 2018, 173 master's, 1 doctorate awarded. Terminal master's awarded for partial completion of doctoral program. *Degree requirements:* For master's, capstone project; for doctorate, thesis/dissertation. *Entrance requirements:* For master's and doctorate, GRE. Additional exam requirements/recommendations for international students: Required—TOEFL. *Application deadline:* Applications are processed on a rolling basis. Electronic applications accepted. *Financial support:* Fellowships, research assistantships with full tuition reimbursements, teaching assistantships with full tuition reimbursements, career-related internships or fieldwork, scholarships/grants, and unspecified assistantships available. Financial award applicants required to submit FAFSA. *Faculty research:* Automotive engineering, design science, energy systems engineering, engineering sustainable systems, financial engineering, global automotive and manufacturing engineering, integrated microsystems, manufacturing engineering, pharmaceutical engineering, robotics and autonomous vehicles. *Total annual research expenditures:* $595,323. *Unit head:* Diann Brei, Department Chair, 734-763-6617, E-mail: drdiannbrei@umich.edu. *Application contact:* Kathy Bishar, Senior Graduate Coordinator, 734-764-3312, E-mail: kbishar@umich.edu. Website: http://www.isd.engin.umich.edu

University of Michigan, College of Engineering, Program in Robotics, Ann Arbor, MI 48109. Offers MS, PhD. *Students:* 93 full-time (18 women), 1 part-time (0 women). 740 applicants, 18% accepted, 49 enrolled. In 2018, 43 master's awarded. *Entrance requirements:* For master's and doctorate, GRE General Test. Additional exam requirements/recommendations for international students: Required—TOEFL. *Faculty research:* Autonomous vehicles, human-robot interaction, legged locomotion, manipulation, manufacturing. *Unit head:* Jessy Grizzle, Director, 734-763-3598, E-mail: grizzle@umich.edu. *Application contact:* Denise Edmund, Graduate Program Coordinator, 734-647-2970, E-mail: dledmund@umich.edu. Website: https://robotics.umich.edu/

University of Nebraska at Omaha, Graduate Studies, College of Information Science and Technology, Department of Computer Science, Omaha, NE 68182. Offers artificial intelligence (Certificate); communication networks (Certificate); computer science (MA, MS); computer science education (MS, Certificate); software engineering (Certificate); system and architecture (Certificate). *Program availability:* Part-time, evening/weekend. *Degree requirements:* For master's, comprehensive exam, thesis (for some programs). *Entrance requirements:* For master's, GRE General Test, minimum GPA of 3.0, prior course work in computer science, official transcripts, resume, 2 letters of recommendation; for Certificate, minimum GPA of 3.0, resume. Additional exam requirements/recommendations for international students: Required—TOEFL, IELTS, PTE. Electronic applications accepted.

University of Pennsylvania, School of Engineering and Applied Science, Program in Robotics, Philadelphia, PA 19104. Offers MSE. *Program availability:* Part-time. *Students:* 38 full-time (5 women), 28 part-time (7 women); includes 13 minority (10 Asian, non-Hispanic/Latino; 1 Hispanic/Latino; 2 Two or more races, non-Hispanic/Latino), 45 international. Average age 24. 542 applicants, 14% accepted, 30 enrolled. In 2018, 69 master's awarded. *Degree requirements:* For master's, comprehensive exam, thesis optional. *Entrance requirements:* For master's, GRE, bachelor's degree, letters of recommendation, resume, personal statement. Additional exam requirements/recommendations for international students: Required—TOEFL (minimum score 100 iBT), IELTS (minimum score 7). *Application deadline:* For fall admission, 2/1 priority date for domestic and international students. Application fee: $80. Electronic applications accepted. *Expenses:* Contact institution. *Faculty research:* Artificial intelligence, computer vision, control systems, machine learning, robotic systems. *Application contact:* William Fenton, Assistant Director of Graduate Admissions, 215-898-4542, Fax: 215-573-5577, E-mail: gradstudies@seas.upenn.edu.
Website: http://www.grasp.upenn.edu

University of Pittsburgh, School of Computing and Information, Intelligent Systems Program, Pittsburgh, PA 15260. Offers MS, PhD. *Program availability:* Part-time, evening/weekend. *Degree requirements:* For master's, research project; for doctorate, comprehensive exam, thesis/dissertation. *Entrance requirements:* For master's, GRE General Test, BS, relevant experience; for doctorate, GRE General Test. Additional exam requirements/recommendations for international students: Required—TOEFL (minimum score 90 iBT), IELTS (minimum score 7). Electronic applications accepted. *Expenses:* Contact institution. *Faculty research:* Artificial intelligence and education, machine learning, natural language processing, biomedical informatics, artificial intelligence and law.

University of Rochester, Hajim School of Engineering and Applied Sciences, Department of Computer Science, Rochester, NY 14627. Offers algorithms and complexity (MS); artificial intelligence and machine learning (MS); computer architecture (MS); computer science (PhD); human computer interaction (MS); natural language processing (MS); programming languages and computer systems (MS). *Faculty:* 18 full-time (1 woman). *Students:* 125 full-time (20 women); includes 7 minority (2 Black or African American, non-Hispanic/Latino; 4 Asian, non-Hispanic/Latino; 1 Two or more races, non-Hispanic/Latino), 103 international. Average age 26. 868 applicants, 16% accepted, 44 enrolled. In 2018, 41 master's, 8 doctorates awarded. Terminal master's awarded for partial completion of doctoral program. *Degree requirements:* For master's, comprehensive exam (for some programs), thesis (for some programs); for doctorate, comprehensive exam, thesis/dissertation, qualifying exam. *Entrance requirements:* For master's and doctorate, GRE General Test, personal statement, transcripts, three letters of recommendation. Additional exam requirements/recommendations for international students: Required—TOEFL, IELTS. *Application deadline:* For fall admission, 1/15 for domestic and international students. Application fee: $60. Electronic applications accepted. *Expenses: Tuition:* Full-time $52,974; part-time $1654 per credit hour. *Required fees:* $612. One-time fee: $30 part-time. Tuition and fees vary according to campus/location and program. *Financial support:* In 2018–19, 68 students received support, including 3 fellowships with full tuition reimbursements available (averaging $33,336 per year), 51 research assistantships with full tuition reimbursements available (averaging $30,720 per year), 14 teaching assistantships with full tuition reimbursements available (averaging $30,720 per year); scholarships/grants, traineeships, health care benefits, and tuition waivers (full and partial) also available. Financial award application deadline: 12/15. *Faculty research:* Artificial intelligence, human-computer interaction, systems research, theory research. *Total annual research expenditures:* $4.1 million. *Unit head:* Sandhya Dwarkadas, Professor and Chair, 585-275-5647, E-mail: sandhya@cs.rochester.edu. *Application contact:* Michelle Kiso, Graduate Coordinator, 585-275-7737, E-mail: mkiso@cs.rochester.edu.
Website: https://www.cs.rochester.edu/graduate/index.html

University of Southern California, Graduate School, Viterbi School of Engineering, Department of Computer Science, Los Angeles, CA 90089. Offers computer networks (MS); computer science (MS, PhD); computer security (MS); game development (MS); high performance computing and simulations (MS); human language technology (MS); intelligent robotics (MS); multimedia and creative technologies (MS); software engineering (MS). *Program availability:* Part-time, evening/weekend, online learning. *Entrance requirements:* For master's and doctorate, GRE General Test. Additional exam requirements/recommendations for international students: Required—TOEFL. Electronic applications accepted. *Faculty research:* Databases, computer graphics and computer vision, software engineering, networks and security, robotics, multimedia and virtual reality.

Villanova University, College of Engineering, Department of Electrical and Computer Engineering, Program in Computer Engineering, Villanova, PA 19085-1699. Offers computer architectures (Certificate); computer engineering (MSCPE); intelligent control systems (Certificate). *Program availability:* Part-time, evening/weekend. *Degree requirements:* For master's, thesis optional. *Entrance requirements:* For master's, GRE General Test (for applicants with degrees from foreign universities), BEE, minimum GPA of 3.0. Additional exam requirements/recommendations for international students: Required—TOEFL (minimum score 600 paper-based; 100 iBT). Electronic applications accepted. *Faculty research:* Expert systems, computer vision, neural networks, image processing, computer architectures.

Villanova University, College of Engineering, Department of Electrical and Computer Engineering, Program in Electrical Engineering, Villanova, PA 19085-1699. Offers electric power systems (Certificate); electrical engineering (MSEE); electro mechanical systems (Certificate); high frequency systems (Certificate); intelligent control systems (Certificate); wireless and digital communications (Certificate). *Program availability:* Part-time, evening/weekend. *Degree requirements:* For master's, thesis optional. *Entrance requirements:* For master's, GRE General Test (for applicants with degrees from foreign universities), BEE, minimum GPA of 3.0. Additional exam requirements/recommendations for international students: Required—TOEFL (minimum score 600 paper-based; 100 iBT). *Faculty research:* Signal processing, communications, antennas, devices.

Worcester Polytechnic Institute, Graduate Admissions, Program in Robotics Engineering, Worcester, MA 01609-2280. Offers robotics engineering (MS). *Program availability:* Part-time, evening/weekend, 100% online, blended/hybrid learning. *Students:* 85 full-time (10 women), 102 part-time (10 women); includes 22 minority (4 Black or African American, non-Hispanic/Latino; 8 Asian, non-Hispanic/Latino; 9 Hispanic/Latino; 1 Two or more races, non-Hispanic/Latino), 111 international. Average age 27. 356 applicants, 59% accepted, 72 enrolled. In 2018, 72 master's, 5 doctorates awarded. Terminal master's awarded for partial completion of doctoral program. *Degree requirements:* For master's, thesis or capstone design project; for doctorate, thesis/dissertation. *Entrance requirements:* For master's and doctorate, GRE, 3 letters of recommendation, statement of purpose. Additional exam requirements/recommendations for international students: Required—TOEFL (minimum score 563 paper-based; 84 iBT), IELTS (minimum score 7). *Application deadline:* For fall admission, 1/1 priority date for domestic and international students; for spring admission, 10/1 priority date for domestic and international students. Applications are processed on a rolling basis. Application fee: $70. Electronic applications accepted. *Financial support:* Fellowships, research assistantships, teaching assistantships, career-related internships or fieldwork, institutionally sponsored loans, scholarships/grants, and unspecified assistantships available. Financial award application deadline: 1/1. *Unit head:* Dr. Jing Xiao, Director, 508-831-6665, Fax: 508-831-6864, E-mail: jxiao2@wpi.edu. *Application contact:* Cagdas Onal, Graduate Coordinator, 508-831-6665, Fax: 508-831-6864, E-mail: cdonal@wpi.edu.
Website: https://www.wpi.edu/academics/departments/robotics-engineering

Bioinformatics

Arizona State University at the Tempe campus, College of Health Solutions, Department of Biomedical Informatics, Phoenix, AZ 85004. Offers MS, PhD. Terminal master's awarded for partial completion of doctoral program. *Degree requirements:* For master's, interactive Program of Study (iPOS) submitted before completing 50 percent of required credit hours; for doctorate, comprehensive exam, thesis/dissertation, interactive Program of Study (iPOS) submitted before completing 50 percent of required credit hours. *Entrance requirements:* For master's, GRE or MCAT, bachelor's degree with minimum GPA of 3.25 in computer science, biology, physiology, nursing, statistics, engineering, related fields, or unrelated fields with appropriate academic backgrounds; resume/curriculum vitae; statement of purpose; 3 letters of recommendation; all official transcripts; for doctorate, GRE or MCAT, bachelor's degree with minimum GPA of 3.5 in computer science, biology, physiology, nursing, statistics, engineering, related fields, or unrelated fields with appropriate academic backgrounds; resume/curriculum vitae; statement of purpose; 3 letters of recommendation; all official transcripts. Additional exam requirements/recommendations for international students: Required—TOEFL (minimum score 550 paper-based; 83 iBT), IELTS (minimum score 6.5). Electronic applications accepted.

Boston University, Graduate School of Arts and Sciences and College of Engineering, Intercollegiate Program in Bioinformatics, Boston, MA 02215. Offers MS, PhD. *Students:* 82 full-time (29 women), 9 part-time (2 women); includes 14 minority (3 Black or African American, non-Hispanic/Latino; 5 Asian, non-Hispanic/Latino; 6 Hispanic/Latino), 41 international. Average age 25. 238 applicants, 34% accepted, 29 enrolled. In 2018, 36 master's, 12 doctorates awarded. Terminal master's awarded for partial completion of doctoral program. *Degree requirements:* For master's, thesis or alternative, internship; for doctorate, comprehensive exam, thesis/dissertation. *Entrance requirements:* For master's, 3 letters of recommendation, transcripts, personal statement, resume; for doctorate, GRE General Test, 3 letters of recommendation, transcripts, personal statement, resume. Additional exam requirements/recommendations for international students: Required—TOEFL (minimum score 550 paper-based; 84 iBT). *Application deadline:* For fall and spring admission, 12/1 for domestic and international students. Application fee: $95. Electronic applications accepted. *Financial support:* In 2018–19, 55 students received support, including 4 fellowships with full tuition reimbursements available (averaging $22,660 per year), 40 research assistantships with full tuition reimbursements available (averaging $22,660 per year); career-related internships or fieldwork, Federal Work-Study, scholarships/grants, traineeships, and health care benefits also available. Financial award application deadline: 12/1. *Unit head:* Tom Tullius, Director, 617-353-2482, E-mail: tullius@bu.edu. *Application contact:* David King, Administrator, 617-358-0751, Fax: 617-353-5929, E-mail: dking@bu.edu.
Website: http://www.bu.edu/bioinformatics

Brandeis University, Rabb School of Continuing Studies, Division of Graduate Professional Studies, Master of Science in Bioinformatics Program, Waltham, MA 02454-9110. Offers MS. *Program availability:* Part-time-only. *Entrance requirements:* For master's, undergraduate-level coursework in molecular biology, organic chemistry, and programming in Java, C++ or C; four-year bachelor's degree from regionally-accredited U.S. institution or equivalent; official transcript(s) from every college or university attended; resume or curriculum vitae; statement of goals; letter of recommendation. Additional exam requirements/recommendations for international students: Required—TWE (minimum score 4.5), TOEFL (minimum scores: 600 paper-based, 100 iBT), IELTS (7), or PTE (68). Electronic applications accepted. *Expenses:* Contact institution.

California State University Channel Islands, Extended University and International Programs, MS Biotechnology & Bioinformatics, Camarillo, CA 93012. Offers biotechnology and bioinformatics (MS); MS/MBA. *Program availability:* Part-time, evening/weekend. *Students:* 66 full-time (33 women); includes 44 minority (1 Black or African American, non-Hispanic/Latino; 28 Asian, non-Hispanic/Latino; 7 Hispanic/Latino; 2 Native Hawaiian or other Pacific Islander, non-Hispanic/Latino; 6 Two or more races, non-Hispanic/Latino). *Degree requirements:* For master's, thesis. *Entrance requirements:* For master's, GRE/GMAT; GMAT can be waived based on certain requirements. Additional exam requirements/recommendations for international students: Required—TOEFL (minimum score 550 paper-based; 80 iBT), IELTS (minimum score 6.5). *Application deadline:* For fall admission, 5/1 for domestic students; for spring admission, 11/1 for domestic students. Application fee: $55. Electronic applications accepted. *Financial support:* Applicants required to submit FAFSA. *Unit head:* Dr. Nitika Parmar, Program Director, 805-437-8873, E-mail: nitika.parmar@csuci.edu. *Application contact:* Andrew Conley, Graduate Program Recruiter, 805-437-2652, E-mail: andrew.conley@csuci.edu.
Website: https://ext.csuci.edu/

California State University, Dominguez Hills, College of Natural and Behavioral Sciences, Department of Biology, Carson, CA 90747-0001. Offers MS. *Program availability:* Part-time, evening/weekend. *Degree requirements:* For master's, thesis. *Entrance requirements:* For master's, minimum GPA of 2.75. Additional exam requirements/recommendations for international students: Required—TOEFL (minimum score 550 paper-based). Electronic applications accepted. *Faculty research:* Cancer biology, infectious diseases, ecology of native plants, remediation, community ecology.

Clemson University, Graduate School, College of Behavioral, Social and Health Sciences, Department of Public Health Sciences, Clemson, SC 29634. Offers applied health research and evaluation (MS, PhD); biomedical data science and informatics (PhD); clinical and translational research (Certificate). *Program availability:* Part-time, 100% online. *Faculty:* 19 full-time (11 women). *Students:* 29 full-time (15 women), 19 part-time (11 women); includes 9 minority (3 Black or African American, non-Hispanic/Latino; 4 Asian, non-Hispanic/Latino; 2 Hispanic/Latino), 10 international. Average age 30. 44 applicants, 82% accepted, 26 enrolled. In 2018, 7 master's, 1 doctorate, 17 other advanced degrees awarded. *Degree requirements:* For doctorate, comprehensive exam, thesis/dissertation. *Entrance requirements:* For master's and Certificate, GRE General Test, curriculum vitae, statement of career goals, letters of recommendation, unofficial transcripts; for doctorate, GRE General Test, MS/MA thesis or publications, curriculum vitae, statement of career goals, letters of recommendation, unofficial transcripts. Additional exam requirements/recommendations for international students: Required—TOEFL (minimum score 80 paper-based; 80 iBT); Recommended—IELTS (minimum score 6.5), TSE (minimum score 54). *Application deadline:* For fall admission, 4/15 for international students; for spring admission, 10/15 for international students. Applications are processed on a rolling basis. Application fee: $80 ($90 for international students). Electronic applications accepted. *Expenses:* $6823 per semester full-time resident, $14023 per semester full-time non-resident, $833 per credit hour part-time resident, $1731 per credit hour part-time non-resident, online $1264 per credit hour, $4938 doctoral programs resident, $10405 doctoral programs non-resident, $1144 full-time graduate assistant, other fees may apply per session. *Financial support:* In 2018–19, 2 students received support, including 1 research assistantship with full and partial tuition reimbursement available (averaging $12,960 per year), 1 teaching assistantship with full and partial tuition reimbursement available (averaging $15,552 per year); career-related internships or fieldwork also available. *Faculty research:* Health promotion and behavior, epidemiology and outcomes research, public health informatics, health policy and health services research, global health, evaluation. *Total annual research expenditures:* $1.6 million. *Unit head:* Dr. Ronald Gimbel, Department Chair, 864-656-1969, E-mail: rgimbel@clemson.edu. *Application contact:* Dr. Lee Crandall, Interim Director of Graduate Studies, 864-656-3082, E-mail: lac@clemson.edu.
Website: http://www.clemson.edu/cbshs/departments/public-health/index.html

Dalhousie University, Faculty of Computer Science, Halifax, NS B3H 1W5, Canada. Offers computational biology and bioinformatics (M Sc); computer science (MA Sc, MC Sc, PhD); electronic commerce (MEC); health informatics (MHI). *Degree requirements:* For master's, thesis (for some programs); for doctorate, thesis/dissertation. *Entrance requirements:* Additional exam requirements/recommendations for international students: Required—1 of 5 approved tests: TOEFL, IELTS, CANTEST, CAEL, Michigan English Language Assessment Battery. Electronic applications accepted.

Duke University, Graduate School, Department of Computational Biology and Bioinformatics, Durham, NC 27708. Offers PhD, Certificate. *Degree requirements:* For doctorate, thesis/dissertation. *Entrance requirements:* For doctorate, GRE General Test. Additional exam requirements/recommendations for international students: Required—TOEFL (minimum score 577 paper-based; 90 iBT) or IELTS (minimum score 7). Electronic applications accepted.

Emory University, Rollins School of Public Health, Department of Biostatistics and Bioinformatics, Atlanta, GA 30322-1100. Offers bioinformatics (PhD); biostatistics (MPH, MSPH); public health informatics (MSPH). PhD offered through the Graduate School of Arts and Sciences. *Program availability:* Part-time. *Degree requirements:* For master's, thesis, practicum. *Entrance requirements:* For master's, GRE General Test. Additional exam requirements/recommendations for international students: Required—TOEFL (minimum score 550 paper-based; 80 iBT). Electronic applications accepted.

Endicott College, Van Loan School of Graduate and Professional Studies, Program in Bioinformatics, Beverly, MA 01915-2096. Offers MS.

George Mason University, College of Science, School of Systems Biology, Manassas, VA 22030. Offers bioinformatics and computational biology (MS, PhD, Certificate); bioinformatics management (MS); biology (MS); biosciences (PhD). *Faculty:* 10 full-time (3 women), 1 part-time/adjunct (0 women). *Students:* 124 full-time (65 women), 91 part-time (46 women); includes 72 minority (16 Black or African American, non-Hispanic/Latino; 1 American Indian or Alaska Native, non-Hispanic/Latino; 29 Asian, non-Hispanic/Latino; 17 Hispanic/Latino; 9 Two or more races, non-Hispanic/Latino), 35 international. Average age 32. 150 applicants, 87% accepted, 84 enrolled. In 2018, 39 master's, 13 doctorates, 1 other advanced degree awarded. *Degree requirements:* For master's, comprehensive exam (for some programs), research project or thesis; for doctorate, comprehensive exam, thesis/dissertation. *Entrance requirements:* For master's, GRE, resume; 3 letters of recommendation; expanded goals statement; 2 copies of official transcripts; bachelor's degree in related field with minimum GPA of 3.0 in last 60 hours; for doctorate, GRE, self-assessment form; resume; 3 letters of recommendation; expanded goals statement; 2 copies of official transcripts; bachelor's degree in related field with minimum GPA of 3.0 in last 60 hours; for Certificate, resume; 2 copies of official transcripts. Additional exam requirements/recommendations for international students: Required—TOEFL (minimum score 575 paper-based; 88 iBT), IELTS (minimum score 6.5), PTE (minimum score 59). Application fee: $75 ($80 for international students). Electronic applications accepted. *Financial support:* In 2018–19, 56 students received support, including 13 research assistantships with tuition reimbursements available (averaging $17,533 per year), 43 teaching assistantships with tuition reimbursements available (averaging $16,983 per year); career-related internships or fieldwork, Federal Work-Study, scholarships/grants, unspecified assistantships, and health care benefits (for full-time research or teaching assistantship recipients) also available. Support available to part-time students. Financial award application deadline: 3/1; financial award applicants required to submit FAFSA. *Faculty research:* Functional genomics of chronic human diseases, ecology of vector-borne infectious diseases, neurogenetics, molecular biology, computational modeling, proteomics, chronic metabolic diseases, nanotechnology. *Total annual research expenditures:* $766,416. *Unit head:* Dr. Iosif Vaisman, Director, 703-993-8431, Fax: 703-993-8976, E-mail: ivaisman@gmu.edu. *Application contact:* Diane St. Germain, Graduate Student Services Coordinator, 703-993-4263, Fax: 703-993-8976, E-mail: dstgerma@gmu.edu.
Website: http://ssb.gmu.edu/

Georgetown University, Graduate School of Arts and Sciences, Department of Biostatistics, Bioinformatics and Biomathematics, Washington, DC 20057-1484. Offers biostatistics (MS, Certificate), including bioinformatics (MS), epidemiology (MS); epidemiology (Certificate). *Entrance requirements:* For master's, GRE General Test. Additional exam requirements/recommendations for international students: Required—TOEFL. *Faculty research:* Occupation epidemiology, cancer.

Georgia Institute of Technology, Graduate Studies, Multidisciplinary Program in Bioinformatics, Atlanta, GA 30332-0001. Offers MS, PhD. Program offered jointly with School of Biology, Wallace H. Coulter Department of Biomedical Engineering, School of Chemistry and Biochemistry, School of Computational Science and Engineering, School of Mathematics, and School of Industrial and Systems Engineering. *Program availability:* Part-time. Terminal master's awarded for partial completion of doctoral program. *Degree requirements:* For master's, research with faculty, professional internships, co-op work experience; for doctorate, comprehensive exam, thesis/dissertation. *Entrance requirements:* For master's and doctorate, GRE General Test. Additional exam requirements/recommendations for international students: Required—TOEFL (minimum score 600 paper-based; 100 iBT). Electronic applications accepted. *Expenses:* Contact institution.

Georgia State University, College of Arts and Sciences, Department of Biology, Program in Applied and Environmental Microbiology, Atlanta, GA 30302-3083. Offers applied and environmental microbiology (MS, PhD); bioinformatics (MS). *Program availability:* Part-time. Terminal master's awarded for partial completion of doctoral program. *Degree requirements:* For master's, comprehensive exam (for some programs), thesis optional; for doctorate, comprehensive exam, thesis/dissertation. *Entrance requirements:* For master's and doctorate, GRE. *Application deadline:* For fall admission, 7/1 priority date for domestic students, 6/1 priority date for international students; for spring admission, 11/15 priority date for domestic students, 10/15 priority date for international students. Applications are processed on a rolling basis. Application fee: $50. Electronic applications accepted. *Expenses: Tuition, area resident:* Full-time $9360; part-time $390 per credit hour. Tuition, state resident: full-time $9360; part-time $390 per credit hour. Tuition, nonresident: full-time $30,024; part-time $1251 per credit hour. *International tuition:* $30,024 full-time. *Required fees:* $2128. *Financial support:* In 2018–19, fellowships with full tuition reimbursements (averaging $22,000 per year), research assistantships with full tuition reimbursements (averaging $20,000 per year) were awarded. Financial award application deadline: 12/3. *Faculty research:* Bioremediation, biofilms, indoor air quality control, environmental toxicology, product biosynthesis. *Unit head:* Dr. Charles Derby, Director of Graduate Studies, 404-413-5393, Fax: 404-413-5446, E-mail: cderby@gsu.edu. *Application contact:* Dr. Charles Derby, Director of Graduate Studies, 404-413-5393, Fax: 404-413-5446, E-mail: cderby@gsu.edu.
Website: http://biology.gsu.edu/

Georgia State University, College of Arts and Sciences, Department of Biology, Program in Cellular and Molecular Biology and Physiology, Atlanta, GA 30302-3083. Offers bioinformatics (MS); cellular and molecular biology and physiology (MS, PhD). *Program availability:* Part-time. Terminal master's awarded for partial completion of doctoral program. *Entrance requirements:* For master's and doctorate, GRE. *Application deadline:* Applications are processed on a rolling basis. Application fee: $50. Electronic applications accepted. *Expenses: Tuition, area resident:* Full-time $9360; part-time $390 per credit hour. Tuition, state resident: full-time $9360; part-time $390 per credit hour. Tuition, nonresident: full-time $30,024; part-time $1251 per credit hour. *International tuition:* $30,024 full-time. *Required fees:* $2128. *Financial support:* Fellowships and research assistantships available. Financial award application deadline: 12/3. *Faculty research:* Membrane transport, viral infection, molecular immunology, protein modeling, gene regulation. *Unit head:* Dr. Charles Derby, Director of Graduate Studies, 404-413-5393, Fax: 404-413-5446, E-mail: cderby@gsu.edu. *Application contact:* Dr. Charles Derby, Director of Graduate Studies, 404-413-5393, Fax: 404-413-5446, E-mail: cderby@gsu.edu.
Website: http://biology.gsu.edu/

Georgia State University, College of Arts and Sciences, Department of Biology, Program in Molecular Genetics and Biochemistry, Atlanta, GA 30302-3083. Offers bioinformatics (MS); molecular genetics and biochemistry (MS, PhD). *Program availability:* Part-time. Terminal master's awarded for partial completion of doctoral program. *Entrance requirements:* For master's and doctorate, GRE. *Application deadline:* Applications are processed on a rolling basis. Application fee: $50. Electronic applications accepted. *Expenses: Tuition, area resident:* Full-time $9360; part-time $390 per credit hour. Tuition, state resident: full-time $9360; part-time $390 per credit hour. Tuition, nonresident: full-time $30,024; part-time $1251 per credit hour. *International tuition:* $30,024 full-time. *Required fees:* $2128. *Financial support:* Fellowships and research assistantships available. Financial award application deadline: 12/3. *Faculty research:* Gene regulation, microbial pathogenesis, molecular transport, protein modeling, viral pathogenesis. *Unit head:* Dr. Charles Derby, Director of Graduate Studies, 404-413-5393, Fax: 404-413-5446, E-mail: cderby@gsu.edu. *Application contact:* Dr. Charles Derby, Director of Graduate Studies, 404-413-5393, Fax: 404-413-5446, E-mail: cderby@gsu.edu.
Website: http://biology.gsu.edu/

Georgia State University, College of Arts and Sciences, Department of Biology, Program in Neurobiology and Behavior, Atlanta, GA 30302-3083. Offers bioinformatics (MS); neurobiology and behavior (MS, PhD). *Program availability:* Part-time. Terminal master's awarded for partial completion of doctoral program. *Entrance requirements:* For master's and doctorate, GRE. *Application deadline:* Applications are processed on a rolling basis. Application fee: $50. Electronic applications accepted. *Expenses: Tuition, area resident:* Full-time $9360; part-time $390 per credit hour. Tuition, state resident: full-time $9360; part-time $390 per credit hour. Tuition, nonresident: full-time $30,024; part-time $1251 per credit hour. *International tuition:* $30,024 full-time. *Required fees:* $2128. *Financial support:* Fellowships and research assistantships available. Financial award application deadline: 12/3. *Faculty research:* Behavior, circadian and circa-annual rhythms, developmental genetics, neuroendocrinology, cytoskeletal dynamics. *Unit head:* Dr. Charles Derby, Director of Graduate Studies, 404-413-5393, Fax: 404-413-5446, E-mail: cderby@gsu.edu. *Application contact:* Dr. Charles Derby, Director of Graduate Studies, 404-413-5393, Fax: 404-413-5446, E-mail: cderby@gsu.edu.
Website: http://biology.gsu.edu/

Georgia State University, College of Arts and Sciences, Department of Chemistry, Atlanta, GA 30302-3083. Offers analytical chemistry (MS, PhD); biochemistry (MS, PhD); bioinformatics (MS, PhD); biophysical chemistry (PhD); computational chemistry (MS, PhD); geochemistry (PhD); organic/medicinal chemistry (MS, PhD); physical chemistry (MS). PhD in geochemistry offered jointly with Department of Geosciences. *Program availability:* Part-time. *Faculty:* 27 full-time (6 women), 1 part-time/adjunct (0 women). *Students:* 147 full-time (59 women), 15 part-time (10 women); includes 37 minority (21 Black or African American, non-Hispanic/Latino; 7 Asian, non-Hispanic/Latino; 4 Hispanic/Latino; 5 Two or more races, non-Hispanic/Latino), 84 international. Average age 29. 106 applicants, 40% accepted, 28 enrolled. In 2018, 37 master's, 13 doctorates awarded. Terminal master's awarded for partial completion of doctoral program. *Degree requirements:* For master's, one foreign language, comprehensive exam (for some programs), thesis (for some programs); for doctorate, one foreign language, comprehensive exam, thesis/dissertation. *Entrance requirements:* For master's and doctorate, GRE. *Application deadline:* For fall admission, 7/1 priority date for domestic and international students; for winter admission, 11/15 priority date for

domestic and international students; for spring admission, 4/15 priority date for domestic and international students. Applications are processed on a rolling basis. Application fee: $50. Electronic applications accepted. *Expenses: Tuition, area resident:* Full-time $9360; part-time $390 per credit hour. Tuition, state resident: full-time $9360; part-time $390 per credit hour. Tuition, nonresident: full-time $30,024; part-time $1251 per credit hour. *International tuition:* $30,024 full-time. *Required fees:* $2128. *Financial support:* Fellowships with full tuition reimbursements, research assistantships with full tuition reimbursements, and teaching assistantships with full tuition reimbursements available. Financial award applicants required to submit FAFSA. *Faculty research:* Analytical chemistry, biological/biochemistry, biophysical/computational chemistry, chemical education, organic/medicinal chemistry. *Unit head:* Dr. Donald Hamelberg, Professor; Chair, 404-413-5564, Fax: 404-413-5505, E-mail: dhamelberg@gsu.edu. *Application contact:* Dr. Donald Hamelberg, Professor; Chair, 404-413-5564, Fax: 404-413-5505, E-mail: dhamelberg@gsu.edu.
Website: http://chemistry.gsu.edu/

Georgia State University, College of Arts and Sciences, Department of Computer Science, Atlanta, GA 30302-3083. Offers bioinformatics (MS, PhD); computer science (MS, PhD). *Program availability:* Part-time. *Faculty:* 29 full-time (6 women), 3 part-time/adjunct (1 woman). *Students:* 166 full-time (63 women), 32 part-time (12 women); includes 25 minority (8 Black or African American, non-Hispanic/Latino; 11 Asian, non-Hispanic/Latino; 3 Hispanic/Latino; 3 Two or more races, non-Hispanic/Latino), 155 international. Average age 29. 331 applicants, 40% accepted, 68 enrolled. In 2018, 67 master's, 14 doctorates awarded. Terminal master's awarded for partial completion of doctoral program. *Entrance requirements:* For master's and doctorate, GRE General Test. Additional exam requirements/recommendations for international students: Required—TOEFL (minimum score 550 paper-based; 80 iBT). *Application deadline:* For fall admission, 3/15 for domestic and international students; for spring admission, 10/15 for domestic and international students. Application fee: $50. Electronic applications accepted. *Expenses: Tuition, area resident:* Full-time $9360; part-time $390 per credit hour. Tuition, state resident: full-time $9360; part-time $390 per credit hour. Tuition, nonresident: full-time $30,024; part-time $1251 per credit hour. *International tuition:* $30,024 full-time. *Required fees:* $2128. *Financial support:* In 2018–19, fellowships with full tuition reimbursements (averaging $22,000 per year), research assistantships with full tuition reimbursements (averaging $16,000 per year), teaching assistantships with full tuition reimbursements (averaging $16,000 per year) were awarded; institutionally sponsored loans, health care benefits, and unspecified assistantships also available. Financial award application deadline: 2/15; financial award applicants required to submit FAFSA. *Faculty research:* Artificial intelligence and computational intelligence, bioinformatics, computer software systems, databases, graphics and human computer interaction, networks and parallel and distributed computing. *Unit head:* Dr. Yi Pan, Regents Professor and Chair, 404-413-5342, Fax: 404-413-5717, E-mail: yipan@gsu.edu. *Application contact:* Dr. Yi Pan, Regents Professor and Chair, 404-413-5342, Fax: 404-413-5717, E-mail: yipan@gsu.edu.
Website: http://www.cs.gsu.edu/

Georgia State University, College of Arts and Sciences, Department of Mathematics and Statistics, Atlanta, GA 30302-3083. Offers bioinformatics (MS, PhD); biostatistics (MS, PhD); discrete mathematics (MS); mathematics (MS, PhD); scientific computing (MS); statistics (MS). *Program availability:* Part-time. *Faculty:* 28 full-time (8 women), 1 part-time/adjunct (0 women). *Students:* 88 full-time (46 women), 15 part-time (8 women); includes 27 minority (7 Black or African American, non-Hispanic/Latino; 14 Asian, non-Hispanic/Latino; 4 Hispanic/Latino; 2 Two or more races, non-Hispanic/Latino), 57 international. Average age 32. 109 applicants, 65% accepted, 37 enrolled. In 2018, 29 master's, 11 doctorates awarded. Terminal master's awarded for partial completion of doctoral program. *Entrance requirements:* For master's and doctorate, GRE. Additional exam requirements/recommendations for international students: Required—TOEFL (minimum score 550 paper-based; 80 iBT). *Application deadline:* For fall admission, 7/1 priority date for domestic and international students; for spring admission, 11/15 priority date for domestic and international students. Application fee: $50. Electronic applications accepted. *Expenses: Tuition, area resident:* Full-time $9360; part-time $390 per credit hour. Tuition, state resident: full-time $9360; part-time $390 per credit hour. Tuition, nonresident: full-time $30,024; part-time $1251 per credit hour. *International tuition:* $30,024 full-time. *Required fees:* $2128. *Financial support:* In 2018–19, fellowships with full tuition reimbursements (averaging $22,000 per year), research assistantships with full tuition reimbursements (averaging $9,000 per year), teaching assistantships with full tuition reimbursements (averaging $9,000 per year) were awarded; institutionally sponsored loans, scholarships/grants, health care benefits, and unspecified assistantships also available. Financial award application deadline: 2/1. *Faculty research:* Algebra, matrix theory, graph theory and combinatorics; applied mathematics and analysis; collegiate mathematics education; statistics, biostatistics and applications; bioinformatics, dynamical systems. *Unit head:* Dr. Guantao Chen, Chair, 404-413-6436, Fax: 404-413-6403, E-mail: gchen@gsu.edu. *Application contact:* Dr. Guantao Chen, Chair, 404-413-6436, Fax: 404-413-6403, E-mail: gchen@gsu.edu.
Website: https://www.mathstat.gsu.edu/

Grand Valley State University, Padnos College of Engineering and Computing, Health Informatics and Bioinformatics Program, Allendale, MI 49401-9403. Offers MS. *Program availability:* Part-time, evening/weekend. *Students:* 15 full-time (6 women), 15 part-time (9 women); includes 4 minority (1 Black or African American, non-Hispanic/Latino; 2 Asian, non-Hispanic/Latino; 1 Two or more races, non-Hispanic/Latino), 10 international. Average age 26. 18 applicants, 100% accepted, 12 enrolled. In 2018, 10 master's awarded. *Entrance requirements:* For master's, GRE or GMAT if undergraduate GPA is less than 3.0, minimum GPA of 3.0, resume, personal statement, minimum of 2 letters of recommendation, previous academic study or work experience. Additional exam requirements/recommendations for international students: Required—TOEFL (minimum iBT score of 80), IELTS (6.5), or Michigan English Language Assessment Battery (77). *Application deadline:* For fall admission, 2/1 priority date for domestic students. Applications are processed on a rolling basis. Application fee: $30. Electronic applications accepted. *Expenses:* $682 per credit hour, 36 credit hours. *Financial support:* In 2018–19, 7 students received support, including 2 fellowships, 5 research assistantships with full and partial tuition reimbursements available (averaging $8,000 per year); career-related internships or fieldwork, tuition waivers (full and partial), and unspecified assistantships also available. *Faculty research:* Biomedical informatics, information visualization, data mining, high-performance computing, computational biology. *Unit head:* Dr. Paul Leidig, Director, 616-331-2060, Fax: 616-331-2144, E-mail: leidigp@gvsu.edu. *Application contact:* Dr. Guenter Tusch, Graduate Program Director, 616-331-2046, Fax: 616-331-2144, E-mail: tuschg@gvsu.edu.

Hood College, Graduate School, Program in Bioinformatics, Frederick, MD 21701-8575. Offers MS, Certificate. *Program availability:* Part-time-only, evening/weekend. *Faculty:* 2 full-time (both women), 4 part-time/adjunct (1 woman). *Students:* 9 full-time (6 women), 19 part-time (12 women); includes 6 minority (2 Black or African American, non-Hispanic/Latino; 2 Asian, non-Hispanic/Latino; 1 Hispanic/Latino; 1 Two or more races, non-Hispanic/Latino), 8 international. Average age 32. 15 applicants, 100% accepted, 10 enrolled. In 2018, 3 master's, 2 other advanced degrees awarded. *Degree requirements:* For master's, capstone project. *Entrance requirements:* For master's, bachelor's degree in life science or computer science field, minimum GPA of 2.75, written statement of intent (250 words). Additional exam requirements/recommendations for international students: Required—TOEFL (minimum score 575 paper-based; 89 iBT), IELTS (minimum score 6.5). *Application deadline:* For fall admission, 8/15 priority date for domestic students, 8/5 for international students; for spring admission, 12/1 priority date for domestic students, 12/1 for international students; for summer admission, 5/1 priority date for domestic students, 4/15 for international students. Applications are processed on a rolling basis. Application fee: $50 ($100 for international students). Electronic applications accepted. *Expenses:* Science Programs: Tuition $535 per credit, Comprehensive fee $115 per semester. *Financial support:* Research assistantships with full tuition reimbursements, tuition waivers (partial), and unspecified assistantships available. Financial award applicants required to submit FAFSA. *Faculty research:* Bioinformatics, gene environmental interactions in psychiatric disease. *Unit head:* Dr. April M. Boulton, Dean of the Graduate School, 301-696-3600, E-mail: gofurther@hood.edu. *Application contact:* Larbi Bricha, Assistant Director of Graduate Admissions, 301-696-3601, E-mail: gofurther@hood.edu.

Hunter College of the City University of New York, Graduate School, School of Arts and Sciences, Department of Mathematics and Statistics, New York, NY 10065-5085. Offers adolescent mathematics education (MA); applied mathematics (MA); bioinformatics (MA); pure mathematics (MA); statistics (MA). *Program availability:* Part-time, evening/weekend. *Degree requirements:* For master's, one foreign language, comprehensive exam, thesis (for some programs). *Entrance requirements:* For master's, GRE General Test, 24 credits in mathematics. Additional exam requirements/recommendations for international students: Required—TOEFL. *Faculty research:* Data analysis, dynamical systems, computer graphics, topology, statistical decision theory.

Indiana University Bloomington, School of Informatics, Computing, and Engineering, Department of Computer Science, Bloomington, IN 47405. Offers bioinformatics (MS); computer science (MS, PhD); cybersecurity risk management (MS); secure computing (MS, Graduate Certificate). MS in cybersecurity risk management offered in partnership with Kelley School of Business and Maurer School of Law. Terminal master's awarded for partial completion of doctoral program. *Degree requirements:* For master's, thesis optional; for doctorate, comprehensive exam, thesis/dissertation, oral and written exams. *Entrance requirements:* For master's and doctorate, GRE General Test, statement of purpose, bachelor's degree. Additional exam requirements/recommendations for international students: Required—TOEFL. Electronic applications accepted. *Faculty research:* Algorithms, applied logic and computational theory, artificial intelligence, bioinformatics, case-based reasoning, chemical informatics, citation analysis, cognitive science, community informatics, compilers, complex networks and systems, computer optimization, computer-supported cooperative work, computer vision, cyberinfrastructure and e-science, database theory and systems, data mining, digital design and preservation, design pedagogy, digital humanities, digital learning environments.

Indiana University Bloomington, School of Informatics, Computing, and Engineering, Program in Informatics, Bloomington, IN 47405. Offers informatics (MS, PhD), including bioinformatics (PhD), complex systems (PhD), computing, culture and society (PhD), health informatics (PhD), human-computer interaction (MS), human-computer interaction design (PhD), music informatics (PhD), security informatics (PhD); visual heritage (PhD). *Program availability:* Part-time. Terminal master's awarded for partial completion of doctoral program. *Degree requirements:* For master's, thesis, capstone project; for doctorate, variable foreign language requirement, comprehensive exam, thesis/dissertation. *Entrance requirements:* For master's and doctorate, GRE, resume/curriculum vitae, transcripts, 3 letters of recommendation. Additional exam requirements/recommendations for international students: Required—TOEFL (minimum score 600 paper-based; 100 iBT). Electronic applications accepted. *Faculty research:* Algorithms, applied logic and computational theory, artificial intelligence, bioinformatics, case-based reasoning, chemical informatics, citation analysis, cognitive science, community informatics, compilers, complex networks and systems, computer optimization, computer-supported cooperative work, computer vision, cyberinfrastructure and e-science, database theory and systems, data mining, digital design and preservation, design pedagogy, digital humanities, digital learning environments.

Indiana University–Purdue University Indianapolis, School of Informatics and Computing, Department of BioHealth Informatics, Indianapolis, IN 46202. Offers bioinformatics (MS, PhD); health informatics (MS, PhD).

Iowa State University of Science and Technology, Bioinformatics and Computational Biology Program, Ames, IA 50011. Offers MS, PhD. *Degree requirements:* For doctorate, thesis/dissertation. *Entrance requirements:* For master's and doctorate, GRE General Test. Additional exam requirements/recommendations for international students: Recommended—TOEFL, IELTS. Electronic applications accepted. *Faculty research:* Functional and structural genomics, genome evolution, macromolecular structure and function, mathematical biology and biological statistics, metabolic and developmental networks.

Johns Hopkins University, Advanced Academic Programs, Program in Bioinformatics, Washington, DC 21218. Offers MS. *Program availability:* Part-time, evening/weekend, 100% online. *Students:* 36 full-time (20 women), 138 part-time (70 women). 88 applicants, 83% accepted, 37 enrolled. In 2018, 39 master's awarded. *Entrance requirements:* For master's, minimum GPA of 3.0; coursework in programming and data structures, biology, and chemistry. Additional exam requirements/recommendations for international students: Required—TOEFL (minimum score 100 iBT). *Application deadline:* For fall admission, 5/31 priority date for domestic students, 4/30 priority date for international students; for spring admission, 10/31 priority date for domestic and international students. Applications are processed on a rolling basis. Application fee: $75. Electronic applications accepted. *Financial support:* Applicants required to submit FAFSA. *Unit head:* Dr. Kristina Obom, Program Director, 301-294-7159, E-mail: kobom@jhu.edu. *Application contact:* Melissa Edwards, Admissions Manager, 202-452-1941, Fax: 202-452-1970, E-mail: aapadmissions@jhu.edu.
Website: http://advanced.jhu.edu/academics/graduate-degree-programs/bioinformatics/

Lawrence Technological University, College of Arts and Sciences, Southfield, MI 48075-1058. Offers bioinformatics (Graduate Certificate); computer science (MS), including data science, big data, and data mining, intelligent systems; educational technology (MA), including robotics; instructional design, communication, and presentation (Graduate Certificate); integrated science (MA); science education (MA); technical and professional communication (MS, Graduate Certificate); writing for the digital age (Graduate Certificate). *Program availability:* Part-time, evening/weekend. *Degree requirements:* For master's, thesis (for some programs). *Entrance requirements:* Additional exam requirements/recommendations for international students: Required—TOEFL (minimum score 550 paper-based; 79 iBT), IELTS (minimum score 6.5). Electronic applications accepted. *Faculty research:* Computer analysis of music, machine learning of literature and lyrics, customer sentiments and response analysis through social media, peta-scale computing in astronomical databases, early detection of diseases with pattern recognition.

Lewis University, College of Arts and Sciences, Program in Data Science, Romeoville, IL 60446. Offers computational biology and bioinformatics (MS); computer science (MS).

Program availability: Part-time, evening/weekend, 100% online, blended/hybrid learning. *Students:* 16 full-time (4 women), 99 part-time (28 women); includes 34 minority (8 Black or African American, non-Hispanic/Latino; 12 Asian, non-Hispanic/Latino; 8 Hispanic/Latino; 1 Native Hawaiian or other Pacific Islander, non-Hispanic/Latino; 5 Two or more races, non-Hispanic/Latino), 2 international. Average age 35. *Entrance requirements:* For master's, bachelor's degree, undergraduate coursework in calculus, minimum undergraduate GPA of 3.0, resume, statement of purpose, two letters of recommendation. Additional exam requirements/recommendations for international students: Required—TOEFL (minimum score 550 paper-based; 79 iBT), IELTS (minimum score 6). *Application deadline:* For fall admission, 5/1 priority date for international students; for winter admission, 11/1 priority date for international students. Applications are processed on a rolling basis. Application fee: $40. Electronic applications accepted. Application fee is waived when completed online. *Financial support:* Federal Work-Study available. Financial award application deadline: 5/1; financial award applicants required to submit FAFSA. *Unit head:* Dr. Piotr Szczurek, Program Director. *Application contact:* Linda Campbell, Graduate Admissions Counselor, 815-836-5610, E-mail: grad@lewisu.edu.
Website: http://www.lewisu.edu/academics/data-science/index.htm

Loyola University Chicago, Graduate School, Program in Bioinformatics, Chicago, IL 60660. Offers thesis (MS). *Program availability:* Part-time. *Faculty:* 19 full-time (6 women). *Students:* 10 full-time (4 women); includes 4 minority (1 Black or African American, non-Hispanic/Latino; 3 Asian, non-Hispanic/Latino), 1 international. Average age 23. 18 applicants, 67% accepted, 4 enrolled. *Degree requirements:* For master's, thesis (for some programs). *Entrance requirements:* For master's, official college transcripts, 2 letters of recommendation, a current resume/CV, brief (500 word maximum) statement of purpose. Additional exam requirements/recommendations for international students: Required—TOEFL (minimum score 79 paper-based; 550 iBT), IELTS (minimum score 6.5), TOEFL or IELTS. *Application deadline:* For fall admission, 3/15 for domestic and international students; for spring admission, 10/15 for domestic and international students. Application fee: $0. Electronic applications accepted. *Expenses: Tuition:* Full-time $1033; part-time $788 per credit hour. *Required fees:* $700; $400 per credit hour. $400. One-time fee: $100. Tuition and fees vary according to course level, course load, degree level, program and student level. *Financial support:* In 2018–19, 4 students received support, including 2 research assistantships with full tuition reimbursements available (averaging $18,000 per year), 2 teaching assistantships with partial tuition reimbursements available (averaging $9,000 per year); Federal Work-Study, scholarships/grants, and health care benefits also available. Financial award application deadline: 2/1. *Faculty research:* Human genetics, microbiology, infectious disease, machine learning, natural language processing. *Unit head:* Dr. Catherine Putonti, Program Director, 773-508-3277, Fax: 773-508-3646, E-mail: cputonti@luc.edu. *Application contact:* Jill Schur, Director of Graduate Enrollment Management, 312-915-8902, E-mail: gradinfo@luc.edu.
Website: https://www.luc.edu/bioinformatics/msinbioinformatics/

Marquette University, Graduate School, College of Arts and Sciences, Department of Mathematics, Statistics, and Computer Science, Milwaukee, WI 53201-1881. Offers bioinformatics (MS); computational sciences (MS, PhD); computing (MS); mathematics education (MS). *Program availability:* Part-time, evening/weekend, online learning. Terminal master's awarded for partial completion of doctoral program. *Degree requirements:* For master's, thesis (for some programs), essay with oral presentation; for doctorate, comprehensive exam, thesis/dissertation, qualifying examination. *Entrance requirements:* For master's, official transcripts from all current and previous colleges/universities except Marquette, three letters of recommendation; for doctorate, GRE General Test, official transcripts from all current and previous colleges/universities except Marquette, three letters of recommendation. Additional exam requirements/recommendations for international students: Required—TOEFL (minimum score 530 paper-based). Electronic applications accepted. *Faculty research:* Models of physiological systems, mathematical immunology, computational group theory, mathematical logic, computational science.

Marquette University, Graduate School, College of Arts and Sciences, Program in Bioinformatics, Milwaukee, WI 53201-1881. Offers MS. Program offered jointly with Medical College of Wisconsin. *Program availability:* Part-time, evening/weekend, online learning. *Degree requirements:* For master's, research practicum or thesis. *Entrance requirements:* For master's, GRE (strongly recommended), official transcripts from all current and previous colleges/universities except Marquette; essay outlining relevant work experience or education, career goals, possible areas of interest, and reasons for seeking admission; three letters of reference. Additional exam requirements/recommendations for international students: Required—TOEFL (minimum score 530 paper-based). Electronic applications accepted.

Massachusetts Institute of Technology, School of Engineering, Harvard-MIT Health Sciences and Technology Program, Cambridge, MA 02139. Offers health sciences and technology (SM, PhD, Sc D), including bioastronautics (PhD, Sc D), bioinformatics and integrative genomics (PhD, Sc D), medical engineering and medical physics (PhD, Sc D), speech and hearing bioscience and technology (PhD, Sc D). Terminal master's awarded for partial completion of doctoral program. *Degree requirements:* For doctorate, comprehensive exam, thesis/dissertation. *Entrance requirements:* For doctorate, GRE General Test. Additional exam requirements/recommendations for international students: Required—TOEFL, IELTS. Electronic applications accepted. *Expenses: Tuition:* Full-time $51,520; part-time $800 per credit hour. *Required fees:* $312. *Faculty research:* Biomedical imaging, drug delivery, medical devices, medical diagnostics, regenerative biomedical technologies.

McGill University, Faculty of Graduate and Postdoctoral Studies, Faculty of Science, Department of Biology, Montréal, QC H3A 2T5, Canada. Offers bioinformatics (M Sc, PhD); environment (M Sc, PhD); neo-tropical environment (M Sc, PhD).

Morgan State University, School of Graduate Studies, School of Computer, Mathematical, and Natural Sciences, Department of Computer Science, Baltimore, MD 21251. Offers bioinformatics (MS); computer science (MS). *Entrance requirements:* Additional exam requirements/recommendations for international students: Required—TOEFL (minimum score 550 paper-based).

New Mexico State University, College of Arts and Sciences, Department of Computer Science, Las Cruces, NM 88003-8001. Offers bioinformatics (MS); computer science (MS, PhD). *Program availability:* Part-time. *Faculty:* 11 full-time (3 women). *Students:* 68 full-time (21 women), 12 part-time (2 women); includes 12 minority (5 Asian, non-Hispanic/Latino; 6 Hispanic/Latino; 1 Two or more races, non-Hispanic/Latino), 57 international. Average age 30. 98 applicants, 56% accepted, 15 enrolled. In 2018, 20 master's, 7 doctorates awarded. Terminal master's awarded for partial completion of doctoral program. *Degree requirements:* For master's, comprehensive exam, thesis or alternative; for doctorate, comprehensive exam, thesis/dissertation, qualifying exam, thesis proposal. *Entrance requirements:* For master's and doctorate, BS in computer science. Additional exam requirements/recommendations for international students: Required—TOEFL (minimum score 550 paper-based; 79 iBT), IELTS (minimum score 6.5). *Application deadline:* For fall admission, 3/1 priority date for domestic and international students; for spring admission, 11/1 priority date for domestic and international students. Applications are processed on a rolling basis. Application fee: $40 ($50 for international students). Electronic applications accepted. *Expenses: Tuition, area resident:* Full-time $4216.70; part-time $252.70 per credit hour. Tuition, state resident: full-time $4216.70; part-time $252.70 per credit hour. Tuition, nonresident: full-time $12,769; part-time $881.10 per credit hour. *International tuition:* $12,769.30 full-time. *Required fees:* $878.40; $48.80 per credit hour. Full-time tuition and fees vary according to course load and reciprocity agreements. *Financial support:* In 2018–19, 55 students received support, including 2 fellowships (averaging $4,548 per year), 13 research assistantships (averaging $16,141 per year), 24 teaching assistantships (averaging $10,014 per year); career-related internships or fieldwork, Federal Work-Study, scholarships/grants, traineeships, health care benefits, and unspecified assistantships also available. Support available to part-time students. Financial award application deadline: 3/1. *Faculty research:* Bioinformatics, database and data mining, networks and systems optimization, artificial intelligence, human factors and user interfaces, computer security, big data, data engineering, software engineering, automata theory, wireless sensor, smart grid, high performance computing, future Internet, automated planning, intelligent agents, logic programming, assistive technology, computer system, data storage. *Total annual research expenditures:* $2 million. *Unit head:* Dr. Son Tran, Department Head, 575-646-3723, Fax: 575-646-1002, E-mail: stran@cs.nmsu.edu. *Application contact:* Dr. Joe Song, Associate Professor, 575-646-3723, Fax: 575-646-1002, E-mail: gradcs@cs.nmsu.edu.
Website: http://www.cs.nmsu.edu/

New York University, Tandon School of Engineering, Department of Computer Science and Engineering, New York, NY 10012-1019. Offers bioinformatics (MS, Advanced Certificate); computer science (MS, PhD); cyber security (MS); cybersecurity risk and strategy (MS); software engineering (Graduate Certificate). *Program availability:* Part-time, evening/weekend. *Faculty:* 33 full-time (8 women), 35 part-time/adjunct (4 women). *Students:* 616 full-time (155 women), 204 part-time (44 women); includes 129 minority (8 Black or African American, non-Hispanic/Latino; 75 Asian, non-Hispanic/Latino; 39 Hispanic/Latino; 7 Two or more races, non-Hispanic/Latino), 561 international. Average age 26. 3,333 applicants, 29% accepted, 414 enrolled. In 2018, 280 master's, 8 doctorates awarded. *Degree requirements:* For master's, comprehensive exam (for some programs), thesis (for some programs); for doctorate, comprehensive exam, thesis/dissertation, qualifying exam. *Entrance requirements:* For master's, BA or BS in computer science, mathematics, science, or engineering; working knowledge of a high-level program; for doctorate, GRE General Test, GRE Subject Test, BA or BS in science, engineering, or management; MS or 1 year of graduate course work. Additional exam requirements/recommendations for international students: Required—TOEFL (minimum score 550 paper-based; 90 iBT); Recommended—IELTS (minimum score 7). *Application deadline:* For fall admission, 2/15 priority date for domestic and international students; for spring admission, 11/1 priority date for domestic and international students. Applications are processed on a rolling basis. Application fee: $75. Electronic applications accepted. *Expenses:* Contact institution. *Financial support:* In 2018–19, 589 students received support, including 6 fellowships with partial tuition reimbursements available (averaging $25,617 per year), 22 research assistantships with tuition reimbursements available (averaging $26,693 per year), 1 teaching assistantship with tuition reimbursement available (averaging $26,572 per year); career-related internships or fieldwork, scholarships/grants, tuition waivers, and unspecified assistantships also available. Support available to part-time students. Financial award application deadline: 2/15. *Faculty research:* Peer-to-peer networking, cloud services, Web search, Web mining, social networks, multi-player games, vulnerability analysis, peer-to-peer security, multimedia forensics, biometrics, watermarking and digital rights management, wireless security, steganography, fault-tolerant distributed cryptography, usable security, computer graphics and visualization, computer vision, image processing, data structures, computational geometry and learning theory, combinational optimization. *Total annual research expenditures:* $12 million. *Unit head:* Dr. Guido Gerig, Head, 646-997-3975, E-mail: gerig@nyu.edu. *Application contact:* Elizabeth Ensweiler, Senior Director of Graduate Enrollment and Graduate Admissions, 646-997-3936, E-mail: elizabeth.ensweiler@nyu.edu.

North Dakota State University, College of Graduate and Interdisciplinary Studies, Interdisciplinary Program in Genomics and Bioinformatics, Fargo, ND 58102. Offers MS, PhD. *Program availability:* Part-time. *Degree requirements:* For master's, thesis; for doctorate, comprehensive exam, thesis/dissertation. *Entrance requirements:* For master's and doctorate, minimum GPA of 3.0. Additional exam requirements/recommendations for international students: Required—TOEFL. Electronic applications accepted.

Northeastern University, College of Science, Boston, MA 02115-5096. Offers applied mathematics (MS); bioinformatics (MS); biology (PhD); biotechnology (MS); chemistry and chemical biology (MS, PhD); environmental science and policy (MS); marine and environmental sciences (PhD); marine biology (MS); mathematics (MS, PhD); operations research (MSOR); physics (MS, PhD); psychology (PhD). *Program availability:* Part-time. Terminal master's awarded for partial completion of doctoral program. *Degree requirements:* For master's, comprehensive exam (for some programs), thesis; for doctorate, comprehensive exam (for some programs), thesis/dissertation. *Entrance requirements:* For master's, GRE General Test. Electronic applications accepted. *Expenses:* Contact institution.

Nova Southeastern University, Dr. Kiran C. Patel College of Osteopathic Medicine, Fort Lauderdale, FL 33328. Offers biomedical informatics (MS, Graduate Certificate), including biomedical informatics (MS), clinical informatics (Graduate Certificate), public health informatics (Graduate Certificate); disaster and emergency management (MS); medical education (MS); nutrition (MS, Graduate Certificate), including functional nutrition and herbal therapy (Graduate Certificate); osteopathic medicine (DO); public health (MPH, Graduate Certificate), including health education (Graduate Certificate); social medicine (Graduate Certificate); DO/DMD. *Accreditation:* AOsA; CEPH. *Degree requirements:* For master's, comprehensive exam (for MPH); field/special projects; for doctorate, comprehensive exam, COMLEX Board Exams; for Graduate Certificate, thesis or alternative. *Entrance requirements:* For master's, GRE; for doctorate, MCAT, coursework in biology, chemistry, organic chemistry, physics (all with labs), biochemistry, and English. Electronic applications accepted. *Expenses:* Contact institution. *Faculty research:* Teaching strategies, simulated patient use, HIV/AIDS education, minority health issues, immune disorders.

Oregon Health & Science University, School of Medicine, Graduate Programs in Medicine, Department of Medical Informatics and Clinical Epidemiology, Portland, OR 97239-3098. Offers bioinformatics and computational biology (MS, PhD); clinical informatics (MBI, MS, PhD, Certificate); health information management (Certificate). *Program availability:* Part-time, online learning. *Faculty:* 12 full-time (6 women), 15 part-time/adjunct (7 women). *Students:* 28 full-time (12 women), 31 part-time (10 women); includes 13 minority (1 Black or African American, non-Hispanic/Latino; 9 Asian, non-Hispanic/Latino; 2 Hispanic/Latino; 1 Two or more races, non-Hispanic/Latino), 8 international. Average age 34. 65 applicants, 54% accepted, 32 enrolled. In 2018, 23 master's, 3 doctorates, 20 other advanced degrees awarded. Terminal master's awarded for partial completion of doctoral program. *Degree requirements:* For master's, thesis or capstone project; for doctorate, comprehensive exam, thesis/dissertation, qualifying exam. *Entrance requirements:* For master's and doctorate, GRE General Test

(minimum scores: 153 Verbal/148 Quantitative/4.5 Analytical), coursework in computer programming, human anatomy and physiology. *Application deadline:* For fall admission, 12/1 for domestic students; for winter admission, 11/1 for domestic students; for spring admission, 2/1 for domestic students. Applications are processed on a rolling basis. Application fee: $70. Electronic applications accepted. *Expenses:* Contact institution. *Financial support:* Fellowships with full tuition reimbursements, research assistantships, Federal Work-Study, scholarships/grants, health care benefits, and full-tuition and stipends (for PhD students) available. Financial award application deadline: 3/1; financial award applicants required to submit FAFSA. *Faculty research:* Clinical informatics, computational biology, health information management, genomics, data analytics. *Unit head:* Dr. William Hersh, Program Director, 503-494-4563, E-mail: somgrad@ohsu.edu. *Application contact:* Lauren Ludwig, Administrative Coordinator, 503-494-2252, E-mail: informat@ohsu.edu.
Website: http://www.ohsu.edu/dmice/

Oregon State University, Interdisciplinary/Institutional Programs, Program in Molecular and Cellular Biology, Corvallis, OR 97331. Offers bioinformatics (PhD); biotechnology (PhD); genome biology (PhD); molecular virology (PhD); plant molecular biology (PhD). *Degree requirements:* For doctorate, thesis/dissertation, oral and written qualifying exams. *Entrance requirements:* For doctorate, GRE. Additional exam requirements/recommendations for international students: Required—TOEFL (minimum score 80 iBT), IELTS (minimum score 6.5).

Penn State Hershey Medical Center, College of Medicine, Graduate School Programs in the Biomedical Sciences, Huck Institutes of the Life Sciences, Intercollege Graduate Program in Bioinformatics and Genomics, Hershey, PA 17033-2360. Offers MS, PhD. Program also offered at University Park location.

Rice University, Graduate Programs, George R. Brown School of Engineering, Department of Statistics, Houston, TX 77251-1892. Offers bioinformatics (PhD); biostatistics (PhD); computational finance (PhD); general statistics (PhD); statistics (M Stat, MA); MBA/M Stat. *Program availability:* Part-time. *Degree requirements:* For master's, comprehensive exam; for doctorate, comprehensive exam, thesis/dissertation. *Entrance requirements:* For master's and doctorate, GRE General Test, minimum GPA of 3.0. Additional exam requirements/recommendations for international students: Required—TOEFL (minimum score 630 paper-based; 90 iBT). Electronic applications accepted. *Faculty research:* Statistical genetics, non parametric function estimation, computational statistics and visualization, stochastic processes.

Rochester Institute of Technology, Graduate Enrollment Services, College of Science, School of Life Sciences, MS Program in Bioinformatics, Rochester, NY 14623-5603. Offers MS. *Program availability:* Part-time. *Students:* 6 full-time (4 women), 8 part-time (2 women), 3 international. Average age 30. 29 applicants, 59% accepted, 2 enrolled. In 2018, 3 master's awarded. *Degree requirements:* For master's, thesis. *Entrance requirements:* For master's, GRE, minimum GPA of 3.2 (recommended), two letters of recommendation. Additional exam requirements/recommendations for international students: Required—TOEFL (minimum score 570 paper-based; 79 iBT), IELTS (minimum score 6.5), PTE (minimum score 58). *Application deadline:* For fall admission, 2/15 priority date for domestic and international students; for spring admission, 12/15 priority date for domestic and international students. Applications are processed on a rolling basis. Application fee: $65. Electronic applications accepted. *Financial support:* In 2018–19, 15 students received support. Research assistantships with partial tuition reimbursements available, teaching assistantships with partial tuition reimbursements available, career-related internships or fieldwork, scholarships/grants, and unspecified assistantships available. Support available to part-time students. Financial award applicants required to submit FAFSA. *Faculty research:* Gene expression analysis, genomic sequence analysis, computational biology and evolution, machine learning of big data in biology, metabolomics. *Unit head:* Dr. Feng Cui, Graduate Program Director, 585-475-4115, Fax: 585-475-6970, E-mail: fxcsbi@rit.edu. *Application contact:* Diane Ellison, Senior Associate Vice President, Graduate Enrollment Services, 585-475-2229, Fax: 585-475-7164, E-mail: gradinfo@rit.edu.
Website: https://www.rit.edu/study/bioinformatics-ms

Rowan University, Graduate School, College of Science and Mathematics, Program in Bioinformatics, Glassboro, NJ 08028-1701. Offers MS. *Entrance requirements:* For master's, GRE, BS in biology, biochemistry, chemistry, computer science, or related field with minimum GPA of 2.5. Additional exam requirements/recommendations for international students: Required—TOEFL. Electronic applications accepted.

Rutgers University–Newark, School of Health Related Professions, Department of Health Informatics, Program in Biomedical Informatics, Newark, NJ 07102. Offers MS, PhD, DMD/MS, MD/MS. *Program availability:* Part-time, evening/weekend, online learning. *Degree requirements:* For master's, thesis; for doctorate, comprehensive exam, thesis/dissertation. *Entrance requirements:* For master's, BS, transcript of highest degree, statement of research interests, curriculum vitae, basic understanding of database concepts and calculus, 3 reference letters; for doctorate, master's degree, transcripts of highest degree, statement of research interests, curriculum vitae, basic understanding of database concepts and calculus, 3 reference letters. Additional exam requirements/recommendations for international students: Required—TOEFL. Electronic applications accepted.

Saint Louis University, Graduate Programs, College of Arts and Sciences, Department of Computer Science, St. Louis, MO 63103. Offers bioinformatics and computational biology (MS); computer science (MS); software engineering (MS). MS in bioinformatics and computational biology offered in coordination with Departments of Biology, Chemistry, and Mathematics and Statistics).

Simon Fraser University, Office of Graduate Studies and Postdoctoral Fellows, Faculty of Science, Department of Biological Sciences, Burnaby, BC V5A 1S6, Canada. Offers bioinformatics (Graduate Diploma); biological sciences (M Sc, PhD); environmental toxicology (MET); pest management (MPM). *Degree requirements:* For master's, thesis; for doctorate, thesis/dissertation, candidacy exam; for Graduate Diploma, practicum. *Entrance requirements:* For master's, minimum GPA of 3.0 (on scale of 4.33) or 3.33 based on last 60 credits of undergraduate courses; for doctorate, minimum GPA of 3.5 (on scale of 4.33); for Graduate Diploma, minimum GPA of 2.5 (on scale of 4.33) or 2.67 based on last 60 credits of undergraduate courses. Additional exam requirements/recommendations for international students: Recommended—TOEFL (minimum score 580 paper-based; 93 iBT), IELTS (minimum score 7), TWE (minimum score 5). Electronic applications accepted. *Faculty research:* Cell biology, wildlife ecology, environmental and evolutionary physiology, environmental toxicology, pest management.

Simon Fraser University, Office of Graduate Studies and Postdoctoral Fellows, Faculty of Science, Department of Molecular Biology and Biochemistry, Burnaby, BC V5A 1S6, Canada. Offers bioinformatics (Graduate Diploma); molecular biology and biochemistry (M Sc, PhD). *Degree requirements:* For master's, thesis; for doctorate, thesis/dissertation; for Graduate Diploma, practicum. *Entrance requirements:* For master's, minimum GPA of 3.0 (on scale of 4.33) or 3.33 based on last 60 credits of undergraduate courses; for doctorate, minimum GPA of 3.5; for Graduate Diploma, minimum GPA of 2.5 (on scale of 4.33) or 2.67 based on last 60 credits of undergraduate courses. Additional exam requirements/recommendations for international students: Recommended—TOEFL (minimum score 580 paper-based; 100 iBT), IELTS (minimum score 7.5), TWE (minimum score 5). Electronic applications accepted. *Faculty research:* Genomics and bioinformatics, cell and developmental biology, structural biology/biochemistry, immunology, nucleic acid function.

State University of New York at Oswego, Graduate Studies, Program in Biomedical and Health Informatics, Oswego, NY 13126. Offers health informatics professional (MS); health informatics: intelligent health systems (MS); health information management: health data science (MS). Program also offered at Syracuse campus. *Program availability:* Online learning. *Entrance requirements:* For master's, GRE (recommended), official transcripts, statement of purpose, resume, two letters of recommendation.

Stony Brook University, State University of New York, Graduate School, College of Engineering and Applied Sciences, Department of Biomedical Informatics, Stony Brook, NY 11794. Offers MS, PhD, AGC. *Faculty:* 3 full-time (0 women). *Students:* 7 full-time (5 women), 2 part-time (0 women); includes 2 minority (1 Black or African American, non-Hispanic/Latino; 1 Hispanic/Latino), 5 international. Average age 28. 28 applicants, 25% accepted, 3 enrolled. *Degree requirements:* For doctorate, thesis/dissertation, qualifying examination, teaching requirement. *Entrance requirements:* For master's, GRE, minimum B average or equivalent, two letters of recommendation; for doctorate, GRE; for AGC, minimum B average or equivalent, statement of purpose, three letters of recommendation. Additional exam requirements/recommendations for international students: Required—TOEFL. *Application deadline:* For fall admission, 1/15 for domestic students; for spring admission, 10/1 for domestic students. *Expenses:* Contact institution. *Financial support:* In 2018–19, 1 fellowship was awarded; research assistantships also available. *Faculty research:* Ecological risk, health care, health care administration, medical informatics, public health. *Total annual research expenditures:* $1.5 million. *Unit head:* Dr. Joel H. Saltz, Professor/Founding Chair, 631-638-1420, Fax: 631-638-1323, E-mail: joel.saltz@stonybrook.edu. *Application contact:* Craig Stewart, Senior Staff Assistant, 631-638-2864, Fax: 631-638-1323, E-mail: craig.stewart@stonybrookmedicine.edu.
Website: http://bmi.stonybrookmedicine.edu/

Tufts University, School of Engineering, Department of Computer Science, Medford, MA 02155. Offers bioengineering (MS), including bioinformatics; cognitive science/computer science (PhD); computer science (MS, PhD); soft material robotics (PhD). *Program availability:* Part-time. Terminal master's awarded for partial completion of doctoral program. *Entrance requirements:* For master's and doctorate, GRE General Test. Additional exam requirements/recommendations for international students: Required—TOEFL (minimum score 550 paper-based; 80 iBT), IELTS (minimum score 6.5). Electronic applications accepted. *Expenses: Tuition:* Full-time $51,288; part-time $1710 per credit hour. *Required fees:* $904. Full-time tuition and fees vary according to degree level, program and student level. Part-time tuition and fees vary according to course load. *Faculty research:* Computational biology, computational geometry, and computational systems biology; cognitive sciences, human-computer interaction, and human-robotic interaction; visualization and graphics, educational technologies; machine learning and data mining; programming languages and systems.

Université de Montréal, Faculty of Medicine, Biochemistry Department, Montréal, QC H3C 3J7, Canada. Offers M Sc, PhD. Electronic applications accepted.

Université de Montréal, Faculty of Medicine, Program in Bioinformatics, Montréal, QC H3C 3J7, Canada. Offers M Sc, PhD.

University at Buffalo, the State University of New York, Graduate School, Jacobs School of Medicine and Biomedical Sciences, Graduate Programs in Medicine and Biomedical Sciences, Program in Genetics, Genomics and Bioinformatics, Buffalo, NY 14203. Offers MS, PhD, MD/PhD. *Faculty:* 59 full-time (16 women). *Students:* 13 full-time (6 women); includes 4 minority (all Asian, non-Hispanic/Latino). Average age 25. 22 applicants, 64% accepted, 5 enrolled. In 2018, 4 master's awarded. Terminal master's awarded for partial completion of doctoral program. *Degree requirements:* For master's, thesis or alternative; for doctorate, thesis/dissertation. *Entrance requirements:* For master's and doctorate, GRE. Additional exam requirements/recommendations for international students: Required—TOEFL (minimum score 100 iBT); Recommended—IELTS (minimum score 6.5). *Application deadline:* For fall admission, 3/1 for domestic and international students. Application fee: $85. Electronic applications accepted. *Faculty research:* Human and medical genetics and genomics, developmental genomics and genetics, microbial genetics and pathogenesis, bioinformatics. *Unit head:* Dr. Richard Gronostajski, Director, 716-829-3471, Fax: 716-849-6655, E-mail: rgron@buffalo.edu. *Application contact:* M. Sara Thomas, Program Administrator, 716-829-3890, E-mail: msthomas@buffalo.edu.
Website: http://medicine.buffalo.edu/education/ggb.html

The University of Alabama at Birmingham, Joint Health Sciences, Genetics, Genomics, and Bioinformatics Theme, Birmingham, AL 35294. Offers PhD. *Students:* Average age 27. 27 applicants, 33% accepted, 3 enrolled. In 2018, 4 doctorates awarded. *Degree requirements:* For doctorate, comprehensive exam, thesis/dissertation. *Entrance requirements:* For doctorate, personal statement, resume or curriculum vitae, letters of recommendation, research experience, interview. Additional exam requirements/recommendations for international students: Required—TOEFL (minimum score 80 iBT), IELTS (minimum score 6.5). *Application deadline:* For fall admission, 12/31 for domestic and international students. Applications are processed on a rolling basis. Electronic applications accepted. *Expenses: Tuition, area resident:* Full-time $8100; part-time $8100 per year. Tuition, state resident: full-time $8100. Tuition, nonresident: full-time $19,188; part-time $19,188 per year. Tuition and fees vary according to program. *Financial support:* In 2018–19, fellowships with full tuition reimbursements (averaging $30,000 per year), research assistantships with full tuition reimbursements (averaging $31,000 per year) were awarded; health care benefits also available. *Unit head:* Dr. Kevin Dybvig, Theme Director, 205-934-9327, E-mail: dybvig@uab.edu. *Application contact:* Alyssa Zasada, Admissions Manager for Graduate Biomedical Sciences, 205-934-3857, E-mail: grad-gbs@uab.edu.
Website: http://www.uab.edu/gbs/home/themes/ggb

University of Arkansas at Little Rock, Graduate School, George W. Donaghey College of Engineering and Information Technology, Program in Bioinformatics, Little Rock, AR 72204-1099. Offers MS, PhD. *Entrance requirements:* For doctorate, MS in bioinformatics. Additional exam requirements/recommendations for international students: Required—TOEFL.

University of Arkansas for Medical Sciences, Graduate School, Little Rock, AR 72205. Offers biochemistry and molecular biology (MS, PhD); bioinformatics (MS, PhD); cellular physiology and molecular biophysics (MS, PhD); clinical nutrition (MS); interdisciplinary biomedical sciences (MS, PhD, Certificate); interdisciplinary toxicology (MS); microbiology and immunology (PhD); neurobiology and developmental sciences (PhD); pharmacology (PhD); MD/PhD. Bioinformatics programs hosted jointly with the University of Arkansas at Little Rock. *Program availability:* Part-time. Terminal master's awarded for partial completion of doctoral program. *Degree requirements:* For master's, comprehensive exam (for some programs), thesis (for some programs); for doctorate, thesis/dissertation. *Entrance requirements:* For master's and doctorate, GRE. Additional exam requirements/recommendations for international students: Required—TOEFL. Electronic applications accepted. *Expenses:* Contact institution.

The University of British Columbia, Faculty of Medicine, Department of Cellular and Physiological Sciences, Vancouver, BC V6T 1Z3, Canada. Offers bioinformatics (M Sc, PhD); cell and developmental biology (M Sc, PhD); genome science and technology (M Sc, PhD); neuroscience (M Sc, PhD). *Degree requirements:* For master's, thesis, oral defense; for doctorate, comprehensive exam, thesis/dissertation, oral defense. *Entrance requirements:* For master's, minimum overall B+ average in third- and fourth-year courses; for doctorate, minimum overall B+ average in master's degree (or equivalent) from approved institution with clear evidence of research ability or potential. Additional exam requirements/recommendations for international students: Required—TOEFL, IELTS. *Expenses:* Contact institution.

University of California, Los Angeles, Graduate Division, College of Letters and Science, Interdepartmental Program in Bioinformatics, Los Angeles, CA 90095. Offers MS, PhD. Terminal master's awarded for partial completion of doctoral program. *Degree requirements:* For master's, comprehensive exam, thesis, one quarter of teaching experience; for doctorate, thesis/dissertation, oral and written qualifying exams; one quarter of teaching experience. *Entrance requirements:* For doctorate, GRE General Test, bachelor's degree; minimum undergraduate GPA of 3.0 (or its equivalent if letter grade system not used). Additional exam requirements/recommendations for international students: Required—TOEFL. Electronic applications accepted.

University of California, Riverside, Graduate Division, Graduate Program in Genetics, Genomics, and Bioinformatics, Riverside, CA 92521-0102. Offers PhD. *Degree requirements:* For doctorate, thesis/dissertation, qualifying exams, teaching experience. *Entrance requirements:* For doctorate, GRE General Test, minimum GPA of 3.2. Additional exam requirements/recommendations for international students: Required—TOEFL (minimum score 550 paper-based, 80 iBT) or IELTS. Electronic applications accepted. *Faculty research:* Molecular genetics, evolution and population genetics, genomics and bioinformatics.

University of California, San Diego, Graduate Division, Program in Bioinformatics and Systems Biology, La Jolla, CA 92093. Offers PhD. *Students:* 82 full-time (24 women), 1 (woman) part-time. 251 applicants, 16% accepted, 22 enrolled. In 2018, 12 doctorates awarded. *Degree requirements:* For doctorate, comprehensive exam, thesis/dissertation, two quarters as teaching assistant. *Entrance requirements:* For doctorate, GRE General Test. Additional exam requirements/recommendations for international students: Required—TOEFL (minimum score 550 paper-based; 80 iBT), IELTS (minimum score 7). *Application deadline:* For fall admission, 12/11 for domestic students. Application fee: $105 ($125 for international students). Electronic applications accepted. *Financial support:* Fellowships, research assistantships, teaching assistantships, scholarships/grants, and traineeships available. Financial award applicants required to submit FAFSA. *Faculty research:* Quantitative foundations of computational biology, structural bioinformatics and systems pharmacology, proteomics and metabolomics, epigenomics and gene expression control, genetic and molecular networks. *Unit head:* Vineet Bafna, Director, 858-822-4978, E-mail: vbafna@ucsd.edu. *Application contact:* Jade Hermes, Graduate Coordinator, 858-822-0831, E-mail: bioinfo@ucsd.edu.
Website: http://bioinformatics.ucsd.edu/

University of California, San Diego, School of Medicine and Graduate Division, Graduate Studies in Biomedical Sciences, La Jolla, CA 92093-0685. Offers anthropogeny (PhD); bioinformatics (PhD); biomedical science (PhD); multi-scale biology (PhD). *Students:* 164 full-time (83 women), 3 part-time (2 women). 537 applicants, 18% accepted, 24 enrolled. In 2018, 32 doctorates awarded. *Degree requirements:* For doctorate, comprehensive exam, thesis/dissertation, 1-quarter teaching assistantship. *Entrance requirements:* For doctorate, As of 2018, applicants are no longer required to submit scores for either the GRE General or Subject Tests. Applicants can optionally submit scores for the GRE General Test (verbal, quantitative, and analytical sections) and/or an applicable GRE Subject Test (Biology, Biochemistry (discontinued December 2016), or Chemistry). Additional exam requirements/recommendations for international students: Required—TOEFL (minimum score 550 paper-based; 80 iBT), IELTS (minimum score 7). *Application deadline:* For fall admission, 4/3 for domestic students. Application fee: $105 ($125 for international students). Electronic applications accepted. *Financial support:* Fellowships, research assistantships, teaching assistantships, scholarships/grants, traineeships, unspecified assistantships, and stipends available. Financial award applicants required to submit FAFSA. *Faculty research:* Anthropogeny; Cancer Biology; Computational and Integrative Biology; Genetics and Genomics; Glycobiology; Immunology; Microbiome and Micbrobial Sciences; Molecular Cell and Developmental Biology; Molecular Pharmacology; Multi-Scale Biology; Neurobiology of Disease; Pharmaceutical Sciences and Drug Development; Physiology and Endocrinology; Quantitative Biology; Stem Cell Biology; Structural and Chemical Biology. *Unit head:* Arshad Desai, Chair, 858-534-9698, E-mail: abdesai@ucsd.edu. *Application contact:* Leanne Nordeman, Graduate Coordinator, 858-534-3982, E-mail: biomedsci@ucsd.edu.
Website: http://biomedsci.ucsd.edu

University of California, San Francisco, School of Pharmacy and Graduate Division, Program in Bioinformatics, San Francisco, CA 94158-2517. Offers PhD. Terminal master's awarded for partial completion of doctoral program. *Degree requirements:* For doctorate, thesis/dissertation, cumulative qualifying exams, proposal defense. *Entrance requirements:* For doctorate, GRE General Test, minimum GPA of 3.0, bachelor's degree. Additional exam requirements/recommendations for international students: Required—TOEFL (minimum score 550 paper-based; 80 iBT). *Faculty research:* Bioinformatics and computational biology, genetics and genomics, systems biology.

University of California, Santa Cruz, Jack Baskin School of Engineering, Program in Biomolecular Engineering and Bioinformatics, Santa Cruz, CA 95064. Offers MS, PhD. Terminal master's awarded for partial completion of doctoral program. *Degree requirements:* For master's, thesis, research project with written report; for doctorate, thesis/dissertation. *Entrance requirements:* For master's and doctorate, GRE General Test. Additional exam requirements/recommendations for international students: Required—TOEFL (minimum score 570 paper-based; 89 iBT); Recommended—IELTS (minimum score 8). Electronic applications accepted. *Faculty research:* Bioinformatics, genomics, stem cell.

University of Chicago, Graham School of Continuing Liberal and Professional Studies, Master of Science Program in Biomedical Informatics, Chicago, IL 60637-1513. Offers M Sc. *Program availability:* Part-time, evening/weekend. *Entrance requirements:* For master's, 3 letters of recommendation, statement of purpose, transcripts, resume or curriculum vitae. Additional exam requirements/recommendations for international students: Required—TOEFL (minimum score 104 iBT), IELTS (minimum score 7). Electronic applications accepted.

University of Cincinnati, Graduate School, College of Medicine, Graduate Programs in Biomedical Sciences, Department of Biomedical Informatics, Cincinnati, OH 45221. Offers PhD, Graduate Certificate. Program offered jointly with Cincinnati Children's Hospital Medical Center. *Program availability:* Part-time. *Degree requirements:* For doctorate, comprehensive exam, thesis/dissertation. *Entrance requirements:* For doctorate and Graduate Certificate, GRE. Additional exam requirements/recommendations for international students: Required—TOEFL (minimum score 520 paper-based; 80 iBT), IELTS (minimum score 6.5). Electronic applications accepted. *Expenses:* Contact institution. *Faculty research:* Clinical informatics; genomics, proteomics, metabolomics, transcriptomics and single-cell analysis; precision medicine; computational biology and bioinformatics; quality improvement, decision support and patient safety.

University of Colorado Denver, School of Medicine, Program in Pharmacology, Aurora, CO 80206. Offers bioinformatics (PhD); biomolecular structure (PhD). *Degree requirements:* For doctorate, comprehensive exam, thesis/dissertation, major seminar, 3 research rotations in the first year, 30 hours each of course work and thesis. *Entrance requirements:* For doctorate, GRE General Test, three letters of recommendation, personal statement. Additional exam requirements/recommendations for international students: Required—TOEFL (minimum score 550 paper-based; 80 iBT). Electronic applications accepted. *Expenses:* Tuition, state resident: full-time $6786; part-time $337 per credit hour. Tuition, nonresident: full-time $22,590; part-time $1255 per credit hour. *Required fees:* $1231; $137 per credit hour. Tuition and fees vary according to program and reciprocity agreements. *Faculty research:* Cancer biology, drugs of abuse, neuroscience, signal transduction, structural biology.

University of Georgia, Institute of Bioinformatics, Athens, GA 30602. Offers MS, PhD.

University of Idaho, College of Graduate Studies, College of Science, Department of Bioinformatics and Computational Biology, Moscow, ID 83844-3051. Offers MS, PhD. *Faculty:* 16. *Students:* 22. Average age 29. In 2018, 3 master's, 4 doctorates awarded. *Degree requirements:* For master's, thesis; for doctorate, thesis/dissertation. *Entrance requirements:* For master's, GRE, minimum GPA of 3.0. Additional exam requirements/recommendations for international students: Required—TOEFL (minimum score 100 iBT). *Application deadline:* For fall admission, 12/15 for domestic students; for spring admission, 9/1 for domestic students. Applications are processed on a rolling basis. Application fee: $60. Electronic applications accepted. *Expenses:* Tuition, state resident: full-time $7266.44; part-time $474.50 per credit hour. Tuition, nonresident: full-time $24,902; part-time $1453.50 per credit hour. *Required fees:* $2085.56; $45.50 per credit hour. *Financial support:* Applicants required to submit FAFSA. *Faculty research:* Ecology and evolutionary biology; computational biology. *Unit head:* Dr. David Tank, Director, 208-885-6010, E-mail: bcb@uidaho.edu. *Application contact:* Dr. David Tank, Director, 208-885-6010, E-mail: bcb@uidaho.edu.
Website: https://www.uidaho.edu/sci/bcb

University of Illinois at Chicago, College of Engineering, Department of Bioengineering, Chicago, IL 60607-7128. Offers MS, PhD. Terminal master's awarded for partial completion of doctoral program. *Degree requirements:* For master's, thesis; for doctorate, thesis/dissertation. *Entrance requirements:* For master's and doctorate, GRE Subject Test, minimum GPA of 3.0. Additional exam requirements/recommendations for international students: Required—TOEFL. Electronic applications accepted. *Expenses:* Contact institution. *Faculty research:* Imaging systems, bioinstrumentation, electrophysiology, biological control, laser scattering.

University of Illinois at Urbana–Champaign, Graduate College, College of Agricultural, Consumer and Environmental Sciences, Department of Crop Sciences, Champaign, IL 61820. Offers bioinformatics: crop sciences (MS); crop sciences (MS, PhD). *Program availability:* Online learning.

University of Illinois at Urbana–Champaign, Graduate College, College of Engineering, Department of Computer Science, Champaign, IL 61820. Offers bioinformatics (MS); computer science (MCS, MS, PhD); MCS/JD; MCS/M Arch; MCS/MBA. *Program availability:* Part-time, evening/weekend, online learning.

University of Illinois at Urbana–Champaign, Graduate College, School of Information Sciences, Champaign, IL 61820. Offers bioinformatics (MS); digital libraries (CAS); information management (MS); library and information science (MS, PhD, CAS). *Accreditation:* ALA (one or more programs are accredited). *Program availability:* Part-time, online learning. *Entrance requirements:* For degree, master's degree in library and information science or related field with minimum GPA of 3.0.

The University of Iowa, Graduate College, Program in Informatics, Iowa City, IA 52242-1316. Offers bioinformatics (MS, PhD); bioinformatics and computational biology (Certificate); geoinformatics (MS, PhD, Certificate); health informatics (MS, PhD, Certificate); information science (MS, PhD, Certificate). *Degree requirements:* For master's, thesis optional; for doctorate, comprehensive exam, thesis/dissertation. *Entrance requirements:* For master's and doctorate, GRE General Test, minimum GPA of 3.0. Additional exam requirements/recommendations for international students: Required—TOEFL (minimum score 550 paper-based; 81 iBT). Electronic applications accepted.

University of Louisville, School of Interdisciplinary and Graduate Studies, Louisville, KY 40292. Offers interdisciplinary studies (MA, MS, PhD), including bioethics and medical humanities (MA), bioinformatics (PhD), sustainability (MA, MS), translational bioengineering (PhD), translational neuroscience (PhD). *Program availability:* Part-time. *Students:* 27 full-time (13 women), 11 part-time (5 women); includes 4 minority (1 Black or African American, non-Hispanic/Latino; 2 Hispanic/Latino; 1 Two or more races, non-Hispanic/Latino), 11 international. Average age 32. 19 applicants, 68% accepted, 8 enrolled. In 2018, 2 master's awarded. *Degree requirements:* For master's, variable foreign language requirement, comprehensive exam (for some programs), thesis (for some programs); for doctorate, variable foreign language requirement, comprehensive exam, thesis/dissertation. *Entrance requirements:* For master's and doctorate, GRE General Test, 3 letters of recommendation, transcripts from previous post-secondary educational institutions. Additional exam requirements/recommendations for international students: Required—TOEFL (minimum score 550 paper-based; 79 iBT), IELTS (minimum score 6.5). *Application deadline:* For fall admission, 12/1 priority date for domestic and international students; for winter admission, 11/1 for domestic students, 6/1 for international students; for spring admission, 11/1 for domestic students, 6/1 for international students; for summer admission, 4/1 for domestic students, 1/1 for international students. Applications are processed on a rolling basis. Application fee: $65. Electronic applications accepted. *Expenses: Tuition, area resident:* Full-time $6500; part-time $723 per credit hour. Tuition, state resident: full-time $6500. Tuition, nonresident: full-time $13,557; part-time $1507 per credit hour. Tuition and fees vary according to course load and program. *Financial support:* In 2018–19, 30 students received support, including 120 fellowships with full tuition reimbursements available (averaging $20,000 per year). Financial award application deadline: 1/15. *Unit head:* Dr. Paul DeMarco, Acting Dean and Acting Vice Provost for Graduate Affairs, 502-852-5110, E-mail: paul.demarco@louisville.edu. *Application contact:* Dr. Barbara Clark, Acting Associate Dean, 502-852-6498, E-mail: gradadm@louisville.edu.
Website: http://www.graduate.louisville.edu

University of Maine, Graduate School, Graduate School of Biomedical Science and Engineering, Orono, ME 04469. Offers bioinformatics (PSM); biomedical engineering (PhD); biomedical science (PhD). *Faculty:* 182 full-time (60 women). *Students:* 46 full-time (25 women), 6 part-time (3 women); includes 2 minority (1 Asian, non-Hispanic/Latino; 1 Two or more races, non-Hispanic/Latino), 9 international. Average age 30. 54 applicants, 20% accepted, 8 enrolled. In 2018, 5 doctorates awarded. *Degree requirements:* For doctorate, comprehensive exam, thesis/dissertation. *Entrance requirements:* For doctorate, GRE General Test, master's degree. Additional exam

requirements/recommendations for international students: Required—TOEFL (minimum score 80 iBT), IELTS (minimum score 6.5), PTE (minimum score 60). *Application deadline:* For fall admission, 1/1 priority date for domestic and international students. Applications are processed on a rolling basis. Application fee: $65. Electronic applications accepted. *Financial support:* In 2018–19, 4 students received support, including 1 research assistantship with full tuition reimbursement available (averaging $18,000 per year), 4 teaching assistantships with full tuition reimbursements available (averaging $15,600 per year); scholarships/grants and unspecified assistantships also available. Financial award application deadline: 3/1. *Faculty research:* Molecular and Cellular Biology, Developmental Biology, Genomics, Neuroscience, Stem Cell Research. *Total annual research expenditures:* $1.6 million. *Unit head:* Dr. David Neivandt, Director, 207-581-2803. *Application contact:* Scott G. Delcourt, Assistant Vice President for Graduate Studies and Senior Associate Dean, 207-581-3291, Fax: 207-581-3232, E-mail: graduate@maine.edu.
Website: http://gsbse.umaine.edu/

The University of Manchester, School of Biological Sciences, Manchester, United Kingdom. Offers adaptive organismal biology (M Phil, PhD); animal biology (M Phil, PhD); biochemistry (M Phil, PhD); bioinformatics (M Phil, PhD); biomolecular sciences (M Phil, PhD); biotechnology (M Phil, PhD); cell biology (M Phil, PhD); cell matrix research (M Phil, PhD); channels and transporters (M Phil, PhD); developmental biology (M Phil, PhD); environmental biology (M Phil, PhD); evolutionary biology (M Phil, PhD); gene expression (M Phil, PhD); genetics (M Phil, PhD); history of science, technology and medicine (M Phil, PhD); immunology (M Phil, PhD); integrative neurobiology and behavior (M Phil, PhD); membrane trafficking (M Phil, PhD); microbiology (M Phil, PhD); molecular and cellular neuroscience (M Phil, PhD); molecular biology (M Phil, PhD); molecular cancer studies (M Phil, PhD); neuroscience (M Phil, PhD); ophthalmology (M Phil, PhD); optometry (M Phil, PhD); organelle function (M Phil, PhD); pharmacology (M Phil, PhD); physiology (M Phil, PhD); plant sciences (M Phil, PhD); stem cell research (M Phil, PhD); structural biology (M Phil, PhD); systems neuroscience (M Phil, PhD); toxicology (M Phil, PhD).

University of Maryland, College Park, Academic Affairs, College of Computer, Mathematical and Natural Sciences, Department of Biology, PhD Program in Biological Sciences, College Park, MD 20742. Offers behavior, ecology, evolution, and systematics (PhD); computational biology, bioinformatics, and genomics (PhD); molecular and cellular biology (PhD); physiological systems (PhD). *Degree requirements:* For doctorate, comprehensive exam, thesis/dissertation, thesis work presentation in seminar. *Entrance requirements:* For doctorate, GRE General Test; GRE Subject Test in biology (recommended), academic transcripts, statement of purpose/research interests, 3 letters of recommendation. Additional exam requirements/recommendations for international students: Required—TOEFL. Electronic applications accepted.

University of Massachusetts Medical School, Graduate School of Biomedical Sciences, Worcester, MA 01655-0115. Offers biomedical sciences (PhD), including biochemistry and molecular pharmacology, bioinformatics and computational biology, cancer biology, immunology and microbiology, interdisciplinary, neuroscience, translational science; biomedical sciences (millennium program) (PhD); clinical and population health research (PhD); clinical investigation (MS). Terminal master's awarded for partial completion of doctoral program. *Degree requirements:* For master's, comprehensive exam, thesis; for doctorate, comprehensive exam, thesis/dissertation. *Entrance requirements:* For master's, MD, PhD, DVM, or PharmD; for doctorate, GRE General Test, bachelor's degree. Additional exam requirements/recommendations for international students: Required—TOEFL (minimum score 90 iBT) or IELTS (minimum score 7.0). Electronic applications accepted. Application fee is waived when completed online. *Expenses:* Contact institution. *Faculty research:* RNA biology, molecular/cell/developmental/metabolic biology, bioinformatics and computational biology, clinical/translational research, infectious disease and immunology.

University of Memphis, Graduate School, College of Arts and Sciences, Department of Computer Science, Memphis, TN 38152. Offers bioinformatics (MS); computer science (MS, PhD). *Students:* 79 full-time (19 women), 21 part-time (4 women); includes 17 minority (7 Black or African American, non-Hispanic/Latino; 9 Asian, non-Hispanic/Latino; 1 Hispanic/Latino; 67 international. Average age 29. 110 applicants, 66% accepted, 29 enrolled. In 2018, 7 master's, 5 doctorates awarded. Terminal master's awarded for partial completion of doctoral program. *Degree requirements:* For master's, comprehensive exam, thesis; for doctorate, comprehensive exam, thesis/dissertation, qualifying exam, final exam. *Entrance requirements:* For master's and doctorate, GRE, letters of recommendation. Additional exam requirements/recommendations for international students: Required—TOEFL (minimum score 550 paper-based; 79 iBT). *Application deadline:* Applications are processed on a rolling basis. Application fee: $35 ($60 for international students). *Expenses: Tuition, area resident:* Full-time $10,240; part-time $503 per credit hour. Tuition, state resident: full-time $10,464. Tuition, nonresident: full-time $20,224; part-time $991 per credit hour. *Required fees:* $850; $106 per credit hour. *Financial support:* Fellowships, research assistantships with full tuition reimbursements, teaching assistantships with full tuition reimbursements, Federal Work-Study, scholarships/grants, and unspecified assistantships available. Financial award application deadline: 2/1; financial award applicants required to submit FAFSA. *Faculty research:* Network security, biomolecular and distributed computing, wireless sensor networks, artificial intelligence. *Unit head:* Dr. Lan Wang, Chair, 901-678-5465, Fax: 901-678-1506, E-mail: lanwang@memphis.edu. *Application contact:* Dr. Scott Fleming, Graduate Studies Coordinator, 901-678-3142, E-mail: info@cs.memphis.edu. Website: https://www.memphis.edu/cs/

University of Michigan, Rackham Graduate School, Program in Biomedical Sciences (PIBS) and Rackham Graduate School, Program in Bioinformatics, Ann Arbor, MI 48109. Offers MS, PhD. *Program availability:* Part-time. Terminal master's awarded for partial completion of doctoral program. *Degree requirements:* For master's, thesis optional, summer internship or rotation; for doctorate, thesis/dissertation, oral defense of dissertation, preliminary exam, two rotations. *Entrance requirements:* For master's and doctorate, GRE or MCAT. Additional exam requirements/recommendations for international students: Required—TOEFL (minimum score 100 iBT). Electronic applications accepted. *Faculty research:* Genomics; regulatory genomics and epigenomics; protein structure; proteomics; alternative splicing; integrative bioinformatics; systems biology and networks analysis; biomedical data science; translational bioinformatics, and pharmacogenomics; methodological development in computational biology; applications to complex genetic diseases.

University of Minnesota Rochester, Graduate Programs, Rochester, MN 55904. Offers bioinformatics and computational biology (MS, PhD); business administration (MBA); occupational therapy (MOT). *Accreditation:* AOTA.

University of Missouri, Office of Research and Graduate Studies, Informatics Institute, Columbia, MO 65211. Offers MS. *Entrance requirements:* Additional exam requirements/recommendations for international students: Required—TOEFL, IELTS. Electronic applications accepted.

University of Missouri–Kansas City, School of Computing and Engineering, Kansas City, MO 64110-2499. Offers civil engineering (MS); computer and electrical engineering (PhD); computer science (MS), including bioinformatics, software engineering, telecommunications networking; computer science and informatics (PhD); computing (PhD); electrical engineering (MS); engineering (PhD); engineering and construction management (Graduate Certificate); mechanical engineering (MS); telecommunications and computer networking (PhD). PhD (interdisciplinary) offered through the School of Graduate Studies. *Program availability:* Part-time. *Degree requirements:* For doctorate, thesis/dissertation. *Entrance requirements:* For master's, GRE General Test, minimum GPA of 3.0, 3 letters of recommendation from professors; for doctorate, GRE General Test, minimum GPA of 3.5. Additional exam requirements/recommendations for international students: Required—TOEFL (minimum score 550 paper-based; 80 iBT). *Faculty research:* Algorithms, bioinformatics and medical informatics, biomechanics/biomaterials, civil engineering materials, networking and telecommunications, thermal science.

University of Nebraska at Omaha, Graduate Studies, College of Information Science and Technology, School of Interdisciplinary Informatics, Omaha, NE 68182. Offers biomedical informatics (MS, PhD); information assurance (MS). *Program availability:* Part-time, evening/weekend. *Degree requirements:* For master's, comprehensive exam, thesis (for some programs); for doctorate, comprehensive exam, thesis/dissertation. *Entrance requirements:* For master's and doctorate, GRE General Test, letters of recommendation, resume, transcripts. Additional exam requirements/recommendations for international students: Required—TOEFL, IELTS, PTE.

University of Nebraska–Lincoln, Graduate College, College of Arts and Sciences and College of Engineering, Department of Computer Science and Engineering, Lincoln, NE 68588. Offers bioinformatics (MS, PhD); computer engineering (MS, PhD); computer science (MS, PhD); information technology (PhD). *Degree requirements:* For master's, thesis optional; for doctorate, comprehensive exam, thesis/dissertation. *Entrance requirements:* For master's and doctorate, GRE General Test. Additional exam requirements/recommendations for international students: Required—TOEFL (minimum score 600 paper-based). Electronic applications accepted. *Faculty research:* Software engineering, geo- and bio-informatics, scientific computation, secure communication.

University of Nebraska Medical Center, Program in Biomedical Informatics, Omaha, NE 68198. Offers MS, PhD. *Program availability:* Part-time. *Faculty:* 29 full-time (7 women). *Students:* 1 full-time (0 women), 6 part-time (2 women); includes 1 minority (Asian, non-Hispanic/Latino), 5 international. Average age 37. In 2018, 2 doctorates awarded. *Degree requirements:* For master's, comprehensive exam, thesis; for doctorate, comprehensive exam, thesis/dissertation. *Entrance requirements:* For master's and doctorate, GRE, clinical training and experience (medicine, nursing, dentistry, or allied health degree). Additional exam requirements/recommendations for international students: Required—TOEFL (minimum score 550 paper-based; 80 iBT), IELTS. *Application deadline:* For fall admission, 6/1 for domestic students, 4/1 for international students; for spring admission, 10/1 for domestic and international students. Applications are processed on a rolling basis. Application fee: $60. Electronic applications accepted. *Expenses:* Contact institution. *Financial support:* In 2018–19, 9 students received support, including 1 fellowship with full tuition reimbursement available (averaging $25,000 per year), 4 research assistantships with full tuition reimbursements available (averaging $25,000 per year); scholarships/grants and unspecified assistantships also available. Financial award application deadline: 2/15; financial award applicants required to submit FAFSA. *Faculty research:* Genomics, bioinformatics, clinical research informatics, health informatics, pathology informatics. *Unit head:* Dr. Jim McClay, Director, 402-559-3587, E-mail: jmcclay@unmc.edu. *Application contact:* Rhonda Sheibal-Carver, Academic Program Coordinator, 402-559-5141, E-mail: rhonda.sheibalcarver@unmc.edu.
Website: http://www.unmc.edu/bmi/

The University of North Carolina at Chapel Hill, School of Medicine and Graduate School, Graduate Programs in Medicine, Curriculum in Bioinformatics and Computational Biology, Chapel Hill, NC 27599. Offers PhD. *Degree requirements:* For doctorate, comprehensive exam, thesis/dissertation. *Entrance requirements:* For doctorate, GRE, minimum GPA of 3.0. Additional exam requirements/recommendations for international students: Required—TOEFL. Electronic applications accepted. *Faculty research:* Protein folding, design and evolution and molecular biophysics of disease; mathematical modeling of signaling pathways and regulatory networks; bioinformatics, medical informatics, user interface design; statistical genetics and genetic epidemiology datamining, classification and clustering analysis of gene-expression data.

The University of North Carolina at Charlotte, College of Computing and Informatics, Department of Bioinformatics and Genomics, Charlotte, NC 28223-0001. Offers bioinformatics (PSM); bioinformatics and computational biology (PhD); bioinformatics applications (Graduate Certificate); bioinformatics technology (Graduate Certificate). *Program availability:* Part-time. *Students:* 44 full-time (22 women), 17 part-time (9 women); includes 19 minority (2 Black or African American, non-Hispanic/Latino; 7 Asian, non-Hispanic/Latino; 8 Hispanic/Latino; 1 Native Hawaiian or other Pacific Islander, non-Hispanic/Latino; 1 Two or more races, non-Hispanic/Latino), 12 international. Average age 29. 41 applicants, 73% accepted, 17 enrolled. In 2018, 7 master's, 2 doctorates, 5 other advanced degrees awarded. Terminal master's awarded for partial completion of doctoral program. *Entrance requirements:* For master's, GRE, baccalaureate degree from accredited college or university in biology, biochemistry, chemistry, physics, mathematics, statistics, computer science, or another related field that provides sound background in life sciences, computing, or both; minimum undergraduate GPA of 3.0 overall and in major; recommendation letters; for doctorate, GRE, baccalaureate degree from recognized institution; adequate preparation in chemistry, biology, mathematics (preferably statistics), and computer science; evidence of scholarly and creative activity; minimum GPA of 3.0; essay; reference letters; for Graduate Certificate, bachelor's degree in related field; practical experience and confidence with computers, for instance use of common Web browsers, word processing, plotting, and spreadsheet applications. Additional exam requirements/recommendations for international students: Required—TOEFL (minimum score 523 paper-based; 70 iBT), IELTS (minimum score 6), TOEFL (minimum score 523 paper-based, 70 iBT) or IELTS (6). *Application deadline:* Applications are processed on a rolling basis. Application fee: $75. Electronic applications accepted. *Expenses:* Contact institution. *Financial support:* Fellowships, research assistantships, teaching assistantships, career-related internships or fieldwork, institutionally sponsored loans, scholarships/grants, unspecified assistantships, and administrative assistantships available. Support available to part-time students. Financial award application deadline: 3/1; financial award applicants required to submit FAFSA. *Total annual research expenditures:* $2.7 million. *Unit head:* Dr. Lawrence Mays, Chair, 704-687-8555, E-mail: lemays@uncc.edu. *Application contact:* Kathy B. Giddings, Director of Graduate Admissions, 704-687-5503, Fax: 704-687-1668, E-mail: gradadm@uncc.edu.
Website: http://bioinformatics.uncc.edu

The University of North Carolina at Charlotte, College of Computing and Informatics, Program in Computing and Information Systems, Charlotte, NC 28223-0001. Offers computing and information systems (PhD), including bioinformatics, business information systems and operations management, computer science, interdisciplinary, software and information systems. *Students:* 99 full-time (27 women), 18 part-time (5 women); includes 4 minority (1 Black or African American, non-Hispanic/Latino; 1 Asian, non-Hispanic/Latino; 1 Hispanic/Latino; 1 Two or more races, non-Hispanic/Latino), 90 international. Average age 30. 86 applicants, 33% accepted, 15 enrolled. In 2018, 17 doctorates awarded. *Entrance requirements:* For doctorate, GRE or GMAT, baccalaureate degree, minimum GPA of 3.0 on courses related to the chosen field of PhD study, essay, reference letters. Additional exam requirements/recommendations for international students: Required—TOEFL (minimum score 523 paper-based; 70 iBT), IELTS (minimum score 6), TOEFL (minimum score 523 paper-based, 70 iBT) or IELTS (6). *Application deadline:* Applications are processed on a rolling basis. Application fee: $75. Electronic applications accepted. Tuition and fees vary according to course load and program. *Financial support:* Career-related internships or fieldwork, institutionally sponsored loans, scholarships/grants, health care benefits, and unspecified assistantships available. Support available to part-time students. Financial award applicants required to submit FAFSA. *Unit head:* Dr. Fatma Mili, Dean, 704-687-8450. *Application contact:* Kathy B. Giddings, Director of Graduate Admissions, 704-687-5503, Fax: 704-687-1668, E-mail: gradadm@uncc.edu.

University of Pittsburgh, School of Medicine, Graduate Programs in Medicine, Biomedical Informatics Programs, Pittsburgh, PA 15260. Offers MS, PhD, Certificate. Terminal master's awarded for partial completion of doctoral program. *Degree requirements:* For master's, comprehensive exam, thesis; for doctorate, comprehensive exam, thesis/dissertation. *Entrance requirements:* For master's and doctorate, GRE, transcripts, letters of recommendation. Additional exam requirements/recommendations for international students: Required—TOEFL (minimum score 600 paper-based; 100 iBT), IELTS (minimum score 7). Electronic applications accepted. *Expenses:* Contact institution. *Faculty research:* Biomedical informatics; machine learning; artificial intelligence; human computer interaction.

University of Rochester, School of Medicine and Dentistry, Graduate Programs in Medicine and Dentistry, Department of Biostatistics and Computational Biology, Programs in Statistics, Rochester, NY 14642. Offers bioinformatics and computational biology (PhD). *Expenses: Tuition:* Full-time $52,974; part-time $1654 per credit hour. *Required fees:* $612. One-time fee: $30 part-time. Tuition and fees vary according to campus/location and program.

University of Southern California, Graduate School, Dana and David Dornsife College of Letters, Arts and Sciences, Department of Biological Sciences, Program in Molecular and Computational Biology, Los Angeles, CA 90089. Offers computational biology and bioinformatics (PhD); molecular biology (PhD). *Degree requirements:* For doctorate, comprehensive exam, thesis/dissertation, qualifying examination, dissertation defense. *Entrance requirements:* For doctorate, GRE, 3 letters of recommendation, personal statement, resume, minimum GPA of 3.0. Additional exam requirements/recommendations for international students: Required—TOEFL (minimum score 600 paper-based; 100 iBT). Electronic applications accepted. *Faculty research:* Biochemistry and molecular biology; genomics; computational biology and bioinformatics; cell and developmental biology, and genetics; DNA replication and repair, and cancer biology.

University of South Florida, Innovative Education, Tampa, FL 33620-9951. Offers adult, career and higher education (Graduate Certificate), including college teaching, leadership in developing human resources, leadership in higher education; Africana studies (Graduate Certificate), including diasporas and health disparities, genocide and human rights; aging studies (Graduate Certificate), including gerontology; art research (Graduate Certificate), including museum studies; business foundations (Graduate Certificate); chemical and biomedical engineering (Graduate Certificate), including materials science and engineering, water, health and sustainability; child and family studies (Graduate Certificate), including positive behavior support; civil and industrial engineering (Graduate Certificate), including transportation systems analysis; community and family health (Graduate Certificate), including maternal and child health, social marketing and public health, violence and injury: prevention and intervention, women's health; criminology (Graduate Certificate), including criminal justice administration; data science for public administration (Graduate Certificate); digital humanities (Graduate Certificate); educational measurement and research (Graduate Certificate), including evaluation; English (Graduate Certificate), including comparative literary studies, creative writing, professional and technical communication; entrepreneurship (Graduate Certificate); environmental health (Graduate Certificate), including safety management; epidemiology and biostatistics (Graduate Certificate), including applied biostatistics, biostatistics, concepts and tools of epidemiology, epidemiology, epidemiology of infectious diseases; geography, environment and planning (Graduate Certificate), including community development, environmental policy and management, geographical information systems; geology (Graduate Certificate), including hydrogeology; global health (Graduate Certificate), including disaster management, global health and Latin American and Caribbean studies, global health practice, humanitarian assistance, infection control; government and international affairs (Graduate Certificate), including Cuban studies, globalization studies; health policy and management (Graduate Certificate), including health management and leadership, public health policy and programs; hearing specialist: early intervention (Graduate Certificate); industrial and management systems engineering (Graduate Certificate), including systems engineering, technology management; information studies (Graduate Certificate), including school library media specialist; information systems/decision sciences (Graduate Certificate), including analytics and business intelligence; instructional technology (Graduate Certificate), including distance education, Florida digital/virtual educator, instructional design, multimedia design, Web design; internal medicine, bioethics and medical humanities (Graduate Certificate), including biomedical ethics; Latin American and Caribbean studies (Graduate Certificate); leadership for coastal resiliency planning (Graduate Certificate); mass communications (Graduate Certificate), including multimedia journalism; mathematics and statistics (Graduate Certificate), including mathematics; medicine (Graduate Certificate), including aging and neuroscience, bioinformatics, biotechnology, brain fitness and memory management, clinical investigation, hand and upper limb rehabilitation, health informatics, health sciences, integrative weight management, intellectual property, medicine and gender, metabolic and nutritional medicine, metabolic cardiology, pharmacy sciences; national and competitive intelligence (Graduate Certificate); nursing (Graduate Certificate), including simulation based academic fellowship in advanced pain management; psychological and social foundations (Graduate Certificate), including career counseling, college teaching, diversity in education, mental health counseling, school counseling; public affairs (Graduate Certificate), including nonprofit management, public management, research administration; public health (Graduate Certificate), including assessing chemical toxicity and public health risks, health equity, pharmacoepidemiology, public health generalist, toxicology, translational research in adolescent behavioral health; public health practices (Graduate Certificate), including planning for healthy communities; rehabilitation and mental health counseling (Graduate Certificate), including integrative mental health care, marriage and family therapy, rehabilitation technology; secondary education (Graduate Certificate), including ESOL, foreign language education: culture and content, foreign language education: professional; social work (Graduate Certificate), including geriatric social work/clinical gerontology; special education (Graduate Certificate), including autism spectrum disorder, disabilities education: severe/profound; world languages (Graduate Certificate), including teaching English as a second language (TESL) or foreign language. *Expenses:* Tuition, state resident: full-time $6350. Tuition, nonresident: full-

time $19,048. *International tuition:* $19,048 full-time. *Required fees:* $2079. *Unit head:* Dr. Cynthia DeLuca, Associate Vice President and Assistant Vice Provost, 813-974-3077, Fax: 813-974-7061, E-mail: deluca@usf.edu. *Application contact:* Owen Hooper, Director, Summer and Alternative Calendar Programs, 813-974-6917, E-mail: hooper@usf.edu.
Website: http://www.usf.edu/innovative-education/

University of South Florida, Morsani College of Medicine and College of Graduate Studies, Graduate Programs in Medical Sciences, Tampa, FL 33620-9951. Offers advanced athletic training (MS); athletic training (MS); bioinformatics and computational biology (MSBCB); biotechnology (MSB); health informatics (MSHI); medical sciences (MSMS, PhD), including aging and neuroscience (MSMS), allergy, immunology and infectious disease (PhD), anatomy, biochemistry and molecular biology, clinical and translational research, health science (MSMS), interdisciplinary medical sciences (MSMS), medical microbiology and immunology (MSMS), metabolic and nutritional medicine (MSMS), microbiology and immunology (PhD), molecular medicine, molecular pharmacology and physiology (PhD), neuroscience (PhD), pathology and cell biology (PhD), women's health (MSMS). *Faculty:* 1 (woman) full-time. *Students:* 355 full-time (207 women), 229 part-time (145 women); includes 283 minority (71 Black or African American, non-Hispanic/Latino; 2 American Indian or Alaska Native, non-Hispanic/Latino; 89 Asian, non-Hispanic/Latino; 103 Hispanic/Latino; 2 Native Hawaiian or other Pacific Islander, non-Hispanic/Latino; 16 Two or more races, non-Hispanic/Latino), 48 international. Average age 28. 898 applicants, 57% accepted, 323 enrolled. In 2018, 227 master's, 13 doctorates awarded. Terminal master's awarded for partial completion of doctoral program. *Degree requirements:* For master's, comprehensive exam, thesis; for doctorate, comprehensive exam, thesis/dissertation. *Entrance requirements:* For master's, GRE General Test or GMAT, bachelor's degree or equivalent from regionally-accredited university with minimum GPA of 3.0 in upper-division sciences coursework; prerequisites in general biology, general chemistry, general physics, organic chemistry, quantitative analysis, and integral and differential calculus; for doctorate, GRE General Test, bachelor's degree from regionally-accredited university with minimum GPA of 3.0 in upper-division sciences coursework; 3 letters of recommendation; personal interview; 1-2 page personal statement; prerequisites in biology, chemistry, physics, organic chemistry, quantitative analysis, and integral/differential calculus. Additional exam requirements/recommendations for international students: Required—TOEFL (minimum score 550 paper-based; 79 iBT) or IELTS (minimum score 6.5). *Application deadline:* For fall admission, 2/1 priority date for domestic students, 2/1 for international students. Application fee: $30. Electronic applications accepted. *Expenses:* Contact institution. *Financial support:* In 2018–19, 106 students received support. *Faculty research:* Anatomy, biochemistry, cancer biology, cardiovascular disease, cell biology, immunology, microbiology, molecular biology, neuroscience, pharmacology, physiology. *Total annual research expenditures:* $50.9 million. *Unit head:* Dr. Michael Barber, Professor/Associate Dean for Graduate and Postdoctoral Affairs, 813-974-9908, Fax: 813-974-4317, E-mail: mbarber@health.usf.edu. *Application contact:* Dr. Eric Bennett, Graduate Director, PhD Program in Medical Sciences, 813-974-1545, Fax: 813-974-4317, E-mail: esbennet@health.usf.edu.
Website: http://health.usf.edu/nocms/medicine/graduatestudies/

The University of Tennessee at Chattanooga, Program in Computer Science, Chattanooga, TN 37403. Offers biomedical informatics (Post Master's Certificate); computer science (MS). *Program availability:* Part-time. *Degree requirements:* For master's, comprehensive exam, thesis. *Entrance requirements:* For master's, GRE General Test, minimum cumulative undergraduate GPA of 2.7 or 3.0 in senior year. Additional exam requirements/recommendations for international students: Required—TOEFL (minimum score 550 paper-based; 79 iBT), IELTS (minimum score 6). Electronic applications accepted. *Expenses:* Contact institution. *Faculty research:* Power systems, computer architecture, pattern recognition, artificial intelligence, statistical data analysis.

The University of Texas at El Paso, Graduate School, College of Science, Department of Biological Sciences, El Paso, TX 79968-0001. Offers bioinformatics (MS); biological sciences (MS, PhD). *Program availability:* Part-time, evening/weekend. *Degree requirements:* For master's, thesis; for doctorate, thesis/dissertation. *Entrance requirements:* For master's, GRE, minimum GPA of 3.0, letters of recommendation; for doctorate, GRE, statement of purpose, letters of recommendation. Additional exam requirements/recommendations for international students: Required—TOEFL; Recommended—IELTS. Electronic applications accepted.

The University of Texas Health Science Center at Houston, School of Biomedical Informatics, Houston, TX 77030. Offers applied biomedical informatics (MS, Certificate); biomedical informatics (MS, PhD, Certificate); health data science (Certificate); public health informatics (Certificate); MPH/MS; MPH/PhD. *Program availability:* Part-time, 100% online, blended/hybrid learning. *Faculty:* 29 full-time (10 women), 11 part-time/adjunct (2 women). *Students:* 62 full-time (42 women), 224 part-time (120 women); includes 152 minority (43 Black or African American, non-Hispanic/Latino; 2 American Indian or Alaska Native, non-Hispanic/Latino; 59 Asian, non-Hispanic/Latino; 42 Hispanic/Latino; 3 Native Hawaiian or other Pacific Islander, non-Hispanic/Latino; 3 Two or more races, non-Hispanic/Latino). Average age 36. 136 applicants, 77% accepted, 52 enrolled. In 2018, 48 master's, 4 doctorates awarded. *Degree requirements:* For master's, thesis or alternative, practicum with capstone report; for doctorate, comprehensive exam, thesis/dissertation. *Entrance requirements:* For master's and doctorate, GRE. Additional exam requirements/recommendations for international students: Required—TOEFL (minimum score 87 iBT), IELTS (minimum score 7). *Application deadline:* For fall admission, 7/1 for domestic and international students; for spring admission, 11/1 for domestic and international students; for summer admission, 3/1 for domestic and international students. Applications are processed on a rolling basis. Application fee: $60. Electronic applications accepted. *Expenses:* Certificate (full-time) - TX Resident: $6,825; Certificate (full-time) non-resident: $16,065 Masters (full-time) resident: $17,955, Masters (full-time) non-resident: $41,980; PhD - TX Resident: $32,325, PhD - non-resident: $89,612; DHI - program starting in Fall 2019. *Financial support:* In 2018–19, 59 students received support, including 50 research assistantships (averaging $22,376 per year), 10 teaching assistantships (averaging $11,600 per year); career-related internships or fieldwork, institutionally sponsored loans, scholarships/grants, health care benefits, and unspecified assistantships also available. Support available to part-time students. Financial award application deadline: 5/1; financial award applicants required to submit FAFSA. *Faculty research:* Health data science, bioinformatics, precision health and human factors engineering. *Total annual research expenditures:* $9.5 million. *Unit head:* Dr. Jiajie Zhang, Dean/Chair in Informatics Excellence, 713-500-3922, E-mail: jiajie.zhang@uth.tmc.edu. *Application contact:* Jaime Hargrave, Director, Student Affairs, 713-500-3920, Fax: 713-500-0360, E-mail: jaime.n.hargrave@uth.tmc.edu.
Website: https://sbmi.uth.edu

The University of Texas Health Science Center at Houston, School of Public Health, Houston, TX 77030. Offers behavioral science (PhD); biostatistics (MPH, MS, PhD); environmental health (MPH); epidemiology (MPH, MS, PhD); general public health (Certificate); genomics and bioinformatics (Certificate); health disparities (Certificate); health promotion/health education (MPH, Dr PH); healthcare management (Certificate); management, policy and community health (MPH, Dr PH, PhD); maternal and child health (Certificate); public health informatics (Certificate); DDS/MPH; JD/MPH; MBA/MPH; MD/MPH; MGPS/MPH; MP Aff/MPH; MS/MPH; MSN/MPH; MSW/MPH; PhD/MPH. Specific programs are offered at each of our six campuses in Texas (Austin, Brownsville, Dallas, El Paso, Houston, and San Antonio). *Accreditation:* CAHME; CEPH. *Program availability:* Part-time. *Degree requirements:* For master's, thesis (for some programs); for doctorate, comprehensive exam, thesis/dissertation. *Entrance requirements:* For master's and doctorate, GRE General Test. Additional exam requirements/recommendations for international students: Required—TOEFL (minimum score 600 paper-based, 100 iBT) or IELTS (7.5). Electronic applications accepted. *Expenses:* Contact institution. *Faculty research:* Chronic and infectious disease epidemiology; health promotion and health education; applied and theoretical biostatistics; healthcare management, policy and economics; environmental and occupational health.

The University of Texas Medical Branch, Graduate School of Biomedical Sciences, Program in Biochemistry and Molecular Biology, Galveston, TX 77555. Offers biochemistry (PhD); bioinformatics (PhD); biophysics (PhD); cell biology (PhD); computational biology (PhD); structural biology (PhD). *Degree requirements:* For doctorate, thesis/dissertation. *Entrance requirements:* Additional exam requirements/recommendations for international students: Required—TOEFL (minimum score 550 paper-based). Electronic applications accepted.

University of the Sciences, Program in Bioinformatics, Philadelphia, PA 19104-4495. Offers MS. *Program availability:* Part-time, evening/weekend. *Entrance requirements:* Additional exam requirements/recommendations for international students: Required—TOEFL, TWE. *Expenses:* Contact institution. *Faculty research:* Genomics, microarray analysis, computer-aided drug design, molecular biophysics, cell structure, molecular dynamics, computational chemistry.

The University of Toledo, College of Graduate Studies, College of Medicine and Life Sciences, Interdepartmental Programs, Toledo, OH 43606-3390. Offers bioinformatics and proteomics/genomics (MSBS); biomarkers and bioinformatics (Certificate); biomarkers and diagnostics (PSM); human donation sciences (MSBS); medical sciences (MSBS); MD/MSBS. *Degree requirements:* For master's, thesis or alternative. *Entrance requirements:* For master's, GRE, minimum undergraduate GPA of 3.0, three letters of recommendation, statement of purpose, transcripts from all prior institutions attended, resume; for Certificate, minimum undergraduate GPA of 3.0, three letters of recommendation, statement of purpose, transcripts from all prior institutions attended, resume. Additional exam requirements/recommendations for international students: Required—TOEFL (minimum score 550 paper-based; 80 iBT). Electronic applications accepted.

University of Utah, School of Medicine and Graduate School, Graduate Programs in Medicine, Department of Biomedical Informatics, Salt Lake City, UT 84112-1107. Offers MS, PhD, Certificate. *Program availability:* Part-time, online learning. *Degree requirements:* For master's, comprehensive exam, thesis; for doctorate, comprehensive exam, thesis/dissertation, qualifying exam. *Entrance requirements:* For master's and doctorate, GRE General Test (minimum 60th percentile), minimum GPA of 3.3. Additional exam requirements/recommendations for international students: Required—TOEFL (minimum score 600 paper-based). Electronic applications accepted. *Expenses: Tuition, area resident:* Full-time $7190.66; part-time $2112.48 per year. Tuition, state resident: full-time $7190.66. Tuition, nonresident: full-time $25,195. *Required fees:* $558; $555.04 per unit. Tuition and fees vary according to course level, course load, degree level, program and student level. *Faculty research:* Health information systems and expert systems, genetic epidemiology, medical imaging, bioinformatics, public health informatics.

University of Washington, Graduate School, School of Medicine, Graduate Programs in Medicine, Department of Medical Education and Biomedical Informatics, Division of Biomedical and Health Informatics, Seattle, WA 98195. Offers MS, PhD. *Entrance requirements:* For master's and doctorate, GRE General Test, minimum GPA of 3.0; previous undergraduate course work in biology, computer programming, and mathematics. Additional exam requirements/recommendations for international students: Required—TOEFL (minimum score 580 paper-based; 70 iBT). Electronic applications accepted. *Faculty research:* Bio-clinical informatics, information retrieval, human-computer interaction, knowledge-based systems, telehealth.

University of Wisconsin–Madison, School of Medicine and Public Health, Biomedical Data Science Graduate Program, Madison, WI 53706-1380. Offers MS, PhD. *Application contact:* Beth Bierman, Student Services Coordinator, 608-265-8649, E-mail: bbierman@wisc.edu.
Website: https://www.biostat.wisc.edu/content/ms_program_in_biomedical_data_science

Vanderbilt University, Department of Biomedical Informatics, Nashville, TN 37240-1001. Offers MS, PhD. *Program availability:* Part-time. *Faculty:* 26 full-time (6 women). *Students:* 18 full-time (6 women); includes 4 minority (1 Black or African American, non-Hispanic/Latino; 3 Asian, non-Hispanic/Latino), 1 international. Average age 31. 51 applicants, 12% accepted, 3 enrolled. In 2018, 5 master's, 2 doctorates awarded. Terminal master's awarded for partial completion of doctoral program. *Degree requirements:* For master's, thesis; for doctorate, thesis/dissertation, final and qualifying exams. *Entrance requirements:* For master's and doctorate, GRE General Test. Additional exam requirements/recommendations for international students: Required—TOEFL (minimum score 570 paper-based; 88 iBT). *Application deadline:* For fall admission, 1/15 for domestic and international students. Electronic applications accepted. *Expenses: Tuition:* Full-time $47,208; part-time $2026 per credit hour. *Required fees:* $478. *Financial support:* Fellowships with tuition reimbursements, research assistantships with tuition reimbursements, teaching assistantships with tuition reimbursements, Federal Work-Study, institutionally sponsored loans, scholarships/grants, traineeships, and health care benefits available. Financial award application deadline: 1/15; financial award applicants required to submit CSS PROFILE or FAFSA. *Faculty research:* Organizational informatics, the application of informatics to the role of information technology in organizational change, clinical research and translational informatics, applications of informatics to facilitating and quota; bench to bedside and quote; translational research. *Unit head:* Dr. Kevin Johnson, Chair, 615-936-1423, Fax: 615-936-1427, E-mail: kevin.johnson@vanderbilt.edu. *Application contact:* Cynthia Gadd, Director of Graduate Studies, 615-936-1050, Fax: 615-936-1427, E-mail: cindy.gadd@vanderbilt.edu.
Website: https://medschool.vanderbilt.edu/dbmi/

Virginia Polytechnic Institute and State University, Graduate School, Intercollege, Blacksburg, VA 24061. Offers genetics, bioinformatics, and computational biology (PhD); information technology (MIT); macromolecular science and engineering (MS, PhD); translational biology, medicine, and health (PhD). *Students:* 189 full-time (92 women), 685 part-time (206 women); includes 260 minority (65 Black or African American, non-Hispanic/Latino; 106 Asian, non-Hispanic/Latino; 54 Hispanic/Latino; 2 Native Hawaiian or other Pacific Islander, non-Hispanic/Latino; 33 Two or more races, non-Hispanic/Latino), 98 international. Average age 33. 531 applicants, 75% accepted, 274 enrolled. In 2018, 138 master's, 20 doctorates awarded. *Degree requirements:* For master's, comprehensive exam (for some programs), thesis (for some programs); for doctorate, comprehensive exam (for some programs), thesis/dissertation (for some programs). *Entrance requirements:* For master's and doctorate, GRE/GMAT. Additional exam requirements/recommendations for international students: Required—TOEFL (minimum score 90 iBT). *Application deadline:* For fall admission, 8/1 for domestic students, 4/1 for international students; for spring admission, 1/1 for domestic students, 9/1 for international students. Applications are processed on a rolling basis. Application fee: $75. Electronic applications accepted. *Expenses:* Tuition, state resident: full-time $15,510; part-time $739.50 per credit hour. Tuition, nonresident: full-time $29,629; part-time $1490.25 per credit hour. *Required fees:* $2804; $550 per semester. Tuition and fees vary according to course load, campus/location and program. *Financial support:* In 2018–19, 3 fellowships with full and partial tuition reimbursements (averaging $18,380 per year), 158 research assistantships with full tuition reimbursements (averaging $22,336 per year), 21 teaching assistantships with full tuition reimbursements (averaging $19,355 per year) were awarded; scholarships/grants also available. Financial award application deadline: 3/1; financial award applicants required to submit FAFSA. *Unit head:* Dr. Karen P. DePauw, Vice President and Dean for Graduate Education, 540-231-7581, Fax: 540-231-1670, E-mail: kpdepauw@vt.edu. *Application contact:* Dr. Karen P. DePauw, Vice President and Dean for Graduate Education, 540-231-7581, Fax: 540-231-1670, E-mail: kpdepauw@vt.edu.

Wayne State University, College of Engineering, Department of Computer Science, Detroit, MI 48202. Offers computer science (MS, PhD), including bioinformatics and computational biology (PhD); data science and business analytics (MS). Application deadline for PhD is February 17. *Faculty:* 23. *Students:* 107 full-time (41 women), 39 part-time (11 women); includes 11 minority (2 Black or African American, non-Hispanic/Latino; 6 Asian, non-Hispanic/Latino; 2 Hispanic/Latino; 1 Two or more races, non-Hispanic/Latino), 99 international. Average age 30. 237 applicants, 28% accepted, 35 enrolled. In 2018, 27 master's, 7 doctorates awarded. *Degree requirements:* For master's, thesis (for some programs), practicum (for MS in data science and business analytics); for doctorate, thesis/dissertation. *Entrance requirements:* For master's, GRE (GMAT accepted for MS in data science and business analytics), minimum GPA of 3.0, three letters of recommendation, adequate preparation in computer science and mathematics courses, personal statement, resume (for MS in data science and business analytics); for doctorate, GRE, bachelor's or master's degree in computer science or related field; minimum GPA of 3.3 in most recent degree; three letters of recommendation; personal statement; adequate preparation in computer science and mathematics courses. Additional exam requirements/recommendations for international students: Required—TOEFL (minimum score 550 paper-based; 79 iBT), TWE (minimum score 5.5); Recommended—IELTS (minimum score 6.5). *Application deadline:* For fall admission, 6/1 priority date for domestic students, 5/1 priority date for international students; for winter admission, 10/1 priority date for domestic students, 9/1 priority date for international students; for spring admission, 2/1 priority date for domestic students, 1/2 priority date for international students. Applications are processed on a rolling basis. Application fee: $50. Electronic applications accepted. *Expenses:* Contact institution. *Financial support:* In 2018–19, 91 students received support, including 5 fellowships with tuition reimbursements available (averaging $20,000 per year), 18 research assistantships with tuition reimbursements available (averaging $20,383 per year), 27 teaching assistantships with tuition reimbursements available (averaging $20,166 per year); scholarships/grants, health care benefits, and unspecified assistantships also available. Financial award application deadline: 2/17; financial award applicants required to submit FAFSA. *Faculty research:* Software engineering, databases, bioinformatics, artificial intelligence, networking, distributed and parallel computing, security, graphics, visualizations. *Total annual research expenditures:* $1.1 million. *Unit head:* Dr. Loren Schwiebert, Chair, 313-577-5474, E-mail: loren@wayne.edu. *Application contact:* Areej Salaymeh, Graduate Advisor, 313-577-2477, E-mail: csgradadvisor@cs.wayne.edu.
Website: http://engineering.wayne.edu/cs/

Wesleyan University, Graduate Studies, Department of Biology, Middletown, CT 06459. Offers cell and developmental biology (PhD); evolution and ecology (PhD); genetics and genomics (PhD), including bioinformatics; neurobiology and behavior (PhD). Terminal master's awarded for partial completion of doctoral program. *Degree requirements:* For doctorate, comprehensive exam, thesis/dissertation, public seminar. *Entrance requirements:* For doctorate, GRE, official transcripts, three recommendation letters, essay. Additional exam requirements/recommendations for international students: Required—TOEFL. Electronic applications accepted. *Faculty research:* Evolution and ecology, neurobiology and behavior, cell and developmental biology, genetics, genomics and bioinformatics.

Worcester Polytechnic Institute, Graduate Admissions, Program in Bioinformatics and Computational Biology, Worcester, MA 01609-2280. Offers bioinformatics & computational biology (PhD). *Program availability:* Evening/weekend. *Students:* 11 full-time (4 women), 4 part-time (2 women), 9 international. Average age 27. 25 applicants, 64% accepted, 4 enrolled. In 2018, 4 master's, 1 doctorate awarded. *Entrance requirements:* For master's and doctorate, GRE, 3 letters of recommendation, statement of purpose. Additional exam requirements/recommendations for international students: Required—TOEFL (minimum score 563 paper-based; 84 iBT), IELTS (minimum score 7). *Application deadline:* For fall admission, 1/1 priority date for domestic and international students; for spring admission, 10/1 priority date for domestic and international students. Applications are processed on a rolling basis. Application fee: $70. Electronic applications accepted. *Financial support:* Fellowships, research assistantships, teaching assistantships, and career-related internships or fieldwork available. Financial award application deadline: 1/1. *Unit head:* Dmitry Korkin, Professor, 508-831-5538, Fax: 508-831-5933, E-mail: dkorkin@wpi.edu. *Application contact:* Barbara Milanese, Administrative Assistant, 508-831-5538, Fax: 508-831-5933, E-mail: milanese@wpi.edu.
Website: https://www.wpi.edu/academics/departments/bioinformatics-computational-biology

Yale University, Yale School of Medicine and Graduate School of Arts and Sciences, Combined Program in Biological and Biomedical Sciences (BBS), Computational Biology and Bioinformatics Track, New Haven, CT 06520. Offers PhD, MD/PhD. *Entrance requirements:* Additional exam requirements/recommendations for international students: Required—TOEFL.

Computer and Information Systems Security

American InterContinental University Online, Program in Information Technology, Schaumburg, IL 60173. Offers Internet security (MIT); IT project management (MIT). *Program availability:* Evening/weekend, online learning. *Entrance requirements:* Additional exam requirements/recommendations for international students: Required—TOEFL (minimum score 550 paper-based). Electronic applications accepted.

American Public University System, AMU/APU Graduate Programs, Charles Town, WV 25414. Offers accounting (MS); applied business analytics (MS); business administration (MBA); criminal justice (MA); cybersecurity studies (MS); educational leadership (M Ed); environmental policy and management (MS); global security (DGS); health information management (MS); history (MA), including American military history, American Revolution, civil war, war since 1945, World War II; information technology (MS); international relations and conflict resolution (MA), including American politics and government, comparative government and development, general, international relations, public policy; national security studies (MA); nursing (MSN); political science (MA); public policy (MPP); reverse logistics management (MA), including comparative and security issues, conflict resolution, international and transnational security issues, peacekeeping; space studies (MS); sports management (MS); strategic intelligence (DSI); teaching (M Ed), including secondary social studies; transportation and logistics management (MA). *Program availability:* Part-time, evening/weekend, online only, 100% online. *Students:* 406 full-time (180 women), 7,826 part-time (3,329 women); includes 2,781 minority (1,438 Black or African American, non-Hispanic/Latino; 44 American Indian or Alaska Native, non-Hispanic/Latino; 193 Asian, non-Hispanic/Latino; 747 Hispanic/Latino; 53 Native Hawaiian or other Pacific Islander, non-Hispanic/Latino; 306 Two or more races, non-Hispanic/Latino), 121 international. Average age 38. In 2018, 2,717 master's awarded. *Degree requirements:* For master's, comprehensive exam or practicum; for doctorate, practicum. *Entrance requirements:* For master's, official transcript showing earned bachelor's degree from institution accredited by recognized accrediting body. Additional exam requirements/recommendations for international students: Required—TOEFL (minimum score 550 paper-based), IELTS (minimum score 6.5). *Application deadline:* Applications are processed on a rolling basis. Application fee: $0. Electronic applications accepted. *Financial support:* Scholarships/grants available. Financial award applicants required to submit FAFSA. *Unit head:* Dr. Wallace Boston, President, 877-468-6268, Fax: 304-728-2348, E-mail: president@apus.edu. *Application contact:* Yoci Deal, Associate Vice President, Graduate and International Admissions, 877-468-6268, Fax: 304-724-3764, E-mail: info@apus.edu.
Website: http://www.apus.edu

Augusta University, Hull College of Business, Augusta, GA 30912. Offers business administration (MBA); information security management (MS). *Accreditation:* AACSB. *Program availability:* Part-time, evening/weekend. *Entrance requirements:* For master's, GMAT.

Austin Peay State University, College of Graduate Studies, College of Science, Technology, Engineering and Mathematics, Professional Science Master's Program, Clarksville, TN 37044. Offers data management and analysis (MS, PSM); information assurance and security (MS, PSM); mathematical finance (MS, PSM); mathematics instruction (MS); predictive analytics (MS, PSM). *Program availability:* Part-time, online learning. *Faculty:* 7 full-time (0 women), 1 part-time/adjunct (0 women). *Students:* 48 full-time (11 women), 72 part-time (29 women); includes 22 minority (9 Black or African American, non-Hispanic/Latino; 5 Asian, non-Hispanic/Latino; 4 Hispanic/Latino; 4 Two or more races, non-Hispanic/Latino), 41 international. Average age 32. 76 applicants, 88% accepted, 41 enrolled. In 2018, 16 master's awarded. *Entrance requirements:* For master's, GRE, minimum undergraduate GPA of 2.5. Additional exam requirements/recommendations for international students: Required—TOEFL (minimum score 500 paper-based). *Application deadline:* For fall admission, 8/21 priority date for domestic students. Applications are processed on a rolling basis. Application fee: $45 ($55 for international students). Electronic applications accepted. *Expenses: Tuition, area resident:* Part-time $450 per credit hour. Tuition, state resident: full-time $5987; part-time $450 per credit hour. Tuition, nonresident: full-time $8757; part-time $806 per credit hour. *Required fees:* $1583; $79.15 per credit hour. *Financial support:* Research assistantships with full tuition reimbursements, career-related internships or fieldwork, Federal Work-Study, institutionally sponsored loans, scholarships/grants, and unspecified assistantships available. Support available to part-time students. Financial award application deadline: 7/1; financial award applicants required to submit FAFSA. *Unit head:* Dr. Matt Jones, Graduate Coordinator, 931-221-7814, E-mail: gradpsm@apsu.edu. *Application contact:* Megan Mitchell, Coordinator of Graduate Admissions, 800-859-4723, Fax: 931-221-7641, E-mail: gradadmissions@apsu.edu.
Website: http://www.apsu.edu/csci/masters_degrees/index.php

Bay Path University, Program in Cybersecurity Management, Longmeadow, MA 01106-2292. Offers MS. *Program availability:* Part-time, evening/weekend, online only, 100% online. *Students:* 9 full-time (6 women), 20 part-time (11 women); includes 14 minority (2 Black or African American, non-Hispanic/Latino; 1 Asian, non-Hispanic/Latino; 8 Hispanic/Latino; 3 Two or more races, non-Hispanic/Latino). Average age 36. *Entrance requirements:* For master's, completed application; official undergraduate and graduate transcripts (a GPA of 3.0 or higher is preferred); original essay of at least 250 words on the topic: "Why the MS in Cybersecurity Management is important to my personal and professional goals"; current resume; 2 recommendations. *Application deadline:* Applications are processed on a rolling basis. Electronic applications accepted. Application fee is waived when completed online. *Expenses:* Contact institution. *Financial support:* Unspecified assistantships available. Financial award applicants required to submit FAFSA. *Unit head:* Dr. Matthew J. Smith, DIRECTOR OF COMPUTER SCIENCE & CYBERSECURITY PROGRAMS, 413-5656828, E-mail: matsmith@baypath.edu. *Application contact:* Sheryl Kosakowski, Executive Director of Graduate Admissions, 413-565-1075, Fax: 413-565-1250, E-mail: skosakowski@baypath.edu.
Website: https://www.baypath.edu/academics/graduate-programs/cybersecurity-management-ms/

Benedictine University, Graduate Programs, Program in Business Administration, Lisle, IL 60532. Offers accounting (MBA); entrepreneurship and managing innovation (MBA); financial management (MBA); health administration (MBA); human resource management (MBA); information systems security (MBA); international business (MBA); management consulting (MBA); management information systems (MBA); marketing management (MBA); operations management and logistics (MBA); organizational leadership (MBA). *Program availability:* Part-time, evening/weekend, 100% online, blended/hybrid learning. *Faculty:* 7 full-time (1 woman), 36 part-time/adjunct (10 women). *Students:* 110 full-time (71 women), 500 part-time (302 women); includes 104 minority (34 Black or African American, non-Hispanic/Latino; 1 American Indian or Alaska Native, non-Hispanic/Latino; 41 Asian, non-Hispanic/Latino; 23 Hispanic/Latino; 5 Native Hawaiian or other Pacific Islander, non-Hispanic/Latino), 7 international. Average age 33. 251 applicants, 84% accepted, 202 enrolled. In 2018, 345 master's awarded. *Entrance requirements:* For master's, GMAT or GRE test scores or completed test waiver form, official transcripts; 2 letters of reference from individuals familiar with the applicant's professional or academic work, excluding family or personal friends; a 1-2 page essay addressing educational and career goals; current résumé listing chronological work history; personal interview may be required prior to an admission decision. Additional exam requirements/recommendations for international students: Required—TOEFL (minimum score 550 paper-based; 79 iBT), IELTS (minimum score 6.5). *Application deadline:* Applications are processed on a rolling basis. Application fee: $40. Electronic applications accepted. *Unit head:* Ricky Holman, Assistant Professor, 630-829-1936, E-mail: rholman@ben.edu. *Application contact:* Ricky Holman, Assistant Professor, 630-829-1936, E-mail: rholman@ben.edu.

Boston University, Graduate School of Arts and Sciences, Department of Computer Science, Boston, MA 02215. Offers computer science (MS, PhD); cyber security (MS); data-centric computing (MS). *Students:* 188 full-time (43 women), 39 part-time (7 women); includes 11 minority (10 Asian, non-Hispanic/Latino; 1 Hispanic/Latino), 185 international. Average age 24. 1,576 applicants, 20% accepted, 95 enrolled. In 2018, 53 master's, 8 doctorates awarded. Terminal master's awarded for partial completion of doctoral program. *Degree requirements:* For master's, thesis optional, project; for doctorate, comprehensive exam, thesis/dissertation. *Entrance requirements:* For master's and doctorate, GRE General Test, 3 letters of recommendation, transcripts, personal statement. Additional exam requirements/recommendations for international students: Required—TOEFL (minimum score 550 paper-based; 84 iBT). *Application deadline:* For fall admission, 12/15 for domestic and international students; for spring admission, 11/1 for domestic and international students. Applications are processed on a rolling basis. Application fee: $95. Electronic applications accepted. *Financial support:* In 2018–19, 95 students received support, including 4 fellowships with full tuition reimbursements available (averaging $22,660 per year), 41 research assistantships with full tuition reimbursements available (averaging $22,660 per year), 37 teaching assistantships with full tuition reimbursements available (averaging $22,660 per year); Federal Work-Study, scholarships/grants, and health care benefits also available. Support available to part-time students. Financial award application deadline: 12/15. *Unit head:* Abraham Matta, Chair, 617-353-8919, Fax: 617-353-6457, E-mail: matta@bu.edu. *Application contact:* Kori MacDonald, Program Coordinator, 617-353-8919, Fax: 617-353-6457, E-mail: korimac@bu.edu.
Website: http://www.bu.edu/cs

Boston University, Metropolitan College, Department of Computer Science, Boston, MA 02215. Offers computer information systems (MS), including computer networks, data analytics, database management and business intelligence, health informatics, IT project management, security, Web application development; computer networks (Certificate); computer science (MS); data analytics (Certificate); digital forensics (Certificate); health informatics (Certificate); information technology project management (Certificate); software development (MS); software engineering in health care systems (Certificate); telecommunications (MS), including security. *Program availability:* Part-time, evening/weekend, online learning. *Faculty:* 16 full-time (3 women), 52 part-time/adjunct (5 women). *Students:* 201 full-time (57 women), 953 part-time (252 women); includes 285 minority (57 Black or African American, non-Hispanic/Latino; 2 American Indian or Alaska Native, non-Hispanic/Latino; 139 Asian, non-Hispanic/Latino; 67 Hispanic/Latino; 1 Native Hawaiian or other Pacific Islander, non-Hispanic/Latino; 19 Two or more races, non-Hispanic/Latino), 333 international. Average age 31. 1,079 applicants, 72% accepted, 297 enrolled. In 2018, 395 master's awarded. *Entrance requirements:* For master's and Certificate, official transcripts from regionally-accredited bachelor's degree program, 3 letters of recommendation, professional resume, personal statement. Additional exam requirements/recommendations for international students: Required—TOEFL (minimum score 84 iBT), IELTS. *Application deadline:* For fall admission, 8/1 priority date for domestic students, 6/1 priority date for international students; for spring admission, 12/1 priority date for domestic students, 11/15 priority date for international students; for summer admission, 4/1 priority date for domestic students, 3/1 priority date for international students. Applications are processed on a rolling basis. Application fee: $85. Electronic applications accepted. *Expenses:* Contact institution. *Financial support:* In 2018–19, 11 research assistantships (averaging $8,400 per year), 23 teaching assistantships (averaging $3,400 per year) were awarded; unspecified assistantships also available. Support available to part-time students. Financial award applicants required to submit FAFSA. *Faculty research:* Artificial intelligence and machine learning, security and forensics, web technologies, software engineering, programming languages, medical informatics, information systems and IT project management. *Unit head:* Dr. Anatoly Temkin, Chair, 617-353-2566, Fax: 617-353-2367, E-mail: csinfo@bu.edu. *Application contact:* Enrollment Services, 617-353-6004, E-mail: met@bu.edu.
Website: http://www.bu.edu/csmet/

Boston University, Metropolitan College, Program in Criminal Justice, Boston, MA 02215. Offers cybercrime investigation and cybersecurity (MCJ); strategic management (MCJ). *Program availability:* Part-time, evening/weekend, online learning. *Faculty:* 5 full-time (2 women), 9 part-time/adjunct (3 women). *Students:* 10 full-time (2 women), 202 part-time (118 women); includes 70 minority (29 Black or African American, non-Hispanic/Latino; 3 American Indian or Alaska Native, non-Hispanic/Latino; 8 Asian, non-Hispanic/Latino; 27 Hispanic/Latino; 3 Two or more races, non-Hispanic/Latino), 18 international. Average age 30. In 2018, 165 master's awarded. *Degree requirements:* For master's, comprehensive examination (for on-campus program only). *Entrance requirements:* Additional exam requirements/recommendations for international students: Required—TOEFL (minimum score 84 iBT). *Application deadline:* For fall admission, 8/1 priority date for domestic students, 6/1 priority date for international students; for spring admission, 12/1 priority date for domestic students, 11/15 priority date for international students; for summer admission, 4/1 priority date for domestic students, 3/1 priority date for international students. Applications are processed on a rolling basis. Application fee: $85. Electronic applications accepted. *Expenses:* Contact institution. *Financial support:* In 2018–19, 8 research assistantships (averaging $4,200 per year) were awarded; scholarships/grants and unspecified assistantships also available. Support available to part-time students. Financial award applicants required to submit FAFSA. *Faculty research:* Criminal justice administration and planning, criminology, police, corrections, collective violence, prison education, cybercrime, forensic psychology, firearm violence. *Unit head:* Dr. Mary Ellen Mastrorilli, Associate Professor of the Practice and Chair, 617-353-3025, Fax: 617-358-3595, E-mail: memastro@bu.edu. *Application contact:* Enrollment Services, 617-353-9185, E-mail: met@bu.edu.
Website: http://www.bu.edu/met/cj/

Brandeis University, Rabb School of Continuing Studies, Division of Graduate Professional Studies, Master of Science in Information Security Leadership Program, Waltham, MA 02454-9110. Offers MS. *Program availability:* Part-time-only. *Entrance* *requirements:* For master's, undergraduate degree with work experience and/or coursework in networking, computer science, and computer security; 4-year bachelor's degree from regionally-accredited U.S. institution or equivalent; official transcript(s) from every college/university attended; resume or curriculum vitae; statement of goals; letter of recommendation. Additional exam requirements/recommendations for international students: Required—TWE (minimum score 4.5), TOEFL (minimum scores: 600 paper-based, 100 iBT), IELTS (7), or PTE (68). Electronic applications accepted. *Expenses:* Contact institution.

California State University, San Bernardino, Graduate Studies, College of Business and Public Administration, Program in Business Administration, San Bernardino, CA 92407. Offers accounting (MBA); entrepreneurship (MBA); finance (MBA); global business (MBA); information management (MBA); information security (MBA); management (MBA); supply chain management (MBA). *Accreditation:* AACSB. *Program availability:* Part-time, evening/weekend, online learning. *Faculty:* 5 full-time (4 women), 7 part-time/adjunct (3 women). *Students:* 40 full-time (14 women), 163 part-time (72 women); includes 99 minority (7 Black or African American, non-Hispanic/Latino; 15 Asian, non-Hispanic/Latino; 71 Hispanic/Latino; 6 Two or more races, non-Hispanic/Latino), 58 international. Average age 32. 342 applicants, 52% accepted, 91 enrolled. In 2018, 106 master's awarded. *Degree requirements:* For master's, comprehensive exam, thesis. *Entrance requirements:* Additional exam requirements/recommendations for international students: Required—TOEFL. *Application deadline:* For fall admission, 7/16 for domestic students, 7/20 for international students; for winter admission, 10/23 for domestic students, 10/20 for international students; for spring admission, 1/22 for domestic students, 1/20 for international students. Application fee: $55. *Expenses:* Contact institution. *Financial support:* Application deadline: 3/1. *Unit head:* Dr. Lawrence C. Rose, Dean, 909-537-3703, Fax: 909-537-7026, E-mail: lrose@csusb.edu. *Application contact:* Ernest Silvers, MBA Program Director, 909-537-5703, E-mail: esilvers@csusb.edu.
Website: http://mba.csusb.edu/

California State University, San Bernardino, Graduate Studies, College of Social and Behavioral Sciences, Program in National Cyber Security Studies, San Bernardino, CA 92407. Offers MA. *Students:* 3 full-time (1 woman), 6 part-time (3 women); includes 4 minority (1 Black or African American, non-Hispanic/Latino; 1 Asian, non-Hispanic/Latino; 2 Hispanic/Latino). Average age 25. 4 applicants, 75% accepted, 2 enrolled. In 2018, 1 master's awarded. *Entrance requirements:* Additional exam requirements/recommendations for international students: Required—TOEFL. *Application deadline:* For fall admission, 4/15 for domestic students; for winter admission, 10/16 for domestic students; for spring admission, 1/22 for domestic students. Application fee: $55. *Financial support:* Unspecified assistantships available. *Unit head:* Dr. Mark Clark, Director, 909-537-5491, E-mail: mtclark@csusb.edu. *Application contact:* Dr. Dorota Huizinga, Dean, 909-537-3064, E-mail: dorota.huizinga@csusb.edu.

California State University, San Marcos, College of Science and Mathematics, Program in Computer Science, San Marcos, CA 92096-0001. Offers computer science (MS); cybersecurity (MS). *Program availability:* Part-time. *Entrance requirements:* For master's, GRE General Test, statement of purpose, letters of recommendation. Additional exam requirements/recommendations for international students: Required—TOEFL (minimum score 550 paper-based; 80 iBT). *Application deadline:* For fall admission, 5/30 for domestic students; for spring admission, 8/30 for domestic students, 11/1 for international students. Application fee: $55. *Faculty research:* Networks, multimedia, parallel algorithms, software engineering, artificial intelligence. *Unit head:* Ahmad Hadaegh, Associate Professor, 760-750-8068, E-mail: ahadaegh@csusm.edu. *Application contact:* Dr. Wesley Schultz, Dean of Office of Graduate Studies and Research, 760-750-8045, Fax: 760-750-8045, E-mail: apply@csusm.edu.

California University of Pennsylvania, School of Graduate Studies and Research, Eberly College of Science and Technology, Program in Cybersecurity, California, PA 15419-1394. Offers PSM.

Capella University, School of Business and Technology, Doctoral Programs in Technology, Minneapolis, MN 55402. Offers general information technology (PhD); global operations and supply chain management (DBA); information assurance and security (PhD); information technology education (PhD); information technology management (DBA, PhD).

Capella University, School of Business and Technology, Master's Programs in Technology, Minneapolis, MN 55402. Offers enterprise software architecture (MS); general information systems and technology management (MS); global operations and supply chain management (MBA); information assurance and security (MS); information technology management (MBA); network management (MS).

Capitol Technology University, Graduate Programs, Laurel, MD 20708-9759. Offers business administration (MBA); computer science (MS); electrical engineering (MS); information and telecommunications systems management (MS); information architecture (MS); network security (MS). *Program availability:* Part-time, evening/weekend, online learning. *Entrance requirements:* For master's, minimum GPA of 3.0. Electronic applications accepted.

Cardinal Stritch University, College of Business and Management, Milwaukee, WI 53217-3985. Offers cyber security (MBA); healthcare management (MBA); justice administration (MBA); marketing (MBA). *Accreditation:* ACBSP. *Program availability:* Part-time, evening/weekend, 100% online, blended/hybrid learning. *Degree requirements:* For master's, thesis. *Entrance requirements:* For master's, 3 years of management or related experience, minimum GPA of 2.5. Additional exam requirements/recommendations for international students: Required—TOEFL (minimum score 79 iBT), IELTS (minimum score 6.5). Electronic applications accepted. *Expenses:* Contact institution.

Carnegie Mellon University, Carnegie Institute of Technology, Information Networking Institute, Pittsburgh, PA 15213. Offers information networking (MS); information security (MS); information technology - information security (MS); information technology - mobility (MS); information technology - software management (MS). *Degree requirements:* For master's, thesis optional. *Entrance requirements:* For master's, GRE General Test, bachelor's degree in computer science, computer engineering, or electrical engineering, or related technology degree; programming skills (C/C++ fluency for some programs). Additional exam requirements/recommendations for international students: Required—TOEFL. *Faculty research:* Computer forensics and incident response; dependable systems, embedded systems, mobile systems, and sensor networks; computer and information networks, network and information security, human and socio-economic factors in secure system design; wireless sensor networks, survivable embedded systems, signal processing/compression; strategic management, international strategic management, group dynamics and decision-making structures, simulated competitive environments.

Carnegie Mellon University, Heinz College, School of Information Systems and Management, Master of Science in Information Security Policy and Management Program, Pittsburgh, PA 15213-3891. Offers MSISPM. *Entrance requirements:* For master's, GRE or GMAT, college-level course in advanced algebra/pre-calculus; college-level courses in economics and statistics (recommended). Additional exam requirements/recommendations for international students: Required—TOEFL or IELTS.

Central Michigan University, Central Michigan University Global Campus, Program in Cybersecurity, Mount Pleasant, MI 48859. Offers Certificate. *Program availability:* Part-time, evening/weekend. Electronic applications accepted.

Champlain College, Graduate Studies, Burlington, VT 05402-0670. Offers business (MBA); digital forensic science (MS); early childhood education (M Ed); emergent media (MFA, MS); executive leadership (MS); health care administration (MS); information security operations (MS); law (MS); mediation and applied conflict studies (MS). MS in emergent media program held in Shanghai. *Program availability:* Part-time, online learning. *Degree requirements:* For master's, capstone project. *Entrance requirements:* Additional exam requirements/recommendations for international students: Required—TOEFL (minimum score 550 paper-based; 80 iBT). Electronic applications accepted.

City University of Seattle, Graduate Division, School of Management, Seattle, WA 98121. Offers accounting (Certificate); change leadership (MBA, Certificate); computer systems (MS); finance (Certificate); financial management (MBA); general management (MBA); general management-Europe (MBA); global marketing (MBA); human resources management (Certificate); individualized study (MBA); information security (MS); information systems (MBA); leadership (MA); marketing (MBA, Certificate); project management (MBA, MS, Certificate); sustainable business (Certificate); technology management (MBA, Certificate). *Program availability:* Part-time, evening/weekend, online learning. *Degree requirements:* For master's, comprehensive exam (for some programs), thesis (for some programs). *Entrance requirements:* For master's, baccalaureate degree or equivalent from an accredited or otherwise recognized institution. Additional exam requirements/recommendations for international students: Required—TOEFL (minimum score 567 paper-based; 87 iBT); Recommended—IELTS. Electronic applications accepted.

Claremont Graduate University, Graduate Programs, Center for Information Systems and Technology, Claremont, CA 91711-6160. Offers cybersecurity and networking (MS); data science and analytics (MS); electronic commerce (PhD); geographic information systems (MS); health informatics (MS); information systems (Certificate); IT strategy and innovation (MS); knowledge management (PhD); systems development (PhD); telecommunications and networking (PhD); MBA/MS. *Program availability:* Part-time. *Degree requirements:* For doctorate, comprehensive exam, thesis/dissertation, portfolio. *Entrance requirements:* For master's and doctorate, GMAT, GRE General Test. Additional exam requirements/recommendations for international students: Required—TOEFL (minimum score 75 iBT). Electronic applications accepted. *Faculty research:* Man-machine interaction, organizational aspects of computing, implementation of information systems, information systems practice.

College of Saint Elizabeth, Program in Justice Administration and Public Service, Morristown, NJ 07960-6989. Offers counter terrorism (Certificate); cyber security investigation (Certificate); justice administration and public service (MA); leadership in community policing (Certificate). *Program availability:* Part-time, 100% online, blended/hybrid learning. *Degree requirements:* For master's, thesis. *Entrance requirements:* Additional exam requirements/recommendations for international students: Required—TOEFL (minimum score 550 paper-based; 79 iBT), IELTS (minimum score 6.5). Electronic applications accepted. Application fee is waived when completed online. *Expenses:* Contact institution.

College of Staten Island of the City University of New York, Graduate Programs, Division of Science and Technology, Program in Computer Science, Staten Island, NY 10314-6600. Offers computer science (MS), including artificial intelligence and data analytics, cloud computing and software engineering, cybersecurity and networks. *Program availability:* Part-time, evening/weekend. *Students:* 35. 48 applicants, 48% accepted, 14 enrolled. In 2018, 17 master's awarded. *Degree requirements:* For master's, thesis optional, a program of 10 courses (30 credits) with at least a 3.0 (B) average. Exceptional students may be permitted to satisfy six credits of the total credit requirement with a master's thesis. *Entrance requirements:* For master's, GRE General Test, BS in Computer Science or related area with a B average (3.0 out of 4.0) overall and in the major. Additional exam requirements/recommendations for international students: Required—TOEFL (minimum score 550 paper-based; 79 iBT), IELTS (minimum score 6.5). *Application deadline:* For fall admission, 7/20 priority date for domestic students, 4/25 for international students; for spring admission, 11/2 priority date for domestic students, 11/2 for international students. Applications are processed on a rolling basis. Application fee: $75. Electronic applications accepted. *Expenses:* *Tuition, area resident:* Full-time $10,770; part-time $455 per credit. Tuition, state resident: full-time $10,770; part-time $455 per credit. Tuition, nonresident: full-time $19,920; part-time $830 per credit. *International tuition:* $19,920 full-time. *Required fees:* $559.20; $181.10 per semester. Tuition and fees vary according to program. *Faculty research:* Big data, pattern recognition, text mining and frequent pattern mining; graph theory; computer vision, image processing pattern recognition and serious game; parallel computing and stimulation; high performance computing and modeling simulation; serious games; security, cryptography and communication networks; scheduling algorithms; scheduling, operations research and graph theory. *Unit head:* Dr. Xiaowen Zhang, Associate Professor, 718-982-3262, E-mail: xiaowen.zhang@csi.cuny.edu. *Application contact:* Sasha Spence, Associate Director for Graduate Admissions, 718-982-2019, Fax: 718-982-2500, E-mail: sasha.spence@csi.cuny.edu.
Website: https://www.csi.cuny.edu/sites/default/files/pdf/admissions/grad/pdf/Computer%20Science%20Fact%20Sheet.pdf

Colorado Christian University, Program in Business Administration, Lakewood, CO 80226. Offers corporate training (MBA); information security (MA); leadership (MBA); project management (MBA). *Program availability:* Part-time, evening/weekend, online learning. *Degree requirements:* For master's, thesis optional. *Entrance requirements:* For master's, GMAT, 2 letters of recommendation, resume. Additional exam requirements/recommendations for international students: Required—TOEFL. Electronic applications accepted. *Expenses:* Contact institution.

Colorado Technical University Aurora, Program in Computer Science, Aurora, CO 80014. Offers computer systems security (MSCS); database systems (MSCS); software engineering (MSCS). *Program availability:* Part-time, evening/weekend. *Degree requirements:* For master's, thesis or alternative. *Entrance requirements:* For master's, minimum undergraduate GPA of 3.0, resume.

Colorado Technical University Aurora, Program in Information Science, Aurora, CO 80014. Offers information systems security (MSM).

Colorado Technical University Colorado Springs, Graduate Studies, Program in Computer Science, Colorado Springs, CO 80907. Offers computer science (DCS); computer systems security (MSCS); database systems (MSCS); software engineering (MSCS). *Program availability:* Part-time, evening/weekend, online learning. *Degree requirements:* For master's, thesis or alternative; for doctorate, thesis/dissertation. *Entrance requirements:* For doctorate, minimum graduate GPA of 3.0, 5 years of related work experience. *Faculty research:* Software engineering, systems engineering.

Colorado Technical University Colorado Springs, Graduate Studies, Program in Information Science, Colorado Springs, CO 80907. Offers information systems security (MSM). *Program availability:* Online learning.

Columbus State University, Graduate Studies, Turner College of Business, Columbus, GA 31907-5645. Offers applied computer science (MS), including informational assurance, modeling and simulation, software development; business administration (MBA); cyber security (MS); human resource management (Certificate); information systems security (Certificate); modeling and simulation (Certificate); organizational leadership (MS), including human resource management, leader development, servant leadership; servant leadership (Certificate). *Accreditation:* AACSB. *Program availability:* Part-time, evening/weekend, 100% online, blended/hybrid learning. *Faculty:* 10 full-time (3 women), 1 part-time/adjunct (0 women). *Students:* 79 full-time (24 women), 136 part-time (47 women); includes 73 minority (40 Black or African American, non-Hispanic/Latino; 1 American Indian or Alaska Native, non-Hispanic/Latino; 8 Asian, non-Hispanic/Latino; 15 Hispanic/Latino; 9 Two or more races, non-Hispanic/Latino), 27 international. Average age 31. 237 applicants, 51% accepted, 64 enrolled. In 2018, 113 master's, 10 other advanced degrees awarded. *Entrance requirements:* For master's, GMAT, GRE, minimum undergraduate GPA of 2.75, letters of recommendation. Additional exam requirements/recommendations for international students: Required—TOEFL (minimum score 550 paper-based; 79 iBT). *Application deadline:* For fall admission, 6/30 for domestic students, 5/1 for international students; for spring admission, 11/1 for domestic and international students; for summer admission, 3/1 for domestic and international students. Applications are processed on a rolling basis. Application fee: $50. Electronic applications accepted. *Expenses:* Contact institution. *Financial support:* In 2018–19, 18 students received support, including 20 research assistantships (averaging $3,000 per year); Federal Work-Study also available. Financial award application deadline: 5/1; financial award applicants required to submit FAFSA. *Unit head:* Dr. Linda U. Hadley, Dean, 706-507-8153, Fax: 706-568-2184, E-mail: hadley_linda@columbusstate.edu. *Application contact:* Catrina Smith-Edmond, Assistant Director for Graduate and Global Admission, 706-507-8824, Fax: 706-568-5091, E-mail: smithedmond_catrina@columbusstate.edu.
Website: http://turner.columbusstate.edu/

Concordia University, School of Graduate Studies, Faculty of Engineering and Computer Science, Concordia Institute for Information Systems Engineering (CIISE), Montréal, QC H3G 1M8, Canada. Offers 3D graphics and game development (Certificate); information and systems engineering (PhD); information systems security (M Eng, MA Sc); quality systems engineering (M Eng, MA Sc); service engineering and network management (Certificate).

Concordia University, Nebraska, Program in Computer Science, Seward, NE 68434. Offers cyber operations (MS). *Program availability:* Online learning.

Concordia University of Edmonton, Program in Information Systems Security Management, Edmonton, AB T5B 4E4, Canada. Offers MA.

Concordia University, St. Paul, College of Business and Technology, St. Paul, MN 55104-5494. Offers business administration (MBA), including cyber-security leadership; health care management (MBA); human resource management (MA); information technology (MBA); leadership and management (MA); strategic communication management (MA). *Accreditation:* ACBSP. *Program availability:* Part-time, evening/weekend, 100% online, blended/hybrid learning. *Faculty:* 12 full-time (5 women), 28 part-time/adjunct (14 women). *Students:* 448 full-time (289 women), 30 part-time (17 women); includes 135 minority (58 Black or African American, non-Hispanic/Latino; 2 American Indian or Alaska Native, non-Hispanic/Latino; 46 Asian, non-Hispanic/Latino; 13 Hispanic/Latino; 16 Two or more races, non-Hispanic/Latino), 40 international. Average age 32. 328 applicants, 96% accepted, 149 enrolled. In 2018, 205 master's awarded. *Degree requirements:* For master's, thesis (for some programs). *Entrance requirements:* For master's, official transcripts from regionally-accredited institution stating the conferral of a bachelor's degree with minimum cumulative GPA of 3.0; personal statement; professional resume. Additional exam requirements/recommendations for international students: Recommended—TOEFL (minimum score 547 paper-based; 78 iBT), IELTS (minimum score 6). *Application deadline:* For fall admission, 8/1 for domestic and international students; for spring admission, 12/1 for domestic and international students; for summer admission, 5/1 for domestic and international students. Applications are processed on a rolling basis. Application fee: $0. Electronic applications accepted. *Expenses:* $625 a credit for 42 credits (for MBA), $475 a credit for 36 credits (for MA/MS). *Financial support:* In 2018–19, 267 students received support. Federal Work-Study, scholarships/grants, and unspecified assistantships available. Financial award applicants required to submit FAFSA. *Faculty research:* Leadership in transition and polarity, managing the evolution of a software product line, decision making and behavioral economics, strength based coaching and the relationship with student success, three-way XML merging. *Unit head:* Dr. Kevin Hall, Dean, 651-603-6165, Fax: 651-641-8807, E-mail: khall@csp.edu. *Application contact:* Amber Faletti, Director of Enrollment Management, 651-641-8838, Fax: 651-603-6320, E-mail: faletti@csp.edu.

Davenport University, Sneden Graduate School, Grand Rapids, MI 49512. Offers accounting (MBA); business administration (EMBA); finance (MBA); health care management (MBA); human resources (MBA); information assurance (MS); occupational therapy (MSOT); public health (MPH); strategic management (MBA). *Program availability:* Evening/weekend. *Entrance requirements:* For master's, GMAT, minimum undergraduate GPA of 2.75. Additional exam requirements/recommendations for international students: Required—TOEFL. Electronic applications accepted. *Faculty research:* Leadership, management, marketing, organizational culture.

DePaul University, College of Computing and Digital Media, Chicago, IL 60604. Offers animation (MA, MFA); applied technology (MS); business information technology (MS); computational finance (MS); computer and information sciences (PhD); computer science (MS); creative producing (MFA); cybersecurity (MS); data science (MS); digital communication and media arts (MA); documentary (MFA); e-commerce technology (MS); experience design (MA); film and television (MS); film and television directing (MFA); game design (MFA); game programming (MS); health informatics (MS); human centered design (PhD); human-computer interaction (MS); information systems (MS); network engineering and security (MS); product innovation and computing (MS); screenwriting (MFA); software engineering (MS); JD/MS. *Program availability:* Part-time, evening/weekend, online learning. *Degree requirements:* For master's, thesis (for some programs); for doctorate, comprehensive exam, thesis/dissertation. *Entrance requirements:* For master's, GRE or GMAT (for MS in computational finance only), bachelor's degree, resume (MS in predictive analytics only), IT experience (MS in information technology project management only), portfolio review (all MFA programs and MA in animation); for doctorate, GRE, master's degree in computer science. Additional exam requirements/recommendations for international students: Required—TOEFL (minimum score 590 paper-based; 80 iBT), IELTS (minimum score 6.5), PTE (minimum score 53). Electronic applications accepted. *Expenses:* Contact institution. *Faculty research:* Data mining, computer science, human-computer interaction, security, animation and film.

DeSales University, Division of Science and Mathematics, Center Valley, PA 18034-9568. Offers cyber security (Postbaccalaureate Certificate); data analytics (Postbaccalaureate Certificate); information systems (MS), including cyber security, digital forensics, healthcare information management, project management. *Program availability:* Part-time, evening/weekend, 100% online, blended/hybrid learning.

Entrance requirements: For master's, GRE or GMAT, bachelor's degree in computer-related discipline from accredited college or university, minimum undergraduate GPA of 3.0, personal statement, three letters of recommendation. Additional exam requirements/recommendations for international students: Required—TOEFL. Electronic applications accepted. *Expenses:* Contact institution.

Drury University, Cybersecurity Leadership Certificate Program, Springfield, MO 65802. Offers Certificate. *Program availability:* Part-time, evening/weekend. *Faculty:* 1 full-time (0 women), 2 part-time/adjunct (1 woman). *Students:* 1 full-time (0 women). Average age 43. 1 applicant, 100% accepted, 1 enrolled. *Entrance requirements:* For degree, bachelor's degree, minimum GPA of 3.0. Additional exam requirements/recommendations for international students: Recommended—TOEFL (minimum score 80 iBT), IELTS (minimum score 6.5). *Application deadline:* For fall admission, 8/4 for domestic and international students; for spring admission, 1/5 for domestic and international students; for summer admission, 5/26 for domestic and international students. Applications are processed on a rolling basis. Application fee: $25. Electronic applications accepted. *Expenses:* CSL tuition is $534/credit hour plus $27 per credit hour in fees. Program is 12 credit hours total. *Financial support:* Career-related internships or fieldwork available. Financial award application deadline: 6/30; financial award applicants required to submit FAFSA. *Faculty research:* Cybersecurity leadership, health care management, cross cultural management, corporate finance, social entrepreneurship. *Unit head:* Dr. Robin Soster, Director, 417-873-7612, E-mail: rsoster@drury.edu. *Application contact:* Dr. Robin Soster, Director, 417-873-7612, E-mail: rsoster@drury.edu.
Website: http://www.drury.edu/cybersecurity

East Carolina University, Graduate School, College of Engineering and Technology, Department of Technology Systems, Greenville, NC 27858-4353. Offers computer network professional (Certificate); cyber security professional (Certificate); information assurance (Certificate); Lean Six Sigma Black Belt (Certificate); network technology (MS), including computer networking management, digital communications technology, information security, Web technologies; occupational safety (MS); technology management (MS, PhD), including industrial distribution and logistics (MS); Website developer (Certificate). *Application deadline:* For fall admission, 6/1 priority date for domestic students. *Expenses:* Tuition, area resident: Full-time $4749. Tuition, state resident: full-time $4749. Tuition, nonresident: full-time $17,898. *International tuition:* $17,898 full-time. *Required fees:* $2787. Part-time tuition and fees vary according to course load and program. *Financial support:* Application deadline: 6/1. *Unit head:* Dr. Tijjani Mohammed, Chair, 252-328-9668, E-mail: mohammedt@ecu.edu. *Application contact:* Graduate School Admissions, 252-328-6012, Fax: 252-328-6071, E-mail: gradschool@ecu.edu.
Website: http://www.ecu.edu/cs-cet/techsystems/index.cfm

Eastern Illinois University, Graduate School, Lumpkin College of Business and Technology, School of Technology, Program in Cybersecurity, Charleston, IL 61920. Offers MS. *Expenses:* Tuition, state resident: part-time $299 per credit hour. Tuition, nonresident: part-time $718 per credit hour. *Required fees:* $214.50 per credit hour.

Eastern Michigan University, Graduate School, College of Engineering and Technology, School of Information Security and Applied Computing, Program in Cybersecurity, Ypsilanti, MI 48197. Offers Graduate Certificate. Application fee: $45. *Application contact:* Dr. Munther Abualkibash, Program Coordinator, 734-487-2490, Fax: 734-483-8755, E-mail: pc_sisac@emich.edu.

EC-Council University, Master of Science in Cyber Security Program, Albuquerque, NM 87109. Offers information assurance management (MSCS). *Program availability:* Part-time, online only, 100% online. *Degree requirements:* For master's, capstone. *Entrance requirements:* Additional exam requirements/recommendations for international students: Required—TOEFL (minimum score 500 paper-based; 71 iBT), IELTS (minimum score 6.1). Electronic applications accepted.

ECPI University, Graduate Programs, Virginia Beach, VA 23462. Offers business administration (MBA); cybersecurity (MS); information systems (MS).

Embry-Riddle Aeronautical University–Daytona, Department of Electrical, Computer, Software and Systems Engineering, Daytona Beach, FL 32114-3900. Offers cybersecurity engineering (MS); electrical and computer engineering (MSECE); software engineering (MSSE); systems engineering (MS). *Degree requirements:* For master's, thesis optional. *Entrance requirements:* For master's, GRE (for some programs). Additional exam requirements/recommendations for international students: Required—TOEFL (minimum score 550 paper-based, 79 iBT) or IELTS (6). Electronic applications accepted.

Embry-Riddle Aeronautical University–Worldwide, Department of Security and Emergency Services, Daytona Beach, FL 32114-3900. Offers cybersecurity management and policy (MSCMP); human security and resilience (MSHSR). *Program availability:* Part-time, evening/weekend, EagleVision Classroom (between classrooms), EagleVision Home (faculty and students at home), and a blend of Classroom or Home. *Degree requirements:* For master's, capstone project (for MSHSR). *Entrance requirements:* Additional exam requirements/recommendations for international students: Required—TOEFL (minimum score 550 paper-based; 79 iBT), IELTS (minimum score 6). Electronic applications accepted. *Expenses:* Tuition: Full-time $7980; part-time $665 per credit hour. Tuition and fees vary according to course load, degree level and program.

Endicott College, Van Loan School of Graduate and Professional Studies, Program in Homeland Security, Beverly, MA 01915-2096. Offers cybersecurity (MS, Postbaccalaureate Certificate); emergency management (MS). *Program availability:* Part-time. *Degree requirements:* For master's, thesis. *Entrance requirements:* For master's, undergraduate transcript, two recommendations, personal statement. Additional exam requirements/recommendations for international students: Required—TOEFL. Electronic applications accepted. *Expenses:* Contact institution.

Fairfield University, School of Engineering, Fairfield, CT 06824. Offers database management (CAS); electrical and computer engineering (MS); information security (CAS); management of technology (MS); mechanical engineering (MS); network technology (CAS); software engineering (MS); Web application development (CAS). *Program availability:* Part-time, evening/weekend. *Degree requirements:* For master's, capstone course. *Entrance requirements:* For master's, resume, 2 recommendations. Additional exam requirements/recommendations for international students: Required—TOEFL (minimum score 550 paper-based; 80 iBT) or IELTS (minimum score 6.5). Electronic applications accepted. *Expenses:* Contact institution. *Faculty research:* Artificial intelligence and information visualization, natural language processing, thermofluids, microwaves and electromagnetics, micro-/nano-manufacturing.

Florida Institute of Technology, College of Engineering and Science, Program in Information Assurance and Cybersecurity, Melbourne, FL 32901-6975. Offers MS. *Program availability:* Part-time, evening/weekend, 100% online. *Students:* 18 full-time (9 women), 10 part-time (2 women); includes 5 minority (1 Black or African American, non-Hispanic/Latino; 2 Asian, non-Hispanic/Latino; 2 Hispanic/Latino), 17 international. Average age 30. 11 applicants, 64% accepted, 3 enrolled. In 2018, 13 master's awarded. *Degree requirements:* For master's, comprehensive exam (for some

programs), thesis optional, minimum of 33 credit hours, capstone project or thesis. *Entrance requirements:* For master's, GRE General Test, transcripts. Additional exam requirements/recommendations for international students: Required—TOEFL (minimum score 550 paper-based; 79 iBT). *Application deadline:* Applications are processed on a rolling basis. Application fee: $50. Electronic applications accepted. *Expenses: Tuition:* Full-time $22,338; part-time $1241 per credit hour. Tuition and fees vary according to degree level, campus/location and program. *Financial support:* Applicants required to submit FAFSA. *Unit head:* Dr. Philip Berhard, Department Head, 321-674-7294, E-mail: pbernhar@fit.edu. *Application contact:* Mike Perry, Executive Director of Admissions, 321-674-7127, E-mail: perrymj@fit.edu.
Website: https://www.fit.edu/programs/information-assurance-and-cybersecurity-ms/

Florida International University, College of Engineering and Computing, School of Computing and Information Sciences, Miami, FL 33199. Offers computer science (MS, PhD); cybersecurity (MS); data science (MS); information technology (MS); telecommunications and networking (MS). *Program availability:* Part-time, evening/weekend. *Faculty:* 49 full-time (13 women), 31 part-time/adjunct (7 women). *Students:* 182 full-time (53 women), 132 part-time (28 women); includes 168 minority (13 Black or African American, non-Hispanic/Latino; 1 American Indian or Alaska Native, non-Hispanic/Latino; 10 Asian, non-Hispanic/Latino; 137 Hispanic/Latino; 7 Two or more races, non-Hispanic/Latino), 123 international. Average age 30. 393 applicants, 47% accepted, 92 enrolled. In 2018, 81 master's, 9 doctorates awarded. *Degree requirements:* For master's, thesis or alternative; for doctorate, comprehensive exam, thesis/dissertation. *Entrance requirements:* For master's and doctorate, GRE General Test, 3 letters of recommendation, minimum GPA of 3.0. Additional exam requirements/recommendations for international students: Required—TOEFL (minimum score 550 paper-based; 80 iBT). *Application deadline:* For fall admission, 6/1 for domestic students, 4/1 for international students; for spring admission, 10/1 for domestic students, 9/1 for international students. Applications are processed on a rolling basis. Application fee: $30. Electronic applications accepted. *Financial support:* Research assistantships, teaching assistantships, institutionally sponsored loans, scholarships/grants, and unspecified assistantships available. Financial award application deadline: 3/1; financial award applicants required to submit FAFSA. *Faculty research:* Database systems, software engineering, operating systems, networks. *Unit head:* Dr. Sundararaj S. Iyengar, Director, 305-348-3947, Fax: 305-348-3549, E-mail: sundararaj.iyengar@fiu.edu. *Application contact:* Nanett Rojas, Manager, Admissions Operations, 305-348-7464, Fax: 305-348-7441, E-mail: gradadm@fiu.edu.

Florida State University, The Graduate School, Department of Anthropology, Department of Computer Science, Tallahassee, FL 32306. Offers computer network and system administration (MS); computer science (MS, PhD); cyber criminology (MS); cyber security (MS). *Program availability:* Part-time. *Faculty:* 32 full-time (5 women), 2 part-time/adjunct (0 women). *Students:* 131 full-time (29 women), 8 part-time (3 women); includes 21 minority (1 Black or African American, non-Hispanic/Latino; 3 Asian, non-Hispanic/Latino; 12 Hispanic/Latino; 5 Two or more races, non-Hispanic/Latino), 82 international. Average age 29. 262 applicants, 52% accepted, 26 enrolled. In 2018, 56 master's, 7 doctorates awarded. Terminal master's awarded for partial completion of doctoral program. *Degree requirements:* For master's, comprehensive exam (for some programs), thesis (for some programs); for doctorate, comprehensive exam, thesis/dissertation, qualifying exam, preliminary exam, prospectus defense. *Entrance requirements:* For master's, GRE General Test, minimum undergraduate GPA of 3.0; for doctorate, GRE General Test, minimum GPA of 3.0. Additional exam requirements/recommendations for international students: Required—TOEFL (minimum score 550 paper-based; 80 iBT), IELTS (minimum score 6.5). *Application deadline:* For fall admission, 6/1 for domestic students, 1/15 priority date for international students; for spring admission, 11/1 for domestic students, 9/1 priority date for international students. Applications are processed on a rolling basis. Application fee: $30. Electronic applications accepted. *Expenses: Tuition, area resident:* Part-time $479.32 per credit hour. Tuition and fees vary according to campus/location and program. *Financial support:* In 2018–19, 121 students received support, including 23 fellowships with full tuition reimbursements available (averaging $36,000 per year), 40 research assistantships with full tuition reimbursements available (averaging $23,800 per year), 60 teaching assistantships with full tuition reimbursements available (averaging $19,725 per year); scholarships/grants, health care benefits, tuition waivers (full), and unspecified assistantships also available. Financial award application deadline: 1/15; financial award applicants required to submit FAFSA. *Faculty research:* Embedded systems, high performance computing, networking, operating systems, security, cryptography, databases, algorithms, big data, AI and machine learning, data science. *Total annual research expenditures:* $2.7 million. *Unit head:* Dr. Xin Yuan, Chairman, 850-644-9133, Fax: 850-644-0058, E-mail: xyuan@cs.fsu.edu. *Application contact:* Daniel B. Clawson, Graduate Coordinator, 850-645-4975, Fax: 850-644-0058, E-mail: clawson@cs.fsu.edu.
Website: http://www.cs.fsu.edu/

George Mason University, School of Business, Program in Management of Secure Information Systems, Fairfax, VA 22030. Offers MS. *Faculty:* 7 full-time (1 woman), 3 part-time/adjunct (1 woman). *Students:* 25 full-time (7 women); includes 9 minority (3 Black or African American, non-Hispanic/Latino; 3 Asian, non-Hispanic/Latino; 2 Hispanic/Latino; 1 Two or more races, non-Hispanic/Latino). Average age 38. In 2018, 18 master's awarded. *Degree requirements:* For master's, thesis, capstone project. *Entrance requirements:* For master's, current resume; official copies of transcripts from all colleges or universities attended; two professional letters of recommendation; goal statement; interview. Additional exam requirements/recommendations for international students: Required—TOEFL (minimum score 650 paper-based; 93 iBT), IELTS, PTE. Application fee: $75 ($80 for international students). Electronic applications accepted. *Expenses:* $1,200 per credit. *Financial support:* Career-related internships or fieldwork, Federal Work-Study, and scholarships/grants available. Support available to part-time students. Financial award applicants required to submit FAFSA. *Unit head:* Kumar Mehta, Director, 703-993-9412, Fax: 703-993-1809, E-mail: kmehta1@gmu.edu. *Application contact:* Jacky Buchy, Assistant Dean of Graduate Enrollment, 703-993-1856, Fax: 703-993-1778, E-mail: jbuchy@gmu.edu.
Website: http://business.gmu.edu/cyber-security-degree/

The George Washington University, School of Engineering and Applied Science, Department of Computer Science, Washington, DC 20052. Offers computer science (MS, D Sc); cybersecurity (MS). *Program availability:* Part-time, evening/weekend. *Faculty:* 14 full-time (6 women), 28 part-time/adjunct (3 women). *Students:* 385 full-time (88 women), 396 part-time (107 women); includes 137 minority (69 Black or African American, non-Hispanic/Latino; 4 American Indian or Alaska Native, non-Hispanic/Latino; 49 Asian, non-Hispanic/Latino; 8 Hispanic/Latino; 7 Two or more races, non-Hispanic/Latino), 379 international. Average age 31. 1,262 applicants, 76% accepted, 287 enrolled. In 2018, 253 master's, 12 doctorates, 13 other advanced degrees awarded. *Degree requirements:* For master's, thesis optional; for doctorate, thesis/dissertation, dissertation defense, qualifying exam. *Entrance requirements:* For master's, appropriate bachelor's degree, minimum GPA of 3.0; for doctorate, GRE (if highest earned degree is BS), appropriate bachelor's or master's degree, minimum GPA of 3.3; for other advanced degree, appropriate master's degree, minimum GPA of 3.4. Additional exam requirements/recommendations for international students: Required—TOEFL or The George Washington University English as a Foreign Language Test. *Application deadline:* For fall admission, 3/1 priority date for domestic students; for spring admission, 10/1 for domestic students. Applications are processed on a rolling basis. Application fee: $75. *Financial support:* In 2018–19, 49 students received support. Fellowships, research assistantships, teaching assistantships, career-related internships or fieldwork, institutionally sponsored loans, and tuition waivers available. Financial award application deadline: 3/1; financial award applicants required to submit FAFSA. *Faculty research:* Computer graphics, multimedia, VLSI, parallel processing. *Unit head:* Prof. Abdou Youssef, Chair, 202-994-4953, E-mail: ayoussef@gwu.edu. *Application contact:* Adina Lav, Marketing, Recruiting and Admissions, 202-994-5827, Fax: 202-994-0909, E-mail: engineering@gwu.edu.
Website: http://www.cs.gwu.edu/

Georgia Institute of Technology, Graduate Studies, College of Computing, Program in Information Security, Atlanta, GA 30332-0001. Offers MS. *Program availability:* Part-time. *Entrance requirements:* For master's, GRE General Test. Additional exam requirements/recommendations for international students: Required—TOEFL (minimum score 600 paper-based; 100 iBT). Electronic applications accepted.

Georgia Southern University, Jack N. Averitt College of Graduate Studies, College of Behavioral and Social Sciences, Program in Criminal Justice and Criminology, Statesboro, GA 30458. Offers criminal justice (MS); cyber crime (Certificate). *Program availability:* Part-time, online learning. *Degree requirements:* For master's, comprehensive exam, field practicum or thesis. *Entrance requirements:* For master's, GRE General Test (minimum score 150 on verbal, 141 on quantitative, or 4 on analytical section) or MAT, minimum GPA of 2.5, 2 letters of recommendation, letter of intent (500-1000 words). Additional exam requirements/recommendations for international students: Required—TOEFL (minimum score 523 paper-based; 70 iBT). Electronic applications accepted. *Expenses: Tuition, area resident:* Part-time $3324 per semester. Tuition, state resident: full-time $5814; part-time $3324 per semester. Tuition, nonresident: full-time $23,204; part-time $13,260 per semester. *Required fees:* $2092; $2092. Tuition and fees vary according to course load, degree level, campus/location and program. *Faculty research:* International crime/globalization, cyber-crime, influence of social science research on judicial decision-making.

Hampton University, School of Science, Department of Computer Science, Program in Information Assurance, Hampton, VA 23668. Offers MS. *Students:* 4 full-time (3 women); all minorities (all Black or African American, non-Hispanic/Latino). Average age 24. 2 applicants, 100% accepted, 1 enrolled. In 2018, 3 master's awarded. *Faculty research:* Artificial intelligence, software development, machine learning, neural networks, parallel processing, natural language processing, distributive agents. *Unit head:* Dr. Chutima Boonthum-Denecke, Director, 757-727-5082. *Application contact:* Dr. Chutima Boonthum-Denecke, Director, 757-727-5082.

Harrisburg University of Science and Technology, Program in Information Systems Engineering and Management, Harrisburg, PA 17101. Offers analytics (MS); digital government (MS); digital health (MS); entrepreneurship (MS); information security (MS); software engineering and systems development (MS). *Program availability:* Part-time, evening/weekend. *Degree requirements:* For master's, thesis optional. *Entrance requirements:* For master's, baccalaureate degree. Additional exam requirements/recommendations for international students: Required—TOEFL (minimum score 520 paper-based; 80 iBT); Recommended—IELTS (minimum score 6). Electronic applications accepted. *Faculty research:* Healthcare Informatics, material analysis, enterprise systems, circuit design, enterprise architectures.

Hofstra University, Fred DeMatteis School of Engineering and Applied Sciences, Hempstead, NY 11549. Offers computer science (MS). *Program availability:* Part-time, evening/weekend, blended/hybrid learning. *Faculty:* 10 full-time (4 women), 5 part-time/adjunct. *Students:* 30 full-time (9 women), 13 part-time (1 woman); includes 11 minority (1 Black or African American, non-Hispanic/Latino; 5 Asian, non-Hispanic/Latino; 5 Hispanic/Latino), 15 international. Average age 27. 82 applicants, 66% accepted, 19 enrolled. In 2018, 18 master's awarded. *Degree requirements:* For master's, thesis optional, 30 credits, minimum GPA of 3.0. *Entrance requirements:* For master's, GRE, minimum GPA of 3.0. Additional exam requirements/recommendations for international students: Required—TOEFL (minimum score 550 paper-based; 80 iBT). *Application deadline:* Applications are processed on a rolling basis. Application fee: $75. Electronic applications accepted. *Financial support:* In 2018–19, 24 students received support, including 11 fellowships with full and partial tuition reimbursements available (averaging $4,482 per year); research assistantships with full and partial tuition reimbursements available, career-related internships or fieldwork, Federal Work-Study, institutionally sponsored loans, scholarships/grants, tuition waivers (full and partial), unspecified assistantships, and scholarships and endowed scholarships also available. Support available to part-time students. Financial award applicants required to submit FAFSA. *Faculty research:* Cognitive neuroscience and artificial intelligence; cyber-security and privacy; cell and tissue engineering; experimental fluid mechanics; STEM education. *Total annual research expenditures:* $716,770. *Unit head:* Dr. Sina Rabbany, Dean, 516-463-6672, E-mail: sina.y.rabbany@hofstra.edu. *Application contact:* Sunil Samuel, Assistant Vice President of Admissions, 516-463-4723, Fax: 516-463-4664, E-mail: graduateadmission@hofstra.edu.
Website: http://www.hofstra.edu/academics/colleges/seas/

Hood College, Graduate School, Programs in Computer and Information Sciences, Frederick, MD 21701-8575. Offers computer science (MS); cybersecurity (MS, Certificate); information technology (MS). *Program availability:* Part-time, evening/weekend, 100% online. *Faculty:* 8 full-time (2 women), 2 part-time/adjunct (0 women). *Students:* 48 full-time (15 women), 64 part-time (17 women); includes 15 minority (7 Black or African American, non-Hispanic/Latino; 2 Asian, non-Hispanic/Latino; 4 Hispanic/Latino; 2 Two or more races, non-Hispanic/Latino), 54 international. Average age 33. 55 applicants, 100% accepted, 26 enrolled. In 2018, 47 master's, 26 other advanced degrees awarded. *Degree requirements:* For master's, thesis optional, capstone (S). *Entrance requirements:* For master's, minimum GPA of 2.75, essay, resume. Additional exam requirements/recommendations for international students: Required—TOEFL (minimum score 575 paper-based; 89 iBT), IELTS (minimum score 6.5). *Application deadline:* For fall admission, 8/15 priority date for domestic students, 8/5 for international students; for spring admission, 12/1 priority date for domestic students, 12/1 for international students; for summer admission, 5/1 for domestic students, 4/15 for international students. Applications are processed on a rolling basis. Application fee: $50 ($100 for international students). Electronic applications accepted. *Expenses:* Science Programs: Tuition $535 per credit hour, Comprehensive Fee $115 per semester. *Financial support:* Tuition waivers (partial) and unspecified assistantships available. Financial award applicants required to submit FAFSA. *Faculty research:* Systems engineering, natural language, processing, database design, artificial intelligence and parallel distributed computing. *Unit head:* Dr. April M. Boulton, Dean of the Graduate School, 301-696-3600, E-mail: gofurther@hood.edu. *Application contact:* Larbi Bricha, Assistant Director of Graduate Admissions, 301-696-3601, E-mail: gofurther@hood.edu.
Website: https://www.hood.edu/graduate

Illinois Institute of Technology, Graduate College, College of Science, Department of Computer Science, Chicago, IL 60616. Offers business (MCS); computational intelligence (MCS); computer science (MCS, MS, PhD); cyber-physical systems (MCS); data analytics (MCS); data science (MAS); database systems (MCS); distributed and cloud computing (MCS); education (MCS); finance (MCS); information security and assurance (MCS); networking and communications (MCS); software engineering (MCS); telecommunications and software engineering (MAS); MS/MAS. *Program availability:* Part-time, evening/weekend, online learning. Terminal master's awarded for partial completion of doctoral program. *Degree requirements:* For master's, thesis optional; for doctorate, comprehensive exam, thesis/dissertation. *Entrance requirements:* For master's, GRE General Test with minimum scores of 298 Quantitative and Verbal, 3.0 Analytical Writing (for MS); GRE General Test with minimum scores of 292 Quantitative and Verbal, 2.5 Analytical Writing (for MAS), minimum undergraduate GPA of 3.0; for doctorate, GRE General Test (minimum scores: 304 Quantitative and Verbal, 3.5 Analytical Writing), minimum undergraduate GPA of 3.0. Additional exam requirements/recommendations for international students: Required—TOEFL (minimum score 523 paper-based; 70 iBT). Electronic applications accepted. *Faculty research:* Parallel and distributed processing, high-performance computing, computational linguistics, information retrieval, data mining, grid computing.

Illinois Institute of Technology, Graduate College, School of Applied Technology, Department of Information Technology and Management, Wheaton, IL 60189. Offers cyber forensics and security (MAS); information technology and management (MAS). *Program availability:* Part-time, evening/weekend, online learning. *Entrance requirements:* For master's, GRE (minimum score 300 Quantitative and Verbal, 2.5 Analytical Writing), bachelor's degree with minimum cumulative undergraduate GPA of 3.0 (or its equivalent) from accredited institution. Additional exam requirements/recommendations for international students: Required—TOEFL (minimum score 523 paper-based; 70 iBT); Recommended—IELTS (minimum score 5.5). Electronic applications accepted. *Faculty research:* Database design, voice over IP, process engineering, object-oriented programming, computer networking, online design, system administration.

Indiana University Bloomington, School of Informatics, Computing, and Engineering, Program in Informatics, Bloomington, IN 47405. Offers informatics (MS, PhD), including bioinformatics (PhD), complex systems (PhD), computing, culture and society (PhD), health informatics (PhD), human-computer interaction (MS), human-computer interaction design (PhD), music informatics (PhD), security informatics (PhD); visual heritage (PhD). *Program availability:* Part-time. Terminal master's awarded for partial completion of doctoral program. *Degree requirements:* For master's, thesis, capstone project; for doctorate, variable foreign language requirement, comprehensive exam, thesis/dissertation. *Entrance requirements:* For master's and doctorate, GRE, resume/curriculum vitae, transcripts, 3 letters of recommendation. Additional exam requirements/recommendations for international students: Required—TOEFL (minimum score 600 paper-based; 100 iBT). Electronic applications accepted. *Faculty research:* Algorithms, applied logic and computational theory, artificial intelligence, bioinformatics, case-based reasoning, chemical informatics, citation analysis, cognitive science, community informatics, compilers, complex networks and systems, computer optimization, computer-supported cooperative work, computer vision, cyberinfrastructure and e-science, database theory and systems, data mining, digital design and preservation, design pedagogy, digital humanities, digital learning environments.

Indiana University–Purdue University Indianapolis, School of Engineering and Technology, MS in Technology Program, Indianapolis, IN 46202. Offers applied data management and analytics (MS); facilities management (MS); information security and assurance (MS); motorsports (MS); organizational leadership (MS); technical communication (MS). *Program availability:* Online learning.

Indiana University–Purdue University Indianapolis, School of Science, Department of Computer and Information Science, Indianapolis, IN 46202-5132. Offers biocomputing (Graduate Certificate); biometrics (Graduate Certificate); computer science (MS, PhD); computer security (Graduate Certificate); databases and data mining (Graduate Certificate); software engineering (Graduate Certificate). *Program availability:* Part-time. Terminal master's awarded for partial completion of doctoral program. *Degree requirements:* For master's and Graduate Certificate, thesis optional; for doctorate, thesis/dissertation. *Entrance requirements:* For master's and doctorate, GRE, BS in computer science or the equivalent with a minimum GPA of 3.0 (or equivalent); for Graduate Certificate, BS in computer science or the equivalent with a minimum GPA of 3.0 (or equivalent). Additional exam requirements/recommendations for international students: Required—PTE (minimum score 58), TOEFL (minimum score 550 paper-based, 79 iBT) or IELTS (6.5). *Faculty research:* Imaging and visualization; networking and security; software engineering; distributed and parallel computing; database, data mining and machine learning.

The Institute of World Politics, Graduate Programs in National Security, Intelligence, and International Affairs, Washington, DC 20036. Offers American foreign policy (Certificate); comparative political culture (Certificate); conflict prevention (Certificate); counterintelligence (Certificate); counterterrorism (Certificate); cyber statecraft (Certificate); economic statecraft (Certificate); homeland security (Certificate); intelligence (Certificate); international politics (Certificate); national security affairs (Executive MA, Certificate); nonviolent conflict (Certificate); peace building, stabilization, and humanitarian affairs (Certificate); public diplomacy and strategic influence (Certificate); statecraft and international affairs (MA); statecraft and national security (MA, DSNS); strategic communication (Certificate); strategic intelligence studies (MA, Professional MA); strategic soft power (Certificate). *Program availability:* Part-time, evening/weekend. *Degree requirements:* For master's, 52 credit hours, comprehensive written and oral exam (for MA); proficiency in critical language (for MA in statecraft and international affairs); 28 credit hours (for Executive MA); 36 credit hours (for Professional MA); for doctorate, comprehensive exam, thesis/dissertation; for Certificate, 20 credit hours. *Entrance requirements:* For master's, resume, personal statement, 3 references, essay; 7-10 years of professional experience (for Executive MA); 5-7 years of professional experience (for Professional MA); for doctorate, MA. Additional exam requirements/recommendations for international students: Required—TOEFL. Electronic applications accepted. *Faculty research:* Intelligence, national security, statecraft, international affairs.

Inter American University of Puerto Rico, Guayama Campus, Department of Natural and Applied Sciences, Guayama, PR 00785. Offers computer security and networks (MS); networking and security (MCS).

Iona College, School of Arts and Science, Department of Computer Science, New Rochelle, NY 10801-1890. Offers computer science (MS); cyber security (MS); game development (MS). *Program availability:* Part-time, evening/weekend. *Faculty:* 8 full-time (4 women), 7 part-time/adjunct (3 women). *Students:* 3 full-time (0 women), 9 part-time (2 women); includes 3 minority (2 Black or African American, non-Hispanic/Latino; 1 Hispanic/Latino), 1 international. Average age 26. 17 applicants, 76% accepted, 3 enrolled. In 2018, 6 master's awarded. *Degree requirements:* For master's, thesis optional. *Entrance requirements:* For master's, minimum GPA of 3.0. Additional exam requirements/recommendations for international students: Required—TOEFL (minimum score 550 paper-based; 80 iBT), IELTS (minimum score 6.5). *Application deadline:* For fall admission, 8/1 priority date for domestic students, 5/1 priority date for international students; for spring admission, 1/1 priority date for domestic students, 9/1 priority date for international students. Applications are processed on a rolling basis. Electronic applications accepted. *Expenses: Tuition:* Full-time $14,064; part-time $7032 per credit. *Required fees:* $245 per semester. One-time fee: $250. Tuition and fees vary according to program. *Financial support:* In 2018–19, 2 students received support, including 2 research assistantships with full and partial tuition reimbursements available (averaging $5,072 per year); tuition waivers (partial) and unspecified assistantships also available. Support available to part-time students. Financial award application deadline: 4/15; financial award applicants required to submit FAFSA. *Faculty research:* Parallel procession, data mining, machine learning, cyber security, medical imaging. *Unit head:* Frances Bailie, PhD, Chair, 914-633-2335, E-mail: fbailie@iona.edu. *Application contact:* Christopher Kash, Assistant Director, Graduate Admissions, 914-633-2403, Fax: 914-633-2277, E-mail: ckash@iona.edu.
Website: http://www.iona.edu/Academics/School-of-Arts-Science/Departments/Computer-Science/Graduate-Programs.aspx

Iona College, School of Arts and Science, Department of Criminal Justice, New Rochelle, NY 10801-1890. Offers criminal justice (MS); cybercrime and security (AC); forensic criminology and criminal justice systems (Certificate). *Program availability:* Part-time, evening/weekend. *Faculty:* 4 full-time (2 women), 11 part-time/adjunct (1 woman). *Students:* 13 full-time (9 women), 6 part-time (5 women); includes 14 minority (5 Black or African American, non-Hispanic/Latino; 9 Hispanic/Latino). Average age 23. 19 applicants, 95% accepted, 10 enrolled. In 2018, 11 master's, 3 other advanced degrees awarded. *Degree requirements:* For master's, thesis (for some programs), thesis or literature review. *Entrance requirements:* For master's, minimum GPA of 3.0. Additional exam requirements/recommendations for international students: Required—TOEFL (minimum score 550 paper-based; 80 iBT), IELTS (minimum score 6.5). *Application deadline:* For fall admission, 8/1 priority date for domestic students, 5/1 priority date for international students; for spring admission, 1/1 priority date for domestic students, 9/1 priority date for international students. Applications are processed on a rolling basis. Electronic applications accepted. *Expenses: Tuition:* Full-time $14,064; part-time $7032 per credit. *Required fees:* $245 per semester. One-time fee: $250. Tuition and fees vary according to program. *Financial support:* In 2018–19, 1 student received support. Unspecified assistantships available. Financial award application deadline: 4/15; financial award applicants required to submit FAFSA. *Faculty research:* Juvenile justice, criminology, victimology, policing, social justice, security threat assessment. *Unit head:* Marcus Aldredge, PhD, Chair, 914-633-2594, E-mail: maldredge@iona.edu. *Application contact:* Christopher Kash, Assistant Director of Graduate Admissions, 914-633-2403, Fax: 914-633-2277, E-mail: ckash@iona.edu.
Website: http://www.iona.edu/Academics/School-of-Arts-Science/Departments/Criminal-Justice/Graduate-Programs.aspx

James Madison University, The Graduate School, College of Integrated Science and Engineering, Program in Computer Science, Harrisonburg, VA 22807. Offers digital forensics (MS); information security (MS). *Program availability:* Online learning. *Students:* 3 full-time (0 women), 48 part-time (10 women); includes 13 minority (7 Black or African American, non-Hispanic/Latino; 3 Asian, non-Hispanic/Latino; 2 Hispanic/Latino; 1 Two or more races, non-Hispanic/Latino), 1 international. Average age 30. In 2018, 5 master's awarded. Electronic applications accepted. *Expenses:* Tuition, state resident: full-time $10,848. Tuition, nonresident: full-time $27,888. *Required fees:* $1128. *Financial support:* In 2018–19, 2 students received support. Fellowships, Federal Work-Study, and assistantships (averaging $7911) available. Financial award application deadline: 3/1; financial award applicants required to submit FAFSA. *Unit head:* Dr. Sharon J. Simmons, Department Head, 540-568-4196, E-mail: simmonsj@jmu.edu. *Application contact:* Lynette D. Michael, Director of Graduate Admissions, 540-568-6131 Ext. 6395, Fax: 540-568-7860, E-mail: michaeld@jmu.edu.
Website: http://www.jmu.edu/cs/

Johns Hopkins University, Engineering Program for Professionals, Part-time Program in Cybersecurity, Baltimore, MD 21218. Offers MS, Post-Master's Certificate. *Program availability:* Part-time, evening/weekend, 100% online, blended/hybrid learning. *Faculty:* 11 part-time/adjunct (1 woman). *Students:* 81 part-time (17 women). 125 applicants, 26% accepted, 21 enrolled. In 2018, 27 master's, 2 other advanced degrees awarded. *Entrance requirements:* Additional exam requirements/recommendations for international students: Required—TOEFL (minimum score 600 paper-based; 100 iBT). Application fee: $0. Electronic applications accepted. *Unit head:* Dr. Lanier Watkins, Program Chair, 443-778-5913, E-mail: Lanier.Watkins@jhuapl.edu. *Application contact:* Doug Schiller, Admissions Director, 410-516-2300, Fax: 410-579-8049, E-mail: schiller@jhu.edu.
Website: http://ep.jhu.edu/graduate-programs/cybersecurity

Johns Hopkins University, G. W. C. Whiting School of Engineering, Master of Science in Security Informatics Program, Baltimore, MD 21218. Offers MSSI. *Faculty:* 1 full-time. *Students:* 57 full-time (15 women), 44 part-time (9 women). 166 applicants, 64% accepted, 61 enrolled. In 2018, 58 master's awarded. *Degree requirements:* For master's, 10 courses, capstone project. *Entrance requirements:* For master's, GRE, minimum GPA of 3.0, 2 letters of recommendation, statement of purpose, transcripts. Additional exam requirements/recommendations for international students: Required—TOEFL (minimum score 600 paper-based, 100 iBT) or IELTS (7). *Application deadline:* For fall admission, 3/1 for domestic and international students; for spring admission, 11/15 for domestic students, 9/15 for international students. Applications are processed on a rolling basis. Application fee: $25. Electronic applications accepted. *Financial support:* In 2018–19, 5 students received support, including 2 fellowships with full tuition reimbursements available (averaging $34,000 per year); career-related internships or fieldwork, Federal Work-Study, institutionally sponsored loans, scholarships/grants, traineeships, health care benefits, tuition waivers (partial), and unspecified assistantships also available. Financial award application deadline: 1/31. *Faculty research:* Cryptography and encryption methodologies; security and privacy in applications such as electronic voting, consumer transactions and electronic medical records; security in healthcare it; bitcoin and electronic currencies; security policy and management. *Unit head:* Dr. Anton Dahbura, Executive Director, 410-516-0211, Fax: 410-516-3301, E-mail: antondahbura@jhu.edu. *Application contact:* Revelie Niles, Academic Program Administrator, 410-516-6282, Fax: 410-516-3301, E-mail: rniles3@jhu.edu.
Website: http://www.jhuisi.jhu.edu/

Johnson & Wales University, Graduate Studies, MBA Program, Providence, RI 02903-3703. Offers accounting (MBA); business administration (MBA); finance (MBA); global fashion merchandising and management (MBA); hospitality (MBA); human resource management (MBA); information security/assurance (MBA); information technology (MBA); nonprofit management (MBA); operations and supply chain management (MBA); organizational leadership (MBA); organizational psychology (MBA); sport leadership (MBA). Program also offered on Denver campus. *Program availability:* Part-time, online learning. *Entrance requirements:* For master's, minimum GPA of 2.75. Additional exam requirements/recommendations for international students: Required—TOEFL (minimum score 550 paper-based); Recommended—IELTS, TWE. *Faculty research:* International banking, global economy, international trade, cultural differences.

Computer and Information Systems Security

Johnson & Wales University, Graduate Studies, MS Program in Information Security/Assurance, Providence, RI 02903-3703. Offers MS. *Program availability:* Online learning.

Keiser University, MS in Information Security Program, Fort Lauderdale, FL 33309. Offers MS.

Kennesaw State University, College of Computing and Software Engineering, Program in Information Technology, Kennesaw, GA 30144. Offers data management and analytics (Graduate Certificate); health information technology (Postbaccalaureate Certificate); information technology (MSIT); information technology foundations (Postbaccalaureate Certificate); information technology security (Graduate Certificate). *Program availability:* Part-time, evening/weekend, blended/hybrid learning. *Students:* 100 full-time (45 women), 195 part-time (76 women); includes 137 minority (75 Black or African American, non-Hispanic/Latino; 42 Asian, non-Hispanic/Latino; 14 Hispanic/Latino; 1 Native Hawaiian or other Pacific Islander, non-Hispanic/Latino; 5 Two or more races, non-Hispanic/Latino), 40 international. Average age 34. 131 applicants, 81% accepted, 81 enrolled. In 2018, 70 master's awarded. *Degree requirements:* For master's, thesis optional. *Entrance requirements:* For master's, minimum GPA of 2.75; for other advanced degree, bachelor's degree. Additional exam requirements/recommendations for international students: Required—TOEFL (minimum score 80 iBT), IELTS (minimum score 6.5). *Application deadline:* For fall admission, 7/1 priority date for domestic students, 5/1 priority date for international students; for spring admission, 11/1 priority date for domestic students, 9/1 priority date for international students; for summer admission, 4/1 priority date for domestic students, 3/1 priority date for international students. Applications are processed on a rolling basis. Application fee: $60. Electronic applications accepted. *Expenses: Tuition, area resident:* Full-time $6960; part-time $290 per credit hour. Tuition, state resident: full-time $6960; part-time $290 per credit hour. Tuition, nonresident: full-time $25,080; part-time $1045 per credit hour. *International tuition:* $25,080 full-time. *Required fees:* $2006; $1706 per semester. $853 per semester. *Financial support:* Research assistantships with full and partial tuition reimbursements, career-related internships or fieldwork, scholarships/grants, and unspecified assistantships available. Support available to part-time students. Financial award applicants required to submit FAFSA. *Application contact:* Admission Counselor, 470-578-4377, Fax: 470-578-9172, E-mail: ksugrad@kennesaw.edu.
Website: http://ccse.kennesaw.edu/it/

Kent State University, College of Communication and Information, School of Digital Sciences, Kent, OH 44242-0001. Offers digital sciences (MDS), including data sciences; digital systems management (MDS); digital systems software development (MDS); digital systems telecommunication network (MDS); digital systems training technology (MDS); enterprise architecture (MDS). *Program availability:* Part-time. *Faculty:* 2 full-time (1 woman), 5 part-time/adjunct (2 women). *Students:* 21 full-time (10 women), 28 part-time (12 women); includes 2 minority (both Black or African American, non-Hispanic/Latino), 28 international. Average age 32. 47 applicants, 72% accepted, 12 enrolled. In 2018, 121 master's awarded. *Degree requirements:* For master's, thesis optional, capstone. *Entrance requirements:* For master's, GRE, minimum GPA of 3.0, transcripts, goal statement, resume, 3 letters of recommendation. may have GRE waived if applicant has 36 months of relevant work experience. Additional exam requirements/recommendations for international students: Required—TOEFL (minimum score 550 paper-based; 79 iBT), IELTS (minimum score 6.5), PTE (minimum score 58), Michigan English Language Assessment Battery (minimum score 77). *Application deadline:* For fall admission, 7/1 for domestic students, 5/15 for international students; for spring admission, 11/15 for domestic students, 10/1 for international students; for summer admission, 4/15 for domestic students, 3/15 for international students. Applications are processed on a rolling basis. Application fee: $45 ($70 for international students). Electronic applications accepted. *Expenses:* Tuition, state resident: full-time $11,766; part-time $536 per credit. Tuition, nonresident: full-time $21,952; part-time $999 per credit. *International tuition:* $21,952 full-time. Tuition and fees vary according to course load. *Financial support:* Career-related internships or fieldwork and scholarships/grants available. *Unit head:* Jeff Fruit, Interim Director, 330-672-9105, E-mail: jfruit@kent.edu. *Application contact:* Amy Copus, Academic Advisor II for Graduate Students, 330-672-9105, E-mail: acopus@kent.edu.
Website: http://www.kent.edu/dsci

Lawrence Technological University, College of Management, Southfield, MI 48075-1058. Offers business administration (MBA, DBA), including business analytics (MBA, MS), cybersecurity (MBA, MS), finance (MBA), information systems (MBA), information technology (MBA), marketing (MBA), project management (MBA, MS); cybersecurity (Graduate Certificate); health IT management (Graduate Certificate); information assurance management (Graduate Certificate); information systems (MS), including enterprise resource planning, enterprise security management, project management (MBA, MS); information technology (MS, DM), including business analytics (MBA, MS), cybersecurity (MBA, MS), information assurance (MS), project management (MBA, MS); management (PhD); nonprofit management and leadership (Graduate Certificate); operations management (MS), including manufacturing operations, service operations; project management (Graduate Certificate). *Accreditation:* ACBSP. *Program availability:* Part-time, evening/weekend, 100% online. Terminal master's awarded for partial completion of doctoral program. *Degree requirements:* For master's, thesis (for some programs); for doctorate, comprehensive exam, thesis/dissertation. *Entrance requirements:* Additional exam requirements/recommendations for international students: Required—TOEFL (minimum score 550 paper-based; 79 iBT), IELTS (minimum score 6.5). Electronic applications accepted. *Faculty research:* Cybersecurity; risk management; IT governance; security controls and countermeasures; threat modeling cyber resilience; autonomous cars; natural language processing; text mining; machine learning; reflective leadership; emerging leadership theories and practice; motivational studies; teaching effectiveness strategies; teamwork; organization development; strategic planning; strengths-based and positive organizational scholarship; global leadership; globalization; corporate governance.

Lewis University, College of Arts and Sciences, Program in Computer Science, Romeoville, IL 60446. Offers cyber security (MS); intelligent systems (MS); software engineering (MS). *Program availability:* Part-time, evening/weekend, 100% online, blended/hybrid learning. *Students:* 23 full-time (5 women), 90 part-time (23 women); includes 34 minority (8 Black or African American, non-Hispanic/Latino; 12 Asian, non-Hispanic/Latino; 9 Hispanic/Latino; 1 Native Hawaiian or other Pacific Islander, non-Hispanic/Latino; 4 Two or more races, non-Hispanic/Latino), 6 international. Average age 32. *Entrance requirements:* For master's, bachelor's degree; minimum undergraduate GPA of 3.0; resume; statement of purpose; two letters of recommendation; undergraduate coursework in discrete mathematics, programming or algorithms. Additional exam requirements/recommendations for international students: Required—TOEFL (minimum score 550 paper-based; 79 iBT), IELTS (minimum score 6). *Application deadline:* For fall admission, 5/1 for international students; for winter admission, 11/15 for international students. Applications are processed on a rolling basis. Application fee: $40. Electronic applications accepted. *Financial support:* Federal Work-Study and unspecified assistantships available. Financial award application deadline: 5/1; financial award applicants required to submit FAFSA. *Unit head:* Dr. Khaled Alzoubi, Program Director. *Application contact:* Linda Campbell, Graduate Admissions Counselor, 815-836-5610, E-mail: grad@lewisu.edu.
Website: http://www.lewisu.edu/academics/mscomputerscience/index.htm

Lewis University, College of Arts and Sciences, Program in Information Security - Technical, Romeoville, IL 60446. Offers technical (MS). *Program availability:* Part-time, evening/weekend, 100% online, blended/hybrid learning. *Students:* 15 full-time (4 women), 24 part-time (6 women); includes 18 minority (5 Black or African American, non-Hispanic/Latino; 7 Asian, non-Hispanic/Latino; 5 Hispanic/Latino; 1 Two or more races, non-Hispanic/Latino), 3 international. Average age 34. *Entrance requirements:* For master's, bachelor's degree, minimum GPA of 3.0, resume, 2-page statement of purpose, 2 letters of recommendation. Additional exam requirements/recommendations for international students: Required—TOEFL (minimum score 550 paper-based; 79 iBT), IELTS (minimum score 6). *Application deadline:* For fall admission, 5/1 priority date for international students; for spring admission, 11/15 priority date for international students. Applications are processed on a rolling basis. Application fee: $40. Electronic applications accepted. *Financial support:* Federal Work-Study and unspecified assistantships available. Financial award application deadline: 5/1; financial award applicants required to submit FAFSA. *Total annual research expenditures:* $33. *Unit head:* Dr. Raymond Klump, Program Director. *Application contact:* Linda Campbell, Graduate Admission Counselor, 815-836-5610, E-mail: grad@lewisu.edu.
Website: http://www.lewisu.edu/academics/msinfosec/index.htm

Lewis University, College of Business, Program in Information Security - Management, Romeoville, IL 60446. Offers MS. *Students:* 6 full-time (1 woman), 16 part-time (5 women); includes 12 minority (6 Black or African American, non-Hispanic/Latino; 3 Asian, non-Hispanic/Latino; 1 Hispanic/Latino; 2 Two or more races, non-Hispanic/Latino), 2 international. Average age 33. *Unit head:* Dr. Ryan Butt, Dean. *Application contact:* Office of Graduate Admission, 815-836-5610, E-mail: grad@lewisu.edu.

Liberty University, School of Business, Lynchburg, VA 24515. Offers accounting (MBA, MS), including audit and financial reporting (MS), business (MS), financial services (MS), forensic accounting (MS), leadership (MS), taxation (MS); cyber security (MS); executive leadership (MA); international business (DBA); leadership (DBA); marketing (MBA, MS, DBA), including digital marketing and advertising (MS), project management (MS), public relations (MS), sports marketing and media (MS); project management (MBA, DBA); public relations (MBA). *Program availability:* Part-time, online learning. *Students:* 2,871 full-time (1,496 women), 4,437 part-time (1,969 women); includes 2,069 minority (1,424 Black or African American, non-Hispanic/Latino; 44 American Indian or Alaska Native, non-Hispanic/Latino; 133 Asian, non-Hispanic/Latino; 282 Hispanic/Latino; 16 Native Hawaiian or other Pacific Islander, non-Hispanic/Latino; 170 Two or more races, non-Hispanic/Latino), 154 international. Average age 36. 8,980 applicants, 45% accepted, 2009 enrolled. In 2018, 1,988 master's, 25 doctorates awarded. *Entrance requirements:* For master's, minimum undergraduate GPA of 3.0, 15 hours of upper-level business courses. Additional exam requirements/recommendations for international students: Required—TOEFL (minimum score 600 paper-based; 100 iBT). *Application deadline:* Applications are processed on a rolling basis. Application fee: $50. Electronic applications accepted. *Expenses:* Contact institution. *Financial support:* In 2018–19, 990 students received support. Teaching assistantships and Federal Work-Study available. Financial award applicants required to submit FAFSA. *Unit head:* Dr. Dave Bratt, Dean, 434-592-7321, E-mail: dabrat@liberty.edu. *Application contact:* Jay Bridge, Director of Graduate Admissions, 800-424-9595, Fax: 800-628-7977, E-mail: gradadmissions@liberty.edu.
Website: https://www.liberty.edu/business/

Lindenwood University, Graduate Programs, School of Accelerated Degree Programs, St. Charles, MO 63301-1695. Offers administration (MSA), including management, marketing, project management; business administration (MBA); communications (MA), including digital and multimedia, media management, promotions, training and development; criminal justice and administration (MS); healthcare administration (MS); human resource management (MS); information technology (Certificate); managing information security (MS); managing information technology (MS); managing virtualization and cloud computing (MS); writing (MFA). *Program availability:* Part-time, evening/weekend, 100% online. *Faculty:* 15 full-time (8 women), 62 part-time/adjunct (22 women). *Students:* 652 full-time (398 women), 66 part-time (45 women); includes 241 minority (182 Black or African American, non-Hispanic/Latino; 1 American Indian or Alaska Native, non-Hispanic/Latino; 8 Asian, non-Hispanic/Latino; 25 Hispanic/Latino; 1 Native Hawaiian or other Pacific Islander, non-Hispanic/Latino; 24 Two or more races, non-Hispanic/Latino), 81 international. Average age 36. 359 applicants, 54% accepted, 170 enrolled. In 2018, 416 master's, 2 other advanced degrees awarded. *Degree requirements:* For master's, thesis (for some programs), minimum cumulative GPA of 3.0; for Certificate, minimum cumulative GPA of 3.0. *Entrance requirements:* For master's, resume, personal statement, official undergraduate transcript, minimum undergraduate cumulative GPA of 3.0. Additional exam requirements/recommendations for international students: Required—TOEFL (minimum score 553 paper-based; 81 iBT); Recommended—IELTS (minimum score 6.5). *Application deadline:* For fall admission, 9/30 priority date for domestic and international students; for winter admission, 1/6 priority date for domestic and international students; for spring admission, 4/6 priority date for domestic and international students; for summer admission, 7/8 priority date for domestic and international students. Applications are processed on a rolling basis. Application fee: $0 ($100 for international students). Electronic applications accepted. *Expenses:* Contact institution. *Financial support:* In 2018–19, 372 students received support. Career-related internships or fieldwork, institutionally sponsored loans, scholarships/grants, tuition waivers (partial), and unspecified assistantships available. Financial award application deadline: 6/30; financial award applicants required to submit FAFSA. *Unit head:* Dr. Gina Ganahl, Dean, Accelerated Degree Programs, 636-949-4501, Fax: 636-949-4505, E-mail: gganahl@lindenwood.edu. *Application contact:* Kara Schilli, Assistant Vice President, University Admissions, 636-949-4349, Fax: 636-949-4109, E-mail: adultadmissions@lindenwood.edu.
Website: https://www.lindenwood.edu/academics/academic-schools/school-of-accelerated-degree-programs/

Lipscomb University, College of Computing and Technology, Nashville, TN 37204-3951. Offers data science (MS, Certificate); information technology (MS, Certificate), including data science (MS), information security (MS), information technology management (MS), software engineering (MS); software engineering (MS, Certificate). *Program availability:* Part-time, evening/weekend. *Degree requirements:* For master's, capstone project. *Entrance requirements:* For master's, GRE, 2 references, transcripts, resume, personal statement. Additional exam requirements/recommendations for international students: Required—TOEFL (minimum score 570 paper-based; 80 iBT). Electronic applications accepted. *Expenses:* Contact institution.

London Metropolitan University, Graduate Programs, London, United Kingdom. Offers applied psychology (M Sc); architecture (MA); biomedical science (M Sc); blood science (M Sc); cancer pharmacology (M Sc); computer networking and cyber security (M Sc); computing and information systems (M Sc); conference interpreting (MA); counter-terrorism studies (M Sc); creative, digital and professional writing (MA); crime, violence and prevention (M Sc); criminology (M Sc); curating contemporary art (MA); data analytics (M Sc); digital media (MA); early childhood studies (MA); education (MA,

Ed D); financial services law, regulation and compliance (LL M); food science (M Sc); forensic psychology (M Sc); health and social care management and policy (M Sc); human nutrition (M Sc); human resource management (MA); human rights and international conflict (MA); information technology (M Sc); intelligence and security studies (M Sc); international oil, gas and energy law (LL M); international relations (MA); interpreting (MA); learning and teaching in higher education (MA); legal practice (LL M); media and entertainment law (LL M); organizational and consumer psychology (M Sc); psychological therapy (M Sc); psychology of mental health (M Sc); public health (M Sc); public policy and management (MPA); security studies (M Sc); social work (M Sc); spatial planning and urban design (MA); sports therapy (M Sc); supporting older children and young people with dyslexia (MA); teaching languages (MA), including Arabic, English; translation (MA); woman and child abuse (MA).

Long Island University–Riverhead, Graduate Programs, Riverhead, NY 11901. Offers applied behavior analysis (Advanced Certificate); childhood education (MS), including grades 1-6; cybersecurity policy (Advanced Certificate); homeland security management (MS, Advanced Certificate); literacy education (MS); literacy education B-6 (MS); teaching students with disabilities (MS), including grades 1-6; TESOL (Advanced Certificate). *Accreditation:* TEAC. *Program availability:* Part-time. *Entrance requirements:* Additional exam requirements/recommendations for international students: Required—TOEFL or IELTS. Electronic applications accepted. *Expenses:* Contact institution.

Louisiana Tech University, Graduate School, College of Business, Ruston, LA 71272. Offers accounting (M Acc, DBA); computer information systems (DBA); finance (MBA, DBA); information assurance (MBA); innovation (MBA); management (DBA); marketing (MBA, DBA). *Accreditation:* AACSB. *Program availability:* Part-time, evening/weekend, 100% online, blended/hybrid learning. *Degree requirements:* For doctorate, thesis/dissertation. *Entrance requirements:* For master's and doctorate, GMAT, transcript with bachelor's degree awarded. Additional exam requirements/recommendations for international students: Required—TOEFL (minimum score 550 paper-based; 80 iBT), IELTS (minimum score 6.5). Electronic applications accepted. *Faculty research:* Consumer environmental behavior; identifying and analyzing current issues and future concerns in real estate; information assurance and related areas in business for Northwest Louisiana and the United States (business continuity, disaster recovery, accounting controls, auditing, computer forensics, and security attribution); value creation driven by the consumer and employee interface within exchange environments.

Marymount University, School of Business and Technology, Program in Cybersecurity, Arlington, VA 22207-4299. Offers cybersecurity (MS), including data science, digital health; cybersecurity with information technology (MS/MS); MS/MS. *Program availability:* Part-time, evening/weekend, 100% online. *Faculty:* 5 full-time (4 women), 5 part-time/adjunct (1 woman). *Students:* 43 full-time (17 women), 75 part-time (21 women); includes 66 minority (23 Black or African American, non-Hispanic/Latino; 25 Asian, non-Hispanic/Latino; 12 Hispanic/Latino; 6 Two or more races, non-Hispanic/Latino), 20 international. Average age 33. 90 applicants, 100% accepted, 58 enrolled. In 2018, 26 master's, 1 other advanced degree awarded. *Degree requirements:* For master's, thesis or alternative. *Entrance requirements:* For master's, resume, certification or demonstrated work experience in computer networking; for doctorate, Three writing samples demonstrating research on a topic in technology. A research statement and personal statement outlining personal goals and research focuses for the program. Additional exam requirements/recommendations for international students: Required—TOEFL (minimum score 600 paper-based; 96 iBT), IELTS (minimum score 6.5), PTE (minimum score 58). *Application deadline:* For fall admission, 7/16 priority date for domestic and international students; for spring admission, 11/16 priority date for domestic and international students; for summer admission, 4/16 priority date for domestic and international students. Applications are processed on a rolling basis. Application fee: $40. Electronic applications accepted. *Expenses:* $1,060 per credit. *Financial support:* In 2018–19, 4 students received support. Research assistantships, teaching assistantships, career-related internships or fieldwork, scholarships/grants, and unspecified assistantships available. Support available to part-time students. Financial award application deadline: 3/1; financial award applicants required to submit FAFSA. *Unit head:* Dr. Diane Murphy, Chair/Director, Information Technology, Management Sciences and Cybersecurity, 703-284-5958, E-mail: diane.murphy@marymount.edu. *Application contact:* Rebecca Esposito, Senior Associate Director, Graduate Admissions, 703-284-5901, Fax: 703-527-3815, E-mail: grad.admissions@marymount.edu.
Website: https://www.marymount.edu/Academics/School-of-Business-and-Technology/Graduate-Programs

Marymount University, School of Business and Technology, Program in Information Technology, Arlington, VA 22207-4299. Offers health care informatics (Certificate); information technology (MS, Certificate), including cybersecurity (MS), health care informatics (MS), project management and technology leadership (MS), software engineering (MS); information technology project management and technology leadership (Certificate); information technology with business administration (MS/MBA); information technology with health care management (MS/MS); MS/MBA; MS/MS. *Program availability:* Part-time, evening/weekend. *Faculty:* 5 full-time (3 women), 7 part-time/adjunct (0 women). *Students:* 29 full-time (17 women), 36 part-time (19 women); includes 25 minority (15 Black or African American, non-Hispanic/Latino; 5 Asian, non-Hispanic/Latino; 5 Hispanic/Latino), 24 international. Average age 30. 66 applicants, 98% accepted, 22 enrolled. In 2018, 35 master's, 3 other advanced degrees awarded. *Degree requirements:* For master's, thesis or alternative. *Entrance requirements:* For master's, resume, bachelor's degree in computer-related field or degree in another subject with a certificate in a computer-related field or related work experience. Software Engineering Track: bachelor's degree in Computer Science or work in software development. Project Mgmt/Tech Leadership Track: minimum 2 years of IT experience. Additional exam requirements/recommendations for international students: Required—TOEFL (minimum score 600 paper-based; 96 iBT), IELTS (minimum score 6.5), PTE (minimum score 58). *Application deadline:* For fall admission, 7/16 priority date for domestic and international students; for spring admission, 11/16 priority date for domestic and international students; for summer admission, 4/16 priority date for domestic and international students. Applications are processed on a rolling basis. Application fee: $40. Electronic applications accepted. *Expenses:* $1,060 per credit. *Financial support:* In 2018–19, 1 student received support. Research assistantships, teaching assistantships, career-related internships or fieldwork, scholarships/grants, and unspecified assistantships available. Support available to part-time students. Financial award application deadline: 3/1; financial award applicants required to submit FAFSA. *Unit head:* Dr. Diane Murphy, Chair/Director, Information Technology, Management Sciences and Cybersecurity, 703-284-5958, E-mail: diane.murphy@marymount.edu. *Application contact:* Rebecca Esposito, Senior Associate Director, Graduate Admissions, 703-284-5901, Fax: 703-527-3815, E-mail: grad.admissions@marymount.edu.
Website: https://www.marymount.edu/Academics/School-of-Business-and-Technology/Graduate-Programs/Information-Technology-(M-S-)

Maryville University of Saint Louis, The John E. Simon School of Business, St. Louis, MO 63141-7299. Offers accounting (MBA, MS, Certificate); business studies (Certificate); cybersecurity (MBA, MS, Certificate); financial services (MBA, Certificate); health administration (MBA); healthcare administration (Certificate); human resource management (MBA); human resources management (Certificate); information technology (MBA); information technology management (Certificate); management (MBA, Certificate); management and leadership (MA); marketing (MBA, Certificate); project management (MBA, Certificate); sport business management (MBA); supply chain management (Certificate); supply chain management/logistics (MBA). *Accreditation:* ACBSP. *Program availability:* Part-time, 100% online, blended/hybrid learning. *Faculty:* 5 full-time (1 woman), 77 part-time/adjunct (19 women). *Students:* 338 full-time (166 women), 739 part-time (356 women); includes 310 minority (161 Black or African American, non-Hispanic/Latino; 6 American Indian or Alaska Native, non-Hispanic/Latino; 59 Asian, non-Hispanic/Latino; 57 Hispanic/Latino; 27 Two or more races, non-Hispanic/Latino), 30 international. Average age 33. In 2018, 143 master's awarded. *Degree requirements:* For master's, capstone course (for MBA). *Entrance requirements:* Additional exam requirements/recommendations for international students: Required—TOEFL (minimum score 563 paper-based; 85 iBT). *Application deadline:* Applications are processed on a rolling basis. Electronic applications accepted. *Expenses:* Tuition varies by program. *Financial support:* Career-related internships or fieldwork, Federal Work-Study, tuition waivers (partial), and campus employment available. Financial award application deadline: 4/1; financial award applicants required to submit FAFSA. *Unit head:* Tammy Gocial, Interim Dean, 314-529-9401, Fax: 314-529-9975, E-mail: tgocial@maryville.edu. *Application contact:* Chris Gourdine, Assistant Dean Business Administration, 314-529-6861, Fax: 314-529-9975, E-mail: cgourdine@maryville.edu.
Website: http://www.maryville.edu/bu/business-administration-masters/

Marywood University, Academic Affairs, Munley College of Liberal Arts and Sciences, Department of Mathematics and Computer Science, Scranton, PA 18509-1598. Offers information security (MS).

Mercy College, School of Liberal Arts, Program in Cybersecurity, Dobbs Ferry, NY 10522-1189. Offers MS. *Program availability:* Part-time, evening/weekend, 100% online, blended/hybrid learning. *Students:* 23 full-time (3 women), 16 part-time (2 women); includes 14 minority (6 Black or African American, non-Hispanic/Latino; 2 Asian, non-Hispanic/Latino; 6 Hispanic/Latino), 5 international. Average age 31. 30 applicants, 63% accepted, 14 enrolled. In 2018, 23 master's awarded. *Degree requirements:* For master's, thesis optional. *Entrance requirements:* For master's, transcript(s); letter of recommendation; CV; plan of study and research; interview may be required. Additional exam requirements/recommendations for international students: Required—TOEFL (minimum score 600 paper-based; 71 iBT), IELTS (minimum score 8). *Application deadline:* Applications are processed on a rolling basis. Application fee: $40. Electronic applications accepted. *Expenses:* Contact institution. *Financial support:* Career-related internships or fieldwork, Federal Work-Study, scholarships/grants, and unspecified assistantships available. Support available to part-time students. Financial award applicants required to submit FAFSA. *Unit head:* Stephen Ward, Interim Dean, School of Liberal Arts, 914-674-7432, Fax: 914-674-7518, E-mail: sward@mercy.edu. *Application contact:* Allison Gurdineer, Executive Director of Admissions, 877-637-2946, Fax: 914-674-7382, E-mail: admissions@mercy.edu.
Website: https://www.mercy.edu/degrees-programs/ms-cybersecurity

Mercyhurst University, Graduate Studies, Program in Data Science, Erie, PA 16546. Offers MS. Electronic applications accepted.

Metropolitan State University, College of Management, St. Paul, MN 55106-5000. Offers business administration (MBA, DBA); business analytics (Graduate Certificate); database administration (Graduate Certificate); global supply chain management (Graduate Certificate); information assurance security (Graduate Certificate); management information systems (MMIS); MIS generalist (Graduate Certificate); MIS systems analysis and design (Graduate Certificate); project management (Graduate Certificate). *Program availability:* Part-time, evening/weekend. *Degree requirements:* For master's, thesis optional, computer language (MMIS). *Entrance requirements:* For master's, GMAT (for MBA), resume. Additional exam requirements/recommendations for international students: Required—TOEFL (minimum score 550 paper-based). Electronic applications accepted. *Faculty research:* Yugoslav economic system, workers' cooperatives, participative management and job enrichment, global business systems.

Middle Georgia State University, Office of Graduate Studies, Macon, GA 31206. Offers adult/gerontology acute care nurse practitioner (MSN); information technology (MS), including health informatics, information security and digital forensics, software development. *Entrance requirements:* For master's, GRE. Additional exam requirements/recommendations for international students: Required—TOEFL (minimum score 523 paper-based; 69 iBT). *Expenses:* Contact institution.

Mississippi College, Graduate School, College of Arts and Sciences, School of Science and Mathematics, Department of Engineering, Computer Science, and Physics, Clinton, MS 39058. Offers computer science (M Ed, MS); cybersecurity and information assurance (MS). *Program availability:* Part-time. *Degree requirements:* For master's, comprehensive exam, thesis or alternative. *Entrance requirements:* For master's, GRE. Additional exam requirements/recommendations for international students: Recommended—TOEFL, IELTS.

Missouri Western State University, CyberSecurity, St. Joseph, MO 64507-2294. Offers MS. *Program availability:* Part-time. *Students:* 9 full-time (2 women), 2 part-time (0 women); includes 1 minority (Asian, non-Hispanic/Latino), 7 international. Average age 27. 30 applicants, 63% accepted, 6 enrolled. In 2018, 6 master's awarded. *Entrance requirements:* For master's, minimum GPA of 3.0. Additional exam requirements/recommendations for international students: Recommended—TOEFL (minimum score 79 iBT), IELTS (minimum score 6). *Application deadline:* For fall admission, 7/15 for domestic and international students; for spring admission, 11/1 for domestic and international students; for summer admission, 4/29 for domestic and international students. Applications are processed on a rolling basis. Application fee: $45 ($50 for international students). Electronic applications accepted. *Expenses: Tuition, area resident:* Part-time $359.39 per credit hour. *Tuition, state resident:* part-time $359.39 per credit hour. *Tuition, nonresident:* part-time $643.39 per credit hour. Tuition and fees vary according to program. *Financial support:* Scholarships/grants and unspecified assistantships available. Support available to part-time students. *Unit head:* Dr. Yipkei Kwok, Assistant Professor, 816-271-4523, E-mail: ykwok@missouriwestern.edu. *Application contact:* Dr. Susan Bashinski, Dean of the Graduate School, 816-271-4394, Fax: 816-271-4525, E-mail: graduate@missouriwestern.edu.
Website: https://www.missouriwestern.edu/itaa/

National University, School of Engineering and Computing, La Jolla, CA 92037-1011. Offers computer science (MS), including advanced computing; cyber security and information assurance (MS); data analytics (MS); electrical engineering (MS); engineering management (MS); information technology management (MS); management information systems (MS); sustainability management (MS). *Program availability:* Part-time, evening/weekend, 100% online, blended/hybrid learning. *Degree requirements:* For master's, thesis (for some programs). *Entrance requirements:* For master's, interview, minimum GPA of 2.5. Additional exam requirements/recommendations for international students:

Required—TOEFL (minimum score 550 paper-based; 79 iBT), IELTS (minimum score 6). Electronic applications accepted. *Expenses: Tuition:* Full-time $10,320; part-time $430 per unit. Tuition and fees vary according to degree level. *Faculty research:* Educational technology, scholarships in science.

Naval Postgraduate School, Departments and Academic Groups, Department of Computer Science, Monterey, CA 93943. Offers computer science (MS, PhD); identity management and cyber security (MA); modeling of virtual environments and simulations (MS, PhD); software engineering (MS, PhD). Program only open to commissioned officers of the United States and friendly nations and selected United States federal civilian employees. *Program availability:* Part-time, online learning. *Degree requirements:* For master's, thesis; for doctorate, thesis/dissertation.

New Jersey City University, College of Professional Studies, Program in National Security Studies, Jersey City, NJ 07305-1597. Offers civil security leadership (D Sc); national security studies (MS, Certificate). *Program availability:* Part-time. *Entrance requirements:* Additional exam requirements/recommendations for international students: Required—TOEFL (minimum score 79 iBT).

New Jersey Institute of Technology, Ying Wu College of Computing, Newark, NJ 07102. Offers big data management and mining (Certificate); business and information systems (Certificate); computer science (PhD); computing and business (MS); data mining (Certificate); data science (MS); information security (Certificate); information systems (PhD); information technology administration and security (MS); IT administration (Certificate); network security and information assurance (Certificate); software engineering (MS), including information systems; software engineering analysis/design (Certificate); Web systems development (Certificate). *Program availability:* Part-time, evening/weekend. *Faculty:* 69 full-time (13 women), 38 part-time/adjunct (4 women). *Students:* 699 full-time (229 women), 269 part-time (67 women); includes 260 minority (44 Black or African American, non-Hispanic/Latino; 145 Asian, non-Hispanic/Latino; 59 Hispanic/Latino; 12 Two or more races, non-Hispanic/Latino), 614 international. Average age 26. 2,216 applicants, 55% accepted, 366 enrolled. In 2018, 418 master's, 5 doctorates, 13 other advanced degrees awarded. Terminal master's awarded for partial completion of doctoral program. *Degree requirements:* For master's, thesis optional; for doctorate, thesis/dissertation. *Entrance requirements:* For master's, GRE General Test; for doctorate, GRE General Test, minimum graduate GPA of 3.5. Additional exam requirements/recommendations for international students: Required—TOEFL (minimum score 550 paper-based; 79 iBT), IELTS (minimum score 6.5). *Application deadline:* For fall admission, 6/1 priority date for domestic students, 5/1 priority date for international students; for spring admission, 11/15 priority date for domestic and international students. Applications are processed on a rolling basis. Application fee: $75. Electronic applications accepted. *Expenses:* $22,690 per year (in-state), $32,136 per year (out-of-state). *Financial support:* In 2018–19, 366 students received support, including 10 fellowships with full tuition reimbursements available (averaging $22,000 per year), 47 research assistantships with full tuition reimbursements available (averaging $22,000 per year), 28 teaching assistantships with full tuition reimbursements available (averaging $22,000 per year); career-related internships or fieldwork, Federal Work-Study, scholarships/grants, and unspecified assistantships also available. Financial award application deadline: 1/15. *Faculty research:* Computer systems, communications and networking, artificial intelligence, database engineering, systems analysis, analytics and optimization in crowdsourcing. *Total annual research expenditures:* $4.9 million. *Unit head:* Dr. Craig Gotsman, Dean, 973-596-3366, Fax: 973-596-5777, E-mail: craig.gotsman@njit.edu. *Application contact:* Stephen Eck, Director of Admissions, 973-596-3300, Fax: 973-596-3461, E-mail: admissions@njit.edu.
Website: http://computing.njit.edu/

New York Institute of Technology, College of Engineering and Computing Sciences, Department of Computer Science, Old Westbury, NY 11568-8000. Offers computer science (MS); information, network, and computer security (MS). *Program availability:* Part-time. *Faculty:* 12 full-time (3 women), 19 part-time/adjunct (3 women). *Students:* 196 full-time (66 women), 94 part-time (33 women); includes 54 minority (12 Black or African American, non-Hispanic/Latino; 27 Asian, non-Hispanic/Latino; 13 Hispanic/Latino; 1 Native Hawaiian or other Pacific Islander, non-Hispanic/Latino; 1 Two or more races, non-Hispanic/Latino), 209 international. Average age 26. 947 applicants, 57% accepted, 68 enrolled. In 2018, 247 master's awarded. *Degree requirements:* For master's, thesis or alternative. *Entrance requirements:* For master's, BS or its equivalent from accredited college or university in computer science, engineering, management, mathematics, information technology, liberal arts, and related areas; minimum undergraduate GPA of 2.85. Additional exam requirements/recommendations for international students: Required—TOEFL (minimum score 79 iBT), IELTS (minimum score 6), PTE (minimum score 53). *Application deadline:* For fall admission, 7/1 for domestic students, 6/1 for international students; for spring admission, 12/1 for domestic and international students. Applications are processed on a rolling basis. Application fee: $50. Electronic applications accepted. *Expenses: Tuition:* Full-time $1285; part-time $1285 per credit. *Required fees:* $215; $175 per unit. Tuition and fees vary according to course load, degree level and campus/location. *Financial support:* Fellowships with partial tuition reimbursements, teaching assistantships with partial tuition reimbursements, career-related internships or fieldwork, Federal Work-Study, scholarships/grants, tuition waivers (full and partial), and unspecified assistantships available. Support available to part-time students. Financial award application deadline: 2/15; financial award applicants required to submit FAFSA. *Faculty research:* Active authentication of mobile users; privacy-preserving authentication protocols; sensing cloud system for cybersecurity; cognitive rhythms as a new modality for continuous authentication; cloud-enabled and cloud source disaster detection. *Unit head:* Dr. Frank Lee, Department Chair, 516-686-7456, Fax: 516-686-7439, E-mail: fli@nyit.edu. *Application contact:* Alice Dolitsky, Director, Graduate Admissions, 516-686-7520, Fax: 516-686-1116, E-mail: admissions@nyit.edu.
Website: http://www.nyit.edu/degrees/computer_science_ms

New York University, Tandon School of Engineering, Department of Computer Science and Engineering, Major in Cyber Security, New York, NY 10012-1019. Offers MS. *Program availability:* Online learning. *Students:* 35 full-time (11 women), 136 part-time (29 women); includes 73 minority (4 Black or African American, non-Hispanic/Latino; 39 Asian, non-Hispanic/Latino; 24 Hispanic/Latino; 6 Two or more races, non-Hispanic/Latino), 26 international. Average age 32. 448 applicants, 43% accepted, 135 enrolled. In 2018, 28 master's awarded. *Degree requirements:* For master's, comprehensive exam (for some programs), thesis (for some programs). *Entrance requirements:* Additional exam requirements/recommendations for international students: Required—TOEFL (minimum score 550 paper-based; 90 iBT); Recommended—IELTS (minimum score 7). *Application deadline:* For fall admission, 2/15 priority date for domestic and international students; for spring admission, 11/1 priority date for domestic and international students. Applications are processed on a rolling basis. Application fee: $75. Electronic applications accepted. *Financial support:* In 2018–19, 146 students received support. Fellowships, research assistantships, teaching assistantships, career-related internships or fieldwork, scholarships/grants, tuition waivers, and unspecified assistantships available. Support available to part-time students. Financial award application deadline: 2/15. *Unit head:* Dr. Nasir Memon, Program Director, 646-997-3970, E-mail: memon@nyu.edu. *Application contact:* Elizabeth Ensweiler, Senior Director of Graduate Enrollment and Graduate Admissions, 646-997-3182, E-mail: elizabeth.ensweiler@nyu.edu.

New York University, Tandon School of Engineering, Department of Computer Science and Engineering, Major in Cybersecurity Risk and Strategy, New York, NY 10012-1019. Offers MS. Program offered jointly with School of Law. *Program availability:* Part-time, online learning. *Degree requirements:* For master's, comprehensive exam (for some programs), thesis (for some programs). *Entrance requirements:* Additional exam requirements/recommendations for international students: Required—TOEFL (minimum score 550 paper-based; 90 iBT); Recommended—IELTS (minimum score 7). *Application deadline:* For fall admission, 2/15 priority date for domestic and international students; for spring admission, 11/1 priority date for domestic and international students. Applications are processed on a rolling basis. Application fee: $75. Electronic applications accepted. *Financial support:* Fellowships, research assistantships, teaching assistantships, career-related internships or fieldwork, scholarships/grants, tuition waivers, and unspecified assistantships available. Support available to part-time students. Financial award application deadline: 2/15. *Unit head:* Dr. Nasir Memon, Head, 646-997-3970, E-mail: memon@nyu.edu. *Application contact:* Elizabeth Ensweiler, Senior Director of Graduate Enrollment and Graduate Admissions, 646-997-3182, E-mail: elizabeth.ensweiler@nyu.edu.

Niagara University, Graduate Division of Arts and Sciences, Program in Information Security and Digital Forensics, Niagara University, NY 14109. Offers MS. *Program availability:* Part-time. *Students:* 14 full-time (6 women), 10 part-time (3 women); includes 6 minority (2 Black or African American, non-Hispanic/Latino; 1 American Indian or Alaska Native, non-Hispanic/Latino; 2 Asian, non-Hispanic/Latino; 1 Hispanic/Latino), 4 international. Average age 30. In 2018, 7 master's awarded. *Entrance requirements:* For master's, GRE. Additional exam requirements/recommendations for international students: Required—TOEFL (minimum score 550 paper-based; 79 iBT), IELTS (minimum score 6). Tuition and fees vary according to program. *Financial support:* Research assistantships, teaching assistantships, career-related internships or fieldwork, Federal Work-Study, scholarships/grants, and unspecified assistantships available. Support available to part-time students. Financial award applicants required to submit FAFSA. *Unit head:* Dr. Peter Butera, Dean, 716-286-8060, Fax: 716-286-8061, E-mail: pbutera@niagara.edu. *Application contact:* Evan Pierce, Associate Dean for Graduate Recruitment, 716-286-8327, Fax: 716-286-8710.
Website: http://www.niagara.edu/isdf

Northcentral University, Graduate Studies, San Diego, CA 92106. Offers business (MBA, DBA, PhD, Postbaccalaureate Certificate); education (M Ed, Ed D, PhD, Ed S, Post-Master's Certificate, Postbaccalaureate Certificate); marriage and family therapy (MA, DMFT, PhD, Post-Master's Certificate, Postbaccalaureate Certificate); psychology (MA, PhD, Post-Master's Certificate, Postbaccalaureate Certificate); technology (MS, PhD), including computer science, cybersecurity (MS), data science, technology and innovation management (PhD). *Program availability:* Part-time, evening/weekend, online only, 100% online. *Faculty:* 98 full-time (63 women), 385 part-time/adjunct (203 women). *Students:* 5,036 full-time (3,291 women), 5,747 part-time (3,977 women); includes 3,777 minority (2,550 Black or African American, non-Hispanic/Latino; 76 American Indian or Alaska Native, non-Hispanic/Latino; 192 Asian, non-Hispanic/Latino; 603 Hispanic/Latino; 39 Native Hawaiian or other Pacific Islander, non-Hispanic/Latino; 317 Two or more races, non-Hispanic/Latino). Average age 45. In 2018, 929 master's, 782 doctorates, 278 other advanced degrees awarded. *Degree requirements:* For doctorate, comprehensive exam, thesis/dissertation. *Entrance requirements:* For master's, bachelor's degree from regionally- or nationally-accredited institution, current resume or curriculum vitae, statement of intent, interview, and background check (for marriage and family therapy); for doctorate, post-baccalaureate master's degree and/or doctoral degree from nationally- or regionally-accredited academic institution; for other advanced degree, bachelor's-level or higher degree from accredited institution or university (for Post-Baccalaureate Certificate); master's and/or doctoral degree from regionally- or nationally-accredited academic institution (for Post-Master's Certificate). Additional exam requirements/recommendations for international students: Required—TOEFL (minimum score 550 paper-based; 79 iBT), IELTS (minimum score 6.5), PTE (minimum score 53). *Application deadline:* Applications are processed on a rolling basis. Application fee: $0. Electronic applications accepted. *Expenses: Tuition:* Full-time $893. *Required fees:* $95. Tuition and fees vary according to degree level and program. *Financial support:* Scholarships/grants available. *Faculty research:* Business management, curriculum and instruction, educational leadership, health psychology, organizational behavior. *Unit head:* Dr. David Harpool, Acting Provost, 888-327-2877 Ext. 8181, E-mail: provost@ncu.edu. *Application contact:* Ken Boutelle, Vice President, Enrollment Services, 888-628-4979, E-mail: enrollmentservices@ncu.edu.

Northeastern University, College of Engineering, Boston, MA 02115-5096. Offers bioengineering (MS, PhD); chemical engineering (MS, PhD); civil engineering (MS, PhD); computer engineering (PhD); computer systems engineering (MS); electrical and computer engineering (MS); electrical and computer engineering leadership (MS); electrical engineering (PhD); energy systems (MS); engineering and public policy (MS); engineering management (MS, Certificate); environmental engineering (MS); industrial engineering (MS, PhD); information assurance (PhD); information systems (MS); interdisciplinary engineering (PhD); mechanical engineering (PhD); operations research (MS); telecommunication systems management (MS). *Program availability:* Part-time, online learning. Electronic applications accepted. *Expenses:* Contact institution.

Northern Kentucky University, Office of Graduate Programs, College of Informatics, Department of Business Informatics, Highland Heights, KY 41099. Offers business informatics (MS, Certificate); corporate information security (Certificate); enterprise resource planning (Certificate). *Program availability:* Part-time, evening/weekend. *Entrance requirements:* For master's, GRE or GMAT. Additional exam requirements/recommendations for international students: Required—TOEFL (minimum score 79 iBT); Recommended—IELTS (minimum score 6.5). Electronic applications accepted. *Faculty research:* Data analytics, cloud computing, healthcare informatics, information systems security.

Northwestern University, School of Professional Studies, Program in Information Systems, Evanston, IL 60208. Offers analytics and business intelligence (MS); database and Internet technologies (MS); information systems (MS); information systems management (MS); information systems security (MS); medical informatics (MS); software project management and development (MS). *Program availability:* Part-time, evening/weekend.

Norwich University, College of Graduate and Continuing Studies, Master of Science in Information Security and Assurance Program, Northfield, VT 05663. Offers information security and assurance (MS), including computer forensic investigation/incident response team management, critical infrastructure protection and cyber crime, cyber law and international perspectives on cyberspace, project management, vulnerability management. *Program availability:* Evening/weekend, online only, mostly all online with a week-long residency requirement. *Entrance requirements:* For master's, minimum undergraduate GPA of 2.75. Additional exam requirements/recommendations for international students: Required—TOEFL (minimum score 550 paper-based; 80 iBT), IELTS (minimum score 6.5). Electronic applications accepted. *Expenses:* Contact institution.

Nova Southeastern University, College of Engineering and Computing, Fort Lauderdale, FL 33314-7796. Offers computer science (MS, PhD); information assurance (PhD); information assurance and cybersecurity (MS); information systems (PhD); information technology (MS); management information systems (MS). *Program availability:* Part-time, evening/weekend, blended/hybrid learning. Terminal master's awarded for partial completion of doctoral program. *Degree requirements:* For master's, thesis optional; for doctorate, thesis/dissertation. *Entrance requirements:* For master's, minimum undergraduate GPA of 2.5; for doctorate, master's degree, minimum graduate GPA of 3.25. Additional exam requirements/recommendations for international students: Required—TOEFL (minimum score 80 iBT), IELTS (minimum score 6), PTE (minimum score 54). Electronic applications accepted. *Expenses:* Contact institution. *Faculty research:* Artificial intelligence, database management, human-computer interaction, business intelligence and data analytics, information assurance and cybersecurity.

Our Lady of the Lake University, School of Business and Leadership, Program in Information Systems and Security, San Antonio, TX 78207-4689. Offers MS. *Program availability:* Part-time, online only, 100% online. *Faculty:* 3 full-time (all women), 1 part-time/adjunct (0 women). *Students:* 28 full-time (11 women), 2 part-time (0 women); includes 16 minority (all Hispanic/Latino). Average age 36. 10 applicants, 100% accepted, 9 enrolled. In 2018, 13 master's awarded. *Entrance requirements:* For master's, GRE or GMAT, official transcripts showing baccalaureate degree from regionally-accredited institution in technical discipline and minimum GPA of 3.0 for cumulative undergraduate work or 3.2 in the major field (technical discipline) of study. Additional exam requirements/recommendations for international students: Required—TOEFL. *Application deadline:* For fall admission, 6/15 for domestic and international students; for spring admission, 11/15 for domestic and international students; for summer admission, 4/15 for domestic and international students. Applications are processed on a rolling basis. Application fee: $40 ($50 for international students). Electronic applications accepted. Application fee is waived when completed online. *Expenses: Tuition:* Full-time $16,326; part-time $907 per credit. *Financial support:* In 2018–19, 9 students received support. Federal Work-Study, scholarships/grants, unspecified assistantships, and tuition discounts available. Support available to part-time students. Financial award application deadline: 5/1; financial award applicants required to submit FAFSA. *Faculty research:* Computer information systems implementation and best practices, computer and network security, cyber security legal issues, information assurance, and information technology education. *Unit head:* Carol Jeffries-Horner, Chair, Computer Information Systems and Security Department, 210-528-6730, E-mail: cjeffries@ollusa.edu. *Application contact:* Office of Graduate Admissions, 210-431-3995, Fax: 210-431-3945, E-mail: gradadm@ollusa.edu.
Website: http://www.ollusa.edu/s/1190/hybrid/default-hybrid-ollu.aspx?sid-1190&gid-1&pgid-7901

Pace University, Seidenberg School of Computer Science and Information Systems, New York, NY 10038. Offers chief information security officer (APC); computer science (MS, PhD); enterprise analytics (MS); information and communication technology strategy and innovation (APC); information systems (MS, APC); information technology (MS); professional studies in computing (DPS); secure software and information engineering (APC); security and information assurance (Certificate); software development and engineering (MS, Certificate); telecommunications systems and networks (MS, Certificate). *Program availability:* Part-time, evening/weekend, online only, 100% online, blended/hybrid learning. *Faculty:* 26 full-time (7 women), 7 part-time/adjunct (2 women). *Students:* 515 full-time (172 women), 288 part-time (90 women); includes 183 minority (67 Black or African American, non-Hispanic/Latino; 3 American Indian or Alaska Native, non-Hispanic/Latino; 50 Asian, non-Hispanic/Latino; 52 Hispanic/Latino; 1 Native Hawaiian or other Pacific Islander, non-Hispanic/Latino; 10 Two or more races, non-Hispanic/Latino), 497 international. Average age 30. 817 applicants, 93% accepted, 235 enrolled. In 2018, 383 master's, 15 doctorates, 1 other advanced degree awarded. *Degree requirements:* For master's, thesis or alternative, capstone course; for doctorate, comprehensive exam (for some programs), thesis/dissertation. *Entrance requirements:* Additional exam requirements/recommendations for international students: Required—TOEFL (minimum score 78 iBT), IELTS (minimum score 6.5) or PTE (minimum score 52). *Application deadline:* For fall admission, 8/1 priority date for domestic students, 6/1 for international students; for spring admission, 12/1 for domestic students, 10/1 for international students. Applications are processed on a rolling basis. Application fee: $70. Electronic applications accepted. *Expenses:* Contact institution. *Financial support:* In 2018–19, 45 students received support. Research assistantships, career-related internships or fieldwork, scholarships/grants, and unspecified assistantships available. Support available to part-time students. Financial award application deadline: 2/15; financial award applicants required to submit FAFSA. *Faculty research:* Cyber security/digital forensics; mobile app development; big data/enterprise analytics; artificial intelligence; software development. *Total annual research expenditures:* $584,594. *Unit head:* Dr. Jonathan Hill, Dean, Seidenberg School of Computer Science and Information Systems, 212-346-1864, E-mail: jhill@pace.edu. *Application contact:* Susan Ford-Goldschein, Director of Graduate Admissions, 914-422-4283, Fax: 212-346-1585, E-mail: graduateadmission@pace.edu.
Website: http://www.pace.edu/seidenberg

Penn State Great Valley, Graduate Studies, Management Division, Malvern, PA 19355-1488. Offers business administration (MBA); cyber security (Certificate); data analytics (MPS, MS, Certificate); distributed energy and grid modernization (Certificate); finance (M Fin); health sector management (Certificate); human resource management (Certificate); information science (MSIS); leadership development (MLD); new ventures and entrepreneurship (Certificate); sustainable management practices (Certificate). *Accreditation:* AACSB.

Portland State University, Graduate Studies, Maseeh College of Engineering and Computer Science, Department of Computer Science, Portland, OR 97207-0751. Offers computer science (MS, PhD); computer security (Certificate). *Program availability:* Part-time. *Degree requirements:* For master's, thesis or alternative; for doctorate, comprehensive exam, thesis/dissertation. *Entrance requirements:* For master's, GRE (minimum scores 60th percentile in Quantitative and 25th percentile in Verbal), BS in engineering field, science or closely-related area; minimum GPA of 3.0 or equivalent; 2 letters of recommendation; personal statement; for doctorate, GRE (minimum scores 60th percentile in Quantitative and 25th percentile in Verbal), MS in computer science or allied field. Additional exam requirements/recommendations for international students: Required—TOEFL (minimum score 550 paper-based). *Expenses:* Contact institution. *Faculty research:* Formal methods, database systems, parallel programming environments, computer security, software tools.

Purdue University, Graduate School, Interdisciplinary Program in Information Security, West Lafayette, IN 47907. Offers MS. *Students:* 3 part-time (1 woman), all international. Average age 30. 9 applicants, 22% accepted, 2 enrolled. *Entrance requirements:* For master's, GRE, minimum undergraduate GPA of 3.0 or equivalent. Additional exam requirements/recommendations for international students: Required—TOEFL (minimum score 550 paper-based; 100 iBT); Recommended—TWE. *Application deadline:* For fall admission, 4/1 priority date for domestic and international students; for spring admission, 10/1 priority date for domestic and international students. Applications are processed on a rolling basis. Application fee: $60 ($75 for international students). Electronic applications accepted. *Unit head:* Dr. Eugene Spafford, Head of the Graduate Program, 765-454-7805, E-mail: advising@cerias.purdue.edu. *Application contact:* Dr. Eugene Spafford, Head of the Graduate Program, 765-454-7805, E-mail: advising@cerias.purdue.edu.
Website: http://www.cerias.purdue.edu/site/education/graduate_program/

Purdue University Global, School of Information Technology, Davenport, IA 52807. Offers decision support systems (MS); information security and assurance (MS). *Program availability:* Part-time, evening/weekend, online learning. *Entrance requirements:* Additional exam requirements/recommendations for international students: Required—TOEFL (minimum score 550 paper-based; 80 iBT).

Quinnipiac University, School of Engineering, Hamden, CT 06518-1940. Offers cybersecurity (MS).

Regent University, Graduate School, Robertson School of Government, Virginia Beach, VA 23464-9800. Offers government (MA), including American government, healthcare policy and ethics (MA, MPA), international relations, law and public policy, national security studies, political communication, political theory, religion and politics; national security studies (MA), including cybersecurity, homeland security, international security, Middle East politics; public administration (MPA), including emergency management and homeland security, federal government, general public administration, healthcare policy and ethics (MA, MPA), law, nonprofit administration and faith-based organizations, public leadership and management, servant leadership. *Program availability:* Part-time, evening/weekend, 100% online, blended/hybrid learning. *Degree requirements:* For master's, thesis optional, internship. *Entrance requirements:* For master's, GRE General Test or LSAT, personal essay, writing sample, resume, college transcripts. Additional exam requirements/recommendations for international students: Required—TOEFL (minimum score 577 paper-based). Electronic applications accepted. *Expenses:* Contact institution. *Faculty research:* International relations and politics, public administration, leadership and ethics, Biblical law, Constitutional law and Supreme Court.

Regis University, College of Computer and Information Sciences, Denver, CO 80221-1099. Offers agile technologies (Certificate); cybersecurity (Certificate); data science (M Sc); database administration with Oracle (Certificate); database development (Certificate); database technologies (M Sc); enterprise Java software development (Certificate); enterprise resource planning (Certificate); executive information technology (Certificate); health care informatics (Certificate); health care informatics and information management (M Sc); information assurance (M Sc); information assurance policy management (Certificate); information technology management (M Sc); mobile software development (Certificate); software engineering (M Sc, Certificate); software engineering and database technology (M Sc); storage area networks (Certificate); systems engineering (M Sc, Certificate). *Program availability:* Part-time, evening/weekend, 100% online, blended/hybrid learning. *Degree requirements:* For master's, thesis (for some programs), final research project. *Entrance requirements:* For master's, official transcript reflecting baccalaureate degree awarded from regionally-accredited college or university, 2 years of related experience, resume, interview. Additional exam requirements/recommendations for international students: Required—TOEFL (minimum score 550 paper-based; 82 iBT). Electronic applications accepted. *Expenses:* Contact institution. *Faculty research:* Information policy, knowledge management, software architectures, data science.

Robert Morris University, School of Informatics, Humanities and Social Sciences, Moon Township, PA 15108-1189. Offers communication and information systems (MS); cyber security (MS); data analytics (MS); information security and assurance (MS); information systems and communications (D Sc); information systems management (MS); information technology project management (MS); Internet information systems (MS); organizational leadership (MS). *Program availability:* Part-time-only, evening/weekend, 100% online. *Faculty:* 22 full-time (7 women), 10 part-time/adjunct (0 women). *Students:* 262 part-time (94 women); includes 57 minority (31 Black or African American, non-Hispanic/Latino; 13 Asian, non-Hispanic/Latino; 8 Hispanic/Latino; 5 Two or more races, non-Hispanic/Latino), 43 international. Average age 35. 150 applicants, 92% accepted, 79 enrolled. In 2018, 133 master's, 11 doctorates awarded. *Degree requirements:* For master's, Completion of 30 credits; for doctorate, thesis/dissertation, Completion of 63 credits. *Entrance requirements:* For doctorate, employer letter of endorsement, interview. Additional exam requirements/recommendations for international students: Required—TOEFL (minimum score 550 paper-based; 79 iBT). *Application deadline:* For fall admission, 7/1 priority date for domestic and international students; for spring admission, 11/1 priority date for domestic and international students. Applications are processed on a rolling basis. Application fee: $35. Electronic applications accepted. Application fee is waived when completed online. *Expenses:* Master's $920/credit plus $80/credit fees; D.Sc. $28,290/year. *Financial support:* Institutionally sponsored loans available. Support available to part-time students. Financial award application deadline: 5/1; financial award applicants required to submit FAFSA. *Unit head:* Jon A. Radermacher, Interim Dean, School of Informatics, Humanities and Social Sciences, 412-397-4088, E-mail: radermacher@rmu.edu. *Application contact:* Jon A. Radermacher, Interim Dean, School of Informatics, Humanities and Social Sciences, 412-397-4088, E-mail: radermacher@rmu.edu.
Website: https://www.rmu.edu/academics/schools/sihss

Robert Morris University Illinois, Morris Graduate School of Management, Chicago, IL 60605. Offers accounting (MBA); accounting/finance (MBA); business analytics (MIS); health care administration (MM); higher education administration (MM); human performance (MS); human resource management (MBA); information security (MIS); information systems management (MIS); law enforcement administration (MM); management (MBA); management/finance (MBA); management/human resource management (MBA); sports administration (MM). *Program availability:* Part-time, evening/weekend. *Entrance requirements:* For master's, official transcripts and letters of recommendation (for some programs); written personal statement. Additional exam requirements/recommendations for international students: Required—TOEFL (minimum score 550 paper-based). Electronic applications accepted.

Rochester Institute of Technology, Graduate Enrollment Services, Golisano College of Computing and Information Sciences, Computing Security Department, Advanced Certificate Program in Cybersecurity, Rochester, NY 14623-5603. Offers Advanced Certificate. *Program availability:* Part-time, 100% online. *Students:* 4 part-time (1 woman). Average age 41. 17 applicants, 47% accepted, 4 enrolled. In 2018, 2 Advanced Certificates awarded. *Entrance requirements:* For degree, GRE required for international students only. However, for students from US universities with a GPA that is lower than required, GRE scores can strengthen their application., minimum GPA of 3.0 (recommended), Have knowledge of computing networking and system administration, and introductory knowledge of computing security. Additional exam requirements/recommendations for international students: Required—TOEFL (minimum score 570 paper-based; 88 iBT), IELTS (minimum score 6.5), PTE (minimum score 61). *Application deadline:* Applications are processed on a rolling basis. Application fee: $65. Electronic applications accepted. *Financial support:* Available to part-time students. Applicants required to submit FAFSA. *Faculty research:* Enterprise level network security and computer system security, forensics. *Unit head:* Sumita Mishra, Graduate Program Director, 585-475-4475, Fax: 585-475-6584, E-mail: sumita.mishra@rit.edu.

Computer and Information Systems Security

Application contact: Diane Ellison, Senior Associate Vice President, Graduate Enrollment Services, 585-475-2229, Fax: 585-475-7164, E-mail: gradinfo@rit.edu.
Website: https://www.rit.edu/study/cybersecurity-adv-cert

Rochester Institute of Technology, Graduate Enrollment Services, Golisano College of Computing and Information Sciences, Computing Security Department, MS Program in Computing Security, Rochester, NY 14623-5603. Offers MS. *Program availability:* Part-time, 100% online. *Students:* 40 full-time (12 women), 12 part-time (2 women); includes 5 minority (4 Asian, non-Hispanic/Latino; 1 Hispanic/Latino), 29 international. Average age 28. 115 applicants, 53% accepted, 17 enrolled. In 2018, 18 master's awarded. *Degree requirements:* For master's, thesis or alternative, Thesis, Project, and Capstone options. *Entrance requirements:* For master's, GRE required for individuals with degrees from international universities., minimum GPA of 3.0 (recommended), Hold a relevant baccalaureate degree, two letters of recommendation. Additional exam requirements/recommendations for international students: Required—TOEFL (minimum score 570 paper-based; 88 iBT), IELTS (minimum score 6.5), PTE (minimum score 61). *Application deadline:* For fall admission, 2/15 priority date for domestic and international students; for spring admission, 12/15 priority date for domestic and international students. Applications are processed on a rolling basis. Application fee: $65. Electronic applications accepted. *Financial support:* In 2018–19, 45 students received support. Research assistantships with partial tuition reimbursements available, teaching assistantships with partial tuition reimbursements available, career-related internships or fieldwork, scholarships/grants, and unspecified assistantships available. Support available to part-time students. Financial award applicants required to submit FAFSA. *Faculty research:* Game-based learning for digital forensics, anonymity and privacy, usable security, security of Internet of things, risk management in information security. *Unit head:* Sumita Mishra, Graduate Program Director, 585-475-4475, Fax: 585-475-6584, E-mail: sumita.mishra@rit.edu. *Application contact:* Diane Ellison, Senior Associate Vice President, Graduate Enrollment Services, 585-475-2229, Fax: 585-475-7164, E-mail: gradinfo@rit.edu.
Website: https://www.rit.edu/study/computing-security-ms

Roger Williams University, School of Justice Studies, Bristol, RI 02809. Offers criminal justice (MS); cybersecurity (MS); leadership (MS), including health care administration (MPA, MS), public management (MPA, MS); public administration (MPA), including health care administration (MPA, MS), public management (MPA, MS); MS/JD. *Program availability:* Part-time, evening/weekend, 100% online, blended/hybrid learning. *Faculty:* 10 full-time (5 women), 3 part-time/adjunct (all women). *Students:* 13 full-time (8 women), 109 part-time (51 women); includes 30 minority (10 Black or African American, non-Hispanic/Latino; 1 Asian, non-Hispanic/Latino; 18 Hispanic/Latino; 1 Two or more races, non-Hispanic/Latino), 2 international. Average age 35. 90 applicants, 71% accepted, 35 enrolled. In 2018, 39 master's awarded. *Degree requirements:* For master's, thesis (for some programs). *Entrance requirements:* For master's, 2 letters of recommendation, college transcript, and resume (for MS in leadership and MPA programs); criminal background check (for MS in cybersecurity). Additional exam requirements/recommendations for international students: Required—TOEFL (minimum score 85 iBT), IELTS (minimum score 6.5). *Application deadline:* For fall admission, 8/1 for domestic students; for spring admission, 1/1 for domestic students. Applications are processed on a rolling basis. Application fee: $50. Electronic applications accepted. Application fee is waived when completed online. *Expenses:* $593 per credit hour for academic year 2018-2019 (for MS in leadership, MPA, individual certificates in Leadership, Public Management, Health Care Administration); $907 per credit hour for academic year 2018-2019 (for MS in criminal justice, MS in cybersecurity, individual certificates in Digital Forensics, Cyber Security, Cyberspecialist); $267 graduate fee for all programs for academic year 2018-2019. *Financial support:* In 2018–19, 2 students received support. Scholarships/grants and unspecified assistantships available. Financial award application deadline: 3/15; financial award applicants required to submit FAFSA. *Faculty research:* Opioid addiction and treatment, community policing. *Unit head:* Dr. Eric Bronson, Dean, 401-254-3336, E-mail: ebronson@rwu.edu. *Application contact:* Marcus Hanscom, Director of Graduate Admission, 401-254-3345, Fax: 401-254-3557, E-mail: gradadmit@rwu.edu.
Website: http://www.rwu.edu/academics/departments/criminaljustice.htm#graduate

Rowan University, Graduate School, College of Science and Mathematics, Networks Certificate of Graduate Study Program, Glassboro, NJ 08028-1701. Offers CGS. Electronic applications accepted.

Sacred Heart University, Graduate Programs, College of Arts and Sciences, Department of Computing, Fairfield, CT 06825. Offers computer science (MS); computer science gaming (MS); cybersecurity (MS); information technology (MS). *Program availability:* Part-time, evening/weekend. *Degree requirements:* For master's, thesis or alternative. *Entrance requirements:* For master's, bachelor's degree, minimum GPA of 3.0. Additional exam requirements/recommendations for international students: Required—TOEFL (minimum score 570 paper-based, 80 iBT), TWE, or IELTS (6.5). Electronic applications accepted. *Expenses:* Contact institution.

Saginaw Valley State University, College of Science, Engineering, and Technology, University Center, MI 48710. Offers computer science and information systems (MS); energy and materials (MS). *Program availability:* Part-time, evening/weekend. *Faculty:* 5 full-time (0 women), 1 part-time/adjunct (0 women). *Students:* 10 full-time (1 woman), 12 part-time (3 women); includes 1 minority (Asian, non-Hispanic/Latino), 8 international. Average age 32. 35 applicants, 80% accepted, 8 enrolled. *Degree requirements:* For master's, field project or thesis work. *Entrance requirements:* For master's, minimum GPA of 3.0. Additional exam requirements/recommendations for international students: Required—TOEFL (minimum score 550 paper-based; 79 iBT). *Application deadline:* For fall admission, 7/15 for international students; for winter admission, 11/15 for international students; for spring admission, 4/15 for international students. Applications are processed on a rolling basis. Application fee: $30 ($90 for international students). Electronic applications accepted. *Expenses: Tuition, area resident:* Full-time $6225; part-time $623 per credit hour. Tuition, state resident: full-time $6225; part-time $623 per credit hour. Tuition, nonresident: full-time $14,215; part-time $1185 per credit hour. *International tuition:* $14,215 full-time. *Required fees:* $263; $14.60 per credit hour. Tuition and fees vary according to degree level. *Financial support:* Federal Work-Study and scholarships/grants available. Support available to part-time students. Financial award application deadline: 4/1; financial award applicants required to submit FAFSA. *Unit head:* Dr. Robert Tuttle, Program Coordinator, 989-964-4144, Fax: 989-964-2717. *Application contact:* Jenna Briggs, Director, Graduate and International Admissions, 989-964-6096, Fax: 989-964-2788, E-mail: gradadm@svsu.edu.
Website: http://www.svsu.edu/collegeofscienceengineeringtechnology/

St. Cloud State University, School of Graduate Studies, College of Science and Engineering, Program in Information Assurance, St. Cloud, MN 56301-4498. Offers MS. *Program availability:* Part-time. *Degree requirements:* For master's, 30 to 33 credits of coursework. *Entrance requirements:* For master's, minimum overall GPA of 2.75 in previous undergraduate and graduate records or in last half of undergraduate work. Electronic applications accepted.

St. Cloud State University, School of Graduate Studies, Herberger Business School, St. Cloud, MN 56301-4498. Offers business administration (MBA); information assurance (MS). *Accreditation:* AACSB. *Program availability:* Part-time, evening/weekend. *Degree requirements:* For master's, thesis or alternative. *Entrance requirements:* For master's, GMAT, minimum GPA of 2.75. Additional exam requirements/recommendations for international students: Required—Michigan English Language Assessment Battery; Recommended—TOEFL (minimum score 550 paper-based), IELTS (minimum score 6.5). Electronic applications accepted. *Expenses:* Contact institution.

Saint Leo University, Graduate Studies in Business, Saint Leo, FL 33574-6665. Offers accounting (M Acc); cybersecurity management (MBA); health care management (MBA); human resource management (MBA); marketing (MBA); marketing research and social media analytics (MBA); software engineering (MS). *Accreditation:* ACBSP. *Program availability:* Part-time, evening/weekend, 100% online, blended/hybrid learning. *Faculty:* 51 full-time (16 women), 54 part-time/adjunct (22 women). *Students:* 8 full-time (3 women), 2,209 part-time (1,288 women); includes 1,046 minority (691 Black or African American, non-Hispanic/Latino; 10 American Indian or Alaska Native, non-Hispanic/Latino; 47 Asian, non-Hispanic/Latino; 249 Hispanic/Latino; 5 Native Hawaiian or other Pacific Islander, non-Hispanic/Latino; 44 Two or more races, non-Hispanic/Latino), 71 international. Average age 37. 760 applicants, 83% accepted, 498 enrolled. In 2018, 763 master's, 14 doctorates awarded. *Degree requirements:* For doctorate, comprehensive exam, thesis/dissertation. *Entrance requirements:* For master's, GMAT with minimum score 500 (for M Acc), official transcripts, current resume, 2 professional recommendations, personal statement, bachelor's degree from regionally-accredited university; undergraduate degree in accounting and minimum undergraduate GPA of 3.0 (for M Acc); minimum undergraduate GPA of 3.0 in final 2 years of undergraduate study and 2 years' work experience (for MBA); for doctorate, GMAT (minimum score of 550) if master's GPA is under 3.25, official transcripts, current resume, 2 professional recommendations, personal statement, master's degree from regionally-accredited university with minimum GPA of 3.25, 3 years' work experience, interview. Additional exam requirements/recommendations for international students: Required—TOEFL (minimum score 550 paper-based; 78 iBT). *Application deadline:* For fall admission, 7/1 priority date for domestic and international students; for spring admission, 11/12 priority date for domestic students, 11/1 for international students. Applications are processed on a rolling basis. Application fee: $80. Electronic applications accepted. *Expenses:* Onground Master of Accounting $555 per credit, Online Master of Accounting $720 per credit, Onground MBA $555 per credit, Onground MBA Intl/Experiential $720 per credit, Online MBA/Cybersecurity military rate $555 per credit, Online MBA civilian rate $720, MS Cybersecurity civilian rate $770, DBA $900 per credit. *Financial support:* In 2018–19, 213 students received support. Scholarships/grants, unspecified assistantships, and tuition remission for Saint Leo employees and their dependents available. Financial award application deadline: 3/1; financial award applicants required to submit FAFSA. *Faculty research:* Servant leadership, work/life balance, emotional intelligence, pricing, marketing. *Unit head:* Dr. Robyn Parker, Dean, School of Business, 352-588-8599, Fax: 352-588-8912, E-mail: mbaslu@saintleo.edu. *Application contact:* Mark Russum, Assistant Vice President, Enrollment, 800-707-8846, Fax: 352-588-7873, E-mail: grad.admissions@saintleo.edu.
Website: https://www.saintleo.edu/college-of-business

St. Mary's University, School of Science, Engineering and Technology, Program in Cybersecurity, San Antonio, TX 78228. Offers MS, Certificate. *Program availability:* Part-time, evening/weekend. *Students:* 6 full-time (0 women), 7 part-time (3 women); includes 9 minority (2 Black or African American, non-Hispanic/Latino; 7 Hispanic/Latino), 4 international. Average age 34. 16 applicants, 63% accepted, 2 enrolled. In 2018, 4 master's, 1 other advanced degree awarded. *Degree requirements:* For master's, project or thesis. *Entrance requirements:* For master's, GRE (minimum quantitative score 152), minimum GPA of 3.0, written statement of purpose indicating applicant's interests and objectives, two letters of recommendation concerning applicant's potential for succeeding in graduate program, official transcripts of all college-level work. Additional exam requirements/recommendations for international students: Required—TOEFL (minimum score 550 paper-based; 80 iBT), IELTS (minimum score 6). *Application deadline:* For fall admission, 7/1 for domestic students; for spring admission, 11/15 for domestic students; for summer admission, 4/1 for domestic students. Applications are processed on a rolling basis. Application fee: $0. Electronic applications accepted. *Expenses: Tuition:* Full-time $16,830; part-time $935 per credit hour. *Required fees:* $1055. Tuition and fees vary according to program. *Financial support:* Application deadline: 3/31; applicants required to submit FAFSA. *Faculty research:* Information and network security, replicating data over cloud servers, cryptographic protocols, data integrity in cloud computing systems, knowledge discovery and data mining. *Unit head:* Dr. Ayad Barsoum, Graduate Program Director, 210-436-3315, E-mail: abarsoum@stmarytx.edu. *Application contact:* Dr. Ayad Barsoum, Graduate Program Director, 210-436-3315, E-mail: abarsoum@stmarytx.edu.
Website: https://www.stmarytx.edu/academics/programs/master-cybersecurity/

Saint Mary's University of Minnesota, Schools of Graduate and Professional Programs, Graduate School of Business and Technology, Cybersecurity Program, Winona, MN 55987-1399. Offers MS. *Unit head:* Don Heier, Director, 507-457-1575, E-mail: dheier@smumn.edu. *Application contact:* Laurie Roy, Director of Admissions of Schools of Graduate and Professional Programs, 507-457-8606, Fax: 612-728-5121, E-mail: lroy@smumn.edu.
Website: https://onlineprograms.smumn.edu/mscs/masters-cybersecurity?_ga=2.250083014.1736907137.1523547391-1359115499.1515170921

Salem International University, School of Business, Salem, WV 26426-0500. Offers information security (MBA); international business (MBA). *Program availability:* Part-time, online learning. *Entrance requirements:* For master's, minimum undergraduate GPA of 2.5, course work in business, resume. Additional exam requirements/recommendations for international students: Recommended—TOEFL (minimum score 550 paper-based), IELTS (minimum score 6.5). Electronic applications accepted. *Expenses:* Contact institution. *Faculty research:* Organizational behavior strategy, marketing services.

Salve Regina University, Program in Administration of Justice and Homeland Security, Newport, RI 02840-4192. Offers administration of justice and homeland security (MS); cybersecurity and intelligence (CGS); digital forensics (CGS); leadership in justice (CGS). *Program availability:* Part-time, evening/weekend, online learning. *Entrance requirements:* For master's, GMAT, GRE General Test, or MAT. Additional exam requirements/recommendations for international students: Required—TOEFL (minimum score 600 paper-based; 100 iBT). Electronic applications accepted. *Expenses: Tuition:* Full-time $10,530; part-time $585 per credit. *Required fees:* $60 per term. Tuition and fees vary according to course level, course load, degree level and program.

Salve Regina University, Program in Business Administration, Newport, RI 02840-4192. Offers cybersecurity issues in business (MBA); entrepreneurial enterprise (MBA); health care administration and management (MBA); nonprofit management (MBA); social ventures (MBA). *Program availability:* Part-time, evening/weekend, online learning. *Entrance requirements:* For master's, GMAT, GRE General Test, or MAT, 6 undergraduate credits each in accounting, economics, quantitative analysis and calculus or statistics. Additional exam requirements/recommendations for international students: Required—TOEFL (minimum score 600 paper-based; 100 iBT) or IELTS. Electronic applications accepted. *Expenses: Tuition:* Full-time $10,530; part-time $585 per credit. *Required fees:* $60 per term. Tuition and fees vary according to course level, course load, degree level and program.

Sam Houston State University, College of Sciences, Department of Computer Science, Huntsville, TX 77341. Offers computing and information science (MS); digital forensics (MS); information assurance and security (MS). *Program availability:* Part-time. *Degree requirements:* For master's, comprehensive exam, thesis optional, internship; for doctorate, comprehensive exam, thesis/dissertation. *Entrance requirements:* For master's, GRE General Test, letters of recommendation. Additional exam requirements/recommendations for international students: Required—TOEFL (minimum score 550 paper-based; 79 iBT), IELTS (minimum score 6.5). Electronic applications accepted.

The SANS Technology Institute, Programs in Information Security, Bethesda, MD 20814. Offers information security engineering (MS); information security management (MS).

Seattle Pacific University, Master of Arts in Management Program, Seattle, WA 98119-1997. Offers business intelligence and data analytics (MA); cybersecurity (MA); faith and business (MA); human resources (MA); social and sustainable management (MA). *Students:* 12 part-time (9 women); includes 3 minority (2 Black or African American, non-Hispanic/Latino; 1 Asian, non-Hispanic/Latino), 4 international. Average age 31. 11 applicants, 45% accepted, 2 enrolled. *Entrance requirements:* For master's, GMAT scores above 500 (25 verbal; 30 quantitative; 4.4 analytical writing) are preferred. https://spu.edu/academics/school-of-business-and-economics/graduate-programs/mba#application, bachelor's degree from accredited college or university, resume, essay, official transcript. *Application deadline:* For fall admission, 8/1 for domestic students, 6/1 for international students; for winter admission, 11/1 for domestic students, 9/1 for international students; for spring admission, 2/1 for domestic students, 12/1 for international students; for summer admission, 5/1 for domestic students. Application fee: $50. Website: http://spu.edu/academics/school-of-business-and-economics/graduate-programs/ma-management

Southern Arkansas University–Magnolia, School of Graduate Studies, Magnolia, AR 71753. Offers agriculture (MS); business administration (MBA), including agribusiness, social entrepreneurship, supply chain management; clinical and mental health counseling (MS); computer and information sciences (MS), including cyber security and privacy, data science, information technology; gifted and talented (M Ed), including curriculum and instruction, educational administration and supervision, gifted and talented P-8/7-12, instructional specialist P-4; higher, adult and lifelong education (M Ed); kinesiology (M Ed), including coaching; library media and information specialist (M Ed); public administration (MPA); school counseling K-12 (M Ed); student affairs and college counseling (M Ed); teaching (MAT). *Accreditation:* NCATE. *Program availability:* Part-time, 100% online, blended/hybrid learning. *Faculty:* 36 full-time (21 women), 32 part-time/adjunct (15 women). *Students:* 164 full-time (77 women), 762 part-time (510 women); includes 192 minority (163 Black or African American, non-Hispanic/Latino; 7 American Indian or Alaska Native, non-Hispanic/Latino; 13 Asian, non-Hispanic/Latino; 1 Hispanic/Latino; 8 Two or more races, non-Hispanic/Latino), 213 international. Average age 28. 363 applicants, 100% accepted, 237 enrolled. In 2018, 716 master's awarded. *Degree requirements:* For master's, comprehensive exam (for some programs), thesis optional. *Entrance requirements:* For master's, GRE, MAT or GMAT, minimum GPA of 2.5. Additional exam requirements/recommendations for international students: Required—TOEFL (minimum score 550 paper-based), IELTS (minimum score 6). *Application deadline:* For fall admission, 8/1 for domestic and international students; for spring admission, 12/1 for domestic students, 11/15 for international students; for summer admission, 4/1 for domestic students, 5/10 for international students. Applications are processed on a rolling basis. Application fee: $25 ($90 for international students). Electronic applications accepted. *Expenses: Tuition, area resident:* Full-time $5130; part-time $3420 per year. Tuition, state resident: full-time $5130; part-time $3420 per year. Tuition, nonresident: full-time $7866; part-time $5244 per year. *International tuition:* $7866 full-time. *Required fees:* $1052; $710 per unit. Tuition and fees vary according to course load. *Financial support:* Career-related internships or fieldwork, Federal Work-Study, scholarships/grants, tuition waivers (full), and unspecified assistantships available. Financial award applicants required to submit FAFSA. *Faculty research:* Alternative certification for teachers, supervision of instruction, instructional leadership, counseling. *Unit head:* Dr. Kim Bloss, Dean, School of Graduate Studies, 870-235-4150, Fax: 870-235-5227, E-mail: kkbloss@saumag.edu. *Application contact:* Talia Jett, Admissions Coordinator, 870-2355450, Fax: 870-235-5227, E-mail: taliajett@saumag.edu. Website: http://www.saumag.edu/graduate

Southern New Hampshire University, School of Arts and Sciences, Manchester, NH 03106-1045. Offers clinical mental health counseling (MS); creative writing (MA); criminal justice (MS); cyber security (MS); English (MA); fiction and nonfiction (MFA); history (MA); political science (MS); psychology (MS). *Program availability:* Part-time, evening/weekend. *Degree requirements:* For master's, one foreign language, thesis. *Entrance requirements:* For master's, minimum GPA of 3.0 (for MFA). Additional exam requirements/recommendations for international students: Required—TOEFL (minimum score 550 paper-based; 79 iBT), IELTS (minimum score 6.5), TWE (minimum score 5). Electronic applications accepted. *Expenses:* Contact institution. *Faculty research:* Action research, state of the art practice in behavioral health services, wraparound approaches to working with youth, learning styles.

Southern Utah University, Program in Cyber Security and Information Assurance, Cedar City, UT 84720-2498. Offers cyber and web security (MS). *Program availability:* Part-time, online only, 100% online. *Faculty:* 2 full-time (1 woman), 3 part-time/adjunct (0 women). *Students:* 5 full-time (1 woman), 26 part-time (3 women); includes 6 minority (1 Black or African American, non-Hispanic/Latino; 1 Asian, non-Hispanic/Latino; 3 Hispanic/Latino; 1 Native Hawaiian or other Pacific Islander, non-Hispanic/Latino). Average age 36. 13 applicants, 54% accepted, 5 enrolled. In 2018, 5 master's awarded. *Degree requirements:* For master's, thesis, if students choose not to work on a capstone project/thesis for their CSIA graduate degree, they can take any two (2) additional courses (6 credits) from either emphasis (Cyber and Web Security or GRC and IS Controls). *Entrance requirements:* For master's, GRE (minimum score of 300), qualifying entrance exam. Additional exam requirements/recommendations for international students: Required—TOEFL (minimum score 550 paper-based; 80 iBT), IELTS (minimum score 6). Application fee: $60 ($65 for international students). Electronic applications accepted. *Expenses:* Contact institution. *Unit head:* Dr. Nathan Barker, Department Chair/Interim Graduate Program Director, 435-586-5414, Fax: 435-865-8444, E-mail: barkern@suu.edu. *Application contact:* Mary Gillins, Administrative Assistant, 435-586-5405, Fax: 435-865-8444, E-mail: marygillins@suu.edu. Website: https://www.suu.edu/cose/csis/masters/

State University of New York Polytechnic Institute, Program in Network and Computer Security, Utica, NY 13502. Offers MS. *Program availability:* Part-time. *Faculty:* 3 full-time (0 women), 3 part-time/adjunct (0 women). *Students:* 15 full-time (1 woman), 13 part-time (3 women); includes 2 minority (1 Asian, non-Hispanic/Latino; 1 Hispanic/Latino), 11 international. Average age 30. 42 applicants, 52% accepted, 14 enrolled. In 2018, 12 master's awarded. *Degree requirements:* For master's, thesis or project. *Entrance requirements:* For master's, GRE or approved GRE waiver, undergraduate prereq in math and computer science. Additional exam requirements/

recommendations for international students: Required—TOEFL (minimum score 79 iBT), IELTS (minimum score 6.5), PTE (minimum score 53), TOEFL, IELTS, or PTE; GRE. *Application deadline:* For fall admission, 7/1 for domestic and international students; for spring admission, 12/1 for domestic students, 11/1 for international students. Applications are processed on a rolling basis. Application fee: $60. Electronic applications accepted. *Expenses: Tuition, area resident:* Full-time $8316; part-time $462 per credit hour. Tuition, nonresident: full-time $16,992; part-time $944 per credit hour. *International tuition:* $16,992 full-time. *Required fees:* $1023; $56.87 per credit hour. Tuition and fees vary according to course load, campus/location and program. *Financial support:* Research assistantships and unspecified assistantships available. Financial award applicants required to submit FAFSA. *Faculty research:* Internet of things (iot) security, network perimeter security, penetration testing, big data and cloud security, intrusion detection and prevention systems, cybersecurity education. *Unit head:* Dr. John Marsh, Chair, NCS Department, 315-792-7125, E-mail: john.marsh@sunypoly.edu. *Application contact:* Alicia Foster, Director of Graduate Admissions, 315-792-7347, E-mail: alicia.foster@sunyit.edu. Website: https://sunypoly.edu/academics/majors-and-programs/ms-network-computer-security.html

Stephen F. Austin State University, Graduate School, College of Sciences and Mathematics, Department of Computer Science, Nacogdoches, TX 75962. Offers cyber security (MS). *Program availability:* Part-time. *Degree requirements:* For master's, comprehensive exam, thesis optional. *Entrance requirements:* For master's, GRE General Test. Additional exam requirements/recommendations for international students: Required—TOEFL.

Stevenson University, Program in Cyber Forensics, Owings Mills, MD 21153. Offers MS. *Program availability:* Part-time, 100% online. *Faculty:* 6 part-time/adjunct (1 woman). *Students:* 16 part-time (5 women); includes 6 minority (4 Black or African American, non-Hispanic/Latino; 1 American Indian or Alaska Native, non-Hispanic/Latino; 1 Asian, non-Hispanic/Latino). Average age 32. 12 applicants, 92% accepted, 7 enrolled. In 2018, 9 master's awarded. *Degree requirements:* For master's, capstone. *Entrance requirements:* For master's, bachelor's degree in a related field and two years of related work experience or a bachelor's degree in an unrelated field with five years of experience in information technology, telecommunication systems, system administration, network management, or information assurance. Additional exam requirements/recommendations for international students: Required—TOEFL, IELTS. *Application deadline:* Applications are processed on a rolling basis. Electronic applications accepted. *Expenses:* Contact institution. *Financial support:* Unspecified assistantships available. Financial award applicants required to submit FAFSA. *Unit head:* Carolyn Johnson, Program Coordinator, E-mail: CHJOHNSON@stevenson.edu. *Application contact:* Amanda Millar, Director, Admissions, 443-334-3334, Fax: 443-394-0538, E-mail: amillar@stevenson.edu. Website: http://www.stevenson.edu

Stratford University, School of Graduate Studies, Falls Church, VA 22043. Offers accounting (MS); business administration (MBA, DBA); cyber security (MS); cyber security leadership and policy (MS); digital forensics (MS); healthcare administration (MS); information systems (MS); information technology (DIT); networking and telecommunications (MS); software engineering (MS). *Program availability:* Part-time, evening/weekend, 100% online, blended/hybrid learning. *Degree requirements:* For master's, comprehensive exam, capstone project. *Entrance requirements:* For master's, GRE or GMAT, baccalaureate degree. Additional exam requirements/recommendations for international students: Required—TOEFL (minimum score 79 iBT), IELTS (minimum score 6.5), PTE (minimum score 5). Electronic applications accepted. *Expenses: Tuition:* Full-time $22,275; part-time $11,137 per year. One-time fee: $385.

Strayer University, Graduate Studies, Washington, DC 20005-2603. Offers accounting (MS); acquisition (MBA); business administration (MBA); communications technology (MS); educational management (M Ed); finance (MBA); health services administration (MHSA); hospitality and tourism management (MBA); human resource management (MBA); information systems (MS), including computer security management, decision support system management, enterprise resource management, network management, software engineering management, systems development management; management (MBA); management information systems (MS); marketing (MBA); professional accounting (MS), including accounting information systems, controllership, taxation; public administration (MPA); supply chain management (MBA); technology in education (M Ed). Programs also offered at campus locations in Birmingham, AL; Chamblee, GA; Cobb County, GA; Morrow, GA; White Marsh, MD; Charleston, SC; Columbia, SC; Greensboro, NC; Greenville, SC; Lexington, KY; Louisville, KY; Nashville, TN; North Raleigh, NC; Washington, DC. *Accreditation:* ACBSP. *Program availability:* Part-time, evening/weekend, online learning. *Degree requirements:* For master's, thesis. *Entrance requirements:* For master's, GMAT, GRE General Test, bachelor's degree from an accredited college or university, minimum undergraduate GPA of 2.75. Electronic applications accepted.

Syracuse University, College of Engineering and Computer Science, Programs in Cybersecurity, Syracuse, NY 13244. Offers MS, CAS. *Program availability:* Part-time, evening/weekend. *Entrance requirements:* For master's, GRE, three letters of recommendation, personal statement, resume, official transcripts. Additional exam requirements/recommendations for international students: Required—TOEFL (minimum score 100 iBT). *Application deadline:* For fall admission, 7/1 priority date for domestic students, 6/1 priority date for international students; for spring admission, 11/15 for domestic students, 10/15 priority date for international students. Applications are processed on a rolling basis. Application fee: $75. Electronic applications accepted. *Financial support:* Fellowships, research assistantships, teaching assistantships, and tuition waivers available. Financial award application deadline: 1/1. *Faculty research:* Design of secure systems that exhibit confidentiality, integrity, and availability through authentication, reference monitoring, and sound design and implementation. *Unit head:* Dr. Jae C. Oh, Professor and Chair, 315-443-2652, E-mail: eccsadmissions@syr.edu. *Application contact:* Kathleen Joyce, Assistant Dean, 315-443-2219, E-mail: topgrads@syr.edu. Website: http://eng-cs.syr.edu/our-departments/electrical-engineering-and-computer-science/

Syracuse University, School of Information Studies, CAS Program in Information Security Management, Syracuse, NY 13244. Offers CAS. *Program availability:* Part-time, evening/weekend, online learning. *Students:* Average age 26. *Entrance requirements:* For degree, resume, personal statement, official transcripts. Additional exam requirements/recommendations for international students: Required—TOEFL (minimum score 100 iBT). *Application deadline:* For fall admission, 1/1 priority date for domestic and international students; for spring admission, 10/15 priority date for domestic and international students; for summer admission, 2/1 priority date for domestic and international students. Applications are processed on a rolling basis. Application fee: $75. Electronic applications accepted. *Financial support:* Application deadline: 1/1. *Faculty research:* Information security, digital forensics, Internet security, risk management, security policy. *Unit head:* Carsten Oesterlund, Program Director, 315-443-2911, E-mail: igrad@syr.edu. *Application contact:* Susan Corieri, Director of Enrollment Management, 315-443-2575, E-mail: ischool@syr.edu. Website: https://ischool.syr.edu/academics/graduate/cas/cas-information-security-management/

Computer and Information Systems Security

Temple University, College of Science and Technology, Department of Computer and Information Sciences, Philadelphia, PA 19122. Offers computational data science (MS); computer and information sciences (PhD), including artificial intelligence, computer and network systems, information systems, software systems; computer science (MS); cyber defense and information assurance (PSM); information science and technology (MS). *Program availability:* Part-time, evening/weekend, online learning. *Faculty:* 31 full-time (7 women), 10 part-time/adjunct (2 women). *Students:* 92 full-time (28 women), 15 part-time (3 women); includes 7 minority (2 Black or African American, non-Hispanic/Latino; 4 Asian, non-Hispanic/Latino; 1 Hispanic/Latino), 82 international. 119 applicants, 43% accepted, 21 enrolled. In 2018, 20 master's, 5 doctorates awarded. *Degree requirements:* For doctorate, thesis/dissertation. *Entrance requirements:* For master's, GRE, 3 letters of recommendation, statement of goals; for doctorate, GRE, 3 letters of recommendation, bachelor's degree in related field, statement of goals, resume. Additional exam requirements/recommendations for international students: Required—TOEFL (minimum score 85 iBT), IELTS (minimum score 6.5), PTE (minimum score 58), one of three is required. *Application deadline:* Applications are processed on a rolling basis. Application fee: $60. Electronic applications accepted. *Expenses:* Contact institution. *Financial support:* Research assistantships, teaching assistantships, health care benefits, and unspecified assistantships available. Financial award applicants required to submit FAFSA. *Faculty research:* Data mining, machine learning, knowledge discovery, computer networks and systems, cyberspace security. *Unit head:* Jamie Payton, Department Chairperson, 215-204-8245, E-mail: Jamie.payton@temple.edu. *Application contact:* Eduard Dragut, Graduate Chair, 215-204-0521, E-mail: cisadmit@temple.edu.
Website: https://cis.temple.edu/

Thomas Edison State University, School of Applied Science and Technology, Trenton, NJ 08608. Offers clinical trials management (MS); cybersecurity (Graduate Certificate); information technology (MS); nuclear energy technology management (MS); technical studies (MS). *Program availability:* Part-time, online learning. *Degree requirements:* For master's, project. *Entrance requirements:* Additional exam requirements/recommendations for international students: Required—TOEFL (minimum score 550 paper-based; 79 iBT). Electronic applications accepted.

Trident University International, College of Business Administration, Program in Business Administration, Cypress, CA 90630. Offers business administration (PhD); conflict and negotiation management (MBA); criminal justice administration (MBA); entrepreneurship (MBA); finance (MBA); general management (MBA); government accounting (MBA); human resource management (MBA); information security and digital assurance management (MBA); information technology management (MBA); international business (MBA); logistics management (MBA); marketing (MBA); project management (MBA); public management (MBA); quality management (MBA); strategic leadership (MBA). *Program availability:* Part-time, evening/weekend, online learning. *Degree requirements:* For doctorate, comprehensive exam, thesis/dissertation, defense of dissertation. *Entrance requirements:* For master's, minimum GPA of 2.5 (students with GPA 3.0 or greater may transfer up to 30% of graduate level credits); for doctorate, minimum GPA of 3.4, curriculum vitae, course work in research methods or statistics. Additional exam requirements/recommendations for international students: Required—TOEFL. Electronic applications accepted.

Tuskegee University, Graduate Programs, Andrew F. Brimmer College of Business and Information Science, Tuskegee, AL 36088. Offers information systems and security management (MS). *Degree requirements:* For master's, thesis. *Entrance requirements:* For master's, GRE or GMAT, baccalaureate degree in computer science, management information systems, accounting, finance, management, information technology, or a closely-related field.

Universidad del Este, Graduate School, Carolina, PR 00984. Offers accounting (MBA); adult education (M Ed); agribusiness (MBA); criminal justice and criminology (MA); curriculum and instruction - early education (M Ed); curriculum and instruction - elementary (M Ed); curriculum and instruction - English (M Ed); curriculum and instruction - Spanish (M Ed); human resources (MBA); information security management (MBA); information technology and Web business development (MBA); management (MBA); public policy (MPA); social work (MA), including clinical social work; special education (M Ed); strategic leadership (MBA).

Université de Sherbrooke, Faculty of Administration, Program in Governance, Audit and Security of Information Technology, Longueuil, QC J4K0A8, Canada. Offers M Adm. *Program availability:* Part-time, evening/weekend, online learning. *Degree requirements:* For master's, thesis. *Entrance requirements:* For master's, bachelor's degree, related work experience. Electronic applications accepted.

University at Albany, State University of New York, College of Emergency Preparedness, Homeland Security and Cybersecurity, Albany, NY 12222-0001. Offers cybersecurity (Certificate); emergency preparedness (Certificate); homeland security (Certificate); information science (MS, PhD). *Faculty:* 14 full-time (6 women), 7 part-time/adjunct (4 women). *Students:* 50 full-time (35 women), 108 part-time (83 women); includes 27 minority (8 Black or African American, non-Hispanic/Latino; 5 Asian, non-Hispanic/Latino; 12 Hispanic/Latino; 2 Two or more races, non-Hispanic/Latino), 13 international. 90 applicants, 67% accepted, 36 enrolled. In 2018, 30 master's, 1 doctorate, 24 other advanced degrees awarded. *Entrance requirements:* Additional exam requirements/recommendations for international students: Required—TOEFL. *Faculty research:* Electrical and computer engineering, environmental and sustainability engineering, computer science. *Unit head:* Dr. Robert Griffin, Dean, 518-442-5258. *Application contact:* Michael DeRensis, Director, Graduate Admissions, 518-442-3980, Fax: 518-442-3922, E-mail: graduate@albany.edu.
Website: http://www.albany.edu/cehc/

University at Albany, State University of New York, School of Business, MBA Programs, Albany, NY 12222-0001. Offers business administration (MBA); cyber security (MBA); entrepreneurship (MBA); finance (MBA); human resource information systems (MBA); information systems and business analytics (MBA); marketing (MBA); JD/MBA. JD/MBA offered jointly with Albany Law School. *Program availability:* Part-time, evening/weekend. *Faculty:* 29 full-time (13 women), 9 part-time/adjunct (2 women). *Students:* 103 full-time (36 women), 188 part-time (69 women); includes 76 minority (27 Black or African American, non-Hispanic/Latino; 33 Asian, non-Hispanic/Latino; 16 Hispanic/Latino), 16 international. Average age 25. 181 applicants, 80% accepted, 114 enrolled. In 2018, 103 master's awarded. *Degree requirements:* For master's, thesis (for some programs), field or research project. *Entrance requirements:* For master's, GMAT, minimum undergraduate GPA of 3.0; 3 letters of recommendation; resume; statement of goals. Additional exam requirements/recommendations for international students: Required—TOEFL (minimum score 100 iBT); Recommended—IELTS (minimum score 7). *Application deadline:* For fall admission, 4/1 priority date for domestic students, 2/15 for international students; for spring admission, 12/1 for domestic students; for summer admission, 5/1 for domestic students. Applications are processed on a rolling basis. Application fee: $75. Electronic applications accepted. *Expenses:* 16818. *Financial support:* In 2018–19, 25 students received support, including 7 fellowships with partial tuition reimbursements available (averaging $6,000 per year), 4 research assistantships with partial tuition reimbursements available, 21 teaching assistantships with partial tuition reimbursements available; unspecified

assistantships also available. Financial award application deadline: 4/1; financial award applicants required to submit FAFSA. *Faculty research:* Social goods, information assurance, social computing, corporate entrepreneurship, asset pricing. *Total annual research expenditures:* $136,000. *Unit head:* Dr. Nilanjan Sen, Dean, 518-956-8370, Fax: 518-442-3273, E-mail: nsen@albany.edu. *Application contact:* Zina Mega Lawrence, Assistant Dean of Graduate Student Services, 518-956-8320, Fax: 518-442-4042, E-mail: zlawrence@albany.edu.
Website: https://graduatebusiness.albany.edu/

University of Advancing Technology, Master of Science Program in Technology, Tempe, AZ 85283-1042. Offers advancing computer science (MS); emerging technologies (MS); game production and management (MS); information assurance (MS); technology leadership (MS). *Degree requirements:* For master's, project or thesis. *Entrance requirements:* Additional exam requirements/recommendations for international students: Required—TOEFL (minimum score 550 paper-based). Electronic applications accepted. *Faculty research:* Artificial intelligence, fractals, organizational management.

The University of Alabama at Birmingham, Collat School of Business, Program in Management Information Systems, Birmingham, AL 35294. Offers management information systems (MS), including cybersecurity management, information technology management. *Program availability:* Part-time, evening/weekend, online only, 100% online. *Faculty:* 7 full-time (1 woman), 4 part-time/adjunct (2 women). *Students:* 8 full-time (0 women), 116 part-time (38 women); includes 49 minority (35 Black or African American, non-Hispanic/Latino; 1 American Indian or Alaska Native, non-Hispanic/Latino; 5 Asian, non-Hispanic/Latino; 3 Hispanic/Latino; 5 Two or more races, non-Hispanic/Latino), 1 international. Average age 37. 47 applicants, 94% accepted, 36 enrolled. In 2018, 35 master's awarded. *Entrance requirements:* For master's, GMAT or GRE. Additional exam requirements/recommendations for international students: Required—TOEFL (minimum score 80 iBT), IELTS (minimum score 6.5). *Application deadline:* For fall admission, 8/1 for domestic and international students; for spring admission, 12/1 for domestic and international students; for summer admission, 5/1 for domestic and international students. Applications are processed on a rolling basis. Application fee: $70 ($85 for international students). Electronic applications accepted. *Expenses: Tuition, area resident:* Full-time $8100; part-time $8100 per year. Tuition, state resident: full-time $8100. Tuition, nonresident: full-time $19,188; part-time $19,188 per year. Tuition and fees vary according to program. *Faculty research:* Open innovation, information security, online communities, privacy, business analytics. *Unit head:* Dr. Jack Howard, Department Chair, 205-934-8846, Fax: 205-934-8886, E-mail: jlhoward@uab.edu. *Application contact:* Wendy England, Online Program Coordinator, 205-934-8813, Fax: 205-975-4429.
Website: https://businessdegrees.uab.edu/mis-degree-masters/

The University of Alabama at Birmingham, College of Arts and Sciences, Program in Computer Forensics and Security Management, Birmingham, AL 35294. Offers MS. Interdisciplinary program offered jointly with College of Arts and Sciences and School of Business. *Degree requirements:* For master's, field practicum (internship). *Entrance requirements:* For master's, GRE General Test (minimum combined score of 320) or GMAT (minimum total score of 550), minimum GPA of 3.0. Electronic applications accepted. *Expenses: Tuition, area resident:* Full-time $8100; part-time $8100 per year. Tuition, state resident: full-time $8100. Tuition, nonresident: full-time $19,188; part-time $19,188 per year. Tuition and fees vary according to program.

The University of Alabama in Huntsville, School of Graduate Studies, College of Business Administration, Programs in Information Systems, Huntsville, AL 35899. Offers cybersecurity (MS, Certificate); enterprise resource planning (Certificate); information systems (MSIS); supply chain and logistics management (MS); supply chain management (Certificate). *Program availability:* Part-time. *Faculty:* 4 full-time. *Students:* 33 full-time (9 women), 89 part-time (34 women); includes 23 minority (13 Black or African American, non-Hispanic/Latino; 3 Asian, non-Hispanic/Latino; 5 Hispanic/Latino; 2 Two or more races, non-Hispanic/Latino), 3 international. Average age 35. 117 applicants, 69% accepted, 46 enrolled. In 2018, 39 master's, 3 other advanced degrees awarded. *Degree requirements:* For master's, comprehensive exam, thesis or alternative. *Entrance requirements:* For master's, GMAT (minimum score 500), minimum AACSB index of 1080. Additional exam requirements/recommendations for international students: Required—TOEFL (minimum score 550 paper-based; 80 iBT), IELTS (minimum score 6.5). *Application deadline:* For fall admission, 7/15 priority date for domestic students, 4/1 priority date for international students; for spring admission, 11/30 priority date for domestic students, 9/1 priority date for international students. Applications are processed on a rolling basis. Application fee: $50. Electronic applications accepted. *Expenses: Tuition, area resident:* Full-time $10,632; part-time $412 per credit hour. Tuition, state resident: full-time $10,632. Tuition, nonresident: full-time $23,604; part-time $412 per credit hour. *Required fees:* $582; $582. Tuition and fees vary according to course load and program. *Financial support:* Research assistantships with full tuition reimbursements, teaching assistantships with full tuition reimbursements, career-related internships or fieldwork, Federal Work-Study, institutionally sponsored loans, scholarships/grants, health care benefits, and unspecified assistantships available. Support available to part-time students. Financial award application deadline: 4/1; financial award applicants required to submit FAFSA. *Faculty research:* Supply chain information systems, information assurance and security, databases and conceptual schema, workflow management, inter-organizational information sharing. *Unit head:* Dr. Fan Tseng, Chair, 256-824-6804, Fax: 256-824-6328, E-mail: fan.tseng@uah.edu. *Application contact:* Jennifer Pettitt, Director of Advising, 256-824-6681, Fax: 256-824-7571, E-mail: jennifer.pettitt@uah.edu.

The University of Alabama in Huntsville, School of Graduate Studies, College of Science, Department of Computer Science, Huntsville, AL 35899. Offers computer science (MS, PhD); cybersecurity (MS); modeling and simulation (MS, PhD, Certificate); software engineering (MSSE, Certificate). *Program availability:* Part-time. *Faculty:* 14 full-time (4 women), 1 part-time/adjunct. *Students:* 67 full-time (16 women), 65 part-time (11 women); includes 14 minority (4 Black or African American, non-Hispanic/Latino; 1 American Indian or Alaska Native, non-Hispanic/Latino; 5 Asian, non-Hispanic/Latino; 3 Hispanic/Latino; 1 Two or more races, non-Hispanic/Latino), 60 international. Average age 33. 219 applicants, 74% accepted, 37 enrolled. In 2018, 47 master's awarded. *Degree requirements:* For master's, comprehensive exam, thesis or alternative, oral and written exams; for doctorate, comprehensive exam, thesis/dissertation, oral and written exams. *Entrance requirements:* For master's, doctorate, and Certificate, GRE General Test, minimum GPA of 3.0. Additional exam requirements/recommendations for international students: Required—TOEFL (minimum score 550 paper-based; 80 iBT), IELTS (minimum score 6.5). *Application deadline:* For fall admission, 7/15 priority date for domestic students, 4/1 priority date for international students; for spring admission, 11/30 priority date for domestic students, 9/1 priority date for international students. Applications are processed on a rolling basis. Application fee: $50. Electronic applications accepted. *Expenses: Tuition, area resident:* Full-time $10,632; part-time $412 per credit hour. Tuition, state resident: full-time $10,632. Tuition, nonresident: full-time $23,604; part-time $412 per credit hour. *Required fees:* $582; $582. Tuition and fees vary according to course load and program. *Financial support:* In 2018–19, 39 students received support, including 18 research assistantships with full tuition

reimbursements available (averaging $6,762 per year), 19 teaching assistantships with full tuition reimbursements available (averaging $6,315 per year); career-related internships or fieldwork, Federal Work-Study, institutionally sponsored loans, scholarships/grants, health care benefits, and unspecified assistantships also available. Support available to part-time students. Financial award application deadline: 4/1; financial award applicants required to submit FAFSA. *Faculty research:* Information assurance and cyber security, modeling and simulation, data science, computer graphics and visualization, multimedia systems. *Unit head:* Dr. Heggere Ranganath, Professor and Chair, 256-824-6088, Fax: 256-824-6239, E-mail: info@cs.uah.edu. *Application contact:* Kim Gray, Graduate Studies Admissions Manager, 256-824-6002, Fax: 256-824-6405, E-mail: deangrad@uah.edu.
Website: http://www.cs.uah.edu

University of Colorado Colorado Springs, College of Engineering and Applied Science, Program in General Engineering, Colorado Springs, CO 80918. Offers computer science (PhD); cybersecurity (ME); energy engineering (ME); engineering management (ME); engineering systems (ME); software engineering (ME); space operations (ME). *Program availability:* Part-time, evening/weekend, blended/hybrid learning. *Faculty:* 1 full-time (0 women), 20 part-time/adjunct (6 women). *Students:* 12 full-time (1 woman), 177 part-time (39 women); includes 38 minority (4 Black or African American, non-Hispanic/Latino; 12 Asian, non-Hispanic/Latino; 12 Hispanic/Latino; 1 Native Hawaiian or other Pacific Islander, non-Hispanic/Latino; 9 Two or more races, non-Hispanic/Latino), 54 international. Average age 35. 44 applicants, 93% accepted, 21 enrolled. In 2018, 24 master's, 15 doctorates awarded. *Degree requirements:* For master's, thesis, portfolio, or project; for doctorate, comprehensive exam, thesis/dissertation. *Entrance requirements:* For master's, GRE may be required based on past academic performance., Professional recommendation letters are required for all applicants.; for doctorate, GRE (minimum score of 148 new grading scale on the quantitative portion if the applicant has not graduated from a program of recognized standing), minimum GPA of 3.3 in the bachelor's or master's degree program attempted. Additional exam requirements/recommendations for international students: Required—TOEFL (minimum score 80 iBT), IELTS (minimum score 6). *Application deadline:* For fall admission, 6/1 for domestic and international students; for spring admission, 11/1 for domestic and international students; for summer admission, 4/15 for domestic and international students. Applications are processed on a rolling basis. Application fee: $60 ($100 for international students). Electronic applications accepted. *Expenses:* Program tuition and fees vary by course load and residency classification. Please visit the University of Colorado Colorado Springs Student Financial Services website to see current program costs: https://www.uccs.edu/bursar/index.php/estimate-your-bill. *Financial support:* In 2018–19, 1 student received support. Career-related internships or fieldwork, Federal Work-Study, scholarships/grants, traineeships, and unspecified assistantships available. Support available to part-time students. Financial award application deadline: 3/1; financial award applicants required to submit FAFSA. *Total annual research expenditures:* $22,249. *Unit head:* Dr. Donald Rabern, Dean of Engineering and Applied Science, 719-255-3543, E-mail: drabern@uccs.edu. *Application contact:* Dawn House, Extended Studies Coordinator, 719-255-3246, E-mail: dhouse@uccs.edu.

University of Dallas, Satish and Yasmin Gupta College of Business, Irving, TX 75062. Offers accounting (MBA, MS); business administration (DBA); business analytics (MS); business management (MBA); corporate finance (MBA); cybersecurity (MS); finance (MS); financial services (MBA); global business (MBA, MS); health services management (MBA); human resource management (MBA); information and technology management (MS); information assurance (MBA); information technology (MBA); information technology service management (MBA); marketing management (MBA); organization development (MBA); project management (MBA); sports and entertainment management (MBA); strategic leadership (MBA); supply chain management (MBA). *Accreditation:* AACSB. *Program availability:* Part-time, evening/weekend, 100% online. *Students:* 147 full-time (56 women), 584 part-time (232 women); includes 402 minority (204 Black or African American, non-Hispanic/Latino; 95 Asian, non-Hispanic/Latino; 92 Hispanic/Latino; 2 Native Hawaiian or other Pacific Islander, non-Hispanic/Latino; 9 Two or more races, non-Hispanic/Latino), 113 international. Average age 34. 992 applicants, 30% accepted, 157 enrolled. In 2018, 336 master's, 5 doctorates awarded. *Degree requirements:* For doctorate, thesis/dissertation. *Entrance requirements:* For master's and doctorate, U.S. bachelor's degree with a minimum cumulative GPA of 2.0 from a regionally accredited college or university (or comparable foreign degree); minimum 3.0 GPA in any graduate-level coursework completed; good academic standing with all colleges attended. Additional exam requirements/recommendations for international students: Required—TOEFL (minimum score 80 iBT), IELTS (minimum score 6.5), PTE (minimum score 67). *Application deadline:* Applications are processed on a rolling basis. Application fee: $50. Electronic applications accepted. *Expenses:* $1250 per credit hour. *Financial support:* In 2018–19, 291 students received support. Research assistantships, teaching assistantships, scholarships/grants, and unspecified assistantships available. Support available to part-time students. Financial award application deadline: 2/15; financial award applicants required to submit FAFSA. *Unit head:* Brett J.L. Landry, Dean, 972-721-5356, E-mail: blandry@udallas.edu. *Application contact:* Breonna Collins, Director, Graduate Admissions, 972-7215304, E-mail: bcollins@udallas.edu.
Website: http://www.udallas.edu/cob/

University of Dayton, School of Business Administration, Dayton, OH 45469. Offers accounting (MBA); cyber security (MBA); finance (MBA); marketing (MBA); JD/MBA. *Accreditation:* AACSB. *Program availability:* Part-time, evening/weekend, blended/hybrid learning. *Entrance requirements:* For master's, GMAT (minimum score of 500 total, 19 verbal); GRE (minimum score of 149 verbal, 146 quantitative), minimum GPA of 3.0, current resume. Additional exam requirements/recommendations for international students: Required—TOEFL (minimum score 550 paper-based; 80 iBT); Recommended—IELTS (minimum score 6.5). Electronic applications accepted. *Expenses:* Contact institution. *Faculty research:* Management information systems, economics, finance, marketing, entrepreneurship, accounting, cyber security, analytics.

University of Denver, Daniel Felix Ritchie School of Engineering and Computer Science, Department of Computer Science, Denver, CO 80210. Offers computer science (MS, PhD); cybersecurity (MS); data science (MS). *Program availability:* Part-time, evening/weekend. *Faculty:* 15 full-time (3 women), 1 (woman) part-time/adjunct. *Students:* 23 full-time (8 women), 91 part-time (29 women); includes 11 minority (5 Asian, non-Hispanic/Latino; 1 Hispanic/Latino; 1 Native Hawaiian or other Pacific Islander, non-Hispanic/Latino; 4 Two or more races, non-Hispanic/Latino), 51 international. Average age 30. 263 applicants, 59% accepted, 79 enrolled. In 2018, 9 master's, 1 doctorate awarded. *Degree requirements:* For doctorate, variable foreign language requirement, comprehensive exam, thesis/dissertation, reading competency in two languages, modern typesetting system, or additional coursework. *Entrance requirements:* For master's and doctorate, GRE General Test, bachelor's degree, transcripts, personal statement, resume or curriculum vitae, three letters of recommendation. Additional exam requirements/recommendations for international students: Required—TOEFL (minimum score 550 paper-based; 80 iBT). *Application deadline:* For fall admission, 1/15 priority date for domestic and international students; for winter admission, 10/25 for domestic and international students; for spring admission, 2/7 for domestic and international students; for summer admission, 4/24 for

domestic and international students. Applications are processed on a rolling basis. Application fee: $65. Electronic applications accepted. *Expenses:* $33,183 per year full-time. *Financial support:* In 2018–19, 98 students received support, including 14 teaching assistantships with tuition reimbursements available (averaging $18,214 per year); research assistantships with tuition reimbursements available, career-related internships or fieldwork, Federal Work-Study, institutionally sponsored loans, scholarships/grants, and unspecified assistantships also available. Financial award application deadline: 2/15; financial award applicants required to submit FAFSA. *Faculty research:* Algorithms, artificial intelligence, databases, game development, robotics. *Unit head:* Dr. Bruce Harmon, Professor of the Practice and Interim Chair, 303-871-6949, E-mail: bruce.harmon@du.edu. *Application contact:* Information Contact, 303-871-2458, E-mail: info@cs.du.edu.
Website: http://ritchieschool.du.edu/departments/computer-science/

University of Detroit Mercy, College of Liberal Arts and Education, Detroit, MI 48221. Offers addiction counseling (MA); addiction studies (Certificate); clinical mental health counseling (MA); clinical psychology (MA, PhD); computer and information systems (MS); criminal justice (MA); curriculum and instruction (MA); economics (MA); educational administration (MA); financial economics (MA); industrial/organizational psychology (MA); information assurance (MS); intelligence analysis (MA); liberal studies (MALS); religious studies (MA); school counseling (MA, Certificate); school psychology (Spec); security administration (MS); special education: emotionally impaired/behaviorally disordered (MA); special education: learning disabilities (MA). *Program availability:* Part-time, evening/weekend. *Degree requirements:* For doctorate, departmental qualifying exam. *Faculty research:* Psychology of aging, history of technology, Renaissance humanism, U.S. and Japanese economic relations.

University of Fairfax, Graduate Programs, Vienna, VA 22182. Offers business administration (DBA); computer science (MCS); cybersecurity (MBA, MS); general business administration (MBA); information technology (MBA); project management (MBA).

University of Houston, College of Technology, Department of Information and Logistics Technology, Houston, TX 77204. Offers information security (MS); supply chain and logistics technology (MS); technology project management (MS). *Program availability:* Part-time. *Degree requirements:* For master's, project or thesis (most programs). *Entrance requirements:* For master's, GMAT. Additional exam requirements/recommendations for international students: Required—TOEFL (minimum score 550 paper-based; 79 iBT). Electronic applications accepted.

University of Louisville, J. B. Speed School of Engineering, Department of Computer Engineering and Computer Science, Louisville, KY 40292-0001. Offers computer engineering and computer science (M Eng); computer science (MS, PhD); cybersecurity (Certificate); data science (Certificate). *Accreditation:* ABET (one or more programs are accredited). *Program availability:* Part-time, 100% online, blended/hybrid learning. *Faculty:* 14 full-time (2 women), 3 part-time/adjunct (0 women). *Students:* 62 full-time (16 women), 124 part-time (31 women); includes 32 minority (4 Black or African American, non-Hispanic/Latino; 14 Asian, non-Hispanic/Latino; 8 Hispanic/Latino; 6 Two or more races, non-Hispanic/Latino), 46 international. Average age 33. 74 applicants, 49% accepted, 25 enrolled. In 2018, 18 master's, 5 doctorates, 7 other advanced degrees awarded. Terminal master's awarded for partial completion of doctoral program. *Degree requirements:* For master's, thesis optional; for doctorate, comprehensive exam, thesis/dissertation. *Entrance requirements:* For master's, GRE, Two letters of recommendation, official final transcripts; for doctorate, GRE, Two letters of recommendation, personal statement, official final transcripts. Additional exam requirements/recommendations for international students: Required—TOEFL (minimum score 550 paper-based; 80 iBT), IELTS (minimum score 6.5), GRE. *Application deadline:* For fall admission, 5/1 priority date for domestic and international students; for spring admission, 11/1 priority date for domestic and international students; for summer admission, 3/1 priority date for domestic and international students. Applications are processed on a rolling basis. Application fee: $65. Electronic applications accepted. *Expenses: Tuition, area resident:* Full-time $6500; part-time $723 per credit hour. Tuition, state resident: full-time $6500. Tuition, nonresident: full-time $13,557; part-time $1507 per credit hour. Tuition and fees vary according to course load and program. *Financial support:* In 2018–19, 78 students received support. Fellowships, research assistantships, teaching assistantships, scholarships/grants, health care benefits, and tuition waivers (full) available. Financial award application deadline: 1/1. *Faculty research:* Artificial Intelligence, Big Data Analytics, Bioinformatics, Cybersecurity, Data Mining. *Total annual research expenditures:* $740,736. *Unit head:* Dr. Wei Zhang, Chair, 502-852-0715, E-mail: wei.zhang@louisville.edu. *Application contact:* Dr. Mehmed Kantardzic, Director of Graduate Studies, 502-852-3703, E-mail: mehmed.kantardzic@louisville.edu.
Website: http://louisville.edu/speed/computer

University of Maryland, Baltimore County, The Graduate School, College of Engineering and Information Technology, Department of Computer Science and Electrical Engineering, Program in Cybersecurity, Baltimore, MD 21250. Offers cybersecurity (MPS); cybersecurity operations (Postbaccalaureate Certificate); cybersecurity strategy and policy (Postbaccalaureate Certificate). *Program availability:* Part-time. *Degree requirements:* For master's, comprehensive exam (for some programs). *Entrance requirements:* For master's, bachelor's degree in computer science, computer engineering, engineering, math, or information systems, or in other field with relevant work experience; curriculum vitae and two letters of recommendation (for international students). Electronic applications accepted. *Expenses:* Contact institution. *Faculty research:* Cybersecurity strategy and policy; cybersecurity operations.

University of Maryland University College, The Graduate School, Cybersecurity Management and Policy Program, Adelphi, MD 20783. Offers MS, Certificate. *Program availability:* Part-time, evening/weekend, online learning. *Students:* 518 part-time (218 women); includes 270 minority (180 Black or African American, non-Hispanic/Latino; 2 American Indian or Alaska Native, non-Hispanic/Latino; 32 Asian, non-Hispanic/Latino; 28 Hispanic/Latino; 28 Two or more races, non-Hispanic/Latino), 5 international. Average age 37. 276 applicants, 100% accepted, 108 enrolled. In 2018, 178 master's, 42 other advanced degrees awarded. *Degree requirements:* For master's, thesis or alternative, capstone course. *Application deadline:* Applications are processed on a rolling basis. Application fee: $50. Electronic applications accepted. *Financial support:* Scholarships/grants available. Support available to part-time students. Financial award application deadline: 6/1; financial award applicants required to submit FAFSA. *Unit head:* Bruce deGrazia, Program Chair, 240-684-2400, E-mail: bruce.degrazia@umuc.edu. *Application contact:* Admissions, 800-888-8682, E-mail: studentsfirst@umuc.edu.
Website: https://www.umuc.edu/academic-programs/masters-degrees/cybersecurity-management-policy-ms.cfm

University of Maryland University College, The Graduate School, Cybersecurity Technology Program, Adelphi, MD 20783. Offers MS, Certificate. *Program availability:* Part-time, evening/weekend, online learning. *Students:* 1 (woman) full-time, 1,291 part-time (371 women); includes 721 minority (464 Black or African American, non-Hispanic/Latino; 4 American Indian or Alaska Native, non-Hispanic/Latino; 105 Asian, non-

Hispanic/Latino; 96 Hispanic/Latino; 2 Native Hawaiian or other Pacific Islander, non-Hispanic/Latino; 50 Two or more races, non-Hispanic/Latino), 14 international. Average age 36. 534 applicants, 100% accepted, 224 enrolled. In 2018, 667 master's, 125 other advanced degrees awarded. *Degree requirements:* For master's, thesis or alternative, capstone course. *Application deadline:* Applications are processed on a rolling basis. Application fee: $50. Electronic applications accepted. *Financial support:* Scholarships/grants available. Support available to part-time students. Financial award application deadline: 6/1; financial award applicants required to submit FAFSA. *Unit head:* Mansur Hasib, Program Chair, 240-684-2400, E-mail: Mansur.Hasib@umuc.edu. *Application contact:* Admissions, 800-888-8682, E-mail: studentsfirst@umuc.edu.
Website: https://www.umuc.edu/academic-programs/masters-degrees/cybersecurity-technology-ms.cfm

University of Maryland University College, The Graduate School, Program in Cloud Computing Architecture, Adelphi, MD 20783. Offers MS. *Program availability:* Part-time, evening/weekend, online learning. *Students:* 170 part-time (39 women); includes 92 minority (66 Black or African American, non-Hispanic/Latino; 15 Asian, non-Hispanic/Latino; 10 Hispanic/Latino; 1 Two or more races, non-Hispanic/Latino), 11 international. Average age 39. 126 applicants, 100% accepted, 54 enrolled. In 2018, 29 master's awarded. *Degree requirements:* For master's, thesis or alternative. *Application deadline:* Applications are processed on a rolling basis. Application fee: $50. Electronic applications accepted. *Financial support:* Scholarships/grants available. Support available to part-time students. Financial award application deadline: 6/1; financial award applicants required to submit FAFSA. *Unit head:* Jeff Tjiputra, Program Chair, 240-684-2840, E-mail: jeff.tjiputra@umuc.edu. *Application contact:* Admissions, 800-888-8682, E-mail: studentsfirst@umuc.edu.
Website: https://www.umuc.edu/academic-programs/masters-degrees/cloud-computing-architecture.cfm

University of Maryland University College, The Graduate School, Program in Digital Forensics and Cyber Investigation, Adelphi, MD 20783. Offers MS, Certificate. *Program availability:* Part-time, evening/weekend, online learning. *Students:* 1 (woman) full-time, 305 part-time (172 women); includes 168 minority (108 Black or African American, non-Hispanic/Latino; 2 American Indian or Alaska Native, non-Hispanic/Latino; 11 Asian, non-Hispanic/Latino; 36 Hispanic/Latino; 11 Two or more races, non-Hispanic/Latino), 3 international. Average age 34. 175 applicants, 100% accepted, 69 enrolled. In 2018, 125 master's, 2 other advanced degrees awarded. *Degree requirements:* For master's, thesis or alternative, capstone course. *Application deadline:* Applications are processed on a rolling basis. Application fee: $50. Electronic applications accepted. *Financial support:* Scholarships/grants available. Support available to part-time students. Financial award application deadline: 6/1; financial award applicants required to submit FAFSA. *Unit head:* Patrick O'Guinn, 240-684-2400, E-mail: patrick.oguinn@umuc.edu. *Application contact:* Admissions, 800-888-8682, E-mail: studentfirst@umuc.edu.
Website: https://www.umuc.edu/academic-programs/masters-degrees/digital-forensics-cyber-investigation-ms.cfm

University of Michigan–Dearborn, College of Engineering and Computer Science, PhD Program in Computer and Information Science, Dearborn, MI 48128. Offers data management (PhD); data science (PhD); software engineering (PhD); systems and security (PhD). *Faculty:* 19 full-time (1 woman), 5 part-time/adjunct (0 women). *Students:* 7 full-time (4 women), 7 part-time (1 woman); includes 1 minority (Asian, non-Hispanic/Latino), 9 international. Average age 30. 22 applicants, 36% accepted, 6 enrolled. In 2018, 1 doctorate awarded. *Degree requirements:* For doctorate, comprehensive exam, thesis/dissertation. *Entrance requirements:* For doctorate, GRE, bachelor's or master's degree in computer science or closely-related field. Additional exam requirements/recommendations for international students: Required—TOEFL (minimum score 560 paper-based; 84 iBT), IELTS (minimum score 6.5). *Application deadline:* For fall admission, 2/1 for domestic and international students. Application fee: $60. Electronic applications accepted. *Expenses:* Tuition, state resident: full-time $15,380; part-time $88 per credit hour. Tuition, nonresident: full-time $23,948; part-time $1377 per credit hour. *Required fees:* $780; $780 $390. Tuition and fees vary according to course level, course load, degree level, program, reciprocity agreements and student level. *Financial support:* In 2018–19, 2 students received support. Research assistantships with full tuition reimbursements available, teaching assistantships with full tuition reimbursements available, scholarships/grants, health care benefits, and unspecified assistantships available. Financial award application deadline: 2/1; financial award applicants required to submit FAFSA. *Faculty research:* Data science, data management, cybersecurity, software engineering, systems. *Unit head:* Dr. Di Ma, Director, 313-583-6737, E-mail: dmadma@umich.edu. *Application contact:* Office of Graduate Studies, 313-583-6321, E-mail: umd-graduatestudies@umich.edu.
Website: https://umdearborn.edu/cecs/departments/computer-and-information-science/graduate-programs/phd-computer-and-information-science

University of Minnesota, Twin Cities Campus, College of Science and Engineering, Technological Leadership Institute, Program in Security Technologies, Minneapolis, MN 55455-0213. Offers MSST. *Program availability:* Part-time. *Degree requirements:* For master's, capstone project. *Entrance requirements:* Additional exam requirements/recommendations for international students: Required—TOEFL (minimum score 580 paper-based; 90 iBT). Electronic applications accepted.

University of Missouri–St. Louis, College of Business Administration, St. Louis, MO 63121. Offers accounting (M Acc); business administration (MBA, DBA, PhD, Certificate), including logistics and supply chain management (PhD); business intelligence (Certificate); cybersecurity (Certificate); digital and social media marketing (Certificate); human resources management (Certificate); information systems (MS); logistics and supply chain management (Certificate); marketing management (Certificate). *Program availability:* Part-time, evening/weekend. *Degree requirements:* For doctorate, thesis/dissertation. *Entrance requirements:* For master's, GMAT, 2 letters of recommendation; for doctorate, GMAT or GRE, 3 letters of recommendation. Additional exam requirements/recommendations for international students: Recommended—TOEFL (minimum score 550 paper-based; 79 iBT), IELTS (minimum score 6.5). Electronic applications accepted. *Faculty research:* Statistical decision aids, commercial banking, corporate finance, operations management, information systems.

University of Nebraska at Omaha, Graduate Studies, College of Information Science and Technology, Department of Information Systems and Quantitative Analysis, Omaha, NE 68182. Offers data analytics (Certificate); information assurance (Certificate); information technology (MIT, PhD); management information systems (MS); project management (Certificate); systems analysis and design (Certificate). *Program availability:* Part-time, evening/weekend. *Degree requirements:* For master's, comprehensive exam, thesis (for some programs); for doctorate, comprehensive exam, thesis/dissertation. *Entrance requirements:* For master's, GRE General Test, minimum GPA of 3.0, 3 letters of recommendation, writing sample, resume, official transcripts; for doctorate, GMAT or GRE General Test, minimum GPA of 3.0, 3 letters of recommendation, writing sample, resume, official transcripts; for Certificate, minimum GPA of 3.0, official transcripts. Additional exam requirements/recommendations for international students: Required—TOEFL, IELTS, PTE. Electronic applications accepted.

University of Nebraska at Omaha, Graduate Studies, College of Information Science and Technology, School of Interdisciplinary Informatics, Omaha, NE 68182. Offers biomedical informatics (MS, PhD); information assurance (MS). *Program availability:* Part-time, evening/weekend. *Degree requirements:* For master's, comprehensive exam, thesis (for some programs); for doctorate, comprehensive exam, thesis/dissertation. *Entrance requirements:* For master's and doctorate, GRE General Test, letters of recommendation, resume, transcripts. Additional exam requirements/recommendations for international students: Required—TOEFL, IELTS, PTE.

University of Nevada, Las Vegas, Graduate College, Greenspun College of Urban Affairs, School of Public Policy and Leadership, Las Vegas, NV 89154-4030. Offers crisis and emergency management (MS); emergency crisis management cybersecurity (Certificate); environmental science (MS, PhD); non-profit management (Certificate); public administration (MPA); public affairs (PhD); public management (Certificate); urban leadership (MA). *Program availability:* Part-time. *Faculty:* 14 full-time (6 women), 11 part-time/adjunct (4 women). *Students:* 61 full-time (33 women), 113 part-time (74 women); includes 95 minority (29 Black or African American, non-Hispanic/Latino; 1 American Indian or Alaska Native, non-Hispanic/Latino; 9 Asian, non-Hispanic/Latino; 41 Hispanic/Latino; 3 Native Hawaiian or other Pacific Islander, non-Hispanic/Latino; 12 Two or more races, non-Hispanic/Latino), 2 international. Average age 37. 96 applicants, 68% accepted, 55 enrolled. In 2018, 59 master's, 6 doctorates, 19 other advanced degrees awarded. *Degree requirements:* For master's, comprehensive exam (for some programs), thesis (for some programs), oral exam; for doctorate, comprehensive exam, thesis/dissertation; for Certificate, portfolio. *Entrance requirements:* For master's, GRE General Test or GMAT, bachelor's degree with minimum GPA 2.75; statement of purpose; 3 letters of recommendation; for doctorate, GRE General Test, master's degree with minimum GPA of 3.5; 3 letters of recommendation; statement of purpose; writing sample; personal interview; for Certificate, bachelor's degree; 2 letters of recommendation; writing sample. Additional exam requirements/recommendations for international students: Required—TOEFL (minimum score 550 paper-based; 80 iBT), IELTS (minimum score 7). *Application deadline:* For fall admission, 6/1 for domestic and international students; for spring admission, 11/1 for domestic and international students; for summer admission, 3/1 for domestic students. Application fee: $60 ($95 for international students). Electronic applications accepted. *Expenses:* Contact institution. *Financial support:* In 2018–19, 23 students received support, including 8 research assistantships with full tuition reimbursements available (averaging $16,719 per year), 15 teaching assistantships with full tuition reimbursements available (averaging $13,500 per year); institutionally sponsored loans, scholarships/grants, health care benefits, and unspecified assistantships also available. Financial award application deadline: 3/15; financial award applicants required to submit FAFSA. *Total annual research expenditures:* $109,177. *Unit head:* Dr. Christopher Stream, Director, 702-895-5120, Fax: 702-895-4436, E-mail: sppl.chair@unlv.edu. *Application contact:* Dr. Jayce Farmer, Graduate Coordinator, 702-895-4828, E-mail: sppl.gradcoord@unlv.edu.
Website: https://www.unlv.edu/publicpolicy

University of New Hampshire, Graduate School Manchester Campus, Manchester, NH 03101. Offers business administration (MBA); cybersecurity policy and risk management (MS); educational administration and supervision (Ed S); educational studies (M Ed); elementary education (M Ed); information technology (MS); public administration (MPA); public health (MPH, Certificate); secondary education (M Ed, MAT); social work (MSW); substance use disorders (Certificate). *Program availability:* Part-time, evening/weekend. *Entrance requirements:* Additional exam requirements/recommendations for international students: Required—TOEFL (minimum score 550 paper-based; 80 iBT). Electronic applications accepted.

University of New Haven, Graduate School, Tagliatela College of Engineering, Program in Cybersecurity and Networks, West Haven, CT 06516. Offers MS. *Students:* 41 full-time (14 women), 15 part-time (4 women); includes 4 minority (1 Black or African American, non-Hispanic/Latino; 1 Asian, non-Hispanic/Latino; 2 Hispanic/Latino), 35 international. Average age 26. 84 applicants, 73% accepted, 20 enrolled. In 2018, 5 master's awarded. *Application deadline:* Applications are processed on a rolling basis. Application fee: $50. *Expenses: Tuition:* Full-time $16,470; part-time $915 per credit hour. *Required fees:* $230; $95 per term. *Financial support:* Applicants required to submit FAFSA. *Unit head:* Dr. David Eggert, Associate Professor, 203-932-7097, E-mail: deggert@newhaven.edu. *Application contact:* Selina O'Toole, Senior Associate Director of Graduate Admissions, 203-932-7337, E-mail: sotoole@newhaven.edu.
Website: http://www.newhaven.edu/engineering/graduate-programs/cybersecurity-networks/

University of New Mexico, Anderson School of Management, Department of Accounting, Albuquerque, NM 87131. Offers accounting (MBA); advanced accounting (M Acct); information assurance (M Acct); professional accounting (M Acct); tax accounting (M Acct); JD/M Acct. *Accreditation:* AACSB. *Program availability:* Part-time, evening/weekend. *Faculty:* 15 full-time (9 women), 5 part-time/adjunct (2 women). *Students:* 69 applicants, 70% accepted, 36 enrolled. In 2018, 52 master's awarded. *Entrance requirements:* For master's, GMAT/GRE (minimum score of 500), minimum GPA of 3.25, 3.0 on last 60 hours of coursework (for M Acct in professional accounting). Additional exam requirements/recommendations for international students: Required—TOEFL (minimum score 550 paper-based; 79 iBT), IELTS (minimum score 6.5). *Application deadline:* For fall admission, 4/1 priority date for domestic and international students; for spring admission, 10/1 priority date for domestic and international students. Applications are processed on a rolling basis. Application fee: $50. Electronic applications accepted. *Expenses:* $531.34 per credit hour resident, $1197.99 per credit hour non-resident. *Financial support:* In 2018–19, 20 students received support, including 5 fellowships (averaging $16,744 per year), 14 research assistantships with partial tuition reimbursements available (averaging $15,345 per year); career-related internships or fieldwork, Federal Work-Study, scholarships/grants, and unspecified assistantships also available. Support available to part-time students. Financial award application deadline: 6/1; financial award applicants required to submit FAFSA. *Faculty research:* Critical accounting, accounting pedagogy, theory, taxation, information fraud. *Unit head:* Dr. Richard Brody, Interim Chair, 505-277-6471, E-mail: tmarmijo@unm.edu. *Application contact:* Dr. Richard Brody, Interim Chair, 505-277-6471, E-mail: tmarmijo@unm.edu.
Website: https://www.mgt.unm.edu/acct/default.asp?mm-faculty

University of New Mexico, Anderson School of Management, Department of Marketing, Information Systems, Information Assurance, and Operations Management, Albuquerque, NM 87131. Offers information assurance (MBA); information systems and assurance (MS); management information systems (MBA); marketing management (MBA); operations management (MBA). *Program availability:* Part-time. *Faculty:* 17 full-time (6 women), 12 part-time/adjunct (5 women). In 2018, 59 master's awarded. *Entrance requirements:* For master's, GMAT or GRE, minimum GPA of 3.0 on last 60 hours of coursework; bachelor's degree from regionally-accredited college or university in U.S. or its equivalent in another country. Additional exam requirements/recommendations for international students: Required—TOEFL (minimum score 550 paper-based; 79 iBT), IELTS (minimum score 6.5). *Application deadline:* For fall admission, 4/1 priority date for domestic and international students; for spring

admission, 10/1 priority date for domestic and international students. Applications are processed on a rolling basis. Application fee: $50. Electronic applications accepted. *Expenses:* $531.34 per credit hour resident, $1197.98 per credit hour non-resident. *Financial support:* In 2018–19, 23 students received support, including 13 fellowships (averaging $16,320 per year), 12 research assistantships with partial tuition reimbursements available (averaging $15,180 per year); career-related internships or fieldwork, Federal Work-Study, scholarships/grants, and unspecified assistantships also available. Support available to part-time students. Financial award application deadline: 6/1; financial award applicants required to submit FAFSA. *Faculty research:* Marketing, operations management, information systems, information assurance. *Unit head:* Dr. Mary Margaret Rogers, Chair, 505-277-6471, E-mail: mmrogers@unm.edu. *Application contact:* Lisa Beauchene-Lawson, Supervisor, Graduate Advisement, 505-277-6471, E-mail: andersongrad@unm.edu.
Website: https://www.mgt.unm.edu/mids/default.asp?mm-faculty

The University of North Carolina at Charlotte, College of Computing and Informatics, Department of Software and Information Systems, Charlotte, NC 28223-0001. Offers advanced databases and knowledge discovery (Graduate Certificate); game design and development (Graduate Certificate); information security and privacy (Graduate Certificate); information technology (MS); management of information technology (Graduate Certificate); network security (Graduate Certificate); secure software development (Graduate Certificate). *Program availability:* Part-time, evening/weekend. *Students:* 122 full-time (57 women), 102 part-time (39 women); includes 44 minority (24 Black or African American, non-Hispanic/Latino; 8 Asian, non-Hispanic/Latino; 10 Hispanic/Latino; 2 Two or more races, non-Hispanic/Latino), 126 international. Average age 28. 308 applicants, 82% accepted, 98 enrolled. In 2018, 107 master's, 18 other advanced degrees awarded. *Entrance requirements:* For master's, GRE or GMAT, undergraduate or equivalent course work in data structures, object-oriented programming in C++, C#, or Java with minimum GPA of 3.0; for Graduate Certificate, bachelor's degree from accredited institution in computing, mathematical, engineering or business discipline with minimum overall GPA of 2.8, junior/senior 3.0; substantial knowledge of data structures and object-oriented programming in C++, C# or Java. Additional exam requirements/recommendations for international students: Required— TOEFL (minimum score 523 paper-based; 70 iBT), IELTS (minimum score 6), TOEFL (minimum score 523 paper-based, 70 iBT) or IELTS (6). *Application deadline:* Applications are processed on a rolling basis. Application fee: $75. Electronic applications accepted. *Expenses:* Contact institution. *Financial support:* Fellowships, research assistantships, teaching assistantships, career-related internships or fieldwork, institutionally sponsored loans, scholarships/grants, and unspecified assistantships available. Support available to part-time students. Financial award application deadline: 3/1; financial award applicants required to submit FAFSA. *Total annual research expenditures:* $3.1 million. *Unit head:* Dr. Mary Lou Maher, Chair, 704-687-1940, E-mail: mmaher9@uncc.edu. *Application contact:* Kathy B. Giddings, Director of Graduate Admissions, 704-687-5503, Fax: 704-687-1668, E-mail: gradadm@uncc.edu.
Website: http://sis.uncc.edu/

The University of North Carolina at Charlotte, College of Computing and Informatics, Program in Computing and Information Systems, Charlotte, NC 28223-0001. Offers computing and information systems (PhD), including bioinformatics, business information systems and operations management, computer science, interdisciplinary, software and information systems. *Students:* 99 full-time (27 women), 18 part-time (5 women); includes 4 minority (1 Black or African American, non-Hispanic/Latino; 1 Asian, non-Hispanic/Latino; 1 Hispanic/Latino; 1 Two or more races, non-Hispanic/Latino), 90 international. Average age 30. 86 applicants, 33% accepted, 15 enrolled. In 2018, 17 doctorates awarded. *Entrance requirements:* For doctorate, GRE or GMAT, baccalaureate degree, minimum GPA of 3.0 on courses related to the chosen field of PhD study, essay, reference letters. Additional exam requirements/recommendations for international students: Required—TOEFL (minimum score 523 paper-based; 70 iBT), IELTS (minimum score 6), TOEFL (minimum score 523 paper-based, 70 iBT) or IELTS (6). *Application deadline:* Applications are processed on a rolling basis. Application fee: $75. Electronic applications accepted. Tuition and fees vary according to course load and program. *Financial support:* Career-related internships or fieldwork, institutionally sponsored loans, scholarships/grants, health care benefits, and unspecified assistantships available. Support available to part-time students. Financial award applicants required to submit FAFSA. *Unit head:* Dr. Fatma Mili, Dean, 704-687-8450. *Application contact:* Kathy B. Giddings, Director of Graduate Admissions, 704-687-5503, Fax: 704-687-1668, E-mail: gradadm@uncc.edu.

University of Rhode Island, Graduate School, College of Arts and Sciences, Department of Computer Science and Statistics, Kingston, RI 02881. Offers computer science (MS, PhD); cyber security (PSM, Graduate Certificate); digital forensics (Graduate Certificate). *Program availability:* Part-time, evening/weekend, 100% online, blended/hybrid learning. *Faculty:* 18 full-time (5 women). *Students:* 27 full-time (15 women), 98 part-time (22 women); includes 16 minority (3 Black or African American, non-Hispanic/Latino; 5 Asian, non-Hispanic/Latino; 8 Hispanic/Latino), 14 international. 78 applicants, 88% accepted, 50 enrolled. In 2018, 34 master's, 2 doctorates, 23 other advanced degrees awarded. Terminal master's awarded for partial completion of doctoral program. *Entrance requirements:* Additional exam requirements/ recommendations for international students: Required—TOEFL. *Application deadline:* For fall admission, 7/15 for domestic students, 2/1 for international students; for spring admission, 11/15 for domestic students, 7/15 for international students. Application fee: $65. Electronic applications accepted. *Expenses: Tuition, area resident:* Full-time $13,226; part-time $735 per credit. *Tuition, state resident:* full-time $13,226; part-time $735 per credit. *Tuition, nonresident:* full-time $25,854; part-time $1436 per credit. *International tuition:* $25,854 full-time. *Required fees:* $1698; $50 per credit. $35 per semester. One-time fee: $165. *Financial support:* In 2018–19, 1 research assistantship with tuition reimbursement (averaging $8,862 per year), 12 teaching assistantships with tuition reimbursements (averaging $16,443 per year) were awarded; unspecified assistantships also available. Financial award application deadline: 2/1; financial award applicants required to submit FAFSA. *Unit head:* Dr. Lisa DiPippo, Chair, 401-874-2701, Fax: 401-874-4617, E-mail: dipippo@cs.uri.edu. *Application contact:* Lutz Hamel, Graduate Program Director, 401-874-2701, E-mail: lutzhamel@uri.edu.
Website: http://www.cs.uri.edu/

University of San Diego, Division of Professional and Continuing Education, San Diego, CA 92110-2492. Offers cyber security operations and leadership (MS); law enforcement and public safety leadership (MS). *Program availability:* Part-time-only, evening/weekend, 100% online. *Faculty:* 1 full-time (0 women), 25 part-time/adjunct (1 woman). *Students:* 331 part-time (83 women); includes 117 minority (16 Black or African American, non-Hispanic/Latino; 1 American Indian or Alaska Native, non-Hispanic/Latino; 22 Asian, non-Hispanic/Latino; 73 Hispanic/Latino; 1 Native Hawaiian or other Pacific Islander, non-Hispanic/Latino; 4 Two or more races, non-Hispanic/Latino), 1 international. Average age 39. 224 applicants, 98% accepted, 159 enrolled. *Entrance requirements:* For master's, GMAT, GRE, or LSAT if GPA is under 2.75. Additional exam requirements/recommendations for international students: Required—TOEFL (minimum score 90 iBT). *Application deadline:* For fall admission, 8/7 for domestic students; for spring admission, 12/3 for domestic students; for summer admission, 4/24 for domestic students. Applications are processed on a rolling basis. Application fee:

$45. Electronic applications accepted. *Financial support:* Application deadline: 4/1; applicants required to submit FAFSA. *Unit head:* Dr. Chell Roberts, Assoc. Provost for Professional Education and Online Dev., 619-260-4585, Fax: 619-260-2961, E-mail: continuinged@sandiego.edu. *Application contact:* Erika Garwood, Associate Director of Graduate Admissions, 619-260-4524, Fax: 619-260-4158, E-mail: grads@sandiego.edu.
Website: http://pce.sandiego.edu.

University of San Diego, Shiley-Marcos School of Engineering, San Diego, CA 92110-2492. Offers cyber security engineering (MS). *Program availability:* Part-time, evening/weekend. *Faculty:* 2 full-time (0 women), 2 part-time/adjunct (1 woman). *Students:* 57 part-time (9 women); includes 34 minority (6 Black or African American, non-Hispanic/Latino; 10 Asian, non-Hispanic/Latino; 16 Hispanic/Latino; 1 Native Hawaiian or other Pacific Islander, non-Hispanic/Latino; 1 Two or more races, non-Hispanic/Latino), 1 international. Average age 33. 47 applicants, 79% accepted, 23 enrolled. In 2018, 3 master's awarded. *Degree requirements:* For master's, capstone course. *Entrance requirements:* For master's, GMAT, GRE, or LSAT if GPA is under 3.0. Additional exam requirements/recommendations for international students: Required—TOEFL (minimum score 120 iBT). *Application deadline:* For fall admission, 8/5 for domestic students; for spring admission, 12/2 for domestic students; for summer admission, 4/24 for domestic students. Applications are processed on a rolling basis. Application fee: $45. Electronic applications accepted. *Financial support:* In 2018–19, 15 students received support. Institutionally sponsored loans and scholarships/grants available. Financial award application deadline: 4/1; financial award applicants required to submit FAFSA. *Unit head:* Dr. Chell Roberts, Dean, 619-260-4627, E-mail: croberts@sandiego.edu. *Application contact:* Erika Garwood, Associate Director of Graduate Admissions, 619-260-4524, Fax: 619-260-4158, E-mail: grads@sandiego.edu.
Website: http://www.sandiego.edu/engineering/

University of Southern California, Graduate School, Viterbi School of Engineering, Department of Computer Science, Los Angeles, CA 90089. Offers computer networks (MS); computer science (MS, PhD); computer security (MS); game development (MS); high performance computing and simulations (MS); human language technology (MS); intelligent robotics (MS); multimedia and creative technologies (MS); software engineering (MS). *Program availability:* Part-time, evening/weekend, online learning. *Entrance requirements:* For master's and doctorate, GRE General Test. Additional exam requirements/recommendations for international students: Required—TOEFL. Electronic applications accepted. *Faculty research:* Databases, computer graphics and computer vision, software engineering, networks and security, robotics, multimedia and virtual reality.

University of South Florida, College of Arts and Sciences, School of Information, Tampa, FL 33620-9951. Offers intelligence studies (MS), including cyber intelligence, strategic intelligence; library and information science (MA). *Accreditation:* ALA (one or more programs are accredited). *Program availability:* Part-time, evening/weekend, online learning. *Faculty:* 15 full-time (7 women). *Students:* 108 full-time (77 women), 182 part-time (137 women); includes 83 minority (23 Black or African American, non-Hispanic/Latino; 7 Asian, non-Hispanic/Latino; 49 Hispanic/Latino; 4 Two or more races, non-Hispanic/Latino). Average age 32. 141 applicants, 86% accepted, 71 enrolled. In 2018, 128 master's awarded. *Degree requirements:* For master's, comprehensive exam, thesis (for some programs). *Entrance requirements:* For master's, GRE not required for Intelligence Studies; GRE required for Library and Information Science with preferred minimum scores of 734d percentile (156v), 10th percentile (141Q). May be waived under certain criteria, goals statement, resume or CV, some programs need understanding of programming/coding, computational problem solving and operating systems (for Intelligence Studies); GRE, writing sample, 3 letters of recommendation, resume, statement of purpose (for Library and Information Science). Additional exam requirements/recommendations for international students: Required—TOEFL, TOEFL (minimum score 550 paper-based; 79 iBT) or IELTS (minimum score 6.5). *Application deadline:* For fall admission, 6/1 priority date for domestic students, 5/1 for international students; for spring admission, 10/15 priority date for domestic students, 9/15 for international students. Applications are processed on a rolling basis. Application fee: $30. Electronic applications accepted. *Expenses:* Tuition, state resident: full-time $6350. Tuition, nonresident: full-time $19,048. *International tuition:* $19,048 full-time. *Required fees:* $2079. *Financial support:* In 2018–19, 62 students received support. Unspecified assistantships available. Financial award application deadline: 6/30. *Faculty research:* Youth services in libraries, community engagement and libraries, information architecture, biomedical informatics, health informatics. *Total annual research expenditures:* $21,733. *Unit head:* Dr. Jim Andrews, Director and Associate Professor, 813-974-2108, Fax: 813-974-6840, E-mail: jimandrews@usf.edu. *Application contact:* Dr. Randy Borum, Graduate Program Director, 813-974-3520, Fax: 813-974-6840, E-mail: wborum@usf.edu.
Website: http://si.usf.edu/

University of South Florida, College of Behavioral and Community Sciences, Department of Criminology, Tampa, FL 33620-9951. Offers criminal justice administration (MA); criminology (MA, PhD); cybercrime (MS). *Faculty:* 13 full-time (5 women). *Students:* 47 full-time (23 women), 56 part-time (32 women); includes 34 minority (12 Black or African American, non-Hispanic/Latino; 1 Asian, non-Hispanic/Latino; 18 Hispanic/Latino; 3 Two or more races, non-Hispanic/Latino), 3 international. Average age 31. 135 applicants, 62% accepted, 59 enrolled. In 2018, 22 master's, 3 doctorates awarded. *Degree requirements:* For master's, comprehensive exam, thesis (for some programs); for doctorate, comprehensive exam, thesis/dissertation. *Entrance requirements:* For master's, GRE (for Criminology), preferred minimum scores of 153V (61st percentile), 144Q (17th percentile) or higher, 2 letters of recommendation; statement of purpose; writing sample (Criminology and Cybercrime); for doctorate, GRE (preferred minimum score of 153 Verbal (61st percentile), 144 Quantitative (17thh percentile) or higher), masters degree with at least 3.4 GPA; 3 letters of recommendation; statement of purpose; writing sample. Additional exam requirements/ recommendations for international students: Required—TOEFL, TOEFL (minimum score 550 paper-based; 79 iBT) or IELTS (minimum score 6.5). *Application deadline:* For fall admission, 1/15 for domestic and international students; for spring admission, 9/30 for domestic students, 9/15 for international students. Application fee: $30. Electronic applications accepted. *Expenses:* Tuition, state resident: full-time $6350. Tuition, nonresident: full-time $19,048. *International tuition:* $19,048 full-time. *Required fees:* $2079. *Financial support:* In 2018–19, 24 students received support, including 2 research assistantships (averaging $14,172 per year), 15 teaching assistantships with tuition reimbursements available (averaging $11,702 per year). *Faculty research:* Juvenile justice and delinquency, substance use and abuse, macro-level models of criminal behavior, race and social control, violence. *Total annual research expenditures:* $195,549. *Unit head:* Dr. Michael Leiber, Professor and Chair, 813-974-9704, Fax: 813-974-2803, E-mail: mjleiber@usf.edu. *Application contact:* Dr. Rachel Powers, Associate Professor and Graduate Director, 813-974-9531, E-mail: powersr@usf.edu.
Website: http://criminology.cbcs.usf.edu/

University of South Florida, College of Graduate Studies, Tampa, FL 33620-9951. Offers cybersecurity (MS), including computer security fundamentals, cyber intelligence, digital forensics, information assurance. *Program availability:* Part-time, evening/weekend,

online learning. *Faculty:* 1 (woman) full-time. *Students:* 69 full-time (19 women), 157 part-time (41 women); includes 103 minority (22 Black or African American, non-Hispanic/Latino; 1 American Indian or Alaska Native, non-Hispanic/Latino; 18 Asian, non-Hispanic/Latino; 55 Hispanic/Latino; 7 Two or more races, non-Hispanic/Latino), 2 international. Average age 35. 135 applicants, 67% accepted, 64 enrolled. In 2018, 124 master's awarded. Terminal master's awarded for partial completion of doctoral program. *Degree requirements:* For master's, variable foreign language requirement, comprehensive exam, thesis (for some programs), practicum. *Entrance requirements:* For master's, GRE General Test, 250-500 word essay in which student describes academic and professional background, reasons for pursuing degree, and professional goals pertaining to cybersecurity; 2 letters of recommendation; current resume or CV. Video or phone interview may be required. Additional exam requirements/recommendations for international students: Required—TOEFL, TOEFL (minimum score 550 paper-based; 79 iBT) or IELTS (minimum score 6.5). *Application deadline:* For fall admission, 2/15 for domestic and international students; for spring admission, 10/15 for domestic students, 9/15 for international students; for summer admission, 2/15 for domestic and international students. Application fee: $30. Electronic applications accepted. *Expenses:* Tuition, state resident: full-time $6350. Tuition, nonresident: full-time $19,048. *International tuition:* $19,048 full-time. *Required fees:* $2079. *Financial support:* In 2018–19, 20 students received support. Teaching assistantships available. Financial award application deadline: 2/1; financial award applicants required to submit FAFSA. *Faculty research:* Integrated neuroscience, diabetes, sustainability of populations/environment, drug design and delivery, marine science. *Total annual research expenditures:* $790,232. *Unit head:* Dr. Dwayne Smith, Senior Vice Provost and Dean of the Office of Graduate Studies, 813-974-7359, Fax: 813-974-5762, E-mail: mdsmith8@usf.edu. *Application contact:* Paul Crawford, Associate Director for Graduate Admissions, 813-974-8800, E-mail: pjcrawford@usf.edu.
Website: https://www.usf.edu/graduate-studies/

The University of Tampa, Sykes College of Business, Tampa, FL 33606-1490. Offers accounting (MS); business analytics (MBA); cybersecurity (MBA, MS); entrepreneurship (MBA, MS); finance (MBA, MS); information systems management (MBA); innovation management (MBA); international business (MBA); marketing (MBA, MS); nonprofit management (MBA, Certificate). *Accreditation:* AACSB. *Program availability:* Part-time, evening/weekend. *Faculty:* 61 full-time (13 women), 11 part-time/adjunct (3 women). *Students:* 361 full-time (153 women), 122 part-time (52 women); includes 101 minority (31 Black or African American, non-Hispanic/Latino; 5 Asian, non-Hispanic/Latino; 57 Hispanic/Latino; 1 Native Hawaiian or other Pacific Islander, non-Hispanic/Latino; 7 Two or more races, non-Hispanic/Latino), 144 international. Average age 29. 1,079 applicants, 57% accepted, 263 enrolled. In 2018, 281 master's, 12 other advanced degrees awarded. *Degree requirements:* For master's, capstone. *Entrance requirements:* For master's, GMAT or GRE, official transcripts from all colleges and/or universities previously attended, resume, personal statement, letters of recommendation. Additional exam requirements/recommendations for international students: Required—TOEFL (minimum score 577 paper-based; 90 iBT), IELTS (minimum score 7.5). *Application deadline:* Applications are processed on a rolling basis. Application fee: $40. Electronic applications accepted. *Expenses:* Contact institution. *Financial support:* In 2018–19, 123 students received support. Career-related internships or fieldwork, scholarships/grants, and unspecified assistantships available. Financial award applicants required to submit FAFSA. *Faculty research:* Job market signaling, on-line shopping behaviors and social media, the Tampa Bay economy, digital literacy, entrepreneurship in small businesses. *Unit head:* Dr. Natasha F. Veltri, Associate Dean, 813-253-6289, E-mail: nveltri@ut.edu. *Application contact:* Ashley Russell, Staff Assistant, Admissions for Graduate and Continuing Studies, 813-253-6249, E-mail: arussell@ut.edu.
Website: http://www.ut.edu/business/

The University of Texas at Austin, Graduate School, School of Information, Austin, TX 78712-1111. Offers identity management and security (MSIMS); information (PhD); information studies (MSIS); MSIS/MA. MSIMS program offered in conjunction with the Center for Identity. *Accreditation:* ALA (one or more programs are accredited). *Program availability:* Part-time. *Degree requirements:* For doctorate, 2 foreign languages, thesis/dissertation. *Entrance requirements:* For master's and doctorate, GRE General Test. Electronic applications accepted. *Faculty research:* Information retrieval and artificial intelligence, library history and administration, classification and cataloguing.

The University of Texas at El Paso, Graduate School, College of Engineering, Department of Computer Science, El Paso, TX 79968-0001. Offers computer science (MS, PhD); cyber security (Graduate Certificate); information technology (MSIT); software engineering (MS). *Program availability:* Part-time, evening/weekend. *Degree requirements:* For master's, thesis optional; for doctorate, thesis/dissertation. *Entrance requirements:* For master's, GRE, minimum GPA of 3.0; for doctorate, GRE, statement of purpose, letters of reference. Additional exam requirements/recommendations for international students: Required—TOEFL; Recommended—IELTS. Electronic applications accepted.

The University of Texas at San Antonio, College of Business, Department of Information Systems and Cyber Security, San Antonio, TX 78249-0617. Offers cyber security (MSIT); information technology (MS, PhD); management of technology (MBA); technology entrepreneurship and management (Certificate). *Program availability:* Part-time, evening/weekend. *Degree requirements:* For master's, comprehensive exam (for some programs), thesis optional; for doctorate, comprehensive exam, thesis/dissertation. *Entrance requirements:* For master's and doctorate, GMAT/GRE, official transcripts, statement of purpose, letters of recommendation. Additional exam requirements/recommendations for international students: Required—TOEFL (minimum score 550 paper-based; 79 iBT), IELTS (minimum score 6.5). Electronic applications accepted. *Expenses:* Contact institution. *Faculty research:* Cyber security, digital forensics, economics of information systems, information systems privacy, information technology adoption.

The University of Texas at Tyler, Soules College of Business, Department of Management and Marketing, Tyler, TX 75799-0001. Offers cyber security (MBA); engineering management (MBA); general management (MBA); healthcare management (MBA); internal assurance and consulting (MBA); marketing (MBA); oil, gas and energy (MBA); organizational development (MBA); quality management (MBA). *Accreditation:* AACSB. *Program availability:* Part-time, online learning. *Students:* Average age 29. 73 applicants, 96% accepted, 35 enrolled. In 2018, 37 master's awarded. *Entrance requirements:* Additional exam requirements/recommendations for international students: Required—TOEFL (minimum score 550 paper-based). *Application deadline:* For fall admission, 8/17 priority date for domestic students, 7/1 priority date for international students; for spring admission, 12/21 priority date for domestic students, 11/1 priority date for international students. Application fee: $25 ($50 for international students). *Faculty research:* General business, inventory control, institutional markets, service marketing, product distribution, accounting fraud, financial reporting and recognition. *Unit head:* Dr. Krist Swimberghe, Chair, 903-565-5803, E-mail: kswimberghe@uttyler.edu. *Application contact:* Dr. Krist Swimberghe, Chair, 903-565-5803, E-mail: kswimberghe@uttyler.edu.
Website: https://www.uttyler.edu/cbt/manamark/

The University of Tulsa, Graduate School, College of Engineering and Natural Sciences, Tandy School of Computer Science, Tulsa, OK 74104-3189. Offers computer science (MS, PhD); cyber security (MS); JD/MS; MBA/MS. *Program availability:* Part-time. *Faculty:* 16 full-time (3 women), 1 part-time/adjunct (0 women). *Students:* 43 full-time (9 women), 20 part-time (6 women); includes 8 minority (2 Black or African American, non-Hispanic/Latino; 1 American Indian or Alaska Native, non-Hispanic/Latino; 2 Asian, non-Hispanic/Latino; 1 Hispanic/Latino; 2 Two or more races, non-Hispanic/Latino), 18 international. Average age 27. 55 applicants, 87% accepted, 20 enrolled. In 2018, 26 master's, 1 doctorate awarded. Terminal master's awarded for partial completion of doctoral program. *Degree requirements:* For master's, thesis (for some programs); for doctorate, comprehensive exam, thesis/dissertation. *Entrance requirements:* For master's and doctorate, GRE General Test. Additional exam requirements/recommendations for international students: Required—TOEFL (minimum score 550 paper-based; 80 iBT), IELTS (minimum score 6). *Application deadline:* Applications are processed on a rolling basis. Application fee: $55. Electronic applications accepted. *Expenses: Tuition:* Full-time $22,230; part-time $1235 per credit hour. *Required fees:* $2100; $6 per credit hour. One-time fee: $400 full-time. Tuition and fees vary according to course level, course load and program. *Financial support:* In 2018–19, 28 students received support, including 4 fellowships with full tuition reimbursements available (averaging $6,178 per year), 24 research assistantships with full tuition reimbursements available (averaging $18,847 per year), 4 teaching assistantships with full tuition reimbursements available (averaging $12,097 per year); career-related internships or fieldwork, Federal Work-Study, scholarships/grants, health care benefits, tuition waivers (full and partial), and unspecified assistantships also available. Support available to part-time students. Financial award application deadline: 2/1; financial award applicants required to submit FAFSA. *Faculty research:* Robotics, human-computer interaction, systems security, information assurance, machine learning, intelligent systems, software engineering, distributed systems, evolutionary computation, computational biology, bioinformatics. *Unit head:* Dr. John Hale, Chairperson, 918-631-3143, E-mail: john-hale@utulsa.edu. *Application contact:* Dr. Mauricio Papa, Advisor, 918-631-2987, Fax: 918-631-3077, E-mail: mauricio-papa@utulsa.edu.
Website: http://engineering.utulsa.edu/academics/computer-science/

University of Utah, Graduate School, David Eccles School of Business, Master of Science in Information Systems Program, Salt Lake City, UT 84112-8939. Offers information systems (MS, Graduate Certificate), including business intelligence and analytics, IT security, product and process management, software and systems architecture. *Program availability:* Part-time, evening/weekend, 100% online, blended/hybrid learning. *Degree requirements:* For master's, capstone project. *Entrance requirements:* For master's, GMAT/GRE, minimum undergraduate GPA of 3.0, 2 letters of recommendation, personal statement, professional resume. Additional exam requirements/recommendations for international students: Required—TOEFL (minimum score 550 paper-based; 80 iBT), IELTS (minimum score 6.5). Electronic applications accepted. *Expenses:* Contact institution. *Faculty research:* Business intelligence and analytics, software and system architecture, product and process management, IT security, Web and data mining, applications and management of IT in healthcare.

University of Washington, Graduate School, Information School, Seattle, WA 98195. Offers information management (MSIM), including business intelligence, data science, information architecture, information consulting, information security, user experience; information science (PhD); library and information science (MLIS). *Accreditation:* ALA (one or more programs are accredited). *Program availability:* Part-time, evening/weekend, 100% online coursework with required attendance at on-campus orientation at start of program. *Faculty:* 51 full-time (23 women), 38 part-time/adjunct (21 women). *Students:* 347 full-time (229 women), 259 part-time (195 women); includes 129 minority (23 Black or African American, non-Hispanic/Latino; 7 American Indian or Alaska Native, non-Hispanic/Latino; 59 Asian, non-Hispanic/Latino; 36 Hispanic/Latino; 4 Native Hawaiian or other Pacific Islander, non-Hispanic/Latino), 160 international. Average age 32. 1,190 applicants, 42% accepted, 264 enrolled. In 2018, 231 master's, 10 doctorates awarded. Terminal master's awarded for partial completion of doctoral program. *Degree requirements:* For master's, comprehensive exam (for some programs), thesis or alternative, capstone or culminating project; for doctorate, comprehensive exam, thesis/dissertation. *Entrance requirements:* For master's, GRE General Test, GMAT; for doctorate, GRE General Test. Additional exam requirements/recommendations for international students: Required—TOEFL (minimum score 590 paper-based; 100 iBT). *Application deadline:* For fall admission, 12/1 priority date for domestic and international students. Application fee: $85. Electronic applications accepted. *Expenses:* MLIS: $825/credit $51,975 approximate tuition without fees; MSIM: $837/credit, $54,405 approximate tuition without fees. *Financial support:* In 2018–19, 73 students received support. Fellowships with full tuition reimbursements available, research assistantships with full tuition reimbursements available, teaching assistantships with full tuition reimbursements available, Federal Work-Study, institutionally sponsored loans, scholarships/grants, health care benefits, tuition waivers (full and partial), and unspecified assistantships available. Support available to part-time students. Financial award application deadline: 10/1; financial award applicants required to submit FAFSA. *Unit head:* Dr. Anind Dey, Dean, E-mail: anind@uw.edu. *Application contact:* Kari Brothers, Admissions Counselor, 206-616-5541, Fax: 206-616-3152, E-mail: kari683@uw.edu.
Website: http://ischool.uw.edu/

University of West Florida, Hal Marcus College of Science and Engineering, Department of Computer Science, Pensacola, FL 32514-5750. Offers computer science (MS), including computer science, database systems, software engineering; information technology (MS), including cybersecurity, database management. *Program availability:* Part-time, evening/weekend. *Degree requirements:* For master's, thesis optional. *Entrance requirements:* For master's, GRE, MAT, or GMAT, official transcripts; minimum undergraduate GPA of 3.0; letter of intent; three letters of recommendation. Additional exam requirements/recommendations for international students: Required—TOEFL (minimum score 550 paper-based).

University of Wisconsin–Madison, Graduate School, Wisconsin School of Business, Wisconsin Full-Time MBA Program, Madison, WI 53706-1380. Offers applied security analysis (MBA); arts administration (MBA); brand and product management (MBA); corporate finance and investment banking (MBA); marketing research (MBA); operations and technology management (MBA); real estate (MBA); risk management and insurance (MBA); strategic human resource management (MBA); supply chain management (MBA). *Faculty:* 137 full-time (36 women), 39 part-time/adjunct (11 women). *Students:* 183 full-time (59 women); includes 31 minority (5 Black or African American, non-Hispanic/Latino; 1 American Indian or Alaska Native, non-Hispanic/Latino; 6 Asian, non-Hispanic/Latino; 13 Hispanic/Latino; 6 Two or more races, non-Hispanic/Latino), 40 international. Average age 28. 465 applicants, 33% accepted, 79 enrolled. In 2018, 104 master's awarded. *Entrance requirements:* For master's, GMAT or GRE, bachelor's or equivalent degree, essay, letter of recommendation, resume. Additional exam requirements/recommendations for international students: Required—TOEFL (minimum score 100 iBT), IELTS (minimum score 7.5), TOEFL is not required for international students whose undergraduate training was in English. *Application deadline:* For fall admission, 11/1 for domestic and international students; for winter

admission, 1/10 for domestic and international students; for spring admission, 3/1 for domestic and international students; for summer admission, 4/10 for domestic students, 4/10 priority date for international students. Applications are processed on a rolling basis. Application fee: $75 ($81 for international students). Electronic applications accepted. *Expenses:* Wisconsin Resident tuition and fees - $39,156; Nonresident tuition and fees - $76,635. *Financial support:* In 2018–19, 148 students received support, including 7 fellowships with full tuition reimbursements available (averaging $25,871 per year), 7 research assistantships with full tuition reimbursements available (averaging $14,832 per year), 47 teaching assistantships with full tuition reimbursements available (averaging $14,832 per year); scholarships/grants, health care benefits, tuition waivers (full and partial), and unspecified assistantships also available. Financial award application deadline: 6/1. *Faculty research:* Ecology, environmental studies, and business; decision making; tax policy; diversity and inclusion in governance boards; marketing and social media. *Unit head:* Dr. Enno Siemsen, Associate Dean of the MBA and Masters Programs, 608-890-3130, E-mail: esiemsen@wisc.edu. *Application contact:* Betsy Kacizak, Director of Admissions and Recruiting, Full-time MBA Program, 608-262-4000, E-mail: betsy.kacizak@wisc.edu.
Website: https://wsb.wisc.edu/

Utah Valley University, Program in Cybersecurity, Orem, UT 84058-5999. Offers Graduate Certificate. *Entrance requirements:* For degree, bachelor's degree; 2 years of IT or IT security industry experience; undergraduate courses in data communication, programming, and servers. *Expenses: Tuition, area resident:* Full-time $7932. Tuition, state resident: full-time $7932. Tuition, nonresident: full-time $19,781. *International tuition:* $19,781 full-time. *Required fees:* $700. Tuition and fees vary according to course load and program.

Utica College, Program in Cybersecurity, Utica, NY 13502-4892. Offers MPS, MS. *Program availability:* Part-time, evening/weekend, 100% online. *Faculty:* 5 full-time (0 women), 8 part-time/adjunct (0 women). *Students:* 280 full-time (75 women), 88 part-time (32 women); includes 97 minority (52 Black or African American, non-Hispanic/Latino; 1 American Indian or Alaska Native, non-Hispanic/Latino; 15 Asian, non-Hispanic/Latino; 23 Hispanic/Latino; 6 Two or more races, non-Hispanic/Latino). Average age 34. 232 applicants, 78% accepted, 148 enrolled. In 2018, 155 master's awarded. *Entrance requirements:* For master's, BS, minimum GPA of 3.0. Additional exam requirements/recommendations for international students: Recommended—TOEFL (minimum score 525 paper-based). *Application deadline:* Applications are processed on a rolling basis. Electronic applications accepted. *Expenses:* Contact institution. *Financial support:* Application deadline: 3/15; applicants required to submit FAFSA. *Faculty research:* Steganography and data hiding, cryptography. *Unit head:* Joseph Giordano, Chair, 315-792-2521. *Application contact:* John D. Rowe, Director of Graduate Admissions, 315-792-3824, Fax: 315-792-3003, E-mail: jrowe@utica.edu.
Website: http://programs.online.utica.edu/programs/masters-cybersecurity.asp

Valparaiso University, Graduate School and Continuing Education, Program in Cyber Security, Valparaiso, IN 46383. Offers MS. *Program availability:* Part-time, evening/weekend, online learning. *Degree requirements:* For master's, internship or research project. *Entrance requirements:* Additional exam requirements/recommendations for international students: Required—TOEFL (minimum score 550 paper-based; 80 iBT), IELTS (minimum score 6). Electronic applications accepted.

Vanderbilt University, School of Engineering, Program in Cyber-Physical Systems, Nashville, TN 37240-1001. Offers M Eng. *Entrance requirements:* For master's, resume or curriculum vitae, three letters of recommendation, statement of purpose. Electronic applications accepted. *Expenses: Tuition:* Full-time $47,208; part-time $2026 per credit hour. *Required fees:* $478.

Virginia International University, School of Computer Information Systems, Fairfax, VA 22030. Offers business intelligence (Graduate Certificate); business intelligence and data analytics (MIS); computer science (MS), including computer animation and gaming, cybersecurity, data management networking, intelligent systems, software applications development, software engineering; cybersecurity (MIS); data management (MIS); enterprise project management (MIS); health informatics (MIS); information assurance (MIS); information systems (Graduate Certificate); information systems management (MS, Graduate Certificate); information technology (MS); information technology audit and compliance (Graduate Certificate); knowledge management (MIS); software engineering (MS). *Program availability:* Part-time, online learning. *Entrance requirements:* For master's, bachelor's degree. Additional exam requirements/recommendations for international students: Required—TOEFL (minimum score 550 paper-based; 80 iBT), IELTS. Electronic applications accepted.

Virginia Polytechnic Institute and State University, VT Online, Blacksburg, VA 24061. Offers advanced transportation systems (Certificate); aerospace engineering (MS); agricultural and life sciences (MSLFS); business information systems (Graduate Certificate); career and technical education (MS); civil engineering (MS); computer engineering (M Eng, MS); decision support systems (Graduate Certificate); eLearning leadership (MA); electrical engineering (M Eng, MS); engineering administration (MEA); environmental engineering (Certificate); environmental politics and policy (Graduate Certificate); environmental sciences and engineering (MS); foundations of political analysis (Graduate Certificate); health product risk management (Graduate Certificate); industrial and systems engineering (MS); information policy and society (Graduate Certificate); information security (Graduate Certificate); information technology (MIT); instructional technology (MA); integrative STEM education (MA Ed); liberal arts (Graduate Certificate); life sciences: health product risk management (MS); natural resources (MNR, Graduate Certificate); networking (Graduate Certificate); nonprofit and nongovernmental organization management (Graduate Certificate); ocean engineering (MS); political science (MA); security studies (Graduate Certificate); software development (Graduate Certificate). *Expenses:* Tuition, state resident: full-time $15,510; part-time $739.50 per credit hour. Tuition, nonresident: full-time $29,629; part-time $1490.25 per credit hour. *Required fees:* $2804; $550 per semester. Tuition and fees vary according to course load, campus/location and program. *Application contact:* Graduate Admissions and Academic Progress, 540-231-8636, E-mail: grads@vt.edu.
Website: http://www.vto.vt.edu/

Walden University, Graduate Programs, School of Information Systems and Technology, Minneapolis, MN 55401. Offers information systems (Graduate Certificate); information systems management (MISM); information technology (MS, DIT), including health informatics (MS), information assurance and cyber security (MS), information systems (MS), software engineering (MS). *Program availability:* Part-time, evening/weekend, online only, 100% online. *Degree requirements:* For doctorate, thesis/dissertation (for some programs), residency. *Entrance requirements:* For master's, bachelor's degree or higher; minimum GPA of 2.5; official transcripts; goal statement (for some programs); access to computer and Internet; for doctorate, master's degree or higher; three years of related professional or academic experience (preferred); minimum GPA of 3.0; goal statement and current resume (for select programs); official transcripts; access to computer and Internet; for Graduate Certificate, relevant work experience; access to computer and Internet. Additional exam requirements/recommendations for international students: Required—TOEFL (minimum score 550 paper-based, 79 iBT), IELTS (minimum score 6.5), Michigan English Language Assessment Battery (minimum score 82), or PTE (minimum score 53). Electronic applications accepted.

Walsh College of Accountancy and Business Administration, Graduate Programs, Program in Information Technology, Troy, MI 48083. Offers chief information officer (MSIT); cybersecurity (MSIT); data science (MSIT); global project and program management (MSIT). *Program availability:* Part-time, evening/weekend. *Faculty:* 2 full-time (1 woman), 10 part-time/adjunct (2 women). *Students:* 3 full-time (1 woman), 66 part-time (25 women); includes 22 minority (14 Black or African American, non-Hispanic/Latino; 4 Asian, non-Hispanic/Latino; 1 Hispanic/Latino; 3 Two or more races, non-Hispanic/Latino), 13 international. Average age 36. 23 applicants, 83% accepted, 13 enrolled. In 2018, 22 master's awarded. *Entrance requirements:* For master's, minimum overall cumulative GPA of 2.75 from all colleges previously attended. Additional exam requirements/recommendations for international students: Required—TOEFL (minimum score 550 paper-based, 79-80 internet based), IELTS (6.5), Michigan Test of English Language Proficiency, or MTELP (80). *Application deadline:* Applications are processed on a rolling basis. Application fee: $35. Electronic applications accepted. *Expenses:* $785 per credit hour plus $175 student support fee per semester. International students pay $785 per credit hour plus $175 student support fee and $275 international student fee per semester. *Financial support:* In 2018–19, 3 students received support. Scholarships/grants and Tuition Exchange Program available. Financial award application deadline: 6/30; financial award applicants required to submit FAFSA. *Faculty research:* Business intelligence, data and decision-making, cyber security, project management, mobile technologies. *Unit head:* Dr. David Schippers, Chair, Information Technology and Decision Sciences, 248-823-1635, Fax: 248-689-0920, E-mail: dschippe@walshcollege.edu. *Application contact:* Karen Mahaffy, Executive Director, Admissions and Enrollment Services, 248-823-1600, Fax: 248-823-1611, E-mail: kmahaffy@walshcollege.edu.

Webster University, George Herbert Walker School of Business and Technology, Department of Mathematics and Computer Science, St. Louis, MO 63119-3194. Offers cybersecurity (MS). *Program availability:* Part-time, evening/weekend, online learning. *Entrance requirements:* For master's, 36 hours of graduate course work. Additional exam requirements/recommendations for international students: Required—TOEFL. *Expenses: Tuition:* Full-time $22,500; part-time $750 per credit hour. Tuition and fees vary according to degree level, campus/location and program. *Faculty research:* Databases, computer information systems networks, operating systems, computer architecture.

West Chester University of Pennsylvania, College of the Sciences and Mathematics, Department of Computer Science, West Chester, PA 19383. Offers computer science (MS); computer security (information assurance) (Certificate); information systems (Certificate); Web technology (Certificate). *Program availability:* Part-time, evening/weekend. *Degree requirements:* For master's, thesis optional, 33 credits; for Certificate, 12 credits. *Entrance requirements:* For master's, GRE, two letters of reference; for Certificate, BS. Additional exam requirements/recommendations for international students: Required—TOEFL or IELTS. Electronic applications accepted. *Faculty research:* Security in mobile ad-hoc networks, intrusion detection, security and trust in pervasive computing, cloud computing, wireless sensor networks, cloud computing and data mining.

Western Governors University, College of Information Technology, Salt Lake City, UT 84107. Offers cybersecurity and information assurance (MS); data analytics (MS); information technology management (MS). *Program availability:* Online learning. *Degree requirements:* For master's, capstone project. Application fee is waived when completed online.

West Virginia University, College of Business and Economics, Morgantown, WV 26506. Offers accountancy (M Acc); accounting (PhD); business administration (MBA); business cyber security management (MS); business data analytics (MS); economics (MA, PhD); finance (MS, PhD); forensic and fraud examination (MS); industrial relations (MS); management (PhD); marketing (PhD). *Program availability:* Part-time, online learning. *Students:* 341 full-time (139 women), 44 part-time (13 women); includes 39 minority (10 Black or African American, non-Hispanic/Latino; 12 Asian, non-Hispanic/Latino; 7 Hispanic/Latino; 10 Two or more races, non-Hispanic/Latino), 40 international. In 2018, 208 master's, 20 doctorates awarded. Terminal master's awarded for partial completion of doctoral program. *Degree requirements:* For master's, thesis optional; for doctorate, comprehensive exam, thesis/dissertation. *Entrance requirements:* For doctorate, GRE General Test, minimum GPA of 3.0. Additional exam requirements/recommendations for international students: Required—TOEFL (minimum score 550 paper-based; 92 iBT). *Application deadline:* For fall admission, 10/15 priority date for domestic and international students; for spring admission, 3/1 priority date for domestic and international students. Applications are processed on a rolling basis. Application fee: $60. Electronic applications accepted. *Expenses:* Contact institution. *Financial support:* Fellowships, research assistantships, teaching assistantships, career-related internships or fieldwork, Federal Work-Study, institutionally sponsored loans, scholarships/grants, health care benefits, tuition waivers (full and partial), unspecified assistantships, and administrative assistantships available. Financial award application deadline: 2/1; financial award applicants required to submit FAFSA. *Faculty research:* Regional labor market studies, economic development, market research, economic forecasting, energy analysis. *Unit head:* Dr. Javier Reyes, Dean, 304-293-7800, Fax: 304-293-4056, E-mail: javier.reyes@mail.wvu.edu. *Application contact:* Dr. Virginia F Kleist, Associate Dean for Graduate Programs, 304-293-7939, Fax: 304-293-7188, E-mail: Virginia.Kleist@mail.wvu.edu.
Website: http://www.be.wvu.edu

Wilmington University, College of Technology, New Castle, DE 19720-6491. Offers cybersecurity (MS); information assurance (MS); information systems technologies (MS); management and management information systems (MS); technology project management (MS); Web design (MS). *Program availability:* Part-time, evening/weekend. *Entrance requirements:* Additional exam requirements/recommendations for international students: Required—TOEFL (minimum score 500 paper-based). Electronic applications accepted.

Computer Science

Acadia University, Faculty of Pure and Applied Science, Jodrey School of Computer Science, Wolfville, NS B4P 2R6, Canada. Offers M Sc. *Entrance requirements:* For master's, honors degree in computer science. Additional exam requirements/recommendations for international students: Required—TOEFL (minimum score 580 paper-based; 93 iBT), IELTS (minimum score 6.5). *Faculty research:* Visual and object-oriented programming, concurrency, artificial intelligence, hypertext and multimedia, algorithm analysis, XML.

Air Force Institute of Technology, Graduate School of Engineering and Management, Department of Electrical and Computer Engineering, Dayton, OH 45433-7765. Offers computer engineering (MS, PhD); computer systems/science (MS); electrical engineering (MS, PhD); electro-optics (MS, PhD). *Accreditation:* ABET (one or more programs are accredited). *Program availability:* Part-time. *Degree requirements:* For master's, thesis; for doctorate, thesis/dissertation. *Entrance requirements:* For master's and doctorate, GRE General Test, minimum GPA of 3.0, U.S. citizenship. *Faculty research:* Remote sensing, information survivability, microelectronics, computer networks, artificial intelligence.

Alabama Agricultural and Mechanical University, School of Graduate Studies, College of Engineering, Technology, and Physical Sciences, Department of Electrical Engineering and Computer Science, Huntsville, AL 35811. Offers computer science (MS); material engineering (M Eng), including electrical engineering. *Program availability:* Evening/weekend. *Degree requirements:* For master's, comprehensive exam, thesis optional. *Entrance requirements:* For master's, GRE General Test. Additional exam requirements/recommendations for international students: Required—TOEFL (minimum score 500 paper-based; 61 iBT). Electronic applications accepted. *Faculty research:* Computer-assisted instruction, database management, software engineering, operating systems, neural networks.

Alcorn State University, School of Graduate Studies, School of Arts and Sciences, Department of Mathematics and Computer Science, Lorman, MS 39096-7500. Offers computer and information science (MS).

American Sentinel University, Graduate Programs, Aurora, CO 80014. Offers business administration (MBA); business intelligence (MS); computer science (MSCS); health information management (MS); healthcare (MBA); information systems (MSIS); nursing (MSN). *Program availability:* Part-time, evening/weekend, online learning. *Entrance requirements:* Additional exam requirements/recommendations for international students: Required—TOEFL (minimum score 600 paper-based). Electronic applications accepted.

The American University in Cairo, School of Sciences and Engineering, Cairo, Egypt. Offers biotechnology (MS); chemistry (MS); computer science (MS); computing (M Comp); construction engineering (M Eng, MS); electronics and communications engineering (M Eng); environmental engineering (MS); environmental system design (M Eng); mechanical engineering (M Eng, MS); nanotechnology (MS); physics (MS); robotics, control and smart systems (MS); sciences and engineering (PhD); sustainable development (MS, Graduate Diploma). *Program availability:* Part-time, evening/weekend. *Degree requirements:* For master's, comprehensive exam (for some programs), thesis (for some programs); for doctorate, comprehensive exam (for some programs), thesis/dissertation. *Entrance requirements:* Additional exam requirements/recommendations for international students: Required—TOEFL (minimum score 450 paper-based; 45 iBT), IELTS (minimum score 5). Electronic applications accepted. *Faculty research:* Construction, mechanical, and electronics engineering; physics; computer science; biotechnology; nanotechnology; chemistry; robotics.

American University of Armenia, Graduate Programs, Yerevan, Armenia. Offers business administration (MBA); computer and information science (MS), including business management, design and manufacturing, energy (ME, MS), industrial engineering and systems management; economics (MS); industrial engineering and systems management (ME), including business, computer aided design/manufacturing, energy (ME, MS), information technology; law (LL M); political science and international affairs (MPSIA); public health (MPH); teaching English as a foreign language (MA). *Program availability:* Part-time, evening/weekend. *Degree requirements:* For master's, thesis (for some programs), capstone/project. *Entrance requirements:* For master's, GRE, GMAT, or LSAT. Additional exam requirements/recommendations for international students: Recommended—TOEFL (minimum score 79 iBT), IELTS (minimum score 6.5). *Faculty research:* Microfinance, finance (rural/development, international, corporate), firm life cycle theory, TESOL, language proficiency testing, public policy, administrative law, economic development, cryptography, artificial intelligence, energy efficiency/renewable energy, computer-aided design/manufacturing, health financing, tuberculosis control, mother/child health, preventive ophthalmology, post-earthquake psychopathological investigations, tobacco control, environmental health risk assessments.

American University of Beirut, Graduate Programs, Faculty of Arts and Sciences, Beirut 1107 2020, Lebanon. Offers anthropology (MA); Arab and Middle Eastern history (PhD); Arabic language and literature (MA, PhD); archaeology (MA); art history and curating (MA); biology (MS); cell and molecular biology (PhD); chemistry (MS); clinical psychology (MA); computational sciences (MS); computer science (MS); economics (MA); education (MA), including administration and policy studies, elementary education, mathematics education, psychology school guidance, psychology test and measurements, science education, teaching English as a foreign language; English language (MA); English literature (MA); environmental policy planning (MS); financial economics (MAFE); general psychology (MA); geology (MS); history (MA); Islamic studies (MA); mathematics (MS); media studies (MA); Middle East studies (MA); philosophy (MA); physics (MS); political studies (MA); public administration (MA); public policy and international affairs (MA); sociology (MA); theoretical physics (PhD). *Program availability:* Part-time. *Faculty:* 187 full-time (64 women), 27 part-time/adjunct (15 women). *Students:* 292 full-time (215 women), 216 part-time (148 women). Average age 27. 422 applicants, 64% accepted, 124 enrolled. In 2018, 90 master's, 3 doctorates awarded. *Degree requirements:* For master's, comprehensive exam, thesis (for some programs), project; for doctorate, comprehensive exam, thesis/dissertation (for some programs). *Entrance requirements:* For master's, GRE General Test (for archaeology, clinical psychology, general psychology, economics, financial economics and biology); for doctorate, GRE General Test for all PhD programs, GRE Subject Test for theoretical physics. Additional exam requirements/recommendations for international students: Required—TOEFL (minimum score 583 paper-based; 97 iBT), IELTS (minimum score 7). *Application deadline:* For fall admission, 3/18 for domestic students; for spring admission, 11/5 for domestic students. Application fee: $50. Electronic applications accepted. *Expenses:* MA/MS: Humanities and social sciences=$912/credit. Sciences=$943/credit. Financial economics=$986/credit. Thesis: Humanities/social sciences=$6565 and sciences=$6865. *Financial support:* In 2018–19, 227 fellowships with full tuition reimbursements, 17 research assistantships with full tuition

reimbursements, 83 teaching assistantships with full tuition reimbursements were awarded; scholarships/grants, tuition waivers (full and partial), and unspecified assistantships also available. Financial award application deadline: 3/18. *Faculty research:* Sciences: Physics: High energy, Particle, Polymer and Soft Matter, Thermal, Plasma; String Theory, Mathematical physics, Astrophysics (stellar evolution, planet and galaxy formation and evolution, astrophysical dynamics), Solid State physics/thin films, Spintronics, Magnetic properties of materials, Mineralogy, Petrology, and Geochemistry of Hard Rocks, Geophysics and Petrophysics, Hydrogeology, Micropaleontology, Sedimentology, and Stratigraphy, Structural Geology and Geotectonics, Renewable en. *Total annual research expenditures:* $4.3 million. *Unit head:* Dr. Nadia Maria El Cheikh, Dean, Faculty of Arts and Sciences, 961-1-350000 Ext. 3800, Fax: 961-1-744461, E-mail: nmcheikh@aub.edu.lb. *Application contact:* Adriana Michelle Zanaty, Curriculum and Graduate Studies Officer, 961-1-350000 Ext. 3833, Fax: 961-1-744461, E-mail: az48@aub.edu.lb.
Website: https://www.aub.edu.lb/fas/Pages/default.aspx

Appalachian State University, Cratis D. Williams School of Graduate Studies, Department of Computer Science, Boone, NC 28608. Offers MS. *Program availability:* Part-time. *Degree requirements:* For master's, comprehensive exam, thesis. *Entrance requirements:* For master's, GRE General Test, 3 letters of recommendation. Additional exam requirements/recommendations for international students: Required—TOEFL (minimum score 570 paper-based; 79 iBT), IELTS (minimum score 6.5). Electronic applications accepted. *Expenses: Tuition, area resident:* Full-time $4839; part-time $237 per credit hour. Tuition, state resident: full-time $4839; part-time $237 per credit hour. Tuition, nonresident: full-time $18,271; part-time $895.50 per credit hour. *Faculty research:* Graph theory, compilers, parallel architecture, image processing.

Arizona State University at the Tempe campus, Ira A. Fulton Schools of Engineering, The Polytechnic School, Department of Engineering, Mesa, AZ 85212. Offers simulation, modeling, and applied cognitive science (PhD). *Program availability:* Part-time. *Degree requirements:* For doctorate, comprehensive exam, thesis/dissertation, interactive Program of Study (iPOS) submitted before completing 50 percent of required credit hours. *Entrance requirements:* For doctorate, GRE, master's degree in psychology, engineering, cognitive science, or computer science; 3 letters of recommendation; statement of research interests. Additional exam requirements/recommendations for international students: Required—TOEFL, IELTS, or PTE. Electronic applications accepted. *Faculty research:* Software process and automated workflow, software architecture, dotal technologies, relational database systems, embedded systems.

Arizona State University at the Tempe campus, Ira A. Fulton Schools of Engineering, School of Computing, Informatics, and Decision Systems Engineering, Tempe, AZ 85287-8809. Offers computer engineering (MS, PhD); computer science (MCS, MS, PhD); industrial engineering (MS, PhD); software engineering (MS). *Program availability:* Part-time, evening/weekend, online learning. Terminal master's awarded for partial completion of doctoral program. *Degree requirements:* For master's, comprehensive exam (for some programs), portfolio (MCS); interactive Program of Study (iPOS) submitted before completing 50 percent of required credit hours; for doctorate, comprehensive exam, thesis/dissertation, interactive Program of Study (iPOS) submitted before completing 50 percent of required credit hours. *Entrance requirements:* For master's, GRE, minimum GPA of 3.0 or equivalent in last 2 years of work leading to bachelor's degree; for doctorate, GRE, minimum GPA of 3.0 in last 2 years of work leading to bachelor's degree. Additional exam requirements/recommendations for international students: Required—TOEFL, IELTS, or PTE. Electronic applications accepted. *Expenses:* Contact institution. *Faculty research:* Artificial intelligence, cyberphysical and embedded systems, health informatics, information assurance and security, information management/multimedia/visualization, network science, personalized learning/educational games, production logistics, software and systems engineering, statistical modeling and data mining.

Arkansas State University, Graduate School, College of Sciences and Mathematics, Department of Computer Science, State University, AR 72467. Offers MS. *Program availability:* Part-time. *Degree requirements:* For master's, comprehensive exam, thesis or alternative. *Entrance requirements:* For master's, GRE General Test or MAT, appropriate bachelor's degree, official transcripts, immunization records. Additional exam requirements/recommendations for international students: Required—TOEFL (minimum score 550 paper-based; 79 iBT), IELTS (minimum score 6), PTE (minimum score 56). Electronic applications accepted.

Auburn University, Graduate School, Ginn College of Engineering, Department of Computer Science and Software Engineering, Auburn University, AL 36849. Offers MS, MSWE, PhD. *Program availability:* Part-time. *Degree requirements:* For master's, thesis (for some programs); for doctorate, thesis/dissertation. *Entrance requirements:* For master's and doctorate, GRE General Test, GRE Subject Test. Electronic applications accepted. *Expenses:* Tuition, state resident: full-time $11,282; part-time $535 per credit hour. Tuition, nonresident: full-time $30,542; part-time $1605 per credit hour. *Required fees:* $826 per semester. Tuition and fees vary according to degree level and program. *Faculty research:* Parallelizable, scalable software translations; graphical representations of algorithms, structures, and processes; graph drawing.

Ball State University, Graduate School, College of Sciences and Humanities, Department of Computer Science, Muncie, IN 47306. Offers computer science (MA, MS). *Program availability:* Part-time. *Entrance requirements:* For master's, GRE General Test, minimum baccalaureate GPA of 2.75 or 3.0 in latter half of baccalaureate, goals statement, three letters of recommendation. Additional exam requirements/recommendations for international students: Required—TOEFL (minimum score 550 paper-based; 79 iBT), IELTS (minimum score 6.5). Electronic applications accepted. *Faculty research:* Numerical methods, programmer productivity, graphics.

Baylor University, Graduate School, School of Engineering and Computer Science, Department of Computer Science, Waco, TX 76798. Offers MS, PhD. *Program availability:* Part-time. *Students:* 18 full-time (3 women), 2 part-time (0 women); includes 1 minority (Asian, non-Hispanic/Latino), 14 international. 30 applicants, 27% accepted, 7 enrolled. In 2018, 6 master's awarded. Terminal master's awarded for partial completion of doctoral program. *Degree requirements:* For master's, thesis (for some programs); for doctorate, comprehensive exam, thesis/dissertation. *Entrance requirements:* For master's and doctorate, GRE, course training in computer science equivalent to BS in computer science from Baylor University. Additional exam requirements/recommendations for international students: Required—TOEFL (minimum score 550 paper-based; 90 iBT). *Application deadline:* For fall admission, 2/15 priority date for domestic and international students; for spring admission, 12/1 priority date for domestic students, 11/1 priority date for international students. Applications are processed on a rolling basis. Application fee: $40. Electronic applications accepted. *Financial support:* In 2018–19, 15 students received support, including 5 research assistantships with full

tuition reimbursements available (averaging $15,600 per year), 10 teaching assistantships with full tuition reimbursements available (averaging $15,600 per year); tuition waivers (full) also available. Financial award application deadline: 2/15. *Faculty research:* Bioinformatics, databases, machine learning, software engineering, networking. *Unit head:* Dr. Eunjee Song, Associate Professor and Graduate Program Director, 254-710-1498, E-mail: eunjee_song@baylor.edu. *Application contact:* Dr. Eunjee Song, Associate Professor and Graduate Program Director, 254-710-1498, E-mail: eunjee_song@baylor.edu.
Website: http://www.ecs.baylor.edu/computerscience

Binghamton University, State University of New York, Graduate School, Thomas J. Watson School of Engineering and Applied Science, Department of Computer Science, Binghamton, NY 13902-6000. Offers MS, PhD. *Program availability:* Part-time, online learning. *Degree requirements:* For master's, comprehensive exam (for some programs), thesis or alternative; for doctorate, comprehensive exam, thesis/dissertation. *Entrance requirements:* For master's and doctorate, GRE General Test. Additional exam requirements/recommendations for international students: Required—TOEFL (minimum score 550 paper-based; 80 iBT). Electronic applications accepted. *Expenses:* Contact institution.

Boise State University, College of Engineering, Department of Computer Science, Boise, ID 83725-0399. Offers computer science (MS); computer science teacher endorsement (Graduate Certificate); STEM education (MS), including computer science. *Program availability:* Part-time. *Degree requirements:* For master's, comprehensive exam, thesis. *Entrance requirements:* For master's, GRE General Test, minimum GPA of 3.0. Additional exam requirements/recommendations for international students: Required—TOEFL (minimum score 550 paper-based; 80 iBT), IELTS (minimum score 6). Electronic applications accepted.

Boston University, Graduate School of Arts and Sciences, Department of Computer Science, Boston, MA 02215. Offers computer science (MS, PhD); cyber security (MS); data-centric computing (MS). *Students:* 188 full-time (43 women), 39 part-time (7 women); includes 11 minority (10 Asian, non-Hispanic/Latino; 1 Hispanic/Latino), 185 international. Average age 24. 1,576 applicants, 20% accepted, 95 enrolled. In 2018, 53 master's, 8 doctorates awarded. Terminal master's awarded for partial completion of doctoral program. *Degree requirements:* For master's, thesis optional, project; for doctorate, comprehensive exam, thesis/dissertation. *Entrance requirements:* For master's and doctorate, GRE General Test, 3 letters of recommendation, transcripts, personal statement. Additional exam requirements/recommendations for international students: Required—TOEFL (minimum score 550 paper-based; 84 iBT). *Application deadline:* For fall admission, 12/15 for domestic and international students; for spring admission, 11/1 for domestic and international students. Applications are processed on a rolling basis. Application fee: $95. Electronic applications accepted. *Financial support:* In 2018–19, 95 students received support, including 4 fellowships with full tuition reimbursements available (averaging $22,660 per year), 41 research assistantships with full tuition reimbursements available (averaging $22,660 per year), 37 teaching assistantships with full tuition reimbursements available (averaging $22,660 per year); Federal Work-Study, scholarships/grants, and health care benefits also available. Support available to part-time students. Financial award application deadline: 12/15. *Unit head:* Abraham Matta, Chair, 617-353-8919, Fax: 617-353-6457, E-mail: matta@bu.edu. *Application contact:* Kori MacDonald, Program Coordinator, 617-353-8919, Fax: 617-353-6457, E-mail: korimac@bu.edu.
Website: http://www.bu.edu/cs

Boston University, Metropolitan College, Department of Computer Science, Boston, MA 02215. Offers computer information systems (MS), including computer networks, data analytics, database management and business intelligence, health informatics, IT project management, security, Web application development; computer networks (Certificate); computer science (MS); data analytics (Certificate); digital forensics (Certificate); health informatics (Certificate); information technology project management (Certificate); software development (MS); software engineering in health care systems (Certificate); telecommunications (MS), including security. *Program availability:* Part-time, evening/weekend, online learning. *Faculty:* 16 full-time (3 women), 52 part-time/adjunct (5 women). *Students:* 201 full-time (57 women), 953 part-time (252 women); includes 285 minority (57 Black or African American, non-Hispanic/Latino; 2 American Indian or Alaska Native, non-Hispanic/Latino; 139 Asian, non-Hispanic/Latino; 67 Hispanic/Latino; 1 Native Hawaiian or other Pacific Islander, non-Hispanic/Latino; 19 Two or more races, non-Hispanic/Latino), 333 international. Average age 31. 1,079 applicants, 72% accepted, 297 enrolled. In 2018, 395 master's awarded. *Entrance requirements:* For master's and Certificate, official transcripts from regionally-accredited bachelor's degree program, 3 letters of recommendation, professional resume, personal statement. Additional exam requirements/recommendations for international students: Required—TOEFL (minimum score 84 iBT), IELTS. *Application deadline:* For fall admission, 8/1 priority date for domestic students, 6/1 priority date for international students; for spring admission, 12/1 priority date for domestic students, 11/15 priority date for international students; for summer admission, 4/1 priority date for domestic students, 3/1 priority date for international students. Applications are processed on a rolling basis. Application fee: $85. Electronic applications accepted. *Expenses:* Contact institution. *Financial support:* In 2018–19, 11 research assistantships (averaging $8,400 per year), 23 teaching assistantships (averaging $3,400 per year) were awarded; unspecified assistantships also available. Support available to part-time students. Financial award applicants required to submit FAFSA. *Faculty research:* Artificial intelligence and machine learning, security and forensics, web technologies, software engineering, programming languages, medical informatics, information systems and IT project management. *Unit head:* Dr. Anatoly Temkin, Chair, 617-353-2566, Fax: 617-353-2367, E-mail: csinfo@bu.edu. *Application contact:* Enrollment Services, 617-353-6004, E-mail: met@bu.edu.
Website: http://www.bu.edu/csmet/

Bowie State University, Graduate Programs, Department of Computer Science, Bowie, MD 20715-9465. Offers MS. *Program availability:* Part-time, evening/weekend. *Degree requirements:* For master's, comprehensive exam, thesis optional, research paper. *Entrance requirements:* For master's, minimum undergraduate GPA of 2.5. Electronic applications accepted. *Faculty research:* Holographics, launch vehicle ground truth ephemera.

Bowie State University, Graduate Programs, Program in Computer Science, Bowie, MD 20715-9465. Offers App Sc D. *Program availability:* Part-time, evening/weekend. Electronic applications accepted.

Bowling Green State University, Graduate College, College of Arts and Sciences, Department of Computer Science, Bowling Green, OH 43403. Offers computer science (MS), including operations research, parallel and distributed computing, software engineering. *Program availability:* Part-time. *Degree requirements:* For master's, thesis or alternative. *Entrance requirements:* For master's, GRE General Test. Additional exam requirements/recommendations for international students: Required—TOEFL. Electronic applications accepted. *Faculty research:* Artificial intelligence, real time and concurrent programming languages, behavioral aspects of computing, network protocols.

Bradley University, The Graduate School, College of Liberal Arts and Sciences, Department of Computer Science and Information Systems, Peoria, IL 61625-0002. Offers computer information systems (MS); computer science (MS). *Program availability:* Part-time, evening/weekend. *Faculty:* 10 full-time (2 women), 1 part-time/adjunct. *Students:* 19 full-time (8 women), 4 part-time (1 woman), 20 international. Average age 25. 99 applicants, 91% accepted, 11 enrolled. In 2018, 11 master's awarded. *Degree requirements:* For master's, comprehensive exam, thesis or alternative, programming test. *Entrance requirements:* For master's, GRE. Additional exam requirements/recommendations for international students: Required—TOEFL (minimum score 550 paper-based; 79 iBT), IELTS (minimum score 6.5). *Application deadline:* For fall admission, 5/15 priority date for domestic and international students; for spring admission, 10/15 priority date for domestic and international students. Applications are processed on a rolling basis. Application fee: $40 ($50 for international students). Electronic applications accepted. *Expenses: Tuition:* Part-time $890 per credit. *Required fees:* $50 per unit. *Financial support:* In 2018–19, 24 students received support, including 1 fellowship with full tuition reimbursement available (averaging $8,010 per year), 11 research assistantships with full and partial tuition reimbursements available (averaging $5,947 per year); teaching assistantships, scholarships/grants, tuition waivers (partial), and unspecified assistantships also available. Support available to part-time students. Financial award application deadline: 4/1. *Unit head:* Dr. Steven Dolins, Chair, 309-677-3284, E-mail: sdolins@bradley.edu. *Application contact:* Rachel Webb, Director of On-Campus Graduate Admissions & International Student and Scholar Services, 309-677-2375, E-mail: rkwebb@bradley.edu.
Website: http://www.bradley.edu/academic/departments/csis/

Brandeis University, Graduate School of Arts and Sciences, Department of Computer Science, Waltham, MA 02454-9110. Offers computer science (PhD). *Program availability:* Part-time. *Faculty:* 15 full-time (4 women). *Students:* 94 full-time (24 women), 1 (woman) part-time; includes 5 minority (2 Asian, non-Hispanic/Latino; 2 Hispanic/Latino; 1 Two or more races, non-Hispanic/Latino), 75 international. Average age 26. 495 applicants, 42% accepted, 57 enrolled. In 2018, 34 master's, 7 doctorates awarded. Terminal master's awarded for partial completion of doctoral program. *Degree requirements:* For master's, thesis (for some programs), thesis, capstone project, or internship for computational linguistics programs; for doctorate, thesis/dissertation, thesis proposal. *Entrance requirements:* For master's and doctorate, GRE, transcripts, statement of purpose, resume, letters of recommendation. Additional exam requirements/recommendations for international students: Required—TOEFL, IELTS, PTE. *Application deadline:* For fall admission, 1/15 priority date for domestic students. Applications are processed on a rolling basis. Application fee: $75. Electronic applications accepted. *Financial support:* In 2018–19, 22 fellowships with full tuition reimbursements (averaging $25,800 per year), 16 research assistantships with full tuition reimbursements (averaging $16,125 per year), 23 teaching assistantships with full tuition reimbursements (averaging $6,400 per year) were awarded; scholarships/grants, health care benefits, and tuition waivers (full and partial) also available. Support available to part-time students. *Faculty research:* Databases, programming languages, artificial intelligence, networks, distributed and parallel computing, data compression, human computer interaction and collaborative technology. *Unit head:* Dr. Nianwen Xue, Director of Graduate Studies, 781-736-2728, E-mail: xuen@brandeis.edu. *Application contact:* Anne Gudaitis, Administrator, 781-736-2723, E-mail: compsci@brandeis.edu.
Website: http://www.brandeis.edu/gsas/programs/computer_science.html

Brandeis University, Graduate School of Arts and Sciences, Program in Computational Linguistics, Waltham, MA 02454-9110. Offers MS. *Faculty:* 14 full-time (3 women), 3 part-time/adjunct (1 woman). *Students:* 43 full-time (31 women); includes 6 minority (1 Black or African American, non-Hispanic/Latino; 2 Asian, non-Hispanic/Latino; 1 Hispanic/Latino; 2 Two or more races, non-Hispanic/Latino), 17 international. Average age 25. 69 applicants, 70% accepted, 29 enrolled. In 2018, 15 master's awarded. *Degree requirements:* For master's, thesis or alternative, internship in computational linguistics or thesis. *Entrance requirements:* For master's, GRE, statement of purpose, letters of recommendation, transcripts, resume. Additional exam requirements/recommendations for international students: Required—TOEFL, IELTS, PTE. *Application deadline:* For fall admission, 1/15 priority date for domestic students. Applications are processed on a rolling basis. Application fee: $75. Electronic applications accepted. *Financial support:* In 2018–19, 2 teaching assistantships (averaging $3,200 per year) were awarded; scholarships/grants and tuition waivers (full and partial) also available. Support available to part-time students. *Faculty research:* Computational linguistics, statistical natural language processing, machine learning, computer science, speech recognition, automated text analysis. *Unit head:* Dr. Lotus Goldberg, Director of Graduate Studies, 781-736-3265, E-mail: lmgold@brandeis.edu. *Application contact:* Anne Gudaitis, Administrator, 781-736-2723, E-mail: compsci@brandeis.edu.
Website: http://www.brandeis.edu/gsas/programs/comp_ling.html

Bridgewater State University, College of Graduate Studies, Bartlett College of Science and Mathematics, Department of Computer Science, Bridgewater, MA 02325. Offers MS.

Brigham Young University, Graduate Studies, College of Physical and Mathematical Sciences, Department of Computer Science, Provo, UT 84602-1001. Offers MS, PhD. *Faculty:* 26 full-time (0 women). *Students:* 99 full-time (12 women); includes 19 minority (15 Asian, non-Hispanic/Latino; 4 Hispanic/Latino). Average age 29. 48 applicants, 88% accepted, 29 enrolled. In 2018, 18 master's, 1 doctorate awarded. Terminal master's awarded for partial completion of doctoral program. *Degree requirements:* For master's, thesis (for some programs); for doctorate, comprehensive exam, thesis/dissertation, residency. *Entrance requirements:* For master's, GRE General Test, minimum GPA of 3.25 in last 60 hours; for doctorate, GRE General Test, minimum GPA of 3.5 in last 60 hours, undergraduate degree in computer science. Additional exam requirements/recommendations for international students: Required—TOEFL (minimum score 600 paper-based; 105 iBT). *Application deadline:* For fall admission, 12/15 for domestic and international students; for winter admission, 7/15 for domestic and international students. Application fee: $50. Electronic applications accepted. *Financial support:* In 2018–19, 3 fellowships with full tuition reimbursements (averaging $32,000 per year), 178 research assistantships (averaging $15,000 per year), 27 teaching assistantships (averaging $13,000 per year) were awarded; scholarships/grants and health care benefits also available. Financial award application deadline: 3/1. *Faculty research:* Graphics/animation and computer vision, artificial intelligence and machine learning, computer networks/systems and security, human-computer interaction and software development, data and text analytics. *Total annual research expenditures:* $665,596. *Unit head:* Dr. Kevin Seppi, Chair, 801-422-4619, Fax: 801-422-0169, E-mail: kseppi@cs.byu.edu. *Application contact:* Dr. Michael Jones, Graduate Coordinator, 801-422-2217, Fax: 801-422-0169, E-mail: jones@cs.byu.edu.
Website: https://cs.byu.edu/

Brock University, Faculty of Graduate Studies, Faculty of Mathematics and Science, Program in Computer Science, St. Catharines, ON L2S 3A1, Canada. Offers MSc. *Program availability:* Part-time. *Degree requirements:* For master's, thesis. *Entrance requirements:* For master's, honors degree. Additional exam requirements/recommendations for international students: Required—TOEFL (minimum score 550 paper-based; 80 iBT), IELTS (minimum score 6.5), TWE (minimum score 4).

Computer Science

Brooklyn College of the City University of New York, School of Natural and Behavioral Sciences, Department of Computer and Information Science, Brooklyn, NY 11210-2889. Offers computer science (MA); health informatics (MS); information systems (MS); parallel and distributed computing (Advanced Certificate). *Program availability:* Part-time, evening/weekend. *Degree requirements:* For master's, comprehensive exam, thesis or alternative. *Entrance requirements:* For master's, previous course work in computer science, 2 letters of recommendation. Additional exam requirements/recommendations for international students: Required—TOEFL (minimum score 525 paper-based; 70 iBT). Electronic applications accepted. *Faculty research:* Networks and distributed systems, programming languages, modeling and computer applications, algorithms, artificial intelligence, theoretical computer science.

Brown University, Graduate School, Department of Computer Science, Providence, RI 02912. Offers Sc M, PhD. *Degree requirements:* For master's, thesis or alternative; for doctorate, one foreign language, comprehensive exam, thesis/dissertation. *Entrance requirements:* For master's and doctorate, GRE General Test, GRE Subject Test.

California Institute of Technology, Division of Engineering and Applied Science, Option in Computer Science, Pasadena, CA 91125-0001. Offers MS, PhD. *Degree requirements:* For master's, thesis; for doctorate, thesis/dissertation. Electronic applications accepted. *Faculty research:* VLSI systems, concurrent computation, high-level programming languages, signal and image processing, graphics.

California Polytechnic State University, San Luis Obispo, College of Engineering, Department of Computer Science, San Luis Obispo, CA 93407. Offers MS. *Program availability:* Part-time. *Faculty:* 15 full-time (2 women). *Students:* 27 full-time (7 women), 11 part-time (2 women); includes 10 minority (5 Asian, non-Hispanic/Latino; 3 Hispanic/Latino; 2 Two or more races, non-Hispanic/Latino), 1 international. Average age 25. 141 applicants, 12% accepted, 11 enrolled. In 2018, 35 master's awarded. *Degree requirements:* For master's, thesis. *Entrance requirements:* For master's, GRE. Additional exam requirements/recommendations for international students: Required— TOEFL (minimum score 80 iBT). *Application deadline:* For fall admission, 2/1 for domestic and international students. Applications are processed on a rolling basis. Application fee: $55. Electronic applications accepted. *Expenses: Tuition, area resident:* Full-time $7176; part-time $4164 per year. Tuition, state resident: full-time $10,965. Tuition, nonresident: full-time $10,965. *Required fees:* $6336; $3711. *Financial support:* Fellowships, research assistantships, teaching assistantships, career-related internships or fieldwork, institutionally sponsored loans, scholarships/grants, and unspecified assistantships available. Financial award application deadline: 3/2; financial award applicants required to submit FAFSA. *Faculty research:* Human-computer interaction, artificial intelligence, programming languages, computer graphics, database systems. *Unit head:* Dr. Zoe Wood, Graduate Coordinator, 805-756-5540, E-mail: zwood@calpoly.edu. *Application contact:* Dr. Zoe Wood, Graduate Coordinator, 805-756-5540, E-mail: zwood@calpoly.edu.
Website: http://www.csc.calpoly.edu/programs/ms-csc/

California State Polytechnic University, Pomona, Program in Computer Science, Pomona, CA 91768-2557. Offers computer science (MS). *Program availability:* Part-time, evening/weekend. *Students:* 25 full-time (7 women), 45 part-time (6 women); includes 37 minority (1 Black or African American, non-Hispanic/Latino; 28 Asian, non-Hispanic/Latino; 7 Hispanic/Latino; 1 Two or more races, non-Hispanic/Latino), 22 international. Average age 28. 184 applicants, 38% accepted, 22 enrolled. In 2018, 39 master's awarded. *Degree requirements:* For master's, thesis. *Entrance requirements:* Additional exam requirements/recommendations for international students: Required— TOEFL (minimum score 550 paper-based). *Application deadline:* Applications are processed on a rolling basis. Application fee: $55. Electronic applications accepted. *Expenses:* Contact institution. *Financial support:* Application deadline: 3/2; applicants required to submit FAFSA. *Unit head:* Dr. Gilbert S. Young, Professor/Graduate Coordinator, 909-869-4413, Fax: 909-869-4733, E-mail: gsyoung@cpp.edu. *Application contact:* Dr. Gilbert S. Young, Professor/Graduate Coordinator, 909-869-4413, Fax: 909-869-4733, E-mail: gsyoung@cpp.edu.
Website: http://www.cpp.edu/~sci/computer-science/prospective-graduate-students/

California State University Channel Islands, Extended University and International Programs, MS Computer Science, Camarillo, CA 93012. Offers MS. *Program availability:* Part-time, evening/weekend. *Students:* 45 full-time (12 women); includes 28 minority (23 Asian, non-Hispanic/Latino; 3 Hispanic/Latino; 2 Two or more races, non-Hispanic/Latino). *Degree requirements:* For master's, thesis. *Entrance requirements:* Additional exam requirements/recommendations for international students: Required— TOEFL (minimum score 550 paper-based; 80 iBT), IELTS (minimum score 6). *Application deadline:* For fall admission, 5/1 for domestic and international students; for spring admission, 11/1 for domestic and international students. Application fee: $55. Electronic applications accepted. *Financial support:* Applicants required to submit FAFSA. *Unit head:* Dr. Michael Soltys, Program Director for Computer Science, 805-437-3713, E-mail: michael.soltys@csuci.edu. *Application contact:* Andrew Conley, Graduate Programs Recruiter, 805-437-2652, E-mail: andrew.conley@csuci.edu.
Website: https://ext.csuci.edu/

California State University, Chico, Office of Graduate Studies, College of Engineering, Computer Science, and Construction Management, Department of Computer Science, Chico, CA 95929-0722. Offers MS. *Program availability:* Online learning. *Faculty:* 1 full-time (0 women), 1 part-time/adjunct (0 women). In 2018, 6 master's awarded. *Degree requirements:* For master's, thesis or project and oral defense. *Entrance requirements:* For master's, GRE General Test (waived if graduated from ABET-accredited institution), fall admissions only; 2 letters of recommendation, statement of purpose, departmental letter of recommendation access waiver form. Additional exam requirements/recommendations for international students: Required—TOEFL (minimum score 550 paper-based; 80 iBT), IELTS (minimum score 6.5). *Application deadline:* For fall admission, 4/1 priority date for domestic and international students. Application fee: $55. Electronic applications accepted. *Expenses: Tuition, area resident:* Full-time $4622; part-time $3116 per unit. Tuition, state resident: full-time $4622; part-time $3116 per unit. Tuition, nonresident: full-time $10,634. *Required fees:* $2160; $1620 per year. Tuition and fees vary according to class time and program. *Financial support:* Fellowships, research assistantships, teaching assistantships, career-related internships or fieldwork, Federal Work-Study, scholarships/grants, traineeships, health care benefits, unspecified assistantships, and stipends available. Support available to part-time students. Financial award application deadline: 3/2; financial award applicants required to submit FAFSA. *Unit head:* Dr. Tyson Henry, Chair, 530-898-6442, Fax: 530-898-5995, E-mail: csci@csuchico.edu. *Application contact:* Micah Lehner, Graduate Admissions Coordinator, 530-898-5416, Fax: 530-898-3342, E-mail: mlehner@csuchico.edu.
Website: http://www.csuchico.edu/csci

California State University, Dominguez Hills, College of Natural and Behavioral Sciences, Department of Computer Science, Carson, CA 90747-0001. Offers MS. *Degree requirements:* For master's, comprehensive exam (for some programs), thesis (for some programs). *Entrance requirements:* For master's, GRE (minimum score 900), minimum GPA of 2.75. Additional exam requirements/recommendations for international students: Required—TOEFL (minimum score 550 paper-based). Electronic applications accepted.

California State University, East Bay, Office of Graduate Studies, College of Science, Department of Computer Science, Hayward, CA 94542-3000. Offers computer networks (MS); computer science (MS). *Program availability:* Part-time. *Degree requirements:* For master's, thesis or capstone experience. *Entrance requirements:* For master's, GRE, minimum GPA of 3.0 in field, 2.75 overall; baccalaureate degree in computer science or related field. Additional exam requirements/recommendations for international students: Required—TOEFL (minimum score 550 paper-based). Electronic applications accepted.

California State University, Fresno, Division of Research and Graduate Studies, College of Science and Mathematics, Department of Computer Science, Fresno, CA 93740-8027. Offers MS. *Program availability:* Part-time, evening/weekend. *Degree requirements:* For master's, thesis or alternative. *Entrance requirements:* For master's, GRE General Test, minimum GPA of 2.75. Additional exam requirements/ recommendations for international students: Required—TOEFL. Electronic applications accepted. *Faculty research:* Software design, parallel processing, computer engineering, auto line research.

California State University, Fullerton, Graduate Studies, College of Engineering and Computer Science, Department of Computer Science, Fullerton, CA 92831-3599. Offers computer science (MS); software engineering (MS). *Program availability:* Part-time, online learning. *Degree requirements:* For master's, comprehensive exam, project or thesis. *Entrance requirements:* For master's, GRE General Test, minimum undergraduate GPA of 2.5. *Faculty research:* Software engineering, development of computer networks.

California State University, Long Beach, Graduate Studies, College of Engineering, Department of Computer Engineering and Computer Science, Long Beach, CA 90840. Offers computer engineering (MSCS); computer science (MSCS). *Program availability:* Part-time. *Degree requirements:* For master's, thesis or alternative. *Entrance requirements:* Additional exam requirements/recommendations for international students: Required—TOEFL. *Application deadline:* For fall admission, 3/1 for domestic students. Application fee: $55. Electronic applications accepted. *Expenses: Required fees:* $2628 per term. Tuition and fees vary according to class time, course level, course load, degree level, campus/location and program. *Financial support:* Teaching assistantships, Federal Work-Study, institutionally sponsored loans, scholarships/grants, and unspecified assistantships available. Financial award application deadline: 3/2; financial award applicants required to submit FAFSA. *Faculty research:* Artificial intelligence, software engineering, computer simulation and modeling, user-interface design, networking. *Unit head:* Mehrdad Aliasgari, Chair, 562-985-4285, E-mail: mehrdad.aliasgari@csulb.edu. *Application contact:* Dr. Bo Fu, Graduate Advisor, 562-985-4386, E-mail: bo.fu@csulb.edu.
Website: http://www.csulb.edu/college-of-engineering/computer-engineering-computer-science

California State University, Los Angeles, Graduate Studies, College of Engineering, Computer Science, and Technology, Department of Computer Science, Los Angeles, CA 90032-8530. Offers MS. *Entrance requirements:* Additional exam requirements/ recommendations for international students: Required—TOEFL (minimum score 550 paper-based). Electronic applications accepted.

California State University, Northridge, Graduate Studies, College of Engineering and Computer Science, Department of Computer Science, Northridge, CA 91330. Offers computer science (MS); software engineering (MS). *Program availability:* Part-time, evening/weekend. *Degree requirements:* For master's, thesis. *Entrance requirements:* For master's, GRE General Test, minimum GPA of 2.5. Additional exam requirements/ recommendations for international students: Required—TOEFL. *Faculty research:* Radar data processing.

California State University, Sacramento, College of Engineering and Computer Science, Department of Computer Science, Sacramento, CA 95819. Offers computer science (MS); software engineering (MS). *Program availability:* Part-time, evening/ weekend. *Degree requirements:* For master's, thesis, project or comprehensive exam; writing proficiency exam. *Entrance requirements:* For master's, GRE, minimum GPA of 3.0 in last 60 units attempted. Additional exam requirements/recommendations for international students: Required—TOEFL (minimum score 550 paper-based; 80 iBT); Recommended—IELTS, TSE. Electronic applications accepted. *Expenses:* Contact institution.

California State University, San Bernardino, Graduate Studies, College of Natural Sciences, Program in Computer Science, San Bernardino, CA 92407. Offers MS. *Faculty:* 2 full-time (0 women). *Students:* 8 full-time (0 women), 7 part-time (1 woman); includes 3 minority (1 Asian, non-Hispanic/Latino; 2 Hispanic/Latino), 10 international. Average age 27. 116 applicants, 14% accepted, 6 enrolled. In 2018, 12 master's awarded. *Entrance requirements:* Additional exam requirements/recommendations for international students: Required—TOEFL. *Application deadline:* For fall admission, 7/16 for domestic students; for winter admission, 10/16 for domestic students; for spring admission, 1/22 for domestic students. Application fee: $55. *Unit head:* Dr. Haiyan Qiao, Director, 909-537-5415, Fax: 909-537-7004, E-mail: hqiao@csusb.edu. *Application contact:* Dr. Dorota Huizinga, Dean of Graduate Studies, 909-537-3064, E-mail: dorota.huizinga@csusb.edu.

California State University, San Marcos, College of Science and Mathematics, Program in Computer Science, San Marcos, CA 92096-0001. Offers computer science (MS); cybersecurity (MS). *Program availability:* Part-time. *Entrance requirements:* For master's, GRE General Test, statement of purpose, letters of recommendation. Additional exam requirements/recommendations for international students: Required— TOEFL (minimum score 550 paper-based; 80 iBT). *Application deadline:* For fall admission, 5/30 for domestic students; for spring admission, 8/30 for domestic students, 11/1 for international students. Application fee: $55. *Faculty research:* Networks, multimedia, parallel algorithms, software engineering, artificial intelligence. *Unit head:* Ahmad Hadaegh, Associate Professor, 760-750-8068, E-mail: ahadaegh@csusm.edu. *Application contact:* Dr. Wesley Schultz, Dean of Office of Graduate Studies and Research, 760-750-8045, Fax: 760-750-8045, E-mail: apply@csusm.edu.

Capitol Technology University, Graduate Programs, Laurel, MD 20708-9759. Offers business administration (MBA); computer science (MS); electrical engineering (MS); information and telecommunications systems management (MS); information architecture (MS); network security (MS). *Program availability:* Part-time, evening/ weekend, online learning. *Entrance requirements:* For master's, minimum GPA of 3.0. Electronic applications accepted.

Carleton University, Faculty of Graduate Studies, Faculty of Science, School of Computer Science, Ottawa, ON K1S 5B6, Canada. Offers computer science (MCS, PhD); information and system science (M Sc). MCS and PhD programs offered jointly with University of Ottawa. *Program availability:* Part-time. *Degree requirements:* For master's, thesis optional, project; for doctorate, comprehensive exam, thesis/ dissertation. *Entrance requirements:* For master's, honors degree. Additional exam requirements/recommendations for international students: Required—TOEFL. *Faculty research:* Programming systems, theory of computing, computer applications, computer systems.

Carnegie Mellon University, School of Computer Science, Department of Computer Science, Pittsburgh, PA 15213-3891. Offers algorithms, combinatorics, and optimization (PhD); computer science (MS, PhD); pure and applied logic (PhD). *Degree requirements:* For doctorate, thesis/dissertation. *Entrance requirements:* For doctorate, GRE General Test, GRE Subject Test, BS in computer science or equivalent. Additional exam requirements/recommendations for international students: Required—TOEFL. *Faculty research:* Software systems, theory of computations, artificial intelligence, computer systems, programming languages.

Carnegie Mellon University, School of Computer Science, Language Technologies Institute, Pittsburgh, PA 15213-3891. Offers MLT, MS, PhD. Terminal master's awarded for partial completion of doctoral program. *Degree requirements:* For doctorate, thesis/dissertation. *Entrance requirements:* For master's and doctorate, GRE General Test, GRE Subject Test. Additional exam requirements/recommendations for international students: Required—TOEFL. *Faculty research:* Machine translation, natural language processing, speech and information retrieval, literacy.

Case Western Reserve University, School of Graduate Studies, Case School of Engineering, Department of Computer and Data Sciences, Cleveland, OH 44106. Offers computer engineering (MS, PhD); computing and information sciences (MS, PhD); electrical engineering (MS, PhD); systems and control engineering (MS, PhD). *Program availability:* Part-time, evening/weekend, online only, 100% online. *Faculty:* 31 full-time (2 women). *Students:* 228 full-time (49 women), 17 part-time (3 women); includes 18 minority (13 Asian, non-Hispanic/Latino; 3 Hispanic/Latino; 2 Two or more races, non-Hispanic/Latino), 180 international. In 2018, 29 master's, 16 doctorates awarded. Terminal master's awarded for partial completion of doctoral program. *Degree requirements:* For master's, thesis; for doctorate, thesis/dissertation, qualifying exam, teaching experience. *Entrance requirements:* For master's and doctorate, GRE General Test. Additional exam requirements/recommendations for international students: Required—TOEFL. *Application deadline:* For fall admission, 2/1 for domestic students; for spring admission, 11/1 for domestic students. Applications are processed on a rolling basis. Application fee: $50. *Expenses: Tuition:* Full-time $45,168; part-time $1939 per credit hour. *Required fees:* $36; $18 per semester. $18 per semester. *Financial support:* In 2018–19, 1 fellowship with tuition reimbursement, 72 research assistantships with tuition reimbursements, 10 teaching assistantships were awarded; career-related internships or fieldwork, Federal Work-Study, and institutionally sponsored loans also available. Support available to part-time students. Financial award application deadline: 3/1; financial award applicants required to submit FAFSA. *Faculty research:* Micro-/nano-systems; robotics and haptics; applied artificial intelligence; automation; computer-aided design and testing of digital systems. *Total annual research expenditures:* $5.1 million. *Unit head:* Jing Li, Interim Department Chair, 216-368-0356, E-mail: jxl175@case.edu. *Application contact:* Angela Beca, Student Affairs Specialist, 216-368-2800, Fax: 216-368-2801, E-mail: angela.beca@case.edu.
Website: www.engineering.case.edu/eecs

The Catholic University of America, School of Engineering, Department of Electrical Engineering and Computer Science, Washington, DC 20064. Offers computer science (MSCS, PhD); electrical engineering (MEE, PhD). *Program availability:* Part-time. *Faculty:* 9 full-time (2 women), 13 part-time/adjunct (0 women). *Students:* 18 full-time (10 women), 65 part-time (19 women); includes 12 minority (3 Black or African American, non-Hispanic/Latino; 4 Asian, non-Hispanic/Latino; 3 Hispanic/Latino; 2 Two or more races, non-Hispanic/Latino), 45 international. Average age 32. 40 applicants, 73% accepted, 15 enrolled. In 2018, 10 master's, 6 doctorates awarded. *Degree requirements:* For master's, thesis or alternative; for doctorate, comprehensive exam, thesis/dissertation, oral exams. *Entrance requirements:* For master's and doctorate, statement of purpose, official copies of academic transcripts, three letters of recommendation. Additional exam requirements/recommendations for international students: Required—TOEFL (minimum score 550 paper-based; 80 iBT). *Application deadline:* For fall admission, 7/15 priority date for domestic students, 7/1 for international students; for spring admission, 11/15 priority date for domestic students, 11/1 for international students. Applications are processed on a rolling basis. Application fee: $55. Electronic applications accepted. *Expenses:* Contact institution. *Financial support:* Fellowships, research assistantships, teaching assistantships, Federal Work-Study, scholarships/grants, tuition waivers (full and partial), and unspecified assistantships available. Financial award application deadline: 2/1; financial award applicants required to submit FAFSA. *Faculty research:* Signal and image processing, computer communications, robotics, intelligent controls, bio-electromagnetics. *Unit head:* Dr. Ozlem Kilic, Chair, 202-319-5879, Fax: 202-319-5195, E-mail: regalia@cua.edu. *Application contact:* Dr. Steven Brown, Director of Graduate Admissions, 202-319-5057, Fax: 202-319-6533, E-mail: cua-admissions@cua.edu.
Website: https://engineering.catholic.edu/eecs/index.html

Central Connecticut State University, School of Graduate Studies, School of Engineering, Science and Technology, Department of Computer Science, New Britain, CT 06050-4010. Offers computer information technology (MS). *Program availability:* Part-time, evening/weekend. *Faculty:* 9 full-time (4 women). *Students:* 24 full-time (9 women), 28 part-time (6 women); includes 15 minority (8 Black or African American, non-Hispanic/Latino; 4 Asian, non-Hispanic/Latino; 2 Hispanic/Latino; 1 Two or more races, non-Hispanic/Latino), 9 international. Average age 31. 53 applicants, 72% accepted, 21 enrolled. In 2018, 20 master's awarded. *Degree requirements:* For master's, thesis or alternative, special project. *Entrance requirements:* For master's, minimum undergraduate GPA of 2.7, letters of recommendation, resume. Additional exam requirements/recommendations for international students: Required—TOEFL (minimum score 550 paper-based; 79 iBT); Recommended—IELTS (minimum score 6.5). *Application deadline:* For fall admission, 6/1 for domestic students, 5/1 for international students; for spring admission, 11/1 for domestic and international students. Applications are processed on a rolling basis. Application fee: $50. Electronic applications accepted. *Expenses: Tuition, area resident:* Full-time $7027; part-time $388 per credit. Tuition, state resident: full-time $9750; part-time $388 per credit. Tuition, nonresident: full-time $18,102; part-time $388 per credit. *International tuition:* $18,102 full-time. *Required fees:* $266 per semester. *Financial support:* In 2018–19, 10 students received support. Career-related internships or fieldwork, Federal Work-Study, scholarships/grants, and unspecified assistantships available. Support available to part-time students. Financial award application deadline: 3/1; financial award applicants required to submit FAFSA. *Unit head:* Dr. Stanislav Kurkovsky, Chair, 860-832-2710, E-mail: kurkovsky@ccsu.edu. *Application contact:* Patricia Gardner, Associate Director of Graduate Studies, 860-832-2350, Fax: 860-832-2362.
Website: http://www.ccsu.edu/cs/

Central Connecticut State University, School of Graduate Studies, School of Engineering, Science and Technology, Department of Mathematical Sciences, New Britain, CT 06050-4010. Offers data mining (MS, Certificate); mathematics (MA, MS), including actuarial science (MA), computer science (MA), statistics (MA); mathematics education leadership (Sixth Year Certificate); mathematics for secondary education (Certificate). *Program availability:* Part-time, evening/weekend, 100% online. *Faculty:* 13 full-time (4 women). *Students:* 14 full-time (9 women), 70 part-time (39 women); includes 21 minority (8 Black or African American, non-Hispanic/Latino; 9 Asian, non-Hispanic/Latino; 3 Hispanic/Latino; 1 Two or more races, non-Hispanic/Latino), 2 international.

Average age 33. 57 applicants, 70% accepted, 20 enrolled. In 2018, 20 master's, 3 other advanced degrees awarded. *Degree requirements:* For master's, comprehensive exam, thesis or alternative, special project; for other advanced degree, qualifying exam. *Entrance requirements:* For master's, minimum undergraduate GPA of 2.7; for other advanced degree, minimum undergraduate GPA of 3.0, essay, letters of recommendation. Additional exam requirements/recommendations for international students: Required—TOEFL (minimum score 550 paper-based; 79 iBT); Recommended—IELTS (minimum score 6.5). *Application deadline:* For fall admission, 6/1 for domestic students, 5/1 for international students; for spring admission, 11/1 for domestic and international students. Applications are processed on a rolling basis. Application fee: $50. Electronic applications accepted. *Expenses: Tuition, area resident:* Full-time $7027; part-time $388 per credit. Tuition, state resident: full-time $9750; part-time $388 per credit. Tuition, nonresident: full-time $18,102; part-time $388 per credit. *International tuition:* $18,102 full-time. *Required fees:* $266 per semester. *Financial support:* In 2018–19, 22 students received support. Career-related internships or fieldwork, Federal Work-Study, scholarships/grants, and unspecified assistantships available. Support available to part-time students. Financial award application deadline: 3/1; financial award applicants required to submit FAFSA. *Faculty research:* Statistics, actuarial mathematics, computer systems and engineering, computer programming techniques, operations research. *Unit head:* Dr. Robin Kalder, Chair, 860-832-2835, E-mail: kalderr@ccsu.edu. *Application contact:* Patricia Gardner, Associate Director of Graduate Studies, 860-832-2350, Fax: 860-832-2362.
Website: http://www.ccsu.edu/mathematics/

Central Michigan University, College of Graduate Studies, College of Science and Engineering, Department of Computer Science, Mount Pleasant, MI 48859. Offers MS. *Program availability:* Part-time. *Degree requirements:* For master's, thesis or alternative. *Entrance requirements:* For master's, bachelor's degree from accredited institution with minimum GPA of 3.0 in last two years of study. Electronic applications accepted. *Faculty research:* Artificial intelligence, biocomputing, data mining, software engineering, operating systems, mobile applications.

Chicago State University, School of Graduate and Professional Studies, College of Arts and Sciences, Department of Mathematics and Computer Science, Chicago, IL 60628. Offers computer science (MS); mathematics (MS). *Degree requirements:* For master's, thesis optional, oral exam. *Entrance requirements:* For master's, minimum GPA of 2.75.

Christopher Newport University, Graduate Studies, Department of Physics, Computer Science, and Engineering, Newport News, VA 23606-3072. Offers applied physics and computer science (MS). *Program availability:* Part-time. *Degree requirements:* For master's, comprehensive exam (for some programs), thesis (for some programs). *Entrance requirements:* For master's, GRE General Test, minimum GPA of 3.0. Additional exam requirements/recommendations for international students: Required—TOEFL (minimum score 580 paper-based; 92 iBT), IELTS (minimum score 7). Electronic applications accepted. *Faculty research:* Advanced programming methodologies, experimental nuclear physics, computer architecture, semiconductor nanophysics, laser and optical fiber sensors.

City College of the City University of New York, Graduate School, Grove School of Engineering, Department of Computer Science, New York, NY 10031-9198. Offers computer science (MS, PhD); information systems (MIS). PhD program offered jointly with Graduate School and University Center of the City University of New York. *Degree requirements:* For master's, thesis optional; for doctorate, one foreign language, comprehensive exam, thesis/dissertation. *Entrance requirements:* For master's and doctorate, GRE General Test. Additional exam requirements/recommendations for international students: Required—TOEFL (minimum score 500 paper-based; 61 iBT). *Faculty research:* Complexities of algebraic research, human issues in computer science, scientific computing, super compilers, parallel algorithms.

City University of Seattle, Graduate Division, School of Management, Seattle, WA 98121. Offers accounting (Certificate); change leadership (MBA, Certificate); computer systems (MS); finance (Certificate); financial management (MBA); general management (MBA); general management-Europe (MBA); global marketing (MBA); human resources management (Certificate); individualized study (MBA); information security (MS); information systems (MBA); leadership (MA); marketing (MBA, Certificate); project management (MBA, MS, Certificate); sustainable business (Certificate); technology management (MBA, Certificate). *Program availability:* Part-time, evening/weekend, online learning. *Degree requirements:* For master's, comprehensive exam (for some programs), thesis (for some programs). *Entrance requirements:* For master's, baccalaureate degree or equivalent from an accredited or otherwise recognized institution. Additional exam requirements/recommendations for international students: Required—TOEFL (minimum score 567 paper-based; 87 iBT); Recommended—IELTS. Electronic applications accepted.

Clark Atlanta University, School of Arts and Sciences, Department of Computer and Information Science, Atlanta, GA 30314. Offers MS. *Program availability:* Part-time. *Degree requirements:* For master's, one foreign language, thesis. *Entrance requirements:* For master's, GRE General Test, minimum GPA of 2.5. Additional exam requirements/recommendations for international students: Required—TOEFL (minimum score 500 paper-based; 61 iBT).

Clarkson University, School of Arts and Sciences, Department of Computer Science, Potsdam, NY 13699. Offers MS, PhD. *Faculty:* 7 full-time (2 women). *Students:* 16 full-time (4 women), 5 part-time (0 women); includes 1 minority (Black or African American, non-Hispanic/Latino), 11 international. 34 applicants, 68% accepted, 5 enrolled. In 2018, 2 master's awarded. *Degree requirements:* For master's, thesis; for doctorate, comprehensive exam, thesis/dissertation. *Entrance requirements:* For master's and doctorate, GRE. Additional exam requirements/recommendations for international students: Required—TOEFL (minimum score 550 paper-based, 80 iBT) or IELTS (6.5). *Application deadline:* Applications are processed on a rolling basis. Application fee: $50. Electronic applications accepted. *Expenses: Tuition:* Full-time $24,984; part-time $1388 per credit hour. *Required fees:* $225. Tuition and fees vary according to campus/location and program. *Financial support:* Scholarships/grants and unspecified assistantships available. *Unit head:* Dr. Christopher Lynch, Chair of Computer Science, 315-268-2395, E-mail: clynch@clarkson.edu. *Application contact:* Dan Capogna, Director of Graduate Admissions & Recruitment, 518-631-9910, E-mail: graduate@clarkson.edu.
Website: https://www.clarkson.edu/academics/graduate

Clemson University, Graduate School, College of Engineering, Computing and Applied Sciences, School of Computing, Clemson, SC 29634. Offers computer science (MS, PhD); digital production arts (MFA); human centered computing (PhD). *Faculty:* 34 full-time (8 women), 1 (woman) part-time/adjunct. *Students:* 185 full-time (60 women), 27 part-time (6 women); includes 26 minority (13 Black or African American, non-Hispanic/Latino; 3 Asian, non-Hispanic/Latino; 8 Hispanic/Latino; 2 Two or more races, non-Hispanic/Latino), 124 international. Average age 26. 454 applicants, 53% accepted, 87 enrolled. In 2018, 85 master's, 4 doctorates awarded. Terminal master's awarded for partial completion of doctoral program. *Degree requirements:* For master's, thesis (for some programs); for doctorate, comprehensive exam, thesis/dissertation. *Entrance requirements:* For master's and doctorate, GRE General Test, unofficial transcripts,

letters of recommendation. Additional exam requirements/recommendations for international students: Required—IELTS (minimum score 6.5); Recommended—TOEFL (minimum score 550 paper-based; 80 iBT), TSE (minimum score 54). *Application deadline:* For fall admission, 5/15 priority date for domestic students, 4/15 priority date for international students; for spring admission, 10/15 priority date for domestic students, 9/15 priority date for international students. Applications are processed on a rolling basis. Application fee: $80 ($90 for international students). Electronic applications accepted. *Expenses:* $6823 per semester full-time resident, $14023 per semester full-time non-resident, $833 per credit hour part-time resident, $1731 per credit hour part-time non-resident, online $1264 per credit hour, $4938 doctoral programs resident, $10405 doctoral programs non-resident, $1144 full-time graduate assistant, other fees may apply per session; Biomedical Data Science & Informatics Ph.D.: $8011 full-time resident, $10823 full-time non-resident, $669 per credit hour part-time resident, $995 part-time non-resident; Digital Production Arts MFA: $14080 full-time, $1565 per credit hour part-time; MS: $12784 full-time, $1420 per credit hour part-time. *Financial support:* In 2018–19, 97 students received support, including 7 fellowships with full and partial tuition reimbursements available (averaging $3,214 per year), 47 research assistantships with full and partial tuition reimbursements available (averaging $17,570 per year), 28 teaching assistantships with full and partial tuition reimbursements available (averaging $19,498 per year); career-related internships or fieldwork, traineeships, and unspecified assistantships also available. Financial award application deadline: 1/1. *Faculty research:* Algorithms and data structures, computer graphics, parallel and distributed computing, security and privacy, software engineering. *Total annual research expenditures:* $2.2 million. *Unit head:* Dr. Amy Apon, Director, 864-656-5769, E-mail: aapon@clemson.edu. *Application contact:* Adam Rollins, Student Services Graduate Program Coordinator, 864-656-5853, E-mail: rollin7@clemson.edu.
Website: https://www.clemson.edu/cecas/departments/computing/index.html

Coastal Carolina University, College of Science, Conway, SC 29528-6054. Offers applied computing and information systems (Certificate); coastal marine and wetland studies (MS); information systems technology (MS); marine science (PhD); sports management (MS). *Program availability:* Part-time, evening/weekend, 100% online. *Degree requirements:* For master's, thesis or internship; for doctorate, comprehensive exam, thesis/dissertation. *Entrance requirements:* For master's, GRE, 3 letters of recommendation, resume, official transcripts, written statement of educational and career goals, baccalaureate degree; for doctorate, GRE, official transcripts; baccalaureate or master's degree; minimum GPA of 3.0 for all collegiate coursework; successful completion of at least two semesters of college-level calculus, physics, and chemistry; 3 letters of recommendation; written statement of educational and career goals; resume; for Certificate, 2 letters of reference, official transcripts, minimum GPA of 3.0 in all computing and information systems courses, documentation of graduation from accredited four-year college or university. Additional exam requirements/recommendations for international students: Required—TOEFL (minimum score 550 paper-based; 79 iBT), IELTS (minimum score 6.5). Electronic applications accepted.

College of Charleston, Graduate School, School of Sciences and Mathematics, Program in Computer and Information Sciences, Charleston, SC 29424-0001. Offers MS. Program offered jointly with The Citadel, The Military College of South Carolina. *Program availability:* Part-time, evening/weekend. *Degree requirements:* For master's, thesis optional. *Entrance requirements:* For master's, GRE. Additional exam requirements/recommendations for international students: Required—TOEFL (minimum score 81 iBT). Electronic applications accepted.

The College of Saint Rose, Graduate Studies, School of Mathematics and Sciences, Program in Computer Information Systems, Albany, NY 12203-1419. Offers MS, Advanced Certificate. *Program availability:* Part-time, evening/weekend. *Students:* 14 full-time (6 women), 25 part-time (7 women); includes 5 minority (4 Asian, non-Hispanic/Latino; 1 Hispanic/Latino), 24 international. Average age 31. 74 applicants, 81% accepted, 16 enrolled. In 2018, 35 master's, 4 other advanced degrees awarded. *Degree requirements:* For master's, comprehensive exam, research component, project. *Entrance requirements:* For master's, minimum GPA of 3.0, 9 undergraduate credits in math. Additional exam requirements/recommendations for international students: Required—TOEFL (minimum score 550 paper-based; 80 iBT), IELTS (minimum score 6), PTE (minimum score 56). *Application deadline:* For fall admission, 4/1 priority date for domestic and international students; for spring admission, 10/15 priority date for domestic and international students; for summer admission, 3/15 priority date for domestic and international students. Applications are processed on a rolling basis. Application fee: $40. Electronic applications accepted. *Expenses: Tuition:* Full-time $14,382; part-time $799 per credit hour. *Required fees:* $924; $408 per credit. $286. *Financial support:* Career-related internships or fieldwork, scholarships/grants, tuition waivers (partial), and unspecified assistantships available. Support available to part-time students. Financial award application deadline: 4/15; financial award applicants required to submit FAFSA. *Unit head:* Dr. John Avitabile, Department Chair, 518-458-5317, E-mail: avitabij@strose.edu. *Application contact:* Daniel Gallagher, Assistant Vice President for Graduate Recruitment and Enrollment, 518-485-3390.
Website: https://www.strose.edu/computer-information-systems/

College of Staten Island of the City University of New York, Graduate Programs, Division of Science and Technology, Program in Computer Science, Staten Island, NY 10314-6600. Offers computer science (MS), including artificial intelligence and data analytics, cloud computing and software engineering, cybersecurity and networks. *Program availability:* Part-time, evening/weekend. *Students:* 35. 48 applicants, 48% accepted, 14 enrolled. In 2018, 17 master's awarded. *Degree requirements:* For master's, thesis optional, a program of 10 courses (30 credits) with at least a 3.0 (B) average. Exceptional students may be permitted to satisfy six credits of the total credit requirement with a master's thesis. *Entrance requirements:* For master's, GRE General Test, BS in Computer Science or related area with a B average (3.0 out of 4.0) overall and in the major. Additional exam requirements/recommendations for international students: Required—TOEFL (minimum score 550 paper-based; 79 iBT), IELTS (minimum score 6.5). *Application deadline:* For fall admission, 7/20 priority date for domestic students, 4/25 for international students; for spring admission, 11/2 priority date for domestic students, 11/2 for international students. Applications are processed on a rolling basis. Application fee: $75. Electronic applications accepted. *Expenses: Tuition, area resident:* Full-time $10,770; part-time $455 per credit. Tuition, state resident: full-time $10,770; part-time $455 per credit. Tuition, nonresident: full-time $19,920; part-time $830 per credit. *International tuition:* $19,920 full-time. *Required fees:* $559.20; $181.10 per semester. Tuition and fees vary according to program. *Faculty research:* Big data, pattern recognition, text mining and frequent pattern mining; graph theory; computer vision, image processing pattern recognition and serious game; parallel computing and stimulation; high performance computing and modeling simulation; serious games; security, cryptography and communication networks; scheduling algorithms; scheduling, operations research and graph theory. *Unit head:* Dr. Xiaowen Zhang, Associate Professor, 718-982-3262, E-mail: xiaowen.zhang@csi.cuny.edu. *Application contact:* Sasha Spence, Associate Director for Graduate Admissions, 718-982-2019, Fax: 718-982-2500, E-mail: sasha.spence@csi.cuny.edu.
Website: https://www.csi.cuny.edu/sites/default/files/pdf/admissions/grad/pdf/Computer%20Science%20Fact%20Sheet.pdf

Colorado School of Mines, Office of Graduate Studies, Department of Electrical Engineering and Computer Science, Golden, CO 80401-1887. Offers electrical engineering (MS, PhD). *Program availability:* Part-time. *Students:* 68 full-time (14 women), 25 part-time (2 women); includes 10 minority (1 Black or African American, non-Hispanic/Latino; 3 Asian, non-Hispanic/Latino; 4 Hispanic/Latino; 2 Two or more races, non-Hispanic/Latino), 40 international. Average age 28. 180 applicants, 67% accepted, 38 enrolled. In 2018, 38 master's, 6 doctorates awarded. *Degree requirements:* For master's, thesis (for some programs); for doctorate, comprehensive exam, thesis/dissertation. *Entrance requirements:* For master's and doctorate, GRE General Test. Additional exam requirements/recommendations for international students: Required—TOEFL (minimum score 550 paper-based; 79 iBT). *Application deadline:* For fall admission, 12/15 priority date for domestic and international students; for spring admission, 9/1 priority date for domestic and international students. Application fee: $60 ($80 for international students). Electronic applications accepted. *Expenses:* Tuition, state resident: full-time $16,650; part-time $925 per contact hour. Tuition, nonresident: full-time $36,270; part-time $2015 per contact hour. *International tuition:* $36,270 full-time. *Required fees:* $2314; $2314 per semester. *Financial support:* In 2018–19, 25 research assistantships with full tuition reimbursements, 11 teaching assistantships with full tuition reimbursements were awarded; fellowships, career-related internships or fieldwork, Federal Work-Study, institutionally sponsored loans, scholarships/grants, health care benefits, and unspecified assistantships also available. Financial award application deadline: 12/15; financial award applicants required to submit FAFSA. *Unit head:* Dr. Peter Aaen, Head, 303-384-2245, E-mail: paaen@mines.edu. *Application contact:* Lori Sisneros, Graduate Program Administrator, 303-384-3658, E-mail: sisneros@mines.edu.
Website: http://eecs.mines.edu/

Colorado State University, College of Natural Sciences, Department of Computer Science, Fort Collins, CO 80523-1873. Offers MCS, MS, PhD. *Program availability:* Part-time, 100% online, blended/hybrid learning. Terminal master's awarded for partial completion of doctoral program. *Degree requirements:* For master's, thesis (for some programs); for doctorate, thesis/dissertation. *Entrance requirements:* For master's, minimum GPA of 3.2, BS in computer science; for doctorate, minimum GPA of 3.2, BS/MS in computer science, research experience. Additional exam requirements/recommendations for international students: Required—TOEFL (minimum score 580 paper-based; 92 iBT), IELTS (minimum score 6.5), PTE (minimum score 62), GRE (without degree from U.S. institution). Electronic applications accepted. *Expenses:* Contact institution. *Faculty research:* Artificial intelligence, software engineering, networks and security, big data/cloud computing, computer vision/graphics.

Colorado Technical University Aurora, Program in Computer Science, Aurora, CO 80014. Offers computer systems security (MSCS); database systems (MSCS); software engineering (MSCS). *Program availability:* Part-time, evening/weekend. *Degree requirements:* For master's, thesis or alternative. *Entrance requirements:* For master's, minimum undergraduate GPA of 3.0, resume.

Colorado Technical University Colorado Springs, Graduate Studies, Program in Computer Science, Colorado Springs, CO 80907. Offers computer science (DCS); computer systems security (MSCS); database systems (MSCS); software engineering (MSCS). *Program availability:* Part-time, evening/weekend, online learning. *Degree requirements:* For master's, thesis or alternative; for doctorate, thesis/dissertation. *Entrance requirements:* For doctorate, minimum graduate GPA of 3.0, 5 years of related work experience. *Faculty research:* Software engineering, systems engineering.

Columbia University, Fu Foundation School of Engineering and Applied Science, Department of Computer Science, New York, NY 10027. Offers computer science (MS, Eng Sc D, PhD). PhD offered through the Graduate School of Arts and Sciences. *Program availability:* Part-time, online learning. Terminal master's awarded for partial completion of doctoral program. *Degree requirements:* For master's, thesis optional; for doctorate, comprehensive exam, thesis/dissertation, candidacy exam. *Entrance requirements:* For master's and doctorate, GRE General Test. Additional exam requirements/recommendations for international students: Required—TOEFL, IELTS, PTE. Electronic applications accepted. *Faculty research:* Natural language processing, machine learning, software systems, network systems, computer security, computational biology, foundations of computer science, vision and graphics.

Columbus State University, Graduate Studies, Turner College of Business, Columbus, GA 31907-5645. Offers applied computer science (MS), including informational assurance, modeling and simulation, software development; business administration (MBA); cyber security (MS); human resource management (Certificate); information systems security (Certificate); modeling and simulation (Certificate); organizational leadership (MS), including human resource management, leader development, servant leadership; servant leadership (Certificate). *Accreditation:* AACSB. *Program availability:* Part-time, evening/weekend, 100% online, blended/hybrid learning. *Faculty:* 10 full-time (3 women), 1 part-time/adjunct (0 women). *Students:* 79 full-time (24 women), 136 part-time (47 women); includes 73 minority (40 Black or African American, non-Hispanic/Latino; 1 American Indian or Alaska Native, non-Hispanic/Latino; 8 Asian, non-Hispanic/Latino; 15 Hispanic/Latino; 9 Two or more races, non-Hispanic/Latino), 27 international. Average age 31. 237 applicants, 51% accepted, 64 enrolled. In 2018, 113 master's, 10 other advanced degrees awarded. *Entrance requirements:* For master's, GMAT, GRE, minimum undergraduate GPA of 2.75, letters of recommendation. Additional exam requirements/recommendations for international students: Required—TOEFL (minimum score 550 paper-based; 79 iBT). *Application deadline:* For fall admission, 6/30 for domestic students, 5/1 for international students; for spring admission, 11/1 for domestic and international students; for summer admission, 3/1 for domestic and international students. Applications are processed on a rolling basis. Application fee: $50. Electronic applications accepted. *Expenses:* Contact institution. *Financial support:* In 2018–19, 18 students received support, including 20 research assistantships (averaging $3,000 per year); Federal Work-Study also available. Financial award application deadline: 5/1; financial award applicants required to submit FAFSA. *Unit head:* Dr. Linda U. Hadley, Dean, 706-507-8153, Fax: 706-568-2184, E-mail: hadley_linda@columbusstate.edu. *Application contact:* Catrina Smith-Edmond, Assistant Director for Graduate and Global Admission, 706-507-8824, Fax: 706-568-5091, E-mail: smithedmond_catrina@columbusstate.edu.
Website: http://turner.columbusstate.edu/

Concordia University, School of Graduate Studies, Faculty of Engineering and Computer Science, Department of Computer Science and Software Engineering, Montréal, QC H3G 1M8, Canada. Offers computer science (M App Comp Sc, M Comp Sc, PhD, Diploma); software engineering (M Eng, MA Sc). *Degree requirements:* For master's, one foreign language, thesis optional; for doctorate, one foreign language, comprehensive exam, thesis/dissertation. *Faculty research:* Computer systems and applications, mathematics of computation, pattern recognition, artificial intelligence and robotics.

Concordia University, Nebraska, Program in Computer Science, Seward, NE 68434. Offers cyber operations (MS). *Program availability:* Online learning.

Cornell University, Graduate School, Graduate Fields of Engineering, Field of Computer Science, Ithaca, NY 14853. Offers algorithms (M Eng, PhD); applied logic and automated reasoning (M Eng, PhD); artificial intelligence (M Eng, PhD); computer graphics (M Eng, PhD); computer science (M Eng, PhD); computer vision (M Eng, PhD); concurrency and distributed computing (M Eng, PhD); information organization and retrieval (M Eng, PhD); operating systems (M Eng, PhD); parallel computing (M Eng, PhD); programming environments (M Eng, PhD); programming languages and methodology (M Eng, PhD); robotics (M Eng, PhD); scientific computing (M Eng, PhD); theory of computation (M Eng, PhD). *Degree requirements:* For doctorate, comprehensive exam, thesis/dissertation. *Entrance requirements:* For master's, GRE General Test, 2 letters of recommendation; for doctorate, GRE General Test, GRE Subject Test (computer science or mathematics), 3 letters of recommendation. Additional exam requirements/recommendations for international students: Required—TOEFL (minimum score 505 paper-based; 77 iBT). Electronic applications accepted. *Faculty research:* Artificial intelligence, operating systems and databases, programming languages and security, scientific computing, theory of computing, computational biology and graphics.

Dakota State University, Beacom College of Computer and Cyber Sciences, Madison, SD 57042-1799. Offers applied computer science (MSACS); banking security (Graduate Certificate); cyber security (D Sc); ethical hacking (Graduate Certificate); information assurance and computer security (MSIA). *Program availability:* Part-time, evening/weekend, online learning. *Faculty:* 15 full-time (3 women). *Students:* 30 full-time (6 women), 101 part-time (14 women); includes 27 minority (7 Black or African American, non-Hispanic/Latino; 3 American Indian or Alaska Native, non-Hispanic/Latino; 8 Asian, non-Hispanic/Latino; 5 Hispanic/Latino; 2 Native Hawaiian or other Pacific Islander, non-Hispanic/Latino; 2 Two or more races, non-Hispanic/Latino), 8 international. Average age 35. 188 applicants, 36% accepted, 40 enrolled. In 2018, 38 master's, 4 other advanced degrees awarded. *Entrance requirements:* Additional exam requirements/recommendations for international students: Required—PTE (minimum score 53), TOEFL (minimum score 550 paper-based, 76 iBT) or IELTS (6.5). *Application deadline:* For fall admission, 6/15 for domestic students, 4/15 for international students; for spring admission, 11/15 for domestic students, 9/15 priority date for international students; for summer admission, 4/15 for domestic and international students. Applications are processed on a rolling basis. Application fee: $35. Electronic applications accepted. *Expenses: Tuition, area resident:* Full-time $7666. Tuition, state resident: full-time $7666. Tuition, nonresident: full-time $14,311. *International tuition:* $14,311 full-time. *Required fees:* $953. *Financial support:* In 2018–19, 4 students received support. Research assistantships with partial tuition reimbursements available, teaching assistantships with partial tuition reimbursements available, career-related internships or fieldwork, Federal Work-Study, scholarships/grants, unspecified assistantships, and administrative Assistantships available. Support available to part-time students. Financial award applicants required to submit FAFSA. *Unit head:* Dr. Richard Hanson, Dean, Beacom College of Computer and Cyber Science, 605-256-5838, E-mail: richard.hanson@dsu.edu. *Application contact:* Erin Blankespoor, Senior Secretary, Office of Graduate Studies and Research, 605-256-5799, E-mail: erin.blankespoor@dsu.edu.
Website: https://dsu.edu/academics/colleges/beacom-college-of-computer-and-cyber-sciences

Dalhousie University, Faculty of Computer Science, Halifax, NS B3H 1W5, Canada. Offers computational biology and bioinformatics (M Sc); computer science (MA Sc, MC Sc, PhD); electronic commerce (MEC); health informatics (MHI). *Degree requirements:* For master's, thesis (for some programs); for doctorate, thesis/dissertation. *Entrance requirements:* Additional exam requirements/recommendations for international students: Required—1 of 5 approved tests: TOEFL, IELTS, CANTEST, CAEL, Michigan English Language Assessment Battery. Electronic applications accepted.

Dartmouth College, Guarini School of Graduate and Advanced Studies, Department of Computer Science, Hanover, NH 03755. Offers MS, PhD. *Faculty:* 23 full-time (2 women), 5 part-time/adjunct (2 women). *Students:* 79 full-time (14 women); includes 6 minority (5 Asian, non-Hispanic/Latino; 1 Hispanic/Latino), 53 international. Average age 26. 350 applicants, 24% accepted, 31 enrolled. In 2018, 36 master's, 1 doctorate awarded. Terminal master's awarded for partial completion of doctoral program. *Entrance requirements:* For master's and doctorate, GRE General Test, GRE Subject Test. Additional exam requirements/recommendations for international students: Required—TOEFL. *Application deadline:* For fall admission, 12/15 for domestic students. Application fee: $60. Electronic applications accepted. *Financial support:* Fellowships, research assistantships, teaching assistantships, career-related internships or fieldwork, institutionally sponsored loans, scholarships/grants, and tuition waivers (full and partial) available. Support available to part-time students. Financial award application deadline: 4/1; financial award applicants required to submit CSS PROFILE or FAFSA. *Faculty research:* Algorithms, computational geometry and learning, computer vision, information retrieval, robotics. *Unit head:* Dr. Hany Farid, Chair, 603-646-2761. *Application contact:* Susan J. Perry, Department Administrator, 603-646-1358.
Website: http://www.cs.dartmouth.edu/

DePaul University, College of Computing and Digital Media, Chicago, IL 60604. Offers animation (MA, MFA); applied technology (MS); business information technology (MS); computational finance (MS); computer and information sciences (PhD); computer science (MS); creative producing (MFA); cybersecurity (MS); data science (MS); digital communication and media arts (MA); documentary (MFA); e-commerce technology (MS); experience design (MA); film and television (MS); film and television directing (MFA); game design (MFA); game programming (MS); health informatics (MS); human centered design (PhD); human-computer interaction (MS); information systems (MS); network engineering and security (MS); product innovation and computing (MS); screenwriting (MFA); software engineering (MS); JD/MS. *Program availability:* Part-time, evening/weekend, online learning. *Degree requirements:* For master's, thesis (for some programs); for doctorate, comprehensive exam, thesis/dissertation. *Entrance requirements:* For master's, GRE or GMAT (for MS in computational finance only), bachelor's degree, resume (MS in predictive analytics only), IT experience (MS in information technology project management only), portfolio review (all MFA programs and MA in animation); for doctorate, GRE, master's degree in computer science. Additional exam requirements/recommendations for international students: Required—TOEFL (minimum score 590 paper-based; 80 iBT), IELTS (minimum score 6.5), PTE (minimum score 53). Electronic applications accepted. *Expenses:* Contact institution. *Faculty research:* Data mining, computer science, human-computer interaction, security, animation and film.

DigiPen Institute of Technology, Graduate Programs, Redmond, WA 98052. Offers computer science (MS); digital art and animation (MFA). *Program availability:* Part-time. *Degree requirements:* For master's, comprehensive exam (for some programs), thesis (for some programs). *Entrance requirements:* For master's, GRE General Test (for MSCS), art portfolio (for MFA); official transcripts from all post-secondary education including final transcript indicating degree earned, statement of purpose, and 2 letters of recommendation. Additional exam requirements/recommendations for international students: Required—TOEFL (minimum score 550 paper-based; 80 iBT). Electronic applications accepted. *Expenses:* Contact institution. *Faculty research:* Procedural modeling, computer graphics and visualization, human-computer interaction, fuzzy numbers and fuzzy analysis, modeling under spistemic uncertainty, nonlinear image processing, mathematical representation of surfaces, advanced computer graphic rendering techniques, mathematical physics, computer music and sound synthesis.

Drexel University, College of Computing and Informatics, Department of Computer Science, Philadelphia, PA 19104-2875. Offers computer science (MS, PhD, Postbaccalaureate Certificate); software engineering (MS). *Program availability:* Part-time, evening/weekend, 100% online. *Faculty:* 23 full-time (3 women), 4 part-time/adjunct (0 women). *Students:* 69 full-time (21 women), 84 part-time (23 women); includes 23 minority (4 Black or African American, non-Hispanic/Latino; 10 Asian, non-Hispanic/Latino; 3 Hispanic/Latino; 6 Two or more races, non-Hispanic/Latino), 43 international. Average age 29. 431 applicants, 34% accepted, 70 enrolled. In 2018, 43 master's, 7 doctorates, 11 other advanced degrees awarded. Terminal master's awarded for partial completion of doctoral program. *Degree requirements:* For doctorate, thesis/dissertation. *Entrance requirements:* For master's and doctorate, GRE General Test. Additional exam requirements/recommendations for international students: Required—TOEFL (minimum score 90 iBT), IELTS (minimum score 6.5). *Application deadline:* For fall admission, 8/15 for domestic students, 7/15 for international students; for spring admission, 3/1 for domestic students, 2/1 for international students. Applications are processed on a rolling basis. Application fee: $65. Electronic applications accepted. *Financial support:* In 2018–19, 41 students received support. Fellowships, research assistantships, teaching assistantships, scholarships/grants, and tuition waivers (partial) available. Financial award application deadline: 3/1; financial award applicants required to submit FAFSA. *Unit head:* Dr. Yi Deng, Dean/Professor, 215-895-2474, Fax: 215-895-2494, E-mail: yd362@drexel.edu. *Application contact:* Matthew Lechtenberg, Director, Recruitment, 215-895-2474, Fax: 215-895-2303, E-mail: cciinfo@drexel.edu.

See Display on the next page and Close-Up on page 309.

Duke University, Graduate School, Department of Computer Science, Durham, NC 27708. Offers MS, PhD. Spring admission applies to MS program only. *Degree requirements:* For doctorate, thesis/dissertation. *Entrance requirements:* For master's, GRE General Test; for doctorate, GRE General Test, GRE Subject Test (recommended). Additional exam requirements/recommendations for international students: Required—TOEFL (minimum score 577 paper-based; 90 iBT) or IELTS (minimum score 7). Electronic applications accepted.

East Carolina University, Graduate School, College of Engineering and Technology, Department of Computer Science, Greenville, NC 27858-4353. Offers computer science (MS); software engineering (MS). *Program availability:* Part-time, evening/weekend. *Application deadline:* For fall admission, 11/1 priority date for domestic students, 10/1 priority date for international students; for spring admission, 3/1 priority date for domestic and international students. *Expenses: Tuition, area resident:* Full-time $4749. Tuition, state resident: full-time $4749. Tuition, nonresident: full-time $17,898. *International tuition:* $17,898 full-time. *Required fees:* $2787. Part-time tuition and fees vary according to course load and program. *Financial support:* Application deadline: 3/1. *Unit head:* Dr. Venkat Gudivada, Chair, 252-328-9693, E-mail: gudivadav15@ecu.edu. *Application contact:* Graduate School Admissions, 252-328-6012, Fax: 252-328-6071, E-mail: gradschool@ecu.edu.
Website: http://www.ecu.edu/cet/csci/index.cfm

East Carolina University, Graduate School, College of Engineering and Technology, Department of Technology Systems, Greenville, NC 27858-4353. Offers computer network professional (Certificate); cyber security professional (Certificate); information assurance (Certificate); Lean Six Sigma Black Belt (Certificate); network technology (MS), including computer networking management, digital communications technology, information security, Web technologies; occupational safety (MS); technology management (MS, PhD), including industrial distribution and logistics (MS); Website developer (Certificate). *Application deadline:* For fall admission, 6/1 priority date for domestic students. *Expenses: Tuition, area resident:* Full-time $4749. Tuition, state resident: full-time $4749. Tuition, nonresident: full-time $17,898. *International tuition:* $17,898 full-time. *Required fees:* $2787. Part-time tuition and fees vary according to course load and program. *Financial support:* Application deadline: 6/1. *Unit head:* Dr. Tijjani Mohammed, Chair, 252-328-9668, E-mail: mohammedt@ecu.edu. *Application contact:* Graduate School Admissions, 252-328-6012, Fax: 252-328-6071, E-mail: gradschool@ecu.edu.
Website: http://www.ecu.edu/cs-cet/techsystems/index.cfm

Eastern Illinois University, Graduate School, Lumpkin College of Business and Technology, School of Technology, Program in Technology, Charleston, IL 61920. Offers MS. *Program availability:* Part-time, evening/weekend. *Degree requirements:* For master's, comprehensive exam (for some programs), thesis (for some programs). *Entrance requirements:* For master's, GMAT or GRE. Additional exam requirements/recommendations for international students: Required—TOEFL (minimum score 500 paper-based; 61 iBT), IELTS (minimum score 6). Electronic applications accepted. *Expenses:* Tuition, state resident: part-time $299 per credit hour. Tuition, nonresident: part-time $718 per credit hour. *Required fees:* $214.50 per credit hour.

Eastern Michigan University, Graduate School, College of Arts and Sciences, Department of Computer Science, Ypsilanti, MI 48197. Offers MS, Graduate Certificate. *Program availability:* Part-time, evening/weekend, online learning. *Faculty:* 16 full-time (7 women). *Students:* 27 full-time (12 women), 20 part-time (9 women); includes 7 minority (1 Black or African American, non-Hispanic/Latino; 4 Asian, non-Hispanic/Latino; 2 Hispanic/Latino), 27 international. Average age 27. 137 applicants, 52% accepted, 19 enrolled. In 2018, 15 master's awarded. *Entrance requirements:* For master's, at least 18 credit hours of computer science courses including data structures, programming languages like java, C or C++, computer organization; courses in discrete mathematics, probability and statistics, linear algebra and calculus; minimum GPA of 2.75 in computer science. Additional exam requirements/recommendations for international students: Required—TOEFL. *Application deadline:* For fall admission, 8/1 for domestic students, 5/1 for international students; for winter admission, 12/1 for domestic students, 10/1 for international students; for spring admission, 4/1 for domestic students, 2/1 for international students. Application fee: $45. *Financial support:* Fellowships, research assistantships with full tuition reimbursements, teaching assistantships with full tuition reimbursements, career-related internships or fieldwork, Federal Work-Study, institutionally sponsored loans, scholarships/grants, tuition waivers (partial), and unspecified assistantships available. Support available to part-time students. Financial award applicants required to submit FAFSA. *Unit head:* Dr. Augstine C. Ikeji, Department Head, 734-487-0056, Fax: 734-487-6824, E-mail: aikeji@emich.edu. *Application contact:* Dr. Krish Narayanan, Graduate Coordinator, 734-487-1256, Fax: 734-487-6824, E-mail: knarayana@emich.edu.
Website: http://www.emich.edu/compsci

Eastern Washington University, Graduate Studies, College of Science, Technology, Engineering and Mathematics, Department of Computer Science, Cheney, WA 99004-2431. Offers computer science (MS). *Program availability:* Part-time. *Degree requirements:* For master's, comprehensive exam, thesis or alternative. *Entrance requirements:* For master's, minimum GPA of 3.0. Additional exam requirements/

Computer Science

recommendations for international students: Required—TOEFL (minimum score 580 paper-based; 92 iBT), IELTS (minimum score 7), PTE (minimum score 63). Electronic applications accepted.

East Stroudsburg University of Pennsylvania, Graduate and Extended Studies, College of Arts and Sciences, Department of Computer Science, East Stroudsburg, PA 18301-2999. Offers MS. *Program availability:* Part-time, evening/weekend. *Faculty:* 3 full-time (1 woman). *Students:* 4 full-time (1 woman), 1 part-time (0 women), 3 international. Average age 29. 5 applicants, 40% accepted, 1 enrolled. In 2018, 5 master's awarded. *Degree requirements:* For master's, comprehensive exam, thesis or alternative. *Entrance requirements:* For master's, bachelor's degree in computer science or related field. Additional exam requirements/recommendations for international students: Recommended—TOEFL (minimum score 560 paper-based; 83 iBT), IELTS. *Application deadline:* For fall admission, 7/31 priority date for domestic students, 6/30 priority date for international students; for spring admission, 11/30 for domestic students, 10/31 for international students. Applications are processed on a rolling basis. Application fee: $50. Electronic applications accepted. *Expenses: Tuition, area resident:* Full-time $9288; part-time $516 per credit. Tuition, state resident: full-time $9288. Tuition, nonresident: full-time $13,932; part-time $774 per credit. *International tuition:* $13,932 full-time. *Required fees:* $2059; $114 per credit. Tuition and fees vary according to course load and degree level. *Financial support:* Research assistantships with tuition reimbursements, career-related internships or fieldwork, Federal Work-Study, and unspecified assistantships available. Support available to part-time students. Financial award application deadline: 3/1; financial award applicants required to submit FAFSA. *Unit head:* Dr. Eun-Joo Lee, Interim Graduate Coordinator, 570-422-2740, E-mail: elee@esu.edu. *Application contact:* Kevin Quintero, Associate Director, Graduate and Extended Studies, 570-422-3890, Fax: 570-422-3711, E-mail: kquintero@esu.edu.
Website: http://www.esu.edu/cpsc/

East Tennessee State University, School of Graduate Studies, College of Business and Technology, Department of Computing, Johnson City, TN 37614. Offers applied computer science (MS); emerging technologies (Postbaccalaureate Certificate); information technology (MS). *Program availability:* Part-time, evening/weekend. *Degree requirements:* For master's, comprehensive exam, thesis optional, capstone, oral exam. *Entrance requirements:* For master's, GRE General Test, minimum GPA of 3.0, three letters of recommendation. Additional exam requirements/recommendations for international students: Required—TOEFL (minimum score 550 paper-based; 79 iBT). Electronic applications accepted. *Faculty research:* Data mining, security and forensics, numerical optimization, computer gaming, enterprise resource planning.

École Polytechnique de Montréal, Graduate Programs, Department of Electrical and Computer Engineering, Montréal, QC H3C 3A7, Canada. Offers automation (M Eng, M Sc A, PhD); computer science (M Eng, M Sc A, PhD); electrical engineering (DESS); electrotechnology (M Eng, M Sc A, PhD); microelectronics (M Eng, M Sc A, PhD); microwave technology (M Eng, M Sc A, PhD). *Program availability:* Part-time, evening/ weekend. *Degree requirements:* For master's, one foreign language, thesis; for doctorate, one foreign language, thesis/dissertation. *Entrance requirements:* For master's, minimum GPA of 2.75; for doctorate, minimum GPA of 3.0. *Faculty research:* Microwaves, telecommunications, software engineering.

Elizabeth City State University, Department of Mathematics and Computer Science, Elizabeth City, NC 27909-7806. Offers mathematics (MS), including applied mathematics, community college teaching, mathematics education, remote sensing. *Program availability:* Part-time, evening/weekend. *Degree requirements:* For master's, thesis. *Entrance requirements:* Additional exam requirements/recommendations for international students: Required—TOEFL. Electronic applications accepted.

Emory University, Laney Graduate School, Department of Mathematics and Computer Science, Atlanta, GA 30322-1100. Offers computer science (MS); computer science and informatics (PhD); mathematics (MS, PhD). Terminal master's awarded for partial completion of doctoral program. *Degree requirements:* For master's, thesis; for doctorate, one foreign language, comprehensive exam, thesis/dissertation. *Entrance requirements:* For master's and doctorate, GRE General Test. Additional exam requirements/recommendations for international students: Recommended—TOEFL. Electronic applications accepted.

Fairleigh Dickinson University, Florham Campus, Maxwell Becton College of Arts and Sciences, Department of Computer Science, Madison, NJ 07940-1099. Offers MS.

Fairleigh Dickinson University, Metropolitan Campus, University College: Arts, Sciences, and Professional Studies, School of Computer Sciences and Engineering, Program in Computer Science, Teaneck, NJ 07666-1914. Offers MS.

Fitchburg State University, Division of Graduate and Continuing Education, Program in Computer Science, Fitchburg, MA 01420-2697. Offers computer science (MS); data science (MS). *Program availability:* Part-time, evening/weekend. *Entrance requirements:* Additional exam requirements/recommendations for international students: Required—TOEFL (minimum score 550 paper-based; 79 iBT). Electronic applications accepted. *Expenses:* Contact institution.

Florida Atlantic University, College of Engineering and Computer Science, Department of Computer and Electrical Engineering and Computer Science, Boca Raton, FL 33431-0991. Offers bioengineering (MS); computer engineering (MS, PhD); computer science (MS, PhD); electrical engineering (MS, PhD). *Program availability:* Part-time, evening/weekend. *Faculty:* 37 full-time (7 women), 2 part-time/adjunct (0 women). *Students:* 85 full-time (18 women), 140 part-time (26 women); includes 86 minority (18 Black or African American, non-Hispanic/Latino; 17 Asian, non-Hispanic/ Latino; 43 Hispanic/Latino; 8 Two or more races, non-Hispanic/Latino), 60 international. Average age 32. 185 applicants, 41% accepted, 69 enrolled. In 2018, 89 master's, 11 doctorates awarded. Terminal master's awarded for partial completion of doctoral program. *Degree requirements:* For master's, thesis optional; for doctorate, thesis/ dissertation, qualifying exam. *Entrance requirements:* For master's, GRE General Test, minimum GPA of 3.0; for doctorate, GRE General Test, master's degree, minimum GPA of 3.5. Additional exam requirements/recommendations for international students: Required—TOEFL (minimum score 500 paper-based; 61 iBT), IELTS (minimum score 6). *Application deadline:* For fall admission, 7/1 priority date for domestic students, 2/15 for international students; for spring admission, 11/1 for domestic students, 7/15 for international students. Applications are processed on a rolling basis. Application fee: $30. *Expenses: Tuition, area resident:* Full-time $7400; part-time $369.82 per credit. Tuition, state resident: full-time $7400; part-time $369.82 per credit. Tuition, nonresident: full-time $20,496; part-time $1024.81 per credit. *Financial support:* Fellowships, research assistantships with partial tuition reimbursements, teaching assistantships with full tuition reimbursements, career-related internships or fieldwork, and Federal Work-Study available. Support available to part-time students. Financial award application deadline: 4/1; financial award applicants required to submit FAFSA. *Faculty research:* VLSI and neural networks, communication networks, software engineering, computer architecture, multimedia and video processing. *Unit head:* Jean Mangiaracina, Graduate Program Administrator, 561-297-6482, E-mail: jmangiar@ fau.edu. *Application contact:* Jean Mangiaracina, Graduate Program Administrator, 561-297-6482, E-mail: jmangiar@fau.edu.
Website: http://www.ceecs.fau.edu/

Florida Institute of Technology, College of Engineering and Science, Program in Computer Science, Melbourne, FL 32901-6975. Offers MS, PhD. *Program availability:* Part-time. *Students:* 49 full-time (13 women), 14 part-time (2 women); includes 4

minority (1 Asian, non-Hispanic/Latino; 2 Hispanic/Latino; 1 Two or more races, non-Hispanic/Latino), 43 international. Average age 30. 61 applicants, 82% accepted, 10 enrolled. In 2018, 19 master's, 11 doctorates awarded. Terminal master's awarded for partial completion of doctoral program. *Degree requirements:* For master's, comprehensive exam (for some programs), thesis optional, minimum of 30 credits; for doctorate, comprehensive exam, thesis/dissertation, minimum of 72 credits beyond bachelor's degree, publications. *Entrance requirements:* For master's, GRE General Test, 3 letters of recommendation, transcript, 12 credits of advanced coursework in computer science; for doctorate, GRE General Test, GRE Subject Test in computer science (recommended), 3 letters of recommendation, minimum GPA of 3.5 in both bachelor's and master's degree in computer science, resume, statement of objectives. Additional exam requirements/recommendations for international students: Required—TOEFL (minimum score 550 paper-based; 79 iBT). *Application deadline:* For fall admission, 4/1 for international students; for spring admission, 9/30 for international students. Applications are processed on a rolling basis. Application fee: $50. Electronic applications accepted. *Expenses:* Tuition: Full-time $22,338; part-time $1241 per credit hour. Tuition and fees vary according to degree level, campus/location and program. *Financial support:* Career-related internships or fieldwork, institutionally sponsored loans, tuition waivers (partial), unspecified assistantships, and tuition remissions available. Support available to part-time students. Financial award application deadline: 3/1; financial award applicants required to submit FAFSA. *Faculty research:* Artificial intelligence, software engineering, management and processes, programming languages, database systems. *Unit head:* Dr. Phillip Bermhard, Department Head, 321-674-7294, E-mail: pbernhar@fit.edu. *Application contact:* Mike Perry, Executive Director of Admissions, 321-674-7127, E-mail: perrymj@fit.edu.
Website: https://www.fit.edu/programs/computer-science-ms/

Florida International University, College of Engineering and Computing, School of Computing and Information Sciences, Miami, FL 33199. Offers computer science (MS, PhD); cybersecurity (MS); data science (MS); information technology (MS); telecommunications and networking (MS). *Program availability:* Part-time, evening/weekend. *Faculty:* 49 full-time (13 women), 31 part-time/adjunct (7 women). *Students:* 182 full-time (53 women), 132 part-time (28 women); includes 168 minority (13 Black or African American, non-Hispanic/Latino; 1 American Indian or Alaska Native, non-Hispanic/Latino; 10 Asian, non-Hispanic/Latino; 137 Hispanic/Latino; 7 Two or more races, non-Hispanic/Latino), 123 international. Average age 30. 393 applicants, 47% accepted, 92 enrolled. In 2018, 81 master's, 9 doctorates awarded. *Degree requirements:* For master's, thesis or alternative; for doctorate, comprehensive exam, thesis/dissertation. *Entrance requirements:* For master's and doctorate, GRE General Test, 3 letters of recommendation, minimum GPA of 3.0. Additional exam requirements/recommendations for international students: Required—TOEFL (minimum score 550 paper-based; 80 iBT). *Application deadline:* For fall admission, 6/1 for domestic students, 4/1 for international students; for spring admission, 10/1 for domestic students, 9/1 for international students. Applications are processed on a rolling basis. Application fee: $30. Electronic applications accepted. *Financial support:* Research assistantships, teaching assistantships, institutionally sponsored loans, scholarships/grants, and unspecified assistantships available. Financial award application deadline: 3/1; financial award applicants required to submit FAFSA. *Faculty research:* Database systems, software engineering, operating systems, networks. *Unit head:* Dr. Sundararaj S. Iyengar, Director, 305-348-3947, Fax: 305-348-3549, E-mail: sundararaj.iyengar@fiu.edu. *Application contact:* Nanett Rojas, Manager, Admissions Operations, 305-348-7464, Fax: 305-348-7441, E-mail: gradadm@fiu.edu.

Florida Polytechnic University, Graduate Programs, Lakeland, FL 33805. Offers computer science (MS); engineering (MS).

Fontbonne University, Graduate Programs, St. Louis, MO 63105-3098. Offers accounting (MBA, MS); art (MA); art (K-12) (MAT); business (MBA); computer science (MS); deaf education (MA); early intervention in deaf education (MA); education (MA), including autism spectrum disorders, curriculum and instruction, diverse learners, early childhood education, reading, special education; elementary education (MAT); family and consumer sciences (MA), including multidisciplinary health communication studies; fine arts (MFA); instructional design and technology (MS); management and leadership (MM); middle school education (MAT); secondary education (MAT); special education (MAT); speech-language pathology (MS); supply chain management (MS); theatre (MA). *Accreditation:* ASHA. *Program availability:* Part-time, evening/weekend, online learning. *Degree requirements:* For master's, comprehensive exam (for some programs), thesis (for some programs). *Entrance requirements:* Additional exam requirements/recommendations for international students: Required—TOEFL (minimum score 500 paper-based; 65 iBT). Electronic applications accepted.

Fordham University, Graduate School of Arts and Sciences, Department of Computer and Information Sciences, New York, NY 10458. Offers computer science (MS); data analytics (MS). *Program availability:* Part-time, evening/weekend. *Faculty:* 11 full-time (1 woman). *Students:* 164 full-time (51 women), 75 part-time (27 women); includes 21 minority (7 Black or African American, non-Hispanic/Latino; 5 Asian, non-Hispanic/Latino; 4 Hispanic/Latino; 5 Two or more races, non-Hispanic/Latino), 102 international. Average age 31. 378 applicants, 71% accepted, 94 enrolled. In 2018, 62 master's awarded. *Degree requirements:* For master's, thesis optional. *Entrance requirements:* For master's, GRE General Test. Additional exam requirements/recommendations for international students: Required—TOEFL (minimum score 550 paper-based). *Application deadline:* For fall admission, 1/4 priority date for domestic students; for spring admission, 11/1 for domestic students. Application fee: $70. Electronic applications accepted. *Financial support:* In 2018–19, 5 students received support, including 3 research assistantships with tuition reimbursements available (averaging $15,000 per year); career-related internships or fieldwork, institutionally sponsored loans, tuition waivers (full and partial), and unspecified assistantships also available. Financial award application deadline: 1/4; financial award applicants required to submit CSS PROFILE or FAFSA. *Faculty research:* Robotics and computer vision, data mining and informatics, information and networking, computation and algorithms, biomedical informatics. *Total annual research expenditures:* $213,000. *Unit head:* Dr. Damian Lyons, Chair, 718-817-4485, Fax: 718-817-4488, E-mail: dlyons@fordham.edu. *Application contact:* Garrett Marino, Director of Graduate Admissions, 718-817-4419, Fax: 718-817-3566, E-mail: gmarino10@fordham.edu.

Franklin University, Computer Science Program, Columbus, OH 43215-5399. Offers MS. *Program availability:* Part-time, evening/weekend. *Entrance requirements:* For master's, minimum undergraduate GPA of 2.75. Additional exam requirements/recommendations for international students: Required—TOEFL (minimum score 550 paper-based). Electronic applications accepted. *Expenses:* Contact institution.

Frostburg State University, College of Liberal Arts and Sciences, Department of Computer Science, Program in Applied Computer Science, Frostburg, MD 21532-1099. Offers MS. *Entrance requirements:* Additional exam requirements/recommendations for international students: Required—TOEFL. Electronic applications accepted.

Gannon University, School of Graduate Studies, College of Engineering and Business, School of Engineering and Computer Science, Program in Computer and Information Science, Erie, PA 16541-0001. Offers information analytics (MSCIS); software engineering (MSCIS). *Program availability:* Part-time, evening/weekend. *Degree*

requirements: For master's, thesis (for some programs), directed research. *Entrance requirements:* For master's, 3 letters of recommendation; resume; transcripts; baccalaureate degree in computer science, information systems, information science, software engineering, or related field from regionally-accredited institution with minimum GPA of 2.5. Additional exam requirements/recommendations for international students: Required—TOEFL (minimum score 79 iBT). Electronic applications accepted. Application fee is waived when completed online.

George Mason University, Volgenau School of Engineering, Department of Computer Science, Fairfax, VA 22030. Offers MS, PhD, Certificate. MS programs offered jointly with Old Dominion University, University of Virginia, Virginia Commonwealth University, and Virginia Polytechnic Institute and State University. *Faculty:* 46 full-time (11 women), 23 part-time/adjunct (2 women). *Students:* 238 full-time (82 women), 191 part-time (45 women); includes 87 minority (10 Black or African American, non-Hispanic/Latino; 56 Asian, non-Hispanic/Latino; 16 Hispanic/Latino; 5 Two or more races, non-Hispanic/Latino), 207 international. Average age 28. 708 applicants, 59% accepted, 121 enrolled. In 2018, 165 master's, 15 doctorates, 9 other advanced degrees awarded. *Degree requirements:* For master's, thesis optional, 30 credits (10 courses); for doctorate, comprehensive exam, thesis/dissertation, 72 credits (includes dissertation research and coursework); for Certificate, 12 credits (4 courses). *Entrance requirements:* For master's and Certificate, GRE (for applicants who have not earned bachelor's degree from U.S. institution), BS in computer science or related field; for doctorate, GRE, personal goals statement; 2 official copies of transcripts; self-evaluation form; 3 letters of recommendation; photocopy of passport; proof of financial support; official bank statement; resume; 4-year baccalaureate degree in computer science or related field. Additional exam requirements/recommendations for international students: Required—TOEFL (minimum score 575 paper-based; 88 iBT), IELTS (minimum score 6.5), PTE (minimum score 59). *Application deadline:* For fall admission, 12/1 priority date for domestic and international students; for spring admission, 8/15 priority date for domestic and international students. Application fee: $75 ($80 for international students). Electronic applications accepted. *Expenses:* $589 per credit in-state, $1,346.75 per credit out-of-state. *Financial support:* In 2018–19, 127 students received support, including 1 fellowship, 36 research assistantships with tuition reimbursements available (averaging $19,341 per year), 91 teaching assistantships with tuition reimbursements available (averaging $12,634 per year); career-related internships or fieldwork, Federal Work-Study, scholarships/grants, unspecified assistantships, and health care benefits (for full-time research or teaching assistantship recipients) also available. Support available to part-time students. Financial award application deadline: 3/1; financial award applicants required to submit FAFSA. *Faculty research:* Computer and network security; machine learning and artificial intelligence; computer systems and networking; software engineering; computer graphics and visual computing. *Total annual research expenditures:* $3.5 million. *Unit head:* Sanjeev Setia, Chair, 703-993-4098, Fax: 703-993-1710, E-mail: setia@gmu.edu. *Application contact:* Michele Pieper, Office Manager, 703-993-9483, Fax: 703-993-1710, E-mail: mpieper@gmu.edu.
Website: http://cs.gmu.edu/

Georgetown University, Graduate School of Arts and Sciences, Department of Computer Science, Washington, DC 20057. Offers MS, PhD. *Program availability:* Part-time, evening/weekend. *Degree requirements:* For master's, thesis optional. *Entrance requirements:* For master's, GRE, basic course work in data structures, advanced math, and programming; 3 letters of recommendation. Additional exam requirements/recommendations for international students: Required—TOEFL. Electronic applications accepted. *Faculty research:* Data mining, artificial intelligence, software engineering, security.

The George Washington University, School of Engineering and Applied Science, Department of Computer Science, Washington, DC 20052. Offers computer science (MS, D Sc); cybersecurity (MS). *Program availability:* Part-time, evening/weekend. *Faculty:* 14 full-time (6 women), 28 part-time/adjunct (3 women). *Students:* 385 full-time (88 women), 396 part-time (107 women); includes 137 minority (69 Black or African American, non-Hispanic/Latino; 4 American Indian or Alaska Native, non-Hispanic/Latino; 49 Asian, non-Hispanic/Latino; 8 Hispanic/Latino; 7 Two or more races, non-Hispanic/Latino), 379 international. Average age 31. 1,262 applicants, 76% accepted, 287 enrolled. In 2018, 253 master's, 12 doctorates, 13 other advanced degrees awarded. *Degree requirements:* For master's, thesis optional; for doctorate, thesis/dissertation, dissertation defense, qualifying exam. *Entrance requirements:* For master's, appropriate bachelor's degree, minimum GPA of 3.0; for doctorate, GRE (if highest earned degree is BS), appropriate bachelor's or master's degree, minimum GPA of 3.3; for other advanced degree, appropriate master's degree, minimum GPA of 3.4. Additional exam requirements/recommendations for international students: Required—TOEFL or The George Washington University English as a Foreign Language Test. *Application deadline:* For fall admission, 3/1 priority date for domestic students; for spring admission, 10/1 for domestic students. Applications are processed on a rolling basis. Application fee: $75. *Financial support:* In 2018–19, 49 students received support. Fellowships, research assistantships, teaching assistantships, career-related internships or fieldwork, institutionally sponsored loans, and tuition waivers available. Financial award application deadline: 3/1; financial award applicants required to submit FAFSA. *Faculty research:* Computer graphics, multimedia, VLSI, parallel processing. *Unit head:* Prof. Abdou Youssef, Chair, 202-994-4953, E-mail: ayoussef@gwu.edu. *Application contact:* Adina Lav, Marketing, Recruiting and Admissions, 202-994-5827, Fax: 202-994-0909, E-mail: engineering@gwu.edu.
Website: http://www.cs.gwu.edu/

Georgia Institute of Technology, Graduate Studies, College of Computing, Program in Computer Science, Atlanta, GA 30332-0001. Offers MS, PhD. *Program availability:* Part-time, online learning. Terminal master's awarded for partial completion of doctoral program. *Degree requirements:* For master's, thesis optional; for doctorate, comprehensive exam, thesis/dissertation. *Entrance requirements:* For master's, GRE General Test, GRE Subject Test (computer science); for doctorate, GRE General Test, GRE Subject Test (computer science, mathematics, or physics). Additional exam requirements/recommendations for international students: Required—TOEFL (minimum score 600 paper-based; 100 iBT). Electronic applications accepted. *Expenses:* Contact institution.

Georgia Southern University, Jack N. Averitt College of Graduate Studies, Allen E. Paulson College of Engineering and Computing, Department of Computer Science, Statesboro, GA 30458. Offers MS. *Program availability:* Part-time, blended/hybrid learning. *Degree requirements:* For master's, comprehensive exam, thesis (for some programs). *Entrance requirements:* For master's, GRE, undergraduate major or equivalent in proposed study area. Additional exam requirements/recommendations for international students: Required—TOEFL (minimum score 550 paper-based; 80 iBT), IELTS (minimum score 6). Electronic applications accepted. *Expenses:* Tuition, area resident: Part-time $3324 per semester. Tuition, state resident: full-time $5814; part-time $3324 per semester. Tuition, nonresident: full-time $23,204; part-time $13,260 per semester. *Required fees:* $2092; $2092. Tuition and fees vary according to course load, degree level, campus/location and program. *Faculty research:* Cyber physical systems, big data, data mining and analytics, cloud computing.

Computer Science

Georgia Southwestern State University, School of Computing and Mathematics, Americus, GA 31709-4693. Offers computer information systems (Graduate Certificate); computer science (MS). *Program availability:* Part-time, 100% online, blended/hybrid learning. *Degree requirements:* For master's, thesis optional, minimum cumulative GPA of 3.0; maximum of 6 credit hours with C grade; no courses with D grade; degree must be completed within 7 calendar years from date of initial enrollment in graduate course work; for Graduate Certificate, minimum cumulative GPA of 3.0; maximum of 6 credit hours with C grade; no courses with D grade; degree must be completed within 7 calendar years from date of initial enrollment in graduate course work. *Entrance requirements:* For master's and Graduate Certificate, GRE, bachelor's degree from regionally-accredited college; minimum undergraduate GPA of 2.5 as reported on official final transcripts from all institutions attended; letters of recommendation. Additional exam requirements/recommendations for international students: Required—TOEFL (minimum score 523 paper-based; 69 iBT), IELTS (minimum score 6.5). Electronic applications accepted. *Expenses:* Contact institution.

Georgia State University, College of Arts and Sciences, Department of Computer Science, Atlanta, GA 30302-3083. Offers bioinformatics (MS, PhD); computer science (MS, PhD). *Program availability:* Part-time. *Faculty:* 29 full-time (6 women), 3 part-time/adjunct (1 woman). *Students:* 166 full-time (63 women), 32 part-time (12 women); includes 25 minority (8 Black or African American, non-Hispanic/Latino; 11 Asian, non-Hispanic/Latino; 3 Hispanic/Latino; 3 Two or more races, non-Hispanic/Latino), 155 international. Average age 29. 331 applicants, 40% accepted, 68 enrolled. In 2018, 67 master's, 14 doctorates awarded. Terminal master's awarded for partial completion of doctoral program. *Entrance requirements:* For master's and doctorate, GRE General Test. Additional exam requirements/recommendations for international students: Required—TOEFL (minimum score 550 paper-based; 80 iBT). *Application deadline:* For fall admission, 3/15 for domestic and international students; for spring admission, 10/15 for domestic and international students. Application fee: $50. Electronic applications accepted. *Expenses: Tuition, area resident:* Full-time $9360; part-time $390 per credit hour. Tuition, state resident: full-time $9360; part-time $390 per credit hour. Tuition, nonresident: full-time $30,024; part-time $1251 per credit hour. *International tuition:* $30,024 full-time. *Required fees:* $2128. *Financial support:* In 2018–19, fellowships with full tuition reimbursements (averaging $22,000 per year), research assistantships with full tuition reimbursements (averaging $16,000 per year), teaching assistantships with full tuition reimbursements (averaging $16,000 per year) were awarded; institutionally sponsored loans, health care benefits, and unspecified assistantships also available. Financial award application deadline: 2/15; financial award applicants required to submit FAFSA. *Faculty research:* Artificial intelligence and computational intelligence, bioinformatics, computer software systems, databases, graphics and human computer interaction, networks and parallel and distributed computing. *Unit head:* Dr. Yi Pan, Regents Professor and Chair, 404-413-5342, Fax: 404-413-5717, E-mail: yipan@gsu.edu. *Application contact:* Dr. Yi Pan, Regents Professor and Chair, 404-413-5342, Fax: 404-413-5717, E-mail: yipan@gsu.edu.
Website: http://www.cs.gsu.edu/

Georgia State University, College of Arts and Sciences, Department of Mathematics and Statistics, Atlanta, GA 30302-3083. Offers bioinformatics (MS, PhD); biostatistics (MS, PhD); discrete mathematics (MS); mathematics (MS, PhD); scientific computing (MS); statistics (MS). *Program availability:* Part-time. *Faculty:* 28 full-time (8 women), 1 part-time/adjunct (0 women). *Students:* 88 full-time (46 women), 15 part-time (8 women); includes 27 minority (7 Black or African American, non-Hispanic/Latino; 14 Asian, non-Hispanic/Latino; 4 Hispanic/Latino; 2 Two or more races, non-Hispanic/Latino), 57 international. Average age 32. 109 applicants, 65% accepted, 37 enrolled. In 2018, 29 master's, 11 doctorates awarded. Terminal master's awarded for partial completion of doctoral program. *Entrance requirements:* For master's and doctorate, GRE. Additional exam requirements/recommendations for international students: Required—TOEFL (minimum score 550 paper-based; 80 iBT). *Application deadline:* For fall admission, 7/1 priority date for domestic and international students; for spring admission, 11/15 priority date for domestic and international students. Application fee: $50. Electronic applications accepted. *Expenses: Tuition, area resident:* Full-time $9360; part-time $390 per credit hour. Tuition, state resident: full-time $9360; part-time $390 per credit hour. Tuition, nonresident: full-time $30,024; part-time $1251 per credit hour. *International tuition:* $30,024 full-time. *Required fees:* $2128. *Financial support:* In 2018–19, fellowships with full tuition reimbursements (averaging $22,000 per year), research assistantships with full tuition reimbursements (averaging $9,000 per year), teaching assistantships with full tuition reimbursements (averaging $9,000 per year) were awarded; institutionally sponsored loans, scholarships/grants, health care benefits, and unspecified assistantships also available. Financial award application deadline: 2/1. *Faculty research:* Algebra, matrix theory, graph theory and combinatorics; applied mathematics and analysis; collegiate mathematics education; statistics, biostatistics and applications; bioinformatics, dynamical systems. *Unit head:* Dr. Guantao Chen, Chair, 404-413-6436, Fax: 404-413-6403, E-mail: gchen@gsu.edu. *Application contact:* Dr. Guantao Chen, Chair, 404-413-6436, Fax: 404-413-6403, E-mail: gchen@gsu.edu.
Website: https://www.mathstat.gsu.edu/

Governors State University, College of Arts and Sciences, Program in Computer Science, University Park, IL 60484. Offers MS. *Program availability:* Part-time. *Faculty:* 39 full-time (14 women), 29 part-time/adjunct (12 women). *Students:* 45 full-time (14 women), 32 part-time (5 women); includes 19 minority (12 Black or African American, non-Hispanic/Latino; 1 Asian, non-Hispanic/Latino; 6 Hispanic/Latino), 50 international. Average age 29. 136 applicants, 74% accepted, 17 enrolled. In 2018, 112 master's awarded. *Application deadline:* For fall admission, 4/1 for domestic students. Applications are processed on a rolling basis. Application fee: $50. Electronic applications accepted. *Financial support:* Application deadline: 5/1; applicants required to submit FAFSA. *Unit head:* Mary Carrington, Interim Chair, Division of Science, Mathematics, and Technology, 708-534-5000 Ext. 4532, E-mail: mcarrington@govst.edu. *Application contact:* Mary Carrington, Interim Chair, Division of Science, Mathematics, and Technology, 708-534-5000 Ext. 4532, E-mail: mcarrington@govst.edu.

The Graduate Center, City University of New York, Graduate Studies, Program in Computer Science, New York, NY 10016-4039. Offers PhD. Program offered jointly with College of Staten Island of the City University of New York. *Degree requirements:* For doctorate, one foreign language, thesis/dissertation. *Entrance requirements:* For doctorate, GRE General Test. Additional exam requirements/recommendations for international students: Required—TOEFL. Electronic applications accepted.

Grand Valley State University, Padnos College of Engineering and Computing, School of Computing and Information Systems, Allendale, MI 49401-9403. Offers computer information systems (MS), including databases, distributed systems, management of information systems, object-oriented systems, software engineering. *Program availability:* Part-time, evening/weekend. *Faculty:* 10 full-time (0 women). *Students:* 26 full-time (10 women), 53 part-time (7 women); includes 10 minority (2 Black or African American, non-Hispanic/Latino; 6 Asian, non-Hispanic/Latino; 1 Hispanic/Latino; 1 Two or more races, non-Hispanic/Latino), 21 international. Average age 29. 56 applicants, 70% accepted, 15 enrolled. In 2018, 23 master's awarded. *Entrance requirements:* For master's, GRE (recommended with GPA below 3.0), minimum GPA of 3.0; knowledge of a programming language; coursework or experience in: computer architecture and/or organization, data structures and algorithms, databases, discrete math, networking, operating systems, and software engineering; minimum of 2 letters of recommendation; resume; personal statement. Additional exam requirements/recommendations for international students: Required—Michigan English Language Assessment Battery (minimum score 77), TOEFL (minimum iBT score of 80), or IELTS (6.5); GRE. *Application deadline:* For fall admission, 6/1 for international students; for winter admission, 9/1 for international students. Applications are processed on a rolling basis. Application fee: $30. Electronic applications accepted. *Expenses:* $712 per credit hour, 33 credit hours. *Financial support:* In 2018–19, 13 students received support, including 6 fellowships, 5 research assistantships with full and partial tuition reimbursements available (averaging $8,000 per year). *Faculty research:* Object technology, distributed computing, information systems management database, software engineering. *Unit head:* Dr. Paul Leidig, Director, 616-331-2060, Fax: 616-331-2144, E-mail: leidigp@gvsu.edu. *Application contact:* Dr. D. Robert Adams, Graduate Program Director, 616-331-3885, Fax: 616-331-2144, E-mail: adamsr@gvsu.edu.
Website: http://www.cis.gvsu.edu/

Hampton University, School of Science, Department of Computer Science, Hampton, VA 23668. Offers computer science (MS); information assurance (MS). *Program availability:* Part-time, evening/weekend. *Students:* 2 full-time (0 women), 2 part-time (1 woman); includes 2 minority (1 Black or African American, non-Hispanic/Latino; 1 Asian, non-Hispanic/Latino), 2 international. Average age 34. 1 applicant, 100% accepted, 1 enrolled. In 2018, 1 master's awarded. *Degree requirements:* For master's, thesis or alternative. *Entrance requirements:* For master's, GRE General Test. Additional exam requirements/recommendations for international students: Required—TOEFL (minimum score 525 paper-based) or IELTS (6.5). *Application deadline:* For fall admission, 6/1 priority date for domestic students, 4/1 priority date for international students; for spring admission, 11/1 priority date for domestic students, 9/1 priority date for international students; for summer admission, 4/1 priority date for domestic students, 2/1 priority date for international students. Applications are processed on a rolling basis. Application fee: $35. Electronic applications accepted. *Financial support:* In 2018–19, 5 fellowships (averaging $38,900 per year), 1 research assistantship were awarded; career-related internships or fieldwork, Federal Work-Study, and scholarships/grants also available. Support available to part-time students. Financial award application deadline: 6/30; financial award applicants required to submit FAFSA. *Faculty research:* Artificial intelligence, software development, machine learning, neural networks, parallel processing, natural language processing, distributive agents. *Unit head:* Dr. Jean Muhammad, Chair, 757-727-5552. *Application contact:* Dr. Jean Muhammad, Chair, 757-727-5552.

Harvard University, Graduate School of Arts and Sciences, Harvard John A. Paulson School of Engineering and Applied Sciences, Cambridge, MA 02138. Offers applied mathematics (PhD); applied physics (PhD); computational science and engineering (ME, SM); computer science (PhD); data science (SM); design engineering (MDE); engineering science (ME), including electrical engineering (ME, SM, PhD); engineering sciences (SM, PhD), including bioengineering (PhD), electrical engineering (ME, SM, PhD), environmental science and engineering (PhD), materials science and mechanical engineering (PhD). MDE offered in collaboration with Graduate School of Design. *Program availability:* Part-time. Terminal master's awarded for partial completion of doctoral program. *Degree requirements:* For master's, thesis (for ME); for doctorate, comprehensive exam, thesis/dissertation. *Entrance requirements:* For master's and doctorate, GRE General Test, GRE Subject Test (recommended), 3 letters of recommendation. Additional exam requirements/recommendations for international students: Required—TOEFL (minimum score 80 iBT). Electronic applications accepted. *Expenses:* Contact institution. *Faculty research:* Applied mathematics, applied physics, computer science and electrical engineering, environmental engineering, mechanical and biomedical engineering.

Hood College, Graduate School, Programs in Computer and Information Sciences, Frederick, MD 21701-8575. Offers computer science (MS); cybersecurity (MS, Certificate); information technology (MS). *Program availability:* Part-time, evening/weekend, 100% online. *Faculty:* 8 full-time (2 women), 2 part-time/adjunct (0 women). *Students:* 48 full-time (15 women), 64 part-time (17 women); includes 15 minority (7 Black or African American, non-Hispanic/Latino; 2 Asian, non-Hispanic/Latino; 4 Hispanic/Latino; 2 Two or more races, non-Hispanic/Latino), 54 international. Average age 33. 55 applicants, 100% accepted, 26 enrolled. In 2018, 47 master's, 26 other advanced degrees awarded. *Degree requirements:* For master's, thesis optional, capstone (S). *Entrance requirements:* For master's, minimum GPA of 2.75, essay, resume. Additional exam requirements/recommendations for international students: Required—TOEFL (minimum score 575 paper-based; 89 iBT), IELTS (minimum score 6.5). *Application deadline:* For fall admission, 8/15 priority date for domestic students, 8/5 for international students; for spring admission, 12/1 priority date for domestic students, 12/1 for international students; for summer admission, 5/1 for domestic students, 4/15 for international students. Applications are processed on a rolling basis. Application fee: $50 ($100 for international students). Electronic applications accepted. *Expenses:* Science Programs: Tuition $535 per credit hour, Comprehensive Fee $115 per semester. *Financial support:* Tuition waivers (partial) and unspecified assistantships available. Financial award applicants required to submit FAFSA. *Faculty research:* Systems engineering, natural language, processing, database design, artificial intelligence and parallel distributed computing. *Unit head:* Dr. April M. Boulton, Dean of the Graduate School, 301-696-3600, E-mail: gofurther@hood.edu. *Application contact:* Larbi Bricha, Assistant Director of Graduate Admissions, 301-696-3601, E-mail: gofurther@hood.edu.
Website: https://www.hood.edu/graduate

Howard University, College of Engineering, Architecture, and Computer Sciences, School of Engineering and Computer Science, Department of Systems and Computer Science, Washington, DC 20059-0002. Offers MCS. Offered through the Graduate School of Arts and Sciences. *Program availability:* Part-time. *Degree requirements:* For master's, thesis. *Entrance requirements:* For master's, GRE General Test, minimum GPA of 3.0. Additional exam requirements/recommendations for international students: Required—TOEFL. Electronic applications accepted. *Faculty research:* Software engineering, software fault-tolerance, software reliability, artificial intelligence.

Illinois Institute of Technology, Graduate College, College of Science, Department of Computer Science, Chicago, IL 60616. Offers business (MCS); computational intelligence (MCS); computer science (MCS, MS, PhD); cyber-physical systems (MCS); data analytics (MCS); data science (MAS); database systems (MCS); distributed and cloud computing (MCS); education (MCS); finance (MCS); information security and assurance (MCS); networking and communications (MCS); software engineering (MCS); telecommunications and software engineering (MAS); MS/MAS. *Program availability:* Part-time, evening/weekend, online learning. Terminal master's awarded for partial completion of doctoral program. *Degree requirements:* For master's, thesis optional; for doctorate, comprehensive exam, thesis/dissertation. *Entrance requirements:* For master's, GRE General Test with minimum scores of 298 Quantitative and Verbal, 3.0 Analytical Writing (for MS); GRE General Test with minimum scores of 292 Quantitative and Verbal, 2.5 Analytical Writing (for MAS), minimum undergraduate

GPA of 3.0; for doctorate, GRE General Test (minimum scores: 304 Quantitative and Verbal, 3.5 Analytical Writing), minimum undergraduate GPA of 3.0. Additional exam requirements/recommendations for international students: Required—TOEFL (minimum score 523 paper-based; 70 iBT). Electronic applications accepted. *Faculty research:* Parallel and distributed processing, high-performance computing, computational linguistics, information retrieval, data mining, grid computing.

Indiana State University, College of Graduate and Professional Studies, College of Arts and Sciences, Department of Mathematics and Computer Science, Terre Haute, IN 47809. Offers computer science (MS); mathematics (MA, MS). *Program availability:* Part-time. *Degree requirements:* For master's, thesis or alternative. *Entrance requirements:* For master's, 24 semester hours of course work in undergraduate mathematics. Electronic applications accepted.

Indiana University Bloomington, School of Informatics, Computing, and Engineering, Department of Computer Science, Bloomington, IN 47405. Offers bioinformatics (MS); computer science (MS, PhD); cybersecurity risk management (MS); secure computing (MS, Graduate Certificate). MS in cybersecurity risk management offered in partnership with Kelley School of Business and Maurer School of Law. Terminal master's awarded for partial completion of doctoral program. *Degree requirements:* For master's, thesis optional; for doctorate, comprehensive exam, thesis/dissertation, oral and written exams. *Entrance requirements:* For master's and doctorate, GRE General Test, statement of purpose, bachelor's degree. Additional exam requirements/recommendations for international students: Required—TOEFL. Electronic applications accepted. *Faculty research:* Algorithms, applied logic and computational theory, artificial intelligence, bioinformatics, case-based reasoning, chemical informatics, citation analysis, cognitive science, community informatics, compilers, complex networks and systems, computer optimization, computer-supported cooperative work, computer vision, cyberinfrastructure and e-science, database theory and systems, data mining, digital design and preservation, design pedagogy, digital humanities, digital learning environments.

Indiana University Bloomington, School of Informatics, Computing, and Engineering, Program in Informatics, Bloomington, IN 47405. Offers informatics (MS, PhD), including bioinformatics (PhD), complex systems (PhD), computing, culture and society (PhD), health informatics (PhD), human-computer interaction (MS), human-computer interaction design (PhD), music informatics (PhD), security informatics (PhD); visual heritage (PhD). *Program availability:* Part-time. Terminal master's awarded for partial completion of doctoral program. *Degree requirements:* For master's, thesis, capstone project; for doctorate, variable foreign language requirement, comprehensive exam, thesis/dissertation. *Entrance requirements:* For master's and doctorate, GRE, resume/curriculum vitae, transcripts, 3 letters of recommendation. Additional exam requirements/recommendations for international students: Required—TOEFL (minimum score 600 paper-based; 100 iBT). Electronic applications accepted. *Faculty research:* Algorithms, applied logic and computational theory, artificial intelligence, bioinformatics, case-based reasoning, chemical informatics, citation analysis, cognitive science, community informatics, compilers, complex networks and systems, computer optimization, computer-supported cooperative work, computer vision, cyberinfrastructure and e-science, database theory and systems, data mining, digital design and preservation, design pedagogy, digital humanities, digital learning environments.

Indiana University–Purdue University Indianapolis, School of Science, Department of Computer and Information Science, Indianapolis, IN 46202-5132. Offers biocomputing (Graduate Certificate); biometrics (Graduate Certificate); computer science (MS, PhD); computer security (Graduate Certificate); databases and data mining (Graduate Certificate); software engineering (Graduate Certificate). *Program availability:* Part-time. Terminal master's awarded for partial completion of doctoral program. *Degree requirements:* For master's and Graduate Certificate, thesis optional; for doctorate, thesis/dissertation. *Entrance requirements:* For master's and doctorate, GRE, BS in computer science or the equivalent with a minimum GPA of 3.0 (or equivalent); for Graduate Certificate, BS in computer science or the equivalent with a minimum GPA of 3.0 (or equivalent). Additional exam requirements/recommendations for international students: Required—PTE (minimum score 58), TOEFL (minimum score 550 paper-based, 79 iBT) or IELTS (6.5). *Faculty research:* Imaging and visualization; networking and security; software engineering; distributed and parallel computing; database, data mining and machine learning.

Indiana University South Bend, College of Liberal Arts and Sciences, South Bend, IN 46615. Offers advanced computer programming (Graduate Certificate); applied informatics (Graduate Certificate); applied mathematics and computer science (MS); behavior modification (Graduate Certificate); computer applications (Graduate Certificate); computer programming (Graduate Certificate); correctional management and supervision (Graduate Certificate); English (MA); health systems management (Graduate Certificate); international studies (Graduate Certificate); liberal studies (MLS); nonprofit management (Graduate Certificate); paralegal studies (Graduate Certificate); professional writing (Graduate Certificate); public affairs (MPA); public management (Graduate Certificate); social and cultural diversity (Graduate Certificate); strategic sustainability leadership (Graduate Certificate); technology for administration (Graduate Certificate). *Program availability:* Part-time, evening/weekend. *Degree requirements:* For master's, variable foreign language requirement, thesis (for some programs). *Entrance requirements:* For master's, minimum GPA of 3.0. Additional exam requirements/recommendations for international students: Required—TOEFL (minimum score 550 paper-based; 80 iBT). *Expenses:* Contact institution. *Faculty research:* Artificial intelligence, bioinformatics, English language and literature, creative writing, computer networks.

Instituto Tecnológico y de Estudios Superiores de Monterrey, Campus Central de Veracruz, Graduate Programs, Córdoba, Mexico. Offers administration (MA); administration of information technologies (MTI); computer sciences (MCC); education (MEE); educational institution administration (MAD); educational technology (MTE); electronic commerce (MCE); finance (MAF); humanistic studies (MEH); international business for Latin America (MNL); marketing (MMT); science (MCP). *Program availability:* Part-time, evening/weekend, online learning. *Degree requirements:* For master's, thesis (for some programs). *Entrance requirements:* For master's, PAEP College Board. Electronic applications accepted.

Instituto Tecnológico y de Estudios Superiores de Monterrey, Campus Ciudad de México, Virtual University Division, Ciudad de Mexico, Mexico. Offers administration of information technologies (MA); computer sciences (MA); education (MA, PhD); educational technology (MA); environmental engineering (MA); environmental systems (MA); humanistic studies (MA); industrial engineering (MA); international business for Latin America (MA); quality systems (MA); quality systems and productivity (MA). *Program availability:* Part-time, evening/weekend, online learning. *Entrance requirements:* For master's and doctorate, Instituto entrance exam. Additional exam requirements/recommendations for international students: Required—TOEFL.

Instituto Tecnológico y de Estudios Superiores de Monterrey, Campus Cuernavaca, Programs in Information Science, Temixco, Mexico. Offers administration of information technology (MATI); computer science (MCC, DCC); information technology (MTI).

Instituto Tecnológico y de Estudios Superiores de Monterrey, Campus Estado de México, Professional and Graduate Division, Estado de Mexico, Mexico. Offers administration of information technologies (MITA); architecture (M Arch); business administration (GMBA, MBA); computer sciences (MCS, PhD); education (M Ed); educational institution administration (MAD); educational technology and innovation (PhD); electronic commerce (MEC); environmental systems (MS); finance (MAF); humanistic studies (MHS); information sciences and knowledge management (MISKM); information systems (MS); manufacturing systems (MS); marketing (MEM); quality systems and productivity (MS); science and materials engineering (PhD); telecommunications management (MTM). *Program availability:* Part-time, online learning. *Degree requirements:* For master's, one foreign language, thesis (for some programs); for doctorate, one foreign language, thesis/dissertation. *Entrance requirements:* For master's, E-PAEP 500, interview; for doctorate, E-PAEP 500, research proposal. Additional exam requirements/recommendations for international students: Required—TOEFL (minimum score 550 paper-based). *Faculty research:* Surface treatments by plasmas, mechanical properties, robotics, graphical computing, mechatronics security protocols.

Instituto Tecnológico y de Estudios Superiores de Monterrey, Campus Irapuato, Graduate Programs, Irapuato, Mexico. Offers administration (MBA); administration of information technology (MAIT); administration of telecommunications (MAT); architecture (M Arch); computer science (MCS); education (M Ed); educational administration (MEA); educational innovation and technology (DEIT); educational technology (MET); electronic commerce (MBA); environmental administration and planning (MEAP); environmental systems (MES); finances (MBA); humanistic studies (MHS); international management for Latin American executives (MIMLAE); library and information science (MLIS); manufacturing quality management (MMQM); marketing research (MBA).

Instituto Tecnológico y de Estudios Superiores de Monterrey, Campus Monterrey, Graduate and Research Division, Program in Computer Science, Monterrey, Mexico. Offers artificial intelligence (PhD); computer science (MS); information systems (MS); information technology (MS). *Program availability:* Part-time. *Degree requirements:* For master's, one foreign language, thesis; for doctorate, one foreign language, thesis/dissertation. *Entrance requirements:* For master's, EXADEP; for doctorate, master's degree in related field. Additional exam requirements/recommendations for international students: Required—TOEFL. *Faculty research:* Distributed systems, software engineering, decision support systems.

Inter American University of Puerto Rico, Fajardo Campus, Graduate Programs, Fajardo, PR 00738-7003. Offers computer science (MS); educational management and leadership (MA Ed); general business (MBA); human resources (MBA); management information systems (MBA); marketing (MBA); special education (MA Ed). *Program availability:* Online learning.

Inter American University of Puerto Rico, Guayama Campus, Department of Natural and Applied Sciences, Guayama, PR 00785. Offers computer security and networks (MS); networking and security (MCS).

Inter American University of Puerto Rico, Metropolitan Campus, Graduate Programs, Program in Open Information Systems, San Juan, PR 00919-1293. Offers MS. *Degree requirements:* For master's, 2 foreign languages.

Iona College, School of Arts and Science, Department of Computer Science, New Rochelle, NY 10801-1890. Offers computer science (MS); cyber security (MS); game development (MS). *Program availability:* Part-time, evening/weekend. *Faculty:* 8 full-time (4 women), 7 part-time/adjunct (3 women). *Students:* 3 full-time (0 women), 9 part-time (2 women); includes 3 minority (2 Black or African American, non-Hispanic/Latino; 1 Hispanic/Latino), 1 international. Average age 26. 17 applicants, 76% accepted, 3 enrolled. In 2018, 6 master's awarded. *Degree requirements:* For master's, thesis optional. *Entrance requirements:* For master's, minimum GPA of 3.0. Additional exam requirements/recommendations for international students: Required—TOEFL (minimum score 550 paper-based; 80 iBT), IELTS (minimum score 6.5). *Application deadline:* For fall admission, 8/1 priority date for domestic students, 5/1 priority date for international students; for spring admission, 1/1 priority date for domestic students, 9/1 priority date for international students. Applications are processed on a rolling basis. Electronic applications accepted. *Expenses: Tuition:* Full-time $14,064; part-time $7032 per credit. *Required fees:* $245 per semester. One-time fee: $250. Tuition and fees vary according to program. *Financial support:* In 2018–19, 2 students received support, including 2 research assistantships with full and partial tuition reimbursements available (averaging $5,072 per year); tuition waivers (partial) and unspecified assistantships also available. Support available to part-time students. Financial award application deadline: 4/15; financial award applicants required to submit FAFSA. *Faculty research:* Parallel procession, data mining, machine learning, cyber security, medical imaging. *Unit head:* Frances Bailie, PhD, Chair, 914-633-2335, E-mail: fbailie@iona.edu. *Application contact:* Christopher Kash, Assistant Director, Graduate Admissions, 914-633-2403, Fax: 914-633-2277, E-mail: ckash@iona.edu.
Website: http://www.iona.edu/Academics/School-of-Arts-Science/Departments/Computer-Science/Graduate-Programs.aspx

Iowa State University of Science and Technology, Department of Computer Science, Ames, IA 50011. Offers MS, PhD. *Degree requirements:* For master's, thesis; for doctorate, thesis/dissertation. *Entrance requirements:* For master's and doctorate, GRE General Test. Additional exam requirements/recommendations for international students: Recommended—TOEFL (minimum score 550 paper-based; 79 iBT), IELTS (minimum score 6.5). Electronic applications accepted.

Jackson State University, Graduate School, College of Science, Engineering and Technology, Department of Computer Science, Jackson, MS 39217. Offers MS. *Program availability:* Part-time, evening/weekend. *Degree requirements:* For master's, comprehensive exam, thesis. *Entrance requirements:* For master's, GRE General Test. Additional exam requirements/recommendations for international students: Required—TOEFL (minimum score 520 paper-based; 67 iBT).

Jacksonville State University, Graduate Studies, School of Science, Program in Computer Systems and Software Design, Jacksonville, AL 36265-1602. Offers MS. *Program availability:* Part-time, evening/weekend. *Degree requirements:* For master's, comprehensive exam, thesis (for some programs). *Entrance requirements:* Additional exam requirements/recommendations for international students: Required—TOEFL (minimum score 500 paper-based; 61 iBT). Electronic applications accepted.

James Madison University, The Graduate School, College of Integrated Science and Engineering, Program in Computer Science, Harrisonburg, VA 22807. Offers digital forensics (MS); information security (MS). *Program availability:* Online learning. *Students:* 3 full-time (0 women), 48 part-time (10 women); includes 13 minority (7 Black or African American, non-Hispanic/Latino; 3 Asian, non-Hispanic/Latino; 2 Hispanic/Latino; 1 Two or more races, non-Hispanic/Latino), 1 international. Average age 30. In 2018, 5 master's awarded. Electronic applications accepted. *Expenses:* Tuition, state resident: full-time $10,848. Tuition, nonresident: full-time $27,888. *Required fees:*

$1128. *Financial support:* In 2018–19, 2 students received support. Fellowships, Federal Work-Study, and assistantships (averaging $7911) available. Financial award application deadline: 3/1; financial award applicants required to submit FAFSA. *Unit head:* Dr. Sharon J. Simmons, Department Head, 540-568-4196, E-mail: simmonsj@jmu.edu. *Application contact:* Lynette D. Michael, Director of Graduate Admissions, 540-568-6131 Ext. 6395, Fax: 540-568-7860, E-mail: michaeld@jmu.edu.
Website: http://www.jmu.edu/cs/

Johns Hopkins University, Engineering Program for Professionals, Part-time Program in Computer Science, Baltimore, MD 21218. Offers communications and networking (MS); computer science (Post-Master's Certificate). *Program availability:* Part-time, evening/weekend, 100% online, blended/hybrid learning. *Faculty:* 63 part-time/adjunct (7 women). *Students:* 407 part-time (79 women). 275 applicants, 39% accepted, 72 enrolled. In 2018, 163 master's awarded. *Entrance requirements:* Additional exam requirements/recommendations for international students: Required—TOEFL (minimum score 600 paper-based; 100 iBT). *Application deadline:* Applications are processed on a rolling basis. Application fee: $0. Electronic applications accepted. *Unit head:* Dr. Lanier A. Watkins, Program Chair, 443-778-5913, E-mail: Lanier.Watkins@jhuapl.edu. *Application contact:* Doug Schiller, Admissions Director, 410-516-2300, Fax: 410-579-8049, E-mail: schiller@jhu.edu.
Website: http://www.ep.jhu.edu/

Johns Hopkins University, Engineering Program for Professionals, Part-time Program in Electrical and Computer Engineering, Baltimore, MD 21218. Offers communications and networking (MS); electrical and computer engineering (Graduate Certificate, Post-Master's Certificate); photonics (MS). *Program availability:* Part-time, evening/weekend, 100% online, blended/hybrid learning. *Faculty:* 1 full-time, 47 part-time/adjunct (2 women). *Students:* 364 part-time (60 women). 119 applicants, 68% accepted, 53 enrolled. In 2018, 101 master's awarded. *Entrance requirements:* Additional exam requirements/recommendations for international students: Required—TOEFL (minimum score 600 paper-based; 100 iBT). *Application deadline:* Applications are processed on a rolling basis. Application fee: $0. Electronic applications accepted. *Unit head:* Dr. Brian Jennison, Program Chair, 443-778-6421, E-mail: brian.jennison@jhuapl.edu. *Application contact:* Doug Schiller, Admissions Director, 410-516-2300, Fax: 410-579-8049, E-mail: schiller@jhu.edu.
Website: http://www.ep.jhu.edu/

Johns Hopkins University, G. W. C. Whiting School of Engineering, Department of Computer Science, Baltimore, MD 21218. Offers MSE, MSSI, PhD. *Faculty:* 34 full-time (6 women), 9 part-time/adjunct (1 woman). *Students:* 245 full-time (52 women), 19 part-time (5 women). 1,140 applicants, 20% accepted, 111 enrolled. In 2018, 98 master's, 21 doctorates awarded. Terminal master's awarded for partial completion of doctoral program. *Degree requirements:* For master's, thesis optional; for doctorate, comprehensive exam, thesis/dissertation, oral exam. *Entrance requirements:* For master's, GRE General Test, 2 letters of recommendation, statement of purpose, transcripts; for doctorate, GRE General Test, 3 letters of recommendation, statement of purpose, transcripts. Additional exam requirements/recommendations for international students: Required—TOEFL (minimum score 600 paper-based, 100 iBT) or IELTS (7). *Application deadline:* For fall admission, 12/15 for domestic students, 2/15 for international students; for spring admission, 11/15 for domestic students, 9/15 for international students. Application fee: $25. Electronic applications accepted. *Financial support:* In 2018–19, 150 students received support, including 10 fellowships with full and partial tuition reimbursements available (averaging $25,497 per year), 115 research assistantships with full tuition reimbursements available (averaging $32,400 per year), 25 teaching assistantships with full tuition reimbursements available (averaging $10,800 per year); institutionally sponsored loans, scholarships/grants, health care benefits, tuition waivers (partial), and unspecified assistantships also available. Financial award application deadline: 12/15. *Faculty research:* Theory and programming languages, systems, information security, machine learning and data intensive computing, language and speech processing, computational biology and medicine, Robotics, Vision and Graphics. *Unit head:* Dr. Randal Burns, Chair, 410-516-8775, Fax: 410-516-6134, E-mail: randal@jhu.edu. *Application contact:* Zach Burwell, Academic Program Administrator, 410-516-7451, Fax: 410-516-6134, E-mail: zburwel1@jhu.edu.
Website: http://www.cs.jhu.edu/

Johns Hopkins University, G. W. C. Whiting School of Engineering, Master of Science in Engineering Management Program, Baltimore, MD 21218. Offers biomaterials (MSEM); civil engineering (MSEM); communications science (MSEM); computer science (MSEM); environmental systems analysis, economics and public policy (MSEM); fluid mechanics (MSEM); materials science and engineering (MSEM); mechanical engineering (MSEM); mechanics and materials (MSEM); nano-biotechnology (MSEM); nanomaterials and nanotechnology (MSEM); operations research (MSEM); probability and statistics (MSEM); smart product and device design (MSEM). *Students:* 34 full-time (12 women), 18 part-time (7 women). 233 applicants, 39% accepted, 33 enrolled. In 2018, 27 master's awarded. *Entrance requirements:* For master's, GRE, 3 letters of recommendation, statement of purpose, transcripts. Additional exam requirements/recommendations for international students: Required—TOEFL (minimum score 600 paper-based, 100 iBT) or IELTS (7). *Application deadline:* For fall admission, 2/15 for domestic and international students. Application fee: $75. Electronic applications accepted. *Financial support:* In 2018–19, 43 research assistantships (averaging $43,344 per year) were awarded; health care benefits also available. *Unit head:* Dr. Pamela Sheff, Director, 410-516-7056, Fax: 410-516-4880, E-mail: pamsheff@gmail.com. *Application contact:* Lindsey Conklin, Sr. Academic Program Coordinator, 410-516-1108, Fax: 410-516-0780, E-mail: lconkli4@jhu.edu.
Website: http://engineering.jhu.edu/msem/

Kansas State University, Graduate School, College of Engineering, Department of Computer Science, Manhattan, KS 66506. Offers MS, MSE, PhD. *Program availability:* Part-time, online learning. Terminal master's awarded for partial completion of doctoral program. *Degree requirements:* For master's, thesis or alternative; for doctorate, thesis/dissertation. *Entrance requirements:* For master's, GRE General Test, bachelor's degree in computer science, minimum GPA of 3.0; for doctorate, GRE General Test, master's degree in computer science or bachelor's degree and strong advanced computer knowledge. Additional exam requirements/recommendations for international students: Required—TOEFL (minimum score 575 paper-based; 90 iBT), IELTS, or PTE. Electronic applications accepted. *Faculty research:* High-assurance software and programming languages, data mining, parallel and distributed computing, computer security, embedded systems.

Kennesaw State University, College of Computing and Software Engineering, Program in Computer Science, Kennesaw, GA 30144. Offers MS. *Program availability:* Part-time, evening/weekend, blended/hybrid learning. *Students:* 81 full-time (33 women), 90 part-time (27 women); includes 61 minority (24 Black or African American, non-Hispanic/Latino; 21 Asian, non-Hispanic/Latino; 10 Hispanic/Latino; 6 Two or more races, non-Hispanic/Latino), 49 international. Average age 30. 119 applicants, 70% accepted, 54 enrolled. In 2018, 29 master's awarded. *Degree requirements:* For master's, thesis optional. *Entrance requirements:* For master's, GMAT or GRE, minimum GPA of 2.75. Additional exam requirements/recommendations for international students: Required—TOEFL (minimum score 80 iBT), IELTS (minimum score 6.5). *Application deadline:* For fall admission, 7/1 priority date for domestic students, 7/1 for international students; for spring admission, 11/1 priority date for domestic students, 11/1 for international students; for summer admission, 4/1 for domestic and international students. Applications are processed on a rolling basis. Application fee: $60. Electronic applications accepted. *Expenses: Tuition, area resident:* Full-time $6960; part-time $290 per credit hour. Tuition, state resident: full-time $6960; part-time $290 per credit hour. Tuition, nonresident: full-time $25,080; part-time $1045 per credit hour. *International tuition:* $25,080 full-time. *Required fees:* $2006; $1706 per semester. $853 per semester. *Financial support:* Research assistantships with full tuition reimbursements, Federal Work-Study, and unspecified assistantships available. Support available to part-time students. Financial award applicants required to submit FAFSA. *Application contact:* Admissions Counselor, 470-578-4377, Fax: 470-578-9172, E-mail: ksugrad@kennesaw.edu.
Website: http://ccse.kennesaw.edu/cs/

Kent State University, College of Arts and Sciences, Department of Computer Science, Kent, OH 44242-0001. Offers MA, MS, PhD. *Program availability:* Part-time. *Faculty:* 16 full-time (1 woman), 3 part-time/adjunct (0 women). *Students:* 88 full-time (32 women), 16 part-time (4 women); includes 2 minority (1 Black or African American, non-Hispanic/Latino; 1 Hispanic/Latino), 86 international. Average age 28. 254 applicants, 56% accepted, 29 enrolled. In 2018, 49 master's, 10 doctorates awarded. *Degree requirements:* For master's, thesis optional; for doctorate, comprehensive exam, thesis/dissertation, preliminary examination, two public presentations of project/research work. *Entrance requirements:* For master's, GRE, transcripts, goal statement, resume, 3 letters of recommendation, core components of an undergraduate computer science curriculum; for doctorate, GRE, transcript, goal statement, 3 letters of recommendation, master's degree in computer science (or closely related field). Additional exam requirements/recommendations for international students: Required—TOEFL (minimum score 525 paper-based, 71 iBT), Michigan English Language Assessment Battery (minimum score 74), IELTS (minimum score 6.0) or PTE (minimum score 50). *Application deadline:* For fall admission, 6/1 for domestic and international students; for spring admission, 10/10 for domestic and international students. Applications are processed on a rolling basis. Application fee: $45 ($70 for international students). Electronic applications accepted. *Expenses:* Tuition, state resident: full-time $11,766; part-time $536 per credit. Tuition, nonresident: full-time $21,952; part-time $999 per credit. *International tuition:* $21,952 full-time. Tuition and fees vary according to course load. *Financial support:* Fellowships with full tuition reimbursements, research assistantships with full tuition reimbursements, teaching assistantships with full tuition reimbursements, Federal Work-Study, and unspecified assistantships available. Financial award application deadline: 1/31. *Unit head:* Dr. Javed Khan, Professor and Chair, 330-672-9055, E-mail: javed@kent.edu. *Application contact:* Dr. Cheng Chang Lu, Professor/Assistant Chair/Graduate Advisor, 330-672-9031, Fax: 330-672-0737, E-mail: clu@kent.edu.
Website: http://www.kent.edu/cs

Kutztown University of Pennsylvania, College of Liberal Arts and Sciences, Program in Computer Science, Kutztown, PA 19530-0730. Offers MS. *Program availability:* Part-time, evening/weekend. *Faculty:* 5 full-time (0 women). *Students:* 8 full-time (0 women), 10 part-time (2 women); includes 1 minority (Asian, non-Hispanic/Latino). Average age 30. 14 applicants, 93% accepted, 8 enrolled. In 2018, 9 master's awarded. *Entrance requirements:* For master's, GRE General Test, 3 letters of recommendation. Additional exam requirements/recommendations for international students: Required—TOEFL (minimum score 550 paper-based, 79 iBT), IELTS (minimum score 6.5), or PTE (minimum score 53). *Application deadline:* For fall admission, 8/1 for domestic and international students; for spring admission, 12/1 for domestic and international students. Application fee: $35. Electronic applications accepted. *Expenses:* Tuition, state resident: part-time $516 per credit. Tuition, nonresident: part-time $774 per credit. *Required fees:* $119 per credit. One-time fee: $50 part-time. Tuition and fees vary according to degree level. *Financial support:* Career-related internships or fieldwork, Federal Work-Study, and unspecified assistantships available. Financial award application deadline: 3/1; financial award applicants required to submit FAFSA. *Faculty research:* Artificial intelligence, expert systems, neural networks. *Unit head:* Dr. Lisa Frye, Chairperson, 610-683-4422, Fax: 610-683-4129, E-mail: frye@kutztown.edu. *Application contact:* Dr. Lisa Frye, Chairperson, 610-683-4422, Fax: 610-683-4129, E-mail: frye@kutztown.edu.
Website: https://www.kutztown.edu/academics/graduate-programs/computer-science.htm

Lakehead University, Graduate Studies, School of Mathematical Sciences, Thunder Bay, ON P7B 5E1, Canada. Offers computer science (M Sc); mathematical science (MA). *Program availability:* Part-time, evening/weekend. *Degree requirements:* For master's, thesis optional. *Entrance requirements:* For master's, minimum B average, honours degree in mathematics or computer science. Additional exam requirements/recommendations for international students: Required—TOEFL. *Faculty research:* Numerical analysis, classical analysis, theoretical computer science, abstract harmonic analysis, functional analysis.

Lamar University, College of Graduate Studies, College of Arts and Sciences, Department of Computer Science, Beaumont, TX 77710. Offers MS. *Program availability:* Part-time. *Faculty:* 13 full-time (3 women), 2 part-time/adjunct (1 woman). *Students:* 59 full-time (19 women), 22 part-time (8 women), 77 international. Average age 26. 129 applicants, 71% accepted, 22 enrolled. In 2018, 67 master's awarded. *Degree requirements:* For master's, comprehensive exams and project or thesis. *Entrance requirements:* For master's, GRE General Test, minimum GPA of 3.3 in last 60 hours of undergraduate course work or 3.0 overall. Additional exam requirements/recommendations for international students: Required—TOEFL (minimum score 527 paper-based; 71 iBT), IELTS (minimum score 6). *Application deadline:* Applications are processed on a rolling basis. Application fee: $25 ($50 for international students). *Expenses:* Tuition, state resident: full-time $6234; part-time $346 per credit hour. Tuition, nonresident: full-time $6852; part-time $761 per credit hour. *International tuition:* $6852 full-time. *Required fees:* $1940; $327 per credit hour. Tuition and fees vary according to course load, campus/location, program and reciprocity agreements. *Financial support:* In 2018–19, 2 research assistantships with partial tuition reimbursements (averaging $6,000 per year), 4 teaching assistantships with partial tuition reimbursements (averaging $6,000 per year) were awarded; institutionally sponsored loans, scholarships/grants, and tuition waivers (partial) also available. Financial award applicants required to submit FAFSA. *Faculty research:* Computer architecture, network security. *Total annual research expenditures:* $52,414. *Unit head:* Dr. Stefan Andrei, Chair, 409-880-8775, Fax: 409-880-2364. *Application contact:* Celeste Contreas, Director, Admissions and Academic Services, 409-880-8888, Fax: 409-880-7419, E-mail: gradmissions@lamar.edu.
Website: http://artssciences.lamar.edu/computer-science

La Salle University, School of Arts and Sciences, Program in Computer Information Science, Philadelphia, PA 19141-1199. Offers application development (Certificate); computer information science (MS). *Program availability:* Part-time, evening/weekend, online only, 100% online. *Degree requirements:* For master's, capstone project. *Entrance requirements:* For master's, GRE, MAT, or GMAT, minimum undergraduate

GPA of 3.0; two letters of recommendation; resume; telephone or in-person interview. Additional exam requirements/recommendations for international students: Required—TOEFL. Electronic applications accepted. Application fee is waived when completed online. *Expenses:* Contact institution. *Faculty research:* Human-computer interaction, networks, technology trends, databases, groupware.

Lawrence Technological University, College of Arts and Sciences, Southfield, MI 48075-1058. Offers bioinformatics (Graduate Certificate); computer science (MS), including data science, big data, and data mining, intelligent systems; educational technology (MA), including robotics; instructional design, communication, and presentation (Graduate Certificate); integrated science (MA); science education (MA); technical and professional communication (MS, Graduate Certificate); writing for the digital age (Graduate Certificate). *Program availability:* Part-time, evening/weekend. *Degree requirements:* For master's, thesis (for some programs). *Entrance requirements:* Additional exam requirements/recommendations for international students: Required—TOEFL (minimum score 550 paper-based; 79 iBT), IELTS (minimum score 6.5). Electronic applications accepted. *Faculty research:* Computer analysis of music, machine learning of literature and lyrics, customer sentiments and response analysis through social media, peta-scale computing in astronomical databases, early detection of diseases with pattern recognition.

Lebanese American University, School of Arts and Sciences, Beirut, Lebanon. Offers computer science (MS); international affairs (MA).

Lehigh University, P.C. Rossin College of Engineering and Applied Science, Department of Computer Science and Engineering, Bethlehem, PA 18015. Offers computer engineering (M Eng, MS, PhD); computer science (M Eng, MS, PhD); MBA/E. Computer engineering program handled through the ECE department. *Program availability:* Part-time. *Faculty:* 15 full-time (2 women), 1 (woman) part-time/adjunct. *Students:* 59 full-time (13 women), 2 part-time (0 women); includes 3 minority (1 Black or African American, non-Hispanic/Latino; 1 Asian, non-Hispanic/Latino; 1 Hispanic/Latino), 49 international. Average age 26. 263 applicants, 36% accepted, 21 enrolled. In 2018, 19 master's, 1 doctorate awarded. Terminal master's awarded for partial completion of doctoral program. *Degree requirements:* For master's, thesis optional, oral presentation of thesis; for doctorate, thesis/dissertation, qualifying, general, and oral exams. *Entrance requirements:* For master's, GRE General Test, minimum GPA of 3.0; for doctorate, GRE General Test, minimum GPA of 3.5. Additional exam requirements/recommendations for international students: Required—TOEFL (minimum score 550 paper-based; 79 iBT), IELTS (minimum score 6.5). *Application deadline:* For fall admission, 4/1 for domestic and international students; for spring admission, 11/1 for domestic and international students. Application fee: $75. Electronic applications accepted. *Expenses:* $1500 per credit. *Financial support:* In 2018–19, 16 students received support, including 3 fellowships with full tuition reimbursements available (averaging $22,325 per year), 7 research assistantships with full tuition reimbursements available (averaging $22,050 per year), 7 teaching assistantships with full tuition reimbursements available (averaging $22,050 per year). Financial award application deadline: 1/15. *Faculty research:* Artificial intelligence, networking-pattern recognition, multimedia e-learning/data mining/Web search, mobile robotics, bioinformatics, computer vision, data science. *Total annual research expenditures:* $1.1 million. *Unit head:* Dr. Daniel P. Lopresti, Chair, 610-758-5782, E-mail: dal9@lehigh.edu. *Application contact:* Heidi Wegrzyn, Graduate Coordinator, 610-758-3065, E-mail: hew207@lehigh.edu.
Website: http://www.cse.lehigh.edu/

Lehman College of the City University of New York, School of Natural and Social Sciences, Department of Mathematics and Computer Science, Program in Computer Science, Bronx, NY 10468-1589. Offers MS. *Degree requirements:* For master's, one foreign language, thesis or alternative.

Lewis University, College of Arts and Sciences, Program in Computer Science, Romeoville, IL 60446. Offers cyber security (MS); intelligent systems (MS); software engineering (MS). *Program availability:* Part-time, evening/weekend, 100% online, blended/hybrid learning. *Students:* 23 full-time (5 women), 90 part-time (23 women); includes 34 minority (8 Black or African American, non-Hispanic/Latino; 12 Asian, non-Hispanic/Latino; 9 Hispanic/Latino; 1 Native Hawaiian or other Pacific Islander, non-Hispanic/Latino; 4 Two or more races, non-Hispanic/Latino), 6 international. Average age 32. *Entrance requirements:* For master's, bachelor's degree; minimum undergraduate GPA of 3.0; resume; statement of purpose; two letters of recommendation; undergraduate coursework in discrete mathematics, programming or algorithms. Additional exam requirements/recommendations for international students: Required—TOEFL (minimum score 550 paper-based; 79 iBT), IELTS (minimum score 6). *Application deadline:* For fall admission, 5/1 for international students; for winter admission, 11/15 for international students. Applications are processed on a rolling basis. Application fee: $40. Electronic applications accepted. *Financial support:* Federal Work-Study and unspecified assistantships available. Financial award application deadline: 5/1; financial award applicants required to submit FAFSA. *Unit head:* Dr. Khaled Alzoubi, Program Director. *Application contact:* Linda Campbell, Graduate Admissions Counselor, 815-836-5610, E-mail: grad@lewisu.edu.
Website: http://www.lewisu.edu/academics/mscomputerscience/index.htm

Lewis University, College of Arts and Sciences, Program in Data Science, Romeoville, IL 60446. Offers computational biology and bioinformatics (MS); computer science (MS). *Program availability:* Part-time, evening/weekend, 100% online, blended/hybrid learning. *Students:* 16 full-time (4 women), 99 part-time (28 women); includes 34 minority (8 Black or African American, non-Hispanic/Latino; 12 Asian, non-Hispanic/Latino; 8 Hispanic/Latino; 1 Native Hawaiian or other Pacific Islander, non-Hispanic/Latino; 5 Two or more races, non-Hispanic/Latino), 2 international. Average age 35. *Entrance requirements:* For master's, bachelor's degree, undergraduate coursework in calculus, minimum undergraduate GPA of 3.0, resume, statement of purpose, two letters of recommendation. Additional exam requirements/recommendations for international students: Required—TOEFL (minimum score 550 paper-based; 79 iBT), IELTS (minimum score 6). *Application deadline:* For fall admission, 5/1 priority date for international students; for winter admission, 11/1 priority date for international students. Applications are processed on a rolling basis. Application fee: $40. Electronic applications accepted. Application fee is waived when completed online. *Financial support:* Federal Work-Study available. Financial award application deadline: 5/1; financial award applicants required to submit FAFSA. *Unit head:* Dr. Piotr Szczurek, Program Director. *Application contact:* Linda Campbell, Graduate Admissions Counselor, 815-836-5610, E-mail: grad@lewisu.edu.
Website: http://www.lewisu.edu/academics/data-science/index.htm

Long Island University–LIU Brooklyn, School of Business, Public Administration and Information Sciences, Brooklyn, NY 11201-8423. Offers accounting (MBA); accounting (MS); business administration (MBA); computer science (MS); gerontology (Advanced Certificate); health administration (MPA); human resources management (MS); not-for-profit management (Advanced Certificate); public administration (MPA); taxation (MS). *Program availability:* Part-time, evening/weekend. *Entrance requirements:* Additional exam requirements/recommendations for international students: Required—TOEFL (minimum score 550 paper-based; 75 iBT). Electronic applications accepted. *Faculty research:* Tax policy; public sector budgeting and gender inequities; technology and innovation; game theory; knowledge management.

Louisiana State University and Agricultural & Mechanical College, Graduate School, College of Engineering, Division of Computer Science, Baton Rouge, LA 70803. Offers computer science (MSSS, PhD); systems science (MSSS).

Louisiana State University in Shreveport, College of Arts and Sciences, Program in Computer Systems Technology, Shreveport, LA 71115-2399. Offers MS. *Program availability:* Part-time, evening/weekend. *Degree requirements:* For master's, comprehensive exam (for some programs), thesis or alternative. *Entrance requirements:* For master's, GRE, programming course in high-level language, interview. Additional exam requirements/recommendations for international students: Required—TOEFL (minimum score 550 paper-based; 80 iBT). Electronic applications accepted.

Louisiana Tech University, Graduate School, College of Engineering and Science, Ruston, LA 71272. Offers applied physics (MS); biomedical engineering (PhD); computer science (MS); engineering (MS, PhD), including cyberspace engineering (PhD), engineering education (PhD), engineering physics (PhD), materials and infrastructure systems (PhD), micro/nanoscale systems (PhD); engineering and technology management (MS); mathematics (MS); molecular science and nanotechnology (MS, PhD). *Program availability:* Part-time-only. Terminal master's awarded for partial completion of doctoral program. *Degree requirements:* For master's, thesis (for some programs); for doctorate, thesis/dissertation. *Entrance requirements:* For master's and Graduate Certificate, GRE General Test, minimum GPA of 3.0 in last 60 hours. Additional exam requirements/recommendations for international students: Required—TOEFL (minimum score 550 paper-based; 80 iBT), IELTS (minimum score 6.5). Electronic applications accepted. *Faculty research:* Trenchless technology, micromanufacturing, radionuclide transport, microbial liquefaction, hazardous waste treatment.

Loyola University Chicago, Graduate School, Department of Computer Science, Chicago, IL 60660. Offers computer science (MS); information technology (MS); software engineering (MS). *Program availability:* Part-time, evening/weekend, 100% online, blended/hybrid learning. *Faculty:* 16 full-time (3 women), 16 part-time/adjunct (2 women). *Students:* 45 full-time (13 women), 40 part-time (11 women); includes 23 minority (7 Black or African American, non-Hispanic/Latino; 15 Asian, non-Hispanic/Latino; 1 Hispanic/Latino), 29 international. Average age 29. 116 applicants, 53% accepted, 29 enrolled. In 2018, 48 master's awarded. *Degree requirements:* For master's, thesis optional, 30 credits/ten courses. *Entrance requirements:* For master's, 2 letters of recommendation, transcripts, statement of purpose. Additional exam requirements/recommendations for international students: Required—TOEFL (minimum score 550 paper-based; 79 iBT), IELTS (minimum score 6.5). *Application deadline:* Applications are processed on a rolling basis. Application fee: $50. Electronic applications accepted. Application fee is waived when completed online. *Expenses:* Contact institution. *Financial support:* In 2018–19, 17 students received support, including 2 fellowships with full tuition reimbursements available, 1 research assistantship with full tuition reimbursement available (averaging $17,000 per year), 11 teaching assistantships with partial tuition reimbursements available (averaging $9,575 per year); career-related internships or fieldwork, Federal Work-Study, health care benefits, and tuition waivers (full and partial) also available. Financial award application deadline: 3/15. *Faculty research:* Software engineering, machine learning, algorithms and complexity, parallel and distributed computing, databases and computer networks, security. *Total annual research expenditures:* $22,000. *Unit head:* Dr. Chandra Sekharan, Chair, 773-508-3572, Fax: 773-508-3739, E-mail: laufer@cs.luc.edu. *Application contact:* Cecilia Murphy, Graduate Program Secretary, 773-508-8035, E-mail: cmurphy@luc.edu.
Website: http://luc.edu/cs

Maharishi University of Management, Graduate Studies, Program in Computer Science, Fairfield, IA 52557. Offers MS. *Degree requirements:* For master's, thesis or alternative. *Entrance requirements:* For master's, GRE General Test, minimum GPA of 3.0. Additional exam requirements/recommendations for international students: Required—TOEFL. *Expenses: Tuition:* Full-time $29,000; part-time $4800 per credit hour. *Required fees:* $530. *Faculty research:* Parallel processing, computer systems in architecture.

Marist College, Graduate Programs, School of Computer Science and Mathematics, Poughkeepsie, NY 12601-1387. Offers business analytics (Adv C); computer science/software development (MS); information systems (MS, Adv C). *Program availability:* Part-time, evening/weekend, online learning. *Entrance requirements:* For master's, resume. Additional exam requirements/recommendations for international students: Required—TOEFL (minimum score 550 paper-based; 80 iBT); Recommended—IELTS (minimum score 6.5). Electronic applications accepted. *Faculty research:* Data quality, artificial intelligence, imaging, analysis of algorithms, distributed systems and applications.

Marquette University, Graduate School, College of Arts and Sciences, Department of Mathematics, Statistics, and Computer Science, Milwaukee, WI 53201-1881. Offers bioinformatics (MS); computational sciences (MS, PhD); computing (MS); mathematics education (MS). *Program availability:* Part-time, evening/weekend, online learning. Terminal master's awarded for partial completion of doctoral program. *Degree requirements:* For master's, thesis (for some programs), essay with oral presentation; for doctorate, comprehensive exam, thesis/dissertation, qualifying examination. *Entrance requirements:* For master's, official transcripts from all current and previous colleges/universities except Marquette, three letters of recommendation; for doctorate, GRE General Test, official transcripts from all current and previous colleges/universities except Marquette, three letters of recommendation. Additional exam requirements/recommendations for international students: Required—TOEFL (minimum score 530 paper-based). Electronic applications accepted. *Faculty research:* Models of physiological systems, mathematical immunology, computational group theory, mathematical logic, computational science.

Marquette University, Graduate School, College of Arts and Sciences, Program in Computing, Milwaukee, WI 53201-1881. Offers MS. *Program availability:* Part-time, evening/weekend, online learning. *Degree requirements:* For master's, thesis optional, enrollment in the Professional Seminar in Computing each term. *Entrance requirements:* For master's, official transcripts from all current and previous colleges/universities except Marquette, essay, three letters of reference. Additional exam requirements/recommendations for international students: Required—TOEFL (minimum score 530 paper-based). Electronic applications accepted.

Marshall University, Academic Affairs Division, College of Information Technology and Engineering, Program in Computer Science, Huntington, WV 25755. Offers MS. *Degree requirements:* For master's, thesis or project. *Entrance requirements:* Additional exam requirements/recommendations for international students: Required—IELTS (minimum score 5.5).

Massachusetts Institute of Technology, School of Engineering, Department of Electrical Engineering and Computer Science, Cambridge, MA 02139. Offers computer science (PhD, Sc D, ECS); computer science and engineering (PhD, Sc D); computer science and molecular biology (M Eng); electrical engineering (PhD, Sc D, EE);

electrical engineering and computer science (M Eng, SM, PhD, Sc D); SM/MBA. *Degree requirements:* For master's and other advanced degree, thesis; for doctorate, comprehensive exam, thesis/dissertation. *Entrance requirements:* Additional exam requirements/recommendations for international students: Required—TOEFL, IELTS. Electronic applications accepted. *Expenses: Tuition:* Full-time $51,520; part-time $800 per credit hour. *Required fees:* $312. *Faculty research:* Information systems, circuits, biomedical sciences and engineering, computer science: artificial intelligence, systems, theory.

McGill University, Faculty of Graduate and Postdoctoral Studies, Faculty of Science, School of Computer Science, Montréal, QC H3A 2T5, Canada. Offers M Sc, PhD.

McMaster University, School of Graduate Studies, Faculty of Engineering, Department of Computing and Software, Hamilton, ON L8S 4M2, Canada. Offers computer science (M Sc, PhD); software engineering (M Eng, MA Sc, PhD). *Program availability:* Part-time. *Degree requirements:* For master's, thesis. *Entrance requirements:* Additional exam requirements/recommendations for international students: Required—TOEFL (minimum score 550 paper-based). *Faculty research:* Software engineering; theory of non-sequential systems; parallel and distributed computing; artificial intelligence; complexity, design, and analysis of algorithms; combinatorial computing, especially applications to molecular biology.

McNeese State University, Doré School of Graduate Studies, College of Science and Agriculture, Department of Mathematical Sciences, Lake Charles, LA 70609. Offers computer science (MS); mathematics (MS); statistics (MS). *Program availability:* Evening/weekend. *Degree requirements:* For master's, comprehensive exam, thesis or alternative, written exam. *Entrance requirements:* For master's, GRE.

Memorial University of Newfoundland, School of Graduate Studies, Department of Computer Science, St. John's, NL A1C 5S7, Canada. Offers M Sc, PhD. *Program availability:* Part-time. *Degree requirements:* For master's, thesis; for doctorate, comprehensive exam, thesis/dissertation, oral thesis defense. *Entrance requirements:* For master's, GRE (strongly recommended), honors degree in computer science or related field; for doctorate, GRE (strongly recommended), master's degree in computer science. Electronic applications accepted. *Faculty research:* Theoretical computer science, parallel and distributed computing, scientific computing, software systems and artificial intelligence.

Merrimack College, School of Science and Engineering, North Andover, MA 01845-5800. Offers civil engineering (MS); computer science (MS); data science (MS); engineering management (MS); mechanical engineering (MS), including engineering management. *Program availability:* Part-time, evening/weekend, 100% online. *Faculty:* 10 full-time (2 women), 6 part-time/adjunct (1 woman). *Students:* 53 full-time (18 women), 17 part-time (5 women); includes 14 minority (6 Black or African American, non-Hispanic/Latino; 6 Asian, non-Hispanic/Latino; 2 Two or more races, non-Hispanic/Latino), 9 international. Average age 34. 183 applicants, 61% accepted, 40 enrolled. In 2018, 27 master's awarded. *Degree requirements:* For master's, comprehensive exam, thesis optional, internship or capstone (for some programs). *Entrance requirements:* For master's, official college transcripts, resume, personal statement, 2 recommendations. Additional exam requirements/recommendations for international students: Required—TOEFL (minimum score 84 iBT), IELTS (minimum score 6.5), PTE (minimum score 56). *Application deadline:* For fall admission, 8/24 for domestic students, 7/30 for international students; for spring admission, 1/10 for domestic students, 12/10 for international students; for summer admission, 5/10 for domestic students, 4/10 for international students. Applications are processed on a rolling basis. Application fee: $0. Electronic applications accepted. Application fee is waived when completed online. *Expenses:* Contact institution. *Financial support:* Career-related internships or fieldwork, scholarships/grants, health care benefits, and unspecified assistantships available. Support available to part-time students. Financial award application deadline: 5/1; financial award applicants required to submit FAFSA. *Unit head:* Dr. Naira Campbell-Kyureghyan, Dean, 978-837-5265, E-mail: campbellnk@merrimack.edu. *Application contact:* Allison Pena, Graduate Admissions Counselor, 978-837-3563, E-mail: penaa@merrimack.edu.
Website: http://www.merrimack.edu/academics/graduate/

Metropolitan State University, College of Sciences, St. Paul, MN 55106-5000. Offers computer science (MS, PSM).

Michigan State University, The Graduate School, College of Engineering, Department of Computer Science and Engineering, East Lansing, MI 48824. Offers computer science (MS, PhD). *Entrance requirements:* Additional exam requirements/recommendations for international students: Required—TOEFL. Electronic applications accepted.

Middle Tennessee State University, College of Graduate Studies, College of Basic and Applied Sciences, Department of Computer Science, Murfreesboro, TN 37132. Offers MS. *Program availability:* Part-time, evening/weekend, online learning. *Degree requirements:* For master's, comprehensive exam, thesis. *Entrance requirements:* For master's, GRE. Additional exam requirements/recommendations for international students: Required—TOEFL (minimum score 525 paper-based; 71 iBT) or IELTS (minimum score 6). Electronic applications accepted. *Faculty research:* Computational science, parallel processing, artificial intelligence.

Midwestern State University, Billie Doris McAda Graduate School, College of Science and Mathematics, Department of Computer Science, Wichita Falls, TX 76308. Offers MS. *Program availability:* Part-time, evening/weekend. *Degree requirements:* For master's, comprehensive exam, thesis. *Entrance requirements:* For master's, GRE General Test. Additional exam requirements/recommendations for international students: Required—TOEFL (minimum score 573 paper-based). Electronic applications accepted. *Faculty research:* Software engineering, genetic algorithms and graphics, computational epidemiology, new ways of using GPS.

Mills College, Graduate Studies, Program in Computer Science, Oakland, CA 94613-1000. Offers computer science (Certificate); interdisciplinary computer science (MA). *Program availability:* Part-time. *Degree requirements:* For master's, thesis. *Entrance requirements:* For master's, three letters of recommendation. Additional exam requirements/recommendations for international students: Required—TOEFL (minimum score 600 paper-based; 100 iBT) or IELTS (minimum score 7). Electronic applications accepted. *Expenses:* Contact institution. *Faculty research:* Dynamical systems, linear programming, theory of computer viruses, interface design, intelligent tutoring systems.

Minnesota State University Mankato, College of Graduate Studies and Research, College of Science, Engineering and Technology, Department of Computer Information Science, Mankato, MN 56001. Offers information technology (MS). *Degree requirements:* For master's, comprehensive exam, thesis or alternative. *Entrance requirements:* For master's, GRE General Test, minimum GPA of 3.0 during previous 2 years. Additional exam requirements/recommendations for international students: Required—TOEFL (minimum score 550 paper-based; 80 iBT). Electronic applications accepted.

Mississippi College, Graduate School, College of Arts and Sciences, School of Science and Mathematics, Department of Engineering, Computer Science, and Physics, Clinton, MS 39058. Offers computer science (M Ed, MS); cybersecurity and information assurance (MS). *Program availability:* Part-time. *Degree requirements:* For master's, comprehensive exam, thesis or alternative. *Entrance requirements:* For master's, GRE. Additional exam requirements/recommendations for international students: Recommended—TOEFL, IELTS.

Mississippi State University, Bagley College of Engineering, Department of Computer Science and Engineering, Mississippi State, MS 39762. Offers MS, PhD. *Program availability:* Part-time, blended/hybrid learning. *Faculty:* 17 full-time (3 women), 2 part-time/adjunct (0 women). *Students:* 65 full-time (17 women), 15 part-time (2 women); includes 13 minority (9 Black or African American, non-Hispanic/Latino; 2 Asian, non-Hispanic/Latino; 2 Hispanic/Latino), 24 international. Average age 28. 102 applicants, 29% accepted, 15 enrolled. In 2018, 19 master's, 3 doctorates awarded. *Degree requirements:* For master's, thesis optional, comprehensive oral exam; for doctorate, thesis/dissertation, comprehensive oral or written exam. *Entrance requirements:* For master's, GRE, minimum GPA of 2.75; for doctorate, GRE. Additional exam requirements/recommendations for international students: Required—TOEFL (minimum score 550 paper-based; 79 iBT); Recommended—IELTS (minimum score 6.5). *Application deadline:* For fall admission, 7/1 for domestic students, 5/1 for international students; for spring admission, 11/1 for domestic students, 9/1 for international students. Applications are processed on a rolling basis. Application fee: $60 ($80 for international students). Electronic applications accepted. *Expenses:* Tuition, state resident: full-time $8450; part-time $360.59 per credit hour. Tuition, nonresident: full-time $23,140; part-time $969.09 per credit hour. *Required fees:* $110. One-time fee: $55 full-time. Part-time tuition and fees vary according to course load, degree level, campus/location and reciprocity agreements. *Financial support:* In 2018–19, 7 research assistantships with full tuition reimbursements (averaging $18,231 per year), 22 teaching assistantships with full tuition reimbursements (averaging $13,820 per year) were awarded; Federal Work-Study, institutionally sponsored loans, and unspecified assistantships also available. Financial award application deadline: 4/1; financial award applicants required to submit FAFSA. *Faculty research:* Artificial intelligence, software engineering, visualization, high performance computing. *Total annual research expenditures:* $6.3 million. *Unit head:* Dr. Shahram Rahimi, Department Head and Professor, 662-325-7450, Fax: 662-325-8997, E-mail: office@cse.msstate.edu. *Application contact:* Angie Campbell, Admissions and Enrollment Assistant, 662-325-9514, E-mail: acampbell@grad.msstate.edu.
Website: http://www.cse.msstate.edu/

Missouri State University, Graduate College, College of Natural and Applied Sciences, Department of Computer Science, Springfield, MO 65897. Offers natural and applied science (MNAS), including computer science. *Program availability:* Part-time. *Faculty:* 6 full-time (1 woman). *Students:* 14 full-time (1 woman), 7 part-time (2 women); includes 3 minority (1 Asian, non-Hispanic/Latino; 1 Hispanic/Latino; 1 Two or more races, non-Hispanic/Latino), 12 international. Average age 25. 21 applicants, 67% accepted. In 2018, 3 master's awarded. *Degree requirements:* For master's, comprehensive exam, thesis or alternative. *Entrance requirements:* For master's, GRE, minimum GPA of 3.0. Additional exam requirements/recommendations for international students: Required—TOEFL (minimum score 550 paper-based; 79 iBT), IELTS (minimum score 6). *Application deadline:* For fall admission, 7/20 priority date for domestic students, 5/1 for international students; for spring admission, 12/20 priority date for domestic students, 9/1 for international students. Applications are processed on a rolling basis. Application fee: $55 ($60 for international students). Electronic applications accepted. Tuition and fees vary according to class time, course level, course load, degree level, campus/location, program and student level. *Financial support:* In 2018–19, 1 teaching assistantship with partial tuition reimbursement (averaging $2,150 per year) was awarded; Federal Work-Study, institutionally sponsored loans, scholarships/grants, and unspecified assistantships also available. Financial award application deadline: 1/31; financial award applicants required to submit FAFSA. *Faculty research:* Floating point numbers, data compression, graph theory. *Unit head:* Dr. Ajay Katangur, Department Head, 417-836-4157, Fax: 417-836-6659, E-mail: computerscience@missouristate.edu. *Application contact:* Lakan Drinker, Director, Graduate Enrollment Management, 417-836-5330, Fax: 417-836-6200, E-mail: lakandrinker@missouristate.edu.
Website: http://computerscience.missouristate.edu/

Missouri University of Science and Technology, Department of Computer Science, Rolla, MO 65401. Offers MS, PhD. *Program availability:* Part-time. Terminal master's awarded for partial completion of doctoral program. *Degree requirements:* For doctorate, thesis/dissertation, departmental qualifying exam. *Entrance requirements:* For master's, GRE General Test (minimum score 700 quantitative, 4 writing); for doctorate, GRE Subject Test (minimum score: quantitative 600, writing 3.5). Additional exam requirements/recommendations for international students: Required—TOEFL (minimum score 550 paper-based). Electronic applications accepted. *Expenses:* Tuition, state resident: full-time $7545.60; part-time $419.20 per credit hour. Tuition, nonresident: full-time $22,169; part-time $1231.60 per credit hour. *International tuition:* $23,518.80 full-time. *Required fees:* $4523.05. Full-time tuition and fees vary according to course load, campus/location, program and reciprocity agreements. *Faculty research:* Intelligent systems, artificial intelligence software engineering, distributed systems, database systems, computer systems.

Monmouth University, Graduate Studies, Program in Computer Science, West Long Branch, NJ 07764-1898. Offers MS. *Program availability:* Part-time, evening/weekend. *Faculty:* 3 full-time (0 women), 5 part-time/adjunct (0 women). *Students:* 30 full-time (10 women), 20 part-time (3 women); includes 6 minority (2 Black or African American, non-Hispanic/Latino; 3 Asian, non-Hispanic/Latino; 1 Hispanic/Latino), 22 international. Average age 28. In 2018, 18 master's awarded. *Degree requirements:* For master's, thesis (for some programs), practicum. *Entrance requirements:* For master's, minimum GPA of 3.0 in major, 2.75 overall; two letters of recommendation; calculus I and II with minimum C grade; two semesters of computer programming within past five years with minimum B grade; undergraduate degree in major that requires substantial component of software development and/or business administration. Additional exam requirements/recommendations for international students: Required—TOEFL (minimum score 550 paper-based, 79 iBT), IELTS (minimum score 6), Michigan English Language Assessment Battery (minimum score 77) or Certificate of Advanced English (minimum score 160). *Application deadline:* For fall admission, 7/15 priority date for domestic students, 6/1 for international students; for spring admission, 12/1 priority date for domestic students, 11/1 for international students; for summer admission, 5/1 for domestic students. Applications are processed on a rolling basis. Application fee: $50. Electronic applications accepted. *Expenses: Tuition:* Part-time $1233 per credit. *Required fees:* $178 per term. *Financial support:* In 2018–19, 41 students received support. Institutionally sponsored loans, scholarships/grants, and unspecified assistantships available. Support available to part-time students. Financial award applicants required to submit FAFSA. *Faculty research:* Databases, natural language processing, protocols, performance analysis, communications networks (systems), cybersecurity. *Unit head:* Dr. Jiacun Wang, Program Director, 732-571-7501, Fax: 732-263-5202, E-mail: jwang@monmouth.edu. *Application contact:* Laurie Kuhn, Associate Director of Graduate Admission, 732-571-3452, Fax: 732-263-5123, E-mail: gradadm@monmouth.edu.
Website: https://www.monmouth.edu/graduate/ms-computer-science/

Monroe College, King Graduate School, Bronx, NY 10468. Offers accounting (MS); business administration (MBA), including entrepreneurship, finance, general business administration, healthcare management, human resources, information technology, marketing; computer science (MS); criminal justice (MS); hospitality management (MS); public health (MPH), including biostatistics and epidemiology, community health, health administration and leadership. *Program availability:* Online learning.

Montana State University, The Graduate School, College of Engineering, Department of Computer Science, Bozeman, MT 59717. Offers computer science (MS, PhD). *Program availability:* Part-time. *Degree requirements:* For master's, comprehensive exam; for doctorate, comprehensive exam, thesis/dissertation. *Entrance requirements:* For master's and doctorate, GRE. Additional exam requirements/recommendations for international students: Required—TOEFL (minimum score 550 paper-based). Electronic applications accepted. *Faculty research:* Applied algorithms, artificial intelligence, data mining, software engineering, Web-based learning, wireless networking and robotics.

Montclair State University, The Graduate School, College of Science and Mathematics, CISCO Certificate Program, Montclair, NJ 07043-1624. Offers Certificate.

Montclair State University, The Graduate School, College of Science and Mathematics, MS Program in Computer Science, Montclair, NJ 07043-1624. Offers computer science (MS); information technology (MS). *Program availability:* Part-time, evening/weekend. *Degree requirements:* For master's, comprehensive exam, thesis or alternative. *Entrance requirements:* For master's, GRE General Test, 2 letters of recommendation, essay. Additional exam requirements/recommendations for international students: Required—TOEFL (minimum score 83 iBT) or IELTS (minimum score 6.5). Electronic applications accepted. *Faculty research:* Software engineering, parallel and distributed systems, artificial intelligence, databases, human-computer interaction.

Morgan State University, School of Graduate Studies, School of Computer, Mathematical, and Natural Sciences, Department of Computer Science, Baltimore, MD 21251. Offers bioinformatics (MS); computer science (MS). *Entrance requirements:* Additional exam requirements/recommendations for international students: Required—TOEFL (minimum score 550 paper-based).

Murray State University, Arthur J. Bauernfeind College of Business, Department of Computer Science and Information Systems, Murray, KY 42071. Offers MSIS. *Program availability:* Part-time, evening/weekend, 100% online, blended/hybrid learning. *Entrance requirements:* For master's, GRE or GMAT, minimum university GPA of 2.75. Additional exam requirements/recommendations for international students: Required—TOEFL (minimum score 527 paper-based; 71 iBT). Electronic applications accepted.

National University, School of Engineering and Computing, La Jolla, CA 92037-1011. Offers computer science (MS), including advanced computing; cyber security and information assurance (MS); data analytics (MS); electrical engineering (MS); engineering management (MS); information technology management (MS); management information systems (MS); sustainability management (MS). *Program availability:* Part-time, evening/weekend, 100% online, blended/hybrid learning. *Degree requirements:* For master's, thesis (for some programs). *Entrance requirements:* For master's, interview, minimum GPA of 2.5. Additional exam requirements/recommendations for international students: Required—TOEFL (minimum score 550 paper-based; 79 iBT), IELTS (minimum score 6). Electronic applications accepted. *Expenses: Tuition:* Full-time $10,320; part-time $430 per unit. Tuition and fees vary according to degree level. *Faculty research:* Educational technology, scholarships in science.

Naval Postgraduate School, Departments and Academic Groups, Department of Computer Science, Monterey, CA 93943. Offers computer science (MS, PhD); identity management and cyber security (MA); modeling of virtual environments and simulations (MS, PhD); software engineering (MS, PhD). Program only open to commissioned officers of the United States and friendly nations and selected United States federal civilian employees. *Program availability:* Part-time, online learning. *Degree requirements:* For master's, thesis; for doctorate, thesis/dissertation.

Naval Postgraduate School, Departments and Academic Groups, Space Systems Academic Group, Monterey, CA 93943. Offers applied physics (MS); astronautical engineering (MS); computer science (MS); electrical engineering (MS); mechanical engineering (MS); space systems (Engr); space systems operations (MS). Program only open to commissioned officers of the United States and friendly nations and selected United States federal civilian employees. *Program availability:* Part-time. *Degree requirements:* For master's and Engr, thesis; for doctorate, thesis/dissertation. *Faculty research:* Military applications for space; space reconnaissance and remote sensing; radiation-hardened electronics for space; design, construction and operations of small satellites; satellite communications systems.

New Jersey Institute of Technology, Ying Wu College of Computing, Newark, NJ 07102. Offers big data management and mining (Certificate); business and information systems (Certificate); computer science (PhD); computing and business (MS); data mining (Certificate); data science (MS); information security (Certificate); information systems (PhD); information technology administration and security (MS); IT administration (Certificate); network security and information assurance (Certificate); software engineering (MS), including information systems; software engineering analysis/design (Certificate); Web systems development (Certificate). *Program availability:* Part-time, evening/weekend. *Faculty:* 69 full-time (13 women), 38 part-time/adjunct (4 women). *Students:* 699 full-time (229 women), 269 part-time (67 women); includes 260 minority (44 Black or African American, non-Hispanic/Latino; 145 Asian, non-Hispanic/Latino; 59 Hispanic/Latino; 12 Two or more races, non-Hispanic/Latino), 614 international. Average age 26. 2,216 applicants, 55% accepted, 366 enrolled. In 2018, 418 master's, 5 doctorates, 13 other advanced degrees awarded. Terminal master's awarded for partial completion of doctoral program. *Degree requirements:* For master's, thesis optional; for doctorate, thesis/dissertation. *Entrance requirements:* For master's, GRE General Test; for doctorate, GRE General Test, minimum graduate GPA of 3.5. Additional exam requirements/recommendations for international students: Required—TOEFL (minimum score 550 paper-based; 79 iBT), IELTS (minimum score 6.5). *Application deadline:* For fall admission, 6/1 priority date for domestic students, 5/1 priority date for international students; for spring admission, 11/15 priority date for domestic and international students. Applications are processed on a rolling basis. Application fee: $75. Electronic applications accepted. *Expenses:* $22,690 per year (in-state), $32,136 per year (out-of-state). *Financial support:* In 2018–19, 366 students received support, including 10 fellowships with full tuition reimbursements available (averaging $22,000 per year), 47 research assistantships with full tuition reimbursements available (averaging $22,000 per year), 28 teaching assistantships with full tuition reimbursements available (averaging $22,000 per year); career-related internships or fieldwork, Federal Work-Study, scholarships/grants, and unspecified assistantships also available. Financial award application deadline: 1/15. *Faculty research:* Computer systems, communications and networking, artificial intelligence, database engineering, systems analysis, analytics and optimization in crowdsourcing. *Total annual research expenditures:* $4.9 million. *Unit head:* Dr. Craig Gotsman, Dean, 973-596-3366, Fax: 973-596-5777, E-mail: craig.gotsman@njit.edu. *Application contact:* Stephen Eck, Director of Admissions, 973-596-3300, Fax: 973-596-3461, E-mail: admissions@njit.edu.
Website: http://computing.njit.edu/

New Mexico Highlands University, Graduate Studies, College of Arts and Sciences, Department of Computer Sciences, Las Vegas, NM 87701. Offers media arts and computer science (MS), including computer science. *Degree requirements:* For master's, comprehensive exam, thesis. *Entrance requirements:* For master's, minimum undergraduate GPA of 3.0. Additional exam requirements/recommendations for international students: Required—TOEFL (minimum score 540 paper-based). *Faculty research:* Advanced digital compositing, photographic installations and exhibition design, pattern recognition, parallel and distributed computing, computer security education.

New Mexico Institute of Mining and Technology, Center for Graduate Studies, Department of Computer Science and Engineering, Socorro, NM 87801. Offers computer science (MS, PhD). *Program availability:* Part-time. *Degree requirements:* For master's, thesis optional; for doctorate, thesis/dissertation. *Entrance requirements:* For master's, GRE General Test; for doctorate, GRE General Test, GRE Subject Test. Additional exam requirements/recommendations for international students: Required—TOEFL. Electronic applications accepted.

New York Institute of Technology, College of Engineering and Computing Sciences, Department of Computer Science, Old Westbury, NY 11568-8000. Offers computer science (MS); information, network, and computer security (MS). *Program availability:* Part-time. *Faculty:* 12 full-time (3 women), 19 part-time/adjunct (3 women). *Students:* 196 full-time (66 women), 94 part-time (33 women); includes 54 minority (12 Black or African American, non-Hispanic/Latino; 27 Asian, non-Hispanic/Latino; 13 Hispanic/Latino; 1 Native Hawaiian or other Pacific Islander, non-Hispanic/Latino; 1 Two or more races, non-Hispanic/Latino), 209 international. Average age 26. 947 applicants, 57% accepted, 68 enrolled. In 2018, 247 master's awarded. *Degree requirements:* For master's, thesis or alternative. *Entrance requirements:* For master's, BS or its equivalent from accredited college or university in computer science, engineering, management, mathematics, information technology, liberal arts, and related areas; minimum undergraduate GPA of 2.85. Additional exam requirements/recommendations for international students: Required—TOEFL (minimum score 79 iBT), IELTS (minimum score 6), PTE (minimum score 53). *Application deadline:* For fall admission, 7/1 for domestic students, 6/1 for international students; for spring admission, 12/1 for domestic and international students. Applications are processed on a rolling basis. Application fee: $50. Electronic applications accepted. *Expenses: Tuition:* Full-time $1285; part-time $1285 per credit. *Required fees:* $215; $175 per unit. Tuition and fees vary according to course load, degree level and campus/location. *Financial support:* Fellowships with partial tuition reimbursements, teaching assistantships with partial tuition reimbursements, career-related internships or fieldwork, Federal Work-Study, scholarships/grants, tuition waivers (full and partial), and unspecified assistantships available. Support available to part-time students. Financial award application deadline: 2/15; financial award applicants required to submit FAFSA. *Faculty research:* Active authentication of mobile users; privacy-preserving authentication protocols; sensing cloud system for cybersecurity; cognitive rhythms as a new modality for continuous authentication; cloud-enabled and cloud source disaster detection. *Unit head:* Dr. Frank Lee, Department Chair, 516-686-7456, Fax: 516-686-7439, E-mail: fli@nyit.edu. *Application contact:* Alice Dolitsky, Director, Graduate Admissions, 516-686-7520, Fax: 516-686-1116, E-mail: admissions@nyit.edu.
Website: http://www.nyit.edu/degrees/computer_science_ms

New York University, Graduate School of Arts and Science, Courant Institute of Mathematical Sciences, Department of Computer Science, New York, NY 10012-1019. Offers computer science (MS, PhD); information systems (MS); scientific computing (MS). *Program availability:* Part-time, evening/weekend. *Students:* 429 full-time (138 women), 79 part-time (21 women); includes 62 minority (3 Black or African American, non-Hispanic/Latino; 1 American Indian or Alaska Native, non-Hispanic/Latino; 45 Asian, non-Hispanic/Latino; 8 Hispanic/Latino; 5 Two or more races, non-Hispanic/Latino), 376 international. Average age 26. 2,226 applicants, 25% accepted, 183 enrolled. In 2018, 198 master's, 7 doctorates awarded. *Degree requirements:* For doctorate, thesis/dissertation, oral and written exams. *Entrance requirements:* For master's and doctorate, GRE General Test. Additional exam requirements/recommendations for international students: Required—TOEFL, IELTS. *Application deadline:* For fall admission, 12/12 for domestic and international students; for spring admission, 10/1 for domestic and international students. Application fee: $110. *Financial support:* Fellowships, research assistantships, teaching assistantships, Federal Work-Study, institutionally sponsored loans, scholarships/grants, health care benefits, and unspecified assistantships available. Financial award application deadline: 12/12; financial award applicants required to submit FAFSA. *Faculty research:* Distributed parallel and secure computing, computer graphics and vision, algorithmic and theory of computation, natural language processing, computational biology. *Unit head:* Oded Regev, Director of Graduate Studies, PhD Program, 212-998-3011, Fax: 212-995-4124, E-mail: admissions@cs.nyu.edu. *Application contact:* Benjamin Goldberg, Director of Graduate Studies, Master's Program, 212-998-3011, Fax: 212-995-4124, E-mail: admissions@cs.nyu.edu.
Website: http://cs.nyu.edu/

New York University, Tandon School of Engineering, Department of Computer Science and Engineering, New York, NY 10012-1019. Offers bioinformatics (MS, Advanced Certificate); computer science (MS, PhD); cyber security (MS); cybersecurity risk and strategy (MS); software engineering (Graduate Certificate). *Program availability:* Part-time, evening/weekend. *Faculty:* 33 full-time (8 women), 35 part-time/adjunct (4 women). *Students:* 616 full-time (155 women), 204 part-time (44 women); includes 129 minority (8 Black or African American, non-Hispanic/Latino; 75 Asian, non-Hispanic/Latino; 39 Hispanic/Latino; 7 Two or more races, non-Hispanic/Latino), 561 international. Average age 26. 3,333 applicants, 29% accepted, 414 enrolled. In 2018, 280 master's, 8 doctorates awarded. *Degree requirements:* For master's, comprehensive exam (for some programs), thesis (for some programs); for doctorate, comprehensive exam, thesis/dissertation, qualifying exam. *Entrance requirements:* For master's, BA or BS in computer science, mathematics, science, or engineering; working knowledge of a high-level program; for doctorate, GRE General Test, GRE Subject Test, BA or BS in science, engineering, or management; MS or 1 year of graduate course work. Additional exam requirements/recommendations for international students: Required—TOEFL (minimum score 550 paper-based; 90 iBT); Recommended—IELTS (minimum score 7). *Application deadline:* For fall admission, 2/15 priority date for domestic and international students; for spring admission, 11/1 priority date for domestic and international students. Applications are processed on a rolling basis. Application fee: $75. Electronic applications accepted. *Expenses:* Contact institution. *Financial support:* In 2018–19, 589 students received support, including 6 fellowships with partial tuition reimbursements available (averaging $25,617 per year), 22 research assistantships with tuition reimbursements available (averaging $26,693 per year), 1 teaching assistantship with tuition reimbursement available (averaging $26,572 per year); career-related internships or fieldwork, scholarships/grants, tuition waivers, and unspecified assistantships also available. Support available to part-time students. Financial award application deadline: 2/15. *Faculty research:* Peer-to-peer networking, cloud services, Web search, Web mining, social networks, multi-player games, vulnerability analysis, peer-to-peer security, multimedia forensics, biometrics, watermarking and digital rights management, wireless security, steganography, fault-tolerant distributed cryptography, usable security, computer graphics and visualization, computer vision, image processing, data structures, computational geometry and learning theory, combinational optimization. *Total annual research expenditures:* $12 million. *Unit head:* Dr. Guido Gerig, Head, 646-997-3975, E-mail: gerig@nyu.edu. *Application contact:* Elizabeth Ensweiler, Senior Director of Graduate Enrollment and Graduate Admissions, 646-997-3936, E-mail: elizabeth.ensweiler@nyu.edu.

Norfolk State University, School of Graduate Studies, School of Science and Technology, Department of Computer Science, Norfolk, VA 23504. Offers MS.

North Carolina Agricultural and Technical State University, The Graduate College, College of Engineering, Department of Computer Science, Greensboro, NC 27411. Offers MSCS, PhD. *Program availability:* Part-time. *Degree requirements:* For master's, thesis optional. *Faculty research:* Object-oriented analysis, artificial intelligence, distributed computing, societal implications of computing, testing.

North Carolina State University, Graduate School, College of Engineering, Department of Computer Science, Raleigh, NC 27695. Offers MC Sc, MS, PhD. *Program availability:* Part-time, online learning. *Degree requirements:* For master's, thesis optional; for doctorate, thesis/dissertation. *Entrance requirements:* For master's, GRE General Test, GRE Subject Test, minimum GPA of 3.0; for doctorate, GRE General Test, GRE Subject Test (recommended), minimum GPA of 3.5. Additional exam requirements/recommendations for international students: Required—TOEFL. Electronic applications accepted. *Faculty research:* Networking and performance analysis, theory and algorithms of computation, data mining, graphics and human computer interaction, software engineering and information security.

North Carolina State University, Graduate School, College of Engineering, Department of Electrical and Computer Engineering and Department of Computer Science, Program in Computer Networking, Raleigh, NC 27695. Offers MS. *Degree requirements:* For master's, thesis optional. *Entrance requirements:* For master's, GRE General Test, GRE Subject Test (recommended). Electronic applications accepted. *Faculty research:* High-speed networks, performance modelling, security, wireless and mobile.

North Central College, School of Graduate and Professional Studies, Department of Computer Science, Naperville, IL 60566-7063. Offers MS. *Program availability:* Part-time, evening/weekend. *Degree requirements:* For master's, thesis optional, project. *Entrance requirements:* For master's, interview. Additional exam requirements/recommendations for international students: Required—TOEFL (minimum score 550 paper-based; 80 iBT), IELTS (minimum score 6.5). Electronic applications accepted. Application fee is waived when completed online. *Expenses:* Contact institution.

Northcentral University, Graduate Studies, San Diego, CA 92106. Offers business (MBA, DBA, PhD, Postbaccalaureate Certificate); education (M Ed, Ed D, PhD, Ed S, Post-Master's Certificate, Postbaccalaureate Certificate); marriage and family therapy (MA, DMFT, PhD, Post-Master's Certificate, Postbaccalaureate Certificate); psychology (MA, PhD, Post-Master's Certificate, Postbaccalaureate Certificate); technology (MS, PhD), including computer science, cybersecurity (MS), data science, technology and innovation management (PhD). *Program availability:* Part-time, evening/weekend, online only, 100% online. *Faculty:* 98 full-time (63 women), 385 part-time/adjunct (203 women). *Students:* 5,036 full-time (3,291 women), 5,747 part-time (3,977 women); includes 3,777 minority (2,550 Black or African American, non-Hispanic/Latino; 76 American Indian or Alaska Native, non-Hispanic/Latino; 192 Asian, non-Hispanic/Latino; 603 Hispanic/Latino; 39 Native Hawaiian or other Pacific Islander, non-Hispanic/Latino; 317 Two or more races, non-Hispanic/Latino). Average age 45. In 2018, 929 master's, 782 doctorates, 278 other advanced degrees awarded. *Degree requirements:* For doctorate, comprehensive exam, thesis/dissertation. *Entrance requirements:* For master's, bachelor's degree from regionally- or nationally-accredited institution, current resume or curriculum vitae, statement of intent, interview, and background check (for marriage and family therapy); for doctorate, post-baccalaureate master's degree and/or doctoral degree from nationally- or regionally-accredited academic institution; for other advanced degree, bachelor's-level or higher degree from accredited institution or university (for Post-Baccalaureate Certificate); master's and/or doctoral degree from regionally- or nationally-accredited academic institution (for Post-Master's Certificate). Additional exam requirements/recommendations for international students: Required—TOEFL (minimum score 550 paper-based; 79 iBT), IELTS (minimum score 6.5), PTE (minimum score 53). *Application deadline:* Applications are processed on a rolling basis. Application fee: $0. Electronic applications accepted. *Expenses: Tuition:* Full-time $893. *Required fees:* $95. Tuition and fees vary according to degree level and program. *Financial support:* Scholarships/grants available. *Faculty research:* Business management, curriculum and instruction, educational leadership, health psychology, organizational behavior. *Unit head:* Dr. David Harpool, Acting Provost, 888-327-2877 Ext. 8181, E-mail: provost@ncu.edu. *Application contact:* Ken Boutelle, Vice President, Enrollment Services, 888-628-4979, E-mail: enrollmentservices@ncu.edu.

North Dakota State University, College of Graduate and Interdisciplinary Studies, College of Science and Mathematics, Department of Computer Science, Fargo, ND 58102. Offers computer science (MS, PhD); software engineering (MS, MSE, PhD, Certificate). *Program availability:* Part-time. *Degree requirements:* For master's, comprehensive exam, thesis optional; for doctorate, thesis/dissertation, qualifying exam. *Entrance requirements:* For master's, minimum GPA of 3.0, BS in computer science or related field; for doctorate, minimum GPA of 3.25, MS in computer science or related field. Additional exam requirements/recommendations for international students: Required—TOEFL (minimum score 550 paper-based; 79 iBT). Electronic applications accepted. *Faculty research:* Networking, software engineering, artificial intelligence, database, programming languages.

Northeastern Illinois University, College of Graduate Studies and Research, College of Arts and Sciences, Program in Computer Science, Chicago, IL 60625. Offers MS. *Program availability:* Part-time, evening/weekend. *Degree requirements:* For master's, comprehensive exam, research project or thesis. *Entrance requirements:* For master's, minimum GPA of 2.75, proficiency in 2 higher-level computer languages, course in discrete mathematics. Additional exam requirements/recommendations for international students: Required—TOEFL (minimum score 550 paper-based; 79 iBT). Electronic applications accepted. *Faculty research:* Telecommunications, database inference problems, decision-making under uncertainty, belief networks, analysis of algorithms.

Northeastern University, College of Computer and Information Science, Boston, MA 02115-5096. Offers computer science (MS, PhD); data science (MS); game science and design (MS); health informatics (MS); information assurance (MS); network science (PhD); personal health informatics (PhD). *Program availability:* Part-time, evening/weekend. Terminal master's awarded for partial completion of doctoral program. *Degree requirements:* For master's, thesis optional; for doctorate, comprehensive exam, thesis/dissertation. Electronic applications accepted. *Expenses:* Contact institution.

Northern Arizona University, College of Engineering, Informatics, and Applied Sciences, School of Informatics, Computing, and Cyber Systems, Flagstaff, AZ 86011. Offers engineering (M Eng), including computer science and engineering, electrical engineering; informatics and computing (PhD). *Program availability:* Part-time. *Degree requirements:* For master's, variable foreign language requirement, comprehensive exam (for some programs), thesis (for some programs); for doctorate, variable foreign language requirement, comprehensive exam (for some programs), thesis/dissertation (for some programs). *Entrance requirements:* Additional exam requirements/recommendations for international students: Required—TOEFL (minimum score 80 iBT), IELTS (minimum score 6.5). Electronic applications accepted.

Northern Illinois University, Graduate School, College of Liberal Arts and Sciences, Department of Computer Science, De Kalb, IL 60115-2854. Offers MS. *Program availability:* Part-time, evening/weekend. *Faculty:* 14 full-time (3 women). *Students:* 112 full-time (46 women), 30 part-time (9 women); includes 6 minority (2 Black or African American, non-Hispanic/Latino; 1 Asian, non-Hispanic/Latino; 2 Hispanic/Latino; 1 Two or more races, non-Hispanic/Latino), 124 international. Average age 25. 231 applicants, 65% accepted, 33 enrolled. In 2018, 101 master's awarded. *Degree requirements:* For master's, comprehensive exam. *Entrance requirements:* For master's, GRE General Test, minimum GPA of 2.75. Additional exam requirements/recommendations for international students: Required—TOEFL (minimum score 550 paper-based). *Application deadline:* For fall admission, 6/1 for domestic students, 5/1 for international students; for spring admission, 11/1 for domestic students, 10/1 for international students. Applications are processed on a rolling basis. Application fee: $40. Electronic applications accepted. *Financial support:* In 2018–19, 9 research assistantships with full tuition reimbursements, 29 teaching assistantships with full tuition reimbursements were awarded; fellowships with full tuition reimbursements, career-related internships or fieldwork, Federal Work-Study, scholarships/grants, tuition waivers (full), and unspecified assistantships also available. Support available to part-time students. Financial award applicants required to submit FAFSA. *Faculty research:* Databases, theorem proving, artificial intelligence, neural networks, computer ethics. *Unit head:* Dr. Nicholas Karonis, Chair, 815-753-0349, Fax: 815-753-0342, E-mail: karonis@niu.edu. *Application contact:* Graduate School Office, 815-753-0395, E-mail: gradsch@niu.edu.
Website: http://www.cs.niu.edu/

Northern Kentucky University, Office of Graduate Programs, College of Informatics, Department of Computer Science, Highland Heights, KY 41099. Offers computer science (MSCS); geographic information systems (Certificate); secure software engineering (Certificate). *Program availability:* Part-time, evening/weekend. *Degree requirements:* For master's, thesis optional. *Entrance requirements:* For master's, GRE, minimum GPA of 3.0, at least 4 semesters of undergraduate study in computer science including intermediate computer programming and data structures, one year of calculus, one course in discrete mathematics. Additional exam requirements/recommendations for international students: Required—TOEFL (minimum score 550 paper-based; 79 iBT); Recommended—IELTS (minimum score 6.5). Electronic applications accepted. *Faculty research:* Data privacy, data mining, wireless security, secure software engineering, secure networking.

Northwestern Polytechnic University, School of Engineering, Fremont, CA 94539-7482. Offers computer engineering (DCE); computer science (MS); computer systems engineering (MS); electrical engineering (MS). *Program availability:* Part-time, evening/weekend. *Degree requirements:* For master's, thesis optional; for doctorate, thesis/dissertation. *Entrance requirements:* For master's, minimum GPA of 3.0. Additional exam requirements/recommendations for international students: Required—TOEFL (minimum score 550 paper-based; 79 iBT). *Faculty research:* Computer networking, database design, Internet technology, software engineering, digital signal processing.

Northwestern University, McCormick School of Engineering and Applied Science, Department of Electrical Engineering and Computer Science, Evanston, IL 60208. Offers computer engineering (MS, PhD); computer science (MS, PhD); electrical engineering (MS, PhD); information technology (MS). MS and PhD admissions and degrees offered through The Graduate School. *Program availability:* Part-time. Terminal master's awarded for partial completion of doctoral program. *Degree requirements:* For master's, comprehensive exam (for some programs), thesis optional; for doctorate, comprehensive exam, thesis/dissertation. *Entrance requirements:* For master's and doctorate, GRE General Test. Additional exam requirements/recommendations for international students: Required—TOEFL (minimum score 577 paper-based; 90 iBT), IELTS (minimum score 7). Electronic applications accepted. *Faculty research:* Solid state and photonics; computing, algorithms, and applications; computer engineering and systems; cognitive systems; graphics and interactive media; signals and systems.

Northwest Missouri State University, Graduate School, School of Computer Science and Information Systems, Maryville, MO 64468-6001. Offers applied computer science (MS); information systems (MS); instructional technology (MS). *Program availability:* Part-time. *Faculty:* 13 full-time (5 women). *Students:* 205 full-time (82 women), 36 part-time (14 women); includes 1 minority (Two or more races, non-Hispanic/Latino), 233 international. Average age 24. 459 applicants, 79% accepted, 116 enrolled. In 2018, 185 master's awarded. *Degree requirements:* For master's, comprehensive exam. *Entrance requirements:* For master's, GRE General Test,, minimum GPA of 3.0. Additional exam requirements/recommendations for international students: Required—TOEFL (minimum score 550 paper-based). *Application deadline:* Applications are processed on a rolling basis. Application fee: $0 ($75 for international students). *Expenses: Tuition, area resident:* Full-time $4551; part-time $252.86 per credit hour. Tuition, state resident: full-time $4551; part-time $252.86 per credit hour. Tuition, nonresident: full-time $9103; part-time $505.72 per credit hour. *International tuition:* $9103 full-time. *Required fees:* $2668; $148.20 per credit hour. Tuition and fees vary according to program. *Financial support:* Research assistantships, teaching assistantships with full tuition reimbursements, and unspecified assistantships available. Financial award application deadline: 4/1; financial award applicants required to submit FAFSA. *Unit head:* Dr. Douglas Hawley, Director of School of Computer Science and Information Systems, 660-562-1200, Fax: 660-562-1963, E-mail: hawley@nwmissouri.edu. *Application contact:* Dr. Gregory Haddock, Dean of Graduate School, 660-562-1145, Fax: 660-562-1096, E-mail: gradsch@nwmissouri.edu.
Website: http://www.nwmissouri.edu/csis/

Notre Dame College, Graduate Programs, South Euclid, OH 44121-4293. Offers mild/moderate needs (M Ed); reading (M Ed); security policy studies (MA, Graduate Certificate); technology (M Ed). *Program availability:* Part-time, evening/weekend. *Degree requirements:* For master's, thesis. *Entrance requirements:* For master's, GRE General Test, MAT, minimum undergraduate GPA of 2.75, valid teaching certificate, bachelor's degree in an education-related field from accredited college or university, official transcripts of most recent college work. *Faculty research:* Cognitive psychology, teaching critical thinking in the classroom.

Nova Southeastern University, College of Engineering and Computing, Fort Lauderdale, FL 33314-7796. Offers computer science (MS, PhD); information assurance (PhD); information assurance and cybersecurity (MS); information systems (PhD); information technology (MS); management information systems (MS). *Program availability:* Part-time, evening/weekend, blended/hybrid learning. Terminal master's awarded for partial completion of doctoral program. *Degree requirements:* For master's, thesis optional; for doctorate, thesis/dissertation. *Entrance requirements:* For master's, minimum undergraduate GPA of 2.5; for doctorate, master's degree, minimum graduate GPA of 3.25. Additional exam requirements/recommendations for international students: Required—TOEFL (minimum score 80 iBT), IELTS (minimum score 6), PTE (minimum score 54). Electronic applications accepted. *Expenses:* Contact institution. *Faculty* *research:* Artificial intelligence, database management, human-computer interaction, business intelligence and data analytics, information assurance and cybersecurity.

Oakland University, Graduate Study and Lifelong Learning, School of Engineering and Computer Science, Department of Computer Science and Engineering, Rochester, MI 48309-4401. Offers computer science (MS); computer science and informatics (PhD); software engineering and information technology (MS). *Program availability:* Part-time, evening/weekend. *Entrance requirements:* For master's, minimum GPA of 3.0. Electronic applications accepted. *Expenses:* Contact institution.

The Ohio State University, Graduate School, College of Engineering, Department of Computer Science and Engineering, Columbus, OH 43210. Offers MS, PhD. *Faculty:* 43. *Students:* 298 (55 women). Average age 26. In 2018, 61 master's, 26 doctorates awarded. *Entrance requirements:* For master's and doctorate, GRE (minimum score Quantitative 750 old, 159 new; Verbal 500 old, 155 new; Analytical Writing 3.0); GRE Subject Test in computer science (strongly recommended for those whose undergraduate degree is not in computer science). Additional exam requirements/recommendations for international students: Required—TOEFL (minimum score 550 paper-based; 79 iBT), Michigan English Language Assessment Battery (minimum score 82); Recommended—IELTS (minimum score 7). *Application deadline:* For fall admission, 12/13 priority date for domestic students, 11/30 priority date for international students. Applications are processed on a rolling basis. Application fee: $60 ($70 for international students). Electronic applications accepted. *Financial support:* Fellowships, research assistantships, teaching assistantships, career-related internships or fieldwork, Federal Work-Study, institutionally sponsored loans, unspecified assistantships, and administrative assistantships available. Support available to part-time students. Financial award application deadline: 1/15. *Unit head:* Dr. Tamal Dey, Interim Chair, 614-688-3029, E-mail: dey.8@osu.edu. *Application contact:* Graduate and Professional Admissions, 614-292-9444, Fax: 614-292-3895, E-mail: gpadmissions@osu.edu.
Website: http://www.cse.osu.edu

Ohio University, Graduate College, Russ College of Engineering and Technology, School of Electrical Engineering and Computer Science, Athens, OH 45701-2979. Offers electrical engineering (MS); electrical engineering and computer science (PhD). *Degree requirements:* For master's, comprehensive exam (for some programs), thesis; for doctorate, comprehensive exam, thesis/dissertation, qualifying exams. *Entrance requirements:* For master's, GRE, BSEE or BSCS, minimum GPA of 3.0; for doctorate, GRE, MSEE or MSCS, minimum GPA of 3.0. Additional exam requirements/recommendations for international students: Required—TOEFL (minimum score 550 paper-based; 80 iBT) or IELTS (minimum score 6.5). Electronic applications accepted. *Faculty research:* Avionics, networking/communications, intelligent distribution, real-time computing, control systems, optical properties of semiconductors.

Oklahoma Christian University, Graduate School of Engineering and Computer Science, Oklahoma City, OK 73136-1100. Offers electrical and computer engineering (MSE); engineering management (MSE); mechanical engineering (MSE); software engineering (MSCS, MSE). *Program availability:* Part-time. *Entrance requirements:* Additional exam requirements/recommendations for international students: Required—TOEFL (minimum score 550 paper-based). Electronic applications accepted. *Expenses:* Contact institution.

Oklahoma City University, Meinders School of Business, Oklahoma City, OK 73106-1402. Offers business (MBA, MSA); computer science (MS); energy legal studies (MS); energy management (MS); JD/MBA. *Program availability:* Part-time, evening/weekend, 100% online. *Degree requirements:* For master's, practicum/capstone. *Entrance requirements:* For master's, undergraduate degree from accredited institution, minimum GPA of 3.0, essay, letters of recommendation. Additional exam requirements/recommendations for international students: Required—TOEFL (minimum score 550 paper-based; 80 iBT). Electronic applications accepted. *Expenses:* Contact institution. *Faculty research:* Group support systems, leadership, decision models in accounting.

Oklahoma State University, College of Arts and Sciences, Department of Computer Science, Stillwater, OK 74078. Offers MS, PhD. *Faculty:* 14 full-time (1 woman). *Students:* 37 full-time (18 women), 26 part-time (5 women); includes 2 minority (1 Asian, non-Hispanic/Latino; 1 Two or more races, non-Hispanic/Latino), 58 international. Average age 26. 168 applicants, 31% accepted, 27 enrolled. In 2018, 32 master's, 4 doctorates awarded. *Entrance requirements:* For master's, GRE; for doctorate, GRE General Test, GRE Subject Test in computer science (recommended), 3 letters of recommendation. Additional exam requirements/recommendations for international students: Required—TOEFL (minimum score 550 paper-based; 79 iBT). *Application deadline:* For fall admission, 3/1 priority date for international students; for spring admission, 8/1 priority date for international students. Applications are processed on a rolling basis. Application fee: $40 ($75 for international students). Electronic applications accepted. *Expenses:* Tuition, area resident: Full-time $4148. Tuition, state resident: full-time $4148. Tuition, nonresident: full-time $10,517. *International tuition:* $10,517 full-time. *Required fees:* $4394; $2929 per credit hour. Tuition and fees vary according to course load and program. *Financial support:* Research assistantships, teaching assistantships, career-related internships or fieldwork, Federal Work-Study, scholarships/grants, health care benefits, tuition waivers (partial), and unspecified assistantships available. Support available to part-time students. Financial award application deadline: 3/1; financial award applicants required to submit FAFSA. *Unit head:* Dr. K. M. George, Department Head, 405-744-5668, Fax: 405-774-9097, E-mail: kmg@cs.okstate.edu. *Application contact:* Dr. Sheryl Tucker, Dean, 405-744-6368, Fax: 405-744-0355, E-mail: gradi@okstate.edu.
Website: http://cs.okstate.edu/

Old Dominion University, College of Sciences, Program in Computer Science, Norfolk, VA 23529. Offers computer information systems (MS); computer science (MS, PhD). *Program availability:* Part-time, 100% online. Terminal master's awarded for partial completion of doctoral program. *Degree requirements:* For master's, comprehensive exam, thesis optional, 34 credit hours; for doctorate, comprehensive exam, thesis/dissertation, 48 credit hours beyond the MS. *Entrance requirements:* For master's, GRE General Test, minimum GPA of 3.0; for doctorate, GRE General Test, MS in computer science. Additional exam requirements/recommendations for international students: Required—TOEFL (minimum score 550 paper-based; 79 iBT), IELTS (minimum score 6.5). Electronic applications accepted. *Faculty research:* Machine intelligence and data science, Web science and digital libraries, cyber-physical systems, bioinformatics, scientific computing.

Oregon Health & Science University, School of Medicine, Graduate Programs in Medicine, Department of Computer Science and Electrical Engineering, Portland, OR 97239-3098. Offers computer science and engineering (MS, PhD); electrical engineering (MS, PhD). *Program availability:* Part-time. *Faculty:* 12 full-time (7 women), 9 part-time/adjunct (0 women). *Students:* 13 full-time (6 women), 12 part-time (1 woman); includes 4 minority (3 Asian, non-Hispanic/Latino; 1 Two or more races, non-Hispanic/Latino), 8 international. Average age 31. 16 applicants, 69% accepted, 11 enrolled. In 2018, 6 master's, 3 doctorates awarded. Terminal master's awarded for partial completion of doctoral program. *Degree requirements:* For master's, thesis (for some programs); for doctorate, comprehensive exam, thesis/dissertation, qualifying

exam. *Entrance requirements:* For master's and doctorate, GRE General Test (minimum scores: 153 Verbal/148 Quantitative/4.5 Analytical). *Application deadline:* For fall admission, 7/15 for domestic students, 5/15 for international students; for winter admission, 10/15 for domestic students, 9/15 for international students; for spring admission, 1/15 for domestic students, 12/15 for international students. Applications are processed on a rolling basis. Application fee: $70. Electronic applications accepted. *Financial support:* Health care benefits, tuition waivers (full), and full-tuition and stipends (for PhD students) available. Financial award applicants required to submit FAFSA. *Faculty research:* Natural language processing, speech signal processing, computational biology, autism spectrum disorders, hearing and speaking disorders. *Unit head:* Dr. Peter Heeman, Program Director, 503-346-3755, E-mail: somgrad@ohsu.edu. *Application contact:* Pat Dickerson, Administrative Coordinator, 503-346-3753, E-mail: somgrad@ohsu.edu.
Website: http://www.ohsu.edu/xd/education/schools/school-of-medicine/departments/basic-science-departments/csee/

Oregon State University, College of Engineering, Program in Computer Science, Corvallis, OR 97331. Offers algorithms and cryptography (M Eng, MS, PhD). *Entrance requirements:* For master's and doctorate, GRE. Additional exam requirements/recommendations for international students: Required—TOEFL (minimum score 600 paper-based; 80 iBT), IELTS (minimum score 6.5). *Expenses:* Contact institution.

Pace University, Seidenberg School of Computer Science and Information Systems, New York, NY 10038. Offers chief information security officer (APC); computer science (MS, PhD); enterprise analytics (MS); information and communication technology strategy and innovation (APC); information systems (MS, APC); information technology (MS); professional studies in computing (DPS); secure software and information engineering (APC); security and information assurance (Certificate); software development and engineering (MS, Certificate); telecommunications systems and networks (MS, Certificate). *Program availability:* Part-time, evening/weekend, online only, 100% online, blended/hybrid learning. *Faculty:* 26 full-time (7 women), 7 part-time/adjunct (2 women). *Students:* 515 full-time (172 women), 288 part-time (90 women); includes 183 minority (67 Black or African American, non-Hispanic/Latino; 3 American Indian or Alaska Native, non-Hispanic/Latino; 50 Asian, non-Hispanic/Latino; 52 Hispanic/Latino; 1 Native Hawaiian or other Pacific Islander, non-Hispanic/Latino; 10 Two or more races, non-Hispanic/Latino), 497 international. Average age 30. 817 applicants, 93% accepted, 235 enrolled. In 2018, 383 master's, 15 doctorates, 1 other advanced degree awarded. *Degree requirements:* For master's, thesis or alternative, capstone course; for doctorate, comprehensive exam (for some programs), thesis/dissertation. *Entrance requirements:* Additional exam requirements/recommendations for international students: Required—TOEFL (minimum score 78 iBT), IELTS (minimum score 6.5) or PTE (minimum score 52). *Application deadline:* For fall admission, 8/1 priority date for domestic students, 6/1 for international students; for spring admission, 12/1 for domestic students, 10/1 for international students. Applications are processed on a rolling basis. Application fee: $70. Electronic applications accepted. *Expenses:* Contact institution. *Financial support:* In 2018–19, 45 students received support. Research assistantships, career-related internships or fieldwork, scholarships/grants, and unspecified assistantships available. Support available to part-time students. Financial award application deadline: 2/15; financial award applicants required to submit FAFSA. *Faculty research:* Cyber security/digital forensics; mobile app development; big data/enterprise analytics; artificial intelligence; software development. *Total annual research expenditures:* $584,594. *Unit head:* Dr. Jonathan Hill, Dean, Seidenberg School of Computer Science and Information Systems, 212-346-1864, E-mail: jhill@pace.edu. *Application contact:* Susan Ford-Goldschein, Director of Graduate Admissions, 914-422-4283, Fax: 212-346-1585, E-mail: graduateadmission@pace.edu.
Website: http://www.pace.edu/seidenberg

Pacific States University, College of Computer Science and Information Systems, Los Angeles, CA 90010. Offers computer science (MS); information systems (MS). *Program availability:* Part-time, evening/weekend. *Entrance requirements:* For master's, bachelor's degree in physics, engineering, computer science, information systems, or applied mathematics; minimum undergraduate GPA of 2.5 during last 90 quarter units of course work. Additional exam requirements/recommendations for international students: Required—TOEFL (minimum score 500 paper-based; 61 iBT), IELTS (minimum score 5.5).

Penn State Harrisburg, Graduate School, School of Science, Engineering and Technology, Middletown, PA 17057. Offers civil engineering (MS); computer science (MS); electrical engineering (M Eng, MS); engineering management (MPS); engineering science (M Eng); environmental engineering (M Eng); environmental pollution control (MEPC, MS); mechanical engineering (MS); structural engineering (Certificate). *Program availability:* Part-time, evening/weekend.

Penn State University Park, Graduate School, College of Engineering, Department of Computer Science and Engineering, University Park, PA 16802. Offers M Eng, MS, PhD.

See Display on the next page and Close-Up on page 311.

Polytechnic University of Puerto Rico, Graduate School, Hato Rey, PR 00918. Offers business administration (MBA), including computer information systems, general management, management of information systems, management of international enterprises; civil engineering (ME, MS); computer engineering (ME, MS); computer science (MCS, MS); electrical engineering (ME, MS); engineering management (MEM); environmental management (MEM); landscape architecture (M Land Arch); manufacturing competitiveness (MMC, MS); manufacturing engineering (ME, MS); mechanical engineering (M Mech E). *Accreditation:* ASLA. *Program availability:* Part-time, evening/weekend. *Entrance requirements:* For master's, 3 letters of recommendation.

Portland State University, Graduate Studies, Maseeh College of Engineering and Computer Science, Department of Computer Science, Portland, OR 97207-0751. Offers computer science (MS, PhD); computer security (Certificate). *Program availability:* Part-time. *Degree requirements:* For master's, thesis or alternative; for doctorate, comprehensive exam, thesis/dissertation. *Entrance requirements:* For master's, GRE (minimum scores 60th percentile in Quantitative and 25th percentile in Verbal), BS in engineering field, science or closely-related area; minimum GPA of 3.0 or equivalent; 2 letters of recommendation; personal statement; for doctorate, GRE (minimum scores 60th percentile in Quantitative and 25th percentile in Verbal), MS in computer science or allied field. Additional exam requirements/recommendations for international students: Required—TOEFL (minimum score 550 paper-based). *Expenses:* Contact institution. *Faculty research:* Formal methods, database systems, parallel programming environments, computer security, software tools.

Prairie View A&M University, College of Engineering, Prairie View, TX 77446. Offers computer information systems (MSCIS); computer science (MSCS); electrical engineering (MSEE, PhDEE); general engineering (MS Engr). *Program availability:* Part-time, evening/weekend. *Faculty:* 29 full-time (8 women), 1 part-time/adjunct (0 women). *Students:* 134 full-time (34 women), 67 part-time (24 women); includes 84 minority (67 Black or African American, non-Hispanic/Latino; 12 Asian, non-Hispanic/Latino; 5 Hispanic/Latino), 102 international. Average age 31. 130 applicants, 80%

Computer Science

accepted, 52 enrolled. In 2018, 67 master's, 3 doctorates awarded. *Degree requirements:* For master's, thesis optional; for doctorate, comprehensive exam, thesis/dissertation. *Entrance requirements:* For master's, GRE General Test (minimum score of 900), bachelor's degree in engineering from ABET-accredited institution; for doctorate, minimum GPA of 3.0. Additional exam requirements/recommendations for international students: Required—TOEFL (minimum score 550 paper-based; 79 iBT). *Application deadline:* For fall admission, 5/1 priority date for domestic and international students; for spring admission, 10/1 priority date for domestic students, 9/1 priority date for international students; for summer admission, 3/1 priority date for domestic students, 2/1 priority date for international students. Applications are processed on a rolling basis. Application fee: $50. Electronic applications accepted. *Expenses: Tuition, area resident:* Full-time $3172; part-time $317 per credit. Tuition, state resident: full-time $3172; part-time $317 per credit. Tuition, nonresident: full-time $7965; part-time $796 per credit. *Required fees:* $4847; $485 per credit. *Financial support:* Fellowships, research assistantships, teaching assistantships, career-related internships or fieldwork, institutionally sponsored loans, scholarships/grants, health care benefits, tuition waivers (full), and unspecified assistantships available. Financial award application deadline: 4/1; financial award applicants required to submit FAFSA. *Faculty research:* Electrical and computer engineering: big data analysis, wireless communications, bioinformatics and computational biology, space radiation; computer science: cloud computing, cyber security; chemical engineering: thermochemical processing of biofuel, photochemical modeling; civil and environmental engineering: environmental sustainability, water resources, structure; mechanical engineering: thermal science, nanocomposites, computational fluid dynamics. *Unit head:* Dr. Pamela H Obiomon, Dean, 936-261-9890, Fax: 936-261-9868, E-mail: phobiomon@pvamu.edu. *Application contact:* Pauline Walker, Administrative Assistant II, Research and Graduate Studies, 936-261-3521, Fax: 936-261-3529, E-mail: gradadmissions@pvamu.edu.

Princeton University, Graduate School, School of Engineering and Applied Science, Department of Computer Science, Princeton, NJ 08544-1019. Offers MSE, PhD. Terminal master's awarded for partial completion of doctoral program. *Degree requirements:* For master's, thesis; for doctorate, thesis/dissertation, general exam. *Entrance requirements:* For master's, GRE General Test, GRE Subject Test (recommended), 3 letters of recommendation; for doctorate, GRE General Test, GRE Subject Test (recommended), official transcript(s), 3 letters of recommendation, personal statement. Additional exam requirements/recommendations for international students: Required—TOEFL. Electronic applications accepted. *Faculty research:* Computational biology and bioinformatics; computer and network systems; graphics, vision, and sound; machine learning, programming languages and security; theory.

Purdue University, Graduate School, College of Science, Department of Computer Sciences, West Lafayette, IN 47907. Offers MS, PhD. *Program availability:* Part-time. *Faculty:* 51 full-time (43 women). *Students:* 222 full-time (45 women), 106 part-time (24 women); includes 21 minority (4 Black or African American, non-Hispanic/Latino; 10 Asian, non-Hispanic/Latino; 6 Hispanic/Latino; 1 Two or more races, non-Hispanic/Latino), 260 international. Average age 27. 1,621 applicants, 9% accepted, 65 enrolled. In 2018, 71 master's, 34 doctorates awarded. Terminal master's awarded for partial completion of doctoral program. *Degree requirements:* For master's, thesis optional; for doctorate, comprehensive exam, thesis/dissertation. *Entrance requirements:* For master's and doctorate, minimum GPA of 3.5. Additional exam requirements/recommendations for international students: Required—TOEFL (minimum score 600 paper-based; 95 iBT), TWE (minimum score 5). *Application deadline:* For fall admission, 12/15 for domestic and international students; for spring admission, 10/1 for domestic and international students. Application fee: $60 ($75 for international students). Electronic applications accepted. *Financial support:* Fellowships with partial tuition reimbursements, research assistantships with partial tuition reimbursements, teaching

assistantships with partial tuition reimbursements, health care benefits, and unspecified assistantships available. Financial award application deadline: 12/15. *Faculty research:* Bioinformatics and computational biology, computational science and engineering, databases, data mining, distributed systems, graphics and visualization, information retrieval, information security and assurance, machine learning, networking and operation systems, programming languages and compilers, software engineering, theory of computing and algorithms. *Unit head:* Prof. Susan Hambrusch Hambrusch, Head, 765-494-6003, E-mail: seh@cs.purdue.edu. *Application contact:* Shelley Straley, Graduate Contact, 765-494-6004, E-mail: sstrale@purdue.edu. Website: http://www.cs.purdue.edu/

Purdue University Fort Wayne, College of Engineering, Technology, and Computer Science, Department of Computer Science, Fort Wayne, IN 46805-1499. Offers applied computer science (MS). *Program availability:* Part-time. *Entrance requirements:* For master's, GRE General Test, minimum GPA of 3.0. Additional exam requirements/recommendations for international students: Required—TOEFL (minimum score 550 paper-based; 79 iBT); Recommended—TWE. Electronic applications accepted. *Faculty research:* Architecture, cloud computing and security.

Purdue University Northwest, Graduate Studies Office, School of Engineering, Mathematics, and Science, Department of Mathematics, Computer Science, and Statistics, Hammond, IN 46323-2094. Offers computer science (MS); mathematics (MAT, MS). *Program availability:* Part-time. *Entrance requirements:* Additional exam requirements/recommendations for international students: Required—TOEFL. *Faculty research:* Topology, analysis, algebra, mathematics education.

Queens College of the City University of New York, Mathematics and Natural Sciences Division, Department of Computer Science, Queens, NY 11367-1597. Offers MA. *Program availability:* Part-time, evening/weekend. *Faculty:* 22 full-time (6 women), 43 part-time/adjunct (11 women). *Students:* 12 full-time (3 women), 68 part-time (23 women); includes 37 minority (5 Black or African American, non-Hispanic/Latino; 20 Asian, non-Hispanic/Latino; 4 Hispanic/Latino; 8 Two or more races, non-Hispanic/Latino), 23 international. Average age 30. 72 applicants, 71% accepted, 26 enrolled. In 2018, 19 master's awarded. *Degree requirements:* For master's, thesis optional. *Entrance requirements:* For master's, minimum GPA of 3.0. Additional exam requirements/recommendations for international students: Required—TOEFL (minimum score 61 iBT), IELTS (minimum score 5). *Application deadline:* For fall admission, 4/1 for domestic students; for spring admission, 11/1 for domestic students. Applications are processed on a rolling basis. Application fee: $125. Electronic applications accepted. *Financial support:* Career-related internships or fieldwork and unspecified assistantships available. Financial award application deadline: 4/1; financial award applicants required to submit FAFSA. *Faculty research:* Algorithms, artificial intelligence, information security, machine learning, natural language processing. *Unit head:* Dr. Zhigang Xiang, Chair, 718-997-3566, E-mail: zhigang.xiang@qc.cuny.edu. *Application contact:* Elizabeth D'Amico-Ramirez, Assistant Director of Graduate Admissions, 718-997-5203, E-mail: elizabeth.damicoramirez@qc.cuny.edu.

Queen's University at Kingston, School of Graduate Studies, Faculty of Arts and Science, School of Computing, Kingston, ON K7L 3N6, Canada. Offers M Sc, PhD. *Degree requirements:* For master's, thesis; for doctorate, comprehensive exam, thesis/dissertation. *Entrance requirements:* For master's, honours B Sc in computer science; for doctorate, M Sc in computer science. Additional exam requirements/recommendations for international students: Required—TOEFL, TWE. *Faculty research:* Software engineering, human computer interaction, data base, networks, computational geometry.

Regis University, College of Computer and Information Sciences, Denver, CO 80221-1099. Offers agile technologies (Certificate); cybersecurity (Certificate); data science

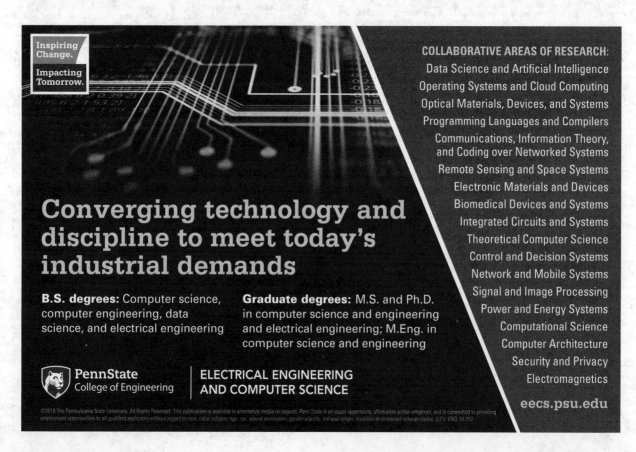

(M Sc); database administration with Oracle (Certificate); database development (Certificate); database technologies (M Sc); enterprise Java software development (Certificate); enterprise resource planning (Certificate); executive information technology (Certificate); health care informatics (Certificate); health care informatics and information management (M Sc); information assurance (M Sc); information assurance policy management (Certificate); information technology management (M Sc); mobile software development (Certificate); software engineering (M Sc, Certificate); software engineering and database technology (M Sc); storage area networks (Certificate); systems engineering (M Sc, Certificate). *Program availability:* Part-time, evening/weekend, 100% online, blended/hybrid learning. *Degree requirements:* For master's, thesis (for some programs), final research project. *Entrance requirements:* For master's, official transcript reflecting baccalaureate degree awarded from regionally-accredited college or university, 2 years of related experience, resume, interview. Additional exam requirements/recommendations for international students: Required—TOEFL (minimum score 550 paper-based; 82 iBT). Electronic applications accepted. *Expenses:* Contact institution. *Faculty research:* Information policy, knowledge management, software architectures, data science.

Rensselaer at Hartford, Department of Computer and Information Science, Hartford, CT 06120-2991. Offers computer science (MS); information technology (MS). *Program availability:* Part-time, evening/weekend. *Degree requirements:* For master's, thesis optional. *Entrance requirements:* For master's, GRE. Additional exam requirements/recommendations for international students: Required—TOEFL (minimum score 600 paper-based; 100 iBT). Electronic applications accepted.

Rensselaer Polytechnic Institute, Graduate School, School of Science, Program in Computer Science, Troy, NY 12180-3590. Offers MS, PhD. *Program availability:* Part-time. *Faculty:* 32 full-time (8 women), 1 (woman) part-time/adjunct. *Students:* 104 full-time (22 women), 6 part-time (0 women); includes 18 minority (5 Black or African American, non-Hispanic/Latino; 8 Asian, non-Hispanic/Latino; 3 Hispanic/Latino; 2 Two or more races, non-Hispanic/Latino), 52 international. Average age 26. 115 applicants, 21% accepted, 7 enrolled. In 2018, 22 master's, 14 doctorates awarded. Terminal master's awarded for partial completion of doctoral program. *Degree requirements:* For master's, thesis; for doctorate, comprehensive exam, thesis/dissertation. *Entrance requirements:* For master's and doctorate, GRE. Additional exam requirements/recommendations for international students: Required—TOEFL (minimum score 570 paper-based; 88 iBT), IELTS (minimum score 6.5), PTE (minimum score 60). *Application deadline:* For fall admission, 1/1 priority date for domestic and international students; for spring admission, 8/15 priority date for domestic and international students. Applications are processed on a rolling basis. Application fee: $75. Electronic applications accepted. *Financial support:* In 2018–19, research assistantships (averaging $23,000 per year), teaching assistantships (averaging $23,000 per year) were awarded; fellowships also available. Financial award application deadline: 1/1. *Faculty research:* Algorithms and theory; artificial intelligence; bioinformatics; computational science and engineering; computer vision, graphics, and robotics; data mining and machine and computational learning; database systems; pervasive computing and networking; programming languages and software engineering; security; social networking. *Total annual research expenditures:* $6.8 million. *Unit head:* Dr. Mohammed Zaki, Graduate Program Director, 518-276-6340, E-mail: sibel@cs.rpi.edu. *Application contact:* Jarron Decker, Director of Graduate Admissions, 518-276-6216, Fax: 518-276-4072, E-mail: gradadmissions@rpi.edu. Website: https://science.rpi.edu/computer-science

Rice University, Graduate Programs, George R. Brown School of Engineering, Department of Computer Science, Houston, TX 77251-1892. Offers MCS, MS, PhD. Terminal master's awarded for partial completion of doctoral program. *Degree requirements:* For master's, comprehensive exam; for doctorate, comprehensive exam, thesis/dissertation. *Entrance requirements:* For master's and doctorate, bachelor's degree. Additional exam requirements/recommendations for international students: Required—TOEFL. Electronic applications accepted. *Faculty research:* Programming languages and compiler construction; robotics, bioinformatics, algorithms - motion planning with emphasis on high-dimensional systems; network protocols, distributed systems, and operating systems - adaptive protocols for wireless; computer architecture, aperating systems - virtual machine monitors; computer graphics - application of computers to geometric problems and centered around general problem of representing geometric shapes.

Rivier University, School of Graduate Studies, Department of Computer Science and Mathematics, Nashua, NH 03060. Offers computer science (MS); mathematics (MAT). *Program availability:* Part-time, evening/weekend. *Entrance requirements:* For master's, GRE Subject Test. Electronic applications accepted.

Rochester Institute of Technology, Graduate Enrollment Services, Golisano College of Computing and Information Sciences, Computer Science Department, MS Program in Computer Science, Rochester, NY 14623-5603. Offers MS. *Program availability:* Part-time. *Students:* 395 full-time (93 women), 41 part-time (11 women); includes 16 minority (2 Black or African American, non-Hispanic/Latino; 9 Asian, non-Hispanic/Latino; 2 Hispanic/Latino; 3 Two or more races, non-Hispanic/Latino), 393 international. Average age 25. 796 applicants, 57% accepted, 170 enrolled. In 2018, 133 master's awarded. *Degree requirements:* For master's, thesis or alternative, Thesis or Project. *Entrance requirements:* For master's, GRE scores are required for students with degrees from international universities, recommended for all other applicants., minimum GPA of 3.0, personal statement, two letters of recommendation. Additional exam requirements/recommendations for international students: Required—TOEFL (minimum score 570 paper-based; 88 iBT), IELTS (minimum score 6.5), PTE (minimum score 61). *Application deadline:* For fall admission, 2/15 priority date for domestic and international students; for spring admission, 12/15 priority date for domestic and international students. Applications are processed on a rolling basis. Application fee: $65. Electronic applications accepted. *Financial support:* In 2018–19, 425 students received support. Research assistantships with partial tuition reimbursements available, teaching assistantships with partial tuition reimbursements available, career-related internships or fieldwork, scholarships/grants, and unspecified assistantships available. Financial award applicants required to submit FAFSA. *Faculty research:* Mobile and pervasive computing, including Internet-of-Things (IoT) and cloud computing for big data analytics; privacy-preserving techniques for cloud computing, specifically homomorphic encryption; norms and normative behavior in AI, reversible computing and reversible logic; graph database; semantic queries with nodes, edges, and properties to represent and store data; machine learning with applications in document recognition and informational retrieval. *Unit head:* Dr. Hans-Peter Bischof, Graduate Program Coordinator, 585-475-2995, Fax: 585-475-4935, E-mail: csdept@cs.rit.edu. *Application contact:* Diane Ellison, Senior Associate Vice President, Graduate Enrollment Services, 585-475-2229, Fax: 585-475-7164, E-mail: gradinfo@rit.edu. Website: https://www.rit.edu/study/computer-science-ms

Rochester Institute of Technology, Graduate Enrollment Services, Golisano College of Computing and Information Sciences, Computing and Information Sciences Department, PhD Program in Computing and Information Sciences, Rochester, NY 14623-5603. Offers PhD. *Program availability:* Part-time. *Students:* 50 full-time (9 women), 20 part-time (5 women); includes 5 minority (1 Asian, non-Hispanic/Latino; 3

Hispanic/Latino; 1 Two or more races, non-Hispanic/Latino), 56 international. Average age 31. 102 applicants, 25% accepted, 17 enrolled. In 2018, 1 doctorate awarded. *Degree requirements:* For doctorate, comprehensive exam, thesis/dissertation. *Entrance requirements:* For doctorate, GRE, minimum GPA of 3.0, statement of purpose, resume, two letters of recommendation, professional or research paper sample(s) (if available). Additional exam requirements/recommendations for international students: Required—TOEFL (minimum score 570 paper-based; 88 iBT), IELTS (minimum score 6.5), PTE (minimum score 61). *Application deadline:* For fall admission, 1/15 priority date for domestic and international students. Applications are processed on a rolling basis. Application fee: $65. Electronic applications accepted. *Expenses:* Contact institution. *Financial support:* In 2018–19, 53 students received support. Research assistantships with full tuition reimbursements available, teaching assistantships with full tuition reimbursements available, career-related internships or fieldwork, scholarships/grants, health care benefits, and unspecified assistantships available. Financial award applicants required to submit FAFSA. *Faculty research:* Accessibility and HCI; algorithm and programming languages; bioinformatics and health IT; cybersecurity; machine learning and data science. *Unit head:* Dr. Pengcheng Shi, Director, 585-475-6147, E-mail: spcast@rit.edu. *Application contact:* Diane Ellison, Senior Associate Vice President, Graduate Enrollment Services, 585-475-2229, Fax: 585-475-7164, E-mail: gradinfo@rit.edu. Website: https://www.rit.edu/study/computing-and-information-sciences-phd

Rochester Institute of Technology, Graduate Enrollment Services, Golisano College of Computing and Information Sciences, Information Science and Technologies Department, MS Program in Networking and Systems Administration, Rochester, NY 14623-5603. Offers MS. *Program availability:* Part-time, 100% online. *Students:* 16 full-time (6 women), 21 part-time (5 women); includes 3 minority (2 Black or African American, non-Hispanic/Latino; 1 Hispanic/Latino), 26 international. Average age 28. 34 applicants, 62% accepted, 8 enrolled. In 2018, 17 master's awarded. *Degree requirements:* For master's, thesis or alternative, Thesis or Project. *Entrance requirements:* For master's, GRE required for individuals with degrees from international universities. The GRE is recommended for students whose GPA is below 3.0., minimum GPA of 3.0, two letters of recommendation. Additional exam requirements/recommendations for international students: Required—TOEFL (minimum score 570 paper-based; 88 iBT), IELTS (minimum score 6.5), PTE (minimum score 61). *Application deadline:* For fall admission, 2/15 priority date for domestic and international students; for spring admission, 12/15 priority date for domestic and international students. Applications are processed on a rolling basis. Application fee: $65. Electronic applications accepted. *Expenses:* Contact institution. *Financial support:* In 2018–19, 26 students received support. Research assistantships with partial tuition reimbursements available, teaching assistantships with partial tuition reimbursements available, career-related internships or fieldwork, scholarships/grants, and unspecified assistantships available. Support available to part-time students. Financial award applicants required to submit FAFSA. *Faculty research:* Vehicle area network, IoT networking and security, future Internet, network protocols and algorithms, cloud computing. *Unit head:* Qi Yu, Graduate Program Director, 585-475-6929, Fax: 585-475-6584, E-mail: qyuvks@rit.edu. *Application contact:* Diane Ellison, Senior Associate Vice President, Graduate Enrollment Services, 585-475-2229, Fax: 585-475-7164, E-mail: gradinfo@rit.edu. Website: https://www.rit.edu/study/networking-and-systems-administration-ms

Roosevelt University, Graduate Division, College of Arts and Sciences, Department of Computer Science and Data Science, Chicago, IL 60605. Offers computer science (MS). *Program availability:* Part-time, evening/weekend. Electronic applications accepted.

Rowan University, Graduate School, College of Science and Mathematics, Program in Computer Science, Glassboro, NJ 08028-1701. Offers MS. *Degree requirements:* For master's, thesis optional. *Entrance requirements:* For master's, bachelor's degree (or its equivalent) in related field from accredited institution; official transcripts from all colleges attended; current professional resume; two letters of recommendation; statement of professional objectives; minimum undergraduate cumulative GPA of 3.0. Electronic applications accepted.

Royal Military College of Canada, Division of Graduate Studies, Faculty of Science, Department of Mathematics and Computer Science, Kingston, ON K7K 7B4, Canada. Offers computer science (M Sc); mathematics (M Sc). *Degree requirements:* For master's, thesis. *Entrance requirements:* For master's, honours degree with second-class standing. Electronic applications accepted.

Rutgers University–Camden, Graduate School of Arts and Sciences, Program in Computer Science, Camden, NJ 08102. Offers MS. *Program availability:* Part-time, evening/weekend. *Degree requirements:* For master's, comprehensive exam, thesis (for some programs), 30 credits. *Entrance requirements:* For master's, GRE, 3 letters of recommendation; statement of personal, professional, and academic goals; computer science undergraduate degree (preferred). Additional exam requirements/recommendations for international students: Required—TOEFL, IELTS. Electronic applications accepted. *Faculty research:* Cryptography and computer security, approximation algorithms, optical networks and wireless communications, computational geometry, data compression and encoding.

Rutgers University–New Brunswick, Graduate School-New Brunswick, Program in Computer Science, Piscataway, NJ 08854-8097. Offers MS, PhD. *Program availability:* Part-time. Terminal master's awarded for partial completion of doctoral program. *Degree requirements:* For master's, comprehensive exam, thesis; for doctorate, comprehensive exam, thesis/dissertation. *Entrance requirements:* For master's and doctorate, GRE General Test, GRE Subject Test. Additional exam requirements/recommendations for international students: Required—TOEFL. *Faculty research:* Artificial intelligence and machine learning, bioinformatics, algorithms and complexity, networking and operating systems, computational graphics and vision.

Sacred Heart University, Graduate Programs, College of Arts and Sciences, Department of Computing, Fairfield, CT 06825. Offers computer science (MS); computer science gaming (MS); cybersecurity (MS); information technology (MS). *Program availability:* Part-time, evening/weekend. *Degree requirements:* For master's, thesis or alternative. *Entrance requirements:* For master's, bachelor's degree, minimum GPA of 3.0. Additional exam requirements/recommendations for international students: Required—TOEFL (minimum score 570 paper-based, 80 iBT), TWE, or IELTS (6.5). Electronic applications accepted. *Expenses:* Contact institution.

Saginaw Valley State University, College of Science, Engineering, and Technology, University Center, MI 48710. Offers computer science and information systems (MS); energy and materials (MS). *Program availability:* Part-time, evening/weekend. *Faculty:* 5 full-time (0 women), 1 part-time/adjunct (0 women). *Students:* 10 full-time (1 woman), 12 part-time (3 women); includes 1 minority (Asian, non-Hispanic/Latino), 8 international. Average age 32. 35 applicants, 80% accepted, 8 enrolled. *Degree requirements:* For master's, field project or thesis work. *Entrance requirements:* For master's, minimum GPA of 3.0. Additional exam requirements/recommendations for international students: Required—TOEFL (minimum score 550 paper-based; 79 iBT). *Application deadline:* For fall admission, 7/15 for international students; for winter admission, 11/15 for international students; for spring admission, 4/15 for international students. Applications

are processed on a rolling basis. Application fee: $30 ($90 for international students). Electronic applications accepted. *Expenses: Tuition, area resident:* Full-time $6225; part-time $623 per credit hour. Tuition, state resident: full-time $6225; part-time $623 per credit hour. Tuition, nonresident: full-time $14,215; part-time $1185 per credit hour. *International tuition:* $14,215 full-time. *Required fees:* $263; $14.60 per credit hour. Tuition and fees vary according to degree level. *Financial support:* Federal Work-Study and scholarships/grants available. Support available to part-time students. Financial award application deadline: 4/1; financial award applicants required to submit FAFSA. *Unit head:* Dr. Robert Tuttle, Program Coordinator, 989-964-4144, Fax: 989-964-2717. *Application contact:* Jenna Briggs, Director, Graduate and International Admissions, 989-964-6096, Fax: 989-964-2788, E-mail: gradadm@svsu.edu.
Website: http://www.svsu.edu/collegeofscienceengineeringtechnology/

St. Cloud State University, School of Graduate Studies, College of Science and Engineering, Department of Computer Science and Information Technology, St. Cloud, MN 56301-4498. Offers computer science (MS); instructional technology (Graduate Certificate). *Degree requirements:* For master's, thesis or alternative. *Entrance requirements:* For master's, GRE General Test, minimum GPA of 2.75. Additional exam requirements/recommendations for international students: Required—Michigan English Language Assessment Battery; Recommended—TOEFL (minimum score 550 paper-based), IELTS (minimum score 6.5). Electronic applications accepted.

St. Francis Xavier University, Graduate Studies, Department of Mathematics, Statistics and Computer Science, Antigonish, NS B2G 2W5, Canada. Offers computer science (M Sc). *Degree requirements:* For master's, thesis. *Entrance requirements:* For master's, bachelor's degree or equivalent in computer science with minimum B average, 2 letters of recommendation. Additional exam requirements/recommendations for international students: Required—TOEFL (minimum score 580 paper-based). *Expenses: Tuition, area resident:* Full-time $7547 Canadian dollars. Tuition, state resident: full-time $7547 Canadian dollars; part-time $804.19 Canadian dollars per course. Tuition, nonresident: full-time $8839 Canadian dollars; part-time $932.49 Canadian dollars per course. *International tuition:* $932.49 Canadian dollars full-time. *Required fees:* $90.20 Canadian dollars; $90.20 Canadian dollars per course. One-time fee: $6 Canadian dollars. Tuition and fees vary according to course load, degree level and program.

Saint Joseph's University, College of Arts and Sciences, Department of Computer Science, Philadelphia, PA 19131-1395. Offers computer science (MS); mathematics and computer science (Post-Master's Certificate). *Program availability:* Part-time, evening/weekend. *Entrance requirements:* For master's, 2 letters of recommendation, resume, personal statement, official transcripts. Additional exam requirements/recommendations for international students: Required—TOEFL (minimum score 550 paper-based; 80 iBT), IELTS (minimum score 6.5). Electronic applications accepted. *Expenses:* Contact institution. *Faculty research:* Computer vision, artificial intelligence, computer graphics, database modelling, computer security.

Saint Louis University, Graduate Programs, College of Arts and Sciences, Department of Computer Science, St. Louis, MO 63103. Offers bioinformatics and computational biology (MS); computer science (MS); software engineering (MS). MS in bioinformatics and computational biology offered in coordination with Departments of Biology, Chemistry, and Mathematics and Statistics).

St. Mary's University, School of Science, Engineering and Technology, Program in Computer Information Systems, San Antonio, TX 78228. Offers MS. *Program availability:* Part-time, evening/weekend. *Students:* 3 full-time (0 women), 2 part-time (1 woman); includes 1 minority (Black or African American, non-Hispanic/Latino), 3 international. Average age 34. 12 applicants, 58% accepted. In 2018, 3 master's awarded. *Degree requirements:* For master's, comprehensive exam, thesis optional. *Entrance requirements:* For master's, GMAT (minimum score of 334) or GRE General Test (minimum quantitative score of 148, analytical writing 2.5), minimum GPA of 3.0 in a bachelor's degree, written statement of purpose indicating interest and objective, two letters of recommendation, official transcripts of all college-level work. Additional exam requirements/recommendations for international students: Required—TOEFL (minimum score 530 paper-based; 80 iBT), IELTS (minimum score 6). *Application deadline:* For fall admission, 7/1 for domestic students; for spring admission, 11/15 for domestic students; for summer admission, 4/1 for domestic students. Applications are processed on a rolling basis. Application fee: $0. Electronic applications accepted. *Expenses: Tuition:* Full-time $16,830; part-time $935 per credit hour. *Required fees:* $1055. Tuition and fees vary according to program. *Financial support:* Career-related internships or fieldwork, Federal Work-Study, institutionally sponsored loans, scholarships/grants, health care benefits, and unspecified assistantships available. Financial award application deadline: 3/31; financial award applicants required to submit FAFSA. *Faculty research:* Artificial intelligence, biological modeling, computer languages, computer security, educational computer gaming. *Unit head:* Dr. Arthur Hanna, Graduate Program Director, 210-431-2021, E-mail: ahanna@stmarytx.edu. *Application contact:* Dr. Arthur Hanna, Graduate Program Director, 210-431-2021, E-mail: ahanna@stmarytx.edu.
Website: https://www.stmarytx.edu/academics/programs/master-computer-information-systems/

St. Mary's University, School of Science, Engineering and Technology, Program in Computer Science, San Antonio, TX 78228. Offers MS. *Program availability:* Part-time, evening/weekend. *Students:* 2 full-time (1 woman), 4 part-time (1 woman), 4 international. Average age 27. 16 applicants, 31% accepted. In 2018, 5 master's awarded. *Degree requirements:* For master's, thesis or project. *Entrance requirements:* For master's, GRE (minimum quantitative score 148, analytical writing 2.5), GMAT (minimum score 334), written statement of purpose indicating interest and objective, two letters of recommendation, official transcripts of all college-level work, minimum GPA of 3.0 in a bachelor's degree. Additional exam requirements/recommendations for international students: Required—TOEFL (minimum score 550 paper-based; 80 iBT), IELTS (minimum score 6). *Application deadline:* For fall admission, 7/1 for domestic students; for spring admission, 11/15 for domestic students; for summer admission, 4/1 for domestic students. Applications are processed on a rolling basis. Application fee: $0. Electronic applications accepted. *Expenses: Tuition:* Full-time $16,830; part-time $935 per credit hour. *Required fees:* $1055. Tuition and fees vary according to program. *Financial support:* Fellowships, research assistantships, career-related internships or fieldwork, Federal Work-Study, institutionally sponsored loans, scholarships/grants, and health care benefits available. Financial award application deadline: 3/31; financial award applicants required to submit FAFSA. *Faculty research:* Artificial intelligence, biological modeling, computer languages, computer security, educational computer gaming. *Unit head:* Dr. Arthur Hanna, Graduate Program Director, 210-431-2021, E-mail: ahanna@stmarytx.edu. *Application contact:* Dr. Arthur Hanna, Graduate Program Director, 210-431-2021, E-mail: ahanna@stmarytx.edu.
Website: https://www.stmarytx.edu/academics/programs/master-computer-science/

Saint Xavier University, Graduate Studies, College of Arts and Sciences, Department of Computer Science, Chicago, IL 60655-3105. Offers MACS. *Degree requirements:* For master's, thesis optional.

Sam Houston State University, College of Sciences, Department of Computer Science, Huntsville, TX 77341. Offers computing and information science (MS); digital forensics (MS); information assurance and security (MS). *Program availability:* Part-time. *Degree requirements:* For master's, comprehensive exam, thesis optional, internship; for doctorate, comprehensive exam, thesis/dissertation. *Entrance requirements:* For master's, GRE General Test, letters of recommendation. Additional exam requirements/recommendations for international students: Required—TOEFL (minimum score 550 paper-based; 79 iBT), IELTS (minimum score 6.5). Electronic applications accepted.

San Diego State University, Graduate and Research Affairs, College of Sciences, Program in Computer Science, San Diego, CA 92182. Offers MS. *Program availability:* Part-time. *Degree requirements:* For master's, comprehensive exam or thesis. *Entrance requirements:* For master's, GRE General Test. Additional exam requirements/recommendations for international students: Required—TOEFL. Electronic applications accepted.

San Francisco State University, Division of Graduate Studies, College of Science and Engineering, Department of Computer Science, San Francisco, CA 94132-1722. Offers MS. *Program availability:* Part-time. *Application deadline:* Applications are processed on a rolling basis. *Unit head:* Dr. Arno Puder, Chair, 415-338-2156, Fax: 415-338-6826, E-mail: arno@sfsu.edu. *Application contact:* Prof. Hui Yang, Graduate Coordinator, 415-338-2221, Fax: 415-338-6826, E-mail: huiyang@sfsu.edu.
Website: http://cs.sfsu.edu/grad/graduate.html

San Francisco State University, Division of Graduate Studies, College of Science and Engineering, School of Engineering, San Francisco, CA 94132-1722. Offers embedded electrical and computer systems (MS); energy systems (MS); structural/earthquake engineering (MS). *Program availability:* Part-time. *Application deadline:* Applications are processed on a rolling basis. Electronic applications accepted. *Unit head:* Dr. Kwok-Siong Teh, Director, 415-338-1228, Fax: 415-338-0525, E-mail: ksteh@sfsu.edu. *Application contact:* Dr. Hamid Shahnasser, Graduate Coordinator, 415-338-2124, Fax: 415-338-0525, E-mail: hamid@sfsu.edu.
Website: http://engineering.sfsu.edu/

Santa Clara University, School of Engineering, Santa Clara, CA 95053. Offers applied mathematics (MS); bioengineering (MS); civil, environmental, and sustainable engineering (MS); computer science and engineering (MS, PhD, Engineer); electrical engineering (MS, PhD, Engineer); engineering management and leadership (MS); mechanical engineering (MS, PhD, Engineer); power systems and sustainable energy (MS); software engineering (MS). *Program availability:* Part-time. *Faculty:* 72 full-time (24 women), 52 part-time/adjunct (9 women). *Students:* 555 full-time (211 women), 269 part-time (91 women); includes 208 minority (8 Black or African American, non-Hispanic/Latino; 1 American Indian or Alaska Native, non-Hispanic/Latino; 145 Asian, non-Hispanic/Latino; 28 Hispanic/Latino; 26 Two or more races, non-Hispanic/Latino), 472 international. Average age 27. 1,309 applicants, 36% accepted, 269 enrolled. In 2018, 320 master's, 7 doctorates awarded. *Entrance requirements:* For master's, GRE, official transcript; for doctorate, GRE, Official transcript, 500 word statement of purpose, three letters of recommendation. Additional exam requirements/recommendations for international students: Required—TOEFL (minimum score 79 iBT), IELTS (minimum score 6.5). *Application deadline:* For fall admission, 6/1 for domestic students; for winter admission, 9/6 for domestic students; for spring admission, 1/10 for domestic students; for summer admission, 3/6 for domestic students. Application fee: $60. Electronic applications accepted. *Financial support:* Fellowships, Federal Work-Study, and scholarships/grants available. Support available to part-time students. Financial award applicants required to submit FAFSA. *Unit head:* Dr. Elaine Scott, Dean, 408-554-3512, E-mail: epscott@scu.edu. *Application contact:* Stacey Tinker, Director of Admissions and Marketing, 408-554-4748, Fax: 408-554-4323, E-mail: stinker@scu.edu.
Website: http://www.scu.edu/engineering/graduate/

Seattle University, College of Science and Engineering, Program in Computer Science, Seattle, WA 98122-1090. Offers MSCS. *Faculty:* 17 full-time (5 women), 2 part-time/adjunct (0 women). *Students:* 71 full-time (29 women), 73 part-time (23 women); includes 33 minority (17 Asian, non-Hispanic/Latino; 11 Hispanic/Latino; 5 Two or more races, non-Hispanic/Latino), 50 international. Average age 28. 125 applicants, 56% accepted, 52 enrolled. In 2018, 7 master's awarded. *Entrance requirements:* For master's, GRE, bachelor's degree in computer science or related discipline from regionally-accredited institution; minimum GPA of 3.0; letter of intent; 2 academic or professional recommendations; official transcripts. Additional exam requirements/recommendations for international students: Required—TOEFL (minimum score 580 paper-based; 92 iBT). *Application deadline:* For fall admission, 7/20 for domestic students, 4/1 for international students; for winter admission, 11/20 for domestic students, 9/1 for international students; for spring admission, 2/20 for domestic students, 12/1 for international students. *Financial support:* In 2018–19, 15 students received support. *Unit head:* Dr. Richard LeBlanc, Chair, 206-296-5510, Fax: 206-296-2071, E-mail: leblanc@seattleu.edu. *Application contact:* Janet Shandley, Director of Graduate Admissions, 206-296-5900, Fax: 206-298-5656, E-mail: grad_admissions@seattleu.edu.
Website: https://www.seattleu.edu/scieng/computer-science/graduate/mscs/

Shippensburg University of Pennsylvania, School of Graduate Studies, College of Arts and Sciences, Department of Computer Science and Engineering, Shippensburg, PA 17257-2299. Offers agile software engineering (Certificate); computer science (MS); IT leadership (Certificate). *Program availability:* Part-time, evening/weekend. *Faculty:* 4 full-time (2 women). *Students:* 5 full-time (3 women), 6 part-time (1 woman); includes 2 minority (both Black or African American, non-Hispanic/Latino), 7 international. Average age 29. 29 applicants, 55% accepted, 5 enrolled. In 2018, 15 master's awarded. *Entrance requirements:* For master's, GRE (if GPA less than 2.75), professional resume. Additional exam requirements/recommendations for international students: Required—TOEFL (minimum score 70 iBT), IELTS (minimum score 6), TOEFL (minimum score 70 iBT) or IELTS (minimum score 6). *Application deadline:* For fall admission, 4/30 for international students. Applications are processed on a rolling basis. Application fee: $45. Electronic applications accepted. *Expenses:* Tuition, state resident: part-time $516 per credit. Tuition, nonresident: part-time $750 per credit. *Required fees:* $149 per credit. *Financial support:* In 2018–19, 4 students received support. Career-related internships or fieldwork, scholarships/grants, unspecified assistantships, and resident hall director and student payroll positions available. Support available to part-time students. Financial award application deadline: 3/1; financial award applicants required to submit FAFSA. *Unit head:* Dr. Jeonghwa Lee, Professor and Director of Graduate Studies, 717-477-1178, Fax: 717-477-4002, E-mail: jlee@ship.edu. *Application contact:* Maya T. Mapp, Director of Admissions, 717-477-1231, Fax: 717-477-4016, E-mail: mtmapp@ship.edu.
Website: http://www.cs.ship.edu/

Simon Fraser University, Office of Graduate Studies and Postdoctoral Fellows, Faculty of Applied Sciences, School of Computing Science, Burnaby, BC V5A 1S6, Canada. Offers M Sc, PhD, M Sc/MSE. M Sc/MSE offered jointly with Zhejiang University. *Degree requirements:* For master's, comprehensive exam, thesis or alternative; for doctorate, comprehensive exam, thesis/dissertation, qualifying exams. *Entrance requirements:* For master's, minimum GPA of 3.0 (on scale of 4.33) or 3.33 based on last 60 credits of undergraduate courses; for doctorate, minimum GPA of 3.5 (on scale of 4.33). Additional exam requirements/recommendations for international students:

Recommended—TOEFL (minimum score 580 paper-based; 93 iBT), IELTS (minimum score 7), TWE (minimum score 5). Electronic applications accepted. *Faculty research:* Artificial intelligence, computer hardware, computer systems, database systems, theory.

Simon Fraser University, Office of Graduate Studies and Postdoctoral Fellows, Faculty of Communication, Art and Technology, School of Interactive Arts and Technology, Surrey, BC V3T 2W1, Canada. Offers M Sc, MA, PhD. *Degree requirements:* For master's, thesis, seminar presentation; for doctorate, comprehensive exam, thesis/dissertation, seminar presentations. *Entrance requirements:* For master's, minimum GPA of 3.0 (on scale of 4.33) or 3.33 based on last 60 credits of undergraduate courses; for doctorate, minimum GPA of 3.5 (on scale of 4.33). Additional exam requirements/recommendations for international students: Required—TOEFL (minimum score 580 paper-based; 93 iBT), IELTS (minimum score 7), TWE (minimum score 5). Electronic applications accepted. *Faculty research:* Media and culture, scientific methods, social and human experience, knowledge computation, media art.

Sofia University, Residential Programs, Palo Alto, CA 94303. Offers clinical psychology (Psy D); computer science (MS); counseling psychology (MA); transpersonal psychology (MA, PhD). *Program availability:* Part-time, evening/weekend. Terminal master's awarded for partial completion of doctoral program. *Degree requirements:* For doctorate, thesis/dissertation. *Entrance requirements:* For master's, bachelor's degree; for doctorate, bachelor's degree; master's degree (for some programs). Electronic applications accepted.

Southern Adventist University, School of Computing, Collegedale, TN 37315-0370. Offers computer science (MS). *Program availability:* Part-time. *Faculty:* 4 full-time (0 women). *Students:* 17 full-time (0 women), 3 part-time (0 women); includes 5 minority (all Hispanic/Latino), 6 international. Average age 27. 5 applicants, 20% accepted, 1 enrolled. In 2018, 4 master's awarded. *Degree requirements:* For master's, professional software development portfolio. *Entrance requirements:* For master's, minimum GPA of 3.0. Additional exam requirements/recommendations for international students: Required—TOEFL (minimum score 80 iBT). *Application deadline:* For fall admission, 3/1 priority date for domestic students, 3/1 for international students; for winter admission, 10/1 priority date for domestic students, 10/1 for international students. Applications are processed on a rolling basis. Application fee: $25. Electronic applications accepted. *Financial support:* Career-related internships or fieldwork, tuition waivers (full and partial), and unspecified assistantships available. Financial award application deadline: 8/1; financial award applicants required to submit FAFSA. *Faculty research:* Component-based technologies, web-based development, large scale systems architecture, database integration. *Unit head:* Rick Halterman, Dean, 423-236-2871, E-mail: halterman@southern.edu. *Application contact:* Tyson Hall, Program Coordinator, 423-236-2916, E-mail: tyson@southern.edu.
Website: http://www.southern.edu/computing/

Southern Arkansas University–Magnolia, School of Graduate Studies, Magnolia, AR 71753. Offers agriculture (MS); business administration (MBA), including agribusiness, social entrepreneurship, supply chain management; clinical and mental health counseling (MS); computer and information sciences (MS), including cyber security and privacy, data science, information technology; gifted and talented (M Ed), including curriculum and instruction, educational administration and supervision, gifted and talented P-8/7-12, instructional specialist P-4; higher, adult and lifelong education (M Ed); kinesiology (M Ed), including coaching; library media and information specialist (M Ed); public administration (MPA); school counseling K-12 (M Ed); student affairs and college counseling (M Ed); teaching (MAT). *Accreditation:* NCATE. *Program availability:* Part-time, 100% online, blended/hybrid learning. *Faculty:* 36 full-time (21 women), 32 part-time/adjunct (15 women). *Students:* 164 full-time (77 women), 762 part-time (510 women); includes 192 minority (163 Black or African American, non-Hispanic/Latino; 7 American Indian or Alaska Native, non-Hispanic/Latino; 13 Asian, non-Hispanic/Latino; 1 Hispanic/Latino; 8 Two or more races, non-Hispanic/Latino), 213 international. Average age 28. 363 applicants, 100% accepted, 237 enrolled. In 2018, 716 master's awarded. *Degree requirements:* For master's, comprehensive exam (for some programs), thesis optional. *Entrance requirements:* For master's, GRE, MAT or GMAT, minimum GPA of 2.5. Additional exam requirements/recommendations for international students: Required—TOEFL (minimum score 550 paper-based), IELTS (minimum score 6). *Application deadline:* For fall admission, 8/1 for domestic and international students; for spring admission, 12/1 for domestic students, 11/15 for international students; for summer admission, 4/1 for domestic students, 5/10 for international students. Applications are processed on a rolling basis. Application fee: $25 ($90 for international students). Electronic applications accepted. *Expenses: Tuition, area resident:* Full-time $5130; part-time $3420 per year. Tuition, state resident: full-time $5130; part-time $3420 per year. Tuition, nonresident: full-time $7866; part-time $5244 per year. *International tuition:* $7866 full-time. *Required fees:* $1052; $710 per unit. Tuition and fees vary according to course load. *Financial support:* Career-related internships or fieldwork, Federal Work-Study, scholarships/grants, tuition waivers (full), and unspecified assistantships available. Financial award applicants required to submit FAFSA. *Faculty research:* Alternative certification for teachers, supervision of instruction, instructional leadership, counseling. *Unit head:* Dr. Kim Bloss, Dean, School of Graduate Studies, 870-235-4150, Fax: 870-235-5227, E-mail: kkbloss@saumag.edu. *Application contact:* Talia Jett, Admissions Coordinator, 870-2355450, Fax: 870-235-5227, E-mail: taliajett@saumag.edu.
Website: http://www.saumag.edu/graduate

Southern Connecticut State University, School of Graduate Studies, School of Arts and Sciences, Department of Computer Science, New Haven, CT 06515-1355. Offers MS. *Program availability:* Part-time, evening/weekend. *Entrance requirements:* For master's, GRE. Electronic applications accepted.

Southern Illinois University Carbondale, Graduate School, College of Science, Department of Computer Science, Carbondale, IL 62901-4701. Offers MS, PhD. *Degree requirements:* For master's, thesis; for doctorate, thesis/dissertation. *Entrance requirements:* For master's, previous undergraduate course work in computer science, minimum GPA of 2.7; for doctorate, GRE General Test, minimum GPA of 3.25. Additional exam requirements/recommendations for international students: Required—TOEFL. *Faculty research:* Analysis of algorithms, VLSI testing, database systems, artificial intelligence, computer architecture.

Southern Illinois University Edwardsville, Graduate School, School of Engineering, Department of Computer Science, Edwardsville, IL 62026. Offers MS. *Program availability:* Part-time, evening/weekend. *Degree requirements:* For master's, thesis (for some programs), final exam, final project. *Entrance requirements:* Additional exam requirements/recommendations for international students: Required—TOEFL (minimum score 550 paper-based; 79 iBT), IELTS (minimum score 6.5). Electronic applications accepted.

Southern Methodist University, Lyle School of Engineering, Department of Computer Science and Engineering, Dallas, TX 75275-0122. Offers computer engineering (MS, PhD); computer science (MS, PhD); security engineering (MS); software engineering (MS, DE). *Program availability:* Part-time, evening/weekend, online learning. Terminal master's awarded for partial completion of doctoral program. *Degree requirements:* For master's, thesis optional; for doctorate, thesis/dissertation, oral and written qualifying

exams, oral final exam (PhD). *Entrance requirements:* For master's, GRE General Test, minimum GPA of 3.0 in last 2 years; bachelor's degree in engineering, mathematics, or sciences; for doctorate, preliminary counseling exam (PhD), minimum GPA of 3.0, bachelor's degree in related field, MA (for DE). Additional exam requirements/recommendations for international students: Required—TOEFL (minimum score 550 paper-based). *Faculty research:* Trusted and high performance network computing, software engineering and management, knowledge engineering and management, computer arithmetic, computer architecture and CAD.

Southern Oregon University, Graduate Studies, Department of Computer Science, Ashland, OR 97520. Offers applied computer science (PSM). *Program availability:* Part-time, online learning. *Degree requirements:* For master's, thesis (for some programs). *Entrance requirements:* For master's, GRE General Test, minimum cumulative GPA of 3.0 in the last 90 quarter credits (60 semester credits) of undergraduate coursework. Additional exam requirements/recommendations for international students: Required—TOEFL (minimum score 540 paper-based; 76 iBT), IELTS (minimum score 6), ELPT (minimum score 964) or ELS (minimum score 112). Electronic applications accepted.

Southern University and Agricultural and Mechanical College, Graduate School, College of Sciences and Engineering, Department of Computer Science, Baton Rouge, LA 70813. Offers information systems (MS); micro/minicomputer architecture (MS); operating systems (MS). *Program availability:* Part-time, online learning. *Degree requirements:* For master's, thesis. *Entrance requirements:* For master's, GRE General Test, minimum GPA of 3.0, bachelor's degree in computer science or related field. Additional exam requirements/recommendations for international students: Required—TOEFL (minimum score 525 paper-based). *Faculty research:* Network theory, computational complexity, high speed computing, neural networking, data warehousing/mining.

Stanford University, School of Engineering, Department of Computer Science, Stanford, CA 94305-2004. Offers MS, PhD. *Expenses: Tuition:* Full-time $50,703; part-time $32,970 per year. *Required fees:* $651.
Website: http://www.cs.stanford.edu/

Stanford University, School of Engineering, Institute for Computational and Mathematical Engineering, Stanford, CA 94305-2004. Offers MS, PhD. *Expenses: Tuition:* Full-time $50,703; part-time $32,970 per year. *Required fees:* $651.
Website: http://icme.stanford.edu/

State University of New York Polytechnic Institute, Program in Computer and Information Science, Utica, NY 13502. Offers MS. *Program availability:* Part-time. *Students:* 78 full-time (18 women), 25 part-time (4 women); includes 7 minority (5 Asian, non-Hispanic/Latino; 2 Hispanic/Latino), 76 international. Average age 24. 153 applicants, 64% accepted, 39 enrolled. In 2018, 36 master's awarded. *Degree requirements:* For master's, thesis, thesis or project. *Entrance requirements:* For master's, GRE or approved GRE waiver, undergraduate prerequisite courses in math and computer science. Additional exam requirements/recommendations for international students: Required—TOEFL (minimum score 79 iBT), IELTS (minimum score 6.5), PTE (minimum score 53), Only ONE of above. *Application deadline:* For fall admission, 7/1 for domestic and international students; for spring admission, 12/1 for domestic students, 11/1 for international students. Applications are processed on a rolling basis. Application fee: $60. Electronic applications accepted. *Expenses: Tuition, area resident:* Full-time $8316; part-time $462 per credit hour. Tuition, nonresident: full-time $16,992; part-time $944 per credit hour. *International tuition:* $16,992 full-time. *Required fees:* $1023; $56.87 per credit hour. Tuition and fees vary according to course load, campus/location and program. *Financial support:* Research assistantships, scholarships/grants, and unspecified assistantships available. Financial award application deadline: 6/1; financial award applicants required to submit FAFSA. *Faculty research:* Computer vision and deep learning, quantum computing, blockchains, artificial intelligence and optimization, and architecture virtualization. *Unit head:* Dr. Roger Cavallo, Program Coordinator, 315-792-7231, E-mail: roger.cavallo@sunypoly.edu. *Application contact:* Alicia Foster, Director of Graduate Admissions, 315-792-7347, E-mail: fostera3@sunypoly.edu.
Website: https://sunypoly.edu/academics/majors-and-programs/ms-computer-information-science.html

Stevens Institute of Technology, Graduate School, Charles V. Schaefer Jr. School of Engineering and Science, Department of Computer Science, Program in Computer Science, Hoboken, NJ 07030. Offers MS, PhD, Certificate. *Program availability:* Part-time, evening/weekend. *Faculty:* 25 full-time (5 women), 7 part-time/adjunct. *Students:* 422 full-time (84 women), 52 part-time (8 women); includes 35 minority (9 Black or African American, non-Hispanic/Latino; 26 Asian, non-Hispanic/Latino), 392 international. Average age 25. In 2018, 289 master's, 5 other advanced degrees awarded. Terminal master's awarded for partial completion of doctoral program. *Degree requirements:* For master's, thesis optional, minimum B average in major field and overall; for doctorate, comprehensive exam (for some programs), thesis/dissertation; for Certificate, minimum B average. *Entrance requirements:* For master's, GRE/GMAT scores: GRE scores are required for all applicants applying to a full-time graduate program in the Schaefer School of Engineering and Science (SES). International applicants must submit TOEFL/IELTS scores and fulfill the English Language Proficiency Requirements in order to be considered. Additional exam requirements/recommendations for international students: Required—TOEFL (minimum score 74 iBT), IELTS (minimum score 6). *Application deadline:* For fall admission, 4/15 for domestic and international students; for spring admission, 11/1 for domestic and international students; for summer admission, 5/1 for domestic students. Applications are processed on a rolling basis. Application fee: $60. Electronic applications accepted. *Expenses: Tuition:* Full-time $35,960; part-time $1620 per credit. *Required fees:* $1290; $600 per semester. Tuition and fees vary according to course load. *Financial support:* Fellowships, research assistantships, teaching assistantships, career-related internships or fieldwork, Federal Work-Study, scholarships/grants, and unspecified assistantships available. Financial award application deadline: 2/15; financial award applicants required to submit FAFSA. *Unit head:* Dr. Jean Zu, Dean of SES, 201-216.8233, Fax: 201-216.8372, E-mail: Jean.Zu@stevens.edu. *Application contact:* Graduate Admissions, 888-783-8367, Fax: 888-511-1306, E-mail: graduate@stevens.edu.

Stevens Institute of Technology, Graduate School, School of Business, Program in Information Systems, Hoboken, NJ 07030. Offers computer science (MS); e-commerce (MS); enterprise systems (MS); entrepreneurial information technology (MS); information architecture (MS); information management (MS, Certificate); information security (MS); information technology in financial services industry (MS); information technology in the pharmaceutical industry (MS); information technology outsourcing management (MS); project management (MS, Certificate); software engineering (MS); telecommunications (MS). *Program availability:* Part-time, evening/weekend. *Students:* 248 full-time (87 women), 54 part-time (20 women); includes 25 minority (8 Black or African American, non-Hispanic/Latino; 17 Asian, non-Hispanic/Latino), 245 international. Average age 27. In 2018, 202 master's, 16 other advanced degrees awarded. Terminal master's awarded for partial completion of doctoral program. *Degree requirements:* For master's, thesis optional, minimum B average in major field and overall; for Certificate, minimum B average. *Entrance requirements:* For master's, GRE/

GMAT scores: GRE scores are required for all applicants applying to a full-time graduate program in the Schaefer School of Engineering and Science (SES). International applicants must submit TOEFL/IELTS scores and fulfill the English Language Proficiency Requirements in order to be considered. Additional exam requirements/recommendations for international students: Required—TOEFL (minimum score 74 iBT), IELTS (minimum score 6). *Application deadline:* For fall admission, 4/1 for domestic and international students; for spring admission, 11/1 for domestic and international students; for summer admission, 5/1 for domestic students. Applications are processed on a rolling basis. Application fee: $60. Electronic applications accepted. *Expenses: Tuition:* Full-time $35,960; part-time $1620 per credit. *Required fees:* $1290; $600 per semester. Tuition and fees vary according to course load. *Financial support:* Fellowships, research assistantships, teaching assistantships, career-related internships or fieldwork, Federal Work-Study, scholarships/grants, and unspecified assistantships available. Financial award application deadline: 2/15; financial award applicants required to submit FAFSA. *Unit head:* Dr. Gregory Prastacos, Dean of SB, 201-216-8366, E-mail: gprastac@stevens.edu. *Application contact:* Graduate Admissions, 888-783-8367, Fax: 888-511-1306, E-mail: graduate@stevens.edu.
Website: https://www.stevens.edu/school-business/masters-programs/information-systems

Stony Brook University, State University of New York, Graduate School, College of Engineering and Applied Sciences, Department of Computer Science, Stony Brook, NY 11794. Offers MS, PhD, Certificate. *Faculty:* 46 full-time (4 women), 4 part-time/adjunct (3 women). *Students:* 475 full-time (104 women), 194 part-time (55 women); includes 31 minority (3 Black or African American, non-Hispanic/Latino; 21 Asian, non-Hispanic/Latino; 7 Hispanic/Latino), 601 international. Average age 26. 1,947 applicants, 30% accepted, 232 enrolled. In 2018, 162 master's, 22 doctorates awarded. Terminal master's awarded for partial completion of doctoral program. *Degree requirements:* For master's, thesis or alternative; for doctorate, comprehensive exam, thesis/dissertation. *Entrance requirements:* For master's and doctorate, GRE General Test. Additional exam requirements/recommendations for international students: Required—TOEFL (minimum score 90 iBT). *Application deadline:* For fall admission, 1/15 for domestic students; for spring admission, 10/1 for domestic students. Application fee: $100. *Expenses:* Contact institution. *Financial support:* In 2018–19, 1 fellowship, 114 research assistantships, 94 teaching assistantships were awarded. *Faculty research:* Cyber security, computer security, computer software, computer operating systems, computer and information sciences. *Total annual research expenditures:* $7.6 million. *Unit head:* Prof. Samir Das, Chair, 631-632-1807, E-mail: samir@cs.stonybrook.edu. *Application contact:* Cynthia Scalzo, Coordinator, 631-632-1521, E-mail: cscalzo@cs.stonybrook.edu.
Website: http://www.cs.sunysb.edu/

Stratford University, School of Graduate Studies, Falls Church, VA 22043. Offers accounting (MS); business administration (MBA, DBA); cyber security (MS); cyber security leadership and policy (MS); digital forensics (MS); healthcare administration (MS); information systems (MS); information technology (DIT); networking and telecommunications (MS); software engineering (MS). *Program availability:* Part-time, evening/weekend, 100% online, blended/hybrid learning. *Degree requirements:* For master's, comprehensive exam, capstone project. *Entrance requirements:* For master's, GRE or GMAT, baccalaureate degree. Additional exam requirements/recommendations for international students: Required—TOEFL (minimum score 79 iBT), IELTS (minimum score 6.5), PTE (minimum score 5). Electronic applications accepted. *Expenses: Tuition:* Full-time $22,275; part-time $11,137 per year. One-time fee: $385.

Syracuse University, College of Engineering and Computer Science, MS Program in Computer Science, Syracuse, NY 13244. Offers MS. *Program availability:* Part-time. *Students:* Average age 25. In 2018, 53 master's awarded. *Degree requirements:* For master's, comprehensive exam (for some programs), thesis (for some programs). *Entrance requirements:* For master's, GRE General Test, three letters of recommendation, resume, personal statement, official transcripts. Additional exam requirements/recommendations for international students: Required—TOEFL (minimum score 100 iBT). *Application deadline:* For fall admission, 7/1 priority date for domestic students, 6/1 priority date for international students; for spring admission, 11/15 priority date for domestic students, 10/15 priority date for international students. Applications are processed on a rolling basis. Application fee: $75. Electronic applications accepted. *Financial support:* Fellowships with full tuition reimbursements, research assistantships, teaching assistantships, and tuition waivers (partial) available. Financial award application deadline: 1/1; financial award applicants required to submit FAFSA. *Faculty research:* Structured programming and formal methods, computer architecture, operating systems, design and analysis of algorithms. *Unit head:* Dr. Qinru Qiu, Program Director, 315-443-2652, E-mail: eecsadmissions@syr.edu. *Application contact:* Kathleen Joyce, Assistant Dean, 315-443-2219, E-mail: topgrads@syr.edu.
Website: http://eng-cs.syr.edu/our-departments/electrical-engineering-and-computer-science/graduate/academic-programs/?programID=1555&degree=masters_program

Télé-université, Graduate Programs, Québec, QC G1K 9H5, Canada. Offers computer science (PhD); corporate finance (MS); distance learning (MS). *Program availability:* Part-time.

Temple University, College of Science and Technology, Department of Computer and Information Sciences, Philadelphia, PA 19122. Offers computational data science (MS); computer and information sciences (PhD), including artificial intelligence, computer and network systems, information systems, software systems; computer science (MS); cyber defense and information assurance (PSM); information science and technology (MS). *Program availability:* Part-time, evening/weekend, online learning. *Faculty:* 31 full-time (7 women), 10 part-time/adjunct (2 women). *Students:* 92 full-time (28 women), 15 part-time (3 women); includes 7 minority (2 Black or African American, non-Hispanic/Latino; 4 Asian, non-Hispanic/Latino; 1 Hispanic/Latino), 82 international. 119 applicants, 43% accepted, 21 enrolled. In 2018, 20 master's, 5 doctorates awarded. *Degree requirements:* For doctorate, thesis/dissertation. *Entrance requirements:* For master's, GRE, 3 letters of recommendation, statement of goals; for doctorate, GRE, 3 letters of recommendation, bachelor's degree in related field, statement of goals, resume. Additional exam requirements/recommendations for international students: Required—TOEFL (minimum score 85 iBT), IELTS (minimum score 6.5), PTE (minimum score 58), one of three is required. *Application deadline:* Applications are processed on a rolling basis. Application fee: $60. Electronic applications accepted. *Expenses:* Contact institution. *Financial support:* Research assistantships, teaching assistantships, health care benefits, and unspecified assistantships available. Financial award applicants required to submit FAFSA. *Faculty research:* Data mining, machine learning, knowledge discovery, computer networks and systems, cyberspace security. *Unit head:* Jamie Payton, Department Chairperson, 215-204-8245, E-mail: Jamie.payton@temple.edu. *Application contact:* Eduard Dragut, Graduate Chair, 215-204-0521, E-mail: cisadmit@temple.edu.
Website: https://cis.temple.edu/

Tennessee Technological University, College of Graduate Studies, College of Engineering, Department of Computer Science, Cookeville, TN 38505. Offers MS, PhD. *Program availability:* Part-time. *Students:* 18 full-time (3 women), 15 part-time (2 women); includes 2 minority (both Black or African American, non-Hispanic/Latino), 8 international. 44 applicants, 66% accepted, 12 enrolled. In 2018, 7 master's awarded. *Degree requirements:* For master's, thesis or alternative. *Entrance requirements:* For master's, GRE. Additional exam requirements/recommendations for international students: Required—TOEFL (minimum score 550 paper-based; 79 iBT), IELTS (minimum score 5.5), PTE (minimum score 53), or TOEIC (Test of English as an International Communication). *Application deadline:* For fall admission, 8/1 for domestic students, 5/1 for international students; for spring admission, 12/1 for domestic students, 10/1 for international students; for summer admission, 5/1 for domestic students, 2/1 for international students. Applications are processed on a rolling basis. Application fee: $35 ($40 for international students). Electronic applications accepted. *Financial support:* Research assistantships and teaching assistantships available. Financial award application deadline: 4/1. *Unit head:* Dr. Jerry Gannod, Chairperson, 931-372-3691, Fax: 931-372-3686, E-mail: jgannod@tntech.edu. *Application contact:* Shelia K. Kendrick, Coordinator of Graduate Studies, 931-372-3808, Fax: 931-372-3497, E-mail: skendrick@tntech.edu.

Texas A&M University, College of Engineering, Department of Computer Science and Engineering, College Station, TX 77843. Offers computer engineering (M Eng, MS); computer science (MCS, MS, PhD). *Program availability:* Part-time. *Faculty:* 52. *Students:* 345 full-time (65 women), 58 part-time (6 women); includes 47 minority (4 Black or African American, non-Hispanic/Latino; 26 Asian, non-Hispanic/Latino; 13 Hispanic/Latino; 1 Native Hawaiian or other Pacific Islander, non-Hispanic/Latino; 3 Two or more races, non-Hispanic/Latino), 296 international. Average age 27. 2,312 applicants, 13% accepted, 125 enrolled. In 2018, 74 master's, 16 doctorates awarded. *Degree requirements:* For master's, thesis (for some programs); for doctorate, thesis/dissertation. *Entrance requirements:* For master's and doctorate, GRE General Test. Additional exam requirements/recommendations for international students: Required—TOEFL (minimum score 550 paper-based; 80 iBT), IELTS (minimum score 6), PTE (minimum score 53). *Application deadline:* For fall admission, 1/1 priority date for domestic and international students; for spring admission, 8/1 priority date for domestic and international students. Applications are processed on a rolling basis. Application fee: $50 ($90 for international students). Electronic applications accepted. *Expenses:* Contact institution. *Financial support:* In 2018–19, 306 students received support, including 10 fellowships with tuition reimbursements available (averaging $22,371 per year), 155 research assistantships with tuition reimbursements available (averaging $13,271 per year), 91 teaching assistantships with tuition reimbursements available (averaging $13,225 per year); career-related internships or fieldwork, institutionally sponsored loans, scholarships/grants, traineeships, health care benefits, tuition waivers (full and partial), and unspecified assistantships also available. Support available to part-time students. Financial award application deadline: 3/15; financial award applicants required to submit FAFSA. *Faculty research:* Software, systems, informatics, human-centered systems, theory. *Unit head:* Dr. Dilma Da Silva, Department Head, 979-845-5820, E-mail: dilma@cse.tamu.edu. *Application contact:* Dr. Duncan M. Walker, Professor and Graduate Advisor, 979-458-4087, E-mail: grad-advisor@cse.tamu.edu.
Website: http://engineering.tamu.edu/cse/

Texas A&M University–Corpus Christi, College of Graduate Studies, College of Science and Engineering, Program in Computer Science, Corpus Christi, TX 78412. Offers MS. *Program availability:* Part-time, evening/weekend. *Degree requirements:* For master's, comprehensive exam (for some programs), thesis (for some programs), thesis or project. *Entrance requirements:* For master's, GRE (taken within 5 years), essay (500-1,000 words). Additional exam requirements/recommendations for international students: Required—TOEFL (minimum score 550 paper-based; 79 iBT), IELTS (minimum score 6.5). Electronic applications accepted.

Texas A&M University–Kingsville, College of Graduate Studies, Frank H. Dotterweich College of Engineering, Department of Electrical Engineering and Computer Science, Program in Computer Science, Kingsville, TX 78363. Offers MS. *Degree requirements:* For master's, variable foreign language requirement, comprehensive exam, thesis (for some programs). *Entrance requirements:* For master's, GRE (minimum Quantitative and Verbal score of 288), MAT, GMAT, minimum undergraduate GPA of 3.0. Additional exam requirements/recommendations for international students: Required—TOEFL (minimum score 550 paper-based; 79 iBT). Electronic applications accepted.

Texas Southern University, School of Science and Technology, Department of Computer Science, Houston, TX 77004-4584. Offers MS. Electronic applications accepted.

Texas State University, The Graduate College, College of Science and Engineering, Doctoral Program in Computer Science, San Marcos, TX 78666. Offers PhD. *Program availability:* Part-time. *Faculty:* 11 full-time (3 women). *Students:* 15 full-time (4 women), 6 part-time; includes 1 minority (Two or more races, non-Hispanic/Latino), 9 international. Average age 31. 41 applicants, 41% accepted, 12 enrolled. *Degree requirements:* For doctorate, comprehensive exam, thesis/dissertation, qualifying exam; dissertation defense; demonstration of significant experience designing and implementing a substantial piece of software. *Entrance requirements:* For doctorate, official GRE (general test only) required with competitive scores in the verbal reasoning and quantitative reasoning sections, baccalaureate degree in computer science with minimum GPA of 3.0 in last 60 hours of undergraduate course work or master's degree in computer science with minimum GPA of 3.3; interview; resume; 3 letters of recommendation from those with knowledge of academic abilities. Additional exam requirements/recommendations for international students: Required—TOEFL (minimum score 85 iBT), IELTS (minimum score 6.5). *Application deadline:* For fall admission, 2/1 priority date for domestic and international students. Applications are processed on a rolling basis. Application fee: $55 ($90 for international students). Electronic applications accepted. *Expenses:* Tuition, state resident: full-time $8102; part-time $4051 per semester. Tuition, nonresident: full-time $18,229; part-time $9115 per semester. *International tuition:* $18,229 full-time. *Required fees:* $2116; $120 per credit hour. Tuition and fees vary according to course load. *Financial support:* In 2018–19, 17 students received support, including 3 research assistantships (averaging $30,000 per year), 11 teaching assistantships (averaging $30,000 per year); scholarships/grants, health care benefits, and unspecified assistantships also available. Financial award application deadline: 1/15; financial award applicants required to submit FAFSA. *Faculty research:* Artificial intelligence, bioinformatics, computer communication and networking, cyber security and trustworthy computing, database and information systems, distributed and parallel computing, high performance computing, human computer interaction, image retrieval, multimedia computing, real time systems, sensor networks, software engineering, and sustainable computing. *Total annual research expenditures:* $261,837. *Unit head:* Dr. Anne Hee-Hiong Ngu, Doctoral Program Director, 512-245-3409, Fax: 512-245-8750, E-mail: cs_phd_advisor@txstate.edu. *Application contact:* Dr. Andrea Golato, Dean of the Graduate College, 512-245-2581.
Website: https://cs.txstate.edu/academics/phd/

Texas State University, The Graduate College, College of Science and Engineering, Master's Program in Computer Science, San Marcos, TX 78666. Offers MA, MS. *Program availability:* Part-time. *Faculty:* 9 full-time (1 woman). *Students:* 69 full-time (38 women), 38 part-time (16 women); includes 15 minority (8 Asian, non-Hispanic/Latino; 7 Hispanic/Latino), 76 international. Average age 27. 162 applicants, 72% accepted, 34 enrolled. In 2018, 55 master's awarded. *Degree requirements:* For master's, comprehensive exam, thesis (for some programs). *Entrance requirements:* For master's, official GRE (general test only) required with competitive scores in the verbal reasoning and quantitative reasoning sections, baccalaureate degree from regionally-accredited university with minimum GPA of 2.75 on last 60 undergraduate semester hours, a copy of an official transcript from each institution where course credit was granted, 3 letters of recommendation, academic vitae (resume), statement of purpose. Additional exam requirements/recommendations for international students: Required—TOEFL (minimum score 550 paper-based; 78 iBT), IELTS (minimum score 6.5). *Application deadline:* For fall admission, 2/15 priority date for domestic and international students; for spring admission, 10/15 for domestic students, 10/1 for international students; for summer admission, 4/15 for domestic students, 3/15 for international students. Applications are processed on a rolling basis. Application fee: $55 ($90 for international students). Electronic applications accepted. *Expenses:* Tuition, state resident: full-time $8102; part-time $4051 per semester. Tuition, nonresident: full-time $18,229; part-time $9115 per semester. *International tuition:* $18,229 full-time. *Required fees:* $2116; $120 per credit hour. Tuition and fees vary according to course load. *Financial support:* In 2018–19, 44 students received support, including 5 research assistantships (averaging $12,651 per year), 23 teaching assistantships (averaging $13,095 per year); Federal Work-Study, institutionally sponsored loans, scholarships/grants, health care benefits, and unspecified assistantships also available. Support available to part-time students. Financial award application deadline: 1/15; financial award applicants required to submit FAFSA. *Faculty research:* Artificial intelligence, computer communication and networking, computer vision, cyber security and trustworthy computing, database and information systems, data mining, distributed and parallel computing, high performance computing, human computer interaction, image retrieval, machine learning, multimedia computing, sensor networks, software engineering, sustainable computing. *Total annual research expenditures:* $294,885. *Unit head:* Dr. Wuxu Peng, Graduate Advisor, 512-245-3874, Fax: 512-245-8750, E-mail: cs_graduateadvisor@txstate.edu. *Application contact:* Dr. Andrea Golato, Dean of the Graduate College, 512-245-2581, E-mail: gradcollege@txstate.edu. Website: https://cs.txstate.edu/academics/graduate_program/

Towson University, Jess and Mildred Fisher College of Science and Mathematics, Program in Computer Science, Towson, MD 21252-0001. Offers MS. *Program availability:* Part-time, evening/weekend. *Degree requirements:* For master's, thesis optional. *Entrance requirements:* For master's, minimum GPA of 3.0, bachelor's degree in computer science or bachelor's degree in any other field and completion of 1-3 preparatory courses. Electronic applications accepted. *Expenses: Tuition, area resident:* Full-time $9196; part-time $418 per unit. Tuition, state resident: full-time $9196; part-time $418 per unit. Tuition, nonresident: full-time $19,030; part-time $865 per unit. *International tuition:* $19,030 full-time. *Required fees:* $3102; $141 per year. $423 per term. Tuition and fees vary according to campus/location and program.

Toyota Technological Institute at Chicago, Program in Computer Science, Chicago, IL 60637. Offers PhD. *Degree requirements:* For doctorate, thesis/dissertation.

Trent University, Graduate Studies, Program in Applications of Modeling in the Natural and Social Sciences, Department of Computer Studies, Peterborough, ON K9J 7B8, Canada. Offers M Sc. *Degree requirements:* For master's, thesis. *Entrance requirements:* For master's, honours degree.

Troy University, Graduate School, College of Arts and Sciences, Program in Computer Science, Troy, AL 36082. Offers MS. *Program availability:* Part-time, evening/weekend. *Faculty:* 7 full-time (2 women). *Students:* 18 full-time (4 women), 17 part-time (3 women); includes 3 minority (1 Black or African American, non-Hispanic/Latino; 1 Asian, non-Hispanic/Latino; 1 Hispanic/Latino), 28 international. Average age 28. 98 applicants, 81% accepted, 7 enrolled. In 2018, 87 master's awarded. *Degree requirements:* For master's, thesis or research paper and comprehensive exam; minimum GPA of 3.0; admission to candidacy. *Entrance requirements:* For master's, GRE (minimum score of 850 on old exam or 286 on new exam), MAT (minimum score of 385) or GMAT (minimum score of 380), bachelor's degree; minimum undergraduate GPA of 2.5 or 3.0 on last 30 semester hours. Additional exam requirements/recommendations for international students: Required—TOEFL (minimum score 523 paper-based; 70 iBT), IELTS (minimum score 6). *Application deadline:* For fall admission, 6/1 for international students; for spring admission, 10/15 for international students. Applications are processed on a rolling basis. Application fee: $50. Electronic applications accepted. *Expenses: Tuition, area resident:* Full-time $425; part-time $425 per credit hour. Tuition, state resident: full-time $425; part-time $425 per credit hour. Tuition, nonresident: full-time $850; part-time $850 per credit hour. *International tuition:* $850 full-time. *Required fees:* $50 per semester. Tuition and fees vary according to campus/location and program. *Financial support:* Fellowships, career-related internships or fieldwork, and scholarships/grants available. Support available to part-time students. Financial award applicants required to submit FAFSA. *Unit head:* Dr. Bill Zhong, Department Chairman/Professor, 334-670-3388, Fax: 334-670-3729, E-mail: jzhong@troy.edu. *Application contact:* Jessica A. Kimbro, Assistant Director of Graduate Programs, 334-670-3189, E-mail: jacord@troy.edu. Website: https://www.troy.edu/academics/academic-programs/computer-science.html

Tufts University, Graduate School of Arts and Sciences, Graduate Certificate Programs, Computer Science Program, Medford, MA 02155. Offers Certificate. *Program availability:* Part-time, evening/weekend. Electronic applications accepted. *Expenses: Tuition:* Full-time $51,288; part-time $1710 per credit hour. *Required fees:* $904. Full-time tuition and fees vary according to degree level, program and student level. Part-time tuition and fees vary according to course load.

Tufts University, Graduate School of Arts and Sciences, Graduate Certificate Programs, Post-Baccalaureate Minor Program in Computer Science, Medford, MA 02155. Offers Certificate. *Program availability:* Part-time, evening/weekend. Electronic applications accepted. *Expenses: Tuition:* Full-time $51,288; part-time $1710 per credit hour. *Required fees:* $904. Full-time tuition and fees vary according to degree level, program and student level. Part-time tuition and fees vary according to course load.

Tufts University, School of Engineering, Department of Computer Science, Medford, MA 02155. Offers bioengineering (MS), including bioinformatics; cognitive science/computer science (PhD); computer science (MS, PhD); soft material robotics (PhD). *Program availability:* Part-time. Terminal master's awarded for partial completion of doctoral program. *Entrance requirements:* For master's and doctorate, GRE General Test. Additional exam requirements/recommendations for international students: Required—TOEFL (minimum score 550 paper-based; 80 iBT), IELTS (minimum score 6.5). Electronic applications accepted. *Expenses: Tuition:* Full-time $51,288; part-time $1710 per credit hour. *Required fees:* $904. Full-time tuition and fees vary according to degree level, program and student level. Part-time tuition and fees vary according to course load. *Faculty research:* Computational biology, computational geometry, and computational systems biology; cognitive sciences, human-computer interaction, and human-robotic interaction; visualization and graphics, educational technologies; machine learning and data mining; programming languages and systems.

Universidad Autonoma de Guadalajara, Graduate Programs, Guadalajara, Mexico. Offers administrative law and justice (LL M); advertising and corporate communications (MA); architecture (M Arch); business (MBA); computational science (MCC); education (Ed M, Ed D); English-Spanish translation (MA); entrepreneurship and management (MBA); integrated management of digital animation (MA); international business (MIB);

international corporate law (LL M); Internet technologies (MS); manufacturing systems (MMS); occupational health (MS); philosophy (MA, PhD); power electronics (MS); quality systems (MQS); renewable energy (MS); social evaluation of projects (MBA); strategic market research (MBA); tax law (MA); teaching mathematics (MA).

Universidad de las Américas Puebla, Division of Graduate Studies, School of Engineering, Program in Computer Engineering, Puebla, Mexico. Offers computer science (MS). *Program availability:* Part-time, evening/weekend. *Degree requirements:* For master's, one foreign language, thesis. *Faculty research:* Computers in education, robotics, artificial intelligence.

Universidad de las Américas Puebla, Division of Graduate Studies, School of Engineering, Program in Computer Science, Puebla, Mexico. Offers PhD.

Université de Moncton, Faculty of Sciences, Information Technology Programs, Moncton, NB E1A 3E9, Canada. Offers M Sc, Certificate, Diploma. *Program availability:* Part-time. *Degree requirements:* For master's, thesis. Electronic applications accepted. *Faculty research:* Programming, databases, networks.

Université de Montréal, Faculty of Arts and Sciences, Department of Computer Science and Operational Research, Montréal, QC H3C 3J7, Canada. Offers computer systems (M Sc, PhD); electronic commerce (M Sc). *Program availability:* Part-time. Terminal master's awarded for partial completion of doctoral program. *Degree requirements:* For master's, one foreign language, thesis; for doctorate, one foreign language, thesis/dissertation, general exam. *Entrance requirements:* For master's, B Sc in related field; for doctorate, MA or M Sc in related field. Electronic applications accepted. *Faculty research:* Optimization statistics, programming languages, telecommunications, theoretical computer science, artificial intelligence.

Université du Québec à Trois-Rivières, Graduate Programs, Program in Mathematics and Computer Science, Trois-Rivières, QC G9A 5H7, Canada. Offers M Sc. *Faculty research:* Probability, statistics.

Université du Québec en Outaouais, Graduate Programs, Program in Computer Network, Gatineau, QC J8X 3X7, Canada. Offers computer science (M Sc, PhD, DESS). *Program availability:* Part-time, evening/weekend. *Degree requirements:* For master's, thesis; for doctorate, thesis/dissertation.

Université Laval, Faculty of Sciences and Engineering, Department of Computer Science, Programs in Computer Science, Québec, QC G1K 7P4, Canada. Offers M Sc, PhD. Terminal master's awarded for partial completion of doctoral program. *Degree requirements:* For master's, thesis; for doctorate, thesis/dissertation. *Entrance requirements:* For master's and doctorate, knowledge of French and English. Electronic applications accepted.

University at Albany, State University of New York, College of Engineering and Applied Sciences, Department of Computer Science, Albany, NY 12222-0001. Offers MS, PhD. *Faculty:* 29 full-time (8 women), 19 part-time/adjunct (3 women). *Students:* 188 full-time (48 women), 69 part-time (22 women); includes 14 minority (1 Black or African American, non-Hispanic/Latino; 9 Asian, non-Hispanic/Latino; 3 Hispanic/Latino; 1 Two or more races, non-Hispanic/Latino), 228 international. Average age 27. 552 applicants, 51% accepted, 193 enrolled. In 2018, 84 master's, 3 doctorates awarded. *Degree requirements:* For master's, comprehensive exam, project or thesis; for doctorate, comprehensive exam, thesis/dissertation, area exams. *Entrance requirements:* For master's and doctorate, GRE General Test. Additional exam requirements/recommendations for international students: Required—TOEFL (minimum score 550 paper-based). *Application deadline:* For fall admission, 8/1 for domestic students, 5/1 for international students; for spring admission, 11/1 for domestic and international students. Applications are processed on a rolling basis. Application fee: $75. Electronic applications accepted. *Financial support:* Fellowships, research assistantships, teaching assistantships, career-related internships or fieldwork, and Federal Work-Study available. Financial award application deadline: 3/1. *Faculty research:* Artificial intelligence, forensics, graphics, modeling and simulation; natural language processing, networks, parallel and distributed processing; security, software engineering practice and principles; algorithms, discrete mathematics; logic and optimization. *Unit head:* Randy Moulic, Chair, 518-956-8242, Fax: 518-442-5638, E-mail: jmoulic@albany.edu. *Application contact:* Randy Moulic, Chair, 518-956-8242, Fax: 518-442-5638, E-mail: jmoulic@albany.edu. Website: http://www.cs.albany.edu/

University at Buffalo, the State University of New York, Graduate School, School of Engineering and Applied Sciences, Department of Computer Science and Engineering, Buffalo, NY 14260. Offers computer science and engineering (MS, PhD); information assurance (Certificate). *Program availability:* Part-time. Terminal master's awarded for partial completion of doctoral program. *Degree requirements:* For master's, thesis or alternative; for doctorate, thesis/dissertation, comprehensive qualifying exam. *Entrance requirements:* For master's and doctorate, GRE General Test. Additional exam requirements/recommendations for international students: Required—TOEFL (minimum score 550 paper-based; 79 iBT). Electronic applications accepted. *Faculty research:* Theory and algorithms, databases and information retrieval, data mining and data science, artificial intelligence and machine learning, computer security and information assurance, computing education, cyber-physical systems (Internet of Things), distributed systems and networks, hardware and architecture, high-performance and computing and computational science, medical applications and bioinformatics, mobile systems, programming languages and software systems.

University of Advancing Technology, Master of Science Program in Technology, Tempe, AZ 85283-1042. Offers advancing computer science (MS); emerging technologies (MS); game production and management (MS); information assurance (MS); technology leadership (MS). *Degree requirements:* For master's, project or thesis. *Entrance requirements:* Additional exam requirements/recommendations for international students: Required—TOEFL (minimum score 550 paper-based). Electronic applications accepted. *Faculty research:* Artificial intelligence, fractals, organizational management.

The University of Akron, Graduate School, Buchtel College of Arts and Sciences, Department of Computer Science, Akron, OH 44325. Offers MS. *Entrance requirements:* For master's, baccalaureate degree in computer science or a related field; three letters of recommendation; statement of purpose; resume; knowledge of one high-level programming language; mathematical maturity; proficiency in data structures, computer organization, and operating systems. Additional exam requirements/recommendations for international students: Required—TOEFL (minimum score 79 iBT), IELTS (minimum score 6.5). Electronic applications accepted. *Faculty research:* Bioinformatics, database/data mining, networking, parallel computing, visualization.

The University of Alabama, Graduate School, College of Engineering, Department of Computer Science, Tuscaloosa, AL 35487-0290. Offers MS, PhD. *Program availability:* Part-time. Terminal master's awarded for partial completion of doctoral program. *Degree requirements:* For master's, comprehensive exam, thesis (for some programs); for doctorate, comprehensive exam, thesis/dissertation. *Entrance requirements:* For master's and doctorate, GRE. Additional exam requirements/recommendations for international students: Required—TOEFL (minimum score 550 paper-based; 79 iBT). Electronic applications accepted. *Faculty research:* Software engineering, networking, database management, robotics, security, algorithms.

Computer Science

The University of Alabama at Birmingham, College of Arts and Sciences, Program in Computer and Information Sciences, Birmingham, AL 35294. Offers MS, PhD. Terminal master's awarded for partial completion of doctoral program. *Degree requirements:* For master's, thesis optional; for doctorate, thesis/dissertation. *Entrance requirements:* For master's, GRE General Test, minimum GPA of 3.0, letters of recommendation; for doctorate, GRE General Test, minimum GPA of 3.5 overall or on last 60 hours; letters of recommendation. Additional exam requirements/recommendations for international students: Required—TOEFL, IELTS. Electronic applications accepted. *Expenses: Tuition, area resident:* Full-time $8100; part-time $8100 per year. Tuition, state resident: full-time $8100. Tuition, nonresident: full-time $19,188; part-time $19,188 per year. Tuition and fees vary according to program. *Faculty research:* Theory and software systems, intelligent systems, systems architecture, high performance computing, computer architecture, computer graphics, data mining, software engineering.

The University of Alabama in Huntsville, School of Graduate Studies, College of Science, Department of Computer Science, Huntsville, AL 35899. Offers computer science (MS, PhD); cybersecurity (MS); modeling and simulation (MS, PhD, Certificate); software engineering (MSSE, Certificate). *Program availability:* Part-time. *Faculty:* 14 full-time (4 women), 1 part-time/adjunct. *Students:* 67 full-time (16 women), 65 part-time (11 women); includes 14 minority (4 Black or African American, non-Hispanic/Latino; 1 American Indian or Alaska Native, non-Hispanic/Latino; 5 Asian, non-Hispanic/Latino; 3 Hispanic/Latino; 1 Two or more races, non-Hispanic/Latino), 60 international. Average age 33. 219 applicants, 74% accepted, 37 enrolled. In 2018, 47 master's awarded. *Degree requirements:* For master's, comprehensive exam, thesis or alternative, oral and written exams; for doctorate, comprehensive exam, thesis/dissertation, oral and written exams. *Entrance requirements:* For master's, doctorate, and Certificate, GRE General Test, minimum GPA of 3.0. Additional exam requirements/recommendations for international students: Required—TOEFL (minimum score 550 paper-based; 80 iBT), IELTS (minimum score 6.5). *Application deadline:* For fall admission, 7/15 priority date for domestic students, 4/1 priority date for international students; for spring admission, 11/30 priority date for domestic students, 9/1 priority date for international students. Applications are processed on a rolling basis. Application fee: $50. Electronic applications accepted. *Expenses: Tuition, area resident:* Full-time $10,632; part-time $412 per credit hour. Tuition, state resident: full-time $10,632. Tuition, nonresident: full-time $23,604; part-time $412 per credit hour. *Required fees:* $582; $582. Tuition and fees vary according to course load and program. *Financial support:* In 2018–19, 39 students received support, including 18 research assistantships with full tuition reimbursements available (averaging $6,762 per year), 19 teaching assistantships with full tuition reimbursements available (averaging $6,315 per year); career-related internships or fieldwork, Federal Work-Study, institutionally sponsored loans, scholarships/grants, health care benefits, and unspecified assistantships also available. Support available to part-time students. Financial award application deadline: 4/1; financial award applicants required to submit FAFSA. *Faculty research:* Information assurance and cyber security, modeling and simulation, data science, computer graphics and visualization, multimedia systems. *Unit head:* Dr. Heggere Ranganath, Professor and Chair, 256-824-6088, Fax: 256-824-6239, E-mail: info@cs.uah.edu. *Application contact:* Kim Gray, Graduate Studies Admissions Manager, 256-824-6002, Fax: 256-824-6405, E-mail: deangrad@uah.edu.
Website: http://www.cs.uah.edu

University of Alaska Fairbanks, College of Engineering and Mines, Department of Computer Science, Fairbanks, AK 99775-6670. Offers MS. *Program availability:* Part-time. *Faculty:* 4 full-time (0 women). *Students:* 4 full-time (0 women), 1 part-time (0 women); includes 1 minority (Two or more races, non-Hispanic/Latino). Average age 25. 12 applicants, 67% accepted, 5 enrolled. In 2018, 1 master's awarded. *Degree requirements:* For master's, comprehensive exam, oral defense of project or thesis. *Entrance requirements:* For master's, GRE General Test, GRE Subject Test (computer science), bachelor's degree from accredited institution with minimum cumulative undergraduate and major GPA of 3.0. Additional exam requirements/recommendations for international students: Required—TOEFL (minimum score 600 paper-based). *Application deadline:* For fall admission, 6/1 for domestic students, 3/1 for international students; for spring admission, 10/15 for domestic students, 9/1 for international students. Applications are processed on a rolling basis. Application fee: $60. Electronic applications accepted. *Expenses:* College of Engineering and Mines (CEM) tuition has a 20% surcharge per credit hour over that for credits of most other UAF colleges. Assuming 60 credits for PhD and 32 for Master's, this augments costs by $6,180 for in-state PhD, $3,296 for in-state Master's, $12,948 for non-resident PhD and $6,912 for non-resident Master's students, respectively. *Financial support:* In 2018–19, 3 research assistantships with full tuition reimbursements (averaging $7,180 per year), 2 teaching assistantships with full tuition reimbursements (averaging $7,629 per year) were awarded; fellowships with full tuition reimbursements, career-related internships or fieldwork, Federal Work-Study, scholarships/grants, health care benefits, and unspecified assistantships also available. Support available to part-time students. Financial award application deadline: 7/1; financial award applicants required to submit FAFSA. *Faculty research:* Interaction with a virtual reality environment, synthetic aperture radar interferometry software. *Unit head:* Dr. Chris Hartman, Department Chair, 907-474-2777, E-mail: uaf-cs-dept@alaska.edu. *Application contact:* Samara Taber, Director of Admissions, 907-474-7500, E-mail: uaf-admissions@alaska.edu.
Website: http://www.cs.uaf.edu

University of Alberta, Faculty of Graduate Studies and Research, Department of Computing Science, Edmonton, AB T6G 2E1, Canada. Offers M Sc, PhD. *Program availability:* Part-time. Terminal master's awarded for partial completion of doctoral program. *Degree requirements:* For master's, thesis (for some programs), oral exam, seminar; for doctorate, thesis/dissertation, oral exam, seminar. *Entrance requirements:* For master's and doctorate, GRE General Test. Additional exam requirements/recommendations for international students: Required—TOEFL. *Faculty research:* Artificial intelligence, multimedia, distributed computing, theory, software engineering.

The University of Arizona, College of Science, Department of Computer Science, Tucson, AZ 85721. Offers MS, PhD. *Program availability:* Part-time. *Faculty:* 18 full-time (2 women). *Students:* 60 full-time (10 women), 6 part-time (3 women); includes 7 minority (3 Asian, non-Hispanic/Latino; 3 Hispanic/Latino; 1 Two or more races, non-Hispanic/Latino), 38 international. Average age 30. 223 applicants, 21% accepted, 12 enrolled. In 2018, 17 master's, 1 doctorate awarded. Terminal master's awarded for partial completion of doctoral program. *Degree requirements:* For master's, thesis optional; for doctorate, comprehensive exam, thesis/dissertation. *Entrance requirements:* For master's, GRE General Test, typical minimum GPA is 3.2; for doctorate, GRE General Test, typical minimum undergraduate GPA is 3.5, graduate GPA is 3.7. Additional exam requirements/recommendations for international students: Required—TOEFL (minimum score 79 iBT). *Application deadline:* For fall admission, 1/15 for domestic and international students. Application fee: $85 ($95 for international students). Electronic applications accepted. *Financial support:* In 2018–19, 61 students received support, including 9 fellowships with full tuition reimbursements available (averaging $6,667 per year), 32 research assistantships with full tuition reimbursements available (averaging $19,200 per year), 20 teaching assistantships with full tuition reimbursements available (averaging $18,400 per year); scholarships/grants, health care benefits, tuition waivers (full and partial), and unspecified assistantships also available. Financial award application deadline: 1/15. *Faculty research:* Algorithms, artificial intelligence, parallel, distributed, and high performance computing, programming languages and compilers, security, systems, visualization and graphics. *Total annual research expenditures:* $3.7 million. *Unit head:* Dr. Todd Proebsting, Department Head, 520-621-4324, Fax: 520-621-0308, E-mail: depthead@cs.arizona.edu. *Application contact:* Chelsea Skotnicki, Graduate Program Coordinator, 520-626-8470, Fax: 520-621-0308, E-mail: gradadvising@cs.arizona.edu.
Website: https://www.cs.arizona.edu/

University of Arkansas, Graduate School, College of Engineering, Department of Computer Science and Computer Engineering, Program in Computer Science, Fayetteville, AR 72701. Offers MS, PhD. *Application deadline:* For fall admission, 8/1 for domestic students, 4/1 for international students; for spring admission, 12/1 for domestic students, 10/1 for international students; for summer admission, 4/15 for domestic students, 3/1 for international students. Applications are processed on a rolling basis. Application fee: $60. Electronic applications accepted. *Financial support:* In 2018–19, 16 research assistantships, 6 teaching assistantships were awarded; fellowships with tuition reimbursements, career-related internships or fieldwork, and Federal Work-Study also available. Support available to part-time students. Financial award application deadline: 4/1; financial award applicants required to submit FAFSA. *Unit head:* Dr. Xiaoqing Liu, Department Head, 479-575-6197, Fax: 479-575-5339, E-mail: frankliu@uark.edu. *Application contact:* Dr. Brajendra Nath Panda, Professor, Associate Department Head for Graduate Program, 479-575-2067, Fax: 479-575-5339, E-mail: bpanda@uark.edu.
Website: https://computer-science-and-computer-engineering.uark.edu/index.php

University of Arkansas at Little Rock, Graduate School, George W. Donaghey College of Engineering and Information Technology, Department of Computer Science, Little Rock, AR 72204-1099. Offers MS, PhD. *Program availability:* Part-time, evening/weekend. *Degree requirements:* For master's, thesis optional. *Entrance requirements:* For master's, GRE General Test, minimum GPA of 3.0; bachelor's degree in computer science, mathematics, or appropriate alternative.

University of Bridgeport, School of Engineering, Departments of Computer Science and Computer Engineering, Bridgeport, CT 06604. Offers computer engineering (MS); computer science (MS); computer science and engineering (PhD). *Degree requirements:* For master's, thesis optional; for doctorate, comprehensive exam, thesis/dissertation. *Entrance requirements:* Additional exam requirements/recommendations for international students: Recommended—TOEFL (minimum score 550 paper-based; 80 iBT), IELTS (minimum score 6.5). Electronic applications accepted. *Expenses:* Contact institution.

The University of British Columbia, Faculty of Science, Department of Computer Science, Vancouver, BC V6T 1Z4, Canada. Offers computer science (M Sc, PhD); data science (MDS). *Program availability:* Part-time. *Degree requirements:* For doctorate, comprehensive exam, thesis/dissertation. *Entrance requirements:* Additional exam requirements/recommendations for international students: Required—TOEFL. Electronic applications accepted. *Expenses:* Contact institution. *Faculty research:* Computational intelligence, data management and mining, theory, graphics, network security and systems.

University of Calgary, Faculty of Graduate Studies, Faculty of Science, Program in Computer Science, Calgary, AB T2N 1N4, Canada. Offers computer science (M Sc, PhD); software engineering (M Sc). *Program availability:* Part-time. *Degree requirements:* For master's, comprehensive exam (for some programs), thesis (for some programs); for doctorate, thesis/dissertation, oral and written departmental exam. *Entrance requirements:* For master's, bachelor's degree in computer science; for doctorate, M Sc in computer science. Additional exam requirements/recommendations for international students: Required—TOEFL (minimum score 600 paper-based); Recommended—TWE. Electronic applications accepted. *Faculty research:* Visual and interactive computing, quantum computing and cryptography, evolutionary software engineering, distributed systems and algorithms.

University of California, Berkeley, Graduate Division, College of Engineering, Department of Electrical Engineering and Computer Sciences, Berkeley, CA 94720. Offers computer science (MS, PhD); electrical engineering (M Eng, MS, PhD). Terminal master's awarded for partial completion of doctoral program. *Degree requirements:* For master's, comprehensive exam (for some programs), thesis (for some programs), comprehensive exam or thesis; for doctorate, thesis/dissertation, qualifying exam. *Entrance requirements:* For master's and doctorate, GRE General Test, minimum GPA of 3.0, 3 letters of recommendation. Additional exam requirements/recommendations for international students: Required—TOEFL (minimum score 570 paper-based; 90 iBT). Electronic applications accepted.

University of California, Davis, College of Engineering, Graduate Group in Computer Science, Davis, CA 95616. Offers MS, PhD. Terminal master's awarded for partial completion of doctoral program. *Degree requirements:* For master's, comprehensive exam (for some programs), thesis optional; for doctorate, comprehensive exam, thesis/dissertation. *Entrance requirements:* For master's and doctorate, GRE General Test, GRE Subject Test, minimum GPA of 3.0. Additional exam requirements/recommendations for international students: Required—TOEFL (minimum score 550 paper-based). Electronic applications accepted. *Faculty research:* Intrusion detection, malicious code detection, next generation light wave computer networks, biological algorithms, parallel processing.

University of California, Irvine, Donald Bren School of Information and Computer Sciences, Department of Computer Science, Irvine, CA 92697. Offers MS, PhD. *Students:* 251 full-time (57 women), 10 part-time (3 women); includes 30 minority (2 Black or African American, non-Hispanic/Latino; 21 Asian, non-Hispanic/Latino; 4 Hispanic/Latino; 3 Two or more races, non-Hispanic/Latino), 183 international. Average age 27. 2,753 applicants, 8% accepted, 86 enrolled. In 2018, 169 master's, 24 doctorates awarded. Application fee: $105 ($125 for international students). *Unit head:* Alexandru Nicolau, Chair, 949-824-4079, E-mail: nicolau@ics.uci.edu. *Application contact:* Holly Byrnes, Department Manager, 949-824-6753, E-mail: hbyrnes@uci.edu.
Website: http://www.cs.uci.edu/

University of California, Irvine, Donald Bren School of Information and Computer Sciences, Program in Networked Systems, Irvine, CA 92697. Offers MS, PhD. *Students:* 42 full-time (12 women), 3 part-time (0 women); includes 1 minority (Asian, non-Hispanic/Latino), 42 international. Average age 25. 159 applicants, 42% accepted, 19 enrolled. In 2018, 13 master's, 1 doctorate awarded. *Application deadline:* For fall admission, 1/15 for domestic students. Application fee: $105 ($125 for international students). *Financial support:* Fellowships, research assistantships, and teaching assistantships available. *Unit head:* Nalini Venkatasubramanian, Director, 949-824-5898, Fax: 949-824-4056, E-mail: nalini@uci.edu. *Application contact:* Athina Markopoulou, Co-Director, 949-824-0357, Fax: 949-824-3203, E-mail: athina@uci.edu.
Website: http://www.networkedsystems.uci.edu/

University of California, Irvine, Samueli School of Engineering, Department of Electrical Engineering and Computer Science, Irvine, CA 92697. Offers electrical engineering and computer science (MS, PhD); networked systems (MS, PhD). *Program availability:* Part-time. *Students:* 292 full-time (77 women), 20 part-time (1 woman);

includes 28 minority (2 Black or African American, non-Hispanic/Latino; 21 Asian, non-Hispanic/Latino; 2 Hispanic/Latino; 3 Two or more races, non-Hispanic/Latino), 253 international. Average age 26. 1,595 applicants, 21% accepted, 99 enrolled. In 2018, 88 master's, 26 doctorates awarded. Terminal master's awarded for partial completion of doctoral program. *Entrance requirements:* For master's and doctorate, GRE General Test, minimum GPA of 3.0, 3 letters of recommendation. Additional exam requirements/recommendations for international students: Required—TOEFL (minimum score 550 paper-based). *Application deadline:* For fall admission, 1/15 priority date for domestic students, 1/15 for international students. Applications are processed on a rolling basis. Application fee: $105 ($125 for international students). Electronic applications accepted. *Financial support:* Fellowships, research assistantships with full tuition reimbursements, teaching assistantships, institutionally sponsored loans, traineeships, health care benefits, and unspecified assistantships available. Financial award application deadline: 3/1; financial award applicants required to submit FAFSA. *Faculty research:* Optics and electronic devices and circuits, signal processing, communications, machine vision, power electronics. *Unit head:* Prof. H. Kumar Wickramasinghe, Chair, 949-824-2213, E-mail: hkwick@uci.edu. *Application contact:* Jean Bennett, Director of Graduate Student Affairs, 949-824-6475, Fax: 949-824-8200, E-mail: jean.bennett@uci.edu. Website: http://www.eng.uci.edu/dept/eecs

University of California, Los Angeles, Graduate Division, Henry Samueli School of Engineering and Applied Science, Department of Computer Science, Los Angeles, CA 90095-1596. Offers MS, PhD, MBA/MS. *Degree requirements:* For master's, comprehensive exam or thesis; for doctorate, thesis/dissertation, qualifying exams. *Entrance requirements:* For master's, GRE General Test, GRE Subject Test, minimum GPA of 3.0; for doctorate, GRE General Test, GRE Subject Test, minimum GPA of 3.25. Additional exam requirements/recommendations for international students: Required—TOEFL (minimum score 560 paper-based; 87 iBT), IELTS (minimum score 7). Electronic applications accepted. *Faculty research:* Artificial intelligence, computational systems biology, computer network systems, computer systems architecture, information and data management.

University of California, Merced, Graduate Division, School of Engineering, Merced, CA 95343. Offers biological engineering and small scale technologies (MS, PhD); electrical engineering and computer science (MS, PhD); environmental systems (MS, PhD); management of innovation, sustainability, and technology (MM); mechanical engineering (MS); mechanical engineering and applied mechanics (PhD). *Faculty:* 60 full-time (16 women). *Students:* 219 full-time (72 women), 1 part-time (0 women); includes 43 minority (2 Black or African American, non-Hispanic/Latino; 17 Asian, non-Hispanic/Latino; 20 Hispanic/Latino; 1 Native Hawaiian or other Pacific Islander, non-Hispanic/Latino; 3 Two or more races, non-Hispanic/Latino), 145 international. Average age 28. 371 applicants, 46% accepted, 75 enrolled. In 2018, 30 master's, 17 doctorates awarded. Terminal master's awarded for partial completion of doctoral program. *Degree requirements:* For master's, variable foreign language requirement, comprehensive exam, thesis or alternative, oral defense; for doctorate, variable foreign language requirement, comprehensive exam, thesis/dissertation, oral defense. *Entrance requirements:* For master's and doctorate, GRE. Additional exam requirements/recommendations for international students: Required—TOEFL (minimum score 550 paper-based; 80 iBT); Recommended—IELTS (minimum score 6.5). *Application deadline:* For fall admission, 1/15 priority date for domestic and international students. Application fee: $105 ($125 for international students). Electronic applications accepted. *Expenses:* In-state tuition $11442 per year; Out-of-state tuition $26544 per year; Student Fees $1765 per year. *Financial support:* In 2018–19, 200 students received support, including 14 fellowships with full tuition reimbursements available (averaging $20,851 per year), 70 research assistantships with full tuition reimbursements available (averaging $18,334 per year), 116 teaching assistantships with full tuition reimbursements available (averaging $19,841 per year); scholarships/grants, traineeships, and health care benefits also available. *Faculty research:* Sustainability systems engineering and resource management: food, energy, water; biomolecular engineering and biotechnology; computational science and data analytics; artificial intelligence, machine learning, internet of things, human computer interface; cyber-physical systems and automation. *Total annual research expenditures:* $3.1 million. *Unit head:* Dr. Mark Matsumoto, Dean, 209-228-4047, Fax: 209-228-4047, E-mail: mmatsumoto@ucmerced.edu. *Application contact:* Tsu Ya, Director of Admissions and Academic Services, 209-228-4521, Fax: 209-228-6906, E-mail: tya@ucmerced.edu.

University of California, Riverside, Graduate Division, Department of Computer Science and Engineering, Riverside, CA 92521. Offers computer engineering (MS); computer science (MS, PhD). Terminal master's awarded for partial completion of doctoral program. *Degree requirements:* For master's, comprehensive exam, project, or thesis; for doctorate, thesis/dissertation, written and oral qualifying exams, dissertation defense. *Entrance requirements:* For master's and doctorate, GRE General Test (minimum expected score of 300 verbal and quantitative combined), minimum GPA of 3.2 in junior/senior years of undergraduate study (last two years). Additional exam requirements/recommendations for international students: Required—TOEFL (minimum score 550 paper-based, 80 iBT) or IELTS (7). Electronic applications accepted. *Expenses:* Contact institution. *Faculty research:* Algorithms, bioinformatics; logic; architecture, compilers, embedded systems; cyber-security; databases, data mining, artificial intelligence; high-performance computing, graphics; programming languages, software engineering; systems, networks.

University of California, San Diego, Graduate Division, Department of Computer Science and Engineering, La Jolla, CA 92093. Offers computer engineering (MS, PhD); computer science (MS, PhD). *Students:* 689 full-time (158 women), 136 part-time (22 women). 5,646 applicants, 15% accepted, 340 enrolled. In 2018, 259 master's, 28 doctorates awarded. Terminal master's awarded for partial completion of doctoral program. *Degree requirements:* For master's, comprehensive exam (for some programs), thesis (for some programs), comprehensive exam or thesis; for doctorate, comprehensive exam, thesis/dissertation, 1-quarter teaching assistantship. *Entrance requirements:* For master's and doctorate, GRE General Test. Additional exam requirements/recommendations for international students: Required—TOEFL (minimum score 550 paper-based; 80 iBT), IELTS (minimum score 7). *Application deadline:* For fall admission, 12/18 for domestic students. Application fee: $105 ($125 for international students). Electronic applications accepted. *Financial support:* Fellowships, research assistantships, teaching assistantships, career-related internships or fieldwork, and scholarships/grants available. Financial award applicants required to submit FAFSA. *Faculty research:* Artificial intelligence and machine learning, bioinformatics, computer architecture and compilers, visual computing, computer graphics, computer vision, databases and information management, embedded systems and software, high-performance computing, human-computer interaction, programming systems, security and cryptography, software engineering, systems and networking, ubiquitous computing and social dynamics, VLSI/CAD. *Unit head:* Dean Tullsen, Chair, 858-534-6181, E-mail: dtullsen@ucsd.edu. *Application contact:* Julie Connor, Graduate Coordinator, 858-534-8872, E-mail: gradinfo@cs.ucsd.edu. Website: http://cse.ucsd.edu

University of California, Santa Barbara, Graduate Division, College of Engineering, Department of Computer Science, Santa Barbara, CA 93106-5110. Offers computer

science (MS, PhD), including cognitive science (PhD), computational science and engineering (PhD), technology and society (PhD). Terminal master's awarded for partial completion of doctoral program. *Degree requirements:* For master's, comprehensive exam (for some programs), thesis (for some programs), project (for some programs); for doctorate, thesis/dissertation. *Entrance requirements:* For master's and doctorate, GRE. Additional exam requirements/recommendations for international students: Required—TOEFL (minimum score 600 paper-based; 100 iBT), IELTS (minimum score 7). Electronic applications accepted. *Faculty research:* Algorithms and theory, computational science and engineering, computer architecture, database and information systems, machine learning and data mining, networking, operating systems and distributed systems, programming languages and software engineering, security and cryptography, social computing, visual computing and interaction.

University of California, Santa Cruz, Jack Baskin School of Engineering, Department of Applied Mathematics, Santa Cruz, CA 95064. Offers scientific computing and applied mathematics (MS); statistics and applied mathematics (MS, PhD), including applied mathematics, statistics. *Program availability:* Part-time. Terminal master's awarded for partial completion of doctoral program. *Degree requirements:* For master's, thesis, seminar, capstone project; for doctorate, thesis/dissertation, seminar, first-year exam, qualifying exam. *Entrance requirements:* For master's and doctorate, GRE General Test; GRE Subject Test in math (recommended). Additional exam requirements/recommendations for international students: Required—TOEFL (minimum score 570 paper-based; 89 iBT); Recommended—IELTS (minimum score 8). Electronic applications accepted. *Expenses:* Contact institution. *Faculty research:* Bayesian nonparametric methods; computationally intensive Bayesian inference, prediction, and decision-making; envirometrics; fluid mechanics; mathematical biology.

University of California, Santa Cruz, Jack Baskin School of Engineering, Program in Computer Science, Santa Cruz, CA 95064. Offers MS, PhD. *Program availability:* Part-time. Terminal master's awarded for partial completion of doctoral program. *Degree requirements:* For master's, thesis, project; for doctorate, one foreign language, thesis/dissertation, qualifying exam. *Entrance requirements:* For master's and doctorate, GRE General Test. Additional exam requirements/recommendations for international students: Required—TOEFL (minimum score 570 paper-based; 89 iBT); Recommended—IELTS (minimum score 8). Electronic applications accepted. *Faculty research:* Algorithm analysis, data science, scientific visualization, machine learning, multimodal human-computer interaction.

University of Central Arkansas, Graduate School, College of Natural Sciences and Math, Department of Applied Computing, Conway, AR 72035-0001. Offers MS. *Entrance requirements:* For master's, GRE, minimum GPA of 2.7. Additional exam requirements/recommendations for international students: Required—TOEFL (minimum score 550 paper-based; 80 iBT). Electronic applications accepted.

University of Central Florida, College of Engineering and Computer Science, Department of Computer Science, Orlando, FL 32816. Offers computer science (MS, PhD). *Program availability:* Part-time, evening/weekend. *Students:* 299 full-time (69 women), 187 part-time (46 women); includes 105 minority (21 Black or African American, non-Hispanic/Latino; 1 American Indian or Alaska Native, non-Hispanic/Latino; 29 Asian, non-Hispanic/Latino; 50 Hispanic/Latino; 4 Two or more races, non-Hispanic/Latino), 219 international. Average age 30. 714 applicants, 58% accepted, 186 enrolled. In 2018, 108 master's, 18 doctorates awarded. *Degree requirements:* For master's, thesis or alternative; for doctorate, thesis/dissertation, candidacy exam, departmental qualifying exam. *Entrance requirements:* For master's, GRE General Test, GRE Subject Test, minimum GPA of 3.0 in last 60 hours, letters of recommendation, resume; for doctorate, GRE Subject Test, minimum GPA of 3.0 in last 60 hours, letters of recommendation, resume, goal statement. Additional exam requirements/recommendations for international students: Required—TOEFL. *Application deadline:* For fall admission, 7/15 for domestic students; for spring admission, 12/1 for domestic students. Application fee: $30. Electronic applications accepted. *Financial support:* In 2018–19, 158 students received support, including 44 fellowships with partial tuition reimbursements available (averaging $11,186 per year), 109 research assistantships with partial tuition reimbursements available (averaging $13,632 per year), 60 teaching assistantships with partial tuition reimbursements available (averaging $12,933 per year); career-related internships or fieldwork, Federal Work-Study, institutionally sponsored loans, health care benefits, tuition waivers (partial), and unspecified assistantships also available. Financial award application deadline: 3/1; financial award applicants required to submit FAFSA. *Faculty research:* Image and video processing, computer vision, artificial intelligence and machine learning, virtual reality, software engineering and systems. *Unit head:* Dr. Gary Leavens, Chair, 407-823-4758, Fax: 407-823-1488, E-mail: leavens@eecs.ucf.edu. *Application contact:* Associate Director, Graduate Admissions, 407-823-2766, Fax: 407-823-6442, E-mail: gradadmissions@ucf.edu.
Website: http://www.cs.ucf.edu/

University of Central Missouri, The Graduate School, Warrensburg, MO 64093. Offers accountancy (MA); accounting (MBA); applied mathematics (MS); aviation safety (MA); biology (MS); business administration (MBA); career and technical education leadership (MS); college student personnel administration (MS); communication (MA); computer science (MS); counseling (MS); criminal justice (MS); educational leadership (Ed D); educational technology (MS); elementary and early childhood education (MSE); English (MA); environmental studies (MA); finance (MBA); history (MA); human services/educational technology (Ed S); human services/learning resources (Ed S); human services/professional counseling (Ed S); industrial hygiene (MS); industrial management (MS); information systems (MBA); information technology (MS); kinesiology (MS); library science and information services (MS); literacy education (MSE); marketing (MBA); mathematics (MS); music (MA); occupational safety management (MS); psychology (MS); rural family nursing (MS); school administration (MSE); social gerontology (MS); sociology (MA); special education (MSE); speech language pathology (MS); superintendency (Ed S); teaching (MAT); teaching English as a second language (MA); technology (MS); technology management (PhD); theatre (MA). *Accreditation:* ASHA. *Program availability:* Part-time, 100% online, blended/hybrid learning. *Degree requirements:* For master's and Ed S, comprehensive exam (for some programs), thesis (for some programs). *Entrance requirements:* Additional exam requirements/recommendations for international students: Required—TOEFL (minimum score 550 paper-based; 79 iBT). Electronic applications accepted.

University of Central Oklahoma, The Jackson College of Graduate Studies, College of Mathematics and Science, Department of Mathematics and Statistics, Edmond, OK 73034-5209. Offers applied mathematical science (MS), including mathematics, statistics, teaching; applied mathematics and computer science (MS). *Program availability:* Part-time. *Degree requirements:* For master's, comprehensive exam (for some programs), thesis (for some programs). *Entrance requirements:* Additional exam requirements/recommendations for international students: Required—TOEFL (minimum score 550 paper-based; 79 iBT), IELTS (minimum score 6.5). Electronic applications accepted.

University of Chicago, Division of the Physical Sciences, Master's Program in Computer Science, Chicago, IL 60637-1513. Offers MS. *Program availability:* Part-time, evening/weekend. *Entrance requirements:* For master's, GRE General Test, personal statement, 3 letters of recommendation, transcripts for all previous degrees and institutions attended. Additional exam requirements/recommendations for international students: Required—TOEFL (minimum score 90 iBT), IELTS (minimum score 7). Electronic applications accepted.

University of Chicago, Division of the Physical Sciences, PhD Program in Computer Science, Chicago, IL 60637. Offers PhD. *Degree requirements:* For doctorate, thesis/dissertation. *Entrance requirements:* For doctorate, GRE General Test, 3 letters of recommendation, statement of purpose, transcripts, resume or curriculum vitae. Additional exam requirements/recommendations for international students: Required—TOEFL (minimum score 104 iBT), IELTS (minimum score 7). Electronic applications accepted. *Faculty research:* Systems, theoretical computer science, machine learning, programming languages, scientific computing and visualization.

University of Cincinnati, Graduate School, College of Engineering and Applied Science, Department of Electrical Engineering and Computing Systems, Program in Computer Science, Cincinnati, OH 45221. Offers MS. *Degree requirements:* For master's, thesis. *Entrance requirements:* For master's, GRE General Test, GRE Subject Test or BS in computer science. Additional exam requirements/recommendations for international students: Required—TOEFL (minimum score 550 paper-based).

University of Cincinnati, Graduate School, College of Engineering and Applied Science, Department of Electrical Engineering and Computing Systems, Program in Computer Science and Engineering, Cincinnati, OH 45221. Offers PhD. *Degree requirements:* For doctorate, thesis/dissertation. *Entrance requirements:* For doctorate, GRE General Test. Additional exam requirements/recommendations for international students: Required—TOEFL.

University of Colorado Boulder, Graduate School, College of Engineering and Applied Science, Department of Computer Science, Boulder, CO 80309. Offers ME, MS, PhD. Terminal master's awarded for partial completion of doctoral program. *Degree requirements:* For master's, comprehensive exam, thesis or alternative; for doctorate, one foreign language, thesis/dissertation. *Entrance requirements:* For master's, minimum undergraduate GPA of 3.0. Electronic applications accepted. Application fee is waived when completed online. *Faculty research:* Computer science; computer interface; artificial intelligence/cybernetics; distributed systems; computer software.

University of Colorado Denver, Business School, Program in Computer Science and Information Systems, Denver, CO 80217. Offers PhD. *Degree requirements:* For doctorate, comprehensive exam, thesis/dissertation. *Entrance requirements:* For doctorate, GMAT or GRE General Test, letters of recommendation, portfolio, essay describing applicant's motivation and initial plan for doctoral study, resume. Additional exam requirements/recommendations for international students: Required—TOEFL (minimum score 525 paper-based; 71 iBT); Recommended—IELTS (minimum score 6.5). Electronic applications accepted. *Expenses:* Contact institution. *Faculty research:* Design science of information systems, information system economics, organizational impacts of information technology, high performance parallel and distributed systems, performance measurement and prediction.

University of Colorado Denver, College of Engineering, Design and Computing, Department of Computer Science and Engineering, Denver, CO 80217. Offers computer science (MS); computer science and engineering (EASPh D); computer science and information systems (PhD). *Program availability:* Part-time, evening/weekend. *Degree requirements:* For master's, thesis or alternative, at least 30 semester hours of computer science courses while maintaining minimum GPA of 3.0; for doctorate, comprehensive exam, thesis/dissertation, at least 60 hours beyond the master's degree level, 30 of which are dissertation research. *Entrance requirements:* For master's, GRE, minimum GPA of 3.0, 10 semester hours of university-level calculus, at least one math course beyond calculus, statement of purpose, letters of recommendation; for doctorate, GRE or GMAT. Additional exam requirements/recommendations for international students: Required—TOEFL (minimum score 537 paper-based; 75 iBT). Electronic applications accepted. *Expenses:* Tuition, state resident: full-time $6786; part-time $337 per credit hour. Tuition, nonresident: full-time $22,590; part-time $1255 per credit hour. *Required fees:* $1231; $137 per credit hour: Tuition and fees vary according to program and reciprocity agreements.

University of Colorado Denver, College of Liberal Arts and Sciences, Program in Integrated Sciences, Denver, CO 80217. Offers applied science (MIS); computer science (MIS); mathematics (MIS). *Program availability:* Part-time, evening/weekend. *Entrance requirements:* For master's, GRE if undergraduate GPA is 3.0 or less, minimum of 40 semester hours in mathematics, computer science, physics, biology, chemistry and/or geology; essay; three letters of recommendation. *Expenses:* Tuition, state resident: full-time $6786; part-time $337 per credit hour. Tuition, nonresident: full-time $22,590; part-time $1255 per credit hour. *Required fees:* $1231; $137 per credit hour. Tuition and fees vary according to program and reciprocity agreements. *Faculty research:* Computer science, applied science, mathematics.

University of Connecticut, Graduate School, School of Engineering, Department of Computer Science and Engineering, Storrs, CT 06269. Offers computer science (MS, PhD), including artificial intelligence, computer architecture, computer science, operating systems, robotics, software engineering. Terminal master's awarded for partial completion of doctoral program. *Degree requirements:* For master's, comprehensive exam, thesis or alternative; for doctorate, thesis/dissertation. *Entrance requirements:* For master's and doctorate, GRE General Test. Additional exam requirements/recommendations for international students: Required—TOEFL (minimum score 550 paper-based). Electronic applications accepted.

University of Dayton, Department of Computer Science, Dayton, OH 45469. Offers MCS. *Program availability:* Part-time. *Degree requirements:* For master's, software project, additional coursework, or thesis. *Entrance requirements:* For master's, minimum GPA of 3.0, undergraduate degree in computer science or related field. Additional exam requirements/recommendations for international students: Required—TOEFL (minimum score 550 paper-based; 80 iBT). Electronic applications accepted. *Faculty research:* Mobile app development, cyber security, data analytics, autonomous systems, virtual reality.

University of Delaware, College of Engineering, Department of Computer and Information Sciences, Newark, DE 19716. Offers MS, PhD. *Program availability:* Part-time. Terminal master's awarded for partial completion of doctoral program. *Degree requirements:* For master's, thesis optional; for doctorate, comprehensive exam, thesis/dissertation. *Entrance requirements:* For master's and doctorate, GRE General Test. Additional exam requirements/recommendations for international students: Required—TOEFL (minimum score 550 paper-based). Electronic applications accepted. *Faculty research:* Artificial intelligence, computational theory, graphics and computer vision, networks, systems.

University of Denver, Daniel Felix Ritchie School of Engineering and Computer Science, Department of Computer Science, Denver, CO 80210. Offers computer science (MS, PhD); cybersecurity (MS); data science (MS). *Program availability:* Part-time, evening/weekend. *Faculty:* 15 full-time (3 women), 1 (woman) part-time/adjunct. *Students:* 23 full-time (8 women), 91 part-time (29 women); includes 11 minority (5 Asian, non-Hispanic/Latino; 1 Hispanic/Latino; 1 Native Hawaiian or other Pacific Islander, non-Hispanic/Latino; 4 Two or more races, non-Hispanic/Latino), 51 international. Average age 30. 263 applicants, 59% accepted, 79 enrolled. In 2018, 9 master's, 1 doctorate awarded. *Degree requirements:* For doctorate, variable foreign language requirement, comprehensive exam, thesis/dissertation, reading competency in two languages, modern typesetting system, or additional coursework. *Entrance requirements:* For master's and doctorate, GRE General Test, bachelor's degree, transcripts, personal statement, resume or curriculum vitae, three letters of recommendation. Additional exam requirements/recommendations for international students: Required—TOEFL (minimum score 550 paper-based; 80 iBT). *Application deadline:* For fall admission, 1/15 priority date for domestic and international students; for winter admission, 10/25 for domestic and international students; for spring admission, 2/7 for domestic and international students; for summer admission, 4/24 for domestic and international students. Applications are processed on a rolling basis. Application fee: $65. Electronic applications accepted. *Expenses:* $33,183 per year full-time. *Financial support:* In 2018–19, 98 students received support, including 14 teaching assistantships with tuition reimbursements available (averaging $18,214 per year); research assistantships with tuition reimbursements available, career-related internships or fieldwork, Federal Work-Study, institutionally sponsored loans, scholarships/grants, and unspecified assistantships also available. Financial award application deadline: 2/15; financial award applicants required to submit FAFSA. *Faculty research:* Algorithms, artificial intelligence, databases, game development, robotics. *Unit head:* Dr. Bruce Harmon, Professor of the Practice and Interim Chair, 303-871-6949, E-mail: bruce.harmon@du.edu. *Application contact:* Information Contact, 303-871-2458, E-mail: info@cs.du.edu.
Website: http://ritchieschool.du.edu/departments/computer-science/

University of Detroit Mercy, College of Liberal Arts and Education, Detroit, MI 48221. Offers addiction counseling (MA); addiction studies (Certificate); clinical mental health counseling (MA); clinical psychology (MA, PhD); computer and information systems (MS); criminal justice (MA); curriculum and instruction (MA); economics (MA); educational administration (MA); financial economics (MA); industrial/organizational psychology (MA); information assurance (MS); intelligence analysis (MA); liberal studies (MALS); religious studies (MA); school counseling (MA, Certificate); school psychology (Spec); security administration (MS); special education: emotionally impaired/behaviorally disordered (MA); special education: learning disabilities (MA). *Program availability:* Part-time, evening/weekend. *Degree requirements:* For doctorate, departmental qualifying exam. *Faculty research:* Psychology of aging, history of technology, Renaissance humanism, U.S. and Japanese economic relations.

University of Fairfax, Graduate Programs, Vienna, VA 22182. Offers business administration (DBA); computer science (MCS); cybersecurity (MBA, MS); general business administration (MBA); information technology (MBA); project management (MBA).

University of Florida, Graduate School, Herbert Wertheim College of Engineering, Department of Computer and Information Science and Engineering, Gainesville, FL 32611. Offers computer engineering (ME, MS, PhD); computer science (MS); digital arts and sciences (MS). *Program availability:* Part-time, online learning. Terminal master's awarded for partial completion of doctoral program. *Degree requirements:* For master's, comprehensive exam, thesis optional; for doctorate, comprehensive exam, thesis/dissertation. *Entrance requirements:* For master's and doctorate, minimum GPA of 3.0. Additional exam requirements/recommendations for international students: Required—TOEFL (minimum score 550 paper-based; 80 iBT), IELTS (minimum score 6). Electronic applications accepted. *Faculty research:* Computer systems and computer networking; high-performance computing and algorithm; database and machine learning; computer graphics, vision, and intelligent systems; human center computing and digital art.

University of Georgia, Franklin College of Arts and Sciences, Department of Computer Science, Athens, GA 30602. Offers applied mathematical science (MAMS); computer science (MS, PhD). *Degree requirements:* For doctorate, thesis/dissertation. *Entrance requirements:* For master's and doctorate, GRE General Test. Electronic applications accepted.

University of Guelph, Office of Graduate and Postdoctoral Studies, College of Physical and Engineering Science, Department of Computing and Information Science, Guelph, ON N1G 2W1, Canada. Offers applied computer science (M Sc); computer science (PhD). *Degree requirements:* For master's, thesis; for doctorate, comprehensive exam, thesis/dissertation. *Entrance requirements:* For master's, major or minor in computer science, honors degree; for doctorate, M Sc in computer science or related discipline. Additional exam requirements/recommendations for international students: Required—TOEFL (minimum score 600 paper-based; 89 iBT), IELTS (minimum score 6.5). Electronic applications accepted. *Faculty research:* Modeling and theory, distributed computing, soft computing, software and information systems, data and knowledge management.

University of Hawaii at Manoa, Office of Graduate Education, College of Natural Sciences, Department of Information and Computer Sciences, Honolulu, HI 96822. Offers computer science (MS, PhD); library and information science (MLI Sc, Graduate Certificate), including advanced library and information science (Graduate Certificate), library and information science (MLI Sc). *Program availability:* Part-time. *Degree requirements:* For master's, thesis optional; for doctorate, comprehensive exam, thesis/dissertation. *Entrance requirements:* For master's and doctorate, GRE. Additional exam requirements/recommendations for international students: Required—TOEFL (minimum score 580 paper-based; 92 iBT), IELTS (minimum score 5). *Faculty research:* Software engineering, telecommunications, artificial intelligence, multimedia.

University of Houston, College of Natural Sciences and Mathematics, Department of Computer Science, Houston, TX 77204. Offers MA, PhD. *Program availability:* Part-time. Terminal master's awarded for partial completion of doctoral program. *Degree requirements:* For master's, thesis or alternative; for doctorate, comprehensive exam, thesis/dissertation. *Entrance requirements:* For master's and doctorate, GRE. Additional exam requirements/recommendations for international students: Required—TOEFL (minimum score 550 paper-based; 79 iBT), IELTS (minimum score 6.5). Electronic applications accepted. *Faculty research:* Databases, networks, image analysis, security, animation.

University of Houston–Clear Lake, School of Science and Computer Engineering, Program in Computer Science, Houston, TX 77058-1002. Offers MS. *Program availability:* Part-time, evening/weekend. *Entrance requirements:* For master's, GRE General Test. Additional exam requirements/recommendations for international students: Required—TOEFL (minimum score 550 paper-based).

University of Houston–Victoria, School of Arts and Sciences, Department of Computer Science, Victoria, TX 77901-4450. Offers computer information systems (MS); computer science (MS). *Program availability:* Part-time, evening/weekend, online learning. *Degree requirements:* For master's, comprehensive exam (for some programs), thesis (for some programs). *Entrance requirements:* For master's, GRE. Additional exam requirements/recommendations for international students: Required—TOEFL (minimum score 550 paper-based). *Expenses: Tuition, area resident:* Full-time $6154; part-time $3077 per semester. Tuition, state resident: full-time $6154; part-time $3077 per semester. Tuition, nonresident: full-time $13,624; part-time $6812 per semester. *International tuition:* $13,624 full-time. *Required fees:* $1405; $847 per semester. $423 per semester. Tuition and fees vary according to program.

University of Idaho, College of Graduate Studies, College of Engineering, Department of Computer Science, Moscow, ID 83844-1010. Offers MS, PhD. *Faculty:* 15 full-time. *Students:* 62 full-time (12 women), 28 part-time (6 women). Average age 32. In 2018, 11 master's, 4 doctorates awarded. *Degree requirements:* For doctorate, thesis/dissertation. *Entrance requirements:* For master's and doctorate, minimum GPA of 3.0. Additional exam requirements/recommendations for international students: Required—TOEFL (minimum score 79 iBT). *Application deadline:* For fall admission, 8/1 for domestic students; for spring admission, 12/15 for domestic students. Applications are processed on a rolling basis. Application fee: $60. Electronic applications accepted. *Expenses:* Tuition, state resident: full-time $7266.44; part-time $474.50 per credit hour. Tuition, nonresident: full-time $24,902; part-time $1453.50 per credit hour. *Required fees:* $2085.56; $45.50 per credit hour. *Financial support:* Research assistantships, teaching assistantships, and career-related internships or fieldwork available. Financial award applicants required to submit FAFSA. *Faculty research:* Information assurance and security, collaborative virtual education, evolutionary computation, bioinformatics. *Unit head:* Dr. Terry Soule, Chair, 208-885-6592, E-mail: csinfo@uidaho.edu. *Application contact:* Dr. Terry Soule, Chair, 208-885-6592, E-mail: csinfo@uidaho.edu. Website: https://www.uidaho.edu/engr/departments/cs

University of Illinois at Chicago, College of Engineering, Department of Computer Science, Chicago, IL 60607-7128. Offers MS, PhD. *Program availability:* Part-time. *Degree requirements:* For master's, thesis or alternative; for doctorate, thesis/dissertation, departmental qualifying exam. *Entrance requirements:* For master's, BS in related field, minimum GPA of 2.75; for doctorate, GRE General Test, minimum GPA of 2.75, MS in related field. Additional exam requirements/recommendations for international students: Required—TOEFL. *Expenses:* Contact institution. *Faculty research:* Artificial intelligence; deployment of natural language discourse/dialogue coordinated with graphics tools; data management and mining, information retrieval; computational techniques for population biology; systems security research; scientific visualization.

University of Illinois at Chicago, College of Liberal Arts and Sciences, Department of Mathematics, Statistics, and Computer Science, Chicago, IL 60607-7128. Offers mathematics (DA); probability and statistics (PhD); secondary school mathematics (MST); statistics (MS). *Program availability:* Part-time. *Degree requirements:* For master's, comprehensive exam; for doctorate, one foreign language, thesis/dissertation. *Entrance requirements:* For master's and doctorate, GRE General Test, minimum GPA of 3.0. Additional exam requirements/recommendations for international students: Required—TOEFL (minimum score 100 iBT). Electronic applications accepted.

University of Illinois at Springfield, Graduate Programs, College of Liberal Arts and Sciences, Program in Computer Science, Springfield, IL 62703-5407. Offers MS. *Program availability:* Part-time, evening/weekend, 100% online, blended/hybrid learning. *Faculty:* 18 full-time (5 women), 2 part-time/adjunct (0 women). *Students:* 141 full-time (38 women), 254 part-time (57 women); includes 83 minority (21 Black or African American, non-Hispanic/Latino; 42 Asian, non-Hispanic/Latino; 11 Hispanic/Latino; 2 Native Hawaiian or other Pacific Islander, non-Hispanic/Latino; 7 Two or more races, non-Hispanic/Latino), 146 international. Average age 31. 604 applicants, 57% accepted, 141 enrolled. In 2018, 338 master's awarded. *Degree requirements:* For master's, comprehensive closure exercise. *Entrance requirements:* For master's, minimum undergraduate GPA of 2.7; bachelor's degree in computer science or the equivalent. Additional exam requirements/recommendations for international students: Required—TOEFL (minimum score 550 paper-based; 79 iBT). *Application deadline:* Applications are processed on a rolling basis. Application fee: $60 ($75 for international students). Electronic applications accepted. *Expenses:* Contact institution. *Financial support:* In 2018–19, research assistantships with full tuition reimbursements (averaging $10,384 per year), teaching assistantships with full tuition reimbursements (averaging $10,303 per year) were awarded; fellowships, career-related internships or fieldwork, Federal Work-Study, scholarships/grants, health care benefits, and unspecified assistantships also available. Support available to part-time students. Financial award application deadline: 11/15; financial award applicants required to submit FAFSA. *Unit head:* Dr. Sviatoslav Braynov, Program Administrator, 217-206-8245, Fax: 217-206-6217, E-mail: sbray2@uis.edu. *Application contact:* Dr. Sviatoslav Braynov, Program Administrator, 217-206-8245, Fax: 217-206-6217, E-mail: sbray2@uis.edu. Website: csc@uis.edu

University of Illinois at Urbana–Champaign, Graduate College, College of Engineering, Department of Computer Science, Champaign, IL 61820. Offers bioinformatics (MS); computer science (MCS, MS, PhD); MCS/JD; MCS/M Arch; MCS/MBA. *Program availability:* Part-time, evening/weekend, online learning.

The University of Iowa, Graduate College, College of Liberal Arts and Sciences, Department of Computer Science, Iowa City, IA 52242-1316. Offers MCS, PhD. *Degree requirements:* For master's, thesis optional, exam; for doctorate, comprehensive exam, thesis/dissertation. *Entrance requirements:* For master's, minimum GPA of 3.0; for doctorate, GRE General Test, minimum GPA of 3.0. Additional exam requirements/recommendations for international students: Required—TOEFL (minimum score 550 paper-based; 81 iBT). Electronic applications accepted.

The University of Kansas, Graduate Studies, School of Engineering, Program in Computer Science, Lawrence, KS 66045. Offers MS, PhD. *Program availability:* Part-time, evening/weekend. *Students:* 49 full-time (11 women), 11 part-time (1 woman); includes 8 minority (2 Black or African American, non-Hispanic/Latino; 2 Asian, non-Hispanic/Latino; 2 Hispanic/Latino; 2 Two or more races, non-Hispanic/Latino), 30 international. Average age 27. 97 applicants, 54% accepted, 12 enrolled. In 2018, 19 master's, 7 doctorates awarded. Terminal master's awarded for partial completion of doctoral program. *Entrance requirements:* For master's, GRE (minimum scores: 146 verbal and 155 quantitative), minimum GPA of 3.0, official transcript, three recommendations, statement of academic objectives, resume; for doctorate, GRE (minimum scores: 146 verbal and 155 quantitative), minimum GPA of 3.5, official transcript, three recommendations, statement of academic objectives, resume. Additional exam requirements/recommendations for international students: Required—TOEFL, IELTS. *Application deadline:* For fall admission, 12/15 priority date for domestic and international students; for spring admission, 10/1 for domestic and international students. Application fee: $65 ($85 for international students). Electronic applications accepted. *Financial support:* Fellowships, research assistantships, teaching assistantships, career-related internships or fieldwork, scholarships/grants, and unspecified assistantships available. Financial award application deadline: 12/15. *Faculty research:* Communication systems and networking, computer systems design, interactive intelligent systems, bioinformatics. *Unit head:* Erik Perrins, Chair, 785-864-4486, E-mail: perrins@ku.edu. *Application contact:* Joy Grisafe-Gross, Graduate Admissions Contact, 785-864-4487, E-mail: jgrisafe@ku.edu.

University of Kentucky, Graduate School, College of Engineering, Program in Computer Science, Lexington, KY 40506-0032. Offers MS, PhD. *Degree requirements:* For master's, comprehensive exam, thesis optional; for doctorate, one foreign language, comprehensive exam, thesis/dissertation. *Entrance requirements:* For master's, GRE

General Test, minimum undergraduate GPA of 2.75; for doctorate, GRE General Test, minimum undergraduate GPA of 3.0. Additional exam requirements/recommendations for international students: Required—TOEFL (minimum score 550 paper-based). Electronic applications accepted. *Faculty research:* Artificial intelligence and databases, communication networks and operating systems, graphics and vision, numerical analysis, theory.

University of Lethbridge, School of Graduate Studies, Lethbridge, AB T1K 3M4, Canada. Offers addictions counseling (M Sc); agricultural biotechnology (M Sc); agricultural studies (M Sc, MA); anthropology (MA); archaeology (M Sc, MA); art (MA, MFA); biochemistry (M Sc); biological sciences (M Sc); biomolecular science (PhD); biosystems and biodiversity (PhD); Canadian studies (MA); chemistry (M Sc); computer science (M Sc); computer science and geographical information science (M Sc); counseling (MC); counseling psychology (M Ed); dramatic arts (MA); earth, space, and physical science (PhD); economics (MA); education (MA, PhD); educational leadership (M Ed); English (MA); environmental science (M Sc); evolution and behavior (PhD); exercise science (M Sc); French (MA); French/German (MA); French/Spanish (MA); general education (M Ed); geography (M Sc, MA); German (MA); health sciences (M Sc); individualized multidisciplinary (M Sc, MA); kinesiology (M Sc, MA); management (M Sc), including accounting, finance, human resource management and labor relations, information systems, international management, marketing, policy and strategy; mathematics (M Sc); music (M Mus, MA); Native American studies (MA); neuroscience (M Sc, PhD); new media (MA, MFA); nursing (M Sc, MN); philosophy (MA); physics (M Sc); political science (MA); psychology (M Sc, MA); religious studies (MA); sociology (MA); theatre and dramatic arts (MFA); theoretical and computational science (PhD); urban and regional studies (MA); women and gender studies (MA). *Program availability:* Part-time, evening/weekend. *Degree requirements:* For master's, thesis (for some programs); for doctorate, comprehensive exam, thesis/dissertation. *Entrance requirements:* For master's, GMAT (for M Sc in management), bachelor's degree in related field, minimum GPA of 3.0 during previous 20 graded semester courses, 2 years' teaching or related experience (M Ed); for doctorate, master's degree, minimum graduate GPA of 3.5. Additional exam requirements/recommendations for international students: Required—TOEFL (minimum score 580 paper-based; 93 iBT). Electronic applications accepted. *Faculty research:* Movement and brain plasticity, gibberellin physiology, photosynthesis, carbon cycling, molecular properties of main-group ring components.

University of Louisville, J. B. Speed School of Engineering, Department of Computer Engineering and Computer Science, Louisville, KY 40292-0001. Offers computer engineering and computer science (M Eng); computer science (MS, PhD); cybersecurity (Certificate); data science (Certificate). *Accreditation:* ABET (one or more programs are accredited). *Program availability:* Part-time, 100% online, blended/hybrid learning. *Faculty:* 14 full-time (2 women), 3 part-time/adjunct (0 women). *Students:* 62 full-time (16 women), 124 part-time (31 women); includes 32 minority (4 Black or African American, non-Hispanic/Latino; 14 Asian, non-Hispanic/Latino; 8 Hispanic/Latino; 6 Two or more races, non-Hispanic/Latino), 46 international. Average age 33. 74 applicants, 49% accepted, 25 enrolled. In 2018, 18 master's, 5 doctorates, 7 other advanced degrees awarded. Terminal master's awarded for partial completion of doctoral program. *Degree requirements:* For master's, thesis optional; for doctorate, comprehensive exam, thesis/dissertation. *Entrance requirements:* For master's, GRE, Two letters of recommendation, official final transcripts; for doctorate, GRE, Two letters of recommendation, personal statement, official final transcripts. Additional exam requirements/recommendations for international students: Required—TOEFL (minimum score 550 paper-based; 80 iBT), IELTS (minimum score 6.5), GRE. *Application deadline:* For fall admission, 5/1 priority date for domestic and international students; for spring admission, 11/1 priority date for domestic and international students; for summer admission, 3/1 priority date for domestic and international students. Applications are processed on a rolling basis. Application fee: $65. Electronic applications accepted. *Expenses: Tuition, area resident:* Full-time $6500; part-time $723 per credit hour. Tuition, state resident: full-time $6500. Tuition, nonresident: full-time $13,557; part-time $1507 per credit hour. Tuition and fees vary according to course load and program. *Financial support:* In 2018–19, 78 students received support. Fellowships, research assistantships, teaching assistantships, scholarships/grants, health care benefits, and tuition waivers (full) available. Financial award application deadline: 1/1. *Faculty research:* Artificial Intelligence, Big Data Analytics, Bioinformatics, Cybersecurity, Data Mining. *Total annual research expenditures:* $740,736. *Unit head:* Dr. Wei Zhang, Chair, 502-852-0715, E-mail: wei.zhang@louisville.edu. *Application contact:* Dr. Mehmed Kantardzic, Director of Graduate Studies, 502-852-3703, E-mail: mehmed.kantardzic@louisville.edu. Website: http://louisville.edu/speed/computer

University of Maine, Graduate School, College of Liberal Arts and Sciences, School of Computing and Information Science, Orono, ME 04469. Offers MS, PhD, CGS. *Program availability:* Part-time. *Faculty:* 13 full-time (2 women), 2 part-time/adjunct (1 woman). *Students:* 18 full-time (3 women), 10 part-time (2 women); includes 3 minority (1 Black or African American, non-Hispanic/Latino; 1 American Indian or Alaska Native, non-Hispanic/Latino; 1 Two or more races, non-Hispanic/Latino), 6 international. Average age 36. 34 applicants, 74% accepted, 10 enrolled. In 2018, 9 master's, 1 doctorate, 2 other advanced degrees awarded. *Degree requirements:* For master's, thesis (for some programs); for doctorate, comprehensive exam, thesis/dissertation. *Entrance requirements:* For master's and doctorate, GRE General Test, GRE Subject Test. Additional exam requirements/recommendations for international students: Required—TOEFL (minimum score 550 paper-based; 80 iBT). *Application deadline:* Applications are processed on a rolling basis. Application fee: $65. Electronic applications accepted. *Financial support:* In 2018–19, 21 students received support, including 1 fellowship (averaging $21,400 per year), 11 research assistantships with full tuition reimbursements available (averaging $17,200 per year), 8 teaching assistantships with full tuition reimbursements available (averaging $15,600 per year); career-related internships or fieldwork, Federal Work-Study, institutionally sponsored loans, tuition waivers (full), and unspecified assistantships also available. Financial award application deadline: 3/1. *Faculty research:* Geographic information science, spatial informatics, scientific computing. *Total annual research expenditures:* $860,302. *Unit head:* Dr. Max Egenhofer, Acting Director, 207-581-2114, Fax: 207-581-2206. *Application contact:* Scott G. Delcourt, Assistant Vice President for Graduate Studies and Senior Associate Dean, 207-581-3291, Fax: 207-581-3232, E-mail: graduate@maine.edu. Website: http://umaine.edu/cis/

University of Management and Technology, Program in Computer Science, Arlington, VA 22209-1609. Offers computer science (MS); information technology (AC); project management (AC); software engineering (MS). *Program availability:* Part-time, evening/weekend, online learning. *Entrance requirements:* For master's, 3 recommendations, resume. Additional exam requirements/recommendations for international students: Required—TOEFL (minimum score 530 paper-based; 71 iBT). Electronic applications accepted. *Expenses: Tuition:* Full-time $7020; part-time $1170 per course.

The University of Manchester, School of Computer Science, Manchester, United Kingdom. Offers M Phil, PhD.

Computer Science

University of Manitoba, Faculty of Graduate Studies, Faculty of Science, Department of Computer Science, Winnipeg, MB R3T 2N2, Canada. Offers M Sc, PhD. *Degree requirements:* For master's, thesis or alternative; for doctorate, thesis/dissertation.

University of Maryland, Baltimore County, The Graduate School, College of Engineering and Information Technology, Department of Computer Science and Electrical Engineering, Program in Computer Science, Baltimore, MD 21250. Offers MS, PhD. *Program availability:* Part-time. *Degree requirements:* For master's, comprehensive exam (for some programs), thesis (for some programs); for doctorate, comprehensive exam, thesis/dissertation. *Entrance requirements:* For master's, GRE General Test, strong background in computer science and math courses; for doctorate, GRE General Test, MS in computer science (strongly recommended). Additional exam requirements/recommendations for international students: Required—TOEFL (minimum score 550 paper-based; 80 iBT). Electronic applications accepted. *Expenses:* Contact institution. *Faculty research:* Artificial intelligence, graphics and visualization, high performance computing, information and knowledge management, networking and systems, security, theory and algorithms.

University of Maryland, Baltimore County, The Graduate School, College of Engineering and Information Technology, Department of Information Systems, Program in Human-Centered Computing, Baltimore, MD 21250. Offers MS, PhD. *Program availability:* Part-time, evening/weekend. Terminal master's awarded for partial completion of doctoral program. *Degree requirements:* For master's, comprehensive exam (for some programs), thesis optional; for doctorate, comprehensive exam, thesis/dissertation. *Entrance requirements:* For master's, minimum GPA of 3.0; for doctorate, GRE General Test or GMAT, competence in statistical analysis and experimental design. Additional exam requirements/recommendations for international students: Required—TOEFL (minimum score 550 paper-based; 80 iBT). Electronic applications accepted. *Expenses:* Contact institution. *Faculty research:* Human-centered computing.

University of Maryland, College Park, Academic Affairs, College of Computer, Mathematical and Natural Sciences, Department of Computer Science, College Park, MD 20742. Offers MS, PhD. *Program availability:* Part-time, evening/weekend. Terminal master's awarded for partial completion of doctoral program. *Degree requirements:* For master's, thesis or scholarly paper and exam; for doctorate, thesis/dissertation. *Entrance requirements:* For master's and doctorate, GRE General Test, GRE Subject Test (recommended), minimum GPA of 3.0, 3 letters of recommendation. Additional exam requirements/recommendations for international students: Required—TOEFL; Recommended—TWE. Electronic applications accepted. *Faculty research:* Artificial intelligence, computer applications, information processing, bioinformatics and computational biology, human-computer interaction.

University of Maryland Eastern Shore, Graduate Programs, Department of Mathematics and Computer Science, Princess Anne, MD 21853. Offers applied computer science (MS). *Program availability:* Part-time, evening/weekend. *Degree requirements:* For master's, thesis or alternative, research project. *Entrance requirements:* For master's, GRE General Test, minimum GPA of 3.0. Additional exam requirements/recommendations for international students: Required—TOEFL (minimum score 80 iBT). Electronic applications accepted.

University of Massachusetts Amherst, Graduate School, College of Natural Sciences, School of Computer Science, Amherst, MA 01003. Offers MS, PhD. *Program availability:* Part-time. Terminal master's awarded for partial completion of doctoral program. *Degree requirements:* For master's, thesis or alternative; for doctorate, comprehensive exam, thesis/dissertation. *Entrance requirements:* For master's and doctorate, GRE General Test. Additional exam requirements/recommendations for international students: Required—TOEFL (minimum score 550 paper-based; 80 iBT), IELTS (minimum score 6.5), TWE. Electronic applications accepted. *Faculty research:* Artificial intelligence, robotics, computer vision, and wearable computing; autonomous and multiagent systems; information retrieval, data mining and machine learning; networking, distributed systems and security.

University of Massachusetts Boston, College of Science and Mathematics, Program in Computer Science, Boston, MA 02125-3393. Offers MS, PhD. *Program availability:* Part-time, evening/weekend. *Faculty:* 20 full-time (4 women), 2 part-time/adjunct (0 women). *Students:* 84 full-time (28 women), 29 part-time (6 women); includes 15 minority (3 Black or African American, non-Hispanic/Latino; 9 Asian, non-Hispanic/Latino; 2 Hispanic/Latino; 1 Two or more races, non-Hispanic/Latino), 84 international. Average age 29. 114 applicants, 60% accepted, 24 enrolled. In 2018, 57 master's, 4 doctorates awarded. *Entrance requirements:* For master's and doctorate, GRE General Test, minimum GPA of 2.75. Additional exam requirements/recommendations for international students: Required—TOEFL (minimum score 80 iBT). *Application deadline:* For fall admission, 6/1 for domestic students; for spring admission, 11/1 for domestic students. *Expenses: Tuition, area resident:* Full-time $17,896. Tuition, state resident: full-time $17,896. Tuition, nonresident: full-time $34,932. International tuition: $34,932 full-time. *Required fees:* $355. *Financial support:* Research assistantships, teaching assistantships, career-related internships or fieldwork, Federal Work-Study, and unspecified assistantships available. Support available to part-time students. Financial award application deadline: 3/1; financial award applicants required to submit FAFSA. *Faculty research:* Queuing theory, database design theory, computer networks, theory of database query languages, real-time systems. *Unit head:* Dr. Dan Simovici, Director, 617-287-6472, E-mail: dsim@cs.umb.edu. *Application contact:* Graduate Admissions Coordinator, 617-287-6400, Fax: 617-287-6236, E-mail: graduate.admissions@umb.edu.

University of Massachusetts Dartmouth, Graduate School, College of Engineering, Department of Computer Science, North Dartmouth, MA 02747-2300. Offers computer science (MS, Graduate Certificate); software development and design (Postbaccalaureate Certificate). *Program availability:* Part-time, 100% online, blended/hybrid learning. *Faculty:* 11 full-time (3 women), 2 part-time/adjunct (0 women). *Students:* 53 full-time (17 women), 48 part-time (7 women); includes 11 minority (2 Black or African American, non-Hispanic/Latino; 4 Asian, non-Hispanic/Latino; 2 Hispanic/Latino; 3 Two or more races, non-Hispanic/Latino), 59 international. Average age 32. 102 applicants, 92% accepted, 34 enrolled. In 2018, 57 master's, 2 other advanced degrees awarded. *Degree requirements:* For master's, thesis, thesis or project. *Entrance requirements:* For master's, GRE unless UMass Dartmouth graduate in computer science, statement of purpose (minimum of 300 words), resume, 3 letters of recommendation, official transcripts; for other advanced degree, statement of purpose (minimum of 300 words), resume, official transcripts. Additional exam requirements/recommendations for international students: Required—TOEFL (minimum score 533 paper-based; 72 iBT), IELTS (minimum score 6). *Application deadline:* For fall admission, 4/15 priority date for domestic students, 3/15 priority date for international students; for spring admission, 11/15 priority date for domestic students, 10/15 priority date for international students. Application fee: $60. Electronic applications accepted. *Financial support:* In 2018–19, 1 research assistantship (averaging $5,192 per year), 10 teaching assistantships (averaging $8,075 per year) were awarded; tuition waivers (full and partial) and unspecified assistantships also available. Support available to part-time students. Financial award application deadline: 3/1; financial award applicants required to submit FAFSA. *Faculty research:* Artificial intelligence, sensor fusion and autonomous underwater vehicles, self organizing feature maps, data mining, development of agent oriented software. *Total annual research expenditures:* $973,000. *Unit head:* Dr. Xiaoqin Zhang, Graduate Program Director, Computer Science, 508-999-8294, E-mail: x2zhang@umassd.edu. *Application contact:* Scott Webster, Director of Graduate studies and Admissions, 508-999-8202, Fax: 508-999-8183, E-mail: graduate@umassd.edu.
Website: http://www.umassd.edu/engineering/cis/graduate

University of Massachusetts Lowell, College of Sciences, Department of Computer Science, Lowell, MA 01854. Offers MS, PhD. *Program availability:* Part-time. *Degree requirements:* For master's, thesis optional; for doctorate, thesis/dissertation. *Entrance requirements:* For master's and doctorate, GRE General Test. *Faculty research:* Networks, multimedia systems, human-computer interaction, graphics and visualization databases.

University of Memphis, Graduate School, College of Arts and Sciences, Department of Computer Science, Memphis, TN 38152. Offers bioinformatics (MS); computer science (MS, PhD). *Students:* 79 full-time (19 women), 21 part-time (4 women); includes 17 minority (7 Black or African American, non-Hispanic/Latino; 9 Asian, non-Hispanic/Latino; 1 Hispanic/Latino), 67 international. Average age 29. 110 applicants, 66% accepted, 29 enrolled. In 2018, 7 master's, 5 doctorates awarded. Terminal master's awarded for partial completion of doctoral program. *Degree requirements:* For master's, comprehensive exam, thesis; for doctorate, comprehensive exam, thesis/dissertation, qualifying exam, final exam. *Entrance requirements:* For master's and doctorate, GRE, letters of recommendation. Additional exam requirements/recommendations for international students: Required—TOEFL (minimum score 550 paper-based; 79 iBT). *Application deadline:* Applications are processed on a rolling basis. Application fee: $35 ($60 for international students). *Expenses:* Tuition, area resident: Full-time $10,240; part-time $503 per credit hour. Tuition, state resident: full-time $10,464. Tuition, nonresident: full-time $20,224; part-time $991 per credit hour. *Required fees:* $850; $106 per credit hour. *Financial support:* Fellowships, research assistantships with full tuition reimbursements, teaching assistantships with full tuition reimbursements, Federal Work-Study, scholarships/grants, and unspecified assistantships available. Financial award application deadline: 2/1; financial award applicants required to submit FAFSA. *Faculty research:* Network security, biomolecular and distributed computing, wireless sensor networks, artificial intelligence. *Unit head:* Dr. Lan Wang, Chair, 901-678-5465, Fax: 901-678-1506, E-mail: lanwang@memphis.edu. *Application contact:* Dr. Scott Fleming, Graduate Studies Coordinator, 901-678-3142, E-mail: info@cs.memphis.edu.
Website: https://www.memphis.edu/cs/

University of Miami, Graduate School, College of Arts and Sciences, Department of Computer Science, Coral Gables, FL 33124. Offers MS, PhD. *Program availability:* Part-time, online learning. *Degree requirements:* For master's, comprehensive exam (for some programs), thesis. *Entrance requirements:* For master's, GRE. Additional exam requirements/recommendations for international students: Required—TOEFL. Electronic applications accepted. *Faculty research:* Algorithm engineering, automated reasoning, computer graphics, cryptography, security network.

University of Michigan, College of Engineering, Department of Computer Science and Engineering, Ann Arbor, MI 48109. Offers MS, MSE, PhD. *Program availability:* Part-time. *Students:* 344 full-time (62 women), 3 part-time (0 women). 2,461 applicants, 15% accepted, 112 enrolled. In 2018, 69 master's, 29 doctorates awarded. *Financial support:* Fellowships, research assistantships, teaching assistantships, career-related internships or fieldwork, Federal Work-Study, institutionally sponsored loans, and health care benefits available. Support available to part-time students. *Faculty research:* Solid state electronics and optics; communications, control, signal process; sensors and integrated circuitry; software systems; artificial intelligence; hardware systems. *Total annual research expenditures:* $28.7 million. *Unit head:* Brian Noble, Department Chair, 734-764-8504, E-mail: bnoble@umich.edu. *Application contact:* Ashley Andreae, Graduate Programs Coordinator, 734-647-1807, E-mail: smash@umich.edu.
Website: http://eecs.umich.edu/cse/

University of Michigan–Dearborn, College of Engineering and Computer Science, PhD Program in Computer and Information Science, Dearborn, MI 48128. Offers data management (PhD); data science (PhD); software engineering (PhD); systems and security (PhD). *Faculty:* 19 full-time (1 woman), 5 part-time/adjunct (0 women). *Students:* 7 full-time (4 women), 7 part-time (1 woman); includes 1 minority (Asian, non-Hispanic/Latino), 9 international. Average age 30. 22 applicants, 36% accepted, 6 enrolled. In 2018, 1 doctorate awarded. *Degree requirements:* For doctorate, comprehensive exam, thesis/dissertation. *Entrance requirements:* For doctorate, GRE, bachelor's or master's degree in computer science or closely-related field. Additional exam requirements/recommendations for international students: Required—TOEFL (minimum score 560 paper-based; 84 iBT), IELTS (minimum score 6.5). *Application deadline:* For fall admission, 2/1 for domestic and international students. Application fee: $60. Electronic applications accepted. *Expenses:* Tuition, state resident: full-time $15,380; part-time $88 per credit hour. Tuition, nonresident: full-time $23,948; part-time $1377 per credit hour. *Required fees:* $780; $780 $390. Tuition and fees vary according to course level, course load, degree level, program, reciprocity agreements and student level. *Financial support:* In 2018–19, 2 students received support. Research assistantships with full tuition reimbursements available, teaching assistantships with full tuition reimbursements available, scholarships/grants, health care benefits, and unspecified assistantships available. Financial award application deadline: 2/1; financial award applicants required to submit FAFSA. *Faculty research:* Data science, data management, cybersecurity, software engineering, systems. *Unit head:* Dr. Di Ma, Director, 313-583-6737, E-mail: dmadma@umich.edu. *Application contact:* Office of Graduate Studies, 313-583-6321, E-mail: umd-graduatestudies@umich.edu.
Website: https://umdearborn.edu/cecs/departments/computer-and-information-science/graduate-programs/phd-computer-and-information-science

University of Michigan–Flint, College of Arts and Sciences, Program in Computer Science and Information Systems, Flint, MI 48502-1950. Offers computer science (MS); information systems (MS), including business information systems, health information systems. *Program availability:* Part-time, evening/weekend, 100% online. *Faculty:* 15 full-time (5 women), 7 part-time/adjunct (3 women). *Students:* 33 full-time (14 women), 56 part-time (17 women); includes 17 minority (4 Black or African American, non-Hispanic/Latino; 1 American Indian or Alaska Native, non-Hispanic/Latino; 3 Asian, non-Hispanic/Latino; 6 Hispanic/Latino; 1 Native Hawaiian or other Pacific Islander, non-Hispanic/Latino; 2 Two or more races, non-Hispanic/Latino), 39 international. Average age 30. 310 applicants, 66% accepted, 21 enrolled. In 2018, 29 master's awarded. *Degree requirements:* For master's, thesis optional, Non Thesis option available. *Entrance requirements:* For master's, BS from regionally-accredited institution in computer science, computer information systems, or computer engineering (preferred); minimum overall undergraduate GPA of 3.0. Additional exam requirements/recommendations for international students: Required—TOEFL (minimum score 84 iBT), IELTS (minimum score 6.5). *Application deadline:* For fall admission, 8/1 for domestic students, 5/1 for international students; for winter admission, 10/1 for domestic students, 8/1 for international students; for spring admission, 3/15 for domestic students, 1/1 for international students. Applications are processed on a rolling basis. Application fee: $55. Electronic applications accepted. *Expenses:* Contact institution. *Financial support:* Federal Work-Study, scholarships/grants, and unspecified assistantships

available. Financial award application deadline: 3/1; financial award applicants required to submit FAFSA. *Faculty research:* Computer network systems, database management systems, artificial intelligence and controlled systems. *Unit head:* Dr. Mike Farmer, Department Chair, 810-762-3423, Fax: 810-766-6780, E-mail: farmerme@umflint.edu. *Application contact:* Matt Bohlen, Director of Graduate Admissions, 810-762-3171, Fax: 810-766-6789, E-mail: mbohlen@umflint.edu.
Website: http://www.umflint.edu/graduateprograms/computer-science-information-systems-ms

University of Minnesota, Duluth, Graduate School, Swenson College of Science and Engineering, Department of Computer Science, Duluth, MN 55812-2496. Offers MS. *Program availability:* Part-time. *Entrance requirements:* For master's, GRE General Test, minimum GPA of 3.0. Additional exam requirements/recommendations for international students: Required—TOEFL (minimum score 550 paper-based). Electronic applications accepted. *Faculty research:* Information retrieval, artificial intelligence, machine learning, parallel/distributed computing, graphics.

University of Minnesota, Twin Cities Campus, College of Science and Engineering, Department of Computer Science and Engineering, Minneapolis, MN 55455-0213. Offers computer science (MCS, MS, PhD); data science (MS); software engineering (MSSE). *Program availability:* Part-time. Terminal master's awarded for partial completion of doctoral program. *Degree requirements:* For doctorate, thesis/dissertation. *Entrance requirements:* For master's and doctorate, GRE General Test. Additional exam requirements/recommendations for international students: Required—TOEFL. Electronic applications accepted. *Faculty research:* Computer architecture, bioinformatics and computational biology, data mining, graphics and visualization, high performance computing, human-computer interaction, networks, software systems, theory, artificial intelligence.

University of Minnesota, Twin Cities Campus, College of Science and Engineering, Scientific Computation Program, Minneapolis, MN 55455-0213. Offers MS, PhD. *Program availability:* Part-time. *Degree requirements:* For master's, thesis; for doctorate, thesis/dissertation. *Entrance requirements:* For master's and doctorate, GRE General Test. Additional exam requirements/recommendations for international students: Required—TOEFL (minimum score 550 paper-based; 79 iBT), IELTS (minimum score 6.5). Electronic applications accepted. *Faculty research:* Parallel computations, quantum mechanical dynamics, computational materials science, computational fluid dynamics, computational neuroscience.

University of Mississippi, Graduate School, School of Engineering, University, MS 38677. Offers aeroacoustics (MS, PhD); chemical engineering (MS, PhD); civil engineering (MS, PhD); computational hydroscience (MS, PhD); computer science (MS, PhD); electrical engineering (MS, PhD); electromagnetics (MS, PhD); environmental engineering (MS, PhD); geology and geological engineering (MS, PhD); hydrology (MS); material science (MS); mechanical engineering (MS, PhD); telecommunications (MS). *Faculty:* 76 full-time (16 women), 3 part-time/adjunct (1 woman). *Students:* 129 full-time (33 women), 21 part-time (5 women); includes 15 minority (7 Black or African American, non-Hispanic/Latino; 6 Asian, non-Hispanic/Latino; 1 Hispanic/Latino; 1 Two or more races, non-Hispanic/Latino), 73 international. Average age 29. In 2018, 36 master's, 17 doctorates awarded. *Entrance requirements:* For master's, GRE General Test, minimum GPA of 3.0; for doctorate, GRE General Test. Additional exam requirements/recommendations for international students: Required—TOEFL. *Application deadline:* Applications are processed on a rolling basis. Application fee: $50. Electronic applications accepted. *Financial support:* Scholarships/grants available. Financial award application deadline: 3/1; financial award applicants required to submit FAFSA. *Unit head:* Dr. David Puleo, Dean, 662-915-5780, Fax: 662-915-5387, E-mail: engineer@olemiss.edu. *Application contact:* Temeka Smith, Graduate Activities Specialist for Admissions, 662-915-7474, Fax: 662-915-7577, E-mail: gschool@olemiss.edu.

University of Missouri, Office of Research and Graduate Studies, College of Engineering, Department of Electrical Engineering and Computer Science, Columbia, MO 65211. Offers computer engineering (MSCE); computer science (MS, PhD); electrical and computer engineering (PhD); electrical engineering (MSEE). *Entrance requirements:* For master's, GRE General Test, minimum GPA of 3.0; for doctorate, GRE General Test, GRE Subject Test, minimum GPA of 3.0. Additional exam requirements/recommendations for international students: Required—TOEFL.

University of Missouri–Kansas City, School of Computing and Engineering, Kansas City, MO 64110-2499. Offers civil engineering (MS); computer and electrical engineering (PhD); computer science (MS), including bioinformatics, software engineering, telecommunications networking; computer science and informatics (PhD); computing (PhD); electrical engineering (MS); engineering (PhD); engineering and construction management (Graduate Certificate); mechanical engineering (MS); telecommunications and computer networking (PhD). PhD (interdisciplinary) offered through the School of Graduate Studies. *Program availability:* Part-time. *Degree requirements:* For doctorate, thesis/dissertation. *Entrance requirements:* For master's, GRE General Test, minimum GPA of 3.0, 3 letters of recommendation from professors; for doctorate, GRE General Test, minimum GPA of 3.5. Additional exam requirements/recommendations for international students: Required—TOEFL (minimum score 550 paper-based; 80 iBT). *Faculty research:* Algorithms, bioinformatics and medical informatics, biomechanics/biomaterials, civil engineering materials, networking and telecommunications, thermal science.

University of Missouri–St. Louis, College of Arts and Sciences, Department of Mathematics and Computer Science, St. Louis, MO 63121. Offers computer science (MS); mathematical and computational sciences (PhD); mathematics (MA). *Program availability:* Part-time, evening/weekend. *Degree requirements:* For master's, thesis optional; for doctorate, thesis/dissertation. *Entrance requirements:* For master's, GRE (for teaching assistantships), 2 letters of recommendation; C programming, C++ or Java (for computer science); for doctorate, GRE General Test, 3 letters of recommendation. Additional exam requirements/recommendations for international students: Required—TOEFL (minimum score 550 paper-based; 79 iBT), IELTS (minimum score 6.5). Electronic applications accepted. *Faculty research:* Probability and statistics; algebra, geometry, and topology; evolutionary computation; computer graphics and image manipulations; networking and communications; computational mathematics; biological data.

University of Montana, Graduate School, College of Humanities and Sciences, Department of Computer Science, Missoula, MT 59812. Offers MS. *Program availability:* Part-time. *Degree requirements:* For master's, project or thesis. *Entrance requirements:* For master's, GRE General Test. Additional exam requirements/recommendations for international students: Required—TOEFL (minimum score 525 paper-based). *Faculty research:* Parallel and distributed systems, neural networks, genetic algorithms, machine learning, data visualization, artificial intelligence.

University of Nebraska at Omaha, Graduate Studies, College of Information Science and Technology, Department of Computer Science, Omaha, NE 68182. Offers artificial intelligence (Certificate); communication networks (Certificate); computer science (MA, MS); computer science education (MS, Certificate); software engineering (Certificate); system and architecture (Certificate). *Program availability:* Part-time, evening/weekend.

Degree requirements: For master's, comprehensive exam, thesis (for some programs). *Entrance requirements:* For master's, GRE General Test, minimum GPA of 3.0, prior course work in computer science, official transcripts, resume, 2 letters of recommendation; for Certificate, minimum GPA of 3.0, resume. Additional exam requirements/recommendations for international students: Required—TOEFL, IELTS, PTE. Electronic applications accepted.

University of Nebraska–Lincoln, Graduate College, College of Arts and Sciences and College of Engineering, Department of Computer Science and Engineering, Lincoln, NE 68588. Offers bioinformatics (MS, PhD); computer engineering (MS, PhD); computer science (MS, PhD); information technology (PhD). *Degree requirements:* For master's, thesis optional; for doctorate, comprehensive exam, thesis/dissertation. *Entrance requirements:* For master's and doctorate, GRE General Test. Additional exam requirements/recommendations for international students: Required—TOEFL (minimum score 600 paper-based). Electronic applications accepted. *Faculty research:* Software engineering, geo- and bio-informatics, scientific computation, secure communication.

University of Nevada, Reno, Graduate School, College of Engineering, Department of Computer Science and Engineering, Reno, NV 89557. Offers MS, PhD. Terminal master's awarded for partial completion of doctoral program. *Degree requirements:* For master's, thesis optional; for doctorate, thesis/dissertation. *Entrance requirements:* For master's, GRE General Test, minimum GPA of 2.75; for doctorate, GRE General Test, minimum GPA of 3.0. Additional exam requirements/recommendations for international students: Required—TOEFL (minimum score 500 paper-based; 61 iBT), IELTS (minimum score 6). Electronic applications accepted. *Faculty research:* Evolutionary computing systems, computer vision/virtual reality, software engineering.

University of New Brunswick Fredericton, School of Graduate Studies, Faculty of Computer Science, Fredericton, NB E3B 5A3, Canada. Offers M Sc CS, PhD. *Program availability:* Part-time. *Degree requirements:* For master's, thesis; for doctorate, comprehensive exam, thesis/dissertation, qualifying exam. *Entrance requirements:* For master's, minimum GPA of 3.0; undergraduate degree with sufficient computer science background; for doctorate, research-based master's degree in computer science or related area. Additional exam requirements/recommendations for international students: Required—TOEFL (minimum score 550 paper-based; 80 iBT), IELTS (minimum score 7), TWE (minimum score 4.5), Michigan English Language Assessment Battery (minimum score 85) or CanTest (minimum score 4.5). Electronic applications accepted. *Faculty research:* Computer hardware, software engineering, embedded systems, e-business, e-learning, security, artificial intelligence, bioinformatics, computer-assisted drug design, high performance computing, Web services.

University of New Hampshire, Graduate School, College of Engineering and Physical Sciences, Department of Computer Science, Durham, NH 03824. Offers MS, PhD. *Program availability:* Part-time, evening/weekend. *Entrance requirements:* For master's and doctorate, GRE General Test. Additional exam requirements/recommendations for international students: Required—TOEFL (minimum score 550 paper-based; 80 iBT), IELTS (minimum score 6.5). Electronic applications accepted.

University of New Haven, Graduate School, Tagliatela College of Engineering, Program in Computer Science, West Haven, CT 06516. Offers computer programming (Graduate Certificate); computer science (MS); network systems (MS); software development (MS). *Program availability:* Part-time, evening/weekend. *Students:* 107 full-time (36 women), 26 part-time (7 women); includes 11 minority (2 Black or African American, non-Hispanic/Latino; 7 Asian, non-Hispanic/Latino; 1 Hispanic/Latino; 1 Two or more races, non-Hispanic/Latino), 104 international. Average age 26. 560 applicants, 61% accepted, 26 enrolled. In 2018, 41 master's awarded. *Degree requirements:* For master's, thesis or alternative. *Entrance requirements:* Additional exam requirements/recommendations for international students: Required—TOEFL (minimum score 75 iBT), IELTS, PTE (minimum score 50). *Application deadline:* Applications are processed on a rolling basis. Application fee: $50. Electronic applications accepted. Application fee is waived when completed online. *Expenses: Tuition:* Full-time $16,470; part-time $915 per credit hour. *Required fees:* $230; $95 per term. *Financial support:* Research assistantships with partial tuition reimbursements, teaching assistantships with partial tuition reimbursements, career-related internships or fieldwork, Federal Work-Study, scholarships/grants, and unspecified assistantships available. Support available to part-time students. Financial award applicants required to submit FAFSA. *Unit head:* Dr. David Eggert, Associate Professor, 203-932-7097, E-mail: deggert@newhaven.edu. *Application contact:* Selina O'Toole, Senior Associate Director of Graduate Admissions, 203-932-7337, E-mail: sotoole@newhaven.edu.
Website: https://www.newhaven.edu/engineering/graduate-programs/computer-science/

University of New Mexico, Graduate Studies, School of Engineering, Program in Computer Science, Albuquerque, NM 87131-2039. Offers MS, PhD. *Program availability:* Part-time. Terminal master's awarded for partial completion of doctoral program. *Entrance requirements:* For master's and doctorate, GRE General Test, minimum GPA of 3.0. Additional exam requirements/recommendations for international students: Required—TOEFL (minimum score 550 paper-based; 79 iBT), IELTS (minimum score 6.5). Electronic applications accepted. *Faculty research:* Artificial life, genetic algorithms, computer security, complexity theory, interactive computer graphics, operating systems and networking, biology and computation, machine learning, automated reasoning, quantum computation.

University of New Orleans, Graduate School, College of Sciences, Department of Computer Science, New Orleans, LA 70148. Offers MS, PhD. *Entrance requirements:* For master's, GRE General Test. Additional exam requirements/recommendations for international students: Required—TOEFL (minimum score 550 paper-based; 79 iBT), IELTS (minimum score 6.5). Electronic applications accepted.

The University of North Carolina at Chapel Hill, Graduate School, College of Arts and Sciences, Department of Computer Science, Chapel Hill, NC 27599. Offers MS, PhD. *Program availability:* Part-time, online learning. Terminal master's awarded for partial completion of doctoral program. *Degree requirements:* For master's, comprehensive exam, thesis or alternative, programming product; for doctorate, comprehensive exam, thesis/dissertation, programming product, teaching requirement. *Entrance requirements:* For master's and doctorate, GRE General Test, minimum GPA of 3.0. Additional exam requirements/recommendations for international students: Required—TOEFL (minimum score 575 paper-based). Electronic applications accepted. *Faculty research:* Bioinformatics, graphics, hardware, systems, theory.

The University of North Carolina at Charlotte, College of Computing and Informatics, Department of Computer Science, Charlotte, NC 28223-0001. Offers computer science (MS). *Program availability:* Part-time, evening/weekend. *Students:* 306 full-time (110 women), 97 part-time (38 women); includes 21 minority (2 Black or African American, non-Hispanic/Latino; 16 Asian, non-Hispanic/Latino; 2 Hispanic/Latino; 1 Two or more races, non-Hispanic/Latino), 360 international. Average age 24. 1,149 applicants, 62% accepted, 222 enrolled. In 2018, 243 master's awarded. *Entrance requirements:* For master's, GRE General Test, knowledge of two higher languages, data structures, algorithm analysis, operating systems or computer architecture, and two additional upper-division computer science courses; knowledge of calculus, discrete mathematics, and linear algebra; minimum undergraduate GPA of 3.0. Additional exam requirements/

recommendations for international students: Required—TOEFL (minimum score 523 paper-based; 70 iBT), IELTS (minimum score 6), TOEFL (minimum score 523 paper-based, 70 iBT) or IELTS (6). *Application deadline:* Applications are processed on a rolling basis. Application fee: $75. Electronic applications accepted. *Expenses:* Contact institution. *Financial support:* Fellowships, research assistantships, teaching assistantships, career-related internships or fieldwork, Federal Work-Study, institutionally sponsored loans, scholarships/grants, unspecified assistantships, and administrative assistantships available. Support available to part-time students. Financial award application deadline: 3/1; financial award applicants required to submit FAFSA. *Total annual research expenditures:* $2.3 million. *Unit head:* Dr. Bojan Cukic, Chair, 704-687-6155, E-mail: bcukic@uncc.edu. *Application contact:* Kathy B. Giddings, Director of Graduate Admissions, 704-687-3366, Fax: 704-687-3279, E-mail: gradadm@uncc.edu.
Website: http://cs.uncc.edu/

The University of North Carolina at Charlotte, College of Computing and Informatics, Program in Computing and Information Systems, Charlotte, NC 28223-0001. Offers computing and information systems (PhD), including bioinformatics, business information systems and operations management, computer science, interdisciplinary, software and information systems. *Students:* 99 full-time (27 women), 18 part-time (5 women); includes 4 minority (1 Black or African American, non-Hispanic/Latino; 1 Asian, non-Hispanic/Latino; 1 Hispanic/Latino; 1 Two or more races, non-Hispanic/Latino), 90 international. Average age 30. 86 applicants, 33% accepted, 15 enrolled. In 2018, 17 doctorates awarded. *Entrance requirements:* For doctorate, GRE or GMAT, baccalaureate degree, minimum GPA of 3.0 on courses related to the chosen field of PhD study, essay, reference letters. Additional exam requirements/recommendations for international students: Required—TOEFL (minimum score 523 paper-based; 70 iBT), IELTS (minimum score 6), TOEFL (minimum score 523 paper-based, 70 iBT) or IELTS (6). *Application deadline:* Applications are processed on a rolling basis. Application fee: $75. Electronic applications accepted. Tuition and fees vary according to course load and program. *Financial support:* Career-related internships or fieldwork, institutionally sponsored loans, scholarships/grants, health care benefits, and unspecified assistantships available. Support available to part-time students. Financial award applicants required to submit FAFSA. *Unit head:* Dr. Fatma Mili, Dean, 704-687-8450. *Application contact:* Kathy B. Giddings, Director of Graduate Admissions, 704-687-5503, Fax: 704-687-1668, E-mail: gradadm@uncc.edu.

The University of North Carolina at Greensboro, Graduate School, College of Arts and Sciences, Department of Computer Science, Greensboro, NC 27412-5001. Offers MS.

The University of North Carolina Wilmington, Interdisciplinary Program in Computer Science and Information Systems, Wilmington, NC 28403-3297. Offers computer science and information systems (MS); data science (MS). *Degree requirements:* For master's, thesis or alternative, research project. *Entrance requirements:* For master's, GMAT or GRE, 3 letters of recommendation, resume, statement of interest; baccalaureate degree in a computational field preferred (for data science). Additional exam requirements/recommendations for international students: Required—TOEFL (minimum score 550 paper-based; 79 iBT), IELTS (minimum score 6.5). Electronic applications accepted. *Expenses:* Contact institution.

University of North Dakota, Graduate School, John D. Odegard School of Aerospace Sciences, Department of Computer Science, Grand Forks, ND 58202. Offers MS. *Program availability:* Part-time. *Degree requirements:* For master's, comprehensive exam, thesis or alternative. *Entrance requirements:* For master's, GRE General Test, minimum GPA of 3.0. Additional exam requirements/recommendations for international students: Required—TOEFL (minimum score 550 paper-based; 79 iBT), IELTS (minimum score 6.5). Electronic applications accepted. *Faculty research:* Operating systems, simulation, parallel computation, hypermedia, graph theory.

University of Northern British Columbia, Office of Graduate Studies, Prince George, BC V2N 4Z9, Canada. Offers business administration (Diploma); community health science (M Sc); disability management (MA); education (M Ed); first nations studies (MA); gender studies (MA); history (MA); interdisciplinary studies (MA); international studies (MA); mathematical, computer and physical sciences (M Sc); natural resources and environmental studies (M Sc, MA, MNRES, PhD); political science (MA); psychology (M Sc, PhD); social work (MSW). *Program availability:* Part-time, evening/weekend, online learning. *Degree requirements:* For master's, thesis; for doctorate, thesis/dissertation. *Entrance requirements:* For master's, GRE, minimum B average in undergraduate course work; for doctorate, candidacy exam, minimum A average in graduate course work.

University of North Florida, College of Computing, Engineering, and Construction, School of Computing, Jacksonville, FL 32224. Offers computer science (MS); information systems (MS); software engineering (MS). *Program availability:* Part-time. *Faculty:* 13 full-time (1 woman). *Students:* 14 full-time (4 women), 35 part-time (9 women); includes 14 minority (1 Black or African American, non-Hispanic/Latino; 8 Asian, non-Hispanic/Latino; 3 Hispanic/Latino; 2 Two or more races, non-Hispanic/Latino), 8 international. Average age 33. 33 applicants, 45% accepted, 11 enrolled. In 2018, 48 master's awarded. *Degree requirements:* For master's, thesis. *Entrance requirements:* For master's, GRE General Test, minimum GPA of 3.0 in last 60 hours of course work. Additional exam requirements/recommendations for international students: Required—TOEFL (minimum score 500 paper-based; 61 iBT). *Application deadline:* For fall admission, 8/1 priority date for domestic students, 5/1 for international students; for spring admission, 12/1 priority date for domestic students, 10/1 for international students; for summer admission, 3/15 priority date for domestic students, 2/1 for international students. Application fee: $30. Electronic applications accepted. *Expenses: Tuition, area resident:* Part-time $408.10 per credit hour. *Tuition, state resident:* part-time $408.10 per credit hour. *Tuition, nonresident:* part-time $932.61 per credit hour. *Required fees:* $111.81 per credit hour. Tuition and fees vary according to course load, campus/location and program. *Financial support:* In 2018–19, 8 students received support, including 6 research assistantships (averaging $3,134 per year), 1 teaching assistantship (averaging $2,666 per year); Federal Work-Study, scholarships/grants, and unspecified assistantships also available. Financial award application deadline: 4/1; financial award applicants required to submit FAFSA. *Total annual research expenditures:* $86,396. *Unit head:* Dr. Sherif Elfayoumy, Director/Professor, 904-620-2985, E-mail: selfayou@unf.edu. *Application contact:* Dr. Amanda Pascale, Director, The Graduate School, 904-620-1360, Fax: 904-620-1362, E-mail: graduateschool@unf.edu.
Website: http://www.unf.edu/ccec/computing/

University of North Texas, Toulouse Graduate School, Denton, TX 76203-5459. Offers accounting (MS); applied anthropology (MA, MS); applied behavior analysis (Certificate); applied geography (MA); applied technology and performance improvement (M Ed, MS); art education (MA); art history (MA); arts leadership (Certificate); audiology (Au D); behavior analysis (MS); behavioral science (PhD); biochemistry and molecular biology (MS); biology (MA, MS); biomedical engineering (MS); business analysis (MS); chemistry (MS); clinical health psychology (PhD); communication studies (MA, MS); computer engineering (MS); computer science (MS); counseling (M Ed, MS), including clinical mental health counseling (MS), college and university counseling, elementary school counseling, secondary school counseling; creative writing (MA); criminal justice (MS); curriculum and instruction (M Ed); decision sciences (MBA); design (MA, MFA), including fashion design (MFA), innovation studies, interior design (MFA); early childhood studies (MS); economics (MS); educational leadership (M Ed, Ed D); educational psychology (MS, PhD), including family studies (MS), gifted and talented (MS), human development (MS), learning and cognition (MS), research, measurement and evaluation (MS); electrical engineering (MS); emergency management (MPA); engineering technology (MS); English (MA); English as a second language (MA); environmental science (MS); finance (MBA, MS); financial management (MPA); French (MA); health services management (MBA); higher education (M Ed, Ed D); history (MA, MS); hospitality management (MS); human resources management (MPA); information science (MS); information systems (PhD); information technologies (MBA); interdisciplinary studies (MA, MS); international studies (MA); international sustainable tourism (MS); jazz studies (MM); journalism (MA, MJ, Graduate Certificate), including interactive and virtual digital communication (Graduate Certificate), narrative journalism (Graduate Certificate), public relations (Graduate Certificate); kinesiology (MS); linguistics (MA); local government management (MPA); logistics (PhD); logistics and supply chain management (MBA); long-term care, senior housing, and aging services (MA); management (PhD); marketing (MBA); mathematics (MA, MS); mechanical and energy engineering (MS, PhD); music (MA), including ethnomusicology, music theory, musicology, performance; music composition (PhD); music education (MM Ed, PhD); nonprofit management (MPA); operations and supply chain management (MBA); performance (MM, DMA); philosophy (MA); political science (MA); professional and technical communication (MA); radio, television and film (MA, MFA); rehabilitation counseling (Certificate); sociology (MA); Spanish (MA); special education (M Ed); speech-language pathology (MA); strategic management (MBA); studio art (MFA); teaching (M Ed); MBA/MS. *Program availability:* Part-time, evening/weekend, online learning. Terminal master's awarded for partial completion of doctoral program. *Degree requirements:* For master's, variable foreign language requirement, comprehensive exam (for some programs), thesis (for some programs); for doctorate, variable foreign language requirement, comprehensive exam (for some programs), thesis/dissertation; for other advanced degree, variable foreign language requirement, comprehensive exam (for some programs). *Entrance requirements:* For master's and doctorate, GRE, GMAT. Additional exam requirements/recommendations for international students: Required—TOEFL (minimum score 550 paper-based; 79 iBT). Electronic applications accepted.

University of Notre Dame, The Graduate School, College of Engineering, Department of Computer Science and Engineering, Notre Dame, IN 46556. Offers MSCSE, PhD. Terminal master's awarded for partial completion of doctoral program. *Degree requirements:* For master's, comprehensive exam; for doctorate, thesis/dissertation, candidacy exam. *Entrance requirements:* For master's and doctorate, GRE General Test. Additional exam requirements/recommendations for international students: Required—TOEFL (minimum score 600 paper-based; 80 iBT). Electronic applications accepted. *Faculty research:* Algorithms and theory of computer science, artificial intelligence, behavior-based robotics, biometrics, computer vision.

University of Oregon, Graduate School, College of Arts and Sciences, Department of Computer and Information Science, Eugene, OR 97403. Offers MA, MS, PhD. *Program availability:* Part-time. Terminal master's awarded for partial completion of doctoral program. *Degree requirements:* For doctorate, thesis/dissertation. *Entrance requirements:* For master's and doctorate, GRE General Test, minimum GPA of 3.0. Additional exam requirements/recommendations for international students: Required—TOEFL. *Faculty research:* Artificial intelligence, graphics, natural-language processing, expert systems, operating systems.

University of Ottawa, Faculty of Graduate and Postdoctoral Studies, Faculty of Engineering, Ottawa-Carleton Institute for Computer Science, Ottawa, ON K1N 6N5, Canada. Offers MCS, PhD. MCS, PhD offered jointly with Carleton University. *Degree requirements:* For master's, thesis or alternative; for doctorate, comprehensive exam, thesis/dissertation, two seminars. *Entrance requirements:* For master's, honors degree or equivalent, minimum B average; for doctorate, minimum B+ average. Electronic applications accepted. *Faculty research:* Knowledge-based and intelligent systems, algorithms, parallel and distributed systems.

University of Pennsylvania, School of Engineering and Applied Science, Department of Computer and Information Science, Philadelphia, PA 19104. Offers computer and information science (MSE, PhD); computer and information technology (MCIT); computer graphics and game technology (MSE). *Program availability:* Part-time. *Students:* Average age 26. 2,559 applicants, 14% accepted, 216 enrolled. In 2018, 130 master's, 15 doctorates awarded. Terminal master's awarded for partial completion of doctoral program. *Degree requirements:* For master's, comprehensive exam, thesis optional; for doctorate, comprehensive exam, thesis/dissertation. *Entrance requirements:* For master's and doctorate, GRE, bachelor's degree, letters of recommendation, resume, personal statement. Additional exam requirements/recommendations for international students: Required—TOEFL (minimum score 100 iBT), IELTS (minimum score 7). *Application deadline:* For fall admission, 12/15 priority date for domestic and international students. Application fee: $80. Electronic applications accepted. *Expenses:* Contact institution. *Faculty research:* Artificial intelligence, bioinformatics and computational biology, embedded and real-time systems, machine learning, security and information assurance. *Application contact:* William Fenton, Assistant Director of Graduate Admissions, 215-898-4542, Fax: 215-573-5577, E-mail: gradstudies@seas.upenn.edu.
Website: http://www.cis.upenn.edu/prospective-students/graduate/

University of Pittsburgh, School of Computing and Information, Department of Computer Science, Pittsburgh, PA 15260. Offers MS, PhD. *Program availability:* Part-time, evening/weekend, online learning. *Degree requirements:* For master's, thesis optional; for doctorate, comprehensive exam, thesis/dissertation, preliminary exam. *Entrance requirements:* For master's, GRE General Test, BS, minimum B average; for doctorate, GRE General Test. Additional exam requirements/recommendations for international students: Required—TOEFL (minimum score 90 iBT), IELTS (minimum score 7), GRE. Electronic applications accepted. *Expenses:* Contact institution. *Faculty research:* Artificial intelligence, mobile interfaces and pedagogical systems, machine learning and user modeling, power aware computing, green computing, real-time and embedded systems, cloud and high performance computing.

University of Portland, Shiley School of Engineering, Portland, OR 97203-5798. Offers biomedical engineering (MBME); civil engineering (ME); computer science (ME); electrical engineering (ME); mechanical engineering (ME). *Program availability:* Part-time, evening/weekend. *Students:* 12 full-time (4 women), 2 part-time (both women); includes 1 minority (Black or African American, non-Hispanic/Latino), 2 international. Average age 24. 43 applicants, 49% accepted, 10 enrolled. In 2018, 6 master's awarded. *Degree requirements:* For master's, thesis optional. *Entrance requirements:* For master's, GRE General Test, minimum GPA of 3.0, 2 letters of recommendation, resume, statement of goals, official transcripts. Additional exam requirements/recommendations for international students: Required—TOEFL (minimum score 80 iBT), IELTS (minimum score 7). *Application deadline:* For fall admission, 7/15 priority date for domestic and international students; for spring admission, 12/15 priority date for

domestic and international students; for summer admission, 4/15 for domestic and international students. Applications are processed on a rolling basis. Electronic applications accepted. *Expenses:* $1,326 per credit plus $50 professional tuition per credit. *Financial support:* Research assistantships, career-related internships or fieldwork, Federal Work-Study, and scholarships/grants available. Support available to part-time students. Financial award application deadline: 3/1; financial award applicants required to submit FAFSA. *Unit head:* Dr. Matthew Kuhn, Dean, 503-943-7361, E-mail: kuhn@up.edu. *Application contact:* Caitlin Biddulph, Graduate Programs and Admissions Specialist, 503-943-7107.
Website: http://engineering.up.edu/default.aspx?cid-6464&pid-2432

University of Puerto Rico–Mayagüez, Graduate Studies, College of Engineering, Computer Science and Engineering Program, Mayagüez, PR 00681-9000. Offers PhD. *Program availability:* Part-time. *Degree requirements:* For doctorate, one foreign language, comprehensive exam, thesis/dissertation. *Entrance requirements:* For doctorate, GRE General Test, BS in engineering or science; undergraduate courses in data structures, programming language, calculus III and linear algebra, or the equivalent. Electronic applications accepted. *Faculty research:* Big data analysis, parallel and distributor processing, mobile computing and networking, remote sensing, channel capacity.

University of Puerto Rico–Mayagüez, Graduate Studies, College of Engineering, Department of Electrical and Computer Engineering, Mayagüez, PR 00681-9000. Offers computer engineering (ME, MS); computing and information sciences and engineering (PhD); electrical engineering (ME, MS). *Program availability:* Part-time. Terminal master's awarded for partial completion of doctoral program. *Degree requirements:* For master's, one foreign language, comprehensive exam, thesis; for doctorate, one foreign language, comprehensive exam, thesis/dissertation. *Entrance requirements:* For master's and doctorate, proficiency in English and Spanish; BS in electrical or computer engineering, or equivalent; minimum GPA of 3.0. Electronic applications accepted. *Faculty research:* Digital signal processing, power electronics, microwave ocean emissivity, parallel and distributed computing, microwave remote sensing.

University of Regina, Faculty of Graduate Studies and Research, Faculty of Science, Department of Computer Science, Regina, SK S4S 0A2, Canada. Offers M Sc, PhD. *Program availability:* Part-time. *Faculty:* 18 full-time (5 women), 9 part-time/adjunct (0 women). *Students:* 138 full-time (46 women), 16 part-time (5 women). Average age 30. 411 applicants, 21% accepted, 20 enrolled. In 2018, 12 master's, 4 doctorates awarded. *Degree requirements:* For master's, thesis (for some programs), project, report; for doctorate, thesis/dissertation. *Entrance requirements:* For master's, 4 years bachelor degree in Computer science or related program; for doctorate, applicants must have obtained a thesis-based master's degree in the discipline to qualify as a doctoral student. Applicants must have academic credentials consistent with being fully-qualified to undertake graduate work at the doctoral level. Additional exam requirements/recommendations for international students: Required—TOEFL (minimum score 580 paper-based; 80 iBT), IELTS (minimum score 6.5), PTE (minimum score 59), options are CAEL, MELAB, Cantest and U of R ESL. *Application deadline:* For fall admission, 3/15 for domestic and international students; for winter admission, 7/15 for domestic and international students; for spring admission, 11/15 for domestic and international students. Application fee: $100. Electronic applications accepted. Tuition and fees vary according to course level, course load, degree level and program. *Financial support:* Fellowships, research assistantships, teaching assistantships, career-related internships or fieldwork, Federal Work-Study, scholarships/grants, unspecified assistantships, and travel award & Graduate Scholarship Base Funds available. Financial award application deadline: 9/30. *Faculty research:* Information retrieval, machine learning, computer visualization, theory and application of rough sets, human-computer interaction. *Unit head:* Dr. David Gerhard, Department Head, 306-585-5227, Fax: 306-585-4745, E-mail: gerhard@cs.uregina.ca. *Application contact:* Dr. Orland Hoeber, Graduate Program Coordinator, 306-585-4598, Fax: 306-585-4745, E-mail: gscoord@cs.uregina.ca.
Website: http://www.cs.uregina.ca

University of Rhode Island, Graduate School, College of Arts and Sciences, Department of Computer Science and Statistics, Kingston, RI 02881. Offers computer science (MS, PhD); cyber security (PSM, Graduate Certificate); digital forensics (Graduate Certificate). *Program availability:* Part-time, evening/weekend, 100% online, blended/hybrid learning. *Faculty:* 18 full-time (5 women). *Students:* 27 full-time (15 women), 98 part-time (22 women); includes 16 minority (3 Black or African American, non-Hispanic/Latino; 5 Asian, non-Hispanic/Latino; 8 Hispanic/Latino), 14 international. 78 applicants, 88% accepted, 50 enrolled. In 2018, 34 master's, 2 doctorates, 23 other advanced degrees awarded. Terminal master's awarded for partial completion of doctoral program. *Entrance requirements:* Additional exam requirements/recommendations for international students: Required—TOEFL. *Application deadline:* For fall admission, 7/15 for domestic students, 2/1 for international students; for spring admission, 11/15 for domestic students, 7/15 for international students. Application fee: $65. Electronic applications accepted. *Expenses: Tuition, area resident:* Full-time $13,226; part-time $735 per credit. Tuition, state resident: full-time $13,226; part-time $735 per credit. Tuition, nonresident: full-time $25,854; part-time $1436 per credit. *International tuition:* $25,854 full-time. *Required fees:* $1698; $50 per credit. $35 per semester. One-time fee: $165. *Financial support:* In 2018–19, 1 research assistantship with tuition reimbursement (averaging $8,862 per year), 12 teaching assistantships with tuition reimbursements (averaging $16,443 per year) were awarded; unspecified assistantships also available. Financial award application deadline: 2/1; financial award applicants required to submit FAFSA. *Unit head:* Dr. Lisa DiPippo, Chair, 401-874-2701, Fax: 401-874-4617, E-mail: dipippo@cs.uri.edu. *Application contact:* Lutz Hamel, Graduate Program Director, 401-874-2701, E-mail: lutzhamel@uri.edu.
Website: http://www.cs.uri.edu/

University of Rochester, Hajim School of Engineering and Applied Sciences, Department of Computer Science, Rochester, NY 14627. Offers algorithms and complexity (MS); artificial intelligence and machine learning (MS); computer architecture (MS); computer science (PhD); human computer interaction (MS); natural language processing (MS); programming languages and computer systems (MS). *Faculty:* 18 full-time (1 woman). *Students:* 125 full-time (20 women); includes 7 minority (2 Black or African American, non-Hispanic/Latino; 4 Asian, non-Hispanic/Latino; 1 Two or more races, non-Hispanic/Latino), 103 international. Average age 26. 868 applicants, 16% accepted, 44 enrolled. In 2018, 41 master's, 8 doctorates awarded. Terminal master's awarded for partial completion of doctoral program. *Degree requirements:* For master's, comprehensive exam (for some programs), thesis (for some programs); for doctorate, comprehensive exam, thesis/dissertation, qualifying exam. *Entrance requirements:* For master's and doctorate, GRE General Test, personal statement, transcripts, three letters of recommendation. Additional exam requirements/recommendations for international students: Required—TOEFL, IELTS. *Application deadline:* For fall admission, 1/15 for domestic and international students. Application fee: $60. Electronic applications accepted. *Expenses: Tuition:* Full-time $52,974; part-time $1654 per credit hour. *Required fees:* $612. One-time fee: $30 part-time. Tuition and fees vary according to campus/location and program. *Financial support:* In 2018–19, 68 students received support, including 3 fellowships with full tuition reimbursements available (averaging $33,336 per year), 51 research assistantships with full tuition reimbursements available (averaging $30,720 per year), 14 teaching assistantships with full tuition reimbursements available (averaging $30,720 per year); scholarships/grants, traineeships, health care benefits, and tuition waivers (full and partial) also available. Financial award application deadline: 12/15. *Faculty research:* Artificial intelligence, human-computer interaction, systems research, theory research. *Total annual research expenditures:* $4.1 million. *Unit head:* Sandhya Dwarkadas, Professor and Chair, 585-275-5647, E-mail: sandhya@cs.rochester.edu. *Application contact:* Michelle Kiso, Graduate Coordinator, 585-275-7737, E-mail: mkiso@cs.rochester.edu.
Website: https://www.cs.rochester.edu/graduate/index.html

University of San Francisco, College of Arts and Sciences, Computer Science Program, San Francisco, CA 94117. Offers MS. *Program availability:* Part-time. *Students:* 102 full-time (34 women), 3 part-time (0 women); includes 16 minority (1 Black or African American, non-Hispanic/Latino; 14 Asian, non-Hispanic/Latino; 1 Hispanic/Latino), 79 international. Average age 26. 275 applicants, 35% accepted, 27 enrolled. In 2018, 32 master's awarded. *Degree requirements:* For master's, thesis optional. *Entrance requirements:* For master's, GRE General Test, GRE Subject Test, BS in computer science or related field. Additional exam requirements/recommendations for international students: Required—TOEFL (minimum score 79 iBT), IELTS (minimum score 6.5), PTE (minimum score 53). *Application deadline:* For fall admission, 3/1 for domestic and international students. Applications are processed on a rolling basis. Application fee: $55. Electronic applications accepted. *Financial support:* In 2018–19, 16 students received support. Fellowships with partial tuition reimbursements available, teaching assistantships, career-related internships or fieldwork, and scholarships/grants available. Financial award applicants required to submit FAFSA. *Faculty research:* Software engineering, computer graphics, computer networks. *Unit head:* Gian Bruno, Graduate Director, 415-422-5247, E-mail: gbruno@usfca.edu. *Application contact:* Information Contact, 415-422-5101, E-mail: asgraduate@usfca.edu.
Website: https://www.usfca.edu/arts-sciences/graduate-programs/computer-science

University of Saskatchewan, College of Graduate and Postdoctoral Studies, College of Arts and Science, Department of Computer Science, Saskatoon, SK S7N 5A2, Canada. Offers M Sc, PhD. *Degree requirements:* For master's, thesis; for doctorate, comprehensive exam (for some programs), thesis/dissertation. *Entrance requirements:* For master's and doctorate, GRE. Additional exam requirements/recommendations for international students: Required—TOEFL (minimum score 80 iBT); Recommended—IELTS (minimum score 6.5). Electronic applications accepted.

University of South Alabama, School of Computing, Mobile, AL 36688. Offers computer science (MS); information systems (MS). *Program availability:* Part-time, evening/weekend. *Degree requirements:* For master's, comprehensive exam, project, thesis, or coursework only with additional credit hours earned; for doctorate, comprehensive exam, thesis/dissertation, minimum GPA of 3.0. *Entrance requirements:* For master's, GRE General Test, undergraduate degree, official transcripts, three letters of recommendation, statement of purpose; for doctorate, GRE, master's degree in related discipline, minimum graduate GPA of 3.5, statement of purpose, three letters of recommendation, curriculum vitae, official transcripts. Additional exam requirements/recommendations for international students: Required—TOEFL (minimum score 525 paper-based; 71 iBT). Electronic applications accepted. *Faculty research:* Artificial intelligence, big data/data mining, STEM education, visual analytics.

University of South Carolina, The Graduate School, College of Engineering and Computing, Department of Computer Science and Engineering, Columbia, SC 29208. Offers computer science and engineering (ME, MS, PhD); software engineering (MS). *Program availability:* Part-time, evening/weekend, online learning. *Degree requirements:* For master's, comprehensive exam, thesis (for some programs); for doctorate, comprehensive exam, thesis/dissertation. *Entrance requirements:* For master's and doctorate, GRE General Test. Additional exam requirements/recommendations for international students: Required—TOEFL (minimum score 570 paper-based). Electronic applications accepted. *Faculty research:* Computer security, computer vision, artificial intelligence, multiagent systems, bioinformatics.

University of South Dakota, Graduate School, College of Arts and Sciences, Department of Computer Science, Vermillion, SD 57069. Offers MS. *Program availability:* Part-time. *Degree requirements:* For master's, thesis optional. *Entrance requirements:* For master's, GRE General Test, GRE Subject Test (recommended), minimum GPA of 2.7. Additional exam requirements/recommendations for international students: Required—TOEFL (minimum score 550 paper-based; 79 iBT). Electronic applications accepted.

University of Southern California, Graduate School, Viterbi School of Engineering, Department of Computer Science, Los Angeles, CA 90089. Offers computer networks (MS); computer science (MS, PhD); computer security (MS); game development (MS); high performance computing and simulations (MS); human language technology (MS); intelligent robotics (MS); multimedia and creative technologies (MS); software engineering (MS). *Program availability:* Part-time, evening/weekend, online learning. *Entrance requirements:* For master's and doctorate, GRE General Test. Additional exam requirements/recommendations for international students: Required—TOEFL. Electronic applications accepted. *Faculty research:* Databases, computer graphics and computer vision, software engineering, networks and security, robotics, multimedia and virtual reality.

University of Southern Maine, College of Science, Technology, and Health, Department of Computer Science, Portland, ME 04103. Offers computer science (MS); software systems (CGS). *Program availability:* Part-time. *Degree requirements:* For master's, thesis. *Entrance requirements:* For master's, GRE General Test, minimum GPA of 3.0. Additional exam requirements/recommendations for international students: Required—TOEFL. Electronic applications accepted. *Faculty research:* Software engineering, database systems, formal methods, object-oriented technology, artificial intelligence, bioinformatics, data analysis and data mining, health information systems.

University of Southern Mississippi, College of Arts and Sciences, School of Computing Sciences and Computer Engineering, Hattiesburg, MS 39406-0001. Offers computational science (MS, PhD); computer science (MS). *Degree requirements:* For master's, comprehensive exam, thesis; for doctorate, comprehensive exam, thesis/dissertation. *Entrance requirements:* For master's, GRE General Test, minimum GPA of 2.75 in last 60 hours; for doctorate, GRE General Test, minimum GPA of 3.5. Additional exam requirements/recommendations for international students: Required—TOEFL, IELTS. Electronic applications accepted. *Faculty research:* Satellite telecommunications, advanced life-support systems, artificial intelligence.

University of South Florida, College of Engineering, Department of Computer Science and Engineering, Tampa, FL 33620-9951. Offers computer engineering (MSCP); computer science (MSCS); computer science and engineering (PhD). *Program availability:* Part-time. *Faculty:* 33 full-time (6 women). *Students:* 177 full-time (57 women), 36 part-time (10 women); includes 30 minority (7 Black or African American, non-Hispanic/Latino; 9 Asian, non-Hispanic/Latino; 13 Hispanic/Latino; 1 Two or more races, non-Hispanic/Latino), 161 international. Average age 27. 595 applicants, 35% accepted, 64 enrolled. In 2018, 56 master's, 11 doctorates awarded. Terminal master's awarded for partial completion of doctoral program. *Degree requirements:* For master's,

comprehensive exam, thesis or alternative; for doctorate, comprehensive exam, thesis/dissertation, teaching of at least one undergraduate computer science and engineering course. *Entrance requirements:* For master's, GRE General Test, minimum GPA of 3.0, three letters of recommendation, statement of purpose, mathematical preparation; for the MSIT, evidence of completion of a defined subset of the required core courses of the USF BSIT; for doctorate, GRE General Test, minimum GPA of 3.0, three letters of recommendation, statement of purpose that includes three areas of research interest, mathematical preparation. Additional exam requirements/recommendations for international students: Required—TOEFL, TOEFL (minimum score 550 paper-based; 79 iBT) or IELTS (minimum score 6.5). *Application deadline:* For fall admission, 2/15 for domestic and international students; for spring admission, 10/15 for domestic students, 9/15 for international students. Application fee: $30. Electronic applications accepted. *Expenses:* Tuition, state resident: full-time $6350. Tuition, nonresident: full-time $19,048. *International tuition:* $19,048 full-time. *Required fees:* $2079. *Financial support:* In 2018–19, 25 students received support, including 30 research assistantships with tuition reimbursements available (averaging $14,942 per year), 35 teaching assistantships with tuition reimbursements available (averaging $14,003 per year); unspecified assistantships also available. Financial award application deadline: 1/1; financial award applicants required to submit FAFSA. *Faculty research:* Artificial intelligence/intelligence systems; computational biology and bioinformatics; computer vision and pattern recognition; databases; distributed systems; graphics; information systems (networks) and location-aware information systems; robotics (biomorphic robotics and robot perception and action); software security; VLSI, computer architecture, and parallel processing. *Total annual research expenditures:* $2.9 million. *Unit head:* Dr. Lawrence Hall, Professor and Department Chair, 813-974-4195, Fax: 813-974-5094, E-mail: hall@cse.usf.edu. *Application contact:* Dr. Yu Sun, Graduate Program Director, 813-974-7508, E-mail: yusun@usf.edu.
Website: http://www.cse.usf.edu/

The University of Tennessee, Graduate School, College of Arts and Sciences, Department of Computer Science, Knoxville, TN 37996. Offers MS, PhD. *Program availability:* Part-time. *Degree requirements:* For master's, thesis or alternative; for doctorate, thesis/dissertation. *Entrance requirements:* For master's and doctorate, GRE General Test, minimum GPA of 2.7. Additional exam requirements/recommendations for international students: Required—TOEFL. Electronic applications accepted.

The University of Tennessee, Graduate School, Tickle College of Engineering, Min H. Kao Department of Electrical Engineering and Computer Science, Program in Computer Science, Knoxville, TN 37996. Offers MS, PhD. *Program availability:* Part-time. *Faculty:* 23 full-time (3 women), 5 part-time/adjunct (2 women). *Students:* 77 full-time (12 women), 11 part-time (2 women); includes 14 minority (3 Black or African American, non-Hispanic/Latino; 8 Asian, non-Hispanic/Latino; 1 Hispanic/Latino; 2 Two or more races, non-Hispanic/Latino), 31 international. Average age 27. 142 applicants, 44% accepted, 23 enrolled. In 2018, 22 master's, 1 doctorate awarded. *Degree requirements:* For master's, thesis or alternative; for doctorate, comprehensive exam, thesis/dissertation. *Entrance requirements:* For master's, GRE General Test (for MS students pursuing research thesis), minimum GPA of 2.7 (for U.S. degree holders), 3.0 (for international degree holders); 3 references; personal statement; for doctorate, GRE General Test, minimum GPA of 3.0 on previous graduate coursework; 3 references; personal statement. Additional exam requirements/recommendations for international students: Required—TOEFL (minimum score 550 paper-based; 80 iBT), IELTS (minimum score 6.5). *Application deadline:* For fall admission, 2/1 priority date for domestic and international students; for spring admission, 6/15 for domestic and international students; for summer admission, 10/15 for domestic and international students. Applications are processed on a rolling basis. Application fee: $60. Electronic applications accepted. *Financial support:* In 2018–19, 98 students received support, including 12 fellowships with full tuition reimbursements available (averaging $9,480 per year), 55 research assistantships with full tuition reimbursements available (averaging $25,996 per year), 31 teaching assistantships with full tuition reimbursements available (averaging $17,130 per year); career-related internships or fieldwork, Federal Work-Study, institutionally sponsored loans, health care benefits, and unspecified assistantships also available. Financial award application deadline: 2/1; financial award applicants required to submit FAFSA. *Unit head:* Dr. Gregory Peterson, PhD, Head, 865-974-3461, Fax: 865-974-5483, E-mail: gdp@utk.edu. *Application contact:* Dr. Jens Gregor, PhD, Associate Head, 865-974-4399, Fax: 865-974-5483, E-mail: jgregor@utk.edu.
Website: http://www.eecs.utk.edu

The University of Tennessee at Chattanooga, Program in Computer Science, Chattanooga, TN 37403. Offers biomedical informatics (Post Master's Certificate); computer science (MS). *Program availability:* Part-time. *Degree requirements:* For master's, comprehensive exam, thesis. *Entrance requirements:* For master's, GRE General Test, minimum cumulative undergraduate GPA of 2.7 or 3.0 in senior year. Additional exam requirements/recommendations for international students: Required—TOEFL (minimum score 550 paper-based; 79 iBT), IELTS (minimum score 6). Electronic applications accepted. *Expenses:* Contact institution. *Faculty research:* Power systems, computer architecture, pattern recognition, artificial intelligence, statistical data analysis.

The University of Texas at Arlington, Graduate School, College of Engineering, Department of Computer Science and Engineering, Arlington, TX 76019. Offers computer engineering (MS, PhD); computer science (MS, PhD); software engineering (MS). *Program availability:* Part-time, online learning. Terminal master's awarded for partial completion of doctoral program. *Degree requirements:* For master's, comprehensive exam (for some programs), thesis; for doctorate, comprehensive exam, thesis/dissertation. *Entrance requirements:* For master's, GRE General Test, minimum GPA of 3.0 (3.2 in computer science-related classes); for doctorate, GRE General Test, minimum GPA of 3.5. Additional exam requirements/recommendations for international students: Required—TOEFL (minimum score 550 paper-based; 92 iBT), IELTS (minimum score 6.5). *Faculty research:* Algorithms, homeland security, mobile pervasive computing, high performance computing bioinformation.

The University of Texas at Austin, Graduate School, College of Natural Sciences, Department of Computer Science, Austin, TX 78712-1111. Offers MSCS, PhD. *Program availability:* Online learning. *Degree requirements:* For master's, thesis optional; for doctorate, thesis/dissertation, oral proposal, final defense. *Entrance requirements:* For master's and doctorate, GRE General Test, GRE Subject Test, bachelor's degree in computer sciences (preferred). Additional exam requirements/recommendations for international students: Required—TOEFL. Electronic applications accepted. *Faculty research:* Artificial intelligence, distributed computing, networks, algorithms, experimental systems.

The University of Texas at Dallas, Erik Jonsson School of Engineering and Computer Science, Department of Computer Science, Richardson, TX 75080. Offers computer science (MSCS, PhD); software engineering (MS, PhD). *Program availability:* Part-time, evening/weekend. *Faculty:* 49 full-time (5 women), 23 part-time/adjunct (6 women). *Students:* 913 full-time (288 women), 291 part-time (75 women); includes 70 minority (5 Black or African American, non-Hispanic/Latino; 45 Asian, non-Hispanic/Latino; 14 Hispanic/Latino; 6 Two or more races, non-Hispanic/Latino), 1,051 international. Average age 27. 3,695 applicants, 38% accepted, 433 enrolled. In 2018, 442 master's, 16 doctorates awarded. *Degree requirements:* For master's, thesis optional; for doctorate, comprehensive exam, thesis/dissertation. *Entrance requirements:* For master's, GRE General Test, minimum GPA of 3.0 in undergraduate course work, 3.3 in quantitative course work; for doctorate, GRE General Test, minimum GPA of 3.5. Additional exam requirements/recommendations for international students: Required—TOEFL (minimum score 550 paper-based). *Application deadline:* For fall admission, 7/15 for domestic students, 5/1 priority date for international students; for spring admission, 11/15 for domestic students, 9/1 priority date for international students. Applications are processed on a rolling basis. Application fee: $50 ($100 for international students). Electronic applications accepted. *Expenses: Tuition, area resident:* Full-time $13,458. Tuition, state resident: full-time $13,458. Tuition, nonresident: full-time $26,852. *International tuition:* $26,852 full-time. Tuition and fees vary according to course load. *Financial support:* In 2018–19, 102 students received support, including 6 fellowships (averaging $1,083 per year), 83 research assistantships with partial tuition reimbursements available (averaging $23,617 per year), 76 teaching assistantships with partial tuition reimbursements available (averaging $17,325 per year); career-related internships or fieldwork, Federal Work-Study, institutionally sponsored loans, and scholarships/grants also available. Support available to part-time students. Financial award application deadline: 4/30; financial award applicants required to submit FAFSA. *Faculty research:* AI-based automated software synthesis and testing, quality of service in computer networks, wireless networks, cloud computing and IT security, speech recognition. *Unit head:* Dr. Gopal Gupta, Department Head, 972-883-4107, Fax: 972-883-2399, E-mail: gupta@utdallas.edu. *Application contact:* Dr. Gopal Gupta, Department Head, 972-883-4107, Fax: 972-883-2399, E-mail: gupta@utdallas.edu.
Website: http://cs.utdallas.edu/

The University of Texas at El Paso, Graduate School, College of Engineering, Department of Computer Science, El Paso, TX 79968-0001. Offers computer science (MS, PhD); cyber security (Graduate Certificate); information technology (MSIT); software engineering (MS). *Program availability:* Part-time, evening/weekend. *Degree requirements:* For master's, thesis optional; for doctorate, thesis/dissertation. *Entrance requirements:* For master's, GRE, minimum GPA of 3.0; for doctorate, GRE, statement of purpose, letters of reference. Additional exam requirements/recommendations for international students: Required—TOEFL; Recommended—IELTS. Electronic applications accepted.

The University of Texas at San Antonio, College of Sciences, Department of Computer Science, San Antonio, TX 78249-0617. Offers MS, PhD. *Program availability:* Part-time. Terminal master's awarded for partial completion of doctoral program. *Degree requirements:* For master's, 36 credits of coursework; thesis or comprehensive exam within 6 years; minimum GPA of 3.0; for doctorate, comprehensive exam, thesis/dissertation, continuous enrollment until time of graduation; admission to candidacy; oral examination; 90 credits of coursework and research; minimum GPA of 3.0 on all coursework. *Entrance requirements:* For master's and doctorate, GRE General Test, bachelor's degree in computer science offered by UTSA or an equivalent academic preparation from an accredited college or university in the United States or a comparable foreign institution; minimum GPA of 3.0; at least 24 semester credit hours in the area (12 of which must be at the upper-division level). Additional exam requirements/recommendations for international students: Required—TOEFL (minimum score 550 paper-based; 79 iBT), IELTS (minimum score 6.5). Electronic applications accepted. *Expenses:* Contact institution. *Faculty research:* Cyber security, cloud computing, software engineering, data science, bioinformatics and computational biology, high performance computing and storage systems, programming languages, operating systems, real-time systems, embedded computing, human-computer Interaction, augmented reality, computer vision and multimedia, wireless networks, artificial intelligence and machine learning.

The University of Texas at Tyler, Soules College of Business, Department of Computer Science, Tyler, TX 75799-0001. Offers MS. *Students:* Average age 25. 28 applicants, 68% accepted, 5 enrolled. In 2018, 10 master's awarded. *Degree requirements:* For master's, comprehensive exam, thesis optional. *Entrance requirements:* For master's, GRE General Test, previous course work in data structures and computer organization, 6 hours of course work in calculus and statistics. Additional exam requirements/recommendations for international students: Required—TOEFL. *Application deadline:* For fall admission, 6/15 priority date for domestic students, 7/1 priority date for international students; for spring admission, 10/15 priority date for domestic students, 11/1 priority date for international students. Applications are processed on a rolling basis. Application fee: $25 ($50 for international students). Electronic applications accepted. *Financial support:* In 2018–19, 5 research assistantships (averaging $2,590 per year), 5 teaching assistantships (averaging $3,090 per year) were awarded; scholarships/grants also available. Financial award application deadline: 7/1; financial award applicants required to submit FAFSA. *Faculty research:* Database design, software engineering, client-server architecture, visual programming, data mining, computer security, digital image processing, simulation and modeling, computer science education. *Total annual research expenditures:* $20,000. *Unit head:* Dr. Stephen Rainwater, Chair, 903-566-7403, E-mail: srainwater@uttyler.edu. *Application contact:* Dr. Stephen Rainwater, Chair, 903-566-7403, E-mail: srainwater@uttyler.edu.
Website: https://www.uttyler.edu/cs

The University of Texas of the Permian Basin, Office of Graduate Studies, College of Arts and Sciences, Department of Math and Computer Science, Odessa, TX 79762-0001. Offers computer science (MS). *Program availability:* Part-time, evening/weekend. *Degree requirements:* For master's, comprehensive exam, thesis or alternative. *Entrance requirements:* For master's, GRE General Test. Additional exam requirements/recommendations for international students: Required—TOEFL (minimum score 550 paper-based).

The University of Texas Rio Grande Valley, College of Engineering and Computer Science, Department of Computer Science, Edinburg, TX 78539. Offers computer science (MS); information technology (MS). *Program availability:* Part-time, evening/weekend, online learning. *Degree requirements:* For master's, comprehensive exam, thesis optional. *Entrance requirements:* For master's, GRE General Test. Additional exam requirements/recommendations for international students: Required—TOEFL (minimum score 550 paper-based, 79 iBT) or IELTS (6.5). Electronic applications accepted. *Expenses: Tuition, area resident:* Full-time $6888. Tuition, state resident: full-time $6888. Tuition, nonresident: full-time $14,484. *International tuition:* $14,484 full-time. *Required fees:* $1468. *Faculty research:* Artificial intelligence, distributed systems, Internet computing, theoretical computer sciences, information visualization.

University of the District of Columbia, School of Engineering and Applied Sciences, Program in Computer Science, Washington, DC 20008-1175. Offers MS, MSCS. *Degree requirements:* For master's, thesis optional.

The University of Toledo, College of Graduate Studies, College of Engineering, Department of Electrical Engineering and Computer Science, Toledo, OH 43606-3390. Offers computer science (MS, PhD); electrical engineering (MS, PhD). *Program availability:* Part-time, evening/weekend. *Degree requirements:* For master's, thesis or alternative; for doctorate, thesis/dissertation, qualifying exam. *Entrance requirements:* For master's, GRE General Test, minimum GPA of 3.0; for doctorate, GRE General

Test, minimum GPA of 3.3. Additional exam requirements/recommendations for international students: Required—TOEFL (minimum score 550 paper-based; 80 iBT). Electronic applications accepted. *Faculty research:* Communication and signal processing, high performance computing systems, intelligent systems, power electronics and energy systems, RF and microwave systems, sensors and medical devices, solid state devices.

University of Toronto, School of Graduate Studies, Faculty of Arts and Science, Department of Computer Science, Toronto, ON M5S 1A1, Canada. Offers applied computing (M Sc AC); computer science (M Sc, PhD). *Program availability:* Part-time. *Degree requirements:* For master's, thesis; for doctorate, thesis/dissertation, thesis defense/oral exam. *Entrance requirements:* For master's, GRE (recommended), minimum B+ average overall and in final year; resume; 3 letters of reference; background in computer science and mathematics (preferred); for doctorate, minimum B+ average overall and in final year; resume; 3 letters of reference; background in computer science and mathematics (preferred). Additional exam requirements/ recommendations for international students: Required—TOEFL (minimum score 580 paper-based), TWE (minimum score 5). Electronic applications accepted.

The University of Tulsa, Graduate School, College of Engineering and Natural Sciences, Tandy School of Computer Science, Tulsa, OK 74104-3189. Offers computer science (MS, PhD); cyber security (MS); JD/MS; MBA/MS. *Program availability:* Part-time. *Faculty:* 16 full-time (3 women), 1 part-time/adjunct (0 women). *Students:* 43 full-time (9 women), 20 part-time (6 women); includes 8 minority (2 Black or African American, non-Hispanic/Latino; 1 American Indian or Alaska Native, non-Hispanic/Latino; 2 Asian, non-Hispanic/Latino; 1 Hispanic/Latino; 2 Two or more races, non-Hispanic/Latino), 18 international. Average age 27. 55 applicants, 87% accepted, 20 enrolled. In 2018, 26 master's, 1 doctorate awarded. Terminal master's awarded for partial completion of doctoral program. *Degree requirements:* For master's, thesis (for some programs); for doctorate, comprehensive exam, thesis/dissertation. *Entrance requirements:* For master's and doctorate, GRE General Test. Additional exam requirements/recommendations for international students: Required—TOEFL (minimum score 550 paper-based; 80 iBT), IELTS (minimum score 6). *Application deadline:* Applications are processed on a rolling basis. *Application fee:* $55. Electronic applications accepted. *Expenses: Tuition:* Full-time $22,230; part-time $1235 per credit hour. *Required fees:* $2100; $6 per credit hour. One-time fee: $400 full-time. Tuition and fees vary according to course level, course load and program. *Financial support:* In 2018–19, 28 students received support, including 4 fellowships with full tuition reimbursements available (averaging $6,178 per year), 24 research assistantships with full tuition reimbursements available (averaging $18,847 per year), 4 teaching assistantships with full tuition reimbursements available (averaging $12,097 per year); career-related internships or fieldwork, Federal Work-Study, scholarships/grants, health care benefits, tuition waivers (full and partial), and unspecified assistantships also available. Support available to part-time students. Financial award application deadline: 2/1; financial award applicants required to submit FAFSA. *Faculty research:* Robotics, human-computer interaction, systems security, information assurance, machine learning, intelligent systems, software engineering, distributed systems, evolutionary computation, computational biology, bioinformatics. *Unit head:* Dr. John Hale, Chairperson, 918-631-3143, E-mail: john-hale@utulsa.edu. *Application contact:* Dr. Mauricio Papa, Advisor, 918-631-2987, Fax: 918-631-3077, E-mail: mauricio-papa@utulsa.edu.
Website: http://engineering.utulsa.edu/academics/computer-science/

University of Utah, Graduate School, College of Engineering, School of Computing, Salt Lake City, UT 84112-9205. Offers computer science (MS, PhD); computing (MS, PhD); software development (MS); MS/MBA. *Faculty:* 40 full-time (6 women), 17 part-time/adjunct (3 women). *Students:* 272 full-time (73 women), 75 part-time (14 women); includes 33 minority (4 Black or African American, non-Hispanic/Latino; 16 Asian, non-Hispanic/Latino; 9 Hispanic/Latino; 4 Two or more races, non-Hispanic/Latino), 199 international. Average age 28. 955 applicants, 22% accepted, 86 enrolled. In 2018, 64 master's, 17 doctorates awarded. Terminal master's awarded for partial completion of doctoral program. *Degree requirements:* For master's, comprehensive exam (for some programs), thesis optional; for doctorate, comprehensive exam, thesis/dissertation. *Entrance requirements:* For master's and doctorate, GRE General Test, minimum GPA of 3.0. Additional exam requirements/recommendations for international students: Required—TOEFL (minimum score 500 paper-based; 61 iBT), IELTS (minimum score 6.5). *Application deadline:* For fall admission, 12/15 for domestic and international students. Application fee: $55 ($65 for international students). Electronic applications accepted. *Expenses:* Contact institution. *Financial support:* In 2018–19, 2 students received support, including 1 fellowship with full tuition reimbursement available (averaging $25,000 per year), 115 research assistantships with full tuition reimbursements available (averaging $35,625 per year), 163 teaching assistantships with full tuition reimbursements available (averaging $15,120 per year); Federal Work-Study, scholarships/grants, health care benefits, and unspecified assistantships also available. Financial award application deadline: 12/15; financial award applicants required to submit FAFSA. *Faculty research:* Operating systems, programming languages, formal methods, natural language processing, architecture, networks, image analysis, data analysis, visualization, graphics, scientific computing, robotics. *Total annual research expenditures:* $7.9 million. *Unit head:* Dr. Ross Whitaker, Director, 801-587-9549, Fax: 801-581-5843, E-mail: whitaker@cs.utah.edu. *Application contact:* Robert Barber, Graduate Advisor, 801-581-3479, Fax: 801-581-5843, E-mail: annc@cs.utah.edu.
Website: http://www.cs.utah.edu

University of Vermont, Graduate College, College of Engineering and Mathematical Sciences, Department of Computer Science, Burlington, VT 05405. Offers MS, PhD. *Degree requirements:* For master's, thesis or alternative. *Entrance requirements:* For master's and doctorate, GRE General Test. Additional exam requirements/ recommendations for international students: Required—TOEFL (minimum score 550 paper-based, 90 iBT) or IELTS (6.5). Electronic applications accepted.

University of Victoria, Faculty of Graduate Studies, Faculty of Engineering, Department of Computer Science, Victoria, BC V8W 2Y2, Canada. Offers M Sc, PhD. *Program availability:* Part-time. Terminal master's awarded for partial completion of doctoral program. *Degree requirements:* For master's, thesis or alternative; for doctorate, thesis/dissertation, candidacy exam. *Entrance requirements:* For master's, GRE (recommended), B Sc in computer science/software engineering or the equivalent or bachelor's degree in mathematics with emphasis on computer science (recommended); for doctorate, GRE (recommended), MS in computer science or equivalent (recommended). Additional exam requirements/recommendations for international students: Required—TOEFL (minimum score 575 paper-based), IELTS (minimum score 7). Electronic applications accepted. *Faculty research:* Functional and logic programming, numerical analysis, parallel and distributed computing, software systems, theoretical computer science, VLSI design and testing.

University of Virginia, School of Engineering and Applied Science, Department of Computer Science, Charlottesville, VA 22903. Offers MCS, MS, PhD. *Degree requirements:* For master's, thesis (for some programs); for doctorate, comprehensive exam, thesis/dissertation. *Entrance requirements:* For master's, GRE General Test, 3

letters of recommendation; for doctorate, GRE General Test, 3 letters of recommendation; essay. Additional exam requirements/recommendations for international students: Required—TOEFL (minimum score 650 paper-based; 90 iBT), IELTS (minimum score 7). Electronic applications accepted. *Faculty research:* Systems programming, operating systems, analysis of programs and computation theory, programming languages, software engineering.

University of Washington, Graduate School, College of Engineering, Paul G. Allen School of Computer Science and Engineering, Seattle, WA 98195-2350. Offers MS, PhD. *Program availability:* Part-time, evening/weekend. In 2018, 107 master's, 18 doctorates awarded. *Degree requirements:* For doctorate, thesis/dissertation, independent project. *Entrance requirements:* For master's, GRE General Test; for doctorate, GRE General Test, minimum GPA of 3.0, statement of purpose, curriculum vitae, letters of recommendation, transcript. Additional exam requirements/ recommendations for international students: Required—TOEFL (minimum score 580 paper-based; 92 iBT); Recommended—IELTS (minimum score 7). *Application deadline:* For fall admission, 12/15 for domestic and international students. Applications are processed on a rolling basis. Application fee: $85. Electronic applications accepted. *Expenses:* Contact institution. *Financial support:* In 2018–19, 248 students received support, including 60 fellowships with full tuition reimbursements available (averaging $36,210 per year), 213 research assistantships with full tuition reimbursements available (averaging $36,120 per year), 95 teaching assistantships with full tuition reimbursements available (averaging $36,210 per year); career-related internships or fieldwork and health care benefits also available. Financial award application deadline: 12/15. *Faculty research:* Theory, systems, artificial intelligence, graphics, databases. *Total annual research expenditures:* $35.9 million. *Unit head:* Henry M. Levy, Director/Chair, 206-543-9204, Fax: 206-543-2969, E-mail: levy@cs.washington.edu. *Application contact:* Elise DeGoede Dorough, Graduate Admissions Information Contact, 206-543-1695, Fax: 206-543-2969, E-mail: elised@cs.washington.edu.
Website: http://www.cs.washington.edu/

University of Waterloo, Graduate Studies and Postdoctoral Affairs, Faculty of Mathematics, David R. Cheriton School of Computer Science, Waterloo, ON N2L 3G1, Canada. Offers computer science (M Math, PhD); software engineering (M Math); statistics and computing (M Math). *Program availability:* Part-time. *Degree requirements:* For master's, research paper or thesis; for doctorate, comprehensive exam, thesis/dissertation. *Entrance requirements:* For master's, honors degree in field, minimum B+ average; for doctorate, master's degree, minimum B+ average. Additional exam requirements/recommendations for international students: Required—TOEFL, IELTS, PTE. Application fee: $125 Canadian dollars. Electronic applications accepted. *Financial support:* Research assistantships, teaching assistantships, scholarships/grants, and unspecified assistantships available. *Faculty research:* Computer graphics, artificial intelligence, algorithms and complexity, distributed computing and networks, software engineering.
Website: https://cs.uwaterloo.ca/

The University of Western Ontario, School of Graduate and Postdoctoral Studies, Faculty of Science, Department of Computer Science, London, ON N6A 3K7, Canada. Offers M Sc, PhD. *Program availability:* Part-time. *Degree requirements:* For master's, thesis, project, or course work; for doctorate, thesis/dissertation. *Entrance requirements:* For master's, B Sc in computer science or comparable academic qualifications; for doctorate, M Sc in computer science or comparable academic qualifications. Additional exam requirements/recommendations for international students: Required—TOEFL. *Faculty research:* Artificial intelligence and logic programming, graphics and image processing, software and systems, theory of computing, symbolic mathematical computation.

University of West Florida, Hal Marcus College of Science and Engineering, Department of Computer Science, Pensacola, FL 32514-5750. Offers computer science (MS), including computer science, database systems, software engineering; information technology (MS), including cybersecurity, database management. *Program availability:* Part-time, evening/weekend. *Degree requirements:* For master's, thesis optional. *Entrance requirements:* For master's, GRE, MAT, or GMAT, official transcripts; minimum undergraduate GPA of 3.0; letter of intent; three letters of recommendation. Additional exam requirements/recommendations for international students: Required—TOEFL (minimum score 550 paper-based).

University of West Georgia, College of Science and Mathematics, Carrollton, GA 30118. Offers biology (MS); computer science (MS); geographic information systems (Postbaccalaureate Certificate); mathematics (MS). *Program availability:* Part-time, evening/weekend, 100% online, blended/hybrid learning. *Faculty:* 47 full-time (16 women). *Students:* 14 full-time (12 women), 93 part-time (26 women); includes 35 minority (21 Black or African American, non-Hispanic/Latino; 1 American Indian or Alaska Native, non-Hispanic/Latino; 7 Asian, non-Hispanic/Latino; 3 Hispanic/Latino; 3 Two or more races, non-Hispanic/Latino), 11 international. Average age 34. 97 applicants, 91% accepted, 71 enrolled. In 2018, 27 master's, 4 other advanced degrees awarded. *Entrance requirements:* Additional exam requirements/recommendations for international students: Required—TOEFL (minimum score 523 paper-based; 69 iBT); Recommended—IELTS (minimum score 6.5). *Application deadline:* For fall admission, 6/1 for domestic and international students; for spring admission, 11/15 for domestic students, 10/15 for international students; for summer admission, 4/1 for domestic students, 3/30 for international students. Applications are processed on a rolling basis. Application fee: $40. Electronic applications accepted. Tuition and fees vary according to course load, degree level, campus/location and program. *Financial support:* Fellowships, research assistantships, teaching assistantships, career-related internships or fieldwork, Federal Work-Study, institutionally sponsored loans, scholarships/grants, and unspecified assistantships available. Support available to part-time students. Financial award application deadline: 4/1; financial award applicants required to submit FAFSA. *Unit head:* Dr. Pauline Gagnon, Interim Dean of Science and Mathematics, Dean of COAH, 678-839-5190, Fax: 678-839-5191, E-mail: pgagnon@westga.edu. *Application contact:* Dr. Toby Ziglar, Assistant Dean of the Graduate School, 678-839-1394, Fax: 678-839-1395, E-mail: graduate@westga.edu.
Website: http://www.westga.edu/cosm

University of Windsor, Faculty of Graduate Studies, Faculty of Science, School of Computer Science, Windsor, ON N9B 3P4, Canada. Offers M Sc, PhD. *Program availability:* Part-time. *Degree requirements:* For master's, thesis; for doctorate, comprehensive exam, thesis/dissertation. *Entrance requirements:* For master's, GRE, minimum B average; for doctorate, master's degree in computer science, minimum B+ average. Additional exam requirements/recommendations for international students: Required—TOEFL (minimum score 580 paper-based). Electronic applications accepted. *Faculty research:* Data mining, distributed query optimization, distributed object based systems, grid computing, querying multimedia database systems.

University of Wisconsin–Madison, Graduate School, College of Letters and Science, Department of Computer Sciences, Madison, WI 53706-1380. Offers MS, PhD. *Program availability:* Part-time. Terminal master's awarded for partial completion of doctoral program. *Degree requirements:* For doctorate, thesis/dissertation. *Entrance requirements:* For master's and doctorate, GRE General Test, GRE Subject Test. Electronic applications accepted.

Computer Science

University of Wisconsin–Milwaukee, Graduate School, College of Engineering and Applied Science, Computer Science Program, Milwaukee, WI 53201-0413. Offers MS. *Program availability:* Part-time. *Students:* 34 full-time (10 women), 18 part-time (4 women); includes 9 minority (5 Asian, non-Hispanic/Latino; 1 Hispanic/Latino; 3 Two or more races, non-Hispanic/Latino), 28 international. Average age 29. 124 applicants, 44% accepted, 16 enrolled. In 2018, 14 master's awarded. *Degree requirements:* For master's, comprehensive exam (for some programs), thesis or alternative. *Entrance requirements:* For master's, GRE, minimum GPA of 2.75. Additional exam requirements/recommendations for international students: Required—TOEFL (minimum score 550 paper-based; 79 iBT), IELTS (minimum score 6.5). *Application deadline:* For fall admission, 1/1 priority date for domestic students; for spring admission, 9/1 for domestic students. Applications are processed on a rolling basis. Application fee: $56 ($96 for international students). Electronic applications accepted. *Financial support:* Fellowships, research assistantships, teaching assistantships, career-related internships or fieldwork, unspecified assistantships, and project assistantships available. Support available to part-time students. Financial award application deadline: 4/15. *Unit head:* John Boyland, PhD, Department Chair, 414-229-6986, E-mail: boyland@uwm.edu. *Application contact:* Engineering and Computer Science Graduate Programs, 414-229-6169, E-mail: ceas-graduate@uwm.edu.
Website: http://uwm.edu/engineering/academics-2/departments/computer-science/

University of Wisconsin–Milwaukee, Graduate School, College of Engineering and Applied Science, Program in Engineering, Milwaukee, WI 53201-0413. Offers biomedical engineering (MS); civil engineering (MS, PhD); computer science (PhD); electrical and computer engineering (MS); electrical engineering (PhD); engineering mechanics (MS); industrial and management engineering (MS); industrial engineering (PhD); manufacturing engineering (MS); materials (PhD); materials engineering (MS); mechanical engineering (MS). *Program availability:* Part-time. *Students:* 174 full-time (41 women), 149 part-time (27 women); includes 31 minority (2 Black or African American, non-Hispanic/Latino; 1 American Indian or Alaska Native, non-Hispanic/Latino; 16 Asian, non-Hispanic/Latino; 4 Hispanic/Latino; 8 Two or more races, non-Hispanic/Latino), 207 international. Average age 31. 343 applicants, 57% accepted, 78 enrolled. In 2018, 73 master's, 24 doctorates awarded. *Degree requirements:* For master's, comprehensive exam (for some programs), thesis or alternative; for doctorate, comprehensive exam, thesis/dissertation, internship. *Entrance requirements:* For master's, GRE, minimum GPA of 2.75; for doctorate, GRE, minimum GPA of 3.5. Additional exam requirements/recommendations for international students: Required—TOEFL (minimum score 550 paper-based; 79 iBT), IELTS (minimum score 6.5). *Application deadline:* For fall admission, 1/1 priority date for domestic students; for spring admission, 9/1 for domestic students. Applications are processed on a rolling basis. Application fee: $56 ($96 for international students). *Financial support:* Fellowships, research assistantships, teaching assistantships, career-related internships or fieldwork, Federal Work-Study, unspecified assistantships, and project assistantships available. Support available to part-time students. Financial award application deadline: 4/15. *Unit head:* David Yu, Representative, 414-229-6169, E-mail: yu@uwm.edu. *Application contact:* Betty Warras, General Information Contact, 414-229-6169, Fax: 414-229-6967, E-mail: bwarras@uwm.edu.
Website: http://www4.uwm.edu/ceas/academics/graduate_programs/

University of Wisconsin–Parkside, College of Business, Economics, and Computing, Program in Computer and Information Systems, Kenosha, WI 53141-2000. Offers MSCIS. *Entrance requirements:* For master's, GRE General Test or GMAT, 3 letters of recommendation, minimum GPA of 3.0. *Faculty research:* Distributed systems, data bases, natural language processing, event-driven systems.

University of Wisconsin–Platteville, School of Graduate Studies, College of Engineering, Mathematics and Science, Program in Computer Science, Platteville, WI 53818-3099. Offers MS. *Program availability:* Part-time. *Degree requirements:* For master's, comprehensive exam, thesis or alternative. *Entrance requirements:* Additional exam requirements/recommendations for international students: Required—TOEFL (minimum score 550 paper-based; 79 iBT), IELTS (minimum score 6.5). Electronic applications accepted.

University of Wyoming, College of Engineering and Applied Science, Department of Computer Science, Laramie, WY 82071. Offers MS, PhD. *Program availability:* Part-time. Terminal master's awarded for partial completion of doctoral program. *Degree requirements:* For master's, thesis; for doctorate, thesis/dissertation. *Entrance requirements:* For master's and doctorate, GRE General Test, minimum GPA of 3.0. Additional exam requirements/recommendations for international students: Required—TOEFL (minimum score 550 paper-based), IELTS (minimum score 6). Electronic applications accepted. *Expenses: Tuition, area resident:* Full-time $6504; part-time $271 per credit hour. Tuition, state resident: full-time $6504; part-time $271 per credit hour. Tuition, nonresident: full-time $19,464; part-time $811 per credit hour. *International tuition:* $19,464 full-time. *Required fees:* $1410.94; $343.82 per semester. $343.82 per semester. Tuition and fees vary according to course load, program and reciprocity agreements. *Faculty research:* Fault-tolerant computing, distributed systems, knowledge representation, automated reasoning, parallel database access, formal methods.

Utah State University, School of Graduate Studies, College of Engineering, Department of Computer Science, Logan, UT 84322. Offers MCS, MS, PhD. *Program availability:* Part-time, evening/weekend, online learning. *Degree requirements:* For master's, thesis (for some programs), research project; for doctorate, thesis/dissertation. *Entrance requirements:* For master's, GRE General Test, GRE Subject Test, minimum GPA of 3.25, prerequisite coursework in math, 3 recommendation letters; for doctorate, GRE General Test, minimum GPA of 3.25, BS or MS. Additional exam requirements/recommendations for international students: Required—TOEFL. Electronic applications accepted. *Faculty research:* Artificial intelligence, software engineering, parallelism.

Vanderbilt University, School of Engineering, Department of Electrical Engineering and Computer Science, Program in Computer Science, Nashville, TN 37240-1001. Offers M Eng, MS, PhD. MS and PhD offered through the Graduate School. *Program availability:* Part-time. Terminal master's awarded for partial completion of doctoral program. *Degree requirements:* For master's, thesis (for some programs); for doctorate, comprehensive exam, thesis/dissertation. *Entrance requirements:* For master's and doctorate, GRE General Test, 3 letters of recommendation. Additional exam requirements/recommendations for international students: Required—TOEFL. Electronic applications accepted. *Expenses: Tuition:* Full-time $47,208; part-time $2026 per credit hour. *Required fees:* $478. *Faculty research:* Artificial intelligence, performance evaluation, databases, software engineering, computational science.

Villanova University, College of Engineering, Department of Electrical and Computer Engineering, Program in Computer Engineering, Villanova, PA 19085-1699. Offers computer architectures (Certificate); computer engineering (MSCPE); intelligent control systems (Certificate). *Program availability:* Part-time, evening/weekend. *Degree requirements:* For master's, thesis optional. *Entrance requirements:* For master's, GRE General Test (for applicants with degrees from foreign universities), BEE, minimum GPA of 3.0. Additional exam requirements/recommendations for international students: Required—TOEFL (minimum score 600 paper-based; 100 iBT). Electronic applications accepted. *Faculty research:* Expert systems, computer vision, neural networks, image processing, computer architectures.

Villanova University, Graduate School of Liberal Arts and Sciences, Department of Computing Sciences, Villanova, PA 19085-1699. Offers computer science (MS). *Program availability:* Part-time, evening/weekend. *Degree requirements:* For master's, thesis optional, independent study project. *Entrance requirements:* For master's, GRE, minimum GPA of 3.0, 3 recommendation letters. Additional exam requirements/recommendations for international students: Required—TOEFL. Electronic applications accepted.

Virginia Commonwealth University, Graduate School, School of Engineering, Department of Computer Science, Richmond, VA 23284-9005. Offers computer science (MS). *Degree requirements:* For master's, thesis optional. *Entrance requirements:* For master's, GRE General Test; for doctorate, GRE. Additional exam requirements/recommendations for international students: Required—TOEFL (minimum score 600 paper-based; 100 iBT). Electronic applications accepted.

Virginia International University, School of Computer Information Systems, Fairfax, VA 22030. Offers business intelligence (Graduate Certificate); business intelligence and data analytics (MIS); computer science (MS), including computer animation and gaming, cybersecurity, data management networking, intelligent systems, software applications development, software engineering; cybersecurity (MIS); data management (MIS); enterprise project management (MIS); health informatics (MIS); information assurance (MIS); information systems (Graduate Certificate); information systems management (MS, Graduate Certificate); information technology (MS); information technology audit and compliance (Graduate Certificate); knowledge management (MIS); software engineering (MS). *Program availability:* Part-time, online learning. *Entrance requirements:* For master's, bachelor's degree. Additional exam requirements/recommendations for international students: Required—TOEFL (minimum score 550 paper-based; 80 iBT), IELTS. Electronic applications accepted.

Virginia Polytechnic Institute and State University, Graduate School, College of Engineering, Blacksburg, VA 24061. Offers aerospace engineering (PhD, M Eng/MS); biological systems engineering (PhD); biomedical engineering (MS, PhD); chemical engineering (PhD); civil engineering (PhD); computer engineering (PhD); computer science and applications (MS); electrical engineering (PhD); engineering education (PhD); M Eng/MS. *Faculty:* 446 full-time (87 women), 7 part-time/adjunct (3 women). *Students:* 1,776 full-time (471 women), 367 part-time (62 women); includes 260 minority (50 Black or African American, non-Hispanic/Latino; 3 American Indian or Alaska Native, non-Hispanic/Latino; 99 Asian, non-Hispanic/Latino; 67 Hispanic/Latino; 41 Two or more races, non-Hispanic/Latino), 1,178 international. Average age 27. 3,798 applicants, 37% accepted, 507 enrolled. In 2018, 489 master's, 200 doctorates awarded. *Degree requirements:* For master's, comprehensive exam (for some programs), thesis (for some programs); for doctorate, comprehensive exam (for some programs), thesis/dissertation (for some programs). *Entrance requirements:* For master's and doctorate, GRE/GMAT. Additional exam requirements/recommendations for international students: Required—TOEFL (minimum score 90 iBT). *Application deadline:* For fall admission, 8/1 for domestic students, 4/1 for international students; for spring admission, 1/1 for domestic students, 9/1 for international students. Applications are processed on a rolling basis. Application fee: $75. Electronic applications accepted. *Expenses:* Tuition, state resident: full-time $15,510; part-time $739.50 per credit hour. Tuition, nonresident: full-time $29,629; part-time $1490.25 per credit hour. *Required fees:* $2804; $550 per semester. Tuition and fees vary according to course load, campus/location and program. *Financial support:* In 2018–19, 37 fellowships with full tuition reimbursements (averaging $24,951 per year), 1,110 research assistantships with full tuition reimbursements (averaging $20,129 per year), 486 teaching assistantships with full tuition reimbursements (averaging $16,192 per year) were awarded; scholarships/grants and unspecified assistantships also available. Financial award application deadline: 3/1; financial award applicants required to submit FAFSA. *Total annual research expenditures:* $96.3 million. *Unit head:* Dr. Julia Ross, Dean, 540-231-9752, Fax: 540-231-3031, E-mail: rjulie@vt.edu. *Application contact:* Linda Perkins, Executive Assistant, 540-231-9752, Fax: 540-231-3031, E-mail: lperkins@vt.edu.
Website: http://www.eng.vt.edu/

Virginia Polytechnic Institute and State University, VT Online, Blacksburg, VA 24061. Offers advanced transportation systems (Certificate); aerospace engineering (MS); agricultural and life sciences (MSLFS); business information systems (Graduate Certificate); career and technical education (MS); civil engineering (MS); computer engineering (M Eng, MS); decision support systems (Graduate Certificate); eLearning leadership (MA); electrical engineering (M Eng, MS); engineering administration (MEA); environmental engineering (Certificate); environmental politics and policy (Graduate Certificate); environmental sciences and engineering (MS); foundations of political analysis (Graduate Certificate); health product risk management (Graduate Certificate); industrial and systems engineering (MS); information policy and society (Graduate Certificate); information security (Graduate Certificate); information technology (MIT); instructional technology (MA); integrative STEM education (MA Ed); liberal arts (Graduate Certificate); life sciences: health product risk management (MS); natural resources (MNR, Graduate Certificate); networking (Graduate Certificate); nonprofit and nongovernmental organization management (Graduate Certificate); ocean engineering (MS); political science (MA); security studies (Graduate Certificate); software development (Graduate Certificate). *Expenses:* Tuition, state resident: full-time $15,510; part-time $739.50 per credit hour. Tuition, nonresident: full-time $29,629; part-time $1490.25 per credit hour. *Required fees:* $2804; $550 per semester. Tuition and fees vary according to course load, campus/location and program. *Application contact:* Graduate Admissions and Academic Progress, 540-231-8636, E-mail: grads@vt.edu.
Website: http://www.vto.vt.edu/

Wake Forest University, Graduate School of Arts and Sciences, Department of Computer Science, Winston-Salem, NC 27109. Offers MS. *Program availability:* Part-time. *Degree requirements:* For master's, one foreign language, thesis optional. *Entrance requirements:* For master's, GRE General Test. Additional exam requirements/recommendations for international students: Required—TOEFL (minimum score 79 iBT). Electronic applications accepted.

Washington State University, Voiland College of Engineering and Architecture, Engineering and Computer Science Programs, Vancouver Campus, Pullman, WA 99164. Offers MS. *Degree requirements:* For master's, comprehensive exam, thesis optional. *Entrance requirements:* For master's, official transcripts from all colleges and universities attended; one-page statement of purpose; three letters of recommendation. Additional exam requirements/recommendations for international students: Required—TOEFL; Recommended—IELTS. Electronic applications accepted. *Faculty research:* High yield production of bioenergy biofuels and bioproducts, nanomaterials, power systems, microfluidics, atmospheric research.

Washington State University, Voiland College of Engineering and Architecture, School of Electrical Engineering and Computer Science, Pullman, WA 99164-2752. Offers computer engineering (MS); computer science (MS); electrical engineering (MS); electrical engineering and computer science (PhD); electrical power engineering (MS). MS programs in computer engineering, computer science and electrical engineering also offered at Tri-Cities campus; MS in electrical power engineering offered at the Global (online) campus. *Program availability:* Part-time. *Degree requirements:* For master's, comprehensive exam (for some programs), thesis or alternative; for doctorate, comprehensive exam, thesis/dissertation. *Entrance requirements:* For master's and doctorate, GRE General Test, minimum GPA of 3.0, 3 letters of recommendation, statement of purpose, transcripts. Additional exam requirements/recommendations for international students: Required—TOEFL (minimum score 580 paper-based). *Faculty research:* Software engineering, networks, distributed computing, computer engineering, electrophysics, artificial intelligence, bioinformatics and computational biology, computer graphics, communications, control systems, signal processing, power systems, microelectronics, algorithms.

Washington University in St. Louis, School of Engineering and Applied Science, Department of Computer Science and Engineering, St. Louis, MO 63130-4899. Offers computer engineering (MS, PhD); computer science (MS, PhD); computer science and engineering (M Eng). *Program availability:* Part-time. Terminal master's awarded for partial completion of doctoral program. *Degree requirements:* For master's, thesis optional; for doctorate, thesis/dissertation. *Entrance requirements:* For doctorate, GRE General Test. Additional exam requirements/recommendations for international students: Required—TOEFL. Electronic applications accepted. *Faculty research:* Artificial intelligence, computational genomics, computer and systems architecture, media and machines, networking and communication, software systems.

Wayne State University, College of Engineering, Department of Computer Science, Detroit, MI 48202. Offers computer science (MS, PhD), including bioinformatics and computational biology (PhD); data science and business analytics (MS). Application deadline for PhD is February 17. *Faculty:* 23. *Students:* 107 full-time (41 women), 39 part-time (11 women); includes 11 minority (2 Black or African American, non-Hispanic/Latino; 6 Asian, non-Hispanic/Latino; 2 Hispanic/Latino; 1 Two or more races, non-Hispanic/Latino), 99 international. Average age 30. 237 applicants, 28% accepted, 35 enrolled. In 2018, 27 master's, 7 doctorates awarded. *Degree requirements:* For master's, thesis (for some programs), practicum (for MS in data science and business analytics); for doctorate, thesis/dissertation. *Entrance requirements:* For master's, GRE (GMAT accepted for MS in data science and business analytics), minimum GPA of 3.0, three letters of recommendation, adequate preparation in computer science and mathematics courses, personal statement, resume (for MS in data science and business analytics); for doctorate, GRE, bachelor's or master's degree in computer science or related field; minimum GPA of 3.3 in most recent degree; three letters of recommendation; personal statement; adequate preparation in computer science and mathematics courses. Additional exam requirements/recommendations for international students: Required—TOEFL (minimum score 550 paper-based; 79 iBT), TWE (minimum score 5.5); Recommended—IELTS (minimum score 6.5). *Application deadline:* For fall admission, 6/1 priority date for domestic students, 5/1 priority date for international students; for winter admission, 10/1 priority date for domestic students, 9/1 priority date for international students; for spring admission, 2/1 priority date for domestic students, 1/2 priority date for international students. Applications are processed on a rolling basis. Application fee: $50. Electronic applications accepted. *Expenses:* Contact institution. *Financial support:* In 2018–19, 91 students received support, including 5 fellowships with tuition reimbursements available (averaging $20,000 per year), 18 research assistantships with tuition reimbursements available (averaging $20,383 per year), 27 teaching assistantships with tuition reimbursements available (averaging $20,166 per year); scholarships/grants, health care benefits, and unspecified assistantships also available. Financial award application deadline: 2/17; financial award applicants required to submit FAFSA. *Faculty research:* Software engineering, databases, bioinformatics, artificial intelligence, networking, distributed and parallel computing, security, graphics, visualizations. *Total annual research expenditures:* $1.1 million. *Unit head:* Dr. Loren Schwiebert, Chair, 313-577-5474, E-mail: loren@wayne.edu. *Application contact:* Areej Salaymeh, Graduate Advisor, 313-577-2477, E-mail: csgradadvisor@cs.wayne.edu. Website: http://engineering.wayne.edu/cs/

Webster University, George Herbert Walker School of Business and Technology, Department of Mathematics and Computer Science, St. Louis, MO 63119-3194. Offers cybersecurity (MS). *Program availability:* Part-time, evening/weekend, online learning. *Entrance requirements:* For master's, 36 hours of graduate course work. Additional exam requirements/recommendations for international students: Required—TOEFL. *Expenses: Tuition:* Full-time $22,500; part-time $750 per credit hour. Tuition and fees vary according to degree level, campus/location and program. *Faculty research:* Databases, computer information systems networks, operating systems, computer architecture.

Wentworth Institute of Technology, Master of Science in Applied Computer Science Program, Boston, MA 02115-5998. Offers MS. *Program availability:* Part-time, online only, 100% online. *Entrance requirements:* Additional exam requirements/recommendations for international students: Recommended—TOEFL (minimum score 550 paper-based). Electronic applications accepted. *Expenses:* Contact institution.

Wesleyan University, Graduate Studies, Department of Mathematics and Computer Science, Middletown, CT 06459. Offers computer science (MA); mathematics (MA, PhD). *Faculty:* 22 full-time (7 women). *Students:* 19 full-time (8 women); includes 3 minority (1 Black or African American, non-Hispanic/Latino; 1 Asian, non-Hispanic/Latino; 1 Hispanic/Latino), 4 international. Average age 25. 66 applicants, 11% accepted, 6 enrolled. In 2018, 4 master's, 2 doctorates awarded. Terminal master's awarded for partial completion of doctoral program. *Degree requirements:* For master's, one foreign language, thesis; for doctorate, 2 foreign languages, comprehensive exam (for some programs), thesis/dissertation. *Entrance requirements:* For master's, GRE General Test, GRE Subject Test; for doctorate, GRE Subject Test. Additional exam requirements/recommendations for international students: Recommended—TOEFL. *Application deadline:* For fall admission, 2/15 for domestic and international students. Applications are processed on a rolling basis. Application fee: $0. Electronic applications accepted. *Financial support:* In 2018–19, 17 teaching assistantships with full tuition reimbursements (averaging $23,000 per year) were awarded; tuition waivers (full) also available. Financial award application deadline: 4/15. *Faculty research:* Topology, analysis, algebra, geometry, number theory. *Unit head:* Dr. Karen Collins, Chair, 860-685-2196, E-mail: kcollins@wesleyan.edu. *Application contact:* Caryn Canalia, Administrative Assistant, 860-685-2182, Fax: 860-685-2571, E-mail: ccanalia@wesleyan.edu.
Website: http://www.wesleyan.edu/mathcs/index.html

West Chester University of Pennsylvania, College of the Sciences and Mathematics, Department of Computer Science, West Chester, PA 19383. Offers computer science (MS); computer security (information assurance) (Certificate); information systems (Certificate); Web technology (Certificate). *Program availability:* Part-time, evening/weekend. *Degree requirements:* For master's, thesis optional, 33 credits; for Certificate, 12 credits. *Entrance requirements:* For master's, GRE, two letters of reference; for Certificate, BS. Additional exam requirements/recommendations for international students: Required—TOEFL or IELTS. Electronic applications accepted. *Faculty research:* Security in mobile ad-hoc networks, intrusion detection, security and trust in pervasive computing, cloud computing, wireless sensor networks, cloud computing and data mining.

Western Illinois University, School of Graduate Studies, College of Business and Technology, School of Computer Science, Macomb, IL 61455-1390. Offers MS. *Program availability:* Part-time. *Students:* 105 full-time (38 women), 15 part-time (7 women); includes 5 minority (4 Black or African American, non-Hispanic/Latino; 1

Hispanic/Latino), 104 international. Average age 25. 56 applicants, 77% accepted, 22 enrolled. In 2018, 82 master's awarded. *Entrance requirements:* For master's, proficiency in Java. Additional exam requirements/recommendations for international students: Required—TOEFL (minimum score 550 paper-based; 80 iBT). *Application deadline:* Applications are processed on a rolling basis. Application fee: $30. Electronic applications accepted. *Financial support:* In 2018–19, teaching assistantships with full tuition reimbursements (averaging $8,688 per year) were awarded; unspecified assistantships also available. Financial award applicants required to submit FAFSA. *Unit head:* Dr. Dennis DeVolder, Program Director, 309-298-1452. *Application contact:* Dr. Mark Mossman, Associate Provost and Director of Graduate Studies, 309-298-1806, Fax: 309-298-2345, E-mail: grad-office@wiu.edu.
Website: http://wiu.edu/computerscience

Western Kentucky University, Graduate School, Ogden College of Science and Engineering, The School of Engineering and Applied Sciences, Bowling Green, KY 42101. Offers computer science (MS); engineering technology management (MS).

Western Michigan University, Graduate College, College of Engineering and Applied Sciences, Department of Computer Science, Kalamazoo, MI 49008. Offers MS, PhD. *Degree requirements:* For master's, thesis optional; for doctorate, 2 foreign languages, thesis/dissertation.

Western Washington University, Graduate School, College of Sciences and Technology, Department of Computer Science, Bellingham, WA 98225-5996. Offers MS. *Program availability:* Part-time. *Degree requirements:* For master's, thesis optional, project. *Entrance requirements:* For master's, GRE General Test, minimum GPA of 3.0 in last 60 semester hours or last 90 quarter hours. Additional exam requirements/recommendations for international students: Required—TOEFL (minimum score 567 paper-based). Electronic applications accepted. *Faculty research:* Distributed operating systems, data mining, machine learning, robotics, information retrieval, graphics and visualization, parallel and distributed computing.

West Virginia University, Statler College of Engineering and Mineral Resources, Morgantown, WV 26506. Offers aerospace engineering (MSAE, PhD); chemical engineering (MS Ch E, PhD); civil engineering (MSCE, PhD); computer engineering (PhD); computer science (MSCS, PhD); electrical engineering (MSEE, PhD); energy systems engineering (MSESE); engineering (MSE); industrial engineering (MSIE, PhD); industrial hygiene (MS); material science and engineering (MSMSE, PhD); mechanical engineering (MSME, PhD); mining engineering (MS Min E, PhD); petroleum and natural gas engineering (MSPNGE, PhD); safety management (MS); software engineering (MSSE). *Program availability:* Part-time. *Students:* 466 full-time (113 women), 154 part-time (27 women); includes 57 minority (22 Black or African American, non-Hispanic/Latino; 1 American Indian or Alaska Native, non-Hispanic/Latino; 8 Asian, non-Hispanic/Latino; 12 Hispanic/Latino; 14 Two or more races, non-Hispanic/Latino), 283 international. In 2018, 179 master's, 39 doctorates awarded. Terminal master's awarded for partial completion of doctoral program. *Degree requirements:* For master's, thesis optional; for doctorate, comprehensive exam, thesis/dissertation. *Entrance requirements:* Additional exam requirements/recommendations for international students: Required—TOEFL (minimum score 550 paper-based). *Application deadline:* For fall admission, 4/1 for international students; for winter admission, 4/1 for international students; for spring admission, 10/1 for international students. Applications are processed on a rolling basis. Application fee: $60. Electronic applications accepted. *Expenses:* Contact institution. *Financial support:* Fellowships, research assistantships, teaching assistantships, career-related internships or fieldwork, Federal Work-Study, institutionally sponsored loans, health care benefits, tuition waivers (full and partial), unspecified assistantships, and administrative assistantships available. Financial award application deadline: 2/1; financial award applicants required to submit FAFSA. *Faculty research:* Composite materials, software engineering, information systems, aerodynamics, vehicle propulsion and emission. *Unit head:* Dr. Earl Scime, Interim Dean, 304-293-4157 Ext. 2237, Fax: 304-293-2037, E-mail: earl.scime@mail.wvu.edu. *Application contact:* Dr. David A. Wyrick, Associate Dean, Academic Affairs, 304-293-4334, Fax: 304-293-5024, E-mail: david.wyrick@mail.wvu.edu.
Website: https://www.statler.wvu.edu

Wichita State University, Graduate School, College of Engineering, Department of Electrical Engineering and Computer Science, Wichita, KS 67260. Offers computer networking (MS); computer science (MS); electrical and computer engineering (MS); electrical engineering and computer science (PhD). *Program availability:* Part-time, evening/weekend. *Unit head:* Dr. Gergely Zaruba, Chair, 316-978-3156, Fax: 316-978-5408, E-mail: gergely.zaruba@wichita.edu. *Application contact:* Jordan Oleson, Admissions Coordinator, 316-978-3095, Fax: 316-978-3253, E-mail: jordan.oleson@wichita.edu.
Website: http://www.wichita.edu/eecs

Winston-Salem State University, Program in Computer Science and Information Technology, Winston-Salem, NC 27110-0003. Offers MS. *Program availability:* Part-time. *Degree requirements:* For master's, thesis optional. *Entrance requirements:* For master's, GRE, resume. Electronic applications accepted. *Faculty research:* Artificial intelligence, network protocols, software engineering.

Worcester Polytechnic Institute, Graduate Admissions, Department of Computer Science, Worcester, MA 01609-2280. Offers computer science (MS, PhD, Advanced Certificate, Graduate Certificate). *Program availability:* Part-time, evening/weekend. *Students:* 81 full-time (23 women), 52 part-time (14 women); includes 11 minority (1 Black or African American, non-Hispanic/Latino; 6 Asian, non-Hispanic/Latino; 4 Hispanic/Latino), 89 international. Average age 29. 625 applicants, 28% accepted, 53 enrolled. In 2018, 47 master's, 7 doctorates, 1 other advanced degree awarded. Terminal master's awarded for partial completion of doctoral program. *Degree requirements:* For master's, thesis optional; for doctorate, comprehensive exam, thesis/dissertation. *Entrance requirements:* For master's and doctorate, GRE General Test recommended for students seeking funding, 3 letters of recommendation, statement of purpose. Additional exam requirements/recommendations for international students: Required—TOEFL (minimum score 563 paper-based; 84 iBT), IELTS (minimum score 7). *Application deadline:* For fall admission, 1/1 priority date for domestic and international students; for spring admission, 10/1 priority date for domestic and international students. Applications are processed on a rolling basis. Application fee: $70. Electronic applications accepted. *Financial support:* Fellowships, research assistantships, teaching assistantships, career-related internships or fieldwork, institutionally sponsored loans, scholarships/grants, and unspecified assistantships available. Financial award application deadline: 1/1. *Unit head:* Dr. Craig Wills, Department Head, 508-831-5357, Fax: 508-831-5776, E-mail: cew@wpi.edu. *Application contact:* Dr. Craig Shue, Graduate Coordinator, 508-831-5357, Fax: 508-831-5776, E-mail: cshue@wpi.edu.
Website: https://www.wpi.edu/academics/departments/computer-science

Wright State University, Graduate School, College of Engineering and Computer Science, Department of Computer Science and Engineering, Computer Science Program, Dayton, OH 45435. Offers MS. *Degree requirements:* For master's, thesis optional. *Entrance requirements:* For master's, GRE General Test, minimum GPA of 3.0 in major, 2.7 overall. Additional exam requirements/recommendations for international students: Required—TOEFL.

Computer Science

Wright State University, Graduate School, College of Engineering and Computer Science, Department of Computer Science and Engineering, Program in Computer Science and Engineering, Dayton, OH 45435. Offers PhD. *Degree requirements:* For doctorate, thesis/dissertation, candidacy and general exams. *Entrance requirements:* For doctorate, GRE General Test, minimum GPA of 3.3. Additional exam requirements/recommendations for international students: Required—TOEFL.

Yale University, Graduate School of Arts and Sciences, Department of Computer Science, New Haven, CT 06520. Offers MS, PhD. *Degree requirements:* For doctorate, thesis/dissertation. *Entrance requirements:* For doctorate, GRE General Test, GRE Subject Test.

York University, Faculty of Graduate Studies, Lassonde School of Engineering, Program in Computer Science, Toronto, ON M3J 1P3, Canada. Offers M Sc, PhD. *Degree requirements:* For master's, thesis or alternative; for doctorate, comprehensive exam, thesis/dissertation, internship or practicum. Electronic applications accepted.

Youngstown State University, College of Graduate Studies, College of Science, Technology, Engineering and Mathematics, Department of Computer Science and Information Systems, Youngstown, OH 44555-0001. Offers computing and information systems (MCIS). *Program availability:* Part-time. *Degree requirements:* For master's, thesis or capstone project. *Entrance requirements:* For master's, GRE or GMAT. Additional exam requirements/recommendations for international students: Required—TOEFL (minimum score 550 paper-based). *Faculty research:* Networking, computational science, graphics and visualization, database and data mining, biometrics, artificial intelligence, online learning environments.

Youngstown State University, College of Graduate Studies, College of Science, Technology, Engineering and Mathematics, Department of Mathematics and Statistics, Youngstown, OH 44555-0001. Offers actuarial science (MS); applied mathematics (MS); computer science (MS); mathematics (MS); secondary/community college mathematics (MS); statistics (MS). *Program availability:* Part-time. *Degree requirements:* For master's, comprehensive exam, thesis optional. *Entrance requirements:* For master's, minimum GPA of 2.7 in computer science and mathematics. Additional exam requirements/recommendations for international students: Required—TOEFL. *Faculty research:* Regression analysis, numerical analysis, statistics, Markov chain, topology and fuzzy sets.

Data Science/Data Analytics

American University, College of Arts and Sciences, Department of Mathematics and Statistics, Washington, DC 22016-8050. Offers applied statistics (Certificate); biostatistics (MS); data science (Certificate); mathematics (MA); professional science: quantitative analysis (MS); statistics (MS). *Program availability:* Part-time, evening/weekend. *Faculty:* 36 full-time (13 women), 8 part-time/adjunct (1 woman). *Students:* 19 full-time (4 women), 21 part-time (9 women); includes 14 minority (7 Black or African American, non-Hispanic/Latino; 2 Asian, non-Hispanic/Latino; 4 Hispanic/Latino; 1 Two or more races, non-Hispanic/Latino), 10 international. Average age 29. 64 applicants, 92% accepted, 19 enrolled. In 2018, 10 master's, 9 other advanced degrees awarded. *Degree requirements:* For master's, comprehensive exam, thesis or alternative. *Entrance requirements:* For master's, GRE; please see website: https://www.american.edu/cas/mathstat/, statement of purpose, transcripts, 2 letters of recommendation, resume; for Certificate, bachelor's degree, statement of purpose, transcripts, resume. Additional exam requirements/recommendations for international students: Required—TOEFL (minimum score 600 paper-based; 100 iBT). Application fee: $55. *Expenses:* Contact institution. *Financial support:* Scholarships/grants and unspecified assistantships available. Financial award applicants required to submit FAFSA. *Unit head:* Dr. Stephen Casey, Department Chair, 202-885-3120, E-mail: mathstat@american.edu. *Application contact:* Jonathan Harper, Assistant Director, Graduate Recruitment, 202-855-3620, E-mail: casgrad@american.edu.
Website: http://www.american.edu/cas/mathstat/

Austin Peay State University, College of Graduate Studies, College of Science, Technology, Engineering and Mathematics, Professional Science Master's Program, Clarksville, TN 37044. Offers data management and analysis (MS, PSM); information assurance and security (MS, PSM); mathematical finance (MS, PSM); mathematics instruction (MS); predictive analytics (MS, PSM). *Program availability:* Part-time, online learning. *Faculty:* 7 full-time (0 women), 1 part-time/adjunct (0 women). *Students:* 48 full-time (11 women), 72 part-time (29 women); includes 22 minority (9 Black or African American, non-Hispanic/Latino; 5 Asian, non-Hispanic/Latino; 4 Hispanic/Latino; 4 Two or more races, non-Hispanic/Latino), 41 international. Average age 32. 76 applicants, 88% accepted, 41 enrolled. In 2018, 16 master's awarded. *Entrance requirements:* For master's, GRE, minimum undergraduate GPA of 2.5. Additional exam requirements/recommendations for international students: Required—TOEFL (minimum score 500 paper-based). *Application deadline:* For fall admission, 8/21 priority date for domestic students. Applications are processed on a rolling basis. Application fee: $45 ($55 for international students). Electronic applications accepted. *Expenses:* Tuition, area resident: Part-time $450 per credit hour. Tuition, state resident: full-time $5987; part-time $450 per credit hour. Tuition, nonresident: full-time $8757; part-time $806 per credit hour. *Required fees:* $1583; $79.15 per credit hour. *Financial support:* Research assistantships with full tuition reimbursements, career-related internships or fieldwork, Federal Work-Study, institutionally sponsored loans, scholarships/grants, and unspecified assistantships available. Support available to part-time students. Financial award application deadline: 7/1; financial award applicants required to submit FAFSA. *Unit head:* Dr. Matt Jones, Graduate Coordinator, 931-221-7814, E-mail: gradpsm@apsu.edu. *Application contact:* Megan Mitchell, Coordinator of Graduate Admissions, 800-859-4723, Fax: 931-221-7641, E-mail: gradadmissions@apsu.edu.
Website: http://www.apsu.edu/csci/masters_degrees/index.php

Azusa Pacific University, School of Behavioral and Applied Sciences, Department of Psychology, Azusa, CA 91702-7000. Offers child life (MS); research psychology and data analytics (MS).

Boston University, Metropolitan College, Department of Computer Science, Boston, MA 02215. Offers computer information systems (MS), including computer networks, data analytics, database management and business intelligence, health informatics, IT project management, security, Web application development; computer networks (Certificate); computer science (MS); data analytics (Certificate); digital forensics (Certificate); health informatics (Certificate); information technology project management (Certificate); software development (MS); software engineering in health care systems (Certificate); telecommunications (MS), including security. *Program availability:* Part-time, evening/weekend, online learning. *Faculty:* 16 full-time (3 women), 52 part-time/adjunct (5 women). *Students:* 201 full-time (57 women), 953 part-time (252 women); includes 285 minority (57 Black or African American, non-Hispanic/Latino; 2 American Indian or Alaska Native, non-Hispanic/Latino; 139 Asian, non-Hispanic/Latino; 67 Hispanic/Latino; 1 Native Hawaiian or other Pacific Islander, non-Hispanic/Latino; 19 Two or more races, non-Hispanic/Latino), 333 international. Average age 31. 1,079 applicants, 72% accepted, 297 enrolled. In 2018, 395 master's awarded. *Entrance requirements:* For master's and Certificate, official transcripts from regionally-accredited bachelor's degree program, 3 letters of recommendation, professional resume, personal statement. Additional exam requirements/recommendations for international students: Required—TOEFL (minimum score 84 iBT), IELTS. *Application deadline:* For fall admission, 8/1 priority date for domestic students, 6/1 priority date for international students; for spring admission, 12/1 priority date for domestic students, 11/15 priority date for international students; for summer admission, 4/1 priority date for domestic students, 3/1 priority date for international students. Applications are processed on a rolling basis. Application fee: $85. Electronic applications accepted. *Expenses:* Contact institution. *Financial support:* In 2018–19, 11 research assistantships (averaging $8,400 per year), 23 teaching assistantships (averaging $3,400 per year) were awarded; unspecified assistantships also available. Support available to part-time students. Financial award applicants required to submit FAFSA. *Faculty research:* Artificial intelligence and machine learning, security and forensics, web technologies, software engineering, programming languages, medical informatics, information systems and IT project management. *Unit head:* Dr. Anatoly Temkin, Chair, 617-353-2566, Fax: 617-353-2367, E-mail: csinfo@bu.edu. *Application contact:* Enrollment Services, 617-353-6004, E-mail: met@bu.edu.
Website: http://www.bu.edu/csmet/

Brandman University, School of Business and Professional Studies, Irvine, CA 92618. Offers accounting (MBA); business administration (MBA); business intelligence and data analytics (MBA); e-business strategic management (MBA); entrepreneurship (MBA); finance (MBA); health administration (MBA); human resources (MBA, MS); international business (MBA); marketing (MBA); organizational leadership (MA, MBA, MPA); public administration (MPA).

Buffalo State College, State University of New York, The Graduate School, Program in Multidisciplinary Studies, Buffalo, NY 14222-1095. Offers data science and analytics (MS); individualized studies (MA, MS); nutrition (MS). *Program availability:* Part-time, evening/weekend. *Degree requirements:* For master's, thesis or project. *Entrance requirements:* For master's, minimum GPA of 2.5. Additional exam requirements/recommendations for international students: Required—TOEFL (minimum score 550 paper-based).

Central European University, Center for Network Science, 1051, Hungary. Offers PhD. *Degree requirements:* For doctorate, comprehensive exam, thesis/dissertation. *Entrance requirements:* For doctorate, master's degree in physics, mathematics, computer science, sociology, political science, economics, or equivalent; two references. Additional exam requirements/recommendations for international students: Required—TOEFL. Electronic applications accepted. *Faculty research:* Social network analysis, complex systems in physics and biology, computational methods.

Claremont Graduate University, Graduate Programs, Center for Information Systems and Technology, Claremont, CA 91711-6160. Offers cybersecurity and networking (MS); data science and analytics (MS); electronic commerce (PhD); geographic information systems (MS); health informatics (MS); information systems (Certificate); IT strategy and innovation (MS); knowledge management (PhD); systems development (PhD); telecommunications and networking (PhD); MBA/MS. *Program availability:* Part-time. *Degree requirements:* For doctorate, comprehensive exam, thesis/dissertation, portfolio. *Entrance requirements:* For master's and doctorate, GMAT, GRE General Test. Additional exam requirements/recommendations for international students: Required—TOEFL (minimum score 75 iBT). Electronic applications accepted. *Faculty research:* Man-machine interaction, organizational aspects of computing, implementation of information systems, information systems practice.

Clarion University of Pennsylvania, College of Business Administration and Information Sciences, MS Program in Applied Data Analytics, Clarion, PA 16214. Offers MS. *Program availability:* Part-time-only, evening/weekend, online only, 100% online. *Faculty:* 1 full-time (0 women). *Students:* 27 part-time (14 women); all minorities (1 Black or African American, non-Hispanic/Latino; 26 American Indian or Alaska Native, non-Hispanic/Latino). Average age 32. 17 applicants, 47% accepted, 8 enrolled. In 2018, 7 master's awarded. *Entrance requirements:* For master's, undergraduate degree with minimum GPA of 3.0, undergraduate programming course, undergraduate statistics course. Additional exam requirements/recommendations for international students: Required—TOEFL (minimum score 550 paper-based; 80 iBT), Or IELTS score of at least 7.0. Bachelor's degree accredited U.S. college or university is acceptable evidence of English language proficiency. *Application deadline:* For fall admission, 8/1 priority date for domestic students, 7/15 priority date for international students. Applications are processed on a rolling basis. Application fee: $40. Electronic applications accepted. *Expenses:* $675.60 per credit including fees, in state. *Financial support:* Federal Work-Study, institutionally sponsored loans, and scholarships/grants available. Financial award application deadline: 3/1; financial award applicants required to submit FAFSA. *Unit head:* Dr. Jon Odonnell, Department Chair, 814-393-2320, E-mail: jodonnell@clarion.edu. *Application contact:* Susan Staub, Graduate Admissions Counselor, 814-393-2337, Fax: 814-393-2722, E-mail: gradstudies@clarion.edu.

College of Saint Elizabeth, Program in Data Analytics, Morristown, NJ 07960-6989. Offers MS. *Program availability:* Part-time. *Degree requirements:* For master's, thesis. *Entrance requirements:* Additional exam requirements/recommendations for international students: Required—TOEFL (minimum score 550 paper-based; 79 iBT), IELTS (minimum score 6.5). Electronic applications accepted. Application fee is waived when completed online.

College of Staten Island of the City University of New York, Graduate Programs, Division of Science and Technology, Program in Computer Science, Staten Island, NY 10314-6600. Offers computer science (MS), including artificial intelligence and data analytics, cloud computing and software engineering, cybersecurity and networks. *Program availability:* Part-time, evening/weekend. *Students:* 35. 48 applicants, 48% accepted, 14 enrolled. In 2018, 17 master's awarded. *Degree requirements:* For master's, thesis optional, a program of 10 courses (30 credits) with at least a 3.0 (B) average. Exceptional students may be permitted to satisfy six credits of the total credit requirement with a master's thesis. *Entrance requirements:* For master's, GRE General Test, BS in Computer Science or related area with a B average (3.0 out of 4.0) overall and in the major. Additional exam requirements/recommendations for international students: Required—TOEFL (minimum score 550 paper-based; 79 iBT), IELTS (minimum score 6.5). *Application deadline:* For fall admission, 7/20 priority date for domestic students, 4/25 for international students; for spring admission, 11/2 priority date for domestic students, 11/2 for international students. Applications are processed on a rolling basis. Application fee: $75. Electronic applications accepted. *Expenses: Tuition,* area resident: Full-time $10,770; part-time $455 per credit. Tuition, state resident: full-time $10,770; part-time $455 per credit. Tuition, nonresident: full-time $19,920; part-time $830 per credit. *International tuition:* $19,920 full-time. *Required fees:* $559.20; $181.10 per semester. Tuition and fees vary according to program. *Faculty research:* Big data, pattern recognition, text mining and frequent pattern mining; graph theory; computer vision, image processing pattern recognition and serious game; parallel computing and stimulation; high performance computing and modeling simulation; serious games; security, cryptography and communication networks; scheduling algorithms; scheduling, operations research and graph theory. *Unit head:* Dr. Xiaowen Zhang, Associate Professor, 718-982-3262, E-mail: xiaowen.zhang@csi.cuny.edu. *Application contact:* Sasha Spence, Associate Director for Graduate Admissions, 718-982-2019, Fax: 718-982-2500, E-mail: sasha.spence@csi.cuny.edu. Website: https://www.csi.cuny.edu/sites/default/files/pdf/admissions/grad/pdf/Computer%20Science%20Fact%20Sheet.pdf

College of Staten Island of the City University of New York, Graduate Programs, School of Business, Program in Business Analytics of Large-Scale Data, Staten Island, NY 10314-6600. Offers Advanced Certificate. *Program availability:* Part-time, evening/weekend. *Degree requirements:* For Advanced Certificate, Students must maintain a GPA of 3.0 to be rewarded the certificate. Students below 3.0 may continue the program but may not be rewarded the certificate. If a grade of 2.0-3.0 is received in a course, s/he will be encouraged to retake the course. minimum GPA of 3.0. *Entrance requirements:* For degree, assessment test in statistical methods, bachelor's degree in business, economics, or a related field, or be in a graduate student program with a GPA of 3.0; 2 letters of recommendation; résumé,; cover letter of the applicants experience. Additional exam requirements/recommendations for international students: Required—TOEFL (minimum score 550 paper-based; 79 iBT), IELTS (minimum score 6.5). *Application deadline:* For fall admission, 4/25 priority date for domestic and international students; for spring admission, 11/25 priority date for domestic and international students. Applications are processed on a rolling basis. Application fee: $125. Electronic applications accepted. *Expenses: Tuition,* area resident: Full-time $10,770; part-time $455 per credit. Tuition, state resident: full-time $10,770; part-time $455 per credit. Tuition, nonresident: full-time $19,920; part-time $830 per credit. *International tuition:* $19,920 full-time. *Required fees:* $559.20; $181.10 per semester. Tuition and fees vary according to program. *Faculty research:* Transportation policy, econometrics. *Unit head:* Prof. Hyuong Suk Shim, Graduate Program Coordinator, 718-982-3309, E-mail: hyoungsuk.shim@csi.cuny.edu. *Application contact:* Sasha Spence, Associate Director for Graduate Admissions, 718-982-2019, Fax: 718-982-2500, E-mail: sasha.spence@csi.cuny.edu. Website: https://www.csi.cuny.edu/sites/default/files/pdf/admissions/grad/pdf/Business%20Analytics%20Fact%20Sheet.pdf

Colorado Technical University Aurora, Program in Computer Science, Aurora, CO 80014. Offers computer systems security (MSCS); database systems (MSCS); software engineering (MSCS). *Program availability:* Part-time, evening/weekend. *Degree requirements:* For master's, thesis or alternative. *Entrance requirements:* For master's, minimum undergraduate GPA of 3.0, resume.

Colorado Technical University Colorado Springs, Graduate Studies, Program in Computer Science, Colorado Springs, CO 80907. Offers computer science (DCS); computer systems security (MSCS); database systems (MSCS); software engineering (MSCS). *Program availability:* Part-time, evening/weekend, online learning. *Degree requirements:* For master's, thesis or alternative; for doctorate, thesis/dissertation. *Entrance requirements:* For doctorate, minimum graduate GPA of 3.0, 5 years of related work experience. *Faculty research:* Software engineering, systems engineering.

Columbia University, Fu Foundation School of Engineering and Applied Science, Data Science Institute, New York, NY 10027. Offers MS. *Program availability:* Part-time. *Entrance requirements:* For master's, GRE General Test. Additional exam requirements/recommendations for international students: Required—TOEFL, IELTS, PTE. *Expenses:* Contact institution. *Faculty research:* Cybersecurity, financial and business analytics, foundations of data science, health analytics, new media, smart cities.

DePaul University, College of Computing and Digital Media, Chicago, IL 60604. Offers animation (MA, MFA); applied technology (MS); business information technology (MS); computational finance (MS); computer and information sciences (PhD); computer science (MS); creative producing (MFA); cybersecurity (MS); data science (MS); digital communication and media arts (MA); documentary (MFA); e-commerce technology (MS); experience design (MA); film and television (MS); film and television directing (MFA); game design (MFA); game programming (MS); health informatics (MS); human centered design (PhD); human-computer interaction (MS); information systems (MS); network engineering and security (MS); product innovation and computing (MS); screenwriting (MFA); software engineering (MS); JD/MS. *Program availability:* Part-time, evening/weekend, online learning. *Degree requirements:* For master's, thesis (for some programs); for doctorate, comprehensive exam, thesis/dissertation. *Entrance requirements:* For master's, GRE or GMAT (for MS in computational finance only), bachelor's degree, resume (MS in predictive analytics only), IT experience (MS in information technology project management only), portfolio review (all MFA programs and MA in animation); for doctorate, GRE, master's degree in computer science. Additional exam requirements/recommendations for international students: Required—TOEFL (minimum score 590 paper-based; 80 iBT), IELTS (minimum score 6.5), PTE (minimum score 53). Electronic applications accepted. *Expenses:* Contact institution. *Faculty research:* Data mining, computer science, human-computer interaction, security, animation and film.

DeSales University, Division of Science and Mathematics, Center Valley, PA 18034-9568. Offers cyber security (Postbaccalaureate Certificate); data analytics (Postbaccalaureate Certificate); information systems (MS), including cyber security, digital forensics, healthcare information management, project management. *Program availability:* Part-time, evening/weekend, 100% online, blended/hybrid learning. *Entrance requirements:* For master's, GRE or GMAT, bachelor's degree in computer-related discipline from accredited college or university, minimum undergraduate GPA of 3.0, personal statement, three letters of recommendation. Additional exam requirements/recommendations for international students: Required—TOEFL. Electronic applications accepted. *Expenses:* Contact institution.

Elmhurst College, Graduate Programs, Program in Data Science, Elmhurst, IL 60126-3296. Offers MS. *Program availability:* Part-time, evening/weekend, 100% online. *Faculty:* 2 full-time (0 women), 2 part-time/adjunct (0 women). *Students:* 1 full-time (0 women), 53 part-time (15 women); includes 15 minority (3 Black or African American, non-Hispanic/Latino; 7 Asian, non-Hispanic/Latino; 4 Hispanic/Latino; 1 Native Hawaiian or other Pacific Islander, non-Hispanic/Latino), 1 international. Average age 31. 77 applicants, 32% accepted, 21 enrolled. In 2018, 12 master's awarded. *Entrance requirements:* For master's, 3 recommendations, resume, statement of purpose, interview. Additional exam requirements/recommendations for international students: Required—TOEFL (minimum score 550 paper-based; 79 iBT). *Application deadline:* Applications are processed on a rolling basis. Application fee: $0. Electronic applications accepted. *Expenses:* $870 per semester hour. *Financial support:* In 2018–19, 14

students received support. Scholarships/grants available. Support available to part-time students. Financial award applicants required to submit FAFSA. *Unit head:* Dr. Jim Kulich, Director, 630-617-3575, E-mail: jimk@elmhurst.edu. *Application contact:* Timothy J. Panfil, Senior Director of Graduate Admission and Enrollment Management, 630-617-3300 Ext. 3256, E-mail: panfilt@elmhurst.edu. Website: http://www.elmhurst.edu/data_science

Fairfield University, School of Engineering, Fairfield, CT 06824. Offers database management (CAS); electrical and computer engineering (MS); information security (CAS); management of technology (MS); mechanical engineering (MS); network technology (CAS); software engineering (MS); Web application development (CAS). *Program availability:* Part-time, evening/weekend. *Degree requirements:* For master's, capstone course. *Entrance requirements:* For master's, resume, 2 recommendations. Additional exam requirements/recommendations for international students: Required—TOEFL (minimum score 550 paper-based; 80 iBT) or IELTS (minimum score 6.5). Electronic applications accepted. *Expenses:* Contact institution. *Faculty research:* Artificial intelligence and information visualization, natural language processing, thermofluids, microwaves and electromagnetics, micro-/nano-manufacturing.

Fitchburg State University, Division of Graduate and Continuing Education, Program in Computer Science, Fitchburg, MA 01420-2697. Offers computer science (MS); data science (MS). *Program availability:* Part-time, evening/weekend. *Entrance requirements:* Additional exam requirements/recommendations for international students: Required—TOEFL (minimum score 550 paper-based; 79 iBT). Electronic applications accepted. *Expenses:* Contact institution.

Florida International University, College of Engineering and Computing, School of Computing and Information Sciences, Miami, FL 33199. Offers computer science (MS, PhD); cybersecurity (MS); data science (MS); information technology (MS); telecommunications and networking (MS). *Program availability:* Part-time, evening/weekend. *Faculty:* 49 full-time (13 women), 31 part-time/adjunct (7 women). *Students:* 182 full-time (53 women), 132 part-time (28 women); includes 168 minority (13 Black or African American, non-Hispanic/Latino; 1 American Indian or Alaska Native, non-Hispanic/Latino; 10 Asian, non-Hispanic/Latino; 137 Hispanic/Latino; 7 Two or more races, non-Hispanic/Latino), 123 international. Average age 30. 393 applicants, 47% accepted, 92 enrolled. In 2018, 81 master's, 9 doctorates awarded. *Degree requirements:* For master's, thesis or alternative; for doctorate, comprehensive exam, thesis/dissertation. *Entrance requirements:* For master's and doctorate, GRE General Test, 3 letters of recommendation, minimum GPA of 3.0. Additional exam requirements/recommendations for international students: Required—TOEFL (minimum score 550 paper-based; 80 iBT). *Application deadline:* For fall admission, 6/1 for domestic students, 4/1 for international students; for spring admission, 10/1 for domestic students, 9/1 for international students. Applications are processed on a rolling basis. Application fee: $30. Electronic applications accepted. *Financial support:* Research assistantships, teaching assistantships, institutionally sponsored loans, scholarships/grants, and unspecified assistantships available. Financial award application deadline: 3/1; financial award applicants required to submit FAFSA. *Faculty research:* Database systems, software engineering, operating systems, networks. *Unit head:* Dr. Sundararaj S. Iyengar, Director, 305-348-3947, Fax: 305-348-3549, E-mail: sundararaj.iyengar@fiu.edu. *Application contact:* Nanett Rojas, Manager, Admissions Operations, 305-348-7464, Fax: 305-348-7441, E-mail: gradadm@fiu.edu.

Fordham University, Graduate School of Arts and Sciences, Department of Computer and Information Sciences, New York, NY 10458. Offers computer science (MS); data analytics (MS). *Program availability:* Part-time, evening/weekend. *Faculty:* 11 full-time (1 woman). *Students:* 164 full-time (51 women), 75 part-time (27 women); includes 21 minority (7 Black or African American, non-Hispanic/Latino; 5 Asian, non-Hispanic/Latino; 4 Hispanic/Latino; 5 Two or more races, non-Hispanic/Latino), 102 international. Average age 31. 378 applicants, 71% accepted, 94 enrolled. In 2018, 62 master's awarded. *Degree requirements:* For master's, thesis optional. *Entrance requirements:* For master's, GRE General Test. Additional exam requirements/recommendations for international students: Required—TOEFL (minimum score 550 paper-based). *Application deadline:* For fall admission, 1/4 priority date for domestic students; for spring admission, 11/1 for domestic students. Application fee: $70. Electronic applications accepted. *Financial support:* In 2018–19, 5 students received support, including 3 research assistantships with tuition reimbursements available (averaging $15,000 per year); career-related internships or fieldwork, institutionally sponsored loans, tuition waivers (full and partial), and unspecified assistantships also available. Financial award application deadline: 1/4; financial award applicants required to submit CSS PROFILE or FAFSA. *Faculty research:* Robotics and computer vision, data mining and informatics, information and networking, computation and algorithms, biomedical informatics. *Total annual research expenditures:* $213,000. *Unit head:* Dr. Damian Lyons, Chair, 718-817-4485, Fax: 718-817-4488, E-mail: dlyons@fordham.edu. *Application contact:* Garrett Marino, Director of Graduate Admissions, 718-817-4419, Fax: 718-817-3566, E-mail: gmarino10@fordham.edu.

George Mason University, College of Health and Human Services, Department of Health Administration and Policy, Fairfax, VA 22030. Offers health and medical policy (MS); health informatics (MS); health informatics and data analytics (Certificate); health services research (PhD); health systems management (MHA); quality improvement and outcomes management in health care systems (Certificate). *Accreditation:* CAHME. *Program availability:* Part-time, evening/weekend, 100% online. *Faculty:* 19 full-time (11 women), 29 part-time/adjunct (11 women). *Students:* 102 full-time (76 women), 165 part-time (129 women); includes 125 minority (54 Black or African American, non-Hispanic/Latino; 53 Asian, non-Hispanic/Latino; 13 Hispanic/Latino; 5 Two or more races, non-Hispanic/Latino), 48 international. Average age 31. 268 applicants, 78% accepted, 116 enrolled. In 2018, 49 master's, 6 other advanced degrees awarded. *Degree requirements:* For master's, comprehensive exam, internship; for doctorate, thesis/dissertation. *Entrance requirements:* For master's, GRE recommended if undergraduate GPA is below 3.0 (for MS in health and medical policy), 2 official transcripts; expanded goals statement; 3 letters of recommendation; resume; 1 year of work experience (for MHA in health systems management); minimum GPA of 3.25 preferred (for MS in health informatics); for doctorate, GRE, professional and volunteer experience, evidence of ability to write and conduct research at the doctoral level, master's degree or equivalent; for Certificate, 2 official transcripts; expanded goals statement; 3 letters of recommendation; resume. Additional exam requirements/recommendations for international students: Required—TOEFL (minimum score 575 paper-based; 88 iBT), IELTS (minimum score 6.5), PTE (minimum score 59). *Application deadline:* For fall admission, 4/1 for domestic and international students; for spring admission, 11/1 for domestic and international students. Application fee: $75 ($80 for international students). Electronic applications accepted. *Expenses:* $564 per credit in-state, $1,421.75 per credit out-of-state. *Financial support:* In 2018–19, 19 students received support, including 15 research assistantships with tuition reimbursements available (averaging $18,185 per year), 5 teaching assistantships (averaging $5,859 per year); career-related internships or fieldwork, Federal Work-Study, scholarships/grants, unspecified assistantships, and health care benefits (for full-time research or teaching assistantship recipients) also available. Support available to part-time students. Financial award application deadline: 3/1; financial award applicants required to submit

FAFSA. *Faculty research:* Universal health care, publications, relationships between malpractice pressure and rates of Cesarean section and VBAC, seniors and Wii gaming, relationships between changes in physician's incomes and practice settings and their care to Medicaid and charity patients. *Total annual research expenditures:* $396,087. *Unit head:* Dr. P.J. Maddox, Chair, 703-993-1982, Fax: 703-993-1953, E-mail: pmaddox@gmu.edu. *Application contact:* Tracy Shevlin, Department Manager, 703-993-1929, Fax: 703-993-1953, E-mail: tshevlin@gmu.edu.
Website: http://chhs.gmu.edu/hap/index

George Mason University, College of Science, Department of Computational and Data Sciences, Fairfax, VA 22030. Offers computational science (MS); computational sciences and informatics (PhD); computational social science (PhD, Certificate); data science (Certificate). *Faculty:* 9 full-time (2 women), 10 part-time/adjunct (1 woman). *Students:* 30 full-time (6 women), 78 part-time (24 women); includes 34 minority (11 Black or African American, non-Hispanic/Latino; 20 Asian, non-Hispanic/Latino; 3 Hispanic/Latino), 19 international. Average age 39. 70 applicants, 63% accepted, 19 enrolled. In 2018, 5 master's, 12 doctorates, 1 other advanced degree awarded. *Degree requirements:* For master's, comprehensive exam (for some programs), thesis optional; for doctorate, comprehensive exam, thesis/dissertation. *Entrance requirements:* For master's, GRE general required for students with degrees outside US. TOEFL required for students with degrees outside US., GPA of at least 3.00 in their last 60 credits of undergraduate study. Applicants should have taken at least one course in differential equations. Applicant should have proficiency in using a high-level computer programming language.; for doctorate, GRE required for students with degrees outside US. TOEFL required for students with degrees outside US., GPA of at least 3.00 in their last 60 credits of undergraduate study. Applicants should have taken at least one course in differential equations. Applicants should have knowledge of a computer programming language such as C, C++, Fortran, Python, etc.; for Certificate, TOEFL required for students with degrees outside US., GPA of at least 3.00 in their last 60 credits of undergraduate study. Applicants should have taken at least one course in differential equation. Applicants should have knowledge of a computer programming language such as C, C++, Fortran, Python, etc. Additional exam requirements/recommendations for international students: Required—TOEFL. *Financial support:* In 2018–19, 12 students received support, including 10 research assistantships (averaging $16,004 per year), 3 teaching assistantships (averaging $14,397 per year); scholarships/grants and unspecified assistantships also available. *Faculty research:* Computational social science; material science; computational science; image analysis; data science. *Total annual research expenditures:* $262,807. *Unit head:* Jason Kinser, Acting Chair, 703-993-3785, E-mail: jkinser@gmu.edu. *Application contact:* Melissa C. Hayes, Graduate Programs Director, 703-993-3430, Fax: 703-993-9033, E-mail: mhayes5@gmu.edu.
Website: http://cos.gmu.edu/cds/

George Mason University, Volgenau School of Engineering, Department of Information Sciences and Technology, Program in Data Analytics Engineering, Fairfax, VA 22030. Offers MS. *Faculty:* 29 full-time (10 women), 67 part-time/adjunct (13 women). *Students:* 196 full-time (106 women), 185 part-time (64 women); includes 99 minority (21 Black or African American, non-Hispanic/Latino; 57 Asian, non-Hispanic/Latino; 17 Hispanic/Latino; 4 Two or more races, non-Hispanic/Latino), 173 international. Average age 29. 302 applicants, 80% accepted, 112 enrolled. In 2018, 119 master's awarded. *Entrance requirements:* For master's, three letters of recommendation; detailed statement of career goals and professional aspiration; self-evaluation form. Additional exam requirements/recommendations for international students: Required—TOEFL (minimum score 575 paper-based; 88 iBT), IELTS (minimum score 6.5), PTE (minimum score 59). *Application deadline:* For fall admission, 12/15 priority date for domestic and international students; for spring admission, 8/15 priority date for domestic and international students. Application fee: $75 ($80 for international students). Electronic applications accepted. *Expenses:* $589 per credit in-state, $1,346.75 per credit out-of-state. *Financial support:* In 2018–19, 42 students received support, including 6 research assistantships (averaging $11,237 per year), 36 teaching assistantships (averaging $6,335 per year); career-related internships or fieldwork, Federal Work-Study, and scholarships/grants also available. Support available to part-time students. Financial award applicants required to submit FAFSA. *Unit head:* Robert Osgood, Director, 703-993-5443, Fax: 703-993-6137, E-mail: rosgood@gmu.edu. *Application contact:* Suddaf Ismail, Director, Graduate Admissions and Recruitment, 703-993-9115, Fax: 703-993-1242, E-mail: sismail@gmu.edu.
Website: http://volgenau.gmu.edu/data-analytics-engineering

The Graduate Center, City University of New York, Graduate Studies, Program in Data Analysis and Visualization, New York, NY 10016-4039. Offers data analysis (MS); data studies (MS); data visualization (MS).

The Graduate Center, City University of New York, Graduate Studies, Program in Data Science, New York, NY 10016-4039. Offers MS.

Grand Canyon University, College of Doctoral Studies, Phoenix, AZ 85017-1097. Offers data analytics (DBA); general psychology (PhD), including cognition and instruction, industrial and organizational psychology, integrating technology, learning, and psychology, performance psychology; management (DBA); marketing (DBA); organizational leadership (Ed D), including behavioral health, Christian ministry, health care administration, organizational development. *Degree requirements:* For doctorate, comprehensive exam, thesis/dissertation. *Entrance requirements:* For doctorate, minimum GPA of 3.4 on earned advanced degree from regionally-accredited institution; transcripts; goals statement.

HEC Montreal, School of Business Administration, Doctoral Program in Administration, Montréal, QC H3T 2A7, Canada. Offers accounting (PhD); applied economics (PhD); data science (PhD); finance (PhD); financial engineering (PhD); information technology (PhD); international business (PhD); logistics and operations management (PhD); management science (PhD); management, strategy and organizations (PhD); marketing (PhD); organizational behaviour and human resources (PhD). Program offered jointly with Concordia University, McGill University, and Universite du Quebec a Montreal. *Accreditation:* AACSB. *Students:* 130 full-time (55 women). 114 applicants, 46% accepted, 31 enrolled. In 2018, 19 doctorates awarded. *Entrance requirements:* For doctorate, TAGE MAGE, GMAT, or GRE, master's degree in administration or related field. *Application deadline:* For fall admission, 1/15 for domestic and international students. Application fee: 91 (191 for international students). Electronic applications accepted. *Expenses: Tuition, area resident:* Full-time $3052.80 Canadian dollars; part-time $84.80 Canadian dollars per credit. Tuition, state resident: full-time $3816 Canadian dollars; part-time $264.67 Canadian dollars per credit. Tuition, nonresident: full-time $11,910 Canadian dollars. *International tuition:* $20,905.20 Canadian dollars full-time. *Required fees:* $1805.34 Canadian dollars; $43.62 Canadian dollars per credit. $71.78 Canadian dollars per term. Tuition and fees vary according to degree level and program. *Financial support:* Research assistantships, teaching assistantships, and scholarships/grants available. Financial award application deadline: 9/2. *Faculty research:* Art management, business policy, entrepreneurship, new technologies, transportation. *Unit head:* Guy Paré, Director, 514-340-6264, E-mail: guy.pare@hec.ca. *Application contact:* Julie Bilodeau, PhD Program Analyst, 514-340-6000, Fax: 514-340-6411, E-mail: analyste.phd@hec.ca.
Website: http://www.hec.ca/en/programs/phd/index.html

IGlobal University, Graduate Programs, Vienna, VA 22182. Offers accounting (MBA); data management and analytics (MSIT); entrepreneurship (MBA); finance (MBA); global business management (MBA); health care management (MBA); hospitality and tourism management (MBA); human resources management (MBA); information technology (MBA); information technology systems and management (MSIT); leadership and management (MBA); project management (MBA); public service and administration (MBA); software design and management (MSIT).

Illinois Institute of Technology, Graduate College, College of Science, Department of Applied Mathematics, Chicago, IL 60616. Offers applied mathematics (MS, PhD); data science (MAS); mathematical finance (MAS). MAS in mathematical finance program held jointly with Stuart School of Business. Terminal master's awarded for partial completion of doctoral program. *Degree requirements:* For master's, comprehensive exam, thesis; for doctorate, comprehensive exam, thesis/dissertation. *Entrance requirements:* For master's, GRE General Test (minimum scores: 304 Quantitative and Verbal, 2.5 Analytical Writing), minimum undergraduate GPA of 3.0; three letters of recommendation; for doctorate, GRE General Test (minimum scores: 304 Quantitative and Verbal, 3.0 Analytical Writing), minimum undergraduate GPA of 3.5; three letters of recommendation. Additional exam requirements/recommendations for international students: Required—TOEFL (minimum score 550 paper-based; 80 iBT). Electronic applications accepted. *Faculty research:* Applied analysis, computational mathematics, discrete applied mathematics, stochastics (including financial mathematics).

Illinois Institute of Technology, Graduate College, College of Science, Department of Computer Science, Chicago, IL 60616. Offers business (MCS); computational intelligence (MCS); computer science (MCS, MS, PhD); cyber-physical systems (MCS); data analytics (MCS); data science (MAS); database systems (MCS); distributed and cloud computing (MCS); education (MCS); finance (MCS); information security and assurance (MCS); networking and communications (MCS); software engineering (MCS); telecommunications and software engineering (MAS); MS/MAS. *Program availability:* Part-time, evening/weekend, online learning. Terminal master's awarded for partial completion of doctoral program. *Degree requirements:* For master's, thesis optional; for doctorate, comprehensive exam, thesis/dissertation. *Entrance requirements:* For master's, GRE General Test with minimum scores of 298 Quantitative and Verbal, 3.0 Analytical Writing (for MS); GRE General Test with minimum scores of 292 Quantitative and Verbal, 2.5 Analytical Writing (for MAS), minimum undergraduate GPA of 3.0; for doctorate, GRE General Test (minimum scores: 304 Quantitative and Verbal, 3.5 Analytical Writing), minimum undergraduate GPA of 3.0. Additional exam requirements/recommendations for international students: Required—TOEFL (minimum score 523 paper-based; 70 iBT). Electronic applications accepted. *Faculty research:* Parallel and distributed processing, high-performance computing, computational linguistics, information retrieval, data mining, grid computing.

Indiana University Bloomington, School of Informatics, Computing, and Engineering, Program in Data Science, Bloomington, IN 47408. Offers MS, Graduate Certificate. *Program availability:* Part-time, evening/weekend, 100% online, blended/hybrid learning. *Entrance requirements:* For master's, GRE, statement of purpose, 3 recommendation letters, transcripts. Additional exam requirements/recommendations for international students: Required—TOEFL (minimum score 100 iBT). Electronic applications accepted. *Expenses:* Contact institution. *Faculty research:* 3D collaborative virtual environments, algorithms for big data, artificial intelligence, astronomy, Bayesian analysis, bioinformatics, case-based reasoning, causal inference, cheminformatics, citation analysis, classical multidimensional scaling, cognitive aspects of data management, cognitive science, complex networks and systems, computational linguistics, computational social science, computer networks, computer vision.

Indiana University–Purdue University Indianapolis, School of Informatics and Computing, Department of Human-Centered Computing, Indianapolis, IN 46202. Offers human-computer interaction (MS, PhD); informatics (MS), including data analytics; media arts and science (MS).

Indiana University–Purdue University Indianapolis, School of Science, Department of Computer and Information Science, Indianapolis, IN 46202-5132. Offers biocomputing (Graduate Certificate); biometrics (Graduate Certificate); computer science (MS, PhD); computer security (Graduate Certificate); databases and data mining (Graduate Certificate); software engineering (Graduate Certificate). *Program availability:* Part-time. Terminal master's awarded for partial completion of doctoral program. *Degree requirements:* For master's and Graduate Certificate, thesis optional; for doctorate, thesis/dissertation. *Entrance requirements:* For master's and doctorate, GRE, BS in computer science or the equivalent with a minimum GPA of 3.0 (or equivalent); for Graduate Certificate, BS in computer science or the equivalent with a minimum GPA of 3.0 (or equivalent). Additional exam requirements/recommendations for international students: Required—PTE (minimum score 58), TOEFL (minimum score 550 paper-based, 79 iBT) or IELTS (6.5). *Faculty research:* Imaging and visualization; networking and security; software engineering; distributed and parallel computing; database, data mining and machine learning.

Johnson & Wales University, Graduate Studies, MS Program in Data Analytics, Providence, RI 02903-3703. Offers MS. *Program availability:* Online learning.

Kansas State University, Graduate School, College of Business, Program in Business Administration, Manhattan, KS 66506. Offers data analytics (MBA); finance (MBA); management (MBA); marketing (MBA); technology entrepreneurship (MBA). *Accreditation:* AACSB. *Program availability:* Part-time, 100% online. *Entrance requirements:* For master's, GMAT (minimum score of 500), minimum undergraduate GPA of 3.0. Additional exam requirements/recommendations for international students: Required—TOEFL (minimum score 550 paper-based; 79 iBT); Recommended—IELTS (minimum score 7). Electronic applications accepted. *Expenses:* Contact institution. *Faculty research:* Organizational citizenship behavior, service marketing, impression management, human resources management, lean manufacturing and supply chain management, financial market behavior and investment management, data analytics, corporate responsibility, technology entrepreneurship.

Keck Graduate Institute, Minerva Schools at KGI, Claremont, CA 91711. Offers decision analysis (MS).

Kennesaw State University, Analytics and Data Science Institute, Kennesaw, GA 30144. Offers PhD. *Students:* 20 full-time (9 women), 1 part-time (0 women); includes 1 minority (Black or African American, non-Hispanic/Latino), 13 international. Average age 33. 52 applicants, 10% accepted, 5 enrolled. *Degree requirements:* For doctorate, comprehensive exam, thesis/dissertation. *Entrance requirements:* For doctorate, GRE, Resume, Statement, Letters of Recommendation, Base SAS Certification, Math through Calculus II. Additional exam requirements/recommendations for international students: Required—TOEFL (minimum score 80 iBT), IELTS (minimum score 6.5). *Application deadline:* For fall admission, 2/1 for domestic and international students. Application fee: $60. Electronic applications accepted. *Expenses: Tuition, area resident:* Full-time $6960; part-time $290 per credit hour. Tuition, state resident: full-time $6960; part-time $290 per credit hour. Tuition, nonresident: full-time $25,080; part-time $1045 per credit hour. *International tuition:* $25,080 full-time. *Required fees:* $2006; $1706 per semester. $853 per semester. *Financial support:* In 2018–19, 5 research assistantships with full and partial tuition reimbursements (averaging $36,000 per year) were awarded. *Unit*

head: Sherrill Hayes, Program Director, 470-578-6499, E-mail: shayes32@kennesaw.edu. *Application contact:* Admissions Counselor, 470-578-4377, Fax: 470-578-9172, E-mail: ksugrad@kennesaw.edu.
Website: http://datascience.kennesaw.edu/

Kennesaw State University, College of Computing and Software Engineering, Program in Information Technology, Kennesaw, GA 30144. Offers data management and analytics (Graduate Certificate); health information technology (Postbaccalaureate Certificate); information technology (MSIT); information technology foundations (Postbaccalaureate Certificate); information technology security (Graduate Certificate). *Program availability:* Part-time, evening/weekend, blended/hybrid learning. *Students:* 100 full-time (45 women), 195 part-time (76 women); includes 137 minority (75 Black or African American, non-Hispanic/Latino; 42 Asian, non-Hispanic/Latino; 14 Hispanic/Latino; 1 Native Hawaiian or other Pacific Islander, non-Hispanic/Latino; 5 Two or more races, non-Hispanic/Latino), 40 international. Average age 34. 131 applicants, 81% accepted, 81 enrolled. In 2018, 70 master's awarded. *Degree requirements:* For master's, thesis optional. *Entrance requirements:* For master's, minimum GPA of 2.75; for other advanced degree, bachelor's degree. Additional exam requirements/recommendations for international students: Required—TOEFL (minimum score 80 iBT), IELTS (minimum score 6.5). *Application deadline:* For fall admission, 7/1 priority date for domestic students, 5/1 priority date for international students; for spring admission, 11/1 priority date for domestic students, 9/1 priority date for international students; for summer admission, 4/1 priority date for domestic students, 3/1 priority date for international students. Applications are processed on a rolling basis. Application fee: $60. Electronic applications accepted. *Expenses: Tuition, area resident:* Full-time $6960; part-time $290 per credit hour. Tuition, state resident: full-time $6960; part-time $290 per credit hour. Tuition, nonresident: full-time $25,080; part-time $1045 per credit hour. *International tuition:* $25,080 full-time. *Required fees:* $2006; $1706 per semester. $853 per semester. *Financial support:* Research assistantships with full and partial tuition reimbursements, career-related internships or fieldwork, scholarships/grants, and unspecified assistantships available. Support available to part-time students. Financial award applicants required to submit FAFSA. *Application contact:* Admission Counselor, 470-578-4377, Fax: 470-578-9172, E-mail: ksugrad@kennesaw.edu.
Website: http://ccse.kennesaw.edu/it/

Lawrence Technological University, College of Arts and Sciences, Southfield, MI 48075-1058. Offers bioinformatics (Graduate Certificate); computer science (MS), including data science, big data, and data mining, intelligent systems; educational technology (MA), including robotics; instructional design, communication, and presentation (Graduate Certificate); integrated science (MA); science education (MA); technical and professional communication (MS, Graduate Certificate); writing for the digital age (Graduate Certificate). *Program availability:* Part-time, evening/weekend. *Degree requirements:* For master's, thesis (for some programs). *Entrance requirements:* Additional exam requirements/recommendations for international students: Required—TOEFL (minimum score 550 paper-based; 79 iBT), IELTS (minimum score 6.5). Electronic applications accepted. *Faculty research:* Computer analysis of music, machine learning of literature and lyrics, customer sentiments and response analysis through social media, peta-scale computing in astronomical databases, early detection of diseases with pattern recognition.

Lewis University, College of Arts and Sciences, Program in Data Science, Romeoville, IL 60446. Offers computational biology and bioinformatics (MS); computer science (MS). *Program availability:* Part-time, evening/weekend, 100% online, blended/hybrid learning. *Students:* 16 full-time (4 women), 99 part-time (28 women); includes 34 minority (8 Black or African American, non-Hispanic/Latino; 12 Asian, non-Hispanic/Latino; 8 Hispanic/Latino; 1 Native Hawaiian or other Pacific Islander, non-Hispanic/Latino; 5 Two or more races, non-Hispanic/Latino), 2 international. Average age 35. *Entrance requirements:* For master's, bachelor's degree, undergraduate coursework in calculus, minimum undergraduate GPA of 3.0, resume, statement of purpose, two letters of recommendation. Additional exam requirements/recommendations for international students: Required—TOEFL (minimum score 550 paper-based; 79 iBT), IELTS (minimum score 6). *Application deadline:* For fall admission, 5/1 priority date for international students; for winter admission, 11/1 priority date for international students. Applications are processed on a rolling basis. Application fee: $40. Electronic applications accepted. Application fee is waived when completed online. *Financial support:* Federal Work-Study available. Financial award application deadline: 5/1; financial award applicants required to submit FAFSA. *Unit head:* Dr. Piotr Szczurek, Program Director. *Application contact:* Linda Campbell, Graduate Admissions Counselor, 815-836-5610, E-mail: grad@lewisu.edu.
Website: http://www.lewisu.edu/academics/data-science/index.htm

Lipscomb University, College of Computing and Technology, Nashville, TN 37204-3951. Offers data science (MS, Certificate); information technology (MS, Certificate), including data science (MS), information security (MS), information technology management (MS), software engineering (MS); software engineering (MS, Certificate). *Program availability:* Part-time, evening/weekend. *Degree requirements:* For master's, capstone project. *Entrance requirements:* For master's, GRE, 2 references, transcripts, resume, personal statement. Additional exam requirements/recommendations for international students: Required—TOEFL (minimum score 570 paper-based; 80 iBT). Electronic applications accepted. *Expenses:* Contact institution.

London Metropolitan University, Graduate Programs, London, United Kingdom. Offers applied psychology (M Sc); architecture (MA); biomedical science (M Sc); blood science (M Sc); cancer pharmacology (M Sc); computer networking and cyber security (M Sc); computing and information systems (M Sc); conference interpreting (MA); counter-terrorism studies (M Sc); creative, digital and professional writing (MA); crime, violence and prevention (M Sc); criminology (M Sc); curating contemporary art (MA); data analytics (M Sc); digital media (MA); early childhood studies (MA); education (MA, Ed D); financial services law, regulation and compliance (LL M); food science (M Sc); forensic psychology (M Sc); health and social care management and policy (M Sc); human nutrition (M Sc); human resource management (MA); human rights and international conflict (MA); information technology (M Sc); intelligence and security studies (M Sc); international oil, gas and energy law (LL M); international relations (MA); interpreting (MA); learning and teaching in higher education (MA); legal practice (LL M); media and entertainment law (LL M); organizational and consumer psychology (M Sc); psychological therapy (M Sc); psychology of mental health (M Sc); public health (M Sc); public policy and management (MPA); security studies (M Sc); social work (M Sc); spatial planning and urban design (MA); sports therapy (M Sc); supporting older children and young people with dyslexia (MA); teaching languages (MA), including Arabic, English; translation (MA); woman and child abuse (MA).

Manhattan College, Graduate Programs, School of Science, Program in Applied Mathematics - Data Analytics, Riverdale, NY 10471. Offers MS. *Program availability:* Part-time. *Faculty:* 10 full-time (4 women). *Students:* 7 full-time (2 women), 3 part-time; includes 4 minority (1 Black or African American, non-Hispanic/Latino; 3 Hispanic/Latino), 2 international. Average age 24. 7 applicants, 86% accepted, 4 enrolled. In 2018, 4 master's awarded. *Degree requirements:* For master's, comprehensive exam. *Entrance requirements:* Additional exam requirements/recommendations for international students: Required—TOEFL (minimum score 550 paper-based; 80 iBT), IELTS (minimum score 6.5), TOEFL or IELTS is required. *Application deadline:* Applications are processed on a rolling basis. Application fee: $75. Electronic applications accepted. *Financial support:* In 2018–19, 4 students received support. Unspecified assistantships available. *Faculty research:* Machine learning, probabilistic modeling, statistical learning, operations research, network theory. *Unit head:* Dr. Constantine Theodosiou, Dean of Science, 718-862-7368, E-mail: constantine.theodosiou@manhattan.edu. *Application contact:* Doina Lawler, Assistant Director of Graduate Admissions, 718-862-8649, E-mail: dlawler01@manhattan.edu.
Website: https://manhattan.edu/academics/5-year-programs/applied-mathematics-data-analytics.php

Maryville University of Saint Louis, College of Arts and Sciences, St. Louis, MO 63141-7299. Offers actuarial science (MS); data science (MS); strategic communication and leadership (MA). *Program availability:* Part-time. *Faculty:* 7 full-time (5 women), 11 part-time/adjunct (5 women). *Students:* 62 full-time (33 women), 37 part-time (28 women); includes 11 minority (5 Black or African American, non-Hispanic/Latino; 3 Asian, non-Hispanic/Latino; 1 Hispanic/Latino; 2 Two or more races, non-Hispanic/Latino), 52 international. Average age 28. In 2018, 32 master's awarded. *Entrance requirements:* For master's, strong mathematics background, 2 letters of recommendation, and personal statement (MS). Additional exam requirements/recommendations for international students: Required—TOEFL (minimum score 550 paper-based; 80 iBT). *Application deadline:* Applications are processed on a rolling basis. Electronic applications accepted. *Expenses:* Tuition varies by program. *Financial support:* Application deadline: 4/1; applicants required to submit FAFSA. *Unit head:* Jennifer Yukna, Interim Dean, 314-529-6858, Fax: 314-529-9965, E-mail: jyukna@maryville.edu. *Application contact:* Shani Lenore-Jenkins, Associate Vice President of Enrollment, 314-529-9359, E-mail: slenore@maryville.edu.
Website: https://www.maryville.edu/as/

Merrimack College, School of Science and Engineering, North Andover, MA 01845-5800. Offers civil engineering (MS); computer science (MS); data science (MS); engineering management (MS); mechanical engineering (MS), including engineering management. *Program availability:* Part-time, evening/weekend, 100% online. *Faculty:* 10 full-time (2 women), 6 part-time/adjunct (1 woman). *Students:* 53 full-time (18 women), 17 part-time (5 women); includes 14 minority (6 Black or African American, non-Hispanic/Latino; 6 Asian, non-Hispanic/Latino; 2 Two or more races, non-Hispanic/Latino), 9 international. Average age 34. 183 applicants, 61% accepted, 40 enrolled. In 2018, 27 master's awarded. *Degree requirements:* For master's, comprehensive exam, thesis optional, internship or capstone (for some programs). *Entrance requirements:* For master's, official college transcripts, resume, personal statement, 2 recommendations. Additional exam requirements/recommendations for international students: Required—TOEFL (minimum score 84 iBT), IELTS (minimum score 6.5), PTE (minimum score 56). *Application deadline:* For fall admission, 8/24 for domestic students, 7/30 for international students; for spring admission, 1/10 for domestic students, 12/10 for international students; for summer admission, 5/10 for domestic students, 4/10 for international students. Applications are processed on a rolling basis. Application fee: $0. Electronic applications accepted. Application fee is waived when completed online. *Expenses:* Contact institution. *Financial support:* Career-related internships or fieldwork, scholarships/grants, health care benefits, and unspecified assistantships available. Support available to part-time students. Financial award application deadline: 5/1; financial award applicants required to submit FAFSA. *Unit head:* Dr. Naira Campbell-Kyureghyan, Dean, 978-837-5265, E-mail: campbellnk@merrimack.edu. *Application contact:* Allison Pena, Graduate Admissions Counselor, 978-837-3563, E-mail: penaa@merrimack.edu.
Website: http://www.merrimack.edu/academics/graduate/

Metropolitan State University, College of Management, St. Paul, MN 55106-5000. Offers business administration (MBA, DBA); business analytics (Graduate Certificate); database administration (Graduate Certificate); global supply chain management (Graduate Certificate); information assurance security (Graduate Certificate); management information systems (MMIS); MIS generalist (Graduate Certificate); MIS systems analysis and design (Graduate Certificate); project management (Graduate Certificate). *Program availability:* Part-time, evening/weekend. *Degree requirements:* For master's, thesis optional, computer language (MMIS). *Entrance requirements:* For master's, GMAT (for MBA), resume. Additional exam requirements/recommendations for international students: Required—TOEFL (minimum score 550 paper-based). Electronic applications accepted. *Faculty research:* Yugoslav economic system, workers' cooperatives, participative management and job enrichment, global business systems.

Michigan Technological University, Graduate School, Interdisciplinary Programs, Houghton, MI 49931. Offers automotive systems and controls (Graduate Certificate); biochemistry and molecular biology (PhD); computational science and engineering (PhD); data science (Graduate Certificate); sustainability (Graduate Certificate). *Program availability:* Part-time. *Faculty:* 120 full-time (25 women), 8 part-time/adjunct. *Students:* 67 full-time (28 women), 24 part-time; includes 5 minority (2 Black or African American, non-Hispanic/Latino; 1 American Indian or Alaska Native, non-Hispanic/Latino; 2 Two or more races, non-Hispanic/Latino), 59 international. Average age 29. 479 applicants, 24% accepted, 17 enrolled. In 2018, 19 master's, 8 doctorates, 10 other advanced degrees awarded. Terminal master's awarded for partial completion of doctoral program. *Degree requirements:* For master's, comprehensive exam (for some programs), thesis (for some programs); for doctorate, comprehensive exam, thesis/dissertation. *Entrance requirements:* For master's, doctorate, and Graduate Certificate, GRE, statement of purpose, personal statement, official transcripts, 2-3 letters of recommendation. Additional exam requirements/recommendations for international students: Required—TOEFL or IELTS. *Application deadline:* Applications are processed on a rolling basis. Electronic applications accepted. *Expenses: Tuition, area resident:* Full-time $18,126; part-time $1007 per credit. Tuition, state resident: full-time $18,126; part-time $1007 per credit. Tuition, nonresident: full-time $18,126; part-time $1007 per credit. *International tuition:* $18,126 full-time. *Required fees:* $248; $124 per semester. Tuition and fees vary according to course load and program. *Financial support:* In 2018–19, 64 students received support, including 14 fellowships with tuition reimbursements available (averaging $16,590 per year), 14 research assistantships with tuition reimbursements available (averaging $16,590 per year), 12 teaching assistantships with tuition reimbursements available (averaging $16,590 per year); career-related internships or fieldwork, Federal Work-Study, scholarships/grants, health care benefits, unspecified assistantships, and cooperative program also available. Financial award applicants required to submit FAFSA. *Faculty research:* Big data, atmospheric sciences, bioinformatics and systems biology, molecular dynamics, environmental studies. *Unit head:* Dr. Pushpalatha Murthy, Dean of the Graduate School/Associate Provost for Graduate Education, 906-487-3007, Fax: 906-487-2284, E-mail: ppmurthy@mtu.edu. *Application contact:* Carol T. Wingerson, Administrative Aide, 906-487-2328, Fax: 906-487-2284, E-mail: gradadms@mtu.edu.

Montclair State University, The Graduate School, College of Humanities and Social Sciences, Data Collection and Management Certificate Program, Montclair, NJ 07043-1624. Offers Certificate.

Data Science/Data Analytics

National University, School of Engineering and Computing, La Jolla, CA 92037-1011. Offers computer science (MS), including advanced computing; cyber security and information assurance (MS); data analytics (MS); electrical engineering (MS); engineering management (MS); information technology management (MS); management information systems (MS); sustainability management (MS). *Program availability:* Part-time, evening/weekend, 100% online, blended/hybrid learning. *Degree requirements:* For master's, thesis (for some programs). *Entrance requirements:* For master's, interview, minimum GPA of 2.5. Additional exam requirements/recommendations for international students: Required—TOEFL (minimum score 550 paper-based; 79 iBT), IELTS (minimum score 6). Electronic applications accepted. *Expenses: Tuition:* Full-time $10,320; part-time $430 per unit. Tuition and fees vary according to degree level. *Faculty research:* Educational technology, scholarships in science.

New College of Florida, Program in Data Science, Sarasota, FL 34243. Offers MDS. *Entrance requirements:* For master's, bachelor's degree, course in linear algebra, programming proficiency. Additional exam requirements/recommendations for international students: Required—TOEFL (minimum score 560 paper-based; 83 iBT), IELTS (minimum score 6.5).

New Jersey Institute of Technology, Ying Wu College of Computing, Newark, NJ 07102. Offers big data management and mining (Certificate); business and information systems (Certificate); computer science (PhD); computing and business (MS); data mining (Certificate); data science (MS); information security (Certificate); information systems (PhD); information technology administration and security (MS); IT administration (Certificate); network security and information assurance (Certificate); software engineering (MS), including information systems; software engineering analysis/design (Certificate); Web systems development (Certificate). *Program availability:* Part-time, evening/weekend. *Faculty:* 69 full-time (13 women), 38 part-time/adjunct (4 women). *Students:* 699 full-time (229 women), 269 part-time (67 women); includes 260 minority (44 Black or African American, non-Hispanic/Latino; 145 Asian, non-Hispanic/Latino; 59 Hispanic/Latino; 12 Two or more races, non-Hispanic/Latino), 614 international. Average age 26. 2,216 applicants, 55% accepted, 366 enrolled. In 2018, 418 master's, 5 doctorates, 13 other advanced degrees awarded. Terminal master's awarded for partial completion of doctoral program. *Degree requirements:* For master's, thesis optional; for doctorate, thesis/dissertation. *Entrance requirements:* For master's, GRE General Test; for doctorate, GRE General Test, minimum graduate GPA of 3.5. Additional exam requirements/recommendations for international students: Required—TOEFL (minimum score 550 paper-based; 79 iBT), IELTS (minimum score 6.5). *Application deadline:* For fall admission, 6/1 priority date for domestic students, 5/1 priority date for international students; for spring admission, 11/15 priority date for domestic and international students. Applications are processed on a rolling basis. Application fee: $75. Electronic applications accepted. *Expenses:* $22,690 per year (in-state), $32,136 per year (out-of-state). *Financial support:* In 2018–19, 366 students received support, including 10 fellowships with full tuition reimbursements available (averaging $22,000 per year), 47 research assistantships with full tuition reimbursements available (averaging $22,000 per year), 28 teaching assistantships with full tuition reimbursements available (averaging $22,000 per year); career-related internships or fieldwork, Federal Work-Study, scholarships/grants, and unspecified assistantships also available. Financial award application deadline: 1/15. *Faculty research:* Computer systems, communications and networking, artificial intelligence, database engineering, systems analysis, analytics and optimization in crowdsourcing. *Total annual research expenditures:* $4.9 million. *Unit head:* Dr. Craig Gotsman, Dean, 973-596-3366, Fax: 973-596-5777, E-mail: craig.gotsman@njit.edu. *Application contact:* Stephen Eck, Director of Admissions, 973-596-3300, Fax: 973-596-3461, E-mail: admissions@njit.edu.
Website: http://computing.njit.edu/

The New School, Parsons School of Design, Program in Data Visualization, New York, NY 10011. Offers MS. *Program availability:* Part-time. *Degree requirements:* For master's, thesis or alternative. *Entrance requirements:* For master's, transcripts, resume, statement of purpose, recommendation letters, portfolio, programming sample and/or writing sample, interview. Additional exam requirements/recommendations for international students: Required—TOEFL (minimum score 92 iBT), IELTS (minimum score 7), PTE (minimum score 63). Electronic applications accepted. *Expenses:* Contact institution.

New York University, Graduate School of Arts and Science, Department of Data Science, New York, NY 10012-1019. Offers MS. *Students:* 225 full-time (97 women), 30 part-time (13 women); includes 28 minority (4 Black or African American, non-Hispanic/Latino; 14 Asian, non-Hispanic/Latino; 6 Hispanic/Latino; 4 Two or more races, non-Hispanic/Latino), 185 international. Average age 25. 2,144 applicants, 19% accepted, 154 enrolled. In 2018, 69 master's awarded. *Entrance requirements:* For master's, GRE or GMAT. Additional exam requirements/recommendations for international students: Required—TOEFL, IELTS. *Application deadline:* For fall admission, 2/4 for domestic and international students. Application fee: $110. Electronic applications accepted. *Financial support:* Application deadline: 2/4; applicants required to submit FAFSA. *Unit head:* Roy Lawrence, Director, 212-998-3401, E-mail: datascience-group@nyu.edu. *Application contact:* Varsha Tiger, Administrator, 212-998-3401, E-mail: datascience-group@nyu.edu.

New York University, School of Professional Studies, Division of Programs in Business, Program in Management and Systems, New York, NY 10012-1019. Offers management and systems (MS), including database technologies, enterprise risk management, strategy and leadership, systems management. *Program availability:* Part-time, evening/weekend, 100% online, blended/hybrid learning. *Degree requirements:* For master's, thesis, capstone project. *Entrance requirements:* For master's, GRE or GMAT (only upon request), bachelor's degree, resume with relevant professional work, internship or volunteer experience, two letters of recommendation, statement of purpose. Additional exam requirements/recommendations for international students: Required—TOEFL (minimum score 600 paper-based; 100 iBT), IELTS (minimum score 7). Electronic applications accepted. *Expenses:* Contact institution.

Northcentral University, Graduate Studies, San Diego, CA 92106. Offers business (MBA, DBA, PhD, Postbaccalaureate Certificate); education (M Ed, Ed D, PhD, Ed S, Post-Master's Certificate, Postbaccalaureate Certificate); marriage and family therapy (MA, DMFT, PhD, Post-Master's Certificate, Postbaccalaureate Certificate); psychology (MA, PhD, Post-Master's Certificate, Postbaccalaureate Certificate); technology (MS, PhD), including computer science, cybersecurity (MS), data science, technology and innovation management (PhD). *Program availability:* Part-time, evening/weekend, online only, 100% online. *Faculty:* 98 full-time (63 women), 385 part-time/adjunct (203 women). *Students:* 5,036 full-time (3,291 women), 5,747 part-time (3,977 women); includes 3,777 minority (2,550 Black or African American, non-Hispanic/Latino; 76 American Indian or Alaska Native, non-Hispanic/Latino; 192 Asian, non-Hispanic/Latino; 603 Hispanic/Latino; 39 Native Hawaiian or other Pacific Islander, non-Hispanic/Latino; 317 Two or more races, non-Hispanic/Latino). Average age 45. In 2018, 929 master's, 782 doctorates, 278 other advanced degrees awarded. *Degree requirements:* For doctorate, comprehensive exam, thesis/dissertation. *Entrance requirements:* For master's, bachelor's degree from regionally- or nationally-accredited institution, current resume or

curriculum vitae, statement of intent, interview, and background check (for marriage and family therapy); for doctorate, post-baccalaureate master's degree and/or doctoral degree from nationally- or regionally-accredited academic institution; for other advanced degree, bachelor's-level or higher degree from accredited institution or university (for Post-Baccalaureate Certificate); master's and/or doctoral degree from regionally- or nationally-accredited academic institution (for Post-Master's Certificate). Additional exam requirements/recommendations for international students: Required—TOEFL (minimum score 550 paper-based; 79 iBT), IELTS (minimum score 6.5), PTE (minimum score 53). *Application deadline:* Applications are processed on a rolling basis. Application fee: $0. Electronic applications accepted. *Expenses: Tuition:* Full-time $893. *Required fees:* $95. Tuition and fees vary according to degree level and program. *Financial support:* Scholarships/grants available. *Faculty research:* Business management, curriculum and instruction, educational leadership, health psychology, organizational behavior. *Unit head:* Dr. David Harpool, Acting Provost, 888-327-2877 Ext. 8181, E-mail: provost@ncu.edu. *Application contact:* Ken Boutelle, Vice President, Enrollment Services, 888-628-4979, E-mail: enrollmentservices@ncu.edu.

Northeastern University, College of Computer and Information Science, Boston, MA 02115-5096. Offers computer science (MS, PhD); data science (MS); game science and design (MS); health informatics (MS); information assurance (MS); network science (PhD); personal health informatics (PhD). *Program availability:* Part-time, evening/weekend. Terminal master's awarded for partial completion of doctoral program. *Degree requirements:* For master's, thesis optional; for doctorate, comprehensive exam, thesis/dissertation. Electronic applications accepted. *Expenses:* Contact institution.

Northwestern University, School of Professional Studies, Program in Data Science, Evanston, IL 60208. Offers computer-based data mining (MS); marketing analytics (MS); predictive modeling (MS); risk analytics (MS); Web analytics (MS). *Program availability:* Online learning. *Entrance requirements:* For master's, official transcripts, two letters of recommendation, statement of purpose, current resume or curriculum vitae. Additional exam requirements/recommendations for international students: Required—TOEFL (minimum score 600 paper-based; 100 iBT) or IELTS (minimum score 7).

Northwestern University, School of Professional Studies, Program in Information Systems, Evanston, IL 60208. Offers analytics and business intelligence (MS); database and Internet technologies (MS); information systems (MS); information systems management (MS); information systems security (MS); medical informatics (MS); software project management and development (MS). *Program availability:* Part-time, evening/weekend.

Ohio Dominican University, Division of Business, Program in Business Administration, Columbus, OH 43219-2099. Offers accounting (MBA); data analytics (MBA); finance (MBA); leadership (MBA); risk management (MBA); sport management (MBA). *Program availability:* Part-time, evening/weekend, 100% online, blended/hybrid learning. *Faculty:* 10 full-time (4 women), 12 part-time/adjunct (1 woman). *Students:* 42 full-time (17 women), 88 part-time (43 women); includes 29 minority (16 Black or African American, non-Hispanic/Latino; 1 American Indian or Alaska Native, non-Hispanic/Latino; 3 Asian, non-Hispanic/Latino; 5 Hispanic/Latino; 4 Two or more races, non-Hispanic/Latino), 14 international. Average age 31. 97 applicants, 44% accepted, 26 enrolled. In 2018, 56 master's awarded. *Entrance requirements:* For master's, minimum overall GPA of 3.0 in undergraduate degree from regionally-accredited institution or 2.75 in last 60 semester hours of bachelor's degree. Additional exam requirements/recommendations for international students: Required—TOEFL (minimum score 550 paper-based), IELTS (minimum score 6.5). *Application deadline:* For fall admission, 8/15 for domestic students, 6/10 for international students; for spring admission, 1/4 for domestic students, 11/2 for international students; for summer admission, 5/30 for domestic students. Applications are processed on a rolling basis. Application fee: $25. Electronic applications accepted. *Expenses: Tuition:* Full-time $10,800; part-time $600 per credit hour. *Required fees:* $450; $225 per semester. Tuition and fees vary according to program. *Financial support:* Applicants required to submit FAFSA. *Unit head:* Dr. Thomas Eveland, Director of Graduate Programs in Business, 614-251-4569, E-mail: evelandt@ohiodominican.edu. *Application contact:* John W. Naughton, Vice President for Enrollment and Student Success, 614-251-4721, Fax: 614-251-6654, E-mail: grad@ohiodominican.edu.
Website: http://www.ohiodominican.edu/academics/graduate/mba

Oregon State University, College of Science, Program in Data Analytics, Corvallis, OR 97331. Offers MS. *Program availability:* Part-time, online only, 100% online. *Expenses:* Contact institution.

Penn State Great Valley, Graduate Studies, Management Division, Malvern, PA 19355-1488. Offers business administration (MBA); cyber security (Certificate); data analytics (MPS, MS, Certificate); distributed energy and grid modernization (Certificate); finance (M Fin); health sector management (Certificate); human resource management (Certificate); information science (MSIS); leadership development (MLD); new ventures and entrepreneurship (Certificate); sustainable management practices (Certificate). *Accreditation:* AACSB.

Queens College of the City University of New York, Division of Social Sciences, Department of Sociology, Queens, NY 11367-1597. Offers data analytics and applied social research (MA). *Program availability:* Part-time, evening/weekend. *Faculty:* 28 full-time (11 women), 52 part-time/adjunct (29 women). *Students:* 5 full-time (4 women), 51 part-time (33 women); includes 32 minority (5 Black or African American, non-Hispanic/Latino; 11 Asian, non-Hispanic/Latino; 16 Hispanic/Latino), 10 international. Average age 30. In 2018, 12 master's awarded. *Entrance requirements:* For master's, minimum GPA of 3.0. Additional exam requirements/recommendations for international students: Required—TOEFL (minimum score 100 iBT), IELTS (minimum score 7). *Application deadline:* For fall admission, 5/15 for domestic students; for spring admission, 12/1 for domestic students. Applications are processed on a rolling basis. Application fee: $125. Electronic applications accepted. *Financial support:* Career-related internships or fieldwork and unspecified assistantships available. Financial award application deadline: 4/1; financial award applicants required to submit FAFSA. *Unit head:* Dr. Andrew Beveridge, Chair, 718-997-2800, E-mail: andrew.beveridge@qc.cuny.edu. *Application contact:* Elizabeth D'Amico-Ramirez, Assistant Director of Graduate Admissions, 718-997-5203, E-mail: elizabeth.damicoramirez@qc.cuny.edu.
Website: http://qcsociology.org/

Radford University, College of Graduate Studies and Research, Program in Data and Information Management, Radford, VA 24142. Offers MS. *Program availability:* Part-time. *Faculty:* 4 full-time (0 women). *Students:* 4 full-time (1 woman), 3 part-time (0 women); includes 1 minority (Asian, non-Hispanic/Latino), 3 international. Average age 30. 4 applicants, 50% accepted, 1 enrolled. In 2018, 5 master's awarded. *Entrance requirements:* For master's, GRE (minimum scores of 152 on quantitative portion and 148 on verbal portion, or 650 and 420, respectively, under old scoring system), minimum GPA of 3.0 overall from accredited educational institution, three letters of reference from faculty members familiar with academic performance in major coursework or from colleagues or supervisors familiar with work. Additional exam requirements/recommendations for international students: Required—TOEFL (minimum score 567 paper-based). *Application deadline:* Applications are processed on a rolling basis. Application fee: $50. Electronic applications accepted. *Expenses: Tuition, area resident:*

Full-time $8915; part-time $371 per credit hour. Tuition, state resident: full-time $8915; part-time $371 per credit hour. Tuition, nonresident: full-time $17,441. *Required fees:* $3288; $138 per credit hour. *Financial support:* In 2018–19, 3 students received support, including 3 teaching assistantships (averaging $10,000 per year); scholarships/grants and unspecified assistantships also available. Support available to part-time students. Financial award application deadline: 3/1; financial award applicants required to submit FAFSA. *Unit head:* Dr. Jeff Pittges, Graduate Coordinator and Director, 540-831-5381, E-mail: jpittges@radford.edu. *Application contact:* Dr. Jeff Pittges, Graduate Coordinator and Director, 540-831-5381, E-mail: jpittges@radford.edu.
Website: http://www.radford.edu/content/csat/home/daim.html

Regis University, College of Computer and Information Sciences, Denver, CO 80221-1099. Offers agile technologies (Certificate); cybersecurity (Certificate); data science (M Sc); database administration with Oracle (Certificate); database development (Certificate); database technologies (M Sc); enterprise Java software development (Certificate); enterprise resource planning (Certificate); executive information technology (Certificate); health care informatics (Certificate); health care informatics and information management (M Sc); information assurance (M Sc); information assurance policy management (Certificate); information technology management (M Sc); mobile software development (Certificate); software engineering (M Sc, Certificate); software engineering and database technology (M Sc); storage area networks (Certificate); systems engineering (M Sc, Certificate). *Program availability:* Part-time, evening/weekend, 100% online, blended/hybrid learning. *Degree requirements:* For master's, thesis (for some programs), final research project. *Entrance requirements:* For master's, official transcript reflecting baccalaureate degree awarded from regionally-accredited college or university, 2 years of related experience, resume, interview. Additional exam requirements/recommendations for international students: Required—TOEFL (minimum score 550 paper-based; 82 iBT). Electronic applications accepted. *Expenses:* Contact institution. *Faculty research:* Information policy, knowledge management, software architectures, data science.

Robert Morris University, School of Informatics, Humanities and Social Sciences, Moon Township, PA 15108-1189. Offers communication and information systems (MS); cyber security (MS); data analytics (MS); information security and assurance (MS); information systems and communications (D Sc); information systems management (MS); information technology project management (MS); Internet information systems (MS); organizational leadership (MS). *Program availability:* Part-time-only, evening/weekend, 100% online. *Faculty:* 22 full-time (7 women), 10 part-time/adjunct (0 women). *Students:* 262 part-time (94 women); includes 57 minority (31 Black or African American, non-Hispanic/Latino; 13 Asian, non-Hispanic/Latino; 8 Hispanic/Latino; 5 Two or more races, non-Hispanic/Latino), 43 international. Average age 35. 150 applicants, 92% accepted, 79 enrolled. In 2018, 133 master's, 11 doctorates awarded. *Degree requirements:* For master's, Completion of 30 credits; for doctorate, thesis/dissertation, Completion of 63 credits. *Entrance requirements:* For doctorate, employer letter of endorsement, interview. Additional exam requirements/recommendations for international students: Required—TOEFL (minimum score 550 paper-based; 79 iBT). *Application deadline:* For fall admission, 7/1 priority date for domestic and international students; for spring admission, 11/1 priority date for domestic and international students. Applications are processed on a rolling basis. Application fee: $35. Electronic applications accepted. Application fee is waived when completed online. *Expenses:* Master's $920/credit plus $80/credit fees; D.Sc. $28,290/year. *Financial support:* Institutionally sponsored loans available. Support available to part-time students. Financial award application deadline: 5/1; financial award applicants required to submit FAFSA. *Unit head:* Jon A. Radermacher, Interim Dean, School of Informatics, Humanities and Social Sciences, 412-397-4088, E-mail: radermacher@rmu.edu. *Application contact:* Jon A. Radermacher, Interim Dean, School of Informatics, Humanities and Social Sciences, 412-397-4088, E-mail: radermacher@rmu.edu.
Website: https://www.rmu.edu/academics/schools/sihss

Rochester Institute of Technology, Graduate Enrollment Services, Golisano College of Computing and Information Sciences, Computer Science Department, Advanced Certificate Program in Big Data Analytics, Rochester, NY 14623-5603. Offers Advanced Certificate. *Program availability:* Part-time, 100% online. *Students:* Average age 38. 1 applicant. In 2018, 59 Advanced Certificates awarded. *Entrance requirements:* For degree, GRE required for applicants with degrees from foreign universities., Personal statement. Two letters of recommendation. Minimum cumulative GPA of 3.0 (or equivalent). Additional exam requirements/recommendations for international students: Required—TOEFL (minimum score 550 paper-based; 79 iBT), IELTS (minimum score 6.5), PTE (minimum score 58). *Application deadline:* Applications are processed on a rolling basis. Application fee: $65. Electronic applications accepted. *Expenses:* Contact institution. *Financial support:* In 2018–19, 32 students received support. Available to part-time students. Applicants required to submit FAFSA. *Faculty research:* Data management, data analytics, data security, data warehousing. *Unit head:* Dr. Hans-Peter Bischof, Graduate Program Director, 585-475-5568, Fax: 585-475-4935, E-mail: hpb@cs.rit.edu. *Application contact:* Diane Ellison, Senior Associate Vice President, Graduate Enrollment Services, 585-475-2229, Fax: 585-475-7164, E-mail: gradinfo@rit.edu.
Website: https://www.rit.edu/study/big-data-analytics-adv-cert

Rockhurst University, Helzberg School of Management, Kansas City, MO 64110-2561. Offers accounting (MBA); business intelligence (MBA, Certificate); business intelligence and analytics (MS); data science (MBA, Certificate); entrepreneurship (MBA); finance (MBA); fundraising leadership (MBA, Certificate); healthcare management (MBA, Certificate); human capital (Certificate); international business (Certificate); management (MA, MBA, Certificate); nonprofit administration (Certificate); organizational development (Certificate); science leadership (Certificate). *Accreditation:* AACSB. *Program availability:* Part-time, evening/weekend. *Entrance requirements:* For master's, GMAT or GRE. Additional exam requirements/recommendations for international students: Required—TOEFL (minimum score 550 paper-based; 79 iBT). Electronic applications accepted. *Faculty research:* Offshoring/outsourcing, systems analysis/synthesis, work teams, multilateral trade, path dependencies/creation.

St. John's University, College of Professional Studies, Department of Computer Science, Mathematics and Science, Queens, NY 11439. Offers data mining and predictive analytics (MS). *Entrance requirements:* For master's, letters of recommendation, transcripts, resume, personal statement, prerequisites: calculus, probability and statistics. Additional exam requirements/recommendations for international students: Required—TOEFL (minimum score 80 iBT), IELTS (minimum score 6.5). Electronic applications accepted.

Saint Mary's College, Graduate Programs, Master of Science Program in Data Science, Notre Dame, IN 46556. Offers MS. *Program availability:* Part-time-only, blended/hybrid learning. *Faculty:* 3 full-time (2 women). *Students:* 6 part-time (4 women); includes 4 minority (3 Black or African American, non-Hispanic/Latino; 1 Hispanic/Latino). Average age 37. 12 applicants, 83% accepted, 6 enrolled. In 2018, 3 master's awarded. *Degree requirements:* For master's, thesis optional, practicum presentation. *Entrance requirements:* For master's, bachelor's degree, official transcripts, current resume or curriculum vitae, letter of recommendation, personal statement. Additional exam requirements/recommendations for international students: Required—TOEFL or IELTS. *Application deadline:* For fall admission, 6/15 priority date for domestic students. Applications are processed on a rolling basis. Application fee: $50. Electronic applications accepted. *Expenses:* $832 per credit hour (36 credits to degree), $475 graduate fee per academic year. *Financial support:* In 2018–19, 2 students received support. Scholarships/grants available. Financial award application deadline: 3/1; financial award applicants required to submit FAFSA. *Faculty research:* Real analysis and number theory, algorithm design and analysis, probability theory and Brownian motion, topological data analysis, data science education. *Unit head:* Kristin Kuter, Program Director, Master of Science in Data Science, 574-284-4458, E-mail: kjehring@saintmarys.edu. *Application contact:* Melissa Fruscione, Graduate Admission, 574-284-5098, E-mail: graduateadmission@saintmarys.edu.
Website: http://grad.saintmarys.edu/academic-programs/ms-data-science

Saint Mary's University of Minnesota, Schools of Graduate and Professional Programs, Graduate School of Business and Technology, Business Intelligence and Data Analytics Program, Winona, MN 55987-1399. Offers MS. *Unit head:* Michael Ratajczyk, Director, 507-457-1698, E-mail: mratajcz@smumn.edu. *Application contact:* Laurie Roy, Director of Admission of Schools of Graduate and Professional Programs, 507-457-8606, Fax: 612-728-5121, E-mail: lroy@smumn.edu.
Website: https://onlineprograms.smumn.edu/msbida/masters-in-business-intelligence-and-analytics?_ga=2.146577908.1736907137.1523547391-1359115499.1515170921

Saint Peter's University, Graduate Business Programs, Program in Data Science, Jersey City, NJ 07306-5997. Offers business analytics (MS). *Program availability:* Part-time. *Entrance requirements:* Additional exam requirements/recommendations for international students: Required—TOEFL (minimum score 550 paper-based; 79 iBT), IELTS (minimum score 6.5).

Seattle Pacific University, Master of Arts in Management Program, Seattle, WA 98119-1997. Offers business intelligence and data analytics (MA); cybersecurity (MA); faith and business (MA); human resources (MA); social and sustainable management (MA). *Students:* 12 part-time (9 women); includes 3 minority (2 Black or African American, non-Hispanic/Latino; 1 Asian, non-Hispanic/Latino), 4 international. Average age 31. 11 applicants, 45% accepted, 2 enrolled. *Entrance requirements:* For master's, GMAT scores above 500 (25 verbal; 30 quantitative; 4.4 analytical writing) are preferred. https://spu.edu/academics/school-of-business-and-economics/graduate-programs/mba#application, bachelor's degree from accredited college or university, resume, essay, official transcript. *Application deadline:* For fall admission, 8/1 for domestic students, 6/1 for international students; for winter admission, 11/1 for domestic students, 9/1 for international students; for spring admission, 2/1 for domestic students, 12/1 for international students; for summer admission, 5/1 for domestic students. Application fee: $50.
Website: http://spu.edu/academics/school-of-business-and-economics/graduate-programs/ma-management

Slippery Rock University of Pennsylvania, Graduate Studies (Recruitment), College of Health, Environment, and Science, Department of Mathematics and Statistics, Slippery Rock, PA 16057-1383. Offers data analytics (MS). *Program availability:* Part-time, blended/hybrid learning. *Faculty:* 3 full-time (1 woman). *Students:* 5 full-time (3 women), 18 part-time (7 women); includes 4 minority (2 Black or African American, non-Hispanic/Latino; 1 Asian, non-Hispanic/Latino; 1 Hispanic/Latino). Average age 31. 37 applicants, 68% accepted, 16 enrolled. In 2018, 13 master's awarded. *Entrance requirements:* For master's, official transcripts; minimum GPA of 3.0; completion of following prerequisite courses with minimum C grade: differential calculus, integral calculus, probability/inferential statistics, and a programming language (C, C++, C#, Java, Python); familiarity with multivariable calculus, linear algebra, and math statistics. Additional exam requirements/recommendations for international students: Required—TOEFL (minimum score 550 paper-based; 80 iBT). *Application deadline:* For fall admission, 5/1 priority date for domestic students, 3/1 priority date for international students; for spring admission, 10/1 priority date for domestic students, 9/1 priority date for international students. Applications are processed on a rolling basis. Application fee: $25 ($30 for international students). Electronic applications accepted. *Expenses:* Contact institution. *Financial support:* In 2018–19, 1 student received support. Career-related internships or fieldwork, Federal Work-Study, institutionally sponsored loans, scholarships/grants, tuition waivers (partial), and unspecified assistantships available. Support available to part-time students. Financial award application deadline: 5/1; financial award applicants required to submit FAFSA. *Unit head:* Dr. Christy Crute, Graduate Coordinator, 724-738-4286, Fax: 724-738-4807, E-mail: christy.crute@sru.edu. *Application contact:* Brandi Weber-Mortimer, Director of Graduate Admissions, 724-738-4340, E-mail: graduate.admissions@sru.edu.
Website: http://www.sru.edu/academics/colleges-and-departments/ches/departments/mathematics-and-statistics

Southern Arkansas University–Magnolia, School of Graduate Studies, Magnolia, AR 71753. Offers agriculture (MS); business administration (MBA), including agribusiness, social entrepreneurship, supply chain management; clinical and mental health counseling (MS); computer and information sciences (MS), including cyber security and privacy, data science, information technology; gifted and talented (M Ed), including curriculum and instruction, educational administration and supervision, gifted and talented P-8/7-12, instructional specialist P-4; higher, adult and lifelong education (M Ed); kinesiology (M Ed), including coaching; library media and information specialist (M Ed); public administration (MPA); school counseling K-12 (M Ed); student affairs and college counseling (M Ed); teaching (MAT). *Accreditation:* NCATE. *Program availability:* Part-time, 100% online, blended/hybrid learning. *Faculty:* 36 full-time (21 women), 32 part-time/adjunct (15 women). *Students:* 164 full-time (77 women), 762 part-time (510 women); includes 192 minority (163 Black or African American, non-Hispanic/Latino; 7 American Indian or Alaska Native, non-Hispanic/Latino; 13 Asian, non-Hispanic/Latino; 1 Hispanic/Latino; 8 Two or more races, non-Hispanic/Latino), 213 international. Average age 28. 363 applicants, 100% accepted, 237 enrolled. In 2018, 716 master's awarded. *Degree requirements:* For master's, comprehensive exam (for some programs), thesis optional. *Entrance requirements:* For master's, GRE, MAT or GMAT, minimum GPA of 2.5. Additional exam requirements/recommendations for international students: Required—TOEFL (minimum score 550 paper-based), IELTS (minimum score 6). *Application deadline:* For fall admission, 8/1 for domestic and international students; for spring admission, 12/1 for domestic students, 11/15 for international students; for summer admission, 4/1 for domestic students, 5/10 for international students. Applications are processed on a rolling basis. Application fee: $25 ($90 for international students). Electronic applications accepted. *Expenses: Tuition, area resident:* Full-time $5130; part-time $3420 per year. Tuition, state resident: full-time $5130; part-time $3420 per year. Tuition, nonresident: full-time $7866; part-time $5244 per year. *International tuition:* $7866 full-time. *Required fees:* $1052; $710 per unit. Tuition and fees vary according to course load. *Financial support:* Career-related internships or fieldwork, Federal Work-Study, scholarships/grants, tuition waivers (full), and unspecified assistantships available. Financial award applicants required to submit FAFSA. *Faculty research:* Alternative certification for teachers, supervision of instruction, instructional leadership, counseling. *Unit head:* Dr. Kim Bloss, Dean, School of Graduate Studies, 870-235-4150, Fax: 870-235-5227, E-mail: kkbloss@saumag.edu. *Application contact:* Talia Jett, Admissions Coordinator, 870-2355450, Fax: 870-235-5227, E-mail: taliajett@saumag.edu.
Website: http://www.saumag.edu/graduate

Data Science/Data Analytics

Southern Methodist University, Dedman College of Humanities and Sciences, Department of Statistical Science, Dallas, TX 75275-0332. Offers applied statistics and data analytics (MS); biostatistics (PhD); statistical science (PhD). *Program availability:* Part-time. *Degree requirements:* For master's, thesis, oral and written exams; for doctorate, thesis/dissertation, oral and written exams. *Entrance requirements:* For master's, GRE General Test, 12 hours of advanced math courses; for doctorate, GRE General Test, minimum GPA of 3.0. Additional exam requirements/recommendations for international students: Required—TOEFL. Electronic applications accepted. *Faculty research:* Regression, time series, linear models sampling, nonparametrics, biostatistics.

Southern Methodist University, Lyle School of Engineering, Department of Multidisciplinary Studies, Dallas, TX 75275. Offers data science (MS), including business analytics, machine learning; datacenter systems engineering (MS); design and innovation (MA). *Program availability:* Part-time, online learning. *Entrance requirements:* For master's, BS in one of the engineering disciplines, computer science, one of the quantitative sciences or mathematics; minimum of two years of college-level mathematics including one year of college-level calculus.

Southern New Hampshire University, School of Business, Manchester, NH 03106-1045. Offers accounting (MBA, Graduate Certificate); accounting finance (MS); accounting/auditing (MS); accounting/forensic accounting (MS); accounting/management accounting (MS); accounting/taxation (MS); applied economics (MS); athletic administration (MBA, Graduate Certificate); business administration (IMBA, Certificate), including business information systems (Certificate), human resource management (Certificate); business analytics (MBA); business intelligence (MBA); communication (MA), including new media and marketing, public relations; community economic development (MBA); criminal justice (MBA); data analytics (MS); economics (MBA); engineering management (MBA); entrepreneurship (MBA); finance (MBA, MS, Graduate Certificate); finance/corporate finance (MS); finance/investments (MS); forensic accounting (MBA); forensic accounting and fraud examination (Graduate Certificate); healthcare informatics (MBA); healthcare management (MBA); human resource management (MS); human resources (MBA); information technology (MS); information technology management (MBA); international business (PhD); Internet marketing (MBA); leadership (MBA); leadership of nonprofit organizations (Graduate Certificate); management (MS); marketing (MBA, MS, Graduate Certificate); music business (MBA); operations and project management (MS); operations and supply chain management (MBA, Graduate Certificate); organizational leadership (MS); project management (MBA, Graduate Certificate); public administration (MBA, Graduate Certificate); quantitative analysis (MBA); Six Sigma (Graduate Certificate); Six Sigma quality (MBA); social media marketing (MBA, Graduate Certificate); sport management (MBA, MS, Graduate Certificate); sustainability and environmental compliance (MBA); MBA/Certificate. *Accreditation:* ACBSP. *Program availability:* Part-time, evening/weekend, online learning. Terminal master's awarded for partial completion of doctoral program. *Degree requirements:* For master's, one foreign language, comprehensive exam (for some programs), thesis or alternative; for doctorate, one foreign language, comprehensive exam, thesis/dissertation. *Entrance requirements:* For master's, minimum GPA of 2.5; for doctorate, GMAT. Additional exam requirements/recommendations for international students: Required—TOEFL (minimum score 500 paper-based). Electronic applications accepted.

Stockton University, Office of Graduate Studies, Program in Data Science and Strategic Analytics, Galloway, NJ 08205-9441. Offers MS. *Program availability:* Part-time, online learning. *Faculty:* 6 full-time (2 women), 3 part-time/adjunct (1 woman). *Students:* 23 full-time (9 women), 8 part-time (3 women); includes 6 minority (1 Black or African American, non-Hispanic/Latino; 4 Asian, non-Hispanic/Latino; 1 Two or more races, non-Hispanic/Latino), 2 international. Average age 30. 41 applicants, 76% accepted, 26 enrolled. *Expenses: Tuition, area resident:* Full-time $11,226; part-time $623.69 per credit hour. Tuition, state resident: full-time $11,226; part-time $623.69 per credit hour. Tuition, nonresident: full-time $17,282; part-time $960.10 per credit hour. *International tuition:* $17,282 full-time. *Required fees:* $3376; $187.56 per credit hour. *Unit head:* Dr. J. Russell Manson, Director, 609-652-4354. *Application contact:* Tara Williams, Assistant Director of Graduate Enrollment, 609-626-3640, Fax: 609-626-6050, E-mail: gradschool@stockton.edu.
Website: https://stockton.edu/graduate/data-science_strategic-analytics.html

Suffolk University, Sawyer Business School, Department of Public Administration, Boston, MA 02108-2770. Offers community health (MPA); information systems, performance management, and big data analytics (MPA); nonprofit management (MPA); state and local government (MPA); JD/MPA; MPA/MS; MPA/MSCJ; MPA/MSMHC; MPA/MSPS. *Accreditation:* NASPAA (one or more programs are accredited). *Program availability:* Part-time, evening/weekend. *Faculty:* 9 full-time (5 women), 4 part-time/adjunct (2 women). *Students:* 21 full-time (14 women), 85 part-time (57 women); includes 37 minority (20 Black or African American, non-Hispanic/Latino; 5 Asian, non-Hispanic/Latino; 9 Hispanic/Latino; 3 Two or more races, non-Hispanic/Latino), 3 international. Average age 35. 106 applicants, 83% accepted, 34 enrolled. In 2018, 42 master's awarded. *Entrance requirements:* Additional exam requirements/recommendations for international students: Required—TOEFL (minimum score 550 paper-based; 80 iBT). *Application deadline:* For fall admission, 3/15 priority date for domestic and international students; for spring admission, 10/15 priority date for domestic and international students. Applications are processed on a rolling basis. Application fee: $50. Electronic applications accepted. *Expenses:* Contact institution. *Financial support:* In 2018–19, 76 students received support, including 2 fellowships (averaging $4,650 per year); career-related internships or fieldwork, Federal Work-Study, institutionally sponsored loans, and scholarships/grants also available. Support available to part-time students. Financial award application deadline: 4/1; financial award applicants required to submit FAFSA. *Faculty research:* Local government, health care, federal policy, mental health, HIV/AIDS. *Unit head:* Brenda Bond, Director/Department Chair, 617-305-1768, E-mail: bbond@suffolk.edu. *Application contact:* Mara Marzocchi, Associate Director of Graduate Admissions, 617-573-8302, Fax: 617-305-1733, E-mail: grad.admission@suffolk.edu.
Website: http://www.suffolk.edu/mpa

Syracuse University, School of Information Studies, CAS Program in Data Science, Syracuse, NY 13244. Offers CAS. *Program availability:* Part-time, evening/weekend, online learning. *Students:* Average age 36. In 2018, 47 CASs awarded. *Entrance requirements:* For degree, resume, personal statement. Additional exam requirements/recommendations for international students: Required—TOEFL (minimum score 100 iBT). *Application deadline:* For fall admission, 1/1 for domestic students, 1/1 priority date for international students; for spring admission, 10/15 for domestic students, 10/15 priority date for international students. Applications are processed on a rolling basis. Application fee: $75. Electronic applications accepted. *Faculty research:* Digital curation, data science education, and information analytics, digital libraries, information assurance. *Unit head:* Carsten Oesterlund, Program Director, 315-443-2911, E-mail: igrad@syr.edu. *Application contact:* Susan Corieri, Director of Enrollment Management, 315-443-2575, E-mail: ischool@syr.edu.
Website: https://ischool.syr.edu/academics/graduate/cas/cas-data-science/

Syracuse University, School of Information Studies, MS Program in Applied Data Science, Syracuse, NY 13244. Offers MS, MS/CAS. *Program availability:* Part-time, evening/weekend, online learning. *Students:* Average age 29. *Entrance requirements:* For master's, GRE General Test, resume. Additional exam requirements/recommendations for international students: Required—TOEFL (minimum score 100 iBT). *Application deadline:* For fall admission, 1/1 priority date for domestic and international students; for spring admission, 10/15 priority date for domestic and international students. Applications are processed on a rolling basis. Application fee: $75. Electronic applications accepted. *Financial support:* Fellowships with full tuition reimbursements, research assistantships with partial tuition reimbursements, teaching assistantships with partial tuition reimbursements, career-related internships or fieldwork, institutionally sponsored loans, and scholarships/grants available. Financial award application deadline: 2/1. *Faculty research:* Multimedia, information resources management, information security, network management. *Unit head:* Carsten Oesterlund, Program Director, 315-443-2911, Fax: 315-443-6886, E-mail: igrad@syr.edu. *Application contact:* Susan Corieri, Assistant Dean for Enrollment Management, 315-443-2575, E-mail: igrad@syr.edu.
Website: https://ischool.syr.edu/academics/graduate/masters-degrees/ms-in-applied-data-science/

Texas Tech University, Rawls College of Business Administration, Lubbock, TX 79409-2101. Offers accounting (MSA, PhD), including audit/financial reporting (MSA), taxation (MSA); data science (MS); finance (PhD); general business (MBA); healthcare management (MS); information systems and operations management (PhD); management (PhD); marketing (PhD); STEM (MBA); JD/MBA; JD/MSA; MBA/M Arch; MBA/MD; MBA/MS; MBA/Pharm D. *Accreditation:* AACSB. *Program availability:* Evening/weekend, 100% online, blended/hybrid learning. *Degree requirements:* For master's, thesis (for MS); capstone course; for doctorate, comprehensive exam, thesis/dissertation, qualifying exams. *Entrance requirements:* For master's, GMAT, GRE, MCAT, PCAT, LSAT, or DAT, holistic review of academic credentials, resume, essay, letters of recommendation; for doctorate, GMAT, GRE, holistic review of academic credentials, resume, statement of purpose, letters of recommendation. Additional exam requirements/recommendations for international students: Required—TOEFL (minimum score 550 paper-based; 79 iBT), IELTS (minimum score 6.5), PTE (minimum score 60). Electronic applications accepted. *Expenses:* Contact institution. *Faculty research:* Governmental and nonprofit accounting, securities and options futures, statistical analysis and design, leadership, consumer behavior.

Tufts University, School of Engineering, Department of Civil and Environmental Engineering, Medford, MA 02155. Offers bioengineering (MS), including environmental biotechnology; civil and environmental engineering (MS, PhD), including applied data science, environmental and water resources engineering, environmental health, geosystems engineering, structural engineering and mechanics; PhD/PhD. *Program availability:* Part-time. Terminal master's awarded for partial completion of doctoral program. *Degree requirements:* For master's, thesis (for some programs); for doctorate, thesis/dissertation. *Entrance requirements:* For master's and doctorate, GRE General Test. Additional exam requirements/recommendations for international students: Required—TOEFL (minimum score 550 paper-based; 80 iBT), IELTS (minimum score 6.5). Electronic applications accepted. *Expenses: Tuition:* Full-time $51,288; part-time $1710 per credit hour. *Required fees:* $904. Full-time tuition and fees vary according to degree level, program and student level. Part-time tuition and fees vary according to course load. *Faculty research:* Environmental and water resources engineering, environmental health, geotechnical and geoenvironmental engineering, structural engineering and mechanics, water diplomacy.

University at Buffalo, the State University of New York, Graduate School, School of Engineering and Applied Sciences, Department of Civil, Structural, and Environmental Engineering, Buffalo, NY 14260. Offers civil engineering (MS, PhD); engineering science (MS), including data sciences, green energy, Internet of Things, nanoelectronics; environmental and water resources engineering (MS). *Program availability:* Part-time, online learning. Terminal master's awarded for partial completion of doctoral program. *Degree requirements:* For master's, project, thesis, or comprehensive exam; for doctorate, thesis/dissertation. *Entrance requirements:* For master's and doctorate, GRE General Test, letters of reference. Additional exam requirements/recommendations for international students: Required—TOEFL (minimum score 550 paper-based; 79 iBT). Electronic applications accepted. *Faculty research:* Structural and earthquake engineering; geomechanics, geotechnical and geoenvironmental engineering; computational engineering mechanics; bridge engineering; environmental and water resources engineering; transportation systems engineering.

The University of Arizona, College of Agriculture and Life Sciences, Department of Agricultural and Resource Economics, Tucson, AZ 85721. Offers applied econometrics and data analytics (MS); applied economics and policy analysis (MS). *Program availability:* Part-time. *Degree requirements:* For master's, thesis or alternative. *Entrance requirements:* For master's, GRE General Test, 3 letters of recommendation, minimum GPA of 3.0. Additional exam requirements/recommendations for international students: Required—TOEFL (minimum score 550 paper-based; 79 iBT). Electronic applications accepted. *Faculty research:* Natural resources, international development trade, production and marketing, agricultural policy, rural development.

University of California, Berkeley, Graduate Division, School of Information, Program in Information and Data Science, Berkeley, CA 94720. Offers MIDS. *Program availability:* Online only, 100% online. *Degree requirements:* For master's, capstone project. Electronic applications accepted.

University of California, San Diego, Graduate Division, Program in Data Science and Engineering, La Jolla, CA 92093. Offers MAS. *Program availability:* Part-time. *Students:* 63 part-time (8 women). 96 applicants, 36% accepted, 31 enrolled. In 2018, 39 master's awarded. *Degree requirements:* For master's, capstone team project. *Entrance requirements:* For master's, 2 letters of recommendation, statement of purpose, resume/curriculum vitae. Additional exam requirements/recommendations for international students: Required—TOEFL (minimum score 550 paper-based; 80 iBT), IELTS (minimum score 7). *Application deadline:* For fall admission, 6/25 for domestic students. Application fee: $105 ($125 for international students). Electronic applications accepted. *Expenses:* Contact institution. *Financial support:* Applicants required to submit FAFSA. *Unit head:* Dr. Yoav Freund, Co-Director, 858-534-0404, E-mail: datasciencemas@eng.ucsd.edu. *Application contact:* Yvonne Wu, Program Coordinator, 858-246-1463, E-mail: yvwu@ucsd.edu.
Website: http://jacobsschool.ucsd.edu/mas/dse/

University of Colorado Denver, Business School, Program in Marketing, Denver, CO 80217. Offers advanced market analytics in a big data world (MS); brand communication in the digital era (MS); global marketing (MS); high-tech and entrepreneurial marketing (MS); marketing and global sustainability (MS); marketing intelligence and strategy in the 21st century (MS); sports and entertainment business (MS). *Program availability:* Part-time, evening/weekend. *Degree requirements:* For master's, 30 semester hours (21 of marketing core courses, 9 of marketing electives). *Entrance requirements:* For master's, GMAT, resume, essay, two letters of recommendation, financial statements (for international applicants). Additional exam requirements/recommendations for international students: Required—TOEFL (minimum score 525 paper-based; 71 iBT); Recommended—IELTS (minimum score 6.5). Electronic applications accepted. *Expenses:* Contact institution. *Faculty research:* Marketing issues in the Chinese environment, impact of individual difference and contextual factors on the risk-taking behaviors of managers making new-business creation decisions, attribution theory perspective of conflict between marketers and engineers, organizational identity and identification, international market entry strategies.

University of Denver, Daniel Felix Ritchie School of Engineering and Computer Science, Department of Computer Science, Denver, CO 80210. Offers computer science (MS, PhD); cybersecurity (MS); data science (MS). *Program availability:* Part-time, evening/weekend. *Faculty:* 15 full-time (3 women), 1 (woman) part-time/adjunct. *Students:* 23 full-time (8 women), 91 part-time (29 women); includes 11 minority (5 Asian, non-Hispanic/Latino; 1 Hispanic/Latino; 1 Native Hawaiian or other Pacific Islander, non-Hispanic/Latino; 4 Two or more races, non-Hispanic/Latino), 51 international. Average age 30. 263 applicants, 59% accepted, 79 enrolled. In 2018, 9 master's, 1 doctorate awarded. *Degree requirements:* For doctorate, variable foreign language requirement, comprehensive exam, thesis/dissertation, reading competency in two languages, modern typesetting system, or additional coursework. *Entrance requirements:* For master's and doctorate, GRE General Test, bachelor's degree, transcripts, personal statement, resume or curriculum vitae, three letters of recommendation. Additional exam requirements/recommendations for international students: Required—TOEFL (minimum score 550 paper-based; 80 iBT). *Application deadline:* For fall admission, 1/15 priority date for domestic and international students; for winter admission, 10/25 for domestic and international students; for spring admission, 2/7 for domestic and international students; for summer admission, 4/24 for domestic and international students. Applications are processed on a rolling basis. Application fee: $65. Electronic applications accepted. *Expenses:* $33,183 per year full-time. *Financial support:* In 2018–19, 98 students received support, including 14 teaching assistantships with tuition reimbursements available (averaging $18,214 per year); research assistantships with tuition reimbursements available, career-related internships or fieldwork, Federal Work-Study, institutionally sponsored loans, scholarships/grants, and unspecified assistantships also available. Financial award application deadline: 2/15; financial award applicants required to submit FAFSA. *Faculty research:* Algorithms, artificial intelligence, databases, game development, robotics. *Unit head:* Dr. Bruce Harmon, Professor of the Practice and Interim Chair, 303-871-6949, E-mail: bruce.harmon@du.edu. *Application contact:* Information Contact, 303-871-2458, E-mail: info@cs.du.edu.
Website: http://ritchieschool.du.edu/departments/computer-science/

University of Houston–Downtown, College of Sciences and Technology, Houston, TX 77002. Offers data analytics (MS). *Program availability:* Part-time, evening/weekend. *Degree requirements:* For master's, capstone course, internship course or approved directed study. *Entrance requirements:* For master's, GRE. Additional exam requirements/recommendations for international students: Required—TOEFL (minimum score 553 paper-based; 81 iBT), IELTS (minimum score 6.5). Electronic applications accepted. *Expenses:* Contact institution.

University of Illinois at Springfield, Graduate Programs, College of Liberal Arts and Sciences, Program in Data Analytics, Springfield, IL 62703-5407. Offers MS. Program administered jointly by the Departments of Computer Science and Mathematical Sciences. *Program availability:* Part-time, evening/weekend, 100% online, blended/hybrid learning. *Faculty:* 6 full-time (2 women), 1 part-time/adjunct (0 women). *Students:* 19 full-time (9 women), 35 part-time (11 women); includes 8 minority (1 Black or African American, non-Hispanic/Latino; 2 Asian, non-Hispanic/Latino; 5 Hispanic/Latino), 22 international. Average age 33. 146 applicants, 38% accepted, 22 enrolled. *Degree requirements:* For master's, thesis or alternative, capstone course. *Entrance requirements:* For master's, bachelor's degree or equivalent with minimum undergraduate GPA of 3.0; completion of all prerequisite courses with minimum grade of B-; written evidence of ability to perform at a high academic level by submitting a personal and academic statement. Additional exam requirements/recommendations for international students: Required—TOEFL (minimum score 500 paper-based; 61 iBT). *Application deadline:* Applications are processed on a rolling basis. Application fee: $60 ($75 for international students). Electronic applications accepted. *Financial support:* In 2018–19, research assistantships with full tuition reimbursements (averaging $10,384 per year), teaching assistantships with full tuition reimbursements (averaging $10,303 per year) were awarded; fellowships, career-related internships or fieldwork, Federal Work-Study, scholarships/grants, health care benefits, and unspecified assistantships also available. Support available to part-time students. Financial award application deadline: 11/15; financial award applicants required to submit FAFSA. *Unit head:* Dr. Hei-Chi Chan, Program Administrator, 217-206-7331, E-mail: hchan1@uis.edu. *Application contact:* Dr. Hei-Chi Chan, Program Administrator, 217-206-7331, E-mail: hchan1@uis.edu.
Website: http://www.uis.edu/dataanalytics/

University of Louisville, J. B. Speed School of Engineering, Department of Computer Engineering and Computer Science, Louisville, KY 40292-0001. Offers computer engineering and computer science (M Eng); computer science (MS, PhD); cybersecurity (Certificate); data science (Certificate). *Accreditation:* ABET (one or more programs are accredited). *Program availability:* Part-time, 100% online, blended/hybrid learning. *Faculty:* 14 full-time (2 women), 3 part-time/adjunct (0 women). *Students:* 62 full-time (16 women), 124 part-time (31 women); includes 32 minority (4 Black or African American, non-Hispanic/Latino; 14 Asian, non-Hispanic/Latino; 8 Hispanic/Latino; 6 Two or more races, non-Hispanic/Latino), 46 international. Average age 33. 74 applicants, 49% accepted, 25 enrolled. In 2018, 18 master's, 5 doctorates, 7 other advanced degrees awarded. Terminal master's awarded for partial completion of doctoral program. *Degree requirements:* For master's, thesis optional; for doctorate, comprehensive exam, thesis/dissertation. *Entrance requirements:* For master's, GRE, Two letters of recommendation, official final transcripts; for doctorate, GRE, Two letters of recommendation, personal statement, official final transcripts. Additional exam requirements/recommendations for international students: Required—TOEFL (minimum score 550 paper-based; 80 iBT), IELTS (minimum score 6.5), GRE. *Application deadline:* For fall admission, 5/1 priority date for domestic and international students; for spring admission, 11/1 priority date for domestic and international students; for summer admission, 3/1 priority date for domestic and international students. Applications are processed on a rolling basis. Application fee: $65. Electronic applications accepted. *Expenses: Tuition, area resident:* Full-time $6500; part-time $723 per credit hour. Tuition, state resident: full-time $6500. Tuition, nonresident: full-time $13,557; part-time $1507 per credit hour. Tuition and fees vary according to course load and program. *Financial support:* In 2018–19, 78 students received support. Fellowships, research assistantships, teaching assistantships, scholarships/grants, health care benefits, and tuition waivers (full) available. Financial award application deadline: 1/1. *Faculty research:* Artificial Intelligence, Big Data Analytics, Bioinformatics, Cybersecurity, Data Mining. *Total annual research expenditures:* $740,736. *Unit head:* Dr. Wei Zhang, Chair, 502-852-0715, E-mail: wei.zhang@louisville.edu. *Application contact:* Dr. Mehmed Kantardzic, Director of Graduate Studies, 502-852-3703, E-mail: mehmed.kantardzic@louisville.edu.
Website: http://louisville.edu/speed/computer

University of Maryland, Baltimore County, The Graduate School, College of Engineering and Information Technology, Department of Computer Science and Electrical Engineering, Program in Data Science, Baltimore, MD 21250. Offers MPS. *Program availability:* Part-time. *Entrance requirements:* For master's, one semester of statistics, calculus I or II (depending upon track), academic or professional experience equivalent to basic programming courses. Additional exam requirements/recommendations for international students: Required—TOEFL (minimum score 550 paper-based; 80 iBT). Electronic applications accepted. *Faculty research:* Data science.

University of Maryland University College, The Graduate School, Program in Data Analytics, Adelphi, MD 20783. Offers MS, Certificate. *Program availability:* Part-time, evening/weekend, online learning. *Students:* 346 part-time (135 women); includes 184 minority (112 Black or African American, non-Hispanic/Latino; 40 Asian, non-Hispanic/Latino; 20 Hispanic/Latino; 12 Two or more races, non-Hispanic/Latino), 19 international. Average age 38. 128 applicants, 100% accepted, 49 enrolled. In 2018, 115 master's, 22 other advanced degrees awarded. *Application deadline:* Applications are processed on a rolling basis. Application fee: $50. Electronic applications accepted. *Financial support:* Scholarships/grants available. Support available to part-time students. Financial award application deadline: 6/1; financial award applicants required to submit FAFSA. *Unit head:* Elena Gortcheva, Program Chair, 240-684-2400, E-mail: elena.gortcheva@umuc.edu. *Application contact:* Admissions, 800-888-8682, Fax: 240-684-2151, E-mail: studentsfirst@umuc.edu.
Website: https://www.umuc.edu/academic-programs/masters-degrees/data-analytics.cfm

University of Massachusetts Dartmouth, Graduate School, Program in Data Science, North Dartmouth, MA 02747-2300. Offers MS. Program offered jointly by the Department of Computer Science and the Department of Mathematics. *Program availability:* Part-time, online learning. *Students:* 8 full-time (6 women), 3 part-time (1 woman), 8 international. Average age 26. 53 applicants, 70% accepted, 5 enrolled. In 2018, 1 master's awarded. *Degree requirements:* For master's, thesis, practicum. *Entrance requirements:* For master's, GRE, statement of purpose (minimum 300 words), resume, official transcripts, 3 letters of recommendation. Additional exam requirements/recommendations for international students: Required—TOEFL (minimum score 533 paper-based; 72 iBT), IELTS (minimum score 6). *Application deadline:* For fall admission, 4/15 priority date for domestic students, 3/15 priority date for international students; for spring admission, 12/15 priority date for domestic students, 11/15 priority date for international students. Application fee: $60. Electronic applications accepted. *Financial support:* In 2018–19, 1 research assistantship (averaging $18,000 per year) was awarded; tuition waivers (full) also available. Financial award application deadline: 3/1; financial award applicants required to submit FAFSA. *Faculty research:* Behavioral trajectory pattern recognition in longitudinal studies, computational partial differential equations, uncertainty quantification, computational general relativity and fluid dynamics, data mining. *Unit head:* Scott Field, Director, College of Engineering Data Science, 508-999-8318, E-mail: sfield@umassd.edu. *Application contact:* Scott Webster, Director of Graduate Studies & Admissions, 508-999-8604, Fax: 508-999-8183, E-mail: graduate@umassd.edu.
Website: http://www.umassd.edu/programs/data-science-ms

University of Michigan, Rackham Graduate School, College of Literature, Science, and the Arts, Department of Statistics, Ann Arbor, MI 48109. Offers applied statistics (MS); data science (MS); statistics (AM, PhD). *Faculty:* 23 full-time (5 women). *Students:* 216 full-time (88 women), 1 part-time (0 women); includes 25 minority (1 Black or African American, non-Hispanic/Latino; 20 Asian, non-Hispanic/Latino; 2 Hispanic/Latino; 2 Two or more races, non-Hispanic/Latino), 157 international. 1,267 applicants, 27% accepted, 102 enrolled. In 2018, 70 master's, 14 doctorates awarded. Terminal master's awarded for partial completion of doctoral program. *Degree requirements:* For doctorate, comprehensive exam, thesis/dissertation, oral defense of dissertation, preliminary exams. *Entrance requirements:* For master's and doctorate, GRE General Test. Additional exam requirements/recommendations for international students: Required—TOEFL (minimum score 560 paper-based; 84 iBT), IELTS (minimum score 6.5). *Application deadline:* For fall admission, 12/31 for domestic and international students. Application fee: $75 ($90 for international students). Electronic applications accepted. *Financial support:* Fellowships, research assistantships, teaching assistantships, career-related internships or fieldwork, Federal Work-Study, institutionally sponsored loans, scholarships/grants, health care benefits, and unspecified assistantships available. *Faculty research:* Reliability and degradation modeling, biological and legal applications, bioinformatics, statistical computing, covariance estimation. *Unit head:* Prof. Xuming He, Chair, 734-7645981, E-mail: statchair@umich.edu. *Application contact:* Andrea Nashar, PhD Program Coordinator, 734-763-3520, E-mail: statsphdprogram@umich.edu.
Website: http://www.lsa.umich.edu/stats/

University of Michigan, Rackham Graduate School, Program in Survey Methodology, Ann Arbor, MI 48109. Offers data science (MS, PhD); social and psychological (MS, PhD); statistical (MS, PhD); survey methodology (Certificate). *Program availability:* Part-time. *Faculty:* 12 full-time (2 women), 8 part-time/adjunct (3 women). *Students:* 26 full-time (16 women), 4 part-time (3 women); includes 24 minority (1 Black or African American, non-Hispanic/Latino; 14 Asian, non-Hispanic/Latino; 1 Hispanic/Latino; 8 Two or more races, non-Hispanic/Latino). Average age 26. 42 applicants, 48% accepted, 13 enrolled. In 2018, 6 master's, 3 doctorates, 2 other advanced degrees awarded. Terminal master's awarded for partial completion of doctoral program. *Degree requirements:* For master's, internships; for doctorate, comprehensive exam, thesis/dissertation. *Entrance requirements:* For master's and doctorate, GRE, 3 letters of recommendation, academic statement of purpose, personal statement, resume or curriculum vitae, academic transcripts; for Certificate, 3 letters of recommendation, academic statement of purpose, personal statement, resume or curriculum vitae, academic transcripts. Additional exam requirements/recommendations for international students: Required—TOEFL (minimum score 560 paper-based; 84 iBT). *Application deadline:* For fall admission, 1/1 for domestic and international students. Application fee: $75 ($90 for international students). Electronic applications accepted. *Expenses:* Contact institution. *Financial support:* In 2018–19, 11 students received support, including 11 research assistantships with full tuition reimbursements available; teaching assistantships, career-related internships or fieldwork, institutionally sponsored loans, scholarships/grants, traineeships, health care benefits, and unspecified assistantships also available. Support available to part-time students. Financial award application deadline: 1/1. *Faculty research:* Survey methodology, web surveys, survey non-response, sample design methods, adaptive survey design. *Total annual research expenditures:* $2.5 million. *Unit head:* Dr. Frederick Conrad, Director, 734-936-1019, Fax: 734-764-8263, E-mail: fconrad@umich.edu. *Application contact:* Jill Esau, Educational Programs Administrator, 734-647-4620, Fax: 734-764-8263, E-mail: jesau@umich.edu.
Website: http://psm.isr.umich.edu/

University of Michigan–Dearborn, College of Engineering and Computer Science, Master of Science in Data Science Program, Dearborn, MI 48128. Offers MS. *Program availability:* Part-time, evening/weekend. *Faculty:* 19 full-time (1 woman), 5 part-time/adjunct (0 women). *Students:* 22 full-time (14 women), 19 part-time (6 women); includes

3 minority (1 Black or African American, non-Hispanic/Latino; 2 Asian, non-Hispanic/Latino), 25 international. Average age 29. 105 applicants, 57% accepted, 26 enrolled. *Entrance requirements:* Additional exam requirements/recommendations for international students: Required—TOEFL (minimum score 560 paper-based; 84 iBT), IELTS (minimum score 6.5). *Application deadline:* For fall admission, 8/1 for domestic students, 5/1 for international students; for winter admission, 12/1 for domestic students, 9/1 for international students; for spring admission, 4/1 for domestic students, 1/1 for international students. Applications are processed on a rolling basis. Application fee: $60. Electronic applications accepted. *Expenses:* Tuition, state resident: full-time $15,380; part-time $88 per credit hour. Tuition, nonresident: full-time $23,948; part-time $1377 per credit hour. *Required fees:* $780; $780 $390. Tuition and fees vary according to course level, course load, degree level, program, reciprocity agreements and student level. *Financial support:* In 2018–19, 24 students received support. Scholarships/grants, unspecified assistantships, and non-resident tuition scholarships available. Support available to part-time students. Financial award application deadline: 3/1; financial award applicants required to submit FAFSA. *Faculty research:* Data analytics for various applications, applied machine learning, natural language processing, optimization, advanced data management. *Unit head:* Dr. William Grosky, Director, 313-583-6424, E-mail: wgrosky@umich.edu. *Application contact:* Office of Graduate Studies, 313-583-6321, E-mail: umd-graduatestudies@umich.edu.
Website: https://umdearborn.edu/cecs/departments/computer-and-information-science/graduate-programs/ms-data-science

University of Michigan–Dearborn, College of Engineering and Computer Science, PhD Program in Computer and Information Science, Dearborn, MI 48128. Offers data management (PhD); data science (PhD); software engineering (PhD); systems and security (PhD). *Faculty:* 19 full-time (1 woman), 5 part-time/adjunct (0 women). *Students:* 7 full-time (4 women), 7 part-time (1 woman); includes 1 minority (Asian, non-Hispanic/Latino), 9 international. Average age 30. 22 applicants, 36% accepted, 6 enrolled. In 2018, 1 doctorate awarded. *Degree requirements:* For doctorate, comprehensive exam, thesis/dissertation. *Entrance requirements:* For doctorate, GRE, bachelor's or master's degree in computer science or closely-related field. Additional exam requirements/recommendations for international students: Required—TOEFL (minimum score 560 paper-based; 84 iBT), IELTS (minimum score 6.5). *Application deadline:* For fall admission, 2/1 for domestic and international students. Application fee: $60. Electronic applications accepted. *Expenses:* Tuition, state resident: full-time $15,380; part-time $88 per credit hour. Tuition, nonresident: full-time $23,948; part-time $1377 per credit hour. *Required fees:* $780; $780 $390. Tuition and fees vary according to course level, course load, degree level, program, reciprocity agreements and student level. *Financial support:* In 2018–19, 2 students received support. Research assistantships with full tuition reimbursements available, teaching assistantships with full tuition reimbursements available, scholarships/grants, health care benefits, and unspecified assistantships available. Financial award application deadline: 2/1; financial award applicants required to submit FAFSA. *Faculty research:* Data science, data management, cybersecurity, software engineering, systems. *Unit head:* Dr. Di Ma, Director, 313-583-6737, E-mail: dmadma@umich.edu. *Application contact:* Office of Graduate Studies, 313-583-6321, E-mail: umd-graduatestudies@umich.edu.
Website: https://umdearborn.edu/cecs/departments/computer-and-information-science/graduate-programs/phd-computer-and-information-science

University of Minnesota, Twin Cities Campus, College of Science and Engineering, Department of Computer Science and Engineering, Program in Data Science, Minneapolis, MN 55455-0213. Offers MS. *Entrance requirements:* For master's, GRE. Additional exam requirements/recommendations for international students: Required—TOEFL. Electronic applications accepted. *Faculty research:* Data collection and management, data analytics, scalable data-driven pattern discovery, and the fundamental algorithmic and statistical concepts behind these methods.

University of Mississippi, Graduate School, School of Accountancy, University, MS 38677. Offers accountancy (M Acc, PhD); accounting and data analytics (MA); taxation accounting (M Tax). *Accreditation:* AACSB. *Faculty:* 20 full-time (6 women), 2 part-time/adjunct (both women). *Students:* 228 full-time (102 women), 4 part-time (2 women); includes 32 minority (16 Black or African American, non-Hispanic/Latino; 4 Asian, non-Hispanic/Latino; 5 Hispanic/Latino; 1 Native Hawaiian or other Pacific Islander, non-Hispanic/Latino; 6 Two or more races, non-Hispanic/Latino), 7 international. Average age 24. In 2018, 131 master's, 2 doctorates awarded. *Entrance requirements:* For master's, GMAT, minimum GPA of 3.0; for doctorate, GMAT. Additional exam requirements/recommendations for international students: Required—TOEFL. *Application deadline:* Applications are processed on a rolling basis. Application fee: $50. Electronic applications accepted. *Financial support:* Scholarships/grants available. Financial award application deadline: 3/1; financial award applicants required to submit FAFSA. *Unit head:* Dr. W. Mark Wilder, Dean, School of Accountancy, 662-915-7468, Fax: 662-915-7483, E-mail: umaccy@olemiss.edu. *Application contact:* Tameka Smith, Graduate Activities Specialist for Admissions, 662-915-7474, Fax: 662-915-7577, E-mail: gschool@olemiss.edu.
Website: https://www.olemiss.edu

University of Nebraska at Omaha, Graduate Studies, College of Information Science and Technology, Department of Information Systems and Quantitative Analysis, Omaha, NE 68182. Offers data analytics (Certificate); information assurance (Certificate); information technology (MIT, PhD); management information systems (MS); project management (Certificate); systems analysis and design (Certificate). *Program availability:* Part-time, evening/weekend. *Degree requirements:* For master's, comprehensive exam, thesis (for some programs); for doctorate, comprehensive exam, thesis/dissertation. *Entrance requirements:* For master's, GRE General Test, minimum GPA of 3.0, 3 letters of recommendation, writing sample, resume, official transcripts; for doctorate, GMAT or GRE General Test, minimum GPA of 3.0, 3 letters of recommendation, writing sample, resume, official transcripts; for Certificate, minimum GPA of 3.0, official transcripts. Additional exam requirements/recommendations for international students: Required—TOEFL, IELTS, PTE. Electronic applications accepted.

University of Nevada, Las Vegas, Graduate College, Lee Business School, Department of Management, Entrepreneurship and Technology, Las Vegas, NV 89154-6034. Offers data analytics (Certificate); data analytics and applied economics (MS); hotel administration/management information systems (MS/MS); management (Certificate); management information systems (MS, Certificate); new venture management (Certificate); MS/MS. *Program availability:* Part-time, evening/weekend. *Faculty:* 10 full-time (1 woman), 1 part-time/adjunct (0 women). *Students:* 59 full-time (21 women), 36 part-time (15 women); includes 27 minority (5 Black or African American, non-Hispanic/Latino; 14 Asian, non-Hispanic/Latino; 4 Hispanic/Latino; 4 Two or more races, non-Hispanic/Latino), 32 international. Average age 30. 85 applicants, 84% accepted, 44 enrolled. In 2018, 28 master's, 5 other advanced degrees awarded. *Degree requirements:* For master's, thesis optional. *Entrance requirements:* For master's, GMAT or GRE, bachelor's degree with minimum GPA 3.0; 2 letters of recommendation; for Certificate, GMAT or GRE. Additional exam requirements/recommendations for international students: Required—TOEFL (minimum score 550 paper-based; 80 iBT), IELTS (minimum score 7). *Application deadline:* For fall admission, 8/1 for domestic students, 5/1 for international students; for spring admission, 11/15 for domestic students, 10/1 for international students. Application fee: $60 ($95 for international students). Electronic applications accepted. *Expenses:* Contact institution. *Financial support:* In 2018–19, 25 students received support, including 8 research assistantships with full tuition reimbursements available (averaging $11,286 per year), 7 teaching assistantships with full tuition reimbursements available (averaging $11,429 per year); institutionally sponsored loans, scholarships/grants, health care benefits, and unspecified assistantships also available. Financial award application deadline: 3/15; financial award applicants required to submit FAFSA. *Faculty research:* Decision-making, publish or perish, ethical issues in information systems, IT-enabled decision making, business ethics. *Total annual research expenditures:* $28,971. *Unit head:* Dr. Rajiv Kishore, Chair/ Professor, 702-895-1709, Fax: 702-895-4370, E-mail: met.chair@unlv.edu. *Application contact:* Dr. Greg Moody, Graduate Coordinator, 702-895-1365, Fax: 702-895-4370, E-mail: met.gradcoord@unlv.edu.
Website: https://www.unlv.edu/met

The University of North Carolina at Charlotte, The Graduate School, Program in Data Science and Business Analytics, Charlotte, NC 28223-0001. Offers MS, PSM, Graduate Certificate. *Program availability:* Part-time, evening/weekend. *Students:* 62 full-time (31 women), 101 part-time (33 women); includes 50 minority (19 Black or African American, non-Hispanic/Latino; 20 Asian, non-Hispanic/Latino; 8 Hispanic/Latino; 3 Two or more races, non-Hispanic/Latino), 52 international. Average age 31. 456 applicants, 32% accepted, 84 enrolled. In 2018, 57 master's, 13 other advanced degrees awarded. *Entrance requirements:* For master's, GRE, GMAT, undergraduate degree in any scientific, engineering or business discipline or a closely-related field; minimum undergraduate GPA of 3.0; three letters of recommendation; statement of purpose outlining goals for pursuing graduate education; current working knowledge of at least one higher-level (procedural) language; for Graduate Certificate, undergraduate degree in any scientific, engineering or business discipline or a closely-related field; minimum undergraduate GPA of 3.0; statement of purpose outlining goals for pursuing graduate education; current working knowledge of at least one higher-level (procedural) language; familiarity with computer applications. Additional exam requirements/recommendations for international students: Required—TOEFL (minimum score 523 paper-based; 70 iBT), IELTS (minimum score 6), TOEFL (minimum score 523 paper-based, 70 iBT) or IELTS (6). *Application deadline:* Applications are processed on a rolling basis. Application fee: $75. Electronic applications accepted. *Expenses:* Contact institution. *Financial support:* Career-related internships or fieldwork, institutionally sponsored loans, scholarships/grants, and unspecified assistantships available. Support available to part-time students. Financial award application deadline: 3/1; financial award applicants required to submit FAFSA. *Unit head:* Carly Mahedy, Director of Student Services, Data Science Initiative, 704-687-0068, E-mail: datascience@uncc.edu. *Application contact:* Kathy B. Giddings, Director of Graduate Admissions, 704-687-5503, Fax: 704-687-1668, E-mail: gradadm@uncc.edu.
Website: http://www.analytics.uncc.edu/

The University of North Carolina Wilmington, Interdisciplinary Program in Computer Science and Information Systems, Wilmington, NC 28403-3297. Offers computer science and information systems (MS); data science (MS). *Degree requirements:* For master's, thesis or alternative, research project. *Entrance requirements:* For master's, GMAT or GRE, 3 letters of recommendation, resume, statement of interest; baccalaureate degree in a computational field preferred (for data science). Additional exam requirements/recommendations for international students: Required—TOEFL (minimum score 550 paper-based; 79 iBT), IELTS (minimum score 6.5). Electronic applications accepted. *Expenses:* Contact institution.

University of Pennsylvania, School of Engineering and Applied Science, Program in Data Science, Philadelphia, PA 19104. Offers MSE. *Program availability:* Part-time. *Students:* 36 full-time (14 women), 17 part-time (3 women); includes 1 minority (Two or more races, non-Hispanic/Latino), 45 international. Average age 24. 747 applicants, 9% accepted, 39 enrolled. In 2018, 6 master's awarded. *Degree requirements:* For master's, comprehensive exam, thesis optional. *Entrance requirements:* For master's, GRE, bachelor's degree, letters of recommendation, resume, personal statement. Additional exam requirements/recommendations for international students: Required—TOEFL (minimum score 100 iBT), IELTS (minimum score 7). *Application deadline:* For fall admission, 3/15 priority date for domestic and international students. Application fee: $80. *Expenses:* Contact institution. *Faculty research:* Machine learning, big data analytics, statistics, biomedical informatics, policy creation. *Application contact:* William Fenton, Assistant Director of Graduate Admissions, 215-898-4542, Fax: 215-573-5577, E-mail: gradstudies@seas.upenn.edu.
Website: https://dats.seas.upenn.edu/

University of Pittsburgh, School of Computing and Information, Department of Informatics and Networked Systems, Pittsburgh, PA 15260. Offers big data analytics (Certificate); information science (MSIS, PhD, Certificate), including telecommunications (PhD); security assurance/information systems (Certificate); telecommunications (MST, Certificate). *Program availability:* Part-time, evening/weekend, 100% online. *Degree requirements:* For master's, thesis optional; for doctorate, comprehensive exam, thesis/dissertation. *Entrance requirements:* For master's, GRE, GMAT, bachelor's degree with minimum GPA of 3.0; previous course work in instructional programming language, statistics, mathematics, and probability; for doctorate, GRE, GMAT, master's degree; minimum GPA of 3.3; course work in programming, cognitive psychology, systems analysis and design, data structures, and statistics or mathematics; for Certificate, master's degree in information science, telecommunications, or related field. Additional exam requirements/recommendations for international students: Required—TOEFL (minimum score 550 paper-based; 80 iBT), IELTS (minimum score 6.5). Electronic applications accepted. *Expenses:* Contact institution. *Faculty research:* Cybersecurity and privacy, social computing and networks, data analytics and data science, human-centered computing, spectrum use and enforcement.

University of Rochester, School of Arts and Sciences, Goergen Institute for Data Science, Rochester, NY 14627. Offers business and social science (MS); computational and statistical methods (MS); health and biomedical sciences (MS). *Students:* 49 full-time (25 women), 7 part-time (3 women); includes 5 minority (1 Black or African American, non-Hispanic/Latino; 2 Asian, non-Hispanic/Latino; 2 Hispanic/Latino), 43 international. Average age 27. 351 applicants, 46% accepted, 37 enrolled. In 2018, 6 master's awarded. *Degree requirements:* For master's, oral exam. *Entrance requirements:* For master's, transcripts, three letters of recommendation, statement of purpose, resume/curriculum vitae. Additional exam requirements/recommendations for international students: Required—TOEFL (minimum score 100 iBT), IELTS (minimum score 7). *Application deadline:* For fall admission, 4/15 priority date for domestic and international students. Application fee: $60. Electronic applications accepted. *Expenses: Tuition:* Full-time $52,974; part-time $1654 per credit hour. *Required fees:* $612. One-time fee: $30 part-time. Tuition and fees vary according to campus/location and program. *Financial support:* In 2018–19, 5 students received support, including 1 fellowship with partial tuition reimbursement available (averaging $2,100 per year), 6 teaching assistantships (averaging $500 per year); tuition waivers (full and partial) also available. *Total annual research expenditures:* $521,652. *Unit head:* Ajay Anand, Deputy Director, 585-276-3149, E-mail: ajay.anand@rochester.edu. *Application contact:*

Lisa Altman, Education Program Coordinator, 585-275-5288, E-mail: lisa.altman@rochester.edu.
Website: http://www.sas.rochester.edu/dsc/graduate/index.html

University of St. Thomas, School of Engineering, St. Paul, MN 55105. Offers data science (MS); electrical engineering (MS); information technology (MS); manufacturing engineering (MS); manufacturing systems (Certificate); mechanical engineering (MS); medical device development (Certificate); regulatory science (MS); software engineering (MS); software management (MS); systems engineering (MS); technology leadership (Certificate); technology management (MS). *Program availability:* Part-time, evening/weekend. *Entrance requirements:* For master's, resume, official transcripts. Additional exam requirements/recommendations for international students: Required—TOEFL (minimum score 80 iBT), IELTS (minimum score 6.5). Electronic applications accepted. *Expenses:* Contact institution.

University of San Francisco, College of Arts and Sciences, Data Science Program, San Francisco, CA 94117. Offers MS. Program offered jointly with School of Management. *Students:* 87 full-time (45 women); includes 22 minority (15 Asian, non-Hispanic/Latino; 3 Hispanic/Latino; 4 Two or more races, non-Hispanic/Latino), 47 international. Average age 25. 657 applicants, 27% accepted, 87 enrolled. In 2018, 59 master's awarded. *Entrance requirements:* For master's, GRE or GMAT, prerequisite courses in inferential statistics, linear algebra, computer programming (Java, Mathematica, Matlab, Python or C++), and a social science course. Additional exam requirements/recommendations for international students: Required—TOEFL (minimum score 90 iBT), IELTS (minimum score 6.5), PTE (minimum score 61). *Application deadline:* For summer admission, 3/1 for domestic and international students. Applications are processed on a rolling basis. Application fee: $55. Electronic applications accepted. *Financial support:* Career-related internships or fieldwork and scholarships/grants available. Financial award applicants required to submit FAFSA. *Faculty research:* Economic development, forecasting and planning, labor markets, Pacific Rim, financial markets. *Unit head:* Kirsten Keihl, Graduate Director, 415-422-2966, E-mail: info@datascience.usfca.edu. *Application contact:* Information Contact, 415-422-5101, Fax: 415-422-2217, E-mail: asgraduate@usfca.edu.
Website: https://www.usfca.edu/arts-sciences/graduate-programs/data-science

University of Southern Indiana, Graduate Studies, Romain College of Business, Program in Business Administration, Evansville, IN 47712-3590. Offers accounting (MBA); data analytics (MBA); engineering management (MBA); general business administration (MBA); healthcare administration (MBA); human resource management (MBA). *Accreditation:* AACSB. *Program availability:* Part-time, evening/weekend, 100% online, blended/hybrid learning. *Entrance requirements:* For master's, GMAT or GRE, minimum GPA of 2.5, resume, 3 professional references. Additional exam requirements/recommendations for international students: Required—TOEFL (minimum score 550 paper-based; 79 iBT), IELTS (minimum score 6). Electronic applications accepted.

University of South Florida, Innovative Education, Tampa, FL 33620-9951. Offers adult, career and higher education (Graduate Certificate), including college teaching, leadership in developing human resources, leadership in higher education; Africana studies (Graduate Certificate), including diasporas and health disparities, genocide and human rights; aging studies (Graduate Certificate), including gerontology; art research (Graduate Certificate), including museum studies; business foundations (Graduate Certificate); chemical and biomedical engineering (Graduate Certificate), including materials science and engineering, water, health and sustainability; child and family studies (Graduate Certificate), including positive behavior support; civil and industrial engineering (Graduate Certificate), including transportation systems analysis; community and family health (Graduate Certificate), including maternal and child health, social marketing and public health, violence and injury: prevention and intervention, women's health; criminology (Graduate Certificate), including criminal justice administration; data science for public administration (Graduate Certificate); digital humanities (Graduate Certificate); educational measurement and research (Graduate Certificate), including evaluation; English (Graduate Certificate), including comparative literary studies, creative writing, professional and technical communication; entrepreneurship (Graduate Certificate); environmental health (Graduate Certificate), including safety management; epidemiology and biostatistics (Graduate Certificate), including applied biostatistics, biostatistics, concepts and tools of epidemiology, epidemiology, epidemiology of infectious diseases; geography, environment and planning (Graduate Certificate), including community development, environmental policy and management, geographical information systems; geology (Graduate Certificate), including hydrogeology; global health (Graduate Certificate), including disaster management, global health and Latin American and Caribbean studies, global health practice, humanitarian assistance, infection control; government and international affairs (Graduate Certificate), including Cuban studies, globalization studies; health policy and management (Graduate Certificate), including health management and leadership, public health policy and programs; hearing specialist: early intervention (Graduate Certificate); industrial and management systems engineering (Graduate Certificate), including systems engineering, technology management; information studies (Graduate Certificate), including school library media specialist; information systems/decision sciences (Graduate Certificate), including analytics and business intelligence; instructional technology (Graduate Certificate), including distance education, Florida digital/virtual educator, instructional design, multimedia design, Web design; internal medicine, bioethics and medical humanities (Graduate Certificate), including biomedical ethics; Latin American and Caribbean studies (Graduate Certificate); leadership for coastal resiliency planning (Graduate Certificate); mass communications (Graduate Certificate), including multimedia journalism; mathematics and statistics (Graduate Certificate), including mathematics; medicine (Graduate Certificate), including aging and neuroscience, bioinformatics, biotechnology, brain fitness and memory management, clinical investigation, hand and upper limb rehabilitation, health informatics, health sciences, integrative weight management, intellectual property, medicine and gender, metabolic and nutritional medicine, metabolic cardiology, pharmacy sciences; national and competitive intelligence (Graduate Certificate); nursing (Graduate Certificate), including simulation based academic fellowship in advanced pain management; psychological and social foundations (Graduate Certificate), including career counseling, college teaching, diversity in education, mental health counseling, school counseling; public affairs (Graduate Certificate), including nonprofit management, public management, research administration; public health (Graduate Certificate), including assessing chemical toxicity and public health risks, health equity, pharmacoepidemiology, public health generalist, toxicology, translational research in adolescent behavioral health; public health practices (Graduate Certificate), including planning for healthy communities; rehabilitation and mental health counseling (Graduate Certificate), including integrative mental health care, marriage and family therapy, rehabilitation technology; secondary education (Graduate Certificate), including ESOL, foreign language education: culture and content, foreign language education: professional; social work (Graduate Certificate), including geriatric social work/clinical gerontology; special education (Graduate Certificate), including autism spectrum disorder, disabilities education: severe/profound; world languages (Graduate Certificate), including teaching English as a second language (TESL) or foreign language. *Expenses:* Tuition, state resident: full-time $6350. Tuition, nonresident: full-time $19,048. *International tuition:* $19,048 full-time. *Required fees:* $2079. *Unit head:*

Dr. Cynthia DeLuca, Associate Vice President and Assistant Vice Provost, 813-974-3077, Fax: 813-974-7061, E-mail: deluca@usf.edu. *Application contact:* Owen Hooper, Director, Summer and Alternative Calendar Programs, 813-974-6917, E-mail: hooper@usf.edu.
Website: http://www.usf.edu/innovative-education/

University of South Florida, Muma College of Business, Department of Information Systems and Decision Sciences, Tampa, FL 33620-9951. Offers business administration (PhD), including information systems; business analytics and information systems (MS), including analytics and business intelligence, information assurance. *Program availability:* Part-time. *Faculty:* 25 full-time (4 women). *Students:* 193 full-time (66 women), 130 part-time (38 women); includes 36 minority (9 Black or African American, non-Hispanic/Latino; 18 Asian, non-Hispanic/Latino; 7 Hispanic/Latino; 2 Two or more races, non-Hispanic/Latino), 245 international. Average age 29. 668 applicants, 65% accepted, 131 enrolled. In 2018, 189 master's awarded. Terminal master's awarded for partial completion of doctoral program. *Degree requirements:* For master's, comprehensive exam, thesis (for some programs), thesis or practicum project; for doctorate, comprehensive exam, thesis/dissertation. *Entrance requirements:* For master's, GMAT, GRE or other standardized scores for graduate programs, letters of recommendation, statement of purpose, relevant work experience; for doctorate, GMAT or GRE, letters of recommendation, personal statement, interview. Additional exam requirements/recommendations for international students: Required—TOEFL, TOEFL (minimum score 550 paper-based; 79 iBT) or IELTS (minimum score 6.5). *Application deadline:* For fall admission, 6/1 for domestic students, 2/1 for international students; for spring admission, 10/15 for domestic students, 9/15 for international students. Applications are processed on a rolling basis. Application fee: $30. Electronic applications accepted. *Expenses:* Tuition, state resident: full-time $6350. Tuition, nonresident: full-time $19,048. *International tuition:* $19,048 full-time. *Required fees:* $2079. *Financial support:* In 2018–19, 43 students received support, including 8 research assistantships with tuition reimbursements available (averaging $11,972 per year), 22 teaching assistantships with tuition reimbursements available (averaging $9,002 per year); scholarships/grants, health care benefits, and unspecified assistantships also available. Financial award applicants required to submit FAFSA. *Faculty research:* Data mining, business intelligence, bioterrorism surveillance, health informatics/informatics, software engineering, agent-based modeling, distributed systems, statistics, electronic markets, e-commerce, business process improvement, operations management, supply chain, LEAN management, global information systems, organizational impacts of IT, enterprise resource planning, business intelligence, Web and mobile technologies, social networks, information security. *Total annual research expenditures:* $423,775. *Unit head:* Dr. Kaushal Chari, Chair and Professor, 813-974-6768, Fax: 813-974-6749, E-mail: kchari@usf.edu. *Application contact:* Barber Warner, 813-974-6776, Fax: 813-974-6749, E-mail: bwarner@usf.edu.
Website: http://business.usf.edu/departments/isds/

The University of Tennessee, Graduate School, Tickle College of Engineering, Bredesen Center for Interdisciplinary Research and Graduate Education, Knoxville, TN 37996. Offers data science and engineering (PhD); energy science and engineering (PhD). *Students:* 70 full-time (24 women); includes 11 minority (2 Black or African American, non-Hispanic/Latino; 5 Asian, non-Hispanic/Latino; 3 Hispanic/Latino; 1 Two or more races, non-Hispanic/Latino), 18 international. Average age 29. 86 applicants, 41% accepted, 24 enrolled. In 2018, 11 doctorates awarded. *Degree requirements:* For doctorate, comprehensive exam, thesis/dissertation, qualifying examination. *Entrance requirements:* For doctorate, GRE General Test, research interest letter, resume/curriculum vitae, 3 letters of recommendation. Additional exam requirements/recommendations for international students: Required—TOEFL (minimum score 550 paper-based; 80 iBT), IELTS (minimum score 6.5). *Application deadline:* For fall admission, 1/31 for domestic and international students. Applications are processed on a rolling basis. Application fee: $60. Electronic applications accepted. *Financial support:* In 2018–19, 70 students received support, including 70 fellowships with full tuition reimbursements available (averaging $28,000 per year); health care benefits also available. Financial award application deadline: 1/31. *Faculty research:* Biomass processing for biofuels, cellulosic ethanol, and lignin repurposing; applied photosynthesis; nuclear fusion, reactor design and modeling; design and distribution of wind power; development of photovoltaic materials; fuel cell and battery design for energy conversion and storage; development of next generation SMART grid systems and novel grid management tools; climate change modeling, environmental, and planetary sciences as they relate to energy usage. *Unit head:* Dr. Sudarsanam Babu, Director, 865-974-7999, Fax: 865-974-9482, E-mail: sbabu@utk.edu. *Application contact:* Dr. Sudarsanam Babu, Director, 865-974-7999, Fax: 865-974-9482, E-mail: sbabu@utk.edu.
Website: http://bredesencenter.utk.edu/

The University of Texas at Dallas, School of Natural Sciences and Mathematics, Department of Mathematical Sciences, Richardson, TX 75080. Offers actuarial science (MS); mathematics (MS, PhD), including applied mathematics, data science (MS), engineering mathematics (MS), mathematics (MS); statistics (MS, PhD). *Program availability:* Part-time, evening/weekend. *Faculty:* 29 full-time (6 women), 3 part-time/adjunct (0 women). *Students:* 155 full-time (58 women), 35 part-time (9 women); includes 34 minority (4 Black or African American, non-Hispanic/Latino; 19 Asian, non-Hispanic/Latino; 7 Hispanic/Latino; 4 Two or more races, non-Hispanic/Latino), 116 international. Average age 32. 264 applicants, 37% accepted, 48 enrolled. In 2018, 48 master's, 11 doctorates awarded. *Degree requirements:* For master's, thesis optional; for doctorate, thesis/dissertation. *Entrance requirements:* For master's, GRE General Test, minimum GPA of 3.0 in upper-level course work in field; for doctorate, GRE General Test, minimum GPA of 3.5 in upper-level course work in field. Additional exam requirements/recommendations for international students: Required—TOEFL (minimum score 550 paper-based). *Application deadline:* For fall admission, 7/15 for domestic students, 5/1 priority date for international students; for spring admission, 11/15 for domestic students, 9/1 priority date for international students. Applications are processed on a rolling basis. Application fee: $50 ($100 for international students). Electronic applications accepted. *Expenses:* Tuition, area resident: Full-time $13,458. Tuition, state resident: full-time $13,458. Tuition, nonresident: full-time $26,852. *International tuition:* $26,852 full-time. Tuition and fees vary according to course load. *Financial support:* In 2018–19, 92 students received support, including 10 research assistantships (averaging $24,110 per year), 89 teaching assistantships with partial tuition reimbursements available (averaging $17,110 per year); fellowships, career-related internships or fieldwork, Federal Work-Study, institutionally sponsored loans, scholarships/grants, and unspecified assistantships also available. Support available to part-time students. Financial award application deadline: 4/30; financial award applicants required to submit FAFSA. *Faculty research:* Sequential analysis, applications in semiconductor manufacturing, medical image analysis, computational anatomy, information theory, probability theory. *Unit head:* Dr. Vladimir Dragovic, Department Head, 972-883-2161, Fax: 972-883-6622, E-mail: utdmath@utdallas.edu. *Application contact:* Evangelina Bustamante, Graduate Student Coordinator, 972-883-2163, Fax: 972-883-6622, E-mail: utdmath@utdallas.edu.
Website: http://www.utdallas.edu/math

Data Science/Data Analytics

The University of Texas Health Science Center at Houston, School of Biomedical Informatics, Houston, TX 77030. Offers applied biomedical informatics (MS, Certificate); biomedical informatics (MS, PhD, Certificate); health data science (Certificate); public health informatics (Certificate); MPH/MS; MPH/PhD. *Program availability:* Part-time, 100% online, blended/hybrid learning. *Faculty:* 29 full-time (10 women), 11 part-time/adjunct (2 women). *Students:* 62 full-time (42 women), 224 part-time (120 women); includes 152 minority (43 Black or African American, non-Hispanic/Latino; 2 American Indian or Alaska Native, non-Hispanic/Latino; 59 Asian, non-Hispanic/Latino; 42 Hispanic/Latino; 3 Native Hawaiian or other Pacific Islander, non-Hispanic/Latino; 3 Two or more races, non-Hispanic/Latino). Average age 36. 136 applicants, 77% accepted, 52 enrolled. In 2018, 48 master's, 4 doctorates awarded. *Degree requirements:* For master's, thesis or alternative, practicum with capstone report; for doctorate, comprehensive exam, thesis/dissertation. *Entrance requirements:* For master's and doctorate, GRE. Additional exam requirements/recommendations for international students: Required—TOEFL (minimum score 87 iBT), IELTS (minimum score 7). *Application deadline:* For fall admission, 7/1 for domestic and international students; for spring admission, 11/1 for domestic and international students; for summer admission, 3/1 for domestic and international students. Applications are processed on a rolling basis. Application fee: $60. Electronic applications accepted. *Expenses:* Certificate (full-time) - TX Resident: $6,825; Certificate (full-time) non-resident: $16,065 Masters (full-time) resident: $17,955, Masters (full-time) non-resident: $41,980; Phd - TX Resident: $32,325, PhD - non-resident: $89,612; DHI - program starting in Fall 2019. *Financial support:* In 2018–19, 59 students received support, including 50 research assistantships (averaging $22,376 per year), 10 teaching assistantships (averaging $11,600 per year); career-related internships or fieldwork, institutionally sponsored loans, scholarships/grants, health care benefits, and unspecified assistantships also available. Support available to part-time students. Financial award application deadline: 5/1; financial award applicants required to submit FAFSA. *Faculty research:* Health data science, bioinformatics, precision health and human factors engineering. *Total annual research expenditures:* $9.5 million. *Unit head:* Dr. Jiajie Zhang, Dean/Chair in Informatics Excellence, 713-500-3922, E-mail: jiajie.zhang@uth.tmc.edu. *Application contact:* Jaime Hargrave, Director, Student Affairs, 713-500-3920, Fax: 713-500-0360, E-mail: jaime.n.hargrave@uth.tmc.edu. Website: https://sbmi.uth.edu/

University of Vermont, Graduate College, College of Engineering and Mathematical Sciences, Program in Complex Systems and Data Science, Burlington, VT 05405. Offers MS, PhD. *Entrance requirements:* Additional exam requirements/recommendations for international students: Required—TOEFL (minimum iBT score of 90) or IELTS (6.5). Electronic applications accepted.

University of Virginia, Data Science Institute, Charlottesville, VA 22903. Offers MS, MBA/MSDS. *Entrance requirements:* For master's, GRE or GMAT, undergraduate degree, personal statement, official transcripts, two letters of recommendation. Additional exam requirements/recommendations for international students: Required—TOEFL or IELTS. *Expenses:* Contact institution.

University of Washington, Graduate School, Information School, Seattle, WA 98195. Offers information management (MSIM), including business intelligence, data science, information architecture, information consulting, information security, user experience; information science (PhD); library and information science (MLIS). *Accreditation:* ALA (one or more programs are accredited). *Program availability:* Part-time, evening/weekend, 100% online coursework with required attendance at on-campus orientation at start of program. *Faculty:* 51 full-time (23 women), 38 part-time/adjunct (21 women). *Students:* 347 full-time (229 women), 259 part-time (195 women); includes 129 minority (23 Black or African American, non-Hispanic/Latino; 7 American Indian or Alaska Native, non-Hispanic/Latino; 59 Asian, non-Hispanic/Latino; 36 Hispanic/Latino; 4 Native Hawaiian or other Pacific Islander, non-Hispanic/Latino), 160 international. Average age 32. 1,190 applicants, 42% accepted, 264 enrolled. In 2018, 231 master's, 10 doctorates awarded. Terminal master's awarded for partial completion of doctoral program. *Degree requirements:* For master's, comprehensive exam (for some programs), thesis or alternative, capstone or culminating project; for doctorate, comprehensive exam, thesis/dissertation. *Entrance requirements:* For master's, GRE General Test, GMAT; for doctorate, GRE General Test. Additional exam requirements/recommendations for international students: Required—TOEFL (minimum score 590 paper-based; 100 iBT). *Application deadline:* For fall admission, 12/1 priority date for domestic and international students. Application fee: $85. Electronic applications accepted. *Expenses:* MLIS: $825/credit $51,975 approximate tuition without fees; MSIM: $837/credit, $54,405 approximate tuition without fees. *Financial support:* In 2018–19, 73 students received support. Fellowships with full tuition reimbursements available, research assistantships with full tuition reimbursements available, teaching assistantships with full tuition reimbursements available, Federal Work-Study, institutionally sponsored loans, scholarships/grants, health care benefits, tuition waivers (full and partial), and unspecified assistantships available. Support available to part-time students. Financial award application deadline: 10/1; financial award applicants required to submit FAFSA. *Unit head:* Dr. Anind Dey, Dean, E-mail: anind@uw.edu. *Application contact:* Kari Brothers, Admissions Counselor, 206-616-5541, Fax: 206-616-3152, E-mail: kari683@uw.edu. Website: http://ischool.uw.edu/

University of West Florida, Hal Marcus College of Science and Engineering, Department of Computer Science, Pensacola, FL 32514-5750. Offers computer science (MS), including computer science, database systems, software engineering; information technology (MS), including cybersecurity, database management. *Program availability:* Part-time, evening/weekend. *Degree requirements:* For master's, thesis optional. *Entrance requirements:* For master's, GRE, MAT, or GMAT, official transcripts; minimum undergraduate GPA of 3.0; letter of intent; three letters of recommendation. Additional exam requirements/recommendations for international students: Required—TOEFL (minimum score 550 paper-based).

University of Wisconsin–La Crosse, College of Science and Health, Department of Mathematics and Statistics, La Crosse, WI 54601-3742. Offers data science (MS). *Program availability:* Part-time, online learning. Electronic applications accepted. *Faculty research:* Scientific computing, inverse problems and uncertainty analysis for environmental computer models, Bayesian optimization.

University of Wisconsin–Stevens Point, College of Letters and Science, Department of Computing and New Media Technologies, Stevens Point, WI 54481-3897. Offers data science (MS).

Virginia International University, School of Computer Information Systems, Fairfax, VA 22030. Offers business intelligence (Graduate Certificate); business intelligence and data analytics (MIS); computer science (MS), including computer animation and gaming, cybersecurity, data management networking, intelligent systems, software applications development, software engineering; cybersecurity (MIS); data management (MIS); enterprise project management (MIS); health informatics (MIS); information assurance (MIS); information systems (Graduate Certificate); information systems management (MS, Graduate Certificate); information technology (MS); information technology audit and compliance (Graduate Certificate); knowledge management (MIS); software engineering (MS). *Program availability:* Part-time, online learning. *Entrance*

requirements: For master's, bachelor's degree. Additional exam requirements/recommendations for international students: Required—TOEFL (minimum score 550 paper-based; 80 iBT), IELTS. Electronic applications accepted.

Walsh College of Accountancy and Business Administration, Graduate Programs, Program in Information Technology, Troy, MI 48083. Offers chief information officer (MSIT); cybersecurity (MSIT); data science (MSIT); global project and program management (MSIT). *Program availability:* Part-time, evening/weekend. *Faculty:* 2 full-time (1 woman), 10 part-time/adjunct (2 women). *Students:* 3 full-time (1 woman), 66 part-time (25 women); includes 22 minority (14 Black or African American, non-Hispanic/Latino; 4 Asian, non-Hispanic/Latino; 1 Hispanic/Latino; 3 Two or more races, non-Hispanic/Latino), 13 international. Average age 36. 23 applicants, 83% accepted, 13 enrolled. In 2018, 22 master's awarded. *Entrance requirements:* For master's, minimum overall cumulative GPA of 2.75 from all colleges previously attended. Additional exam requirements/recommendations for international students: Required—TOEFL (minimum score 550 paper-based, 79-80 internet based), IELTS (6.5), Michigan Test of English Language Proficiency, or MTELP (80). *Application deadline:* Applications are processed on a rolling basis. Application fee: $35. Electronic applications accepted. *Expenses:* $785 per credit hour plus $175 student support fee per semester. International students pay $785 per credit hour plus $175 student support fee and $275 international student fee per semester. *Financial support:* In 2018–19, 3 students received support. Scholarships/grants and Tuition Exchange Program available. Financial award application deadline: 6/30; financial award applicants required to submit FAFSA. *Faculty research:* Business intelligence, data and decision-making, cyber security, project management, mobile technologies. *Unit head:* Dr. David Schippers, Chair, Information Technology and Decision Sciences, 248-823-1635, Fax: 248-689-0920, E-mail: dschippe@walshcollege.edu. *Application contact:* Karen Mahaffy, Executive Director, Admissions and Enrollment Services, 248-823-1600, Fax: 248-823-1611, E-mail: kmahaffy@walshcollege.edu.

Washington University in St. Louis, Olin Business School, Business Analytics, St. Louis, MO 63130-4899. Offers MS. *Program availability:* Part-time. *Faculty:* 85 full-time (16 women), 46 part-time/adjunct (13 women). *Students:* 159 full-time (105 women); includes 3 minority (1 Black or African American, non-Hispanic/Latino; 2 Asian, non-Hispanic/Latino), 150 international. Average age 23. 508 applicants, 23% accepted, 48 enrolled. In 2018, 33 master's awarded. *Degree requirements:* For master's, 39 credit hours. *Entrance requirements:* For master's, GMAT or GRE, U.S. bachelor's degree or equivalent, one letter of recommendation. Additional exam requirements/recommendations for international students: Required—TOEFL, IELTS. *Application deadline:* For fall admission, 10/10 for domestic and international students; for winter admission, 1/15 for domestic students, 1/15 priority date for international students; for spring admission, 3/18 for domestic and international students. Applications are processed on a rolling basis. Application fee: $100. Electronic applications accepted. *Financial support:* Institutionally sponsored loans and scholarships/grants available. Financial award applicants required to submit FAFSA. *Unit head:* Dr. Steve Malter, Senior Associate Dean, Undergrad and Graduate Programs, 314-935-6315, Fax: 314-935-9095, E-mail: malter@wustl.edu. *Application contact:* Ruthie Pyles, Asst Dean & Dir of Grad Admissions & Fin Aid, 314-935-7301, E-mail: olingradadmissions@wustl.edu.

Wayne State University, College of Engineering, Department of Computer Science, Detroit, MI 48202. Offers computer science (MS, PhD), including bioinformatics and computational biology (PhD); data science and business analytics (MS). Application deadline for PhD is February 17. *Faculty:* 23. *Students:* 107 full-time (41 women), 39 part-time (11 women); includes 11 minority (2 Black or African American, non-Hispanic/Latino; 6 Asian, non-Hispanic/Latino; 2 Hispanic/Latino; 1 Two or more races, non-Hispanic/Latino), 99 international. Average age 30. 237 applicants, 28% accepted, 35 enrolled. In 2018, 27 master's, 7 doctorates awarded. *Degree requirements:* For master's, thesis (for some programs), practicum (for MS in data science and business analytics); for doctorate, thesis/dissertation. *Entrance requirements:* For master's, GRE (GMAT accepted for MS in data science and business analytics), minimum GPA of 3.0, three letters of recommendation, adequate preparation in computer science and mathematics courses, personal statement, resume (for MS in data science and business analytics); for doctorate, GRE, bachelor's or master's degree in computer science or related field; minimum GPA of 3.3 in most recent degree; three letters of recommendation; personal statement; adequate preparation in computer science and mathematics courses. Additional exam requirements/recommendations for international students: Required—TOEFL (minimum score 550 paper-based; 79 iBT, TWE (minimum score 5.5); Recommended—IELTS (minimum score 6.5). *Application deadline:* For fall admission, 6/1 priority date for domestic students, 5/1 priority date for international students; for winter admission, 10/1 priority date for domestic students, 9/1 priority date for international students; for spring admission, 2/1 priority date for domestic students, 1/2 priority date for international students. Applications are processed on a rolling basis. Application fee: $50. Electronic applications accepted. *Expenses:* Contact institution. *Financial support:* In 2018–19, 91 students received support, including 5 fellowships with tuition reimbursements available (averaging $20,000 per year), 18 research assistantships with tuition reimbursements available (averaging $20,383 per year), 27 teaching assistantships with tuition reimbursements available (averaging $20,166 per year); scholarships/grants, health care benefits, and unspecified assistantships also available. Financial award application deadline: 2/17; financial award applicants required to submit FAFSA. *Faculty research:* Software engineering, databases, bioinformatics, artificial intelligence, networking, distributed and parallel computing, security, graphics, visualizations. *Total annual research expenditures:* $1.1 million. *Unit head:* Dr. Loren Schwiebert, Chair, 313-577-5474, E-mail: loren@wayne.edu. *Application contact:* Areej Salaymeh, Graduate Advisor, 313-577-2477, E-mail: csgradadvisor@cs.wayne.edu. Website: http://engineering.wayne.edu/cs/

Wayne State University, College of Engineering, Department of Industrial and Systems Engineering, Detroit, MI 48202. Offers data science and business analytics (MS); engineering management (MS); industrial engineering (MS, PhD); manufacturing engineering (MS); systems engineering (Certificate). *Program availability:* Online learning. *Faculty:* 11. *Students:* 178 full-time (40 women), 109 part-time (30 women); includes 42 minority (20 Black or African American, non-Hispanic/Latino; 16 Asian, non-Hispanic/Latino; 6 Hispanic/Latino), 167 international. Average age 29. 539 applicants, 40% accepted, 68 enrolled. In 2018, 172 master's, 9 doctorates awarded. *Entrance requirements:* For master's, GRE or GMAT (for applicants to MS in data science and business analytics), BS from ABET-accredited institution; for doctorate, GRE, graduate degree in engineering or related discipline with minimum graduate GPA of 3.5, statement of purpose, resume/curriculum vitae, three letters of recommendation; for Certificate, GRE (for applicants from non-ABET institutions), BS in engineering or other technical field from ABET-accredited institution with minimum GPA of 3.0 in upper-division course work, at least one year of full-time work experience as practicing engineer or technical leader. Additional exam requirements/recommendations for international students: Required—TOEFL (minimum score 550 paper-based; 79 iBT), TWE (minimum score 5.5), Michigan English Language Assessment Battery (minimum score 85); GRE; Recommended—IELTS (minimum score 6.5). *Application deadline:* Applications are processed on a rolling basis. Application fee: $50. Electronic applications accepted. *Expenses:* Contact institution. *Financial support:* In 2018–19, 135 students received support, including 2 fellowships with tuition reimbursements available (averaging $20,000 per year), 5 research assistantships with tuition reimbursements available (averaging $23,260 per year), 8 teaching assistantships with tuition reimbursements available (averaging $20,166 per year); scholarships/grants, tuition waivers (full), and unspecified assistantships also available. Financial award applicants required to submit FAFSA. *Faculty research:* Manufacturing systems, infrastructure, and management. *Total annual research expenditures:* $320,400. *Unit head:* Dr. Leslie Monplaisir, Associate Professor/Chair, 313-577-3821, Fax: 313-577-8833, E-mail: leslie.monplaisir@wayne.edu. *Application contact:* Eric Scimeca, Graduate Program Coordinator, 313-577-0412, E-mail: eric.scimeca@wayne.edu. Website: http://engineering.wayne.edu/ise/

Wayne State University, Mike Ilitch School of Business, Detroit, MI 48202. Offers accounting (MS, MSA, Postbaccalaureate Certificate); business (EMS, Graduate Certificate); business administration (MBA, PhD); data science (MS), including business analytics; entrepreneurship and innovation (Postbaccalaureate Certificate); finance (MS); information systems management (Postbaccalaureate Certificate); taxation (MST); JD/MBA. Application deadline for PhD is February 15. *Accreditation:* AACSB. *Program availability:* Part-time, evening/weekend. *Faculty:* 31. *Students:* 286 full-time (152 women), 1,166 part-time (533 women); includes 409 minority (236 Black or African American, non-Hispanic/Latino; 83 Asian, non-Hispanic/Latino; 53 Hispanic/Latino; 37 Two or more races, non-Hispanic/Latino; 74 international. Average age 30. 1,212 applicants, 38% accepted, 294 enrolled. In 2018, 285 master's, 6 doctorates, 7 other advanced degrees awarded. *Degree requirements:* For doctorate, thesis/dissertation. *Entrance requirements:* For master's, GMAT, GRE, LSAT, MCAT, at least three years of relevant work experience that shows increased responsibility, or minimum GPA of 3.0 from AACSB-accredited program or 3.2 from regionally-accredited program, undergraduate degree from accredited institution; undergraduate degree in accounting, business administration, or area of business administration (for MS and MST); for doctorate, GMAT (minimum score of 600), minimum undergraduate GPA of 3.0, 3.5 upper-division or graduate; three letters of recommendation; brief essay; undergraduate degree from accredited institution; personal statement; for other advanced degree, bachelor's degree from accredited institution. Additional exam requirements/recommendations for international students: Required—TOEFL (minimum score 550 paper-based; 79 iBT), Michigan English Language Assessment Battery (minimum score 85); Recommended—IELTS (minimum score 6.5), TWE (minimum score 5.5). *Application deadline:* For fall admission, 7/1 for domestic students, 5/1 priority date for international students; for winter admission, 11/1 for domestic students, 9/1 priority date for international students; for spring admission, 3/1 for domestic students, 1/1 priority date for international students. Applications are processed on a rolling basis. Application fee: $50. Electronic applications accepted. *Expenses:* Contact institution. *Financial support:* In 2018–19, 175 students received support, including 1 fellowship with tuition reimbursement available (averaging $20,000 per year), 5 research assistantships with tuition reimbursements available (averaging $21,393 per year); teaching assistantships with tuition reimbursements available, scholarships/grants, health care benefits, and unspecified assistantships also available. Support available to part-time students. Financial award applicants required to submit FAFSA. *Faculty research:* Executive compensation and stock performance, consumer reactions to pricing strategies, communication across the automotive supply chain, performance of firms in sub-Saharan Africa, implementation issues with ERP software. *Unit head:* Dr. Robert Forsythe, Dean, School of Business Administration, 313-577-4501, E-mail: robert.forsythe@wayne.edu. *Application contact:* Kiantee N. Rupert-Jones, Director, 313-577-4511, Fax: 313-577-9442, E-mail: gradbusiness@wayne.edu. Website: http://ilitchbusiness.wayne.edu/

Weill Cornell Medicine, Weill Cornell Graduate School of Medical Sciences, Program in Healthcare Policy and Research, New York, NY 10065. Offers biostatistics and data science (MS); health informatics (MS); health policy and economics (MS). *Program availability:* Part-time. *Students:* 62 full-time, 27 part-time; includes 3 minority (2 Asian, non-Hispanic/Latino; 1 Hispanic/Latino). In 2018, 4 master's awarded. *Degree requirements:* For master's, thesis. *Entrance requirements:* For master's, GRE, MCAT, or GMAT (recommended), official transcripts, resume, personal statement, 3 letters of reference. Additional exam requirements/recommendations for international students: Required—TOEFL. *Application deadline:* For fall admission, 3/1 priority date for domestic and international students. Application fee: $75. *Expenses:* Contact institution. *Unit head:* William Tseng, Admissions Manager, 646-962-8083, E-mail: wit2006@med.cornell.edu. *Application contact:* William Tseng, Admissions Manager, 646-962-8083, E-mail: wit2006@med.cornell.edu. Website: http://hpr.weill.cornell.edu/education/

Western Governors University, College of Information Technology, Salt Lake City, UT 84107. Offers cybersecurity and information assurance (MS); data analytics (MS); information technology management (MS). *Program availability:* Online learning. *Degree requirements:* For master's, capstone project. Application fee is waived when completed online.

Worcester Polytechnic Institute, Graduate Admissions, Program in Data Science, Worcester, MA 01609-2280. Offers data science (Graduate Certificate). *Program availability:* Part-time, evening/weekend, 100% online, blended/hybrid learning. *Students:* 100 full-time (42 women), 47 part-time (16 women); includes 15 minority (1 Black or African American, non-Hispanic/Latino; 7 Asian, non-Hispanic/Latino; 4 Hispanic/Latino; 3 Two or more races, non-Hispanic/Latino; 109 international. Average age 27. 425 applicants, 48% accepted, 59 enrolled. In 2018, 50 master's, 2 doctorates, 1 other advanced degree awarded. *Entrance requirements:* For master's, GRE or GMAT required for all international applicants; recommended for U.S. students., 3 letters of recommendation, statement of purpose; for doctorate, GRE or GMAT required for all international applicants; recommended for U.S. students., 3 letters of recommendation, statement of purpose. Additional exam requirements/recommendations for international students: Required—TOEFL (minimum score 563 paper-based; 84 iBT), IELTS, GRE or GMAT. *Application deadline:* For fall admission, 1/1 for domestic and international students; for spring admission, 10/1 for domestic and international students. Applications are processed on a rolling basis. Application fee: $70. Electronic applications accepted. *Financial support:* Fellowships, research assistantships, teaching assistantships, career-related internships or fieldwork, health care benefits, and unspecified assistantships available. Financial award application deadline: 1/1. *Unit head:* Dr. Elke Rundensteiner, Director, 508-831-4883, Fax: 508-831-5776, E-mail: rundenst@wpi.edu. *Application contact:* Mary Racicot, Administrative Assistant, 508-831-4883, Fax: 508-831-5776, E-mail: mracicot@wpi.edu. Website: https://www.wpi.edu/academics/departments/data-science

Yeshiva University, The Katz School, Program in Data Analytics and Visualization, New York, NY 10033-3201. Offers MS. *Program availability:* Part-time, online learning.

Financial Engineering

Baruch College of the City University of New York, Weissman School of Arts and Sciences, Program in Financial Engineering, New York, NY 10010-5585. Offers MS. *Program availability:* Part-time, evening/weekend. *Entrance requirements:* For master's, 3 recommendations. Electronic applications accepted. *Faculty research:* Two-dimensional random walks; Brownian motion; financial applications of probability; volatility modeling; modeling equity market micro-structure for algorithmic trading; mathematical physics; properties of spatially disordered systems; stochastic processes; interacting particle systems; algebra and number theory; discrete and computational geometry; Ramsey theory; additive number theory; numerical methods for financial applications; option pricing; dynamical systems.

Claremont Graduate University, Graduate Programs, Financial Engineering Program, Claremont, CA 91711-6160. Offers MSFE, MS/EMBA, MS/MBA, MS/PhD. *Entrance requirements:* For master's, GRE General Test or GMAT. Additional exam requirements/recommendations for international students: Required—TOEFL (minimum score 75 iBT). Electronic applications accepted.

Columbia University, Fu Foundation School of Engineering and Applied Science, Department of Industrial Engineering and Operations Research, New York, NY 10027. Offers financial engineering (MS); industrial engineering (MS); industrial engineering and operations research (PhD); management science and engineering (MS); operations research (MS); MS/MBA. *Program availability:* Part-time, evening/weekend, online learning. *Degree requirements:* For doctorate, thesis/dissertation, oral and written qualifying exams. *Entrance requirements:* For master's and doctorate, GRE General Test. Additional exam requirements/recommendations for international students: Required—TOEFL, IELTS, PTE. Electronic applications accepted. *Faculty research:* Applied probability and optimization; financial engineering, modeling risk including credit risk and systemic risk, asset allocation, portfolio execution, behavioral finance, agent-based model in finance; revenue management; management and optimization of service systems, call centers, capacity allocation in healthcare systems, inventory control for vaccines; energy, smart grids, demand shaping, managing renewable energy sources, energy-aware scheduling.

HEC Montreal, School of Business Administration, Doctoral Program in Administration, Montréal, QC H3T 2A7, Canada. Offers accounting (PhD); applied economics (PhD); data science (PhD); finance (PhD); financial engineering (PhD); information technology (PhD); international business (PhD); logistics and operations management (PhD); management science (PhD); management, strategy and organizations (PhD); marketing (PhD); organizational behaviour and human resources (PhD). Program offered jointly with Concordia University, McGill University, and Universite du Quebec a Montreal. *Accreditation:* AACSB. *Students:* 130 full-time (55 women). 114 applicants, 46% accepted, 31 enrolled. In 2018, 19 doctorates awarded. *Entrance requirements:* For doctorate, TAGE MAGE, GMAT, or GRE, master's degree in administration or related field. *Application deadline:* For fall admission, 1/15 for domestic and international students. Application fee: 91 (191 for international students). Electronic applications accepted. *Expenses: Tuition, area resident:* Full-time $3052.80 Canadian dollars; part-time $84.80 Canadian dollars per credit. *Tuition, state resident:* full-time $3816 Canadian dollars; part-time $264.67 Canadian dollars per credit. *Tuition, nonresident:* full-time $11,910 Canadian dollars. *International tuition:* $20,905.20 Canadian dollars full-time. *Required fees:* $1805.34 Canadian dollars; $43.62 Canadian dollars per credit. $71.78 Canadian dollars per term. Tuition and fees vary according to degree level and program. *Financial support:* Research assistantships, teaching assistantships, and scholarships/grants available. Financial award application deadline: 9/2. *Faculty research:* Art management, business policy, entrepreneurship, new technologies, transportation. *Unit head:* Guy Paré, Director, 514-340-6264, E-mail: guy.pare@hec.ca. *Application contact:* Julie Bilodeau, PhD Program Analyst, 514-340-6000, Fax: 514-340-6411, E-mail: analyste.phd@hec.ca. Website: http://www.hec.ca/en/programs/phd/index.html

HEC Montreal, School of Business Administration, Master of Science Programs in Administration, Program in Financial Engineering, Montréal, QC H3T 2A7, Canada. Offers M Sc. Program offered in French (Thesis Stream, Supervised project Stream) and also in English (Thesis Stream). *Students:* 36 full-time (11 women), 11 part-time (0 women). 76 applicants, 67% accepted, 40 enrolled. In 2018, 17 master's awarded. *Entrance requirements:* For master's, BBA, undergraduate degree in another field, degree deemed equivalent by program director and minimum GPA of 3.0 on 4.3 scale. Additional exam requirements/recommendations for international students: Required—TAGE MAGE (minimum recommended score of 300), GMAT (minimum recommended score of 630), or GRE. *Application deadline:* For fall admission, 3/15 for domestic and international students; for winter admission, 9/15 for domestic and international students. Application fee: $91 Canadian dollars ($191 Canadian dollars for international students). Electronic applications accepted. *Expenses: Tuition, area resident:* Full-time $3052.80 Canadian dollars; part-time $84.80 Canadian dollars per credit. *Tuition, state resident:* full-time $3816 Canadian dollars; part-time $264.67 Canadian dollars per credit. *Tuition, nonresident:* full-time $11,910 Canadian dollars. *International tuition:* $20,905.20 Canadian dollars full-time. *Required fees:* $1805.34 Canadian dollars; $43.62 Canadian dollars per credit. $71.78 Canadian dollars per term. Tuition and fees vary according to degree level and program. *Financial support:* Research assistantships, teaching assistantships, and scholarships/grants available. Financial award application deadline: 9/2. *Unit head:* Dr. Sihem Taboubi, Director, 514-340-6428, E-mail: sihem.taboubi@hec.ca. *Application contact:* Marianne de Moura, Administrative Director, 514-340-6000, Fax: 514-340-6411, E-mail: aide@hec.ca. Website: http://www.hec.ca/en/programs/masters/master-financial-engineering/index.html

The International University of Monaco, Graduate Programs, Monte Carlo, Monaco. Offers entrepreneurship (EMBA, MBA); financial engineering (M Sc); hedge fund and private equity (M Sc); international marketing (EMBA, MBA); international wealth management (M Sc); luxury goods and services (EMBA, M Sc, MBA); wealth and asset management (EMBA, MBA). *Program availability:* Part-time. *Degree requirements:* For master's, comprehensive exam (for some programs), applied research project. *Entrance requirements:* Additional exam requirements/recommendations for international students: Required—TOEFL (minimum score 550 paper-based), IELTS. Electronic applications accepted. *Faculty research:* Gaming, leadership, disintermediation.

North Carolina State University, Graduate School, College of Agriculture and Life Sciences and College of Engineering and College of Sciences, Program in Financial Mathematics, Raleigh, NC 27695. Offers MFM. *Program availability:* Part-time. *Degree*

requirements: For master's, thesis optional, project/internship. *Entrance requirements:* For master's, GRE General Test. Additional exam requirements/recommendations for international students: Required—TOEFL (minimum score 550 paper-based). Electronic applications accepted. *Faculty research:* Financial mathematics modeling and computation, futures, options and commodities markets, real options, credit risk, portfolio optimization.

Princeton University, Graduate School, School of Engineering and Applied Science, Department of Operations Research and Financial Engineering, Princeton, NJ 08544-1019. Offers M Eng, MSE, PhD. Terminal master's awarded for partial completion of doctoral program. *Degree requirements:* For master's, thesis (MSE); for doctorate, thesis/dissertation, general exam. *Entrance requirements:* For master's and doctorate, GRE General Test, official transcript(s), 3 letters of recommendation, personal statement. Additional exam requirements/recommendations for international students: Required—TOEFL. Electronic applications accepted. *Faculty research:* Applied and computational mathematics; financial mathematics; optimization, queuing theory, and machine learning; statistics and stochastic analysis; transportation and logistics.

Rensselaer Polytechnic Institute, Graduate School, Lally School of Management, Program in Quantitative Finance and Risk Analytics, Troy, NY 12180-3590. Offers MS, MS/MBA. *Program availability:* Part-time. *Faculty:* 36 full-time (9 women), 5 part-time/adjunct (0 women). *Students:* 73 full-time (29 women), 20 part-time (6 women); includes 3 minority (1 Black or African American, non-Hispanic/Latino; 2 Hispanic/Latino), 81 international. Average age 24. 382 applicants, 61% accepted, 69 enrolled. In 2018, 44 master's awarded. *Entrance requirements:* For master's, GMAT or GRE, personal statement. Additional exam requirements/recommendations for international students: Required—TOEFL (minimum score 570 paper-based; 88 iBT), IELTS (minimum score 6.5), PTE (minimum score 60). *Application deadline:* For fall admission, 1/1 for domestic and international students. Applications are processed on a rolling basis. Application fee: $75. Electronic applications accepted. *Financial support:* Scholarships/grants available. Financial award application deadline: 1/1. *Unit head:* Dr. Qiang Wu, Graduate Program Director, 518-276-3338, E-mail: wuq2@rpi.edu. *Application contact:* Jarron Decker, Director of Graduate Admissions, 518-276-6216, Fax: 518-276-4072, E-mail: gradadmissions@rpi.edu.
Website: https://lallyschool.rpi.edu/graduate-programs/ms-qfra

Stevens Institute of Technology, Graduate School, School of Business, Program in Financial Engineering, Hoboken, NJ 07030. Offers MS, PhD, Certificate. *Program availability:* Part-time, evening/weekend. *Faculty:* 58 full-time (8 women), 18 part-time/adjunct (3 women). *Students:* 196 full-time (51 women), 58 part-time (12 women); includes 28 minority (4 Black or African American, non-Hispanic/Latino; 1 American Indian or Alaska Native, non-Hispanic/Latino; 23 Asian, non-Hispanic/Latino), 187 international. Average age 27. In 2018, 1 master's, 1 doctorate awarded. Terminal master's awarded for partial completion of doctoral program. *Degree requirements:* For master's, thesis optional, minimum B average in major field and overall; for doctorate, comprehensive exam (for some programs), thesis/dissertation; for Certificate, minimum B average. *Entrance requirements:* For master's, GRE/GMAT scores: GRE scores are required for all applicants applying to a full-time graduate program in the Schaefer School of Engineering and Science (SES). International applicants must submit TOEFL/IELTS scores and fulfill the English Language Proficiency Requirements in order to be considered. Additional exam requirements/recommendations for international students: Required—TOEFL (minimum score 74 iBT), IELTS (minimum score 6). *Application deadline:* For fall admission, 4/1 for domestic and international students; for spring admission, 11/1 for domestic and international students; for summer admission, 5/1 for domestic students. Applications are processed on a rolling basis. Application fee: $60. Electronic applications accepted. *Expenses: Tuition:* Full-time $35,960; part-time $1620 per credit. *Required fees:* $1290; $600 per semester. Tuition and fees vary according to course load. *Financial support:* Fellowships, research assistantships, teaching assistantships, career-related internships or fieldwork, Federal Work-Study, scholarships/grants, and unspecified assistantships available. Financial award application deadline: 2/15; financial award applicants required to submit FAFSA. *Faculty research:* Quantitative finance, financial services analytics, financial risk and regulation, financial systems. *Unit head:* Dr. Gregory Prastacos, Dean of SB, 201-216-8366, E-mail: gprastac@stevens.edu. *Application contact:* Graduate Admissions, 888-783-8367, Fax: 888-511-1306, E-mail: graduate@stevens.edu.
Website: https://www.stevens.edu/school-systems-enterprises/masters-degree-programs/financial-engineering

Temple University, Fox School of Business, Specialized Master's Programs, Philadelphia, PA 19122-6096. Offers accountancy (MS); actuarial science (MS); finance (MS); financial engineering (MS); human resource management (MS); innovation management and entrepreneurship (MS); marketing (MS); statistics (MS). MS in innovation management and entrepreneurship delivered jointly with College of Engineering. *Accreditation:* AACSB. *Program availability:* Part-time. *Entrance requirements:* For master's, GRE General Test or GMAT, minimum undergraduate GPA of 3.0. Additional exam requirements/recommendations for international students: Required—TOEFL (minimum score 600 paper-based; 100 iBT), IELTS (minimum score 7.5).

University of California, Berkeley, Graduate Division, Haas School of Business, Master of Financial Engineering Program, Berkeley, CA 94720. Offers MFE. *Degree requirements:* For master's, comprehensive exam, internship/applied finance project. *Entrance requirements:* For master's, GMAT or GRE (waived if candidate holds PhD), bachelor's degree with minimum GPA of 3.0 or equivalent; two recommendation letters; proficiency in math, statistics, computer science, and economics/finance. Additional exam requirements/recommendations for international students: Required—TOEFL (minimum score 570 paper-based, 90 iBT) or IELTS (minimum score 7). Electronic applications accepted. *Expenses:* Contact institution. *Faculty research:* Financial economics, modern portfolio theory, valuation of exotic options, mortgage markets.

University of California, Los Angeles, Graduate Division, UCLA Anderson School of Management, Los Angeles, CA 90095-1481. Offers accounting (PhD); behavioral decision making (PhD); business administration (EMBA, MBA); business administration/computer science (MBA/MSCS); business administration/latin american studies (MBA/MLAS); business administration/law (MBA/JD); business administration/library science (MBA/MLIS); business administration/medicine (MBA/MD); business administration/nursing (MBA/MN); business administration/public health (MBA/MPH); business administration/public policy (MBA/MPP); business administration/urban and regional planning (MBA/MURP); business analytics (MSBA); decisions, operations, and technology management (PhD); finance (PhD); financial engineering (MFE); global economics and management (PhD); management and organizations (PhD); marketing (PhD); strategy and policy (PhD); DDS/MBA; MBA/JD; MBA/MD; MBA/MLAS; MBA/MLIS; MBA/MN; MBA/MPH; MBA/MPP; MBA/MSCS; MBA/MURP. UCLA-NUS EMBA: UCLA Anderson and the National University of Singapore. *Accreditation:* AACSB. *Program availability:* Part-time, evening/weekend. *Faculty:* 86 full-time (19 women), 102 part-time/adjunct (16 women). *Students:* 1,040 full-time (378 women), 1,262 part-time (391 women); includes 784 minority (47 Black or African American, non-Hispanic/Latino; 1 American Indian or Alaska Native, non-Hispanic/Latino; 539 Asian, non-Hispanic/Latino; 116 Hispanic/Latino; 5 Native Hawaiian or other Pacific Islander, non-Hispanic/Latino; 76 Two or more races, non-Hispanic/Latino), 609 international. Average age 31. 6,708 applicants, 27% accepted, 949 enrolled. In 2018, 885 master's, 13 doctorates awarded. Terminal master's awarded for partial completion of doctoral program. *Degree requirements:* For master's, comprehensive exam, field consulting project (for MBA, FEMBA, EMBA, UCLA-NUS EMBA, MFE, and MSBA); internship (for MBA only); for doctorate, comprehensive exam, thesis/dissertation, oral and written qualifying exams. *Entrance requirements:* For master's, GMAT or GRE (for MBA, MFE, MSBA); Executive Assessment (EA) for candidates with 10+ years of work experience (FEMBA); Executive Assessment (EA) or STEM Master's degree or JD, MBA, CPA (EMBA), 4-year bachelor's degree or equivalent; 2 letters of recommendation; interview (invitation only); 2 essays; average 4-8 years of full-time work experience (for FEMBA); minimum 8 years of work experience with at least 3 years at management level (for EMBA); 10 years of full-time high managerial responsibility work experience (UCLA-NUS EMBA); for doctorate, GMAT or GRE, bachelor's degree from college or university of fully-recognized standing, minimum B average during junior and senior undergraduate years, 3 letters of recommendation, statement of purpose. Additional exam requirements/recommendations for international students: Required—TOEFL (minimum score 560 paper-based; 87 iBT), IELTS (minimum score 7), TOEFL with minimum iBT score of 100 (for MSBA). *Application deadline:* For fall admission, 10/2 for domestic and international students; for winter admission, 1/8 for domestic and international students; for spring admission, 4/16 for domestic and international students. Applications are processed on a rolling basis. Application fee: $200. Electronic applications accepted. *Expenses:* Per Year - MBA: $64,292, FEMBA: $42,420, EMBA: $81,120, UCLA-NUS EMBA (UC Portion only): $57,500, MFE: $75,816, MSBA: $64,1,43, PhD: $32,049. *Financial support:* Fellowships, research assistantships with partial tuition reimbursements, teaching assistantships with partial tuition reimbursements, career-related internships or fieldwork, institutionally sponsored loans, and scholarships/grants available. Support available to part-time students. *Faculty research:* Finance/global economics, entrepreneurship, accounting, human resources/organizational behavior, marketing and behavioral decision making. *Total annual research expenditures:* $2 million. *Unit head:* Dr. Antonio Bernardo, Dean & John E. Anderson Chair in Management, 310-825-7982, Fax: 310-206-2073, E-mail: a.bernardo@anderson.ucla.edu. *Application contact:* Alex Lawrence, Assistant Dean and Director of MBA Admissions, 310-825-6944, Fax: 310-825-8582, E-mail: mba.admissions@anderson.ucla.edu.
Website: http://www.anderson.ucla.edu/

University of Illinois at Urbana–Champaign, Graduate College, College of Engineering, Joint Program in Financial Engineering, Champaign, IL 61820. Offers MS. Program offered jointly with College of Business. *Degree requirements:* For master's, thesis or alternative.

Game Design and Development

Academy of Art University, Graduate Programs, School of Game Development, San Francisco, CA 94105-3410. Offers MA, MFA. *Program availability:* Part-time, 100% online. *Degree requirements:* For master's, final review. *Entrance requirements:* For master's, statement of intent; resume; portfolio/reel; official college transcripts. Electronic applications accepted.

Concordia University, School of Graduate Studies, Faculty of Engineering and Computer Science, Concordia Institute for Information Systems Engineering (CIISE), Montréal, QC H3G 1M8, Canada. Offers 3D graphics and game development (Certificate); information and systems engineering (PhD); information systems security (M Eng, MA Sc); quality systems engineering (M Eng, MA Sc); service engineering and network management (Certificate).

DePaul University, College of Computing and Digital Media, Chicago, IL 60604. Offers animation (MA, MFA); applied technology (MS); business information technology (MS); computational finance (MS); computer and information sciences (PhD); computer science (MS); creative producing (MFA); cybersecurity (MS); data science (MS); digital communication and media arts (MA); documentary (MFA); e-commerce technology (MS); experience design (MA); film and television (MS); film and television directing (MFA); game design (MFA); game programming (MS); health informatics (MS); human centered design (PhD); human-computer interaction (MS); information systems (MS); network engineering and security (MS); product innovation and computing (MS); screenwriting (MFA); software engineering (MS); JD/MS. *Program availability:* Part-time, evening/weekend, online learning. *Degree requirements:* For master's, thesis (for some programs); for doctorate, comprehensive exam, thesis/dissertation. *Entrance requirements:* For master's, GRE or GMAT (for MS in computational finance only), bachelor's degree, resume (MS in predictive analytics only), IT experience (MS in information technology project management only), portfolio review (all MFA programs and MA in animation); for doctorate, GRE, master's degree in computer science. Additional exam requirements/recommendations for international students: Required—TOEFL (minimum score 590 paper-based; 80 iBT), IELTS (minimum score 6.5), PTE (minimum score 53). Electronic applications accepted. *Expenses:* Contact institution. *Faculty research:* Data mining, computer science, human-computer interaction, security, animation and film.

Full Sail University, Game Design Master of Science Program - Campus, Winter Park, FL 32792-7437. Offers MS.

Iona College, School of Arts and Science, Department of Computer Science, New Rochelle, NY 10801-1890. Offers computer science (MS); cyber security (MS); game development (MS). *Program availability:* Part-time, evening/weekend. *Faculty:* 8 full-time (4 women), 7 part-time/adjunct (3 women). *Students:* 3 full-time (0 women), 9 part-time (2 women); includes 3 minority (2 Black or African American, non-Hispanic/Latino; 1 Hispanic/Latino), 1 international. Average age 26. 17 applicants, 76% accepted, 3 enrolled. In 2018, 6 master's awarded. *Degree requirements:* For master's, thesis optional. *Entrance requirements:* For master's, minimum GPA of 3.0. Additional exam requirements/recommendations for international students: Required—TOEFL (minimum score 550 paper-based; 80 iBT), IELTS (minimum score 6.5). *Application deadline:* For fall admission, 8/1 priority date for domestic students, 5/1 priority date for international students; for spring admission, 1/1 priority date for domestic students, 9/1 priority date for international students. Applications are processed on a rolling basis. Electronic applications accepted. *Expenses: Tuition:* Full-time $14,064; part-time $7032 per credit.

Required fees: $245 per semester. One-time fee: $250. Tuition and fees vary according to program. *Financial support:* In 2018–19, 2 students received support, including 2 research assistantships with full and partial tuition reimbursements available (averaging $5,072 per year); tuition waivers (partial) and unspecified assistantships also available. Support available to part-time students. Financial award application deadline: 4/15; financial award applicants required to submit FAFSA. *Faculty research:* Parallel procession, data mining, machine learning, cyber security, medical imaging. *Unit head:* Frances Bailie, PhD, Chair, 914-633-2335, E-mail: fbailie@iona.edu. *Application contact:* Christopher Kash, Assistant Director, Graduate Admissions, 914-633-2403, Fax: 914-633-2277, E-mail: ckash@iona.edu.
Website: http://www.iona.edu/Academics/School-of-Arts-Science/Departments/Computer-Science/Graduate-Programs.aspx

Long Island University–LIU Post, College of Arts, Communications and Design, Brookville, NY 11548-1300. Offers art (MA); clinical art therapy (MA); clinical art therapy and counseling (MA); digital game design and development (MA); fine arts and design (MFA); interactive multimedia arts (MA); museum studies (MA); music (MA); theatre (MFA). *Degree requirements:* For master's, variable foreign language requirement, comprehensive exam (for some programs), thesis. *Entrance requirements:* For master's, performance audition or portfolio. Additional exam requirements/recommendations for international students: Required—TOEFL (minimum score 550 paper-based; 79 iBT). Electronic applications accepted. *Faculty research:* Creative writing, playwriting, music composition, music performance, international impact of art therapy, artistic creation.

Michigan State University, The Graduate School, College of Communication Arts and Sciences, Department of Media and Information, East Lansing, MI 48824. Offers media and information management (MA); serious game design (MA). *Entrance requirements:* Additional exam requirements/recommendations for international students: Required—TOEFL. Electronic applications accepted.

New York University, Tisch School of the Arts, Game Center, Brooklyn, NY 11201. Offers game design (MFA). *Faculty:* 11 full-time (4 women), 33 part-time/adjunct (8 women). *Students:* 68 full-time (37 women); includes 51 minority (2 Black or African American, non-Hispanic/Latino; 1 American Indian or Alaska Native, non-Hispanic/Latino; 45 Asian, non-Hispanic/Latino; 3 Hispanic/Latino). Average age 26. 226 applicants, 25% accepted, 33 enrolled. In 2018, 33 master's awarded. *Degree requirements:* For master's, thesis. *Entrance requirements:* Additional exam requirements/recommendations for international students: Required—TOEFL (minimum score 100 paper-based; 100 iBT), IELTS (minimum score 7.5). *Application deadline:* For fall admission, 1/1 for domestic students. Application fee: $65. Electronic applications accepted. *Financial support:* In 2018–19, 52 students received support, including 20 teaching assistantships (averaging $3,600 per year); career-related internships or fieldwork and scholarships/grants also available. Financial award application deadline: 1/1. *Faculty research:* Game design, game studies, game interfaces, art games, strategic depth, game development, programming, multimedia, installation, big games, physical games, card games, board games, game history, artificial intelligence, independent games, audio for games. *Unit head:* Frank Lantz, Director, 646-997-0746, E-mail: frank.lantz@nyu.edu. *Application contact:* Jessica Lam, Department Administrator, 646-9970708, E-mail: gamecenter@nyu.edu.
Website: http://gamecenter.nyu.edu/

Rochester Institute of Technology, Graduate Enrollment Services, Golisano College of Computing and Information Sciences, Interactive Games and Media School, MS Program in Game Design and Development, Rochester, NY 14623-5603. Offers MS. *Students:* 47 full-time (7 women), 5 part-time (1 woman); includes 6 minority (1 Black or African American, non-Hispanic/Latino; 2 Asian, non-Hispanic/Latino; 2 Hispanic/Latino; 1 Two or more races, non-Hispanic/Latino), 38 international. Average age 24. 113 applicants, 52% accepted, 19 enrolled. In 2018, 9 master's awarded. *Degree requirements:* For master's, thesis or alternative, capstone experience. *Entrance requirements:* For master's, GRE required for individuals with degrees from international universities., portfolio, minimum GPA of 3.0 (recommended). Additional exam requirements/recommendations for international students: Required—TOEFL (minimum score 570 paper-based; 88 iBT), IELTS (minimum score 6.5), PTE (minimum score 61). *Application deadline:* For fall admission, 2/15 priority date for domestic and international students. Applications are processed on a rolling basis. Application fee: $65. Electronic applications accepted. *Financial support:* In 2018–19, 51 students received support. Research assistantships with partial tuition reimbursements available, teaching assistantships with partial tuition reimbursements available, career-related internships or fieldwork, scholarships/grants, and unspecified assistantships available. Support available to part-time students. Financial award applicants required to submit FAFSA. *Faculty research:* Game balance, game engines, games for health, graphics, e-sports. *Unit head:* Dr. Jessica Bayliss, Graduate Program Director, 585-475-2507, E-mail: jdbics@rit.edu. *Application contact:* Diane Ellison, Senior Associate Vice President, Graduate Enrollment Services, 585-475-2229, Fax: 585-475-7164, E-mail: gradinfo@rit.edu.
Website: https://www.rit.edu/study/game-design-and-development-ms

Sacred Heart University, Graduate Programs, College of Arts and Sciences, Department of Computing, Fairfield, CT 06825. Offers computer science (MS); computer science gaming (MS); cybersecurity (MS); information technology (MS). *Program availability:* Part-time, evening/weekend. *Degree requirements:* For master's, thesis or alternative. *Entrance requirements:* For master's, bachelor's degree, minimum GPA of 3.0. Additional exam requirements/recommendations for international students: Required—TOEFL (minimum score 570 paper-based, 80 iBT), TWE, or IELTS (6.5). Electronic applications accepted. *Expenses:* Contact institution.

Savannah College of Art and Design, Program in Interactive Design and Game Development, Savannah, GA 31402-3146. Offers MA, MFA. *Program availability:* Part-time, 100% online. *Faculty:* 16 full-time (4 women), 4 part-time/adjunct (1 woman). *Students:* 83 full-time (33 women), 27 part-time (8 women); includes 18 minority (6 Black or African American, non-Hispanic/Latino; 5 Asian, non-Hispanic/Latino; 7 Hispanic/Latino), 67 international. Average age 27. 196 applicants, 43% accepted, 29 enrolled. In 2018, 33 master's awarded. *Degree requirements:* For master's, final project (for MA); thesis (for MFA). *Entrance requirements:* For master's, GRE (recommended), portfolio (submitted in digital format), audition or writing submission, resume, statement of purpose, two letters of recommendation. Additional exam requirements/recommendations for international students: Recommended—TOEFL (minimum score 550 paper-based; 85 iBT), IELTS (minimum score 6.5). *Application deadline:* For fall admission, 4/1 for domestic and international students. Applications are processed on a rolling basis. Application fee: $40. Electronic applications accepted. *Expenses: Tuition:* Full-time $37,530; part-time $4170 per course. One-time fee: $500. *Financial support:* Career-related internships or fieldwork, Federal Work-Study, and scholarships/grants available. Financial award application deadline: 4/1; financial award applicants required to submit FAFSA. *Unit head:* SuAnne Fu, Chair, interactive design and game development. *Application contact:* Jenny Jaquillard, Executive Director of Admission Recruitment, 912-525-5100, E-mail: admission@scad.edu.
Website: http://www.scad.edu/academics/programs/interactive-design-and-game-development

University of Advancing Technology, Master of Science Program in Technology, Tempe, AZ 85283-1042. Offers advancing computer science (MS); emerging technologies (MS); game production and management (MS); information assurance (MS); technology leadership (MS). *Degree requirements:* For master's, project or thesis. *Entrance requirements:* Additional exam requirements/recommendations for international students: Required—TOEFL (minimum score 550 paper-based). Electronic applications accepted. *Faculty research:* Artificial intelligence, fractals, organizational management.

University of California, Santa Cruz, Jack Baskin School of Engineering, Department of Computational Media, Santa Cruz, CA 95064. Offers computational media (MS, PhD); games and playable media (MS).

The University of North Carolina at Charlotte, College of Computing and Informatics, Department of Software and Information Systems, Charlotte, NC 28223-0001. Offers advanced databases and knowledge discovery (Graduate Certificate); game design and development (Graduate Certificate); information security and privacy (Graduate Certificate); information technology (MS); management of information technology (Graduate Certificate); network security (Graduate Certificate); secure software development (Graduate Certificate). *Program availability:* Part-time, evening/weekend. *Students:* 122 full-time (57 women), 102 part-time (39 women); includes 44 minority (24 Black or African American, non-Hispanic/Latino; 8 Asian, non-Hispanic/Latino; 10 Hispanic/Latino; 2 Two or more races, non-Hispanic/Latino), 126 international. Average age 28. 308 applicants, 82% accepted, 98 enrolled. In 2018, 107 master's, 18 other advanced degrees awarded. *Entrance requirements:* For master's, GRE or GMAT, undergraduate or equivalent course work in data structures, object-oriented programming in C++, C#, or Java with minimum GPA of 3.0; for Graduate Certificate, bachelor's degree from accredited institution in computing, mathematical, engineering or business discipline with minimum overall GPA of 2.8, junior/senior 3.0; substantial knowledge of data structures and object-oriented programming in C++, C# or Java. Additional exam requirements/recommendations for international students: Required—TOEFL (minimum score 523 paper-based; 70 iBT), IELTS (minimum score 6), TOEFL (minimum score 523 paper-based, 70 iBT) or IELTS (6). *Application deadline:* Applications are processed on a rolling basis. Application fee: $75. Electronic applications accepted. *Expenses:* Contact institution. *Financial support:* Fellowships, research assistantships, teaching assistantships, career-related internships or fieldwork, institutionally sponsored loans, scholarships/grants, and unspecified assistantships available. Support available to part-time students. Financial award application deadline: 3/1; financial award applicants required to submit FAFSA. *Total annual research expenditures:* $3.1 million. *Unit head:* Dr. Mary Lou Maher, Chair, 704-687-1940, E-mail: mmaher9@uncc.edu. *Application contact:* Kathy B. Giddings, Director of Graduate Admissions, 704-687-5503, Fax: 704-687-1668, E-mail: gradadm@uncc.edu.
Website: http://sis.uncc.edu/

University of Pennsylvania, School of Engineering and Applied Science, Department of Computer and Information Science, Philadelphia, PA 19104. Offers computer and information science (MSE, PhD); computer and information technology (MCIT); computer graphics and game technology (MSE). *Program availability:* Part-time. *Students:* Average age 26. 2,559 applicants, 14% accepted, 216 enrolled. In 2018, 130 master's, 15 doctorates awarded. Terminal master's awarded for partial completion of doctoral program. *Degree requirements:* For master's, comprehensive exam, thesis optional; for doctorate, comprehensive exam, thesis/dissertation. *Entrance requirements:* For master's and doctorate, GRE, bachelor's degree, letters of recommendation, resume, personal statement. Additional exam requirements/recommendations for international students: Required—TOEFL (minimum score 100 iBT), IELTS (minimum score 7). *Application deadline:* For fall admission, 12/15 priority date for domestic and international students. Application fee: $80. Electronic applications accepted. *Expenses:* Contact institution. *Faculty research:* Artificial intelligence, bioinformatics and computational biology, embedded and real-time systems, machine learning, security and information assurance. *Application contact:* William Fenton, Assistant Director of Graduate Admissions, 215-898-4542, Fax: 215-573-5577, E-mail: gradstudies@seas.upenn.edu.
Website: http://www.cis.upenn.edu/prospective-students/graduate/

University of Southern California, Graduate School, School of Cinematic Arts, Interactive Media and Games Division, Los Angeles, CA 90089. Offers interactive media (MFA). *Degree requirements:* For master's, thesis, thesis project. *Entrance requirements:* Additional exam requirements/recommendations for international students: Required—TOEFL (minimum score 600 paper-based; 100 iBT). Electronic applications accepted. *Expenses:* Contact institution. *Faculty research:* Immersive media, mobile media, stereoscopic, game design and development, serious games and games for health and learning, experiments in game play.

University of Southern California, Graduate School, Viterbi School of Engineering, Department of Computer Science, Los Angeles, CA 90089. Offers computer networks (MS); computer science (MS, PhD); computer security (MS); game development (MS); high performance computing and simulations (MS); human language technology (MS); intelligent robotics (MS); multimedia and creative technologies (MS); software engineering (MS). *Program availability:* Part-time, evening/weekend, online learning. *Entrance requirements:* For master's and doctorate, GRE General Test. Additional exam requirements/recommendations for international students: Required—TOEFL. Electronic applications accepted. *Faculty research:* Databases, computer graphics and computer vision, software engineering, networks and security, robotics, multimedia and virtual reality.

University of Utah, Graduate School, College of Engineering, Program in Entertainment Arts and Engineering, Salt Lake City, UT 84112-1107. Offers game art (MEAE); game engineering (MEAE); game production (MEAE); technical art (MEAE). *Faculty:* 10 full-time (1 woman), 14 part-time/adjunct (2 women). *Students:* 117 full-time (29 women), 2 part-time (1 woman); includes 16 minority (3 Black or African American, non-Hispanic/Latino; 4 Asian, non-Hispanic/Latino; 7 Hispanic/Latino; 2 Two or more races, non-Hispanic/Latino), 47 international. Average age 23. 183 applicants, 31% accepted, 54 enrolled. In 2018, 67 master's awarded. *Degree requirements:* For master's, Project/Non-thesis Required. *Entrance requirements:* For master's, GRE (recommended for game engineering and game production track applicants). Additional exam requirements/recommendations for international students: Required—TOEFL (minimum score 600 paper-based; 100 iBT), IELTS (minimum score 7). *Application deadline:* For fall admission, 2/28 for domestic and international students. Application fee: $55 ($65 for international students). Electronic applications accepted. *Expenses:* Contact institution. *Financial support:* In 2018–19, 91 students received support, including 60 research assistantships with partial tuition reimbursements available (averaging $15,500 per year), 80 teaching assistantships with partial tuition reimbursements available (averaging $15,500 per year); scholarships/grants, health care benefits, and unspecified assistantships also available. Financial award application deadline: 2/28; financial award applicants required to submit FAFSA. *Faculty research:* Games for health, simulation, user research/user interface, narrative for games, ethics for games. *Unit head:* Hallie Huber, Academic Program Manager, 801-5815460, E-mail: hallie.huber@utah.edu. *Application contact:* CJ Lederman, Graduate Student Advisor, 801-587-1299, E-mail: cj@eae.utah.edu.
Website: http://eae.utah.edu/

Game Design and Development

Virginia International University, School of Computer Information Systems, Fairfax, VA 22030. Offers business intelligence (Graduate Certificate); business intelligence and data analytics (MIS); computer science (MS), including computer animation and gaming, cybersecurity, data management networking, intelligent systems, software applications development, software engineering; cybersecurity (MIS); data management (MIS); enterprise project management (MIS); health informatics (MIS); information assurance (MIS); information systems (Graduate Certificate); information systems management (MS, Graduate Certificate); information technology (MS); information technology audit and compliance (Graduate Certificate); knowledge management (MIS); software engineering (MS). *Program availability:* Part-time, online learning. *Entrance requirements:* For master's, bachelor's degree. Additional exam requirements/recommendations for international students: Required—TOEFL (minimum score 550 paper-based; 80 iBT), IELTS. Electronic applications accepted.

Worcester Polytechnic Institute, Graduate Admissions, Program in Interactive Media and Game Development, Worcester, MA 01609-2280. Offers interactive media & game development (MS). *Program availability:* Part-time, evening/weekend. *Students:* 13 full-time (4 women), 12 part-time (1 woman); includes 2 minority (1 Asian, non-Hispanic/Latino; 1 Hispanic/Latino), 16 international. Average age 25. 44 applicants, 86% accepted, 15 enrolled. In 2018, 6 master's awarded. *Entrance requirements:* For master's, GRE (recommended), 3 letters of recommendation, statement of purpose, portfolio (recommended). Additional exam requirements/recommendations for international students: Required—TOEFL (minimum score 563 paper-based; 84 iBT), IELTS (minimum score 7). *Application deadline:* For fall admission, 1/1 for domestic and international students; for spring admission, 10/1 for domestic and international students. Applications are processed on a rolling basis. Application fee: $70. Electronic applications accepted. *Financial support:* Research assistantships, teaching assistantships, and health care benefits available. Financial award application deadline: 1/1. *Unit head:* Jennifer DeWinter, Graduate Coordinator, 508-831-4977, Fax: 508-831-5776, E-mail: jdewinter@wpi.edu. *Application contact:* Allison Darling, Administrative Assistant, 508-831-4977, Fax: 508-831-5776, E-mail: ajdarling@wpi.edu.
Website: https://www.wpi.edu/academics/departments/interactive-media-game-development

Health Informatics

Adelphi University, College of Nursing and Public Health, Garden City, NY 11530. Offers adult gerontology primary care nurse practitioner (Advanced Certificate); adult health nurse (MS); nurse practitioner in adult health nursing (Certificate); nursing (PhD); nursing administration (MS, Certificate); nursing education (MS, Certificate); nutrition (MS); public health (MPH). *Accreditation:* AACN. *Program availability:* Part-time, evening/weekend. *Faculty:* 45 full-time (35 women), 228 part-time/adjunct (208 women). *Students:* 35 full-time (27 women), 387 part-time (323 women); includes 260 minority (131 Black or African American, non-Hispanic/Latino; 1 American Indian or Alaska Native, non-Hispanic/Latino; 90 Asian, non-Hispanic/Latino; 29 Hispanic/Latino; 9 Two or more races, non-Hispanic/Latino), 11 international. Average age 36. 510 applicants, 48% accepted, 123 enrolled. In 2018, 112 master's, 4 doctorates, 3 other advanced degrees awarded. *Entrance requirements:* For master's, BSN, clinical experience, course in basic statistics, minimum GPA of 3.0, 2 letters of recommendation, resume or curriculum vitae; for doctorate, GRE, licensure as RN in New York, professional writing sample (scholarly writing), 3 letters of recommendation, resume or curriculum vitae; for other advanced degree, MSN. Additional exam requirements/recommendations for international students: Required—TOEFL (minimum score 550 paper-based; 80 iBT), IELTS (minimum score 6.5). *Application deadline:* Applications are processed on a rolling basis. Application fee: $50. Electronic applications accepted. *Expenses:* Contact institution. *Financial support:* Fellowships, research assistantships, teaching assistantships with full and partial tuition reimbursements, career-related internships or fieldwork, Federal Work-Study, scholarships/grants, traineeships, tuition waivers, unspecified assistantships, and tuition remission for employees available. Support available to part-time students. Financial award application deadline: 1/1; financial award applicants required to submit FAFSA. *Faculty research:* Social practices in healthcare, bereavement, family grief, historiography, gerontology. *Unit head:* Dr. Elaine Smith, Dean, 516-833-8181, E-mail: elsmith@adelphi.edu. *Application contact:* Kristen Capezza, Vice President for Enrollment Management, 516-877-3021, Fax: 516-877-3039, E-mail: graduateadmissions@adelphi.edu.
Website: http://nursing.adelphi.edu/

American Public University System, AMU/APU Graduate Programs, Charles Town, WV 25414. Offers accounting (MS); applied business analytics (MS); business administration (MBA); criminal justice (MA); cybersecurity studies (MS); educational leadership (M Ed); environmental policy and management (MS); global security (DGS); health information management (MS); history (MA), including American military history, American Revolution, civil war, war since 1945, World War II; information technology (MS); international relations and conflict resolution (MA), including American politics and government, comparative government and development, general, international relations, public policy; national security studies (MA); nursing (MSN); political science (MA); public policy (MPP); reverse logistics management (MA), including comparative and security issues, conflict resolution, international and transnational security issues, peacekeeping; space studies (MS); sports management (MS); strategic intelligence (DSI); teaching (M Ed), including secondary social studies; transportation and logistics management (MA). *Program availability:* Part-time, evening/weekend, online only, 100% online. *Students:* 406 full-time (180 women), 7,826 part-time (3,329 women); includes 2,781 minority (1,438 Black or African American, non-Hispanic/Latino; 44 American Indian or Alaska Native, non-Hispanic/Latino; 193 Asian, non-Hispanic/Latino; 747 Hispanic/Latino; 53 Native Hawaiian or other Pacific Islander, non-Hispanic/Latino; 306 Two or more races, non-Hispanic/Latino), 121 international. Average age 38. In 2018, 2,717 master's awarded. *Degree requirements:* For master's, comprehensive exam or practicum; for doctorate, practicum. *Entrance requirements:* For master's, official transcript showing earned bachelor's degree from institution accredited by recognized accrediting body. Additional exam requirements/recommendations for international students: Required—TOEFL (minimum score 550 paper-based), IELTS (minimum score 6.5). *Application deadline:* Applications are processed on a rolling basis. Application fee: $0. Electronic applications accepted. *Financial support:* Scholarships/grants available. Financial award applicants required to submit FAFSA. *Unit head:* Dr. Wallace Boston, President, 877-468-6268, Fax: 304-728-2348, E-mail: president@apus.edu. *Application contact:* Yoci Deal, Associate Vice President, Graduate and International Admissions, 877-468-6268, Fax: 304-724-3764, E-mail: info@apus.edu.
Website: http://www.apus.edu

American Sentinel University, Graduate Programs, Aurora, CO 80014. Offers business administration (MBA); business intelligence (MS); computer science (MSCS); health information management (MS); healthcare (MBA); information systems (MSIS); nursing (MSN). *Program availability:* Part-time, evening/weekend, online learning. *Entrance requirements:* Additional exam requirements/recommendations for international students: Required—TOEFL (minimum score 600 paper-based). Electronic applications accepted.

Arkansas Tech University, College of Natural and Health Sciences, Russellville, AR 72801. Offers fisheries and wildlife biology (MS); health informatics (MS); nursing (MSN). *Program availability:* Part-time, evening/weekend, 100% online, blended/hybrid learning. *Students:* 11 full-time (7 women), 46 part-time (30 women); includes 10 minority (9 Black or African American, non-Hispanic/Latino; 1 Asian, non-Hispanic/Latino), 1 international. Average age 35. In 2018, 22 master's awarded. *Degree requirements:* For master's, thesis (for some programs), project. *Entrance requirements:* Additional exam requirements/recommendations for international students: Required—TOEFL (minimum score 550 paper-based; 79 iBT), IELTS (minimum score 6.5), PTE (minimum score 58). *Application deadline:* For fall admission, 3/1 priority date for domestic students, 5/1 priority date for international students; for spring admission, 10/1

priority date for domestic and international students. Applications are processed on a rolling basis. Application fee: $40 ($90 for international students). Electronic applications accepted. *Expenses: Tuition, area resident:* Full-time $6816; part-time $284 per credit hour. Tuition, state resident: full-time $6816; part-time $284 per credit hour. Tuition, nonresident: full-time $13,632; part-time $568 per credit hour. *International tuition:* $13,632 full-time. *Required fees:* $457.50 per semester. Tuition and fees vary according to course load and degree level. *Financial support:* In 2018–19, research assistantships with full and partial tuition reimbursements (averaging $4,800 per year), teaching assistantships with full and partial tuition reimbursements (averaging $4,800 per year) were awarded; career-related internships or fieldwork, Federal Work-Study, scholarships/grants, health care benefits, and unspecified assistantships also available. Support available to part-time students. Financial award application deadline: 4/15; financial award applicants required to submit FAFSA. *Unit head:* Dr. Jeff Robertson, Dean, 479-968-0498, E-mail: jrobertson@atu.edu. *Application contact:* Dr. Jeff Robertson, Interim Dean of Graduate College, 479-968-0398, Fax: 479-964-0542, E-mail: gradcollege@atu.edu.
Website: http://www.atu.edu/nhs/

Augusta University, College of Allied Health Sciences, Program in Public Health, Augusta, GA 30912. Offers environmental health (MPH); health informatics (MPH); health management (MPH); social and behavioral sciences (MPH). *Accreditation:* CEPH. *Program availability:* Part-time. *Degree requirements:* For master's, thesis (for some programs). *Entrance requirements:* For master's, GRE General Test, three letters of recommendation. Additional exam requirements/recommendations for international students: Required—TOEFL. Electronic applications accepted.

Barry University, College of Health Sciences, Graduate Certificate Programs, Miami Shores, FL 33161-6695. Offers health care leadership (Certificate); health care planning and informatics (Certificate); histotechnology (Certificate); long term care management (Certificate); medical group practice management (Certificate); quality improvement and outcomes management (Certificate).

Bay Path University, Program in Healthcare Management, Longmeadow, MA 01106-2292. Offers health informatics (MS); organizational excellence (MS). *Program availability:* Part-time, online only, 100% online. *Students:* 34 part-time (25 women); includes 11 minority (4 Black or African American, non-Hispanic/Latino; 1 Asian, non-Hispanic/Latino; 4 Hispanic/Latino; 2 Two or more races, non-Hispanic/Latino). Average age 39. *Entrance requirements:* For master's, completed application; official undergraduate and graduate transcripts (a GPA of 3.0 or higher is preferred); original essay of at least 250 words on the topic: "Why the MS in Healthcare Management is important to my personal and professional goals"; current resume; 2 recommendations. *Application deadline:* Applications are processed on a rolling basis. Electronic applications accepted. Application fee is waived when completed online. *Unit head:* Dr. Terry DeVito, Coordinator, E-mail: tdevito@baypath.edu. *Application contact:* Anastasia Spremulli, Assistant Director of Graduate Admissions, 413-565-1340, Fax: 413-565-1250, E-mail: aspremulli@baypath.edu.
Website: https://www.baypath.edu/academics/graduate-programs/healthcare-management-ms/

Belmont University, College of Pharmacy, Nashville, TN 37212. Offers advanced pharmacotherapy (Pharm D); health care informatics (Pharm D); management (Pharm D); missions/public health (Pharm D); Pharm D/MBA. PharmD/MBA offered in collaboration with Jack C. Massey Graduate School of Business. *Accreditation:* ACPE. *Faculty:* 25 full-time (16 women), 3 part-time/adjunct (2 women). *Students:* Average age 25. 638 applicants, 34% accepted, 94 enrolled. In 2018, 65 doctorates awarded. *Degree requirements:* For doctorate, comprehensive exam. *Entrance requirements:* For doctorate, PCAT. Additional exam requirements/recommendations for international students: Required—TOEFL. *Application deadline:* For fall admission, 8/31 priority date for domestic students; for spring admission, 3/1 for domestic students. Applications are processed on a rolling basis. Application fee: $50. Electronic applications accepted. *Expenses:* Contact institution. *Financial support:* In 2018–19, 112 students received support. Career-related internships or fieldwork and scholarships/grants available. Financial award application deadline: 12/1; financial award applicants required to submit FAFSA. *Faculty research:* Academic innovation, cultural competency, medication errors, patient safety. *Unit head:* Dr. David Gregory, Dean, 615-460-6746, Fax: 615-460-6741, E-mail: david.gregory@belmont.edu. *Application contact:* Dr. David Gregory, Dean, 615-460-6746, Fax: 615-460-6741, E-mail: david.gregory@belmont.edu.
Website: http://www.belmont.edu/pharmacy/index.html

Benedictine University, Graduate Programs, Program in Public Health, Lisle, IL 60532. Offers administration of health care institutions (MPH); dietetics (MPH); disaster management (MPH); health education (MPH); health information systems (MPH); management information systems (MPH/MS); MBA/MPH; MPH/MS. *Accreditation:* CEPH. *Program availability:* Part-time, evening/weekend, 100% online. *Faculty:* 8 full-time (5 women), 25 part-time/adjunct (15 women). *Students:* 60 full-time (53 women), 544 part-time (415 women); includes 71 minority (26 Black or African American, non-Hispanic/Latino; 3 American Indian or Alaska Native, non-Hispanic/Latino; 27 Asian, non-Hispanic/Latino; 14 Hispanic/Latino; 1 Native Hawaiian or other Pacific Islander, non-Hispanic/Latino), 11 international. Average age 33. 245 applicants, 84% accepted, 201 enrolled. In 2018, 219 master's awarded. *Entrance requirements:* For master's, GRE, MAT, GMAT, LSAT, DAT or other graduate professional exams, official transcript; 2 letters of recommendation from individuals familiar with the applicant's professional or academic work, excluding family or personal friends; essay describing the candidate's career path. Additional exam requirements/recommendations for international students:

Required—TOEFL (minimum score 600 paper-based; 79 iBT), IELTS (minimum score 6.5). *Application deadline:* Applications are processed on a rolling basis. Application fee: $40. Electronic applications accepted. *Unit head:* Dr. Susan Cheng, Department Chair and Associate Professor, 630-829-6181, E-mail: scheng@ben.edu. *Application contact:* Dr. Susan Cheng, Department Chair and Associate Professor, 630-829-6181, E-mail: scheng@ben.edu.

Boston University, Metropolitan College, Department of Computer Science, Boston, MA 02215. Offers computer information systems (MS), including computer networks, data analytics, database management and business intelligence, health informatics, IT project management, security, Web application development; computer networks (Certificate); computer science (MS); data analytics (Certificate); digital forensics (Certificate); health informatics (Certificate); information technology project management (Certificate); software development (MS); software engineering in health care systems (Certificate); telecommunications (MS), including security. *Program availability:* Part-time, evening/weekend, online learning. *Faculty:* 16 full-time (3 women), 52 part-time/adjunct (5 women). *Students:* 201 full-time (57 women), 953 part-time (252 women); includes 285 minority (57 Black or African American, non-Hispanic/Latino; 2 American Indian or Alaska Native, non-Hispanic/Latino; 139 Asian, non-Hispanic/Latino; 67 Hispanic/Latino; 1 Native Hawaiian or other Pacific Islander, non-Hispanic/Latino; 19 Two or more races, non-Hispanic/Latino), 333 international. Average age 31. 1,079 applicants, 72% accepted, 297 enrolled. In 2018, 395 master's awarded. *Entrance requirements:* For master's and Certificate, official transcripts from regionally-accredited bachelor's degree program, 3 letters of recommendation, professional resume, personal statement. Additional exam requirements/recommendations for international students: Required—TOEFL (minimum score 84 iBT), IELTS. *Application deadline:* For fall admission, 8/1 priority date for domestic students, 6/1 priority date for international students; for spring admission, 12/1 priority date for domestic students, 11/15 priority date for international students; for summer admission, 4/1 priority date for domestic students, 3/1 priority date for international students. Applications are processed on a rolling basis. Application fee: $85. Electronic applications accepted. *Expenses:* Contact institution. *Financial support:* In 2018–19, 11 research assistantships (averaging $8,400 per year), 23 teaching assistantships (averaging $3,400 per year) were awarded; unspecified assistantships also available. Support available to part-time students. Financial award applicants required to submit FAFSA. *Faculty research:* Artificial intelligence and machine learning, security and forensics, web technologies, software engineering, programming languages, medical informatics, information systems and IT project management. *Unit head:* Dr. Anatoly Temkin, Chair, 617-353-2566, Fax: 617-353-2367, E-mail: csinfo@bu.edu. *Application contact:* Enrollment Services, 617-353-6004, E-mail: met@bu.edu.
Website: http://www.bu.edu/csmet/

Brandeis University, Rabb School of Continuing Studies, Division of Graduate Professional Studies, Master of Science in Health and Medical Informatics Program, Waltham, MA 02454-9110. Offers MS. *Program availability:* Part-time-only. *Entrance requirements:* For master's, four-year bachelor's degree from regionally-accredited U.S. institution or equivalent; official transcript(s) from every college or university attended; resume or curriculum vitae; statement of goals; letter of recommendation. Additional exam requirements/recommendations for international students: Required—TWE (minimum score 4.5), TOEFL (minimum scores: 600 paper-based, 100 iBT), IELTS (7), or PTE (68). Electronic applications accepted. *Expenses:* Contact institution.

Brooklyn College of the City University of New York, School of Natural and Behavioral Sciences, Department of Computer and Information Science, Brooklyn, NY 11210-2889. Offers computer science (MA); health informatics (MS); information systems (MS); parallel and distributed computing (Advanced Certificate). *Program availability:* Part-time, evening/weekend. *Degree requirements:* For master's, comprehensive exam, thesis or alternative. *Entrance requirements:* For master's, previous course work in computer science, 2 letters of recommendation. Additional exam requirements/recommendations for international students: Required—TOEFL (minimum score 525 paper-based; 70 iBT). Electronic applications accepted. *Faculty research:* Networks and distributed systems, programming languages, modeling and computer applications, algorithms, artificial intelligence, theoretical computer science.

Canisius College, Graduate Division, School of Education and Human Services, Office of Professional Studies, Buffalo, NY 14208-1098. Offers applied nutrition (MS, Certificate); community and school health (MS); health and human performance (MS); health information technology (MS); respiratory care (MS). *Program availability:* Part-time, evening/weekend, 100% online, blended/hybrid learning. *Faculty:* 3 full-time (0 women), 16 part-time/adjunct (6 women). *Students:* 19 full-time (12 women), 35 part-time (27 women); includes 10 minority (5 Black or African American, non-Hispanic/Latino; 1 Asian, non-Hispanic/Latino; 2 Hispanic/Latino; 2 Two or more races, non-Hispanic/Latino), 2 international. Average age 31. 42 applicants, 81% accepted, 19 enrolled. In 2018, 39 master's awarded. *Degree requirements:* For master's, thesis (for some programs), Programs require Thesis/Project or Internship. *Entrance requirements:* For master's, GRE (recommended), bachelor's degree transcript, two letters of recommendation, current licensure (for applied nutrition), minimum GPA of 2.7, current resume. Additional exam requirements/recommendations for international students: Required—TOEFL (minimum score 550 paper-based, 79 iBT), IELTS (minimum score 6.5), or CAEL (minimum score 70). *Application deadline:* Applications are processed on a rolling basis. Application fee: $0. Electronic applications accepted. *Expenses: Tuition:* Part-time $820 per credit hour. *Required fees:* $25 per semester. One-time fee: $65 part-time. Tuition and fees vary according to program. *Financial support:* In 2018–19, 40 students received support. Career-related internships or fieldwork, Federal Work-Study, scholarships/grants, tuition waivers (partial), and unspecified assistantships available. Support available to part-time students. Financial award application deadline: 4/30; financial award applicants required to submit FAFSA. *Faculty research:* Nutrition, community and school health; community and health; health and human performance applied; nutrition and respiratory care. *Unit head:* Dennis W. Koch, Director, Office of Professional Studies, 716-888-8292, E-mail: koch5@canisius.edu. *Application contact:* Dennis W. Koch, Director, Office of Professional Studies, 716-888-8292, E-mail: koch5@canisius.edu.
Website: http://www.canisius.edu/graduate/

Capella University, School of Public Service Leadership, Master's Programs in Nursing, Minneapolis, MN 55402. Offers diabetes nursing (MSN); general nursing (MSN); gerontology nursing (MSN); health information management (MS); nurse educator (MSN); nursing leadership and administration (MSN). *Accreditation:* AACN.

Chatham University, Program in Healthcare Informatics, Pittsburgh, PA 15232-2826. Offers MHI. *Program availability:* Online learning. *Entrance requirements:* Additional exam requirements/recommendations for international students: Required—TOEFL (minimum score 600 paper-based; 100 iBT), IELTS, TWE. Application fee is waived when completed online.

Claremont Graduate University, Graduate Programs, Center for Information Systems and Technology, Claremont, CA 91711-6160. Offers cybersecurity and networking (MS); data science and analytics (MS); electronic commerce (PhD); geographic information systems (MS); health informatics (MS); information systems (Certificate); IT strategy and innovation (MS); knowledge management (PhD); systems development (PhD);

telecommunications and networking (PhD); MBA/MS. *Program availability:* Part-time. *Degree requirements:* For doctorate, comprehensive exam, thesis/dissertation, portfolio. *Entrance requirements:* For master's and doctorate, GMAT, GRE General Test. Additional exam requirements/recommendations for international students: Required—TOEFL (minimum score 75 iBT). Electronic applications accepted. *Faculty research:* Man-machine interaction, organizational aspects of computing, implementation of information systems, information systems practice.

Clarkson University, Program in Data Analytics, Potsdam, NY 13699. Offers MS. *Program availability:* Part-time, evening/weekend, 100% online. *Students:* 12 full-time (4 women), 16 part-time (4 women); includes 1 minority (Asian, non-Hispanic/Latino), 7 international. 57 applicants, 70% accepted, 18 enrolled. In 2018, 20 master's awarded. *Entrance requirements:* For master's, GMAT or GRE. Additional exam requirements/recommendations for international students: Required—TOEFL (minimum score 550 paper-based, 80 iBT) or IELTS (6.5). *Application deadline:* Applications are processed on a rolling basis. Application fee: $50. Electronic applications accepted. *Expenses:* Contact institution. *Financial support:* Scholarships/grants and unspecified assistantships available. *Unit head:* Dr. Boris Jukic, Director of Business Analytics, 315-268-3884, E-mail: bjukic@clarkson.edu. *Application contact:* Dan Capogna, Director of Graduate Admissions, 518-631-9910, E-mail: graduate@clarkson.edu.
Website: https://www.clarkson.edu/academics/graduate

The College of St. Scholastica, Graduate Studies, Department of Health Information Management, Duluth, MN 55811-4199. Offers MA, Certificate. *Program availability:* Part-time. *Degree requirements:* For master's, thesis. *Entrance requirements:* Additional exam requirements/recommendations for international students: Required—TOEFL (minimum score 550 paper-based; 79 iBT). Electronic applications accepted. *Expenses:* Contact institution. *Faculty research:* Electronic health record implementation, personal health records, Athens Project.

Colorado Mesa University, Department of Health Sciences, Grand Junction, CO 81501-3122. Offers advanced nursing practice (MSN); family nurse practitioner (DNP); health information technology systems (Graduate Certificate); nursing education (MSN). *Accreditation:* AACN. *Program availability:* Part-time, evening/weekend, 100% online, blended/hybrid learning. *Degree requirements:* For master's and doctorate, capstone. *Entrance requirements:* For master's and doctorate, minimum GPA of 3.0 in BSN program. Additional exam requirements/recommendations for international students: Required—TOEFL (minimum score 550 paper-based). Electronic applications accepted.

Dakota State University, College of Business and Information Systems, Madison, SD 57042-1799. Offers analytics (MSA); business analytics (Graduate Certificate); general management (MBA); health informatics (MSHI); information systems (MSIS, D Sc IS); information technology (Graduate Certificate). *Accreditation:* ACBSP. *Program availability:* Part-time, evening/weekend, 100% online, blended/hybrid learning. *Faculty:* 27 full-time (10 women). *Students:* 40 full-time (11 women), 165 part-time (60 women); includes 56 minority (21 Black or African American, non-Hispanic/Latino; 4 American Indian or Alaska Native, non-Hispanic/Latino; 19 Asian, non-Hispanic/Latino; 10 Hispanic/Latino; 1 Native Hawaiian or other Pacific Islander, non-Hispanic/Latino; 1 Two or more races, non-Hispanic/Latino), 38 international. Average age 38. 246 applicants, 47% accepted, 63 enrolled. In 2018, 62 master's, 7 doctorates, 9 other advanced degrees awarded. *Degree requirements:* For master's, comprehensive exam, thesis optional, Examination, integrative project; for doctorate, comprehensive exam, thesis/dissertation, portfolio. *Entrance requirements:* For master's, GRE General Test, Demonstration of information systems skills, minimum GPA of 2.7; for doctorate, GRE General Test, Demonstration of information systems skills; for Graduate Certificate, GMAT. Additional exam requirements/recommendations for international students: Required—PTE (minimum score 53), TOEFL (minimum score 550 paper-based, 76 iBT) or IELTS (6.0). *Application deadline:* For fall admission, 6/15 for domestic students, 4/15 for international students; for spring admission, 11/15 for domestic students, 9/15 priority date for international students; for summer admission, 4/15 for domestic and international students. Applications are processed on a rolling basis. Application fee: $35. Electronic applications accepted. *Expenses:* Contact institution. *Financial support:* In 2018–19, 20 students received support. Research assistantships with partial tuition reimbursements available, teaching assistantships with partial tuition reimbursements available, career-related internships or fieldwork, Federal Work-Study, scholarships/grants, and unspecified assistantships available. Support available to part-time students. Financial award applicants required to submit FAFSA. *Faculty research:* Data mining and analytics, biometrics and information assurance, decision support systems, health informatics, STEM education for K-12 teachers/students and underrepresented populations. *Unit head:* Dr. Dorine Bennett, Dean of College of Business and Information Systems, 605-256-5176, E-mail: dorine.bennett@dsu.edu. *Application contact:* Erin Blankespoor, Senior Secretary, Office of Graduate Studies and Research, 605-256-5799, E-mail: erin.blankespoor@dsu.edu.
Website: http://dsu.edu/academics/colleges/college-of-business-and-information-systems

Dartmouth College, Guarini School of Graduate and Advanced Studies, Institute for Quantitative Biomedical Sciences, Hanover, NH 03755. Offers epidemiology (MS); health data science (MS); quantitative biomedical sciences (PhD). PhD offered in collaboration with the Department of Genetics and the Department of Community and Family Medicine. *Students:* 57 full-time (30 women); includes 10 minority (2 Black or African American, non-Hispanic/Latino; 5 Asian, non-Hispanic/Latino; 2 Hispanic/Latino; 1 Two or more races, non-Hispanic/Latino), 27 international. Average age 26. 155 applicants, 35% accepted, 29 enrolled. In 2018, 1 doctorate awarded. *Entrance requirements:* For doctorate, GRE (minimum scores: 1200 old scoring, 308 new scoring verbal and quantitative; analytical writing 4.5; verbal 500 old scoring, 153 new scoring). *Application deadline:* For fall admission, 3/1 for domestic students. Applications are processed on a rolling basis. Application fee: $75. Electronic applications accepted. *Financial support:* Fellowships available. *Unit head:* Dr. Micheal Whitfield, Director, 603-650-1109. *Application contact:* Gary Hutchins, Assistant Dean, School of Arts and Sciences, 603-646-2107, Fax: 603-646-3488, E-mail: g.hutchins@dartmouth.edu.
Website: https://www.dartmouth.edu/~qbs/index.html

DePaul University, College of Computing and Digital Media, Chicago, IL 60604. Offers animation (MA, MFA); applied technology (MS); business information technology (MS); computational finance (MS); computer and information sciences (PhD); computer science (MS); creative producing (MFA); cybersecurity (MS); data science (MS); digital communication and media arts (MA); documentary (MFA); e-commerce technology (MS); experience design (MA); film and television (MS); film and television directing (MFA); game design (MFA); game programming (MS); health informatics (MS); human centered design (PhD); human-computer interaction (MS); information systems (MS); network engineering and security (MS); product innovation and computing (MS); screenwriting (MFA); software engineering (MS); JD/MS. *Program availability:* Part-time, evening/weekend, online learning. *Degree requirements:* For master's, thesis (for some programs); for doctorate, comprehensive exam, thesis/dissertation. *Entrance requirements:* For master's, GRE or GMAT (for MS in computational finance only), bachelor's degree, resume (MS in predictive analytics only), IT experience (MS in information technology project management only), portfolio review (all MFA programs and MA in animation); for doctorate, GRE, master's degree in computer science.

Health Informatics

Additional exam requirements/recommendations for international students: Required—TOEFL (minimum score 590 paper-based; 80 iBT), IELTS (minimum score 6.5), PTE (minimum score 53). Electronic applications accepted. *Expenses:* Contact institution. *Faculty research:* Data mining, computer science, human-computer interaction, security, animation and film.

DeSales University, Division of Science and Mathematics, Center Valley, PA 18034-9568. Offers cyber security (Postbaccalaureate Certificate); data analytics (Postbaccalaureate Certificate); information systems (MS), including cyber security, digital forensics, healthcare information management, project management. *Program availability:* Part-time, evening/weekend, 100% online, blended/hybrid learning. *Entrance requirements:* For master's, GRE or GMAT, bachelor's degree in computer-related discipline from accredited college or university, minimum undergraduate GPA of 3.0, personal statement, three letters of recommendation. Additional exam requirements/recommendations for international students: Required—TOEFL. Electronic applications accepted. *Expenses:* Contact institution.

Duke University, The Fuqua School of Business, Master of Quantitative Management Program: Health Analytics, Durham, NC 27708. Offers health analytics (MQM). *Faculty:* 9 full-time (1 woman), 6 part-time/adjunct (1 woman). *Students:* 21 full-time (12 women); includes 5 minority (2 Asian, non-Hispanic/Latino; 3 Hispanic/Latino), 5 international. Average age 37. *Entrance requirements:* For master's, GMAT or GRE or waived, transcripts, essays, resume, recommendation letter, interview. *Application deadline:* For fall admission, 10/16 for domestic and international students; for winter admission, 1/22 for domestic and international students; for spring admission, 5/4 for domestic and international students; for summer admission, 8/1 for domestic and international students. Applications are processed on a rolling basis. Application fee: $125. Electronic applications accepted. *Expenses:* Contact institution. *Unit head:* Preyas Desai, Senior Associate Dean for Digital Education, 919-660-2893. *Application contact:* Shari Hubert, Associate Dean, Office of Admissions, 919-660-7705, Fax: 919-681-8026, E-mail: mqmhealthanalytics@fuqua.duke.edu.
Website: https://www.fuqua.duke.edu/programs/mqm-health-analytics

Duke University, School of Medicine, Program in Clinical Informatics, Durham, NC 27710. Offers MS. *Program availability:* Part-time, evening/weekend. *Faculty:* 12 part-time/adjunct (4 women). *Students:* 38 full-time (19 women); includes 16 minority (5 Black or African American, non-Hispanic/Latino; 8 Asian, non-Hispanic/Latino; 3 Hispanic/Latino). 75 applicants, 83% accepted, 37 enrolled. In 2018, 36 master's awarded. *Entrance requirements:* For master's, essay; two letters of recommendation (one addressing work or educational experience and conveying ability to work at the level of a master's program and one addressing interpersonal skills, values, or character); interview with the program director. Additional exam requirements/recommendations for international students: Required—TOEFL, GRE. *Application deadline:* For fall admission, 7/20 for domestic students. Applications are processed on a rolling basis. Electronic applications accepted. *Financial support:* In 2018–19, 34 students received support. Scholarships/grants available. Financial award application deadline: 4/15; financial award applicants required to submit FAFSA. *Unit head:* Randy Sears, Operations Director, 919-681-8817, Fax: 919-681-4569, E-mail: r.sears@dm.duke.edu. *Application contact:* Catherine Diederich, Assistant Director, 919-613-0310, Fax: 919-681-4569, E-mail: catherine.diederich@duke.edu.
Website: http://www.dukemmci.org

East Carolina University, Graduate School, College of Allied Health Sciences, Department of Health Services and Information Management, Greenville, NC 27858-4353. Offers health care administration (Certificate); health care management (Certificate); health informatics (Certificate); health informatics and information management (MS); health information management (Certificate). *Program availability:* Part-time, evening/weekend, online learning. *Degree requirements:* For master's, comprehensive exam, thesis optional. *Entrance requirements:* For master's, GRE General Test or GMAT. Additional exam requirements/recommendations for international students: Recommended—TOEFL, IELTS. *Application deadline:* For fall admission, 5/1 priority date for domestic students; for spring admission, 10/15 priority date for domestic students. Applications are processed on a rolling basis. Electronic applications accepted. *Expenses: Tuition, area resident:* Full-time $4749. Tuition, state resident: Full-time $4749. Tuition, nonresident: full-time $17,898. *International tuition:* $17,898 full-time. *Required fees:* $2787. Part-time tuition and fees vary according to course load and program. *Unit head:* Dr. Xiaoming Zeng, Chair, 252-744-6176, E-mail: zengx@ecu.edu. *Application contact:* Graduate School Admissions, 252-328-6012, Fax: 252-328-6071, E-mail: gradschool@ecu.edu.
Website: http://www.ecu.edu/cs-dhs/hsim/index.cfm

Emory University, Rollins School of Public Health, Department of Biostatistics and Bioinformatics, Atlanta, GA 30322-1100. Offers bioinformatics (PhD); biostatistics (MPH, MSPH); public health informatics (MSPH). PhD offered through the Graduate School of Arts and Sciences. *Program availability:* Part-time. *Degree requirements:* For master's, thesis, practicum. *Entrance requirements:* For master's, GRE General Test. Additional exam requirements/recommendations for international students: Required—TOEFL (minimum score 550 paper-based; 80 iBT). Electronic applications accepted.

Emory University, Rollins School of Public Health, Online Program in Public Health, Atlanta, GA 30322-1100. Offers applied epidemiology (MPH); applied public health informatics (MPH); prevention science (MPH). *Program availability:* Part-time, evening/weekend, online learning. *Degree requirements:* For master's, thesis, practicum. *Entrance requirements:* For master's, GRE. Additional exam requirements/recommendations for international students: Required—TOEFL (minimum score 550 paper-based; 80 iBT). Electronic applications accepted.

George Mason University, College of Health and Human Services, Department of Health Administration and Policy, Fairfax, VA 22030. Offers health and medical policy (MS); health informatics (MS); health informatics and data analytics (Certificate); health services research (PhD); health systems management (MHA); quality improvement and outcomes management in health care systems (Certificate). *Accreditation:* CAHME. *Program availability:* Part-time, evening/weekend, 100% online. *Faculty:* 19 full-time (11 women), 29 part-time/adjunct (11 women). *Students:* 102 full-time (76 women), 165 part-time (129 women); includes 125 minority (54 Black or African American, non-Hispanic/Latino; 53 Asian, non-Hispanic/Latino; 13 Hispanic/Latino; 5 Two or more races, non-Hispanic/Latino), 48 international. Average age 31. 268 applicants, 78% accepted, 116 enrolled. In 2018, 49 master's, 6 other advanced degrees awarded. *Degree requirements:* For master's, comprehensive exam, internship; for doctorate, thesis/dissertation. *Entrance requirements:* For master's, GRE recommended if undergraduate GPA is below 3.0 (for MS in health and medical policy), 2 official transcripts; expanded goals statement; 3 letters of recommendation; resume; 1 year of work experience (for MHA in health systems management); minimum GPA of 3.25 preferred (for MS in health informatics); for doctorate, GRE, professional and volunteer experience, evidence of ability to write and conduct research at the doctoral level, master's degree or equivalent; for Certificate, 2 official transcripts; expanded goals statement; 3 letters of recommendation; resume. Additional exam requirements/recommendations for international students: Required—TOEFL (minimum score 575 paper-based; 88 iBT), IELTS (minimum score 6.5), PTE (minimum score 59). *Application deadline:* For fall admission, 4/1 for domestic and international students; for spring admission, 11/1 for

domestic and international students. Application fee: $75 ($80 for international students). Electronic applications accepted. *Expenses:* $564 per credit in-state, $1,421.75 per credit out-of-state. *Financial support:* In 2018–19, 19 students received support, including 15 research assistantships with tuition reimbursements available (averaging $18,185 per year), 5 teaching assistantships (averaging $5,859 per year); career-related internships or fieldwork, Federal Work-Study, scholarships/grants, unspecified assistantships, and health care benefits (for full-time research or teaching assistantship recipients) also available. Support available to part-time students. Financial award application deadline: 3/1; financial award applicants required to submit FAFSA. *Faculty research:* Universal health care, publications, relationships between malpractice pressure and rates of Cesarean section and VBAC, seniors and Wii gaming, relationships between changes in physician's incomes and practice settings and their care to Medicaid and charity patients. *Total annual research expenditures:* $396,087. *Unit head:* Dr. P.J. Maddox, Chair, 703-993-1982, Fax: 703-993-1953, E-mail: pmaddox@gmu.edu. *Application contact:* Tracy Shevlin, Department Manager, 703-993-1929, Fax: 703-993-1953, E-mail: tshevlin@gmu.edu.
Website: http://chhs.gmu.edu/hap/index

Georgia Southwestern State University, College of Nursing and Health Sciences, Americus, GA 31709-4693. Offers family nurse practitioner (MSN); health informatics (Postbaccalaureate Certificate); nurse educator (Post Master's Certificate); nursing educator (MSN); nursing informatics (MSN); nursing leadership (MSN). MSN program offered by the Georgia Intercollegiate Consortium for Graduate Nursing Education, a partnership with Columbus State University. *Program availability:* Part-time, online only, all theory courses are offered online. *Degree requirements:* For master's, comprehensive exam (for some programs), thesis (for some programs), minimum cumulative GPA of 3.0; maximum of 6 credit hours with C grade and no D grades; degree completed within 7 calendar years from initial enrollment date in graduate courses; for other advanced degree, minimum cumulative GPA of 3.0; maximum of 6 credit hours with C grade and no D grades; degree completed within 7 calendar years from initial enrollment date in graduate courses. *Entrance requirements:* For master's and other advanced degree, baccalaureate degree in nursing from regionally-accredited institution and nationally-accredited nursing program with minimum GPA of 3.0; three professional letters of recommendation; current unencumbered RN license in state where clinical course requirements will be met; background check/drug test; proof of immunizations. Electronic applications accepted. *Expenses:* Contact institution.

Georgia State University, J. Mack Robinson College of Business, Department of Computer Information Systems, Atlanta, GA 30302-3083. Offers computer information systems (PhD); health informatics (MBA, MS); information systems (MSIS, Certificate); information systems development and project management (MBA); information systems management (MBA); managing information technology (Exec MS); the wireless organization (MBA). *Program availability:* Part-time, evening/weekend. *Faculty:* 13 full-time (1 woman), 4 part-time/adjunct (all women). *Students:* 126 full-time (60 women), 6 part-time (0 women); includes 32 minority (20 Black or African American, non-Hispanic/Latino; 9 Asian, non-Hispanic/Latino; 2 Hispanic/Latino; 1 Two or more races, non-Hispanic/Latino), 90 international. Average age 30. 409 applicants, 62% accepted, 86 enrolled. In 2018, 156 master's, 5 doctorates awarded. *Entrance requirements:* For master's, GRE or GMAT, transcripts from all institutions attended, resume, essays; for doctorate, GRE or GMAT, three letters of recommendation, personal statement, transcripts from all institutions attended, resume. Additional exam requirements/recommendations for international students: Required—TOEFL (minimum score 610 paper-based; 101 iBT), IELTS (minimum score 7). *Application deadline:* For fall admission, 5/1 priority date for domestic students, 2/1 priority date for international students; for spring admission, 9/15 priority date for domestic students, 4/1 priority date for international students. Applications are processed on a rolling basis. Application fee: $50. Electronic applications accepted. *Expenses: Tuition, area resident:* Full-time $9360; part-time $390 per credit hour. Tuition, state resident: full-time $9360; part-time $390 per credit hour. Tuition, nonresident: full-time $30,024; part-time $1251 per credit hour. *International tuition:* $30,024 full-time. *Required fees:* $2128. *Financial support:* Research assistantships, teaching assistantships, scholarships/grants, tuition waivers, and unspecified assistantships available. Financial award applicants required to submit FAFSA. *Faculty research:* Process and technological innovation, strategic IT management, intelligent systems, information systems security, software project risk. *Unit head:* Dr. Ephraim R. McLean, Professor/Chair, 404-413-7360, Fax: 404-413-7394. *Application contact:* Toby McChesney, Assistant Dean for Graduate Recruiting and Student Services, 404-413-7167, Fax: 404-413-7167, E-mail: rcbgradadmissions@gsu.edu.
Website: http://cis.robinson.gsu.edu/

Georgia State University, J. Mack Robinson College of Business, Institute of Health Administration, Atlanta, GA 30302-3083. Offers health administration (MBA, MSHA); health informatics (MBA, MSCIS); MBA/MHA; PMBA/MHA. *Accreditation:* CAHME. *Program availability:* Part-time, evening/weekend. *Faculty:* 4 full-time (1 woman). *Students:* 42 full-time (21 women), 14 part-time (6 women); includes 19 minority (8 Black or African American, non-Hispanic/Latino; 9 Asian, non-Hispanic/Latino; 1 Hispanic/Latino; 1 Two or more races, non-Hispanic/Latino), 7 international. Average age 31. 75 applicants, 39% accepted, 24 enrolled. In 2018, 49 master's awarded. *Entrance requirements:* For master's, GRE or GMAT, transcripts from all institutions attended, resume, essays. Additional exam requirements/recommendations for international students: Required—TOEFL (minimum score 610 paper-based; 101 iBT), IELTS (minimum score 7). *Application deadline:* For fall admission, 5/1 priority date for domestic students, 2/1 priority date for international students; for spring admission, 9/15 priority date for domestic students, 4/1 priority date for international students. Applications are processed on a rolling basis. Application fee: $50. Electronic applications accepted. *Expenses: Tuition, area resident:* Full-time $9360; part-time $390 per credit hour. Tuition, state resident: Full-time $9360; part-time $390 per credit hour. Tuition, nonresident: full-time $30,024; part-time $1251 per credit hour. *International tuition:* $30,024 full-time. *Required fees:* $2128. *Financial support:* Research assistantships, teaching assistantships, scholarships/grants, tuition waivers, and unspecified assistantships available. *Faculty research:* Health information technology, health insurance exchanges, health policy and economic impact, healthcare quality, healthcare transformation. *Unit head:* Dr. Andrew T. Sumner, Chair in Health Administration/Director of the Institute of Health, 404-413-7630, Fax: 404-413-7631. *Application contact:* Toby McChesney, Assistant Dean for Graduate Recruiting and Student Services, 404-413-7167, Fax: 404-413-7162, E-mail: rcbgradadmissions@gsu.edu.
Website: http://www.hagsu.org/

Grand Canyon University, College of Nursing and Health Care Professions, Phoenix, AZ 85017-1097. Offers acute care nurse practitioner (MSN, PMC); family nurse practitioner (MSN, PMC); health care administration (MS); health care informatics (MS, MSN); leadership in health care systems (MSN); nursing (DNP); nursing education (MSN, PMC); public health (MPH, MSN); MBA/MSN. *Accreditation:* AACN. *Program availability:* Part-time, evening/weekend, online learning. *Degree requirements:* For master's and PMC, comprehensive exam (for some programs). *Entrance requirements:* For master's, minimum cumulative and science course undergraduate GPA of 3.0.

Additional exam requirements/recommendations for international students: Required—TOEFL (minimum score 575 paper-based; 90 iBT), IELTS (minimum score 7).

Hofstra University, School of Health Professions and Human Services, Programs in Health, Hempstead, NY 11549. Offers foundations of public health (Advanced Certificate); health administration (MHA); health informatics (MS); occupational therapy (MS); public health (MPH); security and privacy in health information systems (Advanced Certificate); sports science (MS); teacher of students with speech-language disabilities (Advanced Certificate). *Program availability:* Part-time, evening/weekend. *Students:* 307 full-time (231 women), 101 part-time (72 women); includes 207 minority (76 Black or African American, non-Hispanic/Latino; 1 American Indian or Alaska Native, non-Hispanic/Latino; 69 Asian, non-Hispanic/Latino; 48 Hispanic/Latino; 9 Native Hawaiian or other Pacific Islander, non-Hispanic/Latino; 4 Two or more races, non-Hispanic/Latino), 21 international. Average age 28. 756 applicants, 46% accepted, 151 enrolled. In 2018, 132 master's, 1 other advanced degree awarded. *Degree requirements:* For master's, internship, minimum GPA of 3.0. *Entrance requirements:* For master's, interview, 2 letters of recommendation, essay, resume. Additional exam requirements/recommendations for international students: Required—TOEFL (minimum score 550 paper-based; 80 iBT). *Application deadline:* Applications are processed on a rolling basis. Application fee: $75. Electronic applications accepted. *Financial support:* In 2018–19, 151 students received support, including 113 fellowships with full and partial tuition reimbursements available (averaging $2,868 per year), 6 research assistantships with full and partial tuition reimbursements available (averaging $4,575 per year); career-related internships or fieldwork, Federal Work-Study, institutionally sponsored loans, scholarships/grants, traineeships, tuition waivers (full and partial), unspecified assistantships, and scholarships and endowed scholarships also available. Support available to part-time students. Financial award applicants required to submit FAFSA. *Faculty research:* Health economics, policy and long-term care; pallative care, neurorehabilitation, neurovision; public health and health inequities, particularly in the american suburbs and minority communities; exercise and nutritional strategies; hiv, sti, sexual health. *Unit head:* Dr. Corinne Kyriacou, Chairperson, 516-463-4553, E-mail: corinne.m.kyriacou@hofstra.edu. *Application contact:* Sunil Samuel, Assistant Vice President of Admissions, 516-463-4723, Fax: 516-463-4664, E-mail: graduateadmission@hofstra.edu.
Website: http://www.hofstra.edu/academics/colleges/healthscienceshumanservices/

Indiana University Bloomington, School of Informatics, Computing, and Engineering, Program in Informatics, Bloomington, IN 47405. Offers informatics (MS, PhD), including bioinformatics (PhD), complex systems (PhD), computing, culture and society (PhD), health informatics (PhD), human-computer interaction (MS), human-computer interaction design (PhD), music informatics (PhD), security informatics (PhD); visual heritage (PhD). *Program availability:* Part-time. Terminal master's awarded for partial completion of doctoral program. *Degree requirements:* For master's, thesis, capstone project; for doctorate, variable foreign language requirement, comprehensive exam, thesis/dissertation. *Entrance requirements:* For master's and doctorate, GRE, resume/curriculum vitae, transcripts, 3 letters of recommendation. Additional exam requirements/recommendations for international students: Required—TOEFL (minimum score 600 paper-based; 100 iBT). Electronic applications accepted. *Faculty research:* Algorithms, applied logic and computational theory, artificial intelligence, bioinformatics, case-based reasoning, chemical informatics, citation analysis, cognitive science, community informatics, compilers, complex networks and systems, computer optimization, computer-supported cooperative work, computer vision, cyberinfrastructure and e-science, database theory and systems, data mining, digital design and preservation, design pedagogy, digital humanities, digital learning environments.

Indiana University–Purdue University Indianapolis, School of Informatics and Computing, Department of BioHealth Informatics, Indianapolis, IN 46202. Offers bioinformatics (MS, PhD); health informatics (MS, PhD).

Jacksonville University, Brooks Rehabilitation College of Healthcare Sciences, School of Applied Health Sciences, Program in Health Informatics, Jacksonville, FL 32211. Offers MS. *Program availability:* Part-time, 100% online, blended/hybrid learning. *Entrance requirements:* For master's, baccalaureate degree in any discipline from regionally-accredited institution with minimum GPA of 3.0; official transcripts; evidence of undergraduate course completion in statistics and college algebra; resume or curriculum vitae demonstrating healthcare experience. Additional exam requirements/recommendations for international students: Required—TOEFL (minimum score 540 paper-based; 76 iBT), IELTS (minimum score 6). Electronic applications accepted. *Expenses:* Contact institution.

Kennesaw State University, Coles College of Business, Program in Health Management and Informatics, Kennesaw, GA 30144. Offers MS. *Program availability:* Part-time-only, evening/weekend, online only, blended/hybrid learning. *Students:* 1 full-time, 60 part-time (41 women); includes 40 minority (25 Black or African American, non-Hispanic/Latino; 2 American Indian or Alaska Native, non-Hispanic/Latino; 7 Asian, non-Hispanic/Latino; 3 Hispanic/Latino; 3 Two or more races, non-Hispanic/Latino), 6 international. Average age 34. 35 applicants, 86% accepted, 26 enrolled. In 2018, 17 master's awarded. *Entrance requirements:* Additional exam requirements/recommendations for international students: Required—TOEFL (minimum score 80 iBT), IELTS (minimum score 6.5). *Application deadline:* For fall admission, 7/1 for domestic and international students. Applications are processed on a rolling basis. Application fee: $60. Electronic applications accepted. *Expenses:* Contact institution. *Unit head:* Dr. Sweta Sneha, Director, 470-578-2436, E-mail: ssneha@kennesaw.edu. *Application contact:* Admissions Counselor, 470-578-4377, Fax: 470-578-9172, E-mail: ksugrad@kennesaw.edu.
Website: http://coles.kennesaw.edu/mshmi/

Kennesaw State University, College of Computing and Software Engineering, Program in Information Technology, Kennesaw, GA 30144. Offers data management and analytics (Graduate Certificate); health information technology (Postbaccalaureate Certificate); information technology (MSIT); information technology foundations (Postbaccalaureate Certificate); information technology security (Graduate Certificate). *Program availability:* Part-time, evening/weekend, blended/hybrid learning. *Students:* 100 full-time (45 women), 195 part-time (76 women); includes 137 minority (75 Black or African American, non-Hispanic/Latino; 42 Asian, non-Hispanic/Latino; 14 Hispanic/Latino; 1 Native Hawaiian or other Pacific Islander, non-Hispanic/Latino; 5 Two or more races, non-Hispanic/Latino), 40 international. Average age 34. 131 applicants, 81% accepted, 81 enrolled. In 2018, 70 master's awarded. *Degree requirements:* For master's, thesis optional. *Entrance requirements:* For master's, minimum GPA of 2.75; for other advanced degree, bachelor's degree. Additional exam requirements/recommendations for international students: Required—TOEFL (minimum score 80 iBT), IELTS (minimum score 6.5). *Application deadline:* For fall admission, 7/1 priority date for domestic students, 5/1 priority date for international students; for spring admission, 11/1 priority date for domestic students, 9/1 priority date for international students; for summer admission, 4/1 priority date for domestic students, 3/1 priority date for international students. Applications are processed on a rolling basis. Application fee: $60. Electronic applications accepted. *Expenses: Tuition, area resident:* Full-time $6960; part-time $290 per credit hour. Tuition, state resident: full-time $6960; part-time $290 per credit hour. Tuition, nonresident: full-time $25,080; part-time $1045 per credit hour. *International tuition:* $25,080 full-time. *Required fees:* $2006; $1706 per semester. $853 per semester. *Financial support:* Research assistantships with full and partial tuition reimbursements, career-related internships or fieldwork, scholarships/grants, and unspecified assistantships available. Support available to part-time students. Financial award applicants required to submit FAFSA. *Application contact:* Admission Counselor, 470-578-4377, Fax: 470-578-9172, E-mail: ksugrad@kennesaw.edu.
Website: http://ccse.kennesaw.edu/it/

Kent State University, College of Communication and Information, School of Information, Kent, OH 44242-0001. Offers health informatics (MS), including health informatics, knowledge management, user experience design; library and information science (MLIS), including K-12 school library media; M Ed/MLIS; MBA/MLIS; MLIS/MS. *Accreditation:* ALA (one or more programs are accredited). *Program availability:* Part-time, 100% online. *Faculty:* 16 full-time (13 women), 10 part-time/adjunct (6 women). *Students:* 114 full-time (91 women), 235 part-time (162 women); includes 52 minority (24 Black or African American, non-Hispanic/Latino; 8 Asian, non-Hispanic/Latino; 15 Hispanic/Latino; 5 Two or more races, non-Hispanic/Latino), 4 international. Average age 32. 212 applicants, 99% accepted, 147 enrolled. In 2018, 308 master's awarded. *Degree requirements:* For master's, portfolio (MLIS); internship, project, paper, or thesis. *Entrance requirements:* For master's, GRE if total GPA is below 3.0 in highest completed degree, minimum GPA of 3.0, statement of purpose, 3 letters of recommendation, curriculum vitae/resume, transcripts, writing sample, personal interview. Additional exam requirements/recommendations for international students: Required—TOEFL (minimum score 587 paper-based, 94 iBT), Michigan English Language Assessment Battery (minimum score 82), IELTS (minimum score 7.0) or PTE (minimum score 65). *Application deadline:* For fall admission, 3/15 priority date for domestic students, 3/15 for international students; for spring admission, 9/15 priority date for domestic students, 9/15 for international students; for summer admission, 1/15 priority date for domestic students, 1/15 for international students. Applications are processed on a rolling basis. Application fee: $45 ($70 for international students). Electronic applications accepted. *Expenses:* Tuition, state resident: full-time $11,766; part-time $536 per credit. Tuition, nonresident: full-time $21,952; part-time $999 per credit. *International tuition:* $21,952 full-time. Tuition and fees vary according to course load. *Financial support:* Fellowships with full tuition reimbursements, research assistantships with full tuition reimbursements, teaching assistantships with full tuition reimbursements, scholarships/grants, and unspecified assistantships available. Financial award application deadline: 3/1. *Unit head:* Dr. Kendra Albright, Director and Professor, 330-672-8535, E-mail: kalbrig7@kent.edu. *Application contact:* Dr. Karen Gracy, Graduate Co-Coordinator/Associate Professor, 330-672-2782, E-mail: kgracy@kent.edu.
Website: https://www.kent.edu/iSchool

Liberty University, School of Health Sciences, Lynchburg, VA 24515. Offers anatomy and cell biology (PhD); biomedical sciences (MS); epidemiology (MPH); exercise science (MS), including clinical, community physical activity, human performance, nutrition; global health (MPH); health promotion (MPH); medical sciences (MA), including biopsychology, business management, health informatics, molecular medicine, public health; nutrition (MPH). *Program availability:* Part-time, online learning. *Students:* 729 full-time (530 women), 760 part-time (555 women); includes 505 minority (327 Black or African American, non-Hispanic/Latino; 9 American Indian or Alaska Native, non-Hispanic/Latino; 38 Asian, non-Hispanic/Latino; 80 Hispanic/Latino; 4 Native Hawaiian or other Pacific Islander, non-Hispanic/Latino; 47 Two or more races, non-Hispanic/Latino), 71 international. Average age 31. 3,363 applicants, 32% accepted, 522 enrolled. In 2018, 373 master's awarded. *Degree requirements:* For master's, thesis (for some programs); for doctorate, thesis/dissertation. *Entrance requirements:* For doctorate, MAT or GRE, minimum GPA of 3.25 in master's program, 2-3 recommendations, writing samples (for some programs), letter of intent, professional vitae. Additional exam requirements/recommendations for international students: Required—TOEFL (minimum score 600 paper-based; 100 iBT). Application fee: $50. *Expenses: Tuition:* Full-time $10,851; part-time $562 per credit hour. *Financial support:* In 2018–19, 918 students received support. Federal Work-Study available. Financial award applicants required to submit FAFSA. *Unit head:* Dr. Ralph Linstra, Dean. *Application contact:* Jay Bridge, Director of Admissions, 800-424-9595, Fax: 800-628-7977, E-mail: gradadmissions@liberty.edu.
Website: https://www.liberty.edu/health-sciences/

Lipscomb University, College of Pharmacy, Nashville, TN 37204-3951. Offers healthcare informatics (MS); pharmacy (Pharm D); Pharm D/MM; Pharm D/MS. *Accreditation:* ACPE. *Degree requirements:* For master's, capstone project; for doctorate, comprehensive exam. *Entrance requirements:* For master's, GRE, 2 references, transcripts, resume, personal statement, eligibility documentation (degree and/or experience in related area); for doctorate, PCAT (minimum 45th percentile), 66 pre-professional semester hours, minimum GPA of 2.5, interview, PharmCAS application (for international students). Additional exam requirements/recommendations for international students: Required—TOEFL (minimum score 550 paper-based; 80 iBT). Electronic applications accepted. *Expenses:* Contact institution.

Logan University, College of Health Sciences, Chesterfield, MO 63017. Offers health informatics (MS); health professions education (DHPE); nutrition and human performance (MS); sports science and rehabilitation (MS). *Program availability:* Part-time, online only, 100% online. *Entrance requirements:* For master's, minimum GPA of 2.5; 6 hours of biology and physical science; bachelor's degree and 9 hours of business health administration (for health informatics). Additional exam requirements/recommendations for international students: Required—TOEFL (minimum score 500 paper-based; 79 iBT); Recommended—IELTS (minimum score 6.5). Electronic applications accepted. *Expenses:* Contact institution. *Faculty research:* Ankle injury prevention in high school athletes, low back pain in college football players, short arc banding and low back pain, the effects of enzymes on inflammatory blood markers, gait analysis in high school and college athletes.

Louisiana Tech University, Graduate School, College of Applied and Natural Sciences, Ruston, LA 71272. Offers biology (MS); dietetics (Graduate Certificate); health informatics (MHI); molecular science and nanotechnology (MS, PhD). *Program availability:* Part-time. *Degree requirements:* For master's, comprehensive exam (for some programs), thesis (for some programs); for doctorate, comprehensive exam, thesis/dissertation. *Entrance requirements:* For master's and doctorate, GRE General Test, transcript with bachelor's degree awarded; for Graduate Certificate, transcript with bachelor's degree awarded. Additional exam requirements/recommendations for international students: Required—TOEFL (minimum score 550 paper-based; 80 iBT), IELTS (minimum score 6.5). Electronic applications accepted. *Faculty research:* Developmentally appropriate practices in early childhood education, maternal and child nutrition, nutrition and cardiovascular disease, and early intervention for infants and toddlers; research in cell and molecular biology; health promotion in emerging adults, insulin pump use, forensic nursing, qualitative research, empathy in nursing students, civility in nursing education, and STI education; gene expression data analysis and data mining, knowledge discovery for health related data.

Health Informatics

Marshall University, Academic Affairs Division, College of Health Professions, Department of Health Informatics, Huntington, WV 25755. Offers MS. Program offered jointly with College of Business and College of Information Technology and Engineering.

Marymount University, School of Business and Technology, Program in Information Technology, Arlington, VA 22207-4299. Offers health care informatics (Certificate); information technology (MS, Certificate), including cybersecurity (MS); health care informatics (MS), project management and technology leadership (MS), software engineering (MS); information technology project management and technology leadership (Certificate); information technology with business administration (MS/MBA); information technology with health care management (MS/MS); MS/MBA; MS/MS. *Program availability:* Part-time, evening/weekend. *Faculty:* 5 full-time (3 women), 7 part-time/adjunct (0 women). *Students:* 29 full-time (17 women), 36 part-time (19 women); includes 25 minority (15 Black or African American, non-Hispanic/Latino; 5 Asian, non-Hispanic/Latino; 5 Hispanic/Latino), 24 international. Average age 30. 66 applicants, 98% accepted, 22 enrolled. In 2018, 35 master's, 3 other advanced degrees awarded. *Degree requirements:* For master's, thesis or alternative. *Entrance requirements:* For master's, resume, bachelor's degree in computer-related field or degree in another subject with a certificate in a computer-related field or related work experience. Software Engineering Track: bachelor's degree in Computer Science or work in software development. Project Mgmt/Tech Leadership Track: minimum 2 years of IT experience. Additional exam requirements/recommendations for international students: Required—TOEFL (minimum score 600 paper-based; 96 iBT), IELTS (minimum score 6.5), PTE (minimum score 58). *Application deadline:* For fall admission, 7/16 priority date for domestic and international students; for spring admission, 11/16 priority date for domestic and international students; for summer admission, 4/16 priority date for domestic and international students. Applications are processed on a rolling basis. Application fee: $40. Electronic applications accepted. *Expenses:* $1,060 per credit. *Financial support:* In 2018–19, 1 student received support. Research assistantships, teaching assistantships, career-related internships or fieldwork, scholarships/grants, and unspecified assistantships available. Support available to part-time students. Financial award application deadline: 3/1; financial award applicants required to submit FAFSA. *Unit head:* Dr. Diane Murphy, Chair/Director, Information Technology, Management Sciences and Cybersecurity, 703-284-5958, E-mail: diane.murphy@marymount.edu. *Application contact:* Rebecca Esposito, Senior Associate Director, Graduate Admissions, 703-284-5901, Fax: 703-527-3815, E-mail: grad.admissions@marymount.edu.
Website: https://www.marymount.edu/Academics/School-of-Business-and-Technology/Graduate-Programs/Information-Technology-(M-S-)

Mercer University, Graduate Studies, Cecil B. Day Campus, Penfield College, Atlanta, GA 30341. Offers certified rehabilitation counseling (MS); clinical mental health (MS); counselor education and supervision (PhD); criminal justice and public safety leadership (MS); health informatics (MS); human services (MS), including child and adolescent services, gerontology services; organizational leadership (MS), including leadership for the health care professional, leadership for the nonprofit organization, organizational development and change; school counseling (MS). *Program availability:* Part-time, evening/weekend, 100% online, blended/hybrid learning. *Degree requirements:* For master's, comprehensive exam (for some programs), thesis (for some programs); for doctorate, thesis/dissertation. *Entrance requirements:* For master's, GRE or MAT, Georgia Professional Standards Commission (GPSC) Certification at the SC-5 level; for doctorate, GRE or MAT. Additional exam requirements/recommendations for international students: Recommended—TOEFL (minimum score 550 paper-based; 80 iBT), IELTS (minimum score 6.5). Electronic applications accepted. Application fee is waived when completed online. *Expenses:* Contact institution. *Faculty research:* Marriage and families issues, leadership and ethics, cyber-bullying, trauma, narrative counseling and theory.

Middle Georgia State University, Office of Graduate Studies, Macon, GA 31206. Offers adult/gerontology acute care nurse practitioner (MSN); information technology (MS), including health informatics, information security and digital forensics, software development. *Entrance requirements:* For master's, GRE. Additional exam requirements/recommendations for international students: Required—TOEFL (minimum score 523 paper-based; 69 iBT). *Expenses:* Contact institution.

Midwestern State University, Billie Doris McAda Graduate School, Robert D. and Carol Gunn College of Health Sciences and Human Services, Department of Criminal Justice and Health Services Administration, Wichita Falls, TX 76308. Offers criminal justice (MA); health information management (MHA); health services administration (Graduate Certificate); medical practice management (MHA); public and community sector health care management (MHA); rural and urban hospital management (MHA). *Program availability:* Part-time, evening/weekend. *Degree requirements:* For master's, comprehensive exam, thesis. *Entrance requirements:* For master's, GRE. Additional exam requirements/recommendations for international students: Required—TOEFL (minimum score 550 paper-based). Electronic applications accepted. *Faculty research:* Universal service policy, telehealth, bullying, healthcare financial management, public health ethics.

Millennia Atlantic University, Graduate Programs, Doral, FL 33178. Offers accounting (MBA); business administration (MBA); health information management (MS); human resource management (MA). *Program availability:* Online learning.

Montana Tech of The University of Montana, Health Care Informatics Program, Butte, MT 59701-8997. Offers Certificate. *Program availability:* Part-time, evening/weekend, online learning. *Entrance requirements:* Additional exam requirements/recommendations for international students: Required—TOEFL (minimum score 545 paper-based; 78 iBT), IELTS (minimum score 6.5). Electronic applications accepted. *Faculty research:* Informatics, healthcare, computer science.

National University, School of Health and Human Services, La Jolla, CA 92037-1011. Offers clinical affairs (MS); clinical regulatory affairs (MS); complementary and integrative healthcare (MS); family nurse practitioner (MSN); health and life science analytics (MS); health informatics (MS, Certificate); healthcare administration (MHA); nurse anesthesia (MSNA); nursing administration (MSN); nursing informatics (MSN); psychiatric-mental health nurse practitioner (MSN); public health (MPH), including health promotion, healthcare administration, mental health. *Accreditation:* CEPH. *Program availability:* Part-time, evening/weekend, 100% online, blended/hybrid learning. *Degree requirements:* For master's, thesis (for some programs). *Entrance requirements:* For master's, interview, minimum GPA of 2.5. Additional exam requirements/recommendations for international students: Required—TOEFL (minimum score 550 paper-based; 79 iBT), IELTS (minimum score 6). Electronic applications accepted. *Expenses:* Tuition: Full-time $10,320; part-time $430 per unit. Tuition and fees vary according to degree level. *Faculty research:* Nursing education, obesity prevention, workforce diversity.

Northeastern University, College of Computer and Information Science, Boston, MA 02115-5096. Offers computer science (MS, PhD); data science (MS); game science and design (MS); health informatics (MS); information assurance (MS); network science (PhD); personal health informatics (PhD). *Program availability:* Part-time, evening/weekend. Terminal master's awarded for partial completion of doctoral program. *Degree*

requirements: For master's, thesis optional; for doctorate, comprehensive exam, thesis/dissertation. Electronic applications accepted. *Expenses:* Contact institution.

Northern Kentucky University, Office of Graduate Programs, College of Informatics, Program in Health Informatics, Highland Heights, KY 41099. Offers MS, Certificate. *Program availability:* Part-time, evening/weekend, online learning. *Degree requirements:* For master's, capstone, electronic portfolio. *Entrance requirements:* For master's, MAT, GRE, or GMAT, official transcripts from accredited college or university, minimum GPA of 3.0, letter of career goals and background, statement addressing computer proficiencies; references (recommended). Additional exam requirements/recommendations for international students: Required—TOEFL (minimum score 79 iBT); Recommended—IELTS (minimum score 6.5). Electronic applications accepted. *Faculty research:* Health informatics course development, healthcare analytics, technology acceptance in healthcare, consumer engagement, population health outcome, systems implementation, healthcare operations.

Northwestern University, Feinberg School of Medicine, Driskill Graduate Program in Life Sciences, Chicago, IL 60611. Offers biostatistics (PhD); epidemiology (PhD); health and biomedical informatics (PhD); health services and outcomes research (PhD); healthcare quality and patient safety (PhD); translational outcomes in science (PhD). *Degree requirements:* For doctorate, comprehensive exam, thesis/dissertation, written and oral qualifying exams. *Entrance requirements:* For doctorate, GRE General Test. Additional exam requirements/recommendations for international students: Required—TOEFL (minimum score 600 paper-based). Electronic applications accepted.

Northwestern University, School of Professional Studies, Program in Health Informatics, Evanston, IL 60208. Offers MS. *Program availability:* Online learning.

Nova Southeastern University, Dr. Kiran C. Patel College of Osteopathic Medicine, Fort Lauderdale, FL 33328. Offers biomedical informatics (MS, Graduate Certificate), including biomedical informatics (MS), clinical informatics (Graduate Certificate), public health informatics (Graduate Certificate); disaster and emergency management (MS); medical education (MS); nutrition (MS, Graduate Certificate), including functional nutrition and herbal therapy (Graduate Certificate); osteopathic medicine (DO); public health (MPH, Graduate Certificate), including health education (Graduate Certificate); social medicine (Graduate Certificate); DO/DMD. *Accreditation:* AOsA; CEPH. *Degree requirements:* For master's, comprehensive exam (for MPH); field/special projects; for doctorate, comprehensive exam, COMLEX Board Exams; for Graduate Certificate, thesis or alternative. *Entrance requirements:* For master's, GRE; for doctorate, MCAT, coursework in biology, chemistry, organic chemistry, physics (all with labs), biochemistry, and English. Electronic applications accepted. *Expenses:* Contact institution. *Faculty research:* Teaching strategies, simulated patient use, HIV/AIDS education, minority health issues, immune disorders.

Oregon Health & Science University, School of Medicine, Graduate Programs in Medicine, Department of Medical Informatics and Clinical Epidemiology, Portland, OR 97239-3098. Offers bioinformatics and computational biology (MS, PhD); clinical informatics (MBI, MS, PhD, Certificate); health information management (Certificate). *Program availability:* Part-time, online learning. *Faculty:* 12 full-time (6 women), 15 part-time/adjunct (7 women). *Students:* 28 full-time (12 women), 31 part-time (10 women); includes 13 minority (1 Black or African American, non-Hispanic/Latino; 9 Asian, non-Hispanic/Latino; 2 Hispanic/Latino; 1 Two or more races, non-Hispanic/Latino), 8 international. Average age 34. 65 applicants, 54% accepted, 32 enrolled. In 2018, 23 master's, 3 doctorates, 20 other advanced degrees awarded. Terminal master's awarded for partial completion of doctoral program. *Degree requirements:* For master's, thesis or capstone project; for doctorate, comprehensive exam, thesis/dissertation, qualifying exam. *Entrance requirements:* For master's and doctorate, GRE General Test (minimum scores: 153 Verbal/148 Quantitative/4.5 Analytical), coursework in computer programming, human anatomy and physiology. *Application deadline:* For fall admission, 12/1 for domestic students; for winter admission, 11/1 for domestic students; for spring admission, 2/1 for domestic students. Applications are processed on a rolling basis. Application fee: $70. Electronic applications accepted. *Expenses:* Contact institution. *Financial support:* Fellowships with full tuition reimbursements, research assistantships, Federal Work-Study, scholarships/grants, health care benefits, and full-tuition and stipends (for PhD students) available. Financial award application deadline: 3/1; financial award applicants required to submit FAFSA. *Faculty research:* Clinical informatics, computational biology, health information management, genomics, data analytics. *Unit head:* Dr. William Hersh, Program Director, 503-494-4563, E-mail: somgrad@ohsu.edu. *Application contact:* Lauren Ludwig, Administrative Coordinator, 503-494-2252, E-mail: informat@ohsu.edu.
Website: http://www.ohsu.edu/dmice/

Regis University, College of Computer and Information Sciences, Denver, CO 80221-1099. Offers agile technologies (Certificate); cybersecurity (Certificate); data science (M Sc); database administration with Oracle (Certificate); database development (Certificate); database technologies (M Sc); enterprise Java software development (Certificate); enterprise resource planning (Certificate); executive information technology (Certificate); health care informatics (Certificate); health care informatics and information management (M Sc); information assurance (M Sc); information assurance policy management (Certificate); information technology management (M Sc); mobile software development (Certificate); software engineering (M Sc, Certificate); software engineering and database technology (M Sc); storage area networks (Certificate); systems engineering (M Sc, Certificate). *Program availability:* Part-time, evening/weekend, 100% online, blended/hybrid learning. *Degree requirements:* For master's, thesis (for some programs), final research project. *Entrance requirements:* For master's, official transcript reflecting baccalaureate degree awarded from regionally-accredited college or university, 2 years of related experience, resume, interview. Additional exam requirements/recommendations for international students: Required—TOEFL (minimum score 550 paper-based; 82 iBT). Electronic applications accepted. *Expenses:* Contact institution. *Faculty research:* Information policy, knowledge management, software architectures, data science.

Roberts Wesleyan College, Health Administration Programs, Rochester, NY 14624-1997. Offers health administration (MS); healthcare informatics administration (MS). *Program availability:* Evening/weekend, online learning. *Degree requirements:* For master's, thesis or alternative. *Entrance requirements:* For master's, minimum GPA of 3.0, verifiable work experience or recommendation.

Rochester Institute of Technology, Graduate Enrollment Services, Golisano College of Computing and Information Sciences, Information Science and Technologies Department, MS Program in Health Informatics, Rochester, NY 14623-5603. Offers MS. *Program availability:* Part-time, evening/weekend, online only, 100% online. *Students:* 1 full-time (0 women), 3 part-time (all women); includes 1 minority (Asian, non-Hispanic/Latino). Average age 36. 5 applicants, 60% accepted, 3 enrolled. *Degree requirements:* For master's, Capstone. *Entrance requirements:* For master's, GRE required for international students only., minimum GPA of 3.0 (preferred), two letters of recommendation, resume, recommended to have a minimum of three years experience in a relevant field, and interview may be required. Additional exam requirements/recommendations for international students: Required—TOEFL (minimum score 88 iBT), IELTS (minimum score 6.5). *Application deadline:* Applications are processed on a

rolling basis. Application fee: $65. Electronic applications accepted. *Expenses:* Contact institution. *Financial support:* Applicants required to submit FAFSA. *Unit head:* Qi Yu, Director, 585-475-6929, E-mail: qyuvks@rit.edu. *Application contact:* Diane Ellison, Senior Associate Vice President, Graduate Enrollment Services, 585-475-2229, Fax: 585-475-7164, E-mail: gradinfo@rit.edu.
Website: https://www.rit.edu/study/health-informatics-ms

Rutgers University–New Brunswick, Edward J. Bloustein School of Planning and Public Policy, Program in Public Informatics, Piscataway, NJ 08854-8097. Offers MPI.

Sacred Heart University, Graduate Programs, College of Health Professions, Department of Health Science, Fairfield, CT 06825. Offers healthcare informatics (MS). *Program availability:* Part-time, evening/weekend. *Degree requirements:* For master's, comprehensive exam (for some programs). *Entrance requirements:* For master's, bachelor's degree, minimum cumulative undergraduate GPA of 3.0, personal essay, two letters of recommendation, resume. Additional exam requirements/recommendations for international students: Required—TOEFL (minimum score 570 paper-based, 80 iBT), TWE, or IELTS (6.5). Electronic applications accepted. *Expenses:* Contact institution.

St. Catherine University, Graduate Programs, Program in Health Informatics, St. Paul, MN 55105. Offers MHI. *Program availability:* Online learning. *Expenses:* Contact institution.

St. Joseph's College, Long Island Campus, Programs in Health Care Administration, Field in Health Care Management - Health Information Systems, Patchogue, NY 11772-2399. Offers MBA. *Program availability:* Part-time, evening/weekend, 100% online, blended/hybrid learning. *Faculty:* 13 full-time (5 women), 23 part-time/adjunct (8 women). *Students:* 6 full-time (4 women), 18 part-time (11 women); includes 6 minority (2 Black or African American, non-Hispanic/Latino; 1 Asian, non-Hispanic/Latino; 3 Hispanic/Latino). Average age 37. 10 applicants, 50% accepted, 2 enrolled. In 2018, 13 master's awarded. *Entrance requirements:* For master's, Application, $25 application fee, official transcripts, two letters of recommendation, current resume, 250 word written statement. Additional exam requirements/recommendations for international students: Required—TOEFL (minimum score 80 iBT). *Application deadline:* Applications are processed on a rolling basis. Application fee: $25. Electronic applications accepted. *Expenses: Tuition:* Full-time $18,450; part-time $1025 per credit. *Required fees:* $414. *Financial support:* In 2018–19, 13 students received support. *Unit head:* John Sardelis, Associate Chair and Professor, 631-687-1493, E-mail: jsardelis@sjcny.edu. *Application contact:* John Sardelis, Associate Chair and Professor, 631-687-1493, E-mail: jsardelis@sjcny.edu.

St. Joseph's College, New York, Programs in Health Care Administration, Field in Health Care Management - Health Information Systems, Brooklyn, NY 11205-3688. Offers MBA. *Program availability:* Part-time, evening/weekend, 100% online, blended/hybrid learning. *Faculty:* 5 part-time/adjunct (4 women). *Students:* 9 part-time (7 women); includes 6 minority (4 Black or African American, non-Hispanic/Latino; 2 Asian, non-Hispanic/Latino). Average age 36. In 2018, 6 master's awarded. *Entrance requirements:* For master's, Application, $25 application fee, two letters of recommendation, current resume, 250 word essay, official transcripts. Additional exam requirements/recommendations for international students: Required—TOEFL (minimum score 80 iBT). *Application deadline:* Applications are processed on a rolling basis. Application fee: $25. Electronic applications accepted. *Expenses: Tuition:* Full-time $18,450; part-time $1025 per credit. *Required fees:* $414. *Financial support:* In 2018–19, 4 students received support. *Unit head:* Lauren Pete, Chair, 718-940-5890, E-mail: lpete@sjcny.edu. *Application contact:* Lauren Pete, Chair, 718-940-5890, E-mail: lpete@sjcny.edu.

Saint Joseph's University, College of Arts and Sciences, Department of Health Services, Philadelphia, PA 19131-1395. Offers health administration (MS); health informatics (MS); organizations development and leadership (MS). *Program availability:* Part-time, evening/weekend. *Entrance requirements:* For master's, GRE (if GPA less than 2.75), 2 letters of recommendation, resume, personal statement, official transcripts. Additional exam requirements/recommendations for international students: Required—TOEFL (minimum score 550 paper-based; 80 iBT), IELTS (minimum score 6.5). Electronic applications accepted. *Expenses:* Contact institution.

Samford University, School of Public Health, Birmingham, AL 35229. Offers health informatics (MSHI); healthcare administration (MHA); nutrition (MS); public health (MPH); social work (MSW). *Accreditation:* CSWE. *Program availability:* Part-time, online only, 100% online. *Faculty:* 18 full-time (11 women), 1 (woman) part-time/adjunct. *Students:* 86 full-time (79 women), 6 part-time (all women); includes 18 minority (15 Black or African American, non-Hispanic/Latino; 1 Hispanic/Latino; 2 Two or more races, non-Hispanic/Latino). Average age 28. 93 applicants, 73% accepted, 30 enrolled. In 2018, 59 master's awarded. *Degree requirements:* For master's, capstone course. *Entrance requirements:* For master's, GRE, MAT, recommendations, resume, personal statement, transcripts, application. Additional exam requirements/recommendations for international students: Required—TOEFL (minimum score 590 paper-based; 90 iBT), IELTS (minimum score 6.5). *Application deadline:* For fall admission, 10/1 for domestic students; for winter admission, 12/1 for domestic students; for spring admission, 5/1 for domestic students. Applications are processed on a rolling basis. Application fee: $75. Electronic applications accepted. *Expenses:* $862 per credit hour. *Financial support:* In 2018–19, 39 students received support. Scholarships/grants available. Financial award application deadline: 5/1; financial award applicants required to submit FAFSA. *Faculty research:* Chronic kidney disease, disasters and vulnerable populations, children's health, obesity, metabolism and diabetes, health policy and health care delivery. *Unit head:* Dr. Keith Elder, Ph.D., Dean, School of Public Health, 205-726-4655, E-mail: kelder@samford.edu. *Application contact:* Dr. Marian Carter, Ed.D, Assistant Dean of Enrollment Management and Student Services, 205-726-2611, E-mail: mwcarter@samford.edu.
Website: http://www.samford.edu/publichealth

Slippery Rock University of Pennsylvania, Graduate Studies (Recruitment), College of Health, Environment, and Science, Department of Computer Science, Slippery Rock, PA 16057-1383. Offers health informatics (MS). *Program availability:* Part-time, evening/weekend, online only, 100% online. *Faculty:* 2 full-time (0 women). *Students:* 6 full-time (1 woman), 14 part-time (7 women); includes 2 minority (both Black or African American, non-Hispanic/Latino), 1 international. Average age 31. 22 applicants, 77% accepted, 13 enrolled. In 2018, 8 master's awarded. *Entrance requirements:* For master's, minimum GPA of 3.0. Additional exam requirements/recommendations for international students: Required—TOEFL (minimum score 550 paper-based; 80 iBT). *Application deadline:* For fall admission, 5/1 priority date for domestic students, 3/1 priority date for international students; for spring admission, 10/1 priority date for domestic students, 9/1 priority date for international students. Applications are processed on a rolling basis. Application fee: $25 ($30 for international students). Electronic applications accepted. *Expenses:* Contact institution. *Financial support:* In 2018–19, 2 students received support. Career-related internships or fieldwork, Federal Work-Study, institutionally sponsored loans, scholarships/grants, tuition waivers (partial), and unspecified assistantships available. Support available to part-time students. Financial award application deadline: 5/1; financial award applicants required to submit FAFSA. *Unit head:* Dr. Sam Thangiah, Department Chair, 724-738-2141, Fax: 724-738-4513, E-mail: sam.thangiah@sru.edu. *Application contact:* Brandi Weber-Mortimer, Director of Graduate Admissions, 724-738-2051, Fax: 724-738-2146, E-mail: graduate.admissions@sru.edu.
Website: http://www.sru.edu/academics/colleges-and-departments/ches/departments/computer-science

Southern Illinois University Edwardsville, Graduate School, Program in Healthcare Informatics, Edwardsville, IL 62026. Offers MS. *Program availability:* Part-time, evening/weekend. *Degree requirements:* For master's, comprehensive exam. *Entrance requirements:* For master's, baccalaureate degree with minimum GPA of 2.75. Additional exam requirements/recommendations for international students: Required—TOEFL (minimum score 550 paper-based; 79 iBT), IELTS (minimum score 6.5). Electronic applications accepted.

Southern New Hampshire University, School of Business, Manchester, NH 03106-1045. Offers accounting (MBA, Graduate Certificate); accounting finance (MS); accounting/auditing (MS); accounting/forensic accounting (MS); accounting/management accounting (MS); accounting/taxation (MS); applied economics (MS); athletic administration (MBA, Graduate Certificate); business administration (IMBA, Certificate), including business information systems (Certificate), human resource management (Certificate); business analytics (MBA); business intelligence (MBA); communication (MA), including new media and marketing, public relations; community economic development (MBA); criminal justice (MBA); data analytics (MS); economics (MBA); engineering management (MBA); entrepreneurship (MBA); finance (MBA, MS, Graduate Certificate); finance/corporate finance (MS); finance/investments (MS); forensic accounting (MBA); forensic accounting and fraud examination (Graduate Certificate); healthcare informatics (MBA); healthcare management (MBA); human resource management (MS); human resources (MBA); information technology (MS); information technology management (MBA); international business (PhD); Internet marketing (MBA); leadership (MBA); leadership of nonprofit organizations (Graduate Certificate); management (MS); marketing (MBA, MS, Graduate Certificate); music business (MBA); operations and project management (MS); operations and supply chain management (MBA, Graduate Certificate); organizational leadership (MS); project management (MBA, Graduate Certificate); public administration (MBA, Graduate Certificate); quantitative analysis (MBA); Six Sigma (Graduate Certificate); Six Sigma quality (MBA); social media marketing (MBA, Graduate Certificate); sport management (MBA, MS, Graduate Certificate); sustainability and environmental compliance (MBA); MBA/Certificate. *Accreditation:* ACBSP. *Program availability:* Part-time, evening/weekend, online learning. Terminal master's awarded for partial completion of doctoral program. *Degree requirements:* For master's, one foreign language, comprehensive exam (for some programs), thesis or alternative; for doctorate, one foreign language, comprehensive exam, thesis/dissertation. *Entrance requirements:* For master's, minimum GPA of 2.5; for doctorate, GMAT. Additional exam requirements/recommendations for international students: Required—TOEFL (minimum score 500 paper-based). Electronic applications accepted.

State University of New York at Oswego, Graduate Studies, Program in Biomedical and Health Informatics, Oswego, NY 13126. Offers health informatics professional (MS); health informatics: intelligent health systems (MS); health information management: health data science (MS). Program also offered at Syracuse campus. *Program availability:* Online learning. *Entrance requirements:* For master's, GRE (recommended), official transcripts, statement of purpose, resume, two letters of recommendation.

Stephens College, Division of Graduate and Continuing Studies, Columbia, MO 65215-0002. Offers counseling (M Ed), including addictions counseling, clinical mental health counseling, school counseling; health information administration (Postbaccalaureate Certificate); physician assistant studies (MPAS); TV and screenwriting (MFA). *Program availability:* Part-time, evening/weekend, online learning. *Entrance requirements:* For master's, minimum GPA of 3.0 in last 60 hours. Additional exam requirements/recommendations for international students: Required—TOEFL (minimum score 79 iBT). Electronic applications accepted. *Faculty research:* Educational psychology, outcomes assessment.

Stony Brook University, State University of New York, Stony Brook Medicine, School of Health Technology and Management, Stony Brook, NY 11794. Offers applied health informatics (MS); disability studies (Certificate); health administration (MHA); health and rehabilitation sciences (PhD); health care management (Advanced Certificate); health care policy and management (MS); occupational therapy (MS); physical therapy (DPT); physician assistant (MS). *Accreditation:* AOTA; APTA. *Faculty:* 61 full-time (41 women), 56 part-time/adjunct (36 women). *Students:* 595 full-time (407 women), 67 part-time (51 women); includes 202 minority (29 Black or African American, non-Hispanic/Latino; 97 Asian, non-Hispanic/Latino; 62 Hispanic/Latino; 1 Native Hawaiian or other Pacific Islander, non-Hispanic/Latino; 13 Two or more races, non-Hispanic/Latino), 13 international. Average age 26. 2,386 applicants, 17% accepted, 256 enrolled. In 2018, 158 master's, 89 doctorates, 27 other advanced degrees awarded. *Entrance requirements:* For master's, GRE General Test, minimum GPA of 3.0, work experience in field, references; for doctorate, GRE, three references, essay. Additional exam requirements/recommendations for international students: Required—TOEFL (minimum score 550 paper-based). *Application deadline:* For fall admission, 1/15 for domestic students; for spring admission, 10/1 for domestic students. Application fee: $100. *Expenses:* Contact institution. *Financial support:* In 2018–19, 1 research assistantship was awarded; fellowships, teaching assistantships, career-related internships or fieldwork, Federal Work-Study, and institutionally sponsored loans also available. Financial award application deadline: 3/15. *Faculty research:* Developmental disabilities, disability studies, health promotion, multiple sclerosis, quality of life program, internal medicine, lung disease, palliative care, respiratory diseases, neuromuscular disorders, orthopedics, physical medicine and rehabilitation, physical therapy, prostheses or implants, advance directives, advocacy alienation, allied health education, allied health occupations, adolescents, adoption, child or adolescent mental health, multiple sclerosis, youth policy. *Total annual research expenditures:* $1.3 million. *Unit head:* Lisa M Johnson, Interim Dean, 631-444-3181, Fax: 631-444-7621, E-mail: lisa.johnson@stonybrook.edu. *Application contact:* Frances Shaw, Department Secretary, 631-444-3240, Fax: 631-444-7621, E-mail: frances.shaw@stonybrook.edu.
Website: http://healthtechnology.stonybrookmedicine.edu/

Temple University, College of Public Health, Department of Health Services Administration and Policy, Philadelphia, PA 19122. Offers health informatics (MS); health policy (PhD); health policy and management (MPH). *Program availability:* Part-time, evening/weekend, online learning. *Faculty:* 10 full-time (6 women), 2 part-time/adjunct (both women). *Students:* 20 full-time (12 women), 45 part-time (35 women); includes 32 minority (13 Black or African American, non-Hispanic/Latino; 13 Asian, non-Hispanic/Latino; 5 Hispanic/Latino; 1 Two or more races, non-Hispanic/Latino), 4 international. 125 applicants, 63% accepted, 28 enrolled. In 2018, 20 master's awarded. *Degree requirements:* For doctorate, comprehensive exam, thesis/dissertation, area paper, oral presentation, article critique. *Entrance requirements:* For master's, GRE, 3 letters of reference, statement of goals, resume, clearances for clinical/field education (M.P.H. only); for doctorate, GRE, 3 letters of reference, statement of goals, resume, writing sample. Additional exam requirements/recommendations for international students: Required—TOEFL (minimum score 79 iBT), IELTS (minimum score 6.5), PTE (minimum score 53), one of three is required. Application fee: $60. Electronic

applications accepted. *Expenses:* Contact institution. *Financial support:* Fellowships, research assistantships, teaching assistantships, Federal Work-Study, scholarships/grants, and health care benefits available. Financial award applicants required to submit FAFSA. *Faculty research:* Behavioral health services, chronic disease, patient-centered decision-making, outcomes research, cancer prevention. *Unit head:* Stephen Lepore, Interim Department Chair, 215-204-9422, E-mail: slepore@temple.edu. *Application contact:* Annemarie Szambelak, Assistant Director of Admissions, 215-204-4526, E-mail: aszambelak@temple.edu.
Website: https://cph.temple.edu/healthadminpolicy/

Texas State University, The Graduate College, College of Health Professions, Program in Health Information Management, San Marcos, TX 78666. Offers MHIIM. *Program availability:* Part-time, evening/weekend. *Faculty:* 6 full-time (3 women), 1 (woman) part-time/adjunct. *Students:* 33 full-time (27 women), 14 part-time (13 women); includes 31 minority (11 Black or African American, non-Hispanic/Latino; 3 Asian, non-Hispanic/Latino; 16 Hispanic/Latino; 1 Two or more races, non-Hispanic/Latino). Average age 33. 48 applicants, 63% accepted, 22 enrolled. In 2018, 13 master's awarded. *Degree requirements:* For master's, comprehensive exam, thesis optional, committee review. *Entrance requirements:* For master's, baccalaureate degree from regionally-accredited institution with minimum GPA of 2.75 on last 60 hours of undergraduate work, 3 letters of reference, written statement of purpose, current resume, background course work in statistics and computer information systems. Additional exam requirements/recommendations for international students: Required—TOEFL (minimum score 550 paper-based; 78 iBT), IELTS (minimum score 6). *Application deadline:* For fall admission, 6/1 for domestic and international students. Applications are processed on a rolling basis. Application fee: $55 ($90 for international students). Electronic applications accepted. *Expenses:* Tuition, state resident: full-time $8102; part-time $4051 per semester. Tuition, nonresident: full-time $18,229; part-time $9115 per semester. *International tuition:* $18,229 full-time. *Required fees:* $2116; $120 per credit hour. Tuition and fees vary according to course load. *Financial support:* In 2018–19, 13 students received support. Research assistantships, teaching assistantships, career-related internships or fieldwork, Federal Work-Study, institutionally sponsored loans, scholarships/grants, and unspecified assistantships available. Support available to part-time students. Financial award application deadline: 1/15; financial award applicants required to submit FAFSA. *Faculty research:* Individual and organizational performance, healthcare information systems, tax and technology and information system security; relational databases, electronically stored information, informatics, and data analytics; securing information systems and electronic health records; Healthcare Management, Health Policy, Health Information Management applications, Electronic Health Records, and Entrepreneurship for Healthcare Professionals. *Total annual research expenditures:* $1,500. *Unit head:* Dr. Tiankai Wang, Graduate Advisor, 512-245-7773, E-mail: tw26@txstate.edu. *Application contact:* Dr. Andrea Golato, Dean of Graduate School, 512-245-2581, Fax: 512-245-8365, E-mail: gradcollege@txstate.edu.
Website: http://www.health.txstate.edu/him/degrees-programs/Master-Degree-in-HIM.html

Trident University International, College of Health Sciences, Program in Health Sciences, Cypress, CA 90630. Offers clinical research administration (MS, Certificate); emergency and disaster management (MS, Certificate); environmental health science (Certificate); health care administration (PhD); health care management (MS), including health informatics; health education (MS, Certificate); health informatics (Certificate); health sciences (PhD); international health (MS); international health: educator or researcher option (PhD); international health: practitioner option (PhD); law and expert witness studies (MS, Certificate); public health (MS); quality assurance (Certificate). *Program availability:* Part-time, evening/weekend, online learning. *Degree requirements:* For doctorate, comprehensive exam, thesis/dissertation, defense of dissertation. *Entrance requirements:* For master's, minimum GPA of 2.5 (students with GPA 3.0 or greater may transfer up to 30% of graduate level credits); for doctorate, minimum GPA of 3.4, curriculum vitae, course work in research methods or statistics. Additional exam requirements/recommendations for international students: Required—TOEFL. Electronic applications accepted.

The University of Alabama at Birmingham, School of Health Professions, Graduate Programs in Health Informatics, Birmingham, AL 35294. Offers data analytics user experience (MSHI). *Program availability:* Fall and Spring Residential Visit. *Faculty:* 7 full-time (5 women), 3 part-time/adjunct (1 woman). *Students:* 48 full-time (22 women); includes 22 minority (16 Black or African American, non-Hispanic/Latino; 6 Asian, non-Hispanic/Latino). Average age 32. 52 applicants, 63% accepted, 30 enrolled. In 2018, 30 master's awarded. *Degree requirements:* For master's, Applied capstone project. *Entrance requirements:* For master's, minimum undergraduate GPA of 3.0, letters of recommendation, interview. Additional exam requirements/recommendations for international students: Required—TOEFL, IELTS. *Application deadline:* For fall admission, 5/31 for domestic students. Application fee: $45 ($60 for international students). Electronic applications accepted. *Expenses: Tuition, area resident:* Full-time $8100; part-time $8100 per year. Tuition, state resident: full-time $8100. Tuition, nonresident: full-time $19,188; part-time $19,188 per year. Tuition and fees vary according to program. *Financial support:* Career-related internships or fieldwork, Federal Work-Study, and Employee tuition assistance available. Financial award applicants required to submit FAFSA. *Faculty research:* Healthcare/medical informatics, health information system development and evaluation, natural language processing, clinical decision support. *Unit head:* Dr. Sue S Feldman, Program Director, 205-9750809. *Application contact:* Misty Altiparmak, Director of Operations, 205-934-3509, E-mail: maltima@uab.edu.
Website: http://www.uab.edu/hi

University of Central Florida, College of Community Innovation and Education, Department of Health Management and Informatics, Orlando, FL 32816. Offers health administration (MHA); health care informatics (MS); health information administration (Certificate). *Accreditation:* CAHME. *Program availability:* Part-time, evening/weekend. *Degree requirements:* For master's, comprehensive exam, thesis or alternative, research report. *Entrance requirements:* For master's, letters of recommendation, resume, goal statement. Additional exam requirements/recommendations for international students: Required—TOEFL. Electronic applications accepted.

University of Cincinnati, Graduate School, College of Allied Health Sciences, Department of Clinical and Health Information Sciences, Cincinnati, OH 45221. Offers health informatics (MHI). *Program availability:* Part-time, online learning.

University of Colorado Denver, Business School, Program in Information Systems, Denver, CO 80217. Offers accounting and information systems audit and control (MS); business intelligence systems (MS); digital health entrepreneurship (MS); enterprise risk management (MS); enterprise technology management (MS); geographic information systems (MS); health information technology (MS); technology innovation and entrepreneurship (MS); Web and mobile computing (MS). *Program availability:* Part-time, evening/weekend, online learning. *Degree requirements:* For master's, 30 credit hours. *Entrance requirements:* For master's, GMAT, resume, essay, two letters of recommendation, financial statements (for international applicants). Additional exam requirements/recommendations for international students: Required—TOEFL (minimum score 525 paper-based; 71 iBT); Recommended—IELTS (minimum score 6.5). Electronic applications accepted. *Expenses:* Contact institution. *Faculty research:* Human-computer interaction, expert systems, database management, electronic commerce, object-oriented software development.

The University of Findlay, Office of Graduate Admissions, Findlay, OH 45840-3653. Offers applied security and analytics (MSAS); athletic training (MAT); business (MBA), including certified management accountant, certified public accountant, health care management, hospitality management; education (MA Ed, Ed D), including children's literature (MA Ed), curriculum and teaching (MA Ed), education (MA Ed), educational administration (MA Ed), human resource development (MA Ed), mathematics (MA Ed), reading (MA Ed), science education (MA Ed), superintendent (Ed D), teaching (Ed D), technology (MA Ed); environmental, safety, and health management (MSEM); health informatics (MS); occupational therapy (MOT); pharmacy (Pharm D); physical therapy (DPT); physician assistant (MPA); rhetoric and writing (MA); teaching English to speakers of other languages (TESOL) and applied linguistics (MA). *Program availability:* Part-time, evening/weekend, 100% online, blended/hybrid learning. *Degree requirements:* For master's, comprehensive exam (for some programs), thesis (for some programs), cumulative project, capstone project; for doctorate, thesis/dissertation (for some programs). *Entrance requirements:* For master's, GRE/GMAT, bachelor's degree from accredited institution, minimum undergraduate GPA of 2.5 in last 64 hours of course work; for doctorate, GRE, MAT, minimum cumulative GPA of 3.0. Additional exam requirements/recommendations for international students: Required—TOEFL (minimum score 79 iBT), IELTS (minimum score 7), PTE (minimum score 61). Electronic applications accepted.

University of Illinois at Chicago, College of Applied Health Sciences, Program in Health Informatics, Chicago, IL 60607-7128. Offers health informatics (MS, CAS); health information management (Certificate). *Program availability:* Part-time, online learning. *Expenses:* Contact institution. *Faculty research:* Information science, computer science, health informatics, health information management.

University of Illinois at Urbana–Champaign, Graduate College, School of Information Sciences, Champaign, IL 61820. Offers bioinformatics (MS); digital libraries (CAS); information management (MS); library and information science (MS, PhD, CAS). *Accreditation:* ALA (one or more programs are accredited). *Program availability:* Part-time, online learning. *Entrance requirements:* For degree, master's degree in library and information science or related field with minimum GPA of 3.0.

The University of Iowa, Graduate College, Program in Informatics, Iowa City, IA 52242-1316. Offers bioinformatics (MS, PhD); bioinformatics and computational biology (Certificate); geoinformatics (MS, PhD, Certificate); health informatics (MS, PhD, Certificate); information science (MS, PhD, Certificate). *Degree requirements:* For master's, thesis optional; for doctorate, comprehensive exam, thesis/dissertation. *Entrance requirements:* For master's and doctorate, GRE General Test, minimum GPA of 3.0. Additional exam requirements/recommendations for international students: Required—TOEFL (minimum score 550 paper-based; 81 iBT). Electronic applications accepted.

The University of Kansas, University of Kansas Medical Center, Interprofessional Program in Health Informatics, Kansas City, KS 66045. Offers MS, Post Master's Certificate. *Program availability:* Part-time, evening/weekend, 100% online, blended/hybrid learning. *Students:* Average age 33. 8 applicants, 63% accepted, 5 enrolled. In 2018, 4 master's awarded. *Degree requirements:* For master's, comprehensive exam, research paper, minimum GPA of 3.0; for Post Master's Certificate, minimum GPA of 3.0. *Entrance requirements:* For master's, minimum GPA of 3.0, official copies of transcripts, 3 references, resume, personal statement; for Post Master's Certificate, minimum cumulative GPA of 3.0, official copies of transcripts, 3 references, resume, personal statement. Additional exam requirements/recommendations for international students: Required—TOEFL or IELTS. *Application deadline:* For fall admission, 4/1 for domestic and international students; for spring admission, 9/1 for domestic and international students. Application fee: $60. Electronic applications accepted. *Financial support:* Application deadline: 3/1; applicants required to submit FAFSA. *Faculty research:* Symbolic representation of health data, inter-professional education and practice, usability of health systems, workforce and staffing, secondary use of data. *Unit head:* Dr. E. LaVerne Manos, Director, 913-588-1671, Fax: 913-588-1660, E-mail: lmanos@kumc.edu. *Application contact:* Teresa Stenner, Program Manager, 913-588-3362, Fax: 913-588-1660, E-mail: healthinformatics@kumc.edu.
Website: http://www.kumc.edu/health-informatics.html

University of Lynchburg, Graduate Studies, Program in Health Informatics Management, Lynchburg, VA 24501-3199. Offers Certificate. *Program availability:* Part-time. *Entrance requirements:* For degree, official transcripts from each college attended indicating all college coursework completed. Additional exam requirements/recommendations for international students: Required—TOEFL (minimum score 550 paper-based; 80 iBT), IELTS (minimum score 6). Electronic applications accepted. Application fee is waived when completed online. *Expenses:* Contact institution.

University of Maryland, Baltimore County, The Graduate School, College of Engineering and Information Technology, Department of Information Systems, Program in Health Information Technology, Baltimore, MD 21250. Offers MPS. *Program availability:* Part-time. *Entrance requirements:* For master's, minimum undergraduate GPA of 3.0. Additional exam requirements/recommendations for international students: Required—TOEFL (minimum score 550 paper-based; 80 iBT), GRE. Electronic applications accepted. *Expenses:* Contact institution. *Faculty research:* Health information technology.

University of Maryland University College, The Graduate School, Health Informatics Administration Program, Adelphi, MD 20783. Offers MS. *Program availability:* Part-time, evening/weekend, online learning. *Students:* 1 (woman) full-time, 481 part-time (346 women); includes 317 minority (221 Black or African American, non-Hispanic/Latino; 2 American Indian or Alaska Native, non-Hispanic/Latino; 53 Asian, non-Hispanic/Latino; 30 Hispanic/Latino; 11 Two or more races, non-Hispanic/Latino), 11 international. Average age 36. 138 applicants, 100% accepted, 92 enrolled. In 2018, 103 master's awarded. *Degree requirements:* For master's, thesis or alternative, capstone course. *Application deadline:* Applications are processed on a rolling basis. Application fee: $50. Electronic applications accepted. *Financial support:* Scholarships/grants available. Support available to part-time students. Financial award application deadline: 6/1; financial award applicants required to submit FAFSA. *Unit head:* Donald Donahue, Program Chair, 240-684-2400, E-mail: Donald.Donahue@umuc.edu. *Application contact:* Admissions, 800-888-8682, E-mail: studentsfirst@umuc.edu.
Website: https://www.umuc.edu/academic-programs/masters-degrees/health-informatics-administration.cfm

University of Michigan, School of Information, Ann Arbor, MI 48109-1285. Offers health informatics (MHI); information (MSI, PhD). *Accreditation:* ALA (one or more programs are accredited). *Program availability:* Part-time. *Students:* 453 full-time (270 women), 32 part-time (20 women); includes 99 minority (16 Black or African American, non-Hispanic/Latino; 49 Asian, non-Hispanic/Latino; 21 Hispanic/Latino; 13 Two or more races, non-Hispanic/Latino), 212 international. Average age 27. 829 applicants, 53% accepted, 199 enrolled. In 2018, 179 master's, 7 doctorates awarded. Terminal master's

awarded for partial completion of doctoral program. *Degree requirements:* For master's, thesis optional, internship; for doctorate, thesis/dissertation. *Entrance requirements:* For master's and doctorate, GRE General Test. Additional exam requirements/recommendations for international students: Required—TOEFL (minimum score 100 iBT). *Application deadline:* Applications are processed on a rolling basis. Application fee: $75 ($90 for international students). Electronic applications accepted. *Expenses:* Contact institution. *Financial support:* In 2018–19, 122 students received support, including 2 fellowships (averaging $28,200 per year), 33 research assistantships (averaging $28,200 per year), 41 teaching assistantships (averaging $28,200 per year); scholarships/grants and tuition waivers (full and partial) also available. *Unit head:* Dr. Thomas A. Finholt, Dean, School of Information, 734-647-3576. *Application contact:* School of Information Admissions, 734-763-2285, Fax: 734-615-3587, E-mail: umsi.admissions@umich.edu.
Website: http://www.si.umich.edu/

University of Michigan–Dearborn, College of Education, Health, and Human Services, Master of Science Program in Health Information Technology, Dearborn, MI 48126. Offers MS. *Program availability:* Part-time, evening/weekend. *Faculty:* 2 part-time/adjunct (both women). *Students:* 3 full-time (all women), 16 part-time (11 women); includes 9 minority (5 Black or African American, non-Hispanic/Latino; 2 Asian, non-Hispanic/Latino; 1 Hispanic/Latino; 1 Two or more races, non-Hispanic/Latino), 4 international. Average age 35. 13 applicants, 46% accepted, 4 enrolled. In 2018, 11 master's awarded. *Entrance requirements:* Additional exam requirements/recommendations for international students: Required—TOEFL (minimum score 560 paper-based; 84 iBT), IELTS (minimum score 6.5). *Application deadline:* For fall admission, 3/1 for domestic and international students. Application fee: $60. Electronic applications accepted. *Expenses:* $12,140 per academic year (typical full-time in-state); $20,708 per academic year (typical full-time out-of-state). *Financial support:* In 2018–19, 5 students received support. Career-related internships or fieldwork and scholarships/grants available. Financial award application deadline: 3/1; financial award applicants required to submit FAFSA. *Faculty research:* Race and health, urban education, data analysis, economics. *Unit head:* Dr. Paul Fossum, Director, Master's Programs, 313-593-0982, E-mail: pfossum@umich.edu. *Application contact:* Office of Graduate Studies, 313-583-6321, E-mail: umd-graduatestudies@umich.edu.
Website: http://umdearborn.edu/cehhs/cehhs_m_hit/

University of Michigan–Flint, College of Arts and Sciences, Program in Computer Science and Information Systems, Flint, MI 48502-1950. Offers computer science (MS); information systems (MS), including business information systems, health information systems. *Program availability:* Part-time, evening/weekend, 100% online. *Faculty:* 15 full-time (5 women), 7 part-time/adjunct (3 women). *Students:* 33 full-time (14 women), 56 part-time (17 women); includes 17 minority (4 Black or African American, non-Hispanic/Latino; 1 American Indian or Alaska Native, non-Hispanic/Latino; 3 Asian, non-Hispanic/Latino; 6 Hispanic/Latino; 1 Native Hawaiian or other Pacific Islander, non-Hispanic/Latino; 2 Two or more races, non-Hispanic/Latino), 39 international. Average age 30. 310 applicants, 66% accepted, 21 enrolled. In 2018, 29 master's awarded. *Degree requirements:* For master's, thesis optional, Non Thesis option available. *Entrance requirements:* For master's, BS from regionally-accredited institution in computer science, computer information systems, or computer engineering (preferred); minimum overall undergraduate GPA of 3.0. Additional exam requirements/recommendations for international students: Required—TOEFL (minimum score 84 iBT), IELTS (minimum score 6.5). *Application deadline:* For fall admission, 8/1 for domestic students, 5/1 for international students; for winter admission, 10/1 for domestic students, 8/1 for international students; for spring admission, 3/15 for domestic students, 1/1 for international students. Applications are processed on a rolling basis. Application fee: $55. Electronic applications accepted. *Expenses:* Contact institution. *Financial support:* Federal Work-Study, scholarships/grants, and unspecified assistantships available. Financial award application deadline: 3/1; financial award applicants required to submit FAFSA. *Faculty research:* Computer network systems, database management systems, artificial intelligence and controlled systems. *Unit head:* Dr. Mike Farmer, Department Chair, 810-762-3423, Fax: 810-766-6780, E-mail: farmerme@umflint.edu. *Application contact:* Matt Bohlen, Director of Graduate Admissions, 810-762-3171, Fax: 810-766-6789, E-mail: mbohlen@umflint.edu.
Website: http://www.umflint.edu/graduateprograms/computer-science-information-systems-ms

University of Minnesota, Twin Cities Campus, Graduate School, Program in Health Informatics, Minneapolis, MN 55455-0213. Offers MHI, MS, PhD, MD/MHI. *Program availability:* Part-time. *Degree requirements:* For master's, thesis or alternative; for doctorate, thesis/dissertation. *Entrance requirements:* For master's and doctorate, GRE General Test, previous course work in life sciences, programming, calculus. Additional exam requirements/recommendations for international students: Required—TOEFL (minimum score 550 paper-based). Electronic applications accepted. *Faculty research:* Medical decision making, physiological control systems, population studies, clinical information systems, telemedicine.

University of Missouri, School of Medicine and Office of Research and Graduate Studies, Graduate Programs in Medicine, Department of Health Management and Informatics, Columbia, MO 65211. Offers health administration (MHA); health informatics (MS, Certificate). *Accreditation:* CAHME. *Program availability:* Part-time. *Entrance requirements:* For master's, GRE General Test or GMAT, minimum GPA of 3.0. Additional exam requirements/recommendations for international students: Required—TOEFL (minimum score 550 paper-based; 80 iBT), IELTS (minimum score 6.5). Electronic applications accepted.

University of New England, College of Graduate and Professional Studies, Portland, ME 04005-9526. Offers advanced educational leadership (CAGS); applied nutrition (MS); career and technical education (MS Ed); curriculum and instruction (MS Ed); education (CAGS, Post-Master's Certificate); educational leadership (MS Ed, Ed D); generalist (MS Ed); health informatics (MS, Graduate Certificate); inclusion education (MS Ed); literacy K-12 (MS Ed); medical education leadership (MMEL); public health (MPH, Graduate Certificate); reading specialist (MS Ed); social work (MSW). *Program availability:* Part-time, evening/weekend, online only, 100% online. *Faculty:* 109 part-time/adjunct (78 women). *Students:* 1,207 full-time (972 women), 561 part-time (450 women); includes 411 minority (280 Black or African American, non-Hispanic/Latino; 17 American Indian or Alaska Native, non-Hispanic/Latino; 74 Asian, non-Hispanic/Latino; 25 Hispanic/Latino; 9 Native Hawaiian or other Pacific Islander, non-Hispanic/Latino; 6 Two or more races, non-Hispanic/Latino). Average age 36. 740 applicants, 92% accepted, 494 enrolled. In 2018, 586 master's, 44 doctorates, 85 other advanced degrees awarded. *Application deadline:* Applications are processed on a rolling basis. Electronic applications accepted. *Financial support:* Application deadline: 5/1; applicants required to submit FAFSA. *Unit head:* Dr. Martha Wilson, Dean of the College of Graduate and Professional Studies, 207-221-4985, E-mail: mwilson13@une.edu. *Application contact:* Nicole Lindsay, Director of Online Admissions, 207-221-4966, E-mail: nlindsay1@une.edu.
Website: http://online.une.edu

The University of North Carolina at Charlotte, The Graduate School, Program in Health Informatics, Charlotte, NC 28223-0001. Offers PSM, Graduate Certificate. *Program availability:* Part-time, evening/weekend. *Students:* 21 full-time (17 women), 23 part-time (18 women); includes 12 minority (6 Black or African American, non-Hispanic/Latino; 3 Asian, non-Hispanic/Latino; 2 Hispanic/Latino; 1 Two or more races, non-Hispanic/Latino), 13 international. Average age 32. 39 applicants, 79% accepted, 18 enrolled. In 2018, 25 master's, 8 Graduate Certificates awarded. *Entrance requirements:* For master's, GRE, undergraduate degree in health, the life sciences, an informatics discipline or closely-related field; minimum undergraduate GPA of 3.0; three letters of recommendation; statement of purpose outlining goals for pursuing graduate education; for Graduate Certificate, bachelor's degree from regionally-accredited university in related field, including, but not limited to, a life science, health science, health administration, business administration, or computing discipline; minimum undergraduate GPA of 2.75; statement of purpose outlining the goals for pursuing a graduate education in health informatics. Additional exam requirements/recommendations for international students: Required—TOEFL (minimum score 523 paper-based; 70 iBT), IELTS (minimum score 6), TOEFL (minimum score 523 paper-based, 70 iBT) or IELTS (6). *Application deadline:* Applications are processed on a rolling basis. Application fee: $75. Electronic applications accepted. *Expenses:* Contact institution. *Financial support:* Career-related internships or fieldwork, institutionally sponsored loans, scholarships/grants, and unspecified assistantships available. Support available to part-time students. Financial award application deadline: 3/1; financial award applicants required to submit FAFSA. *Unit head:* Carly Mahedy, Director of Student Services, 704-687-0068, E-mail: healthinformatics@uncc.edu. *Application contact:* Kathy B. Giddings, Director of Graduate Admissions, 704-687-5503, Fax: 704-687-1668, E-mail: gradadm@uncc.edu.
Website: http://www.hi.uncc.edu/

University of Phoenix–Online Campus, College of Health Sciences and Nursing, Phoenix, AZ 85034-7209. Offers family nurse practitioner (Certificate); health care (Certificate); health care education (Certificate); health care informatics (Certificate); informatics (MSN); nursing (MSN); nursing and health care education (MSN); MSN/MBA; MSN/MHA. *Accreditation:* AACN. *Program availability:* Evening/weekend, online learning. *Entrance requirements:* Additional exam requirements/recommendations for international students: Required—TOEFL, TOEIC (Test of English as an International Communication), Berlitz Online English Proficiency Exam, PTE, or IELTS. Electronic applications accepted. *Expenses:* Contact institution.

University of Pittsburgh, School of Health and Rehabilitation Sciences, Department of Health Information Management, Pittsburgh, PA 15260. Offers health and rehabilitation sciences (MS), including health information systems, healthcare supervision and management. *Accreditation:* APTA. *Program availability:* Part-time. *Degree requirements:* For master's, comprehensive exam, thesis optional. *Entrance requirements:* For master's, minimum GPA of 3.0. Additional exam requirements/recommendations for international students: Required—TOEFL (minimum score 550 paper-based; 80 iBT), IELTS (minimum score 6.5). Electronic applications accepted. *Faculty research:* Effectiveness of technology, mobile health monitoring, independence and self-management using mHealth information and communication technology, telehealth implementation.

University of Puerto Rico–Medical Sciences Campus, School of Health Professions, Program in Health Information Administration, San Juan, PR 00936-5067. Offers MS. *Program availability:* Part-time. *Degree requirements:* For master's, one foreign language, thesis or alternative, internship. *Entrance requirements:* For master's, EXADEP or GRE General Test, minimum GPA of 2.5, interview, fluency in Spanish. *Faculty research:* Quality of medical records, health information data.

University of St. Augustine for Health Sciences, Graduate Programs, Master of Health Science Program, San Marcos, CA 92069. Offers athletic training (MHS); executive leadership (MHS); informatics (MHS); teaching and learning (MHS). *Program availability:* Online learning. *Degree requirements:* For master's, comprehensive project.

University of San Diego, Hahn School of Nursing and Health Science, San Diego, CA 92110-2492. Offers adult-gerontology clinical nurse specialist (MSN); adult-gerontology nurse practitioner/family nurse practitioner (MSN); clinical nurse leader (MSN); executive nurse leader (MSN); family nurse practitioner (MSN); healthcare informatics (MS, MSN); master's entry program in clinical nursing (for non-rns) (MSN); nursing (PhD); nursing informatics (MSN); nursing practice (DNP); psychiatric-mental health nurse practitioner (MSN). *Accreditation:* AACN. *Program availability:* Part-time, evening/weekend. *Faculty:* 28 full-time (24 women), 58 part-time/adjunct (47 women). *Students:* 260 full-time (219 women), 282 part-time (205 women); includes 273 minority (47 Black or African American, non-Hispanic/Latino; 1 American Indian or Alaska Native, non-Hispanic/Latino; 118 Asian, non-Hispanic/Latino; 82 Hispanic/Latino; 25 Two or more races, non-Hispanic/Latino), 19 international. Average age 34. In 2018, 122 master's, 33 doctorates awarded. *Degree requirements:* For doctorate, thesis/dissertation (for some programs), residency (DNP). *Entrance requirements:* For master's, GRE General Test (for entry-level nursing), BSN, current California RN licensure (except for entry-level nursing), minimum GPA of 3.0; for doctorate, minimum GPA of 3.5, MSN, current California RN licensure. Additional exam requirements/recommendations for international students: Required—TOEFL (minimum score 580 paper-based; 83 iBT), TWE. *Application deadline:* Applications are processed on a rolling basis. Application fee: $45. Electronic applications accepted. *Financial support:* In 2018–19, 260 students received support. Institutionally sponsored loans, scholarships/grants, and traineeships available. Support available to part-time students. Financial award application deadline: 4/1; financial award applicants required to submit FAFSA. *Faculty research:* Maternal/neonatal health, palliative and end of life care, adolescent obesity, health disparities, cognitive dysfunction. *Unit head:* Dr. Jane Georges, Dean, 619-260-4550, Fax: 619-260-6814, E-mail: nursing@sandiego.edu. *Application contact:* Erika Garwood, Associate Director of Graduate Admissions, 619-260-4524, Fax: 619-260-4158, E-mail: grads@sandiego.edu.
Website: http://www.sandiego.edu/nursing/

University of San Francisco, School of Nursing and Health Professions, Program in Health Informatics, San Francisco, CA 94117. Offers MS. *Program availability:* Part-time, evening/weekend. *Students:* 32 full-time (19 women), 7 part-time (5 women); includes 12 minority (2 Black or African American, non-Hispanic/Latino; 8 Asian, non-Hispanic/Latino; 2 Two or more races, non-Hispanic/Latino), 17 international. Average age 32. 53 applicants, 72% accepted, 12 enrolled. In 2018, 18 master's awarded. *Entrance requirements:* Additional exam requirements/recommendations for international students: Required—TOEFL (minimum score 600 paper-based; 90 iBT), PTE (minimum score 68). *Application deadline:* For fall admission, 5/15 for domestic students; for spring admission, 11/15 for domestic students. Applications are processed on a rolling basis. Application fee: $55. Electronic applications accepted. *Financial support:* Scholarships/grants available. *Unit head:* Dr. Andrew Nguyen, Program Director, 415-422-6681, E-mail: nursing@usfca.edu. *Application contact:* Carolyn Arroyo, Graduate Enrollment Manager, 415-422-2807, E-mail: carroyo2@usfca.edu.
Website: https://www.usfca.edu/nursing/programs/masters/health-informatics

University of South Carolina Upstate, Graduate Programs, Spartanburg, SC 29303-4999. Offers early childhood education (M Ed); elementary education (M Ed); informatics (MS); special education: visual impairment (M Ed). *Accreditation:* NCATE. *Program availability:* Part-time, evening/weekend. *Degree requirements:* For master's, professional portfolio. *Entrance requirements:* For master's, GRE General Test or MAT, interview, minimum undergraduate GPA of 2.5, teaching certificate, 2 letters of recommendation. *Faculty research:* Promoting university diversity awareness, rough and tumble play, social justice education, American Indian literatures and cultures, diversity and multicultural education, science teaching strategy.

University of South Florida, Innovative Education, Tampa, FL 33620-9951. Offers adult, career and higher education (Graduate Certificate), including college teaching, leadership in developing human resources, leadership in higher education; Africana studies (Graduate Certificate), including diasporas and health disparities, genocide and human rights; aging studies (Graduate Certificate), including gerontology; art research (Graduate Certificate), including museum studies; business foundations (Graduate Certificate); chemical and biomedical engineering (Graduate Certificate), including materials science and engineering, water, health and sustainability; child and family studies (Graduate Certificate), including positive behavior support; civil and industrial engineering (Graduate Certificate), including transportation systems analysis; community and family health (Graduate Certificate), including maternal and child health, social marketing and public health, violence and injury: prevention and intervention, women's health; criminology (Graduate Certificate), including criminal justice administration; data science for public administration (Graduate Certificate); digital humanities (Graduate Certificate); educational measurement and research (Graduate Certificate), including evaluation; English (Graduate Certificate), including comparative literary studies, creative writing, professional and technical communication; entrepreneurship (Graduate Certificate); environmental health (Graduate Certificate), including safety management; epidemiology and biostatistics (Graduate Certificate), including applied biostatistics, biostatistics, concepts and tools of epidemiology, epidemiology, epidemiology of infectious diseases; geography, environment and planning (Graduate Certificate), including community development, environmental policy and management, geographical information systems; geology (Graduate Certificate), including hydrogeology; global health (Graduate Certificate), including disaster management, global health and Latin American and Caribbean studies, global health practice, humanitarian assistance, infection control; government and international affairs (Graduate Certificate), including Cuban studies, globalization studies; health policy and management (Graduate Certificate), including health management and leadership, public health policy and programs; hearing specialist: early intervention (Graduate Certificate); industrial and management systems engineering (Graduate Certificate), including systems engineering, technology management; information studies (Graduate Certificate), including school library media specialist; information systems/decision sciences (Graduate Certificate), including analytics and business intelligence; instructional technology (Graduate Certificate), including distance education, Florida digital/virtual educator, instructional design, multimedia design, Web design; internal medicine, bioethics and medical humanities (Graduate Certificate), including biomedical ethics; Latin American and Caribbean studies (Graduate Certificate); leadership for coastal resiliency planning (Graduate Certificate); mass communications (Graduate Certificate), including multimedia journalism; mathematics and statistics (Graduate Certificate), including mathematics; medicine (Graduate Certificate), including aging and neuroscience, bioinformatics, biotechnology, brain fitness and memory management, clinical investigation, hand and upper limb rehabilitation, health informatics, health sciences, integrative weight management, intellectual property, medicine and gender, metabolic and nutritional medicine, metabolic cardiology, pharmacy sciences; national and competitive intelligence (Graduate Certificate); nursing (Graduate Certificate), including simulation based academic fellowship in advanced pain management; psychological and social foundations (Graduate Certificate), including career counseling, college teaching, diversity in education, mental health counseling, school counseling; public affairs (Graduate Certificate), including nonprofit management, public management, research administration; public health (Graduate Certificate), including assessing chemical toxicity and public health risks, health equity, pharmacoepidemiology, public health generalist, toxicology, translational research in adolescent behavioral health; public health practices (Graduate Certificate), including planning for healthy communities; rehabilitation and mental health counseling (Graduate Certificate), including integrative mental health care, marriage and family therapy, rehabilitation technology; secondary education (Graduate Certificate), including ESOL, foreign language education: culture and content, foreign language education: professional; social work (Graduate Certificate), including geriatric social work/clinical gerontology; special education (Graduate Certificate), including autism spectrum disorder, disabilities education: severe/profound; world languages (Graduate Certificate), including teaching English as a second language (TESL) or foreign language. *Expenses:* Tuition, state resident: full-time $6350. Tuition, nonresident: full-time $19,048. International tuition: $19,048 full-time. *Required fees:* $2079. *Unit head:* Dr. Cynthia DeLuca, Associate Vice President and Assistant Vice Provost, 813-974-3077, Fax: 813-974-7061, E-mail: deluca@usf.edu. *Application contact:* Owen Hooper, Director, Summer and Alternative Calendar Programs, 813-974-6917, E-mail: hooper@usf.edu.
Website: http://www.usf.edu/innovative-education/

University of South Florida, Morsani College of Medicine and College of Graduate Studies, Graduate Programs in Medical Sciences, Tampa, FL 33620-9951. Offers advanced athletic training (MS); athletic training (MS); bioinformatics and computational biology (MSBCB); biotechnology (MSB); health informatics (MSHI); medical sciences (MSMS, PhD), including aging and neuroscience (MSMS), allergy, immunology and infectious disease (PhD), anatomy, biochemistry and molecular biology, clinical and translational research, health science (MSMS), interdisciplinary medical sciences (MSMS), medical microbiology and immunology (MSMS), metabolic and nutritional medicine (MSMS), microbiology and immunology (PhD), molecular medicine, molecular pharmacology and physiology (PhD), neuroscience (PhD), pathology and cell biology (PhD), women's health (MSMS). *Faculty:* 1 (woman) full-time. *Students:* 355 full-time (207 women), 229 part-time (145 women); includes 283 minority (71 Black or African American, non-Hispanic/Latino; 2 American Indian or Alaska Native, non-Hispanic/Latino; 89 Asian, non-Hispanic/Latino; 103 Hispanic/Latino; 2 Native Hawaiian or other Pacific Islander, non-Hispanic/Latino; 16 Two or more races, non-Hispanic/Latino), 48 international. Average age 28. 898 applicants, 57% accepted, 323 enrolled. In 2018, 227 master's, 13 doctorates awarded. Terminal master's awarded for partial completion of doctoral program. *Degree requirements:* For master's, comprehensive exam, thesis; for doctorate, comprehensive exam, thesis/dissertation. *Entrance requirements:* For master's, GRE General Test or GMAT, bachelor's degree or equivalent from regionally-accredited university with minimum GPA of 3.0 in upper-division sciences coursework; prerequisites in general biology, general chemistry, general physics, organic chemistry, quantitative analysis, and integral and differential calculus; for doctorate, GRE General Test, bachelor's degree from regionally-accredited university with minimum GPA of 3.0 in upper-division sciences coursework; 3 letters of recommendation; personal interview; 1-2 page personal statement; prerequisites in biology, chemistry, physics, organic chemistry, quantitative analysis, and integral/differential calculus. Additional exam requirements/recommendations for international students: Required—TOEFL (minimum score 550 paper-based; 79 iBT) or IELTS (minimum score 6.5). *Application deadline:* For fall admission, 2/1 priority date for domestic students, 2/1 for international students. Application fee: $30. Electronic applications accepted. *Expenses:* Contact institution.

Financial support: In 2018–19, 106 students received support. *Faculty research:* Anatomy, biochemistry, cancer biology, cardiovascular disease, cell biology, immunology, microbiology, molecular biology, neuroscience, pharmacology, physiology. *Total annual research expenditures:* $50.9 million. *Unit head:* Dr. Michael Barber, Professor/Associate Dean for Graduate and Postdoctoral Affairs, 813-974-9908, Fax: 813-974-4317, E-mail: mbarber@health.usf.edu. *Application contact:* Dr. Eric Bennett, Graduate Director, PhD Program in Medical Sciences, 813-974-1545, Fax: 813-974-4317, E-mail: esbennet@health.usf.edu.
Website: http://health.usf.edu/nocms/medicine/graduatestudies/

The University of Tennessee Health Science Center, College of Health Professions, Memphis, TN 38163-0002. Offers audiology (MS, Au D); clinical laboratory science (MSCLS); cytopathology practice (MCP); health informatics and information management (MHIIM); occupational therapy (MOT); physical therapy (DPT, ScDPT); physician assistant (MMS); speech-language pathology (MS). *Accreditation:* AOTA; APTA. *Program availability:* Part-time, evening/weekend, online learning. Terminal master's awarded for partial completion of doctoral program. *Degree requirements:* For master's, comprehensive exam, thesis; for doctorate, comprehensive exam, residency. *Entrance requirements:* For master's, GRE (MOT, MSCLS), minimum GPA of 3.0, 3 letters of reference, national accreditation (MSCLS), GRE if GPA is less than 3.0 (MCP); for doctorate, GRE. Additional exam requirements/recommendations for international students: Required—TOEFL (minimum score 550 paper-based; 80 iBT). Electronic applications accepted. *Expenses:* Contact institution. *Faculty research:* Gait deviation, muscular dystrophy and strength, hemophilia and exercise, pediatric neurology, self-efficacy.

The University of Texas Health Science Center at Houston, School of Public Health, Houston, TX 77030. Offers behavioral science (PhD); biostatistics (MPH, MS, PhD); environmental health (MPH); epidemiology (MPH, MS, PhD); general public health (Certificate); genomics and bioinformatics (Certificate); health disparities (Certificate); health promotion/health education (MPH, Dr PH); healthcare management (Certificate); management, policy and community health (MPH, Dr PH, PhD); maternal and child health (Certificate); public health informatics (Certificate); DDS/MPH; JD/MPH; MBA/MPH; MD/MPH; MGPS/MPH; MP Aff/MPH; MS/MPH; MSN/MPH; MSW/MPH; PhD/MPH. Specific programs are offered at each of our six campuses in Texas (Austin, Brownsville, Dallas, El Paso, Houston, and San Antonio). *Accreditation:* CAHME; CEPH. *Program availability:* Part-time. *Degree requirements:* For master's, thesis (for some programs); for doctorate, comprehensive exam, thesis/dissertation. *Entrance requirements:* For master's and doctorate, GRE General Test. Additional exam requirements/recommendations for international students: Required—TOEFL (minimum score 600 paper-based, 100 iBT) or IELTS (7.5). Electronic applications accepted. *Expenses:* Contact institution. *Faculty research:* Chronic and infectious disease epidemiology; health promotion and health education; applied and theoretical biostatistics; healthcare management, policy and economics; environmental and occupational health.

University of Toronto, Faculty of Medicine, Institute of Health Policy, Management and Evaluation, Program in Health Informatics, Toronto, ON M5S 1A1, Canada. Offers MHI. *Entrance requirements:* For master's, minimum B average in last academic year. Additional exam requirements/recommendations for international students: Required—TOEFL (minimum score 580 paper-based; 93 iBT), TWE (minimum score 5). Electronic applications accepted.

University of Victoria, Faculty of Graduate Studies, Faculty of Human and Social Development, School of Health Information Science, Victoria, BC V8W 2Y2, Canada. Offers M Sc. *Degree requirements:* For master's, thesis or research project. *Entrance requirements:* Additional exam requirements/recommendations for international students: Required—TOEFL (minimum score 575 paper-based).

University of Virginia, School of Medicine, Department of Public Health Sciences, Program in Clinical Research, Charlottesville, VA 22903. Offers clinical investigation and patient-oriented research (MS); informatics in medicine (MS). *Program availability:* Part-time. *Degree requirements:* For master's, thesis (for some programs). *Entrance requirements:* For master's, 2 letters of recommendation. Additional exam requirements/recommendations for international students: Required—TOEFL (minimum score 600 paper-based; 90 iBT). Electronic applications accepted.

University of Washington, Graduate School, School of Medicine, Graduate Programs in Medicine, Department of Medical Education and Biomedical Informatics, Division of Biomedical and Health Informatics, Seattle, WA 98195. Offers MS, PhD. *Entrance requirements:* For master's and doctorate, GRE General Test, minimum GPA of 3.0; previous undergraduate course work in biology, computer programming, and mathematics. Additional exam requirements/recommendations for international students: Required—TOEFL (minimum score 580 paper-based; 70 iBT). Electronic applications accepted. *Faculty research:* Bio-clinical informatics, information retrieval, human-computer interaction, knowledge-based systems, telehealth.

University of Washington, Graduate School, School of Public Health, Program in Health Informatics and Health Information Management, Seattle, WA 98195. Offers MHIHIM. *Students:* 37 part-time (28 women); includes 25 minority (6 Black or African American, non-Hispanic/Latino; 2 American Indian or Alaska Native, non-Hispanic/Latino; 15 Asian, non-Hispanic/Latino; 2 Hispanic/Latino), 3 international. Average age 34. 28 applicants, 89% accepted, 20 enrolled. In 2018, 19 master's awarded. *Degree requirements:* For master's, capstone project. Electronic applications accepted. *Expenses:* Contact institution. *Financial support:* Applicants required to submit FAFSA. Website: http://www.health-informatics.uw.edu/

University of Waterloo, Graduate Studies and Postdoctoral Affairs, Faculty of Applied Health Sciences, School of Public Health and Health Systems, Waterloo, ON N2L 3G1, Canada. Offers health evaluation (MHE); health informatics (MHI); health studies and gerontology (M Sc, PhD); public health (MPH). *Program availability:* Part-time. *Degree requirements:* For master's, thesis; for doctorate, comprehensive exam, thesis/dissertation. *Entrance requirements:* For master's, honors degree, minimum B average, resume, writing sample; for doctorate, GRE (recommended), master's degree, minimum B average, resume, writing sample. Additional exam requirements/recommendations for international students: Required—TOEFL, IELTS, PTE. *Application deadline:* For fall admission, 2/1 for domestic and international students. Application fee: $125 Canadian dollars. Electronic applications accepted. *Financial support:* In 2018–19, teaching assistantships (averaging $6,141 per year) were awarded; research assistantships, career-related internships or fieldwork, Federal Work-Study, institutionally sponsored loans, scholarships/grants, and university-sponsored bursaries also available. *Faculty research:* Population health, health promotion and disease prevention, healthy aging, health policy, planning and evaluation, health information management and health informatics, aging, health and well-being, work and health.
Website: https://uwaterloo.ca/public-health-and-health-systems/

University of Wisconsin–Milwaukee, Graduate School, College of Engineering and Applied Science, Biomedical and Health Informatics Program, Milwaukee, WI 53201-0413. Offers health information systems (PhD); health services management and policy (PhD); knowledge based systems (PhD); medical imaging and instrumentation (PhD); public health informatics (PhD). *Students:* 11 full-time (3 women), 10 part-time (3

women); includes 2 minority (both Black or African American, non-Hispanic/Latino), 8 international. Average age 37. 17 applicants, 71% accepted, 4 enrolled. In 2018, 1 doctorate awarded. *Degree requirements:* For doctorate, comprehensive exam, thesis/dissertation. *Entrance requirements:* For doctorate, GRE, GMAT or MCAT. Additional exam requirements/recommendations for international students: Required—TOEFL (minimum score 600 paper-based; 79 iBT), IELTS (minimum score 6.5). Application fee: $56 ($96 for international students). Electronic applications accepted. *Financial support:* Fellowships, research assistantships, teaching assistantships, and project assistantships available. *Unit head:* Devendra Misra, PhD, Chair, 414-229-3327, E-mail: misra@uwm.edu. *Application contact:* Betty Warras, Engineering and Computer Science Graduate Programs, 414-229-6169, E-mail: ceas-graduate@uwm.edu.
Website: http://uwm.edu/engineering/academics-2/departments/biomedical-engineering/

University of Wisconsin–Milwaukee, Graduate School, College of Health Sciences, Department of Health Informatics and Administration, Milwaukee, WI 53201-0413. Offers health care informatics (MS); healthcare administration (MHA). *Students:* 47 full-time (27 women), 20 part-time (12 women); includes 16 minority (6 Black or African American, non-Hispanic/Latino; 3 Asian, non-Hispanic/Latino; 7 Two or more races, non-Hispanic/Latino), 11 international. Average age 33. 67 applicants, 72% accepted, 24 enrolled. In 2018, 25 master's awarded. *Degree requirements:* For master's, comprehensive exam, thesis optional. *Entrance requirements:* For master's, GRE General Test. Additional exam requirements/recommendations for international students: Required—TOEFL (minimum score 550 paper-based; 79 iBT), IELTS (minimum score 6.5). Application fee: $56 ($96 for international students). *Financial support:* Fellowships, research assistantships, and teaching assistantships available. *Unit head:* Priya Nambisan, Department Chair, 414-229-7136, Fax: 414-229-3373, E-mail: nambisap@uwm.edu. *Application contact:* Kathleen M. Olewinski, Educational Coordinator, 414-229-7110, Fax: 414-229-3373, E-mail: kmo@uwm.edu.
Website: http://uwm.edu/healthsciences/academics/health-informatics-administration/

Virginia International University, School of Computer Information Systems, Fairfax, VA 22030. Offers business intelligence (Graduate Certificate); business intelligence and data analytics (MIS); computer science (MS), including computer animation and gaming, cybersecurity, data management networking, intelligent systems, software applications development, software engineering; cybersecurity (MIS); data management (MIS); enterprise project management (MIS); health informatics (MIS); information assurance (MIS); information systems (Graduate Certificate); information systems management (MS, Graduate Certificate); information technology (MS); information technology audit and compliance (Graduate Certificate); knowledge management (MIS); software engineering (MS). *Program availability:* Part-time, online learning. *Entrance requirements:* For master's, bachelor's degree. Additional exam requirements/recommendations for international students: Required—TOEFL (minimum score 550 paper-based; 80 iBT), IELTS. Electronic applications accepted.

Walden University, Graduate Programs, School of Health Sciences, Minneapolis, MN 55401. Offers clinical research administration (MS, Graduate Certificate); health education and promotion (MS, PhD), including behavioral health (PhD), disease surveillance (PhD), emergency preparedness (MS), general (MHA, MS), global health (PhD), health policy (PhD), health policy and advocacy (MS), population health (PhD); health informatics (MS); health services (PhD), including community health, healthcare administration, leadership, public health policy, self-designed; healthcare administration (MHA, DHA), including general (MHA, MS); leadership and organizational development (MHA); public health (MPH, Dr PH, PhD, Graduate Certificate), including community health education (PhD), epidemiology (PhD); systems policy (MHA). *Program availability:* Part-time, evening/weekend, online only, 100% online. *Degree requirements:* For doctorate, thesis/dissertation, residency. *Entrance requirements:* For master's, bachelor's degree or higher; minimum GPA of 2.5; official transcripts; goal statement (for some programs); access to computer and Internet; for doctorate, master's degree or higher; three years of related professional or academic experience (preferred); minimum GPA of 3.0; goal statement and current resume (for select programs); official transcripts; access to computer and Internet; for Graduate Certificate, relevant work experience; access to computer and Internet. Additional exam requirements/recommendations for international students: Required—TOEFL (minimum score 550 paper-based, 79 iBT), IELTS (minimum score 6.5), Michigan English Language Assessment Battery (minimum score 82), or PTE (minimum score 53). Electronic applications accepted.

Walden University, Graduate Programs, School of Information Systems and Technology, Minneapolis, MN 55401. Offers information systems (Graduate Certificate); information systems management (MISM); information technology (MS, DIT), including health informatics (MS), information assurance and cyber security (MS), information systems (MS), software engineering (MS). *Program availability:* Part-time, evening/weekend, online only, 100% online. *Degree requirements:* For doctorate, thesis/dissertation (for some programs), residency. *Entrance requirements:* For master's, bachelor's degree or higher; minimum GPA of 2.5; official transcripts; goal statement (for some programs); access to computer and Internet; for doctorate, master's degree or higher; three years of related professional or academic experience (preferred); minimum GPA of 3.0; goal statement and current resume (for select programs); official transcripts; access to computer and Internet; for Graduate Certificate, relevant work experience; access to computer and Internet. Additional exam requirements/recommendations for international students: Required—TOEFL (minimum score 550 paper-based, 79 iBT), IELTS (minimum score 6.5), Michigan English Language Assessment Battery (minimum score 82), or PTE (minimum score 53). Electronic applications accepted.

Weill Cornell Medicine, Weill Cornell Graduate School of Medical Sciences, Program in Healthcare Policy and Research, New York, NY 10065. Offers biostatistics and data science (MS); health informatics (MS); health policy and economics (MS). *Program availability:* Part-time. *Students:* 62 full-time, 27 part-time; includes 3 minority (2 Asian, non-Hispanic/Latino; 1 Hispanic/Latino). In 2018, 4 master's awarded. *Degree requirements:* For master's, thesis. *Entrance requirements:* For master's, GRE, MCAT, or GMAT (recommended), official transcripts, resume, personal statement, 3 letters of reference. Additional exam requirements/recommendations for international students: Required—TOEFL. *Application deadline:* For fall admission, 3/1 priority date for domestic and international students. Application fee: $75. *Expenses:* Contact institution. *Unit head:* William Tseng, Admissions Manager, 646-962-8083, E-mail: wit2006@med.cornell.edu. *Application contact:* William Tseng, Admissions Manager, 646-962-8083, E-mail: wit2006@med.cornell.edu.
Website: http://hpr.weill.cornell.edu/education/

Human-Computer Interaction

Brandeis University, Rabb School of Continuing Studies, Division of Graduate Professional Studies, Master of Science in User-Centered Design Program, Waltham, MA 02454-9110. Offers MS. *Program availability:* Part-time-only. *Degree requirements:* For master's, capstone. *Entrance requirements:* For master's, four-year bachelor's degree from regionally-accredited U.S. institution or equivalent; official transcript(s) from every college or university attended; resume or curriculum vitae; statement of goals; letter of recommendation. Additional exam requirements/recommendations for international students: Required—TWE (minimum score 4.5), TOEFL (minimum scores: 600 paper-based, 100 iBT), IELTS (7), or PTE (68). Electronic applications accepted. *Expenses:* Contact institution.

Carnegie Mellon University, School of Computer Science, Department of Human-Computer Interaction, Pittsburgh, PA 15213-3891. Offers MHCI, PhD. *Entrance requirements:* For master's, GRE General Test, GRE Subject Test.

Cornell University, Graduate School, Graduate Fields of Agriculture and Life Sciences, Field of Communication, Ithaca, NY 14853. Offers communication (MS, PhD); human-computer interaction (MS, PhD); language and communication (MS, PhD); media communication and society (MS, PhD); organizational communication (MS, PhD); science, environment and health communication (MS, PhD); social psychology of communication (MS, PhD). *Degree requirements:* For master's, thesis (MS); for doctorate, comprehensive exam, thesis/dissertation. *Entrance requirements:* For master's and doctorate, GRE General Test, 3 letters of recommendation. Additional exam requirements/recommendations for international students: Required—TOEFL (minimum score 600 paper-based; 100 iBT). Electronic applications accepted. *Faculty research:* Mass communication, communication technologies, science and environmental communication.

Cornell University, Graduate School, Graduate Fields of Arts and Sciences, Field of Information Science, Ithaca, NY 14853. Offers cognition (PhD); human computer interaction (PhD); information science (PhD); information systems (PhD); social aspects of information (PhD). *Degree requirements:* For doctorate, comprehensive exam, thesis/dissertation. *Entrance requirements:* For doctorate, GRE General Test, 3 letters of recommendation. Additional exam requirements/recommendations for international students: Required—TOEFL (minimum score 550 paper-based; 77 iBT). Electronic applications accepted. *Faculty research:* Digital libraries, game theory, data mining, human-computer interaction, computational linguistics.

Dalhousie University, Faculty of Engineering, Department of Engineering Mathematics and Internetworking, Halifax, NS B3J 2X4, Canada. Offers engineering mathematics (M Sc, PhD); internetworking (M Eng). *Degree requirements:* For master's, thesis; for doctorate, thesis/dissertation. *Entrance requirements:* Additional exam requirements/recommendations for international students: Required—TOEFL, IELTS, CANTEST, CAEL, or Michigan English Language Assessment Battery. Electronic applications accepted. *Faculty research:* Piecewise regression and robust statistics, random field theory, dynamical systems, wave loads on offshore structures, digital signal processing.

DePaul University, College of Computing and Digital Media, Chicago, IL 60604. Offers animation (MA, MFA); applied technology (MS); business information technology (MS); computational finance (MS); computer and information sciences (PhD); computer science (MS); creative producing (MFA); cybersecurity (MS); data science (MS); digital communication and media arts (MA); documentary (MFA); e-commerce technology (MS); experience design (MA); film and television (MS); film and television directing (MFA); game design (MFA); game programming (MS); health informatics (MS); human centered design (PhD); human-computer interaction (MS); information systems (MS); network engineering and security (MS); product innovation and computing (MS); screenwriting (MFA); software engineering (MS); JD/MS. *Program availability:* Part-time, evening/weekend, online learning. *Degree requirements:* For master's, thesis (for some programs); for doctorate, comprehensive exam, thesis/dissertation. *Entrance requirements:* For master's, GRE or GMAT (for MS in computational finance only), bachelor's degree, resume (MS in predictive analytics only), IT experience (MS in information technology project management only), portfolio review (all MFA programs and MA in animation); for doctorate, GRE, master's degree in computer science. Additional exam requirements/recommendations for international students: Required—TOEFL (minimum score 590 paper-based; 80 iBT), IELTS (minimum score 6.5), PTE (minimum score 53). Electronic applications accepted. *Expenses:* Contact institution. *Faculty research:* Data mining, computer science, human-computer interaction, security, animation and film.

Georgia Institute of Technology, Graduate Studies, Multidisciplinary Program in Human Computer Interaction, Atlanta, GA 30332-0001. Offers MS. Program offered jointly with School of Industrial Design, School of Interactive Computing, School of Psychology, and School of Literature, Media, and Communication. *Program availability:* Part-time. *Degree requirements:* For master's, seminar, project. *Entrance requirements:* For master's, GRE General Test. Additional exam requirements/recommendations for international students: Required—TOEFL (minimum score 600 paper-based; 100 iBT). Electronic applications accepted. *Expenses:* Contact institution.

Harrisburg University of Science and Technology, Program in Human-Centered Interaction Design, Philadelphia, PA 19130. Offers MS.

Indiana University Bloomington, School of Informatics, Computing, and Engineering, Program in Informatics, Bloomington, IN 47405. Offers informatics (MS, PhD), including bioinformatics (PhD), complex systems (PhD), computing, culture and society (PhD), health informatics (PhD), human-computer interaction (MS), human-computer interaction design (PhD), music informatics (PhD), security informatics (PhD); visual heritage (PhD). *Program availability:* Part-time. Terminal master's awarded for partial completion of doctoral program. *Degree requirements:* For master's, thesis, capstone project; for doctorate, variable foreign language requirement, comprehensive exam, thesis/dissertation. *Entrance requirements:* For master's and doctorate, GRE, resume/curriculum vitae, transcripts, 3 letters of recommendation. Additional exam requirements/recommendations for international students: Required—TOEFL (minimum score 600 paper-based; 100 iBT). Electronic applications accepted. *Faculty research:* Algorithms, applied logic and computational theory, artificial intelligence, bioinformatics, case-based reasoning, chemical informatics, citation analysis, cognitive science, community informatics, compilers, complex networks and systems, computer optimization, computer-supported cooperative work, computer vision, cyberinfrastructure and e-science, database theory and systems, data mining, digital design and preservation, design pedagogy, digital humanities, digital learning environments.

Indiana University–Purdue University Indianapolis, School of Informatics and Computing, Department of Human-Centered Computing, Indianapolis, IN 46202. Offers human-computer interaction (MS, PhD); informatics (MS), including data analytics; media arts and science (MS).

Human-Computer Interaction

Iowa State University of Science and Technology, Program in Human-Computer Interaction, Ames, IA 50011. Offers MS, PhD. *Degree requirements:* For master's, thesis; for doctorate, thesis/dissertation. *Entrance requirements:* For master's, GRE General Test; for doctorate, GRE General Test, e-portfolio of research. Additional exam requirements/recommendations for international students: Required—TOEFL (minimum score 580 paper-based; 95 iBT), IELTS (minimum score 7). Electronic applications accepted.

Rochester Institute of Technology, Graduate Enrollment Services, Golisano College of Computing and Information Sciences, Information Science and Technologies Department, MS Program in Human Computer Interaction, Rochester, NY 14623-5603. Offers MS. *Program availability:* Part-time, evening/weekend, 100% online. *Students:* 53 full-time (31 women), 17 part-time (8 women); includes 11 minority (2 Black or African American, non-Hispanic/Latino; 6 Asian, non-Hispanic/Latino; 2 Hispanic/Latino; 1 Two or more races, non-Hispanic/Latino), 46 international. Average age 26. 192 applicants, 59% accepted, 22 enrolled. In 2018, 12 master's awarded. *Degree requirements:* For master's, thesis or alternative, Thesis or Capstone. *Entrance requirements:* For master's, GRE required for individuals with degrees from international universities., minimum GPA of 3.0 (if you have less than a 3.0, you are required to submit GRE scores), resume, two letters of recommendation. Additional exam requirements/recommendations for international students: Required—TOEFL (minimum score 570 paper-based; 88 iBT), IELTS (minimum score 6.5), PTE (minimum score 61). *Application deadline:* For fall admission, 2/15 priority date for domestic and international students; for spring admission, 12/15 priority date for domestic and international students. Applications are processed on a rolling basis. Application fee: $65. Electronic applications accepted. *Financial support:* In 2018–19, 66 students received support. Research assistantships with partial tuition reimbursements available, teaching assistantships with partial tuition reimbursements available, career-related internships or fieldwork, scholarships/grants, and unspecified assistantships available. Support available to part-time students. Financial award applicants required to submit FAFSA. *Faculty research:* Ubiquitous and wearable computing, computing accessibility for people with disabilities, social factors influencing technology use, empirical evaluation of human language technologies, personal fabrication technologies. *Unit head:* Qi Yu, Graduate Program Director, 585-475-2700, Fax: 585-475-6584, E-mail: informaticsgrad@rit.edu. *Application contact:* Diane Ellison, Senior Associate Vice President, Graduate Enrollment Services, 585-475-2229, Fax: 585-475-7164, E-mail: gradinfo@rit.edu. Website: https://www.rit.edu/study/human-computer-interaction-ms

State University of New York at Oswego, Graduate Studies, College of Liberal Arts and Sciences, Interdisciplinary Program in Human Computer Interaction, Oswego, NY 13126. Offers MA. *Program availability:* Part-time. *Entrance requirements:* For master's, GRE, minimum GPA of 3.0. Additional exam requirements/recommendations for international students: Required—TOEFL (minimum score 560 paper-based).

Tufts University, Graduate School of Arts and Sciences, Graduate Certificate Programs, Human-Computer Interaction Program, Medford, MA 02155. Offers Certificate. *Program availability:* Part-time, evening/weekend. Electronic applications accepted. *Expenses: Tuition:* Full-time $51,288; part-time $1710 per credit hour. *Required fees:* $904. Full-time tuition and fees vary according to degree level, program and student level. Part-time tuition and fees vary according to course load.

University of Baltimore, Graduate School, Yale Gordon College of Arts and Sciences, Program in Interaction Design and Information Architecture, Baltimore, MD 21201-5779. Offers MS. *Program availability:* Part-time, evening/weekend. *Degree requirements:* For master's, project or thesis. *Entrance requirements:* For master's, GRE General Test or Miller Analogy Test, undergraduate GPA of 3.0.

University of Illinois at Urbana–Champaign, Graduate College, School of Information Sciences, Champaign, IL 61820. Offers bioinformatics (MS); digital libraries (CAS); information management (MS); library and information science (MS, PhD, CAS). *Accreditation:* ALA (one or more programs are accredited). *Program availability:* Part-time, online learning. *Entrance requirements:* For degree, master's degree in library and information science or related field with minimum GPA of 3.0.

University of Rochester, Hajim School of Engineering and Applied Sciences, Department of Computer Science, Rochester, NY 14627. Offers algorithms and complexity (MS); artificial intelligence and machine learning (MS); computer architecture (MS); computer science (PhD); human computer interaction (MS); natural language processing (MS); programming languages and computer systems (MS). *Faculty:* 18 full-time (1 woman). *Students:* 125 full-time (20 women); includes 7 minority (2 Black or African American, non-Hispanic/Latino; 4 Asian, non-Hispanic/Latino; 1 Two or more races, non-Hispanic/Latino), 103 international. Average age 26. 868 applicants, 16% accepted, 44 enrolled. In 2018, 41 master's, 8 doctorates awarded. Terminal master's awarded for partial completion of doctoral program. *Degree requirements:* For master's, comprehensive exam (for some programs), thesis (for some programs); for doctorate, comprehensive exam, thesis/dissertation, qualifying exam. *Entrance requirements:* For master's and doctorate, GRE General Test, personal statement, transcripts, three letters of recommendation. Additional exam requirements/recommendations for international students: Required—TOEFL, IELTS. *Application deadline:* For fall admission, 1/15 for domestic and international students. Application fee: $60. Electronic applications accepted. *Expenses: Tuition:* Full-time $52,974; part-time $1654 per credit hour. *Required fees:* $612. One-time fee: $30 part-time. Tuition and fees vary according to campus/location and program. *Financial support:* In 2018–19, 68 students received support, including 3 fellowships with full tuition reimbursements available (averaging $33,336 per year), 51 research assistantships with full tuition reimbursements available (averaging $30,720 per year), 14 teaching assistantships with full tuition reimbursements available (averaging $30,720 per year); scholarships/grants, traineeships, health care benefits, and tuition waivers (full and partial) also available. Financial award application deadline: 12/15. *Faculty research:* Artificial intelligence, human-computer interaction, systems research, theory research. *Total annual research expenditures:* $4.1 million. *Unit head:* Sandhya Dwarkadas, Professor and Chair, 585-275-5647, E-mail: sandhya@cs.rochester.edu. *Application contact:* Michelle Kiso, Graduate Coordinator, 585-275-7737, E-mail: mkiso@cs.rochester.edu. Website: https://www.cs.rochester.edu/graduate/index.html

University of Washington, Graduate School, College of Engineering, Department of Human Centered Design and Engineering, Seattle, WA 98195-2315. Offers human centered design and engineering (MS, PhD); user centered design (Certificate). *Program availability:* Part-time, evening/weekend. *Faculty:* 9 full-time (3 women). *Students:* 117 full-time (79 women), 171 part-time (103 women); includes 87 minority (6 Black or African American, non-Hispanic/Latino; 1 American Indian or Alaska Native, non-Hispanic/Latino; 50 Asian, non-Hispanic/Latino; 19 Hispanic/Latino; 11 Two or more races, non-Hispanic/Latino), 76 international. Average age 29. 859 applicants, 27% accepted, 130 enrolled. In 2018, 74 master's, 6 doctorates awarded. Terminal master's awarded for partial completion of doctoral program. *Degree requirements:* For master's, thesis or alternative; for doctorate, comprehensive exam, thesis/dissertation, preliminary, general, and final exams. *Entrance requirements:* For master's, minimum GPA of 3.0, transcripts, 3 letters of recommendation, curriculum vitae, personal statement of objectives; for doctorate, GRE General Test, minimum GPA of 3.0, transcripts, 3 letters of recommendation, curriculum vitae, personal statement of objectives. Additional exam requirements/recommendations for international students: Required—TOEFL (minimum score 623 paper-based; 106 iBT); Recommended—IELTS (minimum score 7). *Application deadline:* For fall admission, 1/15 for domestic and international students. Application fee: $85. Electronic applications accepted. *Expenses:* Research-focused Master's and PhD: $18,852 resident; $32,760 nonresident. *Financial support:* In 2018–19, 71 students received support, including 2 fellowships with full tuition reimbursements available (averaging $32,160 per year), 34 research assistantships with full tuition reimbursements available (averaging $32,160 per year), 35 teaching assistantships with full tuition reimbursements available (averaging $32,160 per year); career-related internships or fieldwork, institutionally sponsored loans, and tuition waivers (full) also available. Financial award application deadline: 2/28; financial award applicants required to submit FAFSA. *Faculty research:* Usability testing; rhetorical and empirical exploration of basic communication phenomena; computer documentation; technology assessment; educational assessment; Web, multimedia and user interface design. *Total annual research expenditures:* $4.2 million. *Unit head:* Dr. David McDonald, Professor/Chair, 206-685-2945, Fax: 206-543-8858, E-mail: hcdechr@uw.edu. *Application contact:* Pat Reilly, Academic Services Manager, 206-543-1798, Fax: 206-543-8858, E-mail: preilly@uw.edu. Website: http://www.hcde.washington.edu/

Information Science

Alcorn State University, School of Graduate Studies, School of Arts and Sciences, Department of Mathematics and Computer Science, Lorman, MS 39096-7500. Offers computer and information science (MS).

American InterContinental University Atlanta, Program in Information Technology, Atlanta, GA 30328. Offers MIT. *Program availability:* Part-time, evening/weekend. *Degree requirements:* For master's, technical proficiency demonstration. *Entrance requirements:* For master's, Computer Programmer Aptitude Battery Exam, interview. Electronic applications accepted. *Faculty research:* Operating systems, security issues, networks and routing, computer hardware.

American InterContinental University Online, Program in Information Technology, Schaumburg, IL 60173. Offers Internet security (MIT); IT project management (MIT). *Program availability:* Evening/weekend, online learning. *Entrance requirements:* Additional exam requirements/recommendations for international students: Required—TOEFL (minimum score 550 paper-based). Electronic applications accepted.

American University of Armenia, Graduate Programs, Yerevan, Armenia. Offers business administration (MBA); computer and information science (MS), including business management, design and manufacturing, energy (ME, MS), industrial engineering and systems management; economics (MS); industrial engineering and systems management (ME), including business, computer aided design/manufacturing, energy (ME, MS), information technology; law (LL M); political science and international affairs (MPSIA); public health (MPH); teaching English as a foreign language (MA). *Program availability:* Part-time, evening/weekend. *Degree requirements:* For master's, thesis (for some programs), capstone/project. *Entrance requirements:* For master's, GRE, GMAT, or LSAT. Additional exam requirements/recommendations for international students: Recommended—TOEFL (minimum score 79 iBT), IELTS (minimum score 6.5). *Faculty research:* Microfinance, finance (rural/development, international, corporate), firm life cycle theory, TESOL, language proficiency testing, public policy, administrative law, economic development, cryptography, artificial intelligence, energy efficiency/renewable energy, computer-aided design/manufacturing, health financing, tuberculosis control, mother/child health, preventive ophthalmology, post-earthquake psychopathological investigations, tobacco control, environmental health risk assessments.

Arizona State University at the Tempe campus, Ira A. Fulton Schools of Engineering, The Polytechnic School, Programs in Technology Management, Mesa, AZ 85212. Offers aviation management and human factors (MS); environmental technology management (MS); global technology and development (MS); graphic information technology (MS); management of technology (MS). *Program availability:* Part-time, evening/weekend, online learning. *Degree requirements:* For master's, thesis or applied project and oral defense; interactive Program of Study (iPOS) submitted before completing 50 percent of required credit hours. *Entrance requirements:* For master's, GRE, minimum GPA of 3.0 or equivalent in last 2 years of work leading to bachelor's degree. Additional exam requirements/recommendations for international students: Required—TOEFL, IELTS, or PTE. Electronic applications accepted. *Faculty research:* Digital imaging, digital publishing, Internet development/e-commerce, information aviation human factors, pilot selection, databases, multimedia, commercial digital photography, digital workflow, computer graphics modeling and animation, information design, sociotechnology, visual and technical literacy, environmental management, quality management, project management, industrial ethics, hazardous materials, environmental chemistry.

Arkansas Tech University, College of Engineering and Applied Sciences, Russellville, AR 72801. Offers electrical engineering (M Engr); emergency management (MS); information technology (MS); mechanical engineering (M Engr). *Program availability:* Part-time, evening/weekend, 100% online, blended/hybrid learning. *Students:* 46 full-time (17 women), 39 part-time (16 women); includes 12 minority (7 Black or African American, non-Hispanic/Latino; 1 American Indian or Alaska Native, non-Hispanic/Latino; 1 Asian, non-Hispanic/Latino; 2 Hispanic/Latino; 1 Two or more races, non-Hispanic/Latino), 29 international. Average age 31. In 2018, 54 master's awarded. *Degree requirements:* For master's, comprehensive exam (for some programs), thesis (for some programs). *Entrance requirements:* Additional exam requirements/recommendations for international students: Required—TOEFL (minimum score 550 paper-based; 79 iBT), IELTS (minimum score 6.5), PTE (minimum score 58). *Application deadline:* For fall admission, 3/1 priority date for domestic students, 5/1 priority date for international students; for spring admission, 10/1 priority date for domestic and international students. Applications are processed on a rolling basis. Application fee: $40 ($90 for international students). Electronic applications accepted.

Expenses: Tuition, area resident: Full-time $6816; part-time $284 per credit hour. Tuition, state resident: full-time $6816; part-time $284 per credit hour. Tuition, nonresident: full-time $13,632; part-time $568 per credit hour. *International tuition:* $13,632 full-time. *Required fees:* $457.50 per semester. Tuition and fees vary according to course load and degree level. *Financial support:* In 2018–19, research assistantships with full and partial tuition reimbursements (averaging $4,800 per year), teaching assistantships with full and partial tuition reimbursements (averaging $4,800 per year) were awarded; career-related internships or fieldwork, Federal Work-Study, scholarships/grants, health care benefits, and unspecified assistantships also available. Support available to part-time students. Financial award application deadline: 4/15; financial award applicants required to submit FAFSA. *Unit head:* Dr. Judy Cezeaux, Dean, 479-968-0353, E-mail: jcezeaux@atu.edu. *Application contact:* Dr. Jeff Robertson, Interim Dean of Graduate College, 479-968-0398, Fax: 479-964-0542, E-mail: gradcollege@atu.edu.
Website: http://www.atu.edu/appliedsci/

Aspen University, Program in Information Technology, Denver, CO 80246-1930. Offers MS, Certificate. *Program availability:* Part-time, evening/weekend, online only, 100% online. *Faculty:* 10 part-time/adjunct (5 women). *Students:* Average age 37. *Degree requirements:* For master's, comprehensive exam. *Entrance requirements:* For master's and Certificate, www.aspen.edu, www.aspen.edu. *Application deadline:* Applications are processed on a rolling basis. Application fee: $0. Electronic applications accepted. *Financial support:* Applicants required to submit FAFSA. *Unit head:* Kevin Thrasher, Provost, 602-5706708, E-mail: kevin.thrasher@aspen.edu. *Application contact:* Enrollment Advisor, 800-373-7814.

Ball State University, Graduate School, College of Communication, Information, and Media, Center for Information and Communication Sciences, Muncie, IN 47306. Offers information and communication sciences (MS); information and communication technologies (Certificate). *Program availability:* Part-time, 100% online. *Entrance requirements:* For master's, minimum baccalaureate GPA of 2.75 or 3.0 in latter half of baccalaureate, statement of goals. Additional exam requirements/recommendations for international students: Required—TOEFL (minimum score 550 paper-based; 79 iBT), IELTS (minimum score 6.5). Electronic applications accepted.

Barry University, School of Adult and Continuing Education, Program in Information Technology, Miami Shores, FL 33161-6695. Offers MS. *Program availability:* Part-time, evening/weekend. *Entrance requirements:* For master's, GMAT, GRE or MAT, bachelor's degree in information technology, related area or professional experience. Electronic applications accepted.

Bellevue University, Graduate School, College of Information Technology, Bellevue, NE 68005-3098. Offers computer information systems (MS); cybersecurity (MS); management of information systems (MS); project management (MPM).

Bentley University, McCallum Graduate School of Business, Masters in Digital Innovation, Waltham, MA 02452-4705. Offers MSIT. *Program availability:* Part-time, evening/weekend. *Faculty:* 118 full-time (38 women), 25 part-time/adjunct (4 women). *Students:* 33 full-time (17 women), 19 part-time (8 women); includes 9 minority (2 Black or African American, non-Hispanic/Latino; 5 Asian, non-Hispanic/Latino; 1 Hispanic/Latino; 1 Two or more races, non-Hispanic/Latino), 28 international. Average age 30. 59 applicants, 64% accepted, 10 enrolled. In 2018, 28 master's awarded. *Entrance requirements:* For master's, GMAT or GRE General Test (may be waived for qualified students), Transcripts; Resume; Two essays; Two letters of recommendation; Interview (may be requested by Bentley). Additional exam requirements/recommendations for international students: Required—TOEFL (minimum score 100) or IELTS (minimum score 7). *Application deadline:* For fall admission, 7/31 for domestic students, 6/30 for international students; for spring admission, 1/1 for domestic students, 11/1 for international students. Applications are processed on a rolling basis. Application fee: $150. Electronic applications accepted. *Financial support:* In 2018–19, 18 students received support. Scholarships/grants and unspecified assistantships available. Financial award application deadline: 6/1; financial award applicants required to submit FAFSA. *Faculty research:* Business intelligence and analytics; enterprise networks and services; telemedicine; system usability; information visualization, cybersecurity, system design quality. *Unit head:* Jennifer Xu, Associate Professor and Program Director, 781-891-2711, E-mail: jxu@bentley.edu. *Application contact:* Office of Graduate Admissions, 781-891-2108, E-mail: applygrad@bentley.edu.
Website: https://www.bentley.edu/academics/graduate-programs/masters-digital-innovation

Bradley University, The Graduate School, College of Liberal Arts and Sciences, Department of Computer Science and Information Systems, Peoria, IL 61625-0002. Offers computer information systems (MS); computer science (MS). *Program availability:* Part-time, evening/weekend. *Faculty:* 10 full-time (2 women), 1 part-time/adjunct. *Students:* 19 full-time (8 women), 4 part-time (1 woman), 20 international. Average age 25. 99 applicants, 91% accepted, 11 enrolled. In 2018, 11 master's awarded. *Degree requirements:* For master's, comprehensive exam, thesis or alternative, programming test. *Entrance requirements:* For master's, GRE. Additional exam requirements/recommendations for international students: Required—TOEFL (minimum score 550 paper-based; 79 iBT), IELTS (minimum score 6.5). *Application deadline:* For fall admission, 5/15 priority date for domestic and international students; for spring admission, 10/15 priority date for domestic and international students. Applications are processed on a rolling basis. Application fee: $40 ($50 for international students). Electronic applications accepted. *Expenses: Tuition:* Part-time $890 per credit. *Required fees:* $50 per unit. *Financial support:* In 2018–19, 24 students received support, including 1 fellowship with full tuition reimbursement available (averaging $8,010 per year), 11 research assistantships with full and partial tuition reimbursements available (averaging $5,947 per year); teaching assistantships, scholarships/grants, tuition waivers (partial), and unspecified assistantships also available. Support available to part-time students. Financial award application deadline: 4/1. *Unit head:* Dr. Steven Dolins, Chair, 309-677-3284, E-mail: sdolins@bradley.edu. *Application contact:* Rachel Webb, Director of On-Campus Graduate Admissions & International Student and Scholar Services, 309-677-2375, E-mail: rkwebb@bradley.edu.
Website: http://www.bradley.edu/academic/departments/csis/

Brigham Young University, Graduate Studies, Ira A. Fulton College of Engineering, School of Technology, Provo, UT 84602. Offers construction management (MS); information technology (MS); manufacturing engineering technology (MS); technology and engineering education (MS). *Faculty:* 30 full-time (1 woman), 2 part-time/adjunct (0 women). *Students:* 30 full-time (4 women); includes 6 minority (1 Asian, non-Hispanic/Latino; 1 Hispanic/Latino; 1 Native Hawaiian or other Pacific Islander, non-Hispanic/Latino; 3 Two or more races, non-Hispanic/Latino), 2 international. Average age 28. 14 applicants, 79% accepted, 11 enrolled. In 2018, 29 master's awarded. *Degree requirements:* For master's, thesis. *Entrance requirements:* For master's, GRE General Test; GMAT or GRE (for construction management emphasis), Minimum GPA of 3.0 in last 60 hours of course work. Additional exam requirements/recommendations for international students: Required—TOEFL (minimum score 580 paper-based; 85 iBT). *Application deadline:* For fall admission, 2/15 for domestic and international students; for winter admission, 9/10 for domestic and international students; for spring admission, 2/

15 for domestic and international students; for summer admission, 2/15 for domestic and international students. Application fee: $50. Electronic applications accepted. *Financial support:* In 2018–19, 28 students received support, including 9 research assistantships (averaging $3,496 per year), 11 teaching assistantships (averaging $4,755 per year); scholarships/grants also available. Financial award application deadline: 1/15; financial award applicants required to submit FAFSA. *Faculty research:* Information assurance and security, HEI and databases, manufacturing materials, processes and systems, innovation in construction management scheduling and delivery methods. *Total annual research expenditures:* $67,118. *Unit head:* Dr. Barry M. Lunt, Director, 801-422-6300, Fax: 801-422-0490, E-mail: blunt@byu.edu. *Application contact:* Clifton Farnsworth, Graduate Coordinator, 801-422-6494, Fax: 801-422-0490, E-mail: clifton_farnsworth@byu.edu.
Website: http://www.et.byu.edu/sot/

Brooklyn College of the City University of New York, School of Natural and Behavioral Sciences, Department of Computer and Information Science, Brooklyn, NY 11210-2889. Offers computer science (MA); health informatics (MS); information systems (MS); parallel and distributed computing (Advanced Certificate). *Program availability:* Part-time, evening/weekend. *Degree requirements:* For master's, comprehensive exam, thesis or alternative. *Entrance requirements:* For master's, previous course work in computer science, 2 letters of recommendation. Additional exam requirements/recommendations for international students: Required—TOEFL (minimum score 525 paper-based; 70 iBT). Electronic applications accepted. *Faculty research:* Networks and distributed systems, programming languages, modeling and computer applications, algorithms, artificial intelligence, theoretical computer science.

California State University, Fullerton, Graduate Studies, College of Business and Economics, Department of Information Systems and Decision Sciences, Fullerton, CA 92831-3599. Offers decision science (MBA); information systems (MBA, MS); information systems and decision sciences (MS); information systems and e-commerce (MS); information technology (MS). *Program availability:* Part-time. *Entrance requirements:* For master's, GMAT, minimum AACSB index of 950.

Capitol Technology University, Graduate Programs, Laurel, MD 20708-9759. Offers business administration (MBA); computer science (MS); electrical engineering (MS); information and telecommunications systems management (MS); information architecture (MS); network security (MS). *Program availability:* Part-time, evening/weekend, online learning. *Entrance requirements:* For master's, minimum GPA of 3.0. Electronic applications accepted.

Carleton University, Faculty of Graduate Studies, Faculty of Engineering and Design, Ottawa-Carleton Institute for Electrical Engineering, Department of Systems and Computer Engineering, Program in Information and Systems Science, Ottawa, ON K1S 5B6, Canada. Offers M Sc.

Carleton University, Faculty of Graduate Studies, Faculty of Science, Information and Systems Science Program, Ottawa, ON K1S 5B6, Canada. Offers M Sc. *Degree requirements:* For master's, thesis optional. *Entrance requirements:* For master's, honors degree. Additional exam requirements/recommendations for international students: Required—TOEFL. *Faculty research:* Software engineering, real-time and microprocessor programming, computer communications.

Carleton University, Faculty of Graduate Studies, Faculty of Science, School of Computer Science, Ottawa, ON K1S 5B6, Canada. Offers computer science (MCS, PhD); information and system science (M Sc). MCS and PhD programs offered jointly with University of Ottawa. *Program availability:* Part-time. *Degree requirements:* For master's, thesis optional, project; for doctorate, comprehensive exam, thesis/dissertation. *Entrance requirements:* For master's, honors degree. Additional exam requirements/recommendations for international students: Required—TOEFL. *Faculty research:* Programming systems, theory of computing, computer applications, computer systems.

Carnegie Mellon University, Heinz College Australia, Master of Science in Information Technology Program (Adelaide, South Australia), Adelaide SA 5000, Australia. Offers MSIT. *Entrance requirements:* For master's, GRE or GMAT, college-level course in advanced algebra/pre-calculus; college-level courses in economics and statistics (recommended). Additional exam requirements/recommendations for international students: Required—TOEFL or IELTS.

Carnegie Mellon University, Heinz College, School of Information Systems and Management, Master of Information Systems Management Program, Pittsburgh, PA 15213-3891. Offers MISM. *Entrance requirements:* For master's, GRE or GMAT, college-level course in advanced algebra/pre-calculus; college-level courses in economics and statistics (recommended). Additional exam requirements/recommendations for international students: Required—TOEFL or IELTS.

Carnegie Mellon University, School of Computer Science, Language Technologies Institute, Pittsburgh, PA 15213-3891. Offers MLT, MS, PhD. Terminal master's awarded for partial completion of doctoral program. *Degree requirements:* For doctorate, thesis/dissertation. *Entrance requirements:* For master's and doctorate, GRE General Test, GRE Subject Test. Additional exam requirements/recommendations for international students: Required—TOEFL. *Faculty research:* Machine translation, natural language processing, speech and information retrieval, literacy.

Case Western Reserve University, School of Graduate Studies, Case School of Engineering, Department of Computer and Data Sciences, Cleveland, OH 44106. Offers computer engineering (MS, PhD); computing and information sciences (MS, PhD); electrical engineering (MS, PhD); systems and control engineering (MS, PhD). *Program availability:* Part-time, evening/weekend, online only, 100% online. *Faculty:* 31 full-time (2 women). *Students:* 228 full-time (49 women), 17 part-time (3 women); includes 18 minority (13 Asian, non-Hispanic/Latino; 3 Hispanic/Latino; 2 Two or more races, non-Hispanic/Latino), 180 international. In 2018, 29 master's, 16 doctorates awarded. Terminal master's awarded for partial completion of doctoral program. *Degree requirements:* For master's, thesis; for doctorate, thesis/dissertation, qualifying exam, teaching experience. *Entrance requirements:* For master's and doctorate, GRE General Test. Additional exam requirements/recommendations for international students: Required—TOEFL. *Application deadline:* For fall admission, 2/1 for domestic students; for spring admission, 11/1 for domestic students. Applications are processed on a rolling basis. Application fee: $50. *Expenses: Tuition:* Full-time $45,168; part-time $1939 per credit hour. *Required fees:* $36; $18 per semester. $18 per semester. *Financial support:* In 2018–19, 1 fellowship with tuition reimbursement, 72 research assistantships with tuition reimbursements, 10 teaching assistantships were awarded; career-related internships or fieldwork, Federal Work-Study, and institutionally sponsored loans also available. Support available to part-time students. Financial award application deadline: 3/1; financial award applicants required to submit FAFSA. *Faculty research:* Micro-/nano-systems; robotics and haptics; applied artificial intelligence; automation; computer-aided design and testing of digital systems. *Total annual research expenditures:* $5.1 million. *Unit head:* Jing Li, Interim Department Chair, 216-368-0356, E-mail: jxl175@case.edu. *Application contact:* Angela Beca, Student Affairs Specialist, 216-368-2800, Fax: 216-368-2801, E-mail: angela.beca@case.edu.
Website: www.engineering.case.edu/eecs

Information Science

The Citadel, The Military College of South Carolina, Citadel Graduate College, School of Science and Mathematics, Department of Mathematics and Computer Science, Charleston, SC 29409. Offers computer and information sciences (MS). MS computer and information sciences and cybersecurity graduate certificate offered jointly with the Graduate College of the College of Charleston. *Accreditation:* NCATE (one or more programs are accredited). *Program availability:* Part-time, evening/weekend. *Degree requirements:* For master's, comprehensive exam (for some programs), thesis (for some programs). *Entrance requirements:* For master's, GRE General Test (minimum combined score of 300 on the verbal and quantitative sections, 1000 under the old grading system, 4.0 on the writing assessment for MS); MAT with minimum raw score of 396 (for MA Ed), minimum undergraduate GPA of 3.0 and competency demonstrated through coursework, approved work experience, or a program-administrated competency exam, in the areas of basic computer architecture, object-oriented programming, discrete mathematics, and data structures (for MS). Additional exam requirements/recommendations for international students: Required—TOEFL (minimum score 550 paper-based; 79 iBT). Electronic applications accepted. *Expenses:* Tuition, state resident: part-time $595 per credit hour. Tuition, nonresident: part-time $1020 per credit hour. *Required fees:* $90 per term.

Claremont Graduate University, Graduate Programs, Center for Information Systems and Technology, Claremont, CA 91711-6160. Offers cybersecurity and networking (MS); data science and analytics (MS); electronic commerce (PhD); geographic information systems (MS); health informatics (MS); information systems (Certificate); IT strategy and innovation (MS); knowledge management (PhD); systems development (PhD); telecommunications and networking (PhD); MBA/MS. *Program availability:* Part-time. *Degree requirements:* For doctorate, comprehensive exam, thesis/dissertation, portfolio. *Entrance requirements:* For master's and doctorate, GMAT, GRE General Test. Additional exam requirements/recommendations for international students: Required—TOEFL (minimum score 75 iBT). Electronic applications accepted. *Faculty research:* Man-machine interaction, organizational aspects of computing, implementation of information systems, information systems practice.

Clarion University of Pennsylvania, College of Business Administration and Information Sciences, MSLS Program in Information and Library Science, Clarion, PA 16214. Offers information and library science (MSLS); school library media (MSLS). *Accreditation:* ALA. *Program availability:* Part-time, evening/weekend, online only, 100% online. *Faculty:* 5 full-time (4 women), 5 part-time/adjunct (3 women). *Students:* 117 full-time (97 women), 247 part-time (206 women); includes 55 minority (23 Black or African American, non-Hispanic/Latino; 7 Asian, non-Hispanic/Latino; 19 Hispanic/Latino; 6 Two or more races, non-Hispanic/Latino), 2 international. Average age 33. 239 applicants, 62% accepted, 139 enrolled. In 2018, 129 master's awarded. *Entrance requirements:* For master's, Overall GPA for the bacc degree of at least 3.00 on a 4.00 scale; Or a 3.00 GPA for the last 60 credits of the bacc degree with an overall QPA of at least 2.75; or a 2.75 to 2.99 overall GPA for the bacc degree with a score of at least 412 on the MAT or score of at least 300 on the GRE; or a graduate degree with at least a GPA of 3.00. Additional exam requirements/recommendations for international students: Required—TOEFL (minimum score 80 iBT), International students are required to achieve a minimum score of 213 computer-based or 80 internet-based on the TOEFL MSLS with Pennsylvania. *Application deadline:* For fall admission, 8/1 priority date for domestic students, 7/15 priority date for international students; for winter admission, 11/1 priority date for domestic students; for spring admission, 12/1 priority date for domestic students, 11/15 priority date for international students; for summer admission, 4/1 priority date for domestic students. Applications are processed on a rolling basis. Application fee: $40. Electronic applications accepted. *Expenses:* $675.60 per credit including fees in state. *Financial support:* Career-related internships or fieldwork, institutionally sponsored loans, scholarships/grants, and unspecified assistantships available. Financial award application deadline: 3/1; financial award applicants required to submit FAFSA. *Unit head:* Dr. Linda Lillard, Department Chair, 814-393-2383, E-mail: llillard@clarion.edu. *Application contact:* Susan Staub, Graduate Admissions Counselor, 814-393-2337, Fax: 814-393-2722, E-mail: gradstudies@clarion.edu.
Website: http://www.clarion.edu/academics/colleges-and-schools/college-of-business-administration-and-information-sciences/library-science/

Clark Atlanta University, School of Arts and Sciences, Department of Computer and Information Science, Atlanta, GA 30314. Offers MS. *Program availability:* Part-time. *Degree requirements:* For master's, one foreign language, thesis. *Entrance requirements:* For master's, GRE General Test, minimum GPA of 2.5. Additional exam requirements/recommendations for international students: Required—TOEFL (minimum score 500 paper-based; 61 iBT).

Clark University, Graduate School, School of Professional Studies, Program in Information Technology, Worcester, MA 01610-1477. Offers MSIT. *Program availability:* Part-time, evening/weekend. *Degree requirements:* For master's, thesis or alternative. *Entrance requirements:* For master's, 2 references, resume or curriculum vitae, personal statement. Additional exam requirements/recommendations for international students: Required—TOEFL (minimum score 575 paper-based; 90 iBT), IELTS (minimum score 6.5). Electronic applications accepted. *Expenses:* Contact institution.

The College of Saint Rose, Graduate Studies, School of Mathematics and Sciences, Program in Computer Information Systems, Albany, NY 12203-1419. Offers MS, Advanced Certificate. *Program availability:* Part-time, evening/weekend. *Students:* 14 full-time (6 women), 25 part-time (7 women); includes 5 minority (4 Asian, non-Hispanic/Latino; 1 Hispanic/Latino), 24 international. Average age 31. 74 applicants, 81% accepted, 16 enrolled. In 2018, 35 master's, 4 other advanced degrees awarded. *Degree requirements:* For master's, comprehensive exam, research component, project. *Entrance requirements:* For master's, minimum GPA of 3.0, 9 undergraduate credits in math. Additional exam requirements/recommendations for international students: Required—TOEFL (minimum score 550 paper-based; 80 iBT), IELTS (minimum score 6), PTE (minimum score 56). *Application deadline:* For fall admission, 4/1 priority date for domestic and international students; for spring admission, 10/15 priority date for domestic and international students; for summer admission, 3/15 priority date for domestic and international students. Applications are processed on a rolling basis. Application fee: $40. Electronic applications accepted. *Expenses: Tuition:* Full-time $14,382; part-time $799 per credit hour. *Required fees:* $924; $408 per credit. $286. *Financial support:* Career-related internships or fieldwork, scholarships/grants, tuition waivers (partial), and unspecified assistantships available. Support available to part-time students. Financial award application deadline: 4/15; financial award applicants required to submit FAFSA. *Unit head:* Dr. John Avitabile, Department Chair, 518-458-5317, E-mail: avitabij@strose.edu. *Application contact:* Daniel Gallagher, Assistant Vice President for Graduate Recruitment and Enrollment, 518-485-3390.
Website: https://www.strose.edu/computer-information-systems/

Cornell University, Graduate School, Graduate Fields of Arts and Sciences, Field of Information Science, Ithaca, NY 14853. Offers cognition (PhD); human computer interaction (PhD); information science (PhD); information systems (PhD); social aspects of information (PhD). *Degree requirements:* For doctorate, comprehensive exam, thesis/dissertation. *Entrance requirements:* For doctorate, GRE General Test, 3 letters of recommendation. Additional exam requirements/recommendations for international students: Required—TOEFL (minimum score 550 paper-based; 77 iBT). Electronic applications accepted. *Faculty research:* Digital libraries, game theory, data mining, human-computer interaction, computational linguistics.

Dakota State University, College of Business and Information Systems, Madison, SD 57042-1799. Offers analytics (MSA); business analytics (Graduate Certificate); general management (MBA); health informatics (MSHI); information systems (MSIS, D Sc IS); information technology (Graduate Certificate). *Accreditation:* ACBSP. *Program availability:* Part-time, evening/weekend, 100% online, blended/hybrid learning. *Faculty:* 27 full-time (10 women). *Students:* 40 full-time (11 women), 165 part-time (60 women); includes 56 minority (21 Black or African American, non-Hispanic/Latino; 4 American Indian or Alaska Native, non-Hispanic/Latino; 19 Asian, non-Hispanic/Latino; 10 Hispanic/Latino; 1 Native Hawaiian or other Pacific Islander, non-Hispanic/Latino; 1 Two or more races, non-Hispanic/Latino), 38 international. Average age 38. 246 applicants, 47% accepted, 63 enrolled. In 2018, 62 master's, 7 doctorates, 9 other advanced degrees awarded. *Degree requirements:* For master's, comprehensive exam, thesis optional, Examination, integrative project; for doctorate, comprehensive exam, thesis/dissertation, portfolio. *Entrance requirements:* For master's, GRE General Test, Demonstration of information systems skills, minimum GPA of 2.7; for doctorate, GRE General Test, Demonstration of information systems skills; for Graduate Certificate, GMAT. Additional exam requirements/recommendations for international students: Required—PTE (minimum score 53), TOEFL (minimum score 550 paper-based, 76 iBT) or IELTS (6.0). *Application deadline:* For fall admission, 6/15 for domestic students, 4/15 for international students; for spring admission, 11/15 for domestic students, 9/15 priority date for international students; for summer admission, 4/15 for domestic and international students. Applications are processed on a rolling basis. Application fee: $35. Electronic applications accepted. *Expenses:* Contact institution. *Financial support:* In 2018–19, 20 students received support. Research assistantships with partial tuition reimbursements available, teaching assistantships with partial tuition reimbursements available, career-related internships or fieldwork, Federal Work-Study, scholarships/grants, and unspecified assistantships available. Support available to part-time students. Financial award applicants required to submit FAFSA. *Faculty research:* Data mining and analytics, biometrics and information assurance, decision support systems, health informatics, STEM education for K-12 teachers/students and underrepresented populations. *Unit head:* Dr. Dorine Bennett, Dean of College of Business and Information Systems, 605-256-5176, E-mail: dorine.bennett@dsu.edu. *Application contact:* Erin Blankespoor, Senior Secretary, Office of Graduate Studies and Research, 605-256-5799, E-mail: erin.blankespoor@dsu.edu.
Website: http://dsu.edu/academics/colleges/college-of-business-and-information-systems

DePaul University, College of Computing and Digital Media, Chicago, IL 60604. Offers animation (MA, MFA); applied technology (MS); business information technology (MS); computational finance (MS); computer and information sciences (PhD); computer science (MS); creative producing (MFA); cybersecurity (MS); data science (MS); digital communication and media arts (MA); documentary (MFA); e-commerce technology (MS); experience design (MA); film and television (MS); film and television directing (MFA); game design (MFA); game programming (MS); health informatics (MS); human centered design (PhD); human-computer interaction (MS); information systems (MS); network engineering and security (MS); product innovation and computing (MS); screenwriting (MFA); software engineering (MS); JD/MS. *Program availability:* Part-time, evening/weekend, online learning. *Degree requirements:* For master's, thesis (for some programs); for doctorate, comprehensive exam, thesis/dissertation. *Entrance requirements:* For master's, GRE or GMAT (for MS in computational finance only), bachelor's degree, resume (MS in predictive analytics only), IT experience (MS in information technology project management only), portfolio review (all MFA programs and MA in animation); for doctorate, GRE, master's degree in computer science. Additional exam requirements/recommendations for international students: Required—TOEFL (minimum score 590 paper-based; 80 iBT), IELTS (minimum score 6.5), PTE (minimum score 53). Electronic applications accepted. *Expenses:* Contact institution. *Faculty research:* Data mining, computer science, human-computer interaction, security, animation and film.

Drexel University, College of Computing and Informatics, Department of Information Science, Philadelphia, PA 19104-2875. Offers health informatics (MS); information science (PhD, Post-Master's Certificate, Postbaccalaureate Certificate); information systems (MS); library and information science (MS). *Accreditation:* ALA. *Program availability:* Part-time, evening/weekend, 100% online. *Faculty:* 24 full-time (11 women), 18 part-time/adjunct (9 women). *Students:* 153 full-time (92 women), 212 part-time (137 women); includes 85 minority (29 Black or African American, non-Hispanic/Latino; 22 Asian, non-Hispanic/Latino; 19 Hispanic/Latino; 15 Two or more races, non-Hispanic/Latino), 66 international. Average age 33. 570 applicants, 45% accepted, 136 enrolled. In 2018, 144 master's, 8 doctorates, 8 other advanced degrees awarded. *Degree requirements:* For doctorate, thesis/dissertation. *Entrance requirements:* For master's and doctorate, GRE General Test. Additional exam requirements/recommendations for international students: Required—TOEFL (minimum score 90 iBT), IELTS (minimum score 6.5). *Application deadline:* For fall admission, 8/15 for domestic students, 7/15 for international students; for spring admission, 3/1 for domestic students, 2/1 for international students. Applications are processed on a rolling basis. Application fee: $65. Electronic applications accepted. *Financial support:* Fellowships, research assistantships, teaching assistantships, career-related internships or fieldwork, scholarships/grants, and tuition waivers (partial) available. Support available to part-time students. Financial award application deadline: 3/1; financial award applicants required to submit FAFSA. *Unit head:* Dr. Yi Deng, Dean/Professor, 215-895-2474, Fax: 215-895-2494, E-mail: yd362@drexel.edu. *Application contact:* Matthew Lechtenberg, Director, Recruitment, 215-895-2474, Fax: 215-895-2303, E-mail: cciinfo@drexel.edu.
Website: http://cci.drexel.edu/academics/graduate-programs/ms-in-health-informatics

See Display on page 229 and Close-Up on page 309.

East Tennessee State University, School of Graduate Studies, College of Business and Technology, Department of Computing, Johnson City, TN 37614. Offers applied computer science (MS); emerging technologies (Postbaccalaureate Certificate); information technology (MS). *Program availability:* Part-time, evening/weekend. *Degree requirements:* For master's, comprehensive exam, thesis optional, capstone, oral exam. *Entrance requirements:* For master's, GRE General Test, minimum GPA of 3.0, three letters of recommendation. Additional exam requirements/recommendations for international students: Required—TOEFL (minimum score 550 paper-based; 79 iBT). Electronic applications accepted. *Faculty research:* Data mining, security and forensics, numerical optimization, computer gaming, enterprise resource planning.

Florida Institute of Technology, College of Engineering and Science, Program in Computer Information Systems, Melbourne, FL 32901-6975. Offers MS. *Program availability:* Part-time. *Students:* 33 full-time (11 women), 20 part-time (6 women); includes 1 minority (Asian, non-Hispanic/Latino), 43 international. Average age 28. 48 applicants, 83% accepted, 8 enrolled. In 2018, 32 master's awarded. *Degree requirements:* For master's, comprehensive exam (for some programs), thesis optional,

minimum of 30 credits. *Entrance requirements:* For master's, GRE recommended, 3 letters of recommendation, resume, mathematical proficiency. Additional exam requirements/recommendations for international students: Required—TOEFL (minimum score 550 paper-based; 79 iBT). *Application deadline:* Applications are processed on a rolling basis. Application fee: $50. Electronic applications accepted. *Expenses: Tuition:* Full-time $22,338; part-time $1241 per credit hour. Tuition and fees vary according to degree level, campus/location and program. *Financial support:* Tuition remissions available. Financial award application deadline: 3/1; financial award applicants required to submit FAFSA. *Faculty research:* Artificial intelligence, software engineering, computer graphics, programming languages, database systems. *Unit head:* Dr. Philip Berhard, Department Head, 321-674-7294, E-mail: pbernhar@fit.edu. *Application contact:* Mike Perry, Executive Director of Admissions, 321-674-7127, E-mail: perrymj@fit.edu.
Website: https://www.fit.edu/programs/computer-information-systems-ms/

Florida International University, College of Engineering and Computing, School of Computing and Information Sciences, Miami, FL 33199. Offers computer science (MS, PhD); cybersecurity (MS); data science (MS); information technology (MS); telecommunications and networking (MS). *Program availability:* Part-time, evening/weekend. *Faculty:* 49 full-time (13 women), 31 part-time/adjunct (7 women). *Students:* 182 full-time (53 women), 132 part-time (28 women); includes 168 minority (13 Black or African American, non-Hispanic/Latino; 1 American Indian or Alaska Native, non-Hispanic/Latino; 10 Asian, non-Hispanic/Latino; 137 Hispanic/Latino; 7 Two or more races, non-Hispanic/Latino), 123 international. Average age 30. 393 applicants, 47% accepted, 92 enrolled. In 2018, 81 master's, 9 doctorates awarded. *Degree requirements:* For master's, thesis or alternative; for doctorate, comprehensive exam, thesis/dissertation. *Entrance requirements:* For master's and doctorate, GRE General Test, 3 letters of recommendation, minimum GPA of 3.0. Additional exam requirements/recommendations for international students: Required—TOEFL (minimum score 550 paper-based; 80 iBT). *Application deadline:* For fall admission, 6/1 for domestic students, 4/1 for international students; for spring admission, 10/1 for domestic students, 9/1 for international students. Applications are processed on a rolling basis. Application fee: $30. Electronic applications accepted. *Financial support:* Research assistantships, teaching assistantships, institutionally sponsored loans, scholarships/grants, and unspecified assistantships available. Financial award application deadline: 3/1; financial award applicants required to submit FAFSA. *Faculty research:* Database systems, software engineering, operating systems, networks. *Unit head:* Dr. Sundararaj S. Iyengar, Director, 305-348-3947, Fax: 305-348-3549, E-mail: sundararaj.iyengar@fiu.edu. *Application contact:* Nanett Rojas, Manager, Admissions Operations, 305-348-7464, Fax: 305-348-7441, E-mail: gradadm@fiu.edu.

Gannon University, School of Graduate Studies, College of Engineering and Business, School of Engineering and Computer Science, Program in Computer and Information Science, Erie, PA 16541-0001. Offers information analytics (MSCIS); software engineering (MSCIS). *Program availability:* Part-time, evening/weekend. *Degree requirements:* For master's, thesis (for some programs), directed research. *Entrance requirements:* For master's, 3 letters of recommendation; resume; transcripts; baccalaureate degree in computer science, information systems, information science, software engineering, or related field from regionally-accredited institution with minimum GPA of 2.5. Additional exam requirements/recommendations for international students: Required—TOEFL (minimum score 79 iBT). Electronic applications accepted. Application fee is waived when completed online.

Gannon University, School of Graduate Studies, College of Engineering and Business, School of Engineering and Computer Science, Program in Information Analytics, Erie, PA 16541-0001. Offers MSCIS. *Program availability:* Part-time, evening/weekend. *Entrance requirements:* For master's, baccalaureate degree in computer science, information systems, information science, software engineering, or a related field from regionally-accredited institution with minimum GPA of 2.5; resume; transcripts; 3 letters of recommendation. Additional exam requirements/recommendations for international students: Required—TOEFL (minimum score 79 iBT). Electronic applications accepted. Application fee is waived when completed online.

George Mason University, Volgenau School of Engineering, Department of Information Sciences and Technology, Fairfax, VA 22030. Offers applied information technology (MS); data analytics engineering (MS); information sciences and technology (Certificate). *Program availability:* Evening/weekend, 100% online. *Faculty:* 26 full-time (9 women), 67 part-time/adjunct (13 women). *Students:* 253 full-time (135 women), 330 part-time (108 women); includes 192 minority (36 Black or African American, non-Hispanic/Latino; 125 Asian, non-Hispanic/Latino; 25 Hispanic/Latino; 6 Two or more races, non-Hispanic/Latino), 206 international. Average age 30. 438 applicants, 82% accepted, 176 enrolled. In 2018, 182 master's, 40 other advanced degrees awarded. *Entrance requirements:* For master's, GRE/GMAT, personal goals statement; 2 copies of official transcripts; 3 letters of recommendation; resume; official bank statement; proof of financial support; photocopy of passport; baccalaureate degree from an accredited program with minimum B average in last 60 credit hours. Additional exam requirements/recommendations for international students: Required—TOEFL (minimum score 575 paper-based; 88 iBT), IELTS (minimum score 6.5), PTE (minimum score 59). *Application deadline:* For fall admission, 12/15 priority date for domestic and international students; for spring admission, 8/15 priority date for domestic and international students. Application fee: $75 ($80 for international students). Electronic applications accepted. *Expenses:* $589 per credit in-state, $1,346.75 per credit out-of-state. *Financial support:* In 2018–19, 52 students received support, including 1 fellowship, 7 research assistantships (averaging $12,774 per year), 44 teaching assistantships with tuition reimbursements available (averaging $6,224 per year); career-related internships or fieldwork, Federal Work-Study, scholarships/grants, unspecified assistantships, and health care benefits (for full-time research or teaching assistantship recipients) also available. Support available to part-time students. Financial award application deadline: 3/1; financial award applicants required to submit FAFSA. *Faculty research:* Secure information systems, document forensics, it entrepreneurship, learning agents. *Total annual research expenditures:* $246,221. *Unit head:* Ioulia Rytikova, Associate Chair for Graduate Studies, 703-993-6889, E-mail: irytikov@gmu.edu. *Application contact:* Academic Advisor, 703-993-3565, E-mail: msait@gmu.edu.
Website: http://ist.gmu.edu

George Mason University, Volgenau School of Engineering, Program in Information Technology, Fairfax, VA 22030. Offers PhD. *Faculty:* 82 full-time (19 women), 15 part-time/adjunct (0 women). *Students:* 40 full-time (18 women), 44 part-time (5 women); includes 21 minority (4 Black or African American, non-Hispanic/Latino; 10 Asian, non-Hispanic/Latino; 5 Hispanic/Latino; 2 Two or more races, non-Hispanic/Latino), 36 international. Average age 36. 44 applicants, 66% accepted, 8 enrolled. In 2018, 10 doctorates awarded. *Degree requirements:* For doctorate, comprehensive exam, thesis/dissertation, 18 credits of courses beyond MS; qualifying exams. *Entrance requirements:* For doctorate, GRE, MS and BS in a related field; 2 official copies of transcripts; 3 letters of recommendation; resume; expanded goals statement. Additional exam requirements/recommendations for international students: Required—TOEFL (minimum score 575 paper-based; 88 iBT), IELTS (minimum score 6.5), PTE (minimum

score 59). *Application deadline:* For fall admission, 12/15 priority date for domestic and international students; for spring admission, 8/15 priority date for domestic and international students. Application fee: $75 ($80 for international students). Electronic applications accepted. *Expenses:* $589 per credit in-state, $1,346.75 per credit out-of-state. *Financial support:* In 2018–19, 31 students received support, including 19 research assistantships with tuition reimbursements available (averaging $20,673 per year), 13 teaching assistantships with tuition reimbursements available (averaging $16,455 per year); career-related internships or fieldwork, Federal Work-Study, scholarships/grants, unspecified assistantships, and health care benefits (for full-time research or teaching assistantship recipients) also available. Support available to part-time students. Financial award application deadline: 3/1; financial award applicants required to submit FAFSA. *Faculty research:* Information security and assurance; digital forensics; information systems; software engineering; information sciences and technology. *Unit head:* Stephen Nash, Senior Associate Dean, 703-993-1505, Fax: 703-993-1633, E-mail: snash@gmu.edu. *Application contact:* Jennifer Skorzawski-Ross, Director, Graduate Academic Affairs, 703-993-1505, Fax: 703-993-1633, E-mail: jskorzaw@gmu.edu.
Website: http://volgenau.gmu.edu/students/graduates/phd-in-information-technology

Georgia State University, J. Mack Robinson College of Business, Department of Computer Information Systems, Atlanta, GA 30302-3083. Offers computer information systems (PhD); health informatics (MBA, MS); information systems (MSIS, Certificate); information systems development and project management (MBA); information systems management (MBA); managing information technology (Exec MS); the wireless organization (MBA). *Program availability:* Part-time, evening/weekend. *Faculty:* 13 full-time (1 woman), 4 part-time/adjunct (all women). *Students:* 126 full-time (60 women), 6 part-time (0 women); includes 32 minority (20 Black or African American, non-Hispanic/Latino; 9 Asian, non-Hispanic/Latino; 2 Hispanic/Latino; 1 Two or more races, non-Hispanic/Latino), 90 international. Average age 30. 409 applicants, 62% accepted, 86 enrolled. In 2018, 156 master's, 5 doctorates awarded. *Entrance requirements:* For master's, GRE or GMAT, transcripts from all institutions attended, resume, essays; for doctorate, GRE or GMAT, three letters of recommendation, personal statement, transcripts from all institutions attended, resume. Additional exam requirements/recommendations for international students: Required—TOEFL (minimum score 610 paper-based; 101 iBT), IELTS (minimum score 7). *Application deadline:* For fall admission, 5/1 priority date for domestic students, 2/1 priority date for international students; for spring admission, 9/15 priority date for domestic students, 4/1 priority date for international students. Applications are processed on a rolling basis. Application fee: $50. Electronic applications accepted. *Expenses: Tuition, area resident:* Full-time $9360; part-time $390 per credit hour. Tuition, state resident: full-time $9360; part-time $390 per credit hour. Tuition, nonresident: full-time $30,024; part-time $1251 per credit hour. *International tuition:* $30,024 full-time. *Required fees:* $2128. *Financial support:* Research assistantships, teaching assistantships, scholarships/grants, tuition waivers, and unspecified assistantships available. Financial award applicants required to submit FAFSA. *Faculty research:* Process and technological innovation, strategic IT management, intelligent systems, information systems security, software project risk. *Unit head:* Dr. Ephraim R. McLean, Professor/Chair, 404-413-7360, Fax: 404-413-7394. *Application contact:* Toby McChesney, Assistant Dean for Graduate Recruiting and Student Services, 404-413-7167, Fax: 404-413-7167, E-mail: rcbgradadmissions@gsu.edu.
Website: http://cis.robinson.gsu.edu/

Grand Valley State University, Padnos College of Engineering and Computing, School of Computing and Information Systems, Allendale, MI 49401-9403. Offers computer information systems (MS), including databases, distributed systems, management of information systems, object-oriented systems, software engineering. *Program availability:* Part-time, evening/weekend. *Faculty:* 10 full-time (0 women). *Students:* 26 full-time (10 women), 53 part-time (7 women); includes 10 minority (2 Black or African American, non-Hispanic/Latino; 6 Asian, non-Hispanic/Latino; 1 Hispanic/Latino; 1 Two or more races, non-Hispanic/Latino), 21 international. Average age 29. 56 applicants, 70% accepted, 15 enrolled. In 2018, 23 master's awarded. *Entrance requirements:* For master's, GRE (recommended with GPA below 3.0), minimum GPA of 3.0; knowledge of a programming language; coursework or experience in: computer architecture and/or organization, data structures and algorithms, databases, discrete math, networking, operating systems, and software engineering; minimum of 2 letters of recommendation; resume; personal statement. Additional exam requirements/recommendations for international students: Required—Michigan English Language Assessment Battery (minimum score 77), TOEFL (minimum iBT score of 80), or IELTS (6.5); GRE. *Application deadline:* For fall admission, 6/1 for international students; for winter admission, 9/1 for international students. Applications are processed on a rolling basis. Application fee: $30. Electronic applications accepted. *Expenses:* $712 per credit hour, 33 credit hours. *Financial support:* In 2018–19, 13 students received support, including 6 fellowships, 5 research assistantships with full and partial tuition reimbursements available (averaging $8,000 per year). *Faculty research:* Object technology, distributed computing, information systems management database, software engineering. *Unit head:* Dr. Paul Leidig, Director, 616-331-2060, Fax: 616-331-2144, E-mail: leidigp@gvsu.edu. *Application contact:* Dr. D. Robert Adams, Graduate Program Director, 616-331-3885, Fax: 616-331-2144, E-mail: adamsr@gvsu.edu.
Website: http://www.cis.gvsu.edu/

Hardin-Simmons University, Graduate School, Kelley College of Business, Abilene, TX 79698-0001. Offers business administration (MBA); information science (MS); sports management (MBA). *Accreditation:* ACBSP. *Program availability:* Part-time. *Faculty:* 10 full-time (3 women). *Students:* 32 full-time (6 women), 55 part-time (23 women); includes 16 minority (5 Black or African American, non-Hispanic/Latino; 11 Hispanic/Latino), 2 international. Average age 29. 48 applicants, 96% accepted, 41 enrolled. In 2018, 27 master's awarded. *Degree requirements:* For master's, thesis or alternative. *Entrance requirements:* For master's, GMAT, minimum GPA of 3.0 in upper-level course work, resume, interview. Additional exam requirements/recommendations for international students: Required—TOEFL (minimum score 550 paper-based; 79 iBT). *Application deadline:* For fall admission, 8/15 priority date for domestic students, 4/1 for international students; for spring admission, 1/5 priority date for domestic students, 9/1 for international students. Applications are processed on a rolling basis. Application fee: $50. Electronic applications accepted. *Expenses: Tuition:* Full-time $750; part-time $750 per credit hour. *Required fees:* $1300; $880 per credit. Tuition and fees vary according to degree level and program. *Financial support:* Fellowships and scholarships/grants available. Support available to part-time students. Financial award application deadline: 6/30; financial award applicants required to submit FAFSA. *Unit head:* Dr. Jennifer Plantier, Program Director, 325-671-2166, Fax: 325-670-1523, E-mail: jplantier@hsutx.edu. *Application contact:* Dr. Nancy Kucinski, Dean of Graduate Studies, 325-670-1298, Fax: 325-670-1564, E-mail: gradoff@hsutx.edu.
Website: http://www.hsutx.edu/academics/kelley/graduate/

Harvard University, Extension School, Cambridge, MA 02138-3722. Offers applied sciences (CAS); biotechnology (ALM); educational technologies (ALM); educational technology (CET); English for graduate and professional studies (DGP); environmental management (ALM, CEM); information technology (ALM); journalism (ALM); liberal arts (ALM); management (ALM, CM); mathematics for teaching (ALM); museum studies

(ALM); premedical studies (Diploma); publication and communication (CPC). *Program availability:* Part-time, evening/weekend. *Degree requirements:* For master's, thesis. *Entrance requirements:* For master's, 3 completed graduate courses with grade of B or higher. Additional exam requirements/recommendations for international students: Required—TOEFL (minimum score 600 paper-based), TWE (minimum score 5). *Expenses:* Contact institution.

Harvard University, Graduate School of Arts and Sciences, Program in Information, Technology and Management, Cambridge, MA 02138. Offers PhD.

Hood College, Graduate School, Program in Management Information Systems, Frederick, MD 21701-8575. Offers MS. *Program availability:* Part-time, evening/weekend. *Students:* 21 full-time (8 women), 7 part-time (1 woman); includes 1 minority (Black or African American, non-Hispanic/Latino), 26 international. Average age 30. 16 applicants, 100% accepted, 7 enrolled. In 2018, 11 master's awarded. *Entrance requirements:* For master's, minimum GPA of 2.75, essay, resume. Additional exam requirements/recommendations for international students: Required—TOEFL (minimum score 575 paper-based; 89 iBT), IELTS (minimum score 6.5). *Application deadline:* For fall admission, 8/15 priority date for domestic students, 8/5 for international students; for spring admission, 12/1 priority date for domestic students, 12/1 for international students; for summer admission, 5/1 priority date for domestic students, 4/15 for international students. Applications are processed on a rolling basis. Application fee: $50 ($100 for international students). Electronic applications accepted. *Expenses:* Science Programs: Tuition $535 per credit hour, Comprehensive Fee $115 per semester. *Financial support:* Tuition waivers (partial) and unspecified assistantships available. Financial award applicants required to submit FAFSA. *Faculty research:* Systems engineering, parallel distributed computing, strategy, business ethics, entrepreneurship. *Unit head:* Dr. April M. Boulton, Dean of the Graduate School, 301-696-3600, E-mail: gofurther@hood.edu. *Application contact:* Larbi Bricha, Assistant Director of Graduate Admissions, 301-696-3601, E-mail: gofurther@hood.edu.
Website: http://www.hood.edu/graduate

Hood College, Graduate School, Programs in Computer and Information Sciences, Frederick, MD 21701-8575. Offers computer science (MS); cybersecurity (MS, Certificate); information technology (MS). *Program availability:* Part-time, evening/weekend, 100% online. *Faculty:* 8 full-time (2 women), 2 part-time/adjunct (0 women). *Students:* 48 full-time (15 women), 64 part-time (17 women); includes 15 minority (7 Black or African American, non-Hispanic/Latino; 2 Asian, non-Hispanic/Latino; 4 Hispanic/Latino; 2 Two or more races, non-Hispanic/Latino), 54 international. Average age 33. 55 applicants, 100% accepted, 26 enrolled. In 2018, 47 master's, 26 other advanced degrees awarded. *Degree requirements:* For master's, thesis optional, capstone (S). *Entrance requirements:* For master's, minimum GPA of 2.75, essay, resume. Additional exam requirements/recommendations for international students: Required—TOEFL (minimum score 575 paper-based; 89 iBT), IELTS (minimum score 6.5). *Application deadline:* For fall admission, 8/15 priority date for domestic students, 8/5 for international students; for spring admission, 12/1 priority date for domestic students, 12/1 for international students; for summer admission, 5/1 for domestic students, 4/15 for international students. Applications are processed on a rolling basis. Application fee: $50 ($100 for international students). Electronic applications accepted. *Expenses:* Science Programs: Tuition $535 per credit hour, Comprehensive Fee $115 per semester. *Financial support:* Tuition waivers (partial) and unspecified assistantships available. Financial award applicants required to submit FAFSA. *Faculty research:* Systems engineering, natural language, processing, database design, artificial intelligence and parallel distributed computing. *Unit head:* Dr. April M. Boulton, Dean of the Graduate School, 301-696-3600, E-mail: gofurther@hood.edu. *Application contact:* Larbi Bricha, Assistant Director of Graduate Admissions, 301-696-3601, E-mail: gofurther@hood.edu.
Website: https://www.hood.edu/graduate

Indiana University Bloomington, School of Informatics, Computing, and Engineering, Department of Information and Library Science, Bloomington, IN 47405-3907. Offers information architecture (Graduate Certificate); information science (MIS, PhD); library and information science (Sp LIS); library science (MLS); JD/MLS; MIS/MA; MLS/MA; MPA/MIS; MPA/MLS. *Accreditation:* ALA (one or more programs are accredited). *Program availability:* Part-time. Terminal master's awarded for partial completion of doctoral program. *Degree requirements:* For master's, internship; for doctorate, comprehensive exam, thesis/dissertation. *Entrance requirements:* For master's, GRE General Test (for applicants whose previous undergraduate degree GPA was below 3.0 or previous graduate degree GPA was below 3.2), 3 letters of reference, resume, personal statement (500 words minimum), transcripts; for doctorate, GRE General Test, resume, personal statement (800-1000 words), writing sample, transcripts, 3 letters of reference. Additional exam requirements/recommendations for international students: Required—TOEFL (minimum score 600 paper-based; 100 iBT), IELTS. Electronic applications accepted. *Expenses:* Contact institution. *Faculty research:* Scholarly communication, interface design, library and management policy, computer-mediated communication, information retrieval, documentation, web analysis, e-business, information architecture, social informatics, virtual groups and online communities, online deviant behaviors, knowledge sharing, indexing, philosophy of information, information policy, resource management, research methods digital humanities, digital libraries, semantic web, digital preservation, natural language processing.

Indiana University Bloomington, School of Informatics, Computing, and Engineering, Program in Informatics, Bloomington, IN 47405. Offers informatics (MS, PhD), including bioinformatics (PhD), complex systems (PhD), computing, culture and society (PhD), health informatics (PhD), human-computer interaction (MS), human-computer interaction design (PhD), music informatics (PhD), security informatics (PhD); visual heritage (PhD). *Program availability:* Part-time. Terminal master's awarded for partial completion of doctoral program. *Degree requirements:* For master's, thesis, capstone project; for doctorate, variable foreign language requirement, comprehensive exam, thesis/dissertation. *Entrance requirements:* For master's and doctorate, GRE, resume/curriculum vitae, transcripts, 3 letters of recommendation. Additional exam requirements/recommendations for international students: Required—TOEFL (minimum score 600 paper-based; 100 iBT). Electronic applications accepted. *Faculty research:* Algorithms, applied logic and computational theory, artificial intelligence, bioinformatics, case-based reasoning, chemical informatics, citation analysis, cognitive science, community informatics, compilers, complex networks and systems, computer optimization, computer-supported cooperative work, computer vision, cyberinfrastructure and e-science, database theory and systems, data mining, digital design and preservation, design pedagogy, digital humanities, digital learning environments.

Indiana University–Purdue University Indianapolis, School of Informatics and Computing, Department of Library and Information Science, Indianapolis, IN 46202. Offers MLS. *Accreditation:* ALA. *Program availability:* Part-time, evening/weekend, 100% online. *Entrance requirements:* For master's, GRE General Test. Additional exam requirements/recommendations for international students: Required—TOEFL (minimum score 600 paper-based).

Instituto Tecnologico de Santo Domingo, Graduate School, Area of Engineering, Santo Domingo, Dominican Republic. Offers construction administration (MS, Certificate); data telecommunications (M Eng, MS, Certificate); industrial engineering (M Eng, Certificate); industrial management (M Mgmt); information technology (Certificate); maintenance engineering (M Eng); occupational hazard prevention (M Mgmt); production management (Certificate); quantitative methods (Certificate); sanitary and environmental engineering (M Eng); structural engineering (M Eng); systems engineering and electronic data processing (Certificate); transportation (Certificate).

Instituto Tecnológico y de Estudios Superiores de Monterrey, Campus Cuernavaca, Programs in Information Science, Temixco, Mexico. Offers administration of information technology (MATI); computer science (MCC, DCC); information technology (MTI).

Instituto Tecnológico y de Estudios Superiores de Monterrey, Campus Estado de México, Professional and Graduate Division, Estado de Mexico, Mexico. Offers administration of information technologies (MITA); architecture (M Arch); business administration (GMBA, MBA); computer sciences (MCS, PhD); education (M Ed); educational institution administration (MAD); educational technology and innovation (PhD); electronic commerce (MEC); environmental systems (MS); finance (MAF); humanistic studies (MHS); information sciences and knowledge management (MISKM); information systems (MS); manufacturing systems (MS); marketing (MEM); quality systems and productivity (MS); science and materials engineering (PhD); telecommunications management (MTM). *Program availability:* Part-time, online learning. *Degree requirements:* For master's, one foreign language, thesis (for some programs); for doctorate, one foreign language, thesis/dissertation. *Entrance requirements:* For master's, E-PAEP 500, interview; for doctorate, E-PAEP 500, research proposal. Additional exam requirements/recommendations for international students: Required—TOEFL (minimum score 550 paper-based). *Faculty research:* Surface treatments by plasmas, mechanical properties, robotics, graphical computing, mechatronics security protocols.

Instituto Tecnológico y de Estudios Superiores de Monterrey, Campus Irapuato, Graduate Programs, Irapuato, Mexico. Offers administration (MBA); administration of information technology (MAIT); administration of telecommunications (MAT); architecture (M Arch); computer science (MCS); education (M Ed); educational administration (MEA); educational innovation and technology (DEIT); educational technology (MET); electronic commerce (MBA); environmental administration and planning (MEAP); environmental systems (MES); finances (MBA); humanistic studies (MHS); international management for Latin American executives (MIMLAE); library and information science (MLIS); manufacturing quality management (MMQM); marketing research (MBA).

Instituto Tecnológico y de Estudios Superiores de Monterrey, Campus Monterrey, Graduate and Research Division, Program in Computer Science, Monterrey, Mexico. Offers artificial intelligence (PhD); computer science (MS); information systems (MS); information technology (MS). *Program availability:* Part-time. *Degree requirements:* For master's, one foreign language, thesis; for doctorate, one foreign language, thesis/dissertation. *Entrance requirements:* For master's, EXADEP; for doctorate, master's degree in related field. Additional exam requirements/recommendations for international students: Required—TOEFL. *Faculty research:* Distributed systems, software engineering, decision support systems.

Instituto Tecnológico y de Estudios Superiores de Monterrey, Campus Monterrey, Graduate and Research Division, Program in Informatics, Monterrey, Mexico. Offers PhD. *Program availability:* Part-time. *Degree requirements:* For doctorate, one foreign language, thesis/dissertation, technological project, arbitrated publication of articles. *Entrance requirements:* For doctorate, GRE General Test, GRE Subject Test, master's degree in related field. Additional exam requirements/recommendations for international students: Required—TOEFL. *Faculty research:* Artificial intelligence, distributed systems, software engineering, decision support systems.

Instituto Tecnológico y de Estudios Superiores de Monterrey, Campus Sonora Norte, Program in Technological Information Management, Hermosillo, Mexico. Offers MA.

Iowa State University of Science and Technology, Program in Information Assurance, Ames, IA 50011. Offers M Eng, MS. *Degree requirements:* For master's, thesis or alternative. *Entrance requirements:* For master's, GRE General Test. Additional exam requirements/recommendations for international students: Required—TOEFL (minimum score 570 paper-based; 79 iBT), IELTS (minimum score 6.5). Electronic applications accepted.

Kennesaw State University, Coles College of Business, Program in Information Systems, Kennesaw, GA 30144. Offers MSIS. *Program availability:* Part-time. *Students:* 10 full-time (6 women), 21 part-time (10 women); includes 13 minority (9 Black or African American, non-Hispanic/Latino; 3 Asian, non-Hispanic/Latino; 1 Hispanic/Latino), 5 international. Average age 38. 31 applicants, 42% accepted, 7 enrolled. In 2018, 14 master's awarded. *Entrance requirements:* For master's, GMAT or GRE General Test, minimum GPA of 2.75. Additional exam requirements/recommendations for international students: Required—TOEFL (minimum score 80 iBT), IELTS (minimum score 6.5). *Application deadline:* For fall admission, 7/1 for domestic and international students; for spring admission, 11/1 for domestic and international students; for summer admission, 4/1 for domestic and international students. Applications are processed on a rolling basis. Application fee: $60. Electronic applications accepted. *Expenses: Tuition, area resident:* Full-time $6960; part-time $290 per credit hour. Tuition, state resident: full-time $6960; part-time $290 per credit hour. Tuition, nonresident: full-time $25,080; part-time $1045 per credit hour. *International tuition:* $25,080 full-time. *Required fees:* $2006; $1706 per semester. $853 per semester. *Financial support:* Research assistantships with full tuition reimbursements, Federal Work-Study, and unspecified assistantships available. Support available to part-time students. Financial award application deadline: 4/1; financial award applicants required to submit FAFSA. *Unit head:* Dr. Tridib Bandyopadhyay, Director, 470-578-2144, E-mail: tbandyop@kennesaw.edu. *Application contact:* Admissions Counselor, 470-578-4377, Fax: 770-578-9172, E-mail: ksugrad@kennesaw.edu.
Website: http://coles.kennesaw.edu/msis/

Kennesaw State University, College of Computing and Software Engineering, Program in Information Technology, Kennesaw, GA 30144. Offers data management and analytics (Graduate Certificate); health information technology (Postbaccalaureate Certificate); information technology (MSIT); information technology foundations (Postbaccalaureate Certificate); information technology security (Graduate Certificate). *Program availability:* Part-time, evening/weekend, blended/hybrid learning. *Students:* 100 full-time (45 women), 195 part-time (76 women); includes 137 minority (75 Black or African American, non-Hispanic/Latino; 42 Asian, non-Hispanic/Latino; 14 Hispanic/Latino; 1 Native Hawaiian or other Pacific Islander, non-Hispanic/Latino; 5 Two or more races, non-Hispanic/Latino), 40 international. Average age 34. 131 applicants, 81% accepted, 81 enrolled. In 2018, 70 master's awarded. *Degree requirements:* For master's, thesis optional. *Entrance requirements:* For master's, minimum GPA of 2.75; for other advanced degree, bachelor's degree. Additional exam requirements/recommendations for international students: Required—TOEFL (minimum score 80 iBT), IELTS (minimum score 6.5). *Application deadline:* For fall admission, 7/1 priority

date for domestic students, 5/1 priority date for international students; for spring admission, 11/1 priority date for domestic students, 9/1 priority date for international students; for summer admission, 4/1 priority date for domestic students, 3/1 priority date for international students. Applications are processed on a rolling basis. Application fee: $60. Electronic applications accepted. *Expenses: Tuition, area resident:* Full-time $6960; part-time $290 per credit hour. Tuition, state resident: full-time $6960; part-time $290 per credit hour. Tuition, nonresident: full-time $25,080; part-time $1045 per credit hour. *International tuition:* $25,080 full-time. *Required fees:* $2006; $1706 per semester. $853 per semester. *Financial support:* Research assistantships with full and partial tuition reimbursements, career-related internships or fieldwork, scholarships/grants, and unspecified assistantships available. Support available to part-time students. Financial award applicants required to submit FAFSA. *Application contact:* Admission Counselor, 470-578-4377, Fax: 470-578-9172, E-mail: ksugrad@kennesaw.edu.
Website: http://ccse.kennesaw.edu/it/

Kent State University, College of Communication and Information, School of Information, Kent, OH 44242-0001. Offers health informatics (MS), including health informatics, knowledge management, user experience design; library and information science (MLIS), including K-12 school library media; M Ed/MLIS; MBA/MLIS; MLIS/MS. *Accreditation:* ALA (one or more programs are accredited). *Program availability:* Part-time, 100% online. *Faculty:* 16 full-time (13 women), 10 part-time/adjunct (6 women). *Students:* 114 full-time (91 women), 235 part-time (162 women); includes 52 minority (24 Black or African American, non-Hispanic/Latino; 8 Asian, non-Hispanic/Latino; 15 Hispanic/Latino; 5 Two or more races, non-Hispanic/Latino), 4 international. Average age 32. 212 applicants, 99% accepted, 147 enrolled. In 2018, 308 master's awarded. *Degree requirements:* For master's, portfolio (MLIS); internship, project, paper, or thesis. *Entrance requirements:* For master's, GRE if total GPA is below 3.0 in highest completed degree, minimum GPA of 3.0, statement of purpose, 3 letters of recommendation, curriculum vitae/resume, transcripts, writing sample, personal interview. Additional exam requirements/ recommendations for international students: Required—TOEFL (minimum score 587 paper-based, 94 iBT), Michigan English Language Assessment Battery (minimum score 82), IELTS (minimum score 7.0) or PTE (minimum score 65). *Application deadline:* For fall admission, 3/15 priority date for domestic students, 3/15 for international students; for spring admission, 9/15 priority date for domestic students, 9/15 for international students; for summer admission, 1/15 priority date for domestic students, 1/15 for international students. Applications are processed on a rolling basis. Application fee: $45 ($70 for international students). Electronic applications accepted. *Expenses:* Tuition, state resident: full-time $11,766; part-time $536 per credit. Tuition, nonresident: full-time $21,952; part-time $999 per credit. *International tuition:* $21,952 full-time. Tuition and fees vary according to course load. *Financial support:* Fellowships with full tuition reimbursements, research assistantships with full tuition reimbursements, teaching assistantships with full tuition reimbursements, scholarships/grants, and unspecified assistantships available. Financial award application deadline: 3/1. *Unit head:* Dr. Kendra Albright, Director and Professor, 330-672-8535, E-mail: kalbrig7@kent.edu. *Application contact:* Dr. Karen Gracy, Graduate Co-Coordinator/Associate Professor, 330-672-2782, E-mail: kgracy@kent.edu.
Website: https://www.kent.edu/iSchool

Lawrence Technological University, College of Management, Southfield, MI 48075-1058. Offers business administration (MBA, DBA), including business analytics (MBA, MS), cybersecurity (MBA, MS), finance (MBA), information systems (MBA), information technology (MBA), marketing (MBA), project management (MBA, MS); cybersecurity (Graduate Certificate); health IT management (Graduate Certificate); information assurance management (Graduate Certificate); information systems (MS), including enterprise resource planning, enterprise security management, project management (MBA, MS); information technology (MS, DM), including business analytics (MBA, MS), cybersecurity (MBA, MS), information assurance (MS), project management (MBA, MS); management (PhD); nonprofit management and leadership (Graduate Certificate); operations management (MS), including manufacturing operations, service operations; project management (Graduate Certificate). *Accreditation:* ACBSP. *Program availability:* Part-time, evening/weekend, 100% online. Terminal master's awarded for partial completion of doctoral program. *Degree requirements:* For master's, thesis (for some programs); for doctorate, comprehensive exam, thesis/dissertation. *Entrance requirements:* Additional exam requirements/recommendations for international students: Required—TOEFL (minimum score 550 paper-based; 79 iBT), IELTS (minimum score 6.5). Electronic applications accepted. *Faculty research:* Cybersecurity; risk management; IT governance; security controls and countermeasures; threat modeling cyber resilience; autonomous cars; natural language processing; text mining; machine learning; reflective leadership; emerging leadership theories and practice; motivational studies; teaching effectiveness strategies; teamwork; organization development; strategic planning; strengths-based and positive organizational scholarship; global leadership; globalization; corporate governance.

Lehigh University, College of Business, Department of Accounting, Bethlehem, PA 18015. Offers accounting and information analysis (MS). *Accreditation:* AACSB. *Program availability:* Part-time. *Faculty:* 6 full-time (0 women), 1 (woman) part-time/ adjunct. *Students:* 30 full-time (25 women), 1 part-time (0 women); includes 2 minority (both Asian, non-Hispanic/Latino), 24 international. Average age 24. 68 applicants, 65% accepted, 13 enrolled. In 2018, 24 master's awarded. *Entrance requirements:* For master's, GMAT. Additional exam requirements/recommendations for international students: Required—TOEFL (minimum score 105 iBT). *Application deadline:* For fall admission, 4/15 for domestic and international students. Application fee: $75. *Expenses:* $1280 per credit hour; 30 credits required for degree. *Financial support:* In 2018–19, 19 students received support. Fellowships and scholarships/grants available. Financial award application deadline: 1/15. *Faculty research:* Behavioral accounting, internal control, information systems, supply chain management, financial accounting. *Unit head:* Dr. C. Bryan Cloyd, Chairman, 610-758-2816, Fax: 610-758-6429, E-mail: cbc215@lehigh.edu. *Application contact:* Mary Theresa Taglang, Director of Recruitment and Admissions, 610-758-4386, Fax: 610-758-5283, E-mail: mtt4@ lehigh.edu.
Website: https://cbe.lehigh.edu/academics/graduate/master-accounting-and-information-analysis

Loyola University Chicago, Graduate School, Department of Computer Science, Chicago, IL 60660. Offers computer science (MS); information technology (MS); software engineering (MS). *Program availability:* Part-time, evening/weekend, 100% online, blended/hybrid learning. *Faculty:* 16 full-time (3 women), 16 part-time/adjunct (2 women). *Students:* 45 full-time (13 women), 40 part-time (11 women); includes 23 minority (7 Black or African American, non-Hispanic/Latino; 15 Asian, non-Hispanic/ Latino; 1 Hispanic/Latino), 29 international. Average age 29. 116 applicants, 53% accepted, 29 enrolled. In 2018, 48 master's awarded. *Degree requirements:* For master's, thesis optional, 30 credits/ten courses. *Entrance requirements:* For master's, 2 letters of recommendation, transcripts, statement of purpose. Additional exam requirements/recommendations for international students: Required—TOEFL (minimum score 550 paper-based; 79 iBT), IELTS (minimum score 6.5). *Application deadline:* Applications are processed on a rolling basis. Application fee: $50. Electronic applications accepted. Application fee is waived when completed online. *Expenses:* Contact institution. *Financial support:* In 2018–19, 17 students received support, including 2 fellowships with full tuition reimbursements available, 1 research assistantship with full tuition reimbursement available (averaging $17,000 per year), 11 teaching assistantships with partial tuition reimbursements available (averaging $9,575 per year); career-related internships or fieldwork, Federal Work-Study, health care benefits, and tuition waivers (full and partial) also available. Financial award application deadline: 3/15. *Faculty research:* Software engineering, machine learning, algorithms and complexity, parallel and distributed computing, databases and computer networks, security. *Total annual research expenditures:* $22,000. *Unit head:* Dr. Chandra Sekharan, Chair, 773-508-3572, Fax: 773-508-3739, E-mail: laufer@cs.luc.edu. *Application contact:* Cecilia Murphy, Graduate Program Secretary, 773-508-8035, E-mail: cmurphy@luc.edu.
Website: http://luc.edu/cs

Marshall University, Academic Affairs Division, College of Information Technology and Engineering, Program in Information Systems, Huntington, WV 25755. Offers MS. *Program availability:* Part-time, evening/weekend. *Degree requirements:* For master's, final project, oral exam. *Entrance requirements:* For master's, GRE General Test or MAT, minimum undergraduate GPA of 2.5.

Maryville University of Saint Louis, The John E. Simon School of Business, St. Louis, MO 63141-7299. Offers accounting (MBA, MS, Certificate); business studies (Certificate); cybersecurity (MBA, MS, Certificate); financial services (MBA, Certificate); health administration (MBA); healthcare administration (Certificate); human resource management (MBA); human resources management (Certificate); information technology (MBA); information technology management (Certificate); management (MBA, Certificate); management and leadership (MA); marketing (MBA, Certificate); project management (MBA, Certificate); sport business management (MBA); supply chain management (Certificate); supply chain management/logistics (MBA). *Accreditation:* ACBSP. *Program availability:* Part-time, 100% online, blended/hybrid learning. *Faculty:* 5 full-time (1 woman), 77 part-time/adjunct (19 women). *Students:* 338 full-time (166 women), 739 part-time (356 women); includes 310 minority (161 Black or African American, non-Hispanic/Latino; 6 American Indian or Alaska Native, non-Hispanic/Latino; 59 Asian, non-Hispanic/Latino; 57 Hispanic/Latino; 27 Two or more races, non-Hispanic/Latino), 30 international. Average age 33. In 2018, 143 master's awarded. *Degree requirements:* For master's, capstone course (for MBA). *Entrance requirements:* Additional exam requirements/recommendations for international students: Required—TOEFL (minimum score 563 paper-based; 85 iBT). *Application deadline:* Applications are processed on a rolling basis. Electronic applications accepted. *Expenses:* Tuition varies by program. *Financial support:* Career-related internships or fieldwork, Federal Work-Study, tuition waivers (partial), and campus employment available. Financial award application deadline: 4/1; financial award applicants required to submit FAFSA. *Unit head:* Tammy Gocial, Interim Dean, 314-529-9401, Fax: 314-529-9975, E-mail: tgocial@maryville.edu. *Application contact:* Chris Gourdine, Assistant Dean Business Administration, 314-529-6861, Fax: 314-529-9975, E-mail: cgourdine@maryville.edu.
Website: http://www.maryville.edu/bu/business-administration-masters/

Massachusetts Institute of Technology, School of Engineering, Department of Civil and Environmental Engineering, Cambridge, MA 02139. Offers biological oceanography (PhD, Sc D); chemical oceanography (PhD, Sc D); civil and environmental engineering (M Eng, SM, PhD, Sc D); civil and environmental systems (PhD, Sc D); civil engineering (PhD, Sc D, CE); civil engineering and computation (PhD); coastal engineering (PhD, Sc D); construction engineering and management (PhD, Sc D); environmental biology (PhD, Sc D); environmental chemistry (PhD, Sc D); environmental engineering (PhD, Sc D); environmental engineering and computation (PhD); environmental fluid mechanics (PhD, Sc D); geotechnical and geoenvironmental engineering (PhD, Sc D); hydrology (PhD, Sc D); information technology (PhD, Sc D); oceanographic engineering (PhD, Sc D); structures and materials (PhD, Sc D); transportation (PhD, Sc D); SM/ MBA. *Degree requirements:* For master's, thesis; for doctorate, comprehensive exam, thesis/dissertation; for CE, comprehensive exam, thesis. *Entrance requirements:* For master's, doctorate, and CE, GRE General Test. Additional exam requirements/ recommendations for international students: Required—TOEFL, IELTS. Electronic applications accepted. *Expenses: Tuition:* Full-time $51,520; part-time $800 per credit hour. *Required fees:* $312. *Faculty research:* Environmental chemistry, environmental fluid mechanics and coastal engineering, environmental microbiology, geotechnical engineering and geomechanics, hydrology and hydro climatology, infrastructure systems, mechanics of materials and structures, transportation systems.

Minnesota State University Mankato, College of Graduate Studies and Research, College of Science, Engineering and Technology, Department of Computer Information Science, Mankato, MN 56001. Offers information technology (MS). *Degree requirements:* For master's, comprehensive exam, thesis or alternative. *Entrance requirements:* For master's, GRE General Test, minimum GPA of 3.0 during previous 2 years. Additional exam requirements/recommendations for international students: Required—TOEFL (minimum score 550 paper-based; 80 iBT). Electronic applications accepted.

Missouri University of Science and Technology, Department of Business and Information Technology, Rolla, MO 65401. Offers business administration (MBA); information science and technology (MS). *Degree requirements:* For master's, thesis or alternative. *Entrance requirements:* Additional exam requirements/recommendations for international students: Required—TOEFL (minimum score 600 paper-based); Recommended—IELTS. Electronic applications accepted. *Expenses:* Tuition, state resident: full-time $7545.60; part-time $419.20 per credit hour. Tuition, nonresident: full-time $22,169; part-time $1231.60 per credit hour. *International tuition:* $23,518.80 full-time. *Required fees:* $4523.05. Full-time tuition and fees vary according to course load, campus/location, program and reciprocity agreements.

Monroe College, King Graduate School, Bronx, NY 10468. Offers accounting (MS); business administration (MBA), including entrepreneurship, finance, general business administration, healthcare management, human resources, information technology, marketing; computer science (MS); criminal justice (MS); hospitality management (MS); public health (MPH), including biostatistics and epidemiology, community health, health administration and leadership. *Program availability:* Online learning.

Naval Postgraduate School, Departments and Academic Groups, Department of Information Sciences, Monterey, CA 93943. Offers electronic warfare systems engineering (MS); information sciences (PhD); information systems and operations (MS); information technology management (MS); information warfare systems engineering (MS); knowledge superiority (Certificate); remote sensing intelligence (MS); system technology (command, control and communications) (MS). Program open only to commissioned officers of the United States and friendly nations and selected United States federal civilian employees. *Program availability:* Part-time. *Degree requirements:* For master's, thesis (for some programs); for doctorate, thesis/dissertation. *Faculty research:* Designing inter-organisational collectivities for dynamic fit: stability, manoeuvrability and application in disaster relief endeavours; system self-awareness and related methods for Improving the use and understanding of data within DoD; evaluating a macrocognition model of team collaboration using real-world data from the Haiti relief effort; cyber distortion in command and control; performance and QoS in service-based systems.

Information Science

New Jersey Institute of Technology, Ying Wu College of Computing, Newark, NJ 07102. Offers big data management and mining (Certificate); business and information systems (Certificate); computer science (PhD); computing and business (MS); data mining (Certificate); data science (MS); information security (Certificate); information systems (PhD); information technology administration and security (MS); IT administration (Certificate); network security and information assurance (Certificate); software engineering (MS), including information systems; software engineering analysis/design (Certificate); Web systems development (Certificate). *Program availability:* Part-time, evening/weekend. *Faculty:* 69 full-time (13 women), 38 part-time/adjunct (4 women). *Students:* 699 full-time (229 women), 269 part-time (67 women); includes 260 minority (44 Black or African American, non-Hispanic/Latino; 145 Asian, non-Hispanic/Latino; 59 Hispanic/Latino; 12 Two or more races, non-Hispanic/Latino), 614 international. Average age 26. 2,216 applicants, 55% accepted, 366 enrolled. In 2018, 418 master's, 5 doctorates, 13 other advanced degrees awarded. Terminal master's awarded for partial completion of doctoral program. *Degree requirements:* For master's, thesis optional; for doctorate, thesis/dissertation. *Entrance requirements:* For master's, GRE General Test; for doctorate, GRE General Test, minimum graduate GPA of 3.5. Additional exam requirements/recommendations for international students: Required—TOEFL (minimum score 550 paper-based; 79 iBT), IELTS (minimum score 6.5). *Application deadline:* For fall admission, 6/1 priority date for domestic students, 5/1 priority date for international students; for spring admission, 11/15 priority date for domestic and international students. Applications are processed on a rolling basis. Application fee: $75. Electronic applications accepted. *Expenses:* $22,690 per year (in-state), $32,136 per year (out-of-state). *Financial support:* In 2018–19, 366 students received support, including 10 fellowships with full tuition reimbursements available (averaging $22,000 per year), 47 research assistantships with full tuition reimbursements available (averaging $22,000 per year), 28 teaching assistantships with full tuition reimbursements available (averaging $22,000 per year); career-related internships or fieldwork, Federal Work-Study, scholarships/grants, and unspecified assistantships also available. Financial award application deadline: 1/15. *Faculty research:* Computer systems, communications and networking, artificial intelligence, database engineering, systems analysis, analytics and optimization in crowdsourcing. *Total annual research expenditures:* $4.9 million. *Unit head:* Dr. Craig Gotsman, Dean, 973-596-3366, Fax: 973-596-5777, E-mail: craig.gotsman@njit.edu. *Application contact:* Stephen Eck, Director of Admissions, 973-596-3300, Fax: 973-596-3461, E-mail: admissions@njit.edu.
Website: http://computing.njit.edu/

Northern Kentucky University, Office of Graduate Programs, College of Informatics, Department of Business Informatics, Highland Heights, KY 41099. Offers business informatics (MS, Certificate); corporate information security (Certificate); enterprise resource planning (Certificate). *Program availability:* Part-time, evening/weekend. *Entrance requirements:* For master's, GRE or GMAT. Additional exam requirements/recommendations for international students: Required—TOEFL (minimum score 79 iBT); Recommended—IELTS (minimum score 6.5). Electronic applications accepted. *Faculty research:* Data analytics, cloud computing, healthcare informatics, information systems security.

Northwestern University, McCormick School of Engineering and Applied Science, Department of Electrical Engineering and Computer Science, MS in Information Technology Program, Evanston, IL 60208. Offers MS. *Program availability:* Part-time, evening/weekend. *Entrance requirements:* For master's, GRE (recommended), work experience in an IT-related position. Additional exam requirements/recommendations for international students: Required—TOEFL (minimum score 80 iBT), IELTS (minimum score 7). Electronic applications accepted.

Northwestern University, School of Professional Studies, Program in Information Design and Strategy, Evanston, IL 60208. Offers MS.

Nova Southeastern University, College of Engineering and Computing, Fort Lauderdale, FL 33314-7796. Offers computer science (MS, PhD); information assurance (PhD); information assurance and cybersecurity (MS); information systems (PhD); information technology (MS); management information systems (MS). *Program availability:* Part-time, evening/weekend, blended/hybrid learning. Terminal master's awarded for partial completion of doctoral program. *Degree requirements:* For master's, thesis optional; for doctorate, thesis/dissertation. *Entrance requirements:* For master's, minimum undergraduate GPA of 2.5; for doctorate, master's degree, minimum graduate GPA of 3.25. Additional exam requirements/recommendations for international students: Required—TOEFL (minimum score 80 iBT), IELTS (minimum score 6), PTE (minimum score 54). Electronic applications accepted. *Expenses:* Contact institution. *Faculty research:* Artificial intelligence, database management, human-computer interaction, business intelligence and data analytics, information assurance and cybersecurity.

Oklahoma State University, Spears School of Business, Department of Management Science and Information Systems, Stillwater, OK 74078. Offers management information systems (MS); management science and information systems (PhD); telecommunications management (MS). *Program availability:* Part-time, online learning. *Faculty:* 15 full-time (1 woman), 6 part-time/adjunct (3 women). *Students:* 57 full-time (18 women), 76 part-time (16 women); includes 15 minority (3 Black or African American, non-Hispanic/Latino; 3 American Indian or Alaska Native, non-Hispanic/Latino; 3 Asian, non-Hispanic/Latino; 2 Hispanic/Latino; 1 Native Hawaiian or other Pacific Islander, non-Hispanic/Latino; 3 Two or more races, non-Hispanic/Latino), 73 international. Average age 29. 391 applicants, 27% accepted, 65 enrolled. In 2018, 50 master's awarded. *Entrance requirements:* For master's and doctorate, GRE or GMAT. Additional exam requirements/recommendations for international students: Required—TOEFL (minimum score 550 paper-based; 79 iBT). *Application deadline:* For fall admission, 3/1 priority date for international students; for spring admission, 8/1 priority date for international students. Applications are processed on a rolling basis. Application fee: $40 ($75 for international students). Electronic applications accepted. *Expenses: Tuition, area resident:* Full-time $4148. Tuition, state resident: full-time $4148. Tuition, nonresident: full-time $10,517. *International tuition:* $10,517 full-time. *Required fees:* $4394; $2929 per credit hour. Tuition and fees vary according to course load and program. *Financial support:* Research assistantships, teaching assistantships, career-related internships or fieldwork, Federal Work-Study, scholarships/grants, health care benefits, tuition waivers (partial), and unspecified assistantships available. Support available to part-time students. Financial award application deadline: 3/1; financial award applicants required to submit FAFSA. *Unit head:* Dr. Rick Wilson, Department Head, 405-744-3551, Fax: 405-744-5180, E-mail: rick.wilson@okstate.edu. *Application contact:* Dr. Rathin Sarathy, Graduate Coordinator, 405-744-8646, Fax: 405-744-5180, E-mail: rathin.sarathy@okstate.edu.
Website: https://business.okstate.edu/msis/

Old Dominion University, Strome College of Business, Doctoral Program in Business Administration, Norfolk, VA 23529. Offers business administration (PhD), including finance, IT and supply chain management, marketing, strategic management. *Accreditation:* AACSB. *Degree requirements:* For doctorate, comprehensive exam, thesis/dissertation. *Entrance requirements:* For doctorate, GMAT or GRE. Additional exam requirements/recommendations for international students: Required—TOEFL (minimum score 550 paper-based; 79 iBT). Electronic applications accepted. *Faculty research:* International business, buyer behavior, financial markets, strategy, operations research.

Pace University, Seidenberg School of Computer Science and Information Systems, New York, NY 10038. Offers chief information security officer (APC); computer science (MS, PhD); enterprise analytics (MS); information and communication technology strategy and innovation (APC); information systems (MS, APC); information technology (MS); professional studies in computing (DPS); secure software and information engineering (APC); security and information assurance (Certificate); software development and engineering (MS, Certificate); telecommunications systems and networks (MS, Certificate). *Program availability:* Part-time, evening/weekend, online only, 100% online, blended/hybrid learning. *Faculty:* 26 full-time (7 women), 7 part-time/adjunct (2 women). *Students:* 515 full-time (172 women), 288 part-time (90 women); includes 183 minority (67 Black or African American, non-Hispanic/Latino; 3 American Indian or Alaska Native, non-Hispanic/Latino; 50 Asian, non-Hispanic/Latino; 52 Hispanic/Latino; 1 Native Hawaiian or other Pacific Islander, non-Hispanic/Latino; 10 Two or more races, non-Hispanic/Latino), 497 international. Average age 30. 817 applicants, 93% accepted, 235 enrolled. In 2018, 383 master's, 15 doctorates, 1 other advanced degree awarded. *Degree requirements:* For master's, thesis or alternative, capstone course; for doctorate, comprehensive exam (for some programs), thesis/dissertation. *Entrance requirements:* Additional exam requirements/recommendations for international students: Required—TOEFL (minimum score 78 iBT), IELTS (minimum score 6.5) or PTE (minimum score 52). *Application deadline:* For fall admission, 8/1 priority date for domestic students, 6/1 for international students; for spring admission, 12/1 for domestic students, 10/1 for international students. Applications are processed on a rolling basis. Application fee: $70. Electronic applications accepted. *Expenses:* Contact institution. *Financial support:* In 2018–19, 45 students received support. Research assistantships, career-related internships or fieldwork, scholarships/grants, and unspecified assistantships available. Support available to part-time students. Financial award application deadline: 2/15; financial award applicants required to submit FAFSA. *Faculty research:* Cyber security/digital forensics; mobile app development; big data/enterprise analytics; artificial intelligence; software development. *Total annual research expenditures:* $584,594. *Unit head:* Dr. Jonathan Hill, Dean, Seidenberg School of Computer Science and Information Systems, 212-346-1864, E-mail: jhill@pace.edu. *Application contact:* Susan Ford-Goldschein, Director of Graduate Admissions, 914-422-4283, Fax: 212-346-1585, E-mail: graduateadmission@pace.edu.
Website: http://www.pace.edu/seidenberg

Penn State Great Valley, Graduate Studies, Management Division, Malvern, PA 19355-1488. Offers business administration (MBA); cyber security (Certificate); data analytics (MPS, MS, Certificate); distributed energy and grid modernization (Certificate); finance (M Fin); health sector management (Certificate); human resource management (Certificate); information science (MSIS); leadership development (MLD); new ventures and entrepreneurship (Certificate); sustainable management practices (Certificate). *Accreditation:* AACSB.

Penn State University Park, Graduate School, College of Information Sciences and Technology, University Park, PA 16802. Offers information sciences (MPS); information sciences and technology (MS, PhD). *Program availability:* Part-time, evening/weekend. *Entrance requirements:* Additional exam requirements/recommendations for international students: Required—TOEFL (minimum score 550 paper-based; 80 iBT), IELTS. Electronic applications accepted. *Expenses:* Contact institution.

Purdue University Fort Wayne, College of Engineering, Technology, and Computer Science, Program in Technology, Fort Wayne, IN 46805-1499. Offers facilities/construction management (MS); industrial technology/manufacturing (MS); information technology/advanced computer applications (MS). *Program availability:* Part-time. *Entrance requirements:* For master's, minimum GPA of 3.0. Additional exam requirements/recommendations for international students: Required—TOEFL (minimum score 550 paper-based; 79 iBT), TWE. Electronic applications accepted.

Regis University, College of Computer and Information Sciences, Denver, CO 80221-1099. Offers agile technologies (Certificate); cybersecurity (Certificate); data science (M Sc); database administration with Oracle (Certificate); database development (Certificate); database technologies (M Sc); enterprise Java software development (Certificate); enterprise resource planning (Certificate); executive information technology (Certificate); health care informatics (Certificate); health care informatics and information management (M Sc); information assurance (M Sc); information assurance policy management (Certificate); information technology management (M Sc); mobile software development (Certificate); software engineering (M Sc, Certificate); software engineering and database technology (M Sc); storage area networks (Certificate); systems engineering (M Sc, Certificate). *Program availability:* Part-time, evening/weekend, 100% online, blended/hybrid learning. *Degree requirements:* For master's, thesis (for some programs), final research project. *Entrance requirements:* For master's, official transcript reflecting baccalaureate degree awarded from regionally-accredited college or university, 2 years of related experience, resume, interview. Additional exam requirements/recommendations for international students: Required—TOEFL (minimum score 550 paper-based; 82 iBT). Electronic applications accepted. *Expenses:* Contact institution. *Faculty research:* Information policy, knowledge management, software architectures, data science.

Rensselaer at Hartford, Department of Computer and Information Science, Program in Information Technology, Hartford, CT 06120-2991. Offers MS. *Program availability:* Part-time, evening/weekend. *Entrance requirements:* For master's, GRE. Additional exam requirements/recommendations for international students: Required—TOEFL (minimum score 600 paper-based; 100 iBT). Electronic applications accepted.

Rensselaer Polytechnic Institute, Graduate School, School of Science, Program in Information Technology, Troy, NY 12180-3590. Offers MS. *Program availability:* Part-time. *Faculty:* 5 part-time/adjunct (2 women). *Students:* 45 full-time (17 women), 4 part-time (1 woman); includes 6 minority (3 Asian, non-Hispanic/Latino; 1 Hispanic/Latino; 2 Two or more races, non-Hispanic/Latino), 37 international. Average age 24. 131 applicants, 44% accepted, 20 enrolled. In 2018, 19 master's awarded. *Entrance requirements:* For master's, GRE, IT Background Evaluation Form. Additional exam requirements/recommendations for international students: Required—TOEFL (minimum score 570 paper-based; 88 iBT), IELTS (minimum score 6.5), PTE (minimum score 60). *Application deadline:* For fall admission, 1/1 priority date for domestic and international students; for spring admission, 8/15 priority date for domestic and international students. Applications are processed on a rolling basis. Application fee: $75. Electronic applications accepted. *Financial support:* In 2018–19, teaching assistantships with full tuition reimbursements (averaging $23,000 per year) were awarded. Financial award application deadline: 1/1. *Faculty research:* Database and intelligent systems, data science and analytics, financial engineering, human computer interaction, information dominance, information security, information systems engineering, management information systems, networking, software design and engineering, Web science. *Total annual research expenditures:* $32,893. *Unit head:* Dr. Peter Fox, Graduate Program Director, 518-276-4862, E-mail: pfox@cs.rpi.edu. *Application contact:* Jarron Decker, Director of Graduate Admissions, 518-276-6216, Fax: 518-276-4072, E-mail: gradadmissions@rpi.edu.
Website: https://science.rpi.edu/itws

Robert Morris University, School of Informatics, Humanities and Social Sciences, Moon Township, PA 15108-1189. Offers communication and information systems (MS);

cyber security (MS); data analytics (MS); information security and assurance (MS); information systems and communications (D Sc); information systems management (MS); information technology project management (MS); Internet information systems (MS); organizational leadership (MS). *Program availability:* Part-time-only, evening/weekend, 100% online. *Faculty:* 22 full-time (7 women), 10 part-time/adjunct (0 women). *Students:* 262 part-time (94 women); includes 57 minority (31 Black or African American, non-Hispanic/Latino; 13 Asian, non-Hispanic/Latino; 8 Hispanic/Latino; 5 Two or more races, non-Hispanic/Latino), 43 international. Average age 35. 150 applicants, 92% accepted, 79 enrolled. In 2018, 133 master's, 11 doctorates awarded. *Degree requirements:* For master's, Completion of 30 credits; for doctorate, thesis/dissertation, Completion of 63 credits. *Entrance requirements:* For doctorate, employer letter of endorsement, interview. Additional exam requirements/recommendations for international students: Required—TOEFL (minimum score 550 paper-based; 79 iBT). *Application deadline:* For fall admission, 7/1 priority date for domestic and international students; for spring admission, 11/1 priority date for domestic and international students. Applications are processed on a rolling basis. Application fee: $35. Electronic applications accepted. Application fee is waived when completed online. *Expenses:* Master's $920/credit plus $80/credit fees; D.Sc. $28,290/year. *Financial support:* Institutionally sponsored loans available. Support available to part-time students. Financial award application deadline: 5/1; financial award applicants required to submit FAFSA. *Unit head:* Jon A. Radermacher, Interim Dean, School of Informatics, Humanities and Social Sciences, 412-397-4088, E-mail: radermacher@rmu.edu. *Application contact:* Jon A. Radermacher, Interim Dean, School of Informatics, Humanities and Social Sciences, 412-397-4088, E-mail: radermacher@rmu.edu. Website: https://www.rmu.edu/academics/schools/sihss

Rochester Institute of Technology, Graduate Enrollment Services, Golisano College of Computing and Information Sciences, Computing and Information Sciences Department, PhD Program in Computing and Information Sciences, Rochester, NY 14623-5603. Offers PhD. *Program availability:* Part-time. *Students:* 50 full-time (9 women), 20 part-time (5 women); includes 5 minority (1 Asian, non-Hispanic/Latino; 3 Hispanic/Latino; 1 Two or more races, non-Hispanic/Latino), 56 international. Average age 31. 102 applicants, 25% accepted, 17 enrolled. In 2018, 1 doctorate awarded. *Degree requirements:* For doctorate, comprehensive exam, thesis/dissertation. *Entrance requirements:* For doctorate, GRE, minimum GPA of 3.0, statement of purpose, resume, two letters of recommendation, professional or research paper sample(s) (if available). Additional exam requirements/recommendations for international students: Required—TOEFL (minimum score 570 paper-based; 88 iBT), IELTS (minimum score 6.5), PTE (minimum score 61). *Application deadline:* For fall admission, 1/15 priority date for domestic and international students. Applications are processed on a rolling basis. Application fee: $65. Electronic applications accepted. *Expenses:* Contact institution. *Financial support:* In 2018–19, 53 students received support. Research assistantships with full tuition reimbursements available, teaching assistantships with full tuition reimbursements available, career-related internships or fieldwork, scholarships/grants, health care benefits, and unspecified assistantships available. Financial award applicants required to submit FAFSA. *Faculty research:* Accessibility and HCI; algorithm and programming languages; bioinformatics and health IT; cybersecurity; machine learning and data science. *Unit head:* Dr. Pengcheng Shi, Director, 585-475-6147, E-mail: spcast@rit.edu. *Application contact:* Diane Ellison, Senior Associate Vice President, Graduate Enrollment Services, 585-475-2229, Fax: 585-475-7164, E-mail: gradinfo@rit.edu. Website: https://www.rit.edu/study/computing-and-information-sciences-phd

Rochester Institute of Technology, Graduate Enrollment Services, Golisano College of Computing and Information Sciences, Information Science and Technologies Department, MS Program in Information Sciences and Technologies, Rochester, NY 14623-5603. Offers MS. *Program availability:* Part-time, online learning. *Students:* 62 full-time (26 women), 52 part-time (22 women); includes 3 minority (1 American Indian or Alaska Native, non-Hispanic/Latino; 1 Asian, non-Hispanic/Latino; 1 Two or more races, non-Hispanic/Latino), 103 international. Average age 26. 237 applicants, 57% accepted, 24 enrolled. In 2018, 28 master's awarded. *Degree requirements:* For master's, thesis or alternative, Thesis or Project. *Entrance requirements:* For master's, GRE required for individuals with degrees from international universities. GRE scores are strongly recommended for students whose GPA is below 3.0., minimum GPA of 3.0, resume, two letters of recommendation. Additional exam requirements/recommendations for international students: Required—TOEFL (minimum score 570 paper-based; 88 iBT), IELTS (minimum score 6.5), PTE (minimum score 61). *Application deadline:* For fall admission, 2/15 priority date for domestic and international students; for spring admission, 12/15 priority date for domestic and international students. Applications are processed on a rolling basis. Application fee: $65. Electronic applications accepted. *Financial support:* In 2018–19, 98 students received support. Research assistantships with partial tuition reimbursements available, teaching assistantships with partial tuition reimbursements available, career-related internships or fieldwork, scholarships/grants, and unspecified assistantships available. Support available to part-time students. Financial award applicants required to submit FAFSA. *Faculty research:* Machine learning, data analytics/management, service computing, Web and mobile computing, geographic information science and technology. *Unit head:* Qi Yu, Graduate Program Director, 585-475-6929, E-mail: qyuvks@rit.edu. *Application contact:* Diane Ellison, Senior Associate Vice President, Graduate Enrollment Services, 585-475-2229, Fax: 585-475-7164, E-mail: gradinfo@rit.edu. Website: https://www.rit.edu/study/information-sciences-and-technologies-ms

Rutgers University–New Brunswick, School of Communication and Information, Master of Information, New Brunswick, NJ 08901. Offers MI. *Accreditation:* ALA. *Program availability:* Part-time, online learning. *Entrance requirements:* For master's, GRE General Test. Additional exam requirements/recommendations for international students: Required—TOEFL. Electronic applications accepted. *Faculty research:* Information science, library services, management of information services.

Sacred Heart University, Graduate Programs, College of Arts and Sciences, Department of Computing, Fairfield, CT 06825. Offers computer science (MS); computer science gaming (MS); cybersecurity (MS); information technology (MS). *Program availability:* Part-time, evening/weekend. *Degree requirements:* For master's, thesis or alternative. *Entrance requirements:* For master's, bachelor's degree, minimum GPA of 3.0. Additional exam requirements/recommendations for international students: Required—TOEFL (minimum score 570 paper-based, 80 iBT), TWE, or IELTS (6.5). Electronic applications accepted. *Expenses:* Contact institution.

St. John's University, St. John's College of Liberal Arts and Sciences, Department of Government and Politics and Division of Library and Information Science, Program in Government and Library and Information Science, Queens, NY 11439. Offers MA/MS. *Program availability:* Part-time, evening/weekend. *Entrance requirements:* Additional exam requirements/recommendations for international students: Required—TOEFL (minimum score 80 iBT), IELTS (minimum score 6.5). Electronic applications accepted. *Faculty research:* Presidential leadership, morality and politics, U.S. foreign policy, U.S. national security policy, NY state and local government and politics, state building and social policy, public opinion, campaigns and elections, education politics, North African politics, energy and European Union politics.

St. Mary's University, School of Science, Engineering and Technology, Program in Computer Information Systems, San Antonio, TX 78228. Offers MS. *Program availability:* Part-time, evening/weekend. *Students:* 3 full-time (0 women), 2 part-time (1 woman); includes 1 minority (Black or African American, non-Hispanic/Latino), 3 international. Average age 34. 12 applicants, 58% accepted. In 2018, 3 master's awarded. *Degree requirements:* For master's, comprehensive exam, thesis optional. *Entrance requirements:* For master's, GMAT (minimum score of 334) or GRE General Test (minimum quantitative score of 148, analytical writing 2.5), minimum GPA of 3.0 in a bachelor's degree, written statement of purpose indicating interest and objective, two letters of recommendation, official transcripts of all college-level work. Additional exam requirements/recommendations for international students: Required—TOEFL (minimum score 530 paper-based; 80 iBT), IELTS (minimum score 6). *Application deadline:* For fall admission, 7/1 for domestic students; for spring admission, 11/15 for domestic students; for summer admission, 4/1 for domestic students. Applications are processed on a rolling basis. Application fee: $0. Electronic applications accepted. *Expenses: Tuition:* Full-time $16,830; part-time $935 per credit hour. *Required fees:* $1055. Tuition and fees vary according to program. *Financial support:* Career-related internships or fieldwork, Federal Work-Study, institutionally sponsored loans, scholarships/grants, health care benefits, and unspecified assistantships available. Financial award application deadline: 3/31; financial award applicants required to submit FAFSA. *Faculty research:* Artificial intelligence, biological modeling, computer languages, computer security, educational computer gaming. *Unit head:* Dr. Arthur Hanna, Graduate Program Director, 210-431-2021, E-mail: ahanna@stmarytx.edu. *Application contact:* Dr. Arthur Hanna, Graduate Program Director, 210-431-2021, E-mail: ahanna@stmarytx.edu. Website: https://www.stmarytx.edu/academics/programs/master-computer-information-systems/

Sam Houston State University, College of Sciences, Department of Computer Science, Huntsville, TX 77341. Offers computing and information science (MS); digital forensics (MS); information assurance and security (MS). *Program availability:* Part-time. *Degree requirements:* For master's, comprehensive exam, thesis optional, internship; for doctorate, comprehensive exam, thesis/dissertation. *Entrance requirements:* For master's, GRE General Test, letters of recommendation. Additional exam requirements/recommendations for international students: Required—TOEFL (minimum score 550 paper-based; 79 iBT), IELTS (minimum score 6.5). Electronic applications accepted.

Shippensburg University of Pennsylvania, School of Graduate Studies, College of Arts and Sciences, Department of Computer Science and Engineering, Shippensburg, PA 17257-2299. Offers agile software engineering (Certificate); computer science (MS); IT leadership (Certificate). *Program availability:* Part-time, evening/weekend. *Faculty:* 4 full-time (2 women). *Students:* 5 full-time (3 women), 6 part-time (1 woman); includes 2 minority (both Black or African American, non-Hispanic/Latino), 7 international. Average age 29. 29 applicants, 55% accepted, 5 enrolled. In 2018, 15 master's awarded. *Entrance requirements:* For master's, GRE (if GPA less than 2.75), professional resume. Additional exam requirements/recommendations for international students: Required—TOEFL (minimum score 70 iBT), IELTS (minimum score 6), TOEFL (minimum score 70 iBT) or IELTS (minimum score 6). *Application deadline:* For fall admission, 4/30 for international students. Applications are processed on a rolling basis. Application fee: $45. Electronic applications accepted. *Expenses:* Tuition, state resident: part-time $516 per credit. Tuition, nonresident: part-time $750 per credit. *Required fees:* $149 per credit. *Financial support:* In 2018–19, 4 students received support. Career-related internships or fieldwork, scholarships/grants, unspecified assistantships, and resident hall director and student payroll positions available. Support available to part-time students. Financial award application deadline: 3/1; financial award applicants required to submit FAFSA. *Unit head:* Dr. Jeonghwa Lee, Professor and Director of Graduate Studies, 717-477-1178, Fax: 717-477-4002, E-mail: jlee@ship.edu. *Application contact:* Maya T. Mapp, Director of Admissions, 717-477-1231, Fax: 717-477-4016, E-mail: mtmapp@ship.edu. Website: http://www.cs.ship.edu/

Southern Methodist University, Lyle School of Engineering, Department of Engineering Management, Information, and Systems, Dallas, TX 75275. Offers engineering entrepreneurship (MS); engineering management (MS, DE); information engineering and management (MSIEM); operations research (MS, PhD); systems engineering (MS). MS in engineering entrepreneurship offered in collaboration with the Cox School of Business. *Program availability:* Part-time, evening/weekend, online learning. Terminal master's awarded for partial completion of doctoral program. *Degree requirements:* For master's, thesis optional; for doctorate, thesis/dissertation, oral and written qualifying exams. *Entrance requirements:* For master's, minimum GPA of 3.0 in last 2 years; bachelor's degree in engineering, mathematics, sciences, or technical area; for doctorate, GRE General Test (operations research, engineering management), bachelor's degree in related field. Additional exam requirements/recommendations for international students: Required—TOEFL. *Faculty research:* Telecommunications, decision systems, information engineering, operations research, software.

Southern States University, Graduate Programs, San Diego, CA 92110. Offers business administration (MBA); information technology (MSIT).

State University of New York Polytechnic Institute, Program in Computer and Information Science, Utica, NY 13502. Offers MS. *Program availability:* Part-time. *Students:* 78 full-time (18 women), 25 part-time (4 women); includes 7 minority (5 Asian, non-Hispanic/Latino; 2 Hispanic/Latino), 76 international. Average age 24. 153 applicants, 64% accepted, 39 enrolled. In 2018, 36 master's awarded. *Degree requirements:* For master's, thesis, thesis or project. *Entrance requirements:* For master's, GRE or approved GRE waiver, undergraduate prerequisite courses in math and computer science. Additional exam requirements/recommendations for international students: Required—TOEFL (minimum score 79 iBT), IELTS (minimum score 6.5), PTE (minimum score 53), Only ONE of above. *Application deadline:* For fall admission, 7/1 for domestic and international students; for spring admission, 12/1 for domestic students, 11/1 for international students. Applications are processed on a rolling basis. Application fee: $60. Electronic applications accepted. *Expenses: Tuition, area resident:* Full-time $8316; part-time $462 per credit hour. Tuition, nonresident: full-time $16,992; part-time $944 per credit hour. *International tuition:* $16,992 full-time. *Required fees:* $1023; $56.87 per credit hour. Tuition and fees vary according to course load, campus/location and program. *Financial support:* Research assistantships, scholarships/grants, and unspecified assistantships available. Financial award application deadline: 6/1; financial award applicants required to submit FAFSA. *Faculty research:* Computer vision and deep learning, quantum computing, blockchains, artificial intelligence and optimization, and architecture virtualization. *Unit head:* Dr. Roger Cavallo, Program Coordinator, 315-792-7231, E-mail: roger.cavallo@sunypoly.edu. *Application contact:* Alicia Foster, Director of Graduate Admissions, 315-792-7347, E-mail: fostera3@sunypoly.edu. Website: https://sunypoly.edu/academics/majors-and-programs/ms-computer-information-science.html

State University of New York Polytechnic Institute, Program in Information Design and Technology, Utica, NY 13502. Offers MS. *Program availability:* Part-time. *Students:* 10 full-time (5 women), 55 part-time (27 women); includes 18 minority (4 Black or African

American, non-Hispanic/Latino; 4 Asian, non-Hispanic/Latino; 7 Hispanic/Latino; 3 Two or more races, non-Hispanic/Latino). Average age 36. 26 applicants, 50% accepted, 10 enrolled. In 2018, 21 master's awarded. *Degree requirements:* For master's, project or thesis. *Application deadline:* For fall admission, 7/1 for domestic and international students; for spring admission, 12/1 for domestic students, 11/1 for international students. Applications are processed on a rolling basis. Application fee: $60. Electronic applications accepted. *Expenses: Tuition, area resident:* Full-time $8316; part-time $462 per credit hour. Tuition, nonresident: full-time $16,992; part-time $944 per credit hour. *International tuition:* $16,992 full-time. *Required fees:* $1023; $56.87 per credit hour. Tuition and fees vary according to course load, campus/location and program. *Financial support:* Applicants required to submit FAFSA. *Faculty research:* Information technology, data visualization, visual communication, instructional design, mass communications and mediated memory, video design, digital narratives, online communities, digital archiving, cultural analytics, video game design, ethnographic methods for idt, and the social, cultural, and ethical aspects of information technology. *Unit head:* Dr. Kathryn Stam, Professor, 315-792-7241, E-mail: Kathryn.Stam@sunypoly.edu. *Application contact:* Alicia Foster, Director of Graduate Admissions, 315-792-7347, E-mail: fostera3@sunypoly.edu.
Website: https://sunypoly.edu/academics/majors-and-programs/ms-information-design-technology.html

Stevens Institute of Technology, Graduate School, School of Business, Program in Information Systems, Hoboken, NJ 07030. Offers computer science (MS); e-commerce (MS); enterprise systems (MS); entrepreneurial information technology (MS); information architecture (MS); information management (MS, Certificate); information security (MS); information technology in financial services industry (MS); information technology in the pharmaceutical industry (MS); information technology outsourcing management (MS); project management (MS, Certificate); software engineering (MS); telecommunications (MS). *Program availability:* Part-time, evening/weekend. *Students:* 248 full-time (87 women), 54 part-time (20 women); includes 25 minority (8 Black or African American, non-Hispanic/Latino; 17 Asian, non-Hispanic/Latino), 245 international. Average age 27. In 2018, 202 master's, 16 other advanced degrees awarded. Terminal master's awarded for partial completion of doctoral program. *Degree requirements:* For master's, thesis optional, minimum B average in major field and overall; for Certificate, minimum B average. *Entrance requirements:* For master's, GRE/GMAT scores: GRE scores are required for all applicants applying to a full-time graduate program in the Schaefer School of Engineering and Science (SES). International applicants must submit TOEFL/IELTS scores and fulfill the English Language Proficiency Requirements in order to be considered. Additional exam requirements/recommendations for international students: Required—TOEFL (minimum score 74 iBT), IELTS (minimum score 6). *Application deadline:* For fall admission, 4/1 for domestic and international students; for spring admission, 11/1 for domestic and international students; for summer admission, 5/1 for domestic students. Applications are processed on a rolling basis. Application fee: $60. Electronic applications accepted. *Expenses: Tuition:* Full-time $35,960; part-time $1620 per credit. *Required fees:* $1290; $600 per semester. Tuition and fees vary according to course load. *Financial support:* Fellowships, research assistantships, teaching assistantships, career-related internships or fieldwork, Federal Work-Study, scholarships/grants, and unspecified assistantships available. Financial award application deadline: 2/15; financial award applicants required to submit FAFSA. *Unit head:* Dr. Gregory Prastacos, Dean of SB, 201-216-8366, E-mail: gprastac@stevens.edu. *Application contact:* Graduate Admissions, 888-783-8367, Fax: 888-511-1306, E-mail: graduate@stevens.edu.
Website: https://www.stevens.edu/school-business/masters-programs/information-systems

Strayer University, Graduate Studies, Washington, DC 20005-2603. Offers accounting (MS); acquisition (MBA); business administration (MBA); communications technology (MS); educational management (M Ed); finance (MBA); health services administration (MHSA); hospitality and tourism management (MBA); human resource management (MBA); information systems (MS), including computer security management, decision support system management, enterprise resource management, network management, software engineering management, systems development management; management (MBA); management information systems (MS); marketing (MBA); professional accounting (MS), including accounting information systems, controllership, taxation; public administration (MPA); supply chain management (MBA); technology in education (M Ed). Programs also offered at campus locations in Birmingham, AL; Chamblee, GA; Cobb County, GA; Morrow, GA; White Marsh, MD; Charleston, SC; Columbia, SC; Greensboro, NC; Greenville, SC; Lexington, KY; Louisville, KY; Nashville, TN; North Raleigh, NC; Washington, DC. *Accreditation:* ACBSP. *Program availability:* Part-time, evening/weekend, online learning. *Degree requirements:* For master's, thesis. *Entrance requirements:* For master's, GMAT, GRE General Test, bachelor's degree from an accredited college or university, minimum undergraduate GPA of 2.75. Electronic applications accepted.

Syracuse University, College of Engineering and Computer Science, PhD Program in Computer and Information Science and Engineering, Syracuse, NY 13244. Offers PhD. *Program availability:* Part-time. *Students:* Average age 29. In 2018, 3 doctorates awarded. *Degree requirements:* For doctorate, comprehensive exam, thesis/dissertation. *Entrance requirements:* For doctorate, GRE General Test, GRE Subject Test (computer science), three letters of recommendation, personal statement, official transcripts, resume. Additional exam requirements/recommendations for international students: Required—TOEFL (minimum score 100 iBT). *Application deadline:* For fall admission, 2/1 priority date for domestic and international students. Application fee: $75. Electronic applications accepted. *Financial support:* Fellowships with full tuition reimbursements, research assistantships, teaching assistantships, and tuition waivers (partial) available. Financial award application deadline: 1/1; financial award applicants required to submit FAFSA. *Faculty research:* Computer and information science, software aspects of the computer-engineering field. *Unit head:* Dr. Qinru Qiu, Program Director, 315-443-2652, E-mail: eecsadmissions@syr.edu. *Application contact:* Kathleen Joyce, Assistant Dean, 315-443-2219, E-mail: topgrads@syr.edu.
Website: http://eng-cs.syr.edu/program/computerinformation-science-an-engineering/?degree-doctoral_program

Syracuse University, School of Information Studies, MS Program in Library and Information Science, Syracuse, NY 13244. Offers MS. *Accreditation:* ALA. *Program availability:* Part-time, evening/weekend, online learning. *Students:* Average age 30. *Entrance requirements:* For master's, GRE General Test, two letters of recommendation, personal statement, resume. Additional exam requirements/recommendations for international students: Required—TOEFL (minimum score 100 iBT). *Application deadline:* For fall admission, 2/1 priority date for domestic and international students; for spring admission, 10/15 priority date for domestic and international students. Applications are processed on a rolling basis. Application fee: $75. Electronic applications accepted. *Financial support:* Fellowships with full tuition reimbursements and teaching assistantships available. Financial award application deadline: 1/1; financial award applicants required to submit FAFSA. *Faculty research:* Information environments, library planning and marketing, management principles, information policy. *Unit head:* Prof. Caroline Haythornthwaite, Program Director, 315-443-2911, E-mail: igrad@syr.edu. *Application contact:* Susan Corieri, Director of Enrollment Management, 315-443-1070, E-mail: ischool@syr.edu.
Website: https://ischool.syr.edu/academics/graduate/masters-degrees/ms-library-and-information-science/

Syracuse University, School of Information Studies, PhD Program in Information Science and Technology, Syracuse, NY 13244. Offers PhD. *Students:* Average age 35. In 2018, 4 doctorates awarded. *Degree requirements:* For doctorate, comprehensive exam, thesis/dissertation. *Entrance requirements:* For doctorate, GRE General Test, writing sample, personal statement, three letters of recommendation, official transcripts. Additional exam requirements/recommendations for international students: Required—TOEFL (minimum score 100 iBT). *Application deadline:* For fall admission, 1/3 priority date for domestic and international students. Application fee: $75. Electronic applications accepted. *Financial support:* Fellowships with full tuition reimbursements, research assistantships with partial tuition reimbursements, and teaching assistantships with partial tuition reimbursements available. Financial award application deadline: 1/1. *Faculty research:* Information and public policy, human-computer interaction, emerging technologies, digital literacy. *Unit head:* Dr. Steve Sawyer, Director, 315-443-6147, Fax: 315-443-6886, E-mail: istphd@syr.edu. *Application contact:* Susan Corieri, Director of Enrollment Management, 315-443-2575, E-mail: ischool@syr.edu.
Website: https://ischool.syr.edu/academics/graduate/doctoral/information-science-and-technology/

Temple University, College of Science and Technology, Department of Computer and Information Sciences, Philadelphia, PA 19122. Offers computational data science (MS); computer and information sciences (PhD), including artificial intelligence, computer and network systems, information systems, software systems; computer science (MS); cyber defense and information assurance (PSM); information science and technology (MS). *Program availability:* Part-time, evening/weekend, online learning. *Faculty:* 31 full-time (7 women), 10 part-time/adjunct (2 women). *Students:* 92 full-time (28 women), 15 part-time (3 women); includes 7 minority (2 Black or African American, non-Hispanic/Latino; 4 Asian, non-Hispanic/Latino; 1 Hispanic/Latino), 82 international. 119 applicants, 43% accepted, 21 enrolled. In 2018, 20 master's, 5 doctorates awarded. *Degree requirements:* For doctorate, thesis/dissertation. *Entrance requirements:* For master's, GRE, 3 letters of recommendation, statement of goals; for doctorate, GRE, 3 letters of recommendation, bachelor's degree in related field, statement of goals, resume. Additional exam requirements/recommendations for international students: Required—TOEFL (minimum score 85 iBT), IELTS (minimum score 6.5), PTE (minimum score 58), one of three is required. *Application deadline:* Applications are processed on a rolling basis. Application fee: $60. Electronic applications accepted. *Expenses:* Contact institution. *Financial support:* Research assistantships, teaching assistantships, health care benefits, and unspecified assistantships available. Financial award applicants required to submit FAFSA. *Faculty research:* Data mining, machine learning, knowledge discovery, computer networks and systems, cyberspace security. *Unit head:* Jamie Payton, Department Chairperson, 215-204-8245, E-mail: Jamie.payton@temple.edu. *Application contact:* Eduard Dragut, Graduate Chair, 215-204-0521, E-mail: cisadmit@temple.edu.
Website: https://cis.temple.edu/

Texas Woman's University, Graduate School, College of Arts and Sciences, Department of Mathematics and Computer Science, Denton, TX 76204. Offers emphasis in mathematics or computer science (MAT); informatics (MS); mathematics (MS); mathematics teaching (MS). *Program availability:* Part-time, evening/weekend, blended/hybrid learning. *Faculty:* 11 full-time (7 women), 1 part-time/adjunct (0 women). *Students:* 17 full-time (13 women), 71 part-time (49 women); includes 53 minority (22 Black or African American, non-Hispanic/Latino; 16 Asian, non-Hispanic/Latino; 13 Hispanic/Latino; 2 Two or more races, non-Hispanic/Latino), 2 international. Average age 36. 37 applicants, 78% accepted, 24 enrolled. In 2018, 23 master's awarded. *Degree requirements:* For master's, comprehensive exam, thesis (for some programs), professional paper, capstone or thesis (depending on degree). *Entrance requirements:* For master's, minimum GPA of 3.0 in last 60 undergraduate credit hours, 2 semesters of calculus, 2 additional advanced math courses, 2 letters of reference (for MS in mathematics, mathematics teaching); minimum GPA of 3.0, statement of intent, resume, 2 letters of recommendation (for MS in informatics). Additional exam requirements/recommendations for international students: Required—TOEFL (minimum score 79 iBT); Recommended—IELTS (minimum score 6.5), TSE (minimum score 53). *Application deadline:* Applications are processed on a rolling basis. Application fee: $50 ($75 for international students). Electronic applications accepted. *Expenses: Tuition, area resident:* Full-time $4852; part-time $270 per semester hour. Tuition, state resident: full-time $4852; part-time $270 per semester hour. Tuition, nonresident: full-time $12,322; part-time $685 per semester hour. *International tuition:* $12,322 full-time. *Required fees:* $2714; $113 per semester hour. $296 per semester. Tuition and fees vary according to course level, course load, degree level, campus/location and program. *Financial support:* In 2018–19, 16 students received support, including 12 teaching assistantships (averaging $10,987 per year); career-related internships or fieldwork, Federal Work-Study, institutionally sponsored loans, scholarships/grants, traineeships, health care benefits, and unspecified assistantships also available. Support available to part-time students. Financial award application deadline: 3/1; financial award applicants required to submit FAFSA. *Faculty research:* Optimal control theory and differential games, information security, statistics and modern approaches, knot theory, math and computer science education. *Unit head:* Dr. Don E. Edwards, Chair, 940-898-2166, Fax: 940-898-2179, E-mail: mathcs@twu.edu. *Application contact:* Korie Hawkins, Associate Director of Admissions, Graduate Recruitment, 940-898-3188, Fax: 940-898-3081, E-mail: admissions@twu.edu.
Website: http://www.twu.edu/math-computer-science/

Thomas Edison State University, School of Applied Science and Technology, Trenton, NJ 08608. Offers clinical trials management (MS); cybersecurity (Graduate Certificate); information technology (MS); nuclear energy technology management (MS); technical studies (MS). *Program availability:* Part-time, online learning. *Degree requirements:* For master's, project. *Entrance requirements:* Additional exam requirements/recommendations for international students: Required—TOEFL (minimum score 550 paper-based; 79 iBT). Electronic applications accepted.

Towson University, Jess and Mildred Fisher College of Science and Mathematics, Program in Applied Information Technology, Towson, MD 21252-0001. Offers applied information technology (MS); Internet application development (Postbaccalaureate Certificate). *Entrance requirements:* For master's and Postbaccalaureate Certificate, bachelor's degree, minimum GPA of 3.0. Additional exam requirements/recommendations for international students: Required—TOEFL. Electronic applications accepted. *Expenses: Tuition, area resident:* Full-time $9196; part-time $418 per unit. Tuition, state resident: full-time $9196; part-time $418 per unit. Tuition, nonresident: full-time $19,030; part-time $865 per unit. *International tuition:* $19,030 full-time. *Required fees:* $3102; $141 per year. $423 per term. Tuition and fees vary according to campus/location and program.

Towson University, Jess and Mildred Fisher College of Science and Mathematics, Program in Information Technology, Towson, MD 21252-0001. Offers D Sc. *Entrance requirements:* For doctorate, minimum GPA of 3.0, letter of intent, resume, 2 letters of recommendation, personal assessment forms, official transcripts. Additional exam requirements/recommendations for international students: Required—TOEFL (minimum score 550 paper-based). Electronic applications accepted. *Expenses: Tuition, area resident:* Full-time $9196; part-time $418 per unit. Tuition, state resident: full-time $9196; part-time $418 per unit. Tuition, nonresident: full-time $19,030; part-time $865 per unit. *International tuition:* $19,030 full-time. *Required fees:* $3102; $141 per year. $423 per term. Tuition and fees vary according to campus/location and program.

Trevecca Nazarene University, Graduate Education Program, Nashville, TN 37210-2877. Offers accountability and instructional leadership (Ed S); curriculum and instruction for Christian school educators (M Ed); curriculum and instruction K-12 (M Ed); educational leadership (M Ed); English second language (M Ed); library and information science (MLI Sc); special education: visual impairments (M Ed); teaching (MAT), including teaching 6-12, teaching K-5. *Accreditation:* NCATE. *Program availability:* Part-time, evening/weekend, online learning. *Degree requirements:* For master's, comprehensive exam, exit assessment/e-portfolio. *Entrance requirements:* For master's, GRE or MAT; PRAXIS (for MAT), minimum GPA of 3.0, official transcript from regionally-accredited institution, references, interview, writing sample, at least 3 years' successful teaching experience (for M Ed in educational leadership); for Ed S, GRE or MAT, master's degree with minimum GPA of 3.0, official transcript from regionally accredited institution, at least 3 years' successful teaching experience, interview, writing sample, background and fingerprinting check, recommendations. Additional exam requirements/recommendations for international students: Required—TOEFL (minimum score 550 paper-based). Electronic applications accepted. *Expenses:* Contact institution.

Université de Sherbrooke, Faculty of Sciences, Department of Informatics, Sherbrooke, QC J1K 2R1, Canada. Offers M Sc, PhD. *Degree requirements:* For master's, thesis. Electronic applications accepted.

University at Albany, State University of New York, College of Emergency Preparedness, Homeland Security and Cybersecurity, MS Program in Information Science, Albany, NY 12222-0001. Offers MS. *Accreditation:* ALA. *Faculty:* 10 full-time (5 women), 6 part-time/adjunct (4 women). *Students:* 38 full-time (27 women), 78 part-time (69 women); includes 19 minority (5 Black or African American, non-Hispanic/Latino; 4 Asian, non-Hispanic/Latino; 8 Hispanic/Latino; 2 Two or more races, non-Hispanic/Latino), 2 international. 71 applicants, 70% accepted, 31 enrolled. In 2018, 30 master's awarded. *Entrance requirements:* Additional exam requirements/recommendations for international students: Required—TOEFL. Application fee: $75. *Financial support:* Research assistantships and teaching assistantships available. Financial award applicants required to submit FAFSA. *Faculty research:* Electronic information across technologies system dynamics modeling archives, records administration. *Unit head:* Philip B. Eppard, Chair, 518-442-5119, E-mail: peppard@albany.edu. *Application contact:* Philip B. Eppard, Chair, 518-442-5119, E-mail: peppard@albany.edu. Website: http://www.albany.edu/informationstudies/

University at Albany, State University of New York, College of Emergency Preparedness, Homeland Security and Cybersecurity, PhD Program in Informatics, Albany, NY 12222-0001. Offers PhD. *Faculty:* 4 full-time (1 woman), 1 part-time/adjunct (0 women). *Students:* 11 full-time (7 women), 20 part-time (9 women); includes 6 minority (2 Black or African American, non-Hispanic/Latino; 1 Asian, non-Hispanic/Latino; 3 Hispanic/Latino), 11 international. 19 applicants, 53% accepted, 5 enrolled. In 2018, 1 doctorate awarded. *Degree requirements:* For doctorate, comprehensive exam. *Entrance requirements:* Additional exam requirements/recommendations for international students: Required—TOEFL. Electronic applications accepted. *Unit head:* Randy Moulic, Acting Chair, 518-956-8242, E-mail: jmoulic@albany.edu. *Application contact:* Randy Moulic, Acting Chair, 518-956-8242, E-mail: jmoulic@albany.edu.

The University of Alabama at Birmingham, College of Arts and Sciences, Program in Computer and Information Sciences, Birmingham, AL 35294. Offers MS, PhD. Terminal master's awarded for partial completion of doctoral program. *Degree requirements:* For master's, thesis optional; for doctorate, thesis/dissertation. *Entrance requirements:* For master's, GRE General Test, minimum GPA of 3.0, letters of recommendation; for doctorate, GRE General Test, minimum GPA of 3.5 overall or on last 60 hours; letters of recommendation. Additional exam requirements/recommendations for international students: Required—TOEFL, IELTS. Electronic applications accepted. *Expenses: Tuition, area resident:* Full-time $8100; part-time $8100 per year. Tuition, state resident: full-time $8100. Tuition, nonresident: full-time $19,188; part-time $19,188 per year. Tuition and fees vary according to program. *Faculty research:* Theory and software systems, intelligent systems, systems architecture, high performance computing, computer architecture, computer graphics, data mining, software engineering.

University of Arkansas at Little Rock, Graduate School, George W. Donaghey College of Engineering and Information Technology, Program in Information Quality, Little Rock, AR 72204-1099. Offers MS, PhD, Graduate Certificate.

University of California, Irvine, Donald Bren School of Information and Computer Sciences, Department of Informatics, Irvine, CA 92697. Offers information and computer science (MS, PhD). *Students:* 150 full-time (79 women), 2 part-time (1 woman); includes 35 minority (4 Black or African American, non-Hispanic/Latino; 21 Asian, non-Hispanic/Latino; 5 Hispanic/Latino; 5 Two or more races, non-Hispanic/Latino), 80 international. Average age 29. 581 applicants, 22% accepted, 70 enrolled. In 2018, 52 master's, 8 doctorates awarded. Application fee: $105 ($125 for international students). *Unit head:* Andre van der Hoek, Chair, 949-824-6326, Fax: 949-824-4056, E-mail: andre@uci.edu. *Application contact:* Melissa Mazmanian, Vice Chair for Graduate Affairs, 949-824-9284, Fax: 949-824-2056, E-mail: m.mazmani@ics.uci.edu. Website: http://www.informatics.uci.edu/

University of California, Merced, Graduate Division, School of Social Sciences, Humanities and Arts, Merced, CA 95343. Offers cognitive and information sciences (PhD); interdisciplinary humanities (MA, PhD); psychological sciences (MA, PhD); social sciences (MA, PhD); sociology (MA, PhD). *Faculty:* 113 full-time (57 women). *Students:* 195 full-time (130 women), 4 part-time (3 women); includes 83 minority (6 Black or African American, non-Hispanic/Latino; 21 Asian, non-Hispanic/Latino; 52 Hispanic/Latino; 1 Native Hawaiian or other Pacific Islander, non-Hispanic/Latino; 3 Two or more races, non-Hispanic/Latino), 35 international. Average age 31. 150 applicants, 54% accepted, 36 enrolled. In 2018, 12 master's, 23 doctorates awarded. Terminal master's awarded for partial completion of doctoral program. *Degree requirements:* For master's, variable foreign language requirement, comprehensive exam, thesis or alternative, oral defense; for doctorate, variable foreign language requirement, comprehensive exam, thesis/dissertation, oral defense. *Entrance requirements:* For master's and doctorate, GRE. Additional exam requirements/recommendations for international students: Required—TOEFL (minimum score 550 paper-based; 80 iBT); Recommended—IELTS (minimum score 6.5). *Application deadline:* For fall admission, 1/15 for domestic and international students. Application fee: $105 ($125 for international students). Electronic applications accepted. *Expenses: Tuition, area resident:* Full-time $11,442; part-time $5721 per year. Tuition, state resident: full-time $11,442; part-time $5721 per year. Tuition, nonresident: full-time $26,544; part-time $13,272 per year. *International tuition:* $26,544 full-time. *Required fees:* $1765; $1765 per unit. $883 per semester. *Financial support:* In 2018–19, 193 students received support, including 8 fellowships with full tuition reimbursements available (averaging $21,003 per year), 25 research

assistantships with full tuition reimbursements available (averaging $19,145 per year), 160 teaching assistantships with full tuition reimbursements available (averaging $21,617 per year); scholarships/grants, traineeships, and health care benefits also available. *Faculty research:* Social inequality and disparities; history and world cultures; society, politics and economies; behavioral and health-related sciences; literature, language and fine arts. *Total annual research expenditures:* $566,638. *Unit head:* Dr. Jeffrey Gilger, Interim Dean, 209-228-4343, E-mail: jgilger@ucmerced.edu. *Application contact:* Tsu Ya, Director of Admissions and Academic Services, 209-228-4521, Fax: 209-228-6906, E-mail: tya@ucmerced.edu.

University of Central Missouri, The Graduate School, Warrensburg, MO 64093. Offers accountancy (MA); accounting (MBA); applied mathematics (MS); aviation safety (MA); biology (MS); business administration (MBA); career and technical education leadership (MS); college student personnel administration (MS); communication (MA); computer science (MS); counseling (MS); criminal justice (MS); educational leadership (Ed D); educational technology (MS); elementary and early childhood education (MSE); English (MA); environmental studies (MA); finance (MBA); history (MA); human services/educational technology (Ed S); human services/learning resources (Ed S); human services/professional counseling (Ed S); industrial hygiene (MS); industrial management (MS); information systems (MBA); information technology (MS); kinesiology (MS); library science and information services (MS); literacy education (MSE); marketing (MBA); mathematics (MS); music (MA); occupational safety management (MS); psychology (MS); rural family nursing (MS); school administration (MSE); social gerontology (MS); sociology (MA); special education (MSE); speech language pathology (MS); superintendency (Ed S); teaching (MAT); teaching English as a second language (MA); technology (MS); technology management (PhD); theatre (MA). *Accreditation:* ASHA. *Program availability:* Part-time, 100% online, blended/hybrid learning. *Degree requirements:* For master's and Ed S, comprehensive exam (for some programs), thesis (for some programs). *Entrance requirements:* Additional exam requirements/recommendations for international students: Required—TOEFL (minimum score 550 paper-based; 79 iBT). Electronic applications accepted.

University of Cincinnati, Graduate School, College of Education, Criminal Justice, and Human Services, School of Information Technology, Cincinnati, OH 45221. Offers MS, Graduate Certificate. *Program availability:* Part-time, 100% online, blended/hybrid learning.

University of Colorado Boulder, Graduate School, College of Media, Communication and Information, Department of Information Science, Boulder, CO 80309. Offers PhD. Electronic applications accepted. *Faculty research:* Computer science; information science/systems; data analysis; computer interface; science and technology/mathematics/computer science.

University of Colorado Denver, College of Engineering, Design and Computing, Department of Computer Science and Engineering, Denver, CO 80217. Offers computer science (MS); computer science and engineering (EASPh D); computer science and information systems (PhD). *Program availability:* Part-time, evening/weekend. *Degree requirements:* For master's, thesis or alternative, at least 30 semester hours of computer science courses while maintaining minimum GPA of 3.0; for doctorate, comprehensive exam, thesis/dissertation, at least 60 hours beyond the master's degree level, 30 of which are dissertation research. *Entrance requirements:* For master's, GRE, minimum GPA of 3.0, 10 semester hours of university-level calculus, at least one math course beyond calculus, statement of purpose, letters of recommendation; for doctorate, GRE or GMAT. Additional exam requirements/recommendations for international students: Required—TOEFL (minimum score 537 paper-based; 75 iBT). Electronic applications accepted. *Expenses:* Tuition, state resident: full-time $6786; part-time $337 per credit hour. Tuition, nonresident: full-time $22,590; part-time $1255 per credit hour. *Required fees:* $1231; $137 per credit hour. Tuition and fees vary according to program and reciprocity agreements.

University of Delaware, College of Engineering, Department of Computer and Information Sciences, Newark, DE 19716. Offers MS, PhD. *Program availability:* Part-time. Terminal master's awarded for partial completion of doctoral program. *Degree requirements:* For master's, thesis optional; for doctorate, comprehensive exam, thesis/dissertation. *Entrance requirements:* For master's and doctorate, GRE General Test. Additional exam requirements/recommendations for international students: Required—TOEFL (minimum score 550 paper-based). Electronic applications accepted. *Faculty research:* Artificial intelligence, computational theory, graphics and computer vision, networks, systems.

University of Denver, University College, Denver, CO 80208. Offers arts and culture (MA, Certificate); communication management (MS, Certificate), including translation studies (Certificate); world history and culture (Certificate); environmental policy and management (MS); geographic information systems (MS); global affairs (MA, Certificate), including human capital in organizations (Certificate), philanthropic leadership (Certificate), project management (Certificate), strategic innovation and change (Certificate); healthcare leadership (MS); information communications and technology (MS); leadership and organizations (MS); professional creative writing (MA, Certificate), including emergency planning and response (Certificate), organizational security (Certificate); security management (MS, Certificate); strategic human resources (Certificate). *Program availability:* Part-time, evening/weekend, 100% online, blended/hybrid learning. *Faculty:* 4 full-time (2 women), 108 part-time/adjunct (51 women). *Students:* 51 full-time (26 women), 1,291 part-time (733 women); includes 337 minority (112 Black or African American, non-Hispanic/Latino; 6 American Indian or Alaska Native, non-Hispanic/Latino; 46 Asian, non-Hispanic/Latino; 132 Hispanic/Latino; 3 Native Hawaiian or other Pacific Islander, non-Hispanic/Latino; 38 Two or more races, non-Hispanic/Latino), 75 international. Average age 34. 834 applicants, 87% accepted, 423 enrolled. In 2018, 443 master's, 232 other advanced degrees awarded. *Degree requirements:* For master's, capstone project. *Entrance requirements:* For master's, baccalaureate degree, transcripts, two letters of recommendation, personal statement, resume, writing sample (Master of Arts in Professional Creative Writing). Additional exam requirements/recommendations for international students: Required—TOEFL (minimum score 550 paper-based; 80 iBT). *Application deadline:* For fall admission, 6/19 priority date for domestic students, 6/14 priority date for international students; for winter admission, 10/25 priority date for domestic students, 9/27 priority date for international students; for spring admission, 2/7 priority date for domestic students, 1/10 priority date for international students; for summer admission, 4/24 priority date for domestic students, 3/27 priority date for international students. Applications are processed on a rolling basis. Application fee: $75. Electronic applications accepted. *Expenses:* $8,280 per year half-time. *Financial support:* In 2018–19, 38 students received support. Teaching assistantships available. Financial award applicants required to submit FAFSA. *Unit head:* Dr. Michael McGuire, Dean, 303-871-3518, E-mail: michael.mcguire@du.edu. *Application contact:* Admission Team, 303-871-2291, E-mail: ucoladm@du.edu. Website: http://universitycollege.du.edu/

University of Fairfax, Graduate Programs, Vienna, VA 22182. Offers business administration (DBA); computer science (MCS); cybersecurity (MBA, MS); general business administration (MBA); information technology (MBA); project management (MBA).

Information Science

University of Florida, Graduate School, Herbert Wertheim College of Engineering, Department of Computer and Information Science and Engineering, Gainesville, FL 32611. Offers computer engineering (ME, MS, PhD); computer science (MS); digital arts and sciences (MS). *Program availability:* Part-time, online learning. Terminal master's awarded for partial completion of doctoral program. *Degree requirements:* For master's, comprehensive exam, thesis optional; for doctorate, comprehensive exam, thesis/dissertation. *Entrance requirements:* For master's and doctorate, minimum GPA of 3.0. Additional exam requirements/recommendations for international students: Required—TOEFL (minimum score 550 paper-based; 80 iBT), IELTS (minimum score 6). Electronic applications accepted. *Faculty research:* Computer systems and computer networking; high-performance computing and algorithm; database and machine learning; computer graphics, vision, and intelligent systems; human center computing and digital art.

University of Hawaii at Manoa, Office of Graduate Education, Interdisciplinary Program in Communication and Information Sciences, Honolulu, HI 96822. Offers PhD. *Program availability:* Part-time. *Degree requirements:* For doctorate, comprehensive exam, thesis/dissertation. *Entrance requirements:* For doctorate, GRE or GMAT. Additional exam requirements/recommendations for international students: Required—TOEFL (minimum score 600 paper-based; 100 iBT), IELTS (minimum score 7).

University of Hawaii at Manoa, Office of Graduate Education, Shidler College of Business, Program in Business Administration, Honolulu, HI 96822. Offers Asian business studies (MBA); Chinese business studies (MBA); decision sciences (MBA); entrepreneurship (MBA); finance (MBA); finance and banking (MBA); human resources management (MBA); information management (MBA); information technology (MBA); international business (MBA); Japanese business studies (MBA); marketing (MBA); organizational behavior (MBA); organizational management (MBA); real estate (MBA); student-designed track (MBA). *Accreditation:* AACSB. *Program availability:* Part-time, evening/weekend. *Degree requirements:* For master's, thesis optional. *Entrance requirements:* For master's, GMAT, minimum GPA of 3.0. Additional exam requirements/recommendations for international students: Required—TOEFL (minimum score 600 paper-based; 100 iBT), IELTS (minimum score 7). *Expenses:* Contact institution.

University of Houston, Bauer College of Business, Decision and Information Sciences Program, Houston, TX 77204. Offers PhD. *Program availability:* Evening/weekend.

University of Houston, College of Technology, Department of Information and Logistics Technology, Houston, TX 77204. Offers information security (MS); supply chain and logistics technology (MS); technology project management (MS). *Program availability:* Part-time. *Degree requirements:* For master's, project or thesis (most programs). *Entrance requirements:* For master's, GMAT. Additional exam requirements/recommendations for international students: Required—TOEFL (minimum score 550 paper-based; 79 iBT). Electronic applications accepted.

University of Houston–Clear Lake, School of Science and Computer Engineering, Program in Computer Information Systems, Houston, TX 77058-1002. Offers MS. *Program availability:* Part-time, evening/weekend. *Entrance requirements:* For master's, GRE General Test. Additional exam requirements/recommendations for international students: Required—TOEFL (minimum score 550 paper-based).

University of Illinois at Urbana–Champaign, Graduate College, School of Information Sciences, Champaign, IL 61820. Offers bioinformatics (MS); digital libraries (CAS); information management (MS); library and information science (MS, PhD, CAS). *Accreditation:* ALA (one or more programs are accredited). *Program availability:* Part-time, online learning. *Entrance requirements:* For degree, master's degree in library and information science or related field with minimum GPA of 3.0.

University of Illinois at Urbana–Champaign, Illinois Informatics Institute, Champaign, IL 61820. Offers PhD. *Degree requirements:* For doctorate, thesis/dissertation.

The University of Iowa, Graduate College, Program in Informatics, Iowa City, IA 52242-1316. Offers bioinformatics (MS, PhD); bioinformatics and computational biology (Certificate); geoinformatics (MS, PhD, Certificate); health informatics (MS, PhD, Certificate); information science (MS, PhD, Certificate). *Degree requirements:* For master's, thesis optional; for doctorate, comprehensive exam, thesis/dissertation. *Entrance requirements:* For master's and doctorate, GRE General Test, minimum GPA of 3.0. Additional exam requirements/recommendations for international students: Required—TOEFL (minimum score 550 paper-based; 81 iBT). Electronic applications accepted.

University of Kentucky, Graduate School, College of Communication and Information, Program in Information Communication Technology, Lexington, KY 40506-0032. Offers MA, PhD. *Degree requirements:* For master's, comprehensive exam, thesis optional; for doctorate, comprehensive exam, thesis/dissertation. *Entrance requirements:* For master's, GRE General Test, minimum undergraduate GPA of 2.75; for doctorate, GRE General Test, minimum graduate GPA of 3.0, undergraduate 2.75. Additional exam requirements/recommendations for international students: Required—TOEFL (minimum score 550 paper-based). Electronic applications accepted. *Faculty research:* Public service campaigns, health communication, mass media law and public policy, political communication, international and intercultural communication.

University of Maine, Graduate School, College of Liberal Arts and Sciences, School of Computing and Information Science, Orono, ME 04469. Offers MS, PhD, CGS. *Program availability:* Part-time. *Faculty:* 13 full-time (2 women), 2 part-time/adjunct (1 woman). *Students:* 18 full-time (3 women), 10 part-time (2 women); includes 3 minority (1 Black or African American, non-Hispanic/Latino; 1 American Indian or Alaska Native, non-Hispanic/Latino; 1 Two or more races, non-Hispanic/Latino), 6 international. Average age 36. 34 applicants, 74% accepted, 10 enrolled. In 2018, 9 master's, 1 doctorate, 2 other advanced degrees awarded. *Degree requirements:* For master's, thesis (for some programs); for doctorate, comprehensive exam, thesis/dissertation. *Entrance requirements:* For master's and doctorate, GRE General Test, GRE Subject Test. Additional exam requirements/recommendations for international students: Required—TOEFL (minimum score 550 paper-based; 80 iBT). *Application deadline:* Applications are processed on a rolling basis. Application fee: $65. Electronic applications accepted. *Financial support:* In 2018–19, 21 students received support, including 1 fellowship (averaging $21,400 per year), 11 research assistantships with full tuition reimbursements available (averaging $17,200 per year), 8 teaching assistantships with full tuition reimbursements available (averaging $15,600 per year); career-related internships or fieldwork, Federal Work-Study, institutionally sponsored loans, tuition waivers (full), and unspecified assistantships also available. Financial award application deadline: 3/1. *Faculty research:* Geographic information science, spatial informatics, scientific computing. *Total annual research expenditures:* $860,302. *Unit head:* Dr. Max Egenhofer, Acting Director, 207-581-2114, Fax: 207-581-2206. *Application contact:* Scott G. Delcourt, Assistant Vice President for Graduate Studies and Senior Associate Dean, 207-581-3291, Fax: 207-581-3232, E-mail: graduate@maine.edu.
Website: http://umaine.edu/cis/

University of Maryland, Baltimore County, The Graduate School, College of Engineering and Information Technology, Department of Information Systems, Program in Information Systems, Baltimore, MD 21250. Offers MS, PhD. *Program availability:* Part-time, 100% online. *Degree requirements:* For master's, comprehensive exam (for some programs), thesis optional; for doctorate, comprehensive exam, thesis/dissertation. *Entrance requirements:* For master's, minimum GPA of 3.0; for doctorate, GRE General Test or GMAT, competence in statistical analysis, experimental design, programming, databases, and computer networks. Additional exam requirements/recommendations for international students: Required—TOEFL (minimum score 550 paper-based; 80 iBT). Electronic applications accepted. *Expenses:* Contact institution. *Faculty research:* Artificial intelligence/knowledge management, database/data mining, software engineering.

University of Maryland University College, The Graduate School, Program in Information Technology, Adelphi, MD 20783. Offers MS. *Program availability:* Part-time, evening/weekend, online learning. *Students:* 11 full-time (3 women), 1,030 part-time (368 women); includes 564 minority (382 Black or African American, non-Hispanic/Latino; 2 American Indian or Alaska Native, non-Hispanic/Latino; 77 Asian, non-Hispanic/Latino; 69 Hispanic/Latino; 4 Native Hawaiian or other Pacific Islander, non-Hispanic/Latino; 30 Two or more races, non-Hispanic/Latino), 58 international. Average age 36. 259 applicants, 100% accepted, 174 enrolled. In 2018, 280 master's awarded. *Degree requirements:* For master's, thesis or alternative, capstone course. *Application deadline:* Applications are processed on a rolling basis. Application fee: $50. Electronic applications accepted. *Financial support:* Scholarships/grants available. Support available to part-time students. Financial award application deadline: 6/1; financial award applicants required to submit FAFSA. *Unit head:* Les Pang, Acting Vice Dean, 240-684-2400, E-mail: les.pang@umuc.edu. *Application contact:* Admissions, 800-888-8682, E-mail: studentfirst@umuc.edu.
Website: http://www.umuc.edu/academic-programs/masters-degrees/information-technology.cfm

University of Michigan, School of Information, Ann Arbor, MI 48109-1285. Offers health informatics (MHI); information (MSI, PhD). *Accreditation:* ALA (one or more programs are accredited). *Program availability:* Part-time. *Students:* 453 full-time (270 women), 32 part-time (20 women); includes 99 minority (16 Black or African American, non-Hispanic/Latino; 49 Asian, non-Hispanic/Latino; 21 Hispanic/Latino; 13 Two or more races, non-Hispanic/Latino), 212 international. Average age 27. 829 applicants, 53% accepted, 199 enrolled. In 2018, 179 master's, 7 doctorates awarded. Terminal master's awarded for partial completion of doctoral program. *Degree requirements:* For master's, thesis optional, internship; for doctorate, thesis/dissertation. *Entrance requirements:* For master's and doctorate, GRE General Test. Additional exam requirements/recommendations for international students: Required—TOEFL (minimum score 100 iBT). *Application deadline:* Applications are processed on a rolling basis. Application fee: $75 ($90 for international students). Electronic applications accepted. *Expenses:* Contact institution. *Financial support:* In 2018–19, 122 students received support, including 2 fellowships (averaging $28,200 per year), 33 research assistantships (averaging $28,200 per year), 41 teaching assistantships (averaging $28,200 per year); scholarships/grants and tuition waivers (full and partial) also available. *Unit head:* Dr. Thomas A. Finholt, Dean, School of Information, 734-647-3576. *Application contact:* School of Information Admissions, 734-763-2285, Fax: 734-615-3587, E-mail: umsi.admissions@umich.edu.
Website: http://www.si.umich.edu/

University of Michigan–Dearborn, College of Engineering and Computer Science, Master of Science Program in Computer and Information Science, Dearborn, MI 48128. Offers MS. *Program availability:* Part-time, evening/weekend, 100% online. *Faculty:* 19 full-time (1 woman), 5 part-time/adjunct (0 women). *Students:* 30 full-time (19 women), 46 part-time (10 women); includes 15 minority (4 Black or African American, non-Hispanic/Latino; 6 Asian, non-Hispanic/Latino; 3 Hispanic/Latino; 2 Two or more races, non-Hispanic/Latino), 37 international. Average age 28. 123 applicants, 53% accepted, 24 enrolled. In 2018, 34 master's awarded. *Degree requirements:* For master's, thesis optional. *Entrance requirements:* For master's, bachelor's degree with minimum GPA of 3.0. Additional exam requirements/recommendations for international students: Required—TOEFL (minimum score 560 paper-based; 84 iBT), IELTS (minimum score 6.5). *Application deadline:* For fall admission, 8/1 priority date for domestic students, 5/1 for international students; for winter admission, 12/1 priority date for domestic students, 9/1 for international students; for spring admission, 4/1 priority date for domestic students, 1/1 for international students. Applications are processed on a rolling basis. Application fee: $60. Electronic applications accepted. *Expenses:* Tuition, state resident: full-time $15,380; part-time $88 per credit hour. Tuition, nonresident: full-time $23,948; part-time $1377 per credit hour. *Required fees:* $780; $780 $390. Tuition and fees vary according to course level, course load, degree level, program, reciprocity agreements and student level. *Financial support:* In 2018–19, 27 students received support. Research assistantships with full tuition reimbursements available, teaching assistantships with full tuition reimbursements available, career-related internships or fieldwork, scholarships/grants, unspecified assistantships, and non-resident tuition scholarships available. Support available to part-time students. Financial award application deadline: 3/1; financial award applicants required to submit FAFSA. *Faculty research:* Data science and management, cybersecurity, software engineering, distributed systems, computer graphics and visualization. *Unit head:* Dr. David Yoon, Director, 313-436-9146, E-mail: dhyoon@umich.edu. *Application contact:* Office of Graduate Studies, 313-583-6321, E-mail: umd-graduatestudies@umich.edu.
Website: https://umdearborn.edu/cecs/departments/computer-and-information-science/graduate-programs/masters-computer-and-information-science

University of Michigan–Dearborn, College of Engineering and Computer Science, PhD Program in Computer and Information Science, Dearborn, MI 48128. Offers data management (PhD); data science (PhD); software engineering (PhD); systems and security (PhD). *Faculty:* 19 full-time (1 woman), 5 part-time/adjunct (0 women). *Students:* 7 full-time (4 women), 7 part-time (1 woman); includes 1 minority (Asian, non-Hispanic/Latino), 9 international. Average age 30. 22 applicants, 36% accepted, 6 enrolled. In 2018, 1 doctorate awarded. *Degree requirements:* For doctorate, comprehensive exam, thesis/dissertation. *Entrance requirements:* For doctorate, GRE, bachelor's or master's degree in computer science or closely-related field. Additional exam requirements/recommendations for international students: Required—TOEFL (minimum score 560 paper-based; 84 iBT), IELTS (minimum score 6.5). *Application deadline:* For fall admission, 2/1 for domestic and international students. Application fee: $60. Electronic applications accepted. *Expenses:* Tuition, state resident: full-time $15,380; part-time $88 per credit hour. Tuition, nonresident: full-time $23,948; part-time $1377 per credit hour. *Required fees:* $780; $780 $390. Tuition and fees vary according to course level, course load, degree level, program, reciprocity agreements and student level. *Financial support:* In 2018–19, 2 students received support. Research assistantships with full tuition reimbursements available, teaching assistantships with full tuition reimbursements available, scholarships/grants, health care benefits, and unspecified assistantships available. Financial award application deadline: 2/1; financial award applicants required to submit FAFSA. *Faculty research:* Data science, data management, cybersecurity, software engineering, systems. *Unit head:* Dr. Di Ma, Director, 313-583-6737, E-mail: dmadma@umich.edu. *Application contact:* Office of Graduate Studies, 313-583-6321, E-mail: umd-graduatestudies@umich.edu.
Website: https://umdearborn.edu/cecs/departments/computer-and-information-science/graduate-programs/phd-computer-and-information-science

University of Michigan–Flint, College of Arts and Sciences, Program in Computer Science and Information Systems, Flint, MI 48502-1950. Offers computer science (MS); information systems (MS), including business information systems, health information systems. *Program availability:* Part-time, evening/weekend, 100% online. *Faculty:* 15 full-time (5 women), 7 part-time/adjunct (3 women). *Students:* 33 full-time (14 women), 56 part-time (17 women); includes 17 minority (4 Black or African American, non-Hispanic/Latino; 1 American Indian or Alaska Native, non-Hispanic/Latino; 3 Asian, non-Hispanic/Latino; 6 Hispanic/Latino; 1 Native Hawaiian or other Pacific Islander, non-Hispanic/Latino; 2 Two or more races, non-Hispanic/Latino), 39 international. Average age 30. 310 applicants, 66% accepted, 21 enrolled. In 2018, 29 master's awarded. *Degree requirements:* For master's, thesis optional, Non Thesis option available. *Entrance requirements:* For master's, BS from regionally-accredited institution in computer science, computer information systems, or computer engineering (preferred); minimum overall undergraduate GPA of 3.0. Additional exam requirements/recommendations for international students: Required—TOEFL (minimum score 84 iBT), IELTS (minimum score 6.5). *Application deadline:* For fall admission, 8/1 for domestic students, 5/1 for international students; for winter admission, 10/1 for domestic students, 8/1 for international students; for spring admission, 3/15 for domestic students, 1/1 for international students. Applications are processed on a rolling basis. Application fee: $55. Electronic applications accepted. *Expenses:* Contact institution. *Financial support:* Federal Work-Study, scholarships/grants, and unspecified assistantships available. Financial award application deadline: 3/1; financial award applicants required to submit FAFSA. *Faculty research:* Computer network systems, database management systems, artificial intelligence and controlled systems. *Unit head:* Dr. Mike Farmer, Department Chair, 810-762-3423, Fax: 810-766-6780, E-mail: farmerme@umflint.edu. *Application contact:* Matt Bohlen, Director of Graduate Admissions, 810-762-3171, Fax: 810-766-6789, E-mail: mbohlen@umflint.edu.
Website: http://www.umflint.edu/graduateprograms/computer-science-information-systems-ms

University of Nebraska at Omaha, Graduate Studies, College of Information Science and Technology, Department of Information Systems and Quantitative Analysis, Omaha, NE 68182. Offers data analytics (Certificate); information assurance (Certificate); information technology (MIT, PhD); management information systems (MS); project management (Certificate); systems analysis and design (Certificate). *Program availability:* Part-time, evening/weekend. *Degree requirements:* For master's, comprehensive exam, thesis (for some programs); for doctorate, comprehensive exam, thesis/dissertation. *Entrance requirements:* For master's, GRE General Test, minimum GPA of 3.0, 3 letters of recommendation, writing sample, resume, official transcripts; for doctorate, GMAT or GRE General Test, minimum GPA of 3.0, 3 letters of recommendation, writing sample, resume, official transcripts; for Certificate, minimum GPA of 3.0, official transcripts. Additional exam requirements/recommendations for international students: Required—TOEFL, IELTS, PTE. Electronic applications accepted.

University of Nebraska–Lincoln, Graduate College, College of Arts and Sciences and College of Engineering, Department of Computer Science and Engineering, Lincoln, NE 68588. Offers bioinformatics (MS, PhD); computer engineering (MS, PhD); computer science (MS, PhD); information technology (PhD). *Degree requirements:* For master's, thesis optional; for doctorate, comprehensive exam, thesis/dissertation. *Entrance requirements:* For master's and doctorate, GRE General Test. Additional exam requirements/recommendations for international students: Required—TOEFL (minimum score 600 paper-based). Electronic applications accepted. *Faculty research:* Software engineering, geo- and bio-informatics, scientific computation, secure communication.

University of North Alabama, College of Arts and Sciences, Department of Interdisciplinary and Professional Studies, Florence, AL 35632-0001. Offers professional studies (MPS), including community development, higher education administration, information technology, security and safety leadership. *Program availability:* Part-time, 100% online. *Degree requirements:* For master's, thesis optional. *Entrance requirements:* For master's, ETS PPI, personal statement; three letters of recommendation. Additional exam requirements/recommendations for international students: Required—TOEFL (minimum score 79 iBT), IELTS (minimum score 6), PTE (minimum score 54). Electronic applications accepted.

The University of North Carolina at Charlotte, College of Computing and Informatics, Department of Software and Information Systems, Charlotte, NC 28223-0001. Offers advanced databases and knowledge discovery (Graduate Certificate); game design and development (Graduate Certificate); information security and privacy (Graduate Certificate); information technology (MS); management of information technology (Graduate Certificate); network security (Graduate Certificate); secure software development (Graduate Certificate). *Program availability:* Part-time, evening/weekend. *Students:* 122 full-time (57 women), 102 part-time (39 women); includes 44 minority (24 Black or African American, non-Hispanic/Latino; 8 Asian, non-Hispanic/Latino; 10 Hispanic/Latino; 2 Two or more races, non-Hispanic/Latino), 126 international. Average age 28. 308 applicants, 82% accepted, 98 enrolled. In 2018, 107 master's, 18 other advanced degrees awarded. *Entrance requirements:* For master's, GRE or GMAT, undergraduate or equivalent course work in data structures, object-oriented programming in C++, C#, or Java with minimum GPA of 3.0; for Graduate Certificate, bachelor's degree from accredited institution in computing, mathematical, engineering or business discipline with minimum overall GPA of 2.8, junior/senior 3.0; substantial knowledge of data structures and object-oriented programming in C++, C# or Java. Additional exam requirements/recommendations for international students: Required—TOEFL (minimum score 523 paper-based; 70 iBT), IELTS (minimum score 6), TOEFL (minimum score 523 paper-based, 70 iBT) or IELTS (6). *Application deadline:* Applications are processed on a rolling basis. Application fee: $75. Electronic applications accepted. *Expenses:* Contact institution. *Financial support:* Fellowships, research assistantships, teaching assistantships, career-related internships or fieldwork, institutionally sponsored loans, scholarships/grants, and unspecified assistantships available. Support available to part-time students. Financial award application deadline: 3/1; financial award applicants required to submit FAFSA. *Total annual research expenditures:* $3.1 million. *Unit head:* Dr. Mary Lou Maher, Chair, 704-687-1940, E-mail: mmaher9@uncc.edu. *Application contact:* Kathy B. Giddings, Director of Graduate Admissions, 704-687-5503, Fax: 704-687-1668, E-mail: gradadm@uncc.edu.
Website: http://sis.uncc.edu/

University of North Texas, Toulouse Graduate School, Denton, TX 76203-5459. Offers accounting (MS); applied anthropology (MA, MS); applied behavior analysis (Certificate); applied geography (MA); applied technology and performance improvement (M Ed, MS); art education (MA); art history (MA); arts leadership (Certificate); audiology (Au D); behavior analysis (MS); behavioral science (PhD); biochemistry and molecular biology (MS); biology (MA, MS); biomedical engineering (MS); business analysis (MS); chemistry (MS); clinical health psychology (PhD); communication studies (MA, MS); computer engineering (MS); computer science (MS); counseling (M Ed, MS), including clinical mental health counseling (MS), college and university counseling, elementary school counseling, secondary school counseling; creative writing (MA); criminal justice (MS); curriculum and instruction (M Ed); decision sciences (MBA); design (MA, MFA), including fashion design (MFA), innovation studies,

interior design (MFA); early childhood studies (MS); economics (MS); educational leadership (M Ed, Ed D); educational psychology (MS, PhD), including family studies (MS), gifted and talented (MS), human development (MS), learning and cognition (MS), research, measurement and evaluation (MS); electrical engineering (MS); emergency management (MPA); engineering technology (MS); English (MA); English as a second language (MA); environmental science (MS); finance (MBA, MS); financial management (MPA); French (MA); health services management (MBA); higher education (M Ed, Ed D); history (MA, MS); hospitality management (MS); human resources management (MPA); information science (MS); information systems (PhD); information technologies (MBA); interdisciplinary studies (MA, MS); international studies (MA); international sustainable tourism (MS); jazz studies (MM); journalism (MA, MJ, Graduate Certificate), including interactive and virtual digital communication (Graduate Certificate), narrative journalism (Graduate Certificate); public relations (Graduate Certificate); kinesiology (MS); linguistics (MA); local government management (MPA); logistics (PhD); logistics and supply chain management (MBA); long-term care, senior housing, and aging services (MA); management (PhD); marketing (MBA); mathematics (MA, MS); mechanical and energy engineering (MS, PhD); music (MA), including ethnomusicology, music theory, musicology, performance; music composition (PhD); music education (MM Ed, PhD); nonprofit management (MPA); operations and supply chain management (MBA); performance (MM, DMA); philosophy (MA); political science (MA); professional and technical communication (MA); radio, television and film (MA, MFA); rehabilitation counseling (Certificate); sociology (MA); Spanish (MA); special education (M Ed); speech-language pathology (MA); strategic management (MBA); studio art (MFA); teaching (M Ed); MBA/MS. *Program availability:* Part-time, evening/weekend, online learning. Terminal master's awarded for partial completion of doctoral program. *Degree requirements:* For master's, variable foreign language requirement, comprehensive exam (for some programs), thesis (for some programs); for doctorate, variable foreign language requirement, comprehensive exam (for some programs), thesis/dissertation; for other advanced degree, variable foreign language requirement, comprehensive exam (for some programs). *Entrance requirements:* For master's and doctorate, GRE, GMAT. Additional exam requirements/recommendations for international students: Required—TOEFL (minimum score 550 paper-based; 79 iBT). Electronic applications accepted.

University of Oregon, Graduate School, College of Arts and Sciences, Department of Computer and Information Science, Eugene, OR 97403. Offers MA, MS, PhD. *Program availability:* Part-time. Terminal master's awarded for partial completion of doctoral program. *Degree requirements:* For doctorate, thesis/dissertation. *Entrance requirements:* For master's and doctorate, GRE General Test, minimum GPA of 3.0. Additional exam requirements/recommendations for international students: Required—TOEFL. *Faculty research:* Artificial intelligence, graphics, natural-language processing, expert systems, operating systems.

University of Ottawa, Faculty of Graduate and Postdoctoral Studies, Faculty of Engineering, Engineering Management Program, Ottawa, ON K1N 6N5, Canada. Offers engineering management (M Eng); information technology (Certificate); project management (Certificate). *Degree requirements:* For master's, thesis or alternative. *Entrance requirements:* For master's and Certificate, honors degree or equivalent, minimum B average. Electronic applications accepted.

University of Pennsylvania, School of Engineering and Applied Science, Department of Computer and Information Science, Philadelphia, PA 19104. Offers computer and information science (MSE, PhD); computer and information technology (MCIT); computer graphics and game technology (MSE). *Program availability:* Part-time. *Students:* Average age 26. 2,559 applicants, 14% accepted, 216 enrolled. In 2018, 130 master's, 15 doctorates awarded. Terminal master's awarded for partial completion of doctoral program. *Degree requirements:* For master's, comprehensive exam, thesis optional; for doctorate, comprehensive exam, thesis/dissertation. *Entrance requirements:* For master's and doctorate, GRE, bachelor's degree, letters of recommendation, resume, personal statement. Additional exam requirements/recommendations for international students: Required—TOEFL (minimum score 100 iBT), IELTS (minimum score 7). *Application deadline:* For fall admission, 12/15 priority date for domestic and international students. Application fee: $80. Electronic applications accepted. *Expenses:* Contact institution. *Faculty research:* Artificial intelligence, bioinformatics and computational biology, embedded and real-time systems, machine learning, security and information assurance. *Application contact:* William Fenton, Assistant Director of Graduate Admissions, 215-898-4542, Fax: 215-573-5577, E-mail: gradstudies@seas.upenn.edu.
Website: http://www.cis.upenn.edu/prospective-students/graduate/

University of Pittsburgh, School of Computing and Information, Department of Informatics and Networked Systems, Pittsburgh, PA 15260. Offers big data analytics (Certificate); information science (MSIS, PhD, Certificate), including telecommunications (PhD); security assurance/information systems (Certificate); telecommunications (MST, Certificate). *Program availability:* Part-time, evening/weekend, 100% online. *Degree requirements:* For master's, thesis optional; for doctorate, comprehensive exam, thesis/dissertation. *Entrance requirements:* For master's, GRE, GMAT, bachelor's degree with minimum GPA of 3.0; previous course work in instructional programming language, statistics, mathematics, and probability; for doctorate, GRE, GMAT, master's degree; minimum GPA of 3.3; course work in programming, cognitive psychology, systems analysis and design, data structures, and statistics or mathematics; for Certificate, master's degree in information science, telecommunications, or related field. Additional exam requirements/recommendations for international students: Required—TOEFL (minimum score 550 paper-based; 80 iBT), IELTS (minimum score 6.5). Electronic applications accepted. *Expenses:* Contact institution. *Faculty research:* Cybersecurity and privacy, social computing and networks, data analytics and data science, human-centered computing, spectrum use and enforcement.

University of Pittsburgh, School of Computing and Information, Department of Information Culture and Data Stewardship, Pittsburgh, PA 15260. Offers library and information science (MLIS, PhD). *Accreditation:* ALA. *Program availability:* Part-time, evening/weekend, 100% online. *Degree requirements:* For master's, thesis optional; for doctorate, comprehensive exam, thesis/dissertation. *Entrance requirements:* For master's, GRE General Test, GMAT, MAT, MCAT, LSAT, bachelor's degree with minimum GPA of 3.0; for doctorate, GRE General Test, GMAT, MAT, MCAT, LSAT, master's degree with minimum GPA of 3.5. Additional exam requirements/recommendations for international students: Required—TOEFL (minimum score 550 paper-based; 80 iBT), IELTS (minimum score 6.5). Electronic applications accepted. *Expenses:* Contact institution. *Faculty research:* Data and information, archives and data preservation, information and society, children and youth services, research data management.

University of Puerto Rico–Mayagüez, Graduate Studies, College of Engineering, Department of Electrical and Computer Engineering, Mayagüez, PR 00681-9000. Offers computer engineering (ME, MS); computing and information sciences and engineering (PhD); electrical engineering (ME, MS). *Program availability:* Part-time. Terminal master's awarded for partial completion of doctoral program. *Degree requirements:* For master's, one foreign language, comprehensive exam, thesis; for doctorate, one foreign language, comprehensive exam, thesis/dissertation. *Entrance requirements:* For master's and doctorate, proficiency in English and Spanish; BS in electrical or computer engineering, or equivalent; minimum GPA of 3.0. Electronic applications accepted. *Faculty research:* Digital signal processing, power electronics, microwave ocean emissivity, parallel and distributed computing, microwave remote sensing.

University of Puerto Rico–Río Piedras, Graduate School of Information Sciences and Technologies, San Juan, PR 00931-3300. Offers administration of academic libraries (PMC); administration of public libraries (PMC); administration of special libraries (PMC); consultant in information services (PMC); documents and files administration (Post-Graduate Certificate); electronic information resources analyst (Post-Graduate Certificate); information science (MIS); librarianship and information services (MLS); school librarian (Post-Graduate Certificate); school librarian distance education mode (Post-Graduate Certificate); specialist in legal information (PMC). *Accreditation:* ALA. *Program availability:* Part-time. *Degree requirements:* For master's, comprehensive exam, thesis, portfolio. *Entrance requirements:* For master's, PAEG, GRE, interview, minimum GPA of 3.0, 3 letters of recommendation; for other advanced degree, PAEG, GRE, minimum GPA of 3.0, IST master's degree. *Faculty research:* Investigating the users needs and preferences for a specialized environmental library.

University of St. Thomas, School of Engineering, St. Paul, MN 55105. Offers data science (MS); electrical engineering (MS); information technology (MS); manufacturing engineering (MS); manufacturing systems (Certificate); mechanical engineering (MS); medical device development (Certificate); regulatory science (MS); software engineering (MS); software management (MS); systems engineering (MS); technology leadership (Certificate); technology management (MS). *Program availability:* Part-time, evening/weekend. *Entrance requirements:* For master's, resume, official transcripts. Additional exam requirements/recommendations for international students: Required—TOEFL (minimum score 80 iBT), IELTS (minimum score 6.5). Electronic applications accepted. *Expenses:* Contact institution.

University of South Africa, College of Human Sciences, Pretoria, South Africa. Offers adult education (M Ed); African languages (MA, PhD); African politics (MA, PhD); Afrikaans (MA, PhD); ancient history (MA, PhD); ancient Near Eastern studies (MA, PhD); anthropology (MA, PhD); applied linguistics (MA); Arabic (MA, PhD); archaeology (MA); art history (MA); Biblical archaeology (MA); Biblical studies (M Th, D Th, PhD); Christian spirituality (M Th, D Th); church history (M Th, D Th); classical studies (MA, PhD); clinical psychology (MA); communication (MA, PhD); comparative education (M Ed, Ed D); consulting psychology (D Admin, D Com, PhD); curriculum studies (M Ed, Ed D); development studies (M Admin, MA, D Admin, PhD); didactics (M Ed, Ed D); education (M Tech); education management (M Ed, Ed D); educational psychology (M Ed); English (MA); environmental education (M Ed); French (MA, PhD); German (MA, PhD); Greek (MA); guidance and counseling (M Ed); health studies (MA, PhD), including health sciences education (MA), health services management (MA), medical and surgical nursing science (critical care general) (MA), midwifery and neonatal nursing science (MA), trauma and emergency care (MA); history (MA, PhD); history of education (Ed D); inclusive education (M Ed, Ed D); information and communications technology policy and regulation (MA); information science (MA, MIS, PhD); international politics (MA, PhD); Islamic studies (MA, PhD); Italian (MA, PhD); Judaica (MA, PhD); linguistics (MA, PhD); mathematical education (M Ed); mathematics education (MA); missiology (M Th, D Th); modern Hebrew (MA, PhD); musicology (MA, MMus, D Mus, PhD); natural science education (M Ed); New Testament (M Th, D Th); Old Testament (D Th); pastoral therapy (M Th, D Th); philosophy (MA); philosophy of education (M Ed, Ed D); politics (MA, PhD); Portuguese (MA, PhD); practical theology (M Th, D Th); psychology (MA, MS, PhD); psychology of education (M Ed, Ed D); public health (MA); religious studies (MA, D Th, PhD); Romance languages (MA); Russian (MA, PhD); Semitic languages (MA, PhD); social behavior studies in HIV/AIDS (MA); social science (mental health) (MA); social science in development studies (MA); social science in psychology (MA); social science in social work (MA); social science in sociology (MA); social work (MSW, DSW, PhD); socio-education (M Ed, Ed D); sociolinguistics (MA); sociology (MA, PhD); Spanish (MA, PhD); systematic theology (M Th, D Th); TESOL (teaching English to speakers of other languages) (MA); theological ethics (M Th, D Th); theory of literature (MA, PhD); urban ministries (D Th); urban ministry (M Th).

University of South Carolina Upstate, Graduate Programs, Spartanburg, SC 29303-4999. Offers early childhood education (M Ed); elementary education (M Ed); informatics (MS); special education: visual impairment (M Ed). *Accreditation:* NCATE. *Program availability:* Part-time, evening/weekend. *Degree requirements:* For master's, professional portfolio. *Entrance requirements:* For master's, GRE General Test or MAT, interview, minimum undergraduate GPA of 2.5, teaching certificate, 2 letters of recommendation. *Faculty research:* Promoting university diversity awareness, rough and tumble play, social justice education, American Indian literatures and cultures, diversity and multicultural education, science teaching strategy.

University of Southern Mississippi, College of Education and Human Sciences, School of Library and Information Science, Hattiesburg, MS 39406-0001. Offers library and information science (MLIS); youth services and literature (Graduate Certificate). *Accreditation:* ALA (one or more programs are accredited). *Program availability:* Part-time, evening/weekend, online learning. *Degree requirements:* For master's, comprehensive exam, thesis. *Entrance requirements:* For master's, GRE General Test, minimum GPA of 3.0. Additional exam requirements/recommendations for international students: Required—TOEFL, IELTS. Electronic applications accepted. *Faculty research:* Printing, library history, children's literature, telecommunications, management.

University of South Florida, College of Arts and Sciences, School of Information, Tampa, FL 33620-9951. Offers intelligence studies (MS), including cyber intelligence, strategic intelligence; library and information science (MA). *Accreditation:* ALA (one or more programs are accredited). *Program availability:* Part-time, evening/weekend, online learning. *Faculty:* 15 full-time (7 women). *Students:* 108 full-time (77 women), 182 part-time (137 women); includes 83 minority (23 Black or African American, non-Hispanic/Latino; 7 Asian, non-Hispanic/Latino; 49 Hispanic/Latino; 4 Two or more races, non-Hispanic/Latino). Average age 32. 141 applicants, 86% accepted, 71 enrolled. In 2018, 128 master's awarded. *Degree requirements:* For master's, comprehensive exam, thesis (for some programs). *Entrance requirements:* For master's, GRE not required for Intelligence Studies; GRE required for Library and Information Science with preferred minimum scores of 734d percentile (156v), 10th percentile (141Q). May be waived under certain criteria, goals statement, resume or CV, some programs need understanding of programming/coding, computational problem solving and operating systems (for Intelligence Studies); GRE, writing sample, 3 letters of recommendation, resume, statement of purpose (for Library and Information Science). Additional exam requirements/recommendations for international students: Required—TOEFL, TOEFL (minimum score 550 paper-based; 79 iBT) or IELTS (minimum score 6.5). *Application deadline:* For fall admission, 6/1 priority date for domestic students, 5/1 for international students; for spring admission, 10/15 priority date for domestic students, 9/15 for international students. Applications are processed on a rolling basis. Application fee: $30. Electronic applications accepted. *Expenses:* Tuition, state resident: full-time $6350. Tuition, nonresident: full-time $19,048. *International tuition:* $19,048 full-time. *Required fees:* $2079. *Financial support:* In 2018–19, 62 students received support. Unspecified assistantships available. Financial award application deadline: 6/30. *Faculty research:* Youth services in libraries, community engagement and libraries, information architecture, biomedical informatics, health informatics. *Total annual research expenditures:* $21,733. *Unit head:* Dr. Jim Andrews, Director and Associate Professor, 813-974-2108, Fax: 813-974-6840, E-mail: jimandrews@usf.edu. *Application contact:* Dr. Randy Borum, Graduate Program Director, 813-974-3520, Fax: 813-974-6840, E-mail: wborum@usf.edu.
Website: http://si.usf.edu/

The University of Tennessee, Graduate School, College of Communication and Information, School of Information Sciences, Knoxville, TN 37996. Offers MS, PhD. *Accreditation:* ALA (one or more programs are accredited). *Program availability:* Part-time, evening/weekend, online learning. *Degree requirements:* For master's, 42 semester hours; written comprehensive exam, online e-portfolio, or thesis; for doctorate, thesis/dissertation or alternative. *Entrance requirements:* For master's, GRE General Test, minimum GPA of 2.7; for doctorate, GRE General Test (minimum scores at or above the 50th percentile on the 3 components, taken within the past five years), master's degree; minimum undergraduate GPA of 3.0, graduate 3.5; recommendation letters from at least three former instructors or professional supervisors; personal statement; interview. Additional exam requirements/recommendations for international students: Required—TOEFL. Electronic applications accepted.

The University of Texas at El Paso, Graduate School, College of Engineering, Department of Computer Science, El Paso, TX 79968-0001. Offers computer science (MS, PhD); cyber security (Graduate Certificate); information technology (MSIT); software engineering (MS). *Program availability:* Part-time, evening/weekend. *Degree requirements:* For master's, thesis optional; for doctorate, thesis/dissertation. *Entrance requirements:* For master's, GRE, minimum GPA of 3.0; for doctorate, GRE, statement of purpose, letters of reference. Additional exam requirements/recommendations for international students: Required—TOEFL; Recommended—IELTS. Electronic applications accepted.

The University of Texas at San Antonio, College of Business, Department of Information Systems and Cyber Security, San Antonio, TX 78249-0617. Offers cyber security (MSIT); information technology (MS, PhD); management of technology (MBA); technology entrepreneurship and management (Certificate). *Program availability:* Part-time, evening/weekend. *Degree requirements:* For master's, comprehensive exam (for some programs), thesis optional; for doctorate, comprehensive exam, thesis/dissertation. *Entrance requirements:* For master's and doctorate, GMAT/GRE, official transcripts, statement of purpose, letters of recommendation. Additional exam requirements/recommendations for international students: Required—TOEFL (minimum score 550 paper-based; 79 iBT), IELTS (minimum score 6.5). Electronic applications accepted. *Expenses:* Contact institution. *Faculty research:* Cyber security, digital forensics, economics of information systems, information systems privacy, information technology adoption.

University of the Sacred Heart, Graduate Programs, Department of Business Administration, Program in Information Technology, San Juan, PR 00914-0383. Offers Certificate.

University of Washington, Graduate School, Information School, Seattle, WA 98195. Offers information management (MSIM), including business intelligence, data science, information architecture, information consulting, information security, user experience; information science (PhD); library and information science (MLIS). *Accreditation:* ALA (one or more programs are accredited). *Program availability:* Part-time, evening/weekend, 100% online coursework with required attendance at on-campus orientation at start of program. *Faculty:* 51 full-time (23 women), 38 part-time/adjunct (21 women). *Students:* 347 full-time (229 women), 259 part-time (195 women); includes 129 minority (23 Black or African American, non-Hispanic/Latino; 7 American Indian or Alaska Native, non-Hispanic/Latino; 59 Asian, non-Hispanic/Latino; 36 Hispanic/Latino; 4 Native Hawaiian or other Pacific Islander, non-Hispanic/Latino), 160 international. Average age 32. 1,190 applicants, 42% accepted, 264 enrolled. In 2018, 231 master's, 10 doctorates awarded. Terminal master's awarded for partial completion of doctoral program. *Degree requirements:* For master's, comprehensive exam (for some programs), thesis or alternative, capstone or culminating project; for doctorate, comprehensive exam, thesis/dissertation. *Entrance requirements:* For master's, GRE General Test, GMAT; for doctorate, GRE General Test. Additional exam requirements/recommendations for international students: Required—TOEFL (minimum score 590 paper-based; 100 iBT). *Application deadline:* For fall admission, 12/1 priority date for domestic and international students. Application fee: $85. Electronic applications accepted. *Expenses:* MLIS: $825/credit $51,975 approximate tuition without fees; MSIM: $837/credit, $54,405 approximate tuition without fees. *Financial support:* In 2018–19, 73 students received support. Fellowships with full tuition reimbursements available, research assistantships with full tuition reimbursements available, teaching assistantships with full tuition reimbursements available, Federal Work-Study, institutionally sponsored loans, scholarships/grants, health care benefits, tuition waivers (full and partial), and unspecified assistantships available. Support available to part-time students. Financial award application deadline: 10/1; financial award applicants required to submit FAFSA. *Unit head:* Dr. Anind Dey, Dean, E-mail: anind@uw.edu. *Application contact:* Kari Brothers, Admissions Counselor, 206-616-5541, Fax: 206-616-3152, E-mail: kari683@uw.edu.
Website: http://ischool.uw.edu/

University of Waterloo, Graduate Studies and Postdoctoral Affairs, Faculty of Engineering, Department of Management Sciences, Waterloo, ON N2L 3G1, Canada. Offers applied operations research (MA Sc, MMS, PhD); information systems (MA Sc, MMS, PhD); management of technology (MA Sc, MMS, PhD). *Program availability:* Part-time, online learning. *Degree requirements:* For master's, research paper or thesis; for doctorate, comprehensive exam, thesis/dissertation. *Entrance requirements:* For master's, GMAT or GRE, honors degree, minimum B average, resume; for doctorate, GMAT or GRE, master's degree, minimum A- average, resume. Additional exam requirements/recommendations for international students: Required—TOEFL, IELTS, PTE. *Application deadline:* Applications are processed on a rolling basis. Application fee: $125 Canadian dollars. Electronic applications accepted. *Financial support:* Fellowships, research assistantships, teaching assistantships, career-related internships or fieldwork, and institutionally sponsored loans available. *Faculty research:* Operations research, manufacturing systems, scheduling, information systems.
Website: https://uwaterloo.ca/management-sciences/

University of Wisconsin–Parkside, College of Business, Economics, and Computing, Program in Computer and Information Systems, Kenosha, WI 53141-2000. Offers MSCIS. *Entrance requirements:* For master's, GRE General Test or GMAT, 3 letters of recommendation, minimum GPA of 3.0. *Faculty research:* Distributed systems, data bases, natural language processing, event-driven systems.

University of Wisconsin–Stout, Graduate School, College of Science, Technology, Engineering and Mathematics, Program in Information and Communication Technologies, Menomonie, WI 54751. Offers MS. *Program availability:* Part-time, online learning. *Degree requirements:* For master's, thesis. *Entrance requirements:* For master's, minimum GPA of 2.75. Additional exam requirements/recommendations for international students: Required—TOEFL (minimum score 500 paper-based; 61 iBT). Electronic applications accepted.

Western Governors University, College of Information Technology, Salt Lake City, UT 84107. Offers cybersecurity and information assurance (MS); data analytics (MS); information technology management (MS). *Program availability:* Online learning. *Degree requirements:* For master's, capstone project. Application fee is waived when completed online.

Youngstown State University, College of Graduate Studies, College of Science, Technology, Engineering and Mathematics, Department of Computer Science and Information Systems, Youngstown, OH 44555-0001. Offers computing and information systems (MCIS). *Program availability:* Part-time. *Degree requirements:* For master's, thesis or capstone project. *Entrance requirements:* For master's, GRE or GMAT. Additional exam requirements/recommendations for international students: Required—TOEFL (minimum score 550 paper-based). *Faculty research:* Networking, computational science, graphics and visualization, database and data mining, biometrics, artificial intelligence, online learning environments.

Internet Engineering

Dalhousie University, Faculty of Engineering, Department of Engineering Mathematics and Internetworking, Halifax, NS B3J 2X4, Canada. Offers engineering mathematics (M Sc, PhD); internetworking (M Eng). *Degree requirements:* For master's, thesis; for doctorate, thesis/dissertation. *Entrance requirements:* Additional exam requirements/ recommendations for international students: Required—TOEFL, IELTS, CANTEST, CAEL, or Michigan English Language Assessment Battery. Electronic applications accepted. *Faculty research:* Piecewise regression and robust statistics, random field theory, dynamical systems, wave loads on offshore structures, digital signal processing.

New Jersey Institute of Technology, Newark College of Engineering, Newark, NJ 07102. Offers biomedical engineering (MS, PhD); biopharmaceutical engineering (MS); chemical engineering (MS, PhD); civil engineering (MS, PhD); computer engineering (MS); critical infrastructure systems (MS); electrical engineering (MS, PhD); engineering management (MS); engineering science (MS); environmental engineering (MS, PhD); healthcare systems management (MS); industrial engineering (MS, PhD); internet engineering (MS); manufacturing systems engineering (MS); materials science & engineering (PhD); materials science and engineering (MS); mechanical engineering (MS, PhD); occupational safety and health engineering (MS). *Program availability:* Part-time, evening/weekend. *Faculty:* 147 full-time (26 women), 133 part-time/adjunct (16 women). *Students:* 690 full-time (163 women), 594 part-time (130 women); includes 427 minority (79 Black or African American, non-Hispanic/Latino; 181 Asian, non-Hispanic/ Latino; 140 Hispanic/Latino; 27 Two or more races, non-Hispanic/Latino), 553 international. Average age 27. 2,334 applicants, 57% accepted, 452 enrolled. In 2018, 418 master's, 31 doctorates awarded. Terminal master's awarded for partial completion of doctoral program. *Degree requirements:* For master's, thesis (for some programs); for doctorate, thesis/dissertation. *Entrance requirements:* For master's, GRE General Test, minimum GPA 2.8, personal statement, 1 letter of recommendation, transcripts; for doctorate, GRE General Test, minimum GPA of 3.5, personal statement, 3 letters of recommendation, transcripts. Additional exam requirements/recommendations for international students: Required—TOEFL (minimum score 550 paper-based; 79 iBT), IELTS (minimum score 6.5). *Application deadline:* For fall admission, 6/1 priority date for domestic students, 5/1 priority date for international students; for spring admission, 11/ 15 priority date for domestic and international students. Applications are processed on a rolling basis. Application fee: $75. Electronic applications accepted. *Expenses:* $22,690 per year (in-state), $32,136 per year (out-of-state). *Financial support:* In 2018–19, 396 students received support, including 52 fellowships with full tuition reimbursements available (averaging $22,000 per year), 113 research assistantships with full tuition reimbursements available (averaging $22,000 per year), 101 teaching assistantships with full tuition reimbursements available (averaging $22,000 per year); career-related internships or fieldwork, Federal Work-Study, scholarships/grants, and unspecified assistantships also available. Financial award application deadline: 1/15. *Faculty research:* Nonlinear signal processing, intelligent medical image analysis, calibration issues in coherent localization, computer-aided design, neural network for tool wear measurement. *Total annual research expenditures:* $41.7 million. *Unit head:* Dr. Moshe Kam, Dean, 973-596-5534, Fax: 973-596-2316, E-mail: moshe.kam@njit.edu. *Application contact:* Stephen Eck, Director of Admissions, 973-596-3300, Fax: 973-596-3461, E-mail: admissions@njit.edu.
Website: http://engineering.njit.edu/

Wilmington University, College of Technology, New Castle, DE 19720-6491. Offers cybersecurity (MS); information assurance (MS); information systems technologies (MS); management and management information systems (MS); technology project management (MS); Web design (MS). *Program availability:* Part-time, evening/ weekend. *Entrance requirements:* Additional exam requirements/recommendations for international students: Required—TOEFL (minimum score 500 paper-based). Electronic applications accepted.

Medical Informatics

Arizona State University at the Tempe campus, College of Health Solutions, Department of Biomedical Informatics, Phoenix, AZ 85004. Offers MS, PhD. Terminal master's awarded for partial completion of doctoral program. *Degree requirements:* For master's, interactive Program of Study (iPOS) submitted before completing 50 percent of required credit hours; for doctorate, comprehensive exam, thesis/dissertation, interactive Program of Study (iPOS) submitted before completing 50 percent of required credit hours. *Entrance requirements:* For master's, GRE or MCAT, bachelor's degree with minimum GPA of 3.25 in computer science, biology, physiology, nursing, statistics, engineering, related fields, or unrelated fields with appropriate academic backgrounds; resume/curriculum vitae; statement of purpose; 3 letters of recommendation; all official transcripts; for doctorate, GRE or MCAT, bachelor's degree with minimum GPA of 3.5 in computer science, biology, physiology, nursing, statistics, engineering, related fields, or unrelated fields with appropriate academic backgrounds; resume/curriculum vitae; statement of purpose; 3 letters of recommendation; all official transcripts. Additional exam requirements/recommendations for international students: Required—TOEFL (minimum score 550 paper-based; 83 iBT), IELTS (minimum score 6.5). Electronic applications accepted.

Brandeis University, Rabb School of Continuing Studies, Division of Graduate Professional Studies, Master of Science in Health and Medical Informatics Program, Waltham, MA 02454-9110. Offers MS. *Program availability:* Part-time-only. *Entrance requirements:* For master's, four-year bachelor's degree from regionally-accredited U.S. institution or equivalent; official transcript(s) from every college or university attended; resume or curriculum vitae; statement of goals; letter of recommendation. Additional exam requirements/recommendations for international students: Required—TWE (minimum score 4.5), TOEFL (minimum scores: 600 paper-based, 100 iBT), IELTS (7), or PTE (68). Electronic applications accepted. *Expenses:* Contact institution.

Columbia University, College of Dental Medicine and Graduate School of Arts and Sciences, Programs in Dental Specialties, New York, NY 10027. Offers advanced education in general dentistry (Certificate); biomedical informatics (MA, PhD); endodontics (Certificate); orthodontics (MS, Certificate); periodontics (MS, Certificate); prosthodontics (MS, Certificate); science education (MA). *Degree requirements:* For master's, thesis, presentation of seminar. *Entrance requirements:* For master's, GRE General Test, DDS or equivalent. *Expenses:* Contact institution. *Faculty research:* Analysis of growth/form, pulpal microcirculation, implants, microbiology of oral environment, calcified tissues.

Columbia University, College of Physicians and Surgeons, Department of Biomedical Informatics, New York, NY 10032. Offers M Phil, MA, PhD, MD/PhD. *Degree requirements:* For doctorate, thesis/dissertation. *Entrance requirements:* For master's and doctorate, GRE General Test, knowledge of computational techniques. Additional exam requirements/recommendations for international students: Required—TOEFL. Electronic applications accepted. *Faculty research:* Bioinformatics, bioimaging, clinical informatics, public health informatics.

Dalhousie University, Faculty of Computer Science, Halifax, NS B3H 1W5, Canada. Offers computational biology and bioinformatics (M Sc); computer science (MA Sc, MC Sc, PhD); electronic commerce (MEC); health informatics (MHI). *Degree requirements:* For master's, thesis (for some programs); for doctorate, thesis/ dissertation. *Entrance requirements:* Additional exam requirements/recommendations for international students: Required—1 of 5 approved tests: TOEFL, IELTS, CANTEST, CAEL, Michigan English Language Assessment Battery. Electronic applications accepted.

Grand Valley State University, Padnos College of Engineering and Computing, Health Informatics and Bioinformatics Program, Allendale, MI 49401-9403. Offers MS. *Program availability:* Part-time, evening/weekend. *Students:* 15 full-time (6 women), 15 part-time (9 women); includes 4 minority (1 Black or African American, non-Hispanic/Latino; 2 Asian, non-Hispanic/Latino; 1 Two or more races, non-Hispanic/Latino), 10 international. Average age 26. 18 applicants, 100% accepted, 12 enrolled. In 2018, 10 master's awarded. *Entrance requirements:* For master's, GRE or GMAT if undergraduate GPA is less than 3.0, minimum GPA of 3.0, resume, personal statement, minimum of 2 letters of recommendation, previous academic study or work experience. Additional exam requirements/recommendations for international students: Required—TOEFL (minimum iBT score of 80), IELTS (6.5), or Michigan English Language Assessment Battery (77). *Application deadline:* For fall admission, 2/1 priority date for domestic students. Applications are processed on a rolling basis. Application fee: $30. Electronic applications accepted. *Expenses:* $682 per credit hour, 36 credit hours. *Financial support:* In 2018–19, 7 students received support, including 2 fellowships, 5 research assistantships with full and partial tuition reimbursements available (averaging $8,000 per year); career-related internships or fieldwork, tuition waivers (full and partial), and unspecified assistantships also available. *Faculty research:* Biomedical informatics, information visualization, data mining, high-performance computing, computational biology. *Unit head:* Dr. Paul Leidig, Director, 616-331-2060, Fax: 616-331-2144, E-mail: leidigp@gvsu.edu. *Application contact:* Dr. Guenter Tusch, Graduate Program Director, 616-331-2046, Fax: 616-331-2144, E-mail: tuschg@gvsu.edu.

Middle Tennessee State University, College of Graduate Studies, College of Basic and Applied Sciences, Program in Professional Science, Murfreesboro, TN 37132. Offers actuarial sciences (MS); biostatistics (MS); biotechnology (MS); engineering management (MS); health care informatics (MS). *Program availability:* Part-time, evening/weekend, online learning. *Degree requirements:* For master's, comprehensive exam. *Entrance requirements:* For master's, GRE. Additional exam requirements/ recommendations for international students: Required—TOEFL (minimum score 525 paper-based; 71 iBT) or IELTS (minimum score 6).

Northwestern University, Feinberg School of Medicine, Driskill Graduate Program in Life Sciences, Chicago, IL 60611. Offers biostatistics (PhD); epidemiology (PhD); health and biomedical informatics (PhD); health services and outcomes research (PhD); healthcare quality and patient safety (PhD); translational outcomes in science (PhD). *Degree requirements:* For doctorate, comprehensive exam, thesis/dissertation, written and oral qualifying exams. *Entrance requirements:* For doctorate, GRE General Test. Additional exam requirements/recommendations for international students: Required—TOEFL (minimum score 600 paper-based). Electronic applications accepted.

Northwestern University, School of Professional Studies, Program in Information Systems, Evanston, IL 60208. Offers analytics and business intelligence (MS); database and Internet technologies (MS); information systems (MS); information systems management (MS); information systems security (MS); medical informatics (MS); software project management and development (MS). *Program availability:* Part-time, evening/weekend.

Nova Southeastern University, Dr. Kiran C. Patel College of Osteopathic Medicine, Fort Lauderdale, FL 33328. Offers biomedical informatics (MS, Graduate Certificate), including biomedical informatics (MS), clinical informatics (Graduate Certificate), public health informatics (Graduate Certificate); disaster and emergency management (MS); medical education (MS); nutrition (MS, Graduate Certificate), including functional nutrition and herbal therapy (Graduate Certificate); osteopathic medicine (DO); public health (MPH, Graduate Certificate), including health education (Graduate Certificate); social medicine (Graduate Certificate); DO/DMD. *Accreditation:* AOsA; CEPH. *Degree requirements:* For master's, comprehensive exam (for MPH); field/special projects; for doctorate, comprehensive exam, COMLEX Board Exams; for Graduate Certificate, thesis or alternative. *Entrance requirements:* For master's, GRE; for doctorate, MCAT, coursework in biology, chemistry, organic chemistry, physics (all with labs), biochemistry, and English. Electronic applications accepted. *Expenses:* Contact institution. *Faculty research:* Teaching strategies, simulated patient use, HIV/AIDS education, minority health issues, immune disorders.

Oregon Health & Science University, School of Medicine, Graduate Programs in Medicine, Department of Medical Informatics and Clinical Epidemiology, Portland, OR 97239-3098. Offers bioinformatics and computational biology (MS, PhD); clinical informatics (MBI, MS, PhD, Certificate); health information management (Certificate). *Program availability:* Part-time, online learning. *Faculty:* 12 full-time (6 women), 15 part-time/adjunct (7 women). *Students:* 28 full-time (12 women), 31 part-time (10 women); includes 13 minority (1 Black or African American, non-Hispanic/Latino; 9 Asian, non-Hispanic/Latino; 2 Hispanic/Latino; 1 Two or more races, non-Hispanic/Latino), 8 international. Average age 34. 65 applicants, 54% accepted, 32 enrolled. In 2018, 23 master's, 3 doctorates, 20 other advanced degrees awarded. Terminal master's awarded for partial completion of doctoral program. *Degree requirements:* For master's, thesis or capstone project; for doctorate, comprehensive exam, thesis/dissertation, qualifying exam. *Entrance requirements:* For master's and doctorate, GRE General Test (minimum scores: 153 Verbal/148 Quantitative/4.5 Analytical), coursework in computer programming, human anatomy and physiology. *Application deadline:* For fall admission, 12/1 for domestic students; for winter admission, 11/1 for domestic students; for spring admission, 2/1 for domestic students. Applications are processed on a rolling basis. Application fee: $70. Electronic applications accepted. *Expenses:* Contact institution. *Financial support:* Fellowships with full tuition reimbursements, research assistantships, Federal Work-Study, scholarships/grants, health care benefits, and full-tuition and stipends (for PhD students) available. Financial award application deadline: 3/1; financial award applicants required to submit FAFSA. *Faculty research:* Clinical informatics, computational biology, health information management, genomics, data analytics. *Unit head:* Dr. William Hersh, Program Director, 503-494-4563, E-mail: somgrad@ohsu.edu. *Application contact:* Lauren Ludwig, Administrative Coordinator, 503-494-2252, E-mail: informat@ohsu.edu.
Website: http://www.ohsu.edu/dmice.

Regis University, College of Computer and Information Sciences, Denver, CO 80221-1099. Offers agile technologies (Certificate); cybersecurity (Certificate); data science (M Sc); database administration with Oracle (Certificate); database development (Certificate); database technologies (M Sc); enterprise Java software development (Certificate); enterprise resource planning (Certificate); executive information technology (Certificate); health care informatics (Certificate); health care informatics and information management (M Sc); information assurance (M Sc); information assurance policy management (Certificate); information technology management (M Sc); mobile software development (Certificate); software engineering (M Sc, Certificate); software engineering and database technology (M Sc); storage area networks (Certificate); systems engineering (M Sc, Certificate). *Program availability:* Part-time, evening/weekend, 100% online, blended/hybrid learning. *Degree requirements:* For master's, thesis (for some programs), final research project. *Entrance requirements:* For master's, official transcript reflecting baccalaureate degree awarded from regionally-accredited college or university, 2 years of related experience, resume, interview. Additional exam requirements/recommendations for international students: Required—TOEFL (minimum score 550 paper-based; 82 iBT). Electronic applications accepted. *Expenses:* Contact institution. *Faculty research:* Information policy, knowledge management, software architectures, data science.

Rutgers University–Newark, School of Health Related Professions, Department of Health Informatics, Program in Biomedical Informatics, Newark, NJ 07102. Offers MS, PhD, DMD/MS, MD/MS. *Program availability:* Part-time, evening/weekend, online learning. *Degree requirements:* For master's, thesis; for doctorate, comprehensive exam, thesis/dissertation. *Entrance requirements:* For master's, BS, transcript of highest degree, statement of research interests, curriculum vitae, basic understanding of database concepts and calculus, 3 reference letters; for doctorate, master's degree, transcripts of highest degree, statement of research interests, curriculum vitae, basic understanding of database concepts and calculus, 3 reference letters. Additional exam requirements/recommendations for international students: Required—TOEFL. Electronic applications accepted.

Rutgers University–Newark, School of Health Related Professions, Department of Health Informatics, Program in Health Care Informatics, Newark, NJ 07102. Offers Certificate. *Program availability:* Part-time, evening/weekend, online learning. *Entrance requirements:* For degree, all transcripts, basic proficiency in programming language, BS, 3 reference letters. Additional exam requirements/recommendations for international students: Required—TOEFL (minimum score 500 paper-based; 79 iBT). Electronic applications accepted.

Stanford University, School of Medicine, Stanford Center for Biomedical Informatics Research, Stanford, CA 94305-2004. Offers MS, PhD. *Expenses: Tuition:* Full-time $50,703; part-time $32,970 per year. *Required fees:* $651.
Website: http://bmir.stanford.edu/

University at Buffalo, the State University of New York, Graduate School, Jacobs School of Medicine and Biomedical Sciences, Graduate Programs in Medicine and Biomedical Sciences, Department of Biomedical Informatics, Buffalo, NY 14260. Offers bioinformatics and translational research informatics (PhD); biomedical informatics (MS); biomedical ontology (PhD); clinical informatics and decision support (PhD). *Program availability:* Part-time. *Faculty:* 5 full-time (1 woman), 1 part-time/adjunct (0 women). *Students:* 7 full-time (2 women), 8 part-time (2 women); includes 4 minority (all Asian, non-Hispanic/Latino), 1 international. Average age 32. 16 applicants, 56% accepted, 5 enrolled. Terminal master's awarded for partial completion of doctoral program. *Degree requirements:* For master's, thesis; for doctorate, variable foreign language requirement, comprehensive exam (for some programs), thesis/dissertation. *Entrance requirements:* For master's, 3 letters of recommendation; for doctorate, GRE, MCAT, 3 letters of recommendation. Additional exam requirements/recommendations for international students: Required—TOEFL (minimum score 600 paper-based; 100 iBT), IELTS (minimum score 7.5). *Application deadline:* Applications are processed on a rolling basis. Application fee: $85. Electronic applications accepted. *Financial support:* In 2018–19, 9 students received support, including 2 fellowships with full and partial tuition reimbursements available (averaging $50,000 per year), 5 research assistantships with full and partial tuition reimbursements available (averaging $27,000 per year); traineeships, health care benefits, and unspecified assistantships also available. *Faculty research:* Integrated information systems planning and evaluation, management of knowledge-based information resources, scholarly communication in the health sciences, the economic value of health information, electronic health records, natural language understanding, ontologies, telemedicine/telehealth systems of healthcare, quality management information systems, implementation and evaluation of electronic health record systems, ethical and social issues in informatics. *Unit head:* Dr. Peter L. Elkin, MD, Professor and Chair, 716-816-7292, Fax: 716-842-4170, E-mail: elkinp@buffalo.edu. *Application contact:* Winanne Conway, Assistant to the Chair, 716-888-4858, Fax: 716-842-4170, E-mail: wwconway@buffalo.edu.
Website: http://medicine.buffalo.edu/departments/biomedical-informatics.html

The University of Arizona, College of Nursing, Tucson, AZ 85721. Offers health care informatics (Certificate); nurse practitioner (MS); nursing (DNP, PhD). *Accreditation:* AACN; AANA/CANAEP. *Program availability:* Part-time, online learning. Terminal master's awarded for partial completion of doctoral program. *Degree requirements:* For master's, thesis optional; for doctorate, comprehensive exam, thesis/dissertation. *Entrance requirements:* For master's, BSN, eligibility for RN license; for doctorate, BSN; for Certificate, GRE General Test, Arizona RN license, BSN, minimum GPA of 3.0. Additional exam requirements/recommendations for international students: Required—TOEFL (minimum score 550 paper-based; 79 iBT). Electronic applications accepted. *Expenses:* Contact institution. *Faculty research:* Vulnerable populations, injury mechanisms and biobehavioral responses, health care systems, informatics, rural health.

University of California, Davis, Graduate Studies, Graduate Group in Health Informatics, Davis, CA 95616. Offers MS. *Entrance requirements:* Additional exam requirements/recommendations for international students: Required—TOEFL (minimum score 550 paper-based).

University of Colorado Denver, College of Nursing, Aurora, CO 80045. Offers adult clinical nurse specialist (MS); adult nurse practitioner (MS); family nurse practitioner (MS); family psychiatric mental health nurse practitioner (MS); health care informatics (MS); nurse-midwifery (MS); nursing (DNP, PhD); nursing leadership and health care systems (MS); pediatric nurse practitioner (MS); women's health (MS); MS/PhD. *Accreditation:* ACNM/ACME (one or more programs are accredited). *Program availability:* Part-time, evening/weekend, online learning. *Students:* 468 full-time (407 women), 150 part-time (121 women); includes 111 minority (19 Black or African American, non-Hispanic/Latino; 3 American Indian or Alaska Native, non-Hispanic/Latino; 27 Asian, non-Hispanic/Latino; 47 Hispanic/Latino; 15 Two or more races, non-Hispanic/Latino), 2 international. Average age 38. 370 applicants, 51% accepted, 173 enrolled. In 2018, 157 master's, 25 doctorates awarded. Terminal master's awarded for partial completion of doctoral program. *Degree requirements:* For master's, thesis optional; for doctorate, comprehensive exam, thesis/dissertation, 42 credits of coursework. *Entrance requirements:* For master's, GRE if cumulative undergraduate GPA is less than 3.0, undergraduate nursing degree from ACEN- or CCNE-accredited school or university; completion of research and statistics courses with minimum grade of C; copy of current and unencumbered nursing license; for doctorate, GRE, bachelor's and/or master's degrees in nursing from ACEN- or CCNE-accredited institution; portfolio; minimum undergraduate GPA of 3.0, graduate 3.5; graduate-level intermediate statistics and master's-level nursing theory courses with minimum B grade; interview. Additional exam requirements/recommendations for international students: Required—TOEFL (minimum score 560 paper-based; 83 iBT). *Application deadline:* For fall admission, 2/15 for domestic students, 1/15 for international students; for spring admission, 7/1 for domestic students, 6/1 for international students. Application fee: $50 ($75 for international students). Electronic applications accepted. *Expenses:* Contact institution. *Financial support:* In 2018–19, 232 students received support. *Unit head:* Dr. Elias Provencio-Vasquez, Dean, 303-724-1679, E-mail: Eli.Provencio-Vasquez@ucdenver.edu. *Application contact:* Judy Campbell, Graduate Programs Advisor, 303-724-8503, E-mail: judy.campbell@ucdenver.edu.
Website: http://www.ucdenver.edu/academics/colleges/nursing/Pages/default.aspx

University of Illinois at Urbana–Champaign, Graduate College, School of Information Sciences, Champaign, IL 61820. Offers bioinformatics (MS); digital libraries (CAS); information management (MS); library and information science (MS, PhD, CAS). *Accreditation:* ALA (one or more programs are accredited). *Program availability:* Part-time, online learning. *Entrance requirements:* For degree, master's degree in library and information science or related field with minimum GPA of 3.0.

The University of Kansas, University of Kansas Medical Center, School of Nursing, Kansas City, KS 66045. Offers adult/gerontological clinical nurse specialist (PMC); adult/gerontological nurse practitioner (PMC); health care informatics (PMC); health professions educator (PMC); nurse midwife (PMC); nursing (MS, DNP, PhD); organizational leadership (PMC); psychiatric/mental health nurse practitioner (PMC); public health nursing (PMC). *Accreditation:* AACN; ACNM/ACME. *Program availability:* Part-time, 100% online, blended/hybrid learning. *Faculty:* 56. *Students:* 55 full-time (49 women), 273 part-time (246 women); includes 62 minority (16 Black or African American, non-Hispanic/Latino; 2 American Indian or Alaska Native, non-Hispanic/Latino; 21 Asian, non-Hispanic/Latino; 9 Hispanic/Latino; 14 Two or more races, non-Hispanic/Latino), 1 international. Average age 36. 76 applicants, 93% accepted, 60 enrolled. In 2018, 19 master's, 28 doctorates, 7 other advanced degrees awarded. Terminal master's awarded for partial completion of doctoral program. *Degree requirements:* For master's, comprehensive exam, thesis (for some programs), general oral exam; for doctorate, thesis/dissertation or alternative, comprehensive oral exam (for DNP); comprehensive written and oral exam, or three publications (for PhD). *Entrance requirements:* For master's, bachelor's degree in nursing, minimum GPA of 3.0, 1 year of clinical experience, RN license in KS and MO; for doctorate, GRE General Test (for PhD only), bachelor's degree in nursing, minimum GPA of 3.5, RN license in KS and MO. Additional exam requirements/recommendations for international students: Required—TOEFL. *Application deadline:* For fall admission, 4/1 for domestic and international students; for spring admission, 9/1 for domestic and international students. Application fee: $75. Electronic applications accepted. *Financial support:* In 2018–19, 5 research assistantships with tuition reimbursements (averaging $20,000 per year), 30 teaching assistantships with tuition reimbursements (averaging $20,000 per year) were awarded; scholarships/grants and traineeships also available. Financial award application deadline: 3/1; financial award applicants required to submit FAFSA. *Faculty research:* Breastfeeding practices of teen mothers, national database of nursing quality indicators, caregiving of families of patients using technology in the home, simulation in nursing education, diaphragm fatigue. *Total annual research expenditures:* $3 million. *Unit head:* Dr. Sally Maliski, Dean, 913-588-1601, Fax: 913-588-1660, E-mail: smaliski@kumc.edu. *Application contact:* Dr. Pamela K. Barnes, Associate Dean, Student Affairs, 913-588-1619, Fax: 913-588-1615, E-mail: pbarnes2@kumc.edu.
Website: http://nursing.kumc.edu

University of Phoenix–Phoenix Campus, College of Health Sciences and Nursing, Tempe, AZ 85282-2371. Offers family nurse practitioner (MSN, Certificate); gerontology health care (Certificate); health care education (MSN, Certificate); health care informatics (Certificate); informatics (MSN); nursing (MSN); MSN/MHA. *Program availability:* Evening/weekend, online learning. *Entrance requirements:* Additional exam requirements/recommendations for international students: Required—TOEFL, TOEIC (Test of English as an International Communication), Berlitz Online English Proficiency Exam, PTE, or IELTS. Electronic applications accepted. *Expenses:* Contact institution.

University of Washington, Graduate School, School of Medicine, Graduate Programs in Medicine, Department of Medical Education and Biomedical Informatics, Division of Biomedical and Health Informatics, Seattle, WA 98195. Offers MS, PhD. *Entrance requirements:* For master's and doctorate, GRE General Test, minimum GPA of 3.0; previous undergraduate course work in biology, computer programming, and mathematics. Additional exam requirements/recommendations for international students: Required—TOEFL (minimum score 580 paper-based; 70 iBT). Electronic applications accepted. *Faculty research:* Bio-clinical informatics, information retrieval, human-computer interaction, knowledge-based systems, telehealth.

University of Wisconsin–Milwaukee, Graduate School, College of Health Sciences, Department of Health Informatics and Administration, Milwaukee, WI 53201-0413. Offers health care informatics (MS); healthcare administration (MHA). *Students:* 47 full-time (27 women), 20 part-time (12 women); includes 16 minority (6 Black or African American, non-Hispanic/Latino; 3 Asian, non-Hispanic/Latino; 7 Two or more races, non-Hispanic/Latino), 11 international. Average age 33. 67 applicants, 72% accepted, 24 enrolled. In 2018, 25 master's awarded. *Degree requirements:* For master's,

comprehensive exam, thesis optional. *Entrance requirements:* For master's, GRE General Test. Additional exam requirements/recommendations for international students: Required—TOEFL (minimum score 550 paper-based; 79 iBT), IELTS (minimum score 6.5). Application fee: $56 ($96 for international students). *Financial support:* Fellowships, research assistantships, and teaching assistantships available. *Unit head:* Priya Nambisan, Department Chair, 414-229-7136, Fax: 414-229-3373, E-mail: nambisap@uwm.edu. *Application contact:* Kathleen M. Olewinski, Educational Coordinator, 414-229-7110, Fax: 414-229-3373, E-mail: kmo@uwm.edu. Website: http://uwm.edu/healthsciences/academics/health-informatics-administration/

Modeling and Simulation

Arizona State University at the Tempe campus, Ira A. Fulton Schools of Engineering, ASU Engineering Online Programs, Tempe, AZ 85287. Offers construction (MS); embedded systems (M Eng); enterprise systems innovation and management (MSE); modeling and simulation (M Eng); quality and reliability engineering (M Eng); software engineering (MSE); systems engineering (M Eng).

Arizona State University at the Tempe campus, Ira A. Fulton Schools of Engineering, The Polytechnic School, Department of Engineering, Mesa, AZ 85212. Offers simulation, modeling, and applied cognitive science (PhD). *Program availability:* Part-time. *Degree requirements:* For doctorate, comprehensive exam, thesis/dissertation, interactive Program of Study (iPOS) submitted before completing 50 percent of required credit hours. *Entrance requirements:* For doctorate, GRE, master's degree in psychology, engineering, cognitive science, or computer science; 3 letters of recommendation; statement of research interests. Additional exam requirements/recommendations for international students: Required—TOEFL, IELTS, or PTE. Electronic applications accepted. *Faculty research:* Software process and automated workflow, software architecture, dotal technologies, relational database systems, embedded systems.

Carnegie Mellon University, Carnegie Institute of Technology, Department of Civil and Environmental Engineering, Pittsburgh, PA 15213. Offers advanced infrastructure systems (MS, PhD); advanced infrastructure systems technology development and application (MS); air quality engineering and science (MS); civil and environmental engineering (MS, PhD); civil and environmental engineering/engineering and public policy (PhD); civil engineering (MS, PhD); computational mechanics (MS, PhD); computational modeling and monitoring for resilient structural and material systems (MS); energy infrastructure systems (MS); environmental engineering (MS, PhD); environmental management and science (MS, PhD); IT-based sustainable global infrastructure and construction management (MS); sustainability and green design (MS); water quality engineering and science (MS). *Program availability:* Part-time. *Faculty:* 23 full-time (5 women), 12 part-time/adjunct (3 women). *Students:* 264 full-time (109 women); includes 24 minority (6 Black or African American, non-Hispanic/Latino; 13 Asian, non-Hispanic/Latino; 5 Hispanic/Latino), 208 international. Average age 25. 630 applicants, 64% accepted, 114 enrolled. In 2018, 112 master's, 15 doctorates awarded. Terminal master's awarded for partial completion of doctoral program. *Degree requirements:* For master's, thesis optional; for doctorate, comprehensive exam, thesis/dissertation, two-part qualifying exam, public defense of dissertation. *Entrance requirements:* For master's, GRE General Test, BS in engineering, science or mathematics; for doctorate, GRE General Test, BS or MS in engineering, science or mathematics. Additional exam requirements/recommendations for international students: Required—TOEFL (minimum score 84 iBT), TOEFL (minimum score 84 iBT) or IELTS (7.0). *Application deadline:* For fall admission, 1/5 priority date for domestic and international students; for spring admission, 9/15 priority date for domestic and international students. Applications are processed on a rolling basis. Application fee: $75. Electronic applications accepted. *Expenses:* Contact institution. *Financial support:* In 2018–19, 137 students received support. Fellowships with tuition reimbursements available, research assistantships with tuition reimbursements available, scholarships/grants, health care benefits, tuition waivers (full and partial), unspecified assistantships, and service assistantships available. Financial award application deadline: 1/5. *Faculty research:* Advanced infrastructure systems; environmental engineering, sustainability, and science; mechanics, materials, and computing. *Total annual research expenditures:* $7.4 million. *Unit head:* Dr. David A. Dzombak, Professor and Department Head, 412-268-2941, Fax: 412-268-7813, E-mail: dzombak@cmu.edu. *Application contact:* David A. Vey, Director of Graduate Programs, 412-268-2292, Fax: 412-268-7813, E-mail: dvey@andrew.cmu.edu.
Website: http://www.cmu.edu/cee/

Columbus State University, Graduate Studies, Turner College of Business, Columbus, GA 31907-5645. Offers applied computer science (MS), including informational assurance, modeling and simulation, software development; business administration (MBA); cyber security (MS); human resource management (Certificate); information systems security (Certificate); modeling and simulation (Certificate); organizational leadership (MS), including human resource management, leader development, servant leadership; servant leadership (Certificate). *Accreditation:* AACSB. *Program availability:* Part-time, evening/weekend, 100% online, blended/hybrid learning. *Faculty:* 10 full-time (3 women), 1 part-time/adjunct (0 women). *Students:* 79 full-time (24 women), 136 part-time (47 women); includes 73 minority (40 Black or African American, non-Hispanic/Latino; 1 American Indian or Alaska Native, non-Hispanic/Latino; 8 Asian, non-Hispanic/Latino; 15 Hispanic/Latino; 9 Two or more races, non-Hispanic/Latino), 27 international. Average age 31. 237 applicants, 51% accepted, 64 enrolled. In 2018, 113 master's, 10 other advanced degrees awarded. *Entrance requirements:* For master's, GMAT, GRE, minimum undergraduate GPA of 2.75, letters of recommendation. Additional exam requirements/recommendations for international students: Required—TOEFL (minimum score 550 paper-based; 79 iBT). *Application deadline:* For fall admission, 6/30 for domestic students, 5/1 for international students; for spring admission, 11/1 for domestic and international students; for summer admission, 3/1 for domestic and international students. Applications are processed on a rolling basis. Application fee: $50. Electronic applications accepted. *Expenses:* Contact institution. *Financial support:* In 2018–19, 18 students received support, including 20 research assistantships (averaging $3,000 per year); Federal Work-Study also available. Financial award application deadline: 5/1; financial award applicants required to submit FAFSA. *Unit head:* Dr. Linda U. Hadley, Dean, 706-507-8153, Fax: 706-568-2184, E-mail: hadley_linda@columbusstate.edu. *Application contact:* Catrina Smith-Edmond, Assistant Director for Graduate and Global Admission, 706-507-8824, Fax: 706-568-5091, E-mail: smithedmond_catrina@columbusstate.edu.
Website: http://turner.columbusstate.edu/

Naval Postgraduate School, Departments and Academic Groups, Department of Computer Science, Monterey, CA 93943. Offers computer science (MS, PhD); identity management and cyber security (MA); modeling of virtual environments and simulations

(MS, PhD); software engineering (MS, PhD). Program only open to commissioned officers of the United States and friendly nations and selected United States federal civilian employees. *Program availability:* Part-time, online learning. *Degree requirements:* For master's, thesis; for doctorate, thesis/dissertation.

Old Dominion University, College of Arts and Letters, Graduate Program in International Studies, Norfolk, VA 23529. Offers conflict and cooperation (MA, PhD); interdependence and transnationalism (MA, PhD); international cultural studies (MA, PhD); international political economy and development (MA, PhD); modeling and simulation (MA, PhD); U.S. foreign policy and international relations (MA, PhD). *Program availability:* Part-time. Terminal master's awarded for partial completion of doctoral program. *Degree requirements:* For master's, one foreign language, comprehensive exam, thesis optional; for doctorate, one foreign language, comprehensive exam, thesis/dissertation. *Entrance requirements:* For master's, GRE General Test, sample of written work, 2 letters of recommendation; for doctorate, GRE General Test, sample of written work, 3 letters of recommendation. Additional exam requirements/recommendations for international students: Required—TOEFL (minimum score 570 paper-based). Electronic applications accepted. *Expenses:* Contact institution. *Faculty research:* U.S. foreign policy, international security, transatlantic and transpacific relations, transnational issues, international political economy and development.

Old Dominion University, Frank Batten College of Engineering and Technology, Program in Modeling and Simulation, Norfolk, VA 23529. Offers ME, MS, D Eng, PhD. *Program availability:* Part-time, evening/weekend, 100% online, blended/hybrid learning. Terminal master's awarded for partial completion of doctoral program. *Degree requirements:* For master's, comprehensive exam (for some programs), thesis (for some programs); for doctorate, comprehensive exam, thesis/dissertation, candidacy exam. *Entrance requirements:* For master's, GRE, proficiency in calculus, calculus-based statistics, and computer science; for doctorate, GRE, graduate-level proficiency in calculus, calculus-based statistics, and computer science. Additional exam requirements/recommendations for international students: Required—TOEFL (minimum score 550 paper-based; 79 iBT). Electronic applications accepted. *Faculty research:* Distributed simulation and interoperability, medical modeling and simulation, educational gaming and training, transportation modeling and simulation, cybersecurity.

Portland State University, Graduate Studies, College of Liberal Arts and Sciences, Systems Science Program, Portland, OR 97207-0751. Offers computational intelligence (Certificate); computer modeling and simulation (Certificate); systems science (MS); systems science/anthropology (PhD); systems science/business administration (PhD); systems science/civil engineering (PhD); systems science/economics (PhD); systems science/engineering management (PhD); systems science/general (PhD); systems science/mathematical sciences (PhD); systems science/mechanical engineering (PhD); systems science/psychology (PhD); systems science/sociology (PhD). *Degree requirements:* For master's, comprehensive exam (for some programs), thesis optional; for doctorate, variable foreign language requirement, comprehensive exam (for some programs), thesis/dissertation. *Entrance requirements:* For master's, GRE/GMAT (recommended), minimum GPA of 3.0 on undergraduate or graduate work, 2 letters of recommendation, statement of interest; for doctorate, GMAT, GRE General Test, minimum GPA of 3.0 undergraduate, 3.25 graduate; 3 letters of recommendation; statement of interest. Additional exam requirements/recommendations for international students: Required—TOEFL (minimum score 550 paper-based; 80 iBT). Electronic applications accepted. *Faculty research:* Systems theory and methodology, artificial intelligence neural networks, information theory, nonlinear dynamics/chaos, modeling and simulation.

Rochester Institute of Technology, Graduate Enrollment Services, College of Science, School of Mathematical Sciences, PhD Program in Mathematical Modeling, Rochester, NY 14623-5603. Offers PhD. *Students:* 13 full-time (9 women), 1 part-time (0 women); includes 1 minority (Asian, non-Hispanic/Latino), 3 international. Average age 27. 32 applicants, 25% accepted, 4 enrolled. *Degree requirements:* For doctorate, thesis/dissertation. *Entrance requirements:* For doctorate, GRE, official transcripts, minimum GPA of 3.0 in primary field of study, previous mathematical coursework beyond calculus, two letters of recommendation, personal statement. Additional exam requirements/recommendations for international students: Required—TOEFL (minimum score 100 iBT), IELTS (minimum score 7), PTE (minimum score 68). *Application deadline:* For fall admission, 1/15 priority date for domestic and international students. Applications are processed on a rolling basis. Application fee: $65. Electronic applications accepted. *Expenses:* Contact institution. *Financial support:* In 2018–19, 13 students received support. Research assistantships with full tuition reimbursements available, teaching assistantships with full tuition reimbursements available, career-related internships or fieldwork, scholarships/grants, health care benefits, and unspecified assistantships available. Support available to part-time students. Financial award applicants required to submit FAFSA. *Faculty research:* Mathematical biology; dynamical systems and fluid dynamics; discrete mathematics; applied inverse problems; geometry, relativity and gravitation. *Unit head:* Dr. Elizabeth Cherry, Director, 585-475-4497, E-mail: excsma@rit.edu. *Application contact:* Diane Ellison, Senior Associate Vice President, Graduate Enrollment Services, 585-475-2229, Fax: 585-475-7164, E-mail: gradinfo@rit.edu.
Website: https://www.rit.edu/study/mathematical-modeling-phd

Stevens Institute of Technology, Graduate School, Charles V. Schaefer Jr. School of Engineering and Science, Department of Civil, Environmental, and Ocean Engineering, Program in Civil Engineering, Hoboken, NJ 07030. Offers civil engineering (PhD, Certificate), including geotechnical engineering (Certificate); geotechnical/geoenvironmental engineering (M Eng, Engr); hydrologic modeling (M Eng); stormwater management (M Eng); structural engineering (M Eng, Engr); transportation engineering (M Eng); water resources engineering (M Eng). *Program availability:* Part-time, evening/weekend. *Faculty:* 28 full-time (7 women), 2 part-time/adjunct (1 woman). *Students:* 37 full-time (8 women), 27 part-time (8 women); includes 8 minority (1 Black or African American, non-Hispanic/Latino; 1 American Indian or Alaska Native, non-Hispanic/

Latino; 6 Asian, non-Hispanic/Latino), 30 international. Average age 25. In 2018, 44 master's awarded. Terminal master's awarded for partial completion of doctoral program. *Degree requirements:* For master's, thesis optional, minimum B average in major field and overall; for doctorate, comprehensive exam (for some programs), thesis/dissertation; for other advanced degree, minimum B average. *Entrance requirements:* For master's, GRE/GMAT scores: GRE scores are required for all applicants applying to a full-time graduate program in the Schaefer School of Engineering and Science (SES). International applicants must submit TOEFL/IELTS scores and fulfill the English Language Proficiency Requirements in order to be considered. Additional exam requirements/recommendations for international students: Required—TOEFL (minimum score 74 iBT), IELTS (minimum score 6). *Application deadline:* For fall admission, 4/15 for domestic and international students; for spring admission, 11/1 for domestic and international students; for summer admission, 5/1 for domestic students. Applications are processed on a rolling basis. Application fee: $60. Electronic applications accepted. *Expenses: Tuition:* Full-time $35,960; part-time $1620 per credit. *Required fees:* $1290; $600 per semester. Tuition and fees vary according to course load. *Financial support:* Fellowships, research assistantships, teaching assistantships, career-related internships or fieldwork, Federal Work-Study, scholarships/grants, and unspecified assistantships available. Financial award application deadline: 2/15; financial award applicants required to submit FAFSA. *Unit head:* Dr. Jean Zu, Dean of SES, 201-216.8233, Fax: 201-216.8372, E-mail: Jean.Zu@stevens.edu. *Application contact:* Graduate Admission, 888-783-8367, Fax: 888-511-1306, E-mail: graduate@stevens.edu.

Trent University, Graduate Studies, Program in Applications of Modeling in the Natural and Social Sciences, Peterborough, ON K9J 7B8, Canada. Offers applications of modeling in the natural and social sciences (MA); biology (M Sc, PhD); chemistry (M Sc); computer studies (M Sc); geography (M Sc, PhD); physics (M Sc). *Program availability:* Part-time. *Degree requirements:* For master's, thesis. *Entrance requirements:* For master's, honours degree. *Faculty research:* Computation of heat transfer, atmospheric physics, statistical mechanics, stress and coping, evolutionary ecology.

Université Laval, Faculty of Administrative Sciences, Programs in Business Administration, Québec, QC G1K 7P4, Canada. Offers accounting (MBA); agri-food management (MBA); electronic business (MBA, Diploma); factory management and logistics (MBA); finance (MBA); firm management (MBA); geomatic management (MBA); information technology management (MBA); international management (MBA); management (MBA); management accounting (MBA, Diploma); marketing (MBA); modeling and organizational decision (MBA); occupational health and safety management (MBA); pharmacy management (MBA); social and environmental responsibility (MBA); technological entrepreneurship (Diploma). *Accreditation:* AACSB. *Program availability:* Part-time, evening/weekend, online learning. *Entrance requirements:* For master's and Diploma, knowledge of French and English. Electronic applications accepted.

University at Buffalo, the State University of New York, Graduate School, College of Arts and Sciences, Department of Geography, Buffalo, NY 14260. Offers earth systems science (MA, MS); economic geography and business geographics (MS); environmental modeling and analysis (MA); geographic information science (MA, MS); geography (MA, PhD); health geography (MS); international trade (MA); urban and regional analysis (MA). *Program availability:* Part-time. Terminal master's awarded for partial completion of doctoral program. *Degree requirements:* For master's, thesis (for some programs), project or portfolio; for doctorate, thesis/dissertation. *Entrance requirements:* For master's, GRE General Test, minimum GPA of 2.9; for doctorate, GRE General Test, minimum GPA of 3.0. Additional exam requirements/recommendations for international students: Required—TOEFL (minimum score 550 paper-based; 79 iBT). Electronic applications accepted. *Expenses:* Contact institution. *Faculty research:* International business and world trade, geographic information systems and cartography, transportation, urban and regional analysis, physical and environmental geography.

The University of Alabama in Huntsville, School of Graduate Studies, College of Science, Department of Computer Science, Huntsville, AL 35899. Offers computer science (MS, PhD); cybersecurity (MS); modeling and simulation (MS, PhD, Certificate); software engineering (MSSE, Certificate). *Program availability:* Part-time. *Faculty:* 14 full-time (4 women), 1 part-time/adjunct. *Students:* 67 full-time (16 women), 65 part-time (11 women); includes 14 minority (4 Black or African American, non-Hispanic/Latino; 1 American Indian or Alaska Native, non-Hispanic/Latino; 5 Asian, non-Hispanic/Latino; 3 Hispanic/Latino; 1 Two or more races, non-Hispanic/Latino), 60 international. Average age 33. 219 applicants, 74% accepted, 37 enrolled. In 2018, 47 master's awarded. *Degree requirements:* For master's, comprehensive exam, thesis or alternative, oral and written exams; for doctorate, comprehensive exam, thesis/dissertation, oral and written exams. *Entrance requirements:* For master's, doctorate, and Certificate, GRE General Test, minimum GPA of 3.0. Additional exam requirements/recommendations for international students: Required—TOEFL (minimum score 550 paper-based; 80 iBT), IELTS (minimum score 6.5). *Application deadline:* For fall admission, 7/15 priority date for domestic students, 4/1 priority date for international students; for spring admission, 11/30 priority date for domestic students, 9/1 priority date for international students. Applications are processed on a rolling basis. Application fee: $50. Electronic applications accepted. *Expenses: Tuition, area resident:* Full-time $10,632; part-time $412 per credit hour. Tuition, state resident: full-time $10,632. Tuition, nonresident: full-time $23,604; part-time $412 per credit hour. *Required fees:* $582; $582. Tuition and fees vary according to course load and program. *Financial support:* In 2018–19, 39 students received support, including 18 research assistantships with full tuition reimbursements available (averaging $6,762 per year), 19 teaching assistantships with full tuition reimbursements available (averaging $6,315 per year); career-related internships or fieldwork, Federal Work-Study, institutionally sponsored loans, scholarships/grants, health care benefits, and unspecified assistantships also available. Support available to part-time students. Financial award application deadline: 4/1; financial award applicants required to submit FAFSA. *Faculty research:* Information assurance and cyber security, modeling and simulation, data science, computer graphics and visualization, multimedia systems. *Unit head:* Dr. Heggere Ranganath, Professor and Chair, 256-824-6088, Fax: 256-824-6239, E-mail: info@cs.uah.edu. *Application contact:* Kim Gray, Graduate Studies Admissions Manager, 256-824-6002, Fax: 256-824-6405, E-mail: deangrad@uah.edu.
Website: http://www.cs.uah.edu

University of California, San Diego, Graduate Division, Department of Structural Engineering, La Jolla, CA 92093. Offers structural engineering (MS, PhD); structural health monitoring, prognosis, and validated simulations (MS). PhD in engineering sciences offered jointly with San Diego State University. *Students:* 169 full-time (46 women), 19 part-time (6 women). 391 applicants, 51% accepted, 74 enrolled. In 2018, 84 master's, 5 doctorates awarded. *Degree requirements:* For master's, comprehensive exam (for some programs), thesis (for some programs); for doctorate, comprehensive exam, thesis/dissertation, 1-quarter teaching assistantship. *Entrance requirements:* For master's and doctorate, GRE General Test. Additional exam requirements/recommendations for international students: Required—TOEFL (minimum score 550 paper-based; 80 iBT), IELTS (minimum score 7). *Application deadline:* For fall admission, 1/9 for domestic students. Application fee: $105 ($125 for international students). Electronic applications accepted. *Financial support:* Fellowships, research assistantships, teaching assistantships, scholarships/grants, and readerships available. Financial award applicants required to submit FAFSA. *Faculty research:* Earthquake engineering, advanced composites and aerospace structural systems, geotechnical, marine/offshore engineering; renewal engineering, structural health monitoring, prognosis and validated simulations, structural materials; computational mechanics; solid mechanics. *Unit head:* John McCartney, Chair, 858-534-9630, E-mail: mccartney@eng.ucsd.edu. *Application contact:* Yvonne C. Wollman, Graduate Coordinator, 858-822-1421, E-mail: se-info@ucsd.edu.
Website: http://www.structures.ucsd.edu/

University of Central Florida, College of Graduate Studies, Dean's Office Graduate Studies, Program in Modeling and Simulation, Orlando, FL 32816. Offers modeling and simulation (MS, PhD); modeling and simulation of behavioral cybersecurity (Certificate); modeling and simulation of technical systems (Certificate). *Degree requirements:* For master's, thesis or alternative; for doctorate, comprehensive exam, thesis/dissertation. *Entrance requirements:* For master's, letters of recommendation, resume, goal statement; for doctorate, GRE, letters of recommendation, resume, goal statement. Additional exam requirements/recommendations for international students: Required—TOEFL. Electronic applications accepted.

University of Central Florida, College of Community Innovation and Education, Education Doctoral Programs, Program in Instructional Design and Technology, Orlando, FL 32816. Offers e-learning (Certificate); educational technology (Certificate); instructional design (Certificate); instructional design and technology (MA), including e-learning, educational technology, instructional systems; instructional design for simulations (Certificate). *Program availability:* Part-time. *Students:* 25 full-time (20 women), 127 part-time (93 women); includes 56 minority (19 Black or African American, non-Hispanic/Latino; 1 American Indian or Alaska Native, non-Hispanic/Latino; 6 Asian, non-Hispanic/Latino; 27 Hispanic/Latino; 3 Two or more races, non-Hispanic/Latino), 1 international. Average age 36. 93 applicants, 89% accepted, 57 enrolled. In 2018, 35 master's, 16 other advanced degrees awarded. *Entrance requirements:* For master's, letters of recommendation, resume. Additional exam requirements/recommendations for international students: Required—TOEFL. *Application deadline:* For fall admission, 7/15 for domestic students; for spring admission, 12/1 for domestic students. Application fee: $30. Electronic applications accepted. *Financial support:* In 2018–19, 5 students received support, including 5 research assistantships with partial tuition reimbursements available (averaging $14,317 per year); health care benefits also available. Financial award application deadline: 3/1; financial award applicants required to submit FAFSA. *Unit head:* Dr. Richard Hartshorne, Program Coordinator, 407-823-1861, E-mail: richard.hartshorne@ucf.edu. *Application contact:* Associate Director, Graduate Admissions, 407-823-2766, Fax: 407-823-6442, E-mail: gradadmissions@ucf.edu.
Website: https://edcollege.ucf.edu/insttech/

The University of Manchester, School of Chemical Engineering and Analytical Science, Manchester, United Kingdom. Offers biocatalysis (M Phil, PhD); chemical engineering (M Phil, PhD); chemical engineering and analytical science (M Phil, D Eng, PhD); colloids, crystals, interfaces and materials (M Phil, PhD); environment and sustainable technology (M Phil, PhD); instrumentation (M Phil, PhD); multi-scale modeling (M Phil, PhD); process integration (M Phil, PhD); systems biology (M Phil, PhD).

University of Pittsburgh, School of Computing and Information, Program in Computational Modeling and Simulation, Pittsburgh, PA 15260. Offers biological science (PhD). *Program availability:* Part-time. Terminal master's awarded for partial completion of doctoral program. *Degree requirements:* For master's, comprehensive exam, thesis; for doctorate, comprehensive exam, thesis/dissertation, preliminary exam. *Entrance requirements:* For doctorate, GRE General Test, GRE Subject Test, statement of purpose, transcripts for all college-level institutions attended, three letters of reference. Additional exam requirements/recommendations for international students: Required—TOEFL (minimum score 600 paper-based; 90 iBT), IELTS (minimum score 7). Electronic applications accepted. *Expenses:* Contact institution. *Faculty research:* Modeling of geological systems, electronic structure, chemical reaction mechanisms, computation economics, machine learning methods.

University of Southern California, Graduate School, Viterbi School of Engineering, Department of Computer Science, Los Angeles, CA 90089. Offers computer networks (MS); computer science (MS, PhD); computer security (MS); game development (MS); high performance computing and simulations (MS); human language technology (MS); intelligent robotics (MS); multimedia and creative technologies (MS); software engineering (MS). *Program availability:* Part-time, evening/weekend, online learning. *Entrance requirements:* For master's and doctorate, GRE General Test. Additional exam requirements/recommendations for international students: Required—TOEFL. Electronic applications accepted. *Faculty research:* Databases, computer graphics and computer vision, software engineering, networks and security, robotics, multimedia and virtual reality.

Worcester Polytechnic Institute, Graduate Admissions, Programs in Interdisciplinary Studies, Worcester, MA 01609-2280. Offers bioscience administration (MS); nuclear science and engineering (Graduate Certificate); power systems management (MS); social science (PhD); system dynamics and innovation management (MS, Graduate Certificate); systems modeling (MS). *Program availability:* Part-time, evening/weekend, 100% online. *Students:* 5 full-time (2 women), 49 part-time (17 women); includes 18 minority (6 Black or African American, non-Hispanic/Latino; 4 Asian, non-Hispanic/Latino; 5 Hispanic/Latino; 3 Two or more races, non-Hispanic/Latino), 1 international. Average age 35. 44 applicants, 93% accepted, 34 enrolled. In 2018, 13 master's, 1 doctorate, 21 other advanced degrees awarded. Terminal master's awarded for partial completion of doctoral program. *Degree requirements:* For master's, thesis; for doctorate, comprehensive exam, thesis/dissertation. *Entrance requirements:* For master's and doctorate, 3 letters of recommendation. Additional exam requirements/recommendations for international students: Required—TOEFL (minimum score 563 paper-based; 84 iBT), IELTS (minimum score 7). *Application deadline:* For fall admission, 1/1 priority date for domestic students, 1/1 for international students; for spring admission, 10/1 priority date for domestic students, 10/1 for international students. Applications are processed on a rolling basis. Application fee: $70. Electronic applications accepted. *Financial support:* Institutionally sponsored loans, scholarships/grants, and unspecified assistantships available. Financial award application deadline: 1/1. *Unit head:* Michale McGrade, Dean, 508-831-5301, Fax: 508-831-5717, E-mail: grad@wpi.edu. *Application contact:* Lynne Dougherty, Administrative Assistant, 508-831-5301, Fax: 508-831-5717, E-mail: grad@wpi.edu.

Software Engineering

Arizona State University at the Tempe campus, Ira A. Fulton Schools of Engineering, ASU Engineering Online Programs, Tempe, AZ 85287. Offers construction (MS); embedded systems (M Eng); enterprise systems innovation and management (MSE); modeling and simulation (M Eng); quality and reliability engineering (M Eng); software engineering (MSE); systems engineering (M Eng).

Arizona State University at the Tempe campus, Ira A. Fulton Schools of Engineering, School of Computing, Informatics, and Decision Systems Engineering, Tempe, AZ 85287-8809. Offers computer engineering (MS, PhD); computer science (MCS, MS, PhD); industrial engineering (MS, PhD); software engineering (MS). *Program availability:* Part-time, evening/weekend, online learning. Terminal master's awarded for partial completion of doctoral program. *Degree requirements:* For master's, comprehensive exam (for some programs), portfolio (MCS); interactive Program of Study (iPOS) submitted before completing 50 percent of required credit hours; for doctorate, comprehensive exam, thesis/dissertation, interactive Program of Study (iPOS) submitted before completing 50 percent of required credit hours. *Entrance requirements:* For master's, GRE, minimum GPA of 3.0 or equivalent in last 2 years of work leading to bachelor's degree; for doctorate, GRE, minimum GPA of 3.0 in last 2 years of work leading to bachelor's degree. Additional exam requirements/recommendations for international students: Required—TOEFL, IELTS, or PTE. Electronic applications accepted. *Expenses:* Contact institution. *Faculty research:* Artificial intelligence, cyberphysical and embedded systems, health informatics, information assurance and security, information management/multimedia/visualization, network science, personalized learning/educational games, production logistics, software and systems engineering, statistical modeling and data mining.

Auburn University, Graduate School, Ginn College of Engineering, Department of Computer Science and Software Engineering, Auburn University, AL 36849. Offers MS, MSWE, PhD. *Program availability:* Part-time. *Degree requirements:* For master's, thesis (for some programs); for doctorate, thesis/dissertation. *Entrance requirements:* For master's and doctorate, GRE General Test, GRE Subject Test. Electronic applications accepted. *Expenses:* Tuition, state resident: full-time $11,282; part-time $535 per credit hour. Tuition, nonresident: full-time $30,542; part-time $1605 per credit hour. *Required fees:* $826 per semester. Tuition and fees vary according to degree level and program. *Faculty research:* Parallelizable, scalable software translations; graphical representations of algorithms, structures, and processes; graph drawing.

Boston University, Metropolitan College, Department of Computer Science, Boston, MA 02215. Offers computer information systems (MS), including computer networks, data analytics, database management and business intelligence, health informatics, IT project management, security, Web application development; computer networks (Certificate); computer science (MS); data analytics (Certificate); digital forensics (Certificate); health informatics (Certificate); information technology project management (Certificate); software development (MS); software engineering in health care systems (Certificate); telecommunications (MS), including security. *Program availability:* Part-time, evening/weekend, online learning. *Faculty:* 16 full-time (3 women), 52 part-time/adjunct (5 women). *Students:* 201 full-time (57 women), 953 part-time (252 women); includes 285 minority (57 Black or African American, non-Hispanic/Latino; 2 American Indian or Alaska Native, non-Hispanic/Latino; 139 Asian, non-Hispanic/Latino; 67 Hispanic/Latino; 1 Native Hawaiian or other Pacific Islander, non-Hispanic/Latino; 19 Two or more races, non-Hispanic/Latino), 333 international. Average age 31. 1,079 applicants, 72% accepted, 297 enrolled. In 2018, 395 master's awarded. *Entrance requirements:* For master's and Certificate, official transcripts from regionally-accredited bachelor's degree program, 3 letters of recommendation, professional resume, personal statement. Additional exam requirements/recommendations for international students: Required—TOEFL (minimum score 84 iBT), IELTS. *Application deadline:* For fall admission, 8/1 priority date for domestic students, 6/1 priority date for international students; for spring admission, 12/1 priority date for domestic students, 11/15 priority date for international students; for summer admission, 4/1 priority date for domestic students, 3/1 priority date for international students. Applications are processed on a rolling basis. Application fee: $85. Electronic applications accepted. *Expenses:* Contact institution. *Financial support:* In 2018–19, 11 research assistantships (averaging $8,400 per year), 23 teaching assistantships (averaging $3,400 per year) were awarded; unspecified assistantships also available. Support available to part-time students. Financial award applicants required to submit FAFSA. *Faculty research:* Artificial intelligence and machine learning, security and forensics, web technologies, software engineering, programming languages, medical informatics, information systems and IT project management. *Unit head:* Dr. Anatoly Temkin, Chair, 617-353-2566, Fax: 617-353-2367, E-mail: csinfo@bu.edu. *Application contact:* Enrollment Services, 617-353-6004, E-mail: met@bu.edu.
Website: http://www.bu.edu/csmet/

Bowling Green State University, Graduate College, College of Arts and Sciences, Department of Computer Science, Bowling Green, OH 43403. Offers computer science (MS), including operations research, parallel and distributed computing, software engineering. *Program availability:* Part-time. *Degree requirements:* For master's, thesis or alternative. *Entrance requirements:* For master's, GRE General Test. Additional exam requirements/recommendations for international students: Required—TOEFL. Electronic applications accepted. *Faculty research:* Artificial intelligence, real time and concurrent programming languages, behavioral aspects of computing, network protocols.

Brandeis University, Rabb School of Continuing Studies, Division of Graduate Professional Studies, Master of Science in Robotic Software Engineering Program, Waltham, MA 02454-9110. Offers MS. *Program availability:* Part-time-only. *Entrance requirements:* For master's, bachelor's degree in computer science or software engineering, or 2-3 years of experience in software engineering and undergraduate courses in linear algebra, calculus, and probability/statistics, official transcripts, resume, statement of goals, letter of recommendation. Additional exam requirements/recommendations for international students: Required—TOEFL (minimum score 600 paper-based; 100 iBT), IELTS (minimum score 7), TWE (minimum score 4.5), PTE (minimum score 68). Electronic applications accepted. *Expenses:* Contact institution.

Brandeis University, Rabb School of Continuing Studies, Division of Graduate Professional Studies, Master of Software Engineering Program, Waltham, MA 02454-9110. Offers MSE. *Program availability:* Part-time-only. *Entrance requirements:* For master's, programming language (Java, C++, C), software engineering, and data structures, or equivalent work experience; 4-year bachelor's degree from regionally-accredited U.S. institution or equivalent; official transcript(s) from every college/university attended; resume or curriculum vitae; statement of goals; letter of recommendation. Additional exam requirements/recommendations for international students: Required—TWE (minimum score 4.5), TOEFL (minimum scores: 600 paper-based, 100 iBT), IELTS (7), or PTE (68). Electronic applications accepted. *Expenses:* Contact institution.

California Baptist University, Program in Software Engineering, Riverside, CA 92504-3206. Offers MS. *Program availability:* Part-time. *Faculty:* 4 full-time (1 woman), 2 part-time/adjunct (0 women). *Students:* 13 full-time (6 women), 5 part-time (2 women); includes 2 minority (1 Asian, non-Hispanic/Latino; 1 Two or more races, non-Hispanic/Latino), 14 international. Average age 27. 2 applicants, 100% accepted, 2 enrolled. In 2018, 11 master's awarded. *Entrance requirements:* For master's, minimum undergraduate GPA of 3.0, bachelor's transcripts, three letters of recommendation, essay, resume, interview. Additional exam requirements/recommendations for international students: Required—TOEFL (minimum score 80 iBT). *Application deadline:* For fall admission, 8/1 priority date for domestic students, 7/1 priority date for international students; for spring admission, 12/1 priority date for domestic students, 11/1 priority date for international students. Applications are processed on a rolling basis. Application fee: $45. Electronic applications accepted. *Expenses:* $961 per unit. *Financial support:* In 2018–19, 1 student received support. Federal Work-Study and scholarships/grants available. Financial award applicants required to submit CSS PROFILE or FAFSA. *Faculty research:* Mathematical modeling, computational statistics and programming, agile software development, database management systems. *Unit head:* Dr. Anthony Donaldson, Dean, College of Engineering, 951-343-4841, E-mail: adonaldson@calbaptist.edu. *Application contact:* Larry Clement, Interim Department Chair, Computing, Software, and Data Sciences, 951-343-4471, E-mail: lclement@calbaptist.edu.

California State University, Fullerton, Graduate Studies, College of Engineering and Computer Science, Department of Computer Science, Fullerton, CA 92831-3599. Offers computer science (MS); software engineering (MS). *Program availability:* Part-time, online learning. *Degree requirements:* For master's, comprehensive exam, project or thesis. *Entrance requirements:* For master's, GRE General Test, minimum undergraduate GPA of 2.5. *Faculty research:* Software engineering, development of computer networks.

California State University, Northridge, Graduate Studies, College of Engineering and Computer Science, Department of Computer Science, Northridge, CA 91330. Offers computer science (MS); software engineering (MS). *Program availability:* Part-time, evening/weekend. *Degree requirements:* For master's, thesis. *Entrance requirements:* For master's, GRE General Test, minimum GPA of 2.5. Additional exam requirements/recommendations for international students: Required—TOEFL. *Faculty research:* Radar data processing.

California State University, Sacramento, College of Engineering and Computer Science, Department of Computer Science, Sacramento, CA 95819. Offers computer science (MS); software engineering (MS). *Program availability:* Part-time, evening/weekend. *Degree requirements:* For master's, thesis, project or comprehensive exam; writing proficiency exam. *Entrance requirements:* For master's, GRE, minimum GPA of 3.0 in last 60 units attempted. Additional exam requirements/recommendations for international students: Required—TOEFL (minimum score 550 paper-based; 80 iBT); Recommended—IELTS, TSE. Electronic applications accepted. *Expenses:* Contact institution.

Carnegie Mellon University, Carnegie Institute of Technology, Information Networking Institute, Pittsburgh, PA 15213. Offers information networking (MS); information security (MS); information technology - information security (MS); information technology - mobility (MS); information technology - software management (MS). *Degree requirements:* For master's, thesis optional. *Entrance requirements:* For master's, GRE General Test, bachelor's degree in computer science, computer engineering, or electrical engineering, or related technology degree; programming skills (C/C++ fluency for some programs). Additional exam requirements/recommendations for international students: Required—TOEFL. *Faculty research:* Computer forensics and incident response; dependable systems, embedded systems, mobile systems, and sensor networks; computer and information networks, network and information security, human and socio-economic factors in secure system design; wireless sensor networks, survivable embedded systems, signal processing/compression; strategic management, international strategic management, group dynamics and decision-making structures, simulated competitive environments.

Carnegie Mellon University, School of Computer Science, Software Engineering Program, Pittsburgh, PA 15213-3891. Offers MSE, PhD. *Entrance requirements:* For master's, GRE General Test, GRE Subject Test (computer science), 2 years of experience in large-scale software development project.

Carnegie Mellon University, Tepper School of Business, Pittsburgh, PA 15213-3891. Offers accounting (PhD); business management and software engineering (MBMSE); business technologies (PhD); civil engineering and industrial management (MS); computational finance (MSCF); economics (PhD); environmental engineering and management (MEEM); financial economics (PhD); industrial administration (MBA), including administration and public management; marketing (PhD); mathematical finance (PhD); operations management (PhD); operations research (PhD); organizational behavior and theory (PhD); production and operations management (PhD); public policy and management (MS, MSED); software engineering and business management (MS); JD/MS; JD/MSIA; M Div/MS; MOM/MSIA; MSCF/MSIA. JD/MSIA offered jointly with University of Pittsburgh. *Program availability:* Part-time. Terminal master's awarded for partial completion of doctoral program. *Degree requirements:* For doctorate, thesis/dissertation. *Entrance requirements:* For master's, GMAT. Additional exam requirements/recommendations for international students: Required—TOEFL. *Expenses:* Contact institution.

Carroll University, Program in Software Engineering, Waukesha, WI 53186-5593. Offers MSE. *Program availability:* Part-time, evening/weekend. *Degree requirements:* For master's, professional experience, capstone project. *Entrance requirements:* For master's, BA or BS, 2 years of professional experience. Additional exam requirements/recommendations for international students: Required—TOEFL. Electronic applications accepted. *Faculty research:* Networking, artificial intelligence, virtual reality, effective teaching of software design, computer science pedagogy.

Cleveland State University, College of Graduate Studies, Fenn College of Engineering, Department of Electrical and Computer Engineering, Cleveland, OH 44115. Offers electrical engineering (MS, D Eng); software engineering (MS). *Program availability:* Part-time, evening/weekend. *Faculty:* 15 full-time (2 women), 1 part-time/adjunct (0 women). *Students:* 108 full-time (36 women), 69 part-time (13 women); includes 16 minority (1 Black or African American, non-Hispanic/Latino; 12 Asian, non-Hispanic/Latino; 1 Hispanic/Latino; 2 Two or more races, non-Hispanic/Latino), 115 international. Average age 26. 1,083 applicants, 44% accepted, 89 enrolled. In 2018, 120 master's, 3 doctorates awarded. Terminal master's awarded for partial completion of doctoral program. *Entrance requirements:* For master's, GRE General Test (minimum score 650 quantitative), minimum GPA of 2.75; for doctorate, GRE General Test (minimum quantitative score in 80th percentile), minimum GPA of 3.25. *Application*

deadline: Applications are processed on a rolling basis. Application fee: $40. Electronic applications accepted. *Expenses:* Contact institution. *Financial support:* In 2018–19, 31 students received support, including 14 research assistantships with tuition reimbursements available (averaging $8,300 per year), 16 teaching assistantships with tuition reimbursements available (averaging $9,500 per year); career-related internships or fieldwork, scholarships/grants, and unspecified assistantships also available. Financial award applicants required to submit FAFSA. *Faculty research:* Computer networks, computer security and privacy, mobile computing, distributed computing, software engineering, knowledge-based control systems, artificial intelligence, digital communications, MEMS, sensors, power systems, power electronics. *Total annual research expenditures:* $484,362. *Unit head:* Dr. Chansu Yu, Chairperson, 216-687-2584, Fax: 216-687-5405, E-mail: f.xiong@csuohio.edu. *Application contact:* Deborah L. Brown, Interim Assistant Director, Graduate Admissions, 216-523-7572, Fax: 216-687-9214, E-mail: d.l.brown@csuohio.edu.
Website: http://www.csuohio.edu/ece

College of Staten Island of the City University of New York, Graduate Programs, Division of Science and Technology, Program in Computer Science, Staten Island, NY 10314-6600. Offers computer science (MS), including artificial intelligence and data analytics, cloud computing and software engineering, cybersecurity and networks. *Program availability:* Part-time, evening/weekend. *Students:* 35. 48 applicants, 48% accepted, 14 enrolled. In 2018, 17 master's awarded. *Degree requirements:* For master's, thesis optional, a program of 10 courses (30 credits) with at least a 3.0 (B) average. Exceptional students may be permitted to satisfy six credits of the total credit requirement with a master's thesis. *Entrance requirements:* For master's, GRE General Test, BS in Computer Science or related area with a B average (3.0 out of 4.0) overall and in the major. Additional exam requirements/recommendations for international students: Required—TOEFL (minimum score 550 paper-based; 79 iBT), IELTS (minimum score 6.5). *Application deadline:* For fall admission, 7/20 priority date for domestic students, 4/25 for international students; for spring admission, 11/2 priority date for domestic students, 11/2 for international students. Applications are processed on a rolling basis. Application fee: $75. Electronic applications accepted. *Expenses: Tuition, area resident:* Full-time $10,770; part-time $455 per credit. Tuition, state resident: full-time $10,770; part-time $455 per credit. Tuition, nonresident: full-time $19,920; part-time $830 per credit. *International tuition:* $19,920 full-time. *Required fees:* $559.20; $181.10 per semester. Tuition and fees vary according to program. *Faculty research:* Big data, pattern recognition, text mining and frequent pattern mining; graph theory; computer vision, image processing pattern recognition and serious game; parallel computing and stimulation; high performance computing and modeling simulation; serious games; security, cryptography and communication networks; scheduling algorithms; scheduling, operations research and graph theory. *Unit head:* Dr. Xiaowen Zhang, Associate Professor, 718-982-3262, E-mail: xiaowen.zhang@csi.cuny.edu. *Application contact:* Sasha Spence, Associate Director for Graduate Admissions, 718-982-2019, Fax: 718-982-2500, E-mail: sasha.spence@csi.cuny.edu.
Website: https://www.csi.cuny.edu/sites/default/files/pdf/admissions/grad/pdf/Computer%20Science%20Fact%20Sheet.pdf

Colorado Technical University Aurora, Program in Computer Science, Aurora, CO 80014. Offers computer systems security (MSCS); database systems (MSCS); software engineering (MSCS). *Program availability:* Part-time, evening/weekend. *Degree requirements:* For master's, thesis or alternative. *Entrance requirements:* For master's, minimum undergraduate GPA of 3.0, resume.

Colorado Technical University Colorado Springs, Graduate Studies, Program in Computer Science, Colorado Springs, CO 80907. Offers computer science (DCS); computer systems security (MSCS); database systems (MSCS); software engineering (MSCS). *Program availability:* Part-time, evening/weekend, online learning. *Degree requirements:* For master's, thesis or alternative; for doctorate, thesis/dissertation. *Entrance requirements:* For doctorate, minimum graduate GPA of 3.0, 5 years of related work experience. *Faculty research:* Software engineering, systems engineering.

Concordia University, School of Graduate Studies, Faculty of Engineering and Computer Science, Department of Computer Science and Software Engineering, Montréal, QC H3G 1M8, Canada. Offers computer science (M App Comp Sc, M Comp Sc, PhD, Diploma); software engineering (M Eng, MA Sc). *Degree requirements:* For master's, one foreign language, thesis optional; for doctorate, one foreign language, comprehensive exam, thesis/dissertation. *Faculty research:* Computer systems and applications, mathematics of computation, pattern recognition, artificial intelligence and robotics.

DePaul University, College of Computing and Digital Media, Chicago, IL 60604. Offers animation (MA, MFA); applied technology (MS); business information technology (MS); computational finance (MS); computer and information sciences (PhD); computer science (MS); creative producing (MFA); cybersecurity (MS); data science (MS); digital communication and media arts (MA); documentary (MFA); e-commerce technology (MS); experience design (MA); film and television (MS); film and television directing (MFA); game design (MFA); game programming (MS); health informatics (MS); human centered design (PhD); human-computer interaction (MS); information systems (MS); network engineering and security (MS); product innovation and computing (MS); screenwriting (MFA); software engineering (MS); JD/MS. *Program availability:* Part-time, evening/weekend, online learning. *Degree requirements:* For master's, thesis (for some programs); for doctorate, comprehensive exam, thesis/dissertation. *Entrance requirements:* For master's, GRE or GMAT (for MS in computational finance only), bachelor's degree, resume (MS in predictive analytics only), IT experience (MS in information technology project management only), portfolio review (all MFA programs and MA in animation); for doctorate, GRE, master's degree in computer science. Additional exam requirements/recommendations for international students: Required—TOEFL (minimum score 590 paper-based; 80 iBT), IELTS (minimum score 6.5), PTE (minimum score 53). Electronic applications accepted. *Expenses:* Contact institution. *Faculty research:* Data mining, computer science, human-computer interaction, security, animation and film.

Drexel University, College of Computing and Informatics, Department of Computer Science, Philadelphia, PA 19104-2875. Offers computer science (MS, PhD, Postbaccalaureate Certificate); software engineering (MS). *Program availability:* Part-time, evening/weekend, 100% online. *Faculty:* 23 full-time (3 women), 4 part-time/adjunct (0 women). *Students:* 69 full-time (21 women), 84 part-time (23 women); includes 23 minority (4 Black or African American, non-Hispanic/Latino; 10 Asian, non-Hispanic/Latino; 3 Hispanic/Latino; 6 Two or more races, non-Hispanic/Latino), 43 international. Average age 29. 431 applicants, 34% accepted, 70 enrolled. In 2018, 43 master's, 7 doctorates, 11 other advanced degrees awarded. Terminal master's awarded for partial completion of doctoral program. *Degree requirements:* For doctorate, thesis/dissertation. *Entrance requirements:* For master's and doctorate, GRE General Test. Additional exam requirements/recommendations for international students: Required—TOEFL (minimum score 90 iBT), IELTS (minimum score 6.5). *Application deadline:* For fall admission, 8/15 for domestic students, 7/15 for international students; for spring admission, 3/1 for domestic students, 2/1 for international students. Applications are processed on a rolling basis. Application fee: $65. Electronic applications accepted. *Financial support:* In 2018–19, 41 students received support. Fellowships, research assistantships, teaching assistantships, scholarships/grants, and tuition waivers (partial) available. Financial award application deadline: 3/1; financial award applicants required to submit FAFSA. *Unit head:* Dr. Yi Deng, Dean/Professor, 215-895-2474, Fax: 215-895-2494, E-mail: yd362@drexel.edu. *Application contact:* Matthew Lechtenberg, Director, Recruitment, 215-895-2474, Fax: 215-895-2303, E-mail: cciinfo@drexel.edu.

See Display on page 229 and Close-Up on page 309.

Drexel University, College of Engineering, Department of Electrical and Computer Engineering, Program in Software Engineering, Philadelphia, PA 19104-2875. Offers MSSE. *Entrance requirements:* For master's, GRE. Additional exam requirements/recommendations for international students: Required—TOEFL. Electronic applications accepted.

East Carolina University, Graduate School, College of Engineering and Technology, Department of Computer Science, Greenville, NC 27858-4353. Offers computer science (MS); software engineering (MS). *Program availability:* Part-time, evening/weekend. *Application deadline:* For fall admission, 11/1 priority date for domestic students, 10/1 priority date for international students; for spring admission, 3/1 priority date for domestic and international students. *Expenses: Tuition, area resident:* Full-time $4749. Tuition, state resident: full-time $4749. Tuition, nonresident: full-time $17,898. *International tuition:* $17,898 full-time. *Required fees:* $2787. Part-time tuition and fees vary according to course load and program. *Financial support:* Application deadline: 3/1. *Unit head:* Dr. Venkat Gudivada, Chair, 252-328-9693, E-mail: gudivadav15@ecu.edu. *Application contact:* Graduate School Admissions, 252-328-6012, Fax: 252-328-6071, E-mail: gradschool@ecu.edu.
Website: http://www.ecu.edu/cet/csci/index.cfm

Embry-Riddle Aeronautical University–Daytona, Department of Electrical, Computer, Software and Systems Engineering, Daytona Beach, FL 32114-3900. Offers cybersecurity engineering (MS); electrical and computer engineering (MSECE); software engineering (MSSE); systems engineering (MS). *Degree requirements:* For master's, thesis optional. *Entrance requirements:* For master's, GRE (for some programs). Additional exam requirements/recommendations for international students: Required—TOEFL (minimum score 550 paper-based, 79 iBT) or IELTS (6). Electronic applications accepted.

Fairfield University, School of Engineering, Fairfield, CT 06824. Offers database management (CAS); electrical and computer engineering (MS); information security (CAS); management of technology (MS); mechanical engineering (MS); network technology (CAS); software engineering (MS); Web application development (CAS). *Program availability:* Part-time, evening/weekend. *Degree requirements:* For master's, capstone course. *Entrance requirements:* For master's, resume, 2 recommendations. Additional exam requirements/recommendations for international students: Required—TOEFL (minimum score 550 paper-based; 80 iBT) or IELTS (minimum score 6.5). Electronic applications accepted. *Expenses:* Contact institution. *Faculty research:* Artificial intelligence and information visualization, natural language processing, thermofluids, microwaves and electromagnetics, micro-/nano-manufacturing.

Florida Agricultural and Mechanical University, Division of Graduate Studies, Research, and Continuing Education, College of Science and Technology, Department of Computer Information Sciences, Tallahassee, FL 32307-3200. Offers software engineering (MS). *Entrance requirements:* Additional exam requirements/recommendations for international students: Required—TOEFL.

Florida Institute of Technology, College of Engineering and Science, Program in Software Engineering, Melbourne, FL 32901-6975. Offers MS. *Program availability:* Part-time. *Students:* 5 full-time (3 women), 15 part-time (2 women); includes 5 minority (all Hispanic/Latino), 5 international. Average age 30. 15 applicants, 73% accepted, 1 enrolled. In 2018, 3 master's awarded. *Degree requirements:* For master's, comprehensive exam (for some programs), thesis or alternative, internship, minimum of 30 credit hours. *Entrance requirements:* For master's, GRE General Test, 3 letters of recommendation, specific courses in mathematical studies. Additional exam requirements/recommendations for international students: Required—TOEFL (minimum score 550 paper-based; 79 iBT). *Application deadline:* Applications are processed on a rolling basis. Application fee: $50. Electronic applications accepted. *Expenses: Tuition:* Full-time $22,338; part-time $1241 per credit hour. Tuition and fees vary according to degree level, campus/location and program. *Financial support:* Career-related internships or fieldwork available. Financial award applicants required to submit FAFSA. *Faculty research:* Machine learning, computer vision, biologically inspired computing, data mining, cryptography, speech recognition. *Unit head:* Dr. Philip Bernhard, Department Head, 321-674-7294, E-mail: pbernhar@fit.edu. *Application contact:* Mike Perry, Executive Director of Admissions, 321-674-7127, E-mail: perrymj@fit.edu.
Website: https://www.fit.edu/programs/software-engineering-ms/

Gannon University, School of Graduate Studies, College of Engineering and Business, School of Engineering and Computer Science, Program in Computer and Information Science, Erie, PA 16541-0001. Offers information analytics (MSCIS); software engineering (MSCIS). *Program availability:* Part-time, evening/weekend. *Degree requirements:* For master's, thesis (for some programs), directed research. *Entrance requirements:* For master's, 3 letters of recommendation; resume; transcripts; baccalaureate degree in computer science, information systems, information science, software engineering, or related field from regionally-accredited institution with minimum GPA of 2.5. Additional exam requirements/recommendations for international students: Required—TOEFL (minimum score 79 iBT). Electronic applications accepted. Application fee is waived when completed online.

Gannon University, School of Graduate Studies, College of Engineering and Business, School of Engineering and Computer Science, Program in Electrical and Computer Engineering, Erie, PA 16541-0001. Offers MSEE, MSES. *Program availability:* Part-time, evening/weekend. *Degree requirements:* For master's, thesis (for some programs), oral exam (for some programs), design project (for some programs). *Entrance requirements:* For master's, bachelor's degree in electrical or computer engineering from an ABET-accredited program or its equivalent with minimum GPA of 2.5, transcripts, 3 letters of recommendation. Additional exam requirements/recommendations for international students: Required—TOEFL (minimum score 79 iBT). Electronic applications accepted. Application fee is waived when completed online.

Gannon University, School of Graduate Studies, College of Engineering and Business, School of Engineering and Computer Science, Program in Software Engineering, Erie, PA 16541-0001. Offers MSCIS. *Program availability:* Part-time, evening/weekend. *Entrance requirements:* For master's, baccalaureate degree in computer science, information systems, information science, software engineering, or a related field from regionally-accredited institution with minimum GPA of 2.5; resume; transcripts; 3 letters of recommendation. Additional exam requirements/recommendations for international students: Required—TOEFL (minimum score 79 iBT). Electronic applications accepted. Application fee is waived when completed online.

Grand Valley State University, Padnos College of Engineering and Computing, School of Computing and Information Systems, Allendale, MI 49401-9403. Offers computer information systems (MS), including databases, distributed systems, management of

information systems, object-oriented systems, software engineering. *Program availability:* Part-time, evening/weekend. *Faculty:* 10 full-time (0 women). *Students:* 26 full-time (10 women), 53 part-time (7 women); includes 10 minority (2 Black or African American, non-Hispanic/Latino; 6 Asian, non-Hispanic/Latino; 1 Hispanic/Latino; 1 Two or more races, non-Hispanic/Latino), 21 international. Average age 29. 56 applicants, 70% accepted, 15 enrolled. In 2018, 23 master's awarded. *Entrance requirements:* For master's, GRE (recommended with GPA below 3.0), minimum GPA of 3.0; knowledge of a programming language; coursework or experience in: computer architecture and/or organization, data structures and algorithms, databases, discrete math, networking, operating systems, and software engineering; minimum of 2 letters of recommendation; resume; personal statement. Additional exam requirements/recommendations for international students: Required—Michigan English Language Assessment Battery (minimum score 77), TOEFL (minimum iBT score of 80), or IELTS (6.5); GRE. *Application deadline:* For fall admission, 6/1 for international students; for winter admission, 9/1 for international students. Applications are processed on a rolling basis. Application fee: $30. Electronic applications accepted. *Expenses:* $712 per credit hour, 33 credit hours. *Financial support:* In 2018–19, 13 students received support, including 6 fellowships, 5 research assistantships with full and partial tuition reimbursements available (averaging $8,000 per year). *Faculty research:* Object technology, distributed computing, information systems management database, software engineering. *Unit head:* Dr. Paul Leidig, Director, 616-331-2060, Fax: 616-331-2144, E-mail: leidigp@gvsu.edu. *Application contact:* Dr. D. Robert Adams, Graduate Program Director, 616-331-3885, Fax: 616-331-2144, E-mail: adamsr@gvsu.edu.
Website: http://www.cis.gvsu.edu/

Harrisburg University of Science and Technology, Program in Information Systems Engineering and Management, Harrisburg, PA 17101. Offers analytics (MS); digital government (MS); digital health (MS); entrepreneurship (MS); information security (MS); software engineering and systems development (MS). *Program availability:* Part-time, evening/weekend. *Degree requirements:* For master's, thesis optional. *Entrance requirements:* For master's, baccalaureate degree. Additional exam requirements/recommendations for international students: Required—TOEFL (minimum score 520 paper-based; 80 iBT); Recommended—IELTS (minimum score 6). Electronic applications accepted. *Faculty research:* Healthcare Informatics, material analysis, enterprise systems, circuit design, enterprise architectures.

Illinois Institute of Technology, Graduate College, Armour College of Engineering, Department of Electrical and Computer Engineering, Chicago, IL 60616. Offers biomedical imaging and signals (MAS); computer engineering (MS, PhD); electrical engineering (MS, PhD); electricity markets (MAS); network engineering (MAS); power engineering (MAS); telecommunications and software engineering (MAS); VLSI and microelectronics (MAS); MS/MS. *Program availability:* Part-time, evening/weekend, online learning. Terminal master's awarded for partial completion of doctoral program. *Degree requirements:* For master's, comprehensive exam (for some programs), thesis (for some programs); for doctorate, comprehensive exam, thesis/dissertation. *Entrance requirements:* For master's and doctorate, GRE General Test (minimum score 1100 Quantitative and Verbal, 3.5 Analytical Writing), minimum undergraduate GPA of 3.0. Additional exam requirements/recommendations for international students: Required—TOEFL (minimum score 550 paper-based; 80 iBT); Recommended—IELTS (minimum score 5.5). Electronic applications accepted. *Faculty research:* Communication systems, wireless networks, computer systems, computer networks, wireless security, cloud computing and micro-electronics; electromagnetics and electronics; power and control systems; signal and image processing.

Illinois Institute of Technology, Graduate College, College of Science, Department of Computer Science, Chicago, IL 60616. Offers business (MCS); computational intelligence (MCS); computer science (MCS, MS, PhD); cyber-physical systems (MCS); data analytics (MCS); data science (MAS); database systems (MCS); distributed and cloud computing (MCS); education (MCS); finance (MCS); information security and assurance (MCS); networking and communications (MCS); software engineering (MCS); telecommunications and software engineering (MAS); MS/MAS. *Program availability:* Part-time, evening/weekend, online learning. Terminal master's awarded for partial completion of doctoral program. *Degree requirements:* For master's, thesis optional; for doctorate, comprehensive exam, thesis/dissertation. *Entrance requirements:* For master's, GRE General Test with minimum scores of 298 Quantitative and Verbal, 3.0 Analytical Writing (for MS); GRE General Test with minimum scores of 292 Quantitative and Verbal, 2.5 Analytical Writing (for MAS), minimum undergraduate GPA of 3.0; for doctorate, GRE General Test (minimum scores: 304 Quantitative and Verbal, 3.5 Analytical Writing), minimum undergraduate GPA of 3.0. Additional exam requirements/recommendations for international students: Required—TOEFL (minimum score 523 paper-based; 70 iBT). Electronic applications accepted. *Faculty research:* Parallel and distributed processing, high-performance computing, computational linguistics, information retrieval, data mining, grid computing.

Indiana University–Purdue University Indianapolis, School of Science, Department of Computer and Information Science, Indianapolis, IN 46202-5132. Offers biocomputing (Graduate Certificate); biometrics (Graduate Certificate); computer science (MS, PhD); computer security (Graduate Certificate); databases and data mining (Graduate Certificate); software engineering (Graduate Certificate). *Program availability:* Part-time. Terminal master's awarded for partial completion of doctoral program. *Degree requirements:* For master's and Graduate Certificate, thesis optional; for doctorate, thesis/dissertation. *Entrance requirements:* For master's and doctorate, GRE, BS in computer science or the equivalent with a minimum GPA of 3.0 (or equivalent); for Graduate Certificate, BS in computer science or the equivalent with a minimum GPA of 3.0 (or equivalent). Additional exam requirements/recommendations for international students: Required—PTE (minimum score 58), TOEFL (minimum score 550 paper-based, 79 iBT) or IELTS (6.5). *Faculty research:* Imaging and visualization; networking and security; software engineering; distributed and parallel computing; database, data mining and machine learning.

Instituto Tecnologico de Santo Domingo, Graduate School, Area of Engineering, Santo Domingo, Dominican Republic. Offers construction administration (MS, Certificate); data telecommunications (M Eng, MS, Certificate); industrial engineering (M Eng, Certificate); industrial management (M Mgmt); information technology (Certificate); maintenance engineering (M Eng); occupational hazard prevention (M Mgmt); production management (Certificate); quantitative methods (Certificate); sanitary and environmental engineering (M Eng); structural engineering (M Eng); systems engineering and electronic data processing (Certificate); transportation (Certificate).

International Technological University, Program in Software Engineering, San Jose, CA 95134. Offers MSSE. *Program availability:* Part-time, evening/weekend. *Degree requirements:* For master's, thesis or alternative, capstone project. *Entrance requirements:* Additional exam requirements/recommendations for international students: Required—TOEFL, IELTS. Electronic applications accepted.

Jacksonville State University, Graduate Studies, School of Science, Program in Computer Systems and Software Design, Jacksonville, AL 36265-1602. Offers MS. *Program availability:* Part-time, evening/weekend. *Degree requirements:* For master's, comprehensive exam, thesis (for some programs). *Entrance requirements:* Additional

exam requirements/recommendations for international students: Required—TOEFL (minimum score 500 paper-based; 61 iBT). Electronic applications accepted.

Kennesaw State University, College of Computing and Software Engineering, Program in Software Engineering, Kennesaw, GA 30144. Offers software engineering (MSSWE, Graduate Certificate); software engineering foundations (Graduate Certificate). *Program availability:* Part-time, evening/weekend, blended/hybrid learning. *Students:* 30 full-time (6 women), 69 part-time (11 women); includes 51 minority (30 Black or African American, non-Hispanic/Latino; 14 Asian, non-Hispanic/Latino; 5 Hispanic/Latino; 2 Two or more races, non-Hispanic/Latino), 9 international. Average age 34. 51 applicants, 78% accepted, 29 enrolled. In 2018, 16 master's awarded. *Degree requirements:* For master's, thesis optional, capstone. *Entrance requirements:* For master's, GRE (recommended). Additional exam requirements/recommendations for international students: Required—TOEFL (minimum score 80 iBT), IELTS (minimum score 6.5). *Application deadline:* For fall admission, 7/1 priority date for domestic students, 6/1 priority date for international students; for spring admission, 11/1 priority date for domestic students, 9/1 priority date for international students; for summer admission, 4/1 priority date for domestic students, 3/1 priority date for international students. Applications are processed on a rolling basis. Application fee: $60. Electronic applications accepted. *Expenses: Tuition,* area resident: Full-time $6960; part-time $290 per credit hour. Tuition, state resident: full-time $6960; part-time $290 per credit hour. Tuition, nonresident: full-time $25,080; part-time $1045 per credit hour. *International tuition:* $25,080 full-time. *Required fees:* $2006; $1706 per semester. $853 per semester. *Financial support:* Research assistantships with full tuition reimbursements, teaching assistantships with full tuition reimbursements, career-related internships or fieldwork, scholarships/grants, unspecified assistantships, and cooperative programs available. Financial award applicants required to submit FAFSA. *Application contact:* Admission Counselor, 470-578-4377, Fax: 470-578-9172, E-mail: ksugrad@kennesaw.edu.
Website: http://ccse.kennesaw.edu/swegd/

Lewis University, College of Arts and Sciences, Program in Computer Science, Romeoville, IL 60446. Offers cyber security (MS); intelligent systems (MS); software engineering (MS). *Program availability:* Part-time, evening/weekend, 100% online, blended/hybrid learning. *Students:* 23 full-time (5 women), 90 part-time (23 women); includes 34 minority (8 Black or African American, non-Hispanic/Latino; 12 Asian, non-Hispanic/Latino; 9 Hispanic/Latino; 1 Native Hawaiian or other Pacific Islander, non-Hispanic/Latino; 4 Two or more races, non-Hispanic/Latino), 6 international. Average age 32. *Entrance requirements:* For master's, bachelor's degree; minimum undergraduate GPA of 3.0; resume; statement of purpose; two letters of recommendation; undergraduate coursework in discrete mathematics, programming or algorithms. Additional exam requirements/recommendations for international students: Required—TOEFL (minimum score 550 paper-based; 79 iBT), IELTS (minimum score 6). *Application deadline:* For fall admission, 5/1 for international students; for winter admission, 11/15 for international students. Applications are processed on a rolling basis. Application fee: $40. Electronic applications accepted. *Financial support:* Federal Work-Study and unspecified assistantships available. Financial award application deadline: 5/1; financial award applicants required to submit FAFSA. *Unit head:* Dr. Khaled Alzoubi, Program Director. *Application contact:* Linda Campbell, Graduate Admissions Counselor, 815-836-5610, E-mail: grad@lewisu.edu.
Website: http://www.lewisu.edu/academics/mscomputerscience/index.htm

Lipscomb University, College of Computing and Technology, Nashville, TN 37204-3951. Offers data science (MS, Certificate); information technology (MS, Certificate), including data science (MS), information security (MS), information technology management (MS), software engineering (MS); software engineering (MS, Certificate). *Program availability:* Part-time, evening/weekend. *Degree requirements:* For master's, capstone project. *Entrance requirements:* For master's, GRE, 2 references, transcripts, resume, personal statement. Additional exam requirements/recommendations for international students: Required—TOEFL (minimum score 570 paper-based; 80 iBT). Electronic applications accepted. *Expenses:* Contact institution.

Loyola University Chicago, Graduate School, Department of Computer Science, Chicago, IL 60660. Offers computer science (MS); information technology (MS); software engineering (MS). *Program availability:* Part-time, evening/weekend, 100% online, blended/hybrid learning. *Faculty:* 16 full-time (3 women), 16 part-time/adjunct (2 women). *Students:* 45 full-time (13 women), 40 part-time (11 women); includes 23 minority (7 Black or African American, non-Hispanic/Latino; 15 Asian, non-Hispanic/Latino; 1 Hispanic/Latino), 29 international. Average age 29. 116 applicants, 53% accepted, 29 enrolled. In 2018, 48 master's awarded. *Degree requirements:* For master's, thesis optional, 30 credits/ten courses. *Entrance requirements:* For master's, 2 letters of recommendation, transcripts, statement of purpose. Additional exam requirements/recommendations for international students: Required—TOEFL (minimum score 550 paper-based; 79 iBT), IELTS (minimum score 6.5). *Application deadline:* Applications are processed on a rolling basis. Application fee: $50. Electronic applications accepted. Application fee is waived when completed online. *Expenses:* Contact institution. *Financial support:* In 2018–19, 17 students received support, including 2 fellowships with full tuition reimbursements available, 1 research assistantship with full tuition reimbursement available (averaging $17,000 per year), 11 teaching assistantships with partial tuition reimbursements available (averaging $9,575 per year); career-related internships or fieldwork, Federal Work-Study, health care benefits, and tuition waivers (full and partial) also available. Financial award application deadline: 3/15. *Faculty research:* Software engineering, machine learning, algorithms and complexity, parallel and distributed computing, databases and computer networks, security. *Total annual research expenditures:* $22,000. *Unit head:* Dr. Chandra Sekharan, Chair, 773-508-3572, Fax: 773-508-3739, E-mail: laufer@cs.luc.edu. *Application contact:* Cecilia Murphy, Graduate Program Secretary, 773-508-8035, E-mail: cmurphy@luc.edu.
Website: http://luc.edu/cs

Marist College, Graduate Programs, School of Computer Science and Mathematics, Poughkeepsie, NY 12601-1387. Offers business analytics (Adv C); computer science/software development (MS); information systems (MS, Adv C). *Program availability:* Part-time, evening/weekend, online learning. *Entrance requirements:* For master's, resume. Additional exam requirements/recommendations for international students: Required—TOEFL (minimum score 550 paper-based; 80 iBT); Recommended—IELTS (minimum score 6.5). Electronic applications accepted. *Faculty research:* Data quality, artificial intelligence, imaging, analysis of algorithms, distributed systems and applications.

Marymount University, School of Business and Technology, Program in Information Technology, Arlington, VA 22207-4299. Offers health care informatics (Certificate); information technology (MS, Certificate), including cybersecurity (MS), health care informatics (MS), project management and technology leadership (MS), software engineering (MS); information technology project management and technology leadership (Certificate); information technology with business administration (MS/MBA); information technology with health care management (MS/MS); MS/MBA; MS/MS. *Program availability:* Part-time, evening/weekend. *Faculty:* 5 full-time (3 women), 7 part-time/adjunct (0 women). *Students:* 29 full-time (17 women), 36 part-time (19 women);

includes 25 minority (15 Black or African American, non-Hispanic/Latino; 5 Asian, non-Hispanic/Latino; 5 Hispanic/Latino), 24 international. Average age 30. 66 applicants, 98% accepted, 22 enrolled. In 2018, 35 master's, 3 other advanced degrees awarded. *Degree requirements:* For master's, thesis or alternative. *Entrance requirements:* For master's, resume, bachelor's degree in computer-related field or degree in another subject with a certificate in a computer-related field or related work experience. Software Engineering Track: bachelor's degree in Computer Science or work in software development. Project Mgmt/Tech Leadership Track: minimum 2 years of IT experience. Additional exam requirements/recommendations for international students: Required—TOEFL (minimum score 600 paper-based; 96 iBT), IELTS (minimum score 6.5), PTE (minimum score 58). *Application deadline:* For fall admission, 7/16 priority date for domestic and international students; for spring admission, 11/16 priority date for domestic and international students; for summer admission, 4/16 priority date for domestic and international students. Applications are processed on a rolling basis. Application fee: $40. Electronic applications accepted. *Expenses:* $1,060 per credit. *Financial support:* In 2018–19, 1 student received support. Research assistantships, teaching assistantships, career-related internships or fieldwork, scholarships/grants, and unspecified assistantships available. Support available to part-time students. Financial award application deadline: 3/1; financial award applicants required to submit FAFSA. *Unit head:* Dr. Diane Murphy, Chair/Director, Information Technology, Management Sciences and Cybersecurity, 703-284-5958, E-mail: diane.murphy@marymount.edu. *Application contact:* Rebecca Esposito, Senior Associate Director, Graduate Admissions, 703-284-5901, Fax: 703-527-3815, E-mail: grad.admissions@marymount.edu.
Website: https://www.marymount.edu/Academics/School-of-Business-and-Technology/Graduate-Programs/Information-Technology-(M-S-)

McMaster University, School of Graduate Studies, Faculty of Engineering, Department of Computing and Software, Hamilton, ON L8S 4M2, Canada. Offers computer science (M Sc, PhD); software engineering (M Eng, MA Sc, PhD). *Program availability:* Part-time. *Degree requirements:* For master's, thesis. *Entrance requirements:* Additional exam requirements/recommendations for international students: Required—TOEFL (minimum score 550 paper-based). *Faculty research:* Software engineering; theory of non-sequential systems; parallel and distributed computing; artificial intelligence; complexity, design, and analysis of algorithms; combinatorial computing, especially applications to molecular biology.

Mercer University, Graduate Studies, Macon Campus, School of Engineering, Macon, GA 31207. Offers biomedical engineering (MSE); computer engineering (MSE); electrical engineering (MSE); engineering management (MSE); environmental engineering (MSE); environmental systems (MS); mechanical engineering (MSE); software engineering (MSE); software systems (MS); technical communications management (MS); technical management (MS). *Program availability:* Part-time-only, evening/weekend, online learning. *Degree requirements:* For master's, thesis or alternative. *Entrance requirements:* For master's, GRE (minimum score 300), minimum undergraduate GPA of 3.0. Additional exam requirements/recommendations for international students: Required—TOEFL (minimum score 550 paper-based; 80 iBT). *Expenses:* Contact institution. *Faculty research:* Designing prostheses and orthotics, oxygen transfer and limitations in biological systems, low-cost groundwater development, lung airway and transport, autonomous mobile robots.

Monmouth University, Graduate Studies, Program in Software Engineering, West Long Branch, NJ 07764-1898. Offers MS, Certificate. *Program availability:* Part-time, evening/weekend, online learning. *Faculty:* 3 full-time (1 woman), 5 part-time/adjunct (2 women). *Students:* 10 full-time (2 women), 14 part-time (6 women); includes 2 minority (1 Black or African American, non-Hispanic/Latino; 1 Asian, non-Hispanic/Latino), 15 international. Average age 27. In 2018, 16 master's awarded. *Degree requirements:* For master's, thesis optional, practicum. *Entrance requirements:* For master's and Certificate, bachelor's degree in software engineering, computer science, computer engineering or other engineering-related discipline; minimum GPA of 3.0 in major, 2.5 overall; completed course work in computer programming, data structures and algorithms, and software engineering. Additional exam requirements/recommendations for international students: Required—TOEFL (minimum score 550 paper-based, 79 iBT), IELTS (minimum score 6), Michigan English Language Assessment Battery (minimum score 77) or Certificate of Advanced English (minimum score 160). *Application deadline:* For fall admission, 7/15 priority date for domestic students, 6/1 for international students; for spring admission, 12/1 priority date for domestic students, 11/1 for international students; for summer admission, 5/1 for domestic students. Applications are processed on a rolling basis. Application fee: $50. Electronic applications accepted. *Expenses:* Contact institution. *Financial support:* In 2018–19, 18 students received support. Institutionally sponsored loans, scholarships/grants, and unspecified assistantships available. Support available to part-time students. Financial award applicants required to submit FAFSA. *Faculty research:* Conceptual structures, real time software, business rules, project management, software related to homeland security. *Unit head:* Dr. Jiacun Wang, Program Director, 732-571-7501, Fax: 732-263-5253, E-mail: jwang@monmouth.edu. *Application contact:* Laurie Kuhn, Associate Director of Graduate Admission, 732-571-3452, Fax: 732-263-5123, E-mail: gradadm@monmouth.edu.
Website: http://www.monmouth.edu/graduate_se

Naval Postgraduate School, Departments and Academic Groups, Department of Computer Science, Monterey, CA 93943. Offers computer science (MS, PhD); identity management and cyber security (MA); modeling of virtual environments and simulations (MS, PhD); software engineering (MS, PhD). Program only open to commissioned officers of the United States and friendly nations and selected United States federal civilian employees. *Program availability:* Part-time, online learning. *Degree requirements:* For master's, thesis; for doctorate, thesis/dissertation.

New Jersey Institute of Technology, Ying Wu College of Computing, Newark, NJ 07102. Offers big data management and mining (Certificate); business and information systems (Certificate); computer science (PhD); computing and business (MS); data mining (Certificate); data science (MS); information security (Certificate); information systems (PhD); information technology administration and security (MS); IT administration (Certificate); network security and information assurance (Certificate); software engineering (MS), including information systems; software engineering analysis/design (Certificate); Web systems development (Certificate). *Program availability:* Part-time, evening/weekend. *Faculty:* 69 full-time (13 women), 38 part-time/adjunct (4 women). *Students:* 699 full-time (229 women), 269 part-time (67 women); includes 260 minority (44 Black or African American, non-Hispanic/Latino; 145 Asian, non-Hispanic/Latino; 59 Hispanic/Latino; 12 Two or more races, non-Hispanic/Latino), 614 international. Average age 26. 2,216 applicants, 55% accepted, 366 enrolled. In 2018, 418 master's, 5 doctorates, 13 other advanced degrees awarded. Terminal master's awarded for partial completion of doctoral program. *Degree requirements:* For master's, thesis optional; for doctorate, thesis/dissertation. *Entrance requirements:* For master's, GRE General Test; for doctorate, GRE General Test, minimum graduate GPA of 3.5. Additional exam requirements/recommendations for international students: Required—TOEFL (minimum score 550 paper-based; 79 iBT), IELTS (minimum score 6.5). *Application deadline:* For fall admission, 6/1 priority date for domestic students, 5/1 priority date for international students; for spring admission, 11/15 priority date for domestic and international students. Applications are processed on a rolling basis. Application fee: $75. Electronic applications accepted. *Expenses:* $22,690 per year (in-state), $32,136 per year (out-of-state). *Financial support:* In 2018–19, 366 students received support, including 10 fellowships with full tuition reimbursements available (averaging $22,000 per year), 47 research assistantships with full tuition reimbursements available (averaging $22,000 per year), 28 teaching assistantships with full tuition reimbursements available (averaging $22,000 per year); career-related internships or fieldwork, Federal Work-Study, scholarships/grants, and unspecified assistantships also available. Financial award application deadline: 1/15. *Faculty research:* Computer systems, communications and networking, artificial intelligence, database engineering, systems analysis, analytics and optimization in crowdsourcing. *Total annual research expenditures:* $4.9 million. *Unit head:* Dr. Craig Gotsman, Dean, 973-596-3366, Fax: 973-596-5777, E-mail: craig.gotsman@njit.edu. *Application contact:* Stephen Eck, Director of Admissions, 973-596-3300, Fax: 973-596-3461, E-mail: admissions@njit.edu.
Website: http://computing.njit.edu/

New York University, Tandon School of Engineering, Department of Computer Science and Engineering, Major in Software Engineering, New York, NY 10012-1019. Offers Graduate Certificate. *Students:* Average age 31. 1 applicant. *Application deadline:* For fall admission, 2/15 priority date for domestic and international students; for spring admission, 11/1 priority date for domestic and international students. Applications are processed on a rolling basis. Application fee: $75. Electronic applications accepted. *Financial support:* Fellowships, research assistantships, teaching assistantships, career-related internships or fieldwork, scholarships/grants, tuition waivers, and unspecified assistantships available. Support available to part-time students. Financial award application deadline: 2/15. *Unit head:* Dr. Nasir Memon, Head, 718-260-3970, E-mail: memon@nyu.edu. *Application contact:* Raymond Lutzky, Director, Graduate Enrollment Management, 718-637-5984, Fax: 718-260-3624, E-mail: rlutzky@poly.edu.
Website: http://www.poly.edu/cis/graduate/certificates/

North Dakota State University, College of Graduate and Interdisciplinary Studies, College of Science and Mathematics, Department of Computer Science, Program in Software Engineering, Fargo, ND 58102. Offers MS, MSE, PhD, Certificate. *Program availability:* Part-time, online learning. Terminal master's awarded for partial completion of doctoral program. *Entrance requirements:* Additional exam requirements/recommendations for international students: Required—TOEFL. Electronic applications accepted.

Northern Kentucky University, Office of Graduate Programs, College of Informatics, Department of Computer Science, Highland Heights, KY 41099. Offers computer science (MSCS); geographic information systems (Certificate); secure software engineering (Certificate). *Program availability:* Part-time, evening/weekend. *Degree requirements:* For master's, thesis optional. *Entrance requirements:* For master's, GRE, minimum GPA of 3.0, at least 4 semesters of undergraduate study in computer science including intermediate computer programming and data structures, one year of calculus, one course in discrete mathematics. Additional exam requirements/recommendations for international students: Required—TOEFL (minimum score 550 paper-based; 79 iBT); Recommended—IELTS (minimum score 6.5). Electronic applications accepted. *Faculty research:* Data privacy, data mining, wireless security, secure software engineering, secure networking.

Northwestern University, School of Professional Studies, Program in Information Systems, Evanston, IL 60208. Offers analytics and business intelligence (MS); database and Internet technologies (MS); information systems (MS); information systems management (MS); information systems security (MS); medical informatics (MS); software project management and development (MS). *Program availability:* Part-time, evening/weekend.

Oakland University, Graduate Study and Lifelong Learning, School of Engineering and Computer Science, Department of Computer Science and Engineering, Rochester, MI 48309-4401. Offers computer science (MS); computer science and informatics (PhD); software engineering and information technology (MS). *Program availability:* Part-time, evening/weekend. *Entrance requirements:* For master's, minimum GPA of 3.0. Electronic applications accepted. *Expenses:* Contact institution.

Oklahoma Christian University, Graduate School of Engineering and Computer Science, Oklahoma City, OK 73136-1100. Offers electrical and computer engineering (MSE); engineering management (MSE); mechanical engineering (MSE); software engineering (MSCS, MSE). *Program availability:* Part-time. *Entrance requirements:* Additional exam requirements/recommendations for international students: Required—TOEFL (minimum score 550 paper-based). Electronic applications accepted. *Expenses:* Contact institution.

Pace University, Seidenberg School of Computer Science and Information Systems, New York, NY 10038. Offers chief information security officer (APC); computer science (MS, PhD); enterprise analytics (MS); information and communication technology strategy and innovation (APC); information systems (MS, APC); information technology (MS); professional studies in computing (DPS); secure software and information engineering (APC); security and information assurance (Certificate); software development and engineering (MS, Certificate); telecommunications systems and networks (MS, Certificate). *Program availability:* Part-time, evening/weekend, online only, 100% online, blended/hybrid learning. *Faculty:* 26 full-time (7 women), 7 part-time/adjunct (2 women). *Students:* 515 full-time (172 women), 288 part-time (90 women); includes 183 minority (67 Black or African American, non-Hispanic/Latino; 3 American Indian or Alaska Native, non-Hispanic/Latino; 50 Asian, non-Hispanic/Latino; 52 Hispanic/Latino; 1 Native Hawaiian or other Pacific Islander, non-Hispanic/Latino; 10 Two or more races, non-Hispanic/Latino), 497 international. Average age 30. 817 applicants, 93% accepted, 235 enrolled. In 2018, 383 master's, 15 doctorates, 1 other advanced degree awarded. *Degree requirements:* For master's, thesis or alternative, capstone course; for doctorate, comprehensive exam (for some programs), thesis/dissertation. *Entrance requirements:* Additional exam requirements/recommendations for international students: Required—TOEFL (minimum score 78 iBT), IELTS (minimum score 6.5) or PTE (minimum score 52). *Application deadline:* For fall admission, 8/1 priority date for domestic students, 6/1 for international students; for spring admission, 12/1 for domestic students, 10/1 for international students. Applications are processed on a rolling basis. Application fee: $70. Electronic applications accepted. *Expenses:* Contact institution. *Financial support:* In 2018–19, 45 students received support. Research assistantships, career-related internships or fieldwork, scholarships/grants, and unspecified assistantships available. Support available to part-time students. Financial award application deadline: 2/15; financial award applicants required to submit FAFSA. *Faculty research:* Cyber security/digital forensics; mobile app development; big data/enterprise analytics; artificial intelligence; software development. *Total annual research expenditures:* $584,594. *Unit head:* Dr. Jonathan Hill, Dean, Seidenberg School of Computer Science and Information Systems, 212-346-1864, E-mail: jhill@pace.edu. *Application contact:* Susan Ford-Goldschein, Director of Graduate Admissions, 914-422-4283, Fax: 212-346-1585, E-mail: graduateadmission@pace.edu.
Website: http://www.pace.edu/seidenberg

Penn State Great Valley, Graduate Studies, Engineering Division, Malvern, PA 19355-1488. Offers engineering management (MEM); software engineering (MSE); systems engineering (M Eng, Certificate).

Regis University, College of Computer and Information Sciences, Denver, CO 80221-1099. Offers agile technologies (Certificate); cybersecurity (Certificate); data science (M Sc); database administration with Oracle (Certificate); database development (Certificate); database technologies (M Sc); enterprise Java software development (Certificate); enterprise resource planning (Certificate); executive information technology (Certificate); health care informatics (Certificate); health care informatics and information management (M Sc); information assurance (M Sc); information assurance policy management (Certificate); information technology management (M Sc); mobile software development (Certificate); software engineering (M Sc, Certificate); software engineering and database technology (M Sc); storage area networks (Certificate); systems engineering (M Sc, Certificate). *Program availability:* Part-time, evening/weekend, 100% online, blended/hybrid learning. *Degree requirements:* For master's, thesis (for some programs), final research project. *Entrance requirements:* For master's, official transcript reflecting baccalaureate degree awarded from regionally-accredited college or university, 2 years of related experience, resume, interview. Additional exam requirements/recommendations for international students: Required—TOEFL (minimum score 550 paper-based; 82 iBT). Electronic applications accepted. *Expenses:* Contact institution. *Faculty research:* Information policy, knowledge management, software architectures, data science.

Rochester Institute of Technology, Graduate Enrollment Services, Golisano College of Computing and Information Sciences, Software Engineering Department, MS Program in Software Engineering, Rochester, NY 14623-5603. Offers MS. *Program availability:* Part-time. *Students:* 45 full-time (14 women), 6 part-time (1 woman); includes 2 minority (1 Asian, non-Hispanic/Latino; 1 Hispanic/Latino), 41 international. Average age 26. 73 applicants, 74% accepted, 14 enrolled. In 2018, 17 master's awarded. *Degree requirements:* For master's, thesis or alternative, Thesis or Capstone. *Entrance requirements:* For master's, GRE required for individuals with degrees from international universities., minimum GPA of 3.0 (recommended), professional essay (1-4 pages), resume, two letters of recommendation. Additional exam requirements/recommendations for international students: Required—TOEFL (minimum score 570 paper-based; 88 iBT), IELTS (minimum score 6.5), PTE (minimum score 61). *Application deadline:* For fall admission, 2/15 priority date for domestic and international students; for spring admission, 12/15 priority date for domestic and international students. Applications are processed on a rolling basis. Application fee: $65. Electronic applications accepted. *Financial support:* In 2018–19, 37 students received support. Research assistantships with partial tuition reimbursements available, teaching assistantships with partial tuition reimbursements available, career-related internships or fieldwork, scholarships/grants, and unspecified assistantships available. Support available to part-time students. Financial award applicants required to submit FAFSA. *Faculty research:* Software engineering education, software architecture and design, architectural styles and design patterns, mathematical foundations of software engineering, object-oriented software development, augmented and virtual reality systems, engineering of real-time and embedded software systems, concurrent systems, distributed systems, data communications and networking, programming environments and tools, computer graphics, computer vision. *Unit head:* Dr. J. Scott Hawker, Graduate Program Director, 585-475-2705, E-mail: hawker@se.rit.edu. *Application contact:* Diane Ellison, Senior Associate Vice President, Graduate Enrollment Services, 585-475-2229, Fax: 585-475-7164, E-mail: gradinfo@rit.edu.
Website: https://www.rit.edu/study/software-engineering-ms

Royal Military College of Canada, Division of Graduate Studies, Faculty of Engineering, Department of Electrical and Computer Engineering, Kingston, ON K7K 7B4, Canada. Offers computer engineering (M Eng, PhD); electrical engineering (M Eng, PhD); software engineering (M Eng, PhD). *Degree requirements:* For master's, thesis; for doctorate, comprehensive exam, thesis/dissertation. *Entrance requirements:* For master's, honours degree with second-class standing in the appropriate field; for doctorate, master's degree. Electronic applications accepted.

Saint Louis University, Graduate Programs, College of Arts and Sciences, Department of Computer Science, St. Louis, MO 63103. Offers bioinformatics and computational biology (MS); computer science (MS); software engineering (MS). MS in bioinformatics and computational biology offered in coordination with Departments of Biology, Chemistry, and Mathematics and Statistics).

St. Mary's University, School of Science, Engineering and Technology, Program in Software Engineering, San Antonio, TX 78228. Offers MS, Certificate. *Program availability:* Part-time. *Students:* 11 part-time (4 women); includes 6 minority (1 Asian, non-Hispanic/Latino; 5 Hispanic/Latino). Average age 32. 1 applicant, 100% accepted, 1 enrolled. In 2018, 6 master's, 1 other advanced degree awarded. *Degree requirements:* For master's, thesis (for some programs), thesis or project. *Entrance requirements:* For master's, GRE (minimum quantitative score of 148), bachelor's degree in software engineering, computer science, computer engineering or closely-related discipline; minimum GPA of 3.0. Additional exam requirements/recommendations for international students: Required—TOEFL (minimum score 550 paper-based; 80 iBT), IELTS (minimum score 6.5). *Application deadline:* For fall admission, 7/1 for domestic students; for spring admission, 11/15 for domestic students; for summer admission, 4/1 for domestic students. Applications are processed on a rolling basis. Application fee: $0. Electronic applications accepted. *Expenses: Tuition:* Full-time $16,830; part-time $935 per credit hour. *Required fees:* $1055. Tuition and fees vary according to program. *Financial support:* Career-related internships or fieldwork, Federal Work-Study, institutionally sponsored loans, scholarships/grants, and health care benefits available. Financial award application deadline: 3/31; financial award applicants required to submit FAFSA. *Faculty research:* Software analysis, software metrics, usability of Web applications, component-based software development. *Unit head:* Dr. Ozgur Aktunc, Graduate Program Director, 210-431-2052, E-mail: oaktunc@stmarytx.edu. *Application contact:* Dr. Ozgur Aktunc, Graduate Program Director, 210-431-2052, E-mail: oaktunc@stmarytx.edu.
Website: https://www.stmarytx.edu/academics/programs/master-software-engineering/

San Jose State University, Program in Computer Engineering, San Jose, CA 95192-0001. Offers computer engineering (MS); software engineering (MS). *Degree requirements:* For master's, comprehensive exam, thesis. *Entrance requirements:* For master's, GRE General Test. Electronic applications accepted. *Faculty research:* Robotics, database management systems, computer networks.

Santa Clara University, School of Engineering, Santa Clara, CA 95053. Offers applied mathematics (MS); bioengineering (MS); civil, environmental, and sustainable engineering (MS); computer science and engineering (MS, PhD, Engineer); electrical engineering (MS, PhD, Engineer); engineering management and leadership (MS); mechanical engineering (MS, PhD, Engineer); power systems and sustainable energy (MS); software engineering (MS). *Program availability:* Part-time. *Faculty:* 72 full-time (24 women), 52 part-time/adjunct (9 women). *Students:* 555 full-time (211 women), 269 part-time (91 women); includes 208 minority (8 Black or African American, non-Hispanic/Latino; 1 American Indian or Alaska Native, non-Hispanic/Latino; 145 Asian, non-Hispanic/Latino; 28 Hispanic/Latino; 26 Two or more races, non-Hispanic/Latino), 472 international. Average age 27. 1,309 applicants, 36% accepted, 269 enrolled. In 2018, 320 master's, 7 doctorates awarded. *Entrance requirements:* For master's, GRE, official transcript; for doctorate, GRE, Official transcript, 500 word statement of purpose, three letters of recommendation. Additional exam requirements/recommendations for international students: Required—TOEFL (minimum score 79 iBT), IELTS (minimum score 6.5). *Application deadline:* For fall admission, 6/1 for domestic students; for winter admission, 9/6 for domestic students; for spring admission, 1/10 for domestic students; for summer admission, 3/6 for domestic students. Application fee: $60. Electronic applications accepted. *Financial support:* Fellowships, Federal Work-Study, and scholarships/grants available. Support available to part-time students. Financial award applicants required to submit FAFSA. *Unit head:* Dr. Elaine Scott, Dean, 408-554-3512, E-mail: epscott@scu.edu. *Application contact:* Stacey Tinker, Director of Admissions and Marketing, 408-554-4748, Fax: 408-554-4323, E-mail: stinker@scu.edu.
Website: http://www.scu.edu/engineering/graduate/

Shippensburg University of Pennsylvania, School of Graduate Studies, College of Arts and Sciences, Department of Computer Science and Engineering, Shippensburg, PA 17257-2299. Offers agile software engineering (Certificate); computer science (MS); IT leadership (Certificate). *Program availability:* Part-time, evening/weekend. *Faculty:* 4 full-time (2 women). *Students:* 5 full-time (3 women), 6 part-time (1 woman); includes 2 minority (both Black or African American, non-Hispanic/Latino), 7 international. Average age 29. 29 applicants, 55% accepted, 5 enrolled. In 2018, 15 master's awarded. *Entrance requirements:* For master's, GRE (if GPA less than 2.75), professional resume. Additional exam requirements/recommendations for international students: Required—TOEFL (minimum score 70 iBT), IELTS (minimum score 6), TOEFL (minimum score 70 iBT) or IELTS (minimum score 6). *Application deadline:* For fall admission, 4/30 for international students. Applications are processed on a rolling basis. Application fee: $45. Electronic applications accepted. *Expenses:* Tuition, state resident: part-time $516 per credit. Tuition, nonresident: part-time $750 per credit. *Required fees:* $149 per credit. *Financial support:* In 2018–19, 4 students received support. Career-related internships or fieldwork, scholarships/grants, unspecified assistantships, and resident hall director and student payroll positions available. Support available to part-time students. Financial award application deadline: 3/1; financial award applicants required to submit FAFSA. *Unit head:* Dr. Jeonghwa Lee, Professor and Director of Graduate Studies, 717-477-1178, Fax: 717-477-4002, E-mail: jlee@ship.edu. *Application contact:* Maya T. Mapp, Director of Admissions, 717-477-1231, Fax: 717-477-4016, E-mail: mtmapp@ship.edu.
Website: http://www.cs.ship.edu/

Southern Methodist University, Lyle School of Engineering, Department of Computer Science and Engineering, Dallas, TX 75275-0122. Offers computer engineering (MS, PhD); computer science (MS, PhD); security engineering (MS); software engineering (MS, DE). *Program availability:* Part-time, evening/weekend, online learning. Terminal master's awarded for partial completion of doctoral program. *Degree requirements:* For master's, thesis optional; for doctorate, thesis/dissertation, oral and written qualifying exams, oral final exam (PhD). *Entrance requirements:* For master's, GRE General Test, minimum GPA of 3.0 in last 2 years; bachelor's degree in engineering, mathematics, or sciences; for doctorate, preliminary counseling exam (PhD), minimum GPA of 3.0, bachelor's degree in related field, MA (for DE). Additional exam requirements/recommendations for international students: Required—TOEFL (minimum score 550 paper-based). *Faculty research:* Trusted and high performance network computing, software engineering and management, knowledge engineering and management, computer arithmetic, computer architecture and CAD.

Stevens Institute of Technology, Graduate School, School of Systems and Enterprises, Program in Software Engineering, Hoboken, NJ 07030. Offers MS, Certificate. *Program availability:* Part-time, evening/weekend. *Faculty:* 28 full-time (8 women), 5 part-time/adjunct (1 woman). *Students:* 43 full-time (5 women), 36 part-time (7 women); includes 17 minority (5 Black or African American, non-Hispanic/Latino; 1 American Indian or Alaska Native, non-Hispanic/Latino; 10 Asian, non-Hispanic/Latino; 1 Hispanic/Latino), 39 international. Average age 30. In 2018, 23 master's, 22 other advanced degrees awarded. Terminal master's awarded for partial completion of doctoral program. *Degree requirements:* For master's, thesis optional, minimum B average in major field and overall; for Certificate, minimum B average. *Entrance requirements:* For master's, GRE/GMAT scores: GRE scores are required for all applicants applying to a full-time graduate program in the Schaefer School of Engineering and Science (SES). International applicants must submit TOEFL/IELTS scores and fulfill the English Language Proficiency Requirements in order to be considered. Additional exam requirements/recommendations for international students: Required—TOEFL (minimum score 74 iBT), IELTS (minimum score 6). *Application deadline:* For fall admission, 4/15 for domestic and international students; for spring admission, 11/1 for domestic and international students; for summer admission, 5/1 for domestic students. Applications are processed on a rolling basis. Application fee: $60. Electronic applications accepted. *Expenses: Tuition:* Full-time $35,960; part-time $1620 per credit. *Required fees:* $1290; $600 per semester. Tuition and fees vary according to course load. *Financial support:* Fellowships, research assistantships, teaching assistantships, career-related internships or fieldwork, Federal Work-Study, scholarships/grants, and unspecified assistantships available. Financial award application deadline: 2/15; financial award applicants required to submit FAFSA. *Unit head:* Dr. Yehia Massoud, Dean of SSE, 201-216.8025, E-mail: yehia.massoud@stevens.edu. *Application contact:* Graduate Admissions, 888-783-8367, Fax: 888-511-1306, E-mail: graduate@stevens.edu.

Stratford University, School of Graduate Studies, Falls Church, VA 22043. Offers accounting (MS); business administration (MBA, DBA); cyber security (MS); cyber security leadership and policy (MS); digital forensics (MS); healthcare administration (MS); information systems (MS); information technology (DIT); networking and telecommunications (MS); software engineering (MS). *Program availability:* Part-time, evening/weekend, 100% online, blended/hybrid learning. *Degree requirements:* For master's, comprehensive exam, capstone project. *Entrance requirements:* For master's, GRE or GMAT, baccalaureate degree. Additional exam requirements/recommendations for international students: Required—TOEFL (minimum score 79 iBT), IELTS (minimum score 6.5), PTE (minimum score 5). Electronic applications accepted. *Expenses: Tuition:* Full-time $22,275; part-time $11,137 per year. One-time fee: $385.

Strayer University, Graduate Studies, Washington, DC 20005-2603. Offers accounting (MS); acquisition (MBA); business administration (MBA); communications technology (MS); educational management (M Ed); finance (MBA); health services administration (MHSA); hospitality and tourism management (MBA); human resource management (MBA); information systems (MS), including computer security management, decision support system management, enterprise resource management, network management, software engineering management, systems development management; management (MBA); management information systems (MS); marketing (MBA); professional accounting (MS), including accounting information systems, controllership, taxation; public administration (MPA); supply chain management (MBA); technology in education (M Ed). Programs also offered at campus locations in Birmingham, AL; Chamblee, GA; Cobb County, GA; Morrow, GA; White Marsh, MD; Charleston, SC; Columbia, SC; Greensboro, NC; Greenville, SC; Lexington, KY; Louisville, KY; Nashville, TN; North

Raleigh, NC; Washington, DC. *Accreditation:* ACBSP. *Program availability:* Part-time, evening/weekend, online learning. *Degree requirements:* For master's, thesis. *Entrance requirements:* For master's, GMAT, GRE General Test, bachelor's degree from an accredited college or university, minimum undergraduate GPA of 2.75. Electronic applications accepted.

Texas State University, The Graduate College, College of Science and Engineering, Program in Software Engineering, San Marcos, TX 78666. Offers MS. *Program availability:* Part-time. *Faculty:* 2 full-time (1 woman). *Students:* 7 full-time (4 women), 5 part-time (2 women); includes 2 minority (1 Asian, non-Hispanic/Latino; 1 Hispanic/Latino), 6 international. Average age 29. 20 applicants, 40% accepted, 3 enrolled. In 2018, 1 master's awarded. *Degree requirements:* For master's, comprehensive exam, thesis optional. *Entrance requirements:* For master's, official GRE (general test only) required with competitive scores in the verbal reasoning and quantitative reasoning sections, baccalaureate degree from regionally-accredited university with minimum GPA of 2.75 on last 60 undergraduate semester hours, 3 letters of reference, academic vitae (resume), statement of purpose. Additional exam requirements/recommendations for international students: Required—TOEFL (minimum score 550 paper-based; 78 iBT), IELTS (minimum score 6.5). *Application deadline:* For fall admission, 2/1 priority date for domestic and international students; for spring admission, 10/15 for domestic students, 10/1 for international students; for summer admission, 4/15 for domestic students, 3/15 for international students. Applications are processed on a rolling basis. Application fee: $55 ($90 for international students). Electronic applications accepted. *Expenses:* Tuition, state resident: full-time $8102; part-time $4051 per semester. Tuition, nonresident: full-time $18,229; part-time $9115 per semester. *International tuition:* $18,229 full-time. *Required fees:* $2116; $120 per credit hour. Tuition and fees vary according to course load. *Financial support:* In 2018–19, 2 students received support. Research assistantships, teaching assistantships, Federal Work-Study, institutionally sponsored loans, scholarships/grants, health care benefits, and unspecified assistantships available. Support available to part-time students. Financial award application deadline: 1/15; financial award applicants required to submit FAFSA. *Faculty research:* Ad hoc wireless networks, sensor networks, distributed systems; software verification and testing, software evolution, program analysis, and formal methods. *Total annual research expenditures:* $188,667. *Unit head:* Dr. Wuxu Peng, Graduate Advisor, 512-245-3874, Fax: 512-245-8750, E-mail: cs_graduateadvisor@txstate.edu. *Application contact:* Dr. Andrea Golato, Dean of the Graduate College, 512-245-2581, E-mail: gradcollege@txstate.edu.
Website: http://www.gradcollege.txstate.edu/programs/se.html

Texas Tech University, Graduate School, Edward E. Whitacre Jr. College of Engineering, Department of Computer Science, Lubbock, TX 79409-3104. Offers computer science (MS, PhD); software engineering (MS). *Program availability:* Part-time, blended/hybrid learning. *Faculty:* 15 full-time (3 women). *Students:* 64 full-time (22 women), 44 part-time (8 women); includes 13 minority (1 Black or African American, non-Hispanic/Latino; 8 Asian, non-Hispanic/Latino; 4 Hispanic/Latino), 75 international. Average age 29. 171 applicants, 44% accepted, 35 enrolled. In 2018, 25 master's, 3 doctorates awarded. Terminal master's awarded for partial completion of doctoral program. *Degree requirements:* For master's, comprehensive exam (for some programs), thesis (for some programs); for doctorate, comprehensive exam, thesis/dissertation. *Entrance requirements:* For master's and doctorate, GRE (Verbal and Quantitative). Additional exam requirements/recommendations for international students: Required—TOEFL (minimum score 550 paper-based; 79 iBT). *Application deadline:* For fall admission, 6/1 priority date for domestic students, 1/15 priority date for international students; for spring admission, 9/1 priority date for domestic students, 6/15 priority date for international students. Applications are processed on a rolling basis. Application fee: $65. Electronic applications accepted. *Expenses:* Contact institution. *Financial support:* In 2018–19, 70 students received support, including 66 fellowships (averaging $4,579 per year), 24 research assistantships (averaging $20,054 per year), 11 teaching assistantships (averaging $14,832 per year); scholarships/grants, tuition waivers (partial), and unspecified assistantships also available. Financial award application deadline: 4/15; financial award applicants required to submit FAFSA. *Faculty research:* High performance and parallel computing; cyber security and data science; software engineering (quality assurance, testing, design specification); artificial intelligence (intelligent systems, knowledge representation); mobile and computer networks. *Total annual research expenditures:* $1.1 million. *Unit head:* Dr. Rattikorn Hewett, Department Chair and Professor, 806-742-3527, Fax: 806-742-3519, E-mail: rattikorn.hewett@ttu.edu. *Application contact:* Jeremy Herrera, Staff Graduate Advisor, 806-742-3527, Fax: 806-742-3519, E-mail: jeremy.herrera@ttu.edu.
Website: www.cs.ttu.edu/

Université Laval, Faculty of Sciences and Engineering, Program in Software Engineering, Québec, QC G1K 7P4, Canada. Offers Diploma. *Program availability:* Part-time. *Entrance requirements:* For degree, knowledge of French. Electronic applications accepted.

The University of Alabama in Huntsville, School of Graduate Studies, College of Engineering, Department of Electrical and Computer Engineering, Huntsville, AL 35899. Offers computer engineering (MSE, PhD); electrical engineering (MSE, PhD), including optics and photonics technology (MSE); optical science and engineering (PhD); software engineering (MSSE). *Program availability:* Part-time. *Faculty:* 22 full-time (4 women), 4 part-time/adjunct. *Students:* 65 full-time (12 women), 125 part-time (12 women); includes 12 minority (5 Black or African American, non-Hispanic/Latino; 5 Asian, non-Hispanic/Latino; 2 Hispanic/Latino), 61 international. Average age 31. 199 applicants, 78% accepted, 46 enrolled. In 2018, 42 master's, 11 doctorates awarded. *Degree requirements:* For master's, comprehensive exam, thesis or alternative, oral and written exams; for doctorate, comprehensive exam, thesis/dissertation, oral and written exams. *Entrance requirements:* For master's, GRE General Test, appropriate bachelor's degree, minimum GPA of 3.0; for doctorate, GRE General Test, minimum GPA of 3.0. Additional exam requirements/recommendations for international students: Required—TOEFL (minimum score 500 paper-based; 80 iBT), IELTS (minimum score 6.5). *Application deadline:* For fall admission, 7/15 priority date for domestic students, 4/1 priority date for international students; for spring admission, 11/30 priority date for domestic students, 9/1 priority date for international students. Applications are processed on a rolling basis. Application fee: $50. Electronic applications accepted. *Expenses: Tuition, area resident:* Full-time $10,632; part-time $412 per credit hour. Tuition, state resident: full-time $10,632. Tuition, nonresident: full-time $23,604; part-time $412 per credit hour. *Required fees:* $582; $582. Tuition and fees vary according to course load and program. *Financial support:* In 2018–19, 37 students received support, including 18 research assistantships with full tuition reimbursements available (averaging $5,783 per year), 19 teaching assistantships with full tuition reimbursements available (averaging $5,813 per year); career-related internships or fieldwork, Federal Work-Study, institutionally sponsored loans, scholarships/grants, health care benefits, tuition waivers (full and partial), and unspecified assistantships also available. Support available to part-time students. Financial award application deadline: 4/1; financial award applicants required to submit FAFSA. *Faculty research:* Advanced computer architecture and systems, fault tolerant computing and verification, computational electro-magnetics, nano-photonics and plasmonics, micro electro-mechanical (MEMS) systems. *Unit head:* Dr. Ravi Gorur, Chair, 256-824-6316, Fax: 256-824-6803, E-mail: ravi.gorur@uah.edu. *Application contact:* Kim Gray, Graduate Studies Admissions Coordinator, 256-824-6002, Fax: 256-824-6405, E-mail: deangrad@uah.edu.
Website: http://www.ece.uah.edu/

The University of Alabama in Huntsville, School of Graduate Studies, College of Science, Department of Computer Science, Huntsville, AL 35899. Offers computer science (MS, PhD); cybersecurity (MS); modeling and simulation (MS, PhD, Certificate); software engineering (MSSE, Certificate). *Program availability:* Part-time. *Faculty:* 14 full-time (4 women), 1 part-time/adjunct. *Students:* 67 full-time (16 women), 65 part-time (11 women); includes 14 minority (4 Black or African American, non-Hispanic/Latino; 1 American Indian or Alaska Native, non-Hispanic/Latino; 5 Asian, non-Hispanic/Latino; 3 Hispanic/Latino; 1 Two or more races, non-Hispanic/Latino), 60 international. Average age 33. 219 applicants, 74% accepted, 37 enrolled. In 2018, 47 master's awarded. *Degree requirements:* For master's, comprehensive exam, thesis or alternative, oral and written exams; for doctorate, comprehensive exam, thesis/dissertation, oral and written exams. *Entrance requirements:* For master's, doctorate, and Certificate, GRE General Test, minimum GPA of 3.0. Additional exam requirements/recommendations for international students: Required—TOEFL (minimum score 550 paper-based; 80 iBT), IELTS (minimum score 6.5). *Application deadline:* For fall admission, 7/15 priority date for domestic students, 4/1 priority date for international students; for spring admission, 11/30 priority date for domestic students, 9/1 priority date for international students. Applications are processed on a rolling basis. Application fee: $50. Electronic applications accepted. *Expenses: Tuition, area resident:* Full-time $10,632; part-time $412 per credit hour. Tuition, state resident: full-time $10,632. Tuition, nonresident: full-time $23,604; part-time $412 per credit hour. *Required fees:* $582; $582. Tuition and fees vary according to course load and program. *Financial support:* In 2018–19, 39 students received support, including 18 research assistantships with full tuition reimbursements available (averaging $6,762 per year), 19 teaching assistantships with full tuition reimbursements available (averaging $6,315 per year); career-related internships or fieldwork, Federal Work-Study, institutionally sponsored loans, scholarships/grants, health care benefits, and unspecified assistantships also available. Support available to part-time students. Financial award application deadline: 4/1; financial award applicants required to submit FAFSA. *Faculty research:* Information assurance and cyber security, modeling and simulation, data science, computer graphics and visualization, multimedia systems. *Unit head:* Dr. Heggere Ranganath, Professor and Chair, 256-824-6088, Fax: 256-824-6239, E-mail: info@cs.uah.edu. *Application contact:* Kim Gray, Graduate Studies Admissions Manager, 256-824-6002, Fax: 256-824-6405, E-mail: deangrad@uah.edu.
Website: http://www.cs.uah.edu

University of Calgary, Faculty of Graduate Studies, Faculty of Science, Program in Computer Science, Calgary, AB T2N 1N4, Canada. Offers computer science (M Sc, PhD); software engineering (M Sc). *Program availability:* Part-time. *Degree requirements:* For master's, comprehensive exam (for some programs), thesis (for some programs); for doctorate, thesis/dissertation, oral and written departmental exam. *Entrance requirements:* For master's, bachelor's degree in computer science; for doctorate, M Sc in computer science. Additional exam requirements/recommendations for international students: Required—TOEFL (minimum score 600 paper-based); Recommended—TWE. Electronic applications accepted. *Faculty research:* Visual and interactive computing, quantum computing and cryptography, evolutionary software engineering, distributed systems and algorithms.

University of Colorado Colorado Springs, College of Engineering and Applied Science, Program in General Engineering, Colorado Springs, CO 80918. Offers computer science (PhD); cybersecurity (ME); energy engineering (ME); engineering management (ME); engineering systems (ME); software engineering (ME); space operations (ME). *Program availability:* Part-time, evening/weekend, blended/hybrid learning. *Faculty:* 1 full-time (0 women), 20 part-time/adjunct (6 women). *Students:* 12 full-time (1 woman), 177 part-time (39 women); includes 38 minority (4 Black or African American, non-Hispanic/Latino; 12 Asian, non-Hispanic/Latino; 12 Hispanic/Latino; 1 Native Hawaiian or other Pacific Islander, non-Hispanic/Latino; 9 Two or more races, non-Hispanic/Latino), 54 international. Average age 35. 44 applicants, 93% accepted, 21 enrolled. In 2018, 24 master's, 15 doctorates awarded. *Degree requirements:* For master's, thesis, portfolio, or project; for doctorate, comprehensive exam, thesis/dissertation. *Entrance requirements:* For master's, GRE may be required based on past academic performance., Professional recommendation letters are required for all applicants.; for doctorate, GRE (minimum score of 148 new grading scale on the quantitative portion if the applicant has not graduated from a program of recognized standing), minimum GPA of 3.3 in the bachelor's or master's degree program attempted. Additional exam requirements/recommendations for international students: Required—TOEFL (minimum score 80 iBT), IELTS (minimum score 6). *Application deadline:* For fall admission, 6/1 for domestic and international students; for spring admission, 11/1 for domestic and international students; for summer admission, 4/15 for domestic and international students. Applications are processed on a rolling basis. Application fee: $60 ($100 for international students). Electronic applications accepted. *Expenses:* Program tuition and fees vary by course load and residency classification. Please visit the University of Colorado Colorado Springs Student Financial Services website to see current program costs: https://www.uccs.edu/bursar/index.php/estimate-your-bill. *Financial support:* In 2018–19, 1 student received support. Career-related internships or fieldwork, Federal Work-Study, scholarships/grants, traineeships, and unspecified assistantships available. Support available to part-time students. Financial award application deadline: 3/1; financial award applicants required to submit FAFSA. *Total annual research expenditures:* $22,249. *Unit head:* Dr. Donald Rabern, Dean of Engineering and Applied Science, 719-255-3543, E-mail: drabern@uccs.edu. *Application contact:* Dawn House, Extended Studies Coordinator, 719-255-3246, E-mail: dhouse@uccs.edu.

University of Connecticut, Graduate School, School of Engineering, Department of Computer Science and Engineering, Storrs, CT 06269. Offers computer science (MS, PhD), including artificial intelligence, computer architecture, computer science, operating systems, robotics, software engineering. Terminal master's awarded for partial completion of doctoral program. *Degree requirements:* For master's, comprehensive exam, thesis or alternative; for doctorate, thesis/dissertation. *Entrance requirements:* For master's and doctorate, GRE General Test. Additional exam requirements/recommendations for international students: Required—TOEFL (minimum score 550 paper-based). Electronic applications accepted.

University of Detroit Mercy, College of Engineering and Science, Detroit, MI 48221. Offers chemistry (MS); civil and environmental engineering (DE); electrical and computer engineering (ME); electrical engineering (DE); engineering management (M Eng Mgt); environmental engineering (MEE); mechanical engineering (MME, DE); product development (MS); software engineering (MSSE); teaching of mathematics (MATM). *Program availability:* Part-time, evening/weekend. *Degree requirements:* For doctorate, thesis/dissertation. Electronic applications accepted. Application fee is waived when completed online. *Expenses:* Contact institution.

University of Houston–Clear Lake, School of Science and Computer Engineering, Program in Software Engineering, Houston, TX 77058-1002. Offers MS. *Program availability:* Part-time, evening/weekend. *Entrance requirements:* For master's, GRE General Test. Additional exam requirements/recommendations for international students: Required—TOEFL (minimum score 550 paper-based).

University of Management and Technology, Program in Computer Science, Arlington, VA 22209-1609. Offers computer science (MS); information technology (AC); project management (AC); software engineering (MS). *Program availability:* Part-time, evening/weekend, online learning. *Entrance requirements:* For master's, 3 recommendations, resume. Additional exam requirements/recommendations for international students: Required—TOEFL (minimum score 530 paper-based; 71 iBT). Electronic applications accepted. *Expenses: Tuition:* Full-time $7020; part-time $1170 per course.

University of Massachusetts Dartmouth, Graduate School, College of Engineering, Department of Computer Science, North Dartmouth, MA 02747-2300. Offers computer science (MS, Graduate Certificate); software development and design (Postbaccalaureate Certificate). *Program availability:* Part-time, 100% online, blended/hybrid learning. *Faculty:* 11 full-time (3 women), 2 part-time/adjunct (0 women). *Students:* 53 full-time (17 women), 48 part-time (7 women); includes 11 minority (2 Black or African American, non-Hispanic/Latino; 4 Asian, non-Hispanic/Latino; 2 Hispanic/Latino; 3 Two or more races, non-Hispanic/Latino), 59 international. Average age 32. 102 applicants, 92% accepted, 34 enrolled. In 2018, 57 master's, 2 other advanced degrees awarded. *Degree requirements:* For master's, thesis, thesis or project. *Entrance requirements:* For master's, GRE unless UMass Dartmouth graduate in computer science, statement of purpose (minimum of 300 words), resume, 3 letters of recommendation, official transcripts; for other advanced degree, statement of purpose (minimum of 300 words), resume, official transcripts. Additional exam requirements/recommendations for international students: Required—TOEFL (minimum score 533 paper-based; 72 iBT), IELTS (minimum score 6). *Application deadline:* For fall admission, 4/15 priority date for domestic students, 3/15 priority date for international students; for spring admission, 11/15 priority date for domestic students, 10/15 priority date for international students. Application fee: $60. Electronic applications accepted. *Financial support:* In 2018–19, 1 research assistantship (averaging $5,192 per year), 10 teaching assistantships (averaging $8,075 per year) were awarded; tuition waivers (full and partial) and unspecified assistantships also available. Support available to part-time students. Financial award application deadline: 3/1; financial award applicants required to submit FAFSA. *Faculty research:* Artificial intelligence, sensor fusion and autonomous underwater vehicles, self organizing feature maps, data mining, development of agent oriented software. *Total annual research expenditures:* $973,000. *Unit head:* Dr. Xiaoqin Zhang, Graduate Program Director, Computer Science, 508-999-8294, E-mail: x2zhang@umassd.edu. *Application contact:* Scott Webster, Director of Graduate studies and Admissions, 508-999-8202, Fax: 508-999-8183, E-mail: graduate@umassd.edu.
Website: http://www.umassd.edu/engineering/cis/graduate

University of Michigan–Dearborn, College of Engineering and Computer Science, Master of Science in Software Engineering Program, Dearborn, MI 48128. Offers MS. *Program availability:* Part-time, evening/weekend, 100% online. *Faculty:* 19 full-time (1 woman), 5 part-time/adjunct (0 women). *Students:* 9 full-time (2 women), 27 part-time (5 women); includes 9 minority (1 Black or African American, non-Hispanic/Latino; 6 Asian, non-Hispanic/Latino; 2 Two or more races, non-Hispanic/Latino), 6 international. Average age 30. 23 applicants, 65% accepted, 10 enrolled. In 2018, 10 master's awarded. *Degree requirements:* For master's, thesis optional. *Entrance requirements:* For master's, bachelor's degree in mathematics, computer science or engineering; minimum GPA of 3.0. Additional exam requirements/recommendations for international students: Required—TOEFL (minimum score 560 paper-based; 84 iBT), IELTS (minimum score 6.5). *Application deadline:* For fall admission, 8/1 priority date for domestic students, 5/1 priority date for international students; for winter admission, 12/1 priority date for domestic students, 9/1 priority date for international students; for spring admission, 4/1 priority date for domestic students, 1/1 priority date for international students. Applications are processed on a rolling basis. Application fee: $60. Electronic applications accepted. *Expenses: Tuition:* state resident: full-time $15,380; part-time $88 per credit hour. Tuition, nonresident: full-time $23,948; part-time $1377 per credit hour. *Required fees:* $780; $780 $390. Tuition and fees vary according to course level, course load, degree level, program, reciprocity agreements and student level. *Financial support:* In 2018–19, 1 student received support. Research assistantships with full tuition reimbursements available, teaching assistantships with full tuition reimbursements available, scholarships/grants, health care benefits, and non-resident tuition scholarships available. Support available to part-time students. Financial award application deadline: 3/1; financial award applicants required to submit FAFSA. *Faculty research:* Intelligent software engineering, search-based software engineering, software refactoring, model-driven software engineering, human-computer interaction. *Unit head:* Dr. Zhiwei Xu, Chair, 313-583-6436, E-mail: zwxu@umich.edu. *Application contact:* Office of Graduate Studies, 313-583-6321, E-mail: umd-graduatestudies@umich.edu.
Website: https://umdearborn.edu/cecs/departments/computer-and-information-science/graduate-programs/ms-software-engineering

University of Michigan–Dearborn, College of Engineering and Computer Science, PhD Program in Computer and Information Science, Dearborn, MI 48128. Offers data management (PhD); data science (PhD); software engineering (PhD); systems and security (PhD). *Faculty:* 19 full-time (1 woman), 5 part-time/adjunct (0 women). *Students:* 7 full-time (4 women), 7 part-time (1 woman); includes 1 minority (Asian, non-Hispanic/Latino), 9 international. Average age 30. 22 applicants, 36% accepted, 6 enrolled. In 2018, 1 doctorate awarded. *Degree requirements:* For doctorate, comprehensive exam, thesis/dissertation. *Entrance requirements:* For doctorate, GRE, bachelor's or master's degree in computer science or closely-related field. Additional exam requirements/recommendations for international students: Required—TOEFL (minimum score 560 paper-based; 84 iBT), IELTS (minimum score 6.5). *Application deadline:* For fall admission, 2/1 for domestic and international students. Application fee: $60. Electronic applications accepted. *Expenses: Tuition:* state resident: full-time $15,380; part-time $88 per credit hour. Tuition, nonresident: full-time $23,948; part-time $1377 per credit hour. *Required fees:* $780; $780 $390. Tuition and fees vary according to course level, course load, degree level, program, reciprocity agreements and student level. *Financial support:* In 2018–19, 2 students received support. Research assistantships with full tuition reimbursements available, teaching assistantships with full tuition reimbursements available, scholarships/grants, health care benefits, and unspecified assistantships available. Financial award application deadline: 2/1; financial award applicants required to submit FAFSA. *Faculty research:* Data science, data management, cybersecurity, software engineering, systems. *Unit head:* Dr. Di Ma, Director, 313-583-6737, E-mail: dmadma@umich.edu. *Application contact:* Office of Graduate Studies, 313-583-6321, E-mail: umd-graduatestudies@umich.edu.
Website: https://umdearborn.edu/cecs/departments/computer-and-information-science/graduate-programs/phd-computer-and-information-science

University of Minnesota, Twin Cities Campus, College of Science and Engineering, Department of Computer Science and Engineering, Program in Software Engineering, Minneapolis, MN 55455-0213. Offers MSSE. *Program availability:* Part-time, evening/weekend. *Degree requirements:* For master's, thesis optional, capstone project. *Entrance requirements:* For master's, 1 year of work experience in software field; minimum undergraduate GPA of 3.0. Additional exam requirements/recommendations for international students: Required—TOEFL. Electronic applications accepted. *Faculty*

research: Database systems, human-computer interaction, software development, high performance neural systems, data mining.

University of Missouri–Kansas City, School of Computing and Engineering, Kansas City, MO 64110-2499. Offers civil engineering (MS); computer and electrical engineering (PhD); computer science (MS), including bioinformatics, software engineering, telecommunications networking; computer science and informatics (PhD); computing (PhD); electrical engineering (MS); engineering (PhD); engineering and construction management (Graduate Certificate); mechanical engineering (MS); telecommunications and computer networking (PhD). PhD (interdisciplinary) offered through the School of Graduate Studies. *Program availability:* Part-time. *Degree requirements:* For doctorate, thesis/dissertation. *Entrance requirements:* For master's, GRE General Test, minimum GPA of 3.0, 3 letters of recommendation from professors; for doctorate, GRE General Test, minimum GPA of 3.5. Additional exam requirements/recommendations for international students: Required—TOEFL (minimum score 550 paper-based; 80 iBT). *Faculty research:* Algorithms, bioinformatics and medical informatics, biomechanics/biomaterials, civil engineering materials, networking and telecommunications, thermal science.

University of Nebraska at Omaha, Graduate Studies, College of Information Science and Technology, Department of Computer Science, Omaha, NE 68182. Offers artificial intelligence (Certificate); communication networks (Certificate); computer science (MA, MS); computer science education (MS, Certificate); software engineering (Certificate); system and architecture (Certificate). *Program availability:* Part-time, evening/weekend. *Degree requirements:* For master's, comprehensive exam, thesis (for some programs). *Entrance requirements:* For master's, GRE General Test, minimum GPA of 3.0, prior course work in computer science, official transcripts, resume, 2 letters of recommendation; for Certificate, minimum GPA of 3.0, resume. Additional exam requirements/recommendations for international students: Required—TOEFL, IELTS, PTE. Electronic applications accepted.

University of New Haven, Graduate School, Tagliatela College of Engineering, Program in Computer Science, West Haven, CT 06516. Offers computer programming (Graduate Certificate); computer science (MS); network systems (MS); software development (MS). *Program availability:* Part-time, evening/weekend. *Students:* 107 full-time (36 women), 26 part-time (7 women); includes 11 minority (2 Black or African American, non-Hispanic/Latino; 7 Asian, non-Hispanic/Latino; 1 Hispanic/Latino; 1 Two or more races, non-Hispanic/Latino), 104 international. Average age 26. 560 applicants, 61% accepted, 26 enrolled. In 2018, 41 master's awarded. *Degree requirements:* For master's, thesis or alternative. *Entrance requirements:* Additional exam requirements/recommendations for international students: Required—TOEFL (minimum score 75 iBT), IELTS, PTE (minimum score 50). *Application deadline:* Applications are processed on a rolling basis. Application fee: $50. Electronic applications accepted. Application fee is waived when completed online. *Expenses: Tuition:* Full-time $16,470; part-time $915 per credit hour. *Required fees:* $230; $95 per term. *Financial support:* Research assistantships with partial tuition reimbursements, teaching assistantships with partial tuition reimbursements, career-related internships or fieldwork, Federal Work-Study, scholarships/grants, and unspecified assistantships available. Support available to part-time students. Financial award applicants required to submit FAFSA. *Unit head:* Dr. David Eggert, Associate Professor, 203-932-7097, E-mail: deggert@newhaven.edu. *Application contact:* Selina O'Toole, Senior Associate Director of Graduate Admissions, 203-932-7337, E-mail: sotoole@newhaven.edu.
Website: https://www.newhaven.edu/engineering/graduate-programs/computer-science/

University of North Florida, College of Computing, Engineering, and Construction, School of Computing, Jacksonville, FL 32224. Offers computer science (MS); information systems (MS); software engineering (MS). *Program availability:* Part-time. *Faculty:* 13 full-time (1 woman). *Students:* 14 full-time (4 women), 35 part-time (9 women); includes 14 minority (1 Black or African American, non-Hispanic/Latino; 8 Asian, non-Hispanic/Latino; 3 Hispanic/Latino; 2 Two or more races, non-Hispanic/Latino), 8 international. Average age 33. 33 applicants, 45% accepted, 11 enrolled. In 2018, 48 master's awarded. *Degree requirements:* For master's, thesis. *Entrance requirements:* For master's, GRE General Test, minimum GPA of 3.0 in last 60 hours of course work. Additional exam requirements/recommendations for international students: Required—TOEFL (minimum score 500 paper-based; 61 iBT). *Application deadline:* For fall admission, 8/1 priority date for domestic students, 5/1 for international students; for spring admission, 12/1 priority date for domestic students, 10/1 for international students; for summer admission, 3/15 priority date for domestic students, 2/1 for international students. Application fee: $30. Electronic applications accepted. *Expenses: Tuition,* area resident: Part-time $408.10 per credit hour. Tuition, state resident: part-time $408.10 per credit hour. Tuition, nonresident: part-time $932.61 per credit hour. *Required fees:* $111.81 per credit hour. Tuition and fees vary according to course load, campus/location and program. *Financial support:* In 2018–19, 8 students received support, including 6 research assistantships (averaging $3,134 per year), 1 teaching assistantship (averaging $2,666 per year); Federal Work-Study, scholarships/grants, and unspecified assistantships also available. Financial award application deadline: 4/1; financial award applicants required to submit FAFSA. *Total annual research expenditures:* $86,396. *Unit head:* Dr. Sherif Elfayoumy, Director/Professor, 904-620-2985, E-mail: selfayou@unf.edu. *Application contact:* Dr. Amanda Pascale, Director, The Graduate School, 904-620-1360, Fax: 904-620-1362, E-mail: graduateschool@unf.edu.
Website: http://www.unf.edu/ccec/computing/

University of Regina, Faculty of Graduate Studies and Research, Faculty of Engineering and Applied Science, Program in Software Systems Engineering, Regina, SK S4S 0A2, .Canada. Offers software systems (M Eng, MA Sc, PhD). *Program availability:* Part-time. *Faculty:* 5 full-time (1 woman), 3 part-time/adjunct (0 women). *Students:* 19 full-time (5 women), 6 part-time (1 woman). Average age 30. 105 applicants, 2% accepted, 2 enrolled. In 2018, 7 master's, 3 doctorates awarded. *Degree requirements:* For master's, thesis (for some programs), project, report. coop placement; for doctorate, comprehensive exam, thesis/dissertation. *Entrance requirements:* For master's, minimum graduating average of 70 percent from four-year baccalaureate degree (or equivalent); for doctorate, completion of thesis-based master's degree in engineering or closely-related field. Additional exam requirements/recommendations for international students: Required—TOEFL (minimum score 580 paper-based; 80 iBT), IELTS (minimum score 6.5), PTE (minimum score 59), other options are CAEL, MELAB, Cantest and U of R ESL. *Application deadline:* For fall admission, 3/31 for domestic and international students; for winter admission, 7/31 for domestic and international students; for spring admission, 11/30 for domestic and international students. Application fee: $100 Canadian dollars. Electronic applications accepted. *Expenses:* Estimated tuition and fees for one academic year is 8.379.50 for Master's. The fee will vary base on your choice program. For Doctoral program one academic year is estimated 14,129.40. International students will pay additional 1,191.75 for International surcharge per semester. *Financial support:* Fellowships, research assistantships, teaching assistantships, career-related internships or fieldwork, Federal Work-Study, scholarships/grants, unspecified assistantships, and Travel award and Graduate Scholarship Base funds available. Financial award application deadline: 9/30. *Faculty*

research: Software design and development, network computing, multimedia communication, computational theories to real-life programming techniques, embedded systems construction. *Unit head:* Craig Gelowitz, Program Chair/coordinator, Software Systems Engineering, 306-585-4733, Fax: 306-585-4855, E-mail: craig.gelowitz@uregina.ca. *Application contact:* Craig Gelowitz, Program Chair/coordinator, Software Systems Engineering, 306-585-4733, Fax: 306-585-4855, E-mail: craig.gelowitz@uregina.ca.
Website: http://www.uregina.ca/engineering/

University of St. Thomas, School of Engineering, St. Paul, MN 55105. Offers data science (MS); electrical engineering (MS); information technology (MS); manufacturing engineering (MS); manufacturing systems (Certificate); mechanical engineering (MS); medical device development (Certificate); regulatory science (MS); software engineering (MS); software management (MS); systems engineering (MS); technology leadership (Certificate); technology management (MS). *Program availability:* Part-time, evening/weekend. *Entrance requirements:* For master's, resume, official transcripts. Additional exam requirements/recommendations for international students: Required—TOEFL (minimum score 80 iBT), IELTS (minimum score 6.5). Electronic applications accepted. *Expenses:* Contact institution.

The University of Scranton, Kania School of Management, Program in Software Engineering, Scranton, PA 18510. Offers MS. *Program availability:* Part-time, evening/weekend. *Degree requirements:* For master's, comprehensive exam (for some programs), thesis (for some programs), capstone experience. *Entrance requirements:* For master's, minimum GPA of 3.0, three letters of reference. Additional exam requirements/recommendations for international students: Required—TOEFL (minimum score 500 paper-based; 80 iBT), IELTS (minimum score 6.5). Electronic applications accepted. *Faculty research:* Database, parallel and distributed systems, computer network, real time systems.

University of South Carolina, The Graduate School, College of Engineering and Computing, Department of Computer Science and Engineering, Columbia, SC 29208. Offers computer science and engineering (ME, MS, PhD); software engineering (MS). *Program availability:* Part-time, evening/weekend, online learning. *Degree requirements:* For master's, comprehensive exam, thesis (for some programs); for doctorate, comprehensive exam, thesis/dissertation. *Entrance requirements:* For master's and doctorate, GRE General Test. Additional exam requirements/recommendations for international students: Required—TOEFL (minimum score 570 paper-based). Electronic applications accepted. *Faculty research:* Computer security, computer vision, artificial intelligence, multiagent systems, bioinformatics.

University of Southern California, Graduate School, Viterbi School of Engineering, Department of Computer Science, Los Angeles, CA 90089. Offers computer networks (MS); computer science (MS, PhD); computer security (MS); game development (MS); high performance computing and simulations (MS); human language technology (MS); intelligent robotics (MS); multimedia and creative technologies (MS); software engineering (MS). *Program availability:* Part-time, evening/weekend, online learning. *Entrance requirements:* For master's and doctorate, GRE General Test. Additional exam requirements/recommendations for international students: Required—TOEFL. Electronic applications accepted. *Faculty research:* Databases, computer graphics and computer vision, software engineering, networks and security, robotics, multimedia and virtual reality.

University of Southern Maine, College of Science, Technology, and Health, Department of Computer Science, Portland, ME 04103. Offers computer science (MS); software systems (CGS). *Program availability:* Part-time. *Degree requirements:* For master's, thesis. *Entrance requirements:* For master's, GRE General Test, minimum GPA of 3.0. Additional exam requirements/recommendations for international students: Required—TOEFL. Electronic applications accepted. *Faculty research:* Software engineering, database systems, formal methods, object-oriented technology, artificial intelligence, bioinformatics, data analysis and data mining, health information systems.

The University of Texas at Arlington, Graduate School, College of Engineering, Department of Computer Science and Engineering, Arlington, TX 76019. Offers computer engineering (MS, PhD); computer science (MS, PhD); software engineering (MS). *Program availability:* Part-time, online learning. Terminal master's awarded for partial completion of doctoral program. *Degree requirements:* For master's, comprehensive exam (for some programs), thesis; for doctorate, comprehensive exam, thesis/dissertation. *Entrance requirements:* For master's, GRE General Test, minimum GPA of 3.0 (3.2 in computer science-related classes); for doctorate, GRE General Test, minimum GPA of 3.5. Additional exam requirements/recommendations for international students: Required—TOEFL (minimum score 550 paper-based; 92 iBT), IELTS (minimum score 6.5). *Faculty research:* Algorithms, homeland security, mobile pervasive computing, high performance computing bioinformation.

The University of Texas at Dallas, Erik Jonsson School of Engineering and Computer Science, Department of Computer Science, Richardson, TX 75080. Offers computer science (MSCS, PhD); software engineering (MS, PhD). *Program availability:* Part-time, evening/weekend. *Faculty:* 49 full-time (5 women), 23 part-time/adjunct (6 women). *Students:* 913 full-time (288 women), 291 part-time (75 women); includes 70 minority (5 Black or African American, non-Hispanic/Latino; 45 Asian, non-Hispanic/Latino; 14 Hispanic/Latino; 6 Two or more races, non-Hispanic/Latino), 1,051 international. Average age 27. 3,695 applicants, 38% accepted, 433 enrolled. In 2018, 442 master's, 16 doctorates awarded. *Degree requirements:* For master's, thesis optional; for doctorate, comprehensive exam, thesis/dissertation. *Entrance requirements:* For master's, GRE General Test, minimum GPA of 3.0 in undergraduate course work, 3.3 in quantitative course work; for doctorate, GRE General Test, minimum GPA of 3.5. Additional exam requirements/recommendations for international students: Required—TOEFL (minimum score 550 paper-based). *Application deadline:* For fall admission, 7/15 for domestic students, 5/1 priority date for international students; for spring admission, 11/15 for domestic students, 9/1 priority date for international students. Applications are processed on a rolling basis. Application fee: $50 ($100 for international students). Electronic applications accepted. *Expenses: Tuition, area resident:* Full-time $13,458. *Tuition, state resident:* full-time $13,458. *Tuition, nonresident:* full-time $26,852. *International tuition:* $26,852 full-time. Tuition and fees vary according to course load. *Financial support:* In 2018–19, 102 students received support, including 6 fellowships (averaging $1,083 per year), 83 research assistantships with partial tuition reimbursements available (averaging $23,617 per year), 76 teaching assistantships with partial tuition reimbursements available (averaging $17,325 per year); career-related internships or fieldwork, Federal Work-Study, institutionally sponsored loans, and scholarships/grants also available. Support available to part-time students. Financial award application deadline: 4/30; financial award applicants required to submit FAFSA. *Faculty research:* AI-based automated software synthesis and testing, quality of service in computer networks, wireless networks, cloud computing and IT security, speech recognition. *Unit head:* Dr. Gopal Gupta, Department Head, 972-883-4107, Fax: 972-883-2399, E-mail: gupta@utdallas.edu. *Application contact:* Dr. Gopal Gupta, Department Head, 972-883-4107, Fax: 972-883-2399, E-mail: gupta@utdallas.edu.
Website: http://cs.utdallas.edu/

The University of Texas at El Paso, Graduate School, College of Engineering, Department of Computer Science, El Paso, TX 79968-0001. Offers computer science (MS, PhD); cyber security (Graduate Certificate); information technology (MSIT); software engineering (MS). *Program availability:* Part-time, evening/weekend. *Degree requirements:* For master's, thesis optional; for doctorate, thesis/dissertation. *Entrance requirements:* For master's, GRE, minimum GPA of 3.0; for doctorate, GRE, statement of purpose, letters of reference. Additional exam requirements/recommendations for international students: Required—TOEFL; Recommended—IELTS. Electronic applications accepted.

University of Utah, Graduate School, College of Engineering, School of Computing, Salt Lake City, UT 84112-9205. Offers computer science (MS, PhD); computing (MS, PhD); software development (MS); MS/MBA. *Faculty:* 40 full-time (6 women), 17 part-time/adjunct (3 women). *Students:* 272 full-time (73 women), 75 part-time (14 women); includes 33 minority (4 Black or African American, non-Hispanic/Latino; 16 Asian, non-Hispanic/Latino; 9 Hispanic/Latino; 4 Two or more races, non-Hispanic/Latino), 199 international. Average age 28. 955 applicants, 22% accepted, 86 enrolled. In 2018, 64 master's, 17 doctorates awarded. Terminal master's awarded for partial completion of doctoral program. *Degree requirements:* For master's, comprehensive exam (for some programs), thesis optional; for doctorate, comprehensive exam, thesis/dissertation. *Entrance requirements:* For master's and doctorate, GRE General Test, minimum GPA of 3.0. Additional exam requirements/recommendations for international students: Required—TOEFL (minimum score 500 paper-based; 61 iBT), IELTS (minimum score 6.5). *Application deadline:* For fall admission, 12/15 for domestic and international students. Application fee: $55 ($65 for international students). Electronic applications accepted. *Expenses:* Contact institution. *Financial support:* In 2018–19, 2 students received support, including 1 fellowship with full tuition reimbursement available (averaging $25,000 per year), 115 research assistantships with full tuition reimbursements available (averaging $35,625 per year), 163 teaching assistantships with full tuition reimbursements available (averaging $15,120 per year); Federal Work-Study, scholarships/grants, health care benefits, and unspecified assistantships also available. Financial award application deadline: 12/15; financial award applicants required to submit FAFSA. *Faculty research:* Operating systems, programming languages, formal methods, natural language processing, architecture, networks, image analysis, data analysis, visualization, graphics, scientific computing, robotics. *Total annual research expenditures:* $7.9 million. *Unit head:* Dr. Ross Whitaker, Director, 801-587-9549, Fax: 801-581-5843, E-mail: whitaker@cs.utah.edu. *Application contact:* Robert Barber, Graduate Advisor, 801-581-3479, Fax: 801-581-5843, E-mail: annc@cs.utah.edu.
Website: http://www.cs.utah.edu

University of Utah, Graduate School, David Eccles School of Business, Master of Science in Information Systems Program, Salt Lake City, UT 84112-8939. Offers information systems (MS, Graduate Certificate), including business intelligence and analytics, IT security, product and process management, software and systems architecture. *Program availability:* Part-time, evening/weekend, 100% online, blended/hybrid learning. *Degree requirements:* For master's, capstone project. *Entrance requirements:* For master's, GMAT/GRE, minimum undergraduate GPA of 3.0, 2 letters of recommendation, personal statement, professional resume. Additional exam requirements/recommendations for international students: Required—TOEFL (minimum score 550 paper-based; 80 iBT), IELTS (minimum score 6.5). Electronic applications accepted. *Expenses:* Contact institution. *Faculty research:* Business intelligence and analytics, software and system architecture, product and process management, IT security, Web and data mining, applications and management of IT in healthcare.

University of Washington, Bothell, Program in Computing and Software Systems, Bothell, WA 98011. Offers MS. *Program availability:* Part-time, evening/weekend. *Degree requirements:* For master's, comprehensive exam (for some programs), thesis optional. *Entrance requirements:* For master's, GRE. Additional exam requirements/recommendations for international students: Required—TOEFL (minimum score 580 paper-based; 92 iBT) or IELTS (minimum score 7). Electronic applications accepted. *Expenses:* Contact institution. *Faculty research:* Computer science, software engineering, computer graphics, parallel and distributed systems, computer vision.

University of Washington, Tacoma, Graduate Programs, Program in Computing and Software Systems, Tacoma, WA 98402-3100. Offers MS. *Program availability:* Part-time. *Degree requirements:* For master's, capstone project/thesis or 15 credits elective coursework. *Entrance requirements:* For master's, GRE, personal statement, resume, transcripts, 3 recommendations. Additional exam requirements/recommendations for international students: Required—TOEFL (minimum score 580 paper-based; 92 iBT), IELTS (minimum score 7). Electronic applications accepted. *Faculty research:* Data stream analysis, formal methods, data mining, robotic systems, software development processes.

University of Waterloo, Graduate Studies and Postdoctoral Affairs, Faculty of Mathematics, David R. Cheriton School of Computer Science, Waterloo, ON N2L 3G1, Canada. Offers computer science (M Math, PhD); software engineering (M Math); statistics and computing (M Math). *Program availability:* Part-time. *Degree requirements:* For master's, research paper or thesis; for doctorate, comprehensive exam, thesis/dissertation. *Entrance requirements:* For master's, honors degree in field, minimum B+ average; for doctorate, master's degree, minimum B+ average. Additional exam requirements/recommendations for international students: Required—TOEFL, IELTS, PTE. Application fee: $125 Canadian dollars. Electronic applications accepted. *Financial support:* Research assistantships, teaching assistantships, scholarships/grants, and unspecified assistantships available. *Faculty research:* Computer graphics, artificial intelligence, algorithms and complexity, distributed computing and networks, software engineering.
Website: https://cs.uwaterloo.ca/

University of West Florida, Hal Marcus College of Science and Engineering, Department of Computer Science, Pensacola, FL 32514-5750. Offers computer science (MS), including computer science, database systems, software engineering; information technology (MS), including cybersecurity, database management. *Program availability:* Part-time, evening/weekend. *Degree requirements:* For master's, thesis optional. *Entrance requirements:* For master's, GRE, MAT, or GMAT, official transcripts; minimum undergraduate GPA of 3.0; letter of intent; three letters of recommendation. Additional exam requirements/recommendations for international students: Required—TOEFL (minimum score 550 paper-based).

University of Wisconsin–La Crosse, College of Science and Health, Department of Computer Science, La Crosse, WI 54601-3742. Offers software engineering (MSE). *Program availability:* Part-time. *Degree requirements:* For master's, thesis. *Entrance requirements:* Additional exam requirements/recommendations for international students: Recommended—TOEFL (minimum score 550 paper-based; 79 iBT), IELTS (minimum score 6). Electronic applications accepted.

Vermont Technical College, Program in Computer Software Engineering, Randolph Center, VT 05061-0500. Offers MS.

Virginia International University, School of Computer Information Systems, Fairfax, VA 22030. Offers business intelligence (Graduate Certificate); business intelligence and data analytics (MIS); computer science (MS), including computer animation and gaming, cybersecurity, data management networking, intelligent systems, software applications development, software engineering; cybersecurity (MIS); data management (MIS); enterprise project management (MIS); health informatics (MIS); information assurance (MIS); information systems (Graduate Certificate); information systems management (MS, Graduate Certificate); information technology (MS); information technology audit and compliance (Graduate Certificate); knowledge management (MIS); software engineering (MS). *Program availability:* Part-time, online learning. *Entrance requirements:* For master's, bachelor's degree. Additional exam requirements/recommendations for international students: Required—TOEFL (minimum score 550 paper-based; 80 iBT), IELTS. Electronic applications accepted.

Virginia Polytechnic Institute and State University, VT Online, Blacksburg, VA 24061. Offers advanced transportation systems (Certificate); aerospace engineering (MS); agricultural and life sciences (MSLFS); business information systems (Graduate Certificate); career and technical education (MS); civil engineering (MS); computer engineering (M Eng, MS); decision support systems (Graduate Certificate); eLearning leadership (MA); electrical engineering (M Eng, MS); engineering administration (MEA); environmental engineering (Certificate); environmental politics and policy (Graduate Certificate); environmental sciences and engineering (MS); foundations of political analysis (Graduate Certificate); health product risk management (Graduate Certificate); industrial and systems engineering (MS); information policy and society (Graduate Certificate); information security (Graduate Certificate); information technology (MIT); instructional technology (MA); integrative STEM education (MA Ed); liberal arts (Graduate Certificate); life sciences: health product risk management (MS); natural resources (MNR, Graduate Certificate); networking (Graduate Certificate); nonprofit and nongovernmental organization management (Graduate Certificate); ocean engineering (MS); political science (MA); security studies (Graduate Certificate); software development (Graduate Certificate). *Expenses:* Tuition, state resident: full-time $15,510; part-time $739.50 per credit hour. Tuition, nonresident: full-time $29,629; part-time $1490.25 per credit hour. *Required fees:* $2804; $550 per semester. Tuition and fees vary according to course load, campus/location and program. *Application contact:* Graduate Admissions and Academic Progress, 540-231-8636, E-mail: grads@vt.edu. Website: http://www.vto.vt.edu/

West Virginia University, Statler College of Engineering and Mineral Resources, Morgantown, WV 26506. Offers aerospace engineering (MSAE, PhD); chemical engineering (MS Ch E, PhD); civil engineering (MSCE, PhD); computer engineering (PhD); computer science (MSCS, PhD); electrical engineering (MSEE, PhD); energy systems engineering (MSESE); engineering (MSE); industrial engineering (MSIE, PhD); industrial hygiene (MS); material science and engineering (MSMSE, PhD); mechanical engineering (MSME, PhD); mining engineering (MS Min E, PhD); petroleum and natural gas engineering (MSPNGE, PhD); safety management (MS); software engineering (MSSE). *Program availability:* Part-time. *Students:* 466 full-time (113 women), 154 part-time (27 women); includes 57 minority (22 Black or African American, non-Hispanic/Latino; 1 American Indian or Alaska Native, non-Hispanic/Latino; 8 Asian, non-Hispanic/Latino; 12 Hispanic/Latino; 14 Two or more races, non-Hispanic/Latino), 283 international. In 2018, 179 master's, 39 doctorates awarded. Terminal master's awarded for partial completion of doctoral program. *Degree requirements:* For master's, thesis optional; for doctorate, comprehensive exam, thesis/dissertation. *Entrance requirements:* Additional exam requirements/recommendations for international students: Required—TOEFL (minimum score 550 paper-based). *Application deadline:* For fall admission, 4/1 for international students; for winter admission, 4/1 for international students; for spring admission, 10/1 for international students. Applications are processed on a rolling basis. Application fee: $60. Electronic applications accepted. *Expenses:* Contact institution. *Financial support:* Fellowships, research assistantships, teaching assistantships, career-related internships or fieldwork, Federal Work-Study, institutionally sponsored loans, health care benefits, tuition waivers (full and partial), unspecified assistantships, and administrative assistantships available. Financial award application deadline: 2/1; financial award applicants required to submit FAFSA. *Faculty research:* Composite materials, software engineering, information systems, aerodynamics, vehicle propulsion and emission. *Unit head:* Dr. Earl Scime, Interim Dean, 304-293-4157 Ext. 2237, Fax: 304-293-2037, E-mail: earl.scime@mail.wvu.edu. *Application contact:* Dr. David A. Wyrick, Associate Dean, Academic Affairs, 304-293-4334, Fax: 304-293-5024, E-mail: david.wyrick@mail.wvu.edu. Website: https://www.statler.wvu.edu

Systems Science

Arizona State University at the Tempe campus, College of Liberal Arts and Sciences, School of Life Sciences, Tempe, AZ 85287-4601. Offers animal behavior (PhD); applied ethics (biomedical and health ethics) (MA); biology (MS, PhD), including biology, biology and society, complex adaptive systems science (PhD), plant biology and conservation (MS); environmental life sciences (PhD); evolutionary biology (PhD); history and philosophy of science (PhD); human and social dimensions of science and technology (PhD); microbiology (PhD); molecular and cellular biology (PhD); neuroscience (PhD). Terminal master's awarded for partial completion of doctoral program. *Degree requirements:* For master's, thesis (for some programs), interactive Program of Study (iPOS) submitted before completing 50 percent of required credit hours; for doctorate, variable foreign language requirement, comprehensive exam, thesis/dissertation, interactive Program of Study (iPOS) submitted before completing 50 percent of required credit hours. *Entrance requirements:* For master's and doctorate, GRE, minimum GPA of 3.0 or equivalent in last 2 years of work leading to bachelor's degree. Additional exam requirements/recommendations for international students: Required—TOEFL (minimum score 600 paper-based; 100 iBT). Electronic applications accepted.

Arizona State University at the Tempe campus, Ira A. Fulton Schools of Engineering, ASU Engineering Online Programs, Tempe, AZ 85287. Offers construction (MS); embedded systems (M Eng); enterprise systems innovation and management (MSE); modeling and simulation (M Eng); quality and reliability engineering (M Eng); software engineering (MSE); systems engineering (M Eng).

Binghamton University, State University of New York, Graduate School, Thomas J. Watson School of Engineering and Applied Science, Department of Systems Science and Industrial Engineering, Binghamton, NY 13902-6000. Offers executive health systems (MS); industrial and systems engineering (M Eng); systems science and industrial engineering (MS, PhD). MS in executive health systems also offered in Manhattan. *Program availability:* Part-time, evening/weekend, online learning. *Degree requirements:* For master's, thesis; for doctorate, thesis/dissertation. *Entrance requirements:* For master's and doctorate, GRE General Test. Additional exam requirements/recommendations for international students: Required—TOEFL (minimum score 550 paper-based; 80 iBT). Electronic applications accepted. *Expenses:* Contact institution. *Faculty research:* Problem restructuring, protein modeling.

Carleton University, Faculty of Graduate Studies, Faculty of Engineering and Design, Ottawa-Carleton Institute for Electrical Engineering, Department of Systems and Computer Engineering, Program in Information and Systems Science, Ottawa, ON K1S 5B6, Canada. Offers M Sc.

Carleton University, Faculty of Graduate Studies, Faculty of Science, Information and Systems Science Program, Ottawa, ON K1S 5B6, Canada. Offers M Sc. *Degree requirements:* For master's, thesis optional. *Entrance requirements:* For master's, honors degree. Additional exam requirements/recommendations for international students: Required—TOEFL. *Faculty research:* Software engineering, real-time and microprocessor programming, computer communications.

Carleton University, Faculty of Graduate Studies, Faculty of Science, School of Computer Science, Ottawa, ON K1S 5B6, Canada. Offers computer science (MCS, PhD); information and system science (M Sc). MCS and PhD programs offered jointly with University of Ottawa. *Program availability:* Part-time. *Degree requirements:* For master's, thesis optional, project; for doctorate, comprehensive exam, thesis/dissertation. *Entrance requirements:* For master's, honors degree. Additional exam requirements/recommendations for international students: Required—TOEFL. *Faculty research:* Programming systems, theory of computing, computer applications, computer systems.

Claremont Graduate University, Graduate Programs, Center for Information Systems and Technology, Claremont, CA 91711-6160. Offers cybersecurity and networking (MS); data science and analytics (MS); electronic commerce (PhD); geographic information systems (MS); health informatics (MS); information systems (Certificate); IT strategy and innovation (MS); knowledge management (PhD); systems development (PhD); telecommunications and networking (PhD); MBA/MS. *Program availability:* Part-time. *Degree requirements:* For doctorate, comprehensive exam, thesis/dissertation, portfolio. *Entrance requirements:* For master's and doctorate, GMAT, GRE General Test. Additional exam requirements/recommendations for international students: Required—TOEFL (minimum score 75 iBT). Electronic applications accepted. *Faculty research:*

Man-machine interaction, organizational aspects of computing, implementation of information systems, information systems practice.

Eastern Illinois University, Graduate School, Lumpkin College of Business and Technology, School of Technology, Charleston, IL 61920. Offers computer technology (Certificate); cybersecurity (MS); quality systems (Certificate); sustainable energy (MS); technology (MS); technology security (Certificate); work performance improvement (Certificate); MS/MBA; MS/MS. *Program availability:* Part-time, evening/weekend. *Expenses:* Tuition, state resident: part-time $299 per credit hour. Tuition, nonresident: part-time $718 per credit hour. *Required fees:* $214.50 per credit hour.

Fairleigh Dickinson University, Metropolitan Campus, University College: Arts, Sciences, and Professional Studies, Program in Systems Science, Teaneck, NJ 07666-1914. Offers MS. *Entrance requirements:* For master's, GRE General Test.

Harrisburg University of Science and Technology, Program in Information Systems Engineering and Management, Harrisburg, PA 17101. Offers analytics (MS); digital government (MS); digital health (MS); entrepreneurship (MS); information security (MS); software engineering and systems development (MS). *Program availability:* Part-time, evening/weekend. *Degree requirements:* For master's, thesis optional. *Entrance requirements:* For master's, baccalaureate degree. Additional exam requirements/recommendations for international students: Required—TOEFL (minimum score 520 paper-based; 80 iBT); Recommended—IELTS (minimum score 6). Electronic applications accepted. *Faculty research:* Healthcare Informatics, material analysis, enterprise systems, circuit design, enterprise architectures.

Hood College, Graduate School, Program in Management Information Systems, Frederick, MD 21701-8575. Offers MS. *Program availability:* Part-time, evening/weekend. *Students:* 21 full-time (8 women), 7 part-time (1 woman); includes 1 minority (Black or African American, non-Hispanic/Latino), 26 international. Average age 30. 16 applicants, 100% accepted, 7 enrolled. In 2018, 11 master's awarded. *Entrance requirements:* For master's, minimum GPA of 2.75, essay, resume. Additional exam requirements/recommendations for international students: Required—TOEFL (minimum score 575 paper-based; 89 iBT), IELTS (minimum score 6.5). *Application deadline:* For fall admission, 8/15 priority date for domestic students, 8/5 for international students; for spring admission, 12/1 priority date for domestic students, 12/1 for international students; for summer admission, 5/1 priority date for domestic students, 4/15 for international students. Applications are processed on a rolling basis. Application fee: $50 ($100 for international students). Electronic applications accepted. *Expenses:* Science Programs: Tuition $535 per credit hour, Comprehensive Fee $115 per semester. *Financial support:* Tuition waivers (partial) and unspecified assistantships available. Financial award applicants required to submit FAFSA. *Faculty research:* Systems engineering, parallel distributed computing, strategy, business ethics, entrepreneurship. *Unit head:* Dr. April M. Boulton, Dean of the Graduate School, 301-696-3600, E-mail: gofurther@hood.edu. *Application contact:* Larbi Bricha, Assistant Director of Graduate Admissions, 301-696-3601, E-mail: gofurther@hood.edu. Website: http://www.hood.edu/graduate

Louisiana State University and Agricultural & Mechanical College, Graduate School, College of Engineering, Division of Computer Science, Baton Rouge, LA 70803. Offers computer science (MSSS, PhD); systems science (MSSS).

Louisiana State University in Shreveport, College of Arts and Sciences, Program in Computer Systems Technology, Shreveport, LA 71115-2399. Offers MS. *Program availability:* Part-time, evening/weekend. *Degree requirements:* For master's, comprehensive exam (for some programs), thesis or alternative. *Entrance requirements:* For master's, GRE, programming course in high-level language, interview. Additional exam requirements/recommendations for international students: Required—TOEFL (minimum score 550 paper-based; 80 iBT). Electronic applications accepted.

Miami University, College of Engineering and Computing, Department of Computer Science and Software Engineering, Oxford, OH 45056. Offers computer science (MCS). *Faculty:* 18 full-time (4 women). *Students:* 14 full-time (5 women), 3 part-time (0 women), 10 international. Average age 27. In 2018, 12 master's awarded. *Unit head:* Dr. James Kiper, Chair, 513-529-0340, E-mail: kiperjd@miamioh.edu. *Application contact:* Graduate Director, 513-529-0340, E-mail: cecgrad@miamioh.edu. Website: http://miamioh.edu/cec/academics/departments/cse/

Systems Science

Oakland University, Graduate Study and Lifelong Learning, School of Engineering and Computer Science, Department of Electrical and Computer Engineering, Rochester, MI 48309-4401. Offers electrical and computer engineering (MS, PhD); embedded systems (MS); mechatronics (MS). *Program availability:* Part-time, evening/weekend. *Entrance requirements:* For master's, minimum GPA of 3.0. Additional exam requirements/recommendations for international students: Required—TOEFL (minimum score 550 paper-based). Electronic applications accepted. *Expenses:* Contact institution.

Portland State University, Graduate Studies, College of Liberal Arts and Sciences, Systems Science Program, Portland, OR 97207-0751. Offers computational intelligence (Certificate); computer modeling and simulation (Certificate); systems science (MS); systems science/anthropology (PhD); systems science/business administration (PhD); systems science/civil engineering (PhD); systems science/economics (PhD); systems science/engineering management (PhD); systems science/general (PhD); systems science/mathematical sciences (PhD); systems science/mechanical engineering (PhD); systems science/psychology (PhD); systems science/sociology (PhD). *Degree requirements:* For master's, comprehensive exam (for some programs), thesis optional; for doctorate, variable foreign language requirement, comprehensive exam (for some programs), thesis/dissertation. *Entrance requirements:* For master's, GRE/GMAT (recommended), minimum GPA of 3.0 on undergraduate or graduate work, 2 letters of recommendation, statement of interest; for doctorate, GMAT, GRE General Test, minimum GPA of 3.0 undergraduate, 3.25 graduate; 3 letters of recommendation; statement of interest. Additional exam requirements/recommendations for international students: Required—TOEFL (minimum score 550 paper-based; 80 iBT). Electronic applications accepted. *Faculty research:* Systems theory and methodology, artificial intelligence neural networks, information theory, nonlinear dynamics/chaos, modeling and simulation.

Rensselaer at Hartford, Department of Engineering, Program in Computer and Systems Engineering, Hartford, CT 06120-2991. Offers ME. *Entrance requirements:* For master's, GRE.

Stevens Institute of Technology, Graduate School, Charles V. Schaefer Jr. School of Engineering and Science, Department of Mechanical Engineering, Program in Integrated Product Development, Hoboken, NJ 07030. Offers armament engineering (M Eng); computer and electrical engineering (M Eng); manufacturing technologies (M Eng); systems reliability and design (M Eng). *Program availability:* Part-time, evening/weekend. *Faculty:* 32 full-time (4 women), 10 part-time/adjunct (0 women). *Degree requirements:* For master's, thesis optional, minimum B average in major field and overall. *Entrance requirements:* For master's, GRE/GMAT scores: GRE scores are required for all applicants applying to a full-time graduate program in the Schaefer School of Engineering and Science (SES). International applicants must submit TOEFL/IELTS scores and fulfill the English Language Proficiency Requirements in order to be considered. Additional exam requirements/recommendations for international students: Required—TOEFL (minimum score 74 iBT), IELTS (minimum score 6). *Application deadline:* For fall admission, 4/15 for domestic and international students; for spring admission, 11/1 for domestic and international students; for summer admission, 5/1 for domestic students. Applications are processed on a rolling basis. Application fee: $60. Electronic applications accepted. *Expenses: Tuition:* Full-time $35,960; part-time $1620 per credit. *Required fees:* $1290; $600 per semester. Tuition and fees vary according to course load. *Financial support:* Fellowships, research assistantships, teaching assistantships, career-related internships or fieldwork, Federal Work-Study, scholarships/grants, and unspecified assistantships available. Financial award application deadline: 2/15; financial award applicants required to submit FAFSA. *Unit head:* Dr. Jean Zu, Dean of SES, 201-216.8233, Fax: 201-216.8372, E-mail: Jean.Zu@stevens.edu. *Application contact:* Graduate Admissions, 888-783-8367, Fax: 888-511-1306, E-mail: graduate@stevens.edu.

Stevens Institute of Technology, Graduate School, School of Systems and Enterprises, Program in Socio-Technical Systems, Hoboken, NJ 07030. Offers MS, PhD. *Program availability:* Part-time, evening/weekend. *Faculty:* 28 full-time (8 women), 5 part-time/adjunct (1 woman). *Students:* 2 full-time (1 woman), 1 part-time (0 women); includes 1 minority (Black or African American, non-Hispanic/Latino). Average age 41. *Degree requirements:* For master's, thesis optional, minimum B average in major field and overall; for doctorate, comprehensive exam (for some programs), thesis/dissertation. *Entrance requirements:* For master's, GRE/GMAT scores: GRE scores are required for all applicants applying to a full-time graduate program in the Schaefer School of Engineering and Science (SES). International applicants must submit TOEFL/IELTS scores and fulfill the English Language Proficiency Requirements in order to be considered. Additional exam requirements/recommendations for international students: Required—TOEFL (minimum score 74 iBT), IELTS (minimum score 6). *Application deadline:* For fall admission, 4/15 for domestic and international students; for spring admission, 11/1 for domestic and international students; for summer admission, 5/1 for domestic students. Applications are processed on a rolling basis. Application fee: $60. Electronic applications accepted. *Expenses: Tuition:* Full-time $35,960; part-time $1620 per credit. *Required fees:* $1290; $600 per semester. Tuition and fees vary according to course load. *Financial support:* Fellowships, research assistantships, teaching assistantships, career-related internships or fieldwork, Federal Work-Study, scholarships/grants, and unspecified assistantships available. Financial award application deadline: 2/15; financial award applicants required to submit FAFSA. *Unit head:* Dr. Yehia Massoud, Dean of SSE, 201-216.8025, E-mail: yehia.massoud@stevens.edu. *Application contact:* Graduate Admissions, 888-783-8367, Fax: 888-511-1306, E-mail: graduate@stevens.edu.

Strayer University, Graduate Studies, Washington, DC 20005-2603. Offers accounting (MS); acquisition (MBA); business administration (MBA); communications technology (MS); educational management (M Ed); finance (MBA); health services administration (MHSA); hospitality and tourism management (MBA); human resource management (MBA); information systems (MS), including computer security management, decision support system management, enterprise resource management, network management, software engineering management, systems development management; management (MBA); management information systems (MS); marketing (MBA); professional accounting (MS), including accounting information systems, controllership, taxation; public administration (MPA); supply chain management (MBA); technology in education (M Ed). Programs also offered at campus locations in Birmingham, AL; Chamblee, GA; Cobb County, GA; Morrow, GA; White Marsh, MD; Charleston, SC; Columbia, SC; Greensboro, NC; Greenville, SC; Lexington, KY; Louisville, KY; Nashville, TN; North Raleigh, NC; Washington, DC. *Accreditation:* ACBSP. *Program availability:* Part-time, evening/weekend, online learning. *Degree requirements:* For master's, thesis. *Entrance requirements:* For master's, GMAT, GRE General Test, bachelor's degree from an accredited college or university, minimum undergraduate GPA of 2.75. Electronic applications accepted.

Universidad Autonoma de Guadalajara, Graduate Programs, Guadalajara, Mexico. Offers administrative law and justice (LL M); advertising and corporate communications (MA); architecture (M Arch); business (MBA); computational science (MCC); education (Ed M, Ed D); English-Spanish translation (MA); entrepreneurship and management (MBA); integrated management of digital animation (MA); international business (MIB); international corporate law (LL M); Internet technologies (MS); manufacturing systems (MMS); occupational health (MS); philosophy (MA, PhD); power electronics (MS); quality systems (MQS); renewable energy (MS); social evaluation of projects (MBA); strategic market research (MBA); tax law (MA); teaching mathematics (MA).

University of Michigan, College of Engineering, Department of Integrative Systems and Design, Ann Arbor, MI 48109. Offers automotive engineering (M Eng); design science (MS, PhD); energy systems engineering (M Eng, MS); global automotive and manufacturing engineering (M Eng); manufacturing engineering (M Eng, D Eng); pharmaceutical engineering (M Eng); robotics and autonomous vehicles (M Eng); systems engineering and design (M Eng); MBA/M Eng; MSE/MS. *Program availability:* Part-time, online learning. *Students:* 163 full-time (38 women), 251 part-time (40 women). 282 applicants, 12% accepted, 15 enrolled. In 2018, 173 master's, 1 doctorate awarded. Terminal master's awarded for partial completion of doctoral program. *Degree requirements:* For master's, capstone project; for doctorate, thesis/dissertation. *Entrance requirements:* For master's and doctorate, GRE. Additional exam requirements/recommendations for international students: Required—TOEFL. *Application deadline:* Applications are processed on a rolling basis. Electronic applications accepted. *Financial support:* Fellowships, research assistantships with full tuition reimbursements, teaching assistantships with full tuition reimbursements, career-related internships or fieldwork, scholarships/grants, and unspecified assistantships available. Financial award applicants required to submit FAFSA. *Faculty research:* Automotive engineering, design science, energy systems engineering, engineering sustainable systems, financial engineering, global automotive and manufacturing engineering, integrated microsystems, manufacturing engineering, pharmaceutical engineering, robotics and autonomous vehicles. *Total annual research expenditures:* $595,323. *Unit head:* Diann Brei, Department Chair, 734-763-6617, E-mail: drdiannbrei@umich.edu. *Application contact:* Kathy Bishar, Senior Graduate Coordinator, 734-764-3312, E-mail: kbishar@umich.edu. Website: http://www.isd.engin.umich.edu

University of Ottawa, Faculty of Graduate and Postdoctoral Studies, Interdisciplinary Programs, Ottawa, ON K1N 6N5, Canada. Offers e-business (Certificate); e-commerce (Certificate); finance (Certificate); health services and policies research (Diploma); population health (PhD); population health risk assessment and management (Certificate); public management and governance (Certificate); systems science (Certificate).

University of Ottawa, Faculty of Graduate and Postdoctoral Studies, Systems Science Program, Ottawa, ON K1N 6N5, Canada. Offers M Sc, M Sys Sc, Certificate. *Program availability:* Part-time, evening/weekend. *Degree requirements:* For master's and Certificate, thesis optional. *Entrance requirements:* For master's, bachelor's degree or equivalent, minimum B average; for Certificate, honors degree or equivalent, minimum B average. Additional exam requirements/recommendations for international students: Recommended—TOEFL. Electronic applications accepted. *Faculty research:* Software engineering, communication systems, information systems, production management, corporate managerial modeling.

Worcester Polytechnic Institute, Graduate Admissions, Department of Social Science and Policy Studies, Worcester, MA 01609-2280. Offers interdisciplinary social science (PhD); system dynamics (MS, Graduate Certificate). *Program availability:* Part-time, evening/weekend, 100% online. *Students:* 1 (woman) full-time, 5 part-time (2 women), 1 international. Average age 45. 11 applicants, 73% accepted, 2 enrolled. In 2018, 1 master's awarded. *Entrance requirements:* For master's and doctorate, GRE General Test, 3 letters of recommendation, statement of purpose. Additional exam requirements/recommendations for international students: Required—TOEFL (minimum score 563 paper-based; 84 iBT), IELTS (minimum score 7). *Application deadline:* For fall admission, 1/1 priority date for domestic students, 1/1 for international students; for spring admission, 10/1 priority date for domestic students, 10/1 for international students. Applications are processed on a rolling basis. Application fee: $70. Electronic applications accepted. *Financial support:* Research assistantships, teaching assistantships, career-related internships or fieldwork, institutionally sponsored loans, scholarships/grants, and unspecified assistantships available. Financial award application deadline: 1/1. *Unit head:* Dr. Emily Douglas, Head, 508-831-5296, Fax: 508-831-5896, E-mail: emdouglas@wpi.edu. *Application contact:* Dr. Michael Radzicki, Graduate Coordinator, 508-831-5296, Fax: 508-831-5896, E-mail: mjradz@wpi.edu. Website: https://www.wpi.edu/academics/departments/social-science-policy-studies

DREXEL UNIVERSITY
College of Computing & Informatics

Programs of Study

The College of Computing & Informatics (CCI) is located at Drexel University, a private university in the heart of Philadelphia, Pennsylvania. CCI offers graduate degree programs including the online and on-campus Data Science program; the new online and on-campus Information program; the online and on-campus Computer Science program; the online Health Informatics program; the online and on-campus Information Systems program; the online and on-campus Software Engineering program; and the online and on-campus Cybersecurity program (a joint program with the Electrical & Computer Engineering Department of Drexel's College of Engineering).

Founded in 2013, CCI instills the knowledge and skills necessary for students to lead and innovate across industries in a rapidly evolving technological landscape. Building on Drexel University's exceptional foundation of entrepreneurship and cooperative education, CCI provides unparalleled professional experiences and the on-the-job training that is vital to preparing today's students for tomorrow's world. CCI's unique structure brings computing and informatics together under one roof in a dynamic, collaborative college that allows faculty and students to spot trends before they emerge, to solve problems before they occur, and to build a better tomorrow, starting today.

The graduate programs offered by the College of Computing & Informatics include:

The Master of Science in Data Science (M.S.D.S.) equips students with both the computational and applied knowledge necessary to thrive in the fast-growing, interdisciplinary field of data analytics. Drawing on the interdisciplinary strengths of CCI, the M.S.D.S. provides students with in-depth knowledge of core data science principles and the origin of tools necessary to harness big data.

The Master of Science in Computer Science (M.S.C.S.) offers a multidisciplinary and in-depth understanding of the core and advanced topics in the rapidly growing field of computer science, while placing equal emphasis on theory and practice to prepare students for top professional positions.

The Master of Science in Health Informatics (M.S.H.I.) is an online program that teaches students from diverse academic and professional backgrounds how to use information technology efficiently and responsibly to improve health outcomes. Drexel's M.S.H.I. degree program is accredited by the Commission on Accreditation for Health Informatics and Information Management Education (CAHIIM). Drexel University's educational programs are accredited by MSCHE (Middle States Commission on Higher Education).

The NEW Master of Science in Information (M.S.I) program prepares students to be leaders in the information profession who can lead, collaborate and innovate data-driven solutions to advance society and the economy. Students can select one or two of the following majors: Human-Computer Interaction & User Experience (UX), Library and Information Science (ALA accredited since 1924), and/or Digital Content Management.

The Master of Science in Information Systems (M.S.I.S.) equips students with both the domain knowledge and practical competencies to compete in the ever-changing technical landscape of information system business requirements, software design and management, data-oriented informatics, and user experience design.

The Master of Science in Software Engineering (M.S.S.E.) prepares students to become professional software engineers across a wide variety of industries, and offers students a blend of theory and practice to provide a solid understanding of the fundamentals of software systems as well as a working knowledge of the many languages, methods, and systems used in the field.

The Master of Science in Cybersecurity (M.S.C.) is an interdisciplinary program that prepares students with both the academic and practical training to be competitive in the ever-changing technical landscape of cybersecurity. This is a joint program with the Electrical & Computer Engineering Department of Drexel's College of Engineering.

CCI also offers graduate students the opportunity to pursue a dual master's degree among any of their graduate programs. To be eligible for a dual master's degree program, graduate students must be currently working on their first degree when requesting admission to the second.

CCI offers graduate minors in applied data science, computational data science, computer science, human-computer interaction & user experience, and healthcare informatics. The applied data science minor provides Drexel graduate students an interdisciplinary education in foundational and applied data science, where data science methods are used to help solve problems or gain insights. This minor is ideal for Drexel graduate students (master's or doctoral level) from all backgrounds who are interested in gaining core knowledge of data science's value and wide-ranging applications or used as a launching point for more in depth and expansive knowledge in the field. The computational data science minor provides Drexel graduate students with a strong foundation in the emerging field of data science, with a focus on computational and systems issues. This minor is ideal for Drexel graduate students (master's or doctoral level) who are interested in building on their degree and existing quantitative skills to become leaders in the field of data science. The computer science minor allows Drexel students from all backgrounds to obtain fundamental computer science knowledge as well as an introduction to advanced topics in computer science that will be suitable for their own graduate studies. The program is offered to current Drexel graduate students outside of the College's Computer Science Department. The minor in human-computer interaction & user experience provides skills and training for any graduate or doctoral students who wish to expand their understanding of human-centered design and/or apply design skills in their major area of study. The minor in healthcare informatics provides a basic acquaintance with health informatics principles and practices for students pursuing careers in a wide variety of health-related professions. The program is offered to current Drexel graduate students in good standing (students in the M.S. in Health Informatics program are not eligible).

Graduate Co-op is available for the M.S. in Computer Science and M.S. in Information Systems programs. Graduate Co-op allows graduate students to alternate class terms with a six-month period of hands-on experience, gaining access to employers in their chosen industries.

CCI's interdisciplinary doctoral programs in information science and computer science prepare students for leadership careers in research and education in the information and computer science fields. The College's Ph.D. in Computer Science program is designed to ensure core knowledge of the fundamental computer science areas and to conduct leading-edge research at the forefront of a selected area. Students are prepared for leadership careers in research and education in computer science and interdisciplinary work using computer science. The Ph.D. in Information Science prepares students to become creative, interdisciplinary researchers with foundations in information science, data science, and human-centered computing. The main focus of the program is research with applications that benefit all sectors of society.

The College's professional development programs, such as the new Post-Baccalaureate Certificate in Human-Computer Interaction & User Experience; Post-Baccalaureate Certificates in Applied Data Science and Computational Data Science; Post-Baccalaureate Certificate in Computer Science; Certificate in Healthcare Informatics; and the Advanced Certificate in Information Studies and Technology (ACIST), allow students holding a bachelor's or master's degree in any field to update their education and develop new expertise.

Research Facilities

Research at CCI spans a wide range of areas and topics all related in some way to the exciting world of computing and informatics. This research can be categorized in terms of six major research areas: computer science, computer security, human-centered computing, informatics and data science, library and information science, and systems and software engineering.

CCI is associated with a number of research centers and institutes that house a number of the University's leading-edge research initiatives. Collaboratively led by CCI faculty and members from partner colleges and institutions, these centers and institutes encompass a broad range of research topics and solutions in the computing and informatics fields. Some of those include the Center for the Study of Libraries, Information, & Society; Center for Visual and Decision Informatics (CVDI); the Drexel University Cybersecurity Institute; and the Metadata Research Center.

Financial Aid

There are several options which can help CCI graduate students offset the cost of their studies, including CCI incentives, partner organization discounts, scholarships, student loans, the G.I. Bill for veterans, the Yellow Ribbon program, private scholarships, and employment with the University.

Cost of Study

The tuition rate for the 2019–20 academic year is $1,303 per credit hour plus general student fees.

Living and Housing Costs

On-campus housing is available. One-, two- and three- bedroom suites are available. Ample off-campus housing is also available.

Student Life

Both online and on-campus graduate students have the opportunity to participate in a variety of activities. CCI holds events, workshops, and hosts guest speakers throughout the year. The College also hosts industry workshops and showcases through its Corporate Partners Program, as well as career fairs to enable students to network with future employers and gain insights into different career paths.

CCI graduate students have the opportunity to participate in student groups and professional organizations, many of which have local chapters that hold regular events. Student groups include the Drexel University Libraries & Archives Student Association, Upsilon Pi Epsilon, MCS Society, Women in Computing Society (WiCS), Drexel Game Developers Group (DGDG), and CCI Doctoral Student Association.

From graduate co-op programs and career workshops, to career counseling, career fairs, and national and international hands-on experience, the Steinbright Career Development Center at Drexel University helps give students the edge they need to succeed. Steinbright is also home to Handshake, Drexel's online job board of full-time and paid internship positions for graduating students and recent alum.

Location

Drexel University's lively urban campus is located in one of America's most exciting cities—Philadelphia. In a world-class city for business, art, and education, Philadelphia's skyscrapers are blended with distinct and culturally diverse neighborhoods, creating a unique metropolitan yet intimate urban experience. Surrounded by tree-lined residential blocks just minutes away from Philadelphia's downtown Center City district, Drexel makes its home in the neighborhood of University City. Philadelphia, a city steeped in history and tradition, is one of the nation's up-and-coming hubs for innovation, technology, and economic growth. Home to powerhouse companies such as Comcast and Urban Outfitters, as well as a quickly growing number of energetic start-ups, Philadelphia is a natural fit for Drexel's dynamic community. Philadelphia boasts some of the nation's best historical and cultural attractions and offers the vibrant nightlife, choice restaurants, dynamic arts, and major-league athletics of a first-class city. Drexel's location offers easy access to public transportation and the Drexel shuttle provides convenient, free transportation between campuses for Drexel students. Adjacent to Drexel's University City Campus, Amtrak's 30th Street Station is a hub for trains and buses to the Philadelphia suburbs, New York City, Washington, D.C., and the Philadelphia International Airport.

In April 2019, the College of Computing & Informatics (CCI) relocated to 3675 Market. For the first time in the College's history, all CCI faculty, students and professional staff are housed under one roof. Occupying on two floors in the brand new uCity Square building, CCI's new home offers state-of-the-art technology in our classrooms, labs, meeting areas and collaboration spaces. In fall 2019, the College will expand to the 9th Floor, which will include additional offices, classrooms, a research lab, a maker space, and a ground-breaking CCI Corporate Partner DXC Technology Innovation Lab.

The University

Drexel University is a comprehensive global research university with a unique model of experiential learning that combines academic rigor with one of the nation's premier cooperative education programs. U.S. News & World Report ranked Drexel for the first time in 2018 in the "Most International Students" category under national universities, coming in at number 27 with 13 percent of the University's undergraduate student population enrolled from abroad. Drexel also ranked 13th in the Most Innovative Schools category. For the third annual Wall Street Journal and Times Higher Education College Rankings, Drexel moved ten spots ahead of last year's listing to place 74th out of 968 U.S. colleges and universities. As in the past two years' rankings, Drexel made the top 8 percent of ranked institutions in the country this year. In a 2017 report (Concept to Commercialization: The Best Universities for Technology Transfer) released by the Milken Institute, Drexel was ranked 46th out of 225 universities across the country based on its technology transfer, or ability to translate its academic innovators' research into actual technologies, products, and research-driven startups.

Drexel is known for its leadership in experiential learning and career-minded approach to education. Drexel has built its global reputation on core achievements that include leadership in experiential learning through Drexel Co-op; a history of academic technology firsts; and recognition as a model of best practices in translational, use-inspired research.

The Faculty and Their Research

With an emphasis on experiential learning, CCI's approximately 70 full-time faculty members come from elite universities around the world, including Harvard University, University of Pennsylvania, New York University, Columbia University, University of California – Berkeley, and Brown University. Research is conducted in multidisciplinary clusters that are structured to address vital issues at the forefront of today's leading industries, including key areas such as computer science, computer security, human-centered computing, informatics and data science, library and information science, and systems and software engineering.

CCI faculty are engaged in collaborative, interdisciplinary initiatives in teaching and research among two departments: Computer Science and Information Science. The Department of Computer Science offers undergraduate and graduate degrees in computer science and software engineering, and includes world-class instructors and researchers in the field, integrating foundational computing theory with practical applications. The Department of Information Science leverages faculty research and teaching expertise in areas such as informatics and data science, library and information science, digital content management, computer security, and human-computer interaction and user experience to offer core undergraduate and graduate programs in information science. The department seeks to educate the next generation of informatics, computer, data, and library scientists to solve complex problems in an increasingly information-driven world.

Additional information on faculty members is available at http://drexelcci.info/faculty.

Applying

Specific information about applying to any of the CCI graduate programs can be found at http://drexel.edu/cci/admissions/graduate-professional-development/.

Correspondence and Information

College of Computing & Informatics
3675 Market Street, Suite 1000
Philadelphia, Pennsylvania 19104
United States
Phone: 215-895-2474
E-mail: cciinfo@drexel.edu
Website: http://drexel.edu/cci/

PENN STATE UNIVERSITY PARK

Department of Computer Science and Engineering within the School of Electrical Engineering and Computer Science

PennState
College of Engineering | ELECTRICAL ENGINEERING AND COMPUTER SCIENCE

Programs of Study

The Department of Computer Science and Engineering's (CSE) is housed within the School of Electrical Engineering and Computer Science (EECS). Its mission is to educate computer scientists and computer engineers of the highest caliber, and to discover and disseminate new findings from rigorous research.

The department offers three graduate programs. Students may start in a master's program and then continue in the Ph.D. program. Students from our programs go on to pursue careers as software/hardware engineers, mobile and software application developers, cybersecurity analysts, digital designers, computer architects, and more.

Ph.D. in Computer Science and Engineering: All students in the Ph.D. program are required to pass a qualifying examination within the first three regular semesters, complete 33 credits of course work (21 credits if the student has an M.S. degree), pass a comprehensive examination, conduct research and pass the final defense examination.

Master of Science (M.S.) in Computer Science and Engineering: This program requires the completion of 30 credits including 6 credits of research for an M.S. thesis. Students interested in an M.S. in CSE should have already successfully completed Operating Systems Design and Construction, Introduction to Computer Architecture, Programming Language Concepts, Data Structures and Algorithms, and Logical Design of Digital Systems or Introduction to the Theory of Computation.

Master of Engineering (M.Eng.) in Computer Science and Engineering: This one-year intensive master's degree program is meant to prepare students for work in industry. As such, there is no thesis required, although a final paper is required during the last semester of the program.

Research

Graduate students at Penn State enjoy a supportive research environment that provides modern facilities and sufficient funding to make groundbreaking discoveries. According to National Science Foundation data for 2017, Penn State's computer science and engineering program ranked 9th for research and development expenditures, making research a priority.

The School of Electrical Engineering and Computer Science was created in the spring of 2015 to allow greater access to courses offered by both CSE and Electrical Engineering departments and to foster collaborative re-search. Some of the areas of research, specifically related to CSE, include:

- Communications, information theory, and coding over networked systems
- Computational science
- Computer architecture
- Computer networks and mobile systems
- Computer vision and image processing
- Data science and artificial intelligence
- Electronic materials and devices
- Integrated circuits and systems
- Operating systems and cloud computing
- Programming languages and compilers
- Security and privacy
- Theoretical computer science

The Department hosts prominent large-scale research programs including the Collaborative Research Alliance for the Science of Security, a Collaborative Technology Alliance for Network Science, multiple DARPA awards, and both the prestigious NSF Expedition and an NSF Frontier awards. In addition, most of the faculty are well funded through various grants from several federal and industrial sources. State-of-the-art research labs provide a conducive environment work in many areas such as computer architecture and systems, computer vision and robotics, embedded system design and VLSI, networking and security, high performance computing, bioinformatics and machine learning/data science.

Financial Aid

Graduate students at Penn State often receive research assistantships and teaching assistantships to help fund their education. Approximately 4,000 assistantships are awarded each year. Many research assistantships are 48-week appointments, covering the 36-week period of the academic year and an additional 12 weeks for the two summer session terms.

The majority of CSE Ph.D. students receive research and/or teaching assistantships during their studies.

In addition, paid positions are often available in the department.

Cost of Study

The tuition rate for the 2018–19 academic year is $18,454 per year for Pennsylvania residents and $34,858 per year for non-Pennsylvania residents.

Living and Housing Costs

On-campus housing is available. University Park offers graduate and family housing ranging from single unfurnished apartments up to three-bedroom family apartments. Ample off-campus housing is also popular with graduate students.

Location

The University is located in the beautiful town of State College, which is considered one of the best college towns in the United States. The area has 130,000 residents and offers a wide variety of cultural and outdoor recreational activities, as well as outstanding University events, from collegiate sports to fine arts productions.

The University

Penn State, founded in 1855, is the Commonwealth of Pennsylvania's sole land-grant institution and its largest public university. It is a top twenty-five research university. Penn State's research expenditures for each of the last four years have exceeded $860 million, with $970 million in research expenditures for 2018, making it a leader in research and development across the country. Penn State ranks 20th among public universities nationally, according to U.S. News & World Report, and is ranked 43rd for the best universities in the world for the quality of education of its students and the research prowess of its faculty, according to the Center for World University Rankings.

Faculty

Research plays an important role in CSE graduate education. The 48 faculty members work on some of the most leading-edge research areas in bioinformatics, computational science, computer architecture, communication networks and mobile computing, computer vision, databases, data science and artificial intelligence (AI), embedded and hardware systems, enterprise computing and IT infrastructure management, numerical analysis, operating systems and cloud computing, programming languages and compiler, security and privacy, and theoretical computer science.

A full listing of CSE faculty and their areas of research is available at https://www.eecs.psu.edu/departments/cse-faculty-list.aspx.

Applying

Admission to the CSE department is extremely competitive. Applicants are expected to have a B.S. degree in computer science and engineering, computer engineering, computer science, or a closely related degree. Exceptional candidates from related fields are also welcomed to apply. Only well-prepared and highly competitive candidates should apply to enter the Ph.D. program directly from the B.S. program, because they will be required to take the candidacy examinations within one year after entry into the program.

Applicants are required to complete the University's application form. They must provide formal transcripts, general GRE scores (verbal, quantitative, and analytical writing), letters of reference, and a personal statement of technical interests, goals, and experience.

For consideration as a teaching assistant, an international student whose first language is not English must submit a TOEFL score with a minimum of 80 and a Test of Spoken English (TSE) speaking score of 19 or more. It should be noted that students admitted to the graduate program who do not demonstrate satisfactory proficiency in English will be required to take additional English and/or Speech Communication courses.

Students who intend to continue from the M.S. into the Ph.D. program should apply to resume study at least one semester prior to the transition. An updated personal statement and a letter of reference from a professor should accompany that request. Standards for entry to the Ph.D. program are generally more rigorous than for the M.S. program. Satisfactory completion of the M.S. program does not guarantee admission to the Ph.D. program.

Additional information regarding the application process is available at https://www.eecs.psu.edu/students/graduate/EECS-How-to-apply-CSE .aspx.

Correspondence and Information

Jennifer Houser
School of Electrical Engineering and Computer Science
The Pennsylvania State University
207 Electrical Engineering West
University Park, Pennsylvania 16802
United States
Phone: 814-865-9505
Fax: 814-865-7647
E-mail: jjh2@engr.psu.edu
Website: https://www.eecs.psu.edu/students/graduate/Graduate-Degree-
   Programs-CSE.aspx

Section 9
Electrical and Computer Engineering

This section contains a directory of institutions offering graduate work in electrical and computer engineering, followed by in-depth entries submitted by institutions that chose to prepare detailed program descriptions. Additional information about programs listed in the directory but not augmented by an in-depth entry may be obtained by writing directly to the dean of a graduate school or chair of a department at the address given in the directory.

For programs offering related work, see also in this book *Computer Science and Information Technology, Energy and Power Engineering, Engineering and Applied Sciences, Industrial Engineering,* and *Mechanical Engineering and Mechanics.* In another guide in this series:

Graduate Programs in the Physical Sciences, Mathematics, Agricultural Sciences, the Environment & Natural Resources
See *Mathematical Sciences* and *Physics*

CONTENTS

Program Directories

Featured Schools: Displays and Close-Ups

See:

Computer Engineering

Air Force Institute of Technology, Graduate School of Engineering and Management, Department of Electrical and Computer Engineering, Dayton, OH 45433-7765. Offers computer engineering (MS, PhD); computer systems/science (MS); electrical engineering (MS, PhD); electro-optics (MS, PhD). *Accreditation:* ABET (one or more programs are accredited). *Program availability:* Part-time. *Degree requirements:* For master's, thesis; for doctorate, thesis/dissertation. *Entrance requirements:* For master's and doctorate, GRE General Test, minimum GPA of 3.0, U.S. citizenship. *Faculty research:* Remote sensing, information survivability, microelectronics, computer networks, artificial intelligence.

American University of Beirut, Graduate Programs, Maroun Semaan Faculty of Engineering and Architecture, Beirut, Lebanon. Offers applied energy (ME); civil engineering (PhD); electrical and computer engineering (PhD); energy studies (MS); engineering management (MEM); environmental and water resources (ME); environmental technology (MSES); mechanical engineering (ME, PhD); urban design (MUD); urban planning and policy (MUPP). For progreen diploma: LAU/AUC. *Program availability:* Part-time, 100% online. *Faculty:* 105 full-time (25 women), 102 part-time/adjunct (33 women). *Students:* 380 full-time (186 women), 100 part-time (38 women). Average age 27. 489 applicants, 64% accepted, 127 enrolled. In 2018, 109 master's, 14 doctorates awarded. Terminal master's awarded for partial completion of doctoral program. *Degree requirements:* For master's, one foreign language, comprehensive exam, thesis optional; for doctorate, one foreign language, comprehensive exam, thesis/dissertation. *Entrance requirements:* For doctorate, GRE. Additional exam requirements/recommendations for international students: Required—TOEFL (minimum score 575 paper-based; 88 iBT), AUB-EN; Recommended—IELTS (minimum score 7). *Application deadline:* For fall admission, 4/4 for domestic and international students; for spring admission, 11/3 for domestic and international students; for summer admission, 4/4 for domestic and international students. Application fee: $50. *Expenses: Tuition:* Full-time $17,748; part-time $986 per credit. *Required fees:* $762. Tuition and fees vary according to course load and program. *Financial support:* In 2018–19, 15 students received support, including 92 fellowships with full tuition reimbursements available (averaging $14,400 per year), 80 research assistantships with full and partial tuition reimbursements available (averaging $5,300 per year), 162 teaching assistantships with full and partial tuition reimbursements available (averaging $1,400 per year); scholarships/grants, tuition waivers (full and partial), and unspecified assistantships also available. Financial award application deadline: 4/4. *Faculty research:* All areas in engineering, architecture and design. *Total annual research expenditures:* $1.5 million. *Unit head:* Prof. Alan Shihade, Dean, 961-1-374374 Ext. 3400, Fax: 961-1-744462, E-mail: as20@aub.edu.lb. *Application contact:* Dr. Salim Kanaan, Director, Admissions Office, 961-1-374374 Ext. 2590, Fax: 961-1-750775, E-mail: sk00@aub.edu.lb.
Website: https://www.aub.edu.lb/msfea/pages/default.aspx

American University of Sharjah, Graduate Programs, Sharjah, United Arab Emirates. Offers accounting (MS); biomedical engineering (MSBME); business administration (MBA); chemical engineering (MS Ch E); civil engineering (MSCE); computer engineering (MS); electrical engineering (MSEE); engineering systems management (MS, PhD); mathematics (MS); mechanical engineering (MSME); mechatronics engineering (MS); teaching English to speakers of other languages (MA); translation and interpreting (MA); urban planning (MUP). *Program availability:* Part-time, evening/weekend. *Degree requirements:* For master's, thesis (for some programs). *Entrance requirements:* For master's, GMAT (for MBA). Additional exam requirements/recommendations for international students: Required—TOEFL (minimum score 550 paper-based; 80 iBT), TWE (minimum score 5); Recommended—IELTS (minimum score 6.5). Electronic applications accepted. *Faculty research:* Water pollution, management and waste water treatment, energy and sustainability, air pollution, Islamic finance, family business and small and medium enterprises.

Arizona State University at the Tempe campus, Ira A. Fulton Schools of Engineering, School of Computing, Informatics, and Decision Systems Engineering, Tempe, AZ 85287-8809. Offers computer engineering (MS, PhD); computer science (MCS, MS, PhD); industrial engineering (MS, PhD); software engineering (MS). *Program availability:* Part-time, evening/weekend, online learning. Terminal master's awarded for partial completion of doctoral program. *Degree requirements:* For master's, comprehensive exam (for some programs), portfolio (MCS); interactive Program of Study (iPOS) submitted before completing 50 percent of required credit hours; for doctorate, comprehensive exam, thesis/dissertation, interactive Program of Study (iPOS) submitted before completing 50 percent of required credit hours. *Entrance requirements:* For master's, GRE, minimum GPA of 3.0 or equivalent in last 2 years of work leading to bachelor's degree; for doctorate, GRE, minimum GPA of 3.0 in last 2 years of work leading to bachelor's degree. Additional exam requirements/recommendations for international students: Required—TOEFL, IELTS, or PTE. Electronic applications accepted. *Expenses:* Contact institution. *Faculty research:* Artificial intelligence, cyberphysical and embedded systems, health informatics, information assurance and security, information management/multimedia/visualization, network science, personalized learning/educational games, production logistics, software and systems engineering, statistical modeling and data mining.

Atlantis University, School of Engineering, Miami, FL 33132. Offers computer engineering (MS).

Auburn University, Graduate School, Ginn College of Engineering, Department of Electrical and Computer Engineering, Auburn University, AL 36849. Offers MEE, MS, PhD. *Program availability:* Part-time. *Degree requirements:* For master's, comprehensive exam, thesis (for some programs); for doctorate, thesis/dissertation. *Entrance requirements:* For master's and doctorate, GRE General Test, GRE Subject Test. Electronic applications accepted. *Expenses:* Tuition, state resident: full-time $11,282; part-time $535 per credit hour. Tuition, nonresident: full-time $30,542; part-time $1605 per credit hour. *Required fees:* $826 per semester. Tuition and fees vary according to degree level and program. *Faculty research:* Power systems, energy conversion, electronics, electromagnetics, digital systems.

Baylor University, Graduate School, School of Engineering and Computer Science, Department of Electrical and Computer Engineering, Waco, TX 76798. Offers MS, PhD. *Faculty:* 17 full-time (2 women). *Students:* 43 full-time (7 women), 5 part-time (0 women); includes 28 minority (3 Black or African American, non-Hispanic/Latino; 1 American Indian or Alaska Native, non-Hispanic/Latino; 21 Asian, non-Hispanic/Latino; 3 Hispanic/Latino), 19 international. Average age 28. 47 applicants, 21% accepted, 3 enrolled. In 2018, 8 master's, 3 doctorates awarded. Terminal master's awarded for partial completion of doctoral program. *Degree requirements:* For master's, thesis (for some programs); for doctorate, comprehensive exam, thesis/dissertation. *Entrance requirements:* For master's and doctorate, GRE. Additional exam requirements/recommendations for international students: Required—TOEFL (minimum score 550 paper-based; 100 iBT). *Application deadline:* For fall admission, 2/15 for domestic and international students; for spring admission, 12/1 for domestic and international students. Applications are processed on a rolling basis. Application fee: $50. Electronic applications accepted. *Expenses:* Contact institution. *Financial support:* In 2018–19, 17 students received support, including 22 research assistantships with full tuition reimbursements available (averaging $18,750 per year), 17 teaching assistantships with full tuition reimbursements available (averaging $18,750 per year); fellowships, institutionally sponsored loans, scholarships/grants, health care benefits, and unspecified assistantships also available. Financial award application deadline: 4/15. *Faculty research:* Energy systems, medical devices, biosensors, specialty optical fibers, molecular electronics and theory. *Unit head:* Dr. Kwang Y. Lee, Chair, 254-710-4817, Fax: 254-710-3010, E-mail: kwang_y_lee@baylor.edu. *Application contact:* Dr. Ian Gravagne, Electrical and Computer Engineering Graduate Director, 254-710-4194, Fax: 254-710-3010.
Website: http://www.ecs.baylor.edu/ece/

Baylor University, Graduate School, School of Engineering and Computer Science, Department of Engineering, Waco, TX 76798. Offers biomedical engineering (MSBME); electrical and computer engineering (MSECE, PhD); engineering (ME); mechanical engineering (MSME). *Faculty:* 14 full-time (1 woman). *Students:* 7 full-time (3 women), 4 part-time (0 women); includes 4 minority (2 Asian, non-Hispanic/Latino; 2 Hispanic/Latino), 2 international. In 2018, 14 master's, 8 doctorates awarded. *Unit head:* Dr. Mike Thompson, Graduate Director, 254-710-4188. *Application contact:* Linda Keer, Administrative Assistant, 254-710-4188, Fax: 254-710-3870, E-mail: linda_kerr@baylor.edu.
Website: http://www.ecs.baylor.edu/engineering

Boise State University, College of Engineering, Department of Electrical and Computer Engineering, Boise, ID 83725-0399. Offers M Engr, MS, PhD. *Program availability:* Part-time. Terminal master's awarded for partial completion of doctoral program. *Degree requirements:* For master's, comprehensive exam, thesis (for some programs); for doctorate, thesis/dissertation. *Entrance requirements:* For master's, GRE General Test, minimum GPA of 3.0. Additional exam requirements/recommendations for international students: Required—TOEFL (minimum score 550 paper-based; 80 iBT), IELTS (minimum score 6). Electronic applications accepted.

Boston University, College of Engineering, Department of Electrical and Computer Engineering, Boston, MA 02215. Offers computer engineering (M Eng, MS, PhD). *Program availability:* Part-time. *Students:* 274 full-time (71 women), 76 part-time (23 women); includes 20 minority (2 Black or African American, non-Hispanic/Latino; 16 Asian, non-Hispanic/Latino; 2 Two or more races, non-Hispanic/Latino), 275 international. Average age 24. 1,304 applicants, 38% accepted, 144 enrolled. In 2018, 124 master's, 15 doctorates awarded. Terminal master's awarded for partial completion of doctoral program. *Degree requirements:* For master's, thesis (for some programs); for doctorate, comprehensive exam, thesis/dissertation. *Entrance requirements:* For master's and doctorate, GRE General Test. Additional exam requirements/recommendations for international students: Required—TOEFL (minimum score 90 iBT), IELTS (minimum score 7). *Financial support:* Application deadline: 1/15. *Faculty research:* Communications and computer networks; signal, image, video, and multimedia processing; solid-state materials, devices, and photonics; systems, control, and reliable computing; VLSI, computer engineering and high-performance computing. *Unit head:* Dr. William C. Karl, Interim Chairman, 617-353-9880, Fax: 617-353-6440, E-mail: wckarl@bu.edu. *Application contact:* Dr. William C. Karl, Interim Chairman, 617-353-9880, Fax: 617-353-6440, E-mail: wckarl@bu.edu.
Website: http://www.bu.edu/ece/

Boston University, Metropolitan College, Department of Computer Science, Boston, MA 02215. Offers computer information systems (MS), including computer networks, data analytics, database management and business intelligence, health informatics, IT project management, security, Web application development; computer networks (Certificate); computer science (MS); data analytics (Certificate); digital forensics (Certificate); health informatics (Certificate); information technology project management (Certificate); software development (MS); software engineering in health care systems (Certificate); telecommunications (MS), including security. *Program availability:* Part-time, evening/weekend, online learning. *Faculty:* 16 full-time (3 women), 52 part-time/adjunct (5 women). *Students:* 201 full-time (57 women), 953 part-time (252 women); includes 285 minority (57 Black or African American, non-Hispanic/Latino; 2 American Indian or Alaska Native, non-Hispanic/Latino; 139 Asian, non-Hispanic/Latino; 67 Hispanic/Latino; 1 Native Hawaiian or other Pacific Islander, non-Hispanic/Latino; 19 Two or more races, non-Hispanic/Latino), 333 international. Average age 31. 1,079 applicants, 72% accepted, 297 enrolled. In 2018, 395 master's awarded. *Entrance requirements:* For master's and Certificate, official transcripts from regionally-accredited bachelor's degree program, 3 letters of recommendation, professional resume, personal statement. Additional exam requirements/recommendations for international students: Required—TOEFL (minimum score 84 iBT), IELTS. *Application deadline:* For fall admission, 8/1 priority date for domestic students, 6/1 priority date for international students; for spring admission, 12/1 priority date for domestic students, 11/15 priority date for international students; for summer admission, 4/1 priority date for domestic students, 3/1 priority date for international students. Applications are processed on a rolling basis. Application fee: $85. Electronic applications accepted. *Expenses:* Contact institution. *Financial support:* In 2018–19, 11 research assistantships (averaging $8,400 per year), 23 teaching assistantships (averaging $3,400 per year) were awarded; unspecified assistantships also available. Support available to part-time students. Financial award applicants required to submit FAFSA. *Faculty research:* Artificial intelligence and machine learning, security and forensics, web technologies, software engineering, programming languages, medical informatics, information systems and IT project management. *Unit head:* Dr. Anatoly Temkin, Chair, 617-353-2566, Fax: 617-353-2367, E-mail: csinfo@bu.edu. *Application contact:* Enrollment Services, 617-353-6004, E-mail: met@bu.edu.
Website: http://www.bu.edu/csmet/

Brigham Young University, Graduate Studies, Ira A. Fulton College of Engineering, Department of Electrical and Computer Engineering, Provo, UT 84602. Offers electrical & computer engineering (PhD). *Faculty:* 22 full-time (1 woman), 1 part-time/adjunct (0 women). *Students:* 89 full-time (5 women); includes 4 minority (all Two or more races, non-Hispanic/Latino), 15 international. Average age 28. 40 applicants, 48% accepted, 19 enrolled. In 2018, 27 master's, 9 doctorates awarded. *Degree requirements:* For master's, thesis; for doctorate, comprehensive exam, thesis/dissertation. *Entrance requirements:* For master's and doctorate, GRE General Test, Minimum GPA of 3.2 in last 60 hours of course work. Additional exam requirements/recommendations for international students: Required—TOEFL (minimum score 580 paper-based; 85 iBT). *Application deadline:* For fall admission, 1/15 for domestic and international students; for winter admission, 8/15 for domestic and international students. Application fee: $50. Electronic applications accepted. *Financial support:* In 2018–19, 66 students received support, including 2 fellowships with full tuition reimbursements available (averaging

$21,240 per year), 63 research assistantships with full tuition reimbursements available (averaging $15,360 per year), 12 teaching assistantships with full tuition reimbursements available (averaging $16,200 per year); scholarships/grants also available. Financial award application deadline: 1/15; financial award applicants required to submit FAFSA. *Faculty research:* Microwave earth remote sensing, configurable computing and embedded systems, MEMS semiconductors, integrated electro-optics, multiple-agent intelligent coordinated control systems for unmanned air vehicles. *Total annual research expenditures:* $3.7 million. *Unit head:* Dr. Aaron Hawkins, Department Chair, 801-422-4012, Fax: 801-422-0201, E-mail: hawkins@ee.byu.edu. *Application contact:* Janalyn L. Mergist, Graduate Secretary, 801-422-4013, Fax: 801-422-0201, E-mail: janalyn@ee.byu.edu.
Website: http://www.ee.byu.edu/

Brown University, Graduate School, School of Engineering, Program in Electrical Sciences and Computer Engineering, Providence, RI 02912. Offers Sc M, PhD. *Degree requirements:* For doctorate, thesis/dissertation, preliminary exam.

Bucknell University, Graduate Studies, College of Engineering, Department of Electrical and Computer Engineering, Lewisburg, PA 17837. Offers MSEE. *Program availability:* Part-time. *Degree requirements:* For master's, thesis. *Entrance requirements:* For master's, GRE General Test, minimum GPA of 3.0. Additional exam requirements/recommendations for international students: Required—TOEFL (minimum score 600 paper-based).

California State University, Chico, Office of Graduate Studies, College of Engineering, Computer Science, and Construction Management, Electrical and Computer Engineering Department, Option in Computer Engineering, Chico, CA 95929-0722. Offers MS. *Students:* 9 full-time (2 women), 5 part-time (2 women); includes 5 minority (all Asian, non-Hispanic/Latino). 25 applicants, 72% accepted, 3 enrolled. *Degree requirements:* For master's, comprehensive exam, thesis or project plan. *Entrance requirements:* For master's, GRE General Test, Fall Admissions only. Two letters of recommendation, statement of purpose, departmental letter of recommendation access waiver form. Additional exam requirements/recommendations for international students: Required—TOEFL (minimum score 550 paper-based; 80 iBT), IELTS (minimum score 6.8), PTE (minimum score 59). *Application deadline:* For fall admission, 3/1 priority date for domestic students, 3/1 for international students; for spring admission, 9/15 priority date for domestic students, 9/15 for international students. Applications are processed on a rolling basis. Application fee: $55. Electronic applications accepted. *Expenses: Tuition, area resident:* Full-time $4622; part-time $3116 per unit. *Tuition, state resident:* full-time $4622; part-time $3116 per unit. *Tuition, nonresident:* full-time $10,634. *Required fees:* $2160; $1620 per year. Tuition and fees vary according to class time and program. *Financial support:* Fellowships, research assistantships, teaching assistantships, career-related internships or fieldwork, Federal Work-Study, scholarships/grants, traineeships, health care benefits, unspecified assistantships, and stipends available. Support available to part-time students. Financial award application deadline: 3/2; financial award applicants required to submit FAFSA. *Unit head:* Tyson Henry, Chair, 530-898-6442, Fax: 530-898-5995, E-mail: trhenry@csuchico.edu. *Application contact:* Micah Lehner, Graduate Admissions Coordinator, 530-898-5416, Fax: 530-898-3342, E-mail: mlehner@csuchico.edu.
Website: http://catalog.csuchico.edu/viewer/19/ENGR/CMPENONEBS.html

California State University, Fresno, Division of Research and Graduate Studies, Lyles College of Engineering, Department of Electrical and Computer Engineering, Fresno, CA 93740-8027. Offers computer engineering (MSE); electrical engineering (MSE). *Program availability:* Part-time, evening/weekend. *Degree requirements:* For master's, thesis or alternative. *Entrance requirements:* For master's, GRE General Test, minimum GPA of 2.7. Additional exam requirements/recommendations for international students: Required—TOEFL. Electronic applications accepted. *Faculty research:* Research in electromagnetic devices.

California State University, Fullerton, Graduate Studies, College of Engineering and Computer Science, Program in Computer Engineering, Fullerton, CA 92831-3599. Offers MS.

California State University, Long Beach, Graduate Studies, College of Engineering, Department of Computer Engineering and Computer Science, Long Beach, CA 90840. Offers computer engineering (MSCS); computer science (MSCS). *Program availability:* Part-time. *Degree requirements:* For master's, thesis or alternative. *Entrance requirements:* Additional exam requirements/recommendations for international students: Required—TOEFL. *Application deadline:* For fall admission, 3/1 for domestic students. Application fee: $55. Electronic applications accepted. *Expenses: Required fees:* $2628 per term. Tuition and fees vary according to class time, course level, course load, degree level, campus/location and program. *Financial support:* Teaching assistantships, Federal Work-Study, institutionally sponsored loans, scholarships/grants, and unspecified assistantships available. Financial award application deadline: 3/2; financial award applicants required to submit FAFSA. *Faculty research:* Artificial intelligence, software engineering, computer simulation and modeling, user-interface design, networking. *Unit head:* Mehrdad Aliasgari, Chair, 562-985-4285, E-mail: mehrdad.aliasgari@csulb.edu. *Application contact:* Dr. Bo Fu, Graduate Advisor, 562-985-4386, E-mail: bo.fu@csulb.edu.
Website: http://www.csulb.edu/college-of-engineering/computer-engineering-computer-science

Carnegie Mellon University, Carnegie Institute of Technology, Department of Electrical and Computer Engineering, Pittsburgh, PA 15213-3891. Offers MS, PhD. *Program availability:* Part-time. *Degree requirements:* For master's, thesis; for doctorate, thesis/dissertation, qualifying exam, teaching experience. *Entrance requirements:* For master's and doctorate, GRE General Test. Additional exam requirements/recommendations for international students: Required—TOEFL. *Faculty research:* Computer-aided design, solid-state devices, VLSI, processing, robotics and controls, signal processing, data systems storage.

Case Western Reserve University, School of Graduate Studies, Case School of Engineering, Department of Computer and Data Sciences, Cleveland, OH 44106. Offers computer engineering (MS, PhD); computing and information sciences (MS, PhD); electrical engineering (MS, PhD); systems and control engineering (MS, PhD). *Program availability:* Part-time, evening/weekend, online only, 100% online. *Faculty:* 31 full-time (2 women). *Students:* 228 full-time (49 women), 17 part-time (3 women); includes 18 minority (13 Asian, non-Hispanic/Latino; 3 Hispanic/Latino; 2 Two or more races, non-Hispanic/Latino), 180 international. In 2018, 29 master's, 16 doctorates awarded. Terminal master's awarded for partial completion of doctoral program. *Degree requirements:* For master's, thesis; for doctorate, thesis/dissertation, qualifying exam, teaching experience. *Entrance requirements:* For master's and doctorate, GRE General Test. Additional exam requirements/recommendations for international students: Required—TOEFL. *Application deadline:* For fall admission, 2/1 for domestic students; for spring admission, 11/1 for domestic students. Applications are processed on a rolling basis. Application fee: $50. *Expenses: Tuition:* Full-time $45,168; part-time $1939 per credit hour. *Required fees:* $36; $18 per semester. $18 per semester. *Financial support:* In 2018–19, 1 fellowship with tuition reimbursement, 72 research assistantships with tuition reimbursements, 10 teaching assistantships were awarded; career-related

internships or fieldwork, Federal Work-Study, and institutionally sponsored loans also available. Support available to part-time students. Financial award application deadline: 3/1; financial award applicants required to submit FAFSA. *Faculty research:* Micro-/nano-systems; robotics and haptics; applied artificial intelligence; automation; computer-aided design and testing of digital systems. *Total annual research expenditures:* $5.1 million. *Unit head:* Jing Li, Interim Department Chair, 216-368-0356, E-mail: jxl175@case.edu. *Application contact:* Angela Beca, Student Affairs Specialist, 216-368-2800, Fax: 216-368-2801, E-mail: angela.beca@case.edu.
Website: www.engineering.case.edu/eecs

The Citadel, The Military College of South Carolina, Citadel Graduate College, School of Engineering, Department of Electrical and Computer Engineering, Charleston, SC 29409. Offers computer engineering (Graduate Certificate); electrical engineering (MS). *Program availability:* Part-time, evening/weekend. *Degree requirements:* For master's, 30 hours of coursework with minimum GPA of 3.0 on hours earned at The Citadel. *Entrance requirements:* For master's, GRE, 2 letters of recommendation; official transcript of baccalaureate degree from an ABET accredited engineering program or approved alternative. Additional exam requirements/recommendations for international students: Required—TOEFL (minimum score 550 paper-based; 79 iBT). Electronic applications accepted. *Expenses:* Tuition, state resident: part-time $595 per credit hour. Tuition, nonresident: part-time $1020 per credit hour. *Required fees:* $90 per term.

Clemson University, Graduate School, College of Engineering, Computing and Applied Sciences, Holcombe Department of Electrical and Computer Engineering, Clemson, SC 29634. Offers computer engineering (MS, PhD); electrical engineering (M Engr, MS, PhD). *Program availability:* Part-time, evening/weekend, blended/hybrid learning. *Faculty:* 33 full-time (3 women). *Students:* 139 full-time (24 women), 36 part-time (3 women); includes 9 minority (4 Black or African American, non-Hispanic/Latino; 1 American Indian or Alaska Native, non-Hispanic/Latino; 2 Asian, non-Hispanic/Latino; 1 Hispanic/Latino; 1 Two or more races, non-Hispanic/Latino), 107 international. Average age 27. 393 applicants, 42% accepted, 51 enrolled. In 2018, 34 master's, 14 doctorates awarded. *Degree requirements:* For master's, comprehensive exam (for some programs), thesis (for some programs); for doctorate, comprehensive exam, thesis/dissertation, departmental qualifying exam. *Entrance requirements:* For master's and doctorate, GRE General Test, unofficial transcripts, letters of recommendation. Additional exam requirements/recommendations for international students: Required—TOEFL (minimum score 80 paper-based; 95 iBT); Recommended—IELTS (minimum score 7), TSE (minimum score 54). *Application deadline:* For fall admission, 1/15 priority date for domestic students, 4/15 for international students; for spring admission, 9/15 priority date for domestic students, 9/15 for international students. Applications are processed on a rolling basis. Application fee: $80 ($90 for international students). Electronic applications accepted. *Expenses:* $6,823 per semester full-time resident, $14,023 per semester full-time non-resident, $833 per credit hour part-time resident, $1,731 per credit hour part-time non-resident, online $1,264 per credit hour, $4,938 doctoral programs resident, $10,405 doctoral programs non-resident, $1,144 full-time graduate assistant, other fees may apply per session. *Financial support:* In 2018–19, 176 students received support, including 13 fellowships with full and partial tuition reimbursements available (averaging $4,731 per year), 85 research assistantships with full and partial tuition reimbursements available (averaging $17,365 per year), 59 teaching assistantships with full and partial tuition reimbursements available (averaging $18,536 per year); career-related internships or fieldwork and unspecified assistantships also available. Financial award application deadline: 1/15. *Faculty research:* Applied use of emerging heterogeneous computing architectures; communications theory, coding theory, detecting and estimation theory; cognitive radios; organic electronics: polymer-based devices, micro-optics and nano-photonics. *Total annual research expenditures:* $5.1 million. *Unit head:* Dr. Daniel Noneaker, Department Chair, 864-656-0100, E-mail: dnoneak@clemson.edu. *Application contact:* Dr. Harlan Russell, Graduate Program Coordinator, 864-656-7214, E-mail: harlanr@clemson.edu.
Website: http://www.clemson.edu/cecas/departments/ece/index.html

Colorado Technical University Aurora, Program in Computer Engineering, Aurora, CO 80014. Offers MS.

Colorado Technical University Colorado Springs, Graduate Studies, Program in Computer Engineering, Colorado Springs, CO 80907. Offers MSCE. *Program availability:* Part-time, evening/weekend, online learning. *Degree requirements:* For master's, thesis or alternative.

Columbia University, Fu Foundation School of Engineering and Applied Science, Department of Electrical Engineering, New York, NY 10027. Offers computer engineering (MS); electrical engineering (MS, PhD). PhD offered through the Graduate School of Arts and Sciences. *Program availability:* Part-time, online learning. *Degree requirements:* For doctorate, thesis/dissertation, qualifying exam. *Entrance requirements:* For master's and doctorate, GRE General Test. Additional exam requirements/recommendations for international students: Required—TOEFL, IELTS, PTE. Electronic applications accepted. *Faculty research:* Media informatics and signal processing, integrated circuits and cyberphysical systems, communications systems and networking, nanoscale electronics and photonics, systems biology and neuroengineering.

Concordia University, School of Graduate Studies, Faculty of Engineering and Computer Science, Department of Electrical and Computer Engineering, Montréal, QC H3G 1M8, Canada. Offers M Eng, MA Sc, PhD. *Degree requirements:* For master's, thesis optional; for doctorate, comprehensive exam, thesis/dissertation. *Faculty research:* Computer communications and protocols, circuits and systems, graph theory, VLSI systems, microelectronics.

Cornell University, Graduate School, Graduate Fields of Engineering, Field of Electrical and Computer Engineering, Ithaca, NY 14853. Offers computer engineering (M Eng, PhD); electrical engineering (M Eng, PhD); electrical systems (M Eng, PhD); electrophysics (M Eng, PhD). *Degree requirements:* For doctorate, comprehensive exam, thesis/dissertation. *Entrance requirements:* For master's, GRE General Test, 2 letters of recommendation; for doctorate, GRE General Test, 3 letters of recommendation. Additional exam requirements/recommendations for international students: Required—TOEFL (minimum score 600 paper-based; 77 iBT). Electronic applications accepted. *Faculty research:* Communications, information theory, signal processing and power control, computer engineering, microelectromechanical systems and nanotechnology.

Dalhousie University, Faculty of Engineering, Department of Electrical and Computer Engineering, Halifax, NS B3J 1Z1, Canada. Offers M Eng, MA Sc, PhD. *Degree requirements:* For master's, thesis; for doctorate, thesis/dissertation. *Entrance requirements:* Additional exam requirements/recommendations for international students: Required—TOEFL, IELTS, CANTEST, CAEL, or Michigan English Language Assessment Battery. Electronic applications accepted. *Faculty research:* Communications, computer engineering, power engineering, electronics, systems engineering.

Dartmouth College, Thayer School of Engineering, Program in Electrical and Computer Engineering, Hanover, NH 03755. Offers MS, PhD. *Degree requirements:* For master's, thesis; for doctorate, thesis/dissertation, candidacy oral exam. *Entrance requirements:*

For master's and doctorate, GRE General Test. *Faculty research:* Analog VLSI, electromagnetic fields and waves, electronic instrumentation, microelectromechanical systems, optics, lasers and non-linear optics, power electronics and integrated power converters, networking, parallel and distributed computing, simulation, VLSI design and testing, wireless networking.

Drexel University, College of Engineering, Department of Electrical and Computer Engineering, Program in Computer Engineering, Philadelphia, PA 19104-2875. Offers MS. *Program availability:* Part-time, evening/weekend. *Degree requirements:* For master's, thesis (for some programs). Electronic applications accepted.

Duke University, Graduate School, Pratt School of Engineering, Department of Electrical and Computer Engineering, Durham, NC 27708. Offers M Eng, MS, PhD, JD/MS. Terminal master's awarded for partial completion of doctoral program. *Degree requirements:* For doctorate, thesis/dissertation. *Entrance requirements:* For master's and doctorate, GRE General Test. Additional exam requirements/recommendations for international students: Required—TOEFL (minimum score 90 iBT), IELTS (minimum score 7). Electronic applications accepted. *Faculty research:* Architecture and networking; biological applications circuits and systems; nanosystems, devices and materials; quantum computing and photonics; sensing and signals visualization; waves and metamaterials.

Duke University, Graduate School, Pratt School of Engineering, Master of Engineering Program, Durham, NC 27708-0271. Offers biomedical engineering (M Eng); civil engineering (M Eng); computational mechanics and scientific computing (M Eng); electrical and computer engineering (M Eng); environmental engineering (M Eng); materials science and engineering (M Eng); mechanical engineering (M Eng); photonics and optical sciences (M Eng); risk engineering (M Eng). *Program availability:* Part-time. *Entrance requirements:* For master's, GRE General Test, resume, 3 letters of recommendation, statement of purpose, transcripts. Additional exam requirements/recommendations for international students: Required—TOEFL. Electronic applications accepted.

East Carolina University, Graduate School, College of Engineering and Technology, Greenville, NC 27858-4353. Offers MCM, MS, PhD, Certificate. *Program availability:* Part-time, evening/weekend, online learning. *Application deadline:* For fall admission, 6/1 priority date for domestic students. *Expenses: Tuition, area resident:* Full-time $4749. Tuition, state resident: full-time $4749. Tuition, nonresident: full-time $17,898. *International tuition:* $17,898 full-time. *Required fees:* $2787. Part-time tuition and fees vary according to course load and program. *Financial support:* Application deadline: 6/1. *Unit head:* Dr. Harry Ploehn, Dean, 252-328-9600, E-mail: ploehnh17@ecu.edu. *Application contact:* Graduate School Admissions, 252-328-6012, Fax: 252-328-6071, E-mail: gradschool@ecu.edu.
Website: http://www.ecu.edu/cet/

École Polytechnique de Montréal, Graduate Programs, Department of Electrical and Computer Engineering, Montréal, QC H3C 3A7, Canada. Offers automation (M Eng, M Sc A, PhD); computer science (M Eng, M Sc A, PhD); electrical engineering (DESS); electrotechnology (M Eng, M Sc A, PhD); microelectronics (M Eng, M Sc A, PhD); microwave technology (M Eng, M Sc A, PhD). *Program availability:* Part-time, evening/weekend. *Degree requirements:* For master's, one foreign language, thesis; for doctorate, one foreign language, thesis/dissertation. *Entrance requirements:* For master's, minimum GPA of 2.75; for doctorate, minimum GPA of 3.0. *Faculty research:* Microwaves, telecommunications, software engineering.

Fairfield University, School of Engineering, Fairfield, CT 06824. Offers database management (CAS); electrical and computer engineering (MS); information security (CAS); management of technology (MS); mechanical engineering (MS); network technology (CAS); software engineering (MS); Web application development (CAS). *Program availability:* Part-time, evening/weekend. *Degree requirements:* For master's, capstone course. *Entrance requirements:* For master's, resume, 2 recommendations. Additional exam requirements/recommendations for international students: Required—TOEFL (minimum score 550 paper-based; 80 iBT) or IELTS (minimum score 6.5). Electronic applications accepted. *Expenses:* Contact institution. *Faculty research:* Artificial intelligence and information visualization, natural language processing, thermofluids, microwaves and electromagnetics, micro-/nano-manufacturing.

Fairleigh Dickinson University, Metropolitan Campus, University College: Arts, Sciences, and Professional Studies, School of Computer Sciences and Engineering, Program in Computer Engineering, Teaneck, NJ 07666-1914. Offers MS.

Florida Atlantic University, College of Engineering and Computer Science, Department of Computer and Electrical Engineering and Computer Science, Boca Raton, FL 33431-0991. Offers bioengineering (MS); computer engineering (MS, PhD); computer science (MS, PhD); electrical engineering (MS, PhD). *Program availability:* Part-time, evening/weekend. *Faculty:* 37 full-time (7 women), 2 part-time/adjunct (0 women). *Students:* 85 full-time (18 women), 140 part-time (26 women); includes 86 minority (18 Black or African American, non-Hispanic/Latino; 17 Asian, non-Hispanic/Latino; 43 Hispanic/Latino; 8 Two or more races, non-Hispanic/Latino), 60 international. Average age 32. 185 applicants, 41% accepted, 69 enrolled. In 2018, 89 master's, 11 doctorates awarded. Terminal master's awarded for partial completion of doctoral program. *Degree requirements:* For master's, thesis optional; for doctorate, thesis/dissertation, qualifying exam. *Entrance requirements:* For master's, GRE General Test, minimum GPA of 3.0; for doctorate, GRE General Test, master's degree, minimum GPA of 3.5. Additional exam requirements/recommendations for international students: Required—TOEFL (minimum score 500 paper-based; 61 iBT), IELTS (minimum score 6). *Application deadline:* For fall admission, 7/1 priority date for domestic students, 2/15 for international students; for spring admission, 11/1 for domestic students, 7/15 for international students. Applications are processed on a rolling basis. Application fee: $30. *Expenses: Tuition, area resident:* Full-time $7400; part-time $369.82 per credit. Tuition, state resident: full-time $7400; part-time $369.82 per credit. Tuition, nonresident: full-time $20,496; part-time $1024.81 per credit. *Financial support:* Fellowships, research assistantships with partial tuition reimbursements, teaching assistantships with full tuition reimbursements, career-related internships or fieldwork, and Federal Work-Study available. Support available to part-time students. Financial award application deadline: 4/1; financial award applicants required to submit FAFSA. *Faculty research:* VLSI and neural networks, communication networks, software engineering, computer architecture, multimedia and video processing. *Unit head:* Jean Mangiaracina, Graduate Program Administrator, 561-297-6482, E-mail: jmangiar@fau.edu. *Application contact:* Jean Mangiaracina, Graduate Program Administrator, 561-297-6482, E-mail: jmangiar@fau.edu.
Website: http://www.ceecs.fau.edu/

Florida Institute of Technology, College of Engineering and Science, Program in Computer Engineering, Melbourne, FL 32901-6975. Offers MS, PhD. *Program availability:* Part-time. *Students:* 42 full-time (7 women), 17 part-time (2 women); includes 9 minority (2 Black or African American, non-Hispanic/Latino; 3 Asian, non-Hispanic/Latino; 2 Hispanic/Latino; 1 Native Hawaiian or other Pacific Islander, non-Hispanic/Latino; 1 Two or more races, non-Hispanic/Latino), 39 international. Average age 30. 27 applicants, 81% accepted, 8 enrolled. In 2018, 18 master's, 6 doctorates awarded. Terminal master's awarded for partial completion of doctoral program. *Degree requirements:* For master's, comprehensive exam (for some programs), thesis optional, thesis or final examination, 30 credit hours; for doctorate, thesis/dissertation, 24 credit hours of coursework, 24 credit hours of dissertation, yearly seminar demonstrating progress. *Entrance requirements:* For master's, GRE; for doctorate, GRE, 3 letters of recommendation, resume, statement of objectives. Additional exam requirements/recommendations for international students: Required—TOEFL (minimum score 550 paper-based; 79 iBT). *Application deadline:* Applications are processed on a rolling basis. Application fee: $50. Electronic applications accepted. *Expenses: Tuition:* Full-time $22,338; part-time $1241 per credit hour. Tuition and fees vary according to degree level, campus/location and program. *Financial support:* Research assistantships, teaching assistantships, career-related internships or fieldwork, and tuition remissions available. Financial award application deadline: 3/1; financial award applicants required to submit FAFSA. *Faculty research:* Speech processing, machine learning, image processing, software systems, and wireless communication. *Unit head:* Dr. Philip Bernhard, Department Head, 321-674-7291, E-mail: pbernhar@fit.edu. *Application contact:* Mike Perry, Executive Director of Admissions, 321-674-7127, E-mail: perrymj@fit.edu.
Website: https://www.fit.edu/programs/computer-engineering-ms/

Florida International University, College of Engineering and Computing, Department of Electrical and Computer Engineering, Miami, FL 33175. Offers computer engineering (MS); electrical engineering (MS, PhD). *Program availability:* Part-time, evening/weekend. *Faculty:* 33 full-time (3 women), 17 part-time/adjunct (2 women). *Students:* 156 full-time (36 women), 31 part-time (5 women); includes 62 minority (3 Black or African American, non-Hispanic/Latino; 6 Asian, non-Hispanic/Latino; 51 Hispanic/Latino; 2 Two or more races, non-Hispanic/Latino), 107 international. Average age 29. 204 applicants, 53% accepted, 64 enrolled. In 2018, 49 master's, 22 doctorates awarded. Terminal master's awarded for partial completion of doctoral program. *Degree requirements:* For master's, thesis optional; for doctorate, comprehensive exam, thesis/dissertation. *Entrance requirements:* For master's, minimum undergraduate GPA of 3.0 in upper-level coursework, resume, letters of recommendation, letter of intent; for doctorate, GRE General Test, minimum graduate GPA of 3.3, resume, letters of recommendation, letter of intent. Additional exam requirements/recommendations for international students: Required—TOEFL (minimum score 550 paper-based; 80 iBT). *Application deadline:* For fall admission, 6/1 for domestic students, 4/1 for international students; for spring admission, 10/1 for domestic students, 9/1 for international students. Applications are processed on a rolling basis. Application fee: $30. Electronic applications accepted. *Financial support:* Institutionally sponsored loans, scholarships/grants, and unspecified assistantships available. Financial award application deadline: 3/1; financial award applicants required to submit FAFSA. *Unit head:* Dr. Shekhar Bhansali, Chair, 305-348-4439, Fax: 305-348-3747, E-mail: sbhansa@fiu.edu. *Application contact:* Nanett Rojas, Manager, Admissions Operations, 305-348-7464, Fax: 305-348-7441, E-mail: gradadm@fiu.edu.
Website: http://cec.fiu.edu

George Mason University, Volgenau School of Engineering, Department of Electrical and Computer Engineering, Fairfax, VA 22030. Offers computer engineering (MS); electrical and computer engineering (PhD, Certificate). MS programs offered jointly with Old Dominion University, University of Virginia, Virginia Commonwealth University, and Virginia Polytechnic Institute and State University. *Faculty:* 33 full-time (6 women), 32 part-time/adjunct (7 women). *Students:* 138 full-time (34 women), 176 part-time (33 women); includes 77 minority (28 Black or African American, non-Hispanic/Latino; 26 Asian, non-Hispanic/Latino; 20 Hispanic/Latino; 3 Two or more races, non-Hispanic/Latino), 117 international. Average age 30. 244 applicants, 87% accepted, 76 enrolled. In 2018, 130 master's, 13 doctorates, 33 other advanced degrees awarded. *Degree requirements:* For master's, thesis optional; for doctorate, comprehensive exam, thesis or scholarly paper. *Entrance requirements:* For master's, GRE, personal goals statement; 2 official copies of transcripts; self-evaluation form; 3 letters of recommendation; resume; official bank statement; photocopy of passport; proof of financial support; for doctorate, GRE (waived for GMU electrical and computer engineering master's graduates with minimum GPA of 3.0), personal goals statement; 2 official copies of transcripts; self-evaluation form; 3 letters of recommendation; resume; official bank statement; photocopy of passport; proof of financial support. Additional exam requirements/recommendations for international students: Required—TOEFL (minimum score 575 paper-based; 88 iBT), IELTS (minimum score 6.5), PTE (minimum score 59). *Application deadline:* For fall admission, 12/1 priority date for domestic and international students; for spring admission, 8/15 priority date for domestic and international students. Application fee: $75 ($80 for international students). Electronic applications accepted. *Expenses:* $589 per credit in-state, $1,346.75 per credit out-of-state. *Financial support:* In 2018–19, 77 students received support, including 3 fellowships (averaging $13,200 per year), 33 research assistantships with tuition reimbursements available (averaging $17,231 per year), 42 teaching assistantships with tuition reimbursements available (averaging $12,246 per year); career-related internships or fieldwork, Federal Work-Study, scholarships/grants, unspecified assistantships, and health care benefits (for full-time research or teaching assistantship recipients) also available. Support available to part-time students. Financial award application deadline: 3/1; financial award applicants required to submit FAFSA. *Faculty research:* Communication networks, signal processing, system failure diagnosis, multiprocessors, material processing using microwave energy. *Total annual research expenditures:* $2.8 million. *Unit head:* Monson Hayes, Chair, 703-993-1570, Fax: 703-993-1601, E-mail: hayes@gmu.edu. *Application contact:* Jammie Chang, Academic Program Coordinator, 703-993-1570, Fax: 703-993-1601, E-mail: jchangn@gmu.edu.
Website: http://ece.gmu.edu/

The George Washington University, School of Engineering and Applied Science, Department of Electrical and Computer Engineering, Washington, DC 20052. Offers electrical engineering (MS, PhD); telecommunication and computers (MS). *Program availability:* Part-time, evening/weekend. *Faculty:* 25 full-time (2 women), 9 part-time/adjunct (0 women). *Students:* 221 full-time (34 women), 76 part-time (9 women); includes 13 minority (4 Black or African American, non-Hispanic/Latino; 7 Asian, non-Hispanic/Latino; 1 Hispanic/Latino; 1 Native Hawaiian or other Pacific Islander, non-Hispanic/Latino), 253 international. Average age 26. 601 applicants, 85% accepted, 100 enrolled. In 2018, 93 master's, 7 doctorates awarded. *Degree requirements:* For master's, thesis optional; for doctorate, comprehensive exam, thesis/dissertation, dissertation defense, qualifying exam. *Entrance requirements:* For master's, appropriate bachelor's degree, minimum GPA of 3.0; for doctorate, GRE (if highest earned degree is BS), appropriate bachelor's or master's degree, minimum GPA of 3.3; for other advanced degree, appropriate master's degree, minimum GPA of 3.0. Additional exam requirements/recommendations for international students: Required—TOEFL or The George Washington University English as a Foreign Language Test. *Application deadline:* For fall admission, 3/1 priority date for domestic students; for spring admission, 10/1 for domestic students. Applications are processed on a rolling basis. Application fee: $75. *Financial support:* In 2018–19, 39 students received support. Fellowships, research assistantships, teaching assistantships, career-related internships or fieldwork, and institutionally sponsored loans available. Financial award application deadline: 3/1; financial award applicants required to submit FAFSA. *Faculty research:* Computer graphics, multimedia systems. *Unit head:* Prof. Ahmed Louri, Chair,

202-994-5905, E-mail: louri@gwu.edu. *Application contact:* Adina Lav, Marketing, Recruiting and Admissions, 202-994-5827, Fax: 202-994-0909, E-mail: engineering@gwu.edu.
Website: http://www.ece.gwu.edu/

Georgia Institute of Technology, Graduate Studies, College of Engineering, School of Electrical and Computer Engineering, Atlanta, GA 30332-0001. Offers MS, PhD. *Program availability:* Part-time, online learning. Terminal master's awarded for partial completion of doctoral program. *Degree requirements:* For master's, thesis optional; for doctorate, comprehensive exam, thesis/dissertation. *Entrance requirements:* For master's and doctorate, GRE General Test. Additional exam requirements/recommendations for international students: Required—TOEFL (minimum score 550 paper-based; 79 iBT). Electronic applications accepted. *Expenses:* Contact institution. *Faculty research:* Telecommunications, computer systems, microelectronics, optical engineering, digital signal processing.

Grand Valley State University, Padnos College of Engineering and Computing, School of Engineering, Allendale, MI 49401-9403. Offers electrical and computer engineering (MSE); manufacturing operations (MSE); mechanical engineering (MSE); product design and manufacturing engineering (MSE). *Program availability:* Part-time, evening/weekend. *Faculty:* 19 full-time (5 women). *Students:* 26 full-time (5 women), 50 part-time (7 women); includes 6 minority (1 Black or African American, non-Hispanic/Latino; 2 Asian, non-Hispanic/Latino; 1 Hispanic/Latino; 2 Two or more races, non-Hispanic/Latino), 39 international. Average age 26. 52 applicants, 62% accepted, 13 enrolled. In 2018, 32 master's awarded. *Entrance requirements:* For master's, engineering degree, minimum GPA of 3.0, resume, 3 confidential letters of recommendation, 1-2 page essay, base of underlying relevant knowledge/evidence from academic records or relevant wok experience. Additional exam requirements/recommendations for international students: Required—Michigan English Language Assessment Battery (minimum score 77), TOEFL (minimum iBT score of 80), or IELTS (6.5); GRE. *Application deadline:* Applications are processed on a rolling basis. Application fee: $30. Electronic applications accepted. *Expenses:* $712 per credit hour, 33 credit hours. *Financial support:* In 2018–19, 40 students received support, including 8 fellowships, 34 research assistantships with full and partial tuition reimbursements available (averaging $4,000 per year); career-related internships or fieldwork, Federal Work-Study, institutionally sponsored loans, scholarships/grants, and unspecified assistantships also available. *Faculty research:* Digital signal processing, computer aided design, computer aided manufacturing, manufacturing simulation, biomechanics, product design. *Total annual research expenditures:* $300,000. *Unit head:* Dr. Wael Mokhtar, Director, 616-331-6015, Fax: 616-331-7215, E-mail: mokhtarw@gvsu.edu. *Application contact:* Dr. Shabbir Choudhuri, Graduate Program Director, 616-331-6845, Fax: 616-331-7215, E-mail: choudhus@gvsu.edu.
Website: http://www.engineer.gvsu.edu/

Illinois Institute of Technology, Graduate College, Armour College of Engineering, Department of Electrical and Computer Engineering, Chicago, IL 60616. Offers biomedical imaging and signals (MAS); computer engineering (MS, PhD); electrical engineering (MS, PhD); electricity markets (MAS); network engineering (MAS); power engineering (MAS); telecommunications and software engineering (MAS); VLSI and microelectronics (MAS); MS/MS. *Program availability:* Part-time, evening/weekend, online learning. Terminal master's awarded for partial completion of doctoral program. *Degree requirements:* For master's, comprehensive exam (for some programs), thesis (for some programs); for doctorate, comprehensive exam, thesis/dissertation. *Entrance requirements:* For master's and doctorate, GRE General Test (minimum score 1100 Quantitative and Verbal, 3.5 Analytical Writing), minimum undergraduate GPA of 3.0. Additional exam requirements/recommendations for international students: Required—TOEFL (minimum score 550 paper-based; 80 iBT); Recommended—IELTS (minimum score 5.5). Electronic applications accepted. *Faculty research:* Communication systems, wireless networks, computer systems, computer networks, wireless security, cloud computing and micro-electronics; electromagnetics and electronics; power and control systems; signal and image processing.

Indiana State University, College of Graduate and Professional Studies, College of Technology, Department of Electronics and Computer Engineering Technology, Terre Haute, IN 47809. Offers electronics and computer technology (MS). *Degree requirements:* For master's, thesis or alternative. *Entrance requirements:* For master's, bachelor's degree in industrial technology or related field. Additional exam requirements/recommendations for international students: Required—TOEFL. Electronic applications accepted.

Indiana University–Purdue University Indianapolis, School of Engineering and Technology, Department of Electrical and Computer Engineering, Indianapolis, IN 46202. Offers electrical and computer engineering (MS, PhD); engineering (MSE). *Degree requirements:* For master's, thesis optional; for doctorate, thesis/dissertation. *Entrance requirements:* For master's, GRE, minimum GPA of 3.0, three recommendation letters, statement of purpose/intent; for doctorate, GRE, minimum GPA of 3.0, three recommendation letters, statement of purpose/intent, curriculum vitae. Additional exam requirements/recommendations for international students: Required—TOEFL; Recommended—IELTS, TSE. Electronic applications accepted. *Expenses:* Contact institution. *Faculty research:* Modeling and control of advanced vehicle systems; data analytics and parallel processing; robotics and automation; 3-D imaging algorithms and image processing; signal/video processing and analysis; power electronics an renewable energy.

Instituto Tecnológico y de Estudios Superiores de Monterrey, Campus Chihuahua, Graduate Programs, Chihuahua, Mexico. Offers computer systems engineering (Ingeniero); electrical engineering (Ingeniero); electromechanical engineering (Ingeniero); electronic engineering (Ingeniero); engineering administration (MEA); industrial engineering (MIE, Ingeniero); international trade (MIT); mechanical engineering (Ingeniero).

International Technological University, Program in Computer Engineering, San Jose, CA 95134. Offers MSCE. *Program availability:* Part-time, evening/weekend. *Degree requirements:* For master's, thesis or alternative, capstone project. *Entrance requirements:* Additional exam requirements/recommendations for international students: Required—TOEFL, IELTS. Electronic applications accepted.

Iowa State University of Science and Technology, Department of Electrical and Computer Engineering, Ames, IA 50011. Offers computer engineering (M Eng, MS, PhD); electrical engineering (M Eng, MS, PhD). *Degree requirements:* For master's, thesis or alternative; for doctorate, thesis/dissertation. *Entrance requirements:* For master's and doctorate, GRE General Test. Additional exam requirements/recommendations for international students: Required—TOEFL (minimum score 570 paper-based; 79 iBT), IELTS (minimum score 6.5). Electronic applications accepted.

Iowa State University of Science and Technology, Program in Computer Engineering, Ames, IA 50011. Offers M Eng, MS, PhD. *Entrance requirements:* For master's and doctorate, GRE. Additional exam requirements/recommendations for international students: Required—TOEFL (minimum score 570 paper-based; 79 iBT), IELTS (minimum score 6.5). Electronic applications accepted.

Johns Hopkins University, Engineering Program for Professionals, Part-time Program in Electrical and Computer Engineering, Baltimore, MD 21218. Offers communications and networking (MS); electrical and computer engineering (Graduate Certificate, Post-Master's Certificate); photonics (MS). *Program availability:* Part-time, evening/weekend, 100% online, blended/hybrid learning. *Faculty:* 1 full-time, 47 part-time/adjunct (2 women). *Students:* 364 part-time (60 women). 119 applicants, 68% accepted, 53 enrolled. In 2018, 101 master's awarded. *Entrance requirements:* Additional exam requirements/recommendations for international students: Required—TOEFL (minimum score 600 paper-based; 100 iBT). *Application deadline:* Applications are processed on a rolling basis. Application fee: $0. Electronic applications accepted. *Unit head:* Dr. Brian Jennison, Program Chair, 443-778-6421, E-mail: brian.jennison@jhuapl.edu. *Application contact:* Doug Schiller, Admissions Director, 410-516-2300, Fax: 410-579-8049, E-mail: schiller@jhu.edu.
Website: http://www.ep.jhu.edu/

Johns Hopkins University, G. W. C. Whiting School of Engineering, Department of Electrical and Computer Engineering, Baltimore, MD 21218. Offers MSE, PhD. *Faculty:* 32 full-time (6 women). *Students:* 163 full-time (33 women), 6 part-time (1 woman). 436 applicants, 40% accepted, 57 enrolled. In 2018, 38 master's, 15 doctorates awarded. Terminal master's awarded for partial completion of doctoral program. *Degree requirements:* For master's, thesis optional; for doctorate, thesis/dissertation, qualifying and oral exams, seminar. *Entrance requirements:* For master's and doctorate, GRE General Test, transcripts, 3 letters of recommendation, statement of purpose. Additional exam requirements/recommendations for international students: Required—TOEFL (minimum score 600 paper-based, 100 iBT) or IELTS (7). *Application deadline:* For fall admission, 12/22 for domestic and international students. Application fee: $75. Electronic applications accepted. *Financial support:* In 2018–19, 108 students received support, including 15 fellowships with full tuition reimbursements available (averaging $29,496 per year), 93 research assistantships with full tuition reimbursements available (averaging $26,496 per year); teaching assistantships with full tuition reimbursements available, career-related internships or fieldwork, Federal Work-Study, institutionally sponsored loans, scholarships/grants, health care benefits, tuition waivers (partial), and unspecified assistantships also available. Financial award application deadline: 12/15. *Faculty research:* Microsystems, neuromorphics and brain-machines interface; acoustics, speech and language processing; photonics, biophotonics and optoelectronics; signal processing and imaging science and technology; networks, controls and systems. *Unit head:* Dr. Ralph Etienne-Cummings, Chair, 410-516-7031, Fax: 410-516-5566, E-mail: retienne@jhu.edu. *Application contact:* Belinda Blinkoff, Sr. Academic Program Coordinator, 410-516-4808, Fax: 410-516-5566, E-mail: bblinkoff@jhu.edu.
Website: http://www.ece.jhu.edu/

Kansas State University, Graduate School, College of Engineering, Department of Electrical and Computer Engineering, Manhattan, KS 66506. Offers electrical engineering (MS), including bioengineering, communication systems, design of computer systems, electrical engineering, energy and power systems, integrated circuits and devices, real time embedded systems, renewable energy, signal processing. *Program availability:* Part-time, evening/weekend, online learning. *Degree requirements:* For master's, thesis or alternative, final exam; for doctorate, thesis/dissertation, final exam, preliminary exams. *Entrance requirements:* For master's, GRE General Test, bachelor's degree in electrical engineering or computer science, minimum GPA of 3.0; for doctorate, GRE General Test. Additional exam requirements/recommendations for international students: Required—TOEFL (minimum score 600 paper-based; 85 iBT). Electronic applications accepted. *Faculty research:* Energy systems and renewable energy, computer systems and real time embedded systems, communication systems and signal processing, integrated circuits and devices, bioengineering.

Lakehead University, Graduate Studies, Faculty of Engineering, Thunder Bay, ON P7B 5E1, Canada. Offers control engineering (M Sc Engr); electrical/computer engineering (M Sc Engr); environmental engineering (M Sc Engr). *Program availability:* Part-time. *Degree requirements:* For master's, thesis. *Entrance requirements:* For master's, bachelor's degree in chemical, electrical or mechanical engineering, minimum B average. Additional exam requirements/recommendations for international students: Required—TOEFL. *Faculty research:* Pulp and paper, adaptive/process control, robust/interactive learning control, vibration control.

Lawrence Technological University, College of Engineering, Southfield, MI 48075-1058. Offers architectural engineering (MS); automotive engineering (MS); biomedical engineering (MS); civil engineering (MA, MS, PhD), including environmental engineering (MS), geotechnical engineering (MS), structural engineering (MS), transportation engineering (MS), water resource engineering (MS); construction engineering management (MA); electrical and computer engineering (MS); engineering management (MEM); engineering technology (MS); fire engineering (MS); industrial engineering (MS), including healthcare systems; manufacturing systems (ME); mechanical engineering (MS, DE, PhD), including automotive engineering (MS), energy engineering (MS), manufacturing (DE), solid mechanics (MS), thermal/fluid systems (MS); mechatronic systems engineering (MS). *Program availability:* Part-time, evening/weekend. Terminal master's awarded for partial completion of doctoral program. *Degree requirements:* For master's, thesis optional; for doctorate, comprehensive exam, thesis/dissertation optional. *Entrance requirements:* Additional exam requirements/recommendations for international students: Required—TOEFL (minimum score 550 paper-based; 79 iBT), IELTS (minimum score 6.5). Electronic applications accepted. *Faculty research:* Innovative infrastructure and building structures and materials; connectivity and mobility; automotive systems modeling, simulation and testing; biomedical devices and materials; building mechanical/electrical systems.

Lehigh University, P.C. Rossin College of Engineering and Applied Science, Department of Computer Science and Engineering, Bethlehem, PA 18015. Offers computer engineering (M Eng, MS, PhD); computer science (M Eng, MS, PhD); MBA/E. Computer engineering program handled through the ECE department. *Program availability:* Part-time. *Faculty:* 15 full-time (2 women), 1 (woman) part-time/adjunct. *Students:* 59 full-time (13 women), 2 part-time (0 women); includes 3 minority (1 Black or African American, non-Hispanic/Latino; 1 Asian, non-Hispanic/Latino; 1 Hispanic/Latino), 49 international. Average age 26. 263 applicants, 36% accepted, 21 enrolled. In 2018, 19 master's, 1 doctorate awarded. Terminal master's awarded for partial completion of doctoral program. *Degree requirements:* For master's, thesis optional, oral presentation of thesis; for doctorate, thesis/dissertation, qualifying, general, and oral exams. *Entrance requirements:* For master's, GRE General Test, minimum GPA of 3.0; for doctorate, GRE General Test, minimum GPA of 3.5. Additional exam requirements/recommendations for international students: Required—TOEFL (minimum score 550 paper-based; 79 iBT), IELTS (minimum score 6.5). *Application deadline:* For fall admission, 4/1 for domestic and international students; for spring admission, 11/1 for domestic and international students. Application fee: $75. Electronic applications accepted. *Expenses:* $1500 per credit. *Financial support:* In 2018–19, 16 students received support, including 3 fellowships with full tuition reimbursements available (averaging $22,325 per year), 7 research assistantships with full tuition reimbursements available (averaging $22,050 per year), 7 teaching assistantships with full tuition reimbursements available (averaging $22,050 per year). Financial award application

deadline: 1/15. *Faculty research:* Artificial intelligence, networking-pattern recognition, multimedia e-learning/data mining/Web search, mobile robotics, bioinformatics, computer vision, data science. *Total annual research expenditures:* $1.1 million. *Unit head:* Dr. Daniel P. Lopresti, Chair, 610-758-5782, E-mail: dal9@lehigh.edu. *Application contact:* Heidi Wegrzyn, Graduate Coordinator, 610-758-3065, E-mail: hew207@lehigh.edu.
Website: http://www.cse.lehigh.edu/

Lehigh University, P.C. Rossin College of Engineering and Applied Science, Department of Electrical and Computer Engineering, Bethlehem, PA 18015. Offers electrical engineering (M Eng, MS, PhD); photonics (MS). *Program availability:* Part-time. *Faculty:* 16 full-time (4 women). *Students:* 79 full-time (8 women), 73 international. Average age 25. 269 applicants, 27% accepted, 19 enrolled. In 2018, 35 master's, 7 doctorates awarded. Terminal master's awarded for partial completion of doctoral program. *Degree requirements:* For master's, thesis optional; for doctorate, thesis/dissertation, qualifying or comprehensive exam for all 1st year PhD's; general exam 7 months or more prior to completion/dissertation defense. *Entrance requirements:* For master's and doctorate, GRE General Test, BS in field or related field. Additional exam requirements/recommendations for international students: Required—TOEFL (minimum score 79 iBT), IELTS (minimum score 6.5), TOEFL or IELTS; Recommended—TSE. *Application deadline:* For fall admission, 4/1 for domestic and international students; for spring admission, 11/1 for domestic and international students. Application fee: $75. Electronic applications accepted. Tuition and fees vary according to program. *Financial support:* In 2018–19, 52 students received support, including 5 fellowships with full tuition reimbursements available (averaging $29,400 per year), 40 research assistantships with full tuition reimbursements available (averaging $29,400 per year), 7 teaching assistantships with full tuition reimbursements available (averaging $29,400 per year). Financial award application deadline: 1/15. *Faculty research:* Bio-electrical engineering, communications and signal processing, computer engineering, electric energy, electronics and photonics. *Total annual research expenditures:* $4 million. *Unit head:* Dr. Chengshan Xiao, Chair, 610-758-4069, Fax: 610-758-6279, E-mail: chx417@lehigh.edu. *Application contact:* Diane Hubinsky, Graduate Coordinator, 610-758-4072, Fax: 610-758-6279, E-mail: dih2@lehigh.edu.
Website: http://www.ece.lehigh.edu/

Louisiana State University and Agricultural & Mechanical College, Graduate School, College of Engineering, Division of Electrical and Computer Engineering, Baton Rouge, LA 70803. Offers MSEE, PhD.

Manhattan College, Graduate Programs, School of Engineering, Program in Computer Engineering, Riverdale, NY 10471. Offers MS. *Program availability:* Part-time, evening/weekend. *Degree requirements:* For master's, thesis or alternative. *Entrance requirements:* For master's, GRE (recommended), minimum GPA of 3.0. Additional exam requirements/recommendations for international students: Required—TOEFL (minimum score 550 paper-based; 80 iBT), IELTS (minimum score 6).

Marquette University, Graduate School, College of Engineering, Department of Electrical and Computer Engineering, Milwaukee, WI 53201-1881. Offers digital signal processing (Certificate); electric machines, drives, and controls (Certificate); electrical and computer engineering (MS, PhD); microwaves and antennas (Certificate); sensors and smart systems (Certificate). *Program availability:* Part-time, evening/weekend. Terminal master's awarded for partial completion of doctoral program. *Degree requirements:* For master's, comprehensive exam (for some programs), thesis optional; for doctorate, thesis/dissertation, dissertation defense, qualifying exam. *Entrance requirements:* For master's, GRE General Test (recommended), official transcripts from all current and previous colleges/universities except Marquette, three letters of recommendation; for doctorate, GRE General Test, minimum GPA of 3.0, official transcripts from all current and previous colleges/universities except Marquette, three letters of recommendation, statement of purpose, submission of any English language publications authored by applicant (strongly recommended). Additional exam requirements/recommendations for international students: Required—TOEFL (minimum score 530 paper-based). Electronic applications accepted. *Faculty research:* Electric machines, drives, and controls; applied solid-state electronics; computers and signal processing; microwaves and antennas; solid state devices and acoustic wave sensors.

Marshall University, Academic Affairs Division, College of Information Technology and Engineering, Program in Electrical and Computer Engineering, Huntington, WV 25755. Offers MSEE.

Massachusetts Institute of Technology, School of Engineering, Department of Electrical Engineering and Computer Science, Cambridge, MA 02139. Offers computer science (PhD, Sc D, ECS); computer science and engineering (PhD, Sc D); computer science and molecular biology (M Eng); electrical engineering (PhD, Sc D, EE); electrical engineering and computer science (M Eng, SM, PhD, Sc D); SM/MBA. *Degree requirements:* For master's and other advanced degree, thesis; for doctorate, comprehensive exam, thesis/dissertation. *Entrance requirements:* Additional exam requirements/recommendations for international students: Required—TOEFL, IELTS. Electronic applications accepted. *Expenses: Tuition:* Full-time $51,520; part-time $800 per credit hour. *Required fees:* $312. *Faculty research:* Information systems, circuits, biomedical sciences and engineering, computer science: artificial intelligence, systems, theory.

McGill University, Faculty of Graduate and Postdoctoral Studies, Faculty of Engineering, Department of Electrical and Computer Engineering, Montréal, QC H3A 2T5, Canada. Offers M Eng, PhD.

Memorial University of Newfoundland, School of Graduate Studies, Faculty of Engineering and Applied Science, St. John's, NL A1C 5S7, Canada. Offers civil engineering (M Eng, PhD); electrical and computer engineering (M Eng, PhD); mechanical engineering (M Eng, PhD); ocean and naval architecture engineering (M Eng, PhD). *Program availability:* Part-time. *Degree requirements:* For master's, thesis; for doctorate, comprehensive exam, thesis/dissertation, oral thesis defense. *Entrance requirements:* For master's, 2nd class degree; for doctorate, master's degree in engineering. Electronic applications accepted. *Faculty research:* Engineering analysis, environmental and hydrotechnical studies, manufacturing and robotics, mechanics, structures and materials.

Memorial University of Newfoundland, School of Graduate Studies, Interdisciplinary Program in Computer Engineering, St. John's, NL A1C 5S7, Canada. Offers MA Sc. *Degree requirements:* For master's, project course. *Entrance requirements:* For master's, 2nd class engineering degree. Electronic applications accepted. *Expenses:* Contact institution.

Mercer University, Graduate Studies, Macon Campus, School of Engineering, Macon, GA 31207. Offers biomedical engineering (MSE); computer engineering (MSE); electrical engineering (MSE); engineering management (MSE); environmental engineering (MSE); environmental systems (MS); mechanical engineering (MSE); software engineering (MSE); software systems (MS); technical communications management (MS); technical management (MS). *Program availability:* Part-time-only, evening/weekend, online learning. *Degree requirements:* For master's, thesis or alternative. *Entrance requirements:* For master's, GRE (minimum score 300), minimum undergraduate GPA of 3.0. Additional exam requirements/recommendations for international students: Required—TOEFL (minimum score 550 paper-based; 80 iBT). *Expenses:* Contact institution. *Faculty research:* Designing prostheses and orthotics, oxygen transfer and limitations in biological systems, low-cost groundwater development, lung airway and transport, autonomous mobile robots.

Miami University, College of Engineering and Computing, Department of Electrical and Computer Engineering, Oxford, OH 45056. Offers MS. *Faculty:* 9 full-time (1 woman). *Students:* 15 full-time (2 women), 2 part-time (0 women); includes 1 minority (Black or African American, non-Hispanic/Latino), 10 international. Average age 24. In 2018, 7 master's awarded. *Unit head:* Dr. Q. Herb Zhou, Chair, 513-523-0743, E-mail: zhouq@miamioh.edu. *Application contact:* Dr. Q. Herb Zhou, Chair, 513-523-0743, E-mail: zhouq@miamioh.edu.
Website: http://miamioh.edu/cec/academics/departments/ece/

Michigan Technological University, Graduate School, College of Engineering, Department of Electrical and Computer Engineering, Houghton, MI 49931. Offers advanced electric power engineering (Graduate Certificate); electrical engineering (PhD). *Program availability:* Part-time, 100% online, blended/hybrid learning. *Faculty:* 46 full-time, 7 part-time/adjunct. *Students:* 131 full-time (28 women), 27 part-time; includes 4 minority (1 Black or African American, non-Hispanic/Latino; 1 Asian, non-Hispanic/Latino; 2 Hispanic/Latino), 128 international. Average age 27. 490 applicants, 39% accepted, 42 enrolled. In 2018, 95 master's, 9 doctorates, 34 other advanced degrees awarded. Terminal master's awarded for partial completion of doctoral program. *Degree requirements:* For master's, comprehensive exam (for some programs), thesis (for some programs); for doctorate, comprehensive exam, thesis/dissertation. *Entrance requirements:* For master's, statement of purpose, personal statement, official transcripts, 2 letters of recommendation; for doctorate, GRE, statement of purpose, personal statement, official transcripts, 2 letters of recommendation; for Graduate Certificate, statement of purpose, personal statement, official transcripts. Additional exam requirements/recommendations for international students: Required—TOEFL (recommended minimum score 100 iBT) or IELTS (recommended minimum score of 7.0). *Application deadline:* For fall admission, 2/15 priority date for domestic and international students; for spring admission, 8/15 priority date for domestic and international students. Applications are processed on a rolling basis. Electronic applications accepted. *Expenses:* $1,143 per credit. *Financial support:* In 2018–19, 117 students received support, including 7 fellowships with tuition reimbursements available (averaging $16,590 per year), 23 research assistantships with tuition reimbursements available (averaging $16,590 per year), 23 teaching assistantships with tuition reimbursements available (averaging $16,590 per year); career-related internships or fieldwork, Federal Work-Study, scholarships/grants, health care benefits, unspecified assistantships, and cooperative program also available. Financial award applicants required to submit FAFSA. *Faculty research:* Electrical power systems, optics and photonics, embedded computing systems, computer networks, communication and information theory. *Total annual research expenditures:* $2 million. *Unit head:* Dr. Glen E. Archer, Interim Chair & Principal Lecturer, 906-487-2550, Fax: 906-487-2949, E-mail: gearcher@mtu.edu. *Application contact:* Megan Williamson, Graduate Program Coordinator, 906-487-1995, Fax: 906-487-2949, E-mail: meganwil@mtu.edu.
Website: http://www.mtu.edu/ece/

Michigan Technological University, Graduate School, Interdisciplinary Programs, Houghton, MI 49931. Offers automotive systems and controls (Graduate Certificate); biochemistry and molecular biology (PhD); computational science and engineering (PhD); data science (Graduate Certificate); sustainability (Graduate Certificate). *Program availability:* Part-time. *Faculty:* 120 full-time (25 women), 8 part-time/adjunct. *Students:* 67 full-time (28 women), 24 part-time; includes 5 minority (2 Black or African American, non-Hispanic/Latino; 1 American Indian or Alaska Native, non-Hispanic/Latino; 2 Two or more races, non-Hispanic/Latino), 59 international. Average age 29. 479 applicants, 24% accepted, 17 enrolled. In 2018, 19 master's, 8 doctorates, 10 other advanced degrees awarded. Terminal master's awarded for partial completion of doctoral program. *Degree requirements:* For master's, comprehensive exam (for some programs), thesis (for some programs); for doctorate, comprehensive exam, thesis/dissertation. *Entrance requirements:* For master's, doctorate, and Graduate Certificate, GRE, statement of purpose, personal statement, official transcripts, 2-3 letters of recommendation. Additional exam requirements/recommendations for international students: Required—TOEFL or IELTS. *Application deadline:* Applications are processed on a rolling basis. Electronic applications accepted. *Expenses: Tuition, area resident:* Full-time $18,126; part-time $1007 per credit. Tuition, state resident: full-time $18,126; part-time $1007 per credit. Tuition, nonresident: full-time $18,126; part-time $1007 per credit. *International tuition:* $18,126 full-time. *Required fees:* $248; $124 per semester. Tuition and fees vary according to course load and program. *Financial support:* In 2018–19, 64 students received support, including 14 fellowships with tuition reimbursements available (averaging $16,590 per year), 14 research assistantships with tuition reimbursements available (averaging $16,590 per year), 12 teaching assistantships with tuition reimbursements available (averaging $16,590 per year); career-related internships or fieldwork, Federal Work-Study, scholarships/grants, health care benefits, unspecified assistantships, and cooperative program also available. Financial award applicants required to submit FAFSA. *Faculty research:* Big data, atmospheric sciences, bioinformatics and systems biology, molecular dynamics, environmental studies. *Unit head:* Dr. Pushpalatha Murthy, Dean of the Graduate School/Associate Provost for Graduate Education, 906-487-3007, Fax: 906-487-2284, E-mail: ppmurthy@mtu.edu. *Application contact:* Carol T. Wingerson, Administrative Aide, 906-487-2328, Fax: 906-487-2284, E-mail: gradadms@mtu.edu.

Mississippi State University, Bagley College of Engineering, Department of Electrical and Computer Engineering, Mississippi State, MS 39762. Offers MS, PhD. *Program availability:* Part-time, blended/hybrid learning. *Faculty:* 13 full-time (2 women). *Students:* 50 full-time (8 women), 57 part-time (5 women); includes 18 minority (5 Black or African American, non-Hispanic/Latino; 1 American Indian or Alaska Native, non-Hispanic/Latino; 8 Asian, non-Hispanic/Latino; 4 Hispanic/Latino), 43 international. Average age 31. 90 applicants, 42% accepted, 26 enrolled. In 2018, 18 master's, 9 doctorates awarded. Terminal master's awarded for partial completion of doctoral program. *Degree requirements:* For master's, comprehensive exam, thesis optional; for doctorate, comprehensive exam, thesis/dissertation, written exam, oral preliminary exam. *Entrance requirements:* For master's, GRE (for graduates from program not accredited by EAC/ABET), minimum GPA of 3.0 on BS; for doctorate, GRE (for graduates from program not accredited by EAC/ABET), minimum GPA of 3.5 on BS or MS. Additional exam requirements/recommendations for international students: Required—TOEFL (minimum score 550 paper-based; 79 iBT); Recommended—IELTS (minimum score 6.5). *Application deadline:* For fall admission, 7/1 for domestic students, 5/1 for international students; for spring admission, 11/1 for domestic students, 9/1 for international students. Applications are processed on a rolling basis. Application fee: $60 ($80 for international students). Electronic applications accepted. *Expenses:* Tuition, state resident: full-time $8450; part-time $360.59 per credit hour. Tuition, nonresident: full-time $23,140; part-time $969.09 per credit hour. *Required fees:* $110. One-time fee: $55 full-time. Part-time tuition and fees vary according to course load, degree level, campus/location and reciprocity agreements. *Financial support:* In 2018–19, 13 research assistantships with full tuition reimbursements (averaging $18,877 per year), 21 teaching assistantships with full tuition reimbursements (averaging $15,919 per year) were awarded; Federal Work-Study, institutionally sponsored loans, scholarships/grants, and unspecified assistantships also available. Financial award application deadline: 4/1; financial award applicants required to submit FAFSA. *Faculty research:* Digital computing, power, controls, communication systems, microelectronics. *Total annual research expenditures:* $6.2 million. *Unit head:* Dr. James E. Fowler, Jr., Professor/Interim Department Head, 662-325-3912, Fax: 662-325-2298, E-mail: ecehead@ece.msstate.edu. *Application contact:* Angie Campbell, Admissions and Enrollment Assistant, 662-325-9514, E-mail: acampbell@grad.msstate.edu. Website: http://www.ece.msstate.edu/

Missouri University of Science and Technology, Department of Electrical and Computer Engineering, Rolla, MO 65401. Offers computer engineering (MS, DE, PhD); electrical engineering (MS, DE, PhD). *Program availability:* Part-time, evening/weekend. Terminal master's awarded for partial completion of doctoral program. *Degree requirements:* For master's, thesis optional; for doctorate, comprehensive exam, thesis/dissertation, departmental qualifying exam. *Entrance requirements:* For master's, GRE General Test (minimum score 1100 verbal and quantitative, writing 4.5); for doctorate, GRE General Test (minimum score: verbal and quantitative 1100, writing 3.5). Additional exam requirements/recommendations for international students: Required—TOEFL (minimum score 550 paper-based). Electronic applications accepted. *Expenses:* Tuition, state resident: full-time $7545.60; part-time $419.20 per credit hour. Tuition, nonresident: full-time $22,169; part-time $1231.60 per credit hour. *International tuition:* $23,518.80 full-time. *Required fees:* $4523.05. Full-time tuition and fees vary according to course load, campus/location, program and reciprocity agreements. *Faculty research:* Power systems, computer/communication networks, intelligent control/robotics, robust control, nanotechnologies.

Montana State University, The Graduate School, College of Engineering, Department of Electrical and Computer Engineering, Bozeman, MT 59717. Offers electrical engineering (MS); engineering (PhD), including electrical and computer engineering option. *Program availability:* Part-time. *Degree requirements:* For master's, comprehensive exam, thesis (for some programs); for doctorate, comprehensive exam, thesis/dissertation. *Entrance requirements:* For master's, GRE, BS in electrical or computer engineering or related field; for doctorate, GRE, MS in electrical or computer engineering or related field. Additional exam requirements/recommendations for international students: Required—TOEFL (minimum score 550 paper-based). Electronic applications accepted. *Faculty research:* Optics and optoelectonics, communications and signal processing, microfabrication, complex systems and control, energy systems.

Naval Postgraduate School, Departments and Academic Groups, Department of Electrical and Computer Engineering, Monterey, CA 93943-5216. Offers computer engineering (MS); electrical engineer (EE); electrical engineering (PhD); engineering acoustics (MS); engineering science (MS). Program only open to commissioned officers of the United States and friendly nations and selected United States federal civilian employees. *Program availability:* Part-time, online learning. *Degree requirements:* For master's and EE, thesis (for some programs), capstone project or research/dissertation paper (for some programs); for doctorate, thesis/dissertation. *Faculty research:* Theory and design of digital communication systems; behavior modeling for detection, identification, prediction and reaction in artificial intelligence (AI) systems solutions; waveform design for target class discrimination with closed-loop radar; iterative technique for system identification with adaptive signal design.

New Jersey Institute of Technology, Newark College of Engineering, Newark, NJ 07102. Offers biomedical engineering (MS, PhD); biopharmaceutical engineering (MS); chemical engineering (MS, PhD); civil engineering (MS, PhD); computer engineering (MS); critical infrastructure systems (MS); electrical engineering (MS, PhD); engineering management (MS); engineering science (MS); environmental engineering (MS, PhD); healthcare systems management (MS); industrial engineering (MS, PhD); internet engineering (MS); manufacturing systems engineering (MS); materials science & engineering (PhD); materials science and engineering (MS); mechanical engineering (MS, PhD); occupational safety and health engineering (MS). *Program availability:* Part-time, evening/weekend. *Faculty:* 147 full-time (26 women), 133 part-time/adjunct (16 women). *Students:* 690 full-time (163 women), 594 part-time (130 women); includes 427 minority (79 Black or African American, non-Hispanic/Latino; 181 Asian, non-Hispanic/Latino; 140 Hispanic/Latino; 27 Two or more races, non-Hispanic/Latino), 553 international. Average age 27. 2,334 applicants, 57% accepted, 452 enrolled. In 2018, 418 master's, 31 doctorates awarded. Terminal master's awarded for partial completion of doctoral program. *Degree requirements:* For master's, thesis (for some programs); for doctorate, thesis/dissertation. *Entrance requirements:* For master's, GRE General Test, minimum GPA 2.8, personal statement, 1 letter of recommendation, transcripts; for doctorate, GRE General Test, minimum GPA of 3.5, personal statement, 3 letters of recommendation, transcripts. Additional exam requirements/recommendations for international students: Required—TOEFL (minimum score 550 paper-based; 79 iBT), IELTS (minimum score 6.5). *Application deadline:* For fall admission, 6/1 priority date for domestic students, 5/1 priority date for international students; for spring admission, 11/15 priority date for domestic and international students. Applications are processed on a rolling basis. Application fee: $75. Electronic applications accepted. *Expenses:* $22,690 per year (in-state), $32,136 per year (out-of-state). *Financial support:* In 2018–19, 396 students received support, including 52 fellowships with full tuition reimbursements available (averaging $22,000 per year), 113 research assistantships with full tuition reimbursements available (averaging $22,000 per year), 101 teaching assistantships with full tuition reimbursements available (averaging $22,000 per year); career-related internships or fieldwork, Federal Work-Study, scholarships/grants, and unspecified assistantships also available. Financial award application deadline: 1/15. *Faculty research:* Nonlinear signal processing, intelligent medical image analysis, calibration issues in coherent localization, computer-aided design, neural network for tool wear measurement. *Total annual research expenditures:* $41.7 million. *Unit head:* Dr. Moshe Kam, Dean, 973-596-5534, Fax: 973-596-2316, E-mail: moshe.kam@njit.edu. *Application contact:* Stephen Eck, Director of Admissions, 973-596-3300, Fax: 973-596-3461, E-mail: admissions@njit.edu. Website: http://engineering.njit.edu/

New York Institute of Technology, College of Engineering and Computing Sciences, Department of Electrical and Computer Engineering, Old Westbury, NY 11568-8000. Offers MS. *Program availability:* Part-time, evening/weekend. *Faculty:* 10 full-time (2 women), 8 part-time/adjunct (all women). *Students:* 54 full-time (15 women), 36 part-time (7 women); includes 21 minority (3 Black or African American, non-Hispanic/Latino; 12 Asian, non-Hispanic/Latino; 6 Hispanic/Latino), 59 international. Average age 26. 308 applicants, 59% accepted, 25 enrolled. In 2018, 82 master's awarded. *Degree requirements:* For master's, thesis or alternative. *Entrance requirements:* For master's, BS in electrical or computer engineering or closely-related field; minimum undergraduate GPA of 2.85. Additional exam requirements/recommendations for international students: Required—TOEFL (minimum score 79 iBT), IELTS (minimum score 6), PTE (minimum score 53). *Application deadline:* For fall admission, 7/1 for domestic students, 6/1 for international students; for spring admission, 12/1 for domestic and international students. Applications are processed on a rolling basis. Application fee: $50. Electronic applications accepted. *Expenses:* $1285 per credit plus $215 fees per year (full-time) or $175 fees per year (part-time). *Financial support:* Fellowships with

partial tuition reimbursements, teaching assistantships with partial tuition reimbursements, career-related internships or fieldwork, Federal Work-Study, scholarships/grants, tuition waivers (full and partial), and unspecified assistantships available. Support available to part-time students. Financial award application deadline: 2/15; financial award applicants required to submit FAFSA. *Faculty research:* Securing inter-vehicular networks with time and driver identity considerations; security of mobile devices and wireless networks; implantable wireless system to study gastric neurophysiology; model-based software for configuring single switch scanning systems; family-based framework of quality assurance for biomedical ontologies. *Unit head:* Dr. Aydin Farajidavar, Department Chairperson, 516-686-4014, Fax: 516-686-7439, E-mail: afarajid@nyit.edu. *Application contact:* Alice Dolitsky, Director, Graduate Admissions, 516-686-7520, Fax: 516-686-1116, E-mail: admissions@nyit.edu. Website: http://www.nyit.edu/degrees/electrical_computer_engineering_ms

New York University, Tandon School of Engineering, Department of Electrical and Computer Engineering, New York, NY 10012-1019. Offers computer engineering (MS); electrical engineering (MS, PhD). *Program availability:* Part-time, evening/weekend. *Faculty:* 28 full-time (4 women), 13 part-time/adjunct. *Students:* 549 full-time (122 women), 56 part-time (6 women); includes 36 minority (5 Black or African American, non-Hispanic/Latino; 19 Asian, non-Hispanic/Latino; 7 Hispanic/Latino; 5 Two or more races, non-Hispanic/Latino), 538 international. Average age 25. 1,699 applicants, 63% accepted, 313 enrolled. In 2018, 333 master's, 18 doctorates awarded. *Degree requirements:* For master's, comprehensive exam (for some programs), thesis (for some programs); for doctorate, comprehensive exam, thesis/dissertation, qualifying exam. *Entrance requirements:* For master's, BS in electrical engineering; for doctorate, MS in electrical engineering. Additional exam requirements/recommendations for international students: Required—TOEFL (minimum score 550 paper-based; 90 iBT); Recommended—IELTS (minimum score 7). *Application deadline:* For fall admission, 2/15 priority date for domestic and international students; for spring admission, 11/1 priority date for domestic and international students. Applications are processed on a rolling basis. Application fee: $75. Electronic applications accepted. *Expenses:* Contact institution. *Financial support:* In 2018–19, 269 students received support, including 15 fellowships with partial tuition reimbursements available (averaging $22,178 per year), 33 research assistantships with partial tuition reimbursements available (averaging $23,144 per year), 11 teaching assistantships (averaging $52,614 per year); career-related internships or fieldwork, scholarships/grants, tuition waivers, and unspecified assistantships also available. Support available to part-time students. Financial award application deadline: 2/15. *Faculty research:* Communications, networking, and signal processing; systems, control and robotics; energy systems and power electronics; electromagnetics and analog/radio frequency/biomedical circuits; computer engineering and VLSI. *Total annual research expenditures:* $16.6 million. *Unit head:* Dr. Ivan Selesnick, Department Chair, 646-997-3416, E-mail: iws211@nyu.edu. *Application contact:* Elizabeth Ensweiler, Senior Director of Graduate Enrollment and Graduate Admissions, 646-997-3182, E-mail: elizabeth.ensweiler@nyu.edu.

Norfolk State University, School of Graduate Studies, School of Science and Technology, Program in Electronics Engineering, Norfolk, VA 23504. Offers MS.

North Carolina Agricultural and Technical State University, The Graduate College, College of Engineering, Department of Electrical and Computer Engineering, Greensboro, NC 27411. Offers electrical engineering (MSEE, PhD), including communications and signal processing, computer engineering, electronic and optical materials and devices, power systems and control. *Program availability:* Part-time. *Degree requirements:* For master's, project, thesis defense; for doctorate, thesis/dissertation. *Entrance requirements:* For master's, GRE General Test, GRE Subject Test, minimum GPA of 2.8; for doctorate, GRE General Test, minimum GPA of 3.0. *Faculty research:* Semiconductor compounds, VLSI design, image processing, optical systems and devices, fault-tolerant computing.

North Carolina State University, Graduate School, College of Engineering, Department of Electrical and Computer Engineering, Program in Computer Engineering, Raleigh, NC 27695. Offers MS, PhD. *Degree requirements:* For master's, thesis (for some programs); for doctorate, thesis/dissertation. *Entrance requirements:* For master's and doctorate, GRE. Additional exam requirements/recommendations for international students: Required—TOEFL (minimum score 575 paper-based). Electronic applications accepted. *Faculty research:* Computer architecture, parallel processing, embedded computer systems, VLSI design, computer networking performance and control.

North Dakota State University, College of Graduate and Interdisciplinary Studies, College of Engineering, Department of Electrical and Computer Engineering, Fargo, ND 58102. Offers M Eng, MS, PhD. *Program availability:* Part-time. Terminal master's awarded for partial completion of doctoral program. *Degree requirements:* For master's, comprehensive exam, thesis; for doctorate, comprehensive exam, thesis/dissertation. *Entrance requirements:* Additional exam requirements/recommendations for international students: Required—TOEFL (minimum score 525 paper-based; 71 iBT). Electronic applications accepted. *Faculty research:* Computers, power and control systems, microwaves, communications and signal processing, bioengineering.

Northeastern University, College of Engineering, Boston, MA 02115-5096. Offers bioengineering (MS, PhD); chemical engineering (MS, PhD); civil engineering (MS, PhD); computer engineering (PhD); computer systems engineering (MS); electrical and computer engineering (MS); electrical and computer engineering leadership (MS); electrical engineering (PhD); energy systems (MS); engineering and public policy (MS); engineering management (MS, Certificate); environmental engineering (MS); industrial engineering (MS, PhD); information assurance (PhD); information systems (MS); interdisciplinary engineering (PhD); mechanical engineering (PhD); operations research (MS); telecommunication systems management (MS). *Program availability:* Part-time, online learning. Electronic applications accepted. *Expenses:* Contact institution.

Northern Arizona University, College of Engineering, Informatics, and Applied Sciences, School of Informatics, Computing, and Cyber Systems, Flagstaff, AZ 86011. Offers engineering (M Eng), including computer science and engineering, electrical engineering; informatics and computing (PhD). *Program availability:* Part-time. *Degree requirements:* For master's, variable foreign language requirement, comprehensive exam (for some programs), thesis (for some programs); for doctorate, variable foreign language requirement, comprehensive exam (for some programs), thesis/dissertation (for some programs). *Entrance requirements:* Additional exam requirements/recommendations for international students: Required—TOEFL (minimum score 80 iBT), IELTS (minimum score 6.5). Electronic applications accepted.

Northwestern Polytechnic University, School of Engineering, Fremont, CA 94539-7482. Offers computer engineering (DCE); computer science (MS); computer systems engineering (MS); electrical engineering (MS). *Program availability:* Part-time, evening/weekend. *Degree requirements:* For master's, thesis optional; for doctorate, thesis/dissertation. *Entrance requirements:* For master's, minimum GPA of 3.0. Additional exam requirements/recommendations for international students: Required—TOEFL (minimum score 550 paper-based; 79 iBT). *Faculty research:* Computer networking, database design, Internet technology, software engineering, digital signal processing.

Northwestern University, McCormick School of Engineering and Applied Science, Department of Electrical Engineering and Computer Science, Evanston, IL 60208.

Offers computer engineering (MS, PhD); computer science (MS, PhD); electrical engineering (MS, PhD); information technology (MS). MS and PhD admissions and degrees offered through The Graduate School. *Program availability:* Part-time. Terminal master's awarded for partial completion of doctoral program. *Degree requirements:* For master's, comprehensive exam (for some programs), thesis optional; for doctorate, comprehensive exam, thesis/dissertation. *Entrance requirements:* For master's and doctorate, GRE General Test. Additional exam requirements/recommendations for international students: Required—TOEFL (minimum score 577 paper-based; 90 iBT), IELTS (minimum score 7). Electronic applications accepted. *Faculty research:* Solid state and photonics; computing, algorithms, and applications; computer engineering and systems; cognitive systems; graphics and interactive media; signals and systems.

Oakland University, Graduate Study and Lifelong Learning, School of Engineering and Computer Science, Department of Computer Science and Engineering, Rochester, MI 48309-4401. Offers computer science (MS); computer science and informatics (PhD); software engineering and information technology (MS). *Program availability:* Part-time, evening/weekend. *Entrance requirements:* For master's, minimum GPA of 3.0. Electronic applications accepted. *Expenses:* Contact institution.

Oakland University, Graduate Study and Lifelong Learning, School of Engineering and Computer Science, Department of Electrical and Computer Engineering, Rochester, MI 48309-4401. Offers electrical and computer engineering (MS, PhD); embedded systems (MS); mechatronics (MS). *Program availability:* Part-time, evening/weekend. *Entrance requirements:* For master's, minimum GPA of 3.0. Additional exam requirements/recommendations for international students: Required—TOEFL (minimum score 550 paper-based). Electronic applications accepted. *Expenses:* Contact institution.

The Ohio State University, Graduate School, College of Engineering, Department of Computer Science and Engineering, Columbus, OH 43210. Offers MS, PhD. *Faculty:* 43. *Students:* 298 (55 women). Average age 26. In 2018, 61 master's, 26 doctorates awarded. *Entrance requirements:* For master's and doctorate, GRE (minimum score Quantitative 750 old, 159 new; Verbal 500 old, 155 new; Analytical Writing 3.0); GRE Subject Test in computer science (strongly recommended for those whose undergraduate degree is not in computer science). Additional exam requirements/recommendations for international students: Required—TOEFL (minimum score 550 paper-based; 79 iBT), Michigan English Language Assessment Battery (minimum score 82); Recommended—IELTS (minimum score 7). *Application deadline:* For fall admission, 12/13 priority date for domestic students, 11/30 priority date for international students. Applications are processed on a rolling basis. Application fee: $60 ($70 for international students). Electronic applications accepted. *Financial support:* Fellowships, research assistantships, teaching assistantships, career-related internships or fieldwork, Federal Work-Study, institutionally sponsored loans, unspecified assistantships, and administrative assistantships available. Support available to part-time students. Financial award application deadline: 1/15. *Unit head:* Dr. Tamal Dey, Interim Chair, 614-688-3029, E-mail: dey.8@osu.edu. *Application contact:* Graduate and Professional Admissions, 614-292-9444, Fax: 614-292-3895, E-mail: gpadmissions@osu.edu.
Website: http://www.cse.osu.edu

The Ohio State University, Graduate School, College of Engineering, Department of Electrical and Computer Engineering, Columbus, OH 43210. Offers electrical and computer engineering (MS, PhD); electrical engineering (MS, PhD). *Program availability:* Part-time. *Faculty:* 62. *Students:* 437 (73 women). Average age 25. In 2018, 111 master's, 44 doctorates awarded. Terminal master's awarded for partial completion of doctoral program. *Entrance requirements:* For master's, GRE General Test (for all graduates of foreign universities and for applicants if undergraduate GPA below 3.2); for doctorate, GRE General Test (for all graduates of foreign universities and for applicants if graduate work GPA is below 3.5). Additional exam requirements/recommendations for international students: Required—TOEFL (minimum score 580 paper-based; 92 iBT); Recommended—IELTS (minimum score 7.5). *Application deadline:* For fall admission, 11/30 priority date for domestic and international students. Applications are processed on a rolling basis. Application fee: $60 ($70 for international students). Electronic applications accepted. *Financial support:* Fellowships with full tuition reimbursements, research assistantships with full tuition reimbursements, teaching assistantships with full tuition reimbursements, career-related internships or fieldwork, Federal Work-Study, institutionally sponsored loans, scholarships/grants, traineeships, health care benefits, and unspecified assistantships available. Support available to part-time students. *Unit head:* Dr. Hesham M. El Gamal, Chair, 614-292-4374, E-mail: elgamal.2@osu.edu. *Application contact:* Electrical and Computer Engineering Graduate Program, 614-292-2572, Fax: 614-292-7596, E-mail: ecegrad@ece.osu.edu.
Website: http://ece.osu.edu/

Oklahoma Christian University, Graduate School of Engineering and Computer Science, Oklahoma City, OK 73136-1100. Offers electrical and computer engineering (MSE); engineering management (MSE); mechanical engineering (MSE); software engineering (MSCS, MSE). *Program availability:* Part-time. *Entrance requirements:* Additional exam requirements/recommendations for international students: Required—TOEFL (minimum score 550 paper-based). Electronic applications accepted. *Expenses:* Contact institution.

Oklahoma State University, College of Engineering, Architecture and Technology, School of Electrical and Computer Engineering, Stillwater, OK 74078. Offers MS, PhD. *Program availability:* Online learning. *Faculty:* 20 full-time (2 women), 1 part-time/adjunct (0 women). *Students:* 25 full-time (7 women), 38 part-time (6 women); includes 7 minority (2 Black or African American, non-Hispanic/Latino; 1 Asian, non-Hispanic/Latino; 2 Hispanic/Latino; 2 Two or more races, non-Hispanic/Latino), 50 international. Average age 29. 159 applicants, 23% accepted, 18 enrolled. In 2018, 31 master's, 3 doctorates awarded. *Entrance requirements:* For master's and doctorate, GRE or GMAT. Additional exam requirements/recommendations for international students: Required—TOEFL (minimum score 550 paper-based; 79 iBT). *Application deadline:* For fall admission, 3/1 priority date for international students; for spring admission, 8/1 priority date for international students. Applications are processed on a rolling basis. Application fee: $40 ($75 for international students). Electronic applications accepted. *Expenses: Tuition, area resident:* Full-time $4148. Tuition, state resident: full-time $4148. Tuition, nonresident: full-time $10,517. *International tuition:* $10,517 full-time. *Required fees:* $4394; $2929 per credit hour. Tuition and fees vary according to course load and program. *Financial support:* Research assistantships, teaching assistantships, career-related internships or fieldwork, Federal Work-Study, scholarships/grants, health care benefits, tuition waivers (partial), and unspecified assistantships available. Support available to part-time students. Financial award application deadline: 3/1; financial award applicants required to submit FAFSA. *Unit head:* Dr. Jeffrey Young, Department Head, 405-744-5151, Fax: 405-744-9198, E-mail: jl.young@okstate.edu. *Application contact:* Dr. R. G. Ramakumar, Graduate Coordinator, 405-744-5157, Fax: 405-744-9198, E-mail: ramakum@okstate.edu.
Website: http://ece.okstate.edu

Old Dominion University, Frank Batten College of Engineering and Technology, Graduate Program in Electrical and Computer Engineering, Norfolk, VA 23529. Offers ME, MS, D Eng, PhD. *Program availability:* Part-time, online learning. *Degree requirements:* For master's, comprehensive exam (for some programs), thesis (for some programs); for doctorate, thesis/dissertation, candidacy exam, diagnostic exam, proposal defense. *Entrance requirements:* For master's, GRE, two letters of recommendation, resume, personal statement of objectives; for doctorate, GRE, three letters of recommendation, resume, personal statement of objectives. Additional exam requirements/recommendations for international students: Required—TOEFL (minimum score 550 paper-based; 79 iBT), IELTS (minimum score 6.5). Electronic applications accepted. *Expenses:* Contact institution. *Faculty research:* Cyber-physical systems, cybersecurity, communications and networking, computer vision and computational modeling, controls, hardware, bioelectrics, medical image processing, plasma medicine, signal processing for medical and biological applications, systems biology and computational bioengineering, photovoltaics, plasma processing, thin films and nanotechnology.

Oregon Health & Science University, School of Medicine, Graduate Programs in Medicine, Department of Computer Science and Electrical Engineering, Portland, OR 97239-3098. Offers computer science and engineering (MS, PhD); electrical engineering (MS, PhD). *Program availability:* Part-time. *Faculty:* 12 full-time (7 women), 9 part-time/adjunct (0 women). *Students:* 13 full-time (6 women), 12 part-time (1 woman); includes 4 minority (3 Asian, non-Hispanic/Latino; 1 Two or more races, non-Hispanic/Latino), 8 international. Average age 31. 16 applicants, 69% accepted, 11 enrolled. In 2018, 6 master's, 3 doctorates awarded. Terminal master's awarded for partial completion of doctoral program. *Degree requirements:* For master's, thesis (for some programs); for doctorate, comprehensive exam, thesis/dissertation, qualifying exam. *Entrance requirements:* For master's and doctorate, GRE General Test (minimum scores: 153 Verbal/148 Quantitative/4.5 Analytical). *Application deadline:* For fall admission, 7/15 for domestic students, 5/15 for international students; for winter admission, 10/15 for domestic students, 9/15 for international students; for spring admission, 1/15 for domestic students, 12/15 for international students. Applications are processed on a rolling basis. Application fee: $70. Electronic applications accepted. *Financial support:* Health care benefits, tuition waivers (full), and full-tuition and stipends (for PhD students) available. Financial award applicants required to submit FAFSA. *Faculty research:* Natural language processing, speech signal processing, computational biology, autism spectrum disorders, hearing and speaking disorders. *Unit head:* Dr. Peter Heeman, Program Director, 503-346-3755, E-mail: somgrad@ohsu.edu. *Application contact:* Pat Dickerson, Administrative Coordinator, 503-346-3753, E-mail: somgrad@ohsu.edu.
Website: http://www.ohsu.edu/xd/education/schools/school-of-medicine/departments/basic-science-departments/csee/

Oregon State University, College of Engineering, Program in Electrical and Computer Engineering, Corvallis, OR 97331. Offers M Eng, MS, PhD. *Entrance requirements:* For master's and doctorate, GRE. Additional exam requirements/recommendations for international students: Required—TOEFL (minimum score 600 paper-based; 80 iBT), IELTS (minimum score 7). *Expenses:* Contact institution.

Oregon State University, College of Engineering, Program in Materials Science, Corvallis, OR 97331. Offers chemical engineering (MS, PhD); chemistry (MS, PhD); civil engineering (MS, PhD); electrical and computer engineering (MS, PhD); forest products (MS, PhD); mathematics (MS, PhD); mechanical engineering (MS, PhD); nuclear engineering (MS); physics (MS, PhD). *Entrance requirements:* For master's and doctorate, GRE. Additional exam requirements/recommendations for international students: Required—TOEFL (minimum score 80 iBT), IELTS (minimum score 6.5). *Expenses:* Contact institution.

Penn State University Park, Graduate School, College of Engineering, Department of Computer Science and Engineering, University Park, PA 16802. Offers M Eng, MS, PhD.

See Display on page 239 and Close-Up on page 311.

Polytechnic University of Puerto Rico, Graduate School, Hato Rey, PR 00918. Offers business administration (MBA), including computer information systems, general management, management of information systems, management of international enterprises; civil engineering (ME, MS); computer engineering (ME, MS); computer science (MCS, MS); electrical engineering (ME, MS); engineering management (MEM); environmental management (MEM); landscape architecture (M Land Arch); manufacturing competitiveness (MMC, MS); manufacturing engineering (ME, MS); mechanical engineering (M Mech E). *Accreditation:* ASLA. *Program availability:* Part-time, evening/weekend. *Entrance requirements:* For master's, 3 letters of recommendation.

Portland State University, Graduate Studies, Maseeh College of Engineering and Computer Science, Department of Electrical and Computer Engineering, Portland, OR 97207-0751. Offers MS, PhD. *Program availability:* Part-time, evening/weekend. *Degree requirements:* For master's, variable foreign language requirement, oral exam; for doctorate, one foreign language, comprehensive exam, thesis/dissertation, oral and written exams. *Entrance requirements:* For master's, GRE, minimum GPA of 2.75; for doctorate, GRE General Test, GRE Subject Test, master's degree in electrical engineering or related field, 3 reference letters, statement of purpose, writing sample. Additional exam requirements/recommendations for international students: Required—TOEFL (minimum score 550 paper-based; 80 iBT). *Expenses:* Contact institution. *Faculty research:* Optics and laser systems, design automation, VLSI design, computer systems, power electronics.

Purdue University, College of Engineering, School of Electrical and Computer Engineering, West Lafayette, IN 47907-2035. Offers MSECE, PhD. MS and PhD degree programs in biomedical engineering offered jointly with School of Mechanical Engineering and School of Chemical Engineering. *Program availability:* Part-time, online learning. Terminal master's awarded for partial completion of doctoral program. *Degree requirements:* For master's, thesis optional; for doctorate, thesis/dissertation. *Entrance requirements:* For master's and doctorate, GRE General Test, minimum GPA of 3.25. Electronic applications accepted. *Faculty research:* Automatic control, biomedical imaging and sensing, communications, networking, signal and image processing, computer engineering, education, fields and optics, microelectronics and nanotechnology, power and energy systems, VLSI and circuit design.

Purdue University Fort Wayne, College of Engineering, Technology, and Computer Science, Department of Electrical and Computer Engineering, Fort Wayne, IN 46805-1499. Offers computer engineering (MSE); electrical engineering (MSE); systems engineering (MSE). *Program availability:* Part-time. *Entrance requirements:* For master's, minimum GPA of 3.0, bachelor's degree in engineering discipline. Additional exam requirements/recommendations for international students: Required—TOEFL (minimum score 550 paper-based; 79 iBT); Recommended—TWE. Electronic applications accepted.

Purdue University Northwest, Graduate Studies Office, School of Engineering, Mathematics, and Science, Department of Engineering, Hammond, IN 46323-2094. Offers computer engineering (MSE); electrical engineering (MSE); engineering (MS); mechanical engineering (MSE). *Program availability:* Evening/weekend. *Entrance requirements:* Additional exam requirements/recommendations for international students: Required—TOEFL.

Queen's University at Kingston, School of Graduate Studies, Faculty of Engineering and Applied Science, Department of Electrical and Computer Engineering, Kingston, ON K7L 3N6, Canada. Offers M Eng, M Sc, M Sc Eng, PhD. *Program availability:* Part-time. *Degree requirements:* For master's, thesis optional; for doctorate, comprehensive exam, thesis/dissertation. *Entrance requirements:* Additional exam requirements/recommendations for international students: Required—TOEFL (minimum score 580 paper-based). *Faculty research:* Communications and signal processing systems, computer engineering systems.

Rensselaer at Hartford, Department of Engineering, Program in Computer and Systems Engineering, Hartford, CT 06120-2991. Offers ME. *Entrance requirements:* For master's, GRE.

Rensselaer Polytechnic Institute, Graduate School, School of Engineering, Program in Computer and Systems Engineering, Troy, NY 12180-3590. Offers M Eng, MS, PhD. *Faculty:* 40 full-time (6 women), 1 part-time/adjunct (0 women). *Students:* 18 full-time (3 women), 2 part-time (0 women), 16 international. Average age 25. 61 applicants, 46% accepted, 6 enrolled. In 2018, 7 master's, 2 doctorates awarded. Terminal master's awarded for partial completion of doctoral program. *Degree requirements:* For master's, thesis (for some programs); for doctorate, thesis/dissertation. *Entrance requirements:* For master's and doctorate, GRE. Additional exam requirements/recommendations for international students: Required—TOEFL (minimum score 570 paper-based; 88 iBT), IELTS (minimum score 6.5), PTE (minimum score 60). *Application deadline:* For fall admission, 1/1 priority date for domestic and international students; for spring admission, 8/15 priority date for domestic and international students. Applications are processed on a rolling basis. Application fee: $75. Electronic applications accepted. *Financial support:* In 2018–19, research assistantships (averaging $23,000 per year), teaching assistantships (averaging $23,000 per year) were awarded; fellowships also available. Financial award application deadline: 1/1. *Faculty research:* Communications, information, and signals and systems; computer engineering, hardware, and architecture; computer networking; control, robotics, and automation; energy sources and systems; image science: computer vision, image processing, and geographic information science; microelectronics, photonics, VLSI, and mixed-signal design; plasma science and electromagnetics. *Total annual research expenditures:* $1.5 million. *Unit head:* Dr. Hussein Abouzeid, Graduate Program Director, 518-576-6534, E-mail: abouzeid@ecse.rpi.edu. *Application contact:* Jarron Decker, Director of Graduate Admissions, 518-276-6216, Fax: 518-276-4072, E-mail: gradadmissions@rpi.edu. Website: https://ecse.rpi.edu/

Rice University, Graduate Programs, George R. Brown School of Engineering, Department of Electrical and Computer Engineering, Houston, TX 77251-1892. Offers bioengineering (MS, PhD); circuits, controls, and communication systems (MS, PhD); computer science and engineering (MS, PhD); electrical engineering (MEE); lasers, microwaves, and solid-state electronics (MS, PhD); MBA/MEE. *Program availability:* Part-time. *Degree requirements:* For master's, thesis (for some programs); for doctorate, thesis/dissertation. *Entrance requirements:* For master's and doctorate, GRE General Test, GRE Subject Test, minimum GPA of 3.0. Additional exam requirements/recommendations for international students: Required—TOEFL (minimum score 600 paper-based; 90 iBT). Electronic applications accepted. *Faculty research:* Physical electronics, systems, computer engineering, bioengineering.

Rice University, Graduate Programs, George R. Brown School of Engineering, Program in Computational Science and Engineering, Houston, TX 77251-1892. Offers MCSE.

Rochester Institute of Technology, Graduate Enrollment Services, Kate Gleason College of Engineering, Computer Engineering Department, MS Program in Computer Engineering, Rochester, NY 14623-5603. Offers MS. *Program availability:* Part-time. *Students:* 41 full-time (5 women), 7 part-time (1 woman); includes 2 minority (both Asian, non-Hispanic/Latino), 33 international. Average age 24. 98 applicants, 50% accepted, 15 enrolled. In 2018, 17 master's awarded. *Degree requirements:* For master's, thesis or alternative, Thesis or Project. *Entrance requirements:* For master's, GRE, minimum GPA of 3.0 (recommended), two letters of recommendation. Additional exam requirements/recommendations for international students: Required—TOEFL (minimum score 550 paper-based; 79 iBT), IELTS (minimum score 6.5), PTE (minimum score 58). *Application deadline:* For fall admission, 2/15 priority date for domestic and international students; for spring admission, 12/15 priority date for domestic and international students. Applications are processed on a rolling basis. Application fee: $65. Electronic applications accepted. *Financial support:* In 2018–19, 47 students received support. Fellowships, research assistantships with partial tuition reimbursements available, teaching assistantships with partial tuition reimbursements available, career-related internships or fieldwork, scholarships/grants, and unspecified assistantships available. Support available to part-time students. Financial award applicants required to submit FAFSA. *Faculty research:* Computer architecture; integrated circuits and systems; networks and security; computer vision and machine intelligence; signal processing, controls, and embedded systems. *Unit head:* Andres Kwasinski, Graduate Program Director, 585-475-5134, E-mail: axkeec@rit.edu. *Application contact:* Diane Ellison, Senior Associate Vice President, Graduate Enrollment Services, 585-475-2229, Fax: 585-475-7164, E-mail: gradinfo@rit.edu.
Website: https://www.rit.edu/study/computer-engineering-ms

Rose-Hulman Institute of Technology, Graduate Studies, Department of Electrical and Computer Engineering, Terre Haute, IN 47803-3999. Offers electrical and computer engineering (M Eng); electrical engineering (MS); systems engineering and management (MS). *Program availability:* Part-time. *Faculty:* 19 full-time (2 women), 1 (woman) part-time/adjunct. *Students:* 4 full-time (0 women), 4 part-time (2 women), 7 international. Average age 26. 9 applicants, 44% accepted, 4 enrolled. In 2018, 2 master's awarded. *Degree requirements:* For master's, thesis (for some programs). *Entrance requirements:* For master's, GRE, minimum GPA of 3.0. Additional exam requirements/recommendations for international students: Required—TOEFL (minimum score 580 paper-based; 94 iBT), IELTS (minimum score 7). *Application deadline:* For fall admission, 2/1 priority date for domestic and international students; for winter admission, 10/1 for domestic students, 4/1 for international students; for spring admission, 1/15 for domestic students, 11/1 for international students. Applications are processed on a rolling basis. Application fee: $0. Electronic applications accepted. *Expenses: Tuition:* Full-time $46,641. *Financial support:* In 2018–19, 7 students received support. Fellowships with tuition reimbursements available, research assistantships with tuition reimbursements available, institutionally sponsored loans, scholarships/grants, and tuition waivers (full and partial) available. *Faculty research:* VLSI, power systems, analog electronics, communications, electromagnetics. *Total annual research expenditures:* $55,933. *Unit head:* Dr. Mario Simoni, Department Head, 812-877-8341, Fax: 812-877-8895, E-mail: simoni@rose-hulman.edu. *Application contact:* Dr. Craig Downing, Associate Dean of the Faculty, 812-877-8822, E-mail: downing@rose-hulman.edu.
Website: https://www.rose-hulman.edu/academics/academic-departments/electrical-computer-engineering/index.html

Royal Military College of Canada, Division of Graduate Studies, Faculty of Engineering, Department of Electrical and Computer Engineering, Kingston, ON K7K 7B4, Canada. Offers computer engineering (M Eng, PhD); electrical engineering (M Eng, PhD); software engineering (M Eng, PhD). *Degree requirements:* For master's, thesis; for doctorate, comprehensive exam, thesis/dissertation. *Entrance requirements:* For master's, honours degree with second-class standing in the appropriate field; for doctorate, master's degree. Electronic applications accepted.

Rutgers University–New Brunswick, Graduate School-New Brunswick, Department of Electrical and Computer Engineering, Piscataway, NJ 08854-8097. Offers communications and solid-state electronics (MS, PhD); computer engineering (MS, PhD); control systems (MS, PhD); digital signal processing (MS, PhD). *Program availability:* Part-time. Terminal master's awarded for partial completion of doctoral program. *Degree requirements:* For master's, thesis or alternative; for doctorate, thesis/dissertation. *Entrance requirements:* For master's and doctorate, GRE General Test. Additional exam requirements/recommendations for international students: Required—TOEFL. Electronic applications accepted. *Faculty research:* Communication and information processing, wireless information networks, micro-vacuum devices, machine vision, VLSI design.

St. Mary's University, School of Science, Engineering and Technology, Program in Computer Engineering, San Antonio, TX 78228. Offers MS. *Program availability:* Part-time. *Students:* 3 full-time (1 woman), 2 part-time (both women); includes 2 minority (both Hispanic/Latino), 3 international. Average age 27. 3 applicants, 67% accepted, 1 enrolled. In 2018, 1 master's awarded. *Degree requirements:* For master's, thesis or project. *Entrance requirements:* For master's, GRE (minimum quantitative score of 148), bachelor's degree in computer engineering, electrical engineering or a closely-related discipline; minimum GPA of 3.0; written statement of purpose; two letters of recommendation; official transcripts. Additional exam requirements/recommendations for international students: Required—TOEFL (minimum score 550 paper-based; 80 iBT), IELTS (minimum score 6.5). *Application deadline:* For fall admission, 7/1 for domestic students; for spring admission, 11/15 for domestic students; for summer admission, 4/1 for domestic students. Applications are processed on a rolling basis. Electronic applications accepted. *Expenses: Tuition:* Full-time $16,830; part-time $935 per credit hour. *Required fees:* $1055. Tuition and fees vary according to program. *Financial support:* Research assistantships available. Financial award application deadline: 3/31; financial award applicants required to submit FAFSA. *Faculty research:* Computer security, parallel algorithms for 3-D image representation, computer architecture, computer networking. *Unit head:* Dr. Wenbin Luo, Graduate Program Director, 210-431-5002, E-mail: wluo@stmarytx.edu. *Application contact:* Kim Thornton, Director, Graduate and Adult Enrollment, 210-436-3126, E-mail: kthornton@stmarytx.edu. Website: https://www.stmarytx.edu/academics/programs/master-computer-engineering/

San Jose State University, Program in Computer Engineering, San Jose, CA 95192-0001. Offers computer engineering (MS); software engineering (MS). *Degree requirements:* For master's, comprehensive exam, thesis. *Entrance requirements:* For master's, GRE General Test. Electronic applications accepted. *Faculty research:* Robotics, database management systems, computer networks.

Santa Clara University, School of Engineering, Santa Clara, CA 95053. Offers applied mathematics (MS); bioengineering (MS); civil, environmental, and sustainable engineering (MS); computer science and engineering (MS, PhD, Engineer); electrical engineering (MS, PhD, Engineer); engineering management and leadership (MS); mechanical engineering (MS, PhD, Engineer); power systems and sustainable energy (MS); software engineering (MS). *Program availability:* Part-time. *Faculty:* 72 full-time (24 women), 52 part-time/adjunct (9 women). *Students:* 555 full-time (211 women), 269 part-time (91 women); includes 208 minority (8 Black or African American, non-Hispanic/Latino; 1 American Indian or Alaska Native, non-Hispanic/Latino; 145 Asian, non-Hispanic/Latino; 28 Hispanic/Latino; 26 Two or more races, non-Hispanic/Latino), 472 international. Average age 27. 1,309 applicants, 36% accepted, 269 enrolled. In 2018, 320 master's, 7 doctorates awarded. *Entrance requirements:* For master's, GRE, official transcript; for doctorate, GRE, Official transcript, 500 word statement of purpose, three letters of recommendation. Additional exam requirements/recommendations for international students: Required—TOEFL (minimum score 79 iBT), IELTS (minimum score 6.5). *Application deadline:* For fall admission, 6/1 for domestic students; for winter admission, 9/6 for domestic students; for spring admission, 1/10 for domestic students; for summer admission, 3/6 for domestic students. Application fee: $60. Electronic applications accepted. *Financial support:* Fellowships, Federal Work-Study, and scholarships/grants available. Support available to part-time students. Financial award applicants required to submit FAFSA. *Unit head:* Dr. Elaine Scott, Dean, 408-554-3512, E-mail: epscott@scu.edu. *Application contact:* Stacey Tinker, Director of Admissions and Marketing, 408-554-4748, Fax: 408-554-4323, E-mail: stinker@scu.edu. Website: http://www.scu.edu/engineering/graduate/

Southern Illinois University Carbondale, Graduate School, College of Engineering, Department of Electrical and Computer Engineering, Carbondale, IL 62901-4701. Offers MS, PhD, JD/MS. *Degree requirements:* For master's, comprehensive exam, thesis. *Entrance requirements:* For master's, GRE, minimum GPA of 2.7; for doctorate, GRE, minimum GPA of 3.25. Additional exam requirements/recommendations for international students: Required—TOEFL. *Faculty research:* Circuits and power systems, communications and signal processing, controls and systems, electromagnetics and optics, electronics instrumentation and bioengineering.

Southern Illinois University Carbondale, Graduate School, College of Engineering, Program in Engineering Science, Carbondale, IL 62901-4701. Offers engineering science (PhD), including civil and environmental engineering, electrical and computer engineering, mechanical engineering and energy processes, mining and mineral resources engineering. *Degree requirements:* For doctorate, thesis/dissertation. *Entrance requirements:* For doctorate, GRE General Test, minimum GPA of 3.5. Additional exam requirements/recommendations for international students: Required—TOEFL.

Southern Methodist University, Lyle School of Engineering, Department of Computer Science and Engineering, Dallas, TX 75275-0122. Offers computer engineering (MS, PhD); computer science (MS, PhD); security engineering (MS); software engineering (MS, DE). *Program availability:* Part-time, evening/weekend, online learning. Terminal master's awarded for partial completion of doctoral program. *Degree requirements:* For master's, thesis optional; for doctorate, thesis/dissertation, oral and written qualifying exams, oral final exam (PhD). *Entrance requirements:* For master's, GRE General Test, minimum GPA of 3.0 in last 2 years; bachelor's degree in engineering, mathematics, or sciences; for doctorate, preliminary counseling exam (PhD), minimum GPA of 3.0, bachelor's degree in related field, MA (for DE). Additional exam requirements/recommendations for international students: Required—TOEFL (minimum score 550 paper-based). *Faculty research:* Trusted and high performance network computing, software engineering and management, knowledge engineering and management, computer arithmetic, computer architecture and CAD.

Stevens Institute of Technology, Graduate School, Charles V. Schaefer Jr. School of Engineering and Science, Department of Electrical and Computer Engineering, Program in Computer Engineering, Hoboken, NJ 07030. Offers computer engineering (PhD, Certificate), including digital signal processing (Certificate), digital systems and VLSI design (Certificate), multimedia technology (Certificate), networked information systems (Certificate), real-time and embedded systems (Certificate), secure network systems design (Certificate); computer systems (M Eng); data communications and networks (M Eng); digital systems design (M Eng); engineered software systems (M Eng); image processing and multimedia (M Eng); information system security (M Eng); information systems (M Eng). *Program availability:* Part-time, evening/weekend. *Faculty:* 19 full-time (5 women), 5 part-time/adjunct (1 woman). *Students:* 77 full-time (10 women), 15 part-time (1 woman); includes 8 minority (1 Black or African American, non-Hispanic/Latino; 6 Asian, non-Hispanic/Latino; 1 Hispanic/Latino), 68 international. Average age 26. In 2018, 90 master's, 4 doctorates, 27 other advanced degrees awarded. Terminal master's awarded for partial completion of doctoral program. *Degree requirements:* For master's, thesis optional, minimum B average in major field and overall; for doctorate, comprehensive exam (for some programs), thesis/dissertation; for Certificate, minimum B average. *Entrance requirements:* For master's, GRE/GMAT scores: GRE scores are required for all applicants applying to a full-time graduate program in the Schaefer School of Engineering and Science (SES). International applicants must submit TOEFL/IELTS scores and fulfill the English Language Proficiency Requirements in order to be considered. Additional exam requirements/recommendations for international students: Required—TOEFL (minimum score 74 iBT), IELTS (minimum score 6). *Application deadline:* For fall admission, 4/15 for domestic and international students; for spring admission, 11/1 for domestic and international students; for summer admission, 5/1 for domestic students. Applications are processed on a rolling basis. Application fee: $60. Electronic applications accepted. *Expenses: Tuition:* Full-time $35,960; part-time $1620 per credit. *Required fees:* $1290; $600 per semester. Tuition and fees vary according to course load. *Financial support:* Fellowships, research assistantships, teaching assistantships, career-related internships or fieldwork, Federal Work-Study, scholarships/grants, and unspecified assistantships available. Financial award application deadline: 2/15; financial award applicants required to submit FAFSA. *Unit head:* Dr. Jean Zu, Dean of SES, 201-216.8233, Fax: 201-216.8372, E-mail: Jean.Zu@stevens.edu. *Application contact:* Graduate Admissions, 888-783-8367, Fax: 888-511-1306, E-mail: graduate@stevens.edu.

Stevens Institute of Technology, Graduate School, Charles V. Schaefer Jr. School of Engineering and Science, Department of Mechanical Engineering, Program in Integrated Product Development, Hoboken, NJ 07030. Offers armament engineering (M Eng); computer and electrical engineering (M Eng); manufacturing technologies (M Eng); systems reliability and design (M Eng). *Program availability:* Part-time, evening/weekend. *Faculty:* 32 full-time (4 women), 10 part-time/adjunct (0 women). *Degree requirements:* For master's, thesis optional, minimum B average in major field and overall. *Entrance requirements:* For master's, GRE/GMAT scores: GRE scores are required for all applicants applying to a full-time graduate program in the Schaefer School of Engineering and Science (SES). International applicants must submit TOEFL/IELTS scores and fulfill the English Language Proficiency Requirements in order to be considered. Additional exam requirements/recommendations for international students: Required—TOEFL (minimum score 74 iBT), IELTS (minimum score 6). *Application deadline:* For fall admission, 4/15 for domestic and international students; for spring admission, 11/1 for domestic and international students; for summer admission, 5/1 for domestic students. Applications are processed on a rolling basis. Application fee: $60. Electronic applications accepted. *Expenses: Tuition:* Full-time $35,960; part-time $1620 per credit. *Required fees:* $1290; $600 per semester. Tuition and fees vary according to course load. *Financial support:* Fellowships, research assistantships, teaching assistantships, career-related internships or fieldwork, Federal Work-Study, scholarships/grants, and unspecified assistantships available. Financial award application deadline: 2/15; financial award applicants required to submit FAFSA. *Unit head:* Dr. Jean Zu, Dean of SES, 201-216.8233, Fax: 201-216.8372, E-mail: Jean.Zu@stevens.edu. *Application contact:* Graduate Admissions, 888-783-8367, Fax: 888-511-1306, E-mail: graduate@stevens.edu.

Stony Brook University, State University of New York, Graduate School, College of Engineering and Applied Sciences, Department of Electrical and Computer Engineering, Program in Computer Engineering, Stony Brook, NY 11794. Offers MS, PhD. *Students:* 49 full-time (5 women), 42 part-time (13 women); includes 11 minority (8 Asian, non-Hispanic/Latino; 2 Hispanic/Latino; 1 Two or more races, non-Hispanic/Latino), 74 international. Average age 26. 175 applicants, 84% accepted, 32 enrolled. In 2018, 23 master's, 3 doctorates awarded. *Entrance requirements:* For master's, GRE; for doctorate, GRE, statement of purpose, resume, three recommendation letters. Additional exam requirements/recommendations for international students: Required—TOEFL (minimum score 90 iBT). *Application deadline:* For fall admission, 1/15 for domestic students; for spring admission, 10/1 for domestic students. Application fee: $100. *Expenses:* Contact institution. *Financial support:* Research assistantships and teaching assistantships available. *Unit head:* Prof. Petar M. Djuric, Chair, 631-632-8420, Fax: 631-632-8494, E-mail: petar.djuric@stonybrook.edu. *Application contact:* Angela Scauso, Coordinator, 631-632-8401, Fax: 631-632-8494, E-mail: angela.scauso@stonybrook.edu.

Syracuse University, College of Engineering and Computer Science, MS Program in Computer Engineering, Syracuse, NY 13244. Offers MS. *Program availability:* Part-time. *Students:* Average age 24. *Degree requirements:* For master's, comprehensive exam (for some programs), thesis (for some programs). *Entrance requirements:* For master's, GRE General Test, three letters of recommendation, personal statement, resume, official transcripts. Additional exam requirements/recommendations for international students: Required—TOEFL (minimum score 100 iBT). *Application deadline:* For fall admission, 6/1 priority date for domestic and international students; for spring admission, 11/15 priority date for domestic students, 10/15 priority date for international students. Applications are processed on a rolling basis. Application fee: $75. Electronic applications accepted. *Financial support:* Fellowships with full tuition reimbursements, research assistantships, teaching assistantships, and tuition waivers (partial) available. Financial award application deadline: 1/1; financial award applicants required to submit FAFSA. *Faculty research:* Software systems, hardware systems, security and assurance systems, computer engineering, digital machine design. *Unit head:* Dr. Qinru Qiu, Director, 315-443-1836, Fax: 315-443-2583, E-mail: eecsadmissions@syr.edu. *Application contact:* Kathleen Joyce, Assistant Dean, 315-443-2219, E-mail: topgrads@syr.edu.
Website: http://eng-cs.syr.edu/program/computer-engineering/?degree-masters_program

Syracuse University, College of Engineering and Computer Science, PhD Program in Electrical and Computer Engineering, Syracuse, NY 13244. Offers PhD. *Program availability:* Part-time. *Students:* Average age 29. In 2018, 12 doctorates awarded. *Degree requirements:* For doctorate, comprehensive exam, thesis/dissertation. *Entrance requirements:* For doctorate, GRE General Test, three letters of recommendation, personal statement, resume, official transcripts. Additional exam requirements/recommendations for international students: Required—TOEFL (minimum score 100 iBT). *Application deadline:* For fall admission, 2/1 priority date for domestic and international students. Application fee: $75. Electronic applications accepted. *Financial support:* Fellowships with full tuition reimbursements, research assistantships, and teaching assistantships available. Financial award application deadline: 1/1. *Faculty research:* Electrical engineering, computer engineering hardware. *Unit head:* Dr. Qinru Qiu, Professor, Computer Engineering/Program Director, Electrical Engineering and Computer Science, 315-443-1836, E-mail: eecsadmissions@syr.edu. *Application contact:* Kathleen Joyce, Assistant Dean, 315-443-2219, E-mail: bflowers@syr.edu.
Website: http://eng-cs.syr.edu/program/electrical-and-computer-engineering/?degree-doctoral_program

Tennessee State University, The School of Graduate Studies and Research, College of Engineering, Nashville, TN 37209-1561. Offers biomedical engineering (ME); civil engineering (ME); computer and information systems engineering (MS, PhD); electrical engineering (ME); environmental engineering (ME); manufacturing engineering (ME); mathematical sciences (MS); mechanical engineering (ME). *Program availability:* Part-time, evening/weekend. *Degree requirements:* For master's, project; for doctorate, comprehensive exam, thesis/dissertation. *Entrance requirements:* For doctorate, minimum GPA of 3.3. *Faculty research:* Robotics, intelligent systems, human-computer interaction software systems, biomedical engineering, signal/image processing, probabilistic design, intelligent manufacturing, cooperative mobile robots, condition based maintenance, sensor fusion.

Texas A&M University, College of Engineering, Department of Electrical and Computer Engineering, College Station, TX 77843. Offers computer engineering (M Eng, PhD); electrical engineering (M Eng). *Faculty:* 75. *Students:* 606 full-time (124 women), 138 part-time (34 women); includes 33 minority (2 Black or African American, non-Hispanic/Latino; 18 Asian, non-Hispanic/Latino; 10 Hispanic/Latino; 3 Two or more races, non-Hispanic/Latino), 671 international. Average age 27. 1,676 applicants, 33% accepted, 207 enrolled. In 2018, 159 master's, 59 doctorates awarded. *Degree requirements:* For master's, thesis (MS); for doctorate, thesis/dissertation. *Entrance requirements:* For master's and doctorate, GRE General Test. Additional exam requirements/recommendations for international students: Required—TOEFL (minimum score 550 paper-based; 80 iBT), IELTS (minimum score 6), PTE (minimum score 53). *Application deadline:* For fall admission, 1/1 for domestic students, 2/1 for international students; for spring admission, 10/1 for domestic students, 8/1 for international students. Application fee: $50 ($90 for international students). *Expenses:* Contact institution. *Financial support:* In 2018–19, 471 students received support, including 28 fellowships with tuition reimbursements available (averaging $14,729 per year), 204 research assistantships with tuition reimbursements available (averaging $15,220 per year), 109 teaching assistantships with tuition reimbursements available (averaging $13,216 per year); career-related internships or fieldwork, institutionally sponsored loans, scholarships/grants, traineeships, health care benefits, tuition waivers (full and partial), and unspecified assistantships also available. Support available to part-time students. Financial award application deadline: 3/15; financial award applicants required to submit FAFSA. *Faculty research:* Solid-state, electric power systems, and communications engineering. *Unit head:* Dr. Miroslav M. Begovic, Department Head, 979-862-1553, E-mail: begovic@ece.tamu.edu. *Application contact:* Tammy Carda, Senior Academic Advisor II, 979-845-7467, E-mail: t-carda@tamu.edu.
Website: http://engineering.tamu.edu/electrical/

Universidad del Turabo, Graduate Programs, School of Engineering, Gurabo, PR 00778-3030. Offers computer engineering (M Eng); electrical engineering (M Eng); mechanical engineering (M Eng); telecommunications and network systems administration (M Eng). *Entrance requirements:* For master's, GRE, EXADEP or GMAT, interview, essay, official transcript, recommendation letters. Electronic applications accepted.

The University of Akron, Graduate School, College of Engineering, Department of Electrical and Computer Engineering, Akron, OH 44325. Offers computer engineering (MS, PhD); electrical engineering (MS). *Program availability:* Evening/weekend. *Degree requirements:* For master's, oral comprehensive exam or thesis; for doctorate, one foreign language, thesis/dissertation, candidacy exam, qualifying exam. *Entrance requirements:* For master's, GRE, minimum GPA of 2.75, three letters of recommendation, statement of purpose; for doctorate, GRE, minimum GPA of 3.0 with bachelor's degree, 3.5 with master's degree; three letters of recommendation; statement of purpose; resume. Additional exam requirements/recommendations for international students: Required—TOEFL (minimum score 79 iBT), IELTS (minimum score 6.5). Electronic applications accepted. *Faculty research:* Computational electromagnetics and nondestructive testing, control systems, sensors and actuators applications and networks, alternative energy systems and hybrid vehicles, analog integrated circuit (IC) design, embedded systems.

The University of Alabama, Graduate School, College of Engineering, Department of Electrical and Computer Engineering, Tuscaloosa, AL 35487-0286. Offers electrical engineering (MS, PhD). *Program availability:* Part-time, online learning. *Degree requirements:* For master's, thesis or alternative; for doctorate, one foreign language, comprehensive exam, thesis/dissertation. *Entrance requirements:* For master's, GRE (for students from non ABET-accredited schools), minimum GPA of 3.0 in last 60 hours of course work or overall; for doctorate, GRE (for students from non ABET-accredited schools), minimum GPA of 3.0 overall. Additional exam requirements/recommendations for international students: Required—TOEFL (minimum score 550 paper-based). Electronic applications accepted. *Faculty research:* Devices and materials, electromechanical systems, embedded systems.

The University of Alabama at Birmingham, School of Engineering, Program in Electrical Engineering, Birmingham, AL 35294. Offers computer engineering (PhD); electrical and computer engineering (MSEE). *Program availability:* Part-time. *Faculty:* 8 full-time (0 women), 3 part-time/adjunct (0 women). *Students:* 39 full-time (7 women), 27 part-time (3 women); includes 10 minority (3 Black or African American, non-Hispanic/Latino; 3 Asian, non-Hispanic/Latino; 3 Hispanic/Latino; 1 Two or more races, non-Hispanic/Latino), 42 international. Average age 29. 66 applicants, 67% accepted, 18 enrolled. In 2018, 12 master's, 4 doctorates awarded. *Degree requirements:* For master's, comprehensive exam, thesis (for some programs); for doctorate, comprehensive exam, thesis/dissertation. *Entrance requirements:* For master's, GRE, A 3.0 on a 4.0 scale or better GPA in all junior and senior electrical and computer engineering and mathematics courses attempted;; for doctorate, GRE, An overall GPA of at least 3.0 on a 4.0 point scale, or at least 3.0 for the last 60 semester hours completed; and. Additional exam requirements/recommendations for international students: Required—TOEFL (minimum score 80 iBT), IELTS (minimum score 6.5). *Application deadline:* For fall admission, 8/1 for domestic and international students; for spring admission, 12/1 for domestic and international students; for summer admission, 5/1 for domestic and international students. Applications are processed on a rolling basis. Application fee: $50 ($60 for international students). Electronic applications accepted. *Expenses:* Contact institution. *Financial support:* In 2018–19, 22 students received support, including 4 fellowships with full tuition reimbursements available (averaging $30,500 per year), 9 research assistantships with full and partial tuition reimbursements available, 9 teaching assistantships; unspecified assistantships also available. *Faculty research:* Low-power analog and RF circuit design for sensors and biomedical instrumentation, mathematical foundations of quantum electronics, intelligent control of respiratory therapy, mobile and cloud computing, information theoretical foundations for software. *Total annual research expenditures:* $23,644. *Unit head:* Dr. J Iwan Alexander, Interim Chair, 205-934-8440, E-mail: ialex@uab.edu. *Application contact:* Jesse Keppley, Director of Student and Academic Services, 205-996-5696, E-mail: gradschool@uab.edu.
Website: https://www.uab.edu/engineering/home/graduate#msee

The University of Alabama in Huntsville, School of Graduate Studies, College of Engineering, Department of Electrical and Computer Engineering, Huntsville, AL 35899. Offers computer engineering (MSE, PhD); electrical engineering (MSE, PhD), including optics and photonics technology (MSE); optical science and engineering (PhD); software engineering (MSSE). *Program availability:* Part-time. *Faculty:* 22 full-time (4 women), 4 part-time/adjunct. *Students:* 65 full-time (12 women), 125 part-time (12 women); includes 12 minority (5 Black or African American, non-Hispanic/Latino; 5 Asian, non-Hispanic/Latino; 2 Hispanic/Latino), 61 international. Average age 31. 199 applicants, 78% accepted, 46 enrolled. In 2018, 42 master's, 11 doctorates awarded. *Degree requirements:* For master's, comprehensive exam, thesis or alternative, oral and written exams; for doctorate, comprehensive exam, thesis/dissertation, oral and written exams. *Entrance requirements:* For master's, GRE General Test, appropriate bachelor's degree, minimum GPA of 3.0; for doctorate, GRE General Test, minimum GPA of 3.0. Additional exam requirements/recommendations for international students: Required—TOEFL (minimum score 500 paper-based; 80 iBT), IELTS (minimum score 6.5). *Application deadline:* For fall admission, 7/15 priority date for domestic students, 4/1 priority date for international students; for spring admission, 11/30 priority date for domestic students, 9/1 priority date for international students. Applications are processed on a rolling basis. Application fee: $50. Electronic applications accepted. *Expenses: Tuition, area resident:* Full-time $10,632; part-time $412 per credit hour. Tuition, state resident: full-time $10,632. Tuition, nonresident: full-time $23,604; part-time $412 per credit hour. *Required fees:* $582; $582. Tuition and fees vary according to course load and program. *Financial support:* In 2018–19, 37 students received support, including 18 research assistantships with full tuition reimbursements available (averaging $5,783 per year), 19 teaching assistantships with full tuition reimbursements available (averaging $5,813 per year); career-related internships or fieldwork, Federal Work-Study, institutionally sponsored loans, scholarships/grants, health care benefits, tuition waivers (full and partial), and unspecified assistantships also available. Support available to part-time students. Financial award application deadline: 4/1; financial award applicants required to submit FAFSA. *Faculty research:* Advanced computer architecture and systems, fault tolerant computing and verification, computational electro-magnetics, nano-photonics and plasmonics, micro electro-mechanical (MEMS) systems. *Unit head:* Dr. Ravi Gorur, Chair, 256-824-6316, Fax: 256-824-6803, E-mail: ravi.gorur@uah.edu. *Application contact:* Kim Gray, Graduate Studies Admissions Coordinator, 256-824-6002, Fax: 256-824-6405, E-mail: deangrad@uah.edu. Website: http://www.ece.uah.edu/

University of Alberta, Faculty of Graduate Studies and Research, Department of Electrical and Computer Engineering, Edmonton, AB T6G 2E1, Canada. Offers communications (M Eng, M Sc, PhD); computer engineering (M Eng, M Sc, PhD); electromagnetics (M Eng, M Sc, PhD); nanotechnology and microdevices (M Eng, M Sc, PhD); power/power electronics (M Eng, M Sc, PhD); systems (M Eng, M Sc, PhD). Terminal master's awarded for partial completion of doctoral program. *Degree requirements:* For master's, thesis; for doctorate, thesis/dissertation. *Entrance requirements:* Additional exam requirements/recommendations for international students: Required—TOEFL. Electronic applications accepted. *Faculty research:* Controls, communications, microelectronics, electromagnetics.

The University of Arizona, College of Engineering, Department of Electrical and Computer Engineering, Tucson, AZ 85721. Offers MS, PhD. *Program availability:* Part-time. *Degree requirements:* For master's, thesis (for some programs); for doctorate, thesis/dissertation. *Entrance requirements:* For master's, GRE General Test, 3 letters of recommendation, statement of purpose; for doctorate, GRE General Test, master's degree in related field, 3 letters of recommendation, statement of purpose. Additional exam requirements/recommendations for international students: Required—TOEFL (minimum score 550 paper-based; 79 iBT). Electronic applications accepted. *Faculty research:* Communication systems, control systems, signal processing, computer-aided logic.

University of Arkansas, Graduate School, College of Engineering, Department of Computer Science and Computer Engineering, Program in Computer Engineering, Fayetteville, AR 72701. Offers MS Cmp E, MSE, PhD. In 2018, 13 master's, 3 doctorates awarded. *Degree requirements:* For master's, thesis optional; for doctorate, one foreign language, thesis/dissertation. *Application deadline:* For fall admission, 8/1 for domestic students, 4/1 for international students; for spring admission, 12/1 for domestic students, 10/1 for international students; for summer admission, 4/15 for domestic students, 3/1 for international students. Applications are processed on a rolling basis. Application fee: $60. Electronic applications accepted. *Financial support:* In 2018–19, 8 research assistantships, 2 teaching assistantships were awarded; fellowships with tuition reimbursements, career-related internships or fieldwork, and Federal Work-Study also available. Support available to part-time students. Financial award application deadline: 4/1; financial award applicants required to submit FAFSA. *Unit head:* Dr. Xiaoqing Liu, Department Head, 479-575-6254, Fax: 479-575-5339, E-mail: franKliu@uark.edu. *Application contact:* Dr. Brajendra Nath Panda, Professor, Associate Depart. Head of Grad. Program, 479-575-2067, E-mail: bpanda@uark.edu. Website: https://computer-science-and-computer-engineering.uark.edu/index.php

University of Bridgeport, School of Engineering, Departments of Computer Science and Computer Engineering, Bridgeport, CT 06604. Offers computer engineering (MS); computer science (MS); computer science and engineering (PhD). *Degree requirements:* For master's, thesis optional; for doctorate, comprehensive exam, thesis/ dissertation. *Entrance requirements:* Additional exam requirements/recommendations for international students: Recommended—TOEFL (minimum score 550 paper-based; 80 iBT), IELTS (minimum score 6.5). Electronic applications accepted. *Expenses:* Contact institution.

The University of British Columbia, Faculty of Applied Science, Department of Electrical and Computer Engineering, Vancouver, BC V6T 1Z4, Canada. Offers M Eng, MA Sc, PhD. *Program availability:* Part-time. *Degree requirements:* For master's, thesis (for some programs); for doctorate, thesis/dissertation. *Entrance requirements:* Additional exam requirements/recommendations for international students: Required—TOEFL, IELTS. Electronic applications accepted. *Expenses:* Contact institution. *Faculty research:* Applied electromagnetics, biomedical engineering, communications and signal processing, computer and software engineering, power engineering, robotics, solid-state, systems and control.

University of Calgary, Faculty of Graduate Studies, Schulich School of Engineering, Program in Electrical and Computer Engineering, Calgary, AB T2N 1N4, Canada. Offers M Eng, M Sc, PhD. *Program availability:* Part-time. *Degree requirements:* For master's, thesis (for M Sc); for doctorate, thesis/dissertation, candidacy exam. *Entrance requirements:* For master's, minimum GPA of 3.0; for doctorate, minimum GPA of 3.5. Additional exam requirements/recommendations for international students: Required—TOEFL (minimum score 550 paper-based; 80 iBT) or IELTS (minimum score 7). Electronic applications accepted. *Faculty research:* Biomedical and bioelectrics, telecommunications and signal processing, software and computer engineering, power and control, microelectronics and instrumentation.

University of California, Davis, College of Engineering, Program in Electrical and Computer Engineering, Davis, CA 95616. Offers MS, PhD. Terminal master's awarded for partial completion of doctoral program. *Degree requirements:* For master's,

comprehensive exam (for some programs), thesis (for some programs); for doctorate, thesis/dissertation, preliminary and qualifying exams, thesis defense. *Entrance requirements:* For master's, GRE General Test, minimum GPA of 3.2; for doctorate, GRE, minimum graduate GPA of 3.5. Additional exam requirements/recommendations for international students: Required—TOEFL (minimum score 550 paper-based). Electronic applications accepted.

University of California, Los Angeles, Graduate Division, Henry Samueli School of Engineering and Applied Science, Department of Electrical and Computer Engineering, Los Angeles, CA 90095-1594. Offers MS, PhD. *Degree requirements:* For master's, comprehensive exam or thesis; for doctorate, thesis/dissertation, qualifying exams. *Entrance requirements:* For master's, GRE General Test, minimum GPA of 3.0; for doctorate, GRE General Test, minimum GPA of 3.25. Additional exam requirements/ recommendations for international students: Required—TOEFL (minimum score 560 paper-based; 87 iBT), IELTS (minimum score 7). Electronic applications accepted. *Faculty research:* Circuits and embedded systems, physical and wave electronics, signals and systems.

University of California, Riverside, Graduate Division, Department of Computer Science and Engineering, Computer Engineering Program, Riverside, CA 92521. Offers MS. *Degree requirements:* For master's, comprehensive exam, project, or thesis. *Entrance requirements:* For master's, GRE General Test (minimum expected score of 300 verbal and quantitative combined), minimum GPA of 3.2 in junior/senior years of undergraduate study (last two years). Additional exam requirements/recommendations for international students: Required—TOEFL (minimum score 550 paper-based, 80 iBT) or IELTS (7). Electronic applications accepted. *Expenses:* Contact institution.

University of California, San Diego, Graduate Division, Department of Computer Science and Engineering, La Jolla, CA 92093. Offers computer engineering (MS, PhD); computer science (MS, PhD). *Students:* 689 full-time (158 women), 136 part-time (22 women). 5,646 applicants, 15% accepted, 340 enrolled. In 2018, 259 master's, 28 doctorates awarded. Terminal master's awarded for partial completion of doctoral program. *Degree requirements:* For master's, comprehensive exam (for some programs), thesis (for some programs), comprehensive exam or thesis; for doctorate, comprehensive exam, thesis/dissertation, 1-quarter teaching assistantship. *Entrance requirements:* For master's and doctorate, GRE General Test. Additional exam requirements/recommendations for international students: Required—TOEFL (minimum score 550 paper-based; 80 iBT), IELTS (minimum score 7). *Application deadline:* For fall admission, 12/18 for domestic students. Application fee: $105 ($125 for international students). Electronic applications accepted. *Financial support:* Fellowships, research assistantships, teaching assistantships, career-related internships or fieldwork, and scholarships/grants available. Financial award applicants required to submit FAFSA. *Faculty research:* Artificial intelligence and machine learning, bioinformatics, computer architecture and compilers, visual computing, computer graphics, computer vision, databases and information management, embedded systems and software, high-performance computing, human-computer interaction, programming systems, security and cryptography, software engineering, systems and networking, ubiquitous computing and social dynamics, VLSI/CAD. *Unit head:* Dean Tullsen, Chair, 858-534-6181, E-mail: dtullsen@ucsd.edu. *Application contact:* Julie Connor, Graduate Coordinator, 858-534-8872, E-mail: gradinfo@cs.ucsd.edu. Website: http://cse.ucsd.edu

University of California, San Diego, Graduate Division, Department of Electrical and Computer Engineering, La Jolla, CA 92093. Offers applied ocean science (MS, PhD); applied physics (MS, PhD); communication theory and systems (MS, PhD); computer engineering (MS, PhD); electronic circuits and systems (MS, PhD); intelligent systems, robotics and control (MS, PhD); medical devices and systems (MS, PhD); nanoscale devices and systems (MS, PhD); photonics (MS, PhD); signal and image processing (MS, PhD). Program offered jointly with San Diego State University. *Students:* 830 full-time (174 women), 69 part-time (8 women). 2,810 applicants, 40% accepted, 399 enrolled. In 2018, 226 master's, 42 doctorates awarded. Terminal master's awarded for partial completion of doctoral program. *Degree requirements:* For master's, comprehensive exam (for some programs), thesis (for some programs); for doctorate, comprehensive exam, thesis/dissertation. *Entrance requirements:* For master's and doctorate, GRE General Test, minimum GPA of 3.0, resume or curriculum vitae (recommended). Additional exam requirements/recommendations for international students: Required—TOEFL (minimum score 550 paper-based; 80 iBT), IELTS (minimum score 7), PTE (minimum score 65). *Application deadline:* For fall admission, 12/13 for domestic students. Application fee: $105 ($125 for international students). Electronic applications accepted. *Financial support:* Fellowships, research assistantships, teaching assistantships, scholarships/grants, traineeships, and unspecified assistantships available. Financial award applicants required to submit FAFSA. *Faculty research:* Applied ocean science; applied physics; communication theory and systems; computer engineering; electronic circuits and systems; intelligent systems, robotics and control; medical devices and systems; nanoscale devices and systems; photonics; signal and image processing. *Unit head:* Bill Lin, Chair, 858-822-1383, E-mail: billin@ucsd.edu. *Application contact:* Sean Jones, Graduate Admissions Coordinator, 858-534-3213, E-mail: ecegradapps@ece.ucsd.edu. Website: http://ece.ucsd.edu/

University of California, Santa Barbara, Graduate Division, College of Engineering, Department of Computer Science, Santa Barbara, CA 93106-5110. Offers computer science (MS, PhD), including cognitive science (PhD), computational science and engineering (PhD), technology and society (PhD). Terminal master's awarded for partial completion of doctoral program. *Degree requirements:* For master's, comprehensive exam (for some programs), thesis (for some programs), project (for some programs); for doctorate, thesis/dissertation. *Entrance requirements:* For master's and doctorate, GRE. Additional exam requirements/recommendations for international students: Required—TOEFL (minimum score 600 paper-based; 100 iBT), IELTS (minimum score 7). Electronic applications accepted. *Faculty research:* Algorithms and theory, computational science and engineering, computer architecture, database and information systems, machine learning and data mining, networking, operating systems and distributed systems, programming languages and software engineering, security and cryptography, social computing, visual computing and interaction.

University of California, Santa Barbara, Graduate Division, College of Engineering, Department of Electrical and Computer Engineering, Santa Barbara, CA 93106-2014. Offers communications, control and signal processing (MS, PhD); computer engineering (MS, PhD); electronics and photonics (MS, PhD); MS/PhD. *Degree requirements:* For master's, comprehensive exam, thesis; for doctorate, thesis/dissertation. *Entrance requirements:* For master's and doctorate, GRE General Test. Additional exam requirements/recommendations for international students: Required—TOEFL (minimum score 550 paper-based; 80 iBT), IELTS (minimum score 7). Electronic applications accepted. *Faculty research:* Communications, signal processing, computer engineering, control, electronics and photonics.

University of California, Santa Cruz, Jack Baskin School of Engineering, Program in Computer Engineering, Santa Cruz, CA 95064. Offers computer engineering (MS, PhD). *Program availability:* Part-time. Terminal master's awarded for partial completion of doctoral program. *Degree requirements:* For master's, thesis; for doctorate, thesis/

dissertation, oral qualifying exams. *Entrance requirements:* For master's and doctorate, GRE General Test. Additional exam requirements/recommendations for international students: Required—TOEFL (minimum score 570 paper-based; 89 iBT); Recommended—IELTS (minimum score 8). Electronic applications accepted. *Faculty research:* Computer-aided design of digital systems, networks, robotics and control, sensing and interaction.

University of Central Florida, College of Engineering and Computer Science, Department of Electrical and Computer Engineering, Program in Computer Engineering, Orlando, FL 32816. Offers MS Cp E, PhD. *Program availability:* Part-time, evening/weekend. *Students:* 59 full-time (11 women), 24 part-time (3 women); includes 21 minority (3 Black or African American, non-Hispanic/Latino; 10 Asian, non-Hispanic/Latino; 6 Hispanic/Latino; 2 Two or more races, non-Hispanic/Latino), 47 international. Average age 30. 88 applicants, 72% accepted, 30 enrolled. In 2018, 42 master's, 7 doctorates awarded. *Degree requirements:* For master's, thesis or alternative; for doctorate, thesis/dissertation, departmental qualifying exam, candidacy exam. *Entrance requirements:* For master's and doctorate, GRE General Test, minimum GPA of 3.0 in last 60 hours, letters of recommendation, resume, goal statement. Additional exam requirements/recommendations for international students: Required—TOEFL. *Application deadline:* For fall admission, 7/15 for domestic students; for spring admission, 12/1 for domestic students. Application fee: $30. Electronic applications accepted. *Financial support:* In 2018–19, 40 students received support, including 8 fellowships with partial tuition reimbursements available (averaging $8,100 per year), 40 research assistantships with partial tuition reimbursements available (averaging $10,090 per year), 15 teaching assistantships with partial tuition reimbursements available (averaging $10,207 per year); tuition waivers (partial) also available. Financial award application deadline: 3/1; financial award applicants required to submit FAFSA. *Unit head:* Dr. Kalpathy Sundaram, Graduate Coordinator, 407-823-5326, Fax: 407-823-5835, E-mail: sundaram@eecs.ucf.edu. *Application contact:* Associate Director, Graduate Admissions, 407-823-2766, Fax: 407-823-6442, E-mail: gradadmissions@ucf.edu.
Website: http://www.ece.ucf.edu/

University of Cincinnati, Graduate School, College of Engineering and Applied Science, Department of Electrical Engineering and Computing Systems, Program in Computer Engineering, Cincinnati, OH 45221. Offers MS. *Degree requirements:* For master's, thesis. *Entrance requirements:* For master's, GRE General Test. Additional exam requirements/recommendations for international students: Required—TOEFL (minimum score 550 paper-based). Electronic applications accepted. *Faculty research:* Digital signal processing, large-scale systems, picture processing.

University of Cincinnati, Graduate School, College of Engineering and Applied Science, Department of Electrical Engineering and Computing Systems, Program in Computer Science and Engineering, Cincinnati, OH 45221. Offers PhD. *Degree requirements:* For doctorate, thesis/dissertation. *Entrance requirements:* For doctorate, GRE General Test. Additional exam requirements/recommendations for international students: Required—TOEFL.

University of Colorado Boulder, Graduate School, College of Engineering and Applied Science, Department of Electrical, Computer and Energy Engineering, Boulder, CO 80309. Offers ME, MS, PhD. Terminal master's awarded for partial completion of doctoral program. *Degree requirements:* For master's, thesis or alternative; for doctorate, one foreign language, thesis/dissertation, departmental qualifying exam. *Entrance requirements:* For master's, GRE General Test, minimum undergraduate GPA of 3.0; for doctorate, GRE General Test, minimum undergraduate GPA of 3.5. Electronic applications accepted. Application fee is waived when completed online. *Faculty research:* Electrical engineering/electronics; solid state electronics; electromagnetics; circuits and systems; electromagnetic propagation.

University of Connecticut, Graduate School, School of Engineering, Department of Electrical and Computer Engineering, Storrs, CT 06269. Offers MS, PhD. Terminal master's awarded for partial completion of doctoral program. *Degree requirements:* For master's, comprehensive exam, thesis or alternative; for doctorate, thesis/dissertation. *Entrance requirements:* For master's and doctorate, GRE General Test. Additional exam requirements/recommendations for international students: Required—TOEFL (minimum score 550 paper-based). Electronic applications accepted.

University of Dayton, Department of Electrical and Computer Engineering, Dayton, OH 45469. Offers computer engineering (MS); electrical engineering (MSEE, PhD). *Program availability:* Part-time, blended/hybrid learning. *Degree requirements:* For master's, thesis optional; for doctorate, variable foreign language requirement, thesis/dissertation. *Entrance requirements:* For master's, minimum GPA of 3.2, 3 letters of recommendation, bachelor's degree, transcripts; for doctorate, minimum GPA of 3.2, master's degree, transcripts, 3 letters of recommendation. Additional exam requirements/recommendations for international students: Required—TOEFL (minimum score 550 paper-based; 80 iBT). Electronic applications accepted. *Faculty research:* Electrical engineering, video processing, leaky wave antennas, thin film research.

University of Delaware, College of Engineering, Department of Electrical and Computer Engineering, Newark, DE 19716. Offers MSECE, PhD. *Program availability:* Part-time, online learning. Terminal master's awarded for partial completion of doctoral program. *Degree requirements:* For master's, thesis optional; for doctorate, thesis/dissertation. *Entrance requirements:* For master's, GRE General Test; for doctorate, GRE General Test, qualifying exam. Additional exam requirements/recommendations for international students: Required—TOEFL. Electronic applications accepted. *Faculty research:* HIV evolution during dynamic therapy, compressive sensing in imaging, sensor, networks, and UWB radios, computer network time synchronization, silicon spintronics, devices and imaging in the high-terahertz band.

University of Denver, Daniel Felix Ritchie School of Engineering and Computer Science, Department of Electrical and Computer Engineering, Denver, CO 80208. Offers computer engineering (MS); electrical and computer engineering (PhD); electrical engineering (MS); engineering (MS); mechatronic systems engineering (MS, PhD). *Program availability:* Part-time, evening/weekend. *Faculty:* 11 full-time (1 woman). *Students:* 5 full-time (0 women), 55 part-time (8 women); includes 12 minority (2 Black or African American, non-Hispanic/Latino; 1 American Indian or Alaska Native, non-Hispanic/Latino; 3 Asian, non-Hispanic/Latino; 3 Hispanic/Latino; 3 Two or more races, non-Hispanic/Latino), 22 international. Average age 28. 79 applicants, 54% accepted, 17 enrolled. In 2018, 17 master's, 9 doctorates awarded. Terminal master's awarded for partial completion of doctoral program. *Degree requirements:* For master's, thesis optional; for doctorate, comprehensive exam, thesis/dissertation. *Entrance requirements:* For master's, GRE General Test, bachelor of science degree in computer engineering, electrical engineering, or closely related field, transcripts, personal statement, resume or curriculum vitae, three letters of recommendation; for doctorate, GRE General Test, master of science degree in computer engineering, management science and engineering, electrical engineering, mechanical engineering, or closely related areas, transcripts, personal statement, resume or curriculum vitae, three letters of recommendation. Additional exam requirements/recommendations for international students: Required—TOEFL (minimum score 570 paper-based; 80 iBT). *Application deadline:* For fall admission, 1/15 priority date for domestic and international students; for winter admission, 10/25 for domestic and international students; for spring admission, 2/7 for domestic and international students; for summer admission, 4/24 for domestic and international students. Applications are processed on a rolling basis. Application fee: $65. Electronic applications accepted. *Expenses:* $33,183 per year full-time. *Financial support:* In 2018–19, 31 students received support, including 3 research assistantships with tuition reimbursements available (averaging $18,233 per year), 5 teaching assistantships with tuition reimbursements available (averaging $15,833 per year); Federal Work-Study, scholarships/grants, and unspecified assistantships also available. Financial award application deadline: 2/15; financial award applicants required to submit FAFSA. *Faculty research:* Mechatronic systems, unmanned systems, service robotics, smart grid, sensor fusion. *Unit head:* Dr. Amin Khodaei, Professor and Chair, 303-871-2481, E-mail: amin.khodaei@du.edu. *Application contact:* Dr. Amin Khodaei, Professor and Chair, 303-871-2481, E-mail: amin.khodaei@du.edu.
Website: http://ritchieschool.du.edu/departments/ece/

University of Detroit Mercy, College of Engineering and Science, Detroit, MI 48221. Offers chemistry (MS); civil and environmental engineering (DE); electrical and computer engineering (ME); electrical engineering (DE); engineering management (M Eng Mgt); environmental engineering (MEE); mechanical engineering (MME, DE); product development (MS); software engineering (MSSE); teaching of mathematics (MATM). *Program availability:* Part-time, evening/weekend. *Degree requirements:* For doctorate, thesis/dissertation. Electronic applications accepted. Application fee is waived when completed online. *Expenses:* Contact institution.

University of Florida, Graduate School, Herbert Wertheim College of Engineering, Department of Computer and Information Science and Engineering, Gainesville, FL 32611. Offers computer engineering (ME, MS, PhD); computer science (MS); digital arts and sciences (MS). *Program availability:* Part-time, online learning. Terminal master's awarded for partial completion of doctoral program. *Degree requirements:* For master's, comprehensive exam, thesis optional; for doctorate, comprehensive exam, thesis/dissertation. *Entrance requirements:* For master's and doctorate, minimum GPA of 3.0. Additional exam requirements/recommendations for international students: Required—TOEFL (minimum score 550 paper-based; 80 iBT), IELTS (minimum score 6). Electronic applications accepted. *Faculty research:* Computer systems and computer networking; high-performance computing and algorithm; database and machine learning; computer graphics, vision, and intelligent systems; human center computing and digital art.

University of Florida, Graduate School, Herbert Wertheim College of Engineering, Department of Electrical and Computer Engineering, Gainesville, FL 32611. Offers ME, MS, PhD, JD/MS, MSM/MS. *Program availability:* Part-time, online learning. Terminal master's awarded for partial completion of doctoral program. *Degree requirements:* For master's, comprehensive exam (for some programs), thesis (for some programs); for doctorate, comprehensive exam, thesis/dissertation. *Entrance requirements:* For master's, minimum GPA of 3.0; for doctorate, minimum GPA of 3.5. Additional exam requirements/recommendations for international students: Required—TOEFL (minimum score 550 paper-based; 80 iBT), IELTS (minimum score 6). Electronic applications accepted. *Faculty research:* Computer engineering, devices, electromagnetics and energy systems, electronics and signals and systems.

University of Houston–Clear Lake, School of Science and Computer Engineering, Program in Computer Engineering, Houston, TX 77058-1002. Offers MS. *Program availability:* Part-time, evening/weekend. *Entrance requirements:* For master's, GRE General Test. Additional exam requirements/recommendations for international students: Required—TOEFL (minimum score 550 paper-based).

University of Illinois at Chicago, College of Engineering, Department of Electrical and Computer Engineering, Chicago, IL 60607-7128. Offers MS, PhD. *Program availability:* Part-time. *Degree requirements:* For master's, thesis or alternative; for doctorate, thesis/dissertation, departmental qualifying exam. *Entrance requirements:* For master's, minimum GPA of 2.75, BS in related field; for doctorate, GRE General Test, minimum GPA of 2.75, MS in related field. Additional exam requirements/recommendations for international students: Required—TOEFL. Electronic applications accepted. *Expenses:* Contact institution. *Faculty research:* Bioelectronics and biomimetics, computer engineering, device physics and electronics, information systems.

University of Illinois at Urbana–Champaign, Graduate College, College of Engineering, Department of Electrical and Computer Engineering, Champaign, IL 61820. Offers MS, PhD, MS/MBA.

The University of Iowa, Graduate College, College of Engineering, Department of Electrical and Computer Engineering, Iowa City, IA 52242-1316. Offers MS, PhD. *Program availability:* Part-time. *Degree requirements:* For master's, comprehensive exam, thesis optional; for doctorate, comprehensive exam, thesis/dissertation, qualifying exam. *Entrance requirements:* For master's and doctorate, GRE. Additional exam requirements/recommendations for international students: Required—TOEFL (minimum score 550 paper-based; 81 iBT), IELTS (minimum score 7). Electronic applications accepted. *Faculty research:* Applied optics and nanotechnology, compressive sensing, computational genomics, database management systems, large-scale intelligent and control systems, medical image processing, VLSI design and test.

The University of Kansas, Graduate Studies, School of Engineering, Program in Computer Engineering, Lawrence, KS 66045. Offers MS. *Program availability:* Part-time. *Students:* 9 full-time (2 women), 2 part-time (1 woman), 8 international. Average age 26. 12 applicants, 58% accepted. In 2018, 2 master's awarded. *Entrance requirements:* For master's, GRE, minimum GPA of 3.0, official transcript, three recommendations, statement of academic objectives, resume. Additional exam requirements/recommendations for international students: Required—TOEFL, IELTS. *Application deadline:* For fall admission, 12/15 priority date for domestic and international students; for spring admission, 10/1 for domestic and international students. Application fee: $65 ($85 for international students). Electronic applications accepted. *Financial support:* Fellowships, research assistantships, teaching assistantships, career-related internships or fieldwork, scholarships/grants, and unspecified assistantships available. Financial award application deadline: 12/15. *Faculty research:* Communication systems and networking, computer systems design, interactive intelligent systems, radar systems and remote sensing, bioinformatics. *Unit head:* Erik Perrins, Chair, 785-864-4486, E-mail: perrins@ku.edu. *Application contact:* Joy Grisafe-Gross, Graduate Admissions Contact, 785-864-4487, E-mail: jgrisafe@ku.edu.
Website: http://www.eecs.ku.edu/

University of Louisville, J. B. Speed School of Engineering, Department of Computer Engineering and Computer Science, Louisville, KY 40292-0001. Offers computer engineering and computer science (M Eng); computer science (MS, PhD); cybersecurity (Certificate); data science (Certificate). *Accreditation:* ABET (one or more programs are accredited). *Program availability:* Part-time, 100% online, blended/hybrid learning. *Faculty:* 14 full-time (2 women), 3 part-time/adjunct (0 women). *Students:* 62 full-time (16 women), 124 part-time (31 women); includes 32 minority (4 Black or African American, non-Hispanic/Latino; 14 Asian, non-Hispanic/Latino; 8 Hispanic/Latino; 6 Two or more races, non-Hispanic/Latino), 46 international. Average age 33. 74 applicants, 49% accepted, 25 enrolled. In 2018, 18 master's, 5 doctorates, 7 other advanced degrees awarded. Terminal master's awarded for partial completion of doctoral program. *Degree requirements:* For master's, thesis optional; for doctorate,

comprehensive exam, thesis/dissertation. *Entrance requirements:* For master's, GRE, Two letters of recommendation, official final transcripts; for doctorate, GRE, Two letters of recommendation, personal statement, official final transcripts. Additional exam requirements/recommendations for international students: Required—TOEFL (minimum score 550 paper-based; 80 iBT), IELTS (minimum score 6.5), GRE. *Application deadline:* For fall admission, 5/1 priority date for domestic and international students; for spring admission, 11/1 priority date for domestic and international students; for summer admission, 3/1 priority date for domestic and international students. Applications are processed on a rolling basis. Application fee: $65. Electronic applications accepted. *Expenses: Tuition, area resident:* Full-time $6500; part-time $723 per credit hour. Tuition, state resident: full-time $6500. Tuition, nonresident: full-time $13,557; part-time $1507 per credit hour. Tuition and fees vary according to course load and program. *Financial support:* In 2018–19, 78 students received support. Fellowships, research assistantships, teaching assistantships, scholarships/grants, health care benefits, and tuition waivers (full) available. Financial award application deadline: 1/1. *Faculty research:* Artificial Intelligence, Big Data Analytics, Bioinformatics, Cybersecurity, Data Mining. *Total annual research expenditures:* $740,736. *Unit head:* Dr. Wei Zhang, Chair, 502-852-0715, E-mail: wei.zhang@louisville.edu. *Application contact:* Dr. Mehmed Kantardzic, Director of Graduate Studies, 502-852-3703, E-mail: mehmed.kantardzic@louisville.edu.
Website: http://louisville.edu/speed/computer

University of Louisville, J. B. Speed School of Engineering, Department of Electrical and Computer Engineering, Louisville, KY 40292-0001. Offers M Eng, MS, PhD. *Accreditation:* ABET (one or more programs are accredited). *Faculty:* 14 full-time (2 women), 3 part-time/adjunct (0 women). *Students:* 46 full-time (3 women), 29 part-time (7 women); includes 9 minority (6 Asian, non-Hispanic/Latino; 3 Hispanic/Latino), 26 international. Average age 28. 24 applicants, 54% accepted, 11 enrolled. In 2018, 10 master's, 5 doctorates awarded. *Degree requirements:* For master's, thesis optional; for doctorate, comprehensive exam, thesis/dissertation. *Entrance requirements:* For master's and doctorate, GRE General Test, 2 letters of recommendation, official transcripts. Additional exam requirements/recommendations for international students: Required—TOEFL (minimum score 550 paper-based; 80 iBT), IELTS (minimum score 6.5). *Application deadline:* For fall admission, 5/1 priority date for domestic and international students; for spring admission, 11/1 priority date for domestic and international students; for summer admission, 3/1 priority date for domestic and international students. Applications are processed on a rolling basis. Application fee: $65. Electronic applications accepted. *Expenses: Tuition, area resident:* Full-time $6500; part-time $723 per credit hour. Tuition, state resident: full-time $6500. Tuition, nonresident: full-time $13,557; part-time $1507 per credit hour. Tuition and fees vary according to course load and program. *Financial support:* In 2018–19, 50 students received support. Fellowships, research assistantships, teaching assistantships, scholarships/grants, health care benefits, and tuition waivers (full) available. Financial award application deadline: 1/1; financial award applicants required to submit FAFSA. *Faculty research:* 3D Fingerprint Identification and Biometrics, Active Computer Vision, Adaptive Technology for Individuals with Autism, Micro and Nano Robots, Nanotechnology. *Unit head:* Bruce Alpenhaar, Chair, 502-852-1554, Fax: 502-852-6807, E-mail: bruce.alphenaar@louisville.edu. *Application contact:* John Naber, Director of Graduate Studies, 502-852-7910, E-mail: john.naber@louisville.edu.
Website: http://www.louisville.edu/speed/electrical/

University of Maine, Graduate School, College of Engineering, Department of Electrical and Computer Engineering, Orono, ME 04469. Offers computer engineering (MS); electrical engineering (MS, PhD). *Program availability:* Part-time. *Faculty:* 12 full-time (1 woman), 1 part-time/adjunct (0 women). *Students:* 12 full-time (2 women), 1 part-time (0 women); includes 1 minority (Hispanic/Latino), 6 international. Average age 25. 21 applicants, 67% accepted, 5 enrolled. In 2018, 11 master's, 1 doctorate awarded. Terminal master's awarded for partial completion of doctoral program. *Degree requirements:* For master's, thesis (for some programs); for doctorate, comprehensive exam, thesis/dissertation. *Entrance requirements:* For master's and doctorate, GRE General Test. Additional exam requirements/recommendations for international students: Required—TOEFL. *Application deadline:* For fall admission, 2/1 priority date for domestic students. Applications are processed on a rolling basis. Application fee: $65. Electronic applications accepted. *Financial support:* In 2018–19, 13 students received support, including 7 research assistantships with full tuition reimbursements available (averaging $16,100 per year), 4 teaching assistantships with full tuition reimbursements available (averaging $13,600 per year); fellowships, Federal Work-Study, institutionally sponsored loans, and tuition waivers (full and partial) also available. Financial award application deadline: 3/1. *Faculty research:* Microwave acoustic sensors, semiconductor devices and fabrication, high performance computing, instrumentation and industrial automation, wireless communication. *Total annual research expenditures:* $1.5 million. *Unit head:* Dr. Donald Hummels, Chair, 207-581-2244. *Application contact:* Scott G. Delcourt, Assistant Vice President for Graduate Studies and Senior Associate Dean, 207-581-3291, Fax: 207-581-3232, E-mail: graduate@maine.edu.
Website: http://www.ece.umaine.edu/

University of Manitoba, Faculty of Graduate Studies, Faculty of Engineering, Department of Electrical and Computer Engineering, Winnipeg, MB R3T 2N2, Canada. Offers M Eng, M Sc, PhD. *Degree requirements:* For master's, thesis; for doctorate, thesis/dissertation.

University of Maryland, Baltimore County, The Graduate School, College of Engineering and Information Technology, Department of Computer Science and Electrical Engineering, Program in Computer Engineering, Baltimore, MD 21250. Offers MS, PhD. *Program availability:* Part-time. *Degree requirements:* For master's, comprehensive exam (for some programs), thesis or alternative; for doctorate, comprehensive exam, thesis/dissertation. *Entrance requirements:* For master's, GRE General Test, strong background in computer engineering, computer science, and math courses; for doctorate, GRE General Test, MS in computer science (strongly recommended); strong background in computer engineering, computer science, and mathematics courses. Additional exam requirements/recommendations for international students: Required—TOEFL (minimum score 550 paper-based; 80 iBT). Electronic applications accepted. *Expenses:* Contact institution. *Faculty research:* Communication and signal processing, photonics and micro electronics, sensor systems, signal processing architectures, VLSI design and test.

University of Maryland, College Park, Academic Affairs, A. James Clark School of Engineering, Department of Electrical and Computer Engineering, College Park, MD 20742. Offers electrical and computer engineering (M Eng, MS, PhD); electrical engineering (MS, PhD); telecommunications (MS). *Program availability:* Part-time, evening/weekend, online learning. *Degree requirements:* For master's, thesis optional; for doctorate, thesis/dissertation, oral exam, qualifying exam. *Entrance requirements:* For master's and doctorate, GRE General Test, 3 letters of recommendation. Electronic applications accepted. *Faculty research:* Communications and control, electrophysics, micro-electronics, robotics, computer engineering.

University of Massachusetts Amherst, Graduate School, College of Engineering, Department of Electrical and Computer Engineering, Amherst, MA 01003. Offers MSECE, PhD. *Program availability:* Part-time. Terminal master's awarded for partial completion of doctoral program. *Degree requirements:* For master's, thesis or alternative; for doctorate, comprehensive exam, thesis/dissertation. *Entrance requirements:* For master's and doctorate, GRE General Test. Additional exam requirements/recommendations for international students: Required—TOEFL (minimum score 550 paper-based; 80 iBT), IELTS (minimum score 6.5). Electronic applications accepted.

University of Massachusetts Dartmouth, Graduate School, College of Engineering, Department of Electrical and Computer Engineering, North Dartmouth, MA 02747-2300. Offers communications (Postbaccalaureate Certificate); computing infrastructure security (Postbaccalaureate Certificate); digital signal processing (Postbaccalaureate Certificate); electrical engineering (MS, PhD); electrical engineering systems (Postbaccalaureate Certificate). *Program availability:* Part-time. *Faculty:* 15 full-time (4 women), 1 part-time/adjunct (0 women). *Students:* 21 full-time (5 women), 40 part-time (9 women); includes 12 minority (4 Black or African American, non-Hispanic/Latino; 1 Asian, non-Hispanic/Latino; 5 Hispanic/Latino; 2 Two or more races, non-Hispanic/Latino), 20 international. Average age 31. 48 applicants, 71% accepted, 16 enrolled. In 2018, 23 master's, 5 doctorates, 3 other advanced degrees awarded. Terminal master's awarded for partial completion of doctoral program. *Degree requirements:* For master's, thesis, thesis or project; for doctorate, comprehensive exam, thesis/dissertation. *Entrance requirements:* For master's, GRE unless UMass Dartmouth graduate in computer engineering or electrical engineering, statement of purpose (minimum of 300 words), resume, 3 letters of recommendation, official transcripts; for doctorate, GRE unless UMass Dartmouth graduate in college of engineering major or about to receive electrical graduate certificate, statement of purpose (minimum of 300 words), resume, 3 letters of recommendation, official transcripts; for Postbaccalaureate Certificate, statement of purpose (minimum of 300 words), resume, official transcripts. Additional exam requirements/recommendations for international students: Required—TOEFL (minimum score 550 paper-based; 79 iBT), IELTS (minimum score 6.5). *Application deadline:* For fall admission, 2/15 priority date for domestic students, 1/15 priority date for international students; for spring admission, 11/1 priority date for domestic students, 10/1 priority date for international students. Application fee: $60. Electronic applications accepted. *Financial support:* In 2018–19, 12 research assistantships (averaging $15,187 per year), 10 teaching assistantships (averaging $12,907 per year) were awarded; tuition waivers (full and partial) and dissertation writing support also available. Financial award application deadline: 3/1; financial award applicants required to submit FAFSA. *Faculty research:* Array processing, cyber security, underwater acoustics and animal bio-acoustics, electronics and solid-state devices, photonics. *Total annual research expenditures:* $1.9 million. *Unit head:* Liudong Xing, Graduate Program Director/Electrical & Computer Engineering, 508-999-8883, Fax: 508-999-8489, E-mail: liudong.xing@umassd.edu. *Application contact:* Scott Webster, Director of Graduate Studies & Admissions, 508-999-8604, Fax: 508-999-8183, E-mail: graduate@umassd.edu.
Website: http://www.umassd.edu/engineering/ece/graduate

University of Massachusetts Lowell, Francis College of Engineering, Department of Electrical and Computer Engineering, Program in Computer Engineering, Lowell, MA 01854. Offers MS Eng, PhD. *Degree requirements:* For master's, thesis optional.

University of Memphis, Graduate School, Herff College of Engineering, Department of Electrical and Computer Engineering, Memphis, TN 38152. Offers computer engineering (MS, PhD); electrical engineering (MS, PhD); imaging and signal processing (Graduate Certificate). *Students:* 12 full-time (5 women), 9 part-time (2 women); includes 6 minority (4 Asian, non-Hispanic/Latino; 1 Hispanic/Latino; 1 Two or more races, non-Hispanic/Latino), 13 international. Average age 28. 29 applicants, 79% accepted, 4 enrolled. In 2018, 7 master's awarded. *Degree requirements:* For master's, comprehensive exam, thesis or alternative; for doctorate, comprehensive exam, thesis/dissertation. *Entrance requirements:* For master's and doctorate, GRE General Test, MAT, or GMAT, three letters of recommendation. Additional exam requirements/recommendations for international students: Required—TOEFL (minimum score 550 paper-based; 79 iBT). *Application deadline:* For fall admission, 8/1 for domestic students; for spring admission, 12/1 for domestic students. Application fee: $35 ($60 for international students). Electronic applications accepted. *Expenses: Tuition, area resident:* Full-time $10,240; part-time $503 per credit hour. Tuition, state resident: full-time $10,464. Tuition, nonresident: full-time $20,224; part-time $991 per credit hour. *Required fees:* $850; $106 per credit hour. *Financial support:* Fellowships, research assistantships, teaching assistantships, career-related internships or fieldwork, Federal Work-Study, scholarships/grants, and unspecified assistantships available. Financial award application deadline: 2/1; financial award applicants required to submit FAFSA. *Faculty research:* Image processing, imaging sensors, biomedical systems, intelligent systems. *Unit head:* Dr. Chrysanthe Preza, Chair, 901-678-2175, Fax: 901-678-5469, E-mail: cpreza@memphis.edu. *Application contact:* Dr. Aaron Robinson, Coordinator of Graduate Studies, 901-678-4996, Fax: 901-678-5469, E-mail: alrobins@memphis.edu.
Website: http://www.memphis.edu/eece/

University of Miami, Graduate School, College of Engineering, Department of Electrical and Computer Engineering, Coral Gables, FL 33124. Offers MSECE, PhD. *Program availability:* Part-time. *Degree requirements:* For master's, thesis (for some programs); for doctorate, comprehensive exam, thesis/dissertation, dissertation proposal defense. *Entrance requirements:* For master's, GRE General Test, minimum GPA of 3.0; for doctorate, GRE General Test, minimum undergraduate GPA of 3.3, graduate 3.5. Additional exam requirements/recommendations for international students: Required—TOEFL (minimum score 550 paper-based; 59 iBT), IELTS (minimum score 7). Electronic applications accepted. *Faculty research:* Computer network, image processing, database systems, digital signal processing, machine intelligence.

University of Michigan, College of Engineering, Department of Computer Science and Engineering, Ann Arbor, MI 48109. Offers MS, MSE, PhD. *Program availability:* Part-time. *Students:* 344 full-time (62 women), 3 part-time (0 women). 2,461 applicants, 15% accepted, 112 enrolled. In 2018, 69 master's, 29 doctorates awarded. *Financial support:* Fellowships, research assistantships, teaching assistantships, career-related internships or fieldwork, Federal Work-Study, institutionally sponsored loans, and health care benefits available. Support available to part-time students. *Faculty research:* Solid state electronics and optics; communications, control, signal process; sensors and integrated circuitry; software systems; artificial intelligence; hardware systems. *Total annual research expenditures:* $28.7 million. *Unit head:* Brian Noble, Department Chair, 734-764-8504, E-mail: bnoble@umich.edu. *Application contact:* Ashley Andreae, Graduate Programs Coordinator, 734-647-1807, E-mail: smash@umich.edu.
Website: http://eecs.umich.edu/cse/

University of Michigan, College of Engineering, Department of Electrical and Computer Engineering, Ann Arbor, MI 48109. Offers MS, MSE, PhD. *Program availability:* Part-time. *Students:* 698 full-time (154 women), 19 part-time (3 women). 2,183 applicants, 34% accepted, 248 enrolled. In 2018, 310 master's, 55 doctorates awarded. *Financial support:* Fellowships, research assistantships, teaching assistantships, career-related internships or fieldwork, Federal Work-Study, institutionally sponsored loans, and health care benefits available. Support available to

part-time students. *Faculty research:* Solid state electronics and optics; communications, control, signal process; sensors and integrated circuitry; software systems; artificial intelligence; hardware systems. *Total annual research expenditures:* $43.9 million. *Unit head:* Mingyan Liu, Department Chair, 734-764-9546, Fax: 734-763-1503, E-mail: mingyan@umich.edu. *Application contact:* Johnny Linn, Graduate Coordinator, 734-764-9387, E-mail: johnlinn@umich.edu.
Website: http://eecs.umich.edu/ece/

University of Michigan–Dearborn, College of Engineering and Computer Science, MSE Program in Computer Engineering, Dearborn, MI 48128. Offers MSE. *Program availability:* Part-time, evening/weekend, 100% online. *Faculty:* 22 full-time (2 women), 15 part-time/adjunct (0 women). *Students:* 10 full-time (4 women), 31 part-time (3 women); includes 7 minority (1 Black or African American, non-Hispanic/Latino; 3 Asian, non-Hispanic/Latino; 2 Hispanic/Latino; 1 Two or more races, non-Hispanic/Latino), 13 international. Average age 26. 47 applicants, 62% accepted, 13 enrolled. In 2018, 21 master's awarded. *Degree requirements:* For master's, thesis optional. *Entrance requirements:* For master's, bachelor's degree in electrical and/or computer engineering with minimum overall GPA of 3.0. Additional exam requirements/recommendations for international students: Required—TOEFL (minimum score 560 paper-based; 84 iBT), IELTS (minimum score 6.5). *Application deadline:* For fall admission, 8/1 for domestic students, 5/1 for international students; for winter admission, 12/1 for domestic students, 9/1 for international students; for spring admission, 4/1 for domestic students, 1/1 for international students. Applications are processed on a rolling basis. Application fee: $60. Electronic applications accepted. *Expenses:* Tuition, state resident: full-time $15,380; part-time $88 per credit hour. Tuition, nonresident: full-time $23,948; part-time $1377 per credit hour. *Required fees:* $780; $780 $390. Tuition and fees vary according to course level, course load, degree level, program, reciprocity agreements and student level. *Financial support:* In 2018–19, 7 students received support. Research assistantships with full tuition reimbursements available, teaching assistantships with full tuition reimbursements available, scholarships/grants, unspecified assistantships, and non-resident tuition scholarships available. Financial award application deadline: 3/1; financial award applicants required to submit FAFSA. *Faculty research:* Artificial intelligence, power and energy, nanotechnology and optics, control systems, autonomy: sensing and perception. *Unit head:* Dr. Paul Richardson, Chair, 313-593-5420, E-mail: richarpc@umich.edu. *Application contact:* Office of Graduate Studies, 313-583-6321, E-mail: umd-graduatestudies@umich.edu.
Website: https://umdearborn.edu/cecs/departments/electrical-and-computer-engineering/graduate-programs/mse-computer-engineering

University of Michigan–Dearborn, College of Engineering and Computer Science, PhD Program Electrical, Electronics, and Computer Engineering, Dearborn, MI 48128. Offers PhD. *Faculty:* 22 full-time (2 women), 15 part-time/adjunct (0 women). *Students:* 2 full-time (0 women), 27 part-time (3 women); includes 2 minority (both Asian, non-Hispanic/Latino), 21 international. Average age 32. 38 applicants, 29% accepted, 8 enrolled. *Degree requirements:* For doctorate, thesis/dissertation. *Entrance requirements:* For doctorate, GRE, bachelor's or master's degree in electrical/computer engineering, computer science, physical science, or mathematical science with minimum GPA of 3.2. Additional exam requirements/recommendations for international students: Required—TOEFL (minimum score 560 paper-based; 84 iBT), IELTS (minimum score 6.5). *Application deadline:* For fall admission, 2/1 for domestic and international students. Application fee: $60. Electronic applications accepted. *Expenses:* Tuition, state resident: full-time $15,380; part-time $88 per credit hour. Tuition, nonresident: full-time $23,948; part-time $1377 per credit hour. *Required fees:* $780; $780 $390. Tuition and fees vary according to course level, course load, degree level, program, reciprocity agreements and student level. *Financial support:* Research assistantships with full tuition reimbursements, teaching assistantships with full tuition reimbursements, scholarships/grants, health care benefits, and unspecified assistantships available. Financial award application deadline: 2/1; financial award applicants required to submit FAFSA. *Faculty research:* Artificial intelligence, power and energy, nanotechnology and optics, control systems, autonomy: sensing and perception. *Unit head:* Dr. Alex Yi, Chair, 313-583-6318, E-mail: yashayi@umich.edu. *Application contact:* Office of Graduate Studies, 313-583-6321, E-mail: umd-graduatestudies@umich.edu.
Website: https://umdearborn.edu/cecs/departments/electrical-and-computer-engineering/graduate-programs/phd-electrical-and-computer-engineering

University of Minnesota, Duluth, Graduate School, Swenson College of Science and Engineering, Department of Electrical and Computer Engineering, Duluth, MN 55812-2496. Offers MSECE. *Program availability:* Part-time. *Degree requirements:* For master's, thesis. *Entrance requirements:* Additional exam requirements/recommendations for international students: Recommended—TOEFL, IELTS, TWE. *Faculty research:* Biomedical instrumentation, transportation systems, computer hardware and software, signal processing, optical communications.

University of Minnesota, Twin Cities Campus, College of Science and Engineering, Department of Computer Science and Engineering, Minneapolis, MN 55455-0213. Offers computer science (MCS, MS, PhD); data science (MS); software engineering (MSSE). *Program availability:* Part-time. Terminal master's awarded for partial completion of doctoral program. *Degree requirements:* For doctorate, thesis/dissertation. *Entrance requirements:* For master's and doctorate, GRE General Test. Additional exam requirements/recommendations for international students: Required—TOEFL. Electronic applications accepted. *Faculty research:* Computer architecture, bioinformatics and computational biology, data mining, graphics and visualization, high performance computing, human-computer interaction, networks, software systems, theory, artificial intelligence.

University of Minnesota, Twin Cities Campus, College of Science and Engineering, Department of Electrical and Computer Engineering, Minneapolis, MN 55455-0213. Offers MSEE, PhD. *Program availability:* Part-time. *Degree requirements:* For master's, thesis or alternative; for doctorate, thesis/dissertation. *Entrance requirements:* Additional exam requirements/recommendations for international students: Required—TOEFL (minimum score 550 paper-based). Electronic applications accepted. *Faculty research:* Signal processing, micro- and nano-structures, computers, controls, power electronics.

University of Missouri, Office of Research and Graduate Studies, College of Engineering, Department of Electrical Engineering and Computer Science, Columbia, MO 65211. Offers computer engineering (MSCE); computer science (MS, PhD); electrical and computer engineering (PhD); electrical engineering (MSEE). *Entrance requirements:* For master's, GRE General Test, minimum GPA of 3.0; for doctorate, GRE General Test, GRE Subject Test, minimum GPA of 3.0. Additional exam requirements/recommendations for international students: Required—TOEFL.

University of Missouri–Kansas City, School of Computing and Engineering, Kansas City, MO 64110-2499. Offers civil engineering (MS); computer and electrical engineering (PhD); computer science (MS), including bioinformatics, software engineering, telecommunications networking; computer science and informatics (PhD); computing (PhD); electrical engineering (MS); engineering (PhD); engineering and construction management (Graduate Certificate); mechanical engineering (MS); telecommunications and computer networking (PhD). PhD (interdisciplinary) offered through the School of Graduate Studies. *Program availability:* Part-time. *Degree requirements:* For doctorate, thesis/dissertation. *Entrance requirements:* For master's, GRE General Test, minimum GPA of 3.0, 3 letters of recommendation from professors; for doctorate, GRE General Test, minimum GPA of 3.5. Additional exam requirements/recommendations for international students: Required—TOEFL (minimum score 550 paper-based; 80 iBT). *Faculty research:* Algorithms, bioinformatics and medical informatics, biomechanics/biomaterials, civil engineering materials, networking and telecommunications, thermal science.

University of Nebraska–Lincoln, Graduate College, College of Arts and Sciences and College of Engineering, Department of Computer Science and Engineering, Lincoln, NE 68588. Offers bioinformatics (MS, PhD); computer engineering (MS, PhD); computer science (MS, PhD); information technology (PhD). *Degree requirements:* For master's, thesis optional; for doctorate, comprehensive exam, thesis/dissertation. *Entrance requirements:* For master's and doctorate, GRE General Test. Additional exam requirements/recommendations for international students: Required—TOEFL (minimum score 600 paper-based). Electronic applications accepted. *Faculty research:* Software engineering, geo- and bio-informatics, scientific computation, secure communication.

University of Nevada, Reno, Graduate School, College of Engineering, Department of Computer Science and Engineering, Reno, NV 89557. Offers MS, PhD. Terminal master's awarded for partial completion of doctoral program. *Degree requirements:* For master's, thesis optional; for doctorate, thesis/dissertation. *Entrance requirements:* For master's, GRE General Test, minimum GPA of 2.75; for doctorate, GRE General Test, minimum GPA of 3.0. Additional exam requirements/recommendations for international students: Required—TOEFL (minimum score 500 paper-based; 61 iBT), IELTS (minimum score 6). Electronic applications accepted. *Faculty research:* Evolutionary computing systems, computer vision/virtual reality, software engineering.

University of New Brunswick Fredericton, School of Graduate Studies, Faculty of Engineering, Department of Electrical and Computer Engineering, Fredericton, NB E3B 5A3, Canada. Offers M Eng, M Sc E, PhD. *Program availability:* Part-time. *Degree requirements:* For master's, thesis, research proposal; 10 courses (for M Eng); for doctorate, comprehensive exam, thesis/dissertation, research proposal. *Entrance requirements:* For master's, minimum GPA of 3.3; references; for doctorate, M Sc; minimum GPA of 3.3; previous transcripts; references. Additional exam requirements/recommendations for international students: Required—TOEFL (minimum score 580 paper-based; 93 iBT), IELTS (minimum score 7), TWE (minimum score 4). Electronic applications accepted. *Faculty research:* Biomedical engineering, communications, robotics and control systems, electromagnetic systems, embedded systems, optical fiber systems, sustainable energy and power systems, power electronics, image and signal processing, software systems, electronics and digital systems.

University of New Haven, Graduate School, Tagliatela College of Engineering, Program in Electrical Engineering, West Haven, CT 06516. Offers computer engineering (MS); control systems (MS); digital signal processing and communication (MS); electrical engineering (MS). *Program availability:* Part-time, evening/weekend. *Students:* 46 full-time (17 women), 8 part-time (1 woman); includes 4 minority (1 Black or African American, non-Hispanic/Latino; 1 Asian, non-Hispanic/Latino; 2 Hispanic/Latino), 46 international. Average age 24. 135 applicants, 76% accepted, 10 enrolled. In 2018, 20 master's awarded. *Degree requirements:* For master's, thesis or alternative. *Entrance requirements:* For master's, bachelor's degree in electrical engineering. Additional exam requirements/recommendations for international students: Required—TOEFL (minimum score 75 iBT), IELTS, PTE (minimum score 50). *Application deadline:* Applications are processed on a rolling basis. Application fee: $50. Electronic applications accepted. Application fee is waived when completed online. *Expenses: Tuition:* Full-time $16,470; part-time $915 per credit hour. *Required fees:* $230; $95 per term. *Financial support:* Research assistantships with partial tuition reimbursements, teaching assistantships with partial tuition reimbursements, career-related internships or fieldwork, Federal Work-Study, scholarships/grants, and unspecified assistantships available. Support available to part-time students. Financial award applicants required to submit FAFSA. *Unit head:* Dr. Ali Golbazi, Professor, 203-932-7162, E-mail: agolbazi@newhaven.edu. *Application contact:* Selina O'Toole, Senior Associate Director of Graduate Admissions, 203-932-7337, E-mail: sotoole@newhaven.edu.
Website: https://www.newhaven.edu/engineering/graduate-programs/electrical-engineering/

University of New Mexico, Graduate Studies, School of Engineering, Programs in Computer Engineering, Albuquerque, NM 87131-2039. Offers MS, PhD. *Program availability:* Part-time, evening/weekend, online learning. Terminal master's awarded for partial completion of doctoral program. *Degree requirements:* For master's, thesis; for doctorate, comprehensive exam, thesis/dissertation. *Entrance requirements:* For master's, GRE General Test, minimum GPA of 3.0; for doctorate, GRE General Test, minimum GPA of 3.5. Additional exam requirements/recommendations for international students: Required—TOEFL (minimum score 550 paper-based; 79 iBT). Electronic applications accepted. *Faculty research:* Bioengineering, computational intelligence, computer architecture and VLSI design, computer graphics and vision, computer networks and systems, image processing.

University of New Mexico, Graduate Studies, School of Engineering, Programs in Electrical and Computer Engineering, Albuquerque, NM 87131-2039. Offers MS, PhD. *Program availability:* Part-time, evening/weekend, online learning. Terminal master's awarded for partial completion of doctoral program. *Degree requirements:* For master's, thesis; for doctorate, comprehensive exam, thesis/dissertation. *Entrance requirements:* For master's, GRE General Test, minimum GPA of 3.0; for doctorate, GRE General Test, minimum GPA of 3.5. Additional exam requirements/recommendations for international students: Required—TOEFL (minimum score 550 paper-based; 79 iBT). Electronic applications accepted. *Faculty research:* Applied electromagnetics, biomedical engineering, communications, image processing, microelectronics, optoelectronics, signal processing, systems and controls.

The University of North Carolina at Charlotte, William States Lee College of Engineering, Department of Electrical and Computer Engineering, Charlotte, NC 28223-0001. Offers electrical engineering (MSEE, PhD). *Program availability:* Part-time, evening/weekend. *Students:* 143 full-time (34 women), 43 part-time (6 women); includes 9 minority (4 Black or African American, non-Hispanic/Latino; 1 Asian, non-Hispanic/Latino; 2 Hispanic/Latino; 2 Two or more races, non-Hispanic/Latino), 158 international. Average age 27. 279 applicants, 74% accepted, 50 enrolled. In 2018, 61 master's, 11 doctorates awarded. *Entrance requirements:* For master's, GRE, undergraduate degree in electrical and computer engineering or a closely-related field of engineering or sciences; minimum undergraduate GPA of 3.0; letters of recommendation; statement of purpose; for doctorate, GRE General Test, master's degree in electrical and/or computer engineering or a closely-allied field demonstrating strong academic background for performing research in a chosen area of interest; minimum undergraduate and master's-level GPA of 3.5; letters of recommendation; statement of purpose. Additional exam requirements/recommendations for international students: Required—TOEFL (minimum score 523 paper-based; 70 iBT), IELTS (minimum score 6), TOEFL (minimum score 523 paper-based, 70 iBT) or IELTS (6). *Application deadline:* Applications are processed on a rolling basis. Application fee: $75. Electronic applications accepted. *Expenses:* Contact institution. *Financial support:* Research assistantships, teaching assistantships,

career-related internships or fieldwork, institutionally sponsored loans, scholarships/grants, and unspecified assistantships available. Support available to part-time students. Financial award application deadline: 3/1; financial award applicants required to submit FAFSA. *Total annual research expenditures:* $2 million. *Unit head:* Dr. Asis Nasipuri, Chair, 704-687-8418, E-mail: anasipur@uncc.edu. *Application contact:* Kathy B. Giddings, Director of Graduate Admissions, 704-687-5503, Fax: 704-687-1668, E-mail: gradadm@uncc.edu.
Website: http://ece.uncc.edu/

University of North Texas, Toulouse Graduate School, Denton, TX 76203-5459. Offers accounting (MS); applied anthropology (MA, MS); applied behavior analysis (Certificate); applied geography (MA); applied technology and performance improvement (M Ed, MS); art education (MA); art history (MA); arts leadership (Certificate); audiology (Au D); behavior analysis (MS); behavioral science (PhD); biochemistry and molecular biology (MS); biology (MA, MS); biomedical engineering (MS); business analysis (MS); chemistry (MS); clinical health psychology (PhD); communication studies (MA, MS); computer engineering (MS); computer science (MS); counseling (M Ed, MS), including clinical mental health counseling (MS), college and university counseling, elementary school counseling, secondary school counseling; creative writing (MA); criminal justice (MS); curriculum and instruction (M Ed); decision sciences (MBA); design (MA, MFA), including fashion design (MFA), innovation studies, interior design (MFA); early childhood studies (MS); economics (MS); educational leadership (M Ed, Ed D); educational psychology (MS, PhD), including family studies (MS), gifted and talented (MS), human development (MS), learning and cognition (MS), research, measurement and evaluation (MS); electrical engineering (MS); emergency management (MPA); engineering technology (MS); English (MA); English as a second language (MA); environmental science (MS); finance (MBA, MS); financial management (MPA); French (MA); health services management (MBA); higher education (M Ed, Ed D); history (MA, MS); hospitality management (MS); human resources management (MPA); information science (MS); information systems (PhD); information technologies (MBA); interdisciplinary studies (MA, MS); international studies (MA); international sustainable tourism (MS); jazz studies (MM); journalism (MA, MJ, Graduate Certificate), including interactive and virtual digital communication (Graduate Certificate), narrative journalism (Graduate Certificate), public relations (Graduate Certificate); kinesiology (MS); linguistics (MA); local government management (MPA); logistics (PhD); logistics and supply chain management (MBA); long-term care, senior housing, and aging services (MA); management (PhD); marketing (MBA); mathematics (MA, MS); mechanical and energy engineering (MS, PhD); music (MA), including ethnomusicology, music theory, musicology, performance; music composition (PhD); music education (MM Ed, PhD); nonprofit management (MPA); operations and supply chain management (MBA); performance (MM, DMA); philosophy (MA); political science (MA); professional and technical communication (MA); radio, television and film (MA, MFA); rehabilitation counseling (Certificate); sociology (MA); Spanish (MA); special education (M Ed); speech-language pathology (MA); strategic management (MBA); studio art (MFA); teaching (M Ed); MBA/MS. *Program availability:* Part-time, evening/weekend, online learning. Terminal master's awarded for partial completion of doctoral program. *Degree requirements:* For master's, variable foreign language requirement, comprehensive exam (for some programs), thesis (for some programs); for doctorate, variable foreign language requirement, comprehensive exam (for some programs), thesis/dissertation; for other advanced degree, variable foreign language requirement, comprehensive exam (for some programs). *Entrance requirements:* For master's and doctorate, GRE, GMAT. Additional exam requirements/recommendations for international students: Required—TOEFL (minimum score 550 paper-based; 79 iBT). Electronic applications accepted.

University of Notre Dame, The Graduate School, College of Engineering, Department of Computer Science and Engineering, Notre Dame, IN 46556. Offers MSCSE, PhD. Terminal master's awarded for partial completion of doctoral program. *Degree requirements:* For master's, comprehensive exam; for doctorate, thesis/dissertation, candidacy exam. *Entrance requirements:* For master's and doctorate, GRE General Test. Additional exam requirements/recommendations for international students: Required—TOEFL (minimum score 600 paper-based; 80 iBT). Electronic applications accepted. *Faculty research:* Algorithms and theory of computer science, artificial intelligence, behavior-based robotics, biometrics, computer vision.

University of Oklahoma, Gallogly College of Engineering, School of Electrical and Computer Engineering, Norman, OK 73019. Offers electrical and computer engineering (MS, PhD); telecommunications engineering (MS). *Program availability:* Part-time. *Faculty:* 44 full-time (3 women), 1 part-time/adjunct (0 women). *Students:* 83 full-time (16 women), 40 part-time (9 women); includes 11 minority (1 Black or African American, non-Hispanic/Latino; 1 American Indian or Alaska Native, non-Hispanic/Latino; 3 Asian, non-Hispanic/Latino; 5 Hispanic/Latino; 1 Two or more races, non-Hispanic/Latino), 76 international. Average age 29. 61 applicants, 67% accepted, 14 enrolled. In 2018, 21 master's, 15 doctorates awarded. Terminal master's awarded for partial completion of doctoral program. *Degree requirements:* For master's, comprehensive exam (for some programs), thesis (for some programs); for doctorate, thesis/dissertation, general exam. *Entrance requirements:* For master's and doctorate, GRE, minimum GPA of 3.0. Additional exam requirements/recommendations for international students: Required—TOEFL (minimum score 79 iBT) or IELTS (minimum score 6.5). *Application deadline:* For fall admission, 4/1 for domestic students, 3/1 for international students; for spring admission, 11/1 for domestic students, 10/1 for international students. Applications are processed on a rolling basis. Application fee: $50 ($100 for international students). Electronic applications accepted. *Expenses:* Tuition, state resident: full-time $5683.20; part-time $236.80 per credit hour. Tuition, nonresident: full-time $20,342; part-time $847.60 per credit hour. *International tuition:* $20,342.40 full-time. *Required fees:* $2894.20; $110.05 per credit hour. $126.50 per semester. Tuition and fees vary according to course load and program. *Financial support:* Fellowships, research assistantships, teaching assistantships, career-related internships or fieldwork, scholarships/grants, and health care benefits available. Financial award application deadline: 6/1; financial award applicants required to submit FAFSA. *Faculty research:* Radar engineering, medical imaging, photonics, smart grid, wireless networks. *Unit head:* Dr. J.R. Cruz, Director, 405-325-8131, Fax: 405-325-7066, E-mail: jcruz@ou.edu. *Application contact:* Emily Benton Wilkins, Graduate Programs Coordinator, 405-325-7334, Fax: 405-325-7066, E-mail: emily.d.benton-1@ou.edu.
Website: http://www.ou.edu/coe/ece.html

University of Ottawa, Faculty of Graduate and Postdoctoral Studies, Faculty of Engineering, Ottawa-Carleton Institute for Electrical and Computer Engineering, Ottawa, ON K1N 6N5, Canada. Offers M Eng, MA Sc, PhD. *Degree requirements:* For master's, thesis or alternative, project; for doctorate, comprehensive exam, thesis/dissertation. *Entrance requirements:* For master's, honors degree or equivalent, minimum B average; for doctorate, minimum A- average. Electronic applications accepted. *Faculty research:* CAD, distributed systems.

University of Pittsburgh, Swanson School of Engineering, Department of Electrical and Computer Engineering, Pittsburgh, PA 15260. Offers electrical and computer engineering (MS, PhD). *Program availability:* Part-time, 100% online. Terminal master's awarded for partial completion of doctoral program. *Degree requirements:* For doctorate, comprehensive exam, thesis/dissertation, final oral exams. *Entrance requirements:* For master's and doctorate, GRE General Test, minimum GPA of 3.0. Additional exam requirements/recommendations for international students: Required—TOEFL (minimum score 550 paper-based; 80 iBT). Electronic applications accepted. *Expenses:* Contact institution. *Faculty research:* Computer engineering, image processing, signal processing, electro-optic devices, controls/power.

University of Puerto Rico–Mayagüez, Graduate Studies, College of Engineering, Computer Science and Engineering Program, Mayagüez, PR 00681-9000. Offers PhD. *Program availability:* Part-time. *Degree requirements:* For doctorate, one foreign language, comprehensive exam, thesis/dissertation. *Entrance requirements:* For doctorate, GRE General Test, BS in engineering or science; undergraduate courses in data structures, programming language, calculus III and linear algebra, or the equivalent. Electronic applications accepted. *Faculty research:* Big data analysis, parallel and distributor processing, mobile computing and networking, remote sensing, channel capacity.

University of Puerto Rico–Mayagüez, Graduate Studies, College of Engineering, Department of Electrical and Computer Engineering, Mayagüez, PR 00681-9000. Offers computer engineering (ME, MS); computing and information sciences and engineering (PhD); electrical engineering (ME, MS). *Program availability:* Part-time. Terminal master's awarded for partial completion of doctoral program. *Degree requirements:* For master's, one foreign language, comprehensive exam, thesis; for doctorate, one foreign language, comprehensive exam, thesis/dissertation. *Entrance requirements:* For master's and doctorate, proficiency in English and Spanish; BS in electrical or computer engineering, or equivalent; minimum GPA of 3.0. Electronic applications accepted. *Faculty research:* Digital signal processing, power electronics, microwave ocean emissivity, parallel and distributed computing, microwave remote sensing.

University of Regina, Faculty of Graduate Studies and Research, Faculty of Engineering and Applied Science, Program in Electronic Systems Engineering, Regina, SK S4S 0A2, Canada. Offers electronic systems (M Eng, MA Sc, PhD). *Program availability:* Part-time. *Faculty:* 5 full-time (1 woman), 4 part-time/adjunct (0 women). *Students:* 29 full-time (7 women), 11 part-time (3 women). Average age 30. 198 applicants, 14% accepted. In 2018, 20 master's awarded. *Degree requirements:* For master's, thesis, project, report; for doctorate, comprehensive exam, thesis/dissertation. *Entrance requirements:* For master's, 4 years bachelor degree, at least 70 percent from a four-year baccalaureate degree (or equivalent). Additional exam requirements/recommendations for international students: Required—TOEFL (minimum score 580 paper-based; 80 iBT), IELTS (minimum score 6.5), PTE (minimum score 59), other options are CAEL, MELAB, Cantest and U of R ESL. *Application deadline:* For fall admission, 3/31 for domestic and international students; for winter admission, 7/31 for domestic and international students; for spring admission, 11/30 for domestic and international students. Application fee: $100. Electronic applications accepted. *Expenses:* Estimated tuition and fees for one academic year is 8,379.50 for master's. The fee will vary base on your choice program. For doctoral program, one academic year is estimated 14,129.40. International students will pay additional 1,191.75 for international surcharge per semester. *Financial support:* Fellowships, research assistantships, teaching assistantships, career-related internships or fieldwork, Federal Work-Study, scholarships/grants, unspecified assistantships, and travel award and Graduate Scholarship Base funds available. Financial award application deadline: 9/30. *Faculty research:* Local area networks, digital and data communications systems design, telecommunications and computer networks, image processing, radio frequency (RF) and microwave engineering. *Unit head:* Dr. Paul Laforge, Program Chair, 306-585-5305, Fax: 306-585-4855, E-mail: paul.laforge@uregina.ca. *Application contact:* Dr. Irfan Al-Anbaqi, Graduate Coordinator, 306-585-4703, Fax: 306-585-4855, E-mail: Irfan.Al-Anbagi@uregina.ca.
Website: http://www.uregina.ca/engineering/

University of Rhode Island, Graduate School, College of Engineering, Department of Electrical, Computer and Biomedical Engineering, Kingston, RI 02881. Offers acoustics and underwater acoustics (MS, PhD); biomedical engineering (MS, PhD); circuits and devices (MS); communication theory (MS, PhD); computer architectures and digital systems (MS, PhD); computer networks (MS, PhD); digital signal processing (MS); embedded systems and computer applications (MS, PhD); fault-tolerant computing (MS, PhD); materials and optics (MS, PhD); systems theory (MS, PhD). *Program availability:* Part-time. *Faculty:* 23 full-time (4 women), 1 part-time/adjunct (0 women). *Students:* 41 full-time (7 women), 17 part-time (2 women); includes 8 minority (1 Black or African American, non-Hispanic/Latino; 1 American Indian or Alaska Native, non-Hispanic/Latino; 4 Asian, non-Hispanic/Latino; 2 Hispanic/Latino), 26 international. 44 applicants, 75% accepted, 20 enrolled. In 2018, 14 master's, 3 doctorates awarded. *Entrance requirements:* Additional exam requirements/recommendations for international students: Required—TOEFL. *Application deadline:* For fall admission, 7/15 for domestic students, 2/1 for international students; for spring admission, 11/15 for domestic students, 7/15 for international students; for summer admission, 4/15 for domestic students. Application fee: $65. Electronic applications accepted. *Expenses: Tuition, area resident:* Full-time $13,226; part-time $735 per credit. Tuition, state resident: full-time $13,226; part-time $735 per credit. Tuition, nonresident: full-time $25,854; part-time $1436 per credit. *International tuition:* $25,854 full-time. *Required fees:* $1698; $50 per credit. $35 per semester. One-time fee: $165. *Financial support:* In 2018–19, 22 research assistantships with tuition reimbursements (averaging $10,249 per year), 9 teaching assistantships with tuition reimbursements (averaging $8,477 per year) were awarded. Financial award application deadline: 2/1; financial award applicants required to submit FAFSA. *Unit head:* Dr. Haibo He, Chair, 401-874-5844, E-mail: he@ele.uri.edu. *Application contact:* Dr. Frederick J. Vetter, Graduate Director, 401-874-5141, E-mail: vetter@ele.uri.edu.
Website: http://www.ele.uri.edu/

University of Rochester, Hajim School of Engineering and Applied Sciences, Department of Electrical and Computer Engineering, Rochester, NY 14627. Offers biomedical ultrasound and biomedical engineering (MS); integrated electronics and computer engineering (PhD); musical acoustics and signal processing (MS); physical electronics, electron magnetism, and acoustics (PhD); signal and image processing and communications (MS); signal processing and communications (PhD). *Faculty:* 20 full-time (1 woman). *Students:* 132 full-time (24 women), 1 part-time (0 women); includes 8 minority (4 Black or African American, non-Hispanic/Latino; 2 Asian, non-Hispanic/Latino; 2 Hispanic/Latino), 98 international. Average age 26. 483 applicants, 48% accepted, 56 enrolled. In 2018, 28 master's, 10 doctorates awarded. Terminal master's awarded for partial completion of doctoral program. *Degree requirements:* For master's, thesis optional; for doctorate, comprehensive exam, thesis/dissertation, teaching assistant (two semesters), qualifying exam. *Entrance requirements:* For master's and doctorate, personal statement, three letters of recommendation, official transcripts. Additional exam requirements/recommendations for international students: Required—TOEFL (minimum score 90 paper-based; 90 iBT), IELTS (minimum score 6.5). *Application deadline:* For fall admission, 1/15 for domestic and international students. Applications are processed on a rolling basis. Application fee: $60. Electronic applications accepted. *Expenses: Tuition:* Full-time $52,974; part-time $1654 per credit hour. *Required fees:* $612. One-time fee: $30 part-time. Tuition and fees vary according

to campus/location and program. *Financial support:* In 2018–19, 122 students received support, including 2 fellowships with full tuition reimbursements available (averaging $30,000 per year), 54 research assistantships with full tuition reimbursements available (averaging $30,000 per year), 66 teaching assistantships with full and partial tuition reimbursements available (averaging $12,954 per year); scholarships/grants, tuition waivers (full and partial), and unspecified assistantships also available. *Faculty research:* Bio-informatics and biosensing, communications, signal processing, robotics, wireless networks. *Total annual research expenditures:* $3.8 million. *Unit head:* Mark Bocko, Professor/Chair, 585-275-4879, E-mail: mark.bocko@rochester.edu. *Application contact:* Michele Foster, Graduate Program Coordinator, 585-275-4054, E-mail: michele.foster@rochester.edu.
Website: http://www.hajim.rochester.edu/ece/graduate/index.html

University of San Diego, Shiley-Marcos School of Engineering, San Diego, CA 92110-2492. Offers cyber security engineering (MS). *Program availability:* Part-time, evening/weekend. *Faculty:* 2 full-time (0 women), 2 part-time/adjunct (1 woman). *Students:* 57 part-time (9 women); includes 34 minority (6 Black or African American, non-Hispanic/Latino; 10 Asian, non-Hispanic/Latino; 16 Hispanic/Latino; 1 Native Hawaiian or other Pacific Islander, non-Hispanic/Latino; 1 Two or more races, non-Hispanic/Latino), 1 international. Average age 33. 47 applicants, 79% accepted, 23 enrolled. In 2018, 3 master's awarded. *Degree requirements:* For master's, capstone course. *Entrance requirements:* For master's, GMAT, GRE, or LSAT if GPA is under 3.0. Additional exam requirements/recommendations for international students: Required—TOEFL (minimum score 120 iBT). *Application deadline:* For fall admission, 8/5 for domestic students; for spring admission, 12/2 for domestic students; for summer admission, 4/24 for domestic students. Applications are processed on a rolling basis. Application fee: $45. Electronic applications accepted. *Financial support:* In 2018–19, 15 students received support. Institutionally sponsored loans and scholarships/grants available. Financial award application deadline: 4/1; financial award applicants required to submit FAFSA. *Unit head:* Dr. Chell Roberts, Dean, 619-260-4627, E-mail: croberts@sandiego.edu. *Application contact:* Erika Garwood, Associate Director of Graduate Admissions, 619-260-4524, Fax: 619-260-4158, E-mail: grads@sandiego.edu.
Website: http://www.sandiego.edu/engineering/

University of South Alabama, College of Engineering, Department of Electrical and Computer Engineering, Mobile, AL 36688. Offers computer engineering (MSEE); electrical engineering (MSEE). *Program availability:* Part-time. *Degree requirements:* For master's, comprehensive exam, thesis or project. *Entrance requirements:* For master's, GRE General Test, BS in engineering, minimum GPA of 3.0. Additional exam requirements/recommendations for international students: Required—TOEFL (minimum score 550 paper-based; 79 iBT), IELTS (minimum score 6.5). Electronic applications accepted. *Expenses:* Contact institution. *Faculty research:* Target detection and tracking, space propulsion applications, electrical and computer engineering, intelligent systems, robotics.

University of South Carolina, The Graduate School, College of Engineering and Computing, Department of Computer Science and Engineering, Columbia, SC 29208. Offers computer science and engineering (ME, MS, PhD); software engineering (MS). *Program availability:* Part-time, evening/weekend, online learning. *Degree requirements:* For master's, comprehensive exam, thesis (for some programs); for doctorate, comprehensive exam, thesis/dissertation. *Entrance requirements:* For master's and doctorate, GRE General Test. Additional exam requirements/recommendations for international students: Required—TOEFL (minimum score 570 paper-based). Electronic applications accepted. *Faculty research:* Computer security, computer vision, artificial intelligence, multiagent systems, bioinformatics.

University of Southern California, Graduate School, Viterbi School of Engineering, Department of Computer Science, Los Angeles, CA 90089. Offers computer networks (MS); computer science (MS, PhD); computer security (MS); game development (MS); high performance computing and simulations (MS); human language technology (MS); intelligent robotics (MS); multimedia and creative technologies (MS); software engineering (MS). *Program availability:* Part-time, evening/weekend, online learning. *Entrance requirements:* For master's and doctorate, GRE General Test. Additional exam requirements/recommendations for international students: Required—TOEFL. Electronic applications accepted. *Faculty research:* Databases, computer graphics and computer vision, software engineering, networks and security, robotics, multimedia and virtual reality.

University of Southern California, Graduate School, Viterbi School of Engineering, Ming Hsieh Department of Electrical Engineering, Los Angeles, CA 90089. Offers computer engineering (MS, PhD); electric power (MS); electrical engineering (MS, PhD, Engr); engineering technology commercialization (Graduate Certificate); multimedia and creative technologies (MS); telecommunications (MS); VLSI design (MS); wireless health technology (MS). *Program availability:* Part-time, online learning. Terminal master's awarded for partial completion of doctoral program. *Degree requirements:* For master's, thesis optional; for doctorate, thesis/dissertation. *Entrance requirements:* For master's and doctorate, GRE General Test. Additional exam requirements/recommendations for international students: Recommended—TOEFL. Electronic applications accepted. *Faculty research:* Communications, computer engineering and networks, control systems, integrated circuits and systems, electromagnetics and energy conversion, micro electro-mechanical systems and nanotechnology, photonics and quantum electronics, plasma research, signal and image processing.

University of South Florida, College of Engineering, Department of Computer Science and Engineering, Tampa, FL 33620-9951. Offers computer engineering (MSCP); computer science (MSCS); computer science and engineering (PhD). *Program availability:* Part-time. *Faculty:* 33 full-time (6 women). *Students:* 177 full-time (57 women), 36 part-time (10 women); includes 30 minority (7 Black or African American, non-Hispanic/Latino; 9 Asian, non-Hispanic/Latino; 13 Hispanic/Latino; 1 Two or more races, non-Hispanic/Latino), 161 international. Average age 27. 595 applicants, 35% accepted, 64 enrolled. In 2018, 56 master's, 11 doctorates awarded. Terminal master's awarded for partial completion of doctoral program. *Degree requirements:* For master's, comprehensive exam, thesis or alternative; for doctorate, comprehensive exam, thesis/dissertation, teaching of at least one undergraduate computer science and engineering course. *Entrance requirements:* For master's, GRE General Test, minimum GPA of 3.0, three letters of recommendation, statement of purpose, mathematical preparation; for the MSIT, evidence of completion of a defined subset of the required core courses of the USF BSIT; for doctorate, GRE General Test, minimum GPA of 3.0, three letters of recommendation, statement of purpose that includes three areas of research interest, mathematical preparation. Additional exam requirements/recommendations for international students: Required—TOEFL, TOEFL (minimum score 550 paper-based; 79 iBT) or IELTS (minimum score 6.5). *Application deadline:* For fall admission, 2/15 for domestic and international students; for spring admission, 10/15 for domestic students, 9/15 for international students. Application fee: $30. Electronic applications accepted. *Expenses:* Tuition, state resident: full-time $6350. Tuition, nonresident: full-time $19,048. *International tuition:* $19,048 full-time. *Required fees:* $2079. *Financial support:* In 2018–19, 25 students received support, including 30 research assistantships with tuition reimbursements available (averaging $14,942 per year), 35 teaching assistantships with tuition reimbursements available (averaging $14,003 per year); unspecified assistantships also available. Financial award application deadline: 1/1; financial award applicants required to submit FAFSA. *Faculty research:* Artificial intelligence/intelligence systems; computational biology and bioinformatics; computer vision and pattern recognition; databases; distributed systems; graphics; information systems (networks) and location-aware information systems; robotics (biomorphic robotics and robot perception and action); software security; VLSI, computer architecture, and parallel processing. *Total annual research expenditures:* $2.9 million. *Unit head:* Dr. Lawrence Hall, Professor and Department Chair, 813-974-4195, Fax: 813-974-5094, E-mail: hall@cse.usf.edu. *Application contact:* Dr. Yu Sun, Graduate Program Director, 813-974-7508, E-mail: yusun@usf.edu.
Website: http://www.cse.usf.edu/

The University of Tennessee, Graduate School, Tickle College of Engineering, Min H. Kao Department of Electrical Engineering and Computer Science, Program in Computer Engineering, Knoxville, TN 37996. Offers MS, PhD. *Program availability:* Part-time. *Faculty:* 6 full-time (1 woman). *Students:* 26 full-time (5 women), 8 part-time (1 woman); includes 2 minority (1 Asian, non-Hispanic/Latino; 1 Hispanic/Latino), 19 international. Average age 27. 50 applicants, 42% accepted, 10 enrolled. In 2018, 12 master's, 4 doctorates awarded. *Degree requirements:* For master's, thesis or alternative; for doctorate, comprehensive exam, thesis/dissertation. *Entrance requirements:* For master's, GRE General Test (for MS students pursuing research thesis), minimum GPA of 2.7 (for U.S. degree holders), 3.0 (for international degree holders); 3 references; personal statement; for doctorate, GRE General Test, minimum GPA of 3.0 on previous graduate course work; 3 references; personal statement. Additional exam requirements/recommendations for international students: Required—TOEFL (minimum score 550 paper-based; 80 iBT), IELTS (minimum score 6.5). *Application deadline:* For fall admission, 2/1 priority date for domestic and international students; for spring admission, 6/15 for domestic and international students; for summer admission, 10/15 for domestic and international students. Applications are processed on a rolling basis. Application fee: $60. Electronic applications accepted. *Financial support:* In 2018–19, 29 students received support, including 1 fellowship with full tuition reimbursement available (averaging $9,480 per year), 22 research assistantships with full tuition reimbursements available (averaging $21,751 per year), 6 teaching assistantships with full tuition reimbursements available (averaging $14,914 per year); career-related internships or fieldwork, Federal Work-Study, institutionally sponsored loans, health care benefits, and unspecified assistantships also available. Financial award application deadline: 2/1; financial award applicants required to submit FAFSA. *Unit head:* Dr. Gregory Peterson, PhD, Head, 865-974-3461, Fax: 865-974-5483, E-mail: gdp@utk.edu. *Application contact:* Dr. Jens Gregor, PhD, Associate Head, 865-974-4399, Fax: 865-974-5483, E-mail: jgregor@utk.edu.
Website: http://www.eecs.utk.edu

The University of Texas at Arlington, Graduate School, College of Engineering, Department of Computer Science and Engineering, Arlington, TX 76019. Offers computer engineering (MS, PhD); computer science (MS, PhD); software engineering (MS). *Program availability:* Part-time, online learning. Terminal master's awarded for partial completion of doctoral program. *Degree requirements:* For master's, comprehensive exam (for some programs), thesis; for doctorate, comprehensive exam, thesis/dissertation. *Entrance requirements:* For master's, GRE General Test, minimum GPA of 3.0 (3.2 in computer science-related classes); for doctorate, GRE General Test, minimum GPA of 3.5. Additional exam requirements/recommendations for international students: Required—TOEFL (minimum score 550 paper-based; 92 iBT), IELTS (minimum score 6.5). *Faculty research:* Algorithms, homeland security, mobile pervasive computing, high performance computing bioinformation.

The University of Texas at Austin, Graduate School, Cockrell School of Engineering, Department of Electrical and Computer Engineering, Austin, TX 78712-1111. Offers MS, PhD. *Program availability:* Part-time. *Entrance requirements:* For master's, GRE General Test, minimum GPA of 3.3 in upper-division course work; for doctorate, GRE General Test. Electronic applications accepted.

The University of Texas at Dallas, Erik Jonsson School of Engineering and Computer Science, Department of Electrical and Computer Engineering, Richardson, TX 75080. Offers computer engineering (MS, PhD); electrical engineering (MSEE, PhD); telecommunications engineering (MSTE, PhD). *Program availability:* Part-time, evening/weekend. *Faculty:* 44 full-time (4 women), 10 part-time/adjunct (0 women). *Students:* 452 full-time (98 women), 169 part-time (49 women); includes 44 minority (6 Black or African American, non-Hispanic/Latino; 25 Asian, non-Hispanic/Latino; 7 Hispanic/Latino; 6 Two or more races, non-Hispanic/Latino), 525 international. Average age 28. 1,519 applicants, 46% accepted, 177 enrolled. In 2018, 234 master's, 43 doctorates awarded. *Degree requirements:* For master's, thesis or major design project; for doctorate, thesis/dissertation. *Entrance requirements:* For master's, GRE General Test, minimum GPA of 3.0 in related bachelor's degree; for doctorate, GRE General Test, minimum GPA of 3.5. Additional exam requirements/recommendations for international students: Required—TOEFL (minimum score 550 paper-based). *Application deadline:* For fall admission, 7/15 for domestic students, 5/1 priority date for international students; for spring admission, 11/15 for domestic students, 9/1 priority date for international students. Applications are processed on a rolling basis. Application fee: $50 ($100 for international students). Electronic applications accepted. *Expenses: Tuition, area resident:* Full-time $13,458. Tuition, state resident: full-time $13,458. Tuition, nonresident: full-time $26,852. *International tuition:* $26,852 full-time. Tuition and fees vary according to course load. *Financial support:* In 2018–19, 192 students received support, including 11 fellowships (averaging $3,297 per year), 143 research assistantships with partial tuition reimbursements available (averaging $23,638 per year), 57 teaching assistantships with partial tuition reimbursements available (averaging $17,489 per year); Federal Work-Study, institutionally sponsored loans, scholarships/grants, unspecified assistantships, and cooperative positions also available. Support available to part-time students. Financial award application deadline: 4/30; financial award applicants required to submit FAFSA. *Faculty research:* Semiconductor device manufacturing, photonics devices and systems, signal processing and language technology, nano-fabrication, energy efficient digital systems. *Unit head:* Dr. Lawrence Overzet, Department Head, 972-883-2154, Fax: 972-883-2710, E-mail: overzet@utdallas.edu. *Application contact:* Dr. Lawrence Overzet, Department Head, 972-883-2154, Fax: 972-883-2710, E-mail: overzet@utdallas.edu.
Website: http://ece.utdallas.edu

The University of Texas at El Paso, Graduate School, College of Engineering, Department of Electrical and Computer Engineering, El Paso, TX 79968-0001. Offers computer engineering (MS); electric power and energy systems (Graduate Certificate); electrical and computer engineering (PhD); electrical engineering (MS). *Program availability:* Part-time, evening/weekend. Terminal master's awarded for partial completion of doctoral program. *Degree requirements:* For master's, thesis optional; for doctorate, thesis/dissertation. *Entrance requirements:* For master's, GRE General Test, minimum GPA of 3.0; for doctorate, GRE General Test, minimum graduate GPA of 3.0. Additional exam requirements/recommendations for international students: Required—TOEFL. Electronic applications accepted. *Faculty research:* Signal and image processing, computer architecture, fiber optics, computational electromagnetics, electronic displays and thin films.

The University of Texas at San Antonio, College of Engineering, Department of Electrical and Computer Engineering, San Antonio, TX 78249-0617. Offers advanced materials engineering (MS); computer engineering (MS); electrical engineering (MSEE, PhD). *Program availability:* Part-time. Terminal master's awarded for partial completion of doctoral program. *Degree requirements:* For master's, comprehensive exam, thesis (for some programs); for doctorate, comprehensive exam, thesis/dissertation. *Entrance requirements:* For master's, GRE General Test, bachelor's degree in electrical or computer engineering from ABET-accredited institution of higher education or related field; minimum GPA of 3.0 on the last 60 semester credit hours of undergraduate studies; for doctorate, GRE General Test, master's degree or minimum GPA of 3.3 in last 60 semester credit hours of undergraduate level coursework in electrical engineering; statement of purpose. Additional exam requirements/recommendations for international students: Required—TOEFL (minimum score 550 paper-based; 79 iBT), IELTS (minimum score 6.5). Electronic applications accepted. *Faculty research:* Computer engineering, digital signal processing, systems and controls, communications, electronics materials and devices, electric power engineering.

University of Toronto, School of Graduate Studies, Faculty of Applied Science and Engineering, Department of Electrical and Computer Engineering, Toronto, ON M5S 1A1, Canada. Offers M Eng, MA Sc, PhD. *Program availability:* Part-time. *Degree requirements:* For master's, thesis (for some programs), oral thesis defense (MA Sc); for doctorate, thesis/dissertation, qualifying exam, thesis defense. *Entrance requirements:* For master's, four-year degree in electrical or computer engineering, minimum B average, 2 letters of reference; for doctorate, minimum B+ average, MA Sc in electrical or computer engineering, 2 letters of reference. Additional exam requirements/recommendations for international students: Required—TOEFL (minimum score 580 paper-based; 93 iBT). Electronic applications accepted.

University of Utah, Graduate School, College of Engineering, Department of Electrical and Computer Engineering, Salt Lake City, UT 84112. Offers electrical and computer engineering (MS, PhD); electrical engineering (ME); MS/MBA. *Program availability:* Part-time. *Faculty:* 32 full-time (5 women), 17 part-time/adjunct (3 women). *Students:* 122 full-time (20 women), 47 part-time (3 women); includes 12 minority (7 Asian, non-Hispanic/Latino; 5 Hispanic/Latino), 107 international. Average age 29. 395 applicants, 51% accepted, 61 enrolled. In 2018, 42 master's, 21 doctorates awarded. Terminal master's awarded for partial completion of doctoral program. *Entrance requirements:* For master's, GRE General Test, minimum GPA of 3.2; for doctorate, GRE General Test, minimum GPA of 3.5. Additional exam requirements/recommendations for international students: Required—TOEFL (minimum score 600 paper-based; 100 iBT); Recommended—IELTS (minimum score 7.5). *Application deadline:* For fall admission, 1/15 for domestic and international students; for spring admission, 10/1 for domestic students. Application fee: $10 ($25 for international students). *Expenses:* Contact institution. *Financial support:* In 2018–19, 103 students received support, including 2 fellowships with full tuition reimbursements available (averaging $25,000 per year), 71 research assistantships with full tuition reimbursements available (averaging $22,165 per year), 30 teaching assistantships with full tuition reimbursements available (averaging $19,948 per year); Federal Work-Study, institutionally sponsored loans, health care benefits, and unspecified assistantships also available. Financial award application deadline: 1/15; financial award applicants required to submit FAFSA. *Faculty research:* Semiconductors, VLSI design, control systems, electromagnetics and applied optics, communication theory and digital signal processing, power systems. *Total annual research expenditures:* $6.8 million. *Unit head:* Dr. Gianluca Lazzi, Chair, 801-581-6942, Fax: 801-581-5281, E-mail: lazzi@utah.edu. *Application contact:* Holly Cox, Administrative Manager, 801-581-3843, Fax: 801-581-5281, E-mail: h.cox@utah.edu. Website: http://www.ece.utah.edu/

University of Victoria, Faculty of Graduate Studies, Faculty of Engineering, Department of Electrical and Computer Engineering, Victoria, BC V8W 2Y2, Canada. Offers M Eng, MA Sc, PhD. *Degree requirements:* For master's, thesis; for doctorate, thesis/dissertation, candidacy exam. *Entrance requirements:* For master's, GRE (recommended), bachelor's degree in engineering; for doctorate, GRE (recommended), master's degree. Additional exam requirements/recommendations for international students: Required—TOEFL (minimum score 575 paper-based), IELTS (minimum score 7). Electronic applications accepted. *Faculty research:* Communications and computers; electromagnetics, microwaves, and optics; electronics; power systems, signal processing, and control.

University of Virginia, School of Engineering and Applied Science, Department of Electrical and Computer Engineering, Program in Computer Engineering, Charlottesville, VA 22903. Offers ME, MS, PhD. *Program availability:* Online learning. Terminal master's awarded for partial completion of doctoral program. *Degree requirements:* For master's, thesis (for some programs); for doctorate, comprehensive exam, thesis/dissertation. *Entrance requirements:* For master's, GRE General Test, 3 letters of recommendation; for doctorate, GRE General Test, 3 letters of recommendation; essay. Additional exam requirements/recommendations for international students: Required—TOEFL (minimum score 650 paper-based; 90 iBT), IELTS (minimum score 7). Electronic applications accepted. *Faculty research:* Computer architecture, VLSI, switching theory, operating systems, real-time and embedded systems, compiler, software systems and software engineering, fault-tolerant computing and reliability engineering.

University of Washington, Graduate School, College of Engineering, Paul G. Allen School of Computer Science and Engineering, Seattle, WA 98195-2350. Offers MS, PhD. *Program availability:* Part-time, evening/weekend. In 2018, 107 master's, 18 doctorates awarded. *Degree requirements:* For doctorate, thesis/dissertation, independent project. *Entrance requirements:* For master's, GRE General Test; for doctorate, GRE General Test, minimum GPA of 3.0, statement of purpose, curriculum vitae, letters of recommendation, transcript. Additional exam requirements/recommendations for international students: Required—TOEFL (minimum score 580 paper-based; 92 iBT); Recommended—IELTS (minimum score 7). *Application deadline:* For fall admission, 12/15 for domestic and international students. Applications are processed on a rolling basis. Application fee: $85. Electronic applications accepted. *Expenses:* Contact institution. *Financial support:* In 2018–19, 248 students received support, including 60 fellowships with full tuition reimbursements available (averaging $36,210 per year), 213 research assistantships with full tuition reimbursements available (averaging $36,120 per year), 95 teaching assistantships with full tuition reimbursements available (averaging $36,210 per year); career-related internships or fieldwork and health care benefits also available. Financial award application deadline: 12/15. *Faculty research:* Theory, systems, artificial intelligence, graphics, databases. *Total annual research expenditures:* $35.9 million. *Unit head:* Henry M. Levy, Director/Chair, 206-543-9204, Fax: 206-543-2969, E-mail: levy@cs.washington.edu. *Application contact:* Elise DeGoede Dorough, Graduate Admissions Information Contact, 206-543-1695, Fax: 206-543-2969, E-mail: elised@cs.washington.edu. Website: http://www.cs.washington.edu/

University of Washington, Bothell, Program in Computing and Software Systems, Bothell, WA 98011. Offers MS. *Program availability:* Part-time, evening/weekend. *Degree requirements:* For master's, comprehensive exam (for some programs), thesis optional. *Entrance requirements:* For master's, GRE. Additional exam requirements/ recommendations for international students: Required—TOEFL (minimum score 580 paper-based; 92 iBT) or IELTS (minimum score 7). Electronic applications accepted. *Expenses:* Contact institution. *Faculty research:* Computer science, software engineering, computer graphics, parallel and distributed systems, computer vision.

University of Washington, Tacoma, Graduate Programs, Program in Computing and Software Systems, Tacoma, WA 98402-3100. Offers MS. *Program availability:* Part-time. *Degree requirements:* For master's, capstone project/thesis or 15 credits elective coursework. *Entrance requirements:* For master's, GRE, personal statement, resume, transcripts, 3 recommendations. Additional exam requirements/recommendations for international students: Required—TOEFL (minimum score 580 paper-based; 92 iBT), IELTS (minimum score 7). Electronic applications accepted. *Faculty research:* Data stream analysis, formal methods, data mining, robotic systems, software development processes.

University of Waterloo, Graduate Studies and Postdoctoral Affairs, Faculty of Engineering, Department of Electrical and Computer Engineering, Waterloo, ON N2L 3G1, Canada. Offers M Eng, MA Sc, PhD. *Program availability:* Part-time. *Degree requirements:* For master's, research paper or thesis; for doctorate, comprehensive exam, thesis/dissertation. *Entrance requirements:* For master's, honors degree, minimum B+ average; for doctorate, master's degree, minimum A- average. Additional exam requirements/recommendations for international students: Required—TOEFL, IELTS, PTE. Application fee: $125 Canadian dollars. Electronic applications accepted. *Financial support:* Fellowships, research assistantships, and teaching assistantships available. *Faculty research:* Communications, computers, systems and control, silicon devices, power engineering. Website: https://uwaterloo.ca/electrical-computer-engineering/

The University of Western Ontario, School of Graduate and Postdoctoral Studies, Physical Sciences Division, Faculty of Engineering, London, ON N6A 3K7, Canada. Offers chemical and biochemical engineering (ME Sc, PhD); civil and environmental engineering (M Eng, ME Sc, PhD); electrical and computer engineering (M Eng, ME Sc, PhD); mechanical and materials engineering (M Eng, ME Sc, PhD). *Program availability:* Part-time. Terminal master's awarded for partial completion of doctoral program. *Degree requirements:* For master's, thesis; for doctorate, thesis/dissertation. *Entrance requirements:* For master's, minimum B average; for doctorate, minimum B+ average. *Faculty research:* Wind, geotechnical, chemical reactor engineering, applied electrostatics, biochemical engineering.

University of Wisconsin–Milwaukee, Graduate School, College of Engineering and Applied Science, Program in Engineering, Milwaukee, WI 53201-0413. Offers biomedical engineering (MS); civil engineering (MS, PhD); computer science (PhD); electrical and computer engineering (MS); electrical engineering (PhD); engineering mechanics (MS); industrial and management engineering (MS); industrial engineering (PhD); manufacturing engineering (MS); materials (PhD); materials engineering (MS); mechanical engineering (MS). *Program availability:* Part-time. *Students:* 174 full-time (41 women), 149 part-time (27 women); includes 31 minority (2 Black or African American, non-Hispanic/Latino; 1 American Indian or Alaska Native, non-Hispanic/Latino; 16 Asian, non-Hispanic/Latino; 4 Hispanic/Latino; 8 Two or more races, non-Hispanic/Latino), 207 international. Average age 31. 343 applicants, 57% accepted, 78 enrolled. In 2018, 73 master's, 24 doctorates awarded. *Degree requirements:* For master's, comprehensive exam (for some programs), thesis or alternative; for doctorate, comprehensive exam, thesis/dissertation, internship. *Entrance requirements:* For master's, GRE, minimum GPA of 2.75; for doctorate, GRE, minimum GPA of 3.5. Additional exam requirements/recommendations for international students: Required—TOEFL (minimum score 550 paper-based; 79 iBT), IELTS (minimum score 6.5). *Application deadline:* For fall admission, 1/1 priority date for domestic students; for spring admission, 9/1 for domestic students. Applications are processed on a rolling basis. Application fee: $56 ($96 for international students). *Financial support:* Fellowships, research assistantships, teaching assistantships, career-related internships or fieldwork, Federal Work-Study, unspecified assistantships, and project assistantships available. Support available to part-time students. Financial award application deadline: 4/15. *Unit head:* David Yu, Representative, 414-229-6169, E-mail: yu@uwm.edu. *Application contact:* Betty Warras, General Information Contact, 414-229-6169, Fax: 414-229-6967, E-mail: bwarras@uwm.edu. Website: http://www4.uwm.edu/ceas/academics/graduate_programs/

Villanova University, College of Engineering, Department of Electrical and Computer Engineering, Program in Computer Engineering, Villanova, PA 19085-1699. Offers computer architectures (Certificate); computer engineering (MSCPE); intelligent control systems (Certificate). *Program availability:* Part-time, evening/weekend. *Degree requirements:* For master's, thesis optional. *Entrance requirements:* For master's, GRE General Test (for applicants with degrees from foreign universities), BEE, minimum GPA of 3.0. Additional exam requirements/recommendations for international students: Required—TOEFL (minimum score 600 paper-based; 100 iBT). Electronic applications accepted. *Faculty research:* Expert systems, computer vision, neural networks, image processing, computer architectures.

Virginia Polytechnic Institute and State University, Graduate School, College of Engineering, Blacksburg, VA 24061. Offers aerospace engineering (PhD, M Eng/MS); biological systems engineering (PhD); biomedical engineering (MS, PhD); chemical engineering (PhD); civil engineering (PhD); computer engineering (PhD); computer science and applications (MS); electrical engineering (PhD); engineering education (PhD); M Eng/MS. *Faculty:* 446 full-time (87 women), 7 part-time/adjunct (3 women). *Students:* 1,776 full-time (471 women), 367 part-time (62 women); includes 260 minority (50 Black or African American, non-Hispanic/Latino; 3 American Indian or Alaska Native, non-Hispanic/Latino; 99 Asian, non-Hispanic/Latino; 67 Hispanic/Latino; 41 Two or more races, non-Hispanic/Latino), 1,178 international. Average age 27. 3,798 applicants, 37% accepted, 507 enrolled. In 2018, 489 master's, 200 doctorates awarded. *Degree requirements:* For master's, comprehensive exam (for some programs), thesis (for some programs); for doctorate, comprehensive exam (for some programs), thesis/dissertation (for some programs). *Entrance requirements:* For master's and doctorate, GRE/GMAT. Additional exam requirements/recommendations for international students: Required—TOEFL (minimum score 90 iBT). *Application deadline:* For fall admission, 8/1 for domestic students, 4/1 for international students; for spring admission, 1/1 for domestic students, 9/1 for international students. Applications are processed on a rolling basis. Application fee: $75. Electronic applications accepted. *Expenses:* Tuition, state resident: full-time $15,510; part-time $739.50 per credit hour. Tuition, nonresident: full-time $29,629; part-time $1490.25 per credit hour. *Required fees:* $2804; $550 per semester. Tuition and fees vary according to course load, campus/location and program. *Financial support:* In 2018–19, 37 fellowships with full tuition reimbursements (averaging $24,951 per year), 1,110 research assistantships with full tuition reimbursements (averaging $20,129 per year), 486 teaching assistantships with full tuition reimbursements (averaging $16,192 per year) were awarded; scholarships/grants and unspecified assistantships also available. Financial award application deadline: 3/1; financial award applicants required to submit FAFSA. *Total annual research expenditures:* $96.3 million. *Unit head:* Dr. Julia Ross, Dean, 540-231-9752, Fax: 540-231-3031, E-mail: rjulie@vt.edu. *Application contact:* Linda Perkins, Executive Assistant, 540-231-9752, Fax: 540-231-3031, E-mail: lperkins@vt.edu. Website: http://www.eng.vt.edu/

Computer Engineering

Virginia Polytechnic Institute and State University, VT Online, Blacksburg, VA 24061. Offers advanced transportation systems (Certificate); aerospace engineering (MS); agricultural and life sciences (MSLFS); business information systems (Graduate Certificate); career and technical education (MS); civil engineering (MS); computer engineering (M Eng, MS); decision support systems (Graduate Certificate); eLearning leadership (MA); electrical engineering (M Eng, MS); engineering administration (MEA); environmental engineering (Certificate); environmental politics and policy (Graduate Certificate); environmental sciences and engineering (MS); foundations of political analysis (Graduate Certificate); health product risk management (Graduate Certificate); industrial and systems engineering (MS); information policy and society (Graduate Certificate); information security (Graduate Certificate); information technology (MIT); instructional technology (MA); integrative STEM education (MA Ed); liberal arts (Graduate Certificate); life sciences: health product risk management (MS); natural resources (MNR, Graduate Certificate); networking (Graduate Certificate); nonprofit and nongovernmental organization management (Graduate Certificate); ocean engineering (MS); political science (MA); security studies (Graduate Certificate); software development (Graduate Certificate). *Expenses:* Tuition, state resident: full-time $15,510; part-time $739.50 per credit hour. Tuition, nonresident: full-time $29,629; part-time $1490.25 per credit hour. *Required fees:* $2804; $550 per semester. Tuition and fees vary according to course load, campus/location and program. *Application contact:* Graduate Admissions and Academic Progress, 540-231-8636, E-mail: grads@vt.edu. Website: http://www.vto.vt.edu/

Washington State University, Voiland College of Engineering and Architecture, School of Electrical Engineering and Computer Science, Pullman, WA 99164-2752. Offers computer engineering (MS); computer science (MS); electrical engineering (MS); electrical engineering and computer science (PhD); electrical power engineering (MS). MS programs in computer engineering, computer science and electrical engineering also offered at Tri-Cities campus; MS in electrical power engineering offered at the Global (online) campus. *Program availability:* Part-time. *Degree requirements:* For master's, comprehensive exam (for some programs), thesis or alternative; for doctorate, comprehensive exam, thesis/dissertation. *Entrance requirements:* For master's and doctorate, GRE General Test, minimum GPA of 3.0, 3 letters of recommendation, statement of purpose, transcripts. Additional exam requirements/recommendations for international students: Required—TOEFL (minimum score 580 paper-based). *Faculty research:* Software engineering, networks, distributed computing, computer engineering, electrophysics, artificial intelligence, bioinformatics and computational biology, computer graphics, communications, control systems, signal processing, power systems, microelectronics, algorithms.

Washington University in St. Louis, School of Engineering and Applied Science, Department of Computer Science and Engineering, St. Louis, MO 63130-4899. Offers computer engineering (MS, PhD); computer science (MS, PhD); computer science and engineering (M Eng). *Program availability:* Part-time. Terminal master's awarded for partial completion of doctoral program. *Degree requirements:* For master's, thesis optional; for doctorate, thesis/dissertation. *Entrance requirements:* For doctorate, GRE General Test. Additional exam requirements/recommendations for international students: Required—TOEFL. Electronic applications accepted. *Faculty research:* Artificial intelligence, computational genomics, computer and systems architecture, media and machines, networking and communication, software systems.

Wayne State University, College of Engineering, Department of Electrical and Computer Engineering, Detroit, MI 48202. Offers computer engineering (MS, PhD); electrical engineering (MS, PhD). Application deadline for PhD is February 28 for full funding consideration for fall semester. *Faculty:* 19. *Students:* 107 full-time (27 women), 37 part-time (3 women); includes 14 minority (2 Black or African American, non-Hispanic/Latino; 8 Asian, non-Hispanic/Latino; 3 Hispanic/Latino; 1 Two or more races, non-Hispanic/Latino), 98 international. Average age 27. 270 applicants, 34% accepted, 29 enrolled. In 2018, 107 master's, 9 doctorates awarded. *Entrance requirements:* For master's, GRE (recommended if BS is not from ABET-accredited university), BS from ABET-accredited university; for doctorate, GRE, minimum undergraduate GPA of 3.5 with major or substantial specialized work in proposed doctoral major field, or master's degree in electrical and computer engineering with minimum master's GPA of 3.6. Additional exam requirements/recommendations for international students: Required—TOEFL (minimum score 550 paper-based; 79 iBT), TWE (minimum score 5.5), Michigan English Language Assessment Battery (minimum score 85); Recommended—IELTS (minimum score 6.5). *Application deadline:* For fall admission, 6/1 priority date for domestic students, 5/1 priority date for international students; for winter admission, 10/1 priority date for domestic students, 9/1 priority date for international students; for spring admission, 2/1 priority date for domestic students, 1/1 priority date for international students. Applications are processed on a rolling basis. Application fee: $50. Electronic applications accepted. *Expenses:* Contact institution. *Financial support:* In 2018–19, 58 students received support, including 2 fellowships with tuition reimbursements available (averaging $20,000 per year), 5 research assistantships with tuition reimbursements available (averaging $19,324 per year), 10 teaching assistantships with tuition reimbursements available (averaging $20,272 per year); scholarships/grants, health care benefits, and unspecified assistantships also available. Support available to part-time students. Financial award applicants required to submit FAFSA. *Faculty research:* Bioengineering and bioelectromagnetics; computer engineering; control theory; information and communication theory; networks and computer-aided design; parallel and distributed systems; neural networks (soft computing); optical engineering; power systems; software engineering; solid state devices; smart sensors and VLSI. *Total annual research expenditures:* $1.1 million. *Unit head:* Dr. Mohammed Ismail Elnaggar, Department Chair, 734-284-3100, E-mail: gd8686@wayne.edu. *Application contact:* Eric Scimeca, Graduate Program Coordinator, 313-577-0412, E-mail: eric.scimeca@wayne.edu. Website: http://engineering.wayne.edu/ece/

Weber State University, College of Engineering, Applied Science and Technology, Ogden, UT 84408-1001. Offers computer engineering (MS). *Program availability:* Part-time. *Faculty:* 9 full-time (1 woman). *Students:* 6 full-time (1 woman), 9 part-time (0 women); includes 1 minority (Asian, non-Hispanic/Latino), 1 international. Average age 28. In 2018, 3 master's awarded. *Degree requirements:* For master's, thesis optional. *Entrance requirements:* Additional exam requirements/recommendations for international students: Required—TOEFL (minimum score 79 iBT), IELTS (minimum score 6.5). *Application deadline:* For fall admission, 5/7 for domestic and international students; for spring admission, 11/7 for domestic and international students. Electronic applications accepted. *Financial support:* In 2018–19, 1 student received support. *Unit head:* Dr. David L. Ferro, Dean, 801-626-6303, E-mail: dferro@weber.edu. *Application contact:* Scott Teichert, Director of Admissions, 801-626-7670, Fax: 801-626-6045, E-mail: scottteichert@weber.edu. Website: http://www.weber.edu/east

Western Michigan University, Graduate College, College of Engineering and Applied Sciences, Department of Electrical and Computer Engineering, Kalamazoo, MI 49008. Offers computer engineering (MSE); electrical and computer engineering (PhD); electrical engineering (MSE). *Program availability:* Part-time. *Degree requirements:* For master's, thesis optional.

West Virginia University, Statler College of Engineering and Mineral Resources, Morgantown, WV 26506. Offers aerospace engineering (MSAE, PhD); chemical engineering (MS Ch E, PhD); civil engineering (MSCE, PhD); computer engineering (PhD); computer science (MSCS, PhD); electrical engineering (MSEE, PhD); energy systems engineering (MSESE); engineering (MSE); industrial engineering (MSIE, PhD); industrial hygiene (MS); material science and engineering (MSMSE, PhD); mechanical engineering (MSME, PhD); mining engineering (MS Min E, PhD); petroleum and natural gas engineering (MSPNGE, PhD); safety management (MS); software engineering (MSSE). *Program availability:* Part-time. *Students:* 466 full-time (113 women), 154 part-time (27 women); includes 57 minority (22 Black or African American, non-Hispanic/Latino; 1 American Indian or Alaska Native, non-Hispanic/Latino; 8 Asian, non-Hispanic/Latino; 12 Hispanic/Latino; 14 Two or more races, non-Hispanic/Latino), 283 international. In 2018, 179 master's, 39 doctorates awarded. Terminal master's awarded for partial completion of doctoral program. *Degree requirements:* For master's, thesis optional; for doctorate, comprehensive exam, thesis/dissertation. *Entrance requirements:* Additional exam requirements/recommendations for international students: Required—TOEFL (minimum score 550 paper-based). *Application deadline:* For fall admission, 4/1 for international students; for winter admission, 4/1 for international students; for spring admission, 10/1 for international students. Applications are processed on a rolling basis. Application fee: $60. Electronic applications accepted. *Expenses:* Contact institution. *Financial support:* Fellowships, research assistantships, teaching assistantships, career-related internships or fieldwork, Federal Work-Study, institutionally sponsored loans, health care benefits, tuition waivers (full and partial), unspecified assistantships, and administrative assistantships available. Financial award application deadline: 2/1; financial award applicants required to submit FAFSA. *Faculty research:* Composite materials, software engineering, information systems, aerodynamics, vehicle propulsion and emission. *Unit head:* Dr. Earl Scime, Interim Dean, 304-293-4157 Ext. 2237, Fax: 304-293-2037, E-mail: earl.scime@mail.wvu.edu. *Application contact:* Dr. David A. Wyrick, Associate Dean, Academic Affairs, 304-293-4334, Fax: 304-293-5024, E-mail: david.wyrick@mail.wvu.edu. Website: https://www.statler.wvu.edu

Wichita State University, Graduate School, College of Engineering, Department of Electrical Engineering and Computer Science, Wichita, KS 67260. Offers computer networking (MS); computer science (MS); electrical and computer engineering (MS); electrical engineering and computer science (PhD). *Program availability:* Part-time, evening/weekend. *Unit head:* Dr. Gergely Zaruba, Chair, 316-978-3156, Fax: 316-978-5408, E-mail: gergely.zaruba@wichita.edu. *Application contact:* Jordan Oleson, Admissions Coordinator, 316-978-3095, Fax: 316-978-3253, E-mail: jordan.oleson@wichita.edu.
Website: http://www.wichita.edu/eecs

Worcester Polytechnic Institute, Graduate Admissions, Department of Electrical and Computer Engineering, Worcester, MA 01609-2280. Offers electrical and computer engineering (Advanced Certificate, Graduate Certificate); electrical engineering (M Eng, MS, PhD); power systems engineering (MS). *Program availability:* Part-time, evening/weekend, 100% online, blended/hybrid learning. *Students:* 50 full-time (6 women), 157 part-time (23 women); includes 52 minority (12 Black or African American, non-Hispanic/Latino; 22 Asian, non-Hispanic/Latino; 16 Hispanic/Latino; 2 Two or more races, non-Hispanic/Latino), 69 international. Average age 29. 442 applicants, 45% accepted, 53 enrolled. In 2018, 79 master's, 6 doctorates, 5 other advanced degrees awarded. Terminal master's awarded for partial completion of doctoral program. *Degree requirements:* For master's, thesis optional; for doctorate, comprehensive exam, thesis/dissertation. *Entrance requirements:* For master's, GRE (recommended), 3 letters of recommendation; for doctorate, GRE (recommended), 3 letters of recommendation, statement of purpose. Additional exam requirements/recommendations for international students: Required—TOEFL (minimum score 563 paper-based; 84 iBT), IELTS (minimum score 7), GRE. *Application deadline:* For fall admission, 1/1 priority date for domestic students, 1/1 for international students; for spring admission, 10/1 priority date for domestic students, 10/1 for international students. Applications are processed on a rolling basis. Application fee: $70. Electronic applications accepted. *Financial support:* Fellowships, research assistantships, teaching assistantships, career-related internships or fieldwork, institutionally sponsored loans, scholarships/grants, and unspecified assistantships available. Financial award application deadline: 1/1. *Unit head:* Dr. Donald Brown, Department Head, 508-831-5231, Fax: 508-831-5491, E-mail: drb@wpi.edu. *Application contact:* Dr. Berk Sunar, Graduate Coordinator, 508-831-5231, Fax: 508-831-5491, E-mail: sunar@wpi.edu.
Website: https://www.wpi.edu/academics/departments/electrical-computer-engineering

Wright State University, Graduate School, College of Engineering and Computer Science, Department of Computer Science and Engineering, Computer Engineering Program, Dayton, OH 45435. Offers MS. *Degree requirements:* For master's, thesis optional. *Entrance requirements:* For master's, GRE General Test, minimum GPA of 3.0 in major, 2.7 overall. Additional exam requirements/recommendations for international students: Required—TOEFL. *Faculty research:* Networking and digital communications, parallel and concurrent computing, robotics and control, computer vision, optical computing.

Wright State University, Graduate School, College of Engineering and Computer Science, Department of Computer Science and Engineering, Program in Computer Science and Engineering, Dayton, OH 45435. Offers PhD. *Degree requirements:* For doctorate, thesis/dissertation, candidacy and general exams. *Entrance requirements:* For doctorate, GRE General Test, minimum GPA of 3.3. Additional exam requirements/recommendations for international students: Required—TOEFL.

Youngstown State University, College of Graduate Studies, College of Science, Technology, Engineering and Mathematics, Department of Electrical and Computer Engineering, Youngstown, OH 44555-0001. Offers computer engineering (MSE); electrical engineering (MSE). *Program availability:* Part-time, evening/weekend. *Degree requirements:* For master's, thesis optional. *Entrance requirements:* For master's, minimum GPA of 2.75 in field. Additional exam requirements/recommendations for international students: Required—TOEFL. *Faculty research:* Computer-aided design, power systems, electromagnetic energy conversion, sensors, control systems.

Electrical Engineering

Air Force Institute of Technology, Graduate School of Engineering and Management, Department of Electrical and Computer Engineering, Dayton, OH 45433-7765. Offers computer engineering (MS, PhD); computer systems/science (MS); electrical engineering (MS, PhD); electro-optics (MS, PhD). *Accreditation:* ABET (one or more programs are accredited). *Program availability:* Part-time. *Degree requirements:* For master's, thesis; for doctorate, thesis/dissertation. *Entrance requirements:* For master's and doctorate, GRE General Test, minimum GPA of 3.0, U.S. citizenship. *Faculty research:* Remote sensing, information survivability, microelectronics, computer networks, artificial intelligence.

Alfred University, Graduate School, College of Ceramics, Inamori School of Engineering, Alfred, NY 14802. Offers biomaterials engineering (MS); ceramic engineering (MS, PhD); electrical engineering (MS); glass science (MS, PhD); materials science and engineering (MS, PhD); mechanical engineering (MS). *Program availability:* Part-time. *Degree requirements:* For master's, thesis; for doctorate, thesis/dissertation. *Entrance requirements:* Additional exam requirements/recommendations for international students: Required—TOEFL (minimum score 590 paper-based; 90 iBT), IELTS (minimum score 6.5). Electronic applications accepted. *Expenses:* Contact institution. *Faculty research:* X-ray diffraction, biomaterials and polymers, thin-film processing, electronic and optical ceramics, solid-state chemistry.

The American University in Cairo, School of Sciences and Engineering, Cairo, Egypt. Offers biotechnology (MS); chemistry (MS); computer science (MS); computing (M Comp); construction engineering (M Eng, MS); electronics and communications engineering (M Eng); environmental engineering (MS); environmental system design (M Eng); mechanical engineering (M Eng, MS); nanotechnology (MS); physics (MS); robotics, control and smart systems (MS); sciences and engineering (PhD); sustainable development (MS, Graduate Diploma). *Program availability:* Part-time, evening/weekend. *Degree requirements:* For master's, comprehensive exam (for some programs), thesis (for some programs); for doctorate, comprehensive exam (for some programs), thesis/dissertation. *Entrance requirements:* Additional exam requirements/recommendations for international students: Required—TOEFL (minimum score 450 paper-based; 45 iBT), IELTS (minimum score 5). Electronic applications accepted. *Faculty research:* Construction, mechanical, and electronics engineering; physics; computer science; biotechnology; nanotechnology; chemistry; robotics.

American University of Beirut, Graduate Programs, Maroun Semaan Faculty of Engineering and Architecture, Beirut, Lebanon. Offers applied energy (ME); civil engineering (PhD); electrical and computer engineering (PhD); energy studies (MS); engineering management (MEM); environmental and water resources (ME); environmental technology (MSES); mechanical engineering (ME, PhD); urban design (MUD); urban planning and policy (MUPP). For progreen diploma: LAU/AUC. *Program availability:* Part-time, 100% online. *Faculty:* 105 full-time (25 women), 102 part-time/adjunct (33 women). *Students:* 380 full-time (186 women), 100 part-time (38 women). Average age 27. 489 applicants, 64% accepted, 127 enrolled. In 2018, 109 master's, 14 doctorates awarded. Terminal master's awarded for partial completion of doctoral program. *Degree requirements:* For master's, one foreign language, comprehensive exam, thesis optional; for doctorate, one foreign language, comprehensive exam, thesis/dissertation. *Entrance requirements:* For doctorate, GRE. Additional exam requirements/recommendations for international students: Required—TOEFL (minimum score 575 paper-based; 88 iBT), AUB-EN; Recommended—IELTS (minimum score 7). *Application deadline:* For fall admission, 4/4 for domestic and international students; for spring admission, 11/3 for domestic and international students; for summer admission, 4/4 for domestic and international students. Application fee: $50. *Expenses: Tuition:* Full-time $17,748; part-time $986 per credit. *Required fees:* $762. Tuition and fees vary according to course load and program. *Financial support:* In 2018–19, 15 students received support, including 92 fellowships with full tuition reimbursements available (averaging $14,400 per year), 80 research assistantships with full and partial tuition reimbursements available (averaging $5,300 per year), 162 teaching assistantships with full and partial tuition reimbursements available (averaging $1,400 per year); scholarships/grants, tuition waivers (full and partial), and unspecified assistantships also available. Financial award application deadline: 4/4. *Faculty research:* All areas in engineering, architecture and design. *Total annual research expenditures:* $1.5 million. *Unit head:* Prof. Alan Shihade, Dean, 961-1-374374 Ext. 3400, Fax: 961-1-744462, E-mail: as20@aub.edu.lb. *Application contact:* Dr. Salim Kanaan, Director, Admissions Office, 961-1-374374 Ext. 2590, Fax: 961-1-750775, E-mail: sk00@aub.edu.lb.
Website: https://www.aub.edu.lb/msfea/pages/default.aspx

American University of Sharjah, Graduate Programs, Sharjah, United Arab Emirates. Offers accounting (MS); biomedical engineering (MSBME); business administration (MBA); chemical engineering (MS Ch E); civil engineering (MSCE); computer engineering (MS); electrical engineering (MSEE); engineering systems management (MS, PhD); mathematics (MS); mechanical engineering (MSME); mechatronics engineering (MS); teaching English to speakers of other languages (MA); translation and interpreting (MA); urban planning (MUP). *Program availability:* Part-time, evening/weekend. *Degree requirements:* For master's, thesis (for some programs). *Entrance requirements:* For master's, GMAT (for MBA). Additional exam requirements/recommendations for international students: Required—TOEFL (minimum score 550 paper-based; 80 iBT), TWE (minimum score 5); Recommended—IELTS (minimum score 6.5). Electronic applications accepted. *Faculty research:* Water pollution, management and waste water treatment, energy and sustainability, air pollution, Islamic finance, family business and small and medium enterprises.

Arizona State University at the Tempe campus, Ira A. Fulton Schools of Engineering, School of Electrical, Computer and Energy Engineering, Tempe, AZ 85287-5706. Offers electrical engineering (MS, MSE, PhD); nuclear power generation (Graduate Certificate). *Program availability:* Part-time, evening/weekend, online learning. Terminal master's awarded for partial completion of doctoral program. *Degree requirements:* For master's, thesis and defense (MS); comprehensive exams (MSE); interactive Program of Study (iPOS) submitted before completing 50 percent of required credit hours; for doctorate, comprehensive exam, thesis/dissertation, interactive Program of Study (iPOS) submitted before completing 50 percent of required credit hours. *Entrance requirements:* For master's, GRE, minimum GPA of 3.0 in last 2 years of work leading to bachelor's degree, 3.5 if from non-ABET accredited school; for doctorate, GRE, master's degree with minimum GPA of 3.5 or 3.6 in last 2 years of ABET-accredited undergraduate program. Additional exam requirements/recommendations for international students: Required—TOEFL, IELTS, or PTE. Electronic applications accepted. *Expenses:* Contact institution. *Faculty research:* Power and energy systems, signal processing and communications, solid state devices and modeling, wireless communications and circuits, photovoltaics, biosignatures discovery automation, flexible electronics, nanostructures.

Arkansas Tech University, College of Engineering and Applied Sciences, Russellville, AR 72801. Offers electrical engineering (M Engr); emergency management (MS); information technology (MS); mechanical engineering (M Engr). *Program availability:* Part-time, evening/weekend, 100% online, blended/hybrid learning. *Students:* 46 full-time (17 women), 39 part-time (16 women); includes 12 minority (7 Black or African American, non-Hispanic/Latino; 1 American Indian or Alaska Native, non-Hispanic/Latino; 1 Asian, non-Hispanic/Latino; 2 Hispanic/Latino; 1 Two or more races, non-Hispanic/Latino), 29 international. Average age 31. In 2018, 54 master's awarded. *Degree requirements:* For master's, comprehensive exam (for some programs), thesis (for some programs). *Entrance requirements:* Additional exam requirements/recommendations for international students: Required—TOEFL (minimum score 550 paper-based; 79 iBT), IELTS (minimum score 6.5), PTE (minimum score 58). *Application deadline:* For fall admission, 3/1 priority date for domestic students, 5/1 priority date for international students; for spring admission, 10/1 priority date for domestic and international students. Applications are processed on a rolling basis. Application fee: $40 ($90 for international students). Electronic applications accepted. *Expenses: Tuition, area resident:* Full-time $6816; part-time $284 per credit hour. Tuition, state resident: full-time $6816; part-time $284 per credit hour. Tuition, nonresident: full-time $13,632; part-time $568 per credit hour. *International tuition:* $13,632 full-time. *Required fees:* $457.50 per semester. Tuition and fees vary according to course load and degree level. *Financial support:* In 2018–19, research assistantships with full and partial tuition reimbursements (averaging $4,800 per year), teaching assistantships with full and partial tuition reimbursements (averaging $4,800 per year) were awarded; career-related internships or fieldwork, Federal Work-Study, scholarships/grants, health care benefits, and unspecified assistantships also available. Support available to part-time students. Financial award application deadline: 4/15; financial award applicants required to submit FAFSA. *Unit head:* Dr. Judy Cezeaux, Dean, 479-968-0353, E-mail: jcezeaux@atu.edu. *Application contact:* Dr. Jeff Robertson, Interim Dean of Graduate College, 479-968-0398, Fax: 479-964-0542, E-mail: gradcollege@atu.edu.
Website: http://www.atu.edu/appliedsci/

Auburn University, Graduate School, Ginn College of Engineering, Department of Electrical and Computer Engineering, Auburn University, AL 36849. Offers MEE, MS, PhD. *Program availability:* Part-time. *Degree requirements:* For master's, comprehensive exam, thesis (for some programs); for doctorate, thesis/dissertation. *Entrance requirements:* For master's and doctorate, GRE General Test, GRE Subject Test. Electronic applications accepted. *Expenses:* Tuition, state resident: full-time $11,282; part-time $535 per credit hour. Tuition, nonresident: full-time $30,542; part-time $1605 per credit hour. *Required fees:* $826 per semester. Tuition and fees vary according to degree level and program. *Faculty research:* Power systems, energy conversion, electronics, electromagnetics, digital systems.

Baylor University, Graduate School, School of Engineering and Computer Science, Department of Electrical and Computer Engineering, Waco, TX 76798. Offers MS, PhD. *Faculty:* 17 full-time (2 women). *Students:* 43 full-time (7 women), 5 part-time (0 women); includes 28 minority (3 Black or African American, non-Hispanic/Latino; 1 American Indian or Alaska Native, non-Hispanic/Latino; 21 Asian, non-Hispanic/Latino; 3 Hispanic/Latino), 19 international. Average age 28. 47 applicants, 21% accepted, 3 enrolled. In 2018, 8 master's, 3 doctorates awarded. Terminal master's awarded for partial completion of doctoral program. *Degree requirements:* For master's, thesis (for some programs); for doctorate, comprehensive exam, thesis/dissertation. *Entrance requirements:* For master's and doctorate, GRE. Additional exam requirements/recommendations for international students: Required—TOEFL (minimum score 550 paper-based; 100 iBT). *Application deadline:* For fall admission, 2/15 for domestic and international students; for spring admission, 12/1 for domestic and international students. Applications are processed on a rolling basis. Application fee: $50. Electronic applications accepted. *Expenses:* Contact institution. *Financial support:* In 2018–19, 17 students received support, including 22 research assistantships with full tuition reimbursements available (averaging $18,750 per year), 17 teaching assistantships with full tuition reimbursements available (averaging $18,750 per year); fellowships, institutionally sponsored loans, scholarships/grants, health care benefits, and unspecified assistantships also available. Financial award application deadline: 4/15. *Faculty research:* Energy systems, medical devices, biosensors, specialty optical fibers, molecular electronics and theory. *Unit head:* Dr. Kwang Y. Lee, Chair, 254-710-4817, Fax: 254-710-3010, E-mail: kwang_y_lee@baylor.edu. *Application contact:* Dr. Ian Gravagne, Electrical and Computer Engineering Graduate Director, 254-710-4194, Fax: 254-710-3010.
Website: http://www.ecs.baylor.edu/ece/

Baylor University, Graduate School, School of Engineering and Computer Science, Department of Engineering, Waco, TX 76798. Offers biomedical engineering (MSBME); electrical and computer engineering (MSECE, PhD); engineering (ME); mechanical engineering (MSME). *Faculty:* 14 full-time (1 woman). *Students:* 7 full-time (3 women), 4 part-time (0 women); includes 4 minority (2 Asian, non-Hispanic/Latino; 2 Hispanic/Latino), 2 international. In 2018, 14 master's, 8 doctorates awarded. *Unit head:* Dr. Mike Thompson, Graduate Director, 254-710-4188. *Application contact:* Linda Keer, Administrative Assistant, 254-710-4188, Fax: 254-710-3870, E-mail: linda_kerr@baylor.edu.
Website: http://www.ecs.baylor.edu/engineering

Binghamton University, State University of New York, Graduate School, Thomas J. Watson School of Engineering and Applied Science, Department of Electrical and Computer Engineering, Binghamton, NY 13902-6000. Offers MS, PhD. *Program availability:* Part-time, evening/weekend, online learning. *Degree requirements:* For master's, thesis (for some programs); for doctorate, comprehensive exam, thesis/dissertation. *Entrance requirements:* For master's and doctorate, GRE General Test. Additional exam requirements/recommendations for international students: Required—TOEFL (minimum score 550 paper-based; 80 iBT). Electronic applications accepted. *Expenses:* Contact institution.

Boise State University, College of Engineering, Department of Electrical and Computer Engineering, Boise, ID 83725-0399. Offers M Engr, MS, PhD. *Program availability:* Part-time. Terminal master's awarded for partial completion of doctoral program. *Degree requirements:* For master's, comprehensive exam, thesis (for some programs); for doctorate, thesis/dissertation. *Entrance requirements:* For master's, GRE General Test, minimum GPA of 3.0. Additional exam requirements/recommendations for international students: Required—TOEFL (minimum score 550 paper-based; 80 iBT), IELTS (minimum score 6). Electronic applications accepted.

Boston University, College of Engineering, Department of Electrical and Computer Engineering, Boston, MA 02215. Offers computer engineering (M Eng, MS, PhD). *Program availability:* Part-time. *Students:* 274 full-time (71 women), 76 part-time (23 women); includes 20 minority (2 Black or African American, non-Hispanic/Latino; 16 Asian, non-Hispanic/Latino; 2 Two or more races, non-Hispanic/Latino), 275 international. Average age 24. 1,304 applicants, 38% accepted, 144 enrolled. In 2018,

124 master's, 15 doctorates awarded. Terminal master's awarded for partial completion of doctoral program. *Degree requirements:* For master's, thesis (for some programs); for doctorate, comprehensive exam, thesis/dissertation. *Entrance requirements:* For master's and doctorate, GRE General Test. Additional exam requirements/recommendations for international students: Required—TOEFL (minimum score 90 iBT), IELTS (minimum score 7). *Financial support:* Application deadline: 1/15. *Faculty research:* Communications and computer networks; signal, image, video, and multimedia processing; solid-state materials, devices, and photonics; systems, control, and reliable computing; VLSI, computer engineering and high-performance computing. *Unit head:* Dr. William C. Karl, Interim Chairman, 617-353-9880, Fax: 617-353-6440, E-mail: wckarl@bu.edu. *Application contact:* Dr. William C. Karl, Interim Chairman, 617-353-9880, Fax: 617-353-6440, E-mail: wckarl@bu.edu.
Website: http://www.bu.edu/ece/

Bradley University, The Graduate School, Caterpillar College of Engineering and Technology, Department of Electrical and Computer Engineering, Peoria, IL 61625-0002. Offers MSEE. *Program availability:* Part-time, evening/weekend. *Faculty:* 9 full-time. *Students:* 4 full-time (2 women), 1 (woman) part-time, all international. Average age 23. 32 applicants, 81% accepted, 1 enrolled. In 2018, 4 master's awarded. *Degree requirements:* For master's, comprehensive exam, thesis or alternative. *Entrance requirements:* For master's, GRE, minimum GPA of 3.0, Essays, Recommendation letters, Transcripts. Additional exam requirements/recommendations for international students: Required—TOEFL (minimum score 550 paper-based; 79 iBT), IELTS (minimum score 6.5). *Application deadline:* For fall admission, 5/15 priority date for domestic and international students; for spring admission, 10/15 priority date for domestic and international students. Applications are processed on a rolling basis. Application fee: $40 ($50 for international students). Electronic applications accepted. *Expenses: Tuition:* Part-time $890 per credit. *Required fees:* $50 per unit. *Financial support:* In 2018–19, 8 students received support, including 4 research assistantships with partial tuition reimbursements available (averaging $4,005 per year); teaching assistantships, scholarships/grants, tuition waivers (partial), and unspecified assistantships also available. Support available to part-time students. Financial award application deadline: 4/1. *Faculty research:* Nonlinear systems and controls, autonomous robotics, signal processing and sensor networks, cyber physical systems and smart grids, image processing and machine learning. *Unit head:* Yufeng Lu, Interim Department Chair & Associate Professor, 309-677-3564, E-mail: ylu2@bradley.edu. *Application contact:* Rachel Webb, Director of On-Campus Graduate Admissions & International Student and Scholar Services, 309-677-2375, E-mail: rkwebb@bradley.edu.
Website: http://www.bradley.edu/academic/departments/electrical/

Brigham Young University, Graduate Studies, Ira A. Fulton College of Engineering, Department of Electrical and Computer Engineering, Provo, UT 84602. Offers electrical & computer engineering (PhD). *Faculty:* 22 full-time (1 woman), 1 part-time/adjunct (0 women). *Students:* 89 full-time (5 women); includes 4 minority (all Two or more races, non-Hispanic/Latino), 15 international. Average age 28. 40 applicants, 48% accepted, 19 enrolled. In 2018, 27 master's, 9 doctorates awarded. *Degree requirements:* For master's, thesis; for doctorate, comprehensive exam, thesis/dissertation. *Entrance requirements:* For master's and doctorate, GRE General Test, Minimum GPA of 3.2 in last 60 hours of course work. Additional exam requirements/recommendations for international students: Required—TOEFL (minimum score 580 paper-based; 85 iBT). *Application deadline:* For fall admission, 1/15 for domestic and international students; for winter admission, 8/15 for domestic and international students. Application fee: $50. Electronic applications accepted. *Financial support:* In 2018–19, 66 students received support, including 2 fellowships with full tuition reimbursements available (averaging $21,240 per year), 63 research assistantships with full tuition reimbursements available (averaging $15,360 per year), 12 teaching assistantships with full tuition reimbursements available (averaging $16,200 per year); scholarships/grants also available. Financial award application deadline: 1/15; financial award applicants required to submit FAFSA. *Faculty research:* Microwave earth remote sensing, configurable computing and embedded systems, MEMS semiconductors, integrated electro-optics, multiple-agent intelligent coordinated control systems for unmanned air vehicles. *Total annual research expenditures:* $3.7 million. *Unit head:* Dr. Aaron Hawkins, Department Chair, 801-422-4012, Fax: 801-422-0201, E-mail: hawkins@ee.byu.edu. *Application contact:* Janalyn L. Mergist, Graduate Secretary, 801-422-4013, Fax: 801-422-0201, E-mail: janalyn@ee.byu.edu.
Website: http://www.ee.byu.edu/

Brown University, Graduate School, School of Engineering, Program in Electrical Sciences and Computer Engineering, Providence, RI 02912. Offers Sc M, PhD. *Degree requirements:* For doctorate, thesis/dissertation, preliminary exam.

Bucknell University, Graduate Studies, College of Engineering, Department of Electrical and Computer Engineering, Lewisburg, PA 17837. Offers MSEE. *Program availability:* Part-time. *Degree requirements:* For master's, thesis. *Entrance requirements:* For master's, GRE General Test, minimum GPA of 3.0. Additional exam requirements/recommendations for international students: Required—TOEFL (minimum score 600 paper-based).

California Institute of Technology, Division of Engineering and Applied Science, Option in Electrical Engineering, Pasadena, CA 91125-0001. Offers MS, PhD, Engr. *Degree requirements:* For doctorate, thesis/dissertation. Electronic applications accepted. *Faculty research:* Solid-state electronics, power electronics, communications, controls, submillimeter-wave integrated circuits.

California Polytechnic State University, San Luis Obispo, College of Engineering, Department of Electrical Engineering, San Luis Obispo, CA 93407. Offers MS. *Program availability:* Part-time. *Faculty:* 10 full-time (2 women). *Students:* 24 full-time (2 women), 4 part-time (0 women); includes 11 minority (8 Asian, non-Hispanic/Latino; 3 Hispanic/Latino), 3 international. Average age 24. 57 applicants, 46% accepted, 13 enrolled. In 2018, 31 master's awarded. *Degree requirements:* For master's, comprehensive exam (for some programs), thesis (for some programs). *Entrance requirements:* For master's, GRE. Additional exam requirements/recommendations for international students: Required—TOEFL (minimum score 80 iBT). *Application deadline:* For fall admission, 3/1 for domestic and international students. Applications are processed on a rolling basis. Application fee: $55. Electronic applications accepted. *Expenses: Tuition, area resident:* Full-time $7176; part-time $4164 per year. Tuition, state resident: full-time $10,965. Tuition, nonresident: full-time $10,965. *Required fees:* $6336; $3711. *Financial support:* Fellowships, research assistantships, teaching assistantships, career-related internships or fieldwork, scholarships/grants, and unspecified assistantships available. Financial award application deadline: 3/2; financial award applicants required to submit FAFSA. *Faculty research:* Communications, systems design and analysis, control systems, electronic devices, microprocessors. *Unit head:* Dr. Jane Zhang, Graduate Coordinator, 805-756-7528, E-mail: jzhang@calpoly.edu. *Application contact:* Dr. Jane Zhang, Graduate Coordinator, 805-756-7528, E-mail: jzhang@calpoly.edu.
Website: http://www.ee.calpoly.edu/

California State Polytechnic University, Pomona, Program in Electrical Engineering, Pomona, CA 91768-2557. Offers communication systems (MSEE). *Program availability:* Part-time, evening/weekend. *Students:* 13 full-time (2 women), 42 part-time (7 women); includes 32 minority (18 Asian, non-Hispanic/Latino; 12 Hispanic/Latino; 2 Two or more races, non-Hispanic/Latino), 5 international. Average age 28. 93 applicants, 48% accepted, 23 enrolled. In 2018, 25 master's awarded. *Entrance requirements:* Additional exam requirements/recommendations for international students: Required—TOEFL (minimum score 550 paper-based). *Application deadline:* Applications are processed on a rolling basis. Application fee: $55. Electronic applications accepted. *Expenses:* Contact institution. *Financial support:* Application deadline: 3/2; applicants required to submit FAFSA. *Faculty research:* Digital logic, wind and solar powered systems, photonic systems, radar signal processing. *Unit head:* Dr. Thomas Ketseoglou, Professor/Graduate Program Coordinator, 909-869-3977, Fax: 909-869-4687, E-mail: tketseoglou@cpp.edu. *Application contact:* Dr. Thomas Ketseoglou, Professor/Graduate Program Coordinator, 909-869-3977, Fax: 909-869-4687, E-mail: tketseoglou@cpp.edu.
Website: http://www.cpp.edu/~engineering/ECE/msee.shtml

California State University, Chico, Office of Graduate Studies, College of Engineering, Computer Science, and Construction Management, Electrical and Computer Engineering Department, Option in Electronics Engineering, Chico, CA 95929-0722. Offers electronic engineering (MS). *Students:* 10 full-time (4 women), 11 part-time (6 women); includes 14 minority (all Asian, non-Hispanic/Latino). 64 applicants, 75% accepted, 9 enrolled. *Degree requirements:* For master's, thesis or project plan. *Entrance requirements:* For master's, GRE General Test, Fall Admissions only. Two letters of recommendation, statement of purpose, departmental letter of recommendation access waiver form. Additional exam requirements/recommendations for international students: Required—TOEFL (minimum score 550 paper-based; 80 iBT), IELTS (minimum score 6.5), PTE (minimum score 59). *Application deadline:* For fall admission, 3/1 priority date for domestic students, 3/1 for international students; for spring admission, 9/15 priority date for domestic students, 9/15 for international students. Application fee: $55. Electronic applications accepted. *Expenses: Tuition, area resident:* Full-time $4622; part-time $3116 per unit. Tuition, state resident: full-time $4622; part-time $3116 per unit. Tuition, nonresident: full-time $10,634. *Required fees:* $2160; $1620 per year. Tuition and fees vary according to class time and program. *Financial support:* Fellowships, research assistantships, teaching assistantships, career-related internships or fieldwork, Federal Work-Study, scholarships/grants, traineeships, health care benefits, unspecified assistantships, and stipends available. Support available to part-time students. Financial award application deadline: 3/2; financial award applicants required to submit FAFSA. *Unit head:* Dr. Chuen Hsu, Chair, 530-898-5343, Fax: 530-898-4956, E-mail: elce@csuchico.edu. *Application contact:* Judy L. Morris, Graduate Admissions Coordinator, 530-898-5416, Fax: 530-898-3342, E-mail: jlmorris@csuchico.edu.
Website: http://catalog.csuchico.edu/viewer/19/ENGR/ELCENONEMS.html

California State University, Fresno, Division of Research and Graduate Studies, Lyles College of Engineering, Department of Electrical and Computer Engineering, Fresno, CA 93740-8027. Offers computer engineering (MSE); electrical engineering (MSE). *Program availability:* Part-time, evening/weekend. *Degree requirements:* For master's, thesis or alternative. *Entrance requirements:* For master's, GRE General Test, minimum GPA of 2.7. Additional exam requirements/recommendations for international students: Required—TOEFL. Electronic applications accepted. *Faculty research:* Research in electromagnetic devices.

California State University, Fullerton, Graduate Studies, College of Engineering and Computer Science, Department of Electrical Engineering, Fullerton, CA 92831-3599. Offers electrical engineering (MS); systems engineering (MS). *Program availability:* Part-time. *Degree requirements:* For master's, comprehensive exam, project or thesis. *Entrance requirements:* For master's, GRE General Test, GRE Subject Test, minimum undergraduate GPA of 2.5, 3.0 graduate.

California State University, Long Beach, Graduate Studies, College of Engineering, Department of Electrical Engineering, Long Beach, CA 90840. Offers MSEE. *Program availability:* Part-time. *Degree requirements:* For master's, comprehensive exam or thesis. *Entrance requirements:* Additional exam requirements/recommendations for international students: Required—TOEFL. *Application deadline:* For fall admission, 4/15 for domestic students; for spring admission, 10/1 for domestic students. Application fee: $55. Electronic applications accepted. *Expenses: Required fees:* $2628 per term. Tuition and fees vary according to class time, course level, course load, degree level, campus/location and program. *Financial support:* Teaching assistantships, career-related internships or fieldwork, Federal Work-Study, institutionally sponsored loans, scholarships/grants, and unspecified assistantships available. Financial award application deadline: 3/2; financial award applicants required to submit FAFSA. *Faculty research:* Health care systems, VLSI, communications, CAD/CAM. *Unit head:* Hen-Geul Yeh, Chair, 562-985-5102. *Application contact:* Dr. Mohmmad Mozumdar, Graduate Advisor, 562-985-5106, E-mail: mohammad.mozumdar@csulb.edu.
Website: http://www.csulb.edu/college-of-engineering/electrical-engineering

California State University, Los Angeles, Graduate Studies, College of Engineering, Computer Science, and Technology, Department of Electrical and Computer Engineering, Los Angeles, CA 90032-8530. Offers electrical engineering (MS). *Program availability:* Part-time, evening/weekend. *Degree requirements:* For master's, comprehensive exam or thesis. *Entrance requirements:* For master's, GRE General Test, GRE Subject Test. Additional exam requirements/recommendations for international students: Required—TOEFL (minimum score 550 paper-based). Electronic applications accepted.

California State University, Northridge, Graduate Studies, College of Engineering and Computer Science, Department of Electrical and Computer Engineering, Northridge, CA 91330. Offers electrical engineering (MS). *Program availability:* Part-time, evening/weekend. *Degree requirements:* For master's, thesis or alternative. *Entrance requirements:* For master's, GRE General Test, minimum GPA of 2.75. Additional exam requirements/recommendations for international students: Required—TOEFL. *Faculty research:* Reflector antenna study.

California State University, Sacramento, College of Engineering and Computer Science, Department of Electrical and Electronic Engineering, Sacramento, CA 95819. Offers MS. *Program availability:* Part-time, evening/weekend. *Degree requirements:* For master's, thesis or comprehensive exam, writing proficiency exam. *Entrance requirements:* For master's, minimum GPA of 3.0 in last 60 units of the BS in electrical and electronic engineering or equivalent, 3.25 in electrical and electronic engineering major or equivalent major. Additional exam requirements/recommendations for international students: Required—TOEFL (minimum score 550 paper-based; 80 iBT); Recommended—IELTS, TSE. Electronic applications accepted. *Expenses:* Contact institution.

Capitol Technology University, Graduate Programs, Laurel, MD 20708-9759. Offers business administration (MBA); computer science (MS); electrical engineering (MS); information and telecommunications systems management (MS); information architecture (MS); network security (MS). *Program availability:* Part-time, evening/weekend, online learning. *Entrance requirements:* For master's, minimum GPA of 3.0. Electronic applications accepted.

Carleton University, Faculty of Graduate Studies, Faculty of Engineering and Design, Ottawa-Carleton Institute for Electrical Engineering, Department of Electronics, Ottawa, ON K1S 5B6, Canada. Offers electrical engineering (M Eng, MA Sc, PhD). *Degree requirements:* For master's, thesis optional; for doctorate, comprehensive exam, thesis/dissertation. *Entrance requirements:* For master's, honors degree; for doctorate, MA Sc or M Eng. Additional exam requirements/recommendations for international students: Required—TOEFL.

Carleton University, Faculty of Graduate Studies, Faculty of Engineering and Design, Ottawa-Carleton Institute for Electrical Engineering, Department of Systems and Computer Engineering, Ottawa, ON K1S 5B6, Canada. Offers electrical engineering (MA Sc, PhD); information and systems science (M Sc); technology innovation management (M Eng, MA Sc). PhD program offered jointly with University of Ottawa. *Degree requirements:* For master's, thesis optional. *Entrance requirements:* For master's, honors degree. Additional exam requirements/recommendations for international students: Required—TOEFL. *Faculty research:* Design manufacturing management; network design, protocols, and performance; software engineering; wireless and satellite communications.

Carnegie Mellon University, Carnegie Institute of Technology, Department of Electrical and Computer Engineering, Pittsburgh, PA 15213-3891. Offers MS, PhD. *Program availability:* Part-time. *Degree requirements:* For master's, thesis; for doctorate, thesis/dissertation, qualifying exam, teaching experience. *Entrance requirements:* For master's and doctorate, GRE General Test. Additional exam requirements/recommendations for international students: Required—TOEFL. *Faculty research:* Computer-aided design, solid-state devices, VLSI, processing, robotics and controls, signal processing, data systems storage.

Case Western Reserve University, School of Graduate Studies, Case School of Engineering, Department of Computer and Data Sciences, Cleveland, OH 44106. Offers computer engineering (MS, PhD); computing and information sciences (MS, PhD); electrical engineering (MS, PhD); systems and control engineering (MS, PhD). *Program availability:* Part-time, evening/weekend, online only, 100% online. *Faculty:* 31 full-time (2 women). *Students:* 228 full-time (49 women), 17 part-time (3 women); includes 18 minority (13 Asian, non-Hispanic/Latino; 3 Hispanic/Latino; 2 Two or more races, non-Hispanic/Latino), 180 international. In 2018, 29 master's, 16 doctorates awarded. Terminal master's awarded for partial completion of doctoral program. *Degree requirements:* For master's, thesis; for doctorate, thesis/dissertation, qualifying exam, teaching experience. *Entrance requirements:* For master's and doctorate, GRE General Test. Additional exam requirements/recommendations for international students: Required—TOEFL. *Application deadline:* For fall admission, 2/1 for domestic students; for spring admission, 11/1 for domestic students. Applications are processed on a rolling basis. Application fee: $50. *Expenses: Tuition:* Full-time $45,168; part-time $1939 per credit hour. *Required fees:* $36; $18 per semester. $18 per semester. *Financial support:* In 2018–19, 1 fellowship with tuition reimbursement, 72 research assistantships with tuition reimbursements, 10 teaching assistantships were awarded; career-related internships or fieldwork, Federal Work-Study, and institutionally sponsored loans also available. Support available to part-time students. Financial award application deadline: 3/1; financial award applicants required to submit FAFSA. *Faculty research:* Micro-/nano-systems; robotics and haptics; applied artificial intelligence; automation; computer-aided design and testing of digital systems. *Total annual research expenditures:* $5.1 million. *Unit head:* Jing Li, Interim Department Chair, 216-368-0356, E-mail: jxl175@case.edu. *Application contact:* Angela Beca, Student Affairs Specialist, 216-368-2800, Fax: 216-368-2801, E-mail: angela.beca@case.edu.
Website: www.engineering.case.edu/eecs

The Catholic University of America, School of Engineering, Department of Electrical Engineering and Computer Science, Washington, DC 20064. Offers computer science (MSCS, PhD); electrical engineering (MEE, PhD). *Program availability:* Part-time. *Faculty:* 9 full-time (2 women), 13 part-time/adjunct (0 women). *Students:* 18 full-time (10 women), 65 part-time (19 women); includes 12 minority (3 Black or African American, non-Hispanic/Latino; 4 Asian, non-Hispanic/Latino; 3 Hispanic/Latino; 2 Two or more races, non-Hispanic/Latino), 45 international. Average age 32. 40 applicants, 73% accepted, 15 enrolled. In 2018, 10 master's, 6 doctorates awarded. *Degree requirements:* For master's, thesis or alternative; for doctorate, comprehensive exam, thesis/dissertation, oral exams. *Entrance requirements:* For master's and doctorate, statement of purpose, official copies of academic transcripts, three letters of recommendation. Additional exam requirements/recommendations for international students: Required—TOEFL (minimum score 550 paper-based; 80 iBT). *Application deadline:* For fall admission, 7/15 priority date for domestic students, 7/1 for international students; for spring admission, 11/15 priority date for domestic students, 11/1 for international students. Applications are processed on a rolling basis. Application fee: $55. Electronic applications accepted. *Expenses:* Contact institution. *Financial support:* Fellowships, research assistantships, teaching assistantships, Federal Work-Study, scholarships/grants, tuition waivers (full and partial), and unspecified assistantships available. Financial award application deadline: 2/1; financial award applicants required to submit FAFSA. *Faculty research:* Signal and image processing, computer communications, robotics, intelligent controls, bio-electromagnetics. *Unit head:* Dr. Ozlem Kilic, Chair, 202-319-5879, Fax: 202-319-5195, E-mail: regalia@cua.edu. *Application contact:* Dr. Steven Brown, Director of Graduate Admissions, 202-319-5057, Fax: 202-319-6533, E-mail: cua-admissions@cua.edu.
Website: https://engineering.catholic.edu/eecs/index.html

The Citadel, The Military College of South Carolina, Citadel Graduate College, School of Engineering, Department of Electrical and Computer Engineering, Charleston, SC 29409. Offers computer engineering (Graduate Certificate); electrical engineering (MS). *Program availability:* Part-time, evening/weekend. *Degree requirements:* For master's, 30 hours of coursework with minimum GPA of 3.0 on hours earned at The Citadel. *Entrance requirements:* For master's, GRE, 2 letters of recommendation; official transcript of baccalaureate degree from an ABET accredited engineering program or approved alternative. Additional exam requirements/recommendations for international students: Required—TOEFL (minimum score 550 paper-based; 79 iBT). Electronic applications accepted. *Expenses:* Tuition, state resident: part-time $595 per credit hour. Tuition, nonresident: part-time $1020 per credit hour. *Required fees:* $90 per term.

City College of the City University of New York, Graduate School, Grove School of Engineering, Department of Electrical Engineering, New York, NY 10031-9198. Offers ME, MS, PhD. PhD program offered jointly with Graduate School and University Center of the City University of New York. *Program availability:* Part-time. *Degree requirements:* For master's, thesis optional; for doctorate, one foreign language, comprehensive exam, thesis/dissertation. *Entrance requirements:* For master's and doctorate, GRE General Test. Additional exam requirements/recommendations for international students: Required—TOEFL (minimum score 500 paper-based; 61 iBT). *Faculty research:* Optical electronics, microwaves, communication, signal processing, control systems.

Clarkson University, Wallace H. Coulter School of Engineering, Master's Programs in Energy Systems, Schenectady, NY 13699. Offers electrical engineering (ME), including power engineering; energy systems (MS). *Program availability:* Part-time, evening/weekend. *Students:* 5 full-time (4 women), 3 part-time (0 women); includes 1 minority (Hispanic/Latino). 12 applicants, 58% accepted, 6 enrolled. In 2018, 2 master's

awarded. *Degree requirements:* For master's, project. *Entrance requirements:* Additional exam requirements/recommendations for international students: Required—TOEFL (minimum score 550 paper-based, 80 iBT) or IELTS (6.5). *Application deadline:* Applications are processed on a rolling basis. Application fee: $50. Electronic applications accepted. *Expenses: Tuition:* Full-time $24,984; part-time $1388 per credit hour. *Required fees:* $225. Tuition and fees vary according to campus/location and program. *Financial support:* Scholarships/grants available. *Unit head:* Hugo Irizarry-Quinones, Associate Dean of Engineering, 518-631-9881, E-mail: hirizarr@clarkson.edu. *Application contact:* Dan Capogna, Director of Graduate Admissions, 518-631-9910, E-mail: graduate@clarkson.edu.
Website: https://www.clarkson.edu/academics/graduate

Clemson University, Graduate School, College of Engineering, Computing and Applied Sciences, Holcombe Department of Electrical and Computer Engineering, Clemson, SC 29634. Offers computer engineering (MS, PhD); electrical engineering (M Engr, MS, PhD). *Program availability:* Part-time, evening/weekend, blended/hybrid learning. *Faculty:* 33 full-time (3 women). *Students:* 139 full-time (24 women), 36 part-time (3 women); includes 9 minority (4 Black or African American, non-Hispanic/Latino; 1 American Indian or Alaska Native, non-Hispanic/Latino; 2 Asian, non-Hispanic/Latino; 1 Hispanic/Latino; 1 Two or more races, non-Hispanic/Latino), 107 international. Average age 27. 393 applicants, 42% accepted, 51 enrolled. In 2018, 34 master's, 14 doctorates awarded. *Degree requirements:* For master's, comprehensive exam (for some programs), thesis (for some programs); for doctorate, comprehensive exam, thesis/dissertation, departmental qualifying exam. *Entrance requirements:* For master's and doctorate, GRE General Test, unofficial transcripts, letters of recommendation. Additional exam requirements/recommendations for international students: Required—TOEFL (minimum score 80 paper-based; 95 iBT); Recommended—IELTS (minimum score 7), TSE (minimum score 54). *Application deadline:* For fall admission, 1/15 priority date for domestic students, 4/15 for international students; for spring admission, 9/15 priority date for domestic students, 9/15 for international students. Applications are processed on a rolling basis. Application fee: $80 ($90 for international students). Electronic applications accepted. *Expenses:* $6,823 per semester full-time resident, $14,023 per semester full-time non-resident, $833 per credit hour part-time resident, $1,731 per credit hour part-time non-resident, online $1,264 per credit hour, $4,938 doctoral programs resident, $10,405 doctoral programs non-resident, $1,144 full-time graduate assistant, other fees may apply per session. *Financial support:* In 2018–19, 176 students received support, including 13 fellowships with full and partial tuition reimbursements available (averaging $4,731 per year), 85 research assistantships with full and partial tuition reimbursements available (averaging $17,365 per year), 59 teaching assistantships with full and partial tuition reimbursements available (averaging $18,536 per year); career-related internships or fieldwork and unspecified assistantships also available. Financial award application deadline: 1/15. *Faculty research:* Applied use of emerging heterogeneous computing architectures; communications theory, coding theory, detecting and estimation theory; cognitive radios; organic electronics: polymer-based devices, micro-optics and nano-photonics. *Total annual research expenditures:* $5.1 million. *Unit head:* Dr. Daniel Noneaker, Department Chair, 864-656-0100, E-mail: dnoneak@clemson.edu. *Application contact:* Dr. Harlan Russell, Graduate Program Coordinator, 864-656-7214, E-mail: harlanr@clemson.edu.
Website: http://www.clemson.edu/cecas/departments/ece/index.html

Cleveland State University, College of Graduate Studies, Fenn College of Engineering, Department of Electrical and Computer engineering, Cleveland, OH 44115. Offers electrical engineering (MS, D Eng); software engineering (MS). *Program availability:* Part-time, evening/weekend. *Faculty:* 15 full-time (2 women), 1 part-time/adjunct (0 women). *Students:* 108 full-time (36 women), 69 part-time (13 women); includes 16 minority (1 Black or African American, non-Hispanic/Latino; 12 Asian, non-Hispanic/Latino; 1 Hispanic/Latino; 2 Two or more races, non-Hispanic/Latino), 115 international. Average age 26. 1,083 applicants, 44% accepted, 89 enrolled. In 2018, 120 master's, 3 doctorates awarded. Terminal master's awarded for partial completion of doctoral program. *Entrance requirements:* For master's, GRE General Test (minimum score 650 quantitative), minimum GPA of 2.75; for doctorate, GRE General Test (minimum quantitative score in 80th percentile), minimum GPA of 3.25. *Application deadline:* Applications are processed on a rolling basis. Application fee: $40. Electronic applications accepted. *Expenses:* Contact institution. *Financial support:* In 2018–19, 31 students received support, including 14 research assistantships with tuition reimbursements available (averaging $8,300 per year), 16 teaching assistantships with tuition reimbursements available (averaging $9,500 per year); career-related internships or fieldwork, scholarships/grants, and unspecified assistantships also available. Financial award applicants required to submit FAFSA. *Faculty research:* Computer networks, computer security and privacy, mobile computing, distributed computing, software engineering, knowledge-based control systems, artificial intelligence, digital communications, MEMS, sensors, power systems, power electronics. *Total annual research expenditures:* $484,362. *Unit head:* Dr. Chansu Yu, Chairperson, 216-687-2584, Fax: 216-687-5405, E-mail: f.xiong@csuohio.edu. *Application contact:* Deborah L. Brown, Interim Assistant Director, Graduate Admissions, 216-523-7572, Fax: 216-687-9214, E-mail: d.l.brown@csuohio.edu.
Website: http://www.csuohio.edu/ece

College of Staten Island of the City University of New York, Graduate Programs, Division of Science and Technology, Program in Electrical Engineering, Staten Island, NY 10314-6600. Offers ME. *Program availability:* Part-time, evening/weekend. *Students:* 14. 22 applicants, 55% accepted, 6 enrolled. *Degree requirements:* For master's, thesis or alternative, 30 credits. *Entrance requirements:* For master's, The General Aptitude Test (GRE) is recommended but not required of applicants., BS in Electrical Engineering from an accredited institution (students with a baccalaureate degree in a related field such as Physics, Mathematics, or Computer Science may be accepted). Two letters of recommendation. Applicants must provide a one page personal statement which expresses their goals and philosophy for studying and practicing electrica. Additional exam requirements/recommendations for international students: Required—TOEFL (minimum score 73 iBT), IELTS (minimum score 6). *Application deadline:* For fall admission, 6/30 priority date for domestic students, 6/30 for international students; for spring admission, 11/25 priority date for domestic students, 11/25 for international students. Applications are processed on a rolling basis. Application fee: $75. Electronic applications accepted. *Expenses: Tuition, area resident:* Full-time $10,770; part-time $455 per credit. Tuition, state resident: full-time $10,770; part-time $455 per credit. Tuition, nonresident: full-time $19,920; part-time $830 per credit. *International tuition:* $19,920 full-time. *Required fees:* $559.20; $181.10 per semester. Tuition and fees vary according to program. *Unit head:* Prof. Mark D. Feuer, Coordinator, 718-982-2808, E-mail: mark.feuer@csi.cuny.edu. *Application contact:* Sasha Spence, Associate Director for Graduate Admissions, 718-982-2019, Fax: 718-982-2500, E-mail: sasha.spence@csi.cuny.edu.

Colorado School of Mines, Office of Graduate Studies, Department of Electrical Engineering and Computer Science, Golden, CO 80401-1887. Offers electrical engineering (MS, PhD). *Program availability:* Part-time. *Students:* 68 full-time (14 women), 25 part-time (2 women); includes 10 minority (1 Black or African American, non-Hispanic/Latino; 3 Asian, non-Hispanic/Latino; 4 Hispanic/Latino; 2 Two or more races, non-Hispanic/Latino), 40 international. Average age 28. 180 applicants, 67%

accepted, 38 enrolled. In 2018, 38 master's, 6 doctorates awarded. *Degree requirements:* For master's, thesis (for some programs); for doctorate, comprehensive exam, thesis/dissertation. *Entrance requirements:* For master's and doctorate, GRE General Test. Additional exam requirements/recommendations for international students: Required—TOEFL (minimum score 550 paper-based; 79 iBT). *Application deadline:* For fall admission, 12/15 priority date for domestic and international students; for spring admission, 9/1 priority date for domestic and international students. Application fee: $60 ($80 for international students). Electronic applications accepted. *Expenses:* Tuition, state resident: full-time $16,650; part-time $925 per contact hour. Tuition, nonresident: full-time $36,270; part-time $2015 per contact hour. *International tuition:* $36,270 full-time. *Required fees:* $2314; $2314 per semester. *Financial support:* In 2018–19, 25 research assistantships with full tuition reimbursements, 11 teaching assistantships with full tuition reimbursements were awarded; fellowships, career-related internships or fieldwork, Federal Work-Study, institutionally sponsored loans, scholarships/grants, health care benefits, and unspecified assistantships also available. Financial award application deadline: 12/15; financial award applicants required to submit FAFSA. *Unit head:* Dr. Peter Aaen, Head, 303-384-2245, E-mail: paaen@mines.edu. *Application contact:* Lori Sisneros, Graduate Program Administrator, 303-384-3658, E-mail: sisneros@mines.edu.
Website: http://eecs.mines.edu/

Colorado State University, Walter Scott, Jr. College of Engineering, Department of Electrical and Computer Engineering, Fort Collins, CO 80523-1373. Offers computer engineering (ME, PhD); electrical engineering (MS). *Program availability:* Part-time, online learning. Terminal master's awarded for partial completion of doctoral program. *Degree requirements:* For master's, thesis (for some programs); for doctorate, comprehensive exam, thesis/dissertation. *Entrance requirements:* For master's and doctorate, GRE, minimum GPA of 3.0; transcripts; resume; 3 letters of reference. Additional exam requirements/recommendations for international students: Required—TOEFL (minimum score 80 iBT), IELTS (minimum score 6.5). Electronic applications accepted. *Expenses:* Contact institution. *Faculty research:* Biomedical engineering, systems (communications and signal processing, controls and robotics), computer engineering, electric power and energy systems, lasers/optics and electromagnetics/remote sensing.

Colorado Technical University Aurora, Program in Electrical Engineering, Aurora, CO 80014. Offers MS.

Colorado Technical University Colorado Springs, Graduate Studies, Program in Electrical Engineering, Colorado Springs, CO 80907. Offers MSEE. *Program availability:* Part-time, evening/weekend, online learning. *Degree requirements:* For master's, thesis or alternative. *Faculty research:* Electronic systems design, communication systems design.

Columbia University, Fu Foundation School of Engineering and Applied Science, Department of Electrical Engineering, New York, NY 10027. Offers computer engineering (MS); electrical engineering (MS, PhD). PhD offered through the Graduate School of Arts and Sciences. *Program availability:* Part-time, online learning. *Degree requirements:* For doctorate, thesis/dissertation, qualifying exam. *Entrance requirements:* For master's and doctorate, GRE General Test. Additional exam requirements/recommendations for international students: Required—TOEFL, IELTS, PTE. Electronic applications accepted. *Faculty research:* Media informatics and signal processing, integrated circuits and cyberphysical systems, communications systems and networking, nanoscale electronics and photonics, systems biology and neuroengineering.

Concordia University, School of Graduate Studies, Faculty of Engineering and Computer Science, Department of Electrical and Computer Engineering, Montréal, QC H3G 1M8, Canada. Offers M Eng, MA Sc, PhD. *Degree requirements:* For master's, thesis optional; for doctorate, comprehensive exam, thesis/dissertation. *Faculty research:* Computer communications and protocols, circuits and systems, graph theory, VLSI systems, microelectronics.

Cooper Union for the Advancement of Science and Art, Albert Nerken School of Engineering, New York, NY 10003. Offers chemical engineering (ME); civil engineering (ME); electrical engineering (ME); mechanical engineering (ME). *Program availability:* Part-time. *Degree requirements:* For master's, thesis (for some programs), thesis or special project. *Entrance requirements:* For master's, BE or BS in an engineering discipline; official copies of school transcripts including secondary (high school), college and university work; two letters of recommendation; resume. Additional exam requirements/recommendations for international students: Required—TOEFL (minimum score 600 paper-based; 100 iBT). Electronic applications accepted. *Faculty research:* Analytics, bioengineering, dynamic systems, nanoscience, sustainability, STEM education.

Cornell University, Graduate School, Graduate Fields of Engineering, Field of Electrical and Computer Engineering, Ithaca, NY 14853. Offers computer engineering (M Eng, PhD); electrical engineering (M Eng, PhD); electrical systems (M Eng, PhD); electrophysics (M Eng, PhD). *Degree requirements:* For doctorate, comprehensive exam, thesis/dissertation. *Entrance requirements:* For master's, GRE General Test, 2 letters of recommendation; for doctorate, GRE General Test, 3 letters of recommendation. Additional exam requirements/recommendations for international students: Required—TOEFL (minimum score 600 paper-based; 77 iBT). Electronic applications accepted. *Faculty research:* Communications, information theory, signal processing and power control, computer engineering, microelectromechanical systems and nanotechnology.

Dalhousie University, Faculty of Engineering, Department of Electrical and Computer Engineering, Halifax, NS B3J 1Z1, Canada. Offers M Eng, MA Sc, PhD. *Degree requirements:* For master's, thesis; for doctorate, thesis/dissertation. *Entrance requirements:* Additional exam requirements/recommendations for international students: Required—TOEFL, IELTS, CANTEST, CAEL, or Michigan English Language Assessment Battery. Electronic applications accepted. *Faculty research:* Communications, computer engineering, power engineering, electronics, systems engineering.

Dartmouth College, Thayer School of Engineering, Program in Electrical and Computer Engineering, Hanover, NH 03755. Offers MS, PhD. *Degree requirements:* For master's, thesis; for doctorate, thesis/dissertation, candidacy oral exam. *Entrance requirements:* For master's and doctorate, GRE General Test. *Faculty research:* Analog VLSI, electromagnetic fields and waves, electronic instrumentation, microelectromechanical systems, optics, lasers and non-linear optics, power electronics and integrated power converters, networking, parallel and distributed computing, simulation, VLSI design and testing, wireless networking.

Drexel University, College of Engineering, Department of Electrical and Computer Engineering, Program in Electrical Engineering, Philadelphia, PA 19104-2875. Offers MSEE. *Program availability:* Part-time, evening/weekend. Terminal master's awarded for partial completion of doctoral program. *Degree requirements:* For master's, thesis (for some programs). Electronic applications accepted.

Duke University, Graduate School, Pratt School of Engineering, Department of Electrical and Computer Engineering, Durham, NC 27708. Offers M Eng, MS, PhD, JD/MS. Terminal master's awarded for partial completion of doctoral program. *Degree requirements:* For doctorate, thesis/dissertation. *Entrance requirements:* For master's and doctorate, GRE General Test. Additional exam requirements/recommendations for international students: Required—TOEFL (minimum score 90 iBT), IELTS (minimum score 7). Electronic applications accepted. *Faculty research:* Architecture and networking; biological applications circuits and systems; nanosystems, devices and materials; quantum computing and photonics; sensing and signals visualization; waves and metamaterials.

Duke University, Graduate School, Pratt School of Engineering, Master of Engineering Program, Durham, NC 27708-0271. Offers biomedical engineering (M Eng); civil engineering (M Eng); computational mechanics and scientific computing (M Eng); electrical and computer engineering (M Eng); environmental engineering (M Eng); materials science and engineering (M Eng); mechanical engineering (M Eng); photonics and optical sciences (M Eng); risk engineering (M Eng). *Program availability:* Part-time. *Entrance requirements:* For master's, GRE General Test, resume, 3 letters of recommendation, statement of purpose, transcripts. Additional exam requirements/recommendations for international students: Required—TOEFL. Electronic applications accepted.

École Polytechnique de Montréal, Graduate Programs, Department of Electrical and Computer Engineering, Montréal, QC H3C 3A7, Canada. Offers automation (M Eng, M Sc A, PhD); computer science (M Eng, M Sc A, PhD); electrical engineering (DESS); electrotechnology (M Eng, M Sc A, PhD); microelectronics (M Eng, M Sc A, PhD); microwave technology (M Eng, M Sc A, PhD). *Program availability:* Part-time, evening/weekend. *Degree requirements:* For master's, one foreign language, thesis; for doctorate, one foreign language, thesis/dissertation. *Entrance requirements:* For master's, minimum GPA of 2.75; for doctorate, minimum GPA of 3.0. *Faculty research:* Microwaves, telecommunications, software engineering.

Embry-Riddle Aeronautical University–Daytona, Department of Electrical, Computer, Software and Systems Engineering, Daytona Beach, FL 32114-3900. Offers cybersecurity engineering (MS); electrical and computer engineering (MSECE); software engineering (MSSE); systems engineering (MS). *Degree requirements:* For master's, thesis optional. *Entrance requirements:* For master's, GRE (for some programs). Additional exam requirements/recommendations for international students: Required—TOEFL (minimum score 550 paper-based, 79 iBT) or IELTS (6). Electronic applications accepted.

Fairfield University, School of Engineering, Fairfield, CT 06824. Offers database management (CAS); electrical and computer engineering (MS); information security (CAS); management of technology (MS); mechanical engineering (MS); network technology (CAS); software engineering (MS); Web application development (CAS). *Program availability:* Part-time, evening/weekend. *Degree requirements:* For master's, capstone course. *Entrance requirements:* For master's, resume, 2 recommendations. Additional exam requirements/recommendations for international students: Required—TOEFL (minimum score 550 paper-based; 80 iBT) or IELTS (minimum score 6.5). Electronic applications accepted. *Expenses:* Contact institution. *Faculty research:* Artificial intelligence and information visualization, natural language processing, thermofluids, microwaves and electromagnetics, micro-/nano-manufacturing.

Fairleigh Dickinson University, Metropolitan Campus, University College: Arts, Sciences, and Professional Studies, School of Computer Sciences and Engineering, Program in Electrical Engineering, Teaneck, NJ 07666-1914. Offers MSEE. *Entrance requirements:* For master's, GRE General Test.

Farmingdale State College, Program in Technology Management, Farmingdale, NY 11735. Offers construction management (MS); electrical and mechanical engineering (MS). *Degree requirements:* For master's, project or thesis.

Florida Agricultural and Mechanical University, Division of Graduate Studies, Research, and Continuing Education, FAMU-FSU College of Engineering, Department of Electrical and Computer Engineering, Tallahassee, FL 32307-3200. Offers electrical engineering (MS, PhD). *Degree requirements:* For master's, comprehensive exam, thesis, conference paper; for doctorate, comprehensive exam, thesis/dissertation, publishable paper. *Entrance requirements:* For master's, GRE General Test, minimum GPA of 3.0; for doctorate, minimum GPA of 3.3. Additional exam requirements/recommendations for international students: Required—TOEFL (minimum score 550 paper-based). *Faculty research:* Electromagnetics, computer security, advanced power systems, sensor systems.

Florida Atlantic University, College of Engineering and Computer Science, Department of Computer and Electrical Engineering and Computer Science, Boca Raton, FL 33431-0991. Offers bioengineering (MS); computer engineering (MS, PhD); computer science (MS, PhD); electrical engineering (MS, PhD). *Program availability:* Part-time, evening/weekend. *Faculty:* 37 full-time (7 women), 2 part-time/adjunct (0 women). *Students:* 85 full-time (18 women), 140 part-time (26 women); includes 86 minority (18 Black or African American, non-Hispanic/Latino; 17 Asian, non-Hispanic/Latino; 43 Hispanic/Latino; 8 Two or more races, non-Hispanic/Latino), 60 international. Average age 32. 185 applicants, 41% accepted, 69 enrolled. In 2018, 89 master's, 11 doctorates awarded. Terminal master's awarded for partial completion of doctoral program. *Degree requirements:* For master's, thesis optional; for doctorate, thesis/dissertation, qualifying exam. *Entrance requirements:* For master's, GRE General Test, minimum GPA of 3.0; for doctorate, GRE General Test, master's degree, minimum GPA of 3.5. Additional exam requirements/recommendations for international students: Required—TOEFL (minimum score 500 paper-based; 61 iBT), IELTS (minimum score 6). *Application deadline:* For fall admission, 7/1 priority date for domestic students, 2/15 for international students; for spring admission, 11/1 for domestic students, 7/15 for international students. Applications are processed on a rolling basis. Application fee: $30. *Expenses: Tuition, area resident:* Full-time $7400; part-time $369.82 per credit. Tuition, state resident: full-time $7400; part-time $369.82 per credit. Tuition, nonresident: full-time $20,496; part-time $1024.81 per credit. *Financial support:* Fellowships, research assistantships with partial tuition reimbursements, teaching assistantships with full tuition reimbursements, career-related internships or fieldwork, and Federal Work-Study available. Support available to part-time students. Financial award application deadline: 4/1; financial award applicants required to submit FAFSA. *Faculty research:* VLSI and neural networks, communication networks, software engineering, computer architecture, multimedia and video processing. *Unit head:* Jean Mangiaracina, Graduate Program Administrator, 561-297-6482, E-mail: jmangiar@fau.edu. *Application contact:* Jean Mangiaracina, Graduate Program Administrator, 561-297-6482, E-mail: jmangiar@fau.edu.
Website: http://www.ceecs.fau.edu/

Florida Institute of Technology, College of Engineering and Science, Program in Electrical Engineering, Melbourne, FL 32901-6975. Offers MS, PhD. *Program availability:* Part-time. *Students:* 45 full-time (7 women), 35 part-time (7 women); includes 6 minority (2 Asian, non-Hispanic/Latino; 2 Hispanic/Latino; 2 Two or more races, non-Hispanic/Latino), 52 international. Average age 31. 35 applicants, 71% accepted, 13 enrolled. In 2018, 18 master's, 11 doctorates awarded. *Degree*

requirements: For master's, comprehensive exam (for some programs), thesis optional, 30 credit hours; for doctorate, comprehensive exam, thesis/dissertation, significant original research, publication in professional journal of conference proceedings, minimum of 48 credit hours after master's degree. *Entrance requirements:* For master's, GRE, bachelor's degree from ABET-accredited program; for doctorate, GRE, 3 letters of recommendation, resume, statement of objectives, on-campus interview (highly recommended). Additional exam requirements/recommendations for international students: Required—TOEFL (minimum score 550 paper-based; 79 iBT). *Application deadline:* For fall admission, 4/1 for international students; for spring admission, 9/30 for international students. Applications are processed on a rolling basis. Electronic applications accepted. *Expenses: Tuition:* Full-time $22,338; part-time $1241 per credit hour. Tuition and fees vary according to degree level, campus/location and program. *Financial support:* Career-related internships or fieldwork, institutionally sponsored loans, tuition waivers (partial), unspecified assistantships, and tuition remissions available. Support available to part-time students. Financial award application deadline: 3/1; financial award applicants required to submit FAFSA. *Faculty research:* Electro-optics, electromagnetics, microelectronics, communications, computer architecture, neural networks. *Unit head:* Dr. Philip Bernhard, Department Head, 321-674-7294, E-mail: pbernhar@fit.edu. *Application contact:* Mike Perry, Executive Director of Admissions, 321-674-7127, E-mail: perrymj@fit.edu.
Website: https://www.fit.edu/programs/electrical-engineering-ms/

Florida International University, College of Engineering and Computing, Department of Electrical and Computer Engineering, Miami, FL 33175. Offers computer engineering (MS); electrical engineering (MS, PhD). *Program availability:* Part-time, evening/weekend. *Faculty:* 33 full-time (3 women), 17 part-time/adjunct (2 women). *Students:* 156 full-time (36 women), 31 part-time (5 women); includes 62 minority (3 Black or African American, non-Hispanic/Latino; 6 Asian, non-Hispanic/Latino; 51 Hispanic/Latino; 2 Two or more races, non-Hispanic/Latino), 107 international. Average age 29. 204 applicants, 53% accepted, 64 enrolled. In 2018, 49 master's, 22 doctorates awarded. Terminal master's awarded for partial completion of doctoral program. *Degree requirements:* For master's, thesis optional; for doctorate, comprehensive exam, thesis/dissertation. *Entrance requirements:* For master's, minimum undergraduate GPA of 3.0 in upper-level coursework, resume, letters of recommendation, letter of intent; for doctorate, GRE General Test, minimum graduate GPA of 3.3, resume, letters of recommendation, letter of intent. Additional exam requirements/recommendations for international students: Required—TOEFL (minimum score 550 paper-based; 80 iBT). *Application deadline:* For fall admission, 6/1 for domestic students, 4/1 for international students; for spring admission, 10/1 for domestic students, 9/1 for international students. Applications are processed on a rolling basis. Application fee: $30. Electronic applications accepted. *Financial support:* Institutionally sponsored loans, scholarships/grants, and unspecified assistantships available. Financial award application deadline: 3/1; financial award applicants required to submit FAFSA. *Unit head:* Dr. Shekhar Bhansali, Chair, 305-348-4439, Fax: 305-348-3747, E-mail: sbhansa@fiu.edu. *Application contact:* Nanett Rojas, Manager, Admissions Operations, 305-348-7464, Fax: 305-348-7441, E-mail: gradadm@fiu.edu.
Website: http://cec.fiu.edu

Florida State University, The Graduate School, FAMU-FSU College of Engineering, Department of Electrical and Computer Engineering, Tallahassee, FL 32310. Offers electrical engineering (MS, PhD). *Program availability:* Part-time. *Degree requirements:* For master's, comprehensive exam (for some programs), thesis (for some programs); for doctorate, thesis/dissertation, preliminary exam, qualifying exam. *Entrance requirements:* For master's, GRE General Test, minimum GPA of 3.0, BS in electrical engineering; for doctorate, GRE General Test, minimum graduate GPA of 3.3, MS in electrical engineering. Additional exam requirements/recommendations for international students: Required—TOEFL (minimum score 550 paper-based; 80 iBT); Recommended—IELTS. Electronic applications accepted. *Expenses: Tuition, area resident:* Part-time $479.32 per credit hour. Tuition and fees vary according to campus/location and program. *Faculty research:* Electromagnetics, digital signal processing, computer systems, image processing, laser optics.

Gannon University, School of Graduate Studies, College of Engineering and Business, School of Engineering and Computer Science, Program in Electrical and Computer Engineering, Erie, PA 16541-0001. Offers MSEE, MSES. *Program availability:* Part-time, evening/weekend. *Degree requirements:* For master's, thesis (for some programs), oral exam (for some programs), design project (for some programs). *Entrance requirements:* For master's, bachelor's degree in electrical or computer engineering from an ABET-accredited program or its equivalent with minimum GPA of 2.5, transcripts, 3 letters of recommendation. Additional exam requirements/recommendations for international students: Required—TOEFL (minimum score 79 iBT). Electronic applications accepted. Application fee is waived when completed online.

George Mason University, Volgenau School of Engineering, Department of Electrical and Computer Engineering, Fairfax, VA 22030. Offers computer engineering (MS); electrical and computer engineering (PhD, Certificate). MS programs offered jointly with Old Dominion University, University of Virginia, Virginia Commonwealth University, and Virginia Polytechnic Institute and State University. *Faculty:* 33 full-time (6 women), 32 part-time/adjunct (7 women). *Students:* 138 full-time (34 women), 176 part-time (33 women); includes 77 minority (28 Black or African American, non-Hispanic/Latino; 26 Asian, non-Hispanic/Latino; 20 Hispanic/Latino; 3 Two or more races, non-Hispanic/Latino), 117 international. Average age 30. 244 applicants, 87% accepted, 76 enrolled. In 2018, 130 master's, 13 doctorates, 33 other advanced degrees awarded. *Degree requirements:* For master's, thesis optional; for doctorate, comprehensive exam, thesis or scholarly paper. *Entrance requirements:* For master's, GRE, personal goals statement; 2 official copies of transcripts; self-evaluation form; 3 letters of recommendation; resume; official bank statement; photocopy of passport; proof of financial support; for doctorate, GRE (waived for GMU electrical and computer engineering master's graduates with minimum GPA of 3.0), personal goals statement; 2 official copies of transcripts; self-evaluation form; 3 letters of recommendation; resume; official bank statement; photocopy of passport; proof of financial support. Additional exam requirements/recommendations for international students: Required—TOEFL (minimum score 575 paper-based; 88 iBT), IELTS (minimum score 6.5), PTE (minimum score 59). *Application deadline:* For fall admission, 12/1 priority date for domestic and international students; for spring admission, 8/15 priority date for domestic and international students. Application fee: $75 ($80 for international students). Electronic applications accepted. *Expenses:* $589 per credit in-state, $1,346.75 per credit out-of-state. *Financial support:* In 2018–19, 77 students received support, including 3 fellowships (averaging $13,200 per year), 33 research assistantships with tuition reimbursements available (averaging $17,231 per year), 42 teaching assistantships with tuition reimbursements available (averaging $12,246 per year); career-related internships or fieldwork, Federal Work-Study, scholarships/grants, unspecified assistantships, and health care benefits (for full-time research or teaching assistantship recipients) also available. Support available to part-time students. Financial award application deadline: 3/1; financial award applicants required to submit FAFSA. *Faculty research:* Communication networks, signal processing, system failure diagnosis, multiprocessors, material processing using microwave energy. *Total annual research expenditures:* $2.8 million. *Unit head:* Monson Hayes, Chair, 703-993-1570, Fax: 703-

993-1601, E-mail: hayes@gmu.edu. *Application contact:* Jammie Chang, Academic Program Coordinator, 703-993-1570, Fax: 703-993-1601, E-mail: jchangn@gmu.edu.
Website: http://ece.gmu.edu/

The George Washington University, School of Engineering and Applied Science, Department of Electrical and Computer Engineering, Washington, DC 20052. Offers electrical engineering (MS, PhD); telecommunication and computers (MS). *Program availability:* Part-time, evening/weekend. *Faculty:* 25 full-time (2 women), 9 part-time/adjunct (0 women). *Students:* 221 full-time (34 women), 76 part-time (9 women); includes 13 minority (4 Black or African American, non-Hispanic/Latino; 7 Asian, non-Hispanic/Latino; 1 Hispanic/Latino; 1 Native Hawaiian or other Pacific Islander, non-Hispanic/Latino), 253 international. Average age 26. 601 applicants, 85% accepted, 100 enrolled. In 2018, 93 master's, 7 doctorates awarded. *Degree requirements:* For master's, thesis optional; for doctorate, comprehensive exam, thesis/dissertation, dissertation defense, qualifying exam. *Entrance requirements:* For master's, appropriate bachelor's degree, minimum GPA of 3.0; for doctorate, GRE (if highest earned degree is BS), appropriate bachelor's or master's degree, minimum GPA of 3.3; for other advanced degree, appropriate master's degree, minimum GPA of 3.0. Additional exam requirements/recommendations for international students: Required—TOEFL or The George Washington University English as a Foreign Language Test. *Application deadline:* For fall admission, 3/1 priority date for domestic students; for spring admission, 10/1 for domestic students. Applications are processed on a rolling basis. Application fee: $75. *Financial support:* In 2018–19, 39 students received support. Fellowships, research assistantships, teaching assistantships, career-related internships or fieldwork, and institutionally sponsored loans available. Financial award application deadline: 3/1; financial award applicants required to submit FAFSA. *Faculty research:* Computer graphics, multimedia systems. *Unit head:* Prof. Ahmed Louri, Chair, 202-994-5905, E-mail: louri@gwu.edu. *Application contact:* Adina Lav, Marketing, Recruiting and Admissions, 202-994-5827, Fax: 202-994-0909, E-mail: engineering@gwu.edu.
Website: http://www.ece.gwu.edu/

Georgia Institute of Technology, Graduate Studies, College of Engineering, School of Electrical and Computer Engineering, Atlanta, GA 30332-0001. Offers MS, PhD. *Program availability:* Part-time, online learning. Terminal master's awarded for partial completion of doctoral program. *Degree requirements:* For master's, thesis optional; for doctorate, comprehensive exam, thesis/dissertation. *Entrance requirements:* For master's and doctorate, GRE General Test. Additional exam requirements/recommendations for international students: Required—TOEFL (minimum score 550 paper-based; 79 iBT). Electronic applications accepted. *Expenses:* Contact institution. *Faculty research:* Telecommunications, computer systems, microelectronics, optical engineering, digital signal processing.

Georgia Southern University, Jack N. Averitt College of Graduate Studies, Allen E. Paulson College of Engineering and Computing, Department of Electrical and Computer Engineering, Statesboro, GA 30458. Offers MSAE. *Degree requirements:* For master's, thesis optional. *Entrance requirements:* For master's, GRE, minimum GPA of 2.75. Additional exam requirements/recommendations for international students: Required—TOEFL (minimum score 550 paper-based; 80 iBT), IELTS (minimum score 6). Electronic applications accepted. *Expenses: Tuition, area resident:* Part-time $3324 per semester. Tuition, state resident: full-time $5814; part-time $3324 per semester. Tuition, nonresident: full-time $23,204; part-time $13,260 per semester. *Required fees:* $2092; $2092. Tuition and fees vary according to course load, degree level, campus/location and program. *Faculty research:* Programming, artificial intelligence, Web systems, data mining, database systems.

Grand Valley State University, Padnos College of Engineering and Computing, School of Engineering, Allendale, MI 49401-9403. Offers electrical and computer engineering (MSE); manufacturing operations (MSE); mechanical engineering (MSE); product design and manufacturing engineering (MSE). *Program availability:* Part-time, evening/weekend. *Faculty:* 19 full-time (5 women). *Students:* 26 full-time (5 women), 50 part-time (7 women); includes 6 minority (1 Black or African American, non-Hispanic/Latino; 2 Asian, non-Hispanic/Latino; 1 Hispanic/Latino; 2 Two or more races, non-Hispanic/Latino), 39 international. Average age 26. 52 applicants, 62% accepted, 13 enrolled. In 2018, 32 master's awarded. *Entrance requirements:* For master's, engineering degree, minimum GPA of 3.0, resume, 3 confidential letters of recommendation, 1-2 page essay, base of underlying relevant knowledge/evidence from academic records or relevant wok experience. Additional exam requirements/recommendations for international students: Required—Michigan English Language Assessment Battery (minimum score 77), TOEFL (minimum iBT score of 80), or IELTS (6.5); GRE. *Application deadline:* Applications are processed on a rolling basis. Application fee: $30. Electronic applications accepted. *Expenses:* $712 per credit hour, 33 credit hours. *Financial support:* In 2018–19, 40 students received support, including 8 fellowships, 34 research assistantships with full and partial tuition reimbursements available (averaging $4,000 per year); career-related internships or fieldwork, Federal Work-Study, institutionally sponsored loans, scholarships/grants, and unspecified assistantships also available. *Faculty research:* Digital signal processing, computer aided design, computer aided manufacturing, manufacturing simulation, biomechanics, product design. *Total annual research expenditures:* $300,000. *Unit head:* Dr. Wael Mokhtar, Director, 616-331-6015, Fax: 616-331-7215, E-mail: mokhtarw@gvsu.edu. *Application contact:* Dr. Shabbir Choudhuri, Graduate Program Director, 616-331-6845, Fax: 616-331-7215, E-mail: choudhus@gvsu.edu.
Website: http://www.engineer.gvsu.edu/

Harvard University, Graduate School of Arts and Sciences, Harvard John A. Paulson School of Engineering and Applied Sciences, Cambridge, MA 02138. Offers applied mathematics (PhD); applied physics (PhD); computational science and engineering (ME, SM); computer science (PhD); data science (SM); design engineering (MDE); engineering science (ME), including electrical engineering (ME, SM, PhD); engineering sciences (SM, PhD), including bioengineering (PhD), electrical engineering (ME, SM, PhD), environmental science and engineering (PhD), materials science and mechanical engineering (PhD). MDE offered in collaboration with Graduate School of Design. *Program availability:* Part-time. Terminal master's awarded for partial completion of doctoral program. *Degree requirements:* For master's, thesis (for ME); for doctorate, comprehensive exam, thesis/dissertation. *Entrance requirements:* For master's and doctorate, GRE General Test, GRE Subject Test (recommended), 3 letters of recommendation. Additional exam requirements/recommendations for international students: Required—TOEFL (minimum score 80 iBT). Electronic applications accepted. *Expenses:* Contact institution. *Faculty research:* Applied mathematics, applied physics, computer science and electrical engineering, environmental engineering, mechanical and biomedical engineering.

Howard University, College of Engineering, Architecture, and Computer Sciences, School of Engineering and Computer Science, Department of Electrical Engineering, Washington, DC 20059-0002. Offers M Eng, PhD. Offered through the Graduate School of Arts and Sciences. *Program availability:* Part-time. *Degree requirements:* For master's, thesis (for some programs), qualifying exam; for doctorate, thesis/dissertation, preliminary exam. *Entrance requirements:* For master's, GRE General Test, bachelor's degree in electrical engineering, minimum GPA of 3.0; for doctorate, GRE General Test, minimum GPA of 3.0. Additional exam requirements/recommendations for international students: Required—TOEFL. Electronic applications accepted. *Faculty research:* Solid-state electronics, antennas and microwaves, communications and signal processing, controls and power systems, nanotechnology.

Illinois Institute of Technology, Graduate College, Armour College of Engineering, Department of Electrical and Computer Engineering, Chicago, IL 60616. Offers biomedical imaging and signals (MAS); computer engineering (MS, PhD); electrical engineering (MS, PhD); electricity markets (MAS); network engineering (MAS); power engineering (MAS); telecommunications and software engineering (MAS); VLSI and microelectronics (MAS); MS/MS. *Program availability:* Part-time, evening/weekend, online learning. Terminal master's awarded for partial completion of doctoral program. *Degree requirements:* For master's, comprehensive exam (for some programs), thesis (for some programs); for doctorate, comprehensive exam, thesis/dissertation. *Entrance requirements:* For master's and doctorate, GRE General Test (minimum score 1100 Quantitative and Verbal, 3.5 Analytical Writing), minimum undergraduate GPA of 3.0. Additional exam requirements/recommendations for international students: Required—TOEFL (minimum score 550 paper-based; 80 iBT); Recommended—IELTS (minimum score 5.5). Electronic applications accepted. *Faculty research:* Communication systems, wireless networks, computer systems, computer networks, wireless security, cloud computing and micro-electronics; electromagnetics and electronics; power and control systems; signal and image processing.

Indiana University–Purdue University Indianapolis, School of Engineering and Technology, Department of Electrical and Computer Engineering, Indianapolis, IN 46202. Offers electrical and computer engineering (MS, PhD); engineering (MSE). *Degree requirements:* For master's, thesis optional; for doctorate, thesis/dissertation. *Entrance requirements:* For master's, GRE, minimum GPA of 3.0, three recommendation letters, statement of purpose/intent; for doctorate, GRE, minimum GPA of 3.0, three recommendation letters, statement of purpose/intent, curriculum vitae. Additional exam requirements/recommendations for international students: Required—TOEFL; Recommended—IELTS, TSE. Electronic applications accepted. *Expenses:* Contact institution. *Faculty research:* Modeling and control of advanced vehicle systems; data analytics and parallel processing; robotics and automation; 3-D imaging algorithms and image processing; signal/video processing and analysis; power electronics an renewable energy.

Instituto Tecnológico y de Estudios Superiores de Monterrey, Campus Chihuahua, Graduate Programs, Chihuahua, Mexico. Offers computer systems engineering (Ingeniero); electrical engineering (Ingeniero); electromechanical engineering (Ingeniero); electronic engineering (Ingeniero); engineering administration (MEA); industrial engineering (MIE, Ingeniero); international trade (MIT); mechanical engineering (Ingeniero).

Instituto Tecnológico y de Estudios Superiores de Monterrey, Campus Monterrey, Graduate and Research Division, Programs in Engineering, Monterrey, Mexico. Offers applied statistics (M Eng); artificial intelligence (PhD); automation engineering (M Eng); chemical engineering (M Eng); civil engineering (M Eng); electrical engineering (M Eng); electronic engineering (M Eng); environmental engineering (M Eng); industrial engineering (M Eng, PhD); manufacturing engineering (M Eng); mechanical engineering (M Eng); systems and quality engineering (M Eng). M Eng program offered jointly with University of Waterloo; PhD in industrial engineering with Texas A&M University. *Program availability:* Part-time, evening/weekend. Terminal master's awarded for partial completion of doctoral program. *Degree requirements:* For master's, one foreign language, thesis; for doctorate, one foreign language, thesis/dissertation. *Entrance requirements:* For master's, EXADEP; for doctorate, GRE, master's degree in related field. Additional exam requirements/recommendations for international students: Required—TOEFL. *Faculty research:* Flexible manufacturing cells, materials, statistical methods, environmental prevention, control and evaluation.

Inter American University of Puerto Rico, Bayamón Campus, Graduate School, Bayamón, PR 00957. Offers biology (MS), including environmental sciences and ecology, molecular biotechnology; electrical engineering (ME), including control system, potence system; human resources (MBA); mechanical engineering (ME, MS), including aerospace, energy. *Program availability:* Part-time, evening/weekend. *Degree requirements:* For master's, comprehensive exam, research project. *Entrance requirements:* For master's, EXADEP, GRE General Test, letters of recommendation. *Expenses: Tuition:* Full-time $3816; part-time $1908 per trimester. *Required fees:* $735; $642.

International Technological University, Program in Electrical Engineering, San Jose, CA 95134. Offers MSEE, PhD. *Program availability:* Part-time, evening/weekend. *Degree requirements:* For master's, thesis or capstone project; for doctorate, comprehensive exam, thesis/dissertation. *Entrance requirements:* For master's, 3 semesters of calculus, minimum GPA of 2.5. Additional exam requirements/recommendations for international students: Required—TOEFL, IELTS. Electronic applications accepted.

Iowa State University of Science and Technology, Department of Electrical and Computer Engineering, Ames, IA 50011. Offers computer engineering (M Eng, MS, PhD); electrical engineering (M Eng, MS, PhD). *Degree requirements:* For master's, thesis or alternative; for doctorate, thesis/dissertation. *Entrance requirements:* For master's and doctorate, GRE General Test. Additional exam requirements/recommendations for international students: Required—TOEFL (minimum score 570 paper-based; 79 iBT), IELTS (minimum score 6.5). Electronic applications accepted.

Johns Hopkins University, Engineering Program for Professionals, Part-time Program in Electrical and Computer Engineering, Baltimore, MD 21218. Offers communications and networking (MS); electrical and computer engineering (Graduate Certificate, Post-Master's Certificate); photonics (MS). *Program availability:* Part-time, evening/weekend, 100% online, blended/hybrid learning. *Faculty:* 1 full-time, 47 part-time/adjunct (2 women). *Students:* 364 part-time (60 women). 119 applicants, 68% accepted, 53 enrolled. In 2018, 101 master's awarded. *Entrance requirements:* Additional exam requirements/recommendations for international students: Required—TOEFL (minimum score 600 paper-based; 100 iBT). *Application deadline:* Applications are processed on a rolling basis. Application fee: $0. Electronic applications accepted. *Unit head:* Dr. Brian Jennison, Program Chair, 443-778-6421, E-mail: brian.jennison@jhuapl.edu. *Application contact:* Doug Schiller, Admissions Director, 410-516-2300, Fax: 410-579-8049, E-mail: schiller@jhu.edu.
Website: http://www.ep.jhu.edu/

Johns Hopkins University, G. W. C. Whiting School of Engineering, Department of Electrical and Computer Engineering, Baltimore, MD 21218. Offers MSE, PhD. *Faculty:* 32 full-time (6 women). *Students:* 163 full-time (33 women), 6 part-time (1 woman). 436 applicants, 40% accepted, 57 enrolled. In 2018, 38 master's, 15 doctorates awarded. Terminal master's awarded for partial completion of doctoral program. *Degree requirements:* For master's, thesis optional; for doctorate, thesis/dissertation, qualifying and oral exams, seminar. *Entrance requirements:* For master's and doctorate, GRE General Test, transcripts, 3 letters of recommendation, statement of purpose. Additional exam requirements/recommendations for international students: Required—TOEFL (minimum score 600 paper-based, 100 iBT) or IELTS (7). *Application deadline:* For fall admission, 12/22 for domestic and international students. Application fee: $75. Electronic applications accepted. *Financial support:* In 2018–19, 108 students received support, including 15 fellowships with full tuition reimbursements available (averaging $29,496 per year), 93 research assistantships with full tuition reimbursements available (averaging $26,496 per year); teaching assistantships with full tuition reimbursements available, career-related internships or fieldwork, Federal Work-Study, institutionally sponsored loans, scholarships/grants, health care benefits, tuition waivers (partial), and unspecified assistantships also available. Financial award application deadline: 12/15. *Faculty research:* Microsystems, neuromorphics and brain-machines interface; acoustics, speech and language processing; photonics, biophotonics and optoelectronics; signal processing and imaging science and technology; networks, controls and systems. *Unit head:* Dr. Ralph Etienne-Cummings, Chair, 410-516-7031, Fax: 410-516-5566, E-mail: retienne@jhu.edu. *Application contact:* Belinda Blinkoff, Sr. Academic Program Coordinator, 410-516-4808, Fax: 410-516-5566, E-mail: bblinkoff@jhu.edu.
Website: http://www.ece.jhu.edu/

Kansas State University, Graduate School, College of Engineering, Department of Electrical and Computer Engineering, Manhattan, KS 66506. Offers electrical engineering (MS), including bioengineering, communication systems, design of computer systems, electrical engineering, energy and power systems, integrated circuits and devices, real time embedded systems, renewable energy, signal processing. *Program availability:* Part-time, evening/weekend, online learning. *Degree requirements:* For master's, thesis or alternative, final exam; for doctorate, thesis/dissertation, final exam, preliminary exams. *Entrance requirements:* For master's, GRE General Test, bachelor's degree in electrical engineering or computer science, minimum GPA of 3.0; for doctorate, GRE General Test. Additional exam requirements/recommendations for international students: Required—TOEFL (minimum score 600 paper-based; 85 iBT). Electronic applications accepted. *Faculty research:* Energy systems and renewable energy, computer systems and real time embedded systems, communication systems and signal processing, integrated circuits and devices, bioengineering.

Kennesaw State University, Southern Polytechnic College of Engineering and Engineering Technology, Program in Applied Engineering, Kennesaw, GA 30144. Offers electrical engineering (MS). *Program availability:* Part-time, evening/weekend. *Students:* 1 full-time (0 women), 17 part-time (3 women); includes 10 minority (5 Black or African American, non-Hispanic/Latino; 1 Asian, non-Hispanic/Latino; 3 Hispanic/Latino; 1 Two or more races, non-Hispanic/Latino). Average age 36. 6 applicants, 83% accepted, 4 enrolled. In 2018, 4 master's awarded. *Degree requirements:* For master's, thesis. *Entrance requirements:* For master's, GRE (minimum scores: 147 Verbal, 147 Quantitative, 3.5 Analytical), minimum GPA of 2.7. Additional exam requirements/recommendations for international students: Required—TOEFL (minimum score 550 paper-based; 80 iBT), IELTS (minimum score 6.5). *Application deadline:* For fall admission, 7/1 priority date for domestic students, 5/1 priority date for international students; for spring admission, 11/1 priority date for domestic students, 9/1 priority date for international students. Applications are processed on a rolling basis. Application fee: $60. Electronic applications accepted. *Expenses: Tuition, area resident:* Full-time $6960; part-time $290 per credit hour. Tuition, state resident: full-time $6960; part-time $290 per credit hour. Tuition, nonresident: full-time $25,080; part-time $1045 per credit hour. *International tuition:* $25,080 full-time. *Required fees:* $2006; $1706 per semester. $853 per semester. *Financial support:* Teaching assistantships with partial tuition reimbursements, career-related internships or fieldwork, scholarships/grants, and unspecified assistantships available. Support available to part-time students. Financial award applicants required to submit FAFSA. *Application contact:* Admissions Counselor, 470-578-4377, E-mail: ksugrad@kennesaw.edu.
Website: http://engineering.kennesaw.edu/electrical/degrees/ms-applied-engineering.php

Kettering University, Graduate School, Electrical and Computer Engineering Department, Flint, MI 48504. Offers engineering (MS). *Program availability:* Part-time, evening/weekend, online learning. *Degree requirements:* For master's, thesis optional. *Entrance requirements:* Additional exam requirements/recommendations for international students: Required—TOEFL (minimum score 550 paper-based; 79 iBT). Electronic applications accepted. *Faculty research:* Electric power trains, batteries, motor control, haptics.

Lakehead University, Graduate Studies, Faculty of Engineering, Thunder Bay, ON P7B 5E1, Canada. Offers control engineering (M Sc Engr); electrical/computer engineering (M Sc Engr); environmental engineering (M Sc Engr). *Program availability:* Part-time. *Degree requirements:* For master's, thesis. *Entrance requirements:* For master's, bachelor's degree in chemical, electrical or mechanical engineering, minimum B average. Additional exam requirements/recommendations for international students: Required—TOEFL. *Faculty research:* Pulp and paper, adaptive/process control, robust/interactive learning control, vibration control.

Lamar University, College of Graduate Studies, College of Engineering, Phillip M. Drayer Department of Electrical Engineering, Beaumont, TX 77710. Offers ME, MES, DE. *Program availability:* Part-time. *Faculty:* 12 full-time (1 woman). *Students:* 20 full-time (1 woman), 28 part-time (5 women); includes 2 minority (both Asian, non-Hispanic/Latino), 43 international. Average age 28. 73 applicants, 75% accepted, 9 enrolled. In 2018, 23 master's, 1 doctorate awarded. *Degree requirements:* For master's, thesis (for some programs); for doctorate, thesis/dissertation. *Entrance requirements:* For master's and doctorate, GRE General Test. Additional exam requirements/recommendations for international students: Required—TOEFL (minimum score 550 paper-based; 79 iBT), IELTS (minimum score 6.5). *Application deadline:* Applications are processed on a rolling basis. Application fee: $25 ($50 for international students). Electronic applications accepted. *Expenses:* Tuition, state resident: full-time $6234; part-time $346 per credit hour. Tuition, nonresident: full-time $6852; part-time $761 per credit hour. *International tuition:* $6852 full-time. *Required fees:* $1940; $327 per credit hour. Tuition and fees vary according to course load, campus/location, program and reciprocity agreements. *Financial support:* In 2018–19, 3 students received support, including 2 fellowships with partial tuition reimbursements available (averaging $6,000 per year), 20 research assistantships with partial tuition reimbursements available (averaging $6,000 per year), 2 teaching assistantships with partial tuition reimbursements available (averaging $4,500 per year); tuition waivers (partial) also available. Financial award applicants required to submit FAFSA. *Faculty research:* Video processing, photonics, VLSI design, computer networking. *Unit head:* Dr. Harley Ross Myler, Chair, 409-880-8746, Fax: 409-880-8121. *Application contact:* Celeste Contreas, Director, Admissions and Academic Services, 409-880-8888, Fax: 409-880-7419, E-mail: gradmissions@lamar.edu.
Website: http://engineering.lamar.edu/electrical

Lawrence Technological University, College of Engineering, Southfield, MI 48075-1058. Offers architectural engineering (MS); automotive engineering (MS); biomedical engineering (MS); civil engineering (MA, MS, PhD), including environmental engineering (MS), geotechnical engineering (MS), structural engineering (MS), transportation engineering (MS), water resource engineering (MS); construction engineering management (MA); electrical and computer engineering (MS); engineering management (MEM); engineering technology (MS); fire engineering (MS); industrial engineering (MS), including healthcare systems; manufacturing systems (ME); mechanical engineering

(MS, DE, PhD), including automotive engineering (MS), energy engineering (MS), manufacturing (DE), solid mechanics (MS), thermal/fluid systems (MS); mechatronic systems engineering (MS). *Program availability:* Part-time, evening/weekend. Terminal master's awarded for partial completion of doctoral program. *Degree requirements:* For master's, thesis optional; for doctorate, comprehensive exam, thesis/dissertation optional. *Entrance requirements:* Additional exam requirements/recommendations for international students: Required—TOEFL (minimum score 550 paper-based; 79 iBT), IELTS (minimum score 6.5). Electronic applications accepted. *Faculty research:* Innovative infrastructure and building structures and materials; connectivity and mobility; automotive systems modeling, simulation and testing; biomedical devices and materials; building mechanical/electrical systems.

Lehigh University, P.C. Rossin College of Engineering and Applied Science, Department of Electrical and Computer Engineering, Bethlehem, PA 18015. Offers electrical engineering (M Eng, MS, PhD); photonics (MS). *Program availability:* Part-time. *Faculty:* 16 full-time (4 women). *Students:* 79 full-time (8 women), 73 international. Average age 25. 269 applicants, 27% accepted, 19 enrolled. In 2018, 35 master's, 7 doctorates awarded. Terminal master's awarded for partial completion of doctoral program. *Degree requirements:* For master's, thesis optional; for doctorate, thesis/dissertation, qualifying or comprehensive exam for all 1st year PhD's; general exam 7 months or more prior to completion/dissertation defense. *Entrance requirements:* For master's and doctorate, GRE General Test, BS in field or related field. Additional exam requirements/recommendations for international students: Required—TOEFL (minimum score 79 iBT), IELTS (minimum score 6.5), TOEFL or IELTS; Recommended—TSE. *Application deadline:* For fall admission, 4/1 for domestic and international students; for spring admission, 11/1 for domestic and international students. Application fee: $75. Electronic applications accepted. Tuition and fees vary according to program. *Financial support:* In 2018–19, 52 students received support, including 5 fellowships with full tuition reimbursements available (averaging $29,400 per year), 40 research assistantships with full tuition reimbursements available (averaging $29,400 per year), 7 teaching assistantships with full tuition reimbursements available (averaging $29,400 per year). Financial award application deadline: 1/15. *Faculty research:* Bio-electrical engineering, communications and signal processing, computer engineering, electric energy, electronics and photonics. *Total annual research expenditures:* $4 million. *Unit head:* Dr. Chengshan Xiao, Chair, 610-758-4069, Fax: 610-758-6279, E-mail: chx417@lehigh.edu. *Application contact:* Diane Hubinsky, Graduate Coordinator, 610-758-4072, Fax: 610-758-6279, E-mail: dih2@lehigh.edu.
Website: http://www.ece.lehigh.edu/

Louisiana State University and Agricultural & Mechanical College, Graduate School, College of Engineering, Division of Electrical and Computer Engineering, Baton Rouge, LA 70803. Offers MSEE, PhD.

Loyola Marymount University, Frank R. Seaver College of Science and Engineering, Program in Electrical Engineering, Los Angeles, CA 90045. Offers electrical engineering (MS). *Unit head:* Dr. Gustavo Vejarano, Graduate Program Director, Electrical Engineering, 310-338-5761, E-mail: gustavo.vejarano@lmu.edu. *Application contact:* Ammar Dalal, Assistant Vice Provost for Graduate Enrollment, 310-338-2721, Fax: 310-338-6086, E-mail: graduateinfo@lmu.edu.
Website: http://cse.lmu.edu/graduateprograms/ese

Manhattan College, Graduate Programs, School of Engineering, Program in Electrical Engineering, Riverdale, NY 10471. Offers MS. *Program availability:* Part-time, evening/weekend. *Degree requirements:* For master's, thesis or alternative. *Entrance requirements:* For master's, GRE (recommended), minimum GPA of 3.0. Additional exam requirements/recommendations for international students: Required—TOEFL (minimum score 550 paper-based; 80 iBT), IELTS (minimum score 6). *Faculty research:* Multimedia tools, neural networks, robotic control systems, magnetic resonance imaging, telemedicine, computer-based instruction.

Marquette University, Graduate School, College of Engineering, Department of Electrical and Computer Engineering, Milwaukee, WI 53201-1881. Offers digital signal processing (Certificate); electric machines, drives, and controls (Certificate); electrical and computer engineering (MS, PhD); microwaves and antennas (Certificate); sensors and smart systems (Certificate). *Program availability:* Part-time, evening/weekend. Terminal master's awarded for partial completion of doctoral program. *Degree requirements:* For master's, comprehensive exam (for some programs), thesis optional; for doctorate, thesis/dissertation, dissertation defense, qualifying exam. *Entrance requirements:* For master's, GRE General Test (recommended), official transcripts from all current and previous colleges/universities except Marquette, three letters of recommendation; for doctorate, GRE General Test, minimum GPA of 3.0, official transcripts from all current and previous colleges/universities except Marquette, three letters of recommendation, statement of purpose, submission of any English language publications authored by applicant (strongly recommended). Additional exam requirements/recommendations for international students: Required—TOEFL (minimum score 530 paper-based). Electronic applications accepted. *Faculty research:* Electric machines, drives, and controls; applied solid-state electronics; computers and signal processing; microwaves and antennas; solid state devices and acoustic wave sensors.

Marshall University, Academic Affairs Division, College of Information Technology and Engineering, Program in Electrical and Computer Engineering, Huntington, WV 25755. Offers MSEE.

Massachusetts Institute of Technology, School of Engineering, Department of Electrical Engineering and Computer Science, Cambridge, MA 02139. Offers computer science (PhD, Sc D, ECS); computer science and engineering (PhD, Sc D); computer science and molecular biology (M Eng); electrical engineering (PhD, Sc D, EE); electrical engineering and computer science (M Eng, SM, PhD, Sc D); SM/MBA. *Degree requirements:* For master's and other advanced degree, thesis; for doctorate, comprehensive exam, thesis/dissertation. *Entrance requirements:* Additional exam requirements/recommendations for international students: Required—TOEFL, IELTS. Electronic applications accepted. *Expenses: Tuition:* Full-time $51,520; part-time $800 per credit hour. *Required fees:* $312. *Faculty research:* Information systems, circuits, biomedical sciences and engineering, computer science: artificial intelligence, systems, theory.

McGill University, Faculty of Graduate and Postdoctoral Studies, Faculty of Engineering, Department of Electrical and Computer Engineering, Montréal, QC H3A 2T5, Canada. Offers M Eng, PhD.

McMaster University, School of Graduate Studies, Faculty of Engineering, Department of Electrical and Computer Engineering, Hamilton, ON L8S 4M2, Canada. Offers electrical engineering (M Eng, MA Sc, PhD). *Degree requirements:* For master's, thesis; for doctorate, comprehensive exam, thesis/dissertation. *Entrance requirements:* Additional exam requirements/recommendations for international students: Required—TOEFL (minimum score 550 paper-based). *Faculty research:* Robust and blind adaptive filtering, topics in statistical signal processing, local and metropolitan area networks, smart antennas, embedded wireless communications.

McNeese State University, Doré School of Graduate Studies, College of Engineering and Computer Science, Master of Engineering Program, Lake Charles, LA 70609. Offers chemical engineering (M Eng); civil engineering (M Eng); electrical engineering (M Eng); engineering management (M Eng); mechanical engineering (M Eng). *Program availability:* Part-time, evening/weekend. *Entrance requirements:* For master's, GRE, baccalaureate degree, minimum overall GPA of 3.0. Additional exam requirements/recommendations for international students: Required—TOEFL (minimum score 560 paper-based; 83 iBT).

Memorial University of Newfoundland, School of Graduate Studies, Faculty of Engineering and Applied Science, St. John's, NL A1C 5S7, Canada. Offers civil engineering (M Eng, PhD); electrical and computer engineering (M Eng, PhD); mechanical engineering (M Eng, PhD); ocean and naval architecture engineering (M Eng, PhD). *Program availability:* Part-time. *Degree requirements:* For master's, thesis; for doctorate, comprehensive exam, thesis/dissertation, oral thesis defense. *Entrance requirements:* For master's, 2nd class degree; for doctorate, master's degree in engineering. Electronic applications accepted. *Faculty research:* Engineering analysis, environmental and hydrotechnical studies, manufacturing and robotics, mechanics, structures and materials.

Mercer University, Graduate Studies, Macon Campus, School of Engineering, Macon, GA 31207. Offers biomedical engineering (MSE); computer engineering (MSE); electrical engineering (MSE); engineering management (MSE); environmental engineering (MSE); environmental systems (MS); mechanical engineering (MSE); software engineering (MSE); software systems (MS); technical communications management (MS); technical management (MS). *Program availability:* Part-time-only, evening/weekend, online learning. *Degree requirements:* For master's, thesis or alternative. *Entrance requirements:* For master's, GRE (minimum score 300), minimum undergraduate GPA of 3.0. Additional exam requirements/recommendations for international students: Required—TOEFL (minimum score 550 paper-based; 80 iBT). *Expenses:* Contact institution. *Faculty research:* Designing prostheses and orthotics, oxygen transfer and limitations in biological systems, low-cost groundwater development, lung airway and transport, autonomous mobile robots.

Miami University, College of Engineering and Computing, Department of Electrical and Computer Engineering, Oxford, OH 45056. Offers MS. *Faculty:* 9 full-time (1 woman). *Students:* 15 full-time (2 women), 2 part-time (0 women); includes 1 minority (Black or African American, non-Hispanic/Latino), 10 international. Average age 24. In 2018, 7 master's awarded. *Unit head:* Dr. Q. Herb Zhou, Chair, 513-523-0743, E-mail: zhouq@miamioh.edu. *Application contact:* Dr. Q. Herb Zhou, Chair, 513-523-0743, E-mail: zhouq@miamioh.edu.
Website: http://miamioh.edu/cec/academics/departments/ece/

Michigan State University, The Graduate School, College of Engineering, Department of Electrical and Computer Engineering, East Lansing, MI 48824. Offers electrical engineering (MS, PhD). *Entrance requirements:* Additional exam requirements/recommendations for international students: Required—TOEFL. Electronic applications accepted.

Michigan Technological University, Graduate School, College of Engineering, Department of Electrical and Computer Engineering, Houghton, MI 49931. Offers advanced electric power engineering (Graduate Certificate); electrical engineering (PhD). *Program availability:* Part-time, 100% online, blended/hybrid learning. *Faculty:* 46 full-time, 7 part-time/adjunct. *Students:* 131 full-time (28 women), 27 part-time; includes 4 minority (1 Black or African American, non-Hispanic/Latino; 1 Asian, non-Hispanic/Latino; 2 Hispanic/Latino), 128 international. Average age 27. 490 applicants, 39% accepted, 42 enrolled. In 2018, 95 master's, 9 doctorates, 34 other advanced degrees awarded. Terminal master's awarded for partial completion of doctoral program. *Degree requirements:* For master's, comprehensive exam (for some programs), thesis (for some programs); for doctorate, comprehensive exam, thesis/dissertation. *Entrance requirements:* For master's, statement of purpose, personal statement, official transcripts, 2 letters of recommendation; for doctorate, GRE, statement of purpose, personal statement, official transcripts, 2 letters of recommendation; for Graduate Certificate, statement of purpose, personal statement, official transcripts. Additional exam requirements/recommendations for international students: Required—TOEFL (recommended minimum score 100 iBT) or IELTS (recommended minimum score of 7.0). *Application deadline:* For fall admission, 2/15 priority date for domestic and international students; for spring admission, 8/15 priority date for domestic and international students. Applications are processed on a rolling basis. Electronic applications accepted. *Expenses:* $1,143 per credit. *Financial support:* In 2018–19, 117 students received support, including 7 fellowships with tuition reimbursements available (averaging $16,590 per year), 23 research assistantships with tuition reimbursements available (averaging $16,590 per year), 23 teaching assistantships with tuition reimbursements available (averaging $16,590 per year); career-related internships or fieldwork, Federal Work-Study, scholarships/grants, health care benefits, unspecified assistantships, and cooperative program also available. Financial award applicants required to submit FAFSA. *Faculty research:* Electrical power systems, optics and photonics, embedded computing systems, computer networks, communication and information theory. *Total annual research expenditures:* $2 million. *Unit head:* Dr. Glen E. Archer, Interim Chair & Principal Lecturer, 906-487-2550, Fax: 906-487-2949, E-mail: gearcher@mtu.edu. *Application contact:* Megan Williamson, Graduate Program Coordinator, 906-487-1995, Fax: 906-487-2949, E-mail: meganwil@mtu.edu.
Website: http://www.mtu.edu/ece/

Mississippi State University, Bagley College of Engineering, Department of Electrical and Computer Engineering, Mississippi State, MS 39762. Offers MS, PhD. *Program availability:* Part-time, blended/hybrid learning. *Faculty:* 13 full-time (2 women). *Students:* 50 full-time (8 women), 57 part-time (5 women); includes 18 minority (5 Black or African American, non-Hispanic/Latino; 1 American Indian or Alaska Native, non-Hispanic/Latino; 8 Asian, non-Hispanic/Latino; 4 Hispanic/Latino), 43 international. Average age 31. 90 applicants, 42% accepted, 26 enrolled. In 2018, 18 master's, 9 doctorates awarded. Terminal master's awarded for partial completion of doctoral program. *Degree requirements:* For master's, comprehensive exam, thesis optional; for doctorate, comprehensive exam, thesis/dissertation, written exam, oral preliminary exam. *Entrance requirements:* For master's, GRE (for graduates from program not accredited by EAC/ABET), minimum GPA of 3.0 on BS; for doctorate, GRE (for graduates from program not accredited by EAC/ABET), minimum GPA of 3.5 on BS or MS. Additional exam requirements/recommendations for international students: Required—TOEFL (minimum score 550 paper-based; 79 iBT); Recommended—IELTS (minimum score 6.5). *Application deadline:* For fall admission, 7/1 for domestic students, 5/1 for international students; for spring admission, 11/1 for domestic students, 9/1 for international students. Applications are processed on a rolling basis. Application fee: $60 ($80 for international students). Electronic applications accepted. *Expenses:* Tuition, state resident: full-time $8450; part-time $360.59 per credit hour. Tuition, nonresident: full-time $23,140; part-time $969.09 per credit hour. *Required fees:* $110. One-time fee: $55 full-time. Part-time tuition and fees vary according to course load, degree level, campus/location and reciprocity agreements. *Financial support:* In 2018–19, 13 research assistantships with full tuition reimbursements (averaging $18,877 per year), 21 teaching assistantships with full tuition reimbursements (averaging $15,919 per year) were awarded; Federal Work-Study, institutionally sponsored loans, scholarships/grants, and unspecified assistantships also available. Financial award application deadline: 4/1; financial award applicants required to submit FAFSA. *Faculty*

research: Digital computing, power, controls, communication systems, microelectronics. *Total annual research expenditures:* $6.2 million. *Unit head:* Dr. James E. Fowler, Jr., Professor/Interim Department Head, 662-325-3912, Fax: 662-325-2298, E-mail: ece-head@ece.msstate.edu. *Application contact:* Angie Campbell, Admissions and Enrollment Assistant, 662-325-9514, E-mail: acampbell@grad.msstate.edu.
Website: http://www.ece.msstate.edu/

Missouri University of Science and Technology, Department of Electrical and Computer Engineering, Rolla, MO 65401. Offers computer engineering (MS, DE, PhD); electrical engineering (MS, DE, PhD). *Program availability:* Part-time, evening/weekend. Terminal master's awarded for partial completion of doctoral program. *Degree requirements:* For master's, thesis optional; for doctorate, comprehensive exam, thesis/dissertation, departmental qualifying exam. *Entrance requirements:* For master's, GRE General Test (minimum score 1100 verbal and quantitative, writing 4.5); for doctorate, GRE General Test (minimum score: verbal and quantitative 1100, writing 3.5). Additional exam requirements/recommendations for international students: Required—TOEFL (minimum score 550 paper-based). Electronic applications accepted. *Expenses:* Tuition, state resident: full-time $7545.60; part-time $419.20 per credit hour. Tuition, nonresident: full-time $22,169; part-time $1231.60 per credit hour. *International tuition:* $23,518.80 full-time. *Required fees:* $4523.05. Full-time tuition and fees vary according to course load, campus/location, program and reciprocity agreements. *Faculty research:* Power systems, computer/communication networks, intelligent control/robotics, robust control, nanotechnologies.

Montana State University, The Graduate School, College of Engineering, Department of Electrical and Computer Engineering, Bozeman, MT 59717. Offers electrical engineering (MS); engineering (PhD), including electrical and computer engineering option. *Program availability:* Part-time. *Degree requirements:* For master's, comprehensive exam, thesis (for some programs); for doctorate, comprehensive exam, thesis/dissertation. *Entrance requirements:* For master's, GRE, BS in electrical or computer engineering or related field; for doctorate, GRE, MS in electrical or computer engineering or related field. Additional exam requirements/recommendations for international students: Required—TOEFL (minimum score 550 paper-based). Electronic applications accepted. *Faculty research:* Optics and optoelectonics, communications and signal processing, microfabrication, complex systems and control, energy systems.

Montana Tech of The University of Montana, Electrical Engineering Program, Butte, MT 59701-8997. Offers MS. *Program availability:* Part-time. *Degree requirements:* For master's, comprehensive exam (for some programs), thesis optional. *Entrance requirements:* For master's, minimum GPA of 3.0. Additional exam requirements/recommendations for international students: Required—TOEFL (minimum score 545 paper-based; 78 iBT), IELTS (minimum score 6.5). Electronic applications accepted. *Faculty research:* Energy grid modernization, battery diagnostics instrumentation, wind turbine research, improving energy efficiency.

Morgan State University, School of Graduate Studies, Clarence M. Mitchell, Jr. School of Engineering, Baltimore, MD 21251. Offers civil engineering (M Eng, D Eng); electrical and computer engineering (M Eng, MS, D Eng); industrial and systems engineering (M Eng, D Eng); transportation and urban infrastructure studies (MS, PhD, Postbaccalaureate Certificate), including transportation. *Program availability:* Part-time, evening/weekend. *Degree requirements:* For master's, thesis, comprehensive exam or equivalent; for doctorate, thesis/dissertation, comprehensive exam or equivalent. *Entrance requirements:* For master's, GRE, minimum undergraduate GPA of 2.5; for doctorate, GRE, minimum GPA of 3.0. Additional exam requirements/recommendations for international students: Required—TOEFL (minimum score 550 paper-based).

National University, School of Engineering and Computing, La Jolla, CA 92037-1011. Offers computer science (MS), including advanced computing; cyber security and information assurance (MS); data analytics (MS); electrical engineering (MS); engineering management (MS); information technology management (MS); management information systems (MS); sustainability management (MS). *Program availability:* Part-time, evening/weekend, 100% online, blended/hybrid learning. *Degree requirements:* For master's, thesis (for some programs). *Entrance requirements:* For master's, interview, minimum GPA of 2.5. Additional exam requirements/recommendations for international students: Required—TOEFL (minimum score 550 paper-based; 79 iBT), IELTS (minimum score 6). Electronic applications accepted. *Expenses: Tuition:* Full-time $10,320; part-time $430 per unit. Tuition and fees vary according to degree level. *Faculty research:* Educational technology, scholarships in science.

Naval Postgraduate School, Departments and Academic Groups, Department of Electrical and Computer Engineering, Monterey, CA 93943-5216. Offers computer engineering (MS); electrical engineer (EE); electrical engineering (PhD); engineering acoustics (MS); engineering science (MS). Program only open to commissioned officers of the United States and friendly nations and selected United States federal civilian employees. *Program availability:* Part-time, online learning. *Degree requirements:* For master's and EE, thesis (for some programs), capstone project or research/dissertation paper (for some programs); for doctorate, thesis/dissertation. *Faculty research:* Theory and design of digital communication systems; behavior modeling for detection, identification, prediction and reaction in artificial intelligence (AI) systems solutions; waveform design for target class discrimination with closed-loop radar; iterative technique for system identification with adaptive signal design.

Naval Postgraduate School, Departments and Academic Groups, Space Systems Academic Group, Monterey, CA 93943. Offers applied physics (MS); astronautical engineering (MS); computer science (MS); electrical engineering (MS); mechanical engineering (MS); space systems (Engr); space systems operations (MS). Program only open to commissioned officers of the United States and friendly nations and selected United States federal civilian employees. *Program availability:* Part-time. *Degree requirements:* For master's and Engr, thesis; for doctorate, thesis/dissertation. *Faculty research:* Military applications for space; space reconnaissance and remote sensing; radiation-hardened electronics for space; design, construction and operations of small satellites; satellite communications systems.

Naval Postgraduate School, Departments and Academic Groups, Undersea Warfare Academic Group, Monterey, CA 93943. Offers applied mathematics (MS); applied physics (MS); applied science (MS), including acoustics, operations research, physical oceanography, signal processing; electrical engineering (MS); engineering acoustics (MS, PhD); engineering science (MS), including electrical engineering, mechanical engineering; mechanical engineer (ME); mechanical engineering (MS, MSME); meteorology (MS); operations research (MS); physical oceanography (MS). Program only open to commissioned officers of the United States and friendly nations and selected United States federal civilian employees. *Program availability:* Part-time. *Degree requirements:* For master's, thesis. *Faculty research:* Unmanned/autonomous vehicles, sea mines and countermeasures, submarine warfare in the twentieth and twenty-first centuries.

New Jersey Institute of Technology, Newark College of Engineering, Newark, NJ 07102. Offers biomedical engineering (MS, PhD); biopharmaceutical engineering (MS); chemical engineering (MS, PhD); civil engineering (MS, PhD); computer engineering (MS); critical infrastructure systems (MS); electrical engineering (MS, PhD); engineering management (MS); engineering science (MS); environmental engineering (MS, PhD); healthcare systems management (MS); industrial engineering (MS, PhD); internet engineering (MS); manufacturing systems engineering (MS); materials science & engineering (PhD); materials science and engineering (MS); mechanical engineering (MS, PhD); occupational safety and health engineering (MS). *Program availability:* Part-time, evening/weekend. *Faculty:* 147 full-time (26 women), 133 part-time/adjunct (16 women). *Students:* 690 full-time (163 women), 594 part-time (130 women); includes 427 minority (79 Black or African American, non-Hispanic/Latino; 181 Asian, non-Hispanic/Latino; 140 Hispanic/Latino; 27 Two or more races, non-Hispanic/Latino), 553 international. Average age 27. 2,334 applicants, 57% accepted, 452 enrolled. In 2018, 418 master's, 31 doctorates awarded. Terminal master's awarded for partial completion of doctoral program. *Degree requirements:* For master's, thesis (for some programs); for doctorate, thesis/dissertation. *Entrance requirements:* For master's, GRE General Test, minimum GPA 2.8, personal statement, 1 letter of recommendation, transcripts; for doctorate, GRE General Test, minimum GPA of 3.5, personal statement, 3 letters of recommendation, transcripts. Additional exam requirements/recommendations for international students: Required—TOEFL (minimum score 550 paper-based; 79 iBT), IELTS (minimum score 6.5). *Application deadline:* For fall admission, 6/1 priority date for domestic students, 5/1 priority date for international students; for spring admission, 11/15 priority date for domestic and international students. Applications are processed on a rolling basis. Application fee: $75. Electronic applications accepted. *Expenses:* $22,690 per year (in-state), $32,136 per year (out-of-state). *Financial support:* In 2018–19, 396 students received support, including 52 fellowships with full tuition reimbursements available (averaging $22,000 per year), 113 research assistantships with full tuition reimbursements available (averaging $22,000 per year), 101 teaching assistantships with full tuition reimbursements available (averaging $22,000 per year); career-related internships or fieldwork, Federal Work-Study, scholarships/grants, and unspecified assistantships also available. Financial award application deadline: 1/15. *Faculty research:* Nonlinear signal processing, intelligent medical image analysis, calibration issues in coherent localization, computer-aided design, neural network for tool wear measurement. *Total annual research expenditures:* $41.7 million. *Unit head:* Dr. Moshe Kam, Dean, 973-596-5534, Fax: 973-596-2316, E-mail: moshe.kam@njit.edu. *Application contact:* Stephen Eck, Director of Admissions, 973-596-3300, Fax: 973-596-3461, E-mail: admissions@njit.edu.
Website: http://engineering.njit.edu/

New Mexico Institute of Mining and Technology, Center for Graduate Studies, Department of Electrical Engineering, Socorro, NM 87801. Offers MS. *Entrance requirements:* Additional exam requirements/recommendations for international students: Required—TOEFL (minimum score 540 paper-based). Electronic applications accepted.

New York Institute of Technology, College of Engineering and Computing Sciences, Department of Electrical and Computer Engineering, Old Westbury, NY 11568-8000. Offers MS. *Program availability:* Part-time, evening/weekend. *Faculty:* 10 full-time (2 women), 8 part-time/adjunct (all women). *Students:* 54 full-time (15 women), 36 part-time (7 women); includes 21 minority (3 Black or African American, non-Hispanic/Latino; 12 Asian, non-Hispanic/Latino; 6 Hispanic/Latino), 59 international. Average age 26. 308 applicants, 59% accepted, 25 enrolled. In 2018, 82 master's awarded. *Degree requirements:* For master's, thesis or alternative. *Entrance requirements:* For master's, BS in electrical or computer engineering or closely-related field; minimum undergraduate GPA of 2.85. Additional exam requirements/recommendations for international students: Required—TOEFL (minimum score 79 iBT), IELTS (minimum score 6), PTE (minimum score 53). *Application deadline:* For fall admission, 7/1 for domestic students, 6/1 for international students; for spring admission, 12/1 for domestic and international students. Applications are processed on a rolling basis. Application fee: $50. Electronic applications accepted. *Expenses:* $1285 per credit plus $215 fees per year (full-time) or $175 fees per year (part-time). *Financial support:* Fellowships with partial tuition reimbursements, teaching assistantships with partial tuition reimbursements, career-related internships or fieldwork, Federal Work-Study, scholarships/grants, tuition waivers (full and partial), and unspecified assistantships available. Support available to part-time students. Financial award application deadline: 2/15; financial award applicants required to submit FAFSA. *Faculty research:* Securing inter-vehicular networks with time and driver identity considerations; security of mobile devices and wireless networks; implantable wireless system to study gastric neurophysiology; model-based software for configuring single switch scanning systems; family-based framework of quality assurance for biomedical ontologies. *Unit head:* Dr. Aydin Farajidavar, Department Chairperson, 516-686-4014, Fax: 516-686-7439, E-mail: afarajid@nyit.edu. *Application contact:* Alice Dolitsky, Director, Graduate Admissions, 516-686-7520, Fax: 516-686-1116, E-mail: admissions@nyit.edu.
Website: http://www.nyit.edu/degrees/electrical_computer_engineering_ms

New York University, Tandon School of Engineering, Department of Electrical and Computer Engineering, New York, NY 10012-1019. Offers computer engineering (MS); electrical engineering (MS, PhD). *Program availability:* Part-time, evening/weekend. *Faculty:* 28 full-time (4 women), 13 part-time/adjunct. *Students:* 549 full-time (122 women), 56 part-time (6 women); includes 36 minority (5 Black or African American, non-Hispanic/Latino; 19 Asian, non-Hispanic/Latino; 7 Hispanic/Latino; 5 Two or more races, non-Hispanic/Latino), 538 international. Average age 25. 1,699 applicants, 63% accepted, 313 enrolled. In 2018, 333 master's, 18 doctorates awarded. *Degree requirements:* For master's, comprehensive exam (for some programs), thesis (for some programs); for doctorate, comprehensive exam, thesis/dissertation, qualifying exam. *Entrance requirements:* For master's, BS in electrical engineering; for doctorate, MS in electrical engineering. Additional exam requirements/recommendations for international students: Required—TOEFL (minimum score 550 paper-based; 90 iBT); Recommended—IELTS (minimum score 7). *Application deadline:* For fall admission, 2/15 priority date for domestic and international students; for spring admission, 11/1 priority date for domestic and international students. Applications are processed on a rolling basis. Application fee: $75. Electronic applications accepted. *Expenses:* Contact institution. *Financial support:* In 2018–19, 269 students received support, including 15 fellowships with partial tuition reimbursements available (averaging $22,178 per year), 33 research assistantships with partial tuition reimbursements available (averaging $23,144 per year), 11 teaching assistantships (averaging $52,614 per year); career-related internships or fieldwork, scholarships/grants, tuition waivers, and unspecified assistantships also available. Support available to part-time students. Financial award application deadline: 2/15. *Faculty research:* Communications, networking, and signal processing; systems, control and robotics; energy systems and power electronics; electromagnetics and analog/radio frequency/biomedical circuits; computer engineering and VLSI. *Total annual research expenditures:* $16.6 million. *Unit head:* Dr. Ivan Selesnick, Department Chair, 646-997-3416, E-mail: iws211@nyu.edu. *Application contact:* Elizabeth Ensweiler, Senior Director of Graduate Enrollment and Graduate Admissions, 646-997-3182, E-mail: elizabeth.ensweiler@nyu.edu.

Norfolk State University, School of Graduate Studies, School of Science and Technology, Program in Electronics Engineering, Norfolk, VA 23504. Offers MS.

North Carolina Agricultural and Technical State University, The Graduate College, College of Engineering, Department of Electrical and Computer Engineering,

Greensboro, NC 27411. Offers electrical engineering (MSEE, PhD), including communications and signal processing, computer engineering, electronic and optical materials and devices, power systems and control. *Program availability:* Part-time. *Degree requirements:* For master's, project, thesis defense; for doctorate, thesis/dissertation. *Entrance requirements:* For master's, GRE General Test, GRE Subject Test, minimum GPA of 2.8; for doctorate, GRE General Test, minimum GPA of 3.0. *Faculty research:* Semiconductor compounds, VLSI design, image processing, optical systems and devices, fault-tolerant computing.

North Carolina State University, Graduate School, College of Engineering, Department of Electrical and Computer Engineering, Program in Electrical Engineering, Raleigh, NC 27695. Offers MS, PhD. *Degree requirements:* For master's, thesis (for some programs); for doctorate, thesis/dissertation. *Entrance requirements:* For master's and doctorate, GRE. Additional exam requirements/recommendations for international students: Required—TOEFL (minimum score 575 paper-based). Electronic applications accepted. *Faculty research:* Microwave devices, wireless communications, nanoelectronics and photonics, robotic and mechatronics, power electronics.

North Dakota State University, College of Graduate and Interdisciplinary Studies, College of Engineering, Department of Electrical and Computer Engineering, Fargo, ND 58102. Offers M Eng, MS, PhD. *Program availability:* Part-time. Terminal master's awarded for partial completion of doctoral program. *Degree requirements:* For master's, comprehensive exam, thesis; for doctorate, comprehensive exam, thesis/dissertation. *Entrance requirements:* Additional exam requirements/recommendations for international students: Required—TOEFL (minimum score 525 paper-based; 71 iBT). Electronic applications accepted. *Faculty research:* Computers, power and control systems, microwaves, communications and signal processing, bioengineering.

Northeastern University, College of Engineering, Boston, MA 02115-5096. Offers bioengineering (MS, PhD); chemical engineering (MS, PhD); civil engineering (MS, PhD); computer engineering (PhD); computer systems engineering (MS); electrical and computer engineering (MS); electrical and computer engineering leadership (MS); electrical engineering (PhD); energy systems (MS); engineering and public policy (MS); engineering management (MS, Certificate); environmental engineering (MS); industrial engineering (MS, PhD); information assurance (PhD); information systems (MS); interdisciplinary engineering (PhD); mechanical engineering (PhD); operations research (MS); telecommunication systems management (MS). *Program availability:* Part-time, online learning. Electronic applications accepted. *Expenses:* Contact institution.

Northern Arizona University, College of Engineering, Informatics, and Applied Sciences, School of Informatics, Computing, and Cyber Systems, Flagstaff, AZ 86011. Offers engineering (M Eng), including computer science and engineering, electrical engineering; informatics and computing (PhD). *Program availability:* Part-time. *Degree requirements:* For master's, variable foreign language requirement, comprehensive exam (for some programs), thesis (for some programs); for doctorate, variable foreign language requirement, comprehensive exam (for some programs), thesis/dissertation (for some programs). *Entrance requirements:* Additional exam requirements/recommendations for international students: Required—TOEFL (minimum score 80 iBT), IELTS (minimum score 6.5). Electronic applications accepted.

Northern Illinois University, Graduate School, College of Engineering and Engineering Technology, Department of Electrical Engineering, De Kalb, IL 60115-2854. Offers MS. *Program availability:* Part-time, evening/weekend. *Faculty:* 9 full-time (0 women). *Students:* 29 full-time (8 women), 12 part-time (4 women); includes 4 minority (1 Black or African American, non-Hispanic/Latino; 2 Asian, non-Hispanic/Latino; 1 Hispanic/Latino), 31 international. Average age 27. 68 applicants, 69% accepted, 16 enrolled. In 2018, 13 master's awarded. *Degree requirements:* For master's, comprehensive exam, thesis optional. *Entrance requirements:* For master's, GRE General Test, minimum GPA of 2.75. Additional exam requirements/recommendations for international students: Required—TOEFL (minimum score 550 paper-based). *Application deadline:* For fall admission, 6/1 for domestic students, 5/1 for international students; for spring admission, 11/1 for domestic students, 10/1 for international students. Applications are processed on a rolling basis. Application fee: $40. Electronic applications accepted. *Financial support:* In 2018–19, 4 research assistantships with full tuition reimbursements, 19 teaching assistantships with full tuition reimbursements were awarded; fellowships with full tuition reimbursements, career-related internships or fieldwork, Federal Work-Study, scholarships/grants, tuition waivers (full), and staff assistantships also available. Support available to part-time students. Financial award applicants required to submit FAFSA. *Faculty research:* Digital signal processing, optics, nano-electronic devices, VLSI. *Unit head:* Dr. Mansour Tahernezhadi, Acting Chair, 815-753-1290, Fax: 815-753-1289, E-mail: mtaherne@niu.edu. *Application contact:* Graduate School Office, 815-753-0395, E-mail: gradsch@niu.edu.
Website: http://www.niu.edu/ee/

Northwestern Polytechnic University, School of Engineering, Fremont, CA 94539-7482. Offers computer engineering (DCE); computer science (MS); computer systems engineering (MS); electrical engineering (MS). *Program availability:* Part-time, evening/weekend. *Degree requirements:* For master's, thesis optional; for doctorate, thesis/dissertation. *Entrance requirements:* For master's, minimum GPA of 3.0. Additional exam requirements/recommendations for international students: Required—TOEFL (minimum score 550 paper-based; 79 iBT). *Faculty research:* Computer networking, database design, Internet technology, software engineering, digital signal processing.

Northwestern University, McCormick School of Engineering and Applied Science, Department of Electrical Engineering and Computer Science, Evanston, IL 60208. Offers computer engineering (MS, PhD); computer science (MS, PhD); electrical engineering (MS, PhD); information technology (MS). MS and PhD admissions and degrees offered through The Graduate School. *Program availability:* Part-time. Terminal master's awarded for partial completion of doctoral program. *Degree requirements:* For master's, comprehensive exam (for some programs), thesis optional; for doctorate, comprehensive exam, thesis/dissertation. *Entrance requirements:* For master's and doctorate, GRE General Test. Additional exam requirements/recommendations for international students: Required—TOEFL (minimum score 577 paper-based; 90 iBT), IELTS (minimum score 7). Electronic applications accepted. *Faculty research:* Solid state and photonics; computing, algorithms, and applications; computer engineering and systems; cognitive systems; graphics and interactive media; signals and systems.

Oakland University, Graduate Study and Lifelong Learning, School of Engineering and Computer Science, Department of Electrical and Computer Engineering, Rochester, MI 48309-4401. Offers electrical and computer engineering (MS, PhD); embedded systems (MS); mechatronics (MS). *Program availability:* Part-time, evening/weekend. *Entrance requirements:* For master's, minimum GPA of 3.0. Additional exam requirements/recommendations for international students: Required—TOEFL (minimum score 550 paper-based). Electronic applications accepted. *Expenses:* Contact institution.

The Ohio State University, Graduate School, College of Engineering, Department of Electrical and Computer Engineering, Columbus, OH 43210. Offers electrical and computer engineering (MS, PhD); electrical engineering (MS, PhD). *Program availability:* Part-time. *Faculty:* 62. *Students:* 437 (73 women). Average age 25. In 2018, 111 master's, 44 doctorates awarded. Terminal master's awarded for partial completion of doctoral program. *Entrance requirements:* For master's, GRE General Test (for all graduates of foreign universities and for applicants if undergraduate GPA below 3.2); for doctorate, GRE General Test (for all graduates of foreign universities and for applicants if graduate work GPA is below 3.5). Additional exam requirements/recommendations for international students: Required—TOEFL (minimum score 580 paper-based; 92 iBT); Recommended—IELTS (minimum score 7.5). *Application deadline:* For fall admission, 11/30 priority date for domestic and international students. Applications are processed on a rolling basis. Application fee: $60 ($70 for international students). Electronic applications accepted. *Financial support:* Fellowships with full tuition reimbursements, research assistantships with full tuition reimbursements, teaching assistantships with full tuition reimbursements, career-related internships or fieldwork, Federal Work-Study, institutionally sponsored loans, scholarships/grants, traineeships, health care benefits, and unspecified assistantships available. Support available to part-time students. *Unit head:* Dr. Hesham M. El Gamal, Chair, 614-292-4374, E-mail: elgamal.2@osu.edu. *Application contact:* Electrical and Computer Engineering Graduate Program, 614-292-2572, Fax: 614-292-7596, E-mail: ecegrad@ece.osu.edu.
Website: http://ece.osu.edu/

Ohio University, Graduate College, Russ College of Engineering and Technology, School of Electrical Engineering and Computer Science, Athens, OH 45701-2979. Offers electrical engineering (MS); electrical engineering and computer science (PhD). *Degree requirements:* For master's, comprehensive exam (for some programs), thesis; for doctorate, comprehensive exam, thesis/dissertation, qualifying exams. *Entrance requirements:* For master's, GRE, BSEE or BSCS, minimum GPA of 3.0; for doctorate, GRE, MSEE or MSCS, minimum GPA of 3.0. Additional exam requirements/recommendations for international students: Required—TOEFL (minimum score 550 paper-based; 80 iBT) or IELTS (minimum score 6.5). Electronic applications accepted. *Faculty research:* Avionics, networking/communications, intelligent distribution, real-time computing, control systems, optical properties of semiconductors.

Oklahoma Christian University, Graduate School of Engineering and Computer Science, Oklahoma City, OK 73136-1100. Offers electrical and computer engineering (MSE); engineering management (MSE); mechanical engineering (MSE); software engineering (MSCS, MSE). *Program availability:* Part-time. *Entrance requirements:* Additional exam requirements/recommendations for international students: Required—TOEFL (minimum score 550 paper-based). Electronic applications accepted. *Expenses:* Contact institution.

Oklahoma State University, College of Engineering, Architecture and Technology, School of Electrical and Computer Engineering, Stillwater, OK 74078. Offers MS, PhD. *Program availability:* Online learning. *Faculty:* 20 full-time (2 women), 1 part-time/adjunct (0 women). *Students:* 25 full-time (7 women), 38 part-time (6 women); includes 7 minority (2 Black or African American, non-Hispanic/Latino; 1 Asian, non-Hispanic/Latino; 2 Hispanic/Latino; 2 Two or more races, non-Hispanic/Latino), 50 international. Average age 29. 159 applicants, 23% accepted, 18 enrolled. In 2018, 31 master's, 3 doctorates awarded. *Entrance requirements:* For master's and doctorate, GRE or GMAT. Additional exam requirements/recommendations for international students: Required—TOEFL (minimum score 550 paper-based; 79 iBT). *Application deadline:* For fall admission, 3/1 priority date for international students; for spring admission, 8/1 priority date for international students. Applications are processed on a rolling basis. Application fee: $40 ($75 for international students). Electronic applications accepted. *Expenses: Tuition, area resident:* Full-time $4148. Tuition, state resident: full-time $4148. Tuition, nonresident: full-time $10,517. *International tuition:* $10,517 full-time. *Required fees:* $4394; $2929 per credit hour. Tuition and fees vary according to course load and program. *Financial support:* Research assistantships, teaching assistantships, career-related internships or fieldwork, Federal Work-Study, scholarships/grants, health care benefits, tuition waivers (partial), and unspecified assistantships available. Support available to part-time students. Financial award application deadline: 3/1; financial award applicants required to submit FAFSA. *Unit head:* Dr. Jeffrey Young, Department Head, 405-744-5151, Fax: 405-744-9198, E-mail: jl.young@okstate.edu. *Application contact:* Dr. R. G. Ramakumar, Graduate Coordinator, 405-744-5157, Fax: 405-744-9198, E-mail: ramakum@okstate.edu.
Website: http://ece.okstate.edu

Old Dominion University, Frank Batten College of Engineering and Technology, Graduate Program in Electrical and Computer Engineering, Norfolk, VA 23529. Offers ME, MS, D Eng, PhD. *Program availability:* Part-time, online learning. *Degree requirements:* For master's, comprehensive exam (for some programs), thesis (for some programs); for doctorate, thesis/dissertation, candidacy exam, diagnostic exam, proposal defense. *Entrance requirements:* For master's, GRE, two letters of recommendation, resume, personal statement of objectives; for doctorate, GRE, three letters of recommendation, resume, personal statement of objectives. Additional exam requirements/recommendations for international students: Required—TOEFL (minimum score 550 paper-based; 79 iBT), IELTS (minimum score 6.5). Electronic applications accepted. *Expenses:* Contact institution. *Faculty research:* Cyber-physical systems, cybersecurity, communications and networking, computer vision and computational modeling, controls, hardware, bioelectrics, medical image processing, plasma medicine, signal processing for medical and biological applications, systems biology and computational bioengineering, photovoltaics, plasma processing, thin films and nanotechnology.

Oregon Health & Science University, School of Medicine, Graduate Programs in Medicine, Department of Computer Science and Electrical Engineering, Portland, OR 97239-3098. Offers computer science and engineering (MS, PhD); electrical engineering (MS, PhD). *Program availability:* Part-time. *Faculty:* 12 full-time (7 women), 9 part-time/adjunct (0 women). *Students:* 13 full-time (6 women), 12 part-time (1 woman); includes 4 minority (3 Asian, non-Hispanic/Latino; 1 Two or more races, non-Hispanic/Latino), 8 international. Average age 31. 16 applicants, 69% accepted, 11 enrolled. In 2018, 6 master's, 3 doctorates awarded. Terminal master's awarded for partial completion of doctoral program. *Degree requirements:* For master's, thesis (for some programs); for doctorate, comprehensive exam, thesis/dissertation, qualifying exam. *Entrance requirements:* For master's and doctorate, GRE General Test (minimum scores: 153 Verbal/148 Quantitative/4.5 Analytical). *Application deadline:* For fall admission, 7/15 for domestic students, 5/15 for international students; for winter admission, 10/15 for domestic students, 9/15 for international students; for spring admission, 1/15 for domestic students, 12/15 for international students. Applications are processed on a rolling basis. Application fee: $70. Electronic applications accepted. *Financial support:* Health care benefits, tuition waivers (full), and full-tuition and stipends (for PhD students) available. Financial award applicants required to submit FAFSA. *Faculty research:* Natural language processing, speech signal processing, computational biology, autism spectrum disorders, hearing and speaking disorders. *Unit head:* Dr. Peter Heeman, Program Director, 503-346-3755, E-mail: somgrad@ohsu.edu. *Application contact:* Pat Dickerson, Administrative Coordinator, 503-346-3753, E-mail: somgrad@ohsu.edu.
Website: http://www.ohsu.edu/xd/education/schools/school-of-medicine/departments/basic-science-departments/csee/

Oregon State University, College of Engineering, Program in Electrical and Computer Engineering, Corvallis, OR 97331. Offers M Eng, MS, PhD. *Entrance requirements:* For master's and doctorate, GRE. Additional exam requirements/recommendations for international students: Required—TOEFL (minimum score 600 paper-based; 80 iBT), IELTS (minimum score 7). *Expenses:* Contact institution.

Electrical Engineering

Oregon State University, College of Engineering, Program in Materials Science, Corvallis, OR 97331. Offers chemical engineering (MS, PhD); chemistry (MS, PhD); civil engineering (MS, PhD); electrical and computer engineering (MS, PhD); forest products (MS, PhD); mathematics (MS, PhD); mechanical engineering (MS, PhD); nuclear engineering (MS); physics (MS, PhD). *Entrance requirements:* For master's and doctorate, GRE. Additional exam requirements/recommendations for international students: Required—TOEFL (minimum score 80 iBT), IELTS (minimum score 6.5). *Expenses:* Contact institution.

Penn State Harrisburg, Graduate School, School of Science, Engineering and Technology, Middletown, PA 17057. Offers civil engineering (MS); computer science (MS); electrical engineering (M Eng, MS); engineering management (MPS); engineering science (M Eng); environmental engineering (M Eng); environmental pollution control (MEPC, MS); mechanical engineering (MS); structural engineering (Certificate). *Program availability:* Part-time, evening/weekend.

Penn State University Park, Graduate School, College of Engineering, Department of Electrical Engineering, University Park, PA 16802. Offers MS, PhD.

Pittsburg State University, Graduate School, College of Technology, Department of Engineering Technology, Pittsburg, KS 66762. Offers electrical engineering technology (MET); general engineering technology (MET); manufacturing engineering technology (MET); mechanical engineering technology (MET); plastics engineering technology (MET). *Program availability:* Part-time, 100% online, blended/hybrid learning. *Degree requirements:* For master's, thesis optional. *Entrance requirements:* Additional exam requirements/recommendations for international students: Required—TOEFL (minimum score 550 paper-based; 79 iBT), IELTS (minimum score 6.5), PTE (minimum score 51). Electronic applications accepted. *Expenses:* Contact institution.

Polytechnic University of Puerto Rico, Graduate School, Hato Rey, PR 00918. Offers business administration (MBA), including computer information systems, general management, management of information systems, management of international enterprises; civil engineering (ME, MS); computer engineering (ME, MS); computer science (MCS, MS); electrical engineering (ME, MS); engineering management (MEM); environmental management (MEM); landscape architecture (M Land Arch); manufacturing competitiveness (MMC, MS); manufacturing engineering (ME, MS); mechanical engineering (M Mech E). *Accreditation:* ASLA. *Program availability:* Part-time, evening/weekend. *Entrance requirements:* For master's, 3 letters of recommendation.

Portland State University, Graduate Studies, Maseeh College of Engineering and Computer Science, Department of Electrical and Computer Engineering, Portland, OR 97207-0751. Offers MS, PhD. *Program availability:* Part-time, evening/weekend. *Degree requirements:* For master's, variable foreign language requirement, oral exam; for doctorate, one foreign language, comprehensive exam, thesis/dissertation, oral and written exams. *Entrance requirements:* For master's, GRE, minimum GPA of 2.75; for doctorate, GRE General Test, GRE Subject Test, master's degree in electrical engineering or related field, 3 reference letters, statement of purpose, writing sample. Additional exam requirements/recommendations for international students: Required—TOEFL (minimum score 550 paper-based; 80 iBT). *Expenses:* Contact institution. *Faculty research:* Optics and laser systems, design automation, VLSI design, computer systems, power electronics.

Prairie View A&M University, College of Engineering, Prairie View, TX 77446. Offers computer information systems (MSCIS); computer science (MSCS); electrical engineering (MSEE, PhDEE); general engineering (MS Engr). *Program availability:* Part-time, evening/weekend. *Faculty:* 29 full-time (8 women), 1 part-time/adjunct (0 women). *Students:* 134 full-time (34 women), 67 part-time (24 women); includes 84 minority (67 Black or African American, non-Hispanic/Latino; 12 Asian, non-Hispanic/Latino; 5 Hispanic/Latino), 102 international. Average age 31. 130 applicants, 80% accepted, 52 enrolled. In 2018, 67 master's, 3 doctorates awarded. *Degree requirements:* For master's, thesis optional; for doctorate, comprehensive exam, thesis/dissertation. *Entrance requirements:* For master's, GRE General Test (minimum score of 900), bachelor's degree in engineering from ABET-accredited institution; for doctorate, minimum GPA of 3.0. Additional exam requirements/recommendations for international students: Required—TOEFL (minimum score 550 paper-based; 79 iBT). *Application deadline:* For fall admission, 5/1 priority date for domestic and international students; for spring admission, 10/1 priority date for domestic students, 9/1 priority date for international students; for summer admission, 3/1 priority date for domestic students, 2/1 priority date for international students. Applications are processed on a rolling basis. Application fee: $50. Electronic applications accepted. *Expenses: Tuition, area resident:* Full-time $3172; part-time $317 per credit. Tuition, state resident: full-time $3172; part-time $317 per credit. Tuition, nonresident: full-time $7965; part-time $796 per credit. *Required fees:* $4847; $485 per credit. *Financial support:* Fellowships, research assistantships, teaching assistantships, career-related internships or fieldwork, institutionally sponsored loans, scholarships/grants, health care benefits, tuition waivers (full), and unspecified assistantships available. Financial award application deadline: 4/1; financial award applicants required to submit FAFSA. *Faculty research:* Electrical and computer engineering: big data analysis, wireless communications, bioinformatics and computational biology, space radiation; computer science: cloud computing, cyber security; chemical engineering: thermochemical processing of biofuel, photochemical modeling; civil and environmental engineering: environmental sustainability, water resources, structure; mechanical engineering: thermal science, nanocomposites, computational fluid dynamics. *Unit head:* Dr. Pamela H Obiomon, Dean, 936-261-9890, Fax: 936-261-9868, E-mail: phobiomon@pvamu.edu. *Application contact:* Pauline Walker, Administrative Assistant II, Research and Graduate Studies, 936-261-3521, Fax: 936-261-3529, E-mail: gradadmissions@pvamu.edu.

Princeton University, Graduate School, School of Engineering and Applied Science, Department of Electrical Engineering, Princeton, NJ 08544-1019. Offers M Eng, PhD. Terminal master's awarded for partial completion of doctoral program. *Degree requirements:* For doctorate, thesis/dissertation, general exam. *Entrance requirements:* For master's, GRE General Test, 3 letters of recommendation; for doctorate, GRE General Test, official transcript(s), 3 letters of recommendation, personal statement. Additional exam requirements/recommendations for international students: Required—TOEFL. Electronic applications accepted. *Faculty research:* Computer engineering, electronic materials and devices, information sciences and systems, optics and optical electronics.

Purdue University, College of Engineering, School of Electrical and Computer Engineering, West Lafayette, IN 47907-2035. Offers MSECE, PhD. MS and PhD degree programs in biomedical engineering offered jointly with School of Mechanical Engineering and School of Chemical Engineering. *Program availability:* Part-time, online learning. Terminal master's awarded for partial completion of doctoral program. *Degree requirements:* For master's, thesis optional; for doctorate, thesis/dissertation. *Entrance requirements:* For master's and doctorate, GRE General Test, minimum GPA of 3.25. Electronic applications accepted. *Faculty research:* Automatic control, biomedical imaging and sensing, communications, networking, signal and image processing, computer engineering, education, fields and optics, microelectronics and nanotechnology, power and energy systems, VLSI and circuit design.

Purdue University Fort Wayne, College of Engineering, Technology, and Computer Science, Department of Electrical and Computer Engineering, Fort Wayne, IN 46805-1499. Offers computer engineering (MSE); electrical engineering (MSE); systems engineering (MSE). *Program availability:* Part-time. *Entrance requirements:* For master's, minimum GPA of 3.0, bachelor's degree in engineering discipline. Additional exam requirements/recommendations for international students: Required—TOEFL (minimum score 550 paper-based; 79 iBT); Recommended—TWE. Electronic applications accepted.

Purdue University Northwest, Graduate Studies Office, School of Engineering, Mathematics, and Science, Department of Engineering, Hammond, IN 46323-2094. Offers computer engineering (MSE); electrical engineering (MSE); engineering (MS); mechanical engineering (MSE). *Program availability:* Evening/weekend. *Entrance requirements:* Additional exam requirements/recommendations for international students: Required—TOEFL.

Queen's University at Kingston, School of Graduate Studies, Faculty of Engineering and Applied Science, Department of Electrical and Computer Engineering, Kingston, ON K7L 3N6, Canada. Offers M Eng, M Sc, M Sc Eng, PhD. *Program availability:* Part-time. *Degree requirements:* For master's, thesis optional; for doctorate, comprehensive exam, thesis/dissertation. *Entrance requirements:* Additional exam requirements/recommendations for international students: Required—TOEFL (minimum score 580 paper-based). *Faculty research:* Communications and signal processing systems, computer engineering systems.

Rensselaer at Hartford, Department of Engineering, Program in Electrical Engineering, Hartford, CT 06120-2991. Offers ME, MS. *Program availability:* Part-time, evening/weekend. *Degree requirements:* For master's, thesis optional. *Entrance requirements:* For master's, GRE. Additional exam requirements/recommendations for international students: Required—TOEFL (minimum score 600 paper-based; 100 iBT).

Rensselaer Polytechnic Institute, Graduate School, School of Engineering, Program in Electrical Engineering, Troy, NY 12180-3590. Offers M Eng, MS, PhD. *Faculty:* 40 full-time (7 women), 1 part-time/adjunct (0 women). *Students:* 90 full-time (15 women), 4 part-time (0 women); includes 8 minority (3 Black or African American, non-Hispanic/Latino; 4 Asian, non-Hispanic/Latino; 1 Two or more races, non-Hispanic/Latino), 69 international. Average age 26. 305 applicants, 42% accepted, 28 enrolled. In 2018, 22 master's, 11 doctorates awarded. Terminal master's awarded for partial completion of doctoral program. *Degree requirements:* For master's, thesis (for some programs); for doctorate, thesis/dissertation. *Entrance requirements:* For master's and doctorate, GRE. Additional exam requirements/recommendations for international students: Required—TOEFL (minimum score 570 paper-based; 88 iBT), IELTS (minimum score 6.5), PTE (minimum score 60). *Application deadline:* For fall admission, 1/1 priority date for domestic and international students; for spring admission, 8/15 priority date for domestic and international students. Applications are processed on a rolling basis. Application fee: $75. Electronic applications accepted. *Financial support:* In 2018–19, research assistantships (averaging $23,000 per year), teaching assistantships (averaging $23,000 per year) were awarded; fellowships also available. Financial award application deadline: 1/1. *Faculty research:* Communications, information, and signals and systems; computer engineering, hardware, and architecture; computer networking; control, robotics, and automation; energy sources and systems; image science: computer vision, image processing, and geographic information science; microelectronics, photonics, VLSI, and mixed-signal design; plasma science and electromagnetics. *Total annual research expenditures:* $6.3 million. *Unit head:* Dr. Hussein Abouzeid, Graduate Program Director, 518-276-6534, E-mail: gpd@ecse.rpi.edu. *Application contact:* Jarron Decker, Director of Graduate Admissions, 518-276-6216, Fax: 518-276-4072, E-mail: gradadmissions@rpi.edu.
Website: http://www.ecse.rpi.edu/

Rice University, Graduate Programs, George R. Brown School of Engineering, Department of Electrical and Computer Engineering, Houston, TX 77251-1892. Offers bioengineering (MS, PhD); circuits, controls, and communication systems (MS, PhD); computer science and engineering (MS, PhD); electrical engineering (MEE); lasers, microwaves, and solid-state electronics (MS, PhD); MBA/MEE. *Program availability:* Part-time. *Degree requirements:* For master's, thesis (for some programs); for doctorate, thesis/dissertation. *Entrance requirements:* For master's and doctorate, GRE General Test, GRE Subject Test, minimum GPA of 3.0. Additional exam requirements/recommendations for international students: Required—TOEFL (minimum score 600 paper-based; 90 iBT). Electronic applications accepted. *Faculty research:* Physical electronics, systems, computer engineering, bioengineering.

Rochester Institute of Technology, Graduate Enrollment Services, Kate Gleason College of Engineering, Electrical and Microelectronic Engineering Department, MS Program in Electrical Engineering, Rochester, NY 14623-5603. Offers MS. *Program availability:* Part-time, evening/weekend. *Students:* 113 full-time (27 women), 41 part-time (8 women); includes 2 minority (both Asian, non-Hispanic/Latino), 106 international. Average age 25. 213 applicants, 80% accepted, 54 enrolled. In 2018, 57 master's awarded. *Entrance requirements:* For master's, GRE, baccalaureate degree from accredited university in engineering or related field, official transcripts, minimum GPA of 3.0, two letters of reference. Additional exam requirements/recommendations for international students: Required—TOEFL (minimum score 550 paper-based; 79 iBT), IELTS (minimum score 6.5), PTE (minimum score 58). *Application deadline:* For fall admission, 2/15 priority date for domestic and international students; for spring admission, 12/15 priority date for domestic and international students. Applications are processed on a rolling basis. Application fee: $65. Electronic applications accepted. *Financial support:* In 2018–19, 147 students received support. Research assistantships with partial tuition reimbursements available, teaching assistantships with partial tuition reimbursements available, career-related internships or fieldwork, scholarships/grants, and unspecified assistantships available. Support available to part-time students. Financial award applicants required to submit FAFSA. *Faculty research:* Analog and RF; digital and computer systems; electromagnetics, microwaves, and antennas; energy systems; image, video and computer vision; multi-agent bio-robotics; robotics and control systems; wireless communications. *Unit head:* Dr. Jayanti Venkatraman, Graduate Program Director, 585-475-2143, E-mail: jnveee@rit.edu. *Application contact:* Diane Ellison, Senior Associate Vice President, Graduate Enrollment Services, 585-475-2229, Fax: 585-475-7164, E-mail: gradinfo@rit.edu.
Website: https://www.rit.edu/study/electrical-engineering-ms

Rochester Institute of Technology, Graduate Enrollment Services, Kate Gleason College of Engineering, Electrical and Microelectronic Engineering Department, MS Program in Microelectronic Engineering, Rochester, NY 14623-5603. Offers MS. *Program availability:* Part-time. *Students:* 9 full-time (2 women), 7 part-time (2 women); includes 2 minority (1 Asian, non-Hispanic/Latino; 1 Hispanic/Latino), 10 international. Average age 25. 20 applicants, 60% accepted, 4 enrolled. In 2018, 3 master's awarded. *Degree requirements:* For master's, thesis. *Entrance requirements:* For master's, GRE, minimum GPA of 3.0 (recommended), two letters of recommendation. Additional exam requirements/recommendations for international students: Required—TOEFL (minimum score 550 paper-based; 79 iBT), IELTS (minimum score 6.5), PTE (minimum score 58). *Application deadline:* For fall admission, 2/15 priority date for domestic and international students; for spring admission, 12/15 priority date for domestic and international

students. Applications are processed on a rolling basis. Application fee: $65. Electronic applications accepted. *Expenses:* Contact institution. *Financial support:* In 2018–19, 14 students received support. Research assistantships with partial tuition reimbursements available, teaching assistantships with partial tuition reimbursements available, career-related internships or fieldwork, scholarships/grants, and unspecified assistantships available. Support available to part-time students. Financial award applicants required to submit FAFSA. *Faculty research:* Thin-film electronics and photonics; FinFET manufacturing, process and devices; Gallium Nitride materials, optoelectronics, lasers; tunneling devices, TFETs, nanofabrication; nanomaterials, MEMS, sensors and beyond. *Unit head:* Dr. Robert Pearson, Graduate Program Director, 585-475-2923, Fax: 585-475-5845, E-mail: robert.pearson@rit.edu. *Application contact:* Diane Ellison, Senior Associate Vice President, Graduate Enrollment Services, 585-475-2229, Fax: 585-475-7164, E-mail: gradinfo@rit.edu.
Website: https://www.rit.edu/study/microelectronic-engineering-ms

Rose-Hulman Institute of Technology, Graduate Studies, Department of Electrical and Computer Engineering, Terre Haute, IN 47803-3999. Offers electrical and computer engineering (M Eng); electrical engineering (MS); systems engineering and management (MS). *Program availability:* Part-time. *Faculty:* 19 full-time (2 women), 1 (woman) part-time/adjunct. *Students:* 4 full-time (0 women), 4 part-time (2 women), 7 international. Average age 26. 9 applicants, 44% accepted, 4 enrolled. In 2018, 2 master's awarded. *Degree requirements:* For master's, thesis (for some programs). *Entrance requirements:* For master's, GRE, minimum GPA of 3.0. Additional exam requirements/recommendations for international students: Required—TOEFL (minimum score 580 paper-based; 94 iBT), IELTS (minimum score 7). *Application deadline:* For fall admission, 2/1 priority date for domestic and international students; for winter admission, 10/1 for domestic students, 4/1 for international students; for spring admission, 1/15 for domestic students, 11/1 for international students. Applications are processed on a rolling basis. Application fee: $0. Electronic applications accepted. *Expenses: Tuition:* Full-time $46,641. *Financial support:* In 2018–19, 7 students received support. Fellowships with tuition reimbursements available, research assistantships with tuition reimbursements available, institutionally sponsored loans, scholarships/grants, and tuition waivers (full and partial) available. *Faculty research:* VLSI, power systems, analog electronics, communications, electromagnetics. *Total annual research expenditures:* $55,933. *Unit head:* Dr. Mario Simoni, Department Head, 812-877-8341, Fax: 812-877-8895, E-mail: simoni@rose-hulman.edu. *Application contact:* Dr. Craig Downing, Associate Dean of the Faculty, 812-877-8822, E-mail: downing@rose-hulman.edu.
Website: https://www.rose-hulman.edu/academics/academic-departments/electrical-computer-engineering/index.html

Rowan University, Graduate School, College of Engineering, Department of Electrical Engineering, Glassboro, NJ 08028-1701. Offers MS. Electronic applications accepted.

Royal Military College of Canada, Division of Graduate Studies, Faculty of Engineering, Department of Electrical and Computer Engineering, Kingston, ON K7K 7B4, Canada. Offers computer engineering (M Eng, PhD); electrical engineering (M Eng, PhD); software engineering (M Eng, PhD). *Degree requirements:* For master's, thesis; for doctorate, comprehensive exam, thesis/dissertation. *Entrance requirements:* For master's, honours degree with second-class standing in the appropriate field; for doctorate, master's degree. Electronic applications accepted.

Rutgers University–New Brunswick, Graduate School-New Brunswick, Department of Electrical and Computer Engineering, Piscataway, NJ 08854-8097. Offers communications and solid-state electronics (MS, PhD); computer engineering (MS, PhD); control systems (MS, PhD); digital signal processing (MS, PhD). *Program availability:* Part-time. Terminal master's awarded for partial completion of doctoral program. *Degree requirements:* For master's, thesis or alternative; for doctorate, thesis/dissertation. *Entrance requirements:* For master's and doctorate, GRE General Test. Additional exam requirements/recommendations for international students: Required—TOEFL. Electronic applications accepted. *Faculty research:* Communication and information processing, wireless information networks, micro-vacuum devices, machine vision, VLSI design.

St. Cloud State University, School of Graduate Studies, College of Science and Engineering, Department of Electrical and Computer Engineering, St. Cloud, MN 56301-4498. Offers electrical engineering (MS). *Degree requirements:* For master's, thesis or alternative. *Entrance requirements:* For master's, GRE General Test, minimum GPA of 2.75. Additional exam requirements/recommendations for international students: Required—Michigan English Language Assessment Battery; Recommended—TOEFL (minimum score 550 paper-based), IELTS (minimum score 6.5). Electronic applications accepted.

St. Mary's University, School of Science, Engineering and Technology, Program in Electrical Engineering, San Antonio, TX 78228. Offers MS. *Program availability:* Part-time, evening/weekend. *Students:* 3 full-time (0 women), 3 part-time (0 women); includes 1 minority (Hispanic/Latino), 3 international. Average age 27. 7 applicants, 57% accepted. In 2018, 3 master's awarded. *Degree requirements:* For master's, thesis or project. *Entrance requirements:* For master's, GRE (minimum quantitative score of 148), bachelor's degree in electrical engineering, computer engineering or closely-related discipline; minimum undergraduate GPA of 3.0; written statement of purpose; two letters of recommendation; official transcripts. Additional exam requirements/recommendations for international students: Required—TOEFL (minimum score 550 paper-based; 80 iBT), IELTS (minimum score 6.5). *Application deadline:* For fall admission, 7/1 for domestic students; for spring admission, 11/15 for domestic students; for summer admission, 4/1 for domestic students. Applications are processed on a rolling basis. Application fee: $0. Electronic applications accepted. *Expenses: Tuition:* Full-time $16,830; part-time $935 per credit hour. *Required fees:* $1055. Tuition and fees vary according to program. *Financial support:* Research assistantships, career-related internships or fieldwork, Federal Work-Study, institutionally sponsored loans, scholarships/grants, health care benefits, and stipends available. Financial award application deadline: 3/31; financial award applicants required to submit FAFSA. *Faculty research:* Sequencing, scheduling and professional ethics. *Unit head:* Dr. Wenbin Luo, Graduate Program Director, 210-431-5002, E-mail: wluo@stmarytx.edu. *Application contact:* Dr. Wenbin Luo, Graduate Program Director, 210-431-5002, E-mail: wluo@stmarytx.edu.
Website: https://www.stmarytx.edu/academics/programs/master-electrical-engineering/

San Diego State University, Graduate and Research Affairs, College of Engineering, Department of Electrical and Computer Engineering, San Diego, CA 92182. Offers electrical engineering (MS). *Program availability:* Evening/weekend. *Entrance requirements:* For master's, GRE General Test. Additional exam requirements/recommendations for international students: Required—TOEFL. Electronic applications accepted. *Faculty research:* Ultra-high speed integral circuits and systems, naval command control and ocean surveillance, signal processing and analysis.

San Francisco State University, Division of Graduate Studies, College of Science and Engineering, School of Engineering, San Francisco, CA 94132-1722. Offers embedded electrical and computer systems (MS); energy systems (MS); structural/earthquake engineering (MS). *Program availability:* Part-time. *Application deadline:* Applications are processed on a rolling basis. Electronic applications accepted. *Unit head:* Dr. Kwok-

Siong Teh, Director, 415-338-1228, Fax: 415-338-0525, E-mail: ksteh@sfsu.edu. *Application contact:* Dr. Hamid Shahnasser, Graduate Coordinator, 415-338-2124, Fax: 415-338-0525, E-mail: hamid@sfsu.edu.
Website: http://engineering.sfsu.edu/

San Jose State University, Program in Electrical Engineering, San Jose, CA 95192-0001. Offers MS. *Degree requirements:* For master's, thesis. *Entrance requirements:* For master's, GRE General Test. Electronic applications accepted.

Santa Clara University, School of Engineering, Santa Clara, CA 95053. Offers applied mathematics (MS); bioengineering (MS); civil, environmental, and sustainable engineering (MS); computer science and engineering (MS, PhD, Engineer); electrical engineering (MS, PhD, Engineer); engineering management and leadership (MS); mechanical engineering (MS, PhD, Engineer); power systems and sustainable energy (MS); software engineering (MS). *Program availability:* Part-time. *Faculty:* 72 full-time (24 women), 52 part-time/adjunct (9 women). *Students:* 555 full-time (211 women), 269 part-time (91 women); includes 208 minority (8 Black or African American, non-Hispanic/Latino; 1 American Indian or Alaska Native, non-Hispanic/Latino; 145 Asian, non-Hispanic/Latino; 28 Hispanic/Latino; 26 Two or more races, non-Hispanic/Latino), 472 international. Average age 27. 1,309 applicants, 36% accepted, 269 enrolled. In 2018, 320 master's, 7 doctorates awarded. *Entrance requirements:* For master's, GRE, official transcript; for doctorate, GRE, Official transcript, 500 word statement of purpose, three letters of recommendation. Additional exam requirements/recommendations for international students: Required—TOEFL (minimum score 79 iBT), IELTS (minimum score 6.5). *Application deadline:* For fall admission, 6/1 for domestic students; for winter admission, 9/6 for domestic students; for spring admission, 1/10 for domestic students; for summer admission, 3/6 for domestic students. Application fee: $60. Electronic applications accepted. *Financial support:* Fellowships, Federal Work-Study, and scholarships/grants available. Support available to part-time students. Financial award applicants required to submit FAFSA. *Unit head:* Dr. Elaine Scott, Dean, 408-554-3512, E-mail: epscott@scu.edu. *Application contact:* Stacey Tinker, Director of Admissions and Marketing, 408-554-4748, Fax: 408-554-4323, E-mail: stinker@scu.edu.
Website: http://www.scu.edu/engineering/graduate/

South Dakota School of Mines and Technology, Graduate Division, Program in Electrical Engineering, Rapid City, SD 57701-3995. Offers MS. *Program availability:* Part-time. *Degree requirements:* For master's, thesis. *Entrance requirements:* Additional exam requirements/recommendations for international students: Required—TOEFL (minimum score 520 paper-based; 68 iBT), TWE. Electronic applications accepted.

South Dakota State University, Graduate School, Jerome J. Lohr College of Engineering, Department of Electrical Engineering and Computer Science, Brookings, SD 57007. Offers electrical engineering (PhD); engineering (MS). *Program availability:* Part-time. *Degree requirements:* For master's, thesis (for some programs), oral exam; for doctorate, comprehensive exam, thesis/dissertation, oral exam. *Entrance requirements:* For master's and doctorate, GRE. Additional exam requirements/recommendations for international students: Required—TOEFL (minimum score 575 paper-based). *Faculty research:* Image processing, communications, power systems, electronic materials and devices, nanotechnology, photovoltaics.

Southern Illinois University Carbondale, Graduate School, College of Engineering, Department of Electrical and Computer Engineering, Carbondale, IL 62901-4701. Offers MS, PhD, JD/MS. *Degree requirements:* For master's, comprehensive exam, thesis. *Entrance requirements:* For master's, GRE, minimum GPA of 2.7; for doctorate, GRE, minimum GPA of 3.25. Additional exam requirements/recommendations for international students: Required—TOEFL. *Faculty research:* Circuits and power systems, communications and signal processing, controls and systems, electromagnetics and optics, electronics instrumentation and bioengineering.

Southern Illinois University Carbondale, Graduate School, College of Engineering, Program in Engineering Science, Carbondale, IL 62901-4701. Offers engineering science (PhD), including civil and environmental engineering, electrical and computer engineering, mechanical engineering and energy processes, mining and mineral resources engineering. *Degree requirements:* For doctorate, thesis/dissertation. *Entrance requirements:* For doctorate, GRE General Test, minimum GPA of 3.5. Additional exam requirements/recommendations for international students: Required—TOEFL.

Southern Illinois University Edwardsville, Graduate School, School of Engineering, Department of Electrical and Computer Engineering, Edwardsville, IL 62026. Offers electrical engineering (MS). *Program availability:* Part-time, evening/weekend. *Degree requirements:* For master's, thesis (for some programs), research paper, final exam. *Entrance requirements:* For master's, minimum undergraduate GPA of 2.75 in engineering, mathematics, and science courses. Additional exam requirements/recommendations for international students: Required—TOEFL (minimum score 550 paper-based; 79 iBT), IELTS (minimum score 6.5). Electronic applications accepted.

Southern Methodist University, Lyle School of Engineering, Department of Electrical Engineering, Dallas, TX 75275-0338. Offers electrical engineering (MS, PhD); telecommunications and network engineering (MS). *Program availability:* Part-time, evening/weekend, online learning. Terminal master's awarded for partial completion of doctoral program. *Degree requirements:* For master's, thesis optional; for doctorate, thesis/dissertation, oral and written qualifying exams, oral final exam. *Entrance requirements:* For master's, GRE General Test, minimum GPA of 3.0 in last 2 years; bachelor's degree in engineering, mathematics, or sciences; for doctorate, preliminary counseling exam, minimum GPA of 3.0, bachelor's degree in related field. Additional exam requirements/recommendations for international students: Required—TOEFL. Electronic applications accepted. *Faculty research:* Mobile communications, optical communications, digital signal processing, photonics.

Stanford University, School of Engineering, Department of Electrical Engineering, Stanford, CA 94305-2004. Offers MS, PhD. *Expenses: Tuition:* Full-time $50,703; part-time $32,970 per year. *Required fees:* $651.
Website: http://ee.stanford.edu/

Stevens Institute of Technology, Graduate School, Charles V. Schaefer Jr. School of Engineering and Science, Department of Electrical and Computer Engineering, Program in Electrical Engineering, Hoboken, NJ 07030. Offers autonomous robotics (Certificate); electrical engineering (M Eng, PhD, Certificate), including computer architecture and digital systems (M Eng), microelectronics and photonics science and technology (M Eng), signal processing for communications (M Eng), telecommunications systems engineering (M Eng), wireless communications (M Eng, Certificate). *Program availability:* Part-time, evening/weekend. *Faculty:* 19 full-time (5 women), 5 part-time/adjunct (1 woman). *Students:* 149 full-time (25 women), 23 part-time (4 women); includes 8 minority (1 Black or African American, non-Hispanic/Latino; 6 Asian, non-Hispanic/Latino; 1 Hispanic/Latino), 143 international. Average age 25. In 2018, 68 master's, 1 doctorate, 29 other advanced degrees awarded. Terminal master's awarded for partial completion of doctoral program. *Degree requirements:* For master's, thesis optional, minimum B average in major field and overall; for doctorate, comprehensive exam (for some programs), thesis/dissertation; for Certificate, minimum B average. *Entrance requirements:* For master's, GRE/GMAT scores: GRE scores are required for all applicants applying to a full-time graduate program in the Schaefer School of Engineering and Science (SES). International applicants must submit TOEFL/IELTS scores and fulfill the English Language Proficiency Requirements in order to be considered. Additional exam requirements/recommendations for international students: Required—TOEFL (minimum score 74 iBT), IELTS (minimum score 6). *Application deadline:* For fall admission, 4/15 for domestic and international students; for spring admission, 11/1 for domestic and international students; for summer admission, 5/1 for domestic students. Applications are processed on a rolling basis. Application fee: $60. Electronic applications accepted. *Expenses: Tuition:* Full-time $35,960; part-time $1620 per credit. *Required fees:* $1290; $600 per semester. Tuition and fees vary according to course load. *Financial support:* Fellowships, research assistantships, teaching assistantships, career-related internships or fieldwork, Federal Work-Study, scholarships/grants, and unspecified assistantships available. Financial award application deadline: 2/15; financial award applicants required to submit FAFSA. *Unit head:* Dr. Jean Zu, Dean of SES, 201-216.8233, Fax: 201-216.8372, E-mail: Jean.Zu@stevens.edu. *Application contact:* Graduate Admissions, 888-783-8367, Fax: 888-511-1306, E-mail: graduate@stevens.edu.

Stevens Institute of Technology, Graduate School, Charles V. Schaefer Jr. School of Engineering and Science, Department of Mechanical Engineering, Program in Integrated Product Development, Hoboken, NJ 07030. Offers armament engineering (M Eng); computer and electrical engineering (M Eng); manufacturing technologies (M Eng); systems reliability and design (M Eng). *Program availability:* Part-time, evening/weekend. *Faculty:* 32 full-time (4 women), 10 part-time/adjunct (0 women). *Degree requirements:* For master's, thesis optional, minimum B average in major field and overall. *Entrance requirements:* For master's, GRE/GMAT scores: GRE scores are required for all applicants applying to a full-time graduate program in the Schaefer School of Engineering and Science (SES). International applicants must submit TOEFL/IELTS scores and fulfill the English Language Proficiency Requirements in order to be considered. Additional exam requirements/recommendations for international students: Required—TOEFL (minimum score 74 iBT), IELTS (minimum score 6). *Application deadline:* For fall admission, 4/15 for domestic and international students; for spring admission, 11/1 for domestic and international students; for summer admission, 5/1 for domestic students. Applications are processed on a rolling basis. Application fee: $60. Electronic applications accepted. *Expenses: Tuition:* Full-time $35,960; part-time $1620 per credit. *Required fees:* $1290; $600 per semester. Tuition and fees vary according to course load. *Financial support:* Fellowships, research assistantships, teaching assistantships, career-related internships or fieldwork, Federal Work-Study, scholarships/grants, and unspecified assistantships available. Financial award application deadline: 2/15; financial award applicants required to submit FAFSA. *Unit head:* Dr. Jean Zu, Dean of SES, 201-216.8233, Fax: 201-216.8372, E-mail: Jean.Zu@stevens.edu. *Application contact:* Graduate Admissions, 888-783-8367, Fax: 888-511-1306, E-mail: graduate@stevens.edu.

Stony Brook University, State University of New York, Graduate School, College of Engineering and Applied Sciences, Department of Electrical and Computer Engineering, Program in Electrical Engineering, Stony Brook, NY 11794. Offers MS, PhD. *Faculty:* 28 full-time (6 women), 5 part-time/adjunct (1 woman). *Students:* 109 full-time (23 women), 38 part-time (8 women); includes 18 minority (4 Black or African American, non-Hispanic/Latino; 9 Asian, non-Hispanic/Latino; 2 Hispanic/Latino; 3 Two or more races, non-Hispanic/Latino), 105 international. 240 applicants, 81% accepted, 44 enrolled. In 2018, 24 master's, 6 doctorates awarded. *Entrance requirements:* For doctorate, GRE, two official transcripts, letters of recommendation. Additional exam requirements/recommendations for international students: Required—TOEFL (minimum score 90 iBT). *Application deadline:* For fall admission, 1/15 for domestic students; for spring admission, 10/1 for domestic students. Application fee: $100. *Expenses:* Contact institution. *Financial support:* In 2018–19, 1 fellowship was awarded; research assistantships and teaching assistantships also available. *Total annual research expenditures:* $3.6 million. *Unit head:* Prof. Petar M. Djuric, Chair, 631-632-8420, Fax: 631-632-8494, E-mail: petar.djuric@stonybrook.edu. *Application contact:* Susan Hayden, Coordinator, 631-632-8400, Fax: 631-632-8494, E-mail: susan.hayden@stonybrook.edu.

Syracuse University, College of Engineering and Computer Science, MS Program in Electrical Engineering, Syracuse, NY 13244. Offers MS. *Program availability:* Part-time. *Students:* Average age 24. In 2018, 48 master's awarded. *Entrance requirements:* For master's, GRE General Test, three letters of recommendation, personal statement, resume, official transcripts. Additional exam requirements/recommendations for international students: Required—TOEFL (minimum score 100 iBT). *Application deadline:* For fall admission, 7/1 priority date for domestic students, 6/1 priority date for international students; for spring admission, 10/1 priority date for domestic students, 11/1 priority date for international students. Applications are processed on a rolling basis. Application fee: $75. Electronic applications accepted. *Financial support:* Fellowships with full tuition reimbursements, research assistantships, teaching assistantships, scholarships/grants, and tuition waivers (partial) available. Financial award application deadline: 1/1; financial award applicants required to submit FAFSA. *Faculty research:* Methods of engineering analysis, electromagnetic fields, electromechanical devices. *Unit head:* Dr. Qinru Qiu, Program Director, 315-443-2652, E-mail: eecsadmissions@syr.edu. *Application contact:* Kathleen Joyce, Director of Graduate Recruitment, 315-443-2219, E-mail: topgrads@syr.edu.
Website: http://eng-cs.syr.edu/our-departments/electrical-engineering-and-computer-science/graduate/academic-programs/?programID=1561&degree=masters_program

Syracuse University, College of Engineering and Computer Science, PhD Program in Electrical and Computer Engineering, Syracuse, NY 13244. Offers PhD. *Program availability:* Part-time. *Students:* Average age 29. In 2018, 12 doctorates awarded. *Degree requirements:* For doctorate, comprehensive exam, thesis/dissertation. *Entrance requirements:* For doctorate, GRE General Test, three letters of recommendation, personal statement, resume, official transcripts. Additional exam requirements/recommendations for international students: Required—TOEFL (minimum score 100 iBT). *Application deadline:* For fall admission, 2/1 priority date for domestic and international students. Application fee: $75. Electronic applications accepted. *Financial support:* Fellowships with full tuition reimbursements, research assistantships, and teaching assistantships available. Financial award application deadline: 1/1. *Faculty research:* Electrical engineering, computer engineering hardware. *Unit head:* Dr. Qinru Qiu, Professor, Computer Engineering/Program Director, Electrical Engineering and Computer Science, 315-443-1836, E-mail: eecsadmissions@syr.edu. *Application contact:* Kathleen Joyce, Assistant Dean, 315-443-2219, E-mail: bflowers@syr.edu.
Website: http://eng-cs.syr.edu/program/electrical-and-computer-engineering/?degree=doctoral_program

Temple University, College of Engineering, Department of Electrical and Computer Engineering, Philadelphia, PA 19122-6096. Offers electrical and computer engineering (PhD); electrical engineering (MSEE). *Program availability:* Part-time, evening/weekend. Terminal master's awarded for partial completion of doctoral program. *Degree requirements:* For master's, thesis optional; for doctorate, thesis/dissertation, preliminary exam, dissertation proposal and defense. *Entrance requirements:* For master's, GRE General Test, minimum GPA of 3.0; BS in engineering from ABET-accredited or equivalent institution; resume; goals statement; three letters of reference; official transcripts; for doctorate, GRE General Test, minimum GPA of 3.0; MS in engineering from ABET-accredited or equivalent institution (preferred); resume; goals statement; three letters of reference; official transcripts. Additional exam requirements/recommendations for international students: Required—TOEFL (minimum score 550 paper-based; 79 iBT), IELTS (minimum score 6.5), PTE (minimum score 53). Electronic applications accepted. *Expenses:* Contact institution. *Faculty research:* Embedded systems and system-on-a-chip design, intelligent interactive multimedia, intrusion detection, multisensory fusion, speaker identification, speech processing, visualization and fault detection in multicasting networks.

Temple University, College of Engineering, PhD in Engineering Program, Philadelphia, PA 19122-6096. Offers bioengineering (PhD); civil engineering (PhD); electrical engineering (PhD); environmental engineering (PhD); mechanical engineering (PhD). *Program availability:* Part-time, evening/weekend. *Degree requirements:* For doctorate, thesis/dissertation, preliminary exam, dissertation proposal and defense. *Entrance requirements:* For doctorate, GRE, minimum undergraduate GPA of 3.0; MS in engineering from ABET-accredited or equivalent institution (preferred); resume; goals statement; three letters of reference; official transcripts. Additional exam requirements/recommendations for international students: Required—TOEFL (minimum score 550 paper-based; 79 iBT), IELTS (minimum score 6.5), PTE (minimum score 53). Electronic applications accepted. *Expenses:* Contact institution. *Faculty research:* Advanced/computer-aided manufacturing and advanced materials processing; bioengineering; computer engineering; construction engineering and management; dynamics, controls, and systems; energy and environmental science; engineering physics and engineering mathematics; green engineering; signal processing and communication; transportation engineering; water resources, hydrology, and environmental engineering.

See Display on page 59 and Close-Up on page 73.

Tennessee State University, The School of Graduate Studies and Research, College of Engineering, Nashville, TN 37209-1561. Offers biomedical engineering (ME); civil engineering (ME); computer and information systems engineering (MS, PhD); electrical engineering (ME); environmental engineering (ME); manufacturing engineering (ME); mathematical sciences (MS); mechanical engineering (ME). *Program availability:* Part-time, evening/weekend. *Degree requirements:* For master's, project; for doctorate, comprehensive exam, thesis/dissertation. *Entrance requirements:* For doctorate, minimum GPA of 3.3. *Faculty research:* Robotics, intelligent systems, human-computer interaction software systems, biomedical engineering, signal/image processing, probabilistic design, intelligent manufacturing, cooperative mobile robots, condition based maintenance, sensor fusion.

Tennessee Technological University, College of Graduate Studies, College of Engineering, Department of Electrical and Computer Engineering, Cookeville, TN 38505. Offers MS. *Program availability:* Part-time. *Faculty:* 19 full-time (0 women). *Students:* 3 full-time (1 woman), 8 part-time (1 woman), 6 international. 45 applicants, 58% accepted, 3 enrolled. In 2018, 7 master's awarded. *Degree requirements:* For master's, thesis. *Entrance requirements:* For master's, GRE. Additional exam requirements/recommendations for international students: Required—TOEFL (minimum score 550 paper-based; 79 iBT), IELTS (minimum score 5.5), PTE (minimum score 53), or TOEIC (Test of English as an International Communication). *Application deadline:* For fall admission, 8/1 for domestic students, 5/1 for international students; for spring admission, 12/1 for domestic students, 10/1 for international students; for summer admission, 5/1 for domestic students, 2/1 for international students. Applications are processed on a rolling basis. Application fee: $35 ($40 for international students). Electronic applications accepted. *Financial support:* Fellowships, research assistantships, teaching assistantships, and career-related internships or fieldwork available. Financial award application deadline: 4/1. *Faculty research:* Control, digital, and power systems. *Unit head:* Dr. Satish Mahajan, Chairperson, 931-372-3397, Fax: 931-372-3436, E-mail: smahajan@tntech.edu. *Application contact:* Shelia K. Kendrick, Coordinator of Graduate Studies, 931-372-3808, Fax: 931-372-3497, E-mail: skendrick@tntech.edu.

Texas A&M University, College of Engineering, Department of Electrical and Computer Engineering, College Station, TX 77843. Offers computer engineering (M Eng, PhD); electrical engineering (M Eng). *Faculty:* 75. *Students:* 606 full-time (124 women), 138 part-time (34 women); includes 33 minority (2 Black or African American, non-Hispanic/Latino; 18 Asian, non-Hispanic/Latino; 10 Hispanic/Latino; 3 Two or more races, non-Hispanic/Latino), 671 international. Average age 27. 1,676 applicants, 33% accepted, 207 enrolled. In 2018, 159 master's, 59 doctorates awarded. *Degree requirements:* For master's, thesis (MS); for doctorate, thesis/dissertation. *Entrance requirements:* For master's and doctorate, GRE General Test. Additional exam requirements/recommendations for international students: Required—TOEFL (minimum score 550 paper-based; 80 iBT), IELTS (minimum score 6), PTE (minimum score 53). *Application deadline:* For fall admission, 1/1 for domestic students, 2/1 for international students; for spring admission, 10/1 for domestic students, 8/1 for international students. Application fee: $50 ($90 for international students). *Expenses:* Contact institution. *Financial support:* In 2018–19, 471 students received support, including 28 fellowships with tuition reimbursements available (averaging $14,729 per year), 204 research assistantships with tuition reimbursements available (averaging $15,220 per year), 109 teaching assistantships with tuition reimbursements available (averaging $13,216 per year); career-related internships or fieldwork, institutionally sponsored loans, scholarships/grants, traineeships, health care benefits, tuition waivers (full and partial), and unspecified assistantships also available. Support available to part-time students. Financial award application deadline: 3/15; financial award applicants required to submit FAFSA. *Faculty research:* Solid-state, electric power systems, and communications engineering. *Unit head:* Dr. Miroslav M. Begovic, Department Head, 979-862-1553, E-mail: begovic@ece.tamu.edu. *Application contact:* Tammy Carda, Senior Academic Advisor II, 979-845-7467, E-mail: t-carda@tamu.edu.
Website: http://engineering.tamu.edu/electrical/

Texas A&M University–Kingsville, College of Graduate Studies, Frank H. Dotterweich College of Engineering, Department of Electrical Engineering and Computer Science, Program in Electrical Engineering, Kingsville, TX 78363. Offers ME, MS. *Degree requirements:* For master's, variable foreign language requirement, comprehensive exam, thesis (for some programs). *Entrance requirements:* For master's, GRE (minimum score of 145 quantitative revised score, 800 quantitative and verbal old score), MAT, GMAT. Additional exam requirements/recommendations for international students: Required—TOEFL (minimum score 550 paper-based; 79 iBT). Electronic applications accepted.

Texas State University, The Graduate College, College of Science and Engineering, Program in Engineering, San Marcos, TX 78666. Offers civil engineering (MS); electrical engineering (MS); industrial engineering (MS); mechanical and manufacturing engineering (MS). *Program availability:* Part-time. *Faculty:* 15 full-time (2 women). *Students:* 46 full-time (14 women), 41 part-time (13 women); includes 11 minority (3 Asian, non-Hispanic/Latino; 7 Hispanic/Latino; 1 Two or more races, non-Hispanic/Latino), 67 international. Average age 27. 105 applicants, 64% accepted, 31 enrolled. In 2018, 13 master's awarded. *Degree requirements:* For master's, comprehensive exam,

thesis (for some programs), thesis or research project. *Entrance requirements:* For master's, official GRE (general test only) required with competitive scores in the verbal reasoning and quantitative reasoning sections, baccalaureate degree from regionally-accredited university in engineering, computer science, physics, technology, or closely-related field with minimum GPA of 3.0 on last 60 undergraduate semester hours; resume or curriculum vitae; 2 letters of recommendation; statement of purpose conveying research interest and professional aspirations. Additional exam requirements/recommendations for international students: Required—TOEFL (minimum score 550 paper-based; 78 iBT), IELTS (minimum score 6.5). *Application deadline:* For fall admission, 2/15 priority date for domestic students, 2/1 priority date for international students. Application fee: $55 ($90 for international students). Electronic applications accepted. *Expenses:* Tuition, state resident: full-time $8102; part-time $4051 per semester. Tuition, nonresident: full-time $18,229; part-time $9115 per semester. *International tuition:* $18,229 full-time. *Required fees:* $2116; $120 per credit hour. Tuition and fees vary according to course load. *Financial support:* In 2018–19, 52 students received support, including 14 research assistantships (averaging $12,742 per year), 34 teaching assistantships (averaging $12,483 per year); Federal Work-Study, institutionally sponsored loans, scholarships/grants, health care benefits, and unspecified assistantships also available. Support available to part-time students. Financial award application deadline: 1/15; financial award applicants required to submit FAFSA. *Faculty research:* Computer Architecture & Digital Image Processing; Industrial robotics on a mobile platform; supply chain management optimization modeling and algorithms; Modeling and analysis of manufacturing systems especially semiconductor manufacturing; smart grids for big data analytics and demand response; Digital Signal/Image/Speach Processing & Data Compression; Health care systems engineering and anaylsis of patient flow. *Total annual research expenditures:* $920,229. *Unit head:* Dr. Vishu Viswanathan, Graduate Advisor, 512-245-1826, Fax: 512-245-8365, E-mail: v_v42@txstate.edu. *Application contact:* Dr. Andrea Golato, Dean of Graduate School, 512-245-2581, Fax: 512-245-8365, E-mail: gradcollege@txstate.edu.
Website: http://www.engineering.txstate.edu/Programs/Graduate.html

Tufts University, Graduate School of Arts and Sciences, Graduate Certificate Programs, Microwave and Wireless Engineering Program, Medford, MA 02155. Offers Certificate. *Program availability:* Part-time, evening/weekend. Electronic applications accepted. *Expenses: Tuition:* Full-time $51,288; part-time $1710 per credit hour. *Required fees:* $904. Full-time tuition and fees vary according to degree level, program and student level. Part-time tuition and fees vary according to course load.

Tufts University, School of Engineering, Department of Electrical and Computer Engineering, Medford, MA 02155. Offers bioengineering (MS), including signals and systems; electrical engineering (MS, PhD); PhD/PhD. *Program availability:* Part-time. Terminal master's awarded for partial completion of doctoral program. *Degree requirements:* For master's, thesis or alternative; for doctorate, thesis/dissertation. *Entrance requirements:* For master's and doctorate, GRE General Test. Additional exam requirements/recommendations for international students: Required—TOEFL (minimum score 550 paper-based; 80 iBT), IELTS (minimum score 6.5). Electronic applications accepted. *Expenses: Tuition:* Full-time $51,288; part-time $1710 per credit hour. *Required fees:* $904. Full-time tuition and fees vary according to degree level, program and student level. Part-time tuition and fees vary according to course load. *Faculty research:* Communication theory, networks, protocol, and transmission technology; simulation and modeling; digital processing technology; image and signal processing for security and medical applications; integrated circuits and VLSI.

Tuskegee University, Graduate Programs, College of Engineering, Department of Electrical Engineering, Tuskegee, AL 36088. Offers MSEE. *Degree requirements:* For master's, thesis or alternative. *Entrance requirements:* For master's, GRE General Test, GRE Subject Test. Additional exam requirements/recommendations for international students: Required—TOEFL (minimum score 500 paper-based). *Faculty research:* Photovoltaic insulation, automatic guidance and control, wind energy.

Universidad de las Américas Puebla, Division of Graduate Studies, School of Engineering, Program in Electronic Engineering, Puebla, Mexico. Offers MS. *Program availability:* Part-time, evening/weekend. *Faculty research:* Telecommunications, data processing, digital systems.

Universidad del Turabo, Graduate Programs, School of Engineering, Gurabo, PR 00778-3030. Offers computer engineering (M Eng); electrical engineering (M Eng); mechanical engineering (M Eng); telecommunications and network systems administration (M Eng). *Entrance requirements:* For master's, GRE, EXADEP or GMAT, interview, essay, official transcript, recommendation letters. Electronic applications accepted.

Université de Moncton, Faculty of Engineering, Program in Electrical Engineering, Moncton, NB E1A 3E9, Canada. Offers M Sc A. *Degree requirements:* For master's, thesis, proficiency in French. *Faculty research:* Telecommunications, electronics and instrumentation, analog and digital electronics, electronic control of machines, energy systems, electronic design.

Université de Sherbrooke, Faculty of Engineering, Department of Electrical Engineering and Computer Engineering, Sherbrooke, QC J1K 2R1, Canada. Offers electrical engineering (M Sc A, PhD). *Degree requirements:* For master's, one foreign language, thesis; for doctorate, comprehensive exam, thesis/dissertation. *Entrance requirements:* For master's, bachelor's degree in engineering or equivalent. Electronic applications accepted. *Faculty research:* Minielectronics, biomedical engineering, digital signal prolonging and telecommunications, software engineering and artificial intelligence.

Université du Québec à Trois-Rivières, Graduate Programs, Program in Electrical Engineering, Trois-Rivières, QC G9A 5H7, Canada. Offers M Sc A, PhD. *Program availability:* Part-time. *Degree requirements:* For master's, thesis; for doctorate, thesis/dissertation. *Entrance requirements:* For master's, appropriate bachelor's degree, proficiency in French; for doctorate, appropriate master's degree, proficiency in French. *Faculty research:* Industrial electronics.

Université Laval, Faculty of Sciences and Engineering, Department of Electrical and Computer Engineering, Programs in Electrical Engineering, Québec, QC G1K 7P4, Canada. Offers M Sc, PhD. Terminal master's awarded for partial completion of doctoral program. *Degree requirements:* For master's, thesis (for some programs); for doctorate, thesis/dissertation. *Entrance requirements:* For master's and doctorate, knowledge of French and English. Electronic applications accepted.

University at Buffalo, the State University of New York, Graduate School, School of Engineering and Applied Sciences, Department of Electrical Engineering, Buffalo, NY 14260. Offers ME, MS, PhD. *Program availability:* Part-time. Terminal master's awarded for partial completion of doctoral program. *Degree requirements:* For master's, comprehensive exam (for some programs), thesis or exam; for doctorate, comprehensive exam, thesis/dissertation. *Entrance requirements:* For master's and doctorate, GRE General Test. Additional exam requirements/recommendations for international students: Required—TOEFL (minimum score 550 paper-based; 79 iBT). Electronic applications accepted. *Faculty research:* Signals, communications and networking; optics and photonics; energy systems; solid state electronics.

The University of Akron, Graduate School, College of Engineering, Department of Electrical and Computer Engineering, Akron, OH 44325. Offers computer engineering (MS, PhD); electrical engineering (MS). *Program availability:* Evening/weekend. *Degree requirements:* For master's, oral comprehensive exam or thesis; for doctorate, one foreign language, thesis/dissertation, candidacy exam, qualifying exam. *Entrance requirements:* For master's, GRE, minimum GPA of 2.75, three letters of recommendation, statement of purpose; for doctorate, GRE, minimum GPA of 3.0 with bachelor's degree, 3.5 with master's degree; three letters of recommendation; statement of purpose; resume. Additional exam requirements/recommendations for international students: Required—TOEFL (minimum score 79 iBT), IELTS (minimum score 6.5). Electronic applications accepted. *Faculty research:* Computational electromagnetics and nondestructive testing, control systems, sensors and actuators applications and networks, alternative energy systems and hybrid vehicles, analog integrated circuit (IC) design, embedded systems.

The University of Alabama, Graduate School, College of Engineering, Department of Electrical and Computer Engineering, Tuscaloosa, AL 35487-0286. Offers electrical engineering (MS, PhD). *Program availability:* Part-time, online learning. *Degree requirements:* For master's, thesis or alternative; for doctorate, one foreign language, comprehensive exam, thesis/dissertation. *Entrance requirements:* For master's, GRE (for students from non ABET-accredited schools), minimum GPA of 3.0 in last 60 hours of course work or overall; for doctorate, GRE (for students from non ABET-accredited schools), minimum GPA of 3.0 overall. Additional exam requirements/recommendations for international students: Required—TOEFL (minimum score 550 paper-based). Electronic applications accepted. *Faculty research:* Devices and materials, electromechanical systems, embedded systems.

The University of Alabama at Birmingham, School of Engineering, Program in Electrical Engineering, Birmingham, AL 35294. Offers computer engineering (PhD); electrical and computer engineering (MSEE). *Program availability:* Part-time. *Faculty:* 8 full-time (0 women), 3 part-time/adjunct (0 women). *Students:* 39 full-time (7 women), 27 part-time (3 women); includes 10 minority (3 Black or African American, non-Hispanic/Latino; 3 Asian, non-Hispanic/Latino; 3 Hispanic/Latino; 1 Two or more races, non-Hispanic/Latino), 42 international. Average age 29. 66 applicants, 67% accepted, 18 enrolled. In 2018, 12 master's, 4 doctorates awarded. *Degree requirements:* For master's, comprehensive exam, thesis (for some programs); for doctorate, comprehensive exam, thesis/dissertation. *Entrance requirements:* For master's, GRE, A 3.0 on a 4.0 scale or better GPA in all junior and senior electrical and computer engineering and mathematics courses attempted;; for doctorate, GRE, An overall GPA of at least 3.0 on a 4.0 point scale, or at least 3.0 for the last 60 semester hours completed; and. Additional exam requirements/recommendations for international students: Required—TOEFL (minimum score 80 iBT), IELTS (minimum score 6.5). *Application deadline:* For fall admission, 8/1 for domestic and international students; for spring admission, 12/1 for domestic and international students; for summer admission, 5/1 for domestic and international students. Applications are processed on a rolling basis. Application fee: $50 ($60 for international students). Electronic applications accepted. *Expenses:* Contact institution. *Financial support:* In 2018–19, 22 students received support, including 4 fellowships with full tuition reimbursements available (averaging $30,500 per year), 9 research assistantships with full and partial tuition reimbursements available, 9 teaching assistantships; unspecified assistantships also available. *Faculty research:* Low-power analog and RF circuit design for sensors and biomedical instrumentation, mathematical foundations of quantum electronics, intelligent control of respiratory therapy, mobile and cloud computing, information theoretical foundations for software. *Total annual research expenditures:* $23,644. *Unit head:* Dr. J Iwan Alexander, Interim Chair, 205-934-8440, E-mail: ialex@uab.edu. *Application contact:* Jesse Keppley, Director of Student and Academic Services, 205-996-5696, E-mail: gradschool@uab.edu.
Website: https://www.uab.edu/engineering/home/graduate#msee

The University of Alabama in Huntsville, School of Graduate Studies, College of Engineering, Department of Electrical and Computer Engineering, Huntsville, AL 35899. Offers computer engineering (MSE, PhD); electrical engineering (MSE, PhD), including optics and photonics technology (MSE); optical science and engineering (PhD); software engineering (MSSE). *Program availability:* Part-time. *Faculty:* 22 full-time (4 women), 4 part-time/adjunct. *Students:* 65 full-time (12 women), 125 part-time (12 women); includes 12 minority (5 Black or African American, non-Hispanic/Latino; 5 Asian, non-Hispanic/Latino; 2 Hispanic/Latino), 61 international. Average age 31. 199 applicants, 78% accepted, 46 enrolled. In 2018, 42 master's, 11 doctorates awarded. *Degree requirements:* For master's, comprehensive exam, thesis or alternative, oral and written exams; for doctorate, comprehensive exam, thesis/dissertation, oral and written exams. *Entrance requirements:* For master's, GRE General Test, appropriate bachelor's degree, minimum GPA of 3.0; for doctorate, GRE General Test, minimum GPA of 3.0. Additional exam requirements/recommendations for international students: Required—TOEFL (minimum score 500 paper-based; 80 iBT), IELTS (minimum score 6.5). *Application deadline:* For fall admission, 7/15 priority date for domestic students, 4/1 priority date for international students; for spring admission, 11/30 priority date for domestic students, 9/1 priority date for international students. Applications are processed on a rolling basis. Application fee: $50. Electronic applications accepted. *Expenses: Tuition, area resident:* Full-time $10,632; part-time $412 per credit hour. Tuition, state resident: full-time $10,632. Tuition, nonresident: full-time $23,604; part-time $412 per credit hour. *Required fees:* $582; $582. Tuition and fees vary according to course load and program. *Financial support:* In 2018–19, 37 students received support, including 18 research assistantships with full tuition reimbursements available (averaging $5,783 per year), 19 teaching assistantships with full tuition reimbursements available (averaging $5,813 per year); career-related internships or fieldwork, Federal Work-Study, institutionally sponsored loans, scholarships/grants, health care benefits, tuition waivers (full and partial), and unspecified assistantships also available. Support available to part-time students. Financial award application deadline: 4/1; financial award applicants required to submit FAFSA. *Faculty research:* Advanced computer architecture and systems, fault tolerant computing and verification, computational electro-magnetics, nano-photonics and plasmonics, micro electro-mechanical (MEMS) systems. *Unit head:* Dr. Ravi Gorur, Chair, 256-824-6316, Fax: 256-824-6803, E-mail: ravi.gorur@uah.edu. *Application contact:* Kim Gray, Graduate Studies Admissions Coordinator, 256-824-6002, Fax: 256-824-6405, E-mail: deangrad@uah.edu.
Website: http://www.ece.uah.edu/

University of Alaska Fairbanks, College of Engineering and Mines, Department of Electrical and Computer Engineering, Fairbanks, AK 99775-5915. Offers electrical engineering (MEE, MS). *Program availability:* Part-time. *Faculty:* 8 full-time (1 woman). *Students:* 9 full-time (1 woman), 5 part-time (1 woman); includes 1 minority (Hispanic/Latino), 5 international. Average age 28. 8 applicants, 50% accepted, 2 enrolled. In 2018, 6 master's awarded. *Degree requirements:* For master's, comprehensive exam. *Entrance requirements:* For master's, GRE General Test, bachelor's degree from accredited institution with minimum cumulative undergraduate and major GPA of 3.0. Additional exam requirements/recommendations for international students: Required—TOEFL (minimum score 550 paper-based; 79 iBT), IELTS (minimum score 6.5). *Application deadline:* For fall admission, 6/1 for domestic students, 3/1 for international students; for spring admission, 10/15 for domestic students, 9/1 for international

students. Applications are processed on a rolling basis. Application fee: $60. Electronic applications accepted. *Expenses:* College of Engineering and Mines (CEM) tuition has a 20% surcharge per credit hour over that for credits of most other UAF colleges. Assuming 60 credits for PhD and 32 for Master's, this augments costs by $6,180 for in-state PhD, $3,296 for in-state Master's, $12,948 for non-resident PhD and $6,912 for non-resident Master's students, respectively. *Financial support:* In 2018–19, 1 research assistantship with full tuition reimbursement (averaging $9,404 per year), 8 teaching assistantships with full tuition reimbursements (averaging $7,629 per year) were awarded; fellowships with full tuition reimbursements, career-related internships or fieldwork, Federal Work-Study, scholarships/grants, health care benefits, and unspecified assistantships also available. Support available to part-time students. Financial award application deadline: 7/1; financial award applicants required to submit FAFSA. *Faculty research:* Geomagnetically-induced currents in power lines, electromagnetic wave propagation, laser radar systems, bioinformatics, distributed sensor networks. *Unit head:* Dr. Richard Wies, Chair, 907-474-7071, E-mail: uaf-cem-ece-dept@alaska.edu. *Application contact:* Samara Taber, Director of Admissions, 907-474-7500, E-mail: uaf-admissions@alaska.edu.
Website: http://cem.uaf.edu/ece/

University of Alberta, Faculty of Graduate Studies and Research, Department of Electrical and Computer Engineering, Edmonton, AB T6G 2E1, Canada. Offers communications (M Eng, M Sc, PhD); computer engineering (M Eng, M Sc, PhD); electromagnetics (M Eng, M Sc, PhD); nanotechnology and microdevices (M Eng, M Sc, PhD); power/power electronics (M Eng, M Sc, PhD); systems (M Eng, M Sc, PhD). Terminal master's awarded for partial completion of doctoral program. *Degree requirements:* For master's, thesis; for doctorate, thesis/dissertation. *Entrance requirements:* Additional exam requirements/recommendations for international students: Required—TOEFL. Electronic applications accepted. *Faculty research:* Controls, communications, microelectronics, electromagnetics.

The University of Arizona, College of Engineering, Department of Electrical and Computer Engineering, Tucson, AZ 85721. Offers MS, PhD. *Program availability:* Part-time. *Degree requirements:* For master's, thesis (for some programs); for doctorate, thesis/dissertation. *Entrance requirements:* For master's, GRE General Test, 3 letters of recommendation, statement of purpose; for doctorate, GRE General Test, master's degree in related field, 3 letters of recommendation, statement of purpose. Additional exam requirements/recommendations for international students: Required—TOEFL (minimum score 550 paper-based; 79 iBT). Electronic applications accepted. *Faculty research:* Communication systems, control systems, signal processing, computer-aided logic.

University of Arkansas, Graduate School, College of Engineering, Department of Electrical Engineering, Fayetteville, AR 72701. Offers electrical engineering (MSEE, PhD); telecommunications engineering (MS Tc E). In 2018, 24 master's, 3 doctorates awarded. *Degree requirements:* For master's, thesis optional; for doctorate, one foreign language, thesis/dissertation. *Entrance requirements:* For master's and doctorate, GRE General Test. *Application deadline:* For fall admission, 8/1 for domestic students, 4/1 for international students; for spring admission, 12/1 for domestic students, 10/1 for international students; for summer admission, 4/15 for domestic students, 3/1 for international students. Applications are processed on a rolling basis. Application fee: $60. Electronic applications accepted. *Financial support:* In 2018–19, 48 research assistantships, 8 teaching assistantships were awarded; fellowships with tuition reimbursements, career-related internships or fieldwork, and Federal Work-Study also available. Support available to part-time students. Financial award application deadline: 4/1; financial award applicants required to submit FAFSA. *Unit head:* Dr. Juan Carlos Balda, Department Head, 479-575-3005, Fax: 479-575-7967, E-mail: jbalda@uark.edu. *Application contact:* Dr. Hameed Naseem, Graduate Coordinator, 479-575-6052, Fax: 479-575-7967, E-mail: hnaseem@uark.edu.
Website: https://electrical-engineering.uark.edu/index.php

University of Bridgeport, School of Engineering, Department of Electrical Engineering, Bridgeport, CT 06604. Offers MS. *Program availability:* Part-time, evening/weekend. Terminal master's awarded for partial completion of doctoral program. *Degree requirements:* For master's, thesis optional. *Entrance requirements:* Additional exam requirements/recommendations for international students: Recommended—TOEFL (minimum score 550 paper-based; 80 iBT), IELTS (minimum score 6.5). Electronic applications accepted. *Expenses:* Contact institution.

The University of British Columbia, Faculty of Applied Science, Department of Electrical and Computer Engineering, Vancouver, BC V6T 1Z4, Canada. Offers M Eng, MA Sc, PhD. *Program availability:* Part-time. *Degree requirements:* For master's, thesis (for some programs); for doctorate, thesis/dissertation. *Entrance requirements:* Additional exam requirements/recommendations for international students: Required—TOEFL, IELTS. Electronic applications accepted. *Expenses:* Contact institution. *Faculty research:* Applied electromagnetics, biomedical engineering, communications and signal processing, computer and software engineering, power engineering, robotics, solid-state, systems and control.

University of Calgary, Faculty of Graduate Studies, Schulich School of Engineering, Program in Electrical and Computer Engineering, Calgary, AB T2N 1N4, Canada. Offers M Eng, M Sc, PhD. *Program availability:* Part-time. *Degree requirements:* For master's, thesis (for M Sc); for doctorate, thesis/dissertation, candidacy exam. *Entrance requirements:* For master's, minimum GPA of 3.0; for doctorate, minimum GPA of 3.5. Additional exam requirements/recommendations for international students: Required—TOEFL (minimum score 550 paper-based; 80 iBT) or IELTS (minimum score 7). Electronic applications accepted. *Faculty research:* Biomedical and bioelectrics, telecommunications and signal processing, software and computer engineering, power and control, microelectronics and instrumentation.

University of California, Berkeley, Graduate Division, College of Engineering, Department of Electrical Engineering and Computer Sciences, Berkeley, CA 94720. Offers computer science (MS, PhD); electrical engineering (M Eng, MS, PhD). Terminal master's awarded for partial completion of doctoral program. *Degree requirements:* For master's, comprehensive exam (for some programs), thesis (for some programs), comprehensive exam or thesis; for doctorate, thesis/dissertation, qualifying exam. *Entrance requirements:* For master's and doctorate, GRE General Test, minimum GPA of 3.0, 3 letters of recommendation. Additional exam requirements/recommendations for international students: Required—TOEFL (minimum score 570 paper-based; 90 iBT). Electronic applications accepted.

University of California, Davis, College of Engineering, Program in Electrical and Computer Engineering, Davis, CA 95616. Offers MS, PhD. Terminal master's awarded for partial completion of doctoral program. *Degree requirements:* For master's, comprehensive exam (for some programs), thesis (for some programs); for doctorate, thesis/dissertation, preliminary and qualifying exams, thesis defense. *Entrance requirements:* For master's, GRE General Test, minimum GPA of 3.2; for doctorate, GRE, minimum graduate GPA of 3.5. Additional exam requirements/recommendations for international students: Required—TOEFL (minimum score 550 paper-based). Electronic applications accepted.

University of California, Irvine, Samueli School of Engineering, Department of Electrical Engineering and Computer Science, Irvine, CA 92697. Offers electrical engineering and computer science (MS, PhD); networked systems (MS, PhD). *Program availability:* Part-time. *Students:* 292 full-time (77 women), 20 part-time (1 woman); includes 28 minority (2 Black or African American, non-Hispanic/Latino; 21 Asian, non-Hispanic/Latino; 2 Hispanic/Latino; 3 Two or more races, non-Hispanic/Latino), 253 international. Average age 26. 1,595 applicants, 21% accepted, 99 enrolled. In 2018, 88 master's, 26 doctorates awarded. Terminal master's awarded for partial completion of doctoral program. *Entrance requirements:* For master's and doctorate, GRE General Test, minimum GPA of 3.0, 3 letters of recommendation. Additional exam requirements/recommendations for international students: Required—TOEFL (minimum score 550 paper-based). *Application deadline:* For fall admission, 1/15 priority date for domestic students, 1/15 for international students. Applications are processed on a rolling basis. Application fee: $105 ($125 for international students). Electronic applications accepted. *Financial support:* Fellowships, research assistantships with full tuition reimbursements, teaching assistantships, institutionally sponsored loans, traineeships, health care benefits, and unspecified assistantships available. Financial award application deadline: 3/1; financial award applicants required to submit FAFSA. *Faculty research:* Optics and electronic devices and circuits, signal processing, communications, machine vision, power electronics. *Unit head:* Prof. H. Kumar Wickramasinghe, Chair, 949-824-2213, E-mail: hkwick@uci.edu. *Application contact:* Jean Bennett, Director of Graduate Student Affairs, 949-824-6475, Fax: 949-824-8200, E-mail: jean.bennett@uci.edu.
Website: http://www.eng.uci.edu/dept/eecs

University of California, Los Angeles, Graduate Division, Henry Samueli School of Engineering and Applied Science, Department of Electrical and Computer Engineering, Los Angeles, CA 90095-1594. Offers MS, PhD. *Degree requirements:* For master's, comprehensive exam or thesis; for doctorate, thesis/dissertation, qualifying exams. *Entrance requirements:* For master's, GRE General Test, minimum GPA of 3.0; for doctorate, GRE General Test, minimum GPA of 3.25. Additional exam requirements/recommendations for international students: Required—TOEFL (minimum score 560 paper-based; 87 iBT), IELTS (minimum score 7). Electronic applications accepted. *Faculty research:* Circuits and embedded systems, physical and wave electronics, signals and systems.

University of California, Merced, Graduate Division, School of Engineering, Merced, CA 95343. Offers biological engineering and small scale technologies (MS, PhD); electrical engineering and computer science (MS, PhD); environmental systems (MS, PhD); management of innovation, sustainability, and technology (MM); mechanical engineering (MS); mechanical engineering and applied mechanics (PhD). *Faculty:* 60 full-time (16 women). *Students:* 219 full-time (72 women), 1 part-time (0 women); includes 43 minority (2 Black or African American, non-Hispanic/Latino; 17 Asian, non-Hispanic/Latino; 20 Hispanic/Latino; 1 Native Hawaiian or other Pacific Islander, non-Hispanic/Latino; 3 Two or more races, non-Hispanic/Latino), 145 international. Average age 28. 371 applicants, 46% accepted, 75 enrolled. In 2018, 30 master's, 17 doctorates awarded. Terminal master's awarded for partial completion of doctoral program. *Degree requirements:* For master's, variable foreign language requirement, comprehensive exam, thesis or alternative, oral defense; for doctorate, variable foreign language requirement, comprehensive exam, thesis/dissertation, oral defense. *Entrance requirements:* For master's and doctorate, GRE. Additional exam requirements/recommendations for international students: Required—TOEFL (minimum score 550 paper-based; 80 iBT); Recommended—IELTS (minimum score 6.5). *Application deadline:* For fall admission, 1/15 priority date for domestic and international students. Application fee: $105 ($125 for international students). Electronic applications accepted. *Expenses:* In-state tuition $11442 per year; Out-of-state tuition $26544 per year; Student Fees $1765 per year. *Financial support:* In 2018–19, 200 students received support, including 14 fellowships with full tuition reimbursements available (averaging $20,851 per year), 70 research assistantships with full tuition reimbursements available (averaging $18,334 per year), 116 teaching assistantships with full tuition reimbursements available (averaging $19,841 per year); scholarships/grants, traineeships, and health care benefits also available. *Faculty research:* Sustainability systems engineering and resource management: food, energy, water; biomolecular engineering and biotechnology; computational science and data analytics; artificial intelligence, machine learning, internet of things, human computer interface; cyber-physical systems and automation. *Total annual research expenditures:* $3.1 million. *Unit head:* Dr. Mark Matsumoto, Dean, 209-228-4047, Fax: 209-228-4047, E-mail: mmatsumoto@ucmerced.edu. *Application contact:* Tsu Ya, Director of Admissions and Academic Services, 209-228-4521, Fax: 209-228-6906, E-mail: tya@ucmerced.edu.

University of California, Riverside, Graduate Division, Department of Electrical Engineering, Riverside, CA 92521-0102. Offers electrical engineering (MS, PhD), including computer engineering (MS), control and robotics (PhD). Terminal master's awarded for partial completion of doctoral program. *Degree requirements:* For master's, thesis optional; for doctorate, thesis/dissertation, qualifying exams. *Entrance requirements:* For master's and doctorate, GRE General Test, minimum GPA of 3.25. Additional exam requirements/recommendations for international students: Required—TOEFL (minimum score 550 paper-based; 80 iBT). Electronic applications accepted. *Faculty research:* Solid state devices, integrated circuits, signal processing.

University of California, San Diego, Graduate Division, Department of Electrical and Computer Engineering, La Jolla, CA 92093. Offers applied ocean science (MS, PhD); applied physics (MS, PhD); communication theory and systems (MS, PhD); computer engineering (MS, PhD); electronic circuits and systems (MS, PhD); intelligent systems, robotics and control (MS, PhD); medical devices and systems (MS, PhD); nanoscale devices and systems (MS, PhD); photonics (MS, PhD); signal and image processing (MS, PhD). Program offered jointly with San Diego State University. *Students:* 830 full-time (174 women), 69 part-time (8 women). 2,810 applicants, 40% accepted, 399 enrolled. In 2018, 226 master's, 42 doctorates awarded. Terminal master's awarded for partial completion of doctoral program. *Degree requirements:* For master's, comprehensive exam (for some programs), thesis (for some programs); for doctorate, comprehensive exam, thesis/dissertation. *Entrance requirements:* For master's and doctorate, GRE General Test, minimum GPA of 3.0, resume or curriculum vitae (recommended). Additional exam requirements/recommendations for international students: Required—TOEFL (minimum score 550 paper-based; 80 iBT), IELTS (minimum score 7), PTE (minimum score 65). *Application deadline:* For fall admission, 12/13 for domestic students. Application fee: $105 ($125 for international students). Electronic applications accepted. *Financial support:* Fellowships, research assistantships, teaching assistantships, scholarships/grants, traineeships, and unspecified assistantships available. Financial award applicants required to submit FAFSA. *Faculty research:* Applied ocean science; applied physics; communication theory and systems; computer engineering; electronic circuits and systems; intelligent systems, robotics and control; medical devices and systems; nanoscale devices and systems; photonics; signal and image processing. *Unit head:* Bill Lin, Chair, 858-822-1383, E-mail: billin@ucsd.edu. *Application contact:* Sean Jones, Graduate Admissions Coordinator, 858-534-3213, E-mail: ecegradapps@ece.ucsd.edu.
Website: http://ece.ucsd.edu/

University of California, Santa Barbara, Graduate Division, College of Engineering, Department of Electrical and Computer Engineering, Santa Barbara, CA 93106-2014. Offers communications, control and signal processing (MS, PhD); computer engineering (MS, PhD); electronics and photonics (MS, PhD); MS/PhD. *Degree requirements:* For master's, comprehensive exam, thesis; for doctorate, thesis/dissertation. *Entrance requirements:* For master's and doctorate, GRE General Test. Additional exam requirements/recommendations for international students: Required—TOEFL (minimum score 550 paper-based; 80 iBT), IELTS (minimum score 7). Electronic applications accepted. *Faculty research:* Communications, signal processing, computer engineering, control, electronics and photonics.

University of California, Santa Cruz, Jack Baskin School of Engineering, Program in Electrical Engineering, Santa Cruz, CA 95064. Offers MS, PhD. Terminal master's awarded for partial completion of doctoral program. *Degree requirements:* For master's, thesis or comprehensive exam; for doctorate, thesis/dissertation, qualifying exam. *Entrance requirements:* For master's and doctorate, GRE General Test. Additional exam requirements/recommendations for international students: Required—TOEFL (minimum score 570 paper-based; 89 iBT); Recommended—IELTS (minimum score 8). Electronic applications accepted. *Faculty research:* Photonics and electronics, signal processing and communications, remote sensing, nanotechnology.

University of Central Florida, College of Engineering and Computer Science, Department of Electrical and Computer Engineering, Program in Electrical Engineering, Orlando, FL 32816. Offers MSEE, PhD. *Program availability:* Part-time, evening/weekend. *Students:* 119 full-time (17 women), 46 part-time (4 women); includes 26 minority (4 Black or African American, non-Hispanic/Latino; 8 Asian, non-Hispanic/Latino; 13 Hispanic/Latino; 1 Two or more races, non-Hispanic/Latino), 99 international. Average age 31. 206 applicants, 68% accepted, 35 enrolled. In 2018, 37 master's, 19 doctorates awarded. *Degree requirements:* For master's, thesis or alternative; for doctorate, thesis/dissertation, departmental qualifying exam, candidacy exam. *Entrance requirements:* For master's, GRE General Test, minimum GPA of 3.0 in last 60 hours, letters of recommendation, resume, goal statement; for doctorate, GRE General Test, minimum GPA of 3.5 in last 60 hours, letters of recommendation, resume, goal statement. Additional exam requirements/recommendations for international students: Required—TOEFL. *Application deadline:* For fall admission, 7/15 for domestic students; for spring admission, 12/1 for domestic students. Application fee: $30. Electronic applications accepted. *Financial support:* In 2018–19, 91 students received support, including 29 fellowships with partial tuition reimbursements available (averaging $9,517 per year), 71 research assistantships with partial tuition reimbursements available (averaging $11,073 per year), 41 teaching assistantships with partial tuition reimbursements available (averaging $12,335 per year); health care benefits and tuition waivers (partial) also available. Financial award application deadline: 3/1; financial award applicants required to submit FAFSA. *Unit head:* Dr. Zhihua Qu, Chair, 407-823-5976, Fax: 407-823-5835, E-mail: qu@ucf.edu. *Application contact:* Assistant Director, Graduate Admissions, 407-823-2766, Fax: 407-823-6442, E-mail: gradadmissions@ucf.edu.
Website: http://web.eecs.ucf.edu/

University of Central Oklahoma, The Jackson College of Graduate Studies, College of Mathematics and Science, Department of Engineering and Physics, Edmond, OK 73034-5209. Offers engineering physics (MS), including biomedical engineering, electrical engineering, mechanical systems, physics. *Program availability:* Part-time. *Degree requirements:* For master's, thesis optional. *Entrance requirements:* For master's, GRE, 24 hours of course work in physics or equivalent, mathematics through differential equations, minimum GPA of 2.75 overall and 3.0 in last 60 hours attempted, two letters of recommendation. Additional exam requirements/recommendations for international students: Required—TOEFL (minimum score 550 paper-based; 79 iBT), IELTS (minimum score 6.5). Electronic applications accepted.

University of Cincinnati, Graduate School, College of Engineering and Applied Science, Department of Electrical Engineering and Computing Systems, Program in Electrical Engineering, Cincinnati, OH 45221. Offers MS, PhD. *Degree requirements:* For master's, thesis; for doctorate, thesis/dissertation. *Entrance requirements:* For master's and doctorate, GRE General Test. Additional exam requirements/recommendations for international students: Required—TOEFL (minimum score 550 paper-based). *Faculty research:* Integrated circuits and optical devices, charge-coupled devices, photosensitive devices.

University of Colorado Boulder, Graduate School, College of Engineering and Applied Science, Department of Electrical, Computer and Energy Engineering, Boulder, CO 80309. Offers ME, MS, PhD. Terminal master's awarded for partial completion of doctoral program. *Degree requirements:* For master's, thesis or alternative; for doctorate, one foreign language, thesis/dissertation, departmental qualifying exam. *Entrance requirements:* For master's, GRE General Test, minimum undergraduate GPA of 3.0; for doctorate, GRE General Test, minimum undergraduate GPA of 3.5. Electronic applications accepted. Application fee is waived when completed online. *Faculty research:* Electrical engineering/electronics; solid state electronics; electromagnetics; circuits and systems; electromagnetic propagation.

University of Colorado Denver, College of Engineering, Design and Computing, Department of Electrical Engineering, Denver, CO 80217. Offers MS, EASPh D. *Program availability:* Part-time, evening/weekend. *Degree requirements:* For master's, thesis or project, 30 credit hours; for doctorate, thesis/dissertation, 60 credit hours beyond master's work (30 of which are for dissertation research). *Entrance requirements:* For master's and doctorate, GRE, three letters of recommendation, personal statement. Additional exam requirements/recommendations for international students: Required—TOEFL (minimum score 550 paper-based; 80 iBT), TOEFL (minimum score 600 paper-based) for EAS PhD; Recommended—IELTS (minimum score 6.8). Electronic applications accepted. *Expenses:* Tuition, state resident: full-time $6786; part-time $337 per credit hour. Tuition, nonresident: full-time $22,590; part-time $1255 per credit hour. *Required fees:* $1231; $137 per credit hour. Tuition and fees vary according to program and reciprocity agreements. *Faculty research:* Communication and signal processing, embedded systems, electromagnetic fields and matter, energy and power systems, photonics and biomedical imaging.

University of Colorado Denver, College of Engineering, Design and Computing, Master of Engineering Program, Denver, CO 80217-3364. Offers civil engineering (M Eng), including civil engineering, geographic information systems, transportation systems; electrical engineering (M Eng); mechanical engineering (M Eng). *Program availability:* Part-time. *Entrance requirements:* For master's, GRE (for those with GPA below 2.75), transcripts, references, statement of purpose. *Expenses:* Tuition, state resident: full-time $6786; part-time $337 per credit hour. Tuition, nonresident: full-time $22,590; part-time $1255 per credit hour. *Required fees:* $1231; $137 per credit hour. Tuition and fees vary according to program and reciprocity agreements.

University of Connecticut, Graduate School, School of Engineering, Department of Electrical and Computer Engineering, Storrs, CT 06269. Offers MS, PhD. Terminal master's awarded for partial completion of doctoral program. *Degree requirements:* For master's, comprehensive exam, thesis or alternative; for doctorate, thesis/dissertation. *Entrance requirements:* For master's and doctorate, GRE General Test. Additional exam

requirements/recommendations for international students: Required—TOEFL (minimum score 550 paper-based). Electronic applications accepted.

University of Dayton, Department of Electrical and Computer Engineering, Dayton, OH 45469. Offers computer engineering (MS); electrical engineering (MSEE, PhD). *Program availability:* Part-time, blended/hybrid learning. *Degree requirements:* For master's, thesis optional; for doctorate, variable foreign language requirement, thesis/dissertation. *Entrance requirements:* For master's, minimum GPA of 3.2, 3 letters of recommendation, bachelor's degree, transcripts; for doctorate, minimum GPA of 3.2, master's degree, transcripts, 3 letters of recommendation. Additional exam requirements/recommendations for international students: Required—TOEFL (minimum score 550 paper-based; 80 iBT). Electronic applications accepted. *Faculty research:* Electrical engineering, video processing, leaky wave antennas, thin film research.

University of Delaware, College of Engineering, Department of Electrical and Computer Engineering, Newark, DE 19716. Offers MSECE, PhD. *Program availability:* Part-time, online learning. Terminal master's awarded for partial completion of doctoral program. *Degree requirements:* For master's, thesis optional; for doctorate, thesis/dissertation. *Entrance requirements:* For master's, GRE General Test; for doctorate, GRE General Test, qualifying exam. Additional exam requirements/recommendations for international students: Required—TOEFL. Electronic applications accepted. *Faculty research:* HIV evolution during dynamic therapy, compressive sensing in imaging, sensor, networks, and UWB radios, computer network time synchronization, silicon spintronics, devices and imaging in the high-terahertz band.

University of Denver, Daniel Felix Ritchie School of Engineering and Computer Science, Department of Electrical and Computer Engineering, Denver, CO 80208. Offers computer engineering (MS); electrical and computer engineering (PhD); electrical engineering (MS); engineering (MS); mechatronic systems engineering (MS, PhD). *Program availability:* Part-time, evening/weekend. *Faculty:* 11 full-time (1 woman). *Students:* 5 full-time (0 women), 55 part-time (8 women); includes 12 minority (2 Black or African American, non-Hispanic/Latino; 1 American Indian or Alaska Native, non-Hispanic/Latino; 3 Asian, non-Hispanic/Latino; 3 Hispanic/Latino; 3 Two or more races, non-Hispanic/Latino), 22 international. Average age 28. 79 applicants, 54% accepted, 17 enrolled. In 2018, 17 master's, 9 doctorates awarded. Terminal master's awarded for partial completion of doctoral program. *Degree requirements:* For master's, thesis optional; for doctorate, comprehensive exam, thesis/dissertation. *Entrance requirements:* For master's, GRE General Test, bachelor of science degree in computer engineering, electrical engineering, or closely related field, transcripts, personal statement, resume or curriculum vitae, three letters of recommendation; for doctorate, GRE General Test, master of science degree in computer engineering, management science and engineering, electrical engineering, mechanical engineering, or closely related areas, transcripts, personal statement, resume or curriculum vitae, three letters of recommendation. Additional exam requirements/recommendations for international students: Required—TOEFL (minimum score 570 paper-based; 80 iBT). *Application deadline:* For fall admission, 1/15 priority date for domestic and international students; for winter admission, 10/25 for domestic and international students; for spring admission, 2/7 for domestic and international students; for summer admission, 4/24 for domestic and international students. Applications are processed on a rolling basis. Application fee: $65. Electronic applications accepted. *Expenses:* $33,183 per year full-time. *Financial support:* In 2018–19, 31 students received support, including 3 research assistantships with tuition reimbursements available (averaging $18,233 per year), 5 teaching assistantships with tuition reimbursements available (averaging $15,833 per year); Federal Work-Study, scholarships/grants, and unspecified assistantships also available. Financial award application deadline: 2/15; financial award applicants required to submit FAFSA. *Faculty research:* Mechatronic systems, unmanned systems, service robotics, smart grid, sensor fusion. *Unit head:* Dr. Amin Khodaei, Professor and Chair, 303-871-2481, E-mail: amin.khodaei@du.edu. *Application contact:* Dr. Amin Khodaei, Professor and Chair, 303-871-2481, E-mail: amin.khodaei@du.edu.
Website: http://ritchieschool.du.edu/departments/ece/

University of Detroit Mercy, College of Engineering and Science, Detroit, MI 48221. Offers chemistry (MS); civil and environmental engineering (DE); electrical and computer engineering (ME); electrical engineering (DE); engineering management (M Eng Mgt); environmental engineering (MEE); mechanical engineering (MME, DE); product development (MS); software engineering (MSSE); teaching of mathematics (MATM). *Program availability:* Part-time, evening/weekend. *Degree requirements:* For doctorate, thesis/dissertation. Electronic applications accepted. Application fee is waived when completed online. *Expenses:* Contact institution.

University of Florida, Graduate School, Herbert Wertheim College of Engineering, Department of Electrical and Computer Engineering, Gainesville, FL 32611. Offers ME, MS, PhD, JD/MS, MSM/MS. *Program availability:* Part-time, online learning. Terminal master's awarded for partial completion of doctoral program. *Degree requirements:* For master's, comprehensive exam (for some programs), thesis (for some programs); for doctorate, comprehensive exam, thesis/dissertation. *Entrance requirements:* For master's, minimum GPA of 3.0; for doctorate, minimum GPA of 3.5. Additional exam requirements/recommendations for international students: Required—TOEFL (minimum score 550 paper-based; 80 iBT), IELTS (minimum score 6). Electronic applications accepted. *Faculty research:* Computer engineering, devices, electromagnetics and energy systems, electronics and signals and systems.

University of Hawaii at Manoa, Office of Graduate Education, College of Engineering, Department of Electrical Engineering, Honolulu, HI 96822. Offers MS, PhD. *Program availability:* Part-time. *Degree requirements:* For master's, comprehensive exam, thesis; for doctorate, comprehensive exam, thesis/dissertation. *Entrance requirements:* For master's and doctorate, GRE General Test. Additional exam requirements/recommendations for international students: Required—TOEFL (minimum score 540 paper-based; 76 iBT), IELTS (minimum score 5). *Faculty research:* Computers and artificial intelligence, communication and networking, control theory, physical electronics, VLSI design, micromillimeter waves.

University of Houston, Cullen College of Engineering, Department of Electrical and Computer Engineering, Houston, TX 77204. Offers electrical engineering (MEE, MSEE, PhD). *Program availability:* Part-time. Terminal master's awarded for partial completion of doctoral program. *Degree requirements:* For master's, thesis (for some programs); for doctorate, comprehensive exam, thesis/dissertation. *Entrance requirements:* For master's and doctorate, GRE General Test. Additional exam requirements/recommendations for international students: Required—TOEFL (minimum score 580 paper-based; 92 iBT). Electronic applications accepted. *Faculty research:* Applied electromagnetics and microelectronics, signal and image processing, biomedical engineering, geophysical applications, control engineering.

University of Idaho, College of Graduate Studies, College of Engineering, Department of Electrical and Computer Engineering, Moscow, ID 83844-1023. Offers electrical and computer engineering (MS, PhD); electrical engineering (M Engr). *Faculty:* 19. *Students:* 41 full-time (5 women), 46 part-time (5 women). Average age 32. In 2018, 15 master's, 2 doctorates awarded. *Entrance requirements:* For master's and doctorate, minimum GPA of 3.0. Additional exam requirements/recommendations for international students: Required—TOEFL (minimum score 79 iBT). *Application deadline:* For fall admission, 8/1

for domestic students; for spring admission, 12/15 for domestic students. Applications are processed on a rolling basis. Application fee: $60. Electronic applications accepted. *Expenses:* Tuition, state resident: full-time $7266.44; part-time $474.50 per credit hour. Tuition, nonresident: full-time $24,902; part-time $1453.50 per credit hour. *Required fees:* $2085.56; $45.50 per credit hour. *Financial support:* Fellowships, research assistantships, teaching assistantships, career-related internships or fieldwork, and Federal Work-Study available. Financial award applicants required to submit FAFSA. *Faculty research:* Fault-tolerant systems, analog electronics, intelligent systems research, embedded systems. *Unit head:* Dr. Joe Law, Chair, 208-885-6554, E-mail: ece-info@uidaho.edu. *Application contact:* Dr. Joe Law, Chair, 208-885-6554, E-mail: ece-info@uidaho.edu.
Website: https://www.uidaho.edu/engr/departments/ece

University of Illinois at Chicago, College of Engineering, Department of Electrical and Computer Engineering, Chicago, IL 60607-7128. Offers MS, PhD. *Program availability:* Part-time. *Degree requirements:* For master's, thesis or alternative; for doctorate, thesis/dissertation, departmental qualifying exam. *Entrance requirements:* For master's, minimum GPA of 2.75, BS in related field; for doctorate, GRE General Test, minimum GPA of 2.75, MS in related field. Additional exam requirements/recommendations for international students: Required—TOEFL. Electronic applications accepted. *Expenses:* Contact institution. *Faculty research:* Bioelectronics and biomimetics, computer engineering, device physics and electronics, information systems.

University of Illinois at Urbana–Champaign, Graduate College, College of Engineering, Department of Electrical and Computer Engineering, Champaign, IL 61820. Offers MS, PhD, MS/MBA.

The University of Iowa, Graduate College, College of Engineering, Department of Electrical and Computer Engineering, Iowa City, IA 52242-1316. Offers MS, PhD. *Program availability:* Part-time. *Degree requirements:* For master's, comprehensive exam, thesis optional; for doctorate, comprehensive exam, thesis/dissertation, qualifying exam. *Entrance requirements:* For master's and doctorate, GRE. Additional exam requirements/recommendations for international students: Required—TOEFL (minimum score 550 paper-based; 81 iBT), IELTS (minimum score 7). Electronic applications accepted. *Faculty research:* Applied optics and nanotechnology, compressive sensing, computational genomics, database management systems, large-scale intelligent and control systems, medical image processing, VLSI design and test.

The University of Kansas, Graduate Studies, School of Engineering, Program in Electrical Engineering, Lawrence, KS 66045. Offers MS, PhD. *Program availability:* Part-time. *Students:* 47 full-time (5 women), 7 part-time (1 woman); includes 6 minority (1 Black or African American, non-Hispanic/Latino; 2 Asian, non-Hispanic/Latino; 3 Hispanic/Latino), 31 international. Average age 29. 52 applicants, 62% accepted, 6 enrolled. In 2018, 8 master's, 7 doctorates awarded. Terminal master's awarded for partial completion of doctoral program. *Entrance requirements:* For master's, GRE, minimum GPA of 3.0, official transcript, three recommendations, statement of academic objectives, resume; for doctorate, GRE, minimum GPA of 3.5, official transcript, three recommendations, statement of academic objectives, resume. Additional exam requirements/recommendations for international students: Required—TOEFL, IELTS. *Application deadline:* For fall admission, 12/15 priority date for domestic and international students; for spring admission, 10/1 for domestic and international students. Application fee: $65 ($85 for international students). Electronic applications accepted. *Financial support:* Fellowships, research assistantships, teaching assistantships, career-related internships or fieldwork, scholarships/grants, and unspecified assistantships available. Financial award application deadline: 12/15. *Faculty research:* Communication systems and networking, computer systems design, radar systems and remote sensing. *Unit head:* Erik Perrins, Chair, 785-864-4486, E-mail: perrins@ku.edu. *Application contact:* Joy Grisafe-Gross, Graduate Admissions Contact, 785-864-4487, E-mail: jgrisafe@ku.edu.

University of Kentucky, Graduate School, College of Engineering, Program in Electrical Engineering, Lexington, KY 40506-0032. Offers MSEE, PhD. *Degree requirements:* For master's, comprehensive exam, thesis optional; for doctorate, one foreign language, comprehensive exam, thesis/dissertation. *Entrance requirements:* For master's, GRE General Test, minimum undergraduate GPA of 2.75; for doctorate, GRE General Test, minimum undergraduate GPA of 3.0. Additional exam requirements/recommendations for international students: Required—TOEFL (minimum score 550 paper-based). Electronic applications accepted. *Faculty research:* Signal processing, systems, and control; electromagnetic field theory; power electronics and machines; computer engineering and VLSI; materials and devices.

University of Louisiana at Lafayette, College of Engineering, Department of Electrical and Computer Engineering, Lafayette, LA 70504. Offers electrical engineering (MS); systems engineering (PhD). *Degree requirements:* For master's, thesis or alternative; for doctorate, comprehensive exam, thesis/dissertation, final oral exam. *Entrance requirements:* For master's, GRE General Test, minimum GPA of 2.75. Additional exam requirements/recommendations for international students: Required—TOEFL (minimum score 550 paper-based). Electronic applications accepted.

University of Louisville, J. B. Speed School of Engineering, Department of Electrical and Computer Engineering, Louisville, KY 40292-0001. Offers M Eng, MS, PhD. *Accreditation:* ABET (one or more programs are accredited). *Faculty:* 14 full-time (2 women), 3 part-time/adjunct (0 women). *Students:* 46 full-time (3 women), 29 part-time (7 women); includes 9 minority (6 Asian, non-Hispanic/Latino; 3 Hispanic/Latino), 26 international. Average age 28. 24 applicants, 54% accepted, 11 enrolled. In 2018, 10 master's, 5 doctorates awarded. *Degree requirements:* For master's, thesis optional; for doctorate, comprehensive exam, thesis/dissertation. *Entrance requirements:* For master's and doctorate, GRE General Test, 2 letters of recommendation, official transcripts. Additional exam requirements/recommendations for international students: Required—TOEFL (minimum score 550 paper-based; 80 iBT), IELTS (minimum score 6.5). *Application deadline:* For fall admission, 5/1 priority date for domestic and international students; for spring admission, 11/1 priority date for domestic and international students; for summer admission, 3/1 priority date for domestic and international students. Applications are processed on a rolling basis. Application fee: $65. Electronic applications accepted. *Expenses: Tuition, area resident:* Full-time $6500; part-time $723 per credit hour. Tuition, state resident: full-time $6500. Tuition, nonresident: full-time $13,557; part-time $1507 per credit hour. Tuition and fees vary according to course load and program. *Financial support:* In 2018–19, 50 students received support. Fellowships, research assistantships, teaching assistantships, scholarships/grants, health care benefits, and tuition waivers (full) available. Financial award application deadline: 1/1; financial award applicants required to submit FAFSA. *Faculty research:* 3D Fingerprint Identification and Biometrics, Active Computer Vision, Adaptive Technology for Individuals with Autism, Micro and Nano Robots, Nanotechnology. *Unit head:* Bruce Alpenhaar, Chair, 502-852-1554, Fax: 502-852-6807, E-mail: bruce.alphenaar@louisville.edu. *Application contact:* John Naber, Director of Graduate Studies, 502-852-7910, E-mail: john.naber@louisville.edu.
Website: http://www.louisville.edu/speed/electrical/

University of Maine, Graduate School, College of Engineering, Department of Electrical and Computer Engineering, Orono, ME 04469. Offers computer engineering (MS); electrical engineering (MS, PhD). *Program availability:* Part-time. *Faculty:* 12 full-time (1 woman), 1 part-time/adjunct (0 women). *Students:* 12 full-time (2 women), 1 part-time (0 women); includes 1 minority (Hispanic/Latino), 6 international. Average age 25. 21 applicants, 67% accepted, 5 enrolled. In 2018, 11 master's, 1 doctorate awarded. Terminal master's awarded for partial completion of doctoral program. *Degree requirements:* For master's, thesis (for some programs); for doctorate, comprehensive exam, thesis/dissertation. *Entrance requirements:* For master's and doctorate, GRE General Test. Additional exam requirements/recommendations for international students: Required—TOEFL. *Application deadline:* For fall admission, 2/1 priority date for domestic students. Applications are processed on a rolling basis. Application fee: $65. Electronic applications accepted. *Financial support:* In 2018–19, 13 students received support, including 7 research assistantships with full tuition reimbursements available (averaging $16,100 per year), 4 teaching assistantships with full tuition reimbursements available (averaging $13,600 per year); fellowships, Federal Work-Study, institutionally sponsored loans, and tuition waivers (full and partial) also available. Financial award application deadline: 3/1. *Faculty research:* Microwave acoustic sensors, semiconductor devices and fabrication, high performance computing, instrumentation and industrial automation, wireless communication. *Total annual research expenditures:* $1.5 million. *Unit head:* Dr. Donald Hummels, Chair, 207-581-2244. *Application contact:* Scott G. Delcourt, Assistant Vice President for Graduate Studies and Senior Associate Dean, 207-581-3291, Fax: 207-581-3232, E-mail: graduate@maine.edu.
Website: http://www.ece.umaine.edu/

The University of Manchester, School of Electrical and Electronic Engineering, Manchester, United Kingdom. Offers M Phil, PhD.

University of Manitoba, Faculty of Graduate Studies, Faculty of Engineering, Department of Electrical and Computer Engineering, Winnipeg, MB R3T 2N2, Canada. Offers M Eng, M Sc, PhD. *Degree requirements:* For master's, thesis; for doctorate, thesis/dissertation.

University of Maryland, Baltimore County, The Graduate School, College of Engineering and Information Technology, Department of Computer Science and Electrical Engineering, Program in Electrical Engineering, Baltimore, MD 21250. Offers MS, PhD. *Program availability:* Part-time. *Degree requirements:* For master's, comprehensive exam (for some programs), thesis optional; for doctorate, comprehensive exam, thesis/dissertation. *Entrance requirements:* For master's and doctorate, GRE General Test, BS from ABET-accredited undergraduate program in electrical engineering or strong background in computer science, mathematics, physics, or other areas of engineering or science. Additional exam requirements/recommendations for international students: Required—TOEFL (minimum score 550 paper-based; 80 iBT). Electronic applications accepted. *Expenses:* Contact institution. *Faculty research:* Communication and signal processing, photonics and micro electronics, sensor systems, signal processing architectures, VLSI design and test.

University of Maryland, College Park, Academic Affairs, A. James Clark School of Engineering, Department of Electrical and Computer Engineering, Electrical Engineering Program, College Park, MD 20742. Offers MS, PhD. *Degree requirements:* For master's, thesis or alternative; for doctorate, thesis/dissertation, oral exam, qualifying exam. *Entrance requirements:* For master's and doctorate, GRE General Test, minimum GPA of 3.0. Electronic applications accepted.

University of Massachusetts Amherst, Graduate School, College of Engineering, Department of Electrical and Computer Engineering, Amherst, MA 01003. Offers MSECE, PhD. *Program availability:* Part-time. Terminal master's awarded for partial completion of doctoral program. *Degree requirements:* For master's, thesis or alternative; for doctorate, comprehensive exam, thesis/dissertation. *Entrance requirements:* For master's and doctorate, GRE General Test. Additional exam requirements/recommendations for international students: Required—TOEFL (minimum score 550 paper-based; 80 iBT), IELTS (minimum score 6.5). Electronic applications accepted.

University of Massachusetts Dartmouth, Graduate School, College of Engineering, Department of Electrical and Computer Engineering, North Dartmouth, MA 02747-2300. Offers communications (Postbaccalaureate Certificate); computing infrastructure security (Postbaccalaureate Certificate); digital signal processing (Postbaccalaureate Certificate); electrical engineering (MS, PhD); electrical engineering systems (Postbaccalaureate Certificate). *Program availability:* Part-time. *Faculty:* 15 full-time (4 women), 1 part-time/adjunct (0 women). *Students:* 21 full-time (5 women), 40 part-time (9 women); includes 12 minority (4 Black or African American, non-Hispanic/Latino; 1 Asian, non-Hispanic/Latino; 5 Hispanic/Latino; 2 Two or more races, non-Hispanic/Latino), 20 international. Average age 31. 48 applicants, 71% accepted, 16 enrolled. In 2018, 23 master's, 5 doctorates, 3 other advanced degrees awarded. Terminal master's awarded for partial completion of doctoral program. *Degree requirements:* For master's, thesis, thesis or project; for doctorate, comprehensive exam, thesis/dissertation. *Entrance requirements:* For master's, GRE unless UMass Dartmouth graduate in computer engineering or electrical engineering, statement of purpose (minimum of 300 words), resume, 3 letters of recommendation, official transcripts; for doctorate, GRE unless UMass Dartmouth graduate in college of engineering major or about to receive electrical graduate certificate, statement of purpose (minimum of 300 words), resume, 3 letters of recommendation, official transcripts; for Postbaccalaureate Certificate, statement of purpose (minimum of 300 words), resume, official transcripts. Additional exam requirements/recommendations for international students: Required—TOEFL (minimum score 550 paper-based; 79 iBT), IELTS (minimum score 6.5). *Application deadline:* For fall admission, 2/15 priority date for domestic students, 1/15 priority date for international students; for spring admission, 11/1 priority date for domestic students, 10/1 priority date for international students. Application fee: $60. Electronic applications accepted. *Financial support:* In 2018–19, 12 research assistantships (averaging $15,187 per year), 10 teaching assistantships (averaging $12,907 per year) were awarded; tuition waivers (full and partial) and dissertation writing support also available. Financial award application deadline: 3/1; financial award applicants required to submit FAFSA. *Faculty research:* Array processing, cyber security, underwater acoustics and animal bio-acoustics, electronics and solid-state devices, photonics. *Total annual research expenditures:* $1.9 million. *Unit head:* Liudong Xing, Graduate Program Director/Electrical & Computer Engineering, 508-999-8883, Fax: 508-999-8489, E-mail: liudong.xing@umassd.edu. *Application contact:* Scott Webster, Director of Graduate Studies & Admissions, 508-999-8604, Fax: 508-999-8183, E-mail: graduate@umassd.edu.
Website: http://www.umassd.edu/engineering/ece/graduate

University of Massachusetts Lowell, Francis College of Engineering, Department of Electrical and Computer Engineering, Program in Electrical Engineering, Lowell, MA 01854. Offers MS Eng, PhD. *Program availability:* Part-time, evening/weekend. Terminal master's awarded for partial completion of doctoral program. *Degree requirements:* For master's, thesis; for doctorate, 2 foreign languages, thesis/dissertation. *Entrance requirements:* For master's and doctorate, GRE General Test.

University of Memphis, Graduate School, Herff College of Engineering, Department of Electrical and Computer Engineering, Memphis, TN 38152. Offers computer engineering

(MS, PhD); electrical engineering (MS, PhD); imaging and signal processing (Graduate Certificate). *Students:* 12 full-time (5 women), 9 part-time (2 women); includes 6 minority (4 Asian, non-Hispanic/Latino; 1 Hispanic/Latino; 1 Two or more races, non-Hispanic/Latino), 13 international. Average age 28. 29 applicants, 79% accepted, 4 enrolled. In 2018, 7 master's awarded. *Degree requirements:* For master's, comprehensive exam, thesis or alternative; for doctorate, comprehensive exam, thesis/dissertation. *Entrance requirements:* For master's and doctorate, GRE General Test, MAT, or GMAT, three letters of recommendation. Additional exam requirements/recommendations for international students: Required—TOEFL (minimum score 550 paper-based; 79 iBT). *Application deadline:* For fall admission, 8/1 for domestic students; for spring admission, 12/1 for domestic students. Application fee: $35 ($60 for international students). Electronic applications accepted. *Expenses:* Tuition, area resident: Full-time $10,240; part-time $503 per credit hour. Tuition, state resident: full-time $10,464. Tuition, nonresident: full-time $20,224; part-time $991 per credit hour. *Required fees:* $850; $106 per credit hour. *Financial support:* Fellowships, research assistantships, teaching assistantships, career-related internships or fieldwork, Federal Work-Study, scholarships/grants, and unspecified assistantships available. Financial award application deadline: 2/1; financial award applicants required to submit FAFSA. *Faculty research:* Image processing, imaging sensors, biomedical systems, intelligent systems. *Unit head:* Dr. Chrysanthe Preza, Chair, 901-678-2175, Fax: 901-678-5469, E-mail: cpreza@memphis.edu. *Application contact:* Dr. Aaron Robinson, Coordinator of Graduate Studies, 901-678-4996, Fax: 901-678-5469, E-mail: alrobins@memphis.edu. Website: http://www.memphis.edu/eece/

University of Miami, Graduate School, College of Engineering, Department of Electrical and Computer Engineering, Coral Gables, FL 33124. Offers MSECE, PhD. *Program availability:* Part-time. *Degree requirements:* For master's, thesis (for some programs); for doctorate, comprehensive exam, thesis/dissertation, dissertation proposal defense. *Entrance requirements:* For master's, GRE General Test, minimum GPA of 3.0; for doctorate, GRE General Test, minimum undergraduate GPA of 3.3, graduate 3.5. Additional exam requirements/recommendations for international students: Required—TOEFL (minimum score 550 paper-based; 59 iBT), IELTS (minimum score 7). Electronic applications accepted. *Faculty research:* Computer network, image processing, database systems, digital signal processing, machine intelligence.

University of Michigan, College of Engineering, Department of Electrical and Computer Engineering, Ann Arbor, MI 48109. Offers MS, MSE, PhD. *Program availability:* Part-time. *Students:* 698 full-time (154 women), 19 part-time (3 women). 2,183 applicants, 34% accepted, 248 enrolled. In 2018, 310 master's, 55 doctorates awarded. *Financial support:* Fellowships, research assistantships, teaching assistantships, career-related internships or fieldwork, Federal Work-Study, institutionally sponsored loans, and health care benefits available. Support available to part-time students. *Faculty research:* Solid state electronics and optics; communications, control, signal process; sensors and integrated circuitry; software systems; artificial intelligence; hardware systems. *Total annual research expenditures:* $43.9 million. *Unit head:* Mingyan Liu, Department Chair, 734-764-9546, Fax: 734-763-1503, E-mail: mingyan@umich.edu. *Application contact:* Johnny Linn, Graduate Coordinator, 734-764-9387, E-mail: johnlinn@umich.edu. Website: http://eecs.umich.edu/ece/

University of Michigan–Dearborn, College of Engineering and Computer Science, MSE Program in Electrical Engineering, Dearborn, MI 48128. Offers MSE. *Program availability:* Part-time, evening/weekend, 100% online. *Faculty:* 22 full-time (2 women), 15 part-time/adjunct (0 women). *Students:* 23 full-time (7 women), 157 part-time (29 women); includes 26 minority (4 Black or African American, non-Hispanic/Latino; 1 American Indian or Alaska Native, non-Hispanic/Latino; 16 Asian, non-Hispanic/Latino; 3 Hispanic/Latino; 2 Two or more races, non-Hispanic/Latino), 47 international. Average age 27. 103 applicants, 61% accepted, 34 enrolled. In 2018, 63 master's awarded. *Degree requirements:* For master's, thesis optional. *Entrance requirements:* For master's, bachelor's degree in electrical and/or computer engineering with minimum overall GPA of 3.0. Additional exam requirements/recommendations for international students: Required—TOEFL (minimum score 560 paper-based; 84 iBT), IELTS (minimum score 6.5). *Application deadline:* For fall admission, 8/1 for domestic students, 5/1 for international students; for winter admission, 12/1 for domestic students, 9/1 for international students; for spring admission, 4/1 for domestic students, 1/1 for international students. Applications are processed on a rolling basis. Application fee: $60. Electronic applications accepted. *Expenses:* Tuition, state resident: full-time $15,380; part-time $88 per credit hour. Tuition, nonresident: full-time $23,948; part-time $1377 per credit hour. *Required fees:* $780; $780 $390. Tuition and fees vary according to course level, course load, degree level, program, reciprocity agreements and student level. *Financial support:* In 2018–19, 30 students received support. Research assistantships with full tuition reimbursements available, teaching assistantships with full tuition reimbursements available, scholarships/grants, unspecified assistantships, and non-resident tuition scholarships available. Support available to part-time students. Financial award application deadline: 3/1; financial award applicants required to submit FAFSA. *Faculty research:* Artificial intelligence, power and energy, nanotechnology and optics, control systems, autonomy: sensing and perception. *Unit head:* Dr. Paul Richardson, Chair, 313-593-5420, E-mail: richarpc@umich.edu. *Application contact:* Office of Graduate Studies, 313-583-6321, E-mail: umd-graduatestudies@umich.edu. Website: https://umdearborn.edu/cecs/departments/electrical-and-computer-engineering/graduate-programs/mse-electrical-engineering

University of Michigan–Dearborn, College of Engineering and Computer Science, PhD Program Electrical, Electronics, and Computer Engineering, Dearborn, MI 48128. Offers PhD. *Faculty:* 22 full-time (2 women), 15 part-time/adjunct (0 women). *Students:* 2 full-time (0 women), 27 part-time (3 women); includes 2 minority (both Asian, non-Hispanic/Latino), 21 international. Average age 32. 38 applicants, 29% accepted, 8 enrolled. *Degree requirements:* For doctorate, thesis/dissertation. *Entrance requirements:* For doctorate, GRE, bachelor's or master's degree in electrical/computer engineering, computer science, physical science, or mathematical science with minimum GPA of 3.2. Additional exam requirements/recommendations for international students: Required—TOEFL (minimum score 560 paper-based; 84 iBT), IELTS (minimum score 6.5). *Application deadline:* For fall admission, 2/1 for domestic and international students. Application fee: $60. Electronic applications accepted. *Expenses:* Tuition, state resident: full-time $15,380; part-time $88 per credit hour. Tuition, nonresident: full-time $23,948; part-time $1377 per credit hour. *Required fees:* $780; $780 $390. Tuition and fees vary according to course level, course load, degree level, program, reciprocity agreements and student level. *Financial support:* Research assistantships with full tuition reimbursements, teaching assistantships with full tuition reimbursements, scholarships/grants, health care benefits, and unspecified assistantships available. Financial award application deadline: 2/1; financial award applicants required to submit FAFSA. *Faculty research:* Artificial intelligence, power and energy, nanotechnology and optics, control systems, autonomy: sensing and perception. *Unit head:* Dr. Alex Yi, Chair, 313-583-6318, E-mail: yashayi@umich.edu. *Application contact:* Office of Graduate Studies, 313-583-6321, E-mail: umd-graduatestudies@umich.edu. Website: https://umdearborn.edu/cecs/departments/electrical-and-computer-engineering/graduate-programs/phd-electrical-and-computer-engineering

University of Minnesota, Duluth, Graduate School, Swenson College of Science and Engineering, Department of Electrical and Computer Engineering, Duluth, MN 55812-2496. Offers MSECE. *Program availability:* Part-time. *Degree requirements:* For master's, thesis. *Entrance requirements:* Additional exam requirements/recommendations for international students: Recommended—TOEFL, IELTS, TWE. *Faculty research:* Biomedical instrumentation, transportation systems, computer hardware and software, signal processing, optical communications.

University of Minnesota, Twin Cities Campus, College of Science and Engineering, Department of Electrical and Computer Engineering, Minneapolis, MN 55455-0213. Offers MSEE, PhD. *Program availability:* Part-time. *Degree requirements:* For master's, thesis or alternative; for doctorate, thesis/dissertation. *Entrance requirements:* Additional exam requirements/recommendations for international students: Required—TOEFL (minimum score 550 paper-based). Electronic applications accepted. *Faculty research:* Signal processing, micro- and nano-structures, computers, controls, power electronics.

University of Mississippi, Graduate School, School of Engineering, University, MS 38677. Offers aeroacoustics (MS, PhD); chemical engineering (MS, PhD); civil engineering (MS, PhD); computational hydroscience (MS, PhD); computer science (MS, PhD); electrical engineering (MS, PhD); electromagnetics (MS, PhD); environmental engineering (MS, PhD); geology and geological engineering (MS, PhD); hydrology (MS); material science (MS); mechanical engineering (MS, PhD); telecommunications (MS). *Faculty:* 76 full-time (16 women), 3 part-time/adjunct (1 woman). *Students:* 129 full-time (33 women), 21 part-time (5 women); includes 15 minority (7 Black or African American, non-Hispanic/Latino; 6 Asian, non-Hispanic/Latino; 1 Hispanic/Latino; 1 Two or more races, non-Hispanic/Latino), 73 international. Average age 29. In 2018, 36 master's, 17 doctorates awarded. *Entrance requirements:* For master's, GRE General Test, minimum GPA of 3.0; for doctorate, GRE General Test. Additional exam requirements/recommendations for international students: Required—TOEFL. *Application deadline:* Applications are processed on a rolling basis. Application fee: $50. Electronic applications accepted. *Financial support:* Scholarships/grants available. Financial award application deadline: 3/1; financial award applicants required to submit FAFSA. *Unit head:* Dr. David Puleo, Dean, 662-915-5780, Fax: 662-915-5387, E-mail: engineer@olemiss.edu. *Application contact:* Temeka Smith, Graduate Activities Specialist for Admissions, 662-915-7474, Fax: 662-915-7577, E-mail: gschool@olemiss.edu.

University of Missouri, Office of Research and Graduate Studies, College of Engineering, Department of Electrical Engineering and Computer Science, Columbia, MO 65211. Offers computer engineering (MSCE); computer science (MS, PhD); electrical and computer engineering (PhD); electrical engineering (MSEE). *Entrance requirements:* For master's, GRE General Test, minimum GPA of 3.0; for doctorate, GRE General Test, GRE Subject Test, minimum GPA of 3.0. Additional exam requirements/recommendations for international students: Required—TOEFL.

University of Missouri–Kansas City, School of Computing and Engineering, Kansas City, MO 64110-2499. Offers civil engineering (MS); computer and electrical engineering (PhD); computer science (MS), including bioinformatics, software engineering, telecommunications networking; computer science and informatics (PhD); computing (PhD); electrical engineering (MS); engineering (PhD); engineering and construction management (Graduate Certificate); mechanical engineering (MS); telecommunications and computer networking (PhD). PhD (interdisciplinary) offered through the School of Graduate Studies. *Program availability:* Part-time. *Degree requirements:* For doctorate, thesis/dissertation. *Entrance requirements:* For master's, GRE General Test, minimum GPA of 3.0, 3 letters of recommendation from professors; for doctorate, GRE General Test, minimum GPA of 3.5. Additional exam requirements/recommendations for international students: Required—TOEFL (minimum score 550 paper-based; 80 iBT). *Faculty research:* Algorithms, bioinformatics and medical informatics, biomechanics/biomaterials, civil engineering materials, networking and telecommunications, thermal science.

University of Nebraska–Lincoln, Graduate College, College of Engineering, Department of Electrical Engineering, Lincoln, NE 68588. Offers MS, PhD. *Degree requirements:* For master's, thesis optional; for doctorate, comprehensive exam, thesis/dissertation. *Entrance requirements:* For master's and doctorate, GRE General Test. Additional exam requirements/recommendations for international students: Required—TOEFL (minimum score 550 paper-based). Electronic applications accepted. *Faculty research:* Electromagnetics, communications, biomedical digital signal processing, electrical breakdown of gases, optical properties of microelectronic materials.

University of Nevada, Reno, Graduate School, College of Engineering, Department of Electrical and Biomedical Engineering, Reno, NV 89557. Offers MS, PhD. Terminal master's awarded for partial completion of doctoral program. *Degree requirements:* For master's, thesis optional; for doctorate, thesis/dissertation. *Entrance requirements:* For master's, GRE General Test, minimum GPA of 2.75; for doctorate, GRE General Test, minimum GPA of 3.0. Additional exam requirements/recommendations for international students: Required—TOEFL (minimum score 500 paper-based; 61 iBT), IELTS (minimum score 6). Electronic applications accepted. *Faculty research:* Acoustics, neural networking, synthetic aperture radar simulation, optical fiber communications and sensors.

University of New Brunswick Fredericton, School of Graduate Studies, Faculty of Engineering, Department of Electrical and Computer Engineering, Fredericton, NB E3B 5A3, Canada. Offers M Eng, M Sc E, PhD. *Program availability:* Part-time. *Degree requirements:* For master's, thesis, research proposal; 10 courses (for M Eng); for doctorate, comprehensive exam, thesis/dissertation, research proposal. *Entrance requirements:* For master's, minimum GPA of 3.3; references; for doctorate, M Sc; minimum GPA of 3.3; previous transcripts; references. Additional exam requirements/recommendations for international students: Required—TOEFL (minimum score 580 paper-based; 93 iBT), IELTS (minimum score 7), TWE (minimum score 4). Electronic applications accepted. *Faculty research:* Biomedical engineering, communications, robotics and control systems, electromagnetic systems, embedded systems, optical fiber systems, sustainable energy and power systems, power electronics, image and signal processing, software systems, electronics and digital systems.

University of New Hampshire, Graduate School, College of Engineering and Physical Sciences, Department of Electrical and Computer Engineering, Durham, NH 03824. Offers electrical and computer engineering (MS); electrical engineering (M Engr, PhD); ubiquitous computing (Certificate); wireless communication systems (Certificate). *Program availability:* Part-time, evening/weekend. *Entrance requirements:* For master's and doctorate, GRE (for non-U.S. university bachelor's degree holders). Additional exam requirements/recommendations for international students: Required—TOEFL (minimum score 550 paper-based; 80 iBT). Electronic applications accepted.

University of New Haven, Graduate School, Tagliatela College of Engineering, Program in Electrical Engineering, West Haven, CT 06516. Offers computer engineering (MS); control systems (MS); digital signal processing and communication (MS); electrical engineering (MS). *Program availability:* Part-time, evening/weekend. *Students:* 46 full-time (17 women), 8 part-time (1 woman); includes 4 minority (1 Black or African American, non-Hispanic/Latino; 1 Asian, non-Hispanic/Latino; 2 Hispanic/Latino), 46

international. Average age 24. 135 applicants, 76% accepted, 10 enrolled. In 2018, 20 master's awarded. *Degree requirements:* For master's, thesis or alternative. *Entrance requirements:* For master's, bachelor's degree in electrical engineering. Additional exam requirements/recommendations for international students: Required—TOEFL (minimum score 75 iBT), IELTS, PTE (minimum score 50). *Application deadline:* Applications are processed on a rolling basis. Application fee: $50. Electronic applications accepted. Application fee is waived when completed online. *Expenses: Tuition:* Full-time $16,470; part-time $915 per credit hour. *Required fees:* $230; $95 per term. *Financial support:* Research assistantships with partial tuition reimbursements, teaching assistantships with partial tuition reimbursements, career-related internships or fieldwork, Federal Work-Study, scholarships/grants, and unspecified assistantships available. Support available to part-time students. Financial award applicants required to submit FAFSA. *Unit head:* Dr. Ali Golbazi, Professor, 203-932-7162, E-mail: agolbazi@newhaven.edu. *Application contact:* Selina O'Toole, Senior Associate Director of Graduate Admissions, 203-932-7337, E-mail: sotoole@newhaven.edu.
Website: https://www.newhaven.edu/engineering/graduate-programs/electrical-engineering/

University of New Mexico, Graduate Studies, School of Engineering, Programs in Electrical and Computer Engineering, Albuquerque, NM 87131-2039. Offers MS, PhD. *Program availability:* Part-time, evening/weekend, online learning. Terminal master's awarded for partial completion of doctoral program. *Degree requirements:* For master's, thesis; for doctorate, comprehensive exam, thesis/dissertation. *Entrance requirements:* For master's, GRE General Test, minimum GPA of 3.0; for doctorate, GRE General Test, minimum GPA of 3.5. Additional exam requirements/recommendations for international students: Required—TOEFL (minimum score 550 paper-based; 79 iBT). Electronic applications accepted. *Faculty research:* Applied electromagnetics, biomedical engineering, communications, image processing, microelectronics, optoelectronics, signal processing, systems and controls.

University of New Orleans, Graduate School, College of Engineering, Program in Engineering, New Orleans, LA 70148. Offers civil engineering (MS); electrical engineering (MS); mechanical engineering (MS); naval architecture and marine engineering (MS). *Degree requirements:* For master's, thesis optional. *Entrance requirements:* For master's, GRE General Test, minimum GPA of 3.0. Additional exam requirements/recommendations for international students: Required—TOEFL (minimum score 550 paper-based; 79 iBT). Electronic applications accepted. *Faculty research:* Two-phase flow instabilities, thermal-hydrodynamic modeling, solar energy, heat transfer from sprays, boundary integral techniques in mechanics.

The University of North Carolina at Charlotte, William States Lee College of Engineering, Department of Electrical and Computer Engineering, Charlotte, NC 28223-0001. Offers electrical engineering (MSEE, PhD). *Program availability:* Part-time, evening/weekend. *Students:* 143 full-time (34 women), 43 part-time (6 women); includes 9 minority (4 Black or African American, non-Hispanic/Latino; 1 Asian, non-Hispanic/Latino; 2 Hispanic/Latino; 2 Two or more races, non-Hispanic/Latino), 158 international. Average age 27. 279 applicants, 74% accepted, 50 enrolled. In 2018, 61 master's, 11 doctorates awarded. *Entrance requirements:* For master's, GRE, undergraduate degree in electrical and computer engineering or a closely-related field of engineering or sciences; minimum undergraduate GPA of 3.0; letters of recommendation; statement of purpose; for doctorate, GRE General Test, master's degree in electrical and/or computer engineering or a closely-allied field demonstrating strong academic background for performing research in a chosen area of interest; minimum undergraduate and master's-level GPA of 3.5; letters of recommendation; statement of purpose. Additional exam requirements/recommendations for international students: Required—TOEFL (minimum score 523 paper-based; 70 iBT), IELTS (minimum score 6), TOEFL (minimum score 523 paper-based, 70 iBT) or IELTS (6). *Application deadline:* Applications are processed on a rolling basis. Application fee: $75. Electronic applications accepted. *Expenses:* Contact institution. *Financial support:* Research assistantships, teaching assistantships, career-related internships or fieldwork, institutionally sponsored loans, scholarships/grants, and unspecified assistantships available. Support available to part-time students. Financial award application deadline: 3/1; financial award applicants required to submit FAFSA. *Total annual research expenditures:* $2 million. *Unit head:* Dr. Asis Nasipuri, Chair, 704-687-8418, E-mail: anasipur@uncc.edu. *Application contact:* Kathy B. Giddings, Director of Graduate Admissions, 704-687-5503, Fax: 704-687-1668, E-mail: gradadm@uncc.edu.
Website: http://ece.uncc.edu/

University of North Dakota, Graduate School, School of Engineering and Mines, Department of Electrical Engineering, Grand Forks, ND 58202. Offers M Engr, MS, PhD. *Program availability:* Part-time. *Degree requirements:* For master's, comprehensive exam, thesis or alternative. *Entrance requirements:* For master's, GRE General Test, minimum GPA of 3.0 (MS), 2.5 (M Engr). Additional exam requirements/recommendations for international students: Required—TOEFL (minimum score 550 paper-based; 79 iBT), IELTS (minimum score 6.5). Electronic applications accepted. *Faculty research:* Controls and robotics, signal processing, energy conversion, microwaves, computer engineering.

University of North Florida, College of Computing, Engineering, and Construction, School of Engineering, Jacksonville, FL 32224. Offers MSCE, MSEE, MSME. *Program availability:* Part-time. *Faculty:* 19 full-time (4 women). *Students:* 17 full-time (5 women), 32 part-time (5 women); includes 13 minority (1 Black or African American, non-Hispanic/Latino; 5 Asian, non-Hispanic/Latino; 5 Hispanic/Latino; 2 Two or more races, non-Hispanic/Latino), 9 international. Average age 30. 36 applicants, 58% accepted, 16 enrolled. In 2018, 19 master's awarded. *Application deadline:* For fall admission, 8/1 priority date for domestic students, 5/1 for international students; for spring admission, 12/1 priority date for domestic students, 10/1 for international students; for summer admission, 3/15 priority date for domestic students, 2/1 for international students. Application fee: $30. *Expenses: Tuition, area resident:* Part-time $408.10 per credit hour. Tuition, state resident: part-time $408.10 per credit hour. Tuition, nonresident: part-time $932.61 per credit hour. *Required fees:* $111.81 per credit hour. Tuition and fees vary according to course load, campus/location and program. *Financial support:* In 2018–19, 25 students received support, including 4 research assistantships (averaging $3,161 per year), 2 teaching assistantships (averaging $4,445 per year); Federal Work-Study, scholarships/grants, tuition waivers, and unspecified assistantships also available. Financial award application deadline: 4/1; financial award applicants required to submit FAFSA. *Total annual research expenditures:* $1.1 million. *Unit head:* Dr. Murat Tiryakioglo, Director, 904-620-1393, E-mail: m.tiryakioglu@unf.edu. *Application contact:* Dr. Amanda Pascale, Director, The Graduate School, 904-320-1360, Fax: 904-620-1362, E-mail: graduateschool@unf.edu.
Website: http://www.unf.edu/ccec/engineering/

University of North Texas, Toulouse Graduate School, Denton, TX 76203-5459. Offers accounting (MS); applied anthropology (MA, MS); applied behavior analysis (Certificate); applied geography (MA); applied technology and performance improvement (M Ed, MS); art education (MA); art history (MA); arts leadership (Certificate); audiology (Au D); behavior analysis (MS); behavioral science (PhD); biochemistry and molecular biology (MS); biology (MA, MS); biomedical engineering (MS); business analysis (MS); chemistry (MS); clinical health psychology (PhD); communication studies (MA, MS); computer engineering (MS); computer science (MS); counseling (M Ed, MS), including clinical mental health counseling (MS), college and university counseling, elementary school counseling, secondary school counseling; creative writing (MA); criminal justice (MS); curriculum and instruction (M Ed); decision sciences (MBA); design (MA, MFA), including fashion design (MFA), innovation studies, interior design (MFA); early childhood studies (MS); economics (MS); educational leadership (M Ed, Ed D); educational psychology (MS, PhD), including family studies (MS), gifted and talented (MS), human development (MS), learning and cognition (MS), research, measurement and evaluation (MS); electrical engineering (MS); emergency management (MPA); engineering technology (MS); English (MA); English as a second language (MA); environmental science (MS); finance (MBA, MS); financial management (MPA); French (MA); health services management (MBA); higher education (M Ed, Ed D); history (MA, MS); hospitality management (MS); human resources management (MPA); information science (MS); information systems (PhD); information technologies (MBA); interdisciplinary studies (MA, MS); international studies (MA); international sustainable tourism (MS); jazz studies (MM); journalism (MA, MJ, Graduate Certificate), including interactive and virtual digital communication (Graduate Certificate), narrative journalism (Graduate Certificate), public relations (Graduate Certificate); kinesiology (MS); linguistics (MA); local government management (MPA); logistics (PhD); logistics and supply chain management (MBA); long-term care, senior housing, and aging services (MA); management (PhD); marketing (MBA); mathematics (MA, MS); mechanical and energy engineering (MS, PhD); music (MA), including ethnomusicology, music theory, musicology, performance; music composition (PhD); music education (MM Ed, PhD); nonprofit management (MPA); operations and supply chain management (MBA); performance (MM, DMA); philosophy (MA); political science (MA); professional and technical communication (MA); radio, television and film (MA, MFA); rehabilitation counseling (Certificate); sociology (MA); Spanish (MA); special education (M Ed); speech-language pathology (MA); strategic management (MBA); studio art (MFA); teaching (M Ed); MBA/MS. *Program availability:* Part-time, evening/weekend, online learning. Terminal master's awarded for partial completion of doctoral program. *Degree requirements:* For master's, variable foreign language requirement, comprehensive exam (for some programs), thesis (for some programs); for doctorate, variable foreign language requirement, comprehensive exam (for some programs), thesis/dissertation; for other advanced degree, variable foreign language requirement, comprehensive exam (for some programs). *Entrance requirements:* For master's and doctorate, GRE, GMAT. Additional exam requirements/recommendations for international students: Required—TOEFL (minimum score 550 paper-based; 79 iBT). Electronic applications accepted.

University of Notre Dame, The Graduate School, College of Engineering, Department of Electrical Engineering, Notre Dame, IN 46556. Offers MSEE, PhD. Terminal master's awarded for partial completion of doctoral program. *Degree requirements:* For master's, comprehensive exam; for doctorate, thesis/dissertation, candidacy exam. *Entrance requirements:* For master's and doctorate, GRE General Test. Additional exam requirements/recommendations for international students: Required—TOEFL (minimum score 600 paper-based; 80 iBT). Electronic applications accepted. *Faculty research:* Electronic properties of materials and devices, signal and imaging processing, communication theory, control theory and applications, optoelectronics.

University of Oklahoma, Gallogly College of Engineering, School of Electrical and Computer Engineering, Norman, OK 73019. Offers electrical and computer engineering (MS, PhD); telecommunications engineering (MS). *Program availability:* Part-time. *Faculty:* 44 full-time (3 women), 1 part-time/adjunct (0 women). *Students:* 83 full-time (16 women), 40 part-time (9 women); includes 11 minority (1 Black or African American, non-Hispanic/Latino; 1 American Indian or Alaska Native, non-Hispanic/Latino; 3 Asian, non-Hispanic/Latino; 5 Hispanic/Latino; 1 Two or more races, non-Hispanic/Latino), 76 international. Average age 29. 61 applicants, 67% accepted, 14 enrolled. In 2018, 21 master's, 15 doctorates awarded. Terminal master's awarded for partial completion of doctoral program. *Degree requirements:* For master's, comprehensive exam (for some programs), thesis (for some programs); for doctorate, thesis/dissertation, general exam. *Entrance requirements:* For master's and doctorate, GRE, minimum GPA of 3.0. Additional exam requirements/recommendations for international students: Required—TOEFL (minimum score 79 iBT) or IELTS (minimum score 6.5). *Application deadline:* For fall admission, 4/1 for domestic students, 3/1 for international students; for spring admission, 11/1 for domestic students, 10/1 for international students. Applications are processed on a rolling basis. Application fee: $50 ($100 for international students). Electronic applications accepted. *Expenses:* Tuition, state resident: full-time $5683.20; part-time $236.80 per credit hour. Tuition, nonresident: full-time $20,342; part-time $847.60 per credit hour. *International tuition:* $20,342.40 full-time. *Required fees:* $2894.20; $110.05 per credit hour. $126.50 per semester. Tuition and fees vary according to course load and program. *Financial support:* Fellowships, research assistantships, teaching assistantships, career-related internships or fieldwork, scholarships/grants, and health care benefits available. Financial award application deadline: 6/1; financial award applicants required to submit FAFSA. *Faculty research:* Radar engineering, medical imaging, photonics, smart grid, wireless networks. *Unit head:* Dr. J.R. Cruz, Director, 405-325-8131, Fax: 405-325-7066, E-mail: jcruz@ou.edu. *Application contact:* Emily Benton Wilkins, Graduate Programs Coordinator, 405-325-7334, Fax: 405-325-7066, E-mail: emily.d.benton-1@ou.edu.
Website: http://www.ou.edu/coe/ece.html

University of Ottawa, Faculty of Graduate and Postdoctoral Studies, Faculty of Engineering, Ottawa-Carleton Institute for Electrical and Computer Engineering, Ottawa, ON K1N 6N5, Canada. Offers M Eng, MA Sc, PhD. *Degree requirements:* For master's, thesis or alternative, project; for doctorate, comprehensive exam, thesis/dissertation. *Entrance requirements:* For master's, honors degree or equivalent, minimum B average; for doctorate, minimum A- average. Electronic applications accepted. *Faculty research:* CAD, distributed systems.

University of Pennsylvania, School of Engineering and Applied Science, Department of Electrical and Systems Engineering, Philadelphia, PA 19104. Offers MSE, PhD. *Program availability:* Part-time. *Students:* Average age 25. 1,049 applicants, 40% accepted, 206 enrolled. In 2018, 78 master's, 13 doctorates awarded. Terminal master's awarded for partial completion of doctoral program. *Degree requirements:* For master's, comprehensive exam, thesis optional; for doctorate, comprehensive exam, thesis/dissertation. *Entrance requirements:* For master's and doctorate, GRE, bachelor's degree, letters of recommendation, resume, personal statement. Additional exam requirements/recommendations for international students: Required—TOEFL (minimum score 100 iBT), IELTS (minimum score 7). *Application deadline:* For fall admission, 12/15 priority date for domestic and international students. Application fee: $80. Electronic applications accepted. *Expenses:* Contact institution. *Faculty research:* Circuits and computer engineering, information decision systems, nanodevices and nanosystems. *Application contact:* William Fenton, Assistant Director of Graduate Admissions, 215-898-4542, Fax: 215-573-5577, E-mail: gradstudies@seas.upenn.edu.

University of Pittsburgh, Swanson School of Engineering, Department of Electrical and Computer Engineering, Pittsburgh, PA 15260. Offers electrical and computer engineering (MS, PhD). *Program availability:* Part-time, 100% online. Terminal master's awarded for partial completion of doctoral program. *Degree requirements:* For doctorate, comprehensive exam, thesis/dissertation, final oral exams. *Entrance requirements:* For master's and doctorate, GRE General Test, minimum GPA of 3.0. Additional exam requirements/recommendations for international students: Required—TOEFL (minimum score 550 paper-based; 80 iBT). Electronic applications accepted. *Expenses:* Contact institution. *Faculty research:* Computer engineering, image processing, signal processing, electro-optic devices, controls/power.

University of Portland, Shiley School of Engineering, Portland, OR 97203-5798. Offers biomedical engineering (MBME); civil engineering (ME); computer science (ME); electrical engineering (ME); mechanical engineering (ME). *Program availability:* Part-time, evening/weekend. *Students:* 12 full-time (4 women), 2 part-time (both women); includes 1 minority (Black or African American, non-Hispanic/Latino), 2 international. Average age 24. 43 applicants, 49% accepted, 10 enrolled. In 2018, 6 master's awarded. *Degree requirements:* For master's, thesis optional. *Entrance requirements:* For master's, GRE General Test, minimum GPA of 3.0, 2 letters of recommendation, resume, statement of goals, official transcripts. Additional exam requirements/recommendations for international students: Required—TOEFL (minimum score 80 iBT), IELTS (minimum score 7). *Application deadline:* For fall admission, 7/15 priority date for domestic and international students; for spring admission, 12/15 priority date for domestic and international students; for summer admission, 4/15 for domestic and international students. Applications are processed on a rolling basis. Electronic applications accepted. *Expenses:* $1,326 per credit plus $50 professional tuition per credit. *Financial support:* Research assistantships, career-related internships or fieldwork, Federal Work-Study, and scholarships/grants available. Support available to part-time students. Financial award application deadline: 3/1; financial award applicants required to submit FAFSA. *Unit head:* Dr. Matthew Kuhn, Dean, 503-943-7361, E-mail: kuhn@up.edu. *Application contact:* Caitlin Biddulph, Graduate Programs and Admissions Specialist, 503-943-7107.
Website: http://engineering.up.edu/default.aspx?cid-6464&pid-2432

University of Puerto Rico–Mayagüez, Graduate Studies, College of Engineering, Department of Electrical and Computer Engineering, Mayagüez, PR 00681-9000. Offers computer engineering (ME, MS); computing and information sciences and engineering (PhD); electrical engineering (ME, MS). *Program availability:* Part-time. Terminal master's awarded for partial completion of doctoral program. *Degree requirements:* For master's, one foreign language, comprehensive exam, thesis; for doctorate, one foreign language, comprehensive exam, thesis/dissertation. *Entrance requirements:* For master's and doctorate, proficiency in English and Spanish; BS in electrical or computer engineering, or equivalent; minimum GPA of 3.0. Electronic applications accepted. *Faculty research:* Digital signal processing, power electronics, microwave ocean emissivity, parallel and distributed computing, microwave remote sensing.

University of Rhode Island, Graduate School, College of Engineering, Department of Electrical, Computer and Biomedical Engineering, Kingston, RI 02881. Offers acoustics and underwater acoustics (MS, PhD); biomedical engineering (MS, PhD); circuits and devices (MS); communication theory (MS, PhD); computer architectures and digital systems (MS, PhD); computer networks (MS, PhD); digital signal processing (MS); embedded systems and computer applications (MS, PhD); fault-tolerant computing (MS, PhD); materials and optics (MS, PhD); systems theory (MS, PhD). *Program availability:* Part-time. *Faculty:* 23 full-time (4 women), 1 part-time/adjunct (0 women). *Students:* 41 full-time (7 women), 17 part-time (2 women); includes 8 minority (1 Black or African American, non-Hispanic/Latino; 1 American Indian or Alaska Native, non-Hispanic/Latino; 4 Asian, non-Hispanic/Latino; 2 Hispanic/Latino), 26 international. 44 applicants, 75% accepted, 20 enrolled. In 2018, 14 master's, 3 doctorates awarded. *Entrance requirements:* Additional exam requirements/recommendations for international students: Required—TOEFL. *Application deadline:* For fall admission, 7/15 for domestic students, 2/1 for international students; for spring admission, 11/15 for domestic students, 7/15 for international students; for summer admission, 4/15 for domestic students. Application fee: $65. Electronic applications accepted. *Expenses: Tuition, area resident:* Full-time $13,226; part-time $735 per credit. *Tuition, state resident:* full-time $13,226; part-time $735 per credit. *Tuition, nonresident:* full-time $25,854; part-time $1436 per credit. *International tuition:* $25,854 full-time. *Required fees:* $1698; $50 per credit. $35 per semester. One-time fee: $165. *Financial support:* In 2018–19, 22 research assistantships with tuition reimbursements (averaging $10,249 per year), 9 teaching assistantships with tuition reimbursements (averaging $8,477 per year) were awarded. Financial award application deadline: 2/1; financial award applicants required to submit FAFSA. *Unit head:* Dr. Haibo He, Chair, 401-874-5844, E-mail: he@ele.uri.edu. *Application contact:* Dr. Frederick J. Vetter, Graduate Director, 401-874-5141, E-mail: vetter@ele.uri.edu.
Website: http://www.ele.uri.edu/

University of Rochester, Hajim School of Engineering and Applied Sciences, Department of Electrical and Computer Engineering, Rochester, NY 14627. Offers biomedical ultrasound and biomedical engineering (MS); integrated electronics and computer engineering (PhD); musical acoustics and signal processing (MS); physical electronics, electron magnetism, and acoustics (PhD); signal and image processing and communications (MS); signal processing and communications (PhD). *Faculty:* 20 full-time (1 woman). *Students:* 132 full-time (24 women), 1 part-time (0 women); includes 8 minority (4 Black or African American, non-Hispanic/Latino; 2 Asian, non-Hispanic/Latino; 2 Hispanic/Latino), 98 international. Average age 26. 483 applicants, 48% accepted, 56 enrolled. In 2018, 28 master's, 10 doctorates awarded. Terminal master's awarded for partial completion of doctoral program. *Degree requirements:* For master's, thesis optional; for doctorate, comprehensive exam, thesis/dissertation, teaching assistant (two semesters), qualifying exam. *Entrance requirements:* For master's and doctorate, personal statement, three letters of recommendation, official transcripts. Additional exam requirements/recommendations for international students: Required—TOEFL (minimum score 90 paper-based; 90 iBT), IELTS (minimum score 6.5). *Application deadline:* For fall admission, 1/15 for domestic and international students. Applications are processed on a rolling basis. Application fee: $60. Electronic applications accepted. *Expenses: Tuition:* Full-time $52,974; part-time $1654 per credit hour. *Required fees:* $612. One-time fee: $30 part-time. Tuition and fees vary according to campus/location and program. *Financial support:* In 2018–19, 122 students received support, including 2 fellowships with full tuition reimbursements available (averaging $30,000 per year), 54 research assistantships with full tuition reimbursements available (averaging $30,000 per year), 66 teaching assistantships with full and partial tuition reimbursements available (averaging $12,954 per year); scholarships/grants, tuition waivers (full and partial), and unspecified assistantships also available. *Faculty research:* Bio-informatics and biosensing, communications, signal processing, robotics, wireless networks. *Total annual research expenditures:* $3.8 million. *Unit head:* Mark Bocko, Professor/Chair, 585-275-4879, E-mail: mark.bocko@rochester.edu. *Application contact:* Michele Foster, Graduate Program Coordinator, 585-275-4054, E-mail: michele.foster@rochester.edu.
Website: http://www.hajim.rochester.edu/ece/graduate/index.html

University of St. Thomas, School of Engineering, St. Paul, MN 55105. Offers data science (MS); electrical engineering (MS); information technology (MS); manufacturing engineering (MS); manufacturing systems (Certificate); mechanical engineering (MS); medical device development (Certificate); regulatory science (MS); software engineering (MS); software management (MS); systems engineering (MS); technology leadership (Certificate); technology management (MS). *Program availability:* Part-time, evening/weekend. *Entrance requirements:* For master's, resume, official transcripts. Additional exam requirements/recommendations for international students: Required—TOEFL (minimum score 80 iBT), IELTS (minimum score 6.5). Electronic applications accepted. *Expenses:* Contact institution.

University of Saskatchewan, College of Graduate and Postdoctoral Studies, College of Engineering, Electrical Engineering Program, Saskatoon, SK S7N 5E5, Canada. Offers M Eng, M Sc, PhD, PGD. *Program availability:* Part-time. *Degree requirements:* For master's, 30 credits (for M Eng); thesis and 12 credits (for MS); for doctorate, comprehensive exam, thesis/dissertation, qualifying exam, 18 credits; for PGD, 30 credits. *Entrance requirements:* For master's and doctorate, GRE. Additional exam requirements/recommendations for international students: Required—TOEFL (minimum iBT score of 80), IELTS (6.5), CanTEST (4.5), or PTE (59). Electronic applications accepted. *Faculty research:* Artificial neural networks and fuzzy logic, biomedical microdevices, computer engineering, control systems, digital signal processing, electrical machines and power magnetics, embedded systems, high aspect ratio micro patterning, instrumentation and microprocessor applications, multimedia and video signal processing, optoelectronics and photonics, power system protection and control, power system reliability economics, renewable energy applications, thin films.

University of South Alabama, College of Engineering, Department of Electrical and Computer Engineering, Mobile, AL 36688. Offers computer engineering (MSEE); electrical engineering (MSEE). *Program availability:* Part-time. *Degree requirements:* For master's, comprehensive exam, thesis or project. *Entrance requirements:* For master's, GRE General Test, BS in engineering, minimum GPA of 3.0. Additional exam requirements/recommendations for international students: Required—TOEFL (minimum score 550 paper-based; 79 iBT), IELTS (minimum score 6.5). Electronic applications accepted. *Expenses:* Contact institution. *Faculty research:* Target detection and tracking, space propulsion applications, electrical and computer engineering, intelligent systems, robotics.

University of South Carolina, The Graduate School, College of Engineering and Computing, Department of Electrical Engineering, Columbia, SC 29208. Offers ME, MS, PhD. *Program availability:* Part-time, evening/weekend, online learning. *Degree requirements:* For master's, comprehensive exam, thesis (for some programs); for doctorate, comprehensive exam, thesis/dissertation, qualifying exam. *Entrance requirements:* For master's and doctorate, GRE General Test. Additional exam requirements/recommendations for international students: Required—TOEFL (minimum score 570 paper-based; 88 iBT). Electronic applications accepted. *Faculty research:* Microelectronics, photonics, wireless communications, signal integrity, energy and control systems.

University of Southern California, Graduate School, Viterbi School of Engineering, Ming Hsieh Department of Electrical Engineering, Los Angeles, CA 90089. Offers computer engineering (MS, PhD); electric power (MS); electrical engineering (MS, PhD, Engr); engineering technology commercialization (Graduate Certificate); multimedia and creative technologies (MS); telecommunications (MS); VLSI design (MS); wireless health technology (MS). *Program availability:* Part-time, online learning. Terminal master's awarded for partial completion of doctoral program. *Degree requirements:* For master's, thesis optional; for doctorate, thesis/dissertation. *Entrance requirements:* For master's and doctorate, GRE General Test. Additional exam requirements/recommendations for international students: Recommended—TOEFL. Electronic applications accepted. *Faculty research:* Communications, computer engineering and networks, control systems, integrated circuits and systems, electromagnetics and energy conversion, micro electro-mechanical systems and nanotechnology, photonics and quantum electronics, plasma research, signal and image processing.

University of South Florida, College of Engineering, Department of Electrical Engineering, Tampa, FL 33620-9951. Offers MSEE, PhD. *Program availability:* Part-time, online learning. *Faculty:* 30 full-time (3 women), 1 part-time/adjunct (0 women). *Students:* 264 full-time (56 women), 71 part-time (7 women); includes 29 minority (8 Black or African American, non-Hispanic/Latino; 2 Asian, non-Hispanic/Latino; 18 Hispanic/Latino; 1 Two or more races, non-Hispanic/Latino), 270 international. Average age 27. 394 applicants, 65% accepted, 85 enrolled. In 2018, 121 master's, 16 doctorates awarded. Terminal master's awarded for partial completion of doctoral program. *Degree requirements:* For master's, comprehensive exam, thesis or alternative; for doctorate, comprehensive exam, thesis/dissertation. *Entrance requirements:* For master's, minimum GPA of 3.0, three letters of recommendation, resume, statement or purpose; for doctorate, GRE (with preferred minimum scores of Q> 155 (61%), V>146 (28%)), minimum GPA of 3.0, three letters of recommendation, statement of purpose. Additional exam requirements/recommendations for international students: Required—TOEFL, TOEFL (minimum score 550 paper-based; 79 iBT) or IELTS (minimum score 6.5). *Application deadline:* For fall admission, 2/15 for domestic and international students; for spring admission, 10/15 for domestic students, 9/15 for international students; for summer admission, 2/15 for domestic students, 1/15 for international students. Application fee: $30. Electronic applications accepted. *Expenses:* Tuition, state resident: full-time $6350. Tuition, nonresident: full-time $19,048. *International tuition:* $19,048 full-time. *Required fees:* $2079. *Financial support:* In 2018–19, 38 students received support, including 57 research assistantships (averaging $12,357 per year), 41 teaching assistantships with tuition reimbursements available (averaging $13,528 per year). Financial award applicants required to submit FAFSA. *Faculty research:* Wireless communication and signal processing, surface science, wireless and microwave information systems (WAMI), in vivo Wireless Information Networking (iWINLAB), personalized interactive experiences (PIE), Smart Grid power systems, defense and intelligence. *Total annual research expenditures:* $3.2 million. *Unit head:* Dr. Thomas Weller, Professor and Department Chair, 813-974-2740, E-mail: weller@usf.edu. *Application contact:* Dr. Andrew Hoff, Associate Professor and Graduate Program Director, 813-974-4958, Fax: 813-974-5250, E-mail: hoff@usf.edu.
Website: http://ee.eng.usf.edu/

The University of Tennessee, Graduate School, Tickle College of Engineering, Min H. Kao Department of Electrical Engineering and Computer Science, Program in Electrical Engineering, Knoxville, TN 37996. Offers MS, PhD. *Program availability:* Part-time. *Faculty:* 24 full-time (4 women), 3 part-time/adjunct (0 women). *Students:* 113 full-time (28 women), 24 part-time (3 women); includes 8 minority (2 Black or African American, non-Hispanic/Latino; 3 Asian, non-Hispanic/Latino; 3 Hispanic/Latino), 86 international. Average age 28. 194 applicants, 44% accepted, 27 enrolled. In 2018, 25 master's, 22 doctorates awarded. *Degree requirements:* For master's, thesis or alternative; for doctorate, comprehensive exam, thesis/dissertation. *Entrance requirements:* For master's, GRE General Test (for MS students pursuing research thesis), minimum GPA of 2.7 (for U.S. degree holders), 3.0 (for international degree holders); 3 references; personal statement; for doctorate, GRE General Test, minimum GPA of 3.0 on previous graduate coursework; 3 references; personal statement. Additional exam requirements/recommendations for international students: Required—TOEFL (minimum score 550 paper-based; 80 iBT), IELTS (minimum score 6.5). *Application deadline:* For fall admission, 2/1 priority date for domestic and international students; for spring

admission, 6/15 for domestic and international students; for summer admission, 10/15 for domestic and international students. Applications are processed on a rolling basis. Application fee: $60. Electronic applications accepted. *Financial support:* In 2018–19, 128 students received support, including 16 fellowships with full tuition reimbursements available (averaging $9,480 per year), 81 research assistantships with full tuition reimbursements available (averaging $23,424 per year), 31 teaching assistantships with full tuition reimbursements available (averaging $18,289 per year); career-related internships or fieldwork, Federal Work-Study, institutionally sponsored loans, health care benefits, and unspecified assistantships also available. Financial award application deadline: 2/1; financial award applicants required to submit FAFSA. *Unit head:* Dr. Gregory Peterson, PhD, Head, 865-974-3461, Fax: 865-974-5483, E-mail: gdp@utk.edu. *Application contact:* Dr. Jens Gregor, PhD, Associate Head, 865-974-4399, Fax: 865-974-5483, E-mail: jgregor@utk.edu.
Website: http://www.eecs.utk.edu

The University of Tennessee at Chattanooga, Program in Engineering, Chattanooga, TN 37403. Offers automotive (MS Engr); chemical (MS Engr); civil (MS Engr); electrical (MS Engr); mechanical (MS Engr). *Program availability:* Part-time. *Degree requirements:* For master's, comprehensive exam, thesis or alternative, engineering project. *Entrance requirements:* For master's, GRE General Test, minimum undergraduate GPA of 2.7 or 3.0 in last two years of undergraduate coursework. Additional exam requirements/recommendations for international students: Required—TOEFL (minimum score 550 paper-based; 79 iBT), IELTS (minimum score 6). Electronic applications accepted. *Expenses:* Contact institution. *Faculty research:* Quality control and reliability engineering, financial management, thermal science, energy conservation, structural analysis.

The University of Texas at Arlington, Graduate School, College of Engineering, Department of Electrical Engineering, Arlington, TX 76019. Offers M Engr, MS, PhD. *Program availability:* Part-time, evening/weekend, online learning. Terminal master's awarded for partial completion of doctoral program. *Degree requirements:* For master's, thesis optional; for doctorate, comprehensive exam, thesis/dissertation, written diagnostic exam. *Entrance requirements:* For master's, GRE General Test, minimum GPA of 3.25; for doctorate, GRE General Test, minimum GPA of 3.5. Additional exam requirements/recommendations for international students: Required—TOEFL (minimum score 560 paper-based); Recommended—TWE (minimum score 4). *Faculty research:* Nanotech and microelectromechanical systems (MEMS), digital image processing, telecommunications and optics, energy systems and power electronics, VLSI and semiconductors.

The University of Texas at Austin, Graduate School, Cockrell School of Engineering, Department of Electrical and Computer Engineering, Austin, TX 78712-1111. Offers MS, PhD. *Program availability:* Part-time. *Entrance requirements:* For master's, GRE General Test, minimum GPA of 3.3 in upper-division course work; for doctorate, GRE General Test. Electronic applications accepted.

The University of Texas at Dallas, Erik Jonsson School of Engineering and Computer Science, Department of Electrical and Computer Engineering, Richardson, TX 75080. Offers computer engineering (MS, PhD); electrical engineering (MSEE, PhD); telecommunications engineering (MSTE, PhD). *Program availability:* Part-time, evening/weekend. *Faculty:* 44 full-time (4 women), 10 part-time/adjunct (0 women). *Students:* 452 full-time (98 women), 169 part-time (49 women); includes 44 minority (6 Black or African American, non-Hispanic/Latino; 25 Asian, non-Hispanic/Latino; 7 Hispanic/Latino; 6 Two or more races, non-Hispanic/Latino), 525 international. Average age 28. 1,519 applicants, 46% accepted, 177 enrolled. In 2018, 234 master's, 43 doctorates awarded. *Degree requirements:* For master's, thesis or major design project; for doctorate, thesis/dissertation. *Entrance requirements:* For master's, GRE General Test, minimum GPA of 3.0 in related bachelor's degree; for doctorate, GRE General Test, minimum GPA of 3.5. Additional exam requirements/recommendations for international students: Required—TOEFL (minimum score 550 paper-based). *Application deadline:* For fall admission, 7/15 for domestic students, 5/1 priority date for international students; for spring admission, 11/15 for domestic students, 9/1 priority date for international students. Applications are processed on a rolling basis. Application fee: $50 ($100 for international students). Electronic applications accepted. *Expenses: Tuition, area resident:* Full-time $13,458. Tuition, state resident: full-time $13,458. Tuition, nonresident: full-time $26,852. *International tuition:* $26,852 full-time. Tuition and fees vary according to course load. *Financial support:* In 2018–19, 192 students received support, including 11 fellowships (averaging $3,297 per year), 143 research assistantships with partial tuition reimbursements available (averaging $23,638 per year), 57 teaching assistantships with partial tuition reimbursements available (averaging $17,489 per year); Federal Work-Study, institutionally sponsored loans, scholarships/grants, unspecified assistantships, and cooperative positions also available. Support available to part-time students. Financial award application deadline: 4/30; financial award applicants required to submit FAFSA. *Faculty research:* Semiconductor device manufacturing, photonics devices and systems, signal processing and language technology, nano-fabrication, energy efficient digital systems. *Unit head:* Dr. Lawrence Overzet, Department Head, 972-883-2154, Fax: 972-883-2710, E-mail: overzet@utdallas.edu. *Application contact:* Dr. Lawrence Overzet, Department Head, 972-883-2154, Fax: 972-883-2710, E-mail: overzet@utdallas.edu.
Website: http://ece.utdallas.edu

The University of Texas at El Paso, Graduate School, College of Engineering, Department of Electrical and Computer Engineering, El Paso, TX 79968-0001. Offers computer engineering (MS); electric power and energy systems (Graduate Certificate); electrical and computer engineering (PhD); electrical engineering (MS). *Program availability:* Part-time, evening/weekend. Terminal master's awarded for partial completion of doctoral program. *Degree requirements:* For master's, thesis optional; for doctorate, thesis/dissertation. *Entrance requirements:* For master's, GRE General Test, minimum GPA of 3.0; for doctorate, GRE General Test, minimum graduate GPA of 3.0. Additional exam requirements/recommendations for international students: Required—TOEFL. Electronic applications accepted. *Faculty research:* Signal and image processing, computer architecture, fiber optics, computational electromagnetics, electronic displays and thin films.

The University of Texas at San Antonio, College of Engineering, Department of Electrical and Computer Engineering, San Antonio, TX 78249-0617. Offers advanced materials engineering (MS); computer engineering (MS); electrical engineering (MSEE, PhD). *Program availability:* Part-time. Terminal master's awarded for partial completion of doctoral program. *Degree requirements:* For master's, comprehensive exam, thesis (for some programs); for doctorate, comprehensive exam, thesis/dissertation. *Entrance requirements:* For master's, GRE General Test, bachelor's degree in electrical or computer engineering from ABET-accredited institution of higher education or related field; minimum GPA of 3.0 on the last 60 semester credit hours of undergraduate studies; for doctorate, GRE General Test, master's degree or minimum GPA of 3.3 in last 60 semester credit hours of undergraduate level coursework in electrical engineering; statement of purpose. Additional exam requirements/recommendations for international students: Required—TOEFL (minimum score 550 paper-based; 79 iBT), IELTS (minimum score 6.5). Electronic applications accepted. *Faculty research:* Computer engineering, digital signal processing, systems and controls, communications, electronics materials and devices, electric power engineering.

The University of Texas at Tyler, College of Engineering, Department of Electrical Engineering, Tyler, TX 75799-0001. Offers MS. *Program availability:* Part-time, evening/weekend. *Students:* Average age 26. 27 applicants, 100% accepted, 3 enrolled. In 2018, 3 master's awarded. *Entrance requirements:* For master's, GRE General Test, bachelor's degree in electrical engineering. Additional exam requirements/recommendations for international students: Required—TOEFL. *Application deadline:* For fall admission, 8/17 priority date for domestic students, 7/1 priority date for international students; for spring admission, 12/21 priority date for domestic students, 11/1 priority date for international students. Application fee: $25 ($50 for international students). *Financial support:* In 2018–19, 4 research assistantships (averaging $6,000 per year), 6 teaching assistantships (averaging $6,000 per year) were awarded. Financial award application deadline: 7/1. *Faculty research:* Electronics, digital sign processing, real time systems electromagnetic fields, semiconductor modeling. *Total annual research expenditures:* $1 million. *Unit head:* Dr. Hassan El-Kishky, Chair, 903-565-5580, E-mail: helkishky@uttyler.edu. *Application contact:* Dr. Hassan El-Kishky, Chair, 903-565-5580, E-mail: helkishky@uttyler.edu.
Website: https://www.uttyler.edu/ee/

The University of Texas Rio Grande Valley, College of Engineering and Computer Science, Department of Electrical Engineering, Edinburg, TX 78539. Offers MSE. *Program availability:* Part-time, evening/weekend. *Degree requirements:* For master's, comprehensive exam, thesis optional. *Expenses: Tuition, area resident:* Full-time $6888. Tuition, state resident: full-time $6888. Tuition, nonresident: full-time $14,484. *International tuition:* $14,484 full-time. *Required fees:* $1468.

University of the District of Columbia, School of Engineering and Applied Sciences, Program in Electrical Engineering, Washington, DC 20008-1175. Offers MSEE.

The University of Toledo, College of Graduate Studies, College of Engineering, Department of Electrical Engineering and Computer Science, Toledo, OH 43606-3390. Offers computer science (MS, PhD); electrical engineering (MS, PhD). *Program availability:* Part-time, evening/weekend. *Degree requirements:* For master's, thesis or alternative; for doctorate, thesis/dissertation, qualifying exam. *Entrance requirements:* For master's, GRE General Test, minimum GPA of 3.0; for doctorate, GRE General Test, minimum GPA of 3.3. Additional exam requirements/recommendations for international students: Required—TOEFL (minimum score 550 paper-based; 80 iBT). Electronic applications accepted. *Faculty research:* Communication and signal processing, high performance computing systems, intelligent systems, power electronics and energy systems, RF and microwave systems, sensors and medical devices, solid state devices.

University of Toronto, School of Graduate Studies, Faculty of Applied Science and Engineering, Department of Electrical and Computer Engineering, Toronto, ON M5S 1A1, Canada. Offers M Eng, MA Sc, PhD. *Program availability:* Part-time. *Degree requirements:* For master's, thesis (for some programs), oral thesis defense (MA Sc); for doctorate, thesis/dissertation, qualifying exam, thesis defense. *Entrance requirements:* For master's, four-year degree in electrical or computer engineering, minimum B average, 2 letters of reference; for doctorate, minimum B+ average, MA Sc in electrical or computer engineering, 2 letters of reference. Additional exam requirements/recommendations for international students: Required—TOEFL (minimum score 580 paper-based; 93 iBT). Electronic applications accepted.

The University of Tulsa, Graduate School, College of Engineering and Natural Sciences, Department of Electrical and Computer Engineering, Tulsa, OK 74104-3189. Offers computer engineering (ME, MSE, PhD); electrical engineering (ME, MSE). *Program availability:* Part-time. *Faculty:* 8 full-time (0 women). *Students:* 9 full-time (1 woman), 13 part-time (2 women); includes 2 minority (1 Black or African American, non-Hispanic/Latino; 1 Hispanic/Latino), 5 international. Average age 26. 17 applicants, 71% accepted, 6 enrolled. In 2018, 11 master's awarded. Terminal master's awarded for partial completion of doctoral program. *Degree requirements:* For master's, comprehensive exam (for some programs), design report (ME), thesis (MS); for doctorate, comprehensive exam, thesis/dissertation. *Entrance requirements:* For master's, GRE General Test. Additional exam requirements/recommendations for international students: Required—TOEFL (minimum score 550 paper-based; 80 iBT), IELTS (minimum score 6). *Application deadline:* Applications are processed on a rolling basis. Application fee: $55. Electronic applications accepted. *Expenses: Tuition:* Full-time $22,230; part-time $1235 per credit hour. *Required fees:* $2100; $6 per credit hour. One-time fee: $400 full-time. Tuition and fees vary according to course level, course load and program. *Financial support:* In 2018–19, 11 students received support, including 4 fellowships with tuition reimbursements available (averaging $6,953 per year), 7 research assistantships with full tuition reimbursements available (averaging $12,837 per year), 4 teaching assistantships with full tuition reimbursements available (averaging $11,982 per year); career-related internships or fieldwork, Federal Work-Study, scholarships/grants, health care benefits, tuition waivers (full and partial), and unspecified assistantships also available. Support available to part-time students. Financial award application deadline: 2/1; financial award applicants required to submit FAFSA. *Faculty research:* VLSI microprocessors, intelligent systems, electromagnetics, intrusion detection systems, digital electronics. *Unit head:* Dr. Kaveh Ashenayi, Chairperson, 918-631-3278, Fax: 918-631-3344, E-mail: kash@utulsa.edu. *Application contact:* Dr. Heng-Ming Tai, Adviser, 918-631-3271, Fax: 918-631-3344, E-mail: tai@utulsa.edu.
Website: http://engineering.utulsa.edu/academics/electrical-and-computer-engineering/

University of Utah, Graduate School, College of Engineering, Department of Electrical and Computer Engineering, Salt Lake City, UT 84112. Offers electrical and computer engineering (MS, PhD); electrical engineering (ME); MS/MBA. *Program availability:* Part-time. *Faculty:* 32 full-time (5 women), 17 part-time/adjunct (3 women). *Students:* 122 full-time (20 women), 47 part-time (3 women); includes 12 minority (7 Asian, non-Hispanic/Latino; 5 Hispanic/Latino), 107 international. Average age 29. 395 applicants, 51% accepted, 61 enrolled. In 2018, 42 master's, 21 doctorates awarded. Terminal master's awarded for partial completion of doctoral program. *Entrance requirements:* For master's, GRE General Test, minimum GPA of 3.2; for doctorate, GRE General Test, minimum GPA of 3.5. Additional exam requirements/recommendations for international students: Required—TOEFL (minimum score 600 paper-based; 100 iBT); Recommended—IELTS (minimum score 7.5). *Application deadline:* For fall admission, 1/15 for domestic and international students; for spring admission, 10/1 for domestic students. Application fee: $10 ($25 for international students). *Expenses:* Contact institution. *Financial support:* In 2018–19, 103 students received support, including 2 fellowships with full tuition reimbursements available (averaging $25,000 per year), 71 research assistantships with full tuition reimbursements available (averaging $22,165 per year), 30 teaching assistantships with full tuition reimbursements available (averaging $19,948 per year); Federal Work-Study, institutionally sponsored loans, health care benefits, and unspecified assistantships also available. Financial award application deadline: 1/15; financial award applicants required to submit FAFSA. *Faculty research:* Semiconductors, VLSI design, control systems, electromagnetics and applied optics, communication theory and digital signal processing, power systems. *Total annual research expenditures:* $6.8 million. *Unit head:* Dr. Gianluca Lazzi, Chair, 801-581-6942, Fax: 801-581-5281, E-mail: lazzi@utah.edu. *Application contact:* Holly Cox, Administrative Manager, 801-581-3843, Fax: 801-581-5281, E-mail: h.cox@utah.edu.
Website: http://www.ece.utah.edu/

University of Vermont, Graduate College, College of Engineering and Mathematical Sciences, Program in Electrical Engineering, Burlington, VT 05405-0156. Offers MS, PhD. *Degree requirements:* For master's, thesis or alternative; for doctorate, thesis/dissertation. *Entrance requirements:* For master's, GRE General Test. Additional exam requirements/recommendations for international students: Required—TOEFL (minimum score 550 paper-based, 90 iBT) or IELTS (6.5). Electronic applications accepted.

University of Victoria, Faculty of Graduate Studies, Faculty of Engineering, Department of Electrical and Computer Engineering, Victoria, BC V8W 2Y2, Canada. Offers M Eng, MA Sc, PhD. *Degree requirements:* For master's, thesis; for doctorate, thesis/dissertation, candidacy exam. *Entrance requirements:* For master's, GRE (recommended), bachelor's degree in engineering; for doctorate, GRE (recommended), master's degree. Additional exam requirements/recommendations for international students: Required—TOEFL (minimum score 575 paper-based), IELTS (minimum score 7). Electronic applications accepted. *Faculty research:* Communications and computers; electromagnetics, microwaves, and optics; electronics; power systems, signal processing, and control.

University of Virginia, School of Engineering and Applied Science, Department of Electrical and Computer Engineering, Program in Electrical Engineering, Charlottesville, VA 22903. Offers ME, MS, PhD. *Degree requirements:* For doctorate, thesis/dissertation. *Entrance requirements:* For master's, GRE General Test, 3 letters of recommendation; for doctorate, GRE General Test, 3 letters of recommendation; essay. Additional exam requirements/recommendations for international students: Required—TOEFL (minimum score 650 paper-based; 100 iBT), IELTS (minimum score 7). Electronic applications accepted.

University of Washington, Graduate School, College of Engineering, Department of Electrical and Computer Engineering, Seattle, WA 98195-2500. Offers electrical engineering (MS, PhD); electrical engineering and nanotechnology (PhD). *Program availability:* Part-time, evening/weekend. *Faculty:* 40 full-time (8 women), 39 part-time/adjunct (8 women). *Students:* 247 full-time (59 women), 135 part-time (23 women); includes 67 minority (9 Black or African American, non-Hispanic/Latino; 43 Asian, non-Hispanic/Latino; 10 Hispanic/Latino; 5 Two or more races, non-Hispanic/Latino), 192 international. Average age 27. 1,392 applicants, 34% accepted, 132 enrolled. In 2018, 83 master's, 30 doctorates awarded. Terminal master's awarded for partial completion of doctoral program. *Degree requirements:* For master's, thesis optional; for doctorate, thesis/dissertation, qualifying, general, and final exams. *Entrance requirements:* For master's and doctorate, GRE General Test - Optional (not required), minimum GPA of 3.5 (recommended); resume or curriculum vitae, statement of purpose, 3 letters of recommendation, undergraduate and graduate transcripts. Additional exam requirements/recommendations for international students: Required—TOEFL (minimum score 600 paper-based; 92 iBT). *Application deadline:* For fall admission, 12/15 for domestic and international students. Application fee: $85. Electronic applications accepted. *Expenses:* Research-focused Master's and PhD: $18,852 resident; $32,760 nonresident. *Financial support:* In 2018–19, 154 students received support, including 8 fellowships with full tuition reimbursements available (averaging $32,880 per year), 99 research assistantships with full tuition reimbursements available (averaging $32,880 per year), 47 teaching assistantships with full tuition reimbursements available (averaging $32,880 per year); career-related internships or fieldwork, Federal Work-Study, institutionally sponsored loans, health care benefits, and tuition waivers (full) also available. Financial award application deadline: 12/15; financial award applicants required to submit FAFSA. *Faculty research:* Computing and networking, data sciences, and biosystems, photonics and nano-devices, power and energy systems, robotics and controls. *Total annual research expenditures:* $29 million. *Unit head:* Dr. Radha Poovendran, Professor/Chair, 206-543-6515, Fax: 206-543-3842, E-mail: chair@ece.uw.edu. *Application contact:* Brenda Larson, Lead Academic Counselor, Graduate Programs, 206-616-1351, Fax: 206-543-3842, E-mail: grad@ece.uw.edu.
Website: http://www.ece.uw.edu

University of Waterloo, Graduate Studies and Postdoctoral Affairs, Faculty of Engineering, Department of Electrical and Computer Engineering, Waterloo, ON N2L 3G1, Canada. Offers M Eng, MA Sc, PhD. *Program availability:* Part-time. *Degree requirements:* For master's, research paper or thesis; for doctorate, comprehensive exam, thesis/dissertation. *Entrance requirements:* For master's, honors degree, minimum B+ average; for doctorate, master's degree, minimum A- average. Additional exam requirements/recommendations for international students: Required—TOEFL, IELTS, PTE. Application fee: $125 Canadian dollars. Electronic applications accepted. *Financial support:* Fellowships, research assistantships, and teaching assistantships available. *Faculty research:* Communications, computers, systems and control, silicon devices, power engineering.
Website: https://uwaterloo.ca/electrical-computer-engineering/

The University of Western Ontario, School of Graduate and Postdoctoral Studies, Physical Sciences Division, Faculty of Engineering, London, ON N6A 3K7, Canada. Offers chemical and biochemical engineering (ME Sc, PhD); civil and environmental engineering (M Eng, ME Sc, PhD); electrical and computer engineering (M Eng, ME Sc, PhD); mechanical and materials engineering (M Eng, ME Sc, PhD). *Program availability:* Part-time. Terminal master's awarded for partial completion of doctoral program. *Degree requirements:* For master's, thesis; for doctorate, thesis/dissertation. *Entrance requirements:* For master's, minimum B average; for doctorate, minimum B+ average. *Faculty research:* Wind, geotechnical, chemical reactor engineering, applied electrostatics, biochemical engineering.

University of Windsor, Faculty of Graduate Studies, Faculty of Engineering, Department of Electrical and Computer Engineering, Windsor, ON N9B 3P4, Canada. Offers electrical engineering (M Eng, MA Sc, PhD). *Program availability:* Part-time. *Degree requirements:* For master's, thesis; for doctorate, comprehensive exam, thesis/dissertation. *Entrance requirements:* For master's, minimum B average; for doctorate, master's degree, minimum B+ average. Additional exam requirements/recommendations for international students: Required—TOEFL (minimum score 600 paper-based). Electronic applications accepted. *Faculty research:* Systems, signals, power.

University of Wisconsin–Madison, Graduate School, College of Engineering, Department of Electrical and Computer Engineering, Madison, WI 53706-1380. Offers electrical engineering (MS, PhD); machine learning and signal processing (MS). *Program availability:* Blended/hybrid learning. *Faculty:* 44 full-time (8 women). *Students:* 261 full-time (54 women), 64 part-time (5 women); includes 24 minority (5 Black or African American, non-Hispanic/Latino; 13 Asian, non-Hispanic/Latino; 6 Hispanic/Latino), 207 international. Average age 28. 950 applicants, 29% accepted, 84 enrolled. In 2018, 53 master's, 35 doctorates awarded. Terminal master's awarded for partial completion of doctoral program. *Degree requirements:* For master's, thesis (for some programs), 30 semester hours of credit; 3.0 GPA; for doctorate, comprehensive exam, thesis/dissertation, 51 credits; qualifying and preliminary exams; 3.0 GPA. *Entrance requirements:* For master's and doctorate, GRE General Test, bachelor's degree; minimum GPA of 3.0 on last 60 semester hours. Additional exam requirements/recommendations for international students: Required—TOEFL (minimum score 580 paper-based; 92 iBT), IELTS (minimum score 7). *Application deadline:* For fall admission, 12/15 for domestic and international students. Application fee: $75 ($81 for international students). Electronic applications accepted. *Expenses:* In-state tuition (full-time): $10,728; Out-of-state tuition (full-time): $24,054; Fees: $1282; In-state tuition (per credit): $670; Out-of-state tuition (per credit): $1503; Fees (per credit): $126. *Financial support:* In 2018–19, 193 students received support, including 11 fellowships with full tuition reimbursements available (averaging $23,844 per year), 122 research assistantships with full tuition reimbursements available (averaging $25,020 per year), 48 teaching assistantships with full tuition reimbursements available (averaging $11,124 per year); career-related internships or fieldwork, Federal Work-Study, institutionally sponsored loans, health care benefits, unspecified assistantships, and project assistantships also available. Support available to part-time students. Financial award application deadline: 12/1; financial award applicants required to submit FAFSA. *Faculty research:* Applied physics; computer engineering; electric energy and power systems; information theory and systems engineering. *Total annual research expenditures:* $16.7 million. *Unit head:* Prof. Susan Hagness, Chair, 608-262-3840, E-mail: office@ece.wisc.edu. *Application contact:* Hannah Roberg, Student Services Coordinator, 608-890-2204, E-mail: ecegradadmission@engr.wisc.edu.
Website: https://www.engr.wisc.edu/department/electrical-computer-engineering/

University of Wisconsin–Milwaukee, Graduate School, College of Engineering and Applied Science, Program in Engineering, Milwaukee, WI 53201-0413. Offers biomedical engineering (MS); civil engineering (MS, PhD); computer science (PhD); electrical and computer engineering (MS); electrical engineering (PhD); engineering mechanics (MS); industrial and management engineering (MS); industrial engineering (PhD); manufacturing engineering (MS); materials (PhD); materials engineering (MS); mechanical engineering (MS). *Program availability:* Part-time. *Students:* 174 full-time (41 women), 149 part-time (27 women); includes 31 minority (2 Black or African American, non-Hispanic/Latino; 1 American Indian or Alaska Native, non-Hispanic/Latino; 16 Asian, non-Hispanic/Latino; 4 Hispanic/Latino; 8 Two or more races, non-Hispanic/Latino), 207 international. Average age 31. 343 applicants, 57% accepted, 78 enrolled. In 2018, 73 master's, 24 doctorates awarded. *Degree requirements:* For master's, comprehensive exam (for some programs), thesis or alternative; for doctorate, comprehensive exam, thesis/dissertation, internship. *Entrance requirements:* For master's, GRE, minimum GPA of 2.75; for doctorate, GRE, minimum GPA of 3.5. Additional exam requirements/recommendations for international students: Required—TOEFL (minimum score 550 paper-based; 79 iBT), IELTS (minimum score 6.5). *Application deadline:* For fall admission, 1/1 priority date for domestic students; for spring admission, 9/1 for domestic students. Applications are processed on a rolling basis. Application fee: $56 ($96 for international students). *Financial support:* Fellowships, research assistantships, teaching assistantships, career-related internships or fieldwork, Federal Work-Study, unspecified assistantships, and project assistantships available. Support available to part-time students. Financial award application deadline: 4/15. *Unit head:* David Yu, Representative, 414-229-6169, E-mail: yu@uwm.edu. *Application contact:* Betty Warras, General Information Contact, 414-229-6169, Fax: 414-229-6967, E-mail: bwarras@uwm.edu.
Website: http://www4.uwm.edu/ceas/academics/graduate_programs/

University of Wyoming, College of Engineering and Applied Science, Department of Electrical and Computer Engineering, Laramie, WY 82071. Offers electrical engineering (MS, PhD). *Program availability:* Part-time. *Degree requirements:* For master's, thesis (for some programs); for doctorate, comprehensive exam, thesis/dissertation, dissertation proposal/presentation. *Entrance requirements:* For master's, GRE General Test, minimum undergraduate GPA of 3.0; for doctorate, GRE General Test, minimum GPA of 3.0. Additional exam requirements/recommendations for international students: Required—TOEFL (minimum score 550 paper-based; 79 iBT). Electronic applications accepted. *Expenses:* Tuition, area resident: Full-time $6504; part-time $271 per credit hour. Tuition, state resident: full-time $6504; part-time $271 per credit hour. Tuition, nonresident: full-time $19,464; part-time $811 per credit hour. International tuition: $19,464 full-time. *Required fees:* $1410.94; $343.82 per semester. $343.82 per semester. Tuition and fees vary according to course load, program and reciprocity agreements. *Faculty research:* Robotics and controls, signal and image processing, power electronics, power systems, computer networks, wind energy.

Utah State University, School of Graduate Studies, College of Engineering, Department of Electrical and Computer Engineering, Logan, UT 84322. Offers electrical engineering (ME, MS, PhD). *Program availability:* Part-time. *Degree requirements:* For master's, thesis (for some programs); for doctorate, comprehensive exam, thesis/dissertation. *Entrance requirements:* For master's, GRE General Test, minimum GPA of 3.0, BS in electrical engineering, 3 recommendation letters; for doctorate, GRE General Test, minimum GPA of 3.0, MS in electrical engineering, 3 recommendation letters. Additional exam requirements/recommendations for international students: Required—TOEFL. Electronic applications accepted. *Faculty research:* Parallel processing, networking, control systems, digital signal processing, communications.

Vanderbilt University, School of Engineering, Department of Electrical Engineering and Computer Science, Program in Electrical Engineering, Nashville, TN 37240-1001. Offers M Eng, MS, PhD. MS and PhD offered through the Graduate School. *Program availability:* Part-time. Terminal master's awarded for partial completion of doctoral program. *Degree requirements:* For master's, thesis; for doctorate, comprehensive exam, thesis/dissertation. *Entrance requirements:* For master's and doctorate, GRE General Test, 3 letters of recommendation. Additional exam requirements/recommendations for international students: Required—TOEFL. Electronic applications accepted. *Expenses:* Tuition: Full-time $47,208; part-time $2026 per credit hour. *Required fees:* $478. *Faculty research:* Robotics, microelectronics, signal and image processing, VLSI, solid-state sensors, radiation effects and reliability.

Villanova University, College of Engineering, Department of Electrical and Computer Engineering, Program in Electrical Engineering, Villanova, PA 19085-1699. Offers electric power systems (Certificate); electrical engineering (MSEE); electro mechanical systems (Certificate); high frequency systems (Certificate); intelligent control systems (Certificate); wireless and digital communications (Certificate). *Program availability:* Part-time, evening/weekend. *Degree requirements:* For master's, thesis optional. *Entrance requirements:* For master's, GRE General Test (for applicants with degrees from foreign universities), BEE, minimum GPA of 3.0. Additional exam requirements/recommendations for international students: Required—TOEFL (minimum score 600 paper-based; 100 iBT). *Faculty research:* Signal processing, communications, antennas, devices.

Virginia Polytechnic Institute and State University, Graduate School, College of Engineering, Blacksburg, VA 24061. Offers aerospace engineering (PhD, M Eng/MS); biological systems engineering (PhD); biomedical engineering (MS, PhD); chemical engineering (PhD); civil engineering (PhD); computer engineering (PhD); computer science and applications (MS); electrical engineering (PhD); engineering education (PhD); M Eng/MS. *Faculty:* 446 full-time (87 women), 7 part-time/adjunct (3 women). *Students:* 1,776 full-time (471 women), 367 part-time (62 women); includes 260 minority (50 Black or African American, non-Hispanic/Latino; 3 American Indian or Alaska Native, non-Hispanic/Latino; 99 Asian, non-Hispanic/Latino; 67 Hispanic/Latino; 41 Two or more races, non-Hispanic/Latino), 1,178 international. Average age 27. 3,798 applicants, 37% accepted, 507 enrolled. In 2018, 489 master's, 200 doctorates awarded. *Degree requirements:* For master's, comprehensive exam (for some programs), thesis (for some

programs); for doctorate, comprehensive exam (for some programs), thesis/dissertation (for some programs). *Entrance requirements:* For master's and doctorate, GRE/GMAT. Additional exam requirements/recommendations for international students: Required—TOEFL (minimum score 90 iBT). *Application deadline:* For fall admission, 8/1 for domestic students, 4/1 for international students; for spring admission, 1/1 for domestic students, 9/1 for international students. Applications are processed on a rolling basis. Application fee: $75. Electronic applications accepted. *Expenses:* Tuition, state resident: full-time $15,510; part-time $739.50 per credit hour. Tuition, nonresident: full-time $29,629; part-time $1490.25 per credit hour. *Required fees:* $2804; $550 per semester. Tuition and fees vary according to course load, campus/location and program. *Financial support:* In 2018–19, 37 fellowships with full tuition reimbursements (averaging $24,951 per year), 1,110 research assistantships with full tuition reimbursements (averaging $20,129 per year), 486 teaching assistantships with full tuition reimbursements (averaging $16,192 per year) were awarded; scholarships/grants and unspecified assistantships also available. Financial award application deadline: 3/1; financial award applicants required to submit FAFSA. *Total annual research expenditures:* $96.3 million. *Unit head:* Dr. Julia Ross, Dean, 540-231-9752, Fax: 540-231-3031, E-mail: rjulie@vt.edu. *Application contact:* Linda Perkins, Executive Assistant, 540-231-9752, Fax: 540-231-3031, E-mail: lperkins@vt.edu.
Website: http://www.eng.vt.edu/

Virginia Polytechnic Institute and State University, VT Online, Blacksburg, VA 24061. Offers advanced transportation systems (Certificate); aerospace engineering (MS); agricultural and life sciences (MSLFS); business information systems (Graduate Certificate); career and technical education (MS); civil engineering (MS); computer engineering (M Eng, MS); decision support systems (Graduate Certificate); eLearning leadership (MA); electrical engineering (M Eng, MS); engineering administration (MEA); environmental engineering (Certificate); environmental politics and policy (Graduate Certificate); environmental sciences and engineering (MS); foundations of political analysis (Graduate Certificate); health product risk management (Graduate Certificate); industrial and systems engineering (MS); information policy and society (Graduate Certificate); information security (Graduate Certificate); information technology (MIT); instructional technology (MA); integrative STEM education (MA Ed); liberal arts (Graduate Certificate); life sciences: health product risk management (MS); natural resources (MNR, Graduate Certificate); networking (Graduate Certificate); nonprofit and nongovernmental organization management (Graduate Certificate); ocean engineering (MS); political science (MA); security studies (Graduate Certificate); software development (Graduate Certificate). *Expenses:* Tuition, state resident: full-time $15,510; part-time $739.50 per credit hour. Tuition, nonresident: full-time $29,629; part-time $1490.25 per credit hour. *Required fees:* $2804; $550 per semester. Tuition and fees vary according to course load, campus/location and program. *Application contact:* Graduate Admissions and Academic Progress, 540-231-8636, E-mail: grads@vt.edu.
Website: http://www.vto.vt.edu/

Washington State University, Voiland College of Engineering and Architecture, School of Electrical Engineering and Computer Science, Pullman, WA 99164-2752. Offers computer engineering (MS); computer science (MS); electrical engineering (MS); electrical engineering and computer science (PhD); electrical power engineering (MS). MS programs in computer engineering, computer science and electrical engineering also offered at Tri-Cities campus; MS in electrical power engineering offered at the Global (online) campus. *Program availability:* Part-time. *Degree requirements:* For master's, comprehensive exam (for some programs), thesis or alternative; for doctorate, comprehensive exam, thesis/dissertation. *Entrance requirements:* For master's and doctorate, GRE General Test, minimum GPA of 3.0, 3 letters of recommendation, statement of purpose, transcripts. Additional exam requirements/recommendations for international students: Required—TOEFL (minimum score 580 paper-based). *Faculty research:* Software engineering, networks, distributed computing, computer engineering, electrophysics, artificial intelligence, bioinformatics and computational biology, computer graphics, communications, control systems, signal processing, power systems, microelectronics, algorithms.

Wayne State University, College of Engineering, Department of Electrical and Computer Engineering, Detroit, MI 48202. Offers computer engineering (MS, PhD); electrical engineering (MS, PhD). Application deadline for PhD is February 28 for full funding consideration for fall semester. *Faculty:* 19. *Students:* 107 full-time (27 women), 37 part-time (3 women); includes 14 minority (2 Black or African American, non-Hispanic/Latino; 8 Asian, non-Hispanic/Latino; 3 Hispanic/Latino; 1 Two or more races, non-Hispanic/Latino), 98 international. Average age 27. 270 applicants, 34% accepted, 29 enrolled. In 2018, 107 master's, 9 doctorates awarded. *Entrance requirements:* For master's, GRE (recommended if BS is not from ABET-accredited university), BS from ABET-accredited university; for doctorate, GRE, minimum undergraduate GPA of 3.5 with major or substantial specialized work in proposed doctoral major field, or master's degree in electrical and computer engineering with minimum master's GPA of 3.6. Additional exam requirements/recommendations for international students: Required—TOEFL (minimum score 550 paper-based; 79 iBT), TWE (minimum score 5.5), Michigan English Language Assessment Battery (minimum score 85); Recommended—IELTS (minimum score 6.5). *Application deadline:* For fall admission, 6/1 priority date for domestic students, 5/1 priority date for international students; for winter admission, 10/1 priority date for domestic students, 9/1 priority date for international students; for spring admission, 2/1 priority date for domestic students, 1/1 priority date for international students. Applications are processed on a rolling basis. Application fee: $50. Electronic applications accepted. *Expenses:* Contact institution. *Financial support:* In 2018–19, 58 students received support, including 2 fellowships with tuition reimbursements available (averaging $20,000 per year), 5 research assistantships with tuition reimbursements available (averaging $19,324 per year), 10 teaching assistantships with tuition reimbursements available (averaging $20,272 per year); scholarships/grants, health care benefits, and unspecified assistantships also available. Support available to part-time students. Financial award applicants required to submit FAFSA. *Faculty research:* Bioengineering and bioelectromagnetics; computer engineering; control theory; information and communication theory; networks and computer-aided design; parallel and distributed systems; neural networks (soft computing); optical engineering; power systems; software engineering; solid state devices; smart sensors and VLSI. *Total annual research expenditures:* $1.1 million. *Unit head:* Dr. Mohammed Ismail Elnaggar, Department Chair, 734-284-3100, E-mail: gd8686@wayne.edu. *Application contact:* Eric Scimeca, Graduate Program Coordinator, 313-577-0412, E-mail: eric.scimeca@wayne.edu.
Website: http://engineering.wayne.edu/ece/

Western Michigan University, Graduate College, College of Engineering and Applied Sciences, Department of Electrical and Computer Engineering, Kalamazoo, MI 49008. Offers computer engineering (MSE); electrical and computer engineering (PhD); electrical engineering (MSE). *Program availability:* Part-time. *Degree requirements:* For master's, thesis optional.

Western New England University, College of Engineering, Department of Electrical Engineering, Springfield, MA 01119. Offers MSEE. *Program availability:* Part-time, evening/weekend. *Faculty:* 8 full-time (0 women). *Students:* 10 part-time (3 women); includes 1 minority (Black or African American, non-Hispanic/Latino), 3 international. Average age 27. 73 applicants, 70% accepted, 7 enrolled. In 2018, 6 master's awarded. *Degree requirements:* For master's, comprehensive exam, thesis optional. *Entrance requirements:* For master's, official transcript, bachelor's degree in engineering or related field, two recommendations, resume. Additional exam requirements/recommendations for international students: Required—TOEFL (minimum score 79 iBT). *Application deadline:* Applications are processed on a rolling basis. Application fee: $30. Electronic applications accepted. *Expenses:* Contact institution. *Financial support:* Application deadline: 4/15; applicants required to submit FAFSA. *Faculty research:* Superconductors, microwave cooking, computer voice output, digital filters, computer engineering. *Unit head:* Dr. Neeraj J. Magotra, Chair, 413-782-1274, E-mail: neeraj.magotra@wne.edu. *Application contact:* Matthew Fox, Executive Director of Graduate Admissions, 413-782-1410, Fax: 413-782-1777, E-mail: study@wne.edu.
Website: http://www1.wne.edu/academics/graduate/electrical-engineering.cfm

West Virginia University, Statler College of Engineering and Mineral Resources, Morgantown, WV 26506. Offers aerospace engineering (MSAE, PhD); chemical engineering (MS Ch E, PhD); civil engineering (MSCE, PhD); computer engineering (PhD); computer science (MSCS, PhD); electrical engineering (MSEE, PhD); energy systems engineering (MSESE); engineering (MSE); industrial engineering (MSIE, PhD); industrial hygiene (MS); material science and engineering (MSMSE, PhD); mechanical engineering (MSME, PhD); mining engineering (MS Min E, PhD); petroleum and natural gas engineering (MSPNGE, PhD); safety management (MS); software engineering (MSSE). *Program availability:* Part-time. *Students:* 466 full-time (113 women), 154 part-time (27 women); includes 57 minority (22 Black or African American, non-Hispanic/Latino; 1 American Indian or Alaska Native, non-Hispanic/Latino; 8 Asian, non-Hispanic/Latino; 12 Hispanic/Latino; 14 Two or more races, non-Hispanic/Latino), 283 international. In 2018, 179 master's, 39 doctorates awarded. Terminal master's awarded for partial completion of doctoral program. *Degree requirements:* For master's, thesis optional; for doctorate, comprehensive exam, thesis/dissertation. *Entrance requirements:* Additional exam requirements/recommendations for international students: Required—TOEFL (minimum score 550 paper-based). *Application deadline:* For fall admission, 4/1 for international students; for winter admission, 4/1 for international students; for spring admission, 10/1 for international students. Applications are processed on a rolling basis. Application fee: $60. Electronic applications accepted. *Expenses:* Contact institution. *Financial support:* Fellowships, research assistantships, teaching assistantships, career-related internships or fieldwork, Federal Work-Study, institutionally sponsored loans, health care benefits, tuition waivers (full and partial), unspecified assistantships, and administrative assistantships available. Financial award application deadline: 2/1; financial award applicants required to submit FAFSA. *Faculty research:* Composite materials, software engineering, information systems, aerodynamics, vehicle propulsion and emission. *Unit head:* Dr. Earl Scime, Interim Dean, 304-293-4157 Ext. 2237, Fax: 304-293-2037, E-mail: earl.scime@mail.wvu.edu. *Application contact:* Dr. David A. Wyrick, Associate Dean, Academic Affairs, 304-293-4334, Fax: 304-293-5024, E-mail: david.wyrick@mail.wvu.edu.
Website: https://www.statler.wvu.edu

Wichita State University, Graduate School, College of Engineering, Department of Electrical Engineering and Computer Science, Wichita, KS 67260. Offers computer networking (MS); computer science (MS); electrical and computer engineering (MS); electrical engineering and computer science (PhD). *Program availability:* Part-time, evening/weekend. *Unit head:* Dr. Gergely Zaruba, Chair, 316-978-3156, Fax: 316-978-5408, E-mail: gergely.zaruba@wichita.edu. *Application contact:* Jordan Oleson, Admissions Coordinator, 316-978-3095, Fax: 316-978-3253, E-mail: jordan.oleson@wichita.edu.
Website: http://www.wichita.edu/eecs

Widener University, Graduate Programs in Engineering, Program in Electrical Engineering, Chester, PA 19013. Offers M Eng. *Program availability:* Part-time, evening/weekend. *Degree requirements:* For master's, thesis optional. Electronic applications accepted. *Faculty research:* Signal and image processing, electromagnetics, telecommunications and computer network.

Wilkes University, College of Graduate and Professional Studies, College of Science and Engineering, Department of Electrical Engineering and Physics, Wilkes-Barre, PA 18766-0002. Offers bioengineering (MS); electrical engineering (MSEE). *Program availability:* Part-time. *Students:* 8 full-time (2 women), 4 part-time (1 woman); includes 3 minority (1 Asian, non-Hispanic/Latino; 2 Hispanic/Latino), 1 international. Average age 24. In 2018, 15 master's awarded. *Entrance requirements:* For master's, GRE General Test. Additional exam requirements/recommendations for international students: Required—TOEFL (minimum score 550 paper-based; 79 iBT). *Application deadline:* Applications are processed on a rolling basis. Application fee: $45 ($65 for international students). Electronic applications accepted. Tuition and fees vary according to course load, degree level and program. *Financial support:* Unspecified assistantships available. Financial award application deadline: 3/1; financial award applicants required to submit FAFSA. *Unit head:* Dr. Prahlad Murthy, Interim Dean, 570-408-4600, Fax: 570-408-7846, E-mail: prahlad.murthy@wilkes.edu. *Application contact:* Kristin Donati, Associate Director of Graduate Admissions, 570-408-3338, Fax: 570-408-7846, E-mail: kristin.donati@wilkes.edu.
Website: http://www.wilkes.edu/academics/colleges/science-and-engineering/engineering-physics/electrical-engineering-physics/index.aspx

Worcester Polytechnic Institute, Graduate Admissions, Department of Electrical and Computer Engineering, Worcester, MA 01609-2280. Offers electrical and computer engineering (Advanced Certificate, Graduate Certificate); electrical engineering (M Eng, MS, PhD); power systems engineering (MS). *Program availability:* Part-time, evening/weekend, 100% online, blended/hybrid learning. *Students:* 50 full-time (6 women), 157 part-time (23 women); includes 52 minority (12 Black or African American, non-Hispanic/Latino; 22 Asian, non-Hispanic/Latino; 16 Hispanic/Latino; 2 Two or more races, non-Hispanic/Latino), 69 international. Average age 29. 442 applicants, 45% accepted, 53 enrolled. In 2018, 79 master's, 6 doctorates, 5 other advanced degrees awarded. Terminal master's awarded for partial completion of doctoral program. *Degree requirements:* For master's, thesis optional; for doctorate, comprehensive exam, thesis/dissertation. *Entrance requirements:* For master's, GRE (recommended), 3 letters of recommendation; for doctorate, GRE (recommended), 3 letters of recommendation, statement of purpose. Additional exam requirements/recommendations for international students: Required—TOEFL (minimum score 563 paper-based; 84 iBT), IELTS (minimum score 7), GRE. *Application deadline:* For fall admission, 1/1 priority date for domestic students, 1/1 for international students; for spring admission, 10/1 priority date for domestic students, 10/1 for international students. Applications are processed on a rolling basis. Application fee: $70. Electronic applications accepted. *Financial support:* Fellowships, research assistantships, teaching assistantships, career-related internships or fieldwork, institutionally sponsored loans, scholarships/grants, and unspecified assistantships available. Financial award application deadline: 1/1. *Unit head:* Dr. Donald Brown, Department Head, 508-831-5231, Fax: 508-831-5491, E-mail: drb@wpi.edu. *Application contact:* Dr. Berk Sunar, Graduate Coordinator, 508-831-5231, Fax: 508-831-5491, E-mail: sunar@wpi.edu.
Website: https://www.wpi.edu/academics/departments/electrical-computer-engineering

Wright State University, Graduate School, College of Engineering and Computer Science, Department of Electrical Engineering, Dayton, OH 45435. Offers MS. *Program availability:* Part-time, evening/weekend. *Degree requirements:* For master's, thesis or course option alternative. *Entrance requirements:* Additional exam requirements/recommendations for international students: Required—TOEFL. *Faculty research:* Robotics, circuit design, power electronics, image processing, communication systems.

Yale University, Graduate School of Arts and Sciences, School of Engineering and Applied Science, Department of Electrical Engineering, New Haven, CT 06520. Offers MS, PhD. Terminal master's awarded for partial completion of doctoral program. *Degree requirements:* For doctorate, thesis/dissertation, exam. *Entrance requirements:* For master's and doctorate, GRE General Test. Additional exam requirements/recommendations for international students: Required—TOEFL. *Faculty research:* Signal processing, control, and communications; digital systems and computer engineering; microelectronics and photonics; nanotechnology; computers, sensors, and networking.

Youngstown State University, College of Graduate Studies, College of Science, Technology, Engineering and Mathematics, Department of Electrical and Computer Engineering, Youngstown, OH 44555-0001. Offers computer engineering (MSE); electrical engineering (MSE). *Program availability:* Part-time, evening/weekend. *Degree requirements:* For master's, thesis optional. *Entrance requirements:* For master's, minimum GPA of 2.75 in field. Additional exam requirements/recommendations for international students: Required—TOEFL. *Faculty research:* Computer-aided design, power systems, electromagnetic energy conversion, sensors, control systems.

Section 10
Energy and Power Engineering

This section contains a directory of institutions offering graduate work in energy and power engineering. Additional information about programs listed in the directory may be obtained by writing directly to the dean of a graduate school or chair of a department at the address given in the directory.

For programs offering related work, see also in this book *Computer Science and Information Technology, Engineering and Applied Sciences, Industrial Engineering,* and *Mechanical Engineering and Mechanics.* In another guide in this series:

Graduate Programs in the Physical Sciences, Mathematics, Agricultural Sciences, the Environment & Natural Resources
See *Physics* and *Mathematical Sciences*

CONTENTS

Program Directories

Energy and Power Engineering

Appalachian State University, Cratis D. Williams School of Graduate Studies, Department of Sustainable Technology and the Built Environment, Boone, NC 28608. Offers appropriate technology (MS); renewable energy engineering (MS). *Program availability:* Part-time. *Degree requirements:* For master's, comprehensive exam, thesis optional. *Entrance requirements:* For master's, GRE General Test, 3 letters of recommendation. Additional exam requirements/recommendations for international students: Required—TOEFL (minimum score 550 paper-based; 79 iBT), IELTS (minimum score 6.5). Electronic applications accepted. *Expenses: Tuition, area resident:* Full-time $4839; part-time $237 per credit hour. Tuition, state resident: full-time $4839; part-time $237 per credit hour. Tuition, nonresident: full-time $18,271; part-time $895.50 per credit hour. *Faculty research:* Wind power, biofuels, green construction, solar energy production.

Arizona State University at the Tempe campus, Ira A. Fulton Schools of Engineering, School for Engineering of Matter, Transport and Energy, Tempe, AZ 85281. Offers aerospace engineering (MS, PhD); chemical engineering (MS, PhD); materials science and engineering (MS, PhD); mechanical engineering (MS, PhD); solar energy engineering and commercialization (PSM). *Program availability:* Part-time, evening/weekend, online learning. Terminal master's awarded for partial completion of doctoral program. *Degree requirements:* For master's, thesis and oral defense (MS); applied project or comprehensive exam (MSE); interactive Program of Study (iPOS) submitted before completing 50 percent of required credit hours; for doctorate, comprehensive exam, thesis/dissertation, interactive Program of Study (iPOS) submitted before completing 50 percent of required credit hours. *Entrance requirements:* For master's, GRE, minimum GPA of 3.0 or equivalent in last 2 years of work leading to bachelor's degree; for doctorate, GRE, minimum GPA of 3.0 in last 2 years of work leading to bachelor's degree. Additional exam requirements/recommendations for international students: Required—TOEFL, IELTS, or PTE. Electronic applications accepted. *Expenses:* Contact institution. *Faculty research:* Electronic materials and packaging, materials for energy (batteries), adaptive/intelligent materials and structures, multiscale fluid mechanics, membranes, therapeutics and bioseparations, flexible structures, nanostructured materials, micro-/nano-transport.

Carnegie Mellon University, Carnegie Institute of Technology, Department of Civil and Environmental Engineering, Pittsburgh, PA 15213. Offers advanced infrastructure systems (MS, PhD); advanced infrastructure systems technology development and application (MS); air quality engineering and science (MS); civil and environmental engineering (MS, PhD); civil and environmental engineering/engineering and public policy (PhD); civil engineering (MS, PhD); computational mechanics (MS, PhD); computational modeling and monitoring for resilient structural and material systems (MS); energy infrastructure systems (MS); environmental engineering (MS, PhD); environmental management and science (MS, PhD); IT-based sustainable global infrastructure and construction management (MS); sustainability and green design (MS); water quality engineering and science (MS). *Program availability:* Part-time. *Faculty:* 23 full-time (5 women), 12 part-time/adjunct (3 women). *Students:* 264 full-time (109 women); includes 24 minority (6 Black or African American, non-Hispanic/Latino; 13 Asian, non-Hispanic/Latino; 5 Hispanic/Latino), 208 international. Average age 25. 630 applicants, 64% accepted, 114 enrolled. In 2018, 112 master's, 15 doctorates awarded. Terminal master's awarded for partial completion of doctoral program. *Degree requirements:* For master's, thesis optional; for doctorate, comprehensive exam, thesis/dissertation, two-part qualifying exam, public defense of dissertation. *Entrance requirements:* For master's, GRE General Test, BS in engineering, science or mathematics; for doctorate, GRE General Test, BS or MS in engineering, science or mathematics. Additional exam requirements/recommendations for international students: Required—TOEFL (minimum score 84 iBT), TOEFL (minimum score 84 iBT) or IELTS (7.0). *Application deadline:* For fall admission, 1/5 priority date for domestic and international students; for spring admission, 9/15 priority date for domestic and international students. Applications are processed on a rolling basis. Application fee: $75. Electronic applications accepted. *Expenses:* Contact institution. *Financial support:* In 2018–19, 137 students received support. Fellowships with tuition reimbursements available, research assistantships with tuition reimbursements available, scholarships/grants, health care benefits, tuition waivers (full and partial), unspecified assistantships, and service assistantships available. Financial award application deadline: 1/5. *Faculty research:* Advanced infrastructure systems; environmental engineering, sustainability, and science; mechanics, materials, and computing. *Total annual research expenditures:* $7.4 million. *Unit head:* Dr. David A. Dzombak, Professor and Department Head, 412-268-2941, Fax: 412-268-7813, E-mail: dzombak@cmu.edu. *Application contact:* David A. Vey, Director of Graduate Programs, 412-268-2292, Fax: 412-268-7813, E-mail: dvey@andrew.cmu.edu.
Website: http://www.cmu.edu/cee/

Carnegie Mellon University, Mellon College of Science, Department of Chemistry, Pittsburgh, PA 15213-3891. Offers atmospheric chemistry (PhD); bioinorganic chemistry (PhD); bioorganic chemistry and chemical biology (PhD); biophysical chemistry (PhD); catalysis (PhD); green and environmental chemistry (PhD); materials and nanoscience (PhD); renewable energy (PhD); sensors, probes, and imaging (PhD); spectroscopy and single molecule analysis (PhD); theoretical and computational chemistry (PhD). *Program availability:* Part-time. Terminal master's awarded for partial completion of doctoral program. *Degree requirements:* For doctorate, thesis/dissertation, departmental qualifying and oral exams, teaching experience. *Entrance requirements:* For doctorate, GRE General Test, GRE Subject Test. Additional exam requirements/recommendations for international students: Required—TOEFL. Electronic applications accepted. *Faculty research:* Physical and theoretical chemistry, chemical synthesis, biophysical/bioinorganic chemistry.

The Catholic University of America, School of Engineering, Department of Mechanical Engineering, Washington, DC 20064. Offers energy and environment (MME); general (MME); mechanical engineering (MSE, PhD). *Program availability:* Part-time. *Faculty:* 9 full-time (0 women), 7 part-time/adjunct (0 women). *Students:* 11 full-time (4 women), 32 part-time (8 women); includes 7 minority (1 Black or African American, non-Hispanic/Latino; 1 Asian, non-Hispanic/Latino; 1 Hispanic/Latino; 4 Two or more races, non-Hispanic/Latino), 8 international. Average age 31. 27 applicants, 81% accepted, 8 enrolled. In 2018, 13 master's, 1 doctorate awarded. Terminal master's awarded for partial completion of doctoral program. *Degree requirements:* For master's, thesis (for some programs); for doctorate, comprehensive exam, thesis/dissertation. *Entrance requirements:* For master's and doctorate, statement of purpose, official copies of academic transcripts, three letters of recommendation. Additional exam requirements/recommendations for international students: Required—TOEFL (minimum score 550 paper-based; 80 iBT). *Application deadline:* For fall admission, 7/15 priority date for domestic students, 7/1 for international students; for spring admission, 11/15 priority date for domestic students, 11/1 for international students. Applications are processed on a rolling basis. Application fee: $55. Electronic applications accepted. *Expenses:* Contact institution. *Financial support:* Fellowships, research assistantships, teaching assistantships, Federal Work-Study, scholarships/grants, tuition waivers (full and partial), and unspecified assistantships available. Financial award application deadline: 2/1; financial award applicants required to submit FAFSA. *Faculty research:* Energy and environment, acoustics and vibration, biofabrication and lab-on-chip, experimental mechanics, smart materials. *Unit head:* Dr. Sen Nieh, Chair, 202-319-5170, Fax: 202-319-5173, E-mail: nieh@cua.edu. *Application contact:* Dr. Steven Brown, Director of Graduate Admissions, 202-319-5057, Fax: 202-319-6533, E-mail: cua-admissions@cua.edu.
Website: https://engineering.catholic.edu/mechanical/index.html

Clarkson University, Wallace H. Coulter School of Engineering, Master's Programs in Energy Systems, Schenectady, NY 13699. Offers electrical engineering (ME), including power engineering; energy systems (MS). *Program availability:* Part-time, evening/weekend. *Students:* 5 full-time (4 women), 3 part-time (0 women); includes 1 minority (Hispanic/Latino). 12 applicants, 58% accepted, 6 enrolled. In 2018, 2 master's awarded. *Degree requirements:* For master's, project. *Entrance requirements:* Additional exam requirements/recommendations for international students: Required—TOEFL (minimum score 550 paper-based, 80 iBT) or IELTS (6.5). *Application deadline:* Applications are processed on a rolling basis. Application fee: $50. Electronic applications accepted. *Expenses: Tuition:* Full-time $24,984; part-time $1388 per credit hour. *Required fees:* $225. Tuition and fees vary according to campus/location and program. *Financial support:* Scholarships/grants available. *Unit head:* Hugo Irizarry-Quinones, Associate Dean of Engineering, 518-631-9881, E-mail: hirizarr@clarkson.edu. *Application contact:* Dan Capogna, Director of Graduate Admissions, 518-631-9910, E-mail: graduate@clarkson.edu.
Website: https://www.clarkson.edu/academics/graduate

Cornell University, Graduate School, Graduate Fields of Agriculture and Life Sciences and Graduate Fields of Engineering, Field of Biological and Environmental Engineering, Ithaca, NY 14853. Offers bioenergy and integrated energy systems (M Eng, MPS, MS, PhD); biological engineering (M Eng, MPS, MS, PhD); bioprocess engineering (M Eng, MPS, MS, PhD); ecohydrology (M Eng, MPS, MS, PhD); environmental engineering (M Eng, MPS, MS, PhD); environmental management (MPS); food engineering (M Eng, MPS, MS, PhD); industrial biotechnology (M Eng, MPS, MS, PhD); nanobiotechnology (M Eng, MPS, MS, PhD); sustainable systems (M Eng, MPS, MS, PhD); synthetic biology (MS); syntheticbiology (M Eng, MPS, PhD). Terminal master's awarded for partial completion of doctoral program. *Degree requirements:* For master's, thesis (MS); for doctorate, comprehensive exam, thesis/dissertation. *Entrance requirements:* For master's, letters of recommendation (3 for MS, 2 for M Eng and MPS); for doctorate, GRE General Test, 3 letters of recommendation. Additional exam requirements/recommendations for international students: Required—TOEFL (minimum score 550 paper-based; 77 iBT). Electronic applications accepted. *Faculty research:* Biological and food engineering, environmental, soil and water engineering, international agricultural engineering, structures and controlled environments, machine systems and energy.

Dartmouth College, Thayer School of Engineering, Program in Energy Engineering, Hanover, NH 03755. Offers MS, PhD. *Faculty research:* Resource and environmental analysis, decision theory, risk assessment and public policy, environmental fluid mechanics.

Florida State University, The Graduate School, FAMU-FSU College of Engineering, Department of Mechanical Engineering, Tallahassee, FL 32310-6046. Offers mechanical engineering (MS, PhD); sustainable energy (MS). *Program availability:* Part-time. Terminal master's awarded for partial completion of doctoral program. *Degree requirements:* For master's, thesis optional, 30 credit hours (24 coursework, 6 research); for doctorate, thesis/dissertation, 45 credit hours (21 coursework, 24 research). *Entrance requirements:* For master's and doctorate, GRE General Test (minimum scores: Verbal 150, Quantitative 155), minimum GPA of 3.0, official transcripts, resume, personal statement, 3 letters of recommendation. Additional exam requirements/recommendations for international students: Required—TOEFL (minimum score 550 paper-based; 80 iBT), IELTS (minimum score 6.5). Electronic applications accepted. *Expenses: Tuition, area resident:* Part-time $479.32 per credit hour. Tuition and fees vary according to campus/location and program. *Faculty research:* Aero-propulsion, superconductivity, smart materials, nanomaterials, intelligent robotic systems, robotic locomotion, sustainable energy.

Georgia Southern University, Jack N. Averitt College of Graduate Studies, Allen E. Paulson College of Engineering and Computing, Department of Mechanical Engineering, Program in Engineering/Energy Science, Statesboro, GA 30458. Offers MSAE. *Program availability:* Part-time. *Degree requirements:* For master's, comprehensive exam, thesis optional. *Entrance requirements:* For master's, undergraduate major or equivalent in proposed study area. Additional exam requirements/recommendations for international students: Required—TOEFL (minimum score 550 paper-based; 80 iBT), IELTS (minimum score 6). Electronic applications accepted. *Expenses: Tuition, area resident:* Part-time $3324 per semester. Tuition, state resident: full-time $5814; part-time $3324 per semester. Tuition, nonresident: full-time $23,204; part-time $13,260 per semester. *Required fees:* $2092; $2092. Tuition and fees vary according to course load, degree level, campus/location and program. *Faculty research:* Renewable energy and engines, biomechatronics, digital surface imaging, smart materials, nanocomposite material science.

Instituto Tecnologico de Santo Domingo, Graduate School, Area of Basic And Environmental Sciences, Santo Domingo, Dominican Republic. Offers environmental science (M En S), including environmental education, environmental management, marine resources, natural resources management; mathematics (MS, PhD); renewable energy technology (MS, Certificate).

Inter American University of Puerto Rico, Bayamón Campus, Graduate School, Bayamón, PR 00957. Offers biology (MS), including environmental sciences and ecology, molecular biotechnology; electrical engineering (ME), including control system, potence system; human resources (MBA); mechanical engineering (ME, MS), including aerospace, energy. *Program availability:* Part-time, evening/weekend. *Degree requirements:* For master's, comprehensive exam, research project. *Entrance requirements:* For master's, EXADEP, GRE General Test, letters of recommendation. *Expenses: Tuition:* Full-time $3816; part-time $1908 per trimester. *Required fees:* $735; $642.

Kansas State University, Graduate School, College of Engineering, Department of Electrical and Computer Engineering, Manhattan, KS 66506. Offers electrical engineering (MS), including bioengineering, communication systems, design of computer systems, electrical engineering, energy and power systems, integrated circuits and devices, real time embedded systems, renewable energy, signal processing. *Program availability:* Part-time, evening/weekend, online learning. *Degree requirements:* For master's, thesis or alternative, final exam; for doctorate, thesis/dissertation, final exam, preliminary exams. *Entrance requirements:* For master's, GRE General Test, bachelor's degree in electrical engineering or computer science, minimum GPA of 3.0; for doctorate, GRE General Test. Additional exam requirements/recommendations for international students: Required—TOEFL (minimum score 600 paper-based; 85 iBT). Electronic applications accepted. *Faculty research:* Energy systems and renewable energy, computer systems and real time embedded systems, communication systems and signal processing, integrated circuits and devices, bioengineering.

Lawrence Technological University, College of Engineering, Southfield, MI 48075-1058. Offers architectural engineering (MS); automotive engineering (MS); biomedical engineering (MS); civil engineering (MA, MS, PhD), including environmental engineering (MS), geotechnical engineering (MS), structural engineering (MS), transportation engineering (MS), water resource engineering (MS); construction engineering management (MA); electrical and computer engineering (MS); engineering management (MEM); engineering technology (MS); fire engineering (MS); industrial engineering (MS), including healthcare systems; manufacturing systems (ME); mechanical engineering (MS, DE, PhD), including automotive engineering (MS), energy engineering (MS), manufacturing (DE), solid mechanics (MS), thermal/fluid systems (MS); mechatronic systems engineering (MS). *Program availability:* Part-time, evening/weekend. Terminal master's awarded for partial completion of doctoral program. *Degree requirements:* For master's, thesis optional; for doctorate, comprehensive exam, thesis/dissertation optional. *Entrance requirements:* Additional exam requirements/recommendations for international students: Required—TOEFL (minimum score 550 paper-based; 79 iBT), IELTS (minimum score 6.5). Electronic applications accepted. *Faculty research:* Innovative infrastructure and building structures and materials; connectivity and mobility; automotive systems modeling, simulation and testing; biomedical devices and materials; building mechanical/electrical systems.

Lehigh University, P.C. Rossin College of Engineering and Applied Science, Program in Energy Systems Engineering, Bethlehem, PA 18015. Offers M Eng. *Program availability:* Part-time. *Faculty:* 1 full-time (0 women), 2 part-time/adjunct (0 women). *Students:* 8 full-time (1 woman), 2 part-time (0 women); includes 1 minority (Asian, non-Hispanic/Latino), 2 international. Average age 23. 18 applicants, 94% accepted, 7 enrolled. In 2018, 9 master's awarded. *Entrance requirements:* For master's, GRE. Additional exam requirements/recommendations for international students: Required—TOEFL (minimum score 79 iBT), IELTS (minimum score 6.5), TOEFL or IELTS required. *Application deadline:* For fall admission, 5/15 for domestic and international students. Application fee: $75. *Expenses:* $1500 per credit. *Financial support:* Application deadline: 1/15. *Faculty research:* Machine learning, smart grid, electrification, renewable energy, energy systems. *Unit head:* Prof. Ramesh Shankar, PhD, Director, 610-758-3529, E-mail: ras816@lehigh.edu. *Application contact:* Susan Kanarek, Graduate Coordinator, 610-758-3650, E-mail: sak319@lehigh.edu.
Website: http://www.lehigh.edu/esei

New Jersey Institute of Technology, Newark College of Engineering, Newark, NJ 07102. Offers biomedical engineering (MS, PhD); biopharmaceutical engineering (MS); chemical engineering (MS, PhD); civil engineering (MS, PhD); computer engineering (MS); critical infrastructure systems (MS); electrical engineering (MS, PhD); engineering management (MS); engineering science (MS); environmental engineering (MS, PhD); healthcare systems management (MS); industrial engineering (MS, PhD); internet engineering (MS); manufacturing systems engineering (MS); materials science & engineering (PhD); materials science and engineering (MS); mechanical engineering (MS, PhD); occupational safety and health engineering (MS). *Program availability:* Part-time, evening/weekend. *Faculty:* 147 full-time (26 women), 133 part-time/adjunct (16 women). *Students:* 690 full-time (163 women), 594 part-time (130 women); includes 427 minority (79 Black or African American, non-Hispanic/Latino; 181 Asian, non-Hispanic/Latino; 140 Hispanic/Latino; 27 Two or more races, non-Hispanic/Latino), 553 international. Average age 27. 2,334 applicants, 57% accepted, 452 enrolled. In 2018, 418 master's, 31 doctorates awarded. Terminal master's awarded for partial completion of doctoral program. *Degree requirements:* For master's, thesis (for some programs); for doctorate, thesis/dissertation. *Entrance requirements:* For master's, GRE General Test, minimum GPA 2.8, personal statement, 1 letter of recommendation, transcripts; for doctorate, GRE General Test, minimum GPA of 3.5, personal statement, 3 letters of recommendation, transcripts. Additional exam requirements/recommendations for international students: Required—TOEFL (minimum score 550 paper-based; 79 iBT), IELTS (minimum score 6.5). *Application deadline:* For fall admission, 6/1 priority date for domestic students, 5/1 priority date for international students; for spring admission, 11/15 priority date for domestic and international students. Applications are processed on a rolling basis. Application fee: $75. Electronic applications accepted. *Expenses:* $22,690 per year (in-state), $32,136 per year (out-of-state). *Financial support:* In 2018–19, 396 students received support, including 52 fellowships with full tuition reimbursements available (averaging $22,000 per year), 113 research assistantships with full tuition reimbursements available (averaging $22,000 per year), 101 teaching assistantships with full tuition reimbursements available (averaging $22,000 per year); career-related internships or fieldwork, Federal Work-Study, scholarships/grants, and unspecified assistantships also available. Financial award application deadline: 1/15. *Faculty research:* Nonlinear signal processing, intelligent medical image analysis, calibration issues in coherent localization, computer-aided design, neural network for tool wear measurement. *Total annual research expenditures:* $41.7 million. *Unit head:* Dr. Moshe Kam, Dean, 973-596-5534, Fax: 973-596-2316, E-mail: moshe.kam@njit.edu. *Application contact:* Stephen Eck, Director of Admissions, 973-596-3300, Fax: 973-596-3461, E-mail: admissions@njit.edu.
Website: http://engineering.njit.edu/

New York Institute of Technology, College of Engineering and Computing Sciences, Department of Energy Management, Old Westbury, NY 11568-8000. Offers energy technology (Advanced Certificate); environmental management (Advanced Certificate); facilities management (Advanced Certificate); infrastructure security management (Advanced Certificate). *Program availability:* Part-time, evening/weekend, 100% online, blended/hybrid learning. *Faculty:* 2 full-time (0 women), 6 part-time/adjunct (1 woman). *Students:* 30 full-time (4 women), 46 part-time (11 women); includes 27 minority (7 Black or African American, non-Hispanic/Latino; 10 Asian, non-Hispanic/Latino; 9 Hispanic/Latino; 1 Two or more races, non-Hispanic/Latino), 22 international. Average age 32. 96 applicants, 75% accepted, 24 enrolled. In 2018, 3 Advanced Certificates awarded. *Entrance requirements:* For degree, BS or equivalent; minimum undergraduate GPA of 2.85. Additional exam requirements/recommendations for international students: Required—TOEFL (minimum score 79 iBT), IELTS (minimum score 6), PTE (minimum score 53). *Application deadline:* For fall admission, 7/1 for domestic students, 6/1 for international students; for spring admission, 12/1 for domestic and international students. Applications are processed on a rolling basis. Application fee: $50. Electronic applications accepted. *Expenses: Tuition:* Full-time $1285; part-time $1285 per credit. *Required fees:* $215; $175 per unit. Tuition and fees vary according to course load, degree level and campus/location. *Financial support:* Fellowships with partial tuition reimbursements, teaching assistantships with partial tuition reimbursements, career-related internships or fieldwork, Federal Work-Study, scholarships/grants, tuition waivers (full and partial), and unspecified assistantships available. Support available to part-time students. Financial award application deadline: 2/15; financial award applicants required to submit FAFSA. *Faculty research:* Alternative energy systems; energy policy, master planning, and auditing; facilities management; lighting technology; cogeneration; utility rate structures; smart homes; monitoring systems; building information modeling; sustainability. *Unit head:* Dr. Robert Amundsen, Department Chair, 516-686-7578, E-mail: ramundse@nyit.edu. *Application contact:* Alice Dolitsky, Director, Graduate Admissions, 516-686-7520, Fax: 516-686-1116, E-mail: admissions@nyit.edu.
Website: http://www.nyit.edu/engineering/department_of_energy_management

North Carolina Agricultural and Technical State University, The Graduate College, College of Engineering, Department of Electrical and Computer Engineering, Greensboro, NC 27411. Offers electrical engineering (MSEE, PhD), including communications and signal processing, computer engineering, electronic and optical materials and devices, power systems and control. *Program availability:* Part-time. *Degree requirements:* For master's, project, thesis defense; for doctorate, thesis/dissertation. *Entrance requirements:* For master's, GRE General Test, GRE Subject Test, minimum GPA of 2.8; for doctorate, GRE General Test, minimum GPA of 3.0. *Faculty research:* Semiconductor compounds, VLSI design, image processing, optical systems and devices, fault-tolerant computing.

Northeastern University, College of Engineering, Boston, MA 02115-5096. Offers bioengineering (MS, PhD); chemical engineering (MS, PhD); civil engineering (MS, PhD); computer engineering (PhD); computer systems engineering (MS); electrical and computer engineering (MS); electrical and computer engineering leadership (MS); electrical engineering (PhD); energy systems (MS); engineering and public policy (MS); engineering management (MS, Certificate); environmental engineering (MS); industrial engineering (MS, PhD); information assurance (PhD); information systems (MS); interdisciplinary engineering (PhD); mechanical engineering (PhD); operations research (MS); telecommunication systems management (MS). *Program availability:* Part-time, online learning. Electronic applications accepted. *Expenses:* Contact institution.

Saginaw Valley State University, College of Science, Engineering, and Technology, University Center, MI 48710. Offers computer science and information systems (MS); energy and materials (MS). *Program availability:* Part-time, evening/weekend. *Faculty:* 5 full-time (0 women), 1 part-time/adjunct (0 women). *Students:* 10 full-time (1 woman), 12 part-time (3 women); includes 1 minority (Asian, non-Hispanic/Latino), 8 international. Average age 32. 35 applicants, 80% accepted, 8 enrolled. *Degree requirements:* For master's, field project or thesis work. *Entrance requirements:* For master's, minimum GPA of 3.0. Additional exam requirements/recommendations for international students: Required—TOEFL (minimum score 550 paper-based; 79 iBT). *Application deadline:* For fall admission, 7/15 for international students; for winter admission, 11/15 for international students; for spring admission, 4/15 for international students. Applications are processed on a rolling basis. Application fee: $30 ($90 for international students). Electronic applications accepted. *Expenses: Tuition, area resident:* Full-time $6225; part-time $623 per credit hour. Tuition, state resident: full-time $6225; part-time $623 per credit hour. Tuition, nonresident: full-time $14,215; part-time $1185 per credit hour. *International tuition:* $14,215 full-time. *Required fees:* $263; $14.60 per credit hour. Tuition and fees vary according to degree level. *Financial support:* Federal Work-Study and scholarships/grants available. Support available to part-time students. Financial award application deadline: 4/1; financial award applicants required to submit FAFSA. *Unit head:* Dr. Robert Tuttle, Program Coordinator, 989-964-4144, Fax: 989-964-2717. *Application contact:* Jenna Briggs, Director, Graduate and International Admissions, 989-964-6096, Fax: 989-964-2788, E-mail: gradadm@svsu.edu.
Website: http://www.svsu.edu/collegeofscienceengineeringtechnology/

San Francisco State University, Division of Graduate Studies, College of Science and Engineering, School of Engineering, San Francisco, CA 94132-1722. Offers embedded electrical and computer systems (MS); energy systems (MS); structural/earthquake engineering (MS). *Program availability:* Part-time. *Application deadline:* Applications are processed on a rolling basis. Electronic applications accepted. *Unit head:* Dr. Kwok-Siong Teh, Director, 415-338-1228, Fax: 415-338-0525, E-mail: ksteh@sfsu.edu. *Application contact:* Dr. Hamid Shahnasser, Graduate Coordinator, 415-338-2124, Fax: 415-338-0525, E-mail: hamid@sfsu.edu.
Website: http://engineering.sfsu.edu/

Santa Clara University, School of Engineering, Santa Clara, CA 95053. Offers applied mathematics (MS); bioengineering (MS); civil, environmental, and sustainable engineering (MS); computer science and engineering (MS, PhD, Engineer); electrical engineering (MS, PhD, Engineer); engineering management and leadership (MS); mechanical engineering (MS, PhD, Engineer); power systems and sustainable energy (MS); software engineering (MS). *Program availability:* Part-time. *Faculty:* 72 full-time (24 women), 52 part-time/adjunct (9 women). *Students:* 555 full-time (211 women), 269 part-time (91 women); includes 208 minority (8 Black or African American, non-Hispanic/Latino; 1 American Indian or Alaska Native, non-Hispanic/Latino; 145 Asian, non-Hispanic/Latino; 28 Hispanic/Latino; 26 Two or more races, non-Hispanic/Latino), 472 international. Average age 27. 1,309 applicants, 36% accepted, 269 enrolled. In 2018, 320 master's, 7 doctorates awarded. *Entrance requirements:* For master's, GRE, official transcript; for doctorate, GRE, Official transcript, 500 word statement of purpose, three letters of recommendation. Additional exam requirements/recommendations for international students: Required—TOEFL (minimum score 79 iBT), IELTS (minimum score 6.5). *Application deadline:* For fall admission, 6/1 for domestic students; for winter admission, 9/6 for domestic students; for spring admission, 1/10 for domestic students; for summer admission, 3/6 for domestic students. Application fee: $60. Electronic applications accepted. *Financial support:* Fellowships, Federal Work-Study, and scholarships/grants available. Support available to part-time students. Financial award applicants required to submit FAFSA. *Unit head:* Dr. Elaine Scott, Dean, 408-554-3512, E-mail: epscott@scu.edu. *Application contact:* Stacey Tinker, Director of Admissions and Marketing, 408-554-4748, Fax: 408-554-4323, E-mail: stinker@scu.edu.
Website: http://www.scu.edu/engineering/graduate/

Southern Illinois University Carbondale, Graduate School, College of Engineering, Program in Engineering Science, Carbondale, IL 62901-4701. Offers engineering science (PhD), including civil and environmental engineering, electrical and computer engineering, mechanical engineering and energy processes, mining and mineral resources engineering. *Degree requirements:* For doctorate, thesis/dissertation. *Entrance requirements:* For doctorate, GRE General Test, minimum GPA of 3.5. Additional exam requirements/recommendations for international students: Required—TOEFL.

Stanford University, School of Earth, Energy and Environmental Sciences, Department of Energy Resources Engineering, Stanford, CA 94305-2004. Offers energy resources engineering (MS, PhD, Eng); petroleum engineering (MS, PhD). *Expenses: Tuition:* Full-time $50,703; part-time $32,970 per year. *Required fees:* $651.

Stanford University, School of Engineering, Department of Civil and Environmental Engineering, Stanford, CA 94305-2004. Offers atmosphere and energy (MS, PhD); construction (MS), including construction engineering and management, design-construction integration, sustainable design and construction; environmental engineering and science (MS, PhD, Eng); environmental fluid mechanics and hydrology (PhD); geomechanics (MS); structural engineering (MS). *Expenses: Tuition:* Full-time $50,703; part-time $32,970 per year. *Required fees:* $651.
Website: http://www-ce.stanford.edu/

Energy and Power Engineering

Texas A&M University–Kingsville, College of Graduate Studies, Frank H. Dotterweich College of Engineering, Program in Sustainable Energy Systems Engineering, Kingsville, TX 78363. Offers PhD. *Degree requirements:* For doctorate, variable foreign language requirement, comprehensive exam, thesis/dissertation (for some programs). *Entrance requirements:* For doctorate, GRE, MAT, GMAT, bachelor's or master's degree in engineering or science, curriculum vitae, official transcripts, statement of purpose, three letters of recommendation. Additional exam requirements/ recommendations for international students: Required—TOEFL (minimum score 550 paper-based; 79 iBT). Electronic applications accepted.

Texas Tech University, Graduate School, Interdisciplinary Programs, Lubbock, TX 79409-1030. Offers arid land studies (MS); biotechnology (MS); heritage and museum sciences (MA); interdisciplinary studies (MA, MS); wind science and engineering (PhD); JD/MS. *Program availability:* Part-time, 100% online, blended/hybrid learning. *Faculty:* 10 full-time (5 women). *Students:* 98 full-time (50 women), 82 part-time (52 women); includes 75 minority (33 Black or African American, non-Hispanic/Latino; 1 American Indian or Alaska Native, non-Hispanic/Latino; 7 Asian, non-Hispanic/Latino; 31 Hispanic/ Latino; 3 Two or more races, non-Hispanic/Latino), 19 international. Average age 30. 96 applicants, 76% accepted, 55 enrolled. In 2018, 64 master's, 1 doctorate awarded. Terminal master's awarded for partial completion of doctoral program. *Degree requirements:* For master's, comprehensive exam (for some programs), thesis (for some programs); for doctorate, comprehensive exam, thesis/dissertation (for some programs). *Entrance requirements:* Additional exam requirements/recommendations for international students: Required—TOEFL (minimum score 550 paper-based; 79 iBT), IELTS (minimum score 6.5), PTE (minimum score 60), Cambridge Advanced (B), Cambridge Proficiency (C), ELS English for Academic Purposes (Level 112). *Application deadline:* For fall admission, 6/1 priority date for domestic students, 1/15 priority date for international students; for spring admission, 9/1 priority date for domestic students, 6/15 priority date for international students. Applications are processed on a rolling basis. Application fee: $65. Electronic applications accepted. *Expenses:* Tuition, state resident: full-time $7776; part-time $324 per credit hour. Tuition, nonresident: full-time $17,736; part-time $739 per credit hour. *Required fees:* $2504; $53.50 per credit hour. $610 per semester. Tuition and fees vary according to program. *Financial support:* In 2018–19, 124 students received support, including 111 fellowships (averaging $4,942 per year), 27 research assistantships (averaging $17,595 per year), 8 teaching assistantships (averaging $13,758 per year); scholarships/grants and unspecified assistantships also available. Financial award application deadline: 4/15; financial award applicants required to submit FAFSA. *Total annual research expenditures:* $2.3 million. *Unit head:* Dr. Mark A. Sheridan, Vice Provost for Graduate and Postdoctoral Affairs/ Dean of the Graduate School, 806-742-2787, Fax: 806-742-1746, E-mail: mark.sheridan@ttu.edu. *Application contact:* David Doerfert, Associate Dean, 806-834-4477, Fax: 806-742-4038, E-mail: david.doerfert@ttu.edu.
Website: www.depts.ttu.edu/gradschool/

Universidad Autonoma de Guadalajara, Graduate Programs, Guadalajara, Mexico. Offers administrative law and justice (LL M); advertising and corporate communications (MA); architecture (M Arch); business (MBA); computational science (MCC); education (Ed M, Ed D); English-Spanish translation (MA); entrepreneurship and management (MBA); integrated management of digital animation (MA); international business (MIB); international corporate law (LL M); Internet technologies (MS); manufacturing systems (MMS); occupational health (MS); philosophy (MA, PhD); power electronics (MS); quality systems (MQS); renewable energy (MS); social evaluation of projects (MBA); strategic market research (MBA); tax law (MA); teaching mathematics (MA).

University at Buffalo, the State University of New York, Graduate School, School of Engineering and Applied Sciences, Department of Civil, Structural, and Environmental Engineering, Buffalo, NY 14260. Offers civil engineering (MS, PhD); engineering science (MS), including data sciences, green energy, Internet of Things, nanoelectronics; environmental and water resources engineering (MS). *Program availability:* Part-time, online learning. Terminal master's awarded for partial completion of doctoral program. *Degree requirements:* For master's, project, thesis, or comprehensive exam; for doctorate, thesis/dissertation. *Entrance requirements:* For master's and doctorate, GRE General Test, letters of reference. Additional exam requirements/recommendations for international students: Required—TOEFL (minimum score 550 paper-based; 79 iBT). Electronic applications accepted. *Faculty research:* Structural and earthquake engineering; geomechanics, geotechnical and geoenvironmental engineering; computational engineering mechanics; bridge engineering; environmental and water resources engineering; transportation systems engineering.

University of Alberta, Faculty of Graduate Studies and Research, Department of Electrical and Computer Engineering, Edmonton, AB T6G 2E1, Canada. Offers communications (M Eng, M Sc, PhD); computer engineering (M Eng, M Sc, PhD); electromagnetics (M Eng, M Sc, PhD); nanotechnology and microdevices (M Eng, M Sc, PhD); power/power electronics (M Eng, M Sc, PhD); systems (M Eng, M Sc, PhD). Terminal master's awarded for partial completion of doctoral program. *Degree requirements:* For master's, thesis; for doctorate, thesis/dissertation. *Entrance requirements:* Additional exam requirements/recommendations for international students: Required—TOEFL. Electronic applications accepted. *Faculty research:* Controls, communications, microelectronics, electromagnetics.

The University of British Columbia, Faculty of Applied Science, Clean Energy Research Center, Vancouver, BC V6T 1Z1, Canada. Offers MEL. *Entrance requirements:* For master's, undergraduate degree in engineering or BS in environmental science; undergraduate thermodynamics course; three or more years of relevant work experience.

University of Calgary, Faculty of Graduate Studies, Schulich School of Engineering, Program in Chemical and Petroleum Engineering, Calgary, AB T2N 1N4, Canada. Offers chemical engineering (M Eng, M Sc, PhD); energy and environment engineering (M Eng, M Sc, PhD); energy and environmental systems (M Eng, M Sc, PhD); environmental engineering (M Eng, M Sc, PhD); petroleum engineering (M Eng, M Sc, PhD); reservoir characterization (M Eng, M Sc). *Program availability:* Part-time. *Degree requirements:* For master's, thesis (for some programs); for doctorate, comprehensive exam, thesis/dissertation, candidacy exam. *Entrance requirements:* For master's, minimum GPA of 3.0 or equivalent; for doctorate, minimum GPA of 3.5 or equivalent. Additional exam requirements/recommendations for international students: Required—TOEFL (minimum score 550 paper-based; 80 iBT), IELTS (minimum score 7). Electronic applications accepted. *Faculty research:* Environmental engineering, biomedical engineering modeling, simulation and control, petroleum recovery and reservoir engineering, phase equilibria and transport properties.

University of Calgary, Faculty of Graduate Studies, Schulich School of Engineering, Program in Civil Engineering, Calgary, AB T2N 1N4, Canada. Offers avalanche mechanics (M Sc, PhD); civil engineering (M Eng, M Sc, PhD); energy and environment engineering (M Eng, M Sc, PhD); environmental engineering (M Eng, M Sc, PhD); geotechnical engineering (M Eng, M Sc, PhD); materials science (M Eng, M Sc, PhD); project management (M Eng, M Sc, PhD); structures and solid mechanics (M Eng, M Sc, PhD); transportation engineering (M Eng, M Sc, PhD); water resources (M Eng, M Sc, PhD). *Program availability:* Part-time. *Degree requirements:* For master's, thesis; for doctorate, thesis/dissertation, written and oral candidacy exam. *Entrance requirements:* For master's, minimum GPA of 3.0; for doctorate, minimum GPA of 3.5. Additional exam requirements/recommendations for international students: Required—TOEFL (minimum score 580 paper-based; 93 iBT), IELTS (minimum score 7). Electronic applications accepted. *Faculty research:* Geotechnical engineering, energy and environment, transportation, project management, structures and solid mechanics.

University of Colorado Colorado Springs, College of Engineering and Applied Science, Program in General Engineering, Colorado Springs, CO 80918. Offers computer science (PhD); cybersecurity (ME); energy engineering (ME); engineering management (ME); engineering systems (ME); software engineering (ME); space operations (ME). *Program availability:* Part-time, evening/weekend, blended/hybrid learning. *Faculty:* 1 full-time (0 women), 20 part-time/adjunct (6 women). *Students:* 12 full-time (1 woman), 177 part-time (39 women); includes 38 minority (4 Black or African American, non-Hispanic/Latino; 12 Asian, non-Hispanic/Latino; 12 Hispanic/Latino; 1 Native Hawaiian or other Pacific Islander, non-Hispanic/Latino; 9 Two or more races, non-Hispanic/Latino), 54 international. Average age 35. 44 applicants, 93% accepted, 21 enrolled. In 2018, 24 master's, 15 doctorates awarded. *Degree requirements:* For master's, thesis, portfolio, or project; for doctorate, comprehensive exam, thesis/ dissertation. *Entrance requirements:* For master's, GRE may be required based on past academic performance., Professional recommendation letters are required for all applicants.; for doctorate, GRE (minimum score of 148 new grading scale on the quantitative portion if the applicant has not graduated from a program of recognized standing), minimum GPA of 3.3 in the bachelor's or master's degree program attempted. Additional exam requirements/recommendations for international students: Required—TOEFL (minimum score 80 iBT), IELTS (minimum score 6). *Application deadline:* For fall admission, 6/1 for domestic and international students; for spring admission, 11/1 for domestic and international students; for summer admission, 4/15 for domestic and international students. Applications are processed on a rolling basis. Application fee: $60 ($100 for international students). Electronic applications accepted. *Expenses:* Program tuition and fees vary by course load and residency classification. Please visit the University of Colorado Colorado Springs Student Financial Services website to see current program costs: https://www.uccs.edu/bursar/index.php/estimate-your-bill. *Financial support:* In 2018–19, 1 student received support. Career-related internships or fieldwork, Federal Work-Study, scholarships/grants, traineeships, and unspecified assistantships available. Support available to part-time students. Financial award application deadline: 3/1; financial award applicants required to submit FAFSA. *Total annual research expenditures:* $22,249. *Unit head:* Dr. Donald Rabern, Dean of Engineering and Applied Science, 719-255-3543, E-mail: drabern@uccs.edu. *Application contact:* Dawn House, Extended Studies Coordinator, 719-255-3246, E-mail: dhouse@uccs.edu.

University of Illinois at Urbana–Champaign, Graduate College, College of Engineering, Department of Nuclear, Plasma, and Radiological Engineering, Urbana, IL 61801. Offers energy systems (M Eng); nuclear, plasma, and radiological engineering (MS, PhD). Terminal master's awarded for partial completion of doctoral program.

The University of Iowa, Graduate College, College of Engineering, Department of Mechanical Engineering, Iowa City, IA 52242-1316. Offers energy systems (MS, PhD); engineering design (MS, PhD); fluid dynamics (MS, PhD); materials and manufacturing (MS, PhD); wind energy (MS, PhD). Terminal master's awarded for partial completion of doctoral program. *Degree requirements:* For master's, oral exam or thesis; for doctorate, comprehensive exam, thesis/dissertation. *Entrance requirements:* For master's and doctorate, GRE (minimum Verbal score of 153, Quantitative 151), minimum undergraduate GPA of 3.0. Additional exam requirements/recommendations for international students: Required—TOEFL (minimum score 600 paper-based; 100 iBT), IELTS (minimum score 7). Electronic applications accepted. *Faculty research:* Computer simulation methodology, biomechanics, metal casting, dynamics, laser processing, system reliability, ship hydrodynamics, solid mechanics, fluid dynamics, energy, human modeling and nanotechnology.

University of Massachusetts Lowell, Francis College of Engineering, Program in Energy Engineering, Lowell, MA 01854. Offers MS Eng, PhD. *Degree requirements:* For master's, thesis optional. *Entrance requirements:* For master's, GRE General Test. Additional exam requirements/recommendations for international students: Required—TOEFL.

University of Memphis, Graduate School, Herff College of Engineering, Department of Mechanical Engineering, Memphis, TN 38152. Offers power systems (MS). *Program availability:* Part-time. *Students:* 8 full-time (0 women), 5 part-time (1 woman), 5 international. Average age 28. 18 applicants, 56% accepted, 2 enrolled. In 2018, 6 master's awarded. Terminal master's awarded for partial completion of doctoral program. *Degree requirements:* For master's, comprehensive exam, thesis or alternative; for doctorate, comprehensive exam, thesis/dissertation. *Entrance requirements:* For master's, GRE General Test, MAT, GMAT, BS in mechanical engineering, minimum undergraduate GPA of 3.0, three letters of recommendation; for doctorate, GRE, BS in mechanical engineering, minimum undergraduate GPA of 3.0, three letters of recommendation; for Graduate Certificate, letter of intent, two letters of recommendation. Additional exam requirements/recommendations for international students: Required—TOEFL (minimum score 550 paper-based; 79 iBT). *Application deadline:* For fall admission, 8/1 for domestic students; for spring admission, 12/1 for domestic students. Application fee: $35 ($60 for international students). *Expenses: Tuition, area resident:* Full-time $10,240; part-time $503 per credit hour. Tuition, state resident: full-time $10,464. Tuition, nonresident: full-time $20,224; part-time $991 per credit hour. *Required fees:* $850; $106 per credit hour. *Financial support:* Fellowships with full tuition reimbursements, research assistantships with full tuition reimbursements, teaching assistantships with full tuition reimbursements, career-related internships or fieldwork, Federal Work-Study, scholarships/grants, and unspecified assistantships available. Financial award application deadline: 2/1; financial award applicants required to submit FAFSA. *Faculty research:* Computational fluid dynamics, computational mechanics, integrated design, nondestructive testing, operations research. *Unit head:* Dr. Ali Fatemi, Chair, 901-678-2257, E-mail: afatemi@memphis.edu. *Application contact:* Dr. Teong Tan, Graduate Coordinator, 901-678-2701, Fax: 901-678-5459, E-mail: ttan@memphis.edu.
Website: http://www.memphis.edu/me/

University of Michigan, College of Engineering, Department of Integrative Systems and Design, Ann Arbor, MI 48109. Offers automotive engineering (M Eng); design science (MS, PhD); energy systems engineering (M Eng, MS); global automotive and manufacturing engineering (M Eng); manufacturing engineering (M Eng, D Eng); pharmaceutical engineering (M Eng); robotics and autonomous vehicles (M Eng); systems engineering and design (M Eng); MBA/M Eng; MSE/MS. *Program availability:* Part-time, online learning. *Students:* 163 full-time (38 women), 251 part-time (40 women). 282 applicants, 12% accepted, 15 enrolled. In 2018, 173 master's, 1 doctorate awarded. Terminal master's awarded for partial completion of doctoral program. *Degree requirements:* For master's, capstone project; for doctorate, thesis/dissertation. *Entrance requirements:* For master's and doctorate, GRE. Additional exam requirements/recommendations for international students: Required—TOEFL. *Application deadline:* Applications are processed on a rolling basis. Electronic

applications accepted. *Financial support:* Fellowships, research assistantships with full tuition reimbursements, teaching assistantships with full tuition reimbursements, career-related internships or fieldwork, scholarships/grants, and unspecified assistantships available. Financial award applicants required to submit FAFSA. *Faculty research:* Automotive engineering, design science, energy systems engineering, engineering sustainable systems, financial engineering, global automotive and manufacturing engineering, integrated microsystems, manufacturing engineering, pharmaceutical engineering, robotics and autonomous vehicles. *Total annual research expenditures:* $595,323. *Unit head:* Diann Brei, Department Chair, 734-763-6617, E-mail: drdiannbrei@umich.edu. *Application contact:* Kathy Bishar, Senior Graduate Coordinator, 734-764-3312, E-mail: kbishar@umich.edu.
Website: http://www.isd.engin.umich.edu

University of Michigan–Dearborn, College of Engineering and Computer Science, MSE Program in Energy Systems Engineering, Dearborn, MI 48128. Offers MSE. *Program availability:* Part-time, evening/weekend, 100% online. *Faculty:* 22 full-time (2 women), 15 part-time/adjunct (0 women). *Students:* 3 full-time (1 woman), 38 part-time (10 women); includes 5 minority (2 Black or African American, non-Hispanic/Latino; 2 Asian, non-Hispanic/Latino; 1 Hispanic/Latino), 5 international. Average age 27. 42 applicants, 38% accepted, 6 enrolled. In 2018, 4 master's awarded. *Entrance requirements:* Additional exam requirements/recommendations for international students: Required—TOEFL (minimum score 560 paper-based; 84 iBT), IELTS (minimum score 6.5). *Application deadline:* For fall admission, 8/1 for domestic students, 5/1 for international students; for winter admission, 12/1 for domestic students, 9/1 for international students; for spring admission, 4/1 for domestic students, 1/1 for international students. Applications are processed on a rolling basis. Application fee: $60. Electronic applications accepted. *Expenses:* Tuition, state resident: full-time $15,380; part-time $88 per credit hour. Tuition, nonresident: full-time $23,948; part-time $1377 per credit hour. *Required fees:* $780; $780 $390. Tuition and fees vary according to course level, course load, degree level, program, reciprocity agreements and student level. *Financial support:* Scholarships/grants, unspecified assistantships, and non-resident tuition scholarships available. Support available to part-time students. Financial award application deadline: 3/1; financial award applicants required to submit FAFSA. *Faculty research:* Artificial intelligence, power and energy, nanotechnology and optics, control systems, autonomy: sensing and perception. *Unit head:* Dr. Taehyung Kim, Director/Professor, 313-583-6736, E-mail: taehyung@umich.edu. *Application contact:* Office of Graduate Studies, 313-583-6321, E-mail: umd-graduatestudies@umich.edu.
Website: https://umdearborn.edu/cecs/departments/electrical-and-computer-engineering/graduate-programs/mse-energy-systems-engineering

The University of North Carolina at Charlotte, William States Lee College of Engineering, Department of Engineering Technology and Construction Management, Charlotte, NC 28223-0001. Offers applied energy (Graduate Certificate); applied energy and electromechanical systems (MS); construction and facilities management (MS); fire protection and administration (MS). *Program availability:* Part-time. *Students:* 54 full-time (17 women), 17 part-time (3 women); includes 9 minority (3 Black or African American, non-Hispanic/Latino; 2 Asian, non-Hispanic/Latino; 3 Hispanic/Latino; 1 Two or more races, non-Hispanic/Latino), 40 international. Average age 26. 97 applicants, 81% accepted, 22 enrolled. In 2018, 31 master's awarded. *Entrance requirements:* For master's, GRE, minimum undergraduate GPA of 3.0, recommendations, statistics; integral and differential calculus (for students pursuing fire protection concentration or applied energy and electromechanical systems program); for Graduate Certificate, bachelor's degree in engineering, engineering technology, construction management or a closely-related technical or scientific field; undergraduate coursework of at least 3 semesters in engineering analysis or calculus; minimum GPA of 3.0. Additional exam requirements/recommendations for international students: Required—TOEFL (minimum score 523 paper-based; 70 iBT), IELTS (minimum score 6), TOEFL (minimum score 523 paper-based, 70 iBT) or IELTS (6). *Application deadline:* Applications are processed on a rolling basis. Application fee: $75. Electronic applications accepted. *Expenses:* Contact institution. *Financial support:* Research assistantships, career-related internships or fieldwork, institutionally sponsored loans, scholarships/grants, and unspecified assistantships available. Support available to part-time students. Financial award application deadline: 3/1; financial award applicants required to submit FAFSA. *Total annual research expenditures:* $1.7 million. *Unit head:* Dr. Anthony Brizendine, Chair, 704-687-5050, E-mail: albrizen@uncc.edu. *Application contact:* Kathy B. Giddings, Director of Graduate Admissions, 704-687-5503, Fax: 704-687-1668, E-mail: gradadm@uncc.edu.
Website: http://et.uncc.edu/

The University of North Carolina at Charlotte, William States Lee College of Engineering, Department of Systems Engineering and Engineering Management, Charlotte, NC 28223-0001. Offers energy analytics (Graduate Certificate); engineering management (MSEM); Lean Six Sigma (Graduate Certificate); logistics and supply chains (Graduate Certificate); systems analytics (Graduate Certificate). *Program availability:* Part-time, evening/weekend, 100% online, blended/hybrid learning. *Students:* 27 full-time (8 women), 45 part-time (11 women); includes 15 minority (5 Black or African American, non-Hispanic/Latino; 1 American Indian or Alaska Native, non-Hispanic/Latino; 5 Asian, non-Hispanic/Latino; 2 Hispanic/Latino; 2 Two or more races, non-Hispanic/Latino), 27 international. Average age 29. 112 applicants, 77% accepted, 23 enrolled. In 2018, 38 master's, 3 other advanced degrees awarded. *Entrance requirements:* For master's, GRE or GMAT, bachelor's degree in engineering or a closely-related technical or scientific field, or in business, provided relevant technical course requirements have been met; undergraduate coursework in engineering economics, calculus, or statistics; minimum GPA of 3.0; for Graduate Certificate, bachelor's degree in engineering or closely-related technical or scientific field, or in business, provided relevant technical course requirements have been met; minimum GPA of 3.0; undergraduate coursework in engineering economics, calculus, and statistics; written description of work experience. Additional exam requirements/recommendations for international students: Required—TOEFL (minimum score 523 paper-based; 70 iBT), IELTS (minimum score 6), TOEFL (minimum score 523 paper-based, 70 iBT) or IELTS (6). *Application deadline:* Applications are processed on a rolling basis. Application fee: $75. Electronic applications accepted. *Expenses:* Contact institution. *Financial support:* Career-related internships or fieldwork, institutionally sponsored loans, scholarships/grants, and unspecified assistantships available. Support available to part-time students. Financial award application deadline: 3/1; financial award applicants required to submit FAFSA. *Total annual research expenditures:* $186,132. *Unit head:* Dr. Simon M. Hsiang, Chair, 704-687-1958, E-mail: shsiang1@uncc.edu. *Application contact:* Kathy B. Giddings, Director of Graduate Admissions, 704-687-5503, Fax: 704-687-1668, E-mail: gradadm@uncc.edu.
Website: http://seem.uncc.edu/

University of North Texas, Toulouse Graduate School, Denton, TX 76203-5459. Offers accounting (MS); applied anthropology (MA, MS); applied behavior analysis (Certificate); applied geography (MA); applied technology and performance improvement (M Ed, MS); art education (MA); art history (MA); arts leadership (Certificate); audiology (Au D); behavior analysis (MS); behavioral science (PhD); biochemistry and molecular biology (MS); biology (MA, MS); biomedical engineering (MS); business analysis (MS); chemistry (MS); clinical health psychology (PhD);

communication studies (MA, MS); computer engineering (MS); computer science (MS); counseling (M Ed, MS), including clinical mental health counseling (MS), college and university counseling, elementary school counseling, secondary school counseling; creative writing (MA); criminal justice (MS); curriculum and instruction (M Ed); decision sciences (MBA); design (MA, MFA), including fashion design (MFA), innovation studies, interior design (MFA); early childhood studies (MS); economics (MS); educational leadership (M Ed, Ed D); educational psychology (MS, PhD), including family studies (MS), gifted and talented (MS), human development (MS), learning and cognition (MS), research, measurement and evaluation (MS); electrical engineering (MS); emergency management (MPA); engineering technology (MS); English (MA); English as a second language (MA); environmental science (MS); finance (MBA, MS); financial management (MPA); French (MA); health services management (MBA); higher education (M Ed, Ed D); history (MA, MS); hospitality management (MS); human resources management (MPA); information science (MS); information systems (PhD); information technologies (MBA); interdisciplinary studies (MA, MS); international studies (MA); international sustainable tourism (MS); jazz studies (MM); journalism (MA, MJ, Graduate Certificate), including interactive and virtual digital communication (Graduate Certificate), narrative journalism (Graduate Certificate), public relations (Graduate Certificate); kinesiology (MS); linguistics (MA); local government management (MPA); logistics (PhD); logistics and supply chain management (MBA); long-term care, senior housing, and aging services (MA); management (PhD); marketing (MBA); mathematics (MA, MS); mechanical and energy engineering (MS, PhD); music (MA), including ethnomusicology, music theory, musicology, performance; music composition (PhD); music education (MM Ed, PhD); nonprofit management (MPA); operations and supply chain management (MBA); performance (MM, DMA); philosophy (MA); political science (MA); professional and technical communication (MA); radio, television and film (MA, MFA); rehabilitation counseling (Certificate); sociology (MA); Spanish (MA); special education (M Ed); speech-language pathology (MA); strategic management (MBA); studio art (MFA); teaching (M Ed); MBA/MS. *Program availability:* Part-time, evening/weekend, online learning. Terminal master's awarded for partial completion of doctoral program. *Degree requirements:* For master's, variable foreign language requirement, comprehensive exam (for some programs), thesis (for some programs); for doctorate, variable foreign language requirement, comprehensive exam (for some programs), thesis/dissertation; for other advanced degree, variable foreign language requirement, comprehensive exam (for some programs). *Entrance requirements:* For master's and doctorate, GRE, GMAT. Additional exam requirements/recommendations for international students: Required—TOEFL (minimum score 550 paper-based; 79 iBT). Electronic applications accepted.

University of Puerto Rico–Mayagüez, Graduate Studies, College of Engineering, Department of Mechanical Engineering, Mayagüez, PR 00681-9000. Offers mechanical engineering (ME, MS, PhD), including aerospace and unmanned vehicles (ME), automation/mechatronics, bioengineering, fluid mechanics, heat transfer/energy systems, manufacturing, mechanics of materials, micro and nano engineering. *Program availability:* Part-time. Terminal master's awarded for partial completion of doctoral program. *Degree requirements:* For master's, one foreign language, comprehensive exam, thesis; for doctorate, one foreign language, comprehensive exam, thesis/dissertation. *Entrance requirements:* For master's, BS in mechanical engineering or its equivalent; for doctorate, GRE, BS or MS in mechanical engineering or its equivalent; minimum GPA of 3.0. Additional exam requirements/recommendations for international students: Required—TOEFL (minimum score 80 iBT). Electronic applications accepted. *Faculty research:* Computational fluid dynamics, thermal sciences, mechanical design, material health, microfluidics.

The University of Tennessee, Graduate School, Tickle College of Engineering, Bredesen Center for Interdisciplinary Research and Graduate Education, Knoxville, TN 37996. Offers data science and engineering (PhD); energy science and engineering (PhD). *Students:* 70 full-time (24 women); includes 11 minority (2 Black or African American, non-Hispanic/Latino; 5 Asian, non-Hispanic/Latino; 3 Hispanic/Latino; 1 Two or more races, non-Hispanic/Latino), 18 international. Average age 29. 86 applicants, 41% accepted, 24 enrolled. In 2018, 11 doctorates awarded. *Degree requirements:* For doctorate, comprehensive exam, thesis/dissertation, qualifying examination. *Entrance requirements:* For doctorate, GRE General Test, research interest letter, resume/curriculum vitae, 3 letters of recommendation. Additional exam requirements/recommendations for international students: Required—TOEFL (minimum score 550 paper-based; 80 iBT), IELTS (minimum score 6.5). *Application deadline:* For fall admission, 1/31 for domestic and international students. Applications are processed on a rolling basis. Application fee: $60. Electronic applications accepted. *Financial support:* In 2018–19, 70 students received support, including 70 fellowships with full tuition reimbursements available (averaging $28,000 per year); health care benefits also available. Financial award application deadline: 1/31. *Faculty research:* Biomass processing for biofuels, cellulosic ethanol, and lignin repurposing; applied photosynthesis; nuclear fusion, reactor design and modeling; design and distribution of wind power; development of photovoltaic materials; fuel cell and battery design for energy conversion and storage; development of next generation SMART grid systems and novel grid management tools; climate change modeling, environmental, and planetary sciences as they relate to energy usage. *Unit head:* Dr. Sudarsanam Babu, Director, 865-974-7999, Fax: 865-974-9482, E-mail: sbabu@utk.edu. *Application contact:* Dr. Sudarsanam Babu, Director, 865-974-7999, Fax: 865-974-9482, E-mail: sbabu@utk.edu.
Website: http://bredesencenter.utk.edu

The University of Tennessee at Chattanooga, Engineering Management and Technology Program, Chattanooga, TN 37403. Offers construction management (Graduate Certificate); engineering management (MS); fundamentals of engineering management (Graduate Certificate); leadership and ethics (Graduate Certificate); logistics and supply chain management (Graduate Certificate); power systems management (Graduate Certificate); project and technology management (Graduate Certificate); quality management (Graduate Certificate). *Program availability:* 100% online, blended/hybrid learning. *Degree requirements:* For master's, thesis. *Entrance requirements:* For master's, GRE General Test, letters of recommendation; minimum undergraduate GPA of 2.7 overall or 3.0 in final two years; for Graduate Certificate, baccalaureate degree and professional experience or have already been admitted to engineering/engineering management graduate program. Additional exam requirements/recommendations for international students: Required—TOEFL (minimum score 550 paper-based; 79 iBT), IELTS (minimum score 6). Electronic applications accepted. *Expenses:* Contact institution. *Faculty research:* Plant layout design, lean manufacturing, Six Sigma, value management, product development.

The University of Texas at El Paso, Graduate School, College of Engineering, Department of Electrical and Computer Engineering, El Paso, TX 79968-0001. Offers computer engineering (MS); electric power and energy systems (Graduate Certificate); electrical and computer engineering (PhD); electrical engineering (MS). *Program availability:* Part-time, evening/weekend. Terminal master's awarded for partial completion of doctoral program. *Degree requirements:* For master's, thesis optional; for doctorate, thesis/dissertation. *Entrance requirements:* For master's, GRE General Test, minimum GPA of 3.0; for doctorate, GRE General Test, minimum graduate GPA of 3.0. Additional exam requirements/recommendations for international students: Required—

TOEFL. Electronic applications accepted. *Faculty research:* Signal and image processing, computer architecture, fiber optics, computational electromagnetics, electronic displays and thin films.

Washington State University, Voiland College of Engineering and Architecture, School of Electrical Engineering and Computer Science, Pullman, WA 99164-2752. Offers computer engineering (MS); computer science (MS); electrical engineering (MS); electrical engineering and computer science (PhD); electrical power engineering (MS). MS programs in computer engineering, computer science and electrical engineering also offered at Tri-Cities campus; MS in electrical power engineering offered at the Global (online) campus. *Program availability:* Part-time. *Degree requirements:* For master's, comprehensive exam (for some programs), thesis or alternative; for doctorate, comprehensive exam, thesis/dissertation. *Entrance requirements:* For master's and doctorate, GRE General Test, minimum GPA of 3.0, 3 letters of recommendation, statement of purpose, transcripts. Additional exam requirements/recommendations for international students: Required—TOEFL (minimum score 580 paper-based). *Faculty research:* Software engineering, networks, distributed computing, computer engineering, electrophysics, artificial intelligence, bioinformatics and computational biology, computer graphics, communications, control systems, signal processing, power systems, microelectronics, algorithms.

Wayne State University, College of Engineering, Department of Engineering Dean, Detroit, MI 48202. Offers MS, Graduate Certificate. *Students:* 36 full-time (13 women), 46 part-time (8 women); includes 14 minority (6 Black or African American, non-Hispanic/Latino; 6 Asian, non-Hispanic/Latino; 2 Hispanic/Latino), 44 international. Average age 29. 146 applicants, 55% accepted, 35 enrolled. In 2018, 13 master's awarded. *Degree requirements:* For master's, thesis optional. *Entrance requirements:* For master's, bachelor's degree in engineering; minimum GPA of 3.0 or significant relevant professional experience; for Graduate Certificate, bachelor's degree in engineering; minimum GPA of 2.7 or significant relevant professional experience. Additional exam requirements/recommendations for international students: Required—TOEFL (minimum score 550 paper-based; 79 iBT); Recommended—IELTS (minimum score 6.5). *Application deadline:* For fall admission, 6/1 priority date for domestic students, 5/1 priority date for international students; for winter admission, 10/1 priority date for domestic students, 9/1 priority date for international students; for spring admission, 2/1 priority date for domestic students, 1/1 priority date for international students; for summer admission, 2/1 priority date for domestic students, 1/1 priority date for international students. Applications are processed on a rolling basis. Application fee: $50. Electronic applications accepted. *Expenses:* Contact institution. *Financial support:* In 2018–19, 27 students received support, including 1 fellowship (averaging $20,000 per year), 9 teaching assistantships (averaging $20,396 per year); scholarships/grants also available. Support available to part-time students. Financial award applicants required to submit FAFSA. *Unit head:* Dr. Gene Y. Liao, Program Director, 313-577-8078, E-mail: geneliao@wayne.edu. *Application contact:* Ellen Cope, Graduate Program Coordinator, 313-577-0409, Fax: 313-577-3810, E-mail: escope@wayne.edu.
Website: http://engineering.wayne.edu/aet/

West Virginia University, Statler College of Engineering and Mineral Resources, Morgantown, WV 26506. Offers aerospace engineering (MSAE, PhD); chemical engineering (MS Ch E, PhD); civil engineering (MSCE, PhD); computer engineering (PhD); computer science (MSCS, PhD); electrical engineering (MSEE, PhD); energy systems engineering (MSESE); engineering (MSE); industrial engineering (MSIE, PhD); industrial hygiene (MS); material science and engineering (MSMSE, PhD); mechanical engineering (MSME, PhD); mining engineering (MS Min E, PhD); petroleum and natural gas engineering (MSPNGE, PhD); safety management (MS); software engineering (MSSE). *Program availability:* Part-time. *Students:* 466 full-time (113 women), 154 part-time (27 women); includes 57 minority (22 Black or African American, non-Hispanic/Latino; 1 American Indian or Alaska Native, non-Hispanic/Latino; 8 Asian, non-Hispanic/Latino; 12 Hispanic/Latino; 14 Two or more races, non-Hispanic/Latino), 283 international. In 2018, 179 master's, 39 doctorates awarded. Terminal master's awarded for partial completion of doctoral program. *Degree requirements:* For master's, thesis optional; for doctorate, comprehensive exam, thesis/dissertation. *Entrance requirements:* Additional exam requirements/recommendations for international students: Required—TOEFL (minimum score 550 paper-based). *Application deadline:* For fall admission, 4/1 for international students; for winter admission, 4/1 for international students; for spring admission, 10/1 for international students. Applications are processed on a rolling basis. Application fee: $60. Electronic applications accepted. *Expenses:* Contact institution. *Financial support:* Fellowships, research assistantships, teaching assistantships, career-related internships or fieldwork, Federal Work-Study, institutionally sponsored loans, health care benefits, tuition waivers (full and partial), unspecified assistantships, and administrative assistantships available. Financial award application deadline: 2/1; financial award applicants required to submit FAFSA. *Faculty research:* Composite materials, software engineering, information systems, aerodynamics, vehicle propulsion and emission. *Unit head:* Dr. Earl Scime, Interim Dean, 304-293-4157 Ext. 2237, Fax: 304-293-2037, E-mail: earl.scime@mail.wvu.edu. *Application contact:* Dr. David A. Wyrick, Associate Dean, Academic Affairs, 304-293-4334, Fax: 304-293-5024, E-mail: david.wyrick@mail.wvu.edu.
Website: https://www.statler.wvu.edu

Worcester Polytechnic Institute, Graduate Admissions, Programs in Interdisciplinary Studies, Worcester, MA 01609-2280. Offers bioscience administration (MS); nuclear science and engineering (Graduate Certificate); power systems management (MS); social science (PhD); system dynamics and innovation management (MS, Graduate Certificate); systems modeling (MS). *Program availability:* Part-time, evening/weekend, 100% online. *Students:* 5 full-time (2 women), 49 part-time (17 women); includes 18 minority (6 Black or African American, non-Hispanic/Latino; 4 Asian, non-Hispanic/Latino; 5 Hispanic/Latino; 3 Two or more races, non-Hispanic/Latino), 1 international. Average age 35. 44 applicants, 93% accepted, 34 enrolled. In 2018, 13 master's, 1 doctorate, 21 other advanced degrees awarded. Terminal master's awarded for partial completion of doctoral program. *Degree requirements:* For master's, thesis; for doctorate, comprehensive exam, thesis/dissertation. *Entrance requirements:* For master's and doctorate, 3 letters of recommendation. Additional exam requirements/recommendations for international students: Required—TOEFL (minimum score 563 paper-based; 84 iBT), IELTS (minimum score 7). *Application deadline:* For fall admission, 1/1 priority date for domestic students, 1/1 for international students; for spring admission, 10/1 priority date for domestic students, 10/1 for international students. Applications are processed on a rolling basis. Application fee: $70. Electronic applications accepted. *Financial support:* Institutionally sponsored loans, scholarships/grants, and unspecified assistantships available. Financial award application deadline: 1/1. *Unit head:* Michale McGrade, Dean, 508-831-5301, Fax: 508-831-5717, E-mail: grad@wpi.edu. *Application contact:* Lynne Dougherty, Administrative Assistant, 508-831-5301, Fax: 508-831-5717, E-mail: grad@wpi.edu.

Nuclear Engineering

Air Force Institute of Technology, Graduate School of Engineering and Management, Department of Engineering Physics, Dayton, OH 45433-7765. Offers applied physics (MS, PhD); electro-optics (MS, PhD); materials science (PhD); nuclear engineering (MS, PhD); space physics (MS). *Program availability:* Part-time. *Degree requirements:* For master's, thesis; for doctorate, thesis/dissertation. *Entrance requirements:* For master's and doctorate, GRE General Test, minimum GPA of 3.0, U.S. citizenship. *Faculty research:* High-energy lasers, space physics, nuclear weapon effects, semiconductor physics.

Arizona State University at the Tempe campus, Ira A. Fulton Schools of Engineering, School of Electrical, Computer and Energy Engineering, Tempe, AZ 85287-5706. Offers electrical engineering (MS, MSE, PhD); nuclear power generation (Graduate Certificate). *Program availability:* Part-time, evening/weekend, online learning. Terminal master's awarded for partial completion of doctoral program. *Degree requirements:* For master's, thesis and defense (MS); comprehensive exams (MSE); interactive Program of Study (iPOS) submitted before completing 50 percent of required credit hours; for doctorate, comprehensive exam, thesis/dissertation, interactive Program of Study (iPOS) submitted before completing 50 percent of required credit hours. *Entrance requirements:* For master's, GRE, minimum GPA of 3.0 in last 2 years of work leading to bachelor's degree, 3.5 if from non-ABET accredited school; for doctorate, GRE, master's degree with minimum GPA of 3.5 or 3.6 in last 2 years of ABET-accredited undergraduate program. Additional exam requirements/recommendations for international students: Required—TOEFL, IELTS, or PTE. Electronic applications accepted. *Expenses:* Contact institution. *Faculty research:* Power and energy systems, signal processing and communications, solid state devices and modeling, wireless communications and circuits, photovoltaics, biosignatures discovery automation, flexible electronics, nanostructures.

Colorado School of Mines, Office of Graduate Studies, Department of Physics, Golden, CO 80401. Offers applied physics (MS, PhD); materials science (MS, PhD); nuclear engineering (ME, MS, PhD). *Program availability:* Part-time. *Faculty:* 34 full-time (4 women), 9 part-time/adjunct (3 women). *Students:* 61 full-time (14 women), 5 part-time (1 woman); includes 7 minority (4 Hispanic/Latino; 3 Two or more races, non-Hispanic/Latino), 8 international. Average age 27. 70 applicants, 33% accepted, 15 enrolled. In 2018, 5 master's, 10 doctorates awarded. *Degree requirements:* For master's, thesis (for some programs); for doctorate, comprehensive exam, thesis/dissertation. *Entrance requirements:* For master's and doctorate, GRE General Test, GRE Subject Test. Additional exam requirements/recommendations for international students: Required—TOEFL (minimum score 550 paper-based; 79 iBT). *Application deadline:* For fall admission, 12/15 priority date for domestic and international students; for spring admission, 9/1 priority date for domestic and international students. Application fee: $60 ($80 for international students). Electronic applications accepted. *Expenses:* Tuition, state resident: full-time $16,650; part-time $925 per contact hour. Tuition, nonresident: full-time $36,270; part-time $2015 per contact hour. *International tuition:* $36,270 full-time. *Required fees:* $2314; $2314 per semester. *Financial support:* In 2018–19, 32 research assistantships with full tuition reimbursements, 13 teaching assistantships with full tuition reimbursements were awarded; fellowships, scholarships/grants, health care benefits, and unspecified assistantships also available. Financial award application deadline: 12/15; financial award applicants required to submit FAFSA. *Faculty research:* Light scattering, low-energy nuclear physics, high fusion plasma diagnostics, laser operations, mathematical physics. *Unit head:* Dr. Uwe Greife, Head, 303-273-3618, E-mail: ugreife@mines.edu. *Application contact:* Dr. Kyle Leach, Professor, 303-273-3044, E-mail: kleach@mines.edu.
Website: http://physics.mines.edu

École Polytechnique de Montréal, Graduate Programs, Institute of Nuclear Engineering, Montréal, QC H3C 3A7, Canada. Offers nuclear engineering (M Eng, PhD, DESS); nuclear engineering, socio-economics of energy (M Sc A). *Degree requirements:* For master's, one foreign language, thesis; for doctorate, one foreign language, thesis/dissertation. *Entrance requirements:* For master's, minimum GPA of 2.75; for doctorate, minimum GPA of 3.0. *Faculty research:* Nuclear technology, thermohydraulics.

Georgia Institute of Technology, Graduate Studies, College of Engineering, George W. Woodruff School of Mechanical Engineering, Nuclear and Radiological Engineering and Medical Physics Programs, Atlanta, GA 30332-0001. Offers medical physics (MS, MSMP); nuclear and radiological engineering (PhD); nuclear engineering (MSNE). *Program availability:* Part-time, online learning. Terminal master's awarded for partial completion of doctoral program. *Degree requirements:* For master's, thesis optional; for doctorate, comprehensive exam, thesis/dissertation. *Entrance requirements:* For master's and doctorate, GRE General Test, minimum GPA of 3.0. Additional exam requirements/recommendations for international students: Required—TOEFL (minimum score 580 paper-based; 94 iBT). Electronic applications accepted. *Faculty research:* Reactor physics, nuclear materials, plasma physics, radiation detection, radiological assessment.

Idaho State University, Graduate School, College of Science and Engineering, Department of Nuclear Engineering, Pocatello, ID 83209. Offers nuclear science and engineering (MS, PhD). *Program availability:* Part-time. *Degree requirements:* For master's, comprehensive exam (for some programs), thesis, seminar; for doctorate, comprehensive exam, thesis/dissertation, oral and written exams at the end of 1st year. *Entrance requirements:* For master's, GRE; for doctorate, master's degree in engineering, physics, geosciences, or math; 3 letters of recommendation. Additional exam requirements/recommendations for international students: Required—TOEFL (minimum score 550 paper-based; 80 iBT). Electronic applications accepted.

Kansas State University, Graduate School, College of Engineering, Department of Mechanical and Nuclear Engineering, Manhattan, KS 66506. Offers mechanical engineering (MS); nuclear engineering (PhD). *Degree requirements:* For master's, thesis optional; for doctorate, comprehensive exam, thesis/dissertation. *Entrance requirements:* For master's, GRE General Test; for doctorate, GRE General Test, master's degree in mechanical engineering; minimum GPA of 3.0 overall or last 60 hours in calculus-based engineering or related program. Additional exam requirements/recommendations for international students: Required—TOEFL (minimum score 550 paper-based; 79 iBT). Electronic applications accepted. *Faculty research:* Radiation detection and protection, heat and mass transfer, machine design, control systems, nuclear reactor physics and engineering.

Massachusetts Institute of Technology, School of Engineering, Department of Nuclear Science and Engineering, Cambridge, MA 02139. Offers SM, PhD, Sc D, NE. *Degree requirements:* For master's and NE, thesis; for doctorate, comprehensive exam, thesis/dissertation. *Entrance requirements:* For master's, doctorate, and NE, GRE General Test. Additional exam requirements/recommendations for international students: Required—TOEFL, IELTS. Electronic applications accepted. *Expenses:* Tuition: Full-time $51,520; part-time $800 per credit hour. *Required fees:* $312. *Faculty research:* Advanced fission reactor engineering and innovation; nuclear fuel cycle technology and economics; plasma physics and fusion engineering; advanced computation and simulation; materials in extreme environments; radiation sources, detection, and measurement; quantum engineering; nuclear systems engineering, design, management and policy.

McMaster University, School of Graduate Studies, Faculty of Engineering, Department of Engineering Physics, Hamilton, ON L8S 4M2, Canada. Offers engineering physics (M Eng, MA Sc, PhD); nuclear engineering (PhD). *Degree requirements:* For master's, thesis or alternative; for doctorate, comprehensive exam, thesis/dissertation. *Entrance requirements:* For master's, minimum B average in engineering, mathematics, or physical sciences. Additional exam requirements/recommendations for international students: Required—TOEFL (minimum score 550 paper-based). *Faculty research:* Non-thermal plasmas for pollution control and electrostatic precipitation, bulk and thin film luminescent materials, devices and systems for optical fiber communications, physics and applications of III-V materials and devices, defect spectroscopy in semiconductors.

Missouri University of Science and Technology, Department of Mining and Nuclear Engineering, Rolla, MO 65401. Offers explosives engineering (MS, PhD); mining engineering (MS, DE, PhD); nuclear engineering (MS, DE, PhD). *Degree requirements:* For master's, thesis optional; for doctorate, comprehensive exam. *Entrance requirements:* For master's, GRE (minimum score 600 quantitative, 3 writing); for doctorate, GRE (minimum score: quantitative 600, writing 3.5). Additional exam requirements/recommendations for international students: Required—TOEFL (minimum score 550 paper-based). Electronic applications accepted. *Expenses:* Tuition, state resident: full-time $7545.60; part-time $419.20 per credit hour. Tuition, nonresident: full-time $22,169; part-time $1231.60 per credit hour. *International tuition:* $23,518.80 full-time. *Required fees:* $4523.05. Full-time tuition and fees vary according to course load, campus/location, program and reciprocity agreements. *Faculty research:* Mine health and safety, nuclear radiation transport, modeling of mining operations, radiation effects, blasting.

North Carolina State University, Graduate School, College of Engineering, Department of Nuclear Engineering, Raleigh, NC 27695. Offers MNE, MS, PhD. *Degree requirements:* For master's, thesis (for some programs); for doctorate, thesis/dissertation. *Entrance requirements:* For master's, bachelor's degree in engineering or GRE; for doctorate, engineering degree or GRE. Electronic applications accepted. *Faculty research:* Computational reactor engineering, plasma applications, waste management, materials, radiation applications and measurement.

The Ohio State University, Graduate School, College of Engineering, Department of Mechanical and Aerospace Engineering, Program in Nuclear Engineering, Columbus, OH 43210. Offers MS, PhD. *Students:* 22 full-time (6 women). Average age 28. In 2018, 6 master's, 4 doctorates awarded. *Entrance requirements:* For master's and doctorate, GRE. Additional exam requirements/recommendations for international students: Required—TOEFL (minimum score 550 paper-based; 79 iBT), Michigan English Language Assessment Battery (minimum score 82); Recommended—IELTS (minimum score 7). *Application deadline:* For fall admission, 11/30 priority date for domestic and international students; for spring admission, 10/1 for domestic and international students. Applications are processed on a rolling basis. Application fee: $60 ($70 for international students). Electronic applications accepted. *Financial support:* Fellowships, research assistantships, teaching assistantships, career-related internships or fieldwork, Federal Work-Study, and institutionally sponsored loans available. Support available to part-time students. *Unit head:* Dr. Lei R. Cao, Program Director and Professor, 614-292-3204, E-mail: nuclear@osu.edu. *Application contact:* Janeen Sands, Graduate Programs Coordinator, 614-247-6605, Fax: 614-292-5746, E-mail: nuclear@osu.edu.
Website: http://mae.osu.edu/nuclear

Oregon State University, College of Engineering, Program in Nuclear Engineering, Corvallis, OR 97331. Offers application of nuclear techniques (M Eng, MS, PhD). *Entrance requirements:* For master's and doctorate, GRE. Additional exam requirements/recommendations for international students: Required—TOEFL (minimum score 80 iBT), IELTS (minimum score 6.5). *Expenses:* Contact institution.

Penn State University Park, Graduate School, College of Engineering, Department of Mechanical and Nuclear Engineering, University Park, PA 16802. Offers additive manufacturing and design (MS); mechanical engineering (MS, PhD); nuclear engineering (M Eng, MS, PhD).

Purdue University, College of Engineering, School of Nuclear Engineering, West Lafayette, IN 47907-2017. Offers MS, MSNE, PhD. *Program availability:* Part-time. Terminal master's awarded for partial completion of doctoral program. *Degree requirements:* For master's, thesis optional; for doctorate, thesis/dissertation. *Entrance requirements:* For master's, GRE General Test, minimum GPA of 3.2; for doctorate, GRE General Test, minimum GPA of 3.5. Electronic applications accepted. *Faculty research:* Applied intelligent systems, bioelectrics and electro physics, materials under extreme environment, fuel cycle and waste management, hydrogen and fuel cell, nuclear systems simulation, reactor physics, thermal hydraulics and reactor safety.

Rensselaer Polytechnic Institute, Graduate School, School of Engineering, Program in Nuclear Engineering and Science, Troy, NY 12180-3590. Offers M Eng, MS, D Eng, PhD. *Faculty:* 55 full-time (6 women), 1 part-time/adjunct (0 women). *Students:* 26 full-time (5 women); includes 3 minority (1 Asian, non-Hispanic/Latino; 1 Hispanic/Latino; 1 Two or more races, non-Hispanic/Latino), 11 international. Average age 28. 19 applicants, 47% accepted, 3 enrolled. In 2018, 3 master's, 6 doctorates awarded. Terminal master's awarded for partial completion of doctoral program. *Degree requirements:* For master's, thesis (for some programs); for doctorate, thesis/dissertation. *Entrance requirements:* For master's and doctorate, GRE. Additional exam requirements/recommendations for international students: Required—TOEFL (minimum score 600 paper-based; 100 iBT), IELTS (minimum score 7), PTE (minimum score 68). *Application deadline:* For fall admission, 1/1 priority date for domestic and international students; for spring admission, 8/15 priority date for domestic and international students. Applications are processed on a rolling basis. Application fee: $75. Electronic applications accepted. *Financial support:* In 2018–19, research assistantships (averaging $23,000 per year), teaching assistantships (averaging $23,000 per year) were awarded; fellowships also available. Financial award application deadline: 1/1. *Faculty research:* Design, dynamics and vibrations, fissions systems and radiation transport, fluid mechanics (computational, theoretical, and experimental), heat transfer and energy conversion, manufacturing, medical imaging and health physics, multiscale/computational modeling, nanostructured materials and properties, nuclear physics/nuclear reactor, propulsion. *Total annual research expenditures:* $4.7 million. *Unit head:* Dr. Theo Borca-Tasciuc, Graduate Program Director, 518-276-2627, E-mail: borcat@

rpi.edu. *Application contact:* Jarron Decker, Director of Graduate Admissions, 518-276-6216, Fax: 518-276-4072, E-mail: gradadmissions@rpi.edu.
Website: http://mane.rpi.edu/

Texas A&M University, College of Engineering, Department of Nuclear Engineering, College Station, TX 77843. Offers nuclear engineering (M Eng, PhD). *Faculty:* 16. *Students:* 118 full-time (24 women), 22 part-time (5 women); includes 31 minority (2 Black or African American, non-Hispanic/Latino; 5 Asian, non-Hispanic/Latino; 20 Hispanic/Latino; 4 Two or more races, non-Hispanic/Latino), 39 international. Average age 29. 81 applicants, 56% accepted, 29 enrolled. In 2018, 24 master's, 14 doctorates awarded. *Degree requirements:* For master's, thesis or alternative; for doctorate, thesis/dissertation, departmental qualifying exams. *Entrance requirements:* For master's and doctorate, GRE General Test, 3 letters of recommendation. Additional exam requirements/recommendations for international students: Required—TOEFL (minimum score 550 paper-based; 80 iBT), IELTS (minimum score 6), PTE (minimum score 53). *Application deadline:* For fall admission, 12/1 for domestic and international students; for spring admission, 9/1 for domestic and international students. Applications are processed on a rolling basis. Application fee: $50 ($90 for international students). Electronic applications accepted. *Expenses:* Contact institution. *Financial support:* In 2018–19, 118 students received support, including 12 fellowships with tuition reimbursements available (averaging $31,158 per year), 89 research assistantships with tuition reimbursements available (averaging $17,774 per year), 24 teaching assistantships with tuition reimbursements available (averaging $15,095 per year); career-related internships or fieldwork, institutionally sponsored loans, scholarships/grants, traineeships, health care benefits, tuition waivers (full and partial), and unspecified assistantships also available. Support available to part-time students. Financial award application deadline: 3/15; financial award applicants required to submit FAFSA. *Unit head:* Dr. Yassin A. Hassan, Head, 979-845-7090, E-mail: y-hassan@tamu.edu. *Application contact:* Robb Jenson, Graduate Program Coordinator, 979-458-2072, E-mail: robb.jenson@tamu.edu.
Website: https://engineering.tamu.edu/nuclear

University of California, Berkeley, Graduate Division, College of Engineering, Department of Nuclear Engineering, Berkeley, CA 94720-1730. Offers M Eng, MS, PhD. Terminal master's awarded for partial completion of doctoral program. *Degree requirements:* For master's, comprehensive exam (for some programs), thesis (for some programs), project or thesis; for doctorate, thesis/dissertation, oral exam. *Entrance requirements:* For master's and doctorate, GRE General Test, minimum GPA of 3.0, 3 letters of recommendation. Additional exam requirements/recommendations for international students: Required—TOEFL (minimum score 570 paper-based; 90 iBT). Electronic applications accepted. *Faculty research:* Applied nuclear reactions and instrumentation, fission reactor engineering, fusion reactor technology, nuclear waste and materials management, radiation protection and environmental effects.

University of Cincinnati, Graduate School, College of Engineering and Applied Science, Department of Mechanical and Materials Engineering, Cincinnati, OH 45221. Offers industrial engineering (PhD); mechanical engineering (MS, PhD); nuclear engineering (PhD); MBA/MS. *Program availability:* Part-time, evening/weekend. Terminal master's awarded for partial completion of doctoral program. *Degree requirements:* For doctorate, thesis/dissertation. *Entrance requirements:* For master's and doctorate, GRE General Test. Additional exam requirements/recommendations for international students: Required—TOEFL (minimum score 575 paper-based). Electronic applications accepted.

University of Florida, Graduate School, Herbert Wertheim College of Engineering, Department of Materials Science and Engineering, Nuclear Engineering Program, Gainesville, FL 32611. Offers imaging science and technology (PhD); nuclear engineering sciences (ME, MS, PhD). *Program availability:* Part-time. Terminal master's awarded for partial completion of doctoral program. *Degree requirements:* For master's, comprehensive exam, thesis; for doctorate, comprehensive exam, thesis/dissertation. *Entrance requirements:* For master's and doctorate, minimum GPA of 3.0. Additional exam requirements/recommendations for international students: Required—TOEFL (minimum score 550 paper-based; 80 iBT), IELTS (minimum score 6). Electronic applications accepted. *Faculty research:* Nuclear materials, radiation detection, thermal hydraulics, reactor physics and transport, generation 4 reactor technology.

University of Idaho, College of Graduate Studies, College of Engineering, Program in Nuclear Engineering, Moscow, ID 83844-2282. Offers M Engr, MS, PhD. *Faculty:* 5. *Students:* 10 full-time, 10 part-time. Average age 36. In 2018, 6 master's awarded. *Entrance requirements:* For master's and doctorate, minimum GPA of 3.0. Additional exam requirements/recommendations for international students: Required—TOEFL (minimum score 83 iBT). *Application deadline:* For fall admission, 8/1 for domestic students; for spring admission, 12/15 for domestic students. Applications are processed on a rolling basis. Application fee: $60. Electronic applications accepted. *Expenses:* Tuition, state resident: full-time $7266.44; part-time $474.50 per credit hour. Tuition, nonresident: full-time $24,902; part-time $1453.50 per credit hour. *Required fees:* $2085.56; $45.50 per credit hour. *Financial support:* Applicants required to submit FAFSA. *Faculty research:* Water and nuclear systems, nuclear materials. *Unit head:* Dr. Richard Christensen, Chair, 208-282-6470, E-mail: engr-sss@uidaho.edu. *Application contact:* Dr. Richard Christensen, Chair, 208-282-6470, E-mail: engr-sss@uidaho.edu.

University of Illinois at Urbana–Champaign, Graduate College, College of Engineering, Department of Nuclear, Plasma, and Radiological Engineering, Urbana, IL 61801. Offers energy systems (M Eng); nuclear, plasma, and radiological engineering (MS, PhD). Terminal master's awarded for partial completion of doctoral program.

The University of Manchester, School of Mechanical, Aerospace and Civil Engineering, Manchester, United Kingdom. Offers advanced manufacturing technology (M Ent); aerospace engineering (M Phil, M Sc, PhD); civil engineering (M Phil, M Sc, PhD); environmental engineering (M Phil, PhD); management of projects (M Phil, M Sc, PhD); mechanical engineering (M Phil, M Sc, PhD); mechanical engineering design (M Ent); nuclear engineering (M Phil, D Eng, PhD).

University of Maryland, College Park, Academic Affairs, A. James Clark School of Engineering, Department of Materials Science and Engineering, Nuclear Engineering Program, College Park, MD 20742. Offers ME, MS, PhD. *Program availability:* Part-time, evening/weekend, online learning. *Degree requirements:* For master's, thesis optional; for doctorate, variable foreign language requirement, thesis/dissertation, oral exam. *Entrance requirements:* For master's and doctorate, GRE General Test, minimum GPA of 3.0. Additional exam requirements/recommendations for international students: Required—TOEFL. Electronic applications accepted. *Faculty research:* Reliability and risk assessment, heat transfer and two-phase flow, reactor safety analysis, nuclear reactor, radiation/polymers.

University of Massachusetts Lowell, Francis College of Engineering, Program in Energy Engineering, Lowell, MA 01854. Offers MS Eng, PhD. *Degree requirements:* For master's, thesis optional. *Entrance requirements:* For master's, GRE General Test. Additional exam requirements/recommendations for international students: Required—TOEFL.

University of Michigan, College of Engineering, Department of Nuclear Engineering and Radiological Sciences, Ann Arbor, MI 48109. Offers nuclear engineering (Nuc E);

nuclear engineering and radiological sciences (MSE, PhD); nuclear science (MS, PhD). *Students:* 140 full-time (26 women). 119 applicants, 44% accepted, 31 enrolled. In 2018, 23 master's, 14 doctorates awarded. Terminal master's awarded for partial completion of doctoral program. *Degree requirements:* For master's, thesis optional; for doctorate, thesis/dissertation, oral defense of dissertation, preliminary exams. *Entrance requirements:* For master's and doctorate, GRE General Test. Additional exam requirements/recommendations for international students: Required—TOEFL. *Application deadline:* Applications are processed on a rolling basis. Electronic applications accepted. *Financial support:* Fellowships, research assistantships, teaching assistantships, career-related internships or fieldwork, institutionally sponsored loans, scholarships/grants, traineeships, health care benefits, and unspecified assistantships available. Financial award applicants required to submit FAFSA. *Faculty research:* Radiation safety, environmental sciences, medical physics, fission systems and radiation transport, materials, plasmas and fusion, radiation measurements and imaging. *Total annual research expenditures:* $22 million. *Unit head:* Todd Allen, Department Chair, 734-647-5845, Fax: 734-763-4540, E-mail: traumich@umich.edu. *Application contact:* Garnette Roberts, Graduate Program Manager, 734-615-8810, Fax: 734-763-4540, E-mail: ners-grad-admissions@umich.edu.
Website: https://ners.engin.umich.edu/

University of Nevada, Las Vegas, Graduate College, Howard R. Hughes College of Engineering, Department of Mechanical Engineering, Las Vegas, NV 89154-4027. Offers aerospace engineering (MS); biomedical engineering (MS); materials and nuclear engineering (MS); mechanical engineering (MS, PhD); nuclear criticality safety engineering (Certificate); nuclear safeguards and security (Certificate). *Program availability:* Part-time. *Faculty:* 17 full-time (2 women). *Students:* 50 full-time (18 women), 19 part-time (4 women); includes 19 minority (4 Black or African American, non-Hispanic/Latino; 1 American Indian or Alaska Native, non-Hispanic/Latino; 4 Asian, non-Hispanic/Latino; 7 Hispanic/Latino; 3 Two or more races, non-Hispanic/Latino), 21 international. Average age 29. 63 applicants, 73% accepted, 23 enrolled. In 2018, 15 master's, 5 doctorates, 1 other advanced degree awarded. *Degree requirements:* For master's, thesis optional, design project; for doctorate, comprehensive exam, thesis/dissertation. *Entrance requirements:* For master's, GRE General Test, statement of purpose; 2 letters of recommendation; for doctorate, GRE General Test, 3 letters of recommendation; statement of purpose; bachelor's degree with minimum GPA of 3.5/master's degree with minimum GPA of 3.3. Additional exam requirements/recommendations for international students: Required—TOEFL (minimum score 550 paper-based; 80 iBT), IELTS (minimum score 7). *Application deadline:* For fall admission, 8/1 for domestic students, 5/1 for international students; for spring admission, 12/1 for domestic students, 10/1 for international students. Application fee: $60 ($95 for international students). Electronic applications accepted. *Expenses:* Contact institution. *Financial support:* In 2018–19, 40 students received support, including 1 fellowship with full tuition reimbursement available (averaging $15,000 per year), 17 research assistantships with full tuition reimbursements available (averaging $16,910 per year), 23 teaching assistantships with full tuition reimbursements available (averaging $16,467 per year); institutionally sponsored loans, scholarships/grants, health care benefits, and unspecified assistantships also available. Financial award application deadline: 3/15; financial award applicants required to submit FAFSA. *Faculty research:* Dynamics and control systems; energy systems including renewable and nuclear; computational fluid and solid mechanics; structures, materials and manufacturing; vibrations and acoustics. *Total annual research expenditures:* $4.5 million. *Unit head:* Dr. Brendan O'Toole, Chair/Professor, 702-895-3885, Fax: 702-895-3936, E-mail: mechanical.chair@unlv.edu. *Application contact:* Dr. Hui Zhao, Graduate Coordinator, 702-895-1463, Fax: 702-895-3936, E-mail: mechanical.gradcoord@unlv.edu.
Website: http://me.unlv.edu/

University of New Mexico, Graduate Studies, School of Engineering, Program in Nuclear Engineering, Albuquerque, NM 87131-2039. Offers MS, PhD. *Program availability:* Part-time, online learning. Terminal master's awarded for partial completion of doctoral program. *Degree requirements:* For master's, thesis (for some programs); for doctorate, comprehensive exam, thesis/dissertation. *Entrance requirements:* For master's, GRE General Test, minimum GPA of 3.0, 3 letters of recommendation, letter of intent; for doctorate, GRE General Test, 3 letters of recommendation, letter of intent. Additional exam requirements/recommendations for international students: Required—TOEFL. Electronic applications accepted. *Faculty research:* Plasma science, space power, thermal hydraulics, radiation measurement and protection, fusion plasma measurements, medical physics, nuclear criticality safety, radiation measurements and protection, radiation transport modeling and simulation, Monte Carlo methods.

University of South Carolina, The Graduate School, College of Engineering and Computing, Department of Nuclear Engineering, Columbia, SC 29208. Offers ME, MS, PhD. *Program availability:* Part-time, evening/weekend, online learning. *Degree requirements:* For master's, thesis (for some programs); for doctorate, thesis/dissertation. *Entrance requirements:* For master's and doctorate, GRE General Test. Additional exam requirements/recommendations for international students: Required—TOEFL (minimum score 600 paper-based; 100 iBT). Electronic applications accepted.

The University of Tennessee, Graduate School, Tickle College of Engineering, Department of Nuclear Engineering, Program in Nuclear Engineering, Knoxville, TN 37996. Offers MS, PhD. *Program availability:* Part-time. *Faculty:* 16 full-time (2 women), 5 part-time/adjunct (0 women). *Students:* 111 full-time (21 women), 25 part-time (3 women); includes 13 minority (1 Black or African American, non-Hispanic/Latino; 2 Asian, non-Hispanic/Latino; 8 Hispanic/Latino; 2 Two or more races, non-Hispanic/Latino), 18 international. Average age 27. 72 applicants, 69% accepted, 25 enrolled. In 2018, 24 master's, 20 doctorates awarded. *Degree requirements:* For master's, thesis or alternative; for doctorate, comprehensive exam, thesis/dissertation. *Entrance requirements:* For master's, GRE General Test (for MS students pursuing research thesis), minimum GPA of 2.7 (for U.S. degree holders), 3.0 (for international degree holders); for doctorate, GRE General Test, minimum GPA of 3.0 on previous graduate course work. Additional exam requirements/recommendations for international students: Required—TOEFL (minimum score 550 paper-based; 80 iBT), IELTS (minimum score 6.5). *Application deadline:* For fall admission, 2/1 priority date for domestic and international students; for spring admission, 6/15 for domestic students, 5/15 for international students; for summer admission, 10/15 for domestic and international students. Applications are processed on a rolling basis. Application fee: $60. Electronic applications accepted. *Financial support:* In 2018–19, 114 students received support, including 11 fellowships with full tuition reimbursements available (averaging $25,353 per year), 86 research assistantships with full tuition reimbursements available (averaging $26,368 per year), 17 teaching assistantships with full tuition reimbursements available (averaging $23,919 per year); career-related internships or fieldwork, Federal Work-Study, institutionally sponsored loans, health care benefits, and unspecified assistantships also available. Financial award application deadline: 2/1; financial award applicants required to submit FAFSA. *Faculty research:* Heat transfer and fluid dynamics; instrumentation, sensors and controls; nuclear materials and nuclear security; radiological engineering; reactor system design and safety. *Unit head:* Dr. J. Wesley Hines, Head, 865-974-2525, Fax: 865-974-0668, E-mail: jhines2@utk.edu. *Application contact:* Dr. Jason Hayward, PhD, Professor and Graduate Coordinator, 865-974-2525, E-mail: utne@utk.edu.

University of Utah, Graduate School, College of Engineering, Department of Civil and Environmental Engineering, Program in Nuclear Engineering, Salt Lake City, UT 84112. Offers MS, PhD. *Program availability:* Part-time. *Faculty:* 3 full-time (1 woman), 3 part-time/adjunct (0 women). *Students:* 13 full-time (2 women), 2 part-time (0 women); includes 5 minority (1 Asian, non-Hispanic/Latino; 2 Hispanic/Latino; 2 Two or more races, non-Hispanic/Latino), 1 international. Average age 30. 8 applicants, 63% accepted, 3 enrolled. In 2018, 3 master's, 4 doctorates awarded. Terminal master's awarded for partial completion of doctoral program. *Degree requirements:* For master's, comprehensive exam; for doctorate, comprehensive exam, thesis/dissertation, qualifying exam. *Entrance requirements:* For master's and doctorate, GRE General Test, minimum GPA of 3.0. Additional exam requirements/recommendations for international students: Required—TOEFL (minimum score 550 paper-based; 80 iBT). *Application deadline:* For fall admission, 1/1 for domestic students, 12/1 for international students; for spring admission, 10/1 for domestic and international students. Applications are processed on a rolling basis. Application fee: $0 ($25 for international students). Electronic applications accepted. *Expenses:* Contact institution. *Financial support:* In 2018–19, 15 students received support, including 5 fellowships with full tuition reimbursements available (averaging $27,000 per year), 8 research assistantships with full tuition reimbursements available (averaging $24,714 per year), 2 teaching assistantships with full tuition reimbursements available (averaging $23,400 per year); traineeships, health care benefits, and unspecified assistantships also available. Financial award application deadline: 1/1. *Faculty research:* Radiochemistry, nuclear forensics, security, nuclear medicine, radiation detection. *Total annual research expenditures:* $800,705. *Unit head:* Dr. Michael Barber, Program Director, 801-581-6931, Fax: 801-585-5477, E-mail: barber@civil.utah.edu. *Application contact:* Academic Advisor, 801-581-6678, Fax: 801-585-5477, E-mail: cveen-graduate@utah.edu.
Website: http://www.nuclear.utah.edu/

University of Wisconsin–Madison, Graduate School, College of Engineering, Department of Engineering Physics, Madison, WI 53706-1380. Offers engineering mechanics (MS, PhD), including fundamentals of applied mechanics (MS); nuclear engineering and engineering physics (MS, PhD). *Program availability:* Part-time. *Faculty:* 20 full-time (4 women). *Students:* 103 full-time (17 women), 3 part-time (0 women); includes 16 minority (3 Black or African American, non-Hispanic/Latino; 5 Asian, non-Hispanic/Latino; 6 Hispanic/Latino; 2 Two or more races, non-Hispanic/Latino), 16 international. Average age 26. 169 applicants, 42% accepted, 18 enrolled. In 2018, 28 master's, 12 doctorates awarded. Terminal master's awarded for partial completion of doctoral program. *Degree requirements:* For master's, thesis optional, 30 credits of technical courses; oral exam; minimum GPA of 3.0; for doctorate, comprehensive exam, thesis/dissertation, minimum of 60 credits; minimum GPA of 3.0. *Entrance requirements:* For master's and doctorate, GRE General Test, minimum GPA of 3.0 in last 60 hours, appropriate bachelor's degree. Additional exam requirements/recommendations for international students: Required—TOEFL (minimum score 580 paper-based; 92 iBT), IELTS (minimum score 7). *Application deadline:* For fall admission, 12/15 for domestic and international students; for spring admission, 10/1 for domestic and international students; for summer admission, 12/15 for domestic and international students. Application fee: $75 ($81 for international students). Electronic applications accepted. *Financial support:* In 2018–19, 109 students received support, including 9 fellowships with full tuition reimbursements available (averaging $27,204 per year), 82 research assistantships with full tuition reimbursements available (averaging $27,780 per year), 18 teaching assistantships with full tuition reimbursements available (averaging $23,566 per year); career-related internships or fieldwork, Federal Work-Study, institutionally sponsored loans, unspecified assistantships, and project assistantships also available. Support available to part-time students. Financial award application deadline: 12/1; financial award applicants required to submit FAFSA. *Faculty research:* Bio-/micro-/nano-mechanics; astronautics; fission reactor engineering; fusion science and technology; radiation sciences; mechanics of materials. *Total annual research expenditures:* $13.7 million. *Unit head:* Dr. Paul Wilson, Chair, 608-263-1646, Fax: 608-263-7451, E-mail: office@ep.wisc.edu. *Application contact:* Sara Hladilek, Student Services Coordinator, 608-262-8617, Fax: 608-263-7451, E-mail: shladilek@wisc.edu.
Website: https://www.engr.wisc.edu/department/engineering-physics/

Virginia Commonwealth University, Graduate School, School of Engineering, Department of Mechanical and Nuclear Engineering, Richmond, VA 23284-9005. Offers MS, PhD. *Entrance requirements:* For master's and doctorate, GRE. Additional exam requirements/recommendations for international students: Required—TOEFL (minimum score 600 paper-based; 100 iBT). Electronic applications accepted.

Worcester Polytechnic Institute, Graduate Admissions, Programs in Interdisciplinary Studies, Worcester, MA 01609-2280. Offers bioscience administration (MS); nuclear science and engineering (Graduate Certificate); power systems management (MS); social science (PhD); system dynamics and innovation management (MS, Graduate Certificate); systems modeling (MS). *Program availability:* Part-time, evening/weekend, 100% online. *Students:* 5 full-time (2 women), 49 part-time (17 women); includes 18 minority (6 Black or African American, non-Hispanic/Latino; 4 Asian, non-Hispanic/Latino; 5 Hispanic/Latino; 3 Two or more races, non-Hispanic/Latino), 1 international. Average age 35. 44 applicants, 93% accepted, 34 enrolled. In 2018, 13 master's, 1 doctorate, 21 other advanced degrees awarded. Terminal master's awarded for partial completion of doctoral program. *Degree requirements:* For master's, thesis; for doctorate, comprehensive exam, thesis/dissertation. *Entrance requirements:* For master's and doctorate, 3 letters of recommendation. Additional exam requirements/recommendations for international students: Required—TOEFL (minimum score 563 paper-based; 84 iBT), IELTS (minimum score 7). *Application deadline:* For fall admission, 1/1 priority date for domestic students, 1/1 for international students; for spring admission, 10/1 priority date for domestic students, 10/1 for international students. Applications are processed on a rolling basis. Application fee: $70. Electronic applications accepted. *Financial support:* Institutionally sponsored loans, scholarships/grants, and unspecified assistantships available. Financial award application deadline: 1/1. *Unit head:* Michale McGrade, Dean, 508-831-5301, Fax: 508-831-5717, E-mail: grad@wpi.edu. *Application contact:* Lynne Dougherty, Administrative Assistant, 508-831-5301, Fax: 508-831-5717, E-mail: grad@wpi.edu.

Section 11
Engineering Design

This section contains a directory of institutions offering graduate work in engineering design. Additional information about programs listed in the directory may be obtained by writing directly to the dean of a graduate school or chair of a department at the address given in the directory.

For programs offering related work, see also in this book *Aerospace/ Aeronautical Engineering; Agricultural Engineering and Bioengineering; Biomedical Engineering and Biotechnology; Computer Science and Information Technology; Electrical and Computer Engineering; Energy and Power Engineering; Engineering and Applied Sciences; Industrial Engineering; Management of Engineering and Technology;* and *Mechanical Engineering and Mechanics.* In another guide in this series:

Graduate Programs in the Biological/Biomedical Sciences & Health-Related Medical Professions
See *Biological and Biomedical Sciences*

CONTENTS

Program Directory

Engineering Design

Harvard University, Graduate School of Arts and Sciences, Harvard John A. Paulson School of Engineering and Applied Sciences, Cambridge, MA 02138. Offers applied mathematics (PhD); applied physics (PhD); computational science and engineering (ME, SM); computer science (PhD); data science (SM); design engineering (MDE); engineering science (ME), including electrical engineering (ME, SM, PhD); engineering sciences (SM, PhD), including bioengineering (PhD), electrical engineering (ME, SM, PhD), environmental science and engineering (PhD), materials science and mechanical engineering (PhD). MDE offered in collaboration with Graduate School of Design. *Program availability:* Part-time. Terminal master's awarded for partial completion of doctoral program. *Degree requirements:* For master's, thesis (for ME); for doctorate, comprehensive exam, thesis/dissertation. *Entrance requirements:* For master's and doctorate, GRE General Test, GRE Subject Test (recommended), 3 letters of recommendation. Additional exam requirements/recommendations for international students: Required—TOEFL (minimum score 80 iBT). Electronic applications accepted. *Expenses:* Contact institution. *Faculty research:* Applied mathematics, applied physics, computer science and electrical engineering, environmental engineering, mechanical and biomedical engineering.

Northwestern University, McCormick School of Engineering and Applied Science, Department of Mechanical Engineering, MS in Product Design and Development Management Program, Evanston, IL 60208. Offers MS. *Program availability:* Part-time, evening/weekend. *Entrance requirements:* Additional exam requirements/ recommendations for international students: Required—TOEFL (minimum score 100 iBT), IELTS (minimum score 7). Electronic applications accepted.

Northwestern University, McCormick School of Engineering and Applied Science, Segal Design Institute, MS in Engineering Design and Innovation Program, Evanston, IL 60208. Offers MS. *Entrance requirements:* For master's, GRE General Test, 2 letters of recommendation, portfolio, statement of purpose. Additional exam requirements/ recommendations for international students: Required—TOEFL (minimum score 550 paper-based; 80 iBT) or IELTS (minimum score 7). Electronic applications accepted.

Ohio Dominican University, Division of Business, Columbus, OH 43219-2099. Offers business administration (MBA), including accounting, data analytics, finance, leadership, risk management, sport management; healthcare administration (MS); sport management (MS). *Accreditation:* ACBSP. *Program availability:* Part-time, evening/ weekend, 100% online, blended/hybrid learning. *Faculty:* 13 full-time (4 women), 17 part-time/adjunct (3 women). *Students:* 60 full-time (24 women), 100 part-time (48 women); includes 38 minority (24 Black or African American, non-Hispanic/Latino; 1 American Indian or Alaska Native, non-Hispanic/Latino; 4 Asian, non-Hispanic/Latino; 5 Hispanic/Latino; 4 Two or more races, non-Hispanic/Latino), 22 international. Average age 30. 141 applicants, 43% accepted, 38 enrolled. In 2018, 70 master's awarded. *Degree requirements:* For master's, thesis or alternative. *Entrance requirements:* Additional exam requirements/recommendations for international students: Required— TOEFL (minimum score 550 paper-based), IELTS (minimum score 6.5). *Application deadline:* For fall admission, 8/15 for domestic students, 6/10 for international students; for spring admission, 1/4 for domestic students, 11/2 for international students. Applications are processed on a rolling basis. Application fee: $25. Electronic applications accepted. *Expenses: Tuition:* Full-time $10,800; part-time $600 per credit hour. *Required fees:* $450; $225 per semester. Tuition and fees vary according to program. *Financial support:* Applicants required to submit FAFSA. *Unit head:* Dr. Kenneth C. Fah, Chair, 614-251-4566, E-mail: fahk@ohiodominican.edu. *Application contact:* John W. Naughton, Vice President for Enrollment & Student Success, 614-251-4721, Fax: 614-251-6654, E-mail: grad@ohiodominican.edu.
Website: http://www.ohiodominican.edu/academics/graduate/mba

Penn State University Park, Graduate School, College of Engineering, School of Engineering Design, Technology, and Professional Programs, University Park, PA 16802. Offers engineering design (M Eng, MS).

Rochester Institute of Technology, Graduate Enrollment Services, Kate Gleason College of Engineering, Design, Development and Manufacturing Department, Rochester, NY 14623-5603. Offers manufacturing leadership (MS); product development (MS). *Program availability:* Part-time-only, evening/weekend, 100% online, blended/hybrid learning. *Students:* 2 full-time (1 woman), 41 part-time (7 women); includes 3 minority (2 Black or African American, non-Hispanic/Latino; 1 Hispanic/Latino), 1 international. Average age 36. 31 applicants, 48% accepted, 12 enrolled. In 2018, 8 master's awarded. *Entrance requirements:* For master's, minimum GPA of 2.5, 2 years of related work experience. *Application deadline:* Applications are processed on a rolling basis. Application fee: $65. Electronic applications accepted. *Expenses:* Contact institution. *Financial support:* In 2018–19, 3 students received support. Scholarships/grants available. Support available to part-time students. Financial award applicants required to submit FAFSA. *Faculty research:* Systems engineering; project management; lean product development and lean manufacturing; decision analysis; modeling and simulation; supply chain management. *Unit head:* Mark Smith, Director, 585-475-7102, Fax: 585-475-7955, E-mail: mark.smith@rit.edu. *Application contact:* Diane Ellison, Senior Associate Vice President, Graduate Enrollment Services, 585-475-2229, Fax: 585-475-7164, E-mail: gradinfo@rit.edu.
Website: https://www.rit.edu/kgcoe/

San Diego State University, Graduate and Research Affairs, College of Engineering, Department of Mechanical Engineering, San Diego, CA 92182. Offers engineering sciences and applied mechanics (PhD); manufacture and design (MS); mechanical engineering (MS). PhD offered jointly with University of California, San Diego and Department of Aerospace Engineering and Engineering Mechanics. *Program availability:* Evening/weekend. *Degree requirements:* For master's, comprehensive exam (for some programs), thesis (for some programs); for doctorate, thesis/ dissertation. *Entrance requirements:* For master's, GRE General Test; for doctorate, GRE, 3 letters of recommendation. Additional exam requirements/recommendations for international students: Required—TOEFL. Electronic applications accepted. *Faculty research:* Energy analysis and diagnosis, seawater pump design, space-related research.

Stanford University, School of Engineering, Department of Mechanical Engineering, Stanford, CA 94305-2004. Offers biomechanical engineering (MSE); design impact (MSE); mechanical engineering (MS, PhD, Engr). *Expenses: Tuition:* Full-time $50,703; part-time $32,970 per year. *Required fees:* $651.
Website: http://me.stanford.edu/

Stevens Institute of Technology, Graduate School, Charles V. Schaefer Jr. School of Engineering and Science, Department of Mechanical Engineering, Program in Product Architecture and Engineering, Hoboken, NJ 07030. Offers M Eng. *Program availability:* Part-time, evening/weekend. *Faculty:* 32 full-time (4 women), 10 part-time/adjunct (0

women). *Students:* 3. In 2018, 1 master's awarded. *Degree requirements:* For master's, thesis optional, minimum B average in major field and overall. *Entrance requirements:* For master's, GRE/GMAT scores: GRE scores are required for all applicants applying to a full-time graduate program in the Schaefer School of Engineering and Science (SES). International applicants must submit TOEFL/IELTS scores and fulfill the English Language Proficiency Requirements in order to be considered. Additional exam requirements/recommendations for international students: Required—TOEFL (minimum score 74 iBT), IELTS (minimum score 6). *Application deadline:* For fall admission, 4/1 for domestic students, 4/15 for international students; for spring admission, 11/1 for domestic and international students; for summer admission, 5/1 for domestic students. Applications are processed on a rolling basis. Application fee: $60. Electronic applications accepted. *Expenses: Tuition:* Full-time $35,960; part-time $1620 per credit. *Required fees:* $1290; $600 per semester. Tuition and fees vary according to course load. *Financial support:* Fellowships, research assistantships, teaching assistantships, career-related internships or fieldwork, Federal Work-Study, scholarships/grants, and unspecified assistantships available. Financial award application deadline: 2/15; financial award applicants required to submit FAFSA. *Unit head:* Dr. Jean Zu, Dean of SES, 201-216.8233, Fax: 201-216.8372, E-mail: Jean.Zu@stevens.edu. *Application contact:* Graduate Admissions, 888-783-8367, Fax: 888-511-1306, E-mail: graduate@stevens.edu.

The University of Alabama at Birmingham, School of Engineering, Professional Engineering Degrees, Birmingham, AL 35294. Offers advanced safety engineering and management (M Eng); construction engineering management (M Eng); design and commercialization (M Eng); information engineering management (M Eng); structural engineering (M Eng); sustainable smart cities (M Eng). *Program availability:* Part-time, evening/weekend, online only, 100% online, blended/hybrid learning. *Faculty:* 6 full-time (1 woman), 12 part-time/adjunct (2 women). *Students:* 23 full-time (7 women), 315 part-time (63 women); includes 96 minority (73 Black or African American, non-Hispanic/Latino; 1 American Indian or Alaska Native, non-Hispanic/Latino; 8 Asian, non-Hispanic/Latino; 12 Hispanic/Latino; 2 Two or more races, non-Hispanic/Latino), 12 international. Average age 37. 154 applicants, 84% accepted, 91 enrolled. In 2018, 87 master's awarded. *Entrance requirements:* For master's, 3.0 GPA on 4.0 scale, undergraduate degree from a nationally accredited school. Additional exam requirements/ recommendations for international students: Required—TOEFL (minimum score 80 iBT); Recommended—IELTS (minimum score 6.5). *Application deadline:* For fall admission, 8/1 for domestic and international students; for spring admission, 12/1 for domestic and international students; for summer admission, 5/1 for domestic and international students. Applications are processed on a rolling basis. Application fee: $50 ($60 for international students). Electronic applications accepted. *Expenses:* Contact institution. *Faculty research:* Orthopedic biomechanics, translational rehabilitation and assistive devices, innovation and entrepreneurship, anthropogenic activities and the natural environment, prestressed and spun concrete. *Application contact:* Jesse Kepply, Director of Student and Academic Services, 205-996-5696, E-mail: gradschool@uab.edu.

University of Michigan, College of Engineering, Department of Integrative Systems and Design, Ann Arbor, MI 48109. Offers automotive engineering (M Eng); design science (MS, PhD); energy systems engineering (M Eng, MS); global automotive and manufacturing engineering (M Eng); manufacturing engineering (M Eng, D Eng); pharmaceutical engineering (M Eng); robotics and autonomous vehicles (M Eng); systems engineering and design (M Eng); MBA/M Eng; MSE/MS. *Program availability:* Part-time, online learning. *Students:* 163 full-time (38 women), 251 part-time (40 women). 282 applicants, 12% accepted, 15 enrolled. In 2018, 173 master's, 1 doctorate awarded. Terminal master's awarded for partial completion of doctoral program. *Degree requirements:* For master's, capstone project; for doctorate, thesis/dissertation. *Entrance requirements:* For master's and doctorate, GRE. Additional exam requirements/recommendations for international students: Required—TOEFL. *Application deadline:* Applications are processed on a rolling basis. Electronic applications accepted. *Financial support:* Fellowships, research assistantships with full tuition reimbursements, teaching assistantships with full tuition reimbursements, career-related internships or fieldwork, scholarships/grants, and unspecified assistantships available. Financial award applicants required to submit FAFSA. *Faculty research:* Automotive engineering, design science, energy systems engineering, engineering sustainable systems, financial engineering, global automotive and manufacturing engineering, integrated microsystems, manufacturing engineering, pharmaceutical engineering, robotics and autonomous vehicles. *Total annual research expenditures:* $595,323. *Unit head:* Diann Brei, Department Chair, 734-763-6617, E-mail: drdiannbrei@umich.edu. *Application contact:* Kathy Bishar, Senior Graduate Coordinator, 734-764-3312, E-mail: kbishar@umich.edu.
Website: http://www.isd.engin.umich.edu

Worcester Polytechnic Institute, Graduate Admissions, Foisie Business School, Worcester, MA 01609-2280. Offers business administration (PhD); information technology (MS), including information security management; management (MS, Graduate Certificate); marketing and innovation (MS); operations analytics and management (MS); supply chain management (MS). *Accreditation:* AACSB. *Program availability:* Part-time, evening/weekend, 100% online, blended/hybrid learning. *Students:* 136 full-time (74 women), 214 part-time (85 women); includes 29 minority (4 Black or African American, non-Hispanic/Latino; 11 Asian, non-Hispanic/Latino; 9 Hispanic/Latino; 5 Two or more races, non-Hispanic/Latino), 189 international. Average age 29. 636 applicants, 64% accepted, 104 enrolled. In 2018, 165 master's, 1 doctorate, 10 other advanced degrees awarded. *Degree requirements:* For master's, thesis optional. *Entrance requirements:* For master's and Graduate Certificate, GMAT or GRE General Test, 3 letters of recommendation, statement of purpose, resume. Additional exam requirements/recommendations for international students: Required—TOEFL (minimum score 563 paper-based; 84 iBT), IELTS (minimum score 7). *Application deadline:* For fall admission, 6/1 priority date for domestic and international students; for spring admission, 11/1 priority date for domestic students, 10/1 priority date for international students. Applications are processed on a rolling basis. Application fee: $70. Electronic applications accepted. *Financial support:* Career-related internships or fieldwork, institutionally sponsored loans, scholarships/grants, and unspecified assistantships available. Financial award application deadline: 6/1. *Unit head:* Melissa Terrio, Director of Graduate Recruitment & Admissions, 508-831-4665, Fax: 508-831-5866, E-mail: biz@wpi.edu. *Application contact:* Amy Trakimas, Associate Director of Graduate Recruitment & Admissions, 508-831-4665, Fax: 508-831-5866, E-mail: atrakimas@wpi.edu.
Website: https://www.wpi.edu/academics/business

Section 12
Engineering Physics

This section contains a directory of institutions offering graduate work in engineering physics. Additional information about programs listed in the directory may be obtained by writing directly to the dean of a graduate school or chair of a department at the address given in the directory.

For programs offering related work, see also in this book *Electrical and Computer Engineering, Energy and Power Engineering (Nuclear Engineering), Engineering and Applied Sciences,* and *Materials Sciences and Engineering.* In the other guides in this series:

Graduate Programs in the Biological/Biomedical Sciences & Health-Related Medical Professions
See *Biophysics* and *Health Sciences (Medical Physics)*

Graduate Programs in the Physical Sciences, Mathematics, Agricultural Sciences, the Environment & Natural Resources
See *Physics*

CONTENTS

Program Directory

Engineering Physics

Air Force Institute of Technology, Graduate School of Engineering and Management, Department of Engineering Physics, Dayton, OH 45433-7765. Offers applied physics (MS, PhD); electro-optics (MS, PhD); materials science (PhD); nuclear engineering (MS, PhD); space physics (MS). *Program availability:* Part-time. *Degree requirements:* For master's, thesis; for doctorate, thesis/dissertation. *Entrance requirements:* For master's and doctorate, GRE General Test, minimum GPA of 3.0, U.S. citizenship. *Faculty research:* High-energy lasers, space physics, nuclear weapon effects, semiconductor physics.

Cornell University, Graduate School, Graduate Fields of Engineering, Field of Applied Physics, Ithaca, NY 14853. Offers applied physics (PhD); engineering physics (M Eng). *Degree requirements:* For doctorate, comprehensive exam, thesis/dissertation, written exams. *Entrance requirements:* For master's, GRE General Test, 3 letters of recommendation; for doctorate, GRE General Test, GRE Subject Test (physics), GRE Writing Assessment, 3 letters of recommendation. Additional exam requirements/recommendations for international students: Required—TOEFL (minimum score 600 paper-based; 77 iBT). Electronic applications accepted. *Faculty research:* Quantum and nonlinear optics, plasma physics, solid state physics, condensed matter physics and nanotechnology, electron and X-ray spectroscopy.

École Polytechnique de Montréal, Graduate Programs, Department of Engineering Physics, Montréal, QC H3C 3A7, Canada. Offers optical engineering (M Eng, M Sc A, PhD); solid-state physics and engineering (M Eng, M Sc A, PhD). *Program availability:* Part-time. *Degree requirements:* For master's, one foreign language, thesis; for doctorate, one foreign language, thesis/dissertation. *Entrance requirements:* For master's, minimum GPA of 2.75; for doctorate, minimum GPA of 3.0. *Faculty research:* Optics, thin-film physics, laser spectroscopy, plasmas, photonic devices.

Embry-Riddle Aeronautical University–Daytona, Department of Physical Sciences, Daytona Beach, FL 32114-3900. Offers engineering physics (MS, PhD). *Degree requirements:* For master's, thesis or alternative; for doctorate, comprehensive exam, thesis/dissertation. *Entrance requirements:* For doctorate, GRE. Additional exam requirements/recommendations for international students: Required—TOEFL (minimum score 550 paper-based, 79 iBT) or IELTS (6). Electronic applications accepted.

Louisiana Tech University, Graduate School, College of Engineering and Science, Ruston, LA 71272. Offers applied physics (MS); biomedical engineering (PhD); computer science (MS); engineering (MS, PhD), including cyberspace engineering (PhD), engineering education (PhD), engineering physics (PhD), materials and infrastructure systems (PhD), micro/nanoscale systems (PhD); engineering and technology management (MS); mathematics (MS); molecular science and nanotechnology (MS, PhD). *Program availability:* Part-time-only. Terminal master's awarded for partial completion of doctoral program. *Degree requirements:* For master's, thesis (for some programs); for doctorate, thesis/dissertation. *Entrance requirements:* For master's and Graduate Certificate, GRE General Test, minimum GPA of 3.0 in last 60 hours. Additional exam requirements/recommendations for international students: Required—TOEFL (minimum score 550 paper-based; 80 iBT), IELTS (minimum score 6.5). Electronic applications accepted. *Faculty research:* Trenchless technology, micromanufacturing, radionuclide transport, microbial liquefaction, hazardous waste treatment.

McMaster University, School of Graduate Studies, Faculty of Engineering, Department of Engineering Physics, Hamilton, ON L8S 4M2, Canada. Offers engineering physics (M Eng, MA Sc, PhD); nuclear engineering (PhD). *Degree requirements:* For master's, thesis or alternative; for doctorate, comprehensive exam, thesis/dissertation. *Entrance requirements:* For master's, minimum B average in engineering, mathematics, or physical sciences. Additional exam requirements/recommendations for international students: Required—TOEFL (minimum score 550 paper-based). *Faculty research:* Non-thermal plasmas for pollution control and electrostatic precipitation, bulk and thin film luminescent materials, devices and systems for optical fiber communications, physics and applications of III-V materials and devices, defect spectroscopy in semiconductors.

Queen's University at Kingston, School of Graduate Studies, Faculty of Arts and Science, Department of Physics, Engineering Physics and Astronomy, Kingston, ON K7L 3N6, Canada. Offers M Sc, M Sc Eng, PhD. *Program availability:* Part-time. *Degree requirements:* For master's, thesis; for doctorate, comprehensive exam, thesis/dissertation. *Entrance requirements:* For doctorate, M Sc or M Sc Eng. Additional exam requirements/recommendations for international students: Required—TOEFL (minimum score 550 paper-based). *Faculty research:* Theoretical physics, astronomy and astrophysics, condensed matter.

Rensselaer Polytechnic Institute, Graduate School, School of Engineering, Program in Engineering Physics, Troy, NY 12180-3590. Offers MS, PhD. *Program availability:* Part-time. *Faculty:* 48 full-time (7 women), 1 part-time/adjunct (0 women). *Students:* 1 applicant, 100% accepted. Terminal master's awarded for partial completion of doctoral program. *Degree requirements:* For master's, thesis (for some programs); for doctorate, thesis/dissertation. *Entrance requirements:* For master's and doctorate, GRE. Additional exam requirements/recommendations for international students: Required—TOEFL (minimum score 600 paper-based; 100 iBT), IELTS (minimum score 7), PTE (minimum score 68). *Application deadline:* For fall admission, 1/1 priority date for domestic and international students; for spring admission, 8/15 priority date for domestic and international students. Applications are processed on a rolling basis. Application fee: $75. Electronic applications accepted. *Financial support:* In 2018–19, 1 student received support, including research assistantships (averaging $23,000 per year), teaching assistantships (averaging $23,000 per year); fellowships also available. Financial award application deadline: 1/1. *Faculty research:* Applied radiation, radiation transport, medical physics, multiphase phenomena, sonoluminescence, fusion plasma engineering. *Total annual research expenditures:* $2.3 million. *Unit head:* Dr. Theo Borca-Tasciuc, Graduate Program Director, 518-276-2627, E-mail: borcat@rpi.edu. *Application contact:* Jarron Decker, Director of Graduate Admissions, 518-276-6216, Fax: 518-276-4072, E-mail: gradadmissions@rpi.edu.
Website: http://mane.rpi.edu/

Stanford University, School of Humanities and Sciences, Department of Applied Physics, Stanford, CA 94305-2004. Offers applied and engineering physics (MS); applied physics (PhD). *Expenses: Tuition:* Full-time $50,703; part-time $32,970 per year. *Required fees:* $651.
Website: http://www.stanford.edu/dept/app-physics/

University of California, San Diego, Graduate Division, Department of Mechanical and Aerospace Engineering, Program in Engineering Physics, La Jolla, CA 92093. Offers MS, PhD. *Students:* 16 full-time (1 woman). 21 applicants, 71% accepted, 4 enrolled. In 2018, 3 master's, 8 doctorates awarded. *Degree requirements:* For master's, comprehensive exam (for some programs), thesis (for some programs), comprehensive exam or thesis; for doctorate, comprehensive exam, thesis/dissertation. *Entrance requirements:* For master's and doctorate, GRE General Test, minimum GPA of 3.0. Additional exam requirements/recommendations for international students: Required—TOEFL (minimum score 550 paper-based; 80 iBT), IELTS (minimum score 7). *Application deadline:* For fall admission, 12/18 for domestic students. Application fee: $105 ($125 for international students). Electronic applications accepted. *Financial support:* Fellowships, research assistantships, teaching assistantships, scholarships/grants, and unspecified assistantships available. Financial award applicants required to submit FAFSA. *Faculty research:* Experimental, theoretical, and computational programs addressing turbulent flows; mechanics of two-phase flow; rheology of suspensions; laminar and turbulent combustion; chemical kinetics of combustion systems. *Unit head:* Carlos Coimbra, Chair, 858-534-4285, E-mail: mae-chair-l@ucsd.edu. *Application contact:* Joana Halnez, Graduate Coordinator, 858-534-4387, E-mail: mae-gradadm-l@ucsd.edu.
Website: http://maeweb.ucsd.edu/

University of Central Oklahoma, The Jackson College of Graduate Studies, College of Mathematics and Science, Department of Engineering and Physics, Edmond, OK 73034-5209. Offers engineering physics (MS), including biomedical engineering, electrical engineering, mechanical systems, physics. *Program availability:* Part-time. *Degree requirements:* For master's, thesis optional. *Entrance requirements:* For master's, GRE, 24 hours of course work in physics or equivalent, mathematics through differential equations, minimum GPA of 2.75 overall and 3.0 in last 60 hours attempted, two letters of recommendation. Additional exam requirements/recommendations for international students: Required—TOEFL (minimum score 550 paper-based; 79 iBT), IELTS (minimum score 6.5). Electronic applications accepted.

University of Oklahoma, College of Arts and Sciences, Homer L. Dodge Department of Physics and Astronomy, Norman, OK 73019. Offers engineering physics (MS); physics (MS, PhD). *Faculty:* 27 full-time (3 women). *Students:* 46 full-time (12 women), 10 part-time (1 woman); includes 3 minority (2 Hispanic/Latino; 1 Two or more races, non-Hispanic/Latino), 38 international. Average age 27. 98 applicants, 20% accepted, 18 enrolled. In 2018, 6 master's, 9 doctorates awarded. Terminal master's awarded for partial completion of doctoral program. *Degree requirements:* For master's, comprehensive exam, thesis (for some programs), thesis or qualifying exams; for doctorate, comprehensive exam, thesis/dissertation, qualifying exams. *Entrance requirements:* For master's and doctorate, GRE General Test and GRE Subject Test in physics (recommended), transcripts, statement of purpose, three letters of recommendation. Additional exam requirements/recommendations for international students: Required—TOEFL (minimum score 79 iBT) or IELTS (minimum score 6.5). *Application deadline:* For fall admission, 2/1 for domestic and international students; for spring admission, 9/1 for domestic and international students. Applications are processed on a rolling basis. Application fee: $50 ($100 for international students). Electronic applications accepted. *Expenses:* Tuition, state resident: full-time $5683.20; part-time $236.80 per credit hour. Tuition, nonresident: full-time $20,342; part-time $847.60 per credit hour. *International tuition:* $20,342.40 full-time. *Required fees:* $2894.20; $110.05 per credit hour. $126.50 per semester. Tuition and fees vary according to course load and program. *Financial support:* Fellowships, research assistantships, teaching assistantships, scholarships/grants, health care benefits, and unspecified assistantships available. Financial award application deadline: 6/1; financial award applicants required to submit FAFSA. *Faculty research:* Astrophysics; atomic, molecular, and optical physics; high energy physics; condensed matter physics. *Unit head:* Dr. Phillip Gutierrez, Chair, 405-325-3961, Fax: 405-325-7557, E-mail: chair@nhn.ou.edu. *Application contact:* Dr. Lloyd Bumm, Professor, 405-325-6053, Fax: 405-325-7557, E-mail: grad@nhn.ou.edu.
Website: http://www.nhn.ou.edu

University of Saskatchewan, College of Graduate and Postdoctoral Studies, College of Arts and Science, Department of Physics and Engineering Physics, Saskatoon, SK S7N 5A2, Canada. Offers M Sc, PhD. *Degree requirements:* For master's, thesis; for doctorate, comprehensive exam (for some programs), thesis/dissertation. *Entrance requirements:* Additional exam requirements/recommendations for international students: Required—TOEFL (minimum score 80 iBT); Recommended—IELTS (minimum score 6.5). Electronic applications accepted.

University of Virginia, School of Engineering and Applied Science, Program in Engineering Physics, Charlottesville, VA 22903. Offers ME, MS, PhD. *Program availability:* Online learning. *Degree requirements:* For master's, comprehensive exam; for doctorate, comprehensive exam, thesis/dissertation. *Entrance requirements:* For master's and doctorate, GRE General Test, 3 recommendations. Additional exam requirements/recommendations for international students: Required—TOEFL. Electronic applications accepted. *Faculty research:* Continuum and rarefied gas dynamics, ultracentrifuge isotope enrichment, solid-state physics, atmospheric physics, atomic collisions.

University of Wisconsin–Madison, Graduate School, College of Engineering, Department of Engineering Physics, Madison, WI 53706-1380. Offers engineering mechanics (MS, PhD), including fundamentals of applied mechanics (MS); nuclear engineering and engineering physics (MS, PhD). *Program availability:* Part-time. *Faculty:* 20 full-time (4 women). *Students:* 103 full-time (17 women), 3 part-time (0 women); includes 16 minority (3 Black or African American, non-Hispanic/Latino; 5 Asian, non-Hispanic/Latino; 6 Hispanic/Latino; 2 Two or more races, non-Hispanic/Latino), 16 international. Average age 26. 169 applicants, 42% accepted, 18 enrolled. In 2018, 28 master's, 12 doctorates awarded. Terminal master's awarded for partial completion of doctoral program. *Degree requirements:* For master's, thesis optional, 30 credits of technical courses; oral exam; minimum GPA of 3.0; for doctorate, comprehensive exam, thesis/dissertation, minimum of 60 credits; minimum GPA of 3.0. *Entrance requirements:* For master's and doctorate, GRE General Test, minimum GPA of 3.0 in last 60 hours, appropriate bachelor's degree. Additional exam requirements/recommendations for international students: Required—TOEFL (minimum score 580 paper-based; 92 iBT), IELTS (minimum score 7). *Application deadline:* For fall admission, 12/15 for domestic and international students; for spring admission, 10/1 for domestic and international students; for summer admission, 12/15 for domestic and international students. Application fee: $75 ($81 for international students). Electronic applications accepted. *Financial support:* In 2018–19, 109 students received support, including 9 fellowships with full tuition reimbursements available (averaging $27,204 per year), 82 research assistantships with full tuition reimbursements available (averaging $27,780 per year), 18 teaching assistantships with full tuition reimbursements available (averaging $23,566 per year); career-related internships or fieldwork, Federal Work-Study, institutionally sponsored loans, unspecified assistantships, and project assistantships also available. Support available to part-time students. Financial award application deadline: 12/1; financial award applicants required to submit FAFSA. *Faculty research:* Bio-/micro-/nano-mechanics; astronautics; fission reactor engineering; fusion science and technology; radiation sciences; mechanics of materials. *Total annual research expenditures:* $13.7 million. *Unit head:* Dr. Paul Wilson, Chair, 608-263-1646,

Fax: 608-263-7451, E-mail: office@ep.wisc.edu. *Application contact:* Sara Hladilek, Student Services Coordinator, 608-262-8617, Fax: 608-263-7451, E-mail: shladilek@wisc.edu.
Website: https://www.engr.wisc.edu/department/engineering-physics/

Yale University, Graduate School of Arts and Sciences, School of Engineering and Applied Science, Department of Applied Physics, New Haven, CT 06520. Offers MS, PhD. Terminal master's awarded for partial completion of doctoral program. *Degree requirements:* For doctorate, thesis/dissertation, area exam. *Entrance requirements:* For master's and doctorate, GRE General Test. Additional exam requirements/recommendations for international students: Required—TOEFL. *Faculty research:* Condensed-matter physics, optical physics, materials science.

Section 13
Geological, Mineral/Mining, and Petroleum Engineering

This section contains a directory of institutions offering graduate work in geological, mineral/mining, and petroleum engineering. Additional information about programs listed in the directory may be obtained by writing directly to the dean of a graduate school or chair of a department at the address given in the directory.

For programs offering related work, see also in this book *Chemical Engineering, Civil and Environmental Engineering, Electrical and Computer Engineering, Energy and Power Engineering, Engineering and Applied Sciences, Management of Engineering and Technology,* and *Materials Sciences and Engineering.* In another guide in this series:

Graduate Programs in the Physical Sciences, Mathematics, Agricultural Sciences, the Environment & Natural Resources
See *Geosciences* and *Marine Sciences and Oceanography*

CONTENTS

Program Directories

Geological Engineering

Arizona State University at the Tempe campus, College of Liberal Arts and Sciences, School of Earth and Space Exploration, Tempe, AZ 85287-1404. Offers astrophysics (MS, PhD); exploration systems design (PhD); geological sciences (MS, PhD). PhD in exploration systems design is offered in collaboration with the Ira A. Fulton School of Engineering. Terminal master's awarded for partial completion of doctoral program. *Degree requirements:* For master's, thesis, interactive Program of Study (iPOS) submitted before completing 50 percent of required credit hours; for doctorate, thesis/dissertation, interactive Program of Study (iPOS) submitted before completing 50 percent of required credit hours. *Entrance requirements:* For master's and doctorate, GRE, minimum GPA of 3.0 or equivalent in last 2 years of work leading to bachelor's degree. Additional exam requirements/recommendations for international students: Required—TOEFL, IELTS, or PTE. Electronic applications accepted.

Colorado School of Mines, Office of Graduate Studies, Department of Geology and Geological Engineering, Golden, CO 80401. Offers environmental geochemistry (PMS); geochemistry (MS, PhD); geological engineering (ME, MS, PhD); geology (MS, PhD); hydrology (MS, PhD); mineral exploration (PMS); petroleum reservoir systems (PMS); underground construction and tunneling (MS). *Program availability:* Part-time. *Faculty:* 30 full-time (12 women), 6 part-time/adjunct (5 women). *Students:* 129 full-time (44 women), 32 part-time (12 women); includes 20 minority (1 Black or African American, non-Hispanic/Latino; 2 American Indian or Alaska Native, non-Hispanic/Latino; 3 Asian, non-Hispanic/Latino; 10 Hispanic/Latino; 4 Two or more races, non-Hispanic/Latino), 30 international. Average age 29. 244 applicants, 41% accepted, 54 enrolled. In 2018, 39 master's, 11 doctorates awarded. *Degree requirements:* For master's, thesis (for some programs); for doctorate, comprehensive exam, thesis/dissertation. *Entrance requirements:* For master's and doctorate, GRE General Test. Additional exam requirements/recommendations for international students: Required—TOEFL (minimum score 550 paper-based; 79 iBT). *Application deadline:* For fall admission, 12/15 priority date for domestic and international students; for spring admission, 9/1 priority date for domestic and international students. Application fee: $60 ($80 for international students). Electronic applications accepted. *Expenses:* Tuition, state resident: full-time $16,650; part-time $925 per contact hour. Tuition, nonresident: full-time $36,270; part-time $2015 per contact hour. *International tuition:* $36,270 full-time. *Required fees:* $2314; $2314 per semester. *Financial support:* In 2018–19, 48 research assistantships with full tuition reimbursements, 20 teaching assistantships with full tuition reimbursements were awarded; fellowships, scholarships/grants, health care benefits, and unspecified assistantships also available. Financial award application deadline: 12/15; financial award applicants required to submit FAFSA. *Faculty research:* Predictive sediment modeling, petrophysics, aquifer-contaminant flow modeling, water-rock interactions, geotechnical engineering. *Unit head:* Dr. Wendy Bohrson, Head, 303-273-3066, E-mail: bohrson@mines.edu. *Application contact:* Dr. Christian Shorey, Lecturer/Program Manager, 303-273-3556, E-mail: cshorey@mines.edu.
Website: http://geology.mines.edu

Colorado School of Mines, Office of Graduate Studies, Department of Geophysics, Golden, CO 80401. Offers geophysical engineering (ME, MS, PhD); geophysics (MS, PhD); hydrology (MS, PhD); mineral exploration and mining geosciences (PMS); petroleum reservoir systems (PMS). *Program availability:* Part-time. *Faculty:* 14 full-time (5 women), 4 part-time/adjunct (0 women). *Students:* 62 full-time (17 women), 2 part-time (0 women); includes 5 minority (2 Asian, non-Hispanic/Latino; 1 Hispanic/Latino; 2 Two or more races, non-Hispanic/Latino), 33 international. Average age 28. 142 applicants, 26% accepted, 23 enrolled. In 2018, 12 master's, 12 doctorates awarded. *Degree requirements:* For master's, thesis (for some programs); for doctorate, comprehensive exam, thesis/dissertation. *Entrance requirements:* For master's and doctorate, GRE General Test. Additional exam requirements/recommendations for international students: Required—TOEFL (minimum score 550 paper-based; 79 iBT). *Application deadline:* For fall admission, 12/15 priority date for domestic and international students; for spring admission, 9/1 priority date for domestic students, 9/1 for international students. Application fee: $60 ($80 for international students). Electronic applications accepted. *Expenses:* Tuition, state resident: full-time $16,650; part-time $925 per contact hour. Tuition, nonresident: full-time $36,270; part-time $2015 per contact hour. *International tuition:* $36,270 full-time. *Required fees:* $2314; $2314 per semester. *Financial support:* In 2018–19, 40 research assistantships with full tuition reimbursements, 9 teaching assistantships with full tuition reimbursements were awarded; fellowships, career-related internships or fieldwork, scholarships/grants, health care benefits, and unspecified assistantships also available. Financial award application deadline: 12/15; financial award applicants required to submit FAFSA. *Faculty research:* Seismic exploration, gravity and geomagnetic fields, electrical mapping and sounding, bore hole measurements, environmental physics. *Unit head:* Dr. Paul Sava, Head, 303-384-2362, E-mail: psava@mines.edu. *Application contact:* Michelle Szobody, Program Assistant, 303-273-3935, E-mail: mszobody@mines.edu.
Website: http://geophysics.mines.edu

Missouri University of Science and Technology, Department of Geosciences and Geological and Petroleum Engineering, Rolla, MO 65401. Offers geological engineering (MS, DE, PhD); geology and geophysics (MS, PhD), including geochemistry, geology, geophysics, groundwater and environmental geology; petroleum engineering (MS, DE, PhD). *Program availability:* Part-time. *Degree requirements:* For master's, thesis optional; for doctorate, comprehensive exam, thesis/dissertation. *Entrance requirements:* For master's, GRE General Test (minimum score 600 quantitative, writing 3.5), minimum GPA of 3.0 in last 4 semesters; for doctorate, GRE General Test (minimum scores: Quantitative 600, Writing 3.5). Additional exam requirements/recommendations for international students: Required—TOEFL (minimum score 550 paper-based). Electronic applications accepted. *Expenses:* Tuition, state resident: full-time $7545.60; part-time $419.20 per credit hour. Tuition, nonresident: full-time $22,169; part-time $1231.60 per credit hour. *International tuition:* $23,518.80 full-time. *Required fees:* $4523.05. Full-time tuition and fees vary according to course load, campus/location, program and reciprocity agreements. *Faculty research:* Digital image processing and geographic information systems, mineralogy, igneous and sedimentary petrology-geochemistry, sedimentology groundwater hydrology and contaminant transport.

Montana Tech of The University of Montana, Geosciences Programs, Butte, MT 59701-8997. Offers geochemistry (MS); geological engineering (MS); geology (MS); geophysical engineering (MS); hydrogeological engineering (MS); hydrogeology (MS). *Program availability:* Part-time. *Degree requirements:* For master's, comprehensive exam (for some programs), thesis (for some programs). *Entrance requirements:* For master's, GRE General Test, minimum GPA of 3.0. Additional exam requirements/recommendations for international students: Required—TOEFL (minimum score 545 paper-based; 78 iBT), IELTS (minimum score 6.5). Electronic applications accepted. *Faculty research:* Water resource development, seismic processing, petroleum reservoir characterization, environmental geochemistry, geologic mapping.

New Mexico Institute of Mining and Technology, Center for Graduate Studies, Department of Mineral Engineering, Socorro, NM 87801. Offers explosives engineering (MS); geotechnical engineering (MS); mining engineering (MS). *Degree requirements:* For master's, thesis. *Entrance requirements:* Additional exam requirements/recommendations for international students: Required—TOEFL (minimum score 540 paper-based). *Faculty research:* Drilling and blasting, geological engineering, mine design, applied mineral exploration, rock mechanics.

South Dakota School of Mines and Technology, Graduate Division, Department of Geology and Geological Engineering, Rapid City, SD 57701-3995. Offers geology and geological engineering (MS, PhD); paleontology (MS). *Program availability:* Part-time. *Degree requirements:* For master's, thesis; for doctorate, thesis/dissertation. *Entrance requirements:* For master's and doctorate, GRE General Test, GRE Subject Test. Additional exam requirements/recommendations for international students: Required—TOEFL (minimum score 520 paper-based; 68 iBT), TWE. Electronic applications accepted. *Faculty research:* Contaminants in soil, nitrate leaching, environmental changes, fracture formations, greenhouse effect.

The University of Akron, Graduate School, Buchtel College of Arts and Sciences, Department of Geosciences, Akron, OH 44325. Offers earth science (MS); engineering geology (MS); environmental geology (MS); geology (MS). *Program availability:* Part-time. *Entrance requirements:* For master's, minimum GPA of 2.75, three letters of recommendation, statement of purpose. Additional exam requirements/recommendations for international students: Required—TOEFL (minimum score 79 iBT), IELTS (minimum score 6.5). Electronic applications accepted. *Faculty research:* Terrestrial environmental change, karst hydrogeology, lacustrine paleo environments, environmental magnetism and geophysics.

University of Alaska Fairbanks, College of Engineering and Mines, Department of Mining and Geological Engineering, Fairbanks, AK 99775-5800. Offers geological engineering (MS); mineral preparation engineering (MS); mining engineering (MS). *Program availability:* Part-time. *Faculty:* 7 full-time (1 woman). *Students:* 3 full-time (0 women), 3 part-time (1 woman), 5 international. Average age 30. 11 applicants, 27% accepted, 1 enrolled. In 2018, 2 master's awarded. *Degree requirements:* For master's, comprehensive exam, oral defense of project or thesis. *Entrance requirements:* For master's, GRE General Test (for geological engineering), bachelor's degree from accredited institution with minimum cumulative undergraduate and major GPA of 3.0. Additional exam requirements/recommendations for international students: Required—TOEFL (minimum score 550 paper-based; 79 iBT), IELTS (minimum score 6.5). *Application deadline:* For fall admission, 6/1 for domestic students, 3/1 for international students; for spring admission, 10/15 for domestic students, 9/1 for international students. Applications are processed on a rolling basis. Application fee: $60. Electronic applications accepted. *Expenses:* College of Engineering and Mines (CEM) tuition has a 20% surcharge per credit hour over that for credits of most other UAF colleges. Assuming 60 credits for PhD and 32 for Master's, this augments costs by $6,180 for in-state PhD, $3,296 for in-state Master's, $12,948 for non-resident PhD and $6,912 for non-resident Masters students, respectively. *Financial support:* In 2018–19, 3 research assistantships with full tuition reimbursements (averaging $3,544 per year), 4 teaching assistantships with full tuition reimbursements (averaging $4,768 per year) were awarded; fellowships with full tuition reimbursements, career-related internships or fieldwork, Federal Work-Study, scholarships/grants, health care benefits, and unspecified assistantships also available. Support available to part-time students. Financial award application deadline: 7/1; financial award applicants required to submit FAFSA. *Faculty research:* Underground mining in permafrost, testing of ultra clean diesel, slope stability, fractal and mathematical morphology, soil and rock mechanics. *Total annual research expenditures:* $1.1 million. *Unit head:* Dr. Tathagata Gosh, Chair, 907-474-6917, E-mail: cem.mingeo@alaska.edu. *Application contact:* Samara Taber, Director of Admissions, 907-474-7500, E-mail: uaf-admissions@alaska.edu.
Website: http://cem.uaf.edu/mingeo

The University of Arizona, College of Engineering, Department of Mining and Geological Engineering, Tucson, AZ 85721. Offers mining and geological engineering (MS, PhD); mining engineering (Certificate), including mine health and safety, mine information and production technology, rock mechanics. *Program availability:* Part-time, online learning. *Degree requirements:* For master's, thesis; for doctorate, thesis/dissertation. *Entrance requirements:* For master's, GRE General Test, 3 letters of recommendation; for doctorate, GRE General Test, 3 letters of recommendation, statements of purpose. Additional exam requirements/recommendations for international students: Required—TOEFL (minimum score 550 paper-based; 79 iBT). Electronic applications accepted. *Faculty research:* Geomechanics, mineral processing, information technology, automation, geosensing.

The University of British Columbia, Faculty of Science, Department of Earth, Ocean and Atmospheric Sciences, Vancouver, BC V6T 1Z4, Canada. Offers atmospheric science (M Sc, PhD); geological engineering (M Eng, MA Sc, PhD); geological sciences (M Sc, PhD); geophysics (M Sc, MA Sc, PhD); oceanography (M Sc, PhD). *Degree requirements:* For master's, one foreign language, thesis (for some programs); for doctorate, one foreign language, comprehensive exam, thesis/dissertation. *Entrance requirements:* Additional exam requirements/recommendations for international students: Required—TOEFL. *Expenses:* Contact institution. *Faculty research:* Oceans and atmosphere, environmental earth science, hydro geology, mineral deposits, geophysics.

University of Hawaii at Manoa, Office of Graduate Education, School of Ocean and Earth Science and Technology, Department of Geology and Geophysics, Honolulu, HI 96822. Offers high-pressure geophysics and geochemistry (MS, PhD); hydrogeology and engineering geology (MS, PhD); marine geology and geophysics (MS, PhD); planetary geosciences and remote sensing (MS, PhD); seismology and solid-earth geophysics (MS, PhD); volcanology, petrology, and geochemistry (MS, PhD). *Program availability:* Part-time. Terminal master's awarded for partial completion of doctoral program. *Degree requirements:* For master's, thesis optional; for doctorate, comprehensive exam, thesis/dissertation. *Entrance requirements:* For master's and doctorate, GRE General Test, minimum GPA of 3.0. Additional exam requirements/recommendations for international students: Required—TOEFL (minimum score 580 paper-based; 92 iBT), IELTS (minimum score 5).

University of Idaho, College of Graduate Studies, College of Engineering, Department of Civil and Environmental Engineering, Moscow, ID 83844-1022. Offers civil and environmental engineering (M Engr, PhD); geological engineering (MS). *Faculty:* 15. *Students:* 27 full-time, 38 part-time. Average age 33. In 2018, 21 master's, 1 doctorate awarded. *Entrance requirements:* For master's and doctorate, minimum GPA of 3.0. Additional exam requirements/recommendations for international students: Required—TOEFL (minimum score 550 paper-based; 79 iBT). *Application deadline:* For fall admission, 8/1 for domestic students; for spring admission, 12/15 for domestic students.

Applications are processed on a rolling basis. Application fee: $60. Electronic applications accepted. *Expenses:* Tuition, state resident: full-time $7266.44; part-time $474.50 per credit hour. Tuition, nonresident: full-time $24,902; part-time $1453.50 per credit hour. *Required fees:* $2085.56; $45.50 per credit hour. *Financial support:* Fellowships, research assistantships, teaching assistantships, and career-related internships or fieldwork available. Financial award applicants required to submit FAFSA. *Faculty research:* Transportation cyber security, highway maintenance management systems, river restoration,remediation of organic and metal contaminants in the subsurface, pipeline leak detection. *Unit head:* Patricia Colberg, Department Chair, 208-885-6782, E-mail: cee@uidaho.edu. *Application contact:* Patricia Colberg, Department Chair, 208-885-6782, E-mail: cee@uidaho.edu.
Website: http://www.uidaho.edu/engr/cee

University of Minnesota, Twin Cities Campus, College of Science and Engineering, Department of Civil, Environmental, and Geo-Engineering, Minneapolis, MN 55455-0213. Offers civil engineering (MCE, MS, PhD); geological engineering (M Geo E, MS); stream restoration science and engineering (Certificate). *Program availability:* Part-time. *Degree requirements:* For master's, thesis optional; for doctorate, thesis/dissertation. *Entrance requirements:* For master's and doctorate, GRE General Test. Additional exam requirements/recommendations for international students: Required—TOEFL. Electronic applications accepted. *Faculty research:* Environmental engineering, geomechanics, structural engineering, transportation, water resources.

University of Mississippi, Graduate School, School of Engineering, University, MS 38677. Offers aeroacoustics (MS, PhD); chemical engineering (MS, PhD); civil engineering (MS, PhD); computational hydroscience (MS, PhD); computer science (MS, PhD); electrical engineering (MS, PhD); electromagnetics (MS, PhD); environmental engineering (MS, PhD); geology and geological engineering (MS, PhD); hydrology (MS); material science (MS); mechanical engineering (MS, PhD); telecommunications (MS). *Faculty:* 76 full-time (16 women), 3 part-time/adjunct (1 woman). *Students:* 129 full-time (33 women), 21 part-time (5 women); includes 15 minority (7 Black or African American, non-Hispanic/Latino; 6 Asian, non-Hispanic/Latino; 1 Hispanic/Latino; 1 Two or more races, non-Hispanic/Latino), 73 international. Average age 29. In 2018, 36 master's, 17 doctorates awarded. *Entrance requirements:* For master's, GRE General Test, minimum GPA of 3.0; for doctorate, GRE General Test. Additional exam requirements/recommendations for international students: Required—TOEFL. *Application deadline:* Applications are processed on a rolling basis. Application fee: $50. Electronic applications accepted. *Financial support:* Scholarships/grants available. Financial award application deadline: 3/1; financial award applicants required to submit FAFSA. *Unit head:* Dr. David Puleo, Dean, 662-915-5780, Fax: 662-915-5387, E-mail: engineer@olemiss.edu. *Application contact:* Temeka Smith, Graduate Activities Specialist for Admissions, 662-915-7474, Fax: 662-915-7577, E-mail: gschool@olemiss.edu.

University of Nevada, Reno, Graduate School, College of Science, Mackay School of Earth Sciences and Engineering, Department of Geological Sciences and Engineering, Program in Geological Engineering, Reno, NV 89557. Offers MS, PhD. Terminal master's awarded for partial completion of doctoral program. *Degree requirements:* For master's, thesis optional; for doctorate, thesis/dissertation. *Entrance requirements:* For master's and doctorate, GRE General Test, minimum GPA of 2.75. Additional exam requirements/recommendations for international students: Required—TOEFL (minimum score 500 paper-based; 61 iBT), IELTS (minimum score 6). Electronic applications accepted. *Faculty research:* Reclamation, remediation, restoration.

University of North Dakota, Graduate School, School of Engineering and Mines, Department of Geological Engineering, Grand Forks, ND 58202. Offers MS, PhD. *Degree requirements:* For master's, thesis. *Entrance requirements:* For master's, GRE General Test. Additional exam requirements/recommendations for international students: Required—TOEFL (minimum score 550 paper-based; 79 iBT), IELTS (minimum score 6.5). Electronic applications accepted.

University of Oklahoma, Mewbourne College of Earth and Energy, Mewbourne School of Petroleum and Geological Engineering, Norman, OK 73019. Offers geological engineering (MS, PhD); natural gas engineering and management (MS), including natural gas engineering and management; natural gas technology (Graduate Certificate), including natural gas technology; petroleum engineering (MS, PhD). *Program availability:* Part-time, evening/weekend. *Faculty:* 19 full-time (1 woman), 1 part-time/adjunct (0 women). *Students:* 67 full-time (11 women), 65 part-time (11 women); includes 16 minority (3 Black or African American, non-Hispanic/Latino; 1 American Indian or Alaska Native, non-Hispanic/Latino; 1 Asian, non-Hispanic/Latino; 7 Hispanic/Latino; 4 Two or more races, non-Hispanic/Latino), 86 international. Average age 31. 147 applicants, 39% accepted, 31 enrolled. In 2018, 27 master's, 10 doctorates awarded. *Degree requirements:* For master's, variable foreign language requirement, comprehensive exam (for some programs), thesis (for some programs); for doctorate, variable foreign language requirement, comprehensive exam, thesis/dissertation. *Entrance requirements:* For master's and doctorate, GRE, minimum GPA of 3.2, three letters of recommendation, statement of purpose, resume/curriculum vitae. Additional exam requirements/recommendations for international students: Required—TOEFL (minimum score 79 iBT) or IELTS (minimum score 6.5). *Application deadline:* For fall admission, 3/1 for domestic and international students; for spring admission, 9/1 for domestic and international students. Application fee: $50 ($100 for international students). Electronic applications accepted. *Expenses:* Tuition, state resident: full-time $5683.20; part-time $236.80 per credit hour. Tuition, nonresident: full-time $20,342; part-time $847.60 per credit hour. *International tuition:* $20,342.40 full-time. *Required fees:* $2894.20; $110.05 per credit hour. $126.50 per semester. Tuition and fees vary according to course load and program. *Financial support:* Fellowships, research assistantships, teaching assistantships, and scholarships/grants available. Financial award application deadline: 6/1; financial award applicants required to submit FAFSA. *Faculty research:* Geomechanics applied to petroleum and geothermal reservoir development, unconventional petrophysics and rock physics, well construction, integrity and well control, enhanced oil recovery and high resolution reservoir characterization, machine learning, data analytics and predictive analytics. *Unit head:* Dr. Runar Nygaard, Director, 405-325-2921, E-mail: runar.nygaard@ou.edu. *Application contact:* Danika Hines-Barnett, Graduate Programs Coordinator, 405-325-2921, E-mail: danika@ou.edu.
Website: http://www.ou.edu/mcee/mpge

University of Saskatchewan, College of Graduate and Postdoctoral Studies, College of Engineering, Civil and Geological Engineering Program, Saskatoon, SK S7N 5E5, Canada. Offers M Eng, M Sc, PhD. *Program availability:* Part-time. *Degree requirements:* For master's, 30 credits (for M Eng); thesis and 12 credits (for MS); for doctorate, comprehensive exam, thesis/dissertation, qualifying exam, 18 credits. *Entrance requirements:* For master's, GRE, minimum GPA of 5.0 on an 8.0 scale; for doctorate, GRE. Additional exam requirements/recommendations for international students: Required—TOEFL (minimum iBT score of 80), IELTS (6.5), CanTEST (4.5), or PTE (59). Electronic applications accepted. *Faculty research:* Geotechnical/geo-environmental engineering, structural engineering, water resources engineering, civil engineering materials, environmental/sanitary engineering, hydrogeology, rock mechanics and mining, transportation engineering.

University of Utah, Graduate School, College of Mines and Earth Sciences, Department of Geology and Geophysics, Salt Lake City, UT 84112. Offers geological engineering (ME, MS, PhD); geology (MS, PhD); geophysics (MS, PhD). *Faculty:* 23 full-time (6 women), 15 part-time/adjunct (6 women). *Students:* 53 full-time (22 women), 12 part-time (2 women); includes 11 minority (1 American Indian or Alaska Native, non-Hispanic/Latino; 1 Asian, non-Hispanic/Latino; 8 Hispanic/Latino; 1 Two or more races, non-Hispanic/Latino), 11 international. Average age 25. 228 applicants, 14% accepted, 22 enrolled. In 2018, 12 master's, 2 doctorates awarded. Terminal master's awarded for partial completion of doctoral program. *Entrance requirements:* For master's and doctorate, GRE General Test, minimum GPA of 3.25. Additional exam requirements/recommendations for international students: Required—TOEFL (minimum score 500 paper-based; 61 iBT). Application fee: $55 ($65 for international students). Electronic applications accepted. *Expenses: Tuition, area resident:* Full-time $7190.66; part-time $2112.48 per year. Tuition, state resident: full-time $7190.66. Tuition, nonresident: full-time $25,195. *Required fees:* $558; $555.04 per unit. Tuition and fees vary according to course level, course load, degree level, program and student level. *Financial support:* In 2018–19, 62 students received support, including 14 fellowships with full tuition reimbursements available (averaging $18,500 per year), 32 research assistantships with full tuition reimbursements available (averaging $24,000 per year), 16 teaching assistantships with full tuition reimbursements available (averaging $18,500 per year); career-related internships or fieldwork, institutionally sponsored loans, scholarships/grants, health care benefits, unspecified assistantships, and stipends also available. Financial award application deadline: 1/15; financial award applicants required to submit FAFSA. *Faculty research:* Igneous, metamorphic, and sedimentary petrology; stratigraphy; paleoclimatology; hydrology; seismology. *Total annual research expenditures:* $4.1 million. *Unit head:* Dr. John Bartley, Chair, 801-585-1670, Fax: 801-581-7065, E-mail: john.bartley@utah.edu. *Application contact:* Dr. Gabriel J. Bowen, Director of Graduate Studies, 801-585-7925, Fax: 801-581-7065, E-mail: gabe.bowen@utah.edu.
Website: http://www.earth.utah.edu/

University of Wisconsin–Madison, Graduate School, College of Engineering, Department of Civil and Environmental Engineering, Madison, WI 53706-1380. Offers construction engineering and management (MS); environmental science and engineering (MS); geological/geotechnical engineering (MS); structural engineering (MS); transportation engineering (MS); water resources engineering (MS). *Program availability:* Part-time. *Faculty:* 31 full-time (8 women). *Students:* 97 full-time (28 women), 39 part-time (15 women); includes 12 minority (2 Black or African American, non-Hispanic/Latino; 3 Asian, non-Hispanic/Latino; 6 Hispanic/Latino; 1 Two or more races, non-Hispanic/Latino), 62 international. Average age 28. 261 applicants, 45% accepted, 29 enrolled. In 2018, 33 master's awarded. Terminal master's awarded for partial completion of doctoral program. *Degree requirements:* For master's, thesis (for some programs), minimum of 30 credits; minimum overall GPA of 3.0. *Entrance requirements:* For master's, GRE General Test, bachelor's degree; minimum GPA of 3.0 for last 60 credits of course work. Additional exam requirements/recommendations for international students: Required—TOEFL (minimum score 580 paper-based; 92 iBT). *Application deadline:* For fall admission, 12/15 priority date for domestic and international students; for spring admission, 10/1 for domestic and international students. Application fee: $75 ($81 for international students). Electronic applications accepted. *Expenses:* In-state tuition (Full-time): $10,728; Out-of-state tuition (full-time): $24,054; Fees: $1282; In-state tuition (per credit): $670; Out-of-state tuition (per credit): $1503; Fees (per credit): $126. *Financial support:* In 2018–19, 90 students received support, including 8 fellowships with full tuition reimbursements available (averaging $28,704 per year), 54 research assistantships with full tuition reimbursements available (averaging $23,784 per year), 21 teaching assistantships with full tuition reimbursements available (averaging $16,584 per year); Federal Work-Study, scholarships/grants, health care benefits, unspecified assistantships, and project assistantships also available. Support available to part-time students. Financial award application deadline: 12/1; financial award applicants required to submit FAFSA. *Faculty research:* Construction engineering and management; environmental engineering; structural engineering; transportation and city planning; water resources engineering; water chemistry. *Total annual research expenditures:* $12.5 million. *Unit head:* Dr. William Likos, Chair, 608-263-9490, Fax: 608-262-5199, E-mail: frontdesk@cee.wisc.edu. *Application contact:* Cheryl Loschko, Student Services Coordinator, 608-890-2420, E-mail: loschko@wisc.edu.
Website: https://www.engr.wisc.edu/department/civil-environmental-engineering/academics/ms-phd-civil-and-environmental-engineering/

University of Wisconsin–Madison, Graduate School, College of Engineering, Geological Engineering Program, Madison, WI 53706-1380. Offers geological engineering (MS). *Program availability:* Part-time. *Faculty:* 16 full-time (3 women). *Students:* 14 full-time (8 women); includes 2 minority (1 Black or African American, non-Hispanic/Latino; 1 Two or more races, non-Hispanic/Latino), 6 international. Average age 27. 12 applicants, 58% accepted, 2 enrolled. In 2018, 3 master's, 1 doctorate awarded. Terminal master's awarded for partial completion of doctoral program. *Degree requirements:* For master's, thesis optional, minimum of 30 credits; minimum GPA of 3.0; for doctorate, comprehensive exam, thesis/dissertation, minimum of 51 credits; minimum GPA of 3.0. *Entrance requirements:* For master's and doctorate, GRE, BS; minimum GPA of 3.0. Additional exam requirements/recommendations for international students: Required—TOEFL (minimum score 580 paper-based; 92 iBT), IELTS (minimum score 7). *Application deadline:* For fall admission, 12/15 for domestic and international students; for spring admission, 9/1 for domestic and international students. Application fee: $75 ($81 for international students). Electronic applications accepted. *Financial support:* Fellowships with full tuition reimbursements, research assistantships with full tuition reimbursements, teaching assistantships with full tuition reimbursements, Federal Work-Study, scholarships/grants, and unspecified assistantships available. Support available to part-time students. Financial award application deadline: 12/1; financial award applicants required to submit FAFSA. *Faculty research:* Eoenvironmental engineering, water resources, hydrogeology, hydroecology, rock mechanics, structural geology, geosynthetic engineering, and sensor technology, to foundation engineering, site characterization, slope stability, soil dynamics, non-destructive evaluation, engineering geophysics, and alternative energy systems. *Unit head:* Dr. William Likos, Chair, 608-890-2662, Fax: 608-263-2453, E-mail: likos@wisc.edu. *Application contact:* Cheryl Loschko, Student Services Coordinator, 608-890-2420, E-mail: loschko@wisc.edu.
Website: https://www.engr.wisc.edu/department/civil-environmental-engineering/academics/ms-phd-geological-engineering/

Mineral/Mining Engineering

Colorado School of Mines, Office of Graduate Studies, Department of Geology and Geological Engineering, Golden, CO 80401. Offers environmental geochemistry (PMS); geochemistry (MS, PhD); geological engineering (ME, MS, PhD); geology (MS, PhD); hydrology (MS, PhD); mineral exploration (PMS); petroleum reservoir systems (PMS); underground construction and tunneling (MS). *Program availability:* Part-time. *Faculty:* 30 full-time (12 women), 6 part-time/adjunct (5 women). *Students:* 129 full-time (44 women), 32 part-time (12 women); includes 20 minority (1 Black or African American, non-Hispanic/Latino; 2 American Indian or Alaska Native, non-Hispanic/Latino; 3 Asian, non-Hispanic/Latino; 10 Hispanic/Latino; 4 Two or more races, non-Hispanic/Latino), 30 international. Average age 29. 244 applicants, 41% accepted, 54 enrolled. In 2018, 39 master's, 11 doctorates awarded. *Degree requirements:* For master's, thesis (for some programs); for doctorate, comprehensive exam, thesis/dissertation. *Entrance requirements:* For master's and doctorate, GRE General Test. Additional exam requirements/recommendations for international students: Required—TOEFL (minimum score 550 paper-based; 79 iBT). *Application deadline:* For fall admission, 12/15 priority date for domestic and international students; for spring admission, 9/1 priority date for domestic and international students. Application fee: $60 ($80 for international students). Electronic applications accepted. *Expenses:* Tuition, state resident: full-time $16,650; part-time $925 per contact hour. Tuition, nonresident: full-time $36,270; part-time $2015 per contact hour. *International tuition:* $36,270 full-time. *Required fees:* $2314; $2314 per semester. *Financial support:* In 2018–19, 48 research assistantships with full tuition reimbursements, 20 teaching assistantships with full tuition reimbursements were awarded; fellowships, scholarships/grants, health care benefits, and unspecified assistantships also available. Financial award application deadline: 12/15; financial award applicants required to submit FAFSA. *Faculty research:* Predictive sediment modeling, petrophysics, aquifer-contaminant flow modeling, water-rock interactions, geotechnical engineering. *Unit head:* Dr. Wendy Bohrson, Head, 303-273-3066, E-mail: bohrson@mines.edu. *Application contact:* Dr. Christian Shorey, Lecturer/Program Manager, 303-273-3556, E-mail: cshorey@mines.edu.
Website: http://geology.mines.edu

Colorado School of Mines, Office of Graduate Studies, Department of Geophysics, Golden, CO 80401. Offers geophysical engineering (ME, MS, PhD); geophysics (MS, PhD); hydrology (MS, PhD); mineral exploration and mining geosciences (PMS); petroleum reservoir systems (PMS). *Program availability:* Part-time. *Faculty:* 14 full-time (5 women), 4 part-time/adjunct (0 women). *Students:* 62 full-time (17 women), 2 part-time (0 women); includes 5 minority (2 Asian, non-Hispanic/Latino; 1 Hispanic/Latino; 2 Two or more races, non-Hispanic/Latino), 33 international. Average age 28. 142 applicants, 26% accepted, 23 enrolled. In 2018, 12 master's, 12 doctorates awarded. *Degree requirements:* For master's, thesis (for some programs); for doctorate, comprehensive exam, thesis/dissertation. *Entrance requirements:* For master's and doctorate, GRE General Test. Additional exam requirements/recommendations for international students: Required—TOEFL (minimum score 550 paper-based; 79 iBT). *Application deadline:* For fall admission, 12/15 priority date for domestic and international students; for spring admission, 9/1 priority date for domestic students, 9/1 for international students. Application fee: $60 ($80 for international students). Electronic applications accepted. *Expenses:* Tuition, state resident: full-time $16,650; part-time $925 per contact hour. Tuition, nonresident: full-time $36,270; part-time $2015 per contact hour. *International tuition:* $36,270 full-time. *Required fees:* $2314; $2314 per semester. *Financial support:* In 2018–19, 40 research assistantships with full tuition reimbursements, 9 teaching assistantships with full tuition reimbursements were awarded; fellowships, career-related internships or fieldwork, scholarships/grants, health care benefits, and unspecified assistantships also available. Financial award application deadline: 12/15; financial award applicants required to submit FAFSA. *Faculty research:* Seismic exploration, gravity and geomagnetic fields, electrical mapping and sounding, bore hole measurements, environmental physics. *Unit head:* Dr. Paul Sava, Head, 303-384-2362, E-mail: psava@mines.edu. *Application contact:* Michelle Szobody, Program Assistant, 303-273-3935, E-mail: mszobody@mines.edu.
Website: http://geophysics.mines.edu

Colorado School of Mines, Office of Graduate Studies, Department of Mining Engineering, Golden, CO 80401. Offers mining and earth systems engineering (MS); mining engineering (PhD); underground construction and tunneling (MS, PhD). *Program availability:* Part-time. *Faculty:* 16 full-time (6 women), 10 part-time/adjunct (3 women). *Students:* 34 full-time (8 women), 2 part-time (0 women); includes 3 minority (1 Black or African American, non-Hispanic/Latino; 2 Hispanic/Latino), 25 international. Average age 31. 40 applicants, 75% accepted, 9 enrolled. In 2018, 13 master's, 2 doctorates awarded. *Degree requirements:* For master's, thesis (for some programs); for doctorate, comprehensive exam, thesis/dissertation. *Entrance requirements:* For master's and doctorate, GRE General Test. Additional exam requirements/recommendations for international students: Required—TOEFL (minimum score 550 paper-based; 79 iBT). *Application deadline:* For fall admission, 12/15 priority date for domestic and international students; for spring admission, 9/1 priority date for domestic and international students. Application fee: $60 ($80 for international students). Electronic applications accepted. *Expenses:* Tuition, state resident: full-time $16,650; part-time $925 per contact hour. Tuition, nonresident: full-time $36,270; part-time $2015 per contact hour. *International tuition:* $36,270 full-time. *Required fees:* $2314; $2314 per semester. *Financial support:* In 2018–19, 14 research assistantships with full tuition reimbursements, 5 teaching assistantships with full tuition reimbursements were awarded; fellowships, scholarships/grants, health care benefits, and unspecified assistantships also available. Financial award application deadline: 12/15; financial award applicants required to submit FAFSA. *Faculty research:* Mine evaluation and planning, geostatistics, mining robotics, water jet cutting, rock mechanics. *Unit head:* Dr. Jamal Rostami, Head, 303-273-3041, E-mail: rostami@mines.edu. *Application contact:* Justine Robinson, Program Manager, 303-273-3768, E-mail: justinerobinson@mines.edu.
Website: http://mining.mines.edu

Dalhousie University, Faculty of Engineering, Department of Civil and Resource Engineering, Halifax, NS B3J 2X4, Canada. Offers civil engineering (M Eng, MA Sc, PhD); environmental engineering (M Eng, MA Sc); mineral resource engineering (M Eng, MA Sc, PhD). *Degree requirements:* For master's, thesis; for doctorate, thesis/dissertation. *Entrance requirements:* Additional exam requirements/recommendations for international students: Required—TOEFL, IELTS, CANTEST, CAEL, or Michigan English Language Assessment Battery. Electronic applications accepted. *Faculty research:* Environmental/water resources, bridge engineering, geotechnical engineering, pavement design and management/highway materials, composite materials.

Laurentian University, School of Graduate Studies and Research, Programme in Geology (Earth Sciences), Sudbury, ON P3E 2C6, Canada. Offers geology (M Sc); mineral deposits and precambrian geology (PhD); mineral exploration (M Sc). *Program availability:* Part-time. *Degree requirements:* For master's, thesis. *Entrance requirements:* For master's, honors degree with second class or better. *Faculty research:* Localization and metallogenesis of Ni-Cu-(PGE) sulfide mineralization in the Thompson Nickel Belt, mapping lithology and ore-grade and monitoring dissolved organic carbon in lakes using remote sensing, global reefs, volcanic effects on VMS deposits.

Laurentian University, School of Graduate Studies and Research, School of Engineering, Sudbury, ON P3E 2C6, Canada. Offers mineral resources engineering (M Eng, MA Sc); natural resources engineering (PhD). *Program availability:* Part-time. *Faculty research:* Mining engineering, rock mechanics (tunneling, rockbursts, rock support), metallurgy (mineral processing, hydro and pyrometallurgy), simulations and remote mining, simulations and scheduling.

McGill University, Faculty of Graduate and Postdoctoral Studies, Faculty of Engineering, Department of Mining and Materials Engineering, Montréal, QC H3A 2T5, Canada. Offers materials engineering (M Eng, PhD); mining engineering (M Eng, M Sc, PhD, Diploma).

Missouri University of Science and Technology, Department of Mining and Nuclear Engineering, Rolla, MO 65401. Offers explosives engineering (MS, PhD); mining engineering (MS, DE, PhD); nuclear engineering (MS, DE, PhD). *Degree requirements:* For master's, thesis optional; for doctorate, comprehensive exam. *Entrance requirements:* For master's, GRE (minimum score 600 quantitative, 3 writing); for doctorate, GRE (minimum score: quantitative 600, writing 3.5). Additional exam requirements/recommendations for international students: Required—TOEFL (minimum score 550 paper-based). Electronic applications accepted. *Expenses:* Tuition, state resident: full-time $7545.60; part-time $419.20 per credit hour. Tuition, nonresident: full-time $22,169; part-time $1231.60 per credit hour. *International tuition:* $23,518.80 full-time. *Required fees:* $4523.05. Full-time tuition and fees vary according to course load, campus/location, program and reciprocity agreements. *Faculty research:* Mine health and safety, nuclear radiation transport, modeling of mining operations, radiation effects, blasting.

Montana Tech of The University of Montana, Department of Metallurgical/Mineral Processing Engineering, Butte, MT 59701-8997. Offers MS. *Program availability:* Part-time. *Degree requirements:* For master's, comprehensive exam (for some programs), thesis optional. *Entrance requirements:* For master's, GRE General Test, minimum GPA of 3.0. Additional exam requirements/recommendations for international students: Required—TOEFL (minimum score 545 paper-based; 78 iBT), IELTS (minimum score 6.5). Electronic applications accepted. *Faculty research:* Stabilizing hazardous waste, decontamination of metals by melt refining, ultraviolet enhancement of stabilization reactions, extractive metallurgy, fuel cells.

Montana Tech of The University of Montana, Mining Engineering Program, Butte, MT 59701-8997. Offers MS. *Program availability:* Part-time. *Degree requirements:* For master's, thesis optional. *Entrance requirements:* For master's, minimum GPA of 3.0. Additional exam requirements/recommendations for international students: Required—TOEFL (minimum score 545 paper-based; 78 iBT), IELTS (minimum score 6.5). Electronic applications accepted. *Faculty research:* Geostatistics, geotechnics, mine planning, economic models, equipment selection.

New Mexico Institute of Mining and Technology, Center for Graduate Studies, Department of Mineral Engineering, Socorro, NM 87801. Offers explosives engineering (MS); geotechnical engineering (MS); mining engineering (MS). *Degree requirements:* For master's, thesis. *Entrance requirements:* Additional exam requirements/recommendations for international students: Required—TOEFL (minimum score 540 paper-based). *Faculty research:* Drilling and blasting, geological engineering, mine design, applied mineral exploration, rock mechanics.

Penn State University Park, Graduate School, College of Earth and Mineral Sciences, John and Willie Leone Family Department of Energy and Mineral Engineering, University Park, PA 16802. Offers MS, PhD.

Queen's University at Kingston, School of Graduate Studies, Faculty of Engineering and Applied Science, The Robert M. Buchan Department of Mining, Kingston, ON K7L 3N6, Canada. Offers mining engineering (M Eng, M Sc, M Sc Eng, PhD). *Program availability:* Part-time. *Degree requirements:* For master's, thesis optional; for doctorate, comprehensive exam, thesis/dissertation. *Entrance requirements:* Additional exam requirements/recommendations for international students: Required—TOEFL (minimum score 550 paper-based). Electronic applications accepted. *Faculty research:* Rock mechanics, drilling, ventilation/environmental control, gold extraction.

South Dakota School of Mines and Technology, Graduate Division, Department of Mining Engineering and Management, Rapid City, SD 57701-3995. Offers mining engineering (MS). *Program availability:* Part-time. *Entrance requirements:* For master's, GRE General Test. Additional exam requirements/recommendations for international students: Required—TOEFL (minimum score 520 paper-based; 68 iBT), TWE. Electronic applications accepted.

Southern Illinois University Carbondale, Graduate School, College of Engineering, Department of Mining and Mineral Resources Engineering, Carbondale, IL 62901-4701. Offers mining engineering (MS). *Degree requirements:* For master's, comprehensive exam, thesis. *Entrance requirements:* For master's, GRE (recommended), minimum GPA of 2.7. Additional exam requirements/recommendations for international students: Required—TOEFL. *Faculty research:* Rock mechanics and ground control, mine subsidence, mine systems analysis, fine coal cleaning, surface mine reclamation.

Southern Illinois University Carbondale, Graduate School, College of Engineering, Program in Engineering Science, Carbondale, IL 62901-4701. Offers engineering science (PhD), including civil and environmental engineering, electrical and computer engineering, mechanical engineering and energy processes, mining and mineral resources engineering. *Degree requirements:* For doctorate, thesis/dissertation. *Entrance requirements:* For doctorate, GRE General Test, minimum GPA of 3.5. Additional exam requirements/recommendations for international students: Required—TOEFL.

Université du Québec en Abitibi-Témiscamingue, Graduate Programs, Program in Engineering, Rouyn-Noranda, QC J9X 5E4, Canada. Offers engineering (ME); mineral engineering (ME); mining engineering (DESS).

Université Laval, Faculty of Sciences and Engineering, Department of Mining, Metallurgical and Materials Engineering, Programs in Mining Engineering, Québec, QC G1K 7P4, Canada. Offers M Sc, PhD. Terminal master's awarded for partial completion of doctoral program. *Degree requirements:* For master's, thesis; for doctorate, comprehensive exam, thesis/dissertation. *Entrance requirements:* For master's and doctorate, knowledge of French and English. Electronic applications accepted.

University of Alaska Fairbanks, College of Engineering and Mines, Department of Mining and Geological Engineering, Fairbanks, AK 99775-5800. Offers geological engineering (MS); mineral preparation engineering (MS); mining engineering (MS). *Program availability:* Part-time. *Faculty:* 7 full-time (1 woman). *Students:* 3 full-time (0 women), 3 part-time (1 woman), 5 international. Average age 30. 11 applicants, 27% accepted, 1 enrolled. In 2018, 2 master's awarded. *Degree requirements:* For master's, comprehensive exam, oral defense of project or thesis. *Entrance requirements:* For master's, GRE General Test (for geological engineering), bachelor's degree from accredited institution with minimum cumulative undergraduate and major GPA of 3.0. Additional exam requirements/recommendations for international students: Required—TOEFL (minimum score 550 paper-based; 79 iBT), IELTS (minimum score 6.5). *Application deadline:* For fall admission, 6/1 for domestic students, 3/1 for international students; for spring admission, 10/15 for domestic students, 9/1 for international students. Applications are processed on a rolling basis. Application fee: $60. Electronic applications accepted. *Expenses:* College of Engineering and Mines (CEM) tuition has a 20% surcharge per credit hour over that for credits of most other UAF colleges. Assuming 60 credits for PhD and 32 for Master's, this augments costs by $6,180 for in-state PhD, $3,296 for in-state Master's, $12,948 for non-resident PhD and $6,912 for non-resident Masters students, respectively. *Financial support:* In 2018–19, 3 research assistantships with full tuition reimbursements (averaging $3,544 per year), 4 teaching assistantships with full tuition reimbursements (averaging $4,768 per year) were awarded; fellowships with full tuition reimbursements, career-related internships or fieldwork, Federal Work-Study, scholarships/grants, health care benefits, and unspecified assistantships also available. Support available to part-time students. Financial award application deadline: 7/1; financial award applicants required to submit FAFSA. *Faculty research:* Underground mining in permafrost, testing of ultra clean diesel, slope stability, fractal and mathematical morphology, soil and rock mechanics. *Total annual research expenditures:* $1.1 million. *Unit head:* Dr. Tathagata Gosh, Chair, 907-474-6917, E-mail: cem.mingeo@alaska.edu. *Application contact:* Samara Taber, Director of Admissions, 907-474-7500, E-mail: uaf-admissions@alaska.edu.
Website: http://cem.uaf.edu/mingeo

University of Alberta, Faculty of Graduate Studies and Research, Department of Civil and Environmental Engineering, Edmonton, AB T6G 2E1, Canada. Offers construction engineering and management (M Eng, M Sc, PhD); environmental engineering (M Eng, M Sc, PhD); environmental science (M Sc, PhD); geoenvironmental engineering (M Eng, M Sc, PhD); geotechnical engineering (M Eng, M Sc, PhD); mining engineering (M Eng, M Sc, PhD); petroleum engineering (M Eng, M Sc, PhD); structural engineering (M Eng, M Sc, PhD); water resources (M Eng, M Sc, PhD). *Program availability:* Part-time, online learning. *Degree requirements:* For master's, thesis (for some programs); for doctorate, thesis/dissertation. *Entrance requirements:* For master's, minimum GPA of 3.0 in last 2 years of undergraduate studies; for doctorate, minimum GPA of 3.0. Additional exam requirements/recommendations for international students: Required—TOEFL (minimum score 550 paper-based). Electronic applications accepted. *Faculty research:* Mining.

The University of Arizona, College of Engineering, Department of Mining and Geological Engineering, Tucson, AZ 85721. Offers mining and geological engineering (MS, PhD); mining engineering (Certificate), including mine health and safety, mine information and production technology, rock mechanics. *Program availability:* Part-time, online learning. *Degree requirements:* For master's, thesis; for doctorate, thesis/dissertation. *Entrance requirements:* For master's, GRE General Test, 3 letters of recommendation; for doctorate, GRE General Test, 3 letters of recommendation, statements of purpose. Additional exam requirements/recommendations for international students: Required—TOEFL (minimum score 550 paper-based; 79 iBT). Electronic applications accepted. *Faculty research:* Geomechanics, mineral processing, information technology, automation, geosensing.

The University of British Columbia, Faculty of Applied Science, Department of Mining Engineering, Vancouver, BC V6T 1Z4, Canada. Offers M Eng, MA Sc, PhD. *Degree requirements:* For master's, thesis; for doctorate, thesis/dissertation. *Entrance requirements:* Additional exam requirements/recommendations for international students: Required—TOEFL, IELTS. Electronic applications accepted. *Expenses:* Contact institution. *Faculty research:* Advanced mining methods and automation, rock mechanics, mine economics, operations research, mine waste management, environmental aspects of mining, process control, fine particle processing, surface chemistry.

University of Kentucky, Graduate School, College of Engineering, Program in Mining Engineering, Lexington, KY 40506-0032. Offers MME, MS Min, PhD. *Degree requirements:* For master's, comprehensive exam, thesis optional; for doctorate, one foreign language, comprehensive exam, thesis/dissertation. *Entrance requirements:* For master's, GRE General Test, minimum undergraduate GPA of 2.75; for doctorate, GRE General Test, minimum undergraduate GPA of 3.0. Additional exam requirements/recommendations for international students: Required—TOEFL (minimum score 550 paper-based). Electronic applications accepted. *Faculty research:* Benefication of fine

and ultrafine particles, operation research in mining and mineral processing, land reclamation.

University of Nevada, Reno, Graduate School, College of Science, Mackay School of Earth Sciences and Engineering, Department of Mining and Metallurgical Engineering, Reno, NV 89557. Offers metallurgical engineering (MS); mining engineering (MS, PhD). *Degree requirements:* For master's, thesis optional. *Entrance requirements:* For master's, GRE, minimum GPA of 2.75. Additional exam requirements/recommendations for international students: Required—TOEFL (minimum score 500 paper-based; 61 iBT), IELTS (minimum score 6). Electronic applications accepted. *Faculty research:* Mine ventilation, rock mechanics, mine design.

The University of Texas at Austin, Graduate School, Cockrell School of Engineering, Department of Petroleum and Geosystems Engineering, Program in Energy and Earth Resources, Austin, TX 78712-1111. Offers MA. *Degree requirements:* For master's, thesis, seminar. *Entrance requirements:* For master's, GRE General Test. Additional exam requirements/recommendations for international students: Required—TOEFL. Electronic applications accepted.

University of Utah, Graduate School, College of Mines and Earth Sciences, Department of Mining Engineering, Salt Lake City, UT 84112. Offers ME, MS, PhD. *Program availability:* Part-time. *Faculty:* 5 full-time (1 woman), 2 part-time/adjunct (1 woman). *Students:* 5 full-time (0 women), 2 part-time (both women); includes 2 minority (1 Hispanic/Latino; 1 Two or more races, non-Hispanic/Latino), 1 international. Average age 23. 24 applicants, 21% accepted, 3 enrolled. In 2018, 3 master's awarded. *Entrance requirements:* For master's, minimum undergraduate GPA of 3.0; for doctorate, GRE General Test, minimum undergraduate GPA of 3.0. Additional exam requirements/recommendations for international students: Required—TOEFL (minimum score 550 paper-based; 80 iBT). Application fee: $55 ($65 for international students). Electronic applications accepted. *Expenses:* 4500/semester tuition and fees full time at 12 credit hours/semester. *Financial support:* In 2018–19, 10 students received support, including 2 fellowships with full and partial tuition reimbursements available (averaging $21,750 per year), 4 research assistantships with full and partial tuition reimbursements available (averaging $22,000 per year); teaching assistantships, career-related internships or fieldwork, institutionally sponsored loans, health care benefits, and unspecified assistantships also available. Financial award application deadline: 4/15. *Faculty research:* Blasting, underground coal mine design and operations, rock mechanics, mine ventilation, 2-D and 3-D visualization, mine automation, mine safety. *Total annual research expenditures:* $324,354. *Unit head:* Dr. Michael Gordon Nelson, Chair, 801-585-3064, Fax: 801-585-5410, E-mail: mike.nelson@utah.edu. *Application contact:* Pam Hofmann, Administrative Manager, 801-581-7198, Fax: 801-585-5410, E-mail: pam.hofmann@utah.edu.
Website: http://www.mining.utah.edu/

West Virginia University, Statler College of Engineering and Mineral Resources, Morgantown, WV 26506. Offers aerospace engineering (MSAE, PhD); chemical engineering (MS Ch E, PhD); civil engineering (MSCE, PhD); computer engineering (PhD); computer science (MSCS, PhD); electrical engineering (MSEE, PhD); energy systems engineering (MSESE); engineering (MSE); industrial engineering (MSIE, PhD); industrial hygiene (MS); material science and engineering (MSMSE, PhD); mechanical engineering (MSME, PhD); mining engineering (MS Min E, PhD); petroleum and natural gas engineering (MSPNGE, PhD); safety management (MS); software engineering (MSSE). *Program availability:* Part-time. *Students:* 466 full-time (113 women), 154 part-time (27 women); includes 57 minority (22 Black or African American, non-Hispanic/Latino; 1 American Indian or Alaska Native, non-Hispanic/Latino; 8 Asian, non-Hispanic/Latino; 12 Hispanic/Latino; 14 Two or more races, non-Hispanic/Latino), 283 international. In 2018, 179 master's, 39 doctorates awarded. Terminal master's awarded for partial completion of doctoral program. *Degree requirements:* For master's, thesis optional; for doctorate, comprehensive exam, thesis/dissertation. *Entrance requirements:* Additional exam requirements/recommendations for international students: Required—TOEFL (minimum score 550 paper-based). *Application deadline:* For fall admission, 4/1 for international students; for winter admission, 4/1 for international students; for spring admission, 10/1 for international students. Applications are processed on a rolling basis. Application fee: $60. Electronic applications accepted. *Expenses:* Contact institution. *Financial support:* Fellowships, research assistantships, teaching assistantships, career-related internships or fieldwork, Federal Work-Study, institutionally sponsored loans, health care benefits, tuition waivers (full and partial), unspecified assistantships, and administrative assistantships available. Financial award application deadline: 2/1; financial award applicants required to submit FAFSA. *Faculty research:* Composite materials, software engineering, information systems, aerodynamics, vehicle propulsion and emission. *Unit head:* Dr. Earl Scime, Interim Dean, 304-293-4157 Ext. 2237, Fax: 304-293-2037, E-mail: earl.scime@mail.wvu.edu. *Application contact:* Dr. David A. Wyrick, Associate Dean, Academic Affairs, 304-293-4334, Fax: 304-293-5024, E-mail: david.wyrick@mail.wvu.edu.
Website: https://www.statler.wvu.edu

Petroleum Engineering

Colorado School of Mines, Office of Graduate Studies, Department of Petroleum Engineering, Golden, CO 80401. Offers petroleum engineering (ME, MS, PhD); petroleum reservoir systems (PMS). *Program availability:* Part-time. *Faculty:* 21 full-time (7 women), 2 part-time/adjunct (1 woman). *Students:* 82 full-time (13 women), 11 part-time (2 women); includes 5 minority (1 Black or African American, non-Hispanic/Latino; 2 Asian, non-Hispanic/Latino; 2 Hispanic/Latino), 70 international. Average age 29. 234 applicants, 24% accepted, 21 enrolled. In 2018, 28 master's, 9 doctorates awarded. *Degree requirements:* For master's, thesis (for some programs); for doctorate, comprehensive exam, thesis/dissertation. *Entrance requirements:* For master's and doctorate, GRE General Test. Additional exam requirements/recommendations for international students: Required—TOEFL (minimum score 550 paper-based; 79 iBT). *Application deadline:* For fall admission, 12/15 priority date for domestic and international students; for spring admission, 9/1 priority date for domestic and international students. Application fee: $60 ($80 for international students). Electronic applications accepted. *Expenses:* Tuition, state resident: full-time $16,650; part-time $925 per contact hour. Tuition, nonresident: full-time $36,270; part-time $2015 per contact hour. International tuition: $36,270 full-time. *Required fees:* $2314; $2314 per semester. *Financial support:* In 2018–19, 32 research assistantships with full tuition reimbursements, 13 teaching assistantships with full tuition reimbursements were awarded; fellowships, career-related internships or fieldwork, scholarships/grants, health care benefits, and unspecified assistantships also available. Financial award application deadline: 12/15; financial award applicants required to submit FAFSA. *Faculty research:* Dynamic rock mechanics, deflagration theory, geostatistics, geochemistry, petrophysics. *Unit head:* Dr. Jennifer Miskimins, Head, 303-384-2607, E-mail: jmiskimins@mines.edu.

Application contact: Denise Winn-Bower, Program Assistant, 303-273-3945, Fax: 303-273-3189, E-mail: dwinnbow@mines.edu.
Website: http://petroleum.mines.edu

Louisiana State University and Agricultural & Mechanical College, Graduate School, College of Engineering, Department of Petroleum Engineering, Baton Rouge, LA 70803. Offers MS Pet E, PhD.

Missouri University of Science and Technology, Department of Geosciences and Geological and Petroleum Engineering, Rolla, MO 65401. Offers geological engineering (MS, DE, PhD); geology and geophysics (MS, PhD), including geochemistry, geology, geophysics, groundwater and environmental geology; petroleum engineering (MS, DE, PhD). *Program availability:* Part-time. *Degree requirements:* For master's, thesis optional; for doctorate, comprehensive exam, thesis/dissertation. *Entrance requirements:* For master's, GRE General Test (minimum score 600 quantitative, writing 3.5), minimum GPA of 3.0 in last 4 semesters; for doctorate, GRE General Test (minimum scores: Quantitative 600, Writing 3.5). Additional exam requirements/recommendations for international students: Required—TOEFL (minimum score 550 paper-based). Electronic applications accepted. *Expenses:* Tuition, state resident: full-time $7545.60; part-time $419.20 per credit hour. Tuition, nonresident: full-time $22,169; part-time $1231.60 per credit hour. International tuition: $23,518.80 full-time. *Required fees:* $4523.05. Full-time tuition and fees vary according to course load, campus/location, program and reciprocity agreements. *Faculty research:* Digital image processing and geographic information systems, mineralogy, igneous and sedimentary petrology-geochemistry, sedimentology groundwater hydrology and contaminant transport.

Petroleum Engineering

Montana Tech of The University of Montana, Department of Petroleum Engineering, Butte, MT 59701-8997. Offers MS. *Program availability:* Part-time, evening/weekend. *Degree requirements:* For master's, comprehensive exam, thesis optional. *Entrance requirements:* For master's, minimum GPA of 3.0. Additional exam requirements/recommendations for international students: Required—TOEFL (minimum score 545 paper-based; 78 iBT), IELTS (minimum score 6.5). Electronic applications accepted. *Faculty research:* Reservoir characterization, simulations, near well bore problems, environmental waste.

New Mexico Institute of Mining and Technology, Center for Graduate Studies, Department of Petroleum and Natural Gas Engineering, Socorro, NM 87801. Offers petroleum engineering (MS, PhD). *Degree requirements:* For master's, thesis optional; for doctorate, thesis/dissertation. *Entrance requirements:* For master's, GRE General Test; for doctorate, GRE General Test, GRE Subject Test. Additional exam requirements/recommendations for international students: Required—TOEFL (minimum score 540 paper-based). *Faculty research:* Enhanced recovery processes, drilling and production, reservoir evaluation, produced water management, wettability and phase behavior.

Texas A&M University, College of Engineering, Department of Petroleum Engineering, College Station, TX 77843. Offers petroleum engineering (M Eng). *Program availability:* Part-time, online learning. *Faculty:* 31. *Students:* 164 full-time (27 women), 93 part-time (20 women); includes 43 minority (3 Black or African American, non-Hispanic/Latino; 17 Asian, non-Hispanic/Latino; 22 Hispanic/Latino; 1 Two or more races, non-Hispanic/Latino; 147 international. Average age 30. 199 applicants, 39% accepted, 36 enrolled. In 2018, 80 master's, 27 doctorates awarded. *Degree requirements:* For master's, comprehensive exam, thesis (MS); for doctorate, comprehensive exam, thesis/dissertation. *Entrance requirements:* For master's and doctorate, GRE General Test. Additional exam requirements/recommendations for international students: Required—TOEFL (minimum score 550 paper-based; 80 iBT), IELTS (minimum score 6), PTE (minimum score 53). *Application deadline:* For fall admission, 12/15 for domestic students; for spring admission, 9/1 for domestic students; for summer admission, 11/1 for domestic students. Applications are processed on a rolling basis. Application fee: $50 ($90 for international students). Electronic applications accepted. *Expenses:* Contact institution. *Financial support:* In 2018–19, 175 students received support, including 25 fellowships with tuition reimbursements available (averaging $6,600 per year), 116 research assistantships with tuition reimbursements available (averaging $14,963 per year), 35 teaching assistantships with tuition reimbursements available (averaging $11,940 per year); career-related internships or fieldwork, institutionally sponsored loans, scholarships/grants, traineeships, health care benefits, tuition waivers (full and partial), and unspecified assistantships also available. Support available to part-time students. Financial award application deadline: 3/15; financial award applicants required to submit FAFSA. *Faculty research:* Drilling and well stimulation, well completions and well performance, reservoir modeling and reservoir description, reservoir simulation, improved/enhanced recovery. *Unit head:* Dr. A. Daniel Hill, Department Head, 979-845-2244, E-mail: dan.hill@pe.tamu.edu. *Application contact:* Graduate Advisor, 979-847-9095, E-mail: graduate_program@pe.tamu.edu. Website: http://engineering.tamu.edu/petroleum

Texas A&M University–Kingsville, College of Graduate Studies, Frank H. Dotterweich College of Engineering, Wayne H. King Department of Chemical and Natural Gas Engineering, Program in Natural Gas Engineering, Kingsville, TX 78363. Offers ME, MS. *Degree requirements:* For master's, variable foreign language requirement, comprehensive exam, thesis (for some programs). *Entrance requirements:* For master's, GRE (minimum quantitative score of 150, verbal 145), MAT, GMAT, minimum GPA of 2.7. Additional exam requirements/recommendations for international students: Required—TOEFL (minimum score 550 paper-based; 79 iBT). Electronic applications accepted.

University of Alaska Fairbanks, College of Engineering and Mines, Department of Petroleum Engineering, Fairbanks, AK 99775. Offers MS. *Program availability:* Part-time. *Faculty:* 5 full-time (0 women). *Students:* 9 full-time (1 woman), 11 part-time (0 women); includes 2 minority (1 Asian, non-Hispanic/Latino; 1 Two or more races, non-Hispanic/Latino), 9 international. Average age 30. 24 applicants, 29% accepted, 3 enrolled. In 2018, 6 master's awarded. *Degree requirements:* For master's, comprehensive exam, oral defense of project or thesis. *Entrance requirements:* For master's, bachelor's degree in engineering or the natural sciences with minimum cumulative undergraduate and major GPA of 3.0. Additional exam requirements/recommendations for international students: Required—TOEFL (minimum score 550 paper-based; 79 iBT), IELTS (minimum score 6.5). *Application deadline:* For fall admission, 6/1 for domestic students; 3/1 for international students; for spring admission, 10/15 for domestic students, 9/1 for international students. Applications are processed on a rolling basis. Application fee: $60. Electronic applications accepted. *Expenses:* CEM tuition has a 20% surcharge per credit hour over that for credits of most other UAF colleges. Assuming 60 credits for PhD and 32 for Master's, this augments costs by $6,180 for in-state PhD, $3,296 for in-state Master's, $12,948 for non-resident PhD and $6,912 for non-resident Masters students, respectively. *Financial support:* In 2018–19, 1 research assistantship with full tuition reimbursement (averaging $3,338 per year), 6 teaching assistantships with full tuition reimbursements (averaging $7,311 per year) were awarded; fellowships with full tuition reimbursements, career-related internships or fieldwork, Federal Work-Study, scholarships/grants, health care benefits, and unspecified assistantships also available. Support available to part-time students. Financial award application deadline: 7/1; financial award applicants required to submit FAFSA. *Faculty research:* Gas-to-liquid transportation hydraulics and issues, carbon sequestration, enhanced oil recovery, reservoir engineering, coal bed methane. *Total annual research expenditures:* $497,000. *Unit head:* Dr. Abhijit Dandekar, Chair, 907-474-7734, E-mail: uaf-pete-dept@alaska.edu. *Application contact:* Samara Taber, Director of Admissions, 907-474-7500, E-mail: uaf-admissions@alaska.edu. Website: http://cem.uaf.edu/pete/

University of Alberta, Faculty of Graduate Studies and Research, Department of Civil and Environmental Engineering, Edmonton, AB T6G 2E1, Canada. Offers construction engineering and management (M Eng, M Sc, PhD); environmental engineering (M Eng, M Sc, PhD); environmental science (M Sc, PhD); geoenvironmental engineering (M Eng, M Sc, PhD); geotechnical engineering (M Eng, M Sc, PhD); mining engineering (M Eng, M Sc, PhD); petroleum engineering (M Eng, M Sc, PhD); structural engineering (M Eng, M Sc, PhD); water resources (M Eng, M Sc, PhD). *Program availability:* Part-time, online learning. *Degree requirements:* For master's, thesis (for some programs); for doctorate, thesis/dissertation. *Entrance requirements:* For master's, minimum GPA of 3.0 in last 2 years of undergraduate studies; for doctorate, minimum GPA of 3.0. Additional exam requirements/recommendations for international students: Required—TOEFL (minimum score 550 paper-based). Electronic applications accepted. *Faculty research:* Mining.

University of Calgary, Faculty of Graduate Studies, Schulich School of Engineering, Program in Chemical and Petroleum Engineering, Calgary, AB T2N 1N4, Canada. Offers chemical engineering (M Eng, M Sc, PhD); energy and environment engineering (M Eng, M Sc, PhD); energy and environmental systems (M Eng, M Sc, PhD); environmental engineering (M Eng, M Sc, PhD); petroleum engineering (M Eng, M Sc,

PhD); reservoir characterization (M Eng, M Sc). *Program availability:* Part-time. *Degree requirements:* For master's, thesis (for some programs); for doctorate, comprehensive exam, thesis/dissertation, candidacy exam. *Entrance requirements:* For master's, minimum GPA of 3.0 or equivalent; for doctorate, minimum GPA of 3.5 or equivalent. Additional exam requirements/recommendations for international students: Required—TOEFL (minimum score 550 paper-based; 80 iBT), IELTS (minimum score 7). Electronic applications accepted. *Faculty research:* Environmental engineering, biomedical engineering modeling, simulation and control, petroleum recovery and reservoir engineering, phase equilibria and transport properties.

University of Houston, Cullen College of Engineering, Department of Chemical and Biomolecular Engineering, Houston, TX 77204. Offers chemical engineering (MCHE, PhD); petroleum engineering (M Pet E). *Program availability:* Part-time. Terminal master's awarded for partial completion of doctoral program. *Entrance requirements:* For master's and doctorate, GRE General Test. Additional exam requirements/recommendations for international students: Required—TOEFL (minimum score 550 paper-based; 79 iBT), IELTS (minimum score 6.5). *Faculty research:* Chemical engineering.

The University of Kansas, Graduate Studies, School of Engineering, Program in Chemical and Petroleum Engineering, Lawrence, KS 66045. Offers chemical and petroleum engineering (PhD); chemical engineering (MS); petroleum engineering (MS); petroleum management (Certificate). *Program availability:* Part-time. *Students:* 37 full-time (13 women), 2 part-time (1 woman); includes 1 minority (Black or African American, non-Hispanic/Latino), 31 international. Average age 28. 29 applicants, 41% accepted, 3 enrolled. In 2018, 3 doctorates awarded. *Entrance requirements:* For master's, GRE General Test, minimum GPA of 3.0, resume, personal statement, transcripts, three letters of recommendation; for doctorate, GRE General Test, minimum GPA of 3.5, resume, personal statement, transcripts, three letters of recommendation. Additional exam requirements/recommendations for international students: Required—TOEFL, IELTS. *Application deadline:* For fall admission, 12/15 priority date for domestic and international students; for spring admission, 8/31 priority date for domestic and international students. Application fee: $65 ($85 for international students). Electronic applications accepted. *Financial support:* Fellowships, research assistantships, teaching assistantships, career-related internships or fieldwork, Federal Work-Study, scholarships/grants, traineeships, and unspecified assistantships available. Financial award application deadline: 12/15; financial award applicants required to submit FAFSA. *Faculty research:* Enhanced oil recovery, catalysis and kinetics, electrochemical engineering, biomedical engineering, semiconductor materials processing. *Unit head:* Laurence R Weatherley, Chair, 785-864-3553, E-mail: lweather@ku.edu. *Application contact:* Martha Kehr, Graduate Admission Contact, 785-864-2900, E-mail: cpegrad@ku.edu. Website: http://www.cpe.engr.ku.edu

The University of Kansas, Graduate Studies, School of Engineering, Program in Petroleum Engineering, Lawrence, KS 66045. Offers petroleum engineering (MS); petroleum management (Certificate). *Program availability:* Part-time. *Students:* 6 full-time (1 woman), all international. Average age 26. 9 applicants, 22% accepted, 1 enrolled. In 2018, 7 master's awarded. *Entrance requirements:* For master's, GRE, resume, personal statement, transcripts, three letters of recommendation. Additional exam requirements/recommendations for international students: Required—TOEFL, IELTS. *Application deadline:* For fall admission, 12/15 priority date for domestic and international students; for spring admission, 8/31 priority date for domestic and international students. Application fee: $65 ($85 for international students). Electronic applications accepted. *Financial support:* Research assistantships, teaching assistantships, Federal Work-Study, scholarships/grants, and unspecified assistantships available. Financial award application deadline: 12/15. *Unit head:* Laurence Weatherley, Chair, 785-864-3553, E-mail: lweather@ku.edu. *Application contact:* Martha Kehr, Graduate Admission Contact, 785-864-2900, E-mail: cpegrad@ku.edu. Website: http://www.cpe.engr.ku.edu/

University of Louisiana at Lafayette, College of Engineering, Department of Petroleum Engineering, Lafayette, LA 70504. Offers MSE. *Program availability:* Evening/weekend. *Degree requirements:* For master's, comprehensive exam, thesis or alternative. *Entrance requirements:* For master's, GRE General Test, minimum GPA of 2.85. Electronic applications accepted.

University of Oklahoma, Mewbourne College of Earth and Energy, Mewbourne School of Petroleum and Geological Engineering, Norman, OK 73019. Offers geological engineering (MS, PhD); natural gas engineering and management (MS), including natural gas engineering and management; natural gas technology (Graduate Certificate), including natural gas technology; petroleum engineering (MS, PhD). *Program availability:* Part-time, evening/weekend. *Faculty:* 19 full-time (1 woman), 1 part-time/adjunct (0 women). *Students:* 67 full-time (11 women), 65 part-time (11 women); includes 16 minority (3 Black or African American, non-Hispanic/Latino; 1 American Indian or Alaska Native, non-Hispanic/Latino; 1 Asian, non-Hispanic/Latino; 7 Hispanic/Latino; 4 Two or more races, non-Hispanic/Latino), 86 international. Average age 31. 147 applicants, 39% accepted, 31 enrolled. In 2018, 27 master's, 10 doctorates awarded. *Degree requirements:* For master's, variable foreign language requirement, comprehensive exam (for some programs), thesis (for some programs); for doctorate, variable foreign language requirement, comprehensive exam, thesis/dissertation. *Entrance requirements:* For master's and doctorate, GRE, minimum GPA of 3.2, three letters of recommendation, statement of purpose, resume/curriculum vitae. Additional exam requirements/recommendations for international students: Required—TOEFL (minimum score 79 iBT) or IELTS (minimum score 6.5). *Application deadline:* For fall admission, 3/1 for domestic and international students; for spring admission, 9/1 for domestic and international students. Application fee: $50 ($100 for international students). Electronic applications accepted. *Expenses:* Tuition, state resident: full-time $5683.20; part-time $236.80 per credit hour. Tuition, nonresident: full-time $20,342; part-time $847.60 per credit hour. International tuition: $20,342.40 full-time. *Required fees:* $2894.20; $110.05 per credit hour. $126.50 per semester. Tuition and fees vary according to course load and program. *Financial support:* Fellowships, research assistantships, teaching assistantships, and scholarships/grants available. Financial award application deadline: 6/1; financial award applicants required to submit FAFSA. *Faculty research:* Geomechanics applied to petroleum and geothermal reservoir development, unconventional petrophysics and rock physics, well construction, integrity and well control, enhanced oil recovery and high resolution reservoir characterization, machine learning, data analytics and predictive analytics. *Unit head:* Dr. Runar Nygaard, Director, 405-325-2921, E-mail: runar.nygaard@ou.edu. *Application contact:* Danika Hines-Barnett, Graduate Programs Coordinator, 405-325-2921, E-mail: danika@ou.edu. Website: http://www.ou.edu/mcee/mpge

University of Pittsburgh, Swanson School of Engineering, Department of Chemical and Petroleum Engineering, Pittsburgh, PA 15260. Offers chemical engineering (MS Ch E, PhD); petroleum engineering (MSPE); MS Ch E/MSPE. *Program availability:* Part-time, 100% online. Terminal master's awarded for partial completion of doctoral program. *Degree requirements:* For doctorate, comprehensive exam, thesis/dissertation, final oral exams. *Entrance requirements:* For master's and doctorate, GRE

General Test, minimum GPA of 3.0. Additional exam requirements/recommendations for international students: Required—TOEFL (minimum score 550 paper-based; 80 iBT). Electronic applications accepted. *Expenses:* Contact institution. *Faculty research:* Biotechnology, polymers, catalysis, energy and environment, computational modeling.

University of Regina, Faculty of Graduate Studies and Research, Faculty of Engineering and Applied Science, Program in Petroleum Systems Engineering, Regina, SK S4S 0A2, Canada. Offers petroleum systems (M Eng, MA Sc, PhD). *Program availability:* Part-time. *Faculty:* 8 full-time (1 woman), 1 part-time/adjunct (0 women). *Students:* 47 full-time (13 women), 2 part-time (0 women). Average age 30. 106 applicants, 8% accepted. In 2018, 14 master's, 2 doctorates awarded. *Degree requirements:* For master's, thesis (for some programs), project, report, co-op placement; for doctorate, thesis/dissertation. *Entrance requirements:* For master's, minimum graduating average of 70 percent from four-year baccalaureate degree (or equivalent); for doctorate, completion of thesis-based master's degree in engineering or closely-related field. Additional exam requirements/recommendations for international students: Required—TOEFL (minimum score 580 paper-based; 80 iBT), IELTS (minimum score 6.5), PTE (minimum score 59), other options are CAEL, MELAB, Cantest and U of R ESL. *Application deadline:* For fall admission, 3/31 for domestic and international students; for winter admission, 7/31 for domestic and international students; for spring admission, 11/30 for domestic and international students. Application fee: $100 Canadian dollars. Electronic applications accepted. *Expenses:* Estimated tuition and fees for one academic year is 8.379.50 for master's. The fee will vary base on your choice program. For doctoral program one academic year is estimated 14,129.40. International students will pay additional 1,191.75 for international surcharge per semester. *Financial support:* Fellowships, research assistantships, teaching assistantships, career-related internships or fieldwork, Federal Work-Study, scholarships/grants, unspecified assistantships, and travel award and Graduate Scholarship Base funds available. Support available to part-time students. Financial award application deadline: 9/30. *Faculty research:* Enhanced oil recovery, production engineering, reservoir engineering, surface thermodynamics, geostatistics. *Unit head:* Dr. Na jia, Program Chair, 306-337-3287, Fax: 306-585-4855, E-mail: Na.Jia@uregina.ca. *Application contact:* Dr. Tony Yang, Graduate Coordinator, 306-337-2660, Fax: 306-585-4855, E-mail: tony.Yang@uregina.ca.
Website: http://www.uregina.ca/engineering/

University of Southern California, Graduate School, Viterbi School of Engineering, Mork Family Department of Chemical Engineering and Materials Science, Los Angeles, CA 90089. Offers chemical engineering (MS, PhD, Engr); geoscience technologies (MS); materials engineering (MS); materials science (MS, PhD, Engr); petroleum engineering (MS, PhD, Engr); smart oilfield technologies (MS, Graduate Certificate). Terminal master's awarded for partial completion of doctoral program. *Degree requirements:* For master's, thesis optional; for doctorate, thesis/dissertation. *Entrance requirements:* For master's and doctorate, GRE General Test. Additional exam requirements/recommendations for international students: Recommended—TOEFL. Electronic applications accepted. *Expenses:* Contact institution. *Faculty research:* Heterogeneous materials and porous media, statistical mechanics, molecular simulation, polymer science and engineering, advanced materials, reaction engineering and catalysis, membrane processes and separation, biochemical engineering, cell culture, bioreactor modeling, petroleum engineering.

The University of Texas at Austin, Graduate School, Cockrell School of Engineering, Department of Petroleum and Geosystems Engineering, Austin, TX 78712-1111. Offers energy and earth resources (MA); petroleum engineering (MS, PhD). *Program availability:* Evening/weekend, online learning. *Entrance requirements:* For master's and doctorate, GRE General Test. Electronic applications accepted.

The University of Tulsa, Graduate School, College of Engineering and Natural Sciences, McDougall School of Petroleum Engineering, Tulsa, OK 74104-3189. Offers ME, MSE, PhD. *Program availability:* Part-time. *Faculty:* 14 full-time (0 women). *Students:* 47 full-time (5 women), 28 part-time (6 women); includes 1 minority (Hispanic/Latino), 71 international. Average age 27. 118 applicants, 47% accepted, 12 enrolled. In 2018, 20 master's, 13 doctorates awarded. Terminal master's awarded for partial completion of doctoral program. *Degree requirements:* For master's, thesis (MSE); for doctorate, comprehensive exam, thesis/dissertation. *Entrance requirements:* For master's and doctorate, GRE General Test. Additional exam requirements/recommendations for international students: Required—TOEFL (minimum score 550 paper-based; 80 iBT), IELTS (minimum score 6). *Application deadline:* Applications are processed on a rolling basis. Application fee: $55. Electronic applications accepted. *Expenses: Tuition:* Full-time $22,230; part-time $1235 per credit hour. *Required fees:* $2100; $6 per credit hour. One-time fee: $400 full-time. Tuition and fees vary according to course level, course load and program. *Financial support:* In 2018–19, 32 students received support, including 11 fellowships with full tuition reimbursements available (averaging $5,044 per year), 22 research assistantships with full tuition reimbursements available (averaging $14,887 per year), 10 teaching assistantships with full tuition reimbursements available (averaging $12,492 per year); career-related internships or fieldwork, Federal Work-Study, scholarships/grants, health care benefits, tuition waivers (full and partial), and unspecified assistantships also available. Support available to part-time students. Financial award application deadline: 2/1; financial award applicants required to submit FAFSA. *Faculty research:* Artificial lift, drilling, multiphase flow in pipes, separation technology, horizontal well technology, reservoir characterization, well testing, reservoir simulation, unconventional natural gas. *Unit head:* Dr. Mustafa Onur, Chairperson, 918-631-3059, Fax: 915-631-2059, E-mail: mustafa-onur@utulsa.edu.

Application contact: Dr. Hong-Quan Zhang, Adviser, 918-631-2426, Fax: 918-631-5142, E-mail: hong-quan-zhang@utulsa.edu.
Website: http://engineering.utulsa.edu/academics/petroleum-engineering/

University of Utah, Graduate School, College of Engineering, Department of Chemical Engineering, Salt Lake City, UT 84112-1107. Offers chemical engineering (MS, PhD); petroleum engineering (MS); MS/MBA. *Program availability:* Blended/hybrid learning. *Faculty:* 19 full-time (2 women), 10 part-time/adjunct (2 women). *Students:* 62 full-time (15 women), 32 part-time (5 women); includes 8 minority (1 Black or African American, non-Hispanic/Latino; 2 Asian, non-Hispanic/Latino; 4 Hispanic/Latino; 1 Two or more races, non-Hispanic/Latino), 46 international. Average age 29. 145 applicants, 18% accepted, 23 enrolled. In 2018, 18 master's, 11 doctorates awarded. *Degree requirements:* For master's, comprehensive exam (for some programs), thesis optional; for doctorate, comprehensive exam, thesis/dissertation. *Entrance requirements:* For master's, GRE General Test, minimum GPA of 3.0; for doctorate, GRE General Test, minimum GPA of 3.0, degree or course work in chemical engineering. Additional exam requirements/recommendations for international students: Required—TOEFL (minimum score 550 paper-based; 80 iBT), IELTS (minimum score 6.5). *Application deadline:* For fall admission, 1/15 priority date for domestic and international students; for spring admission, 10/1 priority date for domestic and international students; for summer admission, 2/1 priority date for domestic and international students. Applications are processed on a rolling basis. Application fee: $0 ($15 for international students). Electronic applications accepted. *Expenses:* Contact institution. *Financial support:* In 2018–19, 53 students received support, including 10 fellowships with full tuition reimbursements available (averaging $28,000 per year), 53 research assistantships with full tuition reimbursements available (averaging $28,000 per year), 1 teaching assistantship (averaging $6,848 per year); Federal Work-Study, institutionally sponsored loans, scholarships/grants, health care benefits, and unspecified assistantships also available. Financial award application deadline: 4/15; financial award applicants required to submit FAFSA. *Faculty research:* Drug delivery, fossil fuel and biomass combustion and gasification, oil and gas reservoir characteristics and management, multi-scale simulation, micro-scale synthesis. *Unit head:* Dr. Eric G. Eddings, Chair, 801-581-6915, Fax: 801-585-9291, E-mail: eric.eddings@utah.edu. *Application contact:* Wanda Brown, Graduate Coordinator, 801-585-1181, Fax: 801-585-9291, E-mail: wanda.brown@chemeng.utah.edu.
Website: http://www.che.utah.edu/

University of Wyoming, College of Engineering and Applied Science, Department of Petroleum Engineering, Laramie, WY 82071. Offers MS, PhD. *Program availability:* Part-time. Terminal master's awarded for partial completion of doctoral program. *Degree requirements:* For master's, thesis; for doctorate, thesis/dissertation. *Entrance requirements:* For master's and doctorate, GRE General Test, minimum GPA of 3.0. Additional exam requirements/recommendations for international students: Required—TOEFL (minimum score 600 paper-based). Electronic applications accepted. *Expenses: Tuition, area resident:* Full-time $6504; part-time $271 per credit hour. *Tuition, state resident:* full-time $6504; part-time $271 per credit hour. *Tuition, nonresident:* full-time $19,464; part-time $811 per credit hour. *International tuition:* $19,464 full-time. *Required fees:* $1410.94; $343.82 per semester. $343.82 per semester. Tuition and fees vary according to course load, program and reciprocity agreements. *Faculty research:* Oil recovery methods, oil production, coal bed methane.

West Virginia University, Statler College of Engineering and Mineral Resources, Morgantown, WV 26506. Offers aerospace engineering (MSAE, PhD); chemical engineering (MS Ch E, PhD); civil engineering (MSCE, PhD); computer engineering (PhD); computer science (MSCS, PhD); electrical engineering (MSEE, PhD); energy systems engineering (MSESE); engineering (MSE); industrial engineering (MSIE, PhD); industrial hygiene (MS); material science and engineering (MSMSE, PhD); mechanical engineering (MSME, PhD); mining engineering (MS Min E, PhD); petroleum and natural gas engineering (MSPNGE, PhD); safety management (MS); software engineering (MSSE). *Program availability:* Part-time. *Students:* 466 full-time (113 women), 154 part-time (27 women); includes 57 minority (22 Black or African American, non-Hispanic/Latino; 1 American Indian or Alaska Native, non-Hispanic/Latino; 8 Asian, non-Hispanic/Latino; 12 Hispanic/Latino; 14 Two or more races, non-Hispanic/Latino), 283 international. In 2018, 179 master's, 39 doctorates awarded. Terminal master's awarded for partial completion of doctoral program. *Degree requirements:* For master's, thesis optional; for doctorate, comprehensive exam, thesis/dissertation. *Entrance requirements:* Additional exam requirements/recommendations for international students: Required—TOEFL (minimum score 550 paper-based). *Application deadline:* For fall admission, 4/1 for international students; for winter admission, 4/1 for international students; for spring admission, 10/1 for international students. Applications are processed on a rolling basis. Application fee: $60. Electronic applications accepted. *Expenses:* Contact institution. *Financial support:* Fellowships, research assistantships, teaching assistantships, career-related internships or fieldwork, Federal Work-Study, institutionally sponsored loans, health care benefits, tuition waivers (full and partial), unspecified assistantships, and administrative assistantships available. Financial award application deadline: 2/1; financial award applicants required to submit FAFSA. *Faculty research:* Composite materials, software engineering, information systems, aerodynamics, vehicle propulsion and emission. *Unit head:* Dr. Earl Scime, Interim Dean, 304-293-4157 Ext. 2237, Fax: 304-293-2037, E-mail: earl.scime@mail.wvu.edu. *Application contact:* Dr. David A. Wyrick, Associate Dean, Academic Affairs, 304-293-4334, Fax: 304-293-5024, E-mail: david.wyrick@mail.wvu.edu.
Website: https://www.statler.wvu.edu

Section 14
Industrial Engineering

This section contains a directory of institutions offering graduate work in industrial engineering. Additional information about programs listed in the directory may be obtained by writing directly to the dean of a graduate school or chair of a department at the address given in the directory.

For programs offering related work, see also in this book *Computer Science and Information Technology, Electrical and Computer Engineering, Energy and Power Engineering, Engineering and Applied Sciences,* and *Management of Engineering and Technology.* In the other guides in this series:

Graduate Programs in the Physical Sciences, Mathematics, Agricultural Sciences, the Environment & Natural Resources
See *Mathematical Sciences*

Graduate Programs in Business, Education, Information Studies, Law & Social Work
See *Business Administration and Management*

CONTENTS

Program Directories

Automotive Engineering

Clemson University, Graduate School, College of Engineering, Computing and Applied Sciences, Department of Automotive Engineering, Greenville, SC 29607. Offers MS, PhD, Certificate. *Faculty:* 13 full-time (1 woman), 3 part-time/adjunct (1 woman). *Students:* 155 full-time (11 women), 8 part-time (2 women); includes 2 minority (1 Black or African American, non-Hispanic/Latino; 1 Two or more races, non-Hispanic/Latino), 129 international. Average age 26. 427 applicants, 38% accepted, 66 enrolled. In 2018, 79 master's, 9 doctorates, 3 other advanced degrees awarded. *Degree requirements:* For master's, industrial internship; for doctorate, comprehensive exam, thesis/dissertation. *Entrance requirements:* For master's, doctorate, and Certificate, GRE General Test, unofficial transcripts, letters of recommendation. Additional exam requirements/recommendations for international students: Required—TOEFL (minimum score 80 paper-based; 80 iBT); Recommended—IELTS (minimum score 6.5), TSE (minimum score 54). *Application deadline:* For fall admission, 1/15 priority date for domestic students, 4/30 priority date for international students; for spring admission, 9/1 for domestic and international students. Applications are processed on a rolling basis. Application fee: $80 ($90 for international students). Electronic applications accepted. *Expenses:* $7548 per semester full-time resident, $16098 per semester full-time non-resident, $1039 per credit hour part-time resident, $2261 per credit hour part-time non-resident, $1144 full-time graduate assistant, other fees may apply per session. *Financial support:* In 2018–19, 77 students received support, including 16 fellowships with full and partial tuition reimbursements available (averaging $4,563 per year), 38 research assistantships with full and partial tuition reimbursements available (averaging $19,369 per year), 23 teaching assistantships with full and partial tuition reimbursements available (averaging $17,652 per year); career-related internships or fieldwork also available. Financial award application deadline: 1/15. *Faculty research:* Advanced powertrains, automotive systems integration, manufacturing and materials, vehicle performance, vehicle-to-vehicle and vehicle-infrastructure integration. *Total annual research expenditures:* $4.8 million. *Unit head:* Dr. Zoran Filipi, Chair and Executive Director, 864-283-7222, E-mail: zfilipi@clemson.edu. *Application contact:* Dr. Beshah Ayalew, Graduate Coordinator, 864-283-7228, E-mail: beshah@clemson.edu.
Website: https://www.clemson.edu/cecas/departments/automotive-engineering/

College for Creative Studies, Graduate Programs, Detroit, MI 48202-4034. Offers color and materials design (MFA); integrated design (MFA); interaction design (MFA); transportation design (MFA). *Accreditation:* NASAD.

Lawrence Technological University, College of Engineering, Southfield, MI 48075-1058. Offers architectural engineering (MS); automotive engineering (MS); biomedical engineering (MS); civil engineering (MA, MS, PhD), including environmental engineering (MS), geotechnical engineering (MS), structural engineering (MS), transportation engineering (MS), water resource engineering (MS); construction engineering management (MA); electrical and computer engineering (MS); engineering management (MEM); engineering technology (MS); fire engineering (MS); industrial engineering (MS), including healthcare systems; manufacturing systems (ME); mechanical engineering (MS, DE, PhD), including automotive engineering (MS), energy engineering (MS), manufacturing (DE), solid mechanics (MS), thermal/fluid systems (MS); mechatronic systems engineering (MS). *Program availability:* Part-time, evening/weekend. Terminal master's awarded for partial completion of doctoral program. *Degree requirements:* For master's, thesis optional; for doctorate, comprehensive exam, thesis/dissertation optional. *Entrance requirements:* Additional exam requirements/recommendations for international students: Required—TOEFL (minimum score 550 paper-based; 79 iBT), IELTS (minimum score 6.5). Electronic applications accepted. *Faculty research:* Innovative infrastructure and building structures and materials; connectivity and mobility; automotive systems modeling, simulation and testing; biomedical devices and materials; building mechanical/electrical systems.

Minnesota State University Mankato, College of Graduate Studies and Research, College of Science, Engineering and Technology, Department of Automotive and Manufacturing Engineering Technology, Mankato, MN 56001. Offers manufacturing engineering technology (MS). *Degree requirements:* For master's, comprehensive exam, thesis. *Entrance requirements:* For master's, minimum GPA of 2.75 during previous 2 years. Additional exam requirements/recommendations for international students: Required—TOEFL (minimum score 525 paper-based). Electronic applications accepted.

University of Michigan, College of Engineering, Department of Integrative Systems and Design, Ann Arbor, MI 48109. Offers automotive engineering (M Eng); design science (MS, PhD); energy systems engineering (M Eng, MS); global automotive and manufacturing engineering (M Eng); manufacturing engineering (M Eng, D Eng); pharmaceutical engineering (M Eng); robotics and autonomous vehicles (M Eng); systems engineering and design (M Eng); MBA/M Eng; MSE/MS. *Program availability:* Part-time, online learning. *Students:* 163 full-time (38 women), 251 part-time (40 women). 282 applicants, 12% accepted, 15 enrolled. In 2018, 173 master's, 1 doctorate awarded. Terminal master's awarded for partial completion of doctoral program. *Degree requirements:* For master's, capstone project; for doctorate, thesis/dissertation. *Entrance requirements:* For master's and doctorate, GRE. Additional exam requirements/recommendations for international students: Required—TOEFL. *Application deadline:* Applications are processed on a rolling basis. Electronic applications accepted. *Financial support:* Fellowships, research assistantships with full tuition reimbursements, teaching assistantships with full tuition reimbursements, career-related internships or fieldwork, scholarships/grants, and unspecified assistantships available. Financial award applicants required to submit FAFSA. *Faculty research:* Automotive engineering, design science, energy systems engineering, engineering sustainable systems, financial engineering, global automotive and manufacturing engineering, integrated microsystems, manufacturing engineering, pharmaceutical engineering, robotics and autonomous vehicles. *Total annual research expenditures:* $595,323. *Unit head:* Diann Brei, Department Chair, 734-763-6617, E-mail: drdiannbrei@umich.edu. *Application contact:* Kathy Bishar, Senior Graduate Coordinator, 734-764-3312, E-mail: kbishar@umich.edu.
Website: http://www.isd.engin.umich.edu

University of Michigan–Dearborn, College of Engineering and Computer Science, MSE Program in Automotive Systems Engineering, Dearborn, MI 48128. Offers MSE. *Program availability:* Part-time, evening/weekend, 100% online. *Faculty:* 24 full-time (4 women), 12 part-time/adjunct (2 women). *Students:* 84 full-time (5 women), 127 part-time (9 women); includes 17 minority (3 Black or African American, non-Hispanic/Latino; 9 Asian, non-Hispanic/Latino; 4 Hispanic/Latino; 1 Two or more races, non-Hispanic/Latino), 122 international. Average age 26. 341 applicants, 38% accepted, 64 enrolled. In 2018, 92 master's awarded. *Degree requirements:* For master's, thesis optional. *Entrance requirements:* For master's, BS or equivalent degree in engineering from ABET-accredited program with minimum cumulative GPA of 3.0. Additional exam requirements/recommendations for international students: Required—TOEFL (minimum score 560 paper-based; 84 iBT), IELTS (minimum score 6.5). *Application deadline:* For fall admission, 8/1 priority date for domestic students, 5/1 for international students; for winter admission, 12/1 priority date for domestic students, 9/1 for international students; for spring admission, 4/1 priority date for domestic students, 1/1 for international students. Applications are processed on a rolling basis. Application fee: $60. Electronic applications accepted. *Expenses:* Tuition, state resident: full-time $15,380; part-time $88 per credit hour. Tuition, nonresident: full-time $23,948; part-time $1377 per credit hour. *Required fees:* $780; $780 $390. Tuition and fees vary according to course level, course load, degree level, program, reciprocity agreements and student level. *Financial support:* In 2018–19, 81 students received support. Research assistantships with full tuition reimbursements available, scholarships/grants, unspecified assistantships, and non-resident tuition scholarships available. Financial award application deadline: 3/1; financial award applicants required to submit FAFSA. *Faculty research:* Advanced vehicle control and dynamics, materials and material processing, vehicle sensors and actuators, vehicle electronics, vehicle communications. *Unit head:* Dr. Oleg Zikanov, Chair, 313-593-5582, E-mail: zikanov@umich.edu. *Application contact:* Office of Graduate Studies, 313-583-6321, E-mail: umd-graduatestudies@umich.edu.
Website: https://umdearborn.edu/cecs/departments/mechanical-engineering/graduate-programs/mse-automotive-systems-engineering

The University of Tennessee at Chattanooga, Program in Engineering, Chattanooga, TN 37403. Offers automotive (MS Engr); chemical (MS Engr); civil (MS Engr); electrical (MS Engr); mechanical (MS Engr). *Program availability:* Part-time. *Degree requirements:* For master's, comprehensive exam, thesis or alternative, engineering project. *Entrance requirements:* For master's, GRE General Test, minimum undergraduate GPA of 2.7 or 3.0 in last two years of undergraduate coursework. Additional exam requirements/recommendations for international students: Required—TOEFL (minimum score 550 paper-based; 79 iBT), IELTS (minimum score 6). Electronic applications accepted. *Expenses:* Contact institution. *Faculty research:* Quality control and reliability engineering, financial management, thermal science, energy conservation, structural analysis.

University of Wisconsin–Madison, Graduate School, College of Engineering, Department of Mechanical Engineering, Madison, WI 53706. Offers mechanical engineering (MS, PhD), including automotive engineering (MS), modeling and simulation (MS). *Program availability:* Part-time. *Faculty:* 29 full-time (2 women). *Students:* 198 full-time (33 women), 25 part-time (3 women); includes 34 minority (3 Black or African American, non-Hispanic/Latino; 13 Asian, non-Hispanic/Latino; 16 Hispanic/Latino; 2 Two or more races, non-Hispanic/Latino), 103 international. Average age 27. 537 applicants, 31% accepted, 54 enrolled. In 2018, 42 master's, 15 doctorates awarded. Terminal master's awarded for partial completion of doctoral program. *Degree requirements:* For master's, thesis (for some programs), 30 credits; minimum GPA of 3.0; for doctorate, thesis/dissertation, qualifying exam, preliminary exam, final oral defense, 42 formal course credits, 18 thesis credits, minimum GPA of 3.25. *Entrance requirements:* For master's, GRE, BS in mechanical engineering or related field, minimum GPA of 3.2 in last 60 hours of course work; for doctorate, GRE, BS in mechanical engineering or related field, minimum undergraduate GPA of 3.2 in last 60 hours of course work. Additional exam requirements/recommendations for international students: Required—TOEFL (minimum score 580 paper-based; 92 iBT), IELTS (minimum score 7). *Application deadline:* For fall admission, 12/15 for domestic and international students; for spring admission, 10/1 for domestic and international students; for summer admission, 12/15 for domestic and international students. Application fee: $75 ($81 for international students). Electronic applications accepted. *Financial support:* In 2018–19, 159 students received support, including 14 fellowships with full tuition reimbursements available (averaging $28,536 per year), 89 research assistantships with full tuition reimbursements available (averaging $21,396 per year), 56 teaching assistantships with full tuition reimbursements available (averaging $17,880 per year); career-related internships or fieldwork, institutionally sponsored loans, scholarships/grants, traineeships, health care benefits, and unspecified assistantships also available. Financial award application deadline: 12/1; financial award applicants required to submit FAFSA. *Faculty research:* Polymer engineering; robotics/electromechanical system control; advanced manufacturing and prototype processes; computational mechanics; thermal-fluid systems; engine and vehicle systems. *Total annual research expenditures:* $10.9 million. *Unit head:* Dr. Jaal B. Ghandhi, Chair, 608-262-3543, E-mail: dept@me.engr.wisc.edu. *Application contact:* Sara Hladilek, Student Services Coordinator, 608-262-8617, E-mail: shladilek@wisc.edu.
Website: https://www.engr.wisc.edu/department/mechanical-engineering/

Wayne State University, College of Engineering, Interdisciplinary, Detroit, MI 48202. Offers MS, Graduate Certificate. *Students:* 4 full-time (1 woman), 1 part-time (0 women); includes 1 minority (Black or African American, non-Hispanic/Latino), 2 international. Average age 36. 11 applicants, 64% accepted, 3 enrolled. In 2018, 1 master's, 1 other advanced degree awarded. *Entrance requirements:* For master's, bachelor's degree in engineering from accredited institution with minimum GPA of 3.0, significant professional experience, or enrollment in electric-drive vehicle engineering Graduate Certificate program; for Graduate Certificate, bachelor's degree in engineering from accredited institution with minimum GPA of 2.8 or significant professional experience. Additional exam requirements/recommendations for international students: Required—TOEFL (minimum score 550 paper-based; 79 iBT), TWE (minimum score 5.5), Michigan English Language Assessment Battery (minimum score 85); Recommended—IELTS (minimum score 6.5). *Application deadline:* For fall admission, 6/1 priority date for domestic students, 5/1 priority date for international students; for winter admission, 10/1 priority date for domestic students, 9/1 priority date for international students; for spring admission, 2/1 priority date for domestic students, 1/1 priority date for international students. Applications are processed on a rolling basis. Application fee: $50. Electronic applications accepted. *Expenses:* Contact institution. *Financial support:* In 2018–19, 1 student received support. Scholarships/grants and unspecified assistantships available. Financial award application deadline: 3/31; financial award applicants required to submit FAFSA. *Unit head:* Dr. Ece Yaprak, Division Chair, 313-577-8075, E-mail: yaprak@eng.wayne.edu. *Application contact:* Dr. Ece Yaprak, Division Chair, 313-577-8075, E-mail: yaprak@eng.wayne.edu.
Website: http://engineering.wayne.edu/eve/index.php

Industrial/Management Engineering

American University of Armenia, Graduate Programs, Yerevan, Armenia. Offers business administration (MBA); computer and information science (MS), including business management, design and manufacturing, energy (ME, MS), industrial engineering and systems management; economics (MS); industrial engineering and systems management (ME), including business, computer aided design/manufacturing, energy (ME, MS), information technology; law (LL M); political science and international affairs (MPSIA); public health (MPH); teaching English as a foreign language (MA). *Program availability:* Part-time, evening/weekend. *Degree requirements:* For master's, thesis (for some programs), capstone/project. *Entrance requirements:* For master's, GRE, GMAT, or LSAT. Additional exam requirements/recommendations for international students: Recommended—TOEFL (minimum score 79 iBT), IELTS (minimum score 6.5). *Faculty research:* Microfinance, finance (rural/development, international, corporate), firm life cycle theory, TESOL, language proficiency testing, public policy, administrative law, economic development, cryptography, artificial intelligence, energy efficiency/renewable energy, computer-aided design/manufacturing, health financing, tuberculosis control, mother/child health, preventive ophthalmology, post-earthquake psychopathological investigations, tobacco control, environmental health risk assessments.

Arizona State University at the Tempe campus, Ira A. Fulton Schools of Engineering, School of Computing, Informatics, and Decision Systems Engineering, Tempe, AZ 85287-8809. Offers computer engineering (MS, PhD); computer science (MCS, MS, PhD); industrial engineering (MS, PhD); software engineering (MS). *Program availability:* Part-time, evening/weekend, online learning. Terminal master's awarded for partial completion of doctoral program. *Degree requirements:* For master's, comprehensive exam (for some programs), portfolio (MCS); interactive Program of Study (iPOS) submitted before completing 50 percent of required credit hours; for doctorate, comprehensive exam, thesis/dissertation, interactive Program of Study (iPOS) submitted before completing 50 percent of required credit hours. *Entrance requirements:* For master's, GRE, minimum GPA of 3.0 or equivalent in last 2 years of work leading to bachelor's degree; for doctorate, GRE, minimum GPA of 3.0 in last 2 years of work leading to bachelor's degree. Additional exam requirements/recommendations for international students: Required—TOEFL, IELTS, or PTE. Electronic applications accepted. *Expenses:* Contact institution. *Faculty research:* Artificial intelligence, cyberphysical and embedded systems, health informatics, information assurance and security, information management/multimedia/visualization, network science, personalized learning/educational games, production logistics, software and systems engineering, statistical modeling and data mining.

Auburn University, Graduate School, Ginn College of Engineering, Department of Industrial and Systems Engineering, Auburn University, AL 36849. Offers MISE, MS, PhD, Graduate Certificate. *Program availability:* Part-time. *Degree requirements:* For master's, thesis (MS); for doctorate, thesis/dissertation. *Entrance requirements:* For master's and doctorate, GRE General Test. *Expenses:* Tuition, state resident: full-time $11,282; part-time $535 per credit hour. Tuition, nonresident: full-time $30,542; part-time $1605 per credit hour. *Required fees:* $826 per semester. Tuition and fees vary according to degree level and program.

Binghamton University, State University of New York, Graduate School, Thomas J. Watson School of Engineering and Applied Science, Department of Systems Science and Industrial Engineering, Binghamton, NY 13902-6000. Offers executive health systems (MS); industrial and systems engineering (M Eng); systems science and industrial engineering (MS, PhD). MS in executive health systems also offered in Manhattan. *Program availability:* Part-time, evening/weekend, online learning. *Degree requirements:* For master's, thesis; for doctorate, thesis/dissertation. *Entrance requirements:* For master's and doctorate, GRE General Test. Additional exam requirements/recommendations for international students: Required—TOEFL (minimum score 550 paper-based; 80 iBT). Electronic applications accepted. *Expenses:* Contact institution. *Faculty research:* Problem restructuring, protein modeling.

Bradley University, The Graduate School, Caterpillar College of Engineering and Technology, Department of Industrial and Manufacturing Engineering and Technology, Peoria, IL 61625-0002. Offers industrial engineering (MS); manufacturing engineering (MS). *Program availability:* Part-time, evening/weekend. *Faculty:* 10 full-time (1 woman). *Students:* 10 full-time (0 women), 6 part-time (2 women); includes 1 minority (Black or African American, non-Hispanic/Latino), 14 international. Average age 28. 53 applicants, 83% accepted, 4 enrolled. In 2018, 11 master's awarded. *Degree requirements:* For master's, comprehensive exam, thesis or alternative, project. *Entrance requirements:* For master's, Minimum GPA of 2.5, Essays, Recommendation letters, Transcripts. Additional exam requirements/recommendations for international students: Required—TOEFL (minimum score 550 paper-based; 79 iBT), IELTS (minimum score 6.5). *Application deadline:* For fall admission, 5/15 priority date for domestic and international students; for spring admission, 10/15 priority date for domestic and international students. Applications are processed on a rolling basis. Application fee: $40 ($50 for international students). Electronic applications accepted. *Expenses: Tuition:* Part-time $890 per credit. *Required fees:* $50 per unit. *Financial support:* In 2018–19, 15 students received support, including 6 research assistantships with full and partial tuition reimbursements available (averaging $4,895 per year); scholarships/grants, tuition waivers (partial), and unspecified assistantships also available. Support available to part-time students. Financial award application deadline: 4/1. *Unit head:* Dr. Joseph Chen, Chair, 309-677-2740, E-mail: jchen@bradley.edu. *Application contact:* Rachel Webb, Director of On-Campus Graduate Admissions & International Student and Scholar Services, 309-677-2375, E-mail: rkwebb@bradley.edu.
Website: http://www.bradley.edu/academic/departments/imet/

Buffalo State College, State University of New York, The Graduate School, School of the Professions, Department of Engineering Technology, Program in Industrial Technology, Buffalo, NY 14222-1095. Offers MS. *Degree requirements:* For master's, thesis or project. *Entrance requirements:* For master's, minimum GPA of 2.5. Additional exam requirements/recommendations for international students: Required—TOEFL (minimum score 550 paper-based).

California Polytechnic State University, San Luis Obispo, College of Engineering, Department of Industrial Engineering, San Luis Obispo, CA 93407. Offers MS. *Program availability:* Part-time. *Faculty:* 4 full-time (1 woman), 1 (woman) part-time/adjunct. *Students:* 4 full-time (0 women), 2 part-time (0 women); includes 2 minority (1 Hispanic/Latino; 1 Two or more races, non-Hispanic/Latino), 3 international. Average age 24. 20 applicants, 60% accepted, 1 enrolled. In 2018, 3 master's awarded. *Degree requirements:* For master's, thesis. *Entrance requirements:* For master's, GRE. Additional exam requirements/recommendations for international students: Required—TOEFL (minimum score 80 iBT). *Application deadline:* For fall admission, 3/1 for domestic and international students. Applications are processed on a rolling basis. Application fee: $55. Electronic applications accepted. *Expenses: Tuition, area resident:* Full-time $7176; part-time $4164 per year. Tuition, state resident: full-time $10,965. Tuition, nonresident: full-time $10,965. *Required fees:* $6336; $3711. *Financial support:* Fellowships, research assistantships, teaching assistantships, career-related internships or fieldwork, Federal Work-Study, institutionally sponsored loans, and scholarships/grants available. Support available to part-time students. Financial award application deadline: 3/2; financial award applicants required to submit FAFSA. *Faculty research:* Operations research, simulation, project management, supply chain and logistics, quality engineering. *Unit head:* Dr. Tali Freed, Graduate Coordinator, 805-756-2544, E-mail: tfreed@calpoly.edu. *Application contact:* Dr. Tali Freed, Graduate Coordinator, 805-756-2544, E-mail: tfreed@calpoly.edu.
Website: http://www.ime.calpoly.edu/programs/graduate/

California State University, Fresno, Division of Research and Graduate Studies, Jordan College of Agricultural Sciences and Technology, Department of Industrial Technology, Fresno, CA 93740-8027. Offers MS. *Program availability:* Part-time, evening/weekend. *Degree requirements:* For master's, comprehensive exam (for some programs), thesis (for some programs). *Entrance requirements:* For master's, GRE General Test, minimum GPA of 2.5. Additional exam requirements/recommendations for international students: Required—TOEFL. Electronic applications accepted. *Faculty research:* Fuels/pollution, energy, outdoor storage methods.

California State University, Northridge, Graduate Studies, College of Engineering and Computer Science, Department of Manufacturing Systems Engineering and Management, Northridge, CA 91330. Offers engineering automation (MS); engineering management (MS); manufacturing systems engineering (MS); materials engineering (MS). *Program availability:* Online learning. *Entrance requirements:* For master's, GRE (if cumulative undergraduate GPA less than 3.0).

Clemson University, Graduate School, College of Engineering, Computing and Applied Sciences, Department of Industrial Engineering, Clemson, SC 29634. Offers M Engr, MS, PhD. *Program availability:* Part-time, 100% online. *Faculty:* 11 full-time. *Students:* 130 full-time (26 women), 91 part-time (23 women); includes 11 minority (2 Black or African American, non-Hispanic/Latino; 2 Asian, non-Hispanic/Latino; 3 Hispanic/Latino; 1 Native Hawaiian or other Pacific Islander, non-Hispanic/Latino; 3 Two or more races, non-Hispanic/Latino), 140 international. Average age 28. 390 applicants, 66% accepted, 118 enrolled. In 2018, 49 master's, 7 doctorates awarded. Terminal master's awarded for partial completion of doctoral program. *Degree requirements:* For master's, thesis or alternative; for doctorate, comprehensive exam, thesis/dissertation. *Entrance requirements:* For master's and doctorate, GRE General Test, unofficial transcripts, letters of recommendation. Additional exam requirements/recommendations for international students: Required—TOEFL (minimum score 80 paper-based; 80 iBT); Recommended—IELTS (minimum score 6.5), TSE (minimum score 54). *Application deadline:* For fall admission, 4/1 for domestic students, 1/1 for international students. Applications are processed on a rolling basis. Application fee: $80 ($90 for international students). Electronic applications accepted. *Expenses:* $6823 per semester full-time resident, $14023 per semester full-time non-resident, $833 per credit hour part-time resident, $1731 per credit hour part-time non-resident, online $1264 per credit hour, $4938 doctoral programs resident, $10405 doctoral programs non-resident, $1144 full-time graduate assistant, other fees may apply per session. *Financial support:* In 2018–19, 52 students received support, including 1 fellowship with full and partial tuition reimbursement available (averaging $5,000 per year), 26 research assistantships with full and partial tuition reimbursements available (averaging $19,721 per year), 24 teaching assistantships with full and partial tuition reimbursements available (averaging $15,751 per year); career-related internships or fieldwork and unspecified assistantships also available. Financial award application deadline: 4/1. *Faculty research:* System optimization, health care engineering, human factors and safety, human-computer interaction, quality. *Total annual research expenditures:* $2.4 million. *Unit head:* Dr. Jeffrey Kharoufeh, Department Chair, 864-656-5540, E-mail: kharouf@clemson.edu. *Application contact:* Dr. Scott Mason, Graduate Coordinator, 864-656-5645, E-mail: mason@clemson.edu.
Website: https://www.clemson.edu/cecas/departments/ie/index.html

Colorado State University–Pueblo, College of Education, Engineering and Professional Studies, Department of Engineering, Pueblo, CO 81001-4901. Offers industrial and systems engineering (MS). *Degree requirements:* For master's, thesis optional. *Entrance requirements:* For master's, GRE General Test. Additional exam requirements/recommendations for international students: Required—TOEFL (minimum score 500 paper-based). *Faculty research:* Nanotechnology, applied operations, research transportation, decision analysis.

Columbia University, Fu Foundation School of Engineering and Applied Science, Department of Industrial Engineering and Operations Research, New York, NY 10027. Offers financial engineering (MS); industrial engineering (MS); industrial engineering and operations research (PhD); management science and engineering (MS); operations research (MS); MS/MBA. *Program availability:* Part-time, evening/weekend, online learning. *Degree requirements:* For doctorate, thesis/dissertation, oral and written qualifying exams. *Entrance requirements:* For master's and doctorate, GRE General Test. Additional exam requirements/recommendations for international students: Required—TOEFL, IELTS, PTE. Electronic applications accepted. *Faculty research:* Applied probability and optimization; financial engineering, modeling risk including credit risk and systemic risk, asset allocation, portfolio execution, behavioral finance, agent-based model in finance; revenue management; management and optimization of service systems, call centers, capacity allocation in healthcare systems, inventory control for vaccines; energy, smart grids, demand shaping, managing renewable energy sources, energy-aware scheduling.

Concordia University, School of Graduate Studies, Faculty of Engineering and Computer Science, Department of Mechanical and Industrial Engineering, Montréal, QC H3G 1M8, Canada. Offers industrial engineering (M Eng, MA Sc, PhD); mechanical engineering (M Eng, MA Sc, PhD, Certificate). M Eng in composites program offered jointly with École Polytechnique de Montréal. *Degree requirements:* For master's, variable foreign language requirement, thesis or alternative; for doctorate, comprehensive exam, thesis/dissertation. *Faculty research:* Mechanical systems, fluid control systems, thermofluids engineering and robotics, industrial control systems.

Cornell University, Graduate School, Graduate Fields of Agriculture and Life Sciences and Graduate Fields of Engineering, Field of Biological and Environmental Engineering, Ithaca, NY 14853. Offers bioenergy and integrated energy systems (M Eng, MPS, MS, PhD); biological engineering (M Eng, MPS, MS, PhD); bioprocess engineering (M Eng, MPS, MS, PhD); ecohydrology (M Eng, MPS, MS, PhD); environmental engineering (M Eng, MPS, MS, PhD); environmental management (MPS); food engineering (M Eng, MPS, MS, PhD); industrial biotechnology (M Eng, MPS, MS, PhD); nanobiotechnology (M Eng, MPS, MS, PhD); sustainable systems (M Eng, MPS, MS, PhD); synthetic biology (MS); syntheticbiology (M Eng, MPS, PhD). Terminal master's awarded for partial completion of doctoral program. *Degree requirements:* For master's, thesis (MS);

Industrial/Management Engineering

for doctorate, comprehensive exam, thesis/dissertation. *Entrance requirements:* For master's, letters of recommendation (3 for MS, 2 for M Eng and MPS); for doctorate, GRE General Test, 3 letters of recommendation. Additional exam requirements/recommendations for international students: Required—TOEFL (minimum score 550 paper-based; 77 iBT). Electronic applications accepted. *Faculty research:* Biological and food engineering, environmental, soil and water engineering, international agricultural engineering, structures and controlled environments, machine systems and energy.

Cornell University, Graduate School, Graduate Fields of Engineering, Field of Operations Research and Information Engineering, Ithaca, NY 14853. Offers applied probability and statistics (PhD); manufacturing systems engineering (PhD); mathematical programming (PhD); operations research and industrial engineering (M Eng). *Degree requirements:* For doctorate, comprehensive exam, thesis/dissertation. *Entrance requirements:* For master's and doctorate, GRE General Test, 3 letters of recommendation. Additional exam requirements/recommendations for international students: Required—TOEFL (minimum score 600 paper-based; 100 iBT). Electronic applications accepted. *Faculty research:* Mathematical programming and combinatorial optimization, statistics, stochastic processes, mathematical finance, simulation, manufacturing, e-commerce.

Dalhousie University, Faculty of Engineering, Department of Industrial Engineering, Halifax, NS B3J 2X4, Canada. Offers M Eng, MA Sc, PhD. *Degree requirements:* For master's, thesis; for doctorate, thesis/dissertation. *Entrance requirements:* Additional exam requirements/recommendations for international students: Required—TOEFL, IELTS, CANTEST, CAEL, or Michigan English Language Assessment Battery. Electronic applications accepted. *Faculty research:* Industrial ergonomics, operations research, production manufacturing systems, scheduling stochastic models.

Eastern Kentucky University, The Graduate School, College of Business and Technology, Department of Technology, Program in Industrial Technology, Richmond, KY 40475-3102. Offers MS. *Program availability:* Part-time. *Entrance requirements:* For master's, GRE General Test, minimum GPA of 2.5. *Faculty research:* Quality control, dental implants, manufacturing technology.

École Polytechnique de Montréal, Graduate Programs, Department of Mathematics and Industrial Engineering, Montréal, QC H3C 3A7, Canada. Offers ergonomy (M Eng, M Sc A, DESS); mathematical method in CA engineering (M Eng, M Sc A, PhD); operational research (M Eng, M Sc A, PhD); production (M Eng, M Sc A); technology management (M Eng, M Sc A). DESS program offered jointly with HEC Montreal and Université de Montréal. *Program availability:* Part-time. *Degree requirements:* For master's, one foreign language, thesis. *Entrance requirements:* For master's, minimum GPA of 2.75. *Faculty research:* Use of computers in organizations.

Florida Agricultural and Mechanical University, Division of Graduate Studies, Research, and Continuing Education, FAMU-FSU College of Engineering, Department of Industrial and Manufacturing Engineering, Tallahassee, FL 32307-3200. Offers industrial engineering (MS, PhD). *Degree requirements:* For master's, thesis optional. *Entrance requirements:* For master's, GRE General Test, minimum GPA of 3.0. Additional exam requirements/recommendations for international students: Required—TOEFL (minimum score 550 paper-based). *Faculty research:* Design for environmentally conscious manufacturing, affordable composite manufacturing, integrated product and process design, precision machining research.

Florida State University, The Graduate School, FAMU-FSU College of Engineering, Department of Industrial and Manufacturing Engineering, Tallahassee, FL 32310. Offers industrial engineering (MS, PhD). *Degree requirements:* For master's, thesis, proposal presentation, progress presentation, defense presentation; for doctorate, thesis/dissertation, preliminary exam, proposal exam, defense exam. *Entrance requirements:* For master's, GRE General Test (minimum new score of 146 Verbal and 155 Quantitative), minimum GPA of 3.0; for doctorate, GRE General Test (minimum new score of 146 Verbal and 155 Quantitative), minimum GPA of 3.0 (without MS in industrial engineering), 3.4 (with MS in industrial engineering). Additional exam requirements/recommendations for international students: Required—TOEFL (minimum score 550 paper-based; 80 iBT); Recommended—IELTS (minimum score 6.5). Electronic applications accepted. *Expenses: Tuition, area resident:* Part-time $479.32 per credit hour. Tuition and fees vary according to campus/location and program. *Faculty research:* Precision manufacturing, composite manufacturing, green manufacturing, applied optimization, simulation.

Georgia Institute of Technology, Graduate Studies, College of Engineering, H. Milton Stewart School of Industrial and Systems Engineering, Program in Industrial and Systems Engineering, Atlanta, GA 30332-0001. Offers industrial engineering (MS, PhD). *Program availability:* Part-time, online learning. Terminal master's awarded for partial completion of doctoral program. *Degree requirements:* For master's, thesis optional; for doctorate, comprehensive exam, thesis/dissertation. *Entrance requirements:* For master's and doctorate, GRE General Test. Additional exam requirements/recommendations for international students: Required—TOEFL (minimum score 550 paper-based; 79 iBT). Electronic applications accepted. *Faculty research:* Computer-integrated manufacturing systems, materials handling systems, production and distribution.

Illinois State University, Graduate School, College of Applied Science and Technology, Department of Technology, Normal, IL 61790. Offers MS. *Faculty:* 20 full-time (2 women), 16 part-time/adjunct (1 woman). *Students:* 38 full-time (16 women), 63 part-time (29 women); includes 9 minority (3 Black or African American, non-Hispanic/Latino; 2 Asian, non-Hispanic/Latino; 2 Hispanic/Latino; 2 Two or more races, non-Hispanic/Latino), 30 international. Average age 31. 70 applicants, 84% accepted, 21 enrolled. In 2018, 42 master's awarded. *Degree requirements:* For master's, thesis or alternative. *Entrance requirements:* For master's, GRE General Test, minimum GPA of 2.8. *Application deadline:* Applications are processed on a rolling basis. Application fee: $40. *Expenses: Tuition, area resident:* Full-time $7264.62. Tuition, state resident: full-time $9466. Tuition, nonresident: full-time $17,290. *International tuition:* $15,089.40 full-time. *Required fees:* $1481.04. *Financial support:* In 2018–19, 20 research assistantships were awarded; tuition waivers (full) and unspecified assistantships also available. Financial award application deadline: 4/1. *Faculty research:* Illinois Manufacturing Extension Center Field Office hosting, model for the professional development of K-12 technology education teachers, Illinois State University Illinois Mathematics and Science Partnership, Illinois University council for career and technical education. *Unit head:* Dr. Ted Branoff, Department Chair, 309-438-3661, E-mail: tjbrano@IllinoisState.edu. *Application contact:* Dr. Klaus Scmidt, Graduate Coordinator, 309-438-3502, E-mail: kschmid@ilstu.edu.
Website: http://tec.illinoisstate.edu/

Instituto Tecnologico de Santo Domingo, Graduate School, Area of Engineering, Santo Domingo, Dominican Republic. Offers construction administration (MS, Certificate); data telecommunications (M Eng, MS, Certificate); industrial engineering (M Eng, Certificate); industrial management (M Mgmt); information technology (Certificate); maintenance engineering (M Eng); occupational hazard prevention (M Mgmt); production management (Certificate); quantitative methods (Certificate); sanitary and environmental engineering (M Eng); structural engineering (M Eng); systems engineering and electronic data processing (Certificate); transportation (Certificate).

Instituto Tecnológico y de Estudios Superiores de Monterrey, Campus Chihuahua, Graduate Programs, Chihuahua, Mexico. Offers computer systems engineering (Ingeniero); electrical engineering (Ingeniero); electromechanical engineering (Ingeniero); electronic engineering (Ingeniero); engineering administration (MEA); industrial engineering (MIE, Ingeniero); international trade (MIT); mechanical engineering (Ingeniero).

Instituto Tecnológico y de Estudios Superiores de Monterrey, Campus Ciudad de México, Virtual University Division, Ciudad de Mexico, Mexico. Offers administration of information technologies (MA); computer sciences (MA); education (MA, PhD); educational technology (MA); environmental engineering (MA); environmental systems (MA); humanistic studies (MA); industrial engineering (MA); international business for Latin America (MA); quality systems (MA); quality systems and productivity (MA). *Program availability:* Part-time, evening/weekend, online learning. *Entrance requirements:* For master's and doctorate, Instituto entrance exam. Additional exam requirements/recommendations for international students: Required—TOEFL.

Instituto Tecnológico y de Estudios Superiores de Monterrey, Campus Laguna, Graduate School, Torreón, Mexico. Offers business administration (MBA); industrial engineering (MIE); management information systems (MS). *Program availability:* Part-time. *Entrance requirements:* For master's, GMAT. *Faculty research:* Computer communications from home to the university.

Instituto Tecnológico y de Estudios Superiores de Monterrey, Campus Monterrey, Graduate and Research Division, Programs in Engineering, Monterrey, Mexico. Offers applied statistics (M Eng); artificial intelligence (PhD); automation engineering (M Eng); chemical engineering (M Eng); civil engineering (M Eng); electrical engineering (M Eng); electronic engineering (M Eng); environmental engineering (M Eng); industrial engineering (M Eng, PhD); manufacturing engineering (M Eng); mechanical engineering (M Eng); systems and quality engineering (M Eng). M Eng program offered jointly with University of Waterloo; PhD in industrial engineering with Texas A&M University. *Program availability:* Part-time, evening/weekend. Terminal master's awarded for partial completion of doctoral program. *Degree requirements:* For master's, one foreign language, thesis; for doctorate, one foreign language, thesis/dissertation. *Entrance requirements:* For master's, EXADEP; for doctorate, GRE, master's degree in related field. Additional exam requirements/recommendations for international students: Required—TOEFL. *Faculty research:* Flexible manufacturing cells, materials, statistical methods, environmental prevention, control and evaluation.

Iowa State University of Science and Technology, Department of Industrial and Manufacturing Systems Engineering, Ames, IA 50011. Offers industrial engineering (M Eng, MS, PhD); operations research (MS); systems engineering (M Eng). *Degree requirements:* For master's, thesis or alternative; for doctorate, thesis/dissertation. *Entrance requirements:* For master's and doctorate, GRE General Test. Additional exam requirements/recommendations for international students: Required—TOEFL (minimum score 550 paper-based; 79 iBT), IELTS (minimum score 6.5). Electronic applications accepted. *Faculty research:* Economic modeling, valuation techniques, robotics, digital controls, systems reliability.

Kansas State University, Graduate School, College of Engineering, Department of Industrial and Manufacturing Systems Engineering, Manhattan, KS 66506. Offers engineering management (MEM); industrial engineering (MS); operations research (MS). *Program availability:* Part-time, online learning. *Degree requirements:* For master's, thesis or alternative; for doctorate, thesis/dissertation. *Entrance requirements:* For master's, GRE General Test (minimum score of 750 old version, 159 new format on Quantitative portion of exam), bachelor's degree in engineering, mathematics, or physical science; for doctorate, GRE General Test (minimum score of 770 old version, 164 new format on Quantitative portion of exam), master's degree in engineering or industrial manufacturing. Additional exam requirements/recommendations for international students: Required—PTE (minimum score 58), TOEFL (minimum score 550 paper-based; 79 iBT) or IELTS (minimum score 6.5). Electronic applications accepted. *Faculty research:* Industrial engineering, ergonomics, healthcare systems engineering, manufacturing processes, operations research, engineering management.

Lawrence Technological University, College of Engineering, Southfield, MI 48075-1058. Offers architectural engineering (MS); automotive engineering (MS); biomedical engineering (MS); civil engineering (MA, MS, PhD), including environmental engineering (MS), geotechnical engineering (MS), structural engineering (MS), transportation engineering (MS), water resource engineering (MS); construction engineering management (MA); electrical and computer engineering (MS); engineering management (MEM); engineering technology (MS); fire engineering (MS); industrial engineering (MS), including healthcare systems; manufacturing systems (ME); mechanical engineering (MS, DE, PhD), including automotive engineering (MS), energy engineering (MS), manufacturing (DE), solid mechanics (MS), thermal/fluid systems (MS); mechatronic systems engineering (MS). *Program availability:* Part-time, evening/weekend. Terminal master's awarded for partial completion of doctoral program. *Degree requirements:* For master's, thesis optional; for doctorate, comprehensive exam, thesis/dissertation optional. *Entrance requirements:* Additional exam requirements/recommendations for international students: Required—TOEFL (minimum score 550 paper-based; 79 iBT), IELTS (minimum score 6.5). Electronic applications accepted. *Faculty research:* Innovative infrastructure and building structures and materials; connectivity and mobility; automotive systems modeling, simulation and testing; biomedical devices and materials; building mechanical/electrical systems.

Lehigh University, P.C. Rossin College of Engineering and Applied Science, Department of Industrial and Systems Engineering, Bethlehem, PA 18015. Offers analytical finance (MS); healthcare systems engineering (M Eng, Certificate); industrial and systems engineering (M Eng, MS, PhD); management science and engineering (M Eng, MS); MBA/E. *Program availability:* Part-time, blended/hybrid learning. *Faculty:* 19 full-time (2 women), 1 part-time/adjunct (0 women). *Students:* 90 full-time (17 women), 8 part-time (3 women); includes 1 minority (Asian, non-Hispanic/Latino), 89 international. Average age 26. 318 applicants, 48% accepted, 34 enrolled. In 2018, 53 master's, 6 doctorates awarded. Terminal master's awarded for partial completion of doctoral program. *Degree requirements:* For master's, thesis (MS); project (M Eng); for doctorate, comprehensive exam, thesis/dissertation. *Entrance requirements:* For master's and doctorate, GRE General Test. Additional exam requirements/recommendations for international students: Required—TOEFL (minimum score 550 paper-based; 79 iBT), IELTS (minimum score 6.5), TOEFL or IELTS required. *Application deadline:* For fall admission, 7/15 for domestic and international students; for spring admission, 12/1 for domestic and international students. Application fee: $75. Electronic applications accepted. Tuition and fees vary according to program. *Financial support:* In 2018–19, 33 students received support, including 2 fellowships with full tuition reimbursements available (averaging $20,490 per year), 18 research assistantships with full tuition reimbursements available (averaging $20,490 per year), 11 teaching assistantships with full tuition reimbursements available (averaging $21,105 per year); health care benefits and unspecified assistantships also available. Financial award application deadline: 1/15. *Faculty research:* Mathematical optimization; logistics and service systems, stochastic processes and simulation; computational optimization and high performance computing; financial engineering and robust optimization; machine learning and data mining. *Total annual research expenditures:* $2.1 million.

Unit head: Dr. Luis N. Vicente, Chairperson, 610-758-4050, Fax: 610-758-4886, E-mail: lnv@lehigh.edu. *Application contact:* Ana Quiroz, Graduate Coordinator, 610-758-4051, Fax: 610-758-4886, E-mail: acq217@lehigh.edu.
Website: https://ise.lehigh.edu/

Mississippi State University, Bagley College of Engineering, Department of Industrial and Systems Engineering, Mississippi State, MS 39762. Offers human factors and ergonomics (MS); industrial and systems engineering (PhD); industrial systems (MS); management systems (MS); manufacturing systems (MS); operations research (MS). *Program availability:* Part-time, blended/hybrid learning. *Faculty:* 12 full-time (2 women). *Students:* 35 full-time (13 women), 66 part-time (16 women); includes 20 minority (7 Black or African American, non-Hispanic/Latino; 6 Asian, non-Hispanic/Latino; 5 Hispanic/Latino; 1 Native Hawaiian or other Pacific Islander, non-Hispanic/Latino; 1 Two or more races, non-Hispanic/Latino), 21 international. Average age 36. 67 applicants, 40% accepted, 18 enrolled. In 2018, 16 master's, 9 doctorates awarded. *Degree requirements:* For master's, comprehensive exam (for some programs), thesis optional, comprehensive oral or written exam; for doctorate, comprehensive exam, thesis/dissertation, candidacy exam. *Entrance requirements:* For master's, GRE (for graduates from program not accredited by EAC/ABET), minimum GPA of 3.0 on junior and senior years; for doctorate, GRE (for graduates from program not accredited by EAC/ABET), minimum GPA of 3.5 on master's degree and junior and senior years of BS. Additional exam requirements/recommendations for international students: Required—TOEFL (minimum score 550 paper-based; 79 iBT); Recommended—IELTS (minimum score 6.5). *Application deadline:* For fall admission, 7/1 for domestic students, 5/1 for international students; for spring admission, 11/1 for domestic students, 9/1 for international students. Applications are processed on a rolling basis. Application fee: $60 ($80 for international students). Electronic applications accepted. *Expenses:* Tuition, state resident: full-time $8450; part-time $360.59 per credit hour. Tuition, nonresident: full-time $23,140; part-time $969.09 per credit hour. *Required fees:* $110. One-time fee: $55 full-time. Part-time tuition and fees vary according to course load, degree level, campus/location and reciprocity agreements. *Financial support:* In 2018–19, 18 research assistantships with full tuition reimbursements (averaging $16,905 per year), 3 teaching assistantships with full tuition reimbursements (averaging $16,033 per year) were awarded; Federal Work-Study, institutionally sponsored loans, and unspecified assistantships also available. Financial award application deadline: 4/1; financial award applicants required to submit FAFSA. *Faculty research:* Operations research, ergonomics, production systems, management systems, transportation. *Total annual research expenditures:* $2 million. *Unit head:* Dr. Kari Babski-Reeves, Professor/Interim Head and Associate Dean for Research & Graduate Studies, 662-325-8430, Fax: 662-325-7618, E-mail: kari@ise.msstate.edu. *Application contact:* Ryan King, Admissions and Enrollment Assistant, 662-325-8951, E-mail: rjk101@grad.msstate.edu. Website: http://www.ise.msstate.edu/

Montana State University, The Graduate School, College of Engineering, Department of Mechanical and Industrial Engineering, Bozeman, MT 59717. Offers engineering (PhD), including industrial engineering, mechanical engineering; industrial and management engineering (MS); mechanical engineering (MS). *Program availability:* Part-time. *Degree requirements:* For master's, comprehensive exam, thesis, oral exams; for doctorate, comprehensive exam, thesis/dissertation, qualifying exam. *Entrance requirements:* For master's, GRE, official transcript, minimum GPA of 3.0, demonstrated potential for success, statement of goals, three letters of recommendation, proof of funds affidavit; for doctorate, minimum undergraduate GPA of 3.0, 3.2 graduate; three letters of recommendation; statement of objectives. Additional exam requirements/recommendations for international students: Required—TOEFL or IELTS. Electronic applications accepted. *Faculty research:* Human factors engineering, energy, design and manufacture, systems modeling, materials and structures, measurement systems.

Montana Tech of The University of Montana, Project Engineering and Management Program, Butte, MT 59701-8997. Offers MPEM. *Program availability:* Part-time, evening/weekend, online learning. *Degree requirements:* For master's, comprehensive exam, final project presentation. *Entrance requirements:* For master's, minimum GPA of 3.0. Additional exam requirements/recommendations for international students: Required—TOEFL (minimum score 550 paper-based; 80 iBT), IELTS (minimum score 7). Electronic applications accepted.

Morgan State University, School of Graduate Studies, Clarence M. Mitchell, Jr. School of Engineering, Baltimore, MD 21251. Offers civil engineering (M Eng, D Eng); electrical and computer engineering (M Eng, MS, D Eng); industrial and systems engineering (M Eng, D Eng); transportation and urban infrastructure studies (MS, PhD, Postbaccalaureate Certificate), including transportation. *Program availability:* Part-time, evening/weekend. *Degree requirements:* For master's, thesis, comprehensive exam or equivalent; for doctorate, thesis/dissertation, comprehensive exam or equivalent. *Entrance requirements:* For master's, GRE, minimum undergraduate GPA of 2.5; for doctorate, GRE, minimum GPA of 3.0. Additional exam requirements/recommendations for international students: Required—TOEFL (minimum score 550 paper-based).

New Jersey Institute of Technology, Newark College of Engineering, Newark, NJ 07102. Offers biomedical engineering (MS, PhD); biopharmaceutical engineering (MS); chemical engineering (MS, PhD); civil engineering (MS, PhD); computer engineering (MS); critical infrastructure systems (MS); electrical engineering (MS, PhD); engineering management (MS); engineering science (MS); environmental engineering (MS, PhD); healthcare systems management (MS); industrial engineering (MS, PhD); internet engineering (MS); manufacturing systems engineering (MS); materials science & engineering (PhD); materials science and engineering (MS); mechanical engineering (MS, PhD); occupational safety and health engineering (MS). *Program availability:* Part-time, evening/weekend. *Faculty:* 147 full-time (26 women), 133 part-time/adjunct (16 women). *Students:* 690 full-time (163 women), 594 part-time (130 women); includes 427 minority (79 Black or African American, non-Hispanic/Latino; 181 Asian, non-Hispanic/Latino; 140 Hispanic/Latino; 27 Two or more races, non-Hispanic/Latino), 553 international. Average age 27. 2,334 applicants, 57% accepted, 452 enrolled. In 2018, 418 master's, 31 doctorates awarded. Terminal master's awarded for partial completion of doctoral program. *Degree requirements:* For master's, thesis (for some programs); for doctorate, thesis/dissertation. *Entrance requirements:* For master's, GRE General Test, minimum GPA 2.8, personal statement, 1 letter of recommendation, transcripts; for doctorate, GRE General Test, minimum GPA of 3.5, personal statement, 3 letters of recommendation, transcripts. Additional exam requirements/recommendations for international students: Required—TOEFL (minimum score 550 paper-based; 79 iBT), IELTS (minimum score 6.5). *Application deadline:* For fall admission, 6/1 priority date for domestic students, 5/1 priority date for international students; for spring admission, 11/15 priority date for domestic and international students. Applications are processed on a rolling basis. Application fee: $75. Electronic applications accepted. *Expenses:* $22,690 per year (in-state), $32,136 per year (out-of-state). *Financial support:* In 2018–19, 396 students received support, including 52 fellowships with full tuition reimbursements available (averaging $22,000 per year), 113 research assistantships with full tuition reimbursements available (averaging $22,000 per year), 101 teaching assistantships with full tuition reimbursements available (averaging $22,000 per year); career-related internships or fieldwork, Federal Work-Study, scholarships/grants, and unspecified assistantships also available. Financial award application deadline: 1/15. *Faculty*

research: Nonlinear signal processing, intelligent medical image analysis, calibration issues in coherent localization, computer-aided design, neural network for tool wear measurement. *Total annual research expenditures:* $41.7 million. *Unit head:* Dr. Moshe Kam, Dean, 973-596-5534, Fax: 973-596-2316, E-mail: moshe.kam@njit.edu. *Application contact:* Stephen Eck, Director of Admissions, 973-596-3300, Fax: 973-596-3461, E-mail: admissions@njit.edu.
Website: http://engineering.njit.edu/

North Carolina Agricultural and Technical State University, The Graduate College, College of Engineering, Department of Industrial and Systems Engineering, Greensboro, NC 27411. Offers industrial and systems engineering (PhD); industrial engineering (MSIE). *Program availability:* Part-time. *Degree requirements:* For master's, thesis, project; for doctorate, thesis/dissertation. *Entrance requirements:* For master's, GRE General Test (recommended); for doctorate, GRE General Test, degree in engineering, BS in industrial engineering from ABET-accredited program with minimum cumulative credit point average of 3.7 or MS in discipline related to industrial engineering from college or university recognized by a regional or general accrediting agency with minimum cumulative GPA of 3.3. Additional exam requirements/recommendations for international students: Required—TOEFL (minimum score 550 paper-based; 79 iBT). *Faculty research:* Human-machine systems engineering, management systems engineering, operations research and systems analysis, production systems engineering.

North Carolina State University, Graduate School, College of Engineering, Edward P. Fitts Department of Industrial and Systems Engineering, Raleigh, NC 27695. Offers industrial engineering (MIE, MS, PhD). PhD offered jointly with North Carolina Agricultural and Technical State University and The University of North Carolina at Charlotte. *Program availability:* Part-time. Terminal master's awarded for partial completion of doctoral program. *Entrance requirements:* For master's, GRE General Test, minimum GPA of 3.0; for doctorate, GRE General Test. Additional exam requirements/recommendations for international students: Required—TOEFL. Electronic applications accepted.

North Dakota State University, College of Graduate and Interdisciplinary Studies, College of Engineering, Department of Industrial and Manufacturing Engineering, Fargo, ND 58102. Offers industrial and manufacturing engineering (MS, PhD); manufacturing engineering (MS). *Program availability:* Part-time. *Degree requirements:* For doctorate, comprehensive exam, thesis/dissertation. *Entrance requirements:* For master's, GRE General Test, bachelor's degree in engineering; for doctorate, GRE General Test, master's degree in engineering. Additional exam requirements/recommendations for international students: Required—TOEFL (minimum score 550 paper-based; 79 iBT), TWE (minimum score 4). Electronic applications accepted. *Faculty research:* Electronics manufacturing, quality engineering, manufacturing process science, healthcare, lean manufacturing.

Northeastern University, College of Engineering, Boston, MA 02115-5096. Offers bioengineering (MS, PhD); chemical engineering (MS, PhD); civil engineering (MS, PhD); computer engineering (PhD); computer systems engineering (MS); electrical and computer engineering (MS); electrical and computer engineering leadership (MS); electrical engineering (PhD); energy systems (MS); engineering and public policy (MS); engineering management (MS, Certificate); environmental engineering (MS); industrial engineering (MS, PhD); information assurance (PhD); information systems (MS); interdisciplinary engineering (PhD); mechanical engineering (PhD); operations research (MS); telecommunication systems management (MS). *Program availability:* Part-time, online learning. Electronic applications accepted. *Expenses:* Contact institution.

Northern Illinois University, Graduate School, College of Engineering and Engineering Technology, Department of Industrial Engineering, De Kalb, IL 60115-2854. Offers MS. *Program availability:* Part-time. *Faculty:* 4 full-time (1 woman), 1 part-time/adjunct (0 women). *Students:* 75 full-time (17 women), 50 part-time (9 women); includes 14 minority (4 Black or African American, non-Hispanic/Latino; 4 Asian, non-Hispanic/Latino; 4 Hispanic/Latino; 2 Two or more races, non-Hispanic/Latino), 94 international. Average age 27. 170 applicants, 72% accepted, 33 enrolled. In 2018, 72 master's awarded. *Degree requirements:* For master's, comprehensive exam, thesis optional. *Entrance requirements:* For master's, GRE General Test, minimum GPA of 2.75. Additional exam requirements/recommendations for international students: Required—TOEFL (minimum score 550 paper-based). *Application deadline:* For fall admission, 6/1 for domestic students, 5/1 for international students; for spring admission, 11/1 for domestic students, 10/1 for international students. Applications are processed on a rolling basis. Application fee: $40. Electronic applications accepted. *Financial support:* In 2018–19, 9 research assistantships, 29 teaching assistantships were awarded; fellowships, Federal Work-Study, scholarships/grants, tuition waivers (full), and staff assistantships also available. Support available to part-time students. Financial award applicants required to submit FAFSA. *Faculty research:* Assembly robots, engineering ethics, quality cost models, data mining. *Unit head:* Dr. Purushothaman Damodaran, Chair, 815-753-1349, Fax: 815-753-0823. *Application contact:* Graduate School Office, 815-753-0395, E-mail: gradsch@niu.edu.
Website: http://www.niu.edu/isye

Northwestern University, McCormick School of Engineering and Applied Science, Department of Industrial Engineering and Management Sciences, Evanston, IL 60208. Offers analytics (MS); engineering management (MEM); industrial engineering and management science (MS, PhD). MS and PhD admissions and degrees offered through The Graduate School. Terminal master's awarded for partial completion of doctoral program. *Degree requirements:* For master's, comprehensive exam; for doctorate, comprehensive exam, thesis/dissertation. *Entrance requirements:* For master's and doctorate, GRE General Test. Additional exam requirements/recommendations for international students: Required—TOEFL (minimum score 577 paper-based; 90 iBT), IELTS (minimum score 7). Electronic applications accepted. *Faculty research:* Financial engineering, healthcare engineering, humanitarian systems, optimization, organization behavior and technology management, production and logistics, social and organizational networks, statistics for enterprise engineering, stochastic modeling and simulation.

The Ohio State University, Graduate School, College of Engineering, Department of Integrated Systems Engineering, Columbus, OH 43210. Offers industrial and systems engineering (MS, PhD). *Faculty:* 19. *Students:* 91 (27 women). Average age 28. In 2018, 30 master's, 7 doctorates awarded. *Entrance requirements:* For master's and doctorate, GRE General Test (desired minimum scores: Quantitative 166, Verbal 153, Analytical Writing 4.5). Additional exam requirements/recommendations for international students: Required—TOEFL (minimum score 550 paper-based; 79 iBT), Michigan English Language Assessment Battery (minimum score 82); Recommended—IELTS (minimum score 7). *Application deadline:* For fall admission, 12/13 priority date for domestic students, 11/30 priority date for international students; for spring admission, 12/4 for domestic students, 10/1 for international students; for summer admission, 2/1 for domestic and international students. Applications are processed on a rolling basis. Application fee: $60 ($70 for international students). Electronic applications accepted. *Financial support:* Fellowships with tuition reimbursements, research assistantships with tuition reimbursements, teaching assistantships with tuition reimbursements, career-related internships or fieldwork, Federal Work-Study, institutionally sponsored

loans, and unspecified assistantships available. Support available to part-time students. *Unit head:* Dr. Farhang Pourboghrat, Chair, 614-292-6239, E-mail: pourboghrat.2@osu.edu. *Application contact:* Dr. Jerald Brevik, Graduate Studies Chair, 614-292-0177, Fax: 614-292-7852, E-mail: brevik.1@osu.edu.
Website: http://ise.osu.edu/

Ohio University, Graduate College, Russ College of Engineering and Technology, Department of Industrial and Systems Engineering, Athens, OH 45701-2979. Offers M Eng Mgt, MS. *Program availability:* Part-time, evening/weekend. *Degree requirements:* For master's, comprehensive exam (for some programs), thesis optional, research project. *Entrance requirements:* For master's, GRE General Test. Additional exam requirements/recommendations for international students: Required—TOEFL (minimum score 550 paper-based; 80 iBT) or IELTS (minimum score 6.5). Electronic applications accepted. *Faculty research:* Software systems integration, human factors and ergonomics.

Ohio University, Graduate College, Russ College of Engineering and Technology, Program in Mechanical and Systems Engineering, Athens, OH 45701-2979. Offers industrial and systems engineering (MS); mechanical and systems engineering (PhD). *Degree requirements:* For doctorate, comprehensive exam, thesis/dissertation. *Entrance requirements:* For doctorate, GRE General Test, MS in engineering or related field. Additional exam requirements/recommendations for international students: Required—TOEFL (minimum score 550 paper-based; 80 iBT) or IELTS (minimum score 6.5). Electronic applications accepted. *Faculty research:* Material processing, expert systems, environmental geotechnical manufacturing, thermal systems, robotics.

Oklahoma State University, College of Engineering, Architecture and Technology, School of Industrial Engineering and Management, Stillwater, OK 74078. Offers MS, PhD. *Program availability:* Online learning. *Faculty:* 13 full-time (4 women), 1 part-time/adjunct (0 women). *Students:* 22 full-time (5 women), 107 part-time (17 women); includes 23 minority (5 Black or African American, non-Hispanic/Latino; 1 American Indian or Alaska Native, non-Hispanic/Latino; 5 Asian, non-Hispanic/Latino; 6 Hispanic/Latino; 1 Native Hawaiian or other Pacific Islander, non-Hispanic/Latino; 5 Two or more races, non-Hispanic/Latino), 34 international. Average age 30. 247 applicants, 21% accepted, 44 enrolled. In 2018, 101 master's, 6 doctorates awarded. *Entrance requirements:* For master's and doctorate, GRE or GMAT. Additional exam requirements/recommendations for international students: Required—TOEFL (minimum score 550 paper-based; 79 iBT). *Application deadline:* For fall admission, 3/1 priority date for international students; for spring admission, 8/1 priority date for international students. Applications are processed on a rolling basis. Application fee: $40 ($75 for international students). Electronic applications accepted. *Expenses: Tuition, area resident:* Full-time $4148. Tuition, state resident: full-time $4148. Tuition, nonresident: full-time $10,517. *International tuition:* $10,517 full-time. *Required fees:* $4394; $2929 per credit hour. Tuition and fees vary according to course load and program. *Financial support:* Research assistantships, teaching assistantships, career-related internships or fieldwork, Federal Work-Study, scholarships/grants, health care benefits, tuition waivers (partial), and unspecified assistantships available. Support available to part-time students. Financial award application deadline: 3/1; financial award applicants required to submit FAFSA. *Unit head:* Dr. Sunderesh Heragu, Head, 405-744-6055, Fax: 405-744-4654, E-mail: sunderesh.heragu@okstate.edu. *Application contact:* Dr. Baski Balasundaram, Director of Graduate Program, 405-744-6055, Fax: 405-744-4654, E-mail: baski@okstate.edu.
Website: http://iem.okstate.edu/

Oregon State University, College of Engineering, Program in Industrial Engineering, Corvallis, OR 97331. Offers advanced manufacturing (M Eng, MS, PhD); engineering management (M Eng); human systems engineering (M Eng, MS, PhD); information systems engineering (M Eng, MS, PhD); manufacturing systems engineering (M Eng, MS, PhD). *Program availability:* 100% online. *Entrance requirements:* For master's and doctorate, GRE. Additional exam requirements/recommendations for international students: Required—TOEFL (minimum score 80 iBT), IELTS (minimum score 6.5). *Expenses:* Contact institution.

Penn State University Park, Graduate School, College of Engineering, Department of Industrial and Manufacturing Engineering, University Park, PA 16802. Offers industrial engineering (MS, PhD).

Purdue University, College of Engineering, School of Industrial Engineering, West Lafayette, IN 47907-2023. Offers MS, MSIE, PhD. *Program availability:* Part-time, online learning. Terminal master's awarded for partial completion of doctoral program. *Degree requirements:* For master's, thesis optional; for doctorate, thesis/dissertation. *Entrance requirements:* For master's and doctorate, GRE General Test, minimum GPA of 3.2. Electronic applications accepted. *Faculty research:* Cognition and decision making, next generation products and services, computational industrial engineering, complex systems and networks.

Purdue University Fort Wayne, College of Engineering, Technology, and Computer Science, Program in Technology, Fort Wayne, IN 46805-1499. Offers facilities/construction management (MS); industrial technology/manufacturing (MS); information technology/advanced computer applications (MS). *Program availability:* Part-time. *Entrance requirements:* For master's, minimum GPA of 3.0. Additional exam requirements/recommendations for international students: Required—TOEFL (minimum score 550 paper-based; 79 iBT), TWE. Electronic applications accepted.

Rensselaer Polytechnic Institute, Graduate School, School of Engineering, Program in Decision Sciences and Engineering Systems, Troy, NY 12180-3590. Offers PhD. *Faculty:* 3 full-time (2 women). *Students:* 12 full-time (3 women), 3 part-time (0 women), 11 international. Average age 30. 39 applicants, 21% accepted, 3 enrolled. In 2018, 3 doctorates awarded. Terminal master's awarded for partial completion of doctoral program. *Degree requirements:* For doctorate, thesis/dissertation. *Entrance requirements:* For doctorate, GRE. Additional exam requirements/recommendations for international students: Required—TOEFL (minimum score 570 paper-based; 88 iBT), IELTS (minimum score 6.5), PTE (minimum score 60). *Application deadline:* For fall admission, 1/1 priority date for domestic students, 1/1 for international students. Applications are processed on a rolling basis. Application fee: $75. Electronic applications accepted. *Financial support:* In 2018–19, research assistantships (averaging $23,000 per year), teaching assistantships (averaging $23,000 per year) were awarded; fellowships also available. Financial award application deadline: 1/1. *Faculty research:* Agent-based modeling, computational optimization, data mining, decision analysis, decision technologies, human factors engineering, logistics, network optimization and analysis, scheduling, simulation modeling, statistical analysis, stochastic programming. *Total annual research expenditures:* $231,336. *Unit head:* Dr. Thomas Sharkey, Graduate Program Director, 518-276-2958, E-mail: sharkt@rpi.edu. *Application contact:* Jarron Decker, Director of Graduate Admissions, 518-276-6216, Fax: 518-276-4072, E-mail: gradadmissions@rpi.edu.
Website: http://ise.rpi.edu/

Rensselaer Polytechnic Institute, Graduate School, School of Engineering, Program in Industrial and Management Engineering, Troy, NY 12180-3590. Offers M Eng, MS. *Program availability:* Part-time. *Faculty:* 8 full-time (0 women). *Students:* 3 full-time (2 women), 1 (woman) part-time; includes 1 minority (Black or African American, non-Hispanic/Latino), 2 international. Average age 25. 32 applicants, 31% accepted, 3 enrolled. In 2018, 5 master's awarded. *Degree requirements:* For master's, thesis (for some programs). *Entrance requirements:* For master's, GRE. Additional exam requirements/recommendations for international students: Required—TOEFL (minimum score 570 paper-based; 88 iBT), IELTS (minimum score 6.5), PTE (minimum score 60). *Application deadline:* For fall admission, 1/1 priority date for domestic and international students; for spring admission, 8/15 priority date for domestic and international students. Applications are processed on a rolling basis. Application fee: $75. Electronic applications accepted. *Financial support:* In 2018–19, teaching assistantships (averaging $23,000 per year) were awarded. Financial award application deadline: 1/1. *Faculty research:* Bayesian decision systems; database systems; decision technologies for adaptive supply chains; maritime safety systems; materials flow logistics; network optimization, simulated based optimization; social networks/data mining, soft computing/computational optimization; statistical forecasting/exploratory data analysis; stochastic processes in supply chains. *Total annual research expenditures:* $275,429. *Unit head:* Dr. Thomas Sharkey, Graduate Program Director, 518-276-2958, E-mail: sharkt@rpi.edu. *Application contact:* Jarron Decker, Director of Graduate Admissions, 518-276-6216, Fax: 518-276-4072, E-mail: gradadmissions@rpi.edu.
Website: http://ise.rpi.edu/

Rochester Institute of Technology, Graduate Enrollment Services, Kate Gleason College of Engineering, Industrial and Systems Engineering Department, ME Program in Industrial and Systems Engineering, Rochester, NY 14623-5603. Offers ME. *Program availability:* Part-time. *Students:* 5 full-time (1 woman), 3 part-time (2 women), 1 international. Average age 24. 35 applicants, 17% accepted, 2 enrolled. In 2018, 9 master's awarded. *Degree requirements:* For master's, thesis or alternative, capstone project. *Entrance requirements:* For master's, GRE, minimum GPA of 3.0 (recommended), one-page statement of purpose, two letters of recommendation. Additional exam requirements/recommendations for international students: Required—TOEFL (minimum score 580 paper-based; 90 iBT), IELTS (minimum score 6), PTE (minimum score 58). *Application deadline:* For fall admission, 2/15 priority date for domestic and international students; for spring admission, 12/15 priority date for domestic and international students. Applications are processed on a rolling basis. Application fee: $65. Electronic applications accepted. *Financial support:* In 2018–19, 11 students received support. Research assistantships with partial tuition reimbursements available, teaching assistantships with partial tuition reimbursements available, career-related internships or fieldwork, scholarships/grants, and unspecified assistantships available. Support available to part-time students. Financial award applicants required to submit FAFSA. *Faculty research:* Advanced manufacturing, engineering education, ergonomics and human factors, healthcare delivery systems, operations research and simulation, systems engineering, production and logistics, sustainable engineering. *Unit head:* Michael Kuhl, Graduate Program Director, 585-475-2134, E-mail: mekeie@rit.edu. *Application contact:* Diane Ellison, Senior Associate Vice President, Graduate Enrollment Services, 585-475-2229, Fax: 585-475-7164, E-mail: gradinfo@rit.edu.
Website: https://www.rit.edu/study/industrial-and-systems-engineering-me

Rochester Institute of Technology, Graduate Enrollment Services, Kate Gleason College of Engineering, Industrial and Systems Engineering Department, MS Program in Industrial and Systems Engineering, Rochester, NY 14623-5603. Offers MS. *Program availability:* Part-time. *Students:* 14 full-time, 7 part-time (1 woman), 16 international. Average age 25. 134 applicants, 35% accepted, 6 enrolled. In 2018, 10 master's awarded. *Degree requirements:* For master's, thesis. *Entrance requirements:* For master's, GRE, minimum GPA of 3.0 (recommended), statement of purpose, two letters of recommendation. Additional exam requirements/recommendations for international students: Required—TOEFL (minimum score 580 paper-based; 90 iBT), IELTS (minimum score 6.5), PTE (minimum score 58). *Application deadline:* For fall admission, 2/15 priority date for domestic and international students; for spring admission, 12/15 priority date for domestic and international students. Applications are processed on a rolling basis. Application fee: $65. Electronic applications accepted. *Financial support:* In 2018–19, 17 students received support. Research assistantships with partial tuition reimbursements available, teaching assistantships with partial tuition reimbursements available, career-related internships or fieldwork, scholarships/grants, and unspecified assistantships available. Support available to part-time students. Financial award applicants required to submit FAFSA. *Faculty research:* Advanced manufacturing; health care systems engineering, data analytics, operations research, and simulation; supply chain and logistics systems; biomechanics, ergonomics, safety, and rehabilitation. *Unit head:* Michael Kuhl, Graduate Program Director, 585-475-2134, E-mail: mekeie@rit.edu. *Application contact:* Diane Ellison, Senior Associate Vice President, Graduate Enrollment Services, 585-475-2229, Fax: 585-475-7164, E-mail: gradinfo@rit.edu.
Website: https://www.rit.edu/study/industrial-and-systems-engineering-ms

Rutgers University–New Brunswick, Graduate School-New Brunswick, Department of Industrial and Systems Engineering, Piscataway, NJ 08854-8097. Offers industrial and systems engineering (MS, PhD); information technology (MS); manufacturing systems engineering (MS); quality and reliability engineering (MS). *Program availability:* Part-time, evening/weekend. Terminal master's awarded for partial completion of doctoral program. *Degree requirements:* For master's, thesis or alternative, seminar; for doctorate, comprehensive exam, thesis/dissertation. *Entrance requirements:* For master's and doctorate, GRE General Test. Additional exam requirements/recommendations for international students: Required—TOEFL. *Faculty research:* Production and manufacturing systems, quality and reliability engineering, systems engineering and aviation safety.

St. Mary's University, School of Science, Engineering and Technology, Program in Industrial Engineering, San Antonio, TX 78228. Offers MS. *Program availability:* Part-time, evening/weekend. *Students:* 6 full-time (0 women), 11 part-time (2 women); includes 3 minority (1 Asian, non-Hispanic/Latino; 2 Hispanic/Latino), 13 international. Average age 26. 20 applicants, 65% accepted, 1 enrolled. In 2018, 5 master's awarded. *Degree requirements:* For master's, project or thesis. *Entrance requirements:* For master's, GRE (minimum quantitative score of 148), BS in computer engineering, electrical engineering, or closely-related discipline; minimum GPA of 3.0; written statement of purpose indicating applicant's interests and objectives; two letters of recommendation. Additional exam requirements/recommendations for international students: Required—TOEFL (minimum score 550 paper-based; 80 iBT), IELTS (minimum score 6). *Application deadline:* For fall admission, 7/1 for domestic students; for spring admission, 11/15 for domestic students; for summer admission, 4/1 for domestic students. Applications are processed on a rolling basis. Application fee: $0. Electronic applications accepted. *Expenses: Tuition:* Full-time $16,830; part-time $935 per credit hour. *Required fees:* $1055. Tuition and fees vary according to program. *Financial support:* Career-related internships or fieldwork, Federal Work-Study, institutionally sponsored loans, scholarships/grants, and health care benefits available. Financial award application deadline: 3/31; financial award applicants required to submit FAFSA. *Faculty research:* Supply chain, lean production, engineering ethics, manufacturing engineering, human factors and ergonomics. *Unit head:* Dr. Ozgur Aktunc, Graduate Program Director, 210-431-2052, E-mail: oaktunc@stmarytx.edu. *Application contact:* Dr. Ozgur Aktunc, Graduate Program Director, 210-431-2052, E-mail: oaktunc@stmarytx.edu.
Website: https://www.stmarytx.edu/academics/programs/master-industrial-engineering/

San Jose State University, Program in Industrial and Systems Engineering, San Jose, CA 95192-0001. Offers MS. *Program availability:* Part-time. *Degree requirements:* For master's, comprehensive exam. Electronic applications accepted.

Southern Illinois University Edwardsville, Graduate School, School of Engineering, Department of Mechanical and Industrial Engineering, Program in Industrial Engineering, Edwardsville, IL 62026. Offers MS. *Program availability:* Part-time, evening/weekend. *Degree requirements:* For master's, thesis (for some programs), final exam. *Entrance requirements:* For master's, GRE (for applicants whose degree is from non-ABET accredited institution). Additional exam requirements/recommendations for international students: Required—TOEFL (minimum score 550 paper-based; 79 iBT), IELTS (minimum score 6.5). Electronic applications accepted.

Stanford University, School of Engineering, Department of Management Science and Engineering, Stanford, CA 94305-2004. Offers MS, PhD. *Expenses: Tuition:* Full-time $50,703; part-time $32,970 per year. *Required fees:* $651.
Website: http://www.stanford.edu/dept/MSandE/

Texas A&M University, College of Engineering, Department of Industrial and Systems Engineering, College Station, TX 77843. Offers engineering systems management (MS); industrial engineering (M Eng, MS, PhD). *Program availability:* Part-time, online learning. *Faculty:* 38. *Students:* 268 full-time (58 women), 96 part-time (23 women); includes 28 minority (5 Black or African American, non-Hispanic/Latino; 9 Asian, non-Hispanic/Latino; 13 Hispanic/Latino; 1 Two or more races, non-Hispanic/Latino), 288 international. Average age 26. 677 applicants, 44% accepted, 137 enrolled. In 2018, 105 master's, 6 doctorates awarded. *Degree requirements:* For master's, comprehensive exam (for some programs), thesis optional; for doctorate, comprehensive exam, thesis/dissertation. *Entrance requirements:* For master's and doctorate, GRE General Test. Additional exam requirements/recommendations for international students: Required—TOEFL (minimum score 550 paper-based; 80 iBT), IELTS (minimum score 6), PTE (minimum score 53). *Application deadline:* For fall admission, 6/1 priority date for domestic students, 3/1 priority date for international students; for spring admission, 8/1 priority date for domestic and international students. Applications are processed on a rolling basis. Application fee: $50 ($90 for international students). Electronic applications accepted. *Expenses:* Contact institution. *Financial support:* In 2018–19, 259 students received support, including 7 fellowships with tuition reimbursements available (averaging $22,319 per year), 89 research assistantships with tuition reimbursements available (averaging $11,980 per year), 51 teaching assistantships with tuition reimbursements available (averaging $13,217 per year); career-related internships or fieldwork, institutionally sponsored loans, scholarships/grants, traineeships, health care benefits, tuition waivers (full and partial), and unspecified assistantships also available. Support available to part-time students. Financial award application deadline: 3/15; financial award applicants required to submit FAFSA. *Faculty research:* Manufacturing systems, computer integration, operations research, logistics, simulation. *Unit head:* Dr. Cesar O. Malave, Head, 979-845-5535, Fax: 979-458-4299, E-mail: malave@tamu.edu. *Application contact:* Erin Roady, Graduate Program Coordinator, 979-845-5536, Fax: 979-458-4299, E-mail: erinroady@tamu.edu.
Website: http://engineering.tamu.edu/industrial

Texas A&M University–Kingsville, College of Graduate Studies, Frank H. Dotterweich College of Engineering, Department of Mechanical and Industrial Engineering, Program in Industrial Engineering, Kingsville, TX 78363. Offers ME, MS. *Degree requirements:* For master's, variable foreign language requirement, comprehensive exam, thesis (for some programs). *Entrance requirements:* For master's, GRE (minimum overall old score of 900-1000 depending on GPA), MAT, GMAT. Additional exam requirements/recommendations for international students: Required—TOEFL (minimum score 550 paper-based; 79 iBT). Electronic applications accepted.

Texas Southern University, School of Science and Technology, Department of Industrial Technology, Houston, TX 77004-4584. Offers MS. *Degree requirements:* For master's, comprehensive exam. *Entrance requirements:* For master's, GRE General Test, minimum GPA of 2.5. Additional exam requirements/recommendations for international students: Required—TOEFL. Electronic applications accepted.

Texas State University, The Graduate College, College of Science and Engineering, Program in Engineering, San Marcos, TX 78666. Offers civil engineering (MS); electrical engineering (MS); industrial engineering (MS); mechanical and manufacturing engineering (MS). *Program availability:* Part-time. *Faculty:* 15 full-time (2 women). *Students:* 46 full-time (14 women), 41 part-time (13 women); includes 11 minority (3 Asian, non-Hispanic/Latino; 7 Hispanic/Latino; 1 Two or more races, non-Hispanic/Latino), 67 international. Average age 27. 105 applicants, 64% accepted, 31 enrolled. In 2018, 13 master's awarded. *Degree requirements:* For master's, comprehensive exam, thesis (for some programs), thesis or research project. *Entrance requirements:* For master's, official GRE (general test only) required with competitive scores in the verbal reasoning and quantitative reasoning sections, baccalaureate degree from regionally-accredited university in engineering, computer science, physics, technology, or closely-related field with minimum GPA of 3.0 on last 60 undergraduate semester hours; resume or curriculum vitae; 2 letters of recommendation; statement of purpose conveying research interest and professional aspirations. Additional exam requirements/recommendations for international students: Required—TOEFL (minimum score 550 paper-based; 78 iBT), IELTS (minimum score 6.5). *Application deadline:* For fall admission, 2/15 priority date for domestic students, 2/1 priority date for international students. Application fee: $55 ($90 for international students). Electronic applications accepted. *Expenses: Tuition,* state resident: full-time $8102; part-time $4051 per semester. Tuition, nonresident: full-time $18,229; part-time $9115 per semester. *International tuition:* $18,229 full-time. *Required fees:* $2116; $120 per credit hour. Tuition and fees vary according to course load. *Financial support:* In 2018–19, 52 students received support, including 14 research assistantships (averaging $12,742 per year), 34 teaching assistantships (averaging $12,483 per year); Federal Work-Study, institutionally sponsored loans, scholarships/grants, health care benefits, and unspecified assistantships also available. Support available to part-time students. Financial award application deadline: 1/15; financial award applicants required to submit FAFSA. *Faculty research:* Computer Architecture & Digital Image Processing; Industrial robotics on a mobile platform; supply chain management optimization modeling and algorithms; Modeling and analysis of manufacturing systems especially semiconductor manufacturing; smart grids for big data analytics and demand response; Digital Signal/Image/Speach Processing & Data Compression; Health care systems engineering and anaylsis of patient flow. *Total annual research expenditures:* $920,229. *Unit head:* Dr. Vishu Viswanathan, Graduate Advisor, 512-245-1826, Fax: 512-245-8365, E-mail: v_v42@txstate.edu. *Application contact:* Dr. Andrea Golato, Dean of Graduate School, 512-245-2581, Fax: 512-245-8365, E-mail: gradcollege@txstate.edu.
Website: http://www.engineering.txstate.edu/Programs/Graduate.html

Universidad de las Américas Puebla, Division of Graduate Studies, School of Engineering, Program in Industrial Engineering, Puebla, Mexico. Offers industrial engineering (MS); production management (M Adm). *Program availability:* Part-time, evening/weekend. *Degree requirements:* For master's, one foreign language, thesis. *Faculty research:* Textile industry, quality control.

Université de Moncton, Faculty of Engineering, Program in Industrial Engineering, Moncton, NB E1A 3E9, Canada. Offers M Sc A. *Degree requirements:* For master's, thesis, proficiency in French. *Faculty research:* Production systems, optimization, simulation and expert systems, modeling and warehousing systems, quality control.

Université du Québec à Trois-Rivières, Graduate Programs, Program in Industrial Engineering, Trois-Rivières, QC G9A 5H7, Canada. Offers M Sc, DESS. *Entrance requirements:* For degree, appropriate bachelor's degree, proficiency in French. *Faculty research:* Production.

Université Laval, Faculty of Sciences and Engineering, Programs in Industrial Engineering, Québec, QC G1K 7P4, Canada. Offers Diploma. *Program availability:* Part-time. *Entrance requirements:* For degree, knowledge of French. Electronic applications accepted.

University at Buffalo, the State University of New York, Graduate School, School of Engineering and Applied Sciences, Department of Industrial and Systems Engineering, Buffalo, NY 14260. Offers advanced manufacturing (Certificate); industrial engineering (ME, MS, PhD), including data fusion (ME), engineering management (ME). *Program availability:* Part-time, online learning. Terminal master's awarded for partial completion of doctoral program. *Degree requirements:* For master's, comprehensive exam (for some programs), thesis or alternative; for doctorate, thesis/dissertation. *Entrance requirements:* For master's and doctorate, GRE General Test. Additional exam requirements/recommendations for international students: Required—TOEFL (minimum score 550 paper-based; 79 iBT). Electronic applications accepted. *Faculty research:* Advanced manufacturing and sustainable manufacturing design, health and health systems, security and defense, transportation and logistics.

The University of Alabama in Huntsville, School of Graduate Studies, College of Engineering, Department of Industrial and Systems Engineering and Engineering Management, Huntsville, AL 35899. Offers engineering management (MSE, PhD); industrial engineering (MSE, PhD); operations research (MSOR); systems engineering (MSE, PhD). *Program availability:* Part-time. *Faculty:* 10 full-time (2 women), 1 part-time/adjunct. *Students:* 25 full-time (10 women), 62 part-time (20 women); includes 16 minority (4 Black or African American, non-Hispanic/Latino; 3 American Indian or Alaska Native, non-Hispanic/Latino; 5 Asian, non-Hispanic/Latino; 2 Hispanic/Latino; 2 Two or more races, non-Hispanic/Latino), 17 international. Average age 33. 78 applicants, 37% accepted, 13 enrolled. In 2018, 25 master's, 1 doctorate awarded. *Degree requirements:* For master's, comprehensive exam, thesis or alternative, oral and written exams; for doctorate, comprehensive exam, thesis/dissertation, oral and written exams. *Entrance requirements:* For master's and doctorate, GRE General Test, minimum GPA of 3.0. Additional exam requirements/recommendations for international students: Required—TOEFL (minimum score 500 paper-based; 80 iBT), IELTS (minimum score 6.5). *Application deadline:* For fall admission, 7/15 priority date for domestic students, 4/1 priority date for international students; for spring admission, 11/30 priority date for domestic students, 9/1 priority date for international students. Applications are processed on a rolling basis. Application fee: $50. Electronic applications accepted. *Expenses: Tuition,* area resident: Full-time $10,632; part-time $412 per credit hour. Tuition, state resident: full-time $10,632. Tuition, nonresident: full-time $23,604; part-time $412 per credit hour. *Required fees:* $582; $582. Tuition and fees vary according to course load and program. *Financial support:* In 2018–19, 14 students received support, including 8 research assistantships with full tuition reimbursements available (averaging $7,898 per year), 6 teaching assistantships with full tuition reimbursements available (averaging $5,750 per year); career-related internships or fieldwork, Federal Work-Study, institutionally sponsored loans, scholarships/grants, health care benefits, and unspecified assistantships also available. Support available to part-time students. Financial award application deadline: 4/1; financial award applicants required to submit FAFSA. *Faculty research:* Systems engineering process, electronic manufacturing, heuristic manufacturing, teams and team development. *Unit head:* Dr. James J. Swain, Chair, 256-824-6749, Fax: 256-824-6733, E-mail: james.swain@uah.edu. *Application contact:* Kim Gray, Graduate Studies Admissions Coordinator, 256-824-6002, Fax: 256-824-6405, E-mail: deangrad@uah.edu.
Website: http://www.uah.edu/eng/departments/iseem/

The University of Arizona, College of Engineering, Department of Systems and Industrial Engineering, Tucson, AZ 85721. Offers engineering management (Graduate Certificate); industrial engineering (MS); systems and industrial engineering (MS, PhD); systems engineering (MS, PhD, Graduate Certificate). *Program availability:* Part-time, online learning. *Degree requirements:* For doctorate, thesis/dissertation. *Entrance requirements:* For master's, GRE General Test (minimum score: 500 Verbal, 700 Quantitative), 3 letters of recommendation; for doctorate, GRE General Test (minimum score: 500 Verbal, 700 Quantitative), minimum GPA of 3.5, 3 letters of recommendation, letter of intent. Additional exam requirements/recommendations for international students: Required—TOEFL (minimum score 575 paper-based; 80 iBT). Electronic applications accepted. *Faculty research:* Optimization, systems theory, logistics, transportation, embedded systems.

University of Arkansas, Graduate School, College of Engineering, Department of Industrial Engineering, Program in Industrial Engineering, Fayetteville, AR 72701. Offers MSE, MSIE, PhD. *Students:* 61 applicants, 59% accepted. In 2018, 16 master's, 9 doctorates awarded. *Degree requirements:* For master's, thesis optional; for doctorate, one foreign language, thesis/dissertation. *Application deadline:* For fall admission, 8/1 for domestic students, 4/1 for international students; for spring admission, 12/1 for domestic students, 10/1 for international students; for summer admission, 4/15 for domestic students, 3/1 for international students. Applications are processed on a rolling basis. Application fee: $60. Electronic applications accepted. *Financial support:* In 2018–19, 32 research assistantships were awarded; fellowships, teaching assistantships, career-related internships or fieldwork, and Federal Work-Study also available. Support available to part-time students. Financial award application deadline: 4/1; financial award applicants required to submit FAFSA. *Unit head:* Dr. Edward Pohl, Department Head, 479-575-6029, E-mail: epohl@uark.edu. *Application contact:* Dr. Justin Chimka, Graduate Coordinator, 479-575-7392, E-mail: jchimka@uark.edu.
Website: https://industrial-engineering.uark.edu/

University of California, Berkeley, Graduate Division, College of Engineering, Department of Industrial Engineering and Operations Research, Berkeley, CA 94720. Offers decision analytics (M Eng); industrial engineering and operations research (M Eng, MS, PhD). *Program availability:* Part-time, evening/weekend. Terminal master's awarded for partial completion of doctoral program. *Degree requirements:* For master's, comprehensive exam (for some programs), thesis (for some programs), comprehensive exam or thesis (MS); for doctorate, thesis/dissertation, qualifying exam. *Entrance requirements:* For master's and doctorate, GRE General Test, minimum GPA of 3.0, 3 letters of recommendation. Additional exam requirements/recommendations for international students: Required—TOEFL (minimum score 570 paper-based; 90 iBT). Electronic applications accepted. *Faculty research:* Mathematical programming, robotics and manufacturing, linear and nonlinear optimization, production planning and scheduling, queuing theory.

University of Central Florida, College of Engineering and Computer Science, Department of Industrial Engineering and Management Systems, Orlando, FL 32816.

Industrial/Management Engineering

Offers MS, MSEM, MSIE, PhD, Certificate. *Program availability:* Part-time, evening/weekend. *Students:* 120 full-time (41 women), 261 part-time (96 women); includes 143 minority (49 Black or African American, non-Hispanic/Latino; 1 American Indian or Alaska Native, non-Hispanic/Latino; 20 Asian, non-Hispanic/Latino; 69 Hispanic/Latino; 4 Two or more races, non-Hispanic/Latino; 70 international. Average age 32. 258 applicants, 71% accepted, 117 enrolled. In 2018, 117 master's, 16 doctorates, 18 other advanced degrees awarded. *Degree requirements:* For master's, thesis or alternative; for doctorate, thesis/dissertation, departmental qualifying exam, candidacy exam. *Entrance requirements:* For master's, minimum GPA of 3.0 in last 60 hours of course work, letters of recommendation, goal statement, resume; for doctorate, GRE, minimum GPA of 3.0 in last 60 hours of course work, letters of recommendation, goal statement, resume. Additional exam requirements/recommendations for international students: Required—TOEFL. *Application deadline:* For fall admission, 7/15 for domestic students; for spring admission, 12/1 for domestic students. Application fee: $30. Electronic applications accepted. *Financial support:* In 2018–19, 51 students received support, including 16 fellowships with partial tuition reimbursements available (averaging $4,709 per year), 40 research assistantships with partial tuition reimbursements available (averaging $12,388 per year), 20 teaching assistantships with partial tuition reimbursements available (averaging $10,695 per year); career-related internships or fieldwork, Federal Work-Study, institutionally sponsored loans, health care benefits, tuition waivers (partial), and unspecified assistantships also available. Financial award application deadline: 3/1; financial award applicants required to submit FAFSA. *Unit head:* Dr. Waldemar Karwowski, Chair, 407-823-0042, E-mail: wkar@ucf.edu. *Application contact:* Associate Director, Graduate Admissions, 407-823-2766, Fax: 407-823-6442, E-mail: gradadmissions@ucf.edu.
Website: http://iems.ucf.edu/

University of Cincinnati, Graduate School, College of Engineering and Applied Science, Department of Mechanical and Materials Engineering, Cincinnati, OH 45221. Offers industrial engineering (PhD); mechanical engineering (MS, PhD); nuclear engineering (PhD); MBA/MS. *Program availability:* Part-time, evening/weekend. Terminal master's awarded for partial completion of doctoral program. *Degree requirements:* For doctorate, thesis/dissertation. *Entrance requirements:* For master's and doctorate, GRE General Test. Additional exam requirements/recommendations for international students: Required—TOEFL (minimum score 575 paper-based). Electronic applications accepted.

University of Florida, Graduate School, Herbert Wertheim College of Engineering, Department of Industrial and Systems Engineering, Gainesville, FL 32611. Offers industrial and systems engineering (ME, MS, PhD, Engr); quantitative finance (PhD). *Program availability:* Part-time, evening/weekend, online learning. Terminal master's awarded for partial completion of doctoral program. *Degree requirements:* For master's, thesis (for some programs); for doctorate, comprehensive exam (for some programs), thesis/dissertation (for some programs). *Entrance requirements:* For master's and doctorate, minimum GPA of 3.0; for Engr, GRE General Test. Additional exam requirements/recommendations for international students: Required—TOEFL (minimum score 550 paper-based; 80 iBT), IELTS (minimum score 6). Electronic applications accepted. *Faculty research:* Operations research; financial engineering; logistics and supply chain management; energy, healthcare, and transportation applications of operations research.

University of Houston, Cullen College of Engineering, Department of Industrial Engineering, Houston, TX 77204. Offers MIE, PhD. *Program availability:* Part-time. Terminal master's awarded for partial completion of doctoral program. *Degree requirements:* For master's, thesis (for some programs); for doctorate, thesis/dissertation, departmental qualifying exam. *Entrance requirements:* For master's and doctorate, GRE General Test. Additional exam requirements/recommendations for international students: Required—TOEFL; Recommended—IELTS. Electronic applications accepted.

University of Illinois at Chicago, College of Engineering, Department of Mechanical and Industrial Engineering, Program in Industrial Engineering, Chicago, IL 60607-7128. Offers industrial engineering (MS); industrial engineering and operations research (PhD). *Program availability:* Part-time. *Degree requirements:* For doctorate, thesis/dissertation. *Entrance requirements:* For doctorate, GRE General Test, minimum GPA of 2.75. Additional exam requirements/recommendations for international students: Required—TOEFL. Electronic applications accepted. *Expenses:* Contact institution. *Faculty research:* Manufacturing information systems and manufacturing control, supply chain, logistics, optimization quality control, haptics and virtual reality, industrial automation, safety and reliability engineering, diagnostics, prognostics, controls and statistical modeling.

University of Illinois at Urbana–Champaign, Graduate College, College of Engineering, Department of Industrial and Enterprise Systems Engineering, Urbana, IL 61801. Offers industrial engineering (MS, PhD); systems and entrepreneurial engineering (MS, PhD); MBA/MS.

University of Illinois at Urbana–Champaign, Graduate College, College of Engineering, Department of Mechanical Science and Engineering, Champaign, IL 61820. Offers mechanical engineering (MS, PhD); theoretical and applied mechanics (MS, PhD). Terminal master's awarded for partial completion of doctoral program. *Entrance requirements:* Additional exam requirements/recommendations for international students: Required—TOEFL (minimum score 613 paper-based; 103 iBT), IELTS (minimum score 7).

The University of Iowa, Graduate College, College of Engineering, Department of Industrial Engineering, Iowa City, IA 52242-1316. Offers engineering design and manufacturing (MS, PhD); healthcare systems (MS, PhD); human factors (MS, PhD); information and engineering management (MS, PhD); operations research (MS, PhD); wind energy (MS, PhD). Terminal master's awarded for partial completion of doctoral program. *Degree requirements:* For master's, thesis optional, exam; for doctorate, comprehensive exam, thesis/dissertation, final defense exam. *Entrance requirements:* For master's and doctorate, GRE (minimum Verbal score of 153, Quantitative 151), minimum undergraduate GPA of 3.0. Additional exam requirements/recommendations for international students: Required—TOEFL (minimum score 600 paper-based; 100 iBT), IELTS (minimum score 7). Electronic applications accepted. *Faculty research:* Operations research, informatics, human factors engineering, healthcare systems, bio-manufacturing, manufacturing systems, renewable energy, human-machine interactions.

University of Louisville, J. B. Speed School of Engineering, Department of Industrial Engineering, Louisville, KY 40292-0001. Offers engineering management (M Eng); industrial engineering (M Eng, MS, PhD); logistics and distribution (Certificate). *Accreditation:* ABET (one or more programs are accredited). *Program availability:* 100% online. *Faculty:* 9 full-time (4 women), 8 part-time/adjunct (2 women). *Students:* 64 full-time (22 women), 147 part-time (35 women); includes 32 minority (13 Black or African American, non-Hispanic/Latino; 9 Asian, non-Hispanic/Latino; 6 Hispanic/Latino; 4 Two or more races, non-Hispanic/Latino; 78 international. Average age 31. 98 applicants, 66% accepted, 53 enrolled. In 2018, 30 master's, 3 doctorates awarded. Terminal master's awarded for partial completion of doctoral program. *Degree requirements:* For

master's and Certificate, thesis optional; for doctorate, comprehensive exam, thesis/dissertation. *Entrance requirements:* For master's and doctorate, GRE General Test, two letters of recommendation, official transcripts. Additional exam requirements/recommendations for international students: Required—TOEFL (minimum score 550 paper-based; 80 iBT), IELTS (minimum score 6.5). *Application deadline:* For fall admission, 5/1 priority date for domestic and international students; for spring admission, 11/1 priority date for domestic and international students; for summer admission, 3/1 priority date for domestic and international students. Applications are processed on a rolling basis. Application fee: $65. Electronic applications accepted. *Expenses: Tuition, area resident:* Full-time $6500; part-time $723 per credit hour. Tuition, state resident: full-time $6500. Tuition, nonresident: full-time $13,557; part-time $1507 per credit hour. Tuition and fees vary according to course load and program. *Financial support:* In 2018–19, 38 students received support. Fellowships, research assistantships, teaching assistantships, scholarships/grants, health care benefits, and tuition waivers (full) available. Financial award application deadline: 1/1; financial award applicants required to submit FAFSA. *Faculty research:* Quality and Reliability Assurance, Process Monitoring and Diagnostics, Production Systems Design, Supply Chain Risk Management, Decision Support Systems. *Total annual research expenditures:* $620,986. *Unit head:* Dr. Suraj M. Alexander, Chair, 502-852-6342, Fax: 502-852-5633, E-mail: suraj.alexander@louisville.edu. *Application contact:* Lihui Bai, Director of Graduate Studies, 502-852-1416, E-mail: lihui.bai@louisville.edu. Website: http://www.louisville.edu/speed/industrial/

University of Manitoba, Faculty of Graduate Studies, Faculty of Engineering, Department of Mechanical and Manufacturing Engineering, Winnipeg, MB R3T 2N2, Canada. Offers M Eng, M Sc, PhD. *Degree requirements:* For master's, thesis; for doctorate, thesis/dissertation.

University of Massachusetts Amherst, Graduate School, College of Engineering, Department of Mechanical and Industrial Engineering, Amherst, MA 01003. Offers industrial engineering and operations research (MS, PhD); mechanical engineering (MSME, PhD). *Program availability:* Part-time. Terminal master's awarded for partial completion of doctoral program. *Degree requirements:* For master's, thesis or alternative; for doctorate, comprehensive exam, thesis/dissertation. *Entrance requirements:* For master's and doctorate, GRE General Test. Additional exam requirements/recommendations for international students: Required—TOEFL (minimum score 550 paper-based; 80 iBT), IELTS (minimum score 6.5). Electronic applications accepted.

University of Massachusetts Dartmouth, Graduate School, College of Engineering, Department of Mechanical Engineering, North Dartmouth, MA 02747-2300. Offers industrial and systems engineering (Postbaccalaureate Certificate); mechanical engineering (MS). *Program availability:* Part-time. *Faculty:* 10 full-time (2 women). *Students:* 6 full-time (0 women), 19 part-time (1 woman); includes 4 minority (1 Asian, non-Hispanic/Latino; 1 Hispanic/Latino; 2 Two or more races, non-Hispanic/Latino), 5 international. Average age 25. 42 applicants, 55% accepted, 6 enrolled. In 2018, 9 master's awarded. *Degree requirements:* For master's, thesis, thesis or project. *Entrance requirements:* For master's, GRE unless UMass Dartmouth graduate in mechanical engineering, statement of purpose (minimum of 300 words), resume, 3 letters of recommendation, official transcripts; for Postbaccalaureate Certificate, statement of purpose (minimum of 300 words), resume, 3 letters of recommendation, official transcripts. Additional exam requirements/recommendations for international students: Required—TOEFL (minimum score 533 paper-based; 72 iBT), IELTS (minimum score 6). *Application deadline:* For fall admission, 2/15 priority date for domestic students, 1/15 priority date for international students; for spring admission, 11/15 priority date for domestic students, 10/15 priority date for international students. Application fee: $60. Electronic applications accepted. *Financial support:* In 2018–19, 3 research assistantships (averaging $11,606 per year), 4 teaching assistantships (averaging $14,131 per year) were awarded; tuition waivers (full and partial) also available. Financial award application deadline: 3/1; financial award applicants required to submit FAFSA. *Faculty research:* Computer aided tolerance and optimization; diagnostics in manufacturing; MEMS and nano-manufacturing; modeling, simulation and optimization of manufacturing systems, robotics. *Total annual research expenditures:* $1.7 million. *Unit head:* Wenzhen Huang, Graduate Program Director, Mechanical Engineering, 508-910-6568, E-mail: whuang@umassd.edu. *Application contact:* Scott Webster, Director of Graduate Studies & Admissions, 508-999-8604, Fax: 508-999-8183, E-mail: graduate@umassd.edu.
Website: http://www.umassd.edu/engineering/mne/graduate

University of Massachusetts Lowell, College of Health Sciences, Department of Work Environment, Lowell, MA 01854. Offers cleaner production and pollution prevention (Sc D). *Program availability:* Part-time. Terminal master's awarded for partial completion of doctoral program. *Degree requirements:* For doctorate, thesis/dissertation. *Entrance requirements:* For doctorate, GRE General Test. Additional exam requirements/recommendations for international students: Required—TOEFL.

University of Miami, Graduate School, College of Engineering, Department of Industrial Engineering, Coral Gables, FL 33124. Offers environmental health and safety (MS); ergonomics (PhD); industrial engineering (MSIE, PhD); management of technology (MS); occupational ergonomics and safety (MS, MSOES), including environmental health and safety (MS), occupational ergonomics and safety (MSOES); MBA/MSIE. *Program availability:* Part-time. *Degree requirements:* For master's, thesis (for some programs); for doctorate, comprehensive exam, thesis/dissertation. *Entrance requirements:* For master's and doctorate, GRE General Test, minimum GPA of 3.0. Additional exam requirements/recommendations for international students: Required—TOEFL (minimum score 550 paper-based). *Faculty research:* Logistics, supply chain management, industrial applications of biomechanics and ergonomics, technology management, back pain, aging, operations research, manufacturing, safety, human reliability, energy assessment.

University of Michigan, College of Engineering, Department of Industrial and Operations Engineering, Ann Arbor, MI 48109. Offers MS, MSE, PhD, MBA/MS, MBA/MSE. *Program availability:* Part-time. *Students:* 180 full-time (67 women), 12 part-time (3 women). 635 applicants, 29% accepted, 76 enrolled. In 2018, 101 master's, 10 doctorates awarded. Terminal master's awarded for partial completion of doctoral program. *Degree requirements:* For doctorate, oral defense of dissertation, preliminary exams, qualifying exam. *Entrance requirements:* For master's and doctorate, GRE General Test. Additional exam requirements/recommendations for international students: Required—TOEFL. *Application deadline:* Applications are processed on a rolling basis. Electronic applications accepted. *Financial support:* Fellowships, research assistantships, teaching assistantships, Federal Work-Study, institutionally sponsored loans, scholarships/grants, traineeships, health care benefits, and unspecified assistantships available. Financial award applicants required to submit FAFSA. *Faculty research:* Production/distribution/logistics, financial engineering and enterprise systems, ergonomics (physical and cognitive), stochastic processes, linear and nonlinear optimization, operations research. *Total annual research expenditures:* $7.3 million. *Unit head:* Brian Denton, Department Chair, 734-763-2060, Fax: 734-764-3451, E-mail: btdenton@umich.edu. *Application contact:* Matt Irelan, Graduate Student Advisor/Program Coordinator, 734-764-6480, Fax: 734-764-3451, E-mail: mirelan@umich.edu.
Website: https://ioe.engin.umich.edu/

University of Michigan–Dearborn, College of Engineering and Computer Science, MSE Program in Industrial and Systems Engineering, Dearborn, MI 48128. Offers MSE. *Program availability:* Part-time, evening/weekend, 100% online. *Faculty:* 17 full-time (4 women), 9 part-time/adjunct (1 woman). *Students:* 71 full-time (15 women), 56 part-time (24 women); includes 11 minority (5 Black or African American, non-Hispanic/Latino; 4 Asian, non-Hispanic/Latino; 1 Hispanic/Latino; 1 Native Hawaiian or other Pacific Islander, non-Hispanic/Latino), 90 international. Average age 25. 280 applicants, 48% accepted, 41 enrolled. In 2018, 52 master's awarded. *Entrance requirements:* For master's, bachelor's degree in engineering, a physical science, computer science, or applied mathematics. Additional exam requirements/recommendations for international students: Required—TOEFL (minimum score 560 paper-based; 84 iBT), IELTS (minimum score 6.5). *Application deadline:* For fall admission, 8/1 for domestic students, 5/1 for international students; for winter admission, 12/1 for domestic students, 9/1 for international students; for spring admission, 4/1 for domestic students, 1/1 for international students. Applications are processed on a rolling basis. Application fee: $60. Electronic applications accepted. *Expenses:* Tuition, state resident: full-time $15,380; part-time $88 per credit hour. Tuition, nonresident: full-time $23,948; part-time $1377 per credit hour. *Required fees:* $780; $780 $390. Tuition and fees vary according to course level, course load, degree level, program, reciprocity agreements and student level. *Financial support:* In 2018–19, 65 students received support. Research assistantships with full tuition reimbursements available, teaching assistantships with full tuition reimbursements available, scholarships/grants, and non-resident tuition scholarships available. Support available to part-time students. Financial award application deadline: 3/1; financial award applicants required to submit FAFSA. *Faculty research:* Operations Research and Decision Science, Quality and Reliability Engineering, Manufacturing, Human Factors and Ergonomics, Transportation Safety. *Unit head:* Dr. Armen Zakarian, Chair, 313-593-5361, Fax: 313-593-3692, E-mail: zakarian@umich.edu. *Application contact:* Office of Graduate Studies, 313-583-6321, E-mail: umd-graduatestudies@umich.edu.
Website: https://umdearborn.edu/cecs/departments/industrial-and-manufacturing-systems-engineering/graduate-programs/mse-industrial-systems-engineering

University of Michigan–Dearborn, College of Engineering and Computer Science, PhD Program in Industrial and Systems Engineering, Dearborn, MI 48128. Offers PhD. *Faculty:* 17 full-time (4 women), 9 part-time/adjunct (1 woman). *Students:* 2 full-time (1 woman), 6 part-time (2 women), 7 international. Average age 26. 12 applicants, 58% accepted, 5 enrolled. *Degree requirements:* For doctorate, thesis/dissertation, qualifying and preliminary examinations. *Entrance requirements:* For doctorate, GRE, master's degree in engineering, applied mathematics, computer science, or a physical science from accredited program. Additional exam requirements/recommendations for international students: Required—TOEFL (minimum score 560 paper-based; 84 iBT), IELTS (minimum score 6.5). *Application deadline:* For fall admission, 2/1 for domestic and international students. Application fee: $60. Electronic applications accepted. *Expenses:* Tuition, state resident: full-time $15,380; part-time $88 per credit hour. Tuition, nonresident: full-time $23,948; part-time $1377 per credit hour. *Required fees:* $780; $780 $390. Tuition and fees vary according to course level, course load, degree level, program, reciprocity agreements and student level. *Financial support:* Research assistantships with full tuition reimbursements, teaching assistantships with full tuition reimbursements, scholarships/grants, health care benefits, and unspecified assistantships available. Financial award application deadline: 2/1; financial award applicants required to submit FAFSA. *Faculty research:* Operations Research and Decision Science, Quality and Reliability Engineering, Manufacturing, Human Factors and Ergonomics, Transportation Safety. *Unit head:* Dr. Yubao Chen, Director, 313-593-5579, E-mail: yubao@umich.edu. *Application contact:* Office of Graduate Studies, 313-583-6321, E-mail: umd-graduatestudies@umich.edu.
Website: https://umdearborn.edu/cecs/departments/industrial-and-manufacturing-systems-engineering/graduate-programs/phd-industrial-and-systems-engineering

University of Minnesota, Twin Cities Campus, College of Science and Engineering, Department of Industrial and Systems Engineering, Minneapolis, MN 55455-0213. Offers MS, PhD. *Program availability:* Part-time. *Degree requirements:* For doctorate, thesis/dissertation. *Entrance requirements:* For master's, GRE General Test, minimum GPA of 3.0; for doctorate, GRE General Test. Additional exam requirements/recommendations for international students: Required—TOEFL. Electronic applications accepted. *Faculty research:* Operations research, supply chains and logistics, health care, revenue management, transportation, service and manufacturing operations.

University of Missouri, Office of Research and Graduate Studies, College of Engineering, Department of Industrial and Manufacturing Systems Engineering, Columbia, MO 65211. Offers ME, MS, PhD, MS/MHA. *Degree requirements:* For master's, thesis or alternative; for doctorate, thesis/dissertation. *Entrance requirements:* For master's and doctorate, GRE General Test, minimum GPA of 3.0. Additional exam requirements/recommendations for international students: Required—TOEFL.

University of Nebraska–Lincoln, Graduate College, College of Engineering, Department of Industrial and Management Systems Engineering, Lincoln, NE 68588. Offers engineering management (M Eng); industrial and management systems engineering (MS, PhD); manufacturing systems engineering (MS). *Program availability:* Online learning. *Degree requirements:* For master's, thesis optional; for doctorate, comprehensive exam, thesis/dissertation. *Entrance requirements:* For master's and doctorate, GRE. Additional exam requirements/recommendations for international students: Required—TOEFL (minimum score 525 paper-based). Electronic applications accepted. *Faculty research:* Ergonomics, occupational safety, quality control, industrial packaging, facility design.

University of New Haven, Graduate School, Tagliatela College of Engineering, Program in Industrial Engineering, West Haven, CT 06516. Offers industrial engineering (MSIE); quality engineering (Graduate Certificate); MBA/MSIE. *Program availability:* Part-time, evening/weekend. *Students:* 59 full-time (9 women), 7 part-time (2 women); includes 3 minority (2 Black or African American, non-Hispanic/Latino; 1 Asian, non-Hispanic/Latino), 62 international. Average age 25. 179 applicants, 87% accepted, 23 enrolled. In 2018, 41 master's awarded. *Entrance requirements:* For master's, bachelor's degree in engineering. Additional exam requirements/recommendations for international students: Required—TOEFL (minimum score 75 iBT), IELTS, PTE (minimum score 50). *Application deadline:* Applications are processed on a rolling basis. Application fee: $50. Electronic applications accepted. Application fee is waived when completed online. *Expenses:* Tuition: Full-time $16,470; part-time $915 per credit hour. *Required fees:* $230; $95 per term. *Financial support:* Research assistantships with partial tuition reimbursements, teaching assistantships with partial tuition reimbursements, career-related internships or fieldwork, Federal Work-Study, scholarships/grants, and unspecified assistantships available. Support available to part-time students. Financial award applicants required to submit FAFSA. *Unit head:* Dr. Ali Montazer, Professor, 203-932-7050, E-mail: amontazer@newhaven.edu. *Application contact:* Selina O'Toole, Senior Associate Director of Graduate Admissions, 203-932-7337, E-mail: sotoole@newhaven.edu.
Website: https://www.newhaven.edu/engineering/graduate-programs/industrial-engineering/

University of Pittsburgh, Swanson School of Engineering, Department of Industrial Engineering, Pittsburgh, PA 15260. Offers MSIE, PhD. *Program availability:* Part-time, 100% online. Terminal master's awarded for partial completion of doctoral program. *Degree requirements:* For doctorate, comprehensive exam, thesis/dissertation, final oral exams. *Entrance requirements:* For master's and doctorate, GRE General Test, minimum GPA of 3.0. Additional exam requirements/recommendations for international students: Required—TOEFL (minimum score 550 paper-based; 80 iBT). Electronic applications accepted. *Expenses:* Contact institution. *Faculty research:* Operations research, engineering management; computational intelligence, manufacturing, information systems.

University of Puerto Rico–Mayagüez, Graduate Studies, College of Engineering, Department of Industrial Engineering, Mayagüez, PR 00681-9000. Offers ME, MS. *Program availability:* Part-time. *Degree requirements:* For master's, one foreign language, comprehensive exam, thesis, project. *Entrance requirements:* For master's, minimum GPA of 2.5; proficiency in English and Spanish; BS in engineering. Additional exam requirements/recommendations for international students: Required—TOEFL (minimum score 80 iBT). Electronic applications accepted. *Faculty research:* Systems thinking and systems integration, facilities design, engineering analysis methods, lean logistics, lead data-based biological discovery.

University of Regina, Faculty of Graduate Studies and Research, Faculty of Engineering and Applied Science, Program in Industrial Systems Engineering, Regina, SK S4S 0A2, Canada. Offers industrial systems (M Eng, MA Sc, PhD). *Program availability:* Part-time. *Faculty:* 12 full-time (1 woman), 2 part-time/adjunct (0 women). *Students:* 69 full-time (12 women), 5 part-time (1 woman). Average age 30. 235 applicants, 9% accepted, 5 enrolled. In 2018, 24 master's, 4 doctorates awarded. *Degree requirements:* For master's, thesis, project, report, co-op; for doctorate, comprehensive exam, thesis/dissertation. *Entrance requirements:* For master's, 4 years bachelor degree; at least 70 per cent from a four-year baccalaureate degree (or equivalent). Additional exam requirements/recommendations for international students: Required—TOEFL (minimum score 580 paper-based; 80 iBT), IELTS (minimum score 6.5), PTE (minimum score 59), other options are CAEL, MELAB, Cantest and U of R ESL. *Application deadline:* For fall admission, 3/31 for domestic and international students; for winter admission, 7/31 for domestic and international students; for spring admission, 11/30 for domestic and international students. Application fee: $100. Electronic applications accepted. *Expenses:* Estimated tuition and fees for one academic year is 8.379.50 for Master's. The fee will vary base on your choice program. For Doctoral program one academic year is estimated 14,129.40. International students will pay additional 1,191.75 for International surcharge per semester. *Financial support:* Fellowships, research assistantships, teaching assistantships, career-related internships or fieldwork, Federal Work-Study, scholarships/grants, unspecified assistantships, and travel award and Graduate Scholarship Base Funds available. Support available to part-time students. Financial award application deadline: 9/30. *Faculty research:* Stochastic systems simulation, metallurgy of welding, computer-aided engineering, finite element method of engineering systems, manufacturing systems. *Unit head:* Dr. Adisorn Aroonwilas, Program Chair, 306-337-2469, Fax: 306-585-4855, E-mail: Adisorn.Aroonwilas@uregina.ca. *Application contact:* Dr. Golam Kabir, Graduate Coordinator, 306-585-5271, Fax: 306-585-4855, E-mail: golam.kabir@uregina.ca.
Website: http://www.uregina.ca/engineering/

University of Rhode Island, Graduate School, College of Engineering, Department of Mechanical, Industrial and Systems Engineering, Kingston, RI 02881. Offers industrial and systems engineering (MS, PhD), including manufacturing systems, service and enterprise systems. *Program availability:* Part-time. *Faculty:* 19 full-time (4 women). *Students:* 31 full-time (7 women), 36 part-time (2 women); includes 11 minority (3 Black or African American, non-Hispanic/Latino; 2 Asian, non-Hispanic/Latino; 5 Hispanic/Latino; 1 Two or more races, non-Hispanic/Latino), 21 international. 40 applicants, 73% accepted, 17 enrolled. In 2018, 13 master's, 6 doctorates awarded. *Entrance requirements:* Additional exam requirements/recommendations for international students: Required—TOEFL. *Application deadline:* For fall admission, 6/1 for domestic students, 2/1 for international students; for spring admission, 11/1 for domestic students, 7/1 for international students. Application fee: $65. Electronic applications accepted. *Expenses: Tuition, area resident:* Full-time $13,226; part-time $735 per credit. Tuition, state resident: full-time $13,226; part-time $735 per credit. Tuition, nonresident: full-time $25,854; part-time $1436 per credit. *International tuition:* $25,854 full-time. *Required fees:* $1698; $50 per credit. $35 per semester. One-time fee: $165. *Financial support:* In 2018–19, 6 research assistantships with tuition reimbursements (averaging $10,197 per year), 9 teaching assistantships with tuition reimbursements (averaging $8,496 per year) were awarded. Financial award application deadline: 2/1; financial award applicants required to submit FAFSA. *Unit head:* Dr. Carl-Ernst Rousseau, Chair, 401-874-2542, E-mail: rousseau@uri.edu. *Application contact:* David Chelidze, Graduate Admissions, 401-874-2356, E-mail: chelidze@uri.edu.
Website: http://mcise.uri.edu/

University of Southern California, Graduate School, Viterbi School of Engineering, Daniel J. Epstein Department of Industrial and Systems Engineering, Los Angeles, CA 90089. Offers digital supply chain management (MS); engineering management (MS); engineering technology communication (Graduate Certificate); health systems operations (Graduate Certificate); industrial and systems engineering (MS, PhD, Engr); manufacturing engineering (MS); operations research engineering (MS); optimization and supply chain management (Graduate Certificate); product development engineering (MS); safety systems and security (MS); systems architecting and engineering (MS, Graduate Certificate); systems safety and security (Graduate Certificate); transportation systems (Graduate Certificate); MS/MBA. *Program availability:* Part-time, evening/weekend, online learning. Terminal master's awarded for partial completion of doctoral program. *Degree requirements:* For master's, thesis optional; for doctorate, thesis/dissertation. *Entrance requirements:* For master's and doctorate, GRE General Test. Additional exam requirements/recommendations for international students: Recommended—TOEFL. Electronic applications accepted. *Faculty research:* Health systems, music cognition and retrieval, transportation and logistics, manufacturing and automation, engineering systems design, risk and economic analysis.

University of South Florida, College of Engineering, Department of Industrial and Management Systems Engineering, Tampa, FL 33620-9951. Offers engineering management (MSEM); industrial engineering (MSIE, PhD); information technology (MSIT); materials science and engineering (MSMSE). *Program availability:* Part-time, online learning. *Faculty:* 30 full-time (3 women), 1 part-time/adjunct (0 women). *Students:* 84 full-time (25 women), 60 part-time (15 women); includes 13 minority (2 Black or African American, non-Hispanic/Latino; 4 Asian, non-Hispanic/Latino; 7 Hispanic/Latino), 100 international. Average age 27. 280 applicants, 54% accepted, 37 enrolled. In 2018, 72 master's, 3 doctorates awarded. Terminal master's awarded for partial completion of doctoral program. *Degree requirements:* For master's, comprehensive exam, thesis (for some programs); for doctorate, comprehensive exam, thesis/dissertation, 2 tools of research as specified by dissertation committee. *Entrance requirements:* For master's, GRE General Test, BS in engineering (or equivalent), letters of recommendation, resume, two years professional experience or internship may be required; statement of purpose; for doctorate, GRE General Test, minimum GPA of 3.0,

3 letters of recommendation, statement of purpose, strong background in scientific and engineering principles. Ph.D. students must complete their total doctoral major as full-time Tampa campus students. Additional exam requirements/recommendations for international students: Required—TOEFL, TOEFL (minimum score 550 paper-based; 79 iBT) or IELTS (minimum score 6.5). *Application deadline:* For fall admission, 2/15 for domestic and international students; for spring admission, 10/15 for domestic students, 9/15 for international students; for summer admission, 2/15 for domestic students, 1/15 for international students. Application fee: $30. Electronic applications accepted. *Expenses:* Tuition, state resident: full-time $6350. Tuition, nonresident: full-time $19,048. *International tuition:* $19,048 full-time. *Required fees:* $2079. *Financial support:* In 2018–19, 26 students received support, including 20 research assistantships with partial tuition reimbursements available (averaging $16,748 per year), 11 teaching assistantships with partial tuition reimbursements available (averaging $15,000 per year); tuition waivers (partial) also available. Financial award applicants required to submit FAFSA. *Faculty research:* Healthcare, healthcare systems, public health policies, energy and environment, manufacturing, logistics, transportation. *Total annual research expenditures:* $368,578. *Unit head:* Dr. Tapas K. Das, Professor and Department Chair, 813-974-5585, Fax: 813-974-5953, E-mail: das@usf.edu. *Application contact:* Dr. Alex Savachkin, Associate Professor and Graduate Director, 813-974-5577, Fax: 813-974-5953, E-mail: alexs@usf.edu.
Website: http://imse.eng.usf.edu

University of South Florida, Innovative Education, Tampa, FL 33620-9951. Offers adult, career and higher education (Graduate Certificate), including college teaching, leadership in developing human resources, leadership in higher education; Africana studies (Graduate Certificate), including diasporas and health disparities, genocide and human rights; aging studies (Graduate Certificate), including gerontology; art research (Graduate Certificate), including museum studies; business foundations (Graduate Certificate); chemical and biomedical engineering (Graduate Certificate), including materials science and engineering, water, health and sustainability; child and family studies (Graduate Certificate), including positive behavior support; civil and industrial engineering (Graduate Certificate), including transportation systems analysis; community and family health (Graduate Certificate), including maternal and child health, social marketing and public health, violence and injury: prevention and intervention, women's health; criminology (Graduate Certificate), including criminal justice administration; data science for public administration (Graduate Certificate); digital humanities (Graduate Certificate); educational measurement and research (Graduate Certificate), including evaluation; English (Graduate Certificate), including comparative literary studies, creative writing, professional and technical communication; entrepreneurship (Graduate Certificate); environmental health (Graduate Certificate), including safety management; epidemiology and biostatistics (Graduate Certificate), including applied biostatistics, biostatistics, concepts and tools of epidemiology, epidemiology, epidemiology of infectious diseases; geography, environment and planning (Graduate Certificate), including community development, environmental policy and management, geographical information systems; geology (Graduate Certificate), including hydrogeology; global health (Graduate Certificate), including disaster management, global health and Latin American and Caribbean studies, global health practice, humanitarian assistance, infection control; government and international affairs (Graduate Certificate), including Cuban studies, globalization studies; health policy and management (Graduate Certificate), including health management and leadership, public health policy and programs; hearing specialist: early intervention (Graduate Certificate); industrial and management systems engineering (Graduate Certificate), including systems engineering, technology management; information studies (Graduate Certificate), including school library media specialist; information systems/decision sciences (Graduate Certificate), including analytics and business intelligence; instructional technology (Graduate Certificate), including distance education, Florida digital/virtual educator, instructional design, multimedia design, Web design; internal medicine, bioethics and medical humanities (Graduate Certificate), including biomedical ethics; Latin American and Caribbean studies (Graduate Certificate); leadership for coastal resiliency planning (Graduate Certificate); mass communications (Graduate Certificate), including multimedia journalism; mathematics and statistics (Graduate Certificate), including mathematics; medicine (Graduate Certificate), including aging and neuroscience, bioinformatics, biotechnology, brain fitness and memory management, clinical investigation, hand and upper limb rehabilitation, health informatics, health sciences, integrative weight management, intellectual property, medicine and gender, metabolic and nutritional medicine, metabolic cardiology, pharmacy sciences; national and competitive intelligence (Graduate Certificate); nursing (Graduate Certificate), including simulation based academic fellowship in advanced pain management; psychological and social foundations (Graduate Certificate), including career counseling, college teaching, diversity in education, mental health counseling, school counseling; public affairs (Graduate Certificate), including nonprofit management, public management, research administration; public health (Graduate Certificate), including assessing chemical toxicity and public health risks, health equity, pharmacoepidemiology, public health generalist, toxicology, translational research in adolescent behavioral health; public health practices (Graduate Certificate), including planning for healthy communities; rehabilitation and mental health counseling (Graduate Certificate), including integrative mental health care, marriage and family therapy, rehabilitation technology; secondary education (Graduate Certificate), including ESOL, foreign language education: culture and content, foreign language education: professional; social work (Graduate Certificate), including geriatric social work/clinical gerontology; special education (Graduate Certificate), including autism spectrum disorder, disabilities education: severe/profound; world languages (Graduate Certificate), including teaching English as a second language (TESL) or foreign language. *Expenses:* Tuition, state resident: full-time $6350. Tuition, nonresident: full-time $19,048. *International tuition:* $19,048 full-time. *Required fees:* $2079. *Unit head:* Dr. Cynthia DeLuca, Associate Vice President and Assistant Vice Provost, 813-974-3077, Fax: 813-974-7061, E-mail: deluca@usf.edu. *Application contact:* Owen Hooper, Director, Summer and Alternative Calendar Programs, 813-974-6917, E-mail: hooper@usf.edu.
Website: http://www.usf.edu/innovative-education/

The University of Tennessee, Graduate School, Tickle College of Engineering, Department of Industrial and Systems Engineering, Knoxville, TN 37966. Offers engineering management (MS); industrial engineering (MS, PhD); reliability and maintainability engineering (MS); MS/MBA. *Program availability:* Part-time, online learning. *Faculty:* 10 full-time (1 woman), 3 part-time/adjunct (1 woman). *Students:* 74 full-time (20 women), 76 part-time (18 women); includes 26 minority (10 Black or African American, non-Hispanic/Latino; 1 American Indian or Alaska Native, non-Hispanic/Latino; 8 Asian, non-Hispanic/Latino; 7 Hispanic/Latino), 40 international. Average age 35. 122 applicants, 80% accepted, 47 enrolled. In 2018, 42 master's, 8 doctorates awarded. *Degree requirements:* For master's, thesis or alternative; for doctorate, comprehensive exam, thesis/dissertation. *Entrance requirements:* For master's, GRE General Test (for MS students pursuing research thesis), minimum GPA of 2.7 (for U.S. degree holders), 3.0 (for international degree holders); for doctorate, GRE General Test, minimum GPA of 3.0 on previous graduate course work. Additional exam requirements/recommendations for international students: Required—TOEFL (minimum score 550 paper-based; 80 iBT), IELTS (minimum score 6.5). *Application deadline:* For fall admission, 2/1 priority date for domestic and international students; for spring admission, 6/15 for domestic and international students; for summer admission, 10/15 for domestic and international students. Applications are processed on a rolling basis. Application fee: $60. Electronic applications accepted. *Financial support:* In 2018–19, 59 students received support, including 7 fellowships with full tuition reimbursements available (averaging $10,000 per year), 36 research assistantships with full tuition reimbursements available (averaging $15,462 per year), 16 teaching assistantships with full tuition reimbursements available (averaging $19,545 per year); career-related internships or fieldwork, Federal Work-Study, institutionally sponsored loans, health care benefits, and unspecified assistantships also available. Financial award application deadline: 2/1; financial award applicants required to submit FAFSA. *Faculty research:* Combinatorial optimization; design of lean, reliable systems: energy systems; healthcare analytics; transportation, logistics and supply chain modeling. *Total annual research expenditures:* $1.2 million. *Unit head:* Dr. John Kobza, Department Head, 865-974-3333, Fax: 865-974-0588, E-mail: jkobza@utk.edu. *Application contact:* Dr. Mingzhou Jin, Professor, Associate Head and Director of Graduate Studies, 865-974-9992, E-mail: jin@utk.edu.
Website: http://www.engr.utk.edu/ie/

The University of Tennessee, The University of Tennessee Space Institute, Tullahoma, TN 37388. Offers aerospace engineering (MS, PhD); biomedical engineering (MS, PhD); engineering science (MS, PhD); industrial and systems engineering/engineering management (MS, PhD); mechanical engineering (MS, PhD); physics (MS, PhD). *Program availability:* Part-time, blended/hybrid learning. Terminal master's awarded for partial completion of doctoral program. *Degree requirements:* For doctorate, one foreign language, thesis/dissertation. *Entrance requirements:* Additional exam requirements/recommendations for international students: Required—TOEFL (minimum score 550 paper-based; 80 iBT), IELTS (minimum score 6.5). Electronic applications accepted. *Expenses:* Contact institution. *Faculty research:* Fluid mechanics/aerodynamics, chemical and electric propulsion and laser diagnostics, computational mechanics and simulations, carbon fiber production and composite materials.

The University of Texas at Arlington, Graduate School, College of Engineering, Department of Industrial, Manufacturing, and Systems Engineering, Arlington, TX 76019. Offers engineering management (MS); industrial engineering (MS, PhD); logistics (MS); systems engineering (MS). *Program availability:* Part-time, evening/weekend, online learning. Terminal master's awarded for partial completion of doctoral program. *Degree requirements:* For master's, comprehensive exam, thesis optional; for doctorate, comprehensive exam, thesis/dissertation. *Entrance requirements:* For master's and doctorate, GRE General Test, minimum GPA of 3.0. Additional exam requirements/recommendations for international students: Required—TOEFL (minimum score 550 paper-based). *Faculty research:* Manufacturing, healthcare logistics, environmental systems, operations research, statistics.

The University of Texas at Austin, Graduate School, Cockrell School of Engineering, Department of Mechanical Engineering, Program in Operations Research and Industrial Engineering, Austin, TX 78712-1111. Offers MS, PhD. *Entrance requirements:* For master's and doctorate, GRE General Test. Additional exam requirements/recommendations for international students: Required—TOEFL.

The University of Texas at El Paso, Graduate School, College of Engineering, Department of Industrial, Manufacturing and Systems Engineering, El Paso, TX 79968-0001. Offers industrial engineering (MS); manufacturing engineering (MS); systems engineering (MS). *Program availability:* Part-time, evening/weekend. *Degree requirements:* For master's, thesis optional. *Entrance requirements:* For master's, GRE General Test, minimum GPA of 3.0 in major. Additional exam requirements/recommendations for international students: Required—TOEFL. Electronic applications accepted. *Faculty research:* Computer vision, automated inspection, simulation and modeling.

The University of Toledo, College of Graduate Studies, College of Engineering, Department of Mechanical, Industrial, and Manufacturing Engineering, Toledo, OH 43606-3390. Offers industrial engineering (MS, PhD); mechanical engineering (MS, PhD). *Program availability:* Part-time, online learning. *Degree requirements:* For master's, thesis optional; for doctorate, thesis/dissertation, qualifying exam. *Entrance requirements:* For master's, GRE General Test, minimum GPA of 3.0; for doctorate, GRE General Test, minimum GPA of 3.3. Additional exam requirements/recommendations for international students: Required—TOEFL (minimum score 550 paper-based; 80 iBT). Electronic applications accepted. *Faculty research:* Computational and experimental thermal sciences, manufacturing process and systems, mechanics, materials, design, quality and management engineering systems.

University of Toronto, School of Graduate Studies, Faculty of Applied Science and Engineering, Department of Mechanical and Industrial Engineering, Toronto, ON M5S 1A1, Canada. Offers M Eng, MA Sc, PhD. *Program availability:* Part-time. *Degree requirements:* For master's, thesis (for some programs), oral exam/thesis defense (MA Sc); for doctorate, thesis/dissertation, thesis defense, qualifying examination. *Entrance requirements:* For master's, GRE (recommended), minimum B+ average in last 2 years of undergraduate study, 2 letters of reference, resume, Canadian citizenship or permanent residency (M Eng); for doctorate, GRE (recommended), minimum B+ average, 2 letters of reference, resume. Additional exam requirements/recommendations for international students: Required—TOEFL (minimum score 580 paper-based), Michigan English Language Assessment Battery (minimum score 85), IELTS (minimum score 7), or COPE (minimum score 4). Electronic applications accepted.

University of Washington, Graduate School, College of Engineering, Department of Industrial and Systems Engineering, Seattle, WA 98195-2650. Offers MISE, MS, PhD. *Program availability:* Part-time, online learning. *Faculty:* 10 full-time (5 women). *Students:* 35 full-time (12 women), 39 part-time (12 women); includes 18 minority (2 Black or African American, non-Hispanic/Latino; 1 American Indian or Alaska Native, non-Hispanic/Latino; 9 Asian, non-Hispanic/Latino; 5 Hispanic/Latino; 1 Native Hawaiian or other Pacific Islander, non-Hispanic/Latino), 30 international. Average age 28. 242 applicants, 38% accepted, 31 enrolled. In 2018, 28 master's, 5 doctorates awarded. Terminal master's awarded for partial completion of doctoral program. *Degree requirements:* For master's, thesis optional; for doctorate, comprehensive exam, thesis/dissertation, qualifying, general, and final exams. *Entrance requirements:* For master's, GRE General Test, minimum GPA of 3.0; bachelor's degree in engineering, math, or science; transcripts; letters of recommendation; resume; statement of objectives; for doctorate, GRE General Test, minimum GPA of 3.0; master's degree in engineering, math, or science (preferred); transcripts; letters of recommendation; resume; statement of objectives. Additional exam requirements/recommendations for international students: Required—TOEFL (minimum score 580 paper-based; 92 iBT); Recommended—IELTS (minimum score 7). *Application deadline:* For fall admission, 1/1 priority date for domestic students, 1/1 for international students. Applications are processed on a rolling basis. Application fee: $85. Electronic applications accepted. *Expenses:* Research-focused Master's and PhD: $18,852 resident; $32,760 nonresident. Applied/Professional Master's: $23,070 resident; $35,571 nonresident.

Financial support: In 2018–19, 35 students received support, including 23 research assistantships with full tuition reimbursements available (averaging $29,640 per year), 12 teaching assistantships with full tuition reimbursements available (averaging $29,640 per year); fellowships, career-related internships or fieldwork, scholarships/grants, traineeships, and tuition waivers (full) also available. Financial award application deadline: 2/1; financial award applicants required to submit FAFSA. *Faculty research:* Manufacturing, systems engineering and integration, optimization, human factors, virtual reality, quality and reliability, large-scale assembly, supply chain management, health systems engineering. *Total annual research expenditures:* $2.1 million. *Unit head:* Dr. Linda Ng Boyle, Professor/Chair, 206-543-1427, Fax: 206-685-3072, E-mail: linda@uw.edu. *Application contact:* Jennifer W. Tsai, Academic Counselor, 206-543-5041, Fax: 206-685-3072, E-mail: ieadvise@uw.edu.
Website: http://ise.washington.edu

University of Windsor, Faculty of Graduate Studies, Faculty of Engineering, Department of Industrial and Manufacturing Systems Engineering, Windsor, ON N9B 3P4, Canada. Offers industrial engineering (M Eng, MA Sc); manufacturing systems engineering (PhD). *Program availability:* Part-time. *Degree requirements:* For master's, thesis; for doctorate, comprehensive exam, thesis/dissertation. *Entrance requirements:* For master's, minimum B average; for doctorate, master's degree, minimum B average. Additional exam requirements/recommendations for international students: Required—TOEFL (minimum score 560 paper-based). Electronic applications accepted. *Faculty research:* Human factors, operations research.

University of Wisconsin–Madison, Graduate School, College of Engineering, Department of Industrial and Systems Engineering, Madison, WI 53706. Offers industrial engineering (MS, PhD), including human factors and health systems engineering (MS), systems engineering and analytics (MS). *Program availability:* Part-time. *Faculty:* 20 full-time (6 women). *Students:* 87 full-time (33 women), 12 part-time (8 women); includes 4 minority (1 Black or African American, non-Hispanic/Latino; 3 Asian, non-Hispanic/Latino), 63 international. Average age 26. 372 applicants, 21% accepted, 18 enrolled. In 2018, 35 master's, 9 doctorates awarded. Terminal master's awarded for partial completion of doctoral program. *Degree requirements:* For master's, thesis optional, 30 credits; minimum GPA of 3.0; for doctorate, comprehensive exam, thesis/dissertation, minimum of 51 credits; minimum GPA of 3.0. *Entrance requirements:* For master's and doctorate, GRE General Test, minimum GPA of 3.0, BS in engineering or equivalent, course work in computer programming and statistics. Additional exam requirements/recommendations for international students: Required—TOEFL (minimum score 580 paper-based; 92 iBT), IELTS (minimum score 7). *Application deadline:* For fall admission, 12/15 for domestic and international students; for spring admission, 10/1 for domestic and international students; for summer admission, 12/15 for domestic and international students. Application fee: $75 ($81 for international students). Electronic applications accepted. *Financial support:* In 2018–19, 66 students received support, including 2 fellowships with full tuition reimbursements available (averaging $27,816 per year), 39 research assistantships with full tuition reimbursements available (averaging $24,456 per year), 21 teaching assistantships with full tuition reimbursements available (averaging $19,788 per year); career-related internships or fieldwork, Federal Work-Study, institutionally sponsored loans, scholarships/grants, traineeships, health care benefits, and unspecified assistantships also available. Financial award application deadline: 12/1; financial award applicants required to submit FAFSA. *Faculty research:* Operations research; human factors and ergonomics; health systems engineering; manufacturing and production systems. *Total annual research expenditures:* $13.9 million. *Unit head:* Dr. Jeff Lindroth, Chair, 608-262-2686, E-mail: ie@engr.wisc.edu. *Application contact:* Pam Peterson, Student Services Coordinator, 608-263-4025, Fax: 608-890-2204, E-mail: prpeterson@wisc.edu.
Website: http://www.engr.wisc.edu/department/industrial-systems-engineering/

University of Wisconsin–Milwaukee, Graduate School, College of Engineering and Applied Science, Program in Engineering, Milwaukee, WI 53201-0413. Offers biomedical engineering (MS); civil engineering (MS, PhD); computer science (PhD); electrical and computer engineering (MS); electrical engineering (PhD); engineering mechanics (MS); industrial and management engineering (MS); industrial engineering (PhD); manufacturing engineering (MS); materials (PhD); materials engineering (MS); mechanical engineering (MS). *Program availability:* Part-time. *Students:* 174 full-time (41 women), 149 part-time (27 women); includes 31 minority (2 Black or African American, non-Hispanic/Latino; 1 American Indian or Alaska Native, non-Hispanic/Latino; 16 Asian, non-Hispanic/Latino; 4 Hispanic/Latino; 8 Two or more races, non-Hispanic/Latino), 207 international. Average age 31. 343 applicants, 57% accepted, 78 enrolled. In 2018, 73 master's, 24 doctorates awarded. *Degree requirements:* For master's, comprehensive exam (for some programs), thesis or alternative; for doctorate, comprehensive exam, thesis/dissertation, internship. *Entrance requirements:* For master's, GRE, minimum GPA of 2.75; for doctorate, GRE, minimum GPA of 3.5. Additional exam requirements/recommendations for international students: Required—TOEFL (minimum score 550 paper-based; 79 iBT), IELTS (minimum score 6.5). *Application deadline:* For fall admission, 1/1 priority date for domestic students; for spring admission, 9/1 for domestic students. Applications are processed on a rolling basis. Application fee: $56 ($96 for international students). *Financial support:* Fellowships, research assistantships, teaching assistantships, career-related internships or fieldwork, Federal Work-Study, unspecified assistantships, and project assistantships available. Support available to part-time students. Financial award application deadline: 4/15. *Unit head:* David Yu, Representative, 414-229-6169, E-mail: yu@uwm.edu. *Application contact:* Betty Warras, General Information Contact, 414-229-6169, Fax: 414-229-6967, E-mail: bwarras@uwm.edu.
Website: http://www4.uwm.edu/ceas/academics/graduate_programs/

University of Wisconsin–Stout, Graduate School, College of Management, Program in Risk Control, Menomonie, WI 54751. Offers MS. *Program availability:* Part-time. *Degree requirements:* For master's, thesis. *Entrance requirements:* For master's, minimum GPA of 3.0. Additional exam requirements/recommendations for international students: Required—TOEFL (minimum score 500 paper-based; 61 iBT). Electronic applications accepted. *Faculty research:* Environmental microbiology, water supply safety, facilities planning, industrial ventilation, bioterrorist.

Virginia Polytechnic Institute and State University, VT Online, Blacksburg, VA 24061. Offers advanced transportation systems (Certificate); aerospace engineering (MS); agricultural and life sciences (MSLFS); business information systems (Graduate Certificate); career and technical education (MS); civil engineering (MS); computer engineering (M Eng, MS); decision support systems (Graduate Certificate); eLearning leadership (MA); electrical engineering (M Eng, MS); engineering administration (MEA); environmental engineering (Certificate); environmental politics and policy (Graduate Certificate); environmental sciences and engineering (MS); foundations of political analysis (Graduate Certificate); health product risk management (Graduate Certificate); industrial and systems engineering (MS); information policy and society (Graduate Certificate); information security (Graduate Certificate); information technology (MIT); instructional technology (MA); integrative STEM education (MA Ed); liberal arts (Graduate Certificate); life sciences: health product risk management (MS); natural resources (MNR, Graduate Certificate); networking (Graduate Certificate); nonprofit and nongovernmental organization management (Graduate Certificate); ocean engineering

(MS); political science (MA); security studies (Graduate Certificate); software development (Graduate Certificate). *Expenses:* Tuition, state resident: full-time $15,510; part-time $739.50 per credit hour. Tuition, nonresident: full-time $29,629; part-time $1490.25 per credit hour. *Required fees:* $2804; $550 per semester. Tuition and fees vary according to course load, campus/location and program. *Application contact:* Graduate Admissions and Academic Progress, 540-231-8636, E-mail: grads@vt.edu.
Website: http://www.vto.vt.edu/

Wayne State University, College of Engineering, Department of Industrial and Systems Engineering, Detroit, MI 48202. Offers data science and business analytics (MS); engineering management (MS); industrial engineering (MS, PhD); manufacturing engineering (MS); systems engineering (Certificate). *Program availability:* Online learning. *Faculty:* 11. *Students:* 178 full-time (40 women), 109 part-time (30 women); includes 42 minority (20 Black or African American, non-Hispanic/Latino; 16 Asian, non-Hispanic/Latino; 6 Hispanic/Latino), 167 international. Average age 29. 539 applicants, 40% accepted, 68 enrolled. In 2018, 172 master's, 9 doctorates awarded. *Entrance requirements:* For master's, GRE or GMAT (for applicants to MS in data science and business analytics), BS from ABET-accredited institution; for doctorate, GRE, graduate degree in engineering or related discipline with minimum graduate GPA of 3.5, statement of purpose, resume/curriculum vitae, three letters of recommendation; for Certificate, GRE (for applicants from non-ABET institutions), BS in engineering or other technical field from ABET-accredited institution with minimum GPA of 3.0 in upper-division course work, at least one year of full-time work experience as practicing engineer or technical leader. Additional exam requirements/recommendations for international students: Required—TOEFL (minimum score 550 paper-based; 79 iBT), TWE (minimum score 5.5), Michigan English Language Assessment Battery (minimum score 85); GRE; Recommended—IELTS (minimum score 6.5). *Application deadline:* Applications are processed on a rolling basis. Application fee: $50. Electronic applications accepted. *Expenses:* Contact institution. *Financial support:* In 2018–19, 135 students received support, including 2 fellowships with tuition reimbursements available (averaging $20,000 per year), 5 research assistantships with tuition reimbursements available (averaging $23,260 per year), 8 teaching assistantships with tuition reimbursements available (averaging $20,166 per year); scholarships/grants, tuition waivers (full), and unspecified assistantships also available. Financial award applicants required to submit FAFSA. *Faculty research:* Manufacturing systems, infrastructure, and management. *Total annual research expenditures:* $320,400. *Unit head:* Dr. Leslie Monplaisir, Associate Professor/Chair, 313-577-3821, Fax: 313-577-8833, E-mail: leslie.monplaisir@wayne.edu. *Application contact:* Eric Scimeca, Graduate Program Coordinator, 313-577-0412, E-mail: eric.scimeca@wayne.edu.
Website: http://engineering.wayne.edu/ise/

Western Carolina University, Graduate School, College of Engineering and Technology, School of Engineering and Technology, Cullowhee, NC 28723. Offers technology (MS). *Program availability:* Part-time. *Degree requirements:* For master's, comprehensive exam. *Entrance requirements:* For master's, GRE, appropriate undergraduate degree with minimum GPA of 3.0, 3 letters of recommendation. Additional exam requirements/recommendations for international students: Required—TOEFL (minimum score 550 paper-based; 79 iBT). *Expenses:* Tuition, area resident: Full-time $4435. Tuition, state resident: full-time $4435. Tuition, nonresident: full-time $14,842. *International tuition:* $14,842 full-time. *Required fees:* $2979. Part-time tuition and fees vary according to course load, degree level and program. *Faculty research:* Electrophysiology, 3D graphics, digital signal processing, CAM and advanced machining, fluid power, polymer science, wireless communication.

Western Michigan University, Graduate College, College of Engineering and Applied Sciences, Department of Industrial and Entrepreneurial Engineering and Engineering Management, Kalamazoo, MI 49008. Offers engineering management (MS); industrial engineering (MSE, PhD). *Degree requirements:* For master's, thesis optional.

Western New England University, College of Engineering, Program in Industrial Engineering, Springfield, MA 01119. Offers MS. *Program availability:* Part-time, evening/weekend. *Faculty:* 3 full-time (0 women). *Students:* 4 part-time (1 woman); includes 1 minority (Hispanic/Latino), 1 international. Average age 32. 36 applicants, 58% accepted, 1 enrolled. *Degree requirements:* For master's, comprehensive exam, thesis optional. *Entrance requirements:* For master's, bachelor's degree in engineering or related field, two letters of recommendation, resume, transcript. Additional exam requirements/recommendations for international students: Required—TOEFL (minimum score 79 iBT). *Application deadline:* Applications are processed on a rolling basis. Application fee: $30. Electronic applications accepted. *Expenses:* Contact institution. *Financial support:* Application deadline: 4/15; applicants required to submit FAFSA. *Faculty research:* Project scheduling, flexible manufacturing systems, facility layout, energy management. *Unit head:* Dr. Christian Salmon, Chair and Professor, 413-796-2209, E-mail: christian.salmon@wne.edu. *Application contact:* Matthew Fox, Executive Director of Graduate Admissions, 413-782-1410, Fax: 413-782-1777, E-mail: study@wne.edu.
Website: http://www1.wne.edu/academics/graduate/industrial-engineering-ms.cfm

West Virginia University, Statler College of Engineering and Mineral Resources, Morgantown, WV 26506. Offers aerospace engineering (MSAE, PhD); chemical engineering (MS Ch E, PhD); civil engineering (MSCE, PhD); computer engineering (PhD); computer science (MSCS, PhD); electrical engineering (MSEE, PhD); energy systems engineering (MSESE); engineering (MSE); industrial engineering (MSIE, PhD); industrial hygiene (MS); material science and engineering (MSMSE, PhD); mechanical engineering (MSME, PhD); mining engineering (MS Min E, PhD); petroleum and natural gas engineering (MSPNGE, PhD); safety management (MS); software engineering (MSSE). *Program availability:* Part-time. *Students:* 466 full-time (113 women), 154 part-time (27 women); includes 57 minority (22 Black or African American, non-Hispanic/Latino; 1 American Indian or Alaska Native, non-Hispanic/Latino; 8 Asian, non-Hispanic/Latino; 12 Hispanic/Latino; 14 Two or more races, non-Hispanic/Latino), 283 international. In 2018, 179 master's, 39 doctorates awarded. Terminal master's awarded for partial completion of doctoral program. *Degree requirements:* For master's, thesis optional; for doctorate, comprehensive exam, thesis/dissertation. *Entrance requirements:* Additional exam requirements/recommendations for international students: Required—TOEFL (minimum score 550 paper-based). *Application deadline:* For fall admission, 4/1 for international students; for winter admission, 4/1 for international students; for spring admission, 10/1 for international students. Applications are processed on a rolling basis. Application fee: $60. Electronic applications accepted. *Expenses:* Contact institution. *Financial support:* Fellowships, research assistantships, teaching assistantships, career-related internships or fieldwork, Federal Work-Study, institutionally sponsored loans, health care benefits, tuition waivers (full and partial), unspecified assistantships, and administrative assistantships available. Financial award application deadline: 2/1; financial award applicants required to submit FAFSA. *Faculty research:* Composite materials, software engineering, information systems, aerodynamics, vehicle propulsion and emission. *Unit head:* Dr. Earl Scime, Interim Dean, 304-293-4157 Ext. 2237, Fax: 304-293-2037, E-mail: earl.scime@mail.wvu.edu. *Application contact:* Dr. David A. Wyrick, Associate Dean, Academic Affairs, 304-293-4334, Fax: 304-293-5024, E-mail: david.wyrick@mail.wvu.edu.
Website: https://www.statler.wvu.edu

Wichita State University, Graduate School, College of Engineering, Department of Industrial and Manufacturing Engineering, Wichita, KS 67260. Offers engineering management (MEM); industrial engineering (MS, PhD). *Program availability:* Part-time. In 2018, 37 master's, 3 doctorates awarded. *Entrance requirements:* Additional exam requirements/recommendations for international students: Required—TOEFL. *Financial support:* Teaching assistantships available. *Unit head:* Dr. Krishna Krishnan, Chair, 316-978-3425, Fax: 316-978-3742, E-mail: krishna.krishnan@wichita.edu. *Application contact:* Jordan Oleson, Admissions Coordinator, 316-978-3095, Fax: 316-978-3253, E-mail: jordan.oleson@wichita.edu.
Website: http://www.wichita.edu/ime

Wright State University, Graduate School, College of Engineering and Computer Science, Department of Biomedical, Industrial and Human Factors Engineering, Dayton, OH 45435. Offers biomedical engineering (MS); industrial and human factors engineering (MS). *Program availability:* Part-time. *Degree requirements:* For master's, thesis or course option alternative. *Entrance requirements:* Additional exam requirements/recommendations for international students: Required—TOEFL. *Faculty research:* Medical imaging, functional electrical stimulation, implantable aids, man-machine interfaces, expert systems.

Youngstown State University, College of Graduate Studies, College of Science, Technology, Engineering and Mathematics, Department of Mechanical, Industrial and Manufacturing Engineering, Youngstown, OH 44555-0001. Offers industrial and systems engineering (MSE); mechanical engineering (MSE). *Program availability:* Part-time, evening/weekend. *Degree requirements:* For master's, thesis optional. *Entrance requirements:* For master's, minimum GPA of 2.75 in field. Additional exam requirements/recommendations for international students: Required—TOEFL. *Faculty research:* Kinematics and dynamics of machines, computational and experimental heat transfer, machine controls and mechanical design.

Manufacturing Engineering

American University of Armenia, Graduate Programs, Yerevan, Armenia. Offers business administration (MBA); computer and information science (MS), including business management, design and manufacturing, energy (ME, MS), industrial engineering and systems management; economics (MS); industrial engineering and systems management (ME), including business, computer aided design/manufacturing, energy (ME, MS), information technology; law (LL M); political science and international affairs (MPSIA); public health (MPH); teaching English as a foreign language (MA). *Program availability:* Part-time, evening/weekend. *Degree requirements:* For master's, thesis (for some programs), capstone/project. *Entrance requirements:* For master's, GRE, GMAT, or LSAT. Additional exam requirements/recommendations for international students: Recommended—TOEFL (minimum score 79 iBT), IELTS (minimum score 6.5). *Faculty research:* Microfinance, finance (rural/development, international, corporate), firm life cycle theory, TESOL, language proficiency testing, public policy, administrative law, economic development, cryptography, artificial intelligence, energy efficiency/renewable energy, computer-aided design/manufacturing, health financing, tuberculosis control, mother/child health, preventive ophthalmology, post-earthquake psychopathological investigations, tobacco control, environmental health risk assessments.

Arizona State University at the Tempe campus, Ira A. Fulton Schools of Engineering, The Polytechnic School, Program in Engineering Technology, Mesa, AZ 85212. Offers manufacturing engineering technology (MS). *Program availability:* Part-time, evening/weekend. *Degree requirements:* For master's, thesis or applied project and oral defense, final examination, interactive Program of Study (iPOS) submitted before completing 50 percent of required credit hours. *Entrance requirements:* For master's, bachelor's degree with minimum of 30 credit hours or equivalent in a technology area including course work applicable to the concentration being sought and minimum of 16 credit hours of math and science; industrial experience beyond bachelor's degree (recommended). Additional exam requirements/recommendations for international students: Required—TOEFL, IELTS, or PTE. Electronic applications accepted. *Faculty research:* Manufacturing modeling and simulation &ITsmart&RO and composite materials, optimization of turbine engines, machinability and manufacturing processes design, fuel cells and other alternative energy sources.

Boston University, College of Engineering, Department of Mechanical Engineering, Boston, MA 02215. Offers manufacturing engineering (MS); mechanical engineering (PhD); MS/MBA. *Program availability:* Part-time, 100% online, blended/hybrid learning. *Students:* 185 full-time (44 women), 55 part-time (13 women); includes 35 minority (2 Black or African American, non-Hispanic/Latino; 16 Asian, non-Hispanic/Latino; 12 Hispanic/Latino; 5 Two or more races, non-Hispanic/Latino), 133 international. Average age 24. 576 applicants, 52% accepted, 93 enrolled. In 2018, 103 master's, 8 doctorates awarded. Terminal master's awarded for partial completion of doctoral program. *Degree requirements:* For master's, thesis (for some programs); for doctorate, comprehensive exam, thesis/dissertation. *Entrance requirements:* For master's and doctorate, GRE General Test. Additional exam requirements/recommendations for international students: Required—TOEFL (minimum score 90 iBT), IELTS (minimum score 7). *Faculty research:* Acoustics, ultrasound, and vibrations; biomechanics; dynamics, control, and robotics; energy and thermofluid sciences; MEMS and nanotechnology. *Unit head:* Dr. Alice White, Chairperson, 617-353-2814, Fax: 617-353-5866, E-mail: aew1@bu.edu. *Application contact:* Dr. Alice White, Chairperson, 617-353-2814, Fax: 617-353-5866, E-mail: aew1@bu.edu.
Website: http://www.bu.edu/me/

Bradley University, The Graduate School, Caterpillar College of Engineering and Technology, Department of Industrial and Manufacturing Engineering and Technology, Peoria, IL 61625-0002. Offers industrial engineering (MS); manufacturing engineering (MS). *Program availability:* Part-time, evening/weekend. *Faculty:* 10 full-time (1 woman). *Students:* 10 full-time (0 women), 6 part-time (2 women); includes 1 minority (Black or African American, non-Hispanic/Latino), 14 international. Average age 28. 53 applicants, 83% accepted, 4 enrolled. In 2018, 11 master's awarded. *Degree requirements:* For master's, comprehensive exam, thesis or alternative, project. *Entrance requirements:* For master's, Minimum GPA of 2.5, Essays, Recommendation letters, Transcripts. Additional exam requirements/recommendations for international students: Required—TOEFL (minimum score 550 paper-based; 79 iBT), IELTS (minimum score 6.5). *Application deadline:* For fall admission, 5/15 priority date for domestic and international students; for spring admission, 10/15 priority date for domestic and international students. Applications are processed on a rolling basis. Application fee: $40 ($50 for international students). Electronic applications accepted. *Expenses: Tuition:* Part-time $890 per credit. *Required fees:* $50 per unit. *Financial support:* In 2018–19, 15 students received support, including 6 research assistantships with full and partial tuition reimbursements available (averaging $4,895 per year); scholarships/grants, tuition waivers (partial), and unspecified assistantships also available. Support available to part-time students. Financial award application deadline: 4/1. *Unit head:* Dr. Joseph Chen, Chair, 309-677-2740, E-mail: jchen@bradley.edu. *Application contact:* Rachel Webb, Director of On-Campus Graduate Admissions & International Student and Scholar Services, 309-677-2375, E-mail: rkwebb@bradley.edu.
Website: http://www.bradley.edu/academic/departments/imet/

Brigham Young University, Graduate Studies, Ira A. Fulton College of Engineering, School of Technology, Provo, UT 84602. Offers construction management (MS); information technology (MS); manufacturing engineering technology (MS); technology and engineering education (MS). *Faculty:* 30 full-time (1 woman), 2 part-time/adjunct (0 women). *Students:* 30 full-time (4 women); includes 6 minority (1 Asian, non-Hispanic/Latino; 1 Hispanic/Latino; 1 Native Hawaiian or other Pacific Islander, non-Hispanic/Latino; 3 Two or more races, non-Hispanic/Latino), 2 international. Average age 28. 14 applicants, 79% accepted, 11 enrolled. In 2018, 29 master's awarded. *Degree requirements:* For master's, thesis. *Entrance requirements:* For master's, GRE General Test; GMAT or GRE (for construction management emphasis), Minimum GPA of 3.0 in last 60 hours of course work. Additional exam requirements/recommendations for international students: Required—TOEFL (minimum score 580 paper-based; 85 iBT). *Application deadline:* For fall admission, 2/15 for domestic and international students; for winter admission, 9/10 for domestic and international students; for spring admission, 2/15 for domestic and international students; for summer admission, 2/15 for domestic and international students. Application fee: $50. Electronic applications accepted. *Financial support:* In 2018–19, 28 students received support, including 9 research assistantships (averaging $3,496 per year), 11 teaching assistantships (averaging $4,755 per year); scholarships/grants also available. Financial award application deadline: 1/15; financial award applicants required to submit FAFSA. *Faculty research:* Information assurance and security, HEI and databases, manufacturing materials, processes and systems, innovation in construction management scheduling and delivery methods. *Total annual research expenditures:* $67,118. *Unit head:* Dr. Barry M. Lunt, Director, 801-422-6300, Fax: 801-422-0490, E-mail: blunt@byu.edu. *Application contact:* Clifton Farnsworth, Graduate Coordinator, 801-422-6494, Fax: 801-422-0490, E-mail: clifton_farnsworth@byu.edu.
Website: http://www.et.byu.edu/sot/

Buffalo State College, State University of New York, The Graduate School, School of the Professions, Department of Engineering Technology, Program in Mechanical and Manufacturing Technology, Buffalo, NY 14222-1095. Offers MS. *Accreditation:* NCATE. *Degree requirements:* For master's, thesis or project. *Entrance requirements:* For master's, minimum GPA of 2.5 in last 60 hours, New York teaching certificate. Additional exam requirements/recommendations for international students: Required—TOEFL (minimum score 550 paper-based).

California State University, Northridge, Graduate Studies, College of Engineering and Computer Science, Department of Manufacturing Systems Engineering and Management, Northridge, CA 91330. Offers engineering automation (MS); engineering management (MS); manufacturing systems engineering (MS); materials engineering (MS). *Program availability:* Online learning. *Entrance requirements:* For master's, GRE (if cumulative undergraduate GPA less than 3.0).

The Citadel, The Military College of South Carolina, Citadel Graduate College, School of Engineering, Department of Mechanical Engineering, Charleston, SC 29409. Offers aeronautical engineering (Graduate Certificate); composites engineering (Graduate Certificate); manufacturing engineering (Graduate Certificate); mechanical engineering (MS); mechatronics engineering (Graduate Certificate); power and energy (Graduate Certificate). *Program availability:* Part-time, evening/weekend. *Degree requirements:* For master's, 30 hours of coursework with minimum GPA of 3.0 on hours earned at The Citadel. *Entrance requirements:* For master's, GRE, 2 letters of recommendation; official transcript of baccalaureate degree from an ABET accredited engineering program or approved alternative. Additional exam requirements/recommendations for international students: Required—TOEFL (minimum score 550 paper-based; 79 iBT). Electronic applications accepted. *Expenses:* Tuition, state resident: part-time $595 per credit hour. Tuition, nonresident: part-time $1020 per credit hour. *Required fees:* $90 per term.

Cornell University, Graduate School, Graduate Fields of Engineering, Field of Operations Research and Information Engineering, Ithaca, NY 14853. Offers applied probability and statistics (PhD); manufacturing systems engineering (PhD); mathematical programming (PhD); operations research and industrial engineering (M Eng). *Degree requirements:* For doctorate, comprehensive exam, thesis/dissertation. *Entrance requirements:* For master's and doctorate, GRE General Test, 3 letters of recommendation. Additional exam requirements/recommendations for international students: Required—TOEFL (minimum score 600 paper-based; 100 iBT). Electronic applications accepted. *Faculty research:* Mathematical programming and combinatorial optimization, statistics, stochastic processes, mathematical finance, simulation, manufacturing, e-commerce.

Eastern Kentucky University, The Graduate School, College of Business and Technology, Department of Technology, Richmond, KY 40475-3102. Offers industrial education (MS), including occupational training and development, technical administration, technology education; industrial technology (MS). *Program availability:* Part-time, evening/weekend. *Entrance requirements:* For master's, GRE General Test, minimum GPA of 2.5. *Faculty research:* Lunar excavation, computer networking, integrating academic and vocational education.

East Tennessee State University, School of Graduate Studies, College of Business and Technology, Department of Engineering, Engineering Technology, and Surveying, Johnson City, TN 37614. Offers technology (MS). *Program availability:* Part-time. *Degree requirements:* For master's, comprehensive exam, thesis optional, capstone. *Entrance requirements:* For master's, bachelor's degree in technical or related area, minimum GPA of 3.0, undergraduate course in probability and statistics. Additional exam requirements/recommendations for international students: Required—TOEFL (minimum score 550 paper-based; 79 iBT). Electronic applications accepted. *Faculty research:* Computer-integrated manufacturing, alternative energy, sustainability, CAD/CAM, organizational change.

Florida State University, The Graduate School, FAMU-FSU College of Engineering, Department of Industrial and Manufacturing Engineering, Tallahassee, FL 32310. Offers industrial engineering (MS, PhD). *Degree requirements:* For master's, thesis, proposal presentation, progress presentation, defense presentation; for doctorate, thesis/dissertation, preliminary exam, proposal exam, defense exam. *Entrance requirements:*

For master's, GRE General Test (minimum new score of 146 Verbal and 155 Quantitative), minimum GPA of 3.0; for doctorate, GRE General Test (minimum new score of 146 Verbal and 155 Quantitative), minimum GPA of 3.0 (without MS in industrial engineering), 3.4 (with MS in industrial engineering). Additional exam requirements/ recommendations for international students: Required—TOEFL (minimum score 550 paper-based; 80 iBT); Recommended—IELTS (minimum score 6.5). Electronic applications accepted. *Expenses: Tuition, area resident:* Part-time $479.32 per credit hour. Tuition and fees vary according to campus/location and program. *Faculty research:* Precision manufacturing, composite manufacturing, green manufacturing, applied optimization, simulation.

Georgia Southern University, Jack N. Averitt College of Graduate Studies, Allen E. Paulson College of Engineering and Computing, Department of Mechanical Engineering, Statesboro, GA 30460. Offers engineering and information technology (MSAE), including engineering and information technology; engineering and manufacturing management (Graduate Certificate); engineering/energy science (MSAE); engineering/engineering management (MSAE); engineering/mechatronics (MSAE); occupational safety and environmental compliance (Graduate Certificate). *Program availability:* Part-time, evening/weekend. *Degree requirements:* For master's, comprehensive exam, thesis optional. *Entrance requirements:* For master's, GRE, undergraduate major or equivalent in proposed study area. Additional exam requirements/recommendations for international students: Required—TOEFL (minimum score 550 paper-based; 80 iBT), IELTS (minimum score 6). Electronic applications accepted. *Expenses: Tuition, area resident:* Part-time $3324 per semester. Tuition, state resident: full-time $5814; part-time $3324 per semester. Tuition, nonresident: full-time $23,204; part-time $13,260 per semester. *Required fees:* $2092; $2092. Tuition and fees vary according to course load, degree level, campus/location and program. *Faculty research:* Interdisciplinary research in computational mechanics, experimental and computational biofuel combustion and tribology, mechatronics and control, thermomechanical and thermofluid finite element modeling, information technology, analysis and design of antennas for wireless communications, wireless energy harvest, propagation modeling, RFID, wireless sensors, GPS/GNSS, metamaterials, finite element modeling of bioinstrumentation, embedded systems.

Grand Valley State University, Padnos College of Engineering and Computing, School of Engineering, Allendale, MI 49401-9403. Offers electrical and computer engineering (MSE); manufacturing operations (MSE); mechanical engineering (MSE); product design and manufacturing engineering (MSE). *Program availability:* Part-time, evening/ weekend. *Faculty:* 19 full-time (5 women). *Students:* 26 full-time (5 women), 50 part-time (7 women); includes 6 minority (1 Black or African American, non-Hispanic/Latino; 2 Asian, non-Hispanic/Latino; 1 Hispanic/Latino; 2 Two or more races, non-Hispanic/ Latino), 39 international. Average age 26. 52 applicants, 62% accepted, 13 enrolled. In 2018, 32 master's awarded. *Entrance requirements:* For master's, engineering degree, minimum GPA of 3.0, resume, 3 confidential letters of recommendation, 1-2 page essay, base of underlying relevant knowledge/evidence from academic records or relevant wok experience. Additional exam requirements/recommendations for international students: Required—Michigan English Language Assessment Battery (minimum score 77), TOEFL (minimum iBT score of 80), or IELTS (6.5); GRE. *Application deadline:* Applications are processed on a rolling basis. Application fee: $30. Electronic applications accepted. *Expenses:* $712 per credit hour, 33 credit hours. *Financial support:* In 2018–19, 40 students received support, including 8 fellowships, 34 research assistantships with full and partial tuition reimbursements available (averaging $4,000 per year); career-related internships or fieldwork, Federal Work-Study, institutionally sponsored loans, scholarships/grants, and unspecified assistantships also available. *Faculty research:* Digital signal processing, computer aided design, computer aided manufacturing, manufacturing simulation, biomechanics, product design. *Total annual research expenditures:* $300,000. *Unit head:* Dr. Wael Mokhtar, Director, 616-331-6015, Fax: 616-331-7215, E-mail: mokhtarw@gvsu.edu. *Application contact:* Dr. Shabbir Choudhuri, Graduate Program Director, 616-331-6845, Fax: 616-331-7215, E-mail: choudhus@gvsu.edu.
Website: http://www.engineer.gvsu.edu/

Illinois Institute of Technology, Graduate College, Armour College of Engineering, Department of Mechanical, Materials and Aerospace Engineering, Chicago, IL 60616. Offers manufacturing engineering (MAS, MS); materials science and engineering (MAS, MS, PhD); mechanical and aerospace engineering (MAS, MS, PhD), including economics (MS), energy (MS), environment (MS). *Program availability:* Part-time, evening/weekend, online learning. Terminal master's awarded for partial completion of doctoral program. *Degree requirements:* For master's, comprehensive exam (for some programs), thesis (for some programs); for doctorate, comprehensive exam, thesis/ dissertation. *Entrance requirements:* For master's and doctorate, GRE General Test (minimum score 1000 Quantitative and Verbal, 3.0 Analytical Writing), minimum undergraduate GPA of 3.0. Additional exam requirements/recommendations for international students: Required—TOEFL (minimum score 550 paper-based; 80 iBT). Electronic applications accepted. *Faculty research:* Fluid dynamics, metallurgical and materials engineering, solids and structures, computational mechanics, computer added design and manufacturing, thermal sciences, dynamic analysis and control of complex systems.

Instituto Tecnológico y de Estudios Superiores de Monterrey, Campus Monterrey, Graduate and Research Division, Programs in Engineering, Monterrey, Mexico. Offers applied statistics (M Eng); artificial intelligence (PhD); automation engineering (M Eng); chemical engineering (M Eng); civil engineering (M Eng); electrical engineering (M Eng); electronic engineering (M Eng); environmental engineering (M Eng); industrial engineering (M Eng, PhD); manufacturing engineering (M Eng); mechanical engineering (M Eng); systems and quality engineering (M Eng). M Eng program offered jointly with University of Waterloo; PhD in industrial engineering with Texas A&M University. *Program availability:* Part-time, evening/weekend. Terminal master's awarded for partial completion of doctoral program. *Degree requirements:* For master's, one foreign language, thesis; for doctorate, one foreign language, thesis/dissertation. *Entrance requirements:* For master's, EXADEP; for doctorate, GRE, master's degree in related field. Additional exam requirements/recommendations for international students: Required—TOEFL. *Faculty research:* Flexible manufacturing cells, materials, statistical methods, environmental prevention, control and evaluation.

Kansas State University, Graduate School, College of Engineering, Department of Industrial and Manufacturing Systems Engineering, Manhattan, KS 66506. Offers engineering management (MEM); industrial engineering (MS); operations research (MS). *Program availability:* Part-time, online learning. *Degree requirements:* For master's, thesis or alternative; for doctorate, thesis/dissertation. *Entrance requirements:* For master's, GRE General Test (minimum score of 750 old version, 159 new format on Quantitative portion of exam), bachelor's degree in engineering, mathematics, or physical science; for doctorate, GRE General Test (minimum score of 770 old version, 164 new format on Quantitative portion of exam), master's degree in engineering or industrial manufacturing. Additional exam requirements/recommendations for international students: Required—PTE (minimum score 58), TOEFL (minimum score 550 paper-based; 79 iBT) or IELTS (minimum score 6.5). Electronic applications accepted. *Faculty research:* Industrial engineering, ergonomics, healthcare systems engineering, manufacturing processes, operations research, engineering management.

Kettering University, Graduate School, Department of Industrial and Manufacturing Engineering, Flint, MI 48504. Offers engineering (MS). *Program availability:* Part-time, evening/weekend, online learning. *Degree requirements:* For master's, thesis optional. *Entrance requirements:* Additional exam requirements/recommendations for international students: Required—TOEFL (minimum score 550 paper-based; 79 iBT). Electronic applications accepted. *Faculty research:* Failure analysis, gestural controls.

Lawrence Technological University, College of Engineering, Southfield, MI 48075-1058. Offers architectural engineering (MS); automotive engineering (MS); biomedical engineering (MS); civil engineering (MA, MS, PhD), including environmental engineering (MS), geotechnical engineering (MS), structural engineering (MS), transportation engineering (MS), water resource engineering (MS); construction engineering management (MA); electrical and computer engineering (MS); engineering management (MEM); engineering technology (MS); fire engineering (MS); industrial engineering (MS), including healthcare systems; manufacturing systems (ME); mechanical engineering (MS, DE, PhD), including automotive engineering (MS), energy engineering (MS), manufacturing (DE), solid mechanics (MS), thermal/fluid systems (MS); mechatronic systems engineering (MS). *Program availability:* Part-time, evening/weekend. Terminal master's awarded for partial completion of doctoral program. *Degree requirements:* For master's, thesis optional; for doctorate, comprehensive exam, thesis/dissertation optional. *Entrance requirements:* Additional exam requirements/recommendations for international students: Required—TOEFL (minimum score 550 paper-based; 79 iBT), IELTS (minimum score 6.5). Electronic applications accepted. *Faculty research:* Innovative infrastructure and building structures and materials; connectivity and mobility; automotive systems modeling, simulation and testing; biomedical devices and materials; building mechanical/electrical systems.

Massachusetts Institute of Technology, School of Engineering, Department of Mechanical Engineering, Cambridge, MA 02139. Offers manufacturing (M Eng); mechanical engineering (SM, PhD, Sc D, Mech E); naval architecture and marine engineering (SM, PhD, Sc D); naval engineering (Naval E); ocean engineering (SM, PhD, Sc D); oceanographic engineering (SM, PhD, Sc D); SM/MBA. Terminal master's awarded for partial completion of doctoral program. *Degree requirements:* For master's, thesis; for doctorate, comprehensive exam, thesis/dissertation; for other advanced degree, comprehensive exam, thesis. *Entrance requirements:* For master's, doctorate, and other advanced degree, GRE General Test. Additional exam requirements/ recommendations for international students: Required—TOEFL, IELTS. Electronic applications accepted. *Expenses: Tuition:* Full-time $51,520; part-time $800 per credit hour. *Required fees:* $312. *Faculty research:* Mechanics: modeling, experimentation and computation; design, manufacturing, and product development; controls, instrumentation, and robotics; energy science and engineering; ocean science and engineering; bioengineering; micro- and Nano-engineering.

Michigan State University, The Graduate School, College of Agriculture and Natural Resources, School of Packaging, East Lansing, MI 48824. Offers MS, PhD. *Entrance requirements:* Additional exam requirements/recommendations for international students: Required—TOEFL. Electronic applications accepted.

Minnesota State University Mankato, College of Graduate Studies and Research, College of Science, Engineering and Technology, Department of Automotive and Manufacturing Engineering Technology, Mankato, MN 56001. Offers manufacturing engineering technology (MS). *Degree requirements:* For master's, comprehensive exam, thesis. *Entrance requirements:* For master's, minimum GPA of 2.75 during previous 2 years. Additional exam requirements/recommendations for international students: Required—TOEFL (minimum score 525 paper-based). Electronic applications accepted.

Missouri University of Science and Technology, Department of Mechanical and Aerospace Engineering, Rolla, MO 65401. Offers aerospace engineering (MS, PhD); manufacturing engineering (M Eng, MS); mechanical engineering (MS, PhD). *Program availability:* Part-time, evening/weekend. Terminal master's awarded for partial completion of doctoral program. *Degree requirements:* For master's, thesis optional; for doctorate, comprehensive exam, thesis/dissertation. *Entrance requirements:* For master's, GRE General Test (minimum score 1100 verbal and quantitative, writing 3.5), minimum GPA of 3.0; for doctorate, GRE General Test (minimum score: verbal and quantitative 1100, writing 3.5), minimum GPA of 3.5. Additional exam requirements/ recommendations for international students: Required—TOEFL (minimum score 550 paper-based). Electronic applications accepted. *Expenses:* Tuition, state resident: full-time $7545.60; part-time $419.20 per credit hour. Tuition, nonresident: full-time $22,169; part-time $1231.60 per credit hour. *International tuition:* $23,518.80 full-time. *Required fees:* $4523.05. Full-time tuition and fees vary according to course load, campus/location, program and reciprocity agreements. *Faculty research:* Dynamics and controls, acoustics, computational fluid dynamics, space mechanics, hypersonics.

New Jersey Institute of Technology, Newark College of Engineering, Newark, NJ 07102. Offers biomedical engineering (MS, PhD); biopharmaceutical engineering (MS); chemical engineering (MS, PhD); civil engineering (MS, PhD); computer engineering (MS); critical infrastructure systems (MS); electrical engineering (MS, PhD); engineering management (MS); engineering science (MS); environmental engineering (MS, PhD); healthcare systems management (MS); industrial engineering (MS, PhD); internet engineering (MS); manufacturing systems engineering (MS); materials science & engineering (PhD); materials science and engineering (MS); mechanical engineering (MS, PhD); occupational safety and health engineering (MS). *Program availability:* Part-time, evening/weekend. *Faculty:* 147 full-time (26 women), 133 part-time/adjunct (16 women). *Students:* 690 full-time (163 women), 594 part-time (130 women); includes 427 minority (79 Black or African American, non-Hispanic/Latino; 181 Asian, non-Hispanic/ Latino; 140 Hispanic/Latino; 27 Two or more races, non-Hispanic/Latino), 553 international. Average age 27. 2,334 applicants, 57% accepted, 452 enrolled. In 2018, 418 master's, 31 doctorates awarded. Terminal master's awarded for partial completion of doctoral program. *Degree requirements:* For master's, thesis (for some programs); for doctorate, thesis/dissertation. *Entrance requirements:* For master's, GRE General Test, minimum GPA 2.8, personal statement, 1 letter of recommendation, transcripts; for doctorate, GRE General Test, minimum GPA of 3.5, personal statement, 3 letters of recommendation, transcripts. Additional exam requirements/recommendations for international students: Required—TOEFL (minimum score 550 paper-based; 79 iBT), IELTS (minimum score 6.5). *Application deadline:* For fall admission, 6/1 priority date for domestic students, 5/1 priority date for international students; for spring admission, 11/ 15 priority date for domestic and international students. Applications are processed on a rolling basis. Application fee: $75. Electronic applications accepted. *Expenses:* $22,690 per year (in-state), $32,136 per year (out-of-state). *Financial support:* In 2018–19, 396 students received support, including 52 fellowships with full tuition reimbursements available (averaging $22,000 per year), 113 research assistantships with full tuition reimbursements available (averaging $22,000 per year), 101 teaching assistantships with full tuition reimbursements available (averaging $22,000 per year); career-related internships or fieldwork, Federal Work-Study, scholarships/grants, and unspecified assistantships also available. Financial award application deadline: 1/15. *Faculty research:* Nonlinear signal processing, intelligent medical image analysis, calibration

issues in coherent localization, computer-aided design, neural network for tool wear measurement. *Total annual research expenditures:* $41.7 million. *Unit head:* Dr. Moshe Kam, Dean, 973-596-5534, Fax: 973-596-2316, E-mail: moshe.kam@njit.edu. *Application contact:* Stephen Eck, Director of Admissions, 973-596-3300, Fax: 973-596-3461, E-mail: admissions@njit.edu.
Website: http://engineering.njit.edu/

New York University, Tandon School of Engineering, Department of Technology Management, New York, NY 10012-1019. Offers manufacturing engineering (MS); technology management (PhD). *Program availability:* Part-time, evening/weekend. *Faculty:* 10 full-time (3 women), 30 part-time/adjunct (1 woman). *Students:* 231 full-time (105 women), 95 part-time (38 women); includes 49 minority (11 Black or African American, non-Hispanic/Latino; 22 Asian, non-Hispanic/Latino; 15 Hispanic/Latino; 1 Two or more races, non-Hispanic/Latino), 236 international. Average age 26. 858 applicants, 52% accepted, 136 enrolled. In 2018, 260 master's, 2 doctorates awarded. *Entrance requirements:* For master's, GMAT, minimum B average in undergraduate course work. Additional exam requirements/recommendations for international students: Required—TOEFL (minimum score 550 paper-based; 90 iBT); Recommended—IELTS (minimum score 7). *Application deadline:* For fall admission, 2/15 priority date for domestic and international students; for spring admission, 11/1 priority date for domestic and international students. Applications are processed on a rolling basis. Application fee: $75. Electronic applications accepted. *Expenses:* Contact institution. *Financial support:* In 2018–19, 168 students received support, including 1 fellowship (averaging $26,400 per year); research assistantships, teaching assistantships, career-related internships or fieldwork, scholarships/grants, tuition waivers, and unspecified assistantships also available. Support available to part-time students. Financial award application deadline: 2/15. *Faculty research:* Global innovation and research and development strategy, managing emerging technologies, technology and development, service design and innovation, tech entrepreneurship and commercialization, sustainable and clean-tech innovation, impacts of information technology upon individuals, organizations and society. *Total annual research expenditures:* $1.9 million. *Unit head:* Dr. Jonathan Soffer, Interim Department chair, 997-3617, E-mail: bharat.rao@nyu.edu. *Application contact:* Elizabeth Ensweiler, Senior Director of Graduate Enrollment and Graduate Admissions, 646-997-3182, E-mail: elizabeth.ensweiler@nyu.edu.
Website: http://www.poly.edu/academics/departments/technology/

North Carolina State University, Graduate School, College of Engineering, Integrated Manufacturing Systems Engineering Institute, Raleigh, NC 27695. Offers MIMS. *Program availability:* Part-time. *Degree requirements:* For master's, thesis optional. *Entrance requirements:* For master's, GRE. Additional exam requirements/recommendations for international students: Required—TOEFL. Electronic applications accepted. *Faculty research:* Mechatronics, manufacturing systems modeling, systems integration product and process engineering, logistics.

North Dakota State University, College of Graduate and Interdisciplinary Studies, College of Engineering, Department of Industrial and Manufacturing Engineering, Fargo, ND 58102. Offers industrial and manufacturing engineering (MS, PhD); manufacturing engineering (MS). *Program availability:* Part-time. *Degree requirements:* For doctorate, comprehensive exam, thesis/dissertation. *Entrance requirements:* For master's, GRE General Test, bachelor's degree in engineering; for doctorate, GRE General Test, master's degree in engineering. Additional exam requirements/recommendations for international students: Required—TOEFL (minimum score 550 paper-based; 79 iBT), TWE (minimum score 4). Electronic applications accepted. *Faculty research:* Electronics manufacturing, quality engineering, manufacturing process science, healthcare, lean manufacturing.

Oregon Institute of Technology, Program in Manufacturing Engineering Technology, Klamath Falls, OR 97601-8801. Offers MS. *Program availability:* Part-time, online learning. *Degree requirements:* For master's, one foreign language, project. *Entrance requirements:* For master's, GRE General Test. Electronic applications accepted.

Oregon State University, College of Engineering, Program in Industrial Engineering, Corvallis, OR 97331. Offers advanced manufacturing (M Eng, MS, PhD); engineering management (M Eng); human systems engineering (M Eng, MS, PhD); information systems engineering (M Eng, MS, PhD); manufacturing systems engineering (M Eng, MS, PhD). *Program availability:* 100% online. *Entrance requirements:* For master's and doctorate, GRE. Additional exam requirements/recommendations for international students: Required—TOEFL (minimum score 80 iBT), IELTS (minimum score 6.5). *Expenses:* Contact institution.

Pittsburg State University, Graduate School, College of Technology, Department of Engineering Technology, Pittsburg, KS 66762. Offers electrical engineering technology (MET); general engineering technology (MET); manufacturing engineering technology (MET); mechanical engineering technology (MET); plastics engineering technology (MET). *Program availability:* Part-time, 100% online, blended/hybrid learning. *Degree requirements:* For master's, thesis optional. *Entrance requirements:* Additional exam requirements/recommendations for international students: Required—TOEFL (minimum score 550 paper-based; 79 iBT), IELTS (minimum score 6.5), PTE (minimum score 51). Electronic applications accepted. *Expenses:* Contact institution.

Polytechnic University of Puerto Rico, Graduate School, Hato Rey, PR 00918. Offers business administration (MBA), including computer information systems, general management, management of information systems, management of international enterprises; civil engineering (ME, MS); computer engineering (ME, MS); computer science (MCS, MS); electrical engineering (ME, MS); engineering management (MEM); environmental management (MEM); landscape architecture (M Land Arch); manufacturing competitiveness (MMC, MS); manufacturing engineering (ME, MS); mechanical engineering (M Mech E). *Accreditation:* ASLA. *Program availability:* Part-time, evening/weekend. *Entrance requirements:* For master's, 3 letters of recommendation.

Rochester Institute of Technology, Graduate Enrollment Services, College of Applied Science and Technology, School of Engineering Technology, MS Program in Manufacturing and Mechanical Systems Integration, Rochester, NY 14623-5603. Offers MS. *Program availability:* Part-time, evening/weekend. *Students:* 48 full-time (7 women), 17 part-time (2 women); includes 2 minority (1 Black or African American, non-Hispanic/Latino; 1 Hispanic/Latino), 57 international. Average age 24. 43 applicants, 84% accepted, 8 enrolled. In 2018, 14 master's awarded. *Degree requirements:* For master's, thesis (for some programs). *Entrance requirements:* For master's, GRE required for applicants with degrees from international universities, minimum GPA of 3.0 (recommended). Additional exam requirements/recommendations for international students: Required—TOEFL (minimum score 550 paper-based; 80 iBT), IELTS (minimum score 6.5), PTE (minimum score 58). *Application deadline:* Applications are processed on a rolling basis. Application fee: $65. Electronic applications accepted. *Financial support:* In 2018–19, 63 students received support. Research assistantships with partial tuition reimbursements available, teaching assistantships with partial tuition reimbursements available, career-related internships or fieldwork, scholarships/grants, and unspecified assistantships available. Support available to part-time students. Financial award applicants required to submit FAFSA. *Faculty research:* Advanced manufacturing in electronics/photonics including materials and reliability development; complex rheological fluid spray research and development; system dynamics modeling and control using computer aided engineering; automation (robotics) using cyber-physical systems; the Internet of Things, and cloud computing; applications-focused plastics and polymer composites research. *Unit head:* Dr. Betsy Dell, Graduate Program Director, 585-475-6577, E-mail: emdmet@rit.edu. *Application contact:* Diane Ellison, Senior Associate Vice President, Graduate Enrollment Services, 585-475-2229, Fax: 585-475-7164, E-mail: gradinfo@rit.edu.
Website: https://www.rit.edu/study/manufacturing-and-mechanical-systems-integration-ms

Rochester Institute of Technology, Graduate Enrollment Services, College of Applied Science and Technology, School of Engineering Technology, MS Program in Packaging Science, Rochester, NY 14623-5603. Offers MS. *Program availability:* Part-time. *Students:* 27 full-time (10 women), 2 part-time (both women); includes 3 minority (2 Asian, non-Hispanic/Latino; 1 Hispanic/Latino), 21 international. Average age 25. 29 applicants, 76% accepted, 10 enrolled. In 2018, 17 master's awarded. *Degree requirements:* For master's, comprehensive exam (for some programs), thesis or alternative, thesis, project, or comprehensive exam. *Entrance requirements:* For master's, minimum GPA of 3.0 (recommended) in the final two years of graduate study. Additional exam requirements/recommendations for international students: Required—TOEFL (minimum score 550 paper-based; 79 iBT), IELTS (minimum score 6.5), PTE (minimum score 58). *Application deadline:* Applications are processed on a rolling basis. Application fee: $65. Electronic applications accepted. *Expenses:* Contact institution. *Financial support:* In 2018–19, 26 students received support. Research assistantships with partial tuition reimbursements available, teaching assistantships with partial tuition reimbursements available, career-related internships or fieldwork, scholarships/grants, and unspecified assistantships available. Support available to part-time students. Financial award applicants required to submit FAFSA. *Faculty research:* Protective packaging, modeling and mapping of the packaged products in supply chain; packaging design; shelf life extension of food and pharmaceutical products, interaction between packaging materials and packaged goods; design of bioplastic packaging materials for aerobic and anaerobic end of life scenarios; development and evaluation of active and intelligent packaging components. *Unit head:* Dr. Changfeng Ge, Graduate Program Director, 585-475-5391, E-mail: cfgmet@rit.edu. *Application contact:* Diane Ellison, Senior Associate Vice President, Graduate Enrollment Services, 585-475-2229, Fax: 585-475-7164, E-mail: gradinfo@rit.edu.
Website: https://www.rit.edu/study/packaging-science-ms

Rochester Institute of Technology, Graduate Enrollment Services, Kate Gleason College of Engineering, Design, Development and Manufacturing Department, Rochester, NY 14623-5603. Offers manufacturing leadership (MS); product development (MS). *Program availability:* Part-time-only, evening/weekend, 100% online, blended/hybrid learning. *Students:* 2 full-time (1 woman), 41 part-time (7 women); includes 3 minority (2 Black or African American, non-Hispanic/Latino; 1 Hispanic/Latino), 1 international. Average age 36. 31 applicants, 48% accepted, 12 enrolled. In 2018, 8 master's awarded. *Entrance requirements:* For master's, minimum GPA of 2.5, 2 years of related work experience. *Application deadline:* Applications are processed on a rolling basis. Application fee: $65. Electronic applications accepted. *Expenses:* Contact institution. *Financial support:* In 2018–19, 3 students received support. Scholarships/grants available. Support available to part-time students. Financial award applicants required to submit FAFSA. *Faculty research:* Systems engineering; project management; lean product development and lean manufacturing; decision analysis; modeling and simulation; supply chain management. *Unit head:* Mark Smith, Director, 585-475-7102, Fax: 585-475-7955, E-mail: mark.smith@rit.edu. *Application contact:* Diane Ellison, Senior Associate Vice President, Graduate Enrollment Services, 585-475-2229, Fax: 585-475-7164, E-mail: gradinfo@rit.edu.
Website: https://www.rit.edu/kgcoe/

Rochester Institute of Technology, Graduate Enrollment Services, Kate Gleason College of Engineering, Electrical and Microelectronic Engineering Department, ME Program in Microelectronic Manufacturing Engineering, Rochester, NY 14623-5603. Offers ME. *Program availability:* Part-time, evening/weekend, 100% online. *Students:* 2 full-time (1 woman), 3 part-time (1 woman); includes 2 minority (1 Asian, non-Hispanic/Latino; 1 Hispanic/Latino), 1 international. Average age 31. 6 applicants, 50% accepted, 2 enrolled. In 2018, 3 master's awarded. *Degree requirements:* For master's, Internship. *Entrance requirements:* For master's, minimum GPA of 3.0 (recommended), 2 letters of recommendation, hold a baccalaureate degree from an accredited institution in engineering or a related field. Additional exam requirements/recommendations for international students: Required—TOEFL (minimum score 550 paper-based; 79 iBT), IELTS (minimum score 6.5), PTE (minimum score 28). *Application deadline:* For fall admission, 2/15 priority date for domestic and international students. Applications are processed on a rolling basis. Application fee: $65. Electronic applications accepted. *Expenses:* Contact institution. *Financial support:* In 2018–19, 4 students received support. Research assistantships with partial tuition reimbursements available, teaching assistantships with partial tuition reimbursements available, career-related internships or fieldwork, scholarships/grants, and unspecified assistantships available. Support available to part-time students. Financial award applicants required to submit FAFSA. *Faculty research:* Microlithography and design of experiments; electronic materials for microelectronic photovoltaics devices; semiconductor nanolithography materials and systems; thin film deposition and etching. *Unit head:* Dr. Robert Pearson, Graduate Program Director, 585-475-2923, Fax: 585-475-5845, E-mail: robert.pearson@rit.edu. *Application contact:* Diane Ellison, Senior Associate Vice President, Graduate Enrollment Services, 585-475-2229, Fax: 585-475-7164, E-mail: gradinfo@rit.edu.
Website: https://www.rit.edu/study/microelectronics-manufacturing-engineering-me

Rochester Institute of Technology, Graduate Enrollment Services, Kate Gleason College of Engineering, Industrial and Systems Engineering Department, Rochester, NY 14623-5603. Offers engineering management (ME); industrial and systems engineering (ME, MS); sustainable engineering (ME, MS). *Program availability:* Part-time. *Students:* 46 full-time (14 women), 29 part-time (5 women); includes 7 minority (1 Black or African American, non-Hispanic/Latino; 3 Asian, non-Hispanic/Latino; 2 Hispanic/Latino; 1 Two or more races, non-Hispanic/Latino), 30 international. Average age 25. 461 applicants, 28% accepted, 27 enrolled. In 2018, 49 master's awarded. *Entrance requirements:* For master's, GRE, minimum GPA of 3.0 (recommended). *Application deadline:* For fall admission, 2/15 priority date for domestic and international students; for spring admission, 12/15 priority date for domestic and international students. Applications are processed on a rolling basis. Application fee: $65. Electronic applications accepted. *Expenses:* Contact institution. *Financial support:* In 2018–19, 65 students received support. Research assistantships with partial tuition reimbursements available, teaching assistantships with partial tuition reimbursements available, career-related internships or fieldwork, scholarships/grants, and unspecified assistantships available. Support available to part-time students. Financial award applicants required to submit FAFSA. *Faculty research:* Advanced manufacturing; health systems; statistics/analytics; supply chain, production and logistics systems; systems engineering/product life-cycle management; lean manufacturing; renewable and alternative energies; grid optimization and Smart Grid applications; sanitation, water supply, soil fertility; off grid energy applications; human centered design. *Unit head:* Dr. Scott Grasman, Department Head,

585-475-2598, Fax: 585-475-2520, E-mail: ise@rit.edu. *Application contact:* Diane Ellison, Senior Associate Vice President, Graduate Enrollment Services, 585-475-2229, Fax: 585-475-7164, E-mail: gradinfo@rit.edu.
Website: http://www.rit.edu/kgcoe/ise/

Southern Methodist University, Lyle School of Engineering, Department of Mechanical Engineering, Dallas, TX 75205. Offers manufacturing systems management (MS); mechanical engineering (MS, PhD). *Program availability:* Part-time, evening/weekend, online learning. Terminal master's awarded for partial completion of doctoral program. *Degree requirements:* For master's, thesis optional; for doctorate, thesis/dissertation, oral and written qualifying exams, oral final exam. *Entrance requirements:* For master's, GRE General Test, minimum GPA of 3.0 in last 2 years; bachelor's degree in engineering, mathematics, or sciences; for doctorate, preliminary counseling exam, minimum graduate GPA of 3.0, bachelor's degree in related field. Additional exam requirements/recommendations for international students: Required—TOEFL. *Faculty research:* Design, systems, and controls; thermal and fluid sciences.

Stevens Institute of Technology, Graduate School, Charles V. Schaefer Jr. School of Engineering and Science, Department of Mechanical Engineering, Program in Integrated Product Development, Hoboken, NJ 07030. Offers armament engineering (M Eng); computer and electrical engineering (M Eng); manufacturing technologies (M Eng); systems reliability and design (M Eng). *Program availability:* Part-time, evening/weekend. *Faculty:* 32 full-time (4 women), 10 part-time/adjunct (0 women). *Degree requirements:* For master's, thesis optional, minimum B average in major field and overall. *Entrance requirements:* For master's, GRE/GMAT scores: GRE scores are required for all applicants applying to a full-time graduate program in the Schaefer School of Engineering and Science (SES). International applicants must submit TOEFL/IELTS scores and fulfill the English Language Proficiency Requirements in order to be considered. Additional exam requirements/recommendations for international students: Required—TOEFL (minimum score 74 iBT), IELTS (minimum score 6). *Application deadline:* For fall admission, 4/15 for domestic and international students; for spring admission, 11/1 for domestic and international students; for summer admission, 5/1 for domestic students. Applications are processed on a rolling basis. Application fee: $60. Electronic applications accepted. *Expenses: Tuition:* Full-time $35,960; part-time $1620 per credit. *Required fees:* $1290; $600 per semester. Tuition and fees vary according to course load. *Financial support:* Fellowships, research assistantships, teaching assistantships, career-related internships or fieldwork, Federal Work-Study, scholarships/grants, and unspecified assistantships available. Financial award application deadline: 2/15; financial award applicants required to submit FAFSA. *Unit head:* Dr. Jean Zu, Dean of SES, 201-216.8233, Fax: 201-216.8372, E-mail: Jean.Zu@stevens.edu. *Application contact:* Graduate Admissions, 888-783-8367, Fax: 888-511-1306, E-mail: graduate@stevens.edu.

Tennessee State University, The School of Graduate Studies and Research, College of Engineering, Nashville, TN 37209-1561. Offers biomedical engineering (ME); civil engineering (ME); computer and information systems engineering (MS, PhD); electrical engineering (ME); environmental engineering (ME); manufacturing engineering (ME); mathematical sciences (MS); mechanical engineering (ME). *Program availability:* Part-time, evening/weekend. *Degree requirements:* For master's, project; for doctorate, comprehensive exam, thesis/dissertation. *Entrance requirements:* For doctorate, minimum GPA of 3.3. *Faculty research:* Robotics, intelligent systems, human-computer interaction software systems, biomedical engineering, signal/image processing, probabilistic design, intelligent manufacturing, cooperative mobile robots, condition based maintenance, sensor fusion.

Texas A&M University, College of Engineering, Department of Engineering Technology and Industrial Distribution, College Station, TX 77843. Offers industrial distribution (MID); technical management (METM). *Faculty:* 40. *Students:* 141 full-time (45 women), 5 part-time (1 woman); includes 46 minority (8 Black or African American, non-Hispanic/Latino; 7 Asian, non-Hispanic/Latino; 29 Hispanic/Latino; 2 Two or more races, non-Hispanic/Latino), 3 international. Average age 37. 112 applicants, 94% accepted, 92 enrolled. In 2018, 58 master's awarded. *Entrance requirements:* Additional exam requirements/recommendations for international students: Required—TOEFL (minimum score 550 paper-based; 80 iBT), IELTS (minimum score 6), PTE (minimum score 53). *Application deadline:* For fall admission, 3/1 priority date for domestic and international students; for winter admission, 11/1 for domestic and international students; for spring admission, 8/1 priority date for domestic and international students. Applications are processed on a rolling basis. Application fee: $50 ($90 for international students). Electronic applications accepted. *Expenses:* Contact institution. *Financial support:* In 2018–19, 57 students received support. Application deadline: 3/15; applicants required to submit FAFSA. *Unit head:* Dr. Reza Langari, Department Head, 979-862-4945, E-mail: rlangari@tamu.edu. *Application contact:* Graduate Admissions, 979-458-0427, E-mail: graduate-admissions@tamu.edu.
Website: http://engineering.tamu.edu/etid

Texas State University, The Graduate College, College of Science and Engineering, Program in Engineering, San Marcos, TX 78666. Offers civil engineering (MS); electrical engineering (MS); industrial engineering (MS); mechanical and manufacturing engineering (MS). *Program availability:* Part-time. *Faculty:* 15 full-time (2 women). *Students:* 46 full-time (14 women), 41 part-time (13 women); includes 11 minority (3 Asian, non-Hispanic/Latino; 7 Hispanic/Latino; 1 Two or more races, non-Hispanic/Latino), 67 international. Average age 27. 105 applicants, 64% accepted, 31 enrolled. In 2018, 13 master's awarded. *Degree requirements:* For master's, comprehensive exam, thesis (for some programs), thesis or research project. *Entrance requirements:* For master's, official GRE (general test only) required with competitive scores in the verbal reasoning and quantitative reasoning sections, baccalaureate degree from regionally-accredited university in engineering, computer science, physics, technology, or closely-related field with minimum GPA of 3.0 on last 60 undergraduate semester hours; resume or curriculum vitae; 2 letters of recommendation; statement of purpose conveying research interest and professional aspirations. Additional exam requirements/recommendations for international students: Required—TOEFL (minimum score 550 paper-based; 78 iBT), IELTS (minimum score 6.5). *Application deadline:* For fall admission, 2/15 priority date for domestic students, 2/1 priority date for international students. Application fee: $55 ($90 for international students). Electronic applications accepted. *Expenses:* Tuition, state resident: full-time $8102; part-time $4051 per semester. Tuition, nonresident: full-time $18,229; part-time $9115 per semester. *International tuition:* $18,229 full-time. *Required fees:* $2116; $120 per credit hour. Tuition and fees vary according to course load. *Financial support:* In 2018–19, 52 students received support, including 14 research assistantships (averaging $12,742 per year), 34 teaching assistantships (averaging $12,483 per year); Federal Work-Study, institutionally sponsored loans, scholarships/grants, health care benefits, and unspecified assistantships also available. Support available to part-time students. Financial award application deadline: 1/15; financial award applicants required to submit FAFSA. *Faculty research:* Computer Architecture & Digital Image Processing; Industrial robotics on a mobile platform; supply chain management optimization modeling and algorithms; Modeling and analysis of manufacturing systems especially semiconductor manufacturing; smart grids for big data analytics and demand response; Digital Signal/Image/Speach Processing & Data Compression; Health care systems engineering and anaylsis of patient flow. *Total annual research expenditures:* $920,229. *Unit head:* Dr. Vishu Viswanathan, Graduate Advisor, 512-245-1826, Fax: 512-245-8365, E-mail: v_v42@txstate.edu. *Application contact:* Dr. Andrea Golato, Dean of Graduate School, 512-245-2581, Fax: 512-245-8365, E-mail: gradcollege@txstate.edu.
Website: http://www.engineering.txstate.edu/Programs/Graduate.html

Tufts University, Graduate School of Arts and Sciences, Graduate Certificate Programs, Manufacturing Engineering Program, Medford, MA 02155. Offers Certificate. *Program availability:* Part-time, evening/weekend. Electronic applications accepted. *Expenses: Tuition:* Full-time $51,288; part-time $1710 per credit hour. *Required fees:* $904. Full-time tuition and fees vary according to degree level, program and student level. Part-time tuition and fees vary according to course load.

Universidad Autonoma de Guadalajara, Graduate Programs, Guadalajara, Mexico. Offers administrative law and justice (LL M); advertising and corporate communications (MA); architecture (M Arch); business (MBA); computational science (MCC); education (Ed M, Ed D); English-Spanish translation (MA); entrepreneurship and management (MBA); integrated management of digital animation (MA); international business (MIB); international corporate law (LL M); Internet technologies (MS); manufacturing systems (MMS); occupational health (MS); philosophy (MA, PhD); power electronics (MS); quality systems (MQS); renewable energy (MS); social evaluation of projects (MBA); strategic market research (MBA); tax law (MA); teaching mathematics (MA).

Universidad de las Américas Puebla, Division of Graduate Studies, School of Engineering, Program in Manufacturing Administration, Puebla, Mexico. Offers MS. *Faculty research:* Operations research, construction.

University at Buffalo, the State University of New York, Graduate School, School of Engineering and Applied Sciences, Department of Industrial and Systems Engineering, Buffalo, NY 14260. Offers advanced manufacturing (Certificate); industrial engineering (ME, MS, PhD), including data fusion (ME), engineering management (ME). *Program availability:* Part-time, online learning. Terminal master's awarded for partial completion of doctoral program. *Degree requirements:* For master's, comprehensive exam (for some programs), thesis or alternative; for doctorate, thesis/dissertation. *Entrance requirements:* For master's and doctorate, GRE General Test. Additional exam requirements/recommendations for international students: Required—TOEFL (minimum score 550 paper-based; 79 iBT). Electronic applications accepted. *Faculty research:* Advanced manufacturing and sustainable manufacturing design, health and health systems, security and defense, transportation and logistics.

University of Calgary, Faculty of Graduate Studies, Schulich School of Engineering, Program in Mechanical and Manufacturing Engineering, Calgary, AB T2N 1N4, Canada. Offers M Eng, M Sc, PhD. *Program availability:* Part-time. *Degree requirements:* For master's, thesis (for some programs); for doctorate, thesis/dissertation, candidacy exam. *Entrance requirements:* For master's, minimum GPA of 3.0; for doctorate, minimum GPA of 3.3. Additional exam requirements/recommendations for international students: Required—TOEFL (minimum score 550 paper-based; 80 iBT), IELTS (minimum score 7). *Faculty research:* Thermofluids, solid mechanics, materials, biomechanics, manufacturing.

University of California, Irvine, Samueli School of Engineering, Program in Materials and Manufacturing Technology, Irvine, CA 92697. Offers engineering (MS, PhD). *Program availability:* Part-time. *Students:* 21 full-time (7 women), 4 part-time (2 women); includes 6 minority (3 Asian, non-Hispanic/Latino; 3 Hispanic/Latino), 14 international. Average age 28. 27 applicants, 59% accepted, 10 enrolled. In 2018, 5 master's, 2 doctorates awarded. *Entrance requirements:* For master's and doctorate, GRE General Test, 3 letters of recommendation, minimum GPA of 3.0. Additional exam requirements/recommendations for international students: Required—TOEFL (minimum score 550 paper-based). *Application deadline:* For fall admission, 1/15 priority date for domestic students, 1/15 for international students. Applications are processed on a rolling basis. Application fee: $105 ($125 for international students). Electronic applications accepted. *Financial support:* Fellowships, research assistantships with full tuition reimbursements, teaching assistantships, institutionally sponsored loans, traineeships, health care benefits, and unspecified assistantships available. Financial award application deadline: 3/1; financial award applicants required to submit FAFSA. *Faculty research:* Advanced materials, microelectronic and photonic devices and packaging, biomedical devices, MEMS, thin film materials, nanotechnology. *Application contact:* Connie Cheng, Assistant Director of Graduate Student Affairs, 949-824-3562, Fax: 949-824-8200, E-mail: connie.cheng@uci.edu.
Website: http://www.eng.uci.edu/

University of California, Los Angeles, Graduate Division, Henry Samueli School of Engineering and Applied Science, Department of Mechanical and Aerospace Engineering, Program in Manufacturing Engineering, Los Angeles, CA 90095-1597. Offers MS. *Degree requirements:* For master's, comprehensive exam or thesis. *Entrance requirements:* For master's, GRE General Test, minimum GPA of 3.0. Additional exam requirements/recommendations for international students: Required—TOEFL (minimum score 560 paper-based; 87 iBT), IELTS (minimum score 7). Electronic applications accepted.

The University of Iowa, Graduate College, College of Engineering, Department of Industrial Engineering, Iowa City, IA 52242-1316. Offers engineering design and manufacturing (MS, PhD); healthcare systems (MS, PhD); human factors (MS, PhD); information and engineering management (MS, PhD); operations research (MS, PhD); wind energy (MS, PhD). Terminal master's awarded for partial completion of doctoral program. *Degree requirements:* For master's, thesis optional, exam; for doctorate, comprehensive exam, thesis/dissertation, final defense exam. *Entrance requirements:* For master's and doctorate, GRE (minimum Verbal score of 153, Quantitative 151), minimum undergraduate GPA of 3.0. Additional exam requirements/recommendations for international students: Required—TOEFL (minimum score 600 paper-based; 100 iBT), IELTS (minimum score 7). Electronic applications accepted. *Faculty research:* Operations research, informatics, human factors engineering, healthcare systems, bio-manufacturing, manufacturing systems, renewable energy, human-machine interactions.

The University of Iowa, Graduate College, College of Engineering, Department of Mechanical Engineering, Iowa City, IA 52242-1316. Offers energy systems (MS, PhD); engineering design (MS, PhD); fluid dynamics (MS, PhD); materials and manufacturing (MS, PhD); wind energy (MS, PhD). Terminal master's awarded for partial completion of doctoral program. *Degree requirements:* For master's, oral exam or thesis; for doctorate, comprehensive exam, thesis/dissertation. *Entrance requirements:* For master's and doctorate, GRE (minimum Verbal score of 153, Quantitative 151), minimum undergraduate GPA of 3.0. Additional exam requirements/recommendations for international students: Required—TOEFL (minimum score 600 paper-based; 100 iBT), IELTS (minimum score 7). Electronic applications accepted. *Faculty research:* Computer simulation methodology, biomechanics, metal casting, dynamics, laser processing, system reliability, ship hydrodynamics, solid mechanics, fluid dynamics, energy, human modeling and nanotechnology.

University of Kentucky, Graduate School, College of Engineering, Program in Manufacturing Systems Engineering, Lexington, KY 40506-0032. Offers MSMSE. *Degree requirements:* For master's, comprehensive exam. *Entrance requirements:* For master's, GRE General Test, minimum undergraduate GPA of 2.75. Additional exam requirements/recommendations for international students: Required—TOEFL (minimum score 550 paper-based). Electronic applications accepted. *Faculty research:* Manufacturing processes and equipment, manufacturing systems and control, computer-aided design and manufacturing, automation in manufacturing, electric manufacturing and packaging.

University of Manitoba, Faculty of Graduate Studies, Faculty of Engineering, Department of Mechanical and Manufacturing Engineering, Winnipeg, MB R3T 2N2, Canada. Offers M Eng, M Sc, PhD. *Degree requirements:* For master's, thesis; for doctorate, thesis/dissertation.

University of Maryland, College Park, Academic Affairs, A. James Clark School of Engineering, Department of Mechanical Engineering, College Park, MD 20742. Offers electronic packaging and reliability (MS, PhD); manufacturing and design (MS, PhD); mechanics and materials (MS, PhD); reliability engineering (M Eng, MS, PhD); thermal and fluid sciences (MS, PhD). *Program availability:* Part-time, evening/weekend, online learning. *Degree requirements:* For master's, thesis optional; for doctorate, thesis/dissertation, qualifying exam. *Entrance requirements:* For master's, GRE General Test, 3 letters of recommendation; for doctorate, GRE General Test, minimum GPA of 3.0. Additional exam requirements/recommendations for international students: Required—TOEFL. Electronic applications accepted. *Faculty research:* Injection molding, electronic packaging, fluid mechanics, product engineering.

University of Michigan, College of Engineering, Department of Integrative Systems and Design, Ann Arbor, MI 48109. Offers automotive engineering (M Eng); design science (MS, PhD); energy systems engineering (M Eng, MS); global automotive and manufacturing engineering (M Eng); manufacturing engineering (M Eng, D Eng); pharmaceutical engineering (M Eng); robotics and autonomous vehicles (M Eng); systems engineering and design (M Eng); MBA/M Eng; MSE/MS. *Program availability:* Part-time, online learning. *Students:* 163 full-time (38 women), 251 part-time (40 women). 282 applicants, 12% accepted, 15 enrolled. In 2018, 173 master's, 1 doctorate awarded. Terminal master's awarded for partial completion of doctoral program. *Degree requirements:* For master's, capstone project; for doctorate, thesis/dissertation. *Entrance requirements:* For master's and doctorate, GRE. Additional exam requirements/recommendations for international students: Required—TOEFL. *Application deadline:* Applications are processed on a rolling basis. Electronic applications accepted. *Financial support:* Fellowships, research assistantships with full tuition reimbursements, teaching assistantships with full tuition reimbursements, career-related internships or fieldwork, scholarships/grants, and unspecified assistantships available. Financial award applicants required to submit FAFSA. *Faculty research:* Automotive engineering, design science, energy systems engineering, engineering sustainable systems, financial engineering, global automotive and manufacturing engineering, integrated microsystems, manufacturing engineering, pharmaceutical engineering, robotics and autonomous vehicles. *Total annual research expenditures:* $595,323. *Unit head:* Diann Brei, Department Chair, 734-763-6617, E-mail: drdiannbrei@umich.edu. *Application contact:* Kathy Bishar, Senior Graduate Coordinator, 734-764-3312, E-mail: kbishar@umich.edu.
Website: http://www.isd.engin.umich.edu

University of Michigan–Dearborn, College of Engineering and Computer Science, MSE Program in Manufacturing Systems Engineering, Dearborn, MI 48128. Offers MSE. *Program availability:* Part-time, evening/weekend, 100% online. *Faculty:* 17 full-time (4 women), 9 part-time/adjunct (1 woman). *Students:* 7 full-time (1 woman), 8 part-time (2 women), 10 international. Average age 25. 29 applicants, 45% accepted, 8 enrolled. In 2018, 5 master's awarded. *Degree requirements:* For master's, thesis optional. *Entrance requirements:* For master's, BS in engineering or a physical science from accredited program with minimum B average. Additional exam requirements/recommendations for international students: Required—TOEFL (minimum score 560 paper-based; 84 iBT), IELTS (minimum score 6.5). *Application deadline:* For fall admission, 8/1 priority date for domestic students, 5/1 priority date for international students; for winter admission, 12/1 priority date for domestic students, 9/1 priority date for international students; for spring admission, 4/1 priority date for domestic students, 1/1 priority date for international students. Applications are processed on a rolling basis. Application fee: $60. Electronic applications accepted. *Expenses:* Tuition, state resident: full-time $15,380; part-time $88 per credit hour. Tuition, nonresident: full-time $23,948; part-time $1377 per credit hour. *Required fees:* $780; $780 $390. Tuition and fees vary according to course level, course load, degree level, program, reciprocity agreements and student level. *Financial support:* Scholarships/grants, unspecified assistantships, and non-resident tuition scholarships available. Support available to part-time students. Financial award application deadline: 3/1; financial award applicants required to submit FAFSA. *Faculty research:* Operations Research and Decision Science, Quality and Reliability Engineering, Manufacturing, Human Factors and Ergonomics, Transportation Safety. *Unit head:* Dr. Armen Zakarian, Chair, 313-593-5361, E-mail: zakarian@umich.edu. *Application contact:* Office of Graduate Studies, 313-583-6321, E-mail: umd-graduatestudies@umich.edu.
Website: https://umdearborn.edu/cecs/departments/industrial-and-manufacturing-systems-engineering/graduate-programs/mse-manufacturing-systems-engineering

University of Missouri, Office of Research and Graduate Studies, College of Engineering, Department of Industrial and Manufacturing Systems Engineering, Columbia, MO 65211. Offers ME, MS, PhD, MS/MHA. *Degree requirements:* For master's, thesis or alternative; for doctorate, thesis/dissertation. *Entrance requirements:* For master's and doctorate, GRE General Test, minimum GPA of 3.0. Additional exam requirements/recommendations for international students: Required—TOEFL.

University of Nebraska–Lincoln, Graduate College, College of Engineering, Department of Industrial and Management Systems Engineering, Lincoln, NE 68588. Offers engineering management (M Eng); industrial and management systems engineering (MS, PhD); manufacturing systems engineering (MS). *Program availability:* Online learning. *Degree requirements:* For master's, thesis optional; for doctorate, comprehensive exam, thesis/dissertation. *Entrance requirements:* For master's and doctorate, GRE. Additional exam requirements/recommendations for international students: Required—TOEFL (minimum score 525 paper-based). Electronic applications accepted. *Faculty research:* Ergonomics, occupational safety, quality control, industrial packaging, facility design.

University of New Mexico, Graduate Studies, School of Engineering, Manufacturing Engineering Program, Albuquerque, NM 87131. Offers MEME, MBA/MEME. *Program availability:* Part-time. *Entrance requirements:* For master's, GRE General Test (minimum combined score: 300), minimum GPA of 3.0. Additional exam requirements/recommendations for international students: Required—TOEFL (minimum score 550 paper-based; 79 iBT). Electronic applications accepted. *Faculty research:* Robotics, automation control and machine vision, microsystems and microgrippers, semiconductor manufacturing and metrology, cross-training and operations of technicians and engineers.

University of Puerto Rico–Mayagüez, Graduate Studies, College of Engineering, Department of Mechanical Engineering, Mayagüez, PR 00681-9000. Offers mechanical engineering (ME, MS, PhD), including aerospace and unmanned vehicles (ME), automation/mechatronics, bioengineering, fluid mechanics, heat transfer/energy systems, manufacturing, mechanics of materials, micro and nano engineering. *Program availability:* Part-time. Terminal master's awarded for partial completion of doctoral program. *Degree requirements:* For master's, one foreign language, comprehensive exam, thesis; for doctorate, one foreign language, comprehensive exam, thesis/dissertation. *Entrance requirements:* For master's, BS in mechanical engineering or its equivalent; for doctorate, GRE, BS or MS in mechanical engineering or its equivalent; minimum GPA of 3.0. Additional exam requirements/recommendations for international students: Required—TOEFL (minimum score 80 iBT). Electronic applications accepted. *Faculty research:* Computational fluid dynamics, thermal sciences, mechanical design, material health, microfluidics.

University of St. Thomas, School of Engineering, St. Paul, MN 55105. Offers data science (MS); electrical engineering (MS); information technology (MS); manufacturing engineering (MS); manufacturing systems (Certificate); mechanical engineering (MS); medical device development (Certificate); regulatory science (MS); software engineering (MS); software management (MS); systems engineering (MS); technology leadership (Certificate); technology management (MS). *Program availability:* Part-time, evening/weekend. *Entrance requirements:* For master's, resume, official transcripts. Additional exam requirements/recommendations for international students: Required—TOEFL (minimum score 80 iBT), IELTS (minimum score 6.5). Electronic applications accepted. *Expenses:* Contact institution.

University of Southern California, Graduate School, Viterbi School of Engineering, Daniel J. Epstein Department of Industrial and Systems Engineering, Los Angeles, CA 90089. Offers digital supply chain management (MS); engineering management (MS); engineering technology communication (Graduate Certificate); health systems operations (Graduate Certificate); industrial and systems engineering (MS, PhD, Engr); manufacturing engineering (MS); operations research engineering (MS); optimization and supply chain management (Graduate Certificate); product development engineering (MS); safety systems and security (MS); systems architecting and engineering (MS, Graduate Certificate); systems safety and security (Graduate Certificate); transportation systems (Graduate Certificate); MS/MBA. *Program availability:* Part-time, evening/weekend, online learning. Terminal master's awarded for partial completion of doctoral program. *Degree requirements:* For master's, thesis optional; for doctorate, thesis/dissertation. *Entrance requirements:* For master's and doctorate, GRE General Test. Additional exam requirements/recommendations for international students: Recommended—TOEFL. Electronic applications accepted. *Faculty research:* Health systems, music cognition and retrieval, transportation and logistics, manufacturing and automation, engineering systems design, risk and economic analysis.

The University of Texas at El Paso, Graduate School, College of Engineering, Department of Industrial, Manufacturing and Systems Engineering, El Paso, TX 79968-0001. Offers industrial engineering (MS); manufacturing engineering (MS); systems engineering (MS). *Program availability:* Part-time, evening/weekend. *Degree requirements:* For master's, thesis optional. *Entrance requirements:* For master's, GRE General Test, minimum GPA of 3.0 in major. Additional exam requirements/recommendations for international students: Required—TOEFL. Electronic applications accepted. *Faculty research:* Computer vision, automated inspection, simulation and modeling.

The University of Texas at San Antonio, College of Engineering, Department of Mechanical Engineering, San Antonio, TX 78249-0617. Offers advanced manufacturing and enterprise engineering (MS); mechanical engineering (MS, PhD). *Program availability:* Part-time, evening/weekend. Terminal master's awarded for partial completion of doctoral program. *Degree requirements:* For master's, comprehensive exam, thesis; for doctorate, comprehensive exam, thesis/dissertation. *Entrance requirements:* For master's, GRE General Test, bachelor's degree in mechanical engineering or related field from accredited institution of higher education; for doctorate, GRE General Test, master's degree in mechanical engineering, or exceptionally outstanding undergraduate record in mechanical engineering or related field; minimum GPA of 3.33. Additional exam requirements/recommendations for international students: Required—TOEFL (minimum score 550 paper-based; 79 iBT), IELTS (minimum score 6.5). Electronic applications accepted. *Expenses:* Contact institution. *Faculty research:* Mechanics and materials, advanced manufacturing, wind turbine, computational fluid dynamics, robotics, biomechanics, wind energy.

The University of Texas Rio Grande Valley, College of Engineering and Computer Science, Department of Manufacturing and Industrial Engineering, Edinburg, TX 78539. Offers engineering management (MS); manufacturing engineering (MS), including systems engineering. *Expenses: Tuition, area resident:* Full-time $6888. Tuition, state resident: full-time $6888. Tuition, nonresident: full-time $14,484. *International tuition:* $14,484 full-time. *Required fees:* $1468. *Faculty research:* Manufacturing processes, logistics, quality control, lean manufacturing.

University of Toronto, School of Graduate Studies, Advanced Design and Manufacturing Institute, Toronto, ON M5S 1A1, Canada. Offers M Eng. Program offered jointly with McMaster University, Queen's University, and The University of Western Ontario; available only to Canadian citizens and permanent residents of Canada. *Program availability:* Part-time. *Entrance requirements:* For master's, honours bachelor's degree in engineering with grades equivalent to a mid-B or better. Additional exam requirements/recommendations for international students: Required—TOEFL (minimum score 580 paper-based; 93 iBT), TWE (minimum score 4). Electronic applications accepted.

University of Windsor, Faculty of Graduate Studies, Faculty of Engineering, Department of Industrial and Manufacturing Systems Engineering, Windsor, ON N9B 3P4, Canada. Offers industrial engineering (M Eng, MA Sc); manufacturing systems engineering (PhD). *Program availability:* Part-time. *Degree requirements:* For master's, thesis; for doctorate, comprehensive exam, thesis/dissertation. *Entrance requirements:* For master's, minimum B average; for doctorate, master's degree, minimum B average. Additional exam requirements/recommendations for international students: Required—TOEFL (minimum score 560 paper-based). Electronic applications accepted. *Faculty research:* Human factors, operations research.

University of Wisconsin–Madison, Graduate School, College of Engineering, Manufacturing Systems Engineering Program, Madison, WI 53706. Offers MS. *Program availability:* Part-time. *Faculty:* 7 full-time (0 women). *Students:* 12 full-time (3 women), 10 part-time (2 women); includes 2 minority (1 Asian, non-Hispanic/Latino; 1 Hispanic/Latino), 19 international. Average age 26. 31 applicants, 58% accepted, 6 enrolled. In 2018, 6 master's awarded. *Degree requirements:* For master's, thesis (for some programs), minimum of 30 credits; independent research projects; minimum GPA of 3.0. *Entrance requirements:* For master's, GRE General Test, BS in engineering or physical sciences coupled with industry experience; minimum GPA of 3.0; 2 years of relevant industry experience or project work. Additional exam requirements/recommendations for international students: Required—TOEFL (minimum score 580 paper-based; 92 iBT), IELTS (minimum score 7). *Application deadline:* For fall admission, 12/15 for domestic and international students. Application fee: $75 ($81 for international students). Electronic applications accepted. *Expenses:* In-state tuition (fulltime): $10,728; Out-of-state tuition (fulltime): $24,054; Fees: $1282; In-state tuition (per credit): $670; Out-of-

state tuition (per credit): $1503; fees: $126. *Financial support:* Fellowships with full tuition reimbursements, research assistantships with full tuition reimbursements, teaching assistantships with full tuition reimbursements, career-related internships or fieldwork, institutionally sponsored loans, health care benefits, and unspecified assistantships available. Financial award application deadline: 12/1; financial award applicants required to submit FAFSA. *Faculty research:* Advanced manufacturing, computer-aided manufacturing, rapid prototyping, lead time reduction, quick response manufacturing. *Unit head:* Prof. Frank E. Pfefferkorn, Director, 608-263-2668, E-mail: mse@engr.wisc.edu. *Application contact:* Pam Peterson, Student Status Coordinator, 608-263-4025, Fax: 608-262-8454, E-mail: prpeterson@wisc.edu.
Website: https://www.engr.wisc.edu/academics/graduate-academics/manufacturing-systems-engineering/

University of Wisconsin–Milwaukee, Graduate School, College of Engineering and Applied Science, Program in Engineering, Milwaukee, WI 53201-0413. Offers biomedical engineering (MS); civil engineering (MS, PhD); computer science (PhD); electrical and computer engineering (MS); electrical engineering (PhD); engineering mechanics (MS); industrial and management engineering (MS); industrial engineering (PhD); manufacturing engineering (MS); materials (PhD); materials engineering (MS); mechanical engineering (MS). *Program availability:* Part-time. *Students:* 174 full-time (41 women), 149 part-time (27 women); includes 31 minority (2 Black or African American, non-Hispanic/Latino; 1 American Indian or Alaska Native, non-Hispanic/Latino; 16 Asian, non-Hispanic/Latino; 4 Hispanic/Latino; 8 Two or more races, non-Hispanic/Latino), 207 international. Average age 31. 343 applicants, 57% accepted, 78 enrolled. In 2018, 73 master's, 24 doctorates awarded. *Degree requirements:* For master's, comprehensive exam (for some programs), thesis or alternative; for doctorate, comprehensive exam, thesis/dissertation, internship. *Entrance requirements:* For master's, GRE, minimum GPA of 2.75; for doctorate, GRE, minimum GPA of 3.5. Additional exam requirements/recommendations for international students: Required—TOEFL (minimum score 550 paper-based; 79 iBT), IELTS (minimum score 6.5). *Application deadline:* For fall admission, 1/1 priority date for domestic students; for spring admission, 9/1 for domestic students. Applications are processed on a rolling basis. Application fee: $56 ($96 for international students). *Financial support:* Fellowships, research assistantships, teaching assistantships, career-related internships or fieldwork, Federal Work-Study, unspecified assistantships, and project assistantships available. Support available to part-time students. Financial award application deadline: 4/15. *Unit head:* David Yu, Representative, 414-229-6169, E-mail: yu@uwm.edu. *Application contact:* Betty Warras, General Information Contact, 414-229-6169, Fax: 414-229-6967, E-mail: bwarras@uwm.edu.
Website: http://www4.uwm.edu/ceas/academics/graduate_programs/

University of Wisconsin–Stout, Graduate School, College of Science, Technology, Engineering and Mathematics, Program in Manufacturing Engineering, Menomonie, WI 54751. Offers MS. *Program availability:* Online learning. *Degree requirements:* For master's, thesis. *Entrance requirements:* For master's, minimum GPA of 3.0. Additional exam requirements/recommendations for international students: Required—TOEFL (minimum score 500 paper-based; 61 iBT). Electronic applications accepted. *Faculty research:* General ceramics patents, metal matrix composites, solidification processing, high temperature processing.

Villanova University, College of Engineering, Department of Mechanical Engineering, Villanova, PA 19085-1699. Offers electro-mechanical systems (Certificate); machinery dynamics (Certificate); mechanical engineering (MSME); nonlinear dynamics and control (Certificate); thermofluid systems (Certificate). *Program availability:* Part-time, evening/weekend, online learning. *Degree requirements:* For master's, thesis optional. *Entrance requirements:* For master's, GRE General Test (for applicants with degrees from foreign universities), BME, minimum GPA of 3.0. Additional exam requirements/recommendations for international students: Required—TOEFL (minimum score 600 paper-based; 100 iBT). Electronic applications accepted. *Faculty research:* Composite materials, power plant systems, fluid mechanics, automated manufacturing, dynamic analysis.

Wayne State University, College of Engineering, Department of Industrial and Systems Engineering, Detroit, MI 48202. Offers data science and business analytics (MS); engineering management (MS); industrial engineering (MS, PhD); manufacturing engineering (MS); systems engineering (Certificate). *Program availability:* Online learning. *Faculty:* 11. *Students:* 178 full-time (40 women), 109 part-time (30 women); includes 42 minority (20 Black or African American, non-Hispanic/Latino; 16 Asian, non-Hispanic/Latino; 6 Hispanic/Latino), 167 international. Average age 29. 539 applicants, 40% accepted, 68 enrolled. In 2018, 172 master's, 9 doctorates awarded. *Entrance requirements:* For master's, GRE or GMAT (for applicants to MS in data science and business analytics), BS from ABET-accredited institution; for doctorate, GRE, graduate degree in engineering or related discipline with minimum graduate GPA of 3.5, statement of purpose, resume/curriculum vitae, three letters of recommendation; for Certificate, GRE (for applicants from non-ABET institutions), BS in engineering or other technical field from ABET-accredited institution with minimum GPA of 3.0 in upper-division course work, at least one year of full-time work experience as practicing engineer or technical leader. Additional exam requirements/recommendations for international students: Required—TOEFL (minimum score 550 paper-based; 79 iBT), TWE (minimum score 5.5), Michigan English Language Assessment Battery (minimum score 85); GRE; Recommended—IELTS (minimum score 6.5). *Application deadline:* Applications are processed on a rolling basis. Application fee: $50. Electronic applications accepted. *Expenses:* Contact institution. *Financial support:* In 2018–19, 135 students received support, including 2 fellowships with tuition reimbursements available (averaging $20,000 per year), 5 research assistantships with tuition reimbursements available (averaging $23,260 per year), 8 teaching assistantships with

tuition reimbursements available (averaging $20,166 per year); scholarships/grants, tuition waivers (full), and unspecified assistantships also available. Financial award applicants required to submit FAFSA. *Faculty research:* Manufacturing systems, infrastructure, and management. *Total annual research expenditures:* $320,400. *Unit head:* Dr. Leslie Monplaisir, Associate Professor/Chair, 313-577-3821, Fax: 313-577-8833, E-mail: leslie.monplaisir@wayne.edu. *Application contact:* Eric Scimeca, Graduate Program Coordinator, 313-577-0412, E-mail: eric.scimeca@wayne.edu.
Website: http://engineering.wayne.edu/ise/

Western Illinois University, School of Graduate Studies, College of Business and Technology, Program in Engineering Technology Leadership, Macomb, IL 61455-1390. Offers MS. *Program availability:* Part-time. *Students:* 21 full-time (2 women), 5 part-time (0 women); includes 4 minority (3 Black or African American, non-Hispanic/Latino; 1 Two or more races, non-Hispanic/Latino), 14 international. Average age 27. 33 applicants, 79% accepted, 10 enrolled. In 2018, 11 master's awarded. *Entrance requirements:* Additional exam requirements/recommendations for international students: Required—TOEFL (minimum score 550 paper-based; 80 iBT). *Application deadline:* Applications are processed on a rolling basis. Application fee: $30. Electronic applications accepted. *Financial support:* Teaching assistantships with full tuition reimbursements and unspecified assistantships available. Financial award applicants required to submit FAFSA. *Unit head:* Dr. Rafael Obregon, Chairperson, 309-298-1459. *Application contact:* Dr. Mark Mossman, Associate Provost and Director of Graduate Studies, 309-298-1806, Fax: 309-298-2345, E-mail: grad-office@wiu.edu.
Website: http://wiu.edu/engrtech

Western Michigan University, Graduate College, College of Engineering and Applied Sciences, Department of Engineering Design, Manufacturing, and Management Systems, Kalamazoo, MI 49008. Offers MS.

Western New England University, College of Engineering, Master's Program in Engineering Management, Springfield, MA 01119. Offers business and engineering information systems (MSEM); general engineering management (MSEM); production and manufacturing systems (MSEM); quality engineering (MSEM); MSEM/MBA. *Program availability:* Part-time, evening/weekend, online learning. *Faculty:* 3 full-time (0 women). *Students:* 33 part-time (5 women); includes 3 minority (1 Asian, non-Hispanic/Latino; 2 Hispanic/Latino), 6 international. Average age 30. 73 applicants, 73% accepted, 13 enrolled. In 2018, 22 master's awarded. *Degree requirements:* For master's, thesis optional. *Entrance requirements:* For master's, official transcript, bachelor's degree in engineering or related field, two recommendations, resume. Additional exam requirements/recommendations for international students: Required—TOEFL (minimum score 79 iBT). *Application deadline:* Applications are processed on a rolling basis. Application fee: $30. Electronic applications accepted. *Expenses:* Contact institution. *Financial support:* Application deadline: 4/15; applicants required to submit FAFSA. *Unit head:* Dr. Christian Salmon, Chair and Professor, 413-796-2209, E-mail: christian.salmon@wne.edu. *Application contact:* Matthew Fox, Executive Director of Graduate Admissions, 413-782-1410, Fax: 413-782-1777, E-mail: study@wne.edu.
Website: http://www1.wne.edu/academics/graduate/engineering-management.cfm

Wichita State University, Graduate School, College of Engineering, Department of Industrial and Manufacturing Engineering, Wichita, KS 67260. Offers engineering management (MEM); industrial engineering (MS, PhD). *Program availability:* Part-time. In 2018, 37 master's, 3 doctorates awarded. *Entrance requirements:* Additional exam requirements/recommendations for international students: Required—TOEFL. *Financial support:* Teaching assistantships available. *Unit head:* Dr. Krishna Krishnan, Chair, 316-978-3425, Fax: 316-978-3742, E-mail: krishna.krishnan@wichita.edu. *Application contact:* Jordan Oleson, Admissions Coordinator, 316-978-3095, Fax: 316-978-3253, E-mail: jordan.oleson@wichita.edu.
Website: http://www.wichita.edu/ime

Worcester Polytechnic Institute, Graduate Admissions, Department of Mechanical Engineering, Worcester, MA 01609-2280. Offers manufacturing engineering (MS, PhD); materials process engineering (MS); materials science and engineering (PhD). *Program availability:* Part-time, evening/weekend, 100% online, blended/hybrid learning. *Students:* 53 full-time (14 women), 128 part-time (23 women); includes 25 minority (2 Black or African American, non-Hispanic/Latino; 7 Asian, non-Hispanic/Latino; 13 Hispanic/Latino; 1 Native Hawaiian or other Pacific Islander, non-Hispanic/Latino; 2 Two or more races, non-Hispanic/Latino), 47 international. Average age 26. 278 applicants, 62% accepted, 67 enrolled. In 2018, 88 master's, 4 doctorates, 2 other advanced degrees awarded. Terminal master's awarded for partial completion of doctoral program. *Degree requirements:* For master's, thesis optional; for doctorate, comprehensive exam, thesis/dissertation. *Entrance requirements:* For master's and doctorate, GRE (recommended), 3 letters of recommendation, statement of purpose. Additional exam requirements/recommendations for international students: Required—TOEFL (minimum score 563 paper-based; 84 iBT), IELTS (minimum score 7). *Application deadline:* For fall admission, 1/1 priority date for domestic and international students; for spring admission, 10/1 priority date for domestic and international students. Applications are processed on a rolling basis. Application fee: $70. Electronic applications accepted. *Financial support:* Fellowships, research assistantships, teaching assistantships, career-related internships or fieldwork, institutionally sponsored loans, scholarships/grants, and unspecified assistantships available. Financial award application deadline: 1/1. *Unit head:* Dr. Jamal Yagoobi, Department Head, 508-831-5236, Fax: 508-831-5680, E-mail: jyagoobi@wpi.edu. *Application contact:* Barbara Edilberti, Administrative Assistant, 508-831-5236, Fax: 508-831-5680, E-mail: edilbert@wpi.edu.
Website: https://www.wpi.edu/academics/departments/mechanical-engineering

Pharmaceutical Engineering

New Jersey Institute of Technology, Newark College of Engineering, Newark, NJ 07102. Offers biomedical engineering (MS, PhD); biopharmaceutical engineering (MS); chemical engineering (MS, PhD); civil engineering (MS, PhD); computer engineering (MS); critical infrastructure systems (MS); electrical engineering (MS, PhD); engineering management (MS); engineering science (MS); environmental engineering (MS, PhD); healthcare systems management (MS); industrial engineering (MS, PhD); internet engineering (MS); manufacturing systems engineering (MS); materials science & engineering (PhD); materials science and engineering (MS); mechanical engineering (MS, PhD); occupational safety and health engineering (MS). *Program availability:* Part-time, evening/weekend. *Faculty:* 147 full-time (26 women), 133 part-time/adjunct (16 women). *Students:* 690 full-time (163 women), 594 part-time (130 women); includes 427 minority (79 Black or African American, non-Hispanic/Latino; 181 Asian, non-Hispanic/Latino; 140 Hispanic/Latino; 27 Two or more races, non-Hispanic/Latino), 553

international. Average age 27. 2,334 applicants, 57% accepted, 452 enrolled. In 2018, 418 master's, 31 doctorates awarded. Terminal master's awarded for partial completion of doctoral program. *Degree requirements:* For master's, thesis (for some programs); for doctorate, thesis/dissertation. *Entrance requirements:* For master's, GRE General Test, minimum GPA 2.8, personal statement, 1 letter of recommendation, transcripts; for doctorate, GRE General Test, minimum GPA of 3.5, personal statement, 3 letters of recommendation, transcripts. Additional exam requirements/recommendations for international students: Required—TOEFL (minimum score 550 paper-based; 79 iBT), IELTS (minimum score 6.5). *Application deadline:* For fall admission, 6/1 priority date for domestic students, 5/1 priority date for international students; for spring admission, 11/15 priority date for domestic and international students. Applications are processed on a rolling basis. Application fee: $75. Electronic applications accepted. *Expenses:* $22,690 per year (in-state), $32,136 per year (out-of-state). *Financial support:* In 2018–19, 396

students received support, including 52 fellowships with full tuition reimbursements available (averaging $22,000 per year), 113 research assistantships with full tuition reimbursements available (averaging $22,000 per year), 101 teaching assistantships with full tuition reimbursements available (averaging $22,000 per year); career-related internships or fieldwork, Federal Work-Study, scholarships/grants, and unspecified assistantships also available. Financial award application deadline: 1/15. *Faculty research:* Nonlinear signal processing, intelligent medical image analysis, calibration issues in coherent localization, computer-aided design, neural network for tool wear measurement. *Total annual research expenditures:* $41.7 million. *Unit head:* Dr. Moshe Kam, Dean, 973-596-5534, Fax: 973-596-2316, E-mail: moshe.kam@njit.edu. *Application contact:* Stephen Eck, Director of Admissions, 973-596-3300, Fax: 973-596-3461, E-mail: admissions@njit.edu.
Website: http://engineering.njit.edu/

University of Michigan, College of Engineering, Department of Integrative Systems and Design, Ann Arbor, MI 48109. Offers automotive engineering (M Eng); design science (MS, PhD); energy systems engineering (M Eng, MS); global automotive and manufacturing engineering (M Eng); manufacturing engineering (M Eng, D Eng); pharmaceutical engineering (M Eng); robotics and autonomous vehicles (M Eng); systems engineering and design (M Eng); MBA/M Eng; MSE/MS. *Program availability:* Part-time, online learning. *Students:* 163 full-time (38 women), 251 part-time (40 women). 282 applicants, 12% accepted, 15 enrolled. In 2018, 173 master's, 1 doctorate awarded. Terminal master's awarded for partial completion of doctoral program. *Degree requirements:* For master's, capstone project; for doctorate, thesis/dissertation. *Entrance requirements:* For master's and doctorate, GRE. Additional exam requirements/recommendations for international students: Required—TOEFL. *Application deadline:* Applications are processed on a rolling basis. Electronic applications accepted. *Financial support:* Fellowships, research assistantships with full tuition reimbursements, teaching assistantships with full tuition reimbursements, career-related internships or fieldwork, scholarships/grants, and unspecified assistantships available. Financial award applicants required to submit FAFSA. *Faculty research:* Automotive engineering, design science, energy systems engineering, engineering sustainable systems, financial engineering, global automotive and manufacturing engineering, integrated microsystems, manufacturing engineering, pharmaceutical engineering, robotics and autonomous vehicles. *Total annual research expenditures:* $595,323. *Unit head:* Diann Brei, Department Chair, 734-763-6617, E-mail: drdiannbrei@umich.edu. *Application contact:* Kathy Bishar, Senior Graduate Coordinator, 734-764-3312, E-mail: kbishar@umich.edu.
Website: http://www.isd.engin.umich.edu

Reliability Engineering

Arizona State University at the Tempe campus, Ira A. Fulton Schools of Engineering, ASU Engineering Online Programs, Tempe, AZ 85287. Offers construction (MS); embedded systems (M Eng); enterprise systems innovation and management (MSE); modeling and simulation (M Eng); quality and reliability engineering (M Eng); software engineering (MSE); systems engineering (M Eng).

Rutgers University–New Brunswick, Graduate School-New Brunswick, Department of Industrial and Systems Engineering, Piscataway, NJ 08854-8097. Offers industrial and systems engineering (MS, PhD); information technology (MS); manufacturing systems engineering (MS); quality and reliability engineering (MS). *Program availability:* Part-time, evening/weekend. Terminal master's awarded for partial completion of doctoral program. *Degree requirements:* For master's, thesis or alternative, seminar; for doctorate, comprehensive exam, thesis/dissertation. *Entrance requirements:* For master's and doctorate, GRE General Test. Additional exam requirements/recommendations for international students: Required—TOEFL. *Faculty research:* Production and manufacturing systems, quality and reliability engineering, systems engineering and aviation safety.

University of Maryland, College Park, Academic Affairs, A. James Clark School of Engineering, Department of Mechanical Engineering, Reliability Engineering Program, College Park, MD 20742. Offers M Eng, MS, PhD. *Program availability:* Part-time, evening/weekend, online learning. *Degree requirements:* For master's, thesis optional; for doctorate, thesis/dissertation. *Entrance requirements:* For master's, GRE General Test, 3 letters of recommendation; for doctorate, GRE General Test, minimum GPA of 3.0. Additional exam requirements/recommendations for international students: Required—TOEFL. Electronic applications accepted. *Faculty research:* Electron linear acceleration, x-ray and imaging.

The University of Tennessee, Graduate School, Tickle College of Engineering, Department of Chemical and Biomolecular Engineering, Knoxville, TN 37996. Offers chemical engineering (MS, PhD); reliability and maintainability engineering (MS); MS/MBA. *Program availability:* Part-time. *Faculty:* 17 full-time (1 woman), 4 part-time/adjunct (0 women). *Students:* 46 full-time (9 women), 4 part-time (3 women); includes 5 minority (1 Black or African American, non-Hispanic/Latino; 4 Hispanic/Latino), 20 international. Average age 27. 64 applicants, 27% accepted, 7 enrolled. In 2018, 5 master's, 8 doctorates awarded. *Degree requirements:* For master's, thesis or alternative; for doctorate, comprehensive exam, thesis/dissertation. *Entrance requirements:* For master's, GRE General Test (for MS students pursuing research thesis), minimum GPA of 2.7 (for U.S. degree holders), 3.0 (for international degree holders); for doctorate, GRE General Test, minimum GPA of 3.0 on previous graduate course work. Additional exam requirements/recommendations for international students: Required—TOEFL (minimum score 550 paper-based; 80 iBT), IELTS (minimum score 6.5). *Application deadline:* For fall admission, 2/1 priority date for domestic and international students; for spring admission, 6/15 for domestic and international students; for summer admission, 10/15 for domestic and international students. Applications are processed on a rolling basis. Application fee: $60. Electronic applications accepted. *Financial support:* In 2018–19, 72 students received support, including 8 fellowships (averaging $11,544 per year), 43 research assistantships with full tuition reimbursements available (averaging $26,976 per year), 21 teaching assistantships with full tuition reimbursements available (averaging $22,893 per year); career-related internships or fieldwork, Federal Work-Study, institutionally sponsored loans, health care benefits, and unspecified assistantships also available. Financial award application deadline: 2/1; financial award applicants required to submit FAFSA. *Faculty research:* Bio-fuels; engineering of soft, functional and structural materials; fuel cells and energy storage devices; molecular and cellular bioengineering; molecular modeling and simulations. *Total annual research expenditures:* $5.8 million. *Unit head:* Dr. Bamin Khomami, Head, 865-974-2421, Fax: 865-974-7076, E-mail: bkhomami@utk.edu. *Application contact:* Dr. Cong Trinh, Graduate Recruiting Director, 865-974-2421, Fax: 865-974-7076, E-mail: ctrinh@utk.edu.
Website: http://www.engr.utk.edu/cbe/

The University of Tennessee, Graduate School, Tickle College of Engineering, Department of Industrial and Systems Engineering, Knoxville, TN 37966. Offers engineering management (MS); industrial engineering (MS, PhD); reliability and maintainability engineering (MS); MS/MBA. *Program availability:* Part-time, online learning. *Faculty:* 10 full-time (1 woman), 3 part-time/adjunct (1 woman). *Students:* 74 full-time (20 women), 76 part-time (18 women); includes 26 minority (10 Black or African American, non-Hispanic/Latino; 1 American Indian or Alaska Native, non-Hispanic/Latino; 8 Asian, non-Hispanic/Latino; 7 Hispanic/Latino), 40 international. Average age 35. 122 applicants, 80% accepted, 47 enrolled. In 2018, 42 master's, 8 doctorates awarded. *Degree requirements:* For master's, thesis or alternative; for doctorate, comprehensive exam, thesis/dissertation. *Entrance requirements:* For master's, GRE General Test (for MS students pursuing research thesis), minimum GPA of 2.7 (for U.S. degree holders), 3.0 (for international degree holders); for doctorate, GRE General Test, minimum GPA of 3.0 on previous graduate course work. Additional exam requirements/recommendations for international students: Required—TOEFL (minimum score 550 paper-based; 80 iBT), IELTS (minimum score 6.5). *Application deadline:* For fall admission, 2/1 priority date for domestic and international students; for spring admission, 6/15 for domestic and international students; for summer admission, 10/15 for domestic and international students. Applications are processed on a rolling basis. Application fee: $60. Electronic applications accepted. *Financial support:* In 2018–19, 59 students received support, including 7 fellowships with full tuition reimbursements available (averaging $10,000 per year), 36 research assistantships with full tuition reimbursements available (averaging $15,462 per year), 16 teaching assistantships with full tuition reimbursements available (averaging $19,545 per year); career-related internships or fieldwork, Federal Work-Study, institutionally sponsored loans, health care benefits, and unspecified assistantships also available. Financial award application deadline: 2/1; financial award applicants required to submit FAFSA. *Faculty research:* Combinatorial optimization; design of lean, reliable systems: energy systems; healthcare analytics; transportation, logistics and supply chain modeling. *Total annual research expenditures:* $1.2 million. *Unit head:* Dr. John Kobza, Department Head, 865-974-3333, Fax: 865-974-0588, E-mail: jkobza@utk.edu. *Application contact:* Dr. Mingzhou Jin, Professor, Associate Head and Director of Graduate Studies, 865-974-9992, E-mail: jin@utk.edu.
Website: http://www.engr.utk.edu/ie/

The University of Tennessee, Graduate School, Tickle College of Engineering, Department of Materials Science and Engineering, Knoxville, TN 37996-2200. Offers materials science and engineering (MS, PhD); reliability and maintainability engineering (MS); MS/MBA. *Program availability:* Part-time. *Faculty:* 25 full-time (4 women). *Students:* 85 full-time (28 women), 8 part-time (0 women); includes 5 minority (1 Black or African American, non-Hispanic/Latino; 2 Asian, non-Hispanic/Latino; 2 Hispanic/Latino), 44 international. Average age 27. 74 applicants, 34% accepted, 12 enrolled. In 2018, 6 master's, 9 doctorates awarded. *Degree requirements:* For master's, thesis or alternative; for doctorate, comprehensive exam, thesis/dissertation. *Entrance requirements:* For master's, GRE General Test (for MS students pursuing research thesis), minimum GPA of 2.7 (for U.S. degree holders), 3.0 (for international degree holders); 3 references; for doctorate, GRE General Test, minimum GPA of 3.0 on previous graduate course work; 3 references. Additional exam requirements/recommendations for international students: Required—TOEFL (minimum score 550 paper-based; 80 iBT), IELTS (minimum score 6.5). *Application deadline:* For fall admission, 2/1 priority date for domestic and international students; for spring admission, 6/15 for domestic and international students; for summer admission, 10/15 for domestic and international students. Applications are processed on a rolling basis. Application fee: $60. Electronic applications accepted. *Financial support:* In 2018–19, 114 students received support, including 19 fellowships with full tuition reimbursements available (averaging $12,060 per year), 73 research assistantships with full tuition reimbursements available (averaging $23,497 per year), 22 teaching assistantships with full tuition reimbursements available (averaging $21,010 per year); career-related internships or fieldwork, Federal Work-Study, institutionally sponsored loans, health care benefits, and unspecified assistantships also available. Financial award application deadline: 2/1; financial award applicants required to submit FAFSA. *Faculty research:* Biomaterials; functional materials electronic, magnetic and optical; high temperature materials; mechanical behavior of materials; neutron materials science. *Total annual research expenditures:* $6.4 million. *Unit head:* Dr. Veerle Keppens, Head, 865-974-5336, Fax: 865-974-4115, E-mail: vkeppens@utk.edu. *Application contact:* Dr. Kurt Sickafus, Professor and Director of Graduate Studies, 865-974-4858, E-mail: kurt@utk.edu.
Website: http://www.engr.utk.edu/mse

The University of Tennessee, Graduate School, Tickle College of Engineering, Department of Nuclear Engineering, Program in Reliability and Maintainability Engineering, Knoxville, TN 37996. Offers MS. *Students:* 4 full-time (1 woman), 14 part-time (3 women); includes 5 minority (3 Asian, non-Hispanic/Latino; 1 Hispanic/Latino; 1 Two or more races, non-Hispanic/Latino), 1 international. Average age 35. 10 applicants, 90% accepted, 9 enrolled. In 2018, 2 master's awarded. *Degree requirements:* For master's, thesis or alternative. *Entrance requirements:* For master's, GRE General Test (for MS students pursuing research thesis), minimum GPA of 2.7 (for U.S. degree holders), 3.0 (for international degree holders). Additional exam requirements/recommendations for international students: Required—TOEFL (minimum score 550 paper-based; 80 iBT), IELTS (minimum score 6.5). *Application deadline:* For fall admission, 2/1 priority date for domestic and international students; for spring admission, 6/15 for domestic and international students; for summer admission, 10/15 for domestic and international students. Applications are processed on a rolling basis. Application fee: $60. Electronic applications accepted. *Financial support:* In 2018–19, 1 student received support, including 1 teaching assistantship with full tuition reimbursement available (averaging $24,600 per year); career-related internships or fieldwork, Federal Work-Study, institutionally sponsored loans, health care benefits, and unspecified assistantships also available. Financial award application deadline: 2/1; financial award applicants required to submit FAFSA. *Unit head:* Dr. J. Wesley Hines, PhD, Head, 865-974-2525, Fax: 865-974-0668, E-mail: jhines2@utk.edu. *Application contact:* Dr. Jason Hayward, PhD, Professor and Graduate Coordinator, 865-974-2525, E-mail: utne@utk.edu.
Website: http://www.engr.utk.edu/rme/

The University of Tennessee, Graduate School, Tickle College of Engineering, Min H. Kao Department of Electrical Engineering and Computer Science, Knoxville, TN 37996. Offers computer engineering (MS, PhD); computer science (MS, PhD); electrical engineering (MS, PhD); reliability and maintainability engineering (MS); MS/MBA.

Program availability: Part-time. *Faculty:* 53 full-time (8 women), 8 part-time/adjunct (2 women). *Students:* 216 full-time (45 women), 43 part-time (6 women); includes 24 minority (5 Black or African American, non-Hispanic/Latino; 12 Asian, non-Hispanic/Latino; 5 Hispanic/Latino; 2 Two or more races, non-Hispanic/Latino), 136 international. Average age 27. 386 applicants, 44% accepted, 60 enrolled. In 2018, 59 master's, 27 doctorates awarded. *Degree requirements:* For master's, thesis or alternative; for doctorate, comprehensive exam, thesis/dissertation. *Entrance requirements:* For master's, GRE General Test (for MS students pursuing research thesis), minimum GPA of 2.7 (for U.S. degree holders), 3.0 (for international degree holders); 3 references; personal statement; for doctorate, GRE General Test, minimum GPA of 3.0 on previous graduate course work; 3 references; personal statement. Additional exam requirements/recommendations for international students: Required—TOEFL (minimum score 550 paper-based; 80 iBT), IELTS (minimum score 6.5). *Application deadline:* For fall admission, 2/1 priority date for domestic and international students; for spring admission, 6/15 for domestic and international students; for summer admission, 10/15 for domestic students, 10/16 for international students. Applications are processed on a rolling basis. Application fee: $60. Electronic applications accepted. *Financial support:* In 2018–19, 255 students received support, including 29 fellowships with full tuition reimbursements available (averaging $9,480 per year), 158 research assistantships with full tuition reimbursements available (averaging $24,086 per year), 68 teaching assistantships with full tuition reimbursements available (averaging $17,453 per year); career-related internships or fieldwork, Federal Work-Study, institutionally sponsored loans, health care benefits, and unspecified assistantships also available. Financial award application deadline: 2/1; financial award applicants required to submit FAFSA. *Faculty research:* Artificial intelligence and visualization; microelectronics, mixed-signal electronics, VLSI, embedded systems; scientific and distributed computing; computer vision, robotics, and image processing; power electronics, power systems, communications. *Total annual research expenditures:* $21.1 million. *Unit head:* Dr. Gregory Peterson, PhD, Head, 865-974-3461, Fax: 865-974-5483, E-mail: gdp@utk.edu. *Application contact:* Dr. Jens Gregor, PhD, Associate Head, 865-974-4399, Fax: 865-974-5483, E-mail: jgregor@utk.edu.
Website: http://www.eecs.utk.edu

Safety Engineering

Embry-Riddle Aeronautical University–Prescott, Behavioral and Safety Sciences Department, Prescott, AZ 86301-3720. Offers aviation safety (MSSS). *Degree requirements:* For master's, research project, capstone, or thesis. *Entrance requirements:* For master's, transcripts, statement of goals, letters of recommendation, resume. Additional exam requirements/recommendations for international students: Required—TOEFL (minimum score 550 paper-based; 79 iBT), IELTS (minimum score 6). Electronic applications accepted.

Indiana University Bloomington, School of Public Health, Department of Applied Health Science, Bloomington, IN 47405. Offers behavioral, social, and community health (MPH); family health (MPH); health behavior (PhD); nutrition science (MS); professional health education (MPH); public health administration (MPH); safety management (MS); school and college health education (MS). *Degree requirements:* For master's, thesis optional; for doctorate, comprehensive exam, thesis/dissertation. *Entrance requirements:* For master's, GRE (for MS in nutrition science), 3 recommendations; for doctorate, GRE, 3 recommendations. Additional exam requirements/recommendations for international students: Required—TOEFL (minimum score 550 paper-based; 80 iBT). Electronic applications accepted. *Faculty research:* Cancer education, HIV/AIDS and drug education, public health, parent-child interactions, safety education, obesity, public health policy, public health administration, school health, health education, human development, nutrition, human sexuality, chronic disease, early childhood health.

Murray State University, Jesse D. Jones College of Science, Engineering and Technology, Department of Occupational Safety and Health, Murray, KY 42071. Offers environmental science (MS). *Program availability:* Part-time, evening/weekend, 100% online, blended/hybrid learning. *Entrance requirements:* For master's, GRE or GMAT, minimum university GPA of 2.75. Additional exam requirements/recommendations for international students: Required—TOEFL (minimum score 527 paper-based; 71 iBT). Electronic applications accepted.

New Jersey Institute of Technology, Newark College of Engineering, Newark, NJ 07102. Offers biomedical engineering (MS, PhD); biopharmaceutical engineering (MS); chemical engineering (MS, PhD); civil engineering (MS, PhD); computer engineering (MS); critical infrastructure systems (MS); electrical engineering (MS, PhD); engineering management (MS); engineering science (MS); environmental engineering (MS, PhD); healthcare systems management (MS); industrial engineering (MS, PhD); internet engineering (MS); manufacturing systems engineering (MS); materials science & engineering (PhD); materials science and engineering (MS); mechanical engineering (MS, PhD); occupational safety and health engineering (MS). *Program availability:* Part-time, evening/weekend. *Faculty:* 147 full-time (26 women), 133 part-time/adjunct (16 women). *Students:* 690 full-time (163 women), 594 part-time (130 women); includes 427 minority (79 Black or African American, non-Hispanic/Latino; 181 Asian, non-Hispanic/Latino; 140 Hispanic/Latino; 27 Two or more races, non-Hispanic/Latino), 553 international. Average age 27. 2,334 applicants, 57% accepted, 452 enrolled. In 2018, 418 master's, 31 doctorates awarded. Terminal master's awarded for partial completion of doctoral program. *Degree requirements:* For master's, thesis (for some programs); for doctorate, thesis/dissertation. *Entrance requirements:* For master's, GRE General Test, minimum GPA 2.8, personal statement, 1 letter of recommendation, transcripts; for doctorate, GRE General Test, minimum GPA of 3.5, personal statement, 3 letters of recommendation, transcripts. Additional exam requirements/recommendations for international students: Required—TOEFL (minimum score 550 paper-based; 79 iBT), IELTS (minimum score 6.5). *Application deadline:* For fall admission, 6/1 priority date for domestic students, 5/1 priority date for international students; for spring admission, 11/15 priority date for domestic and international students. Applications are processed on a rolling basis. Application fee: $75. Electronic applications accepted. *Expenses:* $22,690 per year (in-state), $32,136 per year (out-of-state). *Financial support:* In 2018–19, 396 students received support, including 52 fellowships with full tuition reimbursements available (averaging $22,000 per year), 113 research assistantships with full tuition reimbursements available (averaging $22,000 per year), 101 teaching assistantships with full tuition reimbursements available (averaging $22,000 per year); career-related internships or fieldwork, Federal Work-Study, scholarships/grants, and unspecified assistantships also available. Financial award application deadline: 1/15. *Faculty research:* Nonlinear signal processing, intelligent medical image analysis, calibration issues in coherent localization, computer-aided design, neural network for tool wear measurement. *Total annual research expenditures:* $41.7 million. *Unit head:* Dr. Moshe Kam, Dean, 973-596-5534, Fax: 973-596-2316, E-mail: moshe.kam@njit.edu. *Application contact:* Stephen Eck, Director of Admissions, 973-596-3300, Fax: 973-596-3461, E-mail: admissions@njit.edu.
Website: http://engineering.njit.edu/

Rochester Institute of Technology, Graduate Enrollment Services, College of Applied Science and Technology, School of Engineering Technology, MS Program in Environmental, Health and Safety Management, Rochester, NY 14623-5603. Offers MS. *Program availability:* Part-time, evening/weekend, 100% online, blended/hybrid learning. *Students:* 19 full-time (11 women), 20 part-time (5 women); includes 5 minority (2 Black or African American, non-Hispanic/Latino; 1 Asian, non-Hispanic/Latino; 2 Hispanic/Latino), 12 international. Average age 30. 47 applicants, 43% accepted, 9 enrolled. In 2018, 16 master's awarded. *Degree requirements:* For master's, thesis or alternative. *Entrance requirements:* For master's, minimum GPA of 3.0 (recommended). Additional exam requirements/recommendations for international students: Required—TOEFL (minimum score 88 iBT), IELTS (minimum score 6.5), PTE (minimum score 61). *Application deadline:* Applications are processed on a rolling basis. Application fee: $65. Electronic applications accepted. *Expenses:* Contact institution. *Financial support:* In 2018–19, 20 students received support. Research assistantships with partial tuition reimbursements available, teaching assistantships with partial tuition reimbursements available, career-related internships or fieldwork, scholarships/grants, and unspecified assistantships available. Support available to part-time students. Financial award applicants required to submit FAFSA. *Faculty research:* Design and implementation of integrated management systems for environmental sustainability, health and safety (ESHS); multidimensional corporate sustainability; global resilience and disaster science. *Unit head:* Joseph Rosenbeck, Graduate Program Director, 585-475-6469, E-mail: jmrcem@rit.edu. *Application contact:* Diane Ellison, Senior Associate Vice President, Graduate Enrollment Services, 585-475-2229, Fax: 585-475-7164, E-mail: gradinfo@rit.edu.
Website: https://www.rit.edu/study/environmental-health-and-safety-management-ms

The University of Alabama at Birmingham, School of Engineering, Professional Engineering Degrees, Birmingham, AL 35294. Offers advanced safety engineering and management (M Eng); construction engineering management (M Eng); design and commercialization (M Eng); information engineering management (M Eng); structural engineering (M Eng); sustainable smart cities (M Eng). *Program availability:* Part-time, evening/weekend, online only, 100% online, blended/hybrid learning. *Faculty:* 6 full-time (1 woman), 12 part-time/adjunct (2 women). *Students:* 23 full-time (7 women), 315 part-time (63 women); includes 96 minority (73 Black or African American, non-Hispanic/Latino; 1 American Indian or Alaska Native, non-Hispanic/Latino; 8 Asian, non-Hispanic/Latino; 12 Hispanic/Latino; 2 Two or more races, non-Hispanic/Latino), 12 international. Average age 37. 154 applicants, 84% accepted, 91 enrolled. In 2018, 87 master's awarded. *Entrance requirements:* For master's, 3.0 GPA on 4.0 scale, undergraduate degree from a nationally accredited school. Additional exam requirements/recommendations for international students: Required—TOEFL (minimum score 80 iBT); Recommended—IELTS (minimum score 6.5). *Application deadline:* For fall admission, 8/1 for domestic and international students; for spring admission, 12/1 for domestic and international students; for summer admission, 5/1 for domestic and international students. Applications are processed on a rolling basis. Application fee: $50 ($60 for international students). Electronic applications accepted. *Expenses:* Contact institution. *Faculty research:* Orthopedic biomechanics, translational rehabilitation and assistive devices, innovation and entrepreneurship, anthropogenic activities and the natural environment, prestressed and spun concrete. *Application contact:* Jesse Kepply, Director of Student and Academic Services, 205-996-5696, E-mail: gradschool@uab.edu.

University of Minnesota, Duluth, Graduate School, Swenson College of Science and Engineering, Department of Mechanical and Industrial Engineering, Duluth, MN 55812-2496. Offers engineering management (MSEM); environmental health and safety (MEHS). *Program availability:* Part-time, evening/weekend, online learning. *Degree requirements:* For master's, comprehensive exam, thesis or alternative, capstone design project (MSEM), field project (MEHS). *Entrance requirements:* For master's, GRE (MEHS), interview (MEHS), letters of recommendation. Additional exam requirements/recommendations for international students: Required—TOEFL (minimum score 550 paper-based). *Faculty research:* Transportation, ergonomics, toxicology, supply chain management, automation and robotics.

University of Southern California, Graduate School, Viterbi School of Engineering, Daniel J. Epstein Department of Industrial and Systems Engineering, Los Angeles, CA 90089. Offers digital supply chain management (MS); engineering management (MS); engineering technology communication (Graduate Certificate); health systems operations (Graduate Certificate); industrial and systems engineering (MS, PhD, Engr); manufacturing engineering (MS); operations research engineering (MS); optimization and supply chain management (Graduate Certificate); product development engineering (MS); safety systems and security (MS); systems architecting and engineering (MS, Graduate Certificate); systems safety and security (Graduate Certificate); transportation systems (Graduate Certificate); MS/MBA. *Program availability:* Part-time, evening/weekend, online learning. Terminal master's awarded for partial completion of doctoral program. *Degree requirements:* For master's, thesis optional; for doctorate, thesis/dissertation. *Entrance requirements:* For master's and doctorate, GRE General Test. Additional exam requirements/recommendations for international students: Recommended—TOEFL. Electronic applications accepted. *Faculty research:* Health systems, music cognition and retrieval, transportation and logistics, manufacturing and automation, engineering systems design, risk and economic analysis.

West Virginia University, Statler College of Engineering and Mineral Resources, Morgantown, WV 26506. Offers aerospace engineering (MSAE, PhD); chemical engineering (MS Ch E, PhD); civil engineering (MSCE, PhD); computer engineering (PhD); computer science (MSCS, PhD); electrical engineering (MSEE, PhD); energy systems engineering (MSESE); engineering (MSE); industrial engineering (MSIE, PhD); industrial hygiene (MS); material science and engineering (MSMSE, PhD); mechanical engineering (MSME, PhD); mining engineering (MS Min E, PhD); petroleum and natural gas engineering (MSPNGE, PhD); safety management (MS); software engineering (MSSE). *Program availability:* Part-time. *Students:* 466 full-time (113 women), 154 part-time (27 women); includes 57 minority (22 Black or African American, non-Hispanic/Latino; 1 American Indian or Alaska Native, non-Hispanic/Latino; 8 Asian, non-Hispanic/Latino; 12 Hispanic/Latino; 14 Two or more races, non-Hispanic/Latino), 283 international. In 2018, 179 master's, 39 doctorates awarded. Terminal master's awarded for partial completion of doctoral program. *Degree requirements:* For master's, thesis optional; for doctorate, comprehensive exam, thesis/dissertation. *Entrance requirements:* Additional exam requirements/recommendations for international students: Required—TOEFL (minimum score 550 paper-based). *Application deadline:* For fall admission, 4/1 for international students; for winter admission, 4/1 for international students; for spring admission, 10/1 for international students. Applications are processed on a rolling basis. Application fee: $60. Electronic applications accepted. *Expenses:* Contact institution. *Financial support:* Fellowships, research assistantships, teaching assistantships, career-related internships or fieldwork, Federal Work-Study, institutionally sponsored loans, health care benefits, tuition waivers (full and partial), unspecified assistantships, and administrative assistantships available. Financial award

application deadline: 2/1; financial award applicants required to submit FAFSA. *Faculty research:* Composite materials, software engineering, information systems, aerodynamics, vehicle propulsion and emission. *Unit head:* Dr. Earl Scime, Interim Dean, 304-293-4157 Ext. 2237, Fax: 304-293-2037, E-mail: earl.scime@mail.wvu.edu. *Application contact:* Dr. David A. Wyrick, Associate Dean, Academic Affairs, 304-293-4334, Fax: 304-293-5024, E-mail: david.wyrick@mail.wvu.edu. Website: https://www.statler.wvu.edu

Systems Engineering

Air Force Institute of Technology, Graduate School of Engineering and Management, Department of Aeronautics and Astronautics, Dayton, OH 45433-7765. Offers aeronautical engineering (MS, PhD); astronautical engineering (MS, PhD); materials science (MS, PhD); space operations (MS); systems engineering (MS, PhD). *Accreditation:* ABET (one or more programs are accredited). *Program availability:* Part-time. *Degree requirements:* For master's, thesis; for doctorate, thesis/dissertation. *Entrance requirements:* For master's and doctorate, GRE General Test, minimum GPA of 3.0, U.S. citizenship. *Faculty research:* Computational fluid dynamics, experimental aerodynamics, computational structural mechanics, experimental structural mechanics, aircraft and spacecraft stability and control.

Arizona State University at the Tempe campus, Ira A. Fulton Schools of Engineering, ASU Engineering Online Programs, Tempe, AZ 85287. Offers construction (MS); embedded systems (M Eng); enterprise systems innovation and management (MSE); modeling and simulation (M Eng); quality and reliability engineering (M Eng); software engineering (MSE); systems engineering (M Eng).

Auburn University, Graduate School, Ginn College of Engineering, Department of Industrial and Systems Engineering, Auburn University, AL 36849. Offers MISE, MS, PhD, Graduate Certificate. *Program availability:* Part-time. *Degree requirements:* For master's, thesis (MS); for doctorate, thesis/dissertation. *Entrance requirements:* For master's and doctorate, GRE General Test. *Expenses:* Tuition, state resident: full-time $11,282; part-time $535 per credit hour. Tuition, nonresident: full-time $30,542; part-time $1605 per credit hour. *Required fees:* $826 per semester. Tuition and fees vary according to degree level and program.

Boston University, College of Engineering, Division of Systems Engineering, Brookline, MA 02215. Offers systems engineering (M Eng, MS, PhD), including engineering practice (M Eng). *Program availability:* Part-time. *Students:* 55 full-time (17 women), 9 part-time (3 women); includes 2 minority (both Asian, non-Hispanic/Latino), 50 international. Average age 25. 208 applicants, 48% accepted, 24 enrolled. In 2018, 13 master's, 4 doctorates awarded. Terminal master's awarded for partial completion of doctoral program. *Degree requirements:* For master's, thesis (for some programs); for doctorate, comprehensive exam, thesis/dissertation. *Entrance requirements:* For master's and doctorate, GRE General Test. Additional exam requirements/recommendations for international students: Required—TOEFL (minimum score 90 iBT), IELTS (minimum score 7). *Financial support:* Application deadline: 1/15. *Faculty research:* Communication, network, sensing, and information systems; control systems, automation, and robotics; discrete event, queuing, hybrid, and complex systems; optimization and algorithms; production, service, distribution, and energy systems. *Unit head:* Dr. Christos Cassandras, Division Head, 617-353-7154, Fax: 617-353-5548, E-mail: cgc@bu.edu. *Application contact:* Dr. Christos Cassandras, Division Head, 617-353-7154, Fax: 617-353-5548, E-mail: cgc@bu.edu. Website: http://www.bu.edu/se/

California Institute of Technology, Division of Engineering and Applied Science, Option in Control and Dynamical Systems, Pasadena, CA 91125-0001. Offers MS, PhD. *Degree requirements:* For doctorate, thesis/dissertation. *Faculty research:* Robustness, multivariable and nonlinear systems, optimal control, decentralized control, modeling and system identification for robust control.

California State Polytechnic University, Pomona, Program in Systems Engineering, Pomona, CA 91768-2557. Offers systems engineering (MS). *Program availability:* Part-time, evening/weekend. *Students:* 8 full-time (0 women), 1 (woman) part-time; includes 3 minority (1 Asian, non-Hispanic/Latino; 2 Hispanic/Latino), 3 international. Average age 26. 3 applicants, 33% accepted. In 2018, 5 master's awarded. *Entrance requirements:* Additional exam requirements/recommendations for international students: Required—TOEFL (minimum score 550 paper-based). *Application deadline:* Applications are processed on a rolling basis. Application fee: $55. Electronic applications accepted. *Expenses:* Contact institution. *Financial support:* Application deadline: 3/2. *Unit head:* Dr. Kamran Abedini, Professor/MSSE Coordinator, 909-869-2569, Fax: 909-869-2564, E-mail: kabedini@cpp.edu. *Application contact:* Dr. Kamran Abedini, Professor/MSSE Coordinator, 909-869-2569, Fax: 909-869-2564, E-mail: kabedini@cpp.edu. Website: https://www.cpp.edu/~ceu/degree-programs/systems-engineering/index.shtml

California State University, Fullerton, Graduate Studies, College of Engineering and Computer Science, Department of Electrical Engineering, Fullerton, CA 92831-3599. Offers electrical engineering (MS); systems engineering (MS). *Program availability:* Part-time. *Degree requirements:* For master's, comprehensive exam, project or thesis. *Entrance requirements:* For master's, GRE General Test, GRE Subject Test, minimum undergraduate GPA of 2.5, 3.0 graduate.

California State University, Northridge, Graduate Studies, College of Engineering and Computer Science, Department of Manufacturing Systems Engineering and Management, Northridge, CA 91330. Offers engineering automation (MS); engineering management (MS); manufacturing systems engineering (MS); materials engineering (MS). *Program availability:* Online learning. *Entrance requirements:* For master's, GRE (if cumulative undergraduate GPA less than 3.0).

Carleton University, Faculty of Graduate Studies, Faculty of Engineering and Design, Ottawa-Carleton Institute for Electrical Engineering, Department of Systems and Computer Engineering, Ottawa, ON K1S 5B6, Canada. Offers electrical engineering (MA Sc, PhD); information and systems science (M Sc); technology innovation management (M Eng, MA Sc). PhD program offered jointly with University of Ottawa. *Degree requirements:* For master's, thesis optional. *Entrance requirements:* For master's, honors degree. Additional exam requirements/recommendations for international students: Required—TOEFL. *Faculty research:* Design manufacturing management; network design, protocols, and performance; software engineering; wireless and satellite communications.

Carnegie Mellon University, Carnegie Institute of Technology, Information Networking Institute, Pittsburgh, PA 15213. Offers information networking (MS); information security (MS); information technology - information security (MS); information technology - mobility (MS); information technology - software management (MS). *Degree*

requirements: For master's, thesis optional. *Entrance requirements:* For master's, GRE General Test, bachelor's degree in computer science, computer engineering, or electrical engineering, or related technology degree; programming skills (C/C++ fluency for some programs). Additional exam requirements/recommendations for international students: Required—TOEFL. *Faculty research:* Computer forensics and incident response; dependable systems, embedded systems, mobile systems, and sensor networks; computer and information networks, network and information security, human and socio-economic factors in secure system design; wireless sensor networks, survivable embedded systems, signal processing/compression; strategic management, international strategic management, group dynamics and decision-making structures, simulated competitive environments.

Case Western Reserve University, School of Graduate Studies, Case School of Engineering, Department of Computer and Data Sciences, Cleveland, OH 44106. Offers computer engineering (MS, PhD); computing and information sciences (MS, PhD); electrical engineering (MS, PhD); systems and control engineering (MS, PhD). *Program availability:* Part-time, evening/weekend, online only, 100% online. *Faculty:* 31 full-time (2 women). *Students:* 228 full-time (49 women), 17 part-time (3 women); includes 18 minority (13 Asian, non-Hispanic/Latino; 3 Hispanic/Latino; 2 Two or more races, non-Hispanic/Latino), 180 international. In 2018, 29 master's, 16 doctorates awarded. Terminal master's awarded for partial completion of doctoral program. *Degree requirements:* For master's, thesis; for doctorate, thesis/dissertation, qualifying exam, teaching experience. *Entrance requirements:* For master's and doctorate, GRE General Test. Additional exam requirements/recommendations for international students: Required—TOEFL. *Application deadline:* For fall admission, 2/1 for domestic students; for spring admission, 11/1 for domestic students. Applications are processed on a rolling basis. Application fee: $50. *Expenses:* Tuition: Full-time $45,168; part-time $1939 per credit hour. *Required fees:* $36; $18 per semester. $18 per semester. *Financial support:* In 2018–19, 1 fellowship with tuition reimbursement, 72 research assistantships with tuition reimbursements, 10 teaching assistantships were awarded; career-related internships or fieldwork, Federal Work-Study, and institutionally sponsored loans also available. Support available to part-time students. Financial award application deadline: 3/1; financial award applicants required to submit FAFSA. *Faculty research:* Micro-/nano-systems; robotics and haptics; applied artificial intelligence; automation; computer-aided design and testing of digital systems. *Total annual research expenditures:* $5.1 million. *Unit head:* Jing Li, Interim Department Chair, 216-368-0356, E-mail: jxl175@case.edu. *Application contact:* Angela Beca, Student Affairs Specialist, 216-368-2800, Fax: 216-368-2801, E-mail: angela.beca@case.edu. Website: www.engineering.case.edu/eecs

The Catholic University of America, School of Engineering, Program in Engineering Management, Washington, DC 20064. Offers engineering management (MSE, Certificate), including engineering management and organization (MSE), project and systems engineering management (MSE), technology management (MSE); program management (Certificate); systems engineering and management of information technology (Certificate). *Program availability:* Part-time. *Faculty:* 6 part-time/adjunct (1 woman). *Students:* 16 full-time (1 woman), 19 part-time (7 women); includes 3 minority (1 Asian, non-Hispanic/Latino; 2 Two or more races, non-Hispanic/Latino), 17 international. Average age 31. 48 applicants, 85% accepted, 19 enrolled. In 2018, 17 master's awarded. *Degree requirements:* For master's, minimum GPA of 3.0. *Entrance requirements:* For master's and Certificate, statement of purpose, official copies of academic transcripts, two letters of recommendation. Additional exam requirements/recommendations for international students: Required—TOEFL (minimum score 550 paper-based; 80 iBT). *Application deadline:* For fall admission, 7/15 priority date for domestic students, 7/1 for international students; for spring admission, 11/15 priority date for domestic students, 11/1 for international students. Applications are processed on a rolling basis. Application fee: $55. Electronic applications accepted. *Expenses:* Contact institution. *Financial support:* Fellowships, research assistantships, teaching assistantships, Federal Work-Study, scholarships/grants, tuition waivers (full and partial), and unspecified assistantships available. Financial award application deadline: 2/1; financial award applicants required to submit FAFSA. *Faculty research:* Engineering management and organization, project and systems engineering management, technology management. *Unit head:* Melvin G. Williams, Jr., Director, 202-319-5191, Fax: 202-319-6860, E-mail: williamsme@cua.edu. *Application contact:* Dr. Steven Brown, Director of Graduate Admissions, 202-319-5057, Fax: 202-319-6533, E-mail: cua-admissions@cua.edu. Website: https://engineering.catholic.edu/management/index.html

The Citadel, The Military College of South Carolina, Citadel Graduate College, School of Engineering, Department of Engineering Leadership and Program Management, Charleston, SC 29409. Offers project management (MS); systems engineering management (Graduate Certificate); technical program management (Graduate Certificate); technical project management (Graduate Certificate). *Program availability:* Part-time, evening/weekend. *Entrance requirements:* For master's, GRE or GMAT, minimum of one year of professional experience or permission from department head; two letters of reference; resume detailing previous work; for Graduate Certificate, one-page letter of intent; resume detailing previous work. Additional exam requirements/recommendations for international students: Required—TOEFL (minimum score 550 paper-based; 79 iBT). Electronic applications accepted. *Expenses:* Tuition, state resident: part-time $595 per credit hour. Tuition, nonresident: part-time $1020 per credit hour. *Required fees:* $90 per term.

Clarkson University, Wallace H. Coulter School of Engineering, Program in Engineering and Management Systems, Schenectady, NY 13699. Offers engineering and management systems (MS). *Program availability:* Part-time, evening/weekend, 100% online, blended/hybrid learning. *Students:* 3 full-time (0 women), 5 part-time (1 woman); includes 1 minority (Hispanic/Latino), 1 international. 10 applicants, 40% accepted, 2 enrolled. In 2018, 10 master's awarded. *Entrance requirements:* Additional exam requirements/recommendations for international students: Required—TOEFL (minimum score 550 paper-based, 80 iBT) or IELTS (6.5). *Application deadline:* Applications are processed on a rolling basis. Application fee: $50. Electronic

applications accepted. *Expenses: Tuition:* Full-time $24,984; part-time $1388 per credit hour. *Required fees:* $225. Tuition and fees vary according to campus/location and program. *Financial support:* Scholarships/grants available. *Unit head:* Hugo Irizarry-Quinones, Associate Dean of Engineering, 518-631-9881, E-mail: hirizarr@clarkson.edu. *Application contact:* Dan Capogna, Director of Graduate Admissions & Recruitment, 518-631-9910, E-mail: graduate@clarkson.edu.
Website: https://www.clarkson.edu/academics/graduate

Colorado State University, Walter Scott, Jr. College of Engineering, Program in Engineering Science, Fort Collins, CO 80523. Offers engineering education (ME). *Program availability:* Part-time, evening/weekend, 100% online, blended/hybrid learning. Terminal master's awarded for partial completion of doctoral program. *Degree requirements:* For master's, comprehensive exam (for some programs), thesis (for some programs); for doctorate, comprehensive exam, thesis/dissertation. *Entrance requirements:* For master's and doctorate, GRE, relevant degree. Additional exam requirements/recommendations for international students: Required—TOEFL (minimum score 550 paper-based; 80 iBT), IELTS (minimum score 6.5). Electronic applications accepted. *Expenses:* Contact institution.

Colorado State University–Pueblo, College of Education, Engineering and Professional Studies, Department of Engineering, Pueblo, CO 81001-4901. Offers industrial and systems engineering (MS). *Degree requirements:* For master's, thesis optional. *Entrance requirements:* For master's, GRE General Test. Additional exam requirements/recommendations for international students: Required—TOEFL (minimum score 500 paper-based). *Faculty research:* Nanotechnology, applied operations, research transportation, decision analysis.

Colorado Technical University Aurora, Program in Systems Engineering, Aurora, CO 80014. Offers MS.

Colorado Technical University Colorado Springs, Graduate Studies, Program in Systems Engineering, Colorado Springs, CO 80907. Offers MS.

Concordia University, School of Graduate Studies, Faculty of Engineering and Computer Science, Concordia Institute for Information Systems Engineering (CIISE), Montréal, QC H3G 1M8, Canada. Offers 3D graphics and game development (Certificate); information and systems engineering (PhD); information systems security (M Eng, MA Sc); quality systems engineering (M Eng, MA Sc); service engineering and network management (Certificate).

Cornell University, Graduate School, Graduate Fields of Engineering, Field of Systems Engineering, Ithaca, NY 14853. Offers M Eng, PhD. *Degree requirements:* For master's, thesis. *Entrance requirements:* For master's, GRE General Test. Additional exam requirements/recommendations for international students: Required—TOEFL (minimum score 600 paper-based; 77 iBT). *Faculty research:* Space systems, systems engineering of mechanical and aerospace systems, multi-echelon inventory theory, math modeling of complex systems, chain supply integration.

Dartmouth College, Thayer School of Engineering, Program in Mechanical and Systems Engineering, Hanover, NH 03755. Offers MS, PhD. *Degree requirements:* For master's, thesis; for doctorate, thesis/dissertation, candidacy oral exam. *Entrance requirements:* For master's and doctorate, GRE General Test. *Faculty research:* Tribology, dynamics and control systems, thermal science and energy conversion, fluid mechanics and multi-phase flow, mobile robots.

Embry-Riddle Aeronautical University–Daytona, Program in Unmanned and Autonomous Systems Engineering, Daytona Beach, FL 32114-3900. Offers systems engineering (MSUASE); technical (MSUASE); unmanned aircraft systems (MSUASE). *Degree requirements:* For master's, coursework, coursework plus two-semester capstone project, or thesis. *Entrance requirements:* Additional exam requirements/recommendations for international students: Required—TOEFL (minimum score 550 paper-based, 79 iBT) or IELTS (6). Electronic applications accepted.

Embry-Riddle Aeronautical University–Worldwide, Department of Decision Sciences, Daytona Beach, FL 32114-3900. Offers aviation and aerospace (MSPM); aviation/aerospace management (MSEM); financial management (MSEM, MSPM); general management (MSPM); global management (MSPM); human resources management (MSPM); information systems (MSPM); leadership (MSEM, MSPM); logistics and supply chain management (MSEM, MSLSCM, MSPM); management (MSEM, MSPM); project management (MSEM); systems engineering (MSEM, MSPM); technical management (MSPM). *Program availability:* Part-time, evening/weekend, EagleVision Classroom (between classrooms), EagleVision Home (faculty and students at home), and a blend of Classroom or Home. *Degree requirements:* For master's, comprehensive exam (for some programs), thesis (for some programs). *Entrance requirements:* Additional exam requirements/recommendations for international students: Required—TOEFL (minimum score 550 paper-based; 79 iBT), IELTS (minimum score 6). Electronic applications accepted. *Expenses:* Contact institution.

Embry-Riddle Aeronautical University–Worldwide, Department of Engineering and Technology, Daytona Beach, FL 32114-3900. Offers aerospace engineering (MS); entrepreneurship in technology (MS); systems engineering (M Sys E), including engineering management, technical. *Program availability:* Part-time, evening/weekend, 100% online, blended/hybrid learning. *Entrance requirements:* For master's, GRE (for MS in aerospace engineering). Additional exam requirements/recommendations for international students: Required—TOEFL (minimum score 550 paper-based; 79 iBT), IELTS (minimum score 6). Electronic applications accepted. *Expenses:* Contact institution.

Florida Institute of Technology, College of Engineering and Science, Program in Systems Engineering, Melbourne, FL 32901-6975. Offers MS, PhD. *Program availability:* Part-time. *Students:* 18 full-time (2 women), 74 part-time (11 women); includes 17 minority (3 Black or African American, non-Hispanic/Latino; 1 American Indian or Alaska Native, non-Hispanic/Latino; 3 Asian, non-Hispanic/Latino; 7 Hispanic/Latino; 3 Two or more races, non-Hispanic/Latino), 10 international. Average age 29. 18 applicants, 83% accepted, 11 enrolled. In 2018, 14 master's awarded. *Degree requirements:* For master's, comprehensive exam (for some programs), thesis optional, 30 credit hours; for doctorate, comprehensive exam, thesis/dissertation, 24 credit hours of coursework, 24 credit hours of research, technical paper in review for a peer reviewed journal and presented at recognized conference. *Entrance requirements:* For master's, GRE, minimum GPA of 3.0, 3 letters of recommendation, resume, bachelor's degree in engineering from ABET-accredited program, statement of objectives; for doctorate, GRE (minimum score of 315), minimum GPA of 3.5, 3 letters of recommendation, resume, statement of objectives. Additional exam requirements/recommendations for international students: Required—TOEFL (minimum score 550 paper-based; 79 iBT). *Application deadline:* For fall admission, 4/1 for international students; for spring admission, 9/30 for international students. Applications are processed on a rolling basis. Application fee: $50. Electronic applications accepted. *Expenses: Tuition:* Full-time $22,338; part-time $1241 per credit hour. Tuition and fees vary according to degree level, campus/location and program. *Financial support:* Career-related internships or fieldwork, institutionally sponsored loans, unspecified assistantships, and tuition remissions available. Support available to part-time students. Financial award application deadline: 3/1; financial award applicants required to submit FAFSA. *Faculty research:* System/software engineering, simulation and analytical modeling, project management, multimedia tools, quality. *Unit head:* Dr. Philip Bernhard, Department Head, 321-674-7294, E-mail: pbernhar@fit.edu. *Application contact:* Mike Perry, Executive Director of Admissions, 321-674-7027, E-mail: perrymj@fit.edu.
Website: https://www.fit.edu/programs/systems-engineering-ms/

George Mason University, Volgenau School of Engineering, Department of Systems Engineering and Operations Research, Fairfax, VA 22030. Offers operations research (MS); systems engineering and operations research (PhD, Certificate). MS programs offered jointly with Old Dominion University, University of Virginia, Virginia Commonwealth University, and Virginia Polytechnic Institute and State University. *Program availability:* Evening/weekend, 100% online. *Faculty:* 20 full-time (5 women), 15 part-time/adjunct (1 woman). *Students:* 39 full-time (13 women), 80 part-time (17 women); includes 25 minority (1 Black or African American, non-Hispanic/Latino; 15 Asian, non-Hispanic/Latino; 7 Hispanic/Latino; 2 Two or more races, non-Hispanic/Latino), 24 international. Average age 31. 73 applicants, 68% accepted, 24 enrolled. In 2018, 35 master's, 1 doctorate, 2 other advanced degrees awarded. *Degree requirements:* For master's, thesis optional; for doctorate, comprehensive exam, thesis/dissertation, qualifying exams. *Entrance requirements:* For master's, GRE General Test, BS in related field; minimum GPA of 3.0; 3 letters of recommendation; 2 official transcripts; expanded goals statement; proof of financial support; photocopy of passport; official bank statement; multivariable calculus, applied probability, statistics and a computer language course; self-evaluation form; for doctorate, GRE, MS with minimum GPA of 3.5; BS with minimum GPA of 3.0 in systems or operational research; 2 official transcripts; 3 letters of recommendation; resume; expanded goals statement; self evaluation form; photocopy of passport; official bank statement; proof of financial support; for Certificate, personal goals statement; 2 official transcripts; self-evaluation form; letter of recommendation; resume; official bank statement; photocopy of passport; proof of financial support; baccalaureate degree in related field. Additional exam requirements/recommendations for international students: Required—TOEFL (minimum score 575 paper-based; 88 iBT), IELTS (minimum score 6.5), PTE (minimum score 59). *Application deadline:* For fall admission, 12/15 priority date for domestic and international students; for spring admission, 8/15 priority date for domestic and international students. Application fee: $75 ($80 for international students). Electronic applications accepted. *Expenses:* $589 per credit in-state, $1,346.75 per credit out-of-state. *Financial support:* In 2018–19, 18 students received support, including 1 fellowship, 9 research assistantships with tuition reimbursements available (averaging $19,494 per year), 8 teaching assistantships with tuition reimbursements available (averaging $15,078 per year); career-related internships or fieldwork, Federal Work-Study, scholarships/grants, unspecified assistantships, and health care benefits (for full-time research or teaching assistantship recipients) also available. Support available to part-time students. Financial award application deadline: 3/1; financial award applicants required to submit FAFSA. *Faculty research:* Requirements engineering, signal processing, systems architecture, data fusion. *Total annual research expenditures:* $702,968. *Unit head:* Ariela Sofer, Chair, 703-993-1692, Fax: 703-993-1521, E-mail: asofer@gmu.edu. *Application contact:* Andy Loerch, Associate Chair, Graduate Information, 703-993-1657, E-mail: aloerch@gmu.edu.
Website: http://seor.gmu.edu

Georgetown University, Graduate School of Arts and Sciences, School of Continuing Studies, Washington, DC 20057. Offers American studies (MALS); applied intelligence (MPS); Catholic studies (MALS); classical civilizations (MALS); emergency and disaster management (MPS); ethics and the professions (MALS); global strategic communications (MPS); hospitality management (MPS); human resources management (MPS); humanities (MALS); individualized study (MALS); integrated marketing communications (MPS); international affairs (MALS); Islam and Muslim-Christian relations (MALS); journalism (MPS); liberal studies (DLS); literature and society (MALS); medieval and early modern European studies (MALS); public relations and corporate communications (MPS); real estate (MPS); religious studies (MALS); social and public policy (MALS); sports industry management (MPS); systems engineering management (MPS); technology management (MPS); the theory and practice of American democracy (MALS); urban and regional planning (MPS); visual culture (MALS). MPS in systems engineering management offered jointly with Stevens Institute of Technology. *Entrance requirements:* Additional exam requirements/recommendations for international students: Required—TOEFL.

The George Washington University, School of Engineering and Applied Science, Department of Engineering Management and Systems Engineering, Washington, DC 20052. Offers system engineering (PhD). *Program availability:* Part-time, evening/weekend. *Faculty:* 12 full-time (2 women), 41 part-time/adjunct (9 women). *Students:* 150 full-time (47 women), 598 part-time (178 women); includes 228 minority (115 Black or African American, non-Hispanic/Latino; 3 American Indian or Alaska Native, non-Hispanic/Latino; 77 Asian, non-Hispanic/Latino; 23 Hispanic/Latino; 1 Native Hawaiian or other Pacific Islander, non-Hispanic/Latino; 9 Two or more races, non-Hispanic/Latino), 41 international. Average age 35. 648 applicants, 66% accepted, 213 enrolled. In 2018, 190 master's, 131 doctorates, 37 other advanced degrees awarded. *Degree requirements:* For master's, thesis optional; for doctorate, one foreign language, thesis/dissertation, final and qualifying exams, submission of articles; for other advanced degree, professional project. *Entrance requirements:* For master's, appropriate bachelor's degree, minimum GPA of 2.7, second-semester calculus; for doctorate, appropriate master's degree, minimum GPA of 3.5, 2 letters of recommendation; for other advanced degree, appropriate master's degree, minimum GPA of 3.4. Additional exam requirements/recommendations for international students: Required—TOEFL or The George Washington University English as a Foreign Language Test. *Application deadline:* For fall admission, 3/1 for domestic students; for spring admission, 10/1 for domestic students. Applications are processed on a rolling basis. Application fee: $75. *Financial support:* In 2018–19, 35 students received support. Fellowships, research assistantships, teaching assistantships, career-related internships or fieldwork, and institutionally sponsored loans available. Financial award application deadline: 3/1; financial award applicants required to submit FAFSA. *Faculty research:* Artificial intelligence and expert systems, human factors engineering and systems analysis. *Total annual research expenditures:* $421,800. *Unit head:* Dr. Thomas Mazzuchi, Chair, 202-994-4892, E-mail: mazzu@gwu.edu. *Application contact:* Adina Lav, Marketing, Recruiting and Admissions, 202-994-5827, Fax: 202-994-0909, E-mail: engineering@gwu.edu.
Website: http://www.seas.gwu.edu/department-engineering-management-systems-engineering

Georgia Institute of Technology, Graduate Studies, College of Engineering, Professional Master's in Applied Systems Engineering Program, Atlanta, GA 30332-0001. Offers PMS. *Program availability:* Part-time. *Degree requirements:* For master's, capstone project. *Entrance requirements:* Additional exam requirements/recommendations for international students: Required—TOEFL (minimum score 550 paper-based; 79 iBT). Electronic applications accepted.

Georgia Southern University, Jack N. Averitt College of Graduate Studies, Allen E. Paulson College of Engineering and Computing, Department of Electrical and Computer Engineering, Statesboro, GA 30458. Offers MSAE. *Degree requirements:* For master's, thesis optional. *Entrance requirements:* For master's, GRE, minimum GPA of 2.75. Additional exam requirements/recommendations for international students: Required—TOEFL (minimum score 550 paper-based; 80 iBT), IELTS (minimum score 6). Electronic applications accepted. *Expenses: Tuition, area resident:* Part-time $3324 per semester. Tuition, state resident: full-time $5814; part-time $3324 per semester. Tuition, nonresident: full-time $23,204; part-time $13,260 per semester. *Required fees:* $2092; $2092. Tuition and fees vary according to course load, degree level, campus/location and program. *Faculty research:* Programming, artificial intelligence, Web systems, data mining, database systems.

Harrisburg University of Science and Technology, Program in Information Systems Engineering and Management, Harrisburg, PA 17101. Offers analytics (MS); digital government (MS); digital health (MS); entrepreneurship (MS); information security (MS); software engineering and systems development (MS). *Program availability:* Part-time, evening/weekend. *Degree requirements:* For master's, thesis optional. *Entrance requirements:* For master's, baccalaureate degree. Additional exam requirements/recommendations for international students: Required—TOEFL (minimum score 520 paper-based; 80 iBT); Recommended—IELTS (minimum score 6). Electronic applications accepted. *Faculty research:* Healthcare Informatics, material analysis, enterprise systems, circuit design, enterprise architectures.

Indiana University Bloomington, School of Informatics, Computing, and Engineering, Program in Intelligent Systems Engineering, Bloomington, IN 47405-7000. Offers PhD. *Program availability:* Part-time. *Degree requirements:* For doctorate, thesis/dissertation, qualifying exam. *Entrance requirements:* For doctorate, GRE, statement of purpose, curriculum vitae, 3 letters of recommendation, transcripts. Additional exam requirements/recommendations for international students: Required—TOEFL. Electronic applications accepted. *Faculty research:* Data mining, data modeling, computer networks, biophysics, biocomplexity, high performance computing, large scale computing, parallel and distributed computing, bioengineering, systems biology, computational, toxicology, experimental imaging analysis, medical modeling and data analysis, cyberinfrastructure, neuroengineering, 3D pranging, nanoengineering, high performance hardware, computer engineering, intelligent systems multimedia.

Instituto Tecnológico y de Estudios Superiores de Monterrey, Campus Chihuahua, Graduate Programs, Chihuahua, Mexico. Offers computer systems engineering (Ingeniero); electrical engineering (Ingeniero); electromechanical engineering (Ingeniero); electronic engineering (Ingeniero); engineering administration (MEA); industrial engineering (MIE, Ingeniero); international trade (MIT); mechanical engineering (Ingeniero).

Instituto Tecnológico y de Estudios Superiores de Monterrey, Campus Monterrey, Graduate and Research Division, Programs in Engineering, Monterrey, Mexico. Offers applied statistics (M Eng); artificial intelligence (PhD); automation engineering (M Eng); chemical engineering (M Eng); civil engineering (M Eng); electrical engineering (M Eng); electronic engineering (M Eng); environmental engineering (M Eng); industrial engineering (M Eng, PhD); manufacturing engineering (M Eng); mechanical engineering (M Eng); systems and quality engineering (M Eng). M Eng program offered jointly with University of Waterloo; PhD in industrial engineering with Texas A&M University. *Program availability:* Part-time, evening/weekend. Terminal master's awarded for partial completion of doctoral program. *Degree requirements:* For master's, one foreign language, thesis; for doctorate, one foreign language, thesis/dissertation. *Entrance requirements:* For master's, EXADEP; for doctorate, GRE, master's degree in related field. Additional exam requirements/recommendations for international students: Required—TOEFL. *Faculty research:* Flexible manufacturing cells, materials, statistical methods, environmental prevention, control and evaluation.

Iowa State University of Science and Technology, Program in Systems Engineering, Ames, IA 50011. Offers M Eng. *Entrance requirements:* Additional exam requirements/recommendations for international students: Required—TOEFL (minimum score 550 paper-based; 79 iBT), IELTS (minimum score 6.5). Electronic applications accepted.

Johns Hopkins University, Engineering Program for Professionals, Part-time Program in Systems Engineering, Baltimore, MD 21218. Offers MS, MSE, Graduate Certificate, Post-Master's Certificate. *Accreditation:* ABET. *Program availability:* Part-time, evening/weekend, 100% online, blended/hybrid learning. *Faculty:* 48 part-time/adjunct (12 women). *Students:* 502 part-time (122 women). 172 applicants, 74% accepted, 95 enrolled. In 2018, 151 master's, 6 other advanced degrees awarded. *Entrance requirements:* Additional exam requirements/recommendations for international students: Required—TOEFL (minimum score 600 paper-based; 100 iBT). *Application deadline:* Applications are processed on a rolling basis. Application fee: $0. Electronic applications accepted. *Unit head:* Dr. Ronald R. Luman, Program Chair, 443-778-5239, E-mail: ronald.luman@jhuapl.edu. *Application contact:* Doug Schiller, Admissions Director, 410-516-2300, Fax: 410-579-8049, E-mail: schiller@jhu.edu.
Website: http://www.ep.jhu.edu/

Kennesaw State University, Southern Polytechnic College of Engineering and Engineering Technology, Program in Systems Engineering, Kennesaw, GA 30144. Offers systems engineering (MS). *Program availability:* Part-time, evening/weekend, online learning. *Students:* 2 full-time (1 woman), 31 part-time (6 women); includes 16 minority (8 Black or African American, non-Hispanic/Latino; 3 Asian, non-Hispanic/Latino; 2 Hispanic/Latino; 3 Two or more races, non-Hispanic/Latino), 1 international. Average age 33. 22 applicants, 86% accepted, 14 enrolled. In 2018, 17 master's awarded. *Degree requirements:* For master's, thesis optional. *Entrance requirements:* For master's, GRE. Additional exam requirements/recommendations for international students: Required—TOEFL (minimum score 550 paper-based; 80 iBT), IELTS (minimum score 6.5). *Application deadline:* For fall admission, 7/1 priority date for domestic students, 5/1 for international students; for spring admission, 11/1 priority date for domestic students, 9/1 for international students. Applications are processed on a rolling basis. Application fee: $60. Electronic applications accepted. *Expenses: Tuition, area resident:* Full-time $6960; part-time $290 per credit hour. Tuition, state resident: full-time $6960; part-time $290 per credit hour. Tuition, nonresident: full-time $25,080; part-time $1045 per credit hour. *International tuition:* $25,080 full-time. *Required fees:* $2006; $1706 per semester. $853 per semester. *Financial support:* Applicants required to submit FAFSA. *Unit head:* Dr. Gregory Wiles, Department Chair, 470-578-7243, E-mail: gwiles1@kennesaw.edu. *Application contact:* Admissions Counselor, 470-578-4377, E-mail: ksugrad@kennesaw.edu.
Website: http://engineering.kennesaw.edu/systems-industrial/degrees/ms-systems.php

Lehigh University, P.C. Rossin College of Engineering and Applied Science, Department of Industrial and Systems Engineering, Bethlehem, PA 18015. Offers analytical finance (MS); healthcare systems engineering (M Eng, Certificate); industrial and systems engineering (M Eng, MS, PhD); management science and engineering (M Eng, MS); MBA/E. *Program availability:* Part-time, blended/hybrid learning. *Faculty:* 19 full-time (2 women), 1 part-time/adjunct (0 women). *Students:* 90 full-time (17 women), 8 part-time (3 women); includes 1 minority (Asian, non-Hispanic/Latino), 89 international. Average age 26. 318 applicants, 48% accepted, 34 enrolled. In 2018, 53 master's, 6 doctorates awarded. Terminal master's awarded for partial completion of doctoral program. *Degree requirements:* For master's, thesis (MS); project (M Eng); for doctorate, comprehensive exam, thesis/dissertation. *Entrance requirements:* For master's and doctorate, GRE General Test. Additional exam requirements/recommendations for international students: Required—TOEFL (minimum score 550 paper-based; 79 iBT), IELTS (minimum score 6.5), TOEFL or IELTS required. *Application deadline:* For fall admission, 7/15 for domestic and international students; for spring admission, 12/1 for domestic and international students. Application fee: $75. Electronic applications accepted. Tuition and fees vary according to program. *Financial support:* In 2018–19, 33 students received support, including 2 fellowships with full tuition reimbursements available (averaging $20,490 per year), 18 research assistantships with full tuition reimbursements available (averaging $20,490 per year), 11 teaching assistantships with full tuition reimbursements available (averaging $21,105 per year); health care benefits and unspecified assistantships also available. Financial award application deadline: 1/15. *Faculty research:* Mathematical optimization; logistics and service systems, stochastic processes and simulation; computational optimization and high performance computing; financial engineering and robust optimization; machine learning and data mining. *Total annual research expenditures:* $2.1 million. *Unit head:* Dr. Luis N. Vicente, Chairperson, 610-758-4050, Fax: 610-758-4886, E-mail: lnv@lehigh.edu. *Application contact:* Ana Quiroz, Graduate Coordinator, 610-758-4051, Fax: 610-758-4886, E-mail: acq217@lehigh.edu.
Website: https://ise.lehigh.edu/

Loyola Marymount University, Frank R. Seaver College of Science and Engineering, MBA/MS Program in Systems Engineering Leadership, Los Angeles, CA 90045-2659. Offers MBA/MS. *Unit head:* Dr. Claire Leon, Systems Engineering Program Director, 310-338-7878, E-mail: claire.leon@lmu.edu. *Application contact:* Ammar Dalal, Assistant Vice Provost for Graduate Enrollment, 310-338-2721, Fax: 310-338-6086, E-mail: graduateinfo@lmu.edu.

Loyola Marymount University, Frank R. Seaver College of Science and Engineering, Program in Healthcare Systems Engineering, Los Angeles, CA 90045. Offers MS. *Unit head:* Dr. Bohdan W. Oppenheim, Associate Director for Healthcare Systems Engineering, 310-338-2825, E-mail: boppenheim@lmu.edu. *Application contact:* Ammar Dalal, Assistant Vice Provost for Graduate Enrollment, 310-338-2721, Fax: 310-338-6086, E-mail: graduateinfo@lmu.edu.
Website: http://cse.lmu.edu/graduateprograms/msinsystemsengineering/msdegreeprograminhealthcaresystemsengineering/

Loyola Marymount University, Frank R. Seaver College of Science and Engineering, Program in Systems Engineering, Los Angeles, CA 90045. Offers MS. *Unit head:* Dr. Claire Leon, Systems Engineering Program Director, 310-338-7878, E-mail: claire.leon@lmu.edu. *Application contact:* Ammar Dalal, Assistant Vice Provost for Graduate Enrollment, 310-338-2721, Fax: 310-338-6086, E-mail: graduateinfo@lmu.edu.
Website: http://cse.lmu.edu/graduateprograms/msinsystemsengineering

Massachusetts Institute of Technology, School of Engineering, Institute for Data, Systems, and Society, Cambridge, MA 02139. Offers social and engineering systems (PhD); technology and policy (SM). *Degree requirements:* For master's, thesis; for doctorate, comprehensive exam, thesis/dissertation. *Entrance requirements:* For doctorate, GRE General Test. Additional exam requirements/recommendations for international students: Required—IELTS. Electronic applications accepted. *Expenses: Tuition:* Full-time $51,520; part-time $800 per credit hour. *Required fees:* $312. *Faculty research:* Information theory and decision systems; sociotechnical systems; statistics and data science; network science; critical infrastructures; health care delivery; humans and technology; policy and standards; social behavior; uncertainty, risk, and dynamics.

Massachusetts Institute of Technology, School of Engineering, System Design and Management Program, Cambridge, MA 02139-4307. Offers engineering and management (SM). Offered jointly with MIT Sloan School of Management. *Degree requirements:* For master's, thesis. *Expenses: Tuition:* Full-time $51,520; part-time $800 per credit hour. *Required fees:* $312. *Faculty research:* Humans and technology; information theory and decision systems; sociotechnical systems; policy and standards; social behavior; uncertainty, risk, and dynamics.

Mississippi State University, Bagley College of Engineering, Department of Industrial and Systems Engineering, Mississippi State, MS 39762. Offers human factors and ergonomics (MS); industrial and systems engineering (PhD); industrial systems (MS); management systems (MS); manufacturing systems (MS); operations research (MS). *Program availability:* Part-time, blended/hybrid learning. *Faculty:* 12 full-time (2 women). *Students:* 35 full-time (13 women), 66 part-time (16 women); includes 20 minority (7 Black or African American, non-Hispanic/Latino; 6 Asian, non-Hispanic/Latino; 5 Hispanic/Latino; 1 Native Hawaiian or other Pacific Islander, non-Hispanic/Latino; 1 Two or more races, non-Hispanic/Latino), 21 international. Average age 36. 67 applicants, 40% accepted, 18 enrolled. In 2018, 16 master's, 9 doctorates awarded. *Degree requirements:* For master's, comprehensive exam (for some programs), thesis optional, comprehensive oral or written exam; for doctorate, comprehensive exam, thesis/dissertation, candidacy exam. *Entrance requirements:* For master's, GRE (for graduates from program not accredited by EAC/ABET), minimum GPA of 3.0 on junior and senior years; for doctorate, GRE (for graduates from program not accredited by EAC/ABET), minimum GPA of 3.5 on master's degree and junior and senior years of BS. Additional exam requirements/recommendations for international students: Required—TOEFL (minimum score 550 paper-based; 79 iBT); Recommended—IELTS (minimum score 6.5). *Application deadline:* For fall admission, 7/1 for domestic students, 5/1 for international students; for spring admission, 11/1 for domestic students, 9/1 for international students. Applications are processed on a rolling basis. Application fee: $60 ($80 for international students). Electronic applications accepted. *Expenses:* Tuition, state resident: full-time $8450; part-time $360.59 per credit hour. Tuition, nonresident: full-time $23,140; part-time $969.09 per credit hour. *Required fees:* $110. One-time fee: $55 full-time. Part-time tuition and fees vary according to course load, degree level, campus/location and reciprocity agreements. *Financial support:* In 2018–19, 18 research assistantships with full tuition reimbursements (averaging $16,905 per year), 3 teaching assistantships with full tuition reimbursements (averaging $16,033 per year) were awarded; Federal Work-Study, institutionally sponsored loans, and unspecified assistantships also available. Financial award application deadline: 4/1; financial award applicants required to submit FAFSA. *Faculty research:* Operations research, ergonomics, production systems, management systems, transportation. *Total annual research expenditures:* $2 million. *Unit head:* Dr. Kari Babski-Reeves, Professor/Interim Head and Associate Dean for Research & Graduate Studies, 662-325-8430, Fax: 662-325-7618, E-mail: kari@ise.msstate.edu. *Application contact:* Ryan King, Admissions and Enrollment Assistant, 662-325-8951, E-mail: rjk101@grad.msstate.edu.
Website: http://www.ise.msstate.edu/

Missouri University of Science and Technology, Department of Engineering Management and Systems Engineering, Rolla, MO 65401. Offers engineering management (MS, PhD); systems engineering (MS, PhD). *Degree requirements:* For master's, thesis optional; for doctorate, comprehensive exam. *Entrance requirements:* For master's, GRE (minimum score 1150 verbal and quantitative, 4.5 writing); for doctorate, GRE (minimum score: 1100 verbal and quantitative, 3.5 writing). Additional exam requirements/recommendations for international students: Required—TOEFL (minimum score 580 paper-based). Electronic applications accepted. *Expenses:* Tuition, state resident: full-time $7545.60; part-time $419.20 per credit hour. Tuition, nonresident: full-time $22,169; part-time $1231.60 per credit hour. *International tuition:* $23,518.80 full-time. *Required fees:* $4523.05. Full-time tuition and fees vary according to course load, campus/location, program and reciprocity agreements. *Faculty research:* Management of technology, industrial engineering, manufacturing engineering, packaging engineering, quality engineering.

Naval Postgraduate School, Departments and Academic Groups, Department of Systems Engineering, Monterey, CA 93943. Offers engineering systems (MS); product development (MS); systems engineering (MS, PhD, Certificate); systems engineering analysis (MS, PhD); systems engineering management (MS, PhD). Program only open to commissioned officers of the United States and friendly nations and selected United States federal civilian employees. *Program availability:* Part-time. *Degree requirements:* For master's, thesis (for some programs), internal project, capstone project, or research/dissertation paper (for some programs); for doctorate, thesis/dissertation (for some programs), internal project, capstone project, or research/dissertation paper (for some programs). *Faculty research:* Net-centric enterprise systems/services, artificial intelligence (AI) systems engineering, unconventional weapons of mass destruction, complex systems engineering, risk-benefit analysis.

New Mexico Institute of Mining and Technology, Center for Graduate Studies, Department of Mechanical Engineering, Socorro, NM 87801. Offers explosives engineering (MS); fluid and thermal sciences (MS); mechatronics systems engineering (MS); solid mechanics (MS). *Degree requirements:* For master's, thesis (for some programs). *Entrance requirements:* For master's, GRE General Test. Additional exam requirements/recommendations for international students: Required—TOEFL (minimum score 540 paper-based). *Faculty research:* Vibrations, fluid-structure interactions.

New Mexico State University, College of Engineering, Department of Industrial Engineering, Las Cruces, NM 88003-8001. Offers industrial engineering (PhD); master of science (MSIE); systems engineering (Graduate Certificate). *Program availability:* Part-time-only, evening/weekend, 100% online. *Faculty:* 6 full-time (3 women). *Students:* 27 full-time (5 women), 79 part-time (20 women); includes 47 minority (5 Black or African American, non-Hispanic/Latino; 2 American Indian or Alaska Native, non-Hispanic/Latino; 5 Asian, non-Hispanic/Latino; 33 Hispanic/Latino; 2 Two or more races, non-Hispanic/Latino), 19 international. Average age 34. 79 applicants, 48% accepted, 25 enrolled. In 2018, 40 master's, 1 doctorate, 1 other advanced degree awarded. *Degree requirements:* For master's, thesis optional, only exit interview required for master of engineering program, no thesis required; master of science students have a thesis option or a project option, comprehensive exam is required of all MS students; for doctorate, comprehensive exam, thesis/dissertation, qualifying exam. *Entrance requirements:* Additional exam requirements/recommendations for international students: Required—TOEFL (minimum score 550 paper-based; 79 iBT), IELTS (minimum score 6.5). *Application deadline:* For fall admission, 7/1 priority date for domestic students, 3/1 for international students; for spring admission, 11/1 for domestic students, 10/1 for international students. Applications are processed on a rolling basis. Application fee: $40 ($50 for international students). Electronic applications accepted. *Expenses: Tuition, area resident:* Full-time $4216.70; part-time $252.70 per credit hour. Tuition, state resident: full-time $4216.70; part-time $252.70 per credit hour. Tuition, nonresident: full-time $12,769; part-time $881.10 per credit hour. *International tuition:* $12,769.30 full-time. *Required fees:* $878.40; $48.80 per credit hour. Full-time tuition and fees vary according to course load and reciprocity agreements. *Financial support:* In 2018–19, 28 students received support, including 1 fellowship (averaging $4,548 per year), 1 research assistantship (averaging $25,446 per year), 4 teaching assistantships (averaging $17,469 per year); career-related internships or fieldwork, Federal Work-Study, scholarships/grants, traineeships, health care benefits, and unspecified assistantships also available. Support available to part-time students. Financial award application deadline: 3/1. *Faculty research:* Operations research, simulation, manufacturing engineering, systems engineering, applied statistics. *Total annual research expenditures:* $250,014. *Unit head:* Dr. Hansuk Sohn, Interim Department Head, 575-646-4923, Fax: 575-646-2976, E-mail: hsohn@nmsu.edu. *Application contact:* Dr. Hansuk Sohn, Interim Department Head, 575-646-4923, Fax: 575-646-2976, E-mail: hsohn@nmsu.edu.
Website: http://ie.nmsu.edu

North Carolina Agricultural and Technical State University, The Graduate College, College of Engineering, Department of Industrial and Systems Engineering, Greensboro, NC 27411. Offers industrial and systems engineering (PhD); industrial engineering (MSIE). *Program availability:* Part-time. *Degree requirements:* For master's, thesis, project; for doctorate, thesis/dissertation. *Entrance requirements:* For master's, GRE General Test (recommended); for doctorate, GRE General Test, degree in engineering, BS in industrial engineering from ABET-accredited program with minimum cumulative credit point average of 3.7 or MS in discipline related to industrial engineering from college or university recognized by a regional or general accrediting agency with minimum cumulative GPA of 3.3. Additional exam requirements/recommendations for international students: Required—TOEFL (minimum score 550 paper-based; 79 iBT). *Faculty research:* Human-machine systems engineering, management systems engineering, operations research and systems analysis, production systems engineering.

Northeastern University, College of Engineering, Boston, MA 02115-5096. Offers bioengineering (MS, PhD); chemical engineering (MS, PhD); civil engineering (MS, PhD); computer engineering (PhD); computer systems engineering (MS); electrical and computer engineering (MS); electrical and computer engineering leadership (MS); electrical engineering (PhD); energy systems (MS); engineering and public policy (MS); engineering management (MS, Certificate); environmental engineering (MS); industrial engineering (MS, PhD); information assurance (PhD); information systems (MS); interdisciplinary engineering (PhD); mechanical engineering (PhD); operations research (MS); telecommunication systems management (MS). *Program availability:* Part-time, online learning. Electronic applications accepted. *Expenses:* Contact institution.

Oakland University, Graduate Study and Lifelong Learning, School of Engineering and Computer Science, Department of Industrial and Systems Engineering, Program in Systems Engineering, Rochester, MI 48309-4401. Offers MS, PhD. *Degree requirements:* For doctorate, thesis/dissertation. *Entrance requirements:* For master's and doctorate, minimum GPA of 3.0. Additional exam requirements/recommendations for international students: Required—TOEFL (minimum score 550 paper-based). Electronic applications accepted. *Expenses:* Contact institution.

The Ohio State University, Graduate School, College of Engineering, Department of Integrated Systems Engineering, Columbus, OH 43210. Offers industrial and systems engineering (MS, PhD). *Faculty:* 19. *Students:* 91 (27 women). Average age 28. In 2018, 30 master's, 7 doctorates awarded. *Entrance requirements:* For master's and doctorate, GRE General Test (desired minimum scores: Quantitative 166, Verbal 153, Analytical Writing 4.5). Additional exam requirements/recommendations for international students: Required—TOEFL (minimum score 550 paper-based; 79 iBT), Michigan English Language Assessment Battery (minimum score 82); Recommended—IELTS (minimum score 7). *Application deadline:* For fall admission, 12/13 priority date for domestic students, 11/30 priority date for international students; for spring admission, 12/4 for domestic students, 10/1 for international students; for summer admission, 2/1 for domestic and international students. Applications are processed on a rolling basis.

Application fee: $60 ($70 for international students). Electronic applications accepted. *Financial support:* Fellowships with tuition reimbursements, research assistantships with tuition reimbursements, teaching assistantships with tuition reimbursements, career-related internships or fieldwork, Federal Work-Study, institutionally sponsored loans, and unspecified assistantships available. Support available to part-time students. *Unit head:* Dr. Farhang Pourboghrat, Chair, 614-292-6239, E-mail: pourboghrat.2@osu.edu. *Application contact:* Dr. Jerald Brevik, Graduate Studies Chair, 614-292-0177, Fax: 614-292-7852, E-mail: brevik.1@osu.edu.
Website: http://ise.osu.edu/

Ohio University, Graduate College, Russ College of Engineering and Technology, Department of Industrial and Systems Engineering, Athens, OH 45701-2979. Offers M Eng Mgt, MS. *Program availability:* Part-time, evening/weekend. *Degree requirements:* For master's, comprehensive exam (for some programs), thesis optional, research project. *Entrance requirements:* For master's, GRE General Test. Additional exam requirements/recommendations for international students: Required—TOEFL (minimum score 550 paper-based; 80 iBT) or IELTS (minimum score 6.5). Electronic applications accepted. *Faculty research:* Software systems integration, human factors and ergonomics.

Old Dominion University, Frank Batten College of Engineering and Technology, Program in Engineering Management and Systems Engineering, Norfolk, VA 23529. Offers D Eng, PhD. *Program availability:* Part-time, evening/weekend, 100% online, blended/hybrid learning. *Degree requirements:* For doctorate, thesis/dissertation, candidacy exam, project. *Entrance requirements:* For doctorate, GRE, resume, letters of recommendation, minimum GPA of 3.0, interview, essay outlining intended area of specialization. Additional exam requirements/recommendations for international students: Required—TOEFL (minimum score 550 paper-based; 79 iBT). Electronic applications accepted. *Faculty research:* Project management, systems engineering, modeling and simulation, virtual collaboration environments, multidisciplinary designs, human systems engineering, decision analysis.

Old Dominion University, Frank Batten College of Engineering and Technology, Program in Systems Engineering, Norfolk, VA 23529. Offers ME. *Program availability:* Part-time, evening/weekend, 100% online, blended/hybrid learning. *Degree requirements:* For master's, comprehensive exam, project. *Entrance requirements:* For master's, GRE, minimum GPA of 3.0. Additional exam requirements/recommendations for international students: Required—TOEFL (minimum score 550 paper-based; 79 iBT). Electronic applications accepted. *Expenses:* Contact institution. *Faculty research:* Systems engineering design, system of systems engineering, complex system governance, optimization.

Oregon State University, College of Engineering, Program in Industrial Engineering, Corvallis, OR 97331. Offers advanced manufacturing (M Eng, MS, PhD); engineering management (M Eng); human systems engineering (M Eng, MS, PhD); information systems engineering (M Eng, MS, PhD); manufacturing systems engineering (M Eng, MS, PhD). *Program availability:* 100% online. *Entrance requirements:* For master's and doctorate, GRE. Additional exam requirements/recommendations for international students: Required—TOEFL (minimum score 80 iBT), IELTS (minimum score 6.5). *Expenses:* Contact institution.

Penn State Great Valley, Graduate Studies, Engineering Division, Malvern, PA 19355-1488. Offers engineering management (MEM); software engineering (MSE); systems engineering (M Eng, Certificate).

Purdue University Fort Wayne, College of Engineering, Technology, and Computer Science, Department of Electrical and Computer Engineering, Fort Wayne, IN 46805-1499. Offers computer engineering (MSE); electrical engineering (MSE); systems engineering (MSE). *Program availability:* Part-time. *Entrance requirements:* For master's, minimum GPA of 3.0, bachelor's degree in engineering discipline. Additional exam requirements/recommendations for international students: Required—TOEFL (minimum score 550 paper-based; 79 iBT); Recommended—TWE. Electronic applications accepted.

Regis University, College of Computer and Information Sciences, Denver, CO 80221-1099. Offers agile technologies (Certificate); cybersecurity (Certificate); data science (M Sc); database administration with Oracle (Certificate); database development (Certificate); database technologies (M Sc); enterprise Java software development (Certificate); enterprise resource planning (Certificate); executive information technology (Certificate); health care informatics (Certificate); health care informatics and information management (M Sc); information assurance (M Sc); information assurance policy management (Certificate); information technology management (M Sc); mobile software development (Certificate); software engineering (M Sc, Certificate); software engineering and database technology (M Sc); storage area networks (Certificate); systems engineering (M Sc, Certificate). *Program availability:* Part-time, evening/weekend, 100% online, blended/hybrid learning. *Degree requirements:* For master's, thesis (for some programs), final research project. *Entrance requirements:* For master's, official transcript reflecting baccalaureate degree awarded from regionally-accredited college or university, 2 years of related experience, resume, interview. Additional exam requirements/recommendations for international students: Required—TOEFL (minimum score 550 paper-based; 82 iBT). Electronic applications accepted. *Expenses:* Contact institution. *Faculty research:* Information policy, knowledge management, software architectures, data science.

Rensselaer Polytechnic Institute, Graduate School, School of Engineering, Program in Computer and Systems Engineering, Troy, NY 12180-3590. Offers M Eng, MS, PhD. *Faculty:* 40 full-time (6 women), 1 part-time/adjunct (0 women). *Students:* 18 full-time (3 women), 2 part-time (0 women), 16 international. Average age 25. 61 applicants, 46% accepted, 6 enrolled. In 2018, 7 master's, 2 doctorates awarded. Terminal master's awarded for partial completion of doctoral program. *Degree requirements:* For master's, thesis (for some programs); for doctorate, thesis/dissertation. *Entrance requirements:* For master's and doctorate, GRE. Additional exam requirements/recommendations for international students: Required—TOEFL (minimum score 570 paper-based; 88 iBT), IELTS (minimum score 6.5), PTE (minimum score 60). *Application deadline:* For fall admission, 1/1 priority date for domestic and international students; for spring admission, 8/15 priority date for domestic and international students. Applications are processed on a rolling basis. Application fee: $75. Electronic applications accepted. *Financial support:* In 2018–19, research assistantships (averaging $23,000 per year), teaching assistantships (averaging $23,000 per year) were awarded; fellowships also available. Financial award application deadline: 1/1. *Faculty research:* Communications, information, and signals and systems; computer engineering, hardware, and architecture; computer networking; control, robotics, and automation; energy sources and systems; image science: computer vision, image processing, and geographic information science; microelectronics, photonics, VLSI, and mixed-signal design; plasma science and electromagnetics. *Total annual research expenditures:* $1.5 million. *Unit head:* Dr. Hussein Abouzeid, Graduate Program Director, 518-576-6534, E-mail: abouzeid@ecse.rpi.edu. *Application contact:* Jarron Decker, Director of Graduate Admissions, 518-276-6216, Fax: 518-276-4072, E-mail: gradadmissions@rpi.edu.
Website: https://ecse.rpi.edu/

Systems Engineering

Rensselaer Polytechnic Institute, Graduate School, School of Engineering, Program in Decision Sciences and Engineering Systems, Troy, NY 12180-3590. Offers PhD. *Faculty:* 3 full-time (2 women). *Students:* 12 full-time (3 women), 3 part-time (0 women), 11 international. Average age 30. 39 applicants, 21% accepted, 3 enrolled. In 2018, 3 doctorates awarded. Terminal master's awarded for partial completion of doctoral program. *Degree requirements:* For doctorate, thesis/dissertation. *Entrance requirements:* For doctorate, GRE. Additional exam requirements/recommendations for international students: Required—TOEFL (minimum score 570 paper-based; 88 iBT), IELTS (minimum score 6.5), PTE (minimum score 60). *Application deadline:* For fall admission, 1/1 priority date for domestic students, 1/1 for international students. Applications are processed on a rolling basis. Application fee: $75. Electronic applications accepted. *Financial support:* In 2018–19, research assistantships (averaging $23,000 per year), teaching assistantships (averaging $23,000 per year) were awarded; fellowships also available. Financial award application deadline: 1/1. *Faculty research:* Agent-based modeling, computational optimization, data mining, decision analysis, decision technologies, human factors engineering, logistics, network optimization and analysis, scheduling, simulation modeling, statistical analysis, stochastic programming. *Total annual research expenditures:* $231,336. *Unit head:* Dr. Thomas Sharkey, Graduate Program Director, 518-276-2958, E-mail: sharkt@rpi.edu. *Application contact:* Jarron Decker, Director of Graduate Admissions, 518-276-6216, Fax: 518-276-4072, E-mail: gradadmissions@rpi.edu.
Website: http://ise.rpi.edu/

Rensselaer Polytechnic Institute, Graduate School, School of Engineering, Program in Systems Engineering and Technology Management, Troy, NY 12180-3590. Offers M Eng. *Program availability:* Part-time. *Faculty:* 8 full-time (0 women). *Students:* 5 full-time (1 woman), 25 part-time (4 women); includes 7 minority (1 Black or African American, non-Hispanic/Latino; 1 American Indian or Alaska Native, non-Hispanic/Latino; 3 Asian, non-Hispanic/Latino; 2 Hispanic/Latino). Average age 28. 18 applicants, 83% accepted, 12 enrolled. In 2018, 5 master's awarded. *Degree requirements:* For master's, thesis (for some programs). *Entrance requirements:* For master's, GRE. Additional exam requirements/recommendations for international students: Required—TOEFL (minimum score 570 paper-based; 88 iBT), IELTS (minimum score 6.5), PTE (minimum score 60). *Application deadline:* For fall admission, 1/1 priority date for domestic and international students; for spring admission, 8/15 priority date for domestic and international students. Applications are processed on a rolling basis. Application fee: $75. Electronic applications accepted. *Financial support:* Institutionally sponsored loans available. Financial award application deadline: 1/1. *Total annual research expenditures:* $329,367. *Unit head:* Dr. Bill Foley, Graduate Program Director, 518-276-4009, E-mail: foleyw@rpi.edu. *Application contact:* Jarron Decker, Director of Graduate Admissions, 518-276-6216, Fax: 518-276-4072, E-mail: gradadmissions@rpi.edu.
Website: http://ise.rpi.edu/

Rochester Institute of Technology, Graduate Enrollment Services, Kate Gleason College of Engineering, Design, Development and Manufacturing Department, MS Program in Product Development, Rochester, NY 14623-5603. Offers MS. *Program availability:* Part-time, evening/weekend, 100% online, blended/hybrid learning. *Students:* 1 full-time, 22 part-time (4 women); includes 2 minority (both Black or African American, non-Hispanic/Latino), 1 international. Average age 38. 21 applicants, 67% accepted, 11 enrolled. In 2018, 6 master's awarded. *Degree requirements:* For master's, capstone project. *Entrance requirements:* For master's, undergraduate degree in engineering or related field, minimum GPA of 3.0, 2 years of experience in product development, one professional recommendation, resume. Additional exam requirements/recommendations for international students: Required—TOEFL (minimum score 550 paper-based; 79 iBT), IELTS (minimum score 6.5), PTE (minimum score 58). *Application deadline:* Applications are processed on a rolling basis. Application fee: $65. Electronic applications accepted. *Expenses:* Contact institution. *Financial support:* In 2018–19, 6 students received support. Scholarships/grants available. Support available to part-time students. Financial award applicants required to submit FAFSA. *Faculty research:* Systems engineering, lean product development, decision analysis, agile methods, project management. *Unit head:* Christine Fisher, Program Director, 585-475-7971, Fax: 585-475-4080, E-mail: christine.fisher@rit.edu. *Application contact:* Diane Ellison, Senior Associate Vice President, Graduate Enrollment Services, 585-475-2229, Fax: 585-475-7164, E-mail: gradinfo@rit.edu.
Website: https://www.rit.edu/study/product-development-ms

Rochester Institute of Technology, Graduate Enrollment Services, Kate Gleason College of Engineering, Industrial and Systems Engineering Department, ME Program in Industrial and Systems Engineering, Rochester, NY 14623-5603. Offers ME. *Program availability:* Part-time. *Students:* 5 full-time (1 woman), 3 part-time (2 women), 1 international. Average age 24. 35 applicants, 17% accepted, 2 enrolled. In 2018, 9 master's awarded. *Degree requirements:* For master's, thesis or alternative, capstone project. *Entrance requirements:* For master's, GRE, minimum GPA of 3.0 (recommended), one-page statement of purpose, two letters of recommendation. Additional exam requirements/recommendations for international students: Required—TOEFL (minimum score 580 paper-based; 90 iBT), IELTS (minimum score 6), PTE (minimum score 58). *Application deadline:* For fall admission, 2/15 priority date for domestic and international students; for spring admission, 12/15 priority date for domestic and international students. Applications are processed on a rolling basis. Application fee: $65. Electronic applications accepted. *Financial support:* In 2018–19, 11 students received support. Research assistantships with partial tuition reimbursements available, teaching assistantships with partial tuition reimbursements available, career-related internships or fieldwork, scholarships/grants, and unspecified assistantships available. Support available to part-time students. Financial award applicants required to submit FAFSA. *Faculty research:* Advanced manufacturing, engineering education, ergonomics and human factors, healthcare delivery systems, operations research and simulation, systems engineering, production and logistics, sustainable engineering. *Unit head:* Michael Kuhl, Graduate Program Director, 585-475-2134, E-mail: mekeie@rit.edu. *Application contact:* Diane Ellison, Senior Associate Vice President, Graduate Enrollment Services, 585-475-2229, Fax: 585-475-7164, E-mail: gradinfo@rit.edu.
Website: https://www.rit.edu/study/industrial-and-systems-engineering-me

Rochester Institute of Technology, Graduate Enrollment Services, Kate Gleason College of Engineering, Industrial and Systems Engineering Department, MS Program in Industrial and Systems Engineering, Rochester, NY 14623-5603. Offers MS. *Program availability:* Part-time. *Students:* 14 full-time, 7 part-time (1 woman), 16 international. Average age 25. 134 applicants, 35% accepted, 6 enrolled. In 2018, 10 master's awarded. *Degree requirements:* For master's, thesis. *Entrance requirements:* For master's, GRE, minimum GPA of 3.0 (recommended), statement of purpose, two letters of recommendation. Additional exam requirements/recommendations for international students: Required—TOEFL (minimum score 580 paper-based; 90 iBT), IELTS (minimum score 6.5), PTE (minimum score 58). *Application deadline:* For fall admission, 2/15 priority date for domestic and international students; for spring admission, 12/15 priority date for domestic and international students. Applications are processed on a rolling basis. Application fee: $65. Electronic applications accepted. *Financial support:* In 2018–19, 17 students received support. Research assistantships with partial tuition reimbursements available, teaching assistantships with partial tuition reimbursements available, career-related internships or fieldwork, scholarships/grants, and unspecified assistantships available. Support available to part-time students. Financial award applicants required to submit FAFSA. *Faculty research:* Advanced manufacturing; health care systems engineering, data analytics, operations research, and simulation; supply chain and logistics systems; biomechanics, ergonomics, safety, and rehabilitation. *Unit head:* Michael Kuhl, Graduate Program Director, 585-475-2134, E-mail: mekeie@rit.edu. *Application contact:* Diane Ellison, Senior Associate Vice President, Graduate Enrollment Services, 585-475-2229, Fax: 585-475-7164, E-mail: gradinfo@rit.edu.
Website: https://www.rit.edu/study/industrial-and-systems-engineering-ms

Rochester Institute of Technology, Graduate Enrollment Services, Kate Gleason College of Engineering, Microsystems Engineering Department, PhD Program in Microsystems Engineering, Rochester, NY 14623-5603. Offers PhD. *Program availability:* Part-time. *Students:* 40 full-time (12 women), 5 part-time (2 women); includes 3 minority (1 Asian, non-Hispanic/Latino; 2 Hispanic/Latino), 22 international. Average age 28. 43 applicants, 23% accepted, 8 enrolled. In 2018, 4 doctorates awarded. *Degree requirements:* For doctorate, comprehensive exam, thesis/dissertation. *Entrance requirements:* For doctorate, GRE, minimum GPA of 3.0 (recommended), resume, personal statement of educational and research objectives, at least two letters of recommendation. Additional exam requirements/recommendations for international students: Required—TOEFL (minimum score 600 paper-based; 100 iBT), IELTS (minimum score 7), PTE (minimum score 68). *Application deadline:* For fall admission, 1/15 priority date for domestic and international students. Applications are processed on a rolling basis. Application fee: $65. Electronic applications accepted. *Expenses:* Contact institution. *Financial support:* In 2018–19, 52 students received support. Fellowships with full tuition reimbursements available, research assistantships with full tuition reimbursements available, teaching assistantships with full tuition reimbursements available, career-related internships or fieldwork, scholarships/grants, health care benefits, and unspecified assistantships available. Support available to part-time students. Financial award applicants required to submit FAFSA. *Faculty research:* Semiconductor microelectronics and nanoelectronics; photovoltaics, solar cells, and energy; photonics and integrated silicon photonics; nanobiodevices and materials; microfluidics and micromechanical systems. *Unit head:* Dr. Bruce Smith, Director, 585-475-2058, E-mail: bwsemc@rit.edu. *Application contact:* Diane Ellison, Senior Associate Vice President, Graduate Enrollment Services, 585-475-2229, Fax: 585-475-7164, E-mail: gradinfo@rit.edu.
Website: https://www.rit.edu/study/microsystems-engineering-phd

Rose-Hulman Institute of Technology, Graduate Studies, Department of Electrical and Computer Engineering, Terre Haute, IN 47803-3999. Offers electrical and computer engineering (M Eng); electrical engineering (MS); systems engineering and management (MS). *Program availability:* Part-time. *Faculty:* 19 full-time (2 women), 1 (woman) part-time/adjunct. *Students:* 4 full-time (0 women), 4 part-time (2 women), 7 international. Average age 26. 9 applicants, 44% accepted, 4 enrolled. In 2018, 2 master's awarded. *Degree requirements:* For master's, thesis (for some programs). *Entrance requirements:* For master's, GRE, minimum GPA of 3.0. Additional exam requirements/recommendations for international students: Required—TOEFL (minimum score 580 paper-based; 94 iBT), IELTS (minimum score 7). *Application deadline:* For fall admission, 2/1 priority date for domestic and international students; for winter admission, 10/1 for domestic students, 4/1 for international students; for spring admission, 1/15 for domestic students, 11/1 for international students. Applications are processed on a rolling basis. Application fee: $0. Electronic applications accepted. *Expenses: Tuition:* Full-time $46,641. *Financial support:* In 2018–19, 7 students received support. Fellowships with tuition reimbursements available, research assistantships with tuition reimbursements available, institutionally sponsored loans, scholarships/grants, and tuition waivers (full and partial) available. *Faculty research:* VLSI, power systems, analog electronics, communications, electromagnetics. *Total annual research expenditures:* $55,933. *Unit head:* Dr. Mario Simoni, Department Head, 812-877-8341, Fax: 812-877-8895, E-mail: simoni@rose-hulman.edu. *Application contact:* Dr. Craig Downing, Associate Dean of the Faculty, 812-877-8822, E-mail: downing@rose-hulman.edu.
Website: https://www.rose-hulman.edu/academics/academic-departments/electrical-computer-engineering/index.html

Rutgers University–New Brunswick, Graduate School-New Brunswick, Department of Industrial and Systems Engineering, Piscataway, NJ 08854-8097. Offers industrial and systems engineering (MS, PhD); information technology (MS); manufacturing systems engineering (MS); quality and reliability engineering (MS). *Program availability:* Part-time, evening/weekend. Terminal master's awarded for partial completion of doctoral program. *Degree requirements:* For master's, thesis or alternative, seminar; for doctorate, comprehensive exam, thesis/dissertation. *Entrance requirements:* For master's and doctorate, GRE General Test. Additional exam requirements/recommendations for international students: Required—TOEFL. *Faculty research:* Production and manufacturing systems, quality and reliability engineering, systems engineering and aviation safety.

San Jose State University, Program in Industrial and Systems Engineering, San Jose, CA 95192-0001. Offers MS. *Program availability:* Part-time. *Degree requirements:* For master's, comprehensive exam. Electronic applications accepted.

Simon Fraser University, Office of Graduate Studies and Postdoctoral Fellows, Faculty of Applied Sciences, School of Mechatronic Systems Engineering, Burnaby, BC V5A 1S6, Canada. Offers MA Sc, PhD. *Degree requirements:* For master's, one foreign language, thesis; for doctorate, one foreign language, comprehensive exam, thesis/dissertation. *Entrance requirements:* Additional exam requirements/recommendations for international students: Required—TOEFL (minimum score 580 paper-based; 93 iBT), IELTS (minimum score 7), TWE (minimum score 5). Electronic applications accepted. *Faculty research:* Intelligent systems and smart materials, micro-electro mechanical systems (MEMS), biomedical engineering, thermal engineering, alternative energy.

Southern Methodist University, Lyle School of Engineering, Department of Engineering Management, Information, and Systems, Dallas, TX 75275. Offers engineering entrepreneurship (MS); engineering management (MS, DE); information engineering and management (MSIEM); operations research (MS, PhD); systems engineering (MS). MS in engineering entrepreneurship offered in collaboration with the Cox School of Business. *Program availability:* Part-time, evening/weekend, online learning. Terminal master's awarded for partial completion of doctoral program. *Degree requirements:* For master's, thesis optional; for doctorate, thesis/dissertation, oral and written qualifying exams. *Entrance requirements:* For master's, minimum GPA of 3.0 in last 2 years; bachelor's degree in engineering, mathematics, sciences, or technical area; for doctorate, GRE General Test (operations research, engineering management), bachelor's degree in related field. Additional exam requirements/recommendations for international students: Required—TOEFL. *Faculty research:* Telecommunications, decision systems, information engineering, operations research, software.

Southern Methodist University, Lyle School of Engineering, Department of Multidisciplinary Studies, Dallas, TX 75275. Offers data science (MS), including business analytics, machine learning; datacenter systems engineering (MS); design and innovation (MA). *Program availability:* Part-time, online learning. *Entrance requirements:*

For master's, BS in one of the engineering disciplines, computer science, one of the quantitative sciences or mathematics; minimum of two years of college-level mathematics including one year of college-level calculus.

Stevens Institute of Technology, Graduate School, Charles V. Schaefer Jr. School of Engineering and Science, Department of Electrical and Computer Engineering, Program in Networked Information Systems, Hoboken, NJ 07030. Offers MS, Certificate. *Program availability:* Part-time, evening/weekend. *Faculty:* 19 full-time (5 women), 5 part-time/adjunct (1 woman). *Students:* 4 part-time (0 women); includes 1 minority (Black or African American, non-Hispanic/Latino). Average age 40. In 2018, 1 master's awarded. Terminal master's awarded for partial completion of doctoral program. *Degree requirements:* For master's, thesis optional, minimum B average in major field and overall; for Certificate, minimum B average. *Entrance requirements:* For master's, GRE/GMAT scores: GRE scores are required for all applicants applying to a full-time graduate program in the Schaefer School of Engineering and Science (SES). International applicants must submit TOEFL/IELTS scores and fulfill the English Language Proficiency Requirements in order to be considered. Additional exam requirements/recommendations for international students: Required—TOEFL (minimum score 74 iBT), IELTS (minimum score 6). *Application deadline:* For fall admission, 4/15 for domestic and international students; for spring admission, 11/1 for domestic and international students; for summer admission, 5/1 for domestic students. Applications are processed on a rolling basis. Application fee: $60. Electronic applications accepted. *Expenses: Tuition:* Full-time $35,960; part-time $1620 per credit. *Required fees:* $1290; $600 per semester. Tuition and fees vary according to course load. *Financial support:* Fellowships, research assistantships, teaching assistantships, career-related internships or fieldwork, Federal Work-Study, scholarships/grants, and unspecified assistantships available. Financial award application deadline: 2/15; financial award applicants required to submit FAFSA. *Unit head:* Dr. Jean Zu, Dean of SES, 201-216.8233, Fax: 201-216.8372, E-mail: Jean.Zu@stevens.edu. *Application contact:* Graduate Admissions, 888-783-8367, Fax: 201-511-1306, E-mail: graduate@stevens.edu.

Stevens Institute of Technology, Graduate School, School of Systems and Enterprises, Program in Systems Engineering, Hoboken, NJ 07030. Offers systems and supportability engineering (Certificate); systems engineering (M Eng, PhD); systems engineering and architecting (Certificate); systems engineering management (Certificate); systems engineering of embedded/cyber-physical systems (Certificate); systems engineering security (Certificate). *Program availability:* Part-time, evening/weekend. *Faculty:* 28 full-time (8 women), 5 part-time/adjunct (1 woman). *Students:* 55 full-time (11 women), 182 part-time (49 women); includes 19 minority (5 Black or African American, non-Hispanic/Latino; 1 American Indian or Alaska Native, non-Hispanic/Latino; 12 Asian, non-Hispanic/Latino; 1 Hispanic/Latino), 33 international. Average age 32. In 2018, 115 master's, 4 doctorates, 112 other advanced degrees awarded. Terminal master's awarded for partial completion of doctoral program. *Degree requirements:* For master's, thesis optional, minimum B average in major field and overall; for doctorate, comprehensive exam (for some programs), thesis/dissertation; for Certificate, minimum B average. *Entrance requirements:* For master's, GRE/GMAT scores: GRE scores are required for all applicants applying to a full-time graduate program in the Schaefer School of Engineering and Science (SES). International applicants must submit TOEFL/IELTS scores and fulfill the English Language Proficiency Requirements in order to be considered. Additional exam requirements/recommendations for international students: Required—TOEFL (minimum score 74 iBT), IELTS (minimum score 6). *Application deadline:* For fall admission, 4/15 for domestic and international students; for spring admission, 11/1 for domestic and international students; for summer admission, 5/1 for domestic students. Applications are processed on a rolling basis. Application fee: $60. Electronic applications accepted. *Expenses: Tuition:* Full-time $35,960; part-time $1620 per credit. *Required fees:* $1290; $600 per semester. Tuition and fees vary according to course load. *Financial support:* Fellowships, research assistantships, teaching assistantships, career-related internships or fieldwork, Federal Work-Study, scholarships/grants, and unspecified assistantships available. Financial award application deadline: 2/15; financial award applicants required to submit FAFSA. *Unit head:* Dr. Yehia Massoud, Dean of SSE, 201-216.8025, E-mail: yehia.massoud@stevens.edu. *Application contact:* Graduate Admissions, 888-783-8367, Fax: 888-511-1306, E-mail: graduate@stevens.edu.
Website: https://www.stevens.edu/school-systems-enterprises/masters-degree-programs/systems-engineering

Stony Brook University, State University of New York, Graduate School, College of Engineering and Applied Sciences, Department of Computer Science, Program in Information Systems Engineering, Stony Brook, NY 11794. Offers MS. *Entrance requirements:* Additional exam requirements/recommendations for international students: Required—TOEFL. *Application deadline:* For fall admission, 1/15 for domestic students; for spring admission, 10/1 for domestic students. Application fee: $100. *Expenses:* Contact institution. *Unit head:* Prof. Samir Das, Chair, 631-632-1807, Fax: 631-632-8334, E-mail: samir@stonybrook.edu. *Application contact:* Prof. Samir Das, Chair, 631-632-1807, Fax: 631-632-8334, E-mail: samir@stonybrook.edu.

Tennessee State University, The School of Graduate Studies and Research, College of Engineering, Nashville, TN 37209-1561. Offers biomedical engineering (ME); civil engineering (ME); computer and information systems engineering (MS, PhD); electrical engineering (ME); environmental engineering (ME); manufacturing engineering (ME); mathematical sciences (MS); mechanical engineering (ME). *Program availability:* Part-time, evening/weekend. *Degree requirements:* For master's, project; for doctorate, comprehensive exam, thesis/dissertation. *Entrance requirements:* For doctorate, minimum GPA of 3.3. *Faculty research:* Robotics, intelligent systems, human-computer interaction software systems, biomedical engineering, signal/image processing, probabilistic design, intelligent manufacturing, cooperative mobile robots, condition based maintenance, sensor fusion.

Texas A&M University–Kingsville, College of Graduate Studies, Frank H. Dotterweich College of Engineering, Program in Sustainable Energy Systems Engineering, Kingsville, TX 78363. Offers PhD. *Degree requirements:* For doctorate, variable foreign language requirement, comprehensive exam, thesis/dissertation (for some programs). *Entrance requirements:* For doctorate, GRE, MAT, GMAT, bachelor's or master's degree in engineering or science, curriculum vitae, official transcripts, statement of purpose, three letters of recommendation. Additional exam requirements/recommendations for international students: Required—TOEFL (minimum score 550 paper-based; 79 iBT). Electronic applications accepted.

The University of Alabama in Huntsville, School of Graduate Studies, College of Engineering, Department of Industrial and Systems Engineering and Engineering Management, Huntsville, AL 35899. Offers engineering management (MSE, PhD); industrial engineering (MSE, PhD); operations research (MSOR); systems engineering (MSE, PhD). *Program availability:* Part-time. *Faculty:* 10 full-time (2 women), 1 part-time/adjunct. *Students:* 25 full-time (10 women), 62 part-time (20 women); includes 16 minority (4 Black or African American, non-Hispanic/Latino; 3 American Indian or Alaska Native, non-Hispanic/Latino; 5 Asian, non-Hispanic/Latino; 2 Hispanic/Latino; 2 Two or more races, non-Hispanic/Latino), 17 international. Average age 33. 78 applicants, 37% accepted, 13 enrolled. In 2018, 25 master's, 1 doctorate awarded. *Degree requirements:* For master's, comprehensive exam, thesis or alternative, oral and written exams; for doctorate, comprehensive exam, thesis/dissertation, oral and written exams. *Entrance requirements:* For master's and doctorate, GRE General Test, minimum GPA of 3.0. Additional exam requirements/recommendations for international students: Required—TOEFL (minimum score 500 paper-based; 80 iBT), IELTS (minimum score 6.5). *Application deadline:* For fall admission, 7/15 priority date for domestic students, 4/1 priority date for international students; for spring admission, 11/30 priority date for domestic students, 9/1 priority date for international students. Applications are processed on a rolling basis. Application fee: $50. Electronic applications accepted. *Expenses: Tuition, area resident:* Full-time $10,632; part-time $412 per credit hour. Tuition, state resident: full-time $10,632. Tuition, nonresident: full-time $23,604; part-time $412 per credit hour. *Required fees:* $582; $582. Tuition and fees vary according to course load and program. *Financial support:* In 2018–19, 14 students received support, including 8 research assistantships with full tuition reimbursements available (averaging $7,898 per year), 6 teaching assistantships with full tuition reimbursements available (averaging $5,750 per year); career-related internships or fieldwork, Federal Work-Study, institutionally sponsored loans, scholarships/grants, health care benefits, and unspecified assistantships also available. Support available to part-time students. Financial award application deadline: 4/1; financial award applicants required to submit FAFSA. *Faculty research:* Systems engineering process, electronic manufacturing, heuristic manufacturing, teams and team development. *Unit head:* Dr. James J. Swain, Chair, 256-824-6749, Fax: 256-824-6733, E-mail: james.swain@uah.edu. *Application contact:* Kim Gray, Graduate Studies Admissions Coordinator, 256-824-6002, Fax: 256-824-6405, E-mail: deangrad@uah.edu.
Website: http://www.uah.edu/eng/departments/iseem/

University of Alberta, Faculty of Graduate Studies and Research, Department of Electrical and Computer Engineering, Edmonton, AB T6G 2E1, Canada. Offers communications (M Eng, M Sc, PhD); computer engineering (M Eng, M Sc, PhD); electromagnetics (M Eng, M Sc, PhD); nanotechnology and microdevices (M Eng, M Sc, PhD); power/power electronics (M Eng, M Sc, PhD); systems (M Eng, M Sc, PhD). Terminal master's awarded for partial completion of doctoral program. *Degree requirements:* For master's, thesis; for doctorate, thesis/dissertation. *Entrance requirements:* Additional exam requirements/recommendations for international students: Required—TOEFL. Electronic applications accepted. *Faculty research:* Controls, communications, microelectronics, electromagnetics.

The University of Arizona, College of Engineering, Department of Systems and Industrial Engineering, Tucson, AZ 85721. Offers engineering management (Graduate Certificate); industrial engineering (MS); systems and industrial engineering (MS, PhD); systems engineering (MS, PhD, Graduate Certificate). *Program availability:* Part-time, online learning. *Degree requirements:* For doctorate, thesis/dissertation. *Entrance requirements:* For master's, GRE General Test (minimum score: 500 Verbal, 700 Quantitative), 3 letters of recommendation; for doctorate, GRE General Test (minimum score: 500 Verbal, 700 Quantitative), minimum GPA of 3.5, 3 letters of recommendation, letter of intent. Additional exam requirements/recommendations for international students: Required—TOEFL (minimum score 575 paper-based; 80 iBT). Electronic applications accepted. *Faculty research:* Optimization, systems theory, logistics, transportation, embedded systems.

University of Arkansas at Little Rock, Graduate School, George W. Donaghey College of Engineering and Information Technology, Department of Systems Engineering, Little Rock, AR 72204-1099. Offers MS, PhD, Graduate Certificate.

University of California, Merced, Graduate Division, School of Engineering, Merced, CA 95343. Offers biological engineering and small scale technologies (MS, PhD); electrical engineering and computer science (MS, PhD); environmental systems (MS, PhD); management of innovation, sustainability, and technology (MM); mechanical engineering (MS); mechanical engineering and applied mechanics (PhD). *Faculty:* 60 full-time (16 women). *Students:* 219 full-time (72 women), 1 part-time (0 women); includes 43 minority (2 Black or African American, non-Hispanic/Latino; 17 Asian, non-Hispanic/Latino; 20 Hispanic/Latino; 1 Native Hawaiian or other Pacific Islander, non-Hispanic/Latino; 3 Two or more races, non-Hispanic/Latino), 145 international. Average age 28. 371 applicants, 46% accepted, 75 enrolled. In 2018, 30 master's, 17 doctorates awarded. Terminal master's awarded for partial completion of doctoral program. *Degree requirements:* For master's, variable foreign language requirement, comprehensive exam, thesis or alternative, oral defense; for doctorate, variable foreign language requirement, comprehensive exam, thesis/dissertation, oral defense. *Entrance requirements:* For master's and doctorate, GRE. Additional exam requirements/recommendations for international students: Required—TOEFL (minimum score 550 paper-based; 80 iBT); Recommended—IELTS (minimum score 6.5). *Application deadline:* For fall admission, 1/15 priority date for domestic and international students. Application fee: $105 ($125 for international students). Electronic applications accepted. *Expenses:* In-state tuition $11442 per year; Out-of-state tuition $26544 per year; Student Fees $1765 per year. *Financial support:* In 2018–19, 200 students received support, including 14 fellowships with full tuition reimbursements available (averaging $20,851 per year), 70 research assistantships with full tuition reimbursements available (averaging $18,334 per year), 116 teaching assistantships with full tuition reimbursements available (averaging $19,841 per year); scholarships/grants, traineeships, and health care benefits also available. *Faculty research:* Sustainability systems engineering and resource management: food, energy, water; biomolecular engineering and biotechnology; computational science and data analytics; artificial intelligence, machine learning, internet of things, human computer interface; cyber-physical systems and automation. *Total annual research expenditures:* $3.1 million. *Unit head:* Dr. Mark Matsumoto, Dean, 209-228-4047, Fax: 209-228-4047, E-mail: mmatsumoto@ucmerced.edu. *Application contact:* Tsu Ya, Director of Admissions and Academic Services, 209-228-4521, Fax: 209-228-6906, E-mail: tya@ucmerced.edu.

University of Colorado Colorado Springs, College of Engineering and Applied Science, Program in General Engineering, Colorado Springs, CO 80918. Offers computer science (PhD); cybersecurity (ME); energy engineering (ME); engineering management (ME); engineering systems (ME); software engineering (ME); space operations (ME). *Program availability:* Part-time, evening/weekend, blended/hybrid learning. *Faculty:* 1 full-time (0 women), 20 part-time/adjunct (6 women). *Students:* 12 full-time (1 woman), 177 part-time (39 women); includes 38 minority (4 Black or African American, non-Hispanic/Latino; 12 Asian, non-Hispanic/Latino; 12 Hispanic/Latino; 1 Native Hawaiian or other Pacific Islander, non-Hispanic/Latino; 9 Two or more races, non-Hispanic/Latino), 54 international. Average age 35. 44 applicants, 93% accepted, 21 enrolled. In 2018, 24 master's, 15 doctorates awarded. *Degree requirements:* For master's, thesis, portfolio, or project; for doctorate, comprehensive exam, thesis/dissertation. *Entrance requirements:* For master's, GRE may be required based on past academic performance., Professional recommendation letters are required for all applicants.; for doctorate, GRE (minimum score of 148 new grading scale on the quantitative portion if the applicant has not graduated from a program of recognized standing), minimum GPA of 3.3 in the bachelor's or master's degree program attempted. Additional exam requirements/recommendations for international students: Required—TOEFL (minimum score 80 iBT), IELTS (minimum score 6). *Application deadline:* For fall admission, 6/1 for domestic and international students; for spring admission, 11/1 for domestic and international students; for summer admission, 4/15 for domestic and international students. Applications are processed on a rolling basis. Application fee: $60 ($100 for international students). Electronic applications accepted. *Expenses:* Program tuition and fees vary by course load and residency classification. Please visit the University of Colorado Colorado Springs Student Financial Services website to see current program costs: https://www.uccs.edu/bursar/index.php/estimate-your-bill. *Financial support:* In 2018–19, 1 student received support. Career-related internships or fieldwork, Federal Work-Study, scholarships/grants, traineeships, and unspecified assistantships available. Support available to part-time students. Financial award application deadline: 3/1; financial award applicants required to submit FAFSA. *Total annual research expenditures:* $22,249. *Unit head:* Dr. Donald Rabern, Dean of Engineering and Applied Science, 719-255-3543, E-mail: drabern@uccs.edu. *Application contact:* Dawn House, Extended Studies Coordinator, 719-255-3246, E-mail: dhouse@uccs.edu.

University of Florida, Graduate School, Herbert Wertheim College of Engineering, Department of Industrial and Systems Engineering, Gainesville, FL 32611. Offers industrial and systems engineering (ME, MS, PhD, Engr); quantitative finance (PhD). *Program availability:* Part-time, evening/weekend, online learning. Terminal master's awarded for partial completion of doctoral program. *Degree requirements:* For master's, thesis (for some programs); for doctorate, comprehensive exam (for some programs), thesis/dissertation (for some programs). *Entrance requirements:* For master's and doctorate, minimum GPA of 3.0; for Engr, GRE General Test. Additional exam requirements/recommendations for international students: Required—TOEFL (minimum score 550 paper-based; 80 iBT), IELTS (minimum score 6). Electronic applications accepted. *Faculty research:* Operations research; financial engineering; logistics and supply chain management; energy, healthcare, and transportation applications of operations research.

University of Houston–Clear Lake, School of Science and Computer Engineering, Program in System Engineering, Houston, TX 77058-1002. Offers MS. *Entrance requirements:* Additional exam requirements/recommendations for international students: Required—TOEFL (minimum score 550 paper-based).

University of Illinois at Urbana–Champaign, Graduate College, College of Engineering, Department of Industrial and Enterprise Systems Engineering, Urbana, IL 61801. Offers industrial engineering (MS, PhD); systems and entrepreneurial engineering (MS, PhD); MBA/MS.

University of Louisiana at Lafayette, College of Engineering, Department of Electrical and Computer Engineering, Lafayette, LA 70504. Offers electrical engineering (MS); systems engineering (PhD). *Degree requirements:* For master's, thesis or alternative; for doctorate, comprehensive exam, thesis/dissertation, final oral exam. *Entrance requirements:* For master's, GRE General Test, minimum GPA of 2.75. Additional exam requirements/recommendations for international students: Required—TOEFL (minimum score 550 paper-based). Electronic applications accepted.

University of Maryland, Baltimore County, The Graduate School, Program in Systems Engineering, Baltimore, MD 21250. Offers MS, Postbaccalaureate Certificate. *Program availability:* Part-time. *Degree requirements:* For master's, comprehensive exam (for some programs), thesis optional. *Entrance requirements:* For master's, undergraduate degree in engineering or information technology; minimum undergraduate GPA of 3.0. Additional exam requirements/recommendations for international students: Required—TOEFL (minimum score 550 paper-based; 80 iBT), GRE General Test. Electronic applications accepted. *Faculty research:* Systems engineering.

University of Maryland, College Park, Academic Affairs, A. James Clark School of Engineering, Systems Engineering Program, College Park, MD 20742. Offers M Eng, MS. *Program availability:* Part-time, evening/weekend. *Degree requirements:* For master's, thesis optional. *Entrance requirements:* For master's, GRE General Test, minimum GPA of 3.0. Electronic applications accepted. *Faculty research:* Automation, computer, information, manufacturing, and process systems.

University of Massachusetts Dartmouth, Graduate School, College of Engineering, Department of Mechanical Engineering, North Dartmouth, MA 02747-2300. Offers industrial and systems engineering (Postbaccalaureate Certificate); mechanical engineering (MS). *Program availability:* Part-time. *Faculty:* 10 full-time (2 women). *Students:* 6 full-time (0 women), 19 part-time (1 woman); includes 4 minority (1 Asian, non-Hispanic/Latino; 1 Hispanic/Latino; 2 Two or more races, non-Hispanic/Latino), 5 international. Average age 25. 42 applicants, 55% accepted, 6 enrolled. In 2018, 9 master's awarded. *Degree requirements:* For master's, thesis, thesis or project. *Entrance requirements:* For master's, GRE unless UMass Dartmouth graduate in mechanical engineering, statement of purpose (minimum of 300 words), resume, 3 letters of recommendation, official transcripts; for Postbaccalaureate Certificate, statement of purpose (minimum of 300 words), resume, 3 letters of recommendation, official transcripts. Additional exam requirements/recommendations for international students: Required—TOEFL (minimum score 533 paper-based; 72 iBT), IELTS (minimum score 6). *Application deadline:* For fall admission, 2/15 priority date for domestic students, 1/15 priority date for international students; for spring admission, 11/15 priority date for domestic students, 10/15 priority date for international students. Application fee: $60. Electronic applications accepted. *Financial support:* In 2018–19, 3 research assistantships (averaging $11,606 per year), 4 teaching assistantships (averaging $14,131 per year) were awarded; tuition waivers (full and partial) also available. Financial award application deadline: 3/1; financial award applicants required to submit FAFSA. *Faculty research:* Computer aided tolerance and optimization; diagnostics in manufacturing; MEMS and nano-manufacturing; modeling, simulation and optimization of manufacturing systems, robotics. *Total annual research expenditures:* $1.7 million. *Unit head:* Wenzhen Huang, Graduate Program Director, Mechanical Engineering, 508-910-6568, E-mail: whuang@umassd.edu. *Application contact:* Scott Webster, Director of Graduate Studies & Admissions, 508-999-8604, Fax: 508-999-8183, E-mail: graduate@umassd.edu.
Website: http://www.umassd.edu/engineering/mne/graduate

University of Michigan, College of Engineering, Department of Integrative Systems and Design, Ann Arbor, MI 48109. Offers automotive engineering (M Eng); design science (MS, PhD); energy systems engineering (M Eng, MS); global automotive and manufacturing engineering (M Eng); manufacturing engineering (M Eng, D Eng); pharmaceutical engineering (M Eng); robotics and autonomous vehicles (M Eng); systems engineering and design (M Eng); MBA/M Eng; MSE/MS. *Program availability:* Part-time, online learning. *Students:* 163 full-time (38 women), 251 part-time (40 women). 282 applicants, 12% accepted, 15 enrolled. In 2018, 173 master's, 1 doctorate awarded. Terminal master's awarded for partial completion of doctoral program. *Degree requirements:* For master's, capstone project; for doctorate, thesis/dissertation. *Entrance requirements:* For master's and doctorate, GRE. Additional exam requirements/recommendations for international students: Required—TOEFL. *Application deadline:* Applications are processed on a rolling basis. Electronic applications accepted. *Financial support:* Fellowships, research assistantships with full tuition reimbursements, teaching assistantships with full tuition reimbursements, career-related internships or fieldwork, scholarships/grants, and unspecified assistantships available. Financial award applicants required to submit FAFSA. *Faculty research:* Automotive engineering, design science, energy systems engineering, engineering sustainable systems, financial engineering, global automotive and manufacturing engineering, integrated microsystems, manufacturing engineering, pharmaceutical engineering, robotics and autonomous vehicles. *Total annual research expenditures:* $595,323. *Unit head:* Diann Brei, Department Chair, 734-763-6617, E-mail: drdiannbrei@umich.edu. *Application contact:* Kathy Bishar, Senior Graduate Coordinator, 734-764-3312, E-mail: kbishar@umich.edu.
Website: http://www.isd.engin.umich.edu

University of Michigan–Dearborn, College of Engineering and Computer Science, MSE Program in Industrial and Systems Engineering, Dearborn, MI 48128. Offers MSE. *Program availability:* Part-time, evening/weekend, 100% online. *Faculty:* 17 full-time (4 women), 9 part-time/adjunct (1 woman). *Students:* 71 full-time (15 women), 56 part-time (24 women); includes 11 minority (5 Black or African American, non-Hispanic/Latino; 4 Asian, non-Hispanic/Latino; 1 Hispanic/Latino; 1 Native Hawaiian or other Pacific Islander, non-Hispanic/Latino), 90 international. Average age 25. 280 applicants, 48% accepted, 41 enrolled. In 2018, 52 master's awarded. *Entrance requirements:* For master's, bachelor's degree in engineering, a physical science, computer science, or applied mathematics. Additional exam requirements/recommendations for international students: Required—TOEFL (minimum score 560 paper-based; 84 iBT), IELTS (minimum score 6.5). *Application deadline:* For fall admission, 8/1 for domestic students, 5/1 for international students; for winter admission, 12/1 for domestic students, 9/1 for international students; for spring admission, 4/1 for domestic students, 1/1 for international students. Applications are processed on a rolling basis. Application fee: $60. Electronic applications accepted. *Expenses:* Tuition, state resident: full-time $15,380; part-time $88 per credit hour. Tuition, nonresident: full-time $23,948; part-time $1377 per credit hour. *Required fees:* $780; $780 $390. Tuition and fees vary according to course level, course load, degree level, program, reciprocity agreements and student level. *Financial support:* In 2018–19, 65 students received support. Research assistantships with full tuition reimbursements available, teaching assistantships with full tuition reimbursements available, scholarships/grants, and non-resident tuition scholarships available. Support available to part-time students. Financial award application deadline: 3/1; financial award applicants required to submit FAFSA. *Faculty research:* Operations Research and Decision Science, Quality and Reliability Engineering, Manufacturing, Human Factors and Ergonomics, Transportation Safety. *Unit head:* Dr. Armen Zakarian, Chair, 313-593-5361, Fax: 313-593-3692, E-mail: zakarian@umich.edu. *Application contact:* Office of Graduate Studies, 313-583-6321, E-mail: umd-graduatestudies@umich.edu.
Website: https://umdearborn.edu/cecs/departments/industrial-and-manufacturing-systems-engineering/graduate-programs/mse-industrial-systems-engineering

University of Michigan–Dearborn, College of Engineering and Computer Science, PhD Program in Industrial and Systems Engineering, Dearborn, MI 48128. Offers PhD. *Faculty:* 17 full-time (4 women), 9 part-time/adjunct (1 woman). *Students:* 2 full-time (1 woman), 6 part-time (2 women), 7 international. Average age 26. 12 applicants, 58% accepted, 5 enrolled. *Degree requirements:* For doctorate, thesis/dissertation, qualifying and preliminary examinations. *Entrance requirements:* For doctorate, GRE, master's degree in engineering, applied mathematics, computer science, or a physical science from accredited program. Additional exam requirements/recommendations for international students: Required—TOEFL (minimum score 560 paper-based; 84 iBT), IELTS (minimum score 6.5). *Application deadline:* For fall admission, 2/1 for domestic and international students. Application fee: $60. Electronic applications accepted. *Expenses:* Tuition, state resident: full-time $15,380; part-time $88 per credit hour. Tuition, nonresident: full-time $23,948; part-time $1377 per credit hour. *Required fees:* $780; $780 $390. Tuition and fees vary according to course level, course load, degree level, program, reciprocity agreements and student level. *Financial support:* Research assistantships with full tuition reimbursements, teaching assistantships with full tuition reimbursements, scholarships/grants, health care benefits, and unspecified assistantships available. Financial award application deadline: 2/1; financial award applicants required to submit FAFSA. *Faculty research:* Operations Research and Decision Science, Quality and Reliability Engineering, Manufacturing, Human Factors and Ergonomics, Transportation Safety. *Unit head:* Dr. Yubao Chen, Director, 313-593-5579, E-mail: yubao@umich.edu. *Application contact:* Office of Graduate Studies, 313-583-6321, E-mail: umd-graduatestudies@umich.edu.
Website: https://umdearborn.edu/cecs/departments/industrial-and-manufacturing-systems-engineering/graduate-programs/phd-industrial-and-systems-engineering

University of Nebraska at Omaha, Graduate Studies, College of Information Science and Technology, Department of Computer Science, Omaha, NE 68182. Offers artificial intelligence (Certificate); communication networks (Certificate); computer science (MA, MS); computer science education (MS, Certificate); software engineering (Certificate); system and architecture (Certificate). *Program availability:* Part-time, evening/weekend. *Degree requirements:* For master's, comprehensive exam, thesis (for some programs). *Entrance requirements:* For master's, GRE General Test, minimum GPA of 3.0, prior course work in computer science, official transcripts, resume, 2 letters of recommendation; for Certificate, minimum GPA of 3.0, resume. Additional exam requirements/recommendations for international students: Required—TOEFL, IELTS, PTE. Electronic applications accepted.

University of New Mexico, Graduate Studies, School of Engineering, Program in Nanoscience and Microsystems Engineering, Albuquerque, NM 87131. Offers MS, PhD. *Program availability:* Part-time. *Degree requirements:* For master's, comprehensive exam, thesis; for doctorate, comprehensive exam, thesis/dissertation. *Entrance requirements:* For master's and doctorate, GRE. Additional exam requirements/recommendations for international students: Required—TOEFL. Electronic applications accepted.

The University of North Carolina at Charlotte, William States Lee College of Engineering, Department of Civil and Environmental Engineering, Charlotte, NC 28223-0001. Offers civil engineering (MSCE); infrastructure and environmental systems (PhD), including infrastructure and environmental systems design. *Program availability:* Part-time, evening/weekend. *Students:* 61 full-time (18 women), 47 part-time (12 women); includes 9 minority (1 Black or African American, non-Hispanic/Latino; 5 Asian, non-Hispanic/Latino; 2 Hispanic/Latino; 1 Two or more races, non-Hispanic/Latino), 51 international. Average age 30. 89 applicants, 47% accepted, 19 enrolled. In 2018, 16 master's, 6 doctorates awarded. *Entrance requirements:* For master's, GRE, undergraduate degree in civil and environmental engineering or a closely-related field; minimum undergraduate GPA of 3.0; for doctorate, GRE General Test, equivalent to U.S. baccalaureate or master's degree from regionally-accredited college or university in engineering, earth science and geology, chemical and biological sciences or a related field with minimum undergraduate GPA of 3.2, graduate 3.5. Additional exam requirements/recommendations for international students: Required—TOEFL (minimum score 523 paper-based; 70 iBT), IELTS (minimum score 6), TOEFL (minimum score 523 paper-based, 70 iBT) or IELTS (6). *Application deadline:* Applications are processed on a rolling basis. Application fee: $75. Electronic applications accepted. *Expenses:* Contact institution. *Financial support:* Fellowships, research assistantships, teaching assistantships, career-related internships or fieldwork, institutionally sponsored loans,

scholarships/grants, and unspecified assistantships available. Support available to part-time students. Financial award application deadline: 3/1; financial award applicants required to submit FAFSA. *Total annual research expenditures:* $3.4 million. *Unit head:* Dr. James D. Bowen, Interim Chair, 704-687-1215, E-mail: jdbowen@uncc.edu. *Application contact:* Kathy B. Giddings, Director of Graduate Admissions, 704-687-5503, Fax: 704-687-1668, E-mail: gradadm@uncc.edu.
Website: http://cee.uncc.edu/

The University of North Carolina at Charlotte, William States Lee College of Engineering, Department of Systems Engineering and Engineering Management, Charlotte, NC 28223-0001. Offers energy analytics (Graduate Certificate); engineering management (MSEM); Lean Six Sigma (Graduate Certificate); logistics and supply chains (Graduate Certificate); systems analytics (Graduate Certificate). *Program availability:* Part-time, evening/weekend, 100% online, blended/hybrid learning. *Students:* 27 full-time (8 women), 45 part-time (11 women); includes 15 minority (5 Black or African American, non-Hispanic/Latino; 1 American Indian or Alaska Native, non-Hispanic/Latino; 5 Asian, non-Hispanic/Latino; 2 Hispanic/Latino; 2 Two or more races, non-Hispanic/Latino), 27 international. Average age 29. 112 applicants, 77% accepted, 23 enrolled. In 2018, 38 master's, 3 other advanced degrees awarded. *Entrance requirements:* For master's, GRE or GMAT, bachelor's degree in engineering or a closely-related technical or scientific field, or in business, provided relevant technical course requirements have been met; undergraduate coursework in engineering economics, calculus, or statistics; minimum GPA of 3.0; for Graduate Certificate, bachelor's degree in engineering or closely-related technical or scientific field, or in business, provided relevant technical course requirements have been met; minimum GPA of 3.0; undergraduate coursework in engineering economics, calculus, and statistics; written description of work experience. Additional exam requirements/recommendations for international students: Required—TOEFL (minimum score 523 paper-based; 70 iBT), IELTS (minimum score 6), TOEFL (minimum score 523 paper-based, 70 iBT) or IELTS (6). *Application deadline:* Applications are processed on a rolling basis. Application fee: $75. Electronic applications accepted. *Expenses:* Contact institution. *Financial support:* Career-related internships or fieldwork, institutionally sponsored loans, scholarships/grants, and unspecified assistantships available. Support available to part-time students. Financial award application deadline: 3/1; financial award applicants required to submit FAFSA. *Total annual research expenditures:* $186,132. *Unit head:* Dr. Simon M. Hsiang, Chair, 704-687-1958, E-mail: shsiang1@uncc.edu. *Application contact:* Kathy B. Giddings, Director of Graduate Admissions, 704-687-5503, Fax: 704-687-1668, E-mail: gradadm@uncc.edu.
Website: http://seem.uncc.edu/

University of Pennsylvania, School of Engineering and Applied Science, Department of Electrical and Systems Engineering, Philadelphia, PA 19104. Offers MSE, PhD. *Program availability:* Part-time. *Students:* Average age 25. 1,049 applicants, 40% accepted, 206 enrolled. In 2018, 78 master's, 13 doctorates awarded. Terminal master's awarded for partial completion of doctoral program. *Degree requirements:* For master's, comprehensive exam, thesis optional; for doctorate, comprehensive exam, thesis/dissertation. *Entrance requirements:* For master's and doctorate, GRE, bachelor's degree, letters of recommendation, resume, personal statement. Additional exam requirements/recommendations for international students: Required—TOEFL (minimum score 100 iBT), IELTS (minimum score 7). *Application deadline:* For fall admission, 12/15 priority date for domestic and international students. Application fee: $80. Electronic applications accepted. *Expenses:* Contact institution. *Faculty research:* Circuits and computer engineering, information decision systems, nanodevices and nanosystems. *Application contact:* William Fenton, Assistant Director of Graduate Admissions, 215-898-4542, Fax: 215-573-5577, E-mail: gradstudies@seas.upenn.edu.

University of Pennsylvania, School of Engineering and Applied Science, Program in Embedded Systems, Philadelphia, PA 19104. Offers MSE. *Program availability:* Part-time. *Students:* 12 full-time (3 women), 14 part-time (3 women); includes 4 minority (3 Asian, non-Hispanic/Latino; 1 Hispanic/Latino), 16 international. Average age 27. 158 applicants, 15% accepted, 17 enrolled. In 2018, 19 master's awarded. *Degree requirements:* For master's, comprehensive exam, thesis optional. *Entrance requirements:* For master's, GRE, bachelor's degree, letters of recommendation, resume, personal statement. Additional exam requirements/recommendations for international students: Required—TOEFL (minimum score 100 iBT), IELTS (minimum score 7). *Application deadline:* For fall admission, 2/1 priority date for domestic and international students. Application fee: $80. Electronic applications accepted. *Expenses:* Contact institution. *Faculty research:* Embedded control systems, model-based design and verification, real time operating systems, implementation of embedded systems. *Application contact:* William Fenton, Assistant Director of Graduate Admissions, 215-898-4542, Fax: 215-573-5577, E-mail: gradstudies@seas.upenn.edu.
Website: http://www.cis.upenn.edu/prospective-students/graduate/embs.php

University of Regina, Faculty of Graduate Studies and Research, Faculty of Engineering and Applied Science, Program in Industrial Systems Engineering, Regina, SK S4S 0A2, Canada. Offers industrial systems (M Eng, MA Sc, PhD). *Program availability:* Part-time. *Faculty:* 12 full-time (1 woman), 2 part-time/adjunct (0 women). *Students:* 69 full-time (12 women), 5 part-time (1 woman). Average age 30. 235 applicants, 9% accepted, 5 enrolled. In 2018, 24 master's, 4 doctorates awarded. *Degree requirements:* For master's, thesis, project, report, co-op; for doctorate, comprehensive exam, thesis/dissertation. *Entrance requirements:* For master's, 4 years bachelor degree; at least 70 per cent from a four-year baccalaureate degree (or equivalent). Additional exam requirements/recommendations for international students: Required—TOEFL (minimum score 580 paper-based; 80 iBT), IELTS (minimum score 6.5), PTE (minimum score 59), other options are CAEL, MELAB, Cantest and U of R ESL. *Application deadline:* For fall admission, 3/31 for domestic and international students; for winter admission, 7/31 for domestic and international students; for spring admission, 11/30 for domestic and international students. Application fee: $100. Electronic applications accepted. *Expenses:* Estimated tuition and fees for one academic year is 8.379.50 for Master's. The fee will vary base on your choice program. For Doctoral program one academic year is estimated 14,129.40. International students will pay additional 1,191.75 for International surcharge per semester. *Financial support:* Fellowships, research assistantships, teaching assistantships, career-related internships or fieldwork, Federal Work-Study, scholarships/grants, unspecified assistantships, and travel award and Graduate Scholarship Base Funds available. Support available to part-time students. Financial award application deadline: 9/30. *Faculty research:* Stochastic systems simulation, metallurgy of welding, computer-aided engineering, finite element method of engineering systems, manufacturing systems. *Unit head:* Dr. Adisorn Aroonwilas, Program Chair, 306-337-2469, Fax: 306-585-4855, E-mail: Adisorn.Aroonwilas@uregina.ca. *Application contact:* Dr. Golam Kabir, Graduate Coordinator, 306-585-5271, Fax: 306-585-4855, E-mail: golam.kabir@uregina.ca.
Website: http://www.uregina.ca/engineering/

University of Regina, Faculty of Graduate Studies and Research, Faculty of Engineering and Applied Science, Program in Petroleum Systems Engineering, Regina, SK S4S 0A2, Canada. Offers petroleum systems (M Eng, MA Sc, PhD). *Program availability:* Part-time. *Faculty:* 8 full-time (1 woman), 1 part-time/adjunct (0 women). *Students:* 47 full-time (13 women), 2 part-time (0 women). Average age 30. 106 applicants, 8% accepted. In 2018, 14 master's, 2 doctorates awarded. *Degree requirements:* For master's, thesis (for some programs), project, report, co-op placement; for doctorate, thesis/dissertation. *Entrance requirements:* For master's, minimum graduating average of 70 percent from four-year baccalaureate degree (or equivalent); for doctorate, completion of thesis-based master's degree in engineering or closely-related field. Additional exam requirements/recommendations for international students: Required—TOEFL (minimum score 580 paper-based; 80 iBT), IELTS (minimum score 6.5), PTE (minimum score 59), other options are CAEL, MELAB, Cantest and U of R ESL. *Application deadline:* For fall admission, 3/31 for domestic and international students; for winter admission, 7/31 for domestic and international students; for spring admission, 11/30 for domestic and international students. Application fee: $100 Canadian dollars. Electronic applications accepted. *Expenses:* Estimated tuition and fees for one academic year is 8.379.50 for master's. The fee will vary base on your choice program. For doctoral program one academic year is estimated 14,129.40. International students will pay additional 1,191.75 for international surcharge per semester. *Financial support:* Fellowships, research assistantships, teaching assistantships, career-related internships or fieldwork, Federal Work-Study, scholarships/grants, unspecified assistantships, and travel award and Graduate Scholarship Base funds available. Support available to part-time students. Financial award application deadline: 9/30. *Faculty research:* Enhanced oil recovery, production engineering, reservoir engineering, surface thermodynamics, geostatistics. *Unit head:* Dr. Na jia, Program Chair, 306-337-3287, Fax: 306-585-4855, E-mail: Na.Jia@uregina.ca. *Application contact:* Dr. Tony Yang, Graduate Coordinator, 306-337-2660, Fax: 306-585-4855, E-mail: tony.Yang@uregina.ca.
Website: http://www.uregina.ca/engineering/

University of Regina, Faculty of Graduate Studies and Research, Faculty of Engineering and Applied Science, Program in Process Systems Engineering, Regina, SK S4S 0A2, Canada. Offers process systems (M Eng, MA Sc, PhD). *Program availability:* Part-time. *Faculty:* 9 full-time (2 women). *Students:* 29 full-time (2 women), 4 part-time (0 women). Average age 30. 37 applicants, 27% accepted, 3 enrolled. In 2018, 12 master's, 3 doctorates awarded. *Degree requirements:* For master's, thesis (for some programs), project, report, co-op placement; for doctorate, comprehensive exam, thesis/dissertation. *Entrance requirements:* For master's, minimum graduating average of 70 percent from four-year baccalaureate degree (or equivalent); for doctorate, completion of thesis-based master's degree in engineering or closely-related field. Additional exam requirements/recommendations for international students: Required—TOEFL (minimum score 580 paper-based; 80 iBT), IELTS (minimum score 6.5), PTE (minimum score 59), other options are CAEL, MELAB, Cantest and U of R ESL. *Application deadline:* For fall admission, 3/31 for domestic and international students; for winter admission, 7/31 for domestic and international students; for spring admission, 11/30 for domestic and international students. Application fee: $100 Canadian dollars. Electronic applications accepted. *Expenses:* Estimated tuition and fees for one academic year is 8.379.50 for Master's. The fee will vary base on your choice program. For Doctoral program one academic year is estimated 14,129.40. International students will pay additional 1,191.75 for International surcharge per semester. *Financial support:* Fellowships, research assistantships, teaching assistantships, career-related internships or fieldwork, Federal Work-Study, scholarships/grants, unspecified assistantships, and travel award and Graduate Scholarship Base Funds available. Support available to part-time students. Financial award application deadline: 9/30. *Faculty research:* Membrane separation technologies, advanced reaction engineering, advanced transport phenomena, advanced heat transfer, advanced mass transfer. *Unit head:* Dr. Raphael Idem, Program Chair, 306-585-4470, Fax: 306-585-4855, E-mail: Raphael.idem@uregina.ca. *Application contact:* Dr. Hussameldin Ibrahim, Graduate Coordinator, 306-337-3347, Fax: 306-585-4855, E-mail: hussameldin.ibrahim@uregina.ca.
Website: http://www.uregina.ca/engineering/

University of Rhode Island, Graduate School, College of Engineering, Department of Mechanical, Industrial and Systems Engineering, Kingston, RI 02881. Offers industrial and systems engineering (MS, PhD), including manufacturing systems, service and enterprise systems. *Program availability:* Part-time. *Faculty:* 19 full-time (4 women). *Students:* 31 full-time (7 women), 36 part-time (2 women); includes 11 minority (3 Black or African American, non-Hispanic/Latino; 2 Asian, non-Hispanic/Latino; 5 Hispanic/Latino; 1 Two or more races, non-Hispanic/Latino), 21 international. 40 applicants, 73% accepted, 17 enrolled. In 2018, 13 master's, 6 doctorates awarded. *Entrance requirements:* Additional exam requirements/recommendations for international students: Required—TOEFL. *Application deadline:* For fall admission, 6/1 for domestic students, 2/1 for international students; for spring admission, 11/1 for domestic students, 7/1 for international students. Application fee: $65. Electronic applications accepted. *Expenses: Tuition, area resident:* Full-time $13,226; part-time $735 per credit. Tuition, state resident: full-time $13,226; part-time $735 per credit. Tuition, nonresident: full-time $25,854; part-time $1436 per credit. *International tuition:* $25,854 full-time. *Required fees:* $1698; $50 per credit. $35 per semester. One-time fee: $165. *Financial support:* In 2018–19, 6 research assistantships with tuition reimbursements (averaging $10,197 per year), 9 teaching assistantships with tuition reimbursements (averaging $8,496 per year) were awarded. Financial award application deadline: 2/1; financial award applicants required to submit FAFSA. *Unit head:* Dr. Carl-Ernst Rousseau, Chair, 401-874-2542, E-mail: rousseau@uri.edu. *Application contact:* David Chelidze, Graduate Admissions, 401-874-2356, E-mail: chelidze@uri.edu.
Website: http://mcise.uri.edu/

University of St. Thomas, School of Engineering, St. Paul, MN 55105. Offers data science (MS); electrical engineering (MS); information technology (MS); manufacturing engineering (MS); manufacturing systems (Certificate); mechanical engineering (MS); medical device development (Certificate); regulatory science (MS); software engineering (MS); software management (MS); systems engineering (MS); technology leadership (Certificate); technology management (MS). *Program availability:* Part-time, evening/weekend. *Entrance requirements:* For master's, resume, official transcripts. Additional exam requirements/recommendations for international students: Required—TOEFL (minimum score 80 iBT), IELTS (minimum score 6.5). Electronic applications accepted. *Expenses:* Contact institution.

University of South Alabama, College of Engineering, Program in Systems Engineering, Mobile, AL 36688. Offers D Sc. *Degree requirements:* For doctorate, comprehensive exam, thesis/dissertation, qualifying examination. *Entrance requirements:* For doctorate, GRE, MS in engineering, minimum graduate GPA of 3.0. Additional exam requirements/recommendations for international students: Required—TOEFL (minimum score 550 paper-based; 79 iBT). Electronic applications accepted. *Expenses:* Contact institution.

University of Southern California, Graduate School, Viterbi School of Engineering, Daniel J. Epstein Department of Industrial and Systems Engineering, Los Angeles, CA 90089. Offers digital supply chain management (MS); engineering management (MS); engineering technology communication (Graduate Certificate); health systems operations (Graduate Certificate); industrial and systems engineering (MS, PhD, Engr); manufacturing engineering (MS); operations research engineering (MS); optimization and supply chain management (Graduate Certificate); product development engineering (MS); safety systems and security (MS); systems architecting and engineering (MS,

Graduate Certificate); systems safety and security (Graduate Certificate); transportation systems (Graduate Certificate); MS/MBA. *Program availability:* Part-time, evening/weekend, online learning. Terminal master's awarded for partial completion of doctoral program. *Degree requirements:* For master's, thesis optional; for doctorate, thesis/dissertation. *Entrance requirements:* For master's and doctorate, GRE General Test. Additional exam requirements/recommendations for international students: Recommended—TOEFL. Electronic applications accepted. *Faculty research:* Health systems, music cognition and retrieval, transportation and logistics, manufacturing and automation, engineering systems design, risk and economic analysis.

University of South Florida, Innovative Education, Tampa, FL 33620-9951. Offers adult, career and higher education (Graduate Certificate), including college teaching, leadership in developing human resources, leadership in higher education; Africana studies (Graduate Certificate), including diasporas and health disparities, genocide and human rights; aging studies (Graduate Certificate), including gerontology; art research (Graduate Certificate), including museum studies; business foundations (Graduate Certificate); chemical and biomedical engineering (Graduate Certificate), including materials science and engineering, water, health and sustainability; child and family studies (Graduate Certificate), including positive behavior support; civil and industrial engineering (Graduate Certificate), including transportation systems analysis; community and family health (Graduate Certificate), including maternal and child health, social marketing and public health, violence and injury: prevention and intervention, women's health; criminology (Graduate Certificate), including criminal justice administration; data science for public administration (Graduate Certificate); digital humanities (Graduate Certificate); educational measurement and research (Graduate Certificate), including evaluation; English (Graduate Certificate), including comparative literary studies, creative writing, professional and technical communication; entrepreneurship (Graduate Certificate); environmental health (Graduate Certificate), including safety management; epidemiology and biostatistics (Graduate Certificate), including applied biostatistics, biostatistics, concepts and tools of epidemiology, epidemiology, epidemiology of infectious diseases; geography, environment and planning (Graduate Certificate), including community development, environmental policy and management, geographical information systems; geology (Graduate Certificate), including hydrogeology; global health (Graduate Certificate), including disaster management, global health and Latin American and Caribbean studies, global health practice, humanitarian assistance, infection control; government and international affairs (Graduate Certificate), including Cuban studies, globalization studies; health policy and management (Graduate Certificate), including health management and leadership, public health policy and programs; hearing specialist: early intervention (Graduate Certificate); industrial and management systems engineering (Graduate Certificate), including systems engineering, technology management; information studies (Graduate Certificate), including school library media specialist; information systems/decision sciences (Graduate Certificate), including analytics and business intelligence; instructional technology (Graduate Certificate), including distance education, Florida digital/virtual educator, instructional design, multimedia design, Web design; internal medicine, bioethics and medical humanities (Graduate Certificate), including biomedical ethics; Latin American and Caribbean studies (Graduate Certificate); leadership for coastal resiliency planning (Graduate Certificate); mass communications (Graduate Certificate), including multimedia journalism; mathematics and statistics (Graduate Certificate), including mathematics; medicine (Graduate Certificate), including aging and neuroscience, bioinformatics, biotechnology, brain fitness and memory management, clinical investigation, hand and upper limb rehabilitation, health informatics, health sciences, integrative weight management, intellectual property, medicine and gender, metabolic and nutritional medicine, metabolic cardiology, pharmacy sciences; national and competitive intelligence (Graduate Certificate); nursing (Graduate Certificate), including simulation based academic fellowship in advanced pain management; psychological and social foundations (Graduate Certificate), including career counseling, college teaching, diversity in education, mental health counseling, school counseling; public affairs (Graduate Certificate), including nonprofit management, public management, research administration; public health (Graduate Certificate), including assessing chemical toxicity and public health risks, health equity, pharmacoepidemiology, public health generalist, toxicology, translational research in adolescent behavioral health; public health practices (Graduate Certificate), including planning for healthy communities; rehabilitation and mental health counseling (Graduate Certificate), including integrative mental health care, marriage and family therapy, rehabilitation technology; secondary education (Graduate Certificate), including ESOL, foreign language education: culture and content, foreign language education: professional; social work (Graduate Certificate), including geriatric social work/clinical gerontology; special education (Graduate Certificate), including autism spectrum disorder, disabilities education: severe/profound; world languages (Graduate Certificate), including teaching English as a second language (TESL) or foreign language. *Expenses:* Tuition, state resident: full-time $6350. Tuition, nonresident: full-time $19,048. *International tuition:* $19,048 full-time. *Required fees:* $2079. *Unit head:* Dr. Cynthia DeLuca, Associate Vice President and Assistant Vice Provost, 813-974-3077, Fax: 813-974-7061, E-mail: deluca@usf.edu. *Application contact:* Owen Hooper, Director, Summer and Alternative Calendar Programs, 813-974-6917, E-mail: hooper@usf.edu.
Website: http://www.usf.edu/innovative-education/

The University of Texas at Arlington, Graduate School, College of Engineering, Department of Industrial, Manufacturing, and Systems Engineering, Program in Systems Engineering, Arlington, TX 76019. Offers MS.

The University of Texas at Dallas, Erik Jonsson School of Engineering and Computer Science, Department of Systems Engineering, Richardson, TX 75080. Offers systems engineering and management (MS). *Program availability:* Part-time, evening/weekend. *Faculty:* 3 full-time (0 women), 3 part-time/adjunct (0 women). *Students:* 39 full-time (9 women), 29 part-time (8 women); includes 10 minority (2 Black or African American, non-Hispanic/Latino; 5 Asian, non-Hispanic/Latino; 3 Hispanic/Latino), 44 international. Average age 27. 127 applicants, 18% accepted, 23 enrolled. In 2018, 42 master's awarded. *Degree requirements:* For master's, thesis or major design project. *Entrance requirements:* For master's, GRE General Test, minimum GPA of 3.0 in related bachelor's degree. Additional exam requirements/recommendations for international students: Required—TOEFL (minimum score 550 paper-based). *Application deadline:* For fall admission, 7/15 for domestic students, 5/1 priority date for international students; for spring admission, 11/15 for domestic students, 9/1 priority date for international students. Applications are processed on a rolling basis. Application fee: $50 ($100 for international students). Electronic applications accepted. *Expenses: Tuition, area resident:* Full-time $13,458. Tuition, state resident: full-time $13,458. Tuition, nonresident: full-time $26,852. *International tuition:* $26,852 full-time. Tuition and fees vary according to course load. *Financial support:* In 2018–19, 1 student received support, including 1 teaching assistantship with partial tuition reimbursement available (averaging $16,650 per year); fellowships, research assistantships with partial tuition reimbursements available, Federal Work-Study, institutionally sponsored loans, scholarships/grants, unspecified assistantships, and cooperative positions also available. Support available to part-time students. Financial award application deadline: 4/30; financial award applicants required to submit FAFSA. *Unit head:* Dr. Steve Yurkovich, Head, 972-883-2305, E-mail: yurkovich@utdallas.edu. *Application contact:* Dr. Steve Yurkovich, Head, 972-883-2305, E-mail: yurkovich@utdallas.edu.
Website: https://syse.utdallas.edu/

The University of Texas at Dallas, Naveen Jindal School of Management, Program in Organizations, Strategy and International Management, Richardson, TX 75080. Offers business administration (MBA); executive business administration (EMBA); global leadership (EMBA); healthcare leadership and management (MS); healthcare management (EMBA); innovation and entrepreneurship (MS); international management studies (MS, PhD); management science (MS, PhD); project management (EMBA); systems engineering and management (MS); MS/MBA. *Program availability:* Part-time, evening/weekend. *Faculty:* 19 full-time (6 women), 33 part-time/adjunct (12 women). *Students:* 587 full-time (237 women), 777 part-time (361 women); includes 456 minority (83 Black or African American, non-Hispanic/Latino; 226 Asian, non-Hispanic/Latino; 110 Hispanic/Latino; 37 Two or more races, non-Hispanic/Latino), 316 international. Average age 34. 1,452 applicants, 43% accepted, 376 enrolled. In 2018, 556 master's, 23 doctorates awarded. *Degree requirements:* For doctorate, thesis/dissertation. *Entrance requirements:* For master's and doctorate, GMAT. Additional exam requirements/recommendations for international students: Required—TOEFL (minimum score 550 paper-based). *Application deadline:* For fall admission, 7/15 for domestic students, 5/1 priority date for international students; for spring admission, 11/15 for domestic students, 9/1 priority date for international students. Applications are processed on a rolling basis. Application fee: $50 ($100 for international students). Electronic applications accepted. *Expenses: Tuition, area resident:* Full-time $13,458. Tuition, state resident: full-time $13,458. Tuition, nonresident: full-time $26,852. *International tuition:* $26,852 full-time. Tuition and fees vary according to course load. *Financial support:* In 2018–19, 102 students received support, including 24 research assistantships with partial tuition reimbursements available (averaging $37,400 per year), 83 teaching assistantships with partial tuition reimbursements available (averaging $25,119 per year); Federal Work-Study, institutionally sponsored loans, scholarships/grants, and unspecified assistantships also available. Support available to part-time students. Financial award application deadline: 4/30; financial award applicants required to submit FAFSA. *Faculty research:* International accounting, international trade and finance, economic development, international economics. *Unit head:* Dr. Seung-Hyun Lee, Area Coordinator, 972-883-6267, Fax: 972-883-5977, E-mail: sxl029100@utdallas.edu. *Application contact:* Dr. Seung-Hyun Lee, Area Coordinator, 972-883-6267, Fax: 972-883-5977, E-mail: sxl029100@utdallas.edu.
Website: http://jindal.utdallas.edu/osim/

The University of Texas at El Paso, Graduate School, College of Engineering, Department of Industrial, Manufacturing and Systems Engineering, El Paso, TX 79968-0001. Offers industrial engineering (MS); manufacturing engineering (MS); systems engineering (MS). *Program availability:* Part-time, evening/weekend. *Degree requirements:* For master's, thesis optional. *Entrance requirements:* For master's, GRE General Test, minimum GPA of 3.0 in major. Additional exam requirements/recommendations for international students: Required—TOEFL. Electronic applications accepted. *Faculty research:* Computer vision, automated inspection, simulation and modeling.

The University of Texas Rio Grande Valley, College of Engineering and Computer Science, Department of Manufacturing and Industrial Engineering, Edinburg, TX 78539. Offers engineering management (MS); manufacturing engineering (MS), including systems engineering. *Expenses: Tuition, area resident:* Full-time $6888. Tuition, state resident: full-time $6888. Tuition, nonresident: full-time $14,484. *International tuition:* $14,484 full-time. *Required fees:* $1468. *Faculty research:* Manufacturing processes, logistics, quality control, lean manufacturing.

University of Utah, Graduate School, David Eccles School of Business, Master of Science in Information Systems Program, Salt Lake City, UT 84112-8939. Offers information systems (MS, Graduate Certificate), including business intelligence and analytics, IT security, product and process management, software and systems architecture. *Program availability:* Part-time, evening/weekend, 100% online, blended/hybrid learning. *Degree requirements:* For master's, capstone project. *Entrance requirements:* For master's, GMAT/GRE, minimum undergraduate GPA of 3.0, 2 letters of recommendation, personal statement, professional resume. Additional exam requirements/recommendations for international students: Required—TOEFL (minimum score 550 paper-based; 80 iBT), IELTS (minimum score 6.5). Electronic applications accepted. *Expenses:* Contact institution. *Faculty research:* Business intelligence and analytics, software and system architecture, product and process management, IT security, Web and data mining, applications and management of IT in healthcare.

University of Virginia, School of Engineering and Applied Science, Department of Systems and Information Engineering, Charlottesville, VA 22903. Offers ME, MS, PhD, ME/MBA. *Program availability:* Online learning. *Degree requirements:* For master's, comprehensive exam (for some programs); for doctorate, comprehensive exam, thesis/dissertation. *Entrance requirements:* For master's, GRE General Test, 3 letters of recommendation; for doctorate, GRE General Test, 3 letters of recommendation; essay. Additional exam requirements/recommendations for international students: Required—TOEFL (minimum score 650 paper-based; 90 iBT), IELTS (minimum score 7). Electronic applications accepted. *Faculty research:* Systems integration, human factors, computational statistics and simulation, risk and decision analysis, optimization and control.

University of Washington, Graduate School, College of Engineering, Department of Industrial and Systems Engineering, Seattle, WA 98195-2650. Offers MISE, MS, PhD. *Program availability:* Part-time, online learning. *Faculty:* 10 full-time (5 women). *Students:* 35 full-time (12 women), 39 part-time (12 women); includes 18 minority (2 Black or African American, non-Hispanic/Latino; 1 American Indian or Alaska Native, non-Hispanic/Latino; 9 Asian, non-Hispanic/Latino; 5 Hispanic/Latino; 1 Native Hawaiian or other Pacific Islander, non-Hispanic/Latino), 30 international. Average age 28. 242 applicants, 38% accepted, 31 enrolled. In 2018, 28 master's, 5 doctorates awarded. Terminal master's awarded for partial completion of doctoral program. *Degree requirements:* For master's, thesis optional; for doctorate, comprehensive exam, thesis/dissertation, qualifying, general, and final exams. *Entrance requirements:* For master's, GRE General Test, minimum GPA of 3.0; bachelor's degree in engineering, math, or science; transcripts; letters of recommendation; resume; statement of objectives; for doctorate, GRE General Test, minimum GPA of 3.0; master's degree in engineering, math, or science (preferred); transcripts; letters of recommendation; resume; statement of objectives. Additional exam requirements/recommendations for international students: Required—TOEFL (minimum score 580 paper-based; 92 iBT); Recommended—IELTS (minimum score 7). *Application deadline:* For fall admission, 1/1 priority date for domestic students, 1/1 for international students. Applications are processed on a rolling basis. Application fee: $85. Electronic applications accepted. *Expenses:* Research-focused Master's and PhD: $18,852 resident; $32,760 nonresident. Applied/Professional Master's: $23,070 resident; $35,571 nonresident. *Financial support:* In 2018–19, 35 students received support, including 23 research assistantships with full tuition reimbursements available (averaging $29,640 per year), 12 teaching assistantships with full tuition reimbursements available (averaging $29,640 per year); fellowships, career-related internships or fieldwork, scholarships/grants,

traineeships, and tuition waivers (full) also available. Financial award application deadline: 2/1; financial award applicants required to submit FAFSA. *Faculty research:* Manufacturing, systems engineering and integration, optimization, human factors, virtual reality, quality and reliability, large-scale assembly, supply chain management, health systems engineering. *Total annual research expenditures:* $2.1 million. *Unit head:* Dr. Linda Ng Boyle, Professor/Chair, 206-543-1427, Fax: 206-685-3072, E-mail: linda@uw.edu. *Application contact:* Jennifer W. Tsai, Academic Counselor, 206-543-5041, Fax: 206-685-3072, E-mail: ieadvise@uw.edu.
Website: http://ise.washington.edu

University of Waterloo, Graduate Studies and Postdoctoral Affairs, Faculty of Engineering, Department of Systems Design Engineering, Waterloo, ON N2L 3G1, Canada. Offers M Eng, MA Sc, PhD. *Program availability:* Part-time. *Degree requirements:* For master's, research project or thesis; for doctorate, comprehensive exam, thesis/dissertation. *Entrance requirements:* For master's, honors degree, minimum B average, resume; for doctorate, master's degree, minimum A- average. Additional exam requirements/recommendations for international students: Required—TOEFL, IELTS, PTE. *Application deadline:* Applications are processed on a rolling basis. Application fee: $125 Canadian dollars. Electronic applications accepted. *Financial support:* Fellowships, research assistantships, teaching assistantships, and scholarships/grants available. *Faculty research:* Ergonomics, human factors and biomedical engineering, modeling and simulation, pattern analysis, machine intelligence and robotics.
Website: https://uwaterloo.ca/systems-design-engineering/

University of Wisconsin–Madison, Graduate School, College of Engineering, Department of Industrial and Systems Engineering, Madison, WI 53706. Offers industrial engineering (MS, PhD), including human factors and health systems engineering (MS), systems engineering and analytics (PhD). *Program availability:* Part-time. *Faculty:* 20 full-time (6 women). *Students:* 87 full-time (33 women), 12 part-time (8 women); includes 4 minority (1 Black or African American, non-Hispanic/Latino; 3 Asian, non-Hispanic/Latino), 63 international. Average age 26. 372 applicants, 21% accepted, 18 enrolled. In 2018, 35 master's, 9 doctorates awarded. Terminal master's awarded for partial completion of doctoral program. *Degree requirements:* For master's, thesis optional, 30 credits; minimum GPA of 3.0; for doctorate, comprehensive exam, thesis/dissertation, minimum of 51 credits; minimum GPA of 3.0. *Entrance requirements:* For master's and doctorate, GRE General Test, minimum GPA of 3.0, BS in engineering or equivalent, course work in computer programming and statistics. Additional exam requirements/recommendations for international students: Required—TOEFL (minimum score 580 paper-based; 92 iBT), IELTS (minimum score 7). *Application deadline:* For fall admission, 12/15 for domestic and international students; for spring admission, 10/1 for domestic and international students; for summer admission, 12/15 for domestic and international students. Application fee: $75 ($81 for international students). Electronic applications accepted. *Financial support:* In 2018–19, 66 students received support, including 2 fellowships with full tuition reimbursements available (averaging $27,816 per year), 39 research assistantships with full tuition reimbursements available (averaging $24,456 per year), 21 teaching assistantships with full tuition reimbursements available (averaging $19,788 per year); career-related internships or fieldwork, Federal Work-Study, institutionally sponsored loans, scholarships/grants, traineeships, health care benefits, and unspecified assistantships also available. Financial award application deadline: 12/1; financial award applicants required to submit FAFSA. *Faculty research:* Operations research; human factors and ergonomics; health systems engineering; manufacturing and production systems. *Total annual research expenditures:* $13.9 million. *Unit head:* Dr. Jeff Lindroth, Chair, 608-262-2686, E-mail: ie@engr.wisc.edu. *Application contact:* Pam Peterson, Student Services Coordinator, 608-263-4025, Fax: 608-890-2204, E-mail: prpeterson@wisc.edu.
Website: http://www.engr.wisc.edu/department/industrial-systems-engineering/

Virginia Polytechnic Institute and State University, VT Online, Blacksburg, VA 24061. Offers advanced transportation systems (Certificate); aerospace engineering (MS); agricultural and life sciences (MSLFS); business information systems (Graduate Certificate); career and technical education (MS); civil engineering (MS); computer engineering (M Eng, MS); decision support systems (Graduate Certificate); eLearning leadership (MA); electrical engineering (M Eng, MS); engineering administration (MEA); environmental engineering (Certificate); environmental politics and policy (Graduate Certificate); environmental sciences and engineering (MS); foundations of political analysis (Graduate Certificate); health product risk management (Graduate Certificate); industrial and systems engineering (MS); information policy and society (Graduate Certificate); information security (Graduate Certificate); information technology (MIT); instructional technology (MA); integrative STEM education (MA Ed); liberal arts (Graduate Certificate); life sciences: health product risk management (MS); natural resources (MNR, Graduate Certificate); networking (Graduate Certificate); nonprofit and nongovernmental organization management (Graduate Certificate); ocean engineering (MS); political science (MA); security studies (Graduate Certificate); software development (Graduate Certificate). *Expenses:* Tuition, state resident: full-time $15,510; part-time $739.50 per credit hour. Tuition, nonresident: full-time $29,629; part-time $1490.25 per credit hour. *Required fees:* $2804; $550 per semester. Tuition and fees vary according to course load, campus/location and program. *Application contact:* Graduate Admissions and Academic Progress, 540-231-8636, E-mail: grads@vt.edu.
Website: http://www.vto.vt.edu/

Wayne State University, College of Engineering, Department of Industrial and Systems Engineering, Detroit, MI 48202. Offers data science and business analytics (MS); engineering management (MS); industrial engineering (MS, PhD); manufacturing engineering (MS); systems engineering (Certificate). *Program availability:* Online learning. *Faculty:* 11. *Students:* 178 full-time (40 women), 109 part-time (30 women); includes 42 minority (20 Black or African American, non-Hispanic/Latino; 16 Asian, non-Hispanic/Latino; 6 Hispanic/Latino), 167 international. Average age 29. 539 applicants, 40% accepted, 68 enrolled. In 2018, 172 master's, 9 doctorates awarded. *Entrance requirements:* For master's, GRE or GMAT (for applicants to MS in data science and business analytics), BS from ABET-accredited institution; for doctorate, GRE, graduate degree in engineering or related discipline with minimum graduate GPA of 3.5, statement of purpose, resume/curriculum vitae, three letters of recommendation; for Certificate, GRE (for applicants from non-ABET institutions), BS in engineering or other technical field from ABET-accredited institution with minimum GPA of 3.0 in upper-division course work, at least one year of full-time work experience as practicing engineer or technical leader. Additional exam requirements/recommendations for international students: Required—TOEFL (minimum score 550 paper-based; 79 iBT), TWE (minimum score 5.5), Michigan English Language Assessment Battery (minimum score 85); GRE; Recommended—IELTS (minimum score 6.5). *Application deadline:* Applications are processed on a rolling basis. Application fee: $50. Electronic applications accepted. *Expenses:* Contact institution. *Financial support:* In 2018–19, 135 students received support, including 2 fellowships with tuition reimbursements available (averaging $20,000 per year), 5 research assistantships with tuition reimbursements available (averaging $23,260 per year), 8 teaching assistantships with tuition reimbursements available (averaging $20,166 per year); scholarships/grants, tuition waivers (full), and unspecified assistantships also available. Financial award applicants required to submit FAFSA. *Faculty research:* Manufacturing systems, infrastructure, and management. *Total annual research expenditures:* $320,400. *Unit head:* Dr. Leslie Monplaisir, Associate Professor/Chair, 313-577-3821, Fax: 313-577-8833, E-mail: leslie.monplaisir@wayne.edu. *Application contact:* Eric Scimeca, Graduate Program Coordinator, 313-577-0412, E-mail: eric.scimeca@wayne.edu.
Website: http://engineering.wayne.edu/ise/

Worcester Polytechnic Institute, Graduate Admissions, Program in Systems Engineering, Worcester, MA 01609-2280. Offers systems engineering (Graduate Certificate). *Program availability:* Part-time, evening/weekend, online only, 100% online. *Students:* 3 full-time (0 women), 158 part-time (34 women); includes 33 minority (8 Black or African American, non-Hispanic/Latino; 18 Asian, non-Hispanic/Latino; 6 Hispanic/Latino; 1 Two or more races, non-Hispanic/Latino), 1 international. Average age 36. 83 applicants, 75% accepted, 41 enrolled. In 2018, 78 master's, 5 other advanced degrees awarded. *Entrance requirements:* For master's, 3 letters of recommendation, statement of purpose. Additional exam requirements/recommendations for international students: Required—TOEFL (minimum score 563 paper-based; 84 iBT), IELTS (minimum score 7). *Application deadline:* For fall admission, 1/1 for domestic and international students; for spring admission, 10/1 for domestic and international students. Applications are processed on a rolling basis. Application fee: $70. Electronic applications accepted. *Financial support:* Research assistantships and teaching assistantships available. Financial award application deadline: 1/1. *Unit head:* Robert Swarz, Director, 508-831-5231, Fax: 508-831-5694, E-mail: rswarz@wpi.edu. *Application contact:* Colleen Sweeney, Administrative Assistant, 508-831-5517, Fax: 508-831-5694, E-mail: sweeney@wpi.edu.
Website: https://www.wpi.edu/academics/departments/systems-engineering

Youngstown State University, College of Graduate Studies, College of Science, Technology, Engineering and Mathematics, Department of Mechanical, Industrial and Manufacturing Engineering, Youngstown, OH 44555-0001. Offers industrial and systems engineering (MSE); mechanical engineering (MSE). *Program availability:* Part-time, evening/weekend. *Degree requirements:* For master's, thesis optional. *Entrance requirements:* For master's, minimum GPA of 2.75 in field. Additional exam requirements/recommendations for international students: Required—TOEFL. *Faculty research:* Kinematics and dynamics of machines, computational and experimental heat transfer, machine controls and mechanical design.

Section 15
Management of Engineering and Technology

This section contains a directory of institutions offering graduate work in management of engineering and technology. Additional information about programs listed in the directory may be obtained by writing directly to the dean of a graduate school or chair of a department at the address given in the directory.

For programs offering related work, in the other guides in this series:

Graduate Programs in the Humanities, Arts & Social Sciences

See *Applied Arts and Design, Architecture, Economics,* and *Sociology, Anthropology, and Archaeology*

Graduate Programs in the Biological/Biomedical Sciences & Health-Related Medical Professions

See *Biophysics (Radiation Biology); Ecology, Environmental Biology, and Evolutionary Biology;* and *Health Services (Health Services Management and Hospital Administration)*

Graduate Programs in Business, Education, Information Studies, Law & Social Work

See *Business Administration and Management* and *Law*

CONTENTS

Program Directories

Construction Management

The American University in Dubai, Graduate Programs, Dubai, United Arab Emirates. Offers construction management (MS); education (M Ed); finance (MBA); generalist (MBA); marketing (MBA). *Program availability:* Part-time, evening/weekend. *Degree requirements:* For master's, thesis optional. *Entrance requirements:* For master's, GMAT (for MBA); GRE (for M Ed and MS), minimum undergraduate GPA of 3.0, official transcripts, two reference forms, curriculum vitae/resume, statement of career objectives, work experience. Additional exam requirements/recommendations for international students: Required—TOEFL (minimum score 550 paper-based; 79 iBT). Electronic applications accepted.

Arizona State University at the Tempe campus, Ira A. Fulton Schools of Engineering, ASU Engineering Online Programs, Tempe, AZ 85287. Offers construction (MS); embedded systems (M Eng); enterprise systems innovation and management (MSE); modeling and simulation (M Eng); quality and reliability engineering (M Eng); software engineering (MSE); systems engineering (M Eng).

Arizona State University at the Tempe campus, Ira A. Fulton Schools of Engineering, School of Sustainable Engineering and the Built Environment, Tempe, AZ 85287-5306. Offers civil, environmental and sustainable engineering (MS, MSE, PhD); construction engineering (MSE); construction management (MS, PhD). *Program availability:* Part-time, evening/weekend, online learning. Terminal master's awarded for partial completion of doctoral program. *Degree requirements:* For master's, thesis optional, comprehensive exams (MSE); interactive Program of Study (iPOS) submitted before completing 50 percent of required credit hours; for doctorate, comprehensive exam, thesis/dissertation, interactive Program of Study (iPOS) submitted before completing 50 percent of required credit hours. *Entrance requirements:* For master's, GRE, minimum GPA of 3.0 or equivalent in last 2 years of work leading to bachelor's degree; for doctorate, GRE, minimum GPA of 3.0 in last 2 years of work leading to bachelor's degree, 3.2 in all graduate-level coursework with master's degree; 3 letters of recommendation; resume/curriculum vitae; letter of intent; thesis (if applicable); statement of research interests. Additional exam requirements/recommendations for international students: Required—TOEFL, IELTS, or PTE. Electronic applications accepted. *Expenses:* Contact institution. *Faculty research:* Water purification, transportation (safety and materials), construction management, environmental biotechnology, environmental nanotechnology, earth systems engineering and management, SMART innovations, project performance metrics, and underground infrastructure.

Brigham Young University, Graduate Studies, Ira A. Fulton College of Engineering, School of Technology, Provo, UT 84602. Offers construction management (MS); information technology (MS); manufacturing engineering technology (MS); technology and engineering education (MS). *Faculty:* 30 full-time (1 woman), 2 part-time/adjunct (0 women). *Students:* 30 full-time (4 women); includes 6 minority (1 Asian, non-Hispanic/Latino; 1 Hispanic/Latino; 1 Native Hawaiian or other Pacific Islander, non-Hispanic/Latino; 3 Two or more races, non-Hispanic/Latino), 2 international. Average age 28. 14 applicants, 79% accepted, 11 enrolled. In 2018, 29 master's awarded. *Degree requirements:* For master's, thesis. *Entrance requirements:* For master's, GRE General Test; GMAT or GRE (for construction management emphasis), Minimum GPA of 3.0 in last 60 hours of course work. Additional exam requirements/recommendations for international students: Required—TOEFL (minimum score 580 paper-based; 85 iBT). *Application deadline:* For fall admission, 2/15 for domestic and international students; for winter admission, 9/10 for domestic and international students; for spring admission, 2/15 for domestic and international students; for summer admission, 2/15 for domestic and international students. Application fee: $50. Electronic applications accepted. *Financial support:* In 2018–19, 28 students received support, including 9 research assistantships (averaging $3,496 per year), 11 teaching assistantships (averaging $4,755 per year); scholarships/grants also available. Financial award application deadline: 1/15; financial award applicants required to submit FAFSA. *Faculty research:* Information assurance and security, HEI and databases, manufacturing materials, processes and systems, innovation in construction management scheduling and delivery methods. *Total annual research expenditures:* $67,118. *Unit head:* Dr. Barry M. Lunt, Director, 801-422-6300, Fax: 801-422-0490, E-mail: blunt@byu.edu. *Application contact:* Clifton Farnsworth, Graduate Coordinator, 801-422-6494, Fax: 801-422-0490, E-mail: clifton_farnsworth@byu.edu.
Website: http://www.et.byu.edu/sot/

California Baptist University, Program in Business Administration, Riverside, CA 92504-3206. Offers accounting (MBA); construction management (MBA); healthcare management (MBA); management (MBA). *Accreditation:* ACBSP. *Program availability:* Part-time, evening/weekend, 100% online, blended/hybrid learning. *Faculty:* 22 full-time (7 women), 14 part-time/adjunct (3 women). *Students:* 124 full-time (65 women), 71 part-time (38 women); includes 108 minority (16 Black or African American, non-Hispanic/Latino; 11 Asian, non-Hispanic/Latino; 74 Hispanic/Latino; 1 Native Hawaiian or other Pacific Islander, non-Hispanic/Latino; 6 Two or more races, non-Hispanic/Latino), 21 international. Average age 36. 71 applicants, 77% accepted, 55 enrolled. In 2018, 131 master's awarded. *Degree requirements:* For master's, thesis, Interdisciplinary Capstone Project. *Entrance requirements:* For master's, GMAT, minimum GPA of 2.5; two recommendations; comprehensive essay; resume; interview. Additional exam requirements/recommendations for international students: Required—TOEFL (minimum score 80 iBT). *Application deadline:* For fall admission, 8/1 priority date for domestic students, 7/1 for international students; for spring admission, 12/1 priority date for domestic students, 11/1 for international students. Applications are processed on a rolling basis. Application fee: $45. Electronic applications accepted. *Expenses:* $662 per unit. *Financial support:* In 2018–19, 70 students received support. Federal Work-Study and scholarships/grants available. Financial award applicants required to submit CSS PROFILE or FAFSA. *Faculty research:* Behavioral economics, economic indicators, marketing ethics, international business, microfinance. *Unit head:* Dr. Andrea Scott, Dean, School of Business, 951-343-4701, E-mail: ascott@calbaptist.edu. *Application contact:* Dr. Scott Dunbar, Program Director, Online Masters in Business Administration, 951-343-2193, E-mail: sdunbar@calbaptist.edu.
Website: http://www.calbaptist.edu/mba/about/

California State University, Chico, Office of Graduate Studies, College of Engineering, Computer Science, and Construction Management, Chico, CA 95929-0722. Offers MS. *Program availability:* Part-time, online learning. *Faculty:* 7 full-time (1 woman), 3 part-time/adjunct (1 woman). *Students:* 1 full-time (0 women), 4 part-time (0 women); includes 3 minority (2 Asian, non-Hispanic/Latino; 1 Hispanic/Latino). 21 applicants. In 2018, 20 master's awarded. *Degree requirements:* For master's, thesis or project or comprehensive exam. *Entrance requirements:* For master's, GRE, fall admissions only; 2 letters of recommendation, statement of purpose, departmental letter of recommendation access waiver form. Additional exam requirements/recommendations for international students: Required—TOEFL (minimum score 550 paper-based; 80 iBT), IELTS (minimum score 6.5), PTE (minimum score 59). *Application deadline:* For fall admission, 4/1 priority date for domestic and international students. Application fee: $55. Electronic applications accepted. *Expenses: Tuition, area resident:* Full-time $4622; part-time $3116 per unit. Tuition, state resident: full-time $4622; part-time $3116 per unit. Tuition, nonresident: full-time $10,634. *Required fees:* $2160; $1620 per year. Tuition and fees vary according to class time and program. *Financial support:* Fellowships, research assistantships, teaching assistantships, career-related internships or fieldwork, Federal Work-Study, scholarships/grants, traineeships, health care benefits, unspecified assistantships, and stipends available. Support available to part-time students. Financial award application deadline: 3/2; financial award applicants required to submit FAFSA. *Unit head:* Melody Stapleton, Interim Dean, 530-898-5963, Fax: 530-898-4070, E-mail: ecc@csuchico.edu. *Application contact:* Micah Lehner, Graduate Admissions Counselor, 530-898-5416, Fax: 530-898-3342, E-mail: mlehner@csuchico.edu.
Website: http://www.csuchico.edu/ecc/

California State University, East Bay, Office of Graduate Studies, College of Science, School of Engineering, Program in Construction Management, Hayward, CA 94542-3000. Offers MS. *Degree requirements:* For master's, comprehensive exam (for some programs), research project or exam. *Entrance requirements:* For master's, GRE or GMAT, baccalaureate degree from accredited university with minimum overall GPA of 2.5; relevant work experience; college algebra and trigonometry or equivalent level math courses; personal statement; resume; two letters of recommendation. Additional exam requirements/recommendations for international students: Required—TOEFL (minimum score 550 paper-based; 79 iBT). Electronic applications accepted.

California State University, Northridge, Graduate Studies, College of Engineering and Computer Science, Department of Civil Engineering and Construction Management, Northridge, CA 91330. Offers engineering (MS), including structural engineering. *Program availability:* Part-time, evening/weekend. *Degree requirements:* For master's, thesis. *Entrance requirements:* Additional exam requirements/recommendations for international students: Required—TOEFL. *Faculty research:* Composite study.

Carnegie Mellon University, Carnegie Institute of Technology, Department of Civil and Environmental Engineering, Pittsburgh, PA 15213. Offers advanced infrastructure systems (MS, PhD); advanced infrastructure systems technology development and application (MS); air quality engineering and science (MS); civil and environmental engineering (MS, PhD); civil and environmental engineering/engineering and public policy (PhD); civil engineering (MS, PhD); computational mechanics (MS, PhD); computational modeling and monitoring for resilient structural and material systems (MS); energy infrastructure systems (MS); environmental engineering (MS, PhD); environmental management and science (MS, PhD); IT-based sustainable global infrastructure and construction management (MS); sustainability and green design (MS); water quality engineering and science (MS). *Program availability:* Part-time. *Faculty:* 23 full-time (5 women), 12 part-time/adjunct (3 women). *Students:* 264 full-time (109 women); includes 24 minority (6 Black or African American, non-Hispanic/Latino; 13 Asian, non-Hispanic/Latino; 5 Hispanic/Latino), 208 international. Average age 25. 630 applicants, 64% accepted, 114 enrolled. In 2018, 112 master's, 15 doctorates awarded. Terminal master's awarded for partial completion of doctoral program. *Degree requirements:* For master's, thesis optional; for doctorate, comprehensive exam, thesis/dissertation, two-part qualifying exam, public defense of dissertation. *Entrance requirements:* For master's, GRE General Test, BS in engineering, science or mathematics; for doctorate, GRE General Test, BS or MS in engineering, science or mathematics. Additional exam requirements/recommendations for international students: Required—TOEFL (minimum score 84 iBT), TOEFL (minimum score 84 iBT) or IELTS (7.0). *Application deadline:* For fall admission, 1/5 priority date for domestic and international students; for spring admission, 9/15 priority date for domestic and international students. Applications are processed on a rolling basis. Application fee: $75. Electronic applications accepted. *Expenses:* Contact institution. *Financial support:* In 2018–19, 137 students received support. Fellowships with tuition reimbursements available, research assistantships with tuition reimbursements available, scholarships/grants, health care benefits, tuition waivers (full and partial), unspecified assistantships, and service assistantships available. Financial award application deadline: 1/5. *Faculty research:* Advanced infrastructure systems; environmental engineering, sustainability, and science; mechanics, materials, and computing. *Total annual research expenditures:* $7.4 million. *Unit head:* Dr. David A. Dzombak, Professor and Department Head, 412-268-2941, Fax: 412-268-7813, E-mail: dzombak@cmu.edu. *Application contact:* David A. Vey, Director of Graduate Programs, 412-268-2292, Fax: 412-268-7813, E-mail: dvey@andrew.cmu.edu.
Website: http://www.cmu.edu/cee/

Carnegie Mellon University, College of Fine Arts, School of Architecture, Pittsburgh, PA 15213-3891. Offers architecture (MSA); architecture, engineering, and construction management (PhD); building performance and diagnostics (MS, PhD); computational design (MS, PhD); engineering construction management (MSA); tangible interaction design (MTID); urban design (MUD). Terminal master's awarded for partial completion of doctoral program. *Degree requirements:* For doctorate, thesis/dissertation. *Entrance requirements:* For master's and doctorate, GRE General Test. Additional exam requirements/recommendations for international students: Required—TOEFL.

Central Connecticut State University, School of Graduate Studies, School of Engineering, Science and Technology, Department of Manufacturing and Construction Management, New Britain, CT 06050-4010. Offers construction management (MS, Certificate); lean manufacturing and Six Sigma (Certificate); supply chain and logistics (Certificate); technology management (MS). *Program availability:* Part-time, evening/weekend. *Faculty:* 6 full-time (0 women), 2 part-time/adjunct (0 women). *Students:* 14 full-time (7 women), 82 part-time (18 women); includes 28 minority (11 Black or African American, non-Hispanic/Latino; 2 Asian, non-Hispanic/Latino; 12 Hispanic/Latino; 3 Two or more races, non-Hispanic/Latino), 6 international. Average age 32. 70 applicants, 71% accepted, 29 enrolled. In 2018, 51 master's, 5 other advanced degrees awarded. *Degree requirements:* For master's, comprehensive exam, special project; for Certificate, qualifying exam. *Entrance requirements:* For master's, minimum undergraduate GPA of 2.7. Additional exam requirements/recommendations for international students: Required—TOEFL (minimum score 550 paper-based; 79 iBT); Recommended—IELTS (minimum score 6.5). *Application deadline:* For fall admission, 8/1 for domestic students, 5/1 for international students; for spring admission, 12/1 for domestic students, 11/1 for international students; for summer admission, 5/1 for domestic students. Applications are processed on a rolling basis. Application fee: $50. Electronic applications accepted. *Expenses: Tuition, area resident:* Full-time $7027; part-time $388 per credit. Tuition, state resident: full-time $9750; part-time $388 per credit. Tuition, nonresident: full-time $18,102; part-time $388 per credit. *International tuition:* $18,102 full-time. *Required fees:* $266 per semester. *Financial support:* In 2018–19, 7 students received support. Career-related internships or fieldwork, Federal Work-Study, scholarships/grants, and unspecified assistantships available. Support available to part-time students. Financial award application deadline: 3/1; financial award applicants required to submit FAFSA. *Faculty research:* All aspects of middle management, technical supervision in the workplace. *Unit head:* Dr. Ravindra Thamma, Chair, 860-832-1830, E-mail: thammarav@ccsu.edu. *Application contact:* Patricia Gardner, Associate Director of Graduate Studies, 860-832-2350, Fax: 860-832-2362. Website: http://www.ccsu.edu/mcm/

Clemson University, Graduate School, College of Architecture, Arts, and Humanities, Department of Construction Science and Management, Clemson, SC 29634. Offers MCSM. *Program availability:* Part-time, 100% online. *Faculty:* 7 full-time (1 woman). *Students:* 8 full-time (1 woman), 7 part-time (4 women), 6 international. Average age 28. 42 applicants, 93% accepted, 12 enrolled. In 2018, 13 master's awarded. *Degree requirements:* For master's, thesis optional. *Entrance requirements:* For master's, GRE General Test, unofficial transcripts, letters of recommendation. Additional exam requirements/recommendations for international students: Required—TOEFL (minimum score 80 paper-based; 80 iBT); Recommended—IELTS (minimum score 6.5), TSE (minimum score 54). *Application deadline:* For fall admission, 4/15 for international students; for spring admission, 10/15 for international students. Applications are processed on a rolling basis. Application fee: $80 ($90 for international students). Electronic applications accepted. *Expenses:* Tuition, area resident: Full-time $11,270; part-time $8688 per credit hour. Tuition, state resident: full-time $11,796. Tuition, nonresident: full-time $23,802; part-time $17,412 per credit hour. *International tuition:* $23,246 full-time. *Required fees:* $1196; $497 per semester. Tuition and fees vary according to course load, degree level, campus/location and program. *Financial support:* In 2018–19, 9 students received support. Career-related internships or fieldwork and unspecified assistantships available. *Faculty research:* Construction best practices, productivity improvement, women's issues in construction, construction project management. *Total annual research expenditures:* $44,237. *Unit head:* Dr. N. Mike Jackson, Department Chair, 864-656-3878, E-mail: nmjacks@clemson.edu. *Application contact:* Dr. Shima Clarke, Graduate Program Coordinator, 864-656-4498, E-mail: shimac@clemson.edu.
Website: http://www.clemson.edu/caah/csm/

Clemson University, Graduate School, College of Engineering, Computing and Applied Sciences, Glenn Department of Civil Engineering, Clemson, SC 29634. Offers civil engineering (MS, PhD), including construction engineering and management, construction materials, geotechnical engineering, structural engineering, transportation engineering, water resources engineering. *Program availability:* Part-time. *Faculty:* 20 full-time (3 women). *Students:* 109 full-time (23 women), 55 part-time (11 women); includes 9 minority (2 Black or African American, non-Hispanic/Latino; 2 Asian, non-Hispanic/Latino; 4 Hispanic/Latino; 1 Two or more races, non-Hispanic/Latino), 111 international. Average age 28. 283 applicants, 59% accepted, 53 enrolled. In 2018, 31 master's, 11 doctorates awarded. *Degree requirements:* For master's, thesis or alternative, oral exam, seminar; for doctorate, comprehensive exam, thesis/dissertation, oral exam, seminar. *Entrance requirements:* For master's and doctorate, GRE General Test, unofficial transcripts, letters of recommendation, statement of purpose. Additional exam requirements/recommendations for international students: Required—TOEFL (minimum score 80 paper-based; 80 iBT), PTE (minimum score 54); Recommended—IELTS (minimum score 6.5). *Application deadline:* For fall admission, 4/15 for domestic and international students; for spring admission, 9/15 for domestic and international students. Applications are processed on a rolling basis. Application fee: $80 ($90 for international students). Electronic applications accepted. *Expenses:* $6823 per semester full-time resident, $14023 per semester full-time non-resident, $833 per credit hour part-time resident, $1731 per credit hour part-time non-resident, online $1264 per credit hour, $4938 doctoral programs resident, $10405 doctoral programs non-resident, $1144 full-time graduate assistant, other fees may apply per session. *Financial support:* In 2018–19, 104 students received support, including 20 fellowships with full and partial tuition reimbursements available (averaging $4,491 per year), 43 research assistantships with full and partial tuition reimbursements available (averaging $16,364 per year), 1 teaching assistantship with full and partial tuition reimbursement available (averaging $12,750 per year); career-related internships or fieldwork and unspecified assistantships also available. Financial award application deadline: 4/15. *Faculty research:* Applied fluid mechanics, construction materials, project management, structural and geotechnical engineering, transportation. *Total annual research expenditures:* $4.9 million. *Unit head:* Dr. Ronald Andrus, Interim Department Chair, 864-656-0488, E-mail: randrus@clemson.edu. *Application contact:* Dr. Abdul Khan, Graduate Program Coordinator, 864-656-3327, E-mail: abdkhan@clemson.edu.
Website: https://www.clemson.edu/cecas/departments/ce/

Colorado State University, College of Health and Human Sciences, Department of Construction Management, Fort Collins, CO 80523-1584. Offers MS. *Degree requirements:* For master's, thesis (for some programs), professional paper (for some programs); article submission for journal or proceedings with faculty advisor. *Entrance requirements:* For master's, GRE, minimum undergraduate GPA of 3.0 or professional experience; undergraduate degree in a related discipline including construction, engineering, architecture or business; three letters of recommendation; official transcripts; resume; statement of purpose. Additional exam requirements/recommendations for international students: Required—TOEFL (minimum score 550 paper-based; 80 iBT), IELTS (minimum score 6.5). Electronic applications accepted. *Expenses:* Tuition, state resident: full-time $10,520; part-time $4675 per credit hour. Tuition, nonresident: full-time $25,791; part-time $11,462 per credit hour. *International tuition:* $25,791 full-time. *Required fees:* $2392; $576 $288. Tuition and fees vary according to course level, course load, degree level, program and student level. *Faculty research:* Project management; sustainability; construction productivity improvement; building and information modeling (BIM); virtual design and construction.

Columbia University, Fu Foundation School of Engineering and Applied Science, Department of Civil Engineering and Engineering Mechanics, New York, NY 10027. Offers civil engineering (MS, Eng Sc D, PhD); construction engineering and management (MS); engineering mechanics (MS, Eng Sc D, PhD). *Program availability:* Part-time, online learning. Terminal master's awarded for partial completion of doctoral program. *Degree requirements:* For doctorate, thesis/dissertation, qualifying exam. *Entrance requirements:* For master's and doctorate, GRE General Test. Additional exam requirements/recommendations for international students: Required—TOEFL, IELTS, PTE. Electronic applications accepted. *Faculty research:* Structural dynamics, structural health and monitoring, fatigue and fracture mechanics, geo-environmental engineering, multiscale science and engineering.

Columbia University, School of Professional Studies, Program in Construction Administration, New York, NY 10027. Offers MS. *Program availability:* Part-time, evening/weekend. *Degree requirements:* For master's, minimum GPA of 3.0 or internship. *Entrance requirements:* For master's, bachelor's degree, minimum GPA of 3.0. Additional exam requirements/recommendations for international students: Recommended—TOEFL. Electronic applications accepted.

Drexel University, Goodwin College of Professional Studies, School of Technology and Professional Studies, Philadelphia, PA 19104-2875. Offers construction management (MS); creativity and innovation (MS); engineering technology (MS); food science (MS); hospitality management (MS); professional studies: creativity studies (MS); professional

studies: e-learning leadership (MS); professional studies: homeland security management (MS); project management (MS); property management (MS); sport management (MS). *Program availability:* Part-time, evening/weekend. *Entrance requirements:* Additional exam requirements/recommendations for international students: Required—TOEFL, IELTS. Electronic applications accepted. Application fee is waived when completed online.

East Carolina University, Graduate School, College of Engineering and Technology, Department of Construction Management, Greenville, NC 27858-4353. Offers construction management (MCM); residential construction management (Certificate). *Expenses: Tuition, area resident:* Full-time $4749. Tuition, state resident: full-time $4749. Tuition, nonresident: full-time $17,898. *International tuition:* $17,898 full-time. *Required fees:* $2787. Part-time tuition and fees vary according to course load and program. *Unit head:* Dr. Syed M. Ahmed, Chair, 252-328-6958, E-mail: ahmeds@ecu.edu. *Application contact:* Graduate School Admissions, 252-328-6012, Fax: 252-328-6071, E-mail: gradschool@ecu.edu.

Eastern Michigan University, Graduate School, College of Engineering and Technology, School of Visual and Built Environments, Programs in Construction Management, Ypsilanti, MI 48197. Offers construction (Certificate); construction management (MS); project leadership (Certificate); sustainable construction (Certificate). *Program availability:* Part-time, evening/weekend, online learning. *Students:* 12 full-time (3 women), 9 part-time (3 women); includes 5 minority (2 Black or African American, non-Hispanic/Latino; 1 Asian, non-Hispanic/Latino; 2 Two or more races, non-Hispanic/Latino), 7 international. Average age 32. 59 applicants, 53% accepted, 6 enrolled. In 2018, 17 master's awarded. *Entrance requirements:* Additional exam requirements/recommendations for international students: Required—TOEFL. *Application deadline:* Applications are processed on a rolling basis. Application fee: $45. *Financial support:* Fellowships, research assistantships with full tuition reimbursements, teaching assistantships with full tuition reimbursements, career-related internships or fieldwork, Federal Work-Study, institutionally sponsored loans, scholarships/grants, tuition waivers (partial), and unspecified assistantships available. Support available to part-time students. Financial award applicants required to submit FAFSA. *Application contact:* Dr. Armagan Korkmaz, Advisor, 734-487-2492, Fax: 734-487-8755, E-mail: kkorkmaz@emich.edu.

Farmingdale State College, Program in Technology Management, Farmingdale, NY 11735. Offers construction management (MS); electrical and mechanical engineering (MS). *Degree requirements:* For master's, project or thesis.

Florida International University, College of Engineering and Computing, School of Construction, Miami, FL 33175. Offers construction management (MS, PMS). *Program availability:* Part-time, evening/weekend. *Faculty:* 9 full-time (1 woman), 8 part-time/adjunct (0 women). *Students:* 23 full-time (8 women), 32 part-time (9 women); includes 26 minority (4 Black or African American, non-Hispanic/Latino; 2 Asian, non-Hispanic/Latino; 20 Hispanic/Latino), 19 international. Average age 31. 102 applicants, 30% accepted, 11 enrolled. In 2018, 37 master's awarded. *Degree requirements:* For master's, thesis optional. *Entrance requirements:* For master's, minimum GPA of 3.0 in upper-level course work. Additional exam requirements/recommendations for international students: Required—TOEFL (minimum score 550 paper-based; 80 iBT). *Application deadline:* For fall admission, 6/1 for domestic students, 4/1 for international students; for spring admission, 10/1 for domestic students, 9/1 for international students. Applications are processed on a rolling basis. Application fee: $30. Electronic applications accepted. *Financial support:* In 2018–19, 5 students received support. Institutionally sponsored loans, scholarships/grants, and unspecified assistantships available. Financial award application deadline: 3/1; financial award applicants required to submit FAFSA. *Faculty research:* Information technology, construction organizations, contracts and partnerships in construction, construction education, concrete technology. *Unit head:* Dr. Irtishad Ahmad, Director, 305-348-3172, Fax: 305-348-6255, E-mail: ahmadi@fiu.edu. *Application contact:* Nanett Rojas, Manager, Admissions Operations, 305-348-7464, Fax: 305-348-7441, E-mail: gradadm@fiu.edu.
Website: http://cec.fiu.edu

Georgia Southern University, Jack N. Averitt College of Graduate Studies, Allen E. Paulson College of Engineering and Computing, Department of Civil Engineering and Construction, Statesboro, GA 30458. Offers MSAE. *Degree requirements:* For master's, comprehensive exam, thesis (for some programs). *Entrance requirements:* For master's, undergraduate major or equivalent in proposed study area. Additional exam requirements/recommendations for international students: Required—TOEFL (minimum score 550 paper-based; 80 iBT), IELTS (minimum score 6). Electronic applications accepted. *Expenses: Tuition, area resident:* Part-time $3324 per semester. Tuition, state resident: full-time $5814; part-time $3324 per semester. Tuition, nonresident: full-time $23,204; part-time $13,260 per semester. *Required fees:* $2092; $2092. Tuition and fees vary according to course load, degree level, campus/location and program.

Illinois Institute of Technology, Graduate College, Armour College of Engineering, Department of Civil, Architectural and Environmental Engineering, Chicago, IL 60616. Offers architectural engineering (M Arch E); civil engineering (MS, PhD), including architectural engineering (MS), construction engineering and management (MS), geoenvironmental engineering (MS), geotechnical engineering (MS), structural engineering (MS), transportation engineering (MS); construction engineering and management (MCEM); environmental engineering (M Env E, MS, PhD); geoenvironmental engineering (M Geoenv E); geotechnical engineering (MGE); infrastructure engineering and management (MPW); structural engineering (MSE); transportation engineering (M Trans E). *Program availability:* Part-time, evening/weekend, online learning. Terminal master's awarded for partial completion of doctoral program. *Degree requirements:* For master's, thesis (for some programs); for doctorate, comprehensive exam, thesis/dissertation. *Entrance requirements:* For master's, GRE General Test (minimum score 900 Quantitative and Verbal, 2.5 Analytical Writing), minimum undergraduate GPA of 3.0; for doctorate, GRE General Test (minimum score 1000 Quantitative and Verbal, 3.0 Analytical Writing), minimum undergraduate GPA of 3.0. Additional exam requirements/recommendations for international students: Required—TOEFL (minimum score 550 paper-based; 80 iBT). Electronic applications accepted. *Faculty research:* Structural, architectural, geotechnical and geoenvironmental engineering; construction engineering and management; transportation engineering; environmental engineering and public works.

Instituto Tecnologico de Santo Domingo, Graduate School, Area of Engineering, Santo Domingo, Dominican Republic. Offers construction administration (MS, Certificate); data telecommunications (M Eng, MS, Certificate); industrial engineering (M Eng, Certificate); industrial management (M Mgmt); information technology (Certificate); maintenance engineering (M Eng); occupational hazard prevention (M Mgmt); production management (Certificate); quantitative methods (Certificate); sanitary and environmental engineering (M Eng); structural engineering (M Eng); systems engineering and electronic data processing (Certificate); transportation (Certificate).

Kennesaw State University, College of Architecture and Construction Management, Program in Construction Management, Marietta, GA 30144. Offers MS. *Program availability:* Part-time, evening/weekend. *Students:* 4 full-time (1 woman), 10 part-time (3

women); includes 5 minority (3 Black or African American, non-Hispanic/Latino; 1 Asian, non-Hispanic/Latino; 1 Hispanic/Latino), 5 international. Average age 40. 10 applicants, 30% accepted, 3 enrolled. In 2018, 9 master's awarded. *Degree requirements:* For master's, comprehensive exam, thesis or alternative. *Entrance requirements:* For master's, GMAT or GRE, 3 reference forms, minimum GPA of 2.75. Additional exam requirements/recommendations for international students: Required—TOEFL (minimum score 80 iBT), IELTS (minimum score 6.5). *Application deadline:* For fall admission, 7/1 priority date for domestic students, 5/1 priority date for international students; for spring admission, 11/1 priority date for domestic students, 9/1 priority date for international students. Applications are processed on a rolling basis. Application fee: $60. Electronic applications accepted. *Expenses: Tuition, area resident:* Full-time $6960; part-time $290 per credit hour. Tuition, state resident: full-time $6960; part-time $290 per credit hour. Tuition, nonresident: full-time $25,080; part-time $1045 per credit hour. *International tuition:* $25,080 full-time. *Required fees:* $2006; $1706 per semester. $853 per semester. *Financial support:* Research assistantships with tuition reimbursements, career-related internships or fieldwork, scholarships/grants, and unspecified assistantships available. Support available to part-time students. Financial award applicants required to submit FAFSA. *Unit head:* Dr. Khalid M. Siddiqi, Chair, 470-578-4216, E-mail: ksiddiqi@kennesaw.edu. *Application contact:* Admissions Counselor, 470-578-4377, Fax: 470-578-9172, E-mail: ksugrad@kennesaw.edu.
Website: http://cacm.kennesaw.edu/constructionmanagement/

Louisiana State University and Agricultural & Mechanical College, Graduate School, College of Engineering, Department of Construction Management, Baton Rouge, LA 70803. Offers MS, PhD.

Manhattan College, Graduate Programs, School of Engineering, Program in Construction Management, Riverdale, NY 10471. Offers MS.

Marquette University, Graduate School, College of Engineering, Department of Civil and Environmental Engineering, Milwaukee, WI 53201-1881. Offers construction engineering and management (MS, PhD, Certificate); environmental engineering (MS, PhD); structural design (Certificate); structural engineering and structural mechanics (MS, PhD); transportation (Certificate); transportation engineering and materials (MS, PhD); waste and wastewater treatment processes (Certificate); water resources engineering (Certificate). *Program availability:* Part-time, evening/weekend. Terminal master's awarded for partial completion of doctoral program. *Degree requirements:* For master's, comprehensive exam (for some programs), thesis or alternative; for doctorate, thesis/dissertation. *Entrance requirements:* For master's, GRE General Test (recommended), minimum GPA of 3.0, official transcripts from all current and previous colleges/universities except Marquette, three letters of recommendation; for doctorate, GRE General Test, minimum GPA of 3.0, official transcripts from all current and previous colleges/universities except Marquette, three letters of recommendation, brief statement of purpose, submission of any English language publications authored by applicant (strongly recommended). Additional exam requirements/recommendations for international students: Required—TOEFL (minimum score 530 paper-based). Electronic applications accepted. *Faculty research:* Highway safety, highway performance, and intelligent transportation systems; surface mount technology; watershed management.

Michigan State University, The Graduate School, College of Agriculture and Natural Resources and College of Social Science, School of Planning, Design and Construction, East Lansing, MI 48824. Offers construction management (MS, PhD); environmental design (MA); interior design and facilities management (MA); international planning studies (MIPS); urban and regional planning (MURP). *Degree requirements:* For master's, thesis or alternative. *Entrance requirements:* Additional exam requirements/recommendations for international students: Required—TOEFL. Electronic applications accepted.

Missouri State University, Graduate College, College of Business, Department of Technology and Construction Management, Springfield, MO 65897. Offers project management (MS). *Program availability:* Part-time. *Faculty:* 4 full-time (0 women), 2 part-time/adjunct (1 woman). *Students:* 24 full-time (13 women), 46 part-time (20 women); includes 12 minority (5 Black or African American, non-Hispanic/Latino; 1 American Indian or Alaska Native, non-Hispanic/Latino; 6 Hispanic/Latino), 13 international. Average age 26. 44 applicants, 68% accepted. In 2018, 25 master's awarded. *Degree requirements:* For master's, thesis or alternative. *Entrance requirements:* For master's, GRE or GMAT, minimum GPA of 2.75. Additional exam requirements/recommendations for international students: Required—TOEFL (minimum score 550 paper-based; 79 iBT), IELTS (minimum score 6). *Application deadline:* For fall admission, 7/20 priority date for domestic students, 5/1 for international students; for spring admission, 12/20 priority date for domestic students, 9/1 for international students; for summer admission, 5/20 priority date for domestic students. Applications are processed on a rolling basis. Application fee: $55 ($60 for international students). Electronic applications accepted. Tuition and fees vary according to class time, course level, course load, degree level, campus/location, program and student level. *Financial support:* Federal Work-Study, institutionally sponsored loans, scholarships/grants, and unspecified assistantships available. Financial award application deadline: 1/31; financial award applicants required to submit FAFSA. *Unit head:* Dr. Richard N. Callahan, Department Head, 417-836-5121, Fax: 417-836-8556, E-mail: indmgt@missouristate.edu. *Application contact:* Lakan Drinker, Director, Graduate Enrollment Management, 417-836-5330, Fax: 417-836-6200, E-mail: lakandrinker@missouristate.edu.
Website: http://tcm.missouristate.edu/

New England Institute of Technology, Program in Construction Management, East Greenwich, RI 02818. Offers MS. *Program availability:* Part-time, evening/weekend, online only, 100% online, blended/hybrid learning. *Students:* 14 full-time (6 women), 4 part-time (2 women), 5 international. Average age 32. *Entrance requirements:* For master's, Minimum GPA 2.5 awarded Bachelor's degree in related field from an accredited institution plus personal statement. Additional exam requirements/recommendations for international students: Required—TOEFL. *Application deadline:* Applications are processed on a rolling basis. Application fee: $25. Electronic applications accepted. *Expenses:* $495.00 per credit x 45 credits to complete this program. Tuition is $22,275.00. Visit https://www.neit.edu/Financial-Aid/Tuition-and-Fees for more information. *Unit head:* Dr. Douglas H. Sherman, Senior Vice President and Provost, 401-739-5000 Ext. 3481, Fax: 401-886-0859, E-mail: dsherman@neit.edu. *Application contact:* Lynn M Fawthrop, Vice President of Enrollment Management and Marketing, 401-739-5000 Ext. 3315, Fax: 401-886-0859, E-mail: lmfawthrop@neit.edu.
Website: http://www.neit.edu/Programs/Masters-Degree-Programs/Construction-Management-Masters-Degree

NewSchool of Architecture and Design, Program in Construction Management, San Diego, CA 92101-6634. Offers MCM. *Program availability:* Part-time, online learning. *Degree requirements:* For master's, thesis. *Entrance requirements:* For master's, GRE/GMAT. Additional exam requirements/recommendations for international students: Required—TOEFL, IELTS. Electronic applications accepted.

New York University, School of Professional Studies, Schack Institute of Real Estate, Program in Construction Management, New York, NY 10012-1019. Offers MS. *Program availability:* Part-time, evening/weekend. *Degree requirements:* For master's, thesis, capstone project. *Entrance requirements:* For master's, GRE or GMAT (only upon request), bachelor's degree, resume with relevant professional work, internship or volunteer experience, two letters of recommendation, statement of purpose. Additional exam requirements/recommendations for international students: Required—TOEFL (minimum score 600 paper-based; 100 iBT), IELTS (minimum score 7). Electronic applications accepted. *Expenses:* Contact institution.

North Dakota State University, College of Graduate and Interdisciplinary Studies, College of Engineering, Department of Construction Management and Engineering, Fargo, ND 58102. Offers construction management (MCM, MS, Graduate Certificate). *Entrance requirements:* Additional exam requirements/recommendations for international students: Required—TOEFL (minimum score 525 paper-based; 71 iBT). Electronic applications accepted.

Norwich University, College of Graduate and Continuing Studies, Master of Business Administration Program, Northfield, VT 05663. Offers construction management (MBA); energy management (MBA); finance (MBA); logistics (MBA); organizational leadership (MBA); project management (MBA); supply chain management (MBA). *Accreditation:* ACBSP. *Program availability:* Evening/weekend, online only, mostly all online with a week-long residency requirement. *Degree requirements:* For master's, comprehensive exam. *Entrance requirements:* For master's, minimum undergraduate GPA of 2.75. Additional exam requirements/recommendations for international students: Required—TOEFL (minimum score 550 paper-based; 80 iBT), IELTS (minimum score 6.5). Electronic applications accepted. *Expenses:* Contact institution.

Norwich University, College of Graduate and Continuing Studies, Master of Civil Engineering Program, Northfield, VT 05663. Offers construction management (MCE); environmental (MCE); geotechnical (MCE); structural (MCE). *Program availability:* Evening/weekend, online only, mostly all online with a week-long residency requirement. *Degree requirements:* For master's, capstone. *Entrance requirements:* For master's, minimum undergraduate GPA of 2.75. Additional exam requirements/recommendations for international students: Required—TOEFL (minimum score 550 paper-based; 80 iBT), IELTS (minimum score 6.5). Electronic applications accepted. *Expenses:* Contact institution.

Pittsburg State University, Graduate School, College of Technology, Department of Technology and Workforce Learning, Pittsburg, KS 66762. Offers career and technical education (MS); human resource development (MS); technology (MS), including automotive technology, construction management, graphic design, graphics management, information technology, innovation in technology, personnel development, technology management, workforce learning; workforce development and education (Ed S). *Program availability:* Part-time, evening/weekend, 100% online, blended/hybrid learning. *Degree requirements:* For master's, thesis or alternative; for Ed S, thesis optional. *Entrance requirements:* Additional exam requirements/recommendations for international students: Required—TOEFL (minimum score 520 paper-based; 68 iBT), IELTS (minimum score 6), PTE (minimum score 47). Electronic applications accepted. *Expenses:* Contact institution.

Pittsburg State University, Graduate School, College of Technology, School of Construction, Pittsburg, KS 66762. Offers construction engineering technology (MET); construction management (MS). *Program availability:* Part-time, 100% online, blended/hybrid learning. *Degree requirements:* For master's, thesis or alternative. *Entrance requirements:* Additional exam requirements/recommendations for international students: Required—TOEFL (minimum score 550 paper-based; 79 iBT), IELTS (minimum score 6.5), PTE (minimum score 53). Electronic applications accepted. *Expenses:* Contact institution.

Polytechnic University of Puerto Rico, Miami Campus, Graduate School, Miami, FL 33166. Offers accounting (MBA); business administration (MBA); construction management (MEM); environmental management (MEM); finance (MBA); human resources management (MBA); logistics and supply chain management (MBA); management of international enterprises (MBA); manufacturing management (MEM); marketing management (MBA); project management (MBA). *Program availability:* Part-time, evening/weekend, online learning. *Entrance requirements:* For master's, minimum GPA of 3.0. Electronic applications accepted.

Polytechnic University of Puerto Rico, Orlando Campus, Graduate School, Orlando, FL 32825. Offers accounting (MBA); business administration (MBA); construction management (MEM); engineering management (MEM); environmental management (MEM); finance (MBA); human resources management (MBA); management of international enterprises (MBA); management of technology (MBA); manufacturing management (MEM). *Program availability:* Part-time, evening/weekend, online learning. *Entrance requirements:* For master's, minimum GPA of 3.0. Additional exam requirements/recommendations for international students: Recommended—TOEFL. Electronic applications accepted.

Purdue University, Graduate School, Purdue Polytechnic Institute, Department of Building Construction Management, West Lafayette, IN 47907. Offers MS. *Program availability:* Online learning. *Faculty:* 19 full-time (5 women). *Students:* 8 full-time (4 women), 14 part-time (3 women); includes 2 minority (1 Asian, non-Hispanic/Latino; 1 Hispanic/Latino), 12 international. Average age 28. 10 applicants, 10% accepted. In 2018, 18 master's awarded. *Entrance requirements:* For master's, GRE, BS/BA with minimum GPA of 3.0. Additional exam requirements/recommendations for international students: Required—TOEFL (minimum score 550 paper-based; 77 iBT); Recommended—TWE. *Application deadline:* For fall admission, 4/1 for domestic and international students; for spring admission, 10/1 for domestic students, 9/1 for international students; for summer admission, 4/1 for domestic students, 2/15 for international students. Application fee: $60 ($75 for international students). Electronic applications accepted. *Financial support:* Fellowships, research assistantships, and teaching assistantships available. *Unit head:* Robert F. Cox, Head, 765-494-7939, E-mail: rfcox@purdue.edu. *Application contact:* Fran Misch, Graduate Contact, 765-494-2465, E-mail: fran@purdue.edu.
Website: http://www.tech.purdue.edu/bcm/

Purdue University Fort Wayne, College of Engineering, Technology, and Computer Science, Program in Technology, Fort Wayne, IN 46805-1499. Offers facilities/construction management (MS); industrial technology/manufacturing (MS); information technology/advanced computer applications (MS). *Program availability:* Part-time. *Entrance requirements:* For master's, minimum GPA of 3.0. Additional exam requirements/recommendations for international students: Required—TOEFL (minimum score 550 paper-based; 79 iBT), TWE. Electronic applications accepted.

South Dakota School of Mines and Technology, Graduate Division, Program in Construction Engineering Management, Rapid City, SD 57701-3995. Offers MS. *Program availability:* Part-time, evening/weekend, online learning. *Entrance requirements:* For master's, GRE General Test. Additional exam requirements/recommendations for international students: Required—TOEFL (minimum score 520 paper-based; 68 iBT). Electronic applications accepted.

Stevens Institute of Technology, Graduate School, Charles V. Schaefer Jr. School of Engineering and Science, Department of Civil, Environmental, and Ocean Engineering, Program in Construction Management, Hoboken, NJ 07030. Offers construction management (MS, Certificate), including construction accounting/estimating (Certificate), construction engineering (Certificate), construction law/disputes (Certificate), construction/quality management (Certificate). *Program availability:* Part-time, evening/weekend. *Faculty:* 6 part-time/adjunct (1 woman). *Students:* 109 full-time (19 women), 21 part-time (7 women); includes 12 minority (4 Black or African American, non-Hispanic/Latino; 8 Asian, non-Hispanic/Latino), 100 international. Average age 25. In 2018, 49 master's, 3 other advanced degrees awarded. Terminal master's awarded for partial completion of doctoral program. *Degree requirements:* For master's, thesis optional, minimum B average in major field and overall; for Certificate, minimum B average. *Entrance requirements:* For master's, GRE/GMAT scores: GRE scores are required for all applicants applying to a full-time graduate program in the Schaefer School of Engineering and Science (SES). International applicants must submit TOEFL/IELTS scores and fulfill the English Language Proficiency Requirements in order to be considered. Additional exam requirements/recommendations for international students: Required—TOEFL (minimum score 74 iBT), IELTS (minimum score 6). *Application deadline:* For fall admission, 4/15 for domestic and international students; for spring admission, 11/1 for domestic and international students; for summer admission, 5/1 for domestic students. Applications are processed on a rolling basis. Application fee: $60. Electronic applications accepted. *Expenses:* Tuition: Full-time $35,960; part-time $1620 per credit. *Required fees:* $1290; $600 per semester. Tuition and fees vary according to course load. *Financial support:* Fellowships, research assistantships, teaching assistantships, career-related internships or fieldwork, Federal Work-Study, scholarships/grants, and unspecified assistantships available. Financial award application deadline: 2/15; financial award applicants required to submit FAFSA. *Unit head:* Dr. Jean Zu, Dean of SES, 201-216.8233, Fax: 201-216.8372, E-mail: Jean.Zu@stevens.edu. *Application contact:* Graduate Admission, 888-783-8367, Fax: 888-511-1306, E-mail: graduate@stevens.edu.

Texas A&M University, College of Architecture, Department of Construction Science, College Station, TX 77843. Offers construction management (MS). *Faculty:* 18. *Students:* 28 full-time (8 women), 5 part-time (2 women); includes 6 minority (1 Black or African American, non-Hispanic/Latino; 2 Asian, non-Hispanic/Latino; 3 Hispanic/Latino), 23 international. Average age 27. 32 applicants, 97% accepted, 17 enrolled. In 2018, 19 master's awarded. *Degree requirements:* For master's, comprehensive exam. *Entrance requirements:* For master's, GRE General Test, 3 recommendation letters, resume, statement of research interest, minimum undergraduate GPA of 3.0 in last 60 hours of applicant's undergraduate degree. Additional exam requirements/recommendations for international students: Required—TOEFL (minimum score 550 paper-based; 80 iBT), IELTS (minimum score 6), PTE (minimum score 53). *Application deadline:* For fall admission, 2/15 for domestic and international students. Applications are processed on a rolling basis. Application fee: $50 ($90 for international students). Electronic applications accepted. *Expenses:* Contact institution. *Financial support:* In 2018–19, 21 students received support, including 4 fellowships with tuition reimbursements available (averaging $1,000 per year), 10 research assistantships with tuition reimbursements available (averaging $10,370 per year), 11 teaching assistantships with tuition reimbursements available (averaging $6,552 per year); career-related internships or fieldwork, institutionally sponsored loans, scholarships/grants, traineeships, health care benefits, tuition waivers (full and partial), and unspecified assistantships also available. Support available to part-time students. Financial award application deadline: 3/15; financial award applicants required to submit FAFSA. *Faculty research:* Advanced project management, construction operation, construction productivity and labor, facility management, information technology in construction, law and risk management, sustainability. *Unit head:* Prof. Joe Horlen, Head, 979-458-3477, E-mail: jhorlen@tamu.edu. *Application contact:* Ben Bigelow, Graduate Program Coordinator, 979-458-4457, E-mail: bbigelow@arch.tamu.edu. Website: http://cosc.arch.tamu.edu/

Thomas Jefferson University, College of Architecture and the Built Environment, Program in Construction Management, Philadelphia, PA 19107. Offers MS.

Universidad de las Américas Puebla, Division of Graduate Studies, School of Engineering, Program in Construction Management, Puebla, Mexico. Offers M Adm. *Program availability:* Part-time, evening/weekend. *Degree requirements:* For master's, one foreign language, thesis. *Faculty research:* Building structures, budget, project management.

The University of Alabama at Birmingham, School of Engineering, Professional Engineering Degrees, Birmingham, AL 35294. Offers advanced safety engineering and management (M Eng); construction engineering management (M Eng); design and commercialization (M Eng); information engineering management (M Eng); structural engineering (M Eng); sustainable smart cities (M Eng). *Program availability:* Part-time, evening/weekend, online only, 100% online, blended/hybrid learning. *Faculty:* 6 full-time (1 woman), 12 part-time/adjunct (2 women). *Students:* 23 full-time (7 women), 315 part-time (63 women); includes 96 minority (73 Black or African American, non-Hispanic/Latino; 1 American Indian or Alaska Native, non-Hispanic/Latino; 8 Asian, non-Hispanic/Latino; 12 Hispanic/Latino; 2 Two or more races, non-Hispanic/Latino), 12 international. Average age 37. 154 applicants, 84% accepted, 91 enrolled. In 2018, 87 master's awarded. *Entrance requirements:* For master's, 3.0 GPA on 4.0 scale, undergraduate degree from a nationally accredited school. Additional exam requirements/recommendations for international students: Required—TOEFL (minimum score 80 iBT); Recommended—IELTS (minimum score 6.5). *Application deadline:* For fall admission, 8/1 for domestic and international students; for spring admission, 12/1 for domestic and international students; for summer admission, 5/1 for domestic and international students. Applications are processed on a rolling basis. Application fee: $50 ($60 for international students). Electronic applications accepted. *Expenses:* Contact institution. *Faculty research:* Orthopedic biomechanics, translational rehabilitation and assistive devices, innovation and entrepreneurship, anthropogenic activities and the natural environment, prestressed and spun concrete. *Application contact:* Jesse Kepply, Director of Student and Academic Services, 205-996-5696, E-mail: gradschool@uab.edu.

University of Alaska Fairbanks, College of Engineering and Mines, Department of Civil and Environmental Engineering, Fairbanks, AK 99775-5900. Offers civil engineering (MS); design and construction management (Graduate Certificate); environmental engineering (PhD). *Program availability:* Part-time. *Faculty:* 6 full-time (1 woman), 1 (woman) part-time/adjunct. *Students:* 8 full-time (2 women), 7 part-time (2 women); includes 4 minority (1 Black or African American, non-Hispanic/Latino; 1 Asian, non-Hispanic/Latino; 2 Two or more races, non-Hispanic/Latino), 2 international. Average age 27. 10 applicants, 30% accepted, 3 enrolled. In 2018, 4 master's awarded. *Degree requirements:* For master's, comprehensive exam, thesis (for some programs), oral defense of project or thesis; for doctorate, comprehensive exam, thesis/dissertation. *Entrance requirements:* For master's, bachelor's degree from accredited institution with minimum cumulative undergraduate and major GPA of 3.0. Additional exam requirements/recommendations for international students: Required—TOEFL (minimum score 550 paper-based; 79 iBT), IELTS (minimum score 6.5). *Application deadline:* For fall admission, 6/1 for domestic students, 3/1 for international students; for spring admission, 10/15 for domestic students, 9/1 for international students. Applications are processed on a rolling basis. Application fee: $60. Electronic applications accepted.

Expenses: CEM tuition has a 20% surcharge per credit hour over that for credits of most other UAF colleges. Assuming 60 credits for PhD and 32 for Master's, this augments costs by $6,180 for in-state PhD, $3,296 for in-state Master's, $12,948 for non-resident PhD and $6,912 for non-resident Masters students, respectively. *Financial support:* In 2018–19, 7 research assistantships with full tuition reimbursements (averaging $4,557 per year), 6 teaching assistantships with full tuition reimbursements (averaging $5,086 per year) were awarded; fellowships with full tuition reimbursements, career-related internships or fieldwork, Federal Work-Study, scholarships/grants, health care benefits, and unspecified assistantships also available. Support available to part-time students. Financial award application deadline: 7/1; financial award applicants required to submit FAFSA. *Faculty research:* Soils, structures, culvert thawing with solar power, pavement drainage, contaminant hydrogeology. *Unit head:* Dr. Robert Perkins, Department Chair, 907-474-7694, E-mail: fycee@uaf.edu. *Application contact:* Samara Taber, Director of Admissions, 907-474-7500, E-mail: uaf-admissions@alaska.edu.
Website: http://cem.uaf.edu/cee

University of Arkansas at Little Rock, Graduate School, George W. Donaghey College of Engineering and Information Technology, Department of Construction Management and Civil and Construction Engineering, Little Rock, AR 72204-1099. Offers construction management (MS).

University of California, Berkeley, UC Berkeley Extension, Certificate Programs in Engineering, Construction and Facilities Management, Berkeley, CA 94720. Offers construction management (Certificate); HVAC (Certificate); integrated circuit design and techniques (online) (Certificate). *Program availability:* Online learning.

University of Denver, Daniels College of Business, Franklin L. Burns School of Real Estate and Construction Management, Denver, CO 80208. Offers real estate and the built environment (MBA, MS). *Program availability:* Part-time, evening/weekend. *Faculty:* 7 full-time (1 woman), 5 part-time/adjunct (0 women). *Students:* 26 full-time (6 women), 50 part-time (16 women); includes 12 minority (1 Black or African American, non-Hispanic/Latino; 7 Hispanic/Latino; 4 Two or more races, non-Hispanic/Latino). Average age 33. 60 applicants, 78% accepted, 25 enrolled. In 2018, 47 master's awarded. *Entrance requirements:* For master's, GRE General Test or GMAT, bachelor's degree, transcripts, essays, resume, interview. Additional exam requirements/recommendations for international students: Required—TOEFL (minimum score 575 paper-based; 94 iBT), TWE. *Application deadline:* For fall admission, 10/15 priority date for domestic and international students; for spring admission, 9/15 priority date for domestic and international students. Applications are processed on a rolling basis. Application fee: $100. Electronic applications accepted. *Expenses:* $49,695 per year full-time; $1,372 per credit. *Financial support:* In 2018–19, 56 students received support. Teaching assistantships with tuition reimbursements available, Federal Work-Study, institutionally sponsored loans, scholarships/grants, and unspecified assistantships available. Support available to part-time students. Financial award application deadline: 2/15; financial award applicants required to submit FAFSA. *Unit head:* Dr. Barbara Jackson, Associate Professor and Director, 303-871-3470, E-mail: barbara.jackson@du.edu. *Application contact:* Ceci Smith, Assistant to the Director, 303-871-2145, E-mail: ceci.smith@du.edu.
Website: https://daniels.du.edu/burns-school/

University of Florida, Graduate School, College of Design, Construction and Planning, Doctoral Program in Design, Construction and Planning, Gainesville, FL 32611. Offers construction management (PhD); design, construction and planning (PhD); geographic information systems (PhD); historic preservation (PhD); interior design (PhD); landscape architecture (PhD); urban and regional planning (PhD). *Degree requirements:* For doctorate, thesis/dissertation. *Entrance requirements:* For doctorate, GRE General Test, minimum GPA of 3.0. Additional exam requirements/recommendations for international students: Required—TOEFL (minimum score 550 paper-based; 80 iBT), IELTS (minimum score 6). Electronic applications accepted. *Faculty research:* Architecture, building construction, urban and regional planning.

University of Florida, Graduate School, College of Design, Construction and Planning, M.E. Rinker, Sr. School of Construction Management, Gainesville, FL 32611. Offers construction management (MSCM); fire and emergency services (MFES); historic preservation (MSCM); international construction (MICM), including historic preservation; sustainable construction (MSCM); sustainable design (MSCM). *Program availability:* Part-time, online learning. *Degree requirements:* For master's, thesis. *Entrance requirements:* For master's, GRE General Test, minimum GPA of 3.0. Additional exam requirements/recommendations for international students: Required—TOEFL (minimum score 550 paper-based; 80 iBT), IELTS (minimum score 6). Electronic applications accepted. *Faculty research:* Safety, affordable housing, construction management, environmental issues, sustainable construction.

University of Houston, College of Technology, Department of Engineering Technology, Houston, TX 77204. Offers construction management (MS); engineering technology (MS); network communications (M Tech). *Program availability:* Part-time. *Degree requirements:* For master's, project or thesis (most programs). *Entrance requirements:* For master's, GRE. Additional exam requirements/recommendations for international students: Required—TOEFL (minimum score 550 paper-based; 79 iBT). Electronic applications accepted.

The University of Kansas, Graduate Studies, School of Engineering, Program in Construction Management, Lawrence, KS 66045. Offers MCM. *Program availability:* Part-time, evening/weekend. *Students:* 6 full-time (2 women), 6 part-time (0 women); includes 1 minority (Asian, non-Hispanic/Latino), 6 international. Average age 28. 21 applicants, 38% accepted, 2 enrolled. In 2018, 10 master's awarded. *Entrance requirements:* For master's, GRE, two letters of recommendation, statement of purpose, resume. Additional exam requirements/recommendations for international students: Required—TOEFL, IELTS. *Application deadline:* For fall admission, 7/31 for domestic students, 5/15 for international students; for spring admission, 12/30 for domestic students, 10/15 for international students; for summer admission, 5/15 for domestic students. Application fee: $65 ($85 for international students). Electronic applications accepted. *Financial support:* Career-related internships or fieldwork available. Financial award application deadline: 2/7. *Faculty research:* Construction engineering, construction management. *Unit head:* David Darwin, Chair, 785-864-3827, Fax: 785-864-5631, E-mail: daved@ku.edu. *Application contact:* Susan Scott, Administrative Assistant, 785-864-3826, E-mail: s523s307@ku.edu.
Website: http://ceae.ku.edu/overview-6

University of New Mexico, Graduate Studies, School of Engineering, Program in Civil Engineering, Albuquerque, NM 87131-0001. Offers civil engineering (M Eng, MSCE); construction management (MCM); engineering (PhD). *Program availability:* Part-time. Terminal master's awarded for partial completion of doctoral program. *Degree requirements:* For master's, comprehensive exam, thesis (for some programs); for doctorate, comprehensive exam, thesis/dissertation. *Entrance requirements:* For master's, GRE General Test (for MSCE and M Eng); GRE or GMAT (for MCM), minimum GPA of 3.0; for doctorate, GRE General Test, minimum GPA of 3.0. Additional exam requirements/recommendations for international students: Required—TOEFL (minimum score 550 paper-based; 80 iBT), IELTS (minimum score 6.5). Electronic applications accepted. *Faculty research:* Integrating design and construction, project delivery methods, sustainable design and construction, leadership and management in construction, project management and project supervision, production management and improvement.

University of New Mexico, Graduate Studies, School of Engineering, Program in Construction Management, Albuquerque, NM 87131. Offers MCM. *Program availability:* Part-time. *Degree requirements:* For master's, comprehensive exam, thesis optional. *Entrance requirements:* For master's, GMAT (minimum score 500) or GRE (minimum score 294 combined verbal and quantitative), minimum GPA of 3.0; courses in statistics, elements of calculus, engineering economy, and construction contracting. Additional exam requirements/recommendations for international students: Required—TOEFL (minimum score 550 paper-based; 80 iBT), IELTS (minimum score 6.5). Electronic applications accepted. *Faculty research:* Applied industry research and training, integration of the design/construction continuum, leadership in project management, life-cycle costing, production management and productivity management, project delivery methods, sustainable asset management, sustainable design and construction.

The University of North Carolina at Charlotte, William States Lee College of Engineering, Department of Engineering Technology and Construction Management, Charlotte, NC 28223-0001. Offers applied energy (Graduate Certificate); applied energy and electromechanical systems (MS); construction and facilities management (MS); fire protection and administration (MS). *Program availability:* Part-time. *Students:* 54 full-time (17 women), 17 part-time (3 women); includes 9 minority (3 Black or African American, non-Hispanic/Latino; 2 Asian, non-Hispanic/Latino; 3 Hispanic/Latino; 1 Two or more races, non-Hispanic/Latino), 40 international. Average age 26. 97 applicants, 81% accepted, 22 enrolled. In 2018, 31 master's awarded. *Entrance requirements:* For master's, GRE, minimum undergraduate GPA of 3.0, recommendations, statistics; integral and differential calculus (for students pursuing fire protection concentration or applied energy and electromechanical systems program); for Graduate Certificate, bachelor's degree in engineering, engineering technology, construction management or a closely-related technical or scientific field; undergraduate coursework of at least 3 semesters in engineering analysis or calculus; minimum GPA of 3.0. Additional exam requirements/recommendations for international students: Required—TOEFL (minimum score 523 paper-based; 70 iBT), IELTS (minimum score 6), TOEFL (minimum score 523 paper-based, 70 iBT) or IELTS (6). *Application deadline:* Applications are processed on a rolling basis. Application fee: $75. Electronic applications accepted. *Expenses:* Contact institution. *Financial support:* Research assistantships, career-related internships or fieldwork, institutionally sponsored loans, scholarships/grants, and unspecified assistantships available. Support available to part-time students. Financial award application deadline: 3/1; financial award applicants required to submit FAFSA. *Total annual research expenditures:* $1.7 million. *Unit head:* Dr. Anthony Brizendine, Chair, 704-687-5050, E-mail: albrizen@uncc.edu. *Application contact:* Kathy B. Giddings, Director of Graduate Admissions, 704-687-5503, Fax: 704-687-1668, E-mail: gradadm@uncc.edu.
Website: http://et.uncc.edu/

University of North Florida, Coggin College of Business, MBA Program, Jacksonville, FL 32224. Offers accounting (MBA); construction management (MBA); e-commerce (MBA); economics (MBA); finance (MBA); human resource management (MBA); international business (MBA); logistics (MBA); management applications (MBA). *Accreditation:* AACSB. *Program availability:* Part-time, evening/weekend. *Faculty:* 40 full-time (14 women). *Students:* 368 part-time (158 women); includes 83 minority (30 Black or African American, non-Hispanic/Latino; 20 Asian, non-Hispanic/Latino; 16 Hispanic/Latino; 17 Two or more races, non-Hispanic/Latino), 28 international. Average age 30. 311 applicants, 51% accepted, 99 enrolled. In 2018, 151 master's awarded. *Entrance requirements:* For master's, GMAT or GRE, U.S. bachelor's degree from regionally-accredited university or equivalent foreign degree. Additional exam requirements/recommendations for international students: Required—TOEFL (minimum score 550 paper-based; 79 iBT). *Application deadline:* For fall admission, 8/1 priority date for domestic students, 5/1 for international students; for spring admission, 12/1 priority date for domestic students, 10/1 for international students; for summer admission, 4/29 priority date for domestic students, 2/1 for international students. Application fee: $30. *Expenses: Tuition, area resident:* Part-time $408.10 per credit hour. Tuition, state resident: part-time $408.10 per credit hour. Tuition, nonresident: part-time $932.61 per credit hour. *Required fees:* $111.81 per credit hour. Tuition and fees vary according to course load, campus/location and program. *Financial support:* In 2018–19, 41 students received support, including 1 research assistantship (averaging $2,143 per year); teaching assistantships, Federal Work-Study, and tuition waivers (partial) also available. Support available to part-time students. Financial award application deadline: 4/1; financial award applicants required to submit FAFSA. *Faculty research:* Performance measures, costing, and inventory issues in logistics and supply chain management; inter-organizational systems; international management and marketing practices; e-commerce; organizational learning and socialization processes. *Unit head:* Dr. Parvez Ahmed, Graduate Program Director, 904-620-1678, E-mail: pahmed@unf.edu. *Application contact:* Amy Bishop, MSM Advisor, 904-620-2575, Fax: 904-620-2832, E-mail: coggin.students@unf.edu.
Website: http://www.unf.edu/graduateschool/academics/programs/MBA.aspx

University of Southern California, Graduate School, Viterbi School of Engineering, Sonny Astani Department of Civil and Environmental Engineering, Los Angeles, CA 90089. Offers applied mechanics (MS); civil engineering (MS, PhD); computer-aided engineering (ME, Graduate Certificate); construction management (MCM); engineering technology commercialization (Graduate Certificate); environmental engineering (MS, PhD); environmental quality management (ME); structural design (ME); sustainable cities (Graduate Certificate); transportation systems (MS, Graduate Certificate); water

and waste management (MS). *Program availability:* Part-time, evening/weekend. Terminal master's awarded for partial completion of doctoral program. *Degree requirements:* For master's, thesis optional; for doctorate, thesis/dissertation. *Entrance requirements:* For master's and doctorate, GRE General Test. Additional exam requirements/recommendations for international students: Recommended—TOEFL. Electronic applications accepted. *Faculty research:* Geotechnical engineering, transportation engineering, structural engineering, construction management, environmental engineering, water resources.

The University of Tennessee at Chattanooga, Engineering Management and Technology Program, Chattanooga, TN 37403. Offers construction management (Graduate Certificate); engineering management (MS); fundamentals of engineering management (Graduate Certificate); leadership and ethics (Graduate Certificate); logistics and supply chain management (Graduate Certificate); power systems management (Graduate Certificate); project and technology management (Graduate Certificate); quality management (Graduate Certificate). *Program availability:* 100% online, blended/hybrid learning. *Degree requirements:* For master's, thesis. *Entrance requirements:* For master's, GRE General Test, letters of recommendation; minimum undergraduate GPA of 2.7 overall or 3.0 in final two years; for Graduate Certificate, baccalaureate degree and professional experience or have already been admitted to engineering/engineering management graduate program. Additional exam requirements/recommendations for international students: Required—TOEFL (minimum score 550 paper-based; 79 iBT), IELTS (minimum score 6). Electronic applications accepted. *Expenses:* Contact institution. *Faculty research:* Plant layout design, lean manufacturing, Six Sigma, value management, product development.

The University of Texas at Arlington, Graduate School, College of Engineering, Department of Civil Engineering, Arlington, TX 76019. Offers civil engineering (M Engr, MS, PhD); construction management (MCM). *Program availability:* Part-time, evening/weekend, online learning. Terminal master's awarded for partial completion of doctoral program. *Degree requirements:* For master's, comprehensive exam, thesis (for some programs), oral and written exams; for doctorate, comprehensive exam, thesis/dissertation, oral and written defense of dissertation. *Entrance requirements:* For master's, GRE General Test, minimum GPA of 3.0 in last 60 hours of undergraduate course work; for doctorate, GRE General Test, minimum GPA of 3.5. Additional exam requirements/recommendations for international students: Required—TOEFL. Electronic applications accepted. *Faculty research:* Environmental and water resources structures, geotechnical, transportation.

The University of Texas at El Paso, Graduate School, College of Engineering, Department of Civil Engineering, El Paso, TX 79968-0001. Offers civil engineering (MS, PhD); construction management (MS, Certificate); environmental engineering (MEENE, MSENE). *Program availability:* Part-time, evening/weekend. *Degree requirements:* For master's, comprehensive exam, thesis optional; for doctorate, comprehensive exam, thesis/dissertation. *Entrance requirements:* For master's, GRE, minimum GPA of 3.0; for doctorate, GRE. Additional exam requirements/recommendations for international students: Required—TOEFL. Electronic applications accepted. *Faculty research:* Non-destructive testing for geotechnical and pavement applications, transportation systems, wastewater treatment systems, air quality, linear and non-linear modeling of structures, structural reliability.

University of Washington, Graduate School, College of Built Environments, Department of Construction Management, Seattle, WA 98195. Offers MSCM. *Program availability:* Part-time, evening/weekend. *Degree requirements:* For master's, thesis or alternative. *Entrance requirements:* For master's, GRE General Test, minimum GPA of 3.0. Additional exam requirements/recommendations for international students: Required—TOEFL. Electronic applications accepted. *Faculty research:* Business practices, delivery methods, materials, productivity.

University of Wisconsin–Stout, Graduate School, College of Science, Technology, Engineering and Mathematics, Program in Construction Management, Menomonie, WI 54751. Offers MS. *Entrance requirements:* For master's, bachelor's degree in construction or a construction-related field from accredited institution, minimum GPA of 3.0, resume.

Wentworth Institute of Technology, Master of Science in Construction Management Program, Boston, MA 02115-5998. Offers MS. *Program availability:* Part-time-only, evening/weekend, 100% online, blended/hybrid learning. *Degree requirements:* For master's, thesis optional, capstone. *Entrance requirements:* For master's, two recommendations from employer; current resume; bachelor's degree in construction management or bachelor's degree with competencies in construction and statement of purpose; minimum GPA of 3.0. Additional exam requirements/recommendations for international students: Recommended—TOEFL (minimum score 550 paper-based). Electronic applications accepted. *Expenses:* Contact institution.

Western Carolina University, Graduate School, College of Engineering and Technology, Kimmel School of Construction Management, Cullowhee, NC 28723. Offers MCM. *Program availability:* Part-time, evening/weekend, online learning. *Entrance requirements:* For master's, GRE or GMAT, appropriate undergraduate degree, resume, letters of recommendation, work experience. Additional exam requirements/recommendations for international students: Required—TOEFL (minimum score 550 paper-based; 79 iBT). *Expenses: Tuition, area resident:* Full-time $4435. Tuition, state resident: full-time $4435. Tuition, nonresident: full-time $14,842. *International tuition:* $14,842 full-time. *Required fees:* $2979. Part-time tuition and fees vary according to course load, degree level and program. *Faculty research:* Hazardous waste management, energy management and conservation, engineering materials, refrigeration and air conditioning systems.

Energy Management and Policy

American College Dublin, Graduate Programs, Dublin, Ireland. Offers business administration (MBA); creative writing (MFA); international business (MBA); oil and gas management (MBA); performance (MFA).

American University of Armenia, Graduate Programs, Yerevan, Armenia. Offers business administration (MBA); computer and information science (MS), including business management, design and manufacturing, energy (ME, MS), industrial engineering and systems management; economics (MS); industrial engineering and systems management (ME), including business, computer aided design/manufacturing, energy (ME, MS), information technology; law (LL M); political science and international affairs (MPSIA); public health (MPH); teaching English as a foreign language (MA). *Program availability:* Part-time, evening/weekend. *Degree requirements:* For master's, thesis (for some programs), capstone/project. *Entrance requirements:* For master's, GRE, GMAT, or LSAT. Additional exam requirements/recommendations for international students: Recommended—TOEFL (minimum score 79 iBT), IELTS (minimum score

6.5). *Faculty research:* Microfinance, finance (rural/development, international, corporate), firm life cycle theory, TESOL, language proficiency testing, public policy, administrative law, economic development, cryptography, artificial intelligence, energy efficiency/renewable energy, computer-aided design/manufacturing, health financing, tuberculosis control, mother/child health, preventive ophthalmology, post-earthquake psychopathological investigations, tobacco control, environmental health risk assessments.

Boston University, Graduate School of Arts and Sciences, Department of Earth and Environment, Boston, MA 02215. Offers earth and environment (MA, PhD); energy and environment (MA); remote sensing and geospatial sciences (MA). *Students:* 73 full-time (41 women), 5 part-time (3 women); includes 7 minority (3 Asian, non-Hispanic/Latino; 4 Hispanic/Latino), 38 international. Average age 25. 195 applicants, 53% accepted, 31 enrolled. In 2018, 30 master's, 4 doctorates awarded. Terminal master's awarded for partial completion of doctoral program. *Degree requirements:* For master's,

comprehensive exam (for some programs), thesis (for some programs); for doctorate, comprehensive exam, thesis/dissertation. *Entrance requirements:* For master's and doctorate, GRE General Test, 3 letters of recommendation, official transcripts, personal statement. Additional exam requirements/recommendations for international students: Required—TOEFL (minimum score 550 paper-based; 84 iBT). *Application deadline:* For fall admission, 12/19 for domestic and international students; for winter admission, 11/1 for domestic and international students. Application fee: $95. Electronic applications accepted. *Financial support:* In 2018–19, 50 students received support, including 4 fellowships with full tuition reimbursements available (averaging $22,660 per year), 24 research assistantships with full tuition reimbursements available (averaging $22,660 per year), 12 teaching assistantships with full tuition reimbursements available (averaging $22,660 per year); Federal Work-Study, scholarships/grants, traineeships, and health care benefits also available. Financial award application deadline: 12/19. *Faculty research:* Biogeosciences, climate and surface processes; energy, environment and society; geographical sciences; geology, geochemistry and geophysics. *Unit head:* Guido Salvucci, Interim Chair, 617-353-8344, E-mail: gdsalvuc@bu.edu. *Application contact:* Matt DiCintio, Graduate Program Coordinator, 617-353-2529, Fax: 617-353-8399, E-mail: dicintio@bu.edu.
Website: http://www.bu.edu/earth/

Clarkson University, Wallace H. Coulter School of Engineering, Master's Program in the Business of Energy, Schenectady, NY 13699. Offers MS, Advanced Certificate. *Program availability:* Part-time, evening/weekend. *Students:* 3 full-time (0 women), 7 part-time (3 women). 8 applicants, 88% accepted, 7 enrolled. In 2018, 2 master's, 4 other advanced degrees awarded. *Entrance requirements:* Additional exam requirements/recommendations for international students: Required—TOEFL (minimum score 550 paper-based, 80 iBT) or IELTS (6.5). *Application deadline:* Applications are processed on a rolling basis. Application fee: $50. Electronic applications accepted. *Expenses: Tuition:* Full-time $24,984; part-time $1388 per credit hour. *Required fees:* $225. Tuition and fees vary according to campus/location and program. *Financial support:* Scholarships/grants available. *Unit head:* Hugo Irizarry-Quinones, Associate Dean of Engineering, 518-631-9881, E-mail: hirizarr@clarkson.edu. *Application contact:* Dan Capogna, Director of Graduate Admissions & Recruitment, 518-631-9910, E-mail: graduate@clarkson.edu.
Website: https://www.clarkson.edu/academics/graduate

Colorado School of Mines, Office of Graduate Studies, Department of Economics and Business, Golden, CO 80401. Offers engineering and technology management (MS); mineral and energy economics (MS, PhD); operations research and engineering (PhD); petroleum economics and management with mineral and energy economics (MS). *Program availability:* Part-time. *Faculty:* 17 full-time (5 women), 4 part-time/adjunct (1 woman). *Students:* 92 full-time (27 women), 12 part-time (4 women); includes 20 minority (4 Black or African American, non-Hispanic/Latino; 4 Asian, non-Hispanic/Latino; 8 Hispanic/Latino; 1 Native Hawaiian or other Pacific Islander, non-Hispanic/Latino; 3 Two or more races, non-Hispanic/Latino), 33 international. Average age 28. 154 applicants, 82% accepted, 53 enrolled. In 2018, 68 master's, 4 doctorates awarded. *Degree requirements:* For master's, thesis (for some programs); for doctorate, comprehensive exam, thesis/dissertation. *Entrance requirements:* For master's and doctorate, GRE General Test. Additional exam requirements/recommendations for international students: Required—TOEFL (minimum score 550 paper-based; 79 iBT). *Application deadline:* For fall admission, 12/15 priority date for domestic and international students; for spring admission, 9/1 priority date for domestic and international students. Application fee: $60 ($80 for international students). Electronic applications accepted. *Expenses:* Tuition, state resident: full-time $16,650; part-time $925 per contact hour. Tuition, nonresident: full-time $36,270; part-time $2015 per contact hour. International tuition: $36,270 full-time. *Required fees:* $2314; $2314 per semester. *Financial support:* In 2018–19, 7 research assistantships with full tuition reimbursements, 22 teaching assistantships with full tuition reimbursements were awarded; fellowships, scholarships/grants, health care benefits, and unspecified assistantships also available. Financial award application deadline: 12/15; financial award applicants required to submit FAFSA. *Faculty research:* International trade, resource and environmental economics, energy economics, operations research. *Unit head:* Dr. Roderick Eggert, Interim Director, 303-273-3981, E-mail: reggert@mines.edu. *Application contact:* Kathleen Martin, Program Assistant, 303-273-3482, Fax: 303-273-3416, E-mail: kmartin@mines.edu.
Website: http://econbus.mines.edu

Colorado State University, Warner College of Natural Resources, Department of Ecosystem Science and Sustainability, Fort Collins, CO 80523-1476. Offers greenhouse gas management and accounting (MGMA); watershed science (MS). *Degree requirements:* For master's, thesis (for some programs). *Entrance requirements:* For master's, GRE (70th percentile or higher), minimum GPA of 3.0; resume; transcript; letters of recommendation; statement of purpose; undergraduate degree in a related field. Additional exam requirements/recommendations for international students: Required—TOEFL (minimum score 550 paper-based; 80 iBT), IELTS (minimum score 6.5). Electronic applications accepted. *Expenses:* Contact institution. *Faculty research:* Animal-habitat relationships; pastoral ecology and simulation; solving applied problems in ecosystem science and sustainable ecosystem management; intersections and boundaries of human activities, physical processes, and ecosystems; theoretical and applied ecology.

Duke University, The Fuqua School of Business, The Duke MBA-Daytime Program, Durham, NC 27708. Offers academic excellence in finance (Certificate); business administration (MBA); decision sciences (MBA); energy and environment (MBA); energy finance (MBA); entrepreneurship and innovation (MBA); finance (MBA); financial analysis (MBA); health sector management (Certificate); leadership and ethics (MBA); management (MBA); management science and technology management (Certificate); marketing (MBA); operations management (MBA); social entrepreneurship (MBA); strategy (MBA). *Faculty:* 100 full-time (21 women), 55 part-time/adjunct (12 women). *Students:* 875 full-time (335 women); includes 188 minority (44 Black or African American, non-Hispanic/Latino; 4 American Indian or Alaska Native, non-Hispanic/Latino; 90 Asian, non-Hispanic/Latino; 43 Hispanic/Latino; 1 Native Hawaiian or other Pacific Islander, non-Hispanic/Latino; 6 Two or more races, non-Hispanic/Latino), 276 international. Average age 29. In 2018, 429 master's awarded. *Entrance requirements:* For master's, GMAT or GRE, transcripts, essays, resume, recommendation letters, interview. *Application deadline:* For fall admission, 9/19 for domestic and international students; for winter admission, 10/14 for domestic and international students; for spring admission, 1/6 for domestic and international students; for summer admission, 3/11 for domestic and international students. Application fee: $225. Electronic applications accepted. *Expenses:* Contact institution. *Financial support:* Scholarships/grants available. Financial award applicants required to submit FAFSA. *Unit head:* Steve Misuraca, Assistant Dean, Daytime MBA Program. *Application contact:* Shari Hubert, Associate Dean, Office of Admissions, 919-660-7705, Fax: 919-681-8026, E-mail: admissions-info@fuqua.duke.edu.
Website: https://www.fuqua.duke.edu/programs/daytime-mba

Duke University, The Fuqua School of Business, The Duke MBA-Global Executive Program, Durham, NC 27708. Offers business administration (MBA); energy and environment (MBA); entrepreneurship and innovation (MBA); finance (MBA); health sector management (Certificate); marketing (MBA); strategy (MBA). *Faculty:* 100 full-time (21 women), 55 part-time/adjunct (12 women). *Students:* 141 full-time (43 women); includes 43 minority (12 Black or African American, non-Hispanic/Latino; 25 Asian, non-Hispanic/Latino; 4 Hispanic/Latino; 1 Native Hawaiian or other Pacific Islander, non-Hispanic/Latino; 1 Two or more races, non-Hispanic/Latino), 34 international. Average age 35. In 2018, 159 master's awarded. *Entrance requirements:* For master's, Executive Assessment, GMAT, or GRE, or waived, transcripts, essays, resume, recommendation letters, letter of company support, interview. *Application deadline:* For fall admission, 10/16 priority date for domestic and international students; for winter admission, 12/4 priority date for domestic and international students; for spring admission, 3/11 priority date for domestic and international students; for summer admission, 5/27 for domestic and international students. Applications are processed on a rolling basis. Application fee: $225. Electronic applications accepted. *Expenses:* Contact institution. *Financial support:* Scholarships/grants available. Financial award applicants required to submit FAFSA. *Unit head:* Karen Courtney, Associate Dean, Executive Programs. *Application contact:* Shari Hubert, Associate Dean, Office of Admissions, 919-660-7705, Fax: 919-681-8026, E-mail: admissions-info@fuqua.duke.edu.
Website: https://www.fuqua.duke.edu/programs/global-executive-mba

Duke University, The Fuqua School of Business, The Duke MBA-Weekend Executive Program, Durham, NC 27708. Offers business administration (MBA); energy and environment (MBA); entrepreneurship and innovation (MBA); finance (MBA); health sector management (Certificate); marketing (MBA); strategy (MBA). *Faculty:* 100 full-time (21 women), 55 part-time/adjunct (12 women). *Students:* 251 full-time (67 women); includes 79 minority (13 Black or African American, non-Hispanic/Latino; 2 American Indian or Alaska Native, non-Hispanic/Latino; 46 Asian, non-Hispanic/Latino; 12 Hispanic/Latino; 1 Native Hawaiian or other Pacific Islander, non-Hispanic/Latino; 5 Two or more races, non-Hispanic/Latino), 32 international. Average age 35. In 2018, 120 master's awarded. *Entrance requirements:* For master's, Executive Assessment, GMAT, or GRE, or waived, transcripts, essays, resume, recommendation letters, letter of company support, interview. *Application deadline:* For fall admission, 9/18 priority date for domestic and international students; for winter admission, 12/4 priority date for domestic and international students; for spring admission, 1/22 priority date for domestic and international students; for summer admission, 3/11 for domestic and international students. Applications are processed on a rolling basis. Application fee: $225. Electronic applications accepted. *Expenses:* Contact institution. *Financial support:* Scholarships/grants available. Financial award applicants required to submit FAFSA. *Unit head:* Karen Courtney, Associate Dean, Executive Programs. *Application contact:* Shari Hubert, Associate Dean, Office of Admissions, 919-660-7705, Fax: 919-681-8026, E-mail: admissions-info@fuqua.duke.edu.
Website: https://www.fuqua.duke.edu/programs/weekend-executive-mba

Eastern Illinois University, Graduate School, Lumpkin College of Business and Technology, School of Technology, Program in Sustainable Energy, Charleston, IL 61920. Offers MS, MS/MBA, MS/MS. *Program availability:* Part-time, evening/weekend. *Degree requirements:* For master's, comprehensive exam. *Entrance requirements:* For master's, GMAT or GRE. Additional exam requirements/recommendations for international students: Required—TOEFL (minimum score 500 paper-based; 61 iBT), IELTS (minimum score 6). Electronic applications accepted. *Expenses:* Tuition, state resident: part-time $299 per credit hour. Tuition, nonresident: part-time $718 per credit hour. *Required fees:* $214.50 per credit hour.

Franklin Pierce University, Graduate and Professional Studies, Rindge, NH 03461-0060. Offers curriculum and instruction (M Ed); elementary education (MS Ed); emerging network technologies (Graduate Certificate); energy and sustainability studies (MBA, Graduate Certificate); health administration (MBA, Graduate Certificate); human resource management (MBA, Graduate Certificate); information technology (MBA); leadership (MBA); nursing education (MS); nursing leadership (MS); physical therapy (DPT); physician assistant studies (MPAS); special education (M Ed); sports management (MBA). *Accreditation:* APTA. *Program availability:* Part-time, 100% online, blended/hybrid learning. *Degree requirements:* For master's, concentrated original research projects; student teaching; fieldwork and/or internship; leadership project; PRAXIS I and II (for M Ed); for doctorate, concentrated original research projects, clinical fieldwork and/or internship, leadership project. *Entrance requirements:* For master's, minimum GPA of 2.5, 3 letters of recommendation; competencies in accounting, economics, statistics, and computer skills through life experience or undergraduate coursework (for MBA); certification/e-portfolio, minimum C grade in all education courses (for M Ed); license to practice as RN (for MS); for doctorate, GRE, 80 hours of observation/work in PT settings; completion of anatomy, chemistry, physics, and statistics; minimum GPA of 3.0. Additional exam requirements/recommendations for international students: Required—TOEFL (minimum score 550 paper-based; 61 iBT). Electronic applications accepted. *Faculty research:* Evidence-based practice in sports physical therapy, human resource management in economic crisis, leadership in nursing, innovation in sports facility management, differentiated learning and understanding by design.

Indiana University Bloomington, School of Public and Environmental Affairs, Environmental Science Programs, Bloomington, IN 47405. Offers applied ecology (MSES); energy (MSES); environmental chemistry, toxicology, and risk assessment (MSES); environmental science (PhD); hazardous materials management (Certificate); specialized environmental science (MSES); water resources (MSES); JD/MSES; MSES/MA; MSES/MPA; MSES/MS. *Program availability:* Part-time. Terminal master's awarded for partial completion of doctoral program. *Degree requirements:* For master's, capstone or thesis; internship; for doctorate, comprehensive exam, thesis/dissertation. *Entrance requirements:* For master's, GRE General Test or GMAT, official transcripts, 3 letters of recommendation, resume, personal statement; for doctorate, GRE General Test or LSAT, official transcripts, 3 letters of recommendation, resume or curriculum vitae, statement of purpose. Additional exam requirements/recommendations for international students: Required—TOEFL (minimum score 600 paper-based; 96 iBT); Recommended—IELTS (minimum score 7). Electronic applications accepted. *Faculty research:* Applied ecology, bio-geochemistry, toxicology, wetlands ecology, environmental microbiology, forest ecology, environmental chemistry.

Indiana University Bloomington, School of Public and Environmental Affairs, Public Affairs Programs, Bloomington, IN 47405. Offers economic development (MPA); energy (MPA); environmental policy (PhD); environmental policy and natural resource management (MPA); information systems (MPA); international development (MPA); local government management (MPA); nonprofit management (MPA, Certificate); policy analysis (MPA); public budgeting and financial management (Certificate); public finance (PhD); public financial administration (MPA); public management (MPA, PhD, Certificate); public policy analysis (PhD); social entrepreneurship (Certificate); specialized public affairs (MPA); sustainability and sustainable development (MPA); JD/MPA; MPA/MA; MPA/MIS; MPA/MLS; MSES/MPA. *Accreditation:* NASPAA (one or more programs are accredited). *Program availability:* Part-time. *Degree requirements:* For master's, capstone, internship; for doctorate, comprehensive exam, thesis/dissertation. *Entrance requirements:* For master's, GRE General Test or GMAT, official transcripts, 3 letters of recommendation, resume, personal statement; for doctorate,

GRE General Test, official transcripts, 3 letters of recommendation, statement of purpose. Additional exam requirements/recommendations for international students: Required—TOEFL (minimum score 600 paper-based; 96 iBT); Recommended—IELTS (minimum score 7). Electronic applications accepted. *Faculty research:* International development, environmental policy and resource management, policy analysis, public finance, public management, urban management, nonprofit management, energy policy, social policy, public finance.

Instituto Tecnologico de Santo Domingo, Graduate School, Area of Basic And Environmental Sciences, Santo Domingo, Dominican Republic. Offers environmental science (M En S), including environmental education, environmental management, marine resources, natural resources management; mathematics (MS, PhD); renewable energy technology (MS, Certificate).

Johns Hopkins University, Advanced Academic Programs, Program in Environmental Sciences and Policy, Washington, DC 21218. Offers energy policy and climate (MS); environmental sciences (MS); geographic information systems (MS, Certificate). *Program availability:* Part-time, evening/weekend, online learning. *Students:* 13 full-time (11 women), 192 part-time (148 women). 81 applicants, 78% accepted, 36 enrolled. In 2018, 66 master's awarded. *Entrance requirements:* For master's, minimum GPA of 3.0, coursework in chemistry and calculus. Additional exam requirements/recommendations for international students: Required—TOEFL (minimum score 100 iBT). *Application deadline:* For fall admission, 5/31 priority date for domestic students, 4/30 priority date for international students; for spring admission, 10/31 priority date for domestic and international students. Applications are processed on a rolling basis. Application fee: $75. Electronic applications accepted. *Financial support:* Applicants required to submit FAFSA. *Unit head:* Dr. Jerry Burgess, Program Director, 202-452-1915, E-mail: jerry.burgess@jhu.edu. *Application contact:* Melissa Edwards, Admissions Manager, 202-452-1941, Fax: 202-452-1970, E-mail: aapadmissions@jhu.edu.
Website: http://advanced.jhu.edu/academics/graduate-degree-programs/environmental-sciences-and-policy/

Kansas State University, Graduate School, College of Engineering, Department of Electrical and Computer Engineering, Manhattan, KS 66506. Offers electrical engineering (MS), including bioengineering, communication systems, design of computer systems, electrical engineering, energy and power systems, integrated circuits and devices, real time embedded systems, renewable energy, signal processing. *Program availability:* Part-time, evening/weekend, online learning. *Degree requirements:* For master's, thesis or alternative, final exam; for doctorate, thesis/dissertation, final exam, preliminary exams. *Entrance requirements:* For master's, GRE General Test, bachelor's degree in electrical engineering or computer science, minimum GPA of 3.0; for doctorate, GRE General Test. Additional exam requirements/recommendations for international students: Required—TOEFL (minimum score 600 paper-based; 85 iBT). Electronic applications accepted. *Faculty research:* Energy systems and renewable energy, computer systems and real time embedded systems, communication systems and signal processing, integrated circuits and devices, bioengineering.

New York Institute of Technology, College of Engineering and Computing Sciences, Department of Energy Management, Old Westbury, NY 11568-8000. Offers energy technology (Advanced Certificate); environmental management (Advanced Certificate); facilities management (Advanced Certificate); infrastructure security management (Advanced Certificate). *Program availability:* Part-time, evening/weekend, 100% online, blended/hybrid learning. *Faculty:* 2 full-time (0 women), 6 part-time/adjunct (1 woman). *Students:* 30 full-time (4 women), 46 part-time (11 women); includes 27 minority (7 Black or African American, non-Hispanic/Latino; 10 Asian, non-Hispanic/Latino; 9 Hispanic/Latino; 1 Two or more races, non-Hispanic/Latino), 22 international. Average age 32. 96 applicants, 75% accepted, 24 enrolled. In 2018, 3 Advanced Certificates awarded. *Entrance requirements:* For degree, BS or equivalent; minimum undergraduate GPA of 2.85. Additional exam requirements/recommendations for international students: Required—TOEFL (minimum score 79 iBT), IELTS (minimum score 6), PTE (minimum score 53). *Application deadline:* For fall admission, 7/1 for domestic students, 6/1 for international students; for spring admission, 12/1 for domestic and international students. Applications are processed on a rolling basis. Application fee: $50. Electronic applications accepted. *Expenses: Tuition:* Full-time $1285; part-time $1285 per credit. *Required fees:* $215; $175 per unit. Tuition and fees vary according to course load, degree level and campus/location. *Financial support:* Fellowships with partial tuition reimbursements, teaching assistantships with partial tuition reimbursements, career-related internships or fieldwork, Federal Work-Study, scholarships/grants, tuition waivers (full and partial), and unspecified assistantships available. Support available to part-time students. Financial award application deadline: 2/15; financial award applicants required to submit FAFSA. *Faculty research:* Alternative energy systems; energy policy, master planning, and auditing; facilities management; lighting technology; cogeneration; utility rate structures; smart homes; monitoring systems; building information modeling; sustainability. *Unit head:* Dr. Robert Amundsen, Department Chair, 516-686-7578, E-mail: ramundse@nyit.edu. *Application contact:* Alice Dolitsky, Director, Graduate Admissions, 516-686-7520, Fax: 516-686-1116, E-mail: admissions@nyit.edu.
Website: http://www.nyit.edu/engineering/department_of_energy_management

Norwich University, College of Graduate and Continuing Studies, Master of Business Administration Program, Northfield, VT 05663. Offers construction management (MBA); energy management (MBA); finance (MBA); logistics (MBA); organizational leadership (MBA); project management (MBA); supply chain management (MBA). *Accreditation:* ACBSP. *Program availability:* Evening/weekend, online only, mostly all online with a week-long residency requirement. *Degree requirements:* For master's, comprehensive exam. *Entrance requirements:* For master's, minimum undergraduate GPA of 2.75. Additional exam requirements/recommendations for international students: Required—TOEFL (minimum score 550 paper-based; 80 iBT), IELTS (minimum score 6.5). Electronic applications accepted. *Expenses:* Contact institution.

Oklahoma Baptist University, Master of Business Administration in Transformational Leadership, Shawnee, OK 74804. Offers energy management (MBA); transformational leadership (MBA). *Accreditation:* ACBSP. *Program availability:* Part-time, evening/weekend, 100% online, blended/hybrid learning. *Students:* 18 full-time (8 women), 33 part-time (15 women); includes 14 minority (1 Black or African American, non-Hispanic/Latino; 11 American Indian or Alaska Native, non-Hispanic/Latino; 1 Hispanic/Latino; 1 Two or more races, non-Hispanic/Latino), 5 international. Average age 32. *Degree requirements:* For master's, comprehensive exam. *Entrance requirements:* Additional exam requirements/recommendations for international students: Recommended—TOEFL, IELTS. *Application deadline:* Applications are processed on a rolling basis. Application fee: $0. Electronic applications accepted. *Expenses: Tuition:* Full-time $9900; part-time $6600 per credit hour. *Financial support:* Applicants required to submit FAFSA. *Unit head:* Will Brantley, Director of Recruitment, 405-5854607, Fax: 405-5854646, E-mail: will.brantley@okbu.edu. *Application contact:* Will Brantley, Director of Recruitment, 405-5854607, Fax: 405-5854646, E-mail: will.brantley@okbu.edu.
Website: http://www.okbu.edu/graduate/mba/

Oklahoma City University, Meinders School of Business, Oklahoma City, OK 73106-1402. Offers business (MBA, MSA); computer science (MS); energy legal studies (MS); energy management (MS); JD/MBA. *Program availability:* Part-time, evening/weekend, 100% online. *Degree requirements:* For master's, practicum/capstone. *Entrance requirements:* For master's, undergraduate degree from accredited institution, minimum GPA of 3.0, essay, letters of recommendation. Additional exam requirements/recommendations for international students: Required—TOEFL (minimum score 550 paper-based; 80 iBT). Electronic applications accepted. *Expenses:* Contact institution. *Faculty research:* Group support systems, leadership, decision models in accounting.

Portland State University, Graduate Studies, College of Urban and Public Affairs, Hatfield School of Government, Department of Public Administration, Portland, OR 97207-0751. Offers collaborative governance (Certificate); energy policy and management (Certificate); global management and leadership (MPA); health administration (MPA); human resource management (MPA); local government (MPA); natural resource policy and administration (MPA); nonprofit and public management (Certificate); nonprofit management (MPA); public administration (EMPA); public affairs and policy (PhD); sustainable food systems (Certificate). *Accreditation:* CAHME; NASPAA (one or more programs are accredited). *Program availability:* Part-time, evening/weekend. *Degree requirements:* For master's, integrative field experience (MPA), practicum (MPH); for doctorate, comprehensive exam, thesis/dissertation. *Entrance requirements:* For master's, GRE (minimum scores: verbal 150, quantitative 149, and analytic writing 4.5), minimum GPA of 3.0, 3 recommendation letters, resume, 500-word statement of intent; for doctorate, GRE, 3 recommendation letters, resume, 500-word personal essay. Additional exam requirements/recommendations for international students: Required—TOEFL (minimum score 550 paper-based; 80 iBT), IELTS (minimum score 7). *Faculty research:* Public budgeting, program evaluation, nonprofit management, natural resources policy and administration.

Portland State University, Graduate Studies, College of Urban and Public Affairs, Nohad A. Toulan School of Urban Studies and Planning, Portland, OR 97207-0751. Offers applied social demography (Certificate); energy policy and management (Certificate); real estate development (Certificate); sustainable food systems (Certificate); transportation (Certificate); urban design (Certificate); urban studies (PhD); urban studies and planning (MRED, MURP, MUS); urban studies: regional science (PhD). *Program availability:* Part-time, evening/weekend. *Degree requirements:* For doctorate, comprehensive exam, thesis/dissertation, residency. *Entrance requirements:* For doctorate, GRE General Test, minimum GPA of 2.75, statement of purpose, 3 letters of recommendation, resume/curriculum vitae. Additional exam requirements/recommendations for international students: Required—TOEFL (minimum score 550 paper-based; 80 iBT). Electronic applications accepted.

Rice University, Graduate Programs, School of Social Sciences, Department of Economics, Houston, TX 77251-1892. Offers economics (PhD); energy economics (MEECON). *Degree requirements:* For doctorate, comprehensive exam, thesis/dissertation. *Entrance requirements:* For doctorate, GRE. Additional exam requirements/recommendations for international students: Required—TOEFL (minimum score 600 paper-based; 90 iBT). Electronic applications accepted.

Samford University, Howard College of Arts and Sciences, Birmingham, AL 35229. Offers energy (MSEM); environmental management (MSEM); public health (MSEM); JD/MSEM. *Program availability:* Part-time, online only, 100% online. *Faculty:* 8 full-time (2 women), 1 part-time/adjunct (0 women). *Students:* 7 full-time (3 women); includes 4 minority (3 Black or African American, non-Hispanic/Latino; 1 Asian, non-Hispanic/Latino). Average age 28. 18 applicants, 28% accepted, 4 enrolled. In 2018, 4 master's awarded. *Entrance requirements:* For master's, 2 letters of recommendation; minimum overall GPA of 3.0 (3 years or less since undergraduate degree); minimum overall GPA of 2.5 (after 3 years' relevant work experience). Additional exam requirements/recommendations for international students: Required—TOEFL (minimum score 520 paper-based). Application fee: $40. *Expenses: Tuition:* Full-time $17,255; part-time $837 per credit. *Required fees:* $610; $305 per term. Tuition and fees vary according to course load, degree level, program and student level. *Financial support:* Application deadline: 2/15; applicants required to submit FAFSA. *Faculty research:* Genetics, environmental science, animal biology, ecology, biodiversity. *Unit head:* Dr. Anthony Scott Overton, Professor and Chair, 205-726-4537, E-mail: aoverton@samford.edu. *Application contact:* David Frings, Assistant Graduate Director, 205-726-4537, E-mail: dmfrings@samford.edu.
Website: http://howard.samford.edu/

SIT Graduate Institute, Graduate Programs, Master's Program in Climate Change and Global Sustainability, Brattleboro, VT 05302-0676. Offers MA.

Stony Brook University, State University of New York, Graduate School, College of Engineering and Applied Sciences, Department of Technology and Society, Program in Energy Technology and Policy, Stony Brook, NY 11794. Offers MS. *Program availability:* Part-time. *Degree requirements:* For master's, thesis, project. *Entrance requirements:* For master's, GRE. Additional exam requirements/recommendations for international students: Required—TOEFL (minimum score 85 iBT), IELTS (minimum score 6.5). *Application deadline:* For fall admission, 7/2 for domestic students, 4/15 for international students; for spring admission, 12/3 for domestic students, 10/5 for international students; for summer admission, 4/15 for domestic students. Application fee: $100. Electronic applications accepted. *Expenses:* Contact institution. *Financial support:* Research assistantships, teaching assistantships, and career-related internships or fieldwork available. *Unit head:* Dr. Wolf Schäfer, Interim Department Chair, 631-632-7924, E-mail: wolf.schafer@stonybrook.edu. *Application contact:* Marypat Taveras, Coordinator, 631-632-8770, Fax: 631-632-7809, E-mail: marypat.taveras@stonybrook.edu.
Website: https://www.stonybrook.edu/commcms/est/masters/msenergyenv

Tulane University, A. B. Freeman School of Business, New Orleans, LA 70118-5669. Offers accounting (M Acct); analytics (MBA); banking and financial services (M Fin); energy (M Fin, MBA); entrepreneurship (MBA); finance (MBA, PhD); financial accounting (PhD); international business (MBA); international management (MBA); strategic management and leadership (MBA); JD/M Acct; JD/MBA; MBA/M Acc; MBA/MA; MBA/MD; MBA/ME; MBA/MPH. *Accreditation:* AACSB. *Program availability:* Part-time, evening/weekend. *Faculty:* 43 full-time (11 women), 45 part-time/adjunct (8 women). *Students:* 432 full-time (218 women), 533 part-time (262 women); includes 99 minority (32 Black or African American, non-Hispanic/Latino; 1 American Indian or Alaska Native, non-Hispanic/Latino; 26 Asian, non-Hispanic/Latino; 35 Hispanic/Latino; 5 Two or more races, non-Hispanic/Latino), 644 international. Average age 28. 1,911 applicants, 77% accepted, 411 enrolled. In 2018, 728 master's, 4 doctorates awarded. Terminal master's awarded for partial completion of doctoral program. *Degree requirements:* For master's, one foreign language, comprehensive exam (for some programs); for doctorate, one foreign language, comprehensive exam, thesis/dissertation. *Entrance requirements:* For master's and doctorate, GMAT or GRE, interview. Additional exam requirements/recommendations for international students: Required—TOEFL or IELTS. *Application deadline:* For fall admission, 11/1 priority date for domestic students, 11/1 for international students; for winter admission, 1/6 for domestic and international students; for spring admission, 3/1 priority date for domestic students, 3/1 for international students; for summer admission, 5/5 for domestic students. Applications are processed on a rolling basis. Application fee: $125. Electronic applications accepted. *Expenses:* Contact institution. *Financial support:* In 2018–19, 153 students received support. Fellowships with tuition reimbursements available,

research assistantships, teaching assistantships, career-related internships or fieldwork, Federal Work-Study, tuition waivers (full and partial), and unspecified assistantships available. Support available to part-time students. Financial award application deadline: 4/15; financial award applicants required to submit FAFSA. *Faculty research:* Corporate finance, managerial accounting and financial reporting, strategic management and leadership, consumer behavior and decision making, organizational behavior and human resource management. *Unit head:* Ira Solomon, PhD, Dean, 504-865-5407, Fax: 504-865-5491, E-mail: businessdean@tulane.edu. *Application contact:* Melissa Booth, Assistant Dean for Graduate Admissions, 800-223-5402, E-mail: freeman.admissions@tulane.edu.
Website: http://www.freeman.tulane.edu

Université du Québec, Institut National de la Recherche Scientifique, Graduate Programs, Centre for Energie Materiaux Telecommunications, Varennes, QC G1K 9A9, Canada. Offers energy and materials science (M Sc, PhD); telecommunications (M Sc, PhD). *Program availability:* Part-time. *Faculty:* 38 full-time. *Students:* 207 full-time (60 women), 13 part-time (3 women), 186 international. Average age 34. 45 applicants, 87% accepted, 24 enrolled. In 2018, 13 master's, 30 doctorates awarded. *Degree requirements:* For master's, thesis (for some programs); for doctorate, thesis/dissertation. *Entrance requirements:* For master's, appropriate bachelor's degree, proficiency in French; for doctorate, appropriate master's degree, proficiency in French. *Application deadline:* For fall admission, 3/30 for domestic and international students; for winter admission, 11/1 for domestic and international students; for spring admission, 3/1 for domestic and international students. Application fee: $45. Electronic applications accepted. *Financial support:* In 2018–19, fellowships (averaging $16,500 per year) were awarded; research assistantships and scholarships/grants also available. *Faculty research:* New energy sources, plasmas, telecommunications, advanced materials, ultrafast photonics. *Total annual research expenditures:* $11.3 million. *Unit head:* Ana Tavares, Director, 514-228-6947, Fax: 450-929-8102, E-mail: ana.tavares@emt.inrs.ca. *Application contact:* Sean Otto, Registrar, 418-654-2518, Fax: 418-654-3858, E-mail: sean.otto@inrs.ca.
Website: http://www.emt.inrs.ca

University of Calgary, Faculty of Graduate Studies, Schulich School of Engineering, Program in Chemical and Petroleum Engineering, Calgary, AB T2N 1N4, Canada. Offers chemical engineering (M Eng, M Sc, PhD); energy and environment engineering (M Eng, M Sc, PhD); energy and environmental systems (M Eng, M Sc, PhD); environmental engineering (M Eng, M Sc, PhD); petroleum engineering (M Eng, M Sc, PhD); reservoir characterization (M Eng, M Sc). *Program availability:* Part-time. *Degree requirements:* For master's, thesis (for some programs); for doctorate, comprehensive exam, thesis/dissertation, candidacy exam. *Entrance requirements:* For master's, minimum GPA of 3.0 or equivalent; for doctorate, minimum GPA of 3.5 or equivalent. Additional exam requirements/recommendations for international students: Required—TOEFL (minimum score 550 paper-based; 80 iBT), IELTS (minimum score 7). Electronic applications accepted. *Faculty research:* Environmental engineering, biomedical engineering modeling, simulation and control, petroleum recovery and reservoir engineering, phase equilibria and transport properties.

University of California, Berkeley, Graduate Division, College of Natural Resources, Group in Energy and Resources, Berkeley, CA 94720. Offers MA, MS, PhD. *Degree requirements:* For master's, project or thesis; for doctorate, one foreign language, thesis/dissertation, qualifying exam. *Entrance requirements:* For master's and doctorate, GRE General Test, minimum GPA of 3.0, 3 letters of recommendation. Electronic applications accepted. *Faculty research:* Technical, economic, environmental, and institutional aspects of energy conservation in residential and commercial buildings; international patterns of energy use; renewable energy sources; assessment of valuation of energy and environmental resources pricing.

University of California, San Diego, Graduate Division, School of Global Policy and Strategy, Master of Public Policy Program, La Jolla, CA 92093. Offers American policy in global context (MPP); business, government and regulation (MPP); energy and environmental policy (MPP); health policy (MPP); program design and evaluation (MPP); security policy (MPP). *Entrance requirements:* For master's, GMAT or GRE General Test. Additional exam requirements/recommendations for international students: Required—TOEFL (minimum score 90 iBT), IELTS (minimum score 7). Electronic applications accepted. *Expenses:* Contact institution.

University of Colorado Denver, Business School, Program in Global Energy Management, Denver, CO 80217. Offers MS. *Program availability:* Online learning. *Degree requirements:* For master's, 36 semester credit hours. *Entrance requirements:* For master's, GMAT if less than three years of experience in the energy industry (waived for students already holding a graduate degree), minimum of 5 years' experience in energy industry; resume; letters of recommendation; essays. Additional exam requirements/recommendations for international students: Required—TOEFL (minimum score 525 paper-based; 71 iBT); Recommended—IELTS (minimum score 6). Electronic applications accepted. *Expenses:* Contact institution.

University of Delaware, Center for Energy and Environmental Policy, Newark, DE 19716. Offers energy and environmental policy (MA, MEEP, PhD); urban affairs and public policy (PhD), including technology, environment, and society. *Degree requirements:* For master's, analytical paper or thesis; for doctorate, comprehensive exam, thesis/dissertation. *Entrance requirements:* For master's, GRE General Test, minimum GPA of 3.0; for doctorate, GRE General Test, minimum GPA of 3.5. Additional exam requirements/recommendations for international students: Required—TOEFL. Electronic applications accepted. *Faculty research:* Sustainable development, renewable energy, climate change, environmental policy, environmental justice, disaster policy.

University of Illinois at Urbana–Champaign, Graduate College, College of Agricultural, Consumer and Environmental Sciences, Program in Bioenergy, Champaign, IL 61820. Offers PSM. Applications accepted for Fall semester only.

University of Mary, Gary Tharaldson School of Business, Bismarck, ND 58504-9652. Offers business administration (MBA); energy management (MBA, MS); executive (MBA, MS); health care (MBA, MS); human resource management (MBA); project management (MBA, MPM); virtuous leadership (MBA, MPM, MS). *Program availability:* Part-time, evening/weekend. *Entrance requirements:* For master's, minimum GPA of 2.5. Additional exam requirements/recommendations for international students: Required—TOEFL (minimum score 550 paper-based; 80 iBT). Electronic applications accepted.

University of Phoenix–Bay Area Campus, School of Business, San Jose, CA 95134-1805. Offers accountancy (MS); accounting (MBA); business administration (MBA, DBA); energy management (MBA); global management (MBA); health care management (MBA); human resource management (MBA); human resources management (MM); management (MM); marketing (MBA); organizational leadership (DM); project management (MBA); public administration (MPA); technology management (MBA). *Accreditation:* ACBSP. *Program availability:* Evening/weekend, online learning. *Degree requirements:* For master's, thesis (for some programs). *Entrance requirements:* For master's, minimum undergraduate GPA of 3.0, 3 years of work experience. Additional exam requirements/recommendations for international students: Required—TOEFL (minimum score 550 paper-based; 79 iBT). Electronic applications accepted.

University of Phoenix–Online Campus, School of Business, Phoenix, AZ 85034-7209. Offers accountancy (MS); accounting (MBA, Certificate); business administration (MBA); energy management (MBA); global management (MBA); health care management (MBA); human resource management (MBA, Certificate); human resources management (MM); management (MM); marketing (MBA, Certificate); project management (MBA, Certificate); public administration (MBA, MM); technology management (MBA). *Program availability:* Evening/weekend, online learning. *Entrance requirements:* Additional exam requirements/recommendations for international students: Required—TOEFL, TOEIC (Test of English as an International Communication), Berlitz Online English Proficiency Exam, PTE, or IELTS. Electronic applications accepted. *Expenses:* Contact institution.

University of Phoenix–Phoenix Campus, School of Business, Tempe, AZ 85282-2371. Offers accounting (MBA, MS, Certificate); business administration (MBA); energy management (MBA); global management (MBA); health care management (MBA); human resource management (MBA, Certificate); management (MM); marketing (MBA); project management (MBA); technology management (MBA). *Program availability:* Evening/weekend, online learning. *Entrance requirements:* Additional exam requirements/recommendations for international students: Required—TOEFL, TOEIC (Test of English as an International Communication), Berlitz Online English Proficiency Exam, PTE, or IELTS. Electronic applications accepted. *Expenses:* Contact institution.

University of Pittsburgh, Graduate School of Public and International Affairs, Master of Public Administration Program, Pittsburgh, PA 15260. Offers energy and environment (MPA); governance and international public management (MPA); policy research and analysis (MPA); public and nonprofit management (MPA); urban affairs and planning (MPA); JD/MPA; MPH/MPA; MSIS/MPA; MSW/MPA. *Accreditation:* NASPAA. *Program availability:* Part-time, evening/weekend. *Degree requirements:* For master's, thesis optional, capstone seminar. *Entrance requirements:* For master's, GRE General Test or GMAT, 2 letters of recommendation, resume, undergraduate transcripts, personal statement. Additional exam requirements/recommendations for international students: Required—TOEFL (minimum score 80 iBT); Recommended—IELTS (minimum score 7). Electronic applications accepted. *Expenses:* Contact institution. *Faculty research:* Urban affairs and planning, governance and international public management, public and nonprofit management, policy research and analysis, energy and environment.

University of San Francisco, College of Arts and Sciences, Energy Systems Management Program, San Francisco, CA 94117. Offers MS. *Program availability:* Part-time, evening/weekend. *Students:* 40 full-time (9 women); includes 9 minority (2 Black or African American, non-Hispanic/Latino; 3 Asian, non-Hispanic/Latino; 4 Hispanic/Latino), 17 international. Average age 30. 54 applicants, 78% accepted, 20 enrolled. *Entrance requirements:* Additional exam requirements/recommendations for international students: Required—TOEFL (minimum score 90 iBT), IELTS (minimum score 6.5), PTE (minimum score 61). *Application deadline:* For fall admission, 2/15 priority date for domestic and international students. Applications are processed on a rolling basis. Application fee: $55. Electronic applications accepted. *Financial support:* Teaching assistantships with partial tuition reimbursements, career-related internships or fieldwork, and scholarships/grants available. Financial award applicants required to submit FAFSA. *Faculty research:* Quantitative methods, renewable energy economics, energy technologies, energy policy, electricity systems, renewable energy finance, energy law. *Unit head:* Dr. Maggie Winslow, Graduate Director, 415-422-5101, E-mail: mwinslow@usfca.edu. *Application contact:* Dr. Maggie Winslow, Graduate Director, 415-422-5101, E-mail: mwinslow@usfca.edu.
Website: https://www.usfca.edu/arts-sciences/graduate-programs/energy-systems-management

The University of Texas at Tyler, Soules College of Business, Department of Management and Marketing, Tyler, TX 75799-0001. Offers cyber security (MBA); engineering management (MBA); general management (MBA); healthcare management (MBA); internal assurance and consulting (MBA); marketing (MBA); oil, gas and energy (MBA); organizational development (MBA); quality management (MBA). *Accreditation:* AACSB. *Program availability:* Part-time, online learning. *Students:* Average age 29. 73 applicants, 96% accepted, 35 enrolled. In 2018, 37 master's awarded. *Entrance requirements:* Additional exam requirements/recommendations for international students: Required—TOEFL (minimum score 550 paper-based). *Application deadline:* For fall admission, 8/17 priority date for domestic students, 7/1 priority date for international students; for spring admission, 12/21 priority date for domestic students, 11/1 priority date for international students. Application fee: $25 ($50 for international students). *Faculty research:* General business, inventory control, institutional markets, service marketing, product distribution, accounting fraud, financial reporting and recognition. *Unit head:* Dr. Krist Swimberghe, Chair, 903-565-5803, E-mail: kswimberghe@uttyler.edu. *Application contact:* Dr. Krist Swimberghe, Chair, 903-565-5803, E-mail: kswimberghe@uttyler.edu.
Website: https://www.uttyler.edu/cbt/manamark/

The University of Tulsa, Graduate School, Collins College of Business, Online Program in Energy Business, Tulsa, OK 74104-3189. Offers MEB. *Program availability:* Part-time, evening/weekend, online only, 100% online. *Students:* 51 part-time (11 women); includes 4 minority (1 American Indian or Alaska Native, non-Hispanic/Latino; 1 Asian, non-Hispanic/Latino; 2 Hispanic/Latino), 2 international. Average age 36. 17 applicants, 94% accepted, 14 enrolled. In 2018, 31 master's awarded. *Degree requirements:* For master's, thesis optional. *Entrance requirements:* For master's, GMAT. Additional exam requirements/recommendations for international students: Required—TOEFL (minimum score 577 paper-based; 91 iBT), IELTS (minimum score 6.5). *Application deadline:* For fall admission, 7/1 for domestic students. Applications are processed on a rolling basis. Application fee: $55. Electronic applications accepted. *Expenses:* Contact institution. *Financial support:* Fellowships with tuition reimbursements, career-related internships or fieldwork, Federal Work-Study, institutionally sponsored loans, scholarships/grants, health care benefits, and tuition waivers available. Support available to part-time students. Financial award applicants required to submit FAFSA. *Unit head:* Dr. Ralph Jackson, Associate Dean, 918-631-2242, Fax: 918-631-2142, E-mail: ralph-jackson@utulsa.edu. *Application contact:* Morgan Ardrey, Marketing Manager, 918-631-2680, Fax: 918-631-2142, E-mail: graduate-business@utulsa.edu.

Vermont Law School, Graduate and Professional Programs, Master's Programs, South Royalton, VT 05068-0096. Offers American legal studies (LL M); energy law (LL M); energy regulation and law (MERL); environmental law (LL M); environmental law and policy (MELP); food and agriculture law (LL M); food and agriculture law and policy (MFALP); JD/MELP; JD/MERL; JD/MFALP. *Program availability:* Part-time, 100% online, blended/hybrid learning. *Entrance requirements:* Additional exam requirements/recommendations for international students: Required—TOEFL. *Faculty research:* Environment and new economy; takings; international environmental law; interaction among science, law, and environmental policy; climate change and the law.

Waynesburg University, Graduate and Professional Studies, Canonsburg, PA 15370. Offers business (MBA), including energy management, finance, health systems, human resources, leadership, market development; counseling (MA), including addictions counseling, clinical mental health; counselor education and supervision (PhD); criminal investigation (MA); education (M Ed), including autism, curriculum and instruction, educational leadership, online teaching; nursing (MSN), including administration, education, informatics; nursing practice (DNP); special education (M Ed); technology

(M Ed); MSN/MBA. *Accreditation:* AACN. *Program availability:* Part-time, evening/weekend. *Degree requirements:* For doctorate, thesis/dissertation. *Entrance requirements:* Additional exam requirements/recommendations for international students: Required—TOEFL. Electronic applications accepted.

Engineering Management

Air Force Institute of Technology, Graduate School of Engineering and Management, Department of Systems and Engineering Management, Dayton, OH 45433-7765. Offers cost analysis (MS); environmental and engineering management (MS); environmental engineering science (MS); information resource/systems management (MS). *Accreditation:* ABET. *Program availability:* Part-time. *Degree requirements:* For master's, thesis. *Entrance requirements:* For master's, GRE, GMAT, minimum GPA of 3.0.

American University of Beirut, Graduate Programs, Maroun Semaan Faculty of Engineering and Architecture, Beirut, Lebanon. Offers applied energy (ME); civil engineering (PhD); electrical and computer engineering (PhD); energy studies (MS); engineering management (MEM); environmental and water resources (ME); environmental technology (MSES); mechanical engineering (ME, PhD); urban design (MUD); urban planning and policy (MUPP). For progreen diploma: LAU/AUC. *Program availability:* Part-time, 100% online. *Faculty:* 105 full-time (25 women), 102 part-time/adjunct (33 women). *Students:* 380 full-time (186 women), 100 part-time (38 women). Average age 27. 489 applicants, 64% accepted, 127 enrolled. In 2018, 109 master's, 14 doctorates awarded. Terminal master's awarded for partial completion of doctoral program. *Degree requirements:* For master's, one foreign language, comprehensive exam, thesis optional; for doctorate, one foreign language, comprehensive exam, thesis/dissertation. *Entrance requirements:* For doctorate, GRE. Additional exam requirements/recommendations for international students: Required—TOEFL (minimum score 575 paper-based; 88 iBT), AUB-EN; Recommended—IELTS (minimum score 7). *Application deadline:* For fall admission, 4/4 for domestic and international students; for spring admission, 11/3 for domestic and international students; for summer admission, 4/4 for domestic and international students. Application fee: $50. *Expenses: Tuition:* Full-time $17,748; part-time $986 per credit. *Required fees:* $762. Tuition and fees vary according to course load and program. *Financial support:* In 2018–19, 15 students received support, including 92 fellowships with full tuition reimbursements available (averaging $14,400 per year), 80 research assistantships with full and partial tuition reimbursements available (averaging $5,300 per year), 162 teaching assistantships with full and partial tuition reimbursements available (averaging $1,400 per year); scholarships/grants, tuition waivers (full and partial), and unspecified assistantships also available. Financial award application deadline: 4/4. *Faculty research:* All areas in engineering, architecture and design. Total annual research expenditures: $1.5 million. *Unit head:* Prof. Alan Shihade, Dean, 961-1-374374 Ext. 3400, Fax: 961-1-744462, E-mail: as20@aub.edu.lb. *Application contact:* Dr. Salim Kanaan, Director, Admissions Office, 961-1-374374 Ext. 2590, Fax: 961-1-750775, E-mail: sk00@aub.edu.lb. Website: https://www.aub.edu.lb/msfea/pages/default.aspx

American University of Sharjah, Graduate Programs, Sharjah, United Arab Emirates. Offers accounting (MS); biomedical engineering (MSBME); business administration (MBA); chemical engineering (MS Ch E); civil engineering (MSCE); computer engineering (MS); electrical engineering (MSEE); engineering systems management (MS, PhD); mathematics (MS); mechanical engineering (MSME); mechatronics engineering (MS); teaching English to speakers of other languages (MA); translation and interpreting (MA); urban planning (MUP). *Program availability:* Part-time, evening/weekend. *Degree requirements:* For master's, thesis (for some programs). *Entrance requirements:* For master's, GMAT (for MBA). Additional exam requirements/recommendations for international students: Required—TOEFL (minimum score 550 paper-based; 80 iBT), TWE (minimum score 5); Recommended—IELTS (minimum score 6.5). Electronic applications accepted. *Faculty research:* Water pollution, management and waste water treatment, energy and sustainability, air pollution, Islamic finance, family business and small and medium enterprises.

Arkansas State University, Graduate School, College of Engineering, State University, AR 72467. Offers engineering (MS Eng); engineering management (MEM). *Program availability:* Part-time. *Degree requirements:* For master's, comprehensive exam. *Entrance requirements:* For master's, GRE, appropriate bachelor's degree, official transcript, letters of recommendation, resume, immunization records. Additional exam requirements/recommendations for international students: Required—TOEFL (minimum score 550 paper-based; 79 iBT), IELTS (minimum score 6), PTE (minimum score 56). Electronic applications accepted. *Expenses:* Contact institution.

California State Polytechnic University, Pomona, Program in Engineering Management, Pomona, CA 91768-2557. Offers MS. *Program availability:* Part-time, evening/weekend. *Students:* 11 full-time (3 women), 12 part-time (2 women); includes 11 minority (2 Asian, non-Hispanic/Latino; 7 Hispanic/Latino; 2 Two or more races, non-Hispanic/Latino), 7 international. Average age 30. 39 applicants, 54% accepted, 9 enrolled. In 2018, 24 master's awarded. *Entrance requirements:* Additional exam requirements/recommendations for international students: Required—TOEFL (minimum score 550 paper-based). *Application deadline:* Applications are processed on a rolling basis. Application fee: $55. Electronic applications accepted. *Expenses:* Contact institution. *Financial support:* Application deadline: 3/2; applicants required to submit FAFSA. *Unit head:* Dr. Kamran Abedini, Chair/Graduate Coordinator, 909-869-2569, Fax: 909-869-2564, E-mail: kabedini@cpp.edu. *Application contact:* Dr. Kamran Abedini, Chair/Graduate Coordinator, 909-869-2569, Fax: 909-869-2564, E-mail: kabedini@cpp.edu.
Website: http://www.cpp.edu/~engineering/IME/grad.shtml

California State University, East Bay, Office of Graduate Studies, College of Science, School of Engineering, Program in Engineering Management, Hayward, CA 94542-3000. Offers MS. *Degree requirements:* For master's, comprehensive exam (for some programs), research project or exam. *Entrance requirements:* For master's, GRE or GMAT, minimum GPA of 2.5, personal statement, two letters of recommendation, resume, college algebra/trigonometry or equivalent. Additional exam requirements/recommendations for international students: Required—TOEFL (minimum score 550 paper-based). Electronic applications accepted.

California State University, Long Beach, Graduate Studies, College of Engineering, Department of Mechanical and Aerospace Engineering, Long Beach, CA 90840. Offers aerospace engineering (MSAE); engineering and industrial applied mathematics (PhD); interdisciplinary engineering (MSE); management engineering (MSE); mechanical engineering (MSME). *Program availability:* Part-time. *Entrance requirements:* Additional exam requirements/recommendations for international students: Required—TOEFL. *Application deadline:* For fall admission, 4/15 for domestic students; for spring

admission, 10/1 for domestic students. Application fee: $55. Electronic applications accepted. *Expenses: Required fees:* $2628 per term. Tuition and fees vary according to class time, course level, course load, degree level, campus/location and program. *Financial support:* Career-related internships or fieldwork, Federal Work-Study, institutionally sponsored loans, scholarships/grants, and unspecified assistantships available. Financial award application deadline: 3/2; financial award applicants required to submit FAFSA. *Faculty research:* Unsteady turbulent flows, solar energy, energy conversion, CAD/CAM, computer-assisted instruction. *Unit head:* Jalal Torabzadeh, Chair, 562-985-4398, E-mail: leanne.hayes@csulb.edu. *Application contact:* Dr. Jalal Torabzadeh, Graduate Advisor, 562-985-1512, Fax: 562-985-7561, E-mail: leanne.hayes@csulb.edu.
Website: http://www.csulb.edu/college-of-engineering/mechanical-aerospace-engineering

California State University Maritime Academy, Graduate Studies, Vallejo, CA 94590. Offers transportation and engineering management (MS), including engineering management, humanitarian disaster management, transportation. *Program availability:* Evening/weekend, online only, 100% online. *Faculty:* 13 part-time/adjunct (2 women). *Students:* 34 full-time (6 women); includes 10 minority (2 Black or African American, non-Hispanic/Latino; 4 Asian, non-Hispanic/Latino; 4 Hispanic/Latino), 2 international. Average age 38. 21 applicants, 86% accepted, 16 enrolled. In 2018, 19 master's awarded. *Degree requirements:* For master's, comprehensive exam (for some programs), thesis, Minimum GPA of 3.0 in 10 required courses including capstone course and project, demonstrated proficiency in graduate-level writing. *Entrance requirements:* For master's, GMAT/GRE (for applicants with fewer than five years of post-baccalaureate professional experience), Equivalent of four-year U.S. bachelor's degree with minimum GPA of 2.5 during last two years (60 semester units or 90 quarter units) of coursework in degree program. Additional exam requirements/recommendations for international students: Required—TOEFL (minimum score 550 paper-based). *Application deadline:* Applications are processed on a rolling basis. Application fee: $55. Electronic applications accepted. *Financial support:* Applicants required to submit FAFSA. *Unit head:* Dr. Graham Benton, Associate Vice President, Academic Affairs, 707-654-1147, E-mail: gbenton@csum.edu. *Application contact:* Kathy Arnold, Program Coordinator, 707-654-1271, Fax: 707-654-1158, E-mail: karnold@csum.edu.
Website: http://www.csum.edu/web/industry/graduate-studies

California State University, Northridge, Graduate Studies, College of Engineering and Computer Science, Department of Manufacturing Systems Engineering and Management, Northridge, CA 91330. Offers engineering automation (MS); engineering management (MS); manufacturing systems engineering (MS); materials engineering (MS). *Program availability:* Online learning. *Entrance requirements:* For master's, GRE (if cumulative undergraduate GPA less than 3.0).

Case Western Reserve University, School of Graduate Studies, Case School of Engineering, The Institute for Management and Engineering, Cleveland, OH 44106. Offers MEM. *Students:* 32 full-time (11 women); includes 13 minority (2 Black or African American, non-Hispanic/Latino; 5 Asian, non-Hispanic/Latino; 4 Hispanic/Latino; 2 Two or more races, non-Hispanic/Latino), 13 international. In 2018, 38 master's awarded. *Entrance requirements:* Additional exam requirements/recommendations for international students: Required—TOEFL, IELTS (minimum score 7.5). *Application deadline:* For fall admission, 5/1 for domestic students, 2/1 for international students. *Expenses: Tuition:* Full-time $45,168; part-time $1939 per credit hour. *Required fees:* $36; $18 per semester. $18 per semester. *Unit head:* Mindy Bairel, Interim Executive Director, 216-368-0637, Fax: 216-368-0144, E-mail: mmb149@case.edu. *Application contact:* Ramona David, Program Assistant, 216-368-0596, Fax: 216-368-0144, E-mail: rxd47@cwru.edu.
Website: http://www.mem.case.edu

The Catholic University of America, School of Engineering, Program in Engineering Management, Washington, DC 20064. Offers engineering management (MSE, Certificate), including engineering management and organization (MSE), project and systems engineering management (MSE), technology management (MSE); program management (Certificate); systems engineering and management of information technology (Certificate). *Program availability:* Part-time. *Faculty:* 6 part-time/adjunct (1 woman). *Students:* 16 full-time (1 woman), 19 part-time (7 women); includes 3 minority (1 Asian, non-Hispanic/Latino; 2 Two or more races, non-Hispanic/Latino), 17 international. Average age 31. 48 applicants, 85% accepted, 19 enrolled. In 2018, 17 master's awarded. *Degree requirements:* For master's, minimum GPA of 3.0. *Entrance requirements:* For master's and Certificate, statement of purpose, official copies of academic transcripts, two letters of recommendation. Additional exam requirements/recommendations for international students: Required—TOEFL (minimum score 550 paper-based; 80 iBT). *Application deadline:* For fall admission, 7/15 priority date for domestic students, 7/1 for international students; for spring admission, 11/15 priority date for domestic students, 11/1 for international students. Applications are processed on a rolling basis. Application fee: $55. Electronic applications accepted. *Expenses:* Contact institution. *Financial support:* Fellowships, research assistantships, teaching assistantships, Federal Work-Study, scholarships/grants, tuition waivers (full and partial), and unspecified assistantships available. Financial award application deadline: 2/1; financial award applicants required to submit FAFSA. *Faculty research:* Engineering management and organization, project and systems engineering management, technology management. *Unit head:* Melvin G. Williams, Jr., Director, 202-319-5191, Fax: 202-319-6860, E-mail: williamsme@cua.edu. *Application contact:* Dr. Steven Brown, Director of Graduate Admissions, 202-319-5057, Fax: 202-319-6533, E-mail: cua-admissions@cua.edu.
Website: https://engineering.catholic.edu/management/index.html

Central Michigan University, Central Michigan University Global Campus, Program in Administration, Mount Pleasant, MI 48859. Offers acquisitions administration (MSA, Certificate); engineering management administration (MSA, Certificate); general administration (MSA, Certificate); health services administration (MSA, Certificate); human resources administration (MSA, Certificate); information resource management (MSA); information resource management administration (Certificate); international administration (MSA, Certificate); leadership (MSA, Certificate); philanthropy and fundraising administration (MSA, Certificate); public administration (MSA, Certificate);

recreation and park administration (MSA); research administration (MSA, Certificate). *Program availability:* Part-time, evening/weekend, online learning. *Entrance requirements:* For master's, minimum GPA of 2.7 in major. Electronic applications accepted.

The Citadel, The Military College of South Carolina, Citadel Graduate College, School of Engineering, Department of Engineering Leadership and Program Management, Charleston, SC 29409. Offers project management (MS); systems engineering management (Graduate Certificate); technical program management (Graduate Certificate); technical project management (Graduate Certificate). *Program availability:* Part-time, evening/weekend. *Entrance requirements:* For master's, GRE or GMAT, minimum of one year of professional experience or permission from department head; two letters of reference; resume detailing previous work; for Graduate Certificate, one-page letter of intent; resume detailing previous work. Additional exam requirements/recommendations for international students: Required—TOEFL (minimum score 550 paper-based; 79 iBT). Electronic applications accepted. *Expenses:* Tuition, state resident: part-time $595 per credit hour. Tuition, nonresident: part-time $1020 per credit hour. *Required fees:* $90 per term.

Clarkson University, Program in Engineering Management, Potsdam, NY 13699. Offers MS. *Program availability:* Part-time-only, evening/weekend, blended/hybrid learning. *Faculty:* 10 part-time/adjunct (0 women). *Students:* 2 full-time (0 women), 199 part-time (46 women); includes 35 minority (10 Black or African American, non-Hispanic/Latino; 14 Asian, non-Hispanic/Latino; 11 Hispanic/Latino), 19 international. 82 applicants, 95% accepted, 78 enrolled. In 2018, 80 master's awarded. *Degree requirements:* For master's, project. *Entrance requirements:* For master's, GRE or GMAT. Additional exam requirements/recommendations for international students: Required—TOEFL (minimum score 550 paper-based, 80 iBT) or IELTS (6.5). *Application deadline:* Applications are processed on a rolling basis. Application fee: $50. Electronic applications accepted. *Expenses:* Contact institution. *Financial support:* Scholarships/grants available. *Unit head:* Hugo Irizarry-Quinones, Associate Dean of Engineering, 518-631-9881, E-mail: hirizarr@clarkson.edu. *Application contact:* Dan Capogna, Director of Graduate Admissions & Recruitment, 518-631-9910, E-mail: graduate@clarkson.edu.
Website: https://www.clarkson.edu/academics/graduate

Colorado School of Mines, Office of Graduate Studies, Department of Economics and Business, Golden, CO 80401. Offers engineering and technology management (MS); mineral and energy economics (MS, PhD); operations research and engineering (PhD); petroleum economics and management with mineral and energy economics (MS). *Program availability:* Part-time. *Faculty:* 17 full-time (5 women), 4 part-time/adjunct (1 woman). *Students:* 92 full-time (27 women), 12 part-time (4 women); includes 20 minority (4 Black or African American, non-Hispanic/Latino; 4 Asian, non-Hispanic/Latino; 8 Hispanic/Latino; 1 Native Hawaiian or other Pacific Islander, non-Hispanic/Latino; 3 Two or more races, non-Hispanic/Latino), 33 international. Average age 28. 154 applicants, 82% accepted, 53 enrolled. In 2018, 68 master's, 4 doctorates awarded. *Degree requirements:* For master's, thesis (for some programs); for doctorate, comprehensive exam, thesis/dissertation. *Entrance requirements:* For master's and doctorate, GRE General Test. Additional exam requirements/recommendations for international students: Required—TOEFL (minimum score 550 paper-based; 79 iBT). *Application deadline:* For fall admission, 12/15 priority date for domestic and international students; for spring admission, 9/1 priority date for domestic and international students. Application fee: $60 ($80 for international students). Electronic applications accepted. *Expenses:* Tuition, state resident: full-time $16,650; part-time $925 per contact hour. Tuition, nonresident: full-time $36,270; part-time $2015 per contact hour. *International tuition:* $36,270 full-time. *Required fees:* $2314; $2314 per semester. *Financial support:* In 2018–19, 7 research assistantships with full tuition reimbursements, 22 teaching assistantships with full tuition reimbursements were awarded; fellowships, scholarships/grants, health care benefits, and unspecified assistantships also available. Financial award application deadline: 12/15; financial award applicants required to submit FAFSA. *Faculty research:* International trade, resource and environmental economics, energy economics, operations research. *Unit head:* Dr. Roderick Eggert, Interim Director, 303-273-3981, E-mail: reggert@mines.edu. *Application contact:* Kathleen Martin, Program Assistant, 303-273-3482, Fax: 303-273-3416, E-mail: kmartin@mines.edu.
Website: http://econbus.mines.edu

Cornell University, Graduate School, Graduate Fields of Engineering, Field of Civil and Environmental Engineering, Ithaca, NY 14853. Offers engineering management (M Eng, MS, PhD); environmental engineering (M Eng, MS, PhD); environmental fluid mechanics and hydrology (M Eng, MS, PhD); environmental systems engineering (M Eng, MS, PhD); geotechnical engineering (M Eng, MS, PhD); remote sensing (M Eng, MS, PhD); structural engineering (M Eng, MS, PhD); structural mechanics (M Eng, MS); transportation engineering (MS, PhD); transportation systems engineering (M Eng); water resource systems (M Eng, MS, PhD). Terminal master's awarded for partial completion of doctoral program. *Degree requirements:* For master's, thesis (MS); for doctorate, comprehensive exam, thesis/dissertation. *Entrance requirements:* For master's and doctorate, GRE General Test (recommended), 2 letters of recommendation. Additional exam requirements/recommendations for international students: Required—TOEFL (minimum score 600 paper-based; 77 iBT). Electronic applications accepted. *Faculty research:* Environmental engineering, geotechnical engineering, remote sensing, environmental fluid mechanics and hydrology, structural engineering.

Dartmouth College, Thayer School of Engineering, Program in Engineering Management, Hanover, NH 03755. Offers MEM. Program offered in conjunction with Tuck School of Business. *Degree requirements:* For master's, capstone experience. *Entrance requirements:* For master's, GRE General Test. Additional exam requirements/recommendations for international students: Required—TOEFL. *Expenses:* Contact institution.

Drexel University, College of Engineering, Program in Engineering Management, Philadelphia, PA 19104-2875. Offers MS, Certificate. *Program availability:* Part-time, evening/weekend, online learning. *Degree requirements:* For master's, thesis optional. *Entrance requirements:* For master's, minimum GPA of 3.0. Additional exam requirements/recommendations for international students: Required—TOEFL. Electronic applications accepted. *Faculty research:* Quality, operations research and management, ergonomics, applied statistics.

Duke University, Graduate School, Pratt School of Engineering, Distributed Master of Engineering Management Program (d-MEMP), Durham, NC 27708-0271. Offers MEM. *Program availability:* Part-time, evening/weekend, blended/hybrid learning. *Entrance requirements:* For master's, GRE General Test, resume, 3 letters of recommendation, statement of purpose, transcripts. Additional exam requirements/recommendations for international students: Required—TOEFL. Electronic applications accepted. *Expenses:* Contact institution. *Faculty research:* Entrepreneurship, innovation and product development, project management, operations and supply chain management, financial engineering.

Duke University, Graduate School, Pratt School of Engineering, Master of Engineering Management Program, Durham, NC 27708-0271. Offers MEM. *Program availability:* Part-time, blended/hybrid learning. *Entrance requirements:* For master's, GRE General Test, resume, 3 letters of recommendation, statement of purpose, transcripts. Additional exam requirements/recommendations for international students: Required—TOEFL. Electronic applications accepted. *Expenses:* Contact institution. *Faculty research:* Entrepreneurship, innovation and product development, project management, operations and supply chain management, financial engineering.

Eastern Michigan University, Graduate School, College of Engineering and Technology, School of Engineering, Program in Engineering Management, Ypsilanti, MI 48197. Offers MS. *Program availability:* Part-time, evening/weekend, online learning. *Students:* 20 full-time (6 women), 72 part-time (19 women); includes 14 minority (9 Black or African American, non-Hispanic/Latino; 1 Asian, non-Hispanic/Latino; 3 Hispanic/Latino; 1 Two or more races, non-Hispanic/Latino), 20 international. Average age 33. 97 applicants, 40% accepted, 19 enrolled. In 2018, 20 master's awarded. *Entrance requirements:* Additional exam requirements/recommendations for international students: Required—TOEFL. *Application deadline:* Applications are processed on a rolling basis. Application fee: $45. *Financial support:* Fellowships, research assistantships with full tuition reimbursements, teaching assistantships with full tuition reimbursements, career-related internships or fieldwork, Federal Work-Study, institutionally sponsored loans, scholarships/grants, tuition waivers (partial), and unspecified assistantships available. Support available to part-time students. Financial award applicants required to submit FAFSA. *Application contact:* Dr. Bryan Booker, Program Coordinator, 734-487-2040, Fax: 734-487-8755, E-mail: bbooker1@emich.edu.

Embry-Riddle Aeronautical University–Worldwide, Department of Engineering and Technology, Daytona Beach, FL 32114-3900. Offers aerospace engineering (MS); entrepreneurship in technology (MS); systems engineering (M Sys E), including engineering management, technical. *Program availability:* Part-time, evening/weekend, 100% online, blended/hybrid learning. *Entrance requirements:* For master's, GRE (for MS in aerospace engineering). Additional exam requirements/recommendations for international students: Required—TOEFL (minimum score 550 paper-based; 79 iBT), IELTS (minimum score 6). Electronic applications accepted. *Expenses:* Contact institution.

Florida Institute of Technology, College of Engineering and Science, Program in Engineering Management, Melbourne, FL 32901-6975. Offers MS. *Program availability:* Part-time. *Students:* 10 full-time (2 women), 8 part-time (1 woman), 14 international. Average age 26. 26 applicants, 46% accepted, 1 enrolled. In 2018, 13 master's awarded. *Degree requirements:* For master's, comprehensive exam (for some programs), thesis optional, 30 credit hours. *Entrance requirements:* For master's, GRE (minimum score of 300), BS in engineering from ABET-accredited program, minimum GPA of 3.0, 3 letters of recommendation, resume, statement of objectives. Additional exam requirements/recommendations for international students: Required—TOEFL (minimum score 550 paper-based; 79 iBT). *Application deadline:* Applications are processed on a rolling basis. Application fee: $50. Electronic applications accepted. *Expenses:* Tuition: Full-time $22,338; part-time $1241 per credit hour. Tuition and fees vary according to degree level, campus/location and program. *Financial support:* Application deadline: 3/1; applicants required to submit FAFSA. *Unit head:* Dr. Muzaffar A. Shaikh, Department Head, 321-674-7132, E-mail: mshaikh@fit.edu. *Application contact:* Mike Perry, Executive Director of Admission, 321-674-7127, E-mail: perrymj@fit.edu.
Website: http://catalog.fit.edu/preview_program.php?catoid=8&poid=2756

Florida International University, College of Engineering and Computing, Department of Engineering Management, Miami, FL 33199. Offers MS. *Accreditation:* CAHME. *Program availability:* Part-time, evening/weekend. *Faculty:* 3 full-time (1 woman), 1 part-time/adjunct (0 women). *Students:* 78 full-time, 56 part-time; includes 69 minority (15 Black or African American, non-Hispanic/Latino; 5 Asian, non-Hispanic/Latino; 49 Hispanic/Latino), 61 international. Average age 30. 113 applicants, 56% accepted, 41 enrolled. In 2018, 80 master's awarded. *Entrance requirements:* For master's, GRE, minimum GPA of 3.0. Additional exam requirements/recommendations for international students: Required—TOEFL (minimum score 550 paper-based; 80 iBT). *Application deadline:* For fall admission, 6/1 for domestic students, 4/1 for international students; for spring admission, 10/1 for domestic students, 9/1 for international students. Applications are processed on a rolling basis. Application fee: $30. Electronic applications accepted. *Financial support:* Institutionally sponsored loans and scholarships/grants available. Financial award application deadline: 3/1; financial award applicants required to submit FAFSA. *Unit head:* Dr. Chin-Sheng Chen, Director, 305-348-3753 Ext. 305, E-mail: chenc@fiu.edu. *Application contact:* Nanett Rojas, Manager, Admissions Operations, 305-348-7464, Fax: 305-348-7441, E-mail: gradadm@fiu.edu.

Gannon University, School of Graduate Studies, College of Engineering and Business, School of Engineering and Computer Science, Program in Engineering Management, Erie, PA 16541-0001. Offers MSEM. *Program availability:* Part-time, evening/weekend. *Entrance requirements:* For master's, bachelor's degree in engineering from an ABET-accredited program or its equivalent with minimum GPA of 2.5, transcripts, 3 letters of recommendation. Additional exam requirements/recommendations for international students: Required—TOEFL (minimum score 79 iBT). Electronic applications accepted. Application fee is waived when completed online.

The George Washington University, School of Engineering and Applied Science, Department of Engineering Management and Systems Engineering, Washington, DC 20052. Offers system engineering (PhD). *Program availability:* Part-time, evening/weekend. *Faculty:* 12 full-time (2 women), 41 part-time/adjunct (9 women). *Students:* 150 full-time (47 women), 598 part-time (178 women); includes 228 minority (115 Black or African American, non-Hispanic/Latino; 3 American Indian or Alaska Native, non-Hispanic/Latino; 77 Asian, non-Hispanic/Latino; 23 Hispanic/Latino; 1 Native Hawaiian or other Pacific Islander, non-Hispanic/Latino; 9 Two or more races, non-Hispanic/Latino), 41 international. Average age 35. 648 applicants, 66% accepted, 213 enrolled. In 2018, 190 master's, 131 doctorates, 37 other advanced degrees awarded. *Degree requirements:* For master's, thesis optional; for doctorate, one foreign language, thesis/dissertation, final and qualifying exams, submission of articles; for other advanced degree, professional project. *Entrance requirements:* For master's, appropriate bachelor's degree, minimum GPA of 2.7, second-semester calculus; for doctorate, appropriate master's degree, minimum GPA of 3.5, 2 letters of recommendation; for other advanced degree, appropriate master's degree, minimum GPA of 3.4. Additional exam requirements/recommendations for international students: Required—TOEFL or The George Washington University English as a Foreign Language Test. *Application deadline:* For fall admission, 3/1 for domestic students; for spring admission, 10/1 for domestic students. Applications are processed on a rolling basis. Application fee: $75. *Financial support:* In 2018–19, 35 students received support. Fellowships, research assistantships, teaching assistantships, career-related internships or fieldwork, and institutionally sponsored loans available. Financial award application deadline: 3/1; financial award applicants required to submit FAFSA. *Faculty research:* Artificial intelligence and expert systems, human factors engineering and systems analysis. *Total annual research expenditures:* $421,800. *Unit head:* Dr. Thomas Mazzuchi, Chair, 202-

994-4892, E-mail: mazzu@gwu.edu. *Application contact:* Adina Lav, Marketing, Recruiting and Admissions, 202-994-5827, Fax: 202-994-0909, E-mail: engineering@gwu.edu.
Website: http://www.seas.gwu.edu/department-engineering-management-systems-engineering

Georgia Southern University, Jack N. Averitt College of Graduate Studies, Allen E. Paulson College of Engineering and Computing, Department of Manufacturing Engineering, Program in Engineering Management, Statesboro, GA 30458. Offers MSAE. *Degree requirements:* For master's, comprehensive exam, thesis optional. *Entrance requirements:* For master's, undergraduate major or equivalent in proposed study area. Additional exam requirements/recommendations for international students: Required—TOEFL (minimum score 550 paper-based; 80 iBT), IELTS (minimum score 6). Electronic applications accepted. *Expenses: Tuition, area resident:* Part-time $3324 per semester. Tuition, state resident: full-time $5814; part-time $3324 per semester. Tuition, nonresident: full-time $23,204; part-time $13,260 per semester. *Required fees:* $2092; $2092. Tuition and fees vary according to course load, degree level, campus/location and program. *Faculty research:* Business intelligence, data mining and analytics, e-commerce, industrial economics, business continuity and disaster recovery.

Georgia Southern University, Jack N. Averitt College of Graduate Studies, Allen E. Paulson College of Engineering and Computing, Department of Mechanical Engineering, Statesboro, GA 30460. Offers engineering and information technology (MSAE), including engineering and information technology; engineering and manufacturing management (Graduate Certificate); engineering/energy science (MSAE); engineering/engineering management (MSAE); engineering/mechatronics (MSAE); occupational safety and environmental compliance (Graduate Certificate). *Program availability:* Part-time, evening/weekend. *Degree requirements:* For master's, comprehensive exam, thesis optional. *Entrance requirements:* For master's, GRE, undergraduate major or equivalent in proposed study area. Additional exam requirements/recommendations for international students: Required—TOEFL (minimum score 550 paper-based; 80 iBT), IELTS (minimum score 6). Electronic applications accepted. *Expenses: Tuition, area resident:* Part-time $3324 per semester. Tuition, state resident: full-time $5814; part-time $3324 per semester. Tuition, nonresident: full-time $23,204; part-time $13,260 per semester. *Required fees:* $2092; $2092. Tuition and fees vary according to course load, degree level, campus/location and program. *Faculty research:* Interdisciplinary research in computational mechanics, experimental and computational biofuel combustion and tribology, mechatronics and control, thermomechanical and thermofluid finite element modeling, information technology, analysis and design of antennas for wireless communications, wireless energy harvest, propagation modeling, RFID, wireless sensors, GPS/GNSS, metamaterials, finite element modeling of bioinstrumentation, embedded systems.

Indiana Tech, Program in Engineering Management, Fort Wayne, IN 46803-1297. Offers MSE. *Program availability:* Part-time, evening/weekend, online only, 100% online. *Entrance requirements:* For master's, BS in a technical field, minimum GPA of 2.5, one undergraduate course each in accounting and finance. Electronic applications accepted.

Instituto Tecnológico y de Estudios Superiores de Monterrey, Campus Chihuahua, Graduate Programs, Chihuahua, Mexico. Offers computer systems engineering (Ingeniero); electrical engineering (Ingeniero); electromechanical engineering (Ingeniero); electronic engineering (Ingeniero); engineering administration (MEA); industrial engineering (MIE, Ingeniero); international trade (MIT); mechanical engineering (Ingeniero).

International Technological University, Program in Engineering Management, San Jose, CA 95134. Offers MSEM. *Program availability:* Part-time, evening/weekend. *Degree requirements:* For master's, thesis or capstone project. *Entrance requirements:* Additional exam requirements/recommendations for international students: Required—TOEFL, IELTS. Electronic applications accepted.

Johns Hopkins University, Engineering Program for Professionals, Part-time Program in Engineering Management, Baltimore, MD 21218. Offers MEM. *Program availability:* Part-time, evening/weekend, 100% online, blended/hybrid learning. *Students:* 70 part-time (22 women). 30 applicants, 43% accepted, 7 enrolled. In 2018, 28 master's awarded. *Entrance requirements:* Additional exam requirements/recommendations for international students: Required—TOEFL (minimum score 600 paper-based; 100 iBT). *Unit head:* Rick Blank, Interim Program Chair, 240-228-3570, Fax: 410-579-8049, E-mail: rblank5@jhu.edu. *Application contact:* Doug Schiller, Admissions Director, 410-516-2300, Fax: 410-579-8049, E-mail: schiller@jhu.edu.

Johns Hopkins University, G. W. C. Whiting School of Engineering, Master of Science in Engineering Management Program, Baltimore, MD 21218. Offers biomaterials (MSEM); civil engineering (MSEM); communications science (MSEM); computer science (MSEM); environmental systems analysis, economics and public policy (MSEM); fluid mechanics (MSEM); materials science and engineering (MSEM); mechanical engineering (MSEM); mechanics and materials (MSEM); nano-biotechnology (MSEM); nanomaterials and nanotechnology (MSEM); operations research (MSEM); probability and statistics (MSEM); smart product and device design (MSEM). *Students:* 34 full-time (12 women), 18 part-time (7 women). 233 applicants, 39% accepted, 33 enrolled. In 2018, 27 master's awarded. *Entrance requirements:* For master's, GRE, 3 letters of recommendation, statement of purpose, transcripts. Additional exam requirements/recommendations for international students: Required—TOEFL (minimum score 600 paper-based, 100 iBT) or IELTS (7). *Application deadline:* For fall admission, 2/15 for domestic and international students. Application fee: $75. Electronic applications accepted. *Financial support:* In 2018–19, 43 research assistantships (averaging $43,344 per year) were awarded; health care benefits also available. *Unit head:* Dr. Pamela Sheff, Director, 410-516-7056, Fax: 410-516-4880, E-mail: pamsheff@gmail.com. *Application contact:* Lindsey Conklin, Sr. Academic Program Coordinator, 410-516-1108, Fax: 410-516-0780, E-mail: lconkli4@jhu.edu.
Website: http://engineering.jhu.edu/msem/

Kansas State University, Graduate School, College of Engineering, Department of Industrial and Manufacturing Systems Engineering, Manhattan, KS 66506. Offers engineering management (MEM); industrial engineering (MS); operations research (MS). *Program availability:* Part-time, online learning. *Degree requirements:* For master's, thesis or alternative; for doctorate, thesis/dissertation. *Entrance requirements:* For master's, GRE General Test (minimum score of 750 old version, 159 new format on Quantitative portion of exam), bachelor's degree in engineering, mathematics, or physical science; for doctorate, GRE General Test (minimum score of 770 old version, 164 new format on Quantitative portion of exam), master's degree in engineering or industrial manufacturing. Additional exam requirements/recommendations for international students: Required—PTE (minimum score 58), TOEFL (minimum score 550 paper-based; 79 iBT) or IELTS (minimum score 6.5). Electronic applications accepted. *Faculty research:* Industrial engineering, ergonomics, healthcare systems engineering, manufacturing processes, operations research, engineering management.

Kennesaw State University, Southern Polytechnic College of Engineering and Engineering Technology, Program in Engineering Management, Kennesaw, GA 30144. Offers MS. Program offered in partnership with Coles College of Business. *Program availability:* 100% online. *Students:* 6 full-time (0 women), 31 part-time (8 women); includes 12 minority (7 Black or African American, non-Hispanic/Latino; 1 Asian, non-Hispanic/Latino; 4 Hispanic/Latino), 1 international. Average age 36. 24 applicants, 83% accepted, 17 enrolled. In 2018, 1 master's awarded. *Entrance requirements:* Additional exam requirements/recommendations for international students: Required—TOEFL (minimum score 550 paper-based; 80 iBT), IELTS (minimum score 6.5). *Application deadline:* For fall admission, 7/1 for domestic and international students; for spring admission, 11/1 for domestic and international students. Applications are processed on a rolling basis. Application fee: $60. Electronic applications accepted. *Expenses: Tuition, area resident:* Full-time $6960; part-time $290 per credit hour. Tuition, state resident: full-time $6960; part-time $290 per credit hour. Tuition, nonresident: full-time $25,080; part-time $1045 per credit hour. *International tuition:* $25,080 full-time. *Required fees:* $2006; $1706 per semester. $853 per semester. *Application contact:* Admissions Counselor, 470-578-4377, E-mail: ksugrad@kennesaw.ed.
Website: http://engineering.kennesaw.edu/systems-industrial/degrees/ms-engineering-management.php

Kettering University, Graduate School, Department of Business, Flint, MI 48504. Offers MBA, MS. *Accreditation:* ACBSP. *Program availability:* Part-time, evening/weekend, online learning. *Entrance requirements:* Additional exam requirements/recommendations for international students: Required—TOEFL (minimum score 550 paper-based; 79 iBT). Electronic applications accepted.

Lawrence Technological University, College of Engineering, Southfield, MI 48075-1058. Offers architectural engineering (MS); automotive engineering (MS); biomedical engineering (MS); civil engineering (MA, MS, PhD), including environmental engineering (MS), geotechnical engineering (MS), structural engineering (MS), transportation engineering (MS), water resource engineering (MS); construction engineering management (MA); electrical and computer engineering (MS); engineering management (MEM); engineering technology (MS); fire engineering (MS); industrial engineering (MS), including healthcare systems; manufacturing systems (ME); mechanical engineering (MS, DE, PhD), including automotive engineering (MS), energy engineering (MS), manufacturing (DE), solid mechanics (MS), thermal/fluid systems (MS); mechatronic systems engineering (MS). *Program availability:* Part-time, evening/weekend. Terminal master's awarded for partial completion of doctoral program. *Degree requirements:* For master's, thesis optional; for doctorate, comprehensive exam, thesis/dissertation optional. *Entrance requirements:* Additional exam requirements/recommendations for international students: Required—TOEFL (minimum score 550 paper-based; 79 iBT), IELTS (minimum score 6.5). Electronic applications accepted. *Faculty research:* Innovative infrastructure and building structures and materials; connectivity and mobility; automotive systems modeling, simulation and testing; biomedical devices and materials; building mechanical/electrical systems.

Lehigh University, P.C. Rossin College of Engineering and Applied Science, Department of Industrial and Systems Engineering, Bethlehem, PA 18015. Offers analytical finance (MS); healthcare systems engineering (M Eng, Certificate); industrial and systems engineering (M Eng, MS, PhD); management science and engineering (M Eng, MS); MBA/E. *Program availability:* Part-time, blended/hybrid learning. *Faculty:* 19 full-time (2 women), 1 part-time/adjunct (0 women). *Students:* 90 full-time (17 women), 8 part-time (3 women); includes 1 minority (Asian, non-Hispanic/Latino), 89 international. Average age 26. 318 applicants, 48% accepted, 34 enrolled. In 2018, 53 master's, 6 doctorates awarded. Terminal master's awarded for partial completion of doctoral program. *Degree requirements:* For master's, thesis (MS); project (M Eng); for doctorate, comprehensive exam, thesis/dissertation. *Entrance requirements:* For master's and doctorate, GRE General Test. Additional exam requirements/recommendations for international students: Required—TOEFL (minimum score 550 paper-based; 79 iBT), IELTS (minimum score 6.5), TOEFL or IELTS required. *Application deadline:* For fall admission, 7/15 for domestic and international students; for spring admission, 12/1 for domestic and international students. Application fee: $75. Electronic applications accepted. Tuition and fees vary according to program. *Financial support:* In 2018–19, 33 students received support, including 2 fellowships with full tuition reimbursements available (averaging $20,490 per year), 18 research assistantships with full tuition reimbursements available (averaging $20,490 per year), 11 teaching assistantships with full tuition reimbursements available (averaging $21,105 per year); health care benefits and unspecified assistantships also available. Financial award application deadline: 1/15. *Faculty research:* Mathematical optimization; logistics and service systems, stochastic processes and simulation; computational optimization and high performance computing; financial engineering and robust optimization; machine learning and data mining. *Total annual research expenditures:* $2.1 million. *Unit head:* Dr. Luis N. Vicente, Chairperson, 610-758-4050, Fax: 610-758-4886, E-mail: lnv@lehigh.edu. *Application contact:* Ana Quiroz, Graduate Coordinator, 610-758-4051, Fax: 610-758-4886, E-mail: acq217@lehigh.edu.
Website: https://ise.lehigh.edu/

LeTourneau University, Graduate Programs, Longview, TX 75607-7001. Offers business administration (MBA); counseling (MA); curriculum and instruction (M Ed); educational administration (M Ed); engineering (ME, MS); engineering management (MEM); health care administration (MS); marriage and family therapy (MA); psychology (MA); strategic leadership (MSL); teacher leadership (M Ed); teaching and learning (M Ed). *Program availability:* Part-time, 100% online, blended/hybrid learning. *Students:* 61 full-time (47 women), 311 part-time (248 women); includes 184 minority (117 Black or African American, non-Hispanic/Latino; 3 American Indian or Alaska Native, non-Hispanic/Latino; 1 Asian, non-Hispanic/Latino; 35 Hispanic/Latino; 28 Two or more races, non-Hispanic/Latino), 2 international. Average age 37. In 2018, 97 master's awarded. *Entrance requirements:* Additional exam requirements/recommendations for international students: Required—TOEFL (minimum score 525 paper-based; 80 iBT), IELTS (minimum score 6), Either a TOEFL or IELTS is required for graduate students. One or the other. *Application deadline:* Applications are processed on a rolling basis. Electronic applications accepted. *Financial support:* Research assistantships, teaching assistantships, unspecified assistantships, and employee tuition waivers and institutionally sponsored loans available. Financial award applicants required to submit FAFSA.
Website: http://www.letu.edu

Long Island University–LIU Post, College of Management, Brookville, NY 11548-1300. Offers accountancy (MS); finance (MBA); information systems (MS); international business (MBA); management (MBA); management engineering (MS); marketing (MBA); taxation (MS); technical project management (MS); JD/MBA. *Accreditation:* AACSB. *Program availability:* Part-time, evening/weekend, blended/hybrid learning. *Entrance requirements:* For master's, GMAT, GRE, or LSAT. Additional exam requirements/recommendations for international students: Required—TOEFL (minimum score 550 paper-based, 75 iBT) or IELTS. Electronic applications accepted. *Faculty research:* Innovation and property rights, knowledge sourcing, sustainability and firm performance, China and growth markets, corporate social responsibility, workforce compensation and issues.

Louisiana Tech University, Graduate School, College of Engineering and Science, Ruston, LA 71272. Offers applied physics (MS); biomedical engineering (PhD); computer science (MS); engineering (MS, PhD), including cyberspace engineering (PhD), engineering education (PhD), engineering physics (PhD), materials and infrastructure systems (PhD), micro/nanoscale systems (PhD); engineering and technology management (MS); mathematics (MS); molecular science and nanotechnology (MS, PhD). *Program availability:* Part-time-only. Terminal master's awarded for partial completion of doctoral program. *Degree requirements:* For master's, thesis (for some programs); for doctorate, thesis/dissertation. *Entrance requirements:* For master's and Graduate Certificate, GRE General Test, minimum GPA of 3.0 in last 60 hours. Additional exam requirements/recommendations for international students: Required—TOEFL (minimum score 550 paper-based; 80 iBT), IELTS (minimum score 6.5). Electronic applications accepted. *Faculty research:* Trenchless technology, micromanufacturing, radionuclide transport, microbial liquefaction, hazardous waste treatment.

Loyola Marymount University, Frank R. Seaver College of Science and Engineering, MBA/MS Program in Systems Engineering Leadership, Los Angeles, CA 90045-2659. Offers MBA/MS. *Unit head:* Dr. Claire Leon, Systems Engineering Program Director, 310-338-7878, E-mail: claire.leon@lmu.edu. *Application contact:* Ammar Dalal, Assistant Vice Provost for Graduate Enrollment, 310-338-2721, Fax: 310-338-6086, E-mail: graduateinfo@lmu.edu.

Marquette University, Graduate School, College of Engineering, Department of Mechanical Engineering, Milwaukee, WI 53201-1881. Offers engineering innovation (Certificate); engineering management (MSEM); mechanical engineering (MS, PhD); new product and process development (Certificate). *Program availability:* Part-time, evening/weekend. Terminal master's awarded for partial completion of doctoral program. *Degree requirements:* For master's, comprehensive exam, thesis (for some programs); for doctorate, comprehensive exam, thesis/dissertation, qualifying exam. *Entrance requirements:* For master's, GRE General Test, minimum GPA of 3.0, official transcripts from all current and previous colleges/universities except Marquette, three letters of recommendation; for doctorate, GRE General Test, minimum GPA of 3.0, official transcripts from all current and previous colleges/universities except Marquette, three letters of recommendation, statement of purpose, copies of any published work. Additional exam requirements/recommendations for international students: Required—TOEFL (minimum score 530 paper-based). Electronic applications accepted. *Faculty research:* Computer-integrated manufacturing, energy conversion, simulation modeling and optimization, applied mechanics, metallurgy.

Marshall University, Academic Affairs Division, College of Information Technology and Engineering, Program in Engineering, Huntington, WV 25755. Offers engineering management (MSE); environmental engineering (MSE); transportation and infrastructure engineering (MSE). *Program availability:* Part-time, evening/weekend. *Degree requirements:* For master's, final project, oral exam. *Entrance requirements:* For master's, GMAT or GRE General Test, minimum undergraduate GPA of 2.75.

Massachusetts Institute of Technology, School of Engineering, System Design and Management Program, Cambridge, MA 02139-4307. Offers engineering and management (SM). Offered jointly with MIT Sloan School of Management. *Degree requirements:* For master's, thesis. *Expenses: Tuition:* Full-time $51,520; part-time $800 per credit hour. *Required fees:* $312. *Faculty research:* Humans and technology; information theory and decision systems; sociotechnical systems; policy and standards; social behavior; uncertainty, risk, and dynamics.

McNeese State University, Doré School of Graduate Studies, College of Engineering and Computer Science, Master of Engineering Program, Lake Charles, LA 70609. Offers chemical engineering (M Eng); civil engineering (M Eng); electrical engineering (M Eng); engineering management (M Eng); mechanical engineering (M Eng). *Program availability:* Part-time, evening/weekend. *Entrance requirements:* For master's, GRE, baccalaureate degree, minimum overall GPA of 3.0. Additional exam requirements/recommendations for international students: Required—TOEFL (minimum score 560 paper-based; 83 iBT).

Mercer University, Graduate Studies, Macon Campus, School of Engineering, Macon, GA 31207. Offers biomedical engineering (MSE); computer engineering (MSE); electrical engineering (MSE); engineering management (MSE); environmental engineering (MSE); environmental systems (MS); mechanical engineering (MSE); software engineering (MSE); software systems (MS); technical communications management (MS); technical management (MS). *Program availability:* Part-time-only, evening/weekend, online learning. *Degree requirements:* For master's, thesis or alternative. *Entrance requirements:* For master's, GRE (minimum score 300), minimum undergraduate GPA of 3.0. Additional exam requirements/recommendations for international students: Required—TOEFL (minimum score 550 paper-based; 80 iBT). *Expenses:* Contact institution. *Faculty research:* Designing prostheses and orthotics, oxygen transfer and limitations in biological systems, low-cost groundwater development, lung airway and transport, autonomous mobile robots.

Merrimack College, School of Science and Engineering, North Andover, MA 01845-5800. Offers civil engineering (MS); computer science (MS); data science (MS); engineering management (MS); mechanical engineering (MS), including engineering management. *Program availability:* Part-time, evening/weekend, 100% online. *Faculty:* 10 full-time (2 women), 6 part-time/adjunct (1 woman). *Students:* 53 full-time (18 women), 17 part-time (5 women); includes 14 minority (6 Black or African American, non-Hispanic/Latino; 6 Asian, non-Hispanic/Latino; 2 Two or more races, non-Hispanic/Latino), 9 international. Average age 34. 183 applicants, 61% accepted, 40 enrolled. In 2018, 27 master's awarded. *Degree requirements:* For master's, comprehensive exam, thesis optional, internship or capstone (for some programs). *Entrance requirements:* For master's, official college transcripts, resume, personal statement, 2 recommendations. Additional exam requirements/recommendations for international students: Required—TOEFL (minimum score 84 iBT), IELTS (minimum score 6.5), PTE (minimum score 56). *Application deadline:* For fall admission, 8/24 for domestic students, 7/30 for international students; for spring admission, 1/10 for domestic students, 12/10 for international students; for summer admission, 5/10 for domestic students, 4/10 for international students. Applications are processed on a rolling basis. Application fee: $0. Electronic applications accepted. Application fee is waived when completed online. *Expenses:* Contact institution. *Financial support:* Career-related internships or fieldwork, scholarships/grants, health care benefits, and unspecified assistantships available. Support available to part-time students. Financial award application deadline: 5/1; financial award applicants required to submit FAFSA. *Unit head:* Dr. Naira Campbell-Kyureghyan, Dean, 978-837-5265, E-mail: campbellnk@merrimack.edu. *Application contact:* Allison Pena, Graduate Admissions Counselor, 978-837-3563, E-mail: penaa@merrimack.edu.
Website: http://www.merrimack.edu/academics/graduate/

Middle Tennessee State University, College of Graduate Studies, College of Basic and Applied Sciences, Program in Professional Science, Murfreesboro, TN 37132. Offers actuarial sciences (MS); biostatistics (MS); biotechnology (MS); engineering management (MS); health care informatics (MS). *Program availability:* Part-time, evening/weekend, online learning. *Degree requirements:* For master's, comprehensive exam. *Entrance requirements:* For master's, GRE. Additional exam requirements/recommendations for international students: Required—TOEFL (minimum score 525 paper-based; 71 iBT) or IELTS (minimum score 6).

Milwaukee School of Engineering, MBA in STEM Leadership Program, Milwaukee, WI 53202-3109. Offers MBA. *Program availability:* Part-time, evening/weekend. *Degree requirements:* For master's, thesis or alternative. *Entrance requirements:* For master's, GRE or GMAT if GPA is below 3.0, official transcripts, 2 letters of recommendation, personal essay, bachelor's degree from accredited university, 3 years work experience as teacher in a STEM field. Additional exam requirements/recommendations for international students: Required—TOEFL (minimum score 90 iBT), IELTS (minimum score 7). Electronic applications accepted.

Milwaukee School of Engineering, MS Program in Engineering Management, Milwaukee, WI 53202-3109. Offers MS. *Program availability:* Part-time, evening/weekend. *Degree requirements:* For master's, thesis or alternative, thesis defense or capstone project. *Entrance requirements:* For master's, GRE General Test or GMAT if undergraduate GPA less than 2.8, bachelor's degree from accredited university; 2 letters of recommendation; work experience (strongly recommended). Additional exam requirements/recommendations for international students: Required—TOEFL (minimum score 90 iBT), IELTS (minimum score 7). Electronic applications accepted. *Faculty research:* Operations, project management, quality marketing.

Missouri University of Science and Technology, Department of Engineering Management and Systems Engineering, Rolla, MO 65401. Offers engineering management (MS, PhD); systems engineering (MS, PhD). *Degree requirements:* For master's, thesis optional; for doctorate, comprehensive exam. *Entrance requirements:* For master's, GRE (minimum score 1150 verbal and quantitative, 4.5 writing); for doctorate, GRE (minimum score: 1100 verbal and quantitative, 3.5 writing). Additional exam requirements/recommendations for international students: Required—TOEFL (minimum score 580 paper-based). Electronic applications accepted. *Expenses: Tuition,* state resident: full-time $7545.60; part-time $419.20 per credit hour. Tuition, nonresident: full-time $22,169; part-time $1231.60 per credit hour. *International tuition:* $23,518.80 full-time. *Required fees:* $4523.05. Full-time tuition and fees vary according to course load, campus/location, program and reciprocity agreements. *Faculty research:* Management of technology, industrial engineering, manufacturing engineering, packaging engineering, quality engineering.

National University, School of Engineering and Computing, La Jolla, CA 92037-1011. Offers computer science (MS), including advanced computing; cyber security and information assurance (MS); data analytics (MS); electrical engineering (MS); engineering management (MS); information technology management (MS); management information systems (MS); sustainability management (MS). *Program availability:* Part-time, evening/weekend, 100% online, blended/hybrid learning. *Degree requirements:* For master's, thesis (for some programs). *Entrance requirements:* For master's, interview, minimum GPA of 2.5. Additional exam requirements/recommendations for international students: Required—TOEFL (minimum score 550 paper-based; 79 iBT), IELTS (minimum score 6). Electronic applications accepted. *Expenses: Tuition:* Full-time $10,320; part-time $430 per unit. Tuition and fees vary according to degree level. *Faculty research:* Educational technology, scholarships in science.

Naval Postgraduate School, Departments and Academic Groups, Department of Systems Engineering, Monterey, CA 93943. Offers engineering systems (MS); product development (MS); systems engineering (MS, PhD, Certificate); systems engineering analysis (MS, PhD); systems engineering management (MS, PhD). Program only open to commissioned officers of the United States and friendly nations and selected United States federal civilian employees. *Program availability:* Part-time. *Degree requirements:* For master's, thesis (for some programs), internal project, capstone project, or research/dissertation paper (for some programs); for doctorate, thesis/dissertation (for some programs), internal project, capstone project, or research/dissertation paper (for some programs). *Faculty research:* Net-centric enterprise systems/services, artificial intelligence (AI) systems engineering, unconventional weapons of mass destruction, complex systems engineering, risk-benefit analysis.

New England Institute of Technology, Program in Engineering Management, East Greenwich, RI 02818. Offers MSEM. *Program availability:* Part-time, evening/weekend, 100% online, blended/hybrid learning. *Students:* 16 full-time (0 women), 1 (woman) part-time; includes 5 minority (3 Black or African American, non-Hispanic/Latino; 2 Hispanic/Latino), 1 international. Average age 29. *Entrance requirements:* For master's, Minimum GPA of 2.5 awarded Bachelor's degree in related field from accredited institution plus personal statement. Additional exam requirements/recommendations for international students: Required—TOEFL. *Application deadline:* Applications are processed on a rolling basis. Application fee: $25. Electronic applications accepted. *Expenses:* $565.00 x 45 credits to complete this program. Tuition is $25,425.00. Visit https://www.neit.edu/Financial-Aid/Tuition-and-Fees for more information. *Unit head:* Dr. Douglas H. Sherman, Senior Vice President and Provost, 401-739-5000 Ext. 3481, Fax: 401-886-0859, E-mail: dsherman@neit.edu. *Application contact:* Lynn M Fawthrop, Vice President of Enrollment Management and Marketing, 401-739-5000 Ext. 3315, Fax: 401-886-0859, E-mail: lmfawthrop@neit.edu.
Website: https://www.neit.edu/Programs/Online-and-Hybrid-Degree-Programs/Engineering-Management-Masters-Degree

New Jersey Institute of Technology, Newark College of Engineering, Newark, NJ 07102. Offers biomedical engineering (MS, PhD); biopharmaceutical engineering (MS); chemical engineering (MS, PhD); civil engineering (MS, PhD); computer engineering (MS); critical infrastructure systems (MS); electrical engineering (MS, PhD); engineering management (MS); engineering science (MS); environmental engineering (MS, PhD); healthcare systems management (MS); industrial engineering (MS, PhD); internet engineering (MS); manufacturing systems engineering (MS); materials science & engineering (PhD); materials science and engineering (MS); mechanical engineering (MS, PhD); occupational safety and health engineering (MS). *Program availability:* Part-time, evening/weekend. *Faculty:* 147 full-time (26 women), 133 part-time/adjunct (16 women). *Students:* 690 full-time (163 women), 594 part-time (130 women); includes 427 minority (79 Black or African American, non-Hispanic/Latino; 181 Asian, non-Hispanic/Latino; 140 Hispanic/Latino; 27 Two or more races, non-Hispanic/Latino), 553 international. Average age 27. 2,334 applicants, 57% accepted, 452 enrolled. In 2018, 418 master's, 31 doctorates awarded. Terminal master's awarded for partial completion of doctoral program. *Degree requirements:* For master's, thesis (for some programs); for doctorate, thesis/dissertation. *Entrance requirements:* For master's, GRE General Test, minimum GPA 2.8, personal statement, 1 letter of recommendation, transcripts; for doctorate, GRE General Test, minimum GPA of 3.5, personal statement, 3 letters of recommendation, transcripts. Additional exam requirements/recommendations for international students: Required—TOEFL (minimum score 550 paper-based; 79 iBT), IELTS (minimum score 6.5). *Application deadline:* For fall admission, 6/1 priority date for domestic students, 5/1 priority date for international students; for spring admission, 11/15 priority date for domestic and international students. Applications are processed on a rolling basis. Application fee: $75. Electronic applications accepted. *Expenses:* $22,690 per year (in-state), $32,136 per year (out-of-state). *Financial support:* In 2018–19, 396 students received support, including 52 fellowships with full tuition reimbursements available (averaging $22,000 per year), 113 research assistantships with full tuition reimbursements available (averaging $22,000 per year), 101 teaching assistantships with full tuition reimbursements available (averaging $22,000 per year); career-related

internships or fieldwork, Federal Work-Study, scholarships/grants, and unspecified assistantships also available. Financial award application deadline: 1/15. *Faculty research:* Nonlinear signal processing, intelligent medical image analysis, calibration issues in coherent localization, computer-aided design, neural network for tool wear measurement. *Total annual research expenditures:* $41.7 million. *Unit head:* Dr. Moshe Kam, Dean, 973-596-5534, Fax: 973-596-2316, E-mail: moshe.kam@njit.edu. *Application contact:* Stephen Eck, Director of Admissions, 973-596-3300, Fax: 973-596-3461, E-mail: admissions@njit.edu.
Website: http://engineering.njit.edu/

New Mexico Institute of Mining and Technology, Center for Graduate Studies, Department of Management, Socorro, NM 87801. Offers STEM education (MEM). *Program availability:* Part-time.

Northeastern University, College of Engineering, Boston, MA 02115-5096. Offers bioengineering (MS, PhD); chemical engineering (MS, PhD); civil engineering (MS, PhD); computer engineering (PhD); computer systems engineering (MS); electrical and computer engineering (MS); electrical and computer engineering leadership (MS); electrical engineering (PhD); energy systems (MS); engineering and public policy (MS); engineering management (MS, Certificate); environmental engineering (MS); industrial engineering (MS, PhD); information assurance (PhD); information systems (MS); interdisciplinary engineering (PhD); mechanical engineering (PhD); operations research (MS); telecommunication systems management (MS). *Program availability:* Part-time, online learning. Electronic applications accepted. *Expenses:* Contact institution.

Northwestern University, McCormick School of Engineering and Applied Science, Department of Industrial Engineering and Management Sciences, Master's in Engineering Management Program, Evanston, IL 60208. Offers MEM. *Program availability:* Part-time, evening/weekend. *Entrance requirements:* For master's, 3 years of work experience. Additional exam requirements/recommendations for international students: Required—TOEFL (minimum score 100 iBT), IELTS (minimum score 7). Electronic applications accepted. *Expenses:* Contact institution.

Northwestern University, McCormick School of Engineering and Applied Science, MMM Program, Evanston, IL 60208. Offers design innovation (MBA, MS). *Entrance requirements:* For master's, GMAT or GRE, transcripts, two letters of recommendation, resume, evaluative interview report, work experience, two core essays, interest essay, video essay. Additional exam requirements/recommendations for international students: Required—TOEFL, IELTS. *Expenses:* Contact institution.

Oakland University, Graduate Study and Lifelong Learning, School of Engineering and Computer Science, Department of Industrial and Systems Engineering, Program in Engineering Management, Rochester, MI 48309-4401. Offers MS. *Entrance requirements:* Additional exam requirements/recommendations for international students: Required—TOEFL (minimum score 550 paper-based). Electronic applications accepted. *Expenses:* Contact institution.

Oklahoma Christian University, Graduate School of Engineering and Computer Science, Oklahoma City, OK 73136-1100. Offers electrical and computer engineering (MSE); engineering management (MSE); mechanical engineering (MSE); software engineering (MSCS, MSE). *Program availability:* Part-time. *Entrance requirements:* Additional exam requirements/recommendations for international students: Required—TOEFL (minimum score 550 paper-based). Electronic applications accepted. *Expenses:* Contact institution.

Old Dominion University, Frank Batten College of Engineering and Technology, Program in Engineering Management, Norfolk, VA 23529. Offers MEM, MS. *Program availability:* Part-time, evening/weekend, 100% online, blended/hybrid learning, Portable Media. *Degree requirements:* For master's, comprehensive exam, thesis optional, project. *Entrance requirements:* For master's, GRE, minimum GPA of 3.0. Additional exam requirements/recommendations for international students: Required—TOEFL (minimum score 550 paper-based; 79 iBT). Electronic applications accepted. *Expenses:* Contact institution. *Faculty research:* Project management, systems engineering, modeling and simulation, virtual collaborative environments, multidisciplinary designs.

Old Dominion University, Frank Batten College of Engineering and Technology, Program in Engineering Management and Systems Engineering, Norfolk, VA 23529. Offers D Eng, PhD. *Program availability:* Part-time, evening/weekend, 100% online, blended/hybrid learning. *Degree requirements:* For doctorate, thesis/dissertation, candidacy exam, project. *Entrance requirements:* For doctorate, GRE, resume, letters of recommendation, minimum GPA of 3.0, interview, essay outlining intended area of specialization. Additional exam requirements/recommendations for international students: Required—TOEFL (minimum score 550 paper-based; 79 iBT). Electronic applications accepted. *Faculty research:* Project management, systems engineering, modeling and simulation, virtual collaboration environments, multidisciplinary designs, human systems engineering, decision analysis.

Oregon State University, College of Engineering, Program in Industrial Engineering, Corvallis, OR 97331. Offers advanced manufacturing (M Eng, MS, PhD); engineering management (M Eng); human systems engineering (M Eng, MS, PhD); information systems engineering (M Eng, MS, PhD); manufacturing systems engineering (M Eng, MS, PhD). *Program availability:* 100% online. *Entrance requirements:* For master's and doctorate, GRE. Additional exam requirements/recommendations for international students: Required—TOEFL (minimum score 80 iBT), IELTS (minimum score 6.5). *Expenses:* Contact institution.

Penn State Great Valley, Graduate Studies, Engineering Division, Malvern, PA 19355-1488. Offers engineering management (MEM); software engineering (MSE); systems engineering (M Eng, Certificate).

Penn State Harrisburg, Graduate School, School of Science, Engineering and Technology, Middletown, PA 17057. Offers civil engineering (MS); computer science (MS); electrical engineering (M Eng, MS); engineering management (MPS); engineering science (M Eng); environmental engineering (M Eng); environmental pollution control (MEPC, MS); mechanical engineering (MS); structural engineering (Certificate). *Program availability:* Part-time, evening/weekend.

Point Park University, School of Arts and Sciences, Department of Natural Sciences, Engineering and Technology, Pittsburgh, PA 15222-1984. Offers engineering management (MS); environmental studies (MS). *Program availability:* Part-time, evening/weekend. *Degree requirements:* For master's, comprehensive exam (for some programs), thesis or alternative. *Entrance requirements:* For master's, minimum QPA of 2.75, 2 letters of recommendation, minimum B average in engineering technology or a related field, official undergraduate transcript, statement of intent, resume. Additional exam requirements/recommendations for international students: Required—TOEFL. Electronic applications accepted.

Polytechnic University of Puerto Rico, Graduate School, Hato Rey, PR 00918. Offers business administration (MBA), including computer information systems, general management, management of information systems, management of international enterprises; civil engineering (ME, MS); computer engineering (ME, MS); computer science (MCS, MS); electrical engineering (ME, MS); engineering management (MEM); environmental management (MEM); landscape architecture (M Land Arch); manufacturing competitiveness (MMC, MS); manufacturing engineering (ME, MS); mechanical

engineering (M Mech E). *Accreditation:* ASLA. *Program availability:* Part-time, evening/weekend. *Entrance requirements:* For master's, 3 letters of recommendation.

Polytechnic University of Puerto Rico, Orlando Campus, Graduate School, Orlando, FL 32825. Offers accounting (MBA); business administration (MBA); construction management (MEM); engineering management (MEM); environmental management (MEM); finance (MBA); human resources management (MBA); management of international enterprises (MBA); management of technology (MBA); manufacturing management (MEM). *Program availability:* Part-time, evening/weekend, online learning. *Entrance requirements:* For master's, minimum GPA of 3.0. Additional exam requirements/recommendations for international students: Recommended—TOEFL. Electronic applications accepted.

Portland State University, Graduate Studies, College of Liberal Arts and Sciences, Systems Science Program, Portland, OR 97207-0751. Offers computational intelligence (Certificate); computer modeling and simulation (Certificate); systems science (MS); systems science/anthropology (PhD); systems science/business administration (PhD); systems science/civil engineering (PhD); systems science/economics (PhD); systems science/engineering management (PhD); systems science/general (PhD); systems science/mathematical sciences (PhD); systems science/mechanical engineering (PhD); systems science/psychology (PhD); systems science/sociology (PhD). *Degree requirements:* For master's, comprehensive exam (for some programs), thesis optional; for doctorate, variable foreign language requirement, comprehensive exam (for some programs), thesis/dissertation. *Entrance requirements:* For master's, GRE/GMAT (recommended), minimum GPA of 3.0 on undergraduate or graduate work, 2 letters of recommendation, statement of interest; for doctorate, GMAT, GRE General Test, minimum GPA of 3.0 undergraduate, 3.25 graduate; 3 letters of recommendation; statement of interest. Additional exam requirements/recommendations for international students: Required—TOEFL (minimum score 550 paper-based; 80 iBT). Electronic applications accepted. *Faculty research:* Systems theory and methodology, artificial intelligence neural networks, information theory, nonlinear dynamics/chaos, modeling and simulation.

Portland State University, Graduate Studies, Maseeh College of Engineering and Computer Science, Department of Engineering and Technology Management, Portland, OR 97207-0751. Offers engineering and technology management (MS); technology management (PhD); MS/MBA; MS/MS. *Program availability:* Part-time, evening/weekend. *Degree requirements:* For master's, thesis or alternative, capstone; for doctorate, one foreign language, comprehensive exam, thesis/dissertation, oral and written exams. *Entrance requirements:* For master's, degree in engineering or related discipline; minimum GPA of 2.75 undergraduate or 3.0 graduate (at least 12 credits); minimum 4 years of experience in engineering or related discipline; 3 letters of recommendation; background in probability/statistics, differential equations, computer programming and linear algebra; for doctorate, GRE General Test (minimum combined score of 1100 for verbal and quantitative), minimum GPA of 3.0 undergraduate, 3.25 graduate. Additional exam requirements/recommendations for international students: Required—TOEFL (minimum score 550 paper-based; 80 iBT). Electronic applications accepted. *Expenses:* Contact institution. *Faculty research:* Scheduling, hierarchical decision modeling, operations research, knowledge-based information systems.

Robert Morris University, School of Engineering, Mathematics and Science, Moon Township, PA 15108-1189. Offers engineering management (MS). *Program availability:* Part-time-only, evening/weekend, 100% online. *Faculty:* 7 full-time (1 woman), 1 part-time/adjunct (0 women). *Students:* 20 part-time (4 women); includes 1 minority (Black or African American, non-Hispanic/Latino), 9 international. Average age 28. 34 applicants, 18% accepted, 6 enrolled. In 2018, 33 master's awarded. *Degree requirements:* For master's, Completion of 30 credits. *Entrance requirements:* For master's, letters of recommendation. Additional exam requirements/recommendations for international students: Required—TOEFL (minimum score 550 paper-based; 79 iBT). *Application deadline:* For fall admission, 7/1 priority date for domestic and international students; for spring admission, 11/1 priority date for domestic and international students. Applications are processed on a rolling basis. Application fee: $35. Electronic applications accepted. *Expenses:* $980 per credit tuition, $80 per credit fees for 2018-2019. *Financial support:* Federal Work-Study, institutionally sponsored loans, and unspecified assistantships available. Financial award application deadline: 5/1; financial award applicants required to submit FAFSA. *Unit head:* Dr. Maria V. Kalevitch, Dean, 412-397-4020, E-mail: kalevitch@rmu.edu. *Application contact:* Dr. Maria V. Kalevitch, Dean, 412-397-4020, E-mail: kalevitch@rmu.edu.
Website: https://www.rmu.edu/academics/schools/sems

Rochester Institute of Technology, Graduate Enrollment Services, Kate Gleason College of Engineering, Design, Development and Manufacturing Department, MS Program in Product Development, Rochester, NY 14623-5603. Offers MS. *Program availability:* Part-time, evening/weekend, 100% online, blended/hybrid learning. *Students:* 1 full-time, 22 part-time (4 women); includes 2 minority (both Black or African American, non-Hispanic/Latino), 1 international. Average age 38. 21 applicants, 67% accepted, 11 enrolled. In 2018, 6 master's awarded. *Degree requirements:* For master's, capstone project. *Entrance requirements:* For master's, undergraduate degree in engineering or related field, minimum GPA of 3.0, 2 years of experience in product development, one professional recommendation, resume. Additional exam requirements/recommendations for international students: Required—TOEFL (minimum score 550 paper-based; 79 iBT), IELTS (minimum score 6.5), PTE (minimum score 58). *Application deadline:* Applications are processed on a rolling basis. Application fee: $65. Electronic applications accepted. *Expenses:* Contact institution. *Financial support:* In 2018-19, 6 students received support. Scholarships/grants available. Support available to part-time students. Financial award applicants required to submit FAFSA. *Faculty research:* Systems engineering, lean product development, decision analysis, agile methods, project management. *Unit head:* Christine Fisher, Program Director, 585-475-7971, Fax: 585-475-4080, E-mail: christine.fisher@rit.edu. *Application contact:* Diane Ellison, Senior Associate Vice President, Graduate Enrollment Services, 585-475-2229, Fax: 585-475-7164, E-mail: gradinfo@rit.edu.
Website: https://www.rit.edu/study/product-development-ms

Rochester Institute of Technology, Graduate Enrollment Services, Kate Gleason College of Engineering, Industrial and Systems Engineering Department, ME Program in Engineering Management, Rochester, NY 14623-5603. Offers ME. *Program availability:* Part-time. *Students:* 12 full-time (8 women), 17 part-time (1 woman); includes 2 minority (1 Asian, non-Hispanic/Latino; 1 Hispanic/Latino), 5 international. Average age 25. 93 applicants, 31% accepted, 10 enrolled. In 2018, 23 master's awarded. *Degree requirements:* For master's, thesis or alternative, capstone. *Entrance requirements:* For master's, GRE, minimum GPA of 3.0 (recommended), letters of recommendation, one-page statement of purpose. Additional exam requirements/recommendations for international students: Required—TOEFL (minimum score 580 paper-based; 90 iBT), IELTS (minimum score 6.5), PTE (minimum score 58). *Application deadline:* For fall admission, 2/15 priority date for domestic and international students; for spring admission, 12/15 priority date for domestic and international students. Applications are processed on a rolling basis. Application fee: $65. Electronic applications accepted. *Financial support:* In 2018-19, 19 students received support. Research assistantships with partial tuition reimbursements available, teaching assistantships with partial tuition reimbursements available, career-related internships or

fieldwork, scholarships/grants, and unspecified assistantships available. Support available to part-time students. Financial award applicants required to submit FAFSA. *Faculty research:* Systems engineering/product development; lean manufacturing; operations research and simulation; production and logistics; project management. *Unit head:* Michael Kuhl, Graduate Program Director, 585-475-2134, E-mail: mekeie@rit.edu. *Application contact:* Diane Ellison, Senior Associate Vice President, Graduate Enrollment Services, 585-475-2229, Fax: 585-475-7164, E-mail: gradinfo@rit.edu.
Website: https://www.rit.edu/study/engineering-management-me

Rose-Hulman Institute of Technology, Graduate Studies, Department of Engineering Management, Terre Haute, IN 47803-3999. Offers M Eng, MS. *Program availability:* Part-time. *Faculty:* 5 full-time (2 women). *Students:* 11 full-time (3 women), 9 part-time (3 women); includes 3 minority (2 Asian, non-Hispanic/Latino; 1 Two or more races, non-Hispanic/Latino), 6 international. Average age 25. 20 applicants, 65% accepted, 9 enrolled. In 2018, 11 master's awarded. *Degree requirements:* For master's, integrated project. *Entrance requirements:* For master's, GRE, minimum GPA of 3.0. Additional exam requirements/recommendations for international students: Required—TOEFL (minimum score 580 paper-based; 94 iBT), IELTS (minimum score 7). *Application deadline:* For fall admission, 2/1 priority date for domestic and international students; for winter admission, 10/1 for domestic students, 4/1 for international students; for spring admission, 1/15 for domestic students, 11/1 for international students. Applications are processed on a rolling basis. Application fee: $0. Electronic applications accepted. *Expenses: Tuition:* Full-time $46,641. *Financial support:* In 2018–19, 17 students received support. Fellowships with tuition reimbursements available, research assistantships with tuition reimbursements available, institutionally sponsored loans, scholarships/grants, and tuition waivers (full and partial) available. *Faculty research:* Systems engineering, technical entrepreneurship, project management, organizational development and management, manufacturing and supply chain, marketing and new product development. *Unit head:* Dr. Craig Downing, Department Head, 812-877-8822, E-mail: downing@rose-hulman.edu. *Application contact:* Dr. Craig Downing, Department Head, 812-877-8822, E-mail: downing@rose-hulman.edu.
Website: https://www.rose-hulman.edu/academics/academic-departments/engineering-management/index.html

Saint Martin's University, Office of Graduate Studies, Program in Engineering Management, Lacey, WA 98503. Offers M Eng Mgt. *Program availability:* Part-time. *Faculty:* 3 full-time (0 women), 1 part-time/adjunct (0 women). *Students:* 1 (woman) full-time, 5 part-time (1 woman); includes 1 minority (Hispanic/Latino), 3 international. Average age 30. 4 applicants, 50% accepted, 1 enrolled. In 2018, 6 master's awarded. *Degree requirements:* For master's, comprehensive exam (for some programs), thesis optional. *Entrance requirements:* For master's, engineering license examination, minimum GPA of 2.8. Additional exam requirements/recommendations for international students: Required—TOEFL (minimum score 550 paper-based; 79 iBT); Recommended—IELTS (minimum score 6.5). *Application deadline:* For fall admission, 4/1 priority date for domestic and international students; for spring admission, 11/1 priority date for domestic and international students. Applications are processed on a rolling basis. Application fee: $50. Electronic applications accepted. *Expenses: Tuition:* Full-time $22,950; part-time $1275 per credit. Tuition and fees vary according to course load, campus/location and program. *Financial support:* Fellowships, research assistantships, and Federal Work-Study available. Support available to part-time students. Financial award application deadline: 3/1; financial award applicants required to submit FAFSA. *Faculty research:* Highway safety management, transportation, hydraulics, database structure. *Unit head:* Dr. David Olwell, Dean, Hal and Inge Marcus School of Engineering, 360-688-2731, Fax: 360-438-4522, E-mail: dolwell@stmartin.edu. *Application contact:* Chantelle Petron Marker, Senior Recruiter, 360-412-6128, E-mail: cmarker@stmartin.edu.
Website: https://www.stmartin.edu

St. Mary's University, School of Science, Engineering and Technology, Program in Engineering Systems Management, San Antonio, TX 78228. Offers MS. *Program availability:* Part-time, evening/weekend, online learning. *Students:* 15 full-time (5 women), 3 part-time (2 women); includes 8 minority (all Hispanic/Latino), 8 international. Average age 23. 5 applicants, 80% accepted, 2 enrolled. In 2018, 2 master's awarded. *Degree requirements:* For master's, thesis or project. *Entrance requirements:* For master's, GRE (minimum quantitative score of 148), BS in computer engineering, electrical engineering, or closely-related discipline; minimum GPA of 3.0; written statement of purpose indicating applicant's interests and objectives; two letters of recommendation. Additional exam requirements/recommendations for international students: Required—TOEFL (minimum score 550 paper-based; 80 iBT), IELTS (minimum score 6). *Application deadline:* For fall admission, 7/1 for domestic students; for spring admission, 11/15 for domestic students; for summer admission, 4/1 for domestic students. Applications are processed on a rolling basis. Application fee: $0. Electronic applications accepted. *Expenses: Tuition:* Full-time $16,830; part-time $935 per credit hour. *Required fees:* $1055. Tuition and fees vary according to program. *Financial support:* Career-related internships or fieldwork, Federal Work-Study, institutionally sponsored loans, scholarships/grants, and health care benefits available. Financial award application deadline: 3/31; financial award applicants required to submit FAFSA. *Faculty research:* Supply chain, financial factors in supply chains, engineering ethics, high technology and society, lean production. *Unit head:* Dr. Ozgur Aktunc, Graduate Program Director, 210-431-2052, E-mail: oaktunc@stmarytx.edu. *Application contact:* Dr. Ozgur Aktunc, Graduate Program Director, 210-431-2052, E-mail: oaktunc@stmarytx.edu.
Website: https://www.stmarytx.edu/academics/programs/master-engineering-systems-management/

Santa Clara University, School of Engineering, Santa Clara, CA 95053. Offers applied mathematics (MS); bioengineering (MS); civil, environmental, and sustainable engineering (MS); computer science and engineering (MS, PhD, Engineer); electrical engineering (MS, PhD, Engineer); engineering management and leadership (MS); mechanical engineering (MS, PhD, Engineer); power systems and sustainable energy (MS); software engineering (MS). *Program availability:* Part-time. *Faculty:* 72 full-time (24 women), 52 part-time/adjunct (9 women). *Students:* 555 full-time (211 women), 269 part-time (91 women); includes 208 minority (8 Black or African American, non-Hispanic/Latino; 1 American Indian or Alaska Native, non-Hispanic/Latino; 145 Asian, non-Hispanic/Latino; 28 Hispanic/Latino; 26 Two or more races, non-Hispanic/Latino), 472 international. Average age 27. 1,309 applicants, 36% accepted, 269 enrolled. In 2018, 320 master's, 7 doctorates awarded. *Entrance requirements:* For master's, GRE, official transcript; for doctorate, GRE, Official transcript, 500 word statement of purpose, three letters of recommendation. Additional exam requirements/recommendations for international students: Required—TOEFL (minimum score 79 iBT), IELTS (minimum score 6.5). *Application deadline:* For fall admission, 6/1 for domestic students; for winter admission, 9/6 for domestic students; for spring admission, 1/10 for domestic students; for summer admission, 3/6 for domestic students. Application fee: $60. Electronic applications accepted. *Financial support:* Fellowships, Federal Work-Study, and scholarships/grants available. Support available to part-time students. Financial award applicants required to submit FAFSA. *Unit head:* Dr. Elaine Scott, Dean, 408-554-3512, E-mail: epscott@scu.edu. *Application contact:* Stacey Tinker, Director of Admissions and Marketing, 408-554-4748, Fax: 408-554-4323, E-mail: stinker@scu.edu.
Website: http://www.scu.edu/engineering/graduate/

South Dakota School of Mines and Technology, Graduate Division, Program in Construction Engineering Management, Rapid City, SD 57701-3995. Offers MS. *Program availability:* Part-time, evening/weekend, online learning. *Entrance requirements:* For master's, GRE General Test. Additional exam requirements/recommendations for international students: Required—TOEFL (minimum score 520 paper-based; 68 iBT). Electronic applications accepted.

South Dakota School of Mines and Technology, Graduate Division, Program in Engineering Management, Rapid City, SD 57701-3995. Offers MS. Program offered jointly with The University of South Dakota. *Program availability:* Part-time, online learning. *Entrance requirements:* For master's, GMAT. Additional exam requirements/recommendations for international students: Required—TOEFL, TWE. Electronic applications accepted.

Southern Illinois University Carbondale, Graduate School, College of Engineering, Program in Quality Engineering Management, Carbondale, IL 62901-4701. Offers quality engineering and management (MS). *Degree requirements:* For master's, comprehensive exam, thesis. *Entrance requirements:* For master's, minimum GPA of 2.7. Additional exam requirements/recommendations for international students: Required—TOEFL. *Faculty research:* Computer-aided manufacturing, robotics, quality assurance.

Southern Methodist University, Lyle School of Engineering, Department of Engineering Management, Information, and Systems, Dallas, TX 75275. Offers engineering entrepreneurship (MS); engineering management (MS, DE); information engineering and management (MSIEM); operations research (MS, PhD); systems engineering (MS). MS in engineering entrepreneurship offered in collaboration with the Cox School of Business. *Program availability:* Part-time, evening/weekend, online learning. Terminal master's awarded for partial completion of doctoral program. *Degree requirements:* For master's, thesis optional; for doctorate, thesis/dissertation, oral and written qualifying exams. *Entrance requirements:* For master's, minimum GPA of 3.0 in last 2 years; bachelor's degree in engineering, mathematics, sciences, or technical area; for doctorate, GRE General Test (operations research, engineering management), bachelor's degree in related field. Additional exam requirements/recommendations for international students: Required—TOEFL. *Faculty research:* Telecommunications, decision systems, information engineering, operations research, software.

Southern New Hampshire University, School of Business, Manchester, NH 03106-1045. Offers accounting (MBA, Graduate Certificate); accounting finance (MS); accounting/auditing (MS); accounting/forensic accounting (MS); accounting/management accounting (MS); accounting/taxation (MS); applied economics (MS); athletic administration (MBA, Graduate Certificate); business administration (IMBA, Certificate), including business information systems (Certificate), human resource management (Certificate); business analytics (MBA); business intelligence (MBA); communication (MA), including new media and marketing, public relations; community economic development (MBA); criminal justice (MBA); data analytics (MS); economics (MBA); engineering management (MBA); entrepreneurship (MBA); finance (MBA, MS, Graduate Certificate); finance/corporate finance (MS); finance/investments (MS); forensic accounting (MBA); forensic accounting and fraud examination (Graduate Certificate); healthcare informatics (MBA); healthcare management (MBA); human resource management (MS); human resources (MBA); information technology (MS); information technology management (MBA); international business (PhD); Internet marketing (MBA); leadership (MBA); leadership of nonprofit organizations (Graduate Certificate); management (MS); marketing (MBA, MS, Graduate Certificate); music business (MBA); operations and project management (MS); operations and supply chain management (MBA, Graduate Certificate); organizational leadership (MS); project management (MBA, Graduate Certificate); public administration (MBA, Graduate Certificate); quantitative analysis (MBA); Six Sigma (Graduate Certificate); Six Sigma quality (MBA); social media marketing (MBA, Graduate Certificate); sport management (MBA, MS, Graduate Certificate); sustainability and environmental compliance (MBA); MBA/Certificate. *Accreditation:* ACBSP. *Program availability:* Part-time, evening/weekend, online learning. Terminal master's awarded for partial completion of doctoral program. *Degree requirements:* For master's, one foreign language, comprehensive exam (for some programs), thesis or alternative; for doctorate, one foreign language, comprehensive exam, thesis/dissertation. *Entrance requirements:* For master's, minimum GPA of 2.5; for doctorate, GMAT. Additional exam requirements/recommendations for international students: Required—TOEFL (minimum score 500 paper-based). Electronic applications accepted.

Stanford University, School of Engineering, Department of Management Science and Engineering, Stanford, CA 94305-2004. Offers MS, PhD. *Expenses: Tuition:* Full-time $50,703; part-time $32,970 per year. *Required fees:* $651.
Website: http://www.stanford.edu/dept/MSandE/

Stevens Institute of Technology, Graduate School, School of Business, Program in Business Administration, Hoboken, NJ 07030. Offers business intelligence and analytics (MBA); engineering management (MBA); finance (MBA); information systems (MBA); innovation and entrepreneurship (MBA); marketing (MBA); pharmaceutical management (MBA); project management (MBA, Certificate); technology management (MBA); telecommunications management (MBA). *Accreditation:* AACSB. *Program availability:* Part-time, evening/weekend. *Faculty:* 58 full-time (8 women), 18 part-time/adjunct (3 women). *Students:* 44 full-time (23 women), 202 part-time (90 women); includes 56 minority (12 Black or African American, non-Hispanic/Latino; 2 American Indian or Alaska Native, non-Hispanic/Latino; 40 Asian, non-Hispanic/Latino; 2 Hispanic/Latino), 28 international. Average age 37. In 2018, 45 master's awarded. Terminal master's awarded for partial completion of doctoral program. *Degree requirements:* For master's, thesis optional, minimum B average in major field and overall; for Certificate, minimum B average. *Entrance requirements:* For master's, GRE/GMAT scores: GRE scores are required for all applicants applying to a full-time graduate program in the Schaefer School of Engineering and Science (SES). International applicants must submit TOEFL/IELTS scores and fulfill the English Language Proficiency Requirements in order to be considered. Additional exam requirements/recommendations for international students: Required—TOEFL (minimum score 74 iBT), IELTS (minimum score 6). *Application deadline:* For fall admission, 4/1 for domestic and international students; for spring admission, 11/1 for domestic and international students; for summer admission, 5/1 for domestic students. Applications are processed on a rolling basis. Application fee: $60. Electronic applications accepted. *Expenses: Tuition:* Full-time $35,960; part-time $1620 per credit. *Required fees:* $1290; $600 per semester. Tuition and fees vary according to course load. *Financial support:* Fellowships, research assistantships, teaching assistantships, career-related internships or fieldwork, Federal Work-Study, scholarships/grants, and unspecified assistantships available. Financial award application deadline: 2/15; financial award applicants required to submit FAFSA. *Unit head:* Dr. Gregory Prastacos, Dean, 201-216-8366, E-mail: gprastac@stevens.edu. *Application contact:* Graduate Admissions, 888-783-8367, Fax: 888-511-1306, E-mail: graduate@stevens.edu.
Website: https://www.stevens.edu/school-business/masters-programs/mbaemba

Stevens Institute of Technology, Graduate School, School of Systems and Enterprises, Program in Engineering Management, Hoboken, NJ 07030. Offers M Eng, PhD, Certificate. *Program availability:* Part-time, evening/weekend. *Faculty:* 28 full-time

(8 women), 5 part-time/adjunct (1 woman). *Students:* 91 full-time (26 women), 45 part-time (11 women); includes 11 minority (3 Black or African American, non-Hispanic/Latino; 8 Asian, non-Hispanic/Latino), 78 international. Average age 26. In 2018, 83 master's, 1 doctorate, 8 other advanced degrees awarded. Terminal master's awarded for partial completion of doctoral program. *Degree requirements:* For master's, thesis optional, minimum B average in major field and overall; for doctorate, comprehensive exam (for some programs), thesis/dissertation; for Certificate, minimum B average. *Entrance requirements:* For master's, GRE/GMAT scores: GRE scores are required for all applicants applying to a full-time graduate program in the Schaefer School of Engineering and Science (SES). International applicants must submit TOEFL/IELTS scores and fulfill the English Language Proficiency Requirements in order to be considered. Additional exam requirements/recommendations for international students: Required—TOEFL (minimum score 74 iBT), IELTS (minimum score 6). *Application deadline:* For fall admission, 4/15 for domestic and international students; for spring admission, 11/1 for domestic and international students; for summer admission, 5/1 for domestic students. Applications are processed on a rolling basis. Application fee: $60. Electronic applications accepted. *Expenses: Tuition:* Full-time $35,960; part-time $1620 per credit. *Required fees:* $1290; $600 per semester. Tuition and fees vary according to course load. *Financial support:* Fellowships, research assistantships, teaching assistantships, career-related internships or fieldwork, Federal Work-Study, scholarships/grants, and unspecified assistantships available. Financial award application deadline: 2/15; financial award applicants required to submit FAFSA. *Unit head:* Dr. Yehia Massoud, Dean of SSE, 201-216.8025, E-mail: yehia.massoud@stevens.edu. *Application contact:* Graduate Admissions, 888-783-8367, Fax: 888-511-1306, E-mail: graduate@stevens.edu.
Website: https://www.stevens.edu/school-systems-enterprises

Syracuse University, College of Engineering and Computer Science, MS Program in Engineering Management, Syracuse, NY 13244. Offers MS. *Program availability:* Part-time. *Students:* Average age 25. *Entrance requirements:* For master's, GRE, three letters of recommendation, personal statement, resume, official transcripts. Additional exam requirements/recommendations for international students: Required—TOEFL (minimum score 100 iBT). *Application deadline:* For fall admission, 7/1 priority date for domestic students, 6/1 priority date for international students; for spring admission, 10/1 priority date for domestic students, 11/1 priority date for international students. Applications are processed on a rolling basis. Application fee: $75. Electronic applications accepted. *Financial support:* Fellowships, research assistantships, and teaching assistantships available. Financial award application deadline: 1/1. *Faculty research:* Industrial energy systems, engineering education, design methodologies, second-law analysis. *Unit head:* Fred Carranti, Program Director, 315-443-4346, E-mail: carranti@syr.edu. *Application contact:* Kathleen Joyce, Assistant Dean, 315-443-2219, E-mail: topgrads@syr.edu.
Website: http://eng-cs.syr.edu/program/engineering-management/?degree-masters_program

Tarleton State University, College of Graduate Studies, College of Science and Technology, Department of Engineering Technology, Stephenville, TX 76402. Offers quality and engineering management (MS). *Program availability:* Part-time, evening/weekend, 100% online, blended/hybrid learning. *Faculty:* 1 (woman) full-time, 1 part-time/adjunct (0 women). *Students:* 4 full-time (0 women), 36 part-time (7 women). Average age 39. 16 applicants, 94% accepted, 12 enrolled. In 2018, 12 master's awarded. *Degree requirements:* For master's, comprehensive exam, thesis optional. *Entrance requirements:* For master's, GRE General Test, minimum GPA of 3.0. Additional exam requirements/recommendations for international students: Required—TOEFL (minimum score 520 paper-based; 69 iBT); Recommended—IELTS (minimum score 6), TSE (minimum score 50). *Application deadline:* For fall admission, 8/15 for domestic students; for spring admission, 1/7 for domestic students. Applications are processed on a rolling basis. Application fee: $50 ($130 for international students). Electronic applications accepted. *Expenses:* Contact institution. *Financial support:* Application deadline: 5/1; applicants required to submit FAFSA. *Unit head:* Billy Gray, Department Head, 254-968-9374, E-mail: bgray@tarleton.edu. *Application contact:* Information Contact, 254-968-9104, Fax: 254-968-9670, E-mail: gradoffice@tarleton.edu.
Website: http://www.tarleton.edu/degrees/masters/ms-quality-engineering-management/

Temple University, College of Engineering, Program in Engineering Management, Philadelphia, PA 19122-6096. Offers MS, Certificate. Program jointly offered with Fox School of Business. *Program availability:* Part-time, evening/weekend, 100% online, blended/hybrid learning. *Entrance requirements:* For master's, GRE, minimum GPA of 3.0; BS in engineering from ABET-accredited or equivalent institution or related degree; resume; goals statement; three letters of reference; official transcripts. Additional exam requirements/recommendations for international students: Required—TOEFL (minimum score 550 paper-based; 79 iBT), IELTS (minimum score 6.5), PTE (minimum score 53). Electronic applications accepted. *Expenses:* Contact institution.

Texas A&M University, College of Engineering, Department of Industrial and Systems Engineering, College Station, TX 77843. Offers engineering systems management (MS); industrial engineering (M Eng, MS, PhD). *Program availability:* Part-time, online learning. *Faculty:* 38. *Students:* 268 full-time (58 women), 96 part-time (23 women); includes 28 minority (5 Black or African American, non-Hispanic/Latino; 9 Asian, non-Hispanic/Latino; 13 Hispanic/Latino; 1 Two or more races, non-Hispanic/Latino), 288 international. Average age 26. 677 applicants, 44% accepted, 137 enrolled. In 2018, 105 master's, 6 doctorates awarded. *Degree requirements:* For master's, comprehensive exam (for some programs), thesis optional; for doctorate, comprehensive exam, thesis/dissertation. *Entrance requirements:* For master's and doctorate, GRE General Test. Additional exam requirements/recommendations for international students: Required—TOEFL (minimum score 550 paper-based; 80 iBT), IELTS (minimum score 6), PTE (minimum score 53). *Application deadline:* For fall admission, 6/1 priority date for domestic students, 3/1 priority date for international students; for spring admission, 8/1 priority date for domestic and international students. Applications are processed on a rolling basis. Application fee: $50 ($90 for international students). Electronic applications accepted. *Expenses:* Contact institution. *Financial support:* In 2018–19, 259 students received support, including 7 fellowships with tuition reimbursements available (averaging $22,319 per year), 89 research assistantships with tuition reimbursements available (averaging $11,980 per year), 51 teaching assistantships with tuition reimbursements available (averaging $13,217 per year); career-related internships or fieldwork, institutionally sponsored loans, scholarships/grants, traineeships, health care benefits, tuition waivers (full and partial), and unspecified assistantships also available. Support available to part-time students. Financial award application deadline: 3/15; financial award applicants required to submit FAFSA. *Faculty research:* Manufacturing systems, computer integration, operations research, logistics, simulation. *Unit head:* Dr. Cesar O. Malave, Head, 979-845-5535, Fax: 979-458-4299, E-mail: malave@tamu.edu. *Application contact:* Erin Roady, Graduate Program Coordinator, 979-845-5536, Fax: 979-458-4299, E-mail: erinroady@tamu.edu.
Website: http://engineering.tamu.edu/industrial

Texas Tech University, Graduate School, Edward E. Whitacre Jr. College of Engineering, Department of Industrial, Manufacturing, and Systems Engineering, Lubbock, TX 79409-3061. Offers industrial engineering (MSIE, PhD); manufacturing engineering (MS); systems and engineering management (MSSEM). *Program availability:* Part-time, 100% online, blended/hybrid learning. *Faculty:* 17 full-time (4 women). *Students:* 57 full-time (13 women), 89 part-time (18 women); includes 23 minority (7 Black or African American, non-Hispanic/Latino; 1 American Indian or Alaska Native, non-Hispanic/Latino; 3 Asian, non-Hispanic/Latino; 8 Hispanic/Latino; 4 Two or more races, non-Hispanic/Latino), 73 international. Average age 33. 162 applicants, 37% accepted, 27 enrolled. In 2018, 49 master's, 10 doctorates awarded. Terminal master's awarded for partial completion of doctoral program. *Degree requirements:* For master's, comprehensive exam, thesis optional; for doctorate, comprehensive exam, thesis/dissertation. *Entrance requirements:* For master's and doctorate, GRE (Verbal and Quantitative). Additional exam requirements/recommendations for international students: Required—TOEFL (minimum score 550 paper-based; 79 iBT), Other English proficiency exams may be substituted for the TOEFL - see the TTU graduate school website. *Application deadline:* For fall admission, 6/1 priority date for domestic students, 1/15 priority date for international students; for spring admission, 9/1 priority date for domestic students, 6/15 priority date for international students. Applications are processed on a rolling basis. Application fee: $65. Electronic applications accepted. *Expenses:* Contact institution. *Financial support:* In 2018–19, 65 students received support, including 63 fellowships (averaging $3,864 per year), 17 research assistantships (averaging $24,105 per year), 18 teaching assistantships (averaging $19,180 per year); scholarships/grants, tuition waivers (partial), and unspecified assistantships also available. Financial award application deadline: 1/15; financial award applicants required to submit FAFSA. *Faculty research:* Ergonomics and human factors engineering, manufacturing systems, operations research, statistics and quality assurance, systems and engineering management. *Total annual research expenditures:* $419,788. *Unit head:* Dr. Bryan A. Norman, Professor and Department Chair, 806-742-3543, E-mail: bryan.norman@ttu.edu. *Application contact:* Dr. Jennifer Cross, Associate Professor, 806-742-3543, E-mail: grad.imse@ttu.edu.
Website: www.depts.ttu.edu/imse/

Trine University, Program in Engineering Management, Angola, IN 46703-1764. Offers MS.

Tufts University, School of Engineering, The Gordon Institute, Medford, MA 02155. Offers engineering management (MS); innovation and management (MS). *Program availability:* Part-time. *Entrance requirements:* Additional exam requirements/recommendations for international students: Required—TOEFL (minimum score 550 paper-based; 80 iBT), IELTS (minimum score 6.5). Electronic applications accepted. *Expenses:* Contact institution. *Faculty research:* Engineering management, engineering leadership.

Université de Sherbrooke, Faculty of Engineering, Programs in Engineering Management, Sherbrooke, QC J1K 2R1, Canada. Offers M Eng, Diploma. *Program availability:* Part-time, evening/weekend. *Entrance requirements:* For master's and Diploma, bachelor's degree in engineering, 1 year of practical experience. Electronic applications accepted.

University at Buffalo, the State University of New York, Graduate School, School of Engineering and Applied Sciences, Department of Industrial and Systems Engineering, Buffalo, NY 14260. Offers advanced manufacturing (Certificate); industrial engineering (ME, MS, PhD), including data fusion (ME), engineering management (ME). *Program availability:* Part-time, online learning. Terminal master's awarded for partial completion of doctoral program. *Degree requirements:* For master's, comprehensive exam (for some programs), thesis or alternative; for doctorate, thesis/dissertation. *Entrance requirements:* For master's and doctorate, GRE General Test. Additional exam requirements/recommendations for international students: Required—TOEFL (minimum score 550 paper-based; 79 iBT). Electronic applications accepted. *Faculty research:* Advanced manufacturing and sustainable manufacturing design, health and health systems, security and defense, transportation and logistics.

The University of Alabama at Birmingham, School of Engineering, Professional Engineering Degrees, Birmingham, AL 35294. Offers advanced safety engineering and management (M Eng); construction engineering management (M Eng); design and commercialization (M Eng); information engineering management (M Eng); structural engineering (M Eng); sustainable smart cities (M Eng). *Program availability:* Part-time, evening/weekend, online only, 100% online, blended/hybrid learning. *Faculty:* 6 full-time (1 woman), 12 part-time/adjunct (2 women). *Students:* 23 full-time (7 women), 315 part-time (63 women); includes 96 minority (73 Black or African American, non-Hispanic/Latino; 1 American Indian or Alaska Native, non-Hispanic/Latino; 8 Asian, non-Hispanic/Latino; 12 Hispanic/Latino; 2 Two or more races, non-Hispanic/Latino), 12 international. Average age 37. 154 applicants, 84% accepted, 91 enrolled. In 2018, 87 master's awarded. *Entrance requirements:* For master's, 3.0 GPA on 4.0 scale, undergraduate degree from a nationally accredited school. Additional exam requirements/recommendations for international students: Required—TOEFL (minimum score 80 iBT); Recommended—IELTS (minimum score 6.5). *Application deadline:* For fall admission, 8/1 for domestic and international students; for spring admission, 12/1 for domestic and international students; for summer admission, 5/1 for domestic and international students. Applications are processed on a rolling basis. Application fee: $50 ($60 for international students). Electronic applications accepted. *Expenses:* Contact institution. *Faculty research:* Orthopedic biomechanics, translational rehabilitation and assistive devices, innovation and entrepreneurship, anthropogenic activities and the natural environment, prestressed and spun concrete. *Application contact:* Jesse Kepply, Director of Student and Academic Services, 205-996-5696, E-mail: gradschool@uab.edu.

University of Alberta, Faculty of Graduate Studies and Research, Department of Mechanical Engineering, Edmonton, AB T6G 2E1, Canada. Offers engineering management (M Eng); mechanical engineering (M Eng, M Sc, PhD); MBA/M Eng. *Program availability:* Part-time. *Degree requirements:* For master's, thesis; for doctorate, thesis/dissertation. *Entrance requirements:* For master's and doctorate, minimum GPA of 7.0 on a 9.0 scale. Additional exam requirements/recommendations for international students: Required—TOEFL (minimum score 580 paper-based). *Faculty research:* Combustion and environmental issues, advanced materials, computational fluid dynamics, biomedical, acoustics and vibrations.

The University of Arizona, College of Engineering, Department of Systems and Industrial Engineering, Tucson, AZ 85721. Offers engineering management (Graduate Certificate); industrial engineering (MS); systems and industrial engineering (MS, PhD); systems engineering (MS, PhD, Graduate Certificate). *Program availability:* Part-time, online learning. *Degree requirements:* For doctorate, thesis/dissertation. *Entrance requirements:* For master's, GRE General Test (minimum score: 500 Verbal, 700 Quantitative), 3 letters of recommendation; for doctorate, GRE General Test (minimum score: 500 Verbal, 700 Quantitative), minimum GPA of 3.5, 3 letters of recommendation, letter of intent. Additional exam requirements/recommendations for international students: Required—TOEFL (minimum score 575 paper-based; 80 iBT). Electronic applications accepted. *Faculty research:* Optimization, systems theory, logistics, transportation, embedded systems.

University of California, Berkeley, Graduate Division, College of Engineering, Department of Civil and Environmental Engineering, Berkeley, CA 94720. Offers engineering and project management (M Eng, MS, PhD); environmental engineering (M Eng, MS, PhD); geoengineering (M Eng, MS, PhD); structural engineering, mechanics and materials (M Eng, MS, PhD); transportation engineering (M Eng, MS, PhD); M Arch/MS; MCP/MS; MPP/MS. Terminal master's awarded for partial completion of doctoral program. *Degree requirements:* For master's, comprehensive exam (for some programs), thesis (for some programs), comprehensive exam or thesis (MS); for doctorate, thesis/dissertation, qualifying exam. *Entrance requirements:* For master's, GRE General Test, minimum GPA of 3.0, 3 letters of recommendation; for doctorate, GRE General Test, minimum GPA of 3.5, 3 letters of recommendation. Additional exam requirements/recommendations for international students: Required—TOEFL (minimum score 570 paper-based; 90 iBT). Electronic applications accepted.

University of California, Irvine, Samueli School of Engineering, Program in Engineering Management, Irvine, CA 92697. Offers MS. Program offered jointly with The Paul Merage School of Business. *Students:* 15 full-time (7 women); includes 1 minority (Hispanic/Latino), 12 international. Average age 24. 185 applicants, 29% accepted, 15 enrolled. In 2018, 17 master's awarded. *Application deadline:* For fall admission, 1/15 priority date for domestic students. Applications are processed on a rolling basis. Application fee: $105 ($125 for international students). *Application contact:* Jean Bennett, Director of Graduate Student Affairs, 949-824-6475, Fax: 949-824-8200, E-mail: jean.bennett@uci.edu.
Website: http://www.eng.uci.edu/admissions/graduate/programs-and-concentrations/engineering-management

University of Colorado Boulder, Graduate School, College of Engineering and Applied Science, Engineering Management Program, Boulder, CO 80309. Offers ME. *Entrance requirements:* For master's, minimum undergraduate GPA of 3.0. Electronic applications accepted. Application fee is waived when completed online. *Faculty research:* Quality and process, research and development, operations and logistics.

University of Dayton, Department of Engineering Management, Systems and Technology, Dayton, OH 45469. Offers engineering management (MSEM); management science (MSMS). *Program availability:* Part-time, 100% online, blended/hybrid learning. *Degree requirements:* For master's, capstone project. *Entrance requirements:* For master's, bachelor's degree in engineering or other STEM discipline with minimum GPA of 3.0. Additional exam requirements/recommendations for international students: Required—TOEFL (minimum score 550 paper-based; 80 iBT); Recommended—IELTS. Electronic applications accepted. *Faculty research:* Operations research, industrial engineering, Lean Six Sigma, modeling and simulation.

University of Denver, Daniel Felix Ritchie School of Engineering and Computer Science, Department of Mechanical and Materials Engineering, Denver, CO 80208. Offers bioengineering (MS); engineering (MS, PhD), including management; materials science (MS, PhD); mechanical engineering (MS, PhD). *Program availability:* Part-time. *Faculty:* 13 full-time (2 women), 2 part-time/adjunct (1 woman). *Students:* 4 full-time (1 woman), 33 part-time (7 women); includes 5 minority (2 Black or African American, non-Hispanic/Latino; 2 Hispanic/Latino; 1 Two or more races, non-Hispanic/Latino), 11 international. Average age 28. 71 applicants, 63% accepted, 15 enrolled. In 2018, 11 master's, 3 doctorates awarded. Terminal master's awarded for partial completion of doctoral program. *Degree requirements:* For master's, thesis optional; for doctorate, comprehensive exam, thesis/dissertation. *Entrance requirements:* For master's, GRE General Test, bachelor's degree in engineering or closely related field, transcripts, personal statement, resume or curriculum vitae, two letters of recommendation; for doctorate, GRE General Test, master's degree in engineering or closely related field, transcripts, personal statement, resume or curriculum vitae, two letters of recommendation, recommended that applicants find a research advisor before submitting the application. Additional exam requirements/recommendations for international students: Required—TOEFL (minimum score 550 paper-based; 80 iBT). *Application deadline:* For fall admission, 1/15 priority date for domestic and international students; for winter admission, 10/25 for domestic and international students; for spring admission, 2/7 for domestic and international students; for summer admission, 4/24 for domestic and international students. Applications are processed on a rolling basis. Application fee: $65. Electronic applications accepted. *Expenses:* $33,183 per year full-time. *Financial support:* In 2018–19, 25 students received support, including 10 research assistantships with tuition reimbursements available (averaging $12,917 per year), 13 teaching assistantships with tuition reimbursements available (averaging $15,289 per year); Federal Work-Study, institutionally sponsored loans, scholarships/grants, health care benefits, and unspecified assistantships also available. Financial award application deadline: 2/15; financial award applicants required to submit FAFSA. *Faculty research:* Cardiac biomechanics, novel high voltage/temperature materials and structures, high speed stereo radiography, musculoskeletal modeling, composites. *Unit head:* Dr. Matt Gordon, Professor and Chair, 303-871-3580, E-mail: matthew.gordon@du.edu. *Application contact:* Chrissy Alexander, Assistant to the Chair, 303-871-3041, E-mail: Christine.Alexander@du.edu.
Website: http://ritchieschool.du.edu/departments/mme/

University of Detroit Mercy, College of Engineering and Science, Detroit, MI 48221. Offers chemistry (MS); civil and environmental engineering (DE); electrical and computer engineering (ME); electrical engineering (DE); engineering management (M Eng Mgt); environmental engineering (MEE); mechanical engineering (MME, DE); product development (MS); software engineering (MSSE); teaching of mathematics (MATM). *Program availability:* Part-time, evening/weekend. *Degree requirements:* For doctorate, thesis/dissertation. Electronic applications accepted. Application fee is waived when completed online. *Expenses:* Contact institution.

The University of Kansas, Graduate Studies, School of Engineering, Program in Engineering Management, Overland Park, KS 66213. Offers MS, Certificate. *Program availability:* Part-time, evening/weekend, online learning. *Students:* 9 full-time (4 women), 80 part-time (12 women); includes 14 minority (2 Black or African American, non-Hispanic/Latino; 9 Asian, non-Hispanic/Latino; 2 Hispanic/Latino; 1 Two or more races, non-Hispanic/Latino), 15 international. Average age 32. 34 applicants, 82% accepted, 25 enrolled. In 2018, 28 master's awarded. *Entrance requirements:* For master's, minimum GPA of 3.0, 2 years of industrial experience, BS in engineering or related science. Additional exam requirements/recommendations for international students: Required—TOEFL, IELTS. Application fee: $65 ($85 for international students). Electronic applications accepted. *Faculty research:* Project management, systems analysis, high performance teams, manufacturing systems, strategic analysis. *Unit head:* Herbert R. Tuttle, Director, 913-897-8561, E-mail: htuttle@ku.edu. *Application contact:* Parveen Mozaffar, Program Advisor, 913-897-8560, E-mail: parveen@ku.edu.
Website: http://emgt.ku.edu/

University of Louisville, J. B. Speed School of Engineering, Department of Industrial Engineering, Louisville, KY 40292-0001. Offers engineering management (M Eng); industrial engineering (M Eng, MS, PhD); logistics and distribution (Certificate). *Accreditation:* ABET (one or more programs are accredited). *Program availability:* 100% online. *Faculty:* 9 full-time (4 women), 8 part-time/adjunct (2 women). *Students:* 64 full-time (22 women), 147 part-time (35 women); includes 32 minority (13 Black or African

American, non-Hispanic/Latino; 9 Asian, non-Hispanic/Latino; 6 Hispanic/Latino; 4 Two or more races, non-Hispanic/Latino), 78 international. Average age 31. 98 applicants, 66% accepted, 53 enrolled. In 2018, 30 master's, 3 doctorates awarded. Terminal master's awarded for partial completion of doctoral program. *Degree requirements:* For master's and Certificate, thesis optional; for doctorate, comprehensive exam, thesis/dissertation. *Entrance requirements:* For master's and doctorate, GRE General Test, two letters of recommendation, official transcripts. Additional exam requirements/recommendations for international students: Required—TOEFL (minimum score 550 paper-based; 80 iBT), IELTS (minimum score 6.5). *Application deadline:* For fall admission, 5/1 priority date for domestic and international students; for spring admission, 11/1 priority date for domestic and international students; for summer admission, 3/1 priority date for domestic and international students. Applications are processed on a rolling basis. Application fee: $65. Electronic applications accepted. *Expenses: Tuition, area resident:* Full-time $6500; part-time $723 per credit hour. Tuition, state resident: Full-time $6500. Tuition, nonresident: full-time $13,557; part-time $1507 per credit hour. Tuition and fees vary according to course load and program. *Financial support:* In 2018–19, 38 students received support. Fellowships, research assistantships, teaching assistantships, scholarships/grants, health care benefits, and tuition waivers (full) available. Financial award application deadline: 1/1; financial award applicants required to submit FAFSA. *Faculty research:* Quality and Reliability Assurance, Process Monitoring and Diagnostics, Production Systems Design, Supply Chain Risk Management, Decision Support Systems. *Total annual research expenditures:* $620,986. *Unit head:* Dr. Suraj M. Alexander, Chair, 502-852-6342, Fax: 502-852-5633, E-mail: suraj.alexander@louisville.edu. *Application contact:* Lihui Bai, Director of Graduate Studies, 502-852-1416, E-mail: lihui.bai@louisville.edu.
Website: http://www.louisville.edu/speed/industrial/

University of Management and Technology, Program in Engineering Management, Arlington, VA 22209-1609. Offers MS. *Expenses: Tuition:* Full-time $7020; part-time $1170 per course.

The University of Manchester, School of Mechanical, Aerospace and Civil Engineering, Manchester, United Kingdom. Offers advanced manufacturing technology (M Ent); aerospace engineering (M Phil, M Sc, PhD); civil engineering (M Phil, M Sc, PhD); environmental engineering (M Phil, PhD); management of projects (M Phil, M Sc, PhD); mechanical engineering (M Phil, M Sc, PhD); mechanical engineering design (M Ent); nuclear engineering (M Phil, D Eng, PhD).

University of Maryland, Baltimore County, The Graduate School, Program in Engineering Management, Baltimore, MD 21250. Offers MS, Postbaccalaureate Certificate. *Program availability:* Part-time. *Degree requirements:* For master's, comprehensive exam (for some programs), thesis optional. *Entrance requirements:* For master's, BS in engineering, computer science, mathematics, physics, chemistry, or other physical sciences; two letters of recommendation (for international students). Additional exam requirements/recommendations for international students: Required—TOEFL (minimum score 550 paper-based; 80 iBT), GRE General Test. Electronic applications accepted. *Faculty research:* Regulatory engineering, environmental engineering, systems engineering, advanced manufacturing, chemical engineering.

University of Michigan–Dearborn, College of Engineering and Computer Science, MS Program in Engineering Management, Dearborn, MI 48128. Offers MS. *Program availability:* Part-time, evening/weekend, 100% online. *Faculty:* 17 full-time (4 women), 9 part-time/adjunct (1 woman). *Students:* 6 full-time (4 women), 184 part-time (35 women); includes 32 minority (9 Black or African American, non-Hispanic/Latino; 1 American Indian or Alaska Native, non-Hispanic/Latino; 13 Asian, non-Hispanic/Latino; 7 Hispanic/Latino; 2 Two or more races, non-Hispanic/Latino), 20 international. Average age 30. 100 applicants, 52% accepted, 32 enrolled. In 2018, 22 master's awarded. *Entrance requirements:* Additional exam requirements/recommendations for international students: Required—TOEFL (minimum score 560 paper-based; 84 iBT), IELTS (minimum score 6.5). *Application deadline:* For fall admission, 8/1 for domestic students, 5/1 for international students; for winter admission, 12/1 for domestic students, 9/1 for international students; for spring admission, 4/1 for domestic students, 1/1 for international students. Applications are processed on a rolling basis. Application fee: $60. Electronic applications accepted. *Expenses:* Tuition, state resident: full-time $15,380; part-time $88 per credit hour. Tuition, nonresident: full-time $23,948; part-time $1377 per credit hour. *Required fees:* $780; $780 $390. Tuition and fees vary according to course level, course load, degree level, program, reciprocity agreements and student level. *Financial support:* In 2018–19, 8 students received support. Scholarships/grants, unspecified assistantships, and non-resident tuition scholarships available. Support available to part-time students. Financial award application deadline: 3/1; financial award applicants required to submit FAFSA. *Faculty research:* Operations Research and Decision Science, Quality and Reliability Engineering, Manufacturing, Human Factors and Ergonomics, Transportation Safety. *Unit head:* Dr. Armen Zakarian, Chair, 313-593-5361, Fax: 313-593-3692, E-mail: zakarian@umich.edu. *Application contact:* Office of Graduate Studies, 313-583-6321, E-mail: umd-graduatestudies@umich.edu.
Website: https://umdearborn.edu/cecs/departments/industrial-and-manufacturing-systems-engineering/graduate-programs/ms-engineering-management

University of Minnesota, Duluth, Graduate School, Swenson College of Science and Engineering, Department of Mechanical and Industrial Engineering, Duluth, MN 55812-2496. Offers engineering management (MSEM); environmental health and safety (MEHS). *Program availability:* Part-time, evening/weekend, online learning. *Degree requirements:* For master's, comprehensive exam, thesis or alternative, capstone design project (MSEM), field project (MEHS). *Entrance requirements:* For master's, GRE (MEHS), interview (MEHS), letters of recommendation. Additional exam requirements/recommendations for international students: Required—TOEFL (minimum score 550 paper-based). *Faculty research:* Transportation, ergonomics, toxicology, supply chain management, automation and robotics.

University of Missouri–Kansas City, School of Computing and Engineering, Kansas City, MO 64110-2499. Offers civil engineering (MS); computer and electrical engineering (PhD); computer science (MS), including bioinformatics, software engineering, telecommunications networking; computer science and informatics (PhD); computing (PhD); electrical engineering (MS); engineering (PhD); engineering and construction management (Graduate Certificate); mechanical engineering (MS); telecommunications and computer networking (PhD). PhD (interdisciplinary) offered through the School of Graduate Studies. *Program availability:* Part-time. *Degree requirements:* For doctorate, thesis/dissertation. *Entrance requirements:* For master's, GRE General Test, minimum GPA of 3.0, 3 letters of recommendation from professors; for doctorate, GRE General Test, minimum GPA of 3.5. Additional exam requirements/recommendations for international students: Required—TOEFL (minimum score 550 paper-based; 80 iBT). *Faculty research:* Algorithms, bioinformatics and medical informatics, biomechanics/biomaterials, civil engineering materials, networking and telecommunications, thermal science.

University of Nebraska–Lincoln, Graduate College, College of Engineering, Department of Industrial and Management Systems Engineering, Lincoln, NE 68588. Offers engineering management (M Eng); industrial and management systems engineering (MS, PhD); manufacturing systems engineering (MS). *Program availability:* Online learning. *Degree requirements:* For master's, thesis optional; for doctorate, comprehensive exam, thesis/dissertation. *Entrance requirements:* For master's and doctorate, GRE. Additional exam requirements/recommendations for international students: Required—TOEFL (minimum score 525 paper-based). Electronic applications accepted. *Faculty research:* Ergonomics, occupational safety, quality control, industrial packaging, facility design.

University of New Brunswick Fredericton, School of Graduate Studies, Faculty of Business Administration, Fredericton, NB E3B 5A3, Canada. Offers business administration (MBA); engineering management (MBA); entrepreneurship (MBA); sports and recreation management (MBA); MBA/LL B. *Program availability:* Part-time. *Degree requirements:* For master's, thesis optional. *Entrance requirements:* For master's, GMAT (minimum score 550), minimum GPA of 3.0; 3-5 years of work experience; 3 letters of reference with at least one academic reference. Additional exam requirements/recommendations for international students: Required—TOEFL (minimum score 580 paper-based; 92 iBT) or IELTS (minimum score 7). Electronic applications accepted. *Faculty research:* Entrepreneurship, finance, law, sport and recreation management, engineering management.

University of New Haven, Graduate School, Tagliatela College of Engineering, Program in Engineering and Operations Management, West Haven, CT 06516. Offers engineering and operations management (MS); engineering management (MS); Lean Six Sigma (Graduate Certificate). *Program availability:* Part-time. *Students:* 59 full-time (11 women), 25 part-time (3 women); includes 4 minority (2 Black or African American, non-Hispanic/Latino; 1 American Indian or Alaska Native, non-Hispanic/Latino; 1 Asian, non-Hispanic/Latino), 59 international. Average age 27. 288 applicants, 86% accepted, 26 enrolled. In 2018, 45 master's awarded. *Entrance requirements:* Additional exam requirements/recommendations for international students: Required—TOEFL (minimum score 75 iBT), IELTS, PTE (minimum score 50). *Application deadline:* Applications are processed on a rolling basis. Application fee: $50. Electronic applications accepted. Application fee is waived when completed online. *Expenses: Tuition:* Full-time $16,470; part-time $915 per credit hour. *Required fees:* $230; $95 per term. *Financial support:* Applicants required to submit FAFSA. *Unit head:* Dr. Ali Montazer, Professor, 203-932-7050, E-mail: amontazer@newhaven.edu. *Application contact:* Selina O'Toole, Senior Associate Director of Graduate Admissions, 203-932-7337, E-mail: sotoole@newhaven.edu.
Website: https://www.newhaven.edu/engineering/graduate-programs/operations-management/

University of New Orleans, Graduate School, College of Engineering, Program in Engineering Management, New Orleans, LA 70148. Offers MS. *Degree requirements:* For master's, thesis optional. *Entrance requirements:* For master's, GRE General Test, minimum GPA of 3.0. Additional exam requirements/recommendations for international students: Required—TOEFL (minimum score 550 paper-based; 79 iBT). Electronic applications accepted.

The University of North Carolina at Charlotte, William States Lee College of Engineering, Department of Systems Engineering and Engineering Management, Charlotte, NC 28223-0001. Offers energy analytics (Graduate Certificate); engineering management (MSEM); Lean Six Sigma (Graduate Certificate); logistics and supply chains (Graduate Certificate); systems analytics (Graduate Certificate). *Program availability:* Part-time, evening/weekend, 100% online, blended/hybrid learning. *Students:* 27 full-time (8 women), 45 part-time (11 women); includes 15 minority (5 Black or African American, non-Hispanic/Latino; 1 American Indian or Alaska Native, non-Hispanic/Latino; 5 Asian, non-Hispanic/Latino; 2 Hispanic/Latino; 2 Two or more races, non-Hispanic/Latino), 27 international. Average age 29. 112 applicants, 77% accepted, 23 enrolled. In 2018, 38 master's, 3 other advanced degrees awarded. *Entrance requirements:* For master's, GRE or GMAT, bachelor's degree in engineering or a closely-related technical or scientific field, or in business, provided relevant technical course requirements have been met; undergraduate coursework in engineering economics, calculus, or statistics; minimum GPA of 3.0; for Graduate Certificate, bachelor's degree in engineering or closely-related technical or scientific field, or in business, provided relevant technical course requirements have been met; minimum GPA of 3.0; undergraduate coursework in engineering economics, calculus, and statistics; written description of work experience. Additional exam requirements/recommendations for international students: Required—TOEFL (minimum score 523 paper-based; 70 iBT), IELTS (minimum score 6), TOEFL (minimum score 523 paper-based, 70 iBT) or IELTS (6). *Application deadline:* Applications are processed on a rolling basis. Application fee: $75. Electronic applications accepted. *Expenses:* Contact institution. *Financial support:* Career-related internships or fieldwork, institutionally sponsored loans, scholarships/grants, and unspecified assistantships available. Support available to part-time students. Financial award application deadline: 3/1; financial award applicants required to submit FAFSA. *Total annual research expenditures:* $186,132. *Unit head:* Dr. Simon M. Hsiang, Chair, 704-687-1958, E-mail: shsiang1@uncc.edu. *Application contact:* Kathy B. Giddings, Director of Graduate Admissions, 704-687-5503, Fax: 704-687-1668, E-mail: gradadm@uncc.edu.
Website: http://seem.uncc.edu/

University of Ottawa, Faculty of Graduate and Postdoctoral Studies, Faculty of Engineering, Engineering Management Program, Ottawa, ON K1N 6N5, Canada. Offers engineering management (M Eng); information technology (Certificate); project management (Certificate). *Degree requirements:* For master's, thesis or alternative. *Entrance requirements:* For master's and Certificate, honors degree or equivalent, minimum B average. Electronic applications accepted.

University of Puerto Rico–Mayagüez, Graduate Studies, College of Engineering, Department of Civil Engineering and Surveying, Mayagüez, PR 00681-9000. Offers civil engineering (ME, MS, PhD), including construction engineering and management (ME, MS), environmental engineering, geotechnical engineering (ME, MS), structural engineering, transportation engineering. *Program availability:* Part-time. Terminal master's awarded for partial completion of doctoral program. *Degree requirements:* For master's, one foreign language, thesis; for doctorate, one foreign language, comprehensive exam, thesis/dissertation, qualifying exams. *Entrance requirements:* For master's, proficiency in English and Spanish; BS in civil engineering or its equivalent; for doctorate, proficiency in English and Spanish. Electronic applications accepted. *Faculty research:* Structural design, concrete structure, finite elements, dynamic analysis, transportation, soils.

University of Regina, Faculty of Graduate Studies and Research, Kenneth Levene Graduate School of Business, Program in Business Administration, Regina, SK S4S 0A2, Canada. Offers business foundations (PGD); engineering management (MBA); executive business administration (EMBA); international business (MBA); leadership (M Admin); organizational leadership (Master's Certificate); project management (Master's Certificate); public safety management (MBA). *Program availability:* Part-time, evening/weekend. *Students:* 30 full-time (14 women), 9 part-time (5 women). Average age 30. In 2018, 23 master's awarded. *Degree requirements:* For master's, project (for some programs). workplacement for Co-op concentration. *Entrance requirements:* For master's, GMAT, 3 years of relevant work experience, four-year undergraduate degree, post secondary transcript, 2 letters of recommendation; for other advanced degree, GMAT (for PGD), four-year undergraduate degree and 2 years of relevant work experience (for Master's Certificate); 3 years' work experience (for PGD). Additional exam requirements/recommendations for international students: Required—TOEFL (minimum score 580 paper-based; 80 iBT), IELTS (minimum score 6.5), PTE (minimum score 59), other options are CAEL, MELAB, CANTEST or U of R ESI; GMAT is mandatory. *Application deadline:* For fall admission, 3/1 for domestic and international students; for winter admission, 7/1 for domestic and international students; for spring admission, 10/1 for domestic and international students; for summer admission, 10/1 for domestic and international students. Applications are processed on a rolling basis. Application fee: $100. Electronic applications accepted. *Expenses:* One academic year is 18,752. International students will pay additional 1,191.75 for International surcharge per semester. *Financial support:* Fellowships, research assistantships, teaching assistantships, career-related internships or fieldwork, Federal Work-Study, scholarships/grants, unspecified assistantships, and travel award and Graduate scholarship Base Funds available. Support available to part-time students. Financial award application deadline: 9/30. *Faculty research:* Business policy and strategy, production and operations management, human behavior in organizations, financial management, social issues in business. *Unit head:* Dr. Gina Grandy, Dean, 306-585-4435, Fax: 306-585-5361, E-mail: business.dean@uregina.ca. *Application contact:* Adrian Pitariu, Associate Dean, Research and Graduate Programs, 306-585-6294, Fax: 306-585-5361, E-mail: business.AD.levene@uregina.ca.
Website: http://www.uregina.ca/business/levene/

University of St. Thomas, School of Engineering, St. Paul, MN 55105. Offers data science (MS); electrical engineering (MS); information technology (MS); manufacturing engineering (MS); manufacturing systems (Certificate); mechanical engineering (MS); medical device development (Certificate); regulatory science (MS); software engineering (MS); software management (MS); systems engineering (MS); technology leadership (Certificate); technology management (MS). *Program availability:* Part-time, evening/weekend. *Entrance requirements:* For master's, resume, official transcripts. Additional exam requirements/recommendations for international students: Required—TOEFL (minimum score 80 iBT), IELTS (minimum score 6.5). Electronic applications accepted. *Expenses:* Contact institution.

University of Southern California, Graduate School, Viterbi School of Engineering, Daniel J. Epstein Department of Industrial and Systems Engineering, Los Angeles, CA 90089. Offers digital supply chain management (MS); engineering management (MS); engineering technology communication (Graduate Certificate); health systems operations (Graduate Certificate); industrial and systems engineering (MS, PhD, Engr); manufacturing engineering (MS); operations research engineering (MS); optimization and supply chain management (Graduate Certificate); product development engineering (MS); safety systems and security (MS); systems architecting and engineering (MS, Graduate Certificate); systems safety and security (Graduate Certificate); transportation systems (Graduate Certificate); MS/MBA. *Program availability:* Part-time, evening/weekend, online learning. Terminal master's awarded for partial completion of doctoral program. *Degree requirements:* For master's, thesis optional; for doctorate, thesis/dissertation. *Entrance requirements:* For master's and doctorate, GRE General Test. Additional exam requirements/recommendations for international students: Recommended—TOEFL. Electronic applications accepted. *Faculty research:* Health systems, music cognition and retrieval, transportation and logistics, manufacturing and automation, engineering systems design, risk and economic analysis.

University of Southern California, Graduate School, Viterbi School of Engineering, Department of Aerospace and Mechanical Engineering, Los Angeles, CA 90089. Offers aerospace and mechanical engineering: computational fluid and solid mechanics (MS); aerospace and mechanical engineering: dynamics and control (MS); aerospace engineering (MS, PhD, Engr), including aerospace engineering (PhD, Engr); green technologies (MS); mechanical engineering (MS, PhD, Engr), including energy conversion (MS), mechanical engineering (PhD, Engr), nuclear power (MS); product development engineering (MS). *Program availability:* Part-time, evening/weekend, online learning. Terminal master's awarded for partial completion of doctoral program. *Degree requirements:* For master's, thesis optional; for doctorate, thesis/dissertation. *Entrance requirements:* For master's, doctorate, and Engr, GRE General Test. Additional exam requirements/recommendations for international students: Recommended—TOEFL. Electronic applications accepted. *Faculty research:* Mechanics and materials, aerodynamics of air/ground vehicles, gas dynamics, aerosols, astronautics and space science, geophysical and microgravity flows, planetary physics, power MEMs and MEMS vacuum pumps, heat transfer and combustion.

University of Southern Indiana, Graduate Studies, Romain College of Business, Program in Business Administration, Evansville, IN 47712-3590. Offers accounting (MBA); data analytics (MBA); engineering management (MBA); general business administration (MBA); healthcare administration (MBA); human resource management (MBA). *Accreditation:* AACSB. *Program availability:* Part-time, evening/weekend, 100% online, blended/hybrid learning. *Entrance requirements:* For master's, GMAT or GRE, minimum GPA of 2.5, resume, 3 professional references. Additional exam requirements/recommendations for international students: Required—TOEFL (minimum score 550 paper-based; 79 iBT), IELTS (minimum score 6). Electronic applications accepted.

University of South Florida, College of Engineering, Department of Industrial and Management Systems Engineering, Tampa, FL 33620-9951. Offers engineering management (MSEM); industrial engineering (MSIE, PhD); information technology (MSIT); materials science and engineering (MSMSE). *Program availability:* Part-time, online learning. *Faculty:* 30 full-time (3 women), 1 part-time/adjunct (0 women). *Students:* 84 full-time (25 women), 60 part-time (15 women); includes 13 minority (2 Black or African American, non-Hispanic/Latino; 4 Asian, non-Hispanic/Latino; 7 Hispanic/Latino), 100 international. Average age 27. 280 applicants, 54% accepted, 37 enrolled. In 2018, 72 master's, 3 doctorates awarded. Terminal master's awarded for partial completion of doctoral program. *Degree requirements:* For master's, comprehensive exam, thesis (for some programs); for doctorate, comprehensive exam, thesis/dissertation, 2 tools of research as specified by dissertation committee. *Entrance requirements:* For master's, GRE General Test, BS in engineering (or equivalent), letters of recommendation, resume, two years professional experience or internship may be required; statement of purpose; for doctorate, GRE General Test, minimum GPA of 3.0, 3 letters of recommendation, statement of purpose, strong background in scientific and engineering principles. Ph.D. students must complete their total doctoral major as full-time Tampa campus students. Additional exam requirements/recommendations for international students: Required—TOEFL, TOEFL (minimum score 550 paper-based; 79 iBT) or IELTS (minimum score 6.5). *Application deadline:* For fall admission, 2/15 for domestic and international students; for spring admission, 10/15 for domestic students, 9/15 for international students; for summer admission, 2/15 for domestic students, 1/15 for international students. Application fee: $30. Electronic applications accepted. *Expenses:* Tuition, state resident: full-time $6350. Tuition, nonresident: full-time $19,048. *International tuition:* $19,048 full-time. *Required fees:* $2079. *Financial support:* In 2018–19, 26 students received support, including 20 research assistantships with partial tuition reimbursements available (averaging $16,748 per year), 11 teaching assistantships with partial tuition reimbursements available (averaging $15,000 per year); tuition waivers (partial) also available. Financial award applicants required to submit FAFSA. *Faculty research:* Healthcare, healthcare systems, public health policies, energy and environment, manufacturing, logistics, transportation.

Total annual research expenditures: $368,578. *Unit head:* Dr. Tapas K. Das, Professor and Department Chair, 813-974-5585, Fax: 813-974-5953, E-mail: das@usf.edu. *Application contact:* Dr. Alex Savachkin, Associate Professor and Graduate Director, 813-974-5577, Fax: 813-974-5953, E-mail: alexs@usf.edu.
Website: http://imse.eng.usf.edu

The University of Tennessee, Graduate School, Tickle College of Engineering, Department of Industrial and Systems Engineering, Knoxville, TN 37966. Offers engineering management (MS); industrial engineering (MS, PhD); reliability and maintainability engineering (MS); MS/MBA. *Program availability:* Part-time, online learning. *Faculty:* 10 full-time (1 woman), 3 part-time/adjunct (1 woman). *Students:* 74 full-time (20 women), 76 part-time (18 women); includes 26 minority (10 Black or African American, non-Hispanic/Latino; 1 American Indian or Alaska Native, non-Hispanic/Latino; 8 Asian, non-Hispanic/Latino; 7 Hispanic/Latino), 40 international. Average age 35. 122 applicants, 80% accepted, 47 enrolled. In 2018, 42 master's, 8 doctorates awarded. *Degree requirements:* For master's, thesis or alternative; for doctorate, comprehensive exam, thesis/dissertation. *Entrance requirements:* For master's, GRE General Test (for MS students pursuing research thesis), minimum GPA of 2.7 (for U.S. degree holders), 3.0 (for international degree holders); for doctorate, GRE General Test, minimum GPA of 3.0 on previous graduate course work. Additional exam requirements/recommendations for international students: Required—TOEFL (minimum score 550 paper-based; 80 iBT), IELTS (minimum score 6.5). *Application deadline:* For fall admission, 2/1 priority date for domestic and international students; for spring admission, 6/15 for domestic and international students; for summer admission, 10/15 for domestic and international students. Applications are processed on a rolling basis. Application fee: $60. Electronic applications accepted. *Financial support:* In 2018–19, 59 students received support, including 7 fellowships with full tuition reimbursements available (averaging $10,000 per year), 36 research assistantships with full tuition reimbursements available (averaging $15,462 per year), 16 teaching assistantships with full tuition reimbursements available (averaging $19,545 per year); career-related internships or fieldwork, Federal Work-Study, institutionally sponsored loans, health care benefits, and unspecified assistantships also available. Financial award application deadline: 2/1; financial award applicants required to submit FAFSA. *Faculty research:* Combinatorial optimization; design of lean, reliable systems: energy systems; healthcare analytics; transportation, logistics and supply chain modeling. *Total annual research expenditures:* $1.2 million. *Unit head:* Dr. John Kobza, Department Head, 865-974-3333, Fax: 865-974-0588, E-mail: jkobza@utk.edu. *Application contact:* Dr. Mingzhou Jin, Professor, Associate Head and Director of Graduate Studies, 865-974-9992, E-mail: jin@utk.edu.
Website: http://www.engr.utk.edu/ie/

The University of Tennessee, The University of Tennessee Space Institute, Tullahoma, TN 37388. Offers aerospace engineering (MS, PhD); biomedical engineering (MS, PhD); engineering science (MS, PhD); industrial and systems engineering/engineering management (MS, PhD); mechanical engineering (MS, PhD); physics (MS, PhD). *Program availability:* Part-time, blended/hybrid learning. Terminal master's awarded for partial completion of doctoral program. *Degree requirements:* For doctorate, one foreign language, thesis/dissertation. *Entrance requirements:* Additional exam requirements/recommendations for international students: Required—TOEFL (minimum score 550 paper-based; 80 iBT), IELTS (minimum score 6.5). Electronic applications accepted. *Expenses:* Contact institution. *Faculty research:* Fluid mechanics/aerodynamics, chemical and electric propulsion and laser diagnostics, computational mechanics and simulations, carbon fiber production and composite materials.

The University of Tennessee at Chattanooga, Engineering Management and Technology Program, Chattanooga, TN 37403. Offers construction management (Graduate Certificate); engineering management (MS); fundamentals of engineering management (Graduate Certificate); leadership and ethics (Graduate Certificate); logistics and supply chain management (Graduate Certificate); power systems management (Graduate Certificate); project and technology management (Graduate Certificate); quality management (Graduate Certificate). *Program availability:* 100% online, blended/hybrid learning. *Degree requirements:* For master's, thesis. *Entrance requirements:* For master's, GRE General Test, letters of recommendation; minimum undergraduate GPA of 2.7 overall or 3.0 in final two years; for Graduate Certificate, baccalaureate degree and professional experience or have already been admitted to engineering/engineering management graduate program. Additional exam requirements/recommendations for international students: Required—TOEFL (minimum score 550 paper-based; 79 iBT), IELTS (minimum score 6). Electronic applications accepted. *Expenses:* Contact institution. *Faculty research:* Plant layout design, lean manufacturing, Six Sigma, value management, product development.

The University of Texas at Arlington, Graduate School, College of Engineering, Department of Industrial, Manufacturing, and Systems Engineering, Program in Engineering Management, Arlington, TX 76019. Offers MS. *Program availability:* Part-time, evening/weekend, online learning. *Degree requirements:* For master's, comprehensive exam, thesis optional. *Entrance requirements:* For master's, GRE, 3 years of full-time work experience, minimum GPA of 3.0. Additional exam requirements/recommendations for international students: Required—TOEFL (minimum score 550 paper-based).

The University of Texas at Tyler, Soules College of Business, Department of Management and Marketing, Tyler, TX 75799-0001. Offers cyber security (MBA); engineering management (MBA); general management (MBA); healthcare management (MBA); internal assurance and consulting (MBA); marketing (MBA); oil, gas and energy (MBA); organizational development (MBA); quality management (MBA). *Accreditation:* AACSB. *Program availability:* Part-time, online learning. *Students:* Average age 29. 73 applicants, 96% accepted, 35 enrolled. In 2018, 37 master's awarded. *Entrance requirements:* Additional exam requirements/recommendations for international students: Required—TOEFL (minimum score 550 paper-based). *Application deadline:* For fall admission, 8/17 priority date for domestic students, 7/1 priority date for international students; for spring admission, 12/21 priority date for domestic students, 11/1 priority date for international students. Application fee: $25 ($50 for international students). *Faculty research:* General business, inventory control, institutional markets, service marketing, product distribution, accounting fraud, financial reporting and recognition. *Unit head:* Dr. Krist Swimberghe, Chair, 903-565-5803, E-mail: kswimberghe@uttyler.edu. *Application contact:* Dr. Krist Swimberghe, Chair, 903-565-5803, E-mail: kswimberghe@uttyler.edu.
Website: https://www.uttyler.edu/cbt/manamark/

The University of Texas Rio Grande Valley, College of Engineering and Computer Science, Department of Manufacturing and Industrial Engineering, Edinburg, TX 78539. Offers engineering management (MS); manufacturing engineering (MS), including systems engineering. *Expenses:* Tuition, area resident: Full-time $6888. Tuition, state resident: full-time $6888. Tuition, nonresident: full-time $14,484. *International tuition:* $14,484 full-time. *Required fees:* $1468. *Faculty research:* Manufacturing processes, logistics, quality control, lean manufacturing.

University of Vermont, Graduate College, College of Engineering and Mathematical Sciences, Program in Engineering Management, Burlington, VT 05405. Offers MS.

Entrance requirements: Additional exam requirements/recommendations for international students: Required—TOEFL (minimum iBT score of 90) or IELTS (6.5).

University of Waterloo, Graduate Studies and Postdoctoral Affairs, Faculty of Engineering, Department of Management Sciences, Waterloo, ON N2L 3G1, Canada. Offers applied operations research (MA Sc, MMS, PhD); information systems (MA Sc, MMS, PhD); management of technology (MA Sc, MMS, PhD). *Program availability:* Part-time, online learning. *Degree requirements:* For master's, research paper or thesis; for doctorate, comprehensive exam, thesis/dissertation. *Entrance requirements:* For master's, GMAT or GRE, honors degree, minimum B average, resume; for doctorate, GMAT or GRE, master's degree, minimum A- average, resume. Additional exam requirements/recommendations for international students: Required—TOEFL, IELTS, PTE. *Application deadline:* Applications are processed on a rolling basis. Application fee: $125 Canadian dollars. Electronic applications accepted. *Financial support:* Fellowships, research assistantships, teaching assistantships, career-related internships or fieldwork, and institutionally sponsored loans available. *Faculty research:* Operations research, manufacturing systems, scheduling, information systems.
Website: https://uwaterloo.ca/management-sciences/

Valparaiso University, Graduate School and Continuing Education, College of Business, Valparaiso, IN 46383. Offers business administration (MBA); business decision-making (Certificate); business intelligence (Certificate); engineering management (Certificate); finance (Certificate); general business (Certificate); leading the global enterprise (Certificate); management (Certificate); JD/MBA; MSN/MBA. *Accreditation:* AACSB. *Program availability:* Part-time, evening/weekend, online learning. *Students:* 7 full-time (5 women), 43 part-time (16 women); includes 5 minority (4 Black or African American, non-Hispanic/Latino; 1 Two or more races, non-Hispanic/Latino). Average age 31. *Entrance requirements:* For master's, GMAT, GRE, minimum GPA of 3.0. Additional exam requirements/recommendations for international students: Required—TOEFL (minimum score 550 paper-based; 80 iBT), IELTS (minimum score 6). *Application deadline:* Applications are processed on a rolling basis. Application fee: $30 ($50 for international students). Electronic applications accepted. *Expenses:* Contact institution. *Financial support:* Available to part-time students. Applicants required to submit FAFSA. *Unit head:* Jim Brodzinski, Dean, 219-464-5035, E-mail: jim.brodzinski@valpo.edu. *Application contact:* Cindy Scanlan, Director of Graduate Programs in Management, 219-465-7952, Fax: 219-464-5789, E-mail: cindy.scanlan@valpo.edu.
Website: http://www.valpo.edu/college-of-business/

Virginia Polytechnic Institute and State University, VT Online, Blacksburg, VA 24061. Offers advanced transportation systems (Certificate); aerospace engineering (MS); agricultural and life sciences (MSLFS); business information systems (Graduate Certificate); career and technical education (MS); civil engineering (MS); computer engineering (M Eng, MS); decision support systems (Graduate Certificate); eLearning leadership (MA); electrical engineering (M Eng, MS); engineering administration (MEA); environmental engineering (Certificate); environmental politics and policy (Graduate Certificate); environmental sciences and engineering (MS); foundations of political analysis (Graduate Certificate); health product risk management (Graduate Certificate); industrial and systems engineering (MS); information policy and society (Graduate Certificate); information security (Graduate Certificate); information technology (MIT); instructional technology (MA); integrative STEM education (MA Ed); liberal arts (Graduate Certificate); life sciences: health product risk management (MS); natural resources (MNR, Graduate Certificate); networking (Graduate Certificate); nonprofit and nongovernmental organization management (Graduate Certificate); ocean engineering (MS); political science (MA); security studies (Graduate Certificate); software development (Graduate Certificate). *Expenses:* Tuition, state resident: full-time $15,510; part-time $739.50 per credit hour. Tuition, nonresident: full-time $29,629; part-time $1490.25 per credit hour. *Required fees:* $2804; $550 per semester. Tuition and fees vary according to course load, campus/location and program. *Application contact:* Graduate Admissions and Academic Progress, 540-231-8636, E-mail: grads@vt.edu.
Website: http://www.vto.vt.edu/

Washington State University, Voiland College of Engineering and Architecture, Program in Engineering and Technology Management, Pullman, WA 99164-2785. Offers METM, Certificate. Program offered through the Global (online) campus. *Program availability:* Part-time, evening/weekend, online learning. *Degree requirements:* For master's, one foreign language, comprehensive exam (for some programs). *Entrance requirements:* Additional exam requirements/recommendations for international students: Required—TOEFL. Electronic applications accepted. *Faculty research:* Constraints management, Six Sigma quality management, supply chain management, project management, construction management, systems engineering management, manufacturing leadership.

Wayne State University, College of Engineering, Department of Industrial and Systems Engineering, Detroit, MI 48202. Offers data science and business analytics (MS); engineering management (MS); industrial engineering (MS, PhD); manufacturing engineering (MS); systems engineering (Certificate). *Program availability:* Online learning. *Faculty:* 11. *Students:* 178 full-time (40 women), 109 part-time (30 women); includes 42 minority (20 Black or African American, non-Hispanic/Latino; 16 Asian, non-Hispanic/Latino; 6 Hispanic/Latino), 167 international. Average age 29. 539 applicants, 40% accepted, 68 enrolled. In 2018, 172 master's, 9 doctorates awarded. *Entrance requirements:* For master's, GRE or GMAT (for applicants to MS in data science and business analytics), BS from ABET-accredited institution; for doctorate, GRE, graduate degree in engineering or related discipline with minimum graduate GPA of 3.5, statement of purpose, resume/curriculum vitae, three letters of recommendation; for Certificate, GRE (for applicants from non-ABET institutions), BS in engineering or other technical field from ABET-accredited institution with minimum GPA of 3.0 in upper-division course work, at least one year of full-time work experience as practicing engineer or technical leader. Additional exam requirements/recommendations for international students: Required—TOEFL (minimum score 550 paper-based; 79 iBT), TWE (minimum score 5.5), Michigan English Language Assessment Battery (minimum score 85); GRE; Recommended—IELTS (minimum score 6.5). *Application deadline:* Applications are processed on a rolling basis. Application fee: $50. Electronic applications accepted. *Expenses:* Contact institution. *Financial support:* In 2018–19, 135 students received support, including 2 fellowships with tuition reimbursements available (averaging $20,000 per year), 5 research assistantships with tuition reimbursements available (averaging $23,260 per year), 8 teaching assistantships with tuition reimbursements available (averaging $20,166 per year); scholarships/grants, tuition waivers (full), and unspecified assistantships also available. Financial award applicants required to submit FAFSA. *Faculty research:* Manufacturing systems, infrastructure, and management. *Total annual research expenditures:* $320,400. *Unit head:* Dr. Leslie Monplaisir, Associate Professor/Chair, 313-577-3821, Fax: 313-577-8833, E-mail: leslie.monplaisir@wayne.edu. *Application contact:* Eric Scimeca, Graduate Program Coordinator, 313-577-0412, E-mail: eric.scimeca@wayne.edu.
Website: http://engineering.wayne.edu/ise/

Western Michigan University, Graduate College, College of Engineering and Applied Sciences, Department of Industrial and Entrepreneurial Engineering and Engineering

Management, Kalamazoo, MI 49008. Offers engineering management (MS); industrial engineering (MSE, PhD). *Degree requirements:* For master's, thesis optional.

Western New England University, College of Engineering, Master's Program in Engineering Management, Springfield, MA 01119. Offers business and engineering information systems (MSEM); general engineering management (MSEM); production and manufacturing systems (MSEM); quality engineering (MSEM); MSEM/MBA. *Program availability:* Part-time, evening/weekend, online learning. *Faculty:* 3 full-time (0 women). *Students:* 33 part-time (5 women); includes 3 minority (1 Asian, non-Hispanic/ Latino; 2 Hispanic/Latino), 6 international. Average age 30. 73 applicants, 73% accepted, 13 enrolled. In 2018, 22 master's awarded. *Degree requirements:* For master's, thesis optional. *Entrance requirements:* For master's, official transcript, bachelor's degree in engineering or related field, two recommendations, resume. Additional exam requirements/recommendations for international students: Required—TOEFL (minimum score 79 iBT). *Application deadline:* Applications are processed on a rolling basis. Application fee: $30. Electronic applications accepted. *Expenses:* Contact institution. *Financial support:* Application deadline: 4/15; applicants required to submit FAFSA. *Unit head:* Dr. Christian Salmon, Chair and Professor, 413-796-2209, E-mail: christian.salmon@wne.edu. *Application contact:* Matthew Fox, Executive Director of Graduate Admissions, 413-782-1410, Fax: 413-782-1777, E-mail: study@wne.edu.
Website: http://www1.wne.edu/academics/graduate/engineering-management.cfm

Western New England University, College of Engineering, PhD Program in Engineering Management, Springfield, MA 01119. Offers PhD. *Program availability:* Part-time, evening/weekend. *Faculty:* 3 full-time (0 women). *Students:* 8 part-time (2 women), 4 international. Average age 33. 14 applicants, 71% accepted, 3 enrolled. In 2018, 2 doctorates awarded. *Degree requirements:* For doctorate, comprehensive exam, thesis/dissertation. *Entrance requirements:* For doctorate, GRE, official transcript, bachelor's or master's degree in engineering or related field, two letters of recommendation, minimum GPA of 3.5. Additional exam requirements/ recommendations for international students: Required—TOEFL (minimum score 550 paper-based; 79 iBT). *Application deadline:* For fall admission, 1/15 priority date for domestic students. Applications are processed on a rolling basis. Application fee: $30. Electronic applications accepted. *Expenses:* Contact institution. *Financial support:* In 2018–19, 6 fellowships with tuition reimbursements were awarded. Financial award application deadline: 4/15; financial award applicants required to submit FAFSA. *Unit head:* Dr. Christian Salmon, Chair and Professor, 413-796-2209, E-mail: christian.salmon@wne.edu. *Application contact:* Matthew Fox, Executive Director of Graduate Admissions, 413-782-1410, Fax: 413-782-1777, E-mail: study@wne.edu.
Website: http://www1.wne.edu/academics/graduate/engineering-management-phd.cfm

Wichita State University, Graduate School, College of Engineering, Department of Industrial and Manufacturing Engineering, Wichita, KS 67260. Offers engineering management (MEM); industrial engineering (MS, PhD). *Program availability:* Part-time. In 2018, 37 master's, 3 doctorates awarded. *Entrance requirements:* Additional exam requirements/recommendations for international students: Required—TOEFL. *Financial support:* Teaching assistantships available. *Unit head:* Dr. Krishna Krishnan, Chair, 316-978-3425, Fax: 316-978-3742, E-mail: krishna.krishnan@wichita.edu. *Application contact:* Jordan Oleson, Admissions Coordinator, 316-978-3095, Fax: 316-978-3253, E-mail: jordan.oleson@wichita.edu.
Website: http://www.wichita.edu/ime

Widener University, Graduate Programs in Engineering, Program in Engineering Management, Chester, PA 19013. Offers M Eng. *Program availability:* Part-time, evening/weekend. *Degree requirements:* For master's, thesis optional. Electronic applications accepted.

Wilkes University, College of Graduate and Professional Studies, College of Science and Engineering, Department of Mechanical Engineering and Engineering Management, Wilkes-Barre, PA 18766-0002. Offers engineering management (MS); mechanical engineering (MS). *Program availability:* Part-time. *Students:* 2 full-time (0 women), 2 part-time (0 women); includes 3 minority (1 Hispanic/Latino; 2 Two or more races, non-Hispanic/Latino). Average age 29. In 2018, 12 master's awarded. *Application deadline:* Applications are processed on a rolling basis. Application fee: $45 ($65 for international students). Electronic applications accepted. Tuition and fees vary according to course load, degree level and program. *Financial support:* Institutionally sponsored loans and unspecified assistantships available. *Unit head:* Dr. Prahlad Murthy, Interim Dean, 570-408-4600, Fax: 570-408-7860, E-mail: prahlad.murthy@wilkes.edu. *Application contact:* Kristin Donati, Associate Director of Graduate Admissions, 570-408-3338, Fax: 570-408-7846, E-mail: kristin.donati@wilkes.edu.
Website: http://www.wilkes.edu/academics/colleges/science-and-engineering/mechanical-engineering-engineering-management-applied-and-engineering-sciences/

Ergonomics and Human Factors

Arizona State University at the Tempe campus, Ira A. Fulton Schools of Engineering, The Polytechnic School, Programs in Technology Management, Mesa, AZ 85212. Offers aviation management and human factors (MS); environmental technology management (MS); global technology and development (MS); graphic information technology (MS); management of technology (MS). *Program availability:* Part-time, evening/weekend, online learning. *Degree requirements:* For master's, thesis or applied project and oral defense; interactive Program of Study (iPOS) submitted before completing 50 percent of required credit hours. *Entrance requirements:* For master's, GRE, minimum GPA of 3.0 or equivalent in last 2 years of work leading to bachelor's degree. Additional exam requirements/recommendations for international students: Required—TOEFL, IELTS, or PTE. Electronic applications accepted. *Faculty research:* Digital imaging, digital publishing, Internet development/e-commerce, information aviation human factors, pilot selection, databases, multimedia, commercial digital photography, digital workflow, computer graphics modeling and animation, information design, sociotechnology, visual and technical literacy, environmental management, quality management, project management, industrial ethics, hazardous materials, environmental chemistry.

Bentley University, McCallum Graduate School of Business, Masters in Human Factors in Information Design, Waltham, MA 02452-4705. Offers MSHFID. *Program availability:* Part-time, evening/weekend, 100% online, blended/hybrid learning. *Faculty:* 118 full-time (38 women), 25 part-time/adjunct (4 women). *Students:* 37 full-time (27 women), 73 part-time (54 women); includes 23 minority (3 Black or African American, non-Hispanic/Latino; 12 Asian, non-Hispanic/Latino; 3 Hispanic/Latino; 5 Two or more races, non-Hispanic/Latino), 21 international. Average age 32. 113 applicants, 63% accepted, 45 enrolled. In 2018, 47 master's awarded. *Entrance requirements:* For master's, GMAT or GRE General Test (may be waived for qualified applicants), Transcripts; Resume; Two essays; Two letters of recommendation; Interview (may be requested by Bentley). Additional exam requirements/recommendations for international students: Required—TOEFL (minimum score 100) or IELTS (minimum score 7). *Application deadline:* For fall admission, 7/31 for domestic students, 6/30 for international students; for spring admission, 1/1 for domestic students, 11/1 for international students. Applications are processed on a rolling basis. Application fee: $150. Electronic applications accepted. *Financial support:* In 2018–19, 57 students received support. Scholarships/grants and unspecified assistantships available. Financial award application deadline: 6/1; financial award applicants required to submit FAFSA. *Faculty research:* Ethnography; human-computer interaction; virtual reality; user experience; haptics. *Unit head:* Dr. William M. Gribbons, Professor and MSHFID Director, 781-891-2926, E-mail: wgribbons@bentley.edu. *Application contact:* Office of Graduate Admissions, 781-891-2108, E-mail: applygrad@bentley.edu.
Website: https://www.bentley.edu/academics/graduate-programs/masters-human-factors

California State University, Long Beach, Graduate Studies, College of Liberal Arts, Department of Psychology, Long Beach, CA 90840. Offers human factors (MS); industrial/organizational psychology (MS); psychology (MA). *Program availability:* Part-time, evening/weekend. *Degree requirements:* For master's, comprehensive exam, thesis. *Entrance requirements:* For master's, GRE General Test, GRE Subject Test. *Application deadline:* Applications are processed on a rolling basis. Application fee: $55. Electronic applications accepted. *Expenses: Required fees:* $2628 per term. Tuition and fees vary according to class time, course level, course load, degree level, campus/ location and program. *Financial support:* Federal Work-Study, institutionally sponsored loans, and scholarships/grants available. Financial award application deadline: 3/2; financial award applicants required to submit FAFSA. *Faculty research:* Physiological psychology, social and personality psychology, community-clinical psychology, industrial-organizational psychology, developmental psychology. *Unit head:* Sherry A. Span, Chair, 562-985-5001, Fax: 562-985-8004. *Application contact:* Dr. Diane Roe, Graduate Advisor, 562-985-5000, E-mail: diane.roe@csulb.edu.
Website: http://www.cla.csulb.edu/departments/psychology/

The Catholic University of America, School of Arts and Sciences, Department of Psychology, Washington, DC 20064. Offers applied experimental psychology (PhD); clinical psychology (PhD); general psychology (MA); human development psychology (PhD); human factors (MA); MA/JD. MA/JD offered jointly with Columbus School of Law. *Accreditation:* APA (one or more programs are accredited). *Program availability:* Part-time. *Faculty:* 11 full-time (6 women), 12 part-time/adjunct (8 women). *Students:* 32 full-time (27 women), 40 part-time (31 women); includes 19 minority (5 Asian, non-Hispanic/ Latino; 5 Hispanic/Latino; 9 Two or more races, non-Hispanic/Latino), 6 international. Average age 28. 172 applicants, 24% accepted, 19 enrolled. In 2018, 16 master's, 7 doctorates awarded. *Degree requirements:* For master's, comprehensive exam, thesis (for some programs); for doctorate, comprehensive exam, thesis/dissertation. *Entrance requirements:* For master's, GRE General Test, statement of purpose, official copies of academic transcripts, three letters of recommendation; for doctorate, GRE General Test, GRE Subject Test, statement of purpose, official copies of academic transcripts, three letters of recommendation. Additional exam requirements/recommendations for international students: Required—TOEFL (minimum score 550 paper-based; 80 iBT). *Application deadline:* For fall admission, 7/15 priority date for domestic students, 7/1 for international students; for spring admission, 11/15 priority date for domestic students, 11/1 for international students. Applications are processed on a rolling basis. Application fee: $55. Electronic applications accepted. *Expenses:* Contact institution. *Financial support:* Fellowships, research assistantships, teaching assistantships, Federal Work-Study, scholarships/grants, tuition waivers (full and partial), and unspecified assistantships available. Financial award application deadline: 2/1; financial award applicants required to submit FAFSA. *Faculty research:* Clinical psychology, applied cognitive science, psychopathology, cognitive neuroscience, psychotherapy. *Unit head:* Dr. Brendan Rich, Chair, 202-319-5823, Fax: 202-319-6263, E-mail: richb@cua.edu. *Application contact:* Dr. Steven Brown, Director of Graduate Admissions, 202-319-5057, Fax: 202-319-6533, E-mail: cua-admissions@cua.edu.
Website: http://psychology.cua.edu/

Clemson University, Graduate School, College of Behavioral, Social and Health Sciences, Department of Psychology, Clemson, SC 29634. Offers applied psychology (MS); human factors psychology (PhD); industrial-organizational psychology (PhD). *Faculty:* 25 full-time (9 women). *Students:* 38 full-time (22 women), 3 part-time (2 women); includes 6 minority (2 Black or African American, non-Hispanic/Latino; 4 Hispanic/Latino). Average age 26. 227 applicants, 10% accepted, 10 enrolled. In 2018, 4 master's, 12 doctorates awarded. *Degree requirements:* For master's, thesis; for doctorate, comprehensive exam, thesis/dissertation. *Entrance requirements:* For master's and doctorate, GRE General Test, unofficial transcripts, letters of recommendation, statement of intent. Additional exam requirements/recommendations for international students: Required—TOEFL (minimum score 80 paper-based; 80 iBT); Recommended—IELTS (minimum score 7), TSE (minimum score 54). *Application deadline:* For fall admission, 4/15 priority date for international students; for spring admission, 10/15 for international students. Applications are processed on a rolling basis. Application fee: $80 ($90 for international students). Electronic applications accepted. *Expenses:* $6823 per semester full-time resident, $14023 per semester full-time non-resident, $833 per credit hour part-time resident, $1731 per credit hour part-time non-resident, online $1264 per credit hour, $4938 doctoral programs resident, $10405 doctoral programs non-resident, $1144 full-time graduate assistant, other fees may apply per session. *Financial support:* In 2018–19, 43 students received support, including 3 fellowships with full and partial tuition reimbursements available (averaging $5,000 per year), 5 research assistantships with full and partial tuition reimbursements available (averaging $14,794 per year), 31 teaching assistantships with full and partial tuition reimbursements available (averaging $13,774 per year); career-related internships or fieldwork and unspecified assistantships also available. *Faculty research:* Occupational health and organizational psychology; transportation safety; human factors in health care; ergonomics and human-computer interaction; aging, retirement, and return to work. *Total annual research expenditures:* $538,726. *Unit head:* Dr. Patrick Raymark, Chair, 864-656-4715, E-mail: praymar@clemson.edu. *Application contact:* Dr. Robert Sinclair, Graduate Program Coordinator, 864-656-3931, E-mail: rsincla@clemson.edu.
Website: http://www.clemson.edu/cbshs/departments/psychology/index.html

Cornell University, Graduate School, Graduate Fields of Human Ecology, Field of Design and Environmental Analysis, Ithaca, NY 14853. Offers applied research in human-environment relations (MS); facilities planning and management (MS); housing and design (MS); human factors and ergonomics (MS); human-environment relations

(MS); interior design (MA, MPS). *Degree requirements:* For master's, thesis. *Entrance requirements:* For master's, GRE General Test, portfolio or slides of recent work; bachelor's degree in interior design, architecture or related design discipline; 2 letters of recommendation. Additional exam requirements/recommendations for international students: Required—TOEFL (minimum score 600 paper-based; 105 iBT). Electronic applications accepted. *Faculty research:* Facility planning and management, environmental psychology, housing, interior design, ergonomics and human factors.

Embry-Riddle Aeronautical University–Daytona, Department of Human Factors and Behavioral Neurobiology, Daytona Beach, FL 32114-3900. Offers human factors (PhD). *Degree requirements:* For master's, thesis or alternative; for doctorate, comprehensive exam, thesis/dissertation. *Entrance requirements:* For doctorate, GRE. Additional exam requirements/recommendations for international students: Required—TOEFL (minimum score 550 paper-based, 79 iBT) or IELTS (6). Electronic applications accepted. *Faculty research:* Aerospace human factors, game-based education, healthcare human factors, applied cognition and training, user experience.

Georgia Institute of Technology, Graduate Studies, College of Computing, Program in Human-Centered Computing, Atlanta, GA 30332-0001. Offers MS, PhD. *Program availability:* Part-time. *Degree requirements:* For doctorate, comprehensive exam, thesis/dissertation, research project, teaching requirement. *Entrance requirements:* For doctorate, GRE General Test. Additional exam requirements/recommendations for international students: Required—TOEFL (minimum score 600 paper-based; 100 iBT). Electronic applications accepted.

Harvard University, Harvard T.H. Chan School of Public Health, Department of Environmental Health, Boston, MA 02115-6096. Offers environmental epidemiology (SM); environmental exposure assessment (SM); ergonomics and safety (SM); occupational health (SM); occupational hygiene (SM); population health sciences (PhD); risk and decision science (SM). *Program availability:* Part-time. *Faculty:* 41 full-time (13 women), 16 part-time/adjunct (3 women). *Students:* 45 full-time (35 women); includes 10 minority (2 Black or African American, non-Hispanic/Latino; 4 Asian, non-Hispanic/Latino; 1 Hispanic/Latino; 3 Two or more races, non-Hispanic/Latino), 24 international. Average age 29. 48 applicants, 67% accepted, 19 enrolled. In 2018, 10 master's, 12 doctorates awarded. *Degree requirements:* For doctorate, thesis/dissertation, qualifying exam. *Entrance requirements:* For master's, GRE, MCAT; for doctorate, GRE. Additional exam requirements/recommendations for international students: Recommended—TOEFL (minimum score 600 paper-based; 100 iBT), IELTS (minimum score 7). *Application deadline:* For fall admission, 12/1 for domestic and international students. Application fee: $135. Electronic applications accepted. *Financial support:* Fellowships, research assistantships, teaching assistantships, career-related internships or fieldwork, Federal Work-Study, scholarships/grants, traineeships, and unspecified assistantships available. Support available to part-time students. Financial award application deadline: 2/15; financial award applicants required to submit FAFSA. *Faculty research:* Exposure assessment, epidemiology, risk assessment, environmental epidemiology, ergonomics and safety, environmental exposure assessment, occupational hygiene, industrial hygiene and occupational safety, population genetics, indoor and outdoor air pollution, cell and molecular biology of the lungs, infectious diseases. *Unit head:* Dr. Russ Hauser, Chairman, 617-432-1270, Fax: 617-432-6913. *Application contact:* Vincent W. James, Director of Admissions, 617-432-1031, Fax: 617-432-7080, E-mail: admissions@hsph.harvard.edu.
Website: http://www.hsph.harvard.edu/environmental-health/

Indiana University Bloomington, School of Public Health, Department of Kinesiology, Bloomington, IN 47405. Offers applied sport science (MS); athletic administration/sport management (MS); athletic training (MS); biomechanics (MS); ergonomics (MS); exercise physiology (MS); human performance (PhD), including biomechanics, exercise physiology, motor learning/control, sport management; motor learning/control (MS); physical activity (MPH); physical activity, fitness and wellness (MS). *Program availability:* Part-time. Terminal master's awarded for partial completion of doctoral program. *Degree requirements:* For master's, thesis optional; for doctorate, variable foreign language requirement, comprehensive exam, thesis/dissertation. *Entrance requirements:* For master's, GRE General Test, minimum GPA of 2.8; for doctorate, GRE General Test, minimum graduate GPA of 3.5, undergraduate 3.0. Additional exam requirements/recommendations for international students: Required—TOEFL (minimum score 80 iBT). *Faculty research:* Exercise physiology and biochemistry, sports biomechanics, human motor control, adaptation of fitness and exercise to special populations.

Michigan Technological University, Graduate School, College of Sciences and Arts, Department of Cognitive and Learning Sciences, Houghton, MI 49931. Offers applied cognitive science and human factors (MS, PhD); applied science education (MS); post-secondary STEM education (Graduate Certificate). *Program availability:* Part-time, blended/hybrid learning. *Faculty:* 21 full-time (9 women), 6 part-time/adjunct. *Students:* 12 full-time (7 women), 22 part-time (16 women); includes 4 minority (3 Black or African American, non-Hispanic/Latino; 1 Two or more races, non-Hispanic/Latino), 5 international. Average age 35. 55 applicants, 38% accepted, 11 enrolled. In 2018, 6 master's, 1 doctorate, 2 other advanced degrees awarded. Terminal master's awarded for partial completion of doctoral program. *Degree requirements:* For master's, comprehensive exam (for some programs), thesis (for some programs); for doctorate, comprehensive exam, thesis/dissertation, applied internship experience. *Entrance requirements:* For master's, GRE (for applied cognitive science and human factors program only), statement of purpose, personal statement, official transcripts, 3 letters of recommendation, resume/curriculum vitae; for doctorate, GRE, statement of purpose, personal statement, official transcripts, 3 letters of recommendation, resume/curriculum vitae. Additional exam requirements/recommendations for international students: Required—TOEFL, TOEFL (recommended minimum score 90 iBT) or IELTS. *Application deadline:* For fall admission, 2/1 priority date for domestic and international students. Applications are processed on a rolling basis. Electronic applications accepted. *Expenses: Tuition, area resident:* Full-time $18,126; part-time $1007 per credit. Tuition, state resident: full-time $18,126; part-time $1007 per credit. Tuition, nonresident: full-time $18,126; part-time $1007 per credit. *International tuition:* $18,126 full-time. *Required fees:* $248; $124 per semester. Tuition and fees vary according to course load and program. *Financial support:* In 2018–19, 20 students received support, including 2 fellowships (averaging $16,590 per year), 3 research assistantships with tuition reimbursements available (averaging $16,590 per year), 5 teaching assistantships (averaging $16,590 per year); career-related internships or fieldwork, scholarships/grants, health care benefits, unspecified assistantships, and adjunct instructor positions also available. Financial award application deadline: 12/15; financial award applicants required to submit FAFSA. *Faculty research:* Human-computer interaction, models of aging in motor movements, cognitive task analyses, decision support technologies, cognitive workload and computational mental modeling. *Total annual research expenditures:* $474,263. *Unit head:* Dr. Susan L. Amato-Henderson, Chair, 906-487-2536, Fax: 906-487-2468, E-mail: slamato@mtu.edu. *Application contact:* Dr. Kelly S. Steelman, Graduate Program Director, 906-487-2792, Fax: 906-487-2468, E-mail: steelman@mtu.edu.
Website: http://www.mtu.edu/cls/

Mississippi State University, Bagley College of Engineering, Department of Industrial and Systems Engineering, Mississippi State, MS 39762. Offers human factors and ergonomics (MS); industrial and systems engineering (PhD); industrial systems (MS); management systems (MS); manufacturing systems (MS); operations research (MS). *Program availability:* Part-time, blended/hybrid learning. *Faculty:* 12 full-time (2 women). *Students:* 35 full-time (13 women), 66 part-time (16 women); includes 20 minority (7 Black or African American, non-Hispanic/Latino; 6 Asian, non-Hispanic/Latino; 5 Hispanic/Latino; 1 Native Hawaiian or other Pacific Islander, non-Hispanic/Latino; 1 Two or more races, non-Hispanic/Latino), 21 international. Average age 36. 67 applicants, 40% accepted, 18 enrolled. In 2018, 16 master's, 9 doctorates awarded. *Degree requirements:* For master's, comprehensive exam (for some programs), thesis optional, comprehensive oral or written exam; for doctorate, comprehensive exam, thesis/dissertation, candidacy exam. *Entrance requirements:* For master's, GRE (for graduates from program not accredited by EAC/ABET), minimum GPA of 3.0 on junior and senior years; for doctorate, GRE (for graduates from program not accredited by EAC/ABET), minimum GPA of 3.5 on master's degree and junior and senior years of BS. Additional exam requirements/recommendations for international students: Required—TOEFL (minimum score 550 paper-based; 79 iBT); Recommended—IELTS (minimum score 6.5). *Application deadline:* For fall admission, 7/1 for domestic students, 5/1 for international students; for spring admission, 11/1 for domestic students, 9/1 for international students. Applications are processed on a rolling basis. Application fee: $60 ($80 for international students). Electronic applications accepted. *Expenses:* Tuition, state resident: full-time $8450; part-time $360.59 per credit hour. Tuition, nonresident: full-time $23,140; part-time $969.09 per credit hour. *Required fees:* $110. One-time fee: $55 full-time. Part-time tuition and fees vary according to course load, degree level, campus/location and reciprocity agreements. *Financial support:* In 2018–19, 18 research assistantships with full tuition reimbursements (averaging $16,905 per year), 3 teaching assistantships with full tuition reimbursements (averaging $16,033 per year) were awarded; Federal Work-Study, institutionally sponsored loans, and unspecified assistantships also available. Financial award application deadline: 4/1; financial award applicants required to submit FAFSA. *Faculty research:* Operations research, ergonomics, production systems, management systems, transportation. *Total annual research expenditures:* $2 million. *Unit head:* Dr. Kari Babski-Reeves, Professor/Interim Head and Associate Dean for Research & Graduate Studies, 662-325-8430, Fax: 662-325-7618, E-mail: kari@ise.msstate.edu. *Application contact:* Ryan King, Admissions and Enrollment Assistant, 662-325-8951, E-mail: rjk101@grad.msstate.edu.
Website: http://www.ise.msstate.edu/

North Carolina State University, Graduate School, College of Humanities and Social Sciences, Department of Psychology, Raleigh, NC 27695. Offers applied social and community psychology (PhD); human factors and applied cognition (PhD); industrial/organizational psychology (PhD); lifespan developmental psychology (PhD); school psychology (PhD). *Accreditation:* APA. *Degree requirements:* For doctorate, comprehensive exam, thesis/dissertation. *Entrance requirements:* For doctorate, GRE General Test, GRE Subject Test (industrial/organizational psychology), MAT (recommended), minimum GPA of 3.0 in major. Electronic applications accepted. *Faculty research:* Cognitive and social development (human factors, families, the workplace, community issues and health, aging).

Old Dominion University, College of Sciences, Doctoral Program in Psychology, Norfolk, VA 23529. Offers applied psychological sciences (PhD); human factors psychology (PhD); industrial/organizational psychology (PhD). *Degree requirements:* For doctorate, comprehensive exam, thesis/dissertation, candidacy exam. *Entrance requirements:* For doctorate, GRE General Test, GRE Subject Test, 3 recommendation letters. Additional exam requirements/recommendations for international students: Required—TOEFL. Electronic applications accepted. *Expenses:* Contact institution. *Faculty research:* Human factors, industrial psychology, organizational psychology, applied psychological sciences (health, developmental, community, quantitative).

Purdue University, Graduate School, College of Health and Human Sciences, School of Health Sciences, West Lafayette, IN 47907. Offers health physics (MS, PhD); medical physics (MS, PhD); occupational and environmental health science (MS, PhD), including aerosol deposition and lung disease, ergonomics, exposure and risk assessment, indoor air quality and bioaerosols (PhD), liver/lung toxicology; radiological health (PhD); toxicology (PhD); MS/PhD. *Program availability:* Part-time. *Faculty:* 15 full-time (6 women). *Students:* 41 full-time (22 women), 7 part-time (2 women); includes 11 minority (2 Black or African American, non-Hispanic/Latino; 5 Asian, non-Hispanic/Latino; 1 Hispanic/Latino; 3 Two or more races, non-Hispanic/Latino), 12 international. Average age 28. 61 applicants, 41% accepted, 14 enrolled. In 2018, 4 master's, 9 doctorates awarded. *Degree requirements:* For master's, thesis optional; for doctorate, one foreign language, thesis/dissertation. *Entrance requirements:* For master's and doctorate, GRE General Test, minimum undergraduate GPA of 3.0 or equivalent. Additional exam requirements/recommendations for international students: Required—TOEFL (minimum score 550 paper-based; 77 iBT); Recommended—TWE. *Application deadline:* For fall admission, 5/15 for domestic and international students; for spring admission, 10/15 for domestic and international students. Applications are processed on a rolling basis. Application fee: $60 ($75 for international students). Electronic applications accepted. *Financial support:* In 2018–19, fellowships with tuition reimbursements (averaging $14,400 per year), research assistantships with tuition reimbursements (averaging $12,000 per year), teaching assistantships with tuition reimbursements (averaging $12,000 per year) were awarded; career-related internships or fieldwork and traineeships also available. Support available to part-time students. Financial award applicants required to submit FAFSA. *Faculty research:* Environmental toxicology, industrial hygiene, radiation dosimetry. *Unit head:* Aaron Bowman, Head of the Graduate Program, 765-494-2684, E-mail: bowma117@purdue.edu. *Application contact:* Karen E. Walker, Graduate Contact, 765-494-1419, E-mail: kwalker@purdue.edu.
Website: https://www.purdue.edu/hhs/hsci/

Queen's University at Kingston, School of Graduate Studies, School of Kinesiology and Health Studies, Kingston, ON K7L 3N6, Canada. Offers biomechanics and ergonomics (M Sc, PhD); exercise physiology (M Sc, PhD); health promotion (M Sc, PhD); physical activity epidemiology (M Sc, PhD); sociocultural studies of sport, health and the body (MA, PhD); sport psychology (M Sc, PhD). *Program availability:* Part-time. *Degree requirements:* For master's, thesis (for some programs); for doctorate, comprehensive exam, thesis/dissertation. *Entrance requirements:* For master's and doctorate, minimum B+ average. Additional exam requirements/recommendations for international students: Required—TOEFL. Electronic applications accepted. *Faculty research:* Expert performance ergonomics, obesity research, pregnancy and exercise, gender and sport participation.

Tufts University, School of Engineering, Department of Mechanical Engineering, Medford, MA 02155. Offers human factors (MS); mechanical engineering (MS, PhD); PhD/PhD. *Program availability:* Part-time. Terminal master's awarded for partial completion of doctoral program. *Degree requirements:* For master's, thesis; for doctorate, thesis/dissertation. *Entrance requirements:* For master's and doctorate, GRE General Test. Additional exam requirements/recommendations for international students: Required—TOEFL (minimum score 550 paper-based; 80 iBT), IELTS (minimum score 6.5). Electronic applications accepted. *Expenses: Tuition:* Full-time

$51,288; part-time $1710 per credit hour. *Required fees:* $904. Full-time tuition and fees vary according to degree level, program and student level. Part-time tuition and fees vary according to course load. *Faculty research:* Applied mechanics, biomaterials, controls/robotics, design/systems, human factors.

Université de Montréal, Faculty of Medicine, Programs in Ergonomics, Montréal, QC H3C 3J7, Canada. Offers occupational therapy (DESS). Program offered jointly with École Polytechnique de Montréal.

Université du Québec à Montréal, Graduate Programs, Program in Ergonomics in Occupational Health and Safety, Montréal, QC H3C 3P8, Canada. Offers Diploma. *Program availability:* Part-time. *Entrance requirements:* For degree, appropriate bachelor's degree or equivalent, proficiency in French.

The University of Alabama, Graduate School, College of Human Environmental Sciences, Program in Human Environmental Science, Tuscaloosa, AL 35487. Offers interactive technology (MS); quality management (MS); restaurant and meeting management (MS); rural community health (MS); sport management (MS). *Program availability:* Part-time, evening/weekend, online learning. *Degree requirements:* For master's, comprehensive exam. *Entrance requirements:* For master's, GRE (for some specializations), minimum GPA of 3.0. Additional exam requirements/recommendations for international students: Required—TOEFL. Electronic applications accepted. *Faculty research:* Rural health, hospitality management, sport management, interactive technology, consumer quality management, environmental health and safety.

University of Cincinnati, Graduate School, College of Medicine, Graduate Programs in Biomedical Sciences, Department of Environmental Health, Cincinnati, OH 45221. Offers environmental and industrial hygiene (MS, PhD); environmental and occupational medicine (MS); environmental genetics and molecular toxicology (MS, PhD); epidemiology and biostatistics (MS, PhD); occupational safety and ergonomics (MS, PhD). *Accreditation:* ABET (one or more programs are accredited); CEPH. Terminal master's awarded for partial completion of doctoral program. *Degree requirements:* For master's, thesis; for doctorate, thesis/dissertation, qualifying exam. *Entrance requirements:* For master's, GRE General Test, bachelor's degree in science; for doctorate, GRE General Test. Additional exam requirements/recommendations for international students: Required—TOEFL (minimum score 600 paper-based; 100 iBT). Electronic applications accepted. *Faculty research:* Carcinogens and mutagenesis, pulmonary studies, reproduction and development.

The University of Iowa, Graduate College, College of Engineering, Department of Industrial Engineering, Iowa City, IA 52242-1316. Offers engineering design and manufacturing (MS, PhD); healthcare systems (MS, PhD); human factors (MS, PhD); information and engineering management (MS, PhD); operations research (MS, PhD); wind energy (MS, PhD). Terminal master's awarded for partial completion of doctoral program. *Degree requirements:* For master's, thesis optional, exam; for doctorate, comprehensive exam, thesis/dissertation, final defense exam. *Entrance requirements:* For master's and doctorate, GRE (minimum Verbal score of 153, Quantitative 151), minimum undergraduate GPA of 3.0. Additional exam requirements/recommendations for international students: Required—TOEFL (minimum score 600 paper-based; 100 iBT), IELTS (minimum score 7). Electronic applications accepted. *Faculty research:* Operations research, informatics, human factors engineering, healthcare systems, bio-manufacturing, manufacturing systems, renewable energy, human-machine interactions.

The University of Iowa, Graduate College, College of Public Health, Department of Occupational and Environmental Health, Iowa City, IA 52242-1316. Offers agricultural safety and health (MS, PhD); ergonomics (MPH); industrial hygiene (MS, PhD); occupational and environmental health (MPH, MS, PhD, Certificate); MS/MA; MS/MS. *Accreditation:* ABET (one or more programs are accredited). *Degree requirements:* For master's, thesis optional, exam; for doctorate, comprehensive exam, thesis/dissertation. *Entrance requirements:* For master's and doctorate, GRE General Test, minimum GPA of 3.0. Additional exam requirements/recommendations for international students: Required—TOEFL (minimum score 600 paper-based; 100 iBT). Electronic applications accepted.

University of Miami, Graduate School, College of Engineering, Department of Industrial Engineering, Program in Occupational Ergonomics and Safety, Coral Gables, FL 33124. Offers environmental health and safety (MS); occupational ergonomics and safety (MSOES). *Program availability:* Part-time. *Degree requirements:* For master's, thesis optional. *Entrance requirements:* For master's, GRE General Test, minimum GPA of 3.0. Additional exam requirements/recommendations for international students: Required—TOEFL (minimum score 550 paper-based). Electronic applications accepted. *Faculty research:* Noise, heat stress, water pollution.

University of Wisconsin–Madison, Graduate School, College of Engineering, Department of Industrial and Systems Engineering, Madison, WI 53706. Offers industrial engineering (MS, PhD), including human factors and health systems engineering (MS), systems engineering and analytics (MS). *Program availability:* Part-time. *Faculty:* 20 full-time (6 women). *Students:* 87 full-time (33 women), 12 part-time (8 women); includes 4 minority (1 Black or African American, non-Hispanic/Latino; 3 Asian, non-Hispanic/Latino), 63 international. Average age 26. 372 applicants, 21% accepted, 18 enrolled. In 2018, 35 master's, 9 doctorates awarded. Terminal master's awarded for partial completion of doctoral program. *Degree requirements:* For master's, thesis optional, 30 credits; minimum GPA of 3.0; for doctorate, comprehensive exam, thesis/dissertation, minimum of 51 credits; minimum GPA of 3.0. *Entrance requirements:* For master's and doctorate, GRE General Test, minimum GPA of 3.0, BS in engineering or equivalent, course work in computer programming and statistics. Additional exam requirements/recommendations for international students: Required—TOEFL (minimum score 580 paper-based; 92 iBT), IELTS (minimum score 7). *Application deadline:* For fall admission, 12/15 for domestic and international students; for spring admission, 10/1 for domestic and international students; for summer admission, 12/15 for domestic and international students. Application fee: $75 ($81 for international students). Electronic applications accepted. *Financial support:* In 2018–19, 66 students received support, including 2 fellowships with full tuition reimbursements available (averaging $27,816 per year), 39 research assistantships with full tuition reimbursements available (averaging $24,456 per year), 21 teaching assistantships with full tuition reimbursements available (averaging $19,788 per year); career-related internships or fieldwork, Federal Work-Study, institutionally sponsored loans, scholarships/grants, traineeships, health care benefits, and unspecified assistantships also available. Financial award application deadline: 12/1; financial award applicants required to submit FAFSA. *Faculty research:* Operations research; human factors and ergonomics; health systems engineering; manufacturing and production systems. *Total annual research expenditures:* $13.9 million. *Unit head:* Dr. Jeff Lindroth, Chair, 608-262-2686, E-mail: ie@engr.wisc.edu. *Application contact:* Pam Peterson, Student Services Coordinator, 608-263-4025, Fax: 608-890-2204, E-mail: prpeterson@wisc.edu.
Website: http://www.engr.wisc.edu/department/industrial-systems-engineering/

University of Wisconsin–Milwaukee, Graduate School, College of Health Sciences, Department of Occupational Science and Technology, Milwaukee, WI 53201-0413. Offers assistive technology and design (MS); disability and occupation (MS); ergonomics (MS); therapeutic recreation (MS). *Accreditation:* AOTA. *Students:* 96 full-time (85 women), 2 part-time (both women); includes 13 minority (4 Asian, non-Hispanic/Latino; 2 Hispanic/Latino; 7 Two or more races, non-Hispanic/Latino), 2 international. Average age 28. 131 applicants, 28% accepted, 33 enrolled. In 2018, 34 master's awarded. *Entrance requirements:* Additional exam requirements/recommendations for international students: Required—TOEFL (minimum score 550 paper-based; 79 iBT), IELTS (minimum score 6.5). *Application deadline:* For fall admission, 1/1 priority date for domestic students; for spring admission, 9/1 for domestic students. Applications are processed on a rolling basis. Application fee: $56 ($75 for international students). *Financial support:* Fellowships, research assistantships, teaching assistantships, and unspecified assistantships available. Support available to part-time students. Financial award application deadline: 4/15. *Unit head:* Jay Kapellusch, PhD, Department Chair, 414-229-5292, Fax: 414-229-2619, E-mail: kap@uwm.edu. *Application contact:* Bhagwant S. Sindhu, PhD, Graduate Program Coordinator, 414-229-1180, Fax: 414-229-5100, E-mail: sindhu@uwm.edu.
Website: http://uwm.edu/healthsciences/academics/occupational-science-technology/

Wright State University, Graduate School, College of Engineering and Computer Science, Department of Biomedical, Industrial and Human Factors Engineering, Dayton, OH 45435. Offers biomedical engineering (MS); industrial and human factors engineering (MS). *Program availability:* Part-time. *Degree requirements:* For master's, thesis or course option alternative. *Entrance requirements:* Additional exam requirements/recommendations for international students: Required—TOEFL. *Faculty research:* Medical imaging, functional electrical stimulation, implantable aids, man-machine interfaces, expert systems.

Wright State University, Graduate School, College of Science and Mathematics, Department of Psychology, Program in Human Factors and Industrial/Organizational Psychology, Dayton, OH 45435. Offers MS, PhD. *Degree requirements:* For master's, thesis; for doctorate, thesis/dissertation.

Management of Technology

Air Force Institute of Technology, Graduate School of Engineering and Management, Department of Operational Sciences, Dayton, OH 45433-7765. Offers logistics management (MS); operations research (MS, PhD); space operations (MS). *Program availability:* Part-time. *Degree requirements:* For master's, thesis; for doctorate, thesis/dissertation. *Entrance requirements:* For doctorate, GRE General Test, minimum GPA of 3.0, U.S. citizenship. *Faculty research:* Optimization, simulation, combat modeling and analysis, reliability and maintainability, resource scheduling.

Arizona State University at the Tempe campus, Ira A. Fulton Schools of Engineering, The Polytechnic School, Programs in Technology Management, Mesa, AZ 85212. Offers aviation management and human factors (MS); environmental technology management (MS); global technology and development (MS); graphic information technology (MS); management of technology (MS). *Program availability:* Part-time, evening/weekend, online learning. *Degree requirements:* For master's, thesis or applied project and oral defense; interactive Program of Study (iPOS) submitted before completing 50 percent of required credit hours. *Entrance requirements:* For master's, GRE, minimum GPA of 3.0 or equivalent in last 2 years of work leading to bachelor's degree. Additional exam requirements/recommendations for international students: Required—TOEFL, IELTS, or PTE. Electronic applications accepted. *Faculty research:* Digital imaging, digital publishing, Internet development/e-commerce, information aviation human factors, pilot selection, databases, multimedia, commercial digital photography, digital workflow, computer graphics modeling and animation, information design, sociotechnology, visual and technical literacy, environmental management, quality management, project management, industrial ethics, hazardous materials, environmental chemistry.

Athabasca University, Faculty of Business, Edmonton, AB T5L 4W1, Canada. Offers business administration (MBA); information technology management (MBA), including policing concentration; innovative management (DBA); management (GDM); project management (MBA, GDM). *Program availability:* Part-time, evening/weekend, online learning. *Degree requirements:* For master's, thesis or alternative, applied project. *Entrance requirements:* For master's, 3-8 years of managerial experience, 3 years with undergraduate degree, 5 years' managerial experience with professional designation, 8-10 years' management experience (on exception). Electronic applications accepted. *Expenses:* Contact institution. *Faculty research:* Human resources, project management, operations research, information technology management, corporate stewardship, energy management.

Atlantis University, School of Computer Science and Information Technology, Miami, FL 33132. Offers information technology (MIT).

Boston University, Metropolitan College, Department of Administrative Sciences, Boston, MA 02215. Offers applied business analytics (MS); economic development and tourism management (MSAS); enterprise risk management (MS); financial management (MS); global marketing management (MS); innovation and technology (MSAS); insurance management (MS); project management (MS); supply chain management (MS). *Accreditation:* AACSB. *Program availability:* Part-time, evening/weekend, 100% online, blended/hybrid learning. *Faculty:* 27 full-time (5 women), 39 part-time/adjunct (5 women). *Students:* 617 full-time (351 women), 574 part-time (290 women); includes 196 minority (47 Black or African American, non-Hispanic/Latino; 2 American Indian or Alaska Native, non-Hispanic/Latino; 75 Asian, non-Hispanic/Latino; 60 Hispanic/Latino; 12 Two or more races, non-Hispanic/Latino), 730 international. Average age 28. 2,259 applicants, 76% accepted, 594 enrolled. In 2018, 441 master's awarded. *Degree requirements:* For master's, thesis optional. *Entrance requirements:* For master's, 1 year of work experience, minimum GPA of 3.0. Additional exam requirements/recommendations for international students: Required—TOEFL (minimum score 84 iBT). *Application deadline:* For fall admission, 8/1 priority date for domestic students, 6/1 priority date for international students; for spring admission, 12/1 priority date for domestic students, 11/15 priority date for international students; for summer admission, 4/1 priority date for domestic students, 3/1 priority date for international students. Applications are processed on a rolling basis. Application fee: $85. Electronic applications accepted. *Expenses:* Contact institution. *Financial support:* In 2018–19, 15 students received support, including 16 research assistantships (averaging $8,400 per year), 30 teaching assistantships (averaging $3,400 per year); career-related internships

or fieldwork, Federal Work-Study, and unspecified assistantships also available. Financial award applicants required to submit FAFSA. *Faculty research:* International business, innovative process. *Unit head:* Dr. John Sullivan, Chair, 617-353-3016, E-mail: adminsc@bu.edu. *Application contact:* Enrollment Services, 617-358-8162, E-mail: met@bu.edu.
Website: http://www.bu.edu/met/academic-community/departments/administrative-sciences/

California Lutheran University, Graduate Studies, School of Management, Thousand Oaks, CA 91360-2787. Offers business (IMBA); entrepreneurship (MBA, Certificate); finance (MBA, Certificate); financial planning (MBA, MS, Certificate); human capital management (MBA, Certificate); information technology (MS); information technology management (MBA, Certificate); international business (MBA, Certificate); management (MS); marketing (MBA, Certificate); public policy and administration (MPPA); quantitative economics (MS). *Program availability:* Part-time, evening/weekend, 100% online, blended/hybrid learning. *Degree requirements:* For master's, comprehensive exam (for some programs). *Entrance requirements:* For master's, GMAT, interview, minimum GPA of 3.0. Electronic applications accepted. *Expenses:* Contact institution.

California State University, Los Angeles, Graduate Studies, College of Engineering, Computer Science, and Technology, Department of Technology, Los Angeles, CA 90032-8530. Offers industrial and technical studies (MA). *Program availability:* Part-time, evening/weekend. *Entrance requirements:* For master's, minimum GPA of 2.5. Additional exam requirements/recommendations for international students: Required—TOEFL (minimum score 550 paper-based).

Cambridge College, School of Management, Boston, MA 02129. Offers business administration (MBA); business negotiation and conflict resolution (M Mgt); general business (M Mgt); health care (MBA); health care management (M Mgt); small business development (M Mgt); technology management (M Mgt). *Program availability:* Part-time, evening/weekend, 100% online, blended/hybrid learning. *Degree requirements:* For master's, thesis, seminars. *Entrance requirements:* For master's, resume, 2 professional references. Additional exam requirements/recommendations for international students: Required—TOEFL (minimum score 550 paper-based; 79 iBT), Michigan English Language Assessment Battery (minimum score 85); Recommended—IELTS (minimum score 6). *Application deadline:* Applications are processed on a rolling basis. Application fee: $50 ($100 for international students). Electronic applications accepted. *Expenses:* Contact institution. *Financial support:* Career-related internships or fieldwork, Federal Work-Study, and scholarships/grants available. Financial award applicants required to submit FAFSA. *Faculty research:* Negotiation, mediation and conflict resolution; leadership; management of diverse organizations; case studies and simulation methodologies for management education, digital as a second language: social networking for digital immigrants, non-profit and public management. *Unit head:* Joseph Miglio, Interim Dean, E-mail: joseph.miglio@cambridgecollege.edu. *Application contact:* Salvadore Liberto, Interim Assistant Vice President of Enrollment, 800-877-4723, E-mail: admissions@cambridgecollege.edu.
Website: https://www.cambridgecollege.edu/school/school-management

Campbellsville University, School of Business, Economics, and Technology, Campbellsville, KY 42718-2799. Offers business administration (MBA, Professional MBA); information technology management (MS); management (PhD); management and leadership (MML). *Program availability:* Part-time, evening/weekend, 100% online, blended/hybrid learning. *Faculty:* 62 full-time (29 women), 28 part-time/adjunct (14 women). *Students:* 6,515 full-time (1,494 women), 134 part-time (35 women); includes 19 minority (16 Black or African American, non-Hispanic/Latino; 1 American Indian or Alaska Native, non-Hispanic/Latino; 1 Asian, non-Hispanic/Latino; 1 Hispanic/Latino), 6,524 international. Average age 28. 3,512 applicants, 85% accepted, 2026 enrolled. In 2018, 1,102 master's awarded. *Degree requirements:* For master's, comprehensive exam (for some programs), thesis optional; for doctorate, comprehensive exam, thesis/dissertation. *Entrance requirements:* For master's, GRE or GMAT, letters of recommendation, college transcripts; for doctorate, GMAT, resume, official transcripts, references, personal essay, interview, completion of course in statistics and research methods. Additional exam requirements/recommendations for international students: Required—TOEFL (minimum score 550 paper-based; 79 iBT); Recommended—IELTS (minimum score 6). *Application deadline:* Applications are processed on a rolling basis. Application fee: $25. Electronic applications accepted. Application fee is waived when completed online. *Expenses:* $479-$525 per credit hour (for master's); $699 per credit hour (for PhD). *Financial support:* Unspecified assistantships available. Financial award application deadline: 6/1; financial award applicants required to submit FAFSA. *Unit head:* Dr. Patricia H. Cowherd, Dean of School of Business, Economics, and Technology, 270-789-5553, Fax: 270-789-5066, E-mail: phcowherd@campbellsville.edu. *Application contact:* Monica Bamwine, Director of Graduate Admissions, 270-789-5221, Fax: 270-789-5071, E-mail: mkbamwine@campbellsville.edu.
Website: http://www.campbellsville.edu

Capella University, School of Business and Technology, Doctoral Programs in Technology, Minneapolis, MN 55402. Offers general information technology (PhD); global operations and supply chain management (DBA); information assurance and security (PhD); information technology education (PhD); information technology management (DBA, PhD).

Capella University, School of Business and Technology, Master's Programs in Technology, Minneapolis, MN 55402. Offers enterprise software architecture (MS); general information systems and technology management (MS); global operations and supply chain management (MBA); information assurance and security (MS); information technology management (MBA); network management (MS).

Carleton University, Faculty of Graduate Studies, Faculty of Engineering and Design, Ottawa-Carleton Institute for Electrical Engineering, Department of Systems and Computer Engineering, Program in Technology Innovation Management, Ottawa, ON K1S 5B6, Canada. Offers M Eng, MA Sc. *Degree requirements:* For master's, thesis optional. *Entrance requirements:* For master's, honors degree. Additional exam requirements/recommendations for international students: Required—TOEFL.

The Catholic University of America, School of Engineering, Program in Engineering Management, Washington, DC 20064. Offers engineering management (MSE, Certificate), including engineering management and organization (MSE), project and systems engineering management (MSE), technology management (MSE); program management (Certificate); systems engineering and management of information technology (Certificate). *Program availability:* Part-time. *Faculty:* 6 part-time/adjunct (1 woman). *Students:* 16 full-time (1 woman), 19 part-time (7 women); includes 3 minority (1 Asian, non-Hispanic/Latino; 2 Two or more races, non-Hispanic/Latino), 17 international. Average age 31. 48 applicants, 85% accepted, 19 enrolled. In 2018, 17 master's awarded. *Degree requirements:* For master's, minimum GPA of 3.0. *Entrance requirements:* For master's and Certificate, statement of purpose, official copies of academic transcripts, two letters of recommendation. Additional exam requirements/recommendations for international students: Required—TOEFL (minimum score 550 paper-based; 80 iBT). *Application deadline:* For fall admission, 7/15 priority date for domestic students, 7/1 for international students; for spring admission, 11/15 priority

date for domestic students, 11/1 for international students. Applications are processed on a rolling basis. Application fee: $55. Electronic applications accepted. *Expenses:* Contact institution. *Financial support:* Fellowships, research assistantships, teaching assistantships, Federal Work-Study, scholarships/grants, tuition waivers (full and partial), and unspecified assistantships available. Financial award application deadline: 2/1; financial award applicants required to submit FAFSA. *Faculty research:* Engineering management and organization, project and systems engineering management, technology management. *Unit head:* Melvin G. Williams, Jr., Director, 202-319-5191, Fax: 202-319-6860, E-mail: williamsme@cua.edu. *Application contact:* Dr. Steven Brown, Director of Graduate Admissions, 202-319-5057, Fax: 202-319-6533, E-mail: cua-admissions@cua.edu.
Website: https://engineering.catholic.edu/management/index.html

Central Connecticut State University, School of Graduate Studies, School of Engineering, Science and Technology, Department of Manufacturing and Construction Management, New Britain, CT 06050-4010. Offers construction management (MS, Certificate); lean manufacturing and Six Sigma (Certificate); supply chain and logistics (Certificate); technology management (MS). *Program availability:* Part-time, evening/weekend. *Faculty:* 6 full-time (0 women), 2 part-time/adjunct (0 women). *Students:* 14 full-time (7 women), 82 part-time (18 women); includes 28 minority (11 Black or African American, non-Hispanic/Latino; 2 Asian, non-Hispanic/Latino; 12 Hispanic/Latino; 3 Two or more races, non-Hispanic/Latino), 6 international. Average age 32. 70 applicants, 71% accepted, 29 enrolled. In 2018, 51 master's, 5 other advanced degrees awarded. *Degree requirements:* For master's, comprehensive exam, special project; for Certificate, qualifying exam. *Entrance requirements:* For master's, minimum undergraduate GPA of 2.7. Additional exam requirements/recommendations for international students: Required—TOEFL (minimum score 550 paper-based; 79 iBT); Recommended—IELTS (minimum score 6.5). *Application deadline:* For fall admission, 8/1 for domestic students, 5/1 for international students; for spring admission, 12/1 for domestic students, 11/1 for international students; for summer admission, 5/1 for domestic students. Applications are processed on a rolling basis. Application fee: $50. Electronic applications accepted. *Expenses: Tuition, area resident:* Full-time $7027; part-time $388 per credit. Tuition, state resident: full-time $9750; part-time $388 per credit. Tuition, nonresident: full-time $18,102; part-time $388 per credit. *International tuition:* $18,102 full-time. *Required fees:* $266 per semester. *Financial support:* In 2018–19, 7 students received support. Career-related internships or fieldwork, Federal Work-Study, scholarships/grants, and unspecified assistantships available. Support available to part-time students. Financial award application deadline: 3/1; financial award applicants required to submit FAFSA. *Faculty research:* All aspects of middle management, technical supervision in the workplace. *Unit head:* Dr. Ravindra Thamma, Chair, 860-832-1830, E-mail: thammarav@ccsu.edu. *Application contact:* Patricia Gardner, Associate Director of Graduate Studies, 860-832-2350, Fax: 860-832-2362.
Website: http://www.ccsu.edu/mcm/

Central European University, Department of Economics, 1051, Hungary. Offers business administration (PhD); business analytics (M Sc); economic policy in global markets (MA); economics (MA, PhD); finance (MS); global economic relations (MA); technology management and innovation (MS). *Program availability:* Part-time. *Degree requirements:* For master's, one foreign language, thesis; for doctorate, one foreign language, comprehensive exam, thesis/dissertation. *Entrance requirements:* For master's and doctorate, interview. Additional exam requirements/recommendations for international students: Required—TOEFL (minimum score 570 paper-based); Recommended—IELTS (minimum score 6.5). Electronic applications accepted. *Faculty research:* Economic theory (microeconomics and macroeconomics) and econometrics, as well as study of many applied fields, including labor economics, health economics and economics of education, industrial organization, monetary economics, international economics, law and economics, comparative institutional economics, corporate governance, and economics of transition.

Champlain College, Graduate Studies, Burlington, VT 05402-0670. Offers business (MBA); digital forensic science (MS); early childhood education (M Ed); emergent media (MFA, MS); executive leadership (MS); health care administration (MS); information security operations (MS); law (MS); mediation and applied conflict studies (MS). MS in emergent media program held in Shanghai. *Program availability:* Part-time, online learning. *Degree requirements:* For master's, capstone project. *Entrance requirements:* Additional exam requirements/recommendations for international students: Required—TOEFL (minimum score 550 paper-based; 80 iBT). Electronic applications accepted.

City University of Seattle, Graduate Division, School of Management, Seattle, WA 98121. Offers accounting (Certificate); change leadership (MBA, Certificate); computer systems (MS); finance (Certificate); financial management (MBA); general management (MBA); general management-Europe (MBA); global marketing (MBA); human resources management (Certificate); individualized study (MBA); information security (MS); information systems (MBA); leadership (MA); marketing (MBA, Certificate); project management (MBA, MS, Certificate); sustainable business (Certificate); technology management (MBA, Certificate). *Program availability:* Part-time, evening/weekend, online learning. *Degree requirements:* For master's, comprehensive exam (for some programs), thesis (for some programs). *Entrance requirements:* For master's, baccalaureate degree or equivalent from an accredited or otherwise recognized institution. Additional exam requirements/recommendations for international students: Required—TOEFL (minimum score 567 paper-based; 87 iBT); Recommended—IELTS. Electronic applications accepted.

Colorado School of Mines, Office of Graduate Studies, Department of Economics and Business, Golden, CO 80401. Offers engineering and technology management (MS); mineral and energy economics (MS, PhD); operations research and engineering (PhD); petroleum economics and management with mineral and energy economics (MS). *Program availability:* Part-time. *Faculty:* 17 full-time (5 women), 4 part-time/adjunct (1 woman). *Students:* 92 full-time (27 women), 12 part-time (4 women); includes 20 minority (4 Black or African American, non-Hispanic/Latino; 4 Asian, non-Hispanic/Latino; 8 Hispanic/Latino; 1 Native Hawaiian or other Pacific Islander, non-Hispanic/Latino; 3 Two or more races, non-Hispanic/Latino), 33 international. Average age 28. 154 applicants, 82% accepted, 53 enrolled. In 2018, 68 master's, 4 doctorates awarded. *Degree requirements:* For master's, thesis (for some programs); for doctorate, comprehensive exam, thesis/dissertation. *Entrance requirements:* For master's and doctorate, GRE General Test. Additional exam requirements/recommendations for international students: Required—TOEFL (minimum score 550 paper-based; 79 iBT). *Application deadline:* For fall admission, 12/15 priority date for domestic and international students; for spring admission, 9/1 priority date for domestic and international students. Application fee: $60 ($80 for international students). Electronic applications accepted. *Expenses:* Tuition, state resident: full-time $16,650; part-time $925 per contact hour. Tuition, nonresident: full-time $36,270; part-time $2015 per contact hour. *International tuition:* $36,270 full-time. *Required fees:* $2314; $2314 per semester. *Financial support:* In 2018–19, 7 research assistantships with full tuition reimbursements, 22 teaching assistantships with full tuition reimbursements were awarded; fellowships, scholarships/grants, health care benefits, and unspecified assistantships also available. Financial award application deadline: 12/15; financial award applicants required to submit FAFSA. *Faculty research:* International trade,

resource and environmental economics, energy economics, operations research. *Unit head:* Dr. Roderick Eggert, Interim Director, 303-273-3981, E-mail: reggert@mines.edu. *Application contact:* Kathleen Martin, Program Assistant, 303-273-3482, Fax: 303-273-3416, E-mail: kmartin@mines.edu.
Website: http://econbus.mines.edu

Colorado Technical University Aurora, Programs in Business Administration and Management, Aurora, CO 80014. Offers accounting (MBA); business administration (MBA); business administration and management (EMBA); finance (MBA); human resource management (MBA); marketing (MBA); mediation and dispute resolution (MBA); operations management (MBA); project management (MBA); technology management (MBA). *Program availability:* Part-time, evening/weekend. *Degree requirements:* For master's, thesis or alternative. *Entrance requirements:* For master's, minimum undergraduate GPA of 3.0, resume.

Colorado Technical University Colorado Springs, Graduate Studies, Program in Management, Colorado Springs, CO 80907. Offers accounting (MBA, MSA); business administration (MBA); finance (MBA); human resources management (MBA); logistics/supply chain management (MBA); management (DM); marketing (MBA); mediation and dispute resolution (MBA); operations management (MBA); project management (MBA); technology management (MBA). *Accreditation:* ACBSP. *Program availability:* Part-time, evening/weekend, online learning. *Degree requirements:* For master's, thesis or alternative; for doctorate, thesis/dissertation. *Entrance requirements:* For doctorate, minimum graduate GPA of 3.0, 5 years of related work experience. *Faculty research:* Sexual harassment, performance evaluation, critical thinking.

Columbia University, School of Professional Studies, Program in Technology Management, New York, NY 10027. Offers Exec MS. *Program availability:* Part-time, evening/weekend. *Entrance requirements:* For master's, minimum undergraduate GPA of 3.0. Additional exam requirements/recommendations for international students: Required—American Language Program placement test. Electronic applications accepted. *Faculty research:* Information systems, management.

Duke University, The Fuqua School of Business, The Duke MBA-Daytime Program, Durham, NC 27708. Offers academic excellence in finance (Certificate); business administration (MBA); decision sciences (MBA); energy and environment (MBA); energy finance (MBA); entrepreneurship and innovation (MBA); finance (MBA); financial analysis (MBA); health sector management (Certificate); leadership and ethics (MBA); management (MBA); management science and technology management (Certificate); marketing (MBA); operations management (MBA); social entrepreneurship (MBA); strategy (MBA). *Faculty:* 100 full-time (21 women), 55 part-time/adjunct (12 women). *Students:* 875 full-time (335 women); includes 188 minority (44 Black or African American, non-Hispanic/Latino; 4 American Indian or Alaska Native, non-Hispanic/Latino; 90 Asian, non-Hispanic/Latino; 43 Hispanic/Latino; 1 Native Hawaiian or other Pacific Islander, non-Hispanic/Latino; 6 Two or more races, non-Hispanic/Latino), 276 international. Average age 29. In 2018, 429 master's awarded. *Entrance requirements:* For master's, GMAT or GRE, transcripts, essays, resume, recommendation letters, interview. *Application deadline:* For fall admission, 9/19 for domestic and international students; for winter admission, 10/14 for domestic and international students; for spring admission, 1/6 for domestic and international students; for summer admission, 3/11 for domestic and international students. Application fee: $225. Electronic applications accepted. *Expenses:* Contact institution. *Financial support:* Scholarships/grants available. Financial award applicants required to submit FAFSA. *Unit head:* Steve Misuraca, Assistant Dean, Daytime MBA Program. *Application contact:* Shari Hubert, Associate Dean, Office of Admissions, 919-660-7705, Fax: 919-681-8026, E-mail: admissions-info@fuqua.duke.edu.
Website: https://www.fuqua.duke.edu/programs/daytime-mba

East Carolina University, Graduate School, College of Engineering and Technology, Department of Technology Systems, Greenville, NC 27858-4353. Offers computer network professional (Certificate); cyber security professional (Certificate); information assurance (Certificate); Lean Six Sigma Black Belt (Certificate); network technology (MS), including computer networking management, digital communications technology, information security, Web technologies; occupational safety (MS); technology management (MS, PhD), including industrial distribution and logistics (MS); Website developer (Certificate). *Application deadline:* For fall admission, 6/1 priority date for domestic students. *Expenses: Tuition, area resident:* Full-time $4749. Tuition, state resident: full-time $4749. Tuition, nonresident: full-time $17,898. *International tuition:* $17,898 full-time. *Required fees:* $2787. Part-time tuition and fees vary according to course load and program. *Financial support:* Application deadline: 6/1. *Unit head:* Dr. Tijjani Mohammed, Chair, 252-328-9668, E-mail: mohammedt@ecu.edu. *Application contact:* Graduate School Admissions, 252-328-6012, Fax: 252-328-6071, E-mail: gradschool@ecu.edu.
Website: http://www.ecu.edu/cs-cet/techsystems/index.cfm

Eastern Michigan University, Graduate School, College of Engineering and Technology, Program in Technology, Ypsilanti, MI 48197. Offers PhD. *Program availability:* Part-time, evening/weekend. *Students:* 8 full-time (3 women), 32 part-time (17 women); includes 8 minority (7 Black or African American, non-Hispanic/Latino; 1 Asian, non-Hispanic/Latino), 18 international. Average age 41. 17 applicants, 47% accepted, 5 enrolled. In 2018, 15 doctorates awarded. *Degree requirements:* For doctorate, comprehensive exam, thesis/dissertation. *Entrance requirements:* For doctorate, GRE. Additional exam requirements/recommendations for international students: Required—TOEFL. *Application deadline:* For fall admission, 5/15 priority date for domestic students, 2/15 priority date for international students; for winter admission, 10/15 priority date for domestic students, 9/1 priority date for international students; for summer admission, 3/15 priority date for domestic students, 3/1 priority date for international students. Applications are processed on a rolling basis. Application fee: $45. *Financial support:* Fellowships, research assistantships with tuition reimbursements, teaching assistantships with tuition reimbursements, career-related internships or fieldwork, Federal Work-Study, institutionally sponsored loans, scholarships/grants, tuition waivers (partial), and unspecified assistantships available. Support available to part-time students. Financial award applicants required to submit FAFSA. *Application contact:* Dr. Dorothy McAllen, Advisor, 734-487-4694, Fax: 734-487-0843, E-mail: dmcallen@emich.edu.

École Polytechnique de Montréal, Graduate Programs, Department of Mathematics and Industrial Engineering, Montréal, QC H3C 3A7, Canada. Offers ergonomy (M Eng, M Sc A, DESS); mathematical method in CA engineering (M Eng, M Sc A, PhD); operational research (M Eng, M Sc A, PhD); production (M Eng, M Sc A); technology management (M Eng, M Sc A). DESS program offered jointly with HEC Montreal and Université de Montréal. *Program availability:* Part-time. *Degree requirements:* For master's, one foreign language, thesis. *Entrance requirements:* For master's, minimum GPA of 2.75. *Faculty research:* Use of computers in organizations.

Embry-Riddle Aeronautical University–Worldwide, Department of Decision Sciences, Daytona Beach, FL 32114-3900. Offers aviation and aerospace (MSPM); aviation/aerospace management (MSEM); financial management (MSEM, MSPM); general management (MSPM); global management (MSPM); human resources management (MSPM); information systems (MSPM); leadership (MSEM, MSPM); logistics and supply chain management (MSEM, MSLSCM, MSPM); management (MSEM, MSPM); project management (MSEM); systems engineering (MSEM, MSPM); technical management (MSPM). *Program availability:* Part-time, evening/weekend, EagleVision Classroom (between classrooms), EagleVision Home (faculty and students at home), and a blend of Classroom or Home. *Degree requirements:* For master's, comprehensive exam (for some programs), thesis (for some programs). *Entrance requirements:* Additional exam requirements/recommendations for international students: Required—TOEFL (minimum score 550 paper-based; 79 iBT), IELTS (minimum score 6). Electronic applications accepted. *Expenses:* Contact institution.

Embry-Riddle Aeronautical University–Worldwide, Department of Technology Management, Daytona Beach, FL 32114-3900. Offers information and security assurance (MS); management information systems (MS). *Program availability:* Part-time, evening/weekend, EagleVision Classroom (between classrooms), EagleVision Home (faculty and students at home), and a blend of Classroom or Home. *Entrance requirements:* Additional exam requirements/recommendations for international students: Required—TOEFL (minimum score 550 paper-based; 79 iBT), IELTS (minimum score 6). Electronic applications accepted. *Expenses: Tuition:* Full-time $7980; part-time $665 per credit hour. Tuition and fees vary according to course load, degree level and program.

Fairfield University, School of Engineering, Fairfield, CT 06824. Offers database management (CAS); electrical and computer engineering (MS); information security (CAS); management of technology (MS); mechanical engineering (MS); network technology (CAS); software engineering (MS); Web application development (CAS). *Program availability:* Part-time, evening/weekend. *Degree requirements:* For master's, capstone course. *Entrance requirements:* For master's, resume, 2 recommendations. Additional exam requirements/recommendations for international students: Required—TOEFL (minimum score 550 paper-based; 80 iBT) or IELTS (minimum score 6.5). Electronic applications accepted. *Expenses:* Contact institution. *Faculty research:* Artificial intelligence and information visualization, natural language processing, thermofluids, microwaves and electromagnetics, micro-/nano-manufacturing.

Fairleigh Dickinson University, Florham Campus, Silberman College of Business, Departments of Management, Marketing, and Entrepreneurial Studies, Program in Management, Madison, NJ 07940-1099. Offers evolving technology (Certificate); management (MBA); MBA/MA.

Farmingdale State College, Program in Technology Management, Farmingdale, NY 11735. Offers construction management (MS); electrical and mechanical engineering (MS). *Degree requirements:* For master's, project or thesis.

George Mason University, School of Business, Program in Technology Management, Fairfax, VA 22030. Offers MS. *Faculty:* 7 full-time (1 woman), 1 part-time/adjunct (0 women). *Students:* 18 full-time (5 women), 1 part-time (0 women); includes 7 minority (1 Black or African American, non-Hispanic/Latino; 3 Asian, non-Hispanic/Latino; 2 Hispanic/Latino; 1 Two or more races, non-Hispanic/Latino), 2 international. Average age 35. In 2018, 19 master's awarded. *Entrance requirements:* For master's, GMAT/GRE, resume; official transcripts; 2 professional letters of recommendation; professional essay; expanded goals statement; interview. Additional exam requirements/recommendations for international students: Required—TOEFL (minimum score 575 paper-based; 93 iBT), IELTS (minimum score 7), PTE (minimum score 59). Application fee: $75 ($80 for international students). Electronic applications accepted. *Expenses:* $1,058.25 per credit. *Financial support:* Career-related internships or fieldwork, Federal Work-Study, and scholarships/grants available. Financial award application deadline: 3/1; financial award applicants required to submit FAFSA. *Faculty research:* Leadership careers in technology-oriented businesses, achieving success in the technology marketplace, emphasizing technology leadership and management, technology innovation, commercialization, methods and approaches of systems thinking. *Unit head:* Kumar Mehta, Director, 703-993-9412, E-mail: kmehta1@gmu.edu. *Application contact:* Jacky Buchy, Assistant Dean, Graduate Enrollment, 703-993-1856, Fax: 703-993-1778, E-mail: jbuchy@gmu.edu.
Website: http://business.gmu.edu/masters-in-technology-management/

Georgetown University, Graduate School of Arts and Sciences, School of Continuing Studies, Washington, DC 20057. Offers American studies (MALS); applied intelligence (MPS); Catholic studies (MALS); classical civilizations (MALS); emergency and disaster management (MPS); ethics and the professions (MALS); global strategic communications (MPS); hospitality management (MPS); human resources management (MPS); humanities (MALS); individualized study (MALS); integrated marketing communications (MPS); international affairs (MALS); Islam and Muslim-Christian relations (MALS); journalism (MPS); liberal studies (DLS); literature and society (MALS); medieval and early modern European studies (MALS); public relations and corporate communications (MPS); real estate (MPS); religious studies (MALS); social and public policy (MALS); sports industry management (MPS); systems engineering management (MPS); technology management (MPS); the theory and practice of American democracy (MALS); urban and regional planning (MPS); visual culture (MALS). MPS in systems engineering management offered jointly with Stevens Institute of Technology. *Entrance requirements:* Additional exam requirements/recommendations for international students: Required—TOEFL.

The George Washington University, School of Business, Department of Information Systems and Technology Management, Washington, DC 20052. Offers information and decision systems (PhD); information systems (MSIST); information systems development (MSIST); information systems management (MBA); information systems project management (MSIST); management information systems (MSIST); management of science, technology, and innovation (MBA, PhD). Programs also offered in Ashburn and Arlington, VA. *Program availability:* Part-time, evening/weekend, online learning. *Students:* 98 full-time (49 women), 47 part-time (19 women); includes 33 minority (12 Black or African American, non-Hispanic/Latino; 14 Asian, non-Hispanic/Latino; 2 Hispanic/Latino; 5 Two or more races, non-Hispanic/Latino), 91 international. Average age 29. 328 applicants, 67% accepted, 55 enrolled. In 2018, 98 master's awarded. *Entrance requirements:* For master's, GMAT. Additional exam requirements/recommendations for international students: Required—TOEFL. *Application deadline:* For fall admission, 4/1 priority date for domestic students; for spring admission, 10/1 for domestic students. Applications are processed on a rolling basis. Application fee: $75. *Financial support:* In 2018–19, 35 students received support. Fellowships, teaching assistantships, career-related internships or fieldwork, Federal Work-Study, institutionally sponsored loans, and tuition waivers available. Financial award application deadline: 4/1. *Faculty research:* Expert systems, decision support systems. *Unit head:* Richard Donnelly, Chair, 202-994-7155, E-mail: rgd@gwu.edu. *Application contact:* Christopher Storer, Executive Director, Graduate Admissions, 202-994-1212, E-mail: gwmba@gwu.edu.

Golden Gate University, Ageno School of Business, San Francisco, CA 94105-2968. Offers accounting (MBA); adaptive leadership (MBA); advanced financial planning (MS); business administration (EMBA, MBA, DBA); business analytics (MBA, MS); entrepreneurship (MBA); finance (MBA, MS, Certificate); financial life planning (Certificate); financial planning (MS, Certificate); global supply chain management (MBA, Certificate); human resource management (MBA, MS, Certificate); information technology management (MBA, MS, Certificate); international business (MBA); marketing (MBA, MS, Certificate); project management (MBA, MS, Certificate); psychology (MA, Certificate); public administration (EMPA, MBA); public administration leadership (Certificate); JD/MBA. *Program availability:* Part-time, evening/weekend. *Degree requirements:* For doctorate, thesis/dissertation, qualifying examination. *Entrance requirements:* For master's, GMAT (for MBA), minimum GPA of 2.5 (MS). Additional exam requirements/recommendations for international students: Required—TOEFL (minimum score 550 paper-based; 79 iBT). Electronic applications accepted. *Expenses:* Contact institution.

Grand Canyon University, Colangelo College of Business, Phoenix, AZ 85017-1097. Offers accounting (MBA, MS); business analytics (MS); disaster preparedness and executive fire service leadership (MS); finance (MBA); general management (MBA); health systems management (MBA); information technology management (MS); leadership (MBA, MS); marketing (MBA); organizational leadership and entrepreneurship (MS); project management (MBA); sports business (MBA); strategic human resource management (MBA). *Accreditation:* ACBSP. *Program availability:* Part-time, evening/weekend, online learning. *Entrance requirements:* For master's, equivalent of two years' full-time professional work experience. Additional exam requirements/recommendations for international students: Required—TOEFL (minimum score 575 paper-based; 90 iBT), IELTS (minimum score 7). Electronic applications accepted.

Harrisburg University of Science and Technology, Program in Project Management, Harrisburg, PA 17101. Offers information technology (MS). *Program availability:* Part-time, evening/weekend. *Degree requirements:* For master's, thesis optional. *Entrance requirements:* For master's, baccalaureate degree. Additional exam requirements/recommendations for international students: Required—TOEFL (minimum score 520 paper-based; 80 iBT); Recommended—IELTS (minimum score 6). Electronic applications accepted. *Faculty research:* Strategic planning, organizational development.

Harvard University, Graduate School of Arts and Sciences, Program in Information, Technology and Management, Cambridge, MA 02138. Offers PhD.

Harvard University, Harvard Business School, Doctoral Programs in Management, Boston, MA 02163. Offers accounting and management (DBA); business economics (PhD); health policy management (PhD); management (DBA); marketing (DBA); organizational behavior (PhD); science, technology and management (PhD); strategy (DBA); technology and operations management (DBA). *Degree requirements:* For doctorate, comprehensive exam (for some programs), thesis/dissertation. *Entrance requirements:* For doctorate, GRE General Test or GMAT. Additional exam requirements/recommendations for international students: Required—TOEFL.

Herzing University Online, Program in Business Administration, Menomonee Falls, WI 53051. Offers accounting (MBA); business administration (MBA); business management (MBA); healthcare management (MBA); human resources (MBA); marketing (MBA); project management (MBA); technology management (MBA). *Program availability:* Online learning.

Illinois State University, Graduate School, College of Applied Science and Technology, Department of Technology, Normal, IL 61790. Offers MS. *Faculty:* 20 full-time (2 women), 16 part-time/adjunct (1 woman). *Students:* 38 full-time (16 women), 63 part-time (29 women); includes 9 minority (3 Black or African American, non-Hispanic/Latino; 2 Asian, non-Hispanic/Latino; 2 Hispanic/Latino; 2 Two or more races, non-Hispanic/Latino), 30 international. Average age 31. 70 applicants, 84% accepted, 21 enrolled. In 2018, 42 master's awarded. *Degree requirements:* For master's, thesis or alternative. *Entrance requirements:* For master's, GRE General Test, minimum GPA of 2.8. *Application deadline:* Applications are processed on a rolling basis. Application fee: $40. *Expenses: Tuition, area resident:* Full-time $7264.62. Tuition, state resident: full-time $9466. Tuition, nonresident: full-time $17,290. *International tuition:* $15,089.40 full-time. *Required fees:* $1481.04. *Financial support:* In 2018–19, 20 research assistantships were awarded; tuition waivers (full) and unspecified assistantships also available. Financial award application deadline: 4/1. *Faculty research:* Illinois Manufacturing Extension Center Field Office hosting, model for the professional development of K-12 technology education teachers, Illinois State University Illinois Mathematics and Science Partnership, Illinois University council for career and technical education. *Unit head:* Dr. Ted Branoff, Department Chair, 309-438-3661, E-mail: tjbrano@IllinoisState.edu. *Application contact:* Dr. Klaus Scmidt, Graduate Coordinator, 309-438-3502, E-mail: kschmid@ilstu.edu.
Website: http://tec.illinoisstate.edu/

Indiana State University, College of Graduate and Professional Studies, College of Technology, Department of Applied Engineering and Technology Management, Terre Haute, IN 47809. Offers technology management (MS); MA/MS. *Accreditation:* NCATE (one or more programs are accredited). *Entrance requirements:* For master's, bachelor's degree in industrial technology or related field. Additional exam requirements/recommendations for international students: Required—TOEFL. Electronic applications accepted.

Indiana State University, College of Graduate and Professional Studies, Program in Technology Management, Terre Haute, IN 47809. Offers PhD. Program part of consortium with North Carolina Agricultural and Technical University, University of Central Missouri, Bowling Green State University, and East Carolina University. *Program availability:* Online learning. *Degree requirements:* For doctorate, thesis/dissertation. *Entrance requirements:* For doctorate, GRE or GMAT, minimum graduate GPA of 3.5, 6000 hours of occupational experience. Electronic applications accepted. *Faculty research:* Production management, quality control, human resource development, construction project management, lean manufacturing.

Indiana University–Purdue University Indianapolis, School of Engineering and Technology, MS in Technology Program, Indianapolis, IN 46202. Offers applied data management and analytics (MS); facilities management (MS); information security and assurance (MS); motorsports (MS); organizational leadership (MS); technical communication (MS). *Program availability:* Online learning.

Instituto Centroamericano de Administración de Empresas, Graduate Programs, La Garita, Costa Rica. Offers agribusiness management (MIAM); business administration (EMBA); finance (MBA); real estate management (MGREM); sustainable development (MBA); technology (MBA). *Degree requirements:* For master's, comprehensive exam, essay. *Entrance requirements:* For master's, GMAT or GRE General Test, fluency in Spanish, interview, letters of recommendation, minimum 1 year of work experience. Additional exam requirements/recommendations for international students: Recommended—TOEFL. Electronic applications accepted. *Faculty research:* Competitiveness, production.

Instituto Tecnológico y de Estudios Superiores de Monterrey, Campus Cuernavaca, Programs in Information Science, Temixco, Mexico. Offers administration of information technology (MATI); computer science (MCC, DCC); information technology (MTI).

Instituto Tecnológico y de Estudios Superiores de Monterrey, Campus Irapuato, Graduate Programs, Irapuato, Mexico. Offers administration (MBA); administration of information technology (MAIT); administration of telecommunications (MAT); architecture (M Arch); computer science (MCS); education (M Ed); educational administration (MEA); educational innovation and technology (DEIT); educational technology (MET); electronic commerce (MBA); environmental administration and planning (MEAP); environmental systems (MES); finances (MBA); humanistic studies (MHS); international management for Latin American executives (MIMLAE); library and information science (MLIS); manufacturing quality management (MMQM); marketing research (MBA).

Iona College, School of Business, Department of Information Systems, New Rochelle, NY 10801-1890. Offers accounting and information systems (MS); business continuity and risk management (AC); information systems (MBA, MS, PMC); project management (MS). *Program availability:* Part-time, evening/weekend. *Faculty:* 5 full-time (0 women). *Students:* 12 full-time (7 women), 9 part-time (4 women); includes 7 minority (3 Black or African American, non-Hispanic/Latino; 2 Asian, non-Hispanic/Latino; 2 Hispanic/Latino), 1 international. Average age 28. 9 applicants, 89% accepted, 2 enrolled. In 2018, 12 master's awarded. *Entrance requirements:* For master's, GMAT, 2 letters of recommendation, minimum GPA of 3.0; for other advanced degree, GMAT, minimum GPA of 3.0. Additional exam requirements/recommendations for international students: Required—TOEFL (minimum score 550 paper-based; 80 iBT), IELTS (minimum score 6.5). *Application deadline:* For fall admission, 8/15 priority date for domestic students, 8/1 priority date for international students; for winter admission, 11/15 priority date for domestic students, 11/1 priority date for international students; for spring admission, 2/15 priority date for domestic students, 2/1 priority date for international students; for summer admission, 5/15 priority date for domestic students, 5/1 priority date for international students. Applications are processed on a rolling basis. Application fee: $50. Electronic applications accepted. *Expenses:* Contact institution. *Financial support:* In 2018–19, 12 students received support. Scholarships/grants, tuition waivers (partial), and unspecified assistantships available. Support available to part-time students. Financial award application deadline: 4/15; financial award applicants required to submit FAFSA. *Faculty research:* Fuzzy sets, risk management, computer security, competence set analysis, investment strategies. *Unit head:* Dr. Shoshana Altschuller, Department Chair, 914-637-7726, E-mail: saltschuller@iona.edu. *Application contact:* Kimberly Kelly, Director of Graduate Business Admissions, 914-633-2271, Fax: 914-633-2012, E-mail: kkelly@iona.edu.
Website: http://www.iona.edu/Academics/Hagan-School-of-Business/Departments/Information-Systems/Graduate-Programs.aspx

John F. Kennedy University, College of Business and Professional Studies, Program in Business Administration, Pleasant Hill, CA 94523-4817. Offers business administration (MBA); finance (MBA); health care (MBA); human resources (MBA); information technology (MBA); management (MBA); sales management (MBA); strategic management (MBA). *Program availability:* Part-time, evening/weekend, online learning. *Degree requirements:* For master's, thesis or alternative. *Entrance requirements:* For master's, interview. Additional exam requirements/recommendations for international students: Required—TOEFL.

Johns Hopkins University, Engineering Program for Professionals, Part-time Program in Technical Management, Baltimore, MD 21218. Offers MS, Graduate Certificate, Post-Master's Certificate. *Program availability:* Part-time, evening/weekend, 100% online, blended/hybrid learning. *Faculty:* 26 part-time/adjunct (4 women). *Students:* 91 part-time (36 women). 20 applicants, 65% accepted, 7 enrolled. In 2018, 42 master's, 2 other advanced degrees awarded. *Entrance requirements:* Additional exam requirements/recommendations for international students: Required—TOEFL (minimum score 600 paper-based; 100 iBT). *Application deadline:* Applications are processed on a rolling basis. Application fee: $0. Electronic applications accepted. *Unit head:* Rick Blank, Interim Program Chair, 240-228-3570, E-mail: rblank5@jhu.edu. *Application contact:* Doug Schiller, Admissions Director, 410-516-2300, Fax: 410-579-8049, E-mail: schiller@jhu.edu.
Website: http://www.ep.jhu.edu/

Kansas State University, Graduate School, College of Technology and Aviation, Salina, KS 67401. Offers MT. *Program availability:* Part-time, evening/weekend, 100% online. *Entrance requirements:* For master's, GRE. Additional exam requirements/recommendations for international students: Required—TOEFL (minimum score 550 paper-based; 79 iBT), IELTS (minimum score 6.5), TWE, or PTE. Electronic applications accepted.

Keiser University, Master of Business Administration Program, Fort Lauderdale, FL 33309. Offers accounting (MBA); health services administration (MBA); international business (MBA); management (MBA); marketing (MBA); technology management (MBA). All concentrations except technology management also offered in Mandarin. *Program availability:* Part-time, online learning.

Kennesaw State University, Southern Polytechnic College of Engineering and Engineering Technology, Program in Quality Assurance, Kennesaw, GA 30144. Offers MS. *Program availability:* Online learning. *Students:* 4 full-time (3 women), 30 part-time (20 women); includes 15 minority (5 Black or African American, non-Hispanic/Latino; 6 Asian, non-Hispanic/Latino; 3 Hispanic/Latino; 1 Two or more races, non-Hispanic/Latino), 1 international. Average age 39. 6 applicants, 83% accepted, 5 enrolled. In 2018, 19 master's awarded. *Entrance requirements:* Additional exam requirements/recommendations for international students: Required—TOEFL (minimum score 550 paper-based; 80 iBT), IELTS (minimum score 6.5). *Application deadline:* For fall admission, 7/1 for domestic and international students; for spring admission, 11/1 for domestic and international students. Applications are processed on a rolling basis. Application fee: $60. Electronic applications accepted. *Expenses: Tuition, area resident:* Full-time $6960; part-time $290 per credit hour. Tuition, state resident: full-time $6960; part-time $290 per credit hour. Tuition, nonresident: full-time $25,080; part-time $1045 per credit hour. *International tuition:* $25,080 full-time. *Required fees:* $2006; $1706 per semester. $853 per semester. *Financial support:* Applicants required to submit FAFSA. *Application contact:* Admissions Counselor, 470-578-4377, E-mail: ksugrad@kennesaw.edu.
Website: http://engineering.kennesaw.edu/systems-industrial/degrees/ms-quality-assurance.php

La Salle University, School of Arts and Sciences, Program in Information Technology Leadership, Philadelphia, PA 19141-1199. Offers information technology leadership (MS); software project leadership (Certificate). *Program availability:* Part-time, evening/weekend, online only, 100% online. *Degree requirements:* For master's, capstone course. *Entrance requirements:* For master's, GRE, GMAT, or MAT, two letters of recommendation; background in computer science or equivalent other training; professional resume; interview; for Certificate, two letters of recommendation; background in computer science or equivalent other training; professional resume; interview. Additional exam requirements/recommendations for international students: Required—TOEFL. Electronic applications accepted. Application fee is waived when completed online. *Expenses:* Contact institution.

Lewis University, College of Business, Program in Business Administration, Romeoville, IL 60446. Offers accounting (MBA); custom elective option (MBA); e-business (MBA); finance (MBA); healthcare management (MBA); human resources management (MBA); international business (MBA); management information systems (MBA); marketing (MBA); project management (MBA); technology and operations management (MBA). *Program availability:* Part-time, evening/weekend. *Students:* 114 full-time (72 women), 143 part-time (87 women); includes 84 minority (21 Black or African American, non-Hispanic/Latino; 2 American Indian or Alaska Native, non-Hispanic/Latino; 11 Asian, non-Hispanic/Latino; 45 Hispanic/Latino; 5 Two or more races, non-Hispanic/Latino), 17 international. Average age 31. In 2018, 99 master's awarded. *Entrance requirements:* For master's, interview, bachelor's degree, resume, two recommendations. Additional exam requirements/recommendations for international students: Required—TOEFL (minimum score 550 paper-based), IELTS. *Application deadline:* For fall admission, 8/15 priority date for domestic students, 5/1 priority date for international students; for spring admission, 11/15 priority date for international students. Applications are processed on a rolling basis. Application fee: $40. Electronic applications accepted. *Financial support:* Career-related internships or fieldwork, Federal Work-Study, scholarships/grants, and unspecified assistantships available. Financial award application deadline: 5/1; financial award applicants required to submit FAFSA. *Unit head:* Dr. Maureen Culleeney, Academic Program Director, 815-838-0500 Ext. 5631, E-mail: culleema@lewisu.edu. *Application contact:* Michele Ryan, Director of Admission, 815-838-0500 Ext. 5384, E-mail: ryanml@lewisu.edu.

Lipscomb University, College of Computing and Technology, Nashville, TN 37204-3951. Offers data science (MS, Certificate); information technology (MS, Certificate), including data science (MS), information security (MS), information technology management (MS), software engineering (MS); software engineering (MS, Certificate). *Program availability:* Part-time, evening/weekend. *Degree requirements:* For master's, capstone project. *Entrance requirements:* For master's, GRE, 2 references, transcripts, resume, personal statement. Additional exam requirements/recommendations for international students: Required—TOEFL (minimum score 570 paper-based; 80 iBT). Electronic applications accepted. *Expenses:* Contact institution.

London Metropolitan University, Graduate Programs, London, United Kingdom. Offers applied psychology (M Sc); architecture (MA); biomedical science (M Sc); blood science (M Sc); cancer pharmacology (M Sc); computer networking and cyber security (M Sc); computing and information systems (M Sc); conference interpreting (MA); counter-terrorism studies (M Sc); creative, digital and professional writing (MA); crime, violence and prevention (M Sc); criminology (M Sc); curating contemporary art (MA); data analytics (M Sc); digital media (MA); early childhood studies (MA); education (MA, Ed D); financial services law, regulation and compliance (LL M); food science (M Sc); forensic psychology (M Sc); health and social care management and policy (M Sc); human nutrition (M Sc); human resource management (MA); human rights and international conflict (MA); information technology (M Sc); intelligence and security studies (M Sc); international oil, gas and energy law (LL M); international relations (MA); interpreting (MA); learning and teaching in higher education (MA); legal practice (LL M); media and entertainment law (LL M); organizational and consumer psychology (M Sc); psychological therapy (M Sc); psychology of mental health (M Sc); public health (M Sc); public policy and management (MPA); security studies (M Sc); social work (M Sc); spatial planning and urban design (MA); sports therapy (M Sc); supporting older children and young people with dyslexia (MA); teaching languages (MA), including Arabic, English; translation (MA); woman and child abuse (MA).

Louisiana Tech University, Graduate School, College of Engineering and Science, Ruston, LA 71272. Offers applied physics (MS); biomedical engineering (PhD); computer science (MS); engineering (MS, PhD), including cyberspace engineering (PhD), engineering education (PhD), engineering physics (PhD), materials and infrastructure systems (PhD), micro/nanoscale systems (PhD); engineering and technology management (MS); mathematics (MS); molecular science and nanotechnology (MS, PhD). *Program availability:* Part-time-only. Terminal master's awarded for partial completion of doctoral program. *Degree requirements:* For master's, thesis (for some programs); for doctorate, thesis/dissertation. *Entrance requirements:* For master's and Graduate Certificate, GRE General Test, minimum GPA of 3.0 in last 60 hours. Additional exam requirements/recommendations for international students: Required—TOEFL (minimum score 550 paper-based; 80 iBT), IELTS (minimum score 6.5). Electronic applications accepted. *Faculty research:* Trenchless technology, micromanufacturing, radionuclide transport, microbial liquefaction, hazardous waste treatment.

Marquette University, Graduate School, College of Engineering, Department of Biomedical Engineering, Milwaukee, WI 53201-1881. Offers biocomputing (ME); bioimaging (ME); bioinstrumentation (ME); bioinstrumentation/computers (MS, PhD); biomechanics (ME); biomechanics/biomaterials (MS, PhD); biorehabilitation (ME); functional imaging (PhD); healthcare technologies management (MS); rehabilitation bioengineering (PhD); systems physiology (MS, PhD). *Program availability:* Part-time, evening/weekend. Terminal master's awarded for partial completion of doctoral program. *Degree requirements:* For master's, comprehensive exam, thesis; for doctorate, comprehensive exam, thesis/dissertation, dissertation defense, qualifying exam. *Entrance requirements:* For master's, GRE General Test, minimum GPA of 3.0, official transcripts from all current and previous colleges/universities except Marquette, three letters of recommendation, brief statement of purpose that includes proposed area of research specialization, interview with program director (for ME), one year of post-baccalaureate professional work experience; for doctorate, GRE General Test, minimum GPA of 3.0, official transcripts from all current and previous colleges/universities except Marquette, three letters of recommendation, brief statement of purpose that includes proposed area of research specialization. Additional exam requirements/recommendations for international students: Required—TOEFL (minimum score 530 paper-based). Electronic applications accepted. *Faculty research:* Cell and organ physiology, signal processing, gait analysis, orthopedic rehabilitation engineering, telemedicine.

Marshall University, Academic Affairs Division, College of Information Technology and Engineering, Division of Applied Science and Technology, Program in Technology Management, Huntington, WV 25755. Offers MS, Certificate. *Program availability:* Part-time, evening/weekend. *Degree requirements:* For master's, final project, oral exam. *Entrance requirements:* For master's, GRE General Test or GMAT, minimum undergraduate GPA of 2.5.

Mercer University, Graduate Studies, Macon Campus, School of Engineering, Macon, GA 31207. Offers biomedical engineering (MSE); computer engineering (MSE); electrical engineering (MSE); engineering management (MSE); environmental engineering (MSE); environmental systems (MS); mechanical engineering (MSE); software engineering (MSE); software systems (MS); technical communications management (MS); technical management (MS). *Program availability:* Part-time-only, evening/weekend, online learning. *Degree requirements:* For master's, thesis or alternative. *Entrance requirements:* For master's, GRE (minimum score 300), minimum undergraduate GPA of 3.0. Additional exam requirements/recommendations for international students: Required—TOEFL (minimum score 550 paper-based; 80 iBT). *Expenses:* Contact institution. *Faculty research:* Designing prostheses and orthotics, oxygen transfer and limitations in biological systems, low-cost groundwater development, lung airway and transport, autonomous mobile robots.

Montclair State University, The Graduate School, Feliciano School of Business, General MBA Program, Montclair, NJ 07043-1624. Offers accounting (MBA); business analytics (MBA); digital marketing (MBA); finance (MBA); general business administration (MBA); human resources management (MBA); management (MBA); management of information and technology (MBA); marketing (MBA); project management (MBA). *Program availability:* Part-time, evening/weekend. *Degree requirements:* For master's, culminating experience. *Entrance requirements:* For master's, GMAT or GRE General Test, 2 letters of recommendation, resume, essay. Additional exam requirements/recommendations for international students: Required—TOEFL (minimum score 83 iBT), IELTS (minimum score 6.5). Electronic applications accepted. *Faculty research:* Accounting, management, marketing.

National University, School of Engineering and Computing, La Jolla, CA 92037-1011. Offers computer science (MS), including advanced computing; cyber security and information assurance (MS); data analytics (MS); electrical engineering (MS); engineering management (MS); information technology management (MS); management information systems (MS); sustainability management (MS). *Program availability:* Part-time, evening/weekend, 100% online, blended/hybrid learning. *Degree requirements:* For master's, thesis (for some programs). *Entrance requirements:* For master's, interview, minimum GPA of 2.5. Additional exam requirements/recommendations for international students: Required—TOEFL (minimum score 550 paper-based; 79 iBT), IELTS (minimum score 6). Electronic applications accepted. *Expenses: Tuition:* Full-time $10,320; part-time $430 per unit. Tuition and fees vary according to degree level. *Faculty research:* Educational technology, scholarships in science.

New Jersey Institute of Technology, Martin Tuchman School of Management, Newark, NJ 07102. Offers business data science (PhD); management (MS); management of technology (MBA, Certificate). *Accreditation:* AACSB. *Program availability:* Part-time, evening/weekend. *Faculty:* 32 full-time (8 women), 22 part-time/adjunct (6 women). *Students:* 132 full-time (30 women), 128 part-time (67 women); includes 141 minority (39 Black or African American, non-Hispanic/Latino; 1 American Indian or Alaska Native, non-Hispanic/Latino; 51 Asian, non-Hispanic/Latino; 44 Hispanic/Latino; 6 Two or more races, non-Hispanic/Latino), 37 international. Average age 30. 339 applicants, 57% accepted, 88 enrolled. In 2018, 82 master's, 11 other advanced degrees awarded. Terminal master's awarded for partial completion of doctoral program. *Degree requirements:* For doctorate, thesis/dissertation. *Entrance requirements:* For master's, GRE General Test/GMAT, minimum GPA 2.8, personal statement, 1 letter of recommendation, transcripts, resume; for doctorate, GRE General Test/GMAT, minimum GPA 3.2, personal statement, 3 letters of recommendation, transcripts, CV. Additional exam requirements/recommendations for international students: Required—TOEFL (minimum score 550 paper-based; 79 iBT), IELTS (minimum score 6.5). *Application deadline:* For fall admission, 6/1 priority date for domestic students, 5/1 priority date for international students; for spring admission, 11/15 priority date for domestic and international students. Applications are processed on a rolling basis. Application fee: $75. Electronic applications accepted. *Expenses:* $22,690 per year (in-state), $32,136 per year (out-of-state). *Financial support:* In 2018–19, 37 students received support, including 6 fellowships with full tuition reimbursements available (averaging $22,000 per year), 9 research assistantships with full tuition reimbursements available (averaging $22,000 per year), 10 teaching assistantships (averaging $22,000 per year); career-related internships or fieldwork, Federal Work-Study, scholarships/grants, and unspecified assistantships also available. Financial award application deadline: 1/15. *Faculty research:* Manufacturing systems analysis, earnings management, knowledge-based view of the firm, data envelopment analysis, human factors in human/machine systems. *Total annual research expenditures:* $687,000. *Unit head:* Dr. Oya Tukel, Dean, 973-596-3248, Fax: 973-596-3074, E-mail: oya.i.tukel@njit.edu. *Application contact:* Stephen Eck, Director of Admissions, 973-596-3300, Fax: 973-596-3461, E-mail: admissions@njit.edu.
Website: http://management.njit.edu

North Carolina State University, Graduate School, Wilson College of Textiles, Department of Textile Engineering, Chemistry, and Science, Raleigh, NC 27695. Offers fiber and polymer science (PhD); textile chemistry (MS); textile engineering (MS); textile technology management (PhD). *Degree requirements:* For master's, thesis optional. Electronic applications accepted.

North Carolina State University, Graduate School, Wilson College of Textiles, Program in Textile Technology Management, Raleigh, NC 27695. Offers PhD. *Degree requirements:* For doctorate, one foreign language, thesis/dissertation, cumulative exams. *Entrance requirements:* For doctorate, GRE or GMAT. Electronic applications accepted. *Faculty research:* Niche markets, supply chain, globalization, logistics.

Northern Kentucky University, Office of Graduate Programs, College of Informatics, Program in Computer Information Technology, Highland Heights, KY 41099. Offers MSCIT. *Program availability:* Part-time, evening/weekend. *Degree requirements:* For master's, comprehensive exam (for some programs), thesis or alternative. *Entrance requirements:* For master's, GRE (waived for undergraduates with GPA greater than 3.0 from a STEM discipline), resume, transcripts. Additional exam requirements/recommendations for international students: Required—TOEFL (minimum score 79 iBT); Recommended—IELTS (minimum score 6.5). Electronic applications accepted. *Faculty research:* Data privacy, security, cloud computing, social networks, intrusion detection.

Pacific States University, College of Business, Los Angeles, CA 90010. Offers accounting (MBA, Certificate); beauty management (MBA); finance (MBA); international business (MBA); management of information technology (MBA); project management (Certificate); real estate management (MBA). *Program availability:* Part-time, evening/weekend, online learning. *Entrance requirements:* For master's, minimum undergraduate GPA of 2.5 during last 90 quarter units of course work, bachelor's degree in business administration or economics. Additional exam requirements/recommendations for international students: Required—TOEFL (minimum score 500 paper-based; 61 iBT), IELTS (minimum score 5.5).

Pittsburg State University, Graduate School, College of Technology, Department of Technology and Workforce Learning, Pittsburg, KS 66762. Offers career and technical education (MS); human resource development (MS); technology (MS), including automotive technology, construction management, graphic design, graphics management, information technology, innovation in technology, personnel development, technology management, workforce learning; workforce development and education (Ed S). *Program availability:* Part-time, evening/weekend, 100% online, blended/hybrid learning. *Degree requirements:* For master's, thesis or alternative; for Ed S, thesis optional. *Entrance requirements:* Additional exam requirements/recommendations for international students: Required—TOEFL (minimum score 520 paper-based; 68 iBT), IELTS (minimum score 6), PTE (minimum score 47). Electronic applications accepted. *Expenses:* Contact institution.

Polytechnic University of Puerto Rico, Graduate School, Hato Rey, PR 00918. Offers business administration (MBA), including computer information systems, general management, management of information systems, management of international enterprises; civil engineering (ME, MS); computer engineering (ME, MS); computer science (MCS, MS); electrical engineering (ME, MS); engineering management (MEM); environmental management (MEM); landscape architecture (M Land Arch); manufacturing competitiveness (MMC, MS); manufacturing engineering (ME, MS); mechanical engineering (M Mech E). *Accreditation:* ASLA. *Program availability:* Part-time, evening/weekend. *Entrance requirements:* For master's, 3 letters of recommendation.

Polytechnic University of Puerto Rico, Orlando Campus, Graduate School, Orlando, FL 32825. Offers accounting (MBA); business administration (MBA); construction management (MEM); engineering management (MEM); environmental management (MEM); finance (MBA); human resources management (MBA); management of international enterprises (MBA); management of technology (MBA); manufacturing management (MEM). *Program availability:* Part-time, evening/weekend, online learning. *Entrance requirements:* For master's, minimum GPA of 3.0. Additional exam requirements/recommendations for international students: Recommended—TOEFL. Electronic applications accepted.

Portland State University, Graduate Studies, Maseeh College of Engineering and Computer Science, Department of Engineering and Technology Management, Portland, OR 97207-0751. Offers engineering and technology management (MS); technology management (PhD); MS/MBA; MS/MS. *Program availability:* Part-time, evening/weekend. *Degree requirements:* For master's, thesis or alternative, capstone; for doctorate, one foreign language, comprehensive exam, thesis/dissertation, oral and written exams. *Entrance requirements:* For master's, degree in engineering or related discipline; minimum GPA of 2.75 undergraduate or 3.0 graduate (at least 12 credits); minimum 4 years of experience in engineering or related discipline; 3 letters of recommendation; background in probability/statistics, differential equations, computer programming and linear algebra; for doctorate, GRE General Test (minimum combined score of 1100 for verbal and quantitative), minimum GPA of 3.0 undergraduate, 3.25 graduate. Additional exam requirements/recommendations for international students: Required—TOEFL (minimum score 550 paper-based; 80 iBT). Electronic applications accepted. *Expenses:* Contact institution. *Faculty research:* Scheduling, hierarchical decision modeling, operations research, knowledge-based information systems.

Purdue University, Graduate School, Purdue Polytechnic Institute, Department of Technology Leadership and Innovation, West Lafayette, IN 47907. Offers leadership (MS, PhD); organizational leadership (MS); technology innovation (MS). *Program availability:* Part-time, evening/weekend, online learning. *Faculty:* 19 full-time (9 women). *Students:* 41 full-time (19 women), 74 part-time (35 women); includes 22 minority (8 Black or African American, non-Hispanic/Latino; 1 American Indian or Alaska Native, non-Hispanic/Latino; 5 Asian, non-Hispanic/Latino; 7 Hispanic/Latino; 1 Two or more races, non-Hispanic/Latino), 15 international. Average age 35. 44 applicants, 77% accepted, 21 enrolled. In 2018, 69 master's awarded. *Entrance requirements:* For master's, GRE General Test, minimum GPA of 3.0. Additional exam requirements/recommendations for international students: Required—TOEFL (minimum score 550 paper-based; 77 iBT); Recommended—TWE. *Application deadline:* For fall admission, 4/1 for domestic and international students; for spring admission, 10/1 for domestic students, 9/1 for international students. Applications are processed on a rolling basis. Application fee: $60 ($75 for international students). Electronic applications accepted. *Financial support:* Fellowships and teaching assistantships available. Support available to part-time students. Financial award applicants required to submit FAFSA. *Unit head:* Patrick E. Connolly, Department Head, 765-494-4585, E-mail: connollp@purdue.edu. *Application contact:* Stephanie Schmidt, Graduate Contact, 765-494-5599, E-mail: sjschmid@purdue.edu.
Website: http://www.tech.purdue.edu/TLI/

Rutgers University–Newark, Rutgers Business School–Newark and New Brunswick, Doctoral Programs in Management, Newark, NJ 07102. Offers accounting (PhD); accounting information systems (PhD); economics (PhD); finance (PhD); individualized study (PhD); information technology (PhD); international business (PhD); management science (PhD); marketing science (PhD); organizational management (PhD); science, technology and management (PhD); supply chain management (PhD). *Degree requirements:* For doctorate, comprehensive exam, thesis/dissertation. *Entrance requirements:* For doctorate, GRE or GMAT. Additional exam requirements/recommendations for international students: Required—TOEFL (minimum score 550 paper-based; 79 iBT). Electronic applications accepted.

Ryerson University, School of Graduate Studies, Ted Rogers School of Management, Toronto, ON M5B 2K3, Canada. Offers global business administration (MBA); management (MSM); management of technology and innovation (MBA).

St. Ambrose University, College of Arts and Sciences, Program in Information Technology Management, Davenport, IA 52803-2898. Offers MSITM. *Program availability:* Part-time. *Degree requirements:* For master's, thesis (for some programs), practica. *Entrance requirements:* For master's, GRE or GMAT, minimum GPA of 2.8. Additional exam requirements/recommendations for international students: Required—TOEFL. Electronic applications accepted.

Seton Hall University, Stillman School of Business, Programs in Business Administration, South Orange, NJ 07079-2697. Offers accounting (MBA); entrepreneurial studies (Certificate); finance (MBA); financial decision making (Certificate); information technology management (MBA); international business (MBA); management (MBA); marketing (MBA); sport management (MBA); supply chain management (MBA, Certificate). *Program availability:* Part-time, evening/weekend. *Faculty:* 27 full-time (5 women), 18 part-time/adjunct (2 women). *Students:* 85 full-time (40 women), 363 part-time (147 women); includes 78 minority (22 Black or African American, non-Hispanic/Latino; 4 Asian, non-Hispanic/Latino; 18 Hispanic/Latino; 29 Native Hawaiian or other Pacific Islander, non-Hispanic/Latino; 5 Two or more races, non-Hispanic/Latino), 282 international. Average age 34. 483 applicants, 85% accepted, 302 enrolled. In 2018, 96 master's awarded. *Degree requirements:* For master's, 20 hours of community service (Social Responsibility Project). *Entrance requirements:* For master's, GMAT or CPA, GRE (waived based on work experience or advanced degree from AACSB institution), MS in business discipline, professional degree or designation (MD, JD, PhD, DVM, DDS, CPA, etc.), minimum undergraduate GPA of 3.0. Additional exam requirements/recommendations for international students: Required—TOEFL (minimum score 607 paper-based; 80 iBT), IELTS (minimum score 6), PTE. *Application deadline:* For fall admission, 5/31 priority date for domestic students, 4/30 priority date for international students; for spring admission, 10/31 priority date for domestic students, 9/30 priority date for international students; for summer admission, 3/31 priority date for domestic students. Applications are processed on a rolling basis. Application fee: $75. Electronic applications accepted. Application fee is waived when completed online. *Expenses:* Tuition is $1,305 per credit hour and the overall MBA is a 40 credit hour program. University fees are $115 per semester. The university also has a technology that is $125 per semester. *Financial support:* In 2018–19, 44 students received support, including 25 research assistantships with partial tuition reimbursements available (averaging $3,644 per year); career-related internships or fieldwork, scholarships/grants, and unspecified assistantships also available. Financial award application deadline: 6/30; financial award applicants required to submit FAFSA. *Faculty research:* Sport, hedge funds, executive compensation, social media, legal studies. *Unit head:* Dr. Joyce Strawser, Dean, 973-761-9013, Fax: 973-761-9217, E-mail: joyce.strawser@

shu.edu. *Application contact:* Alfred Ayoub, Director of Graduate Admissions, 973-761-9262, Fax: 973-761-9208, E-mail: alfred.ayoub@shu.edu.
Website: http://www.shu.edu/business/mba-programs.cfm

Simon Fraser University, Office of Graduate Studies and Postdoctoral Fellows, Faculty of Business Administration, Vancouver, BC V6B 5K3, Canada. Offers business administration (EMBA, PhD, Graduate Diploma); finance (M Sc); management of technology (MBA); management of technology/biotechnology (MBA). *Program availability:* Online learning. *Degree requirements:* For master's, thesis (for some programs); for doctorate, comprehensive exam, thesis/dissertation. *Entrance requirements:* For master's, GMAT, minimum GPA of 3.0 (on scale of 4.33) or 3.33 based on last 60 credits of undergraduate courses; for doctorate, minimum GPA of 3.5 (on scale of 4.33); for Graduate Diploma, minimum GPA of 2.5 (on scale of 4.33) or 2.67 based on last 60 credits of undergraduate courses. Additional exam requirements/recommendations for international students: Recommended—TOEFL (minimum score 580 paper-based; 93 iBT), IELTS (minimum score 7), TWE (minimum score 5). *Expenses:* Contact institution. *Faculty research:* Accounting, management and organizational studies, technology and operations management, finance, international business.

South Dakota School of Mines and Technology, Graduate Division, Program in Engineering Management, Rapid City, SD 57701-3995. Offers MS. Program offered jointly with The University of South Dakota. *Program availability:* Part-time, online learning. *Entrance requirements:* For master's, GMAT. Additional exam requirements/recommendations for international students: Required—TOEFL, TWE. Electronic applications accepted.

Southeast Missouri State University, School of Graduate Studies, Department of Engineering and Technology, Cape Girardeau, MO 63701-4799. Offers MS. *Program availability:* Part-time, evening/weekend, online learning. *Faculty:* 13 full-time (3 women). *Students:* 36 full-time (9 women), 23 part-time (8 women); includes 6 minority (1 Black or African American, non-Hispanic/Latino; 1 American Indian or Alaska Native, non-Hispanic/Latino; 3 Asian, non-Hispanic/Latino; 1 Hispanic/Latino), 39 international. Average age 29. 19 applicants, 100% accepted, 19 enrolled. In 2018, 45 master's awarded. *Degree requirements:* For master's, comprehensive exam (for some programs), thesis or alternative. *Entrance requirements:* Additional exam requirements/recommendations for international students: Required—TOEFL (minimum score 550 paper-based; 79 iBT), IELTS (minimum score 6), PTE (minimum score 53). *Application deadline:* For fall admission, 8/1 for domestic students, 5/1 for international students; for spring admission, 11/1 for domestic students, 10/1 for international students. Applications are processed on a rolling basis. Application fee: $30 ($40 for international students). Electronic applications accepted. *Expenses:* Contact institution. *Financial support:* In 2018–19, 20 students received support. Career-related internships or fieldwork, Federal Work-Study, scholarships/grants, traineeships, tuition waivers (full), and unspecified assistantships available. Financial award application deadline: 6/30; financial award applicants required to submit FAFSA. *Faculty research:* Technology management, mechanical engineering, electrical engineering, industrial engineering, network administration. *Total annual research expenditures:* $25,000. *Unit head:* Dr. Brad Deken, Department Chair, 573-651-2104, Fax: 573-986-6174, E-mail: bdeken@semo.edu. *Application contact:* Dr. Brad Deken, Department Chair, 573-651-2104, Fax: 573-986-6174, E-mail: bdeken@semo.edu.
Website: http://www.semo.edu/polytech/

State University of New York Polytechnic Institute, MBA Program in Technology Management, Utica, NY 13502. Offers accounting and finance (MBA); business management (MBA); health informatics (MBA); human resource management (MBA); marketing management (MBA). *Program availability:* Part-time, 100% online. *Students:* 29 full-time (13 women), 85 part-time (41 women); includes 18 minority (4 Black or African American, non-Hispanic/Latino; 8 Asian, non-Hispanic/Latino; 6 Hispanic/Latino). Average age 32. 54 applicants, 54% accepted, 26 enrolled. In 2018, 29 master's awarded. *Degree requirements:* For master's, comprehensive exam, capstone project. *Entrance requirements:* For master's, GMAT or approved GMAT waiver, resume, letter of reference. Additional exam requirements/recommendations for international students: Required—TOEFL (minimum score 79 iBT), IELTS (minimum score 6.5), PTE (minimum score 53), TOEFL, IELTS, or PTE; GMAT or approved GMAT waiver. *Application deadline:* For fall admission, 7/1 priority date for domestic students, 7/1 for international students; for spring admission, 12/1 for domestic students, 11/1 for international students. Applications are processed on a rolling basis. Application fee: $60. Electronic applications accepted. *Expenses:* Contact institution. *Financial support:* Fellowships, research assistantships, and unspecified assistantships available. Financial award application deadline: 6/1; financial award applicants required to submit FAFSA. *Faculty research:* Entrepreneurial capacity development. *Unit head:* Dr. Rafael Romero, Coordinator, 315-792-7207, E-mail: rafael.romero@sunypoly.edu. *Application contact:* Alicia Foster, Director of Graduate Admissions, 315-792-7347, E-mail: fostera3@sunypoly.edu.
Website: https://sunypoly.edu/academics/majors-and-programs/technology-management.html

Stevens Institute of Technology, Graduate School, School of Business, Program in Business Administration for Experienced Professionals, Hoboken, NJ 07030. Offers business administration (EMBA); technology management (EMBA). *Program availability:* Part-time, evening/weekend. *Faculty:* 58 full-time (8 women), 18 part-time/adjunct (3 women). *Students:* 2 full-time (0 women), 32 part-time (9 women); includes 11 minority (2 Black or African American, non-Hispanic/Latino; 1 American Indian or Alaska Native, non-Hispanic/Latino; 7 Asian, non-Hispanic/Latino; 1 Hispanic/Latino), 3 international. Average age 37. 16 applicants, 81% accepted, 9 enrolled. In 2018, 9 master's awarded. *Degree requirements:* For master's, thesis optional, minimum B average in major field and overall. *Entrance requirements:* For master's, GRE/GMAT scores: GRE scores are required for all applicants applying to a full-time graduate program in the Schaefer School of Engineering and Science (SES). International applicants must submit TOEFL/IELTS scores and fulfill the English Language Proficiency Requirements in order to be considered. Additional exam requirements/recommendations for international students: Required—TOEFL (minimum score 74 iBT), IELTS (minimum score 6). *Application deadline:* For fall admission, 7/1 for domestic students, 4/15 for international students; for spring admission, 12/1 for domestic and international students. Applications are processed on a rolling basis. Application fee: $60. Electronic applications accepted. *Expenses:* Tuition: Full-time $35,960; part-time $1620 per credit. *Required fees:* $1290; $600 per semester. Tuition and fees vary according to course load. *Financial support:* Fellowships, research assistantships, teaching assistantships, career-related internships or fieldwork, Federal Work-Study, scholarships/grants, and unspecified assistantships available. Financial award application deadline: 2/15; financial award applicants required to submit FAFSA. *Unit head:* Dr. Gregory Prastacos, Dean, 201-216-5366, E-mail: gprastac@stevens.edu. *Application contact:* Graduate Admissions, 888-783-8367, Fax: 888-511-1306, E-mail: graduate@stevens.edu.
Website: https://www.stevens.edu/school-business/masters-programs/mbaemba

Stevens Institute of Technology, Graduate School, School of Business, Program in Management, Hoboken, NJ 07030. Offers general management (MS); global innovation

management (MS); human resource management (MS); information management (MS); project management (MS); technology commercialization (MS); technology management (MS). *Program availability:* Part-time, evening/weekend. *Faculty:* 58 full-time (8 women), 18 part-time/adjunct (3 women). *Students:* 101 full-time (41 women), 66 part-time (34 women); includes 14 minority (4 Black or African American, non-Hispanic/Latino; 9 Asian, non-Hispanic/Latino; 1 Hispanic/Latino), 115 international. Average age 28. In 2018, 70 master's awarded. Terminal master's awarded for partial completion of doctoral program. *Degree requirements:* For master's, thesis optional, minimum B average in major field and overall. *Entrance requirements:* For master's, GRE/GMAT scores: GRE scores are required for all applicants applying to a full-time graduate program in the Schaefer School of Engineering and Science (SES). International applicants must submit TOEFL/IELTS scores and fulfill the English Language Proficiency Requirements in order to be considered. Additional exam requirements/recommendations for international students: Required—TOEFL (minimum score 74 iBT), IELTS (minimum score 6). *Application deadline:* For fall admission, 4/1 for domestic and international students; for spring admission, 11/1 for domestic and international students; for summer admission, 5/1 for domestic students. Applications are processed on a rolling basis. Application fee: $60. Electronic applications accepted. *Expenses: Tuition:* Full-time $35,960; part-time $1620 per credit. *Required fees:* $1290; $600 per semester. Tuition and fees vary according to course load. *Financial support:* Fellowships, research assistantships, teaching assistantships, career-related internships or fieldwork, Federal Work-Study, scholarships/grants, and unspecified assistantships available. Financial award application deadline: 2/15; financial award applicants required to submit FAFSA. *Unit head:* Dr. Gregory Prascatos, Dean of SB, 201-216 8366, E-mail: gprastac@stevens.edu. *Application contact:* Graduate Admissions, 888-783-8367, Fax: 888-511-1306, E-mail: graduate@stevens.edu.
Website: https://www.stevens.edu/school-business/masters-programs/management

Stevens Institute of Technology, Graduate School, School of Business, Program in Technology Management, Hoboken, NJ 07030. Offers information management (PhD); technology management (PhD); telecommunications management (PhD). *Program availability:* Part-time, evening/weekend, online learning. *Faculty:* 58 full-time (8 women), 18 part-time/adjunct (3 women). *Students:* 6 full-time (0 women), 23 part-time (6 women); includes 10 minority (4 Black or African American, non-Hispanic/Latino; 6 Asian, non-Hispanic/Latino), 4 international. Average age 38. In 2018, 1 doctorate awarded. Terminal master's awarded for partial completion of doctoral program. *Degree requirements:* For doctorate, comprehensive exam (for some programs), thesis/dissertation. *Entrance requirements:* Additional exam requirements/recommendations for international students: Required—TOEFL (minimum score 74 iBT), IELTS (minimum score 6). *Application deadline:* For fall admission, 4/1 for domestic and international students; for spring admission, 11/1 for domestic and international students; for summer admission, 5/1 for domestic students. Applications are processed on a rolling basis. Application fee: $60. Electronic applications accepted. *Expenses: Tuition:* Full-time $35,960; part-time $1620 per credit. *Required fees:* $1290; $600 per semester. Tuition and fees vary according to course load. *Financial support:* Fellowships, research assistantships, teaching assistantships, career-related internships or fieldwork, Federal Work-Study, scholarships/grants, and unspecified assistantships available. Financial award application deadline: 2/15; financial award applicants required to submit FAFSA. *Unit head:* Dr. Gregory Prascatos, Dean of SB, 201-216 8366, Fax: 201-216-5385, E-mail: gprastac@stevens.edu. *Application contact:* Graduate Admissions, 888-783-8367, Fax: 888-511-1306, E-mail: graduate@stevens.edu.
Website: https://www.stevens.edu/school-business/phd-business-administration

Stevens Institute of Technology, Graduate School, School of Business, Program in Telecommunications Management, Hoboken, NJ 07030. Offers business (MS); global innovation management (MS); management of wireless networks (MS); online security, technology and business (MS); project management (MS); technical management (MS); telecommunications management (PhD, Certificate). *Program availability:* Part-time, evening/weekend. *Faculty:* 58 full-time (8 women), 18 part-time/adjunct (3 women). *Students:* 6 part-time (2 women); includes 1 minority (Asian, non-Hispanic/Latino). Average age 43. In 2018, 11 master's awarded. *Degree requirements:* For master's, thesis optional, minimum B average in major field and overall; for doctorate, comprehensive exam (for some programs), thesis/dissertation; for Certificate, minimum B average. *Entrance requirements:* For master's, GRE/GMAT scores: GRE scores are required for all applicants applying to a full-time graduate program in the Schaefer School of Engineering and Science (SES). International applicants must submit TOEFL/IELTS scores and fulfill the English Language Proficiency Requirements in order to be considered. Additional exam requirements/recommendations for international students: Required—TOEFL (minimum score 74 iBT), IELTS (minimum score 6). *Application deadline:* For fall admission, 4/1 for domestic and international students; for spring admission, 11/1 for domestic and international students; for summer admission, 5/1 for domestic students. Applications are processed on a rolling basis. Application fee: $60. Electronic applications accepted. *Expenses: Tuition:* Full-time $35,960; part-time $1620 per credit. *Required fees:* $1290; $600 per semester. Tuition and fees vary according to course load. *Financial support:* Fellowships, research assistantships, teaching assistantships, career-related internships or fieldwork, Federal Work-Study, scholarships/grants, health care benefits, and unspecified assistantships available. Financial award application deadline: 2/15; financial award applicants required to submit FAFSA. *Unit head:* Dr. Gregory Prastacos, Dean of SB, 201-216-8366, E-mail: gprastac@stevens.edu. *Application contact:* Graduate Admission, 888-783-8367, Fax: 888-511-1306, E-mail: graduate@stevens.edu.
Website: https://www.stevens.edu/school-business/masters-programs/network-communication-management-services

Stevenson University, Program in Business and Technology Management, Owings Mills, MD 21153. Offers emerging technology (MS); innovative leadership (MS). *Program availability:* Part-time, online only, 100% online. *Faculty:* 1 full-time (0 women), 9 part-time/adjunct (2 women). *Students:* 26 full-time (7 women), 82 part-time (45 women); includes 42 minority (32 Black or African American, non-Hispanic/Latino; 3 American Indian or Alaska Native, non-Hispanic/Latino; 3 Asian, non-Hispanic/Latino; 4 Hispanic/Latino). Average age 29. 37 applicants, 49% accepted, 16 enrolled. In 2018, 66 master's awarded. *Degree requirements:* For master's, capstone course. *Entrance requirements:* For master's, bachelor's degree from regionally-accredited institution, official college transcripts from all previous academic work, minimum cumulative GPA of 3.0 in past academic work, personal statement (250-350 words). *Application deadline:* Applications are processed on a rolling basis. Application fee: $0. Electronic applications accepted. *Expenses:* Contact institution. *Financial support:* Unspecified assistantships available. Financial award applicants required to submit FAFSA. *Unit head:* Steven Engorn, Coordinator, 443-352-4220, Fax: 443-394-0538, E-mail: sengorn@stevenson.edu. *Application contact:* Amanda Millar, Director, Admissions, 443-352-4058, Fax: 443-394-0538, E-mail: amillar@stevenson.edu.
Website: http://www.stevenson.edu

Stony Brook University, State University of New York, Graduate School, College of Engineering and Applied Sciences, Department of Technology and Society, Program in Global Technology Management, Stony Brook, NY 11794. Offers MS. *Program availability:* Online learning. *Entrance requirements:* For master's, GRE. Additional exam requirements/recommendations for international students: Required—TOEFL (minimum score 85 iBT), IELTS (minimum score 6.5). *Application deadline:* For fall admission, 7/2 for domestic students, 4/15 for international students; for spring admission, 12/3 for domestic students, 10/5 for international students; for summer admission, 4/15 for domestic students. Application fee: $100. Electronic applications accepted. *Expenses:* Contact institution. *Unit head:* Dr. Wolf Schafer, Interim Department Chair, 631-632-7924, E-mail: wolf.schafer@stonybrook.edu. *Application contact:* Marypat Taveras, Coordinator, 631-632-8762, Fax: 631-632-7809, E-mail: marypat.taveras@stonybrook.edu.
Website: https://www.stonybrook.edu/commcms/est/masters/msgtm.php

Stratford University, School of Graduate Studies, Falls Church, VA 22043. Offers accounting (MS); business administration (MBA, DBA); cyber security (MS); cyber security leadership and policy (MS); digital forensics (MS); healthcare administration (MS); information systems (MS); information technology (DIT); networking and telecommunications (MS); software engineering (MS). *Program availability:* Part-time, evening/weekend, 100% online, blended/hybrid learning. *Degree requirements:* For master's, comprehensive exam, capstone project. *Entrance requirements:* For master's, GRE or GMAT, baccalaureate degree. Additional exam requirements/recommendations for international students: Required—TOEFL (minimum score 79 iBT), IELTS (minimum score 6.5), PTE (minimum score 5). Electronic applications accepted. *Expenses: Tuition:* Full-time $22,275; part-time $11,137 per year. One-time fee: $385.

Texas A&M University–Commerce, College of Science and Engineering, Commerce, TX 75429. Offers biological sciences (MS); broadfield science biology (MS); broadfield science chemistry (MS); broadfield science physics (MS); chemistry (MS); computational linguistics (Graduate Certificate); computational science (MS); computer science (MS); environmental science (Graduate Certificate); mathematics (MS); physics (MS); technology management (MS). *Program availability:* Part-time. *Faculty:* 44 full-time (7 women), 7 part-time/adjunct (0 women). *Students:* 178 full-time (67 women), 234 part-time (104 women); includes 82 minority (19 Black or African American, non-Hispanic/Latino; 1 American Indian or Alaska Native, non-Hispanic/Latino; 14 Asian, non-Hispanic/Latino; 37 Hispanic/Latino; 11 Two or more races, non-Hispanic/Latino), 158 international. Average age 30. 481 applicants, 52% accepted, 105 enrolled. In 2018, 218 master's awarded. *Degree requirements:* For master's, comprehensive exam, thesis optional. *Entrance requirements:* For master's, GRE, official transcripts, letters of recommendation, resume, statement of goals. Additional exam requirements/recommendations for international students: Required—TOEFL (minimum score 550 paper-based; 79 iBT), IELTS (minimum score 6), PTE (minimum score 53). *Application deadline:* For fall admission, 6/1 priority date for international students; for spring admission, 10/15 priority date for international students; for summer admission, 3/15 priority date for international students. Applications are processed on a rolling basis. Application fee: $50 ($75 for international students). Electronic applications accepted. *Expenses:* Contact institution. *Financial support:* In 2018–19, 46 students received support, including 43 research assistantships with partial tuition reimbursements available (averaging $2,418 per year), 135 teaching assistantships with partial tuition reimbursements available (averaging $3,376 per year); scholarships/grants, health care benefits, and unspecified assistantships also available. Financial award application deadline: 5/1; financial award applicants required to submit FAFSA. *Faculty research:* Biomedical, Catalytic Material & Processes, Nuclear Theory/Astrophysics, Cybersecurity, STEM Education. *Total annual research expenditures:* $1.8 million. *Unit head:* Dr. Brent L. Donham, Dean, 903-886-5321, Fax: 903-886-5199, E-mail: brent.donham@tamuc.edu. *Application contact:* Dayla Burgin, Graduate Student Services Coordinator, 903-886-5134, E-mail: dayla.burgin@tamuc.edu.
Website: https://new.tamuc.edu/science-engineering/

Texas State University, The Graduate College, College of Science and Engineering, Program in Technology Management, San Marcos, TX 78666. Offers MS. *Program availability:* Part-time, evening/weekend. *Faculty:* 15 full-time (2 women). *Students:* 13 full-time (4 women), 8 part-time (1 woman); includes 2 minority (both Hispanic/Latino), 10 international. Average age 29. 34 applicants, 62% accepted, 9 enrolled. In 2018, 13 master's awarded. *Degree requirements:* For master's, comprehensive exam, thesis optional. *Entrance requirements:* For master's, baccalaureate degree from regionally-accredited university with minimum GPA of 2.75 on last 60 undergraduate semester hours, statement of purpose stating interest in technology management degree, and resume/CV. Additional exam requirements/recommendations for international students: Required—TOEFL (minimum score 550 paper-based; 78 iBT), IELTS (minimum score 6.5). *Application deadline:* For fall admission, 2/1 priority date for domestic and international students; for spring admission, 10/15 for domestic students, 10/1 for international students; for summer admission, 4/15 for domestic students, 3/15 for international students. Applications are processed on a rolling basis. Application fee: $55 ($90 for international students). Electronic applications accepted. *Expenses:* Tuition, state resident: full-time $8102; part-time $4051 per semester. Tuition, nonresident: full-time $18,229; part-time $9115 per semester. *International tuition:* $18,229 full-time. *Required fees:* $2116; $120 per credit hour. Tuition and fees vary according to course load. *Financial support:* In 2018–19, 12 students received support, including 3 research assistantships (averaging $9,661 per year), 3 teaching assistantships (averaging $13,226 per year); career-related internships or fieldwork, Federal Work-Study, and institutionally sponsored loans also available. Support available to part-time students. Financial award application deadline: 1/15; financial award applicants required to submit FAFSA. *Faculty research:* Concrete Technology and Materials; Concrete Modeling and stuctural Analysis; Fracture and Fatigue Behavior of Concrete; Asphalt technology; innovative construction materials; nondestructive testing of infrastructure; Pavement technology and materials; sustainable construction materials. *Total annual research expenditures:* $280,086. *Unit head:* Dr. Farhad Ameri, Graduate Advisor, 512-245-1984, Fax: 512-245-3052, E-mail: fa11@txstate.edu. *Application contact:* Dr. Andrea Golato, Dean of the Graduate College, 512-245-2581, E-mail: gradcollege@txstate.edu.
Website: http://www.txstate.edu/technology/degrees-programs/graduate.html

Towson University, College of Business and Economics, Program in e-Business and Technology Management, Towson, MD 21252-0001. Offers project, program and portfolio management (Postbaccalaureate Certificate); supply chain management (MS). *Entrance requirements:* For master's and Postbaccalaureate Certificate, GRE or GMAT, bachelor's degree in relevant field and/or three years of post-bachelor's experience working in supply chain related areas; minimum cumulative GPA of 3.0; resume; 2 reference letters. Additional exam requirements/recommendations for international students: Required—TOEFL (minimum score 550 paper-based). Electronic applications accepted. *Expenses: Tuition, area resident:* Full-time $9196; part-time $418 per unit. Tuition, state resident: full-time $9196; part-time $418 per unit. Tuition, nonresident: full-time $19,030; part-time $865 per unit. *International tuition:* $19,030 full-time. *Required fees:* $3102; $141 per year. $423 per term. Tuition and fees vary according to campus/location and program.

University of Advancing Technology, Master of Science Program in Technology, Tempe, AZ 85283-1042. Offers advancing computer science (MS); emerging technologies (MS); game production and management (MS); information assurance (MS); technology leadership (MS). *Degree requirements:* For master's, project or thesis. *Entrance requirements:* Additional exam requirements/recommendations for international students: Required—TOEFL (minimum score 550 paper-based). Electronic applications accepted. *Faculty research:* Artificial intelligence, fractals, organizational management.

The University of Alabama in Huntsville, School of Graduate Studies, College of Business Administration, Programs in Business and Management, Huntsville, AL 35899. Offers business analytics (MSMS); federal contracting and procurement management (Certificate); human resource management (MSM); management (MBA), including acquisition management, entrepreneurship, federal contract accounting, finance, human resource management, logistics and supply chain management, marketing, project management; supply chain management (Certificate); technology and innovation management (Certificate). *Accreditation:* AACSB. *Program availability:* Part-time. *Faculty:* 8 full-time (3 women). *Students:* 57 full-time (25 women), 152 part-time (76 women); includes 37 minority (20 Black or African American, non-Hispanic/Latino; 2 American Indian or Alaska Native, non-Hispanic/Latino; 6 Asian, non-Hispanic/Latino; 8 Hispanic/Latino; 1 Two or more races, non-Hispanic/Latino), 24 international. Average age 33. 178 applicants, 80% accepted, 84 enrolled. In 2018, 96 master's, 1 other advanced degree awarded. *Degree requirements:* For master's, comprehensive exam, thesis or alternative. *Entrance requirements:* For master's, GMAT, minimum score 500), minimum AACSB index of 1080. Additional exam requirements/recommendations for international students: Required—TOEFL (minimum score 550 paper-based; 80 iBT), IELTS (minimum score 6.5). *Application deadline:* For fall admission, 7/15 priority date for domestic students, 4/1 priority date for international students; for spring admission, 11/30 priority date for domestic students, 9/1 priority date for international students. Applications are processed on a rolling basis. Application fee: $50. Electronic applications accepted. *Expenses: Tuition, area resident:* Full-time $10,632; part-time $412 per credit hour. Tuition, state resident: full-time $10,632. Tuition, nonresident: full-time $23,604; part-time $412 per credit hour. *Required fees:* $582; $582. Tuition and fees vary according to course load and program. *Financial support:* In 2018–19, 15 students received support, including 15 teaching assistantships with full tuition reimbursements available (averaging $4,871 per year); research assistantships with full tuition reimbursements available, career-related internships or fieldwork, Federal Work-Study, institutionally sponsored loans, scholarships/grants, health care benefits, tuition waivers (full and partial), and unspecified assistantships also available. Support available to part-time students. Financial award application deadline: 4/1; financial award applicants required to submit FAFSA. *Faculty research:* Supply chain management, management of research and development, international marketing and branding, organizational behavior and human resource management, social networks and computational economics. *Unit head:* Dr. Fan Tseng, Chair, 256-824-6804, Fax: 256-824-6328, E-mail: fan.tseng@uah.edu. *Application contact:* Jennifer Pettitt, Director of Advising, 256-824-6681, Fax: 256-824-7571, E-mail: jennifer.pettitt@uah.edu.

University of Bridgeport, School of Engineering, Department of Technology Management, Bridgeport, CT 06604. Offers MS, PhD. *Degree requirements:* For master's, thesis optional. *Entrance requirements:* Additional exam requirements/recommendations for international students: Recommended—TOEFL (minimum score 550 paper-based; 80 iBT), IELTS (minimum score 6.5). Electronic applications accepted. *Expenses:* Contact institution.

University of California, Los Angeles, Graduate Division, UCLA Anderson School of Management, Los Angeles, CA 90095-1481. Offers accounting (PhD); behavioral decision making (PhD); business administration (EMBA, MBA); business administration/computer science (MBA/MSCS); business administration/latin american studies (MBA/MLAS); business administration/law (MBA/JD); business administration/library science (MBA/MLIS); business administration/medicine (MBA/MD); business administration/nursing (MBA/MN); business administration/public health (MBA/MPH); business administration/public policy (MBA/MPP); business administration/urban and regional planning (MBA/MURP); business analytics (MSBA); decisions, operations, and technology management (PhD); finance (PhD); financial engineering (MFE); global economics and management (PhD); management and organizations (PhD); marketing (PhD); strategy and policy (PhD); DDS/MBA; MBA/JD; MBA/MD; MBA/MLAS; MBA/MLIS; MBA/MN; MBA/MPH; MBA/MPP; MBA/MSCS; MBA/MURP. UCLA-NUS EMBA: UCLA Anderson and the National University of Singapore. *Accreditation:* AACSB. *Program availability:* Part-time, evening/weekend. *Faculty:* 86 full-time (19 women), 102 part-time/adjunct (16 women). *Students:* 1,040 full-time (378 women), 1,262 part-time (391 women); includes 784 minority (47 Black or African American, non-Hispanic/Latino; 1 American Indian or Alaska Native, non-Hispanic/Latino; 539 Asian, non-Hispanic/Latino; 116 Hispanic/Latino; 5 Native Hawaiian or other Pacific Islander, non-Hispanic/Latino; 76 Two or more races, non-Hispanic/Latino), 609 international. Average age 31. 6,708 applicants, 27% accepted, 949 enrolled. In 2018, 885 master's, 13 doctorates awarded. Terminal master's awarded for partial completion of doctoral program. *Degree requirements:* For master's, comprehensive exam, field consulting project (for MBA, FEMBA, EMBA, UCLA-NUS EMBA, MFE, and MSBA); internship (for MBA only); for doctorate, comprehensive exam, thesis/dissertation, oral and written qualifying exams. *Entrance requirements:* For master's, GMAT or GRE (for MBA, MFE, MSBA); Executive Assessment (EA) for candidates with 10+ years of work experience (FEMBA); Executive Assessment (EA) or STEM Master's degree or JD, MBA, CPA (EMBA), 4-year bachelor's degree or equivalent; 2 letters of recommendation; interview (invitation only); 2 essays; average 4-8 years of full-time work experience (for FEMBA); minimum 8 years of work experience with at least 3 years at management level (for EMBA); 10 years of full-time high managerial responsibility work experience (UCLA-NUS EMBA); for doctorate, GMAT or GRE, bachelor's degree from college or university of fully-recognized standing, minimum B average during junior and senior undergraduate years, 3 letters of recommendation, statement of purpose. Additional exam requirements/recommendations for international students: Required—TOEFL (minimum score 560 paper-based; 87 iBT), IELTS (minimum score 7), TOEFL with minimum iBT score of 100 (for MSBA). *Application deadline:* For fall admission, 10/2 for domestic and international students; for winter admission, 1/8 for domestic and international students; for spring admission, 4/16 for domestic and international students. Applications are processed on a rolling basis. Application fee: $200. Electronic applications accepted. *Expenses:* Per Year - MBA: $64,292, FEMBA: $42,420, EMBA: $81,120, UCLA-NUS EMBA (UC Portion only): $57,500, MFE: $75,816, MSBA: $64,1,43, PhD: $32,049. *Financial support:* Fellowships, research assistantships with partial tuition reimbursements, teaching assistantships with partial tuition reimbursements, career-related internships or fieldwork, institutionally sponsored loans, and scholarships/grants available. Support available to part-time students. *Faculty research:* Finance/global economics, entrepreneurship, accounting, human resources/organizational behavior, marketing and behavioral decision making. Total annual research expenditures: $2 million. *Unit head:* Dr. Antonio Bernardo, Dean & John E. Anderson Chair in Management, 310-825-7982, Fax: 310-206-2073, E-mail: a.bernardo@anderson.ucla.edu. *Application contact:* Alex Lawrence, Assistant Dean and Director of MBA Admissions, 310-825-6944, Fax: 310-825-8582, E-mail: mba.admissions@anderson.ucla.edu.
Website: http://www.anderson.ucla.edu/

University of California, Santa Barbara, Graduate Division, College of Engineering, Program in Technology Management, Santa Barbara, CA 93106-2014. Offers MTM.

University of Central Missouri, The Graduate School, Warrensburg, MO 64093. Offers accountancy (MA); accounting (MBA); applied mathematics (MS); aviation safety (MA); biology (MS); business administration (MBA); career and technical education leadership (MS); college student personnel administration (MS); communication (MA); computer science (MS); counseling (MS); criminal justice (MS); educational leadership (Ed D); educational technology (MS); elementary and early childhood education (MSE); English (MA); environmental studies (MA); finance (MBA); history (MA); human services/educational technology (Ed S); human services/learning resources (Ed S); human services/professional counseling (Ed S); industrial hygiene (MS); industrial management (MS); information systems (MBA); information technology (MS); kinesiology (MS); library science and information services (MS); literacy education (MSE); marketing (MBA); mathematics (MS); music (MA); occupational safety management (MS); psychology (MS); rural family nursing (MS); school administration (MSE); social gerontology (MS); sociology (MA); special education (MSE); speech language pathology (MS); superintendency (Ed S); teaching (MAT); teaching English as a second language (MA); technology (MS); technology management (PhD); theatre (MA). *Accreditation:* ASHA. *Program availability:* Part-time, 100% online, blended/hybrid learning. *Degree requirements:* For master's and Ed S, comprehensive exam (for some programs), thesis (for some programs). *Entrance requirements:* Additional exam requirements/recommendations for international students: Required—TOEFL (minimum score 550 paper-based; 79 iBT). Electronic applications accepted.

University of Colorado Denver, Business School, Program in Information Systems, Denver, CO 80217. Offers accounting and information systems audit and control (MS); business intelligence systems (MS); digital health entrepreneurship (MS); enterprise risk management (MS); enterprise technology management (MS); geographic information systems (MS); health information technology (MS); technology innovation and entrepreneurship (MS); Web and mobile computing (MS). *Program availability:* Part-time, evening/weekend, online learning. *Degree requirements:* For master's, 30 credit hours. *Entrance requirements:* For master's, GMAT, resume, essay, two letters of recommendation, financial statements (for international applicants). Additional exam requirements/recommendations for international students: Required—TOEFL (minimum score 525 paper-based; 71 iBT); Recommended—IELTS (minimum score 6.5). Electronic applications accepted. *Expenses:* Contact institution. *Faculty research:* Human-computer interaction, expert systems, database management, electronic commerce, object-oriented software development.

University of Colorado Denver, Business School, Program in Management and Organization, Denver, CO 80217. Offers business strategy (MS); change and innovation (MS); enterprise technology management (MS); entrepreneurship and innovation (MS); global management (MS); leadership (MS); managing for sustainability (MS); managing human resources (MS); sports and entertainment (MS); strategic management (MS). *Accreditation:* AACSB. *Program availability:* Part-time, evening/weekend, online learning. *Degree requirements:* For master's, 30 semester hours (12 of required courses, 12 of management electives, and 6 of free electives). *Entrance requirements:* For master's, GMAT, resume, two letters of recommendation, essay, financial statements (for international applicants). Additional exam requirements/recommendations for international students: Required—TOEFL (minimum score 525 paper-based; 71 iBT); Recommended—IELTS (minimum score 6.5). Electronic applications accepted. *Expenses:* Contact institution. *Faculty research:* Human resource management, management of catastrophe, turnaround strategies.

University of Dallas, Satish and Yasmin Gupta College of Business, Irving, TX 75062. Offers accounting (MBA, MS); business administration (DBA); business analytics (MS); business management (MBA); corporate finance (MBA); cybersecurity (MS); finance (MS); financial services (MBA); global business (MBA, MS); health services management (MBA); human resource management (MBA); information and technology management (MS); information assurance (MBA); information technology (MBA); information technology service management (MBA); marketing management (MBA); organization development (MBA); project management (MBA); sports and entertainment management (MBA); strategic leadership (MBA); supply chain management (MBA). *Accreditation:* AACSB. *Program availability:* Part-time, evening/weekend, 100% online. *Students:* 147 full-time (56 women), 584 part-time (232 women); includes 402 minority (204 Black or African American, non-Hispanic/Latino; 95 Asian, non-Hispanic/Latino; 92 Hispanic/Latino; 2 Native Hawaiian or other Pacific Islander, non-Hispanic/Latino; 9 Two or more races, non-Hispanic/Latino), 113 international. Average age 34. 992 applicants, 30% accepted, 157 enrolled. In 2018, 336 master's, 5 doctorates awarded. *Degree requirements:* For doctorate, thesis/dissertation. *Entrance requirements:* For master's and doctorate, U.S. bachelor's degree with a minimum cumulative GPA of 2.0 from a regionally accredited college or university (or comparable foreign degree); minimum 3.0 GPA in any graduate-level coursework completed; good academic standing with all colleges attended. Additional exam requirements/recommendations for international students: Required—TOEFL (minimum score 80 iBT), IELTS (minimum score 6.5), PTE (minimum score 67). *Application deadline:* Applications are processed on a rolling basis. Application fee: $50. Electronic applications accepted. *Expenses:* $1250 per credit hour. *Financial support:* In 2018–19, 291 students received support. Research assistantships, teaching assistantships, scholarships/grants, and unspecified assistantships available. Support available to part-time students. Financial award application deadline: 2/15; financial award applicants required to submit FAFSA. *Unit head:* Brett J.L. Landry, Dean, 972-721-5356, E-mail: blandry@udallas.edu. *Application contact:* Breonna Collins, Director, Graduate Admissions, 972-7215304, E-mail: bcollins@udallas.edu. Website: http://www.udallas.edu/cob/

University of Delaware, Alfred Lerner College of Business and Economics, Department of Accounting and Management Information Systems and Department of Electrical and Computer Engineering, Program in Information Systems and Technology Management, Newark, DE 19716. Offers MS. *Program availability:* Part-time, evening/weekend. *Entrance requirements:* For master's, GRE or GMAT, 2 letters of recommendation, resume, minimum GPA of 2.75. Additional exam requirements/recommendations for international students: Required—TOEFL (minimum score 600 paper-based). *Faculty research:* Security, developer trust, XML.

University of Illinois at Urbana–Champaign, Graduate College, College of Agricultural, Consumer and Environmental Sciences, Department of Agricultural and Biological Engineering, Champaign, IL 61820. Offers agricultural and biological engineering (MS, PhD); technical systems management (MS, PSM).

University of Illinois at Urbana–Champaign, Graduate College, Gies College of Business, Department of Business Administration, Champaign, IL 61820. Offers business administration (MS, PhD); technology management (MS). *Accreditation:* AACSB. *Expenses:* Contact institution.

University of Maryland, Baltimore County, The Graduate School, College of Engineering and Information Technology, Department of Computer Science and Electrical Engineering, Program in Technical Management, Baltimore, MD 21250. Offers MPS. *Program availability:* Part-time. *Entrance requirements:* For master's, bachelor's degree in a science, technology, engineering, or mathematics related field; minimum undergraduate GPA of 3.0; minimum of two years' experience in a technical field; official transcripts; resume. Additional exam requirements/recommendations for international students: Required—TOEFL (minimum score 550 paper-based; 80 iBT), IELTS. Electronic applications accepted. *Expenses:* Contact institution.

University of Massachusetts Dartmouth, Graduate School, Charlton College of Business, Department of Decision and Information Sciences, North Dartmouth, MA 02747-2300. Offers healthcare management (MS); technology management (MS).

Management of Technology

Program availability: Part-time, 100% online, blended/hybrid learning. *Faculty:* 12 full-time (3 women), 7 part-time/adjunct (3 women). *Students:* 16 full-time (8 women), 45 part-time (32 women); includes 12 minority (3 Black or African American, non-Hispanic/Latino; 1 American Indian or Alaska Native, non-Hispanic/Latino; 7 Asian, non-Hispanic/Latino; 1 Hispanic/Latino), 17 international. Average age 32. 47 applicants, 89% accepted, 22 enrolled. In 2018, 17 master's awarded. *Degree requirements:* For master's, thesis (for some programs), thesis or project (for healthcare management), e-portfolio for business administration. *Entrance requirements:* For master's, GMAT (or waiver), statement of purpose (minimum 300 words), resume, official transcripts, 2 letters of recommendation. Additional exam requirements/recommendations for international students: Required—TOEFL (minimum score 550 paper-based; 80 iBT), IELTS (minimum score 6.5). *Application deadline:* For fall admission, 7/1 priority date for domestic students, 6/1 priority date for international students; for spring admission, 12/1 priority date for domestic students, 11/1 priority date for international students. Application fee: $60. Electronic applications accepted. *Financial support:* Scholarships/grants available. Financial award application deadline: 3/1; financial award applicants required to submit FAFSA. *Faculty research:* Effects of managerial behaviors and personality on strategic decision making, asset pricing, applications in multivariate diagnosis, pattern recognition and dat mining, sustainable development, social media marketing. *Unit head:* Melissa Pacheco, Assistant Dean of Graduate Programs, 508-999-8543, Fax: 508-999-8646, E-mail: mpacheco@umassd.edu. *Application contact:* Scott Webster, Director of Graduate Studies and Admissions, 508-999-8604, Fax: 508-999-8183, E-mail: graduate@umassd.edu.
Website: http://www.umassd.edu/charlton/programs/graduate

University of Miami, Graduate School, College of Engineering, Department of Industrial Engineering, Coral Gables, FL 33124. Offers environmental health and safety (MS); ergonomics (PhD); industrial engineering (MSIE, PhD); management of technology (MS); occupational ergonomics and safety (MS, MSOES), including environmental health and safety (MS), occupational ergonomics and safety (MSOES); MBA/MSIE. *Program availability:* Part-time. *Degree requirements:* For master's, thesis (for some programs); for doctorate, comprehensive exam, thesis/dissertation. *Entrance requirements:* For master's and doctorate, GRE General Test, minimum GPA of 3.0. Additional exam requirements/recommendations for international students: Required—TOEFL (minimum score 550 paper-based). *Faculty research:* Logistics, supply chain management, industrial applications of biomechanics and ergonomics, technology management, back pain, aging, operations research, manufacturing, safety, human reliability, energy assessment.

University of Minnesota, Twin Cities Campus, College of Science and Engineering, Technological Leadership Institute, Program in Management of Technology, Minneapolis, MN 55455-0213. Offers MSMOT. *Program availability:* Evening/weekend. *Degree requirements:* For master's, thesis, capstone project. *Entrance requirements:* For master's, 5 years of work experience in high-tech company, preferably in Twin Cities area; demonstrated technological leadership ability. Additional exam requirements/recommendations for international students: Required—TOEFL (minimum score 580 paper-based; 90 iBT). Electronic applications accepted. *Expenses:* Contact institution. *Faculty research:* Operations management, strategic management, technology foresight, marketing, business analysis.

University of New Mexico, Anderson School of Management, Department of Finance, International, Technology and Entrepreneurship, Albuquerque, NM 87131-1221. Offers entrepreneurship (MBA); finance (MBA); international management (MBA); international management in Latin America (MBA); management of technology (MBA). *Program availability:* Part-time. *Faculty:* 15 full-time (1 woman), 8 part-time/adjunct (2 women). In 2018, 29 master's awarded. *Entrance requirements:* For master's, GMAT or GRE, minimum GPA of 3.0 on last 60 hours of coursework; bachelor's degree from regionally-accredited college or university in U.S. or its equivalent in another country. Additional exam requirements/recommendations for international students: Required—TOEFL (minimum score 550 paper-based; 79 iBT), IELTS (minimum score 6.5). *Application deadline:* For fall admission, 4/1 priority date for domestic and international students; for spring admission, 10/1 priority date for domestic and international students. Applications are processed on a rolling basis. Application fee: $50. Electronic applications accepted. *Expenses:* For MBA (not EMBA): $531.34 per credit hour resident, $1197.98 per credit hour non-resident. *Financial support:* In 2018–19, 17 students received support, including 9 fellowships (averaging $18,720 per year), 12 research assistantships with partial tuition reimbursements available (averaging $15,291 per year); career-related internships or fieldwork, Federal Work-Study, scholarships/grants, and unspecified assistantships also available. Support available to part-time students. Financial award application deadline: 6/1; financial award applicants required to submit FAFSA. *Faculty research:* Corporate finance, investments, management in Latin America, management of technology, entrepreneurship. *Unit head:* Dr. Raul Gouvea, Chair, 505-277-6471, E-mail: rauldg@unm.edu. *Application contact:* Lisa Beauchene, Student Recruitment Specialist, 505-277-6471, E-mail: andersonadvising@unm.edu.
Website: https://www.mgt.unm.edu/fite/default.asp?mm-faculty

University of Phoenix–Bay Area Campus, School of Business, San Jose, CA 95134-1805. Offers accountancy (MS); accounting (MBA); business administration (MBA, DBA); energy management (MBA); global management (MBA); health care management (MBA); human resource management (MBA); human resources management (MM); management (MM); marketing (MBA); organizational leadership (DM); project management (MBA); public administration (MPA); technology management (MBA). *Accreditation:* ACBSP. *Program availability:* Evening/weekend, online learning. *Degree requirements:* For master's, thesis (for some programs). *Entrance requirements:* For master's, minimum undergraduate GPA of 3.0, 3 years of work experience. Additional exam requirements/recommendations for international students: Required—TOEFL (minimum score 550 paper-based; 79 iBT). Electronic applications accepted.

University of Phoenix–Central Valley Campus, College of Information Systems and Technology, Fresno, CA 93720-1552. Offers information systems (MIS); technology management (MBA).

University of Phoenix–Dallas Campus, College of Information Systems and Technology, Dallas, TX 75251. Offers e-business (MBA); information systems (MIS); technology management (MBA). *Program availability:* Evening/weekend. *Degree requirements:* For master's, thesis (for some programs). *Entrance requirements:* For master's, minimum undergraduate GPA of 3.0, 3 years of work experience. Additional exam requirements/recommendations for international students: Required—TOEFL (minimum score 550 paper-based; 79 iBT). Electronic applications accepted.

University of Phoenix–Hawaii Campus, College of Information Systems and Technology, Honolulu, HI 96813-3800. Offers information systems (MIS); technology management (MBA). *Program availability:* Evening/weekend. *Degree requirements:* For master's, thesis (for some programs). *Entrance requirements:* For master's, minimum undergraduate GPA of 3.0, 3 years of work experience. Additional exam requirements/recommendations for international students: Required—TOEFL (minimum score 550 paper-based; 79 iBT). Electronic applications accepted.

University of Phoenix–Houston Campus, College of Information Systems and Technology, Houston, TX 77079-2004. Offers e-business (MBA); information systems (MIS); technology management (MBA). *Program availability:* Evening/weekend, online learning. *Degree requirements:* For master's, comprehensive exam (for some programs), thesis. *Entrance requirements:* For master's, minimum undergraduate GPA of 3.0, 3 years of work experience. Additional exam requirements/recommendations for international students: Required—TOEFL (minimum score 550 paper-based; 79 iBT). Electronic applications accepted.

University of Phoenix–Las Vegas Campus, College of Information Systems and Technology, Las Vegas, NV 89135. Offers information systems (MIS); technology management (MBA). *Program availability:* Evening/weekend. *Degree requirements:* For master's, thesis (for some programs). *Entrance requirements:* For master's, minimum undergraduate GPA of 3.0, 3 years of work experience. Additional exam requirements/recommendations for international students: Required—TOEFL (minimum score 550 paper-based; 79 iBT). Electronic applications accepted.

University of Phoenix–Online Campus, School of Business, Phoenix, AZ 85034-7209. Offers accountancy (MS); accounting (MBA, Certificate); business administration (MBA); energy management (MBA); global management (MBA); health care management (MBA); human resource management (MBA, Certificate); human resources management (MM); management (MM); marketing (MBA, Certificate); project management (MBA, Certificate); public administration (MBA, MM); technology management (MBA). *Program availability:* Evening/weekend, online learning. *Entrance requirements:* Additional exam requirements/recommendations for international students: Required—TOEFL, TOEIC (Test of English as an International Communication), Berlitz Online English Proficiency Exam, PTE, or IELTS. Electronic applications accepted. *Expenses:* Contact institution.

University of Phoenix–Phoenix Campus, School of Business, Tempe, AZ 85282-2371. Offers accounting (MBA, MS, Certificate); business administration (MBA); energy management (MBA); global management (MBA); health care management (MBA); human resource management (MBA, Certificate); management (MM); marketing (MBA); project management (MBA); technology management (MBA). *Program availability:* Evening/weekend, online learning. *Entrance requirements:* Additional exam requirements/recommendations for international students: Required—TOEFL, TOEIC (Test of English as an International Communication), Berlitz Online English Proficiency Exam, PTE, or IELTS. Electronic applications accepted. *Expenses:* Contact institution.

University of Phoenix–Sacramento Valley Campus, College of Information Systems and Technology, Sacramento, CA 95833-4334. Offers management (MIS); technology management (MBA). *Program availability:* Evening/weekend. *Degree requirements:* For master's, thesis (for some programs). *Entrance requirements:* For master's, minimum undergraduate GPA of 3.0, 3 years work experience. Additional exam requirements/recommendations for international students: Required—TOEFL (minimum score 550 paper-based; 79 iBT). Electronic applications accepted.

University of Phoenix–San Antonio Campus, College of Information Systems and Technology, San Antonio, TX 78230. Offers information systems (MIS); technology management (MBA).

University of Phoenix–San Diego Campus, College of Information Systems and Technology, San Diego, CA 92123. Offers management (MIS); technology management (MBA). *Program availability:* Evening/weekend. *Degree requirements:* For master's, thesis (for some programs). *Entrance requirements:* For master's, minimum undergraduate GPA of 3.0, 3 years work experience. Additional exam requirements/recommendations for international students: Required—TOEFL (minimum score 550 paper-based; 79 iBT). Electronic applications accepted.

University of Portland, Dr. Robert B. Pamplin, Jr. School of Business, Portland, OR 97203-5798. Offers entrepreneurship (MBA); finance (MBA, MS); health care management (MBA); marketing (MBA); nonprofit management (EMBA); operations and technology management (MBA, MS); sustainability (MBA). *Accreditation:* AACSB. *Program availability:* Part-time, evening/weekend. *Faculty:* 26 full-time (5 women), 8 part-time/adjunct (1 woman). *Students:* 35 full-time (16 women), 114 part-time (47 women); includes 21 minority (3 Black or African American, non-Hispanic/Latino; 2 American Indian or Alaska Native, non-Hispanic/Latino; 8 Asian, non-Hispanic/Latino; 8 Hispanic/Latino), 24 international. Average age 32. In 2018, 55 master's awarded. *Entrance requirements:* For master's, GMAT or GRE, minimum GPA of 3.0, resume, statement of goals, 2 letters of recommendation. Additional exam requirements/recommendations for international students: Required—TOEFL (minimum score 88 iBT), IELTS (minimum score 7). *Application deadline:* For fall admission, 7/19 priority date for domestic and international students; for spring admission, 12/7 priority date for domestic and international students; for summer admission, 4/12 priority date for domestic and international students. Applications are processed on a rolling basis. Application fee: $0. Electronic applications accepted. *Expenses:* Contact institution. *Financial support:* Application deadline: 3/1; applicants required to submit FAFSA. *Unit head:* Melissa McCarthy, Director, 503-943-7224, E-mail: mba-up@up.edu. *Application contact:* Melissa McCarthy, Director, 503-943-7224, E-mail: mba-up@up.edu.

University of St. Thomas, School of Engineering, St. Paul, MN 55105. Offers data science (MS); electrical engineering (MS); information technology (MS); manufacturing engineering (MS); manufacturing systems (Certificate); mechanical engineering (MS); medical device development (Certificate); regulatory science (MS); software engineering (MS); software management (MS); systems engineering (MS); technology leadership (Certificate); technology management (MS). *Program availability:* Part-time, evening/weekend. *Entrance requirements:* For master's, resume, official transcripts. Additional exam requirements/recommendations for international students: Required—TOEFL (minimum score 80 iBT), IELTS (minimum score 6.5). Electronic applications accepted. *Expenses:* Contact institution.

University of South Florida, Innovative Education, Tampa, FL 33620-9951. Offers adult, career and higher education (Graduate Certificate), including college teaching, leadership in developing human resources, leadership in higher education; Africana studies (Graduate Certificate), including diasporas and health disparities, genocide and human rights; aging studies (Graduate Certificate), including gerontology; art research (Graduate Certificate), including museum studies; business foundations (Graduate Certificate); chemical and biomedical engineering (Graduate Certificate), including materials science and engineering, water, health and sustainability; child and family studies (Graduate Certificate), including positive behavior support; civil and industrial engineering (Graduate Certificate), including transportation systems analysis; community and family health (Graduate Certificate), including maternal and child health, social marketing and public health, violence and injury: prevention and intervention, women's health; criminology (Graduate Certificate), including criminal justice administration; data science for public administration (Graduate Certificate); digital humanities (Graduate Certificate); educational measurement and research (Graduate Certificate), including evaluation; English (Graduate Certificate), including comparative literary studies, creative writing, professional and technical communication; entrepreneurship (Graduate Certificate); environmental health (Graduate Certificate), including safety management; epidemiology and biostatistics (Graduate Certificate), including applied biostatistics, biostatistics, concepts and tools of epidemiology,

epidemiology, epidemiology of infectious diseases; geography, environment and planning (Graduate Certificate), including community development, environmental policy and management, geographical information systems; geology (Graduate Certificate), including hydrogeology; global health (Graduate Certificate), including disaster management, global health and Latin American and Caribbean studies, global health practice, humanitarian assistance, infection control; government and international affairs (Graduate Certificate), including Cuban studies, globalization studies; health policy and management (Graduate Certificate), including health management and leadership, public health policy and programs; hearing specialist: early intervention (Graduate Certificate); industrial and management systems engineering (Graduate Certificate), including systems engineering, technology management; information studies (Graduate Certificate), including school library media specialist; information systems/decision sciences (Graduate Certificate), including analytics and business intelligence; instructional technology (Graduate Certificate), including distance education, Florida digital/virtual educator, instructional design, multimedia design, Web design; internal medicine, bioethics and medical humanities (Graduate Certificate), including biomedical ethics; Latin American and Caribbean studies (Graduate Certificate); leadership for coastal resiliency planning (Graduate Certificate); mass communications (Graduate Certificate), including multimedia journalism; mathematics and statistics (Graduate Certificate), including mathematics; medicine (Graduate Certificate), including aging and neuroscience, bioinformatics, biotechnology, brain fitness and memory management, clinical investigation, hand and upper limb rehabilitation, health informatics, health sciences, integrative weight management, intellectual property, medicine and gender, metabolic and nutritional medicine, metabolic cardiology, pharmacy sciences; national and competitive intelligence (Graduate Certificate); nursing (Graduate Certificate), including simulation based academic fellowship in advanced pain management; psychological and social foundations (Graduate Certificate), including career counseling, college teaching, diversity in education, mental health counseling, school counseling; public affairs (Graduate Certificate), including nonprofit management, public management, research administration; public health (Graduate Certificate), including assessing chemical toxicity and public health risks, health equity, pharmacoepidemiology, public health generalist, toxicology, translational research in adolescent behavioral health; public health practices (Graduate Certificate), including planning for healthy communities; rehabilitation and mental health counseling (Graduate Certificate), including integrative mental health care, marriage and family therapy, rehabilitation technology; secondary education (Graduate Certificate), including ESOL, foreign language education: culture and content, foreign language education: professional; social work (Graduate Certificate), including geriatric social work/clinical gerontology; special education (Graduate Certificate), including autism spectrum disorder, disabilities education: severe/profound; world languages (Graduate Certificate), including teaching English as a second language (TESL) or foreign language. *Expenses:* Tuition, state resident: full-time $6350. Tuition, nonresident: full-time $19,048. *International tuition:* $19,048 full-time. *Required fees:* $2079. *Unit head:* Dr. Cynthia DeLuca, Associate Vice President and Assistant Vice Provost, 813-974-3077, Fax: 813-974-7061, E-mail: deluca@usf.edu. *Application contact:* Owen Hooper, Director, Summer and Alternative Calendar Programs, 813-974-6917, E-mail: hooper@usf.edu.
Website: http://www.usf.edu/innovative-education/

The University of Texas at Dallas, Naveen Jindal School of Management, Program in Information Systems, Richardson, TX 75080. Offers business analytics (MS); information technology and management (MS). *Program availability:* Part-time, evening/weekend. *Faculty:* 19 full-time (2 women), 29 part-time/adjunct (5 women). *Students:* 1,313 full-time (523 women), 504 part-time (202 women); includes 177 minority (16 Black or African American, non-Hispanic/Latino; 128 Asian, non-Hispanic/Latino; 28 Hispanic/Latino; 1 Native Hawaiian or other Pacific Islander, non-Hispanic/Latino; 4 Two or more races, non-Hispanic/Latino), 1,523 international. Average age 27. 2,623 applicants, 76% accepted, 760 enrolled. In 2018, 983 master's awarded. *Degree requirements:* For master's, thesis optional. *Entrance requirements:* For master's, GMAT. Additional exam requirements/recommendations for international students: Required—TOEFL (minimum score 550 paper-based). *Application deadline:* For fall admission, 7/15 for domestic students, 5/1 priority date for international students; for spring admission, 11/15 for domestic students, 9/1 priority date for international students. Applications are processed on a rolling basis. Application fee: $50 ($100 for international students). Electronic applications accepted. *Expenses: Tuition, area resident:* Full-time $13,458. Tuition, state resident: full-time $13,458. Tuition, nonresident: full-time $26,852. *International tuition:* $26,852 full-time. Tuition and fees vary according to course load. *Financial support:* In 2018–19, 1 research assistantship with partial tuition reimbursement (averaging $13,400 per year), 26 teaching assistantships with partial tuition reimbursements (averaging $10,050 per year) were awarded; career-related internships or fieldwork, Federal Work-Study, institutionally sponsored loans, scholarships/grants, and unspecified assistantships also available. Support available to part-time students. Financial award application deadline: 4/30; financial award applicants required to submit FAFSA. *Faculty research:* Electronic commerce, decision support systems, data quality. *Unit head:* Dr. Syam Menon, Area Coordinator, 972-883-4779, E-mail: syam@utdallas.edu. *Application contact:* Dr. Syam Menon, Area Coordinator, 972-883-4779, E-mail: syam@utdallas.edu.
Website: https://jindal.utdallas.edu/information-systems-programs/

The University of Texas at San Antonio, College of Business, Department of Information Systems and Cyber Security, San Antonio, TX 78249-0617. Offers cyber security (MSIT); information technology (MS, PhD); management of technology (MBA); technology entrepreneurship and management (Certificate). *Program availability:* Part-time, evening/weekend. *Degree requirements:* For master's, comprehensive exam for some programs), thesis optional; for doctorate, comprehensive exam, thesis/dissertation. *Entrance requirements:* For master's and doctorate, GMAT/GRE, official transcripts, statement of purpose, letters of recommendation. Additional exam requirements/recommendations for international students: Required—TOEFL (minimum score 550 paper-based; 79 iBT), IELTS (minimum score 6.5). Electronic applications accepted. *Expenses:* Contact institution. *Faculty research:* Cyber security, digital forensics, economics of information systems, information systems privacy, information technology adoption.

University of Toronto, Faculty of Medicine, Program in Management of Innovation, Toronto, ON M5S 1A1, Canada. Offers MMI. *Entrance requirements:* For master's, GMAT, minimum B+ average, 2 reference letters, resume/curriculum vitae. Additional exam requirements/recommendations for international students: Required—TOEFL (minimum score 580 paper-based; 93 iBT), TWE (minimum score 5). Electronic applications accepted.

University of Virginia, McIntire School of Commerce, M.S. in the Management of IT Program, Charlottesville, VA 22903. Offers MS. *Program availability:* Evening/weekend. *Faculty:* 15 full-time (3 women). *Students:* 72 full-time (27 women); includes 29 minority (11 Black or African American, non-Hispanic/Latino; 11 Asian, non-Hispanic/Latino; 5 Hispanic/Latino; 1 Native Hawaiian or other Pacific Islander, non-Hispanic/Latino; 1 Two or more races, non-Hispanic/Latino). Average age 38. 209 applicants, 30% accepted, 54 enrolled. In 2018, 71 master's awarded. *Entrance requirements:* For master's, 1 recommendation letters. bachelor's degree, interview, essay. Additional exam

requirements/recommendations for international students: Required—TOEFL (minimum score 620 paper-based). *Application deadline:* For fall admission, 11/1 for domestic students; for winter admission, 2/1 for domestic students; for spring admission, 3/1 priority date for domestic students; for summer admission, 5/1 for domestic students. Applications are processed on a rolling basis. Application fee: $75. Electronic applications accepted. *Expenses:* Contact institution. *Financial support:* Federal Work-Study and scholarships/grants available. Financial award application deadline: 3/1; financial award applicants required to submit FAFSA. *Unit head:* Stefano Grazioli, Director, 434-982-2973, E-mail: grazioli@virginia.edu. *Application contact:* Lizzie Batman, Assistant Director, Graduate Recruiting and Admissions, 434-982-6920, Fax: 434-924-4511, E-mail: msmit@virginia.edu.
Website: http://www.commerce.virginia.edu/msmit/Pages/default.aspx

University of Washington, Graduate School, Michael G. Foster School of Business, Seattle, WA 98195-3200. Offers auditing and assurance (MP Acc); business administration (MBA, PhD); entrepreneurship (MS); executive business administration (MBA); global executive business administration (MBA); information systems (MSIS); supply chain management (MSSCM); taxation (MP Acc); technology management (MBA); JD/MBA; MBA/MAIS; MBA/MHA. *Accreditation:* AACSB. *Program availability:* Part-time, evening/weekend, blended/hybrid learning. Terminal master's awarded for partial completion of doctoral program. *Degree requirements:* For doctorate, comprehensive exam, thesis/dissertation. *Entrance requirements:* For master's and doctorate, GMAT, GRE. Additional exam requirements/recommendations for international students: Required—TOEFL (minimum score 600 paper-based; 100 iBT). Electronic applications accepted. *Expenses:* Contact institution. *Faculty research:* Finance, consumer behavior, marketing analytics, technology management, supply chain.

University of Waterloo, Graduate Studies and Postdoctoral Affairs, Faculty of Engineering, Conrad School of Entrepreneurship and Business, Waterloo, ON N2L 3G1, Canada. Offers MBET. *Entrance requirements:* For master's, honors degree. Additional exam requirements/recommendations for international students: Required—TOEFL (minimum score 90 iBT), IELTS (minimum score 7), PTE (minimum score 63). *Application deadline:* Applications are processed on a rolling basis. Application fee: $125. Electronic applications accepted. *Application contact:* Tracie Wilkinson, Administrative Liaison and Support, 519-888-4567 Ext. 37167, Fax: 519-747-7287, E-mail: twilkins@uwaterloo.ca.
Website: https://uwaterloo.ca/conrad-business-entrepreneurship-technology/

University of Waterloo, Graduate Studies and Postdoctoral Affairs, Faculty of Engineering, Department of Management Sciences, Waterloo, ON N2L 3G1, Canada. Offers applied operations research (MA Sc, MMS, PhD); information systems (MA Sc, MMS, PhD); management of technology (MA Sc, MMS, PhD). *Program availability:* Part-time, online learning. *Degree requirements:* For master's, research paper or thesis; for doctorate, comprehensive exam, thesis/dissertation. *Entrance requirements:* For master's, GMAT or GRE, honors degree, minimum B average, resume; for doctorate, GMAT or GRE, master's degree, minimum A- average, resume. Additional exam requirements/recommendations for international students: Required—TOEFL, IELTS, PTE. *Application deadline:* Applications are processed on a rolling basis. Application fee: $125 Canadian dollars. Electronic applications accepted. *Financial support:* Fellowships, research assistantships, teaching assistantships, career-related internships or fieldwork, and institutionally sponsored loans available. *Faculty research:* Operations research, manufacturing systems, scheduling, information systems.
Website: https://uwaterloo.ca/management-sciences/

University of Wisconsin–Madison, Graduate School, Wisconsin School of Business, Wisconsin Full-Time MBA Program, Madison, WI 53706-1380. Offers applied security analysis (MBA); arts administration (MBA); brand and product management (MBA); corporate finance and investment banking (MBA); marketing research (MBA); operations and technology management (MBA); real estate (MBA); risk management and insurance (MBA); strategic human resource management (MBA); supply chain management (MBA). *Faculty:* 137 full-time (36 women), 39 part-time/adjunct (11 women). *Students:* 183 full-time (59 women); includes 31 minority (5 Black or African American, non-Hispanic/Latino; 1 American Indian or Alaska Native, non-Hispanic/Latino; 6 Asian, non-Hispanic/Latino; 13 Hispanic/Latino; 6 Two or more races, non-Hispanic/Latino), 40 international. Average age 28. 465 applicants, 33% accepted, 79 enrolled. In 2018, 104 master's awarded. *Entrance requirements:* For master's, GMAT or GRE, bachelor's or equivalent degree, essay, letter of recommendation, resume. Additional exam requirements/recommendations for international students: Required—TOEFL (minimum score 100 iBT), IELTS (minimum score 7.5), TOEFL is not required for international students whose undergraduate training was in English. *Application deadline:* For fall admission, 11/1 for domestic and international students; for winter admission, 1/10 for domestic and international students; for spring admission, 3/1 for domestic and international students; for summer admission, 4/10 for domestic students, 4/10 priority date for international students. Applications are processed on a rolling basis. Application fee: $75 ($81 for international students). Electronic applications accepted. *Expenses:* Wisconsin Resident tuition and fees - $39,156; Nonresident tuition and fees - $76,635. *Financial support:* In 2018–19, 148 students received support, including 7 fellowships with full tuition reimbursements available (averaging $25,871 per year), 7 research assistantships with full tuition reimbursements available (averaging $14,832 per year), 47 teaching assistantships with full tuition reimbursements available (averaging $14,832 per year); scholarships/grants, health care benefits, tuition waivers (full and partial), and unspecified assistantships also available. Financial award application deadline: 6/1. *Faculty research:* Ecology, environmental studies, and business; decision making; tax policy; diversity and inclusion in governance boards; marketing and social media. *Unit head:* Dr. Enno Siemsen, Associate Dean of the MBA and Masters Programs, 608-890-3130, E-mail: esiemsen@wisc.edu. *Application contact:* Betsy Kacizak, Director of Admissions and Recruiting, Full-time MBA Program, 608-262-4000, E-mail: betsy.kacizak@wisc.edu.
Website: https://wsb.wisc.edu/

University of Wisconsin–Milwaukee, Graduate School, Lubar School of Business, Other Business Programs, Milwaukee, WI 53201-0413. Offers business analytics (Graduate Certificate); enterprise resource planning (Graduate Certificate); information technology management (MS); investment management (Graduate Certificate); nonprofit management (Graduate Certificate); nonprofit management and leadership (MS); state and local taxation (Graduate Certificate). *Students:* 132 full-time (63 women), 120 part-time (58 women); includes 45 minority (11 Black or African American, non-Hispanic/Latino; 15 Asian, non-Hispanic/Latino; 4 Hispanic/Latino; 15 Two or more races, non-Hispanic/Latino), 52 international. Average age 31. 196 applicants, 63% accepted, 80 enrolled. In 2018, 108 master's, 18 other advanced degrees awarded. *Entrance requirements:* Additional exam requirements/recommendations for international students: Required—TOEFL (minimum score 550 paper-based; 79 iBT), IELTS (minimum score 6.5). Application fee: $56 ($96 for international students). Electronic applications accepted. *Financial support:* Fellowships, research assistantships, teaching assistantships, health care benefits, unspecified assistantships, and project assistantships available. Financial award applicants required to submit FAFSA. *Application contact:* General Information Contact, 414-229-4982, Fax: 414-229-6967, E-mail: gradschool@uwm.edu.

Washington State University, Voiland College of Engineering and Architecture, Program in Engineering and Technology Management, Pullman, WA 99164-2785. Offers METM, Certificate. Program offered through the Global (online) campus. *Program availability:* Part-time, evening/weekend, online learning. *Degree requirements:* For master's, one foreign language, comprehensive exam (for some programs). *Entrance requirements:* Additional exam requirements/recommendations for international students: Required—TOEFL. Electronic applications accepted. *Faculty research:* Constraints management, Six Sigma quality management, supply chain management, project management, construction management, systems engineering management, manufacturing leadership.

Webster University, George Herbert Walker School of Business and Technology, Department of Management, St. Louis, MO 63119-3194. Offers business and organizational security management (MA); digital marketing management (Graduate Certificate); government contracting (Graduate Certificate); health administration (MHA); health care management (MA); health services management (MA); human resources development (MA); human resources management (MA); information technology management (MA, MS); management (D Mgt); management and leadership (MA); marketing (MA); nonprofit leadership (MA); nonprofit revenue development (Graduate Certificate); organizational development (Graduate Certificate); procurement and acquisitions management (MA); public administration (MPA); space systems operations management (MS). *Program availability:* Part-time, evening/weekend, online learning. *Degree requirements:* For master's, thesis (for some programs); for doctorate, thesis/dissertation, written exam. *Entrance requirements:* For doctorate, GMAT, 3 years of work experience, MBA. Additional exam requirements/recommendations for international students: Required—TOEFL. *Expenses: Tuition:* Full-time $22,500; part-time $750 per credit hour. Tuition and fees vary according to degree level, campus/location and program.

Wentworth Institute of Technology, Online Master of Science in Technology Management Program, Boston, MA 02115-5998. Offers MS. *Program availability:* Part-time-only, evening/weekend, online only, 100% online. *Degree requirements:* For master's, thesis optional, capstone. *Entrance requirements:* For master's, resume, official transcripts, two professional recommendations, BA or BS, one year of professional experience in a technical role and/or technical organization, statement of purpose, minimum GPA of 3.0. Additional exam requirements/recommendations for international students: Recommended—TOEFL (minimum score 550 paper-based). Electronic applications accepted. *Expenses:* Contact institution.

Western Kentucky University, Graduate School, Ogden College of Science and Engineering, The School of Engineering and Applied Sciences, Bowling Green, KY 42101. Offers computer science (MS); engineering technology management (MS).

Wilfrid Laurier University, Faculty of Graduate and Postdoctoral Studies, Lazaridis School of Business and Economics, Department of Business, Waterloo, ON N2L 3C5, Canada. Offers accounting (PhD); finance (M Fin); financial economics (PhD); marketing (PhD); operations and supply chain management (PhD); organizational behavior and human resource management (M Sc); organizational behaviour and human resource management (PhD); supply chain management (M Sc); technology management (EMTM). *Accreditation:* AACSB. *Program availability:* Part-time, evening/weekend. *Degree requirements:* For master's, thesis optional; for doctorate, comprehensive exam, thesis/dissertation. *Entrance requirements:* For master's, GMAT, 4-year honors degree with minimum B+ average; for doctorate, GMAT, master's degree, minimum B+ average. Additional exam requirements/recommendations for international students: Required—TOEFL (minimum score 89 iBT). Electronic applications accepted. *Faculty research:* Financial economics, management and organizational behavior, operations and supply chain management.

Operations Research

Air Force Institute of Technology, Graduate School of Engineering and Management, Department of Operational Sciences, Dayton, OH 45433-7765. Offers logistics management (MS); operations research (MS, PhD); space operations (MS). *Program availability:* Part-time. *Degree requirements:* For master's, thesis; for doctorate, thesis/dissertation. *Entrance requirements:* For doctorate, GRE General Test, minimum GPA of 3.0, U.S. citizenship. *Faculty research:* Optimization, simulation, combat modeling and analysis, reliability and maintainability, resource scheduling.

Bowling Green State University, Graduate College, College of Arts and Sciences, Department of Computer Science, Bowling Green, OH 43403. Offers computer science (MS), including operations research, parallel and distributed computing, software engineering. *Program availability:* Part-time. *Degree requirements:* For master's, thesis or alternative. *Entrance requirements:* For master's, GRE General Test. Additional exam requirements/recommendations for international students: Required—TOEFL. Electronic applications accepted. *Faculty research:* Artificial intelligence, real time and concurrent programming languages, behavioral aspects of computing, network protocols.

Capella University, School of Business and Technology, Master's Programs in Business, Minneapolis, MN 55402. Offers accounting (MBA); business analysis (MS); business intelligence (MBA); entrepreneurship (MBA); finance (MBA); general business administration (MBA); general human resource management (MS); general leadership (MS); health care management (MBA); human resource management (MBA); marketing (MBA); project management (MBA, MS). *Accreditation:* ACBSP.

Carnegie Mellon University, Tepper School of Business, Program in Operations Research, Pittsburgh, PA 15213-3891. Offers PhD. *Degree requirements:* For doctorate, thesis/dissertation. *Entrance requirements:* For doctorate, GMAT or GRE General Test.

Case Western Reserve University, Weatherhead School of Management, Department of Operations, Cleveland, OH 44106. Offers operations and supply chain management (MSM); operations research (PhD); MBA/MSM. *Program availability:* Part-time. *Degree requirements:* For doctorate, thesis/dissertation. *Entrance requirements:* For master's, GRE General Test; for doctorate, GMAT, GRE General Test. *Expenses: Tuition:* Full-time $45,168; part-time $1939 per credit hour. *Required fees:* $36; $18 per semester. $18 per semester. *Faculty research:* Mathematical finance, mathematical programming, scheduling, stochastic optimization, environmental/energy models.

Claremont Graduate University, Graduate Programs, Institute of Mathematical Sciences, Claremont, CA 91711-6160. Offers computational and systems biology (PhD); computational mathematics and numerical analysis (MA, MS); computational science (PhD); engineering and industrial applied mathematics (PhD); mathematics (PhD); operations research and statistics (MA, MS); physical applied mathematics (MA, MS); pure mathematics (MA, MS); scientific computing (MA, MS); systems and control theory (MA, MS). PhD programs offered jointly with San Diego State University and California State University, Long Beach. *Program availability:* Part-time. Terminal master's awarded for partial completion of doctoral program. *Entrance requirements:* For master's and doctorate, GRE General Test. Additional exam requirements/recommendations for international students: Required—TOEFL (minimum score 75 iBT). Electronic applications accepted.

Colorado School of Mines, Office of Graduate Studies, Department of Economics and Business, Golden, CO 80401. Offers engineering and technology management (MS); mineral and energy economics (MS, PhD); operations research and engineering (PhD); petroleum economics and management with mineral and energy economics (MS). *Program availability:* Part-time. *Faculty:* 17 full-time (5 women), 4 part-time/adjunct (1 woman). *Students:* 92 full-time (27 women), 12 part-time (4 women); includes 20 minority (4 Black or African American, non-Hispanic/Latino; 4 Asian, non-Hispanic/Latino; 8 Hispanic/Latino; 1 Native Hawaiian or other Pacific Islander, non-Hispanic/Latino; 3 Two or more races, non-Hispanic/Latino), 33 international. Average age 28. 154 applicants, 82% accepted, 53 enrolled. In 2018, 68 master's, 4 doctorates awarded. *Degree requirements:* For master's, thesis (for some programs); for doctorate, comprehensive exam, thesis/dissertation. *Entrance requirements:* For master's and doctorate, GRE General Test. Additional exam requirements/recommendations for international students: Required—TOEFL (minimum score 550 paper-based; 79 iBT). *Application deadline:* For fall admission, 12/15 priority date for domestic and international students; for spring admission, 9/1 priority date for domestic and international students. Application fee: $60 ($80 for international students). Electronic applications accepted. *Expenses:* Tuition, state resident: full-time $16,650; part-time $925 per contact hour. Tuition, nonresident: full-time $36,270; part-time $2015 per contact hour. *International tuition:* $36,270 full-time. *Required fees:* $2314; $2314 per semester. *Financial support:* In 2018–19, 7 research assistantships with full tuition reimbursements, 22 teaching assistantships with full tuition reimbursements were awarded; fellowships, scholarships/grants, health care benefits, and unspecified assistantships also available. Financial award application deadline: 12/15; financial award applicants required to submit FAFSA. *Faculty research:* International trade, resource and environmental economics, energy economics, operations research. *Unit head:* Dr. Roderick Eggert, Interim Director, 303-273-3981, E-mail: reggert@mines.edu. *Application contact:* Kathleen Martin, Program Assistant, 303-273-3482, Fax: 303-273-3416, E-mail: kmartin@mines.edu.
Website: http://econbus.mines.edu

Columbia University, Fu Foundation School of Engineering and Applied Science, Department of Industrial Engineering and Operations Research, New York, NY 10027. Offers financial engineering (MS); industrial engineering (MS); industrial engineering and operations research (PhD); management science and engineering (MS); operations research (MS); MS/MBA. *Program availability:* Part-time, evening/weekend, online learning. *Degree requirements:* For doctorate, thesis/dissertation, oral and written qualifying exams. *Entrance requirements:* For master's and doctorate, GRE General Test. Additional exam requirements/recommendations for international students: Required—TOEFL, IELTS, PTE. Electronic applications accepted. *Faculty research:* Applied probability and optimization; financial engineering, modeling risk including credit risk and systemic risk, asset allocation, portfolio execution, behavioral finance, agent-based model in finance; revenue management; management and optimization of service systems, call centers, capacity allocation in healthcare systems, inventory control for vaccines; energy, smart grids, demand shaping, managing renewable energy sources, energy-aware scheduling.

Cornell University, Graduate School, Graduate Fields of Engineering, Field of Operations Research and Information Engineering, Ithaca, NY 14853. Offers applied probability and statistics (PhD); manufacturing systems engineering (PhD); mathematical programming (PhD); operations research and industrial engineering (M Eng). *Degree requirements:* For doctorate, comprehensive exam, thesis/dissertation. *Entrance requirements:* For master's and doctorate, GRE General Test, 3 letters of recommendation. Additional exam requirements/recommendations for international students: Required—TOEFL (minimum score 600 paper-based; 100 iBT). Electronic applications accepted. *Faculty research:* Mathematical programming and combinatorial optimization, statistics, stochastic processes, mathematical finance, simulation, manufacturing, e-commerce.

École Polytechnique de Montréal, Graduate Programs, Department of Mathematics and Industrial Engineering, Montréal, QC H3C 3A7, Canada. Offers ergonomy (M Eng, M Sc A, DESS); mathematical method in CA engineering (M Eng, M Sc A, PhD); operational research (M Eng, M Sc A, PhD); production (M Eng, M Sc A); technology management (M Eng, M Sc A). DESS program offered jointly with HEC Montreal and Université de Montréal. *Program availability:* Part-time. *Degree requirements:* For master's, one foreign language, thesis. *Entrance requirements:* For master's, minimum GPA of 2.75. *Faculty research:* Use of computers in organizations.

Florida Institute of Technology, Aberdeen Education Center (Maryland), Program in Management, Melbourne, FL 32901-6975. Offers acquisition and contract management (MS, PMBA); business administration (MS, PMBA); contracts management (PMBA); financial management (MPA); global management (PMBA); health management (MS); human resources management (MS, PMBA); information systems (PMBA); logistics management (MS); management (MS), including information systems, operations research; materials acquisition management (MS); operations research (MS); public administration (MPA); research (PMBA); space systems (MS); space systems management (MS). *Expenses: Tuition:* Full-time $22,338; part-time $1241 per credit hour. Tuition and fees vary according to degree level, campus/location and program. *Financial support:* Application deadline: 3/1. *Application contact:* Online Learning and Off-Campus Programs Admissions, 321-674-8263, E-mail: gradadm-olocp@fit.edu.
Website: https://www.fit.edu/education-centers/degrees-and-programs/management-ms/

Florida Institute of Technology, College of Engineering and Science, Program in Operations Research, Melbourne, FL 32901-6975. Offers MS, PhD. *Program availability:* Part-time, evening/weekend. *Students:* 21 part-time (9 women); includes 7 minority (3 Black or African American, non-Hispanic/Latino; 1 Asian, non-Hispanic/Latino; 2 Hispanic/Latino; 1 Two or more races, non-Hispanic/Latino). Average age 40. 3 applicants, 100% accepted, 1 enrolled. In 2018, 8 master's awarded. Terminal master's awarded for partial completion of doctoral program. *Degree requirements:* For master's, comprehensive exam (for some programs), thesis or final exam, 30 credit hours; for doctorate, comprehensive exam, thesis/dissertation, 42 credit hours after the masters, virtual written grant proposal and oral defense, written dissertation and oral defense, dissertation research, written qualifying exam. *Entrance requirements:* For master's, undergraduate degree in related field and strong math background. Additional exam

requirements/recommendations for international students: Required—TOEFL (minimum score 550 paper-based; 79 iBT). *Application deadline:* Applications are processed on a rolling basis. Application fee: $50. Electronic applications accepted. *Expenses: Tuition:* Full-time $22,338; part-time $1241 per credit hour. Tuition and fees vary according to degree level, campus/location and program. *Financial support:* In 2018–19, 1 student received support. Research assistantships, teaching assistantships, career-related internships or fieldwork, and tuition remissions available. Financial award application deadline: 3/1; financial award applicants required to submit FAFSA. *Unit head:* Dr. Munevver Subasi, Interim Department Head, 321-674-7486, E-mail: msubasi@fit.edu. *Application contact:* Mike Perry, Executive Director of Admissions, 321-674-8098, E-mail: dbatcheldor@fit.edu.
Website: https://www.fit.edu/programs/operations-research-ms/

George Mason University, Volgenau School of Engineering, Department of Systems Engineering and Operations Research, Fairfax, VA 22030. Offers operations research (MS); systems engineering and operations research (PhD, Certificate). MS programs offered jointly with Old Dominion University, University of Virginia, Virginia Commonwealth University, and Virginia Polytechnic Institute and State University. *Program availability:* Evening/weekend, 100% online. *Faculty:* 20 full-time (5 women), 15 part-time/adjunct (1 woman). *Students:* 39 full-time (13 women), 80 part-time (17 women); includes 25 minority (1 Black or African American, non-Hispanic/Latino; 15 Asian, non-Hispanic/Latino; 7 Hispanic/Latino; 2 Two or more races, non-Hispanic/Latino), 24 international. Average age 31. 73 applicants, 68% accepted, 24 enrolled. In 2018, 35 master's, 1 doctorate, 2 other advanced degrees awarded. *Degree requirements:* For master's, thesis optional; for doctorate, comprehensive exam, thesis/dissertation, qualifying exams. *Entrance requirements:* For master's, GRE General Test, BS in related field; minimum GPA of 3.0; 3 letters of recommendation; 2 official transcripts; expanded goals statement; proof of financial support; photocopy of passport; official bank statement; multivariable calculus, applied probability, statistics and a computer language course; self-evaluation form; for doctorate, GRE, MS with minimum GPA of 3.5; BS with minimum GPA of 3.0 in systems or operational research; 2 official transcripts; 3 letters of recommendation; resume; expanded goals statement; self evaluation form; photocopy of passport; official bank statement; proof of financial support; for Certificate, personal goals statement; 2 official transcripts; self-evaluation form; letter of recommendation; resume; official bank statement; photocopy of passport; proof of financial support; baccalaureate degree in related field. Additional exam requirements/recommendations for international students: Required—TOEFL (minimum score 575 paper-based; 88 iBT), IELTS (minimum score 6.5), PTE (minimum score 59). *Application deadline:* For fall admission, 12/15 priority date for domestic and international students; for spring admission, 8/15 priority date for domestic and international students. Application fee: $75 ($80 for international students). Electronic applications accepted. *Expenses:* $589 per credit in-state, $1,346.75 per credit out-of-state. *Financial support:* In 2018–19, 18 students received support, including 1 fellowship, 9 research assistantships with tuition reimbursements available (averaging $19,494 per year), 8 teaching assistantships with tuition reimbursements available (averaging $15,078 per year); career-related internships or fieldwork, Federal Work-Study, scholarships/grants, unspecified assistantships, and health care benefits (for full-time research or teaching assistantship recipients) also available. Support available to part-time students. Financial award application deadline: 3/1; financial award applicants required to submit FAFSA. *Faculty research:* Requirements engineering, signal processing, systems architecture, data fusion. *Total annual research expenditures:* $702,968. *Unit head:* Ariela Sofer, Chair, 703-993-1692, Fax: 703-993-1521, E-mail: asofer@gmu.edu. *Application contact:* Andy Loerch, Associate Chair, Graduate Information, 703-993-1657, E-mail: aloerch@gmu.edu.
Website: http://seor.gmu.edu

Georgia Institute of Technology, Graduate Studies, College of Engineering, H. Milton Stewart School of Industrial and Systems Engineering, Program in Operations Research, Atlanta, GA 30332-0001. Offers MS, PhD. *Program availability:* Part-time, online learning. *Degree requirements:* For doctorate, comprehensive exam. *Entrance requirements:* For master's and doctorate, GRE General Test. Additional exam requirements/recommendations for international students: Required—TOEFL (minimum score 550 paper-based; 79 iBT). Electronic applications accepted. *Faculty research:* Linear and nonlinear deterministic models in operations research, mathematical statistics, design of experiments.

Georgia State University, J. Mack Robinson College of Business, Department of Managerial Sciences, Atlanta, GA 30302-3083. Offers business analysis (MBA, MS); entrepreneurship (MBA); human resources management (MBA, MS); operations management (MBA, MS); organization behavior/human resource management (PhD); organization management (MBA); organizational change (MS); strategic management (PhD). *Accreditation:* AACSB. *Program availability:* Part-time, evening/weekend. *Faculty:* 11 full-time (2 women), 1 part-time/adjunct (0 women). *Students:* 11 full-time (6 women); includes 5 minority (3 Black or African American, non-Hispanic/Latino; 1 Asian, non-Hispanic/Latino; 1 Two or more races, non-Hispanic/Latino), 3 international. Average age 29. 54 applicants, 20% accepted, 8 enrolled. In 2018, 9 master's, 3 doctorates awarded. *Entrance requirements:* For master's, GRE or GMAT, transcripts from all institutions attended, resume, essays; for doctorate, GMAT, three letters of recommendation, personal statement, transcripts from all institutions attended, resume. Additional exam requirements/recommendations for international students: Required—TOEFL (minimum score 610 paper-based; 101 iBT), IELTS (minimum score 7). *Application deadline:* For fall admission, 5/1 priority date for domestic students, 2/1 priority date for international students; for spring admission, 9/15 priority date for domestic students, 4/1 priority date for international students. Applications are processed on a rolling basis. Application fee: $50. Electronic applications accepted. *Expenses: Tuition, area resident:* Full-time $9360; part-time $390 per credit hour. Tuition, state resident: full-time $9360; part-time $390 per credit hour. Tuition, nonresident: full-time $30,024; part-time $1251 per credit hour. *International tuition:* $30,024 full-time. *Required fees:* $2128. *Financial support:* Research assistantships, teaching assistantships, scholarships/grants, tuition waivers, and unspecified assistantships available. Financial award applicants required to submit FAFSA. *Faculty research:* Entrepreneurship and innovation; strategy process; workplace interactions, relationships, and processes; leadership and culture; supply chain management. *Unit head:* Dr. Pamela S. Barr, Chair, 404-413-7525, Fax: 404-413-7571. *Application contact:* Toby McChesney, Assistant Dean for Graduate Recruiting and Student Services, 404-413-7167, Fax: 404-413-7162, E-mail: rcbgradadmissions@gsu.edu.
Website: http://mgmt.robinson.gsu.edu/

HEC Montreal, School of Business Administration, Graduate Diploma Programs in Administration, Montréal, QC H3T 2A7, Canada. Offers business administration (Graduate Diploma); business analysis - information technology (Graduate Diploma); e-business (Graduate Diploma); entrepreneurship (Graduate Diploma); financial professions (Graduate Diploma); human resources (Graduate Diploma); management (Graduate Diploma); management and sustainable development (Graduate Diploma); management of cultural organizations (Graduate Diploma); marketing communication (Graduate Diploma); organizational development (Graduate Diploma); professional accounting (Graduate Diploma); supply chain management (Graduate Diploma); taxation (Graduate Diploma). All courses are given in French. *Students:* 412 full-time

(242 women), 885 part-time (552 women). 834 applicants, 65% accepted, 351 enrolled. In 2018, 611 Graduate Diplomas awarded. *Entrance requirements:* For degree, bachelor's degree. Application fee: $91 Canadian dollars ($191 Canadian dollars for international students). Electronic applications accepted. *Expenses: Tuition, area resident:* Full-time $3052.80 Canadian dollars; part-time $84.80 Canadian dollars per credit. Tuition, state resident: full-time $3816 Canadian dollars; part-time $264.67 Canadian dollars per credit. Tuition, nonresident: full-time $11,910 Canadian dollars. *International tuition:* $20,905.20 Canadian dollars full-time. *Required fees:* $1805.34 Canadian dollars; $43.62 Canadian dollars per credit. $71.78 Canadian dollars per term. Tuition and fees vary according to degree level and program. *Financial support:* Research assistantships, teaching assistantships, and scholarships/grants available. Financial award application deadline: 9/2. *Faculty research:* Art management; business policy, entrepreneurship, new technologies, transportation. *Unit head:* Renaud Lachance, Director, 514-340-6428, E-mail: renaud.lachance@hec.ca. *Application contact:* Anny Caron, Administrative Director, 514-340-6000, Fax: 514-340-6411, E-mail: aide@hec.ca.
Website: http://www.hec.ca/programmes/dess/index.html

Idaho State University, Graduate School, College of Science and Engineering, Department of Mechanical Engineering, Pocatello, ID 83209-8060. Offers measurement and control engineering (MS); mechanical engineering (MS). *Program availability:* Part-time. *Degree requirements:* For master's, comprehensive exam (for some programs), 2 semesters of seminar; thesis or project. *Entrance requirements:* For master's, GRE. Additional exam requirements/recommendations for international students: Required—TOEFL (minimum score 550 paper-based; 80 iBT). Electronic applications accepted. *Faculty research:* Modeling and identification of biomedical systems, intelligent systems and adaptive control, active flow control of turbo machinery, validation of advanced computational codes for thermal fluid interactions, development of methodologies for the assessment of passive safety system performance in advanced reactors, alternative energy research (wind, solar, hydrogen).

Iowa State University of Science and Technology, Department of Industrial and Manufacturing Systems Engineering, Ames, IA 50011. Offers industrial engineering (M Eng, MS, PhD); operations research (MS); systems engineering (M Eng). *Degree requirements:* For master's, thesis or alternative; for doctorate, thesis/dissertation. *Entrance requirements:* For master's and doctorate, GRE General Test. Additional exam requirements/recommendations for international students: Required—TOEFL (minimum score 550 paper-based; 79 iBT), IELTS (minimum score 6.5). Electronic applications accepted. *Faculty research:* Economic modeling, valuation techniques, robotics, digital controls, systems reliability.

Johns Hopkins University, G. W. C. Whiting School of Engineering, Department of Applied Mathematics and Statistics, Baltimore, MD 21218. Offers computational medicine (PhD); discrete mathematics (MA, MSE, PhD); financial mathematics (MSE); operations research/optimization (MA, MSE, PhD); statistics/probability (MA, MSE, PhD). *Faculty:* 25 full-time (4 women). *Students:* 173 full-time (67 women), 13 part-time (10 women). 1,406 applicants, 25% accepted, 89 enrolled. In 2018, 60 master's, 5 doctorates awarded. Terminal master's awarded for partial completion of doctoral program. *Degree requirements:* For master's, thesis (for some programs); for doctorate, thesis/dissertation, oral exam, introductory exam. *Entrance requirements:* For master's and doctorate, GRE General Test, 3 letters of recommendation, statement of purpose, transcripts. Additional exam requirements/recommendations for international students: Required—TOEFL (minimum score 600 paper-based; 100 iBT), IELTS (minimum score 7). *Application deadline:* For fall admission, 1/15 for domestic and international students; for spring admission, 9/15 for domestic and international students. Application fee: $75. Electronic applications accepted. *Financial support:* In 2018–19, 57 students received support, including 14 fellowships with full tuition reimbursements available (averaging $24,750 per year), 13 research assistantships with full tuition reimbursements available (averaging $23,000 per year), 30 teaching assistantships with full tuition reimbursements available (averaging $2,300 per year); Federal Work-Study, health care benefits, and tuition waivers (full and partial) also available. Financial award application deadline: 1/15; financial award applicants required to submit FAFSA. *Faculty research:* Matrix and numerical analysis, differential equation modeling, optimization and operations research, probability and statistics, discrete mathematics, financial mathematics. *Unit head:* Dr. Laurent Younes, Chair, 410-516-5103, Fax: 410-516-7459, E-mail: laurent.younes@jhu.edu. *Application contact:* Kristin Bechtel, Academic Program Coordinator, 410-516-7198, Fax: 410-516-7459, E-mail: kbechtel@jhu.edu.
Website: http://engineering.jhu.edu/ams

Johns Hopkins University, G. W. C. Whiting School of Engineering, Master of Science in Engineering Management Program, Baltimore, MD 21218. Offers biomaterials (MSEM); civil engineering (MSEM); communications science (MSEM); computer science (MSEM); environmental systems analysis, economics and public policy (MSEM); fluid mechanics (MSEM); materials science and engineering (MSEM); mechanical engineering (MSEM); mechanics and materials (MSEM); nano-biotechnology (MSEM); nanomaterials and nanotechnology (MSEM); operations research (MSEM); probability and statistics (MSEM); smart product and device design (MSEM). *Students:* 34 full-time (12 women), 18 part-time (7 women). 233 applicants, 39% accepted, 33 enrolled. In 2018, 27 master's awarded. *Entrance requirements:* For master's, GRE, 3 letters of recommendation, statement of purpose, transcripts. Additional exam requirements/recommendations for international students: Required—TOEFL (minimum score 600 paper-based, 100 iBT) or IELTS (7). *Application deadline:* For fall admission, 2/15 for domestic and international students. Application fee: $75. Electronic applications accepted. *Financial support:* In 2018–19, 43 research assistantships (averaging $43,344 per year) were awarded; health care benefits also available. *Unit head:* Dr. Pamela Sheff, Director, 410-516-7056, Fax: 410-516-4880, E-mail: pamsheff@gmail.com. *Application contact:* Lindsey Conklin, Sr. Academic Program Coordinator, 410-516-1108, Fax: 410-516-0780, E-mail: lconkli4@jhu.edu.
Website: http://engineering.jhu.edu/msem/

Kansas State University, Graduate School, College of Engineering, Department of Industrial and Manufacturing Systems Engineering, Manhattan, KS 66506. Offers engineering management (MEM); industrial engineering (MS); operations research (MS). *Program availability:* Part-time, online learning. *Degree requirements:* For master's, thesis or alternative; for doctorate, thesis/dissertation. *Entrance requirements:* For master's, GRE General Test (minimum score of 750 old version, 159 new format on Quantitative portion of exam), bachelor's degree in engineering, mathematics, or physical science; for doctorate, GRE General Test (minimum score of 770 old version, 164 new format on Quantitative portion of exam), master's degree in engineering or industrial manufacturing. Additional exam requirements/recommendations for international students: Required—PTE (minimum score 58), TOEFL (minimum score 550 paper-based; 79 iBT) or IELTS (minimum score 6.5). Electronic applications accepted. *Faculty research:* Industrial engineering, ergonomics, healthcare systems engineering, manufacturing processes, operations research, engineering management.

Massachusetts Institute of Technology, Operations Research Center, Cambridge, MA 02139. Offers SM, PhD. Terminal master's awarded for partial completion of doctoral program. *Degree requirements:* For master's, thesis; for doctorate, comprehensive exam, thesis/dissertation. *Entrance requirements:* For master's and doctorate, GRE General Test. Additional exam requirements/recommendations for international students: Required—TOEFL, IELTS. Electronic applications accepted. *Expenses:* Tuition: Full-time $51,520; part-time $800 per credit hour. *Required fees:* $312. *Faculty research:* Probability; optimization; statistics; stochastic processes; analytics.

Mississippi State University, Bagley College of Engineering, Department of Industrial and Systems Engineering, Mississippi State, MS 39762. Offers human factors and ergonomics (MS); industrial and systems engineering (PhD); industrial systems (MS); management systems (MS); manufacturing systems (MS); operations research (MS). *Program availability:* Part-time, blended/hybrid learning. *Faculty:* 12 full-time (2 women). *Students:* 35 full-time (13 women), 66 part-time (16 women); includes 20 minority (7 Black or African American, non-Hispanic/Latino; 6 Asian, non-Hispanic/Latino; 5 Hispanic/Latino; 1 Native Hawaiian or other Pacific Islander, non-Hispanic/Latino; 1 Two or more races, non-Hispanic/Latino), 21 international. Average age 36. 67 applicants, 40% accepted, 18 enrolled. In 2018, 16 master's, 9 doctorates awarded. *Degree requirements:* For master's, comprehensive exam (for some programs), thesis optional, comprehensive oral or written exam; for doctorate, comprehensive exam, thesis/dissertation, candidacy exam. *Entrance requirements:* For master's, GRE (for graduates from program not accredited by EAC/ABET), minimum GPA of 3.0 on junior and senior years; for doctorate, GRE (for graduates from program not accredited by EAC/ABET), minimum GPA of 3.5 on master's degree and junior and senior years of BS. Additional exam requirements/recommendations for international students: Required—TOEFL (minimum score 550 paper-based; 79 iBT); Recommended—IELTS (minimum score 6.5). *Application deadline:* For fall admission, 7/1 for domestic students, 5/1 for international students; for spring admission, 11/1 for domestic students, 9/1 for international students. Applications are processed on a rolling basis. Application fee: $60 ($80 for international students). Electronic applications accepted. *Expenses:* Tuition, state resident: full-time $8450; part-time $360.59 per credit hour. Tuition, nonresident: full-time $23,140; part-time $969.09 per credit hour. *Required fees:* $110. One-time fee: $55 full-time. Part-time tuition and fees vary according to course load, degree level, campus/location and reciprocity agreements. *Financial support:* In 2018–19, 18 research assistantships with full tuition reimbursements (averaging $16,905 per year), 3 teaching assistantships with full tuition reimbursements (averaging $16,033 per year) were awarded; Federal Work-Study, institutionally sponsored loans, and unspecified assistantships also available. Financial award application deadline: 4/1; financial award applicants required to submit FAFSA. *Faculty research:* Operations research, ergonomics, production systems, management systems, transportation. *Total annual research expenditures:* $2 million. *Unit head:* Dr. Kari Babski-Reeves, Professor/Interim Head and Associate Dean for Research & Graduate Studies, 662-325-8430, Fax: 662-325-7618, E-mail: kari@ise.msstate.edu. *Application contact:* Ryan King, Admissions and Enrollment Assistant, 662-325-8951, E-mail: rjk101@grad.msstate.edu. Website: http://www.ise.msstate.edu/

Naval Postgraduate School, Departments and Academic Groups, Department of Operations Research, Monterey, CA 93943. Offers applied science (MS), including operations research; cost estimating analysis (MS); human systems integration (MS); operations research (MS, PhD); systems analysis (MS). Program only open to commissioned officers of the United States and friendly nations and selected United States federal civilian employees. *Program availability:* Part-time. *Degree requirements:* For master's, thesis (for some programs); for doctorate, thesis/dissertation. *Faculty research:* Next generation network science, performance analysis of ground solider mobile ad-hoc networks, irregular warfare methods and tools, human social cultural behavior modeling, large-scale optimization.

Naval Postgraduate School, Departments and Academic Groups, Undersea Warfare Academic Group, Monterey, CA 93943. Offers applied mathematics (MS); applied physics (MS); applied science (MS), including acoustics, operations research, physical oceanography, signal processing; electrical engineering (MS); engineering acoustics (MS, PhD); engineering science (MS), including electrical engineering, mechanical engineering; mechanical engineer (ME); mechanical engineering (MS, MSME); meteorology (MS); operations research (MS); physical oceanography (MS). Program only open to commissioned officers of the United States and friendly nations and selected United States federal civilian employees. *Program availability:* Part-time. *Degree requirements:* For master's, thesis. *Faculty research:* Unmanned/autonomous vehicles, sea mines and countermeasures, submarine warfare in the twentieth and twenty-first centuries.

New Mexico Institute of Mining and Technology, Center for Graduate Studies, Department of Mathematics, Socorro, NM 87801. Offers applied and industrial mathematics (PhD); industrial mathematics (MS); mathematics (MS); operations research and statistics (MS). *Degree requirements:* For master's, thesis optional; for doctorate, thesis/dissertation. *Entrance requirements:* For master's, GRE General Test. Additional exam requirements/recommendations for international students: Required—TOEFL (minimum score 540 paper-based). *Faculty research:* Applied mathematics, differential equations, industrial mathematics, numerical analysis, stochastic processes.

North Carolina State University, Graduate School, College of Engineering and College of Sciences, Program in Operations Research, Raleigh, NC 27695. Offers MOR, MS, PhD. *Program availability:* Part-time. *Degree requirements:* For master's, thesis (MS); for doctorate, thesis/dissertation, comprehensive oral and written exams. *Entrance requirements:* For master's, GRE General Test, minimum GPA of 2.7; for doctorate, GRE General Test, minimum GPA of 3.0. Additional exam requirements/recommendations for international students: Required—TOEFL. Electronic applications accepted. *Faculty research:* Queuing analysis, simulation, inventory theory, supply chain management, mathematical programming.

Northeastern University, College of Engineering, Boston, MA 02115-5096. Offers bioengineering (MS, PhD); chemical engineering (MS, PhD); civil engineering (MS, PhD); computer engineering (PhD); computer systems engineering (MS); electrical and computer engineering (MS); electrical and computer engineering leadership (MS); electrical engineering (PhD); energy systems (MS); engineering and public policy (MS); engineering management (MS, Certificate); environmental engineering (MS); industrial engineering (MS, PhD); information assurance (PhD); information systems (MS); interdisciplinary engineering (PhD); mechanical engineering (PhD); operations research (MS); telecommunication systems management (MS). *Program availability:* Part-time, online learning. Electronic applications accepted. *Expenses:* Contact institution.

Northeastern University, College of Science, Boston, MA 02115-5096. Offers applied mathematics (MS); bioinformatics (MS); biology (PhD); biotechnology (MS); chemistry and chemical biology (MS, PhD); environmental science and policy (MS); marine and environmental sciences (PhD); marine biology (MS); mathematics (MS, PhD); operations research (MSOR); physics (MS, PhD); psychology (PhD). *Program availability:* Part-time. Terminal master's awarded for partial completion of doctoral program. *Degree requirements:* For master's, comprehensive exam (for some programs), thesis; for doctorate, comprehensive exam (for some programs), thesis/dissertation. *Entrance requirements:* For master's, GRE General Test. Electronic applications accepted. *Expenses:* Contact institution.

The Ohio State University, Graduate School, Max M. Fisher College of Business, Program in Business Operational Excellence, Columbus, OH 43210. Offers MBOE. *Program availability:* Online learning. *Students:* 24 full-time (13 women). Average age 39. In 2018, 38 master's awarded. *Entrance requirements:* For master's, GMAT if undergraduate GPA is below a 3.0, bachelor's degree from accredited university; at least 3-5 years of successful work experience in which managing processes are part of the job; recommendation by an executive sponsor. Additional exam requirements/recommendations for international students: Required—TOEFL (minimum score 550 paper-based; 79 iBT), Michigan English Language Assessment Battery (minimum score 82); Recommended—IELTS (minimum score 7). *Application deadline:* For fall and spring admission, 6/30 priority date for domestic and international students. Application fee: $60 ($70 for international students). *Unit head:* Laurie Spadaro, Program Director, 614-292-4209, E-mail: spadaro.8@osu.edu. *Application contact:* Graduate and Professional Admissions, 614-292-9444, Fax: 614-292-3895, E-mail: gpadmissions@osu.edu.
Website: http://fisher.osu.edu/mboe

Princeton University, Graduate School, School of Engineering and Applied Science, Department of Operations Research and Financial Engineering, Princeton, NJ 08544-1019. Offers M Eng, MSE, PhD. Terminal master's awarded for partial completion of doctoral program. *Degree requirements:* For master's, thesis (MSE); for doctorate, thesis/dissertation, general exam. *Entrance requirements:* For master's and doctorate, GRE General Test, official transcript(s), 3 letters of recommendation, personal statement. Additional exam requirements/recommendations for international students: Required—TOEFL. Electronic applications accepted. *Faculty research:* Applied and computational mathematics; financial mathematics; optimization, queuing theory, and machine learning; statistics and stochastic analysis; transportation and logistics.

Purdue University Fort Wayne, College of Arts and Sciences, Department of Mathematical Sciences, Fort Wayne, IN 46805-1499. Offers applied mathematics (MS); applied statistics (Certificate); mathematics (MS); operations research (MS); teaching (MAT). *Program availability:* Part-time, evening/weekend. *Entrance requirements:* For master's, minimum GPA of 3.0, major or minor in mathematics, three letters of recommendation. Additional exam requirements/recommendations for international students: Required—TOEFL (minimum score 550 paper-based; 79 iBT); Recommended—TWE. Electronic applications accepted. *Faculty research:* Eves' Theorem, paired-placements for student teaching, holomorphic maps.

Rutgers University–New Brunswick, Graduate School-New Brunswick, Program in Operations Research, Piscataway, NJ 08854-8097. Offers PhD. *Program availability:* Part-time. *Degree requirements:* For doctorate, comprehensive exam, thesis/dissertation, qualifying exam. *Entrance requirements:* For doctorate, GRE General Test, GRE Subject Test. Electronic applications accepted. *Faculty research:* Mathematical programming, combinatorial optimization, graph theory, stochastic modeling, queuing theory.

Simon Fraser University, Office of Graduate Studies and Postdoctoral Fellows, Faculty of Science, Department of Mathematics, Burnaby, BC V5A 1S6, Canada. Offers applied and computational mathematics (M Sc, PhD); mathematics (M Sc, PhD); operations research (M Sc, PhD). *Degree requirements:* For master's, thesis or alternative; for doctorate, comprehensive exam, thesis/dissertation. *Entrance requirements:* For master's, GRE General Test, GRE Subject Test (mathematics), minimum GPA of 3.0 (on scale of 4.33) or 3.33 based on last 60 credits of undergraduate courses; for doctorate, GRE General Test, GRE Subject Test (mathematics), minimum GPA of 3.5 (on scale of 4.33). Additional exam requirements/recommendations for international students: Recommended—TOEFL (minimum score 580 paper-based; 93 iBT), IELTS (minimum score 7), TWE (minimum score 5). Electronic applications accepted. *Faculty research:* Computer algebra, discrete mathematics, fluid dynamics, nonlinear partial differential equations and variation methods, numerical analysis and scientific computing.

South Dakota State University, Graduate School, Jerome J. Lohr College of Engineering, Department of Construction and Operations Management, Brookings, SD 57007. Offers operations management (MS). *Degree requirements:* For master's, comprehensive exam, thesis (for some programs), oral exam. *Entrance requirements:* Additional exam requirements/recommendations for international students: Required—TOEFL (minimum score 575 paper-based). *Faculty research:* Query, economic development, statistical process control, foreign business plans, operations management.

Southern Illinois University Edwardsville, Graduate School, College of Arts and Sciences, Department of Mathematics and Statistics, Program in Statistics and Operations Research, Edwardsville, IL 62026. Offers MS. *Program availability:* Part-time. *Degree requirements:* For master's, thesis (for some programs), special project. *Entrance requirements:* Additional exam requirements/recommendations for international students: Required—TOEFL (minimum score 550 paper-based, 79 iBT), IELTS (minimum score 6.5), Michigan Test of English Language Proficiency or PTE. Electronic applications accepted.

Southern Methodist University, Lyle School of Engineering, Department of Engineering Management, Information, and Systems, Dallas, TX 75275. Offers engineering entrepreneurship (MS); engineering management (MS, DE); information engineering and management (MSIEM); operations research (MS, PhD); systems engineering (MS). MS in engineering entrepreneurship offered in collaboration with the Cox School of Business. *Program availability:* Part-time, evening/weekend, online learning. Terminal master's awarded for partial completion of doctoral program. *Degree requirements:* For master's, thesis optional; for doctorate, thesis/dissertation, oral and written qualifying exams. *Entrance requirements:* For master's, minimum GPA of 3.0 in last 2 years; bachelor's degree in engineering, mathematics, sciences, or technical area; for doctorate, GRE General Test (operations research, engineering management), bachelor's degree in related field. Additional exam requirements/recommendations for international students: Required—TOEFL. *Faculty research:* Telecommunications, decision systems, information engineering, operations research, software.

The University of Alabama in Huntsville, School of Graduate Studies, College of Engineering, Department of Industrial and Systems Engineering and Engineering Management, Huntsville, AL 35899. Offers engineering management (MSE, PhD); industrial engineering (MSE, PhD); operations research (MSOR); systems engineering (MSE, PhD). *Program availability:* Part-time. *Faculty:* 10 full-time (2 women), 1 part-time/adjunct. *Students:* 25 full-time (10 women), 62 part-time (20 women); includes 16 minority (4 Black or African American, non-Hispanic/Latino; 3 American Indian or Alaska Native, non-Hispanic/Latino; 5 Asian, non-Hispanic/Latino; 2 Hispanic/Latino; 2 Two or more races, non-Hispanic/Latino), 17 international. Average age 33. 78 applicants, 37% accepted, 13 enrolled. In 2018, 25 master's, 1 doctorate awarded. *Degree requirements:* For master's, comprehensive exam, thesis or alternative, oral and written exams; for doctorate, comprehensive exam, thesis/dissertation, oral and written exams. *Entrance requirements:* For master's and doctorate, GRE General Test, minimum GPA of 3.0. Additional exam requirements/recommendations for international students: Required—TOEFL (minimum score 500 paper-based; 80 iBT), IELTS (minimum score 6.5). *Application deadline:* For fall admission, 7/15 priority date for domestic students, 4/1

priority date for international students; for spring admission, 11/30 priority date for domestic students, 9/1 priority date for international students. Applications are processed on a rolling basis. Application fee: $50. Electronic applications accepted. *Expenses: Tuition, area resident:* Full-time $10,632; part-time $412 per credit hour. Tuition, state resident: full-time $10,632. Tuition, nonresident: full-time $23,604; part-time $412 per credit hour. *Required fees:* $582; $582. Tuition and fees vary according to course load and program. *Financial support:* In 2018–19, 14 students received support, including 8 research assistantships with full tuition reimbursements available (averaging $7,898 per year), 6 teaching assistantships with full tuition reimbursements available (averaging $5,750 per year); career-related internships or fieldwork, Federal Work-Study, institutionally sponsored loans, scholarships/grants, health care benefits, and unspecified assistantships also available. Support available to part-time students. Financial award application deadline: 4/1; financial award applicants required to submit FAFSA. *Faculty research:* Systems engineering process, electronic manufacturing, heuristic manufacturing, teams and team development. *Unit head:* Dr. James J. Swain, Chair, 256-824-6749, Fax: 256-824-6733, E-mail: james.swain@uah.edu. *Application contact:* Kim Gray, Graduate Studies Admissions Coordinator, 256-824-6002, Fax: 256-824-6405, E-mail: deangrad@uah.edu.
Website: http://www.uah.edu/eng/departments/iseem/

University of California, Berkeley, Graduate Division, College of Engineering, Department of Industrial Engineering and Operations Research, Berkeley, CA 94720. Offers decision analytics (M Eng); industrial engineering and operations research (M Eng, MS, PhD). *Program availability:* Part-time, evening/weekend. Terminal master's awarded for partial completion of doctoral program. *Degree requirements:* For master's, comprehensive exam (for some programs), thesis (for some programs), comprehensive exam or thesis (MS); for doctorate, thesis/dissertation, qualifying exam. *Entrance requirements:* For master's and doctorate, GRE General Test, minimum GPA of 3.0, 3 letters of recommendation. Additional exam requirements/recommendations for international students: Required—TOEFL (minimum score 570 paper-based; 90 iBT). Electronic applications accepted. *Faculty research:* Mathematical programming, robotics and manufacturing, linear and nonlinear optimization, production planning and scheduling, queuing theory.

University of Colorado Denver, College of Liberal Arts and Sciences, Department of Mathematical and Statistical Sciences, Denver, CO 80217. Offers applied mathematics (MS, PhD), including applied mathematics, applied probability (MS), applied statistics (MS), computational biology (PhD), computational mathematics (PhD), discrete mathematics, finite geometry (PhD), mathematics education (PhD), mathematics of engineering and science (MS), numerical analysis, operations research (MS), optimization and operations research (PhD), probability (PhD), statistics (PhD). *Program availability:* Part-time. *Degree requirements:* For master's, comprehensive exam, thesis optional, 30 hours of course work with minimum GPA of 3.0; for doctorate, comprehensive exam, thesis/dissertation, 42 hours of course work with minimum GPA of 3.25. *Entrance requirements:* For master's, GRE General Test; GRE Subject Test in math (recommended), 30 hours of course work in mathematics (24 of which must be upper-division mathematics), bachelor's degree with minimum GPA of 3.0; for doctorate, GRE General Test; GRE Subject Test in math (recommended), 30 hours of course work in mathematics (24 of which must be upper-division mathematics), master's degree with minimum GPA of 3.25. Additional exam requirements/recommendations for international students: Required—TOEFL (minimum score 537 paper-based; 75 iBT); Recommended—IELTS (minimum score 6.5). Electronic applications accepted. *Expenses:* Tuition, state resident: full-time $6786; part-time $337 per credit hour. Tuition, nonresident: full-time $22,590; part-time $1255 per credit hour. *Required fees:* $1231; $137 per credit hour. Tuition and fees vary according to program and reciprocity agreements. *Faculty research:* Computational mathematics, computational biology, discrete mathematics and geometry, probability and statistics, optimization.

University of Delaware, College of Agriculture and Natural Resources, Department of Food and Resource Economics, Operations Research Program, Newark, DE 19716. Offers MS. *Program availability:* Part-time. *Degree requirements:* For master's, thesis, oral exam. *Entrance requirements:* For master's, GRE General Test, 3 letters of recommendation, program language/s, engineering calculus. Additional exam requirements/recommendations for international students: Required—TOEFL. Electronic applications accepted. *Faculty research:* Simulation and modeling-production scheduling and optimization, agricultural production and resource economics, transportation engineering, statistical quality control.

University of Illinois at Chicago, College of Engineering, Department of Mechanical and Industrial Engineering, Program in Industrial Engineering, Chicago, IL 60607-7128. Offers industrial engineering (MS); industrial engineering and operations research (PhD). *Program availability:* Part-time. *Degree requirements:* For doctorate, thesis/dissertation. *Entrance requirements:* For doctorate, GRE General Test, minimum GPA of 2.75. Additional exam requirements/recommendations for international students: Required—TOEFL. Electronic applications accepted. *Expenses:* Contact institution. *Faculty research:* Manufacturing information systems and manufacturing control, supply chain, logistics, optimization quality control, haptics and virtual reality, industrial automation, safety and reliability engineering, diagnostics, prognostics, controls and statistical modeling.

The University of Iowa, Graduate College, College of Engineering, Department of Industrial Engineering, Iowa City, IA 52242-1316. Offers engineering design and manufacturing (MS, PhD); healthcare systems (MS, PhD); human factors (MS, PhD); information and engineering management (MS, PhD); operations research (MS, PhD); wind energy (MS, PhD). Terminal master's awarded for partial completion of doctoral program. *Degree requirements:* For master's, thesis optional, exam; for doctorate, comprehensive exam, thesis/dissertation, final defense exam. *Entrance requirements:*

For master's and doctorate, GRE (minimum Verbal score of 153, Quantitative 151), minimum undergraduate GPA of 3.0. Additional exam requirements/recommendations for international students: Required—TOEFL (minimum score 600 paper-based; 100 iBT), IELTS (minimum score 7). Electronic applications accepted. *Faculty research:* Operations research, informatics, human factors engineering, healthcare systems, bio-manufacturing, manufacturing systems, renewable energy, human-machine interactions.

University of Massachusetts Amherst, Graduate School, College of Engineering, Department of Mechanical and Industrial Engineering, Amherst, MA 01003. Offers industrial engineering and operations research (MS, PhD); mechanical engineering (MSME, PhD). *Program availability:* Part-time. Terminal master's awarded for partial completion of doctoral program. *Degree requirements:* For master's, thesis or alternative; for doctorate, comprehensive exam, thesis/dissertation. *Entrance requirements:* For master's and doctorate, GRE General Test. Additional exam requirements/recommendations for international students: Required—TOEFL (minimum score 550 paper-based; 80 iBT), IELTS (minimum score 6.5). Electronic applications accepted.

University of Michigan, College of Engineering, Department of Industrial and Operations Engineering, Ann Arbor, MI 48109. Offers MS, MSE, PhD, MBA/MS, MBA/MSE. *Program availability:* Part-time. *Students:* 180 full-time (67 women), 12 part-time (3 women). 635 applicants, 29% accepted, 76 enrolled. In 2018, 101 master's, 10 doctorates awarded. Terminal master's awarded for partial completion of doctoral program. *Degree requirements:* For doctorate, oral defense of dissertation, preliminary exams, qualifying exam. *Entrance requirements:* For master's and doctorate, GRE General Test. Additional exam requirements/recommendations for international students: Required—TOEFL. *Application deadline:* Applications are processed on a rolling basis. Electronic applications accepted. *Financial support:* Fellowships, research assistantships, teaching assistantships, Federal Work-Study, institutionally sponsored loans, scholarships/grants, traineeships, health care benefits, and unspecified assistantships available. Financial award applicants required to submit FAFSA. *Faculty research:* Production/distribution/logistics, financial engineering and enterprise systems, ergonomics (physical and cognitive), stochastic processes, linear and nonlinear optimization, operations research. *Total annual research expenditures:* $7.3 million. *Unit head:* Brian Denton, Department Chair, 734-763-2060, Fax: 734-764-3451, E-mail: btdenton@umich.edu. *Application contact:* Matt Irelan, Graduate Student Advisor/Program Coordinator, 734-764-6480, Fax: 734-764-3451, E-mail: mirelan@umich.edu. Website: https://ioe.engin.umich.edu/

The University of North Carolina at Chapel Hill, Graduate School, College of Arts and Sciences, Department of Statistics and Operations Research, Chapel Hill, NC 27599. Offers operations research (MS, PhD); statistics (MS, PhD). *Degree requirements:* For master's, comprehensive exam, essay or thesis; for doctorate, comprehensive exam, thesis/dissertation. *Entrance requirements:* For master's and doctorate, GRE General Test, GRE Subject Test, minimum GPA of 3.0. Additional exam requirements/recommendations for international students: Required—TOEFL.

University of Southern California, Graduate School, Viterbi School of Engineering, Daniel J. Epstein Department of Industrial and Systems Engineering, Los Angeles, CA 90089. Offers digital supply chain management (MS); engineering management (MS); engineering technology communication (Graduate Certificate); health systems operations (Graduate Certificate); industrial and systems engineering (MS, PhD, Engr); manufacturing engineering (MS); operations research engineering (MS); optimization and supply chain management (Graduate Certificate); product development engineering (MS); safety systems and security (MS); systems architecting and engineering (MS, Graduate Certificate); systems safety and security (Graduate Certificate); transportation systems (Graduate Certificate); MS/MBA. *Program availability:* Part-time, evening/weekend, online learning. Terminal master's awarded for partial completion of doctoral program. *Degree requirements:* For master's, thesis optional; for doctorate, thesis/dissertation. *Entrance requirements:* For master's and doctorate, GRE General Test. Additional exam requirements/recommendations for international students: Recommended—TOEFL. Electronic applications accepted. *Faculty research:* Health systems, music cognition and retrieval, transportation and logistics, manufacturing and automation, engineering systems design, risk and economic analysis.

The University of Texas at Austin, Graduate School, Cockrell School of Engineering, Department of Mechanical Engineering, Program in Operations Research and Industrial Engineering, Austin, TX 78712-1111. Offers MS, PhD. *Entrance requirements:* For master's and doctorate, GRE General Test. Additional exam requirements/recommendations for international students: Required—TOEFL.

University of Waterloo, Graduate Studies and Postdoctoral Affairs, Faculty of Engineering, Department of Management Sciences, Waterloo, ON N2L 3G1, Canada. Offers applied operations research (MA Sc, MMS, PhD); information systems (MA Sc, MMS, PhD); management of technology (MA Sc, MMS, PhD). *Program availability:* Part-time, online learning. *Degree requirements:* For master's, research paper or thesis; for doctorate, comprehensive exam, thesis/dissertation. *Entrance requirements:* For master's, GMAT or GRE, honors degree, minimum B average, resume; for doctorate, GMAT or GRE, master's degree, minimum A- average, resume. Additional exam requirements/recommendations for international students: Required—TOEFL, IELTS, PTE. *Application deadline:* Applications are processed on a rolling basis. Application fee: $125 Canadian dollars. Electronic applications accepted. *Financial support:* Fellowships, research assistantships, teaching assistantships, career-related internships or fieldwork, and institutionally sponsored loans available. *Faculty research:* Operations research, manufacturing systems, scheduling, information systems. Website: https://uwaterloo.ca/management-sciences/

Technology and Public Policy

Arizona State University at the Tempe campus, College of Liberal Arts and Sciences, Program in Science and Technology Policy, Tempe, AZ 85287-6505. Offers MS. Fall admission only. *Degree requirements:* For master's, thesis or alternative, internship, applied project, interactive Program of Study (iPOS) submitted before completing 50 percent of required credit hours. *Entrance requirements:* For master's, GRE, bachelor's degree (or equivalent) or graduate degree from regionally-accredited college or university or of recognized standing; minimum GPA of 3.0 or equivalent in last 2 years of work leading to bachelor's degree; 3 letters of recommendation; personal statement; current resume. Additional exam requirements/recommendations for international students: Required—TOEFL, IELTS, or PTE. Electronic applications accepted. *Expenses:* Contact institution.

Carnegie Mellon University, Carnegie Institute of Technology, Department of Civil and Environmental Engineering, Pittsburgh, PA 15213. Offers advanced infrastructure

systems (MS, PhD); advanced infrastructure systems technology development and application (MS); air quality engineering and science (MS); civil and environmental engineering (MS, PhD); civil and environmental engineering/engineering and public policy (PhD); civil engineering (MS, PhD); computational mechanics (MS, PhD); computational modeling and monitoring for resilient structural and material systems (MS); energy infrastructure systems (MS); environmental engineering (MS, PhD); environmental management and science (MS, PhD); IT-based sustainable global infrastructure and construction management (MS); sustainability and green design (MS); water quality engineering and science (MS). *Program availability:* Part-time. *Faculty:* 23 full-time (5 women), 12 part-time/adjunct (3 women). *Students:* 264 full-time (109 women); includes 24 minority (6 Black or African American, non-Hispanic/Latino; 13 Asian, non-Hispanic/Latino; 5 Hispanic/Latino), 208 international. Average age 25. 630 applicants, 64% accepted, 114 enrolled. In 2018, 112 master's, 15 doctorates awarded.

Technology and Public Policy

Terminal master's awarded for partial completion of doctoral program. *Degree requirements:* For master's, thesis optional; for doctorate, comprehensive exam, thesis/dissertation, two-part qualifying exam, public defense of dissertation. *Entrance requirements:* For master's, GRE General Test, BS in engineering, science or mathematics; for doctorate, GRE General Test, BS or MS in engineering, science or mathematics. Additional exam requirements/recommendations for international students: Required—TOEFL (minimum score 84 iBT), TOEFL (minimum score 84 iBT) or IELTS (7.0). *Application deadline:* For fall admission, 1/5 priority date for domestic and international students; for spring admission, 9/15 priority date for domestic and international students. Applications are processed on a rolling basis. Application fee: $75. Electronic applications accepted. *Expenses:* Contact institution. *Financial support:* In 2018–19, 137 students received support. Fellowships with tuition reimbursements available, research assistantships with tuition reimbursements available, scholarships/grants, health care benefits, tuition waivers (full and partial), unspecified assistantships, and service assistantships available. Financial award application deadline: 1/5. *Faculty research:* Advanced infrastructure systems; environmental engineering, sustainability, and science; mechanics, materials, and computing. *Total annual research expenditures:* $7.4 million. *Unit head:* Dr. David A. Dzombak, Professor and Department Head, 412-268-2941, Fax: 412-268-7813, E-mail: dzombak@cmu.edu. *Application contact:* David A. Vey, Director of Graduate Programs, 412-268-2292, Fax: 412-268-7813, E-mail: dvey@andrew.cmu.edu.
Website: http://www.cmu.edu/cee/

Carnegie Mellon University, Carnegie Institute of Technology, Department of Engineering and Public Policy, Pittsburgh, PA 15213-3891. Offers PhD. *Degree requirements:* For doctorate, thesis/dissertation. *Entrance requirements:* For doctorate, GRE General Test, BS in physical sciences or engineering. Additional exam requirements/recommendations for international students: Required—TOEFL. *Faculty research:* Issues in energy and environmental policy, IT and telecommunications policy, risk analysis and communication, management of technological innovation, security and engineered civil systems.

Eastern Michigan University, Graduate School, College of Engineering and Technology, School of Technology and Professional Services Management, Program in Technology Studies, Ypsilanti, MI 48197. Offers MS. *Program availability:* Part-time, evening/weekend, online learning. *Students:* 9 full-time (3 women), 49 part-time (10 women); includes 16 minority (8 Black or African American, non-Hispanic/Latino; 1 American Indian or Alaska Native, non-Hispanic/Latino; 1 Asian, non-Hispanic/Latino; 2 Hispanic/Latino; 4 Two or more races, non-Hispanic/Latino), 4 international. Average age 38. 33 applicants, 61% accepted, 11 enrolled. In 2018, 37 master's awarded. *Entrance requirements:* For master's, GRE General Test, minimum GPA of 2.6. Additional exam requirements/recommendations for international students: Required—TOEFL. *Application deadline:* Applications are processed on a rolling basis. Application fee: $45. *Financial support:* Fellowships, research assistantships with full tuition reimbursements, teaching assistantships with full tuition reimbursements, career-related internships or fieldwork, Federal Work-Study, institutionally sponsored loans, scholarships/grants, tuition waivers (partial), and unspecified assistantships available. Support available to part-time students. Financial award applicants required to submit FAFSA. *Application contact:* Dr. Denise Pilato, Program Coordinator, 734-487-1167, Fax: 734-487-7690, E-mail: cot_msts@emich.edu.

The George Washington University, Elliott School of International Affairs, Program in International Science and Technology Policy, Washington, DC 20052. Offers MA, Graduate Certificate. *Program availability:* Part-time. *Students:* 20 full-time (7 women), 10 part-time (5 women); includes 8 minority (1 Black or African American, non-Hispanic/Latino; 5 Hispanic/Latino; 2 Two or more races, non-Hispanic/Latino), 3 international. Average age 29. 48 applicants, 79% accepted, 13 enrolled. In 2018, 8 master's, 2 other advanced degrees awarded. *Degree requirements:* For master's, one foreign language, capstone project. *Entrance requirements:* For master's, GRE General Test. Additional exam requirements/recommendations for international students: Required—TOEFL (minimum score 100 iBT), IELTS (minimum score 7). *Application deadline:* For fall admission, 1/15 priority date for domestic and international students; for spring admission, 10/1 for domestic students. Application fee: $75. Electronic applications accepted. *Financial support:* In 2018–19, 15 students received support. Fellowships with partial tuition reimbursements available, Federal Work-Study, and scholarships/grants available. Financial award application deadline: 1/15; financial award applicants required to submit FAFSA. *Faculty research:* Science policy, space policy, risk assessment, technology transfer, energy policy. *Unit head:* Prof. Allison Macfarlane, Director, 202-994-7292, E-mail: amacfarlane@gwu.edu. *Application contact:* Nicole A. Campbell, Director of Graduate Admissions, 202-994-7050, Fax: 202-994-9537, E-mail: esiagrad@gwu.edu.
Website: http://elliott.gwu.edu/international-science-and-technology-policy

Massachusetts Institute of Technology, School of Engineering, Institute for Data, Systems, and Society, Cambridge, MA 02139. Offers social and engineering systems (PhD); technology and policy (SM). *Degree requirements:* For master's, thesis; for doctorate, comprehensive exam, thesis/dissertation. *Entrance requirements:* For doctorate, GRE General Test. Additional exam requirements/recommendations for international students: Required—IELTS. Electronic applications accepted. *Expenses:* Tuition: Full-time $51,520; part-time $800 per credit hour. *Required fees:* $312. *Faculty research:* Information theory and decision systems; sociotechnical systems; statistics and data science; network science; critical infrastructures; health care delivery; humans and technology; policy and standards; social behavior; uncertainty, risk, and dynamics.

Massachusetts Institute of Technology, School of Humanities, Arts, and Social Sciences, Program in Science, Technology, and Society, Cambridge, MA 02139. Offers history, anthropology, and science, technology and society (PhD). *Degree requirements:* For doctorate, one foreign language, comprehensive exam, thesis/dissertation. *Entrance requirements:* For doctorate, GRE General Test. Additional exam requirements/recommendations for international students: Required—TOEFL, IELTS. Electronic applications accepted. *Expenses:* Tuition: Full-time $51,520; part-time $800 per credit hour. *Required fees:* $312. *Faculty research:* History of science; history of technology; sociology of science and technology; anthropology of science and technology; science, technology, and society.

Rensselaer Polytechnic Institute, Graduate School, School of Humanities, Arts, and Social Sciences, Program in Science and Technology Studies, Troy, NY 12180-3590. Offers MS, PhD. *Faculty:* 15 full-time (5 women), 1 part-time/adjunct (0 women). *Students:* 21 full-time (10 women), 1 part-time (0 women); includes 1 minority (Hispanic/Latino), 4 international. Average age 29. 24 applicants, 50% accepted, 7 enrolled. In 2018, 2 master's, 5 doctorates awarded. Terminal master's awarded for partial

completion of doctoral program. *Degree requirements:* For master's, thesis (for some programs); for doctorate, comprehensive exam, thesis/dissertation. *Entrance requirements:* For master's and doctorate, GRE, writing sample. Additional exam requirements/recommendations for international students: Required—TOEFL (minimum score 600 paper-based; 100 iBT), IELTS (minimum score 7), PTE (minimum score 68). *Application deadline:* For fall admission, 1/1 priority date for domestic and international students; for spring admission, 8/15 priority date for domestic and international students. Applications are processed on a rolling basis. Application fee: $75. Electronic applications accepted. *Financial support:* In 2018–19, research assistantships (averaging $23,000 per year), teaching assistantships (averaging $23,000 per year) were awarded; fellowships also available. Financial award application deadline: 1/1. *Faculty research:* Policy studies, science studies, technology studies. *Total annual research expenditures:* $30,324. *Unit head:* Dr. Atsushi Akera, Graduate Program Director, 518-276-2314, E-mail: akeraa@rpi.edu. *Application contact:* Jarron Decker, Director of Graduate Admissions, 518-276-6216, Fax: 518-276-4072, E-mail: gradadmissions@rpi.edu.
Website: http://www.sts.rpi.edu/pl/graduate-programs-sts

Rochester Institute of Technology, Graduate Enrollment Services, College of Liberal Arts, Department of Public Policy, MS Program in Science, Technology and Public Policy, Rochester, NY 14623-5603. Offers MS. *Program availability:* Part-time. *Students:* 4 full-time (2 women), 2 part-time (both women), 2 international. Average age 27. 3 applicants, 33% accepted, 1 enrolled. In 2018, 7 master's awarded. *Degree requirements:* For master's, thesis or alternative, Thesis or comprehensive exam plus 2 graduate electives. *Entrance requirements:* For master's, GRE, minimum GPA of 3.0 (recommended), completed course work in calculus and statistics, two writing samples, two letters of recommendation. Additional exam requirements/recommendations for international students: Required—TOEFL (minimum score 570 paper-based; 88 iBT), IELTS (minimum score 6.5), PTE (minimum score 61). *Application deadline:* For fall admission, 2/15 priority date for domestic and international students; for spring admission, 12/15 priority date for domestic and international students. Applications are processed on a rolling basis. Application fee: $65. Electronic applications accepted. *Expenses:* Contact institution. *Financial support:* In 2018–19, 9 students received support. Research assistantships with partial tuition reimbursements available, teaching assistantships with partial tuition reimbursements available, career-related internships or fieldwork, scholarships/grants, and unspecified assistantships available. Support available to part-time students. Financial award applicants required to submit FAFSA. *Faculty research:* Environmental management, innovation, and policy; technological innovation, environmental economics and policy; alternative energy and climate change; cybersecurity economics and Internet policy; e-democracy and digital government. *Unit head:* Dr. Eric Hittinger, Graduate Program Director, E-mail: eshgpt@rit.edu. *Application contact:* Diane Ellison, Senior Associate Vice President, Graduate Enrollment Services, 585-475-2229, Fax: 585-475-7164, E-mail: gradinfo@rit.edu.
Website: https://www.rit.edu/study/science-technology-and-public-policy-ms

University of Minnesota, Twin Cities Campus, Graduate School, Humphrey School of Public Affairs, Program in Science, Technology, and Environmental Policy, Minneapolis, MN 55455. Offers MS, JD/MS. *Program availability:* Part-time. *Degree requirements:* For master's, thesis. *Entrance requirements:* For master's, GRE General Test, undergraduate training in the biological or physical sciences or engineering, minimum undergraduate GPA of 3.0. Additional exam requirements/recommendations for international students: Required—TOEFL (minimum score 600 paper-based; 100 iBT), IELTS (minimum score 7). Electronic applications accepted. *Expenses:* Contact institution. *Faculty research:* Economics, history, philosophy, and politics of science and technology; organization and management of science and technology.

University of South Africa, College of Human Sciences, Pretoria, South Africa. Offers adult education (M Ed); African languages (MA, PhD); African politics (MA, PhD); Afrikaans (MA, PhD); ancient history (MA, PhD); ancient Near Eastern studies (MA, PhD); anthropology (MA, PhD); applied linguistics (MA); Arabic (MA, PhD); archaeology (MA); art history (MA); Biblical archaeology (MA); Biblical studies (M Th, D Th, PhD); Christian spirituality (M Th, D Th); church history (M Th, D Th); classical studies (MA, PhD); clinical psychology (MA); communication (MA, PhD); comparative education (M Ed, Ed D); consulting psychology (D Admin, D Com, PhD); curriculum studies (M Ed, Ed D); development studies (M Admin, MA, D Admin, PhD); didactics (M Ed, Ed D); education (M Tech); education management (M Ed, Ed D); educational psychology (M Ed); English (MA); environmental education (M Ed); French (MA, PhD); German (MA, PhD); Greek (MA); guidance and counseling (M Ed); health studies (MA, PhD), including health sciences education (MA), health services management (MA), medical and surgical nursing science (critical care general) (MA), midwifery and neonatal nursing science (MA), trauma and emergency care (MA); history (MA, PhD); history of education (Ed D); inclusive education (M Ed, Ed D); information and communications technology policy and regulation (MA); information science (MA, MIS, PhD); international politics (MA, PhD); Islamic studies (MA, PhD); Italian (MA, PhD); Judaica (MA, PhD); linguistics (MA, PhD); mathematical education (M Ed); mathematics education (MA); missiology (M Th, D Th); modern Hebrew (MA, PhD); musicology (MA, MMus, D Mus, PhD); natural science education (M Ed); New Testament (M Th, D Th); Old Testament (D Th); pastoral therapy (M Th, D Th); philosophy (MA); philosophy of education (M Ed, Ed D); politics (MA, PhD); Portuguese (MA, PhD); practical theology (M Th, D Th); psychology (MA, MS, PhD); psychology of education (M Ed, Ed D); public health (MA); religious studies (MA, D Th, PhD); Romance languages (MA); Russian (MA, PhD); Semitic languages (MA, PhD); social behavior studies in HIV/AIDS (MA); social science (mental health) (MA); social science in development studies (MA); social science in psychology (MA); social science in social work (MA); social science in sociology (MA); social work (MSW, DSW, PhD); socio-education (M Ed, Ed D); sociolinguistics (MA); sociology (MA, PhD); Spanish (MA, PhD); systematic theology (M Th, D Th); TESOL (teaching English to speakers of other languages) (MA); theological ethics (M Th, D Th); theory of literature (MA, PhD); urban ministries (D Th); urban ministry (M Th).

The University of Texas at Austin, Graduate School, McCombs School of Business, Program in Technology Commercialization, Austin, TX 78712-1111. Offers MS. Twelve-month program, beginning in May, with classes held every other Friday and Saturday. *Program availability:* Evening/weekend, online learning. *Degree requirements:* For master's, year-long global teaming project. *Entrance requirements:* For master's, GRE General Test or GMAT. Additional exam requirements/recommendations for international students: Required—TOEFL (minimum score 550 paper-based; 79 iBT). Electronic applications accepted. *Expenses:* Contact institution. *Faculty research:* Technology transfer; entrepreneurship; commercialization; research, development and innovation.

Section 16
Materials Sciences and Engineering

This section contains a directory of institutions offering graduate work in materials sciences and engineering, followed by an in-depth entry submitted by an institution that chose to prepare a detailed program description. Additional information about programs listed in the directory but not augmented by an in-depth entry may be obtained by writing directly to the dean of a graduate school or chair of a department at the address given in the directory.

For programs offering related work, see also in this book *Agricultural Engineering and Bioengineering, Biomedical Engineering and Biotechnology, Engineering and Applied Sciences,* and *Geological, Mineral/Mining, and Petroleum Engineering.* In another guide in this series:

Graduate Programs in the Physical Sciences, Mathematics, Agricultural Sciences, the Environment & Natural Resources
  See *Chemistry* and *Geosciences*

CONTENTS

Program Directories

Ceramic Sciences and Engineering

Alfred University, Graduate School, College of Ceramics, Inamori School of Engineering, Alfred, NY 14802. Offers biomaterials engineering (MS); ceramic engineering (MS, PhD); electrical engineering (MS); glass science (MS, PhD); materials science and engineering (MS, PhD); mechanical engineering (MS). *Program availability:* Part-time. *Degree requirements:* For master's, thesis; for doctorate, thesis/dissertation. *Entrance requirements:* Additional exam requirements/recommendations for international students: Required—TOEFL (minimum score 590 paper-based; 90 iBT), IELTS (minimum score 6.5). Electronic applications accepted. *Expenses:* Contact institution. *Faculty research:* X-ray diffraction, biomaterials and polymers, thin-film processing, electronic and optical ceramics, solid-state chemistry.

Missouri University of Science and Technology, Department of Materials Science and Engineering, Rolla, MO 65401. Offers ceramic engineering (MS, PhD); materials science and engineering (MS, PhD); metallurgical engineering (MS, PhD). *Degree requirements:* For master's, thesis optional; for doctorate, comprehensive exam. *Entrance requirements:* For master's, GRE (minimum combined score 1100, 600 verbal, 3.5 writing); for doctorate, GRE (minimum score: quantitative 600, writing 3.5). Additional exam requirements/recommendations for international students: Required—TOEFL (minimum score 570 paper-based). Electronic applications accepted. *Expenses:* Tuition, state resident: full-time $7545.60; part-time $419.20 per credit hour. Tuition, nonresident: full-time $22,169; part-time $1231.60 per credit hour. *International tuition:* $23,518.80 full-time. *Required fees:* $4523.05. Full-time tuition and fees vary according to course load, campus/location, program and reciprocity agreements.

Electronic Materials

Colorado School of Mines, Office of Graduate Studies, Department of Metallurgical and Materials Engineering, Golden, CO 80401. Offers materials science (MS, PhD); metallurgical and materials engineering (ME, MS, PhD). *Program availability:* Part-time. *Faculty:* 36 full-time (6 women), 10 part-time/adjunct (1 woman). *Students:* 115 full-time (35 women), 10 part-time (4 women); includes 13 minority (1 Asian, non-Hispanic/Latino; 8 Hispanic/Latino; 4 Two or more races, non-Hispanic/Latino), 29 international. Average age 27. 153 applicants, 50% accepted, 41 enrolled. In 2018, 21 master's, 15 doctorates awarded. *Degree requirements:* For master's, thesis (for some programs); for doctorate, comprehensive exam, thesis/dissertation. *Entrance requirements:* For master's and doctorate, GRE General Test. Additional exam requirements/recommendations for international students: Required—TOEFL (minimum score 550 paper-based; 79 iBT). *Application deadline:* For fall admission, 12/15 priority date for domestic and international students; for spring admission, 9/1 priority date for domestic and international students. Application fee: $60 ($80 for international students). Electronic applications accepted. *Expenses:* Tuition, state resident: full-time $16,650; part-time $925 per contact hour. Tuition, nonresident: full-time $36,270; part-time $2015 per contact hour. *International tuition:* $36,270 full-time. *Required fees:* $2314; $2314 per semester. *Financial support:* In 2018–19, 81 research assistantships with full tuition reimbursements, 15 teaching assistantships with full tuition reimbursements were awarded; fellowships, scholarships/grants, health care benefits, and unspecified assistantships also available. Financial award application deadline: 12/15; financial award applicants required to submit FAFSA. *Unit head:* Dr. Angus Rockett, Head, 303-384-2244, E-mail: arockett@mines.edu. *Application contact:* Megan Steelman, Program Assistant, 303-273-3640, E-mail: msteelman@mines.edu.
Website: http://metallurgy.mines.edu

Princeton University, Princeton Institute for the Science and Technology of Materials (PRISM), Princeton, NJ 08544-1019. Offers materials (PhD).

University of Arkansas, Graduate School, Interdisciplinary Program in Microelectronics and Photonics, Fayetteville, AR 72701. Offers MS, PhD. In 2018, 5 master's, 6 doctorates awarded. *Application deadline:* For fall admission, 8/1 for domestic students, 4/1 for international students; for spring admission, 12/1 for domestic students, 10/1 for international students; for summer admission, 4/15 for domestic students, 3/1 for international students. Applications are processed on a rolling basis. Application fee: $60. Electronic applications accepted. *Financial support:* In 2018–19, 25 research assistantships, 4 teaching assistantships were awarded; fellowships with tuition reimbursements also available. Financial award application deadline: 4/1; financial award applicants required to submit FAFSA. *Unit head:* Dr. Rick Wise, Director, 479-575-2875, E-mail: rickwise@uark.edu. *Application contact:* Dr. Rick Wise, Director, 479-575-2875, E-mail: rickwise@uark.edu.
Website: https://microelectronics-photonics.uark.edu/

University of Memphis, Graduate School, Herff College of Engineering, Department of Engineering Technology, Memphis, TN 38152. Offers applied lean leadership (Graduate Certificate); engineering technology (MS). *Program availability:* Part-time, evening/weekend. *Students:* 7 part-time (2 women); includes 3 minority (all Black or African American, non-Hispanic/Latino). Average age 35. 9 applicants, 89% accepted, 2 enrolled. In 2018, 1 master's, 3 other advanced degrees awarded. *Degree requirements:* For master's, comprehensive exam, thesis optional. *Entrance requirements:* For master's, GRE General Test, GMAT, MAT, three letters of recommendation; for Graduate Certificate, letter of intent. Additional exam requirements/recommendations for international students: Required—TOEFL (minimum score 550 paper-based; 70 iBT). *Application deadline:* For fall admission, 8/1 for domestic students; for spring admission, 12/1 for domestic students. Applications are processed on a rolling basis. Application fee: $35 ($60 for international students). Electronic applications accepted. *Expenses: Tuition, area resident:* Full-time $10,240; part-time $503 per credit hour. Tuition, state resident: full-time $10,464. Tuition, nonresident: full-time $20,224; part-time $991 per credit hour. *Required fees:* $850; $106 per credit hour. *Financial support:* Research assistantships with full tuition reimbursements, career-related internships or fieldwork, Federal Work-Study, scholarships/grants, and unspecified assistantships available. Financial award application deadline: 2/1; financial award applicants required to submit FAFSA. *Faculty research:* Teacher education services-technology education; flexible manufacturing control systems; embedded, dedicated, and real-time computer systems; network, Internet, and Web-based programming; analog and digital electronic communication systems. *Unit head:* Scott Southall, Chair, 901-678-3980, Fax: 901-678-4180, E-mail: ssouthll@memphis.edu. *Application contact:* Carl Williams, Graduate Program Coordinator, 901-678-3320, Fax: 901-678-4180, E-mail: crwillia@memphis.edu.
Website: http://www.memphis.edu/et

Wayne State University, College of Engineering, Division of Engineering Technology, Detroit, MI 48202. Offers MSET. *Faculty:* 4. *Students:* 10 full-time (0 women), 8 part-time (1 woman); includes 7 minority (5 Black or African American, non-Hispanic/Latino; 1 Asian, non-Hispanic/Latino; 1 Hispanic/Latino), 4 international. Average age 35. 23 applicants, 57% accepted, 6 enrolled. In 2018, 6 master's awarded. *Degree requirements:* For master's, thesis (for some programs), project. *Entrance requirements:* For master's, bachelor's degree in engineering technology or related field with minimum GPA of 3.0, 2 letters of recommendation, preliminary proposal for intended plan of study. Additional exam requirements/recommendations for international students: Required—TOEFL (minimum score 550 paper-based; 79 iBT), TWE (minimum score 5.5), Michigan English Language Assessment Battery (minimum score 85); Recommended—IELTS (minimum score 6.5). *Application deadline:* For fall admission, 6/1 priority date for domestic students, 5/1 priority date for international students; for winter admission, 10/1 priority date for domestic students, 9/1 priority date for international students; for spring admission, 2/1 priority date for domestic students, 1/1 priority date for international students. Applications are processed on a rolling basis. Application fee: $50. Electronic applications accepted. *Expenses:* Contact institution. *Financial support:* In 2018–19, 7 students received support. Career-related internships or fieldwork and scholarships/grants available. Financial award applicants required to submit FAFSA. *Faculty research:* Combustion, control systems, autonomous vehicle technology, industrial robots kinematics, hybrid and electric vehicle modeling and analysis, manufacturing systems, vehicle networking, and machine vision and image processing. *Unit head:* Dr. Ece Yaprak, Division Chair, 313-577-0875, E-mail: yaprak@eng.wayne.edu. *Application contact:* Ellen Cope, Graduate Program Coordinator, 313-577-0409, E-mail: escope@wayne.edu.
Website: http://engineering.wayne.edu/et/

Materials Engineering

Alabama Agricultural and Mechanical University, School of Graduate Studies, College of Engineering, Technology, and Physical Sciences, Department of Mechanical and Civil Engineering, Huntsville, AL 35811. Offers material engineering (M Eng), including civil engineering, mechanical engineering.

Arizona State University at the Tempe campus, Ira A. Fulton Schools of Engineering, School for Engineering of Matter, Transport and Energy, Tempe, AZ 85281. Offers aerospace engineering (MS, PhD); chemical engineering (MS, PhD); materials science and engineering (MS, PhD); mechanical engineering (MS, PhD); solar energy engineering and commercialization (PSM). *Program availability:* Part-time, evening/weekend, online learning. Terminal master's awarded for partial completion of doctoral program. *Degree requirements:* For master's, thesis and oral defense (MS); applied project or comprehensive exam (MSE); interactive Program of Study (iPOS) submitted before completing 50 percent of required credit hours; for doctorate, comprehensive exam, thesis/dissertation, interactive Program of Study (iPOS) submitted before completing 50 percent of required credit hours. *Entrance requirements:* For master's, GRE, minimum GPA of 3.0 or equivalent in last 2 years of work leading to bachelor's degree; for doctorate, GRE, minimum GPA of 3.0 in last 2 years of work leading to bachelor's degree. Additional exam requirements/recommendations for international students: Required—TOEFL, IELTS, or PTE. Electronic applications accepted. *Expenses:* Contact institution. *Faculty research:* Electronic materials and packaging, materials for energy (batteries), adaptive/intelligent materials and structures, multiscale fluid mechanics, membranes, therapeutics and bioseparations, flexible structures, nanostructured materials, micro-/nano-transport.

Auburn University, Graduate School, Ginn College of Engineering, Department of Mechanical Engineering, Program in Materials Engineering, Auburn University, AL 36849. Offers M Mtl E, MS, PhD. *Degree requirements:* For master's, thesis (MS), oral exam; for doctorate, one foreign language, thesis/dissertation. *Entrance requirements:* For master's and doctorate, GRE General Test. Electronic applications accepted. *Expenses:* Tuition, state resident: full-time $11,282; part-time $535 per credit hour. Tuition, nonresident: full-time $30,542; part-time $1605 per credit hour. *Required fees:* $826 per semester. Tuition and fees vary according to degree level and program. *Faculty research:* Smart materials.

Binghamton University, State University of New York, Graduate School, Materials Science and Engineering Program, Binghamton, NY 13902-6000. Offers MS, PhD. *Program availability:* Part-time, online learning. *Degree requirements:* For master's, thesis; for doctorate, comprehensive exam, thesis/dissertation. *Entrance requirements:* For master's and doctorate, GRE General Test. Additional exam requirements/recommendations for international students: Required—TOEFL (minimum score 550 paper-based; 80 iBT). Electronic applications accepted. *Expenses:* Contact institution.

Boise State University, College of Engineering, Micron School of Materials Science and Engineering, Boise, ID 83725-0399. Offers materials science and engineering (M Engr, MS, PhD). Terminal master's awarded for partial completion of doctoral program. *Degree requirements:* For master's, comprehensive exam, thesis (for some programs). *Entrance requirements:* For master's, GRE General Test. Additional exam requirements/recommendations for international students: Required—TOEFL (minimum score 550 paper-based; 80 iBT), IELTS (minimum score 6). Electronic applications accepted.

Boston University, College of Engineering, Division of Materials Science and Engineering, Brookline, MA 02215. Offers materials science and engineering (M Eng, MS, PhD). *Program availability:* Part-time. *Students:* 91 full-time (33 women), 9 part-time (1 woman); includes 8 minority (1 Black or African American, non-Hispanic/Latino; 5 Asian, non-Hispanic/Latino; 2 Two or more races, non-Hispanic/Latino), 72 international. Average age 24. 290 applicants, 53% accepted, 24 enrolled. In 2018, 22 master's, 6 doctorates awarded. Terminal master's awarded for partial completion of doctoral program. *Degree requirements:* For master's, thesis (for some programs); for doctorate, comprehensive exam, thesis/dissertation. *Entrance requirements:* For master's and doctorate, GRE General Test. Additional exam requirements/recommendations for international students: Required—TOEFL (minimum score 90 iBT), IELTS (minimum score 7). *Financial support:* Application deadline: 1/15. *Faculty research:* Biomaterials, electronic and photonic materials, materials for energy and environment, nanomaterials. *Unit head:* Dr. David Bishop, Division Head, 617-353-8899, Fax: 617-353-5548, E-mail: djb1@bu.edu. *Application contact:* Dr. David Bishop, Division Head, 617-353-8899, Fax: 617-353-5548, E-mail: djb1@bu.edu.
Website: http://www.bu.edu/mse/

California State University, Northridge, Graduate Studies, College of Engineering and Computer Science, Department of Manufacturing Systems Engineering and Management, Northridge, CA 91330. Offers engineering automation (MS); engineering management (MS); manufacturing systems engineering (MS); materials engineering (MS). *Program availability:* Online learning. *Entrance requirements:* For master's, GRE (if cumulative undergraduate GPA less than 3.0).

Carleton University, Faculty of Graduate Studies, Faculty of Engineering and Design, Department of Mechanical and Aerospace Engineering, Ottawa, ON K1S 5B6, Canada. Offers aerospace engineering (M Eng, MA Sc, PhD); materials engineering (M Eng, MA Sc); mechanical engineering (M Eng, MA Sc, PhD). *Degree requirements:* For master's, thesis optional; for doctorate, thesis/dissertation. *Entrance requirements:* For master's, honors degree; for doctorate, MA Sc or M Eng. Additional exam requirements/recommendations for international students: Required—TOEFL. *Faculty research:* Thermal fluids engineering, heat transfer, vehicle engineering.

Carnegie Mellon University, Carnegie Institute of Technology, Department of Materials Science and Engineering, Pittsburgh, PA 15213-3891. Offers MS, PhD. *Program availability:* Part-time. Terminal master's awarded for partial completion of doctoral program. *Degree requirements:* For master's, exam; for doctorate, thesis/dissertation, qualifying exam. *Entrance requirements:* For master's and doctorate, GRE General Test. Additional exam requirements/recommendations for international students: Required—TOEFL. *Faculty research:* Materials characterization, process metallurgy, high strength alloys, growth kinetics, ceramics.

Case Western Reserve University, School of Graduate Studies, Case School of Engineering, Department of Materials Science and Engineering, Cleveland, OH 44106. Offers materials science and engineering (MS, PhD). *Program availability:* Part-time, online learning. *Faculty:* 12 full-time (1 woman). *Students:* 28 full-time (7 women), 6 part-time (3 women); includes 5 minority (all Asian, non-Hispanic/Latino), 14 international. In 2018, 13 master's, 5 doctorates awarded. Terminal master's awarded for partial completion of doctoral program. *Degree requirements:* For master's, thesis (for some programs); for doctorate, thesis/dissertation, qualifying exam, teaching experience. *Entrance requirements:* For master's and doctorate, GRE General Test. Additional exam requirements/recommendations for international students: Required—TOEFL. *Application deadline:* For fall admission, 2/15 priority date for domestic students; for spring admission, 9/15 for domestic students. Applications are processed on a rolling basis. Application fee: $50. *Expenses: Tuition:* Full-time $45,168; part-time $1939 per credit hour. *Required fees:* $36; $18 per semester. $18 per semester. *Financial support:* In 2018–19, 23 students received support, including 1 fellowship with tuition reimbursement available, 22 research assistantships with tuition reimbursements available. Financial award application deadline: 4/30; financial award applicants required to submit FAFSA. *Faculty research:* Surface hardening of steels and other alloys, chemistry and structure of surfaces, microstructural and mechanical property characterization, materials for energy applications, thermodynamics and kinetics of materials, performance and reliability of materials. *Total annual research expenditures:* $4.2 million. *Unit head:* Dr. Frank Ernst, Department Chair, 216-368-0611, Fax: 216-368-4224, E-mail: emse.info@case.edu. *Application contact:* Theresa Claytor, Student Affairs Coordinator, 216-368-8555, Fax: 216-368-8555, E-mail: esme.info@case.edu.
Website: http://engineering.case.edu/emse/

The Catholic University of America, School of Engineering, Department of Materials Science and Engineering, Washington, DC 20064. Offers MS. *Program availability:* Part-time. *Faculty:* 1 full-time (0 women), 2 part-time/adjunct (0 women). *Students:* 5 part-time (2 women); includes 1 minority (Black or African American, non-Hispanic/Latino). Average age 27. 2 applicants, 100% accepted, 1 enrolled. In 2018, 6 master's awarded. *Degree requirements:* For master's, thesis optional. *Entrance requirements:* For master's, GRE (minimum score 1250), minimum GPA of 3.0, statement of purpose, official copies of academic transcripts. Additional exam requirements/recommendations for international students: Required—TOEFL (minimum score 550 paper-based; 80 iBT). *Application deadline:* For fall admission, 7/15 for domestic students, 7/1 for international students; for spring admission, 11/15 for domestic students, 11/1 for international students. Applications are processed on a rolling basis. Application fee: $55. Electronic applications accepted. *Expenses:* Contact institution. *Financial support:* Fellowships, research assistantships, teaching assistantships, Federal Work-Study, scholarships/grants, tuition waivers (full and partial), and unspecified assistantships available. Financial award application deadline: 2/1; financial award applicants required to submit FAFSA. *Faculty research:* Nanotechnology, biomaterials, magnetic and optical materials, glass, ceramics, and metallurgy processing and instrumentation. *Unit head:* Mel Williams, Director, 202-319-5191, Fax: 202-319-4469, E-mail: williamsme@cua.edu. *Application contact:* Dr. Steven Brown, Director of Graduate Admissions, 202-319-5057, Fax: 202-319-6533, E-mail: cua-admissions@cua.edu.
Website: https://engineering.catholic.edu/materials-science/index.html

Clarkson University, Wallace H. Coulter School of Engineering, Program in Materials Science and Engineering, Potsdam, NY 13699. Offers PhD. *Students:* 5 full-time (1 woman); includes 1 minority (Asian, non-Hispanic/Latino), 4 international. 14 applicants, 50% accepted, 1 enrolled. *Degree requirements:* For doctorate, comprehensive exam, thesis/dissertation. *Entrance requirements:* For doctorate, GRE. Additional exam requirements/recommendations for international students: Required—TOEFL (minimum score 550 paper-based, 80 iBT) or IELTS (6.5). *Application deadline:* Applications are processed on a rolling basis. Application fee: $50. Electronic applications accepted. *Expenses: Tuition:* Full-time $24,984; part-time $1388 per credit hour. *Required fees:* $225. Tuition and fees vary according to campus/location and program. *Financial support:* Scholarships/grants and unspecified assistantships available. *Unit head:* Dr. Silvana Andreescu, Professor / Egon Matijevic Chair of Chemistry / Co-Director of CAMP, 315-268-2394, E-mail: wjemison@clarkson.edu. *Application contact:* Dan Capogna, Director of Graduate Admissions & Recruitment, 518-631-9910, E-mail: graduate@clarkson.edu.
Website: https://www.clarkson.edu/academics/graduate

Clemson University, Graduate School, College of Engineering, Computing and Applied Sciences, Department of Materials Science and Engineering, Clemson, SC 29634. Offers MS, PhD. *Program availability:* Part-time. *Faculty:* 16 full-time (2 women). *Students:* 53 full-time (17 women), 5 part-time (0 women); includes 3 minority (1 Black or African American, non-Hispanic/Latino; 1 Asian, non-Hispanic/Latino; 1 Hispanic/Latino), 32 international. Average age 26. 109 applicants, 29% accepted, 15 enrolled. In 2018, 6 master's, 9 doctorates awarded. Terminal master's awarded for partial completion of doctoral program. *Degree requirements:* For master's, thesis; for doctorate, comprehensive exam, thesis/dissertation. *Entrance requirements:* For master's and doctorate, GRE General Test, unofficial transcripts, letters of recommendation. Additional exam requirements/recommendations for international students: Required—TOEFL (minimum score 80 paper-based; 80 iBT); Recommended—IELTS (minimum score 6.5), TSE (minimum score 54). *Application deadline:* For fall admission, 2/1 priority date for domestic and international students; for spring admission, 9/1 priority date for domestic and international students. Applications are processed on a rolling basis. Application fee: $80 ($90 for international students). Electronic applications accepted. *Expenses:* $6823 per semester full-time resident, $14023 per semester full-time non-resident, $833 per credit hour part-time resident, $1731 per credit hour part-time non-resident, online $1264 per credit hour, $4938 doctoral programs resident, $10405 doctoral programs non-resident, $1144 full-time graduate assistant, other fees may apply per session. *Financial support:* In 2018–19, 52 students received support, including 2 fellowships with full and partial tuition reimbursements available (averaging $1,000 per year), 28 research assistantships with full and partial tuition reimbursements available (averaging $20,518 per year); career-related internships or fieldwork and unspecified assistantships also available. Financial award application deadline: 2/1. *Faculty research:* Polymers, ceramics, nanoparticles, biomimetic materials, optical fibers. *Total annual research expenditures:* $2.5 million. *Unit head:* Dr. Kyle Brinkman, Department Chair, 864-656-1405, E-mail: ksbrink@clemson.edu. *Application contact:* Dr. Igor Luzinov, Graduate Program Coordinator, 864-656-5958, E-mail: luzinov@clemson.edu.
Website: https://www.clemson.edu/cecas/departments/mse/index.html

Colorado School of Mines, Office of Graduate Studies, Department of Metallurgical and Materials Engineering, Golden, CO 80401. Offers materials science (MS, PhD); metallurgical and materials engineering (ME, MS, PhD). *Program availability:* Part-time. *Faculty:* 36 full-time (6 women), 10 part-time/adjunct (1 woman). *Students:* 115 full-time (35 women), 10 part-time (4 women); includes 13 minority (1 Asian, non-Hispanic/Latino; 8 Hispanic/Latino; 4 Two or more races, non-Hispanic/Latino), 29 international. Average age 27. 153 applicants, 50% accepted, 41 enrolled. In 2018, 21 master's, 15 doctorates awarded. *Degree requirements:* For master's, thesis (for some programs); for doctorate, comprehensive exam, thesis/dissertation. *Entrance requirements:* For master's and doctorate, GRE General Test. Additional exam requirements/recommendations for international students: Required—TOEFL (minimum score 550 paper-based; 79 iBT). *Application deadline:* For fall admission, 12/15 priority date for domestic and international students; for spring admission, 9/1 priority date for domestic and international students. Application fee: $60 ($80 for international students). Electronic applications accepted. *Expenses:* Tuition, state resident: full-time $16,650; part-time $925 per contact hour. Tuition, nonresident: full-time $36,270; part-time $2015 per contact hour. *International tuition:* $36,270 full-time. *Required fees:* $2314; $2314 per semester. *Financial support:* In 2018–19, 81 research assistantships with full tuition reimbursements, 15 teaching assistantships with full tuition reimbursements were awarded; fellowships, scholarships/grants, health care benefits, and unspecified assistantships also available. Financial award application deadline: 12/15; financial award applicants required to submit FAFSA. *Unit head:* Dr. Angus Rockett, Head, 303-384-2244, E-mail: arockett@mines.edu. *Application contact:* Megan Steelman, Program Assistant, 303-273-3640, E-mail: msteelman@mines.edu.
Website: http://metallurgy.mines.edu

Columbia University, Fu Foundation School of Engineering and Applied Science, Department of Applied Physics and Applied Mathematics, New York, NY 10027. Offers applied mathematics (MS, Eng Sc D, PhD); applied physics (MS, Eng Sc D, PhD); materials science and engineering (MS, Eng Sc D, PhD); medical physics (MS). *Program availability:* Part-time, online learning. Terminal master's awarded for partial completion of doctoral program. *Degree requirements:* For master's, comprehensive exam; for doctorate, thesis/dissertation, qualifying exam. *Entrance requirements:* For master's, GRE General Test, GRE Subject Test (strongly recommended); for doctorate, GRE General Test, GRE Subject Test (applied physics). Additional exam requirements/recommendations for international students: Required—TOEFL, IELTS, PTE. Electronic applications accepted. *Faculty research:* Plasma physics and fusion energy; optical and laser physics; atmospheric, oceanic and earth physics; applied mathematics; solid state science and processing of materials, their properties, and their structure; medical physics.

Cornell University, Graduate School, Graduate Fields of Engineering, Field of Materials Science and Engineering, Ithaca, NY 14853. Offers materials engineering (M Eng, PhD); materials science (M Eng, PhD). *Degree requirements:* For doctorate, comprehensive exam, thesis/dissertation. *Entrance requirements:* For master's and doctorate, GRE General Test, 3 letters of recommendation. Additional exam requirements/recommendations for international students: Required—TOEFL (minimum score 550 paper-based; 77 iBT). Electronic applications accepted. *Faculty research:* Ceramics, complex fluids, glass, metals, polymers semiconductors.

Dartmouth College, Thayer School of Engineering, Program in Materials Sciences and Engineering, Hanover, NH 03755. Offers MS, PhD. *Degree requirements:* For master's, thesis; for doctorate, thesis/dissertation, candidacy oral exam. *Entrance requirements:* For master's and doctorate, GRE General Test. *Faculty research:* Electronic and magnetic materials, microstructural evolution, biomaterials and nanostructures, laser-material interactions, nanocomposites.

Drexel University, College of Engineering, Department of Materials Engineering, Philadelphia, PA 19104-2875. Offers MS, PhD. *Program availability:* Part-time, evening/weekend. Terminal master's awarded for partial completion of doctoral program. *Degree requirements:* For master's, thesis or alternative; for doctorate, thesis/dissertation. *Entrance requirements:* For master's, minimum GPA of 3.0; for doctorate, minimum GPA of 3.0, MS. Additional exam requirements/recommendations for international students: Required—TOEFL. Electronic applications accepted. *Faculty research:* Composite science; polymer and biomedical engineering; solidification; near net shape processing, including powder metallurgy.

Duke University, Graduate School, Pratt School of Engineering, Master of Engineering Program, Durham, NC 27708-0271. Offers biomedical engineering (M Eng); civil engineering (M Eng); computational mechanics and scientific computing (M Eng); electrical and computer engineering (M Eng); environmental engineering (M Eng); materials science and engineering (M Eng); mechanical engineering (M Eng); photonics and optical sciences (M Eng); risk engineering (M Eng). *Program availability:* Part-time. *Entrance requirements:* For master's, GRE General Test, resume, 3 letters of recommendation, statement of purpose, transcripts. Additional exam requirements/recommendations for international students: Required—TOEFL. Electronic applications accepted.

Materials Engineering

Florida International University, College of Engineering and Computing, Department of Mechanical and Materials Engineering, Miami, FL 33199. Offers materials science and engineering (MS, PhD); mechanical engineering (MS, PhD). *Program availability:* Part-time, evening/weekend. *Faculty:* 22 full-time (4 women), 6 part-time/adjunct (1 woman). *Students:* 49 full-time (12 women), 8 part-time (0 women); includes 20 minority (4 Black or African American, non-Hispanic/Latino; 14 Hispanic/Latino; 2 Two or more races, non-Hispanic/Latino), 33 international. Average age 30. 98 applicants, 45% accepted, 13 enrolled. In 2018, 11 master's, 8 doctorates awarded. Terminal master's awarded for partial completion of doctoral program. *Degree requirements:* For master's, thesis or alternative; for doctorate, comprehensive exam, thesis/dissertation. *Entrance requirements:* For master's, GRE (depending on program), 3 letters of recommendation, minimum undergraduate GPA of 3.0 in upper-level course work; for doctorate, GRE (minimum combined score of 1150, verbal 450, quantitative 650), minimum undergraduate GPA of 3.0 in upper-level coursework with BS, 3.3 with MS; 3 letters of recommendation; letter of intent. Additional exam requirements/recommendations for international students: Required—TOEFL (minimum score 550 paper-based; 80 iBT) or IELTS (minimum score 6.5). *Application deadline:* For fall admission, 6/1 for domestic students, 4/1 for international students; for spring admission, 10/1 for domestic students, 9/1 for international students. Applications are processed on a rolling basis. Application fee: $30. Electronic applications accepted. *Financial support:* Institutionally sponsored loans, scholarships/grants, and unspecified assistantships available. Financial award application deadline: 3/1; financial award applicants required to submit FAFSA. *Faculty research:* Mechanics and materials, fluid/thermal/energy, design and manufacturing, materials science engineering. *Unit head:* Dr. ARVIND AGARWAL, Chair, 305-348-1701, Fax: 305-348-1932, E-mail: Arvind.Agarwal@fiu.edu. *Application contact:* Nanett Rojas, Manager, Admissions Operations, 305-348-7464, Fax: 305-348-7441, E-mail: gradadm@fiu.edu.
Website: http://cec.fiu.edu

Florida State University, The Graduate School, Materials Science and Engineering Program, Tallahassee, FL 32306. Offers MS, PhD. *Faculty:* 37 full-time (6 women). *Students:* 18 full-time (8 women); includes 1 minority (Hispanic/Latino), 14 international. Average age 28. 27 applicants, 26% accepted, 4 enrolled. In 2018, 3 master's awarded. Terminal master's awarded for partial completion of doctoral program. *Degree requirements:* For master's, thesis; for doctorate, comprehensive exam, thesis/dissertation. *Entrance requirements:* For master's and doctorate, GRE General Test (minimum new format 55th percentile Verbal, 75th percentile Quantitative, old version 1100 combined Verbal and Quantitative), minimum GPA of 3.0, 3 letters of recommendation. Additional exam requirements/recommendations for international students: Required—TOEFL (minimum score 80 iBT). *Application deadline:* For fall admission, 5/1 for domestic and international students; for spring admission, 9/1 for domestic and international students; for summer admission, 1/1 for domestic and international students. Applications are processed on a rolling basis. Application fee: $30. Electronic applications accepted. *Expenses: Tuition, area resident:* Part-time $479.32 per credit hour. Tuition and fees vary according to campus/location and program. *Financial support:* In 2018–19, 18 students received support, including 18 research assistantships with full tuition reimbursements available (averaging $23,104 per year); partial payment of required health insurance also available. Financial award application deadline: 12/15. *Faculty research:* Magnetism and magnetic materials, composites, superconductors, polymers, computations, nanotechnology. *Unit head:* Prof. Eric Hellstrom, Director, 850-645-7489, Fax: 850-645-7754, E-mail: hellstrom@asc.magnet.fsu.edu. *Application contact:* Judy Gardner, Admissions Coordinator, 850-645-8980, Fax: 850-645-9123, E-mail: jdgardner@fsu.edu.
Website: http://materials.fsu.edu

Georgia Institute of Technology, Graduate Studies, College of Engineering, School of Materials Science and Engineering, Atlanta, GA 30332-0001. Offers MS, PhD. *Program availability:* Part-time. Terminal master's awarded for partial completion of doctoral program. *Degree requirements:* For master's, thesis optional; for doctorate, comprehensive exam, thesis/dissertation, teaching assignment. *Entrance requirements:* For master's and doctorate, GRE General Test. Additional exam requirements/recommendations for international students: Required—TOEFL (minimum score 620 paper-based; 105 iBT). Electronic applications accepted. *Faculty research:* Nanomaterials, biomaterials, computational materials science, mechanical behavior, advanced engineering materials.

Illinois Institute of Technology, Graduate College, Armour College of Engineering, Department of Mechanical, Materials and Aerospace Engineering, Chicago, IL 60616. Offers manufacturing engineering (MAS, MS); materials science and engineering (MAS, MS, PhD); mechanical and aerospace engineering (MAS, MS, PhD), including economics (MS), energy (MS), environment (MS). *Program availability:* Part-time, evening/weekend, online learning. Terminal master's awarded for partial completion of doctoral program. *Degree requirements:* For master's, comprehensive exam (for some programs), thesis (for some programs); for doctorate, comprehensive exam, thesis/dissertation. *Entrance requirements:* For master's and doctorate, GRE General Test (minimum score 1000 Quantitative and Verbal, 3.0 Analytical Writing), minimum undergraduate GPA of 3.0. Additional exam requirements/recommendations for international students: Required—TOEFL (minimum score 550 paper-based; 80 iBT). Electronic applications accepted. *Faculty research:* Fluid dynamics, metallurgical and materials engineering, solids and structures, computational mechanics, computer added design and manufacturing, thermal sciences, dynamic analysis and control of complex systems.

Instituto Tecnológico y de Estudios Superiores de Monterrey, Campus Estado de México, Professional and Graduate Division, Estado de Mexico, Mexico. Offers administration of information technologies (MITA); architecture (M Arch); business administration (GMBA, MBA); computer sciences (MCS, PhD); education (M Ed); educational institution administration (MAD); educational technology and innovation (PhD); electronic commerce (MEC); environmental systems (MS); finance (MAF); humanistic studies (MHS); information sciences and knowledge management (MISKM); information systems (MS); manufacturing systems (MS); marketing (MEM); quality systems and productivity (MS); science and materials engineering (PhD); telecommunications management (MTM). *Program availability:* Part-time, online learning. *Degree requirements:* For master's, one foreign language, thesis (for some programs); for doctorate, one foreign language, thesis/dissertation. *Entrance requirements:* For master's, E-PAEP 500, interview; for doctorate, E-PAEP 500, research proposal. Additional exam requirements/recommendations for international students: Required—TOEFL (minimum score 550 paper-based). *Faculty research:* Surface treatments by plasmas, mechanical properties, robotics, graphical computing, mechatronics security protocols.

Iowa State University of Science and Technology, Department of Materials Science and Engineering, Ames, IA 50011. Offers M Eng, MS, PhD. *Entrance requirements:* For master's and doctorate, GRE General Test. Additional exam requirements/recommendations for international students: Required—TOEFL (minimum score 550 paper-based; 79 iBT), IELTS (minimum score 6.5). Electronic applications accepted.

Johns Hopkins University, Engineering Program for Professionals, Part-time Program in Materials Science and Engineering, Baltimore, MD 21218. Offers nanotechnology (M Mat SE). *Program availability:* Part-time, evening/weekend. *Faculty:* 1 full-time, 4 part-time/adjunct (2 women). *Students:* 13 part-time (5 women). 14 applicants, 29% accepted, 3 enrolled. In 2018, 8 master's awarded. *Entrance requirements:* Additional exam requirements/recommendations for international students: Required—TOEFL (minimum score 600 paper-based; 100 iBT). *Application deadline:* Applications are processed on a rolling basis. Application fee: $0. Electronic applications accepted. *Unit head:* Dr. James Spicer, Program Chair, 410-516-8524, E-mail: spicer@jhu.edu. *Application contact:* Doug Schiller, Admissions Director, 410-516-2300, Fax: 410-579-8049, E-mail: schiller@jhu.edu.
Website: http://www.ep.jhu.edu

Johns Hopkins University, G. W. C. Whiting School of Engineering, Department of Materials Science and Engineering, Baltimore, MD 21218. Offers M Mat SE, MSE, PhD. *Faculty:* 22 full-time (3 women). *Students:* 78 full-time (24 women), 1 part-time. 303 applicants, 34% accepted, 31 enrolled. In 2018, 21 master's, 11 doctorates awarded. Terminal master's awarded for partial completion of doctoral program. *Degree requirements:* For master's, thesis; for doctorate, thesis/dissertation, oral exam, thesis defense. *Entrance requirements:* For master's and doctorate, GRE General Test, 2 letters of recommendation, statement of purpose, transcripts. Additional exam requirements/recommendations for international students: Required—TOEFL (minimum score 600 paper-based, 100 iBT) or IELTS (7). *Application deadline:* For fall admission, 12/15 priority date for domestic and international students; for spring admission, 10/15 priority date for domestic and international students. Application fee: $0 ($75 for international students). Electronic applications accepted. *Financial support:* In 2018–19, 56 students received support, including 5 fellowships with full tuition reimbursements available (averaging $30,200 per year), 51 research assistantships with full tuition reimbursements available (averaging $30,200 per year), teaching assistantships with full tuition reimbursements available (averaging $30,200 per year); Federal Work-Study, institutionally sponsored loans, health care benefits, tuition waivers (full), and unspecified assistantships also available. Financial award application deadline: 3/15. *Faculty research:* Biomaterials; computational materials science; materials for energy; nanomaterials; optoelectronic and magnetic materials; structural materials. *Unit head:* Dr. Jonah Erlebacher, Chair, 410-516-6141, Fax: 410-516-5293, E-mail: jonah.erlebacher@jhu.edu. *Application contact:* Jeanine Majewski, Academic Coordinator, 410-516-8760, Fax: 410-516-5293, E-mail: dmse-gradadmissions@jhu.edu.
Website: http://engineering.jhu.edu/materials/

Johns Hopkins University, G. W. C. Whiting School of Engineering, Master of Science in Engineering Management Program, Baltimore, MD 21218. Offers biomaterials (MSEM); civil engineering (MSEM); communications science (MSEM); computer science (MSEM); environmental systems analysis, economics and public policy (MSEM); fluid mechanics (MSEM); materials science and engineering (MSEM); mechanical engineering (MSEM); mechanics and materials (MSEM); nanobiotechnology (MSEM); nanomaterials and nanotechnology (MSEM); operations research (MSEM); probability and statistics (MSEM); smart product and device design (MSEM). *Students:* 34 full-time (12 women), 18 part-time (7 women). 233 applicants, 39% accepted, 33 enrolled. In 2018, 27 master's awarded. *Entrance requirements:* For master's, GRE, 3 letters of recommendation, statement of purpose, transcripts. Additional exam requirements/recommendations for international students: Required—TOEFL (minimum score 600 paper-based, 100 iBT) or IELTS (7). *Application deadline:* For fall admission, 2/15 for domestic and international students. Application fee: $75. Electronic applications accepted. *Financial support:* In 2018–19, 43 research assistantships (averaging $43,344 per year) were awarded; health care benefits also available. *Unit head:* Dr. Pamela Sheff, Director, 410-516-7056, Fax: 410-516-4880, E-mail: pamsheff@gmail.com. *Application contact:* Lindsey Conklin, Sr. Academic Program Coordinator, 410-516-1108, Fax: 410-516-0780, E-mail: lconkli4@jhu.edu.
Website: http://engineering.jhu.edu/msem/

Lehigh University, P.C. Rossin College of Engineering and Applied Science, Department of Materials Science and Engineering, Bethlehem, PA 18015. Offers materials science and engineering (M Eng, MS, PhD); photonics (MS); polymer science/engineering (M Eng, MS, PhD); MBA/E. *Program availability:* Part-time. *Faculty:* 16 full-time (4 women). *Students:* 24 full-time (6 women), 2 part-time (1 woman); includes 4 minority (1 Black or African American, non-Hispanic/Latino; 1 Hispanic/Latino; 2 Two or more races, non-Hispanic/Latino), 5 international. Average age 25. 107 applicants, 19% accepted, 8 enrolled. In 2018, 4 master's, 7 doctorates awarded. *Degree requirements:* For master's, thesis; for doctorate, comprehensive exam, thesis/dissertation. *Entrance requirements:* For master's and doctorate, GRE General Test, minimum GPA of 3.60. Additional exam requirements/recommendations for international students: Required—TOEFL (minimum score 487 paper-based; 85 iBT), IELTS (minimum score 6.5), TOEFL or IELTS required. *Application deadline:* For fall admission, 1/15 priority date for domestic students, 1/15 for international students; for spring admission, 12/1 priority date for domestic students, 12/1 for international students. Application fee: $75. Tuition and fees vary according to program. *Financial support:* In 2018–19, 26 students received support, including 9 fellowships with tuition reimbursements available (averaging $12,848 per year), 14 research assistantships with tuition reimbursements available (averaging $29,640 per year), 12 teaching assistantships with tuition reimbursements available (averaging $7,350 per year); scholarships/grants and health care benefits also available. Financial award application deadline: 1/15. *Faculty research:* Metals, ceramics, crystals, polymers, fatigue crack propagation, biomaterials. *Total annual research expenditures:* $2.7 million. *Unit head:* Dr. Wojciech Misiolek, Chairperson, 610-758-4252, Fax: 610-758-4244, E-mail: wzm2@lehigh.edu. *Application contact:* Lisa Carreras Arechiga, Graduate Administrative Coordinator, 610-758-4222, Fax: 610-758-4244, E-mail: lia4@lehigh.edu.
Website: https://engineering.lehigh.edu/matsci

Massachusetts Institute of Technology, School of Engineering, Department of Civil and Environmental Engineering, Cambridge, MA 02139. Offers biological oceanography (PhD, Sc D); chemical oceanography (PhD, Sc D); civil and environmental engineering (M Eng, SM, PhD, Sc D); civil and environmental systems (PhD, Sc D); civil engineering (PhD, Sc D, CE); civil engineering and computation (PhD); coastal engineering (PhD, Sc D); construction engineering and management (PhD, Sc D); environmental biology (PhD, Sc D); environmental chemistry (PhD, Sc D); environmental engineering (PhD, Sc D); environmental engineering and computation (PhD); environmental fluid mechanics (PhD, Sc D); geotechnical and geoenvironmental engineering (PhD, Sc D); hydrology (PhD, Sc D); information technology (PhD, Sc D); oceanographic engineering (PhD, Sc D); structures and materials (PhD, Sc D); transportation (PhD, Sc D); SM/MBA. *Degree requirements:* For master's, thesis; for doctorate, comprehensive exam, thesis/dissertation; for CE, comprehensive exam, thesis. *Entrance requirements:* For master's, doctorate, and CE, GRE General Test. Additional exam requirements/recommendations for international students: Required—TOEFL, IELTS. Electronic applications accepted. *Expenses: Tuition:* Full-time $51,520; part-time $800 per credit hour. *Required fees:* $312. *Faculty research:* Environmental chemistry, environmental fluid mechanics and coastal engineering, environmental microbiology, geotechnical engineering and geomechanics, hydrology and hydro climatology, infrastructure systems, mechanics of materials and structures, transportation systems.

Massachusetts Institute of Technology, School of Engineering, Department of Materials Science and Engineering, Cambridge, MA 02139. Offers archaeological materials (PhD, Sc D); materials engineering (Mat E); materials science and engineering (SM, PhD, Sc D). *Degree requirements:* For master's, thesis; for doctorate, comprehensive exam, thesis/dissertation; for Mat E, comprehensive exam, thesis. *Entrance requirements:* For master's and doctorate, GRE General Test. Additional exam requirements/recommendations for international students: Required—IELTS. Electronic applications accepted. *Expenses: Tuition:* Full-time $51,520; part-time $800 per credit hour. *Required fees:* $312. *Faculty research:* Thermodynamics and kinetics of materials; structure, processing and properties of materials; electronic, structural and biological materials engineering; computational materials science; materials in energy, medicine, nanotechnology and the environment.

McGill University, Faculty of Graduate and Postdoctoral Studies, Faculty of Engineering, Department of Civil Engineering and Applied Mechanics, Montréal, QC H3A 2T5, Canada. Offers environmental engineering (M Eng, M Sc, PhD); fluid mechanics (M Sc); fluid mechanics and hydraulic engineering (M Eng, PhD); materials engineering (M Eng, PhD); rehabilitation of urban infrastructure (M Eng, PhD); soil behavior (M Eng, PhD); soil mechanics and foundations (M Eng, PhD); structures and structural mechanics (M Eng, PhD); water resources (M Sc); water resources engineering (M Eng, PhD).

McGill University, Faculty of Graduate and Postdoctoral Studies, Faculty of Engineering, Department of Mining and Materials Engineering, Montréal, QC H3A 2T5, Canada. Offers materials engineering (M Eng, PhD); mining engineering (M Eng, M Sc, PhD, Diploma).

McMaster University, School of Graduate Studies, Faculty of Engineering, Department of Materials Science and Engineering, Hamilton, ON L8S 4M2, Canada. Offers materials engineering (M Eng, MA Sc, PhD); materials science (M Eng, PhD). *Degree requirements:* For master's, thesis; for doctorate, comprehensive exam, thesis/dissertation. *Entrance requirements:* Additional exam requirements/recommendations for international students: Required—TOEFL (minimum score 550 paper-based). *Faculty research:* Localized corrosion of metals and alloys, electron microscopy, polymer synthesis and characterization, polymer reaction kinetics and engineering, polymer process modeling.

Michigan State University, The Graduate School, College of Engineering, Department of Chemical Engineering and Materials Science, East Lansing, MI 48824. Offers chemical engineering (MS, PhD); materials science and engineering (MS, PhD). *Entrance requirements:* Additional exam requirements/recommendations for international students: Required—TOEFL. Electronic applications accepted.

Michigan Technological University, Graduate School, College of Engineering, Department of Materials Science and Engineering, Houghton, MI 49931. Offers MS, PhD. *Program availability:* Part-time, 100% online, blended/hybrid learning. *Faculty:* 33 full-time (7 women), 12 part-time/adjunct (3 women). *Students:* 30 full-time (9 women), 8 part-time (3 women); includes 1 minority (Two or more races, non-Hispanic/Latino), 24 international. Average age 27. 135 applicants, 30% accepted, 7 enrolled. In 2018, 8 master's, 2 doctorates awarded. Terminal master's awarded for partial completion of doctoral program. *Degree requirements:* For master's, comprehensive exam (for some programs), thesis (for some programs); for doctorate, comprehensive exam, thesis/dissertation. *Entrance requirements:* For master's and doctorate, GRE (domestic students from ABET-accredited programs exempt), statement of purpose, personal statement, official transcripts, 3 letters of recommendation. Additional exam requirements/recommendations for international students: Required—TOEFL (minimum score 79 iBT), IELTS (minimum score 6.5), TOEFL (minimum score 79 iBT) or IELTS (minimum score of 6.5). *Application deadline:* For fall admission, 2/1 priority date for domestic and international students; for spring admission, 9/1 priority date for domestic and international students. Applications are processed on a rolling basis. Electronic applications accepted. *Expenses:* $1,143 per credit. *Financial support:* In 2018–19, 26 students received support, including 4 fellowships with tuition reimbursements available (averaging $16,590 per year), 18 research assistantships with tuition reimbursements available (averaging $16,590 per year); teaching assistantships, career-related internships or fieldwork, Federal Work-Study, scholarships/grants, health care benefits, unspecified assistantships, and cooperative program also available. Financial award applicants required to submit FAFSA. *Faculty research:* Structure/property/processing relationships, microstructural characterization, alloy design, electronic/magnetic/photonic materials, materials and manufacturing processes. *Total annual research expenditures:* $2.1 million. *Unit head:* Dr. Stephen L. Kampe, Chair, 906-487-2036, Fax: 906-487-2934, E-mail: kampe@mtu.edu. *Application contact:* Valentina O'Kane, Department Coordinator, 906-487-4326, Fax: 906-487-2934, E-mail: vokane@mtu.edu. Website: http://www.mtu.edu/materials/

Missouri University of Science and Technology, Department of Materials Science and Engineering, Rolla, MO 65401. Offers ceramic engineering (MS, PhD); materials science and engineering (MS, PhD); metallurgical engineering (MS, PhD). *Degree requirements:* For master's, thesis optional; for doctorate, comprehensive exam. *Entrance requirements:* For master's, GRE (minimum combined score 1100, 600 verbal, 3.5 writing); for doctorate, GRE (minimum score: quantitative 600, writing 3.5). Additional exam requirements/recommendations for international students: Required—TOEFL (minimum score 570 paper-based). Electronic applications accepted. *Expenses:* Tuition, state resident: full-time $7545.60; part-time $419.20 per credit hour. Tuition, nonresident: full-time $22,169; part-time $1231.60 per credit hour. *International tuition:* $23,518.80 full-time. *Required fees:* $4523.05. Full-time tuition and fees vary according to course load, campus/location, program and reciprocity agreements.

New Jersey Institute of Technology, College of Science and Liberal Arts, Newark, NJ 07102. Offers applied mathematics (MS); applied physics (MS, PhD); applied statistics (MS, Certificate); biology (MS, PhD); biostatistics (MS); chemistry (MS, PhD); environmental and sustainability policy (MS); environmental science (MS, PhD); history (MA, MAT); materials science and engineering (MS, PhD); mathematical and computational finance (MS); mathematical sciences (PhD); pharmaceutical chemistry (MS); professional and technical communications (MS); technical communication essentials (Certificate). *Program availability:* Part-time, evening/weekend. *Faculty:* 150 full-time (43 women), 115 part-time/adjunct (47 women). *Students:* 200 full-time (79 women), 63 part-time (29 women); includes 61 minority (17 Black or African American, non-Hispanic/Latino; 29 Asian, non-Hispanic/Latino; 11 Hispanic/Latino; 4 Two or more races, non-Hispanic/Latino), 136 international. Average age 28. 429 applicants, 49% accepted, 89 enrolled. In 2018, 43 master's, 16 doctorates, 2 other advanced degrees awarded. Terminal master's awarded for partial completion of doctoral program. *Degree requirements:* For master's, thesis (for some programs); for doctorate, thesis/dissertation. *Entrance requirements:* For master's and doctorate, GRE General Test, Minimum GPA of 3.0, personal statement, 3 letters of recommendation, and transcripts. Additional exam requirements/recommendations for international students: Required—TOEFL (minimum score 550 paper-based; 79 iBT), IELTS (minimum score 6.5). *Application deadline:* For fall admission, 6/1 priority date for domestic students, 5/1 priority date for international students; for spring admission, 11/15 priority date for domestic and international students. Applications are processed on a rolling basis. Application fee: $75. Electronic applications accepted. *Expenses:* $22,690 per year (in-state), $32,136 per year (out-of-state). *Financial support:* In 2018–19, 134 students received support, including 17 fellowships with full tuition reimbursements available (averaging $22,000 per year), 74 research assistantships with full tuition reimbursements available (averaging $22,000 per year), 71 teaching assistantships with full tuition reimbursements available (averaging $22,000 per year); scholarships/grants, traineeships, health care benefits, and unspecified assistantships also available. Financial award application deadline: 1/15. *Faculty research:* Biophotonics and bioimaging, morphogenetic patterning, embryogenesis, biological fluid dynamics, applied research in the mathematical sciences. *Total annual research expenditures:* $29.2 million. *Unit head:* Dr. Kevin Belfield, Dean, 973-596-3676, Fax: 973-565-0586, E-mail: kevin.d.belfield@njit.edu. *Application contact:* Stephen Eck, Director of Admissions, 973-596-3300, Fax: 973-596-3461, E-mail: admissions@njit.edu. Website: http://csla.njit.edu/

New Mexico Institute of Mining and Technology, Center for Graduate Studies, Department of Materials Engineering, Socorro, NM 87801. Offers MS, PhD. *Degree requirements:* For master's, thesis; for doctorate, thesis/dissertation. *Entrance requirements:* For master's, GRE General Test; for doctorate, GRE General Test, GRE Subject Test. Additional exam requirements/recommendations for international students: Required—TOEFL (minimum score 540 paper-based). *Faculty research:* Thin films, ceramics, damage studies from radiation, corrosion shock.

North Carolina State University, Graduate School, College of Engineering, Department of Materials Science and Engineering, Raleigh, NC 27695. Offers MMSE, MNAE, MS, PhD. PhD offered jointly with The University of North Carolina at Charlotte. *Degree requirements:* For master's, thesis; for doctorate, thesis/dissertation. Electronic applications accepted. *Faculty research:* Processing and properties of wide band gap semiconductors, ferroelectric thin-film materials, ductility of nanocrystalline materials, computational materials science, defects in silicon-based devices.

Northwestern University, McCormick School of Engineering and Applied Science, Department of Materials Science and Engineering, Evanston, IL 60208. Offers integrated computational materials engineering (Certificate); materials science and engineering (MS, PhD). Admissions and degrees offered through The Graduate School. *Program availability:* Part-time. Terminal master's awarded for partial completion of doctoral program. *Degree requirements:* For master's, thesis optional, oral thesis defense; for doctorate, comprehensive exam, thesis/dissertation, oral defense of dissertation, preliminary evaluation, qualifying exam. *Entrance requirements:* For master's and doctorate, GRE General Test. Additional exam requirements/recommendations for international students: Required—TOEFL (minimum score 577 paper-based; 90 iBT), IELTS (minimum score 7). Electronic applications accepted. *Faculty research:* Art conservation science; biomaterials; ceramics; composites; energy; magnetic materials; materials for electronics and photonics; materials synthesis and processing; materials theory, computation, and design; metals; nanomaterials; polymers, self-assembly, and surfaces and interfaces.

The Ohio State University, Graduate School, College of Engineering, Department of Materials Science and Engineering, Columbus, OH 43210. Offers materials science and engineering (MS, PhD); welding engineering (MS, PhD). *Faculty:* 38. *Students:* 157 full-time (40 women), 51 part-time (7 women). Average age 29. In 2018, 38 master's, 16 doctorates awarded. *Entrance requirements:* For master's and doctorate, GRE (for graduates of foreign universities and holders of non-engineering degrees). Additional exam requirements/recommendations for international students: Required—TOEFL (minimum score 550 paper-based; 79 iBT), Michigan English Language Assessment Battery (minimum score 82); Recommended—IELTS (minimum score 7). *Application deadline:* For fall admission, 12/13 priority date for domestic students, 11/30 priority date for international students; for spring admission, 12/14 for domestic students, 11/12 for international students; for summer admission, 5/15 for domestic students, 4/14 for international students. Applications are processed on a rolling basis. Application fee: $60 ($70 for international students). Electronic applications accepted. *Financial support:* Fellowships, research assistantships, teaching assistantships, career-related internships or fieldwork, scholarships/grants, and unspecified assistantships available. *Faculty research:* Computational materials modeling, biomaterials, metallurgy, ceramics, advanced alloys/composites. *Unit head:* Dr. Peter Anderson, Chair, 614-292-6255, E-mail: anderson.1@osu.edu. *Application contact:* Mark Cooper, Graduate Studies Coordinator, 614-292-7280, Fax: 614-292-1357, E-mail: mse@osu.edu. Website: http://mse.osu.edu/

Oklahoma State University, College of Engineering, Architecture and Technology, School of Materials Science and Engineering, Stillwater, OK 74078. Offers MS, PhD. *Faculty:* 7 full-time (0 women), 2 part-time/adjunct (0 women). *Students:* 2 full-time (0 women), 16 part-time (4 women); includes 4 minority (2 American Indian or Alaska Native, non-Hispanic/Latino; 1 Asian, non-Hispanic/Latino; 1 Two or more races, non-Hispanic/Latino), 7 international. Average age 29. 14 applicants, 29% accepted, 4 enrolled. In 2018, 3 master's, 1 doctorate awarded. *Entrance requirements:* Additional exam requirements/recommendations for international students: Required—TOEFL. *Application deadline:* For fall admission, 3/1 for domestic students; for spring admission, 8/1 for domestic students. Application fee: $40 ($75 for international students). Electronic applications accepted. *Expenses: Tuition, area resident:* Full-time $4148. Tuition, state resident: full-time $4148. Tuition, nonresident: full-time $10,517. *International tuition:* $10,517 full-time. *Required fees:* $4394; $2929 per credit hour. Tuition and fees vary according to course load and program. *Financial support:* Research assistantships and teaching assistantships available. *Unit head:* Dr. Raman P Singh, Head, 918-594-8155, E-mail: raman.singh@okstate.edu. *Application contact:* Dr. Sheryl Tucker, Dean, 405-744-6368, Fax: 405-744-0355, E-mail: gradi@okstate.edu. Website: http://mse.okstate.edu/

Penn State University Park, Graduate School, Intercollege Graduate Programs, Intercollege Graduate Program in Materials Science and Engineering, University Park, PA 16802. Offers MS, PhD.

Portland State University, Graduate Studies, Maseeh College of Engineering and Computer Science, Department of Mechanical and Materials Engineering, Portland, OR 97207-0751. Offers mechanical engineering (PhD). *Program availability:* Part-time, evening/weekend. *Degree requirements:* For master's, thesis or alternative; for doctorate, one foreign language, thesis/dissertation, oral and written exams. *Entrance requirements:* For master's, minimum GPA of 3.0 in upper-division course work, BS in mechanical engineering or allied field, 3 letters of recommendation, statement of purpose, resume/curriculum vitae; for doctorate, GRE General Test, GRE Subject Test, MS, minimum GPA of 3.0 in upper-division course work, 3 letters of recommendation. Additional exam requirements/recommendations for international students: Required—TOEFL (minimum score 550 paper-based; 80 iBT). Electronic applications accepted. *Expenses:* Contact institution. *Faculty research:* Mechanical system modeling, indoor air quality, manufacturing process, computational fluid dynamics, building science.

Purdue University, College of Engineering, School of Materials Engineering, West Lafayette, IN 47907. Offers MSMSE, PhD. *Program availability:* Part-time. *Degree requirements:* For master's, thesis optional; for doctorate, thesis/dissertation. *Entrance requirements:* For master's and doctorate, GRE (highly recommended), minimum GPA of 3.0. Additional exam requirements/recommendations for international students:

Required—GRE. Electronic applications accepted. *Faculty research:* Processing, characterization, properties, and modeling of metals, electronics, ceramics, biomaterials, polymers/soft matter and composites.

Queen's University at Kingston, School of Graduate Studies, Faculty of Engineering and Applied Science, Department of Mechanical and Materials Engineering, Kingston, ON K7L 3N6, Canada. Offers M Eng, M Sc, M Sc Eng, PhD. *Program availability:* Part-time. *Degree requirements:* For master's, thesis optional; for doctorate, comprehensive exam, thesis/dissertation. *Entrance requirements:* Additional exam requirements/recommendations for international students: Required—TOEFL. Electronic applications accepted. *Faculty research:* Dynamics and control systems, manufacturing and design, materials and engineering, heat transferring fluid dynamics, energy systems and combustion.

Rensselaer Polytechnic Institute, Graduate School, School of Engineering, Program in Materials Engineering, Troy, NY 12180. Offers M Eng, MS, D Eng, PhD. *Faculty:* 19 full-time (4 women). *Students:* 53 full-time (14 women), 2 part-time (1 woman); includes 2 minority (both Two or more races, non-Hispanic/Latino), 35 international. Average age 25. 177 applicants, 18% accepted, 9 enrolled. In 2018, 5 master's, 6 doctorates awarded. Terminal master's awarded for partial completion of doctoral program. *Degree requirements:* For master's, thesis; for doctorate, comprehensive exam, thesis/dissertation. *Entrance requirements:* For master's and doctorate, GRE. Additional exam requirements/recommendations for international students: Required—TOEFL (minimum score 600 paper-based; 100 iBT), IELTS (minimum score 7), PTE (minimum score 68). *Application deadline:* For fall admission, 1/1 priority date for domestic and international students; for spring admission, 8/15 priority date for domestic and international students. Applications are processed on a rolling basis. Application fee: $75. Electronic applications accepted. *Financial support:* In 2018–19, research assistantships with full tuition reimbursements (averaging $23,000 per year), teaching assistantships with full tuition reimbursements (averaging $23,000 per year) were awarded; fellowships also available. Financial award application deadline: 1/1. *Faculty research:* Advanced processing and synthesis, composites, computational materials, corrosion/electrochemical materials, electronic materials, glasses/ceramics, materials characterization, materials for energy, materials/biology interface, metals, nanomaterials, polymeric materials. *Total annual research expenditures:* $1.8 million. *Unit head:* Dr. Minoru Tomozawa, Graduate Program Director, 518-276-6659, E-mail: tomozm@rpi.edu. *Application contact:* Jarron Decker, Director of Graduate Admissions, 518-276-6216, Fax: 518-276-4072, E-mail: gradadmissions@rpi.edu.
Website: http://mse.rpi.edu/graduate

Rochester Institute of Technology, Graduate Enrollment Services, College of Science, School of Chemistry and Materials Science, MS Program in Materials Science and Engineering, Rochester, NY 14623-5603. Offers MS. Program offered jointly with Kate Gleason College of Engineering. *Program availability:* Part-time, evening/weekend. *Students:* 15 full-time (9 women), 5 part-time (2 women); includes 5 minority (1 Black or African American, non-Hispanic/Latino; 2 Asian, non-Hispanic/Latino; 2 Hispanic/Latino), 1 international. Average age 24. 32 applicants, 84% accepted, 7 enrolled. In 2018, 8 master's awarded. *Degree requirements:* For master's, thesis or project. *Entrance requirements:* For master's, minimum GPA of 3.0 (recommended), two letters of recommendation. Additional exam requirements/recommendations for international students: Required—TOEFL (minimum score 575 paper-based; 90 iBT), IELTS (minimum score 6.5), PTE (minimum score 62). *Application deadline:* Applications are processed on a rolling basis. Application fee: $65. Electronic applications accepted. *Financial support:* In 2018–19, 22 students received support. Research assistantships with partial tuition reimbursements available, teaching assistantships with partial tuition reimbursements available, career-related internships or fieldwork, scholarships/grants, and unspecified assistantships available. Support available to part-time students. Financial award applicants required to submit FAFSA. *Faculty research:* Magnetism and magnetic materials, photovoltaics and batteries, electronic materials, functional nanomaterials, 3D printing and additive manufacturing. *Unit head:* Michael Pierce, PhD, Department Chair, 585-475-2089, E-mail: mspsps@rit.edu. *Application contact:* Diane Ellison, Senior Associate Vice President, Graduate Enrollment Services, 585-475-2229, Fax: 585-475-7164, E-mail: gradinfo@rit.edu.
Website: https://www.rit.edu/study/materials-science-and-engineering-ms

Rutgers University–New Brunswick, Graduate School-New Brunswick, Program in Materials Science and Engineering, Piscataway, NJ 08854-8097. Offers MS, PhD. *Program availability:* Part-time. *Degree requirements:* For master's, thesis; for doctorate, comprehensive exam, thesis/dissertation. *Entrance requirements:* For master's and doctorate, GRE General Test. Additional exam requirements/recommendations for international students: Recommended—TOEFL. Electronic applications accepted. *Faculty research:* Ceramic processing, nanostructured materials, electrical and structural ceramics, fiber optics.

San Jose State University, Program in Chemical & Materials Engineering, San Jose, CA 95192-0001. Offers chemical engineering (MS); materials engineering (MS). *Program availability:* Part-time. *Degree requirements:* For master's, thesis or alternative. Electronic applications accepted.

South Dakota School of Mines and Technology, Graduate Division, Doctoral Program in Materials Engineering and Science, Rapid City, SD 57701-3995. Offers PhD. *Program availability:* Part-time. *Degree requirements:* For doctorate, thesis/dissertation. *Entrance requirements:* For doctorate, GRE General Test, minimum graduate GPA of 3.0, 3 letters of recommendation. Additional exam requirements/recommendations for international students: Required—TOEFL (minimum score 520 paper-based; 68 iBT), TWE. Electronic applications accepted.

South Dakota School of Mines and Technology, Graduate Division, Master's Program in Materials Engineering and Science, Rapid City, SD 57701-3995. Offers MS. *Degree requirements:* For master's, thesis (for some programs). *Entrance requirements:* For master's, GRE General Test. Additional exam requirements/recommendations for international students: Required—TOEFL (minimum score 520 paper-based; 68 iBT), TWE. Electronic applications accepted.

Stanford University, School of Engineering, Department of Materials Science and Engineering, Stanford, CA 94305-2004. Offers MS, PhD, Engr. *Expenses: Tuition:* Full-time $50,703; part-time $32,970 per year. *Required fees:* $651.
Website: https://mse.stanford.edu/

Stevens Institute of Technology, Graduate School, Charles V. Schaefer Jr. School of Engineering and Science, Department of Chemical Engineering and Materials Science, Program in Materials Science and Engineering, Hoboken, NJ 07030. Offers M Eng, PhD. *Program availability:* Part-time, evening/weekend. *Faculty:* 1 part-time/adjunct. *Students:* 53 full-time (14 women), 1 (woman) part-time, 50 international. Average age 25. In 2018, 33 master's, 3 doctorates awarded. Terminal master's awarded for partial completion of doctoral program. *Degree requirements:* For master's, thesis optional, minimum B average in major field and overall; for doctorate, comprehensive exam (for some programs), thesis/dissertation. *Entrance requirements:* For master's, GRE/GMAT scores: GRE scores are required for all applicants applying to a full-time graduate program in the Schaefer School of Engineering and Science (SES). International applicants must submit TOEFL/IELTS scores and fulfill the English Language Proficiency Requirements in order to be considered. Additional exam requirements/recommendations for international students: Required—TOEFL (minimum score 74 iBT), IELTS (minimum score 6). *Application deadline:* For fall admission, 4/15 for domestic and international students; for spring admission, 11/1 for domestic and international students; for summer admission, 5/1 for domestic students. Applications are processed on a rolling basis. Application fee: $60. Electronic applications accepted. *Expenses: Tuition:* Full-time $35,960; part-time $1620 per credit. *Required fees:* $1290; $600 per semester. Tuition and fees vary according to course load. *Financial support:* Fellowships, research assistantships, teaching assistantships, career-related internships or fieldwork, Federal Work-Study, scholarships/grants, and unspecified assistantships available. Financial award application deadline: 2/15; financial award applicants required to submit FAFSA. *Unit head:* Dr. Jean Zu, Dean of SES, 201-216.8233, Fax: 201-216.8372, E-mail: Jean.Zu@stevens.edu. *Application contact:* Graduate Admissions, 888-783-8367, Fax: 888-511-1306, E-mail: graduate@stevens.edu.

Stony Brook University, State University of New York, Graduate School, College of Engineering and Applied Sciences, Department of Materials Science & Chemical Engineering, Stony Brook, NY 11794. Offers MS, PhD. *Faculty:* 19 full-time (5 women), 6 part-time/adjunct (3 women). *Students:* 75 full-time (21 women), 4 part-time (1 woman); includes 11 minority (6 Asian, non-Hispanic/Latino; 4 Hispanic/Latino; 1 Two or more races, non-Hispanic/Latino), 56 international. Average age 26. 151 applicants, 67% accepted, 15 enrolled. In 2018, 21 master's, 13 doctorates awarded. *Degree requirements:* For master's, thesis or alternative; for doctorate, comprehensive exam, thesis/dissertation. *Entrance requirements:* For master's and doctorate, GRE General Test, minimum undergraduate GPA of 3.0. Additional exam requirements/recommendations for international students: Required—TOEFL (minimum score 90 iBT). *Application deadline:* For fall admission, 1/15 for domestic students; for spring admission, 10/1 for domestic students. Application fee: $100. *Expenses:* Contact institution. *Financial support:* In 2018–19, 30 research assistantships, 14 teaching assistantships were awarded; fellowships also available. *Faculty research:* Crystal growth, crystallography, semiconductors, synchrotron X-rays or radiation, fuel cells. *Total annual research expenditures:* $3.7 million. *Unit head:* Dr. Dilip Gersappe, Professor and Interim Chair, 631-632-8500, Fax: 631-632-8052, E-mail: dilip.gersappe@stonybrook.edu. *Application contact:* Kaitlyn Cozier, Coordinator, 631-632-6269, Fax: 631-632-8052, E-mail: Kaitlyn.Cozier@stonybrook.edu.
Website: http://www.stonybrook.edu/commcms/matscieng/index.html

Texas A&M University, College of Engineering, Department of Materials Science and Engineering, College Station, TX 77843. Offers materials science and engineering (M Eng). *Faculty:* 20. *Students:* 157 full-time (51 women), 7 part-time (0 women); includes 30 minority (1 Black or African American, non-Hispanic/Latino; 14 Asian, non-Hispanic/Latino; 10 Hispanic/Latino; 5 Two or more races, non-Hispanic/Latino), 100 international. Average age 28. 221 applicants, 36% accepted, 31 enrolled. In 2018, 10 master's, 14 doctorates awarded. *Degree requirements:* For master's, thesis (MS); for doctorate, thesis/dissertation. *Entrance requirements:* For master's and doctorate, GRE General Test. Additional exam requirements/recommendations for international students: Required—TOEFL (minimum score 550 paper-based; 80 iBT), IELTS (minimum score 6), PTE (minimum score 53). *Application deadline:* For fall admission, 2/28 for domestic and international students; for spring admission, 7/31 for domestic students, 6/1 for international students. Application fee: $50 ($90 for international students). *Expenses:* Contact institution. *Financial support:* In 2018–19, 157 students received support, including 26 fellowships with tuition reimbursements available (averaging $23,103 per year), 119 research assistantships with tuition reimbursements available (averaging $15,964 per year), 15 teaching assistantships with tuition reimbursements available (averaging $12,565 per year); career-related internships or fieldwork, institutionally sponsored loans, scholarships/grants, traineeships, health care benefits, tuition waivers (full and partial), and unspecified assistantships also available. Support available to part-time students. Financial award application deadline: 3/15; financial award applicants required to submit FAFSA. *Faculty research:* Innovative design methods, pavement distress characterization, materials property, characterization and modeling recyclable materials. *Unit head:* Ibrahim Karaman, Department Head, 979-862-3923, E-mail: ikaraman@tamu.edu. *Application contact:* Mildan Radovic, Associate Department Head, 979-845-5114, E-mail: mradovic@tamu.edu.
Website: http://engineering.tamu.edu/materials

Texas State University, The Graduate College, College of Science and Engineering, PhD Program in Materials Science, Engineering, and Commercialization, San Marcos, TX 78666. Offers PhD. *Faculty:* 13 full-time (4 women). *Students:* 38 full-time (13 women), 2 part-time (both women); includes 6 minority (2 Black or African American, non-Hispanic/Latino; 2 Asian, non-Hispanic/Latino; 2 Hispanic/Latino), 25 international. Average age 32. 42 applicants, 14% accepted, 4 enrolled. In 2018, 7 doctorates awarded. *Degree requirements:* For doctorate, comprehensive exam, thesis/dissertation. *Entrance requirements:* For doctorate, GRE (for applicants who have not received a master's degree from a U.S. institution), baccalaureate and master's degrees from regionally-accredited college or university in biology, chemistry, engineering, materials science, physics, technology, or closely-related field with minimum GPA of 3.5 in graduate work; interviews with core doctoral faculty; statement of purpose; 3 letters of recommendation; curriculum vitae or resume. Additional exam requirements/recommendations for international students: Required—TOEFL (minimum score 550 paper-based; 78 iBT); Recommended—IELTS (minimum score 6.5). *Application deadline:* For fall admission, 2/1 priority date for domestic and international students. Application fee: $55 ($90 for international students). Electronic applications accepted. *Expenses:* Tuition, state resident: full-time $8102; part-time $4051 per semester. Tuition, nonresident: full-time $18,229; part-time $9115 per semester. *International tuition:* $18,229 full-time. *Required fees:* $2116; $120 per credit hour. Tuition and fees vary according to course load. *Financial support:* In 2018–19, 38 students received support, including 9 research assistantships (averaging $30,911 per year), 24 teaching assistantships (averaging $33,907 per year); scholarships/grants, health care benefits, and unspecified assistantships also available. Support available to part-time students. Financial award application deadline: 1/15; financial award applicants required to submit FAFSA. *Faculty research:* Materials characterization using RSC, industrial process pollution by development of amorphous biogenic silica, cadmium telluride surface and interface passivation by molecular beam epitaxy, micro power chip prototype development, development materials and processes in compound semiconductor epitaxy and deposition. *Total annual research expenditures:* $840,784. *Unit head:* Dr. Jennifer Irvin, PhD Program Director, 512-245-7875, Fax: 512-245-8365, E-mail: ji12@txstate.edu. *Application contact:* Dr. Andrea Golato, Dean of Graduate School, 512-245-7875, Fax: 512-245-8365, E-mail: gradcollege@txstate.edu.
Website: http://www.msec.txstate.edu/

Tuskegee University, Graduate Programs, College of Engineering, Department of Materials Science and Engineering, Tuskegee, AL 36088. Offers PhD. *Entrance requirements:* Additional exam requirements/recommendations for international students: Required—TOEFL (minimum score 500 paper-based).

The University of Alabama, Graduate School, College of Engineering, Department of Metallurgical and Materials Engineering, Tuscaloosa, AL 35487. Offers MS Met E, PhD. PhD offered jointly with The University of Alabama at Birmingham. *Degree requirements:* For master's, thesis or alternative; for doctorate, thesis/dissertation. *Entrance requirements:* For master's, GRE General Test, minimum GPA of 3.0 in last 60 hours; for doctorate, GRE General Test, minimum graduate GPA of 3.0, graduate degree. Additional exam requirements/recommendations for international students: Required—TOEFL (minimum score 550 paper-based). Electronic applications accepted. *Faculty research:* Thermodynamics, molten metals processing, casting and solidification, mechanical properties of materials, thin films and nanostructures, electrochemistry, corrosion and alloy development.

The University of Alabama at Birmingham, School of Engineering, Program in Materials Engineering, Birmingham, AL 35294. Offers MS Mt E, PhD. PhD offered jointly with The University of Alabama (Tuscaloosa). *Faculty:* 7 full-time (2 women). *Students:* 28 full-time (9 women), 6 part-time (1 woman); includes 6 minority (4 Black or African American, non-Hispanic/Latino; 1 Asian, non-Hispanic/Latino; 1 Hispanic/Latino), 21 international. Average age 28. 30 applicants, 70% accepted, 11 enrolled. In 2018, 10 master's, 4 doctorates awarded. *Degree requirements:* For master's, comprehensive exam, thesis (for some programs), project/thesis; for doctorate, comprehensive exam, thesis/dissertation. *Entrance requirements:* For master's, GRE General Test, minimum GPA of 3.0 on all undergraduate degree major courses attempted; for doctorate, GRE General Test (minimum quantitative score of 156), minimum GPA of 3.0 on all undergraduate degree major courses attempted. Additional exam requirements/recommendations for international students: Required—TOEFL (minimum score 80 iBT); Recommended—IELTS (minimum score 6.5). *Application deadline:* For fall admission, 8/1 for domestic and international students; for spring admission, 12/1 for domestic and international students; for summer admission, 5/1 for domestic and international students. Applications are processed on a rolling basis. Application fee: $50 ($60 for international students). Electronic applications accepted. *Expenses:* Contact institution. *Financial support:* In 2018–19, 35 students received support, including 10 fellowships with full tuition reimbursements available (averaging $26,700 per year), 14 research assistantships with full tuition reimbursements available; unspecified assistantships also available. *Faculty research:* Metal solidification and processing, polymer composite processing, high temperature materials and coatings, nano-sensor development, biomaterial development. *Total annual research expenditures:* $995,168. *Unit head:* Dr. Selvum Pillay, Department Chair, 205-934-8450, E-mail: pillay@uab.edu. *Application contact:* Jesse Keppley, Director of Academic and Student Services, 205-996-5696, E-mail: gradschool@uab.edu.
Website: https://www.uab.edu/engineering/home/departments-research/mse/grad

University of Alberta, Faculty of Graduate Studies and Research, Department of Chemical and Materials Engineering, Edmonton, AB T6G 2E1, Canada. Offers chemical engineering (M Eng, M Sc, PhD); materials engineering (M Eng, M Sc, PhD); process control (M Eng, M Sc, PhD); welding (M Eng). *Program availability:* Part-time, online learning. Terminal master's awarded for partial completion of doctoral program. *Degree requirements:* For master's, thesis; for doctorate, thesis/dissertation. *Faculty research:* Advanced materials and polymers, catalytic and reaction engineering, mineral processing, physical metallurgy, fluid mechanics.

The University of Arizona, College of Engineering, Department of Materials Science and Engineering, Tucson, AZ 85721. Offers MS, PhD. *Program availability:* Part-time. *Degree requirements:* For master's, thesis (for some programs); for doctorate, comprehensive exam, thesis/dissertation. *Entrance requirements:* For master's and doctorate, GRE General Test, 3 letters of recommendation, statement of purpose. Additional exam requirements/recommendations for international students: Required—TOEFL (minimum score 550 paper-based; 79 iBT). Electronic applications accepted. *Faculty research:* High-technology ceramics, optical materials, electronic materials, chemical metallurgy, science of materials.

The University of British Columbia, Faculty of Applied Science, Department of Materials Engineering, Vancouver, BC V6T 1Z4, Canada. Offers M Sc, MA Sc, PhD. *Degree requirements:* For master's, comprehensive exam, thesis; for doctorate, comprehensive exam, thesis/dissertation. *Entrance requirements:* Additional exam requirements/recommendations for international students: Required—TOEFL. Electronic applications accepted. *Expenses:* Contact institution. *Faculty research:* Electroslag melting, mathematical modeling, solidification and hydrometallurgy.

University of California, Berkeley, Graduate Division, College of Engineering, Department of Materials Science and Engineering, Berkeley, CA 94720. Offers engineering science (M Eng, MS, PhD). Terminal master's awarded for partial completion of doctoral program. *Degree requirements:* For master's, comprehensive exam (for some programs), thesis (for some programs), comprehensive exam or thesis (MS); for doctorate, comprehensive exam, thesis/dissertation, qualifying exam. *Entrance requirements:* For master's and doctorate, GRE General Test, minimum GPA of 3.0, 3 letters of recommendation. Additional exam requirements/recommendations for international students: Required—TOEFL (minimum score 570 paper-based; 90 iBT). Electronic applications accepted. *Faculty research:* Ceramics, biomaterials, structural, electronic, magnetic and optical materials.

University of California, Davis, College of Engineering, Program in Materials Science and Engineering, Davis, CA 95616. Offers MS, PhD. Terminal master's awarded for partial completion of doctoral program. *Degree requirements:* For master's, comprehensive exam (for some programs), thesis (for some programs); for doctorate, comprehensive exam, thesis/dissertation. *Entrance requirements:* Additional exam requirements/recommendations for international students: Required—TOEFL (minimum score 550 paper-based).

University of California, Irvine, Samueli School of Engineering, Department of Chemical Engineering and Materials Science, Irvine, CA 92697. Offers chemical and biochemical engineering (MS, PhD); materials science and engineering (MS, PhD). *Program availability:* Part-time. *Students:* 133 full-time (57 women), 2 part-time (0 women); includes 36 minority (3 Black or African American, non-Hispanic/Latino; 26 Asian, non-Hispanic/Latino; 5 Hispanic/Latino; 2 Two or more races, non-Hispanic/Latino), 51 international. Average age 26. 417 applicants, 35% accepted, 36 enrolled. In 2018, 30 master's, 26 doctorates awarded. Terminal master's awarded for partial completion of doctoral program. *Entrance requirements:* For master's and doctorate, GRE General Test, minimum GPA of 3.0, 3 letters of recommendation. Additional exam requirements/recommendations for international students: Required—TOEFL (minimum score 550 paper-based). *Application deadline:* For fall admission, 1/15 priority date for domestic students, 1/15 for international students. Applications are processed on a rolling basis. Application fee: $105 ($125 for international students). Electronic applications accepted. *Financial support:* Fellowships, research assistantships with full tuition reimbursements, teaching assistantships, institutionally sponsored loans, traineeships, health care benefits, and unspecified assistantships available. Financial award application deadline: 3/1; financial award applicants required to submit FAFSA. *Faculty research:* Molecular biotechnology, nanobiomaterials, biophotonics, synthesis, super plasticity and mechanical behavior, characterization of advanced and nanostructural materials. *Unit head:* Prof. Vasan Venugopalan, Chair, 949-824-5802, Fax: 949-824-2541, E-mail: vvenugop@uci.edu. *Application contact:* Grace Chau, Academic Program and Graduate Admission Coordinator, 949-824-3887, Fax: 949-824-2541, E-mail: chaug@uci.edu.
Website: http://www.eng.uci.edu/dept/chems

University of California, Irvine, Samueli School of Engineering, Program in Materials and Manufacturing Technology, Irvine, CA 92697. Offers engineering (MS, PhD). *Program availability:* Part-time. *Students:* 21 full-time (7 women), 4 part-time (2 women); includes 6 minority (3 Asian, non-Hispanic/Latino; 3 Hispanic/Latino), 14 international. Average age 28. 27 applicants, 59% accepted, 10 enrolled. In 2018, 5 master's, 2 doctorates awarded. *Entrance requirements:* For master's and doctorate, GRE General Test, 3 letters of recommendation, minimum GPA of 3.0. Additional exam requirements/recommendations for international students: Required—TOEFL (minimum score 550 paper-based). *Application deadline:* For fall admission, 1/15 priority date for domestic students, 1/15 for international students. Applications are processed on a rolling basis. Application fee: $105 ($125 for international students). Electronic applications accepted. *Financial support:* Fellowships, research assistantships with full tuition reimbursements, teaching assistantships, institutionally sponsored loans, traineeships, health care benefits, and unspecified assistantships available. Financial award application deadline: 3/1; financial award applicants required to submit FAFSA. *Faculty research:* Advanced materials, microelectronic and photonic devices and packaging, biomedical devices, MEMS, thin film materials, nanotechnology. *Application contact:* Connie Cheng, Assistant Director of Graduate Student Affairs, 949-824-3562, Fax: 949-824-8200, E-mail: connie.cheng@uci.edu.
Website: http://www.eng.uci.edu/

University of California, Los Angeles, Graduate Division, Henry Samueli School of Engineering and Applied Science, Department of Materials Science and Engineering, Los Angeles, CA 90095-1595. Offers MS, PhD. *Degree requirements:* For master's, comprehensive exam or thesis; for doctorate, thesis/dissertation, qualifying exams. *Entrance requirements:* For master's, GRE General Test, minimum GPA of 3.0; for doctorate, GRE General Test, minimum GPA of 3.25. Additional exam requirements/recommendations for international students: Required—TOEFL (minimum score 560 paper-based; 87 iBT), IELTS (minimum score 7). Electronic applications accepted. *Faculty research:* Ceramics and ceramic processing, electronic and optical materials, structural materials.

University of California, Riverside, Graduate Division, Materials Science and Engineering Program, Riverside, CA 92521. Offers MS. *Entrance requirements:* For master's, GRE. Additional exam requirements/recommendations for international students: Required—TOEFL (minimum score 550 paper-based; 80 iBT). Electronic applications accepted.

University of California, Santa Barbara, Graduate Division, College of Engineering, Department of Materials, Santa Barbara, CA 93106-5050. Offers MS, PhD, MS/PhD. Terminal master's awarded for partial completion of doctoral program. *Degree requirements:* For master's, variable foreign language requirement, comprehensive exam, thesis; for doctorate, variable foreign language requirement, comprehensive exam, thesis/dissertation. *Entrance requirements:* For master's and doctorate, GRE General Test. Additional exam requirements/recommendations for international students: Required—TOEFL (minimum score 600 paper-based; 100 iBT), IELTS (minimum score 7). Electronic applications accepted. *Faculty research:* Electronic and photonic materials, inorganic materials, macromolecular and biomolecular materials, structural materials.

University of Central Florida, College of Engineering and Computer Science, Department of Materials Science and Engineering, Orlando, FL 32816. Offers MSMSE, PhD. *Students:* 50 full-time (20 women), 16 part-time (8 women); includes 5 minority (2 Asian, non-Hispanic/Latino; 2 Hispanic/Latino; 1 Two or more races, non-Hispanic/Latino), 36 international. Average age 29. 64 applicants, 41% accepted, 17 enrolled. In 2018, 8 master's, 5 doctorates awarded. *Degree requirements:* For master's, thesis or alternative; for doctorate, thesis/dissertation, candidacy exam, departmental qualifying exam. *Entrance requirements;* For master's, resume, goal statement; for doctorate, GRE, letters of recommendation, resume, goal statement. Additional exam requirements/recommendations for international students: Required—TOEFL. *Application deadline:* For fall admission, 7/15 for domestic students; for spring admission, 12/1 for domestic students. Application fee: $30. Electronic applications accepted. *Financial support:* In 2018–19, 45 students received support, including 11 fellowships with tuition reimbursements available (averaging $11,891 per year), 47 research assistantships (averaging $11,177 per year), 6 teaching assistantships (averaging $13,327 per year); health care benefits also available. Financial award application deadline: 3/1; financial award applicants required to submit FAFSA. *Unit head:* Dr. Sudipta Seal, Chair, 407-823-5277, E-mail: sseal@ucf.edu. *Application contact:* Associate Director, Graduate Admissions, 407-823-2766, Fax: 407-823-6442, E-mail: gradadmissions@ucf.edu.
Website: http://mse.ucf.edu/

University of Cincinnati, Graduate School, College of Engineering and Applied Science, Department of Mechanical and Materials Engineering, Program in Materials Science and Engineering, Cincinnati, OH 45221. Offers MS, PhD. *Program availability:* Evening/weekend. *Degree requirements:* For master's, thesis optional; for doctorate, one foreign language, comprehensive exam, thesis/dissertation, oral English proficiency exam. *Entrance requirements:* For master's and doctorate, GRE General Test, BS in related field, minimum undergraduate GPA of 3.0. Additional exam requirements/recommendations for international students: Required—TOEFL. Electronic applications accepted. *Faculty research:* Polymer characterization, surface analysis, and adhesion; mechanical behavior of high-temperature materials; composites; electrochemistry of materials.

University of Colorado Boulder, Graduate School, Materials Science and Engineering Program, Boulder, CO 80309. Offers MS, PhD. Electronic applications accepted.

University of Connecticut, Graduate School, School of Engineering, Department of Materials Science and Engineering, Storrs, CT 06269. Offers M Eng. Terminal master's awarded for partial completion of doctoral program. *Degree requirements:* For master's, comprehensive exam, thesis or alternative. *Entrance requirements:* For master's, GRE General Test, GRE Subject Test. Additional exam requirements/recommendations for international students: Required—TOEFL (minimum score 550 paper-based). Electronic applications accepted.

University of Dayton, Program in Materials Engineering, Dayton, OH 45469. Offers MS, DE, PhD. *Program availability:* Part-time, evening/weekend, blended/hybrid learning. Terminal master's awarded for partial completion of doctoral program. *Degree requirements:* For master's, thesis optional; for doctorate, comprehensive exam, thesis/dissertation, departmental qualifying exam. *Entrance requirements:* Additional exam requirements/recommendations for international students: Required—TOEFL (minimum score 550 paper-based; 80 iBT). Electronic applications accepted. *Faculty research:* Nano-materials, composite materials, carbon materials, 3D printed metals and plastics, 2D nano-materials.

University of Delaware, College of Engineering, Department of Materials Science and Engineering, Newark, DE 19716. Offers MMSE, PhD. Terminal master's awarded for partial completion of doctoral program. *Degree requirements:* For master's, thesis; for doctorate, thesis/dissertation. *Entrance requirements:* For master's and doctorate, GRE General Test, 3 letters of recommendation, minimum GPA of 3.2. Additional exam requirements/recommendations for international students: Required—TOEFL. Electronic applications accepted. *Faculty research:* Thin films and self assembly, drug delivery and tissue engineering, biomaterials and nanocomposites, semiconductor and oxide interfaces, electronic and magnetic materials.

University of Denver, Daniel Felix Ritchie School of Engineering and Computer Science, Department of Mechanical and Materials Engineering, Denver, CO 80208. Offers bioengineering (MS); engineering (MS, PhD), including management; materials science (MS, PhD); mechanical engineering (MS, PhD). *Program availability:* Part-time. *Faculty:* 13 full-time (2 women), 2 part-time/adjunct (1 woman). *Students:* 4 full-time (1 woman), 33 part-time (7 women); includes 5 minority (2 Black or African American, non-Hispanic/Latino; 2 Hispanic/Latino; 1 Two or more races, non-Hispanic/Latino), 11 international. Average age 28. 71 applicants, 63% accepted, 15 enrolled. In 2018, 11 master's, 3 doctorates awarded. Terminal master's awarded for partial completion of doctoral program. *Degree requirements:* For master's, thesis optional; for doctorate, comprehensive exam, thesis/dissertation. *Entrance requirements:* For master's, GRE General Test, bachelor's degree in engineering or closely related field, transcripts, personal statement, resume or curriculum vitae, two letters of recommendation; for doctorate, GRE General Test, master's degree in engineering or closely related field, transcripts, personal statement, resume or curriculum vitae, two letters of recommendation, recommended that applicants find a research advisor before submitting the application. Additional exam requirements/recommendations for international students: Required—TOEFL (minimum score 550 paper-based; 80 iBT). *Application deadline:* For fall admission, 1/15 priority date for domestic and international students; for winter admission, 10/25 for domestic and international students; for spring admission, 2/7 for domestic and international students; for summer admission, 4/24 for domestic and international students. Applications are processed on a rolling basis. Application fee: $65. Electronic applications accepted. *Expenses:* $33,183 per year full-time. *Financial support:* In 2018–19, 25 students received support, including 10 research assistantships with tuition reimbursements available (averaging $12,917 per year), 13 teaching assistantships with tuition reimbursements available (averaging $15,289 per year); Federal Work-Study, institutionally sponsored loans, scholarships/grants, health care benefits, and unspecified assistantships also available. Financial award application deadline: 2/15; financial award applicants required to submit FAFSA. *Faculty research:* Cardiac biomechanics, novel high voltage/temperature materials and structures, high speed stereo radiography, musculoskeletal modeling, composites. *Unit head:* Dr. Matt Gordon, Professor and Chair, 303-871-3580, E-mail: matthew.gordon@du.edu. *Application contact:* Chrissy Alexander, Assistant to the Chair, 303-871-3041, E-mail: Christine.Alexander@du.edu.
Website: http://ritchieschool.du.edu/departments/mme/

University of Florida, Graduate School, Herbert Wertheim College of Engineering, Department of Materials Science and Engineering, Gainesville, FL 32611. Offers material science and engineering (MS), including clinical and translational science; materials science and engineering (ME, PhD); nuclear engineering (ME, PhD), including imaging science and technology (PhD), nuclear engineering sciences (ME, MS, PhD); nuclear engineering (MS), including nuclear engineering sciences (ME, MS, PhD); JD/MS. *Program availability:* Part-time, online learning. Terminal master's awarded for partial completion of doctoral program. *Degree requirements:* For master's, comprehensive exam, thesis; for doctorate, comprehensive exam, thesis/dissertation. *Entrance requirements:* For master's and doctorate, minimum GPA of 3.0. Additional exam requirements/recommendations for international students: Required—TOEFL (minimum score 550 paper-based; 80 iBT), IELTS (minimum score 6). Electronic applications accepted. *Faculty research:* Polymeric system, biomaterials and biomimetics; inorganic and organic electronic materials; functional ceramic materials for energy systems and microelectronic applications; advanced metallic systems for aerospace, transportation and biological applications; nuclear materials.

University of Illinois at Chicago, College of Engineering, Department of Civil and Materials Engineering, Chicago, IL 60607-7128. Offers MS, PhD. *Program availability:* Evening/weekend. *Degree requirements:* For master's, thesis (for some programs); for doctorate, thesis/dissertation, preliminary and qualifying exams. *Entrance requirements:* For master's and doctorate, GRE General Test, minimum GPA of 3.0. Additional exam requirements/recommendations for international students: Required—TOEFL. Electronic applications accepted. *Expenses:* Contact institution. *Faculty research:* Integrated fiber optic, acoustic emission and MEMS-based sensors development; monitoring the state of repaired and strengthened structures; development of weigh-in-motion (WIM) systems; image processing techniques for characterization of concrete entrained air bubble systems.

University of Illinois at Urbana–Champaign, Graduate College, College of Engineering, Department of Materials Science and Engineering, Champaign, IL 61820. Offers M Eng, MS, PhD, MS/MBA, PhD/MBA.

The University of Iowa, Graduate College, College of Engineering, Department of Mechanical Engineering, Iowa City, IA 52242-1316. Offers energy systems (MS, PhD); engineering design (MS, PhD); fluid dynamics (MS, PhD); materials and manufacturing (MS, PhD); wind energy (MS, PhD). Terminal master's awarded for partial completion of doctoral program. *Degree requirements:* For master's, oral exam or thesis; for doctorate, comprehensive exam, thesis/dissertation. *Entrance requirements:* For master's and doctorate, GRE (minimum Verbal score of 153, Quantitative 151), minimum undergraduate GPA of 3.0. Additional exam requirements/recommendations for international students: Required—TOEFL (minimum score 600 paper-based; 100 iBT), IELTS (minimum score 7). Electronic applications accepted. *Faculty research:* Computer simulation methodology, biomechanics, metal casting, dynamics, laser processing, system reliability, ship hydrodynamics, solid mechanics, fluid dynamics, energy, human modeling and nanotechnology.

University of Kentucky, Graduate School, College of Engineering, Program in Materials Science and Engineering, Lexington, KY 40506-0032. Offers MS, PhD. *Degree requirements:* For master's, comprehensive exam, thesis optional; for doctorate, comprehensive exam, thesis/dissertation. *Entrance requirements:* For master's, GRE General Test, minimum undergraduate GPA of 2.75; for doctorate, GRE General Test, minimum undergraduate GPA of 3.0. Additional exam requirements/recommendations for international students: Required—TOEFL (minimum score 550 paper-based). Electronic applications accepted. *Faculty research:* Physical and mechanical metallurgy, computational material engineering, polymers and composites, high-temperature ceramics, powder metallurgy.

University of Maryland, College Park, Academic Affairs, A. James Clark School of Engineering, Department of Materials Science and Engineering, Materials Science and Engineering Program, College Park, MD 20742. Offers MS, PhD. *Program availability:* Part-time, evening/weekend, online learning. *Degree requirements:* For master's, comprehensive exam, thesis optional, research paper; for doctorate, thesis/dissertation, oral exam. *Entrance requirements:* For master's and doctorate, GRE General Test, minimum B+ average in undergraduate course work. Additional exam requirements/recommendations for international students: Required—TOEFL. Electronic applications accepted.

University of Maryland, College Park, Academic Affairs, A. James Clark School of Engineering, Department of Mechanical Engineering, College Park, MD 20742. Offers electronic packaging and reliability (MS, PhD); manufacturing and design (MS, PhD); mechanics and materials (MS, PhD); reliability engineering (M Eng, MS, PhD); thermal and fluid sciences (MS, PhD). *Program availability:* Part-time, evening/weekend, online learning. *Degree requirements:* For master's, thesis optional; for doctorate, thesis/dissertation, qualifying exam. *Entrance requirements:* For master's, GRE General Test, 3 letters of recommendation; for doctorate, GRE General Test, minimum GPA of 3.0. Additional exam requirements/recommendations for international students: Required—TOEFL. Electronic applications accepted. *Faculty research:* Injection molding, electronic packaging, fluid mechanics, product engineering.

University of Michigan, College of Engineering, Department of Materials Science and Engineering, Ann Arbor, MI 48109. Offers MS, MSE, PhD. *Program availability:* Part-time. *Students:* 176 full-time (71 women), 5 part-time (2 women). 668 applicants, 22% accepted, 48 enrolled. In 2018, 31 master's, 28 doctorates awarded. Terminal master's awarded for partial completion of doctoral program. *Degree requirements:* For master's, thesis, oral defense of thesis; for doctorate, thesis/dissertation, oral defense of dissertation, written exam. *Entrance requirements:* For master's and doctorate, GRE General Test. Additional exam requirements/recommendations for international students: Required—TOEFL. *Application deadline:* Applications are processed on a rolling basis. Electronic applications accepted. *Financial support:* Fellowships, research assistantships, and teaching assistantships available. Financial award applicants required to submit FAFSA. *Faculty research:* Soft materials (polymers, biomaterials), computational materials science, structural materials, electronic and optical materials, nanocomposite materials. *Total annual research expenditures:* $10.3 million. *Unit head:* Amit Misra, Department Chair, 734-763-2445, E-mail: amitmis@umich.edu. *Application contact:* Renee Hilgendorf, Graduate Program Coordinator, 734-763-9790, E-mail: reneeh@umich.edu.
Website: http://www.mse.engin.umich.edu

University of Minnesota, Twin Cities Campus, College of Science and Engineering, Department of Chemical Engineering and Materials Science, Program in Materials Science and Engineering, Minneapolis, MN 55455-0132. Offers M Mat SE, MS Mat SE, PhD. *Program availability:* Part-time. Terminal master's awarded for partial completion of doctoral program. *Degree requirements:* For master's, thesis; for doctorate, thesis/dissertation. *Entrance requirements:* For master's and doctorate, GRE General Test. Additional exam requirements/recommendations for international students: Required—TOEFL. Electronic applications accepted. *Faculty research:* Ceramics and metals; coating processes and interfacial engineering; crystal growth and design; polymers; electronic, photonic and magnetic materials.

University of Nebraska–Lincoln, Graduate College, College of Engineering, Department of Mechanical and Materials Engineering, Lincoln, NE 68588-0526. Offers biomedical engineering (PhD); engineering mechanics (MS); materials engineering (PhD); mechanical engineering (MS), including materials science engineering, metallurgical engineering; mechanical engineering and applied mechanics (PhD); MS/MS. MS/MS offered with University of Rouen-France. *Degree requirements:* For master's, thesis optional; for doctorate, comprehensive exam, thesis/dissertation. *Entrance requirements:* For master's and doctorate, GRE General Test. Additional exam requirements/recommendations for international students: Required—TOEFL (minimum score 550 paper-based). Electronic applications accepted. *Faculty research:* Medical robotics, rehabilitation dynamics, and design; combustion, fluid mechanics, and heat transfer; nano-materials, manufacturing, and devices; fiber, tissue, bio-polymer, and adaptive composites; blast, impact, fracture, and failure; electro-active and magnetic materials and devices; functional materials, design, and added manufacturing; materials characterization, modeling, and computational simulation.

University of Nevada, Las Vegas, Graduate College, Howard R. Hughes College of Engineering, Department of Mechanical Engineering, Las Vegas, NV 89154-4027. Offers aerospace engineering (MS); biomedical engineering (MS); materials and nuclear engineering (MS); mechanical engineering (MS, PhD); nuclear criticality safety engineering (Certificate); nuclear safeguards and security (Certificate). *Program availability:* Part-time. *Faculty:* 17 full-time (2 women). *Students:* 50 full-time (18 women), 19 part-time (4 women); includes 19 minority (4 Black or African American, non-Hispanic/Latino; 1 American Indian or Alaska Native, non-Hispanic/Latino; 4 Asian, non-Hispanic/Latino; 7 Hispanic/Latino; 3 Two or more races, non-Hispanic/Latino), 21 international. Average age 29. 63 applicants, 73% accepted, 23 enrolled. In 2018, 15 master's, 5 doctorates, 1 other advanced degree awarded. *Degree requirements:* For master's, thesis optional, design project; for doctorate, comprehensive exam, thesis/dissertation. *Entrance requirements:* For master's, GRE General Test, statement of purpose; 2 letters of recommendation; for doctorate, GRE General Test, 3 letters of recommendation; statement of purpose; bachelor's degree with minimum GPA of 3.5/master's degree with minimum GPA of 3.3. Additional exam requirements/recommendations for international students: Required—TOEFL (minimum score 550 paper-based; 80 iBT), IELTS (minimum score 7). *Application deadline:* For fall admission, 8/1 for domestic students, 5/1 for international students; for spring admission, 12/1 for domestic students, 10/1 for international students. Application fee: $60 ($95 for international students). Electronic applications accepted. *Expenses:* Contact institution. *Financial support:* In 2018–19, 40 students received support, including 1 fellowship with full tuition reimbursement available (averaging $15,000 per year), 17 research assistantships with full tuition reimbursements available (averaging $16,910 per year), 23 teaching assistantships with full tuition reimbursements available (averaging $16,467 per year); institutionally sponsored loans, scholarships/grants, health care benefits, and unspecified assistantships also available. Financial award application deadline: 3/15; financial award applicants required to submit FAFSA. *Faculty research:* Dynamics and control systems; energy systems including renewable and nuclear; computational fluid and solid mechanics; structures, materials and manufacturing; vibrations and acoustics. *Total annual research expenditures:* $4.5 million. *Unit head:* Dr. Brendan O'Toole, Chair/Professor, 702-895-3885, Fax: 702-895-3936, E-mail: mechanical.chair@unlv.edu. *Application contact:* Dr. Hui Zhao, Graduate Coordinator, 702-895-1463, Fax: 702-895-3936, E-mail: mechanical.gradcoord@unlv.edu.
Website: http://me.unlv.edu/

University of Nevada, Reno, Graduate School, College of Engineering, Department of Chemical and Materials Engineering, Program in Materials Science and Engineering, Reno, NV 89557. Offers MS, PhD. Terminal master's awarded for partial completion of doctoral program. *Degree requirements:* For master's, thesis; for doctorate, one foreign language, thesis/dissertation. *Entrance requirements:* For master's, minimum GPA of 2.75; for doctorate, GRE, minimum GPA of 3.0. Additional exam requirements/recommendations for international students: Required—TOEFL (minimum score 500 paper-based; 61 iBT), IELTS (minimum score 6). Electronic applications accepted. *Faculty research:* Hydrometallurgy, applied surface chemistry, mineral processing, mineral bioprocessing, ceramics.

University of New Hampshire, Graduate School, College of Engineering and Physical Sciences, Program in Materials Science, Durham, NH 03824. Offers materials science (MS); materials science and engineering (PhD). *Entrance requirements:* For master's and doctorate, GRE. Additional exam requirements/recommendations for international students: Required—TOEFL (minimum score 550 paper-based; 80 iBT). Electronic applications accepted.

University of Pennsylvania, School of Engineering and Applied Science, Department of Materials Science and Engineering, Philadelphia, PA 19104. Offers MSE, PhD. *Program availability:* Part-time. *Students:* Average age 24. 541 applicants, 30% accepted, 83 enrolled. In 2018, 28 master's, 5 doctorates awarded. *Degree requirements:* For master's, comprehensive exam, thesis optional; for doctorate, comprehensive exam, thesis/dissertation. *Entrance requirements:* For master's and doctorate, GRE, bachelor's degree, letters of recommendation, resume, personal statement. Additional exam requirements/recommendations for international students: Required—TOEFL (minimum score 100 iBT), IELTS (minimum score 7). *Application deadline:* For fall admission, 12/15 priority date for domestic and international students. Application fee: $80. Electronic applications accepted. *Expenses:* Contact institution. *Faculty research:* Biomaterials, ceramics, electronic and optical properties, nanostructured materials, surfaces and interfaces. *Application contact:* William Fenton, Assistant Director of Graduate Admissions, 215-898-4542, Fax: 215-573-5577, E-mail: gradstudies@seas.upenn.edu.
Website: http://www.mse.seas.upenn.edu/current-students/masters/index.php

University of Puerto Rico–Mayagüez, Graduate Studies, College of Engineering, Department of Engineering Sciences and Materials, Mayagüez, PR 00681-9000. Offers materials science and engineering (MS).

University of Puerto Rico–Mayagüez, Graduate Studies, College of Engineering, Department of Mechanical Engineering, Mayagüez, PR 00681-9000. Offers mechanical engineering (ME, MS, PhD), including aerospace and unmanned vehicles (ME), automation/mechatronics, bioengineering, fluid mechanics, heat transfer/energy systems, manufacturing, mechanics of materials, micro and nano engineering. *Program availability:* Part-time. Terminal master's awarded for partial completion of doctoral program. *Degree requirements:* For master's, one foreign language, comprehensive exam, thesis; for doctorate, one foreign language, comprehensive exam, thesis/dissertation. *Entrance requirements:* For master's, BS in mechanical engineering or its equivalent; for doctorate, GRE, BS or MS in mechanical engineering or its equivalent; minimum GPA of 3.0. Additional exam requirements/recommendations for international students: Required—TOEFL (minimum score 80 iBT). Electronic applications accepted. *Faculty research:* Computational fluid dynamics, thermal sciences, mechanical design, material health, microfluidics.

University of Southern California, Graduate School, Viterbi School of Engineering, Mork Family Department of Chemical Engineering and Materials Science, Los Angeles, CA 90089. Offers chemical engineering (MS, PhD, Engr); geoscience technologies (MS); materials engineering (MS); materials science (MS, PhD, Engr); petroleum engineering (MS, PhD, Engr); smart oilfield technologies (MS, Graduate Certificate). Terminal master's awarded for partial completion of doctoral program. *Degree requirements:* For master's, thesis optional; for doctorate, thesis/dissertation. *Entrance requirements:* For master's and doctorate, GRE General Test. Additional exam requirements/recommendations for international students: Recommended—TOEFL. Electronic applications accepted. *Expenses:* Contact institution. *Faculty research:* Heterogeneous materials and porous media, statistical mechanics, molecular simulation, polymer science and engineering, advanced materials, reaction engineering and catalysis, membrane processes and separation, biochemical engineering, cell culture, bioreactor modeling, petroleum engineering.

University of South Florida, College of Engineering, Department of Civil and Environmental Engineering, Tampa, FL 33620-9951. Offers civil engineering (MCE, MSCE, PhD), including geotechnical engineering, materials science and engineering, structures engineering, transportation engineering, water resources; environmental engineering (MEVE, MSEV, PhD), including engineering for international development (MSEV). *Program availability:* Part-time. *Faculty:* 19 full-time (5 women). *Students:* 144 full-time (46 women), 76 part-time (22 women); includes 35 minority (8 Black or African American, non-Hispanic/Latino; 5 Asian, non-Hispanic/Latino; 18 Hispanic/Latino; 4 Two or more races, non-Hispanic/Latino), 123 international. Average age 28. 220 applicants, 65% accepted, 59 enrolled. In 2018, 82 master's, 15 doctorates awarded. Terminal master's awarded for partial completion of doctoral program. *Degree requirements:* For master's, comprehensive exam, thesis (for some programs); for doctorate, comprehensive exam, thesis/dissertation. *Entrance requirements:* For master's, GRE required, bachelor's degree in appropriate field, minimum GPA of 3.0 in major, letters of reference, statement of purpose, resume, intake form; for doctorate, GRE with V (45th percentile), Q (75th percentile), and AW (55th percentile), letters of recommendation, statement of purpose, resume, intake form. Additional exam requirements/recommendations for international students: Required—TOEFL, TOEFL (minimum score 550 paper-based; 79 iBT) or IELTS (minimum score 6.5). *Application deadline:* For fall admission, 2/15 for domestic students, 2/15 priority date for international students; for spring admission, 10/15 for domestic students, 9/15 priority date for international students. Application fee: $30. Electronic applications accepted. *Expenses:* Tuition, state resident: full-time $6350. Tuition, nonresident: full-time $19,048. *International tuition:* $19,048 full-time. *Required fees:* $2079. *Financial support:* In 2018–19, 45 students received support, including 44 research assistantships (averaging $14,123 per year), 21 teaching assistantships with tuition reimbursements available (averaging $15,329 per year). *Faculty research:* Environmental and water resources engineering, geotechnics and geoenvironmental systems, structures and materials systems, transportation systems. *Total annual research expenditures:* $3.7 million. *Unit head:* Dr. Manjriker Gunaratne, Professor and Department Chair, 813-974-5818, Fax: 813-974-2957, E-mail: gunaratn@usf.edu. *Application contact:* Dr. Sarina J. Ergas, Professor and Graduate Program Coordinator, 813-974-1119, Fax: 813-974-2957, E-mail: sergas@usf.edu.
Website: http://www.usf.edu/engineering/cee/

University of South Florida, Innovative Education, Tampa, FL 33620-9951. Offers adult, career and higher education (Graduate Certificate), including college teaching, leadership in developing human resources, leadership in higher education; Africana studies (Graduate Certificate), including diasporas and health disparities, genocide and human rights; aging studies (Graduate Certificate), including gerontology; art research (Graduate Certificate), including museum studies; business foundations (Graduate Certificate); chemical and biomedical engineering (Graduate Certificate), including materials science and engineering, water, health and sustainability; child and family studies (Graduate Certificate), including positive behavior support; civil and industrial engineering (Graduate Certificate), including transportation systems analysis; community and family health (Graduate Certificate), including maternal and child health, social marketing and public health, violence and injury: prevention and intervention, women's health; criminology (Graduate Certificate), including criminal justice administration; data science for public administration (Graduate Certificate); digital humanities (Graduate Certificate); educational measurement and research (Graduate Certificate), including evaluation; English (Graduate Certificate), including comparative literary studies, creative writing, professional and technical communication; entrepreneurship (Graduate Certificate); environmental health (Graduate Certificate), including safety management; epidemiology and biostatistics (Graduate Certificate),

including applied biostatistics, biostatistics, concepts and tools of epidemiology, epidemiology, epidemiology of infectious diseases; geography, environment and planning (Graduate Certificate), including community development, environmental policy and management, geographical information systems; geology (Graduate Certificate), including hydrogeology; global health (Graduate Certificate), including disaster management, global health and Latin American and Caribbean studies, global health practice, humanitarian assistance, infection control; government and international affairs (Graduate Certificate), including Cuban studies, globalization studies; health policy and management (Graduate Certificate), including health management and leadership, public health policy and programs; hearing specialist: early intervention (Graduate Certificate); industrial and management systems engineering (Graduate Certificate), including systems engineering, technology management; information studies (Graduate Certificate), including school library media specialist; information systems/decision sciences (Graduate Certificate), including analytics and business intelligence; instructional technology (Graduate Certificate), including distance education, Florida digital/virtual educator, instructional design, multimedia design, Web design; internal medicine, bioethics and medical humanities (Graduate Certificate), including biomedical ethics; Latin American and Caribbean studies (Graduate Certificate); leadership for coastal resiliency planning (Graduate Certificate); mass communications (Graduate Certificate), including multimedia journalism; mathematics and statistics (Graduate Certificate), including mathematics; medicine (Graduate Certificate), including aging and neuroscience, bioinformatics, biotechnology, brain fitness and memory management, clinical investigation, hand and upper limb rehabilitation, health informatics, health sciences, integrative weight management, intellectual property, medicine and gender, metabolic and nutritional medicine, metabolic cardiology, pharmacy sciences; national and competitive intelligence (Graduate Certificate); nursing (Graduate Certificate), including simulation based academic fellowship in advanced pain management; psychological and social foundations (Graduate Certificate), including career counseling, college teaching, diversity in education, mental health counseling, school counseling; public affairs (Graduate Certificate), including nonprofit management, public management, research administration; public health (Graduate Certificate), including assessing chemical toxicity and public health risks, health equity, pharmacoepidemiology, public health generalist, toxicology, translational research in adolescent behavioral health; public health practices (Graduate Certificate), including planning for healthy communities; rehabilitation and mental health counseling (Graduate Certificate), including integrative mental health care, marriage and family therapy, rehabilitation technology; secondary education (Graduate Certificate), including ESOL, foreign language education: culture and content, foreign language education: professional; social work (Graduate Certificate), including geriatric social work/clinical gerontology; special education (Graduate Certificate), including autism spectrum disorder, disabilities education: severe/profound; world languages (Graduate Certificate), including teaching English as a second language (TESL) or foreign language. *Expenses:* Tuition, state resident: full-time $6350. Tuition, nonresident: full-time $19,048. *International tuition:* $19,048 full-time. *Required fees:* $2079. *Unit head:* Dr. Cynthia DeLuca, Associate Vice President and Assistant Vice Provost, 813-974-3077, Fax: 813-974-7061, E-mail: deluca@usf.edu. *Application contact:* Owen Hooper, Director, Summer and Alternative Calendar Programs, 813-974-6917, E-mail: hooper@usf.edu.
Website: http://www.usf.edu/innovative-education/

The University of Tennessee, Graduate School, Tickle College of Engineering, Department of Materials Science and Engineering, Knoxville, TN 37996-2200. Offers materials science and engineering (MS, PhD); reliability and maintainability engineering (MS); MS/MBA. *Program availability:* Part-time. *Faculty:* 25 full-time (4 women). *Students:* 85 full-time (28 women), 8 part-time (0 women); includes 5 minority (1 Black or African American, non-Hispanic/Latino; 2 Asian, non-Hispanic/Latino; 2 Hispanic/Latino), 44 international. Average age 27. 74 applicants, 34% accepted, 12 enrolled. In 2018, 6 master's, 9 doctorates awarded. *Degree requirements:* For master's, thesis or alternative; for doctorate, comprehensive exam, thesis/dissertation. *Entrance requirements:* For master's, GRE General Test (for MS students pursuing research thesis), minimum GPA of 2.7 (for U.S. degree holders), 3.0 (for international degree holders); 3 references; for doctorate, GRE General Test, minimum GPA of 3.0 on previous graduate course work; 3 references. Additional exam requirements/recommendations for international students: Required—TOEFL (minimum score 550 paper-based; 80 iBT), IELTS (minimum score 6.5). *Application deadline:* For fall admission, 2/1 priority date for domestic and international students; for spring admission, 6/15 for domestic and international students; for summer admission, 10/15 for domestic and international students. Applications are processed on a rolling basis. Application fee: $60. Electronic applications accepted. *Financial support:* In 2018–19, 114 students received support, including 19 fellowships with full tuition reimbursements available (averaging $12,060 per year), 73 research assistantships with full tuition reimbursements available (averaging $23,497 per year), 22 teaching assistantships with full tuition reimbursements available (averaging $21,010 per year); career-related internships or fieldwork, Federal Work-Study, institutionally sponsored loans, health care benefits, and unspecified assistantships also available. Financial award application deadline: 2/1; financial award applicants required to submit FAFSA. *Faculty research:* Biomaterials; functional materials electronic, magnetic and optical; high temperature materials; mechanical behavior of materials; neutron materials science. *Total annual research expenditures:* $6.4 million. *Unit head:* Dr. Veerle Keppens, Head, 865-974-5336, Fax: 865-974-4115, E-mail: vkeppens@utk.edu. *Application contact:* Dr. Kurt Sickafus, Professor and Director of Graduate Studies, 865-974-4858, E-mail: kurt@utk.edu.
Website: http://www.engr.utk.edu/mse

The University of Texas at Arlington, Graduate School, College of Engineering, Department of Materials Science and Engineering, Arlington, TX 76019. Offers M Engr, MS, PhD. Terminal master's awarded for partial completion of doctoral program. *Degree requirements:* For master's, comprehensive exam (for some programs), thesis optional; for doctorate, comprehensive exam, thesis/dissertation optional. *Entrance requirements:* For master's, GRE General Test, minimum GPA of 3.0; for doctorate, GRE General Test, minimum GPA of 3.5. Additional exam requirements/recommendations for international students: Required—TOEFL (minimum score 550 paper-based; 79 iBT), IELTS. *Faculty research:* Electronic materials, conductive polymer, composites biomaterial, structural materials.

The University of Texas at Austin, Graduate School, Cockrell School of Engineering, Program in Materials Science and Engineering, Austin, TX 78712-1111. Offers MS, PhD. *Program availability:* Part-time. *Degree requirements:* For master's, thesis (for some programs); for doctorate, thesis/dissertation. *Entrance requirements:* For master's and doctorate, GRE General Test. Additional exam requirements/recommendations for international students: Required—TOEFL (minimum score 550 paper-based). Electronic applications accepted.

The University of Texas at Dallas, Erik Jonsson School of Engineering and Computer Science, Department of Materials Science and Engineering, Richardson, TX 75080. Offers MS, PhD. *Program availability:* Part-time, evening/weekend. *Faculty:* 13 full-time (2 women), 1 part-time/adjunct (0 women). *Students:* 59 full-time (12 women), 6 part-time (2 women); includes 9 minority (1 Black or African American, non-Hispanic/Latino;

4 Asian, non-Hispanic/Latino; 4 Hispanic/Latino), 43 international. Average age 29. 94 applicants, 35% accepted, 10 enrolled. In 2018, 11 master's, 10 doctorates awarded. *Degree requirements:* For master's, thesis or major design project; for doctorate, thesis/dissertation. *Entrance requirements:* For master's, GRE General Test, minimum GPA of 3.0 in related bachelor's degree; for doctorate, GRE General Test, minimum GPA of 3.5. Additional exam requirements/recommendations for international students: Required—TOEFL (minimum score 550 paper-based). *Application deadline:* For fall admission, 7/15 for domestic students, 5/1 priority date for international students; for spring admission, 11/15 for domestic students, 9/1 priority date for international students. Applications are processed on a rolling basis. Application fee: $50 ($100 for international students). Electronic applications accepted. *Expenses: Tuition, area resident:* Full-time $13,458. Tuition, state resident: full-time $13,458. Tuition, nonresident: full-time $26,852. *International tuition:* $26,852 full-time. Tuition and fees vary according to course load. *Financial support:* In 2018–19, 41 students received support, including 2 fellowships (averaging $7,535 per year), 41 research assistantships with partial tuition reimbursements available (averaging $25,755 per year), 4 teaching assistantships with partial tuition reimbursements available (averaging $18,225 per year); career-related internships or fieldwork, Federal Work-Study, institutionally sponsored loans, scholarships/grants, and unspecified assistantships also available. Support available to part-time students. Financial award application deadline: 4/30; financial award applicants required to submit FAFSA. *Faculty research:* Graphene-based semiconducting materials, neuro-inspired computational paradigms, electronic materials with emphasis on dielectrics, energy harvesting (photovoltaics, lithium-ion batteries), biosensors and hydrogen storage materials. *Unit head:* Dr. Amy Walker, Interim Department Head, 972-883-5780, Fax: 972-883-5725, E-mail: amy.walker@utdallas.edu. *Application contact:* Dr. Lev Gelb, Associate Department Head, 972-883-5644, Fax: 972-883-5725, E-mail: mseadmissions@utdallas.edu.
Website: http://mse.utdallas.edu/

The University of Texas at El Paso, Graduate School, College of Engineering, Department of Metallurgical and Materials Engineering, El Paso, TX 79968-0001. Offers materials science and engineering (PhD); metallurgical and materials engineering (MS). *Program availability:* Part-time, evening/weekend. *Degree requirements:* For master's, thesis. *Entrance requirements:* For master's, GRE General Test. Additional exam requirements/recommendations for international students: Required—TOEFL. Electronic applications accepted.

The University of Texas at San Antonio, College of Engineering, Department of Electrical and Computer Engineering, San Antonio, TX 78249-0617. Offers advanced materials engineering (MS); computer engineering (MS); electrical engineering (MSEE, PhD). *Program availability:* Part-time. Terminal master's awarded for partial completion of doctoral program. *Degree requirements:* For master's, comprehensive exam, thesis (for some programs); for doctorate, comprehensive exam, thesis/dissertation. *Entrance requirements:* For master's, GRE General Test, bachelor's degree in electrical or computer engineering from ABET-accredited institution of higher education or related field; minimum GPA of 3.0 on the last 60 semester credit hours of undergraduate studies; for doctorate, GRE General Test, master's degree or minimum GPA of 3.3 in last 60 semester credit hours of undergraduate level coursework in electrical engineering; statement of purpose. Additional exam requirements/recommendations for international students: Required—TOEFL (minimum score 550 paper-based; 79 iBT), IELTS (minimum score 6.5). Electronic applications accepted. *Faculty research:* Computer engineering, digital signal processing, systems and controls, communications, electronics materials and devices, electric power engineering.

University of Toronto, School of Graduate Studies, Faculty of Applied Science and Engineering, Department of Materials Science and Engineering, Toronto, ON M5S 1A1, Canada. Offers M Eng, MA Sc, PhD. *Program availability:* Part-time. *Degree requirements:* For master's, thesis (for some programs), oral presentation/thesis defense (MA Sc), qualifying exam; for doctorate, thesis/dissertation. *Entrance requirements:* For master's, BA Sc or B Sc in materials science and engineering, 2 letters of reference; for doctorate, MA Sc or equivalent, 2 letters of reference, minimum B+ average in last 2 years. Additional exam requirements/recommendations for international students: Required—TOEFL (minimum score 580 paper-based), TWE (minimum score 4). Electronic applications accepted.

University of Utah, Graduate School, College of Engineering, Department of Materials Science and Engineering, Salt Lake City, UT 84112. Offers MS, PhD. *Faculty:* 7 full-time (0 women), 3 part-time/adjunct (0 women). *Students:* 21 full-time (7 women), 5 part-time (0 women); includes 3 minority (1 Hispanic/Latino; 1 Native Hawaiian or other Pacific Islander, non-Hispanic/Latino; 1 Two or more races, non-Hispanic/Latino), 8 international. Average age 27. 80 applicants, 8% accepted, 5 enrolled. In 2018, 3 master's, 1 doctorate awarded. *Degree requirements:* For master's, thesis or alternative; for doctorate, thesis/dissertation or alternative. *Entrance requirements:* For master's and doctorate, GRE General Test, minimum GPA of 3.0. Additional exam requirements/recommendations for international students: Required—TOEFL (minimum score 570 paper-based; 88 iBT), IELTS (minimum score 7). *Application deadline:* For fall admission, 1/15 for domestic students, 12/15 for international students. Application fee: $30 ($25 for international students). Electronic applications accepted. *Expenses:* Contact institution. *Financial support:* In 2018–19, 1 fellowship with full tuition reimbursement (averaging $26,780 per year), 18 research assistantships with full tuition reimbursements (averaging $23,000 per year) were awarded; teaching assistantships with full tuition reimbursements also available. Financial award application deadline: 2/1; financial award applicants required to submit FAFSA. *Faculty research:* Solid oxide fuel cells, computational nanostructures, solar cells, nano-sensors, batteries: renewable energy. *Total annual research expenditures:* $1.3 million. *Unit head:* Dr. Feng Liu, Chair, 801-581-6863, Fax: 801-581-4816, E-mail: fliu@eng.utah.edu. *Application contact:* Marcie Leek, Academic Advisor, 801-581-6863, Fax: 801-581-4816, E-mail: marcie.leek@utah.edu.
Website: http://www.mse.utah.edu/

University of Washington, Graduate School, College of Engineering, Department of Materials Science and Engineering, Seattle, WA 98195-2120. Offers applied materials science and engineering (MS); materials science and engineering (MS, PhD); materials science and engineering and nanotechnology (PhD); materials science and engineering, nanotechnology, and molecular engineering (PhD). *Program availability:* Part-time. *Faculty:* 12 full-time (2 women). *Students:* 110 full-time (32 women), 24 part-time (9 women); includes 34 minority (3 Black or African American, non-Hispanic/Latino; 14 Asian, non-Hispanic/Latino; 9 Hispanic/Latino; 1 Native Hawaiian or other Pacific Islander, non-Hispanic/Latino; 7 Two or more races, non-Hispanic/Latino), 60 international. Average age 25. 456 applicants, 37% accepted, 57 enrolled. In 2018, 35 master's, 12 doctorates awarded. Terminal master's awarded for partial completion of doctoral program. *Degree requirements:* For master's, comprehensive exam, final paper or thesis and presentation; for doctorate, comprehensive exam, thesis/dissertation, qualifying evaluation, general and final exams. *Entrance requirements:* For master's and doctorate, GRE General Test, minimum GPA of 3.0, resume/curriculum vitae, letters of recommendation, statement of purpose, transcripts. Additional exam requirements/recommendations for international students: Required—TOEFL (minimum score 92 iBT). *Application deadline:* For fall admission, 1/4 for domestic and international students. Application fee: $85. Electronic applications accepted. *Expenses:* Contact institution. *Financial support:* In 2018–19, 65 students received support, including 42 research assistantships with full tuition reimbursements available (averaging $30,660 per year), 20 teaching assistantships with full tuition reimbursements available (averaging $30,660 per year); fellowships with full tuition reimbursements available, career-related internships or fieldwork, Federal Work-Study, institutionally sponsored loans, scholarships/grants, health care benefits, unspecified assistantships, and stipend supplements also available. Financial award application deadline: 1/1; financial award applicants required to submit FAFSA. *Faculty research:* Synthesis/structure/property and processing, biomaterials and biomimetics, solar energy and battery materials, materials chemistry and characterization, optical and electronic materials. *Total annual research expenditures:* $6.5 million. *Unit head:* Dr. Jihui Yang, Professor/Chair, 206-543-7090, Fax: 206-221-4934, E-mail: jihuiy@uw.edu. *Application contact:* Karen Wetterhahn, Academic Counselor, 206-543-2740, Fax: 206-543-3100, E-mail: karenlw@uw.edu.
Website: http://mse.washington.edu

The University of Western Ontario, School of Graduate and Postdoctoral Studies, Physical Sciences Division, Faculty of Engineering, London, ON N6A 3K7, Canada. Offers chemical and biochemical engineering (ME Sc, PhD); civil and environmental engineering (M Eng, ME Sc, PhD); electrical and computer engineering (M Eng, ME Sc, PhD); mechanical and materials engineering (M Eng, ME Sc, PhD). *Program availability:* Part-time. Terminal master's awarded for partial completion of doctoral program. *Degree requirements:* For master's, thesis; for doctorate, thesis/dissertation. *Entrance requirements:* For master's, minimum B average; for doctorate, minimum B+ average. *Faculty research:* Wind, geotechnical, chemical reactor engineering, applied electrostatics, biochemical engineering.

University of Windsor, Faculty of Graduate Studies, Faculty of Engineering, Department of Mechanical, Automotive, and Materials Engineering, Windsor, ON N9B 3P4, Canada. Offers engineering materials (M Eng, MA Sc, PhD); mechanical engineering (M Eng, MA Sc, PhD). *Program availability:* Part-time. *Degree requirements:* For master's, thesis; for doctorate, comprehensive exam, thesis/dissertation. *Entrance requirements:* For master's, minimum B average; for doctorate, master's degree, minimum B average. Additional exam requirements/recommendations for international students: Required—TOEFL (minimum score 600 paper-based). Electronic applications accepted. *Faculty research:* Thermofluids, applied mechanics, materials engineering.

University of Wisconsin–Madison, Graduate School, College of Engineering, Department of Materials Science and Engineering, Madison, WI 53706-1380. Offers materials science and engineering (MS). *Program availability:* Part-time. *Faculty:* 16 full-time (3 women). *Students:* 107 full-time (25 women), 6 part-time (3 women); includes 16 minority (1 Black or African American, non-Hispanic/Latino; 2 Asian, non-Hispanic/Latino; 9 Hispanic/Latino; 4 Two or more races, non-Hispanic/Latino), 64 international. Average age 27. 346 applicants, 24% accepted, 27 enrolled. In 2018, 18 master's, 22 doctorates awarded. Terminal master's awarded for partial completion of doctoral program. *Degree requirements:* For master's, thesis, minimum of 30 credits; minimum GPA of 3.0; for doctorate, comprehensive exam, thesis/dissertation, minimum of 51 credits; minimum GPA of 3.0. *Entrance requirements:* For master's and doctorate, GRE General Test, BS in physical sciences or engineering; minimum GPA of 3.0. Additional exam requirements/recommendations for international students: Required—TOEFL (minimum score 580 paper-based; 92 iBT), IELTS (minimum score 7). *Application deadline:* For fall admission, 12/15 for domestic and international students; for spring admission, 10/1 for domestic and international students. Application fee: $75 ($81 for international students). Electronic applications accepted. *Financial support:* In 2018–19, 72 students received support, including 6 fellowships with full tuition reimbursements available (averaging $31,728 per year), 55 research assistantships with full tuition reimbursements available (averaging $28,200 per year), 11 teaching assistantships with full tuition reimbursements available (averaging $1,770 per year); career-related internships or fieldwork, traineeships, health care benefits, tuition waivers (full), and unspecified assistantships also available. Financial award application deadline: 12/1; financial award applicants required to submit FAFSA. *Faculty research:* Thin film deposition, electron microscopy, applied superconductivity, micromechanical properties, rapid solidification and solidification processin. *Total annual research expenditures:* $10.1 million. *Unit head:* Dr. Susan Babcock, Chair, 608-262-3732, E-mail: msaedept@engr.wisc.edu. *Application contact:* Janna Pollock, Student Services Coordinator, 608-890-2756, E-mail: janna.pollock@wisc.edu.
Website: https://www.engr.wisc.edu/department/materials-science-engineering/academics/ms/

University of Wisconsin–Milwaukee, Graduate School, College of Engineering and Applied Science, Program in Engineering, Milwaukee, WI 53201-0413. Offers biomedical engineering (MS); civil engineering (MS, PhD); computer science (PhD); electrical and computer engineering (MS); electrical engineering (PhD); engineering mechanics (MS); industrial and management engineering (MS); industrial engineering (PhD); manufacturing engineering (MS); materials (PhD); materials engineering (MS); mechanical engineering (MS). *Program availability:* Part-time. *Students:* 174 full-time (41 women), 149 part-time (27 women); includes 31 minority (2 Black or African American, non-Hispanic/Latino; 1 American Indian or Alaska Native, non-Hispanic/Latino; 16 Asian, non-Hispanic/Latino; 4 Hispanic/Latino; 8 Two or more races, non-Hispanic/Latino), 207 international. Average age 31. 343 applicants, 57% accepted, 78 enrolled. In 2018, 73 master's, 24 doctorates awarded. *Degree requirements:* For master's, comprehensive exam (for some programs), thesis or alternative; for doctorate, comprehensive exam, thesis/dissertation, internship. *Entrance requirements:* For master's, GRE, minimum GPA of 2.75; for doctorate, GRE, minimum GPA of 3.5. Additional exam requirements/recommendations for international students: Required—TOEFL (minimum score 550 paper-based; 79 iBT), IELTS (minimum score 6.5). *Application deadline:* For fall admission, 1/1 priority date for domestic students; for spring admission, 9/1 for domestic students. Applications are processed on a rolling basis. Application fee: $56 ($96 for international students). *Financial support:* Fellowships, research assistantships, teaching assistantships, career-related internships or fieldwork, Federal Work-Study, unspecified assistantships, and project assistantships available. Support available to part-time students. Financial award application deadline: 4/15. *Unit head:* David Yu, Representative, 414-229-6169, E-mail: yu@uwm.edu. *Application contact:* Betty Warras, General Information Contact, 414-229-6169, Fax: 414-229-6967, E-mail: bwarras@uwm.edu.
Website: http://www4.uwm.edu/ceas/academics/graduate_programs/

Washington State University, Voiland College of Engineering and Architecture, School of Mechanical and Materials Engineering, Pullman, WA 99164-2920. Offers materials science and engineering (MS, PhD); mechanical engineering (MS, PhD). MS programs also offered at Tri-Cities campus. *Program availability:* Part-time. Terminal master's awarded for partial completion of doctoral program. *Degree requirements:* For master's, comprehensive exam, thesis; for doctorate, comprehensive exam, thesis/dissertation, preliminary exam. *Entrance requirements:* For master's, GRE, bachelor's degree, minimum GPA of 3.0, resume, statement of purpose, 3 letters of recommendation, official transcripts, Student Interest Profile form; for doctorate, GRE, bachelor's degree, minimum GPA of 3.4, resume, statement of purpose, 3 letters of recommendation, official transcripts, Student Interest Profile form. Additional exam requirements/ recommendations for international students: Required—TOEFL (minimum score 500 paper-based), IELTS. Electronic applications accepted. *Faculty research:* Multiscale modeling and characterization of materials; advanced energy; bioengineering; engineering education and curricular innovation; modeling and visualization in the areas of product realization, materials, and processes.

West Virginia University, Statler College of Engineering and Mineral Resources, Morgantown, WV 26506. Offers aerospace engineering (MSAE, PhD); chemical engineering (MS Ch E, PhD); civil engineering (MSCE, PhD); computer engineering (PhD); computer science (MSCS, PhD); electrical engineering (MSEE, PhD); energy systems engineering (MSESE); engineering (MSE); industrial engineering (MSIE, PhD); industrial hygiene (MS); material science and engineering (MSMSE, PhD); mechanical engineering (MSME, PhD); mining engineering (MS Min E, PhD); petroleum and natural gas engineering (MSPNGE, PhD); safety management (MS); software engineering (MSSE). *Program availability:* Part-time. *Students:* 466 full-time (113 women), 154 part-time (27 women); includes 57 minority (22 Black or African American, non-Hispanic/ Latino; 1 American Indian or Alaska Native, non-Hispanic/Latino; 8 Asian, non-Hispanic/ Latino; 12 Hispanic/Latino; 14 Two or more races, non-Hispanic/Latino), 283 international. In 2018, 179 master's, 39 doctorates awarded. Terminal master's awarded for partial completion of doctoral program. *Degree requirements:* For master's, thesis optional; for doctorate, comprehensive exam, thesis/dissertation. *Entrance requirements:* Additional exam requirements/recommendations for international students: Required—TOEFL (minimum score 550 paper-based). *Application deadline:* For fall admission, 4/1 for international students; for winter admission, 4/1 for international students; for spring admission, 10/1 for international students. Applications are processed on a rolling basis. Application fee: $60. Electronic applications accepted. *Expenses:* Contact institution. *Financial support:* Fellowships, research assistantships, teaching assistantships, career-related internships or fieldwork, Federal Work-Study, institutionally sponsored loans, health care benefits, tuition waivers (full and partial), unspecified assistantships, and administrative assistantships available. Financial award application deadline: 2/1; financial award applicants required to submit FAFSA. *Faculty research:* Composite materials, software engineering, information systems, aerodynamics, vehicle propulsion and emission. *Unit head:* Dr. Earl Scime, Interim Dean, 304-293-4157 Ext. 2237, Fax: 304-293-2037, E-mail: earl.scime@mail.wvu.edu. *Application contact:* Dr. David A. Wyrick, Associate Dean, Academic Affairs, 304-293-4334, Fax: 304-293-5024, E-mail: david.wyrick@mail.wvu.edu.
Website: https://www.statler.wvu.edu

Worcester Polytechnic Institute, Graduate Admissions, Department of Mechanical Engineering, Worcester, MA 01609-2280. Offers manufacturing engineering (MS, PhD); materials process engineering (MS); materials science and engineering (PhD). *Program availability:* Part-time, evening/weekend, 100% online, blended/hybrid learning. *Students:* 53 full-time (14 women), 128 part-time (23 women); includes 25 minority (2 Black or African American, non-Hispanic/Latino; 7 Asian, non-Hispanic/Latino; 13 Hispanic/Latino; 1 Native Hawaiian or other Pacific Islander, non-Hispanic/Latino; 2 Two or more races, non-Hispanic/Latino), 47 international. Average age 26. 278 applicants, 62% accepted, 67 enrolled. In 2018, 88 master's, 4 doctorates, 2 other advanced degrees awarded. Terminal master's awarded for partial completion of doctoral program. *Degree requirements:* For master's, thesis optional; for doctorate, comprehensive exam, thesis/dissertation. *Entrance requirements:* For master's and doctorate, GRE (recommended), 3 letters of recommendation, statement of purpose. Additional exam requirements/recommendations for international students: Required—TOEFL (minimum score 563 paper-based; 84 iBT), IELTS (minimum score 7). *Application deadline:* For fall admission, 1/1 priority date for domestic and international students; for spring admission, 10/1 priority date for domestic and international students. Applications are processed on a rolling basis. Application fee: $70. Electronic applications accepted. *Financial support:* Fellowships, research assistantships, teaching assistantships, career-related internships or fieldwork, institutionally sponsored loans, scholarships/grants, and unspecified assistantships available. Financial award application deadline: 1/1. *Unit head:* Dr. Jamal Yagoobi, Department Head, 508-831-5236, Fax: 508-831-5680, E-mail: jyagoobi@wpi.edu. *Application contact:* Barbara Edilberti, Administrative Assistant, 508-831-5236, Fax: 508-831-5680, E-mail: edilbert@wpi.edu.
Website: https://www.wpi.edu/academics/departments/mechanical-engineering

Wright State University, Graduate School, College of Engineering and Computer Science, Department of Mechanical and Materials Engineering, Dayton, OH 45435. Offers aerospace systems engineering (MS); materials science and engineering (MS); mechanical engineering (MS); renewable and clean energy (MS). *Degree requirements:* For master's, thesis or course option alternative. *Entrance requirements:* Additional exam requirements/recommendations for international students: Required—TOEFL.

Materials Sciences

Air Force Institute of Technology, Graduate School of Engineering and Management, Department of Aeronautics and Astronautics, Dayton, OH 45433-7765. Offers aeronautical engineering (MS, PhD); astronautical engineering (MS, PhD); materials science (MS, PhD); space operations (MS); systems engineering (MS, PhD). *Accreditation:* ABET (one or more programs are accredited). *Program availability:* Part-time. *Degree requirements:* For master's, thesis; for doctorate, thesis/dissertation. *Entrance requirements:* For master's and doctorate, GRE General Test, minimum GPA of 3.0, U.S. citizenship. *Faculty research:* Computational fluid dynamics, experimental aerodynamics, computational structural mechanics, experimental structural mechanics, aircraft and spacecraft stability and control.

Air Force Institute of Technology, Graduate School of Engineering and Management, Department of Engineering Physics, Dayton, OH 45433-7765. Offers applied physics (MS, PhD); electro-optics (MS, PhD); materials science (PhD); nuclear engineering (MS, PhD); space physics (MS). *Program availability:* Part-time. *Degree requirements:* For master's, thesis; for doctorate, thesis/dissertation. *Entrance requirements:* For master's and doctorate, GRE General Test, minimum GPA of 3.0, U.S. citizenship. *Faculty research:* High-energy lasers, space physics, nuclear weapon effects, semiconductor physics.

Alabama Agricultural and Mechanical University, School of Graduate Studies, College of Engineering, Technology, and Physical Sciences, Department of Physics, Chemistry and Mathematics, Huntsville, AL 35811. Offers physics (MS, PhD), including materials science (PhD), optics/lasers (PhD), space science (PhD). *Program availability:* Part-time, evening/weekend. *Degree requirements:* For doctorate, thesis/dissertation. *Entrance requirements:* For master's and doctorate, GRE General Test. Additional exam requirements/recommendations for international students: Required—TOEFL (minimum score 500 paper-based; 61 iBT). Electronic applications accepted.

Alfred University, Graduate School, College of Ceramics, Inamori School of Engineering, Alfred, NY 14802. Offers biomaterials engineering (MS); ceramic engineering (MS, PhD); electrical engineering (MS); glass science (MS, PhD); materials science and engineering (MS, PhD); mechanical engineering (MS). *Program availability:* Part-time. *Degree requirements:* For master's, thesis; for doctorate, thesis/dissertation. *Entrance requirements:* Additional exam requirements/recommendations for international students: Required—TOEFL (minimum score 590 paper-based; 90 iBT), IELTS (minimum score 6.5). Electronic applications accepted. *Expenses:* Contact institution. *Faculty research:* X-ray diffraction, biomaterials and polymers, thin-film processing, electronic and optical ceramics, solid-state chemistry.

Arizona State University at the Tempe campus, Ira A. Fulton Schools of Engineering, School for Engineering of Matter, Transport and Energy, Tempe, AZ 85281. Offers aerospace engineering (MS, PhD); chemical engineering (MS, PhD); materials science and engineering (MS, PhD); mechanical engineering (MS, PhD); solar energy engineering and commercialization (PSM). *Program availability:* Part-time, evening/ weekend, online learning. Terminal master's awarded for partial completion of doctoral program. *Degree requirements:* For master's, thesis and oral defense (MS); applied project or comprehensive exam (MSE); interactive Program of Study (iPOS) submitted before completing 50 percent of required credit hours; for doctorate, comprehensive exam, thesis/dissertation, interactive Program of Study (iPOS) submitted before completing 50 percent of required credit hours. *Entrance requirements:* For master's, GRE, minimum GPA of 3.0 or equivalent in last 2 years of work leading to bachelor's degree; for doctorate, GRE, minimum GPA of 3.0 in last 2 years of work leading to bachelor's degree. Additional exam requirements/recommendations for international students: Required—TOEFL, IELTS, or PTE. Electronic applications accepted. *Expenses:* Contact institution. *Faculty research:* Electronic materials and packaging, materials for energy (batteries), adaptive/intelligent materials and structures, multiscale fluid mechanics, membranes, therapeutics and bioseparations, flexible structures, nanostructured materials, micro-/nano-transport.

Binghamton University, State University of New York, Graduate School, Materials Science and Engineering Program, Binghamton, NY 13902-6000. Offers MS, PhD. *Program availability:* Part-time, online learning. *Degree requirements:* For master's, thesis; for doctorate, comprehensive exam, thesis/dissertation. *Entrance requirements:* For master's and doctorate, GRE General Test. Additional exam requirements/ recommendations for international students: Required—TOEFL (minimum score 550 paper-based; 80 iBT). Electronic applications accepted. *Expenses:* Contact institution.

Boston University, College of Engineering, Division of Materials Science and Engineering, Brookline, MA 02215. Offers materials science and engineering (M Eng, MS, PhD). *Program availability:* Part-time. *Students:* 91 full-time (33 women), 9 part-time (1 woman); includes 8 minority (1 Black or African American, non-Hispanic/Latino; 5 Asian, non-Hispanic/Latino; 2 Two or more races, non-Hispanic/Latino), 72 international. Average age 24. 290 applicants, 53% accepted, 24 enrolled. In 2018, 22 master's, 6 doctorates awarded. Terminal master's awarded for partial completion of doctoral program. *Degree requirements:* For master's, thesis (for some programs); for doctorate, comprehensive exam, thesis/dissertation. *Entrance requirements:* For master's and doctorate, GRE General Test. Additional exam requirements/recommendations for international students: Required—TOEFL (minimum score 90 iBT), IELTS (minimum score 7). *Financial support:* Application deadline: 1/15. *Faculty research:* Biomaterials, electronic and photonic materials, materials for energy and environment, nanomaterials. *Unit head:* Dr. David Bishop, Division Head, 617-353-8899, Fax: 617-353-5548, E-mail: djb1@bu.edu. *Application contact:* Dr. David Bishop, Division Head, 617-353-8899, Fax: 617-353-5548, E-mail: djb1@bu.edu.
Website: http://www.bu.edu/mse/

Brown University, Graduate School, School of Engineering, Program in Materials Science and Engineering, Providence, RI 02912. Offers Sc M, PhD. *Degree requirements:* For doctorate, thesis/dissertation, preliminary exam.

California Institute of Technology, Division of Engineering and Applied Science, Option in Materials Science, Pasadena, CA 91125-0001. Offers MS, PhD. *Degree requirements:* For doctorate, thesis/dissertation. *Faculty research:* Mechanical properties, physical properties, kinetics of phase transformations, metastable phases, transmission electron microscopy.

Carnegie Mellon University, Carnegie Institute of Technology, Department of Materials Science and Engineering, Pittsburgh, PA 15213-3891. Offers MS, PhD. *Program availability:* Part-time. Terminal master's awarded for partial completion of doctoral program. *Degree requirements:* For master's, exam; for doctorate, thesis/dissertation, qualifying exam. *Entrance requirements:* For master's and doctorate, GRE General Test. Additional exam requirements/recommendations for international students: Required—TOEFL. *Faculty research:* Materials characterization, process metallurgy, high strength alloys, growth kinetics, ceramics.

Case Western Reserve University, School of Graduate Studies, Case School of Engineering, Department of Materials Science and Engineering, Cleveland, OH 44106. Offers materials science and engineering (MS, PhD). *Program availability:* Part-time, online learning. *Faculty:* 12 full-time (1 woman). *Students:* 28 full-time (7 women), 6 part-time (3 women); includes 5 minority (all Asian, non-Hispanic/Latino), 14 international. In 2018, 13 master's, 5 doctorates awarded. Terminal master's awarded for partial completion of doctoral program. *Degree requirements:* For master's, thesis (for some programs); for doctorate, thesis/dissertation, qualifying exam, teaching experience. *Entrance requirements:* For master's and doctorate, GRE General Test. Additional exam requirements/recommendations for international students: Required—TOEFL. *Application deadline:* For fall admission, 2/15 priority date for domestic students; for spring admission, 9/15 for domestic students. Applications are processed on a rolling basis. Application fee: $50. *Expenses: Tuition:* Full-time $45,168; part-time $1939 per credit hour. *Required fees:* $36; $18 per semester. $18 per semester. *Financial support:* In 2018–19, 23 students received support, including 1 fellowship with tuition reimbursement available, 22 research assistantships with tuition reimbursements available. Financial award application deadline: 4/30; financial award applicants required to submit FAFSA. *Faculty research:* Surface hardening of steels and other alloys, chemistry and structure of surfaces, microstructural and mechanical property characterization, materials for energy applications, thermodynamics and kinetics of materials, performance and reliability of materials. *Total annual research expenditures:* $4.2 million. *Unit head:* Dr. Frank Ernst, Department Chair, 216-368-0611, Fax: 216-368-4224, E-mail: emse.info@case.edu. *Application contact:* Theresa Claytor, Student Affairs Coordinator, 216-368-8555, Fax: 216-368-8555, E-mail: esme.info@case.edu.
Website: http://engineering.case.edu/emse/

Materials Sciences

The Catholic University of America, School of Engineering, Department of Materials Science and Engineering, Washington, DC 20064. Offers MS. *Program availability:* Part-time. *Faculty:* 1 full-time (0 women), 2 part-time/adjunct (0 women). *Students:* 5 part-time (2 women); includes 1 minority (Black or African American, non-Hispanic/Latino). Average age 27. 2 applicants, 100% accepted, 1 enrolled. In 2018, 6 master's awarded. *Degree requirements:* For master's, thesis optional. *Entrance requirements:* For master's, GRE (minimum score 1250), minimum GPA of 3.0, statement of purpose, official copies of academic transcripts. Additional exam requirements/recommendations for international students: Required—TOEFL (minimum score 550 paper-based; 80 iBT). *Application deadline:* For fall admission, 7/15 for domestic students, 7/1 for international students; for spring admission, 11/15 for domestic students, 11/1 for international students. Applications are processed on a rolling basis. Application fee: $55. Electronic applications accepted. *Expenses:* Contact institution. *Financial support:* Fellowships, research assistantships, teaching assistantships, Federal Work-Study, scholarships/grants, tuition waivers (full and partial), and unspecified assistantships available. Financial award application deadline: 2/1; financial award applicants required to submit FAFSA. *Faculty research:* Nanotechnology, biomaterials, magnetic and optical materials, glass, ceramics, and metallurgy processing and instrumentation. *Unit head:* Mel Williams, Director, 202-319-5191, Fax: 202-319-4469, E-mail: williamsme@cua.edu. *Application contact:* Dr. Steven Brown, Director of Graduate Admissions, 202-319-5057, Fax: 202-319-6533, E-mail: cua-admissions@cua.edu.
Website: https://engineering.catholic.edu/materials-science/index.html

Central Michigan University, College of Graduate Studies, College of Science and Engineering, Department of Physics, Program in the Science of Advanced Materials, Mount Pleasant, MI 48859. Offers PhD. *Degree requirements:* For doctorate, comprehensive exam, thesis/dissertation. *Entrance requirements:* For doctorate, GRE. Electronic applications accepted. *Faculty research:* Electronic properties of nanomaterials, polymers for energy and for environmental applications, inorganic materials synthesis, magnetic properties from first-principles, nanodevices for biomedical applications and environmental remediation.

Clarkson University, Wallace H. Coulter School of Engineering, Program in Materials Science and Engineering, Potsdam, NY 13699. Offers PhD. *Students:* 5 full-time (1 woman); includes 1 minority (Asian, non-Hispanic/Latino), 4 international. 14 applicants, 50% accepted, 1 enrolled. *Degree requirements:* For doctorate, comprehensive exam, thesis/dissertation. *Entrance requirements:* For doctorate, GRE. Additional exam requirements/recommendations for international students: Required—TOEFL (minimum score 550 paper-based, 80 iBT) or IELTS (6.5). *Application deadline:* Applications are processed on a rolling basis. Application fee: $50. Electronic applications accepted. *Expenses: Tuition:* Full-time $24,984; part-time $1388 per credit hour. *Required fees:* $225. Tuition and fees vary according to campus/location and program. *Financial support:* Scholarships/grants and unspecified assistantships available. *Unit head:* Dr. Silvana Andreescu, Professor / Egon Matijevic Chair of Chemistry / Co-Director of CAMP, 315-268-2394, E-mail: wjemison@clarkson.edu. *Application contact:* Dan Capogna, Director of Graduate Admissions & Recruitment, 518-631-9910, E-mail: graduate@clarkson.edu.
Website: https://www.clarkson.edu/academics/graduate

Clemson University, Graduate School, College of Engineering, Computing and Applied Sciences, Department of Materials Science and Engineering, Clemson, SC 29634. Offers MS, PhD. *Program availability:* Part-time. *Faculty:* 16 full-time (2 women). *Students:* 53 full-time (17 women), 5 part-time (0 women); includes 3 minority (1 Black or African American, non-Hispanic/Latino; 1 Asian, non-Hispanic/Latino; 1 Hispanic/Latino), 32 international. Average age 26. 109 applicants, 29% accepted, 15 enrolled. In 2018, 6 master's, 9 doctorates awarded. Terminal master's awarded for partial completion of doctoral program. *Degree requirements:* For master's, thesis; for doctorate, comprehensive exam, thesis/dissertation. *Entrance requirements:* For master's and doctorate, GRE General Test, unofficial transcripts, letters of recommendation. Additional exam requirements/recommendations for international students: Required—TOEFL (minimum score 80 paper-based; 80 iBT); Recommended—IELTS (minimum score 6.5), TSE (minimum score 54). *Application deadline:* For fall admission, 2/1 priority date for domestic and international students; for spring admission, 9/1 priority date for domestic and international students. Applications are processed on a rolling basis. Application fee: $80 ($90 for international students). Electronic applications accepted. *Expenses:* $6823 per semester full-time resident, $14023 per semester full-time non-resident, $833 per credit hour part-time resident, $1731 per credit hour part-time non-resident, online $1264 per credit hour, $4938 doctoral programs resident, $10405 doctoral programs non-resident, $1144 full-time graduate assistant, other fees may apply per session. *Financial support:* In 2018–19, 52 students received support, including 2 fellowships with full and partial tuition reimbursements available (averaging $1,000 per year), 28 research assistantships with full and partial tuition reimbursements available (averaging $20,518 per year); career-related internships or fieldwork and unspecified assistantships also available. Financial award application deadline: 2/1. *Faculty research:* Polymers, ceramics, nanoparticles, biomimetic materials, optical fibers. *Total annual research expenditures:* $2.5 million. *Unit head:* Dr. Kyle Brinkman, Department Chair, 864-656-1405, E-mail: ksbrink@clemson.edu. *Application contact:* Dr. Igor Luzinov, Graduate Program Coordinator, 864-656-5958, E-mail: luzinov@clemson.edu.
Website: https://www.clemson.edu/cecas/departments/mse/index.html

Colorado School of Mines, Office of Graduate Studies, Department of Metallurgical and Materials Engineering, Golden, CO 80401. Offers materials science (MS, PhD); metallurgical and materials engineering (ME, MS, PhD). *Program availability:* Part-time. *Faculty:* 36 full-time (6 women), 10 part-time/adjunct (1 woman). *Students:* 115 full-time (35 women), 10 part-time (4 women); includes 13 minority (1 Asian, non-Hispanic/Latino; 8 Hispanic/Latino; 4 Two or more races, non-Hispanic/Latino), 29 international. Average age 27. 153 applicants, 50% accepted, 41 enrolled. In 2018, 21 master's, 15 doctorates awarded. *Degree requirements:* For master's, thesis (for some programs); for doctorate, comprehensive exam, thesis/dissertation. *Entrance requirements:* For master's and doctorate, GRE General Test. Additional exam requirements/recommendations for international students: Required—TOEFL (minimum score 550 paper-based; 79 iBT). *Application deadline:* For fall admission, 12/15 priority date for domestic and international students; for spring admission, 9/1 priority date for domestic and international students. Application fee: $60 ($80 for international students). Electronic applications accepted. *Expenses:* Tuition, state resident: full-time $16,650; part-time $925 per contact hour. Tuition, nonresident: full-time $36,270; part-time $2015 per contact hour. *International tuition:* $36,270 full-time. *Required fees:* $2314; $2314 per semester. *Financial support:* In 2018–19, 81 research assistantships with full tuition reimbursements, 15 teaching assistantships with full tuition reimbursements were awarded; fellowships, scholarships/grants, health care benefits, and unspecified assistantships also available. Financial award application deadline: 12/15; financial award applicants required to submit FAFSA. *Unit head:* Dr. Angus Rockett, Head, 303-384-2244, E-mail: arockett@mines.edu. *Application contact:* Megan Steelman, Program Assistant, 303-273-3640, E-mail: msteelman@mines.edu.
Website: http://metallurgy.mines.edu

Colorado State University, College of Natural Sciences, Programs in Natural Sciences Education, Fort Collins, CO 80523. Offers material science and engineering (PhD); natural science education (MNSE); zoo, aquarium, and animal shelter management (MS). *Program availability:* 100% online. *Degree requirements:* For master's, comprehensive exam (for some programs), thesis (for some programs); for doctorate, comprehensive exam (for some programs), thesis/dissertation. *Entrance requirements:* Additional exam requirements/recommendations for international students: Required—TOEFL (minimum score 550 paper-based). Electronic applications accepted. *Expenses:* Contact institution.

Columbia University, Fu Foundation School of Engineering and Applied Science, Department of Applied Physics and Applied Mathematics, New York, NY 10027. Offers applied mathematics (MS, Eng Sc D, PhD); applied physics (MS, Eng Sc D, PhD); materials science and engineering (MS, Eng Sc D, PhD); medical physics (MS). *Program availability:* Part-time, online learning. Terminal master's awarded for partial completion of doctoral program. *Degree requirements:* For master's, comprehensive exam; for doctorate, thesis/dissertation, qualifying exam. *Entrance requirements:* For master's, GRE General Test, GRE Subject Test (strongly recommended); for doctorate, GRE General Test, GRE Subject Test (applied physics). Additional exam requirements/recommendations for international students: Required—TOEFL, IELTS, PTE. Electronic applications accepted. *Faculty research:* Plasma physics and fusion energy; optical and laser physics; atmospheric, oceanic and earth physics; applied mathematics; solid state science and processing of materials, their properties, and their structure; medical physics.

Cornell University, Graduate School, Graduate Fields of Engineering, Field of Materials Science and Engineering, Ithaca, NY 14853. Offers materials engineering (M Eng, PhD); materials science (M Eng, PhD). *Degree requirements:* For doctorate, comprehensive exam, thesis/dissertation. *Entrance requirements:* For master's and doctorate, GRE General Test, 3 letters of recommendation. Additional exam requirements/recommendations for international students: Required—TOEFL (minimum score 550 paper-based; 77 iBT). Electronic applications accepted. *Faculty research:* Ceramics, complex fluids, glass, metals, polymers semiconductors.

Dartmouth College, Thayer School of Engineering, Program in Materials Sciences and Engineering, Hanover, NH 03755. Offers MS, PhD. *Degree requirements:* For master's, thesis; for doctorate, thesis/dissertation, candidacy oral exam. *Entrance requirements:* For master's and doctorate, GRE General Test. *Faculty research:* Electronic and magnetic materials, microstructural evolution, biomaterials and nanostructures, laser-material interactions, nanocomposites.

Duke University, Graduate School, Pratt School of Engineering, Department of Mechanical Engineering and Materials Science, Durham, NC 27708. Offers materials science (M Eng, MS, PhD); mechanical engineering (M Eng, MS, PhD); JD/MS. Terminal master's awarded for partial completion of doctoral program. *Degree requirements:* For master's, thesis optional; for doctorate, thesis/dissertation. *Entrance requirements:* For master's and doctorate, GRE General Test. Additional exam requirements/recommendations for international students: Required—TOEFL (minimum score 90 iBT), IELTS (minimum score 7). Electronic applications accepted.

Duke University, Graduate School, Pratt School of Engineering, Master of Engineering Program, Durham, NC 27708-0271. Offers biomedical engineering (M Eng); civil engineering (M Eng); computational mechanics and scientific computing (M Eng); electrical and computer engineering (M Eng); environmental engineering (M Eng); materials science and engineering (M Eng); mechanical engineering (M Eng); photonics and optical sciences (M Eng); risk engineering (M Eng). *Program availability:* Part-time. *Entrance requirements:* For master's, GRE General Test, resume, 3 letters of recommendation, statement of purpose, transcripts. Additional exam requirements/recommendations for international students: Required—TOEFL. Electronic applications accepted.

Florida International University, College of Engineering and Computing, Department of Mechanical and Materials Engineering, Miami, FL 33199. Offers materials science and engineering (MS, PhD); mechanical engineering (MS, PhD). *Program availability:* Part-time, evening/weekend. *Faculty:* 22 full-time (4 women), 6 part-time/adjunct (1 woman). *Students:* 49 full-time (12 women), 8 part-time (0 women); includes 20 minority (4 Black or African American, non-Hispanic/Latino; 14 Hispanic/Latino; 2 Two or more races, non-Hispanic/Latino), 33 international. Average age 30. 98 applicants, 45% accepted, 13 enrolled. In 2018, 11 master's, 8 doctorates awarded. Terminal master's awarded for partial completion of doctoral program. *Degree requirements:* For master's, thesis or alternative; for doctorate, comprehensive exam, thesis/dissertation. *Entrance requirements:* For master's, GRE (depending on program), 3 letters of recommendation, minimum undergraduate GPA of 3.0 in upper-level course work; for doctorate, GRE (minimum combined score of 1150, verbal 450, quantitative 650), minimum undergraduate GPA of 3.0 in upper-level coursework with BS, 3.3 with MS; 3 letters of recommendation; letter of intent. Additional exam requirements/recommendations for international students: Required—TOEFL (minimum score 550 paper-based; 80 iBT) or IELTS (minimum score 6.5). *Application deadline:* For fall admission, 6/1 for domestic students, 4/1 for international students; for spring admission, 10/1 for domestic students, 9/1 for international students. Applications are processed on a rolling basis. Application fee: $30. Electronic applications accepted. *Financial support:* Institutionally sponsored loans, scholarships/grants, and unspecified assistantships available. Financial award application deadline: 3/1; financial award applicants required to submit FAFSA. *Faculty research:* Mechanics and materials, fluid/thermal/energy, design and manufacturing, materials science engineering. *Unit head:* Dr. ARVIND AGARWAL, Chair, 305-348-1701, Fax: 305-348-1932, E-mail: Arvind.Agarwal@fiu.edu. *Application contact:* Nanett Rojas, Manager, Admissions Operations, 305-348-7464, Fax: 305-348-7441, E-mail: gradadm@fiu.edu.
Website: http://cec.fiu.edu

Florida State University, The Graduate School, Department of Anthropology, Department of Chemistry and Biochemistry, Tallahassee, FL 32306-4390. Offers analytical chemistry (MS, PhD); biochemistry (MS, PhD); inorganic chemistry (MS, PhD); materials chemistry (PhD); organic chemistry (MS, PhD); physical chemistry (MS, PhD). *Faculty:* 29 full-time (4 women). *Students:* 159 full-time (57 women), 2 part-time (1 woman); includes 73 minority (9 Black or African American, non-Hispanic/Latino; 46 Asian, non-Hispanic/Latino; 9 Hispanic/Latino; 3 Native Hawaiian or other Pacific Islander, non-Hispanic/Latino; 6 Two or more races, non-Hispanic/Latino). Average age 26. 215 applicants, 49% accepted, 35 enrolled. In 2018, 33 master's, 30 doctorates awarded. Terminal master's awarded for partial completion of doctoral program. *Degree requirements:* For master's, thesis (for some programs); for doctorate, thesis/dissertation. *Entrance requirements:* For master's and doctorate, GRE General Test (minimum scores: 150 verbal, 151 quantitative), minimum upper-division GPA of 3.1 in undergraduate course work. Additional exam requirements/recommendations for international students: Required—TOEFL (minimum score 80 iBT). *Application deadline:* For fall admission, 12/15 priority date for domestic and international students. Applications are processed on a rolling basis. Application fee: $30. Electronic applications accepted. *Expenses: Tuition, area resident:* Part-time $479.32 per credit hour. Tuition and fees vary according to campus/location and program. *Financial support:* In 2018–19, 163 students received support, including 4 fellowships with full

tuition reimbursements available (averaging $24,241 per year), 59 research assistantships with full tuition reimbursements available (averaging $24,241 per year), 102 teaching assistantships with full tuition reimbursements available (averaging $24,241 per year). Financial award application deadline: 12/15; financial award applicants required to submit FAFSA. *Faculty research:* Bioanalytical chemistry, separations, microfluidics, petroleomics; materials chemistry, solid state materials, magnets, polymers, catalysts, advanced spectroscopic methods, NMR and EPR, ultrafast, Raman, and mass spectrometry; organic synthesis, natural products, photochemistry, and supramolecular chemistry; biochemistry, structural biology, metabolomics, and anticancer drugs; nanochemistry, applications in energy, sustainability, biology, and technology development; radiochemistry. *Total annual research expenditures:* $7.1 million. *Unit head:* Dr. Geoffrey Strouse, Chairman, 850-644-1244, Fax: 850-644-8281, E-mail: gradinfo@chem.fsu.edu. *Application contact:* Dr. Wei Yang, Associate Chair for Graduate Studies, 850-645-6884, Fax: 850-644-8281, E-mail: gradinfo@chem.fsu.edu.
Website: http://www.chem.fsu.edu/

Florida State University, The Graduate School, Department of Anthropology, Department of Scientific Computing, Tallahassee, FL 32306-4120. Offers computational science (MS, PhD), including atmospheric science (PhD), biochemistry (PhD), biological science (PhD), computational science (PhD), geological science (PhD), materials science (PhD), physics (PhD). *Program availability:* Part-time. *Faculty:* 9 full-time (1 woman), 2 part-time/adjunct (1 woman). *Students:* 34 full-time (6 women); includes 17 minority (10 Asian, non-Hispanic/Latino; 3 Hispanic/Latino; 4 Two or more races, non-Hispanic/Latino), 13 international. Average age 26. 64 applicants, 23% accepted, 6 enrolled. In 2018, 10 master's, 8 doctorates awarded. Terminal master's awarded for partial completion of doctoral program. *Degree requirements:* For master's, comprehensive exam, thesis (for some programs); for doctorate, comprehensive exam, thesis/dissertation. *Entrance requirements:* For master's and doctorate, GRE General Test, knowledge of at least one object-oriented computing language, 3 letters of recommendation, resume, statement of purpose. Additional exam requirements/recommendations for international students: Required—TOEFL (minimum score 550 paper-based; 80 iBT). *Application deadline:* For fall admission, 1/15 for domestic and international students. Applications are processed on a rolling basis. Application fee: $30. Electronic applications accepted. *Expenses: Tuition,* area resident: Part-time $479.32 per credit hour. Tuition and fees vary according to campus/location and program. *Financial support:* In 2018–19, 32 students received support, including 10 research assistantships with full tuition reimbursements available (averaging $26,670 per year), 23 teaching assistantships with full tuition reimbursements available (averaging $23,000 per year); scholarships/grants, health care benefits, tuition waivers (full), and unspecified assistantships also available. Financial award application deadline: 1/15. *Faculty research:* Morphometrics, mathematical and systems biology, mining proteomic and metabolic data, computational materials research, computational fluid dynamics, astrophysics, deep learning, computational neuroscience. *Total annual research expenditures:* $500,000. *Unit head:* Dr. Gordon Erlebacher, Chair, 850-644-7024, E-mail: gerlebacher@fsu.edu. *Application contact:* Karey Fowler, Academic Program Specialist, 850-644-0143, Fax: 850-644-0098, E-mail: kgfowler@fsu.edu.
Website: http://www.sc.fsu.edu

Florida State University, The Graduate School, Materials Science and Engineering Program, Tallahassee, FL 32306. Offers MS, PhD. *Faculty:* 37 full-time (6 women). *Students:* 18 full-time (8 women); includes 1 minority (Hispanic/Latino), 14 international. Average age 28. 27 applicants, 26% accepted, 4 enrolled. In 2018, 3 master's awarded. Terminal master's awarded for partial completion of doctoral program. *Degree requirements:* For master's, thesis; for doctorate, comprehensive exam, thesis/dissertation. *Entrance requirements:* For master's and doctorate, GRE General Test (minimum new format 55th percentile Verbal, 75th percentile Quantitative, old version 1100 combined Verbal and Quantitative), minimum GPA of 3.0, 3 letters of recommendation. Additional exam requirements/recommendations for international students: Required—TOEFL (minimum score 80 iBT). *Application deadline:* For fall admission, 5/1 for domestic and international students; for spring admission, 9/1 for domestic and international students; for summer admission, 1/1 for domestic and international students. Applications are processed on a rolling basis. Application fee: $30. Electronic applications accepted. *Expenses: Tuition,* area resident: Part-time $479.32 per credit hour. Tuition and fees vary according to campus/location and program. *Financial support:* In 2018–19, 18 students received support, including 18 research assistantships with full tuition reimbursements available (averaging $23,104 per year); partial payment of required health insurance also available. Financial award application deadline: 12/15. *Faculty research:* Magnetism and magnetic materials, composites, superconductors, polymers, computations, nanotechnology. *Unit head:* Prof. Eric Hellstrom, Director, 850-645-7489, Fax: 850-645-7754, E-mail: hellstrom@asc.magnet.fsu.edu. *Application contact:* Judy Gardner, Admissions Coordinator, 850-645-8980, Fax: 850-645-9123, E-mail: jdgardner@fsu.edu.
Website: http://materials.fsu.edu

Georgetown University, Graduate School of Arts and Sciences, Department of Chemistry, Washington, DC 20057. Offers analytical chemistry (PhD); biochemistry (PhD); computational chemistry (PhD); inorganic chemistry (PhD); materials chemistry (PhD); organic chemistry (PhD); theoretical chemistry (PhD). Terminal master's awarded for partial completion of doctoral program. *Degree requirements:* For doctorate, comprehensive exam, thesis/dissertation. *Entrance requirements:* For doctorate, GRE General Test. Additional exam requirements/recommendations for international students: Required—TOEFL.

The George Washington University, Columbian College of Arts and Sciences, Department of Chemistry, Washington, DC 20052. Offers analytical chemistry (MS, PhD); inorganic chemistry (MS, PhD); materials science (MS, PhD); organic chemistry (MS, PhD); physical chemistry (MS, PhD). *Program availability:* Part-time, evening/weekend. *Students:* 29 full-time (15 women), 8 part-time (5 women); includes 3 minority (1 Black or African American, non-Hispanic/Latino; 2 Hispanic/Latino), 5 international. Average age 27. 96 applicants, 47% accepted, 9 enrolled. In 2018, 9 master's, 6 doctorates awarded. Terminal master's awarded for partial completion of doctoral program. *Degree requirements:* For master's, comprehensive exam, thesis or alternative; for doctorate, thesis/dissertation, general exam. *Entrance requirements:* For master's and doctorate, GRE General Test, interview, minimum GPA of 3.0. Additional exam requirements/recommendations for international students: Required—TOEFL (minimum score 550 paper-based; 80 iBT). *Application deadline:* For fall admission, 1/15 priority date for domestic and international students; for spring admission, 9/1 priority date for domestic and international students. Applications are processed on a rolling basis. Application fee: $75. Electronic applications accepted. *Financial support:* In 2018–19, 27 students received support. Fellowships, research assistantships, teaching assistantships, Federal Work-Study, and tuition waivers available. Financial award application deadline: 1/15. *Unit head:* Dr. Michael King, Chair, 202-994-6488. *Application contact:* Information Contact, 202-994-6121, E-mail: gwchem@gwu.edu.
Website: http://chemistry.columbian.gwu.edu/

Harvard University, Graduate School of Arts and Sciences, Harvard John A. Paulson School of Engineering and Applied Sciences, Cambridge, MA 02138. Offers applied mathematics (PhD); applied physics (PhD); computational science and engineering (ME, SM); computer science (PhD); data science (SM); design engineering (MDE); engineering science (ME), including electrical engineering (ME, SM, PhD); engineering sciences (SM, PhD), including bioengineering (PhD), electrical engineering (ME, SM, PhD), environmental science and engineering (PhD), materials science and mechanical engineering (PhD). MDE offered in collaboration with Graduate School of Design. *Program availability:* Part-time. Terminal master's awarded for partial completion of doctoral program. *Degree requirements:* For master's, thesis (for ME); for doctorate, comprehensive exam, thesis/dissertation. *Entrance requirements:* For master's and doctorate, GRE General Test, GRE Subject Test (recommended), 3 letters of recommendation. Additional exam requirements/recommendations for international students: Required—TOEFL (minimum score 80 iBT). Electronic applications accepted. *Expenses:* Contact institution. *Faculty research:* Applied mathematics, applied physics, computer science and electrical engineering, environmental engineering, mechanical and biomedical engineering.

Illinois Institute of Technology, Graduate College, Armour College of Engineering, Department of Mechanical, Materials and Aerospace Engineering, Chicago, IL 60616. Offers manufacturing engineering (MAS, MS); materials science and engineering (MAS, MS, PhD); mechanical and aerospace engineering (MAS, MS, PhD), including economics (MS), energy (MS), environment (MS). *Program availability:* Part-time, evening/weekend, online learning. Terminal master's awarded for partial completion of doctoral program. *Degree requirements:* For master's, comprehensive exam (for some programs), thesis (for some programs); for doctorate, comprehensive exam, thesis/dissertation. *Entrance requirements:* For master's and doctorate, GRE General Test (minimum score 1000 Quantitative and Verbal, 3.0 Analytical Writing), minimum undergraduate GPA of 3.0. Additional exam requirements/recommendations for international students: Required—TOEFL (minimum score 550 paper-based; 80 iBT). Electronic applications accepted. *Faculty research:* Fluid dynamics, metallurgical and materials engineering, solids and structures, computational mechanics, computer added design and manufacturing, thermal sciences, dynamic analysis and control of complex systems.

Illinois Institute of Technology, Graduate College, College of Science, Department of Chemistry, Chicago, IL 60616. Offers analytical chemistry (MAS); chemistry (MAS, MS, PhD); materials chemistry (MAS), including inorganic, organic, or polymeric materials. *Program availability:* Part-time, evening/weekend, online learning. Terminal master's awarded for partial completion of doctoral program. *Degree requirements:* For master's, comprehensive exam, thesis (for some programs); for doctorate, comprehensive exam, thesis/dissertation. *Entrance requirements:* For master's, GRE General Test (minimum score 300 Quantitative and Verbal, 2.5 Analytical Writing), minimum undergraduate GPA of 3.0; for doctorate, GRE General Test (minimum score 310 Quantitative and Verbal, 3.0 Analytical Writing), GRE Subject Test, minimum undergraduate GPA of 3.0. Additional exam requirements/recommendations for international students: Required—TOEFL (minimum score 550 paper-based; 80 iBT); Recommended—IELTS. Electronic applications accepted. *Faculty research:* Materials science, biological chemistry, synthetic chemistry, computational chemistry, energy, sensor science and technology, scholarship of teaching and learning.

Indiana University Bloomington, University Graduate School, College of Arts and Sciences, Department of Chemistry, Bloomington, IN 47405. Offers analytical chemistry (PhD); chemical biology (PhD); chemistry (MAT); inorganic chemistry (PhD); materials chemistry (PhD); organic chemistry (PhD); physical chemistry (PhD); MSES/MS. Terminal master's awarded for partial completion of doctoral program. *Degree requirements:* For master's, thesis; for doctorate, thesis/dissertation. *Entrance requirements:* For master's and doctorate, GRE General Test, GRE Subject Test. Additional exam requirements/recommendations for international students: Required—TOEFL. Electronic applications accepted. *Faculty research:* Synthesis of complex natural products, organic reaction mechanisms, organic electrochemistry, transitive-metal chemistry, solid-state and surface chemistry.

Instituto Tecnológico y de Estudios Superiores de Monterrey, Campus Estado de México, Professional and Graduate Division, Estado de Mexico, Mexico. Offers administration of information technologies (MITA); architecture (M Arch); business administration (GMBA, MBA); computer sciences (MCS, PhD); education (M Ed); educational institution administration (MAD); educational technology and innovation (PhD); electronic commerce (MEC); environmental systems (MS); finance (MAF); humanistic studies (MHS); information sciences and knowledge management (MISKM); information systems (MS); manufacturing systems (MS); marketing (MEM); quality systems and productivity (MS); science and materials engineering (PhD); telecommunications management (MTM). *Program availability:* Part-time, online learning. *Degree requirements:* For master's, one foreign language, thesis (for some programs); for doctorate, one foreign language, thesis/dissertation. *Entrance requirements:* For master's, E-PAEP 500, interview; for doctorate, E-PAEP 500, research proposal. Additional exam requirements/recommendations for international students: Required—TOEFL (minimum score 550 paper-based). *Faculty research:* Surface treatments by plasmas, mechanical properties, robotics, graphical computing, mechatronics security protocols.

Iowa State University of Science and Technology, Department of Materials Science and Engineering, Ames, IA 50011. Offers M Eng, MS, PhD. *Entrance requirements:* For master's and doctorate, GRE General Test. Additional exam requirements/recommendations for international students: Required—TOEFL (minimum score 550 paper-based; 79 iBT), IELTS (minimum score 6.5). Electronic applications accepted.

Jackson State University, Graduate School, College of Science, Engineering and Technology, Department of Civil and Environmental Engineering and Industrial Systems and Technology, Jackson, MS 39217. Offers civil engineering (MS, PhD); coastal engineering (MS, PhD); environmental engineering (MS, PhD); hazardous materials management (MS); technology education (MS Ed). *Program availability:* Part-time, evening/weekend. *Degree requirements:* For master's, comprehensive exam, thesis or alternative. *Entrance requirements:* For master's, GRE General Test. Additional exam requirements/recommendations for international students: Required—TOEFL (minimum score 520 paper-based; 67 iBT).

Johns Hopkins University, Engineering Program for Professionals, Part-time Program in Materials Science and Engineering, Baltimore, MD 21218. Offers nanotechnology (M Mat SE). *Program availability:* Part-time, evening/weekend. *Faculty:* 1 full-time, 4 part-time/adjunct (2 women). *Students:* 13 part-time (5 women). 14 applicants, 29% accepted, 3 enrolled. In 2018, 8 master's awarded. *Entrance requirements:* Additional exam requirements/recommendations for international students: Required—TOEFL (minimum score 600 paper-based; 100 iBT). *Application deadline:* Applications are processed on a rolling basis. Application fee: $0. Electronic applications accepted. *Unit head:* Dr. James Spicer, Program Chair, 410-516-8524, E-mail: spicer@jhu.edu. *Application contact:* Doug Schiller, Admissions Director, 410-516-2300, Fax: 410-579-8049, E-mail: schiller@jhu.edu.
Website: http://www.ep.jhu.edu

Johns Hopkins University, G. W. C. Whiting School of Engineering, Department of Materials Science and Engineering, Baltimore, MD 21218. Offers M Mat SE, MSE, PhD.

Faculty: 22 full-time (3 women). *Students:* 78 full-time (24 women), 1 part-time. 303 applicants, 34% accepted, 31 enrolled. In 2018, 21 master's, 11 doctorates awarded. Terminal master's awarded for partial completion of doctoral program. *Degree requirements:* For master's, thesis; for doctorate, thesis/dissertation, oral exam, thesis defense. *Entrance requirements:* For master's and doctorate, GRE General Test, 2 letters of recommendation, statement of purpose, transcripts. Additional exam requirements/recommendations for international students: Required—TOEFL (minimum score 600 paper-based, 100 iBT) or IELTS (7). *Application deadline:* For fall admission, 12/15 priority date for domestic and international students; for spring admission, 10/15 priority date for domestic and international students. Application fee: $0 ($75 for international students). Electronic applications accepted. *Financial support:* In 2018–19, 56 students received support, including 5 fellowships with full tuition reimbursements available (averaging $30,200 per year), 51 research assistantships with full tuition reimbursements available (averaging $30,200 per year), teaching assistantships with full tuition reimbursements available (averaging $30,200 per year); Federal Work-Study, institutionally sponsored loans, health care benefits, tuition waivers (full), and unspecified assistantships also available. Financial award application deadline: 3/15. *Faculty research:* Biomaterials; computational materials science; materials for energy; nanomaterials; optoelectronic and magnetic materials; structural materials. *Unit head:* Dr. Jonah Erlebacher, Chair, 410-516-6141, Fax: 410-516-5293, E-mail: jonah.erlebacher@jhu.edu. *Application contact:* Jeanine Majewski, Academic Coordinator, 410-516-8760, Fax: 410-516-5293, E-mail: dmse-gradadmissions@jhu.edu.
Website: http://engineering.jhu.edu/materials/

Johns Hopkins University, G. W. C. Whiting School of Engineering, Master of Science in Engineering Management Program, Baltimore, MD 21218. Offers biomaterials (MSEM); civil engineering (MSEM); communications science (MSEM); computer science (MSEM); environmental systems analysis, economics and public policy (MSEM); fluid mechanics (MSEM); materials science and engineering (MSEM); mechanical engineering (MSEM); mechanics and materials (MSEM); nanobiotechnology (MSEM); nanomaterials and nanotechnology (MSEM); operations research (MSEM); probability and statistics (MSEM); smart product and device design (MSEM). *Students:* 34 full-time (12 women), 18 part-time (7 women). 233 applicants, 39% accepted, 33 enrolled. In 2018, 27 master's awarded. *Entrance requirements:* For master's, GRE, 3 letters of recommendation, statement of purpose, transcripts. Additional exam requirements/recommendations for international students: Required—TOEFL (minimum score 600 paper-based, 100 iBT) or IELTS (7). *Application deadline:* For fall admission, 2/15 for domestic and international students. Application fee: $75. Electronic applications accepted. *Financial support:* In 2018–19, 43 research assistantships (averaging $43,344 per year) were awarded; health care benefits also available. *Unit head:* Dr. Pamela Sheff, Director, 410-516-7056, Fax: 410-516-4880, E-mail: pamsheff@gmail.com. *Application contact:* Lindsey Conklin, Sr. Academic Program Coordinator, 410-516-1108, Fax: 410-516-0780, E-mail: lconkli4@jhu.edu.
Website: http://engineering.jhu.edu/msem/

Lehigh University, P.C. Rossin College of Engineering and Applied Science, Department of Materials Science and Engineering, Bethlehem, PA 18015. Offers materials science and engineering (M Eng, MS, PhD); photonics (MS); polymer science/engineering (M Eng, MS, PhD); MBA/E. *Program availability:* Part-time. *Faculty:* 16 full-time (4 women). *Students:* 24 full-time (6 women), 2 part-time (1 woman); includes 4 minority (1 Black or African American, non-Hispanic/Latino; 1 Hispanic/Latino; 2 Two or more races, non-Hispanic/Latino), 5 international. Average age 25. 107 applicants, 19% accepted, 8 enrolled. In 2018, 4 master's, 7 doctorates awarded. *Degree requirements:* For master's, thesis; for doctorate, comprehensive exam, thesis/dissertation. *Entrance requirements:* For master's and doctorate, GRE General Test, minimum GPA of 3.60. Additional exam requirements/recommendations for international students: Required—TOEFL (minimum score 487 paper-based; 85 iBT), IELTS (minimum score 6.5), TOEFL or IELTS required. *Application deadline:* For fall admission, 1/15 priority date for domestic students, 1/15 for international students; for spring admission, 12/1 priority date for domestic students, 12/1 for international students. Application fee: $75. Tuition and fees vary according to program. *Financial support:* In 2018–19, 26 students received support, including 9 fellowships with tuition reimbursements available (averaging $12,848 per year), 14 research assistantships with tuition reimbursements available (averaging $29,640 per year), 12 teaching assistantships with tuition reimbursements available (averaging $7,350 per year); scholarships/grants and health care benefits also available. Financial award application deadline: 1/15. *Faculty research:* Metals, ceramics, crystals, polymers, fatigue crack propagation, biomaterials. *Total annual research expenditures:* $2.7 million. *Unit head:* Dr. Wojciech Misiolek, Chairperson, 610-758-4252, Fax: 610-758-4244, E-mail: wzm2@lehigh.edu. *Application contact:* Lisa Carreras Arechiga, Graduate Administrative Coordinator, 610-758-4222, Fax: 610-758-4244, E-mail: lia4@lehigh.edu.
Website: https://engineering.lehigh.edu/matsci

Louisiana Tech University, Graduate School, College of Engineering and Science, Ruston, LA 71272. Offers applied physics (MS); biomedical engineering (PhD); computer science (MS); engineering (MS, PhD), including cyberspace engineering (PhD), engineering education (PhD), engineering physics (PhD), materials and infrastructure systems (PhD), micro/nanoscale systems (PhD); engineering and technology management (MS); mathematics (MS); molecular science and nanotechnology (MS, PhD). *Program availability:* Part-time-only. Terminal master's awarded for partial completion of doctoral program. *Degree requirements:* For master's, thesis (for some programs); for doctorate, thesis/dissertation. *Entrance requirements:* For master's and Graduate Certificate, GRE General Test, minimum GPA of 3.0 in last 60 hours. Additional exam requirements/recommendations for international students: Required—TOEFL (minimum score 550 paper-based; 80 iBT), IELTS (minimum score 6.5). Electronic applications accepted. *Faculty research:* Trenchless technology, micromanufacturing, radionuclide transport, microbial liquefaction, hazardous waste treatment.

Massachusetts Institute of Technology, School of Engineering, Department of Materials Science and Engineering, Cambridge, MA 02139. Offers archaeological materials (PhD, Sc D); materials engineering (Mat E); materials science and engineering (SM, PhD, Sc D). *Degree requirements:* For master's, thesis; for doctorate, comprehensive exam, thesis/dissertation; for Mat E, comprehensive exam, thesis. *Entrance requirements:* For master's and doctorate, GRE General Test. Additional exam requirements/recommendations for international students: Required—IELTS. Electronic applications accepted. *Expenses: Tuition:* Full-time $51,520; part-time $800 per credit hour. *Required fees:* $312. *Faculty research:* Thermodynamics and kinetics of materials; structure, processing and properties of materials; electronic, structural and biological materials engineering; computational materials science; materials in energy, medicine, nanotechnology and the environment.

McMaster University, School of Graduate Studies, Faculty of Engineering, Department of Materials Science and Engineering, Hamilton, ON L8S 4M2, Canada. Offers materials engineering (M Eng, MA Sc, PhD); materials science (M Eng, PhD). *Degree requirements:* For master's, thesis; for doctorate, comprehensive exam, thesis/dissertation. *Entrance requirements:* Additional exam requirements/recommendations for international students: Required—TOEFL (minimum score 550 paper-based). *Faculty research:* Localized corrosion of metals and alloys, electron microscopy, polymer synthesis and characterization, polymer reaction kinetics and engineering, polymer process modeling.

Michigan State University, The Graduate School, College of Engineering, Department of Chemical Engineering and Materials Science, East Lansing, MI 48824. Offers chemical engineering (MS, PhD); materials science and engineering (MS, PhD). *Entrance requirements:* Additional exam requirements/recommendations for international students: Required—TOEFL. Electronic applications accepted.

Missouri State University, Graduate College, College of Natural and Applied Sciences, Department of Physics, Astronomy, and Materials Science, Springfield, MO 65897. Offers materials science (MS); natural and applied science (MNAS), including physics (MNAS, MS Ed); secondary education (MS Ed), including physics (MNAS, MS Ed). *Program availability:* Part-time. *Faculty:* 9 full-time (0 women). *Students:* 11 full-time (1 woman), 4 part-time (1 woman); includes 1 minority (Hispanic/Latino), 13 international. Average age 26. 12 applicants, 92% accepted. In 2018, 9 master's awarded. *Degree requirements:* For master's, comprehensive exam, thesis. *Entrance requirements:* For master's, GRE (MS, MNAS), minimum undergraduate GPA of 3.0 (MS and MNAS), 9-12 teaching certification (MS Ed). Additional exam requirements/recommendations for international students: Required—TOEFL (minimum score 550 paper-based; 79 iBT), IELTS (minimum score 6). *Application deadline:* For fall admission, 7/20 priority date for domestic students, 5/1 for international students; for spring admission, 12/20 priority date for domestic students, 9/1 for international students. Applications are processed on a rolling basis. Application fee: $55 ($60 for international students). Electronic applications accepted. Tuition and fees vary according to class time, course level, course load, degree level, campus/location, program and student level. *Financial support:* In 2018–19, 6 research assistantships with full tuition reimbursements (averaging $10,672 per year), 11 teaching assistantships with full tuition reimbursements (averaging $10,672 per year) were awarded; Federal Work-Study, institutionally sponsored loans, scholarships/grants, and unspecified assistantships also available. Financial award application deadline: 1/31; financial award applicants required to submit FAFSA. *Faculty research:* Nanocomposites, ferroelectricity, infrared focal plane array sensors, biosensors, pulsating stars. *Unit head:* Dr. Robert Mayanovic, Department Head, 417-836-5131, Fax: 417-836-6226, E-mail: physics@missouristate.edu. *Application contact:* Lakan Drinker, Director, Graduate Enrollment Management, 417-836-5330, Fax: 417-836-6200, E-mail: lakandrinker@missouristate.edu.
Website: http://physics.missouristate.edu/

Missouri University of Science and Technology, Department of Materials Science and Engineering, Rolla, MO 65401. Offers ceramic engineering (MS, PhD); materials science and engineering (MS, PhD); metallurgical engineering (MS, PhD). *Degree requirements:* For master's, thesis optional; for doctorate, comprehensive exam. *Entrance requirements:* For master's, GRE (minimum combined score 1100, 600 verbal, 3.5 writing); for doctorate, GRE (minimum score: quantitative 600, writing 3.5). Additional exam requirements/recommendations for international students: Required—TOEFL (minimum score 570 paper-based). Electronic applications accepted. *Expenses:* Tuition, state resident: full-time $7545.60; part-time $419.20 per credit hour. Tuition, nonresident: full-time $22,169; part-time $1231.60 per credit hour. *International tuition:* $23,518.80 full-time. *Required fees:* $4523.05. Full-time tuition and fees vary according to course load, campus/location, program and reciprocity agreements.

Montana Tech of The University of Montana, Program in Materials Science, Butte, MT 59701-8997. Offers PhD. *Degree requirements:* For doctorate, thesis/dissertation optional. *Entrance requirements:* Additional exam requirements/recommendations for international students: Required—TOEFL (minimum score 600 paper-based; 90 iBT), IELTS (minimum score 7).

New Jersey Institute of Technology, College of Science and Liberal Arts, Newark, NJ 07102. Offers applied mathematics (MS); applied physics (MS, PhD); applied statistics (MS, Certificate); biology (MS, PhD); biostatistics (MS); chemistry (MS, PhD); environmental and sustainability policy (MS); environmental science (MS, PhD); history (MA, MAT); materials science and engineering (MS, PhD); mathematical and computational finance (MS); mathematical sciences (PhD); pharmaceutical chemistry (MS); professional and technical communications (MS); technical communication essentials (Certificate). *Program availability:* Part-time, evening/weekend. *Faculty:* 150 full-time (43 women), 115 part-time/adjunct (47 women). *Students:* 200 full-time (79 women), 63 part-time (29 women); includes 61 minority (17 Black or African American, non-Hispanic/Latino; 29 Asian, non-Hispanic/Latino; 11 Hispanic/Latino; 4 Two or more races, non-Hispanic/Latino), 136 international. Average age 28. 429 applicants, 49% accepted, 89 enrolled. In 2018, 43 master's, 16 doctorates, 2 other advanced degrees awarded. Terminal master's awarded for partial completion of doctoral program. *Degree requirements:* For master's, thesis (for some programs); for doctorate, thesis/dissertation. *Entrance requirements:* For master's and doctorate, GRE General Test, Minimum GPA of 3.0, personal statement, 3 letters of recommendation, and transcripts. Additional exam requirements/recommendations for international students: Required—TOEFL (minimum score 550 paper-based; 79 iBT), IELTS (minimum score 6.5). *Application deadline:* For fall admission, 6/1 priority date for domestic students, 5/1 priority date for international students; for spring admission, 11/15 priority date for domestic and international students. Applications are processed on a rolling basis. Application fee: $75. Electronic applications accepted. *Expenses:* $22,690 per year (in-state), $32,136 per year (out-of-state). *Financial support:* In 2018–19, 134 students received support, including 17 fellowships with full tuition reimbursements available (averaging $22,000 per year), 74 research assistantships with full tuition reimbursements available (averaging $22,000 per year), 71 teaching assistantships with full tuition reimbursements available (averaging $22,000 per year); scholarships/grants, traineeships, health care benefits, and unspecified assistantships also available. Financial award application deadline: 1/15. *Faculty research:* Biophotonics and bioimaging, morphogenetic patterning, embryogenesis, biological fluid dynamics, applied research in the mathematical sciences. *Total annual research expenditures:* $29.2 million. *Unit head:* Dr. Kevin Belfield, Dean, 973-596-3676, Fax: 973-565-0586, E-mail: kevin.d.belfield@njit.edu. *Application contact:* Stephen Eck, Director of Admissions, 973-596-3300, Fax: 973-596-3461, E-mail: admissions@njit.edu.
Website: http://csla.njit.edu/

Norfolk State University, School of Graduate Studies, School of Science and Technology, Department of Chemistry, Norfolk, VA 23504. Offers materials science (MS). *Entrance requirements:* Additional exam requirements/recommendations for international students: Required—TOEFL (minimum score 500 paper-based).

North Carolina State University, Graduate School, College of Engineering, Department of Materials Science and Engineering, Raleigh, NC 27695. Offers MMSE, MNAE, MS, PhD. PhD offered jointly with The University of North Carolina at Charlotte. *Degree requirements:* For master's, thesis; for doctorate, thesis/dissertation. Electronic applications accepted. *Faculty research:* Processing and properties of wide band gap semiconductors, ferroelectric thin-film materials, ductility of nanocrystalline materials, computational materials science, defects in silicon-based devices.

North Dakota State University, College of Graduate and Interdisciplinary Studies, Interdisciplinary Program in Materials and Nanotechnology, Fargo, ND 58102. Offers MS, PhD. *Entrance requirements:* For doctorate, GRE General Test. Additional exam requirements/recommendations for international students: Required—TOEFL.

Northwestern University, McCormick School of Engineering and Applied Science, Department of Civil and Environmental Engineering, Evanston, IL 60208-3109. Offers environmental engineering and science (MS, PhD); geotechnical engineering (MS, PhD); mechanics of materials and solids (MS, PhD); project management (MS); structural engineering and materials (MS, PhD); transportation systems analysis and planning (MS, PhD). MS and PhD admissions and degrees offered through The Graduate School. *Program availability:* Part-time. Terminal master's awarded for partial completion of doctoral program. *Degree requirements:* For master's, comprehensive exam (for some programs), thesis (for some programs); for doctorate, comprehensive exam, thesis/dissertation. *Entrance requirements:* For master's and doctorate, GRE General Test, minimum 2 letters of recommendation, transcripts from all academic institutions attended. Additional exam requirements/recommendations for international students: Required—TOEFL (minimum score 577 paper-based; 90 iBT), IELTS (minimum score 7). Electronic applications accepted. *Faculty research:* Environmental engineering and science, geotechnics, mechanics, materials, structures, and transportation systems analysis and planning.

Northwestern University, McCormick School of Engineering and Applied Science, Department of Materials Science and Engineering, Evanston, IL 60208. Offers integrated computational materials engineering (Certificate); materials science and engineering (MS, PhD). Admissions and degrees offered through The Graduate School. *Program availability:* Part-time. Terminal master's awarded for partial completion of doctoral program. *Degree requirements:* For master's, thesis optional, oral thesis defense; for doctorate, comprehensive exam, thesis/dissertation, oral defense of dissertation, preliminary evaluation, qualifying exam. *Entrance requirements:* For master's and doctorate, GRE General Test. Additional exam requirements/recommendations for international students: Required—TOEFL (minimum score 577 paper-based; 90 iBT), IELTS (minimum score 7). Electronic applications accepted. *Faculty research:* Art conservation science; biomaterials; ceramics; composites; energy; magnetic materials; materials for electronics and photonics; materials synthesis and processing; materials theory, computation, and design; metals; nanomaterials; polymers, self-assembly, and surfaces and interfaces.

The Ohio State University, Graduate School, College of Engineering, Department of Materials Science and Engineering, Columbus, OH 43210. Offers materials science and engineering (MS, PhD); welding engineering (MS, PhD). *Faculty:* 38. *Students:* 157 full-time (40 women), 51 part-time (7 women). Average age 29. In 2018, 38 master's, 16 doctorates awarded. *Entrance requirements:* For master's and doctorate, GRE (for graduates of foreign universities and holders of non-engineering degrees). Additional exam requirements/recommendations for international students: Required—TOEFL (minimum score 550 paper-based; 79 iBT), Michigan English Language Assessment Battery (minimum score 82); Recommended—IELTS (minimum score 7). *Application deadline:* For fall admission, 12/13 priority date for domestic students, 11/30 priority date for international students; for spring admission, 12/14 for domestic students, 11/12 for international students; for summer admission, 5/15 for domestic students, 4/14 for international students. Applications are processed on a rolling basis. Application fee: $60 ($70 for international students). Electronic applications accepted. *Financial support:* Fellowships, research assistantships, teaching assistantships, career-related internships or fieldwork, scholarships/grants, and unspecified assistantships available. *Faculty research:* Computational materials modeling, biomaterials, metallurgy, ceramics, advanced alloys/composites. *Unit head:* Dr. Peter Anderson, Chair, 614-292-6255, E-mail: anderson.1@osu.edu. *Application contact:* Mark Cooper, Graduate Studies Coordinator, 614-292-7280, Fax: 614-292-1357, E-mail: mse@osu.edu. Website: http://mse.osu.edu/

Oklahoma State University, College of Engineering, Architecture and Technology, School of Materials Science and Engineering, Stillwater, OK 74078. Offers MS, PhD. *Faculty:* 7 full-time (0 women), 2 part-time/adjunct (0 women). *Students:* 2 full-time (0 women), 16 part-time (4 women); includes 4 minority (2 American Indian or Alaska Native, non-Hispanic/Latino; 1 Asian, non-Hispanic/Latino; 1 Two or more races, non-Hispanic/Latino), 7 international. Average age 29. 14 applicants, 29% accepted, 4 enrolled. In 2018, 3 master's, 1 doctorate awarded. *Entrance requirements:* Additional exam requirements/recommendations for international students: Required—TOEFL. *Application deadline:* For fall admission, 3/1 for domestic students; for spring admission, 8/1 for domestic students. Application fee: $40 ($75 for international students). Electronic applications accepted. *Expenses: Tuition, area resident:* Full-time $4148. Tuition, state resident: full-time $4148. Tuition, nonresident: full-time $10,517. *International tuition:* $10,517 full-time. *Required fees:* $4394; $2929 per credit hour. Tuition and fees vary according to course load and program. *Financial support:* Research assistantships and teaching assistantships available. *Unit head:* Dr. Raman P Singh, Head, 918-594-8155, E-mail: raman.singh@okstate.edu. *Application contact:* Dr. Sheryl Tucker, Dean, 405-744-6368, Fax: 405-744-0355, E-mail: gradi@okstate.edu. Website: http://mse.okstate.edu/

Oregon State University, College of Engineering, Program in Materials Science, Corvallis, OR 97331. Offers chemical engineering (MS, PhD); chemistry (MS, PhD); civil engineering (MS, PhD); electrical and computer engineering (MS, PhD); forest products (MS, PhD); mathematics (MS, PhD); mechanical engineering (MS, PhD); nuclear engineering (MS); physics (MS, PhD). *Entrance requirements:* For master's and doctorate, GRE. Additional exam requirements/recommendations for international students: Required—TOEFL (minimum score 80 iBT), IELTS (minimum score 6.5). *Expenses:* Contact institution.

Penn State University Park, Graduate School, Intercollege Graduate Programs, Intercollege Graduate Program in Materials Science and Engineering, University Park, PA 16802. Offers MS, PhD.

Princeton University, Princeton Institute for the Science and Technology of Materials (PRISM), Princeton, NJ 08544-1019. Offers materials (PhD).

Rice University, Graduate Programs, George R. Brown School of Engineering, Department of Mechanical Engineering and Materials Science, Houston, TX 77251-1892. Offers materials science (MMS, MS, PhD); mechanical engineering (MME, MS, PhD); MBA/ME. *Program availability:* Part-time. Terminal master's awarded for partial completion of doctoral program. *Degree requirements:* For master's, comprehensive exam, thesis; for doctorate, comprehensive exam, thesis/dissertation. *Entrance requirements:* For master's and doctorate, GRE General Test, minimum GPA of 3.0. Additional exam requirements/recommendations for international students: Required—TOEFL (minimum score 600 paper-based; 90 iBT), IELTS (minimum score 7). Electronic applications accepted. *Faculty research:* Heat transfer, biomedical engineering, fluid dynamics, aero-astronautics, control systems/robotics, materials science.

Rochester Institute of Technology, Graduate Enrollment Services, College of Science, School of Chemistry and Materials Science, MS Program in Materials Science and Engineering, Rochester, NY 14623-5603. Offers MS. Program offered jointly with Kate Gleason College of Engineering. *Program availability:* Part-time, evening/weekend.

Students: 15 full-time (9 women), 5 part-time (2 women); includes 5 minority (1 Black or African American, non-Hispanic/Latino; 2 Asian, non-Hispanic/Latino; 2 Hispanic/Latino), 1 international. Average age 24. 32 applicants, 84% accepted, 7 enrolled. In 2018, 8 master's awarded. *Degree requirements:* For master's, thesis or project. *Entrance requirements:* For master's, minimum GPA of 3.0 (recommended), two letters of recommendation. Additional exam requirements/recommendations for international students: Required—TOEFL (minimum score 575 paper-based; 90 iBT), IELTS (minimum score 6.5), PTE (minimum score 62). *Application deadline:* Applications are processed on a rolling basis. Application fee: $65. Electronic applications accepted. *Financial support:* In 2018–19, 22 students received support. Research assistantships with partial tuition reimbursements available, teaching assistantships with partial tuition reimbursements available, career-related internships or fieldwork, scholarships/grants, and unspecified assistantships available. Support available to part-time students. Financial award applicants required to submit FAFSA. *Faculty research:* Magnetism and magnetic materials, photovoltaics and batteries, electronic materials, functional nanomaterials, 3D printing and additive manufacturing. *Unit head:* Michael Pierce, PhD, Department Chair, 585-475-2089, E-mail: mspsps@rit.edu. *Application contact:* Diane Ellison, Senior Associate Vice President, Graduate Enrollment Services, 585-475-2229, Fax: 585-475-7164, E-mail: gradinfo@rit.edu.
Website: https://www.rit.edu/study/materials-science-and-engineering-ms

Rutgers University–New Brunswick, Graduate School-New Brunswick, Program in Materials Science and Engineering, Piscataway, NJ 08854-8097. Offers MS, PhD. *Program availability:* Part-time. *Degree requirements:* For master's, thesis; for doctorate, comprehensive exam, thesis/dissertation. *Entrance requirements:* For master's and doctorate, GRE General Test. Additional exam requirements/recommendations for international students: Recommended—TOEFL. Electronic applications accepted. *Faculty research:* Ceramic processing, nanostructured materials, electrical and structural ceramics, fiber optics.

South Dakota School of Mines and Technology, Graduate Division, Doctoral Program in Materials Engineering and Science, Rapid City, SD 57701-3995. Offers PhD. *Program availability:* Part-time. *Degree requirements:* For doctorate, thesis/dissertation. *Entrance requirements:* For doctorate, GRE General Test, minimum graduate GPA of 3.0, 3 letters of recommendation. Additional exam requirements/recommendations for international students: Required—TOEFL (minimum score 520 paper-based; 68 iBT), TWE. Electronic applications accepted.

South Dakota School of Mines and Technology, Graduate Division, Master's Program in Materials Engineering and Science, Rapid City, SD 57701-3995. Offers MS. *Degree requirements:* For master's, thesis (for some programs). *Entrance requirements:* For master's, GRE General Test. Additional exam requirements/recommendations for international students: Required—TOEFL (minimum score 520 paper-based; 68 iBT), TWE. Electronic applications accepted.

Stanford University, School of Engineering, Department of Materials Science and Engineering, Stanford, CA 94305-2004. Offers MS, PhD, Engr. *Expenses: Tuition:* Full-time $50,703; part-time $32,970 per year. *Required fees:* $651.
Website: https://mse.stanford.edu/

State University of New York College of Environmental Science and Forestry, Department of Paper and Bioprocess Engineering, Syracuse, NY 13210-2779. Offers biomaterials engineering (MS, PhD); bioprocess engineering (MPS, MS, PhD); bioprocessing (Advanced Certificate); paper science and engineering (MPS, MS, PhD); sustainable engineering management (MPS). *Program availability:* Part-time. *Faculty:* 13 full-time (2 women), 1 part-time/adjunct (0 women). *Students:* 20 full-time (11 women), 1 part-time (0 women); includes 29 minority (28 American Indian or Alaska Native, non-Hispanic/Latino; 1 Hispanic/Latino), 14 international. Average age 28. 18 applicants, 100% accepted, 11 enrolled. In 2018, 2 master's awarded. Terminal master's awarded for partial completion of doctoral program. *Degree requirements:* For master's, thesis; for doctorate, comprehensive exam, thesis/dissertation; for Advanced Certificate, 15 credit hours. *Entrance requirements:* For master's and doctorate, GRE General Test, minimum GPA of 3.0; for Advanced Certificate, BS, calculus plus science major. Additional exam requirements/recommendations for international students: Required—TOEFL (minimum score 550 paper-based; 80 iBT), IELTS (minimum score 6). *Application deadline:* For fall admission, 2/1 priority date for domestic and international students; for spring admission, 11/1 priority date for domestic and international students. Applications are processed on a rolling basis. Application fee: $60. Electronic applications accepted. *Expenses: Tuition, area resident:* Full-time $11,090; part-time $462 per credit hour. Tuition, state resident: full-time $11,090; part-time $462 per credit hour. Tuition, nonresident: full-time $22,650; part-time $944 per credit hour. *International tuition:* $22,650 full-time. *Required fees:* $1733; $178.58 per credit hour. *Financial support:* In 2018–19, 17 students received support. Unspecified assistantships available. Financial award application deadline: 6/30; financial award applicants required to submit FAFSA. *Faculty research:* Sustainable products and processes, biorefinery, pulping and papermaking, nanocellulose, bioconversions, process control and modeling. *Total annual research expenditures:* $237,793. *Unit head:* Dr. Bandaru Ramarao, Interim Chair, 315-470-6502, Fax: 315-470-6945, E-mail: bvramara@esf.edu. *Application contact:* Scott Shannon, Associate Provost and Dean, Instruction and Graduate Studies, 315-470-6599, Fax: 315-470-6978, E-mail: esfgrad@esf.edu.
Website: http://www.esf.edu/pbe/

Stevens Institute of Technology, Graduate School, Charles V. Schaefer Jr. School of Engineering and Science, Department of Chemical Engineering and Materials Science, Program in Materials Science and Engineering, Hoboken, NJ 07030. Offers M Eng, PhD. *Program availability:* Part-time, evening/weekend. *Faculty:* 1 part-time/adjunct. *Students:* 53 full-time (14 women), 1 (woman) part-time, 50 international. Average age 25. In 2018, 33 master's, 3 doctorates awarded. Terminal master's awarded for partial completion of doctoral program. *Degree requirements:* For master's, thesis optional, minimum B average in major field and overall; for doctorate, comprehensive exam (for some programs), thesis/dissertation. *Entrance requirements:* For master's, GRE/GMAT scores: GRE scores are required for all applicants applying to a full-time graduate program in the Schaefer School of Engineering and Science (SES). International applicants must submit TOEFL/IELTS scores and fulfill the English Language Proficiency Requirements in order to be considered. Additional exam requirements/recommendations for international students: Required—TOEFL (minimum score 74 iBT), IELTS (minimum score 6). *Application deadline:* For fall admission, 4/15 for domestic and international students; for spring admission, 11/1 for domestic and international students; for summer admission, 5/1 for domestic students. Applications are processed on a rolling basis. Application fee: $60. Electronic applications accepted. *Expenses: Tuition:* Full-time $35,960; part-time $1620 per credit. *Required fees:* $1290; $600 per semester. Tuition and fees vary according to course load. *Financial support:* Fellowships, research assistantships, teaching assistantships, career-related internships or fieldwork, Federal Work-Study, scholarships/grants, and unspecified assistantships available. Financial award application deadline: 2/15; financial award applicants required to submit FAFSA. *Unit head:* Dr. Jean Zu, Dean of SES, 201-216.8233, Fax: 201-216.8372, E-mail: Jean.Zu@stevens.edu. *Application contact:* Graduate Admissions, 888-783-8367, Fax: 888-511-1306, E-mail: graduate@stevens.edu.

Materials Sciences

Stony Brook University, State University of New York, Graduate School, College of Engineering and Applied Sciences, Department of Materials Science & Chemical Engineering, Stony Brook, NY 11794. Offers MS, PhD. *Faculty:* 19 full-time (5 women), 6 part-time/adjunct (3 women). *Students:* 75 full-time (21 women), 4 part-time (1 woman); includes 11 minority (6 Asian, non-Hispanic/Latino; 4 Hispanic/Latino; 1 Two or more races, non-Hispanic/Latino), 56 international. Average age 26. 151 applicants, 67% accepted, 15 enrolled. In 2018, 21 master's, 13 doctorates awarded. *Degree requirements:* For master's, thesis or alternative; for doctorate, comprehensive exam, thesis/dissertation. *Entrance requirements:* For master's and doctorate, GRE General Test, minimum undergraduate GPA of 3.0. Additional exam requirements/recommendations for international students: Required—TOEFL (minimum score 90 iBT). *Application deadline:* For fall admission, 1/15 for domestic students; for spring admission, 10/1 for domestic students. Application fee: $100. *Expenses:* Contact institution. *Financial support:* In 2018–19, 30 research assistantships, 14 teaching assistantships were awarded; fellowships also available. *Faculty research:* Crystal growth, crystallography, semiconductors, synchrotron X-rays or radiation, fuel cells. *Total annual research expenditures:* $3.7 million. *Unit head:* Dr. Dilip Gersappe, Professor and Interim Chair, 631-632-8500, Fax: 631-632-8052, E-mail: dilip.gersappe@stonybrook.edu. *Application contact:* Kaitlyn Cozier, Coordinator, 631-632-6269, Fax: 631-632-8052, E-mail: Kaitlyn.Cozier@stonybrook.edu. Website: http://www.stonybrook.edu/commcms/matscieng/index.html

Texas A&M University, College of Engineering, Department of Materials Science and Engineering, College Station, TX 77843. Offers materials science and engineering (M Eng). *Faculty:* 20. *Students:* 157 full-time (51 women), 7 part-time (0 women); includes 30 minority (1 Black or African American, non-Hispanic/Latino; 14 Asian, non-Hispanic/Latino; 10 Hispanic/Latino; 5 Two or more races, non-Hispanic/Latino), 100 international. Average age 28. 221 applicants, 36% accepted, 31 enrolled. In 2018, 10 master's, 14 doctorates awarded. *Degree requirements:* For master's, thesis (MS); for doctorate, thesis/dissertation. *Entrance requirements:* For master's and doctorate, GRE General Test. Additional exam requirements/recommendations for international students: Required—TOEFL (minimum score 550 paper-based; 80 iBT), IELTS (minimum score 6), PTE (minimum score 53). *Application deadline:* For fall admission, 2/28 for domestic and international students; for spring admission, 7/31 for domestic students, 6/1 for international students. Application fee: $50 ($90 for international students). *Expenses:* Contact institution. *Financial support:* In 2018–19, 157 students received support, including 26 fellowships with tuition reimbursements available (averaging $23,103 per year), 119 research assistantships with tuition reimbursements available (averaging $15,964 per year), 15 teaching assistantships with tuition reimbursements available (averaging $12,565 per year); career-related internships or fieldwork, institutionally sponsored loans, scholarships/grants, traineeships, health care benefits, tuition waivers (full and partial), and unspecified assistantships also available. Support available to part-time students. Financial award application deadline: 3/15; financial award applicants required to submit FAFSA. *Faculty research:* Innovative design methods, pavement distress characterization, materials property, characterization and modeling recyclable materials. *Unit head:* Ibrahim Karaman, Department Head, 979-862-3923, E-mail: ikaraman@tamu.edu. *Application contact:* Mildan Radovic, Associate Department Head, 979-845-5114, E-mail: mradovic@tamu.edu. Website: http://engineering.tamu.edu/materials

Texas State University, The Graduate College, College of Science and Engineering, PhD Program in Materials Science, Engineering, and Commercialization, San Marcos, TX 78666. Offers PhD. *Faculty:* 13 full-time (4 women). *Students:* 38 full-time (13 women), 2 part-time (both women); includes 6 minority (2 Black or African American, non-Hispanic/Latino; 2 Asian, non-Hispanic/Latino; 2 Hispanic/Latino), 25 international. Average age 32. 42 applicants, 14% accepted, 4 enrolled. In 2018, 7 doctorates awarded. *Degree requirements:* For doctorate, comprehensive exam, thesis/dissertation. *Entrance requirements:* For doctorate, GRE (for applicants who have not received a master's degree from a U.S. institution), baccalaureate and master's degrees from regionally-accredited college or university in biology, chemistry, engineering, materials science, physics, technology, or closely-related field with minimum GPA of 3.5 in graduate work; interviews with core doctoral faculty; statement of purpose; 3 letters of recommendation; curriculum vitae or resume. Additional exam requirements/recommendations for international students: Required—TOEFL (minimum score 550 paper-based; 78 iBT); Recommended—IELTS (minimum score 6.5). *Application deadline:* For fall admission, 2/1 priority date for domestic and international students. Application fee: $55 ($90 for international students). Electronic applications accepted. *Expenses:* Tuition, state resident: full-time $8102; part-time $4051 per semester. Tuition, nonresident: full-time $18,229; part-time $9115 per semester. *International tuition:* $18,229 full-time. *Required fees:* $2116; $120 per credit hour. Tuition and fees vary according to course load. *Financial support:* In 2018–19, 38 students received support, including 9 research assistantships (averaging $30,911 per year), 24 teaching assistantships (averaging $33,907 per year); scholarships/grants, health care benefits, and unspecified assistantships also available. Support available to part-time students. Financial award application deadline: 1/15; financial award applicants required to submit FAFSA. *Faculty research:* Materials characterization using RSC, industrial process pollution by development of amorphous biogenic silica, cadmium telluride surface and interface passivation by molecular beam epitaxy, micro power chip prototype development, development materials and processes in compound semiconductor epitaxy and deposition. *Total annual research expenditures:* $840,784. *Unit head:* Dr. Jennifer Irvin, PhD Program Director, 512-245-7875, Fax: 512-245-8365, E-mail: ji12@txstate.edu. *Application contact:* Dr. Andrea Golato, Dean of Graduate School, 512-245-7875, Fax: 512-245-8365, E-mail: gradcollege@txstate.edu. Website: http://www.msec.txstate.edu/

Trent University, Graduate Studies, Program in Materials Science, Peterborough, ON K9J 7B8, Canada. Offers M Sc.

Université du Québec, Institut National de la Recherche Scientifique, Graduate Programs, Centre for Energie Materiaux Telecommunications, Varennes, QC G1K 9A9, Canada. Offers energy and materials science (M Sc, PhD); telecommunications (M Sc, PhD). *Program availability:* Part-time. *Faculty:* 38 full-time. *Students:* 207 full-time (60 women), 13 part-time (3 women), 186 international. Average age 34. 45 applicants, 87% accepted, 24 enrolled. In 2018, 13 master's, 30 doctorates awarded. *Degree requirements:* For master's, thesis (for some programs); for doctorate, thesis/dissertation. *Entrance requirements:* For master's, appropriate bachelor's degree, proficiency in French; for doctorate, appropriate master's degree, proficiency in French. *Application deadline:* For fall admission, 3/30 for domestic and international students; for winter admission, 11/1 for domestic and international students; for spring admission, 3/1 for domestic and international students. Application fee: $45. Electronic applications accepted. *Financial support:* In 2018–19, fellowships (averaging $16,500 per year) were awarded; research assistantships and scholarships/grants also available. *Faculty research:* New energy sources, plasmas, telecommunications, advanced materials, ultrafast photonics. *Total annual research expenditures:* $11.3 million. *Unit head:* Ana Tavares, Director, 514-228-6947, Fax: 450-929-8102, E-mail: ana.tavares@emt.inrs.ca. *Application contact:* Sean Otto, Registrar, 418-654-2518, Fax: 418-654-3858, E-mail: sean.otto@inrs.ca. Website: http://www.emt.inrs.ca

University at Buffalo, the State University of New York, Graduate School, School of Engineering and Applied Sciences, Department of Materials Design and Innovation, Buffalo, NY 14260. Offers MS, PhD.

The University of Alabama, Graduate School, College of Engineering and College of Arts and Sciences, Tri-Campus Materials Science PhD Program, Tuscaloosa, AL 35487. Offers PhD. Program offered jointly with The University of Alabama at Birmingham and The University of Alabama in Huntsville. *Degree requirements:* For doctorate, comprehensive exam, thesis/dissertation. *Entrance requirements:* For doctorate, GRE General Test. Additional exam requirements/recommendations for international students: Required—TOEFL (minimum score 550 paper-based). Electronic applications accepted. *Faculty research:* Magnetic multilayers, metals casting, molecular electronics, conducting polymers, metals physics, electrodeposition.

The University of Alabama in Huntsville, School of Graduate Studies, College of Engineering, Department of Chemical and Materials Engineering, Huntsville, AL 35899. Offers biotechnology science and engineering (PhD); chemical and materials engineering (MSE); materials science (PhD); mechanical engineering (PhD), including chemical engineering. *Program availability:* Part-time. *Faculty:* 3 full-time (1 woman), 1 part-time/adjunct. *Students:* 5 full-time (1 woman), 4 part-time (1 woman); includes 1 minority (Asian, non-Hispanic/Latino), 1 international. Average age 25. 12 applicants, 25% accepted, 2 enrolled. In 2018, 2 master's awarded. *Degree requirements:* For master's, comprehensive exam, thesis or alternative, oral and written exams; for doctorate, comprehensive exam, thesis/dissertation. *Entrance requirements:* For master's, GRE General Test, appropriate bachelor's degree, minimum GPA of 3.0; for doctorate, GRE General Test, minimum GPA of 3.0. Additional exam requirements/recommendations for international students: Required—TOEFL (minimum score 500 paper-based; 80 iBT), IELTS (minimum score 6.5). *Application deadline:* For fall admission, 7/15 priority date for domestic students, 4/1 priority date for international students; for spring admission, 11/30 priority date for domestic students, 9/1 priority date for international students. Applications are processed on a rolling basis. Application fee: $50. Electronic applications accepted. *Expenses: Tuition, area resident:* Full-time $10,632; part-time $412 per credit hour. Tuition, state resident: full-time $10,632. Tuition, nonresident: full-time $23,604; part-time $412 per credit hour. *Required fees:* $582; $582. Tuition and fees vary according to course load and program. *Financial support:* In 2018–19, 4 students received support, including 1 research assistantship with full tuition reimbursement available (averaging $2,500 per year), 3 teaching assistantships with full tuition reimbursements available (averaging $5,500 per year); career-related internships or fieldwork, Federal Work-Study, institutionally sponsored loans, scholarships/grants, health care benefits, and unspecified assistantships also available. Support available to part-time students. Financial award application deadline: 4/1; financial award applicants required to submit FAFSA. *Faculty research:* Ultrathin films for optical, sensor and biological applications; materials processing including low gravity; hypergolic reactants; computational fluid dynamics; biofuels and renewable resources. *Unit head:* Dr. Anuradha Subramanian, Chair, 256-824-6194, Fax: 256-824-6839, E-mail: anu.subramanian@uah.edu. *Application contact:* Kim Gray, Graduate Studies Admissions Coordinator, 256-824-6002, Fax: 256-824-6405, E-mail: deangrad@uah.edu. Website: http://www.cme.uah.edu/

The University of Alabama in Huntsville, School of Graduate Studies, College of Science, Department of Chemistry, Huntsville, AL 35899. Offers biotechnology science and engineering (PhD); chemistry (MS); education (MS); materials science (MS, PhD). *Program availability:* Part-time. *Faculty:* 5 full-time (3 women). *Students:* 14 full-time (5 women), 8 part-time (5 women); includes 5 minority (all Black or African American, non-Hispanic/Latino), 4 international. Average age 29. 26 applicants, 77% accepted, 9 enrolled. In 2018, 3 master's awarded. *Degree requirements:* For master's, comprehensive exam, thesis or alternative, oral and written exams. *Entrance requirements:* For master's, GRE General Test, minimum GPA of 3.0. Additional exam requirements/recommendations for international students: Required—TOEFL (minimum score 550 paper-based; 80 iBT), IELTS (minimum score 6.5). *Application deadline:* For fall admission, 7/15 priority date for domestic students, 4/1 priority date for international students; for spring admission, 11/30 priority date for domestic students, 9/1 priority date for international students. Applications are processed on a rolling basis. Application fee: $50. Electronic applications accepted. *Expenses: Tuition, area resident:* Full-time $10,632; part-time $412 per credit hour. Tuition, state resident: full-time $10,632. Tuition, nonresident: full-time $23,604; part-time $412 per credit hour. *Required fees:* $582; $582. Tuition and fees vary according to course load and program. *Financial support:* In 2018–19, 8 students received support, including 1 research assistantship with full tuition reimbursement available (averaging $6,000 per year), 7 teaching assistantships with full tuition reimbursements available (averaging $6,000 per year); career-related internships or fieldwork, Federal Work-Study, institutionally sponsored loans, scholarships/grants, health care benefits, tuition waivers (full and partial), and unspecified assistantships also available. Support available to part-time students. Financial award application deadline: 4/1; financial award applicants required to submit FAFSA. *Faculty research:* Natural products drug discovery, protein biochemistry, macromolecular biophysics, polymer synthesis, surface modification and analysis of materials. *Unit head:* Dr. John Foster, Professor and Chair, 256-824-6253, Fax: 256-824-6349, E-mail: john.foster@uah.edu. *Application contact:* Kim Gray, Graduate Studies Admissions Coordinator, 256-824-6002, Fax: 256-824-6405, E-mail: deangrad@uah.edu. Website: http://chemistry.uah.edu

The University of Arizona, College of Engineering, Department of Materials Science and Engineering, Tucson, AZ 85721. Offers MS, PhD. *Program availability:* Part-time. *Degree requirements:* For master's, thesis (for some programs); for doctorate, comprehensive exam, thesis/dissertation. *Entrance requirements:* For master's and doctorate, GRE General Test, 3 letters of recommendation, statement of purpose. Additional exam requirements/recommendations for international students: Required—TOEFL (minimum score 550 paper-based; 79 iBT). Electronic applications accepted. *Faculty research:* High-technology ceramics, optical materials, electronic materials, chemical metallurgy, science of materials.

University of Calgary, Faculty of Graduate Studies, Schulich School of Engineering, Program in Civil Engineering, Calgary, AB T2N 1N4, Canada. Offers avalanche mechanics (M Sc, PhD); civil engineering (M Eng, M Sc, PhD); energy and environment engineering (M Eng, M Sc, PhD); environmental engineering (M Eng, M Sc, PhD); geotechnical engineering (M Eng, M Sc, PhD); materials science (M Eng, M Sc, PhD); project management (M Eng, M Sc, PhD); structures and solid mechanics (M Eng, M Sc, PhD); transportation engineering (M Eng, M Sc, PhD); water resources (M Eng, M Sc, PhD). *Program availability:* Part-time. *Degree requirements:* For master's, thesis; for doctorate, thesis/dissertation, written and oral candidacy exam. *Entrance requirements:* For master's, minimum GPA of 3.0; for doctorate, minimum GPA of 3.5. Additional exam requirements/recommendations for international students: Required—TOEFL (minimum score 580 paper-based; 93 iBT), IELTS (minimum score 7). Electronic applications accepted. *Faculty research:* Geotechnical engineering, energy and environment, transportation, project management, structures and solid mechanics.

University of California, Berkeley, Graduate Division, College of Engineering, Department of Materials Science and Engineering, Berkeley, CA 94720. Offers engineering science (M Eng, MS, PhD). Terminal master's awarded for partial completion of doctoral program. *Degree requirements:* For master's, comprehensive exam (for some programs), thesis (for some programs), comprehensive exam or thesis (MS); for doctorate, comprehensive exam, thesis/dissertation, qualifying exam. *Entrance requirements:* For master's and doctorate, GRE General Test, minimum GPA of 3.0, 3 letters of recommendation. Additional exam requirements/recommendations for international students: Required—TOEFL (minimum score 570 paper-based; 90 iBT). Electronic applications accepted. *Faculty research:* Ceramics, biomaterials, structural, electronic, magnetic and optical materials.

University of California, Davis, College of Engineering, Program in Materials Science and Engineering, Davis, CA 95616. Offers MS, PhD. Terminal master's awarded for partial completion of doctoral program. *Degree requirements:* For master's, comprehensive exam (for some programs), thesis (for some programs); for doctorate, comprehensive exam, thesis/dissertation. *Entrance requirements:* Additional exam requirements/recommendations for international students: Required—TOEFL (minimum score 550 paper-based).

University of California, Irvine, Samueli School of Engineering, Department of Chemical Engineering and Materials Science, Irvine, CA 92697. Offers chemical and biochemical engineering (MS, PhD); materials science and engineering (MS, PhD). *Program availability:* Part-time. *Students:* 133 full-time (57 women), 2 part-time (0 women); includes 36 minority (3 Black or African American, non-Hispanic/Latino; 26 Asian, non-Hispanic/Latino; 5 Hispanic/Latino; 2 Two or more races, non-Hispanic/Latino), 51 international. Average age 26. 417 applicants, 35% accepted, 36 enrolled. In 2018, 30 master's, 26 doctorates awarded. Terminal master's awarded for partial completion of doctoral program. *Entrance requirements:* For master's and doctorate, GRE General Test, minimum GPA of 3.0, 3 letters of recommendation. Additional exam requirements/recommendations for international students: Required—TOEFL (minimum score 550 paper-based). *Application deadline:* For fall admission, 1/15 priority date for domestic students, 1/15 for international students. Applications are processed on a rolling basis. Application fee: $105 ($125 for international students). Electronic applications accepted. *Financial support:* Fellowships, research assistantships with full tuition reimbursements, teaching assistantships, institutionally sponsored loans, traineeships, health care benefits, and unspecified assistantships available. Financial award application deadline: 3/1; financial award applicants required to submit FAFSA. *Faculty research:* Molecular biotechnology, nanobiomaterials, biophotonics, synthesis, super plasticity and mechanical behavior, characterization of advanced and nanostructural materials. *Unit head:* Prof. Vasan Venugopalan, Chair, 949-824-5802, Fax: 949-824-2541, E-mail: vvenugop@uci.edu. *Application contact:* Grace Chau, Academic Program and Graduate Admission Coordinator, 949-824-3887, Fax: 949-824-2541, E-mail: chaug@uci.edu.
Website: http://www.eng.uci.edu/dept/chems

University of California, Irvine, School of Physical Sciences, Program in Chemical and Materials Physics (CHAMP), Irvine, CA 92697. Offers MS, PhD. *Students:* 37 full-time (8 women); includes 13 minority (7 Asian, non-Hispanic/Latino; 4 Hispanic/Latino; 2 Two or more races, non-Hispanic/Latino), 6 international. Average age 27. 40 applicants, 40% accepted, 5 enrolled. In 2018, 7 master's, 11 doctorates awarded. *Entrance requirements:* For master's and doctorate, GRE General Test, GRE Subject Test, minimum GPA of 3.0. *Application deadline:* For fall admission, 1/15 priority date for domestic students, 1/15 for international students. Applications are processed on a rolling basis. Application fee: $105 ($125 for international students). Electronic applications accepted. *Financial support:* Fellowships, research assistantships with full tuition reimbursements, teaching assistantships, institutionally sponsored loans, traineeships, health care benefits, and unspecified assistantships available. Financial award application deadline: 3/1; financial award applicants required to submit FAFSA. *Unit head:* A.J. Shaka, Co-Director, 949-824-8509, E-mail: ajshaka@uci.edu. *Application contact:* Jaime M. Albano, Student Affairs Manager, 949-824-4261, Fax: 949-824-8571, E-mail: jmalbano@uci.edu.

University of California, Los Angeles, Graduate Division, Henry Samueli School of Engineering and Applied Science, Department of Materials Science and Engineering, Los Angeles, CA 90095-1595. Offers MS, PhD. *Degree requirements:* For master's, comprehensive exam or thesis; for doctorate, thesis/dissertation, qualifying exams. *Entrance requirements:* For master's, GRE General Test, minimum GPA of 3.0; for doctorate, GRE General Test, minimum GPA of 3.25. Additional exam requirements/recommendations for international students: Required—TOEFL (minimum score 560 paper-based; 87 iBT), IELTS (minimum score 7). Electronic applications accepted. *Faculty research:* Ceramics and ceramic processing, electronic and optical materials, structural materials.

University of California, Riverside, Graduate Division, Materials Science and Engineering Program, Riverside, CA 92521. Offers MS. *Entrance requirements:* For master's, GRE. Additional exam requirements/recommendations for international students: Required—TOEFL (minimum score 550 paper-based; 80 iBT). Electronic applications accepted.

University of California, San Diego, Graduate Division, Program in Materials Science and Engineering, La Jolla, CA 92093. Offers MS, PhD. *Students:* 184 full-time (53 women), 12 part-time (4 women). 469 applicants, 59% accepted, 61 enrolled. In 2018, 50 master's, 21 doctorates awarded. *Degree requirements:* For master's, comprehensive exam (for some programs), thesis (for some programs), thesis or comprehensive exam; for doctorate, comprehensive exam, thesis/dissertation. *Entrance requirements:* For master's and doctorate, GRE General Test, minimum GPA of 3.2. Additional exam requirements/recommendations for international students: Required—TOEFL (minimum score 550 paper-based; 80 iBT), IELTS (minimum score 7). *Application deadline:* For fall admission, 1/8 for domestic students. Application fee: $105 ($125 for international students). Electronic applications accepted. *Financial support:* Fellowships, research assistantships, and teaching assistantships available. Financial award applicants required to submit FAFSA. *Faculty research:* Magnetic and nanomaterials, structural materials, electronic materials and interfaces, biomaterials, energy materials and applications. *Unit head:* Prabhakar Banderu, Director, 858-534-5325, E-mail: pbandaru@ucsd.edu. *Application contact:* Sandra de Sousa, Graduate Coordinator, 858-822-1421, E-mail: mats-gradadm@eng.ucsd.edu.
Website: http://matsci.ucsd.edu/

University of California, Santa Barbara, Graduate Division, College of Engineering, Department of Materials, Santa Barbara, CA 93106-5050. Offers MS, PhD, MS/PhD. Terminal master's awarded for partial completion of doctoral program. *Degree requirements:* For master's, variable foreign language requirement, comprehensive exam, thesis; for doctorate, variable foreign language requirement, comprehensive exam, thesis/dissertation. *Entrance requirements:* For master's and doctorate, GRE General Test. Additional exam requirements/recommendations for international students: Required—TOEFL (minimum score 600 paper-based; 100 iBT), IELTS (minimum score 7). Electronic applications accepted. *Faculty research:* Electronic and photonic materials, inorganic materials, macromolecular and biomolecular materials, structural materials.

University of Central Florida, College of Engineering and Computer Science, Department of Materials Science and Engineering, Orlando, FL 32816. Offers MSMSE, PhD. *Students:* 50 full-time (20 women), 16 part-time (8 women); includes 5 minority (2 Asian, non-Hispanic/Latino; 2 Hispanic/Latino; 1 Two or more races, non-Hispanic/Latino), 36 international. Average age 29. 64 applicants, 41% accepted, 17 enrolled. In 2018, 8 master's, 5 doctorates awarded. *Degree requirements:* For master's, thesis or alternative; for doctorate, thesis/dissertation, candidacy exam, departmental qualifying exam. *Entrance requirements:* For master's, resume, goal statement; for doctorate, GRE, letters of recommendation, resume, goal statement. Additional exam requirements/recommendations for international students: Required—TOEFL. *Application deadline:* For fall admission, 7/15 for domestic students; for spring admission, 12/1 for domestic students. Application fee: $30. Electronic applications accepted. *Financial support:* In 2018–19, 45 students received support, including 11 fellowships with tuition reimbursements available (averaging $11,891 per year), 47 research assistantships (averaging $11,177 per year), 6 teaching assistantships (averaging $13,327 per year); health care benefits also available. Financial award application deadline: 3/1; financial award applicants required to submit FAFSA. *Unit head:* Dr. Sudipta Seal, Chair, 407-823-5277, E-mail: sseal@ucf.edu. *Application contact:* Associate Director, Graduate Admissions, 407-823-2766, Fax: 407-823-6442, E-mail: gradadmissions@ucf.edu.
Website: http://mse.ucf.edu/

University of Cincinnati, Graduate School, College of Engineering and Applied Science, Department of Mechanical and Materials Engineering, Program in Materials Science and Engineering, Cincinnati, OH 45221. Offers MS, PhD. *Program availability:* Evening/weekend. *Degree requirements:* For master's, thesis optional; for doctorate, one foreign language, comprehensive exam, thesis/dissertation, oral English proficiency exam. *Entrance requirements:* For master's and doctorate, GRE General Test, BS in related field, minimum undergraduate GPA of 3.0. Additional exam requirements/recommendations for international students: Required—TOEFL. Electronic applications accepted. *Faculty research:* Polymer characterization, surface analysis, and adhesion; mechanical behavior of high-temperature materials; composites; electrochemistry of materials.

University of Colorado Boulder, Graduate School, Materials Science and Engineering Program, Boulder, CO 80309. Offers MS, PhD. Electronic applications accepted.

University of Connecticut, Graduate School, School of Engineering, Department of Materials Science and Engineering, Storrs, CT 06269. Offers M Eng. Terminal master's awarded for partial completion of doctoral program. *Degree requirements:* For master's, comprehensive exam, thesis or alternative. *Entrance requirements:* For master's, GRE General Test, GRE Subject Test. Additional exam requirements/recommendations for international students: Required—TOEFL (minimum score 550 paper-based). Electronic applications accepted.

University of Connecticut, Institute of Materials Science, Storrs, CT 06269. Offers MS, PhD.

University of Delaware, College of Engineering, Department of Materials Science and Engineering, Newark, DE 19716. Offers MMSE, PhD. Terminal master's awarded for partial completion of doctoral program. *Degree requirements:* For master's, thesis; for doctorate, thesis/dissertation. *Entrance requirements:* For master's and doctorate, GRE General Test, 3 letters of recommendation, minimum GPA of 3.2. Additional exam requirements/recommendations for international students: Required—TOEFL. Electronic applications accepted. *Faculty research:* Thin films and self assembly, drug delivery and tissue engineering, biomaterials and nanocomposites, semiconductor and oxide interfaces, electronic and magnetic materials.

University of Denver, Daniel Felix Ritchie School of Engineering and Computer Science, Department of Mechanical and Materials Engineering, Denver, CO 80208. Offers bioengineering (MS); engineering (MS, PhD), including management; materials science (MS, PhD); mechanical engineering (MS, PhD). *Program availability:* Part-time. *Faculty:* 13 full-time (2 women), 2 part-time/adjunct (1 woman). *Students:* 4 full-time (1 woman), 33 part-time (7 women); includes 5 minority (2 Black or African American, non-Hispanic/Latino; 2 Hispanic/Latino; 1 Two or more races, non-Hispanic/Latino), 11 international. Average age 28. 71 applicants, 63% accepted, 15 enrolled. In 2018, 11 master's, 3 doctorates awarded. Terminal master's awarded for partial completion of doctoral program. *Degree requirements:* For master's, thesis optional; for doctorate, comprehensive exam, thesis/dissertation. *Entrance requirements:* For master's, GRE General Test, bachelor's degree in engineering or closely related field, transcripts, personal statement, resume or curriculum vitae, two letters of recommendation; for doctorate, GRE General Test, master's degree in engineering or closely related field, transcripts, personal statement, resume or curriculum vitae, two letters of recommendation, recommended that applicants find a research advisor before submitting the application. Additional exam requirements/recommendations for international students: Required—TOEFL (minimum score 550 paper-based; 80 iBT). *Application deadline:* For fall admission, 1/15 priority date for domestic and international students; for winter admission, 10/25 for domestic and international students; for spring admission, 2/7 for domestic and international students; for summer admission, 4/24 for domestic and international students. Applications are processed on a rolling basis. Application fee: $65. Electronic applications accepted. *Expenses:* $33,183 per year full-time. *Financial support:* In 2018–19, 25 students received support, including 10 research assistantships with tuition reimbursements available (averaging $12,917 per year), 13 teaching assistantships with tuition reimbursements available (averaging $15,289 per year); Federal Work-Study, institutionally sponsored loans, scholarships/grants, health care benefits, and unspecified assistantships also available. Financial award application deadline: 2/15; financial award applicants required to submit FAFSA. *Faculty research:* Cardiac biomechanics, novel high voltage/temperature materials and structures, high speed stereo radiography, musculoskeletal modeling, composites. *Unit head:* Dr. Matt Gordon, Professor and Chair, 303-871-3580, E-mail: matthew.gordon@du.edu. *Application contact:* Chrissy Alexander, Assistant to the Chair, 303-871-3041, E-mail: Christine.Alexander@du.edu.
Website: http://ritchieschool.du.edu/departments/mme/

University of Florida, Graduate School, Herbert Wertheim College of Engineering, Department of Materials Science and Engineering, Gainesville, FL 32611. Offers material science and engineering (MS), including clinical and translational science; materials science and engineering (ME, PhD); nuclear engineering (ME, PhD), including imaging science and technology (PhD), nuclear engineering sciences (ME, MS, PhD); nuclear engineering (MS), including nuclear engineering sciences (ME, MS, PhD); JD/MS. *Program availability:* Part-time, online learning. Terminal master's awarded for partial completion of doctoral program. *Degree requirements:* For master's, comprehensive exam, thesis; for doctorate, comprehensive exam, thesis/dissertation. *Entrance requirements:* For master's and doctorate, minimum GPA of 3.0. Additional exam requirements/recommendations for international students: Required—TOEFL (minimum score 550 paper-based; 80 iBT), IELTS (minimum score 6). Electronic applications accepted. *Faculty research:* Polymeric system, biomaterials and biomimetics; inorganic and organic electronic materials; functional ceramic materials for energy systems and microelectronic applications; advanced metallic systems for aerospace, transportation and biological applications; nuclear materials.

Materials Sciences

University of Idaho, College of Graduate Studies, College of Engineering, Department of Chemical and Materials Engineering, Moscow, ID 83844-1021. Offers chemical engineering (M Engr, MS, PhD); materials science and engineering (PhD). *Faculty:* 14. *Students:* 27 full-time (5 women), 6 part-time (0 women). Average age 30. In 2018, 7 master's, 1 doctorate awarded. *Entrance requirements:* For master's and doctorate, GRE, minimum GPA of 3.0. Additional exam requirements/recommendations for international students: Required—TOEFL (minimum score 79 iBT). *Application deadline:* For fall admission, 8/1 for domestic students; for spring admission, 12/15 for domestic students. Applications are processed on a rolling basis. Application fee: $60. Electronic applications accepted. *Expenses:* Tuition, state resident: full-time $7266.44; part-time $474.50 per credit hour. Tuition, nonresident: full-time $24,902; part-time $1453.50 per credit hour. *Required fees:* $2085.56; $45.50 per credit hour. *Financial support:* Fellowships, research assistantships, and teaching assistantships available. Financial award applicants required to submit FAFSA. *Faculty research:* High temperature mechanical behavior of materials, polyampholyte polymers, multi-scale modeling of materials. *Unit head:* Dr. Eric Aston, Department Chair, 208-885-7572, E-mail: che@uidaho.edu. *Application contact:* Dr. Eric Aston, Department Chair, 208-885-7572, E-mail: che@uidaho.edu.
Website: https://www.uidaho.edu/engr/departments/cme

University of Illinois at Urbana–Champaign, Graduate College, College of Engineering, Department of Materials Science and Engineering, Champaign, IL 61820. Offers M Eng, MS, PhD, MS/MBA, PhD/MBA.

University of Kentucky, Graduate School, College of Engineering, Program in Materials Science and Engineering, Lexington, KY 40506-0032. Offers MS, PhD. *Degree requirements:* For master's, comprehensive exam, thesis optional; for doctorate, comprehensive exam, thesis/dissertation. *Entrance requirements:* For master's, GRE General Test, minimum undergraduate GPA of 2.75; for doctorate, GRE General Test, minimum undergraduate GPA of 3.0. Additional exam requirements/recommendations for international students: Required—TOEFL (minimum score 550 paper-based). Electronic applications accepted. *Faculty research:* Physical and mechanical metallurgy, computational material engineering, polymers and composites, high-temperature ceramics, powder metallurgy.

The University of Manchester, School of Chemistry, Manchester, United Kingdom. Offers biological chemistry (PhD); chemistry (M Ent, M Phil, M Sc, D Ent, PhD); inorganic chemistry (PhD); materials chemistry (PhD); nanoscience (PhD); nuclear fission (PhD); organic chemistry (PhD); physical chemistry (PhD); theoretical chemistry (PhD).

The University of Manchester, School of Materials, Manchester, United Kingdom. Offers advanced aerospace materials engineering (M Sc); advanced metallic systems (PhD); biomedical materials (M Phil, M Sc, PhD); ceramics and glass (M Phil, M Sc, PhD); composite materials (M Sc, PhD); corrosion and protection (M Phil, M Sc, PhD); materials (M Phil, PhD); metallic materials (M Phil, M Sc, PhD); nanostructural materials (M Phil, M Sc, PhD); paper science (M Phil, M Sc, PhD); polymer science and engineering (M Phil, M Sc, PhD); technical textiles (M Sc); textile design, fashion and management (M Phil, M Sc, PhD); textile science and technology (M Phil, M Sc, PhD); textiles (M Phil, PhD); textiles and fashion (M Ent).

University of Maryland, College Park, Academic Affairs, A. James Clark School of Engineering, Department of Materials Science and Engineering, Materials Science and Engineering Program, College Park, MD 20742. Offers MS, PhD. *Program availability:* Part-time, evening/weekend, online learning. *Degree requirements:* For master's, comprehensive exam, thesis optional, research paper; for doctorate, thesis/dissertation, oral exam. *Entrance requirements:* For master's and doctorate, GRE General Test, minimum B+ average in undergraduate course work. Additional exam requirements/recommendations for international students: Required—TOEFL. Electronic applications accepted.

University of Michigan, College of Engineering, Department of Materials Science and Engineering, Ann Arbor, MI 48109. Offers MS, MSE, PhD. *Program availability:* Part-time. *Students:* 176 full-time (71 women), 5 part-time (2 women). 668 applicants, 22% accepted, 48 enrolled. In 2018, 31 master's, 28 doctorates awarded. Terminal master's awarded for partial completion of doctoral program. *Degree requirements:* For master's, thesis, oral defense of thesis; for doctorate, thesis/dissertation, oral defense of dissertation, written exam. *Entrance requirements:* For master's and doctorate, GRE General Test. Additional exam requirements/recommendations for international students: Required—TOEFL. *Application deadline:* Applications are processed on a rolling basis. Electronic applications accepted. *Financial support:* Fellowships, research assistantships, and teaching assistantships available. Financial award applicants required to submit FAFSA. *Faculty research:* Soft materials (polymers, biomaterials), computational materials science, structural materials, electronic and optical materials, nanocomposite materials. *Total annual research expenditures:* $10.3 million. *Unit head:* Amit Misra, Department Chair, 734-763-2445, E-mail: amitmis@umich.edu. *Application contact:* Renee Hilgendorf, Graduate Program Coordinator, 734-763-9790, E-mail: reneeh@umich.edu.
Website: http://www.mse.engin.umich.edu

University of Michigan, Rackham Graduate School, College of Literature, Science, and the Arts, Department of Chemistry, Ann Arbor, MI 48109-1055. Offers analytical chemistry (PhD); chemical biology (PhD); chemical sciences (MS); inorganic chemistry (PhD); materials chemistry (PhD); organic chemistry (PhD); physical chemistry (PhD). *Program availability:* Part-time. *Faculty:* 40 full-time (14 women), 7 part-time/adjunct (3 women). *Students:* 262 full-time (112 women), 4 part-time (all women); includes 44 minority (11 Black or African American, non-Hispanic/Latino; 11 Asian, non-Hispanic/Latino; 19 Hispanic/Latino; 1 Native Hawaiian or other Pacific Islander, non-Hispanic/Latino; 2 Two or more races, non-Hispanic/Latino), 61 international. 692 applicants, 71 enrolled. In 2018, 47 master's, 46 doctorates awarded. *Degree requirements:* For doctorate, comprehensive exam, thesis/dissertation, oral defense of dissertation, organic cumulative proficiency exams. *Entrance requirements:* For master's, bachelor's degree, 3 letters of recommendation, personal statement; for doctorate, bachelor's degree, 3 letters of recommendation, personal statement, curriculum vitae/resume. Additional exam requirements/recommendations for international students: Required—TOEFL (minimum score 560 paper-based; 84 iBT) or IELTS. *Application deadline:* For fall admission, 12/1 for domestic and international students. Application fee: $0 ($90 for international students). Electronic applications accepted. *Financial support:* In 2018–19, 269 students received support, including 50 fellowships with full tuition reimbursements available (averaging $31,625 per year), 84 research assistantships with full tuition reimbursements available (averaging $31,625 per year), 133 teaching assistantships with full tuition reimbursements available (averaging $31,625 per year); career-related internships or fieldwork, Federal Work-Study, scholarships/grants, traineeships, health care benefits, tuition waivers (full), and unspecified assistantships also available. *Faculty research:* Biological catalysis, protein engineering, chemical sensors, de novo metalloprotein design, supramolecular architecture. *Total annual research expenditures:* $19.6 million. *Unit head:* Dr. Robert Kennedy, Professor of Chemistry/Chair, 734-763-9681, Fax: 734-647-4847. *Application contact:* Elizabeth Oxford, Graduate Program Coordinator, 734-764-7278, Fax: 734-647-4865, E-mail: chemadmissions@umich.edu.
Website: http://www.lsa.umich.edu/chem/

University of Minnesota, Twin Cities Campus, College of Science and Engineering, Department of Chemical Engineering and Materials Science, Program in Materials Science and Engineering, Minneapolis, MN 55455-0132. Offers M Mat SE, MS Mat SE, PhD. *Program availability:* Part-time. Terminal master's awarded for partial completion of doctoral program. *Degree requirements:* For master's, thesis; for doctorate, thesis/dissertation. *Entrance requirements:* For master's and doctorate, GRE General Test. Additional exam requirements/recommendations for international students: Required—TOEFL. Electronic applications accepted. *Faculty research:* Ceramics and metals; coating processes and interfacial engineering; crystal growth and design; polymers; electronic, photonic and magnetic materials.

University of Mississippi Medical Center, School of Graduate Studies in Health Sciences, Program in Biomedical Materials Science, Jackson, MS 39216-4505. Offers MS, PhD. Terminal master's awarded for partial completion of doctoral program. *Degree requirements:* For master's, thesis; for doctorate, comprehensive exam, thesis/dissertation. *Entrance requirements:* For master's, GRE, BS; for doctorate, GRE, BS, MS (preferred). Additional exam requirements/recommendations for international students: Required—TOEFL (minimum score 105 iBT). Electronic applications accepted. *Faculty research:* Tissue engineering, fatigue life prediction, metallurgy and alloy development, dental implant design and testing, ceramics, materials for dental applications.

University of Nebraska–Lincoln, Graduate College, College of Arts and Sciences, Department of Chemistry, Lincoln, NE 68588. Offers analytical chemistry (PhD); biochemistry (PhD); chemistry (MS); inorganic chemistry (PhD); materials chemistry (PhD); organic chemistry (PhD); physical chemistry (PhD). *Degree requirements:* For master's, one foreign language, thesis optional, departmental qualifying exam; for doctorate, one foreign language, comprehensive exam, thesis/dissertation, departmental qualifying exams. *Entrance requirements:* For master's and doctorate, GRE. Additional exam requirements/recommendations for international students: Required—TOEFL (minimum score 550 paper-based). Electronic applications accepted. *Faculty research:* Bioorganic and bioinorganic chemistry, biophysical and bioanalytical chemistry, structure-function of DNA and proteins, organometallics, mass spectrometry.

University of New Brunswick Fredericton, School of Graduate Studies, Faculty of Engineering, Department of Civil Engineering, Fredericton, NB E3B 5A3, Canada. Offers construction engineering and management (M Eng, M Sc E, PhD); environmental engineering (M Eng, M Sc E, PhD); environmental studies (M Eng); geotechnical engineering (M Eng, M Sc E, PhD); groundwater/hydrology (M Eng, M Sc E, PhD); materials (M Eng, M Sc E, PhD); pavements (M Eng, M Sc E, PhD); structures (M Eng, M Sc E, PhD); transportation (M Eng, M Sc E, PhD). *Program availability:* Part-time. *Degree requirements:* For master's, thesis; for doctorate, comprehensive exam, thesis/dissertation, qualifying exam; 27 credit hours of courses. *Entrance requirements:* For master's, minimum GPA of 3.0; B Sc E in civil engineering or related engineering degree; for doctorate, minimum GPA of 3.0; graduate degree in engineering or applied science. Additional exam requirements/recommendations for international students: Required—IELTS (minimum score 7.5), TWE (minimum score 4), Michigan English Language Assessment Battery (minimum score 85) or CanTest (minimum score 4.5); Recommended—TOEFL (minimum score 580 paper-based). Electronic applications accepted. *Faculty research:* Construction engineering and management; engineering materials and infrastructure renewal; highway and pavement research; structures and solid mechanics; geotechnical and geoenvironmental engineering; structure interaction; transportation and planning; environment, solid waste management; structural engineering; water and environmental engineering.

University of New Hampshire, Graduate School, College of Engineering and Physical Sciences, Program in Materials Science, Durham, NH 03824. Offers materials science (MS); materials science and engineering (PhD). *Entrance requirements:* For master's and doctorate, GRE. Additional exam requirements/recommendations for international students: Required—TOEFL (minimum score 550 paper-based; 80 iBT). Electronic applications accepted.

University of Pennsylvania, School of Engineering and Applied Science, Department of Materials Science and Engineering, Philadelphia, PA 19104. Offers MSE, PhD. *Program availability:* Part-time. *Students:* Average age 24. 541 applicants, 30% accepted, 83 enrolled. In 2018, 28 master's, 5 doctorates awarded. *Degree requirements:* For master's, comprehensive exam, thesis optional; for doctorate, comprehensive exam, thesis/dissertation. *Entrance requirements:* For master's and doctorate, GRE, bachelor's degree, letters of recommendation, resume, personal statement. Additional exam requirements/recommendations for international students: Required—TOEFL (minimum score 100 iBT), IELTS (minimum score 7). *Application deadline:* For fall admission, 12/15 priority date for domestic and international students. Application fee: $80. Electronic applications accepted. *Expenses:* Contact institution. *Faculty research:* Biomaterials, ceramics, electronic and optical properties, nanostructured materials, surfaces and interfaces. *Application contact:* William Fenton, Assistant Director of Graduate Admissions, 215-898-4542, Fax: 215-573-5577, E-mail: gradstudies@seas.upenn.edu.
Website: http://www.mse.seas.upenn.edu/current-students/masters/index.php

University of Pittsburgh, Swanson School of Engineering, Department of Mechanical Engineering and Materials Science, Pittsburgh, PA 15260. Offers MSME, MSNE, PhD. *Program availability:* Part-time, 100% online. Terminal master's awarded for partial completion of doctoral program. *Degree requirements:* For doctorate, comprehensive exam, thesis/dissertation, final oral exams. *Entrance requirements:* For master's and doctorate, minimum GPA of 3.0. Additional exam requirements/recommendations for international students: Required—TOEFL (minimum score 550 paper-based; 80 iBT). Electronic applications accepted. *Expenses:* Contact institution. *Faculty research:* Smart materials and structure solid mechanics, computational fluid dynamics, multiphase bio-fluid dynamics, mechanical vibration analysis.

University of Puerto Rico–Mayagüez, Graduate Studies, College of Arts and Sciences, Department of Chemistry, Mayagüez, PR 00681-9000. Offers applied chemistry (MS, PhD), including biophysical chemistry (PhD), chemistry of materials (PhD), environmental chemistry (PhD). *Program availability:* Part-time. Terminal master's awarded for partial completion of doctoral program. *Degree requirements:* For master's, one foreign language, comprehensive exam, thesis; for doctorate, one foreign language, comprehensive exam, thesis/dissertation. *Entrance requirements:* For master's, GRE General Test or minimum GPA of 2.0, BS in chemistry or the equivalent; minimum GPA of 2.8; for doctorate, GRE General Test or minimum GPA of 2.0. Electronic applications accepted. *Faculty research:* Synthesis of heterocyclic moieties, protein structure and function, chemistry of explosives, bio-nanocomposites, process analytical technology.

University of Puerto Rico–Mayagüez, Graduate Studies, College of Engineering, Department of Engineering Sciences and Materials, Mayagüez, PR 00681-9000. Offers materials science and engineering (MS).

University of Rochester, Hajim School of Engineering and Applied Sciences, Program in Materials Science, Rochester, NY 14627. Offers MS, PhD. *Students:* 32 full-time (10 women), 1 part-time (0 women); includes 3 minority (2 Black or African American, non-Hispanic/Latino; 1 American Indian or Alaska Native, non-Hispanic/Latino), 23

international. Average age 27. 118 applicants, 51% accepted, 10 enrolled. In 2018, 7 master's, 4 doctorates awarded. Terminal master's awarded for partial completion of doctoral program. *Degree requirements:* For master's, comprehensive exam, thesis (for some programs); for doctorate, comprehensive exam, thesis/dissertation, qualifying exam. *Entrance requirements:* For master's, personal statement, transcripts, resume/curriculum vitae, three letters of recommendation; for doctorate, GRE, personal statement, transcripts, resume/curriculum vitae, three letters of recommendation. Additional exam requirements/recommendations for international students: Required—TOEFL (minimum score 95 iBT), IELTS (minimum score 7). *Application deadline:* For fall admission, 1/15 for domestic and international students. Application fee: $60. Electronic applications accepted. *Expenses: Tuition:* Full-time $52,974; part-time $1654 per credit hour. *Required fees:* $612. One-time fee: $30 part-time. Tuition and fees vary according to campus/location and program. *Financial support:* In 2018–19, 4 students received support, including 4 research assistantships (averaging $27,000 per year); scholarships/grants also available. Financial award application deadline: 1/15. *Unit head:* Lewis J. Rothberg, Professor and Director, 585-273-4725, E-mail: lewis.rothberg@rochester.edu. *Application contact:* Gina Eagan, Administrative Assistant, 585-275-1626, E-mail: gina.eagan@rochester.edu.
Website: http://www.rochester.edu/college/matsci/

University of Southern California, Graduate School, Viterbi School of Engineering, Mork Family Department of Chemical Engineering and Materials Science, Los Angeles, CA 90089. Offers chemical engineering (MS, PhD, Engr); geoscience technologies (MS); materials engineering (MS); materials science (MS, PhD, Engr); petroleum engineering (MS, PhD, Engr); smart oilfield technologies (MS, Graduate Certificate). Terminal master's awarded for partial completion of doctoral program. *Degree requirements:* For master's, thesis optional; for doctorate, thesis/dissertation. *Entrance requirements:* For master's and doctorate, GRE General Test. Additional exam requirements/recommendations for international students: Recommended—TOEFL. Electronic applications accepted. *Expenses:* Contact institution. *Faculty research:* Heterogeneous materials and porous media, statistical mechanics, molecular simulation, polymer science and engineering, advanced materials, reaction engineering and catalysis, membrane processes and separation, biochemical engineering, cell culture, bioreactor modeling, petroleum engineering.

University of South Florida, College of Engineering, Department of Industrial and Management Systems Engineering, Tampa, FL 33620-9951. Offers engineering management (MSEM); industrial engineering (MSIE, PhD); information technology (MSIT); materials science and engineering (MSMSE). *Program availability:* Part-time, online learning. *Faculty:* 30 full-time (3 women), 1 part-time/adjunct (0 women). *Students:* 84 full-time (25 women), 60 part-time (15 women); includes 13 minority (2 Black or African American, non-Hispanic/Latino; 4 Asian, non-Hispanic/Latino; 7 Hispanic/Latino), 100 international. Average age 27. 280 applicants, 54% accepted, 37 enrolled. In 2018, 72 master's, 3 doctorates awarded. Terminal master's awarded for partial completion of doctoral program. *Degree requirements:* For master's, comprehensive exam, thesis (for some programs); for doctorate, comprehensive exam, thesis/dissertation, 2 tools of research as specified by dissertation committee. *Entrance requirements:* For master's, GRE General Test, BS in engineering (or equivalent), letters of recommendation, resume, two years professional experience or internship may be required; statement of purpose; for doctorate, GRE General Test, minimum GPA of 3.0, 3 letters of recommendation, statement of purpose, strong background in scientific and engineering principles. Ph.D. students must complete their total doctoral major as full-time Tampa campus students. Additional exam requirements/recommendations for international students: Required—TOEFL, TOEFL (minimum score 550 paper-based; 79 iBT) or IELTS (minimum score 6.5). *Application deadline:* For fall admission, 2/15 for domestic and international students; for spring admission, 10/15 for domestic students, 9/15 for international students; for summer admission, 2/15 for domestic students, 1/15 for international students. Application fee: $30. Electronic applications accepted. *Expenses:* Tuition, state resident: full-time $6350. Tuition, nonresident: full-time $19,048. *International tuition:* $19,048 full-time. *Required fees:* $2079. *Financial support:* In 2018–19, 26 students received support, including 20 research assistantships with partial tuition reimbursements available (averaging $16,748 per year), 11 teaching assistantships with partial tuition reimbursements available (averaging $15,000 per year); tuition waivers (partial) also available. Financial award applicants required to submit FAFSA. *Faculty research:* Healthcare, healthcare systems, public health policies, energy and environment, manufacturing, logistics, transportation. *Total annual research expenditures:* $368,578. *Unit head:* Dr. Tapas K. Das, Professor and Department Chair, 813-974-5585, Fax: 813-974-5953, E-mail: das@usf.edu. *Application contact:* Dr. Alex Savachkin, Associate Professor and Graduate Director, 813-974-5577, Fax: 813-974-5953, E-mail: alexs@usf.edu.
Website: http://imse.eng.usf.edu

University of South Florida, Innovative Education, Tampa, FL 33620-9951. Offers adult, career and higher education (Graduate Certificate), including college teaching, leadership in developing human resources, leadership in higher education; Africana studies (Graduate Certificate), including diasporas and health disparities, genocide and human rights; aging studies (Graduate Certificate), including gerontology; art research (Graduate Certificate), including museum studies; business foundations (Graduate Certificate); chemical and biomedical engineering (Graduate Certificate), including materials science and engineering, water, health and sustainability; child and family studies (Graduate Certificate), including positive behavior support; civil and industrial engineering (Graduate Certificate), including transportation systems analysis; community and family health (Graduate Certificate), including maternal and child health, social marketing and public health, violence and injury: prevention and intervention, women's health; criminology (Graduate Certificate), including criminal justice administration; data science for public administration (Graduate Certificate); digital humanities (Graduate Certificate); educational measurement and research (Graduate Certificate), including evaluation; English (Graduate Certificate), including comparative literary studies, creative writing, professional and technical communication; entrepreneurship (Graduate Certificate); environmental health (Graduate Certificate), including safety management; epidemiology and biostatistics (Graduate Certificate), including applied biostatistics, biostatistics, concepts and tools of epidemiology, epidemiology, epidemiology of infectious diseases; geography, environment and planning (Graduate Certificate), including community development, environmental policy and management, geographical information systems; geology (Graduate Certificate), including hydrogeology; global health (Graduate Certificate), including disaster management, global health and Latin American and Caribbean studies, global health practice, humanitarian assistance, infection control; government and international affairs (Graduate Certificate), including Cuban studies, globalization studies; health policy and management (Graduate Certificate), including health management and leadership, public health policy and programs; hearing specialist: early intervention (Graduate Certificate); industrial and management systems engineering (Graduate Certificate), including systems engineering, technology management; information studies (Graduate Certificate), including school library media specialist; information systems/decision sciences (Graduate Certificate), including analytics and business intelligence; instructional technology (Graduate Certificate), including distance education, Florida digital/virtual educator, instructional design, multimedia design, Web design; internal

medicine, bioethics and medical humanities (Graduate Certificate), including biomedical ethics; Latin American and Caribbean studies (Graduate Certificate); leadership for coastal resiliency planning (Graduate Certificate); mass communications (Graduate Certificate), including multimedia journalism; mathematics and statistics (Graduate Certificate), including mathematics; medicine (Graduate Certificate), including aging and neuroscience, bioinformatics, biotechnology, brain fitness and memory management, clinical investigation, hand and upper limb rehabilitation, health informatics, health sciences, integrative weight management, intellectual property, medicine and gender, metabolic and nutritional medicine, metabolic cardiology, pharmacy sciences; national and competitive intelligence (Graduate Certificate); nursing (Graduate Certificate), including simulation based academic fellowship in advanced pain management; psychological and social foundations (Graduate Certificate), including career counseling, college teaching, diversity in education, mental health counseling, school counseling; public affairs (Graduate Certificate), including nonprofit management, public management, research administration; public health (Graduate Certificate), including assessing chemical toxicity and public health risks, health equity, pharmacoepidemiology, public health generalist, toxicology, translational research in adolescent behavioral health; public health practices (Graduate Certificate), including planning for healthy communities; rehabilitation and mental health counseling (Graduate Certificate), including integrative mental health care, marriage and family therapy, rehabilitation technology; secondary education (Graduate Certificate), including ESOL, foreign language education: culture and content, foreign language education: professional; social work (Graduate Certificate), including geriatric social work/clinical gerontology; special education (Graduate Certificate), including autism spectrum disorder, disabilities education: severe/profound; world languages (Graduate Certificate), including teaching English as a second language (TESL) or foreign language. *Expenses:* Tuition, state resident: full-time $6350. Tuition, nonresident: full-time $19,048. *International tuition:* $19,048 full-time. *Required fees:* $2079. *Unit head:* Dr. Cynthia DeLuca, Associate Vice President and Assistant Vice Provost, 813-974-3077, Fax: 813-974-7061, E-mail: deluca@usf.edu. *Application contact:* Owen Hooper, Director, Summer and Alternative Calendar Programs, 813-974-6917, E-mail: hooper@usf.edu.
Website: http://www.usf.edu/innovative-education/

The University of Tennessee, Graduate School, Tickle College of Engineering, Department of Materials Science and Engineering, Knoxville, TN 37996-2200. Offers materials science and engineering (MS, PhD); reliability and maintainability engineering (MS); MS/MBA. *Program availability:* Part-time. *Faculty:* 25 full-time (4 women). *Students:* 85 full-time (28 women), 8 part-time (0 women); includes 5 minority (1 Black or African American, non-Hispanic/Latino; 2 Asian, non-Hispanic/Latino; 2 Hispanic/Latino), 44 international. Average age 27. 74 applicants, 34% accepted, 12 enrolled. In 2018, 6 master's, 9 doctorates awarded. *Degree requirements:* For master's, thesis or alternative; for doctorate, comprehensive exam, thesis/dissertation. *Entrance requirements:* For master's, GRE General Test (for MS students pursuing research thesis), minimum GPA of 2.7 (for U.S. degree holders), 3.0 (for international degree holders); 3 references; for doctorate, GRE General Test, minimum GPA of 3.0 on previous graduate course work; 3 references. Additional exam requirements/recommendations for international students: Required—TOEFL (minimum score 550 paper-based; 80 iBT), IELTS (minimum score 6.5). *Application deadline:* For fall admission, 2/1 priority date for domestic and international students; for spring admission, 6/15 for domestic and international students; for summer admission, 10/15 for domestic and international students. Applications are processed on a rolling basis. Application fee: $60. Electronic applications accepted. *Financial support:* In 2018–19, 114 students received support, including 19 fellowships with full tuition reimbursements available (averaging $12,060 per year), 73 research assistantships with full tuition reimbursements available (averaging $23,497 per year), 22 teaching assistantships with full tuition reimbursements available (averaging $21,010 per year); career-related internships or fieldwork, Federal Work-Study, institutionally sponsored loans, health care benefits, and unspecified assistantships also available. Financial award application deadline: 2/1; financial award applicants required to submit FAFSA. *Faculty research:* Biomaterials; functional materials electronic, magnetic and optical; high temperature materials; mechanical behavior of materials; neutron materials science. *Total annual research expenditures:* $6.4 million. *Unit head:* Dr. Veerle Keppens, Head, 865-974-5336, Fax: 865-974-4115, E-mail: vkeppens@utk.edu. *Application contact:* Dr. Kurt Sickafus, Professor and Director of Graduate Studies, 865-974-4858, E-mail: kurt@utk.edu.
Website: http://www.engr.utk.edu/mse

The University of Texas at Arlington, Graduate School, College of Engineering, Department of Materials Science and Engineering, Arlington, TX 76019. Offers M Engr, MS, PhD. Terminal master's awarded for partial completion of doctoral program. *Degree requirements:* For master's, comprehensive exam (for some programs), thesis optional; for doctorate, comprehensive exam, thesis/dissertation optional. *Entrance requirements:* For master's, GRE General Test, minimum GPA of 3.0; for doctorate, GRE General Test, minimum GPA of 3.5. Additional exam requirements/recommendations for international students: Required—TOEFL (minimum score 550 paper-based; 79 iBT), IELTS. *Faculty research:* Electronic materials, conductive polymer, composites biomaterial, structural materials.

The University of Texas at Austin, Graduate School, Cockrell School of Engineering, Program in Materials Science and Engineering, Austin, TX 78712-1111. Offers MS, PhD. *Program availability:* Part-time. *Degree requirements:* For master's, thesis (for some programs); for doctorate, thesis/dissertation. *Entrance requirements:* For master's and doctorate, GRE General Test. Additional exam requirements/recommendations for international students: Required—TOEFL (minimum score 550 paper-based). Electronic applications accepted.

The University of Texas at Dallas, Erik Jonsson School of Engineering and Computer Science, Department of Materials Science and Engineering, Richardson, TX 75080. Offers MS, PhD. *Program availability:* Part-time, evening/weekend. *Faculty:* 13 full-time (2 women), 1 part-time/adjunct (0 women). *Students:* 59 full-time (12 women), 6 part-time (2 women); includes 9 minority (1 Black or African American, non-Hispanic/Latino; 4 Asian, non-Hispanic/Latino; 4 Hispanic/Latino), 43 international. Average age 29. 94 applicants, 35% accepted, 10 enrolled. In 2018, 11 master's, 10 doctorates awarded. *Degree requirements:* For master's, thesis or major design project; for doctorate, thesis/dissertation. *Entrance requirements:* For master's, GRE General Test, minimum GPA of 3.0 in related bachelor's degree; for doctorate, GRE General Test, minimum GPA of 3.5. Additional exam requirements/recommendations for international students: Required—TOEFL (minimum score 550 paper-based). *Application deadline:* For fall admission, 7/15 for domestic students, 5/1 priority date for international students; for spring admission, 11/15 for domestic students, 9/1 priority date for international students. Applications are processed on a rolling basis. Application fee: $50 ($100 for international students). Electronic applications accepted. *Expenses: Tuition, area resident:* full-time $13,458. Tuition, state resident: full-time $13,458. Tuition, nonresident: full-time $26,852. *International tuition:* $26,852 full-time. Tuition and fees vary according to course load. *Financial support:* In 2018–19, 41 students received support, including 2 fellowships (averaging $7,535 per year), 41 research assistantships with partial tuition reimbursements available (averaging $25,755 per year), 4 teaching assistantships with

partial tuition reimbursements available (averaging $18,225 per year); career-related internships or fieldwork, Federal Work-Study, institutionally sponsored loans, scholarships/grants, and unspecified assistantships also available. Support available to part-time students. Financial award application deadline: 4/30; financial award applicants required to submit FAFSA. *Faculty research:* Graphene-based semiconducting materials, neuro-inspired computational paradigms, electronic materials with emphasis on dielectrics, energy harvesting (photovoltaics, lithium-ion batteries), biosensors and hydrogen storage materials. *Unit head:* Dr. Amy Walker, Interim Department Head, 972-883-5780, Fax: 972-883-5725, E-mail: amy.walker@utdallas.edu. *Application contact:* Dr. Lev Gelb, Associate Department Head, 972-883-5644, Fax: 972-883-5725, E-mail: mseadmissions@utdallas.edu.
Website: http://mse.utdallas.edu/

The University of Texas at El Paso, Graduate School, College of Engineering, Department of Metallurgical and Materials Engineering, El Paso, TX 79968-0001. Offers materials science and engineering (PhD); metallurgical and materials engineering (MS). *Program availability:* Part-time, evening/weekend. *Degree requirements:* For master's, thesis. *Entrance requirements:* For master's, GRE General Test. Additional exam requirements/recommendations for international students: Required—TOEFL. Electronic applications accepted.

The University of Toledo, College of Graduate Studies, College of Natural Sciences and Mathematics, Department of Physics and Astronomy, Toledo, OH 43606-3390. Offers photovoltaics (PSM); physics (MS, PhD), including astrophysics (PhD), materials science, medical physics (PhD); MS/PhD. *Degree requirements:* For master's, thesis; for doctorate, thesis/dissertation, departmental qualifying exam. *Entrance requirements:* For master's and doctorate, GRE General Test, GRE Subject Test, minimum cumulative point-hour ratio of 2.7 for all previous academic work, three letters of recommendation, statement of purpose, transcripts from all prior institutions attended. Additional exam requirements/recommendations for international students: Required—TOEFL (minimum score 550 paper-based; 80 iBT). Electronic applications accepted. *Faculty research:* Atomic physics, solid-state physics, materials science, astrophysics.

University of Toronto, School of Graduate Studies, Faculty of Applied Science and Engineering, Department of Materials Science and Engineering, Toronto, ON M5S 1A1, Canada. Offers M Eng, MA Sc, PhD. *Program availability:* Part-time. *Degree requirements:* For master's, thesis (for some programs), oral presentation/thesis defense (MA Sc), qualifying exam; for doctorate, thesis/dissertation. *Entrance requirements:* For master's, BA Sc or B Sc in materials science and engineering, 2 letters of reference; for doctorate, MA Sc or equivalent, 2 letters of reference, minimum B+ average in last 2 years. Additional exam requirements/recommendations for international students: Required—TOEFL (minimum score 580 paper-based), TWE (minimum score 4). Electronic applications accepted.

University of Utah, Graduate School, College of Engineering, Department of Materials Science and Engineering, Salt Lake City, UT 84112. Offers MS, PhD. *Faculty:* 7 full-time (0 women), 3 part-time/adjunct (0 women). *Students:* 21 full-time (7 women), 5 part-time (0 women); includes 3 minority (1 Hispanic/Latino; 1 Native Hawaiian or other Pacific Islander, non-Hispanic/Latino; 1 Two or more races, non-Hispanic/Latino), 8 international. Average age 27. 80 applicants, 8% accepted, 5 enrolled. In 2018, 3 master's, 1 doctorate awarded. *Degree requirements:* For master's, thesis or alternative; for doctorate, thesis/dissertation or alternative. *Entrance requirements:* For master's and doctorate, GRE General Test, minimum GPA of 3.0. Additional exam requirements/recommendations for international students: Required—TOEFL (minimum score 570 paper-based; 88 iBT), IELTS (minimum score 7). *Application deadline:* For fall admission, 1/15 for domestic students, 12/15 for international students. Application fee: $30 ($25 for international students). Electronic applications accepted. *Expenses:* Contact institution. *Financial support:* In 2018–19, 1 fellowship with full tuition reimbursement (averaging $26,780 per year), 18 research assistantships with full tuition reimbursements (averaging $23,000 per year) were awarded; teaching assistantships with full tuition reimbursements also available. Financial award application deadline: 2/1; financial award applicants required to submit FAFSA. *Faculty research:* Solid oxide fuel cells, computational nanostructures, solar cells, nano-sensors, batteries: renewable energy. *Total annual research expenditures:* $1.3 million. *Unit head:* Dr. Feng Liu, Chair, 801-581-6863, Fax: 801-581-4816, E-mail: fliu@eng.utah.edu. *Application contact:* Marcie Leek, Academic Advisor, 801-581-6863, Fax: 801-581-4816, E-mail: marcie.leek@utah.edu.
Website: http://www.mse.utah.edu/

University of Vermont, Graduate College, Cross-College Interdisciplinary Program, Program in Materials Science, Burlington, VT 05405. Offers MS, PhD. *Degree requirements:* For master's, thesis or alternative; for doctorate, thesis/dissertation. *Entrance requirements:* For master's and doctorate, GRE General Test. Additional exam requirements/recommendations for international students: Required—TOEFL (minimum score 550 paper-based; 90 iBT). Electronic applications accepted.

University of Virginia, School of Engineering and Applied Science, Department of Materials Science and Engineering, Charlottesville, VA 22903. Offers materials science (MMSE, MS, PhD). *Program availability:* Part-time, online learning. Terminal master's awarded for partial completion of doctoral program. *Degree requirements:* For master's, comprehensive exam, thesis (for some programs); for doctorate, comprehensive exam, thesis/dissertation. *Entrance requirements:* For master's and doctorate, GRE General Test, three recommendations. Additional exam requirements/recommendations for international students: Required—TOEFL. Electronic applications accepted. *Faculty research:* Environmental effects on material behavior, electronic materials, metals, polymers, tribology.

University of Washington, Graduate School, College of Engineering, Department of Materials Science and Engineering, Seattle, WA 98195-2120. Offers applied materials science and engineering (MS); materials science and engineering (MS, PhD); materials science and engineering and nanotechnology (PhD); materials science and engineering, nanotechnology, and molecular engineering (PhD). *Program availability:* Part-time. *Faculty:* 12 full-time (2 women). *Students:* 110 full-time (32 women), 24 part-time (9 women); includes 34 minority (3 Black or African American, non-Hispanic/Latino; 14 Asian, non-Hispanic/Latino; 9 Hispanic/Latino; 1 Native Hawaiian or other Pacific Islander, non-Hispanic/Latino; 7 Two or more races, non-Hispanic/Latino), 60 international. Average age 25. 456 applicants, 37% accepted, 57 enrolled. In 2018, 35 master's, 12 doctorates awarded. Terminal master's awarded for partial completion of doctoral program. *Degree requirements:* For master's, comprehensive exam, final paper or thesis and presentation; for doctorate, comprehensive exam, thesis/dissertation, qualifying evaluation, general and final exams. *Entrance requirements:* For master's and doctorate, GRE General Test, minimum GPA of 3.0, resume/curriculum vitae, letters of recommendation, statement of purpose, transcripts. Additional exam requirements/recommendations for international students: Required—TOEFL (minimum score 92 iBT). *Application deadline:* For fall admission, 1/4 for domestic and international students. Application fee: $85. Electronic applications accepted. *Expenses:* Contact institution. *Financial support:* In 2018–19, 65 students received support, including 42 research assistantships with full tuition reimbursements available (averaging $30,660 per year), 20 teaching assistantships with full tuition reimbursements available (averaging $30,660 per year); fellowships with full tuition reimbursements available, career-related internships or fieldwork, Federal Work-Study, institutionally sponsored loans, scholarships/grants, health care benefits, unspecified assistantships, and stipend supplements also available. Financial award application deadline: 1/1; financial award applicants required to submit FAFSA. *Faculty research:* Synthesis/structure/property and processing, biomaterials and biomimetics, solar energy and battery materials, materials chemistry and characterization, optical and electronic materials. *Total annual research expenditures:* $6.5 million. *Unit head:* Dr. Jihui Yang, Professor/Chair, 206-543-7090, Fax: 206-221-4934, E-mail: jihuiy@uw.edu. *Application contact:* Karen Wetterhahn, Academic Counselor, 206-543-2740, Fax: 206-543-3100, E-mail: karenlw@uw.edu.
Website: http://mse.washington.edu

Vanderbilt University, School of Engineering, Interdisciplinary Program in Materials Science, Nashville, TN 37240-1001. Offers M Eng, MS, PhD. *Program availability:* Part-time. Terminal master's awarded for partial completion of doctoral program. *Degree requirements:* For master's, thesis; for doctorate, thesis/dissertation. *Entrance requirements:* For master's and doctorate, GRE General Test. Electronic applications accepted. *Expenses: Tuition:* Full-time $47,208; part-time $2026 per credit hour. *Required fees:* $478. *Faculty research:* Nanostructure materials, materials physics, surface and interface science, materials synthesis, biomaterials.

Washington State University, Voiland College of Engineering and Architecture, School of Mechanical and Materials Engineering, Pullman, WA 99164-2920. Offers materials science and engineering (MS, PhD); mechanical engineering (MS, PhD). MS programs also offered at Tri-Cities campus. *Program availability:* Part-time. Terminal master's awarded for partial completion of doctoral program. *Degree requirements:* For master's, comprehensive exam, thesis; for doctorate, comprehensive exam, thesis/dissertation, preliminary exam. *Entrance requirements:* For master's, GRE, bachelor's degree, minimum GPA of 3.0, resume, statement of purpose, 3 letters of recommendation, official transcripts, Student Interest Profile form; for doctorate, GRE, bachelor's degree, minimum GPA of 3.4, resume, statement of purpose, 3 letters of recommendation, official transcripts, Student Interest Profile form. Additional exam requirements/recommendations for international students: Required—TOEFL (minimum score 500 paper-based), IELTS. Electronic applications accepted. *Faculty research:* Multiscale modeling and characterization of materials; advanced energy; bioengineering; engineering education and curricular innovation; modeling and visualization in the areas of product realization, materials, and processes.

Washington University in St. Louis, School of Engineering and Applied Science, Department of Mechanical Engineering and Materials Science, St. Louis, MO 63130-4899. Offers aerospace engineering (MS, PhD); materials science (MS); mechanical engineering (M Eng, MS, PhD). *Program availability:* Part-time. Terminal master's awarded for partial completion of doctoral program. *Degree requirements:* For master's, thesis optional; for doctorate, thesis/dissertation optional. *Entrance requirements:* For master's, GRE; for doctorate, GRE General Test, departmental qualifying exam. *Faculty research:* Aerosols science and technology, applied mechanics, biomechanics and biomedical engineering, design, dynamic systems, combustion science, composite materials, materials science.

Wayne State University, College of Engineering, Department of Chemical Engineering and Materials Science, Detroit, MI 48202. Offers chemical engineering (MS, PhD); materials science and engineering (MS, PhD), including materials science and engineering; polymer engineering (Graduate Certificate), including polymer engineering. *Program availability:* Part-time. *Faculty:* 15. *Students:* 39 full-time (11 women), 32 part-time (10 women); includes 6 minority (2 Black or African American, non-Hispanic/Latino; 2 Asian, non-Hispanic/Latino; 1 Hispanic/Latino; 1 Two or more races, non-Hispanic/Latino), 36 international. Average age 27. 127 applicants, 28% accepted, 16 enrolled. In 2018, 7 master's, 5 doctorates awarded. *Entrance requirements:* For master's, three letters of recommendation (at least two from the applicant's academic institution); personal statement; resume; for doctorate, GRE, three letters of recommendation (at least two from the applicant's academic institution); personal statement; resume; for Graduate Certificate, bachelor's degree in engineering or other mathematics-based sciences in exceptional cases. Additional exam requirements/recommendations for international students: Required—TOEFL (minimum score 550 paper-based; 79 iBT), TWE (minimum score 5.5), Michigan English Language Assessment Battery (minimum score 85); Recommended—IELTS (minimum score 6.5). *Application deadline:* For fall admission, 3/1 priority date for domestic and international students; for winter admission, 10/1 priority date for domestic students, 9/1 priority date for international students; for spring admission, 2/1 priority date for domestic and international students; for summer admission, 2/1 priority date for domestic and international students. Application fee: $50. Electronic applications accepted. *Expenses:* Contact institution. *Financial support:* In 2018–19, 36 students received support, including 3 fellowships with tuition reimbursements available (averaging $20,000 per year), 16 research assistantships with tuition reimbursements available (averaging $21,307 per year), 6 teaching assistantships with tuition reimbursements available (averaging $20,166 per year); scholarships/grants, health care benefits, and unspecified assistantships also available. Support available to part-time students. Financial award applicants required to submit FAFSA. *Faculty research:* Environmental transport and management of hazardous waste; process design and synthesis based on waste minimization; biocatalysis in multiphase systems; biomaterials and tissue engineering. *Total annual research expenditures:* $1.6 million. *Unit head:* Dr. Guangzhao Mao, Professor and Chair, 313-577-3804, E-mail: gzmao@eng.wayne.edu. *Application contact:* Ellen Cope, Graduate Program Coordinator, 313-577-0409, E-mail: escope@wayne.edu.
Website: http://engineering.wayne.edu/che/

West Virginia University, Statler College of Engineering and Mineral Resources, Morgantown, WV 26506. Offers aerospace engineering (MSAE, PhD); chemical engineering (MS Ch E, PhD); civil engineering (MSCE, PhD); computer engineering (PhD); computer science (MSCS, PhD); electrical engineering (MSEE, PhD); energy systems engineering (MSESE); engineering (MSE); industrial engineering (MSIE, PhD); industrial hygiene (MS); material science and engineering (MSMSE, PhD); mechanical engineering (MSME, PhD); mining engineering (MS Min E, PhD); petroleum and natural gas engineering (MSPNGE, PhD); safety management (MS); software engineering (MSSE). *Program availability:* Part-time. *Students:* 466 full-time (113 women), 154 part-time (27 women); includes 57 minority (22 Black or African American, non-Hispanic/Latino; 1 American Indian or Alaska Native, non-Hispanic/Latino; 8 Asian, non-Hispanic/Latino; 12 Hispanic/Latino; 14 Two or more races, non-Hispanic/Latino), 283 international. In 2018, 179 master's, 39 doctorates awarded. Terminal master's awarded for partial completion of doctoral program. *Degree requirements:* For master's, thesis optional; for doctorate, comprehensive exam, thesis/dissertation. *Entrance requirements:* Additional exam requirements/recommendations for international students: Required—TOEFL (minimum score 550 paper-based). *Application deadline:* For fall admission, 4/1 for international students; for winter admission, 4/1 for international students; for spring admission, 10/1 for international students. Applications are processed on a rolling basis. Application fee: $60. Electronic applications accepted. *Expenses:* Contact institution. *Financial support:* Fellowships, research assistantships, teaching assistantships, career-related internships or fieldwork, Federal Work-Study, institutionally sponsored loans, health care benefits, tuition waivers (full and partial), unspecified assistantships, and administrative assistantships available. Financial award

application deadline: 2/1; financial award applicants required to submit FAFSA. *Faculty research:* Composite materials, software engineering, information systems, aerodynamics, vehicle propulsion and emission. *Unit head:* Dr. Earl Scime, Interim Dean, 304-293-4157 Ext. 2237, Fax: 304-293-2037, E-mail: earl.scime@mail.wvu.edu. *Application contact:* Dr. David A. Wyrick, Associate Dean, Academic Affairs, 304-293-4334, Fax: 304-293-5024, E-mail: david.wyrick@mail.wvu.edu.
Website: https://www.statler.wvu.edu

William Paterson University of New Jersey, College of Science and Health, Wayne, NJ 07470-8420. Offers adult gerontology nurse practitioner (Certificate); adult nurse practitioner (Certificate); biology (MS); biotechnology (MS); communication disorders (MS); exercise and sport studies (MS); materials chemistry (MS); nursing (MSN); nursing education (Certificate); nursing practice (DNP); school nurse instructional (Certificate). *Accreditation:* ASHA. *Program availability:* Part-time. *Faculty:* 34 full-time (20 women), 24 part-time/adjunct (19 women). *Students:* 62 full-time (49 women), 236 part-time (203 women); includes 135 minority (22 Black or African American, non-Hispanic/Latino; 48 Asian, non-Hispanic/Latino; 57 Hispanic/Latino; 8 Two or more races, non-Hispanic/Latino), 4 international. Average age 33. 546 applicants, 47% accepted, 151 enrolled. In 2018, 75 master's, 8 doctorates awarded. *Degree requirements:* For master's, Programs Differ see: https://academiccatalog.wpunj.edu/content.php?catoid=1&navoid=68. *Entrance requirements:* For master's, program details: https://www.wpunj.edu/admissions/graduate/admission-deadlines-and-requirements/. Additional exam requirements/recommendations for international students: Required—TOEFL (minimum score 550 paper-based; 79 iBT), IELTS (minimum score 6). *Application deadline:* For fall admission, 6/1 for domestic students, 3/1 for international students; for spring admission, 11/1 for domestic students, 10/1 for international students. Applications are processed on a rolling basis. Application fee: $50. Electronic applications accepted. *Expenses: Tuition, area resident:* Full-time $14,714; part-time $727 per credit. Tuition, state resident: full-time $14,714; part-time $727 per credit. Tuition, nonresident: full-time $22,952; part-time $727 per credit. *International tuition:* $22,952 full-time. *Required fees:* $4 per semester. Tuition and fees vary according to course load, degree level and program. *Financial support:* In 2018–19, 18 students received support. Career-related internships or fieldwork, Federal Work-Study, scholarships/grants, tuition waivers, and unspecified assistantships available. Support available to part-time students. Financial award application deadline: 3/15; financial award applicants required to submit FAFSA. *Faculty research:* Behaviors of American long-eared bats, postpartum fatigue, methodologies for coating carbon nanotubes, paleo climatology, prelinguistic gestures in children with language disorders. *Total annual research expenditures:* $248,283. *Unit head:* Dr. Venkat Sharma, Dean, 973-720-2194, Fax: 973-720-3414, E-mail: sharmav@wpunj.edu. *Application contact:* Christina Aiello, Assistant Director, Graduate Admissions, 973-720-2506, Fax: 973-720-2035, E-mail: aielloc@wpunj.edu.
Website: http://www.wpunj.edu/cosh

Worcester Polytechnic Institute, Graduate Admissions, Department of Mechanical Engineering, Worcester, MA 01609-2280. Offers manufacturing engineering (MS, PhD); materials process engineering (MS); materials science and engineering (PhD). *Program availability:* Part-time, evening/weekend, 100% online, blended/hybrid learning. *Students:* 53 full-time (14 women), 128 part-time (23 women); includes 25 minority (2 Black or African American, non-Hispanic/Latino; 7 Asian, non-Hispanic/Latino; 13 Hispanic/Latino; 1 Native Hawaiian or other Pacific Islander, non-Hispanic/Latino; 2 Two or more races, non-Hispanic/Latino), 47 international. Average age 26. 278 applicants, 62% accepted, 67 enrolled. In 2018, 88 master's, 4 doctorates, 2 other advanced degrees awarded. Terminal master's awarded for partial completion of doctoral program. *Degree requirements:* For master's, thesis optional; for doctorate, comprehensive exam, thesis/dissertation. *Entrance requirements:* For master's and doctorate, GRE (recommended), 3 letters of recommendation, statement of purpose. Additional exam requirements/recommendations for international students: Required—TOEFL (minimum score 563 paper-based; 84 iBT), IELTS (minimum score 7). *Application deadline:* For fall admission, 1/1 priority date for domestic and international students; for spring admission, 10/1 priority date for domestic and international students. Applications are processed on a rolling basis. Application fee: $70. Electronic applications accepted. *Financial support:* Fellowships, research assistantships, teaching assistantships, career-related internships or fieldwork, institutionally sponsored loans, scholarships/grants, and unspecified assistantships available. Financial award application deadline: 1/1. *Unit head:* Dr. Jamal Yagoobi, Department Head, 508-831-5236, Fax: 508-831-5680, E-mail: jyagoobi@wpi.edu. *Application contact:* Barbara Edilberti, Administrative Assistant, 508-831-5236, Fax: 508-831-5680, E-mail: edilbert@wpi.edu.
Website: https://www.wpi.edu/academics/departments/mechanical-engineering

Wright State University, Graduate School, College of Engineering and Computer Science, Department of Mechanical and Materials Engineering, Dayton, OH 45435. Offers aerospace systems engineering (MS); materials science and engineering (MS); mechanical engineering (MS); renewable and clean energy (MS). *Degree requirements:* For master's, thesis or course option alternative. *Entrance requirements:* Additional exam requirements/recommendations for international students: Required—TOEFL.

Metallurgical Engineering and Metallurgy

Colorado School of Mines, Office of Graduate Studies, Department of Metallurgical and Materials Engineering, Golden, CO 80401. Offers materials science (MS, PhD); metallurgical and materials engineering (ME, MS, PhD). *Program availability:* Part-time. *Faculty:* 36 full-time (6 women), 10 part-time/adjunct (1 woman). *Students:* 115 full-time (35 women), 10 part-time (4 women); includes 13 minority (1 Asian, non-Hispanic/Latino; 8 Hispanic/Latino; 4 Two or more races, non-Hispanic/Latino), 29 international. Average age 27. 153 applicants, 50% accepted, 41 enrolled. In 2018, 21 master's, 15 doctorates awarded. *Degree requirements:* For master's, thesis (for some programs); for doctorate, comprehensive exam, thesis/dissertation. *Entrance requirements:* For master's and doctorate, GRE General Test. Additional exam requirements/recommendations for international students: Required—TOEFL (minimum score 550 paper-based; 79 iBT). *Application deadline:* For fall admission, 12/15 priority date for domestic and international students; for spring admission, 9/1 priority date for domestic and international students. Application fee: $60 ($80 for international students). Electronic applications accepted. *Expenses:* Tuition, state resident: full-time $16,650; part-time $925 per contact hour. Tuition, nonresident: full-time $36,270; part-time $2015 per contact hour. *International tuition:* $36,270 full-time. *Required fees:* $2314; $2314 per semester. *Financial support:* In 2018–19, 81 research assistantships with full tuition reimbursements, 15 teaching assistantships with full tuition reimbursements were awarded; fellowships, scholarships/grants, health care benefits, and unspecified assistantships also available. Financial award application deadline: 12/15; financial award applicants required to submit FAFSA. *Unit head:* Dr. Angus Rockett, Head, 303-384-2244, E-mail: arockett@mines.edu. *Application contact:* Megan Steelman, Program Assistant, 303-273-3640, E-mail: msteelman@mines.edu.
Website: http://metallurgy.mines.edu

Michigan Technological University, Graduate School, College of Engineering, Department of Materials Science and Engineering, Houghton, MI 49931. Offers MS, PhD. *Program availability:* Part-time, 100% online, blended/hybrid learning. *Faculty:* 33 full-time (7 women), 12 part-time/adjunct (3 women). *Students:* 30 full-time (9 women), 8 part-time (3 women); includes 1 minority (Two or more races, non-Hispanic/Latino), 24 international. Average age 27. 135 applicants, 30% accepted, 7 enrolled. In 2018, 8 master's, 2 doctorates awarded. Terminal master's awarded for partial completion of doctoral program. *Degree requirements:* For master's, comprehensive exam (for some programs), thesis (for some programs); for doctorate, comprehensive exam, thesis/dissertation. *Entrance requirements:* For master's and doctorate, GRE (domestic students from ABET-accredited programs exempt), statement of purpose, personal statement, official transcripts, 3 letters of recommendation. Additional exam requirements/recommendations for international students: Required—TOEFL (minimum score 79 iBT), IELTS (minimum score 6.5), TOEFL (minimum score 79 iBT) or IELTS (minimum score of 6.5). *Application deadline:* For fall admission, 2/1 priority date for domestic and international students; for spring admission, 9/1 priority date for domestic and international students. Applications are processed on a rolling basis. Electronic applications accepted. *Expenses:* $1,143 per credit. *Financial support:* In 2018–19, 26 students received support, including 4 fellowships with tuition reimbursements available (averaging $16,590 per year), 18 research assistantships with tuition reimbursements available (averaging $16,590 per year); teaching assistantships, career-related internships or fieldwork, Federal Work-Study, scholarships/grants, health care benefits, unspecified assistantships, and cooperative program also available. Financial award applicants required to submit FAFSA. *Faculty research:* Structure/property/processing relationships, microstructural characterization, alloy design, electronic/magnetic/photonic materials, materials and manufacturing processes. *Total annual research expenditures:* $2.1 million. *Unit head:* Dr. Stephen L. Kampe, Chair, 906-487-2036, Fax: 906-487-2934, E-mail: kampe@mtu.edu. *Application contact:* Valentina O'Kane, Department Coordinator, 906-487-4326, Fax: 906-487-2934, E-mail: vokane@mtu.edu.
Website: http://www.mtu.edu/materials/

Missouri University of Science and Technology, Department of Materials Science and Engineering, Rolla, MO 65401. Offers ceramic engineering (MS, PhD); materials science and engineering (MS, PhD); metallurgical engineering (MS, PhD). *Degree requirements:* For master's, thesis optional; for doctorate, comprehensive exam. *Entrance requirements:* For master's, GRE (minimum combined score 1100, 600 verbal, 3.5 writing); for doctorate, GRE (minimum score: quantitative 600, writing 3.5). Additional exam requirements/recommendations for international students: Required—TOEFL (minimum score 570 paper-based). Electronic applications accepted. *Expenses:* Tuition, state resident: full-time $7545.60; part-time $419.20 per credit hour. Tuition, nonresident: full-time $22,169; part-time $1231.60 per credit hour. *International tuition:* $23,518.80 full-time. *Required fees:* $4523.05. Full-time tuition and fees vary according to course load, campus/location, program and reciprocity agreements.

Montana Tech of The University of Montana, Department of Metallurgical/Mineral Processing Engineering, Butte, MT 59701-8997. Offers MS. *Program availability:* Part-time. *Degree requirements:* For master's, comprehensive exam (for some programs), thesis optional. *Entrance requirements:* For master's, GRE General Test, minimum GPA of 3.0. Additional exam requirements/recommendations for international students: Required—TOEFL (minimum score 545 paper-based; 78 iBT), IELTS (minimum score 6.5). Electronic applications accepted. *Faculty research:* Stabilizing hazardous waste, decontamination of metals by melt refining, ultraviolet enhancement of stabilization reactions, extractive metallurgy, fuel cells.

The Ohio State University, Graduate School, College of Engineering, Department of Materials Science and Engineering, Program in Welding Engineering, Columbus, OH 43210. Offers MS, PhD. *Program availability:* Part-time, online learning. *Students:* 34 full-time (3 women), 47 part-time (7 women). Average age 32. In 2018, 17 master's, 4 doctorates awarded. *Entrance requirements:* For master's and doctorate, GRE General Test (for all with undergraduate GPA less than 3.0 or with a non-ABET accredited degree). Additional exam requirements/recommendations for international students: Required—TOEFL (minimum score 550 paper-based; 79 iBT), Michigan English Language Assessment Battery (minimum score 82); Recommended—IELTS (minimum score 7). *Application deadline:* For fall admission, 12/1 priority date for domestic students, 11/30 priority date for international students. Applications are processed on a rolling basis. Application fee: $60 ($70 for international students). Electronic applications accepted. *Financial support:* Fellowships, research assistantships, teaching assistantships, Federal Work-Study, and institutionally sponsored loans available. Support available to part-time students. *Unit head:* Dr. Antonio J. Ramirez Londono, Graduate Studies Committee Chair, 614-292-8662, E-mail: ramirezlondono.1@osu.edu. *Application contact:* Mark Cooper, Graduate Studies Coordinator, 614-292-7280, Fax: 614-292-1537, E-mail: cooper.73@osu.edu.
Website: http://engineering.osu.edu/graduate/welding

Université Laval, Faculty of Sciences and Engineering, Department of Mining, Metallurgical and Materials Engineering, Programs in Metallurgical Engineering, Québec, QC G1K 7P4, Canada. Offers M Sc, PhD. Terminal master's awarded for partial completion of doctoral program. *Degree requirements:* For master's, thesis; for doctorate, comprehensive exam, thesis/dissertation. *Entrance requirements:* For master's and doctorate, knowledge of French and English. Electronic applications accepted.

The University of Alabama, Graduate School, College of Engineering, Department of Metallurgical and Materials Engineering, Tuscaloosa, AL 35487. Offers MS Met E, PhD. PhD offered jointly with The University of Alabama at Birmingham. *Degree requirements:* For master's, thesis or alternative; for doctorate, thesis/dissertation. *Entrance requirements:* For master's, GRE General Test, minimum GPA of 3.0 in last 60 hours; for doctorate, GRE General Test, minimum graduate GPA of 3.0, graduate degree. Additional exam requirements/recommendations for international students: Required—TOEFL (minimum score 550 paper-based). Electronic applications accepted. *Faculty research:* Thermodynamics, molten metals processing, casting and solidification, mechanical properties of materials, thin films and nanostructures, electrochemistry, corrosion and alloy development.

The University of Manchester, School of Materials, Manchester, United Kingdom. Offers advanced aerospace materials engineering (M Sc); advanced metallic systems (PhD); biomedical materials (M Phil, M Sc, PhD); ceramics and glass (M Phil, M Sc, PhD); composite materials (M Sc, PhD); corrosion and protection (M Phil, M Sc, PhD); materials (M Phil, PhD); metallic materials (M Phil, M Sc, PhD); nanostructural materials

(M Phil, M Sc, PhD); paper science (M Phil, M Sc, PhD); polymer science and engineering (M Phil, M Sc, PhD); technical textiles (M Sc); textile design, fashion and management (M Phil, M Sc, PhD); textile science and technology (M Phil, M Sc, PhD); textiles (M Phil, PhD); textiles and fashion (M Ent).

University of Nebraska–Lincoln, Graduate College, College of Engineering, Department of Mechanical and Materials Engineering, Lincoln, NE 68588-0526. Offers biomedical engineering (PhD); engineering mechanics (MS); materials engineering (PhD); mechanical engineering (MS), including materials science engineering, metallurgical engineering; mechanical engineering and applied mechanics (PhD); MS/MS. MS/MS offered with University of Rouen-France. *Degree requirements:* For master's, thesis optional; for doctorate, comprehensive exam, thesis/dissertation. *Entrance requirements:* For master's and doctorate, GRE General Test. Additional exam requirements/recommendations for international students: Required—TOEFL (minimum score 550 paper-based). Electronic applications accepted. *Faculty research:* Medical robotics, rehabilitation dynamics, and design; combustion, fluid mechanics, and heat transfer; nano-materials, manufacturing, and devices; fiber, tissue, bio-polymer, and adaptive composites; blast, impact, fracture, and failure; electro-active and magnetic materials and devices; functional materials, design, and added manufacturing; materials characterization, modeling, and computational simulation.

University of Nevada, Reno, Graduate School, College of Engineering, Department of Chemical and Materials Engineering, Program in Materials Science and Engineering, Reno, NV 89557. Offers MS, PhD. Terminal master's awarded for partial completion of doctoral program. *Degree requirements:* For master's, thesis; for doctorate, one foreign language, thesis/dissertation. *Entrance requirements:* For master's, minimum GPA of 2.75; for doctorate, GRE, minimum GPA of 3.0. Additional exam requirements/recommendations for international students: Required—TOEFL (minimum score 500 paper-based; 61 iBT), IELTS (minimum score 6). Electronic applications accepted. *Faculty research:* Hydrometallurgy, applied surface chemistry, mineral processing, mineral bioprocessing, ceramics.

University of Nevada, Reno, Graduate School, College of Science, Mackay School of Earth Sciences and Engineering, Department of Mining and Metallurgical Engineering, Reno, NV 89557. Offers metallurgical engineering (MS); mining engineering (MS, PhD). *Degree requirements:* For master's, thesis optional. *Entrance requirements:* For master's, GRE, minimum GPA of 2.75. Additional exam requirements/recommendations for international students: Required—TOEFL (minimum score 500 paper-based; 61 iBT), IELTS (minimum score 6). Electronic applications accepted. *Faculty research:* Mine ventilation, rock mechanics, mine design.

The University of Texas at El Paso, Graduate School, College of Engineering, Department of Metallurgical and Materials Engineering, El Paso, TX 79968-0001. Offers materials science and engineering (PhD); metallurgical and materials engineering (MS). *Program availability:* Part-time, evening/weekend. *Degree requirements:* For master's, thesis. *Entrance requirements:* For master's, GRE General Test. Additional exam requirements/recommendations for international students: Required—TOEFL. Electronic applications accepted.

University of Utah, Graduate School, College of Mines and Earth Sciences, Department of Metallurgical Engineering, Salt Lake City, UT 84112. Offers ME, MS, PhD. *Faculty:* 11 full-time (1 woman), 6 part-time/adjunct (0 women). *Students:* 33 full-time (6 women), 1 part-time (0 women); includes 3 minority (2 Asian, non-Hispanic/Latino; 1 Hispanic/Latino), 17 international. Average age 28. 14 applicants, 71% accepted, 5 enrolled. In 2018, 8 master's, 11 doctorates awarded. Terminal master's awarded for partial completion of doctoral program. *Degree requirements:* For master's, thesis, 20 hours of coursework, 10 hours' thesis research, minimum B average, seminar presentation; for doctorate, comprehensive exam, thesis/dissertation, 33 hours of coursework, 34 hours' thesis research, minimum B average, seminar presentation. *Entrance requirements:* For master's and doctorate, GRE General Test, minimum GPA of 3.0. Additional exam requirements/recommendations for international students: Required—TOEFL (minimum score 550 paper-based; 80 iBT); Recommended—IELTS (minimum score 6.5). *Application deadline:* For fall admission, 4/1 priority date for domestic students, 2/1 priority date for international students; for spring admission, 11/1 priority date for domestic students, 9/1 priority date for international students; for summer admission, 3/15 priority date for domestic students, 1/15 priority date for international students. Applications are processed on a rolling basis. Application fee: $55 ($65 for international students). Electronic applications accepted. *Expenses:* Contact institution. *Financial support:* In 2018–19, 31 students received support, including 4 fellowships with full tuition reimbursements available (averaging $20,000 per year); teaching assistantships, institutionally sponsored loans, and tuition waivers (full) also available. Financial award application deadline: 5/31; financial award applicants required to submit FAFSA. *Faculty research:* Physical metallurgy, mathematical modeling, mineral processing, chemical metallurgy nanoscience and technology. *Total annual research expenditures:* $4.7 million. *Unit head:* Dr. Michael Simpson, Chair, 801-581-4013, Fax: 801-581-4937, E-mail: michael.simpson@utah.edu. *Application contact:* Sara J. Wilson, Administrative Manager, 801-581-6386, Fax: 801-581-4937, E-mail: sara.j.wilson@utah.edu.
Website: http://www.metallurgy.utah.edu/

Polymer Science and Engineering

Auburn University, Graduate School, Ginn College of Engineering, Department of Polymer and Fiber Engineering, Auburn University, AL 36849. Offers MS, PhD. *Degree requirements:* For master's, thesis optional. *Expenses:* Tuition, state resident: full-time $11,282; part-time $535 per credit hour. Tuition, nonresident: full-time $30,542; part-time $1605 per credit hour. *Required fees:* $826 per semester. Tuition and fees vary according to degree level and program.

California Polytechnic State University, San Luis Obispo, College of Science and Mathematics, Department of Chemistry and Biochemistry, San Luis Obispo, CA 93407. Offers polymers and coating science (MS). *Program availability:* Part-time. *Faculty:* 3 full-time (1 woman). *Students:* 5 full-time (1 woman), 2 part-time (0 women); includes 4 minority (1 Asian, non-Hispanic/Latino; 3 Hispanic/Latino), 1 international. Average age 24. 7 applicants, 71% accepted, 3 enrolled. In 2018, 5 master's awarded. *Degree requirements:* For master's, thesis. *Entrance requirements:* For master's, GRE. Additional exam requirements/recommendations for international students: Required—TOEFL (minimum score 80 iBT). *Application deadline:* For fall admission, 4/1 for domestic and international students; for spring admission, 2/1 for domestic students. Applications are processed on a rolling basis. Application fee: $55. Electronic applications accepted. *Expenses: Tuition, area resident:* Full-time $7176; part-time $4164 per year. Tuition, state resident: full-time $10,965. Tuition, nonresident: full-time $10,965. *Required fees:* $6336; $3711. *Financial support:* Fellowships, research assistantships, career-related internships or fieldwork, Federal Work-Study, and scholarships/grants available. Support available to part-time students. Financial award application deadline: 3/2; financial award applicants required to submit FAFSA. *Faculty research:* Polymer physical chemistry and analysis, polymer synthesis, coatings formulation. *Unit head:* Dr. Raymond Fernando, Graduate Coordinator, 805-756-2395, E-mail: rhfernan@calpoly.edu. *Application contact:* Dr. Raymond Fernando, Graduate Coordinator, 805-756-2395, E-mail: rhfernan@calpoly.edu.
Website: http://www.chemistry.calpoly.edu/

Carnegie Mellon University, Carnegie Institute of Technology, Department of Chemical Engineering and Department of Chemistry, Program in Colloids, Polymers and Surfaces, Pittsburgh, PA 15213-3891. Offers MS. *Program availability:* Part-time, evening/weekend. *Entrance requirements:* For master's, GRE General Test, GRE Subject Test. Additional exam requirements/recommendations for international students: Required—TOEFL. *Faculty research:* Surface phenomena, polymer rheology, solubilization phenomena, colloid transport phenomena, polymer synthesis.

Case Western Reserve University, School of Graduate Studies, Case School of Engineering, Department of Macromolecular Science and Engineering, Cleveland, OH 44106. Offers MS, PhD. *Program availability:* Part-time. *Faculty:* 11 full-time (1 woman). *Students:* 70 full-time (27 women), 5 part-time (1 woman); includes 9 minority (1 Black or African American, non-Hispanic/Latino; 5 Asian, non-Hispanic/Latino; 2 Hispanic/Latino; 1 Two or more races, non-Hispanic/Latino), 54 international. In 2018, 17 master's, 11 doctorates awarded. Terminal master's awarded for partial completion of doctoral program. *Degree requirements:* For master's, thesis; for doctorate, thesis/dissertation, qualifying exam, teaching experience. *Entrance requirements:* For master's and doctorate, GRE General Test. Additional exam requirements/recommendations for international students: Required—TOEFL. *Application deadline:* For fall admission, 2/28 priority date for domestic students; for spring admission, 10/1 priority date for domestic students. Applications are processed on a rolling basis. Application fee: $50. *Expenses: Tuition:* Full-time $45,168; part-time $1939 per credit hour. *Required fees:* $36; $18 per semester. $18 per semester. *Financial support:* In 2018–19, 37 students received support, including 37 fellowships. Financial award applicants required to submit FAFSA. *Faculty research:* Synthesis and molecular design; processing, modeling and simulation, structure-property relationships. *Total annual research expenditures:* $4.6 million. *Unit head:* Gary Wnek, Department Chair, 216-368-4243, Fax: 216-368-3116, E-mail: gew5@case.edu. *Application contact:* Theresa Claytor, Student Affairs Coordinator, 216-368-8555, Fax: 216-368-8555, E-mail: theresa.claytor@case.edu.
Website: http://engineering.case.edu/macromolecular-science-and-engineering

Cornell University, Graduate School, Graduate Fields of Engineering, Field of Chemical Engineering, Ithaca, NY 14853. Offers advanced materials processing (M Eng, MS, PhD); applied mathematics and computational methods (M Eng, MS, PhD); biochemical engineering (M Eng, MS, PhD); chemical reaction engineering (M Eng, MS, PhD); classical and statistical thermodynamics (M Eng, MS, PhD); fluid dynamics, rheology and biorheology (M Eng, MS, PhD); heat and mass transfer (M Eng, MS, PhD); kinetics and catalysis (M Eng, MS, PhD); polymers (M Eng, MS, PhD); surface science (M Eng, MS, PhD). *Degree requirements:* For master's, thesis (MS); for doctorate, comprehensive exam, thesis/dissertation. *Entrance requirements:* For master's and doctorate, GRE General Test, 2 letters of recommendation. Additional exam requirements/recommendations for international students: Required—TOEFL (minimum score 600 paper-based; 77 iBT). Electronic applications accepted. *Faculty research:* Biochemical, biomedical and metabolic engineering; fluid and polymer dynamics; surface science and chemical kinetics; electronics materials; microchemical systems and nanotechnology.

Cornell University, Graduate School, Graduate Fields of Human Ecology, Field of Fiber Science and Apparel Design, Ithaca, NY 14853. Offers apparel design (MA, MPS); fiber science (MS, PhD); polymer science (MS, PhD); textile science (MS, PhD). *Degree requirements:* For master's, thesis (MA, MS), project paper (MPS); for doctorate, comprehensive exam, thesis/dissertation. *Entrance requirements:* For master's, GRE General Test, 2 letters of recommendation, portfolio (for functional apparel design); for doctorate, GRE General Test, 2 letters of recommendation. Additional exam requirements/recommendations for international students: Required—TOEFL (minimum score 600 paper-based; 77 iBT). Electronic applications accepted. *Faculty research:* Apparel design, consumption, mass customization, 3-D body scanning.

DePaul University, College of Science and Health, Chicago, IL 60604-2287. Offers applied mathematics (MS); applied statistics (MS); biological sciences (MA, MS); chemistry (MS); environmental science (MS); mathematics education (MA); mathematics for teaching (MS); nursing (MS); nursing practice (DNP); physics (MS); polymer and coatings science (MS); psychology (MS); pure mathematics (MS); science education (MS); MA/PhD. *Accreditation:* AACN. Electronic applications accepted.

Eastern Michigan University, Graduate School, College of Engineering and Technology, School of Engineering, Programs in Polymers and Coatings Technology, Ypsilanti, MI 48197. Offers MS, Postbaccalaureate Certificate. *Program availability:* Part-time, evening/weekend, online learning. *Students:* 1 full-time (0 women), 25 part-time (10 women); includes 3 minority (all Asian, non-Hispanic/Latino), 12 international. Average age 27. 20 applicants, 85% accepted, 11 enrolled. In 2018, 7 master's awarded. *Entrance requirements:* For master's, GRE General Test, BS in chemistry, minimum GPA of 2.6. Additional exam requirements/recommendations for international students: Required—TOEFL. *Application deadline:* Applications are processed on a rolling basis. Application fee: $45. *Financial support:* Fellowships, research assistantships with full tuition reimbursements, teaching assistantships with full tuition reimbursements, career-related internships or fieldwork, Federal Work-Study, institutionally sponsored loans, scholarships/grants, tuition waivers (partial), and unspecified assistantships available. Support available to part-time students. Financial award applicants required to submit FAFSA. *Application contact:* Dr. Vijay Mannari, Program Coordinator, 734-487-2040, Fax: 734-487-8755, E-mail: vmannari@emich.edu.

Lehigh University, P.C. Rossin College of Engineering and Applied Science, Center for Polymer Science and Engineering, Bethlehem, PA 18015. Offers M Eng, MS, PhD. *Program availability:* Part-time, evening/weekend, 100% online, blended/hybrid learning. *Students:* 10 full-time (5 women), 35 part-time (14 women); includes 13 minority (3 Black or African American, non-Hispanic/Latino; 6 Asian, non-Hispanic/Latino; 3 Hispanic/Latino; 1 Native Hawaiian or other Pacific Islander, non-Hispanic/Latino), 5 international. Average age 31. 47 applicants, 36% accepted, 14 enrolled. In 2018, 6 master's awarded. Terminal master's awarded for partial completion of doctoral program. *Degree requirements:* For master's, thesis (for some programs); for doctorate, thesis/

dissertation. *Entrance requirements:* For master's and doctorate, GRE General Test. Additional exam requirements/recommendations for international students: Required—TOEFL (minimum score 487 paper-based; 85 iBT), IELTS (minimum score 6.5), TOEFL or IELTS required. *Application deadline:* For fall admission, 7/15 for domestic students, 1/15 for international students; for spring admission, 12/1 for domestic and international students; for summer admission, 4/30 for domestic and international students. Applications are processed on a rolling basis. Application fee: $75. Electronic applications accepted. Tuition and fees vary according to program. *Financial support:* In 2018–19, 1 research assistantship with full tuition reimbursement (averaging $11,025 per year), 1 teaching assistantship with full tuition reimbursement (averaging $11,025 per year) were awarded; health care benefits also available. Financial award application deadline: 1/15. *Faculty research:* Polymer colloids, polymer coatings, blends and composites, polymer interfaces, emulsion polymer. *Unit head:* Dr. Raymond A. Pearson, Director, 610-758-3857, Fax: 610-758-3526, E-mail: rp02@lehigh.edu. *Application contact:* James E. Roberts, Chair, Polymer Education Committee, 610-758-4841, Fax: 610-758-6536, E-mail: jer1@lehigh.edu.
Website: http://www.lehihttps://engineering.lehigh.edu/academics/graduate/research-based/polymer-science-gh.edu/~inpcreng/academics/graduate/polymerscieng.html

Lehigh University, P.C. Rossin College of Engineering and Applied Science, Department of Materials Science and Engineering, Bethlehem, PA 18015. Offers materials science and engineering (M Eng, MS, PhD); photonics (MS); polymer science/engineering (M Eng, MS, PhD); MBA/E. *Program availability:* Part-time. *Faculty:* 16 full-time (4 women). *Students:* 24 full-time (6 women), 2 part-time (1 woman); includes 4 minority (1 Black or African American, non-Hispanic/Latino; 1 Hispanic/Latino; 2 Two or more races, non-Hispanic/Latino), 5 international. Average age 25. 107 applicants, 19% accepted, 8 enrolled. In 2018, 4 master's, 7 doctorates awarded. *Degree requirements:* For master's, thesis; for doctorate, comprehensive exam, thesis/dissertation. *Entrance requirements:* For master's and doctorate, GRE General Test, minimum GPA of 3.60. Additional exam requirements/recommendations for international students: Required—TOEFL (minimum score 487 paper-based; 85 iBT), IELTS (minimum score 6.5), TOEFL or IELTS required. *Application deadline:* For fall admission, 1/15 priority date for domestic students, 1/15 for international students; for spring admission, 12/1 priority date for domestic students, 12/1 for international students. Application fee: $75. Tuition and fees vary according to program. *Financial support:* In 2018–19, 26 students received support, including 9 fellowships with tuition reimbursements available (averaging $12,848 per year), 14 research assistantships with tuition reimbursements available (averaging $29,640 per year), 12 teaching assistantships with tuition reimbursements available (averaging $7,350 per year); scholarships/grants and health care benefits also available. Financial award application deadline: 1/15. *Faculty research:* Metals, ceramics, crystals, polymers, fatigue crack propagation, biomaterials. *Total annual research expenditures:* $2.7 million. *Unit head:* Dr. Wojciech Misiolek, Chairperson, 610-758-4252, Fax: 610-758-4244, E-mail: wzm2@lehigh.edu. *Application contact:* Lisa Carreras Arechiga, Graduate Administrative Coordinator, 610-758-4222, Fax: 610-758-4244, E-mail: lia4@lehigh.edu.
Website: https://engineering.lehigh.edu/matsci

North Carolina State University, Graduate School, Wilson College of Textiles, Department of Textile Engineering, Chemistry, and Science, Raleigh, NC 27695. Offers fiber and polymer science (PhD); textile chemistry (MS); textile engineering (MS); textile technology management (PhD). *Degree requirements:* For master's, thesis optional. Electronic applications accepted.

North Carolina State University, Graduate School, Wilson College of Textiles, Program in Fiber and Polymer Science, Raleigh, NC 27695. Offers PhD. *Degree requirements:* For doctorate, one foreign language, thesis/dissertation, cumulative exams. *Entrance requirements:* For doctorate, GRE. Electronic applications accepted. *Faculty research:* Polymer science, fiber mechanics, medical textiles, nanotechnology.

North Dakota State University, College of Graduate and Interdisciplinary Studies, College of Science and Mathematics, Department of Coatings and Polymeric Materials, Fargo, ND 58102. Offers MS, PhD. *Program availability:* Part-time. Terminal master's awarded for partial completion of doctoral program. *Degree requirements:* For master's, thesis, cumulative exams; for doctorate, comprehensive exam, thesis/dissertation, cumulative exams. *Entrance requirements:* For master's and doctorate, BS in chemistry or chemical engineering, minimum GPA of 3.0. Additional exam requirements/recommendations for international students: Required—TOEFL (minimum score 550 paper-based). Electronic applications accepted. *Faculty research:* Nanomaterials, combinatorial materials science.

Pittsburg State University, Graduate School, College of Arts and Sciences, Department of Chemistry, Pittsburg, KS 66762. Offers chemistry (MS); polymer chemistry (MS). *Degree requirements:* For master's, comprehensive exam (for some programs), thesis or alternative. *Entrance requirements:* Additional exam requirements/recommendations for international students: Required—TOEFL (minimum score 520 paper-based; 68 iBT), IELTS (minimum score 6), PTE (minimum score 47). Electronic applications accepted. *Expenses:* Contact institution.

Pittsburg State University, Graduate School, College of Technology, Department of Engineering Technology, Pittsburg, KS 66762. Offers electrical engineering technology (MET); general engineering technology (MET); manufacturing engineering technology (MET); mechanical engineering technology (MET); plastics engineering technology (MET). *Program availability:* Part-time, 100% online, blended/hybrid learning. *Degree requirements:* For master's, thesis optional. *Entrance requirements:* Additional exam requirements/recommendations for international students: Required—TOEFL (minimum score 550 paper-based; 79 iBT), IELTS (minimum score 6.5), PTE (minimum score 51). Electronic applications accepted. *Expenses:* Contact institution.

The University of Akron, Graduate School, College of Polymer Science and Polymer Engineering, Department of Polymer Engineering, Akron, OH 44325. Offers MS, PhD. *Program availability:* Part-time, evening/weekend. *Degree requirements:* For master's, thesis; for doctorate, one foreign language, thesis/dissertation, candidacy exam. *Entrance requirements:* For master's and doctorate, GRE, bachelor's degree in engineering or physical science, minimum GPA of 3.0, three letters of recommendation, statement of purpose. Additional exam requirements/recommendations for international students: Required—TOEFL (minimum score 79 iBT), IELTS (minimum score 6.5). Electronic applications accepted. *Faculty research:* Processing and properties of multi-functional polymeric materials, nanomaterials and nanocomposites, micro- and nano-scale materials processing, novel self-assembled polymeric materials for energy applications, coating materials and coating technology.

The University of Akron, Graduate School, College of Polymer Science and Polymer Engineering, Department of Polymer Science, Akron, OH 44325. Offers MS, PhD. *Program availability:* Part-time, evening/weekend. Terminal master's awarded for partial completion of doctoral program. *Degree requirements:* For master's, thesis; for doctorate, one foreign language, thesis/dissertation, cumulative exam, seminars. *Entrance requirements:* For master's and doctorate, GRE, minimum GPA of 3.0, three letters of recommendation, statement of purpose. Additional exam requirements/recommendations for international students: Required—TOEFL (minimum score 79 iBT), IELTS (minimum score 6.5). Electronic applications accepted. *Faculty research:* Synthesis of polymers, structure of polymers, physical properties of polymers, engineering and technological properties of polymers, elastomers.

University of Connecticut, Institute of Materials Science, Polymer Program, Storrs, CT 06269-3136. Offers polymer science and engineering (MS, PhD). *Program availability:* Part-time. Terminal master's awarded for partial completion of doctoral program. *Degree requirements:* For master's, thesis (for some programs); for doctorate, one foreign language, comprehensive exam, thesis/dissertation. *Entrance requirements:* For master's and doctorate, GRE General Test. Additional exam requirements/recommendations for international students: Required—TOEFL (minimum score 550 paper-based; 80 iBT), IELTS (minimum score 6.5). Electronic applications accepted.

The University of Manchester, School of Materials, Manchester, United Kingdom. Offers advanced aerospace materials engineering (M Sc); advanced metallic systems (PhD); biomedical materials (M Phil, M Sc, PhD); ceramics and glass (M Phil, M Sc, PhD); composite materials (M Sc, PhD); corrosion and protection (M Phil, M Sc, PhD); materials (M Phil, PhD); metallic materials (M Phil, M Sc, PhD); nanostructural materials (M Phil, M Sc, PhD); paper science (M Phil, M Sc, PhD); polymer science and engineering (M Phil, M Sc, PhD); technical textiles (M Sc); textile design, fashion and management (M Phil, M Sc, PhD); textile science and technology (M Phil, M Sc, PhD); textiles (M Phil, PhD); textiles and fashion (M Ent).

University of Massachusetts Amherst, Graduate School, College of Natural Sciences, Department of Polymer Science and Engineering, Amherst, MA 01003. Offers MS, PhD. Terminal master's awarded for partial completion of doctoral program. *Degree requirements:* For master's, thesis or alternative; for doctorate, comprehensive exam, thesis/dissertation. *Entrance requirements:* For master's and doctorate, GRE General Test. Additional exam requirements/recommendations for international students: Required—TOEFL (minimum score 550 paper-based; 80 iBT), IELTS (minimum score 6.5). Electronic applications accepted.

University of Massachusetts Lowell, College of Sciences, Department of Chemistry, Program in Polymer Science, Lowell, MA 01854. Offers PhD. Electronic applications accepted.

University of Massachusetts Lowell, Francis College of Engineering, Department of Plastics Engineering, Lowell, MA 01854. Offers plastics engineering (MS Eng, PhD), including coatings and adhesives (MS Eng). *Program availability:* Part-time. Terminal master's awarded for partial completion of doctoral program. *Degree requirements:* For master's, thesis optional; for doctorate, comprehensive exam, thesis/dissertation. *Entrance requirements:* For master's and doctorate, GRE General Test. Additional exam requirements/recommendations for international students: Required—TOEFL.

University of Missouri–Kansas City, College of Arts and Sciences, Department of Chemistry, Kansas City, MO 64110-2499. Offers analytical chemistry (PhD); inorganic chemistry (PhD); organic chemistry (PhD); physical chemistry (PhD); polymer chemistry (MS, PhD). PhD (interdisciplinary) offered through the School of Graduate Studies. *Program availability:* Part-time, evening/weekend. *Degree requirements:* For master's, thesis (for some programs); for doctorate, thesis/dissertation. *Entrance requirements:* For master's, equivalent of American Chemical Society approved bachelor's degree in chemistry; for doctorate, GRE General Test, equivalent of American Chemical Society approved bachelor's degree in chemistry. Additional exam requirements/recommendations for international students: Required—TOEFL (minimum score 550 paper-based; 80 iBT), TWE. Electronic applications accepted. *Faculty research:* Molecular spectroscopy, characterization and synthesis of materials and compounds, computational chemistry, natural products, drug delivery systems and anti-tumor agents.

University of Southern Mississippi, College of Arts and Sciences, School of Polymer Science and Engineering, Hattiesburg, MS 39406-0001. Offers polymer science and engineering (MS, PhD), including polymer science and engineering (PhD). Terminal master's awarded for partial completion of doctoral program. *Degree requirements:* For master's, comprehensive exam, thesis; for doctorate, comprehensive exam, thesis/dissertation, original proposal. *Entrance requirements:* For master's, GRE General Test, minimum GPA of 2.75; for doctorate, GRE General Test, minimum GPA of 3.5. Additional exam requirements/recommendations for international students: Required—TOEFL, IELTS. Electronic applications accepted. *Faculty research:* Water-soluble polymers; polymer composites; coatings; solid-state, laser-initiated polymerization.

Wayne State University, College of Engineering, Department of Chemical Engineering and Materials Science, Detroit, MI 48202. Offers chemical engineering (MS, PhD); materials science and engineering (MS, PhD), including materials science and engineering; polymer engineering (Graduate Certificate), including polymer engineering. *Program availability:* Part-time. *Faculty:* 15. *Students:* 39 full-time (11 women), 32 part-time (10 women); includes 6 minority (2 Black or African American, non-Hispanic/Latino; 2 Asian, non-Hispanic/Latino; 1 Hispanic/Latino; 1 Two or more races, non-Hispanic/Latino), 36 international. Average age 27. 127 applicants, 28% accepted, 16 enrolled. In 2018, 7 master's, 5 doctorates awarded. *Entrance requirements:* For master's, three letters of recommendation (at least two from the applicant's academic institution); personal statement; resume; for doctorate, GRE, three letters of recommendation (at least two from the applicant's academic institution); personal statement; resume; for Graduate Certificate, bachelor's degree in engineering or other mathematics-based sciences in exceptional cases. Additional exam requirements/recommendations for international students: Required—TOEFL (minimum score 550 paper-based; 79 iBT), TWE (minimum score 5.5), Michigan English Language Assessment Battery (minimum score 85); Recommended—IELTS (minimum score 6.5). *Application deadline:* For fall admission, 3/1 priority date for domestic and international students; for winter admission, 10/1 priority date for domestic students, 9/1 priority date for international students; for spring admission, 2/1 priority date for domestic and international students; for summer admission, 2/1 priority date for domestic and international students. Application fee: $50. Electronic applications accepted. *Expenses:* Contact institution. *Financial support:* In 2018–19, 36 students received support, including 3 fellowships with tuition reimbursements available (averaging $20,000 per year), 16 research assistantships with tuition reimbursements available (averaging $21,307 per year), 6 teaching assistantships with tuition reimbursements available (averaging $20,166 per year); scholarships/grants, health care benefits, and unspecified assistantships also available. Support available to part-time students. Financial award applicants required to submit FAFSA. *Faculty research:* Environmental transport and management of hazardous waste; process design and synthesis based on waste minimization; biocatalysis in multiphase systems; biomaterials and tissue engineering. *Total annual research expenditures:* $1.6 million. *Unit head:* Dr. Guangzhao Mao, Professor and Chair, 313-577-3804, E-mail: gzmao@eng.wayne.edu. *Application contact:* Ellen Cope, Graduate Program Coordinator, 313-577-0409, E-mail: escope@wayne.edu.
Website: http://engineering.wayne.edu/che/

Section 17
Mechanical Engineering and Mechanics

This section contains a directory of institutions offering graduate work in mechanical engineering and mechanics. Additional information about programs listed in the directory may be obtained by writing directly to the dean of a graduate school or chair of a department at the address given in the directory.

For programs offering related work, see also in this book *Engineering and Applied Sciences, Management of Engineering and Technology,* and *Materials Sciences and Engineering.* In another guide in this series:

Graduate Programs in the Physical Sciences, Mathematics, Agricultural Sciences, the Environment & Natural Resources
See *Geosciences* and *Physics*

CONTENTS

Program Directories

Featured School: Display and Close-Up

See:

Mechanical Engineering

Alfred University, Graduate School, College of Ceramics, Inamori School of Engineering, Alfred, NY 14802. Offers biomaterials engineering (MS); ceramic engineering (MS, PhD); electrical engineering (MS); glass science (MS, PhD); materials science and engineering (MS, PhD); mechanical engineering (MS). *Program availability:* Part-time. *Degree requirements:* For master's, thesis; for doctorate, thesis/dissertation. *Entrance requirements:* Additional exam requirements/recommendations for international students: Required—TOEFL (minimum score 590 paper-based; 90 iBT), IELTS (minimum score 6.5). Electronic applications accepted. *Expenses:* Contact institution. *Faculty research:* X-ray diffraction, biomaterials and polymers, thin-film processing, electronic and optical ceramics, solid-state chemistry.

The American University in Cairo, School of Sciences and Engineering, Cairo, Egypt. Offers biotechnology (MS); chemistry (MS); computer science (MS); computing (M Comp); construction engineering (M Eng, MS); electronics and communications engineering (M Eng); environmental engineering (MS); environmental system design (M Eng); mechanical engineering (M Eng, MS); nanotechnology (MS); physics (MS); robotics, control and smart systems (MS); sciences and engineering (PhD); sustainable development (MS, Graduate Diploma). *Program availability:* Part-time, evening/weekend. *Degree requirements:* For master's, comprehensive exam (for some programs), thesis (for some programs); for doctorate, comprehensive exam (for some programs), thesis/dissertation. *Entrance requirements:* Additional exam requirements/recommendations for international students: Required—TOEFL (minimum score 450 paper-based; 45 iBT), IELTS (minimum score 5). Electronic applications accepted. *Faculty research:* Construction, mechanical, and electronics engineering; physics; computer science; biotechnology; nanotechnology; chemistry; robotics.

American University of Beirut, Graduate Programs, Maroun Semaan Faculty of Engineering and Architecture, Beirut, Lebanon. Offers applied energy (ME); civil engineering (PhD); electrical and computer engineering (PhD); energy studies (MS); engineering management (MEM); environmental and water resources (ME); environmental technology (MSES); mechanical engineering (ME, PhD); urban design (MUD); urban planning and policy (MUPP). For progreen diploma: LAU/AUC. *Program availability:* Part-time, 100% online. *Faculty:* 105 full-time (25 women), 102 part-time/adjunct (33 women). *Students:* 380 full-time (186 women), 100 part-time (38 women). Average age 27. 489 applicants, 64% accepted, 127 enrolled. In 2018, 109 master's, 14 doctorates awarded. Terminal master's awarded for partial completion of doctoral program. *Degree requirements:* For master's, one foreign language, comprehensive exam, thesis optional; for doctorate, one foreign language, comprehensive exam, thesis/dissertation. *Entrance requirements:* For doctorate, GRE. Additional exam requirements/recommendations for international students: Required—TOEFL (minimum score 575 paper-based; 88 iBT), AUB-EN; Recommended—IELTS (minimum score 7). *Application deadline:* For fall admission, 4/4 for domestic and international students; for spring admission, 11/3 for domestic and international students; for summer admission, 4/4 for domestic and international students. Application fee: $50. *Expenses: Tuition:* Full-time $17,748; part-time $986 per credit. *Required fees:* $762. Tuition and fees vary according to course load and program. *Financial support:* In 2018–19, 15 students received support, including 92 fellowships with full tuition reimbursements available (averaging $14,400 per year), 80 research assistantships with full and partial tuition reimbursements available (averaging $5,300 per year), 162 teaching assistantships with full and partial tuition reimbursements available (averaging $1,400 per year); scholarships/grants, tuition waivers (full and partial), and unspecified assistantships also available. Financial award application deadline: 4/4. *Faculty research:* All areas in engineering, architecture and design. Total annual research expenditures: $1.5 million. *Unit head:* Prof. Alan Shihade, Dean, 961-1-374374 Ext. 3400, Fax: 961-1-744462, E-mail: as20@aub.edu.lb. *Application contact:* Dr. Salim Kanaan, Director, Admissions Office, 961-1-374374 Ext. 2590, Fax: 961-1-750775, E-mail: sk00@aub.edu.lb. Website: https://www.aub.edu.lb/msfea/pages/default.aspx

American University of Sharjah, Graduate Programs, Sharjah, United Arab Emirates. Offers accounting (MS); biomedical engineering (MSBME); business administration (MBA); chemical engineering (MS Ch E); civil engineering (MSCE); computer engineering (MS); electrical engineering (MSEE); engineering systems management (MS, PhD); mathematics (MS); mechanical engineering (MSME); mechatronics engineering (MS); teaching English to speakers of other languages (MA); translation and interpreting (MA); urban planning (MUP). *Program availability:* Part-time, evening/weekend. *Degree requirements:* For master's, thesis (for some programs). *Entrance requirements:* For master's, GMAT (for MBA). Additional exam requirements/recommendations for international students: Required—TOEFL (minimum score 550 paper-based; 80 iBT), TWE (minimum score 5); Recommended—IELTS (minimum score 6.5). Electronic applications accepted. *Faculty research:* Water pollution, management and waste water treatment, energy and sustainability, air pollution, Islamic finance, family business and small and medium enterprises.

Arizona State University at the Tempe campus, Ira A. Fulton Schools of Engineering, The Polytechnic School, Program in Engineering Technology, Mesa, AZ 85212. Offers manufacturing engineering technology (MS). *Program availability:* Part-time, evening/weekend. *Degree requirements:* For master's, thesis or applied project and oral defense, final examination, interactive Program of Study (iPOS) submitted before completing 50 percent of required credit hours. *Entrance requirements:* For master's, bachelor's degree with minimum of 30 credit hours or equivalent in a technology area including course work applicable to the concentration being sought and minimum of 16 credit hours of math and science; industrial experience beyond bachelor's degree (recommended). Additional exam requirements/recommendations for international students: Required—TOEFL, IELTS, or PTE. Electronic applications accepted. *Faculty research:* Manufacturing modeling and simulation &ITsmart&RO and composite materials, optimization of turbine engines, machinability and manufacturing processes design, fuel cells and other alternative energy sources.

Arizona State University at the Tempe campus, Ira A. Fulton Schools of Engineering, School for Engineering of Matter, Transport and Energy, Tempe, AZ 85281. Offers aerospace engineering (MS, PhD); chemical engineering (MS, PhD); materials science and engineering (MS, PhD); mechanical engineering (MS, PhD); solar energy engineering and commercialization (PSM). *Program availability:* Part-time, evening/weekend, online learning. Terminal master's awarded for partial completion of doctoral program. *Degree requirements:* For master's, thesis and oral defense (MS); applied project or comprehensive exam (MSE); interactive Program of Study (iPOS) submitted before completing 50 percent of required credit hours; for doctorate, comprehensive exam, thesis/dissertation, interactive Program of Study (iPOS) submitted before completing 50 percent of required credit hours. *Entrance requirements:* For master's, GRE, minimum GPA of 3.0 or equivalent in last 2 years of work leading to bachelor's degree; for doctorate, GRE, minimum GPA of 3.0 in last 2 years of work leading to bachelor's degree. Additional exam requirements/recommendations for international students: Required—TOEFL, IELTS, or PTE. Electronic applications accepted.

Expenses: Contact institution. *Faculty research:* Electronic materials and packaging, materials for energy (batteries), adaptive/intelligent materials and structures, multiscale fluid mechanics, membranes, therapeutics and bioseparations, flexible structures, nanostructured materials, micro-/nano-transport.

Arkansas Tech University, College of Engineering and Applied Sciences, Russellville, AR 72801. Offers electrical engineering (M Engr); emergency management (MS); information technology (MS); mechanical engineering (M Engr). *Program availability:* Part-time, evening/weekend, 100% online, blended/hybrid learning. *Students:* 46 full-time (17 women), 39 part-time (16 women); includes 12 minority (7 Black or African American, non-Hispanic/Latino; 1 American Indian or Alaska Native, non-Hispanic/Latino; 1 Asian, non-Hispanic/Latino; 2 Hispanic/Latino; 1 Two or more races, non-Hispanic/Latino), 29 international. Average age 31. In 2018, 54 master's awarded. *Degree requirements:* For master's, comprehensive exam (for some programs), thesis (for some programs). *Entrance requirements:* Additional exam requirements/recommendations for international students: Required—TOEFL (minimum score 550 paper-based; 79 iBT), IELTS (minimum score 6.5), PTE (minimum score 58). *Application deadline:* For fall admission, 3/1 priority date for domestic students, 5/1 priority date for international students; for spring admission, 10/1 priority date for domestic and international students. Applications are processed on a rolling basis. Application fee: $40 ($90 for international students). Electronic applications accepted. *Expenses: Tuition, area resident:* Full-time $6816; part-time $284 per credit hour. Tuition, state resident: full-time $6816; part-time $284 per credit hour. Tuition, nonresident: full-time $13,632; part-time $568 per credit hour. *International tuition:* $13,632 full-time. *Required fees:* $457.50 per semester. Tuition and fees vary according to course load and degree level. *Financial support:* In 2018–19, research assistantships with full and partial tuition reimbursements (averaging $4,800 per year), teaching assistantships with full and partial tuition reimbursements (averaging $4,800 per year) were awarded; career-related internships or fieldwork, Federal Work-Study, scholarships/grants, health care benefits, and unspecified assistantships also available. Support available to part-time students. Financial award application deadline: 4/15; financial award applicants required to submit FAFSA. *Unit head:* Dr. Judy Cezeaux, Dean, 479-968-0353, E-mail: jcezeaux@atu.edu. *Application contact:* Dr. Jeff Robertson, Interim Dean of Graduate College, 479-968-0398, Fax: 479-964-0542, E-mail: gradcollege@atu.edu.
Website: http://www.atu.edu/appliedsci/

Auburn University, Graduate School, Ginn College of Engineering, Department of Mechanical Engineering, Auburn University, AL 36849. Offers M Mtl E, MME, MS, PhD. *Program availability:* Part-time. *Degree requirements:* For master's, thesis (for some programs); for doctorate, one foreign language, thesis/dissertation. *Entrance requirements:* For master's and doctorate, GRE General Test. *Expenses:* Tuition, state resident: full-time $11,282; part-time $535 per credit hour. Tuition, nonresident: full-time $30,542; part-time $1605 per credit hour. *Required fees:* $826 per semester. Tuition and fees vary according to degree level and program. *Faculty research:* Engineering mechanics, experimental mechanics, engineering design, engineering acoustics, engineering optics.

Baylor University, Graduate School, School of Engineering and Computer Science, Department of Engineering, Waco, TX 76798. Offers biomedical engineering (MSBME); electrical and computer engineering (MSECE, PhD); engineering (ME); mechanical engineering (MSME). *Faculty:* 14 full-time (1 woman). *Students:* 7 full-time (3 women), 4 part-time (0 women); includes 4 minority (2 Asian, non-Hispanic/Latino; 2 Hispanic/Latino), 2 international. In 2018, 14 master's, 8 doctorates awarded. *Unit head:* Dr. Mike Thompson, Graduate Director, 254-710-4188. *Application contact:* Linda Keer, Administrative Assistant, 254-710-4188, Fax: 254-710-3870, E-mail: linda_kerr@baylor.edu.
Website: http://www.ecs.baylor.edu/engineering

Baylor University, Graduate School, School of Engineering and Computer Science, Department of Mechanical Engineering, Waco, TX 76798. Offers biomedical engineering (MSBME); engineering (ME); mechanical engineering (MS, PhD). *Program availability:* Part-time. *Faculty:* 15 full-time (2 women). *Students:* 25 full-time (4 women), 2 part-time (0 women); includes 3 minority (1 Asian, non-Hispanic/Latino; 2 Two or more races, non-Hispanic/Latino), 10 international. Average age 26. 47 applicants, 40% accepted, 11 enrolled. In 2018, 9 master's awarded. *Degree requirements:* For master's, thesis (for some programs), 30 credits including 24 coursework and 6 research (for MS); 33 coursework credits or 6 project credits and 27 coursework credits (for ME); for doctorate, thesis/dissertation (for some programs), 48 semester hours of approved course work and research hours beyond the master's degree. *Entrance requirements:* For master's, GRE. Additional exam requirements/recommendations for international students: Required—TOEFL (minimum score 550 paper-based; 80 iBT), IELTS (minimum score 6.5). *Application deadline:* For fall admission, 1/15 priority date for domestic and international students; for spring admission, 12/1 priority date for domestic and international students; for summer admission, 5/1 priority date for domestic students. Application fee: $50. Electronic applications accepted. *Expenses:* Contact institution. *Financial support:* In 2018–19, 33 students received support, including 17 research assistantships with full tuition reimbursements available (averaging $16,400 per year), 15 teaching assistantships with full tuition reimbursements available (averaging $17,100 per year); health care benefits and unspecified assistantships also available. Financial award application deadline: 1/15; financial award applicants required to submit FAFSA. *Faculty research:* Bone biomechanics, control strategies for multi-segmented motion, orthopedics and rehabilitation, film cooling for gas turbines, airfoils and combustor liners, convective heat transfer from realistic ice accretion roughness, fiber orientation prediction models for fiber-filled thermoplastic composites, modeling and simulation, the electrical and thermal behavior of carbon nanotube networks. *Unit head:* Dr. Dennis L. O'Neal, Dean, 254-710-3871, Fax: 254-710-3839, E-mail: dennis_oneal@baylor.edu. *Application contact:* Dr. Douglas E. Smith, Associate Professor and Graduate Program Director, 254-710-6830, Fax: 254-710-3360, E-mail: douglas_e_smith@baylor.edu.
Website: http://www.ecs.baylor.edu/mechanicalengineering/

Binghamton University, State University of New York, Graduate School, Thomas J. Watson School of Engineering and Applied Science, Department of Mechanical Engineering, Binghamton, NY 13902-6000. Offers M Eng, MS, PhD. *Program availability:* Part-time, evening/weekend, online learning. *Degree requirements:* For master's, thesis (for some programs); for doctorate, comprehensive exam, thesis/dissertation. *Entrance requirements:* For master's and doctorate, GRE General Test. Additional exam requirements/recommendations for international students: Required—TOEFL (minimum score 550 paper-based; 80 iBT). Electronic applications accepted. *Expenses:* Contact institution.

Boise State University, College of Engineering, Department of Mechanical and Biomedical Engineering, Boise, ID 83725-0399. Offers mechanical engineering (M Engr,

MS). *Program availability:* Part-time. *Degree requirements:* For master's, comprehensive exam, thesis (for some programs). *Entrance requirements:* For master's, GRE General Test, minimum GPA of 3.0. Additional exam requirements/recommendations for international students: Required—TOEFL (minimum score 550 paper-based; 80 iBT), IELTS (minimum score 6). Electronic applications accepted.

Boston University, College of Engineering, Department of Mechanical Engineering, Boston, MA 02215. Offers manufacturing engineering (MS); mechanical engineering (PhD); MS/MBA. *Program availability:* Part-time, 100% online, blended/hybrid learning. *Students:* 185 full-time (44 women), 55 part-time (13 women); includes 35 minority (2 Black or African American, non-Hispanic/Latino; 16 Asian, non-Hispanic/Latino; 12 Hispanic/Latino; 5 Two or more races, non-Hispanic/Latino), 133 international. Average age 24. 576 applicants, 52% accepted, 93 enrolled. In 2018, 103 master's, 8 doctorates awarded. Terminal master's awarded for partial completion of doctoral program. *Degree requirements:* For master's, thesis (for some programs); for doctorate, comprehensive exam, thesis/dissertation. *Entrance requirements:* For master's and doctorate, GRE General Test. Additional exam requirements/recommendations for international students: Required—TOEFL (minimum score 90 iBT), IELTS (minimum score 7). *Faculty research:* Acoustics, ultrasound, and vibrations; biomechanics; dynamics, control, and robotics; energy and thermofluid sciences; MEMS and nanotechnology. *Unit head:* Dr. Alice White, Chairperson, 617-353-2814, Fax: 617-353-5866, E-mail: aew1@bu.edu. *Application contact:* Dr. Alice White, Chairperson, 617-353-2814, Fax: 617-353-5866, E-mail: aew1@bu.edu.
Website: http://www.bu.edu/me/

Bradley University, The Graduate School, Caterpillar College of Engineering and Technology, Department of Mechanical Engineering, Peoria, IL 61625-0002. Offers MSME. *Program availability:* Part-time, evening/weekend. *Faculty:* 15 full-time (3 women), 1 part-time/adjunct. *Students:* 14 full-time (0 women), 7 part-time (1 woman), 16 international. Average age 25. 48 applicants, 83% accepted, 4 enrolled. In 2018, 8 master's awarded. *Degree requirements:* For master's, comprehensive exam, thesis optional. *Entrance requirements:* For master's, Minimum GPA of 2.5, Essays, Recommendation letters, Transcripts. Additional exam requirements/recommendations for international students: Required—TOEFL (minimum score 550 paper-based; 79 iBT), IELTS (minimum score 6.5). *Application deadline:* For fall admission, 5/15 priority date for domestic and international students; for spring admission, 10/15 priority date for domestic and international students. Applications are processed on a rolling basis. Application fee: $40 ($50 for international students). Electronic applications accepted. *Expenses: Tuition:* Part-time $890 per credit. *Required fees:* $50 per unit. *Financial support:* In 2018–19, 17 students received support, including 4 research assistantships with partial tuition reimbursements available (averaging $6,675 per year); teaching assistantships, scholarships/grants, tuition waivers (partial), and unspecified assistantships also available. Support available to part-time students. Financial award application deadline: 4/1. *Faculty research:* Ground-coupled heat pumps, robotic end-effectors, power plant optimization. *Unit head:* Dr. Ahmad Fakheri, Chairperson, 309-677-2719. *Application contact:* Rachel Webb, Director of On-Campus Graduate Admissions & International Student and Scholar Services, 309-677-2375, E-mail: rkwebb@bradley.edu.
Website: http://www.bradley.edu/academic/departments/mechanical/

Brigham Young University, Graduate Studies, Ira A. Fulton College of Engineering, Department of Mechanical Engineering, Provo, UT 84602. Offers mechanical engineering (PhD). *Faculty:* 27 full-time (1 woman), 2 part-time/adjunct (0 women). *Students:* 123 full-time (9 women); includes 10 minority (2 Asian, non-Hispanic/Latino; 2 Hispanic/Latino; 6 Two or more races, non-Hispanic/Latino), 7 international. Average age 28. 59 applicants, 41% accepted, 23 enrolled. In 2018, 35 master's, 2 doctorates awarded. Terminal master's awarded for partial completion of doctoral program. *Degree requirements:* For master's, thesis; for doctorate, comprehensive exam, thesis/dissertation. *Entrance requirements:* For master's and doctorate, GRE General Test, minimum GPA of 3.0 in undergraduate degree course work, 3 letters of recommendation, personal statement of intent, resume. Additional exam requirements/recommendations for international students: Required—TOEFL (minimum score 580 paper-based; 85 iBT), IELTS (minimum score 7). *Application deadline:* For fall admission, 1/15 for domestic and international students; for winter admission, 9/1 for domestic and international students. Application fee: $50. Electronic applications accepted. *Financial support:* In 2018–19, 123 students received support, including 8 fellowships with full and partial tuition reimbursements available (averaging $12,441 per year), 156 research assistantships with full and partial tuition reimbursements available (averaging $18,048 per year), 66 teaching assistantships with full and partial tuition reimbursements available (averaging $8,280 per year); scholarships/grants also available. Financial award application deadline: 1/1; financial award applicants required to submit FAFSA. *Faculty research:* Computational and experimental fluid mechanics, dynamic and mechatronic systems and controls, product design and development, manufacturing systems and processes, materials and bio-mechanics. *Total annual research expenditures:* $6.1 million. *Unit head:* Dr. Dale R. Tree, Chair, 801-422-2626, Fax: 801-422-0516, E-mail: treed@byu.edu. *Application contact:* Janelle Harkness, Graduate Advisor, 801-422-1650, Fax: 801-422-0516, E-mail: jharkness@byu.edu.
Website: http://me.byu.edu

Brown University, Graduate School, School of Engineering, Program in Mechanics of Solids and Structures, Providence, RI 02912. Offers Sc M, PhD. *Degree requirements:* For doctorate, thesis/dissertation, preliminary exam.

Bucknell University, Graduate Studies, College of Engineering, Department of Mechanical Engineering, Lewisburg, PA 17837. Offers MSME. *Program availability:* Part-time. *Degree requirements:* For master's, thesis. *Entrance requirements:* For master's, GRE General Test, minimum GPA of 3.0. Additional exam requirements/recommendations for international students: Required—TOEFL (minimum score 600 paper-based). *Faculty research:* Heat pump performance, microprocessors in heat engine testing, computer-aided design.

Buffalo State College, State University of New York, The Graduate School, School of the Professions, Department of Engineering Technology, Program in Mechanical and Manufacturing Technology, Buffalo, NY 14222-1095. Offers MS. *Accreditation:* NCATE. *Degree requirements:* For master's, thesis or project. *Entrance requirements:* For master's, minimum GPA of 2.5 in last 60 hours, New York teaching certificate. Additional exam requirements/recommendations for international students: Required—TOEFL (minimum score 550 paper-based).

California Baptist University, Program in Mechanical Engineering, Riverside, CA 92504-3206. Offers MS. *Program availability:* Part-time. *Faculty:* 10 full-time (3 women). *Students:* 9 full-time (0 women), 4 part-time (1 woman); includes 3 minority (1 Black or African American, non-Hispanic/Latino; 2 Two or more races, non-Hispanic/Latino), 10 international. Average age 25. 1 applicant, 100% accepted, 1 enrolled. In 2018, 6 master's awarded. *Entrance requirements:* For master's, minimum undergraduate GPA of 3.0, bachelor's transcripts, three letters of recommendation, essay, resume, interview. Additional exam requirements/recommendations for international students: Required—TOEFL (minimum score 80 iBT). *Application deadline:* For fall admission, 8/1 priority date for domestic students, 7/1 priority date for international students; for spring admission, 12/1 priority date for domestic students, 11/1 priority date for international

students. Applications are processed on a rolling basis. Application fee: $45. Electronic applications accepted. *Expenses:* $858 per unit. *Financial support:* In 2018–19, 4 students received support. Federal Work-Study and scholarships/grants available. Financial award applicants required to submit CSS PROFILE or FAFSA. *Faculty research:* Conduction, internal mixed convection, absorption refrigeration, biomechanics, dynamics. *Unit head:* Dr. Anthony Donaldson, Dean, College of Engineering, 951-343-4841, E-mail: adonaldson@calbaptist.edu. *Application contact:* Dr. Xiuhua "April" Si, Department Chair, Aerospace, Industrial, and Mechanical Engineering, 951-552-8479, E-mail: asi@calbaptist.edu.
Website: https://calbaptist.edu/programs/master-of-science-mechanical-engineering/

California Institute of Technology, Division of Engineering and Applied Science, Option in Mechanical Engineering, Pasadena, CA 91125-0001. Offers MS, PhD, Engr. *Degree requirements:* For doctorate, thesis/dissertation. *Faculty research:* Design, mechanics, thermal and fluids engineering, jet propulsion.

California Polytechnic State University, San Luis Obispo, College of Engineering, Department of Mechanical Engineering, San Luis Obispo, CA 93407. Offers MS. *Program availability:* Part-time. *Faculty:* 6 full-time (0 women), 1 part-time/adjunct (0 women). *Students:* 20 full-time (2 women), 37 part-time (7 women); includes 14 minority (1 American Indian or Alaska Native, non-Hispanic/Latino; 4 Asian, non-Hispanic/Latino; 6 Hispanic/Latino; 3 Two or more races, non-Hispanic/Latino). Average age 31. 59 applicants, 47% accepted, 10 enrolled. In 2018, 43 master's awarded. *Degree requirements:* For master's, comprehensive exam (for some programs), thesis (for some programs). *Entrance requirements:* For master's, GRE. Additional exam requirements/recommendations for international students: Required—TOEFL (minimum score 80 iBT). *Application deadline:* For fall admission, 1/4 for domestic and international students. Applications are processed on a rolling basis. Application fee: $55. Electronic applications accepted. *Expenses: Tuition, area resident:* Full-time $7176; part-time $4164 per year. *Tuition, state resident:* full-time $10,965. *Tuition, nonresident:* full-time $10,965. *Required fees:* $6336; $3711. *Financial support:* Fellowships, research assistantships, teaching assistantships, career-related internships or fieldwork, Federal Work-Study, and scholarships/grants available. Support available to part-time students. Financial award application deadline: 3/2; financial award applicants required to submit FAFSA. *Faculty research:* Mechatronics, robotics, thermosciences, mechanics and stress analysis, composite materials. *Unit head:* Dr. Kim Shollenberger, Graduate Coordinator, 805-756-1379, E-mail: kshollen@calpoly.edu. *Application contact:* Dr. Kim Shollenberger, Graduate Coordinator, 805-756-1379, E-mail: kshollen@calpoly.edu.
Website: http://me.calpoly.edu

California State Polytechnic University, Pomona, Program in Mechanical Engineering, Pomona, CA 91768-2557. Offers mechanical engineering (MS). *Program availability:* Part-time, evening/weekend. *Students:* 11 full-time (5 women), 54 part-time (9 women); includes 35 minority (2 Black or African American, non-Hispanic/Latino; 17 Asian, non-Hispanic/Latino; 15 Hispanic/Latino; 1 Two or more races, non-Hispanic/Latino), 8 international. Average age 28. 79 applicants, 54% accepted, 13 enrolled. In 2018, 28 master's awarded. *Entrance requirements:* Additional exam requirements/recommendations for international students: Required—TOEFL (minimum score 550 paper-based). *Application deadline:* Applications are processed on a rolling basis. Application fee: $55. Electronic applications accepted. *Expenses:* Contact institution. *Financial support:* Application deadline: 3/2; applicants required to submit FAFSA. *Unit head:* Dr. Henry Xue, Graduate Coordinator, 909-869-4304, Fax: 909-869-4341, E-mail: hxue@cpp.edu. *Application contact:* Dr. Henry Xue, Graduate Coordinator, 909-869-4304, Fax: 909-869-4341, E-mail: hxue@cpp.edu.
Website: http://www.cpp.edu/~engineering/ME/masters.shtml

California State University, Fresno, Division of Research and Graduate Studies, Lyles College of Engineering, Department of Mechanical Engineering, Fresno, CA 93740-8027. Offers MS. *Program availability:* Part-time. *Degree requirements:* For master's, thesis or alternative. *Entrance requirements:* For master's, GRE General Test, minimum GPA of 2.7. Additional exam requirements/recommendations for international students: Required—TOEFL. Electronic applications accepted. *Faculty research:* Flowmeter calibration, digital camera calibration.

California State University, Fullerton, Graduate Studies, College of Engineering and Computer Science, Department of Mechanical Engineering, Fullerton, CA 92831-3599. Offers MS. *Program availability:* Part-time. *Degree requirements:* For master's, comprehensive exam, project or thesis. *Entrance requirements:* For master's, minimum undergraduate GPA of 2.5.

California State University, Long Beach, Graduate Studies, College of Engineering, Department of Mechanical and Aerospace Engineering, Long Beach, CA 90840. Offers aerospace engineering (MSAE); engineering and industrial applied mathematics (PhD); interdisciplinary engineering (MSE); management engineering (MSE); mechanical engineering (MSME). *Program availability:* Part-time. *Entrance requirements:* Additional exam requirements/recommendations for international students: Required—TOEFL. *Application deadline:* For fall admission, 4/15 for domestic students; for spring admission, 10/1 for domestic students. Application fee: $55. Electronic applications accepted. *Expenses: Required fees:* $2628 per term. Tuition and fees vary according to class time, course level, course load, degree level, campus/location and program. *Financial support:* Career-related internships or fieldwork, Federal Work-Study, institutionally sponsored loans, scholarships/grants, and unspecified assistantships available. Financial award application deadline: 3/2; financial award applicants required to submit FAFSA. *Faculty research:* Unsteady turbulent flows, solar energy, energy conversion, CAD/CAM, computer-assisted instruction. *Unit head:* Jalal Torabzadeh, Chair, 562-985-4398, E-mail: leanne.hayes@csulb.edu. *Application contact:* Dr. Jalal Torabzadeh, Graduate Advisor, 562-985-1512, Fax: 562-985-7561, E-mail: leanne.hayes@csulb.edu.
Website: http://www.csulb.edu/college-of-engineering/mechanical-aerospace-engineering

California State University, Los Angeles, Graduate Studies, College of Engineering, Computer Science, and Technology, Department of Mechanical Engineering, Los Angeles, CA 90032-8530. Offers MS. *Program availability:* Part-time, evening/weekend. *Degree requirements:* For master's, comprehensive exam or thesis. *Entrance requirements:* For master's, minimum GPA of 2.75. Additional exam requirements/recommendations for international students: Required—TOEFL (minimum score 550 paper-based). Electronic applications accepted. *Faculty research:* Mechanical design, thermal systems, solar-powered vehicle.

California State University, Northridge, Graduate Studies, College of Engineering and Computer Science, Department of Mechanical Engineering, Northridge, CA 91330. Offers MS. *Program availability:* Part-time, evening/weekend. *Degree requirements:* For master's, thesis or project. *Entrance requirements:* Additional exam requirements/recommendations for international students: Required—TOEFL.

California State University, Sacramento, College of Engineering and Computer Science, Department of Mechanical Engineering, Sacramento, CA 95819. Offers MS. *Program availability:* Part-time, evening/weekend. *Degree requirements:* For master's, thesis, project. *Entrance requirements:* For master's, minimum GPA of 3.0 in upper-division engineering coursework. Additional exam requirements/recommendations for international students: Required—TOEFL (minimum score 550 paper-based; 80 iBT); Recommended—IELTS, TSE. Electronic applications accepted. *Expenses:* Contact institution.

Carleton University, Faculty of Graduate Studies, Faculty of Engineering and Design, Department of Mechanical and Aerospace Engineering, Ottawa, ON K1S 5B6, Canada. Offers aerospace engineering (M Eng, MA Sc, PhD); materials engineering (M Eng, MA Sc); mechanical engineering (M Eng, MA Sc, PhD). *Degree requirements:* For master's, thesis optional; for doctorate, thesis/dissertation. *Entrance requirements:* For master's, honors degree; for doctorate, MA Sc or M Eng. Additional exam requirements/ recommendations for international students: Required—TOEFL. *Faculty research:* Thermal fluids engineering, heat transfer, vehicle engineering.

Carnegie Mellon University, Carnegie Institute of Technology, Department of Mechanical Engineering, Pittsburgh, PA 15213-3891. Offers MS, PhD. *Program availability:* Part-time, evening/weekend. Terminal master's awarded for partial completion of doctoral program. *Degree requirements:* For master's, thesis (for some programs); for doctorate, thesis/dissertation (for some programs), qualifying exam. *Entrance requirements:* For master's and doctorate, GRE General Test. Additional exam requirements/recommendations for international students: Required—TOEFL. *Faculty research:* Combustion, design, fluid, and thermal sciences; computational fluid dynamics; energy and environment; solid mechanics; systems and controls; materials and manufacturing.

Case Western Reserve University, School of Graduate Studies, Case School of Engineering, Department of Mechanical and Aerospace Engineering, Cleveland, OH 44106. Offers MS, PhD. *Program availability:* Part-time, 100% online. *Faculty:* 15 full-time (5 women). *Students:* 86 full-time (17 women), 3 part-time (1 woman); includes 10 minority (2 Black or African American, non-Hispanic/Latino; 5 Asian, non-Hispanic/ Latino; 3 Hispanic/Latino), 55 international. In 2018, 24 master's, 9 doctorates awarded. *Degree requirements:* For master's, thesis (for some programs); for doctorate, thesis/ dissertation, qualifying exam, teaching experience. *Entrance requirements:* For master's and doctorate, GRE General Test. Additional exam requirements/recommendations for international students: Required—TOEFL. *Application deadline:* For fall admission, 7/1 priority date for domestic students. Applications are processed on a rolling basis. Application fee: $50. *Expenses: Tuition:* Full-time $45,168; part-time $1939 per credit hour. *Required fees:* $36; $18 per semester. $18 per semester. *Financial support:* In 2018–19, 60 students received support, including 4 fellowships with tuition reimbursements available, 26 research assistantships with tuition reimbursements available, 30 teaching assistantships; institutionally sponsored loans and tuition waivers (full and partial) also available. Financial award application deadline: 3/1; financial award applicants required to submit FAFSA. *Faculty research:* Musculoskeletal biomechanics, combustion diagnostics and computation, mechanical behavior of advanced materials and nanostructures, biorobotics. *Total annual research expenditures:* $6.2 million. *Unit head:* Dr. Robert Gao, Department Chair, 216-368-6045, Fax: 216-368-6445, E-mail: robert.gao@case.edu. *Application contact:* Carla Wilson, Student Affairs Coordinator, 216-368-4580, Fax: 216-368-3007, E-mail: cxw75@case.edu.
Website: http://www.engineering.case.edu/emae

The Catholic University of America, School of Engineering, Department of Mechanical Engineering, Washington, DC 20064. Offers energy and environment (MME); general (MME); mechanical engineering (MSE, PhD). *Program availability:* Part-time. *Faculty:* 9 full-time (0 women), 7 part-time/adjunct (0 women). *Students:* 11 full-time (4 women), 32 part-time (8 women); includes 7 minority (1 Black or African American, non-Hispanic/Latino; 1 Asian, non-Hispanic/Latino; 1 Hispanic/Latino; 4 Two or more races, non-Hispanic/Latino), 8 international. Average age 31. 27 applicants, 81% accepted, 8 enrolled. In 2018, 13 master's, 1 doctorate awarded. Terminal master's awarded for partial completion of doctoral program. *Degree requirements:* For master's, thesis (for some programs); for doctorate, comprehensive exam, thesis/dissertation. *Entrance requirements:* For master's and doctorate, statement of purpose, official copies of academic transcripts, three letters of recommendation. Additional exam requirements/recommendations for international students: Required—TOEFL (minimum score 550 paper-based; 80 iBT). *Application deadline:* For fall admission, 7/15 priority date for domestic students, 7/1 for international students; for spring admission, 11/15 priority date for domestic students, 11/1 for international students. Applications are processed on a rolling basis. Application fee: $55. Electronic applications accepted. *Expenses:* Contact institution. *Financial support:* Fellowships, research assistantships, teaching assistantships, Federal Work-Study, scholarships/grants, tuition waivers (full and partial), and unspecified assistantships available. Financial award application deadline: 2/1; financial award applicants required to submit FAFSA. *Faculty research:* Energy and environment, acoustics and vibration, biofabrication and lab-on-chip, experimental mechanics, smart materials. *Unit head:* Dr. Sen Nieh, Chair, 202-319-5170, Fax: 202-319-5173, E-mail: nieh@cua.edu. *Application contact:* Dr. Steven Brown, Director of Graduate Admissions, 202-319-5057, Fax: 202-319-6533, E-mail: cua-admissions@cua.edu.
Website: https://engineering.catholic.edu/mechanical/index.html

The Citadel, The Military College of South Carolina, Citadel Graduate College, School of Engineering, Department of Mechanical Engineering, Charleston, SC 29409. Offers aeronautical engineering (Graduate Certificate); composites engineering (Graduate Certificate); manufacturing engineering (Graduate Certificate); mechanical engineering (MS); mechatronics engineering (Graduate Certificate); power and energy (Graduate Certificate). *Program availability:* Part-time, evening/weekend. *Degree requirements:* For master's, 30 hours of coursework with minimum GPA of 3.0 on hours earned at The Citadel. *Entrance requirements:* For master's, GRE, 2 letters of recommendation; official transcript of baccalaureate degree from an ABET accredited engineering program or approved alternative. Additional exam requirements/ recommendations for international students: Required—TOEFL (minimum score 550 paper-based; 79 iBT). Electronic applications accepted. *Expenses:* Tuition, state resident: part-time $595 per credit hour. Tuition, nonresident: part-time $1020 per credit hour. *Required fees:* $90 per term.

City College of the City University of New York, Graduate School, Grove School of Engineering, Department of Mechanical Engineering, New York, NY 10031-9198. Offers ME, MS, PhD. PhD program offered jointly with Graduate School and University Center of the City University of New York. *Program availability:* Part-time. *Degree requirements:* For master's, thesis optional; for doctorate, one foreign language, comprehensive exam, thesis/dissertation. *Entrance requirements:* For master's and doctorate, GRE General Test. Additional exam requirements/recommendations for international students: Required—TOEFL (minimum score 500 paper-based). *Faculty research:* Bio-heat and mass transfer, bone mechanics, fracture mechanics, heat transfer in computer parts, mechanisms design.

Clarkson University, Wallace H. Coulter School of Engineering, Department of Mechanical and Aeronautical Engineering, Potsdam, NY 13699. Offers mechanical engineering (ME, MS, PhD). *Program availability:* Part-time, evening/weekend. *Faculty:* 22 full-time (2 women), 5 part-time/adjunct (1 woman). *Students:* 43 full-time (6 women), 54 part-time (5 women); includes 11 minority (3 Black or African American, non-Hispanic/Latino; 2 Asian, non-Hispanic/Latino; 4 Hispanic/Latino; 2 Two or more races, non-Hispanic/Latino), 24 international. 86 applicants, 59% accepted, 26 enrolled. In 2018, 33 master's, 8 doctorates awarded. *Degree requirements:* For master's, thesis (for some programs), thesis or project (for MS); project (for ME); for doctorate, comprehensive exam, thesis/dissertation. *Entrance requirements:* For master's and doctorate, GRE. Additional exam requirements/recommendations for international students: Required—TOEFL (minimum score 550 paper-based, 80 iBT) or IELTS (6.5). *Application deadline:* Applications are processed on a rolling basis. Application fee: $50. Electronic applications accepted. *Expenses: Tuition:* Full-time $24,984; part-time $1388 per credit hour. *Required fees:* $225. Tuition and fees vary according to campus/location and program. *Financial support:* Scholarships/grants and unspecified assistantships available. *Unit head:* Dr. Brian Helenbrook, Chair of Mechanical & Aeronautical Engineering, 315-268-6586, E-mail: bhelenbr@clarkson.edu. *Application contact:* Dan Capogna, Director of Graduate Admissions & Recruitment, 518-631-9910, E-mail: graduate@clarkson.edu.
Website: https://www.clarkson.edu/academics/graduate

Clemson University, Graduate School, College of Engineering, Computing and Applied Sciences, Department of Mechanical Engineering, Clemson, SC 29634. Offers MS, PhD. *Program availability:* Part-time, evening/weekend, blended/hybrid learning. *Faculty:* 28 full-time (2 women). *Students:* 174 full-time (28 women), 27 part-time (6 women); includes 18 minority (7 Black or African American, non-Hispanic/Latino; 3 Asian, non-Hispanic/Latino; 6 Hispanic/Latino; 2 Two or more races, non-Hispanic/ Latino), 96 international. Average age 25. 402 applicants, 55% accepted, 81 enrolled. In 2018, 47 master's, 7 doctorates awarded. Terminal master's awarded for partial completion of doctoral program. *Degree requirements:* For master's, thesis (for some programs); for doctorate, comprehensive exam, thesis/dissertation. *Entrance requirements:* For master's and doctorate, GRE General Test, unofficial transcripts, letters of recommendation. Additional exam requirements/recommendations for international students: Required—TOEFL (minimum score 80 paper-based; 80 iBT); Recommended—IELTS (minimum score 6.5), TSE (minimum score 54). *Application deadline:* For fall admission, 2/15 for domestic and international students; for spring admission, 9/15 for domestic and international students. Applications are processed on a rolling basis. Application fee: $80 ($90 for international students). Electronic applications accepted. *Expenses:* $6823 per semester full-time resident, $14023 per semester full-time non-resident, $833 per credit hour part-time resident, $1731 per credit hour part-time non-resident, online $1264 per credit hour, $4938 doctoral programs resident, $10405 doctoral programs non-resident, $1144 full-time graduate assistant, other fees may apply per session. *Financial support:* In 2018–19, 108 students received support, including 4 fellowships with full and partial tuition reimbursements available (averaging $1,000 per year), 38 research assistantships with full and partial tuition reimbursements available (averaging $17,710 per year), 2 teaching assistantships with full and partial tuition reimbursements available (averaging $21,500 per year); career-related internships or fieldwork and unspecified assistantships also available. Financial award application deadline: 2/15. *Faculty research:* Engineering design, thermal and fluid sciences, automated manufacturing, dynamical systems and robotics, engineering mechanics and materials. *Total annual research expenditures:* $2.4 million. *Unit head:* Dr. Atul Kelkar, Department Chair, 864-656-5620, E-mail: agkelka@clemson.edu. *Application contact:* Dr. Joshua Summers, Graduate Program Coordinator, 864-656-3295, E-mail: jsummer@clemson.edu.
Website: https://www.clemson.edu/cecas/departments/me/

Cleveland State University, College of Graduate Studies, Fenn College of Engineering, Department of Mechanical Engineering, Cleveland, OH 44115. Offers MS, D Eng. *Program availability:* Part-time. *Faculty:* 8 full-time (0 women). *Students:* 33 full-time (4 women), 40 part-time (8 women); includes 8 minority (2 Black or African American, non-Hispanic/Latino; 3 Asian, non-Hispanic/Latino; 1 Hispanic/Latino; 2 Two or more races, non-Hispanic/Latino), 20 international. Average age 26. 428 applicants, 21% accepted, 19 enrolled. In 2018, 46 master's, 1 doctorate awarded. *Entrance requirements:* For master's, GRE General Test, minimum GPA of 3.0; for doctorate, GRE General Test, minimum GPA of 3.25. Additional exam requirements/ recommendations for international students: Required—TOEFL (minimum score 550 paper-based; 78 iBT). *Application deadline:* Applications are processed on a rolling basis. Application fee: $40. Electronic applications accepted. *Expenses:* Tuition, state resident: full-time $7232.55; part-time $6676 per credit hour. Tuition, nonresident: full-time $12,375. *International tuition:* $18,914 full-time. *Required fees:* $80; $80 $40. Tuition and fees vary according to program. *Financial support:* In 2018–19, 22 students received support. Research assistantships, teaching assistantships, career-related internships or fieldwork, Federal Work-Study, institutionally sponsored loans, and unspecified assistantships available. Support available to part-time students. Financial award applicants required to submit FAFSA. *Faculty research:* Fluid piezoelectric sensors, laser-optical inspection simulation of forging and forming processes, multiphase flow and heat transfer, turbulent flows. *Unit head:* Dr. William J. Atherton, Interim Chair, 216-687-2595, Fax: 216-687-5375, E-mail: w.atherton@csuohio.edu. *Application contact:* Deborah L. Brown, Interim Assistant Director, Graduate Admissions, 216-523-7572, Fax: 216-687-9214, E-mail: d.l.brown@csuohio.edu.
Website: http://www.csuohio.edu/engineering/mce/

Colorado School of Mines, Office of Graduate Studies, Department of Mechanical Engineering, Golden, CO 80401-1887. Offers mechanical engineering (MS, PhD). *Program availability:* Part-time. *Faculty:* 41 full-time (9 women), 10 part-time/adjunct (0 women). *Students:* 151 full-time (27 women), 26 part-time (5 women); includes 25 minority (1 Black or African American, non-Hispanic/Latino; 1 American Indian or Alaska Native, non-Hispanic/Latino; 9 Asian, non-Hispanic/Latino; 10 Hispanic/Latino; 4 Two or more races, non-Hispanic/Latino), 44 international. Average age 26. 359 applicants, 70% accepted, 91 enrolled. In 2018, 67 master's, 7 doctorates awarded. *Degree requirements:* For master's, thesis (for some programs); for doctorate, comprehensive exam, thesis/dissertation. *Entrance requirements:* For master's and doctorate, GRE General Test. Additional exam requirements/recommendations for international students: Required—TOEFL (minimum score 550 paper-based; 79 iBT). *Application deadline:* For fall admission, 12/15 priority date for domestic and international students; for spring admission, 9/1 priority date for domestic and international students. Application fee: $60 ($80 for international students). Electronic applications accepted. *Expenses:* Tuition, state resident: full-time $16,650; part-time $925 per contact hour. Tuition, nonresident: full-time $36,270; part-time $2015 per contact hour. *International tuition:* $36,270 full-time. *Required fees:* $2314; $2314 per semester. *Financial support:* In 2018–19, 52 research assistantships with full tuition reimbursements, 17 teaching assistantships with full tuition reimbursements were awarded; fellowships, career-related internships or fieldwork, Federal Work-Study, institutionally sponsored loans, scholarships/grants, health care benefits, and unspecified assistantships also available. Financial award application deadline: 12/15; financial award applicants required to submit FAFSA. *Faculty research:* Biomechanics; robotics, automation, and design; solid mechanics and materials; thermal science and engineering. *Unit head:* Dr. John Berger, Department Head, 303-273-3682, E-mail: jberger@mines.edu. *Application contact:* Lori Sisneros, Program Assistant, 303-273-3658, E-mail: sisneros@mines.edu.
Website: http://mechanical.mines.edu/

Colorado State University, Walter Scott, Jr. College of Engineering, Department of Mechanical Engineering, Fort Collins, CO 80523-1374. Offers MS, PhD. *Program availability:* Part-time. *Degree requirements:* For master's, thesis (for some programs), publication, seminar; for doctorate, comprehensive exam, thesis/dissertation, publication, seminar. *Entrance requirements:* For master's, GRE (minimum scores of 150 Verbal, 155 Quantitative, 3.5 Analytical), bachelor's degree in engineering-related field; minimum GPA of 3.0; for doctorate, GRE (minimum scores of 150 Verbal, 155 Quantitative, 3.5 Analytical), bachelor's degree in engineering-related field; minimum GPA of 3.25. Additional exam requirements/recommendations for international students: Required—TOEFL (minimum score 550 paper-based; 80 iBT), IELTS (minimum score 6.5). Electronic applications accepted. *Expenses:* Contact institution. *Faculty research:* Health, energy, materials.

Columbia University, Fu Foundation School of Engineering and Applied Science, Department of Mechanical Engineering, New York, NY 10027. Offers MS, Eng Sc D, PhD. PhD offered through the Graduate School of Arts and Sciences. *Program availability:* Part-time, online learning. *Degree requirements:* For doctorate, thesis/dissertation, qualifying exam. *Entrance requirements:* For master's, GRE General Test, minimum GPA of 3.3; for doctorate, GRE General Test. Additional exam requirements/recommendations for international students: Required—TOEFL, IELTS, PTE. Electronic applications accepted. *Faculty research:* Biomechanics and soft tissue mechanics; control, design, robotics, and manufacturing; energy, fluid mechanics, and heat transfer; micro-electromechanical systems and nanotechnology; bioengineering and biomechanics.

Concordia University, School of Graduate Studies, Faculty of Engineering and Computer Science, Department of Mechanical and Industrial Engineering, Montréal, QC H3G 1M8, Canada. Offers industrial engineering (M Eng, MA Sc, PhD); mechanical engineering (M Eng, MA Sc, PhD, Certificate). M Eng in composites program offered jointly with École Polytechnique de Montréal. *Degree requirements:* For master's, variable foreign language requirement, thesis or alternative; for doctorate, comprehensive exam, thesis/dissertation. *Faculty research:* Mechanical systems, fluid control systems, thermofluids engineering and robotics, industrial control systems.

Cooper Union for the Advancement of Science and Art, Albert Nerken School of Engineering, New York, NY 10003. Offers chemical engineering (ME); civil engineering (ME); electrical engineering (ME); mechanical engineering (ME). *Program availability:* Part-time. *Degree requirements:* For master's, thesis (for some programs), thesis or special project. *Entrance requirements:* For master's, BE or BS in an engineering discipline; official copies of school transcripts including secondary (high school), college and university work; two letters of recommendation; resume. Additional exam requirements/recommendations for international students: Required—TOEFL (minimum score 600 paper-based; 100 iBT). Electronic applications accepted. *Faculty research:* Analytics, bioengineering, dynamic systems, nanoscience, sustainability, STEM education.

Cornell University, Graduate School, Graduate Fields of Engineering, Field of Mechanical Engineering, Ithaca, NY 14853. Offers biomechanical engineering (M Eng, MS, PhD); combustion (M Eng, MS, PhD); energy and power systems (M Eng, MS, PhD); fluid mechanics (M Eng, MS, PhD); heat transfer (M Eng, MS, PhD); materials and manufacturing engineering (M Eng, MS, PhD); mechanical systems and design (M Eng, MS, PhD); multiphase flows (M Eng, MS, PhD). Terminal master's awarded for partial completion of doctoral program. *Degree requirements:* For master's, project (M Eng), thesis (MS); for doctorate, one foreign language, comprehensive exam, thesis/dissertation, 2 semesters of teaching experience. *Entrance requirements:* For master's and doctorate, GRE General Test, 3 letters of recommendation. Additional exam requirements/recommendations for international students: Required—TOEFL (minimum score 550 paper-based; 77 iBT). Electronic applications accepted. *Faculty research:* Combustion and heat transfer, fluid mechanics and computational fluid mechanics, system dynamics and control, biomechanics, manufacturing.

Dalhousie University, Faculty of Engineering, Department of Mechanical Engineering, Halifax, NS B3J 2X4, Canada. Offers M Eng, MA Sc, PhD. *Degree requirements:* For master's, thesis; for doctorate, thesis/dissertation. *Entrance requirements:* Additional exam requirements/recommendations for international students: Required—TOEFL, IELTS, CANTEST, CAEL, or Michigan English Language Assessment Battery. Electronic applications accepted. *Faculty research:* Fluid dynamics and energy, system dynamics, naval architecture, MEMS, space structures.

Dartmouth College, Thayer School of Engineering, Program in Mechanical and Systems Engineering, Hanover, NH 03755. Offers MS, PhD. *Degree requirements:* For master's, thesis; for doctorate, thesis/dissertation, candidacy oral exam. *Entrance requirements:* For master's and doctorate, GRE General Test. *Faculty research:* Tribology, dynamics and control systems, thermal science and energy conversion, fluid mechanics and multi-phase flow, mobile robots.

Drexel University, College of Engineering, Department of Mechanical Engineering and Mechanics, Philadelphia, PA 19104-2875. Offers mechanical engineering (MS, PhD). *Program availability:* Part-time, evening/weekend. Terminal master's awarded for partial completion of doctoral program. *Degree requirements:* For master's, thesis optional; for doctorate, thesis/dissertation. *Entrance requirements:* For master's, minimum GPA of 3.0, BS in engineering or science; for doctorate, minimum GPA of 3.5, MS in engineering or science. Additional exam requirements/recommendations for international students: Required—TOEFL. Electronic applications accepted. *Faculty research:* Composites, dynamic systems and control, combustion and fuels, biomechanics, mechanics and thermal fluid sciences.

Duke University, Graduate School, Pratt School of Engineering, Department of Mechanical Engineering and Materials Science, Durham, NC 27708. Offers materials science (M Eng, MS, PhD); mechanical engineering (M Eng, MS, PhD); JD/MS. Terminal master's awarded for partial completion of doctoral program. *Degree requirements:* For master's, thesis optional; for doctorate, thesis/dissertation. *Entrance requirements:* For master's and doctorate, GRE General Test. Additional exam requirements/recommendations for international students: Required—TOEFL (minimum score 90 iBT), IELTS (minimum score 7). Electronic applications accepted.

Duke University, Graduate School, Pratt School of Engineering, Master of Engineering Program, Durham, NC 27708-0271. Offers biomedical engineering (M Eng); civil engineering (M Eng); computational mechanics and scientific computing (M Eng); electrical and computer engineering (M Eng); environmental engineering (M Eng); materials science and engineering (M Eng); mechanical engineering (M Eng); photonics and optical sciences (M Eng); risk engineering (M Eng). *Program availability:* Part-time. *Entrance requirements:* For master's, GRE General Test, resume, 3 letters of recommendation, statement of purpose, transcripts. Additional exam requirements/recommendations for international students: Required—TOEFL. Electronic applications accepted.

École Polytechnique de Montréal, Graduate Programs, Department of Mechanical Engineering, Montréal, QC H3C 3A7, Canada. Offers aerothermics (M Eng, M Sc A, PhD); applied mechanics (M Eng, M Sc A, PhD); tool design (M Eng, M Sc A, PhD). *Program availability:* Part-time, evening/weekend. *Degree requirements:* For master's, one foreign language, thesis; for doctorate, one foreign language, thesis/dissertation. *Entrance requirements:* For master's, minimum GPA of 2.75; for doctorate, minimum GPA of 3.0. *Faculty research:* Noise control and vibration, fatigue and creep, aerodynamics, composite materials, biomechanics, robotics.

Embry-Riddle Aeronautical University–Daytona, Department of Mechanical Engineering, Daytona Beach, FL 32114-3900. Offers high performance vehicles (MSME); mechanical engineering (PhD); mechanical systems (MSME). *Degree requirements:* For master's, thesis optional; for doctorate, comprehensive exam, thesis/dissertation. *Entrance requirements:* For doctorate, GRE. Additional exam requirements/recommendations for international students: Required—TOEFL (minimum score 550 paper-based, 79 iBT) or IELTS (6). Electronic applications accepted.

Fairfield University, School of Engineering, Fairfield, CT 06824. Offers database management (CAS); electrical and computer engineering (MS); information security (CAS); management of technology (MS); mechanical engineering (MS); network technology (CAS); software engineering (MS); Web application development (CAS). *Program availability:* Part-time, evening/weekend. *Degree requirements:* For master's, capstone course. *Entrance requirements:* For master's, resume, 2 recommendations. Additional exam requirements/recommendations for international students: Required—TOEFL (minimum score 550 paper-based; 80 iBT) or IELTS (minimum score 6.5). Electronic applications accepted. *Expenses:* Contact institution. *Faculty research:* Artificial intelligence and information visualization, natural language processing, thermofluids, microwaves and electromagnetics, micro-/nano-manufacturing.

Farmingdale State College, Program in Technology Management, Farmingdale, NY 11735. Offers construction management (MS); electrical and mechanical engineering (MS). *Degree requirements:* For master's, project or thesis.

Florida Agricultural and Mechanical University, Division of Graduate Studies, Research, and Continuing Education, FAMU-FSU College of Engineering, Department of Mechanical Engineering, Tallahassee, FL 32307-3200. Offers MS, PhD. *Degree requirements:* For master's, thesis optional; for doctorate, comprehensive exam, thesis/dissertation. *Entrance requirements:* For master's, GRE General Test, minimum GPA of 3.0. Additional exam requirements/recommendations for international students: Required—TOEFL (minimum score 550 paper-based). *Faculty research:* Fluid mechanical and heat transfer, thermodynamics, dynamics and controls, mechanics and materials.

Florida Atlantic University, College of Engineering and Computer Science, Department of Ocean and Mechanical Engineering, Boca Raton, FL 33431-0991. Offers mechanical engineering (MS, PhD). *Program availability:* Part-time, evening/weekend. *Faculty:* 23 full-time (1 woman), 1 part-time/adjunct (0 women). *Students:* 42 full-time (6 women), 59 part-time (11 women); includes 17 minority (1 Black or African American, non-Hispanic/Latino; 2 Asian, non-Hispanic/Latino; 14 Hispanic/Latino), 43 international. Average age 30. 67 applicants, 66% accepted, 28 enrolled. In 2018, 34 master's, 4 doctorates awarded. Terminal master's awarded for partial completion of doctoral program. *Degree requirements:* For master's, thesis (for some programs); for doctorate, comprehensive exam, thesis/dissertation, qualifying exam. *Entrance requirements:* For master's and doctorate, GRE General Test, minimum GPA of 3.0. Additional exam requirements/recommendations for international students: Required—TOEFL (minimum score 500 paper-based; 61 iBT), IELTS (minimum score 6). *Application deadline:* For fall admission, 7/1 priority date for domestic students, 2/15 for international students; for spring admission, 11/1 for domestic students, 7/15 for international students. Applications are processed on a rolling basis. Application fee: $30. *Expenses:* Tuition, area resident: Full-time $7400; part-time $369.82 per credit. Tuition, state resident: full-time $7400; part-time $369.82 per credit. Tuition, nonresident: full-time $20,496; part-time $1024.81 per credit. *Financial support:* Research assistantships, career-related internships or fieldwork, Federal Work-Study, scholarships/grants, and unspecified assistantships available. Financial award application deadline: 1/10; financial award applicants required to submit FAFSA. *Faculty research:* Marine materials and corrosion, ocean structures, marine vehicles, acoustics and vibrations, hydrodynamics, coastal engineering. *Unit head:* Manhar Dhanak, Chair, 561-297-2827, E-mail: dhanak@fau.edu. *Application contact:* Manhar Dhanak, Chair, 561-297-2827, E-mail: dhanak@fau.edu.
Website: http://www.ome.fau.edu/

Florida Institute of Technology, College of Engineering and Science, Program in Mechanical Engineering, Melbourne, FL 32901-6975. Offers MS, PhD. *Program availability:* Part-time. *Students:* 52 full-time (6 women), 23 part-time (4 women); includes 11 minority (5 Black or African American, non-Hispanic/Latino; 2 Asian, non-Hispanic/Latino; 3 Hispanic/Latino; 1 Two or more races, non-Hispanic/Latino), 40 international. Average age 27. 43 applicants, 65% accepted, 13 enrolled. In 2018, 23 master's, 6 doctorates awarded. Terminal master's awarded for partial completion of doctoral program. *Degree requirements:* For master's, thesis, 30 credit hours; for doctorate, comprehensive exam, thesis/dissertation. *Entrance requirements:* For master's, GRE General Test, bachelor's degree from an ABET-accredited program, transcripts; for doctorate, GRE General Test, 3 letters of recommendation, minimum GPA of 3.5, resume, statement of objectives, master's degree. Additional exam requirements/recommendations for international students: Required—TOEFL (minimum score 550 paper-based; 79 iBT). *Application deadline:* For fall admission, 4/1 for international students; for spring admission, 9/30 for international students. Applications are processed on a rolling basis. Application fee: $50. Electronic applications accepted. *Expenses:* Tuition: Full-time $22,338; part-time $1241 per credit hour. Tuition and fees vary according to degree level, campus/location and program. *Financial support:* Career-related internships or fieldwork, institutionally sponsored loans, tuition waivers (partial), unspecified assistantships, and tuition remissions available. Support available to part-time students. Financial award application deadline: 3/1; financial award applicants required to submit FAFSA. *Faculty research:* Dynamic systems, robotics, and controls; structures, solid mechanics, and materials; thermal-fluid sciences, optical tomography, composite/recycled materials. *Unit head:* Dr. Ashok Pandit, Department Head, 321-674-7151, E-mail: apandit@fit.edu. *Application contact:* Mike Perry, Executive Director of Admission, 321-674-7127, E-mail: perrymj@fit.edu.
Website: https://www.fit.edu/programs/mechanical-engineering-ms/

Florida International University, College of Engineering and Computing, Department of Mechanical and Materials Engineering, Miami, FL 33199. Offers materials science and engineering (MS, PhD); mechanical engineering (MS, PhD). *Program availability:* Part-time, evening/weekend. *Faculty:* 22 full-time (4 women), 6 part-time/adjunct (1 woman). *Students:* 49 full-time (12 women), 8 part-time (0 women); includes 20 minority (4 Black or African American, non-Hispanic/Latino; 14 Hispanic/Latino; 2 Two or more races, non-Hispanic/Latino), 33 international. Average age 30. 98 applicants, 45% accepted, 13 enrolled. In 2018, 11 master's, 8 doctorates awarded. Terminal master's awarded for partial completion of doctoral program. *Degree requirements:* For master's, thesis or alternative; for doctorate, comprehensive exam, thesis/dissertation. *Entrance requirements:* For master's, GRE (depending on program), 3 letters of recommendation, minimum undergraduate GPA of 3.0 in upper-level course work; for doctorate, GRE (minimum combined score of 1150, verbal 450, quantitative 650), minimum undergraduate GPA of 3.0 in upper-level coursework with BS, 3.3 with MS; 3 letters of recommendation; letter of intent. Additional exam requirements/recommendations for international students: Required—TOEFL (minimum score 550 paper-based; 80 iBT) or IELTS (minimum score 6.5). *Application deadline:* For fall admission, 6/1 for domestic students, 4/1 for international students; for spring admission, 10/1 for domestic students, 9/1 for international students. Applications are processed on a rolling basis. Application

fee: $30. Electronic applications accepted. *Financial support:* Institutionally sponsored loans, scholarships/grants, and unspecified assistantships available. Financial award application deadline: 3/1; financial award applicants required to submit FAFSA. *Faculty research:* Mechanics and materials, fluid/thermal/energy, design and manufacturing, materials science engineering. *Unit head:* Dr. ARVIND AGARWAL, Chair, 305-348-1701, Fax: 305-348-1932, E-mail: Arvind.Agarwal@fiu.edu. *Application contact:* Nanett Rojas, Manager, Admissions Operations, 305-348-7464, Fax: 305-348-7441, E-mail: gradadm@fiu.edu.
Website: http://cec.fiu.edu

Florida State University, The Graduate School, FAMU-FSU College of Engineering, Department of Mechanical Engineering, Tallahassee, FL 32310-6046. Offers mechanical engineering (MS, PhD); sustainable energy (MS). *Program availability:* Part-time. Terminal master's awarded for partial completion of doctoral program. *Degree requirements:* For master's, thesis optional, 30 credit hours (24 coursework, 6 research); for doctorate, thesis/dissertation, 45 credit hours (21 coursework, 24 research). *Entrance requirements:* For master's and doctorate, GRE General Test (minimum scores: Verbal 150, Quantitative 155), minimum GPA of 3.0, official transcripts, resume, personal statement, 3 letters of recommendation. Additional exam requirements/recommendations for international students: Required—TOEFL (minimum score 550 paper-based; 80 iBT), IELTS (minimum score 6.5). Electronic applications accepted. *Expenses: Tuition, area resident:* Part-time $479.32 per credit hour. Tuition and fees vary according to campus/location and program. *Faculty research:* Aero-propulsion, superconductivity, smart materials, nanomaterials, intelligent robotic systems, robotic locomotion, sustainable energy.

Gannon University, School of Graduate Studies, College of Engineering and Business, School of Engineering and Computer Science, Program in Mechanical Engineering, Erie, PA 16541-0001. Offers MSME. *Program availability:* Part-time, evening/weekend. *Degree requirements:* For master's, comprehensive exam, thesis (for some programs), oral exam (for some programs), design project (for some programs). *Entrance requirements:* For master's, bachelor's degree in mechanical engineering from an ABET-accredited program or its equivalent with minimum GPA of 2.5, transcript, 3 letters of recommendation. Additional exam requirements/recommendations for international students: Required—TOEFL (minimum score 79 iBT). Electronic applications accepted. Application fee is waived when completed online.

The George Washington University, School of Engineering and Applied Science, Department of Mechanical and Aerospace Engineering, Washington, DC 20052. Offers MS, PhD, App Sc, Engr, Graduate Certificate. *Program availability:* Part-time, evening/weekend. *Faculty:* 23 full-time (4 women), 11 part-time/adjunct (1 woman). *Students:* 92 full-time (11 women), 37 part-time (6 women); includes 8 minority (1 Black or African American, non-Hispanic/Latino; 1 American Indian or Alaska Native, non-Hispanic/Latino; 2 Asian, non-Hispanic/Latino; 2 Hispanic/Latino; 2 Two or more races, non-Hispanic/Latino), 98 international. Average age 26. 301 applicants, 73% accepted, 42 enrolled. In 2018, 40 master's, 13 doctorates awarded. *Degree requirements:* For master's, thesis optional; for doctorate, thesis/dissertation, final and qualifying exams. *Entrance requirements:* For master's, appropriate bachelor's degree, minimum GPA of 3.0; for doctorate, GRE (if highest earned degree is BS), appropriate bachelor's or master's degree, minimum GPA of 3.4; for other advanced degree, appropriate master's degree, minimum GPA of 3.0. Additional exam requirements/recommendations for international students: Required—TOEFL or The George Washington University English as a Foreign Language Test. *Application deadline:* For fall admission, 3/1 priority date for domestic students; for spring admission, 10/1 for domestic students. Applications are processed on a rolling basis. Application fee: $75. *Financial support:* In 2018–19, 51 students received support. Fellowships, research assistantships, teaching assistantships, career-related internships or fieldwork, and institutionally sponsored loans available. Financial award application deadline: 3/1; financial award applicants required to submit FAFSA. *Unit head:* Dr. Michael Plesniak, Chair, 202-994-9800, E-mail: maeng@gwu.edu. *Application contact:* Adina Lav, Marketing, Recruiting and Admissions, 202-994-5827, Fax: 202-994-0909, E-mail: engineering@gwu.edu.

Georgia Institute of Technology, Graduate Studies, College of Engineering, George W. Woodruff School of Mechanical Engineering, Program in Mechanical Engineering, Atlanta, GA 30332-0001. Offers MS, MSME, MSMP, MSNE, PhD. *Program availability:* Part-time, online learning. Terminal master's awarded for partial completion of doctoral program. *Degree requirements:* For master's, thesis; for doctorate, comprehensive exam, thesis/dissertation. *Entrance requirements:* For master's and doctorate, GRE General Test, minimum GPA of 3.3. Additional exam requirements/recommendations for international students: Required—TOEFL (minimum score 580 paper-based; 94 iBT). Electronic applications accepted. *Faculty research:* Automation and mechatronics; computer-aided engineering and design; micro-electronic mechanical systems; heat transfer, combustion and energy systems; fluid mechanics.

Georgia Southern University, Jack N. Averitt College of Graduate Studies, Allen E. Paulson College of Engineering and Computing, Department of Mechanical Engineering, Program in Engineering/Mechatronics, Statesboro, GA 30458. Offers MSAE. *Degree requirements:* For master's, thesis optional. *Entrance requirements:* Additional exam requirements/recommendations for international students: Required—TOEFL (minimum score 80 iBT). Electronic applications accepted. *Expenses: Tuition, area resident:* Part-time $3324 per semester. Tuition, state resident: full-time $5814; part-time $3324 per semester. Tuition, nonresident: full-time $23,204; part-time $13,260 per semester. *Required fees:* $2092; $2092. Tuition and fees vary according to course load, degree level, campus/location and program. *Faculty research:* Biomechatronics, electromagnetics, smart antennas, wireless communication systems and networks, wireless sensor and actuator networks.

Grand Valley State University, Padnos College of Engineering and Computing, School of Engineering, Allendale, MI 49401-9403. Offers electrical and computer engineering (MSE); manufacturing operations (MSE); mechanical engineering (MSE); product design and manufacturing engineering (MSE). *Program availability:* Part-time, evening/weekend. *Faculty:* 19 full-time (5 women). *Students:* 26 full-time (5 women), 50 part-time (7 women); includes 6 minority (1 Black or African American, non-Hispanic/Latino; 2 Asian, non-Hispanic/Latino; 1 Hispanic/Latino; 2 Two or more races, non-Hispanic/Latino), 39 international. Average age 26. 52 applicants, 62% accepted, 13 enrolled. In 2018, 32 master's awarded. *Entrance requirements:* For master's, engineering degree, minimum GPA of 3.0, resume, 3 confidential letters of recommendation, 1-2 page essay, base of underlying relevant knowledge/evidence from academic records or relevant wok experience. Additional exam requirements/recommendations for international students: Required—Michigan English Language Assessment Battery (minimum score 77), TOEFL (minimum iBT score of 80), or IELTS (6.5); GRE. *Application deadline:* Applications are processed on a rolling basis. Application fee: $30. Electronic applications accepted. *Expenses:* $712 per credit hour, 33 credit hours. *Financial support:* In 2018–19, 40 students received support, including 8 fellowships, 34 research assistantships with full and partial tuition reimbursements available (averaging $4,000 per year); career-related internships or fieldwork, Federal Work-Study, institutionally sponsored loans, scholarships/grants, and unspecified assistantships also available. *Faculty research:* Digital signal processing, computer aided design, computer aided manufacturing, manufacturing simulation, biomechanics, product design. *Total annual research expenditures:* $300,000. *Unit head:* Dr. Wael Mokhtar, Director, 616-331-6015, Fax: 616-331-7215, E-mail: mokhtarw@gvsu.edu. *Application contact:* Dr. Shabbir Choudhuri, Graduate Program Director, 616-331-6845, Fax: 616-331-7215, E-mail: choudhus@gvsu.edu.
Website: http://www.engineer.gvsu.edu/

Harvard University, Graduate School of Arts and Sciences, Harvard John A. Paulson School of Engineering and Applied Sciences, Cambridge, MA 02138. Offers applied mathematics (PhD); applied physics (PhD); computational science and engineering (ME, SM); computer science (PhD); data science (SM); design engineering (MDE); engineering science (ME), including electrical engineering (ME, SM, PhD); engineering sciences (SM, PhD), including bioengineering (PhD), electrical engineering (ME, SM, PhD), environmental science and engineering (PhD), materials science and mechanical engineering (PhD). MDE offered in collaboration with Graduate School of Design. *Program availability:* Part-time. Terminal master's awarded for partial completion of doctoral program. *Degree requirements:* For master's, thesis (for ME); for doctorate, comprehensive exam, thesis/dissertation. *Entrance requirements:* For master's and doctorate, GRE General Test, GRE Subject Test (recommended), 3 letters of recommendation. Additional exam requirements/recommendations for international students: Required—TOEFL (minimum score 80 iBT). Electronic applications accepted. *Expenses:* Contact institution. *Faculty research:* Applied mathematics, applied physics, computer science and electrical engineering, environmental engineering, mechanical and biomedical engineering.

Howard University, College of Engineering, Architecture, and Computer Sciences, School of Engineering and Computer Science, Department of Mechanical Engineering, Washington, DC 20059-0002. Offers M Eng, PhD. *Degree requirements:* For master's, comprehensive exam, thesis; for doctorate, one foreign language, comprehensive exam, thesis/dissertation, 2 terms of residency. *Entrance requirements:* For master's and doctorate, GRE General Test, minimum GPA of 3.0. Additional exam requirements/recommendations for international students: Required—TOEFL. Electronic applications accepted. *Faculty research:* The dynamics and control of large flexible space structures, optimization of space structures.

Idaho State University, Graduate School, College of Science and Engineering, Department of Mechanical Engineering, Pocatello, ID 83209-8060. Offers measurement and control engineering (MS); mechanical engineering (MS). *Program availability:* Part-time. *Degree requirements:* For master's, comprehensive exam (for some programs), 2 semesters of seminar; thesis or project. *Entrance requirements:* For master's, GRE. Additional exam requirements/recommendations for international students: Required—TOEFL (minimum score 550 paper-based; 80 iBT). Electronic applications accepted. *Faculty research:* Modeling and identification of biomedical systems, intelligent systems and adaptive control, active flow control of turbo machinery, validation of advanced computational codes for thermal fluid interactions, development of methodologies for the assessment of passive safety system performance in advanced reactors, alternative energy research (wind, solar, hydrogen).

Illinois Institute of Technology, Graduate College, Armour College of Engineering, Department of Mechanical, Materials and Aerospace Engineering, Chicago, IL 60616. Offers manufacturing engineering (MAS, MS); materials science and engineering (MAS, MS, PhD); mechanical and aerospace engineering (MAS, MS, PhD), including economics (MS), energy (MS), environment (MS). *Program availability:* Part-time, evening/weekend, online learning. Terminal master's awarded for partial completion of doctoral program. *Degree requirements:* For master's, comprehensive exam (for some programs), thesis (for some programs); for doctorate, comprehensive exam, thesis/dissertation. *Entrance requirements:* For master's and doctorate, GRE General Test (minimum score 1000 Quantitative and Verbal, 3.0 Analytical Writing), minimum undergraduate GPA of 3.0. Additional exam requirements/recommendations for international students: Required—TOEFL (minimum score 550 paper-based; 80 iBT). Electronic applications accepted. *Faculty research:* Fluid dynamics, metallurgical and materials engineering, solids and structures, computational mechanics, computer added design and manufacturing, thermal sciences, dynamic analysis and control of complex systems.

Indiana University–Purdue University Indianapolis, School of Engineering and Technology, Department of Mechanical Engineering, Indianapolis, IN 46202. Offers engineering (MSE); mechanical engineering (MSME, PhD). *Program availability:* Part-time. *Degree requirements:* For master's, thesis optional; for doctorate, thesis/dissertation. *Entrance requirements:* For master's, GRE, minimum GPA of 3.0, three recommendation letters, statement of purpose/intent; for doctorate, GRE, minimum GPA of 3.0, three recommendation letters, statement of purpose/intent, curriculum vitae. Additional exam requirements/recommendations for international students: Required—TOEFL (minimum score 550 paper-based; 79 iBT); Recommended—IELTS (minimum score 6.5), TSE (minimum score 58). Electronic applications accepted. *Expenses:* Contact institution. *Faculty research:* Computational fluid dynamics and finite element methods; heat transfer; composites and materials; biomechanics; and mechatronics.

Instituto Tecnológico y de Estudios Superiores de Monterrey, Campus Chihuahua, Graduate Programs, Chihuahua, Mexico. Offers computer systems engineering (Ingeniero); electrical engineering (Ingeniero); electromechanical engineering (Ingeniero); electronic engineering (Ingeniero); engineering administration (MEA); industrial engineering (MIE, Ingeniero); international trade (MIT); mechanical engineering (Ingeniero).

Instituto Tecnológico y de Estudios Superiores de Monterrey, Campus Monterrey, Graduate and Research Division, Programs in Engineering, Monterrey, Mexico. Offers applied statistics (M Eng); artificial intelligence (PhD); automation engineering (M Eng); chemical engineering (M Eng); civil engineering (M Eng); electrical engineering (M Eng); electronic engineering (M Eng); environmental engineering (M Eng); industrial engineering (M Eng, PhD); manufacturing engineering (M Eng); mechanical engineering (M Eng); systems and quality engineering (M Eng). M Eng program offered jointly with University of Waterloo; PhD in industrial engineering with Texas A&M University. *Program availability:* Part-time, evening/weekend. Terminal master's awarded for partial completion of doctoral program. *Degree requirements:* For master's, one foreign language, thesis; for doctorate, one foreign language, thesis/dissertation. *Entrance requirements:* For master's, EXADEP; for doctorate, GRE, master's degree in related field. Additional exam requirements/recommendations for international students: Required—TOEFL. *Faculty research:* Flexible manufacturing cells, materials, statistical methods, environmental prevention, control and evaluation.

Inter American University of Puerto Rico, Bayamón Campus, Graduate School, Bayamón, PR 00957. Offers biology (MS), including environmental sciences and ecology, molecular biotechnology; electrical engineering (ME), including control system, potence system; human resources (MBA); mechanical engineering (ME, MS), including aerospace, energy. *Program availability:* Part-time, evening/weekend. *Degree requirements:* For master's, comprehensive exam, research project. *Entrance requirements:* For master's, EXADEP, GRE General Test, letters of recommendation. *Expenses: Tuition:* Full-time $3816; part-time $1908 per trimester. *Required fees:* $735; $642.

Iowa State University of Science and Technology, Department of Mechanical Engineering, Ames, IA 50011. Offers mechanical engineering (M Eng, MS, PhD); systems engineering (M Eng). *Degree requirements:* For master's, thesis or alternative; for doctorate, thesis/dissertation. *Entrance requirements:* For master's and doctorate, GRE General Test, resume. Additional exam requirements/recommendations for international students: Required—TOEFL (minimum score 570 paper-based; 79 iBT), IELTS (minimum score 6.5). Electronic applications accepted.

Johns Hopkins University, Engineering Program for Professionals, Part-time Program in Mechanical Engineering, Baltimore, MD 21218. Offers MME, Post Master's Certificate. *Program availability:* Part-time, evening/weekend, 100% online, blended/hybrid learning. *Faculty:* 12 part-time/adjunct. *Students:* 196 part-time (44 women). 68 applicants, 68% accepted, 27 enrolled. In 2018, 49 master's awarded. *Entrance requirements:* Additional exam requirements/recommendations for international students: Required—TOEFL (minimum score 600 paper-based; 100 iBT). *Application deadline:* Applications are processed on a rolling basis. Application fee: $0. Electronic applications accepted. *Unit head:* Dr. Jaafar El-Awady, Program Chair, 410-516-6683, E-mail: jelawady@jhu.edu. *Application contact:* Doug Schiller, Admissions Director, 410-516-2300, Fax: 410-579-8049, E-mail: schiller@jhu.edu.

Johns Hopkins University, G. W. C. Whiting School of Engineering, Department of Mechanical Engineering, Baltimore, MD 21218-2681. Offers MSE, PhD. *Faculty:* 40 full-time (7 women). *Students:* 163 full-time (28 women), 6 part-time (1 woman). 591 applicants, 31% accepted, 80 enrolled. In 2018, 38 master's, 18 doctorates awarded. Terminal master's awarded for partial completion of doctoral program. *Degree requirements:* For master's, thesis optional; for doctorate, comprehensive exam, thesis/dissertation, oral exam. *Entrance requirements:* For master's and doctorate, GRE General Test, 3 letters of recommendation, statement of purpose, transcripts. Additional exam requirements/recommendations for international students: Required—TOEFL (minimum score 600 paper-based, 100 iBT) or IELTS (7). *Application deadline:* For fall admission, 12/15 priority date for domestic and international students; for spring admission, 10/15 priority date for domestic and international students. Application fee: $25. Electronic applications accepted. *Financial support:* In 2018–19, 115 students received support, including 11 fellowships with full tuition reimbursements available (averaging $31,212 per year), 104 research assistantships with full tuition reimbursements available (averaging $31,212 per year); Federal Work-Study, institutionally sponsored loans, scholarships/grants, health care benefits, tuition waivers (partial), and unspecified assistantships also available. Support available to part-time students. Financial award application deadline: 12/15. *Faculty research:* Mechanical engineering in biology and medicine; energy and the environment; fluid mechanics and heat transfer; mechanics and materials; micro/nanoscale science and technology; systems, controls, and modeling; robotics. *Unit head:* Dr. Gretar Tryggvason, Department Head, 410-516-5970, Fax: 410-516-7254, E-mail: gtryggv1@jhu.edu. *Application contact:* Mike Bernard, Academic Program Manager, 410-516-7154, Fax: 410-516-7254, E-mail: me-academic@jhu.edu.
Website: http://www.me.jhu.edu/

Johns Hopkins University, G. W. C. Whiting School of Engineering, Master of Science in Engineering Management Program, Baltimore, MD 21218. Offers biomaterials (MSEM); civil engineering (MSEM); communications science (MSEM); computer science (MSEM); environmental systems analysis, economics and public policy (MSEM); fluid mechanics (MSEM); materials science and engineering (MSEM); mechanical engineering (MSEM); mechanics and materials (MSEM); nano-biotechnology (MSEM); nanomaterials and nanotechnology (MSEM); operations research (MSEM); probability and statistics (MSEM); smart product and device design (MSEM). *Students:* 34 full-time (12 women), 18 part-time (7 women). 233 applicants, 39% accepted, 33 enrolled. In 2018, 27 master's awarded. *Entrance requirements:* For master's, GRE, 3 letters of recommendation, statement of purpose, transcripts. Additional exam requirements/recommendations for international students: Required—TOEFL (minimum score 600 paper-based, 100 iBT) or IELTS (7). *Application deadline:* For fall admission, 2/15 for domestic and international students. Application fee: $75. Electronic applications accepted. *Financial support:* In 2018–19, 43 research assistantships (averaging $43,344 per year) were awarded; health care benefits also available. *Unit head:* Dr. Pamela Sheff, Director, 410-516-7056, Fax: 410-516-4880, E-mail: pamsheff@gmail.com. *Application contact:* Lindsey Conklin, Sr. Academic Program Coordinator, 410-516-1108, Fax: 410-516-0780, E-mail: lconkli4@jhu.edu.
Website: http://engineering.jhu.edu/msem/

Kansas State University, Graduate School, College of Engineering, Department of Mechanical and Nuclear Engineering, Manhattan, KS 66506. Offers mechanical engineering (MS); nuclear engineering (PhD). *Degree requirements:* For master's, thesis optional; for doctorate, comprehensive exam, thesis/dissertation. *Entrance requirements:* For master's, GRE General Test; for doctorate, GRE General Test, master's degree in mechanical engineering; minimum GPA of 3.0 overall or last 60 hours in calculus-based engineering or related program. Additional exam requirements/recommendations for international students: Required—TOEFL (minimum score 550 paper-based; 79 iBT). Electronic applications accepted. *Faculty research:* Radiation detection and protection, heat and mass transfer, machine design, control systems, nuclear reactor physics and engineering.

Kennesaw State University, Southern Polytechnic College of Engineering and Engineering Technology, Program in Mechanical Engineering, Kennesaw, GA 30144. Offers MS. *Program availability:* Online learning. *Students:* 5 full-time (3 women), 22 part-time (2 women); includes 5 minority (4 Black or African American, non-Hispanic/Latino; 1 Asian, non-Hispanic/Latino), 3 international. Average age 32. 20 applicants, 95% accepted, 15 enrolled. *Entrance requirements:* Additional exam requirements/recommendations for international students: Required—TOEFL (minimum score 550 paper-based; 80 iBT), IELTS (minimum score 6.5). *Application deadline:* For fall admission, 7/1 for domestic and international students; for spring admission, 11/1 for domestic and international students. Applications are processed on a rolling basis. Application fee: $60. Electronic applications accepted. *Expenses: Tuition, area resident:* Full-time $6960; part-time $290 per credit hour. Tuition, state resident: full-time $6960; part-time $290 per credit hour. Tuition, nonresident: full-time $25,080; part-time $1045 per credit hour. *International tuition:* $25,080 full-time. *Required fees:* $2006; $1706 per semester. $853 per semester. *Financial support:* Applicants required to submit FAFSA. *Application contact:* Admissions Counselor, 470-578-4377, E-mail: ksugrad@kennesaw.edu.
Website: http://engineering.kennesaw.edu/mechanical/degrees/ms-mechanical.php

Kettering University, Graduate School, Mechanical Engineering Department, Flint, MI 48504. Offers engineering (MS). *Program availability:* Part-time, evening/weekend, online learning. *Degree requirements:* For master's, thesis optional. *Entrance requirements:* Additional exam requirements/recommendations for international students: Required—TOEFL (minimum score 550 paper-based; 79 iBT). Electronic applications accepted. *Faculty research:* Occupant protection crash safety, biomechanics, alternative energy systems, advanced auto powertrain.

Lamar University, College of Graduate Studies, College of Engineering, Department of Mechanical Engineering, Beaumont, TX 77710. Offers ME, MES, DE. *Program availability:* Part-time. *Faculty:* 7 full-time (1 woman). *Students:* 28 full-time (3 women), 12 part-time (2 women); includes 2 minority (both Asian, non-Hispanic/Latino), 36 international. Average age 26. 74 applicants, 77% accepted, 9 enrolled. In 2018, 55 master's, 2 doctorates awarded. Terminal master's awarded for partial completion of doctoral program. *Degree requirements:* For master's, comprehensive exam (for some programs), thesis (for some programs); for doctorate, thesis/dissertation. *Entrance requirements:* For master's and doctorate, GRE General Test. Additional exam requirements/recommendations for international students: Required—TOEFL (minimum score 550 paper-based; 79 iBT), IELTS (minimum score 6.5). *Application deadline:* Applications are processed on a rolling basis. Application fee: $25 ($50 for international students). Electronic applications accepted. *Expenses:* Tuition, state resident: full-time $6234; part-time $346 per credit hour. Tuition, nonresident: full-time $6852; part-time $761 per credit hour. *International tuition:* $6852 full-time. *Required fees:* $1940; $327 per credit hour. Tuition and fees vary according to course load, campus/location, program and reciprocity agreements. *Financial support:* In 2018–19, 2 students received support, including 2 fellowships (averaging $7,200 per year); research assistantships, teaching assistantships, and tuition waivers (partial) also available. Financial award applicants required to submit FAFSA. *Faculty research:* Materials combustion, mechanical and multiphysics study in micro-electronics, structural instability/reliability, mechanics of micro electronics. *Total annual research expenditures:* $607,264. *Unit head:* Dr. Hsing-Wei Chu, Chair, 409-880-8094, Fax: 409-880-8121. *Application contact:* Celeste Contreas, Director, Admissions and Academic Services, 409-880-8888, Fax: 409-880-7419, E-mail: gradmissions@lamar.edu.
Website: http://engineering.lamar.edu/mechanical

Lawrence Technological University, College of Engineering, Southfield, MI 48075-1058. Offers architectural engineering (MS); automotive engineering (MS); biomedical engineering (MS); civil engineering (MA, MS, PhD), including environmental engineering (MS), geotechnical engineering (MS), structural engineering (MS), transportation engineering (MS), water resource engineering (MS); construction engineering management (MA); electrical and computer engineering (MS); engineering management (MEM); engineering technology (MS); fire engineering (MS); industrial engineering (MS), including healthcare systems; manufacturing systems (ME); mechanical engineering (MS, DE, PhD), including automotive engineering (MS), energy engineering (MS), manufacturing (DE), solid mechanics (MS), thermal/fluid systems (MS); mechatronic systems engineering (MS). *Program availability:* Part-time, evening/weekend. Terminal master's awarded for partial completion of doctoral program. *Degree requirements:* For master's, thesis optional; for doctorate, comprehensive exam, thesis/dissertation optional. *Entrance requirements:* Additional exam requirements/recommendations for international students: Required—TOEFL (minimum score 550 paper-based; 79 iBT), IELTS (minimum score 6.5). Electronic applications accepted. *Faculty research:* Innovative infrastructure and building structures and materials; connectivity and mobility; automotive systems modeling, simulation and testing; biomedical devices and materials; building mechanical/electrical systems.

Lehigh University, P.C. Rossin College of Engineering and Applied Science, Department of Mechanical Engineering and Mechanics, Bethlehem, PA 18015. Offers mechanical engineering (M Eng, MS, PhD); MBA/E. *Program availability:* Part-time, 100% online, blended/hybrid learning. *Faculty:* 23 full-time (2 women), 1 part-time/adjunct (0 women). *Students:* 123 full-time (11 women), 18 part-time (3 women); includes 5 minority (3 Hispanic/Latino; 1 Native Hawaiian or other Pacific Islander, non-Hispanic/Latino; 1 Two or more races, non-Hispanic/Latino), 96 international. Average age 28. 189 applicants, 38% accepted, 29 enrolled. In 2018, 45 master's, 22 doctorates awarded. Terminal master's awarded for partial completion of doctoral program. *Degree requirements:* For master's, thesis, there are 4 tracks for the MS degree, thesis; for doctorate, thesis/dissertation, general exam, proposal, dissertation. *Entrance requirements:* Additional exam requirements/recommendations for international students: Required—TOEFL (minimum score 550 paper-based; 79 iBT), IELTS (minimum score 6.5), GRE. *Application deadline:* For fall admission, 7/15 for domestic students, 6/20 for international students; for spring admission, 12/1 for domestic and international students. Applications are processed on a rolling basis. Application fee: $75. Electronic applications accepted. Tuition and fees vary according to program. *Financial support:* In 2018–19, 88 students received support, including fellowships with full tuition reimbursements available (averaging $29,400 per year), 69 research assistantships with full tuition reimbursements available (averaging $27,999 per year), 13 teaching assistantships with full tuition reimbursements available (averaging $29,400 per year); unspecified assistantships also available. Support available to part-time students. Financial award application deadline: 1/15. *Faculty research:* Solid mechanics, controls and robotics, thermo-heat transfer, fluid mechanics, mathematical methods, biomechanics. *Total annual research expenditures:* $4.6 million. *Unit head:* Dr. D. Gary Harlow, Chairman, 610-758-4102, Fax: 610-758-6224, E-mail: dgh0@lehigh.edu. *Application contact:* Allison B. Marsteller, Graduate Coordinator, 610-758-4107, Fax: 610-758-6224, E-mail: alm513@lehigh.edu.
Website: http://www.lehigh.edu/~inmem/

Louisiana State University and Agricultural & Mechanical College, Graduate School, College of Engineering, Department of Mechanical and Industrial Engineering, Baton Rouge, LA 70803. Offers MSME, PhD.

Loyola Marymount University, Frank R. Seaver College of Science and Engineering, Program in Mechanical Engineering, Los Angeles, CA 90045-2659. Offers MSE. *Unit head:* Dr. Rafiqul Noorani, Graduate Program Director, Mechanical Engineering, 310-338-2831, E-mail: rafiqul.noorani@lmu.edu. *Application contact:* Ammar Dalal, Assistant Vice Provost for Graduate Enrollment, 310-338-2721, Fax: 310-338-6086, E-mail: graduateinfo@lmu.edu.
Website: http://cse.lmu.edu/graduateprograms/mechanicalengineeringgraduateprogram

Manhattan College, Graduate Programs, School of Engineering, Program in Mechanical Engineering, Riverdale, NY 10471. Offers MS. *Program availability:* Part-time, evening/weekend. *Degree requirements:* For master's, thesis optional. *Entrance requirements:* For master's, GRE (recommended), minimum GPA of 3.0. Additional exam requirements/recommendations for international students: Required—TOEFL (minimum score 550 paper-based; 80 iBT), IELTS (minimum score 6). *Faculty research:* Thermal analysis of rocket thrust chambers, quality of wood, biomechanics/structural analysis of cacti, orthodontic research.

Marquette University, Graduate School, College of Engineering, Department of Mechanical Engineering, Milwaukee, WI 53201-1881. Offers engineering innovation (Certificate); engineering management (MSEM); mechanical engineering (MS, PhD); new product and process development (Certificate). *Program availability:* Part-time, evening/weekend. Terminal master's awarded for partial completion of doctoral program. *Degree requirements:* For master's, comprehensive exam, thesis (for some programs); for doctorate, comprehensive exam, thesis/dissertation, qualifying exam. *Entrance requirements:* For master's, GRE General Test, minimum GPA of 3.0, official transcripts from all current and previous colleges/universities except Marquette, three letters of recommendation; for doctorate, GRE General Test, minimum GPA of 3.0, official transcripts from all current and previous colleges/universities except Marquette, three letters of recommendation, statement of purpose, copies of any published work. Additional exam requirements/recommendations for international students: Required—TOEFL (minimum score 530 paper-based). Electronic applications accepted. *Faculty research:* Computer-integrated manufacturing, energy conversion, simulation modeling and optimization, applied mechanics, metallurgy.

Mechanical Engineering

Marshall University, Academic Affairs Division, College of Information Technology and Engineering, Program in Mechanical Engineering, Huntington, WV 25755. Offers MSME.

Massachusetts Institute of Technology, School of Engineering, Department of Mechanical Engineering, Cambridge, MA 02139. Offers manufacturing (M Eng); mechanical engineering (SM, PhD, Sc D, Mech E); naval architecture and marine engineering (SM, PhD, Sc D); naval engineering (Naval E); ocean engineering (SM, PhD, Sc D); oceanographic engineering (SM, PhD, Sc D); SM/MBA. Terminal master's awarded for partial completion of doctoral program. *Degree requirements:* For master's, thesis; for doctorate, comprehensive exam, thesis/dissertation; for other advanced degree, comprehensive exam, thesis. *Entrance requirements:* For master's, doctorate, and other advanced degree, GRE General Test. Additional exam requirements/recommendations for international students: Required—TOEFL, IELTS. Electronic applications accepted. *Expenses: Tuition:* Full-time $51,520; part-time $800 per credit hour. *Required fees:* $312. *Faculty research:* Mechanics: modeling, experimentation and computation; design, manufacturing, and product development; controls, instrumentation, and robotics; energy science and engineering; ocean science and engineering; bioengineering; micro- and Nano-engineering.

McGill University, Faculty of Graduate and Postdoctoral Studies, Faculty of Engineering, Department of Mechanical Engineering, Montréal, QC H3A 2T5, Canada. Offers aerospace (M Eng); manufacturing management (MMM); mechanical engineering (M Eng, M Sc, PhD).

McMaster University, School of Graduate Studies, Faculty of Engineering, Department of Mechanical Engineering, Hamilton, ON L8S 4M2, Canada. Offers M Eng, MA Sc, PhD. M Eng degree offered as part of the Advanced Design and Manufacturing Institute (ADMI) group collaboration with the University of Toronto, University of Western Ontario, and University of Waterloo. *Degree requirements:* For master's, thesis; for doctorate, comprehensive exam, thesis/dissertation. *Entrance requirements:* Additional exam requirements/recommendations for international students: Required—TOEFL (minimum score 550 paper-based). *Faculty research:* Manufacturing engineering, dimensional metrology, micro-fluidics, multi-phase flow and heat transfer, process modeling simulation.

McNeese State University, Doré School of Graduate Studies, College of Engineering and Computer Science, Master of Engineering Program, Lake Charles, LA 70609. Offers chemical engineering (M Eng); civil engineering (M Eng); electrical engineering (M Eng); engineering management (M Eng); mechanical engineering (M Eng). *Program availability:* Part-time, evening/weekend. *Entrance requirements:* For master's, GRE, baccalaureate degree, minimum overall GPA of 3.0. Additional exam requirements/recommendations for international students: Required—TOEFL (minimum score 560 paper-based; 83 iBT).

Memorial University of Newfoundland, School of Graduate Studies, Faculty of Engineering and Applied Science, St. John's, NL A1C 5S7, Canada. Offers civil engineering (M Eng, PhD); electrical and computer engineering (M Eng, PhD); mechanical engineering (M Eng, PhD); ocean and naval architecture engineering (M Eng, PhD). *Program availability:* Part-time. *Degree requirements:* For master's, thesis; for doctorate, comprehensive exam, thesis/dissertation, oral thesis defense. *Entrance requirements:* For master's, 2nd class degree; for doctorate, master's degree in engineering. Electronic applications accepted. *Faculty research:* Engineering analysis, environmental and hydrotechnical studies, manufacturing and robotics, mechanics, structures and materials.

Mercer University, Graduate Studies, Macon Campus, School of Engineering, Macon, GA 31207. Offers biomedical engineering (MSE); computer engineering (MSE); electrical engineering (MSE); engineering management (MSE); environmental engineering (MSE); environmental systems (MS); mechanical engineering (MSE); software engineering (MSE); software systems (MS); technical communications management (MS); technical management (MS). *Program availability:* Part-time-only, evening/weekend, online learning. *Degree requirements:* For master's, thesis or alternative. *Entrance requirements:* For master's, GRE (minimum score 300), minimum undergraduate GPA of 3.0. Additional exam requirements/recommendations for international students: Required—TOEFL (minimum score 550 paper-based; 80 iBT). *Expenses:* Contact institution. *Faculty research:* Designing prostheses and orthotics, oxygen transfer and limitations in biological systems, low-cost groundwater development, lung airway and transport, autonomous mobile robots.

Merrimack College, School of Science and Engineering, North Andover, MA 01845-5800. Offers civil engineering (MS); computer science (MS); data science (MS); engineering management (MS); mechanical engineering (MS), including engineering management. *Program availability:* Part-time, evening/weekend, 100% online. *Faculty:* 10 full-time (2 women), 6 part-time/adjunct (1 woman). *Students:* 53 full-time (18 women), 17 part-time (5 women); includes 14 minority (6 Black or African American, non-Hispanic/Latino; 6 Asian, non-Hispanic/Latino; 2 Two or more races, non-Hispanic/Latino), 9 international. Average age 34. 183 applicants, 61% accepted, 40 enrolled. In 2018, 27 master's awarded. *Degree requirements:* For master's, comprehensive exam, thesis optional, internship or capstone (for some programs). *Entrance requirements:* For master's, official college transcripts, resume, personal statement, 2 recommendations. Additional exam requirements/recommendations for international students: Required—TOEFL (minimum score 84 iBT), IELTS (minimum score 6.5), PTE (minimum score 56). *Application deadline:* For fall admission, 8/24 for domestic students, 7/30 for international students; for spring admission, 1/10 for domestic students, 12/10 for international students; for summer admission, 5/10 for domestic students, 4/10 for international students. Applications are processed on a rolling basis. Application fee: $0. Electronic applications accepted. Application fee is waived when completed online. *Expenses:* Contact institution. *Financial support:* Career-related internships or fieldwork, scholarships/grants, health care benefits, and unspecified assistantships available. Support available to part-time students. Financial award application deadline: 5/1; financial award applicants required to submit FAFSA. *Unit head:* Dr. Naira Campbell-Kyureghyan, Dean, 978-837-5265, E-mail: campbellnk@merrimack.edu. *Application contact:* Allison Pena, Graduate Admissions Counselor, 978-837-3563, E-mail: penaa@merrimack.edu.
Website: http://www.merrimack.edu/academics/graduate/

Miami University, College of Engineering and Computing, Department of Mechanical and Manufacturing Engineering, Oxford, OH 45056. Offers MS. *Faculty:* 19 full-time (1 woman). *Students:* 18 full-time (4 women); includes 1 minority (Hispanic/Latino), 8 international. Average age 24. In 2018, 8 master's awarded. *Unit head:* Dr. Amit Shukla, Interim Chair/Professor, 513-529-0713, E-mail: shuklaa@miamioh.edu. *Application contact:* Dr. Amit Shukla, Interim Chair/Professor, 513-529-0713, E-mail: shuklaa@miamioh.edu.
Website: http://miamioh.edu/cec/academics/departments/mme/

Michigan State University, The Graduate School, College of Engineering, Department of Mechanical Engineering, East Lansing, MI 48824. Offers engineering mechanics (MS, PhD); mechanical engineering (MS, PhD). *Entrance requirements:* For master's, GRE General Test. Additional exam requirements/recommendations for international students: Required—TOEFL. Electronic applications accepted.

Michigan Technological University, Graduate School, College of Engineering, Department of Mechanical Engineering-Engineering Mechanics, Houghton, MI 49931. Offers engineering mechanics (MS); hybrid electric drive vehicle engineering (Graduate Certificate); mechanical engineering-engineering mechanics (PhD). *Program availability:* Part-time, evening/weekend, 100% online, blended/hybrid learning. *Faculty:* 70 full-time, 43 part-time/adjunct. *Students:* 307 full-time, 77 part-time; includes 10 minority (3 Black or African American, non-Hispanic/Latino; 3 Asian, non-Hispanic/Latino; 4 Hispanic/Latino), 290 international. Average age 27. 1,021 applicants, 42% accepted, 116 enrolled. In 2018, 119 master's, 20 doctorates, 27 other advanced degrees awarded. Terminal master's awarded for partial completion of doctoral program. *Degree requirements:* For master's, thesis (for some programs); for doctorate, comprehensive exam, thesis/dissertation. *Entrance requirements:* For master's, GRE (Michigan Tech and online students exempt), statement of purpose, personal statement, official transcripts, 2 letters of recommendation, resume/curriculum vitae; for doctorate, GRE (Michigan Tech and online students exempt), MS (preferred), statement of purpose, official transcripts, 2 letters of recommendation, resume/curriculum vitae; for Graduate Certificate, statement of purpose, official transcripts, BS in engineering. Additional exam requirements/recommendations for international students: Required—TOEFL (minimum score 90 iBT) or IELTS (minimum score 7.0). *Application deadline:* For fall admission, 3/1 priority date for domestic and international students; for spring admission, 8/1 priority date for domestic and international students. Applications are processed on a rolling basis. Electronic applications accepted. *Expenses:* $1,143 per credit. *Financial support:* In 2018–19, 262 students received support, including 22 fellowships with tuition reimbursements available (averaging $16,590 per year), 50 research assistantships with tuition reimbursements available (averaging $16,590 per year), 29 teaching assistantships with tuition reimbursements available (averaging $16,590 per year); career-related internships or fieldwork, Federal Work-Study, scholarships/grants, health care benefits, unspecified assistantships, and cooperative program also available. Financial award applicants required to submit FAFSA. *Faculty research:* Mobility and autonomy, complex systems and controls, multi-scale materials and mechanics, thermo-fluids and energy conversion, human-centered engineering. *Total annual research expenditures:* $7.6 million. *Unit head:* Dr. William W. Predebon, Chair, 906-487-2551, Fax: 906-487-2822, E-mail: wwpredeb@mtu.edu. *Application contact:* Cindy Wadaga, Graduate Program Assistant, 906-487-2551, Fax: 906-487-2822, E-mail: cawadaga@mtu.edu.
Website: http://www.mtu.edu/mechanical/

Mississippi State University, Bagley College of Engineering, Department of Mechanical Engineering, Mississippi State, MS 39762. Offers mechanical engineering (MS). *Program availability:* Part-time, blended/hybrid learning. *Faculty:* 22 full-time (5 women), 1 part-time/adjunct (0 women). *Students:* 64 full-time (13 women), 44 part-time (9 women); includes 13 minority (3 Black or African American, non-Hispanic/Latino; 5 Asian, non-Hispanic/Latino; 4 Hispanic/Latino; 1 Two or more races, non-Hispanic/Latino), 31 international. Average age 28. 91 applicants, 67% accepted, 26 enrolled. In 2018, 16 master's, 7 doctorates awarded. *Degree requirements:* For master's, thesis optional, oral exam; for doctorate, thesis/dissertation, qualifying exam, preliminary exam, dissertation defense. *Entrance requirements:* For master's, GRE (for graduates from program not accredited by EAC/ABET), minimum GPA of 2.75; for doctorate, GRE, minimum GPA of 2.75. Additional exam requirements/recommendations for international students: Required—TOEFL (minimum score 550 paper-based; 79 iBT); Recommended—IELTS (minimum score 6.5). *Application deadline:* For fall admission, 7/1 for domestic students, 5/1 for international students; for spring admission, 11/1 for domestic students, 9/1 for international students. Applications are processed on a rolling basis. Application fee: $60 ($80 for international students). Electronic applications accepted. *Expenses:* Tuition, state resident: full-time $8450; part-time $360.59 per credit hour. Tuition, nonresident: full-time $23,140; part-time $969.09 per credit hour. *Required fees:* $110. One-time fee: $55 full-time. Part-time tuition and fees vary according to course load, degree level, campus/location and reciprocity agreements. *Financial support:* In 2018–19, 11 research assistantships with full tuition reimbursements (averaging $15,631 per year), 6 teaching assistantships with full tuition reimbursements (averaging $16,035 per year) were awarded; career-related internships or fieldwork, Federal Work-Study, institutionally sponsored loans, scholarships/grants, and unspecified assistantships also available. Financial award application deadline: 4/1; financial award applicants required to submit FAFSA. *Faculty research:* Fatigue and fracture, heat transfer, fluid dynamics, manufacturing systems, materials. *Total annual research expenditures:* $10.8 million. *Unit head:* Dr. Pedro Mago, Professor/Head, 662-325-6602, Fax: 662-325-7223, E-mail: mago@me.msstate.edu. *Application contact:* Robbie Salters, Admissions and Enrollment Assistant, 662-325-8951, E-mail: gradapps@grad.msstate.edu.
Website: http://www.me.msstate.edu/

Missouri University of Science and Technology, Department of Mechanical and Aerospace Engineering, Rolla, MO 65401. Offers aerospace engineering (MS, PhD); manufacturing engineering (M Eng, MS); mechanical engineering (MS, PhD). *Program availability:* Part-time, evening/weekend. Terminal master's awarded for partial completion of doctoral program. *Degree requirements:* For master's, thesis optional; for doctorate, comprehensive exam, thesis/dissertation. *Entrance requirements:* For master's, GRE General Test (minimum score 1100 verbal and quantitative, writing 3.5), minimum GPA of 3.0; for doctorate, GRE General Test (minimum score: verbal and quantitative 1100, writing 3.5), minimum GPA of 3.5. Additional exam requirements/recommendations for international students: Required—TOEFL (minimum score 550 paper-based). Electronic applications accepted. *Expenses:* Tuition, state resident: full-time $7545.60; part-time $419.20 per credit hour. Tuition, nonresident: full-time $22,169; part-time $1231.60 per credit hour. *International tuition:* $23,518.80 full-time. *Required fees:* $4523.05. Full-time tuition and fees vary according to course load, campus/location, program and reciprocity agreements. *Faculty research:* Dynamics and controls, acoustics, computational fluid dynamics, space mechanics, hypersonics.

Montana State University, The Graduate School, College of Engineering, Department of Mechanical and Industrial Engineering, Bozeman, MT 59717. Offers engineering (PhD), including industrial engineering, mechanical engineering; industrial and management engineering (MS); mechanical engineering (MS). *Program availability:* Part-time. *Degree requirements:* For master's, comprehensive exam, thesis, oral exams; for doctorate, comprehensive exam, thesis/dissertation, qualifying exam. *Entrance requirements:* For master's, GRE, official transcript, minimum GPA of 3.0, demonstrated potential for success, statement of goals, three letters of recommendation, proof of funds affidavit; for doctorate, minimum undergraduate GPA of 3.0, 3.2 graduate; three letters of recommendation; statement of objectives. Additional exam requirements/recommendations for international students: Required—TOEFL or IELTS. Electronic applications accepted. *Faculty research:* Human factors engineering, energy, design and manufacture, systems modeling, materials and structures, measurement systems.

Naval Postgraduate School, Departments and Academic Groups, Department of Mechanical and Aerospace Engineering, Monterey, CA 93943. Offers astronautical engineer (AstE); astronautical engineering (MS); engineering science (MS), including astronautical engineering, mechanical engineering; mechanical and aerospace engineering (PhD); mechanical engineering (MS). Program only open to commissioned officers of the United States and friendly nations and selected United States federal civilian employees. *Program availability:* Part-time, online learning. *Degree requirements:* For master's, thesis (for some programs), capstone or research/dissertation paper (for some programs); for doctorate, thesis/dissertation; for AstE, thesis. *Faculty research:* Sensors and actuators, new materials and methods, mechanics of materials, laser and material interaction, energy harvesting and storage.

Naval Postgraduate School, Departments and Academic Groups, Space Systems Academic Group, Monterey, CA 93943. Offers applied physics (MS); astronautical engineering (MS); computer science (MS); electrical engineering (MS); mechanical engineering (MS); space systems (Engr); space systems operations (MS). Program only open to commissioned officers of the United States and friendly nations and selected United States federal civilian employees. *Program availability:* Part-time. *Degree requirements:* For master's and Engr, thesis; for doctorate, thesis/dissertation. *Faculty research:* Military applications for space; space reconnaissance and remote sensing; radiation-hardened electronics for space; design, construction and operations of small satellites; satellite communications systems.

Naval Postgraduate School, Departments and Academic Groups, Undersea Warfare Academic Group, Monterey, CA 93943. Offers applied mathematics (MS); applied physics (MS); applied science (MS), including acoustics, operations research, physical oceanography, signal processing; electrical engineering (MS); engineering acoustics (MS, PhD); engineering science (MS), including electrical engineering, mechanical engineering; mechanical engineer (ME); mechanical engineering (MS, MSME); meteorology (MS); operations research (MS); physical oceanography (MS). Program only open to commissioned officers of the United States and friendly nations and selected United States federal civilian employees. *Program availability:* Part-time. *Degree requirements:* For master's, thesis. *Faculty research:* Unmanned/autonomous vehicles, sea mines and countermeasures, submarine warfare in the twentieth and twenty-first centuries.

New Jersey Institute of Technology, Newark College of Engineering, Newark, NJ 07102. Offers biomedical engineering (MS, PhD); biopharmaceutical engineering (MS); chemical engineering (MS, PhD); civil engineering (MS, PhD); computer engineering (MS); critical infrastructure systems (MS); electrical engineering (MS, PhD); engineering management (MS); engineering science (MS); environmental engineering (MS, PhD); healthcare systems management (MS); industrial engineering (MS, PhD); internet engineering (MS); manufacturing systems engineering (MS); materials science & engineering (PhD); materials science and engineering (MS); mechanical engineering (MS, PhD); occupational safety and health engineering (MS). *Program availability:* Part-time, evening/weekend. *Faculty:* 147 full-time (26 women), 133 part-time/adjunct (16 women). *Students:* 690 full-time (163 women), 594 part-time (130 women); includes 427 minority (79 Black or African American, non-Hispanic/Latino; 181 Asian, non-Hispanic/Latino; 140 Hispanic/Latino; 27 Two or more races, non-Hispanic/Latino), 553 international. Average age 27. 2,334 applicants, 57% accepted, 452 enrolled. In 2018, 418 master's, 31 doctorates awarded. Terminal master's awarded for partial completion of doctoral program. *Degree requirements:* For master's, thesis (for some programs); for doctorate, thesis/dissertation. *Entrance requirements:* For master's, GRE General Test, minimum GPA 2.8, personal statement, 1 letter of recommendation, transcripts; for doctorate, GRE General Test, minimum GPA of 3.5, personal statement, 3 letters of recommendation, transcripts. Additional exam requirements/recommendations for international students: Required—TOEFL (minimum score 550 paper-based; 79 iBT), IELTS (minimum score 6.5). *Application deadline:* For fall admission, 6/1 priority date for domestic students, 5/1 priority date for international students; for spring admission, 11/15 priority date for domestic and international students. Applications are processed on a rolling basis. Application fee: $75. Electronic applications accepted. *Expenses:* $22,690 per year (in-state), $32,136 per year (out-of-state). *Financial support:* In 2018–19, 396 students received support, including 52 fellowships with full tuition reimbursements available (averaging $22,000 per year), 113 research assistantships with full tuition reimbursements available (averaging $22,000 per year), 101 teaching assistantships with full tuition reimbursements available (averaging $22,000 per year); career-related internships or fieldwork, Federal Work-Study, scholarships/grants, and unspecified assistantships also available. Financial award application deadline: 1/15. *Faculty research:* Nonlinear signal processing, intelligent medical image analysis, calibration issues in coherent localization, computer-aided design, neural network for tool wear measurement. *Total annual research expenditures:* $41.7 million. *Unit head:* Dr. Moshe Kam, Dean, 973-596-5534, Fax: 973-596-2316, E-mail: moshe.kam@njit.edu. *Application contact:* Stephen Eck, Director of Admissions, 973-596-3300, Fax: 973-596-3461, E-mail: admissions@njit.edu. Website: http://engineering.njit.edu/

New Mexico Institute of Mining and Technology, Center for Graduate Studies, Department of Mechanical Engineering, Socorro, NM 87801. Offers explosives engineering (MS); fluid and thermal sciences (MS); mechatronics systems engineering (MS); solid mechanics (MS). *Degree requirements:* For master's, thesis (for some programs). *Entrance requirements:* For master's, GRE General Test. Additional exam requirements/recommendations for international students: Required—TOEFL (minimum score 540 paper-based). *Faculty research:* Vibrations, fluid-structure interactions.

New York Institute of Technology, College of Engineering and Computing Sciences, Department of Mechanical Engineering, Old Westbury, NY 11568-8000. Offers MS. *Program availability:* Part-time. *Faculty:* 9 full-time (2 women), 2 part-time/adjunct (0 women). *Students:* 46 full-time (2 women), 14 part-time (0 women); includes 10 minority (3 Black or African American, non-Hispanic/Latino; 3 Asian, non-Hispanic/Latino; 2 Hispanic/Latino; 2 Two or more races, non-Hispanic/Latino), 40 international. Average age 24. 207 applicants, 52% accepted, 23 enrolled. In 2018, 2 master's awarded. *Degree requirements:* For master's, thesis or alternative. *Entrance requirements:* For master's, BS in mechanical engineering or closely-related field with appropriate prerequisite courses approved by department chairperson; minimum undergraduate GPA of 2.85. Additional exam requirements/recommendations for international students: Required—TOEFL (minimum score 79 iBT), IELTS (minimum score 6), PTE (minimum score 53). *Application deadline:* Applications are processed on a rolling basis. Application fee: $50. Electronic applications accepted. *Expenses: Tuition:* Full-time $1285; part-time $1285 per credit. *Required fees:* $215; $175 per unit. Tuition and fees vary according to course load, degree level and campus/location. *Financial support:* Fellowships with partial tuition reimbursements, teaching assistantships with partial tuition reimbursements, career-related internships or fieldwork, Federal Work-Study, scholarships/grants, tuition waivers (full and partial), and unspecified assistantships available. Support available to part-time students. Financial award application deadline: 2/15; financial award applicants required to submit FAFSA. *Faculty research:* Sensors and actuators; biomechanics and biomedical devices; thermal systems; nanotechnology and nanodevices; dynamic systems and controls. *Unit head:* Dr. Xun Yu, Chair, 516-686-7829, E-mail: xyu13@nyit.edu. *Application contact:* Alice Dolitsky, Director, Graduate Admissions, 516-686-7520, Fax: 516-686-1116, E-mail: admissions@nyit.edu. Website: https://www.nyit.edu/degrees/mechanical_engineering_ms

New York University, Tandon School of Engineering, Department of Mechanical and Aerospace Engineering, New York, NY 10012-1019. Offers mechanical engineering (MS, PhD); mechatronics and robotics (MS). *Program availability:* Part-time, evening/weekend. *Faculty:* 18 full-time (2 women), 11 part-time/adjunct (3 women). *Students:* 116 full-time (22 women), 15 part-time (3 women); includes 12 minority (8 Asian, non-Hispanic/Latino; 3 Hispanic/Latino; 1 Two or more races, non-Hispanic/Latino), 98 international. Average age 25. 563 applicants, 45% accepted, 59 enrolled. In 2018, 66 master's, 3 doctorates awarded. *Degree requirements:* For master's, comprehensive exam (for some programs), thesis (for some programs); for doctorate, comprehensive exam, thesis/dissertation. *Entrance requirements:* Additional exam requirements/recommendations for international students: Required—TOEFL (minimum score 550 paper-based; 90 iBT); Recommended—IELTS (minimum score 7). *Application deadline:* For fall admission, 2/15 priority date for domestic and international students; for spring admission, 11/1 priority date for domestic and international students. Applications are processed on a rolling basis. Application fee: $75. Electronic applications accepted. *Expenses:* Contact institution. *Financial support:* In 2018–19, 74 students received support. Fellowships, research assistantships, teaching assistantships, career-related internships or fieldwork, scholarships/grants, tuition waivers, and unspecified assistantships available. Support available to part-time students. Financial award application deadline: 2/15. *Faculty research:* Underwater applications of dynamical systems, systems science approaches to understanding variation in state traffic and alcohol policies, development of ankle instability rehabilitation robot, synthetic osteochondral grafts for knee osteoarthritis. *Total annual research expenditures:* $11.8 million. *Unit head:* Dr. Richard S. Thorsen, Department Chair, 646-997-3090, E-mail: rthorsen@nyu.edu. *Application contact:* Elizabeth Ensweiler, Senior Director of Graduate Enrollment and Graduate Admissions, 646-997-3182, E-mail: elizabeth.ensweiler@nyu.edu.

North Carolina Agricultural and Technical State University, The Graduate College, College of Engineering, Department of Mechanical Engineering, Greensboro, NC 27411. Offers MSME, PhD. *Program availability:* Part-time. *Degree requirements:* For master's, thesis, qualifying exam, thesis defense; for doctorate, thesis/dissertation. *Entrance requirements:* For master's, BS in mechanical engineering from accredited institution with minimum overall GPA of 3.0; for doctorate, GRE, MS in mechanical engineering or closely-related field with minimum GPA of 3.3. *Faculty research:* Composites, smart materials and sensors, mechanical systems modeling and finite element analysis, computational fluid dynamics and engine research, design and manufacturing.

North Carolina State University, Graduate School, College of Engineering, Department of Mechanical and Aerospace Engineering, Program in Mechanical Engineering, Raleigh, NC 27695. Offers MS, PhD. *Program availability:* Part-time, online learning. *Degree requirements:* For master's, thesis optional, oral exam; for doctorate, thesis/dissertation, oral and preliminary exams. *Entrance requirements:* For master's and doctorate, GRE General Test. Additional exam requirements/recommendations for international students: Required—TOEFL (minimum score 550 paper-based). Electronic applications accepted. *Faculty research:* Vibration and control, fluid dynamics, thermal sciences, structures and materials, aerodynamics acoustics.

North Dakota State University, College of Graduate and Interdisciplinary Studies, College of Engineering, Department of Mechanical Engineering, Fargo, ND 58102. Offers MS, PhD. *Program availability:* Part-time. *Degree requirements:* For master's, thesis; for doctorate, comprehensive exam, thesis/dissertation. *Entrance requirements:* For master's and doctorate, minimum GPA of 3.0. Additional exam requirements/recommendations for international students: Required—TOEFL (minimum score 550 paper-based). Electronic applications accepted. *Faculty research:* Thermodynamics, finite element analysis, automotive systems, robotics, nanotechnology.

Northeastern University, College of Engineering, Boston, MA 02115-5096. Offers bioengineering (MS, PhD); chemical engineering (MS, PhD); civil engineering (MS, PhD); computer engineering (PhD); computer systems engineering (MS); electrical and computer engineering (MS); electrical and computer engineering leadership (MS); electrical engineering (PhD); energy systems (MS); engineering and public policy (MS); engineering management (MS, Certificate); environmental engineering (MS); industrial engineering (MS, PhD); information assurance (PhD); information systems (MS); interdisciplinary engineering (PhD); mechanical engineering (PhD); operations research (MS); telecommunication systems management (MS). *Program availability:* Part-time, online learning. Electronic applications accepted. *Expenses:* Contact institution.

Northern Arizona University, College of Engineering, Informatics, and Applied Sciences, Department of Mechanical Engineering, Flagstaff, AZ 86011. Offers bioengineering (PhD); engineering (M Eng), including mechanical engineering. *Program availability:* Part-time. *Degree requirements:* For master's, variable foreign language requirement, comprehensive exam (for some programs), thesis (for some programs); for doctorate, variable foreign language requirement, comprehensive exam (for some programs), thesis/dissertation (for some programs). *Entrance requirements:* For master's and doctorate, GRE General Test. Additional exam requirements/recommendations for international students: Required—TOEFL (minimum score 80 iBT), IELTS (minimum score 6.5). Electronic applications accepted.

Northern Illinois University, Graduate School, College of Engineering and Engineering Technology, Department of Mechanical Engineering, De Kalb, IL 60115-2854. Offers MS. *Program availability:* Part-time. *Faculty:* 9 full-time (0 women). *Students:* 20 full-time (4 women), 45 part-time (2 women); includes 11 minority (3 Black or African American, non-Hispanic/Latino; 5 Asian, non-Hispanic/Latino; 3 Hispanic/Latino), 22 international. Average age 28. 88 applicants, 36% accepted, 15 enrolled. In 2018, 30 master's awarded. *Degree requirements:* For master's, comprehensive exam, thesis optional. *Entrance requirements:* For master's, GRE General Test, minimum GPA of 2.75. Additional exam requirements/recommendations for international students: Required—TOEFL (minimum score 550 paper-based). *Application deadline:* For fall admission, 6/1 for domestic students, 5/1 for international students; for spring admission, 11/1 for domestic students, 10/1 for international students. Applications are processed on a rolling basis. Application fee: $40. Electronic applications accepted. *Financial support:* In 2018–19, 8 research assistantships with full tuition reimbursements, 38 teaching assistantships with full tuition reimbursements were awarded; fellowships with full tuition reimbursements, Federal Work-Study, scholarships/grants, tuition waivers (full), and staff assistantships also available. Support available to part-time students. Financial award applicants required to submit FAFSA. *Faculty research:* Robotics, nonlinear dynamic systems, piezo mechanics, quartz resonators, sheet metal forming. *Unit head:* Dr. Federico Sciammarella, Interim Chair, 815-753-9970, Fax: 815-753-0416, E-mail: sciammarella@niu.edu. *Application contact:* Graduate School Office, 815-753-0395, E-mail: gradsch@niu.edu. Website: http://www.niu.edu/me/graduate/

Northwestern University, McCormick School of Engineering and Applied Science, Department of Mechanical Engineering, Evanston, IL 60208. Offers MS, PhD. MS and PhD offered through the Graduate School. *Program availability:* Part-time. Terminal master's awarded for partial completion of doctoral program. *Degree requirements:* For master's, thesis optional; for doctorate, comprehensive exam, thesis/dissertation. *Entrance requirements:* For master's and doctorate, GRE General Test. Additional exam requirements/recommendations for international students: Required—TOEFL (minimum score 577 paper-based; 90 iBT), IELTS (minimum score 7). Electronic applications accepted. *Faculty research:* MEMS/nanotechnology, robotics, virtual design and manufacturing, tribology, microfluidics, computational solid and fluid mechanics, composite materials, nondestructive materials characterization and structural reliability, neuromechanics, biomimetics, energy, sustainability, multiscale simulation.

Oakland University, Graduate Study and Lifelong Learning, School of Engineering and Computer Science, Department of Mechanical Engineering, Rochester, MI 48309-4401. Offers MS, PhD. *Program availability:* Part-time, evening/weekend. *Entrance requirements:* For master's, minimum GPA of 3.0. Additional exam requirements/recommendations for international students: Required—TOEFL (minimum score 550 paper-based). Electronic applications accepted. *Expenses:* Contact institution.

The Ohio State University, Graduate School, College of Engineering, Department of Mechanical and Aerospace Engineering, Columbus, OH 43210. Offers aerospace engineering (MS, PhD); mechanical engineering (MS, PhD); nuclear engineering (MS, PhD). *Faculty:* 67. *Students:* 367 (56 women). Average age 25. In 2018, 100 master's, 29 doctorates awarded. *Entrance requirements:* For master's and doctorate, GRE. Additional exam requirements/recommendations for international students: Required—TOEFL (minimum score 550 paper-based; 79 iBT), Michigan English Language Assessment Battery (minimum score 82); Recommended—IELTS (minimum score 7). *Application deadline:* For fall admission, 11/30 priority date for domestic and international students; for spring admission, 10/1 for domestic and international students. Applications are processed on a rolling basis. Application fee: $60 ($70 for international students). Electronic applications accepted. *Financial support:* Fellowships, research assistantships, teaching assistantships, career-related internships or fieldwork, Federal Work-Study, institutionally sponsored loans, and unspecified assistantships available. Support available to part-time students. *Unit head:* Dr. Vish Subramaniam, Chair, 614-292-6096, E-mail: subramaniam.1@osu.edu. *Application contact:* Janeen Sands, Graduate Program Administrator, 614-247-6605, Fax: 614-292-3656, E-mail: maegradadmissions@osu.edu.
Website: http://mae.osu.edu/

Ohio University, Graduate College, Russ College of Engineering and Technology, Department of Mechanical Engineering, Athens, OH 45701-2979. Offers biomedical engineering (MS); mechanical engineering (MS), including CAD/CAM, design, energy, manufacturing, materials, robotics, thermofluids. *Program availability:* Part-time. *Degree requirements:* For master's, comprehensive exam (for some programs), thesis. *Entrance requirements:* For master's, GRE, BS in engineering or science, minimum GPA of 2.8. Additional exam requirements/recommendations for international students: Required—TOEFL (minimum score 550 paper-based; 80 iBT) or IELTS (minimum score 6.5). Electronic applications accepted. *Faculty research:* Biomedical, energy and the environment, materials and manufacturing, bioengineering.

Oklahoma Christian University, Graduate School of Engineering and Computer Science, Oklahoma City, OK 73136-1100. Offers electrical and computer engineering (MSE); engineering management (MSE); mechanical engineering (MSE); software engineering (MSCS, MSE). *Program availability:* Part-time. *Entrance requirements:* Additional exam requirements/recommendations for international students: Required—TOEFL (minimum score 550 paper-based). Electronic applications accepted. *Expenses:* Contact institution.

Oklahoma State University, College of Engineering, Architecture and Technology, School of Mechanical and Aerospace Engineering, Stillwater, OK 74078. Offers mechanical and aerospace engineering (MS, PhD). *Program availability:* Online learning. *Faculty:* 31 full-time (1 woman), 3 part-time/adjunct (1 woman). *Students:* 25 full-time (1 woman), 92 part-time (14 women); includes 14 minority (3 American Indian or Alaska Native, non-Hispanic/Latino; 4 Asian, non-Hispanic/Latino; 2 Hispanic/Latino; 5 Two or more races, non-Hispanic/Latino), 50 international. Average age 26. 181 applicants, 22% accepted, 37 enrolled. In 2018, 25 master's, 4 doctorates awarded. *Entrance requirements:* For master's and doctorate, GRE or GMAT. Additional exam requirements/recommendations for international students: Required—TOEFL (minimum score 550 paper-based; 79 iBT). *Application deadline:* For fall admission, 3/1 priority date for international students; for spring admission, 8/1 priority date for international students. Applications are processed on a rolling basis. Application fee: $40 ($75 for international students). Electronic applications accepted. *Expenses: Tuition, area resident:* Full-time $4148. Tuition, state resident: full-time $4148. Tuition, nonresident: full-time $10,517. *International tuition:* $10,517 full-time. *Required fees:* $4394; $2929 per credit hour. Tuition and fees vary according to course load and program. *Financial support:* Research assistantships, teaching assistantships, career-related internships or fieldwork, Federal Work-Study, scholarships/grants, health care benefits, tuition waivers (partial), and unspecified assistantships available. Support available to part-time students. Financial award application deadline: 3/1; financial award applicants required to submit FAFSA. *Unit head:* Dr. Daniel E. Fisher, Department Head, 405-744-5900, Fax: 405-744-7873, E-mail: maehead@okstate.edu. *Application contact:* Dr. Charlotte Fore, Manager of Graduate Studies and Research Development, 405-744-5900, Fax: 405-744-7873, E-mail: charlotte.fore@okstate.edu.
Website: http://mae.okstate.edu

Old Dominion University, Frank Batten College of Engineering and Technology, Program in Mechanical Engineering, Norfolk, VA 23529. Offers ME, MS, D Eng, PhD. *Program availability:* Part-time, 100% online, blended/hybrid learning. *Degree requirements:* For master's, comprehensive exam (for some programs), thesis (for some programs); for doctorate, thesis/dissertation, diagnostic exam, candidacy exam. *Entrance requirements:* For master's, GRE, minimum GPA of 3.0; for doctorate, GRE, minimum GPA of 3.5. Additional exam requirements/recommendations for international students: Required—TOEFL (minimum score 550 paper-based; 79 iBT), IELTS (minimum score 6.5). Electronic applications accepted. *Faculty research:* Computational applied mechanics, manufacturing, experimental stress analysis, systems dynamics and control, mechanical design.

Oregon State University, College of Engineering, Program in Materials Science, Corvallis, OR 97331. Offers chemical engineering (MS, PhD); chemistry (MS, PhD); civil engineering (MS, PhD); electrical and computer engineering (MS, PhD); forest products (MS, PhD); mathematics (MS, PhD); mechanical engineering (MS, PhD); nuclear engineering (MS); physics (MS, PhD). *Entrance requirements:* For master's and doctorate, GRE. Additional exam requirements/recommendations for international students: Required—TOEFL (minimum score 80 iBT), IELTS (minimum score 6.5). *Expenses:* Contact institution.

Oregon State University, College of Engineering, Program in Mechanical Engineering, Corvallis, OR 97331. Offers M Eng, MS, PhD. *Program availability:* Part-time. *Entrance requirements:* For master's and doctorate, GRE. Additional exam requirements/recommendations for international students: Required—TOEFL (minimum score 80 iBT), IELTS (minimum score 6.5). *Expenses:* Contact institution.

Penn State Harrisburg, Graduate School, School of Science, Engineering and Technology, Middletown, PA 17057. Offers civil engineering (MS); computer science (MS); electrical engineering (M Eng, MS); engineering management (MPS); engineering science (M Eng); environmental engineering (M Eng); environmental pollution control (MEPC, MS); mechanical engineering (MS); structural engineering (Certificate). *Program availability:* Part-time, evening/weekend.

Penn State University Park, Graduate School, College of Engineering, Department of Mechanical and Nuclear Engineering, University Park, PA 16802. Offers additive manufacturing and design (MS); mechanical engineering (MS, PhD); nuclear engineering (M Eng, MS, PhD).

Pittsburg State University, Graduate School, College of Technology, Department of Engineering Technology, Pittsburg, KS 66762. Offers electrical engineering technology (MET); general engineering technology (MET); manufacturing engineering technology (MET); mechanical engineering technology (MET); plastics engineering technology (MET). *Program availability:* Part-time, 100% online, blended/hybrid learning. *Degree requirements:* For master's, thesis optional. *Entrance requirements:* Additional exam requirements/recommendations for international students: Required—TOEFL (minimum score 550 paper-based; 79 iBT), IELTS (minimum score 6.5), PTE (minimum score 51). Electronic applications accepted. *Expenses:* Contact institution.

Polytechnic University of Puerto Rico, Graduate School, Hato Rey, PR 00918. Offers business administration (MBA), including computer information systems, general management, management of information systems, management of international enterprises; civil engineering (ME, MS); computer engineering (ME, MS); computer science (MCS, MS); electrical engineering (ME, MS); engineering management (MEM); environmental management (MEM); landscape architecture (M Land Arch); manufacturing competitiveness (MMC, MS); manufacturing engineering (ME, MS); mechanical engineering (M Mech E). *Accreditation:* ASLA. *Program availability:* Part-time, evening/weekend. *Entrance requirements:* For master's, 3 letters of recommendation.

Portland State University, Graduate Studies, College of Liberal Arts and Sciences, Systems Science Program, Portland, OR 97207-0751. Offers computational intelligence (Certificate); computer modeling and simulation (Certificate); systems science (MS); systems science/anthropology (PhD); systems science/business administration (PhD); systems science/civil engineering (PhD); systems science/economics (PhD); systems science/engineering management (PhD); systems science/general (PhD); systems science/mathematical sciences (PhD); systems science/mechanical engineering (PhD); systems science/psychology (PhD); systems science/sociology (PhD). *Degree requirements:* For master's, comprehensive exam (for some programs), thesis optional; for doctorate, variable foreign language requirement, comprehensive exam (for some programs), thesis/dissertation. *Entrance requirements:* For master's, GRE/GMAT (recommended), minimum GPA of 3.0 on undergraduate or graduate work, 2 letters of recommendation, statement of interest; for doctorate, GMAT, GRE General Test, minimum GPA of 3.0 undergraduate, 3.25 graduate; 3 letters of recommendation; statement of interest. Additional exam requirements/recommendations for international students: Required—TOEFL (minimum score 550 paper-based; 80 iBT). Electronic applications accepted. *Faculty research:* Systems theory and methodology, artificial intelligence neural networks, information theory, nonlinear dynamics/chaos, modeling and simulation.

Portland State University, Graduate Studies, Maseeh College of Engineering and Computer Science, Department of Mechanical and Materials Engineering, Portland, OR 97207-0751. Offers mechanical engineering (PhD). *Program availability:* Part-time, evening/weekend. *Degree requirements:* For master's, thesis or alternative; for doctorate, one foreign language, thesis/dissertation, oral and written exams. *Entrance requirements:* For master's, minimum GPA of 3.0 in upper-division course work, BS in mechanical engineering or allied field, 3 letters of recommendation, statement of purpose, resume/curriculum vitae; for doctorate, GRE General Test, GRE Subject Test, MS, minimum GPA of 3.0 in upper-division course work, 3 letters of recommendation. Additional exam requirements/recommendations for international students: Required—TOEFL (minimum score 550 paper-based; 80 iBT). Electronic applications accepted. *Expenses:* Contact institution. *Faculty research:* Mechanical system modeling, indoor air quality, manufacturing process, computational fluid dynamics, building science.

Princeton University, Graduate School, School of Engineering and Applied Science, Department of Mechanical and Aerospace Engineering, Princeton, NJ 08544. Offers M Eng, MSE, PhD. Terminal master's awarded for partial completion of doctoral program. *Degree requirements:* For master's, thesis (MSE); for doctorate, thesis/dissertation, general exam. *Entrance requirements:* For master's, GRE General Test, 3 letters of recommendation; for doctorate, GRE General Test, official transcript(s), 3 letters of recommendation, personal statement. Additional exam requirements/recommendations for international students: Required—TOEFL. Electronic applications accepted. *Faculty research:* Bioengineering and biomechanics; combustion, energy conversion, and climate; fluid mechanics, dynamics, and control systems; lasers and applied physics; materials and mechanical systems.

Purdue University, College of Engineering, School of Mechanical Engineering, West Lafayette, IN 47907-2088. Offers MS, MSE, MSME, PhD, Certificate. MS and PhD degree programs in biomedical engineering offered jointly with School of Electrical and Computer Engineering and School of Chemical Engineering. *Program availability:* Part-time, online learning. Terminal master's awarded for partial completion of doctoral program. *Degree requirements:* For master's, thesis optional; for doctorate, thesis/dissertation. *Entrance requirements:* For master's and doctorate, GRE General Test, minimum GPA of 3.2. Electronic applications accepted. *Faculty research:* Acoustics, bioengineering, combustion, design, fluid mechanics, heat transfer, manufacturing and materials, mechanics and vibration, nanotechnology, robotics, systems, measurement, and control, thermal systems.

Purdue University Fort Wayne, College of Engineering, Technology, and Computer Science, Department of Civil and Mechanical Engineering, Fort Wayne, IN 46805-1499. Offers civil engineering (MSE); mechanical engineering (MSE). *Program availability:* Part-time. *Entrance requirements:* For master's, minimum GPA of 3.0, bachelor's degree in engineering discipline. Additional exam requirements/recommendations for international students: Required—TOEFL (minimum score 550 paper-based; 79 iBT); Recommended—TWE. Electronic applications accepted. *Faculty research:* Continuous space language model, sensor networks, wireless cloud architecture.

Purdue University Northwest, Graduate Studies Office, School of Engineering, Mathematics, and Science, Department of Engineering, Hammond, IN 46323-2094. Offers computer engineering (MSE); electrical engineering (MSE); engineering (MS); mechanical engineering (MSE). *Program availability:* Evening/weekend. *Entrance requirements:* Additional exam requirements/recommendations for international students: Required—TOEFL.

Queen's University at Kingston, School of Graduate Studies, Faculty of Engineering and Applied Science, Department of Mechanical and Materials Engineering, Kingston, ON K7L 3N6, Canada. Offers M Eng, M Sc, M Sc Eng, PhD. *Program availability:* Part-time. *Degree requirements:* For master's, thesis optional; for doctorate, comprehensive exam, thesis/dissertation. *Entrance requirements:* Additional exam requirements/recommendations for international students: Required—TOEFL. Electronic applications accepted. *Faculty research:* Dynamics and control systems, manufacturing and design, materials and engineering, heat transferring fluid dynamics, energy systems and combustion.

Rensselaer at Hartford, Department of Engineering, Program in Mechanical Engineering, Hartford, CT 06120-2991. Offers ME, MS. *Program availability:* Part-time, evening/weekend. *Degree requirements:* For master's, thesis optional. *Entrance requirements:* For master's, GRE. Additional exam requirements/recommendations for international students: Required—TOEFL (minimum score 600 paper-based; 100 iBT).

Rensselaer Polytechnic Institute, Graduate School, School of Engineering, Program in Mechanical Engineering, Troy, NY 12180-3590. Offers M Eng, MS, D Eng, PhD. *Faculty:* 55 full-time (6 women), 1 part-time/adjunct (0 women). *Students:* 104 full-time (17 women), 42 part-time (4 women); includes 18 minority (3 Black or African American, non-Hispanic/Latino; 5 Asian, non-Hispanic/Latino; 4 Hispanic/Latino; 6 Two or more races, non-Hispanic/Latino), 61 international. Average age 27. 253 applicants, 42% accepted, 40 enrolled. In 2018, 35 master's, 24 doctorates awarded. *Degree requirements:* For master's, thesis (for some programs); for doctorate, thesis/dissertation. *Entrance requirements:* For master's and doctorate, GRE. Additional exam requirements/recommendations for international students: Required—TOEFL (minimum score 600 paper-based; 100 iBT), IELTS (minimum score 7), PTE (minimum score 68). *Application deadline:* For fall admission, 1/1 priority date for domestic and international students; for spring admission, 8/15 priority date for domestic and international students. Applications are processed on a rolling basis. Application fee: $75. Electronic applications accepted. *Financial support:* In 2018–19, research assistantships (averaging $23,000 per year) teaching assistantships (averaging $23,000 per year) were awarded; fellowships also available. Financial award application deadline: 1/1. *Faculty research:* Advanced nuclear materials; aerodynamics; design; dynamics and vibrations, fission systems and radiation transport; fluid mechanics (computational, theoretical, and experimental); heat transfer and energy conversion; manufacturing; medical imaging and health physics; multiscale/computational modeling; nanostructured materials and properties; nuclear physics/nuclear reactor; propulsion. *Total annual research expenditures:* $5.4 million. *Unit head:* Dr. Theo Borca-Tasciuc, Graduate Program Director, 518-276-2627, E-mail: borcat@rpi.edu. *Application contact:* Jarron Decker, Director of Graduate Admissions, 518-276-6216, Fax: 518-276-4072, E-mail: gradadmissions@rpi.edu.
Website: http://mane.rpi.edu/

Rice University, Graduate Programs, George R. Brown School of Engineering, Department of Mechanical Engineering and Materials Science, Houston, TX 77251-1892. Offers materials science (MMS, MS, PhD); mechanical engineering (MME, MS, PhD); MBA/ME. *Program availability:* Part-time. Terminal master's awarded for partial completion of doctoral program. *Degree requirements:* For master's, comprehensive exam, thesis; for doctorate, comprehensive exam, thesis/dissertation. *Entrance requirements:* For master's and doctorate, GRE General Test, minimum GPA of 3.0. Additional exam requirements/recommendations for international students: Required—TOEFL (minimum score 600 paper-based; 90 iBT), IELTS (minimum score 7). Electronic applications accepted. *Faculty research:* Heat transfer, biomedical engineering, fluid dynamics, aero-astronautics, control systems/robotics, materials science.

Rochester Institute of Technology, Graduate Enrollment Services, College of Applied Science and Technology, School of Engineering Technology, MS Program in Manufacturing and Mechanical Systems Integration, Rochester, NY 14623-5603. Offers MS. *Program availability:* Part-time, evening/weekend. *Students:* 48 full-time (7 women), 17 part-time (2 women); includes 2 minority (1 Black or African American, non-Hispanic/Latino; 1 Hispanic/Latino), 57 international. Average age 24. 43 applicants, 84% accepted, 8 enrolled. In 2018, 14 master's awarded. *Degree requirements:* For master's, thesis (for some programs). *Entrance requirements:* For master's, GRE required for applicants with degrees from international universities, minimum GPA of 3.0 (recommended). Additional exam requirements/recommendations for international students: Required—TOEFL (minimum score 550 paper-based; 80 iBT), IELTS (minimum score 6.5), PTE (minimum score 58). *Application deadline:* Applications are processed on a rolling basis. Application fee: $65. Electronic applications accepted. *Financial support:* In 2018–19, 63 students received support. Research assistantships with partial tuition reimbursements available, teaching assistantships with partial tuition reimbursements available, career-related internships or fieldwork, scholarships/grants, and unspecified assistantships available. Support available to part-time students. Financial award applicants required to submit FAFSA. *Faculty research:* Advanced manufacturing in electronics/photonics including materials and reliability development; complex rheological fluid spray research and development; system dynamics modeling and control using computer aided engineering; automation (robotics) using cyber-physical systems; the Internet of Things, and cloud computing; applications-focused plastics and polymer composites research. *Unit head:* Dr. Betsy Dell, Graduate Program Director, 585-475-6577, E-mail: emdmet@rit.edu. *Application contact:* Diane Ellison, Senior Associate Vice President, Graduate Enrollment Services, 585-475-2229, Fax: 585-475-7164, E-mail: gradinfo@rit.edu.
Website: https://www.rit.edu/study/manufacturing-and-mechanical-systems-integration-ms

Rochester Institute of Technology, Graduate Enrollment Services, Kate Gleason College of Engineering, Mechanical Engineering Department, ME Program in Mechanical Engineering, Rochester, NY 14623-5603. Offers ME. *Program availability:* Part-time. *Students:* 102 full-time (10 women), 31 part-time (1 woman); includes 6 minority (1 Black or African American, non-Hispanic/Latino; 2 Asian, non-Hispanic/Latino; 3 Hispanic/Latino), 63 international. Average age 25. 138 applicants, 86% accepted, 44 enrolled. In 2018, 55 master's awarded. *Degree requirements:* For master's, Internship or Project with paper options. *Entrance requirements:* For master's, GRE, minimum GPA of 3.0 (recommended), 2 letters of recommendation. Additional exam requirements/recommendations for international students: Required—TOEFL (minimum score 550 paper-based; 79 iBT), IELTS (minimum score 6.5), PTE (minimum score 58). *Application deadline:* For fall admission, 2/15 priority date for domestic and international students; for spring admission, 12/15 priority date for domestic and international students. Applications are processed on a rolling basis. Application fee: $65. Electronic applications accepted. *Financial support:* In 2018–19, 127 students received support. Research assistantships with partial tuition reimbursements available, teaching assistantships with partial tuition reimbursements available, career-related internships or fieldwork, scholarships/grants, and unspecified assistantships available. Support available to part-time students. Financial award applicants required to submit FAFSA. *Faculty research:* Transportation, energy, communications, healthcare, nano-science and engineering, unmanned aircraft systems, biomedical applications. *Unit head:* Risa Robinson, Graduate Director, 585-475-6445, E-mail: rjreme@rit.edu. *Application contact:* Diane Ellison, Senior Associate Vice President, Graduate Enrollment Services, 585-475-2229, Fax: 585-475-7164, E-mail: gradinfo@rit.edu.
Website: https://www.rit.edu/study/mechanical-engineering-me

Rochester Institute of Technology, Graduate Enrollment Services, Kate Gleason College of Engineering, Mechanical Engineering Department, MS Program in Mechanical Engineering, Rochester, NY 14623-5603. Offers MS. *Program availability:* Part-time. *Students:* 10 full-time (2 women), 4 part-time (1 woman), 10 international. Average age 24. 37 applicants, 3% accepted. In 2018, 8 master's awarded. *Degree requirements:* For master's, thesis. *Entrance requirements:* For master's, GRE, minimum GPA of 3.0 (recommended), two letters of recommendation. Additional exam requirements/recommendations for international students: Required—TOEFL (minimum score 550 paper-based; 79 iBT), IELTS (minimum score 6.5), PTE (minimum score 58).

Application deadline: For fall admission, 2/15 priority date for domestic and international students; for spring admission, 12/15 priority date for domestic and international students. Applications are processed on a rolling basis. Application fee: $65. Electronic applications accepted. *Financial support:* In 2018–19, 17 students received support. Research assistantships with partial tuition reimbursements available, teaching assistantships with partial tuition reimbursements available, career-related internships or fieldwork, scholarships/grants, and unspecified assistantships available. Support available to part-time students. Financial award applicants required to submit FAFSA. *Faculty research:* Transportation, energy, communications, healthcare, nano-science and engineering, unmanned aircraft systems, biomedical applications, aerosol mechanics, interface mechanics during rapid evaporation, low SWAP-C inertial navigation systems. *Unit head:* Risa Robinson, Graduate Director, 585-475-6445, E-mail: rjreme@rit.edu. *Application contact:* Diane Ellison, Senior Associate Vice President, Graduate Enrollment Services, 585-475-2229, Fax: 585-475-7164, E-mail: gradinfo@rit.edu.
Website: https://www.rit.edu/study/mechanical-engineering-ms

Rose-Hulman Institute of Technology, Graduate Studies, Department of Mechanical Engineering, Terre Haute, IN 47803-3999. Offers M Eng, MS. *Program availability:* Part-time. *Faculty:* 29 full-time (6 women). *Students:* 5 full-time (0 women), 2 part-time (0 women); includes 2 minority (both Hispanic/Latino), 1 international. Average age 23. 5 applicants, 80% accepted. In 2018, 4 master's awarded. *Degree requirements:* For master's, thesis. *Entrance requirements:* For master's, GRE, minimum GPA of 3.0. Additional exam requirements/recommendations for international students: Required—TOEFL (minimum score 580 paper-based; 94 iBT), IELTS (minimum score 7). *Application deadline:* For fall admission, 2/1 priority date for domestic and international students; for winter admission, 10/1 for domestic students, 4/1 for international students; for spring admission, 1/15 for domestic students, 11/1 for international students. Applications are processed on a rolling basis. Application fee: $0. Electronic applications accepted. *Expenses:* Tuition: Full-time $46,641. *Financial support:* In 2018–19, 6 students received support. Fellowships with tuition reimbursements available, research assistantships with tuition reimbursements available, institutionally sponsored loans, scholarships/grants, and tuition waivers (full and partial) available. *Faculty research:* Finite elements, MEMS, thermodynamics, heat transfer, design methods, noise and vibration analysis. *Total annual research expenditures:* $253,852. *Unit head:* Dr. Richard Onyancha, Department Head, 812-877-8601, Fax: 812-877-3198, E-mail: onyancha@rose-hulman.edu. *Application contact:* Dr. Craig Downing, Associate Dean of Lifelong Learning, 812-877-8822, E-mail: downing@rose-hulman.edu.
Website: https://www.rose-hulman.edu/academics/academic-departments/mechanical-engineering/index.html

Rowan University, Graduate School, College of Engineering, Department of Mechanical Engineering, Glassboro, NJ 08028-1701. Offers MS. Electronic applications accepted.

Royal Military College of Canada, Division of Graduate Studies, Faculty of Engineering, Department of Mechanical Engineering, Kingston, ON K7K 7B4, Canada. Offers M Eng, MA Sc, PhD. *Degree requirements:* For master's, thesis; for doctorate, comprehensive exam, thesis/dissertation. *Entrance requirements:* For master's, honours degree with second-class standing; for doctorate, master's degree. Electronic applications accepted.

Rutgers University–New Brunswick, Graduate School-New Brunswick, Program in Mechanical and Aerospace Engineering, Piscataway, NJ 08854-8097. Offers design and control (MS, PhD); fluid mechanics (MS, PhD); solid mechanics (MS, PhD); thermal sciences (MS, PhD). *Program availability:* Part-time, evening/weekend. *Degree requirements:* For master's, thesis (for some programs); for doctorate, thesis/dissertation. *Entrance requirements:* For master's, GRE General Test, BS in mechanical/aerospace engineering or related field; for doctorate, GRE General Test, MS in mechanical/aerospace engineering or related field. Additional exam requirements/recommendations for international students: Required—TOEFL. Electronic applications accepted. *Faculty research:* Combustion, propulsion, thermal transport, crystal plasticity, optimization, fabrication, nanoidentation.

Saint Martin's University, Office of Graduate Studies, Program in Mechanical Engineering, Lacey, WA 98503. Offers MME. *Program availability:* Part-time. *Faculty:* 6 full-time (0 women), 1 (woman) part-time/adjunct. *Students:* 1 full-time (0 women), 7 part-time (1 woman); includes 1 minority (Two or more races, non-Hispanic/Latino), 1 international. Average age 34. 10 applicants, 60% accepted, 4 enrolled. In 2018, 5 master's awarded. *Degree requirements:* For master's, thesis optional. *Entrance requirements:* For master's, official transcripts from all colleges and universities attended, three letters of recommendation (preferably from professors, registered engineers or supervisors). Additional exam requirements/recommendations for international students: Required—TOEFL (minimum score 550 paper-based, 79 iBT) or IELTS (minimum score 6.5). *Application deadline:* For fall admission, 4/1 priority date for domestic and international students; for spring admission, 11/1 priority date for domestic and international students. Applications are processed on a rolling basis. Application fee: $50. Electronic applications accepted. *Expenses:* Tuition: Full-time $22,950; part-time $1275 per credit. Tuition and fees vary according to course load, campus/location and program. *Financial support:* Unspecified assistantships available. Financial award application deadline: 3/1; financial award applicants required to submit FAFSA. *Unit head:* Dr. Shawn Duan, Chair, Mechanical Engineering, 360-688-2745, E-mail: sduan@stmartin.edu. *Application contact:* Chantelle Petron Marker, Senior Recruiter, 360-412-6128, E-mail: cmarker@stmartin.edu.
Website: https://www.stmartin.edu

San Diego State University, Graduate and Research Affairs, College of Engineering, Department of Mechanical Engineering, San Diego, CA 92182. Offers engineering sciences and applied mechanics (PhD); manufacture and design (MS); mechanical engineering (MS). PhD offered jointly with University of California, San Diego and Department of Aerospace Engineering and Engineering Mechanics. *Program availability:* Evening/weekend. *Degree requirements:* For master's, comprehensive exam (for some programs), thesis (for some programs); for doctorate, thesis/dissertation. *Entrance requirements:* For master's, GRE General Test; for doctorate, GRE, 3 letters of recommendation. Additional exam requirements/recommendations for international students: Required—TOEFL. Electronic applications accepted. *Faculty research:* Energy analysis and diagnosis, seawater pump design, space-related research.

San Jose State University, Program in Mechanical and Aerospace Engineering, San Jose, CA 95192-0001. Offers aerospace engineering (MS); mechanical engineering (MS). *Program availability:* Part-time. *Entrance requirements:* For master's, GRE. Electronic applications accepted.

Santa Clara University, School of Engineering, Santa Clara, CA 95053. Offers applied mathematics (MS); bioengineering (MS); civil, environmental, and sustainable engineering (MS); computer science and engineering (MS, PhD, Engineer); electrical engineering (MS, PhD, Engineer); engineering management and leadership (MS); mechanical engineering (MS, PhD, Engineer); power systems and sustainable energy (MS); software engineering (MS). *Program availability:* Part-time. *Faculty:* 72 full-time

(24 women), 52 part-time/adjunct (9 women). *Students:* 555 full-time (211 women), 269 part-time (91 women); includes 208 minority (8 Black or African American, non-Hispanic/Latino; 1 American Indian or Alaska Native, non-Hispanic/Latino; 145 Asian, non-Hispanic/Latino; 28 Hispanic/Latino; 26 Two or more races, non-Hispanic/Latino), 472 international. Average age 27. 1,309 applicants, 36% accepted, 269 enrolled. In 2018, 320 master's, 7 doctorates awarded. *Entrance requirements:* For master's, GRE, official transcript; for doctorate, GRE, Official transcript, 500 word statement of purpose, three letters of recommendation. Additional exam requirements/recommendations for international students: Required—TOEFL (minimum score 79 iBT), IELTS (minimum score 6.5). *Application deadline:* For fall admission, 6/1 for domestic students; for winter admission, 9/6 for domestic students; for spring admission, 1/10 for domestic students; for summer admission, 3/6 for domestic students. Application fee: $60. Electronic applications accepted. *Financial support:* Fellowships, Federal Work-Study, and scholarships/grants available. Support available to part-time students. Financial award applicants required to submit FAFSA. *Unit head:* Dr. Elaine Scott, Dean, 408-554-3512, E-mail: epscott@scu.edu. *Application contact:* Stacey Tinker, Director of Admissions and Marketing, 408-554-4748, Fax: 408-554-4323, E-mail: stinker@scu.edu.
Website: http://www.scu.edu/engineering/graduate/

Simon Fraser University, Office of Graduate Studies and Postdoctoral Fellows, Faculty of Applied Sciences, School of Mechatronic Systems Engineering, Burnaby, BC V5A 1S6, Canada. Offers MA Sc, PhD. *Degree requirements:* For master's, one foreign language, thesis; for doctorate, one foreign language, comprehensive exam, thesis/dissertation. *Entrance requirements:* Additional exam requirements/recommendations for international students: Required—TOEFL (minimum score 580 paper-based; 93 iBT), IELTS (minimum score 7), TWE (minimum score 5). Electronic applications accepted. *Faculty research:* Intelligent systems and smart materials, micro-electro mechanical systems (MEMS), biomedical engineering, thermal engineering, alternative energy.

South Carolina State University, College of Graduate and Professional Studies, Department of Civil and Mechanical Engineering Technology, Orangeburg, SC 29117-0001. Offers transportation (MS). *Program availability:* Part-time, evening/weekend. *Faculty:* 4 full-time (2 women). *Students:* 11 full-time (1 woman); includes 10 minority (9 Black or African American, non-Hispanic/Latino; 1 Asian, non-Hispanic/Latino), 1 international. Average age 27. 8 applicants, 88% accepted, 7 enrolled. In 2018, 1 master's awarded. *Degree requirements:* For master's, comprehensive exam, thesis, departmental qualifying exam. *Entrance requirements:* For master's, GRE. Additional exam requirements/recommendations for international students: Recommended—TOEFL. *Application deadline:* For fall admission, 6/15 for domestic and international students; for spring admission, 11/1 for domestic and international students. Application fee: $25. Electronic applications accepted. *Expenses: Tuition, area resident:* Full-time $9928; part-time $552 per credit hour. Tuition, state resident: full-time $9928. Tuition, nonresident: full-time $21,038; part-time $1169 per credit hour. *Required fees:* $1532; $85 per credit hour. *Financial support:* Fellowships, research assistantships, career-related internships or fieldwork, Federal Work-Study, scholarships/grants, and unspecified assistantships available. Financial award application deadline: 6/1. *Unit head:* Dr. Stanley Ihekweazu, Chair, 803-536-7117, Fax: 803-516-4607, E-mail: sihekwea@scsu.edu. *Application contact:* Curtis Foskey, Coordinator of Graduate Admission, 803-536-8419, Fax: 803-536-8812, E-mail: cfoskey@scsu.edu.
Website: http://www.scsu.edu/schoolofgraduatestudies.aspx

South Dakota School of Mines and Technology, Graduate Division, Department of Mechanical Engineering, Rapid City, SD 57701-3995. Offers MS, PhD. *Program availability:* Part-time. *Degree requirements:* For master's, thesis (for some programs); for doctorate, thesis/dissertation. *Entrance requirements:* For master's, GRE General Test. Additional exam requirements/recommendations for international students: Required—TOEFL (minimum score 520 paper-based; 68 iBT), TWE. Electronic applications accepted.

South Dakota State University, Graduate School, Jerome J. Lohr College of Engineering, Department of Mechanical Engineering, Brookings, SD 57007. Offers agricultural, biosystems and mechanical engineering (PhD); mechanical engineering (MS). PhD offered jointly with the Department of Agricultural and Biosystems Engineering. *Program availability:* Part-time. *Degree requirements:* For master's, thesis (for some programs), oral exam. *Entrance requirements:* Additional exam requirements/recommendations for international students: Required—TOEFL (minimum score 525 paper-based; 71 iBT). *Faculty research:* Thermo-fluid science, solid mechanics and dynamics, industrial and quality control engineering, bioenergy.

Southern Illinois University Carbondale, Graduate School, College of Engineering, Department of Mechanical Engineering and Energy Processes, Carbondale, IL 62901-4701. Offers engineering sciences (PhD), including mechanical engineering and energy processes; mechanical engineering (MS). *Degree requirements:* For master's, comprehensive exam, thesis or alternative. *Entrance requirements:* For master's, GRE General Test, minimum GPA of 2.7. Additional exam requirements/recommendations for international students: Required—TOEFL. *Faculty research:* Coal conversion and processing, combustion, materials science and engineering, mechanical system dynamics.

Southern Illinois University Carbondale, Graduate School, College of Engineering, Program in Engineering Science, Carbondale, IL 62901-4701. Offers engineering science (PhD), including civil and environmental engineering, electrical and computer engineering, mechanical engineering and energy processes, mining and mineral resources engineering. *Degree requirements:* For doctorate, thesis/dissertation. *Entrance requirements:* For doctorate, GRE General Test, minimum GPA of 3.5. Additional exam requirements/recommendations for international students: Required—TOEFL.

Southern Illinois University Edwardsville, Graduate School, School of Engineering, Department of Mechanical and Industrial Engineering, Program in Mechanical Engineering, Edwardsville, IL 62026. Offers MS. *Program availability:* Part-time, evening/weekend. *Degree requirements:* For master's, comprehensive exam (for some programs), thesis (for some programs). *Entrance requirements:* Additional exam requirements/recommendations for international students: Required—TOEFL (minimum score 550 paper-based; 79 iBT), IELTS (minimum score 6.5). Electronic applications accepted.

Southern Methodist University, Lyle School of Engineering, Department of Mechanical Engineering, Dallas, TX 75205. Offers manufacturing systems management (MS); mechanical engineering (MS, PhD). *Program availability:* Part-time, evening/weekend, online learning. Terminal master's awarded for partial completion of doctoral program. *Degree requirements:* For master's, thesis optional; for doctorate, thesis/dissertation, oral and written qualifying exams, oral final exam. *Entrance requirements:* For master's, GRE General Test, minimum GPA of 3.0 in last 2 years; bachelor's degree in engineering, mathematics, or sciences; for doctorate, preliminary counseling exam, minimum graduate GPA of 3.0, bachelor's degree in related field. Additional exam requirements/recommendations for international students: Required—TOEFL. *Faculty research:* Design, systems, and controls; thermal and fluid sciences.

Stanford University, School of Engineering, Department of Mechanical Engineering, Stanford, CA 94305-2004. Offers biomechanical engineering (MSE); design impact (MSE); mechanical engineering (MS, PhD, Engr). *Expenses: Tuition:* Full-time $50,703; part-time $32,970 per year. *Required fees:* $651.
Website: http://me.stanford.edu/

Stevens Institute of Technology, Graduate School, Charles V. Schaefer Jr. School of Engineering and Science, Department of Mechanical Engineering, Program in Mechanical Engineering, Hoboken, NJ 07030. Offers M Eng, PhD, Eng. *Program availability:* Part-time, evening/weekend. *Faculty:* 32 full-time (4 women), 10 part-time/adjunct (0 women). *Students:* 101 full-time (20 women), 50 part-time (9 women); includes 18 minority (3 Black or African American, non-Hispanic/Latino; 15 Asian, non-Hispanic/Latino), 60 international. Average age 26. In 2018, 74 master's, 8 doctorates, 39 other advanced degrees awarded. Terminal master's awarded for partial completion of doctoral program. *Degree requirements:* For master's, thesis optional, minimum B average in major field and overall; for doctorate, comprehensive exam (for some programs), thesis/dissertation; for Eng, minimum B average. *Entrance requirements:* For master's, GRE/GMAT scores: GRE scores are required for all applicants applying to a full-time graduate program in the Schaefer School of Engineering and Science (SES). International applicants must submit TOEFL/IELTS scores and fulfill the English Language Proficiency Requirements in order to be considered. Additional exam requirements/recommendations for international students: Required—TOEFL (minimum score 74 iBT), IELTS (minimum score 6). *Application deadline:* For fall admission, 4/15 for domestic and international students; for spring admission, 11/1 for domestic and international students; for summer admission, 5/1 for domestic students. Applications are processed on a rolling basis. Application fee: $60. Electronic applications accepted. *Expenses: Tuition:* Full-time $35,960; part-time $1620 per credit. *Required fees:* $1290; $600 per semester. Tuition and fees vary according to course load. *Financial support:* Fellowships, research assistantships, teaching assistantships, career-related internships or fieldwork, Federal Work-Study, scholarships/grants, and unspecified assistantships available. Financial award application deadline: 2/15; financial award applicants required to submit FAFSA. *Unit head:* Dr. Jean Zu, Dean of SES, 201-216.8233, Fax: 201-216.8372, E-mail: Jean.Zu@stevens.edu. *Application contact:* Graduate Admissions, 888-783-8367, Fax: 888-511-1306, E-mail: graduate@stevens.edu.

Stony Brook University, State University of New York, Graduate School, College of Engineering and Applied Sciences, Department of Mechanical Engineering, Stony Brook, NY 11794. Offers MS, PhD. *Program availability:* Part-time, evening/weekend. *Faculty:* 20 full-time (1 woman), 4 part-time/adjunct (1 woman). *Students:* 120 full-time (20 women), 22 part-time (2 women); includes 33 minority (4 Black or African American, non-Hispanic/Latino; 16 Asian, non-Hispanic/Latino; 12 Hispanic/Latino; 1 Two or more races, non-Hispanic/Latino), 80 international. Average age 25. 190 applicants, 67% accepted, 55 enrolled. In 2018, 49 master's, 4 doctorates awarded. Terminal master's awarded for partial completion of doctoral program. *Degree requirements:* For master's, thesis or alternative; for doctorate, comprehensive exam, thesis/dissertation. *Entrance requirements:* For master's, GRE General Test, minimum GPA of 3.0; for doctorate, GRE General Test, minimum GPA of 3.5. Additional exam requirements/recommendations for international students: Required—TOEFL (minimum score 90 iBT). *Application deadline:* For fall admission, 1/15 for domestic students; for spring admission, 10/1 for domestic students. Application fee: $100. *Expenses:* Contact institution. *Financial support:* In 2018–19, 16 research assistantships, 23 teaching assistantships were awarded; fellowships also available. *Faculty research:* Solid mechanics, composite materials, elastomers or coatings, high temperature coatings, thin films. *Total annual research expenditures:* $3.1 million. *Unit head:* Dr. Jeffrey Q. Ge, Chair, 631-632-8305, Fax: 631-632-8544, E-mail: qiaode.ge@stonybrook.edu. *Application contact:* Dianna Berger, Coordinator, 631-632-8340, Fax: 631-632-8544, E-mail: mechanicaengineeringgraduate@stonybrook.edu.
Website: http://me.eng.sunysb.edu/

Syracuse University, College of Engineering and Computer Science, Programs in Mechanical and Aerospace Engineering, Syracuse, NY 13244. Offers MS, PhD. *Program availability:* Part-time. *Students:* Average age 25. In 2018, 55 master's, 8 doctorates awarded. *Degree requirements:* For master's, project or thesis; for doctorate, comprehensive exam, thesis/dissertation. *Entrance requirements:* For master's and doctorate, GRE General Test, official transcripts, personal statement, three letters of recommendation, resume. Additional exam requirements/recommendations for international students: Required—TOEFL (minimum score 100 iBT). *Application deadline:* For fall admission, 7/1 priority date for domestic students, 6/1 priority date for international students; for spring admission, 11/15 priority date for domestic students, 10/15 priority date for international students. Applications are processed on a rolling basis. Application fee: $75. Electronic applications accepted. *Financial support:* Fellowships with full tuition reimbursements, research assistantships, teaching assistantships, scholarships/grants, and tuition waivers (partial) available. Financial award application deadline: 1/1. *Faculty research:* Solid mechanics and materials, fluid mechanics, thermal sciences, controls and robotics. *Unit head:* Dr. Young Bai Moon, III, Department Chair, 315-443-4366, E-mail: gradinfo@syr.edu. *Application contact:* Kathleen Joyce, Assistant Dean, 315-443-2219, E-mail: topgrads@syr.edu.
Website: http://eng-cs.syr.edu/our-departments/mechanical-and-aerospace-engineering/

Temple University, College of Engineering, Department of Mechanical Engineering, Philadelphia, PA 19122-6096. Offers MSME. *Program availability:* Part-time, evening/weekend. Terminal master's awarded for partial completion of doctoral program. *Degree requirements:* For master's, thesis optional. *Entrance requirements:* For master's, GRE General Test, minimum GPA of 3.0; BS in engineering from ABET-accredited or equivalent institution; resume; goals statement; three letters of reference; official transcripts. Additional exam requirements/recommendations for international students: Required—TOEFL (minimum score 550 paper-based; 79 iBT), IELTS (minimum score 6.5), PTE (minimum score 53). Electronic applications accepted. *Expenses:* Contact institution. *Faculty research:* Renewable and alternative energy, advanced materials, nanotechnology, dynamic systems and controls, thin film photovoltaics, thermal and fluid engineering, biomechanics and biofluid mechanics.

Temple University, College of Engineering, PhD in Engineering Program, Philadelphia, PA 19122-6096. Offers bioengineering (PhD); civil engineering (PhD); electrical engineering (PhD); environmental engineering (PhD); mechanical engineering (PhD). *Program availability:* Part-time, evening/weekend. *Degree requirements:* For doctorate, thesis/dissertation, preliminary exam, dissertation proposal and defense. *Entrance requirements:* For doctorate, GRE, minimum undergraduate GPA of 3.0; MS in engineering from ABET-accredited or equivalent institution (preferred); resume; goals statement; three letters of reference; official transcripts. Additional exam requirements/recommendations for international students: Required—TOEFL (minimum score 550 paper-based; 79 iBT), IELTS (minimum score 6.5), PTE (minimum score 53). Electronic applications accepted. *Expenses:* Contact institution. *Faculty research:* Advanced/computer-aided manufacturing and advanced materials processing; bioengineering; computer engineering; construction engineering and management; dynamics, controls, and systems; energy and environmental science; engineering physics and engineering mathematics; green engineering; signal processing and communication; transportation engineering; water resources, hydrology, and environmental engineering.

See Display on page 59 and Close-Up on page 73.

Tennessee State University, The School of Graduate Studies and Research, College of Engineering, Nashville, TN 37209-1561. Offers biomedical engineering (ME); civil engineering (ME); computer and information systems engineering (MS, PhD); electrical engineering (ME); environmental engineering (ME); manufacturing engineering (ME); mathematical sciences (MS); mechanical engineering (ME). *Program availability:* Part-time, evening/weekend. *Degree requirements:* For master's, project; for doctorate, comprehensive exam, thesis/dissertation. *Entrance requirements:* For doctorate, minimum GPA of 3.3. *Faculty research:* Robotics, intelligent systems, human-computer interaction software systems, biomedical engineering, signal/image processing, probabilistic design, intelligent manufacturing, cooperative mobile robots, condition based maintenance, sensor fusion.

Tennessee Technological University, College of Graduate Studies, College of Engineering, Department of Mechanical Engineering, Cookeville, TN 38505. Offers MS. *Program availability:* Part-time. *Faculty:* 25 full-time (2 women). *Students:* 10 full-time (0 women), 28 part-time (1 woman); includes 1 minority (Asian, non-Hispanic/Latino), 8 international. 43 applicants, 74% accepted, 13 enrolled. In 2018, 20 master's awarded. *Degree requirements:* For master's, thesis. *Entrance requirements:* For master's, GRE. Additional exam requirements/recommendations for international students: Required—TOEFL (minimum score 550 paper-based; 79 iBT), IELTS (minimum score 5.5), PTE (minimum score 53), or TOEIC (Test of English as an International Communication). *Application deadline:* For fall admission, 8/1 for domestic students, 5/1 for international students; for spring admission, 12/1 for domestic students, 10/1 for international students; for summer admission, 5/1 for domestic students, 2/1 for international students. Applications are processed on a rolling basis. Application fee: $35 ($40 for international students). Electronic applications accepted. *Financial support:* Fellowships, research assistantships, and teaching assistantships available. Financial award application deadline: 4/1. *Faculty research:* Energy-related systems, design, acoustics and acoustical systems. *Unit head:* Dr. Mohan Rao, Chairperson, 931-372-3254, Fax: 931-372-6340, E-mail: mrao@tntech.edu. *Application contact:* Shelia K. Kendrick, Coordinator of Graduate Studies, 931-372-3808, Fax: 931-372-3497, E-mail: skendrick@tntech.edu.

Texas A&M University, College of Engineering, Department of Mechanical Engineering, College Station, TX 77843. Offers mechanical engineering (PhD). *Faculty:* 63. *Students:* 399 full-time (52 women), 69 part-time (9 women); includes 51 minority (6 Black or African American, non-Hispanic/Latino; 17 Asian, non-Hispanic/Latino; 21 Hispanic/Latino; 7 Two or more races, non-Hispanic/Latino), 311 international. Average age 27. 1,026 applicants, 30% accepted, 130 enrolled. In 2018, 103 master's, 35 doctorates awarded. *Degree requirements:* For master's, thesis (for MS); for doctorate, thesis/dissertation. *Entrance requirements:* For master's, GRE General Test, minimum undergraduate GPA of 3.0; for doctorate, GRE General Test, minimum graduate GPA of 3.5. Additional exam requirements/recommendations for international students: Required—TOEFL (minimum score 570 paper-based; 80 iBT), IELTS (minimum score 6), PTE (minimum score 53). *Application deadline:* For fall admission, 3/1 priority date for domestic students, 3/1 for international students; for winter admission, 11/1 for domestic and international students; for spring admission, 8/1 for domestic and international students. Applications are processed on a rolling basis. Application fee: $50 ($90 for international students). Electronic applications accepted. *Expenses:* Contact institution. *Financial support:* In 2018–19, 369 students received support, including 57 fellowships with tuition reimbursements available (averaging $7,815 per year), 244 research assistantships with tuition reimbursements available (averaging $14,644 per year), 121 teaching assistantships with tuition reimbursements available (averaging $12,953 per year); career-related internships or fieldwork, institutionally sponsored loans, scholarships/grants, traineeships, health care benefits, tuition waivers (full and partial), and unspecified assistantships also available. Support available to part-time students. Financial award application deadline: 3/15; financial award applicants required to submit FAFSA. *Faculty research:* Thermal/fluid sciences, materials/manufacturing and controls systems. *Unit head:* Dr. Andreas A. Polycarpou, Department Head, 979-845-5337, E-mail: apolycarpou@tamu.edu. *Application contact:* Dr. Daniel A. McAdams, Graduate Program Director, 979-862-7834, E-mail: dmcadams@tamu.edu.
Website: http://engineering.tamu.edu/mechanical

Texas A&M University–Kingsville, College of Graduate Studies, Frank H. Dotterweich College of Engineering, Department of Mechanical and Industrial Engineering, Program in Mechanical Engineering, Kingsville, TX 78363. Offers ME, MS. *Degree requirements:* For master's, variable foreign language requirement, comprehensive exam, thesis (for some programs). *Entrance requirements:* For master's, GRE (minimum score quantitative and verbal 950 on old scale), MAT, GMAT, minimum GPA 2.6. Additional exam requirements/recommendations for international students: Required—TOEFL (minimum score 550 paper-based; 79 iBT). Electronic applications accepted.

Texas State University, The Graduate College, College of Science and Engineering, Program in Engineering, San Marcos, TX 78666. Offers civil engineering (MS); electrical engineering (MS); industrial engineering (MS); mechanical and manufacturing engineering (MS). *Program availability:* Part-time. *Faculty:* 15 full-time (2 women). *Students:* 46 full-time (14 women), 41 part-time (13 women); includes 11 minority (3 Asian, non-Hispanic/Latino; 7 Hispanic/Latino; 1 Two or more races, non-Hispanic/Latino), 67 international. Average age 27. 105 applicants, 64% accepted, 31 enrolled. In 2018, 13 master's awarded. *Degree requirements:* For master's, comprehensive exam, thesis (for some programs), thesis or research project. *Entrance requirements:* For master's, official GRE (general test only) required with competitive scores in the verbal reasoning and quantitative reasoning sections, baccalaureate degree from regionally-accredited university in engineering, computer science, physics, technology, or closely-related field with minimum GPA of 3.0 on last 60 undergraduate semester hours; resume or curriculum vitae; 2 letters of recommendation; statement of purpose conveying research interest and professional aspirations. Additional exam requirements/recommendations for international students: Required—TOEFL (minimum score 550 paper-based; 78 iBT), IELTS (minimum score 6.5). *Application deadline:* For fall admission, 2/15 priority date for domestic students, 2/1 priority date for international students. Application fee: $55 ($90 for international students). Electronic applications accepted. *Expenses:* Tuition, state resident: full-time $8102; part-time $4051 per semester. Tuition, nonresident: full-time $18,229; part-time $9115 per semester. *International tuition:* $18,229 full-time. *Required fees:* $2116; $120 per credit hour. Tuition and fees vary according to course load. *Financial support:* In 2018–19, 52 students received support, including 14 research assistantships (averaging $12,742 per year), 34 teaching assistantships (averaging $12,483 per year); Federal Work-Study, institutionally sponsored loans, scholarships/grants, health care benefits, and unspecified assistantships also available. Support available to part-time students. Financial award application deadline: 1/15; financial award applicants required to submit FAFSA. *Faculty research:* Computer Architecture & Digital Image Processing; Industrial robotics on a mobile platform; supply chain management optimization modeling and algorithms; Modeling and analysis of manufacturing systems especially semiconductor manufacturing; smart grids for big data analytics and demand response; Digital Signal/Image/Speach Processing & Data Compression; Health care systems engineering and anaylsis of patient flow. *Total annual research expenditures:* $920,229. *Unit head:* Dr. Vishu Viswanathan, Graduate Advisor, 512-245-1826, Fax: 512-245-8365, E-mail: v_v42@txstate.edu. *Application contact:* Dr. Andrea Golato, Dean of Graduate School, 512-245-2581, Fax: 512-245-8365, E-mail: gradcollege@txstate.edu.
Website: http://www.engineering.txstate.edu/Programs/Graduate.html

Tufts University, School of Engineering, Department of Mechanical Engineering, Medford, MA 02155. Offers human factors (MS); mechanical engineering (MS, PhD); PhD/PhD. *Program availability:* Part-time. Terminal master's awarded for partial completion of doctoral program. *Degree requirements:* For master's, thesis; for doctorate, thesis/dissertation. *Entrance requirements:* For master's and doctorate, GRE General Test. Additional exam requirements/recommendations for international students: Required—TOEFL (minimum score 550 paper-based; 80 iBT), IELTS (minimum score 6.5). Electronic applications accepted. *Expenses: Tuition:* Full-time $51,288; part-time $1710 per credit hour. *Required fees:* $904. Full-time tuition and fees vary according to degree level, program and student level. Part-time tuition and fees vary according to course load. *Faculty research:* Applied mechanics, biomaterials, controls/robotics, design/systems, human factors.

Tuskegee University, Graduate Programs, College of Engineering, Department of Mechanical Engineering, Tuskegee, AL 36088. Offers MSME. *Degree requirements:* For master's, thesis or alternative. *Entrance requirements:* For master's, GRE General Test, GRE Subject Test. Additional exam requirements/recommendations for international students: Required—TOEFL (minimum score 500 paper-based). *Faculty research:* Superalloys, fatigue and surface machinery, energy management, solar energy.

Universidad del Turabo, Graduate Programs, School of Engineering, Gurabo, PR 00778-3030. Offers computer engineering (M Eng); electrical engineering (M Eng); mechanical engineering (M Eng); telecommunications and network systems administration (M Eng). *Entrance requirements:* For master's, GRE, EXADEP or GMAT, interview, essay, official transcript, recommendation letters. Electronic applications accepted.

Université de Moncton, Faculty of Engineering, Program in Mechanical Engineering, Moncton, NB E1A 3E9, Canada. Offers M Sc A. *Degree requirements:* For master's, thesis, proficiency in French. *Faculty research:* Composite materials, thermal energy systems, control systems, fluid mechanics and heat transfer, CAD/CAM and robotics.

Université de Sherbrooke, Faculty of Engineering, Department of Mechanical Engineering, Sherbrooke, QC J1K 2R1, Canada. Offers M Sc A, PhD. *Degree requirements:* For master's, one foreign language, thesis; for doctorate, comprehensive exam, thesis/dissertation. *Entrance requirements:* For master's, bachelor's degree in engineering or equivalent; for doctorate, master's degree in engineering or equivalent. Electronic applications accepted. *Faculty research:* Acoustics, aerodynamics, vehicle dynamics, composite materials, heat transfer.

Université Laval, Faculty of Sciences and Engineering, Department of Mechanical Engineering, Programs in Mechanical Engineering, Québec, QC G1K 7P4, Canada. Offers M Sc, PhD. *Program availability:* Part-time. Terminal master's awarded for partial completion of doctoral program. *Degree requirements:* For master's, thesis; for doctorate, comprehensive exam, thesis/dissertation. *Entrance requirements:* For master's and doctorate, knowledge of French. Electronic applications accepted.

University at Buffalo, the State University of New York, Graduate School, School of Engineering and Applied Sciences, Department of Mechanical and Aerospace Engineering, Buffalo, NY 14260. Offers aerospace engineering (MS, PhD); mechanical engineering (MS, PhD). *Program availability:* Part-time. Terminal master's awarded for partial completion of doctoral program. *Degree requirements:* For master's, comprehensive exam, project or thesis; for doctorate, thesis/dissertation. *Entrance requirements:* For master's and doctorate, GRE General Test, GRE Subject Test. Additional exam requirements/recommendations for international students: Required—TOEFL (minimum score 79 iBT). Electronic applications accepted. *Faculty research:* Fluid and thermal sciences; computational and applied mechanics; materials; bioengineering; design and manufacturing; dynamics, control and mechatronics.

The University of Akron, Graduate School, College of Engineering, Department of Mechanical Engineering, Akron, OH 44325. Offers engineering (PhD); mechanical engineering (MS). *Program availability:* Part-time, evening/weekend. Terminal master's awarded for partial completion of doctoral program. *Degree requirements:* For master's, thesis optional; for doctorate, one foreign language, thesis/dissertation, candidacy exam, qualifying exam. *Entrance requirements:* For master's, GRE, minimum GPA of 2.75, baccalaureate degree in engineering, three letters of recommendation, statement of purpose; for doctorate, GRE, minimum GPA of 3.0 with bachelor's degree, 3.5 with master's degree; three letters of recommendation; statement of purpose; resume. Additional exam requirements/recommendations for international students: Required—TOEFL (minimum score 79 iBT), IELTS (minimum score 6.5). Electronic applications accepted. *Faculty research:* Materials science, tribology and lubrication, vibration and dynamic analysis, solid mechanics, micro and nanoelectromechanical systems (MEMS and NEMS), bio-mechanics.

The University of Alabama, Graduate School, College of Engineering, Department of Mechanical Engineering, Tuscaloosa, AL 35487. Offers MS, PhD. *Program availability:* Part-time, online learning. Terminal master's awarded for partial completion of doctoral program. *Degree requirements:* For master's, comprehensive exam, thesis (for some programs); for doctorate, comprehensive exam, thesis/dissertation. *Entrance requirements:* For master's, GRE General Test, minimum GPA of 3.0; for doctorate, GRE General Test, minimum GPA of 3.0 with MS, 3.3 without MS. Additional exam requirements/recommendations for international students: Required—TOEFL (minimum score 600 paper-based). Electronic applications accepted. *Faculty research:* Thermal/fluids, robotics, numerical modeling, energy conservation, energy and combustion systems, internal combustion engines, heating, ventilation and air conditioning, medical devices, manufacturing, vehicular systems, controls, acoustics solid mechanics and materials.

The University of Alabama at Birmingham, School of Engineering, Program in Mechanical Engineering, Birmingham, AL 35294. Offers mechanical engineering (MSME). *Faculty:* 7 full-time (0 women), 3 part-time/adjunct (1 woman). *Students:* 30 full-time (1 woman), 17 part-time (2 women); includes 4 minority (3 Black or African American, non-Hispanic/Latino; 1 Two or more races, non-Hispanic/Latino), 34 international. Average age 26. 57 applicants, 70% accepted, 14 enrolled. In 2018, 19 master's awarded. *Degree requirements:* For master's, thesis (for some programs). *Entrance requirements:* For master's, GRE (minimum 50th percentile ranking on Quantitative and Verbal sections), minimum GPA of 3.0 overall or over last 60 semester hours of earned credit. Additional exam requirements/recommendations for international students: Required—TOEFL (minimum score 80 iBT). *Application deadline:* For fall admission, 8/1 for domestic and international students; for spring admission, 12/1 for domestic and international students; for summer admission, 5/1 for domestic and international students. Applications are processed on a rolling basis. Application fee: $50 ($60 for international students). Electronic applications accepted. *Expenses:* Contact institution. *Financial support:* In 2018–19, 18 students received support, including 1 fellowship with full tuition reimbursement available (averaging $29,000 per year), 9 research assistantships with full tuition reimbursements available, 8 teaching assistantships. *Faculty research:* Computational mechanics, manufacturing and robotics, vehicle dynamics and drive train engineering, power generation and renewable energy, medical device engineering. *Total annual research expenditures:* $2.2 million. *Unit head:* Dr. David Littlefield, Graduate Program Director, 205-934-8460, E-mail: littlefield@uab.edu. *Application contact:* Jesse Keppley, Director of Academic and Student Services, 205-996-5696, E-mail: gradschool@uab.edu.
Website: http://www.uab.edu/engineering/home/departments-research/me/graduate

Mechanical Engineering

The University of Alabama in Huntsville, School of Graduate Studies, College of Engineering, Department of Chemical and Materials Engineering, Huntsville, AL 35899. Offers biotechnology science and engineering (PhD); chemical and materials engineering (MSE); materials science (PhD); mechanical engineering (PhD), including chemical engineering. *Program availability:* Part-time. *Faculty:* 3 full-time (1 woman), 1 part-time/adjunct. *Students:* 5 full-time (1 woman), 4 part-time (1 woman); includes 1 minority (Asian, non-Hispanic/Latino), 1 international. Average age 25. 12 applicants, 25% accepted, 2 enrolled. In 2018, 2 master's awarded. *Degree requirements:* For master's, comprehensive exam, thesis or alternative, oral and written exams; for doctorate, comprehensive exam, thesis/dissertation. *Entrance requirements:* For master's, GRE General Test, appropriate bachelor's degree, minimum GPA of 3.0; for doctorate, GRE General Test, minimum GPA of 3.0. Additional exam requirements/recommendations for international students: Required—TOEFL (minimum score 500 paper-based; 80 iBT), IELTS (minimum score 6.5). *Application deadline:* For fall admission, 7/15 priority date for domestic students, 4/1 priority date for international students; for spring admission, 11/30 priority date for domestic students, 9/1 priority date for international students. Applications are processed on a rolling basis. Application fee: $50. Electronic applications accepted. *Expenses: Tuition, area resident:* Full-time $10,632; part-time $412 per credit hour. Tuition, state resident: full-time $10,632. Tuition, nonresident: full-time $23,604; part-time $412 per credit hour. *Required fees:* $582; $582. Tuition and fees vary according to course load and program. *Financial support:* In 2018–19, 4 students received support, including 1 research assistantship with full tuition reimbursement available (averaging $2,500 per year), 3 teaching assistantships with full tuition reimbursements available (averaging $5,500 per year); career-related internships or fieldwork, Federal Work-Study, institutionally sponsored loans, scholarships/grants, health care benefits, and unspecified assistantships also available. Support available to part-time students. Financial award application deadline: 4/1; financial award applicants required to submit FAFSA. *Faculty research:* Ultrathin films for optical, sensor and biological applications; materials processing including low gravity; hypergolic reactants; computational fluid dynamics; biofuels and renewable resources. *Unit head:* Dr. Anuradha Subramanian, Chair, 256-824-6194, Fax: 256-824-6839, E-mail: anu.subramanian@uah.edu. *Application contact:* Kim Gray, Graduate Studies Admissions Coordinator, 256-824-6002, Fax: 256-824-6405, E-mail: deangrad@uah.edu.
Website: http://www.cme.uah.edu/

The University of Alabama in Huntsville, School of Graduate Studies, College of Engineering, Department of Mechanical and Aerospace Engineering, Huntsville, AL 35899. Offers aerospace systems engineering (MS, PhD). *Program availability:* Part-time. *Faculty:* 18 full-time (1 woman), 1 part-time/adjunct. *Students:* 75 full-time (11 women), 87 part-time (8 women); includes 20 minority (6 Black or African American, non-Hispanic/Latino; 4 American Indian or Alaska Native, non-Hispanic/Latino; 8 Asian, non-Hispanic/Latino; 1 Hispanic/Latino; 1 Two or more races, non-Hispanic/Latino), 31 international. Average age 29. 167 applicants, 57% accepted, 40 enrolled. In 2018, 33 master's, 7 doctorates awarded. *Degree requirements:* For master's, comprehensive exam, thesis or alternative, oral and written exams; for doctorate, comprehensive exam, thesis/dissertation, oral and written exams. *Entrance requirements:* For master's, GRE General Test, BSE, minimum GPA of 3.0; for doctorate, GRE General Test, minimum GPA of 3.0. Additional exam requirements/recommendations for international students: Required—TOEFL (minimum score 500 paper-based; 80 iBT), IELTS (minimum score 6.5). *Application deadline:* For fall admission, 7/15 priority date for domestic students, 4/1 for international students; for spring admission, 11/30 for domestic students, 9/1 for international students. Applications are processed on a rolling basis. Application fee: $50. Electronic applications accepted. *Expenses: Tuition, area resident:* Full-time $10,632; part-time $412 per credit hour. Tuition, state resident: full-time $10,632. Tuition, nonresident: full-time $23,604; part-time $412 per credit hour. *Required fees:* $582; $582. Tuition and fees vary according to course load and program. *Financial support:* In 2018–19, 70 students received support, including 43 research assistantships with full tuition reimbursements available (averaging $6,736 per year), 27 teaching assistantships with full tuition reimbursements available (averaging $5,609 per year); career-related internships or fieldwork, Federal Work-Study, institutionally sponsored loans, scholarships/grants, health care benefits, and unspecified assistantships also available. Support available to part-time students. Financial award application deadline: 4/1; financial award applicants required to submit FAFSA. *Faculty research:* Rocket propulsion and plasma engineering, materials engineering and solid mechanics, energy conversion, transport, and storage. *Unit head:* Dr. Keith Hollingsworth, Chair, 256-824-5421, Fax: 256-824-6758, E-mail: keith.hollingsworth@uah.edu. *Application contact:* Kim Gray, Graduate Studies Admissions Coordinator, 256-824-6002, Fax: 256-824-6405, E-mail: deangrad@uah.edu.
Website: http://www.mae.uah.edu/graduate.shtml

University of Alaska Fairbanks, College of Engineering and Mines, Department of Mechanical Engineering, Fairbanks, AK 99775-5905. Offers MS. *Program availability:* Part-time. *Faculty:* 6 full-time (1 woman). *Students:* 3 full-time (2 women), 2 part-time (0 women); includes 2 minority (1 Hispanic/Latino; 1 Two or more races, non-Hispanic/Latino). Average age 28. 14 applicants, 57% accepted, 2 enrolled. In 2018, 4 master's awarded. *Degree requirements:* For master's, comprehensive exam, oral defense of project or thesis. *Entrance requirements:* For master's, GRE General Test, bachelor's degree from accredited institution with minimum cumulative undergraduate and major GPA of 3.0. Additional exam requirements/recommendations for international students: Required—TOEFL (minimum score 550 paper-based; 79 iBT), IELTS (minimum score 6.5). *Application deadline:* For fall admission, 6/1 for domestic students, 3/1 for international students; for spring admission, 10/15 for domestic students, 9/1 for international students. Applications are processed on a rolling basis. Application fee: $60. Electronic applications accepted. *Expenses:* College of Engineering and Mines (CEM) tuition has a 20% surcharge per credit hour over that for credits of most other UAF colleges. Assuming 60 credits for PhD and 32 for Master's, this augments costs by $6,180 for in-state PhD, $3,296 for in-state Master's, $12,948 for non-resident PhD and $6,912 for non-resident Masters students, respectively. *Financial support:* In 2018–19, 2 research assistantships with full tuition reimbursements (averaging $12,295 per year), 1 teaching assistantship with full tuition reimbursement (averaging $7,629 per year) were awarded; fellowships with full tuition reimbursements, career-related internships or fieldwork, Federal Work-Study, scholarships/grants, health care benefits, and unspecified assistantships also available. Support available to part-time students. Financial award application deadline: 7/1; financial award applicants required to submit FAFSA. *Faculty research:* Cold regions engineering, fluid mechanics, heat transfer, energy systems, indoor air quality. *Unit head:* Dr. Rorik Peterson, Department Chair, 907-474-7136, E-mail: fymech@uaf.edu. *Application contact:* Samara Taber, Director of Admissions, 907-474-7500, E-mail: uaf-admissions@alaska.edu.
Website: http://cem.uaf.edu/me/

University of Alberta, Faculty of Graduate Studies and Research, Department of Mechanical Engineering, Edmonton, AB T6G 2E1, Canada. Offers engineering management (M Eng); mechanical engineering (M Eng, M Sc, PhD); MBA/M Eng. *Program availability:* Part-time. *Degree requirements:* For master's, thesis; for doctorate, thesis/dissertation. *Entrance requirements:* For master's and doctorate, minimum GPA of 7.0 on a 9.0 scale. Additional exam requirements/recommendations for international students: Required—TOEFL (minimum score 580 paper-based). *Faculty research:* Combustion and environmental issues, advanced materials, computational fluid dynamics, biomedical, acoustics and vibrations.

The University of Arizona, College of Engineering, Department of Aerospace and Mechanical Engineering, Tucson, AZ 85721. Offers aerospace engineering (MS, PhD); mechanical engineering (MS, PhD). *Program availability:* Part-time. *Degree requirements:* For master's, thesis or alternative; for doctorate, thesis/dissertation. *Entrance requirements:* For master's, GRE General Test, 3 letters of recommendation; for doctorate, GRE General Test, 3 letters of recommendation, statement of purpose. Additional exam requirements/recommendations for international students: Required—TOEFL (minimum score 550 paper-based; 79 iBT). Electronic applications accepted.

University of Arkansas, Graduate School, College of Engineering, Department of Mechanical Engineering, Fayetteville, AR 72701. Offers MSE, MSME, PhD. *Program availability:* Part-time, online learning. *Students:* 40 applicants, 65% accepted. In 2018, 7 master's, 4 doctorates awarded. *Degree requirements:* For master's, thesis optional; for doctorate, one foreign language, thesis/dissertation. *Application deadline:* For fall admission, 8/1 for domestic students, 4/1 for international students; for spring admission, 12/1 for domestic students, 10/1 for international students; for summer admission, 4/15 for domestic students, 3/1 for international students. Applications are processed on a rolling basis. Application fee: $60. Electronic applications accepted. *Financial support:* In 2018–19, 16 research assistantships, 1 teaching assistantship were awarded; fellowships, career-related internships or fieldwork, and Federal Work-Study also available. Support available to part-time students. Financial award application deadline: 4/1; financial award applicants required to submit FAFSA. *Unit head:* Dr. Darin Nutter, Department Head, 479-575-4503, E-mail: dnutter@uark.edu. *Application contact:* Dr. Steve Tung, Graduate Programs Coordinator and Curriculum Committee Chair, 479-575-5557, E-mail: chstung@uark.edu.
Website: https://mechanical-engineering.uark.edu/

University of Bridgeport, School of Engineering, Department of Mechanical Engineering, Bridgeport, CT 06604. Offers MS. *Degree requirements:* For master's, thesis optional. *Entrance requirements:* Additional exam requirements/recommendations for international students: Recommended—TOEFL (minimum score 550 paper-based; 80 iBT), IELTS (minimum score 6.5). Electronic applications accepted.

The University of British Columbia, Faculty of Applied Science, Department of Mechanical Engineering, Vancouver, BC V6T 1Z4, Canada. Offers M Eng, MA Sc, PhD. *Degree requirements:* For master's, thesis; for doctorate, comprehensive exam, thesis/dissertation. *Entrance requirements:* For master's, bachelor's degree, minimum B+ average; for doctorate, master's degree, minimum B+ average. Additional exam requirements/recommendations for international students: Required—TOEFL (minimum score 93 iBT), IELTS; Recommended—TWE. Electronic applications accepted. *Expenses:* Contact institution. *Faculty research:* Applied mechanics, manufacturing, robotics and controls, thermodynamics and combustion, fluid/aerodynamics, acoustics.

University of Calgary, Faculty of Graduate Studies, Schulich School of Engineering, Program in Mechanical and Manufacturing Engineering, Calgary, AB T2N 1N4, Canada. Offers M Eng, M Sc, PhD. *Program availability:* Part-time. *Degree requirements:* For master's, thesis (for some programs); for doctorate, thesis/dissertation, candidacy exam. *Entrance requirements:* For master's, minimum GPA of 3.0; for doctorate, minimum GPA of 3.3. Additional exam requirements/recommendations for international students: Required—TOEFL (minimum score 550 paper-based; 80 iBT), IELTS (minimum score 7). *Faculty research:* Thermofluids, solid mechanics, materials, biomechanics, manufacturing.

University of California, Berkeley, Graduate Division, College of Engineering, Department of Mechanical Engineering, Berkeley, CA 94720. Offers M Eng, MS, PhD. Terminal master's awarded for partial completion of doctoral program. *Degree requirements:* For master's, comprehensive exam (for some programs), thesis (for some programs), comprehensive exam or thesis (MS); for doctorate, thesis/dissertation, preliminary and qualifying exams. *Entrance requirements:* For master's and doctorate, GRE General Test, minimum GPA of 3.0, 3 letters of recommendation. Additional exam requirements/recommendations for international students: Required—TOEFL (minimum score 570 paper-based; 90 iBT). Electronic applications accepted.

University of California, Davis, College of Engineering, Program in Mechanical and Aeronautical Engineering, Davis, CA 95616. Offers aeronautical engineering (M Engr, MS, D Engr, PhD, Certificate); mechanical engineering (M Engr, MS, D Engr, PhD, Certificate); M Engr/MBA. *Degree requirements:* For master's, comprehensive exam (for some programs), thesis (for some programs); for doctorate, thesis/dissertation. *Entrance requirements:* For master's and doctorate, GRE General Test, minimum GPA of 3.0. Additional exam requirements/recommendations for international students: Required—TOEFL (minimum score 550 paper-based). Electronic applications accepted.

University of California, Irvine, Samueli School of Engineering, Department of Mechanical and Aerospace Engineering, Irvine, CA 92697. Offers MS, PhD. *Program availability:* Part-time. *Students:* 137 full-time (37 women), 12 part-time (2 women); includes 30 minority (4 Black or African American, non-Hispanic/Latino; 13 Asian, non-Hispanic/Latino; 9 Hispanic/Latino; 4 Two or more races, non-Hispanic/Latino), 90 international. Average age 27. 517 applicants, 25% accepted, 46 enrolled. In 2018, 29 master's, 5 doctorates awarded. Terminal master's awarded for partial completion of doctoral program. *Entrance requirements:* For master's and doctorate, GRE General Test, minimum GPA of 3.0, 3 letters of recommendation. Additional exam requirements/recommendations for international students: Required—TOEFL (minimum score 550 paper-based). *Application deadline:* For fall admission, 1/15 priority date for domestic students, 1/15 for international students. Applications are processed on a rolling basis. Application fee: $105 ($125 for international students). Electronic applications accepted. *Financial support:* Fellowships, research assistantships with full tuition reimbursements, teaching assistantships, institutionally sponsored loans, traineeships, health care benefits, and unspecified assistantships available. Financial award application deadline: 3/1; financial award applicants required to submit FAFSA. *Faculty research:* Thermal and fluid sciences, combustion and propulsion, control systems, robotics, lightweight structures. *Unit head:* Prof. Kenneth Mease, Chair, 949-824-5855, Fax: 949-824-8585, E-mail: kmease@uci.edu. *Application contact:* Prof. Roger Rangel, Graduate Admissions Advisor, 949-824-4033, Fax: 949-824-8585, E-mail: rhrangel@uci.edu.
Website: http://mae.eng.uci.edu/

University of California, Los Angeles, Graduate Division, Henry Samueli School of Engineering and Applied Science, Department of Mechanical and Aerospace Engineering, Program in Mechanical Engineering, Los Angeles, CA 90095-1597. Offers MS, PhD. *Degree requirements:* For master's, comprehensive exam or thesis; for doctorate, thesis/dissertation, qualifying exams. *Entrance requirements:* For master's, GRE General Test, minimum GPA of 3.0; for doctorate, GRE General Test, minimum GPA of 3.25. Additional exam requirements/recommendations for international students: Required—TOEFL (minimum score 560 paper-based; 87 iBT), IELTS (minimum score 7). Electronic applications accepted. *Faculty research:* Applied mathematics, applied plasma physics, dynamics, fluid mechanics, heat and mass transfer, design, robotics and manufacturing, nanoelectromechanical/microelectromechanical systems (NEMS/MEMS), structural and solid mechanics, systems and control.

University of California, Merced, Graduate Division, School of Engineering, Merced, CA 95343. Offers biological engineering and small scale technologies (MS, PhD); electrical engineering and computer science (MS, PhD); environmental systems (MS, PhD); management of innovation, sustainability, and technology (MM); mechanical engineering (MS); mechanical engineering and applied mechanics (PhD). *Faculty:* 60 full-time (16 women). *Students:* 219 full-time (72 women), 1 part-time (0 women); includes 43 minority (2 Black or African American, non-Hispanic/Latino; 17 Asian, non-Hispanic/Latino; 20 Hispanic/Latino; 1 Native Hawaiian or other Pacific Islander, non-Hispanic/Latino; 3 Two or more races, non-Hispanic/Latino), 145 international. Average age 28. 371 applicants, 46% accepted, 75 enrolled. In 2018, 30 master's, 17 doctorates awarded. Terminal master's awarded for partial completion of doctoral program. *Degree requirements:* For master's, variable foreign language requirement, comprehensive exam, thesis or alternative, oral defense; for doctorate, variable foreign language requirement, comprehensive exam, thesis/dissertation, oral defense. *Entrance requirements:* For master's and doctorate, GRE. Additional exam requirements/recommendations for international students: Required—TOEFL (minimum score 550 paper-based; 80 iBT); Recommended—IELTS (minimum score 6.5). *Application deadline:* For fall admission, 1/15 priority date for domestic and international students. Application fee: $105 ($125 for international students). Electronic applications accepted. *Expenses:* In-state tuition $11442 per year; Out-of-state tuition $26544 per year; Student Fees $1765 per year. *Financial support:* In 2018–19, 200 students received support, including 14 fellowships with full tuition reimbursements available (averaging $20,851 per year), 70 research assistantships with full tuition reimbursements available (averaging $18,334 per year), 116 teaching assistantships with full tuition reimbursements available (averaging $19,841 per year); scholarships/grants, traineeships, and health care benefits also available. *Faculty research:* Sustainability systems engineering and resource management: food, energy, water; biomolecular engineering and biotechnology; computational science and data analytics; artificial intelligence, machine learning, internet of things, human computer interface; cyber-physical systems and automation. *Total annual research expenditures:* $3.1 million. *Unit head:* Dr. Mark Matsumoto, Dean, 209-228-4047, Fax: 209-228-4047, E-mail: mmatsumoto@ucmerced.edu. *Application contact:* Tsu Ya, Director of Admissions and Academic Services, 209-228-4521, Fax: 209-228-6906, E-mail: tya@ucmerced.edu.

University of California, Riverside, Graduate Division, Department of Mechanical Engineering, Riverside, CA 92521. Offers MS, PhD. *Program availability:* Part-time. Terminal master's awarded for partial completion of doctoral program. *Degree requirements:* For master's, comprehensive exam or thesis, seminar in mechanical engineering; for doctorate, comprehensive exam, thesis/dissertation, seminar in mechanical engineering. *Entrance requirements:* Additional exam requirements/recommendations for international students: Required—TOEFL (minimum score 550 paper-based; 80 iBT). *Faculty research:* Advanced robotics and machine design, air quality modeling group, computational fluid dynamics, computational mechanics and materials, biomaterials and nanotechnology laboratory.

University of California, San Diego, Graduate Division, Department of Mechanical and Aerospace Engineering, Program in Mechanical Engineering, La Jolla, CA 92093. Offers MS, PhD. *Students:* 233 full-time (53 women), 30 part-time (8 women). 716 applicants, 47% accepted, 115 enrolled. In 2018, 65 master's, 20 doctorates awarded. *Degree requirements:* For master's, comprehensive exam (for some programs), thesis (for some programs), comprehensive exam or thesis; for doctorate, comprehensive exam, thesis/dissertation. *Entrance requirements:* For master's and doctorate, GRE General Test, minimum GPA of 3.0. Additional exam requirements/recommendations for international students: Required—TOEFL (minimum score 550 paper-based; 80 iBT), IELTS (minimum score 7). *Application deadline:* For fall admission, 12/18 for domestic students. Application fee: $105 ($125 for international students). Electronic applications accepted. *Financial support:* Fellowships, research assistantships, teaching assistantships, scholarships/grants, and unspecified assistantships available. Financial award applicants required to submit FAFSA. *Faculty research:* Mechatronics, sensor integration, robotics, vehicle design in water/land/air, medical devices. *Unit head:* Carlos Coimbra, Chair, 858-534-4285, E-mail: mae-chair-l@ucsd.edu. *Application contact:* Joana Halnez, Graduate Coordinator, 858-534-4387, E-mail: mae-gradadm-l@ucsd.edu.
Website: http://maeweb.ucsd.edu/

University of California, Santa Barbara, Graduate Division, College of Engineering, Department of Mechanical Engineering, Santa Barbara, CA 93106-5070. Offers bioengineering (PhD); mechanical engineering (MS); MS/PhD. Terminal master's awarded for partial completion of doctoral program. *Degree requirements:* For master's, thesis optional; for doctorate, comprehensive exam, thesis/dissertation. *Entrance requirements:* For master's and doctorate, GRE. Additional exam requirements/recommendations for international students: Required—TOEFL (minimum score 550 paper-based; 80 iBT), IELTS (minimum score 7). Electronic applications accepted. *Faculty research:* Micro/nanoscale technology; bioengineering and systems biology; computational science and engineering; dynamics systems, controls and robotics; thermofluid sciences; solid mechanics, materials, and structures.

University of Central Florida, College of Engineering and Computer Science, Department of Mechanical and Aerospace Engineering, Program in Mechanical Engineering, Orlando, FL 32816. Offers MSME, PhD. *Students:* 149 full-time (19 women), 87 part-time (9 women); includes 69 minority (3 Black or African American, non-Hispanic/Latino; 21 Asian, non-Hispanic/Latino; 43 Hispanic/Latino; 2 Two or more races, non-Hispanic/Latino), 86 international. Average age 28. 204 applicants, 45% accepted, 55 enrolled. In 2018, 34 master's, 15 doctorates awarded. *Degree requirements:* For master's, thesis or alternative; for doctorate, thesis/dissertation, candidacy exam, departmental qualifying exam. *Entrance requirements:* For master's, goal statement, resume; for doctorate, GRE, letters of recommendation, goal statement, resume. Additional exam requirements/recommendations for international students: Required—TOEFL. *Application deadline:* For fall admission, 7/15 for domestic students; for spring admission, 12/1 for domestic students. Application fee: $30. Electronic applications accepted. *Financial support:* In 2018–19, 119 students received support, including 34 fellowships with partial tuition reimbursements available (averaging $11,212 per year), 77 research assistantships with partial tuition reimbursements available (averaging $14,373 per year), 49 teaching assistantships with partial tuition reimbursements available (averaging $10,997 per year); career-related internships or fieldwork, institutionally sponsored loans, scholarships/grants, health care benefits, tuition waivers (partial), and unspecified assistantships also available. Financial award application deadline: 3/1; financial award applicants required to submit FAFSA. *Unit head:* Dr. Jihua Gou, Program Coordinator, 407-823-2155, E-mail: jihua.gou@ucf.edu. *Application contact:* Associate Director, Graduate Admissions, 407-823-2766, Fax: 407-823-6442, E-mail: gradadmissions@ucf.edu.
Website: http://mae.ucf.edu/academics/graduate/

University of Central Oklahoma, The Jackson College of Graduate Studies, College of Mathematics and Science, Department of Engineering and Physics, Edmond, OK 73034-5209. Offers engineering physics (MS), including biomedical engineering, electrical engineering, mechanical systems, physics. *Program availability:* Part-time. *Degree requirements:* For master's, thesis optional. *Entrance requirements:* For master's, GRE, 24 hours of course work in physics or equivalent, mathematics through differential equations, minimum GPA of 2.75 overall and 3.0 in last 60 hours attempted, two letters of recommendation. Additional exam requirements/recommendations for international students: Required—TOEFL (minimum score 550 paper-based; 79 iBT), IELTS (minimum score 6.5). Electronic applications accepted.

University of Cincinnati, Graduate School, College of Engineering and Applied Science, Department of Mechanical and Materials Engineering, Program in Mechanical Engineering, Cincinnati, OH 45221. Offers MS, PhD. *Program availability:* Evening/weekend. Terminal master's awarded for partial completion of doctoral program. *Degree requirements:* For master's, oral exam or thesis defense; for doctorate, variable foreign language requirement, thesis/dissertation. *Entrance requirements:* For master's and doctorate, GRE General Test. Additional exam requirements/recommendations for international students: Required—TOEFL (minimum score 575 paper-based). Electronic applications accepted. *Faculty research:* Signature analysis, structural analysis, energy, design, robotics.

University of Colorado Boulder, Graduate School, College of Engineering and Applied Science, Department of Mechanical Engineering, Boulder, CO 80309. Offers ME, MS, PhD. Terminal master's awarded for partial completion of doctoral program. *Degree requirements:* For master's, comprehensive exam, thesis optional; for doctorate, comprehensive exam, thesis/dissertation, final and preliminary exams. *Entrance requirements:* For master's and doctorate, minimum undergraduate GPA of 3.0. Additional exam requirements/recommendations for international students: Required—TOEFL. Electronic applications accepted. Application fee is waived when completed online. *Faculty research:* Mechanical engineering; nanotechnology; materials engineering; materials sciences; materials: engineering properties.

University of Colorado Denver, College of Engineering, Design and Computing, Department of Mechanical Engineering, Denver, CO 80217. Offers mechanical engineering (MS); mechanics (MS); thermal sciences (MS). *Program availability:* Part-time, evening/weekend. *Degree requirements:* For master's, comprehensive exam, 30 credit hours, project or thesis. *Entrance requirements:* For master's, GRE, three letters of recommendation, personal statement. Additional exam requirements/recommendations for international students: Required—TOEFL (minimum score 537 paper-based; 75 iBT); Recommended—IELTS (minimum score 6.8). *Expenses:* Tuition, state resident: full-time $6786; part-time $337 per credit hour. Tuition, nonresident: full-time $22,590; part-time $1255 per credit hour. *Required fees:* $1231; $137 per credit hour. Tuition and fees vary according to program and reciprocity agreements.

University of Colorado Denver, College of Engineering, Design and Computing, Master of Engineering Program, Denver, CO 80217-3364. Offers civil engineering (M Eng), including civil engineering, geographic information systems, transportation systems; electrical engineering (M Eng); mechanical engineering (M Eng). *Program availability:* Part-time. *Entrance requirements:* For master's, GRE (for those with GPA below 2.75), transcripts, references, statement of purpose. *Expenses:* Tuition, state resident: full-time $6786; part-time $337 per credit hour. Tuition, nonresident: full-time $22,590; part-time $1255 per credit hour. *Required fees:* $1231; $137 per credit hour. Tuition and fees vary according to program and reciprocity agreements.

University of Connecticut, Graduate School, School of Engineering, Department of Mechanical Engineering, Storrs, CT 06269. Offers MS, PhD. Terminal master's awarded for partial completion of doctoral program. *Degree requirements:* For master's, comprehensive exam, thesis or alternative; for doctorate, thesis/dissertation. *Entrance requirements:* For master's and doctorate, GRE General Test, GRE Subject Test. Additional exam requirements/recommendations for international students: Required—TOEFL (minimum score 550 paper-based). Electronic applications accepted.

University of Dayton, Department of Mechanical and Aerospace Engineering, Dayton, OH 45469. Offers aerospace engineering (MSAE, PhD); mechanical engineering (MSME, PhD); renewable and clean energy (MS). *Program availability:* Part-time, 100% online, blended/hybrid learning. *Degree requirements:* For master's, variable foreign language requirement, comprehensive exam (for some programs), thesis; for doctorate, variable foreign language requirement, comprehensive exam, thesis/dissertation, departmental qualifying exam. *Entrance requirements:* For master's, BS in engineering, math, or physics; minimum GPA of 3.0; for doctorate, GRE. Additional exam requirements/recommendations for international students: Required—TOEFL (minimum score 550 paper-based; 80 iBT), IELTS (minimum score 6.5). Electronic applications accepted. *Faculty research:* Biomechanics, combustion, renewable energy, mechatronics, aerodynamics.

University of Delaware, College of Engineering, Department of Mechanical Engineering, Newark, DE 19716. Offers MEM, MSME, PhD. *Program availability:* Part-time. Terminal master's awarded for partial completion of doctoral program. *Degree requirements:* For master's, thesis (for some programs); for doctorate, thesis/dissertation. *Entrance requirements:* For master's and doctorate, GRE General Test. Additional exam requirements/recommendations for international students: Required—TOEFL (minimum score 600 paper-based). Electronic applications accepted. *Faculty research:* Biomedical engineering, clean energy, composites and nanotechnology, robotics and controls, fluid mechanics.

University of Denver, Daniel Felix Ritchie School of Engineering and Computer Science, Department of Mechanical and Materials Engineering, Denver, CO 80208. Offers bioengineering (MS); engineering (MS, PhD), including management; materials science (MS, PhD); mechanical engineering (MS, PhD). *Program availability:* Part-time. *Faculty:* 13 full-time (2 women), 2 part-time/adjunct (1 woman). *Students:* 4 full-time (1 woman), 33 part-time (7 women); includes 5 minority (2 Black or African American, non-Hispanic/Latino; 2 Hispanic/Latino; 1 Two or more races, non-Hispanic/Latino), 11 international. Average age 28. 71 applicants, 63% accepted, 15 enrolled. In 2018, 11 master's, 3 doctorates awarded. Terminal master's awarded for partial completion of doctoral program. *Degree requirements:* For master's, thesis optional; for doctorate, comprehensive exam, thesis/dissertation. *Entrance requirements:* For master's, GRE General Test, bachelor's degree in engineering or closely related field, transcripts, personal statement, resume or curriculum vitae, two letters of recommendation; for doctorate, GRE General Test, master's degree in engineering or closely related field, transcripts, personal statement, resume or curriculum vitae, two letters of recommendation, recommended that applicants find a research advisor before submitting the application. Additional exam requirements/recommendations for international students: Required—TOEFL (minimum score 550 paper-based; 80 iBT). *Application deadline:* For fall admission, 1/15 priority date for domestic and international students; for winter admission, 10/25 for domestic and international students; for spring admission, 2/7 for domestic and international students; for summer admission, 4/24 for domestic and international students. Applications are processed on a rolling basis. Application fee: $65. Electronic applications accepted. *Expenses:* $33,183 per year full-time. *Financial support:* In 2018–19, 25 students received support, including 10 research assistantships with tuition reimbursements available (averaging $12,917 per year), 13 teaching assistantships with tuition reimbursements available (averaging $15,289 per year); Federal Work-Study, institutionally sponsored loans, scholarships/grants, health care benefits, and unspecified assistantships also available. Financial award application deadline: 2/15; financial award applicants required to submit FAFSA.

Mechanical Engineering

Faculty research: Cardiac biomechanics, novel high voltage/temperature materials and structures, high speed stereo radiography, musculoskeletal modeling, composites. *Unit head:* Dr. Matt Gordon, Professor and Chair, 303-871-3580, E-mail: matthew.gordon@du.edu. *Application contact:* Chrissy Alexander, Assistant to the Chair, 303-871-3041, E-mail: Christine.Alexander@du.edu.
Website: http://ritchieschool.du.edu/departments/mme/

University of Detroit Mercy, College of Engineering and Science, Detroit, MI 48221. Offers chemistry (MS); civil and environmental engineering (DE); electrical and computer engineering (ME); electrical engineering (DE); engineering management (M Eng Mgt); environmental engineering (MEE); mechanical engineering (MME, DE); product development (MS); software engineering (MSSE); teaching of mathematics (MATM). *Program availability:* Part-time, evening/weekend. *Degree requirements:* For doctorate, thesis/dissertation. Electronic applications accepted. Application fee is waived when completed online. *Expenses:* Contact institution.

University of Florida, Graduate School, Herbert Wertheim College of Engineering, Department of Mechanical and Aerospace Engineering, Gainesville, FL 32611. Offers aerospace engineering (ME, MS, PhD); mechanical engineering (ME, MS, PhD). *Program availability:* Part-time, online learning. *Degree requirements:* For master's, thesis (for some programs); for doctorate, comprehensive exam, thesis/dissertation. *Entrance requirements:* For master's and doctorate, minimum GPA of 3.0. Additional exam requirements/recommendations for international students: Required—TOEFL (minimum score 550 paper-based; 80 iBT), IELTS (minimum score 6). Electronic applications accepted. *Faculty research:* Thermal sciences, design, controls and robotics, manufacturing, energy transport and utilization.

University of Hawaii at Manoa, Office of Graduate Education, College of Engineering, Department of Mechanical Engineering, Honolulu, HI 96822. Offers MS, PhD. *Program availability:* Part-time. *Degree requirements:* For master's, comprehensive exam, thesis; for doctorate, comprehensive exam, thesis/dissertation. *Entrance requirements:* For master's and doctorate, GRE General Test. Additional exam requirements/recommendations for international students: Required—TOEFL (minimum score 550 paper-based; 79 iBT), IELTS (minimum score 5). *Faculty research:* Materials and manufacturing; mechanics, systems and control; thermal and fluid sciences.

University of Houston, Cullen College of Engineering, Department of Mechanical Engineering, Houston, TX 77204. Offers MME, MSME, PhD. *Program availability:* Part-time. Terminal master's awarded for partial completion of doctoral program. *Degree requirements:* For master's, thesis (for some programs); for doctorate, thesis/dissertation, departmental qualifying exam. *Entrance requirements:* For master's and doctorate, GRE General Test. Additional exam requirements/recommendations for international students: Required—TOEFL.

University of Idaho, College of Graduate Studies, College of Engineering, Department of Mechanical Engineering, Moscow, ID 83844-0902. Offers M Engr, MS, PhD. *Faculty:* 21. *Students:* 38 full-time, 21 part-time. Average age 29. In 2018, 14 master's, 2 doctorates awarded. *Entrance requirements:* For master's and doctorate, minimum GPA of 3.0. Additional exam requirements/recommendations for international students: Required—TOEFL (minimum score 79 iBT). *Application deadline:* For fall admission, 8/1 for domestic students; for spring admission, 12/15 for domestic students. Applications are processed on a rolling basis. Application fee: $60. Electronic applications accepted. *Expenses:* Tuition, state resident: full-time $7266.44; part-time $474.50 per credit hour. Tuition, nonresident: full-time $24,902; part-time $1453.50 per credit hour. *Required fees:* $2085.56; $45.50 per credit hour. *Financial support:* Research assistantships and teaching assistantships available. Financial award applicants required to submit FAFSA. *Faculty research:* Experimental and theoretical fluid dynamics, defect behavior in crystalline materials, engine modeling, vehicle design, molecular modeling. *Unit head:* Dr. Steven Beyerlein, Chair, 208-885-6579, E-mail: medept@uidaho.edu. *Application contact:* Dr. Steven Beyerlein, Chair, 208-885-6579, E-mail: medept@uidaho.edu.
Website: https://www.uidaho.edu/engr/departments/me

University of Illinois at Chicago, College of Engineering, Department of Mechanical and Industrial Engineering, Program in Mechanical Engineering, Chicago, IL 60607-7128. Offers fluids engineering (MS, PhD); mechanical analysis and design (MS, PhD); thermomechanical and power engineering (MS, PhD). *Program availability:* Part-time. *Degree requirements:* For master's, thesis. *Entrance requirements:* For master's, GRE General Test, minimum GPA of 2.75. Additional exam requirements/recommendations for international students: Required—TOEFL. Electronic applications accepted. *Expenses:* Contact institution. *Faculty research:* Micro/nanoelectromechanical systems (MEMS/NEMS), micro/nanomanipulation, nanoparticle, nanofluidics, microtransducers and micromechanisms, electrospinning, acoustics, dynamics and vibration, medical imaging and diagnostics, biomechanics and computational mechanics, product design, mechatronics and automatic control, multi-body systems and vehicle dynamics, IC engines, combustors, plasma, combustion, heat transfer, turbulence, multi-phase flows, molecular dynamics and air pollution control.

University of Illinois at Urbana–Champaign, Graduate College, College of Engineering, Department of Mechanical Science and Engineering, Champaign, IL 61820. Offers mechanical engineering (MS, PhD); theoretical and applied mechanics (MS, PhD). Terminal master's awarded for partial completion of doctoral program. *Entrance requirements:* Additional exam requirements/recommendations for international students: Required—TOEFL (minimum score 613 paper-based; 103 iBT), IELTS (minimum score 7).

The University of Iowa, Graduate College, College of Engineering, Department of Mechanical Engineering, Iowa City, IA 52242-1316. Offers energy systems (MS, PhD); engineering design (MS, PhD); fluid dynamics (MS, PhD); materials and manufacturing (MS, PhD); wind energy (MS, PhD). Terminal master's awarded for partial completion of doctoral program. *Degree requirements:* For master's, oral exam or thesis; for doctorate, comprehensive exam, thesis/dissertation. *Entrance requirements:* For master's and doctorate, GRE (minimum Verbal score of 153, Quantitative 151), minimum undergraduate GPA of 3.0. Additional exam requirements/recommendations for international students: Required—TOEFL (minimum score 600 paper-based; 100 iBT), IELTS (minimum score 7). Electronic applications accepted. *Faculty research:* Computer simulation methodology, biomechanics, metal casting, dynamics, laser processing, system reliability, ship hydrodynamics, solid mechanics, fluid dynamics, energy, human modeling and nanotechnology.

The University of Kansas, Graduate Studies, School of Engineering, Department of Mechanical Engineering, Lawrence, KS 66045. Offers MS, PhD. *Program availability:* Part-time. *Students:* 43 full-time (6 women), 7 part-time (2 women); includes 7 minority (1 Asian, non-Hispanic/Latino; 4 Hispanic/Latino; 2 Two or more races, non-Hispanic/Latino), 23 international. Average age 26. 74 applicants, 47% accepted, 13 enrolled. In 2018, 11 master's, 2 doctorates awarded. Terminal master's awarded for partial completion of doctoral program. *Entrance requirements:* For master's, GRE, minimum GPA of 3.0, 3 letters of recommendation, official transcript, statement of purpose (one-page maximum); for doctorate, GRE, minimum GPA of 3.5, 3 letters of recommendation, official transcript, statement of purpose (one-page maximum). Additional exam requirements/recommendations for international students: Required—TOEFL, IELTS. *Application deadline:* For fall admission, 12/15 priority date for domestic and international students; for spring admission, 11/1 for domestic students, 9/30 for international students; for summer admission, 5/1 for domestic and international students. Application fee: $65 ($85 for international students). Electronic applications accepted. *Financial support:* Fellowships, research assistantships, teaching assistantships, career-related internships or fieldwork, and scholarships/grants available. Financial award application deadline: 12/15. *Faculty research:* Automotive industry, plant operations, manufacturing, power generation, aerospace industry, transportation, bioengineering, oil and gas industry. *Unit head:* Theodore Bergman, Chair, 785-864-3181, E-mail: tlbergman@ku.edu. *Application contact:* Kate Maisch, Graduate Admissions Contact, 785-864-3181, E-mail: k223m620@ku.edu.
Website: http://www.me.engr.ku.edu/

University of Kentucky, Graduate School, College of Engineering, Program in Mechanical Engineering, Lexington, KY 40506-0032. Offers MSME, PhD. *Degree requirements:* For master's, comprehensive exam, thesis optional; for doctorate, comprehensive exam, thesis/dissertation. *Entrance requirements:* For master's, GRE General Test, minimum undergraduate GPA of 2.75; for doctorate, GRE General Test, minimum undergraduate GPA of 3.0. Additional exam requirements/recommendations for international students: Required—TOEFL (minimum score 550 paper-based). Electronic applications accepted. *Faculty research:* Combustion, computational fluid dynamics, design and systems, manufacturing, thermal and fluid sciences.

University of Louisiana at Lafayette, College of Engineering, Department of Mechanical Engineering, Lafayette, LA 70504. Offers MSE. *Program availability:* Evening/weekend. *Degree requirements:* For master's, comprehensive exam, thesis or alternative. *Entrance requirements:* For master's, GRE General Test, BS in mechanical engineering, minimum GPA of 2.85. Additional exam requirements/recommendations for international students: Required—TOEFL (minimum score 550 paper-based). Electronic applications accepted. *Faculty research:* CAD/CAM, machine design and vibration, thermal science.

University of Louisville, J. B. Speed School of Engineering, Department of Mechanical Engineering, Louisville, KY 40292-0001. Offers M Eng, MS, PhD. *Accreditation:* ABET (one or more programs are accredited). *Faculty:* 16 full-time (2 women), 2 part-time/adjunct (0 women). *Students:* 47 full-time (7 women), 55 part-time (10 women); includes 18 minority (6 Black or African American, non-Hispanic/Latino; 6 Asian, non-Hispanic/Latino; 3 Hispanic/Latino; 3 Two or more races, non-Hispanic/Latino), 22 international. Average age 27. 31 applicants, 48% accepted, 11 enrolled. In 2018, 24 master's, 1 doctorate awarded. *Degree requirements:* For master's, thesis optional; for doctorate, comprehensive exam, thesis/dissertation. *Entrance requirements:* For master's and doctorate, GRE General Test, two letters of recommendation, official transcripts. Additional exam requirements/recommendations for international students: Required—TOEFL (minimum score 550 paper-based; 80 iBT), IELTS (minimum score 6.5). *Application deadline:* For fall admission, 5/1 priority date for domestic and international students; for spring admission, 11/1 priority date for domestic and international students; for summer admission, 3/1 priority date for domestic and international students. Applications are processed on a rolling basis. Application fee: $65. Electronic applications accepted. *Expenses:* Tuition, area resident: Full-time $6500; part-time $723 per credit hour. Tuition, state resident: full-time $6500. Tuition, nonresident: full-time $13,557; part-time $1507 per credit hour. Tuition and fees vary according to course load and program. *Financial support:* In 2018–19, 52 students received support. Fellowships, research assistantships, teaching assistantships, scholarships/grants, health care benefits, and tuition waivers (full) available. Financial award application deadline: 1/1; financial award applicants required to submit FAFSA. *Faculty research:* Additive Manufacturing Process Development, 3D printing, Advanced Manufacturing, Energy Storage Materials and Systems, Digital Design and Manufacturing. *Unit head:* Dr. Kevin Murphy, Jr., Chair, 502-852-6332, E-mail: kevin.murphy@louisville.edu. *Application contact:* Peter Quesada, Director of Graduate Studies, 502-852-5981, E-mail: peter.quesada@louisville.edu.
Website: http://www.louisville.edu/speed/mechanical

University of Maine, Graduate School, College of Engineering, Department of Mechanical Engineering, Orono, ME 04469. Offers MS, PSM, PhD. *Program availability:* Part-time. *Faculty:* 18 full-time (2 women), 3 part-time/adjunct (0 women). *Students:* 36 full-time (4 women), 9 part-time (1 woman); includes 1 minority (Black or African American, non-Hispanic/Latino), 14 international. Average age 29. 44 applicants, 91% accepted, 13 enrolled. In 2018, 6 master's, 3 doctorates awarded. *Degree requirements:* For master's, thesis (for some programs); for doctorate, comprehensive exam, thesis/dissertation. *Entrance requirements:* For master's and doctorate, GRE General Test. Additional exam requirements/recommendations for international students: Required—TOEFL (minimum score 80 iBT), IELTS (minimum score 6.5), PTE (minimum score 60). *Application deadline:* For fall admission, 2/15 for domestic and international students; for spring admission, 7/31 for domestic and international students. Applications are processed on a rolling basis. Application fee: $65. Electronic applications accepted. *Financial support:* In 2018–19, 80 students received support, including 4 fellowships with full tuition reimbursements available (averaging $17,600 per year), 32 research assistantships with full tuition reimbursements available (averaging $16,250 per year), 10 teaching assistantships with full tuition reimbursements available (averaging $15,000 per year); Federal Work-Study and tuition waivers (full and partial) also available. Financial award application deadline: 3/1. *Faculty research:* Additive manufacturing; biomedical engineering; engineering mechanics; simulation and design; renewable energy. *Total annual research expenditures:* $1.5 million. *Unit head:* Dr. Senthil Vel, Chair, 207-581-2777, Fax: 207-581-2379, E-mail: senthil.vel@maine.edu. *Application contact:* Scott G. Delcourt, Assistant Vice President for Graduate Studies and Senior Associate Dean, 207-581-3291, Fax: 207-581-3232, E-mail: graduate@maine.edu.
Website: http://umaine.edu/mecheng/

The University of Manchester, School of Mechanical, Aerospace and Civil Engineering, Manchester, United Kingdom. Offers advanced manufacturing technology (M Ent); aerospace engineering (M Phil, M Sc, PhD); civil engineering (M Phil, M Sc, PhD); environmental engineering (M Phil, PhD); management of projects (M Phil, M Sc, PhD); mechanical engineering (M Phil, M Sc, PhD); mechanical engineering design (M Ent); nuclear engineering (M Phil, D Eng, PhD).

University of Manitoba, Faculty of Graduate Studies, Faculty of Engineering, Department of Mechanical and Manufacturing Engineering, Winnipeg, MB R3T 2N2, Canada. Offers M Eng, M Sc, PhD. *Degree requirements:* For master's, thesis; for doctorate, thesis/dissertation.

University of Maryland, Baltimore County, The Graduate School, College of Engineering and Information Technology, Department of Mechanical Engineering, Program in Mechanical Engineering, Baltimore, MD 21250. Offers MS, PhD. *Program availability:* Part-time. *Degree requirements:* For master's, comprehensive exam (for some programs), thesis (for some programs); for doctorate, comprehensive exam, thesis/dissertation. *Entrance requirements:* For master's, GRE General Test (strongly recommended for applicants from ABET-accredited schools in U.S.), minimum GPA of 3.0; undergraduate degree in mechanical, aerospace, environmental, or chemical engineering (strongly recommended); for doctorate, GRE General Test (strongly recommended for applicants from ABET-accredited schools in U.S.), minimum overall GPA of 3.3; bachelor's degree in mechanical, aerospace, civil, industrial, or chemical engineering. Additional exam requirements/recommendations for international students: Required—TOEFL (minimum score 550 paper-based; 80 iBT), GRE General Test. Electronic applications accepted. *Expenses:* Contact institution. *Faculty research:* Solid mechanics and materials sciences, thermal/fluids sciences, design-manufacturing and systems, bio-mechanical engineering, engineering education.

University of Maryland, College Park, Academic Affairs, A. James Clark School of Engineering, Department of Mechanical Engineering, College Park, MD 20742. Offers electronic packaging and reliability (MS, PhD); manufacturing and design (MS, PhD); mechanics and materials (MS, PhD); reliability engineering (M Eng, MS, PhD); thermal and fluid sciences (MS, PhD). *Program availability:* Part-time, evening/weekend, online learning. *Degree requirements:* For master's, thesis optional; for doctorate, thesis/dissertation, qualifying exam. *Entrance requirements:* For master's, GRE General Test, 3 letters of recommendation; for doctorate, GRE General Test, minimum GPA of 3.0. Additional exam requirements/recommendations for international students: Required—TOEFL. Electronic applications accepted. *Faculty research:* Injection molding, electronic packaging, fluid mechanics, product engineering.

University of Massachusetts Amherst, Graduate School, College of Engineering, Department of Mechanical and Industrial Engineering, Amherst, MA 01003. Offers industrial engineering and operations research (MS, PhD); mechanical engineering (MSME, PhD). *Program availability:* Part-time. Terminal master's awarded for partial completion of doctoral program. *Degree requirements:* For master's, thesis or alternative; for doctorate, comprehensive exam, thesis/dissertation. *Entrance requirements:* For master's and doctorate, GRE General Test. Additional exam requirements/recommendations for international students: Required—TOEFL (minimum score 550 paper-based; 80 iBT), IELTS (minimum score 6.5). Electronic applications accepted.

University of Massachusetts Dartmouth, Graduate School, College of Engineering, Department of Mechanical Engineering, North Dartmouth, MA 02747-2300. Offers industrial and systems engineering (Postbaccalaureate Certificate); mechanical engineering (MS). *Program availability:* Part-time. *Faculty:* 10 full-time (2 women). *Students:* 6 full-time (0 women), 19 part-time (1 woman); includes 4 minority (1 Asian, non-Hispanic/Latino; 1 Hispanic/Latino; 2 Two or more races, non-Hispanic/Latino), 5 international. Average age 25. 42 applicants, 55% accepted, 6 enrolled. In 2018, 9 master's awarded. *Degree requirements:* For master's, thesis, thesis or project. *Entrance requirements:* For master's, GRE unless UMass Dartmouth graduate in mechanical engineering, statement of purpose (minimum of 300 words), resume, 3 letters of recommendation, official transcripts; for Postbaccalaureate Certificate, statement of purpose (minimum of 300 words), resume, 3 letters of recommendation, official transcripts. Additional exam requirements/recommendations for international students: Required—TOEFL (minimum score 533 paper-based; 72 iBT), IELTS (minimum score 6). *Application deadline:* For fall admission, 2/15 priority date for domestic students, 1/15 priority date for international students; for spring admission, 11/15 priority date for domestic students, 10/15 priority date for international students. Application fee: $60. Electronic applications accepted. *Financial support:* In 2018–19, 3 research assistantships (averaging $11,606 per year), 4 teaching assistantships (averaging $14,131 per year) were awarded; tuition waivers (full and partial) also available. Financial award application deadline: 3/1; financial award applicants required to submit FAFSA. *Faculty research:* Computer aided tolerance and optimization; diagnostics in manufacturing; MEMS and nano-manufacturing; modeling, simulation and optimization of manufacturing systems, robotics. *Total annual research expenditures:* $1.7 million. *Unit head:* Wenzhen Huang, Graduate Program Director, Mechanical Engineering, 508-910-6568, E-mail: whuang@umassd.edu. *Application contact:* Scott Webster, Director of Graduate Studies & Admissions, 508-999-8604, Fax: 508-999-8183, E-mail: graduate@umassd.edu.
Website: http://www.umassd.edu/engineering/mne/graduate

University of Massachusetts Lowell, Francis College of Engineering, Department of Mechanical Engineering, Lowell, MA 01854. Offers MS Eng, PhD. *Program availability:* Part-time. *Degree requirements:* For master's, thesis or alternative; for doctorate, 2 foreign languages, comprehensive exam, thesis/dissertation. *Entrance requirements:* For master's and doctorate, GRE General Test. Additional exam requirements/recommendations for international students: Required—TOEFL (minimum score 560 paper-based). Electronic applications accepted. *Faculty research:* Composites, heat transfer.

University of Memphis, Graduate School, Herff College of Engineering, Department of Mechanical Engineering, Memphis, TN 38152. Offers power systems (MS). *Program availability:* Part-time. *Students:* 8 full-time (0 women), 5 part-time (1 woman), 5 international. Average age 28. 18 applicants, 56% accepted, 2 enrolled. In 2018, 6 master's awarded. Terminal master's awarded for partial completion of doctoral program. *Degree requirements:* For master's, comprehensive exam, thesis or alternative; for doctorate, comprehensive exam, thesis/dissertation. *Entrance requirements:* For master's, GRE General Test, MAT, GMAT, BS in mechanical engineering, minimum undergraduate GPA of 3.0, three letters of recommendation; for doctorate, GRE, BS in mechanical engineering, minimum undergraduate GPA of 3.0, three letters of recommendation; for Graduate Certificate, letter of intent, two letters of recommendation. Additional exam requirements/recommendations for international students: Required—TOEFL (minimum score 550 paper-based; 79 iBT). *Application deadline:* For fall admission, 8/1 for domestic students; for spring admission, 12/1 for domestic students. Application fee: $35 ($60 for international students). *Expenses: Tuition, area resident:* Full-time $10,240; part-time $503 per credit hour. Tuition, state resident: full-time $10,464. Tuition, nonresident: full-time $20,224; part-time $991 per credit hour. *Required fees:* $850; $106 per credit hour. *Financial support:* Fellowships with full tuition reimbursements, research assistantships with full tuition reimbursements, teaching assistantships with full tuition reimbursements, career-related internships or fieldwork, Federal Work-Study, scholarships/grants, and unspecified assistantships available. Financial award application deadline: 2/1; financial award applicants required to submit FAFSA. *Faculty research:* Computational fluid dynamics, computational mechanics, integrated design, nondestructive testing, operations research. *Unit head:* Dr. Ali Fatemi, Chair, 901-678-2257, E-mail: afatemi@memphis.edu. *Application contact:* Dr. Teong Tan, Graduate Coordinator, 901-678-2701, Fax: 901-678-5459, E-mail: ttan@memphis.edu.
Website: http://www.memphis.edu/me/

University of Miami, Graduate School, College of Engineering, Department of Mechanical and Aerospace Engineering, Coral Gables, FL 33124. Offers MSME, PhD. *Program availability:* Part-time. *Degree requirements:* For master's, thesis (for some programs); for doctorate, comprehensive exam, thesis/dissertation. *Entrance requirements:* For master's and doctorate, GRE General Test, minimum GPA of 3.0. Additional exam requirements/recommendations for international students: Required—TOEFL (minimum score 550 paper-based). Electronic applications accepted. *Faculty research:* Internal combustion engines, heat transfer, hydrogen energy, controls, fuel cells.

University of Michigan, College of Engineering, Department of Mechanical Engineering, Ann Arbor, MI 48109. Offers MSE, PhD. *Program availability:* Part-time. *Students:* 490 full-time (113 women), 11 part-time (2 women). 1,500 applicants, 24% accepted, 170 enrolled. In 2018, 186 master's, 39 doctorates awarded. Terminal master's awarded for partial completion of doctoral program. *Degree requirements:* For master's, thesis optional; for doctorate, thesis/dissertation, oral defense of dissertation, preliminary and qualifying exams. *Entrance requirements:* For master's, GRE General Test, undergraduate degree in same or relevant field; for doctorate, GRE General Test. Additional exam requirements/recommendations for international students: Required—TOEFL. *Application deadline:* Applications are processed on a rolling basis. Electronic applications accepted. *Financial support:* Fellowships, research assistantships, teaching assistantships, institutionally sponsored loans, health care benefits, tuition waivers (full), and unspecified assistantships available. Financial award applicants required to submit FAFSA. *Faculty research:* Design and manufacturing, systems and controls, combustion and heat transfer, materials and solid mechanics, dynamics and vibrations, biosystems, fluid mechanics, microsystems, environmental sustainabilities. *Total annual research expenditures:* $37.3 million. *Unit head:* Ellen Arruda, Department Chair, 734-763-5328, E-mail: arruda-chair@umich.edu. *Application contact:* Adam Mael, Graduate Coordinator, 734-615-7024, E-mail: amael@umich.edu.
Website: https://me.engin.umich.edu/

University of Michigan–Dearborn, College of Engineering and Computer Science, MSE Program in Mechanical Engineering, Dearborn, MI 48128. Offers MSE. *Program availability:* Part-time, evening/weekend, 100% online. *Faculty:* 24 full-time (4 women), 12 part-time/adjunct (2 women). *Students:* 47 full-time (11 women), 190 part-time (22 women); includes 37 minority (6 Black or African American, non-Hispanic/Latino; 1 American Indian or Alaska Native, non-Hispanic/Latino; 15 Asian, non-Hispanic/Latino; 13 Hispanic/Latino; 2 Two or more races, non-Hispanic/Latino), 60 international. Average age 26. 252 applicants, 40% accepted, 55 enrolled. In 2018, 110 master's awarded. *Degree requirements:* For master's, thesis optional. *Entrance requirements:* For master's, BS in mechanical engineering or equivalent from accredited school with minimum GPA of 3.0. Additional exam requirements/recommendations for international students: Required—TOEFL (minimum score 560 paper-based; 84 iBT), IELTS (minimum score 6.5). *Application deadline:* For fall admission, 8/1 priority date for domestic students, 5/1 for international students; for winter admission, 12/1 priority date for domestic students, 9/1 for international students; for spring admission, 4/1 priority date for domestic students, 1/1 for international students. Applications are processed on a rolling basis. Application fee: $60. Electronic applications accepted. *Expenses:* Tuition, state resident: full-time $15,380; part-time $88 per credit hour. Tuition, nonresident: full-time $23,948; part-time $1377 per credit hour. *Required fees:* $780; $780 $390. Tuition and fees vary according to course level, course load, degree level, program, reciprocity agreements and student level. *Financial support:* In 2018–19, 45 students received support. Research assistantships with full tuition reimbursements available, teaching assistantships with full tuition reimbursements available, health care benefits, unspecified assistantships, and non-resident tuition scholarships available. Financial award application deadline: 3/1; financial award applicants required to submit FAFSA. *Faculty research:* Materials processing, magneto hydrodynamics flows for energy generation and storage, nanomaterials for energy and biosystems, energy management for automobiles, manufacturing. *Unit head:* Dr. Oleg Zikanov, Chair, 313-593-5241, E-mail: zikanov@umich.edu. *Application contact:* Office of Graduate Studies, 313-583-6321, E-mail: umd-graduatestudies@umich.edu.
Website: https://umdearborn.edu/cecs/departments/mechanical-engineering/graduate-programs/mse-mechanical-engineering

University of Michigan–Dearborn, College of Engineering and Computer Science, PhD Program in Mechanical Sciences and Engineering, Dearborn, MI 48128. Offers PhD. *Faculty:* 24 full-time (4 women), 12 part-time/adjunct (2 women). *Students:* 3 full-time (0 women), 13 part-time (2 women); includes 1 minority (Asian, non-Hispanic/Latino), 13 international. Average age 26. 19 applicants, 58% accepted, 11 enrolled. *Degree requirements:* For doctorate, thesis/dissertation. *Entrance requirements:* For doctorate, GRE, bachelor's or master's degree in engineering, applied math, computer science, or physical science. Additional exam requirements/recommendations for international students: Required—TOEFL (minimum score 560 paper-based; 84 iBT), IELTS (minimum score 6.5). *Application deadline:* For fall admission, 2/1 for domestic and international students. Application fee: $60. Electronic applications accepted. *Expenses:* Tuition, state resident: full-time $15,380; part-time $88 per credit hour. Tuition, nonresident: full-time $23,948; part-time $1377 per credit hour. *Required fees:* $780; $780 $390. Tuition and fees vary according to course level, course load, degree level, program, reciprocity agreements and student level. *Financial support:* In 2018–19, 4 students received support. Research assistantships with full tuition reimbursements available, teaching assistantships with full tuition reimbursements available, scholarships/grants, health care benefits, and unspecified assistantships available. Financial award application deadline: 2/1; financial award applicants required to submit FAFSA. *Faculty research:* Materials processing and manufacturing; nanomaterials for energy and biosystems; energy generation, storage, and management; tissue engineering and biomimetics; microfluidics, drug delivery, and biomechanics. *Unit head:* Dr. Dewey Dohoy Jung, Director, 313-436-9137, E-mail: dohoy@umich.edu. *Application contact:* Office of Graduate Studies Staff, 313-583-6321, E-mail: umd-graduatestudies@umich.edu.
Website: https://umdearborn.edu/cecs/departments/mechanical-engineering/graduate-programs/phd-mechanical-sciences-and-engineering

University of Michigan–Flint, College of Arts and Sciences, Program in Mechanical Engineering, Flint, MI 48502-1950. Offers MSE. *Program availability:* Part-time. *Faculty:* 8 full-time (2 women), 2 part-time/adjunct (0 women). *Students:* 2 full-time (0 women), 5 part-time (0 women), all international. Average age 23. 80 applicants, 35% accepted, 7 enrolled. *Degree requirements:* For master's, thesis optional. *Entrance requirements:* For master's, GRE, bachelor's degree in mechanical engineering from regionally-accredited college or university, minimum overall undergraduate GPA of 3.0 on 4.0 scale. Additional exam requirements/recommendations for international students: Required—TOEFL (minimum score 84 iBT), IELTS (minimum score 6.5). *Application deadline:* For fall admission, 8/1 for domestic students, 5/1 for international students; for winter admission, 11/15 for domestic students, 8/1 for international students. Applications are processed on a rolling basis. Application fee: $55. Electronic applications accepted. *Expenses:* Contact institution. *Financial support:* Federal Work-Study, scholarships/grants, and unspecified assistantships available. Support available to part-time students. Financial award application deadline: 3/1; financial award applicants required to submit FAFSA. *Unit head:* Susie Churchill, Program Manager, 810-762-0916, E-mail: vissers@umflint.edu. *Application contact:* Matt Bohlen, Director of Graduate Admissions, 810-762-3171, Fax: 810-766-6789, E-mail: mbohlen@umflint.edu.
Website: https://www.umflint.edu/graduateprograms/master-science-engineering-mse

University of Minnesota, Twin Cities Campus, College of Science and Engineering, Department of Mechanical Engineering, Minneapolis, MN 55455-0213. Offers MSME, PhD. *Program availability:* Part-time. *Degree requirements:* For doctorate, thesis/dissertation. *Entrance requirements:* For master's, GRE General Test, minimum GPA of 3.0; for doctorate, GRE General Test. Additional exam requirements/recommendations for international students: Required—TOEFL. Electronic applications accepted. *Faculty research:* Particle technology, solar energy, controls, heat transfer, fluid power, plasmas, medical devices, bioengineering, nanotechnology, intelligent vehicles.

Mechanical Engineering

University of Mississippi, Graduate School, School of Engineering, University, MS 38677. Offers aeroacoustics (MS, PhD); chemical engineering (MS, PhD); civil engineering (MS, PhD); computational hydroscience (MS, PhD); computer science (MS, PhD); electrical engineering (MS, PhD); electromagnetics (MS, PhD); environmental engineering (MS, PhD); geology and geological engineering (MS, PhD); hydrology (MS); material science (MS); mechanical engineering (MS, PhD); telecommunications (MS). *Faculty:* 76 full-time (16 women), 3 part-time/adjunct (1 woman). *Students:* 129 full-time (33 women), 21 part-time (5 women); includes 15 minority (7 Black or African American, non-Hispanic/Latino; 6 Asian, non-Hispanic/Latino; 1 Hispanic/Latino; 1 Two or more races, non-Hispanic/Latino), 73 international. Average age 29. In 2018, 36 master's, 17 doctorates awarded. *Entrance requirements:* For master's, GRE General Test, minimum GPA of 3.0; for doctorate, GRE General Test. Additional exam requirements/recommendations for international students: Required—TOEFL. *Application deadline:* Applications are processed on a rolling basis. Application fee: $50. Electronic applications accepted. *Financial support:* Scholarships/grants available. Financial award application deadline: 3/1; financial award applicants required to submit FAFSA. *Unit head:* Dr. David Puleo, Dean, 662-915-5780, Fax: 662-915-5387, E-mail: engineer@olemiss.edu. *Application contact:* Temeka Smith, Graduate Activities Specialist for Admissions, 662-915-7474, Fax: 662-915-7577, E-mail: gschool@olemiss.edu.

University of Missouri, Office of Research and Graduate Studies, College of Engineering, Department of Mechanical and Aerospace Engineering, Columbia, MO 65211. Offers ME, MS, PhD. *Entrance requirements:* For master's and doctorate, GRE General Test, minimum GPA of 3.0.

University of Missouri–Kansas City, School of Computing and Engineering, Kansas City, MO 64110-2499. Offers civil engineering (MS); computer and electrical engineering (PhD); computer science (MS), including bioinformatics, software engineering, telecommunications networking; computer science and informatics (PhD); computing (PhD); electrical engineering (MS); engineering (PhD); engineering and construction management (Graduate Certificate); mechanical engineering (MS); telecommunications and computer networking (PhD). PhD (interdisciplinary) offered through the School of Graduate Studies. *Program availability:* Part-time. *Degree requirements:* For doctorate, thesis/dissertation. *Entrance requirements:* For master's, GRE General Test, minimum GPA of 3.0, 3 letters of recommendation from professors; for doctorate, GRE General Test, minimum GPA of 3.5. Additional exam requirements/recommendations for international students: Required—TOEFL (minimum score 550 paper-based; 80 iBT). *Faculty research:* Algorithms, bioinformatics and medical informatics, biomechanics/biomaterials, civil engineering materials, networking and telecommunications, thermal science.

University of Nebraska–Lincoln, Graduate College, College of Engineering, Department of Mechanical and Materials Engineering, Lincoln, NE 68588-0526. Offers biomedical engineering (PhD); engineering mechanics (MS); materials engineering (PhD); mechanical engineering (MS), including materials science engineering, metallurgical engineering; mechanical engineering and applied mechanics (PhD); MS/MS. MS/MS offered with University of Rouen-France. *Degree requirements:* For master's, thesis optional; for doctorate, comprehensive exam, thesis/dissertation. *Entrance requirements:* For master's and doctorate, GRE General Test. Additional exam requirements/recommendations for international students: Required—TOEFL (minimum score 550 paper-based). Electronic applications accepted. *Faculty research:* Medical robotics, rehabilitation dynamics, and design; combustion, fluid mechanics, and heat transfer; nano-materials, manufacturing, and devices; fiber, tissue, bio-polymer, and adaptive composites; blast, impact, fracture, and failure; electro-active and magnetic materials and devices; functional materials, design, and added manufacturing; materials characterization, modeling, and computational simulation.

University of Nevada, Reno, Graduate School, College of Engineering, Department of Mechanical Engineering, Reno, NV 89557. Offers MS, PhD. Terminal master's awarded for partial completion of doctoral program. *Degree requirements:* For master's, thesis optional; for doctorate, thesis/dissertation. *Entrance requirements:* For master's, GRE General Test, minimum GPA of 2.75; for doctorate, GRE General Test, minimum GPA of 3.0. Additional exam requirements/recommendations for international students: Required—TOEFL (minimum score 500 paper-based; 61 iBT), IELTS (minimum score 6). Electronic applications accepted. *Faculty research:* Composite, solid, fluid, thermal, and smart materials.

University of New Brunswick Fredericton, School of Graduate Studies, Faculty of Engineering, Department of Mechanical Engineering, Fredericton, NB E3B 5A3, Canada. Offers applied mechanics (M Eng, M Sc E, PhD); mechanical engineering (M Eng, M Sc E, PhD). *Program availability:* Part-time. *Degree requirements:* For master's, thesis; for doctorate, comprehensive exam, thesis/dissertation, qualifying exam. *Entrance requirements:* For master's, minimum GPA of 3.0; B Sc E; for doctorate, minimum GPA of 3.0; M Sc E. Additional exam requirements/recommendations for international students: Required—TOEFL (minimum score 580 paper-based; 80 iBT), IELTS (minimum score 7), TWE (minimum score 4), Michigan English Language Assessment Battery (minimum score 85) or CanTest (minimum score 4.5). Electronic applications accepted. *Faculty research:* Acoustics and vibration, biomedical, manufacturing and materials processing, mechatronics and design, nuclear and threat detection, renewable energy systems, robotics and applied mechanics, thermofluids and aerodynamics.

University of New Hampshire, Graduate School, College of Engineering and Physical Sciences, Department of Mechanical Engineering, Durham, NH 03824. Offers mechanical engineering (M Engr, MS, PhD). *Program availability:* Part-time. *Entrance requirements:* For master's and doctorate, GRE. Additional exam requirements/recommendations for international students: Required—TOEFL (minimum score 550 paper-based; 80 iBT). Electronic applications accepted.

University of New Haven, Graduate School, Tagliatela College of Engineering, Program in Mechanical Engineering, West Haven, CT 06516. Offers MS. *Program availability:* Part-time, evening/weekend. *Students:* 34 full-time (4 women), 12 part-time (5 women); includes 4 minority (2 Asian, non-Hispanic/Latino; 2 Hispanic/Latino), 34 international. Average age 25. 104 applicants, 72% accepted, 13 enrolled. In 2018, 24 master's awarded. *Entrance requirements:* Additional exam requirements/recommendations for international students: Required—TOEFL (minimum score 75 iBT), IELTS, PTE (minimum score 50). *Application deadline:* Applications are processed on a rolling basis. Application fee: $50. Electronic applications accepted. Application fee is waived when completed online. *Expenses: Tuition:* Full-time $16,470; part-time $915 per credit hour. *Required fees:* $230; $95 per term. *Financial support:* Research assistantships with partial tuition reimbursements, teaching assistantships with partial tuition reimbursements, career-related internships or fieldwork, Federal Work-Study, scholarships/grants, and unspecified assistantships available. Support available to part-time students. Financial award applicants required to submit FAFSA. *Unit head:* Dr. Eric Dieckman, Assistant Professor, 203-479-4249, E-mail: edieckman@newhaven.edu. *Application contact:* Selina O'Toole, Senior Associate Director of Graduate Admissions, 203-932-7337, E-mail: sotoole@newhaven.edu.
Website: https://www.newhaven.edu/engineering/graduate-programs/mechanical-engineering/

University of New Mexico, Graduate Studies, School of Engineering, Program in Mechanical Engineering, Albuquerque, NM 87131-2039. Offers MS, PhD. *Program availability:* Part-time. *Degree requirements:* For master's, thesis optional; for doctorate, comprehensive exam, thesis/dissertation. *Entrance requirements:* For master's and doctorate, GRE. Additional exam requirements/recommendations for international students: Required—TOEFL (minimum score 550 paper-based; 80 iBT). Electronic applications accepted. *Faculty research:* Engineering mechanics and materials (including solid mechanics and materials science), mechanical sciences and engineering (including dynamic systems, controls and robotics), thermal sciences and engineering.

University of New Orleans, Graduate School, College of Engineering, Program in Engineering, New Orleans, LA 70148. Offers civil engineering (MS); electrical engineering (MS); mechanical engineering (MS); naval architecture and marine engineering (MS). *Degree requirements:* For master's, thesis optional. *Entrance requirements:* For master's, GRE General Test, minimum GPA of 3.0. Additional exam requirements/recommendations for international students: Required—TOEFL (minimum score 550 paper-based; 79 iBT). Electronic applications accepted. *Faculty research:* Two-phase flow instabilities, thermal-hydrodynamic modeling, solar energy, heat transfer from sprays, boundary integral techniques in mechanics.

The University of North Carolina at Charlotte, William States Lee College of Engineering, Department of Mechanical Engineering and Engineering Science, Charlotte, NC 28223-0001. Offers mechanical engineering (MSME, PhD). *Program availability:* Part-time, evening/weekend. *Students:* 108 full-time (12 women), 46 part-time (3 women); includes 5 minority (3 Asian, non-Hispanic/Latino; 2 Hispanic/Latino), 94 international. Average age 27. 161 applicants, 75% accepted, 36 enrolled. In 2018, 47 master's, 16 doctorates awarded. *Entrance requirements:* For master's, GRE, baccalaureate degree from accredited institution in some area of engineering, minimum GPA of 3.0; for doctorate, GRE General Test, master's degree in engineering or a closely-allied field; minimum GPA of 3.5; letters of reference. Additional exam requirements/recommendations for international students: Required—TOEFL, IELTS, TOEFL (minimum score 523 paper-based, 70 iBT) or IELTS (6). *Application deadline:* Applications are processed on a rolling basis. Application fee: $75. Electronic applications accepted. *Expenses:* Contact institution. *Financial support:* Fellowships, research assistantships, teaching assistantships, career-related internships or fieldwork, institutionally sponsored loans, scholarships/grants, and unspecified assistantships available. Support available to part-time students. Financial award application deadline: 3/1; financial award applicants required to submit FAFSA. *Total annual research expenditures:* $2.9 million. *Unit head:* Dr. Scott Smith, Department Chair, 704-687-8350, E-mail: kssmith@uncc.edu. *Application contact:* Kathy B. Giddings, Director of Graduate Admissions, 704-687-5503, Fax: 704-687-1668, E-mail: gradadm@uncc.edu.
Website: http://mees.uncc.edu/

University of North Dakota, Graduate School, School of Engineering and Mines, Department of Mechanical Engineering, Grand Forks, ND 58202. Offers M Engr, MS, PhD. *Program availability:* Part-time. *Degree requirements:* For master's, comprehensive exam, thesis or alternative. *Entrance requirements:* For master's, GRE General Test, minimum GPA of 3.0 (MS), 2.5 (M Engr). Additional exam requirements/recommendations for international students: Required—TOEFL (minimum score 550 paper-based; 79 iBT), IELTS (minimum score 6.5). Electronic applications accepted. *Faculty research:* Energy conversion, dynamics, control, manufacturing processes with special emphasis on machining, stress vibration analysis.

University of North Florida, College of Computing, Engineering, and Construction, School of Engineering, Jacksonville, FL 32224. Offers MSCE, MSEE, MSME. *Program availability:* Part-time. *Faculty:* 19 full-time (4 women). *Students:* 17 full-time (5 women), 32 part-time (5 women); includes 13 minority (1 Black or African American, non-Hispanic/Latino; 5 Asian, non-Hispanic/Latino; 5 Hispanic/Latino; 2 Two or more races, non-Hispanic/Latino), 9 international. Average age 30. 36 applicants, 58% accepted, 16 enrolled. In 2018, 19 master's awarded. *Application deadline:* For fall admission, 8/1 priority date for domestic students, 5/1 for international students; for spring admission, 12/1 priority date for domestic students, 10/1 for international students; for summer admission, 3/15 priority date for domestic students, 2/1 for international students. Application fee: $30. *Expenses: Tuition, area resident:* Part-time $408.10 per credit hour. Tuition, state resident: part-time $408.10 per credit hour. Tuition, nonresident: part-time $932.61 per credit hour. *Required fees:* $111.81 per credit hour. Tuition and fees vary according to course load, campus/location and program. *Financial support:* In 2018–19, 25 students received support, including 4 research assistantships (averaging $3,161 per year), 2 teaching assistantships (averaging $4,445 per year); Federal Work-Study, scholarships/grants, tuition waivers, and unspecified assistantships also available. Financial award application deadline: 4/1; financial award applicants required to submit FAFSA. *Total annual research expenditures:* $1.1 million. *Unit head:* Dr. Murat Tiryakioglo, Director, 904-620-1393, E-mail: m.tiryakioglu@unf.edu. *Application contact:* Dr. Amanda Pascale, Director, The Graduate School, 904-320-1360, Fax: 904-620-1362, E-mail: graduateschool@unf.edu.
Website: http://www.unf.edu/ccec/engineering/

University of North Texas, Toulouse Graduate School, Denton, TX 76203-5459. Offers accounting (MS); applied anthropology (MA, MS); applied behavior analysis (Certificate); applied geography (MA); applied technology and performance improvement (M Ed, MS); art education (MA); art history (MA); arts leadership (Certificate); audiology (Au D); behavior analysis (MS); behavioral science (PhD); biochemistry and molecular biology (MS); biology (MA, MS); biomedical engineering (MS); business analysis (MS); chemistry (MS); clinical health psychology (PhD); communication studies (MA, MS); computer engineering (MS); computer science (MS); counseling (M Ed, MS), including clinical mental health counseling (MS), college and university counseling, elementary school counseling, secondary school counseling; creative writing (MA); criminal justice (MS); curriculum and instruction (M Ed); decision sciences (MBA); design (MA, MFA), including fashion design (MFA), innovation studies, interior design (MFA); early childhood studies (MS); economics (MS); educational leadership (M Ed, Ed D); educational psychology (MS, PhD), including family studies (MS), gifted and talented (MS), human development (MS), learning and cognition (MS), research, measurement and evaluation (MS); electrical engineering (MS); emergency management (MPA); engineering technology (MS); English (MA); English as a second language (MA); environmental science (MS); finance (MBA, MS); financial management (MPA); French (MA); health services management (MBA); higher education (M Ed, Ed D); history (MA, MS); hospitality management (MS); human resources management (MPA); information science (MS); information systems (PhD); information technologies (MBA); interdisciplinary studies (MA, MS); international studies (MA); international sustainable tourism (MS); jazz studies (MM); journalism (MA, MJ, Graduate Certificate), including interactive and virtual digital communication (Graduate Certificate), narrative journalism (Graduate Certificate), public relations (Graduate Certificate); kinesiology (MS); linguistics (MA); local government management (MPA); logistics (PhD); logistics and supply chain management (MBA); long-term care, senior housing, and aging services (MA); management (PhD); marketing (MBA); mathematics (MA, MS); mechanical and energy engineering (MS, PhD); music (MA), including ethnomusicology, music theory, musicology, performance; music composition (PhD); music education

(MM Ed, PhD); nonprofit management (MPA); operations and supply chain management (MBA); performance (MM, DMA); philosophy (MA); political science (MA); professional and technical communication (MA); radio, television and film (MA, MFA); rehabilitation counseling (Certificate); sociology (MA); Spanish (MA); special education (M Ed); speech-language pathology (MA); strategic management (MBA); studio art (MFA); teaching (M Ed); MBA/MS. *Program availability:* Part-time, evening/weekend, online learning. Terminal master's awarded for partial completion of doctoral program. *Degree requirements:* For master's, variable foreign language requirement, comprehensive exam (for some programs), thesis (for some programs); for doctorate, variable foreign language requirement, comprehensive exam (for some programs), thesis/dissertation; for other advanced degree, variable foreign language requirement, comprehensive exam (for some programs). *Entrance requirements:* For master's and doctorate, GRE, GMAT. Additional exam requirements/recommendations for international students: Required—TOEFL (minimum score 550 paper-based; 79 iBT). Electronic applications accepted.

University of Notre Dame, The Graduate School, College of Engineering, Department of Aerospace and Mechanical Engineering, Notre Dame, IN 46556. Offers aerospace and mechanical engineering (M Eng, PhD); aerospace engineering (MS Aero E); mechanical engineering (MEME, MSME). Terminal master's awarded for partial completion of doctoral program. *Degree requirements:* For master's, comprehensive exam, thesis or alternative; for doctorate, thesis/dissertation, candidacy exam. *Entrance requirements:* For master's and doctorate, GRE General Test. Additional exam requirements/recommendations for international students: Required—TOEFL (minimum score 600 paper-based; 80 iBT). Electronic applications accepted. *Faculty research:* Aerodynamics/fluid dynamics, design and manufacturing, controls/robotics, solid mechanics or biomechanics/biomaterials.

University of Oklahoma, Gallogly College of Engineering, School of Aerospace and Mechanical Engineering, Norman, OK 73019. Offers aerospace engineering (MS, PhD), including aerospace engineering-general; mechanical engineering (MS, PhD), including mechanical engineering-general. *Program availability:* Part-time. *Faculty:* 28 full-time (3 women). *Students:* 46 full-time (12 women), 18 part-time (5 women); includes 8 minority (1 Black or African American, non-Hispanic/Latino; 1 American Indian or Alaska Native, non-Hispanic/Latino; 2 Asian, non-Hispanic/Latino; 1 Hispanic/Latino; 3 Two or more races, non-Hispanic/Latino), 38 international. Average age 28. 33 applicants, 73% accepted, 14 enrolled. In 2018, 15 master's, 8 doctorates awarded. *Degree requirements:* For master's, comprehensive exam (for some programs), thesis (for some programs); for doctorate, comprehensive exam, thesis/dissertation, general exam. *Entrance requirements:* For master's and doctorate, GRE, letters of reference, resume, statement of purpose. Additional exam requirements/recommendations for international students: Required—TOEFL (minimum score 79 iBT) or IELTS (minimum score 6.5). *Application deadline:* For fall admission, 1/15 for domestic and international students; for spring admission, 9/1 for domestic and international students. Application fee: $50 ($100 for international students). Electronic applications accepted. *Expenses:* Tuition, state resident: full-time $5683.20; part-time $236.80 per credit hour. Tuition, nonresident: full-time $20,342; part-time $847.60 per credit hour. *International tuition:* $20,342.40 full-time. *Required fees:* $2894.20; $110.05 per credit hour. $126.50 per semester. Tuition and fees vary according to course load and program. *Financial support:* Fellowships, research assistantships, teaching assistantships, and scholarships/grants available. Financial award application deadline: 6/1; financial award applicants required to submit FAFSA. *Faculty research:* Unmanned aerial vehicles, advanced materials, energy systems, design and manufacturing, biomechanics. *Unit head:* Zahed Siddique, Director, 405-325-5011, Fax: 405-325-1088, E-mail: zsiddique@ou.edu. *Application contact:* Bethany Burklund, AME Student Services Coordinator, 405-325-5013, Fax: 405-325-1088, E-mail: bethanyhb@ou.edu.
Website: http://www.ou.edu/coe/ame.html

University of Ottawa, Faculty of Graduate and Postdoctoral Studies, Faculty of Engineering, Ottawa-Carleton Institute for Mechanical and Aerospace Engineering, Ottawa, ON K1N 6N5, Canada. Offers M Eng, MA Sc, PhD. MA Sc, M Eng, PhD offered jointly with Carleton University. *Degree requirements:* For master's, thesis or alternative; for doctorate, thesis/dissertation, seminar series, qualifying exam. *Entrance requirements:* For master's, honors degree or equivalent, minimum B average; for doctorate, master's degree, minimum B+ average. Electronic applications accepted. *Faculty research:* Fluid mechanics-heat transfer, solid mechanics, design, manufacturing and control.

University of Pennsylvania, School of Engineering and Applied Science, Department of Mechanical Engineering and Applied Mechanics, Philadelphia, PA 19104. Offers MSE, PhD. *Program availability:* Part-time. *Faculty:* 38 full-time (8 women), 11 part-time/adjunct (2 women). *Students:* 156 full-time (34 women), 21 part-time (3 women); includes 24 minority (3 Black or African American, non-Hispanic/Latino; 10 Asian, non-Hispanic/Latino; 7 Hispanic/Latino; 4 Two or more races, non-Hispanic/Latino), 111 international. Average age 25. 612 applicants, 33% accepted, 109 enrolled. In 2018, 41 master's, 7 doctorates awarded. Terminal master's awarded for partial completion of doctoral program. *Degree requirements:* For master's, comprehensive exam, thesis optional; for doctorate, comprehensive exam, thesis/dissertation. *Entrance requirements:* For master's and doctorate, GRE, bachelor's degree, letters of recommendation, resume, personal statement. Additional exam requirements/recommendations for international students: Required—TOEFL (minimum score 100 iBT), IELTS (minimum score 7). *Application deadline:* For fall admission, 12/15 priority date for domestic students, 12/15 for international students. Application fee: $80. Electronic applications accepted. *Expenses:* Contact institution. *Faculty research:* Design and manufacturing, heat transfer, fluid mechanics and energy, mechanics of materials, mechatronics and robotics systems, micro- and nano-systems. *Application contact:* William Fenton, Assistant Director of Graduate Admissions, 215-898-4542, Fax: 215-573-5577, E-mail: gradstudies@seas.upenn.edu.
Website: http://www.me.upenn.edu/prospective-students/masters/masters-degrees.php

University of Pittsburgh, Swanson School of Engineering, Department of Mechanical Engineering and Materials Science, Pittsburgh, PA 15260. Offers MSME, MSNE, PhD. *Program availability:* Part-time, 100% online. Terminal master's awarded for partial completion of doctoral program. *Degree requirements:* For doctorate, comprehensive exam, thesis/dissertation, final oral exams. *Entrance requirements:* For master's and doctorate, minimum GPA of 3.0. Additional exam requirements/recommendations for international students: Required—TOEFL (minimum score 550 paper-based; 80 iBT). Electronic applications accepted. *Expenses:* Contact institution. *Faculty research:* Smart materials and structure solid mechanics, computational fluid dynamics, multiphase bio-fluid dynamics, mechanical vibration analysis.

University of Portland, Shiley School of Engineering, Portland, OR 97203-5798. Offers biomedical engineering (MBME); civil engineering (ME); computer science (ME); electrical engineering (ME); mechanical engineering (ME). *Program availability:* Part-time, evening/weekend. *Students:* 12 full-time (4 women), 2 part-time (both women); includes 1 minority (Black or African American, non-Hispanic/Latino), 2 international. Average age 24. 43 applicants, 49% accepted, 10 enrolled. In 2018, 6 master's awarded. *Degree requirements:* For master's, thesis optional. *Entrance requirements:* For master's, GRE General Test, minimum GPA of 3.0, 2 letters of recommendation, resume, statement of goals, official transcripts. Additional exam requirements/recommendations for international students: Required—TOEFL (minimum score 80 iBT), IELTS (minimum score 7). *Application deadline:* For fall admission, 7/15 priority date for domestic and international students; for spring admission, 12/15 priority date for domestic and international students; for summer admission, 4/15 for domestic and international students. Applications are processed on a rolling basis. Electronic applications accepted. *Expenses:* $1,326 per credit plus $50 professional tuition per credit. *Financial support:* Research assistantships, career-related internships or fieldwork, Federal Work-Study, and scholarships/grants available. Support available to part-time students. Financial award application deadline: 3/1; financial award applicants required to submit FAFSA. *Unit head:* Dr. Matthew Kuhn, Dean, 503-943-7361, E-mail: kuhn@up.edu. *Application contact:* Caitlin Biddulph, Graduate Programs and Admissions Specialist, 503-943-7107.
Website: http://engineering.up.edu/default.aspx?cid-6464&pid-2432

University of Puerto Rico–Mayagüez, Graduate Studies, College of Engineering, Department of Mechanical Engineering, Mayagüez, PR 00681-9000. Offers mechanical engineering (ME, MS, PhD), including aerospace and unmanned vehicles (ME), automation/mechatronics, bioengineering, fluid mechanics, heat transfer/energy systems, manufacturing, mechanics of materials, micro and nano engineering. *Program availability:* Part-time. Terminal master's awarded for partial completion of doctoral program. *Degree requirements:* For master's, one foreign language, comprehensive exam, thesis; for doctorate, one foreign language, comprehensive exam, thesis/dissertation. *Entrance requirements:* For master's, BS in mechanical engineering or its equivalent; for doctorate, GRE, BS or MS in mechanical engineering or its equivalent; minimum GPA of 3.0. Additional exam requirements/recommendations for international students: Required—TOEFL (minimum score 80 iBT). Electronic applications accepted. *Faculty research:* Computational fluid dynamics, thermal sciences, mechanical design, material health, microfluidics.

University of Rochester, Hajim School of Engineering and Applied Sciences, Department of Mechanical Engineering, Rochester, NY 14627. Offers MS, PhD. *Faculty:* 15 full-time (2 women). *Students:* 46 full-time (8 women), 3 part-time (0 women); includes 2 minority (both Hispanic/Latino), 31 international. Average age 27. 111 applicants, 48% accepted, 15 enrolled. In 2018, 8 master's, 3 doctorates awarded. Terminal master's awarded for partial completion of doctoral program. *Degree requirements:* For master's, comprehensive exam, thesis (for some programs); for doctorate, comprehensive exam, thesis/dissertation, qualifying exam. *Entrance requirements:* For master's and doctorate, GRE, personal statement, official transcripts, three letters of recommendation. Additional exam requirements/recommendations for international students: Required—TOEFL (minimum score 95 paper-based), IELTS (minimum score 6). *Application deadline:* For fall admission, 1/1 for domestic and international students. Application fee: $60. Electronic applications accepted. *Expenses: Tuition:* Full-time $52,974; part-time $1654 per credit hour. *Required fees:* $612. One-time fee: $30 part-time. Tuition and fees vary according to campus/location and program. *Financial support:* In 2018–19, 12 students received support, including 1 fellowship with tuition reimbursement available (averaging $28,500 per year), 11 teaching assistantships with tuition reimbursements available (averaging $28,500 per year); tuition waivers (full and partial) also available. *Faculty research:* Fluid and solid mechanics, biomechanics, fusion/plasma, materials science, precision machining and optics manufacturing. *Total annual research expenditures:* $1.8 million. *Unit head:* Renato Perucchio, Chair, 585-275-4071, E-mail: rlp@me.rochester.edu. *Application contact:* Sarah Ansini, Graduate Program Coordinator, 585-275-2849, E-mail: sarah.ansini@rochester.edu.
Website: http://www.hajim.rochester.edu/me/graduate/index.html

University of St. Thomas, School of Engineering, St. Paul, MN 55105. Offers data science (MS); electrical engineering (MS); information technology (MS); manufacturing engineering (MS); manufacturing systems (Certificate); mechanical engineering (MS); medical device development (Certificate); regulatory science (MS); software engineering (MS); software management (MS); systems engineering (MS); technology leadership (Certificate); technology management (MS). *Program availability:* Part-time, evening/weekend. *Entrance requirements:* For master's, resume, official transcripts. Additional exam requirements/recommendations for international students: Required—TOEFL (minimum score 80 iBT), IELTS (minimum score 6.5). Electronic applications accepted. *Expenses:* Contact institution.

University of Saskatchewan, College of Graduate and Postdoctoral Studies, College of Engineering, Mechanical Engineering Program, Saskatoon, SK S7N 5E5, Canada. Offers M Eng, M Sc, PhD. *Program availability:* Part-time. *Degree requirements:* For master's, 30 credits (for M Eng); thesis and 12 credits (for MS); for doctorate, comprehensive exam, thesis/dissertation, qualifying exam, 18 credits. *Entrance requirements:* For master's and doctorate, GRE. Additional exam requirements/recommendations for international students: Required—TOEFL (minimum iBT score of 80), IELTS (6.5), CanTEST (4.5), or PTE (59). Electronic applications accepted. *Faculty research:* Advanced engineering design and manufacturing, advanced materials for clean energy, applied mechanics and machine design, bioengineering, control systems, fluid power, fluid dynamics, material science and metallurgy, robotics, thermal science and energy.

University of South Alabama, College of Engineering, Department of Mechanical Engineering, Mobile, AL 36688. Offers MSME. *Degree requirements:* For master's, comprehensive exam, project or thesis. *Entrance requirements:* For master's, GRE General Test, BS in engineering, minimum GPA of 3.0. Additional exam requirements/recommendations for international students: Required—TOEFL (minimum score 550 paper-based; 79 iBT), IELTS (minimum score 6.5). Electronic applications accepted. *Expenses:* Contact institution. *Faculty research:* Composite microstructure - property relationships, transport phenomena in porous media, hybrid micro-fiber/nano-particle composites, thermal dilution measurement of cardiac output.

University of South Carolina, The Graduate School, College of Engineering and Computing, Department of Mechanical Engineering, Columbia, SC 29208. Offers ME, MS, PhD. *Program availability:* Part-time, evening/weekend, online learning. *Degree requirements:* For master's, thesis (for some programs); for doctorate, thesis/dissertation. *Entrance requirements:* For master's and doctorate, GRE General Test. Additional exam requirements/recommendations for international students: Required—TOEFL (minimum score 600 paper-based). Electronic applications accepted. *Faculty research:* Heat exchangers, computer vision measurements in solid mechanics and biomechanics, robot dynamics and control.

University of Southern California, Graduate School, Viterbi School of Engineering, Department of Aerospace and Mechanical Engineering, Los Angeles, CA 90089. Offers aerospace and mechanical engineering: computational fluid and solid mechanics (MS); aerospace and mechanical engineering: dynamics and control (MS); aerospace engineering (MS, PhD, Engr), including aerospace engineering (PhD, Engr); green technologies (MS); mechanical engineering (MS, PhD, Engr), including energy conversion (MS), mechanical engineering (PhD, Engr), nuclear power (MS); product development engineering (MS). *Program availability:* Part-time, evening/weekend, online learning. Terminal master's awarded for partial completion of doctoral program. *Degree requirements:* For master's, thesis optional; for doctorate, thesis/dissertation.

Mechanical Engineering

Entrance requirements: For master's, doctorate, and Engr, GRE General Test. Additional exam requirements/recommendations for international students: Recommended—TOEFL. Electronic applications accepted. *Faculty research:* Mechanics and materials, aerodynamics of air/ground vehicles, gas dynamics, aerosols, astronautics and space science, geophysical and microgravity flows, planetary physics, power MEMs and MEMS vacuum pumps, heat transfer and combustion.

University of South Florida, College of Engineering, Department of Mechanical Engineering, Tampa, FL 33620-9951. Offers mechanical engineering (MSME, PhD), including mechanical engineering (PhD). *Program availability:* Part-time. *Faculty:* 15 full-time (2 women). *Students:* 122 full-time (10 women), 37 part-time (3 women); includes 15 minority (2 Black or African American, non-Hispanic/Latino; 3 Asian, non-Hispanic/Latino; 8 Hispanic/Latino; 2 Two or more races, non-Hispanic/Latino), 118 international. Average age 25. 162 applicants, 46% accepted, 38 enrolled. In 2018, 83 master's, 11 doctorates awarded. Terminal master's awarded for partial completion of doctoral program. *Degree requirements:* For master's, comprehensive exam, thesis or alternative; for doctorate, comprehensive exam, thesis/dissertation, 2 tools of research as specified by dissertation committee. *Entrance requirements:* For master's, RE required, with minimum percentile rank of 50% on the quantitative portion and a minimum average percentile rank of 50% in verbal and quantitative., BS in Mechanical Eng or related field; 3.00 GPA for last 2 years of coursework from an ABET accredited engineering major. 2 letters of recommendation; statement of purpose; prerequisite coursework required.; for doctorate, GRE required, with minimum percentile rank of 60% on the quantitative portion and a minimum average percentile rank of 60% in verbal and quantitative., MS in mechanical engineering or closely-related field (preferred); one-page statement of purpose and research interests; 3 letters of recommendation; minimum of 3.00 GPA for last 2 years of coursework from an ABET accredited engineering major; prerequisite coursework required. Additional exam requirements/recommendations for international students: Required—TOEFL, TOEFL (minimum score 550 paper-based; 79 iBT) or IELTS (minimum score 6.5). *Application deadline:* For fall admission, 2/15 for domestic and international students; for spring admission, 10/15 for domestic students, 9/15 for international students; for summer admission, 2/15 for domestic students, 1/15 for international students. Application fee: $30. Electronic applications accepted. *Expenses:* Tuition, state resident: full-time $6350. Tuition, nonresident: full-time $19,048. *International tuition:* $19,048 full-time. *Required fees:* $2079. *Financial support:* In 2018–19, 11 students received support, including 42 research assistantships with tuition reimbursements available (averaging $12,819 per year), 22 teaching assistantships with partial tuition reimbursements available (averaging $14,017 per year). Financial award applicants required to submit FAFSA. *Faculty research:* Acoustic transducers, cellular mechanotransduction and biomaterials, computational fluid dynamics and heat transfer, computational methods research and education, environmentally benign design and manufacturing, micro-/nano-integration, nano-chemical testing, rehabilitation engineering and electromechanical design, rehabilitation robotics, vibrations/dynamic systems. *Total annual research expenditures:* $3.1 million. *Unit head:* Dr. Rajiv Dubey, Professor and Department Chair, 813-974-5619, Fax: 813-974-3539, E-mail: dubey@usf.edu. *Application contact:* Dr. Delcie Durham, Professor and Graduate Program Director, 813-974-5656, Fax: 813-974-3539, E-mail: drdurham@usf.edu.
Website: http://me.eng.usf.edu/

The University of Tennessee, Graduate School, Tickle College of Engineering, Department of Mechanical, Aerospace and Biomedical Engineering, Program in Mechanical Engineering, Knoxville, TN 37996. Offers MS, PhD, MS/MBA. *Program availability:* Part-time, online learning. *Faculty:* 32 full-time (1 woman), 1 part-time/adjunct (0 women). *Students:* 92 full-time (9 women), 28 part-time (3 women); includes 9 minority (2 Black or African American, non-Hispanic/Latino; 2 Asian, non-Hispanic/Latino; 1 Hispanic/Latino; 4 Two or more races, non-Hispanic/Latino), 44 international. Average age 27. 120 applicants, 36% accepted, 23 enrolled. In 2018, 25 master's, 11 doctorates awarded. *Degree requirements:* For master's, thesis or alternative; for doctorate, comprehensive exam, thesis/dissertation. *Entrance requirements:* For master's, GRE General Test (for MS students pursuing research thesis), minimum GPA of 2.7 (for U.S. degree holders), 3.0 (for international degree holders); 3 references; statement of purpose; for doctorate, GRE General Test, minimum GPA of 3.0 on previous graduate course work; 3 references; statement of purpose. Additional exam requirements/recommendations for international students: Required—TOEFL (minimum score 550 paper-based; 80 iBT), IELTS (minimum score 6.5). *Application deadline:* For fall admission, 2/1 priority date for domestic and international students; for spring admission, 6/15 for domestic and international students; for summer admission, 10/15 for domestic and international students. Applications are processed on a rolling basis. Application fee: $60. Electronic applications accepted. *Financial support:* In 2018–19, 88 students received support, including 10 fellowships with full and partial tuition reimbursements available (averaging $9,616 per year), 54 research assistantships with full tuition reimbursements available (averaging $22,028 per year), 24 teaching assistantships with full tuition reimbursements available (averaging $19,468 per year); career-related internships or fieldwork, Federal Work-Study, institutionally sponsored loans, health care benefits, and unspecified assistantships also available. Financial award application deadline: 2/1; financial award applicants required to submit FAFSA. *Faculty research:* Automotive systems and technology; combustion and emissions; alternative fuels; electromechanical actuators; nanomechanics, nanomaterials, and nanotechnology. *Unit head:* Dr. Matthew Mench, Head, 865-974-5115, Fax: 865-974-5274, E-mail: mmench@utk.edu. *Application contact:* Dr. Kivanc Ekici, Associate Professor/Graduate Program Director, 865-974-6016, Fax: 865-974-5274, E-mail: ekici@utk.edu.
Website: http://www.engr.utk.edu/mabe

The University of Tennessee, The University of Tennessee Space Institute, Tullahoma, TN 37388. Offers aerospace engineering (MS, PhD); biomedical engineering (MS, PhD); engineering science (MS, PhD); industrial and systems engineering/engineering management (MS, PhD); mechanical engineering (MS, PhD); physics (MS, PhD). *Program availability:* Part-time, blended/hybrid learning. Terminal master's awarded for partial completion of doctoral program. *Degree requirements:* For doctorate, one foreign language, thesis/dissertation. *Entrance requirements:* Additional exam requirements/recommendations for international students: Required—TOEFL (minimum score 550 paper-based; 80 iBT), IELTS (minimum score 6.5). Electronic applications accepted. *Expenses:* Contact institution. *Faculty research:* Fluid mechanics/aerodynamics, chemical and electric propulsion and laser diagnostics, computational mechanics and simulations, carbon fiber production and composite materials.

The University of Tennessee at Chattanooga, Program in Engineering, Chattanooga, TN 37403. Offers automotive (MS Engr); chemical (MS Engr); civil (MS Engr); electrical (MS Engr); mechanical (MS Engr). *Program availability:* Part-time. *Degree requirements:* For master's, comprehensive exam, thesis or alternative, engineering project. *Entrance requirements:* For master's, GRE General Test, minimum undergraduate GPA of 2.7 or 3.0 in last two years of undergraduate coursework. Additional exam requirements/recommendations for international students: Required—TOEFL (minimum score 550 paper-based; 79 iBT), IELTS (minimum score 6). Electronic applications accepted. *Expenses:* Contact institution. *Faculty research:* Quality control and reliability engineering, financial management, thermal science, energy conservation, structural analysis.

The University of Texas at Arlington, Graduate School, College of Engineering, Department of Mechanical and Aerospace Engineering, Program in Mechanical Engineering, Arlington, TX 76019. Offers M Engr, MS, PhD. *Program availability:* Part-time, evening/weekend, online learning. Terminal master's awarded for partial completion of doctoral program. *Degree requirements:* For master's, thesis optional; for doctorate, comprehensive exam, thesis/dissertation. *Entrance requirements:* For master's and doctorate, GRE General Test, minimum GPA of 3.0. Additional exam requirements/recommendations for international students: Required—TOEFL (minimum score 550 paper-based).

The University of Texas at Austin, Graduate School, Cockrell School of Engineering, Department of Mechanical Engineering, Austin, TX 78712-1111. Offers mechanical engineering (MS, PhD); operations research and industrial engineering (MS, PhD); MBA/MSE; MP Aff/MSE. *Entrance requirements:* For master's and doctorate, GRE General Test. Additional exam requirements/recommendations for international students: Required—TOEFL.

The University of Texas at Dallas, Erik Jonsson School of Engineering and Computer Science, Department of Mechanical Engineering, Richardson, TX 75080. Offers MS, PhD. *Program availability:* Part-time, evening/weekend. *Faculty:* 25 full-time (2 women). *Students:* 153 full-time (19 women), 23 part-time (3 women); includes 17 minority (1 Black or African American, non-Hispanic/Latino; 6 Asian, non-Hispanic/Latino; 9 Hispanic/Latino; 1 Two or more races, non-Hispanic/Latino), 125 international. Average age 28. 332 applicants, 49% accepted, 43 enrolled. In 2018, 60 master's, 16 doctorates awarded. *Degree requirements:* For master's, thesis or major design project; for doctorate, comprehensive exam, thesis/dissertation, final exam, research project, qualifying exam. *Entrance requirements:* For master's, GRE General Test, minimum GPA of 3.0 in related bachelor's degree; for doctorate, GRE General Test, essay. Additional exam requirements/recommendations for international students: Required—TOEFL (minimum score 550 paper-based). *Application deadline:* For fall admission, 7/15 for domestic students, 5/1 priority date for international students; for spring admission, 11/15 for domestic students, 9/1 priority date for international students. Applications are processed on a rolling basis. Application fee: $50 ($100 for international students). Electronic applications accepted. *Expenses: Tuition, area resident:* Full-time $13,458. Tuition, state resident: full-time $13,458. Tuition, nonresident: full-time $26,852. *International tuition:* $26,852 full-time. Tuition and fees vary according to course load. *Financial support:* In 2018–19, 91 students received support, including 6 fellowships (averaging $1,333 per year), 62 research assistantships with partial tuition reimbursements available (averaging $23,913 per year), 29 teaching assistantships with partial tuition reimbursements available (averaging $17,224 per year); career-related internships or fieldwork, Federal Work-Study, institutionally sponsored loans, scholarships/grants, and unspecified assistantships also available. Support available to part-time students. Financial award application deadline: 4/30; financial award applicants required to submit FAFSA. *Faculty research:* Nano-materials and nano-electronic devices, biomedical devices, nonlinear systems and controls, semiconductor and oxide surfaces, flexible electronics. *Unit head:* Dr. Mario Rotea, Department Head, 972-883-2720, Fax: 972-883-2813, E-mail: rotea@utdallas.edu. *Application contact:* Dr. Hongbing Lu, Associate Department Head, 972-883-4647, Fax: 972-883-2813, E-mail: contactme@utdallas.edu.
Website: http://me.utdallas.edu

The University of Texas at El Paso, Graduate School, College of Engineering, Department of Mechanical Engineering, El Paso, TX 79968-0001. Offers environmental science and engineering (PhD); mechanical engineering (MS). *Program availability:* Part-time. *Degree requirements:* For master's, thesis optional; for doctorate, thesis/dissertation. *Entrance requirements:* For master's, GRE, minimum GPA of 3.0, letter of reference; for doctorate, GRE, minimum GPA of 3.5, letters of reference, BS or equivalent. Additional exam requirements/recommendations for international students: Required—TOEFL; Recommended—IELTS. Electronic applications accepted. *Faculty research:* Aerospace, energy, combustion and propulsion, design engineering, high temperature materials.

The University of Texas at San Antonio, College of Engineering, Department of Mechanical Engineering, San Antonio, TX 78249-0617. Offers advanced manufacturing and enterprise engineering (MS); mechanical engineering (MS, PhD). *Program availability:* Part-time, evening/weekend. Terminal master's awarded for partial completion of doctoral program. *Degree requirements:* For master's, comprehensive exam, thesis; for doctorate, comprehensive exam, thesis/dissertation. *Entrance requirements:* For master's, GRE General Test, bachelor's degree in mechanical engineering or related field from accredited institution of higher education; for doctorate, GRE General Test, master's degree in mechanical engineering, or exceptionally outstanding undergraduate record in mechanical engineering or related field; minimum GPA of 3.33. Additional exam requirements/recommendations for international students: Required—TOEFL (minimum score 550 paper-based; 79 iBT), IELTS (minimum score 6.5). Electronic applications accepted. *Expenses:* Contact institution. *Faculty research:* Mechanics and materials, advanced manufacturing, wind turbine, computational fluid dynamics, robotics, biomechanics, wind energy.

The University of Texas at Tyler, College of Engineering, Department of Mechanical Engineering, Tyler, TX 75799-0001. Offers MS. *Program availability:* Part-time, evening/weekend. *Students:* Average age 30. 7 applicants, 71% accepted, 1 enrolled. In 2018, 1 master's awarded. *Entrance requirements:* For master's, GRE or GMAT, bachelor's degree in engineering. *Application deadline:* For fall admission, 10/30 for domestic students; for spring admission, 5/30 for domestic students. Applications are processed on a rolling basis. Application fee: $0 ($50 for international students). *Financial support:* Research assistantships with partial tuition reimbursements and scholarships/grants available. Financial award application deadline: 7/1; financial award applicants required to submit FAFSA. *Faculty research:* Mechatronics vibration analysis, fluid dynamics, electronics and instrumentation, manufacturing processes, optics, computational fluid dynamics, signal processing, high voltage related studies, real time systems, semiconductors. *Total annual research expenditures:* $100,000. *Unit head:* Dr. Nael Barakat, Chair, 903-566-7003, E-mail: nbarakat@uttyler.edu. *Application contact:* Dr. Nael Barakat, Chair, 903-566-7003, E-mail: nbarakat@uttyler.edu.
Website: https://www.uttyler.edu/me/

The University of Texas Rio Grande Valley, College of Engineering and Computer Science, Department of Mechanical Engineering, Edinburg, TX 78539. Offers MSE. *Degree requirements:* For master's, comprehensive exam, thesis (for some programs). *Entrance requirements:* For master's, GRE General Test. Additional exam requirements/recommendations for international students: Required—TOEFL (minimum score 550 paper-based; 79 iBT) or IELTS (6.5). *Expenses: Tuition, area resident:* Full-time $6888. Tuition, state resident: full-time $6888. Tuition, nonresident: full-time $14,484. *International tuition:* $14,484 full-time. *Required fees:* $1468.

The University of Toledo, College of Graduate Studies, College of Engineering, Department of Mechanical, Industrial, and Manufacturing Engineering, Toledo, OH 43606-3390. Offers industrial engineering (MS, PhD); mechanical engineering (MS, PhD). *Program availability:* Part-time, online learning. *Degree requirements:* For master's, thesis optional; for doctorate, thesis/dissertation, qualifying exam. *Entrance requirements:* For master's, GRE General Test, minimum GPA of 3.0; for doctorate,

GRE General Test, minimum GPA of 3.3. Additional exam requirements/recommendations for international students: Required—TOEFL (minimum score 550 paper-based; 80 iBT). Electronic applications accepted. *Faculty research:* Computational and experimental thermal sciences, manufacturing process and systems, mechanics, materials, design, quality and management engineering systems.

University of Toronto, School of Graduate Studies, Faculty of Applied Science and Engineering, Department of Mechanical and Industrial Engineering, Toronto, ON M5S 1A1, Canada. Offers M Eng, MA Sc, PhD. *Program availability:* Part-time. *Degree requirements:* For master's, thesis (for some programs), oral exam/thesis defense (MA Sc); for doctorate, thesis/dissertation, thesis defense, qualifying examination. *Entrance requirements:* For master's, GRE (recommended), minimum B+ average in last 2 years of undergraduate study, 2 letters of reference, resume, Canadian citizenship or permanent residency (M Eng); for doctorate, GRE (recommended), minimum B+ average, 2 letters of reference, resume. Additional exam requirements/recommendations for international students: Required—TOEFL (minimum score 580 paper-based), Michigan English Language Assessment Battery (minimum score 85), IELTS (minimum score 7), or COPE (minimum score 4). Electronic applications accepted.

The University of Tulsa, Graduate School, College of Engineering and Natural Sciences, Department of Mechanical Engineering, Tulsa, OK 74104-3189. Offers ME, MSE, PhD. *Program availability:* Part-time. *Faculty:* 12 full-time (0 women), 8 part-time/adjunct (3 women). *Students:* 32 full-time (7 women), 12 part-time (2 women); includes 4 minority (2 Hispanic/Latino; 2 Two or more races, non-Hispanic/Latino), 17 international. Average age 27. 31 applicants, 74% accepted, 9 enrolled. In 2018, 14 master's, 3 doctorates awarded. Terminal master's awarded for partial completion of doctoral program. *Degree requirements:* For master's, thesis (MSE); for doctorate, comprehensive exam, thesis/dissertation. *Entrance requirements:* For master's and doctorate, GRE General Test. Additional exam requirements/recommendations for international students: Required—TOEFL (minimum score 550 paper-based; 80 iBT), IELTS (minimum score 6). *Application deadline:* Applications are processed on a rolling basis. Application fee: $55. Electronic applications accepted. *Expenses: Tuition:* Full-time $22,230; part-time $1235 per credit hour. *Required fees:* $2100; $6 per credit hour. One-time fee: $400 full-time. Tuition and fees vary according to course level, course load and program. *Financial support:* In 2018–19, 27 students received support, including 4 fellowships with full tuition reimbursements available (averaging $4,250 per year), 27 research assistantships with full tuition reimbursements available (averaging $15,121 per year), 10 teaching assistantships with full tuition reimbursements available (averaging $9,581 per year); career-related internships or fieldwork, Federal Work-Study, health care benefits, tuition waivers (full and partial), and unspecified assistantships also available. Support available to part-time students. Financial award application deadline: 2/1; financial award applicants required to submit FAFSA. *Faculty research:* Erosion and corrosion, solid mechanics, composite material, computational fluid dynamics, coiled tubing mechanics. *Unit head:* Dr. John Henshaw, Chairperson, 918-631-3002, Fax: 918-631-2397, E-mail: john-henshaw@utulsa.edu. *Application contact:* Dr. Siamack A. Shirazi, Adviser, 918-631-3001, Fax: 918-631-2397, E-mail: grad@utulsa.edu.
Website: http://engineering.utulsa.edu/academics/mechanical-engineering/

University of Utah, Graduate School, College of Engineering, Department of Mechanical Engineering, Salt Lake City, UT 84112. Offers MS, PhD, MS/MBA. *Program availability:* Part-time, blended/hybrid learning. *Faculty:* 36 full-time (7 women), 10 part-time/adjunct (1 woman). *Students:* 172 full-time (21 women), 65 part-time (7 women); includes 23 minority (2 Black or African American, non-Hispanic/Latino; 8 Asian, non-Hispanic/Latino; 5 Hispanic/Latino; 8 Two or more races, non-Hispanic/Latino), 62 international. Average age 28. 415 applicants, 27% accepted, 69 enrolled. In 2018, 62 master's, 18 doctorates awarded. Terminal master's awarded for partial completion of doctoral program. *Degree requirements:* For master's, comprehensive exam (for some programs), thesis (for some programs); for doctorate, thesis/dissertation. *Entrance requirements:* For master's and doctorate, GRE General Test, minimum GPA of 3.0, statement of purpose, 3 letters of recommendation, curriculum vitae/resume, transcripts. Additional exam requirements/recommendations for international students: Required—TOEFL (minimum score 550 paper-based; 80 iBT), IELTS (minimum score 6.5). *Application deadline:* For fall admission, 1/1 priority date for domestic students, 12/1 priority date for international students; for spring admission, 10/1 priority date for domestic students; for summer admission, 2/15 priority date for domestic students. Application fee: $0 ($30 for international students). Electronic applications accepted. *Expenses:* $9,323/yr state resident full-time; $26,194/yr nonresident full-time. *Financial support:* In 2018–19, 150 students received support, including 13 fellowships with full tuition reimbursements available (averaging $25,000 per year), 92 research assistantships with full and partial tuition reimbursements available (averaging $22,500 per year), 52 teaching assistantships with full and partial tuition reimbursements available (averaging $15,500 per year); institutionally sponsored loans, scholarships/grants, traineeships, health care benefits, and unspecified assistantships also available. Financial award application deadline: 1/15. *Faculty research:* Design, ergonomics, manufacturing and systems; robotics, controls and mechatronics; solid mechanics; thermal fluids and energy systems. *Total annual research expenditures:* $4.8 million. *Unit head:* Dr. Bruce Gale, Chair, 801-585-5944, Fax: 801-585-9826, E-mail: bruce.gale@utah.edu. *Application contact:* Dr. Mark Fehlberg, Director of Graduate Studies, 801-585-9293, Fax: 801-585-9826, E-mail: m.fehlberg@utah.edu.
Website: http://www.mech.utah.edu/

University of Vermont, Graduate College, College of Engineering and Mathematical Sciences, Department of Mechanical Engineering, Burlington, VT 05405-0156. Offers MS, PhD. *Degree requirements:* For master's, thesis; for doctorate, thesis/dissertation. *Entrance requirements:* For master's and doctorate, GRE General Test (for research assistant or teaching assistant funding). Additional exam requirements/recommendations for international students: Required—TOEFL (minimum score 550 paper-based; 90 iBT), IELTS (minimum score 6.5). Electronic applications accepted.

University of Victoria, Faculty of Graduate Studies, Faculty of Engineering, Department of Mechanical Engineering, Victoria, BC V8W 2Y2, Canada. Offers M Eng, MA Sc, PhD. *Program availability:* Part-time. *Degree requirements:* For master's, thesis (for some programs); for doctorate, thesis/dissertation, candidacy exam. *Entrance requirements:* For master's, minimum B average in undergraduate course work. Additional exam requirements/recommendations for international students: Required—TOEFL (minimum score 575 paper-based), IELTS (minimum score 7). Electronic applications accepted. *Faculty research:* CAD/CAM, energy systems, cryofuels, fuel cell technology, computational mechanics.

University of Virginia, School of Engineering and Applied Science, Department of Mechanical and Aerospace Engineering, Charlottesville, VA 22903. Offers ME, MS, PhD. *Program availability:* Online learning. *Degree requirements:* For master's, thesis (MS); for doctorate, comprehensive exam, thesis/dissertation. *Entrance requirements:* For master's and doctorate, GRE General Test, 3 letters of recommendation. Additional exam requirements/recommendations for international students: Required—TOEFL (minimum score 650 paper-based; 90 iBT), IELTS (minimum score 7). Electronic applications accepted. *Faculty research:* Solid mechanics, dynamical systems and control, thermofluids.

University of Washington, Graduate School, College of Engineering, Department of Mechanical Engineering, Seattle, WA 98195-2600. Offers MSE, MSME, PhD. *Program availability:* Part-time, blended/hybrid learning. *Faculty:* 37 full-time (5 women), 7 part-time/adjunct (2 women). *Students:* 268 full-time (58 women), 104 part-time (15 women); includes 38 minority (1 Black or African American, non-Hispanic/Latino; 22 Asian, non-Hispanic/Latino; 5 Hispanic/Latino; 1 Native Hawaiian or other Pacific Islander, non-Hispanic/Latino; 9 Two or more races, non-Hispanic/Latino), 184 international. Average age 26. 662 applicants, 70% accepted, 124 enrolled. In 2018, 106 master's, 12 doctorates awarded. *Degree requirements:* For master's, thesis optional; for doctorate, comprehensive exam, thesis/dissertation, qualifying, general, and final exams. *Entrance requirements:* For master's, GRE General Test (minimum scores: 150 Verbal, 155 Quantitative, and 4.0 Analytical Writing), minimum GPA of 3.0 (overall undergraduate GPA of 3.3 preferred); 3 letters of recommendation; statement of purpose; for doctorate, GRE General Test (minimum scores: 150 Verbal, 155 Quantitative, and 4.0 Analytical Writing), minimum GPA of 3.0 (overall undergraduate GPA of 3.3, graduate 3.5 preferred); letters of recommendation; statement of purpose. Additional exam requirements/recommendations for international students: Required—TOEFL (minimum score 580 paper-based; 92 iBT). *Application deadline:* For fall admission, 12/15 priority date for domestic and international students; for winter admission, 11/1 for domestic students; for spring admission, 2/1 for domestic students; for summer admission, 4/1 for domestic students. Applications are processed on a rolling basis. Application fee: $85. Electronic applications accepted. *Expenses:* PhD annual tuition: $18,852 (resident rate) and $32,760 (non-resident rate); Professional/Applied Master's degree tuition: $535 per credit (resident rate) and $985 per credit (non-resident rate). *Financial support:* In 2018–19, 147 students received support, including 18 fellowships with full tuition reimbursements available (averaging $30,540 per year), 69 research assistantships with full tuition reimbursements available (averaging $30,540 per year), 34 teaching assistantships with full tuition reimbursements available (averaging $30,540 per year); scholarships/grants, health care benefits, tuition waivers (full), and unspecified assistantships also available. Financial award application deadline: 12/15; financial award applicants required to submit FAFSA. *Faculty research:* Environmentally-friendly energy conversion, mechanics and advanced material systems, system and dynamics, bio-health systems. *Total annual research expenditures:* $19.5 million. *Unit head:* Dr. Per Reinhall, Professor/Chair, 206-543-5090, Fax: 206-685-8047, E-mail: reinhall@uw.edu. *Application contact:* Wanwisa Kisalang, Graduate Academic Adviser, 206-543-7963, Fax: 206-685-8047, E-mail: megrad@uw.edu.
Website: http://www.me.washington.edu

University of Waterloo, Graduate Studies and Postdoctoral Affairs, Faculty of Engineering, Department of Mechanical and Mechatronics Engineering, Waterloo, ON N2L 3G1, Canada. Offers mechanical engineering (M Eng, MA Sc, PhD); mechanical engineering design and manufacturing (M Eng). *Program availability:* Part-time, evening/weekend. *Degree requirements:* For master's, research paper or thesis; for doctorate, comprehensive exam, thesis/dissertation. *Entrance requirements:* For master's, honors degree, minimum B average, resume; for doctorate, master's degree, minimum A- average, resume. Additional exam requirements/recommendations for international students: Required—TOEFL, IELTS, PTE. *Application deadline:* Applications are processed on a rolling basis. Application fee: $125 Canadian dollars. Electronic applications accepted. *Financial support:* Research assistantships and teaching assistantships available. *Faculty research:* Fluid mechanics, thermal engineering, solid mechanics, automation and control, materials engineering.
Website: https://uwaterloo.ca/mechanical-mechatronics-engineering/

The University of Western Ontario, School of Graduate and Postdoctoral Studies, Physical Sciences Division, Faculty of Engineering, London, ON N6A 3K7, Canada. Offers chemical and biochemical engineering (ME Sc, PhD); civil and environmental engineering (M Eng, ME Sc, PhD); electrical and computer engineering (M Eng, ME Sc, PhD); mechanical and materials engineering (M Eng, ME Sc, PhD). *Program availability:* Part-time. Terminal master's awarded for partial completion of doctoral program. *Degree requirements:* For master's, thesis; for doctorate, thesis/dissertation. *Entrance requirements:* For master's, minimum B average; for doctorate, minimum B+ average. *Faculty research:* Wind, geotechnical, chemical reactor engineering, applied electrostatics, biochemical engineering.

University of Windsor, Faculty of Graduate Studies, Faculty of Engineering, Department of Mechanical, Automotive, and Materials Engineering, Windsor, ON N9B 3P4, Canada. Offers engineering materials (M Eng, MA Sc, PhD); mechanical engineering (M Eng, MA Sc, PhD). *Program availability:* Part-time. *Degree requirements:* For master's, thesis; for doctorate, comprehensive exam, thesis/dissertation. *Entrance requirements:* For master's, minimum B average; for doctorate, master's degree, minimum B average. Additional exam requirements/recommendations for international students: Required—TOEFL (minimum score 600 paper-based). Electronic applications accepted. *Faculty research:* Thermofluids, applied mechanics, materials engineering.

University of Wisconsin–Madison, Graduate School, College of Engineering, Department of Mechanical Engineering, Madison, WI 53706. Offers mechanical engineering (MS, PhD), including automotive engineering (MS), modeling and simulation (MS). *Program availability:* Part-time. *Faculty:* 29 full-time (2 women). *Students:* 198 full-time (33 women), 25 part-time (3 women); includes 34 minority (3 Black or African American, non-Hispanic/Latino; 13 Asian, non-Hispanic/Latino; 16 Hispanic/Latino; 2 Two or more races, non-Hispanic/Latino), 103 international. Average age 27. 537 applicants, 31% accepted, 54 enrolled. In 2018, 42 master's, 15 doctorates awarded. Terminal master's awarded for partial completion of doctoral program. *Degree requirements:* For master's, thesis (for some programs), 30 credits; minimum GPA of 3.0; for doctorate, thesis/dissertation, qualifying exam, preliminary exam, final oral defense, 42 formal course credits, 18 thesis credits, minimum GPA of 3.25. *Entrance requirements:* For master's, GRE, BS in mechanical engineering or related field, minimum GPA of 3.2 in last 60 hours of course work; for doctorate, GRE, BS in mechanical engineering or related field, minimum undergraduate GPA of 3.2 in last 60 hours of course work. Additional exam requirements/recommendations for international students: Required—TOEFL (minimum score 580 paper-based; 92 iBT), IELTS (minimum score 7). *Application deadline:* For fall admission, 12/15 for domestic and international students; for spring admission, 10/1 for domestic and international students; for summer admission, 12/15 for domestic and international students. Application fee: $75 ($81 for international students). Electronic applications accepted. *Financial support:* In 2018–19, 159 students received support, including 14 fellowships with full tuition reimbursements available (averaging $28,536 per year), 89 research assistantships with full tuition reimbursements available (averaging $21,396 per year), 56 teaching assistantships with full tuition reimbursements available (averaging $17,880 per year); career-related internships or fieldwork, institutionally sponsored loans, scholarships/grants, traineeships, health care benefits, and unspecified assistantships also available. Financial award application deadline: 12/1; financial award applicants required to submit FAFSA. *Faculty research:* Polymer engineering; robotics/electromechanical system control; advanced manufacturing and prototype processes; computational mechanics; thermal-fluid systems; engine and vehicle systems. *Total annual research expenditures:* $10.9 million. *Unit head:* Dr. Jaal B. Ghandhi, Chair, 608-262-3543, E-mail: dept@me.engr.wisc.edu. *Application contact:* Sara Hladilek, Student Services Coordinator, 608-262-8617, E-mail: shladilek@wisc.edu.
Website: https://www.engr.wisc.edu/department/mechanical-engineering/

Mechanical Engineering

University of Wisconsin–Milwaukee, Graduate School, College of Engineering and Applied Science, Program in Engineering, Milwaukee, WI 53201-0413. Offers biomedical engineering (MS); civil engineering (MS, PhD); computer science (PhD); electrical and computer engineering (MS); electrical engineering (PhD); engineering mechanics (MS); industrial and management engineering (MS); industrial engineering (PhD); manufacturing engineering (MS); materials (PhD); materials engineering (MS); mechanical engineering (MS). *Program availability:* Part-time. *Students:* 174 full-time (41 women), 149 part-time (27 women); includes 31 minority (2 Black or African American, non-Hispanic/Latino; 1 American Indian or Alaska Native, non-Hispanic/Latino; 16 Asian, non-Hispanic/Latino; 4 Hispanic/Latino; 8 Two or more races, non-Hispanic/Latino), 207 international. Average age 31. 343 applicants, 57% accepted, 78 enrolled. In 2018, 73 master's, 24 doctorates awarded. *Degree requirements:* For master's, comprehensive exam (for some programs), thesis or alternative; for doctorate, comprehensive exam, thesis/dissertation, internship. *Entrance requirements:* For master's, GRE, minimum GPA of 2.75; for doctorate, GRE, minimum GPA of 3.5. Additional exam requirements/recommendations for international students: Required—TOEFL (minimum score 550 paper-based; 79 iBT), IELTS (minimum score 6.5). *Application deadline:* For fall admission, 1/1 priority date for domestic students; for spring admission, 9/1 for domestic students. Applications are processed on a rolling basis. Application fee: $56 ($96 for international students). *Financial support:* Fellowships, research assistantships, teaching assistantships, career-related internships or fieldwork, Federal Work-Study, unspecified assistantships, and project assistantships available. Support available to part-time students. Financial award application deadline: 4/15. *Unit head:* David Yu, Representative, 414-229-6169, E-mail: yu@uwm.edu. *Application contact:* Betty Warras, General Information Contact, 414-229-6169, Fax: 414-229-6967, E-mail: bwarras@uwm.edu.
Website: http://www4.uwm.edu/ceas/academics/graduate_programs/

University of Wyoming, College of Engineering and Applied Science, Department of Mechanical and Energy Systems Engineering, Laramie, WY 82071. Offers MS, PhD. Terminal master's awarded for partial completion of doctoral program. *Degree requirements:* For master's, thesis; for doctorate, thesis/dissertation. *Entrance requirements:* For master's, GRE General Test (minimum score 900), minimum GPA of 3.0; for doctorate, GRE General Test (minimum score: 1000), minimum GPA of 3.0. Additional exam requirements/recommendations for international students: Required—TOEFL (minimum score 550 paper-based). Electronic applications accepted. *Expenses: Tuition, area resident:* Full-time $6504; part-time $271 per credit hour. *Tuition, state resident:* full-time $6504; part-time $271 per credit hour. *Tuition, nonresident:* full-time $19,464; part-time $811 per credit hour. *International tuition:* $19,464 full-time. *Required fees:* $1410.94; $343.82 per semester. $343.82 per semester. Tuition and fees vary according to course load, program and reciprocity agreements. *Faculty research:* Composite materials, thermal and fluid sciences, continuum mechanics, material science.

Utah State University, School of Graduate Studies, College of Engineering, Department of Mechanical and Aerospace Engineering, Logan, UT 84322. Offers aerospace engineering (MS, PhD); mechanical engineering (ME, MS, PhD). Terminal master's awarded for partial completion of doctoral program. *Degree requirements:* For master's, thesis (for some programs); for doctorate, thesis/dissertation. *Entrance requirements:* For master's, GRE General Test, minimum GPA of 3.0; for doctorate, GRE General Test, minimum GPA of 3.3. Additional exam requirements/recommendations for international students: Required—TOEFL. *Faculty research:* In-space instruments, cryogenic cooling, thermal science, space structures, composite materials.

Vanderbilt University, School of Engineering, Department of Mechanical Engineering, Nashville, TN 37240-1001. Offers M Eng, MS, PhD. MS and PhD offered through the Graduate School. *Program availability:* Part-time. Terminal master's awarded for partial completion of doctoral program. *Degree requirements:* For master's, comprehensive exam, thesis; for doctorate, comprehensive exam, thesis/dissertation. *Entrance requirements:* For master's and doctorate, GRE General Test. Additional exam requirements/recommendations for international students: Required—TOEFL (minimum score 550 paper-based); Recommended—TWE (minimum score 4). Electronic applications accepted. *Expenses: Tuition:* Full-time $47,208; part-time $2026 per credit hour. *Required fees:* $478. *Faculty research:* Active noise and vibration control, robotics, mesoscale and microscale energy conversions, laser diagnostics, combustion.

Villanova University, College of Engineering, Department of Electrical and Computer Engineering, Program in Electrical Engineering, Villanova, PA 19085-1699. Offers electric power systems (Certificate); electrical engineering (MSEE); electro mechanical systems (Certificate); high frequency systems (Certificate); intelligent control systems (Certificate); wireless and digital communications (Certificate). *Program availability:* Part-time, evening/weekend. *Degree requirements:* For master's, thesis optional. *Entrance requirements:* For master's, GRE General Test (for applicants with degrees from foreign universities), BEE, minimum GPA of 3.0. Additional exam requirements/recommendations for international students: Required—TOEFL (minimum score 600 paper-based; 100 iBT). *Faculty research:* Signal processing, communications, antennas, devices.

Villanova University, College of Engineering, Department of Mechanical Engineering, Villanova, PA 19085-1699. Offers electro-mechanical systems (Certificate); machinery dynamics (Certificate); mechanical engineering (MSME); nonlinear dynamics and control (Certificate); thermofluid systems (Certificate). *Program availability:* Part-time, evening/weekend, online learning. *Degree requirements:* For master's, thesis optional. *Entrance requirements:* For master's, GRE General Test (for applicants with degrees from foreign universities), BME, minimum GPA of 3.0. Additional exam requirements/recommendations for international students: Required—TOEFL (minimum score 600 paper-based; 100 iBT). Electronic applications accepted. *Faculty research:* Composite materials, power plant systems, fluid mechanics, automated manufacturing, dynamic analysis.

Virginia Commonwealth University, Graduate School, School of Engineering, Department of Mechanical and Nuclear Engineering, Richmond, VA 23284-9005. Offers MS, PhD. *Entrance requirements:* For master's and doctorate, GRE. Additional exam requirements/recommendations for international students: Required—TOEFL (minimum score 600 paper-based; 100 iBT). Electronic applications accepted.

Washington State University, Voiland College of Engineering and Architecture, Engineering and Computer Science Programs, Vancouver Campus, Pullman, WA 99164. Offers MS. *Degree requirements:* For master's, comprehensive exam, thesis optional. *Entrance requirements:* For master's, official transcripts from all colleges and universities attended; one-page statement of purpose; three letters of recommendation. Additional exam requirements/recommendations for international students: Required—TOEFL; Recommended—IELTS. Electronic applications accepted. *Faculty research:* High yield production of bioenergy biofuels and bioproducts, nanomaterials, power systems, microfluidics, atmospheric research.

Washington State University, Voiland College of Engineering and Architecture, School of Mechanical and Materials Engineering, Pullman, WA 99164-2920. Offers materials science and engineering (MS, PhD); mechanical engineering (MS, PhD). MS programs also offered at Tri-Cities campus. *Program availability:* Part-time. Terminal master's awarded for partial completion of doctoral program. *Degree requirements:* For master's, comprehensive exam, thesis; for doctorate, comprehensive exam, thesis/dissertation, preliminary exam. *Entrance requirements:* For master's, GRE, bachelor's degree, minimum GPA of 3.0, resume, statement of purpose, 3 letters of recommendation, official transcripts, Student Interest Profile form; for doctorate, GRE, bachelor's degree, minimum GPA of 3.4, resume, statement of purpose, 3 letters of recommendation, official transcripts, Student Interest Profile form. Additional exam requirements/recommendations for international students: Required—TOEFL (minimum score 500 paper-based), IELTS. Electronic applications accepted. *Faculty research:* Multiscale modeling and characterization of materials; advanced energy; bioengineering; engineering education and curricular innovation; modeling and visualization in the areas of product realization, materials, and processes.

Washington University in St. Louis, School of Engineering and Applied Science, Department of Mechanical Engineering and Materials Science, St. Louis, MO 63130-4899. Offers aerospace engineering (MS, PhD); materials science (MS); mechanical engineering (M Eng, MS, PhD). *Program availability:* Part-time. Terminal master's awarded for partial completion of doctoral program. *Degree requirements:* For master's, thesis optional; for doctorate, thesis/dissertation optional. *Entrance requirements:* For master's, GRE; for doctorate, GRE General Test, departmental qualifying exam. *Faculty research:* Aerosols science and technology, applied mechanics, biomechanics and biomedical engineering, design, dynamic systems, combustion science, composite materials, materials science.

Wayne State University, College of Engineering, Department of Mechanical Engineering, Detroit, MI 48202. Offers MS, PhD. *Faculty:* 13. *Students:* 157 full-time (20 women), 46 part-time (6 women); includes 21 minority (2 Black or African American, non-Hispanic/Latino; 14 Asian, non-Hispanic/Latino; 4 Hispanic/Latino; 1 Two or more races, non-Hispanic/Latino), 142 international. Average age 26. 354 applicants, 49% accepted, 58 enrolled. In 2018, 169 master's, 6 doctorates awarded. *Entrance requirements:* For master's, GRE (if BS is not from ABET-accredited university), minimum undergraduate GPA of 3.0, bachelor's degree in mechanical engineering or very similar field; for doctorate, GRE, minimum graduate or undergraduate upper-division GPA of 3.5, undergraduate major or substantial specialized work in proposed doctoral field. Additional exam requirements/recommendations for international students: Required—TOEFL (minimum score 550 paper-based; 79 iBT, TWE (minimum score 5.5), Michigan English Language Assessment Battery (minimum score 85); Recommended—IELTS (minimum score 6.5). *Application deadline:* For fall admission, 3/1 priority date for domestic and international students; for winter admission, 10/1 priority date for domestic students, 9/1 priority date for international students; for spring admission, 2/1 priority date for domestic students, 1/1 priority date for international students. Applications are processed on a rolling basis. Application fee: $50. Electronic applications accepted. *Expenses:* Contact institution. *Financial support:* In 2018–19, 103 students received support, including 3 fellowships with tuition reimbursements available (averaging $20,000 per year), 10 research assistantships with tuition reimbursements available (averaging $21,573 per year), 9 teaching assistantships with tuition reimbursements available (averaging $20,166 per year); scholarships/grants and unspecified assistantships also available. Financial award applicants required to submit FAFSA. *Faculty research:* Manufacturing processes; composite material behavior; combustion; acoustics and noise control; vibrations; laser diagnostics; biomechanics; mechanical systems control. *Total annual research expenditures:* $1.1 million. *Unit head:* Dr. Nabil Chalhoub, Chairman/Professor, 313-577-3753, E-mail: ab9714@wayne.edu. *Application contact:* Ellen Cope, Graduate Program Coordinator, 313-577-0409, E-mail: escope@wayne.edu.
Website: http://engineering.wayne.edu/me/

Western Michigan University, Graduate College, College of Engineering and Applied Sciences, Department of Mechanical and Aerospace Engineering, Kalamazoo, MI 49008. Offers mechanical engineering (MSE, PhD). *Program availability:* Part-time. *Degree requirements:* For master's, thesis optional; for doctorate, thesis/dissertation.

Western New England University, College of Engineering, Department of Mechanical Engineering, Springfield, MA 01119. Offers MSME. *Program availability:* Part-time, evening/weekend. *Faculty:* 9 full-time (1 woman). *Students:* 21 part-time (2 women); includes 1 minority (Asian, non-Hispanic/Latino), 3 international. Average age 25. 68 applicants, 76% accepted, 10 enrolled. In 2018, 12 master's awarded. *Degree requirements:* For master's, comprehensive exam, thesis optional. *Entrance requirements:* For master's, official transcript, bachelor's degree in engineering or related field, two recommendations, resume. Additional exam requirements/recommendations for international students: Required—TOEFL (minimum score 79 iBT). *Application deadline:* Applications are processed on a rolling basis. Application fee: $30. Electronic applications accepted. *Expenses:* Contact institution. *Financial support:* Application deadline: 4/15; applicants required to submit FAFSA. *Faculty research:* Low-loss fluid mixing, flow separation delay and alleviation, high-lift airfoils, ejector research, compact heat exchangers. *Unit head:* Dr. Said Dini, Chair, 413-782-1498, E-mail: said.dini@wne.edu. *Application contact:* Matthew Fox, Executive Director of Graduate Admissions, 413-782-1410, Fax: 413-782-1777, E-mail: study@wne.edu.
Website: http://www1.wne.edu/academics/graduate/mechanical-engineering-ms.cfm

West Virginia University, Statler College of Engineering and Mineral Resources, Morgantown, WV 26506. Offers aerospace engineering (MSAE, PhD); chemical engineering (MS Ch E, PhD); civil engineering (MSCE, PhD); computer engineering (PhD); computer science (MSCS, PhD); electrical engineering (MSEE, PhD); energy systems engineering (MSESE); engineering (MSE); industrial engineering (MSIE, PhD); industrial hygiene (MS); material science and engineering (MSMSE, PhD); mechanical engineering (MSME, PhD); mining engineering (MS Min E, PhD); petroleum and natural gas engineering (MSPNGE, PhD); safety management (MS); software engineering (MSSE). *Program availability:* Part-time. *Students:* 466 full-time (113 women), 154 part-time (27 women); includes 57 minority (22 Black or African American, non-Hispanic/Latino; 1 American Indian or Alaska Native, non-Hispanic/Latino; 8 Asian, non-Hispanic/Latino; 12 Hispanic/Latino; 14 Two or more races, non-Hispanic/Latino), 283 international. In 2018, 179 master's, 39 doctorates awarded. Terminal master's awarded for partial completion of doctoral program. *Degree requirements:* For master's, thesis optional; for doctorate, comprehensive exam, thesis/dissertation. *Entrance requirements:* Additional exam requirements/recommendations for international students: Required—TOEFL (minimum score 550 paper-based). *Application deadline:* For fall admission, 4/1 for international students; for winter admission, 4/1 for international students; for spring admission, 10/1 for international students. Applications are processed on a rolling basis. Application fee: $60. Electronic applications accepted. *Expenses:* Contact institution. *Financial support:* Fellowships, research assistantships, teaching assistantships, career-related internships or fieldwork, Federal Work-Study, institutionally sponsored loans, health care benefits, tuition waivers (full and partial), unspecified assistantships, and administrative assistantships available. Financial award application deadline: 2/1; financial award applicants required to submit FAFSA. *Faculty research:* Composite materials, software engineering, information systems, aerodynamics, vehicle propulsion and emission. *Unit head:* Dr. Earl Scime, Interim Dean, 304-293-4157 Ext. 2237, Fax: 304-293-2037, E-mail: earl.scime@mail.wvu.edu.

Application contact: Dr. David A. Wyrick, Associate Dean, Academic Affairs, 304-293-4334, Fax: 304-293-5024, E-mail: david.wyrick@mail.wvu.edu.
Website: https://www.statler.wvu.edu

Wichita State University, Graduate School, College of Engineering, Department of Mechanical Engineering, Wichita, KS 67260. Offers MS, PhD. *Program availability:* Part-time. *Unit head:* Dr. TS Ravi, Chair, 316-978-3402, Fax: 316-978-3236, E-mail: ts.ravi@wichita.edu. *Application contact:* Jordan Oleson, Admission Coordinator, 316-978-3095, Fax: 316-978-3253, E-mail: jordan.oleson@wichita.edu.
Website: http://www.wichita.edu/mechanical

Widener University, Graduate Programs in Engineering, Program in Mechanical Engineering, Chester, PA 19013. Offers M Eng. *Program availability:* Part-time, evening/weekend. *Degree requirements:* For master's, thesis optional. Electronic applications accepted. *Faculty research:* Computational fluid mechanics, thermal and solar engineering, energy conversion, composite materials, solid mechanics.

Wilkes University, College of Graduate and Professional Studies, College of Science and Engineering, Department of Mechanical Engineering and Engineering Management, Wilkes-Barre, PA 18766-0002. Offers engineering management (MS); mechanical engineering (MS). *Program availability:* Part-time. *Students:* 2 full-time (0 women), 2 part-time (0 women); includes 3 minority (1 Hispanic/Latino; 2 Two or more races, non-Hispanic/Latino). Average age 29. In 2018, 12 master's awarded. *Application deadline:* Applications are processed on a rolling basis. Application fee: $45 ($65 for international students). Electronic applications accepted. Tuition and fees vary according to course load, degree level and program. *Financial support:* Institutionally sponsored loans and unspecified assistantships available. *Unit head:* Dr. Prahlad Murthy, Interim Dean, 570-408-4600, Fax: 570-408-7860, E-mail: prahlad.murthy@wilkes.edu. *Application contact:* Kristin Donati, Associate Director of Graduate Admissions, 570-408-3338, Fax: 570-408-7846, E-mail: kristin.donati@wilkes.edu.
Website: http://www.wilkes.edu/academics/colleges/science-and-engineering/mechanical-engineering-engineering-management-applied-and-engineering-sciences/

Worcester Polytechnic Institute, Graduate Admissions, Department of Mechanical Engineering, Worcester, MA 01609-2280. Offers manufacturing engineering (MS, PhD); materials process engineering (MS); materials science and engineering (PhD). *Program availability:* Part-time, evening/weekend, 100% online, blended/hybrid learning. *Students:* 53 full-time (14 women), 128 part-time (23 women); includes 25 minority (2 Black or African American, non-Hispanic/Latino; 7 Asian, non-Hispanic/Latino; 13 Hispanic/Latino; 1 Native Hawaiian or other Pacific Islander, non-Hispanic/Latino; 2 Two or more races, non-Hispanic/Latino), 47 international. Average age 26. 278 applicants, 62% accepted, 67 enrolled. In 2018, 88 master's, 4 doctorates, 2 other advanced degrees awarded. Terminal master's awarded for partial completion of doctoral program. *Degree requirements:* For master's, thesis optional; for doctorate, comprehensive exam, thesis/dissertation. *Entrance requirements:* For master's and doctorate, GRE (recommended), 3 letters of recommendation, statement of purpose. Additional exam requirements/recommendations for international students: Required—TOEFL (minimum score 563 paper-based; 84 iBT), IELTS (minimum score 7). *Application deadline:* For fall admission, 1/1 priority date for domestic and international students; for spring admission, 10/1 priority date for domestic and international students. Applications are processed on a rolling basis. Application fee: $70. Electronic applications accepted. *Financial support:* Fellowships, research assistantships, teaching assistantships, career-related internships or fieldwork, institutionally sponsored loans, scholarships/grants, and unspecified assistantships available. Financial award application deadline: 1/1. *Unit head:* Dr. Jamal Yagoobi, Department Head, 508-831-5236, Fax: 508-831-5680, E-mail: jyagoobi@wpi.edu. *Application contact:* Barbara Edilberti, Administrative Assistant, 508-831-5236, Fax: 508-831-5680, E-mail: edilbert@wpi.edu.
Website: https://www.wpi.edu/academics/departments/mechanical-engineering

Wright State University, Graduate School, College of Engineering and Computer Science, Department of Mechanical and Materials Engineering, Dayton, OH 45435. Offers aerospace systems engineering (MS); materials science and engineering (MS); mechanical engineering (MS); renewable and clean energy (MS). *Degree requirements:* For master's, thesis or course option alternative. *Entrance requirements:* Additional exam requirements/recommendations for international students: Required—TOEFL.

Yale University, Graduate School of Arts and Sciences, School of Engineering and Applied Science, Department of Mechanical Engineering, New Haven, CT 06520. Offers MS, PhD. Terminal master's awarded for partial completion of doctoral program. *Degree requirements:* For doctorate, thesis/dissertation, exam. *Entrance requirements:* For master's and doctorate, GRE General Test. Additional exam requirements/recommendations for international students: Required—TOEFL. *Faculty research:* Mechanics of fluids, mechanics of solids/material science.

Youngstown State University, College of Graduate Studies, College of Science, Technology, Engineering and Mathematics, Department of Mechanical, Industrial and Manufacturing Engineering, Youngstown, OH 44555-0001. Offers industrial and systems engineering (MSE); mechanical engineering (MSE). *Program availability:* Part-time, evening/weekend. *Degree requirements:* For master's, thesis optional. *Entrance requirements:* For master's, minimum GPA of 2.75 in field. Additional exam requirements/recommendations for international students: Required—TOEFL. *Faculty research:* Kinematics and dynamics of machines, computational and experimental heat transfer, machine controls and mechanical design.

Mechanics

Brown University, Graduate School, School of Engineering, Program in Mechanics of Solids and Structures, Providence, RI 02912. Offers Sc M, PhD. *Degree requirements:* For doctorate, thesis/dissertation, preliminary exam.

California Institute of Technology, Division of Engineering and Applied Science, Option in Applied Mechanics, Pasadena, CA 91125-0001. Offers MS, PhD. *Degree requirements:* For doctorate, thesis/dissertation. *Faculty research:* Elasticity, mechanics of quasi-static and dynamic fracture, dynamics and mechanical vibrations, stability and control.

Carnegie Mellon University, Carnegie Institute of Technology, Department of Civil and Environmental Engineering, Pittsburgh, PA 15213. Offers advanced infrastructure systems (MS, PhD); advanced infrastructure systems technology development and application (MS); air quality engineering and science (MS); civil and environmental engineering (MS, PhD); civil and environmental engineering/engineering and public policy (PhD); civil engineering (MS, PhD); computational mechanics (MS, PhD); computational modeling and monitoring for resilient structural and material systems (MS); energy infrastructure systems (MS); environmental engineering (MS, PhD); environmental management and science (MS, PhD); IT-based sustainable global infrastructure and construction management (MS); sustainability and green design (MS); water quality engineering and science (MS). *Program availability:* Part-time. *Faculty:* 23 full-time (5 women), 12 part-time/adjunct (3 women). *Students:* 264 full-time (109 women); includes 24 minority (6 Black or African American, non-Hispanic/Latino; 13 Asian, non-Hispanic/Latino; 5 Hispanic/Latino), 208 international. Average age 25. 630 applicants, 64% accepted, 114 enrolled. In 2018, 112 master's, 15 doctorates awarded. Terminal master's awarded for partial completion of doctoral program. *Degree requirements:* For master's, thesis optional; for doctorate, comprehensive exam, thesis/dissertation, two-part qualifying exam, public defense of dissertation. *Entrance requirements:* For master's, GRE General Test, BS in engineering, science or mathematics; for doctorate, GRE General Test, BS or MS in engineering, science or mathematics. Additional exam requirements/recommendations for international students: Required—TOEFL (minimum score 84 iBT), TOEFL (minimum score 84 iBT) or IELTS (7.0). *Application deadline:* For fall admission, 1/5 priority date for domestic and international students; for spring admission, 9/15 priority date for domestic and international students. Applications are processed on a rolling basis. Application fee: $75. Electronic applications accepted. *Expenses:* Contact institution. *Financial support:* In 2018–19, 137 students received support. Fellowships with tuition reimbursements available, research assistantships with tuition reimbursements available, scholarships/grants, health care benefits, tuition waivers (full and partial), unspecified assistantships, and service assistantships available. Financial award application deadline: 1/5. *Faculty research:* Advanced infrastructure systems; environmental engineering, sustainability, and science; mechanics, materials, and computing. *Total annual research expenditures:* $7.4 million. *Unit head:* Dr. David A. Dzombak, Professor and Department Head, 412-268-2941, Fax: 412-268-7813, E-mail: dzombak@cmu.edu. *Application contact:* David A. Vey, Director of Graduate Programs, 412-268-2292, Fax: 412-268-7813, E-mail: dvey@andrew.cmu.edu.
Website: http://www.cmu.edu/cee/

Columbia University, Fu Foundation School of Engineering and Applied Science, Department of Civil Engineering and Engineering Mechanics, New York, NY 10027. Offers civil engineering (MS, Eng Sc D, PhD); construction engineering and management (MS); engineering mechanics (MS, Eng Sc D, PhD). *Program availability:* Part-time, online learning. Terminal master's awarded for partial completion of doctoral program. *Degree requirements:* For doctorate, thesis/dissertation, qualifying exam. *Entrance requirements:* For master's and doctorate, GRE General Test. Additional exam requirements/recommendations for international students: Required—TOEFL, IELTS, PTE. Electronic applications accepted. *Faculty research:* Structural dynamics, structural health and monitoring, fatigue and fracture mechanics, geo-environmental engineering, multiscale science and engineering.

Cornell University, Graduate School, Graduate Fields of Engineering, Field of Theoretical and Applied Mechanics, Ithaca, NY 14853. Offers advanced composites and structures (M Eng); dynamics and space mechanics (MS, PhD); fluid mechanics (MS, PhD); mechanics of materials (MS, PhD); solid mechanics (MS, PhD). *Degree requirements:* For master's, thesis (MS); for doctorate, one foreign language, comprehensive exam, thesis/dissertation, teaching experience. *Entrance requirements:* For master's and doctorate, GRE General Test, 3 letters of recommendation. Additional exam requirements/recommendations for international students: Required—TOEFL (minimum score 600 paper-based; 77 iBT). Electronic applications accepted. *Faculty research:* Biomathematics, bio-fluids, animal locomotion; non-linear dynamics, celestial mechanics, control; mechanics of materials, computational mechanics; experimental mechanics; non-linear elasticity, granular materials, phase transitions.

Drexel University, College of Engineering, Department of Mechanical Engineering and Mechanics, Philadelphia, PA 19104-2875. Offers mechanical engineering (MS, PhD). *Program availability:* Part-time, evening/weekend. Terminal master's awarded for partial completion of doctoral program. *Degree requirements:* For master's, thesis optional; for doctorate, thesis/dissertation. *Entrance requirements:* For master's, minimum GPA of 3.0, BS in engineering or science; for doctorate, minimum GPA of 3.5, MS in engineering or science. Additional exam requirements/recommendations for international students: Required—TOEFL. Electronic applications accepted. *Faculty research:* Composites, dynamic systems and control, combustion and fuels, biomechanics, mechanics and thermal fluid sciences.

École Polytechnique de Montréal, Graduate Programs, Department of Mechanical Engineering, Montréal, QC H3C 3A7, Canada. Offers aerothermics (M Eng, M Sc A, PhD); applied mechanics (M Eng, M Sc A, PhD); tool design (M Eng, M Sc A, PhD). *Program availability:* Part-time, evening/weekend. *Degree requirements:* For master's, one foreign language, thesis; for doctorate, one foreign language, thesis/dissertation. *Entrance requirements:* For master's, minimum GPA of 2.75; for doctorate, minimum GPA of 3.0. *Faculty research:* Noise control and vibration, fatigue and creep, aerodynamics, composite materials, biomechanics, robotics.

Georgia Institute of Technology, Graduate Studies, College of Engineering, School of Civil and Environmental Engineering, Program in Engineering Science and Mechanics, Atlanta, GA 30332-0001. Offers MS. Terminal master's awarded for partial completion of doctoral program. *Degree requirements:* For master's, thesis optional. *Entrance requirements:* For master's, GRE. Additional exam requirements/recommendations for international students: Required—TOEFL (minimum score 550 paper-based; 79 iBT). Electronic applications accepted. *Faculty research:* Bioengineering, structural mechanics, solid mechanics, dynamics.

Iowa State University of Science and Technology, Program in Engineering Mechanics, Ames, IA 50011. Offers M Eng, MS, PhD. *Entrance requirements:* For master's and doctorate, GRE. Additional exam requirements/recommendations for international students: Required—TOEFL (minimum score 550 paper-based; 80 iBT), IELTS (minimum score 6.5). Electronic applications accepted.

Johns Hopkins University, G. W. C. Whiting School of Engineering, Master of Science in Engineering Management Program, Baltimore, MD 21218. Offers biomaterials (MSEM); civil engineering (MSEM); communications science (MSEM); computer science (MSEM); environmental systems analysis, economics and public policy (MSEM); fluid mechanics (MSEM); materials science and engineering (MSEM); mechanical engineering (MSEM); mechanics and materials (MSEM); nano-biotechnology (MSEM); nanomaterials and nanotechnology (MSEM); operations research (MSEM); probability and statistics (MSEM); smart product and device design (MSEM). *Students:* 34 full-time (12 women), 18 part-time (7 women). 233 applicants,

39% accepted, 33 enrolled. In 2018, 27 master's awarded. *Entrance requirements:* For master's, GRE, 3 letters of recommendation, statement of purpose, transcripts. Additional exam requirements/recommendations for international students: Required—TOEFL (minimum score 600 paper-based, 100 iBT) or IELTS (7). *Application deadline:* For fall admission, 2/15 for domestic and international students. Application fee: $75. Electronic applications accepted. *Financial support:* In 2018–19, 43 research assistantships (averaging $43,344 per year) were awarded; health care benefits also available. *Unit head:* Dr. Pamela Sheff, Director, 410-516-7056, Fax: 410-516-4880, E-mail: pamsheff@gmail.com. *Application contact:* Lindsey Conklin, Sr. Academic Program Coordinator, 410-516-1108, Fax: 410-516-0780, E-mail: lconkli4@jhu.edu.
Website: http://engineering.jhu.edu/msem/

Lehigh University, P.C. Rossin College of Engineering and Applied Science, Department of Mechanical Engineering and Mechanics, Bethlehem, PA 18015. Offers mechanical engineering (M Eng, MS, PhD); MBA/E. *Program availability:* Part-time, 100% online, blended/hybrid learning. *Faculty:* 23 full-time (2 women), 1 part-time/adjunct (0 women). *Students:* 123 full-time (11 women), 18 part-time (3 women); includes 5 minority (3 Hispanic/Latino; 1 Native Hawaiian or other Pacific Islander, non-Hispanic/Latino; 1 Two or more races, non-Hispanic/Latino), 96 international. Average age 28. 189 applicants, 38% accepted, 29 enrolled. In 2018, 45 master's, 22 doctorates awarded. Terminal master's awarded for partial completion of doctoral program. *Degree requirements:* For master's, thesis, there are 4 tracks for the MS degree, thesis; for doctorate, thesis/dissertation, general exam, proposal, dissertation. *Entrance requirements:* Additional exam requirements/recommendations for international students: Required—TOEFL (minimum score 550 paper-based; 79 iBT), IELTS (minimum score 6.5), GRE. *Application deadline:* For fall admission, 7/15 for domestic students, 6/20 for international students; for spring admission, 12/1 for domestic and international students. Applications are processed on a rolling basis. Application fee: $75. Electronic applications accepted. Tuition and fees vary according to program. *Financial support:* In 2018–19, 88 students received support, including fellowships with full tuition reimbursements available (averaging $29,400 per year), 69 research assistantships with full tuition reimbursements available (averaging $27,999 per year), 13 teaching assistantships with full tuition reimbursements available (averaging $29,400 per year); unspecified assistantships also available. Support available to part-time students. Financial award application deadline: 1/15. *Faculty research:* Solid mechanics, controls and robotics, thermo-heat transfer, fluid mechanics, mathematical methods, biomechanics. *Total annual research expenditures:* $4.6 million. *Unit head:* Dr. D. Gary Harlow, Chairman, 610-758-4102, Fax: 610-758-6224, E-mail: dgh0@lehigh.edu. *Application contact:* Allison B. Marsteller, Graduate Coordinator, 610-758-4107, Fax: 610-758-6224, E-mail: alm513@lehigh.edu.
Website: http://www.lehigh.edu/~inmem/

Louisiana State University and Agricultural & Mechanical College, Graduate School, College of Engineering, Department of Civil and Environmental Engineering, Baton Rouge, LA 70803. Offers environmental engineering (MSCE, PhD); geotechnical engineering (MSCE, PhD); structural engineering and mechanics (MSCE, PhD); transportation engineering (MSCE, PhD); water resources (MSCE, PhD).

McGill University, Faculty of Graduate and Postdoctoral Studies, Faculty of Engineering, Department of Civil Engineering and Applied Mechanics, Montréal, QC H3A 2T5, Canada. Offers environmental engineering (M Eng, M Sc, PhD); fluid mechanics (M Sc); fluid mechanics and hydraulic engineering (M Eng, PhD); materials engineering (M Eng, PhD); rehabilitation of urban infrastructure (M Eng, PhD); soil behavior (M Eng, PhD); soil mechanics and foundations (M Eng, PhD); structures and structural mechanics (M Eng, PhD); water resources (M Sc); water resources engineering (M Eng, PhD).

Michigan State University, The Graduate School, College of Engineering, Department of Mechanical Engineering, East Lansing, MI 48824. Offers engineering mechanics (MS, PhD); mechanical engineering (MS, PhD). *Entrance requirements:* For master's, GRE General Test. Additional exam requirements/recommendations for international students: Required—TOEFL. Electronic applications accepted.

Michigan Technological University, Graduate School, College of Engineering, Department of Mechanical Engineering-Engineering Mechanics, Houghton, MI 49931. Offers engineering mechanics (MS); hybrid electric drive vehicle engineering (Graduate Certificate); mechanical engineering-engineering mechanics (PhD). *Program availability:* Part-time, evening/weekend, 100% online, blended/hybrid learning. *Faculty:* 70 full-time, 43 part-time/adjunct. *Students:* 307 full-time, 77 part-time; includes 10 minority (3 Black or African American, non-Hispanic/Latino; 3 Asian, non-Hispanic/Latino; 4 Hispanic/Latino), 290 international. Average age 27. 1,021 applicants, 42% accepted, 116 enrolled. In 2018, 119 master's, 20 doctorates, 27 other advanced degrees awarded. Terminal master's awarded for partial completion of doctoral program. *Degree requirements:* For master's, thesis (for some programs); for doctorate, comprehensive exam, thesis/dissertation. *Entrance requirements:* For master's, GRE (Michigan Tech and online students exempt), statement of purpose, personal statement, official transcripts, 2 letters of recommendation, resume/curriculum vitae; for doctorate, GRE (Michigan Tech and online students exempt), MS (preferred), statement of purpose, official transcripts, 2 letters of recommendation, resume/curriculum vitae; for Graduate Certificate, statement of purpose, official transcripts, BS in engineering. Additional exam requirements/recommendations for international students: Required—TOEFL (minimum score 90 iBT) or IELTS (minimum score 7.0). *Application deadline:* For fall admission, 3/1 priority date for domestic and international students; for spring admission, 8/1 priority date for domestic and international students. Applications are processed on a rolling basis. Electronic applications accepted. *Expenses:* $1,143 per credit. *Financial support:* In 2018–19, 262 students received support, including 22 fellowships with tuition reimbursements available (averaging $16,590 per year), 50 research assistantships with tuition reimbursements available (averaging $16,590 per year), 29 teaching assistantships with tuition reimbursements available (averaging $16,590 per year); career-related internships or fieldwork, Federal Work-Study, scholarships/grants, health care benefits, unspecified assistantships, and cooperative program also available. Financial award applicants required to submit FAFSA. *Faculty research:* Mobility and autonomy, complex systems and controls, multi-scale materials and mechanics, thermo-fluids and energy conversion, human-centered engineering. *Total annual research expenditures:* $7.6 million. *Unit head:* Dr. William W. Predebon, Chair, 906-487-2551, Fax: 906-487-2822, E-mail: wwpredeb@mtu.edu. *Application contact:* Cindy Wadaga, Graduate Program Assistant, 906-487-2551, Fax: 906-487-2822, E-mail: cawadaga@mtu.edu.
Website: http://www.mtu.edu/mechanical/

Montana State University, The Graduate School, College of Engineering, Department of Civil Engineering, Bozeman, MT 59717. Offers civil engineering (MS); construction engineering management (MCEM); engineering (PhD), including applied mechanics option, civil engineering option. *Program availability:* Part-time. *Degree requirements:* For master's, comprehensive exam, thesis (for some programs); for doctorate, comprehensive exam, thesis/dissertation. *Entrance requirements:* For master's and doctorate, GRE General Test. Additional exam requirements/recommendations for international students: Required—TOEFL (minimum score 550 paper-based). Electronic applications accepted. *Faculty research:* Snow and ice mechanics, biofilm engineering, transportation, structural and geo materials, water resources.

New Mexico Institute of Mining and Technology, Center for Graduate Studies, Department of Mechanical Engineering, Socorro, NM 87801. Offers explosives engineering (MS); fluid and thermal sciences (MS); mechatronics systems engineering (MS); solid mechanics (MS). *Degree requirements:* For master's, thesis (for some programs). *Entrance requirements:* For master's, GRE General Test. Additional exam requirements/recommendations for international students: Required—TOEFL (minimum score 540 paper-based). *Faculty research:* Vibrations, fluid-structure interactions.

Northwestern University, McCormick School of Engineering and Applied Science, Program in Theoretical and Applied Mechanics, Evanston, IL 60208. Offers MS, PhD. Admissions and degrees offered through The Graduate School. Terminal master's awarded for partial completion of doctoral program. *Degree requirements:* For master's, thesis optional; for doctorate, comprehensive exam, thesis/dissertation. *Entrance requirements:* For master's and doctorate, GRE General Test, minimum 2 letters of recommendation, transcripts from all academic institutions attended. Additional exam requirements/recommendations for international students: Required—TOEFL (minimum score 577 paper-based; 90 iBT), IELTS (minimum score 7). Electronic applications accepted. *Faculty research:* Computational mechanics, mechanics in biology and fluids, micro/nanomechanics, multifunctional materials, geomechanics, structural reliability and nondestructive characterization.

Ohio University, Graduate College, Russ College of Engineering and Technology, Department of Civil Engineering, Athens, OH 45701-2979. Offers civil engineering (PhD); construction engineering and management (MS); environmental (MS); geoenvironmental (MS); geotechnical (MS); mechanics (MS); structures (MS); transportation (MS); water resources (MS). *Program availability:* Part-time. *Degree requirements:* For master's, comprehensive exam (for some programs), thesis or alternative; for doctorate, comprehensive exam, thesis/dissertation. *Entrance requirements:* For master's, GRE General Test, minimum GPA of 3.0, 3 letters of recommendation; for doctorate, GRE General Test. Additional exam requirements/recommendations for international students: Required—TOEFL (minimum score 550 paper-based; 80 iBT) or IELTS (minimum score 6.5). Electronic applications accepted. *Faculty research:* Noise abatement, materials and environment, highway infrastructure, subsurface investigation (pavements, pipes, bridges).

Penn State University Park, Graduate School, College of Engineering, Department of Engineering Science and Mechanics, University Park, PA 16802. Offers engineering at the nano-scale (MS); engineering mechanics (M Eng); engineering science and mechanics (MS, PhD).

Rutgers University–New Brunswick, Graduate School-New Brunswick, Program in Mechanics, Piscataway, NJ 08854-8097. Offers MS, PhD. *Program availability:* Part-time. Terminal master's awarded for partial completion of doctoral program. *Degree requirements:* For master's, thesis optional, qualifying exam; for doctorate, thesis/dissertation, qualifying exam. *Entrance requirements:* For master's and doctorate, GRE General Test, GRE Subject Test (recommended). Additional exam requirements/recommendations for international students: Required—TOEFL. Electronic applications accepted. *Faculty research:* Continuum mechanics, constitutive theory, thermodynamics, visolasticity, liquid crystal theory.

San Diego State University, Graduate and Research Affairs, College of Engineering, Department of Aerospace Engineering and Engineering Mechanics, San Diego, CA 92182. Offers aerospace engineering (MS); engineering mechanics (MS); engineering sciences and applied mechanics (PhD); flight dynamics (MS); fluid dynamics (MS). PhD offered jointly with University of California, San Diego and Department of Mechanical Engineering. Terminal master's awarded for partial completion of doctoral program. *Degree requirements:* For master's, comprehensive exam (for some programs), thesis (for some programs); for doctorate, thesis/dissertation. *Entrance requirements:* For master's, GRE General Test; for doctorate, GRE, 3 letters of recommendation. Additional exam requirements/recommendations for international students: Required—TOEFL. Electronic applications accepted. *Faculty research:* Organized structures in post-stall flow over wings/three dimensional separated flow, airfoil growth effect, probabilities, structural mechanics.

Southern Illinois University Carbondale, Graduate School, College of Engineering, Department of Civil and Environmental Engineering, Carbondale, IL 62901-4701. Offers civil and environmental engineering (ME); civil engineering (MS). *Degree requirements:* For master's, comprehensive exam, thesis. *Entrance requirements:* For master's, GRE, minimum GPA of 2.7. Additional exam requirements/recommendations for international students: Required—TOEFL. *Faculty research:* Composite materials, wastewater treatment, solid waste disposal, slurry transport, geotechnical engineering.

Stanford University, School of Engineering, Department of Civil and Environmental Engineering, Stanford, CA 94305-2004. Offers atmosphere and energy (MS, PhD); construction (MS), including construction engineering and management, design-construction integration, sustainable design and construction; environmental engineering and science (MS, PhD, Eng); environmental fluid mechanics and hydrology (PhD); geomechanics (MS); structural engineering (MS). *Expenses: Tuition:* Full-time $50,703; part-time $32,970 per year. *Required fees:* $651.
Website: http://www-ce.stanford.edu/

The University of Alabama, Graduate School, College of Engineering, Department of Aerospace Engineering and Mechanics, Tuscaloosa, AL 35487. Offers aerospace engineering (MSAEM); engineering science and mechanics (PhD). *Program availability:* Part-time, online learning. Terminal master's awarded for partial completion of doctoral program. *Degree requirements:* For master's, comprehensive exam (for some programs), thesis (for some programs); for doctorate, comprehensive exam, thesis/dissertation, 1-year residency. *Entrance requirements:* For master's, GRE, BS in engineering or physics; for doctorate, GRE, BS or MS in engineering or physics. Additional exam requirements/recommendations for international students: Required—TOEFL (minimum score 550 paper-based; 79 iBT). Electronic applications accepted. *Faculty research:* Aeronautics, astronautics, solid mechanics, fluid mechanics, computational modeling.

University of Calgary, Faculty of Graduate Studies, Schulich School of Engineering, Program in Civil Engineering, Calgary, AB T2N 1N4, Canada. Offers avalanche mechanics (M Sc, PhD); civil engineering (M Eng, M Sc, PhD); energy and environment engineering (M Eng, M Sc, PhD); environmental engineering (M Eng, M Sc, PhD); geotechnical engineering (M Eng, M Sc, PhD); materials science (M Eng, M Sc, PhD); project management (M Eng, M Sc, PhD); structures and solid mechanics (M Eng, M Sc, PhD); transportation engineering (M Eng, M Sc, PhD); water resources (M Eng, M Sc, PhD). *Program availability:* Part-time. *Degree requirements:* For master's, thesis; for doctorate, thesis/dissertation, written and oral candidacy exam. *Entrance requirements:* For master's, minimum GPA of 3.0; for doctorate, minimum GPA of 3.5. Additional exam requirements/recommendations for international students: Required—TOEFL (minimum score 580 paper-based; 93 iBT), IELTS (minimum score 7). Electronic applications accepted. *Faculty research:* Geotechnical engineering, energy and environment, transportation, project management, structures and solid mechanics.

University of California, Berkeley, Graduate Division, College of Engineering, Department of Civil and Environmental Engineering, Berkeley, CA 94720. Offers engineering and project management (M Eng, MS, PhD); environmental engineering (M Eng, MS, PhD); geoengineering (M Eng, MS, PhD); structural engineering, mechanics and materials (M Eng, MS, PhD); transportation engineering (M Eng, MS, PhD); M Arch/MS; MCP/MS; MPP/MS. Terminal master's awarded for partial completion of doctoral program. *Degree requirements:* For master's, comprehensive exam (for some programs), thesis (for some programs), comprehensive exam or thesis (MS); for doctorate, thesis/dissertation, qualifying exam. *Entrance requirements:* For master's, GRE General Test, minimum GPA of 3.0, 3 letters of recommendation; for doctorate, GRE General Test, minimum GPA of 3.5, 3 letters of recommendation. Additional exam requirements/recommendations for international students: Required—TOEFL (minimum score 570 paper-based; 90 iBT). Electronic applications accepted.

University of California, Merced, Graduate Division, School of Engineering, Merced, CA 95343. Offers biological engineering and small scale technologies (MS, PhD); electrical engineering and computer science (MS, PhD); environmental systems (MS, PhD); management of innovation, sustainability, and technology (MM); mechanical engineering (MS); mechanical engineering and applied mechanics (PhD). *Faculty:* 60 full-time (16 women). *Students:* 219 full-time (72 women), 1 part-time (0 women); includes 43 minority (2 Black or African American, non-Hispanic/Latino; 17 Asian, non-Hispanic/Latino; 20 Hispanic/Latino; 1 Native Hawaiian or other Pacific Islander, non-Hispanic/Latino; 3 Two or more races, non-Hispanic/Latino), 145 international. Average age 28. 371 applicants, 46% accepted, 75 enrolled. In 2018, 30 master's, 17 doctorates awarded. Terminal master's awarded for partial completion of doctoral program. *Degree requirements:* For master's, variable foreign language requirement, comprehensive exam, thesis or alternative, oral defense; for doctorate, variable foreign language requirement, comprehensive exam, thesis/dissertation, oral defense. *Entrance requirements:* For master's and doctorate, GRE. Additional exam requirements/recommendations for international students: Required—TOEFL (minimum score 550 paper-based; 80 iBT); Recommended—IELTS (minimum score 6.5). *Application deadline:* For fall admission, 1/15 priority date for domestic and international students. Application fee: $105 ($125 for international students). Electronic applications accepted. *Expenses:* In-state tuition $11442 per year; Out-of-state tuition $26544 per year; Student Fees $1765 per year. *Financial support:* In 2018–19, 200 students received support, including 14 fellowships with full tuition reimbursements available (averaging $20,851 per year), 70 research assistantships with full tuition reimbursements available (averaging $18,334 per year), 116 teaching assistantships with full tuition reimbursements available (averaging $19,841 per year); scholarships/grants, traineeships, and health care benefits also available. *Faculty research:* Sustainability systems engineering and resource management: food, energy, water; biomolecular engineering and biotechnology; computational science and data analytics; artificial intelligence, machine learning, internet of things, human computer interface; cyber-physical systems and automation. *Total annual research expenditures:* $3.1 million. *Unit head:* Dr. Mark Matsumoto, Dean, 209-228-4047, Fax: 209-228-4047, E-mail: mmatsumoto@ucmerced.edu. *Application contact:* Tsu Ya, Director of Admissions and Academic Services, 209-228-4521, Fax: 209-228-6906, E-mail: tya@ucmerced.edu.

University of California, San Diego, Graduate Division, Department of Mechanical and Aerospace Engineering, Program in Applied Mechanics, La Jolla, CA 92093. Offers MS, PhD. *Students:* 11 full-time (1 woman). 13 applicants, 46% accepted, 3 enrolled. In 2018, 1 doctorate awarded. *Degree requirements:* For master's, comprehensive exam (for some programs), thesis (for some programs), comprehensive exam or thesis; for doctorate, comprehensive exam, thesis/dissertation. *Entrance requirements:* For master's and doctorate, GRE General Test, minimum GPA of 3.0. Additional exam requirements/recommendations for international students: Required—TOEFL (minimum score 550 paper-based; 80 iBT), IELTS (minimum score 7). *Application deadline:* For fall admission, 12/18 for domestic students. Application fee: $105 ($125 for international students). Electronic applications accepted. *Financial support:* Fellowships, research assistantships, teaching assistantships, scholarships/grants, and unspecified assistantships available. Financial award applicants required to submit FAFSA. *Faculty research:* Interfacial properties, durability, aging, and failure of composites; granular materials, rocks, and centimentious materials; computational methods for materials processing; advanced analytical methods in the theory of elasticity; synthesis, processing, and characterization of advanced ceramics, metals, and composites; shock synthesis and compaction. *Unit head:* Carlos Coimbra, Chair, 858-534-4285, E-mail: mae-chair-l@ucsd.edu. *Application contact:* Joana Halnez, Graduate Coordinator, 858-534-4387, E-mail: mae-gradadm-l@ucsd.edu.
Website: http://maeweb.ucsd.edu/

University of Cincinnati, Graduate School, College of Engineering and Applied Science, Department of Aerospace Engineering and Engineering Mechanics, Cincinnati, OH 45221-0070. Offers M Eng, MS, PhD. *Program availability:* Part-time. Terminal master's awarded for partial completion of doctoral program. *Degree requirements:* For master's, thesis; for doctorate, thesis/dissertation. *Entrance requirements:* For master's and doctorate, GRE General Test. Additional exam requirements/recommendations for international students: Required—TOEFL (minimum iBT score 90), IELTS (6.5), or PTE (47). Electronic applications accepted. *Faculty research:* Computational fluid mechanics/propulsion, large space structures, dynamics and guidance of VTOL vehicles, unmanned aerial vehicles, space robotics, aero-acoustics, thermal management, gas turbine simulation, combustion and rocket propulsion, ultrasonic imaging, nondestructive evaluation, finite element simulation.

University of Colorado Denver, College of Engineering, Design and Computing, Department of Mechanical Engineering, Denver, CO 80217. Offers mechanical engineering (MS); mechanics (MS); thermal sciences (MS). *Program availability:* Part-time, evening/weekend. *Degree requirements:* For master's, comprehensive exam, 30 credit hours, project or thesis. *Entrance requirements:* For master's, GRE, three letters of recommendation, personal statement. Additional exam requirements/recommendations for international students: Required—TOEFL (minimum score 537 paper-based; 75 iBT); Recommended—IELTS (minimum score 6.8). *Expenses:* Tuition, state resident: full-time $6786; part-time $337 per credit hour. Tuition, nonresident: full-time $22,590; part-time $1255 per credit hour. *Required fees:* $1231; $137 per credit hour. Tuition and fees vary according to program and reciprocity agreements.

University of Dayton, Department of Civil and Environmental Engineering and Engineering Mechanics, Dayton, OH 45469. Offers engineering mechanics (MSEM); environmental engineering (MSCE); geotechnical engineering (MSCE); structural engineering (MSCE); transportation engineering (MSCE); water resources engineering (MSCE). *Program availability:* Part-time, blended/hybrid learning. *Degree requirements:* For master's, thesis or alternative. *Entrance requirements:* For master's, minimum GPA of 3.0 in undergraduate work. Additional exam requirements/recommendations for international students: Required—TOEFL (minimum score 550 paper-based; 80 iBT); Recommended—IELTS (minimum score 6.5), TSE (minimum score 60). Electronic applications accepted. *Faculty research:* Infrastructure, environmental composite, reliability, computer simulation.

University of Illinois at Urbana–Champaign, Graduate College, College of Engineering, Department of Mechanical Science and Engineering, Champaign, IL 61820. Offers mechanical engineering (MS, PhD); theoretical and applied mechanics (MS, PhD). Terminal master's awarded for partial completion of doctoral program. *Entrance requirements:* Additional exam requirements/recommendations for international students: Required—TOEFL (minimum score 613 paper-based; 103 iBT), IELTS (minimum score 7).

University of Maryland, Baltimore County, The Graduate School, College of Engineering and Information Technology, Department of Mechanical Engineering, Post Baccalaureate Certificate Program in Computational Thermal Fluid Dynamics, Baltimore, MD 21250. Offers Postbaccalaureate Certificate. *Expenses:* Contact institution.

University of Maryland, Baltimore County, The Graduate School, College of Engineering and Information Technology, Department of Mechanical Engineering, Post Baccalaureate Certificate Program in Mechatronics, Baltimore, MD 21250. Offers Postbaccalaureate Certificate. *Program availability:* Part-time. Electronic applications accepted. *Expenses:* Contact institution.

University of Maryland, College Park, Academic Affairs, A. James Clark School of Engineering, Department of Mechanical Engineering, College Park, MD 20742. Offers electronic packaging and reliability (MS, PhD); manufacturing and design (MS, PhD); mechanics and materials (MS, PhD); reliability engineering (M Eng, MS, PhD); thermal and fluid sciences (MS, PhD). *Program availability:* Part-time, evening/weekend, online learning. *Degree requirements:* For master's, thesis optional; for doctorate, thesis/dissertation, qualifying exam. *Entrance requirements:* For master's, GRE General Test, 3 letters of recommendation; for doctorate, GRE General Test, minimum GPA of 3.0. Additional exam requirements/recommendations for international students: Required—TOEFL. Electronic applications accepted. *Faculty research:* Injection molding, electronic packaging, fluid mechanics, product engineering.

University of Massachusetts Amherst, Graduate School, College of Engineering, Department of Civil and Environmental Engineering, Amherst, MA 01003. Offers civil engineering (MSCE, PhD); environmental and water resources engineering (MSCE); geotechnical engineering (MSCE); structural engineering and mechanics (MSCE); transportation engineering (MSCE). *Program availability:* Part-time. Terminal master's awarded for partial completion of doctoral program. *Degree requirements:* For master's, thesis or alternative; for doctorate, comprehensive exam, thesis/dissertation. *Entrance requirements:* For master's and doctorate, GRE General Test. Additional exam requirements/recommendations for international students: Required—TOEFL (minimum score 550 paper-based; 80 iBT), IELTS (minimum score 6.5). Electronic applications accepted.

University of Minnesota, Twin Cities Campus, College of Science and Engineering, Department of Aerospace Engineering and Mechanics, Minneapolis, MN 55455-0213. Offers MS, PhD. *Program availability:* Part-time. *Degree requirements:* For doctorate, thesis/dissertation. *Entrance requirements:* Additional exam requirements/recommendations for international students: Required—TOEFL (minimum score 550 paper-based). Electronic applications accepted. *Faculty research:* Fluid mechanics, solid mechanics and materials, aerospace systems, nanotechnology.

University of Nebraska–Lincoln, Graduate College, College of Engineering, Department of Engineering Mechanics, Lincoln, NE 68588. Offers MS, PhD. *Degree requirements:* For master's, thesis optional; for doctorate, comprehensive exam, thesis/dissertation. *Entrance requirements:* For master's and doctorate, GRE. Additional exam requirements/recommendations for international students: Required—TOEFL (minimum score 550 paper-based). Electronic applications accepted. *Faculty research:* Polymer mechanics, piezoelectric materials, meshless methods, smart materials, fracture mechanics.

University of Nebraska–Lincoln, Graduate College, College of Engineering, Department of Mechanical and Materials Engineering, Lincoln, NE 68588-0526. Offers biomedical engineering (PhD); engineering mechanics (MS); materials engineering (PhD); mechanical engineering (MS), including materials science engineering, metallurgical engineering; mechanical engineering and applied mechanics (PhD); MS/MS. MS/MS offered with University of Rouen-France. *Degree requirements:* For master's, thesis optional; for doctorate, comprehensive exam, thesis/dissertation. *Entrance requirements:* For master's and doctorate, GRE General Test. Additional exam requirements/recommendations for international students: Required—TOEFL (minimum score 550 paper-based). Electronic applications accepted. *Faculty research:* Medical robotics, rehabilitation dynamics, and design; combustion, fluid mechanics, and heat transfer; nano-materials, manufacturing, and devices; fiber, tissue, bio-polymer, and adaptive composites; blast, impact, fracture, and failure; electro-active and magnetic materials and devices; functional materials, design, and added manufacturing; materials characterization, modeling, and computational simulation.

University of New Brunswick Fredericton, School of Graduate Studies, Faculty of Engineering, Department of Mechanical Engineering, Fredericton, NB E3B 5A3, Canada. Offers applied mechanics (M Eng, M Sc E, PhD); mechanical engineering (M Eng, M Sc E, PhD). *Program availability:* Part-time. *Degree requirements:* For master's, thesis; for doctorate, comprehensive exam, thesis/dissertation, qualifying exam. *Entrance requirements:* For master's, minimum GPA of 3.0; B Sc E; for doctorate, minimum GPA of 3.0; M Sc E. Additional exam requirements/recommendations for international students: Required—TOEFL (minimum score 580 paper-based; 80 iBT), IELTS (minimum score 7), TWE (minimum score 4), Michigan English Language Assessment Battery (minimum score 85) or CanTest (minimum score 4.5). Electronic applications accepted. *Faculty research:* Acoustics and vibration, biomedical, manufacturing and materials processing, mechatronics and design, nuclear and threat detection, renewable energy systems, robotics and applied mechanics, thermofluids and aerodynamics.

University of Pennsylvania, School of Engineering and Applied Science, Department of Mechanical Engineering and Applied Mechanics, Philadelphia, PA 19104. Offers MSE, PhD. *Program availability:* Part-time. *Faculty:* 38 full-time (8 women), 11 part-time/adjunct (2 women). *Students:* 156 full-time (34 women), 21 part-time (3 women); includes 24 minority (3 Black or African American, non-Hispanic/Latino; 10 Asian, non-Hispanic/Latino; 7 Hispanic/Latino; 4 Two or more races, non-Hispanic/Latino), 111 international. Average age 25. 612 applicants, 33% accepted, 109 enrolled. In 2018, 41 master's, 7 doctorates awarded. Terminal master's awarded for partial completion of doctoral program. *Degree requirements:* For master's, comprehensive exam, thesis optional; for doctorate, comprehensive exam, thesis/dissertation. *Entrance requirements:* For master's and doctorate, GRE, bachelor's degree, letters of recommendation, resume, personal statement. Additional exam requirements/recommendations for international students: Required—TOEFL (minimum score 100 iBT), IELTS (minimum score 7). *Application deadline:* For fall admission, 12/15 priority date for domestic students, 12/15 for international students. Application fee: $80. Electronic applications accepted. *Expenses:* Contact institution. *Faculty research:* Design and manufacturing, heat transfer, fluid mechanics and energy, mechanics of materials, mechatronics and robotics systems, micro- and nano-systems. *Application contact:* William Fenton, Assistant Director of Graduate Admissions, 215-898-4542, Fax: 215-573-5577, E-mail: gradstudies@seas.upenn.edu.
Website: http://www.me.upenn.edu/prospective-students/masters/masters-degrees.php

Mechanics

University of Southern California, Graduate School, Viterbi School of Engineering, Sonny Astani Department of Civil and Environmental Engineering, Los Angeles, CA 90089. Offers applied mechanics (MS); civil engineering (MS, PhD); computer-aided engineering (ME, Graduate Certificate); construction management (MCM); engineering technology commercialization (Graduate Certificate); environmental engineering (MS, PhD); environmental quality management (ME); structural design (ME); sustainable cities (Graduate Certificate); transportation systems (MS, Graduate Certificate); water and waste management (MS). *Program availability:* Part-time, evening/weekend. Terminal master's awarded for partial completion of doctoral program. *Degree requirements:* For master's, thesis optional; for doctorate, thesis/dissertation. *Entrance requirements:* For master's and doctorate, GRE General Test. Additional exam requirements/recommendations for international students: Recommended—TOEFL. Electronic applications accepted. *Faculty research:* Geotechnical engineering, transportation engineering, structural engineering, construction management, environmental engineering, water resources.

The University of Texas at Austin, Graduate School, Cockrell School of Engineering, Department of Aerospace Engineering and Engineering Mechanics, Program in Engineering Mechanics, Austin, TX 78712-1111. Offers MS, PhD. *Degree requirements:* For doctorate, one foreign language, thesis/dissertation, qualifying exam. *Entrance requirements:* For master's and doctorate, GRE General Test.

University of Washington, Graduate School, College of Engineering, Department of Civil and Environmental Engineering, Seattle, WA 98195-2700. Offers construction engineering (MSCE, PhD); environmental engineering (MSCE, PhD); geotechnical engineering (MSCE, PhD); hydrology and hydrodynamics (MSCE, PhD); structural engineering and mechanics (MSCE, PhD); transportation engineering (MSCE, PhD). *Program availability:* Part-time, 100% online. *Faculty:* 38 full-time (10 women). *Students:* 239 full-time (104 women), 172 part-time (51 women); includes 91 minority (3 Black or African American, non-Hispanic/Latino; 2 American Indian or Alaska Native, non-Hispanic/Latino; 42 Asian, non-Hispanic/Latino; 26 Hispanic/Latino; 18 Two or more races, non-Hispanic/Latino), 120 international. Average age 28. 787 applicants, 57% accepted, 163 enrolled. In 2018, 161 master's, 11 doctorates awarded. Terminal master's awarded for partial completion of doctoral program. *Degree requirements:* For master's, thesis optional; for doctorate, comprehensive exam, thesis/dissertation, qualifying, general and final exams; completion of degree within 10 years. *Entrance requirements:* For master's, GRE General Test, minimum GPA of 3.0, statement of purpose, letters of recommendation, transcripts; for doctorate, GRE General Test, minimum GPA of 3.5, statement of purpose, letters of recommendation, transcripts, resume. Additional exam requirements/recommendations for international students: Required—TOEFL (minimum score 580 paper-based; 92 iBT); Recommended—IELTS (minimum score 7), TSE. *Application deadline:* For fall admission, 12/15 for domestic and international students. Applications are processed on a rolling basis. Application fee: $85. Electronic applications accepted. *Expenses:* Research-focused Master's and PhD: $18,852 resident; $32,760 nonresident. *Financial support:* In 2018–19, 120 students received support, including 23 fellowships with tuition reimbursements available (averaging $30,240 per year), 78 research assistantships with full tuition reimbursements available (averaging $30,240 per year), 28 teaching assistantships with full tuition reimbursements available (averaging $30,240 per year); scholarships/grants also available. Financial award application deadline: 12/15; financial award applicants required to submit FAFSA. *Faculty research:* Structural and geotechnical engineering, transportation and construction engineering, water and environmental engineering. *Total annual research expenditures:* $16.4 million. *Unit head:* Dr. Timothy V. Larson, Professor/Chair, 206-543-6815, Fax: 206-543-1543, E-mail: tlarson@uw.edu. *Application contact:* Melissa Pritchard, Graduate Adviser, 206-543-2574, Fax: 206-543-1543, E-mail: ceginfo@u.washington.edu.
Website: http://www.ce.washington.edu/

University of Wisconsin–Madison, Graduate School, College of Engineering, Department of Engineering Physics, Madison, WI 53706-1380. Offers engineering mechanics (MS, PhD), including fundamentals of applied mechanics (MS); nuclear engineering and engineering physics (MS, PhD). *Program availability:* Part-time. *Faculty:* 20 full-time (4 women). *Students:* 103 full-time (17 women), 3 part-time (0 women); includes 16 minority (3 Black or African American, non-Hispanic/Latino; 5 Asian, non-Hispanic/Latino; 6 Hispanic/Latino; 2 Two or more races, non-Hispanic/Latino), 16 international. Average age 26. 169 applicants, 42% accepted, 18 enrolled. In 2018, 28 master's, 12 doctorates awarded. Terminal master's awarded for partial completion of doctoral program. *Degree requirements:* For master's, thesis optional, 30 credits of technical courses; oral exam; for doctorate, comprehensive exam, thesis/dissertation, minimum of 60 credits; minimum GPA of 3.0. *Entrance requirements:* For master's and doctorate, GRE General Test, minimum GPA of 3.0 in last 60 hours, appropriate bachelor's degree. Additional exam requirements/recommendations for international students: Required—TOEFL (minimum score 580 paper-based; 92 iBT), IELTS (minimum score 7). *Application deadline:* For fall admission, 12/15 for domestic and international students; for spring admission, 10/1 for domestic and international students; for summer admission, 12/15 for domestic and international students. Application fee: $75 ($81 for international students). Electronic applications accepted. *Financial support:* In 2018–19, 109 students received support, including 9 fellowships with full tuition reimbursements available (averaging $27,204 per year), 82 research assistantships with full tuition reimbursements available (averaging $27,780 per year), 18 teaching assistantships with full tuition reimbursements available (averaging $23,566 per year); career-related internships or fieldwork, Federal Work-Study, institutionally sponsored loans, unspecified assistantships, and project assistantships also available. Support available to part-time students. Financial award application deadline: 12/1; financial award applicants required to submit FAFSA. *Faculty research:* Bio-/micro-/nano-mechanics; astronautics; fission reactor engineering; fusion science and technology; radiation sciences; mechanics of materials. *Total annual research expenditures:* $13.7 million. *Unit head:* Dr. Paul Wilson, Chair, 608-263-1646, Fax: 608-263-7451, E-mail: office@ep.wisc.edu. *Application contact:* Sara Hladilek, Student Services Coordinator, 608-262-8617, Fax: 608-263-7451, E-mail: shladilek@wisc.edu.
Website: https://www.engr.wisc.edu/department/engineering-physics/

University of Wisconsin–Milwaukee, Graduate School, College of Engineering and Applied Science, Program in Engineering, Milwaukee, WI 53201-0413. Offers biomedical engineering (MS); civil engineering (MS, PhD); computer science (PhD); electrical and computer engineering (MS); electrical engineering (PhD); engineering mechanics (MS); industrial and management engineering (MS); industrial engineering (PhD); manufacturing engineering (MS); materials (PhD); materials engineering (MS); mechanical engineering (MS). *Program availability:* Part-time. *Students:* 174 full-time (41 women), 149 part-time (27 women); includes 31 minority (2 Black or African American, non-Hispanic/Latino; 1 American Indian or Alaska Native, non-Hispanic/Latino; 16 Asian, non-Hispanic/Latino; 4 Hispanic/Latino; 8 Two or more races, non-Hispanic/Latino), 207 international. Average age 31. 343 applicants, 57% accepted, 78 enrolled. In 2018, 73 master's, 24 doctorates awarded. *Degree requirements:* For master's, comprehensive exam (for some programs), thesis or alternative; for doctorate, comprehensive exam, thesis/dissertation, internship. *Entrance requirements:* For master's, GRE, minimum GPA of 2.75; for doctorate, GRE, minimum GPA of 3.5. Additional exam requirements/recommendations for international students: Required—TOEFL (minimum score 550 paper-based; 79 iBT), IELTS (minimum score 6.5). *Application deadline:* For fall admission, 1/1 priority date for domestic students; for spring admission, 9/1 for domestic students. Applications are processed on a rolling basis. Application fee: $56 ($96 for international students). *Financial support:* Fellowships, research assistantships, teaching assistantships, career-related internships or fieldwork, Federal Work-Study, unspecified assistantships, and project assistantships available. Support available to part-time students. Financial award application deadline: 4/15. *Unit head:* David Yu, Representative, 414-229-6169, E-mail: yu@uwm.edu. *Application contact:* Betty Warras, General Information Contact, 414-229-6169, Fax: 414-229-6967, E-mail: bwarras@uwm.edu.
Website: http://www4.uwm.edu/ceas/academics/graduate_programs/

Section 18
Ocean Engineering

This section contains a directory of institutions offering graduate work in ocean engineering. Additional information about programs listed in the directory may be obtained by writing directly to the dean of a graduate school or chair of a department at the address given in the directory.

For programs offering related work, see also in this book *Civil and Environmental Engineering* and *Engineering and Applied Sciences.* In the other guides in this series:

Graduate Programs in the Biological/Biomedical Sciences & Health-Related Medical Professions
See *Marine Biology*

Graduate Programs in the Physical Sciences, Mathematics, Agricultural Sciences, the Environment & Natural Resources
See *Environmental Sciences and Management* and *Marine Sciences and Oceanography*

CONTENTS

Program Directory

Ocean Engineering

Florida Atlantic University, College of Engineering and Computer Science, Department of Ocean and Mechanical Engineering, Boca Raton, FL 33431-0991. Offers mechanical engineering (MS, PhD). *Program availability:* Part-time, evening/weekend. *Faculty:* 23 full-time (1 woman), 1 part-time/adjunct (0 women). *Students:* 42 full-time (6 women), 59 part-time (11 women); includes 17 minority (1 Black or African American, non-Hispanic/Latino; 2 Asian, non-Hispanic/Latino; 14 Hispanic/Latino), 43 international. Average age 30. 67 applicants, 66% accepted, 28 enrolled. In 2018, 34 master's, 4 doctorates awarded. Terminal master's awarded for partial completion of doctoral program. *Degree requirements:* For master's, thesis (for some programs); for doctorate, comprehensive exam, thesis/dissertation, qualifying exam. *Entrance requirements:* For master's and doctorate, GRE General Test, minimum GPA of 3.0. Additional exam requirements/recommendations for international students: Required—TOEFL (minimum score 500 paper-based; 61 iBT), IELTS (minimum score 6). *Application deadline:* For fall admission, 7/1 priority date for domestic students, 2/15 for international students; for spring admission, 11/1 for domestic students, 7/15 for international students. Applications are processed on a rolling basis. Application fee: $30. *Expenses: Tuition, area resident:* Full-time $7400; part-time $369.82 per credit. Tuition, state resident: full-time $7400; part-time $369.82 per credit. Tuition, nonresident: full-time $20,496; part-time $1024.81 per credit. *Financial support:* Research assistantships, career-related internships or fieldwork, Federal Work-Study, scholarships/grants, and unspecified assistantships available. Financial award application deadline: 1/10; financial award applicants required to submit FAFSA. *Faculty research:* Marine materials and corrosion, ocean structures, marine vehicles, acoustics and vibrations, hydrodynamics, coastal engineering. *Unit head:* Manhar Dhanak, Chair, 561-297-2827, E-mail: dhanak@fau.edu. *Application contact:* Manhar Dhanak, Chair, 561-297-2827, E-mail: dhanak@fau.edu.
Website: http://www.ome.fau.edu/

Florida Institute of Technology, College of Engineering and Science, Program in Ocean Engineering, Melbourne, FL 32901-6975. Offers MS, PhD. *Program availability:* Part-time. *Students:* 25 full-time (9 women), 6 part-time (2 women); includes 3 minority (1 Asian, non-Hispanic/Latino; 2 Hispanic/Latino), 12 international. Average age 29. 9 applicants, 89% accepted, 4 enrolled. In 2018, 10 master's, 1 doctorate awarded. Terminal master's awarded for partial completion of doctoral program. *Degree requirements:* For master's, comprehensive exam (for some programs), thesis optional, 30 credit hours (thesis), 33 credit hours (non-thesis) with technical paper; for doctorate, comprehensive exam, thesis/dissertation, research program and publication. *Entrance requirements:* For master's, GRE General Test, 3 letters of recommendation, resume, transcripts, statement of objectives, undergraduate degree in physical sciences or engineering, on-campus interview (highly recommended); for doctorate, GRE General Test, minimum GPA of 3.3, resume, 3 letters of recommendation, statement of objectives. Additional exam requirements/recommendations for international students: Required—TOEFL (minimum score 550 paper-based; 79 iBT). *Application deadline:* Applications are processed on a rolling basis. Application fee: $0. Electronic applications accepted. *Expenses: Tuition:* Full-time $22,338; part-time $1241 per credit hour. Tuition and fees vary according to degree level, campus/location and program. *Financial support:* Career-related internships or fieldwork, institutionally sponsored loans, tuition waivers (partial), unspecified assistantships, and tuition remissions available. Support available to part-time students. Financial award application deadline: 3/1; financial award applicants required to submit FAFSA. *Faculty research:* Autonomous underwater and surface vehicles; remote operated underwater and surface vehicles; ocean energy systems via waves and currents; coastal engineering; ocean, estuary, and storm modeling; ship design&—high-speed small craft to large-scale ships; reef and beach restoration; underwater archaeology engineering; corrosion and anti-biofouling studies. *Unit head:* Dr. Richard Aronson, Department Head, 321-674-8034, E-mail: oems@fit.edu. *Application contact:* Mike Perry, Executive Director of Admissions, E-mail: perrymj@fit.edu.
Website: https://www.fit.edu/programs/ocean-engineering-ms/

Massachusetts Institute of Technology, School of Engineering, Department of Mechanical Engineering, Cambridge, MA 02139. Offers manufacturing (M Eng); mechanical engineering (SM, PhD, Sc D, Mech E); naval architecture and marine engineering (SM, PhD, Sc D); naval engineering (Naval E); ocean engineering (SM, PhD, Sc D); oceanographic engineering (SM, PhD, Sc D); SM/MBA. Terminal master's awarded for partial completion of doctoral program. *Degree requirements:* For master's, thesis; for doctorate, comprehensive exam, thesis/dissertation; for other advanced degree, comprehensive exam, thesis. *Entrance requirements:* For master's, doctorate, and other advanced degree, GRE General Test. Additional exam requirements/recommendations for international students: Required—TOEFL, IELTS. Electronic applications accepted. *Expenses: Tuition:* Full-time $51,520; part-time $800 per credit hour. *Required fees:* $312. *Faculty research:* Mechanics: modeling, experimentation and computation; design, manufacturing, and product development; controls, instrumentation, and robotics; energy science and engineering; ocean science and engineering; bioengineering; micro- and Nano-engineering.

Memorial University of Newfoundland, School of Graduate Studies, Faculty of Engineering and Applied Science, St. John's, NL A1C 5S7, Canada. Offers civil engineering (M Eng, PhD); electrical and computer engineering (M Eng, PhD); mechanical engineering (M Eng, PhD); ocean and naval architecture engineering (M Eng, PhD). *Program availability:* Part-time. *Degree requirements:* For master's, thesis; for doctorate, comprehensive exam, thesis/dissertation, oral thesis defense. *Entrance requirements:* For master's, 2nd class degree; for doctorate, master's degree in engineering. Electronic applications accepted. *Faculty research:* Engineering analysis, environmental and hydrotechnical studies, manufacturing and robotics, mechanics, structures and materials.

Oregon State University, College of Engineering, Program in Civil Engineering, Corvallis, OR 97331. Offers civil engineering (M Eng, MS, PhD); coastal and ocean engineering (M Eng, MS, PhD); construction engineering management (M Eng, MS, PhD); engineering education (M Eng, MS, PhD); geomatics (M Eng, MS, PhD); geotechnical engineering (M Eng, MS, PhD); infrastructure materials (M Eng, MS, PhD); structural engineering (M Eng, MS, PhD); transportation engineering (M Eng). *Entrance requirements:* For master's and doctorate, GRE. Additional exam requirements/recommendations for international students: Required—TOEFL (minimum score 80 iBT), IELTS (minimum score 6.5). *Expenses:* Contact institution.

Princeton University, Graduate School, Department of Geosciences, Princeton, NJ 08544-1019. Offers atmospheric and oceanic sciences (PhD); geosciences (PhD); ocean sciences and marine biology (PhD). *Degree requirements:* For doctorate, one foreign language, thesis/dissertation. *Entrance requirements:* For doctorate, GRE General Test. Additional exam requirements/recommendations for international students: Required—TOEFL (minimum score 600 paper-based). Electronic applications accepted. *Faculty research:* Biogeochemistry, climate science, earth history, regional geology and tectonics, solid–earth geophysics.

Stevens Institute of Technology, Graduate School, Charles V. Schaefer Jr. School of Engineering and Science, Department of Civil, Environmental, and Ocean Engineering, Program in Ocean Engineering, Hoboken, NJ 07030. Offers M Eng, PhD. *Program availability:* Part-time, evening/weekend. *Faculty:* 28 full-time (7 women), 2 part-time/adjunct (1 woman). *Students:* 15 full-time (7 women), 5 part-time (1 woman); includes 2 minority (1 Black or African American, non-Hispanic/Latino; 1 Asian, non-Hispanic/Latino), 10 international. Average age 29. In 2018, 10 master's, 4 doctorates awarded. Terminal master's awarded for partial completion of doctoral program. *Degree requirements:* For master's, thesis optional, minimum B average in major field and overall; for doctorate, comprehensive exam (for some programs), thesis/dissertation. *Entrance requirements:* For master's, GRE/GMAT scores: GRE scores are required for all applicants applying to a full-time graduate program in the Schaefer School of Engineering and Science (SES). International applicants must submit TOEFL/IELTS scores and fulfill the English Language Proficiency Requirements in order to be considered. Additional exam requirements/recommendations for international students: Required—TOEFL (minimum score 74 iBT), IELTS (minimum score 6). *Application deadline:* For fall admission, 4/15 for domestic and international students; for spring admission, 11/1 for domestic and international students; for summer admission, 5/1 for domestic students. Applications are processed on a rolling basis. Application fee: $60. Electronic applications accepted. *Expenses: Tuition:* Full-time $35,960; part-time $1620 per credit. *Required fees:* $1290; $600 per semester. Tuition and fees vary according to course load. *Financial support:* Fellowships, research assistantships, teaching assistantships, career-related internships or fieldwork, Federal Work-Study, scholarships/grants, and unspecified assistantships available. Financial award application deadline: 2/15; financial award applicants required to submit FAFSA. *Unit head:* Dr. Jean Zu, Dean of SES, 201-216.8233, Fax: 201-216.8372, E-mail: Jean.Zu@stevens.edu. *Application contact:* Graduate Admission, 888-783-8367, Fax: 888-511-1306, E-mail: graduate@stevens.edu.

University of California, San Diego, Graduate Division, Department of Electrical and Computer Engineering, La Jolla, CA 92093. Offers applied ocean science (MS, PhD); applied physics (MS, PhD); communication theory and systems (MS, PhD); computer engineering (MS, PhD); electronic circuits and systems (MS, PhD); intelligent systems, robotics and control (MS, PhD); medical devices and systems (MS, PhD); nanoscale devices and systems (MS, PhD); photonics (MS, PhD); signal and image processing (MS, PhD). Program offered jointly with San Diego State University. *Students:* 830 full-time (174 women), 69 part-time (8 women). 2,810 applicants, 40% accepted, 399 enrolled. In 2018, 226 master's, 42 doctorates awarded. Terminal master's awarded for partial completion of doctoral program. *Degree requirements:* For master's, comprehensive exam (for some programs), thesis (for some programs); for doctorate, comprehensive exam, thesis/dissertation. *Entrance requirements:* For master's and doctorate, GRE General Test, minimum GPA of 3.0, resume or curriculum vitae (recommended). Additional exam requirements/recommendations for international students: Required—TOEFL (minimum score 550 paper-based; 80 iBT), IELTS (minimum score 7), PTE (minimum score 65). *Application deadline:* For fall admission, 12/13 for domestic students. Application fee: $105 ($125 for international students). Electronic applications accepted. *Financial support:* Fellowships, research assistantships, teaching assistantships, scholarships/grants, traineeships, and unspecified assistantships available. Financial award applicants required to submit FAFSA. *Faculty research:* Applied ocean science; applied physics; communication theory and systems; computer engineering; electronic circuits and systems; intelligent systems, robotics and control; medical devices and systems; nanoscale devices and systems; photonics; signal and image processing. *Unit head:* Bill Lin, Chair, 858-822-1383, E-mail: billin@ucsd.edu. *Application contact:* Sean Jones, Graduate Admissions Coordinator, 858-534-3213, E-mail: ecegradapps@ece.ucsd.edu.
Website: http://ece.ucsd.edu/

University of California, San Diego, Graduate Division, Department of Mechanical and Aerospace Engineering, Program in Applied Ocean Science, La Jolla, CA 92093. Offers MS, PhD. *Students:* 2 full-time (0 women). 6 applicants, 33% accepted, 1 enrolled. *Degree requirements:* For master's, comprehensive exam (for some programs), thesis (for some programs), comprehensive exam or thesis; for doctorate, comprehensive exam, thesis/dissertation. *Entrance requirements:* For master's and doctorate, GRE General Test, minimum GPA of 3.0. Additional exam requirements/recommendations for international students: Required—TOEFL (minimum score 550 paper-based; 80 iBT), IELTS (minimum score 7). *Application deadline:* For fall admission, 12/18 for domestic students. Application fee: $105 ($125 for international students). Electronic applications accepted. *Financial support:* Fellowships, research assistantships, teaching assistantships, scholarships/grants, and unspecified assistantships available. Financial award applicants required to submit FAFSA. *Faculty research:* Water quality in the coastal ocean and subsurface resources; internal waves, gravity currents, wake flows; ocean process modeling. *Unit head:* Carlos Coimbra, Chair, 858-534-4285, E-mail: mae-chair-l@ucsd.edu. *Application contact:* Joana Halnez, Graduate Coordinator, 858-534-4387, E-mail: mae-gradadm-l@ucsd.edu.
Website: http://maeweb.ucsd.edu/

University of Delaware, College of Earth, Ocean, and Environment, School of Marine Science and Policy, Newark, DE 19716. Offers marine policy (MMP); marine studies (MS, PhD), including marine biosciences, oceanography, physical ocean science and engineering; oceanography (PhD).

University of Delaware, College of Engineering, Department of Civil and Environmental Engineering, Newark, DE 19716. Offers environmental engineering (MAS, MCE, PhD); geotechnical engineering (MAS, MCE, PhD); ocean engineering (MAS, MCE, PhD); structural engineering (MAS, MCE, PhD); transportation engineering (MAS, MCE, PhD); water resource engineering (MAS, MCE, PhD). *Program availability:* Part-time. Terminal master's awarded for partial completion of doctoral program. *Degree requirements:* For master's, thesis; for doctorate, thesis/dissertation. *Entrance requirements:* For master's and doctorate, GRE General Test. Additional exam requirements/recommendations for international students: Required—TOEFL. Electronic applications accepted. *Faculty research:* Structural engineering and mechanics; transportation engineering; ocean engineering; soil mechanics and foundation; water resources and environmental engineering.

University of Florida, Graduate School, Herbert Wertheim College of Engineering, Department of Civil and Coastal Engineering, Gainesville, FL 32611. Offers civil engineering (ME, MS, PhD); coastal and oceanographic engineering (ME, MS, PhD); geographic information systems (ME, MS, PhD); hydrologic sciences (ME, MS, PhD); structural engineering (ME, MS); wetland sciences (ME, MS, PhD). *Program availability:* Part-time, online learning. Terminal master's awarded for partial completion of doctoral program. *Degree requirements:* For master's, thesis (for some programs); for doctorate, comprehensive exam, thesis/dissertation. *Entrance requirements:* For master's and doctorate, minimum GPA of 3.0. Additional exam requirements/recommendations for international students: Required—TOEFL (minimum score 550 paper-based; 80 iBT), IELTS (minimum score 6). Electronic applications accepted. *Faculty research:* Traffic congestion mitigation, wind mitigation, sustainable infrastructure materials, improved sensors for in situ measurements, storm surge modeling.

University of Hawaii at Manoa, Office of Graduate Education, School of Ocean and Earth Science and Technology, Department of Ocean and Resources Engineering, Honolulu, HI 96822. Offers MS, PhD. *Accreditation:* ABET (one or more programs are accredited). *Program availability:* Part-time. *Degree requirements:* For master's, thesis optional, exams; for doctorate, comprehensive exam, thesis/dissertation, exams. *Entrance requirements:* For master's and doctorate, GRE General Test. Additional exam requirements/recommendations for international students: Required—TOEFL (minimum score 560 paper-based; 83 iBT), IELTS (minimum score 5). *Faculty research:* Coastal and harbor engineering, near shore environmental ocean engineering, marine structures/naval architecture.

University of Michigan, College of Engineering, Department of Naval Architecture and Marine Engineering, Ann Arbor, MI 48109. Offers MS, MSE, PhD, Mar Eng, Nav Arch, MBA/MSE. *Program availability:* Part-time. *Students:* 72 full-time (18 women), 3 part-time (0 women). 80 applicants, 53% accepted, 26 enrolled. In 2018, 25 master's, 7 doctorates awarded. Terminal master's awarded for partial completion of doctoral program. *Degree requirements:* For master's, thesis (for some programs); for doctorate, comprehensive exam, thesis/dissertation, oral defense of dissertation, written and oral preliminary exams; for other advanced degree, comprehensive exam, thesis, oral defense of thesis. *Entrance requirements:* For doctorate, GRE General Test, master's degree; for other advanced degree, GRE General Test. Additional exam requirements/recommendations for international students: Required—TOEFL. *Application deadline:* Applications are processed on a rolling basis. Electronic applications accepted. *Financial support:* Fellowships, research assistantships, teaching assistantships, career-related internships or fieldwork, Federal Work-Study, institutionally sponsored loans, scholarships/grants, and unspecified assistantships available. Financial award applicants required to submit FAFSA. *Faculty research:* System and structural reliability, design and analysis of offshore structures and vehicles, marine systems design, remote sensing of ship wakes and sea surfaces, marine hydrodynamics, nonlinear seakeeping analysis. *Total annual research expenditures:* $8.2 million. *Unit head:* Jing Sun, Department Chair, 734-615-8061, E-mail: jingsun@umich.edu. *Application contact:* Nathalie Fiveland, Graduate Student Advisor/Program Coordinator, 734-936-0566, Fax: 734-936-8820, E-mail: fiveland@umich.edu.
Website: https://name.engin.umich.edu/

University of New Hampshire, Graduate School, School of Marine Science and Ocean Engineering, Durham, NH 03824. Offers ocean engineering (MS, PhD); ocean mapping (MS, Postbaccalaureate Certificate). *Degree requirements:* For master's, thesis. *Entrance requirements:* Additional exam requirements/recommendations for international students: Required—TOEFL (minimum score 550 paper-based; 80 iBT). Electronic applications accepted.

University of Rhode Island, Graduate School, College of Engineering, Department of Ocean Engineering, Narragansett, RI 02882. Offers ocean engineering (MS, PhD), including acoustics, geomechanics (MS), hydrodynamics (MS), ocean instrumentation (MS), offshore energy (MS), offshore structures (MS), water wave mechanics (MS).

Program availability: Part-time. *Faculty:* 9 full-time (1 woman). *Students:* 24 full-time (6 women), 19 part-time (4 women); includes 2 minority (both Asian, non-Hispanic/Latino), 6 international. 27 applicants, 70% accepted, 9 enrolled. In 2018, 10 master's, 1 doctorate awarded. *Entrance requirements:* Additional exam requirements/recommendations for international students: Required—TOEFL. *Application deadline:* For fall admission, 7/15 for domestic students, 2/1 for international students; for spring admission, 11/15 for domestic students, 7/15 for international students; for summer admission, 4/15 for domestic students. Application fee: $65. Electronic applications accepted. *Expenses: Tuition, area resident:* Full-time $13,226; part-time $735 per credit. Tuition, state resident: full-time $13,226; part-time $735 per credit. Tuition, nonresident: full-time $25,854; part-time $1436 per credit. *International tuition:* $25,854 full-time. *Required fees:* $1698; $50 per credit. $35 per semester. One-time fee: $165. *Financial support:* In 2018–19, 8 research assistantships with tuition reimbursements (averaging $9,512 per year), 3 teaching assistantships with tuition reimbursements (averaging $13,338 per year) were awarded. Financial award application deadline: 2/1; financial award applicants required to submit FAFSA. *Unit head:* Dr. Stephen Grilli, Chairman, 401-874-6636, E-mail: grilli@uri.edu. *Application contact:* Christopher Baxter, Graduate Program Director, 401-874-6575, E-mail: cbaxter@uri.edu.
Website: http://www.oce.uri.edu/

Virginia Polytechnic Institute and State University, VT Online, Blacksburg, VA 24061. Offers advanced transportation systems (Certificate); aerospace engineering (MS); agricultural and life sciences (MSLFS); business information systems (Graduate Certificate); career and technical education (MS); civil engineering (MS); computer engineering (M Eng, MS); decision support systems (Graduate Certificate); eLearning leadership (MA); electrical engineering (M Eng, MS); engineering administration (MEA); environmental engineering (Certificate); environmental politics and policy (Graduate Certificate); environmental sciences and engineering (MS); foundations of political analysis (Graduate Certificate); health product risk management (Graduate Certificate); industrial and systems engineering (MS); information policy and society (Graduate Certificate); information security (Graduate Certificate); information technology (MIT); instructional technology (MA); integrative STEM education (MA Ed); liberal arts (Graduate Certificate); life sciences: health product risk management (MS); natural resources (MNR, Graduate Certificate); networking (Graduate Certificate); nonprofit and nongovernmental organization management (Graduate Certificate); ocean engineering (MS); political science (MA); security studies (Graduate Certificate); software development (Graduate Certificate). *Expenses:* Tuition, state resident: full-time $15,510; part-time $739.50 per credit hour. Tuition, nonresident: full-time $29,629; part-time $1490.25 per credit hour. *Required fees:* $2804; $550 per semester. Tuition and fees vary according to course load, campus/location and program. *Application contact:* Graduate Admissions and Academic Progress, 540-231-8636, E-mail: grads@vt.edu.
Website: http://www.vto.vt.edu/

Woods Hole Oceanographic Institution, MIT/WHOI Joint Program in Oceanography/Applied Ocean Science and Engineering, Woods Hole, MA 02543-1541. Offers applied ocean science and engineering (PhD); biological oceanography (PhD); chemical oceanography (PhD); marine geology and geophysics (PhD); physical oceanography (PhD). Program offered jointly with Massachusetts Institute of Technology. *Degree requirements:* For doctorate, thesis/dissertation. *Entrance requirements:* For doctorate, GRE General Test. Additional exam requirements/recommendations for international students: Required—TOEFL or IELTS. Electronic applications accepted.

Section 19
Paper and Textile Engineering

This section contains a directory of institutions offering graduate work in paper and textile engineering. Additional information about programs listed in the directory may be obtained by writing directly to the dean of a graduate school or chair of a department at the address given in the directory.

For programs offering related work, see also in this book *Engineering and Applied Sciences* and *Materials Sciences and Engineering.* In another guide in this series:

Graduate Programs in the Humanities, Arts & Social Sciences
See *Family and Consumer Sciences (Clothing and Textiles)*

CONTENTS

Paper and Pulp Engineering

Georgia Institute of Technology, Graduate Studies, Multidisciplinary Program in Paper Science and Engineering, Atlanta, GA 30318-5794. Offers MS, PhD. Program offered jointly with School of Chemical and Biomolecular Engineering, School of Chemistry and Biochemistry, School of Materials Science and Engineering, and George W. Woodruff School of Mechanical Engineering. *Program availability:* Part-time. Terminal master's awarded for partial completion of doctoral program. *Degree requirements:* For master's, thesis; for doctorate, comprehensive exam, thesis/dissertation. *Entrance requirements:* For master's and doctorate, GRE General Test. Additional exam requirements/recommendations for international students: Required—TOEFL (minimum score 620 paper-based; 105 iBT). Electronic applications accepted.

State University of New York College of Environmental Science and Forestry, Department of Paper and Bioprocess Engineering, Syracuse, NY 13210-2779. Offers biomaterials engineering (MS, PhD); bioprocess engineering (MPS, MS, PhD); bioprocessing (Advanced Certificate); paper science and engineering (MPS, MS, PhD); sustainable engineering management (MPS). *Program availability:* Part-time. *Faculty:* 13 full-time (2 women), 1 part-time/adjunct (0 women). *Students:* 20 full-time (11 women), 1 part-time (0 women); includes 29 minority (28 American Indian or Alaska Native, non-Hispanic/Latino; 1 Hispanic/Latino), 14 international. Average age 28. 18 applicants, 100% accepted, 11 enrolled. In 2018, 2 master's awarded. Terminal master's awarded for partial completion of doctoral program. *Degree requirements:* For master's, thesis; for doctorate, comprehensive exam, thesis/dissertation; for Advanced Certificate, 15 credit hours. *Entrance requirements:* For master's and doctorate, GRE General Test, minimum GPA of 3.0; for Advanced Certificate, BS, calculus plus science major. Additional exam requirements/recommendations for international students: Required—TOEFL (minimum score 550 paper-based; 80 iBT), IELTS (minimum score 6). *Application deadline:* For fall admission, 2/1 priority date for domestic and international students; for spring admission, 11/1 priority date for domestic and international students. Applications are processed on a rolling basis. Application fee: $60. Electronic applications accepted. *Expenses: Tuition, area resident:* Full-time $11,090; part-time $462 per credit hour. Tuition, state resident: full-time $11,090; part-time $462 per credit hour. Tuition, nonresident: full-time $22,650; part-time $944 per credit hour. *International tuition:* $22,650 full-time. *Required fees:* $1733; $178.58 per credit hour. *Financial support:* In 2018–19, 17 students received support. Unspecified assistantships available. Financial award application deadline: 6/30; financial award applicants required to submit FAFSA. *Faculty research:* Sustainable products and processes, biorefinery, pulping and papermaking, nanocellulose, bioconversions, process control and modeling. *Total annual research expenditures:* $237,793. *Unit head:* Dr. Bandaru Ramarao, Interim Chair, 315-470-6502, Fax: 315-470-6945, E-mail: bvramara@esf.edu. *Application contact:* Scott Shannon, Associate Provost and Dean, Instruction and Graduate Studies, 315-470-6599, Fax: 315-470-6978, E-mail: esfgrad@esf.edu.
Website: http://www.esf.edu/pbe/

The University of Manchester, School of Materials, Manchester, United Kingdom. Offers advanced aerospace materials engineering (M Sc); advanced metallic systems (PhD); biomedical materials (M Phil, M Sc, PhD); ceramics and glass (M Phil, M Sc, PhD); composite materials (M Sc, PhD); corrosion and protection (M Phil, M Sc, PhD); materials (M Phil, PhD); metallic materials (M Phil, M Sc, PhD); nanostructural materials (M Phil, M Sc, PhD); paper science (M Phil, M Sc, PhD); polymer science and engineering (M Phil, M Sc, PhD); technical textiles (M Sc); textile design, fashion and management (M Phil, M Sc, PhD); textile science and technology (M Phil, M Sc, PhD); textiles (M Phil, PhD); textiles and fashion (M Ent).

University of Minnesota, Twin Cities Campus, Graduate School, College of Food, Agricultural and Natural Resource Sciences, Program in Natural Resources Science and Management, St. Paul, MN 55108. Offers assessment, monitoring, and geospatial analysis (MS, PhD); economics, policy, management, and society (MS, PhD); forest hydrology and watershed management (MS, PhD); forest products (MS, PhD); forests: biology, ecology, conservation, and management (MS, PhD); natural resources science and management (MS, PhD); paper science and engineering (MS, PhD); recreation resources, tourism, and environmental education (MS, PhD). *Program availability:* Part-time. Terminal master's awarded for partial completion of doctoral program. *Degree requirements:* For master's, comprehensive exam, thesis (for some programs); for doctorate, comprehensive exam, thesis/dissertation. *Entrance requirements:* For master's and doctorate, GRE General Test. Additional exam requirements/recommendations for international students: Required—TOEFL (minimum score 550 paper-based; 79 iBT); Recommended—IELTS (minimum score 6.5). Electronic applications accepted. *Faculty research:* Forest hydrology, biology, ecology, conservation, and management; recreation resources and environmental education; wildlife ecology; economics, policy, and society; geographic information systems (GIS); forest products and paper science.

Western Michigan University, Graduate College, College of Engineering and Applied Sciences, Department of Chemical and Paper Engineering, Kalamazoo, MI 49008. Offers MS, MSE, PhD. *Degree requirements:* For master's, thesis optional; for doctorate, one foreign language, comprehensive exam, thesis/dissertation.

Textile Sciences and Engineering

Cornell University, Graduate School, Graduate Fields of Human Ecology, Field of Fiber Science and Apparel Design, Ithaca, NY 14853. Offers apparel design (MA, MPS); fiber science (MS, PhD); polymer science (MS, PhD); textile science (MS, PhD). *Degree requirements:* For master's, thesis (MA, MS), project paper (MPS); for doctorate, comprehensive exam, thesis/dissertation. *Entrance requirements:* For master's, GRE General Test, 2 letters of recommendation, portfolio (for functional apparel design); for doctorate, GRE General Test, 2 letters of recommendation. Additional exam requirements/recommendations for international students: Required—TOEFL (minimum score 600 paper-based; 77 iBT). Electronic applications accepted. *Faculty research:* Apparel design, consumption, mass customization, 3-D body scanning.

North Carolina State University, Graduate School, Wilson College of Textiles, Department of Textile and Apparel Technology and Management, Raleigh, NC 27695. Offers MS, MT. *Degree requirements:* For master's, thesis optional. *Entrance requirements:* For master's, GRE. Electronic applications accepted. *Faculty research:* Textile and apparel products and processes, management systems, nonwovens, process simulation, structure design and analysis.

North Carolina State University, Graduate School, Wilson College of Textiles, Department of Textile Engineering, Chemistry, and Science, Program in Textile Chemistry, Raleigh, NC 27695. Offers MS. *Degree requirements:* For master's, thesis optional. *Entrance requirements:* For master's, GRE. Electronic applications accepted. *Faculty research:* Color science, polymer science, dye chemistry, fiber formation, wet processing technology.

North Carolina State University, Graduate School, Wilson College of Textiles, Department of Textile Engineering, Chemistry, and Science, Program in Textile Engineering, Raleigh, NC 27695. Offers MS. *Degree requirements:* For master's, thesis optional. *Entrance requirements:* For master's, GRE. Electronic applications accepted. *Faculty research:* Electro-mechanical design, inventory and supply chain control, textile composites, biomedical textile applications, pollution prevention.

North Carolina State University, Graduate School, Wilson College of Textiles, Program in Fiber and Polymer Science, Raleigh, NC 27695. Offers PhD. *Degree requirements:* For doctorate, one foreign language, thesis/dissertation, cumulative exams. *Entrance requirements:* For doctorate, GRE. Electronic applications accepted. *Faculty research:* Polymer science, fiber mechanics, medical textiles, nanotechnology.

Thomas Jefferson University, Kanbar College of Design, Engineering and Commerce, PhD Program in Textile Engineering and Sciences, Philadelphia, PA 19107. Offers PhD.

Thomas Jefferson University, Kanbar College of Design, Engineering and Commerce, Program in Textile Engineering, Philadelphia, PA 19107. Offers MS. *Program availability:* Part-time. *Degree requirements:* For master's, thesis. *Entrance requirements:* For master's, GRE, minimum GPA of 2.8. Additional exam requirements/recommendations for international students: Required—TOEFL (minimum score 550 paper-based; 79 iBT). Electronic applications accepted.

The University of Texas at Austin, Graduate School, College of Natural Sciences, School of Human Ecology, Program in Textile and Apparel Technology, Austin, TX 78712-1111. Offers MS.

Section 20
Telecommunications

This section contains a directory of institutions offering graduate work in telecommunications. Additional information about programs listed in the directory may be obtained by writing directly to the dean of a graduate school or chair of a department at the address given in the directory.

For programs offering related work, see also in this book *Computer Science and Information Technology* and *Engineering and Applied Sciences*. In the other guides in this series:

Graduate Programs in the Humanities, Arts & Social Sciences
See *Communication and Media*

Graduate Programs in Business, Education, Information Studies, Law & Social Work
See *Business Administration and Management*

CONTENTS

Program Directories

Telecommunications

Ball State University, Graduate School, College of Communication, Information, and Media, Department of Telecommunications, Muncie, IN 47306. Offers telecommunications (MA), including digital storytelling. *Program availability:* Part-time. *Entrance requirements:* For master's, minimum baccalaureate GPA of 2.75 or 3.0 in latter half of baccalaureate. Additional exam requirements/recommendations for international students: Required—TOEFL (minimum score 550 paper-based; 79 iBT), IELTS (minimum score 6.5). Electronic applications accepted.

Boston University, Metropolitan College, Department of Computer Science, Boston, MA 02215. Offers computer information systems (MS), including computer networks, data analytics, database management and business intelligence, health informatics, IT project management, security, Web application development; computer networks (Certificate); computer science (MS); data analytics (Certificate); digital forensics (Certificate); health informatics (Certificate); information technology project management (Certificate); software development (MS); software engineering in health care systems (Certificate); telecommunications (MS), including security. *Program availability:* Part-time, evening/weekend, online learning. *Faculty:* 16 full-time (3 women), 52 part-time/adjunct (5 women). *Students:* 201 full-time (57 women), 953 part-time (252 women); includes 285 minority (57 Black or African American, non-Hispanic/Latino; 2 American Indian or Alaska Native, non-Hispanic/Latino; 139 Asian, non-Hispanic/Latino; 67 Hispanic/Latino; 1 Native Hawaiian or other Pacific Islander, non-Hispanic/Latino; 19 Two or more races, non-Hispanic/Latino), 333 international. Average age 31. 1,079 applicants, 72% accepted, 297 enrolled. In 2018, 395 master's awarded. *Entrance requirements:* For master's and Certificate, official transcripts from regionally-accredited bachelor's degree program, 3 letters of recommendation, professional resume, personal statement. Additional exam requirements/recommendations for international students: Required—TOEFL (minimum score 84 iBT), IELTS. *Application deadline:* For fall admission, 8/1 priority date for domestic students, 6/1 priority date for international students; for spring admission, 12/1 priority date for domestic students, 11/15 priority date for international students; for summer admission, 4/1 priority date for domestic students, 3/1 priority date for international students. Applications are processed on a rolling basis. Application fee: $85. Electronic applications accepted. *Expenses:* Contact institution. *Financial support:* In 2018–19, 11 research assistantships (averaging $8,400 per year), 23 teaching assistantships (averaging $3,400 per year) were awarded; unspecified assistantships also available. Support available to part-time students. Financial award applicants required to submit FAFSA. *Faculty research:* Artificial intelligence and machine learning, security and forensics, web technologies, software engineering, programming languages, medical informatics, information systems and IT project management. *Unit head:* Dr. Anatoly Temkin, Chair, 617-353-2566, Fax: 617-353-2367, E-mail: csinfo@bu.edu. *Application contact:* Enrollment Services, 617-353-6004, E-mail: met@bu.edu.
Website: http://www.bu.edu/csmet/

California Miramar University, Program in Telecommunications Management, San Diego, CA 92108. Offers MST.

Claremont Graduate University, Graduate Programs, Center for Information Systems and Technology, Claremont, CA 91711-6160. Offers cybersecurity and networking (MS); data science and analytics (MS); electronic commerce (PhD); geographic information systems (MS); health informatics (MS); information systems (Certificate); IT strategy and innovation (MS); knowledge management (PhD); systems development (PhD); telecommunications and networking (PhD); MBA/MS. *Program availability:* Part-time. *Degree requirements:* For doctorate, comprehensive exam, thesis/dissertation, portfolio. *Entrance requirements:* For master's and doctorate, GMAT, GRE General Test. Additional exam requirements/recommendations for international students: Required—TOEFL (minimum score 75 iBT). Electronic applications accepted. *Faculty research:* Man-machine interaction, organizational aspects of computing, implementation of information systems, information systems practice.

Drexel University, College of Engineering, Department of Electrical and Computer Engineering, Program in Telecommunications Engineering, Philadelphia, PA 19104-2875. Offers MSEE. *Entrance requirements:* For master's, BS in electrical engineering or physics, minimum GPA of 3.0. Additional exam requirements/recommendations for international students: Required—TOEFL. Electronic applications accepted.

Fairfield University, School of Engineering, Fairfield, CT 06824. Offers database management (CAS); electrical and computer engineering (MS); information security (CAS); management of technology (MS); mechanical engineering (MS); network technology (CAS); software engineering (MS); Web application development (CAS). *Program availability:* Part-time, evening/weekend. *Degree requirements:* For master's, capstone course. *Entrance requirements:* For master's, resume, 2 recommendations. Additional exam requirements/recommendations for international students: Required—TOEFL (minimum score 550 paper-based; 80 iBT) or IELTS (minimum score 6.5). Electronic applications accepted. *Expenses:* Contact institution. *Faculty research:* Artificial intelligence and information visualization, natural language processing, thermofluids, microwaves and electromagnetics, micro-/nano-manufacturing.

Florida International University, College of Engineering and Computing, School of Computing and Information Sciences, Miami, FL 33199. Offers computer science (MS, PhD); cybersecurity (MS); data science (MS); information technology (MS); telecommunications and networking (MS). *Program availability:* Part-time, evening/weekend. *Faculty:* 49 full-time (13 women), 31 part-time/adjunct (7 women). *Students:* 182 full-time (53 women), 132 part-time (28 women); includes 168 minority (13 Black or African American, non-Hispanic/Latino; 1 American Indian or Alaska Native, non-Hispanic/Latino; 10 Asian, non-Hispanic/Latino; 137 Hispanic/Latino; 7 Two or more races, non-Hispanic/Latino), 123 international. Average age 30. 393 applicants, 47% accepted, 92 enrolled. In 2018, 81 master's, 9 doctorates awarded. *Degree requirements:* For master's, thesis or alternative; for doctorate, comprehensive exam, thesis/dissertation. *Entrance requirements:* For master's and doctorate, GRE General Test, 3 letters of recommendation, minimum GPA of 3.0. Additional exam requirements/recommendations for international students: Required—TOEFL (minimum score 550 paper-based; 80 iBT). *Application deadline:* For fall admission, 6/1 for domestic students, 4/1 for international students; for spring admission, 10/1 for domestic students, 9/1 for international students. Applications are processed on a rolling basis. Application fee: $30. Electronic applications accepted. *Financial support:* Research assistantships, teaching assistantships, institutionally sponsored loans, scholarships/grants, and unspecified assistantships available. Financial award application deadline: 3/1; financial award applicants required to submit FAFSA. *Faculty research:* Database systems, software engineering, operating systems, networks. *Unit head:* Dr. Sundararaj S. Iyengar, Director, 305-348-3947, Fax: 305-348-3549, E-mail: sundararaj.iyengar@fiu.edu. *Application contact:* Nanett Rojas, Manager, Admissions Operations, 305-348-7464, Fax: 305-348-7441, E-mail: gradadm@fiu.edu.

Franklin Pierce University, Graduate and Professional Studies, Rindge, NH 03461-0060. Offers curriculum and instruction (M Ed); elementary education (MS Ed); emerging network technologies (Graduate Certificate); energy and sustainability studies (MBA, Graduate Certificate); health administration (MBA, Graduate Certificate); human resource management (MBA, Graduate Certificate); information technology (MBA); leadership (MBA); nursing education (MS); nursing leadership (MS); physical therapy (DPT); physician assistant studies (MPAS); special education (M Ed); sports management (MBA). *Accreditation:* APTA. *Program availability:* Part-time, 100% online, blended/hybrid learning. *Degree requirements:* For master's, concentrated original research projects; student teaching; fieldwork and/or internship; leadership project; PRAXIS I and II (for M Ed); for doctorate, concentrated original research projects, clinical fieldwork and/or internship, leadership project. *Entrance requirements:* For master's, minimum GPA of 2.5, 3 letters of recommendation; competencies in accounting, economics, statistics, and computer skills through life experience or undergraduate coursework (for MBA); certification/e-portfolio, minimum C grade in all education courses (for M Ed); license to practice as RN (for MS); for doctorate, GRE, 80 hours of observation/work in PT settings; completion of anatomy, chemistry, physics, and statistics; minimum GPA of 3.0. Additional exam requirements/recommendations for international students: Required—TOEFL (minimum score 550 paper-based; 61 iBT). Electronic applications accepted. *Faculty research:* Evidence-based practice in sports physical therapy, human resource management in economic crisis, leadership in nursing, innovation in sports facility management, differentiated learning and understanding by design.

The George Washington University, School of Engineering and Applied Science, Department of Electrical and Computer Engineering, Washington, DC 20052. Offers electrical engineering (MS, PhD); telecommunication and computers (MS). *Program availability:* Part-time, evening/weekend. *Faculty:* 25 full-time (2 women), 9 part-time/adjunct (0 women). *Students:* 221 full-time (34 women), 76 part-time (9 women); includes 13 minority (4 Black or African American, non-Hispanic/Latino; 7 Asian, non-Hispanic/Latino; 1 Hispanic/Latino; 1 Native Hawaiian or other Pacific Islander, non-Hispanic/Latino), 253 international. Average age 26. 601 applicants, 85% accepted, 100 enrolled. In 2018, 93 master's, 7 doctorates awarded. *Degree requirements:* For master's, thesis optional; for doctorate, comprehensive exam, thesis/dissertation, dissertation defense, qualifying exam. *Entrance requirements:* For master's, appropriate bachelor's degree, minimum GPA of 3.0; for doctorate, GRE (if highest earned degree is BS), appropriate bachelor's or master's degree, minimum GPA of 3.3; for other advanced degree, appropriate master's degree, minimum GPA of 3.0. Additional exam requirements/recommendations for international students: Required—TOEFL or The George Washington University English as a Foreign Language Test. *Application deadline:* For fall admission, 3/1 priority date for domestic students; for spring admission, 10/1 for domestic students. Applications are processed on a rolling basis. Application fee: $75. *Financial support:* In 2018–19, 39 students received support. Fellowships, research assistantships, teaching assistantships, career-related internships or fieldwork, and institutionally sponsored loans available. Financial award application deadline: 3/1; financial award applicants required to submit FAFSA. *Faculty research:* Computer graphics, multimedia systems. *Unit head:* Prof. Ahmed Louri, Chair, 202-994-5905, E-mail: louri@gwu.edu. *Application contact:* Adina Lav, Marketing, Recruiting and Admissions, 202-994-5827, Fax: 202-994-0909, E-mail: engineering@gwu.edu.
Website: http://www.ece.gwu.edu/

Illinois Institute of Technology, Graduate College, Armour College of Engineering, Department of Electrical and Computer Engineering, Chicago, IL 60616. Offers biomedical imaging and signals (MAS); computer engineering (MS, PhD); electrical engineering (MS, PhD); electricity markets (MAS); network engineering (MAS); power engineering (MAS); telecommunications and software engineering (MAS); VLSI and microelectronics (MAS); MS/MS. *Program availability:* Part-time, evening/weekend, online learning. Terminal master's awarded for partial completion of doctoral program. *Degree requirements:* For master's, comprehensive exam (for some programs), thesis (for some programs); for doctorate, comprehensive exam, thesis/dissertation. *Entrance requirements:* For master's and doctorate, GRE General Test (minimum score 1100 Quantitative and Verbal, 3.5 Analytical Writing), minimum undergraduate GPA of 3.0. Additional exam requirements/recommendations for international students: Required—TOEFL (minimum score 550 paper-based; 80 iBT); Recommended—IELTS (minimum score 5.5). Electronic applications accepted. *Faculty research:* Communication systems, wireless networks, computer systems, computer networks, wireless security, cloud computing and micro-electronics; electromagnetics and electronics; power and control systems; signal and image processing.

Illinois Institute of Technology, Graduate College, College of Science, Department of Computer Science, Chicago, IL 60616. Offers business (MCS); computational intelligence (MCS); computer science (MCS, MS, PhD); cyber-physical systems (MCS); data analytics (MCS); data science (MAS); database systems (MCS); distributed and cloud computing (MCS); education (MCS); finance (MCS); information security and assurance (MCS); networking and communications (MCS); software engineering (MCS); telecommunications and software engineering (MAS); MS/MAS. *Program availability:* Part-time, evening/weekend, online learning. Terminal master's awarded for partial completion of doctoral program. *Degree requirements:* For master's, thesis optional; for doctorate, comprehensive exam, thesis/dissertation. *Entrance requirements:* For master's, GRE General Test with minimum scores of 298 Quantitative and Verbal, 3.0 Analytical Writing (for MS); GRE General Test with minimum scores of 292 Quantitative and Verbal, 2.5 Analytical Writing (for MAS), minimum undergraduate GPA of 3.0; for doctorate, GRE General Test (minimum scores: 304 Quantitative and Verbal, 3.5 Analytical Writing), minimum undergraduate GPA of 3.0. Additional exam requirements/recommendations for international students: Required—TOEFL (minimum score 523 paper-based; 70 iBT). Electronic applications accepted. *Faculty research:* Parallel and distributed processing, high-performance computing, computational linguistics, information retrieval, data mining, grid computing.

Instituto Tecnologico de Santo Domingo, Graduate School, Area of Engineering, Santo Domingo, Dominican Republic. Offers construction administration (MS, Certificate); data telecommunications (M Eng, MS, Certificate); industrial engineering (M Eng, Certificate); industrial management (M Mgmt); information technology (Certificate); maintenance engineering (M Eng); occupational hazard prevention (M Mgmt); production management (Certificate); quantitative methods (Certificate); sanitary and environmental engineering (M Eng); structural engineering (M Eng); systems engineering and electronic data processing (Certificate); transportation (Certificate).

New Jersey Institute of Technology, Newark College of Engineering, Newark, NJ 07102. Offers biomedical engineering (MS, PhD); biopharmaceutical engineering (MS); chemical engineering (MS, PhD); civil engineering (MS, PhD); computer engineering

(MS); critical infrastructure systems (MS); electrical engineering (MS, PhD); engineering management (MS); engineering science (MS); environmental engineering (MS, PhD); healthcare systems management (MS); industrial engineering (MS, PhD); internet engineering (MS); manufacturing systems engineering (MS); materials science & engineering (PhD); materials science and engineering (MS); mechanical engineering (MS, PhD); occupational safety and health engineering (MS). *Program availability:* Part-time, evening/weekend. *Faculty:* 147 full-time (26 women), 133 part-time/adjunct (16 women). *Students:* 690 full-time (163 women), 594 part-time (130 women); includes 427 minority (79 Black or African American, non-Hispanic/Latino; 181 Asian, non-Hispanic/Latino; 140 Hispanic/Latino; 27 Two or more races, non-Hispanic/Latino; 553 international. Average age 27. 2,334 applicants, 57% accepted, 452 enrolled. In 2018, 418 master's, 31 doctorates awarded. Terminal master's awarded for partial completion of doctoral program. *Degree requirements:* For master's, thesis (for some programs); for doctorate, thesis/dissertation. *Entrance requirements:* For master's, GRE General Test, minimum GPA 2.8, personal statement, 1 letter of recommendation, transcripts; for doctorate, GRE General Test, minimum GPA of 3.5, personal statement, 3 letters of recommendation, transcripts. Additional exam requirements/recommendations for international students: Required—TOEFL (minimum score 550 paper-based; 79 iBT), IELTS (minimum score 6.5). *Application deadline:* For fall admission, 6/1 priority date for domestic students, 5/1 priority date for international students; for spring admission, 11/15 priority date for domestic and international students. Applications are processed on a rolling basis. Application fee: $75. Electronic applications accepted. *Expenses:* $22,690 per year (in-state), $32,136 per year (out-of-state). *Financial support:* In 2018–19, 396 students received support, including 52 fellowships with full tuition reimbursements available (averaging $22,000 per year), 113 research assistantships with full tuition reimbursements available (averaging $22,000 per year), 101 teaching assistantships with full tuition reimbursements available (averaging $22,000 per year); career-related internships or fieldwork, Federal Work-Study, scholarships/grants, and unspecified assistantships also available. Financial award application deadline: 1/15. *Faculty research:* Nonlinear signal processing, intelligent medical image analysis, calibration issues in coherent localization, computer-aided design, neural network for tool wear measurement. *Total annual research expenditures:* $41.7 million. *Unit head:* Dr. Moshe Kam, Dean, 973-596-5534, Fax: 973-596-2316, E-mail: moshe.kam@njit.edu. *Application contact:* Stephen Eck, Director of Admissions, 973-596-3300, Fax: 973-596-3461, E-mail: admissions@njit.edu.
Website: http://engineering.njit.edu/

Northeastern University, College of Engineering, Boston, MA 02115-5096. Offers bioengineering (MS, PhD); chemical engineering (MS, PhD); civil engineering (MS, PhD); computer engineering (PhD); computer systems engineering (MS); electrical and computer engineering (MS); electrical and computer engineering leadership (MS); electrical engineering (PhD); energy systems (MS); engineering and public policy (MS); engineering management (MS, Certificate); environmental engineering (MS); industrial engineering (MS, PhD); information assurance (PhD); information systems (MS); interdisciplinary engineering (PhD); mechanical engineering (PhD); operations research (MS); telecommunication systems management (MS). *Program availability:* Part-time, online learning. Electronic applications accepted. *Expenses:* Contact institution.

Ohio University, Graduate College, Scripps College of Communication, J. Warren McClure School of Information and Telecommunication Systems, Athens, OH 45701-2979. Offers MCTP. *Program availability:* Part-time. *Degree requirements:* For master's, comprehensive exam (for some programs), thesis (for some programs). *Entrance requirements:* For master's, GRE or GMAT, minimum cumulative GPA of 3.0. Additional exam requirements/recommendations for international students: Required—TOEFL (minimum score 550 paper-based; 80 iBT) or IELTS (minimum score 6.5). Electronic applications accepted. *Faculty research:* Voice and data networks, with special emphasis on the interaction of technology and policy issues in the successful design, deployment, and operation of complex networks and information systems.

Pace University, Seidenberg School of Computer Science and Information Systems, New York, NY 10038. Offers chief information security officer (APC); computer science (MS, PhD); enterprise analytics (MS); information and communication technology strategy and innovation (APC); information systems (MS, APC); information technology (MS); professional studies in computing (DPS); secure software and information engineering (APC); security and information assurance (Certificate); software development and engineering (MS, Certificate); telecommunications systems and networks (MS, Certificate). *Program availability:* Part-time, evening/weekend, online only, 100% online, blended/hybrid learning. *Faculty:* 26 full-time (7 women), 7 part-time/adjunct (2 women). *Students:* 515 full-time (172 women), 288 part-time (90 women); includes 183 minority (67 Black or African American, non-Hispanic/Latino; 3 American Indian or Alaska Native, non-Hispanic/Latino; 50 Asian, non-Hispanic/Latino; 52 Hispanic/Latino; 1 Native Hawaiian or other Pacific Islander, non-Hispanic/Latino; 10 Two or more races, non-Hispanic/Latino), 497 international. Average age 30. 817 applicants, 93% accepted, 235 enrolled. In 2018, 383 master's, 15 doctorates, 1 other advanced degree awarded. *Degree requirements:* For master's, thesis or alternative, capstone course; for doctorate, comprehensive exam (for some programs), thesis/dissertation. *Entrance requirements:* Additional exam requirements/recommendations for international students: Required—TOEFL (minimum score 78 iBT), IELTS (minimum score 6.5) or PTE (minimum score 52). *Application deadline:* For fall admission, 8/1 priority date for domestic students, 6/1 for international students; for spring admission, 12/1 for domestic students, 10/1 for international students. Applications are processed on a rolling basis. Application fee: $70. Electronic applications accepted. *Expenses:* Contact institution. *Financial support:* In 2018–19, 45 students received support. Research assistantships, career-related internships or fieldwork, scholarships/grants, and unspecified assistantships available. Support available to part-time students. Financial award application deadline: 2/15; financial award applicants required to submit FAFSA. *Faculty research:* Cyber security/digital forensics; mobile app development; big data/enterprise analytics; artificial intelligence; software development. *Total annual research expenditures:* $584,594. *Unit head:* Dr. Jonathan Hill, Dean, Seidenberg School of Computer Science and Information Systems, 212-346-1864, E-mail: jhill@pace.edu. *Application contact:* Susan Ford-Goldschein, Director of Graduate Admissions, 914-422-4283, Fax: 212-346-1585, E-mail: graduateadmission@pace.edu.
Website: http://www.pace.edu/seidenberg

Rochester Institute of Technology, Graduate Enrollment Services, College of Applied Science and Technology, School of Engineering Technology, MS Program in Telecommunications Engineering Technology, Rochester, NY 14623-5603. Offers MS. *Program availability:* Part-time. *Students:* 61 full-time (16 women), 13 part-time (2 women); includes 4 minority (2 Black or African American, non-Hispanic/Latino; 1 Asian, non-Hispanic/Latino; 1 Hispanic/Latino), 69 international. Average age 25. 96 applicants, 92% accepted, 24 enrolled. In 2018, 25 master's awarded. *Degree requirements:* For master's, comprehensive exam (for some programs), thesis or alternative, Thesis, project, or exam options. *Entrance requirements:* For master's, GRE required for individuals with degrees from international universities, minimum GPA of 3.0 (recommended). Additional exam requirements/recommendations for international students: Required—TOEFL (minimum score 570 paper-based; 88 iBT), IELTS (minimum score 6.5), PTE (minimum score 61). *Application deadline:* For fall admission, 2/15 priority date for domestic and international students; for spring admission, 12/15

priority date for domestic and international students. Applications are processed on a rolling basis. Application fee: $65. Electronic applications accepted. *Expenses:* Contact institution. *Financial support:* In 2018–19, 64 students received support. Research assistantships with partial tuition reimbursements available, teaching assistantships with partial tuition reimbursements available, career-related internships or fieldwork, scholarships/grants, and unspecified assistantships available. Support available to part-time students. Financial award applicants required to submit FAFSA. *Faculty research:* Wireless networks, fiber-optic networks, software-defined networks, telecommunications policy and regulations, network quality of service. *Unit head:* William P. Johnson, Graduate Program Director, 585-475-2140, E-mail: wpjiee@rit.edu. *Application contact:* Diane Ellison, Senior Associate Vice President, Graduate Enrollment Services, 585-475-2229, Fax: 585-475-7164, E-mail: gradinfo@rit.edu.
Website: https://www.rit.edu/study/telecommunications-engineering-technology-ms

Southern Methodist University, Lyle School of Engineering, Department of Electrical Engineering, Dallas, TX 75275-0338. Offers electrical engineering (MS, PhD); telecommunications and network engineering (MS). *Program availability:* Part-time, evening/weekend, online learning. Terminal master's awarded for partial completion of doctoral program. *Degree requirements:* For master's, thesis optional; for doctorate, thesis/dissertation, oral and written qualifying exams, oral final exam. *Entrance requirements:* For master's, GRE General Test, minimum GPA of 3.0 in last 2 years; bachelor's degree in engineering, mathematics, or sciences; for doctorate, preliminary counseling exam, minimum GPA of 3.0, bachelor's degree in related field. Additional exam requirements/recommendations for international students: Required—TOEFL. Electronic applications accepted. *Faculty research:* Mobile communications, optical communications, digital signal processing, photonics.

Stevens Institute of Technology, Graduate School, School of Business, Program in Telecommunications Management, Hoboken, NJ 07030. Offers business (MS); global innovation management (MS); management of wireless networks (MS); online security, technology and business (MS); project management (MS); technical management (MS); telecommunications management (PhD, Certificate). *Program availability:* Part-time, evening/weekend. *Faculty:* 58 full-time (8 women), 18 part-time/adjunct (3 women). *Students:* 6 part-time (2 women); includes 1 minority (Asian, non-Hispanic/Latino). Average age 43. In 2018, 11 master's awarded. *Degree requirements:* For master's, thesis optional, minimum B average in major field and overall; for doctorate, comprehensive exam (for some programs), thesis/dissertation; for Certificate, minimum B average. *Entrance requirements:* For master's, GRE/GMAT scores: GRE scores are required for all applicants applying to a full-time graduate program in the Schaefer School of Engineering and Science (SES). International applicants must submit TOEFL/IELTS scores and fulfill the English Language Proficiency Requirements in order to be considered. Additional exam requirements/recommendations for international students: Required—TOEFL (minimum score 74 iBT), IELTS (minimum score 6). *Application deadline:* For fall admission, 4/1 for domestic and international students; for spring admission, 11/1 for domestic and international students; for summer admission, 5/1 for domestic students. Applications are processed on a rolling basis. Application fee: $60. Electronic applications accepted. *Expenses: Tuition:* Full-time $35,960; part-time $1620 per credit. *Required fees:* $1290; $600 per semester. Tuition and fees vary according to course load. *Financial support:* Fellowships, research assistantships, teaching assistantships, career-related internships or fieldwork, Federal Work-Study, scholarships/grants, health care benefits, and unspecified assistantships available. Financial award application deadline: 2/15; financial award applicants required to submit FAFSA. *Unit head:* Dr. Gregory Prastacos, Dean of SB, 201-216-8366, E-mail: gprastac@stevens.edu. *Application contact:* Graduate Admission, 888-783-8367, Fax: 888-511-1306, E-mail: graduate@stevens.edu.
Website: https://www.stevens.edu/school-business/masters-programs/network-communication-management-services

Stony Brook University, State University of New York, Graduate School, College of Engineering and Applied Sciences, Department of Electrical and Computer Engineering, Stony Brook, NY 11794. Offers computer engineering (MS, PhD); electrical engineering (MS, PhD); networking and wireless communications (Certificate). *Program availability:* Evening/weekend. *Faculty:* 28 full-time (6 women), 5 part-time/adjunct (1 woman). *Students:* 158 full-time (28 women), 80 part-time (21 women); includes 29 minority (4 Black or African American, non-Hispanic/Latino; 17 Asian, non-Hispanic/Latino; 4 Hispanic/Latino; 4 Two or more races, non-Hispanic/Latino), 179 international. Average age 25. 415 applicants, 82% accepted, 76 enrolled. In 2018, 47 master's, 9 doctorates, 4 other advanced degrees awarded. *Degree requirements:* For master's, thesis or alternative; for doctorate, comprehensive exam, thesis/dissertation. *Entrance requirements:* For master's and doctorate, GRE General Test. Additional exam requirements/recommendations for international students: Required—TOEFL (minimum score 90 iBT). *Application deadline:* For fall admission, 1/15 for domestic students; for spring admission, 10/1 for domestic students. Application fee: $100. *Expenses:* Contact institution. *Financial support:* In 2018–19, 2 fellowships, 25 research assistantships, 19 teaching assistantships were awarded. *Faculty research:* Lasers and masers, optoelectronics, semiconductors, laser physics, heterostructures. *Total annual research expenditures:* $3.3 million. *Unit head:* Prof. Petar M. Djuric, Chair, 631-632-8420, Fax: 631-632-8494, E-mail: petar.djuric@stonybrook.edu. *Application contact:* Angela Scauso, Coordinator, 631-632-8401, E-mail: angela.scauso@stonybrook.edu.
Website: http://www.stonybrook.edu/commcms/electrical/

Stratford University, School of Graduate Studies, Falls Church, VA 22043. Offers accounting (MS); business administration (MBA, DBA); cyber security (MS); cyber security leadership and policy (MS); digital forensics (MS); healthcare administration (MS); information systems (MS); information technology (DIT); networking and telecommunications (MS); software engineering (MS). *Program availability:* Part-time, evening/weekend, 100% online, blended/hybrid learning. *Degree requirements:* For master's, comprehensive exam, capstone project. *Entrance requirements:* For master's, GRE or GMAT, baccalaureate degree. Additional exam requirements/recommendations for international students: Required—TOEFL (minimum score 79 iBT), IELTS (minimum score 6.5), PTE (minimum score 5). Electronic applications accepted. *Expenses: Tuition:* Full-time $22,275; part-time $11,137 per year. One-time fee: $385.

Universidad del Turabo, Graduate Programs, School of Engineering, Program in Telecommunications and Network Systems Administration, Gurabo, PR 00778-3030. Offers M Eng. *Entrance requirements:* For master's, GRE, EXADEP or GMAT, interview, essay, official transcript, recommendation letters. Electronic applications accepted.

Université du Québec, Institut National de la Recherche Scientifique, Graduate Programs, Centre for Energie Materiaux Telecommunications, Varennes, QC G1K 9A9, Canada. Offers energy and materials science (M Sc, PhD); telecommunications (M Sc, PhD). *Program availability:* Part-time. *Faculty:* 38 full-time. *Students:* 207 full-time (60 women), 13 part-time (3 women), 186 international. Average age 34. 45 applicants, 87% accepted, 24 enrolled. In 2018, 13 master's, 30 doctorates awarded. *Degree requirements:* For master's, thesis (for some programs); for doctorate, thesis/dissertation. *Entrance requirements:* For master's, appropriate bachelor's degree, proficiency in French; for doctorate, appropriate master's degree, proficiency in French. *Application deadline:* For fall admission, 3/30 for domestic and international students; for

winter admission, 11/1 for domestic and international students; for spring admission, 3/1 for domestic and international students. Application fee: $45. Electronic applications accepted. *Financial support:* In 2018–19, fellowships (averaging $16,500 per year) were awarded; research assistantships and scholarships/grants also available. *Faculty research:* New energy sources, plasmas, telecommunications, advanced materials, ultrafast photonics. *Total annual research expenditures:* $11.3 million. *Unit head:* Ana Tavares, Director, 514-228-6947, Fax: 450-929-8102, E-mail: ana.tavares@emt.inrs.ca. *Application contact:* Sean Otto, Registrar, 418-654-2518, Fax: 418-654-3858, E-mail: sean.otto@inrs.ca.
Website: http://www.emt.inrs.ca

University of Alberta, Faculty of Graduate Studies and Research, Department of Electrical and Computer Engineering, Edmonton, AB T6G 2E1, Canada. Offers communications (M Eng, M Sc, PhD); computer engineering (M Eng, M Sc, PhD); electromagnetics (M Eng, M Sc, PhD); nanotechnology and microdevices (M Eng, M Sc, PhD); power/power electronics (M Eng, M Sc, PhD); systems (M Eng, M Sc, PhD). Terminal master's awarded for partial completion of doctoral program. *Degree requirements:* For master's, thesis; for doctorate, thesis/dissertation. *Entrance requirements:* Additional exam requirements/recommendations for international students: Required—TOEFL. Electronic applications accepted. *Faculty research:* Controls, communications, microelectronics, electromagnetics.

University of Arkansas, Graduate School, College of Engineering, Department of Electrical Engineering, Fayetteville, AR 72701. Offers electrical engineering (MSEE, PhD); telecommunications engineering (MS Tc E). In 2018, 24 master's, 3 doctorates awarded. *Degree requirements:* For master's, thesis optional; for doctorate, one foreign language, thesis/dissertation. *Entrance requirements:* For master's and doctorate, GRE General Test. *Application deadline:* For fall admission, 8/1 for domestic students, 4/1 for international students; for spring admission, 12/1 for domestic students, 10/1 for international students; for summer admission, 4/15 for domestic students, 3/1 for international students. Applications are processed on a rolling basis. Application fee: $60. Electronic applications accepted. *Financial support:* In 2018–19, 48 research assistantships, 8 teaching assistantships were awarded; fellowships with tuition reimbursements, career-related internships or fieldwork, and Federal Work-Study also available. Support available to part-time students. Financial award application deadline: 4/1; financial award applicants required to submit FAFSA. *Unit head:* Dr. Juan Carlos Balda, Department Head, 479-575-3005, Fax: 479-575-7967, E-mail: jbalda@uark.edu. *Application contact:* Dr. Hameed Naseem, Graduate Coordinator, 479-575-6052, Fax: 479-575-7967, E-mail: hnaseem@uark.edu.
Website: https://electrical-engineering.uark.edu/index.php

University of California, San Diego, Graduate Division, Department of Electrical and Computer Engineering, La Jolla, CA 92093. Offers applied ocean science (MS, PhD); applied physics (MS, PhD); communication theory and systems (MS, PhD); computer engineering (MS, PhD); electronic circuits and systems (MS, PhD); intelligent systems, robotics and control (MS, PhD); medical devices and systems (MS, PhD); nanoscale devices and systems (MS, PhD); photonics (MS, PhD); signal and image processing (MS, PhD). Program offered jointly with San Diego State University. *Students:* 830 full-time (174 women), 69 part-time (8 women). 2,810 applicants, 40% accepted, 399 enrolled. In 2018, 226 master's, 42 doctorates awarded. Terminal master's awarded for partial completion of doctoral program. *Degree requirements:* For master's, comprehensive exam (for some programs), thesis (for some programs); for doctorate, comprehensive exam, thesis/dissertation. *Entrance requirements:* For master's and doctorate, GRE General Test, minimum GPA of 3.0, resume or curriculum vitae (recommended). Additional exam requirements/recommendations for international students: Required—TOEFL (minimum score 550 paper-based; 80 iBT), IELTS (minimum score 7), PTE (minimum score 65). *Application deadline:* For fall admission, 12/13 for domestic students. Application fee: $105 ($125 for international students). Electronic applications accepted. *Financial support:* Fellowships, research assistantships, teaching assistantships, scholarships/grants, traineeships, and unspecified assistantships available. Financial award applicants required to submit FAFSA. *Faculty research:* Applied ocean science; applied physics; communication theory and systems; computer engineering; electronic circuits and systems; intelligent systems, robotics and control; medical devices and systems; nanoscale devices and systems; photonics; signal and image processing. *Unit head:* Bill Lin, Chair, 858-822-1383, E-mail: billin@ucsd.edu. *Application contact:* Sean Jones, Graduate Admissions Coordinator, 858-534-3213, E-mail: ecegradapps@ece.ucsd.edu.
Website: http://ece.ucsd.edu/

University of California, San Diego, Graduate Division, Program in Wireless Embedded Systems, La Jolla, CA 92093. Offers MAS. *Program availability:* Part-time. *Students:* 12 full-time (1 woman). In 2018, 23 master's awarded. *Degree requirements:* For master's, capstone project. *Entrance requirements:* For master's, GRE General Test (if applicant possesses fewer than 2 years' work experience), 3 letters of recommendation, statement of purpose, resume or curriculum vitae. Additional exam requirements/recommendations for international students: Required—TOEFL (minimum score 550 paper-based; 80 iBT), IELTS (minimum score 7). *Application deadline:* For fall admission, 6/25 for domestic students. Application fee: $105 ($125 for international students). Electronic applications accepted. *Expenses:* Contact institution. *Financial support:* Applicants required to submit FAFSA. *Faculty research:* Systems, software, hardware and communication theory and algorithms. *Unit head:* George Papen, Director, 858-822-1728, E-mail: gpapen@ucsd.edu. *Application contact:* Yvonne Wu, Graduate Coordinator, 858-246-1463, E-mail: wes-mas@ucsd.edu.
Website: http://maseng.ucsd.edu/wes

University of Colorado Boulder, Graduate School, College of Engineering and Applied Science, Interdisciplinary Telecommunications Program, Boulder, CO 80309. Offers MS, JD/MS, MBA/MS. Terminal master's awarded for partial completion of doctoral program. *Degree requirements:* For master's, comprehensive exam, thesis or alternative. *Entrance requirements:* For master's, minimum undergraduate GPA of 3.0. Electronic applications accepted. Application fee is waived when completed online.

University of Florida, Graduate School, College of Journalism and Communications, Program in Mass Communication, Gainesville, FL 32611. Offers international/intercultural communication (MAMC); journalism (MAMC); mass communication (MAMC, PhD), including clinical translational science (MAMC); public relations (MAMC); science/health communication (MAMC); telecommunication (MAMC). *Entrance requirements:* For master's and doctorate, GRE General Test, minimum GPA of 3.0.

University of Hawaii at Manoa, Office of Graduate Education, College of Social Sciences, School of Communications, Program in Telecommunication and Information Resource Management, Honolulu, HI 96822. Offers Graduate Certificate. *Program availability:* Part-time. *Entrance requirements:* Additional exam requirements/recommendations for international students: Required—TOEFL (minimum score 500 paper-based; 61 iBT), IELTS (minimum score 5).

University of Houston, College of Technology, Department of Engineering Technology, Houston, TX 77204. Offers construction management (MS); engineering technology (MS); network communications (M Tech). *Program availability:* Part-time. *Degree requirements:* For master's, project or thesis (most programs). *Entrance requirements:* For master's, GRE. Additional exam requirements/recommendations for international students: Required—TOEFL (minimum score 550 paper-based; 79 iBT). Electronic applications accepted.

University of Maryland, College Park, Academic Affairs, A. James Clark School of Engineering, Department of Electrical and Computer Engineering, Program in Telecommunications, College Park, MD 20742. Offers MS. *Program availability:* Part-time, evening/weekend. *Degree requirements:* For master's, thesis or alternative. *Entrance requirements:* For master's, GRE General Test, minimum GPA of 3.0, professional experience. Additional exam requirements/recommendations for international students: Required—TOEFL. Electronic applications accepted.

University of Massachusetts Dartmouth, Graduate School, College of Engineering, Department of Electrical and Computer Engineering, North Dartmouth, MA 02747-2300. Offers communications (Postbaccalaureate Certificate); computing infrastructure security (Postbaccalaureate Certificate); digital signal processing (Postbaccalaureate Certificate); electrical engineering (MS, PhD); electrical engineering systems (Postbaccalaureate Certificate). *Program availability:* Part-time. *Faculty:* 15 full-time (4 women), 1 part-time/adjunct (0 women). *Students:* 21 full-time (5 women), 40 part-time (9 women); includes 12 minority (4 Black or African American, non-Hispanic/Latino; 1 Asian, non-Hispanic/Latino; 5 Hispanic/Latino; 2 Two or more races, non-Hispanic/Latino), 20 international. Average age 31. 48 applicants, 71% accepted, 16 enrolled. In 2018, 23 master's, 5 doctorates, 3 other advanced degrees awarded. Terminal master's awarded for partial completion of doctoral program. *Degree requirements:* For master's, thesis, thesis or project; for doctorate, comprehensive exam, thesis/dissertation. *Entrance requirements:* For master's, GRE unless UMass Dartmouth graduate in computer engineering or electrical engineering, statement of purpose (minimum of 300 words), resume, 3 letters of recommendation, official transcripts; for doctorate, GRE unless UMass Dartmouth graduate in college of engineering major or about to receive electrical graduate certificate, statement of purpose (minimum of 300 words), resume, 3 letters of recommendation, official transcripts; for Postbaccalaureate Certificate, statement of purpose (minimum of 300 words), resume, official transcripts. Additional exam requirements/recommendations for international students: Required—TOEFL (minimum score 550 paper-based; 79 iBT), IELTS (minimum score 6.5). *Application deadline:* For fall admission, 2/15 priority date for domestic students, 1/15 priority date for international students; for spring admission, 11/1 priority date for domestic students, 10/1 priority date for international students. Application fee: $60. Electronic applications accepted. *Financial support:* In 2018–19, 12 research assistantships (averaging $15,187 per year), 10 teaching assistantships (averaging $12,907 per year) were awarded; tuition waivers (full and partial) and dissertation writing support also available. Financial award application deadline: 3/1; financial award applicants required to submit FAFSA. *Faculty research:* Array processing, cyber security, underwater acoustics and animal bio-acoustics, electronics and solid-state devices, photonics. *Total annual research expenditures:* $1.9 million. *Unit head:* Liudong Xing, Graduate Program Director/Electrical & Computer Engineering, 508-999-8883, Fax: 508-999-8489, E-mail: liudong.xing@umassd.edu. *Application contact:* Scott Webster, Director of Graduate Studies & Admissions, 508-999-8604, Fax: 508-999-8183, E-mail: graduate@umassd.edu.
Website: http://www.umassd.edu/engineering/ece/graduate

University of Mississippi, Graduate School, School of Engineering, University, MS 38677. Offers aeroacoustics (MS, PhD); chemical engineering (MS, PhD); civil engineering (MS, PhD); computational hydroscience (MS, PhD); computer science (MS, PhD); electrical engineering (MS, PhD); electromagnetics (MS, PhD); environmental engineering (MS, PhD); geology and geological engineering (MS, PhD); hydrology (MS); material science (MS); mechanical engineering (MS, PhD); telecommunications (MS). *Faculty:* 76 full-time (16 women), 3 part-time/adjunct (1 woman). *Students:* 129 full-time (33 women), 21 part-time (5 women); includes 15 minority (7 Black or African American, non-Hispanic/Latino; 6 Asian, non-Hispanic/Latino; 1 Hispanic/Latino; 1 Two or more races, non-Hispanic/Latino), 73 international. Average age 29. In 2018, 36 master's, 17 doctorates awarded. *Entrance requirements:* For master's, GRE General Test, minimum GPA of 3.0; for doctorate, GRE General Test. Additional exam requirements/recommendations for international students: Required—TOEFL. *Application deadline:* Applications are processed on a rolling basis. Application fee: $50. Electronic applications accepted. *Financial support:* Scholarships/grants available. Financial award application deadline: 3/1; financial award applicants required to submit FAFSA. *Unit head:* Dr. David Puleo, Dean, 662-915-5780, Fax: 662-915-5387, E-mail: engineer@olemiss.edu. *Application contact:* Temeka Smith, Graduate Activities Specialist for Admissions, 662-915-7474, Fax: 662-915-7577, E-mail: gschool@olemiss.edu.

University of Missouri–Kansas City, School of Computing and Engineering, Kansas City, MO 64110-2499. Offers civil engineering (MS); computer and electrical engineering (PhD); computer science (MS), including bioinformatics, software engineering, telecommunications networking; computer science and informatics (PhD); computing (PhD); electrical engineering (MS); engineering (PhD); engineering and construction management (Graduate Certificate); mechanical engineering (MS); telecommunications and computer networking (PhD). PhD (interdisciplinary) offered through the School of Graduate Studies. *Program availability:* Part-time. *Degree requirements:* For doctorate, thesis/dissertation. *Entrance requirements:* For master's, GRE General Test, minimum GPA of 3.0, 3 letters of recommendation from professors; for doctorate, GRE General Test, minimum GPA of 3.5. Additional exam requirements/recommendations for international students: Required—TOEFL (minimum score 550 paper-based; 80 iBT). *Faculty research:* Algorithms, bioinformatics and medical informatics, biomechanics/biomaterials, civil engineering materials, networking and telecommunications, thermal science.

The University of North Carolina at Chapel Hill, Graduate School, Hussman School of Journalism and Media, Chapel Hill, NC 27599. Offers digital communication (MA, Certificate); media and communication (MA, PhD), including interdisciplinary health communication (MA), journalism (MA), strategic communication (MA), theory and research (MA), visual communication (MA); JD/PhD; MA/JD. MA/JD and JD/PhD offered jointly with School of Law. *Accreditation:* ACEJMC (one or more programs are accredited). *Program availability:* Part-time, all course instruction online, plus two on-campus experiences totaling seven days. *Degree requirements:* For master's, comprehensive exam, thesis; for doctorate, comprehensive exam, thesis/dissertation. *Entrance requirements:* For master's and doctorate, GRE General Test, minimum GPA of 3.0. Additional exam requirements/recommendations for international students: Required—TOEFL (minimum iBT score of 105) or IELTS (7.5). Electronic applications accepted. *Expenses:* Contact institution. *Faculty research:* Media processes and production; legal and regulatory issues in communication; media uses and effects; health communication; political, social, and strategic communication.

University of Oklahoma, Gallogly College of Engineering, School of Electrical and Computer Engineering, Norman, OK 73019. Offers electrical and computer engineering (MS, PhD); telecommunications engineering (MS). *Program availability:* Part-time. *Faculty:* 44 full-time (3 women), 1 part-time/adjunct (0 women). *Students:* 83 full-time (16 women), 40 part-time (9 women); includes 11 minority (1 Black or African American, non-Hispanic/Latino; 1 American Indian or Alaska Native, non-Hispanic/Latino; 3 Asian,

non-Hispanic/Latino; 5 Hispanic/Latino; 1 Two or more races, non-Hispanic/Latino), 76 international. Average age 29. 61 applicants, 67% accepted, 14 enrolled. In 2018, 21 master's, 15 doctorates awarded. Terminal master's awarded for partial completion of doctoral program. *Degree requirements:* For master's, comprehensive exam (for some programs), thesis (for some programs); for doctorate, thesis/dissertation, general exam. *Entrance requirements:* For master's and doctorate, GRE, minimum GPA of 3.0. Additional exam requirements/recommendations for international students: Required—TOEFL (minimum score 79 iBT) or IELTS (minimum score 6.5). *Application deadline:* For fall admission, 4/1 for domestic students, 3/1 for international students; for spring admission, 11/1 for domestic students, 10/1 for international students. Applications are processed on a rolling basis. Application fee: $50 ($100 for international students). Electronic applications accepted. *Expenses:* Tuition, state resident: full-time $5683.20; part-time $236.80 per credit hour. Tuition, nonresident: full-time $20,342; part-time $847.60 per credit hour. *International tuition:* $20,342.40 full-time. *Required fees:* $2894.20; $110.05 per credit hour. $126.50 per semester. Tuition and fees vary according to course load and program. *Financial support:* Fellowships, research assistantships, teaching assistantships, career-related internships or fieldwork, scholarships/grants, and health care benefits available. Financial award application deadline: 6/1; financial award applicants required to submit FAFSA. *Faculty research:* Radar engineering, medical imaging, photonics, smart grid, wireless networks. *Unit head:* Dr. J.R. Cruz, Director, 405-325-8131, Fax: 405-325-7066, E-mail: jcruz@ou.edu. *Application contact:* Emily Benton Wilkins, Graduate Programs Coordinator, 405-325-7334, Fax: 405-325-7066, E-mail: emily.d.benton-1@ou.edu.
Website: http://www.ou.edu/coe/ece.html

University of Southern California, Graduate School, Viterbi School of Engineering, Daniel J. Epstein Department of Industrial and Systems Engineering, Los Angeles, CA 90089. Offers digital supply chain management (MS); engineering management (MS); engineering technology communication (Graduate Certificate); health systems operations (Graduate Certificate); industrial and systems engineering (MS, PhD, Engr); manufacturing engineering (MS); operations research engineering (MS); optimization and supply chain management (Graduate Certificate); product development engineering (MS); safety systems and security (MS); systems architecting and engineering (MS, Graduate Certificate); systems safety and security (Graduate Certificate); transportation systems (Graduate Certificate); MS/MBA. *Program availability:* Part-time, evening/weekend, online learning. Terminal master's awarded for partial completion of doctoral program. *Degree requirements:* For master's, thesis optional; for doctorate, thesis/dissertation. *Entrance requirements:* For master's and doctorate, GRE General Test. Additional exam requirements/recommendations for international students: Recommended—TOEFL. Electronic applications accepted. *Faculty research:* Health systems, music cognition and retrieval, transportation and logistics, manufacturing and automation, engineering systems design, risk and economic analysis.

University of Southern California, Graduate School, Viterbi School of Engineering, Ming Hsieh Department of Electrical Engineering, Los Angeles, CA 90089. Offers computer engineering (MS, PhD); electric power (MS); electrical engineering (MS, PhD, Engr); engineering technology commercialization (Graduate Certificate); multimedia and creative technologies (MS); telecommunications (MS); VLSI design (MS); wireless health technology (MS). *Program availability:* Part-time, online learning. Terminal master's awarded for partial completion of doctoral program. *Degree requirements:* For master's, thesis optional; for doctorate, thesis/dissertation. *Entrance requirements:* For master's and doctorate, GRE General Test. Additional exam requirements/recommendations for international students: Recommended—TOEFL. Electronic applications accepted. *Faculty research:* Communications, computer engineering and networks, control systems, integrated circuits and systems, electromagnetics and energy conversion, micro electro-mechanical systems and nanotechnology, photonics and quantum electronics, plasma research, signal and image processing.

The University of Texas at Dallas, Erik Jonsson School of Engineering and Computer Science, Department of Electrical and Computer Engineering, Richardson, TX 75080. Offers computer engineering (MS, PhD); electrical engineering (MSEE, PhD); telecommunications engineering (MSTE, PhD). *Program availability:* Part-time, evening/weekend. *Faculty:* 44 full-time (4 women), 10 part-time/adjunct (0 women). *Students:* 452 full-time (98 women), 169 part-time (49 women); includes 44 minority (6 Black or African American, non-Hispanic/Latino; 25 Asian, non-Hispanic/Latino; 7 Hispanic/Latino; 6 Two or more races, non-Hispanic/Latino), 525 international. Average age 28. 1,519 applicants, 46% accepted, 177 enrolled. In 2018, 234 master's, 43 doctorates awarded. *Degree requirements:* For master's, thesis or major design project; for doctorate, thesis/dissertation. *Entrance requirements:* For master's, GRE General Test, minimum GPA of 3.0 in related bachelor's degree; for doctorate, GRE General Test, minimum GPA of 3.5. Additional exam requirements/recommendations for international students: Required—TOEFL (minimum score 550 paper-based). *Application deadline:* For fall admission, 7/15 for domestic students, 5/1 priority date for international students; for spring admission, 11/15 for domestic students, 9/1 priority date for international students. Applications are processed on a rolling basis. Application fee: $50 ($100 for international students). Electronic applications accepted. *Expenses: Tuition, area resident:* Full-time $13,458. Tuition, state resident: full-time $13,458. Tuition, nonresident: full-time $26,852. *International tuition:* $26,852 full-time. Tuition and fees vary according to course load. *Financial support:* In 2018–19, 192 students received support, including 11 fellowships (averaging $3,297 per year), 143 research assistantships with partial tuition reimbursements available (averaging $23,638 per year), 57 teaching assistantships with partial tuition reimbursements available (averaging $17,489 per year); Federal Work-Study, institutionally sponsored loans, scholarships/grants, unspecified assistantships, and cooperative positions also available. Support available to part-time students. Financial award application deadline: 4/30; financial award applicants required to submit FAFSA. *Faculty research:* Semiconductor device manufacturing, photonics devices and systems, signal processing and language technology, nano-fabrication, energy efficient digital systems. *Unit head:* Dr. Lawrence Overzet, Department Head, 972-883-2154, Fax: 972-883-2710, E-mail: overzet@utdallas.edu. *Application contact:* Dr. Lawrence Overzet, Department Head, 972-883-2154, Fax: 972-883-2710, E-mail: overzet@utdallas.edu.
Website: http://ece.utdallas.edu

Telecommunications Management

Alaska Pacific University, Graduate Programs, Business Administration Department, Programs in Information and Communication Technology, Anchorage, AK 99508-4672. Offers MBAICT. *Program availability:* Part-time, evening/weekend. *Degree requirements:* For master's, capstone course. *Entrance requirements:* For master's, GMAT or GRE General Test, minimum GPA of 3.0.

Boston University, Metropolitan College, Department of Computer Science, Boston, MA 02215. Offers computer information systems (MS), including computer networks, data analytics, database management and business intelligence, health informatics, IT project management, security, Web application development; computer networks (Certificate); computer science (MS); data analytics (Certificate); digital forensics (Certificate); health informatics (Certificate); information technology project management (Certificate); software development (MS); software engineering in health care systems (Certificate); telecommunications (MS), including security. *Program availability:* Part-time, evening/weekend, online learning. *Faculty:* 16 full-time (3 women), 52 part-time/adjunct (5 women). *Students:* 201 full-time (57 women), 953 part-time (252 women); includes 285 minority (57 Black or African American, non-Hispanic/Latino; 2 American Indian or Alaska Native, non-Hispanic/Latino; 139 Asian, non-Hispanic/Latino; 67 Hispanic/Latino; 1 Native Hawaiian or other Pacific Islander, non-Hispanic/Latino; 19 Two or more races, non-Hispanic/Latino), 333 international. Average age 31. 1,079 applicants, 72% accepted, 297 enrolled. In 2018, 395 master's awarded. *Entrance requirements:* For master's and Certificate, official transcripts from regionally-accredited bachelor's degree program, 3 letters of recommendation, professional resume, personal statement. Additional exam requirements/recommendations for international students: Required—TOEFL (minimum score 84 iBT), IELTS. *Application deadline:* For fall admission, 8/1 priority date for domestic students, 6/1 priority date for international students; for spring admission, 12/1 priority date for domestic students, 11/15 priority date for international students; for summer admission, 4/1 priority date for domestic students, 3/1 priority date for international students. Applications are processed on a rolling basis. Application fee: $85. Electronic applications accepted. *Expenses:* Contact institution. *Financial support:* In 2018–19, 11 research assistantships (averaging $8,400 per year), 23 teaching assistantships (averaging $3,400 per year) were awarded; unspecified assistantships also available. Support available to part-time students. Financial award applicants required to submit FAFSA. *Faculty research:* Artificial intelligence and machine learning, security and forensics, web technologies, software engineering, programming languages, medical informatics, information systems and IT project management. *Unit head:* Dr. Anatoly Temkin, Chair, 617-353-2566, Fax: 617-353-2367, E-mail: csinfo@bu.edu. *Application contact:* Enrollment Services, 617-353-6004, E-mail: met@bu.edu.
Website: http://www.bu.edu/csmet/

California Miramar University, Program in Telecommunications Management, San Diego, CA 92108. Offers MST.

Capitol Technology University, Graduate Programs, Laurel, MD 20708-9759. Offers business administration (MBA); computer science (MS); electrical engineering (MS); information and telecommunications systems management (MS); information architecture (MS); network security (MS). *Program availability:* Part-time, evening/weekend, online learning. *Entrance requirements:* For master's, minimum GPA of 3.0. Electronic applications accepted.

Carnegie Mellon University, Carnegie Institute of Technology, Information Networking Institute, Pittsburgh, PA 15213. Offers information networking (MS); information security (MS); information technology - information security (MS); information technology - mobility (MS); information technology - software management (MS). *Degree requirements:* For master's, thesis optional. *Entrance requirements:* For master's, GRE General Test, bachelor's degree in computer science, computer engineering, or electrical engineering, or related technology degree; programming skills (C/C++ fluency for some programs). Additional exam requirements/recommendations for international students: Required—TOEFL. *Faculty research:* Computer forensics and incident response; dependable systems, embedded systems, mobile systems, and sensor networks; computer and information networks, network and information security, human and socio-economic factors in secure system design; wireless sensor networks, survivable embedded systems, signal processing/compression; strategic management, international strategic management, group dynamics and decision-making structures, simulated competitive environments.

Concordia University, School of Graduate Studies, Faculty of Engineering and Computer Science, Concordia Institute for Information Systems Engineering (CIISE), Montréal, QC H3G 1M8, Canada. Offers 3D graphics and game development (Certificate); information and systems engineering (PhD); information systems security (M Eng, MA Sc); quality systems engineering (M Eng, MA Sc); service engineering and network management (Certificate).

East Carolina University, Graduate School, College of Engineering and Technology, Department of Technology Systems, Greenville, NC 27858-4353. Offers computer network professional (Certificate); cyber security professional (Certificate); information assurance (Certificate); Lean Six Sigma Black Belt (Certificate); network technology (MS), including computer networking management, digital communications technology, information security, Web technologies; occupational safety (MS); technology management (MS, PhD), including industrial distribution and logistics (MS); Website developer (Certificate). *Application deadline:* For fall admission, 6/1 priority date for domestic students. *Expenses: Tuition, area resident:* Full-time $4749. Tuition, state resident: full-time $4749. Tuition, nonresident: full-time $17,898. *International tuition:* $17,898 full-time. *Required fees:* $2787. Part-time tuition and fees vary according to course load and program. *Financial support:* Application deadline: 6/1. *Unit head:* Dr. Tijjani Mohammed, Chair, 252-328-9668, E-mail: mohammedt@ecu.edu. *Application contact:* Graduate School Admissions, 252-328-6012, Fax: 252-328-6071, E-mail: gradschool@ecu.edu.
Website: http://www.ecu.edu/cs-cet/techsystems/index.cfm

Instituto Tecnológico y de Estudios Superiores de Monterrey, Campus Ciudad de México, School of Design, Engineering and Architecture, Ciudad de Mexico, Mexico. Offers management (MA); telecommunications (MA). *Program availability:* Part-time, evening/weekend, online learning. *Faculty research:* Telecommunications; informatics; technology development; computer systems.

Instituto Tecnológico y de Estudios Superiores de Monterrey, Campus Ciudad Obregón, Program in Administration of Telecommunications, Ciudad Obregón, Mexico. Offers MAT.

Instituto Tecnológico y de Estudios Superiores de Monterrey, Campus Estado de México, Professional and Graduate Division, Estado de Mexico, Mexico. Offers administration of information technologies (MITA); architecture (M Arch); business administration (GMBA, MBA); computer sciences (MCS, PhD); education (M Ed); educational institution administration (MAD); educational technology and innovation (PhD); electronic commerce (MEC); environmental systems (MS); finance (MAF); humanistic studies (MHS); information sciences and knowledge management (MISKM);

information systems (MS); manufacturing systems (MS); marketing (MEM); quality systems and productivity (MS); science and materials engineering (PhD); telecommunications management (MTM). *Program availability:* Part-time, online learning. *Degree requirements:* For master's, one foreign language, thesis (for some programs); for doctorate, one foreign language, thesis/dissertation. *Entrance requirements:* For master's, E-PAEP 500, interview; for doctorate, E-PAEP 500, research proposal. Additional exam requirements/recommendations for international students: Required—TOEFL (minimum score 550 paper-based). *Faculty research:* Surface treatments by plasmas, mechanical properties, robotics, graphical computing, mechatronics security protocols.

Instituto Tecnológico y de Estudios Superiores de Monterrey, Campus Irapuato, Graduate Programs, Irapuato, Mexico. Offers administration (MBA); administration of information technology (MAIT); administration of telecommunications (MAT); architecture (M Arch); computer science (MCS); education (M Ed); educational administration (MEA); educational innovation and technology (DEIT); educational technology (MET); electronic commerce (MBA); environmental administration and planning (MEAP); environmental systems (MES); finances (MBA); humanistic studies (MHS); international management for Latin American executives (MIMLAE); library and information science (MLIS); manufacturing quality management (MMQM); marketing research (MBA).

Murray State University, Jesse D. Jones College of Science, Engineering and Technology, Institute of Engineering, Program in Telecommunications Systems Management, Murray, KY 42071. Offers MS. MS in telecommunications systems management is an interdisciplinary program in conjunction with the Arthur J. Bauernfeind College of Business. *Program availability:* Part-time, evening/weekend, 100% online, blended/hybrid learning. *Entrance requirements:* For master's, GRE or GMAT, minimum university GPA of 2.75. Additional exam requirements/recommendations for international students: Required—TOEFL (minimum score 527 paper-based; 71 iBT). Electronic applications accepted. *Faculty research:* Network security, emergency management communications, network economies.

Oklahoma State University, Graduate College, Stillwater, OK 74078. Offers aerospace security (Graduate Certificate); bioenergy and sustainable technology (Graduate Certificate); business data mining (Graduate Certificate); business sustainability (Graduate Certificate); environmental science (MS); international studies (MS); non-profit management (Graduate Certificate); teaching English to speakers of other languages (Graduate Certificate); telecommunications management (MS). Programs are interdisciplinary. *Degree requirements:* For master's, thesis (for some programs); for doctorate, comprehensive exam, thesis/dissertation. *Entrance requirements:* For master's and doctorate, GRE or GMAT. Additional exam requirements/recommendations for international students: Required—TOEFL (minimum score 550 paper-based; 79 iBT). Electronic applications accepted. *Expenses: Tuition, area resident:* Full-time $4148. Tuition, state resident: full-time $4148. Tuition, nonresident: full-time $10,517. *International tuition:* $10,517 full-time. *Required fees:* $4394; $2929 per credit hour. Tuition and fees vary according to course load and program.

Oklahoma State University, Spears School of Business, Department of Management Science and Information Systems, Stillwater, OK 74078. Offers management information systems (MS); management science and information systems (PhD); telecommunications management (MS). *Program availability:* Part-time, online learning. *Faculty:* 15 full-time (1 woman), 6 part-time/adjunct (3 women). *Students:* 57 full-time (18 women), 76 part-time (16 women); includes 15 minority (3 Black or African American, non-Hispanic/Latino; 3 American Indian or Alaska Native, non-Hispanic/Latino; 3 Asian, non-Hispanic/Latino; 2 Hispanic/Latino; 1 Native Hawaiian or other Pacific Islander, non-Hispanic/Latino; 3 Two or more races, non-Hispanic/Latino), 73 international. Average age 29. 391 applicants, 27% accepted, 65 enrolled. In 2018, 50 master's awarded. *Entrance requirements:* For master's and doctorate, GRE or GMAT. Additional exam requirements/recommendations for international students: Required—TOEFL (minimum score 550 paper-based; 79 iBT). *Application deadline:* For fall admission, 3/1 priority date for international students; for spring admission, 8/1 priority date for international students. Applications are processed on a rolling basis. Application fee: $40 ($75 for international students). Electronic applications accepted. *Expenses: Tuition, area resident:* Full-time $4148. Tuition, state resident: full-time $4148. Tuition, nonresident: full-time $10,517. *International tuition:* $10,517 full-time. *Required fees:* $4394; $2929 per credit hour. Tuition and fees vary according to course load and program. *Financial support:* Research assistantships, teaching assistantships, career-related internships or fieldwork, Federal Work-Study, scholarships/grants, health care benefits, tuition waivers (partial), and unspecified assistantships available. Support available to part-time students. Financial award application deadline: 3/1; financial award applicants required to submit FAFSA. *Unit head:* Dr. Rick Wilson, Department Head, 405-744-3551, Fax: 405-744-5180, E-mail: rick.wilson@okstate.edu. *Application contact:* Dr. Rathin Sarathy, Graduate Coordinator, 405-744-8646, Fax: 405-744-5180, E-mail: rathin.sarathy@okstate.edu.
Website: https://business.okstate.edu/msis/

San Diego State University, Graduate and Research Affairs, College of Professional Studies and Fine Arts, School of Communication, San Diego, CA 92182. Offers advertising and public relations (MA); critical-cultural studies (MA); interaction studies (MA); intercultural and international studies (MA); new media studies (MA); news and information studies (MA); telecommunications and media management (MA). *Degree requirements:* For master's, thesis. *Entrance requirements:* For master's, GRE General Test, 3 letters of recommendation. Additional exam requirements/recommendations for international students: Required—TOEFL. Electronic applications accepted.

Stevens Institute of Technology, Graduate School, School of Business, Program in Business Administration, Hoboken, NJ 07030. Offers business intelligence and analytics (MBA); engineering management (MBA); finance (MBA); information systems (MBA); innovation and entrepreneurship (MBA); marketing (MBA); pharmaceutical management (MBA); project management (MBA, Certificate); technology management (MBA); telecommunications management (MBA). *Accreditation:* AACSB. *Program availability:* Part-time, evening/weekend. *Faculty:* 58 full-time (8 women), 18 part-time/adjunct (3 women). *Students:* 44 full-time (23 women), 202 part-time (90 women); includes 56 minority (12 Black or African American, non-Hispanic/Latino; 2 American Indian or Alaska Native, non-Hispanic/Latino; 40 Asian, non-Hispanic/Latino; 2 Hispanic/Latino), 28 international. Average age 37. In 2018, 45 master's awarded. Terminal master's awarded for partial completion of doctoral program. *Degree requirements:* For master's, thesis optional, minimum B average in major field and overall; for Certificate, minimum B average. *Entrance requirements:* For master's, GRE/GMAT scores: GRE scores are required for all applicants applying to a full-time graduate program in the Schaefer School of Engineering and Science (SES). International applicants must submit TOEFL/IELTS scores and fulfill the English Language Proficiency Requirements in order to be considered. Additional exam requirements/recommendations for international students: Required—TOEFL (minimum score 74 iBT), IELTS (minimum score 6). *Application deadline:* For fall admission, 4/1 for domestic and international students; for spring admission, 11/1 for domestic and international students; for summer admission, 5/1 for domestic students. Applications are processed on a rolling basis. Application fee: $60. Electronic applications accepted. *Expenses: Tuition:* Full-time $35,960; part-time $1620 per credit. *Required fees:* $1290; $600 per semester. Tuition and fees vary according to course load. *Financial support:* Fellowships, research assistantships, teaching assistantships, career-related internships or fieldwork, Federal Work-Study, scholarships/grants, and unspecified assistantships available. Financial award application deadline: 2/15; financial award applicants required to submit FAFSA. *Unit head:* Dr. Gregory Prastacos, Dean, 201-216-8366, E-mail: gprastac@stevens.edu. *Application contact:* Graduate Admissions, 888-783-8367, Fax: 888-511-1306, E-mail: graduate@stevens.edu.
Website: https://www.stevens.edu/school-business/masters-programs/mbaemba

Stevens Institute of Technology, Graduate School, School of Business, Program in Information Systems, Hoboken, NJ 07030. Offers computer science (MS); e-commerce (MS); enterprise systems (MS); entrepreneurial information technology (MS); information architecture (MS); information management (MS, Certificate); information security (MS); information technology in financial services industry (MS); information technology in the pharmaceutical industry (MS); information technology outsourcing management (MS); project management (MS, Certificate); software engineering (MS); telecommunications (MS). *Program availability:* Part-time, evening/weekend. *Students:* 248 full-time (87 women), 54 part-time (20 women); includes 25 minority (8 Black or African American, non-Hispanic/Latino; 17 Asian, non-Hispanic/Latino), 245 international. Average age 27. In 2018, 202 master's, 16 other advanced degrees awarded. Terminal master's awarded for partial completion of doctoral program. *Degree requirements:* For master's, thesis optional, minimum B average in major field and overall; for Certificate, minimum B average. *Entrance requirements:* For master's, GRE/GMAT scores: GRE scores are required for all applicants applying to a full-time graduate program in the Schaefer School of Engineering and Science (SES). International applicants must submit TOEFL/IELTS scores and fulfill the English Language Proficiency Requirements in order to be considered. Additional exam requirements/recommendations for international students: Required—TOEFL (minimum score 74 iBT), IELTS (minimum score 6). *Application deadline:* For fall admission, 4/1 for domestic and international students; for spring admission, 11/1 for domestic and international students; for summer admission, 5/1 for domestic students. Applications are processed on a rolling basis. Application fee: $60. Electronic applications accepted. *Expenses: Tuition:* Full-time $35,960; part-time $1620 per credit. *Required fees:* $1290; $600 per semester. Tuition and fees vary according to course load. *Financial support:* Fellowships, research assistantships, teaching assistantships, career-related internships or fieldwork, Federal Work-Study, scholarships/grants, and unspecified assistantships available. Financial award application deadline: 2/15; financial award applicants required to submit FAFSA. *Unit head:* Dr. Gregory Prastacos, Dean of SB, 201-216-8366, E-mail: gprastac@stevens.edu. *Application contact:* Graduate Admissions, 888-783-8367, Fax: 888-511-1306, E-mail: graduate@stevens.edu.
Website: https://www.stevens.edu/school-business/masters-programs/information-systems

Stevens Institute of Technology, Graduate School, School of Business, Program in Network and Communication Management and Services, Hoboken, NJ 07030. Offers MS. *Program availability:* Part-time, evening/weekend. *Faculty:* 58 full-time (8 women), 18 part-time/adjunct (3 women). *Students:* 20 full-time (3 women), 35 part-time (6 women); includes 10 minority (4 Black or African American, non-Hispanic/Latino; 5 Asian, non-Hispanic/Latino; 1 Hispanic/Latino), 19 international. Average age 36. In 2018, 24 master's awarded. *Degree requirements:* For master's, thesis optional, minimum B average in major field and overall. *Entrance requirements:* For master's, GRE/GMAT scores: GRE scores are required for all applicants applying to a full-time graduate program in the Schaefer School of Engineering and Science (SES). International applicants must submit TOEFL/IELTS scores and fulfill the English Language Proficiency Requirements in order to be considered. Additional exam requirements/recommendations for international students: Required—TOEFL (minimum score 74 iBT), IELTS (minimum score 6). *Application deadline:* For fall admission, 7/1 for domestic students, 4/1 for international students; for spring admission, 11/1 for domestic and international students; for summer admission, 5/1 for domestic students. Applications are processed on a rolling basis. Application fee: $60. Electronic applications accepted. *Expenses: Tuition:* Full-time $35,960; part-time $1620 per credit. *Required fees:* $1290; $600 per semester. Tuition and fees vary according to course load. *Financial support:* Fellowships, research assistantships, teaching assistantships, career-related internships or fieldwork, Federal Work-Study, scholarships/grants, and unspecified assistantships available. Financial award application deadline: 2/15; financial award applicants required to submit FAFSA. *Unit head:* Dr. Gregory Prastacos, Dean of SB, 201-216-8366, E-mail: gprastac@stevens.edu. *Application contact:* Graduate Admissions, 888-793-8367, Fax: 888-511-1306, E-mail: graduate@stevens.edu.
Website: http://www.stevens.edu/school-business/masters-programs/network-communication-management-services

Stevens Institute of Technology, Graduate School, School of Business, Program in Technology Management, Hoboken, NJ 07030. Offers information management (PhD); technology management (PhD); telecommunications management (PhD). *Program availability:* Part-time, evening/weekend, online learning. *Faculty:* 58 full-time (8 women), 18 part-time/adjunct (3 women). *Students:* 6 full-time (0 women), 23 part-time (6 women); includes 10 minority (4 Black or African American, non-Hispanic/Latino; 6 Asian, non-Hispanic/Latino), 4 international. Average age 38. In 2018, 1 doctorate awarded. Terminal master's awarded for partial completion of doctoral program. *Degree requirements:* For doctorate, comprehensive exam (for some programs), thesis/dissertation. *Entrance requirements:* Additional exam requirements/recommendations for international students: Required—TOEFL (minimum score 74 iBT), IELTS (minimum score 6). *Application deadline:* For fall admission, 4/1 for domestic and international students; for spring admission, 11/1 for domestic and international students; for summer admission, 5/1 for domestic students. Applications are processed on a rolling basis. Application fee: $60. Electronic applications accepted. *Expenses: Tuition:* Full-time $35,960; part-time $1620 per credit. *Required fees:* $1290; $600 per semester. Tuition and fees vary according to course load. *Financial support:* Fellowships, research assistantships, teaching assistantships, career-related internships or fieldwork, Federal Work-Study, scholarships/grants, and unspecified assistantships available. Financial award application deadline: 2/15; financial award applicants required to submit FAFSA. *Unit head:* Dr. Gregory Prascatos, Dean of SB, 201-216 8366, Fax: 201-216-5385, E-mail: gprastac@stevens.edu. *Application contact:* Graduate Admissions, 888-783-8367, Fax: 888-511-1306, E-mail: graduate@stevens.edu.
Website: https://www.stevens.edu/school-business/phd-business-administration

Stevens Institute of Technology, Graduate School, School of Business, Program in Telecommunications Management, Hoboken, NJ 07030. Offers business (MS); global innovation management (MS); management of wireless networks (MS); online security, technology and business (MS); project management (MS); technical management (MS); telecommunications management (PhD, Certificate). *Program availability:* Part-time, evening/weekend. *Faculty:* 58 full-time (8 women), 18 part-time/adjunct (3 women). *Students:* 6 part-time (2 women); includes 1 minority (Asian, non-Hispanic/Latino). Average age 43. In 2018, 11 master's awarded. *Degree requirements:* For master's, thesis optional, minimum B average in major field and overall; for doctorate, comprehensive exam (for some programs), thesis/dissertation; for Certificate, minimum

B average. *Entrance requirements:* For master's, GRE/GMAT scores: GRE scores are required for all applicants applying to a full-time graduate program in the Schaefer School of Engineering and Science (SES). International applicants must submit TOEFL/IELTS scores and fulfill the English Language Proficiency Requirements in order to be considered. Additional exam requirements/recommendations for international students: Required—TOEFL (minimum score 74 iBT), IELTS (minimum score 6). *Application deadline:* For fall admission, 4/1 for domestic and international students; for spring admission, 11/1 for domestic and international students; for summer admission, 5/1 for domestic students. Applications are processed on a rolling basis. Application fee: $60. Electronic applications accepted. *Expenses: Tuition:* Full-time $35,960; part-time $1620 per credit. *Required fees:* $1290; $600 per semester. Tuition and fees vary according to course load. *Financial support:* Fellowships, research assistantships, teaching assistantships, career-related internships or fieldwork, Federal Work-Study, scholarships/grants, health care benefits, and unspecified assistantships available. Financial award application deadline: 2/15; financial award applicants required to submit FAFSA. *Unit head:* Dr. Gregory Prastacos, Dean of SB, 201-216-8366, E-mail: gprastac@stevens.edu. *Application contact:* Graduate Admission, 888-783-8367, Fax: 888-511-1306, E-mail: graduate@stevens.edu.
Website: https://www.stevens.edu/school-business/masters-programs/network-communication-management-services

Strayer University, Graduate Studies, Washington, DC 20005-2603. Offers accounting (MS); acquisition (MBA); business administration (MBA); communications technology (MS); educational management (M Ed); finance (MBA); health services administration (MHSA); hospitality and tourism management (MBA); human resource management (MBA); information systems (MS), including computer security management, decision support system management, enterprise resource management, network management, software engineering management, systems development management; management (MBA); management information systems (MS); marketing (MBA); professional accounting (MS), including accounting information systems, controllership, taxation; public administration (MPA); supply chain management (MBA); technology in education (M Ed). Programs also offered at campus locations in Birmingham, AL; Chamblee, GA; Cobb County, GA; Morrow, GA; White Marsh, MD; Charleston, SC; Columbia, SC; Greensboro, NC; Greenville, SC; Lexington, KY; Louisville, KY; Nashville, TN; North Raleigh, NC; Washington, DC. *Accreditation:* ACBSP. *Program availability:* Part-time, evening/weekend, online learning. *Degree requirements:* For master's, thesis. *Entrance requirements:* For master's, GMAT, GRE General Test, bachelor's degree from an accredited college or university, minimum undergraduate GPA of 2.75. Electronic applications accepted.

University of Colorado Boulder, Graduate School, College of Engineering and Applied Science, Interdisciplinary Telecommunications Program, Boulder, CO 80309. Offers MS, JD/MS, MBA/MS. Terminal master's awarded for partial completion of doctoral program. *Degree requirements:* For master's, comprehensive exam, thesis or alternative. *Entrance requirements:* For master's, minimum undergraduate GPA of 3.0. Electronic applications accepted. Application fee is waived when completed online.

University of South Africa, College of Human Sciences, Pretoria, South Africa. Offers adult education (M Ed); African languages (MA, PhD); African politics (MA, PhD); Afrikaans (MA, PhD); ancient history (MA, PhD); ancient Near Eastern studies (MA, PhD); anthropology (MA, PhD); applied linguistics (MA); Arabic (MA, PhD); archaeology (MA); art history (MA); Biblical archaeology (MA); Biblical studies (M Th, D Th, PhD); Christian spirituality (M Th, D Th); church history (M Th, D Th); classical studies (MA, PhD); clinical psychology (MA); communication (MA, PhD); comparative education (M Ed, Ed D); consulting psychology (D Admin, D Com, PhD); curriculum studies (M Ed, Ed D); development studies (M Admin, MA, D Admin, PhD); didactics (M Ed, Ed D); education (M Tech); education management (M Ed, Ed D); educational psychology (M Ed); English (MA); environmental education (M Ed); French (MA, PhD); German (MA, PhD); Greek (MA); guidance and counseling (M Ed); health studies (MA, PhD); including health sciences education (MA), health services management (MA), medical and surgical nursing science (critical care general) (MA), midwifery and neonatal nursing science (MA), trauma and emergency care (MA); history (MA, PhD); history of education (Ed D); inclusive education (M Ed, Ed D); information and communications technology policy and regulation (MA); information science (MA, MIS, PhD); international politics (MA, PhD); Islamic studies (MA, PhD); Italian (MA, PhD); Judaica (MA, PhD); linguistics (MA, PhD); mathematical education (M Ed); mathematics education (MA); missiology (M Th, D Th); modern Hebrew (MA, PhD); musicology (MA, MMus, D Mus, PhD); natural science education (M Ed); New Testament (M Th, D Th); Old Testament (D Th); pastoral therapy (M Th, D Th); philosophy (MA); philosophy of education (M Ed, Ed D); politics (MA, PhD); Portuguese (MA, PhD); practical theology (M Th, D Th); psychology (MA, MS, PhD); psychology of education (M Ed, Ed D); public health (MA); religious studies (MA, D Th, PhD); Romance languages (MA); Russian (MA, PhD); Semitic languages (MA, PhD); social behavior studies in HIV/AIDS (MA); social science (mental health) (MA); social science in development studies (MA); social science in psychology (MA); social science in social work (MA); social science in sociology (MA); social work (MSW, DSW, PhD); socio-education (M Ed, Ed D); sociolinguistics (MA); sociology (MA, PhD); Spanish (MA, PhD); systematic theology (M Th, D Th); TESOL (teaching English to speakers of other languages) (MA); theological ethics (M Th, D Th); theory of literature (MA, PhD); urban ministries (D Th); urban ministry (M Th).

University of Wisconsin–Stout, Graduate School, College of Science, Technology, Engineering and Mathematics, Program in Information and Communication Technologies, Menomonie, WI 54751. Offers MS. *Program availability:* Part-time, online learning. *Degree requirements:* For master's, thesis. *Entrance requirements:* For master's, minimum GPA of 2.75. Additional exam requirements/recommendations for international students: Required—TOEFL (minimum score 500 paper-based; 61 iBT). Electronic applications accepted.

APPENDIXES

Institutional Changes
Since the 2019 Edition

Following is an alphabetical listing of institutions that have recently closed, merged with other institutions, or changed their names or status. In the case of a name change, the former name appears first, followed by the new name.

Argosy University, Dallas (Farmers Branch, TX): *closed.*

Argosy University, Denver (Denver, CO): *closed.*

Argosy University, Inland Empire (Ontario, CA): *closed.*

Argosy University, Nashville (Nashville, TN): *closed.*

Argosy University, Salt Lake City (Draper, UT): *closed.*

Argosy University, San Diego (San Diego, CA): *closed.*

Argosy University, San Francisco Bay Area (Alameda, CA): *closed.*

Argosy University, Sarasota (Sarasota, FL): *closed.*

Argosy University, Schaumburg (Schaumburg, IL): *closed.*

Arlington Baptist College (Arlington, TX): *name changed to Arlington Baptist University.*

Armstrong State University (Savannah, GA): *name changed to Georgia Southern University–Armstrong Campus.*

Art Center College of Design (Pasadena, CA): *name changed to ArtCenter College of Design.*

The Art Institute of California–San Francisco, a campus of Argosy University (San Francisco, CA): *closed.*

Augsburg College (Minneapolis, MN): *name changed to Augsburg University.*

Bristol University (Anaheim, CA): *closed.*

Claremont McKenna College (Claremont, CA): *merged into The Claremont Colleges (Claremont, CA).*

Coleman University (San Diego, CA): *closed.*

Digital Media Arts College (Boca Raton, FL): *closed.*

Everest University (Tampa, FL): *no longer offers graduate degrees.*

Fairleigh Dickinson University, College at Florham (Madison, NJ): *name changed to Fairleigh Dickinson University, Florham Campus.*

Faith Evangelical College & Seminary (Tacoma, WA): *name changed to Faith International University.*

Frank Lloyd Wright School of Architecture (Scottsdale, AZ): *name changed to School of Architecture at Taliesin.*

Future Generations Graduate School (Franklin, WV): *name changed to Future Generations University.*

Grace University (Omaha, NE): *closed.*

Greenville College (Greenville, IL): *name changed to Greenville University.*

Hazelden Graduate School of Addiction Studies (Center City, MN): *name changed to Hazelden Betty Ford Graduate School of Addiction.*

Henley-Putnam University (San Jose, CA): *name changed to Henley-Putnam School of Strategic Security.*

Huntington College of Health Sciences (Knoxville, TN): *name changed to Huntington University of Health Sciences.*

The Institute for the Psychological Sciences (Arlington, VA): *name changed to Divine Mercy University.*

International College of the Cayman Islands (Newlands, Cayman Islands): *not accredited by an agency recognized by USDE or CHEA at the time of publication.*

Johnson State College (Johnson, VT): *name changed to Northern Vermont University–Johnson.*

John Wesley University (High Point, NC): *closed.*

Kaplan University, Davenport Campus (Davenport, IA): *name changed to Purdue University Global.*

Knowledge Systems Institute (Skokie, IL): *no longer degree granting.*

Long Island University–Hudson at Westchester (Purchase, NY): *name changed to Long Island University–Hudson.*

Lutheran Theological Seminary at Gettysburg (Gettysburg, PA): *name changed to United Lutheran Seminary.*

Lynchburg College (Lynchburg, VA): *name changed to University of Lynchburg.*

Lyndon State College (Lyndonville, VT): *name changed to Northern Vermont University–Lyndon.*

Marylhurst University (Marylhurst, OR): *closed.*

McNally Smith College of Music (Saint Paul, MN): *closed.*

Memphis College of Art (Memphis, TN): *closed.*

Mirrer Yeshiva (Brooklyn, NY): *name changed to Mirrer Yeshiva Central Institute.*

Moody Theological Seminary–Michigan (Plymouth, MI): *name changed to Moody Theological Seminary Michigan.*

Mount Ida College (Newton, MA): *closed.*

National American University (Rapid City, SD): *no longer offers graduate degrees.*

The Ohio State University–Mansfield Campus (Mansfield, OH): *name changed to The Ohio State University at Mansfield.*

The Ohio State University–Newark Campus (Newark, OH): *name changed to The Ohio State University at Newark.*

Our Lady of the Lake College (Baton Rouge, LA): *name changed to Franciscan Missionaries of Our Lady University.*

Philadelphia University (Philadelphia, PA): *closed.*

Rudolf Steiner College (Fair Oaks, CA): *not accredited by an agency recognized by USDE or CHEA at the time of publication.*

Sacred Heart School of Theology (Hales Corners, WI): *name changed to Sacred Heart Seminary and School of Theology.*

Sewanee: The University of the South (Sewanee, TN): *name changed to The University of the South.*

Shepherd University (Los Angeles, CA): *closed.*

Silicon Valley University (San Jose, CA): *closed.*

South University (Novi, MI): *closed.*

South University (High Point, NC): *closed.*

South University (Cleveland, OH): *closed.*

University of Great Falls (Great Falls, MT): *name changed to University of Providence.*

University of Phoenix–Atlanta Campus (Sandy Springs, GA): *closed.*

University of Phoenix–Augusta Campus (Augusta, GA): *closed.*

University of Phoenix–Central Florida Campus (Orlando, FL): *closed.*

University of Phoenix–Charlotte Campus (Charlotte, NC): *closed.*

University of Phoenix–Colorado Campus (Lone Tree, CO): *closed.*

University of Phoenix–Colorado Springs Downtown Campus (Colorado Springs, CO): *closed.*

University of Phoenix–Columbus Georgia Campus (Columbus, GA): *closed.*

University of Phoenix–Jersey City Campus (Jersey City, NJ): *closed.*

University of Phoenix–New Mexico Campus (Albuquerque, NM): *closed.*

University of Phoenix–North Florida Campus (Jacksonville, FL): *closed.*

University of Phoenix–Southern Arizona Campus (Tucson, AZ): *closed.*

University of Phoenix–Southern California Campus (Costa Mesa, CA): *closed.*

University of Phoenix–South Florida Campus (Miramar, FL): *closed.*

University of Phoenix–Utah Campus (Salt Lake City, UT): *closed.*

University of Phoenix–Washington D.C. Campus (Washington, DC): *closed.*

University of Phoenix–Western Washington Campus (Tukwila, WA): *closed.*

University of Puerto Rico, Mayagüez Campus (Mayagüez, PR): *name changed to University of Puerto Rico–Mayagüez.*

University of Puerto Rico, Medical Sciences Campus (San Juan, PR): *name changed to University of Puerto Rico–Medical Sciences Campus.*

University of Puerto Rico, Río Piedras Campus (San Juan, PR): *name changed to University of Puerto Rico–Río Piedras.*

The University of South Dakota (Vermillion, SD): *name changed to University of South Dakota.*

Urbana University (Urbana, OH): *name changed to Urbana University–A Branch Campus of Franklin University.*

Virginia College in Birmingham (Birmingham, AL): *closed.*

Warner Pacific College (Portland, OR): *name changed to Warner Pacific University.*

Wheelock College (Boston, MA): *merged into Boston University (Boston, MA).*

Wright Institute (Berkeley, CA): *name changed to The Wright Institute.*

Yeshiva Karlin Stolin Rabbinical Institute (Brooklyn, NY): *name changed to Yeshiva Karlin Stolin.*

Abbreviations Used in the Guides

The following list includes abbreviations of degree names used in the profiles in the 2020 edition of the guides. Because some degrees (e.g., Doctor of Education) can be abbreviated in more than one way (e.g., D.Ed. or Ed.D.), and because the abbreviations used in the guides reflect the preferences of the individual colleges and universities, the list may include two or more abbreviations for a single degree.

DEGREES

A Mus D	Doctor of Musical Arts
AC	Advanced Certificate
AD	Artist's Diploma
	Doctor of Arts
ADP	Artist's Diploma
Adv C	Advanced Certificate
AGC	Advanced Graduate Certificate
AGSC	Advanced Graduate Specialist Certificate
ALM	Master of Liberal Arts
AM	Master of Arts
AMBA	Accelerated Master of Business Administration
APC	Advanced Professional Certificate
APMPH	Advanced Professional Master of Public Health
App Sc	Applied Scientist
App Sc D	Doctor of Applied Science
AstE	Astronautical Engineer
ATC	Advanced Training Certificate
Au D	Doctor of Audiology
B Th	Bachelor of Theology
CAES	Certificate of Advanced Educational Specialization
CAGS	Certificate of Advanced Graduate Studies
CAL	Certificate in Applied Linguistics
CAPS	Certificate of Advanced Professional Studies
CAS	Certificate of Advanced Studies
CATS	Certificate of Achievement in Theological Studies
CE	Civil Engineer
CEM	Certificate of Environmental Management
CET	Certificate in Educational Technologies
CGS	Certificate of Graduate Studies
Ch E	Chemical Engineer
Clin Sc D	Doctor of Clinical Science
CM	Certificate in Management
CMH	Certificate in Medical Humanities
CMM	Master of Church Ministries
CMS	Certificate in Ministerial Studies
CNM	Certificate in Nonprofit Management
CPC	Certificate in Publication and Communication
CPH	Certificate in Public Health
CPS	Certificate of Professional Studies
CScD	Doctor of Clinical Science
CSD	Certificate in Spiritual Direction
CSS	Certificate of Special Studies
CTS	Certificate of Theological Studies
D Ac	Doctor of Acupuncture
D Admin	Doctor of Administration
D Arch	Doctor of Architecture
D Be	Doctor in Bioethics
D Com	Doctor of Commerce
D Couns	Doctor of Counseling
D Des	Doctorate of Design
D Div	Doctor of Divinity
D Ed	Doctor of Education
D Ed Min	Doctor of Educational Ministry
D Eng	Doctor of Engineering
D Engr	Doctor of Engineering
D Ent	Doctor of Enterprise
D Env	Doctor of Environment
D Law	Doctor of Law
D Litt	Doctor of Letters
D Med Sc	Doctor of Medical Science
D Mgt	Doctor of Management
D Min	Doctor of Ministry
D Miss	Doctor of Missiology
D Mus	Doctor of Music
D Mus A	Doctor of Musical Arts
D Phil	Doctor of Philosophy
D Prof	Doctor of Professional Studies
D Ps	Doctor of Psychology
D Sc	Doctor of Science
D Sc D	Doctor of Science in Dentistry
D Sc IS	Doctor of Science in Information Systems
D Sc PA	Doctor of Science in Physician Assistant Studies
D Th	Doctor of Theology
D Th P	Doctor of Practical Theology
DA	Doctor of Accounting
	Doctor of Arts
DACM	Doctor of Acupuncture and Chinese Medicine
DAIS	Doctor of Applied Intercultural Studies
DAOM	Doctorate in Acupuncture and Oriental Medicine
DAT	Doctorate of Athletic Training
	Professional Doctor of Art Therapy
DBA	Doctor of Business Administration
DBH	Doctor of Behavioral Health
DBL	Doctor of Business Leadership
DC	Doctor of Chiropractic
DCC	Doctor of Computer Science
DCD	Doctor of Communications Design
DCE	Doctor of Computer Engineering
DCJ	Doctor of Criminal Justice
DCL	Doctor of Civil Law
	Doctor of Comparative Law
DCM	Doctor of Church Music
DCN	Doctor of Clinical Nutrition
DCS	Doctor of Computer Science
DDN	Diplôme du Droit Notarial
DDS	Doctor of Dental Surgery
DE	Doctor of Education
	Doctor of Engineering
DED	Doctor of Economic Development
DEIT	Doctor of Educational Innovation and Technology
DEL	Doctor of Executive Leadership
DEM	Doctor of Educational Ministry
DEPD	Diplôme Études Spécialisées
DES	Doctor of Engineering Science
DESS	Diplôme Études Supérieures Spécialisées
DET	Doctor of Educational Technology
DFA	Doctor of Fine Arts
DGP	Diploma in Graduate and Professional Studies
DGS	Doctor of Global Security
DH Sc	Doctor of Health Sciences
DHA	Doctor of Health Administration
DHCE	Doctor of Health Care Ethics
DHL	Doctor of Hebrew Letters
DHPE	Doctorate of Health Professionals Education
DHS	Doctor of Health Science
DHSc	Doctor of Health Science
DIT	Doctor of Industrial Technology

	Doctor of Information Technology	EMFA	Executive Master of Forensic Accounting
DJS	Doctor of Jewish Studies	EMHA	Executive Master of Health Administration
DLS	Doctor of Liberal Studies	EMHCL	Executive Master in Healthcare Leadership
DM	Doctor of Management	EMIB	Executive Master of International Business
	Doctor of Music	EMIR	Executive Master in International Relations
DMA	Doctor of Musical Arts	EML	Executive Master of Leadership
DMD	Doctor of Dental Medicine	EMPA	Executive Master of Public Administration
DME	Doctor of Manufacturing Management	EMPL	Executive Master in Policy Leadership
	Doctor of Music Education		Executive Master in Public Leadership
DMFT	Doctor of Marital and Family Therapy	EMS	Executive Master of Science
DMH	Doctor of Medical Humanities	EMTM	Executive Master of Technology Management
DML	Doctor of Modern Languages	Eng	Engineer
DMP	Doctorate in Medical Physics	Eng Sc D	Doctor of Engineering Science
DMPNA	Doctor of Management Practice in Nurse Anesthesia	Engr	Engineer
DN Sc	Doctor of Nursing Science	Exec MHA	Executive Master of Health Administration
DNAP	Doctor of Nurse Anesthesia Practice	Exec Ed D	Executive Doctor of Education
DNP	Doctor of Nursing Practice	Exec MBA	Executive Master of Business Administration
DNP-A	Doctor of Nursing Practice - Anesthesia	Exec MPA	Executive Master of Public Administration
DNS	Doctor of Nursing Science	Exec MPH	Executive Master of Public Health
DO	Doctor of Osteopathy	Exec MS	Executive Master of Science
DOL	Doctorate of Organizational Leadership	Executive MA	Executive Master of Arts
DOM	Doctor of Oriental Medicine	G Dip	Graduate Diploma
DOT	Doctor of Occupational Therapy	GBC	Graduate Business Certificate
DPA	Diploma in Public Administration	GDM	Graduate Diploma in Management
	Doctor of Public Administration	GDPA	Graduate Diploma in Public Administration
DPDS	Doctor of Planning and Development Studies	GEMBA	Global Executive Master of Business Administration
DPH	Doctor of Public Health	GM Acc	Graduate Master of Accountancy
DPM	Doctor of Plant Medicine	GMBA	Global Master of Business Administration
	Doctor of Podiatric Medicine	GP LL M	Global Professional Master of Laws
DPPD	Doctor of Policy, Planning, and Development	GPD	Graduate Performance Diploma
DPS	Doctor of Professional Studies	GSS	Graduate Special Certificate for Students in Special Situations
DPT	Doctor of Physical Therapy	IEMBA	International Executive Master of Business Administration
DPTSc	Doctor of Physical Therapy Science		
Dr DES	Doctor of Design	IMA	Interdisciplinary Master of Arts
Dr NP	Doctor of Nursing Practice	IMBA	International Master of Business Administration
Dr OT	Doctor of Occupational Therapy	IMES	International Master's in Environmental Studies
Dr PH	Doctor of Public Health		
Dr Sc PT	Doctor of Science in Physical Therapy	Ingeniero	Engineer
DRSc	Doctor of Regulatory Science	JCD	Doctor of Canon Law
DS	Doctor of Science	JCL	Licentiate in Canon Law
DS Sc	Doctor of Social Science	JD	Juris Doctor
DScPT	Doctor of Science in Physical Therapy	JM	Juris Master
DSI	Doctor of Strategic Intelligence	JSD	Doctor of Juridical Science
DSJS	Doctor of Science in Jewish Studies		Doctor of Jurisprudence
DSL	Doctor of Strategic Leadership		Doctor of the Science of Law
DSNS	Doctorate of Statecraft and National Security	JSM	Master of the Science of Law
DSS	Doctor of Strategic Security	L Th	Licentiate in Theology
DSW	Doctor of Social Work	LL B	Bachelor of Laws
DTL	Doctor of Talmudic Law	LL CM	Master of Comparative Law
	Doctor of Transformational Leadership	LL D	Doctor of Laws
DV Sc	Doctor of Veterinary Science	LL M	Master of Laws
DVM	Doctor of Veterinary Medicine	LL M in Tax	Master of Laws in Taxation
DWS	Doctor of Worship Studies	LL M CL	Master of Laws in Common Law
EAA	Engineer in Aeronautics and Astronautics	M Ac	Master of Accountancy
EASPh D	Engineering and Applied Science Doctor of Philosophy		Master of Accounting
			Master of Acupuncture
ECS	Engineer in Computer Science	M Ac OM	Master of Acupuncture and Oriental Medicine
Ed D	Doctor of Education	M Acc	Master of Accountancy
Ed DCT	Doctor of Education in College Teaching		Master of Accounting
Ed L D	Doctor of Education Leadership	M Acct	Master of Accountancy
Ed M	Master of Education		Master of Accounting
Ed S	Specialist in Education	M Accy	Master of Accountancy
Ed Sp	Specialist in Education	M Actg	Master of Accounting
EDB	Executive Doctorate in Business	M Acy	Master of Accountancy
EDM	Executive Doctorate in Management	M Ad	Master of Administration
EE	Electrical Engineer	M Ad Ed	Master of Adult Education
EJD	Executive Juris Doctor	M Adm	Master of Administration
EMBA	Executive Master of Business Administration		

M Adm Mgt	Master of Administrative Management
M Admin	Master of Administration
M ADU	Master of Architectural Design and Urbanism
M Adv	Master of Advertising
M Ag	Master of Agriculture
M Ag Ed	Master of Agricultural Education
M Agr	Master of Agriculture
M App Comp Sc	Master of Applied Computer Science
M App St	Master of Applied Statistics
M Appl Stat	Master of Applied Statistics
M Aq	Master of Aquaculture
M Ar	Master of Architecture
M Arch	Master of Architecture
M Arch I	Master of Architecture I
M Arch II	Master of Architecture II
M Arch E	Master of Architectural Engineering
M Arch H	Master of Architectural History
M Bioethics	Master in Bioethics
M Cat	Master of Catechesis
M Ch E	Master of Chemical Engineering
M Cl D	Master of Clinical Dentistry
M Cl Sc	Master of Clinical Science
M Comm	Master of Communication
M Comp	Master of Computing
M Comp Sc	Master of Computer Science
M Coun	Master of Counseling
M Dent	Master of Dentistry
M Dent Sc	Master of Dental Sciences
M Des	Master of Design
M Des S	Master of Design Studies
M Div	Master of Divinity
M E Sci	Master of Earth Science
M Ec	Master of Economics
M Econ	Master of Economics
M Ed	Master of Education
M Ed T	Master of Education in Teaching
M En	Master of Engineering
M En S	Master of Environmental Sciences
M Eng	Master of Engineering
M Eng Mgt	Master of Engineering Management
M Engr	Master of Engineering
M Ent	Master of Enterprise
M Env	Master of Environment
M Env Des	Master of Environmental Design
M Env E	Master of Environmental Engineering
M Env Sc	Master of Environmental Science
M Ext Ed	Master of Extension Education
M Fin	Master of Finance
M Geo E	Master of Geological Engineering
M Geoenv E	Master of Geoenvironmental Engineering
M Geog	Master of Geography
M Hum	Master of Humanities
M IDST	Master's in Interdisciplinary Studies
M Jur	Master of Jurisprudence
M Kin	Master of Kinesiology
M Land Arch	Master of Landscape Architecture
M Litt	Master of Letters
M Mark	Master of Marketing
M Mat SE	Master of Material Science and Engineering
M Math	Master of Mathematics
M Mech E	Master of Mechanical Engineering
M Med Sc	Master of Medical Science
M Mgmt	Master of Management
M Mgt	Master of Management
M Min	Master of Ministries
M Mtl E	Master of Materials Engineering
M Mu	Master of Music
M Mus	Master of Music
M Mus Ed	Master of Music Education
M Music	Master of Music
M Pet E	Master of Petroleum Engineering
M Pharm	Master of Pharmacy
M Phil	Master of Philosophy
M Phil F	Master of Philosophical Foundations
M Pl	Master of Planning
M Plan	Master of Planning
M Pol	Master of Political Science
M Pr Met	Master of Professional Meteorology
M Prob S	Master of Probability and Statistics
M Psych	Master of Psychology
M Pub	Master of Publishing
M Rel	Master of Religion
M Sc	Master of Science
M Sc A	Master of Science (Applied)
M Sc AC	Master of Science in Applied Computing
M Sc AHN	Master of Science in Applied Human Nutrition
M Sc BMC	Master of Science in Biomedical Communications
M Sc CS	Master of Science in Computer Science
M Sc E	Master of Science in Engineering
M Sc Eng	Master of Science in Engineering
M Sc Engr	Master of Science in Engineering
M Sc F	Master of Science in Forestry
M Sc FE	Master of Science in Forest Engineering
M Sc Geogr	Master of Science in Geography
M Sc N	Master of Science in Nursing
M Sc OT	Master of Science in Occupational Therapy
M Sc P	Master of Science in Planning
M Sc Pl	Master of Science in Planning
M Sc PT	Master of Science in Physical Therapy
M Sc T	Master of Science in Teaching
M SEM	Master of Sustainable Environmental Management
M Serv Soc	Master of Social Service
M Soc	Master of Sociology
M Sp Ed	Master of Special Education
M Stat	Master of Statistics
M Sys E	Master of Systems Engineering
M Sys Sc	Master of Systems Science
M Tax	Master of Taxation
M Tech	Master of Technology
M Th	Master of Theology
M Trans E	Master of Transportation Engineering
M U Ed	Master of Urban Education
M Urb	Master of Urban Planning
M Vet Sc	Master of Veterinary Science
MA	Master of Accounting
	Master of Administration
	Master of Arts
MA Comm	Master of Arts in Communication
MA Ed	Master of Arts in Education
MA Ed/HD	Master of Arts in Education and Human Development
MA Islamic	Master of Arts in Islamic Studies
MA Min	Master of Arts in Ministry
MA Miss	Master of Arts in Missiology
MA Past St	Master of Arts in Pastoral Studies
MA Ph	Master of Arts in Philosophy
MA Psych	Master of Arts in Psychology
MA Sc	Master of Applied Science
MA Sp	Master of Arts (Spirituality)
MA Th	Master of Arts in Theology
MA-R	Master of Arts (Research)
MAA	Master of Applied Anthropology
	Master of Applied Arts
	Master of Arts in Administration
MAAA	Master of Arts in Arts Administration

MAAD	Master of Advanced Architectural Design
MAAE	Master of Arts in Art Education
MAAPPS	Master of Arts in Asia Pacific Policy Studies
MAAS	Master of Arts in Aging and Spirituality
MAASJ	Master of Arts in Applied Social Justice
MAAT	Master of Arts in Applied Theology
MAB	Master of Agribusiness
	Master of Applied Bioengineering
	Master of Arts in Business
MABA	Master's in Applied Behavior Analysis
MABC	Master of Arts in Biblical Counseling
MABE	Master of Arts in Bible Exposition
MABL	Master of Arts in Biblical Languages
MABM	Master of Agribusiness Management
MABS	Master of Arts in Biblical Studies
MABT	Master of Arts in Bible Teaching
MAC	Master of Accountancy
	Master of Accounting
	Master of Arts in Communication
	Master of Arts in Counseling
MACC	Master of Arts in Christian Counseling
MACCT	Master of Accounting
MACD	Master of Arts in Christian Doctrine
MACE	Master of Arts in Christian Education
MACH	Master of Arts in Church History
MACI	Master of Arts in Curriculum and Instruction
MACIS	Master of Accounting and Information Systems
MACJ	Master of Arts in Criminal Justice
MACL	Master of Arts in Christian Leadership
	Master of Arts in Community Leadership
MACM	Master of Arts in Christian Ministries
	Master of Arts in Christian Ministry
	Master of Arts in Church Music
	Master of Arts in Counseling Ministries
MACML	Master of Arts in Christian Ministry and Leadership
MACN	Master of Arts in Counseling
MACO	Master of Arts in Counseling
MAcOM	Master of Acupuncture and Oriental Medicine
MACP	Master of Arts in Christian Practice
	Master of Arts in Church Planting
	Master of Arts in Counseling Psychology
MACS	Master of Applied Computer Science
	Master of Arts in Catholic Studies
	Master of Arts in Christian Studies
MACSE	Master of Arts in Christian School Education
MACT	Master of Arts in Communications and Technology
MAD	Master in Educational Institution Administration
	Master of Art and Design
MADR	Master of Arts in Dispute Resolution
MADS	Master of Applied Disability Studies
MAE	Master of Aerospace Engineering
	Master of Agricultural Economics
	Master of Agricultural Education
	Master of Applied Economics
	Master of Architectural Engineering
	Master of Art Education
	Master of Arts in Education
	Master of Arts in English
MAEd	Master of Arts Education
MAEE	Master of Agricultural and Extension Education
MAEL	Master of Arts in Educational Leadership
MAEM	Master of Arts in Educational Ministries
MAEP	Master of Arts in Economic Policy
	Master of Arts in Educational Psychology
MAES	Master of Arts in Environmental Sciences
MAET	Master of Arts in English Teaching

MAF	Master of Arts in Finance
MAFE	Master of Arts in Financial Economics
MAFM	Master of Accounting and Financial Management
MAFS	Master of Arts in Family Studies
MAG	Master of Applied Geography
MAGU	Master of Urban Analysis and Management
MAH	Master of Arts in Humanities
MAHA	Master of Arts in Humanitarian Assistance
MAHCM	Master of Arts in Health Care Mission
MAHG	Master of American History and Government
MAHL	Master of Arts in Hebrew Letters
MAHN	Master of Applied Human Nutrition
MAHR	Master of Applied Historical Research
MAHS	Master of Arts in Human Services
MAHSR	Master in Applied Health Services Research
MAIA	Master of Arts in International Administration
	Master of Arts in International Affairs
MAICS	Master of Arts in Intercultural Studies
MAIDM	Master of Arts in Interior Design and Merchandising
MAIH	Master of Arts in Interdisciplinary Humanities
MAIOP	Master of Applied Industrial/Organizational Psychology
MAIS	Master of Arts in Intercultural Studies
	Master of Arts in Interdisciplinary Studies
	Master of Arts in International Studies
MAIT	Master of Administration in Information Technology
MAJ	Master of Arts in Journalism
MAJCS	Master of Arts in Jewish Communal Service
MAJPS	Master of Arts in Jewish Professional Studies
MAJS	Master of Arts in Jewish Studies
MAL	Master of Athletic Leadership
MALA	Master of Arts in Liberal Arts
MALCM	Master in Arts Leadership and Cultural Management
MALD	Master of Arts in Law and Diplomacy
MALER	Master of Arts in Labor and Employment Relations
MALL	Master of Arts in Language Learning
MALLT	Master of Arts in Language, Literature, and Translation
MALP	Master of Arts in Language Pedagogy
MALS	Master of Arts in Liberal Studies
MAM	Master of Acquisition Management
	Master of Agriculture and Management
	Master of Applied Mathematics
	Master of Arts in Management
	Master of Arts in Ministry
	Master of Arts Management
	Master of Aviation Management
MAMC	Master of Arts in Mass Communication
	Master of Arts in Ministry and Culture
	Master of Arts in Ministry for a Multicultural Church
MAME	Master of Arts in Missions/Evangelism
MAMFC	Master of Arts in Marriage and Family Counseling
MAMFT	Master of Arts in Marriage and Family Therapy
MAMHC	Master of Arts in Mental Health Counseling
MAMS	Master of Applied Mathematical Sciences
	Master of Arts in Ministerial Studies
	Master of Arts in Ministry and Spirituality
MAMT	Master of Arts in Mathematics Teaching
MAN	Master of Applied Nutrition
MANT	Master of Arts in New Testament
MAOL	Master of Arts in Organizational Leadership
MAOM	Master of Acupuncture and Oriental Medicine
	Master of Arts in Organizational Management

MAOT	Master of Arts in Old Testament
MAP	Master of Applied Politics
	Master of Applied Psychology
	Master of Arts in Planning
	Master of Psychology
	Master of Public Administration
MAP Min	Master of Arts in Pastoral Ministry
MAPA	Master of Arts in Public Administration
MAPC	Master of Arts in Pastoral Counseling
MAPE	Master of Arts in Physics Education
MAPM	Master of Arts in Pastoral Ministry
	Master of Arts in Pastoral Music
	Master of Arts in Practical Ministry
MAPP	Master of Arts in Public Policy
MAPS	Master of Applied Psychological Sciences
	Master of Arts in Pastoral Studies
	Master of Arts in Public Service
MAPW	Master of Arts in Professional Writing
MAQRM	Master's of Actuarial and Quantitative Risk Management
MAR	Master of Arts in Reading
	Master of Arts in Religion
Mar Eng	Marine Engineer
MARC	Master of Arts in Rehabilitation Counseling
MARE	Master of Arts in Religious Education
MARL	Master of Arts in Religious Leadership
MARS	Master of Arts in Religious Studies
MAS	Master of Accounting Science
	Master of Actuarial Science
	Master of Administrative Science
	Master of Advanced Study
	Master of American Studies
	Master of Animal Science
	Master of Applied Science
	Master of Applied Statistics
	Master of Archival Studies
MASA	Master of Advanced Studies in Architecture
MASC	Master of Arts in School Counseling
MASD	Master of Arts in Spiritual Direction
MASE	Master of Arts in Special Education
MASF	Master of Arts in Spiritual Formation
MASJ	Master of Arts in Systems of Justice
MASLA	Master of Advanced Studies in Landscape Architecture
MASM	Master of Aging Services Management
	Master of Arts in Specialized Ministries
MASS	Master of Applied Social Science
MASW	Master of Aboriginal Social Work
MAT	Master of Arts in Teaching
	Master of Arts in Theology
	Master of Athletic Training
	Master's in Administration of Telecommunications
Mat E	Materials Engineer
MATCM	Master of Acupuncture and Traditional Chinese Medicine
MATDE	Master of Arts in Theology, Development, and Evangelism
MATDR	Master of Territorial Management and Regional Development
MATE	Master of Arts for the Teaching of English
MATESL	Master of Arts in Teaching English as a Second Language
MATESOL	Master of Arts in Teaching English to Speakers of Other Languages
MATF	Master of Arts in Teaching English as a Foreign Language/Intercultural Studies
MATFL	Master of Arts in Teaching Foreign Language
MATH	Master of Arts in Therapy

MATI	Master of Administration of Information Technology
MATL	Master of Arts in Teaching of Languages
	Master of Arts in Transformational Leadership
MATM	Master of Arts in Teaching of Mathematics
MATRN	Master of Athletic Training
MATS	Master of Arts in Theological Studies
	Master of Arts in Transforming Spirituality
MAUA	Master of Arts in Urban Affairs
MAUD	Master of Arts in Urban Design
MAURP	Master of Arts in Urban and Regional Planning
MAW	Master of Arts in Worship
MAWSHP	Master of Arts in Worship
MAYM	Master of Arts in Youth Ministry
MB	Master of Bioinformatics
MBA	Master of Business Administration
MBA-AM	Master of Business Administration in Aviation Management
MBA-EP	Master of Business Administration– Experienced Professionals
MBAA	Master of Business Administration in Aviation
MBAE	Master of Biological and Agricultural Engineering
	Master of Biosystems and Agricultural Engineering
MBAH	Master of Business Administration in Health
MBAi	Master of Business Administration– International
MBAICT	Master of Business Administration in Information and Communication Technology
MBC	Master of Building Construction
MBE	Master of Bilingual Education
	Master of Bioengineering
	Master of Bioethics
	Master of Biomedical Engineering
	Master of Business Economics
	Master of Business Education
MBEE	Master in Biotechnology Enterprise and Entrepreneurship
MBET	Master of Business, Entrepreneurship and Technology
MBI	Master in Business Informatics
MBIOT	Master of Biotechnology
MBiotech	Master of Biotechnology
MBL	Master of Business Leadership
MBLE	Master in Business Logistics Engineering
MBME	Master's in Biomedical Engineering
MBMSE	Master of Business Management and Software Engineering
MBOE	Master of Business Operational Excellence
MBS	Master of Biblical Studies
	Master of Biological Science
	Master of Biomedical Sciences
	Master of Bioscience
	Master of Building Science
	Master of Business and Science
	Master of Business Statistics
MBST	Master of Biostatistics
MBT	Master of Biomedical Technology
	Master of Biotechnology
	Master of Business Taxation
MBV	Master of Business for Veterans
MC	Master of Classics
	Master of Communication
	Master of Counseling
MC Ed	Master of Continuing Education
MC Sc	Master of Computer Science
MCA	Master of Commercial Aviation
	Master of Communication Arts
	Master of Criminology (Applied)

MCAM	Master of Computational and Applied Mathematics
MCC	Master of Computer Science
MCD	Master of Communications Disorders
	Master of Community Development
MCE	Master in Electronic Commerce
	Master of Chemistry Education
	Master of Christian Education
	Master of Civil Engineering
	Master of Control Engineering
MCEM	Master of Construction Engineering Management
MCEPA	Master of Chinese Economic and Political Affairs
MCHE	Master of Chemical Engineering
MCIS	Master of Communication and Information Studies
	Master of Computer and Information Science
	Master of Computer Information Systems
MCIT	Master of Computer and Information Technology
MCJ	Master of Criminal Justice
MCL	Master in Communication Leadership
	Master of Canon Law
	Master of Christian Leadership
	Master of Comparative Law
MCM	Master of Christian Ministry
	Master of Church Music
	Master of Communication Management
	Master of Community Medicine
	Master of Construction Management
	Master of Contract Management
MCMin	Master of Christian Ministry
MCMM	Master in Communications and Media Management
MCMP	Master of City and Metropolitan Planning
MCMS	Master of Clinical Medical Science
MCN	Master of Clinical Nutrition
MCOL	Master of Arts in Community and Organizational Leadership
MCP	Master of City Planning
	Master of Community Planning
	Master of Counseling Psychology
	Master of Cytopathology Practice
	Master of Science in Quality Systems and Productivity
MCPD	Master of Community Planning and Development
MCR	Master in Clinical Research
MCRP	Master of City and Regional Planning
	Master of Community and Regional Planning
MCRS	Master of City and Regional Studies
MCS	Master of Chemical Sciences
	Master of Christian Studies
	Master of Clinical Science
	Master of Combined Sciences
	Master of Communication Studies
	Master of Computer Science
	Master of Consumer Science
MCSE	Master of Computer Science and Engineering
MCSL	Master of Catholic School Leadership
MCSM	Master of Construction Science and Management
MCT	Master of Commerce and Technology
MCTM	Master of Clinical Translation Management
MCTP	Master of Communication Technology and Policy
MCTS	Master of Clinical and Translational Science
MCVS	Master of Cardiovascular Science
MD	Doctor of Medicine
MDA	Master of Dietetic Administration
MDB	Master of Design-Build
MDE	Master in Design Engineering
	Master of Developmental Economics
	Master of Distance Education
	Master of the Education of the Deaf
MDH	Master of Dental Hygiene
MDI	Master of Disruptive Innovation
MDM	Master of Design Methods
	Master of Digital Media
MDP	Master in Sustainable Development Practice
	Master of Development Practice
MDR	Master of Dispute Resolution
MDS	Master in Data Science
	Master of Dental Surgery
	Master of Design Studies
	Master of Digital Sciences
MDSPP	Master in Data Science for Public Policy
ME	Master of Education
	Master of Engineering
	Master of Entrepreneurship
ME Sc	Master of Engineering Science
ME-PD	Master of Education–Professional Development
MEA	Master of Educational Administration
	Master of Engineering Administration
MEAE	Master of Entertainment Arts and Engineering
MEAP	Master of Environmental Administration and Planning
MEB	Master of Energy Business
MEBD	Master in Environmental Building Design
MEBT	Master in Electronic Business Technologies
MEC	Master of Electronic Commerce
Mech E	Mechanical Engineer
MEDS	Master of Environmental Design Studies
MEE	Master in Education
	Master of Electrical Engineering
	Master of Energy Engineering
	Master of Environmental Engineering
MEECON	Master of Energy Economics
MEEM	Master of Environmental Engineering and Management
MEENE	Master of Engineering in Environmental Engineering
MEEP	Master of Environmental and Energy Policy
MEERM	Master of Earth and Environmental Resource Management
MEH	Master in Humanistic Studies
	Master of Environmental Health
	Master of Environmental Horticulture
MEHS	Master of Environmental Health and Safety
MEIM	Master of Entertainment Industry Management
	Master of Equine Industry Management
MEL	Master of Educational Leadership
	Master of Engineering Leadership
	Master of English Literature
MELP	Master of Environmental Law and Policy
MEM	Master of Engineering Management
	Master of Environmental Management
	Master of Marketing
MEME	Master of Engineering in Manufacturing Engineering
	Master of Engineering in Mechanical Engineering
MENR	Master of Environment and Natural Resources
MENVEGR	Master of Environmental Engineering
MEP	Master of Engineering Physics
MEPC	Master of Environmental Pollution Control
MEPD	Master of Environmental Planning and Design
MER	Master of Employment Relations

MERE	Master of Entrepreneurial Real Estate
MERL	Master of Energy Regulation and Law
MES	Master of Education and Science
	Master of Engineering Science
	Master of Environment and Sustainability
	Master of Environmental Science
	Master of Environmental Studies
	Master of Environmental Systems
MESM	Master of Environmental Science and Management
MET	Master of Educational Technology
	Master of Engineering Technology
	Master of Entertainment Technology
	Master of Environmental Toxicology
METM	Master of Engineering and Technology Management
MEVE	Master of Environmental Engineering
MF	Master of Finance
	Master of Forestry
MFA	Master of Financial Administration
	Master of Fine Arts
MFALP	Master of Food and Agriculture Law and Policy
MFAS	Master of Fisheries and Aquatic Science
MFC	Master of Forest Conservation
MFCS	Master of Family and Consumer Sciences
MFE	Master of Financial Economics
	Master of Financial Engineering
	Master of Forest Engineering
MFES	Master of Fire and Emergency Services
MFG	Master of Functional Genomics
MFHD	Master of Family and Human Development
MFM	Master of Financial Management
	Master of Financial Mathematics
MFPE	Master of Food Process Engineering
MFR	Master of Forest Resources
MFRC	Master of Forest Resources and Conservation
MFRE	Master of Food and Resource Economics
MFS	Master of Food Science
	Master of Forensic Sciences
	Master of Forest Science
	Master of Forest Studies
	Master of French Studies
MFST	Master of Food Safety and Technology
MFT	Master of Family Therapy
MFWCB	Master of Fish, Wildlife and Conservation Biology
MFYCS	Master of Family, Youth and Community Sciences
MGA	Master of Global Affairs
	Master of Government Administration
	Master of Governmental Administration
MGBA	Master of Global Business Administration
MGC	Master of Genetic Counseling
MGCS	Master of Genetic Counselor Studies
MGD	Master of Graphic Design
MGE	Master of Geotechnical Engineering
MGEM	Master of Geomatics for Environmental Management
	Master of Global Entrepreneurship and Management
MGIS	Master of Geographic Information Science
	Master of Geographic Information Systems
MGM	Master of Global Management
MGMA	Master of Greenhouse Gas Management and Accounting
MGP	Master of Gestion de Projet
MGPS	Master of Global Policy Studies
MGREM	Master of Global Real Estate Management
MGS	Master of Gender Studies
	Master of Gerontological Studies

	Master of Global Studies
MH	Master of Humanities
MH Sc	Master of Health Sciences
MHA	Master of Health Administration
	Master of Healthcare Administration
	Master of Hospital Administration
	Master of Hospitality Administration
MHB	Master of Human Behavior
MHC	Master of Mental Health Counseling
MHCA	Master of Health Care Administration
MHCD	Master of Health Care Design
MHCI	Master of Human-Computer Interaction
MHCL	Master of Health Care Leadership
MHCM	Master of Health Care Management
MHE	Master of Health Education
	Master of Higher Education
	Master of Human Ecology
MHE Ed	Master of Home Economics Education
MHEA	Master of Higher Education Administration
MHHS	Master of Health and Human Services
MHI	Master of Health Informatics
	Master of Healthcare Innovation
MHID	Master of Healthcare Interior Design
MHIHIM	Master of Health Informatics and Health Information Management
MHIIM	Master of Health Informatics and Information Management
MHK	Master of Human Kinetics
MHM	Master of Healthcare Management
MHMS	Master of Health Management Systems
MHP	Master of Health Physics
	Master of Heritage Preservation
	Master of Historic Preservation
MHPA	Master of Heath Policy and Administration
MHPCTL	Master of High Performance Coaching and Technical Leadership
MHPE	Master of Health Professions Education
MHR	Master of Human Resources
MHRD	Master in Human Resource Development
MHRIR	Master of Human Resources and Industrial Relations
MHRLR	Master of Human Resources and Labor Relations
MHRM	Master of Human Resources Management
MHS	Master of Health Science
	Master of Health Sciences
	Master of Health Studies
	Master of Hispanic Studies
	Master of Human Services
	Master of Humanistic Studies
MHSA	Master of Health Services Administration
MHSM	Master of Health Systems Management
MI	Master of Information
	Master of Instruction
MI Arch	Master of Interior Architecture
MIA	Master of Interior Architecture
	Master of International Affairs
MIAA	Master of International Affairs and Administration
MIAM	Master of International Agribusiness Management
MIAPD	Master of Interior Architecture and Product Design
MIB	Master of International Business
MIBS	Master of International Business Studies
MICLJ	Master of International Criminal Law and Justice
MICM	Master of International Construction Management
MID	Master of Industrial Design

	Master of Industrial Distribution
	Master of Innovation Design
	Master of Interior Design
	Master of International Development
MIDA	Master of International Development Administration
MIDP	Master of International Development Policy
MIDS	Master of Information and Data Science
MIE	Master of Industrial Engineering
MIF	Master of International Forestry
MIHTM	Master of International Hospitality and Tourism Management
MIJ	Master of International Journalism
MILR	Master of Industrial and Labor Relations
MIM	Master in Ministry
	Master of Information Management
	Master of International Management
	Master of International Marketing
MIMFA	Master of Investment Management and Financial Analysis
MIMLAE	Master of International Management for Latin American Executives
MIMS	Master of Information Management and Systems
	Master of Integrated Manufacturing Systems
MIP	Master of Infrastructure Planning
	Master of Intellectual Property
	Master of International Policy
MIPA	Master of International Public Affairs
MIPD	Master of Integrated Product Design
MIPER	Master of International Political Economy of Resources
MIPM	Master of International Policy Management
MIPP	Master of International Policy and Practice
	Master of International Public Policy
MIPS	Master of International Planning Studies
MIR	Master of Industrial Relations
	Master of International Relations
MIRD	Master of International Relations and Diplomacy
MIRHR	Master of Industrial Relations and Human Resources
MIS	Master of Imaging Science
	Master of Industrial Statistics
	Master of Information Science
	Master of Information Systems
	Master of Integrated Science
	Master of Interdisciplinary Studies
	Master of International Service
	Master of International Studies
MISE	Master of Industrial and Systems Engineering
MISKM	Master of Information Sciences and Knowledge Management
MISM	Master of Information Systems Management
MISW	Master of Indigenous Social Work
MIT	Master in Teaching
	Master of Industrial Technology
	Master of Information Technology
	Master of Initial Teaching
	Master of International Trade
MITA	Master of Information Technology Administration
MITM	Master of Information Technology and Management
MJ	Master of Journalism
	Master of Jurisprudence
MJ Ed	Master of Jewish Education
MJA	Master of Justice Administration
MJM	Master of Justice Management
MJS	Master of Judaic Studies

	Master of Judicial Studies
	Master of Juridical Studies
MK	Master of Kinesiology
MKM	Master of Knowledge Management
ML	Master of Latin
	Master of Law
ML Arch	Master of Landscape Architecture
MLA	Master of Landscape Architecture
	Master of Liberal Arts
MLAS	Master of Laboratory Animal Science
	Master of Liberal Arts and Sciences
MLAUD	Master of Landscape Architecture in Urban Development
MLD	Master of Leadership Development
	Master of Leadership Studies
MLE	Master of Applied Linguistics and Exegesis
MLER	Master of Labor and Employment Relations
MLI Sc	Master of Library and Information Science
MLIS	Master of Library and Information Science
	Master of Library and Information Studies
MLM	Master of Leadership in Ministry
MLPD	Master of Land and Property Development
MLRHR	Master of Labor Relations and Human Resources
MLS	Master of Leadership Studies
	Master of Legal Studies
	Master of Liberal Studies
	Master of Library Science
	Master of Life Sciences
	Master of Medical Laboratory Sciences
MLSCM	Master of Logistics and Supply Chain Management
MLT	Master of Language Technologies
MLTCA	Master of Long Term Care Administration
MLW	Master of Studies in Law
MLWS	Master of Land and Water Systems
MM	Master of Management
	Master of Mediation
	Master of Ministry
	Master of Music
MM Ed	Master of Music Education
MM Sc	Master of Medical Science
MM St	Master of Museum Studies
MMA	Master of Marine Affairs
	Master of Media Arts
	Master of Musical Arts
MMAL	Master of Maritime Administration and Logistics
MMAS	Master of Military Art and Science
MMB	Master of Microbial Biotechnology
MMC	Master of Manufacturing Competitiveness
	Master of Mass Communications
MMCM	Master of Music in Church Music
MMCSS	Master of Mathematical Computational and Statistical Sciences
MME	Master of Management in Energy
	Master of Manufacturing Engineering
	Master of Mathematics Education
	Master of Mathematics for Educators
	Master of Mechanical Engineering
	Master of Mining Engineering
	Master of Music Education
MMEL	Master's in Medical Education Leadership
MMF	Master of Mathematical Finance
MMFC/T	Master of Marriage and Family Counseling/ Therapy
MMFT	Master of Marriage and Family Therapy
MMG	Master of Management
MMH	Master of Management in Hospitality

	Master of Medical Humanities
MMI	Master of Management of Innovation
MMIS	Master of Management Information Systems
MML	Master of Managerial Logistics
MMM	Master of Manufacturing Management
	Master of Marine Management
	Master of Medical Management
MMP	Master of Marine Policy
	Master of Medical Physics
	Master of Music Performance
MMPA	Master of Management and Professional Accounting
MMQM	Master of Manufacturing Quality Management
MMR	Master of Marketing Research
MMRM	Master of Marine Resources Management
MMS	Master in Migration Studies
	Master of Management Science
	Master of Management Studies
	Master of Manufacturing Systems
	Master of Marine Studies
	Master of Materials Science
	Master of Mathematical Sciences
	Master of Medical Science
	Master of Medieval Studies
MMSE	Master of Manufacturing Systems Engineering
MMSM	Master of Music in Sacred Music
MMT	Master in Marketing
	Master of Math for Teaching
	Master of Music Therapy
	Master's in Marketing Technology
MMus	Master of Music
MN	Master of Nursing
	Master of Nutrition
MN NP	Master of Nursing in Nurse Practitioner
MNA	Master of Nonprofit Administration
	Master of Nurse Anesthesia
MNAE	Master of Nanoengineering
MNAL	Master of Nonprofit Administration and Leadership
MNAS	Master of Natural and Applied Science
MNCL	Master of Nonprofit and Civic Leadership
MNCM	Master of Network and Communications Management
MNE	Master of Nuclear Engineering
MNL	Master in International Business for Latin America
MNM	Master of Nonprofit Management
MNO	Master of Nonprofit Organization
MNPL	Master of Not-for-Profit Leadership
MNpS	Master of Nonprofit Studies
MNR	Master of Natural Resources
MNRD	Master of Natural Resources Development
MNRES	Master of Natural Resources and Environmental Studies
MNRM	Master of Natural Resource Management
MNRMG	Master of Natural Resource Management and Geography
MNRS	Master of Natural Resource Stewardship
MNS	Master of Natural Science
MNSE	Master of Natural Sciences Education
MO	Master of Oceanography
MOD	Master of Organizational Development
MOGS	Master of Oil and Gas Studies
MOL	Master of Organizational Leadership
MOM	Master of Organizational Management
	Master of Oriental Medicine
MOR	Master of Operations Research
MOT	Master of Occupational Therapy
MP	Master of Physiology

	Master of Planning
MP Ac	Master of Professional Accountancy
MP Acc	Master of Professional Accountancy
	Master of Professional Accounting
	Master of Public Accounting
MP Aff	Master of Public Affairs
MP Th	Master of Pastoral Theology
MPA	Master of Performing Arts
	Master of Physician Assistant
	Master of Professional Accountancy
	Master of Professional Accounting
	Master of Public Administration
	Master of Public Affairs
MPAC	Master of Professional Accounting
MPAID	Master of Public Administration and International Development
MPAP	Master of Physician Assistant Practice
	Master of Public Administration and Policy
	Master of Public Affairs and Politics
MPAS	Master of Physician Assistant Science
	Master of Physician Assistant Studies
MPC	Master of Professional Communication
MPD	Master of Product Development
	Master of Public Diplomacy
MPDS	Master of Planning and Development Studies
MPE	Master of Physical Education
MPEM	Master of Project Engineering and Management
MPFM	Master of Public Financial Management
MPH	Master of Public Health
MPHE	Master of Public Health Education
MPHM	Master in Plant Health Management
MPHS	Master of Population Health Sciences
MPHTM	Master of Public Health and Tropical Medicine
MPI	Master of Public Informatics
MPIA	Master of Public and International Affairs
MPL	Master of Pastoral Leadership
MPM	Master of Pastoral Ministry
	Master of Pest Management
	Master of Policy Management
	Master of Practical Ministries
	Master of Professional Management
	Master of Project Management
	Master of Public Management
MPNA	Master of Public and Nonprofit Administration
MPNL	Master of Philanthropy and Nonprofit Leadership
MPO	Master of Prosthetics and Orthotics
MPOD	Master of Positive Organizational Development
MPP	Master of Public Policy
MPPA	Master of Public Policy Administration
	Master of Public Policy and Administration
MPPAL	Master of Public Policy, Administration and Law
MPPGA	Master of Public Policy and Global Affairs
MPPM	Master of Public Policy and Management
MPR	Master of Public Relations
MPRTM	Master of Parks, Recreation, and Tourism Management
MPS	Master of Pastoral Studies
	Master of Perfusion Science
	Master of Planning Studies
	Master of Political Science
	Master of Preservation Studies
	Master of Prevention Science
	Master of Professional Studies
	Master of Public Service
MPSA	Master of Public Service Administration
MPSG	Master of Population and Social Gerontology

MPSIA	Master of Political Science and International Affairs
MPSL	Master of Public Safety Leadership
MPT	Master of Pastoral Theology
	Master of Physical Therapy
	Master of Practical Theology
MPVM	Master of Preventive Veterinary Medicine
MPW	Master of Professional Writing
	Master of Public Works
MQF	Master of Quantitative Finance
MQM	Master of Quality Management
	Master of Quantitative Management
MQS	Master of Quality Systems
MR	Master of Recreation
	Master of Retailing
MRA	Master in Research Administration
	Master of Regulatory Affairs
MRC	Master of Rehabilitation Counseling
MRCP	Master of Regional and City Planning
	Master of Regional and Community Planning
MRD	Master of Rural Development
MRE	Master of Real Estate
	Master of Religious Education
MRED	Master of Real Estate Development
MREM	Master of Resource and Environmental Management
MRLS	Master of Resources Law Studies
MRM	Master of Resources Management
MRP	Master of Regional Planning
MRRD	Master in Recreation Resource Development
MRS	Master of Religious Studies
MRSc	Master of Rehabilitation Science
MRUD	Master of Resilient Design
MS	Master of Science
MS Cmp E	Master of Science in Computer Engineering
MS Kin	Master of Science in Kinesiology
MS Acct	Master of Science in Accounting
MS Accy	Master of Science in Accountancy
MS Aero E	Master of Science in Aerospace Engineering
MS Ag	Master of Science in Agriculture
MS Arch	Master of Science in Architecture
MS Arch St	Master of Science in Architectural Studies
MS Bio E	Master of Science in Bioengineering
MS Bm E	Master of Science in Biomedical Engineering
MS Ch E	Master of Science in Chemical Engineering
MS Cp E	Master of Science in Computer Engineering
MS Eco	Master of Science in Economics
MS Econ	Master of Science in Economics
MS Ed	Master of Science in Education
MS Ed Admin	Master of Science in Educational Administration
MS El	Master of Science in Educational Leadership and Administration
MS En E	Master of Science in Environmental Engineering
MS Eng	Master of Science in Engineering
MS Engr	Master of Science in Engineering
MS Env E	Master of Science in Environmental Engineering
MS Exp Surg	Master of Science in Experimental Surgery
MS Mat SE	Master of Science in Material Science and Engineering
MS Met E	Master of Science in Metallurgical Engineering
MS Mgt	Master of Science in Management
MS Min	Master of Science in Mining
MS Min E	Master of Science in Mining Engineering
MS Mt E	Master of Science in Materials Engineering
MS Otol	Master of Science in Otolaryngology
MS Pet E	Master of Science in Petroleum Engineering
MS Sc	Master of Social Science

MS Sp Ed	Master of Science in Special Education
MS Stat	Master of Science in Statistics
MS Surg	Master of Science in Surgery
MS Tax	Master of Science in Taxation
MS Tc E	Master of Science in Telecommunications Engineering
MS-R	Master of Science (Research)
MSA	Master of School Administration
	Master of Science in Accountancy
	Master of Science in Accounting
	Master of Science in Administration
	Master of Science in Aeronautics
	Master of Science in Agriculture
	Master of Science in Analytics
	Master of Science in Anesthesia
	Master of Science in Architecture
	Master of Science in Aviation
	Master of Sports Administration
	Master of Surgical Assisting
MSAA	Master of Science in Astronautics and Aeronautics
MSABE	Master of Science in Agricultural and Biological Engineering
MSAC	Master of Science in Acupuncture
MSACC	Master of Science in Accounting
MSACS	Master of Science in Applied Computer Science
MSAE	Master of Science in Aeronautical Engineering
	Master of Science in Aerospace Engineering
	Master of Science in Applied Economics
	Master of Science in Applied Engineering
	Master of Science in Architectural Engineering
MSAEM	Master of Science in Aerospace Engineering and Mechanics
MSAF	Master of Science in Aviation Finance
MSAG	Master of Science in Applied Geosciences
MSAH	Master of Science in Allied Health
MSAL	Master of Sport Administration and Leadership
MSAM	Master of Science in Applied Mathematics
MSANR	Master of Science in Agriculture and Natural Resources
MSAS	Master of Science in Administrative Studies
	Master of Science in Applied Statistics
	Master of Science in Architectural Studies
MSAT	Master of Science in Accounting and Taxation
	Master of Science in Advanced Technology
	Master of Science in Athletic Training
MSB	Master of Science in Biotechnology
MSBA	Master of Science in Business Administration
	Master of Science in Business Analysis
MSBAE	Master of Science in Biological and Agricultural Engineering
	Master of Science in Biosystems and Agricultural Engineering
MSBCB	Master's in Bioinformatics and Computational Biology
MSBE	Master of Science in Biological Engineering
	Master of Science in Biomedical Engineering
MSBENG	Master of Science in Bioengineering
MSBH	Master of Science in Behavioral Health
MSBM	Master of Sport Business Management
MSBME	Master of Science in Biomedical Engineering
MSBMS	Master of Science in Basic Medical Science
MSBS	Master of Science in Biomedical Sciences
MSBTM	Master of Science in Biotechnology and Management
MSC	Master of Science in Commerce
	Master of Science in Communication
	Master of Science in Counseling
	Master of Science in Criminology
	Master of Strategic Communication

MSCC	Master of Science in Community Counseling
MSCD	Master of Science in Communication Disorders
	Master of Science in Community Development
MSCE	Master of Science in Chemistry Education
	Master of Science in Civil Engineering
	Master of Science in Clinical Epidemiology
	Master of Science in Computer Engineering
	Master of Science in Continuing Education
MSCEE	Master of Science in Civil and Environmental Engineering
MSCF	Master of Science in Computational Finance
MSCH	Master of Science in Chemical Engineering
MSChE	Master of Science in Chemical Engineering
MSCI	Master of Science in Clinical Investigation
MSCID	Master of Science in Community and International Development
MSCIS	Master of Science in Computer and Information Science
	Master of Science in Computer and Information Systems
	Master of Science in Computer Information Science
	Master of Science in Computer Information Systems
MSCIT	Master of Science in Computer Information Technology
MSCJ	Master of Science in Criminal Justice
MSCJA	Master of Science in Criminal Justice Administration
MSCJS	Master of Science in Crime and Justice Studies
MSCLS	Master of Science in Clinical Laboratory Studies
MSCM	Master of Science in Church Management
	Master of Science in Conflict Management
	Master of Science in Construction Management
	Master of Supply Chain Management
MSCMP	Master of Science in Cybersecurity Management and Policy
MSCNU	Master of Science in Clinical Nutrition
MSCP	Master of Science in Clinical Psychology
	Master of Science in Community Psychology
	Master of Science in Computer Engineering
	Master of Science in Counseling Psychology
MSCPE	Master of Science in Computer Engineering
MSCPharm	Master of Science in Pharmacy
MSCR	Master of Science in Clinical Research
MSCRP	Master of Science in City and Regional Planning
	Master of Science in Community and Regional Planning
MSCS	Master of Science in Clinical Science
	Master of Science in Computer Science
	Master of Science in Cyber Security
MSCSD	Master of Science in Communication Sciences and Disorders
MSCSE	Master of Science in Computer Science and Engineering
MSCTE	Master of Science in Career and Technical Education
MSD	Master of Science in Dentistry
	Master of Science in Design
	Master of Science in Dietetics
MSDM	Master of Security and Disaster Management
MSE	Master of Science Education
	Master of Science in Economics
	Master of Science in Education
	Master of Science in Engineering
	Master of Science in Engineering Management
	Master of Software Engineering
	Master of Special Education
	Master of Structural Engineering

MSECE	Master of Science in Electrical and Computer Engineering
MSED	Master of Sustainable Economic Development
MSEE	Master of Science in Electrical Engineering
	Master of Science in Environmental Engineering
MSEH	Master of Science in Environmental Health
MSEL	Master of Science in Educational Leadership
MSEM	Master of Science in Engineering and Management
	Master of Science in Engineering Management
	Master of Science in Engineering Mechanics
	Master of Science in Environmental Management
MSENE	Master of Science in Environmental Engineering
MSEO	Master of Science in Electro-Optics
MSES	Master of Science in Embedded Software Engineering
	Master of Science in Engineering Science
	Master of Science in Environmental Science
	Master of Science in Environmental Studies
	Master of Science in Exercise Science
MSESE	Master of Science in Energy Systems Engineering
MSET	Master of Science in Educational Technology
	Master of Science in Engineering Technology
MSEV	Master of Science in Environmental Engineering
MSF	Master of Science in Finance
	Master of Science in Forestry
MSFA	Master of Science in Financial Analysis
MSFCS	Master of Science in Family and Consumer Science
MSFE	Master of Science in Financial Engineering
MSFM	Master of Sustainable Forest Management
MSFOR	Master of Science in Forestry
MSFP	Master of Science in Financial Planning
MSFS	Master of Science in Financial Sciences
	Master of Science in Forensic Science
MSFSB	Master of Science in Financial Services and Banking
MSFT	Master of Science in Family Therapy
MSGC	Master of Science in Genetic Counseling
MSH	Master of Science in Health
	Master of Science in Hospice
MSHA	Master of Science in Health Administration
MSHCA	Master of Science in Health Care Administration
MSHCPM	Master of Science in Health Care Policy and Management
MSHE	Master of Science in Health Education
MSHES	Master of Science in Human Environmental Sciences
MSHFID	Master of Science in Human Factors in Information Design
MSHFS	Master of Science in Human Factors and Systems
MSHI	Master of Science in Health Informatics
MSHP	Master of Science in Health Professions
MSHR	Master of Science in Human Resources
MSHRL	Master of Science in Human Resource Leadership
MSHRM	Master of Science in Human Resource Management
MSHROD	Master of Science in Human Resources and Organizational Development
MSHS	Master of Science in Health Science
	Master of Science in Health Services
	Master of Science in Homeland Security
MSHSR	Master of Science in Human Security and Resilience

MSI	Master of Science in Information
	Master of Science in Instruction
	Master of System Integration
MSIA	Master of Science in Industrial Administration
	Master of Science in Information Assurance
MSIDM	Master of Science in Interior Design and Merchandising
MSIE	Master of Science in Industrial Engineering
MSIEM	Master of Science in Information Engineering and Management
MSIM	Master of Science in Industrial Management
	Master of Science in Information Management
	Master of Science in International Management
MSIMC	Master of Science in Integrated Marketing Communications
MSIMS	Master of Science in Identity Management and Security
MSIS	Master of Science in Information Science
	Master of Science in Information Studies
	Master of Science in Information Systems
	Master of Science in Interdisciplinary Studies
MSISE	Master of Science in Infrastructure Systems Engineering
MSISM	Master of Science in Information Systems Management
MSISPM	Master of Science in Information Security Policy and Management
MSIST	Master of Science in Information Systems Technology
MSIT	Master of Science in Industrial Technology
	Master of Science in Information Technology
	Master of Science in Instructional Technology
MSITM	Master of Science in Information Technology Management
MSJ	Master of Science in Journalism
	Master of Science in Jurisprudence
MSJC	Master of Social Justice and Criminology
MSJFP	Master of Science in Juvenile Forensic Psychology
MSJJ	Master of Science in Juvenile Justice
MSJPS	Master of Science in Justice and Public Safety
MSK	Master of Science in Kinesiology
MSL	Master in the Study of Law
	Master of School Leadership
	Master of Science in Leadership
	Master of Science in Limnology
	Master of Sports Leadership
	Master of Strategic Leadership
	Master of Studies in Law
MSLA	Master of Science in Legal Administration
MSLB	Master of Sports Law and Business
MSLFS	Master of Science in Life Sciences
MSLP	Master of Speech-Language Pathology
MSLS	Master of Science in Library Science
MSLSCM	Master of Science in Logistics and Supply Chain Management
MSLT	Master of Second Language Teaching
MSM	Master of Sacred Ministry
	Master of Sacred Music
	Master of School Mathematics
	Master of Science in Management
	Master of Science in Medicine
	Master of Science in Organization Management
	Master of Security Management
	Master of Strategic Ministry
	Master of Supply Management
MSMA	Master of Science in Marketing Analysis
MSMAE	Master of Science in Materials Engineering
MSMC	Master of Science in Management and Communications
	Master of Science in Mass Communications

MSME	Master of Science in Mathematics Education
	Master of Science in Mechanical Engineering
	Master of Science in Medical Ethics
MSMHC	Master of Science in Mental Health Counseling
MSMIT	Master of Science in Management and Information Technology
MSMLS	Master of Science in Medical Laboratory Science
MSMOT	Master of Science in Management of Technology
MSMP	Master of Science in Medical Physics
	Master of Science in Molecular Pathology
MSMS	Master of Science in Management Science
	Master of Science in Marine Science
	Master of Science in Medical Sciences
MSMSE	Master of Science in Manufacturing Systems Engineering
	Master of Science in Material Science and Engineering
	Master of Science in Material Science Engineering
	Master of Science in Mathematics and Science Education
MSMus	Master of Sacred Music
MSN	Master of Science in Nursing
MSNA	Master of Science in Nurse Anesthesia
MSNE	Master of Science in Nuclear Engineering
MSNS	Master of Science in Natural Science
	Master of Science in Nutritional Science
MSOD	Master of Science in Organization Development
	Master of Science in Organizational Development
MSOEE	Master of Science in Outdoor and Environmental Education
MSOES	Master of Science in Occupational Ergonomics and Safety
MSOH	Master of Science in Occupational Health
MSOL	Master of Science in Organizational Leadership
MSOM	Master of Science in Oriental Medicine
MSOR	Master of Science in Operations Research
MSOT	Master of Science in Occupational Technology
	Master of Science in Occupational Therapy
MSP	Master of Science in Pharmacy
	Master of Science in Planning
	Master of Speech Pathology
	Master of Sustainable Peacebuilding
MSPA	Master of Science in Physician Assistant
MSPAS	Master of Science in Physician Assistant Studies
MSPC	Master of Science in Professional Communications
MSPE	Master of Science in Petroleum Engineering
MSPH	Master of Science in Public Health
MSPHR	Master of Science in Pharmacy
MSPM	Master of Science in Professional Management
	Master of Science in Project Management
MSPNGE	Master of Science in Petroleum and Natural Gas Engineering
MSPPM	Master of Science in Public Policy and Management
MSPS	Master of Science in Pharmaceutical Science
	Master of Science in Political Science
	Master of Science in Psychological Services
MSPT	Master of Science in Physical Therapy
MSRA	Master of Science in Recreation Administration
MSRE	Master of Science in Real Estate
	Master of Science in Religious Education
MSRED	Master of Science in Real Estate Development
	Master of Sustainable Real Estate Development
MSRLS	Master of Science in Recreation and Leisure Studies

MSRM	Master of Science in Risk Management	MTCM	Master of Traditional Chinese Medicine
MSRMP	Master of Science in Radiological Medical Physics	MTD	Master of Training and Development
		MTE	Master in Educational Technology
MSRS	Master of Science in Radiological Sciences		Master of Technological Entrepreneurship
	Master of Science in Rehabilitation Science	MTESOL	Master in Teaching English to Speakers of Other Languages
MSS	Master of Security Studies		
	Master of Social Science	MTHM	Master of Tourism and Hospitality Management
	Master of Social Services	MTI	Master of Information Technology
	Master of Sports Science	MTID	Master of Tangible Interaction Design
	Master of Strategic Studies	MTL	Master of Talmudic Law
	Master's in Statistical Science	MTM	Master of Technology Management
MSSA	Master of Science in Social Administration		Master of Telecommunications Management
MSSCM	Master of Science in Supply Chain Management		Master of the Teaching of Mathematics
MSSD	Master of Arts in Software Driven Systems Design		Master of Transformative Ministry
			Master of Translational Medicine
	Master of Science in Sustainable Design	MTMH	Master of Tropical Medicine and Hygiene
MSSE	Master of Science in Software Engineering	MTMS	Master in Teaching Mathematics and Science
	Master of Science in Special Education	MTOM	Master of Traditional Oriental Medicine
MSSEM	Master of Science in Systems and Engineering Management	MTPC	Master of Technical and Professional Communication
MSSI	Master of Science in Security Informatics	MTR	Master of Translational Research
	Master of Science in Strategic Intelligence	MTS	Master of Theatre Studies
MSSIS	Master of Science in Security and Intelligence Studies		Master of Theological Studies
		MTW	Master of Teaching Writing
MSSL	Master of Science in School Leadership	MTWM	Master of Trust and Wealth Management
MSSLP	Master of Science in Speech-Language Pathology	MUA	Master of Urban Affairs
		MUAP	Master's of Urban Affairs and Policy
MSSM	Master of Science in Sports Medicine	MUCD	Master of Urban and Community Design
	Master of Science in Systems Management	MUD	Master of Urban Design
MSSP	Master of Science in Social Policy	MUDS	Master of Urban Design Studies
MSSS	Master of Science in Safety Science	MUEP	Master of Urban and Environmental Planning
	Master of Science in Systems Science	MUP	Master of Urban Planning
MSST	Master of Science in Security Technologies	MUPD	Master of Urban Planning and Development
MSSW	Master of Science in Social Work	MUPP	Master of Urban Planning and Policy
MSSWE	Master of Science in Software Engineering	MUPRED	Master of Urban Planning and Real Estate Development
MST	Master of Science and Technology		
	Master of Science in Taxation	MURP	Master of Urban and Regional Planning
	Master of Science in Teaching		Master of Urban and Rural Planning
	Master of Science in Technology	MURPL	Master of Urban and Regional Planning
	Master of Science in Telecommunications	MUS	Master of Urban Studies
	Master of Science Teaching	Mus M	Master of Music
MSTC	Master of Science in Technical Communication	MUSA	Master of Urban Spatial Analytics
	Master of Science in Telecommunications	MVP	Master of Voice Pedagogy
MSTCM	Master of Science in Traditional Chinese Medicine	MVS	Master of Visual Studies
		MWBS	Master of Won Buddhist Studies
MSTE	Master of Science in Telecommunications Engineering	MWC	Master of Wildlife Conservation
		MWR	Master of Water Resources
	Master of Science in Transportation Engineering	MWS	Master of Women's Studies
			Master of Worship Studies
MSTL	Master of Science in Teacher Leadership	MWSc	Master of Wildlife Science
MSTM	Master of Science in Technology Management	Nav Arch	Naval Architecture
	Master of Science in Transfusion Medicine	Naval E	Naval Engineer
MSTOM	Master of Science in Traditional Oriental Medicine	ND	Doctor of Naturopathic Medicine
			Doctor of Nursing
MSUASE	Master of Science in Unmanned and Autonomous Systems Engineering	NE	Nuclear Engineer
		Nuc E	Nuclear Engineer
MSUD	Master of Science in Urban Design	OD	Doctor of Optometry
MSUS	Master of Science in Urban Studies	OTD	Doctor of Occupational Therapy
MSW	Master of Social Work	PBME	Professional Master of Biomedical Engineering
MSWE	Master of Software Engineering	PC	Performer's Certificate
MSWREE	Master of Science in Water Resources and Environmental Engineering	PD	Professional Diploma
		PGC	Post-Graduate Certificate
MT	Master of Taxation	PGD	Postgraduate Diploma
	Master of Teaching	Ph L	Licentiate of Philosophy
	Master of Technology	Pharm D	Doctor of Pharmacy
	Master of Textiles	PhD	Doctor of Philosophy
MTA	Master of Tax Accounting	PhD Otol	Doctor of Philosophy in Otolaryngology
	Master of Teaching Arts	PhD Surg	Doctor of Philosophy in Surgery
	Master of Tourism Administration	PhDEE	Doctor of Philosophy in Electrical Engineering
MTC	Master of Technical Communications		

PMBA	Professional Master of Business Administration
PMC	Post Master Certificate
PMD	Post-Master's Diploma
PMS	Professional Master of Science
	Professional Master's
Post-Doctoral MS	Post-Doctoral Master of Science
Post-MSN Certificate	Post-Master of Science in Nursing Certificate
PPDPT	Postprofessional Doctor of Physical Therapy
Pro-MS	Professional Science Master's
Professional MA	Professional Master of Arts
Professional MBA	Professional Master of Business Administration
Professional MS	Professional Master of Science
PSM	Professional Master of Science
	Professional Science Master's
Psy D	Doctor of Psychology
Psy M	Master of Psychology
Psy S	Specialist in Psychology
Psya D	Doctor of Psychoanalysis
S Psy S	Specialist in Psychological Services
Sc D	Doctor of Science
Sc M	Master of Science
SCCT	Specialist in Community College Teaching
ScDPT	Doctor of Physical Therapy Science
SD	Specialist Degree
SJD	Doctor of Juridical Sciences
SLPD	Doctor of Speech-Language Pathology

SM	Master of Science
SM Arch S	Master of Science in Architectural Studies
SMACT	Master of Science in Art, Culture and Technology
SMBT	Master of Science in Building Technology
SP	Specialist Degree
Sp Ed	Specialist in Education
Sp LIS	Specialist in Library and Information Science
SPA	Specialist in Arts
Spec	Specialist's Certificate
Spec M	Specialist in Music
Spt	Specialist Degree
SSP	Specialist in School Psychology
STB	Bachelor of Sacred Theology
STD	Doctor of Sacred Theology
STL	Licentiate of Sacred Theology
STM	Master of Sacred Theology
tDACM	Transitional Doctor of Acupuncture and Chinese Medicine
TDPT	Transitional Doctor of Physical Therapy
Th D	Doctor of Theology
Th M	Master of Theology
TOTD	Transitional Doctor of Occupational Therapy
VMD	Doctor of Veterinary Medicine
WEMBA	Weekend Executive Master of Business Administration
XMA	Executive Master of Arts

INDEXES

Displays and Close-Ups

Directories and Subject Areas

Following is an alphabetical listing of directories and subject areas. Also listed are cross-references for subject area names not used in the directory structure of the guides, for example, "City and Regional Planning (*see* Urban and Regional Planning)."

Graduate Programs in the Humanities, Arts & Social Sciences

Addictions/Substance Abuse Counseling
Administration (*see* Arts Administration; Public Administration)
African-American Studies
African Languages and Literatures (*see* African Studies)
African Studies
Agribusiness (*see* Agricultural Economics and Agribusiness)
Agricultural Economics and Agribusiness
Alcohol Abuse Counseling (*see* Addictions/Substance Abuse Counseling)
American Indian/Native American Studies
American Studies
Anthropology
Applied Arts and Design—General
Applied Behavior Analysis
Applied Economics
Applied History (*see* Public History)
Applied Psychology
Applied Social Research
Arabic (*see* Near and Middle Eastern Languages)
Arab Studies (*see* Near and Middle Eastern Studies)
Archaeology
Architectural History
Architecture
Archives Administration (*see* Public History)
Area and Cultural Studies (*see* African-American Studies; African Studies; American Indian/Native American Studies; American Studies; Asian-American Studies; Asian Studies; Canadian Studies; Cultural Studies; East European and Russian Studies; Ethnic Studies; Folklore; Gender Studies; Hispanic Studies; Holocaust Studies; Jewish Studies; Latin American Studies; Near and Middle Eastern Studies; Northern Studies; Pacific Area/Pacific Rim Studies; Western European Studies; Women's Studies)
Art/Fine Arts
Art History
Arts Administration
Arts Journalism
Art Therapy
Asian-American Studies
Asian Languages
Asian Studies
Behavioral Sciences (*see* Psychology)
Bible Studies (*see* Religion; Theology)
Biological Anthropology
Black Studies (*see* African-American Studies)
Broadcasting (*see* Communication; Film, Television, and Video Production)
Broadcast Journalism
Building Science
Canadian Studies
Celtic Languages
Ceramics (*see* Art/Fine Arts)
Child and Family Studies
Child Development
Chinese
Chinese Studies (*see* Asian Languages; Asian Studies)
Christian Studies (*see* Missions and Missiology; Religion; Theology)
Cinema (*see* Film, Television, and Video Production)
City and Regional Planning (*see* Urban and Regional Planning)
Classical Languages and Literatures (*see* Classics)
Classics

Clinical Psychology
Clothing and Textiles
Cognitive Psychology (*see* Psychology—General; Cognitive Sciences)
Cognitive Sciences
Communication—General
Community Affairs (*see* Urban and Regional Planning; Urban Studies)
Community Planning (*see* Architecture; Environmental Design; Urban and Regional Planning; Urban Design; Urban Studies)
Community Psychology (*see* Social Psychology)
Comparative and Interdisciplinary Arts
Comparative Literature
Composition (*see* Music)
Computer Art and Design
Conflict Resolution and Mediation/Peace Studies
Consumer Economics
Corporate and Organizational Communication
Corrections (*see* Criminal Justice and Criminology)
Counseling (*see* Counseling Psychology; Pastoral Ministry and Counseling)
Counseling Psychology
Crafts (*see* Art/Fine Arts)
Creative Arts Therapies (*see* Art Therapy; Therapies—Dance, Drama, and Music)
Criminal Justice and Criminology
Cultural Anthropology
Cultural Studies
Dance
Decorative Arts
Demography and Population Studies
Design (*see* Applied Arts and Design; Architecture; Art/Fine Arts; Environmental Design; Graphic Design; Industrial Design; Interior Design; Textile Design; Urban Design)
Developmental Psychology
Diplomacy (*see* International Affairs)
Disability Studies
Drama Therapy (*see* Therapies—Dance, Drama, and Music)
Dramatic Arts (*see* Theater)
Drawing (*see* Art/Fine Arts)
Drug Abuse Counseling (*see* Addictions/Substance Abuse Counseling)
Drug and Alcohol Abuse Counseling (*see* Addictions/Substance Abuse Counseling)
East Asian Studies (*see* Asian Studies)
East European and Russian Studies
Economic Development
Economics
Educational Theater (*see* Theater; Therapies—Dance, Drama, and Music)
Emergency Management
English
Environmental Design
Ethics
Ethnic Studies
Ethnomusicology (*see* Music)
Experimental Psychology
Family and Consumer Sciences—General
Family Studies (*see* Child and Family Studies)
Family Therapy (*see* Child and Family Studies; Clinical Psychology; Counseling Psychology; Marriage and Family Therapy)
Filmmaking (*see* Film, Television, and Video Production)
Film Studies (*see* Film, Television, and Video Production)
Film, Television, and Video Production
Film, Television, and Video Theory and Criticism
Fine Arts (*see* Art/Fine Arts)
Folklore
Foreign Languages (*see* specific language)
Foreign Service (*see* International Affairs; International Development)
Forensic Psychology
Forensic Sciences
Forensics (*see* Speech and Interpersonal Communication)
French

Gender Studies
General Studies (*see* Liberal Studies)
Genetic Counseling
Geographic Information Systems
Geography
German
Gerontology
Graphic Design
Greek (*see* Classics)
Health Communication
Health Psychology
Hebrew (*see* Near and Middle Eastern Languages)
Hebrew Studies (*see* Jewish Studies)
Hispanic and Latin American Languages
Hispanic Studies
Historic Preservation
History
History of Art (*see* Art History)
History of Medicine
History of Science and Technology
Holocaust and Genocide Studies
Home Economics (*see* Family and Consumer Sciences—General)
Homeland Security
Household Economics, Sciences, and Management (*see* Family and Consumer Sciences—General)
Human Development
Humanities
Illustration
Industrial and Labor Relations
Industrial and Organizational Psychology
Industrial Design
Interdisciplinary Studies
Interior Design
International Affairs
International Development
International Economics
International Service (*see* International Affairs; International Development)
International Trade Policy
Internet and Interactive Multimedia
Interpersonal Communication (*see* Speech and Interpersonal Communication)
Interpretation (*see* Translation and Interpretation)
Islamic Studies (*see* Near and Middle Eastern Studies; Religion)
Italian
Japanese
Japanese Studies (*see* Asian Languages; Asian Studies; Japanese)
Jewelry (*see* Art/Fine Arts)
Jewish Studies
Journalism
Judaic Studies (*see* Jewish Studies; Religion)
Labor Relations (*see* Industrial and Labor Relations)
Landscape Architecture
Latin American Studies
Latin (*see* Classics)
Law Enforcement (*see* Criminal Justice and Criminology)
Liberal Studies
Lighting Design
Linguistics
Literature (*see* Classics; Comparative Literature; specific language)
Marriage and Family Therapy
Mass Communication
Media Studies
Medical Illustration
Medieval and Renaissance Studies
Metalsmithing (*see* Art/Fine Arts)
Middle Eastern Studies (*see* Near and Middle Eastern Studies)
Military and Defense Studies
Mineral Economics
Ministry (*see* Pastoral Ministry and Counseling; Theology)
Missions and Missiology
Motion Pictures (*see* Film, Television, and Video Production)
Museum Studies
Music
Musicology (*see* Music)
Music Therapy (*see* Therapies—Dance, Drama, and Music)

National Security
Native American Studies (*see* American Indian/Native American Studies)
Near and Middle Eastern Languages
Near and Middle Eastern Studies
Northern Studies
Organizational Psychology (*see* Industrial and Organizational Psychology)
Oriental Languages (*see* Asian Languages)
Oriental Studies (*see* Asian Studies)
Pacific Area/Pacific Rim Studies
Painting (*see* Art/Fine Arts)
Pastoral Ministry and Counseling
Philanthropic Studies
Philosophy
Photography
Playwriting (*see* Theater; Writing)
Policy Studies (*see* Public Policy)
Political Science
Population Studies (*see* Demography and Population Studies)
Portuguese
Printmaking (*see* Art/Fine Arts)
Product Design (*see* Industrial Design)
Psychoanalysis and Psychotherapy
Psychology—General
Public Administration
Public Affairs
Public History
Public Policy
Public Speaking (*see* Mass Communication; Rhetoric; Speech and Interpersonal Communication)
Publishing
Regional Planning (*see* Architecture; Urban and Regional Planning; Urban Design; Urban Studies)
Rehabilitation Counseling
Religion
Renaissance Studies (*see* Medieval and Renaissance Studies)
Rhetoric
Romance Languages
Romance Literatures (*see* Romance Languages)
Rural Planning and Studies
Rural Sociology
Russian
Scandinavian Languages
School Psychology
Sculpture (*see* Art/Fine Arts)
Security Administration (*see* Criminal Justice and Criminology)
Slavic Languages
Slavic Studies (*see* East European and Russian Studies; Slavic Languages)
Social Psychology
Social Sciences
Sociology
Southeast Asian Studies (*see* Asian Studies)
Soviet Studies (*see* East European and Russian Studies; Russian)
Spanish
Speech and Interpersonal Communication
Sport Psychology
Studio Art (*see* Art/Fine Arts)
Substance Abuse Counseling (*see* Addictions/Substance Abuse Counseling)
Survey Methodology
Sustainable Development
Technical Communication
Technical Writing
Telecommunications (*see* Film, Television, and Video Production)
Television (*see* Film, Television, and Video Production)
Textile Design
Textiles (*see* Clothing and Textiles; Textile Design)
Thanatology
Theater
Theater Arts (*see* Theater)
Theology
Therapies—Dance, Drama, and Music
Translation and Interpretation
Transpersonal and Humanistic Psychology

Urban and Regional Planning
Urban Design
Urban Planning (*see* Architecture; Urban and Regional Planning;
    Urban Design; Urban Studies)
Urban Studies
Video (*see* Film, Television, and Video Production)
Visual Arts (*see* Applied Arts and Design; Art/Fine Arts; Film,
    Television, and Video Production; Graphic Design; Illustration;
    Photography)
Western European Studies
Women's Studies
World Wide Web (*see* Internet and Interactive Multimedia)
Writing

Graduate Programs in the Biological/ Biomedical Sciences & Health-Related Medical Professions

Acupuncture and Oriental Medicine
Acute Care/Critical Care Nursing Administration (*see* Health Services
    Management and Hospital Administration; Nursing and Healthcare
    Administration; Pharmaceutical Administration)
Adult Nursing
Advanced Practice Nursing (*see* Family Nurse Practitioner Studies)
Allied Health—General
Allied Health Professions (*see* Clinical Laboratory Sciences/Medical
    Technology; Clinical Research; Communication Disorders; Dental
    Hygiene; Emergency Medical Services; Occupational Therapy;
    Physical Therapy; Physician Assistant Studies; Rehabilitation
    Sciences)
Allopathic Medicine
Anatomy
Anesthesiologist Assistant Studies
Animal Behavior
Bacteriology
Behavioral Sciences (*see* Biopsychology; Neuroscience; Zoology)
Biochemistry
Bioethics
Biological and Biomedical Sciences—General Biological Chemistry
    (*see* Biochemistry)
Biological Oceanography (*see* Marine Biology)
Biophysics
Biopsychology
Botany
Breeding (*see* Botany; Plant Biology; Genetics)
Cancer Biology/Oncology
Cardiovascular Sciences
Cell Biology
Cellular Physiology (*see* Cell Biology; Physiology)
Child-Care Nursing (*see* Maternal and Child/Neonatal Nursing)
Chiropractic
Clinical Laboratory Sciences/Medical Technology
Clinical Research
Community Health
Community Health Nursing
Computational Biology
Conservation (*see* Conservation Biology; Environmental Biology)
Conservation Biology
Crop Sciences (*see* Botany; Plant Biology)
Cytology (*see* Cell Biology)
Dental and Oral Surgery (*see* Oral and Dental Sciences)
Dental Assistant Studies (*see* Dental Hygiene)
Dental Hygiene
Dental Services (*see* Dental Hygiene)
Dentistry
Developmental Biology Dietetics (*see* Nutrition)
Ecology
Embryology (*see* Developmental Biology)
Emergency Medical Services
Endocrinology (*see* Physiology)
Entomology
Environmental Biology

Environmental and Occupational Health
Epidemiology
Evolutionary Biology
Family Nurse Practitioner Studies
Foods (*see* Nutrition)
Forensic Nursing
Genetics
Genomic Sciences
Gerontological Nursing
Health Physics/Radiological Health
Health Promotion
Health-Related Professions (*see* individual allied health professions)
Health Services Management and Hospital Administration
Health Services Research
Histology (*see* Anatomy; Cell Biology)
HIV/AIDS Nursing
Hospice Nursing
Hospital Administration (*see* Health Services Management and
    Hospital Administration)
Human Genetics
Immunology
Industrial Hygiene
Infectious Diseases
International Health
Laboratory Medicine (*see* Clinical Laboratory Sciences/Medical
    Technology; Immunology; Microbiology; Pathology)
Life Sciences (*see* Biological and Biomedical Sciences)
Marine Biology
Maternal and Child Health
Maternal and Child/Neonatal Nursing
Medical Imaging
Medical Microbiology
Medical Nursing (*see* Medical/Surgical Nursing)
Medical Physics
Medical/Surgical Nursing
Medical Technology (*see* Clinical Laboratory Sciences/Medical
    Technology)
Medical Sciences (*see* Biological and Biomedical Sciences)
Medical Science Training Programs (*see* Biological and Biomedical
    Sciences)
Medicinal and Pharmaceutical Chemistry
Medicinal Chemistry (*see* Medicinal and Pharmaceutical Chemistry)
Medicine (*see* Allopathic Medicine; Naturopathic Medicine;
    Osteopathic Medicine; Podiatric Medicine)
Microbiology
Midwifery (*see* Nurse Midwifery)
Molecular Biology
Molecular Biophysics
Molecular Genetics
Molecular Medicine
Molecular Pathogenesis
Molecular Pathology
Molecular Pharmacology
Molecular Physiology
Molecular Toxicology
Naturopathic Medicine
Neural Sciences (*see* Biopsychology; Neurobiology; Neuroscience)
Neurobiology
Neuroendocrinology (*see* Biopsychology; Neurobiology; Neuroscience;
    Physiology)
Neuropharmacology (*see* Biopsychology; Neurobiology; Neuroscience;
    Pharmacology)
Neurophysiology (*see* Biopsychology; Neurobiology; Neuroscience;
    Physiology)
Neuroscience
Nuclear Medical Technology (*see* Clinical Laboratory Sciences/
    Medical Technology)
Nurse Anesthesia
Nurse Midwifery
Nurse Practitioner Studies (*see* Family Nurse Practitioner Studies)
Nursing Administration (*see* Nursing and Healthcare Administration)
Nursing and Healthcare Administration
Nursing Education
Nursing—General
Nursing Informatics
Nutrition

Occupational Health (*see* Environmental and Occupational Health; Occupational Health Nursing)
Occupational Health Nursing
Occupational Therapy
Oncology (*see* Cancer Biology/Oncology)
Oncology Nursing
Optometry
Oral and Dental Sciences
Oral Biology (*see* Oral and Dental Sciences)
Oral Pathology (*see* Oral and Dental Sciences)
Organismal Biology (*see* Biological and Biomedical Sciences; Zoology)
Oriental Medicine and Acupuncture (*see* Acupuncture and Oriental Medicine)
Orthodontics (*see* Oral and Dental Sciences)
Osteopathic Medicine
Parasitology
Pathobiology
Pathology
Pediatric Nursing
Pedontics (*see* Oral and Dental Sciences)
Perfusion
Pharmaceutical Administration
Pharmaceutical Chemistry (*see* Medicinal and Pharmaceutical Chemistry)
Pharmaceutical Sciences
Pharmacology
Pharmacy
Photobiology of Cells and Organelles (*see* Botany; Cell Biology; Plant Biology)
Physical Therapy
Physician Assistant Studies
Physiological Optics (*see* Vision Sciences)
Podiatric Medicine
Preventive Medicine (*see* Community Health and Public Health)
Physiological Optics (*see* Physiology)
Physiology
Plant Biology
Plant Molecular Biology
Plant Pathology
Plant Physiology
Pomology (*see* Botany; Plant Biology)
Psychiatric Nursing
Public Health—General
Public Health Nursing (*see* Community Health Nursing)
Psychiatric Nursing
Psychobiology (*see* Biopsychology)
Psychopharmacology (*see* Biopsychology; Neuroscience; Pharmacology)
Radiation Biology
Radiological Health (*see* Health Physics/Radiological Health)
Rehabilitation Nursing
Rehabilitation Sciences
Rehabilitation Therapy (*see* Physical Therapy)
Reproductive Biology
School Nursing
Sociobiology (*see* Evolutionary Biology)
Structural Biology
Surgical Nursing (*see* Medical/Surgical Nursing)
Systems Biology
Teratology
Therapeutics
Theoretical Biology (*see* Biological and Biomedical Sciences)
Therapeutics (*see* Pharmaceutical Sciences; Pharmacology; Pharmacy)
Toxicology
Transcultural Nursing
Translational Biology
Tropical Medicine (*see* Parasitology)
Veterinary Medicine
Veterinary Sciences
Virology
Vision Sciences
Wildlife Biology (*see* Zoology)
Women's Health Nursing
Zoology

Graduate Programs in the Physical Sciences, Mathematics, Agricultural Sciences, the Environment & Natural Resources

Acoustics
Agricultural Sciences
Agronomy and Soil Sciences
Analytical Chemistry
Animal Sciences
Applied Mathematics
Applied Physics
Applied Statistics
Aquaculture
Astronomy
Astrophysical Sciences (*see* Astrophysics; Atmospheric Sciences; Meteorology; Planetary and Space Sciences)
Astrophysics
Atmospheric Sciences
Biological Oceanography (*see* Marine Affairs; Marine Sciences; Oceanography)
Biomathematics
Biometry
Biostatistics
Chemical Physics
Chemistry
Computational Sciences
Condensed Matter Physics
Dairy Science (*see* Animal Sciences)
Earth Sciences (*see* Geosciences)
Environmental Management and Policy
Environmental Sciences
Environmental Studies (*see* Environmental Management and Policy)
Experimental Statistics (*see* Statistics)
Fish, Game, and Wildlife Management
Food Science and Technology
Forestry
General Science (*see* specific topics)
Geochemistry
Geodetic Sciences
Geological Engineering (*see* Geology)
Geological Sciences (*see* Geology)
Geology
Geophysical Fluid Dynamics (*see* Geophysics)
Geophysics
Geosciences
Horticulture
Hydrogeology
Hydrology
Inorganic Chemistry
Limnology
Marine Affairs
Marine Geology
Marine Sciences
Marine Studies (*see* Marine Affairs; Marine Geology; Marine Sciences; Oceanography)
Mathematical and Computational Finance
Mathematical Physics
Mathematical Statistics (*see* Applied Statistics; Statistics)
Mathematics
Meteorology
Mineralogy
Natural Resource Management (*see* Environmental Management and Policy; Natural Resources)
Natural Resources
Nuclear Physics (*see* Physics)
Ocean Engineering (*see* Marine Affairs; Marine Geology; Marine Sciences; Oceanography)
Oceanography
Optical Sciences
Optical Technologies (*see* Optical Sciences)
Optics (*see* Applied Physics; Optical Sciences; Physics)
Organic Chemistry

Paleontology
Paper Chemistry (*see* Chemistry)
Photonics
Physical Chemistry
Physics
Planetary and Space Sciences
Plant Sciences
Plasma Physics
Poultry Science (*see* Animal Sciences)
Radiological Physics (*see* Physics)
Range Management (*see* Range Science)
Range Science
Resource Management (*see* Environmental Management and Policy; Natural Resources)
Solid-Earth Sciences (*see* Geosciences)
Space Sciences (*see* Planetary and Space Sciences)
Statistics
Theoretical Chemistry
Theoretical Physics
Viticulture and Enology
Water Resources

Graduate Programs in Engineering & Applied Sciences

Aeronautical Engineering (*see* Aerospace/Aeronautical Engineering)
Aerospace/Aeronautical Engineering
Aerospace Studies (*see* Aerospace/Aeronautical Engineering)
Agricultural Engineering
Applied Mechanics (*see* Mechanics)
Applied Science and Technology
Architectural Engineering
Artificial Intelligence/Robotics
Astronautical Engineering (*see* Aerospace/Aeronautical Engineering)
Automotive Engineering
Aviation
Biochemical Engineering
Bioengineering
Bioinformatics
Biological Engineering (*see* Bioengineering)
Biomedical Engineering
Biosystems Engineering
Biotechnology
Ceramic Engineering (*see* Ceramic Sciences and Engineering)
Ceramic Sciences and Engineering
Ceramics (*see* Ceramic Sciences and Engineering)
Chemical Engineering
Civil Engineering
Computer and Information Systems Security
Computer Engineering
Computer Science
Computing Technology (*see* Computer Science)
Construction Engineering
Construction Management
Database Systems
Electrical Engineering
Electronic Materials
Electronics Engineering (*see* Electrical Engineering)
Energy and Power Engineering
Energy Management and Policy
Engineering and Applied Sciences
Engineering and Public Affairs (*see* Technology and Public Policy)
Engineering and Public Policy (*see* Energy Management and Policy; Technology and Public Policy)
Engineering Design
Engineering Management
Engineering Mechanics (*see* Mechanics)
Engineering Metallurgy (*see* Metallurgical Engineering and Metallurgy)

Engineering Physics
Environmental Design (*see* Environmental Engineering)
Environmental Engineering
Ergonomics and Human Factors
Financial Engineering
Fire Protection Engineering
Food Engineering (*see* Agricultural Engineering)
Game Design and Development
Gas Engineering (*see* Petroleum Engineering)
Geological Engineering
Geophysics Engineering (*see* Geological Engineering)
Geotechnical Engineering
Hazardous Materials Management
Health Informatics
Health Systems (*see* Safety Engineering; Systems Engineering)
Highway Engineering (*see* Transportation and Highway Engineering)
Human-Computer Interaction
Human Factors (*see* Ergonomics and Human Factors)
Hydraulics
Hydrology (*see* Water Resources Engineering)
Industrial Engineering (*see* Industrial/Management Engineering)
Industrial/Management Engineering
Information Science
Internet Engineering
Macromolecular Science (*see* Polymer Science and Engineering)
Management Engineering (*see* Engineering Management; Industrial/Management Engineering)
Management of Technology
Manufacturing Engineering
Marine Engineering (*see* Civil Engineering)
Materials Engineering
Materials Sciences
Mechanical Engineering
Mechanics
Medical Informatics
Metallurgical Engineering and Metallurgy
Metallurgy (*see* Metallurgical Engineering and Metallurgy)
Mineral/Mining Engineering
Modeling and Simulation
Nanotechnology
Nuclear Engineering
Ocean Engineering
Operations Research
Paper and Pulp Engineering
Petroleum Engineering
Pharmaceutical Engineering
Plastics Engineering (*see* Polymer Science and Engineering)
Polymer Science and Engineering
Public Policy (*see* Energy Management and Policy; Technology and Public Policy)
Reliability Engineering
Robotics (*see* Artificial Intelligence/Robotics)
Safety Engineering
Software Engineering
Solid-State Sciences (*see* Materials Sciences)
Structural Engineering
Surveying Science and Engineering
Systems Analysis (*see* Systems Engineering)
Systems Engineering
Systems Science
Technology and Public Policy
Telecommunications
Telecommunications Management
Textile Sciences and Engineering
Textiles (*see* Textile Sciences and Engineering)
Transportation and Highway Engineering
Urban Systems Engineering (*see* Systems Engineering)
Waste Management (*see* Hazardous Materials Management)
Water Resources Engineering

Graduate Programs in Business, Education, Information Studies, Law & Social Work

Accounting
Actuarial Science
Adult Education
Advertising and Public Relations
Agricultural Education
Alcohol Abuse Counseling (*see* Counselor Education)
Archival Management and Studies
Art Education
Athletics Administration (*see* Kinesiology and Movement Studies)
Athletic Training and Sports Medicine
Audiology (*see* Communication Disorders)
Aviation Management
Banking (*see* Finance and Banking)
Business Administration and Management—General
Business Education
Communication Disorders
Community College Education
Computer Education
Continuing Education (*see* Adult Education)
Counseling (*see* Counselor Education)
Counselor Education
Curriculum and Instruction
Developmental Education
Distance Education Development
Drug Abuse Counseling (*see* Counselor Education)
Early Childhood Education
Educational Leadership and Administration
Educational Measurement and Evaluation
Educational Media/Instructional Technology
Educational Policy
Educational Psychology
Education—General
Education of the Blind (*see* Special Education)
Education of the Deaf (*see* Special Education)
Education of the Gifted
Education of the Hearing Impaired (*see* Special Education)
Education of the Learning Disabled (*see* Special Education)
Education of the Mentally Retarded (*see* Special Education)
Education of the Physically Handicapped (*see* Special Education)
Education of Students with Severe/Multiple Disabilities
Education of the Visually Handicapped (*see* Special Education)
Electronic Commerce
Elementary Education
English as a Second Language
English Education
Entertainment Management
Entrepreneurship
Environmental Education
Environmental Law
Exercise and Sports Science
Exercise Physiology (*see* Kinesiology and Movement Studies)
Facilities and Entertainment Management
Finance and Banking
Food Services Management (*see* Hospitality Management)
Foreign Languages Education
Foundations and Philosophy of Education
Guidance and Counseling (*see* Counselor Education)
Health Education
Health Law
Hearing Sciences (*see* Communication Disorders)
Higher Education
Home Economics Education
Hospitality Management
Hotel Management (*see* Travel and Tourism)
Human Resources Development
Human Resources Management
Human Services
Industrial Administration (*see* Industrial and Manufacturing Management)
Industrial and Manufacturing Management

Industrial Education (*see* Vocational and Technical Education)
Information Studies
Instructional Technology (*see* Educational Media/Instructional Technology)
Insurance
Intellectual Property Law
International and Comparative Education
International Business
International Commerce (*see* International Business)
International Economics (*see* International Business)
International Trade (*see* International Business)
Investment and Securities (*see* Business Administration and Management; Finance and Banking; Investment Management)
Investment Management
Junior College Education (*see* Community College Education)
Kinesiology and Movement Studies
Law
Legal and Justice Studies
Leisure Services (*see* Recreation and Park Management)
Leisure Studies
Library Science
Logistics
Management (*see* Business Administration and Management)
Management Information Systems
Management Strategy and Policy
Marketing
Marketing Research
Mathematics Education
Middle School Education
Movement Studies (*see* Kinesiology and Movement Studies)
Multilingual and Multicultural Education
Museum Education
Music Education
Nonprofit Management
Nursery School Education (*see* Early Childhood Education)
Occupational Education (*see* Vocational and Technical Education)
Organizational Behavior
Organizational Management
Parks Administration (*see* Recreation and Park Management)
Personnel (*see* Human Resources Development; Human Resources Management; Organizational Behavior; Organizational Management; Student Affairs)
Philosophy of Education (*see* Foundations and Philosophy of Education)
Physical Education
Project Management
Public Relations (*see* Advertising and Public Relations)
Quality Management
Quantitative Analysis
Reading Education
Real Estate
Recreation and Park Management
Recreation Therapy (*see* Recreation and Park Management)
Religious Education
Remedial Education (*see* Special Education)
Restaurant Administration (*see* Hospitality Management)
Science Education
Secondary Education
Social Sciences Education
Social Studies Education (*see* Social Sciences Education)
Social Work
Special Education
Speech-Language Pathology and Audiology (*see* Communication Disorders)
Sports Management
Sports Medicine (*see* Athletic Training and Sports Medicine)
Sports Psychology and Sociology (*see* Kinesiology and Movement Studies)
Student Affairs
Substance Abuse Counseling (*see* Counselor Education)
Supply Chain Management
Sustainability Management
Systems Management (*see* Management Information Systems)
Taxation
Teacher Education (*see* specific subject areas)

Teaching English as a Second Language (*see* English as a Second Language)

Technical Education (*see* Vocational and Technical Education)

Transportation Management

Travel and Tourism

Urban Education

Vocational and Technical Education

Vocational Counseling (*see* Counselor Education)

Directories and Subject Areas in this Book

NOTES

NOTES

NOTES

NOTES

NOTES

NOTES